A Concise Dictionary of Slang
and Unconventional English

Works by Eric Partridge

A DICTIONARY OF SLANG
AND UNCONVENTIONAL ENGLISH

ORIGINS
An Etymological Dictionary of Modern English

A DICTIONARY OF THE UNDERWORLD

A DICTIONARY OF CATCH PHRASES
British and American: from the Sixteenth Century to the Present Day

A DICTIONARY OF HISTORICAL SLANG
that is, up to 1914, ed. Jacqueline Simpson

A SMALLER SLANG DICTIONARY

SHAKESPEARE'S BAWDY
An Essay and a Glossary

A DICTIONARY OF CLICHÉS

COMIC ALPHABETS
A Light-hearted History

SWIFT'S POLITE CONVERSATION
A Commentary Edition

CHAMBER OF HORRORS
Officialese, British and American

USAGE AND ABUSAGE
A Guide to Good English

Edited by PAUL BEALE

A Concise Dictionary of Slang and Unconventional English

From *A Dictionary of Slang and Unconventional English* by Eric Partridge

Macmillan Publishing Company
New York

Macmillan Publishing Company
866 Third Avenue, New York, NY 10022

Collier Macmillan Canada, Inc.
1200 Eglinton Avenue East, Suite 200
Don Mills, Ontario M3C 3N1

First published in 1989 by Routledge, 11 New Fetter Lane, London EC4P 4EE

Library of Congress Cataloging-in-Publication Data
Partridge, Eric, 1894–1979.
    A concise dictionary of slang and unconventional English; from a Dictionary of slang and unconventional English by Eric Partridge / edited by Paul Beale.—1st American ed.
        p.   cm.
    Includes bibliographical references.

    1. English language—Slang—Dictionaries.   I. Beale, Paul.
II. Partridge, Eric, 1894–1979. Dictionary of slang and unconventional English.   III. Title.
PE3721.P3   1990   90-38042   CIP
427′.003—dc20

Printed in the United States of America

Contents

To the memory of
Eric Partridge's greatest helpers in his later editions

Laurie Atkinson   Vernon Noble   Albert Petch   Barry Prentice

And for Robert Claiborne, whose initials appear on so many
pages of this dictionary, with gratitude.

Preface

This concise version of Eric Partridge's *Dictionary of Slang and Unconventional English* arose from a desire to make his work as widely available as possible, especially to those for whom the price of the full volume is impossibly steep. It is therefore based closely on the Eighth Edition of the full volume, but with new material reflecting changes in the language since that edition went to press. Of course, much has had to be left out: the main thing I must stress about this concise version of Eric Partridge's *Dictionary of Slang & Unconventional English*, 8th ed. (*DSUE8*) is that it contains only terms known to have arisen in the Twentieth Century; it is intended as a complement to two other books, Partridge's *Dictionary of Historical Slang*, edited by Jacqueline Simpson, 1972 (*DHS*), and my own edition of Partridge's *Dictionary of Catch Phrases*, 1985. The three volumes between them include almost all the material in *DSUE8*; the only omission is military slang of the earlier C.20, largely and separately covered by B. & P. (see Bibliography), and even then I have included those terms that have since come into civilian use.

A surprise that emerged for me in editing Partridge's work was to find how *old* some of our everyday slang really is. While many terms from earlier C.20 already have a dated air – even vogue-words from the 'Swinging Sixties' feel lifeless – a multitude of others more vivid, familiar, and still in current use, were coined as early as C.17, but because of their racy flavour and their informality they are still regarded as slang today. When we refer, for instance, to food as *grub*, it is perhaps hard to realise that the word goes back to Oliver Cromwell's time; from early C.18 come *mob*, and also *knock off*, to finish; and from early C.19, the sarcastic use of *clear as mud*. It is worth remembering that the famous Cockney rhyming slang was in full flow by the 1850s: the first example to be written down (in 1839) was *Lord o' the manor*, a *tanner*, itself slang for our old, pre-decimal silver sixpence, a $2\frac{1}{2}$p piece. So please, before you angrily denounce this dictionary for omitting your own favourite informal usage, pause to reflect: the word may be much older than you think. Check in *DSUE8* or *DHS* before you write to complain of my negligence. On the other hand, I do not pretend to have been anything like exhaustive in my search for new words, and notice of my failure to cover any C.20 items will be warmly welcomed.

A disturbingly high proportion of the new terms that have come to light since *DSUE8* went to the printers in 1983, and are now recorded here, concern narcotics and the drug trade. But it should be remarked that in the centuries covered by *DHS* the abuse of alcohol was every bit as disastrous for its victims, and its vocabulary was just as preponderant in works of this sort: where *white* once meant gin, now it means cocaine. If the nature of humankind is changing for the better, it is a sadly and imperceptibly slow process.

A word about datings. If none is given, it is because there was none in *DSUE8*. Instead of following E.P.'s 'informed guesstimation', setting first use a few years back from the date of the first citation, I have left it to readers' own judgments. A dating, e.g. 'since ca. 1930', means that E.P. knew, or guessed, that the word in question was first used about then; the word's lifespan must again in most instances be left to readers' own knowledge – and again I shall be grateful for any help that readers can give me on this. It is usually easier to decide when a usage begins than when it ends, unless it is obviously topical/ephemeral, or another term has since taken its place. Partridge died on 1st June 1979; entries with dates since then are my responsibility, and where I know certain words were not in use before ca. 1970, I have labelled them 'later C.20'. The editorial 'I' throughout the main text and appendix is Eric Partridge's, unless shown otherwise by my initials.

P.B.
June 1988

Abbreviations and Signs

AA	anti-aircraft
AIF	Australian Imperial Force
abbr.	abbreviation, or shortening; abbreviated, abridged
adj.	adjective; adjectival(ly)
adv.	adverb; adverbial(ly)
after	after the fashion of; on the analogy of
anon.	anonymous
app.	apparently
Aus.	Australia(n)
BWI	British West Indies
Brit.	British; Britain
c.	cant, i.e. language of the underworld
C.	century
c.p.	a catch-phrase
c. and low	cant and low slang
ca.	about (the year . . .)
Can.	Canada; Canadian
cf.	compare
coll.	colloquial(ism); colloquially
d.	died
derog.	derogatory
dial.	dialect; dialectal(ly)
Dict.	Dictionary
E.P.	Eric Partridge
ed.	edition
elab.	elaborate(s or d); elaboration
Eng.	English
esp.	especially
etym.	etymology; etymological(ly)
euph.	euphemism; euphemistic(ally)
ex	from; derived from
exclam.	exclamation
FAA	Fleet Air Arm
fem.	feminine
fig.	figurative(ly)
fl.	flourished
Fr.	French
gen.	general(ly); usual(ly)
Ger.	German
Gr.	Greek
Ibid.	in the same authority or book
id.	the same
imm.	immediate(ly)
interj.	interjection
It.	Italian
j.	jargon, i.e. technical(ity)
joc.	jocular(ly); humorous
L.	Latin
lit.	literal(ly)
literary	Literary English; i.e. unused in ordinary speech
M.C.P.	male chauvinist pig
M.E.	Middle English
MN	Merchant Navy
military	mainly army usage, perhaps including naval; cf. later 'Services'
mod.	modern
n.	noun
N.	North, in N. Africa; N. Country (of England)
N. Am.	North America
N.B.	note carefully
NZ	New Zealand
non-aristocratic	P.B.: I take this to mean what is, in later C.20, known as 'non-U'
O.E.	Old English; i.e. before ca. 1150
ob.	obsolescent
occ.	occasional(ly)
on	on the analogy of
opp.	opposite; as opposed to
orig.	original(ly); originate(d), or -ing
pej.	pejorative(ly)
pl.	plural; in the plural
Port.	Portuguese
poss.	possible; possibly
ppl	participle; participial
prec.	preceded; preceding (cf. prec. = compare the preceding entry)
prob.	probable; probably
pron.	pronounced; pronunciation
pub.	published
quot'n	quotation
q.v.	which see!
RAF	Royal Air Force
RFC	Royal Flying Corps (1912–18)
RM	Royal Marines
RN	Royal Navy
RNAS	Royal Navy Air Service (1914–18)
ref.	reference
Regt or regt	Regiment
resp.	respective(ly)
rev.	revised
s.	slang
S.E.	Standard English
s.v.	see at
sc.	supply!; understand!
Scot.	Scottish
Services	the Armed Forces of the Crown
sing.	singular
sol.	solecism; solecistic
Sp.	Spanish
synon.	synonymous(ly)
temp.	in or at the time of
US	the United States of America; American
usu.	usual(ly)
v.	verb
v.i.	intransitive verb
v.t.	transitive verb
var.	variant; variation
vbl n.	verbal noun
vulg.	vulgarism
WRNS	Women's Royal Naval Service
WW1	The First World War, 1914–19
WW2	The Second World War, 1939–45
>	become(s); became
=	equal(s); equal to; equivalent to
†	obsolete, except in historical use
+; −	in, e.g. 1930+: for a short time after 1930; −1930: arose sometime before 1930

Acknowledgements and Bibliography

Here follow the expanded sources of all citations used in the dictionary. A few of the sources given in DSUE8 were found, on checking in the British Museum Catalogue of Printed Books, and in other bibliographical reference works, to be slightly misprinted; corrected versions have been included below. Those untraced are marked '(u/t)' and are, I believe, mostly Australian or Canadian. Where no source other than name is given, the references are to private communication, oral or written, up to ca. 1979 to E.P., thereafter to me.

I take this opportunity to thank again most warmly all those people who have helped me in any way with new material for this work: their names are included in the list below (and, of course, at their particular contributions in the main text). I thank especially David Stockley and the Central Drug Squad at New Scotland Yard for permission to draw freely on their excellent *Drug Warning* (published by Macdonald); and Michael Munro, for the same privilege with his delightful and informative guide to current Glasgow 'unconventional usage'.

Paul Beale, 1989

Aaron, 1982. H.A., *Pillar to Post*

Abrahams, 1938. A.A., in *Observer*, 25 Sep.

Ackerley, 1968. J.R.A., *My Father and Myself*

Adams, 1979. Douglas A., *The Hitchhiker's Guide to the Galaxy* (the book)
1931. Herbert A., *The Crooked Lip*, 1926

Adkin, 1983. F.J.A., *From the Ground Up*

Adrian, 1958. Vincent A., *End of a Summer's Day*

Aird, 1970. Catherine A., *A Late Phoenix*

Aldiss, 1978. Brian W.A.

Aldridge, 1942. James A., *Signed with their Honour*

Alexander, 1939. Niall A.

Allen, 1975. Charles A., ed., *Plain Tales from the Raj*
1983. *Tales from the South China Seas*
1972. Richard A., *Boot Boys* (u/t)

Allingham, 1930. Margery A., *Mystery Mile*
1931. *Look to the Lady*
1933. *Sweet Danger*
1936. *Flowers for the Judge*
1938. *The Fashion in Shrouds*
1945. *Coroner's Pidgin*
1947. *More Work for the Undertaker*
1955. *The Beckoning Lady*
1963. *The China Governess*
1934. Philip A., in (London) *Evening News*, 9 July. See also GRAFTERS', and PARLYAREE, in the Appx.

Allison, 1986. Lincoln A., in *New Society*, 8 Aug. See also HAULAGE BASHERS', in Appx.

Althill. See Atthill

Amis, 1969. Kingsley A., *The Green Man*
1986. Quoted in *Radio Times*, 8 Mar.
1977. Martin A., in *Observer*, 19 June

Anderson, 1973. P. Howard A., *Forgotten Railways: the East Midlands*
1965. Mrs Verily A.; and, with Rachel A., *Guide to the Beatniks* (u/t)

Anson, 1985. Victoria A., of Mark Cross, E. Sussex

APOD, 1976. *Australian Pocket Oxford Dict.*

Apt, 1978. Adam J.A.

Archer, 1946. C.S.A., *China Servant*

Armstrong, 1937. Anthony A., *Captain Bayonet*
1941. *Village at War*
1985. G.A., in *New Society*, article on Sheffield United AFC's fans, 9 May

Arnold, 1980. Sue A., in *Observer Mag.*, 28 June
1986. Ibid., 9 Mar.

Arnold-Foster, 1931. D.A.-F., *The Ways of the Navy*

Arthur, 1941. Frank A., *The Suva Harbour Mystery*, 1940

Ascherson, 1985. N.A., reviewing *Secret Service*, by C. Andrew, in *Observer*, Oct.

Ash. Tom A., *Childhood Days: the Docks and Dock Slang* n.d., ca. 1980

Ashley, 1982– Prof. L.R.N.A., of New York

Atkinson, 1961. Hugh A., *Low Company*

Atthill, 1967. Robin A., *The Somerset and Dorset Railway*

Auden, 1935. W.H.A. & C. Isherwood, *The Dog Under the Skin*

B., 1941. Sidney J.B., *New Zealand Slang*
1942. *Australian Slang*
1943. *Aus. S.*, 3rd ed.
1945. *The Australian Language*
1953. *Australia Speaks*
1959. *The Drum*

B & L. Barrère & Leland, *A Dict. of Slang, Jargon and Cant*, 1889–90

B & P. John B., & Eric Partridge, *Songs and Slang of the British Soldier, 1914–18* (3rd ed., 1931). Republished by A. Deutsch as *The Long Trail*, 1965

Bacon, 1986. Mrs Rachel B., of Loughborough

Badges, 1974. *Badges and Insignia of the British Armed Forces*

Bagley, 1968. Desmond B., *The Vivero Letter*

Baglin, 1973. Douglas B. & Barbara Mullins, *Rough as Guts*

Bailey, 1934. F.E.B., *Fleet Street Girl* (u/t)
1937. *Treat Them Gently* (u/t)
1932. H.C.B., *Mr Fortune Wonders*
1970. Paul B., *Trespasses*

Baker, 1931. George B., *Ebenezer Walks with God*
1938. Sidney J. B., letter in *Observer*, 13 Nov. See also B., 1941, etc.

Balchin, 1945. Nigel B., *Mine Own Executioner*

Ball, 1962. Ian M.B., in *Sunday Times*, 21 Jan.

Barber, 1979. Lynn B., in *Telegraph Sunday Mag.*, 2 Dec.
1984. In *Sunday Express Mag.*, 4 Nov.

Barclay, 1982. John B., of Sydney
1968. Stephen B., *Sex Slavery*

Barefoot, 1977. Patricia B. & R.J. Cunningham, *Community Services*

Barker, 1979. Ronnie B., *Fletcher's Book of Rhyming Slang*
1988. Paul B., in *Telegraph Sunday Mag.*, 28 Feb.

Barlay. See Barclay, 1968

Barling, 1973. Tom B., *Bergman's Blitz*

Barlow, 1968. James B., *The Burden of Proof*
1971. *In all Good Faith*

Barltrop, 1985. Robert B., *A Funny Age*; private, since 1979. See also COCKNEY, in Appx.

Barnes, 1979. Julian B., in *New Statesman*, 30 Mar.
1976. Ron B., *Coronation Cups and Jam Jars*
1983. Simon B., in *The Times*, 12 Nov.

Barnett, 1978. James B., *Head of the Force*

Barnhart, 1. *Dictionary of New English*, 1973
2. *Second Barnhart Dict. of New English*, 1980

Baron, 1948. Alexander B., *From the City, from the Plough*
1950. *There's No Home*

Barr, 1933. Cecil B., *'Amour' French for Love* (u/t)
1935. *It's Hard to Sin* (u/t)
1965. David B., of Canada
1983. John B., in the *Guardian*, 16 Sept.

Barrass, 1987. Mrs Hazel B., of Leicester, market traders' argot

Barrett, 1880. D.W.B., *Navvies*

'Bartimeus', 1915. *A Tall Ship*

Bartlett, 1986. Patrick B., Oxford University
1940. Vernon B., *No Man's Land*, 1930

Basic Beatnik, 1959. Article sub-titled *A Square's Guide to Hip Talk*, in (Victoria, BC) *Daily Colonist*, 16 Apr.

Bason, 1952. Fred B., *Second Diary*

Bassett, 1977. Ron B., *The Tinfish Run*
1979. *Neptune Landing*, 1980

Bates, 1955. H.E.B., *The Darling Buds of May*, 1958

Baxter, 1934. Alastair B.
1951. Walter B., *Look Down in Mercy*

Baynham, 1969. H.B., *From the Lower Deck*

Beames, 1932. John B., *Gateway*

Beard, 1940. Sgt-Pilot John B.,DFM, in Michie, 1940 (see below)

Beatles, 1975. Roy Carr & Tony Tyler

Beckett, 1931. Capt. W.N.B., *A Few Naval Customs*

Beede, 1970. John B., *They Hosed Them Out*, 1969

Beeding, 1932. Francis B., *Take It Crooked*

Beevor, 1983. A.B., *Faustian Pact*

Behan, 1958. Brendan B., *Borstal Boy*

Beilby, 1970. R.B., *No Medals for Aphrodite*, 1971

Bell, 1937. Josephine B., *Murder in Hospital*
1942. *Trouble at Wrekin Farm*
1950. *The Summer School Mystery*
1931. Neil B., *Andrew Otway* (u/t)
1934. *Winding Road*
1935. *The Years Dividing* (u/t)
1936. *Crocus*
1946. *Alpha and Omega*

1950. *I Am Legion*
1954. *Many Waters*
1982– Steve B., cartoonist, in the *Guardian*
Benge, 1969. R.C.B., *Libraries*
Bennett, 1919. Mark B., *Under the Periscope*
Benney, 1936. Mark B., *Low Company*
1938. *The Scapegoat Dances*
1940. *The Big Wheel*
Benson, 1910. E.F.B., *The Osbournes*
1916. *David Blaize*
1924. *David of King's*
1933. *Travail of Gold*
Benstead, 1930. Charles R.B., *Retreat: a Story of 1918*
Bentley, 1955. Nicholas B.
Benton, 1973. Kenneth B., *Craig and the Jaguar*
Berkeley, 1929. Anthony B., *The Piccadilly Murder*
1934. *Panic Party*
1937. *Trial and Error*
Bernstein, 1971. Theodore B., in the *Bulletin*, Apr.
Berrey, 1940. Lester V.B., 'English War Slang', in *Nation*, 9 Nov.
Berry, 1979. George B., in *Sunday Times*, 6 Aug.
1958. Rev. P.M.B., as reported in *Daily Telegraph*, 4 June
Betts, 1967. Alan B., *The Awful Punter's Book*
Bevan, 1953. Ian B., ed., *The Sunburnt Country*
Bhatia, 1983. Shyam B., in *Observer*, 20 Mar.
Bickers, 1965. R.T.B., *The Hellions*
Bigam, 1975. Capt. James A.G.B., RAMC, formerly of the Intelligence Corps
Bingham, 1968. John B., *I Love, I Kill*
Binsted, 1899. Arthur M. Binstead, *Gal's Gossip*
1903. *Pitcher in Paradise*
Binyon, 1983. T.J.B., In *The TLS*, 30 Sept.
Birkenhead, 1978. Lord B., *Rudyard Kipling*
Bishop, 1958– Capt. Edward W.B., of Southampton
1982. Patrick B., reporting the Falklands War, in *Observer*, 11 July
BJP. *British Journal of Photography*
Blair, 1947. Elgin B.
'Blake', 1941. Ronald Adams, *Readiness at Dawn*
Blake, 1935. Nicholas B., *A Question of Proof*
1936. *Thou Shell of Death*
1948. *Head of a Traveller*, 1949
1954. *The Whisper in the Gloom*
1964. *The Sad Variety*
1968. *The Private Wound*
Blaker, 1930. Richard B., *Medal Without Bar*
1934. *Night-Shift*
1935. *Here Lies a Most Beautiful Lady*
Bleasdale, 1983. Alan B., *The Boys From The Black Stuff*: 5 Plays for TV
Blight, 1952. Leslie B., *Love and Idleness*, 1958
Bliss, 1980. George B., of Kirby Lonsdale
Bloodworth, 1975. Dennis B., *An Eye for the Dragon*, 1970
Bloor, 1934. J.A.B., in *Passing Show*, 7 July
Blunden, 1935. Godfrey B., *No More Reality*
Blyth Ridley, 1984. The 'O' Level English Set, Blyth Ridley County High School, Northumberland
Blythe, 1979. Ronald B., ed., *The View in Winter*
Bodkin, 1945. Thomas B., *The Approach to Painting*, rev. ed.
Bolitho, 1941. Hector B., in *The English Digest*, Feb.
Bolster, 1945. David B., *Roll on My Twelve !*
Bolt (misprint: see Betts)

Bonham-Carter, 1965. Lady Violet B.-C., *Churchill as I Knew Him*
Boswall, 1970. Jeffrey B., ed., *Private Lives*
Boswell, 1959. John B., *Lost Girl*
Bosworth, 1932. G.H.B., *Prelude*
Bottrall, 1945. Ronald B., *Farewell and Hail*
Bowater, 1979. Mrs Janet B., of Shepshed, Leics.
Bowen, 1929. Frank B., *Sea Slang*
Bower, 1957. Dallas B.
Boycott, 1938. J.A.B.
Boyd, 1965. Martin B., *Day of My Delight*
Boyle, 1962. Andrew B., *Trenchard*
B.P., 1964– Barry Prentice, of Rodd Point, NSW
Bracey, 1934. Axel B., *Public Enemies* and *School for Scoundrels*
Braddon, 1977. Russell B., *The Finalists*
Bradhurst, 1937. Joseph F. Broadhurst, *From Vine Street to Jerusalem*, 1936
Brady, 1924. E.J.B., *Land of the Sun*
Branch, 1951. Pamela B., *The Wooden Overcoat*
Brand, 1941. Christianna B., *Death in High Heels*
1945. *Green for Danger*
1949. *Death of Jezebel*
Brandon, 1931. John G.B., *Th' Big City*, 1930
1933. *West End*
1934. *The One-Minute Murder*
1936. *The Pawnshop Murder* and *The 'Snatch' Game*
Brasch, 1983. Walter M.B., *Cartoon Monickers* (USA)
Brett, 1975. Simon B., *Cast, in Order of Disappearance*
1978. *An Amateur Corpse*
Brewer. *Brewer's Dict. of Phrase & Fable*, ed.
Brewster, 1944. H.C.B., *King's Cross Calling* (u/t)
Brickhill, 1946. B. & Norton, *Escape to Danger*
Brinklow, 1967. Douglas J.A.B., of Cheltenham
Brittain, 1933. *Testament of Youth*
Brock, 1970– Rear-Adm. P.W.B., CB, DSO
Brockman, 1937. Henrietta Drake B., *The Blister* (u/t)
1938. *Men Without Wives* (u/t)
1940. *Hot Gold* (u/t)
1947. *The Fatal Days*
1948. *Sydney or the Bush*
Bronsteen, 1967. Ruth B., *The Hippy's Handbook*, 1968
Brook, 1979. J.C.W.B., *Dream of Murder* (a broadcast play)
Brooke, 1948. Jocelyn B., *The Military Orchid*
Brookes, Ruby B., letter in *Telegraph Sunday Mag.*, 29 May 1988
Brooks, 1935. W. Collin B., *Frame-Up*
1951. *The Swimming Frog*
Broom, 1981. David B., in BBC Radio 4 'Desert Island Discs', 14 Feb.
Brophy, 1932. John B., *English Prose*
1934. *Waterfront*
1937. *Behold the Judge*
1944. *Target Island*
(See also B. & P.)
Brown, 1934. Denis B., in *Spectator*, 5 Jan.
1946. Jane B., *I Had a Pitch on the Stones*
1968. Malcolm B. & P. Meehan, *Scapa Flow*
1934. Percy B., *Blind Alleys* (u/t)
Browne, 1934. K.G.R.B., in The *Humorist*, 26 May & 28 July
Bruce, 1974. Leo B., *Death of a Bovver Boy*
Bruckshaw, 1987. Dr B.B., of Chepstow
Bryant, 1958. Vice-Adm. Ben B., *Submarine Commander* (USA)
Buchan, 1986. Alasdair B., letter in *Guardian*, 7 Nov.
1982. William B., *John Buchan*
Buchanan-Taylor, 1943. W.B.-T., *Shake It Again*
Buckley, 1947. Christopher B., *Rain Before Seven*
Bullion, 1988. A. Hogg, et. al., *Bullion: Brinks-Mat, the Story of Britain's Biggest Gold Robbery*

Burchill, 1978. Julie B. & T. Parsons, *The Boy Looked at Johnny*
 1986. J.B., *Damaged Gods*
Burgess, 1966. Anthony B., *Tremor of Intent*
 1967. Private
 1970. Reviewing *DSUE7*, in *TLS*, 16 Oct.
 1977. *Beard's Roman Women*
 1961. Eric B., *A Killing Frost*
Burland, 1968. Brian B., *Fall from Aloft*
Burn, 1980. Gordon B., in *Listener*, 8 June
 1981. in *Sunday Times Mag.*, 1 Mar.
 1983. in *Listener*, 28 Apr.
 1987. in *Listener*, 12 July
Burrow, 1912. S.E.B., *Friend or Foe*
Burt, 1980– Tony, Helen, Lewis & Julian B., of Sileby, Leics.
Burt, 1942. Cyril B., *The Case of the Fast Young Lady*
Burton, 1818. Alfred B., *Johnny Newcome*
 1932. Miles B., *Murder at the Moorings*
 1934. *To Catch a Thief*
Busby, 1978. Roger B., *Garvey's Code*
Bush, 1936. Christopher B., *The Case of the Monday Murders*
Butcher, 1979. D.B., *The Driftermen*
 1980. *The Trawlermen*
 1979. Maurice B., of Loughborough
Butterworth, 1968. Michael B., *Walk Softly in Fear*
Buzo, 1968. Alex B., *Norm and Ahmed*
 1969. *Rooted*
 1971. *The Roy Murphy Show*
Bygraves, 1976. Max B., *I Wanna Tell You a Story*
Byrde, 1979. Penelope B., *The Male Image*
Cable, 1938. Boyd C., in *Observer*, 30 Oct.
Caddie, 1953. *C., a Sydney Barmaid*
Cadell, 1953. Sir Patrick C. in *Jnl of Soc. for Army Historical Research*, 31
Calder, 1967. Nigel C., ed., *Unless Peace Comes*, 1968
Callow, 1968. Philip C., *Going to the Moon*
 1969. *The Bliss Body*
Cameron, 1937. D.S.C., Librarian, Univ. of Alberta
 1929. Isabel C., *Boysie*
 1979. James C., in *Telegraph Sunday Mag.*, 18 Feb.
Campbell, 1934. Alice C., *Desire to Kill*
 1960. Patrick C., *Come Here Till I Tell You*
 1964. in *Sunday Times*, 12 Apr.
 1916. Capt. R.W.C., *Private Spud Tamson*, 1915
 1964. Ross C., *Mummy, Who Is Your Husband?*
Campion, 1942. Sarah C., *Bonanza*
Canning, 1935. Victor C., *Polycarp's Progress*
Cantwell, 1963. John C., *No Stranger to the Flame*
Cardus, 1934. Neville C., *Good Days*
Carew, 1967. Maj. Tim C., *Korea: The Commonwealth at War*
Carlin, 1927. Francis C., *Reminiscences of an Ex-Detective*
Carmichael, 1983. Kay C., in *New Society*, 1 Sep.
Carr, 1956. John Dickson C., *Patrick Butler for the Defence*
 1930. W.G.C., *By Guess and by God*
 1936. *Brass Hats . . .*
Carrick, 1985. Miss Elizabeth C., MBE, of Carlisle
Carrott, 1982. Jasper C., *Sweet and Sour Labrador*
Carter, 1971. Angela C., *Love*
 1979. in *New Society*, 20 Dec.
 1980. 'The Language of Sisterhood', in *State of the Language*
 1979. Howard C., of Loughborough College of Art
 1988. Dr Toby C.C. of Crewkerne, formerly Wg Cdr RAFVR, who served in the Radio (i.e. Radar) Branch, WW2
Carty, 1983. CSM C., Welsh Gds, quoted in *Observer Mag.*, Feb.
Cary, 1948. Clif C., *Cricket Controversy*

Casey, 1942. Gavin C., *It's Harder for Girls*
 1945. *Downhill Is Easier*
 1947. *The Wits Are Out*
Cash, 1977. Anthony C., in *Gypsy Lore Soc. Jnl.*, vol I, pt 3
Cavanagh, 1965. A.J. M. Cavenagh, *Airborne to Suez*
Cecil, 1964. Lord David C., *Max*
Chamberlain, 1976. Audrey C., in *New Society*, 15 July
Chambers, 1980. Peter C., of London SW11
Chance, 1935. John Newton C., *Wheels in the Forest*
Chancellor, 1982. Julian C., of the Soc. of Authors, quoted in *New Society*, 10 June
Chapman, 1949. F. Spencer S., *The Jungle Is Neutral*
 1986. See *NEW DAS*
Chappell, 1980– Helen C., in *New Society*, 18 Sep.; 8 Oct '81; 24 June & 1 July '82
Cheapjack. Philip Allingham, 1934
Cheney, 1943. Peter Cheyney, *The Stars Are Dark*
Chenhalls. Alfred T.C., ca. 1935
Chine, 1933. See Clunes
Christie, 1926. Agatha C., *The Murder of Roger Ackroyd*
 1939. *Murder at the Vicarage*
 1944. *Towards Zero*
Church, 1986. Roy C., 'It's a Steal', in *You*, 16 Nov.
Claiborne, See R.C., below
Clapin, 1903. Sylva C., *New Dict. of Americanisms*
Clapperton, 1970. Richard C., *Victims Unknown*
 1976. *The Sentimental Kill*
Clark, 1964. Capt. D.M.J.C., *Suez Touchdown*
 1962. Robert C., *The Dogman and Other Poems*
 1975. Douglas C., *Premeditated Murder*
 1976. *Dread and Water*
 1980. *Golden Rain*
 1980(2). *Poacher's Bag*
 1981. *Roast Eggs*
 1982. *Shelf Life*
Clarke, 1948. Dudley C., *Seven Assignments*
 1934. F. Keston C., in *Humorist*, 21 & 28 July
 1980. Keith C., of Loughborough
Clayton, 1970. Tom C., *Men in Prison*
Cleary, 1949. Jon C., *The Long Shadow* and *You Can't See Round Corners*
 1950. *Just Let Me Be*
 1952. *The Sundowners*
 1954. *The Climate of Courage*
 1955. *Justin Bayard*
 1959. *Back of Sunset*
Clement, 1977. Dick C. & Ian Le Frenais, *A Further Stir of Porridge*
 1978. *Going Straight*
Cleugh, 1934. James C., *Orgy by Numbers*
Clifford, 1970. See Gifford
Clouston. J. Storer C.
Clunes, 1933. Frank Clune, *Try Anything Once*
Cobb, 1949. Belton C., *No Last Words*
 1975. Richard C., *A Sense of Place*; and privately
Cochran, 1945. Charles B.C., *A Showman Looks On*
Cockitt, 1988. Heather C., of Loughborough College of Art
Cody, 1985. Liza C., *Head Case*
Cohen, 1965. Morton C., ed., *Rudyard Kipling to Rider Haggard . . .*
Cohn, 1971. Nik C., *Today There Are No Gentlemen*
Coke, 1908. Desmond C., *The House Prefect*
 1910. *The School across the Road*
 1911. *Wilson's*
Cole, 1928. G.D.H., & M.C., *Superintendent Wilson's Holiday*
 1930. *Burglars in Bucks*
 1935. *Scandal at School*
 1980. Harry C., *Policeman's Progress*
 1986– John C., in *Listener*, 27 Mar.; 3 Dec. 1987

Coleman, 1978– John C., in *New Statesman*, 21 Apr.; 21 Mar. 1988
Coles, 1946. Manning C., *The Fifth Man*
Collinson, W.E.C., *Contemporary English*, 1927
Colquhoun, 1796. Patrick C., *Police of the Metropolis*
Connell, 1969. John C., *Wavell: Supreme Commander*
Connington, 1931. J.J.C., *The Sweepstake Murders*
  1937. *A Minor Operation*
  1938. *Truth Comes Limping*
Cook, 1962. Robin C., *The Crust on Its Uppers*
Cooke, 1911. A.S.C., *Off the Beaten Track in Sussex*
Coppard, 1921. A.E.C., *Adam and Eve and Pinch Me*
Cooper, 1925. Courtney R.C., *Lions 'n' Tigers 'n' Everything*, 1924
Cooper, 1980. Jilly C.
Coren, 1975. Alan C., in the *Times*, 8 May
Corrigan, 1979. Paul C., in *New Society*, 5 July
Courtier, 1960. S.H.C., *Gently Dust the Corpse*
  1964. *A Corpse Won't Sing*
Cove-Smith, 1970. C.C-S., *Pilotage on Inland Waterways*
Cowan, 1982. Rex C., in *Illus. London News*, July
  1937. W.L. Gibson C., *Loud Report* (u/t)
Coward, 1923. Noël C., *There's Life in the Old Girl Yet* (u/t)
  1928. *Shop Girls* (u/t)
  1930. *Private Lives*
  1933. *Design for Living*
  1939. *The Step Aside*
  1952. *Relative Values*
  1960. *Pomp and Circumstance*
Cowdy, 1965. Anthony C., in *Sunday Times* col. supp., 24 Oct.
Cown. See Cowan, W.
Cracknell, 1979– Rev. Kenneth R.C., of the British Council of Churches
Craig, 1935. C.W. Thurlow C., *Paraguayan Interlude*
  1976. David C., *Faith, Hope and Death*
Crapp, 1944. B.C., *Shark Hunters* (u/t)
Crawford, 1966. Iain C., *Scare the Gentle Citizen*
Crawley, 1971, William C., *Is It Genuine?*
Creasey, 1949. John C., *Battle for Inspector West*, 1948
Crick, 1980. Bernard C., *George Orwell*; and in *Weekly Guardian* 8 June
Crisp, 1976. N.J.C., *The Gotland Deal*
  1978. *The London Deal*
Crispin, 1950. Edmund C., *Frequent Hearses*
  1977. *Glimpses of the Moon*
Critchley, 1981. Julian C., in *Illus. London News*, Sep.
Crofts, 1931. Freeman W.C., *Mystery in the Channel*
  1942. *Fear Comes to Chalfont*
Crookston, 1967. Peter C., *Villain*
Cropper, 1987. Martin C., of London
Cross, 1984– Morgan C., of BBC Radio Leicester
'Crosstalk', 1984– 'Phone-in' programme on BBC Radio Leicester, 10 Oct.; 13 Feb. '85
Crozier, 1937. Brig.-Gen. Frank C., *The Men I Killed*
Crump, 1960. B.J.C., *A Good Keen Man* (u/t)
Cuddon, 1967. J.A.C., *The Bride of Battersea*
Culotta, 1960. Nino C., *Cop This Lot*
  1963. *Gone Fishin'*
Cunliffe, 1965. L.J.C., *Having It Away*
Curtis, 1937. James C., *You're in the Racket Too*
  1938. *They Drive by Night*
  1939. *What Immortal Hand*
  (See *Gilt Kid*.)
Cusack, 1951. Dymphna C., *Come in Spinner* and *Say No to Death*
  1953. *Southern Steel*
Cutland, 1985. Linda C., *Kick Heroin*
Dadomo, 1979. Giovannia D., in *Time Out*, 7 Dec.
Dalton, 1951. Dr H.W.D.
  1728. James D., *Narrative of a Street Robber*

Daniells, 1978– Red D., in *Brit. Jnl. of Photography*; and privately
Dark, 1959. Eleanor D., *Lantana Lane*
Dartmoor, 1932. Anon., *Dartmoor from Within*
Darwin, Bernard D., *Golf Between Two Wars*, 1944
Davenport, 1982. Hugo D., in *Observer*, 12 Sep.
Davidson, 1978. Lionel D., *The Chelsea Murders*
Davies, 1982. Staff Nurse Catrin D., quoted in *Guardian*, 20 July
  1970. Hunter D., *The Rise and Fall of Jake Sullivan*
  1967– John D., civil engineer
  1961. John D., *See Naples and Die*
  1908. W.H.D., *Autobiography of a Super-Tramp*
  1909. *Beggars*
  1933. in *New Statesman*, 18 Mar.
Davis, 1939. Val D., *Gentlemen of the Broad Arrows*
  1941. *Phenomena in Crime*
Davison, 1942. R.M.D., or Robert M. Dawson
Dawson, 1913. A.H.D., *Dict. of Slang*
  1946. John D'Arcy D., *European Victory*, 1945
DCCU A Dict. of Contemporary and Colloquial Usage, 1971
DCpp E.P., *A Dict. of Catch Phrases*, 2nd ed., 1985
Dean, 1985. Peter D., quoted in *You*, 17 Feb.
De Bunsen, 1960. Mary de B., *Mount up with Wings*
Deeping, 1925. Warwick D., *Sorrell and Son*
  1927. *Kitty*
  1944. *Mr Gurney and Mr Slade*
Deere, 1959. Gp Capt Alan D., *Nine Lives*
Deghy, 1957. Guy D., 'Leave Me the Noshers', in *Observer*, 3 Nov.
Dehn, 1983– Conrad D., of Inner Temple
Deighton, 1968. Len D., *Only When I Larf*
  1970. *Bomber*
  1971. *Declaration of War*
  1975. *Yesterday's Spy*
Delafield, 1933. E.M.D., *Gay Life*
  1935. in *Time & Tide*, 21 Sep.
De Lisle, 1982. Tim de L., 'Rock'n'Stroll', in *Observer*, 1 Aug.
Dempsey, 1975. H.D., Bob Edwards (u/t)
Dempster, 1979. Nigel D., in *Telegraph Sunday Mag.*, 11 Mar.; Ibid., 22 Apr '84
Denby, 1911. Jay D., *Letters of a Shanghai Griffin*, 1910
Dennis, 1916. C.J.D., *The Moods of Ginger Mick*
  1934. Geoffrey D.
  1961, Nigel D., 'Fancy Lingo', in *Sunday Telegraph*, 9 July
Denselow, 1983. Robin D., in *Listener*, 28 July
Dent, 1917. Olive D., *A V.A.D. in France*
De Selincourt, 1924. Hugh de S., *The Cricket Match*
Devanney, 1926. Jean D., *Lenore Divine* and *The Butcher Shop*
  1927. *Old Savage*, etc.
  1928. *Dawn Beloved*
  1929. *Riven*
  1930. *Bushman Burke*
  1938. *Paradise Flow*
  1944. *By Tropic Sea and Jungle*
  1951. *Travels in North Queensland*
Devine, 1968. Dominic D., *The Sleeping Tiger*
Diamant, 1982. John D., in *Time Out*, 3 Dec.
Dick, 1965. William D., *A Bunch of Ratbags*
Dickens, 1945. Monica D., *Thursday Afternoons*
  1946. *The Happy Prisoner*
  1964. in *Women's Own*, 31 Oct.
Dickey, 1986. Bob D., of Alberta, via R. Leech
Dickinson, 1975. Peter D., *The Lively Dead*
  1979. *One Foot in the Grave*
  1982. *The Seventh Raven*
Dickson, 1937. Grierson D., *Design for Treason*
Dilke-Wing, 1975– Mrs Hazel D.-W., of Mountsorrel, Leics.

Diment, 1967. A.D., *The Dolly Dolly Spy*
  1968. *The Bang Bang Birds*
Dixey, 1934. H.G.D.
Doncaster, 1947. Patrick D., *A Sigh for a Drum-Beat*
Don't Cry, 1983. R. McGowan & J. Hands, *Don't Cry for Me, Sergeant-Major*
Doone, 1926. Jice D., *Timely Tips for New Australians*
Douglas, 1947. Keith D., *Alamein to Zem Zem*, 1946
Dovkants, 1988. Keith D., 'Confessions of a Mugger', in London *Evening Standard Mag.*, Feb.
Dowell, 1975. J.D., *Look-Off Bear*, 1974
Downer *or* Downing, 1919. W.H.D., *Digger Dialects* (u/t)
Drage, 1954. Charles D., *Two-Gun Cohen*
  1963. *General of Fortune*
Drake-Brockman, 1937. See Brockman
Draper, 1970. Alfred D., *Swansong for a Rare Bird*
Driberg, 1946. Tom D., in *Reynolds News*, 10 Mar. and 28 Apr.
Driscoll, 1973. Peter D., *The Wilby Conspiracy*
Drummond, 1967. Charles D., *Death at the Furlong Post*
  1969. *The Odds on Death*
  1963. John Dorman D., *Gap of Danger*
  1969. June D., *The People in the Glass House*
Ducange Anglicus *The Vulgar Tongue*, 1857
Duffy, 1978. Maureen D., *Housespy*
Du Maurier, 1938. Daphne du M., *Rebecca*
Duncan, 1979. Andrew D., in *Telegraph Sunday Mag.*, 23 Dec.
  1960. Jane D., *My Friend Monica*
Dunford, 1979. Douglas D., of Southampton
  1984. Dunford 2: a 2nd list of motorcycling terms
Dunn, 1984. F.D., *Speck in the Sky* (u/t)
  1946. James D., in *World's Press News*, 21 Nov.
  1981. Peter D., in *Sunday Times Mag.*, 18 Oct.
Durack, 1955. Mary D., *Keep Him My Country*
Dures, 1982. George D., *Who's Talking About an Arrest*, play broadcast on BBC Radio 4, 14 Aug.
Dyer, 1978. G.D., in *Screen Education*, Summer
Dyke. Roy D., Newfoundland, via R. Leech, ca. 1985
Dyker, 1934. Bob D., *Get Your Man*
Dyson, 1901. Edward D., *The Gold Stealers*
  1906. *Fact'ry 'Ands* (u/t)
Eagar, 1922. W. McG. E., in *Contemporary Review*
East, 1989. Miss Paddy E., of Loughborough, Leics.
EDD. Joseph Wright, *The English Dialect Dict.*, 1898–1905
Edmonds, 1986. Frances E., *Another Bloody Tour*
Edwards, 1961. Courtney E., in *Sunday Telegraph*, 24 Sep.
  1974. Gillian E., *Hobgoblin and Sweet Puck*
  1939. Lt Cdr K.E., *We Dive at Dawn*
  1983. M.E. & R. Holdstock, *Realms of Fantasy*, 1984
Egan, 1832. Pierce E., *Book of Sports*
Eliot, 1935. T.S.E., in *Time & Tide*, 5 Jan.
Elliott, C.M.L.E., OBE, West Australia
  1988. Christopher E., in *Sunday Telegraph*, 14 Feb.
Elting, 1984. Col. John R.E., USA ret'd, et al., *A Dict. of Soldier Talk*
Emanuel. Sgt G.E., RAF
Emerson, 1893. P.H.E., *Signor Lippo* and *On English Lagoons*
Enemy. *The Enemy Within: the Pit Villages and the Miners' Strike, 1984–5*, ed. R. Samuel, *et al.*
England, 1963. Barry E., *Figures in a Landscape*, 1968
English, 1955. L.E.F.E., *Historic Newfoundland*
E.P., 1942. Eric Partridge, in *New Statesman*, 1 Aug. and 19 Sep.
  1948. See P-G-R.
Epton, 1960. Nina E., *Love and the English*
Estevé-Coll, 1985. Mrs Elizabeth E.-C., of the Victoria & Albert Museum
Evans, 1923. Caradoc E., *Taffy*
  1970. George E.E., *Where Beards Wag All*
  1975. *The Days that We Have Seen*
  1979. Hilary E., *The Oldest Profession*

  1983. John E., in *Weekend*, 16 Mar.
  1983. Peter E., *Englishman's Daughter*
Everly, 1966. Record sleeve of the Everly Brothers, 'Two Yanks in Britain'
Ewart, 1921. Wilfred E., *The Way of Revelation*
F. & G. Fraser & Gibbons, *Soldier and Sailor Words and Phrases*, 1925
F. & H. Farmer & Henley, *Slang and its Analogues*, 7 vols, 1890–1904
Fabian, 1954. Robert F., *London After Dark*
Fairborn, 1976. See Freeborn
Fane, 1936. Michael F., *Racecourse Swindlers*
Farley. Sgt R.F., RAF
Farmer, 1945. Rhodes F., *Shanghai Harvest*
Farrell, 1963. A.E.F., *The Vengeance*
Fassnidge, 1981. H.C.L.F., letter in The *Times*, 20 Mar.
Fearon, 1984– Eric F., of London
Fehrenbach, 1966. T.R.F., *The Gnomes of Zurich*
Fellowes, 1934. Gordon F., *They took Me for a Ride*
Fellowship, 1984. News mag. of the Fellowship of Old Time Cyclists, by courtesy of the editor, Derek Roberts
Felton, 1975. Felton & Fowler, *Most Unusual* (u/t)
Ferdinand the Bull, 1936. Munro Leaf, illus. R. Lawson (u/t)
Ferguson, 1942. Rachel F., *Evenfield*
  1939. Ruby F., in the *Queen's Book of the Red Cross* (u/t)
  1936. W.B.M.F., *Somewhere off Borneo*
  1939. *London Lamb*
Field, 1963. Xenia F., *Under Lock and Key*
Fielding, 1932. A.F., *Death of John Tait*
Fighter Pilot, 1981. Colin Strong & Duff Hart-Davis
Finn-Smith, 1942. Grenfell F.-S.
Fitt, 1949. Mary F., *The Banquet Ceases*
Fitter, 1966. R.S.F., *Britain's Wild Life*
Fitzgerald, 1958. Nigel F., *The Student Body*
Fleming, 1964. Ian F., *You Only Live Twice*
  1968. Joan F., *Kill and Cure*
  1957. Peter F., *Invasion, 1940*
Flynt, 1900. Josiah F. & F. Walton, *The Powers that Prey*
  1901. *The World of Graft*
Forbes, 1942. Athol F. & H.R. Allen, *Ten Fighter Boys* (66 Sqn, RAF, 1939–41)
Fordyce, 1956. L.F., letter in *Observer*, 23 Sep.
Forester, 1943. C.S.F., *The Ship*
  1975. Tom F., in *New Society*, 7 Aug.
Forster, 1970. W.F., ed., *Pit-Talk*
Forsyth, 1976. Bruce F., in *Telegraph Sunday Mag.*, 24 Jan.
  1974. Frederick F., *The Dogs of War*
Forwood, 1962. George F., in Hong Kong
Foster, 1968. Brian F., *The Changing English Language*
  1931. D.A.F., *The Ways of the Navy*
Foster-Carter, 1982. Aidan F.-C., in *New Society*, 14 Oct.
Fox, 1982. Robert F., in *Listener*, 1 and 8 July
Francis, 1962. Dick F., *Dead Cert*
  1964. *Nerve*
  1968. *Forfeit*
  1970. *Rat Race*
Frankau, 1920. Gilbert F., *Peter Jackson, Cigar Merchant*
Franklin, 1951. Charles F., *Escape to Death*
  1931. Miles F., *Old Blastus of Bandicoot*
  1956. *Laughter, not for a Cage*
  1982. Norman F., Chairman of RKP
Franklyn, 1934. Julian F., *This Gutter Life*
  2. *Dict. of Rhyming Slang*, 2nd ed., 1961. (See also *Rhyming*)
Fraser, 1986– David F., of Connaught 69, Nottingham
Frater, 1977. Alexander F., in *Telegraph Sunday Mag.*, 9 Oct.
Freeborn, 1976. Bruce F., *Good Luck, Mister Cain*
French, 1977. F.J.F., of Tonbridge
Frome, 1932. David F., *The By-Pass Murder*
  1933. *Mr Simpson Finds a Body*

1934. *That's Your Man, Inspector*
1935. *The Body in the Turl*
Fry, 1950. Christopher F., in *Sunday Times*, 28 May
Fryer, 1967. Peter F., 'A Toz of "Zowie" ', in *Observer* col. supp., 3 Dec.
Fullarton, 1943. J.H.F., *Troop Target*, 1944
Fussell, 1975. Paul F., *The Great War and Modern Memory*
Gadd, 1949. Col. A.L.G.
Gaffin, 1984. Rachel G., letter in *New Society*, 3 May
Gagg, 1972. J.G., *The Canaller's Bedside Book*, 1973
Galsworthy, 1924. John G., *The White Monkey*
1926. *The Silver Spoon*
Gamble, 1977. Tom G., of Shepshed, Leics.
Gander, 1949. L.M.G., *After These Many Quests*
'Ganpat', 1933. *Out of Evil*
Gape, 1936. W.A.G., *Half a Million Tramps*
Garden, 1949. John G., *All on a Summer's Day*
Gardner, 1932. Arthur G., *Tinker's Kitchen*
1972. Charles G., 'Spot the Trog', in *Telegraph Sunday Mag.*, June
1978– David B.G., of Preston
1967. John G., *Madrigal*
1976. *To Run a Little Faster*
1831. John L.G., *Sketch-Book* (II, 68)
Garstin, 1984. D.J.G., letter in *Listener*, 1 Mar.
Garve, 1968. Andrew G., *The Long Short Cut*
Gash, 1978. Jonathan G., *Gold from Gemini*
1983. *Sleepers of Erin*
Gaye, 1959. Phoebe F.G., *Treen and the Wild Horses*
Gaylor, 1977. John G., *Military Badge Collecting*
Gell, 1979– Eric G., of Loughborough College of Art
George, 1986. M.F.A.G., letter in *Guardian*, 27 Aug.
1911. W.L.G., *A Bed of Roses*
1914. *The Making of an Englishman*
1924. *The Triumph of Gallio*
Gibbs, 1934. Anthony G., *London Symphony*
1909. Phillip G., *The Street of Adventure*
Gibson, 1946. Wg Cdr Guy G., VC, *Enemy Coast Ahead*
Gielgud, 1949. Val G., *Fall of a Sparrow*
1969. *A Necessary End*
Gifford, 1970. Colin G., *Each a Glimpse*
Gilbert, 1949. Michael G., *The Doors Open*
1952. *Death in Captivity*
Gilderdale, 1958. Michael G., 'A Glossary of Our Times', in *News Chronicle*, 22 May and (2) 23 May
Giles, 1900. Herbert G., *A Glossary on Subjects Connected with the Far East*
Gilt Kid. James Curtis (see above), 1936
Gladwin, 1973. D.D.G., *Canals of Britain*
Glascock, 1829. W.N.G., *Sailors and Saints*
Glassop, 1949. Lawson G., *Lucky Palmer* (u/t); see also *Rats*
Gloag, 1962. John G., *Unlawful Justice*
Glover, 1985. B.G., *Camra Dict. of Beer*
Glynn, 1972. S/Ldr Ron G., RAF ret'd., of Stamford
1978. Mne Vaughan G., RM
Godbolt, 1985– Jim G., of Ronnie Scott's Jazz Club
Godfrey, 1949. Denis G., *A Tale That Is Told*
1979. Peter G., in *New Society*, 19 July
Gofton, 1983. L.G., in *New Society*, 17 Nov., and 22 Nov. '84
Goodenough, 1900. Rev. George G., *The Handy Man Afloat*
Goodsall, 1925. R.A.G., *Palestine Memories*
Gordon, 1978. Mrs Harry G., of Markfield, Leics.
1939. Sir Home G., *The Background of Cricket*
1950. Jane G., *Married to Charles*
1953. Richard G., *Doctor at Sea*
Gorell, 1935. *Red Lilac* (u/t)
Gosling, 1959. John G., *The Ghost Squad*
1960. J.G. & D. Warner, *Shame of a City*
1982. Ray G., in *Listener*, 22 July
Gosse, 1934. Philip G., *Memoirs of a Camp-Follower*

Graham, 1980. Capt. E.T.G., RN, letter in the *Times*, 25 July
1919. Stephen G., *A Private in the Guards*
1967. Winston G., *The Walking Stick*
Graham-Ranger, 1981. Clive G.-R., in *Sunday Times Mag.*, 9 Aug.
Granville, 1949. Wilfred G., *Sea Slang of C.20th*
Graves, 1943. Charles G., *Seven Pilots*
Gray, 1969. Arthur G.
1946. Berkeley G., *Mr Ball of Fire*
Gray, 1964. Dulcie G., *No Quarter for a Star*
1952. Felicity G., *Ballet for Beginners*
Green, 1976. Gerald G., *The Hostage Heart*
1974. Jonathon G., *Newspeak: a Dictionary of Jargon*; and Green (2), *A Dict. of Contemporary Slang*
Greenberg, 1986. Susannah G., in *Guardian*, 4 Dec.
Greene, 1938. Graham G., *Brighton Rock*
1978. *The Human Factor*
Greenwood, 1965. Dinah G.
1884. J.G., *The Little Ragamuffins*
1938. Walter G., *Only Mugs Work*
Grey, 1976. Anthony G., *The Bulgarian Exclusive*
1977. 'Flying a Jaguar', in *Illus. London News*, Jan.
Grierson, 1924. Francis D.G., *The Limping Man*
1931. *Mystery in Red*
1934. *Murder at Lancaster Gate*
Griffin, 1985. C.G., *Typical Girls?*
Griffiths, 1970. Harold G.
Grindley, 1977. Ian G., Governor of Pentridge Gaol, Melbourne
Grinsted, 1943. Roger Grinstead, *Some Talk of Alexander*
1946. *They Dug a Hole*
Groupie. Jenny Fabian & J. Byrne, 1968
'Gunbuster', 1941. *Battledress*
H. John Camden Hotten, *The Slang Dictionary*, 1859, 1860, etc.
H.W., 1942. H.W., *What's the Gen?*
Haacke, 1987. Miss Kathleen H., MBE, of London
Hackforth-Jones, 1943. Gilbert H.–J., *Submarine Alone*
1948. *Sixteen Bells*, 1946
1970. *Security Risk*
Haden-Guest, 1972. Anthony H.-G., in *Telegraph mag.*, 17 Dec.
Haggard, 1958. William H., *The Telemann Touch*
1964. *The Antagonists*
Haines, 1962– Edwin H., of Sedbergh and Buenos Aires
Hall, 1966. Adam H., *The Ninth Directive*
1975. *The Mandarin Cipher*
1976. *The Kobra Manifesto*
Hall, 1974. Angus H., *On the Run*
1950. John H., in *Daily Mail*, 24 May
1978. Stuart H., *Policing the Crisis*
1959. Willis H., *The Long and the Short and the Tall*
Halliday, 1970. Dorothy H., *Dolly and the Cookie Bird*, 1971
Hamblin, 1988. Prof. T.J.H., of Bournemouth
Hamer. Prof. Douglas H.
Hamilton, 1946. Bruce H., *Pro*
1959. Gerard H., *Summer Glare*
1965. Ian H., *The Persecutor*
1967. *The Man with the Brown Paper Face*
Handley, 1988. Maurice H., of Loughborough
Hanley, 1946. Gerald H., *Monsoon Victory*
Hannabuss, 1976. C.S.H., in *Signal*, May
Harbinson, 1961. Robert H., *Up Spake the Cabin-Boy*
Hardcastle, 1913. Marjory H., *Halfpenny Alley*
Harding, 1981. Mike H., in *Weekly Guardian*, 22 Mar.
Hardman, 1977. Mr & Mrs David H.
Hardy, 1985. Bert H., *My Life*
1979. Clive H., of Derby
1967. Frank H., *Billy Borker Yarns Again* (u/t)

Hargrave, 1925. Basil H., *Origins and Meanings of Popular Phrases . . .* , rev. ed.

Hargreaves, 1954. Elizabeth H., *A Handful of Silver*

Harling, 1946. Robert H., *The Steep Atlantick Stream*

Harney, 1947. W.E.H., *North of 23°*

Harré, 1979. H., Morgan, & O'Neill, *Nicknames*

Harris, 1958. A.M.H., *The Tall Man*

1985. Max H., in *Weekend Australian*, 13 Apr.

1979. Roy H., quoting a bus-driver, in *Guardian*, 10 Dec.

Harrison, 1962– Maj. Christopher H., Int Corps

1978. Matthew H., Loughborough Univ.

1934. Michael H., *Weep for Lycidas*

1935. *Spring in Tartarus*

1936. *All the Trees Were Green*

1939. *Vernal Equinox* and *What Are We Waiting for?*

1943. *Reported Safe Arrival*

1947. Privately

1983. Paul H., quoting the 'Hoxton Creeper', in *New Society*, 18 Aug.

Hart, 1959. Sir Basil H. Liddell H., *The Tanks*, vol. 2

1970. *History of the First World War*

Hart-Davis, 1972. Duff H.-D., *Spider in the Morning*

Hartog, 1966. Jan De H., *The Captain*

Harvey, 1936. Richmond H., *Prison from Within*, 1937

Harwood, 1927. H.M.H., *Transit of Venus*

Hastings, 1947. Lewis H., *Dragons Are Extra*

Hatton, 1930. S.F.H., *The Yarn of a Yeoman*

Hawke, 1979. Christopher H., *For Campaign Service*

Hawkins, 1987– Richard H., of Dublin

Hay, 1907. Ian H., *Pip*

1914. *The Lighter Side of School Life*

1917. *Carrying On*

1934. *David and Destiny* and *The Housemaster*, 1936

Hayes, 1970. Douglas H., *The War of '39*

1971. *Tomorrow the Apricots*

1972. *A Player's Hide*

1973. *Quite a Good Address*

Hayward, 1978. Brig. Pat H., of Norwich

Heading, 1945. Wg Cdr F.J.H.H.

Heart. Colin Evans, *The Heart of Standing*, 1962

Hebden, 1973. Mark H., *Dark Side of the Island*

1974. *A Pride of Dolphins*

1983. *Pel and the Bombers*

Hebdige, 1979. Dick H., *Subcultures*

Hedges, 1982. H. & Beynon, *Born to Work*

Heffernan, 1984. Sandra H., of Loughborough College of Art and NZ

Heller, 1987. Richard H., in the *Times*, 10 June

Hemming, 1979– Anthony H., of Hendon

Hemmingway, 1944. Kenneth Hemingway, *Wings Over Burma*

Henderson, 1967. Hamish H., poem 'Alamein, October 23, 1942', rev. ed., in *Sunday Telegraph*, 22 Oct.

1945. J.H.H., *Inglorious Gunner* (u/t)

1968. Laurence H., *With Intent*

Hennessy, 1979. Val. H., in *Guardian*, 21 Sep.

1982. in *New Society*, 23 Dec.

Henry, 1942. Jack H., *Detective-Inspector Henry's Famous Cases*

1960. Margaret H., *Unlucky Dip*

Herbert, 1935. A.P.H., *Holy Deadlock*

1936. *Mild and Bitter*

1969. Nicholas H., in the *Times Saturday Review*, 14 June

1939. Xavier H., *Capricornia*

1961. *Soldiers' Women*, 1962

Herd, 1957. Richard H., in the (London) *Evening News*, 12 Nov.

Hesling, 1954. Bernard H., *Little and Orphan*

1963. *The Dinkumization* . . . ., 1964

Heyer, 1933. Georgette H., *Why Shoot a Butler?*

1935. *Death in the Stocks*

1936. *Behold, Here's Poison*

1938. *A Blunt Instrument*

Hibbert, 1983. Tom H., *Rockspeak* [a fascinating and valuable compilation]

Hichens, 1933. R.H., *The Paradine Case*

Hickey, 1945. William H., in *Daily Express*, 26 Nov.

Hildick, 1976. Wallace H., *Bracknell's Law*

Hill, 1974. See Hall, 1974

1973. Archie H., *A Cage of Shadows*

1951. Ernestine H., *The Territory*

1978. Peter H., *The Enthusiast*

1978. Reginald H., *A Pinch of Snuff*

Hillaby, 1950. John H., privately

1968. *Journey through Britain*

Hillary, 1942. Richard H., *The Last Enemy*

Hillman, 1974. David H., of Geneva

Hinde, 1945. Fg Off Robert H., RAF

Hindley, 1876. C.H., ed., *The Life and Adventures of a Cheap Jack*, by Walter Green

Hinton, 1958. Norman D.H., 'Language of Jazz Musicians', in *Jnl. American Dialect Soc.*, Nov.

Hitchens, 1980. Christopher H., in *New Statesman*, 18 Jan.

Hjort, 1967. Ronald H.

Hobhouse, 1939. Christopher H., Oxford

Hobson, 1959. Hank H., *Mission House Murder*

Hoby, 1946. Alan H., in the *People*, 7 Apr.

Hodge, 1938. Herbert H., *It's Draughty in Front*

1939. *Cab, Sir?*

Hodson, 1945. J.L.H., *The Sea and the Land*

Hoggart, 1982. Simon H., in *Observer*, 15 Aug.

1983. In *New Society*, 10 Mar.

1984. 'The Wallies of Westminster', in *Guardian*, 19 Aug.

Hollaway, 1986. Dr S.H., quoted in *Sunday Express Mag.*, 24 Aug.

Holland, 1968. Julián H.

Hollander, 1975. Xaviera H., *The Best Part of a Man*

Holliday, 1984. David H., Letter in *Listener*, 1 Mar.

1963. John H., 'Bingo!', in *Sunday Telegraph*, 18 Aug.

Hollis, 1983. Henry H. and Dan Wooding, *Farewell, Leicester Square*

Holloway, 1967. David H., in *Daily Telegraph*, 23 Feb.

Holm, 1981. Ian H., interviewed by S. Morley, in *Guardian*, 11 July

Holman, 1944. Gordon H., *Stand By to Beach*

Holmes, 1869. Oliver W.H., *Guardian Angel*, 1867

Holt, 1936. A.H.H., *Phrase Origins*

1932. Gavin H., *Drums Beat at Midnight*

1934. *Trafalgar Square*

1936. *The Murder Train*

1950. *No Curtain for Cora*

1978. Peter F.H., letter in *Guardian*

Home Office. *Glossary of Terms and Slang Common in Penal Establishments*, issued July 1978 by the Board of Visitors Section, P4 Div.

Horler, 1938. Sydney H., *The Dark Journey*

Horn, 1976. Maurice H., ed. *The World Encyc. of Comics*

Hornadge, 1980. Bill H., *The Australian Slanguage*

Horne, 1923. Eric H., *What the Butler Winked at*

Horsley, 1877. J.W.H., *Jottings from Jail*

1912. *I Remember*, 1911

Houghton, 1946. Claude H., *Transformation Scene*

Hoult, 1933. Norah H., *Youth Can't Be Served*

Howard, 1978. Philip H., in *U and Non-U Revisited*, ed. R. Buckle

1984. Privately

1987. In the *Times*, 5 Feb., and Ibid., 10 May 1988

1934. W.S.H., *You're Telling Me!* (u/t)

Hudson, 1979. Kenneth H., quoted in *Radio Times*, 27 Oct.

Huelin, 1973. Frank H., *Keep Moving*

Hughes, 1984. Joyce H., of Hathern, Leics.

1980. Patricia H., on BBC Radio 3, 26 Aug.

Huie, 1960. W.B.H., *The Americanization of Emily*

Hulme, 1984. Liz H., in *Illus. London News*, July

Hume, 1935. David H.: 5 of his books pub'd in 1935
  1942. *Requiem for Rogues*
  1944. *Toast to a Corpse*
Humphries, 1980. Barry H., in *Sunday Times Mag.*, 22 June
  1982. *A Nice Night's Entertainment*
Hungerford, 1952. T.A.G.H., *The Ridge and the River* (u/t)
  1953. *Riverslake*
Hunt, 1974. William R.H., *North of 53°: Alaska-Yukon Mining, 1870–1914*
Hunter, 1955. Alan H., *Gently Does It*
  1956. *Gently by the Shore*
  1957. *G. down the Stream*
  1960. *G. with the Painters*
  1962. *G. Where the Roads Go*
  1963. *G. Floating*
  1964. *G. Sahib*
  1969. *G. Coloured*
  1971. *G. at a Gallop*
  1974. *G. in Trees*
  1977. *G. Instrumental*
  1981. *Fields of Heather*
  1984. *The Unhung Man*
Hurt, 1984. Rudy H., of Shepshed, Leics.
Huston, 1975– Mr & Mrs Colin H., of Thurmaston, Leics.
Hutchinson, 1908. A.S.M.H., *Once Aboard the Lugger*
  1932. Ray C.H., *The Answering Glory*
Hyder, 1934. Alan H., *Black-Girl, White-Lady*
Iddiwah. See Korean War, in Appx.
Idriess, 1931. Ion L.I., *Lasseter's Last Ride*
  1932. *Flynn of the Inland* and *The Desert Column* and *Men of the Jungle*
  1934. *The Yellow Joss*
  1935. *Man Tracks*
Iles, 1932. Francis I., *Before the Fact*
Ince, 1932. Richard I., *Shadow-Show*
Inglis, 1977. Brian I., in *Spectator*, 15 Jan.
Ingram, 1933. George I., *Stir*
  1935. *Cockney Cavalcade*
  1936. *The Muffled Man*
Irving, 1946. John J., *Royal Navalese*
Irwin, 1975– Chris L.I., of Loughborough and Ravenstonedale
Isherwood, 1933. Christopher I., in *New Country*
Jack, 1979. Ian J., in *Sunday Times Mag.*, 13 Aug. and Ibid., 13 Mar. 1983
Jackson, 1945. C.H. Ward-J., *Airman's Songbook*
  1931. Gibbard J., *Twenty Six Sea Yarns*
  1946. Stanley J., *An Indiscreet Guide to Soho*
Jacobs, 1937. Naomi Jacob, *The Lenient God*
Jaffe, 1959. Jacob J.
James, 1980. Clive J., in *Observer* supp., 10 Feb.
  1986. Ibid., 6 Apr.
  1929. Norah J., *Sleeveless Errand*
  1963. P.D.J., *A Mind to Murder*
Janssen, 1978– Paul J., of Liège, Belgium
Jarram, 1978. A.P.J., *Brush Aircraft Production at Loughborough*
Jarvis, 1925. See Jervis
Jay, 1968. Simon J., *Sleepers Can Kill*
Jefferies, 1958. Ian J., *Thirteen Days*
  1962. See Jeffries
Jefferson, 1983. S.G.J., letter in the *Times*, 18 July
Jeffries, 1962. Roderic J., *Exhibit No. 13*
  1968. *A Traitor's Crime*
Jenkins, 1959. Geoffrey J., *A Twist of Sand*
  1966. *Hunter Killer*
Jenkinson, 1975– Phillip J., reviewing films to be shown on TV, in *Radio Times*
Jennings, 1926. Frank J., *In London's Shadows*
  1932. *Tramping with Tramps*
  1959. Paul J., 'Knight Driving'., collected in *Idly Oddly*

Jerome, 1886. Jerome K.J., *The Idle Thoughts of an Idle Fellow*
Jervis, 1925. Eustace J., *Twenty Five Years in Six Prisons*
Johns, 1933. W.E.J., in *Popular Flying*, May, quoted in Ellis & Williams, *By Jove !, Biggles*, 1985
Johnson, 1978. Brian J., *Secret War*
  1973. B.S.J. ed., *All Bull : the National Servicemen*
  1987. Colleen J. & J. Lloyd, 'The Sun says knickers', in *New Statesman*, 13 Mar.
  1980. Diane J., 'Doctor Talk', in *The State of the Language*
  1980. Frank J., in *Now !*, 16 May
  1987. R.W.J., in *London Review of Books*, 3 Sept.
  1976. Roderick J.
Johnston, 1971. George J., *A Cartload of Clay*
Jones, 1974. A.G.E.J.
  1926. Ada E.J., *In Darkest London*
  1931. *Women of the Underworld*
  1937. David J., *In Parenthesis*
Jones, 1970. See Hackforth-Jones
  1971. Jack J., ed., *Rhyming Cockney Slang*
  1953. Mervyn J., *The New Town*
  1957– Peter J.E.J., Int Corps
Jope-Slade, 1934. Christine J.-S., in *The Passing Show*, 24 Feb.
Jordan, 1935. Humfrey J., *Roundabout*
  1937. *Sea Way*
  1946. *Landfall then Departure*
Jorre, 1967. John de St J., in *Observer* supp., 11 June
Joseph, 1934. George J., in *Everyman*, 5 Jan.
Joyce, 1916. James J., *A Portrait of the Artist*
  1922. *Ulysses*
  1910. P.W.J., *English as We Speak it in Ireland*
Juniper, 1933. William J., *The True Drunkard's Delight*
Karlin, 1986. D.K., letter in *Guardian*, 14 Jan.
Karlsson, 1966. E.K., *Pully-Haul*
Kavanagh, 1980. D.K., *Duffy*
  1987. *Going to the Dogs*
Kay. See Jay
Keable, 1924. Robert K., *Recompence*
Keating, 1981. Frank K., in *Guardian*, 4 Jan.
  1978. H.R.F.K., in the *Times*, 16 Nov.
Kee, 1947. Robert K., *A Crowd Is Not Company*
Keeley, 1985. M.P.K., book review in *The Educationalist*, Spring
Keene, 1980. K. & Haynes, *Spyship*
Keeping, 1975. Charles K., *Cockney Ding-Dong* (u/t)
Kelly, 1955. Vince K., *The Shadow*
  1958. *The Greedy Ones*
Kendall, 1980. Ena K., in *Observer*, 13 July
  1984. Nickie K., of NZ and Loughborough
Keneally, 1964. T.K., *The Place at Whitton*
Kennaway, 1967. James K., *Some Gorgeous Accident*
Kennedy, 1902. Bart K., *A Sailor Tramp*
  1981. Paul K., in *New Society*, 29 Jan.
Kenyon, 1977. Michael K., *The Rapist*
  1978. *Deep Pocket*
Kersh, 1938. Gerald K., *Night and the City*
  1939. *I Got References*
  1941. *They Die with Their Boots Clean*
  1942. *The Nine Lives of Bill Nelson*
  1944. *Faces in a Dusty Picture*
  1946. *Clean, Bright and Slightly Oiled*
  1956. *Fowler's End*, 1958
Kerslake, 1985. Harry K., of Loughborough
Kettle, 1980. Martin K., in *New Society*, 7 Feb.
Keverne, 1926. Richard K., *Carteret's Cure*
  1928. *The Havering Plot*
  1930. *The Man in the Red Hat*
  1933. *Menace*
Keyes, 1966. Thorn K., *All Night Stand*
Keynes, 1981. Sir Geoffrey K., *Gates of Memory*

Kilduff, 1985. Gp Capt J.E.K., RAF ret'd, letter in the *Times*, 6 Sept.

Kimmins, 1960. Anthony K., *Lugs O'Leary*

Kipling, 1910. Rudyard K., *The Horse Marines* and *My Son's Wife*
1925. Letter to Rider Haggard, in Morton Cohen's ed. of the letters, 1965

Kitchin, 1949. C.H.B.K., *The Cornish Fox*

Klickman, 1919. Flora K., *The Lure of the Pen*

Knight, 1984– Andrew K., of Portsmouth
1936. Laura K., *Oil Paint and Grease Paint*

Knock, 1932. Sidney K., *'Clear Lower Deck'*

Knox, 1933. Ronald K., *The Body in the Silo*
1934. *Still Dead*
1937. *Double Cross Purposes*

Krzymowski, 1978. Dr George A.K., of New Orleans

L.A., 1948– Laurie Atkinson, of London

L.L.G. *The London Literary Gazette*

La Bern, 1947. Arthur L.B., *Night Darkens the Street*
1950. *Pennygreen Street*

Laffin, 1969. John L., *Jack Tar*

Laing, 1934. Allan M.L.

Lamb. Cdr Charles L., DSO DSC

Lambert, 1975. Derek L., *Touch the Lion's Paw*
1951. Elizabeth L., *The Sleeping House Party*
1968. Royston L. & S. Millham, *The Hothouse Society*

Lancaster, 1904. G.B.L., *Sons o' Men*

Landy, 1971. Eugene E.L., *The Underground Dictionary*

Lane, 1938. Margaret L., *Edgar Wallace*

Langford, 1941. Mrs C.H.L.

Langmaid, 1935. Margaret L., *The Yes Man*

Lardner, 1949. John L., in *Newsweek*, 21 Nov.
1951. *Strong Cigars and Lovely Women*

Larkin, 1980. Philip L., in *Guardian*, 23 Mar.

Laski, 1944. Marghanita L., *Love on the Super-Tax*

Lawrence, 1961. John L., in *Sunday Telegraph*, 13 Aug.
1955. T.E.L., *The Mint* (written ca. 1922)

Lawson, 1932. Jack L.

Leach, 1933. Charles E.L., *On Top of the Underworld*
1981. in *Now !*, 10 Apr.

Le Carré, 1968. John Le C., *A Small Town in Germany*
1977. *The Honourable Schoolboy*
1983. Quoted in *Observer Mag.*, 6 Mar.

Leech, 1972. Frances L., Canada
1974– Robin L., of Edmonton, Alberta

Leechman, 1959– Douglas L., Canada

Lees-Milne, 1975. James L.-M., *Ancestral Voices*

Leeson, 1934. B.L., *Lost London*

Leitch, 1973. David L., *God Stand up for Bastards*
1979. In *Sunday Times Mag.*, 9 Dec.
1965. Maurice L., *The Liberty Lad*

Lejeune, 1967. Anthony L., in *Telegraph* col. supp., 10 Mar.

Lester, 1937. Sidney L., *Vardi the Palarey*

Lewis, 1936. Cecil A.L., *Sagittarius Rising*
1943. *Pathfinders*
1945. Hilda L., *Strange Story*
1816. J.H.L., *Lectures on the Art of Writing*, 7th ed. (u/t)
1978. John L., *Rowland Hilder : Painter and Illustrator*
1976. Roy L., *A Distant Banner* and *Witness My Death*
1922. Sinclair L., *Babbitt*

Lillington, 1936. C. Lillingston, *His Patients Died*

Lincoln, 1933. Maurice L., *Oh! Definitely*

Lindall, 1959. Edward L., *No Place to Hide*

Lindrum, 1935. Horace L., in *Lyons' Sports Sheet*, 23 Dec.

Lindsay, 1933. Norman L., *'Saturdee'*

Lindsey, 1980. R.L., *The Falcon and the Snowman*

Linklater, 1934. Eric L., *Magnus Merriman*

Lipsey, 1979. David L., in *New Society*, 22 Nov.

Little, 1958. Lawrence L., *The Dear Boys*

Littmoden, 1936– Mrs Jane L., née Beale, of Mark Cross, E. Sussex

Llewellyn, 1943. Richard L., *None but the Lonely Heart*
1968. *The End of the Rug*, 1969

Lobley, –1937. J. Hodgson L., RBA

Loder, 1937. Vernon L., *Choose Your Weapon*

Lodge, 1936. Graveney L., in London *Evening News*, 9 Dec.

London, 1903. Jack L., *The People of the Abyss*

Londres, 1928. Albert L., *The Road to Buenos Aires*

Longmate, 1971. Norman L., *How We Lived Then*

Lorac, 1935. E.C.R.L., *Death of an Author*
1942. *Death Before Dinner*, 1948
1943. *Death Came Softly*

Lorimer, 1939. E.O.L., *Language Hunting in the Karakoram*

Lowell, 1929. Joan L., *Child of the Deep*

Lower, 1945. L.W.L., *Lennie Lower's Sidesplitters* (u/t)

Lowndes, 1937. Mrs Belloc L., *The House by the Sea*

Luard, 1933. L.L., *All Hands*
1935. *Conquering Seas*
1967. Nicholas L., *The Warm and Golden War*

Luckham, 1982. Claire L., *Trafford Tanzi*, prod. 1982

Ludditt, 1974. F.L., *Campfire Sketches* (u/t)

Ludlow, 1938. Capt R. Marleigh-L., in *News of the World*, 28 Aug.

Lunn, 1913. Arnold L., *The Harrovians*
1919. *Loose Ends*

Lustig, 1984. R.L., in *Observer*, 1 Apr.

Lyall, 1961. Gavin L., in *Sunday Times*, 13 Aug.
1981. S.L., in *New Society*, 26 Nov.

Lyell. T.L., *Slang, Phrase and Idiom in Colloquial English*, 1931

Lynch, 1987. Tony L., letter in *Listener*, 4 June

Lynd, 1945. Robert L., *Things One Hears*

Lyndon, 1980. Neil L., in *Sunday Times Mag.*, 2 Mar.

Lyons, 1902. A. Neil L., *Hookey*
1909. *Sixpenny Pieces*
1912. *Clara*
1914. *Simple Simon*
1916. *Moby Lane*
1908. Albert E.L., *Arthur's*
1986. Dr Mary L., of Dublin

M.T. See GRAFTERS, in Appx.

MacArthur. Alex M. & H.K. Long, *No Mean City*, 1935

Macarthney, 1936. Wilfred Macartney, *Walls Have Mouths*

Macaulay, 1937. Rose M., *I Would Be Private*

McCabe, 1937. Cameron McC., *The Face on the Cutting Room Floor*
1972. Peter M. & R. Schonfeld, *Apple to the Core*

McClure, 1977. James M., *The Sunday Hangman*
1980. *Spike Island*

McConnell, 1967. J.D.R.M., *Eton : How It Works*

Macdonald, 1907. Alexander M., *In the Land of Pearl and Gold*
1930. Phillip M., *The Rynox Mystery*
1932. *Rope to Spare*
1933. *R.I.P.*
1933. Archie G.M., *England, Their England*

McFee, 1930. William M., *Sailors of Fortune*, 1929
1930. *North of Suez*
1935. *The Beachcomber*
1947. *In the First Watch*

MacGill, 1920. Patrick M., *Fear!*

MacGowan, 1963. Cathy M., in *TV Times*, 29 Nov.

MacInnes, 1952. Colin M., *June in Her Spring*

McIntosh, 1963. Wg Cdr R.H.M., DFC AFC, *All-Weather Mac*

Mackail, 1921. Denis M., *Romance to the Rescue*
1924. *The 'Majestic' Mystery*
1925. *Greenery Street*
1930. *The Young Livingstones*
1934. *'Summer Leaves'*, and in *Strand Magazine*, Apr.
1937. *Jacinth*

McKenna, 1970. Frank M., *A Glossary of Railwaymen's Talk*
  1980. *The Railway Workers, 1840–1970*
  1937. Stephen M., *Last Confession*
MacKenzie, 1913. Compton M., *Sinister Street*
  1933. *Water on the Brain*
  1956. *Thin Ice*
  1967. *Octave Six*
  1976. Donald M., *Raven in Flight*
  1980. *Raven and the Paperhangers*
  1936. Kenneth M., *Living Rough*
  1932. T.B.G.M., in *Fortnightly Review*, Mar.
Mackie, 1946. Prof. W.S.M., in *Cape Argus*, 4 July
Maclaren, 1929. Hamish M., *The Private Opinions of a British Blue-Jacket*
Maclaren-Ross, 1954. J.M.–R., 'Bop', in *Laugh with Me!*
McLaughlin, 1976. Terence M., in *Daily Telegraph Mag.*, 6 Feb.
MacLean, 1977. Alistair M., *Seawitch*
McLean, 1954. Donald M., *Nature's Second Sun*
McLeod, 1988. Lt Col M.M., RM, quoted in *Radio Times*, 5 Mar.
McMurdo, 1937. Norman T.M.
McNab, 1938. R.G.C.M., in *The Press*, Christchurch, NZ, 2 Apr.
McNeil. Glossary to *The Chocolate Frog* and *The Old Familiar Juice*, two plays pub'd in Sydney and London, 1973
McPheely, 1976. David & Robin M., of Loughborough
McShane, 1960. Mark M., *The Straight and the Crooked*
  1961. *The Passing of Evil*
McVicar, 1974. John M., *McVicar by Himself*
  1979. In *Listener*, 8 Mar.
  1982. In *New Statesman*, 20 Aug.
  1987. In *Sunday Telegraph*, 22 Mar.
Mainprice, 1975. J.L.M., of British Museum Dept. of Printed Books
Mais, 1918. S.P.B.M., *A Schoolmaster's Diary*
  1948. *Caper Sauce*
Malin, 1979– Ex-Petty Officer John M., of Canterbury
Mallalieu, 1944. J.P.W.M., *Very Ordinary Seaman*
Manchon, J.M., *Le Slang*, 1923.
'Mandrake', 1975. In *Sunday Telegraph*, 23 Nov.
Mann, 1984– David M., banker, of Basel
  1972. H.P.M.
  1937. Leonard M., *A Murder in Sydney*
  1939. *Mountain Flat*
  1942. *The Go-Getter*
Manning, 1930. Frederick M., *Her Privates We*
March, 1934. Norah M., in London *Evening Standard*, 28 May
March-Phillipps, 1938. G.M.–P., *Ace High*
Marks, 1977. Alfred M., in *Next Move*
Marling, 1984. Susan M., in *Listener*, 16 Aug.
Marlowe, 1937. Dave M., *Coming, Sir!*
Marples. Morris M., *Public School Slang*, 1940; and Marples, 2, *University Slang*, 1950
Marquand, 1943. John P.M., *So Little Time* (u/t)
Marryat, 1829. F.M., *Frank Mildmay*
Mars, 1984. Mars & Nicod, *The World of Waiters*
Marsh, 1986– Colin M., of Kirby Muxloe, Leics.
  1935. Ngaio M., *Enter a Murderer*
  1938. *Vintage Murder*, 1937
  1938. *Death in a White Tie*
  1939. *Overture to Death*
  1940. *Death at the Bar*
  1945. *Died in the Wool*
  1949. *Swing, Brother, Swing*
  1967. *Death at the Dolphin*
  1968. *Clutch of Constables*
  1976. Peter M., in *New Society*, 13 May
Marshall, 1946. Alan M., *These Are My People*
  1934. Bruce M., *Prayer for the Living*
  1919. J. Vance M., *The World of the Living Dead*
  1962. Jock M. & R. Drysdale, *Journey among Men*

1933. Matt M., *Tramp Royal on the Toby*
  1976. William M., *Hatchet Man*
Martin, 1937. A.A.M.
  1975. Ian K.M., *Regan*
  1984– Michael & Joanna (née Williamson, q.v.), of Wingerworth, Derbys.
  1983. Peter M., in *You*, 13 Nov.
  1984. 'The Third Sex', in *You*, 16 Sept.
  1957. Shane M., *Twelve Girls in the Garden*
Masefield, 1919. John M., *Reynard the Fox*
  1933. *The Conway*
Mason, 1928. A.E.W.M., *The Prisoner in the Opal*
  1930. *The Dean's Elbow*
  1933. *The Sapphire*
  1924. Michael M., *The Arctic Forests*
  1974. Philip M., *A Matter of Honour*
  1978. *A Shaft of Sunlight*
Massingham, 1936. Hugh M., *I Took off My Tie*
Masterman, 1933. J.C.M., *An Oxford Tragedy*
  1935. *Fate Cannot Harm Me*
Mather, 1968. Berkeley M., *The Springers*
  1977. *The Memsahib*
Mathews. Mitford M.M., *Dict. of Americanisms*, 1946
Matthew, 1983. Christopher M., in *Observer Mag.*, 6 Feb.
Matthews, 1938. William M., *Cockney Past and Present*
Maugham, 1897. W. Somerset M., *Liza of Lambeth*
  1921. *The Circle* (u/t)
  1924. *The Lion's Skin* (u/t)
  1930. *Cakes and Ale*
  1937. *Theatre*
  1941. *Up at the Villa*
May, 1985. Derwent M., in D.J. Enright, ed., *Fair of Speech*
Mays, 1969. Spike M., *Fall Out the Officers* and *Reuben's Corner*
  1971. *No More Soldiering for Me*
  1975. *The Band Rats*
Mead, 1967. Brig. P.M., *Soldiers in the Air*
Measures, 1985. Mrs Kate M.
Mellar. See Millar, R.
Melly, 1979. George M., in *London Magazine*, Feb.
Menkes, 1967. Suzy M., 'Switched on Jargon', in the *Times*, 3 July
Merrick, 1911. Leonard M., *The Position of Peggy Harper*
Merrow-Smith, 1962. L.W. M.–S. & J. Harris, *Prison Screw*
Merry. Richard M.
Meynell, 1937. Laurence M., *The House in the Hills*
  1950. *The Lady on Platform One*
Michie, 1940. M. & Graebner, *Their Finest Hour*
  1941. *The Lights of Freedom*
Middlebrook, 1976. M.M., *Convoy*
Millar, 1980. Gavin M., in *Listener*, 18 Dec.
  1966. Robert M., *The New Classes*
Miller, 1934. Henry M., *Tropic of Cancer*
  1935. Ian M., *School Tie*
Milne, 1926. A.A.M., *Winnie-the-Pooh*
  1928. *The House at Pooh Corner*
  1931. *Two People*
  1920. D.G.M., *Wings of Wrath*, [?1920] (u/t)
  1902. James M., *Epistles of Atkins*
Mindel, 1975– J.B. Yehouda M., of Kfar Tabor, Israel
Mitchell, 1930. Gladys M., *The Longer Bodies*
  1945. *The Rising of the Moon*
Mitford, 1960. Jessica M., *Hons and Rebels*
  1960. Nancy M., *The Pursuit of Love*
  1960. *Don't Tell Alfred*
  1969. W.M., *Lovely She Goes*
Moe, 1959– Col. Albert F.M., USMC ret'd
Mogridge, 1950. Stephen M., *Talking Shop*
Moncrieff, 1932. G. Scott M., *Café Bar*
Money, 1871. C.L.M., *Knocking About in New Zealand* (u/t)
Monks, 1940. Noel M., *Squadrons Up*

Monsarrat, 1951. Nicholas M., *The Cruel Sea*
   1960. *The Nylon Pirates*
Montague, 1910. C.E.M., *A Hind Let Loose*
   1923. *Fiery Particles*
Moody, 1984. Susan M., *Penny Dreadful*
   1985. *Penny Post*
Moore, 1960. Brian M., *The Luck of Ginger Coffey*
   1983. Gordon M., *Prelude to Battle* (Brit. Army, 1941–44)
   1942. John M., in *Observer*, 4 Oct.
   1965. Patrick M., *Survey of the Moon*
Moorehead, 1944. Alan M., *African Trilogy*
Moorhouse, 1980. Gerald M., on BBC Radio 4, 19 June
Moran, 1959. J.W.G.M., *Spearhead in Malaya*
Morgan, 1945. Guy M., *Only Ghosts Can Live*
   1977. Harry M., 'Britain's Inland Oil Search', in *Illus. London News*, May
Morice, 1977. Anne M., *Murder in Mimicry*
Morlock. See Mortlock
Morris, 1977. Desmond M., *Man-Watching*
   1965. James M., *Oxford*
Morrisby, 1958. Edwin M.
Morrison, 1896. A.M., *A Child of the Jago*
   1976. Allan M., in the *Times*, 10 Mar.
Morse-Boycott, 1931. Desmond M.–B., *We Do See Life*
Mortimer, 1985. James M., in *Spectator*, 17 Aug.
   1971. John M., *Come as You Are*
   1937. Raymond M., in *Listener*, 10 Mar.
Mortlock, 1965. J.F.M., *Experiences of a Convict*
Moseley, 1935. Sydney A.M., *The Truth about a Journalist*
   1952. *'God Help America!'*
Mosley, 1982. Nicholas M., *Rules of the Game*
Moss, 1969. Stirling M., in a TV programme, 30 May
Mottram, 1934. R.H.M., *Bumphrey's*
Moyes, 1964. Philip J.R.M., *Bomber Squadrons of the RAF*
   1967. Patricia M., *Murder Fantastical*
Moynahan, 1969. Brian M., in *Sunday Times*, 11 May
Muggeridge, 1940. Malcolm M., *The Thirties*
Muir, 1917. Ward M., *Observations of an Orderly*
Mulgan, 1934. Alan M., *Spur of the Morning*
   1939. John M., *Man Alone*
Munroe, 1918. Jack M., *Mopping Up!* (u/t)
Murray, 1933. D.L.M., *The English Family Robinson*
   1965. Fiona M., *Invitation to Danger*
   1977. K.M.E.M., *Caught in the Web of Words*
Musings. 'Guns, Q.F.C. & Phyl Theeluker', *Middle Watch Musings*, 4th ed., ca.1912
Muvver. Robert Barltrop & J. Wolveridge, *The Muvver Tongue*, 1980
Naipaul, 1976. Shiva N., 'London's No-Man's-Land', in *Illus. London News*, June
Nally, 1979. Michael N., 'Hunt the Ripper', in *New Society*, 14 June
Nash, 1985. Walter N., *The Language of Humour*
Naughton, 1966. Bill N., *One Small Boy*, 1967
   1970. *Alfie Darling*
Neil, 1932. A.F.N., *Forty Years of Man-Hunting*
Nelson, 1980. Keith N., in *Amateur Photographer*, 26 July
New DAS. The New Dictionary of American Slang, ed. Robert L. Chapman, 1987
Newman, 1970. G.F.N., *Sir, You Bastard*
   1977. *The Guvnor*
Newport, 1982. Rod N., of Loughborough
Niland, 1955. D'Arcy N., *The Shiralee*
   1958. *Call Me When the Cross Turns Over*
   1959. *The Big Smoke*
Niven, 1927. Frederick N., *Wild Honey*
Nixon, 1975. Graham N., in *Lore & Language*, Jan.
'No 747' Francis Wylde Carew, *'No 747': Being the Autobiography of a Gypsy*, 1891
Noble, 1945. Vernon N., journalist

Norman, 1958. Frank N., *Bang to Rights*
   1959. 'Delinquently Yours' in *Lilliput*, Feb., and in *Encounter*
Norris, 1933. Kathleen N., in *The Passing Show*, 6 Dec.
North, 1960. Eric N., *Nobody Stops Me*
Nowell, 1983. Robert N., letter in *Guardian*, 17 Dec.
Nuttall, 1979. Jeff N., *King Twist*, 1978
Oaksey, 1977. John O., in *Sunday Telegraph*, 22 May, and privately
Oasis. From Oasis to Italy, 1984, an anthology of WW2 writings
O'Casey, 1924. Sean O'C., *Juno and the Paycock*
O'Connor, 1962. Elizabeth O'Connor, *Steak for Breakfast*, 1958
O'Donnell, 1978. Peter O'D., *Dragon's Claw*
O'Flaherty, 1925. Liam O'F., *The Informer*
O'Grady, 1965. John O'G., *Aussie English*
   1972. *It's Your Shout, Mate!*
O'Hanlon, 1984. Redmond O'H., *Into the Heart of Borneo*
Oldham, 1978– Eric O., of Loughborough
Oliver, 1937. H.J.O., in *Bull. of the Aus. Eng. Ass.*, July
   1948. E.J.O., *Not Long to Wait*
Ommanney, 1939. F.D.O., *North Cape*
O'Neill, 1959. Desmond O'N., *Life Has No Price*
   1988. J.T.O'N., letter in *Telegraph Sunday Mag.*, 21 Feb.
Onions, 1939. Dr C.T.O., of the *OED*
   1923. Oliver O., *Peace in Our Time*
   1930. *The Open Secret*
Opie, 1959. Iona & Peter O., *The Lore and Language of Schoolchildren*
Oppenheim, 1934. E. Phillips O., *The Bank Manager*
   1935. *The Strange Boarders of Palace Crescent*
Orme, 1979. Steve O., in *Loughborough Trader*, 15 Aug.
Ortzen, 1938. Len O., *Down Donkey Row*
Orwell, 1933. George O., *Down and Out in Paris and London*
   1935. *Burmese Days*
Osborne, 1978. John O., programme note to *A Night with Dame Edna*, London
O'Shaughnessy, 1979. Patrick O'S., privately; see also *M.T.*
Osmond, 1948. Humphry O., formerly Surgeon Lt., RN
Pahl, 1978. R.E.P., in *New Society*, 2 Nov.
Page, 1973. Martin P., *Kiss Me Goodnight, Sergeant Major*
   1976. *For Gawdsake Don't Take Me*
Pain, 1902. Barry P., *The One Before*
   1912. *Stories in Grey*, 1911
Paine, 1978. Terence P., JP, of Loughborough
Palmer, 1974. Raymond., in *Sunday Times*, 25 Aug.
   1923. Vance P. (as 'Rann Daly'), *The Enchanted Island*
   1924. (Id.), *The Outpost*
   1930. *The Passage* (u/t; but BMC has *The Palmer*)
   1931. *Separate Lives*
   1932. *Daybreak*
   1934. *The Swayne Family*
   1937. *Legend for Sanderson*
   1948. *Golconda*
   1955. *Let the Birds Fly*
   1957. *Seedtime*
Park, 1948. Ruth P., *The Harp in the South*
   1950. *Poor Man's Orange*
   1952. *The Witch's Thorn*
   1953. *A Power of Roses*
   1955. *Pink Flannel*
   1961. *The Good-Looking Women*
Parker, 1986. John S.F.P., of Univ. of York
   1965. Tony P., *The Plough Boy*
   1985. *Soldier, Soldier*
Parkinson, 1969. G.P., in *New Society*, 22 May
   1982. 'Tailgunner' P., Ibid., 19 Aug.
Parkman, 1946. Sydney P., *Captain Bowker*
Parr, 1964. Eric P., *Grafters All*

Parry, 1982. Gareth P., in *Guardian*, 2 & 3 July, on the Falklands War

Parry-Jones, 1981. Elwyn P.–J., in *Listener*, 19 Feb.

Parsons, 1970– Cdr., C.P. RN ret'd

Partridge, 1945. Eric P., *A Dict. of RAF Slang*
   1979– Mike P., of Shepshed, Leics.

Paterson, 1911. Sir Alexander P., *Across the Bridges*
   1975– Rev. David P., of Loughborough

Patten, 1979. Bob P., via John Smith

Patterson, 1984. B.H.P., *A Dict. of Dockyard Language* [Portsmouth]
   1885. Brunlees P., *Life in the Ranks* (u/t)

Paul, 1982. Barbara P., *Your Eyelids Are Growing Heavy*

Pawle, 1976. Gerald P., *The Secret War*, 1972

P.B. Paul Beale, editor of this Dictionary

Peachment, 1983. Chris P., in *Time Out*, 11 Mar.

Pearce, 1982. Edward P., in *Daily Telegraph*, 8 July

Pearl, 1967. Cyril P., *Morrison of Peking*

Pearsall, 1957– Ronald & Corrie P., of Newbiggin-on-Lune, and their sons Michael and Ian
   1978. Mr and Mrs R.F.P., of Lanscove, Devon

Pearson, 1932. Scott P., *To the Streets and Back*

Pearson-Rogers, 1981. Gp Capt H.W.P.–R., letter in the *Times*, 28 Feb.

Peebles, 1959. Ian P., in *Sunday Times*, 31 May

Peniakoff, 1950. Vladimir P., *Popski's Private Army*

Penton, 1936. Brian P., *Inheritors*

Peppitt, 1970– Lt Cdr Frank P., RNR

Petch, 1945– Albert E.P., of Bournemouth

P–G–R. Eric Partridge, W. Granville, F. Roberts, *A Dict. of Forces' Slang, 1939–1945*, 1948

Phantom. Robert Prest, *F4 Phantom : A Pilot's Story*, 1979

Phelan, 1938. Jim P., *Lifer*
   1939. *In the Can*
   1940. *Jail Journey*
   1941. *Murder by Numbers*
   1943. *Letters from the Big House*
   1953. *The Underworld*
   1954. *Tramp at Anchor*
   1957. *Fetters for Twenty*

Phelps, 1946. Anthony P., *I Couldn't Care Less*

Phillips, 1976. G. & P.P., letter in *Radio Times*, 21 Feb.
   1931. I.P., *Dict. of Rhyming Slang* (see also 'P.P.')
   1979. Pearson P., in *Telegraph Sunday Mag.*, 19 Aug.

Phythian, 1986. Brian A.P., *A Concise Dict. of Eng. Slang*, 3rd ed.

Pilkington, 1980. Margaret P., of Kirby Lonsdale
   1985. Sue P., in *Guardian*, 11 Dec., quoting from the long-running TV serial *Coronation Street*

Pinder, 1975– Mrs Patricia P., of Loughborough

Piper, 1974. Steven P., *The North Ships*

Pitman, 1967. Robert P., in *Daily Express*, 2 Mar.

Playfair, 1977– Sir Edward P., of London SW6

Poole, 1986– Andew P., of Braunstone, Leics.
   1935. Michael P., *Revolution at Redways*

Pope, 1915. Jessie P., *Simple Rhymes*, 1916

Postgate, 1940. Raymond P., *Verdict of Twelve*

Pound, 1964. Reginald P., *The Lost Generation*
   1976. *A.P. Herbert*

Powell, 1969. Margaret P., *Climbing the Stairs*
   1970. *The Treasure Upstairs*

Power, 1976. Garry P., letter in *Daily Mirror*, 12 Nov.

Powis, 1977. DAC David P., OBE QPM, *The Signs of Crime*

P.P., 1932. (pseud., i.e. I. Phillips, q.v.), *Rhyming Slang*

Prebble, 1947. John P., *The Edge of Darkness*

Price, 1982. Anthony P., *The Old 'Vengeful'*
   1957. R.G.G.P., *A History of Punch*

Prichard, 1920. Katharine S.P., *Coonardo*, 1929
   1921. *The Black Opal*
   1926. *Working Bullocks*
   1929. *Tornado* (u/t ; ?= *Coonardo*)
   1930. *Haxby's Circus* and *Kiss on the Lips*

   1937. *Intimate Strangers*
   1948. *Golden Miles*
   1950. *Winged Seeds*

Priest, 1983. Christopher P., in *New Statesman*, 18 Mar.

Priestley, 1959– Prof. F.E.L.P., of Canada
   1929. J.B.P., *The Good Companions*
   1936. *They Walk in the City*
   1945. *Three Men in New Suits*

Prior, 1937. Charles P., *So I Wrote It*

Proctor, 1958. Maurice Procter, *Man in Ambush*
   1966. *His Weight in Gold*

Progl, 1964. Zoe P., *Woman of the Underworld*

Pudney, 1945. Sqn Ldr John P., RAF

Pugh, 1895. Edwin P., *A Street in Suburbia*
   1898. *Tony Drum*
   1912. *Harry the Cockney*
   1914. *The Cockney at Home*

Punshon, 1933. E.R.P., *Information Received*

Purser, 1981. Philip P., in *Illus. London News*, Feb.

Pylypiac, 1984. Mrs Mabel P., of Loughborough

Quayle, 1945. Anthony Q., *Eight Hours from England*

Quill, 1936. 'Christopher Q.', in *Books of Today . . .* , Oct.

Quin, 1980. E.G.Q., Assoc. Prof. of Celtic Languages, Univ. of Dublin

Quinn, 1899. T.Q., *The Well Sinkers* (u/t)

Raab, 1978– Mrs Camilla R., of Hampstead Garden Suburb

Railway. Harvey Sheppard, *Dict. of Railway Slang*, 1964; and 2nd ed., 1966

Radcliffe, 1934. Garnett R., in *Passing Show*, 27 Jan.

Ralph, 1901. Julian R., *War's Brighter Side*

Raper. T.C.H.R.

Raphaely, 1987. Vanessa R., in *Sunday Express Mag.*, 12 July

Rathbone, 1968. Julian R., *Hand Out*

Rats, 1944. Lawson Glassop (q.v.), *We Were the Rats*

Rattigan, 1943. Terence R., *While the Sun Shines*
   1950. *Who Is Sylvia?*
   1957. In intro. to Mander & Mitchenson, *Theatrical Companion to Coward*
   1958. *Variations on a Theme*

Rawnsley, 1986. J.R., in *Reform* (the URC mag.), Apr.

Raybold, 1987. John R., of Northants

Raymond, 1929. Ernest R., *A Family That Was*
   1930. *The Jesting Army*
   1931. *Mary Leith*

R.C., 1966– Robert Claiborne, author, of New York and Cape Cod

Read, 1978. Piers Paul R., 'The Great Train Robbers', in *Observer* supp., 16 Apr.

Reed, 1979– Mrs Gwynneth, and Phillip R., of Quorn, Leics

Rees, 1979. Nigel R., *Graffiti Lives, OK*
   1980. *Very Interesting . . . but Stupid*
   1987. *Why Do We Say . . . ?*

Reid, 1970. Adrian R., *Confessions of a Hitch-Hiker*
   1980. Maggie R., in *Observer* supp., 13 July

Rendell, 1980. Douglas R., in *Brit. Jnl. Photography*, 13 June

Reyburn, 1962. Wallace R., in *Sunday Times Mag.*, 8 July

Reynolds, 1979. Peter R.

Rhodes, 1942. Sgt-Pilot F.R., RAF

Richards, 1933. Frank R., *Old Soldiers Never Die*
   1983. Mrs Malvene R., of Warrington and Loughborough

Ridge, 1895. W. Pett R., *Minor Dialogues*

Rigg, 1984. Diana R., quoted in *You*, 20 May

Riley, 1916. William R., *Netherleigh*
   1933. *Old Obbut*

Rimmer, 1986. D.R., in *Listener*, 18 Dec.

Ritchie. Charles R., *The Siren Years : Diaries 1937–45* (u/t)

Rivett, 1946. Rohan D.R., *Behind Bamboo*

Roberts, 1934. C.E. Bechofer R., in *Passing Show*, 16 June
  1974– Derek R., of Mitcham, Surrey; see also *Fellowship*
  1951. Senior Comm. Bo'sun L.D.M.R., MBE, RN
  1938. Frank R., in *The Cottonian*, Autumn; see also P–G–R
  1933. R. Ellis R.
  1971. Robert R., *A Ragged Schooling*
  1976. *The Classic Slum*
  1982. Yvonne R., in *New Society*, 5 Aug.
Robertson, 1985. Rear-Adm. A.R., RAN ret'd, in *The Australian*, 22 Apr.
  1973. Heather R., *Grass Roots*
Robey, 1922. George R., *An Honest Living*
Robinson, 1946. Ray R., *Between Wickets*
Robson, 1980. David R., in *Sunday Times*, 23 Mar.
Robyns, 1949. Gwen R., 'Holiday City', in London *Evening News*, 16 Feb.
Rodd, 1981. Alan R., in *Observer* supp., 31 May
Rodgers, 1972. Bruce R., *The Queens' Vernacular: a Gay Lexicon*
  1983. Christine R., letter in *Guardian*, 10 Mar.
Roeves, 1958. A.T.R., letter in *Manchester Guardian*, 11 Sept.
Rogers, 1980. Bob R., of Loughborough College of Art
  1967. Ronald K.R.
Rogerson, 1984. K.H.R., letter in *Guardian*, 18 Sept.
  1933. Sidney R., *Twelve Days*
Rolling, 1971. R.R., 'I Was a Hell-Driver', in *Guardian Weekly*, 27 Mar.
Rolo, 1944. C.J.R., *Wingate's Raiders*
Rolph, 1954. 'C.H. Rolph', in *News Chronicle*, 15 Mar.
  1980. *London Particulars*
  1987. *Further Particulars*
Rolt, 1944. L.T.C.R., *Narrow Boat*
Ronan, 1954. Tom R., *Vision Splendid*
  1956. *Moleskin Midas*
  1961. *Only a Short Walk*
  1966. *Once There Was a Bagman*
Rook, 1899. Clarence R., *The Hooligan Nights*
Ross, 1956. Prof. A.S.C.R., in *Sunday Times*, 15 July
  1978. In *U and Non-U Revisited*, ed. R. Buckle
  1977. Frank R., *Dead Runner*
  1978. *Sleeping Dogs*
Rosten, 1967. Leo R., *The Joys of Yiddish*, 1968
Roulstone, 1986– Mrs Sue R., of Sutton Bonington, S. Notts.
'Round the Horne' BBC Radio comedy series with Kenneth Horne, Kenneth Williams, et al. See also Took.
Rowbotham, 1987– Colin R., of London
Rowles, 1948. G.E.R., *The 'Line' Is on*
R.S., 1950– Ramsey Spencer
Ruck, 1935. Berta R., *A Story-Teller Tells the Truth*
  1940. *Pennies from Heaven*
Rudd, 1911. Steele R., *The Dashwoods* (u/t)
Rusbridger, 1985. A.R., in *Guardian*, 22 Oct.
Russell 1934. Archer R., *A Tramp Royal in Wild Australia*
  1936. *Gone Nomad*
  1979. Audrey R., MVO, in *Sunday Telegraph Mag.*, 26 Aug.
Ryan, 1935. Desmond R., *St Eustace and the Albatross*
Ryott, 1985. Mrs R., of Hathern, Leics.
Safire, 1968. William S., *The New Language of Politics*
Samuel, 1981. Ralphael S., ed., *East End Underworld*
Sanders, 1967. Peter S., in *Sunday Times Mag.*, 10 Sept.; and privately, 1965
Sandilands, 1984. J.S., in *You*, 4 Mar.
Sangster, 1968. Jimmy S., *Foreign Exchange*
'Sapper', 1924. *The Third Round*
Sargeson, 1940. Frank S., *A Man and His Wife* (u/t)
Sarl, 1938. Arthur J.S., *Gamblers of the Turf*
Sassoon, 1928. Siegfried S., *Memoirs of a Fox-Hunting Man*
  1930. *Memoirs of an Infantry Officer*
Sauce, 1978. A Miscellany, ed. by Ronnie Barker
Sava, 1945. George S., *A Land Fit for Heroes*
Sayers, 1927. Dorothy L.S., *Unnatural Death*
  1928. *The Unpleasantness at the Bellona Club*

  1930. With R. Eustace, *The Documents in the Case*
  1931. *The Five Red Herrings*
  1932. *Have His Carcase*
  1933. *Murder Must Advertise*
  1936. In *Six Against the Yard* (u/t)
  1937. *Busman's Honeymoon*
  1984– Keith S., of Yorkshire and W. Aus.
Scaduto, 1974. Anthony S., *Mick Jagger*
Schofield, 1984. Jack S., in *Guardian*, 16 Feb.
Schroeder, 1976. A.S., *Shaking It Rough*
Schwitzer, 1985. J.S., in *Hornsey Historical Bull.*, No 26
Scott, 1979. Jack S.S., *A Clutch of Vipers*
  1982. *The Local Lads*
  1946. James M.S., *The Other Side of the Moon*
  1977. Jeffrey S., 'Wheelman for the Cleaners', in *John Creasey's Crime Collection*
  1984. Patrice S., of Loughborough Library School
  1971. Paul S., *The Towers of Silence*
  1977. *Staying On*
  1905. R.F.S., *The Voyage of the 'Discovery'*
  1825. Sir Walter S., *St Ronan's Well*, 1824
  1934. Will S., in *The Humorist*, 10 Feb.
  1977. See Stone
'Sea Lion', 1946. *The Phantom Fleet*
Seabrook, 1967. Jeremy S., *The Unprivileged*
  1977. 'The Costa Geriatrica', in *New Society*, 21 Apr.
  1986– Mike S., of King's Langley and Sheringham
  1987. *Coppers*
Seago, 1933. Edward S., *Circus Company*
  1934. *Sons of Sawdust*
Seccombe, 1936. Lionel S., commentating on the Foord–Neusel fight, 18 Nov.
Sells, 1923. Dorothy S., *The British Trade Boards System*
Seton, 1935. Graham S., *Pelican Row*
Seymour, 1966. John S., *Voyage into England*
Shame, 1960. John Gosling & D. Warner, *The Shame of a City*
Shanks, 1933. Edward S., *The Enchanted Village*
Sharpe, 1938. F.D.S., *Sharpe of the Flying Squad*
  1976. Tom S., *Wilt*
Sharpley, 1964. Anne S., 'London's Hidden Problems' series, in *Evening Standard*, 20–24 July
Shaw, 1932. Frank Hubert S., *Atlantic Murder*
  1960– Frank S., of Liverpool
Sheard, 1976– Rev. Ernest S., of Birstall, Leics.
Shepard, 1934. Graham S., *Tea-Tray in the Sky*
Sherwood, 1961. John S., *The Half-Hunter*
Short, 1978. David S.
Shute, 1944. Nevil S., *Pastoral*
  1951. *Round the Bend*
  1954. *Slide Rule*
Sigal, 1959. Clancy S., 'The Punchers' Night Out', in *Observer*, 1 Mar.
Sillitoe, 1959. Alan S., *The Loneliness of the Long-Distance Runner*
Silverlight, 1983– John S., His 'Words' column in *Observer*; and privately
Simmonds, 1980– Posy S., her cartoons in *Guardian*; and privately
Sims, 1880. George S., *How the Poor Live*
Sinclair, 1959. Andrew S., *The Breaking of Bumbo*
  1977. In *The World of the Public School*, ed. G.M. Fraser
Singer, 1980. Angela S., in *Guardian*, 5 May
Skeats, 1963. Thomas S., barrow-boy, reported in *Daily Mail*, 24 July
Slang. E. Partridge, *Slang Today and Yesterday*, r.e. 1935
Slater, 1950– Jack S., of Oldham
Slatter (u/t)
Smith, 1985. C.S., in *Observer*, 26 May
  1979– John B.S., of Bath Univ., in *Somerset Notes & Queries*, 1979; and privately
  1982. Donald J.S., *Horse on the Cut*
  1987. Douglas S., of Southampton, via E.W. Bishop

1969. P.A.S., *Folklore of the Australian Railwaymen* (u/t)
1981. Sam S., in *Illus. London News*, May
1977. Wilbur S., *A Sparrow Falls*
1978. *Hungry as the Sea*
Smollett, 1771. Tobias S., *The Expedition of Humphry Clinker*
Sorenson, 1925. E.S.S., *Murty Brown* (u/t)
Spain, 1949. Nancy S., *Poison for Teacher*
Sparling, 1946. R.A.S., ?in *Answers*, 16 Feb.
Spenser, 1933. James S., *Limey*
1934. *Limey Breaks in*
1948. *The Awkward Marine*
Springer, 1923. Norman S., *The Blood Ship*
Spy II. C.E. Westmacott, *The English Spy*, vol. 2, 1826
St Clair, 1976. Leonard St C., *A Fortune in Death*
St John-Brooks, 1981. Caroline St J.–B., in *New Society*, 5 Mar.
St Pierre, 1970. P. St P., *Chillicotin Holiday* (u/t)
Stalker, 1988. John S., *Stalker*
Stamper, 1931. J.S., *Less than the Dust*
Stanners, 1937. H.H.S., *At the Tenth Clue*
Stead, 1934. Christina S., *Seven Poor Men of Sydney*
Steevens, 1896. G.W.S., *With Kitchener to Khartum*, 1898
Stephens, 1912. James S., *The Crock of Gold*
Stevens, 1942. Kate S., *Typewriting Self-Taught*
Stewart, 1961. J.I.M.S., *The Man Who Won the Pools*
Stilwell Papers, 1949. Theodore H. White, ed., 1st UK edn
Stimoon, 1946. G.S., *Thousand Things*, (u/t)
Stivens, 1946. Dal S., *The Courtship of Uncle Henry*
1951. *Jimmy Brockett*
1953. *The Gambling Ghost*
1958. *The Scholarly Mouse*
Stockholm, 1899. John S., *Navy and Army Illustrated*, Dec.
Stokes, 1950. Sewell S., *Court Circular*
Stone, 1977. Zachary S., *Paper Money*
Story, 1959. Jack Trevor S., *Mix Me a Person*
Stott, 1981. Catherine S., in *Sunday Telegraph*, 23 Aug.
Straker, 1968. J.F.S., *Sin and Johnny Inch*
Strange, 1930. J.D.S., *The Price of Victory*
Stuart, 1971. Alex S., *The Bikers*
1942. Warren S., *The Sword and the Net*
Summers, 1966. D.L.S., *HMS 'Ganges'*
Sutcliff, 1962– Rosemary S., OBE, of Walberton, W. Sx
Sutherland, 1941. Dr J.W.S.
Sutton, 1946. Barry S., *Jungle Pilot*
Swanton, 1946. E.W.S., in *Daily Telegraph*, 6 May & 26 Oct.
Sweeney, 1904. John S., *At Scotland Yard*
1984. J.S., in *New Society*, 22 Nov.
Sykes, 1975– Dr John S., of OUP
Synge, 1988. Hugh S., quoted in *Guardian*, 17 Aug. 1987
Symons, 1950. J.S., *The Thirtyfirst of February*
1958. *The Gigantic Shadow*
1976. Penny S., in the *Times*, 9 Apr.
'Taffrail', 1916. [Capt. H. Taprell Dorling, DSO, RN] *Carry On!* and *Pincher Martin*
1917. *The Sub.* and *Sea Spray* and *Spindrift*
1933. *The Man from Scapa Flow*
1936. *Mystery at Milford Haven* (u/t)
Tait, 1912. R.S.T., *Scotty Mac, Shearer*
Tansey, 1984– Ernest T., of Stony Stanton, Leics
Taylor, 1986– Ean T., in *English Today*, Oct. '86; and privately
1982. Prof. Laurie T., in *New Society*, 4 Nov., 11 Nov., 23 Dec.
1983. Ibid., 6 Jan.
1987. In *Illus. London News*, Oct.
1980. Robert T., 'The Tory Wets', in *New Society*, 17 Apr.
Tempest, 1950. Paul T., *Lag's Lexicon*
Tennant, 1920. J.E.T., *In the Clouds above Baghdad*
1939. Kylie T., *Foveaux*
1941. *The Battlers*
1943. *Ride on, Stranger*
1947. *Lost Haven*

1953. *The Joyful Condemned*
1956. *The Honey Flow* (u/t)
Terkel, 1984. 'Studs' T., *The Good War'*
Tey, 1927. [As Gordon Daviot] *The Man in the Queue*
1929. *Kif*
1936. As J.T., *A Shilling for Candles*
1946. *Miss Pym Disposes*
1952. *The Singing Sands*
Thirkell, 1937. Angela. T., *Summer Half*
Thirsk, 1979. Simon T., in *Guardian*, 27 Apr.
Thomas, 1978. Craig T., *Wolfsbane*
1983. Irene T., in 'Transatlantic Quiz', BBC Radio 4, 18 Oct.
1976. 'Jonathan T.', *English as She Is Fraught*
1966. Leslie T., *The Virgin Soldiers*
1972. *Arthur McCann and All His Women*
1936. Sir William Beach T., *Hunting England*
Thompson, 1985. Julian T., *No Picnic*
1979. Michael T., *Rubbish Theory*
1935. R. Aubrey T., in *Observer*, 3 Mar.
Thomson, 1932. Edward John Thompson, *Lament for Adonis*
Thornton, 1912. R.H.T., *American Glossary*
Tilsley, 1978. Paul T., in *Listener*, 13 July
Tinniswood, 1969. Peter T., *A Touch of Daniel*
1985. *Call It a Canary*
Toby, 1979. *Toby : A Bristol Tramp Tells His Story*
Tod. A.H.T., *Charterhouse*, 1900
Took, 1974. Barry T. & Marty Feldman, *Round the Horne*
1976. B.T., *Laughter in the Air*
Towler, 1979. Robert T. & A. Coxon, *The Fate of the Anglican Clergy*
Toynbee, 1984. Polly T., in *Guardian*, 1 Oct.
Tracy, 1973. Honor T., in *Sunday Telegraph*, 12 Aug.
1975. *In a Year of Grace*
1976. Hugh T., *Death in Reserve*
Traill, 1936. Peter T., *Half Mast*
Train, 1912. A.T., *Courts, Criminals and the Camorra*
Travers, 1973. Ben T., *Turkey Time*, 1934, BBC broadcast 3 Oct '73
Tredrey, 1939. F.D.T., *Pilot's Summer* (set in 1935)
Trevor, 1956. Elleston T., *Gale Force*
1966. *The Shoot*
1967. *Freebooters*
1968. *A Place for the Wicked*
Trevor-Roper, 1980. Hugh T.–R., in valedictory lecture on resigning the Oxford Chair of History, 20 May
Trist, 1945. Margaret T., *Now That We're Laughing*
Triston, 1938. H.U.T., *Men in Cages*
Truck. 'Bill Truck: Man o' War', in *Blackwood's Magazine*, 1821–26
Turner, 1968. Bill T., *The Sex Trap*
1986. Charles T., of Stockport
1983. Glenn T., *Social World of the Comprehensive School*, 1986
1982. Stephanie T., ' "Juliet Bravo" ', in *Radio Times*, 4 Sep.
Turnill, 1970. Reginald T., *The Language of Space*
Tute, 1975. Warren T., *The Rock*, 1971
Tweedie, 1979. Jill T., in *Guardian*, 18 Jan.
1980. In *Illus. London News*, Jan.
Tyler, 1982. Andrew T., 'Piccadilly Rent Boy', in *New Society*, 22 Dec.
1986. 'Crisis at the Met', in *Time Out*, 14–20 May
1987– Phil T., BA, of London
Underworld. E. Partridge, *A Dict. of the Underworld*, 1949
Upfield, 1932. Arthur U., *A Royal Abduction*
1937. *Murder Down Under* (u/t)
1956. *The Battling Prophet*
V.G., 1942. 'V.G.', a verse in *Punch*, 7 Jan.
Vachell, 1913. H.A.V., *Loot from the Temple of Fortune*
1914. *Quinney's*

1934. *Martha Penny* (u/t) and *Moonhills*, 1935
1938. *Quinney's for Quality*
Valtin, 1941. Jan V., *Out of the Night*
Van Dulken, 1987– Geoffrey Van D., of Emeworth, Hants.
Van Greenaway, 1978. P.v. G., *A Man Called Scavener*
Vaughan, 1978. Paul V., in *Listener*, 18 May
Verney, 1955. John V., *Going to the Wars*
Vickers, 1955. F.B.V., *First Place to the Stranger*, 1956
1949. Roy V., *The Department of Dead Ends*
Vivian, 1933. E.C.V., *Ladies in the Case*
Vosburgh, 1980. Dick V., quoted in *Telegraph Sunday Mag.*, 24 Feb.
Vosper, 1929. Frank V., *Murder on the Second Floor*
W. Ernest Weekley, *Etymological Dict. of Modern English*, 1921
W. & F. Wentworth & Flexner, *Dict. of American Slang*, 2nd Supplemented edn., 1975
Wade, 1934. Henry W., *Constable Guard Thyself!*
Wain, 1982. Christopher W., in *Listener*, 17 June
Wainwright, 1965. John W., *Death in a Sleeping City*
1967. *The Worms Must Wait*
1968. *Edge of Destruction*
1971. *The Last Buccaneer* and (2) *Dig the Grave and Let Him Lie*
1975. *Coppers Don't Cry* and *Death of a Big Man*
Wakeman, 1980. Geoffrey W., of the Plough Press
Walker, 1968. David W., *Devil's Plunge*
1979–81. Ian W., in *New Society*, 13 Sept. '79; 26 June '80; 12 Mar., 21 May, 3 Sept. '81
1982. Ted W., *High Path*
Wall, 1939. Prof. Arnold W., review of *DSUE3*, in *The Press*, Christchurch, NZ; and privately, 1945
Wallace, 1912. Edgar W., *Private Selby*
1923. *The Clue of the New Pin* and *The Missing Million*
1924. *Room 13* and *Educated Evans*
1925. *The Mind of Mr J.G.Reader*
1926. *The Avenger* and *The Door With Seven Locks*
1927. *The Mixer* and *The Squeaker* and *The Brigand*
1928. *Elegant Edward* and *The Flying Squad* and *The Gunner* and *The Double*
1929. *Again the Ringer*
Wallinger, 1979. Sue W., Loughborough Library School
Walton, 1977– John W., FLA, of Birstall, Leics.
Walpole, 1933. Hugh W., *Vanessa*
Warburg, 1970. Frederic W., in transcript of a BBC TV programme, in Coppard & Crick, *Orwell Remembered*, 1984
Ward, 1976. Edmund W., *The Hanged Man*
Ware. J. Redding W., *Passing English of the Victorian Era*, 1909
Warner, 1961. Douglas W., *Death of a Snout*
Warren, 1976. P.W. & M. Linskey, *Taxicabs*
Warwick, 1968. Michael W., 'Theatrical Jargon of the Old Days', in *Stage*, 3 Oct.
Waters, 1973. Ivor W., *Folklore & Dialect of the Lower Wye Valley*
Watkins, 1987. G.M.W., letter in *Guardian*, 16 Oct.
Watson, 1979. B.J.W., letter in *Radio Times*, 1 Dec.
1980. Ian W., in *New Society*, 31 Jan.
Watts, 1987– The brothers, Simon G.W., of Loughborough, and Martin N.W., of London
Alec Waugh, 1917. *The Loom of Youth*
1922. *Public School Life*
1928. *Going Their Own Ways*, 1938
1932. *Thirteen Such Years*
1934. *The Balliols*
1936. *Jill Somerset*
1959. *Fuel for the Flame*, 1960
Evelyn Waugh, 1928. *Decline and Fall*
1930. *Vile Bodies*
1932. *Black Mischief*
1934. *A Handful of Dust*
1936. *Mr Loveday's Little Outing*

1942. *Put Out More Flags*
1957. *The Ordeal of Gilbert Pinfold*
Webb, 1945. Duncan W., in *Daily Express*, 11 & 17 Sept.
Weekley, 1937. Ernest W., in *Observer*, 21 Feb.; see also W.
Weighell, 1983. Sid W., in 'Talk of the Town . . .', BBC Radio 4, 25 Sept.
Weightman, 1977. Gavin W., 'God Lets Me Pickpocket', in *New Society*, 7 July
1979. 'Glitching on the Beacon', Ibid., 20 Sept.
Weir, 1980. Stuart W., in *New Society*, 24 Jan.
Welcome, 1965. John W., in *Wanted for Killing*
1968. *Hell Is Where You Find It*
Weldon, 1925. L.B.W., *'Hard Lying'*
Wells, 1909. H.G.W., *Tono Bungay*
1911. *The New Machiavelli*
1912. *Marriage*
1918. *Joan and Peter*
Wensley, 1931. Frederick P.W., *Detective Days*
West, 1956. Morris W., *Gallows on the Sand*
1936. Rebecca W., *The Thinking Reed*
1985. Richard W., in *Spectator*, 15 June, quoting an anecdote of the 1960s
Westbury, 1930. G.H.W., *Misadventures in Canada*
Westerby, 1937. Robert W., *Wide Boys Never Work*
Westerman, 1927. Percy F.W., *The Terror of the Seas*
Westerway, 1963. J.R.W., 'The Rockers', in *The* (Sydney) *Bulletin*, 6 Apr.
Weymouth, 1936. Anthony W., *Hard Liver*
1937. *Tempt Me Not*
Whaley, 1936. F.J.W., *Trouble in College*
Wharton, 1965. David W.
What I Know, by a Philosophic Punter, 1928
White. Col. Archie W., VC
1976. David W., 'Magazine Moneychase', in *New Society*, 12 Aug.
1981. In *New Society*, 11 June; and Ibid., 15 Sept. 1983
Whitlock, 1976. Lt Cdr Peter W., in *Globe & Laurel*, Sept.
Wicks, 1938. H.W., *The Prisoner Speaks*
Wilce, 1977. Hilary W., in *New Society*, 2 Feb.
Wild, 1943. Roland W., *The Rest of the Day's Your Own*
Wilkes. G.A.W., *A Dict. of Australian Colloquialisms*, 1978
Williams, 1932. Charles W., *The Greater Trumps*
1987– David E.W., of Chelmsford
1970. Gordon M.W., *The Upper Pleasure Garden*
1980. Kenneth W., the actor
1983– Mrs Susan, Thomas and Chloe W. of Loughborough
Williamson, 1972. David W., *The Removalist*
1959. H.D.W., *Sammy Anderson, Commercial Traveller*
1984. Havard W., in *New Society*, 21 June
1979– James W., of Eastbourne
1979– Joanna W., BEd. See also Martin
Willis. J. Judfield W.
1976. Paul W., 'Lads, Lobes and Labour', in *New Society*, 20 May
1975. Ted W., *The Left-Handed Sleeper*
1976. *Man-Eater*
1985– Lord Willis, of Chislehurst
Wilson, 1949. Angus W., *The Wrong Set*
1950. *Such Darling Dodos*
1952. *Hemlock and After*
1956. *Anglo-Saxon Attitudes*
1957. *A Bit off the Map*
1979. Sqn Ldr G.D.W., RAF Leuchars
1980. James W., in *Social Work Today*, 22 Jan.
Winchester, 1977. Simon W., in *Overseas Guardian*, 4 Sep.
Wingate, 1976. John W., *Oil Strike*
1981. *Carrier*
Winn, 1965. Godfrey W., in *Woman*, 11 Dec.
Winsor, 1972. Diana W., *Red on Wight*
Winterborn, 1977. Merrilyn W., in *New Society*, 11 Aug.
Winton, 1959. John W., *We Joined the Navy*
1960. *We Saw the Sea*

1963. *Never Go to Sea*
1964. *All the Nice Girls*
1967. *HMS Leviathan*
1971. *The Fighting Temeraire*
1976– In *Illus. London News*, Oct. '76, June '77, May '78
1979. In *Telegraph Sunday Mag.*, 8 Apr.
Witherow, 1982. W. & Bishop, in the *Times*, 4 Sept.
Wober, 1971. Mallory W., *English Girls' Boarding Schools*
Woddis, 1977. Roger W., Cockney-style verse 'Tom Brahn's Schooldays', in *Punch*, 6 July
Wodehouse, 1902. *The Pothunters*
    1903. P.G.W., *Tales of St Austin's*
    1906. *Love Among the Chickens*
    1907. With H.W. Westbrook, *Not George Washington*
    1909. *Mike*
    1910. *Psmith in the City*
    1924. *Ukridge*
    1936. *Young Man in Spats*
Wolfe, 1968. B.H.W., *The Hippies*
Wollaston, 1965. Nicholas W., *Winter in England*
Wolveridge, 1978. Jim W., *He Don't Know 'A' from a Bull's Foot*; see also *Muvver*
Wood, 1980. Christopher W., in *Telegraph Sunday Mag.*, 14 Sept.
    1978– Margo W., BA ALA, formerly Ldg Writer, WRNS
    1932. 'Stuart W.', *Shades of the Prison House*
    1936. Thomas W., *True Thomas*
Woods, 1983. Peter W., in *New Society*, 24 Mar.
Woodward, 1929. Edward E.W., *The House of Terror*
Words! E. Partridge, *Words, Words, Words!*, 1933

Woodworth, 1974– David P.W., BA FLA, of Ashby de la Zouch
Worby, 1937. John W., *The Other Half*
    1939. *Spiv's Progress*
Worsley, 1948. Francis W., *ITMA*
Worsthorne, 1977. Peregrine W., in *The World of the Public School*, ed. G.M. Fraser
Wren, 1934. P.C.W., in *Passing Show*, 18 Aug.
Wright, 1981. Peter W., *Cockney Dialect and Slang*
Wyatt, 1973. John W., *Talking about Drugs*
Wylie, 1965. P.W., *They Were Both Naked* (u/t)
Wyndham, 1899. Horace W., *The Queen's Service*
Wyndham-Lewis, 1968. D.B.W.-L., in *Universe*, 9 Feb.
Y. & B. Henry Yule & A.C. Burnell, *Hobson-Jobson*, r.e., 1903
Yates, 1966. John A.Y.
    1930. Dornford Y., *As Other Men Are*, 1925
Yeates, 1934. V.M.Y., *Winged Victory*
York, 1967. Andrew Y., *The Co-Ordinator*
    1976– Peter Y., collected in *Style Wars*, 1980
Young, 1924. Francis Brett Y., *Woodsmoke*
    1930. *Jim Redlake*
    1934. *This Little World*
    1935. *White Ladies*
    1938. *Dr Bradley Remembers*
    1985. Toby Y., 'The Shock of the Old', in *New Society*, 14 Feb.
    1986. 'The Fashion Victims', Ibid., 14 Mar.
Yuill, 1974. P.B.Y., *Hazell Plays Solomon*

A

a. Amphetamine: drugs c. (Stockley, 1986.) US since—1967 (Spears).

A.B.C. An *A*ustralian-*b*orn *C*hinese: Aus. and Far East: since ca. 1950, perhaps earlier. Also *A*merican-*b*orn *C*hinese. (P.B.)

a.b.f. A final 'last drink': from ca. 1915. I.e. an *a*bsolutely *b*loody *f*inal drink.

AC – DC or **A.C. – D.C.** (Usu. of male) both heterosexual and homosexual: adopted, ca. 1959, ex US. A pun on electricity's '*A.C.* or *D.C.*': alternating current or direct current. Cf. **plug in both ways**.

A/C Plonk. An Aircraftman 2nd class (AC2): RAF: since early 1920s. (*New Statesman*, 30 Aug. 1941; Jackson.) Ex *plonk*, mud. Cf. **P/O Prune**, Plonk's superior officer.

a cooloo. All; everything: RAF, esp. regulars with service in the Middle East: ca. 1925–50 – but since ca. 1914 in army usage. (Jackson, 1945.) Prob. ex Arabic *cooloo*, all.

a–crash of, go. To assault (a person): low coll.:—1923 (Manchon).

A.I.F. Deaf: Aus. r.s.: later C.20. (McNeil.) *AIF* orig. = Australian Imperial Forces.

a.k.a. ' "a.k.a."—"also known as"—is New Wave, or rock press, for "formerly" ' (York, 1977). Ex police j. Later found in more gen. use. (P.B.)

à la . . . In the fashion of; in such-and-such a way or manner: coll.: late C.19–20. 'Trying to bring his entire family into politics *à la* So-and-So' (B.P.).—2. In *very à la*, absolutely in fashion: often used ironically, disparagingly or contemptuously: 'She thought she was the cat's whiskers—oh, very à la!': middle-class feminine: mid-C.20. (P.B.)

à la cart – and horse. 'A jocular perversion of *à la carte*' (Petch).

A over T. See **arse over tip** at **arse over . . .**

a.p. The right procedure, the correct thing to do: RN College, Dartmouth: from ca. 1930. (Granville.) I.e. *A*dmiralty *p*attern.

a.w.o.l. As an acronym, and pron. *ay-wol*, 'it gets used beyond its proper role, to mean anyone missing when there is work to be done' (Sayers, 1985). Ex the military '(go/have gone) a.w.o.l.' = absent without leave.

abaccering. Loafing: canalmen's. (Gladwin.) Peppitt suggests 'perhaps for abackering'; P.B.: or ex smoking, or chewing, (to)bacco?

Abadan. 'When Persia nationalised her oil wells under President Mossadeq [ca. 1952] any driver who was too liberal with engine oil was nicknamed "Abadan" ' (McKenna): railwaymen's.

Abbeville Kids, the. Focke-Wulf pilots (or pilots and planes): RAF: 1942; ob. by 1946. Partridge, 1945, 'Our airmen first met them over or near Abbeville and . . . like the Dead End Kids of cinematic fame, they had no very rosy future'.

Abby, pl **Abbies.** An Abyssinian cat: domestic. Bournemouth *Echo*, 18 Jan. 1968.

abdabs. In *don't come*—or, *give me—the old abdabs*, don't tell me the tale: C.20, esp. WW2. By itself, *abdabs* was, in WW2, occ. used for 'afters'.—2. In *the screaming abdabs*, an attack of *delirium tremens*: since late 1930s. Since ca. 1942, *abdabs* has sometimes been *hab-dabs*. This is prob. the orig. of the *abdabs* 'given' in sense 1.—3. In *have the screaming abdabs*, to be in a state of enraged frustration: RN, MN: since ca. 1950. (Peppitt.)

abdominal. An abdominal case: medical coll. (Herbert, 1934.) P.B.: obviously other parts of the body could be used as appropriate.

Aberdeen booster. See *Scotsman's fifth* at HAULIERS', in Appx.

abfab. 'They looked real "abfab" (absolutely fabulous), another of our bodgie [q.v.] words' (Dick): Aus. teenagers': mid-1950s.

abo, Abo. Australian Aboriginal: Aus. coll.: mid-C.19–20. Wilkes, 'Not always intended as derogatory, but now [1977] increasingly taken to be so.' Cf:—

aboliar (or **A–**); properly **abo-liar**. A regular writer on Aborigine lore or of Aborigine stories: s. (from ca. 1910) >, by 1925 coll. and by 1936 virtually j. It is a coinage of the (Sydney) *Bulletin*. Cognate, and from the same mint, is *aboriginality*, a (preferably *original*) contribution to *Aborigine* lore: Aus. coll. Gen. in pl, in which shape it heads a column in the *Bulletin*.

abolished. Ironically, punished very lightly: a pun on *admonished*: Army: since late 1940s. (P.B.)

abominable 'no'-man, the. One who persists in failing to conform: ca. 1955+. A pun on 'the abominable *snow*-man'.

aboriginality. See **aboliar**.

abortion. As in 'That hat's an abortion'—ludicrous, or very ugly: Aus., since late 1940s (B.P.): also some Brit. usage (P.B.).

Abortion Express, the. See **Leaping Lena**.

about the traps. See **around the traps**.

above. The earnings of any gambling enterprise that are listed for tax and other legal purposes: gamblers': later C.20. Green.—2. An overfed, under-exercised horse; one that has not been adequately trained for a specific race: turf: later C.20. Green.

above oneself. Too ambitious or confident, not by nature but momentarily.

Abrahampstead; Cricklewitch; Goldbergs Green; Yidsbury. London Jewish self-mocking nicknames for the districts of

Hampstead, Cricklewood, Golders Green, and Finsbury: later C.20. (Mindel, 1981.)

absent rider. 'A man who has not turned up for duty. This is based on a race-course term for the jockey who fails to arrive at the course' (McKenna, 1970): railwaymen's: mid-C.20.

absoballylutely; absobloodylutely. Absolutely, utterly: late C.19–20; C.20. The former occurs in George, 1914, and both were, by 1940, rather ob. Note that *absobloodylutely* is the most frequent of the *bloody* interpolations, as *not fucking likely* is of the *fucking* interpolations.

absolute, an. An absolute certainty: coll.: early C.20.—2. In *on the absolute*, on the granting of the decree absolute: divorce-agency coll. Herbert, 1934.

absolutely! Certainly! Coll. intensification of 'yes'.

abstain from beans. To take no part in politics: not very gen.:—1923 (Manchon); ob. by 1930.

absurd is coll. in its loose, Society usage: from ca. 1920. Mackail, 1925, 'Besides, *caveat emptor* and—generally speaking—don't be absurd.'

Abyssinia! I'll be seeing you!: since mid-1930s. (Harrison, 1939.) By a pun. P.B.: and prob. from several decades earlier.

ac. Accumulator: electricians': C.20. (Partridge, 1945.) E.g. in *trolley-ac*, an accumulator on wheels, used for starting aircraft engines: RAF: since mid-C.20. (P.B.)

Academy. Abbr. *Academy-figure*, a 'half-life' drawing from the nude: artists'.

Acca. In *Meanjin* (Melbourne), 1/1977, Dr K.S. Inglis has an article titled 'Accas and Ockers: Australia's New Dictionaries'. To the title, the editor, Jim Davidson, subjoins this footnote: '*ăćca* (slightly derog.) 1, *n*. An academic rather than an intellectual, particularly adept at manipulating trendiologies, usually with full scholarly apparatus. Hence 2, *n*. A particularly sterile piece of academic writing.' But no indication about date of orig. Prompted by **Ocker**, q.v.

accident. See **street accident**.

accrue chocolate. 'To make oneself popular with the officers' (Bowen): RN: early C.20. Cf. **brown-nose**.

ace, n. A showy airman: RFC/RAF (ironic) coll.: since ca. 1918. (F. & G.) Ex the lit. S.E. sense, a crack fighter-pilot.—2. A flagship or other 'key' vessel: RN: from ca. 1914. Ex card-games. See **guard the ace**.—3. 'One bad peach—we call it an "ace"—turns the whole lot bad. We say, "Get that bleedin' ace out" ' (Skeats, 1963): street-traders': since ca. 1920. (Also applied to any other fruit.) A singleton.—4. In *on* (one's) *ace*, alone: Aus. Wilkes.—5. A cannabis cigarette: drugs c. (Stockley, 1986.) US since–1938 (Spears).

ace, adj. Excellent; 'star': coll.: from ca. 1932. *Daily Express*, 20 Apr. 1937, speaking of an orchestra: 'London's ace players improvising hot numbers'. Winton, 1967, of its RN—esp. its FAA—use, writes, 'The word "ace" meant anything superlative, desirable, well planned or well executed. "Dank" was its antonym and "fat" almost its synonym, meaning satisfied, ready, in a good or advantageous position.' P.B.: *ace* was still in use, as an adj. of high praise, in the RAF, early 1970s, and among comprehensive school youngsters in 1978. The latter gave even higher praise to anything by describing it as *pearly ace*.

ace-high. As high as possible: coll.: adopted, ex US, ca. 1925. Campbell, 1934, 'Ace-high in public esteem'. Ex card-games.

ace in the hole. A hidden asset, to be produced when necessary for best advantage: coll. when used gen.: since mid-C.20, when adopted ex US poker-players. Hunter, 1964.

Ace King Queen Jack. A widow's pension: RN: from ca. 1930. P-G-R.

ace of spades. See **black as the ace . . .**

ace of trouble. The ace of spades: late C.19–mid-20. (Petch.)

achage. An aching state: joc. coll. After *breakage*. *SOD*.

acher. A painful blow or kick, esp. in the testicles: since ca. 1960. Thomas.—2. See **acre**.

acid. 'Heavy sarcasm; scornful criticism' (Granville): RN > gen. (esp. in **come the (old) acid**, q.v.).—2. LSD, the psychedelic drug: Can., from 1966 (Leechman); by 1967 also Brit.

(Diment.) Whence, *acid-head*, a user thereof (Ibid.). Both of these terms occur also in Fryer, 1967.—3. In, e.g., ' "Don't give me the old acid." Don't try to fool me with a lot of nonsense' (Thomas): later C.20. See **come the acid.**—4. In *put the acid on*, 'To make the kind of demand (for money, information, or sex) that will either yield results or eliminate that possibility. Ex acid test' (Wilkes): Aus., NZ. Cf. **hard word on.**—5. See **put the acid in**.

acid rock. 'Modern music which, when accompanied by unusual lighting and extreme amplification, is evocative of LSD hallucinations' (Powis): later C.20.

ack, n. An airman, esp. AC1 (Aircraftman 1st Class) or AC2: RAF College, Cranwell: ca. 1920–30. (Gp Capt A. Wall, 1945.) A vocalisation of *ac*.—2. Assistant: Army: from ca. 1940. E.g. *Ack Adj*, the assistant adjutant (P-G-R); *Ack IG*, an assistant instructor of gunnery (P.B.: still current early 1970s, where ack adj was ob. by 1950). Ex the orig. signallers' PHONETIC ALPHABET, q.v. in Appx.

ack, v. To *acknowledge*, e.g. a letter or signal: Forces' and Civil Service > gen. clerical.

ack-ack. Anti-aircraft guns and gunfire: Services': WW2. Hence *Ack-Ack*, AA Command (H. & P., 1943). *Reader's Digest*, Feb. 1941, 'To avoid the "ack-acks" (anti-aircraft guns).'—2. As challenge, with response *beer-beer*, a joc. of early WW2. For both, see PHONETIC ALPHABET, in Appx.

ack adj. See **ack, n, 2**.

Ack and Quack. The A & Q (Adjutant and Quartermaster) Department: Army: ca. 1925–50. P-G-R.

ack-charlie. To 'arse-crawl'; an 'arse-crawler': = sycophant: Services', esp. army: WW2. Ex the signalese for *a–c*. P-G-R.

ack emma. Air Mechanic: RFC, 1912–18, and RAF, 1918. The rank became, in Jan. 1919, aircraftman. Jackson, 1945.—2. A.m.: Services': from 1915. For both, see PHONETIC ALPHABET, in Appx.

ack over toc(k). See **arse over . . .**

ack Willie. Absent without leave: Aus. Army: WW2. (B., 1943.) Signalese for first two letters of AWOL, the official abbr.

ackermaracker. Tea (the beverage): low: since ca. 1920. (Curtis, 1938.) I tentatively suggest that s. *char*, tea, has been back-slanged to *rach* and then elaborated.—2. As *ackamaraka*, in ' "Don't give me the old ackamaraka" = don't tell me tall yarns, don't try to bluff me' (Tempest, 1950): prisons' s.: mid-C.20.

ackers. Activity at physical exercises: Pangbourne Nautical College: since ca. 1950. (Peppitt.) The 'OXFORD/RN *-ER(s)*'.—2. See **Akkas**.

'ackin' corf. A hacking cough: 'pseudo-vulgarly in jest' (Collinson, 1927); i.e. coll. when joc., illiterate when serious.

ackle. To fit, or function, properly, esp. as in 'It (or she) won't ackle': Blaker, 1930, puts it in the mouth of a gunner, ca. 1916; it was also popular in the RFC/RAF; perhaps orig. ex dial.; still current late 1970s, and has long been gen. Also 'Can you ackle it?' = can you make it work? (E.P.; P.B.)

acky. Dirty; nasty: mostly childish and domestic: prob. dial. > s. 'Ugh! Nasty! Acky! Put it down at once!' Perhaps prompted by *cacky*. (P.B.)—2. See **Akky**.

acquire. To steal: coll. Not euph., for it is used joc. But cf.:— To obtain illicitly or deviously: Army euph. coll.: WW2. P-G-R.

acre. Buttocks, backside: Aus.: since late 1930s. Wilkes.

acro. An acrobat: circus peoples': late C.19–20.

across. In *get across*, v.t., to irritate or offend (a person): coll.—2. See **put it across**.

across the pavement. Underworld term for 'a street situation, e.g., "Let's do one across the pavement" may mean "Let's commit a robbery in the street" ' (Powis): since (?) ca. 1960. Elliott, 1988, of a petty criminal, has, 'in [his] case "going to work" meant a traditional "across-the-pavement job" for a bag of money being delivered to a frozen food firm.'

act bored, superior, etc. To behave as if bored, superior, etc.: Can., orig. (ca. 1920) sol., but by 1955, coll. (Leechman.)

act green. To feign ignorance, as of a recruit: coll.: late C.19–20. Mostly, or orig., RN lowerdeck, as in Knock, 1932.

act the angora. To play the fool: Aus. (B., 1942.) Elab. of . . . *goat.*

acting dish. A dish resembling an old favourite; *acting rabbit-pie* is made of beef: RN. (Bowen.) Ex *acting officer.*

acting Jack. An acting sergeant: police. (*Free-Lance Writer*, April 1948.) Cf. the Army's *acting lance-jack*, an acting lance corporal.

acting rabbit-pie. See **acting dish**, and cf.:–

acting scran. 'Food substituted for that promised on the mess menu' (P-G-R): RN officers': since ca. 1920.

acting the maggot, vbl n. and ppl adj. Shirking work: (mostly Anglo-Irish) bank-clerks':—1935.

action. Activity, esp. if great; excitement, as in 'Where's the action?' Adopted, ca. 1968, by British 'underground' (non-Establishment; not drug addicts').—2. Sexual intercourse, as in 'He got all the action he wanted' (Hollander): adopted, ca. 1970, ex US. *DCCU*, 1971; W. & F. record it as used in print in 1968.

action(-)man. A sarcastically derogatory term for one who is really or only apparently over-efficient and military, enjoying route marches, assault courses and the like: Services': since ca. 1960. Ex the 'Action-man' doll, which can be dressed in all sorts of uniforms and fighting gear. (P.B.)

active tack. Active service: Guardsmen's: 1939+. Grinstead, 1946.

actor. 'A bluffer, a spiv [q.v.]' (Tempest): prisons' s.: mid-C.20.

actor-proof was, ca. 1870–1940, applied to an actor who tried hard and selfishly for laughs and for rounds of applause: theatrical. Warwick, 1968.

actor's Bible, the. *The Stage*: theatrical coll. (Green.)

actressy. Characteristic of an actress; theatrical or somewhat melodramatic in manner: coll.: late C.19–20. Shanks, 1933.

actual, your. See **yer actual.**

Adam, adam. In full, *Adam and Eve*, to leave: r.s.: late C.19–20. (Birmingham) *Evening Despatch*, 19 July 1937. Also, to depart (hurriedly): r.s. on *leave*: since ca. 1920. (Franklyn, 2nd.)

Adam and Eve ball. A Cinderella dance: since ca. 1925.

Adam and Eve on a raft. Eggs on toast: mostly military. (F. & G). L.A. adds 'Hoxtonian [Inner London] for fried eggs on toast. T.E. Lawrence, *The Mint.* Not only RAF, but in my experience: Services' and non-aristocratic.' Leechman, however, writes (1959) from Canada, 'Properly two poached eggs on toast, one egg being alone on a raft....it is firmly entrenched as "Short order" restaurant slang'. Cf:–

Adam and Eve wrecked. Scrambled eggs: mostly Army. F. & G.

Adamatical. Naked. 'This', remarks one of my correspondents, 'is Standard English, but I can find no dictionary giving this definition'; neither can I, but then I classify it as jocularly erudite coll.—probably on the analogy of such words as *problematical* and *sabbatical.*

add. In *it doesn't add up*, it fails to make sense: coll. Hence, *it all adds up*, it does make sense—at last (Petch).

adj. (or **A.**), n. Adjutant; esp. *the Adj.*, one's adjutant: Army officers', and later, the Other Ranks'. (Blaker.) Also used in the vocative. Hence:–

adj. (or **A.**), v. Army officers' s., from ca. 1910 as in Blaker, ' "Yes," said the Colonel. "You're all right. That's why I want you to Adj. for me." '

Adji, the. The RAF's shape of **adj.** Partridge, 1945.

adjutant's at. 'A blonde member of the Auxiliary Territorial Service': Army: WW2. P-G-R.

admen. (Singular, little used.) Advertising managers of periodicals and large firms; executive employees of advertising agencies: since ca. 1955: orig. s.: by 1965, coll.

Admin. Administration; administrative: Services' coll.: since 1939. (P-G-R.) By later C.20, much more widespread.

admiral. As the *Admiral*, the officer-in-charge of RAF Air/Sea Rescue Boats: from ca. 1930. (H. & P.) Cf. **airmaids.**—2. See **next in line for admiral.**

Admiral Browning. Human excrement: RN. Personified colour.

Admiral's broom. 'Used humorously to give the Navy an equivalent of the Field Marshal's baton' (Petch, 1946): coll. 'This goes back to the Dutch Admiral Martin Tromp (the elder), who beat the English Fleet under Blake at the Battle of Dungeness in Nov. 1652. The *Encyclopedia Britannica* says that the statement that he sailed up the Channel with a broom at his masthead in token of his ability to sweep the seas is probably mythical. I think it was Newbolt who wrote a song called "The Admiral's Broom" about the turn of this century.' (R.S., 1967.)

Admiral's Mate, the. 'A boastful, know-all rating': RN. (Granville.) Ironic.

Admiralty brown. Toilet paper: R Aus. N: since ca. 1910. Issue and colour.

Admiralty clown. A Naval physical-training instructor: RN: since ca. 1945.

Admiralty-made coffin. An Armed Merchant Cruiser; collectively, such ships formed *the Suicide Squadron*: RN: WW2. Many were sunk during the first two or three years of WW2. (Granville.)

admiration. Abbr. *note of admiration, admiration-mark* (written!): coll.: mainly printers', publishers', authors': rare.

adorable. Vachell, 1933, 'a much debased word; a diabolical twin of "deavie" ': upper and upper-middle class: from ca. 1925.

Ados (pron. *Aydoss*). Assistant Director of Ordnance Services: Army (H. & P.): WW2 and later. His Deputy was, of course, called 'Daydoss'. Simple acronyms.

adrift. Temporarily missing or absent without leave (mid-C.19–20); wide of the mark, confused (C.20: coll.). Nautical. Bowen records the second sense. In the 'absent without leave' nuance, it has, since ca. 1920, been current among RAF regulars.—2. (Of a knot) undone: RN. Granville.—3. (Of kit) missing: id. 'If there's anything adrift it will come off your slop chit, nobody else's. All right?' (*Heart*) See also quot'n at **knickers in a twist** for its application to people. (P.B.)

advertising. Given to seeking publicity—and using it: coll. As in 'He's an advertising (sort of) blighter.' Abbr. *self-advertising.*

aerated, esp as 'Don't get aerated!'—excited or angry: since ca. 1930. (Petch.) Sometimes heard as 'aeriated'.

aerated amateurs. Pre-WW2 Auxiliaries of the RAF—in 1947, recognised as the Royal Auxiliary Air Force. (P.B.)

aerial coolies. Those airmen who dropped supplies to the Chindits in Burma: Army and RAF: 1943–5. P-G-R.

aerial ping-pong. Australian Rules Football: Sydneysiders': since ca. 1950. Mostly in ref. to the game in Victoria. (B.P.)

aeroplanes. A bow tie: Aus.: since ca. 1938. B., 1942.

affair. One's current lover: homosexuals': current 1970.

affluence of incohol, esp. **under the . . .** The influence of alcohol: jocularly intentional spoonerism: Aus. since late 1950s. (B.P.) But Aus. owes it to 'the legion of North Country comedians who have used the phrase in their "drunk" sketches for years' (Holloway, 1967).

affluent society, the. In 1958 Prof. J. K. Galbraith pub'd his book so titled and almost immediately the phrase became a c.p., both in the UK and in the USA. By some people, the *un*-thinkers, it has been held to synonymise 'the welfare state'; by many, to be basically optimistic, whereas, in the fact, the book is only mildly so. Safire.

Affs, the. Black Africans: since ca. 1960—and far commoner in South Africa than in Britain. (Johnson, 1976.)

Africa speaks. Strong liquor from S. Africa: Aus. and NZ. (B., 1941 and 1942.) In *The Drum*, 1959, B. defines it as 'cheap fortified wine'.

African. 'A tailor-made cigarette' (B., 1959): Aus.: since late 1940.

African harp. See **fish-horn.**

African Woodbine. Marijuana cigarette: drug addicts': 1970s. (Home Office.) *Woodbine* = a well-known brand of cheaper cigarette.

Afro. 'Having the hair in a spherical, bushy and tightly curled mass, in the style of certain Negroes' (Powis, 1977). A style much imitated, for a while in the 1970s, by 'Whitey' youth: adopted, early 1970, ex US. *DCCU*, 1971.

aft. Afternoon, as in 'this aft'. Mostly lower-middle class. Also Can.: since ca. 1910. Moore, 1960.—2. In *be taken aft*, to go, as a defaulter, before the Commander: RN coll. Granville.—3. See **carry both sheets aft.**

after. Afternoon: Aus. (Cf. **afto**.) Brockman, 1947, 'Did you see Mr Scrown this after, Les?' A much earlier example occurs in Dyson, 1906. See also **arvo**.

after game, come the. To say, 'I told you so': Aus. coll.: since ca. 1925. B., 1942.

afters. The second course, if any; thus 'Any afters?' = 'Any pudding?': Army. (F. & G.) Also RN lowerdeck, as in Knock, 1932. By 1945, at latest, it had become gen. 'Often with sexual implication, as "What's for afters?"—used by a male at evening meal.' (Petch.)

afto. Afternoon: Aus.: since ca. 1920. B., 1942. See also **arvo**.

Ag and Fish. See **Min. of Ag.**

-age. A beatnik suffix, as in *dressage* (clothes)—*understandage* (understanding)—*workage* (employment): ca. 1959+. (Anderson, 1965.)

agen, agin (esp. *the government*). Against; in late C.19–20, sol.; earlier, S.E. These are Southern forms of the † *again*, against. (W.) P.B.: in later C.20 sometimes used for deliberate, humorous, effect.

agent, n. One in charge of the job; esp. an 'outside' (not an office) man: Public Works' coll.:—1935.

agent, v. To act as literary agent for (an author or his work): authors' coll.: since ca. 1930. Lorac, 1961.

agents. In *have* (one's) *agents*, to be well-informed: Army and RAF: since ca. 1939. (Rivett; E. P., 1948.) With an allusion to secret agents. Cf. **my spies.**

-agger. Mostly in Charterhouse words. E.g. *combinaggers*, a combination suit (esp. of football attire). From ca. 1890. (Tod, 1900.) This prefix is very common in Oxford *-er* words, e.g. *Jaggers*. P.B.: by mid-1980s surviving only in such joc. anachronisms as *indijaggers*, indigestion. See OXFORD *-ER*(s) in Appx.

Aggie. Any ship named *Agamemnon*: RN: C.19–20. Bowen.—2. Agoraphobia: sufferers' and associates': later C.20. *Community Care*, 12 June 1980. (P.B.)

Aggie-on-a-horse, or **Aggie-on-horseback.** HMS *Weston-super-Mare*: RN. (Granville.) 'Weston' evokes the 'Aggie' of '**Aggie Weston's**', below. A. Knight: the sloop, in commission 1932–47, was renamed HMS *Weston*.

Aggie Weston's. The Agnes Weston Sailors' Home: nautical: late C.19–20. Cf.:–

Aggie's. A Sailor's Rest House: RN. 'These Rest Houses were founded by the late Dame Agnes Weston—the "Mother of the Navy"—at Portsmouth and Devonport' (Granville).

aggranoy or **agronoy; aggrovoke** or **agrovoke.** To annoy; to irritate: Aus.: since ca. 1920. (B., 1942.) The former, however, is also Cockney of ca. 1880+. Blend of *aggravate*, *annoy* and *provoke*.

aggravation. A station: r.s.: earlier C.20. F. & G.

aggro. Now usu. n., but earlier also adj.: trouble-making; aggression and aggressiveness; aggravation or annoyance: orig. hippies', hence their allies': since ca. 1965; by 1969, gen., as in 'Don't be so bloody aggro, man!'; 'The aggressive side of his personality . . . his aggro, as he called it' (*Groupie*, 1968). Influenced by other words ending, whether deliberately or, as in *demo*, accidentally with *-o*, it has been a useful portmanteau word for a blend of all that is threatening about a mob. In Hart-Davis, 1972, one of the characters defines and derives it thus: ' "Aggro"? Big trouble. It's short for "aggravation". Opposite of "hassle", which is small.' But by 1978 the sense had weakened for some, so that an apology for a minor inconvenience could be phrased 'I'm sorry to give you this aggro.'

aggy. 'A grouser': RN. Perhaps ex 'agony column'.

Agile and Suffering, the. The Argyll & Sutherland Highlanders: Army, by friendly perversion.

agin. See **agen.**

agolopise. See **ajolopise.**

agonised buttons. Anodised, of military 'brass' buttons given a permanent shine: Army: since ca. 1960. By Hobson-Jobson. (P.B.)

agony. Difficulty, problem; story one has to tell: c.: from ca. 1930. (*Gilt Kid*.) Ex *Conway* Training Ship s.: late C.19–earlier 20. Masefield, 1933.

agony-bags. Scottish bagpipes: English (not Scottish) Army officers': from ca. 1912.

agony column. The letters-and-answers page of women's magazines. (Petch.) Since ca. 1950. Orig., the personal column in a newspaper's advertisements, from ca. 1870.

agony stroke. 'This normally refers to an incident at a critical time, such as when a ship is dry docking and is on the point of sewing (grounding on the blocks). The foreman will want her moved up the dock a few inches. "Cor! Right on the agony stroke he wanted her moved!" ' (Patterson, 1984): Portsmouth dockers'. For etym. cf. **paradise strokes.**

agreement. See **three nines agreement.**

agricultural. See **cow-shot.** Prob. influenced also by *mow*, n. and v., in cricket j.

agricultural stroke. There are variants, as in 'the terms "rustic stroke" and "cow shot" are still in use as deprecatory epithets' (*New Society*, 22 July 1982).

Aintree iron. 'Character or resolution stiffener: Liverpool: 1950s. Brought to a puzzled audience's notice by a Merseyside pop group's hit song [early 1970s]' (Fearon).

air. As in 'left in the air', without support: Army coll.: since ca. 1940. P-G-R.—2. In *on the air*, (wireless telegraphy) on the 'wireless' [i.e. radio] programme; if applied to a person, it often connotes that he—or she—is important, or notorious, as news or publicity: resp. 1927 (*OED*) and 1930: coll.; by 1935, verging S.E.—3. Hence, *on the air*, by radio: since ca. 1935: coll. >, ca. 1955, familiar S.E. 'I heard it on the air.' See **give the air; hot air; lay on air.**

air and exercise. A short term in jail: Aus. (B., 1942.) From the C.19 c. for penal servitude.

air (one's) **bum.** See **airing.**

air commode. An Air Commodore: RAF s.: since ca. 1925. Jackson, 1945.

air disturber. A telegraphist rating: RN: since ca. 1930. (Granville.) Cf. such derogatory terms, as *grub-spoiler*, a Navy cook, and:–

air head. 'Not very bright [person]; does not have all his oars in the water. Poss., dullness caused by drugs. Recent in Can., ex US. Synon. is *space cadet*' (Leech, 1985). Soon reached UK: *Sunday Express Mag.*, 7 Feb. 1988, in a quot'n from a Liverpool teenager.

Air House, the. The Air Ministry: RAF officers': from ca. 1919. (Jackson, 1945.) On the analogy of the army *War House*.

air pie and a walk around. A clerk's lunch: from ca. 1880. Wolveridge, 1978, writing about Stepney in the 1930s, adds the moving comment 'Expressions like "I'm living on Air Pie" for "I'm going hungry", "I haven't had bit nor bite all day", or "I've seen more dinner times than dinners" . . . were said in a wryly humorous way, but the bitter reality behind them was a long way from funny.'

air-pill. A bomb dropped from an aircraft: Services': from ca. 1916; ob. by WW2. F. & G.

air (one's) **pores.** To be naked: earlier C.20. Barr, 1933.

air raid committee. 'A popular term for the Area Committee which would be sent when a dispute on a ship occurred' (Ash): London dockers': post-WW2.

air shot. 'Intercourse without ejaculation. After the tube drill where firing is carried out but without a torpedo in the tube' (Malin, 1979): RN Submariners': mid-C.20.—2. A fart, or a failed attempt to defecate. (Watts, 1988.)

air-to-mud. Air-to-ground, as 'a very small spread in the bullet group—fine for air-to-air, but not so good for air-to-mud' (*Phantom*): RAF aircrews': later C.20. Cf. **mud-movers**, bomber crews.

Air Works, the. The Royal Air Force: RAF: since ca. 1935. 'Not contemptuous' (L.A.).

airing. In *give* (one's) *bum an airing*, to visit the w.c.: low: mid-C.20. One woman day-tripper to another, getting off a coach, ca. 1950, 'Shan't be a moment, Florrie. Must just go and give me bum an airin' ' (P.B.).

airmaids. Crew of the Air/Sea Rescue boats: RAF: WW2. (H. & P.) Cf. **admiral**. ?Suggested by 'mermaids'.

airmen of the shufty. Airmen of the watch (in the watch tower on the station): RAF: from ca. 1938. (Jackson, 1945.) See **shufty**.

airs and graces. Faces: r.s.—2. Braces (for trousers): not very common r.s.—3. The Epsom Races: id. Jones, 1971.

Airships, their. The Air Council: RAF: 1947+. ('Peterborough' in the *Daily Telegraph*, 11 Sep. 1947.) A skit on the RN *their Lordships*, the various 'Lords' at the Admiralty.

airy. Ventilator: prison s.: later C.20. McVicar, 1974.

airy-fairies. (Large) feet: Cockney: C.20. (London *Evening News*, 20 Nov. 1937.) Cf. the adj.—2. See:–

Airy-Fairy, n. A member of the RNAS; later, Fleet Air Arm: RN: since WW1. (Gell, 1979.)

airy-fairy, adj. Shallowly and unthinkingly fanciful, e.g. in argument: coll.: since mid-1920s, I seem to remember; certainly common by ca. 1935.

airyard matey. A civilian mechanic in a Naval Air Station: RN: 1940+. (P-G-R.) Cf. the much older *dockyard matey*.

airyvated, ppl adj. Excited; worked-up: low: 1930s. (*Gilt Kid*.) Ex synon. *aerated* or *aereated*.

ajay. An amateur journalist: schools of authorship and journalism: ca. 1920+.

ajolopise; more correctly **agolopise.** To apologise: non-U, joc. perversion: earlier C.20.

aka. See **a.k.a.**

akka. An Egyptian piastre: Army: since WW1 and perhaps since late C.19. Ex the slang of Egyptian beggars: *piastre* corrupted. In the plural *akkas*, it = money, 'cash'; in this sense it reached the regulars in the RAF by 1925 at the latest (Jackson, 1945). 8th Army N. Africa veterans campaigning later in Italy enjoyed the macaronic *Quanta costa in akkas?*, popularised, if not invented, by their favourite cartoonist, 'Jon' (Wm J.P. Jones).—2. Hence, a Palestinian piastre: Services': since ca. 1920.

Akkas (or **Ackers**). A familiar term of address to a unit's pay-sergeant: Army: since ca. 1950, or perhaps earlier. Ex prec. (P.B.)

Akky. '[The lorry driver] has been driving for over 20 years, and he's had this Atkinson truck (he calls it "an Akky") for 3' (Walker, 1981).—2. See **acky**.

ala kefak (or **kefik**). As in 'I'm (or he's) ala kefak', I'm 'easy' (see **easy**, adj.): Army, in Near and Middle East: ca. 1940–55. Ex Arabic. 'Major Wilmott was *alakefak*: so much so, that it was difficult to get him to do any work at all' (Brooke, 1948.).

Alan Whickers; short form *Alans*. Feminine knickers (panties): r.s.: not before 1965, nor very gen. before 1968 or 1969. Ex the BBC broadcaster, known esp. for his series 'Whicker's World'. Haden-Guest, 1971.

Alans. See prec.

alarm and despondency. War-time depression: 1940+. Ex speech by Sir Winston Churchill, KG. Esp. *(to) spread a. and d.* In ref. to early 1942: 'I was pressed to return urgently to the theatre of my operations and to prepare myself to spread "alarm and despondency" (an expression that was just then coming into fashion)' (Peniakoff, 1950): Army, hence Navy and RAF, mostly among officers; since 1945, reminiscent and usu. joc.

Alaska Highway. Broad deck outboard of the island superstructure of an aircraft carrier, for handling aircraft: RN: since ca. 1960. (Knight, 1984.)

Alb. An Albanian: since ca. 1941. Quayle, 1945.

albatross. A hole played in 3 under bogey: golfers', adopted in 1933 ex US (cf. 'birdie', 1 below, and 'eagle', 2 below, bogey). *Evening News,* 13 Aug. 1937.

alberts. 'Toe-rags as worn by dead-beats and tramps of low degree' (B., 1942): Aus. Worn instead of socks. Also known as *Prince-Alberts* (Wilkes).

Albert Docks. Pox: r.s. (Hollis.) Cf. synon. **Whitehaven Docks.**

alc. Alcohol: from ca. 1930. (Not very gen.)

alcoholic constipation. 'Inability to *pass* a public-house: undergraduates': 1920–30' (R.S.).

Aldershot ladies. A double four at darts: darts players'. See TOMBOLA, in Appx., for explanation.

Alec. See **smart Alec.**—2. Hence, a dupe, esp. a swindler's dupe: Aus.: since ca. 1925. (B., 1942.) Ironically derived from sense 1. Also *Alex* (Trist, 1946).

alert! 'Officer or N.C.O. approaching' (H. & P.): Services': WW2. Ex the air-raid warning.

Alex. See **Alec,** 2.

Alf (or **ocker,** q.v.). Of *ocker*, B.P., 1976, remarks that 'The word was probably coined by a journalist to replace "Alf", which was an exact synonym . . . "Alf" has fallen out of favour because of the English TV character, Alf Garnett, who has some, but not all, of the characteristics of the Australian "Alf" or "ocker". I have never encountered "Alf" as "a heterosexual male" as defined by the late Mr Baker in *The Australian Language*.' See esp. Wilkes.

Alf's peed again. An occ. Hobson-Jobson of *auf Wiedersehen*, 'be seeing you': Brit. Forces in Germany: since (?)ca. 1945. (P.B.)

Ali Babas, the. Australian troops in N. Africa, 1942–3. Ex the name bestowed by 'Lord Haw-Haw' (William Joyce). Page, 1973.

alias man. 'A criminal, especially a morally worthless cheat or hypocrite (West Indian term, originally an eighteenth century English expression)' (Powis, 1977).

alibi. Merely an excuse: since ca. 1935. A slovenliness from the US.

Alice. As *The Alice*: Alice Springs: Aus. coll.: late C.19–20. Russell, 1934.

Alice Springs, via. 'Where have you been all this time? Did you go *via* Alice Springs?' = by a devious route: Aus. since ca. 1945. This town—Nevil Shute's *A Town Like Alice*, 1950—is, roughly, in the centre of Australia. (B.P.)

Alick. Var. (B., 1943) of **Alec,** 2.

aliveo. Lively; sprightly: (low) coll.: late C.19–20. Clouston, 1932, 'Mrs. Morgan considered herself quite as aliveo and beanful as these young chits with no figures.'

alkie, -y. An alcoholic: adopted, ca. 1943, ex US. (B.P.) Cf. **lush.**

all about. Alert; very efficient: mostly RN. (Irving, 1946.) Cook, 1962, uses the elab. *all about trout*. Contrast:–

all about – like shit in a field. 'The rider [to prec.] brings a corrective bathos which may be closer to the truth' (L.A.): RN. Cf. *all over the place*.

all afloat. A boat: r.s. (Haden-Guest, 1971.) Var. of *I'm afloat*.

all-Aloney, the. The Cunard liner *Alaunia*: nautical: earlier C.20. Bowen.

all anyhow, adj. and adv. Disordered; chaotic: late (?mid-) C.19–20. 'Taffrail', 1916.

all balls and bang-me-arse. A post-WW2 intensive of *all balls*, q.v. at **balls.** (R.S., 1969.)

all ballsed-up. Bungled; confused; wrong: Services'; also Aus.: adopted, ca. 1944, ex US servicemen. Cf. **balls-up.**

all bent out of shape. Chagrined; confused, 'knickers in a twist' [q.v.]. 'Widespread usage but becoming obs.; it was popular in the '50s. May be used in two ways: as an order, or as an observation: "Now don't get all bent out of shape when I tell you this, but . . ."; and "He's been all bent out of shape ever since he found out I laid his girl before he did" ' (Leech): Can. P.B.: cf., for the observation, the Brit. Services' 1950s–60s synon. *all bitter and twisted*, used of someone badly warped by

A

life's mishaps. Sometimes said compassionately, but more often unthinkingly and insensitively.

all clear. An all-clear signal: coll.: from 1918. Often fig.; orig. in respect of hostile aircraft.

all cut. Confused; upset; excited: Army: earlier C.20. F. & G.

all dolled up like a barber's cat. Dressed resplendently: Can. (Leechman.)

all down the line. In every way and thoroughly, as in 'They'd been seen off [outwitted] all down the line' (Wingate): coll.: later C.20.

all ends up. Easily: coll.: from ca. 1920. (*OED* Sup.) With a play on *anyhow*.

all fits within limits. 'Engineering way of saying the job meets the specifications' (Fearon): mid-C.20.

all for it, be. To be entirely in favour of it; hence, over-keen: RN coll.; by 1925, at latest, gen. coll.

all g. y. All awry or askew: since ca. 1942.

all gone daft! 'A facetious reply to the command "Let go aft!"'—obviously to be used only when the boat's crew know each other well' (Sayers): RN: mid-C.20.

all gong and no dinner. All talk and no action: coll.: BBC Radio 4, 'The Archers' serial, 13 Oct. 1981.

all hot and bothered. Very agitated, excited, or nervous: coll.: from ca. 1920. *The Times*, 15 Feb. 1937, in leader on this dictionary. Ex the physical and emotional manifestations of haste.

all-in, n. An all-in assurance policy: insurance-world coll.: from ca. 1927.

all in, adj. (Stock Exchange) depressed (of the market): coll.: mid-C.19–20; opp. *all out*. These are also terms shouted by dealers when prices are, esp., falling or rising.—2. Hence, in C.20, *all in* (of persons, occ. of animals) = exhausted.—3. 'Without limit or restriction' (Dennis, 1916): Aus. coll. Cf. S.E. nuance, 'inclusive of all'.

all kiff. All right, all correct: Army,—1914 >, by 1920, fairly gen.; ob. by 1940. (F. & G.; Manchon.) Perhaps ex Fr. s. *kif-kif*.

all marked. 'Jocular for Hall-marked, generally for inferior articles which would hardly be of the hallmarked class' (Petch): since late 1940s.

all my whiskers. Nonsense: from ca. 1920; ob. by ca. 1940. Sayers, 1926, 'All that stuff about his bein' so upset . . . was all my whiskers.' On earlier synon. *all my eye*.

all night in. 'For watch-keeping sailors, the occasion on which they enjoyed an entire night in their hammocks. Ashore, all night abed with a woman' (Bassett): RN: WW2.

all-nighter. 'Prostitutes still classify their clients as "short-timers" and "all-nighters" ' (Gosling, 1960): late C.19–20.

all (one's) oars in the water. Usu. in neg., e.g., 'He hasn't got all his . . .', he is of less than average intelligence: Can.: since ca. 1975. 'Still current' (Leech, 1986).

all of a doodah. Nervous: See **doodah**.—2. Hence, esp. 'of an aeroplane pilot getting nervous in mid-air': RFC/RAF, soon > gen.: from 1915. (F. & G.) P.B.: a var. is *all of a hoo-ha*.

all of a tiswas (or **tizwas**). Very much excited; utterly confused: perhaps orig. RAF, from early 1940s; soon > gen. Occ. as in, e.g., 'She was in a bit of a tiswas', i.e. not quite so agitated as *all of a* . . . Perhaps an elab. of *tizzy*, n., q.v., or a blend of *it is*, *it was*; cf. the later Shell Petrol advertising slogan 'That's Shell—that was!'

all over. In *be all over*, to make a great fuss of, esp. with caresses. (Of a monkey) 'He'll be all over you as soon as he gets to know you,' which indicates the semantics: *The Humorist*, 28 July 1934 (Lyell).—2. Hence, to be infatuated with: from ca. 1925.

all over (one)self. Very much pleased; over-confident: earlier C.20, esp. Army. Lyell.

all over the auction. 'All over the place': Cockney and Aus.: since ca. 1910. (Prichard.) Var. of earlier synon. *all over the shop*.

all present and correct. All correct: coll.: from ca. 1918. Knox, 1934, ' "Is that all present and correct?" "Couldn't be

better." ' Ex the military phrase (applied by a sergeant-major to a parade).

all poshed up. See **all spruced up**.

all revved-up. See **revved-up**.

all round the option. All over the place: coll.: since ca. 1950, perhaps earlier. Hunter, 1957, 'the Old Man was still phoning all round the option . . .' Var. of *all over the auction*, itself prob. a var. of later C.19 *all over the shop*. (P.B.)

all same. All the same; like; equal: pidgin: mid-C.19–20. (B. & L.) In Hong Kong, among Servicemen, 1960s, often *all same like* . . .

all shot (or hyphenated). Rendered useless or inoperative: RN, and later, occ. Army: late C.19–mid–20. (Carr, 1939.) In short, 'all shot up' or 'shot to pieces'.

all-singing all-dancing. Describes anything, esp. a piece of equipment, that is particularly spectacular and/or versatile: Services': since ca. 1970. 'The new tank . . . is expected to be the last word in tank design: an all-singing, all-dancing model which will make [its rivals] look like museum pieces by comparison' (*Listener*, 22 Feb. 1979). Ex musical extravaganza. (P.B.)

all smart. Everything's all right: Army: early C.20.

All Souls' Parish Magazine. *The Times*: University of Oxford: ca. 1920–40. Hobhouse, 1939, says that the Editor and his associates, who were Fellows of the College, often met there in order to discuss policy.

all spruced up – poshed up – togged up. Smartened up, esp. to meet someone: resp. coll., s. (not before 1915), and s. (late C.19–20); the second was orig. Army (F. & G.). In later C.20, *all dolled* or *tarted up*.

all taut. Prepared for anything: RN. (Granville.) Ex:—2. Everything ready: RN coll.: late C.19–20.

all that. Short for *all that sort of thing*, it has, esp. since ca. 1920, become narrowed to 'sex' in general and to 'sexual caresses', and esp. to copulation: partly euph. and partly coll. Powell, 1970, 'She was . . . a virgin when she married and she knew nothing about "all that", so the honeymoon was a revolting experience, ruined by "all that", and since then she has never been able to do with "all that" '—which must surely form the *locus classicus* for this phrase.—2. In *not all that*, mostly with 'bad' or 'good', as in 'Seen a lot of people lately, and my memory isn't all that [good]' (Lorac, 1943): working-class, esp. Cockney, coll.: since ca. 1910.—3. See **give it all that**.

all the . . . See TOMBOLA, in the Appx.

all the best. Elliptical for 'I wish you all the best of everything'. 'A form of leave-taking, meant to be informal, . . . casual but sincere' (L.A.): coll. Callow, 1968, 'He was rocklike, sunny, he stood for something in my eyes . . . Outside we said all the best and went off in different directions. I never saw him again.'

all the shoot. Occ. var., earlier C.20, of (the) **whole shooting-match**.

all the year round. A twelve-months' prison sentence: Aus. c.: since ca. 1925. B., 1943.

all tickettyboo. See **tickettyboo**.

all to buggery. See **buggery**.

all to cock. Awry; (of a statement) inaccurate; (of work) bungled; utterly confused, all mixed-up: coll. Cf. **all to buggery**, and **cock**, n., 2.

all togged up. See **all spruced up**.

all unnecessary. In (*make* one) *come over* (or *go*) *all unnecessary*, to excite, to become excited, esp. sexually, by a member of the opposite sex: since ca. 1930. 'Ooh, the beast! He made me come over all unnecessary.' Cf. synon. **do things to** or **for**. The implications are functional.

all ye in. 'Schoolboys' call when school is going in from play or when players in game must gather' (L.A.).

alleluia! 'A call to shut the tap when boiler washing' (*Railway*, 2nd): railwaymen's: earlier C.20.

alley. A two-up school: Aus. B., 1943.—2. In *up your alley!*, a rude retort (Thomas, 1976). Cf. **up your gonga** or **pipe, up yours!**, etc.

A

alley cat. A girl, a woman, of loose, or no, morals: adopted, ca. 1960, ex US. *DCCU*, 1971.

alley-marble. In, e.g. 'that's just my alley-marble', it is entirely welcome and exactly suitable: coll.: since ca. 1920. An alley-marble was the best sort of toy marble.

alley up. To pay one's share: Aus. (B., 1942.) Ex the game of marbles.

allez oop! Up with you. (Branch, 1951.) 'Also used by acrobats when one of them has to be thrown high. First heard in childhood, ca. 1895' (Leechman).

alligator. Later: r.s. Franklyn.—2. A horse: Aus.: since ca. 1925. B., 1943.

alligator boots. Boots with 'uppers parted from sides, due to soaking up diesel oil' (McKenna, 1970): railwaymen's: since mid-C.20. Ex appearance.

alligator bull. 'Nonsense, senseless chatter' (B., 1942): Aus.: since ca. 1920. There are no alligators in N. Australia. See **bullshit**.

Ally Pally. Alexandra Palace, London (was HQ of television): 1937+. Earlier is the sense 'Alexandra Park race-course'.

ally slope, do an. To make off. (Jarvis, 1925.) (WW1, = go away!) A fusion of *ally* and *Ally Sloper*, that buffoon who named a pre-WW1 comic paper. The name prob. contains a pun on Fr. *allez!*, go, and Eng. *slope*, to go away, decamp furtively.

Ally Sloper's Favourite Relish. 'A particularly racy bottled sauce, available from ship's stores, reputed to be excellent for cleaning brasswork' (Bassett): RN: WW2. See prec.: the name lingered on!

Alma Gray. A threepenny piece: Aus. (B., 1942.) Rhyming on *tray*, since C.18. Parlyaree for three.

almond rocks. Socks: r.s.: late C.19–20. Since 1914 among soldiers: *Army rocks*. (B. & P.) Also C.20 Aus. (McNeil).

almonds. Abbr. of **almond rocks**. P.P., 1932.

alone on a raft is one poached egg on toast, *Adam and Eve on a raft* is two.

aloofer. One aloof and 'superior' in attitude: coll.: ca. 1950 +.

alp bash. A hill climb contest: motorcyclists': since ca. 1950. (Dunford.) Cf. **bash**, n., 2, and **mud-plug**.

Alphabetical. Nickname for anyone with more than two initials to his surname: Services': since ca. 1930. P-G-R.

Alphonse. A 'ponce': r.s. Phelan, 1943.

Alps, the. The 'Carlisle to Stranraer line' (*Railway*, 2nd): railwaymen's: since late 1940s. It has some steep gradients.—2. See **over the Alps**.

also ran, an. A nonentity: mostly Aus. (– 1916) >, by 1918, gen. Dennis, 1916; Collinson. Ex horse-racing.—2. In theatrical circles, a supporting, or bit, part: later C.20. Green.

alter. Unpleasant; e.g. 'We had an alter parade this morning': military (not officers'): from ca. 1930; † by 1950. Perhaps ex (– 1898) Hampshire dial. *alteration* and (– 1898) Berkshire dial. *altery*, (of weather that is) uncertain, tending to rain. (*EDD*.)

altifrontal. High-brow: 1932; somewhat pej., 'Is he intelligent?—Oh, very altifrontal, I'd say.' London authors', reviewers', and publishers'.

altitude. In *grabbing for a.*, striving for height: RAF: since ca. 1925. In WW2 it was used with the connotation 'in order to gain an advantage in aerial combat' (Partridge, 1945). See also **grappling hooks**.—2. Hence, becoming very angry: aircraft engineers': from ca. 1932. *Daily Herald*, 1 Aug. 1936.

Altmark. 'A ship or a Shore Establishment in which discipline is exceptionally severe': RN: 1942+. Granville, 'From the German Prison Ship of that name'.

am and **is** used jocularly. 'There are some jocular and ungrammatical uses of these, as "There you is", "There you am" and "That am so" ' (Petch, 1966): since ca. 1930. Cf. **used to was**.

'Am and Tripe, the. HMS *Amphitrite*: RN: earlier C.20. Bowen.

Amami night. 'Any more or less regular time for searching prisoners, cells, or workshops' (Tempest): prisons' s.: mid-C.20. Ex a popular shampoo of the period, advertised by the slogan 'Friday night is Amami night'. (P.B.)

amateur, or **enthusiastic amateur.** A girl that frequently, promiscuously copulates 'for love': coll.: since ca. 1916.

amber. See **shoot the amber**.

ambidextrous. Both hetero- and homosexual: since ca. 1935. Cf. **AC-DC**.

ambish. Ambition: from ca. 1925. E.g. Radcliffe, 1934.

ambulance chasers. A disreputable firm of solicitors specialising in accident claims: adopted, ca. 1940, ex US.

ameche. A telephone: Can. teenagers': adopted ex US, where current since early 1945. Ex a film in which the actor Don Ameche (pron. am-ee-chee) appeared in 1944–5. The film portrayed the life of Alexander Graham Bell, inventor of the telephone. See CANADIAN ADOLESCENTS in Appx.

amen Theatre Royal. A church: low:—1909 (Ware); ob. by 1930. Why? Perhaps it was orig. theatrical: touring players perform frequently at Theatres Royal.

ameri-can. An *American* petrol *can*: Army: 1942–5. Punning *American* and formed after **jerrican**. P-G-R.

American Workhouse, the. The Park Lane Hotel, London: taxi-drivers': since 1917. (Hodge, 1939.) Ironic: palatial, it caravanserais many rich Americans.

ammo. Ammunition (n. and adj.): military.—2. Hence, *ammos*, ammunition boots, the ordinary army boots: from 1915. (F. & G.) The term *ammo boots*, i.e. those with bradded soles and metalled heels, was still in use in 1950s. Contrast **cobbly-wobbly**, and cf. **tackety boots**.

ammunition. A sanitary tampon or towel; such tampons or towels collectively: feminine: since ca. 1940.

Amorous Military Gentlemen on Tour. The personnel of AMGOT (Allied *Military Government of Occupied Territory*): military and political: 1945–7.

Amos and Andy. Brandy: r.s.: Amos and Andy were coloured American radio comedians, popular during WW2. (Hillman, 1974.) From ca. 1944.

amp. An amputation: medical students':—1933 (*Slang*, p. 190).—2. An 'amputee': Can. (med. and hospital): since ca. 1946.—3. An ampère: electricians' coll.: since ca. 1910; by 1950 > S.E.—4. An ampoule of drug: mostly addicts': since early 1950s. Janssen, 1968; W. & F., 1975 ed.

amphets. Amphetamine: drugs c. Stockley, 1986.

'Ampsteads or **Ampstids**, i.e. *Hampsteads*. Teeth. See **Hampstead Heath**. '*Ampstids*' is the 'deep Cockney' form. (Harrison, 1947.)

ampster or **amster** or **Amsterdam**. A confidence trickster's confederate: Aus.: since ca. 1925. (B., 1942.) It rhymes on **ram**, as Franklyn has noted.

amput. See PRISONER-OF-WAR SLANG, §12, in Appx.

amscray. To depart, make off: Aus.: adopted, ca. 1944, ex US Servicemen. (Park, 1953.) US centre s. on *scram*. 'Like *igaretsay*, it is Pig Latin' (Claiborne)—which owes something to back-s. Cf. *ixnay*, 'nix' = nothing.

anarchists. 'Matches, especially wax vestas' (B., 1942): Aus. Apt to 'blow up'.

anarf = *an'alf = a half*, i.e. ten shillings (50p), the half of £1: London's East End: since ca. 1945. Likewise, *arfundred* = £50. Richard Herd in *Evening News*, 12 Nov. 1957.—2. 'Also a halfpenny. I was told of it in London while at home on leave in 1917. Somebody was told the bus fare was "one anarf"—that is, three ha'pence' (Leechman).

anatomical. Bawdy; sexual: artists': from ca. 1920. E.g. 'anatomical stories, jokes, humour, wit'.

ancestral home. Merely home: joc. coll.: university and Society.

anchor. 'A parachutist who waits overlong before jumping' (Jackson, 1945): RAF: ca. 1930–50.—2. A brake: motorists': since ca. 1930. See **anchors**; and HAULIERS', in Appx. The Regional wireless programme, 23 Nov. 1936, had *drop the anchor*, a busmen's phrase for 'to brake'.

anchor-faced. Derogatory of a sailor loving the Navy and, without questioning, religiously obeying all rules and regulations: RN, WRNS, FAA: since ca. 1950, at latest. (Wood, 1978.) Peppitt adds, 'behaving in a Naval manner in non-Naval surroundings.' Cf. **pusserised**, and the Army's **khaki-brained**.

anchors. Brakes: busmen's: from ca. 1930. (*Daily Herald*, 5 Aug. 1936.) P.B.: by mid-C.20, gen. among motorists, as in, e.g., 'so I slammed the anchors on real hard' = I brought the vehicle to an abrupt halt. Cf. **anchor**, 2.—2. As exclam., soon commoner than the orig. *Whoa, anchors!*, a request to the driver of a vehicle to stop; hence to a speaker to stop, so that a point may be dealt with: RAF: since late 1940s.—3. In *keep* and *put the anchors on*, so to control oneself or one's partner in intercourse as to delay *the final gallop* or orgasm: since ca. 1950. Naughton, 1970, has both *keep* . . . and *final gallop*.

ancient and modern. A hymn-book, as in 'Lend me your ancient and modern': coll. Ex *Hymns, Ancient and Modern*.

Ancient and Tattered Airmen or **Aviators.** The *A*ir *T*ransport *A*uxiliary pilots' name for themselves: 1939–45. The ATA, the ferry-pilots whose task was to fly aircraft from the factories to the RAF, were a gallant band drawn from the ranks of fliers barred from fighting in WW2 by their sex, age, or medical condition. (P.B.)

Ancient Military Gentlemen on Tour. Var. of **Amorous Military** . . . , q.v.

and omitted. A post-WW2 coll. Leechman comments, 1967: 'An Americanism that has spread deep into Canada. "Go feather your nest." "Come see Jimmy swim." "Go tell him hello." "Come have a drink." '

and all that (= and all such things); **all that.** These phrases used to be 'perfectly good English', but since late 1929, when Robert Graves' notable War-book appeared, or mid-1930, when Albert Perceval Graves' *To Return to All That* somewhat modified that picture, they have been so coll. as to verge on s.

and and and. Coll. var. of 'and so on', as in 'Oh, there are a million and one reasons why we can't go: the car's on the blink, and we can't find a baby-sitter, and, and, and': from ca. 1978. (P.B.)

and cakes. 'A supplementary allowance that may be part of the actor's main contract. It means that management either supplies or pays for board and lodging' (Green): theatrical.

and call it 'it'. See **call it 'it'.**

and Co. And the rest; et cetera: RN lowerdeck: from ca. 1912. Maclaren, 1929, 'Sor some nise eye-lands and come after spisse knut mags [*spice, nutmegs*] and co—some times purls'. See also **co.**

and no messing about. A low intensive: since ca. 1930. 'You can lose half a streatch remishion and no messing about' (Norman).

and that. And that sort of thing: coll.: mid(?)C.19–20. Claiborne, 1977, remarks, 'Interestingly, American slang now includes *and like that* with the same meaning. I think a parallel development, since *and that* was never in use here.' This sort of phrase tends to be the most tardily recognised by the dictionaries. (My note: 21 June 1977!). Cf. **and all that.**

and the rest? or **!** A retort on incompleteness or reticence, or of sheer disbelief: since ca. 1860. Still current, later C.20. Cf.:–

and the suet! Midlands var. of the prec. (R. Lucas, on BBC Radio Leicester, 20 June 1984.) Confirmed by Fearon, '1930s or earlier, but not so common now' (of the W. Midlands).

Andrew Makins, (stop your). (Stop your) goings-on or fooling: Anglo-Irish. Is there an allusion to merry Andrews?: cf. the Essex and Sussex *Andrew*, a clown.

Andy McNish. Fish: r.s. Franklyn, 'Either raw or fried'.

anfo. 'Ammonium Nitrate/Fuel Oil (illegal explosive)' (Hawke); Brig. Pat Hayward, 1978, however supplies the alternative translation, 'Any nuisance of foreign origin': Army in N. Ireland: 1970s.

angel. A sandwich-man: c.: earlier C.20. Ex *wings*, the boards. Jennings, 1932.—2. Any outsider that finances a play: theatrical s. > coll. George Orwell, letter 21 Mar 1948 to Julian Symons, uses it for journalism: 'The trouble always is that you must have an angel or you can't keep the magazine alive'.—3. (Also *angie*.) Cocaine: Aus.: since ca. 1925. B., 1942.—4. See **angels**.

angel dust. PCP, phencyclidine: drugs c. (Stockley, 1986.) US since—1969 (Spears).

angels. 'All unidentified dots [on the radar-screen] were originally dubbed "angels" by the radar men . . . Dots in circles that move outwards like ripples on a pond are known as "ring-angels" ' (Boswall, 1970).—2. Amytal: drugs c. Stockley, 1986.

anger. In *in anger*, in earnest, properly, as in 'Once the hassle of the [police driving-]course is over . . . comes the first day actually driving the car in anger' (Cole, 1980): coll.: since later 1970s. Ex S.E. *shots fired in anger*. (P.B.)

angie. See **angel, 3.**

angle-iron pudding. 'A term [formerly] used to describe bread pudding served in Dockyard canteens' (Patterson, 1984): Portsmouth Dockers'.

Angle-irons, the. The Royal Anglian Regiment, formed in 1964 by the amalgamation of the old R. Norfolk Regt., R. Lincolnshire Regt., Suffolk Regt., R. Leicestershire Regt., and the Northamptonshire Regt.: Army. Also known as *the Royal Anglicans*. (P.B.)

angler. See **lens louse.**

Anglo-Banglo, n. (mostly) and adj. Any Anglo-Indian (i.e., of mixed parentage): Army: since ca. 1950; by 1975, ob. (P.B.)

Anglo-Indian back, have an. (Of a girl) to have dead leaves adhering to the back of her dress as she returns from a stroll: Can.: since ca. 1908.

angora. See **act the angora.**

angry man; up with the angry men or **where the angry men are; see an angry bullet.** A serviceman, esp. a soldier, in a battle area; in the battle area; to do service in one: among Aus. servicemen in New Guinea: 1942–5. (B., 1953.) This could form the source of the *angry young men* of whom, since ca. 1957, one has heard far too much.

anguish, be. To be objectionable or deplorable or extremely boring: smart set and BBC 'types': ca. 1946–57. Prompted by 'a *pain* in the neck'?

animal. A policeman: low: from ca. 1919.—2. 'A term of [strong] contempt, esp. since WW2' (Wilkes). Aus. P.B.: also Brit., same period.—3. A professional bully or 'heavy', 'on the Casino payroll to collect outstanding debts and ensure no-one falls out of line on the premises'.

animal run. 'To let your hair down off-duty' (*Mail on Sunday*, 8 Nov. 1987): RM. P.B. The definition is presumably euph.—and the Royal Marines are not notably long-haired.

ankle-biters. Young children: widespread Can. and US: since ca. 1960. Cf. *rug rats*. (Leech, 1986.) An Aus. var. is *ankle-snappers*: later C.20. (Sayers, 1985.) 'Heard of small and unruly children in a Dublin public house, 1961' (Van Dulken, 1988).

Anna May Wong. Stink: r.s. on *pong*: e.g., 'Cor, it dun 'arf Anna May in 'ere, dunnit!' Anna May Wong was an Oriental, silent-film actress, so dating is prob. since 1920s. (Hillman, 1974.)

Annie. An Anson aircraft, 'now used as a Trainer' (H. & P., 1943). Sgt-Pilot Rhodes, 1942, 'The Anson is "limping Annie" from the uneven engine note, or just "Annie" for short.' Jackson, 1943, '*Annie, Old Annie*, the A.V. Roe "Anson" Bomber and Trainer, now obsolescent. Sometimes called "Old Faithful".' (The name *Anson* constitutes a pun on the latter part of 'A. V. Roe *and Son*'.)—2. HMS *Anson*: RN: since ca. 1940. Granville.

Annie Laurie. A 3-ton lorry: r.s. (of an unusual kind): military: ca. 1914–20. (Franklyn.)—2. A bus-conductress: WW2. See **whistler, 4.**

Annie Oakley. 'A free pass to the theatre. Named for the markswoman Annie Oakley (Phoebe Ann Mozee Butler 1860–1912): the holes punched in the tickets supposedly resemble those aces out of which Ms Oakley had shot the pips' (Green): theatrical.

Annie's Bar. 'A place of comfort and refreshment leading off the Members' Lobby' (in the House of Commons): Parliamentary coll. *Time and Tide*, 1 June 1935.

annihilate. To direct a withering glance at; reprimand severely: coll.

annual. A bath (the immersion): Aus. (B., 1942.) Ironic.

anonski; esp. in 'I'll see you *anonski*': Aus. c.p. of ca. 1930–60. After **cheerioski.** (B.P.)

anorak. 'Person, usu. of left of centre political belief, with an interest in "pirate" radio, particularly "off-shore pirates", hence broadcast by Radio Caroline [disc jockeys]: "Some anoraks have just sailed out to visit us" ' (Turner, 1986): ex the customary—and appropriate—dress.

another pair of sleeves, that's. That's another matter: Aus.: since ca. 1925. B., 1943.

Another Place. 'How the Lords and Commons refer to each other's place of discussion' (Raab): Houses of Parliament.

answer the bugle. To fall in with the defaulters: RN coll.: late C.19–20. Irving.

answer to a maiden's prayer. An eligible young bachelor: joc. coll.

ante up. To hand over, surrender (a thing): Services': from not later than 1915. (F. & G.) Ex US poker j.

Anthony Eden. A black felt hat in the upper Civil Service style: coll.: since ca. 1936. Of the kind favoured by the Rt Hon. Anthony Eden.

anti-guggler. 'A straw or tube . . . for sucking liquor out of casks or bottles' (Bowen): nautical coll.

anti-nuke. See **nuke**, n.

anti-wank. Anti-tank: army r.s.: WW2. P-G-R.

antics. Tactical exercises: RN coll. (Bowen.) Also *steam antics*.

antiquarianise. To play at being an antiquary: coll.

ants in (one's: male or female) **pants, have.** To be excited, restless: an Americanism adopted in England in 1938, but not gen. until 1942. Cf.:-

antsy. Restless; nervous: adopted, ca. 1975, ex US; even in 1977, limited use. Ex prec.

anty. Sugar: Army: earlier C.20. (F. & G.) Possibly ex the sweetness of gifts from Anty or Auntie. P.B.: or perhaps simply because, in hot climates, it has an inevitable attraction for ants, and the old Army of the Empire would be only too aware of this.

any. Not any, nothing; none: RN. Ex the abbreviation *N.E.*, not eligible for pay. (Capt. R.J.B. Kenderdine, RN.)

any amount. Much; a *large* amount: coll. 'Have you any sugar?' 'Any amount.'

Any Bloody (occ. **Blooming**) **How, the.** HMS *Howe,* 'which always steered like a dray': RN. Bowen.

any God's quantity. Many; very many: coll.: late C.19–20. 'Any God's quantity of cocked hats and boleros and trunk-hose' (Joyce, 1922). Cf. **any amount.**

any how, anyhow. See **all anyhow.**

any joy? Elliptical for 'Did you have/get any joy (from it/out of them, etc.)?'; 'did you have any luck?': adopted, ex US (?)WW2.

any old how. Haphazardly; unsystematically: coll.: prob. since mid-C.19; certainly C.20.

any old (e.g. **thing**). Any . . . whatsoever: US (ca. 1910), anglicised ca. 1914. W.J. Locke, 1918, 'Mate, Bill, Joe—any old name.' *OED.*

any plum? See **plum pud.**

any Wee Georgie? Any good?: Aus. r.s.: since ca. 1920. (B., 1942.) On 'Wee Georgie Wood', the popular comedian.

anything. In *so help me anything!*: non-U euph. coll.:—1923 (Manchon).

anything else but. See **nothing but.**

Anzac picket, be on (**the**). To be 'dodging the column' at the Anzac Hostel, El Kantara, Egypt. Aus. soldiers': 1940–2. B., 1942.

Anzac poker. See **kangaroo poker.**

Anzac tile. An army biscuit: military: 1915–18.—2. Hence, any very hard biscuit: since 1919; by 1967, ob. (*TV Times,* 27 May 1967.)

ape. Low coll. if applied pej. to a person. Cf. *baboon.*—2. £50; also £500: Aus. (B., 1942.) Suggested by **monkey.**—3. In *go ape*, to be reduced to basic animal instincts by the force of sexual attraction: a girl says '*He's* the one I go ape for' of her boyfriend: since late 1950s. (P.B.)—4. Also *go ape*, (of persons) to go wrong, emotionally or mentally; of things, to go wrong, to fail dismally: adopted, early 1970s, ex US. *Observer,* Dec. 1974, of business or events.

ape hangers (or one word). Highly raised, curved handlebars on a motorcycle: motorcyclists': adopted, with the fashion, ex US, late 1960s. Barnhart cites a US ref. in print, 1965; an early Brit. one occurs in Stuart, 1971. (P.B.)

apeshit. Esp. *go apeshit*, to become very angry: 'Two weeks ago I called him an ugly little f . . . And Steven went *apeshit*' (film actor Harrison Ford, quoted in *Time Out,* 10 Sep. 1982, p.21). Prob. elab. of **ape**, 4, q.v.

apoplectic. Choleric; violent-tempered: coll.

apostle's pinch. A pinch of a very indelicate nature: low.

apothecary. As *the a-*, the ship's surgeon: RN, esp. lowerdeck: ca. 1890–1930. Knock.

app. An *app*lication to, e.g., Governor, chaplain, welfare, etc.: Borstals' and detention centres': current in 1970s. Home Office.

appalling. Objectionable; ugly; noticeable, marked: Society and middle-class coll. Cf.:-

appallingly. Very: coll. Ex last nuance of prec.

apple. A non-addict (of drugs): drugs c. (Stockley, 1986.) US since —1981 (Spears).

apple and pip. To sip: r.s. (Haden-Guest, 1971.) Cf. **apple-pips.**

applebox. 'A small podium hidden from the camera which raises the height either of short actors or of props' (Green): TV.

apple core. £20: r.s., on *score*: since (?)ca. 1950. (Hillman, 1974.)

Apple Corps, the. 'Footplatemen from Yeovil, Somerset' (McKenna, 1970): railwaymen's: mid-C.20. A pun on 'the cider country'.

apple daddy. 'Merchant Navy s. for dried apple rings soaked and cooked in a pastry case, and issued as a pudding on Tuesdays and Thursdays to the apprentices, bosun, etc. Considered a great delicacy, they were liable to be stolen from the galley by ordinary seamen, if they were left unattended while soaking': nautical. (R.S.)

apple fritter. A bitter (ale): r.s.: late C.19–20.

apple pie. Sky: since ca. 1940; rare since 1946. Franklyn.

apple-pips. Lips: r.s., mostly theatrical. (Franklyn.) Cf. **apple and pip.**

apple-polishing. Toadying: Can. Before giving the apple to teacher, a pupil—sometimes ostentatiously—polishes it.

apples. 'In good order, under control' (Wilkes): Aus.: since mid-C.20. As in, e.g., 'How's it going? Everything apples?' Usu. as *she'll be apples.*—2. A shortening of *apples and pears,* trad. r.s. for stairs. It does not predominate over the full term, yet is fairly common: witness Lester.

apples and rice. 'Oh ve-ry nice, oh ve-ry apples and rice,' Harrison, 1943: r.s.: late C.19–20.

'Appy Day. A pessimistic and inveterate 'grouser': RN. (Granville.) Ironic. See **happy.**

April fools. (Football) pools: r.s.: since ca. 1930. Franklyn, 2nd.

April Showers. Flowers: r.s. Franklyn, 2nd.

apron. The tarmac surround of a hangar: RAF: since ca. 1930. Jackson, 1945.

Aqui, the. The *Aquitania*: seamen's coll.: 1914–50, then reminiscent.

Arba Rifles, the. 'A force of Pioneers, pressed into service as front-line troops, at the time of the German break-through near Kasserine (in Tunisia)': Army in N. Africa: WW2. Ex the Souk el Arba. P-G-R.

arch. Archbishop: clerical: late C.19–20.—2. As for 1, always *the a-.* Headmaster: Tonbridge School: late C.19–mid-20.

arch it. 'Gay [= male homosexual] prostitutes who solicit from alleyways or archways [are said to be *arching it*]' (Green): c.: later C.20.

Arch Tiffy, the. The Warrant Engineer: RN: since ca. 1920. (Granville.) See **tiffy**, 1.

archbeak or **archbeako.** Headmaster: some English preparatory schools. See, e.g., the novels of Anthony Buckeridge.

Archbishop Laud, often shortened to *Archbishop.* Fraud: r.s.: since ca. 1945—by 1965, also low s. Cook, 1962.

Archbishop of Cant, the. Any Anglican archbishop; not necessarily Canterbury: since the late 1930s.

archdeacon. As *the Archdeacon,* HMS *Venerable*: RN. (Bowen.) Ex that dignitary's 'style'.

Archibald. The air-bump over the corner of the Brooklands aerodrome next to the sewage-farm: aviation: ca. 1910–14. Ex youth's fondness for bestowing proper names on inanimate objects. W.

Archie. A young station hand, learning his job: Aus. rural (B., 1942.)

are you fit? Are you ready?: orig. RAF, since ca. 1915; by ca. 1950, at very latest, also Army: coll. Perhaps elliptical for 'are you ready and fit for action?' Partridge, 1945; P.B.

arena rat. A 'fan' or an *habitué* or an idler hanging about ice-hockey arenas: Can. sporting circles': since 1957. (Leechman.)

Argate. Joke placename, used in response to the question 'Where did you go for your holidays?': NW England, perhaps wider afield. I.e. 'Our gate'. (Reed, 1980.)

arge. 'Silver (from *argent*)' (Tempest): c.: mid-C.20.

Argie-nought. 'The frigate *Argonaut* was affectionately known by the Paras [q.v.] as "Argie-Nought", and the . . . P. & O. liner *Uganda*, used as a hospital ship, was referred to lovingly as "The Mother Hen" ' (*Don't Cry*): Services': Falklands War. A Hobson-Jobson pun on:-

Argies, the. (Usu. pl.) Argentinians: orig. Falkland Islanders' coll., given wide publicity in the crisis of 1982. *Daily Telegraph,* 6 Apr. 1982. Also *Argie,-y,* adj.

argue the toss. 'To dispute loudly and long': low: since ca. 1910. B.&P. L.A. adds, 1976: 'Assertion and counter-assertion, with varying circumstantial details, on any topic; from "who called heads and who tails" at toss of coin, or "which way it fell".'

argy-bargy, n. and v. Argument, to argue, 'over a point of fact or opinion, esp. of group, even leading to pushing and shoving, to enforce contention'; cf. *barge,* older s. for 'to move roughly and clumsily', and **barge in.** (L.A.).

Ari. Short for **Aristotle**: also spelt *'Arry,* as in Franklyn, 2nd.

arigoni. Tinned tomatoes: RN: later C.20. Ex supplier's name on tin, A. Rigoni (Smith, 1987.)

Aris. Short for **Aristotle,** a bottle. Lester.—2. See **'Arris.**

arisings. Left-overs (as of food): RN. ('Bartimeus'.) Ex official *arisings,* residues proving proper use of expendable stores.

Aristotle. A bottle: r.s.: late C.19–earlier 20. The Sydney *Bulletin,* 7 Aug. 1897; the London *Evening News,* 19 Aug. 1931.—2. Hence, usu. in shortened form *arris* (q.v. at **'Arris**). courage, nerve. This is a double rhyme: *Aristotle* = bottle; *bottle* short for *bottle and glass* = *arse,* s. for 'guts': later C.20, when this *Aristotle* is as likely to be thought of as Aristotle Onassis, the Greek shipping tycoon, rather than the famous philosopher. Howard, 1984, notes that he has even met 'a bit of rhyming slang three times removed, in which *Paris* (*plaster of Paris*) [= *Arris*] = *Aristotle* = *bottle*'.

arith. Arithmetic: schoolchildren's: mid-C.19–20.

ark. In *be,* or *have come, out of the ark,* to be very old or very stale: coll. Lyell, 'Good Heavens! This cheese must have *come out of the Ark!'*—2. As *the Ark,* the aircraft-carrier HMS *Ark Royal*: RN: ca. 1950–80. (A. Knight.)

arm. Influence, power, 'hold': advertising circles': since ca. 1960. 'What sort of arm have you got over them?' (BBC Radio 4, 'You and Yours', 22 May 1975: P.B.)—2. See **long as (one's) arm; not off; under the arm.**

armed begging. 'Demanding money at the pistol point. A hold up' (Tempest): ironic c.: mid-C.20.

Armies. 'Name given generically to *Armament* ratings' (Granville): RN: since ca. 1920.

arms and legs(, all). Weak beer: without *body.* C.19–20.—2. Hence, weak tea: military. F. & G.

Armstrong's patent. Drill that was 'sheer hard labour, needing patience and stamina' and unnecessary: lowerdeck: ?ca. 1850–1920. (Knock.) *Armstrong,* because it required one: not a merely arbitrary surname.

army. As *the Army,* the Salvation Army: coll.

army and navy. Gravy: r.s. Franklyn.

army-barmy. Very keen on, dedicated to, the military life in all its aspects: Army s.: since ca. 1955. Cf. **khaki-brained** and **anchor-faced.** (P.B.)

Army Form blank. Toilet paper: Army (mostly officers'): WW2. P-G-R.

Army tank (usu. in pl). An American serviceman: Aus. prisoners of war in the Far East: 1942–5. (*Sydney Sun,* 22 Sep. 1945; B., 1953.) Rhyming on *Yank*; cf. **Sherman tank.**

aromatic bomb. Atomic bomb: Army, officers' ephemeral pun: late 1945–6. *People,* 2 Sep. 1945.

aroo! See **hooroo!**

around the traps. In (*somewhere*) *around the traps,* somewhere about the place, or around where similar work, e.g. engineering, construction, etc., is being carried on: 'Oh yes, I've been around the traps for a while now': Aus. (Sayers, 1985.) In the *Australian,* 29 Oct. 1986, occurs 'Over the years she worked about the traps . . .', in an article about an actress.

'Arris, 'a-. Esp. in *lose* (one's) *'arris,* to lose one's nerve, to 'chicken out': r.s.: since ca. 1950, or perhaps much earlier. Also spelt *aris,* it is a shortening of **Aristotle,** q.v., r.s. for 'bottle', itself a shortening of *bottle and glass* = **arse,** n., 2 = courage, impudence. There may also be a straight pun on *aris/arse.*

arrival. A landing of the completest mediocrity: RAF: from ca. 1932. H. & P., 1943, gloss as 'The safe landing of an aircraft'; more accurately it should be 'a poor landing, likely to have been troublesome. Thus "Bill's made an arrival" ' (Jackson, rather later in 1943).

arrow. A dart: darts-players' s. > coll.: since ca. 1880. (P. Chamberlain.) A pun. Hence, *in good arrow,* in good dart-playing form.

'Arry. A familiar form of **Aristotle,** q.v. (Franklyn.) Cf. **Ari.**

'Arry's gators. Thank you: Aus.: since ca. 1943. A Hobson-Jobson of Japanese *arrigato.* (Morrisby, 1958.)

arse, n. Posterior: buttocks. Until ca. 1660, S.E.; then a vulg. Ca. 1700–1930, rarely printed in full: even B.E. (1690) on one occasion prints as 'ar—', and Grose often omits the *r,* while Frederic Manning (d. Feb. 1935) was in Jan. 1930 considered extremely daring to give its four letters in his magnificent war-novel, *Her Privates We.*—2. Impudence: Aus.: since ca. 1940. Nino Culotta, *Cop This Lot,* 1960, 'He laughs and says . . . a man would need plenty of arse to pinch another man's book.' I think so too. P.B.: since ca. 1950, and prob. earlier, also Brit. low. See **'Arris,** and cf. **balls** in this sense, of 'nerve, courage'. An elab. occurs in, e.g. 'But it's the kind of movie which is brave, or stupid, enough to ask the meaning of life without having enough arse in its breeches to warrant a reply' (Peachment, 1983).—3. Any person or place the speaker rates as objectionable: see AUSTRALIAN UNDERWORLD, in Appx.—4. In *give* (someone or -thing) *the arse,* to get rid of that person or thing, as in 'She was a pain in the bum, so we gave her the arse': Aus.: since (?)ca. 1950. Cf. the v. (P.B.)—5. See **pain; tear the arse . . . ;** the **arse** entries at KNOW, in Appx.

arse, v.t. To kick (C.19–20); to dismiss, esp. from a job (WW1): s. Cf. **arse,** n., 4.—2. 'One of the blokes said, "Arse her [a lorry] up here." I backed her up against one of the Railway arches' (Gosling, 1959): low.

arse about. To fool about, waste time.

arse about face. Often *it's* or *you've got it* . . . , back to front; all wrong: low coll.: since late C.19. Cf. the early C.20 Services' *arse a-peak,* topsy-turvy.

arse bandit. A notorious sodomite: low. Also *arse brigand*; arse king: earlier C.20. Cf. synon. **turd-burglar.**—2. Hence, 'Among boarding-school boys, one who makes play with homosexual inclinations' (L.A., 1976): since ca. 1910.

arse bit. See **put on the arse bit,** in AUSTRALIAN UNDERWORLD in the Appx.

arse brigand. See **arse bandit.**

arse-end Charlie 'is the man who weaves backwards and forwards above and behind the Squadron to protect them from attack from the rear' (Hillary): RAF: 1939+. Synon. with **tail-end Charlie,** 2.

arse-hole. See **arsehole.**

arse in a sling. See **eye in a sling.**

arse king. See **arse bandit.**

arse-licker. A sycophant: low coll. (Roberts, 1984.)

arse man – leg man – tit man (or hyphenated). Such a male as esteems and enjoys a female's bottom, or legs, or breasts, as her most attractive physical characteristic: coll.: somewhat raffish: the second and third since the late 1940s, although doubtless employed, occ., a decade or two earlier. Of the three, the first term is the least used; also, it arose the latest—not, I think, before ca. 1955.—2. *Arse(-)man.* An active male homosexual: low.

arse of the ship, the. The stern: RN: mid-C.19–20. Granville.

arse off or **out.** See **tear** (one's) **arse off; tear the arse out of it.**

arse over . . . Head over heels; in combinations . . . *over ballocks*: Cockney > gen. low: C.20; . . . *over kettle*: Can.: C.20; . . . *over tip*: low coll.: C.20; . . . *over tit*: Aus. and Brit.: since ca. 1910; . . . *over tits; tock; tuck*: since ca. 1920, perhaps earlier; . . . *over turkey*: late C.19–earlier 20. In Army, esp. officers' s., it > *A over T* and, in WW1, *ack over toc(k)*. All the *arse over t-* perhaps orig. ex . . . *over top*. Cf. **arse upwards.**

arse-party, the. Those who, in any ship, are known to be homosexuals: RN: since ca. 1920.

arse-perisher. See **bum-freezer,** 2.

arse-polishing. An office job: RAF: 1939+. P-G-R.

arse (something) **up.** To bungle: low. To get it the wrong way up. Cf.:-

arse up with care. Applied, as adj. or as adv., to a thorough mess, a real bungle, chaos: low.

arse upwards. In good luck; luckily: coll.: C.17–20. Esp. *rise with one's . . .* (Ray.) Cockneys pronounce it *arsuppards*, whence the punning *Mr R. Suppards*, a very lucky fellow: C.19–20 pron.; C.20 pun.—2. The wrong way round; upside down: Cockneys': C.20. (L.A.)

arse-wiper. A workman that toadies to the boss; a servant to the mistress: low coll.

arse-wise, adj. or adv. Inept; preposterous; awry: low coll.

arsehole, n. Anus: a coll. vulgarism: C.19 (?18)—20.—2. In *I (he,* etc.) *don't* (or *doesn't*) *give an* (or *a cat's) arsehole,* a RN c.p. assertion, either of bravado or of imperturability.

arsehole, v. To dismiss (someone) peremptorily: Aus. low: since mid-C.20. Wilkes.—2. To go up, as in 'Where are you arse-holing off to?' (Parkinson, 1982): Services': mid-C.20.

arsehole bandit. Var. of **arse bandit.**

arsehole going sixpence – half-a-crown. 'Palpitating with fear: RN lowerdeck: 1950s' (Peppitt). Dating, I'd say, ca. 1940–70. Ex the smallest and largest 'silver' coins in circulation during the period. P.B.: an army var. was, e.g. *my arse'ole went like that!,* with finger-tips opening and closing in illustration.

arsehole lucky. Extremely lucky: low: since ca. 1950. Even lower is the mainly Suffolk c.p. it has evoked: *yeah, bending over again.* (F. Leech, 1972.) Cf. **arsy.**

Arsehole Square. Boyish and youthful 'wit' in parroted reply to 'Where?': mostly London: late C.19–20.

arsehole street. In *be in* or *up . . . ,* to be in serious trouble; synon. with *in the shit:* low: since ca. 1950. (L.A.)

arseholed or **arseholes.** Extremely drunk: since ca. 1940. Ex the earlier, low, *pissed as arseholes:* from late C.19.

arser. A fall on one's behind: mostly hunting and turf. Waugh, 1934, 'You just opened your bloody legs and took an arser.'

arsey. See **arsy.**

arso. *Ar*mament *S*upply *O*fficer: RN: WW2. P-G-R.

arsy. (Very) lucky: Aus.: since ca. 1935. (B., 1953.) Ex *tin-arsed,* q.v. at **tin-arse;** cf. also **arsehole lucky.**

arsy-versy. A 'mocking term for a male homosexual's [tendencies]; jocularly contemptuous of [a] thwarting [of] nature': adj. and adv.: (?)since late 1950s. L. A. cites, from the *Sunday Times,* 22 Aug. 1976, a letter in which *gay* is preferred to *arsy-versy.*

arterial. Abbr. arterial road: 1931: coll. E.P.'s orig. comment was 'Soon, prob., to be S.E.' but in the latter half of C.20 the idea is expressed as *motorway.* (P.B.)

Arthur. Arsine gas. H. & P.—2. A simpleton, a dupe: mock-auction promoters': since ca. 1946. Perhaps ex Arthur regarded, by the ignorant, as a 'sissy' name.—3. A (money) bank: r.s. (Powis, 1977): on (*J.*) *Arthur Rank* (1888–1972), the film and flour millionaire.—4. Arthritis: trawlermen's. C.20. Piper, 1974.—5. For *not know whether* (one) *is Arthur or Martha,* see KNOW, in Appx; see also **pair of Arthurs.**

Arthur's fliers. See **fliers.**

artic. An *artic*ulated lorry: since 1938, when the RAF used it of their **Queen Mary** lorries, q.v.; but much more widespread since ca. 1960, with the greatly increased use of this form of transport.

artichoke. A dissolute, debauched old woman: Aus. low B., 1942.

article. 'Used by Wellington to Creevey in Brussels a few weeks before Waterloo: "It all depends on that article there" (pointing to an off-duty, sight-seeing private of one of the line regiments)' (R.S.). Later in C.19, and still (late 1970s), used contemptuously of any person: coll. Ex 'its common use in trade for an item of commodity, as in the phr[ase] "What's the next article?" of the mod. shopkeeper' (*EDD*). Examples heard by me during the 1950s: *nosey article,* inquisitive; *sloppy article; toffee-nosed article.*—2. A woman exported to the Argentine to become a prostitute: white-slavers' c. Londres.—3. A chamber-pot: domestic: mid-C.19–20. It probably arose, as a euph., from 'article of furniture'. Note the story of that bishop, who, to another, complained that his house contained forty bedrooms, to which his guest replied, 'Very awkward, for you have only Thirty-Nine Articles'.

artificial. Usu. in pl, artificial manures: gardening coll.

artillery. (Ones's) *artillery,* one's revolver: Army officers' joc.: WW2. ?Ex US. P-G-R.—2. A full equipment of necessaries for drug injections: addicts': adopted, ca. 1965, ex US. (*DCCU,* 1971.) Cf. synon. **the works.**—3. As *the (heavy) artillery,* 'Big wigs'; convincing or very important persons: coll.: from late 1916; ob. by 1930. In later C.20, sometimes used fig., as in 'Then the Liberals brought their heavy artillery into play, in the shape of Cyril Smith'.

artist. A person; 'chap', 'fellow': from ca. 1905. Hence, by specialisation: an expert, a specialist: since ca. 1918.—2. Hence, 'One who indulges in excesses, e.g., "bilge artist", "booze artist", "bull artist" ' (B., 1942): orig. Aus.; since ca. 1920. But by 1950, at latest, widespread in the Brit. Services, particularly in *piss artist,* a habitual drinker.

Artists, the. The Artists' Rifles: Army coll.

arty, n. Artillery: Aus. Army: WW2. (*Rats.*) Ex the standard Services' abbr. (P.B.)

arty, adj. Artistic; esp. spuriously or affectedly artistic in practice, theory, or manners: coll. Cf.:-

arty-and-crafty; arty-crafty. Artistic but not notably useful or comfortable: coll.: resp. 1902 and ca. 1920. *OED.*

Arty Bishops, the. See **Bishops, the.**

arty roller. A collar: Aus. r.s.: since ca. 1910. B.,1945.

arvo. Afternoon: Aus. (B., 1942.) Cf. **afto.** Usu. as *this arvo,* contracted to '*sarvo.*

Aryan; non-Aryan. Non-Jewish; Jewish: catachreses (of Hitlerite origin) dating, in England, from 1936. This is a particularly crass and barbarous misusage of a useful pair of complementaries.

as – as a –. Similes thus constructed may be found at the appropriate adj., e.g. **easy as** . . . , since, in conversation, the initial *as* is so often dropped.

as-is. Feminine knickers: ca. 1920–40. Lowell, 1929.

as per usual. As usual: coll.: 1874 (W.S. Gilbert). Occ., later, *per usual* (*OED*); another occ. var. is *as per use* (pron. *yews*): non-U: from ca. 1902 (George, 1914). Ex, and perhaps orig. joc. on, the commercial use of *per*, perhaps influenced by Fr. *comme par ordinaire* (W.).

as rotten. (The score) as written: Aus. musicians'. B., 1942.

ash-cash. 'The fee that is paid for signing the doctor's certificate allowing cremation of a dead body: medical s.: since 1967, prob. earlier' (Hamblin, 1988).

Ash Wednesday. The day GHQ Cairo was filled with burning documents on the approach of Rommel.

ashboxing. 'his wife used to go "ashboxing" . . . which involved foraging for food and firewood in the dustbins outside the big houses' (Seabrook, 1967).

ashcan. That's no good, that shot: cinema: since ca. 1925. (London *Evening News*, 7 Nov. 1939.) I.e., put it in the dustbin!— 2. Hence (?), wasted time: Services': WW2. H. & P.—3. A depth charge; orig. its container (ex its appearance): RN: 1939+. Granville.—4. See **put a jelly** . . .

ashcat (or hyphenated). (Usu. in pl.) An engineer, mostly on destroyers: RN: since ca. 1935. Less gen. than synon. *plumber*.

ashed. Drunk; may be intensified *ashed as a rat*—very drunk: Army Signals Regiments': 1960s. Echoic, from the slurred splutterings of a drunkard, 'ash . . . ash . . . ash . . .' (P.B.)

Ashmogger, the. The Ashmolean Museum: Oxford undergraduates':—1920; little used after 1940. Marples, 2.

Ashtip, Mrs. See **Greenfields.**

ask for (one's) **cards.** To leave a job: non-managerial coll.: since ca. 1940, or earlier, to 1974–5: 'I'd just about had enough, so I asked for my cards.' On being paid off, a workman received his insurance cards.

asparagus bed. A kind of anti-tank obstacle: Army: 1939+. H. & P.

aspect. (A look of) ardour; hence, impudence: Hatton Garden District of London:—1909 (Ware). Ex It. *aspetto!*

aspi or **aspy.** An aspidistra: non-U; non-cultured. A modern wit has summarised his life of toil, ending in straitened circumstances, in the epigram: *Per ardua ad aspidistra*.

Aspro. A vocalising of *SPRO*, Services' Public Relations Officer: Army: 1941+. P-G-R.—2. A professional male homosexual: low: since ca. 1940. ?*Ex arse 'pro'*.

Asquith. A French match: Army: WW1. Ex Asquith's too-famous 'Wait and see': such matches often failed to light.

ass. Female pudend: low Can.: late C.19–20. By 1945, partly— by 1960, fairly well, but even by 1987, not fully—adopted in Britain.

ass about. A post-1918 var. of *arse about*. US influence.

ass in a sling. ' "I've got my ass in a sling" or "It's my ass that will be in the sling": means that I'm the one that will be the fall guy [q.v.], my responsibility' (Leech, 1981): Can., ex US: later C.20. Cf. **eye in a sling.**

assap. A vocalising of *ASAP*, as soon as possible: Services': since ca. 1950. Cf. **weff.** (P.B.)

asshole, ass-hole. Arsehole, q.v.; usu. in sense 'a foolish, or objectionable, fellow': adopted, late 1970s, ex US. Philip Howard, in *The Times, passim*.

Assistance, the. National Assistance: poorer classes' coll.: since ca. 1945.

assy. Asphalt: schoolboys'.

astard-ba. Bastard: low: earlier C.20. (*Gilt Kid.*) By transposition.

astern of station. 'Behindhand with a programme or ignorant of the latest intelligence' (Granville): RN coll.: since ca. 1920.

astonisher. An exclamation mark: book-world's: from ca. 1925. Cf. synon. **Christer.**

astronomical. (Esp. in statistics and in sums of money) huge, immense: cultured coll.: since ca. 1938. In ref. to stellar distances and times, and owing much to the vogue of the popular works on astronomy by Eddington and Jeans.

At. A member of the ATS, the [Women's] *A*uxiliary *T*erritorial *S*ervice; as a vocalised acronym it sounded like a natural pl, and so a single member would just as naturally be *an at*: orig. (1939) military. (H. & P.) The ATS became the Women's Royal Army Corps on 1 Feb. 1949. (P.B.) Cf. **Wren; Waaf.**

at it. 'Operating something illegal' (Newman, 1970): police s.: since ca. 1950.—2. (Usu. with *again*.) Indulging once more in sexual intercourse: coll.: late C.19–20. (L.A.) ' "Three minutes pleasure and nine months pain;/another three months and we're at it again./It's a helluva life!" Says the Queen of Spain . . .' (anon.)

at the dip! 'Was a response when addressed or called; an acknowledgment of another' (Bassett, 1979): RN: WW2.

at the high port. At once; vigorously; unhesitatingly; very much: military: from ca. 1925. The name of the position in which a rifle is carried by a soldier who is 'doubling'—running; hence the idea of speed and dash.

atch. To arrest: tramps' c.:—1923 (Manchon). Ex Romany (?): but it may abbr.:-

atchker. To arrest: central s. (–1923) on *catch*. Manchon.

Ath, the. The Athenaeum Club: the world of learning, and that of clubs.

atmospherics. A coll. abbr. of *atmospheric disturbances* ('wireless'): 1928+; by 1935, almost S.E. Hence, fig., an irritable or quarrelsome or highly strung atmosphere: 1932+.

atom-bombo. Cheap but very potent wine: Aus.: since 1945. (B., 1953.) A pun on S.E. *atom bomb* and s. **bombo,** 2.

atomaniac; usually *atomaniacs*. People that would like to use the atom bomb on those they dislike: 1945+.

Ats, the. See **At.**

Atsie, -y. An affectionate var. of **At** (P-G-R.): Army 1939–49, then nostalgic.

attack of the week's (or **month's**) **end, an.** Lack of funds, according as one is paid one's wages or salary every week or every month: joc. coll.: ca. 1890–1915. F. & H.

attention. In *jump* or *spring to* . . . , '(Of men) drill and parade terms used for erection: WW2' (L.A.): Services' joc.

atterise or **-ize.** To staff with ATS or a proportion of ATS; 'to man static gun sites with mixed batteries' (H. & P., 1943): military (orig. joc.). Cf. **waafise** and:-

Attery. Living quarters occupied by *Ats*: 1941–8. (H. & P.) See **At.**

attic. Top deck of a bus: busmen's: from ca. 1920. *Daily Herald*, 5 Aug. 1936.

au reservoir! Au revoir. Orig. US, adopted ca. 1880. In C.20 often *au rev*.

auction. See **all over the auction.**

audies. An ephemeral early name for motion-pictures with sound added: journalistic: 1928. (Hughes, 1980.) Cf. **phonie, talkies.**

aufwiederchooce. 'A fairly recent BAOR corruption, a blending of "Cheers" with *auf Wiedersehen*, for "farewell!" ' (Jones, 1978). Cf. **Alf's peed again.**

Auguste. Orig. (later C.19), a 'feed' or stooge to the white-faced (chief) clown, 'Joey'; later C.20, the principal clown, 'fed' by the ring-master: circus. The name was brought, from the Continent, later C.19, by the clown Thomas Belling, who encouraged the audience to call out '*Auguste idiot*' when he fell over. *Auguste* is Fr. for a type of clown (*Dict. Robert*). (Barltrop; Raab.)

auld case or **gib.** An elderly man: Glasgow coll.:—1934. Ex *gib*, a tom-cat.

aunt. As *the aunt*, the women's lavatory: upper-class feminine: since ca. 1920. Ex:—2. In *go to see* (one's) *aunt* or *auntie*, to visit the w.c.: euph., mostly women's: from ca. 1850. Cf. *Mrs Jones*, which is occ. *Aunt Jones* (H., 5th ed.).

Aunt Edna. 'Slightly derogatory description of traditional theatre-goer of safely conservative tastes' (Green): theatrical.

Aunt Emma. 'In croquet, a typically unenterprising player, or play' (Green).

Aunt Fanny, (e.g. *my* or *his*). Indicates either disbelief or negation: since ca. 1930. Dickens, 1945, 'She's got no more idea how to run this house than my Aunt Fanny.' Also as exclam. of disbelief, etc. A euph. elab. of *fanny*, the backside.

Aunt Maria. A fire: r.s.: late C.19–20. Var. of *Anna Maria.* Franklyn 2nd.

Auntie or **Aunty.** The British Broadcasting Corporation: since ca. 1945; by 1965, slightly ob. Short for *Auntie BBC.* In later C.20, also the Australian Broadcasting Commission (Wilkes). Ex respectability.—2. A mature man kindly—but from suspect tendencies—disposed towards younger men and boys: since ca. 1950 (?much earlier). In e.g., Little, 1958. Green, 1984, more directly: 'an ageing homosexual'. —3. In *'don't be Auntie!'*, Don't be silly: Aus.: since ca. 1920. Prompted by 'Don't be Uncle Willie!' (B., 1959.) Cf. **Uncle Willie**, 1.

Auntie Adas. High rubber overboots, equipment now replaced by leather or plastic riding boots: motorcyclists'. (Dunford.) Mid-C.20: r.s. on *waders*.

Auntie Beeb. See **Auntie**, 1, and **Beeb, the.**

Auntie (or **auntie**) **Ella.** An umbrella: r.s., 'used almost exclusively by women, at the suburban Cockney level' (Franklyn 2nd): since ca. 1946.

Auntie Flo. The Foreign Office: Civil Service, esp. the Diplomatic. Martin, 1957.

Auntie (or **-y**) **May's.** 'Long woollen stockings knitted for the Red Cross, etc., to be issued as "Comforts" to seamen on Russian convoys in WW2'—as in Brown, 1968.

Auntie (or **auntie**) **Nellie.** Belly: r.s. Franklyn 2nd.

auntie's (or **-y's**) **ruin.** A disreputable mess of a man, scheming and seedy: by 1975, virtually †. (Allingham, 1948.) Claiborne suggests, perhaps influenced by **mother's ruin**, q.v.

aurev! Au revoir: from ca. 1920. Galsworthy, 1924. Cf. **au reservoir**.

Aussie, occ. **Aussey.** Australia: from ca. 1895. An Australian: from ca. 1905. Both coll. and orig. Aus.; popularised by WW1. From 1914, also adj.

Aussie rules. Australian football: Aus. coll.: late C.19–20. (B., 1942.) Played under Australian rules.

Aussieland. An occ. var. of *Aussie.* Rare among Australians.

Austin Seven. A 'class B Midland freight locomotive' (*Railway,* 2nd): (?)ca. 1950. Ex its appearance, resembling that of one of the smallest and most famous of the popular saloon cars of the mid-C.20.

Australian adjective, the (often **the great . . .**). 'Bloody': since late C.19. Wilkes.

Australian cigs. In UK, during the cigarette shortage of WW2, cigarettes kept under the counter: ca. 1940–5, then historical. By a pun on *down under*.

Australian days. Night-work: railwaymen's. McKenna, 1970.

Australian salute, the. 'The movement of the hand in brushing away flies' (Wilkes): Aus.: late C.20. Also known as *the Barcoo salute.*

Australian surfing and **Australian** later C.20 underworld terms. See Appx.

Australorp. The Australian 'utility type of Black Orpington fowl' (B., 1959): Aus. coll.: since ca. 1930. A blend of *Australian Orp*ington'.

auto. An automatic revolver: since ca. 1915. (Brandon.) More usu.:-

automatic. Abbr. *automatic revolver*; coll. > S.E. Esp. in WW1.

avast heaving there! 'Stop pulling my leg!': RN lowerdeck: late C.19-mid 20. (Carr.)

'ave a Jew boy's. Weight: joc. Cockney: from ca. 1910. Punning *avoirdupois* and often directed at a fat man.

Ave Maria. A fire: r.s.: late C.19–20. More usu. *Anna Maria.*

avenue. Possibility, as in *explore every avenue*, to try all possible means; mainly political, journalistic, and commercial: soon > coll.; perhaps soon to > S.E.

aviary. 'Chorus girls' dressing room—for the "birds" ' (Green): theatrical.

aviate. To fly, esp. to fly showily, ostentatiously: RAF: since 1938 or 1939 in the latter nuance, since ca. 1936 in the former; joc. and resp. mildly or intensely contemptuous. (Jackson, 1945.) Ex *aviator.*

avit. See PRISONER-OF-WAR SLANG, §12, in Appx.

away. To depart: theatrical: ca. 1905–14. (Ware.) Ex melodramatic *away!* P.B.: since mid-C.20 at latest > gen. (usu. joc.) coll., as in 'Well, I must away!'—2. See **have it away** and the entries following that one.

away all lefts. 'Deprived of badges' (Knock): RN lowerdeck: late C.19-mid 20. Rank, skill and good conduct badges are worn on the left sleeve; perhaps orig. by a pun on the order 'Away all boats!'

away for slates or **away like a mad dog.** (Adj. and adv.) Departing hastily: Liverpool. Cf. **off like a long-dog**, the Sussex version.

away racing. Absent at a race-course: coll., in London's East End: since ca. 1945. Herd, 1957.

away the trip. Pregnant: Scottish working-classes'.

awesome(, totally awesome). 'A youth's expression meaning "wonderful": late 1970s–early 80s: US and Can., at least in the major cities' (Leech, 1985).

awful people, the; Mr. Cochran's young ladies in blue. The police, as in 'Then the awful people arrived': cultured: since ca. 1945, by 1960, the latter slightly ob.

axe. As *the axe*, reduction of expenses, mainly in personnel, in the public services: since 1922; later extended to cuts also in the private sector.—2. Hence, *the axe*, a body of officials (*quis custodiet ipsos custodes*) effecting these reductions: coll., from 1922; 1 and 2 S.E. by 1925, and both ex *the Geddes axe*, that reduction of public-service expenses which was recommended in 1922 by Sir Eric Geddes, who aimed at the *size* of the various staffs: recorded in 1923: coll.; by 1925, S.E. and historical. Prob. ex:—3. In *get* or *give the axe*, to be dismissed, or to dismiss, from employment: coll. until ca. 1945, then S.E. Cf. **get the chop.**—4. 'The extraction of a cut from a player's bet by whoever is running the card or dice game' (Green): gamblers'.—5. 'A performer's musical instrument; usually guitar' (Green): rock musicians'.

axle-grease. Money: Aus.: since ca. 1925. B., 1943.—2. Thick hair-oil; Brilliantine: mostly Aus. schoolchildren's and teenagers': since late 1930. (B.P.) And British too: id. (P.B.)

Ayrab. See **genuwine Bedoowine** . . .

Aztec two-step, the. 'The condition known as "travellers' diarrhoea" ' (Dr Tony Duggan, 1979): gen. among those who suffer the ailment: 1970s. A later var. of *Montezuma's revenge.*

B

b. A euph. for *bastard*, n. and adj., and also for *bloody*, adj.: Aus.: since ca. 1920. 'You'd think the b. lion'd sleep sometimes' (Brockman). P.B.: also some Brit. usage, as in, e.g. 'What a b. nuisance the man is!': perhaps all C.20.

B.A. Buenos Aires: nautical coll.: late C.19–20. (McFee, 1935.) Since mid-C.20, more gen. and widespread.—2. See **Sweet B.A.** where B.A. = *bugger all* = nothing.

b. and m. A mixture of *brown ale and mild bitter*: spivs': since late 1940s. (*Picture Post*, 2 Jan. 1954, article on young spivs.) Cf. the C.19 *b. and s.*, brandy and soda.

B.B. Gen. pl **B.B.s.** A bluejacket: RN: early C.20. (F. & G.) Ex '*British Blue*', with a non-drawing-room pun.—2. Bloody bastard.—3. A bust bodice: feminine coll.: since ca. 1920.—4. A *bitter* and Burton: public houses': late C.19–20. *Fortnightly Review*, Aug. 1937.

b.b.a. *Born before arrival*: medical students'. *Slang*, p. 189.

B.B.C. The British Broadcasting Corporation (founded ca. 1924): coll.: by 1933, S.E.—2. Any broadcasting corporation: 1933 (*Daily Telegraph*, early Aug.): coll.—3. As *the B.B.C.*, the 2.10 a.m. freight express train from London to Wolverhampton: railwaymen's joc.: from ca. 1929. (*Daily Telegraph*, 15 Aug. 1936.) It passes through *B*asingstoke, *B*irmingham, and *C*rewe. Cf. **the Bacca**.—4. See **talk BBC**.

b.d.v. or **B.D.V.** A picked-up stump of a cigarette: tramps' c.: from ca. 1920. Lit., a bend-down Virginia: punning *B.D.V.*, a brand of tobacco. Also called a *stooper*.

B.E.M.s. '*B*ug-eyed *m*onsters', a derogatory epithet for a certain genre of 'pulp' science-fiction: since ca. 1955, the full phrase; the use of initials, soon afterwards. Cf. *little green men*. (Bishop, 1977.) Moore, 1965, writes *the Bems*. R.C. 1976, notes that, as *Bems*, 'it was current among US science-fiction "fen" (i.e. "fans") as early as 1940s.'

b.f. or **B.F.** *Bloody fool*: coll. euph.: C.20; rare before WW1. Lyell.

B.F.N. 'Bye for now!': since ca. 1940. (Petch.) Cf. *T.T.F.N.*, *Ta-ta for now*, 'Mrs Mopp's' famous farewell—c.p. in the Tommy Handley radio comedy show 'Itma', dating from the same time.

b.h. *Bloody hell*: 1928 (*OED* Sup.). Also *bee aitch*.—2. 'Bung-hole', i.e. cheese: Army: from ca. 1918; † by 1950 at latest.

b.i.d. *Brought in dead* (to the hospital): medical students'. Cf. **b.b.a.**

B.M. Abbr. B.M.W. (*Bayerische Motoren Werke*) motorcycle, in production since 1923: motorcyclists'. (Dunford.) Also *Bee Em*.

b.n. *B*loody *n*uisance: coll. euph.: earlier C.20. Cf. **b.f.; b.p.n**

B.O. *B*ody *o*dour: advertisers', and hence gen.: since ca. 1950. (P.B.)—2. (As an imperative.) Run away (and stop bothering me)!: since ca. 1955: abbr. of *bugger off!*

b.o.f. *B*oring *o*ld *f*art: adolescents' term of abuse and contempt for most people older than themselves: from later 1970s; the full term, more widespread.

B.O.L.T.O.P. See LOVERS' ACRONYMS, in Appx.

B.P. The *B*ritish *P*ublic: theatrical (1867) >, by 1910, gen. coll. (Ware.) P.B.: in C.20 usu. G.B.P., the Great . . . ; often ironic.

b.p.n. A *b*loody *p*ublic *n*uisance: earlier C.20. Cf. **b.f.**

B.Q. *B*efore *q*ueues: 1944 (Bason.): WW2 ephemeral.

b.r. or **B.R.** A *b*edroom steward, in the First Class of a passenger liner: nautical. Bowen, 1929.

b.s. A euph. for **bullshit**, q.v.: 'goes back at least to 1908 in British Columbia' (Leechman).

B.S.A. 'The result of too much riding on a bad saddle', i.e. a *bloody sore arse*: club cyclists'. (*Fellowship*, 1984.) A pun on famous make of motorcycle, from the Birmingham Small Arms works.

B.S.H.s. *B*ritish *S*tandard *H*andfuls—a woman's breasts: raffish joc.: later C.20. (Powis.) A pun on BSIs, the coll. ref. to the standards laid down by the British Standards Institution.

B-squared. A brassiere: schoolgirls': since late 1930s. (Wober, 1971). Cf. **B.B.** 3.

b.y.t. '*B*right young *t*hings' or the younger set: ca. 1946–51.

ba-ha. Bronchitis: tailors': from the 1890s; ob. by 1935. By deliberate slurring.

baa-baa. In *go baa-baa* (*black sheep*), to *bar* the favourite: turf s.:—1932. (*Slang*, pp. 242, 246.) There is, further, an allusion to the nursery rhyme.

Baa-Baas, the. The Barbarian Rugby Football team: sporting: from ca. 1924. Also known as *the Barbers* (Bishop, 1984).

baa-lamb. (With capitals) HMS *Barham*: RN.—2. A tram: r.s.—3. A euph. for *bastard*: since ca. 1918.

babbler. Aus. and Brit. var. of **babbling brook**, n. 1: WW1 military > gen.

babbling. Cooking: Aus.: later C.20. Ex prec. and next. Wilkes.

babbling brook, n. A cook: r.s.: Aus. and Brit. (B. & P.; Wilkes). Cf. prec.—2. A criminal: id., on *crook*: later C.20. Aus. and Brit.

babbling brook, adj. Unwell: Aus. r.s., on synon. *crook*: since ca. 1920. Cf. n., 2.

babe in the woods. 'An innocent; inexperienced, untried. As in "I dunno. He's pretty much a babe in the woods about race car driving." Widespread West N.Am.: since 1940s, at latest' (Leech, 1986).—2. In pl. = dice.

babes. As *the Babes*, Charlton Athletic Association Football Club: sporting: from ca. 1925. It is the youngest London club.

babies' cries. A var. of **baby's cries**, q.v.

babies' heads. See **baby's head**.

Babus, The. The Royal Army Pay Corps: a nickname sometimes bestowed upon them by soldiers who had served in India. (Carew): (?)late C.19–mid-20. Ex Hindustani. Y. & B., 'the word has come often to signify "a native clerk who writes English" .'

baby blues. The postnatal depression unhappily suffered by some new mothers: coll.: since mid-1970s. An article on the subject appeared thus titled in *New Society*, 5 Apr. 1979 (P.B.).

baby bonus. A maternity allowance: Aus. coll.: since ca. 1945. (B.P.) 'Common in Canada also; Family Allowance Act passed in 1944' (Leechman).

baby couldn't help it. Minced meat and brown sauce: Marlborough College: from ca. 1920.

baby-farmer or **-stealer.** A male or a female courter or lover of one much younger, very young: C.20. Cf. **baby-snatcher**, now, later C.20, the more usual term.

baby services, the. The pre-service boys' military cadet corps: SCC; ACF; ATC; and CCF: coll.: Services': 1970s. (Peppitt.) An 'in' term.

baby-snatcher. One who marries a person much younger: joc. coll.:—1927 (Collinson). Hence, also, v. and vbl n., *baby-snatch* and *baby-snatching*. Cf. **baby-farmer** and *cradle-snatcher*.

baby spot. See MOVING-PICTURE SLANG, in Appx.

Babylon. The Establishment, esp. the police: the latter, among hippy communes and West Indian Cockneys; the former, in the higher journalism and other forms of the media. Since ca. 1974. (R.S., 1975 and 1976; Powis, 1977.)

baby's bottom. In *smooth as a*, or *like a, baby's . . .* , very smooth and pink, esp. of a face after shaving: coll. Raab recalls 'smooth as a . . . ', a slogan referring to a make of pipe tobacco, mid-C.20. Sidney Morgan, Cardiff, 1977, notes the Welsh var. . . . *bum*.—2. Only as *like a baby's bottom*: expressionless; characterless: since ca. 1925. (L.A.) Cf., for the first nuance, the synon. **po-faced**.

baby's cries. Eyes: r.s.: from ca. 1920. Hyder.

baby's done it. One of the names for the number *two* in TOM-BOLA, q.v. in Appx.

baby's head. A steak-and-kidney pudding: RN, and soon more gen. F. & G., 'Suggested by its smooth, round appearance.' Still current, later C.20. witness John Winton, in an article about RN nuclear submarines, *Illustrated London News*, Oct. 1976, p. 73. Also known as *Dead Baby* (Bassett).

baby's pram. Jam: r.s. (L.A., 1978.)

baby's yellow. (Mainly infantile) excrement: nursery coll.: C.19–20. Cf. **gipsy's ginger**.

Bacca, the. The express goods-train carrying tobacco (including cigarettes) from Bristol to London: railwaymen's: from ca. 1910. (*Daily Telegraph*, 15 Aug. 1936.) Cf. **the Biscuit, the Flying Pig, the Leek, the Magic Carpet, the Sparagras, the Spud**; also **the Early Bird, the Early Riser, the Farmer's Boy, the Feeder**, and **the Mopper Up**. These railwaymen's nicknames were recognised as official in the GWR's *Guide to Economical Transport*, issued in August 1936.

bacca-, more gen. **baccy-box.** The mouth; the nose: low:—1923 (Manchon). Ex *bacca*, s., since C.18, for tobacco.

bacca firm. A small group that deals in tobacco: RN lowerdeck: ca. 1880–1930. (Knock.) A practice not unknown in long-term prisons.

bach. A bachelor: in US in 1850s; anglicised ca. 1900. Ware prefers *bache*. Cf.:—2. 'Camelford's residence was not in a boarding-house, but what is generally known in the Antipodes as a "bach" (or a "batch", if you prefer to maintain fiercely that the word is derived, not from the first syllable of the word "bachelor", but from the idea of a number of similar things being grouped together)' (Arthur, 1941): Aus., NZ, Fijian.—3. Hence, a holiday cottage: NZ, esp. the North Island: later C.20. (M. Moore, 1980.) Var. of Aus. **batch**.

bachelors' buttons. Buttons with small rings on the back, that can be fastened to a garment with a nail or matchstick, as a 'temporary' measure, to avoid the chore of sewing. Brewer, 1970 ed., defines them as 'a type of press-stud'—but the key point is the avoidance of needle and thread. (P.B.)

back. In *get on* (someone's) *back*, to bully; to urge on: Aus.: since ca. 1925. (B., 1959.)—2. Hence, *get off* (someone's) *back*, to cease from nagging or criticising or urging, as in the exasperated 'Get off my back, will you!': since ca. 1930. (Common also in US.)—3. In *be on* (someone's) *back about*, to reprimand concerning, speak sternly to about (something): Aus.: since ca. 1910. ' "You know bloody well you're supposed to re-stock as soon as you run low on anything," said Billy. "The doc was on your back about this before" ' (Cleary, 1959). Cf. sense 1.—4. In *that's what gets up my back!*, that's what angers me: since ca. 1930.—5. In *at the back*, 'where one drug is taken after another' (Dr T.H. Bewlay): addicts': later C.20.

back a tail. To commit sodomy: Aus. low: later C.20. McNeil.

Back-ah-yard. 'The Caribbean generally; an expression, roughly translated as "back home", used by homesick West Indians' (Powis, 1977). Cf. the American and Aus. use of *yard* for what the British call 'garden'.

back board. A distant signal: railwaymen's. (Railway, 2nd.) Cf. **back stick**.

back burner, n. In e.g. *put on the back burner*, to allot a low priority to, as in 'We'll put that one on the back burner, and deal with this one at hand straightaway'. 'Prob. since the advent of gas and/or electric cookers: widespread West US and Can.: poss. back to the 1920s or 30s. The usage is common at almost all social levels' (Leech, 1986). Some Brit. aping of the idiom since ca. 1980; it may also mean the relegation of something from a previously high position to one of comparative obscurity. (P.B.)

back-burner, v. To postpone, hold in abeyance, something non-urgent: ex US c.p. (since ca. 1930) *put it on the back burner*, adopted in UK later C20, and now used thus elliptically. (Watts, 1988.)

back-cloth star. An actor or actress that plays up-stage, thus forcing the others to turn their backs to the audience: theatrical:—1935.

back(-)door (or solid) **entry.** 'The gaining of a commission in the Army by any means other than by passing through the Royal Military Academy, Sandhurst. The term was certainly in common use in the mid–1920s. I suspect not before WW1, as the only entry, as far as I know, other than through RMA/RMC [Royal Mil. College, Woolwich] was through the Militia' (Hayward).

back double. A back street: Cockney: late C.19–20. (Kersh, 1938; Powis, 1977.) Ex **double, 1**.

back duck (usually in pl). A piece of fried bread: RN (lower-deck). (Granville.) Ironic.

back garden. 'The end pages of a magazine, devoted to advertisements inserted between columns of "spill over" from articles and stories in the front of the "book" ' (Leechman): Can. publishers' and journalists': since ca. 1910.

back-hand! Get out of the way!: ships' stokers'.

back-hander. A drink either additional or out of turn: coll.: ca. 1850–1900. Ex:—2. A blow with the back of the hand: coll. >, by 1870, S.E.: 1836, Marryat; Farrar.—3. Hence, a tip or bribe made surreptitiously: since ca. 1915. In later C.20 usu. written solid, as in, e.g. Piper, 1974. Cf. **backhanding**.

back in circulation is applied to a female jilted or divorced or widowed and therefore free from a male tie: coll.: since ca. 1945.

back-mark. See **back-marked**.—2. Hence to outdistance (easily): sporting: 1928 (*OED* Sup.).

back-marked, be. To have one's athletic handicap reduced: late C.19–20 coll., ob. Rare in active voice.

B

back number. (Of a person) a 'has been': coll.: US (1890: *OED* Sup.) anglicised ca. 1905; by 1935, S.E. Prob. ex the back numbers of periodicals.

back of an (or **the**) **envelope.** Used of 'simple and speedy calculations: from the cliché portrait of genius/absent-minded professor scribbling great notions on a scrap of paper' (Green): scientific circles'.

back pedal. 'Withdraw from a previously adopted position or attitude; stop; pause' (Phythian): since ca. 1910. Often in the imperative. Ex cycling.

back-room boy. Usu. pl, . . . *boys*, inventors and theoretical technicians, working for one of the combatant Services: journalistic j. (1941) >, in 1943, a gen. coll.—in 1943–5, mostly Services'. They worked for or the limelight and often literally in back-rooms or back-washes. P.B.: in later C.20 as one word, and also adj., as in 'a new breakthrough in the backroomboy part of the competition' (Phillips, 1979).

back-seat driver. Someone who gives unwanted, and usu. irritatingly unnecessary, advice to the person in control: prob. since soon after motorcars were equipped with rear seats. (P.B.)

back shift. Late turn (of duty): railwaymen's coll. *Railway*, 2nd.

back stick (GWR); **back 'un; brown one** or **'un; ginger one.** A distant signal: railwaymen's. *Railway*, 1964.

back-to-backs, the. Mean, small, thickly set, parallel-ranged houses in slums and mining towns: coll.

back-up. A 'chain' copulation with one girl: Aus. teenage gangsters': ?adopted, ca. 1945, ex US. (Dick.)—2. A second helping of food: Aus., esp. W.Aus. Ronan, 1961.

backblock. Of the backblocks or 'the bush': Aus. coll.: since ca. 1920. B., 1943.

backblocker or **backblockser.** One who lives in a remote rural area: Aus. coll.: since ca. 1920. (B., 1943.) Also (*back-blocker*) NZ coll., as in Devanney, 1928.

backer-up; backing-up. 'The accomplice of a woman who *works a ginger* on a client—i.e. robs him—is a *backer-up* and the practice is called *backing-up*' (B., 1943): Aus. c.: since ca. 1920.

backhanding. Giving gratuities: lower classes'. See **backhander**, 3.

backhouse flush. A very poor hand: Can. poker players': since ca. 1955. 'Fit only for the privy' (*backhouse*, US and Can.). Leechman.

backing dog. 'A sheepdog that will run across the backs of sheep to aid mustering or droving' (B., 1959): Aus. rural coll.: late C.19–20.

backtrack. 'To withdraw plunger of needle, drawing blood into syringe' (Stockley, 1986): drugs c. US since–1959 (Spears).

backyard. Small; insignificant; 'operating on a shoestring': Aus. coll.: since ca. 1925. 'A backyard publishing company.' (B.P.)

bacon and egg tube. 'Fitted as an experiment to Submarine L4 about 1930. It was a flexible hose which could be attached to the hull by divers, and in the event of mishap supplies could be passed down it' (Edwards): RN.

bacon and eggs. Legs: r.s., Aus. and Eng. (B., 1942; Jones, 1971, 'Wot smashin' bacons'.) Cf. **Scotch eggs**.

bacon-and-bull's-eye offices. Country sub-post-offices, combining postal with general-store business: Post Office staff's coll.: since ca. 1930. (L.A., 1976.)

bacon bonce. 'A dull fellow, one whose reactions are slow like those of a country yokel' (Berry, 1958): Borstal, but also gen.—2. A man with a head partially or, esp., wholly bald. (L.A.)

bacon-hole. Mouth: mostly RAF: since ca. 1940. Cf. **cake-hole**.

bacon-slicer. 'Outside flywheel as fitted to some Douglas and Blackburne [motorcycle] engines. Named after its appearance—a large spinning disc' (Partridge, 1979): motorcyclists': ca. 1910–40.

bad. 'Good; the inference being that the individual/object so defined is bad in Establishment eyes and thus good in those

of any outlaw—criminal, drug, minority—culture, esp. in Black use' (Green, 2): some UK adoption ex US, later C.20.

bad break. A stroke of bad luck, or series of misfortunes: coll.: adopted by Can., ca. 1910, ex US—and fairly common in UK since ca. 1919. (Leechman.)

bad dog. An unpaid debt: Aus.: since ca. 1945. (B., 1953.) Cf. **tie up a dog**.

bad mixer. See **mixer**.

bad-mouth. To malign; to run down; criticise adversely: journalistic: copied, ex (orig. Black) US, later 1970s. (Raab.)

bad news. Of a person or a fact, incident, state of things, and always used predicatively, as in 'He's bad news' = he's either dangerous or boring or very unlikeable; and in 'Driving a faulty car in bad conditions is bad news': adopted, late 1960s, ex US. In short, *news* is here either unnecessary or even misleading. (P.B.)

Bad O. The town and barracks of *Bad* Oeynhausen, Westphalia, the seat—1945 onwards—of British military administration in West Germany: esp. among troops of the BAOR: coll., not s. (P.B.)

bad patchville. A period of bad luck: racing: since ca. 1960. Francis, 1964. ' "Pay no attention," he said. " . . . It's bad-patchville, that's all".' The *-ville*, a very popular suffix in the US, was adopted in the late 1950s. Ibid., ' "Strictly dooms-ville, us." ' See also **-ville**.

bad scene. Unpleasantness; a grave disappointment: adopted by teenagers, ex US, ca. 1970.

bad show. See **show**, n., 1.

bad smash. Counterfeit coin: c. Hume.

bad trot. A *run* of bad luck: Aus.: since ca. 1925. Cleary, 1949.—2. A 'rough spin' or 'raw deal': Aus. Ex the game of two-up. (B.P.)

bad types. Service personnel not keen on their work; also objectionable: RAF: WW2. (H. & P.) See **type**, 2.

bad with, get in. To get into bad odour with (e.g. the police): coll. Wallace, 1928.

badders. Something (event, news, etc.) bad or unpleasant: from ca. 1925. (Waugh, 1934.) The 'OXFORD -ER'.

baddie, -y. A bad, an evil, person: mostly schoolchildren's: since late 1950s.—2. A villain in, e.g., a film; the 'bad guy', as in 'You can always tell the baddies because they're the ones dressed in black': adopted, ca. 1960, ex US. *DCCU*, 1971.

badgeman. 'Someone [a rating] with one or more Good Conduct Badges' (Malin, 1979): RN coll. > j.

badger-game. A form of blackmail, based upon timely arrival of 'injured husband': Can. c.: adopted, ca. 1910, ex US. (See *Underworld*.)

badgy. An enlisted boy; **badgy fiddler,** a boy trumpeter: military: ca. 1850–1905. (F. & G.) P.B.: *Badg(e)y* for a boy soldier was still current in 1950s.

badster. A bad one (any living thing): Aus. coll.: since ca. 1925. Devanney, 1944, 'He'—a mate—'was a badster, a soul killer.' After *youngster, oldster, etc.*

Baedeker is a coll. shortening of *Baedeker*, a raid on a place of historic interest rather than of military importance: 1942–4. (Jackson.) See esp. E.P.'s *Name into Word*, 1949.

Baedeker Invasion, the. The invasion of Sicily during WW2: Army coll. Ex the booklets issued beforehand to the troops. (P-G-R.) Cf. prec.

baffle. Elaborate Field Security measure(s): military, esp. Royal Corps of Signals: since 1939. H. & P.

baffs. Pron. of acronym BAFV, *British Armed Forces'* Vouchers, military paper money for use in NAAFI canteens, etc.; they were last used in the Suez expedition, 1956. (P.B.)

bag, n. A parachute: orig., ca. 1930, RAF; by 1944 also Army. (H. & P.) Pej. ?Carried in a bag.—2. A coll. ellipsis of *breathalyser bag*: since ca. 1965. Bournemouth *Echo*, 16 Nov. 1967.—3. A way of life; one's professional or social or other 'circle' or *milieu*: adopted, ca. 1961, ex US.—4. One's

B

current hobby or main interest: adopted, ca. 1962, ex US. (Both 3 and 4 are owed to Janssen, 1968; and both derive from musicians' use of *bag*, a 'school', also a style, of jazz music.)—5. In *in the bag*, (of a situation, a plan, etc.) well in hand; fully arranged; a virtual certainty: Services': since ca. 1925. (H. & P.) Ex game-shooting.—6. Hence, *in the bag*, easy: Army: since ca. 1935.—7. To *be in the bag*, to be a prisoner-of-war: Army: WW1 & 2.—8. Of a horse, *in the bag* = not intended to run: Aus.: turf. B., 1942.—9. As *the bag*, money: Scot., esp. Glasgow lower classes': late C.19–20. MacArthur.—10. In *a bag of*, enough; plenty of: Army: early C.20 (F. & G.) Poss. suggested by *bag of beer*; cf. **bags of**.—11. In *get* or *have a bag on*, to be sulky, peevish, irritable: Leics teenagers'. (Burt, 1988.)—12. See **come the bag; hold the bag**.

bag, v. To shoot down (a 'plane): RAF: 1939+. (Jackson, 1945.) I.e., to add to one's game bag.—2. 'To get unbroken horses used to being touched and rubbed with a *bag* before trying to put on a saddle' (Elliott, 1970): Aus. rural: coll. rather than s.—3. To criticise adversely; disparage, 'knock': Aus.: later C.20. McNeil.—4. 'Sometimes [doctors' talk] is made up of peculiar verbs originating from the apparatus with which they treat people: "Well, we've bronched him, tubed him, bagged him, [and] cathed him" . . . ("We've explored his airways with a bronchoscope, inserted an endotracheal tube, provided assisted ventilation with a resuscitation bag, [and] positioned a catheter in his bladder to monitor his urinary output")' (D. Johnson, 1980).

bag and hammock. A RN coll. var. of S.E. *bag and baggage*: since ca. 1960. (Peppitt.) I.e., entirely; leaving nothing.

bag-lady. 'A dispossessed elderly lady, homeless, who sleeps on the streets [and who keeps all her poor possessions in paper or plastic bags]: New York City orig.: prob. since early 1970s. Understood widely, but applied only in NYC' (Leech, 1986). P.B.: Some journalistic use in UK by 1986; see also **bagman**, 1.

bag of bones. A 'bush pilot' aeroplane: Can.: since ca. 1942. (Leechman.)

bag of flour. A bathroom shower: r.s.: later C.20. (Daniells, 1980.)

bag of fruit. A suit (of clothes): Aus.: since ca. 1945, adopted ex US. Cf. synon. **whistle and flute**.

bag of gold. 'The roes are one of the valuable extras [the cod] provides and are collected by trawlermen in little sacks . . . "bags of gold", these are called' (Piper, 1974): trawlermen's.

bag of nails, a. A state of confusion: Aus. (B., 1942.) Higgledy-piggledy.—2. A noisy, rattly engine: motorcyclists': later C.20. (Bishop, 1987.)

bag of shit tied up with string. Applied to any person, clumsy, shapeless or 'scruffy': mostly military; contemptuous, as in 'She looks like a . . . ': since ca. 1950. (P.B.)

bag of snakes. A pendulous breast: Aus.: ca. 1910–60.—2. (?Hence) a girl, esp. a very lively one: Can.: since ca. 1955. (Leechman.)

bag of tricks. A bag of tools; also *box of tricks*, a box containing anything, esp. tools, needed for any purpose: since ca. 1910. (Petch, 1969.)

bag-shanty. A brothel: RN lowerdeck.

bag-swinger. A bookmaker: Aus.: since ca. 1930. B., 1943.—2. See **swing a bag**.

baggage. 'An observer of a game who does not himself play' (Green): gamblers'. Cf. **kibitzer**.—2. 'Anyone who does not earn enough to pay his own way' (Ibid.): id.

baggage (box) boy. 'Homosexual prostitute who offers only active intercourse or fellatio to his clients' (Green): c.

bagged. Imprisoned: Aus.: since ca. 1925. (B., 1943.) Cf. **bag**, n., 7.

bagged out. 'Tired out, worn out; rather like "fagged out": West Can. and US, esp. among young people: prob. mid-1970s' (Leech, 1986).

bagged up. In cells, as in '[The prisoners] would rather be bagged up than all milling around where the warders can see

them' (BBC Radio 3, 'The Prisoners', broadcast 25 May 1978, a 'documentary' programme). Cf. prec. and **banged up**.

bagger. See **single-bagger**.

baggies. 'Oversize boxer trunks, long in leg' (*Pix*, 28 Sept. 1963): Aus. surfers': since ca. 1955.

baglet. See HAULAGE, in Appx.

bagman. An apparent revival, later C.20, of Aus. late C.19 term for a tramp; but better understood now, and so used on BBC Radio 4, 'Quote, Unquote', 13 Aug. 1985, as the male equivalent of **bag-lady**, q.v.—2. 'A man who collects extortion or bribe money for mobsters or other such groups: since 1952 (W. & F., 1967): widespread in N. Am.' (Leech, 1986).—3. A drug supplier: drugs c. (Stockley, 1986.) US since—1968 (Spears).

Bagman's Gazette, The, or **The Drover's Guide.** An imaginary periodical quoted as the source of a rumour: Aus.: since ca. 1920. (B., 1959.) See **bagman**, 1.

bagpipe. 'Sexual intercourse between the penis and the armpit, considered to be the province of the homosexual world' (Green).

bags of. Much, plenty; many. E.g. 'bags of time'. (B. & P.; Lyell.) Cecil Litchfield entitled his first, and wittily funny, novel: *Bags of Blackmail*. Cf. **bag**, n., 10. P.B.: hence simply *bags*, as in 'Have you got enough? Because I've got bags here—bags to spare.'

bags of brace. 'Drill bombardier's exhortation to his squad' (H. & P.): Royal Artillery: since ca. 1920. Ex the idea of bracing oneself to make a special effort. P.B.: prob., rather, keeping the back erect. Cf. **bags of swank**.

bags of bull. Excessive spit and polish and/or parading: RAF: since ca. 1938; thence to the other services. Partridge, 1945.

bags of panic. Very pronounced nervousness: RAF: since ca. 1938. (Partridge, 1945.) Since WW2, more gen., as in 'So, of course, there was bags of panic all round.'

bags of swank. Synon. with **bags of brace**: Army: WW2 (?and before). 'Right! Let's have you! Bags of swank as you pass the saluting base'—the cry of any drill-instructor anxious to make an impression with 'his' men. (P.B.)

bagsy. Unshapely: Glasgow coll.:—1934. I.e. with as much delicacy of shape as a bag.

bail up. To corner or accost (a person): Aus. B., 1943.

Bailey, the. The Old Bailey (the Central Criminal Court, London): police coll.: mid-C19–20.

bait. Food: railwaymen's, esp. of those on a Pullman-provided train: from ca. 1920. *Daily Herald*, 5 Aug. 1936. Ex C.16 S.E. (by C.20 > dial.) *bait*, provender.—2. A sexually very attractive girl: teenagers': since late 1950s. Variants: *bedbait, jail-bait, johnnybait*. *Sunday Times*, 8 Sep. 1963.

bait-layer. A station cook: rural Aus. since ca. 1925. (B., 1943.) Cf. RN derog. **grub-spoiler**.

bake. The head: an earlier C.20 military corruption of *boco*, C.19 s. for the head. F. & G.—2. A fiasco; a useless act: low and military: earlier C.20. Richards, 'I found a stretcher-bearer already attending to Smith . . . and he informed me that it was a bloody bake, as Smith had stopped it through the pound.' With *bake*, cf. Fr. *four*, an utter failure theatrically; *pound* is *pound of lead*, r.s. for 'head': late C.19–20 (cf. C.19 *lump of lead*).—3. Hence(?), a bore, a nuisance: RAF in India, ca. 1925–35. (Wall.) Cf. the RAF **bind**, n. and v.—4. A disappointment: RN: since ca. 1920. Granville.—5. A malicious description of one's character. See AUSTRALIAN UNDERWORLD TERMS.

bake-out. The disinfection of clothes in an oven: c.: from ca. 1920. Harrison, 1934. Sc.: *of lice*.

bake up, v.; **bake-up**, n. See **stove up**.

baked. (Of persons) extremely hot: coll. A natural extension of *baking*, said of very hot weather, since ca. 1850.

baked bean. HM the Queen: r.s. 'I just can't get the old baked bean in the paper these days. It's all Di [Princess of Wales] and Fergie [Duchess of York]' ('one of the pop reporters', quoted in *Observer*, 13 Sep. 1987).

B

bakshee (C.20 only), backshee; ba(c)ksheesh (most gen. from earlier C.20); buckshee (usu. form later C.20); bucksheesh; buckshish. A tip; gratuity; Near Eastern and Anglo-Indian: from mid-C.18. Popularised by the British Army in India and Egypt, esp. in WW1, though it was fairly gen. even by 1800. The forms in -ee are the more coll. Ex the Persian (thence Arabic, Urdu and Turkish) word for a present. See esp. *OED* and Y. & B.—2. Adj. and adv., free, costing nothing: late C.19–20: orig. and mainly Army. As *buckshees*, its commonest late C.20 sense.—3. Hence, additional; unexpected: Army.

bakshee (gen. buckshee) king. A paymaster: Army: earlier C.20. (F. & G.) Ex prec.

bakshee lance-Jack. A lance-corporal: Army: esp. Aus. and NZ, WW1 (E.P.)—and British Army until at least 1975 (P.B.).

balance. (Of a bookmaker) to cheat: Aus. Hence *balancer, balancing.* B., 1942.

Balbo. 'A large formation of aircraft, so called after the famous flight, Dec. 1930, of the Italian Air Armada from Italy to South America, led by the late Marshal of that name' (H. & P., 1943).

balcony. Female breasts, esp. when displayed as a bulging ridge: Aus. since late 1940s. Perhaps suggested by the Fr. *elle a du monde au balcon.*

bald. Bad: itinerant entertainers'. Lester has 'Bad, *Bald; coteva*'.

bald as a bandicoot. Utterly bald: Aus. coll.: since ca. 1910. (B., 1943.) Can. prefers . . . *billiard ball*: adopted ex US, prob. early C.20. (Leech, 1986.)

bald-tyre bandits. Traffic patrol police (Powis, 1977): since ca. 1960. Either slanderous, or because they are keen to point out the offence of driving a vehicle with 'bald' tyres—old tyres from which the tread has worn right away.

baldy. Usu. in pl *baldies*, white Hereford cattle: Aus. rural. Devanney, 1944.—2. An artist's model denuded of pubic hair: painters' and sculptors': since ca. 1950.—4. See:-

baldy! I refuse (cf. English schoolboy's 'fain I'): NZ juvenile: late C.19–20. (B., 1941.) No hairs on one's head: nothing to offer.

bale. 'A measure of marijuana: either one pound (aka one *weight*) or half a kilo' (Green): drugs world.

bale out. To make a parachute descent from a 'plane: RAF coll. (—1939) > j. by 1942. (Jackson, 1945) Prob. an intransitive development of 'to bale out (a boat)': as a boat is emptied of water, so is an aircraft of its crew.—2. Hence, to depart hurriedly from a tank or a self-propelled gun: Army: since ca. 1940. (P-G-R.)—3. To 'ditch' the weight-belt and rise to the surface as quickly as possible: skin divers': since ca. 1950. Ex sense 1.

balk. To use as cover. See AUSTRALIAN UNDERWORLD.

ball, n. In *have a ball*, to have a thoroughly good time: Can., Aus.; adopted ca. 1935, 1950, 1955, resp., ex US. Cf. *a real gone ball*, a superlatively good party or dance or reception: Aus., bodgies' (q.v.): early 1950s. Dick.—2. In *on the ball*, alert; esp., ready to grasp an opportunity: coll.: since ca. 1925.—3. Short for **ball o'chalk**, 2.

ball, v. To coït with a girl: adopted, late 1960s, ex US, orig. by teenagers. (*Observer* colour mag., 17 June 1974.) Ex *balls*, testicles. See **brewed**.—2. Hence, v.i., and of both sexes, to make love; also, of a female, to fondle a man's genitals: since ca. 1967. Earliest Brit. example I've seen: Wolfe, 1968. Cf. **ball off**.

ball and bat. Hat: r.s.:—1914 (F. & G.). Cf. commoner synon. *tit for tat*.

ball and chain. A wife: Can., adopted ex US. Ex convicts' gyves. P.B.: also some Brit. joc. use.

ball-bearing mousetrap. An ungelded male cat: low pun: since ca. 1950. (B.P.) But beyond the pun, in W. Can. the phrase is used to mean 'something very expensive, or of high qual-

ity, perhaps needlessly designed or needlessly expensive: since the 1950s at latest' (Leech, 1986).

ball-bearings in (one's) feet, have. To be habitually restless: RAF, since ca. 1930; by 1942 also RN. Cf. to have **itchy feet**.

ball-breaker. One who demands or actively exacts an extremely difficult task: adopted, late 1974, ex US, where *ball-buster* is or was more frequent. (See W. & F., 1960.) A British example occurs in the *Observer*, 21 Dec. 1975. Ex the task itself—a strain on the testicles. Cf. **ball-tearer**.

ball-dozed. Drunk; fuddled or muddled: Aus.: ca. 1942+. (B., 1943.) Prompted by *bull-dozed*.

ball is in your court, the. It is your turn; it is up to you: poss. mainly Services': since ca. 1955. The phrase is variable, e.g., 'Well, the ball's in their court now; let's see what *they* make of it.' (P.B.)

ball o(f) chalk. To talk: r.s.: *Evening News* (London), 13 Nov. 1936.—2. A walk: r.s. Also used of things, e.g., 'Now where's me ruddy pen? Gone for a ball o'chalk, I suppose', i.e., it is missing, perhaps stolen. Cf. **penn'orth of chalk**.

ball of fire. As *the Ball of Fire*: the 2nd New Zealand Division: Army in N. Africa: 1941–3.—2. A notably energetic and effectual person (usually male); often sarcastically in negative: Can.: adopted, ca. 1930, ex US. (Leechman.)

ball of lead. Head: r.s., mostly and orig. (—1914) military. F. & G.

ball of muscle(, be a). Energetic: very lively. Aus.: since ca. 1930. B., 1943.

ball of spirit, be a. (Esp. of a horse) to be very high-spirited: Aus.: since ca. 1918. Prichard, 1926.

ball(-)off, n. and v. (To commit) masturbation: men's low. Cf. **ball**, v.

ball-park figures. Rough figures, a 'gues(s)timation': NZ civil engineers': mid-1970s. (John Davies, 1977.) Prob. ex US. Cf. the RAF, 1970s, use of *ball-park*, 'Generally in the right place, as "the target was in the ball-park" ' (Wilson, 1979).

ball-tearer. A physically very demanding task: Aus. military: 1960s. Hence adj., *ball-tearing*, as in 'They sent us off for three weeks in the bush on this bloody great ball-tearing exercise.' Cf. **ball-breaker**. (P.B.)—2. 'An ironic term . . . for a violent person' (McNeil): Aus. low: later C.20.

ball-trap. An at times unexpectedly collapsible seat, esp. in an aircraft: RAF: since ca. 1940. Also, since ca. 1945, Aus. civilian for tractor seats, etc. (B.P.)

ball-up. A kick-about at Association football: Charterhouse.

ballock; now gen. bollock, n. A testicle; gen. in pl. A very old word, S.E. until ca. 1840, then a vulg.—2. 'Ball [dance], as in hunt bollock, charity bollock' (*Sunday Express* supp., 11 Oct. 1982): Sloane Rangers' (q.v.).

ballock, v. To reprimand, reprove, scold: c.: from ca. 1910; by 1920, low s. *Ballocking*, vbl n. With pun on *balls* and *bawl*. Hence:-

ballock drill. Custard and rhubarb: RN lowerdeck. See **rhubarb**.

ballock-naked. (Of both men and women) stark-naked: low.

ballocker. A radar testing-device that resembled an ordinary light-bulb at the end of a long stick: RAF: ca. 1941–5. If you don't 'see' the origin, I can't very well explain it.

ballocks, n. Nonsense: late C.19–20. Now gen. *bollocks*. Cf. **balls**, and *cods*; occ. with *all*. Cf. also **boloney**.—2. (Usu. *bollocks*.) Muddle, confusion; an instance thereof: Army: since ca. 1915.

ballocks, v. To spoil or ruin (a thing or plan): Aus. (Baker, letter to E.P.) Also, sometimes with *up*, British military. (P.B.)

ballocks about. To play the fool, esp. in horseplay; to be indecisive: low.

ballocks in brackets. A low term of address to a bow-legged man. Cowan, 1937.

ballocks in the right place, he has (or he's got) his. He is a sensible, sound fellow: male coll. (L.A., 1974.)

ballocks'd. Thwarted; in a dilemma: low. Cf. **ballocks,** v.

balloon, n. A high and easy catch: cricketers': from ca. 1925. Masterman, 1935, 'And then like an ass I missed a balloon this afternoon—just in front of the pavilion too.'—2. Engineshed 'foremen varied from the type known as "The Whip", to that of "The Balloon", whose plea was always, "Don't let me down boys" ' (McKenna, 1): railwaymen's.—3. See **balloon car.**

balloon, v. 'To forget one's lines or business' (Green): theatrical. Cf. synon. **make an ascension.**—2. 'For a plane to bounce badly on landing when the pilot has failed to master either the controls or the state of the runway' (Ibid.): airlines'.

balloon car. A saloon bar: r.s.: earlier C.20. (Franklyn.) Usu. shortened to *balloon.*

balloonatic. A Services' punning blend of *balloon* + *lunatic:* applied in WW2 to 'anyone on the strength of a Balloon Command unit or squadron' (Jackson, 1945): RAF.

balls. Nonsense: low coll.: since—1890. Also often *all balls.* In Feb. 1929, it was held to be obscene; by 1931 it had > permissible in print. For semantics, cf. **boloney** (orig. US), also the US *nerts* (as an interjection).—2. 'Masculine courage, "He's got balls, all right", and by extension, masterfulness. The term can be used to describe a dominant woman in a home, e.g., "She's the one with the balls in that family" ' (Powis): low > gen. raffish: later C.20. Cf. 'Deke [Arlon] says she'll get there [to stardom] because she's got what the greats have all got, balls. "Liza's got balls; Streisand's got great balls, hasn't she? Well, so's this lady" ' (Burn, 1981). May be elab. as in 'It's probably one of those civil servants again, leaking [news] to the defence correspondents, just to show they're in on the act and have got balls as big as aircraft tyres' (Fox, 1982).—3. Short for **balls-up,** q.v., esp. as in, e.g., 'Well, they've made a right balls of it *this* time': low coll.: since—1890. Ex 1.—4. In *have (got) someone by the balls,* to have utterly in one's power, esp. of women over men: low: late C.19–20. (Kersh, 1944.) P.B.: all senses derive, however inappropriately, ex *balls,* low S.E. = testicles.

balls-ache, n. See **pain,** 2. A *balls-aching talk* is a tedious disquisition: since ca. 1918.—2. As *Balls-ache,* Balzac: schoolboys' and students': late C.19–20. By deliberate distortion. (L.A.)

balls-ache, v. To complain; to nag: low. Cf. the C.19–20 synon. *belly-ache,* from which it prob. derives.

Balls and Bullshit parade, the. The British officers stationed in the Indian peninsula: ca. 1880–1947, then nostalgically; by the richer, more important civilians. Mather, 1977.

balls are bigger than his brains, his (also in vocative). 'Said of, or to, a man apt to plunge into a situation without due thought; by analogy with "your eyes are bigger than your belly!" ' (L.A., 1978): mid-C.20.

balls chewed off, have (one's). To be (severely) reprimanded or taken to task: low.

balls for a necktie, have (one's). A var. of *guts for garters . . .* (Parsons, 1973.)

balls in an uproar, get (one's). To become unduly excited: Can. Army: WW1. Hence also to the British Army where it was still current in the early 1970s, esp. in 'Don't get your balls . . .'

balls in the right place. See **ballocks in . . .**

balls(-)out, adv., synonymises **flat out,** q.v. at **flat,** adv.: WW2 and after: '*Very* commonly used.' (Parsons; French.)

balls to that lark! Nothing doing!: NZ c.p.: since ca. 1920. (Slatter.) An elab. of *balls to that!,* common to all the Commonwealth countries and current since late C.19. Cf.:–

balls to you! Rats to you!: low: late C.19–20. (Cf. **balls.**) Manchon.

balls-up, n. A 'mess', a bungling, confusion: low: since ca. 1910. (Wilson, 1957.) Since mid-C.20, at latest, often shortened to *a balls.* See **balls,** 3.

balls-up, v. To make a mess or a blunder of; to confuse inextricably; misunderstand wholly; do altogether wrongly: low.

Cf. US *ball-up* and (also for *balls-up*) the somewhat rare *ball,* to clog, gen. of a horse getting its feet clogged with balls of clay or snow.

ballsy. 'Tough, masculine, courageous' (Green, 2), as in 'A diminutive Southern belle who scandalised Atlanta Society in the [19]20s by becoming a ballsy, hard-drinking reporter' (*Books & Bookmen,* Feb. 1985): adopted ex US, ca. 1980. Cf. **balls,** 2.

ballyhoo. An abbr. (orig.—ca. 1913—US) of, and from ca. 1925 more gen. than, *ballyhooly:* s. >, by 1930, coll.; now verging on S.E. 'The now recognised term for eloquence aimed at the pocket-book', *TLS,* 19 July 1934.

ballyhooly. Copy-writers' or politicians' exaggeration; 'advance publicity of a vulgar or misleading kind' (H. G. Le Mesurier): from ca. 1910; coll. by 1925. Abbr. *Ballyhooly truth,* a ca. 1880–5 music-hall tag perhaps ex *whole bloody truth* (W.).

balmy breeze. Cheese: (not very common) r.s. Franklyn, 2nd.

baloney, or **-ie.** See **bolon(e)y.**

Balt. 'This was the most common term for New Australians from about 1946 to 1952 and will be found in the Australian literature of the period. It was based on the mistaken belief that they came mainly from the Baltic countries' (B.P., 1963).—2. The Martin *Balt*imore, US light bomber: airmen's: WW2.

bamboo. Inside information; a rumour: Army: 1940+. Ex makeshift aerials. Cf. **jungle wireless.**

bamboo presento. A beating with a bamboo. See PRISONER-OF-WAR SLANG, §15, in Appx.

bambora. 'The spot of light reflected by a mirror held in the hand' (Dalton, 1951): Anglo-Irish. Origin?

ban. (Mostly in pl *bans.*) A banana: greengrocers': since ca. 1910.

banana. A £1 note: Aus.: mid-C.20. (B., 1953.) Sweet and acceptable.—2. A surf board with a raised front: Aus. surfers': since late 1950s. (B.P.)—3. A foolish person; a 'softie': since ca. 1950. Ex the softness of a ripe banana. The shortened *nana* exists mainly as in 'She's a right nana' or 'I felt a right nana'.—4. See **tummy banana.**

banana balancer. An officer's steward; a wardroom waiter: RN. Granville.

Banana Bender. A Queenslander: Aus. (Sayers, 1985.) Cf. the later C.19–earlier 20 *Bananaland(er)* = Queensland(er).

banana boat. An invasion barge: Services': 1943+. H. & P.—2. An aircraft carrier: RAF: 1941+. Partridge, 1945.

Banana Bomber, the. A Buccaneer aircraft: RAF: later C.20. (*Phantom.*) Ex shape of fuselage.

banana farm, the. An asylum for the insane: among Britons in tropical or semi-tropical countries: later C.20. (Marshall, 1976.) Cf. synon. **funny farm.**

Banana-Squeezer. A Hispano-Suiza motorcar or engine: motorists'. (J. Paterson.) Joc. Hobson-Jobson.

banana van. A 'bogie carriage on wooden frame sagging in the middle' (*Railway,* 2nd): railwaymen's: since ca. 1950.

bananabill. See BIRD-WATCHERS, in Appx.

bananas. In *go bananas,* to become, almost or even wholly, madly excited about something: adopted ex US, partially by 1974, widely by 1976. *DCCU,* 1971; W. & F., ed. of 1975—but without ref. to *banana,* hence the orig., 'to go all mushy with emotion, esp. with excitement'. R.S. cites an Eng. example: Kathleen Whitehorn in the *Observer,* 22 Feb. 1976; Leech, 1980, adds ' "To go bananas" was in vogue here [Edmonton, Alberta] during the summer of 1975 and up to about 1976 or early 1977.'—2. Hence, of machines, to go wrong, or to behave oddly, as in 'Help! The damn' photocopier's gone bananas again': coll.: later 1970s.—3. 'Nickname for the Kalashnikov AK–47 [rifle], brandished in myriad revolutionary posters, and so named for the shape of its curving ammunition clip' (Green): military.

band. A prostitute: Aus.: since ca. 1920. B., 1942.

band in the box. Pox: later C.20. Jones, 1971.

B

band moll. 'A delightful creature who travels around the countryside with a group of musicians and singers and satisfies their sexual needs if nothing better turns up' (B.P., 1969): Aus. Cf. **groupie**.

Band of Hope. Lemon syrup: Aus. (Baker.) Ex name of the Temperance Society.—2. Soap: r.s.: late C.19–20. (Ortzen, 1938.) Also Aus.: see **bander**.

bander. Soap: Aus. Baker. Truncated r.s. on prec., 2.

bandicoot. In *poor as a bandicoot*, extremely poor: Aus. coll.: late C.19–20. In *The Drum*, 1959, S.J. Baker lists also the foll. self-explanatory phrases: *bald as a bandicoot*, *bandy as . . .*, *barmy as . . .*, *lousy . . .*, *miserable . . .*, and *not the brains of . . .*

bandicooting. 'The practice of stealing tuberous vegetables, especially potatoes, out of the soil without removing the tops' (B., 1943), i.e. with the tops left: Aus.: since ca. 1920. As bandicoots do.

bandit. 'A term sometimes used ironically in conjunction with other words, e.g., "one of a gang of international milk bandits"—near-vagrant labourers, who steal milk left outside dwellings, esp. when down on their luck' (Powis): police s.: since ca. 1955. Cf. **piss-hole bandit**, **gas-meter b.**, **knickers b.**—2. Elliptical for **one-armed bandit**: Aus.: since late 1950s. (B.P.)

bandmaster, the. A pig's head: RN lowerdeck. Granville.

bandok. See **bundook**.

bandstand. A cruet: Services'. F. & G., 'From its shape.'—2. 'In Ack Ack [anti-aircraft gunnery] the Command post of a gun position' (H. & P.): WW2.

bandwagon, hop (or, in UK, mostly **jump**) **on the.** To join a majority, once it's known to be a majority; to favour someone only after the public has made him or her a favourite: adopted, ca. 1955, ex US; by 1966, coll. (Reyburn.) Foster, 1968, gives several citations.

bang, n. A piece of sexual intercourse; whence a female in the act: *have a bang*, *be a good bang*: low. Cf. etym. of **fuck**.—2. A brothel: low Aus.: since ca. 1920. B., 1942.—3. A stir or considerable movement in stocks and shares, esp. downward: Stock Exchange: ca. 1810–70. *Spy*, II, 1826. P.B.: this piece of historical s. has been retained here because of the excitement caused in 'The City' (the financial world) by the 'big bang' of Autumn 1986, when the Stock Exchange underwent a technological upheaval, and dealing methods were revolutionised. However the etym. of that *big bang* is more prob. to be found in astronomical theories of the origin of the Universe than in 'Spy's' usage.—4. A popular schoolgirl: 1960s. Wober, 1971, quotes a 13-year-old girl who lists all the attributes which give rise to popularity, ending 'If you do what I say you will be a BANG.'—5. In *have a bang*, to make an attempt (at): Services': since ca. 1939. (P-G-R.) Cf. **have a bash**.—6. See **full bang**.

bang, v. To have sexual intercourse (v.t. and with a woman). A usage rare in UK, but very common, esp. among manual workers, in Aus., where also used intransitively. (P.B.) Also common still in Can. (Leechman.) See also **bang like . . .** —2. To go ahead with a robbery or a theft, despite the odds against success: c.: since late 1940s. (Norman, 1959.) Often it implies failure.—3. To inject drugs: drugs c. (Stockley, 1986.) US since 1930s (Spears).

bang-bag. A case of cordite: R Aus. N: since ca. 1925. B., 1943.

bang-box. The turret of a 6-inch gun: R Aus. N: since ca. 1925. B., 1943.

Bang Gang, the. 321 Explosive Ordnance Disposal Company, RAOC: Army in N. Ireland: later C.20. (Knight, 1984.)

bang in. See **banged up**.

bang like a hammer on a nail or **like a rattlesnake** or **like a shithouse door; go pop like a paper bag; ride like a town bike.** To copulate vigorously; *bang* referring to men, and *pop* and *ride* to women: low Aus., esp. Sydney: *bang*, C.20; *ride* since ca. 1925; *pop* since ca. 1950. A further var., contributed 1977: *she bangs like a shithouse rat*.

bang on, v. To talk lengthily, loudly, recklessly; but also, to get on with, to tackle something: Army, mostly officers': since ca. 1960. (P.B.)

bang(-)on. Everything is all right; correct: RAF bomber crews': since 1940. (H. & P.) I.e. bang on the target. As 'dead accurate, strikingly apposite', it was adopted by civilians in 1945. Blake, 1948.

bang-out, n. The informal yet ritualistic ceremony performed for an apprentice compositor to mark the end of his 'time'; the actual ceremony can take several forms, but all involve a great deal of noise generated by the banging of composing sticks on whatever sounds loudest: (?)C.19–20. (David Severn, 'banged-out' printer, 1978.) *Banging out* or *bang 'im out* is performed also when a 'retiring man leaves his place of work for the last time' at Portsmouth Royal Dockyard; Patterson, 1984, remarks sadly, 'In present times, a familiar sound'. See:-

bang-out, v. The v. from the prec. entry: to perform the ceremony. In C.19, known as *hammer out*.

bang-seat. 'A crew member's seat in a jet aircraft (but recently developed for helicopters)—which, for emergency escape, is blown from the aircraft by an explosive charge (which, incidentally, the seat occupant does not hear)'—as a flight lieutenant informs me, late in 1961. Since the mid-1950s: orig. FAA, hence gen. aeronautical.

bang-shoot, the whole. See **whole shebang**.

bang-stick. A rifle: partly marksmen's, partly Services': since ca. 1925. Cf. **shooting-iron**.

bang-tail. Usu. pl *bang-tails*, cattle, 'whence *bang tail muster*, a periodical counting of herds' (B., 1959): Aus. rural: since ca. 1930. Contrast the American *bangtail*, a horse, esp. a racehorse. Now mostly written as one word.

bang to rights. 'An expression of satisfaction, as in "Now we've got everything bang to rights, we can lay off for a bit and have a smoke"' (Franklyn, letter, 1962): since the late 1940s.

bang up. 'Taking coal from railway wagons meant instant dismissal, so engine-men shunting coal wagons would "bang up" the wagons to create spillage, and this was dutifully collected in the signal-box scuttle by the signal-box boy' (McKenna, 1980.): railwaymen's: earlier C.20.—2. To inject heroin into the veins: drugs world: later C.20. *Guardian*, 2 Nov. 1982.—3. See **banged up**.

bang water. Petrol: Can. (also *firewater*): since ca. 1920. H. & P.

banged up and **banged in.** 'There is a very slight difference in meaning between these expressions, which, generally speaking, mean "locked up" or "locked in cell". If a man, at the end of the working day and not attending classes, is locked in his cell in the usual way he may be spoken of as being "banged in". If, on the other hand, a man is rude or disobedient to an officer, who takes him from work or class for the purpose of locking him in his cell . . . , he is spoken of as having been "banged up"' (Tempest): prisoners': since 1930s.

banger. A sausage: perhaps orig. nautical, esp. RN; but by WW2 gen. and widespread, particularly in 'bangers and mash[ed potatoes]'. (*Musings*, 1942.) Good ones explode, if unpricked, when fried. Cf. *barker*.—2. A detonator: railwaymen's: C.20. (*Railway*.) Also *cracker* and *fog*.—3. (Often *old banger*.) An old, near derelict motorcar: motorists': since ca. 1955.—4. Hence, an old and worn-out motorcycle: motorcyclists': id. (Dunford.)—5. Elliptical for **cattle-banger**. B., 1943.—6. Usu. in pl: billiard balls; testicles.—7. In *drop a banger*, make a mistake. See **drop a ballock**; cf. synon. **drop a clanger**.—8. A hypodermic needle: drugs c. (Stockley, 1986.) US since~1950 (Spears). See **bang, v.**, 3.

bangers and red lead. Tinned sausages-and-tomato-sauce: mostly the Services': since ca. 1925.

bang(g)otcher. A Wild West film: Aus. juvenile: since ca. 1946. (B., 1953.) 'Bang! Got you!'

banging. Under the influence of drugs. Stockley, 1986.

banging-off. Sexual intercourse: RN, all branches: since ca. 1950, at latest.

Bangkok bowler. A Thailander's bamboo hat. See PRISONER-OF-WAR SLANG, in Appx.

bangle. A piston ring: motorcyclists': since ca. 1950. (Dunford.)

banjax. To ruin, to defeat, to destroy: Anglo-Irish. (O'Neill, 1959.) Cf.:-

banjaxed. Broken, smashed, out of order: Anglo-Irish intensive: since ca. 1920. Blend of '*banged* about' + '*smashed*'? Given fresh impetus, 1970s, in England by the popular Irish broadcaster Terry Wogan.

banjo, n. A shovel: Durham miners'; builders'; also Aus. Hence, in WW1, an entrenching tool.—2. A sandwich; usu. 'a cob or roll cut in halves with something eatable between the halves; a rather outsize sandwich' (Tempest): c., low, and Army: since ca. 1919. In Malaya and in Cyprus, 1950s, it was in very common use among Army Other Ranks, as in *egg banjo*, *chip banjo*, etc., produced at all hours by the camp *char-wallah* (P.B.). It has, among trawlermen, the nuance 'a large, thick slice of bread topped with a thick slice of cheese' (Mitford, 1969); and as 'sandwich', was still current among RM in N. Ireland, early 1970s (Hawke).—3. Hence, 'any food stolen from the cookhouse. Any "dodgy grub"—food that has been smuggled out of the kitchen or officers' Mess' (Tempest): prisoners' c.: mid-C.20.—4. A shoulder of mutton: Aus.: since ca. 1920. B., 1942.—5. A fireman's shovel: railwaymen's: since ca. 1945. (*Railway*, 2nd.) Cf. sense 1; orig. an American tramps' term.—6. A 'disc signal repeater with black line and white background' (*Railway*, 2nd): railwaymen's: since ca. 1955.—7. A frying pan: Aus.: since late C.19.—8. In Aus., *Banjo* is a nickname for any man surnamed Pat(t)erson: since early C.20. Ex the famous poet, A. B. 'Banjo' Paterson (1864–1941).

banjo, v. To force a door or a window: c.: later C.20. *Now!*, 10 Apr. 1981.—2. To smash or defeat: Parachute Regt, in the Falkland Is.: 1982. (Fox, 1982.) Cf. synon. RM **wellie** and SAS **mallet**.

bank. In *on the bank*, subsisting on bank loans: Aus. coll. Vickers, 1955, 'Chris Cotter came over to Jingiddy on train days and saw the farmers who were "on the bank" then, instead of as before touring round the farms.'—2. See **go to the bank.**

Bank of England Team. See ASSOCIATION FOOTBALL, in Appx.

banker. A river running flush—or almost flush—with the top of its banks: Aus.:—1888; coll. by 1890 and 'accepted' by 1900—if not before. Hence *come a banker*, '(of a river) to become flooded' (B., 1959); and *run a banker*, q.v.: both Aus. coll., the latter, judging by Wilkes's quot'ns, the commoner.—2. An 'assisting locomotive' (*Railway*, 2nd): railwaymen's coll. > j.—3. 'The man who holds a stock of forged notes for those who give them out or try to do so' (Petch, 1966): c.—4. 'One of a series of routes that are most often requested by passengers, [e.g.] Heathrow [Airport] to the Hilton [Hotel], etc.' (Green, 2): London taxi-drivers': later C.20. Ex the gambling j., something solid and reliable—and presumably more lucrative than most other routes.

banks. Rag shops: Aus. (B., 1942.) By inversion from mid-C.19 London s., where *rag shop* = bank.

banner. See **carry the banner.**

banshee wail. An air-raid warning; the moaning of the siren: coll.: WW2, then nostalgic.

banter (someone) **down.** To persuade him to lower his price: market traders'. *M.T.*

Bappo. A baptist: Aus.: since ca. 1925. (B., 1953.) Cf. *Congo*, *Metho*, *Presbo*, the other main Nonconformist sects.

bar. One pound sterling; orig. a sovereign: c. and low: late C.19–20. (Horsley, 1912.) Hence *half a bar*, ten shillings, then 50 pence. Direct ex Romany; the gipsies' *bar* prob. derives ex Romany *bauro*, heavy or big—cf. Gr. βούς.—

2. An excuse; a yarn, a 'tale': Army: but esp. in the Guards: since ca. 1910. Kersh, 1942, 'He had a good bar though, it was on his pass. He'd been trying to get some geezer out of a shelter'; Grinstead, 1943 and 1946, records *soft bar* (a persuasive story), *cakey bar* (a downright lie) and *to spin the bar*. Ex *debar(ring)*?—3. As *the Bar*, Marble Bar, a township in N.W. Australia: Aus. coll.: from ca. 1910. (Idriess, 1932.) Cf. **the Alice.**—4. In *have a bar* (*on*), to have an erection: low. Ex hardness.—5. In *can't stand* or *won't* or *wouldn't have a bar of*, to detest; deny or reject; to be unable to tolerate: Aus. coll.: since the 1930s. Trist, 1945; Buzo, 1969, where Bentley remarks, 'The bloke got all excited . . . saying it was Hammo's fault . . . Hammo wouldn't have a bar of that. "My fault?" he said, "That's a laugh." ' Wilkes suggests perhaps ex musical *bar*.

Bar Abbas and **Bar Jonas.** The two coffee-bars, in the Vatican, for the immured Cardinals and their subordinates: the English-speaking Cardinals': since ca. 1950.

bar-fly. 'A frequenter of bars and saloons, beer parlours, etc.' (Leechman, 1976): Can., adopted ca. 1930, ex US; not unknown elsewhere in the Commonwealth.

bar hustler. 'Prostitute, male or female, who solicits in bars' (Green): adopted ex US later C.20.

bar of chocolate. In *get a bar of . . .*, to receive praise from a senior officer: RN: since ca. 1941. (Granville.) Cf. the army synon. **strawberry.**

bar of soap. Dope (drugs): r.s.: later C.20. Haden-Guest, 1972.

bar-steward. A bastard: joc., orig. mostly Londoners'; common in Forces: since late 1920s. Euph. or polite.

bar-stock, be on the. To carry 'the daily supply of liquor from the store-room to the bar': (liners') nautical coll. Bowen.

barb. A barbiturate: addicts' coll.: adopted, ca. 1950, ex US.

barbary. Difficult in a tough way: Army in N. Africa and N.W. Europe, 1942–5, and in the Army generally for at least three decades afterwards. A *barbary bugger* was a tough and bloody-minded officer or NCO; (of the enemy) 'They're a bit barbary tonight' (inflicting harassing fire, etc.); or, to an equal: 'Don't get barbary with *me*, mate' ('or else . . . !', implied). Perhaps ex 'the Barbary Coast', but certainly influenced by:-

barbary (or **bobbery**) **wallah.** An ill-tempered person: Army and RAF: late C.19–earlier 20. (Jackson.) L.A. noted 'used esp. by and to English-speaking Irakis [in 1941–5].' Prob. from *bobbery*, a C.19 Anglo-Indian word for a noise or squabble, ex Hindi exclam. *Bap re!*, Oh, father; and influenced by *Barbary pirates*.

barbed-wire blues (or **fever**). Prisoner-of-war camp despondency or disgust: prisoner-of-war: 1941–5. The former is an adaptation of George Gershwin's famous title *Rhapsody in Blue*. Cf. **wire-happy.**

barber. A hotel-keeper: Aus.: since ca. 1925. A gossip.—2. A tramp: Aus.: since ca. 1930. B., 1943.—3. See:-

barber a joint. To rob a bedroom while the occupant sleeps: c. Also *barber*, one who does this.

barber-shop harmony. 'Said derisively of male quartets. From 1909 at latest' (Leechman): Can. coll.: by 1962, S.E. (Priestley, 1965).

barberiser. A deck-planing machine: nautical. (Bowen.) Because it 'shaves' so delicately.

Barbers, the. See **Baa-Baas.**

barber's chair. 'A tree which, when cut, breaks off, leaving a tall, jagged strip attached above the stump (often the tree falls unpredictably, endangering the logger): W. Can. and US Forestry Industry' (Leech, 1985).

barbie. A barbecue: Aus.: later C.20. (Wilkes.) Whence the phrase indicating stupidity, *two* (or *three*) *bangers* [sausages] *short of a barbie*. (Raab, 1985.)

Barclay's Bank, often shortened to **Barclay,** or even **barclay.** Of the male, to masturbate: since ca. 1930: r.s. on *w(h)ank*.

Bardia Bill. The 6-inch gun that, in 1941, bombarded Tobruk pretty regularly: Services': 1941, then ob. Granville.

bardies. See **starve the bardies.**

B

bare-bum. A dinner-jacket, as opp. to *tails*, the full-dress evening coat: Aus. low.

bare decker. 'Clearing the tender to the last scrap of [coal-]dust was known as creating "a bare decker" ' (McKenna, 1980): railwaymen's: earlier C.20.

bare navy (or **N.**). The rigid scale of preserved rations, without fresh meat or supplementaries: naval: late C.19–20. Bowen.—2. Hence, applied to a 'mess member who feeds solely on Service rations' (A. Knight): RN.

bareback riding; or **roughriding.** Coïtion without contraceptive: male.

barf. To vomit; to be sea- (or air-)sick: Can., prob. ex US: since (?)ca. 1950. Echoic. (Tuchman, 1976.)

barge. A crowd, a mellay: Scottish Public Schools'. Miller, 1935.—2. Hence, the crowd in an RFC (later, RAF) mess: since ca. 1916. Milne, ca. 1920.—3. A straw hat: Cranbrook, Tonbridge and prob. other Public Schools'. Cf. the S.E. *boater*.

barge at. To argue roughly with: Cockneys': late C.19–20.

barge in. To intrude; to interfere, esp. if rudely or clumsily. (Manchon.) Cf.:-

barge into. To collide with: orig. Uppingham School (—1890). In C.20, gen., and often = meet, encounter esp. if unexpectedly. Cf. prec.

barge the point. To 'argue the toss'. (Brandon.) Cf. **barge at.**

barging match. A loud argument: RN lowerdeck: late C.19–20. 'Taffrail', *Stand By!*, 1916.—2. A collision: lowerdeck. 'Taffrail', *Pincher Martin, O.D.*, 1916.

barker. A sausage: lower classes' and soldiers': earlier C.20. Ex that once excessively popular song, 'Oh vare, and oh vare, is my leedle vee dog? Oh vare, oh vare, is he gone?' (F. & G.) Cf. **banger.**

barking. Raving mad: since ca. 1965. Welcome, 1968, 'She had something, that girl. She's mad, that's the worst of it. Bonkers, barking, round the bend.' Ex dogs suffering from rabies'. P.B.: David Hare, in *Plenty*, prod. and pub. 1978, at sc. 7 set in 1956, has a senior diplomat say: 'Some of the senior men, their wives are absolutely barking.'

barking belly. A 4-inch anti-aircraft gun: R Aus. N: WW2. B., 1943.

barking(-)dog navigator, mostly in pl. 'A term of abuse (or of respect) for those unschooled coasting [coastal] skippers who navigate by the different sounds of the local dogs barking. [In] R. Ruark, "The Long Voyage Home", [n.d.]' (Peppitt.) mainly MN, and prob. throughout C.20.

Barlinnie drumstick. ' "Piece of leadpipe with a few nails in it. If you're caught in possession, you kid on you're a plumber on his way home." Barlinnie is Glasgow's rightly dreaded prison' (Ward, 1976): Glasgow c.: since ca. 1930 or a little earlier.

barmaid's blush. 'A drink of port and lemonade, or rum and raspberry' (B., 1942): Aus. Ex its vivid colour.—2. That special shade of pink paint which, used on invasion craft, was suggested by Lord Louis Mountbatten and therefore known, semi-officially, as *Mountbatten pink*: Services': ca. 1943–5. P-G-R.

barmpot. A person slightly deranged: since ca. 1950. *Sunday Times*, 14 July 1963 (competition). A blend of *barmy* + *potty*.

Barn dance, the; also **the scramble.** Pedestrians scurrying across a street diagonally as soon as the indicator says 'Go' or 'Cross': at crossings where all traffic halts: Aus. and NZ: since ca. 1950. The former was named after Commissioner Barnes—Traffic Commissioner of New York City—the inventor of the buzz crossing; origin of latter, obvious.

barn-stormer. One who, ca. 1919–22, did acrobatics, wing-walking, etc., on aeroplanes; also, any pilot who put on a show for the small-town people of the country: Can. (Leechman.) Adopted in Britain, and still (1979) current.

barn-storming. The corresponding n. of the activities and practices of **barn-stormers.**

Barnaby Rudge. A judge: r.s. Franklyn.

barndook. See **bundook.**

Barnet cut. A haircut, esp. in prison; one such cut indicates a short sentence: since ca. 1940: low s., verging on c. (Norman, 1959.) Ex:-

Barnet Fair. The hair: r.s., orig. (—1857) thieves'. 'Ducange Anglicus'. In C.20, often *Barnet*.

barney, n. A quarrel; a fight: proletarian: since late C.19. (*Cheapjack*.) Often *a bit of a barney*, a scuffle, fight or heated argument; esp. rowdyism in a public house: late C.19–20. In later C.20 this is the predominant sense. Prob ex C.19 s. for 'a jollification, esp. if rowdy' (H., 1st edn.). Ultimately, perhaps, ex *Barney*, typical of a noisy Irishman.—2. As *Barney*, 'inevitable' Aus. nickname of men surnamed Allen. Ex Barney Allen, a famous and very wealthy Australian bookmaker.

barney, v. To argue (*about* something): Aus. (B., 1942.) Ex n., 1.

Barney Dillon. A shillin(g): Scots r.s. *Daily Telegraph*, 8 Mar. 1935.

Barney moke. A pocket: r.s. (on *poke*): orig. (—1941) c.; by 1950, low s.—2. (N. and v.) Poke, both literally and sexually: r.s.: late C.19–20.

barney over (something). To quarrel about it: Aus. (B., 1959.) Cf. **barney,** v.

barns. Shorts; trousers: Marlborough College: since ca. 1920.

baron. 'Anything free in the Navy is said to be "on the Baron" or "Harry Freemans" ' (Granville). Bassett defines a *baron* in WW2 RN as 'One with modest accumulation of money, usually by saving, and a target for borrowers'. Joc.—2. A recognised businessman, or boss, among the prisoners: prison c.: since ca. 1930. (Norman.)—3. One who has money: beatniks': since late 1950s. (Anderson, 1965.) Cf. sense 1.

baron-strangling. 'On visiting terms with a fairly well-off family in a foreign port, distinct from "up-homers" and "feet under the table" where such hospitality was due to a girl friend . . . M N, 1950s' (Peppitt); also RN, since—1935 (Malin, 1979). Cf. **baron,** 1, and **jam-strangling bastard.**

baroning. 'Trafficking. Buying and selling prohibited articles, etc.' (Tempest): prison c.: mid-C.20. See **baron,** 2.

barossa. A girl: Aus. r.s., on *Barossa Pearl* (a popular sweet white wine): later C.20. Hornadge, 1980.

barouche. A motorcar: joc. anachronism: earlier 1940s. 'The trip to dispersal [area] in my old barouche was made in record time' (Deere).

barrack ranger. A seaman, that in RN Barracks is awaiting draft to a ship: RN: since ca. 1920. (Granville.) Cf.:-

barrack stanchion. 'Someone who spends a lot of time in shore bases' (Malin, 1979): RN ironic.

Barrack (or **Barrick**) **Stove, the.** Aden: Services': 1950s. (Sanders.) An extremely hot station.

barrel, n. A nickname for a round-bellied male: coll.—2. In *right into* or *up*, one's) *barrel*, decidedly one's interest, concern, business: Aus. (B., 1942.) Cf. *right up* (one's) *alley* or *street*, synon.—3. 'The body or ribcage of a horse, donkey or mule' (Smith, 1982): inland waterways.—4. See **have over a barrel.**

barrel, v. To move rapidly (and usu. dangerously) with motion of a rolling barrel, as 'these damn great lorries come barrelling down the High Street—sure as fate there'll be an accident one of these days': coll.: since (?)mid-C.20. (P.B.)—2. See AUSTRALIAN UNDERWORLD, in Appx.

barrel-fever. Ill health, disease, caused by excessive drinking: late C.18–20; ob. Grose, 3rd ed., 'He died of the barrel fever'.—2. Hence, delirium tremens: Aus. B., 1943.

barrel of butter. A small rock just awash in the middle of Scapa Flow; hence, *back to the barrel*, back to the anchorage in the Flow: RN: since ca. 1910. Granville, 1962.

barrel of fat. A hat: Aus. r.s. Franklyn 2nd.

barren Joey. A prostitute: NSW, low. B., 1942.

barring. For sure, certainly, indubitably: tailors': earlier C.20. *Tailor and Cutter*, 29 Nov. 1928, 'A powerful shiner, barring'. Abbr. *barring none*.

barrow. A 'Black Maria': Aus. B., 1942.—2. 'To the bus conductor your ticket is a "brief" and his vehicle a "tub", "kite" or "barrow" ' (*Evening News*, 27 Apr. 1954): since ca. 1945.—3. (Mostly in the Cockney pron., *barrer*.) A motor-car: esp. in the secondhand-car business: since ca. 1955. Prob. ex sense 2.—4. In *on my barrow*, giving me trouble: coll.:—1956 (Hunter, 1956).—4. In *into* (one's) *barrow*, and *right up* (one's) *barrow*, variants of **barrel**, n., 2. B., 1959.—5. A pedal tricycle: club cyclists': earlier C.20. (*Fellowship*.) Hence *long barrow*, a tandem bicycle.

barrow wheels. 'Cast metal spoked wheels' (Dunford): motor-cyclists': since ca. 1950.

bars. Handlebars: cyclists' coll.: late C.19–20.

bart. Joc. coll., esp. in address (as in Galsworthy, 1924), for a *baronet*, which it abbr. in superscriptions, *Bart* being much more frequent, formal and polite than *Bt*.—2. A girl: Aus.: since ca. 1920; 'now practically obsolete', says Baker in 1943. Orig. obscure, unless—as Franklyn has suggested—it rhymes on *tart*.

bary. 'Gorgeous', a superlative: Northumberland teenagers': 1984. (Blyth Ridley County High School.)

bas, pron. *bahss* or *bass* (and often so written). A 'bastard': low: since ca. 1920 or earlier. Newman, 1977.

base over apex is a refined version of **arse over tip**: from ca. 1925.

base wallah. A soldier employed behind the lines; orig. and esp. at a Base: military coll.: 1915–18. (F. & G.) Cf. *wallah*, aka *base pup*. Cf. later C.20 synon. **Remf**.

base-walloper. The New Zealanders' preferred version of the prec. entry. As *base-wallopers* it meant the Staff in general to Australian soldiers in WW2. Page, 1973.

basengro. A shepherd: tramps' c.:—1923 (Manchon). Ex Romany, in which *-engro* (man) is a frequent suffix.

bash, n. Brutality: Aus.: since ca. 1925. (B., 1953.)—2. A long—esp. if fast and arduous—ride: cyclists': since ca. 1930. 'The Brighton bash' = London to Brighton and back.—3. In *have a bash*, to make an attempt; to help; to take part: since ca. 1925. L.A. adds, ' "Oh, go on—have a bash!" was frequently used as an encouragement, particularly to someone reluctant to risk the effort': since ca. 1940; by 1980 perhaps slightly ob. Cf. **bash on**.—4. A lively visit or experience or time: Can.: since ca. 1955. *Daily Colonist*, 2 Apr. 1967. 'The party of 48 chartered a bus for a night on the town including a bash at the Old Forge.' (Leechman.)—5. A copulation: low: since ca. 1930. Jones, 1953.—6. A route march, particularly that forming part of the annual fitness tests, as '5-mile bash', '9-mile bash': Army: since late 1940s. Cf. sense 2. (P.B.)—7. In (to be) *on the bash*, to be a prostitute: c. Prob. suggested by synon. *on the batter*.—8. In *on the bash*, on a drunken spree. Campbell, 1916.—9. As *the bash*, smash and grab: c.: from ca. 1920.

bash, v.i. To ply as a prostitute: c. > , by 1930, low s. Kersh, 1938. Ex **bash**, n., 7.—2. To sell (personal possessions or Red Cross gifts): prisoners of war: WW2. (Morgan, 1945.) Prompted by synon. *flog*.—3. See:—

bash; bash it; give it a bash. 'To indulge in a bout of heavy drinking' (B., 1953): Aus.: since ca. 1935. Casey, 1947, 'A man's gotta drink . . . But you can't bash it all the time, the way he does, if you want to get anywhere.'—2. To live gaily, have a good time: general: since ca. 1940. Story, 1959, has 'bash it around'.

bash into. To meet (a person) by chance: low: from ca. 1920. (*Gilt Kid*.) Cf. synon. *bump into*.

bash on. To 'carry on', bravely and doggedly: orig., soldiers' (1940); then, by 1946, gen. Hence, by 1946, attribute, as in 'the bash-on spirit' (*Leader Magazine*, 4 Mar. 1950). P.B.: in 1940s–50s often in *bash on regardless*, a var. of the earlier synon. *press on regardless*.

bash up. To 'beat up', to assault, someone: schoolboys', since ca. 1940; also Aus., since ca. 1945. (P.B.; B.P.)

basha. A hut built from bamboo and *attap*: Army: since ca. 1942. Orig. in South-East Asia, and ex Malay: here it may be considered an S.E. borrowing, but it had, by ca. 1955, been transferred, orig. coll. > j., to other parts of the world, e.g. 'sleeping in self-built shelters, or "bashas", of birch boughs and snow' (Winton, 1979)—which is enough to make a purist shudder! In later C.20 it is sometimes spelt *basher*, e.g. in Green. (P.B.)

basher. A boater hat: Bedford, Rugby, and prob. several other Public Schools'. Cf. **hard-hitter** and **barge**, 3. See also **straw-basher**.—2. A Physical Training Instructor: Services' since ca. 1920. (H. & P.) Cf. *buster* in this sense.—3. 'Buster or basher is very common for mechanics, as in *compass-basher*, *instrument-basher*' (Rhodes, 1942): RAF: since ca. 1930.—4. Indeed *basher* has often, since 1941, meant little more than 'fellow', 'chap'. (Partridge, 1945.) P.B.: ob. by 1950, except in compounds: see **gravel-basher, square-bashing, swede-basher, haulage-basher**.—5. A fornicator: RAF: from ca. 1935. Yet another sexual sadism.—6. A hoodlum: Aus.: since ca. 1920. (B., 1943.)—7. 'A young sailor. An old tar's protégé' (Knock): RN lowerdeck: C.19–20.—8. Incorrect spelling of **basha**.

bashing. The loud, vigorous, cheerful playing of dance music; an engagement at which such music is demanded: dance bands': since ca. 1930.—2. Prostitution: low. (Kersh, 1938.) See **bash**, n. 7.—3. Short for *bashing the bishop*, since late C. 19, low s., at first esp. Army, for male masturbation: since ca. 1920. The full phrase may have arisen as an alliterative var. of mid-C.18–19 nautical synon. *box the Jesuit*.—4. In *get*, or *take*, *a bashing*, to suffer heavy losses: Services': 1939–45, and after. P-G-R.—5. A beating-up, as in *Paki-bashing, queer-bashing*: since ca. 1955.

basic. 'Used to describe a low sort of person, one with rather animal tendencies' (P.B., 1974): since ca. 1955, in the Services.—2. See PUBLIC . . . SCHOOL SLANG in Appx.

basic English. 'Plain' English, esp. as used by workmen not averse from vulgarity and obscenity: since ca. 1945. (Petch.) A pun on S.E. *Basic English*.

basil. As *Basil*, a fat man: Liverpool s.:—1952. Why?

Basil dress. ENSA uniform: a WW2 pun. Ex the Director of Entertainments National Service Association, Basil Dean, on *battle dress*.

basin of gravy. A baby: (defective) r.s.

basinful, a. Of trouble, hardship, labour, etc. Hence, *get* (one's) *basinful*, to receive a severe—esp., a fatal—wound: mostly Army: WW1 and 2. Kersh, 1941, 'Poor old Pete got his basinful somewhere near Hell-Fire.' Only slightly less serious is the 1930s London sense, in Wolveridge, ' "I've had a basinful" meant "I've had all I can take." ' In this latter, 'fed-up' sense, it occurs in, e.g. Allingham, 1955.

basis. The woman a pimp intends to marry when he retires from business: white-slavers' c.: earlier C.20. Londres.

baskervilles. A 'dog' (see **dog**, 6): Aus. c.: later C.20. An elab., ex A. Conan Doyle's *The Hound of the Baskervilles*, 1902. McNeil.

basket. Occ. used joc. as euph. for *bastard* (in the vocative): from ca. 1930. P.B.: also otherwise than vocative, as 'That basket So-and-So'.—2. Disrespectful term for an elderly woman, as 'Silly old basket, always poking her nose into other people's affairs': coll. (P.B.)

basking shark. DS/ID Citroën car: car-dealers'. (Graham-Ranger, 1981.) Ex shape and appearance.

basset, make a. To blunder: racing:—1932 (*Slang*, p. 245.)

bastard. A fellow, chap, man, with no pej. connotation: coll.: chiefly Aus., perhaps ex US; see esp. Grose, P., and cf. the colourless use of **bugger**, q.v.—2. Fig. of a thing, an incident, a situation: low coll. Curtis.—3. As in 'This oppo of Ted's was waiting. He'd got a bit of a bastard on by then and said that if we didn't hurry up it'd be no go' (*Heart*, 1962); i.e.

angry or upset: RN: later C.20.—4. For fig. use as adj., see quot'n at **shattered.**

baste-up. A half-wit; an objectionable fellow: tailors' (*Tailor and Cutter*, 29 Nov. 1928.) Ex tailors' j., wherein it = half-made.

baster. A house thief: Aus. low. B., 1942.

bat, n. A prostitute favouring the night: C.17—early 19. But, in C.20., merely any ill-favoured, disagreeable, middle-aged or elderly woman. Perhaps by association of bats with witches.—2. A drinking bout; esp. *go on the bat*, on the spree: Can. (ex US): late C.19–20. P.B.: perhaps short for *batter*, as Tempest suggests, giving its use also as Brit. c.—3. Price; *come the bat*, to mention the price: grafters':—1934 (*Cheapjack*).—4. Hence, a sale: grafters': 28 Aug. 1938, *News of the World.*—5. 'A whip carried by a horse-rider. Also *mop* and *stick*' (B., 1959): Aus.: since ca. 1930.

bat, v. Military, mostly officers', from late 1914, as in Blaker, ' "That fellow Jackman that Reynolds has produced from his section to 'bat' for you is rather an object, isn't he?" '—2. 'To put an aircraft through its aero*bat*ic paces; to perform aero*bat*ics.' (Parsons): since late 1930s.

bat an eyelid, doesn't or **don't.** (She, etc.) show(s) no emotion at something either startling or shocking: coll. Cf. the S.E. *bat the eyes.*

bat and wicket. A ticket: r.s. B. & P.

bat for. To make one's price at (such and such a sum): show-men's. *Night and Day*, 22 July 1937. 'Most crocus bat for a dena . . . or . . . a two ender . . . but to "bat 'em for a straight tosh" is something to be proud about' (P. Allingham in a letter, 1937). Cf. **bat,** n., 3,4.

bat house. A brothel: Aus. low. (Baker.) Cf. **bat,** n., 1, and **cat house.**

bat on a (very) sticky wicket. To contend with great difficulties: coll.: since ca. 1948. (*National News Letter*, 24 Jan. 1952.) Ex cricket.

bat out of hell, go like a. To go extremely fast: coll.:—1908 (Leechman). In the sense of *to fly* extremely fast, it quickly, in WW1, > RFC coll. (F. & G.) Still heard occ., later C.20.

bat phone. 'Policeman's small personal radio set' (Powis, 1977): since ca. 1960. Ex the equipment of the American cartoon character *Batman*. Seabrook, 1987, notes 'known [thus, early 1970s], though the jargon has changed now'.

bat the breeze. To chatter; to talk: Aus. Army: since ca. 1939. B., 1943.

batarlies. Shoes: parlyaree. (Hollis.) Cf. **bats,** 3.

batch. A small cottage; a shack: Aus.: since ca. 1920. (B., 1942.) Cf. **bach,** 3. Ex:-

batcher. One who lives alone: Aus. Baker.

batchy. Silly; mad: Army, C.19–20; RN, since ca. 1910; thence to the RAF, who gave it as a nickname to the (then) Fg. Off. R.L.R. 'Batchy' Atcherley: as a member of the Schneider Trophy team, he broke the existing air-speed record in 1929.

bate up. A sexual copulation: low. Orig. obscure.

Bath bun. A son: r.s.: late C.19–20.—2. Jones, 1971, equates it to 'sun'.

bath-tub cabbage. 'Cabbage boiled until it is tasteless and almost colourless, as served in schools and boarding-houses' (Sanders): since ca. 1920.

bathers. A bathing costume: Aus. coll. (Baker); and Brit. perhaps later.

bathing beauty. Blancmange: RN lowerdeck: since ca. 1930. Granville.

Batmen, the. The *British Army* Training team seconded to the Sheikhdom of Oman: Army: early 1970s. Ex the heroic *Batman* of the American comic cartoon-strip, by a pun on the initials. (P.B.)

Bats, bats. British American Tobacco Company shares: Stock Exchange: since ca. 1930.—2. The deck-landing officer in an aircraft carrier: RN: since ca. 1938. 'From the bats he carries' (Granville). Cf. **guns, torps:** the Gunnery and Torpedo officers.—3. A pair of bad boots: c. or low s.: ca. 1855–1930. (H., 1st ed.; Manchon.) Cf. **batarlies.**

bats, adj. Very eccentric; mad, to any degree. Ex:–

bats in the belfry(, orig. have; later **to be).** As prec.: late C.19–20.

batter, n. Wear and tear: coll.: C.19–20. 'He can't stand the batter' (H., 1864).—2. In (*go*) *on the batter*, (to walk the streets) as a harlot, to be debauched; to be on a riotous spree: since late 1830s. H. Rodger, 1839 (*OED*); H., 1st ed.; Whiteing, 1899; Tempest, 1950: 'On the "razzle". A pub and/or brothel crawl.' Presumably cognate with US *bat* (1848); cf. **bait** and **bat,** n., 2.—3. On the run, from police or as a deserter: c.: mid-C.20. Tempest.

batter, v. To copulate: low: since ca. 1920. (Kersh, 1938.) Ex prec., 2.

Battersea Dogs' Home (here)! A 'humorous' answer to a phone-call: Army: ca. 1950–70. (P.B.)

battery girl. A prostitute, usu. one of a 'stable', operating in return for sustenance, (a little) pocket money—and drugs, measured to keep her quiet and esp. to increase her sexual desire and ability, much as battery hens are reared and treated: since ca. 1960 at latest, and world-wide. In, e.g., *The Penthouse Sexindex*, 1975, and notably in Barclay, 1968 (Janssen). Clearly s. in origin, it no less clearly became, very rapidly, coll. and then, by late 1977, S.E.: naturally so, because of its felicitous precision, pertinence and pictur-esqueness.

batting and bowling, adj. and n. Participating in both hetero- and homosexual acts: very British: since ca. 1950. Cf. **ambi-dextrous.**

battle. To 'get by' on one's wits: v.t., to obtain, esp. if deviously, the use of: Aus. c. (since ca. 1919) > by 1940, low s. Hence, **battler,** one who 'gets by' on odd jobs and alone; a tramp; a hawker; both v. and n. occur in Tennant's fine novel, *The Battlers*, 1941. The v. occurs earlier in Idriess, 1934. Ex the influence of WW1. A *battler* is also 'a hard-up horse trainer . . . a broken-down punter' (Baker).—2. In *on the battle*, an Aus. synon. of 'on the batter', engaged in pros-titution: low: since ca. 1920. Glassop, *Rats*.

battle-axe. See **old battle-axe.**

battle blouse. A battledress tunic: army: WW2. (P-G-R.) If orig. s., then soon > j.; the garment was always known as a *blouse*, or a *B.D.* [battledress] *blouse*, until replaced by a new style of uniform in the early 1960s. (P.B.)

battle buggy. A jeep: army: 1943—ca. 1950.

battle cruiser. A public house: r.s., on *boozer*: since ca. 1940. (Franklyn.) See **battleship and cruiser.**

battle dress. Pyjamas: RAF: 1940+. (Emanuel, 1945.) Ex amorous 'combat'.

battle of the bulge, the. The struggle against 'middle-aged spread': since 1945. Ex the WW2 battle so named.

Battle of Waterloo. A stew: r.s.: mid-C.19–20.

battle the rattler. To travel on a railway without paying: Aus. c.: since ca. 1920. See **rattler.**

battle the subs. To hawk goods in the suburbs: since ca. 1920: Aus. c. > by 1940, low s. Baker.

battle wag(g)on. A battleship: RN since ca. 1925, RAF since ca. 1930. H. & P.—2. An expensive motor-car: Army since ca. 1940. H. & P.

battler. A prostitute working independently of brothel or ponce: Aus. c.: since ca. 1925. (B., 1953.) See **battle.**—2. A var. of **battle waggon,** 1: RN: since ca. 1930. P-G-R.

battleship and cruiser; soon **battle and cruiser.** Synon. with **battle cruiser:** since ca. 1914. *This Week*, 10 Mar. 1968.

batty, n. A batman or batwoman: Services': since ca. 1925. H. & P.

batty, adj. Mad, crazy: perhaps orig. Services', but soon > gen. Prob. ex **bats in the belfry,** q.v., but cf. also synon. **batchy.**

battyman. 'A male homosexual. South London expression, of West Indian origin' (Powis, 1977).

Batu Road 'flu. Venereal disease: Army in Malaya: 1950s. *Batu Road* was the old name for the main street in Kuala Lumpur. Cf. *Barnwell ague* for the same thing, three centuries before. (P.B.)

baubles, bangles and beads mob. See **Whizz Kids**.

bawl. 'To suck or swallow': East End of London c.:—1933 (Orwell).

bawl out. To upbraid vigorously: Can. coll.: adopted ex US ca. 1910. (Leechman.) Hence a *bawling-out*.

Bayreuth hush. 'The moment of silence when the conductor lifts his baton prior to commencing the performance' (Green): opera circles'. A.k.a. *Glyndebourne silence*.

Bays. Or *The Baze*, the Bayswater Road (London, W.2): low s., and c. Norman.

baywindow, n. A belly protuberant through either pregnancy or obesity: mid-C.19–20.—2. Hence, and ex the baywindows of clubs: talk imitative of that of clubmen: artisans':—1935. Cf.:-

baywindow (or hyphenated), adj. Smart, fashionable: lower-middle class: since ca. 1910. Mais, 1948.

bazazz. Occ. spelling of **bezazz**.

bazooka. Petting. See **high**, adj., 3, and cf. **bazookas**. Since the introduction, in WW2, of an infantry anti-tank weapon of this name, it has become the normal spelling of **bazooker**.

bazookas. Woman's breasts: male medical students'. In, e.g., the Independent Television series 'Doctor in the House', 1973. (L.A.) Perhaps influenced by *bosom*.

bazooker. A thing, esp. if mechanical (e.g. a motor-car): low: C.20. (Blaker, 1934.) An artificial word: cf. **ooja-ka-piv**.

bazooms. See quot'n at **jujubes**. *Time Out*, 25 Oct. 1984, had 'her huge ripe bazoomas bouncing'.

be-in. A hippies' gathering where, with aid of drugs, one 'really' exists: ca. 1963–72. (Janssen.)

be mother. For a person of either sex to assume responsibility for dispensing (usu.) hot drinks, as in 'Shall I be mother, then?', e.g. when teapot and cups are brought in in a café, office, etc.: coll.: since (?)ca. 1950. Ex mother's role at the traditional tea-table. Cf. **do the honours**, which applies to any sort of drink. (P.B.)

be on. To watch; to look at (someone) and see, or understand, what he is doing: Aus.: since ca. 1930. Culotta, 1960, 'The barman . . . pointed to us. "Be on 'im," Joe said. "Dobbin' us in." ' Cf. **be on to**.

be on about. To talk at some length in a way (boring, nagging, etc.) displeasing, because not entirely understood, to the listener, as in 'Oh, good grief! What's he on about *now*?': coll.: since ca. 1950. Also used if the listener has not heard what has been said so far, when another listener may be asked 'What's he [the speaker] on about?' Cf. and contrast *go on*, and *go on about*.

be on to. To be aware of or alert to (a person or plan): coll.: perhaps since mid-C.19 and certainly since late C.19. Adopted by US.

beach. In *put* or *shoved on the beach*, 'Discharged [for a civil offence] ashore' (Knock): RN lowerdeck: ca. 1890–1939.—2. In *take the beach*, to go ashore: RN: late C.19–earlier 20. 'Taffrail', 1917.—3. As *the beach*, land as opposed to sea: Services': WW2. (H. & P.) Cf. **drink**, 2.

beach-bash. To lie on the sand, esp. nocturnally and amorously: Aus. Services': WW2. (B., 1953.) Whence n. *beach-bashing*. Joc. on, e.g., *square-bashing*.

beach-buggy. 'Open motor-vehicle used across sand-dunes for transporting bathers and surf-boards: since 1960' (A.C. Partridge, 1968): S. African coll. >, by ca. 1970, S.E. P.B.: prob. orig. US; cf. the trade name *Dune-buggy*.

beach bunny. A usu. non-surfing girl addicted to watching the surfers surfing: Aus. surfers', esp. teenagers', adopted ex US: since ca. 1960. Also called a *femlin*, a *female gremlin*. Regarded as a hanger-on. (P.B.) Cf. **snow-bunny**, 2.

beach-comber. A white man living with an Eskimo woman: Canadian Arctic: heard, there, by Leechman in 1913; by 1960, slightly ob.

beacher. A quick 'run ashore': RN: since ca. 1920. P-G-R.

beadle. A member of the London Dock Police: dockers': mid-C.20. Ash.

beagle, n. A steward: R Aus. N: since ca. 1925. B., 1943.

beagle, v.i, esp. as vbl n., **beagling**. To pickpocket: London c. of ca. 1965–75. *New Society*, 7 July 1977. (P.B.)

beam. In *off*, or *on, the beam*, failing to understand, or fully understanding: RAF, since ca. 1938 >, by 1943, also civilian. Ex that wireless or radar beam that, in bad visibility, guided a pilot to an airfield.—2. In *on the beam*, 'straight and true; direct. Britain, Canada, elsewhere' (Leechman): since late 1940s.—3. As '*Beam*, a Sunbeam motorcycle (in production 1912–57): motorcyclists'. (Partridge, 1979.)

beamer. A fast, esp. a very fast, ball so delivered by the intimidatory bowler that it bounces head-high and causes, or should cause, the batsman to duck: cricketers': since ca. 1956. 'Right on the beam'; form suggested by *seamer*.

bean, n. The head: late C.19–20. Ex shape (very approximate!). Whence:—2. (Gen. **old bean**, q.v.) A man, chap, fellow. (Manchon.) P.B.: but in *Punch's Almanack for 1861*, pub. late 1860, there is a paragraph headed 'Bricks and Beans', which says: 'These terms are very respectable slang . . . Both "Brick" and "Bean" signify a good fellow . . . Bean, a philanthropist; a beany fellow; one who is a bene-factor to his species.'

bean, v. To hit (someone) on the head: ca. 1916–50. (Loder, 1937.) Ex **bean**, n., 1. Cf. **nut**, v., to hit someone with one's own head.

bean-counting. 'Does strategic intelligence involve merely "bean-counting"—i.e., totals of armed strength?' (Kennedy, 1981). ?Ex *how many beans make five?* (P.B.)

bean-eaters. ' "Argies" and "bean-eaters" had been derisive nicknames for the enemy [Argentinians], on the long voyage south' (Parry, 1982): Services': Falklands War.

bean-feast. Sexual intercourse: raffish: earlier C.20.

bean-stealer. 'A married man living in the mess' (Wilson): RAF officers': late 1970s.

beanie. 'A tight-fitting cap, often made from the crown of an old felt hat. The edge is cut, by the exhibitionists, into a zig-zag. Worn by adolescents' (Leechman): Can.: since ca. 1946(?). Perhaps because it fits as snug as a bean-pod does the beans; also, there is a reference to s. *bean*, the head.

beano. Communion: Cheltenham College: earlier C.20. Marples.—2. A bayonet: Shrewsbury: 1938+. Marples.

beans. In *not to amount to a row of beans*, to be of no account: coll.: adopted, ca. 1910, ex US. (Moe.)—2. Money: teenagers': early 1980s. (Joanna Williamson, 1982.) Cf. synon. **yackers**.

bear. A policeman: Can. and Aus. s.: late 1970s. (Leechman; Wilkes.) Ex US lorry-drivers' argot, whence also its use on Brit. Citizens' Band radio, esp. in such phrases as *bear in the air*, and *wall-to-wall bears*, police everywhere.

bear in the air (or **sky**). A police helicopter: Can. s.: adopted, ex US truck-drivers' argot, late 1970s. (Leechman.) See prec.

bear-leader. A control responsible for, at least superior in rank to, the run-of-the-mill operative: espionage: since (?)ca. 1945. Le Carré, 1977.

bear pit; beerage; brickyard. Steerage: ships' stewards'. (Marlowe, 1937.) In mid-C.20 RN, bear-pit = 'stokers' messdeck' (Bassett, 1979). Cf. **Snake-Pit**.

bearded clam, the. The female pudend: Services', in Far East, perhaps ex Aus.: 1960s. Cf. **velvet glove** or **vice**. (P.B.)

bearded lady, the. A searchlight with diffused beams: WW2. Berrey, 1940.

beardie, -y (or **B.**). A Christian Israelite: a Victorian (Aus.) nickname: 1875. (*OED* Sup.) A sect that let its hair grow.—2. Hence, any man with a beard or long hair: Aus. coll.—3. A ling: Aus. fishermen's. Culotta, 1963.—4. A male beatnik: since ca. 1959. (Anderson, 1965).

beärgered. Drunk: low coll.:—1859 (H., 1st ed.; Ware). Also spelt *biargered*, and still widely in use in late 1930s (Lester).

bearing up. A common answer to 'How are you?' or 'How's things with you?': since ca. 1960. Usu. 'Oh, bearing up, you know', prob. elliptical for 'bearing up under the strain'. (P.B.)

25

bearings. The stomach: Aus. (B., 1943.) It needs constant oiling? (P.B.)

beast. A girl; a young lady: beatniks': 1960s. (Anderson, 1965.) Cf. **beastie**.

beastie. A girl; a young lady: RN: late 1950s. A petty officer of my acquaintance, gazing admiringly at a retreating beauty, could be heard muttering 'Oh, you gorgeous, long-leggedy beastie!' (P.B.)

beasting. Harsh treatment of recruits which, if endured successfully, will turn them into first-class, fit, disciplined soldiers: Army, later C.20. Parker, 1985.

beat, n. A newspaper 'scoop': journalistic: from ca. 1925. Keverne, 1930.—2. A beatnik: since late 1950s. Claiborne, 1976, glosses it thus: 'Not, I think, a shortening of Beatnik [E.P.'s orig. tentative etym.], which is rather an elaboration (with Yiddish suffix) of beat. Ultimate derivation is, I think, less from jazz "beat" than from *beat,* exhausted. The "beats" of the 1950s did indeed suffer from mental exhaustion.'—3. Esp. in *have (got) a beat on,* to have an erection: low.—4. In *off the beat,* out of the usual routine: Aus. coll.:—1916 (Dennis). Cf. S.E. *off the beaten track,* and:—5. As *the beat,* the musical rhythms of jazz: Can. jazz-musicians' and -lovers' coll.: adopted, ca. 1950, ex US. 'Basic Beatnik', 1959, speaks of 'the Beat fraternity'. The term is a specialisation of the conventional musical sense of *beat.* Cf. **Beatnik**.

beat, v. 'To swindle somebody out of drugs or money' (Stockley, 1986): drugs c. US since—1967 (Spears).

beat (one's) **gums.** To be loquacious: Can.: adopted, ca. 1945, ex US.

beat it. (Of criminals) to run away: mostly NZ. Ex US coll. >, by mid-C.20, Brit. s., *beat it,* to depart. Cf. the coll. *beat the hoof* of C.17–18. It has, in Can. usage and since late 1950s, sometimes been elab. as *put an egg in your hat and beat it!* (Leechman, 1961).—2. To defeat an indictment: Aus. prison c.: later C.20. (McNeil.) Cf. US synon. *beat the rap.*—3. In *can you beat it?!,* 'Well, I'm dashed! (damned!, etc.)': coll.

beat it while the beating's, or **the going's, good.** To depart at ease or without trouble. An elab. of prec., 1.

beat (one's) **meat.** (Of a man) to masturbate: low: late C.19–20.

beat (one) **to it.** To forestall: coll.: since ca. 1910; by ca. 1970, informal S.E.

beat the bag(s) off. To defeat ignominiously: ca. 1920–50.

beat the clock. To cease duty before the prescribed time: Services', esp. RAF: since ca. 1930. Occ. *beat the gong.* Cf. **clock in**.—2. 'The names of those [SAS men] killed in action are inscribed on the clock tower at the SAS barracks in Hereford. [They] talk of coming back alive from a particular mission as "beating the clock" ' (*Harper & Queens,* Nov. 1980): Special Air Service Regiment: later C.20.

beat the gun. (Of a female) to have intercourse with her fiancé, esp. if she becomes pregnant by him: Aus.: since late 1940s. Ex athletics. (B.P.) Also Brit.; cf. **beat the starter**.

beat the starter. To become pregnant before the wedding: since late 1940s. (Petch.) Ex athletics. Cf. **beat the gun**.

beat the tar out of. To thrash soundly: from ca. 1920. Harrison, 1935.

beat the tracks. To walk, esp. a long way and over rough ground: Aus. coll. Russell, 1934.

beat-up, n. Ground strafing; hence a lively visit to 'the local' or a good party in the Mess: RAF: since 1940. (H. & P.) From US; imm. ex the v.—2. See **tear-up**.

beat up, v. 'To stunt-fly, at low level, about (a place)' (Partridge, 1945): RAF: since 1940. Adopted from American fliers.

beat-up, adj. Decrepit, dilapidated, worn(-out): adopted, ex US, later C.20 (W & F date it to ca. 1951). As in, e.g., 'a beat-up old banger', a well used car in poor condition. (Fearon, 1984.)

beat up for (one's) **brass-hat.** (Of a Lieutenant-Commander, RN) to seek promotion to Commander: RN. (P-G-R.) See **beating up**.

beat up (one's) **chops.** See JIVE, in Appx.

beating, or **lashing, up.** 'A Lieutenant-Commander is thought to be beating-up for his "brass-hat" (promotion to Commander) when he becomes particularly "taut-handed" and pays great attention to his job' (Granville): RN. Ex beating up against the wind?

Beatnik, usu. **beatnik.** 'Generic term coined by the San Francisco press for members of the Beat fraternity living in North Beach area and abhorred by all Beatniks' ('Basic Beatnik', 1959.) Apparently the term arose in 1957 or perhaps in 1956. See **beat,** n., 2, 5.

Beattie and Babs. Body lice: since ca. 1930. Rhyming on *crabs.* (One of the penalties of a wide and deserved popularity.)

Beatty tilt is a var. of *Beatty angle,* that at which a cap is worn with a slight tilt to starboard: RN: since ca. 1915. A characteristic of Earl Beatty.

Beau. A *Beau*fighter aircraft: RAF: WW2, then historical. Cf. **Whispering Death**.

beaucoup; often spelt **bokoo.** Plenty of; many: military: late 1914–18, then as survival. E.g. *beaucoup beer* or *cigarettes.* Direct ex Fr. (B. & P.) Dent, 1917, notes a 'Tommies' saying': *merci bocoa, merci cocoa*—a good instance of soldiers' macaronic, for 'many thanks'.

beaut, n. and v. A 'beauty' (rarely of persons, at least in the purely aesthetic sense): prob. orig. Cockney or, anyway, 'non-aristocratic'; now chiefly Aus. and, since ca. 1950, NZ. (Prichard, 1921.) A Cockney example occurs in Hardcastle, 1913, concerning a young child, ' "Ain't 'e a *bute*?" answered 'Tilda proudly.' Hence, since ca. 1920, also an adj., as in 'It's a beaut day'. Also ironic, as in the very Aus. 'Oh, you beaut!'

beautiful and . . . ; or, **lovely and . . .** A C.19–20 Cockney synonym of *nice and* in the sense of 'very'; they also = 'satisfactorily'. Franklyn, in a communication of early 1939, adduces the examples, "E 'ad 'is barf beautiful an' quick; and so 'e should 'a' done, the wa'er was lovely an' 'ot'; 'My neighbour's baby is lovely an' quiet, since I hit it beautiful and hard.'

beautiful but dumb. Orig. (?late 1920s) US, became Can. in the late 1930s; foisted on far too many 'dizzy blondes' less stupid than they seemed to be. (Leechman.)

beautiful people, the, defined as 'the wealthy, fashionable people of high society and the arts who set the trend in beauty and elegance' (Barnhart, 1973): US, since earlyish 1960s, soon adopted in Britain; it occurs in, e.g., McCabe's *Apple to the Core* (about the Beatles), 1972: s. that, by 1973 or so, was coll. everywhere. Orig. ironic and somewhat sardonic. An early example: a Beatles' song, 'Baby You're a Rich Man', released on 7 July 1967, has 'How does it feel to be one of the beautiful people?' (Janssen.)

beautifuls. In address, beautiful: feminine: since ca. 1920. Addressed to babies, it tends to emerge as 'boofuls'. Cf. **ducks,** 1.

beauty. As exclam., denotes a thing of beauty and connotes extreme approval: since (?)ca. 1930. 'A pause and then that word of special Aussie approbation. "Beauty!"—but the Chief [Engineer] pronounced it in three distinct syllables, "Be—yew—ty!" ' (Smith, 1978).—2. Hence: Thank you!: non-cultured Aus., esp. Sydney-siders': since late 1940s. (B.P.)

beaver, n. As a beard, hence a bearded man, decidedly s.; esp., shouted after, or at, a bearded man in the street by 'nasty boys': ca. 1907–30, then historical. (Leslie S. Beale.)—2. Hence, a no-score at skittles: from ca. 1926; ob. 'When the nought is chalked up, people sometimes draw a face in the circle and attach a beard or "beaver" to it' (Brian Frith, 1935).—3. Pubic hair, esp. a girl's; hence *split beaver,* overt vulva: photographers' and creators of pornography: since early 1970s. (White, 1976.)

beaver, v. (often with *away at* or *on*). To work hard and diligently, as in 'There's Eric Partridge, over 85 now and *still* beavering away at his dictionaries in spite of everything':

coll.: since late 1960s. (P.B.) An early printed source: *Guardian Weekly*, 3 Apr. 1971, Robert Skidelsky writes of 'young historians who have been beavering away in the Beaverbrook Library', punning on an 'in' phrase.

beazel. A girl: since ca. 1930 (Wodehouse). An arbitrary formation—prob. euph. for *bitch*.

bed and breakfast. 26: darts and tombola players'. Ex tariff, *two* (shillings) and *six* (pence); hence also *half a crown*; and *Southend*—it was once the fare from London. The London *Evening News*, 2 July 1937.—2. A cardboard box container for a parachuted pigeon: RAF: mid–1944–5.—3. In *take* (or *get*) *more than bed and breakfast*, to share the bed as well as the board of one's landlady or her daughter: Aus.: since ca. 1930. (B.P.)—4. Short term funds invested at the close of business one day and taken out again first thing the next: London money market. (Sayers, 1985.)

bed-bait (or unhyphenated). See **bait**, 2.

bed-down, n.; **bed down,** v. A going to bed; to go to bed: Services' coll.: since ca. 1920. (H. & P.) Horses are 'bedded down' for the night. P.B. notes: still current in the Services in the 1970s, as in 'The M.O.'s given me bed-down for 3 days.'

Bed-pan. See **Bedpan**.

bed-rollers. Youths, or young men, travelling the country during summer and sleeping rough: since ca. 1950. Ex the bed-rolls they carry.

bed-sit. A common contraction of the next entry: since ca. 1960. 'Poor little temps [girls in temporary office work] living in bed-sit-land.' (P.B.)

bed-sitter. A bed-sitting room: s. (from ca. 1890) >, ca. 1930, coll. (Collinson.) OXFORD -ER.

bed-spring gymnastics. 'Comment from wire mattress at domestic marital exchange' (L.A.): since ca. 1950.

bed-springs. A guitar. See **fish-horn**.

Beddo. A Bedouin: Services' (N. Africa): 1940+. P-G-R.

beddy-byes. Sleep; *beddy-byes!*, go to sleep!: nursery: C. 19–20.

Bedpan (Line), the. The railway line between *Bed*ford and St *Pan*cras terminus, London, that took 7 years to electrify: commuters': later C.20. *Bedford Times*, 1983.

bedside virgin. Synon. with **prick teaser**: Army: WW2. (Van Dulken, 1988.)

bedworthy. (Of a woman) sexually desirable: upper- and middle-class coll.: since ca. 1925.

bee. A slangy euphemism for *bugger*: since ca. 1920. (Marsh, 1949, 'The old bee.') But also for *bastard*.—2. In *put on the bee*, v.t., *put the bee on*, to ask for a loan or a gift of money: c.: from ca. 1930. (*Gilt Kid*.) For semantics, cf. the corresponding v., *sting*, s. since later C.19.

bee aitch. Bloody hell! See **b.h.**

bee emm. A B.M.W. motorcycle. See **B.M.**

bee fool. A bloody fool. (Galsworthy, 1926.) See **B.F.**

bee in a treacle-pot. See **busy as . . .**

bee-stings. (A woman's) small breasts: Aus. low: adopted ex US late C. 20. (Hornadge, 1980.) P.B.: Cf. the jibe at puny muscles, *sparrow's kneecaps*.

Beeb, the. The BBC: coll.: since late 1920s. Cf. **Auntie**.

beech. 'A railway (or station) marked down for closure is said to be "due for beeching". A railway (or station) closed is "beeched"; and axed personnel are described as "on the beech" ' (a pun on *on the beach*): Sean Fielding, letter to Press, Feb. 1964. Current in late 1963–5, but already ob. by the end of 1965. Richard *Beech*ing was chairman of British Rail Board 1963–5, during which period the railway services in Brit. were drastically reduced. Life Peer in 1965.

Beecham. A bill (list of performers): theatrical: late C. 19–20. Cf. **Beecham's (pills)**.

Beecham's pill. A simpleton; a dupe: Aus. c.: since ca. 1920. (B., 1953.) Rhyming synon. *dil(l)*.—2. A photographic still: r.s.: the film world: since ca. 1950. (Haden-Guest, 1971.)

Beecham's (pills). Bills, placards, etc., showing that one is an ex-soldier: tramps' c.:—1935: r.s. on *bills*.—2. R.s. for 'testicles', mispronounced *testikills*: late C.19–20. Probably suggested by the synon. s. *pills*.

beef, n. 'An alternative term for the famous "*bind*", but only applicable to the crime itself, of boring one's colleagues by retailing shop-news and stale information' (H. & P., 1943): Services'. Adopted from US. As 'a complaint', *beef* has been common in Can. since early C.20., and was adopted in UK ca. 1942; e.g., 'What's his beef?' But see also **beef**, v.—2. A male homosexual: RN lowerdeck: since mid-C.20. (*Heart*, 1962.) Also as adj.—3. A *chief* officer: abbr. r.s. ex synon. *bully* or *corned beef*: prisons'. (Green.)

beef, v. To 'grouse': Army and RAF. (Manchon.) Cf. n. —2. To hit, punch, someone: low: earlier C.20. Hyder, 1934.—3. (Of a male) to coït: low: since mid–1940s. Newman, 1977, 'There were sounds from Connell's bedroom . . . Connell was beefing her.'

beef, adj. Homosexual (male): RN lowerdeck: since mid–C.20. (*Heart*, 1962.). Cf. **beefer**.

beef bayonet. The penis: raffish joc.: later C.20. 'Brandish the . . . !' (Simmonds, 1981). Ex the Aus. satire 'Barry McKenzie' (Barry Humphries). Cf. synon. **mutton dagger** and **pork sword**.

beef-chit. The wardroom menu: RN: since ca. 1920. (Granville.) 'Beef stands for all types of meat in RN' (Green).

beef-heart. (Gen. pl.) A bean: low: late C.19–20. (B. & P.) Rhyming on *fart*: ex the effect of (peas and) beans.—2. Hence, a breaking of wind: low r.s. Franklyn.

beef into it, put some. (Gen., imperative.) To try or work hard: coll.

beef-screen, the. The meat stores: RN: since ca. 1920. (Granville, letter, 1947.) Ex the screen to keep the flies off?

beef to the heels. 'A derisive description of a girl's thick ankles, which run from calf to heel in one sad, straight line' (Leechman): Can.: since ca. 1910.

beef up. To strengthen; enhance; improve to make more attractive: coll. Ex C.19 sense of *beef* as strength, effort.

beef (one's) way through. To force one's way through: Rugby football coll.

beefcake. See **cheesecake**.

beefer. A male homosexual: RN: since mid–C.20. ' "You got a crush on that beefer in the N.A.A.F.I., that's what it is" ' (*Heart*, 1962, p. 87). Cf. **beef**, n., 2. (P.B.)

beefsteak. A harlot in the service of a pimp: white-slavers' c. Londres.

beehive. A fighter-escorted close formation of bombers: RAF: since 1940. (H. & P.) The box-like formation of bombers is the hive, and the fighters buzz around it.—2. Five; esp., £5: rhyming: since ca. 1920: c. >, by 1940, s. Cook, 1962.

been-to. A West African, esp. a Ghanaian or Nigerian, who has 'been to' England, usu. for study, and whose social status has been greatly enhanced thereby: coll.: post-WW2. In later C.20, the term has been extended to include Brit. academics who have 'been to' the more prestigious US universities. The *Guardian*, Nov. 1982, refers to 'young lecturers self-consciously emphasising their "been-to" status on return from Stanford or Berkeley'.

Beer, beer. Burton-on-Trent: railwaymen's: since ca. 1920. (*Daily Herald*, 5 Aug. 1936.) So much beer is brewed there.—2. See **Ack**; and PHONETIC ALPHABET, in Appx.

beer-barrel. A Brewster 'Buffalo' fighter aircraft: RAF: WW2. (Jackson, 1945.) Ex the shape of the fuselage.

beer-beer. A balloon barrage: early WW2, until *beer* was replaced by *baker* in the PHONETIC ALPHABET, in Appx. Cf. **ack-ack**.

beer-bottle label or simply **beer label.** Coat-of-arms on Warrant-Officer's sleeve: RAF: since ca. 1930, ob. by 1950. Cf. **fighting cats**.

beer, bum and bacca. The reputed, almost legendary, pleasures of a sailor's life: since ca. 1870. Since ca. 1910 there has existed the var. *rum, bum and bacca* (-y).

beer is best. 'Chest. "That'll put some barnet [hair] on your beer" ' (Daniells, 1980): r.s.: later C.20.

beer-lever. 'Part of the controls of an aircraft' (H. & P.): RAF: since 1930. Cf. synon. **joy-stick**.

beer-off. A public-house off-licence department: coll. *Nottingham Journal*, 15 Mar. 1939, 'Children and beer-off' (caption). P.B.: also any off-licence establishment selling alcohol. Perhaps mainly East Midlands coll.

beer-spanner. A bottle-opener: RAF: ca. 1919–39, and prob. since. (P.B.)

beer-stain. 'R.A.F., 1939–45. The tiny bronze oak-leaf worn to indicate a mention in despatches. When the wearer had no medal ribbon [to form a background] . . . its appearance on the slaty-blue uniform did indeed suggest carelessness. Cf. *canteen medal*, 2' (R.S., 1971).

beer-trap. Mouth: late C.19–mid-20. *Sapper's War Stories.* (Petch.)

beer-up, n. and occ. v. A drinking: Aus., and Brit. (Army), coll.

beerage. Steerage. See **bear pit**.—2. See:-

beerocracy. Brewers and publicans: coined in either 1880 or 1881. This might be described as pedantic coll.; the likewise coll. *beerage*, which, esp. as *beerage and peerage*, was much neater and much more viable, was ob. as a phrase by ca. 1900. However, as *the beerage*, a collective for those powerful leaders of the brewing industry who have entered public life and the nobility, it has remained in journalistic use into the late 1970s. (Partly P.B.)

beery buff. A fool: r.s. on *muff*.

bees. Money: short for the next.—2. As *the Bees*, the Brentford 'soccer' team: sporting.

bees and honey. Money: r.s.: since—1892 (*EDD*).

bee's knees, the. The acme of perfection, beauty, attractiveness, skill, desirability, etc.: from ca. 1930. In 1939 I heard a girl described as 'a screamer, a smasher, a—oh! the bee's knees'. Cf. *the cat's pyjamas*.

bees wingers. Fingers: r.s.: later C.20. 'Always used in full, as *Bees* was, of course, money' (Daniells, 1980).

beetle, n. The original Volkswagen car, and later editions of the same shape: by 1960, at the latest, the nickname was in worldwide usage, and by the 1970s featured in advertisements for the vehicle. Ex the distinctive shape. Cf. **Volks** and **Vee Wee**. (P.B.)

beetle, v. See **beetle off**.

beetle belch. That unearthly hour even earlier than **sparrowfart**, 2: RAF: from ca. 1935. (Van Dulken, 1988.) Cf. **oh Christ double o**.

beetle juice. Betelgeuse—a star used in astral observation: RAF aircrews': since 1938. (Jackson, 1945.) By Hobson-Jobson.

beetle off. To fly straight in departure: RFC: 1915. F. & G. 'As a beetle flies'. Since WW1, *beetle about*, to wander about actively, as frequently in Brandon, 1934, and *beetle off*, to depart, as in Mackail, 1934. By ca. 1940, also *beetle across, over, up to*, etc. Its popularity does not fade: *beetle* was defined in the Sunday Express supp., 11 Oct. 1982: 'Go. Sloanes [see **Sloane Rangers**] don't like the word "go"—too boring. They substitute beetle, whizz, zoom, toddle—almost anything but go'.

beetle's (or beetles') blood. Stout (the drink): Anglo-Irish:—1935. Ex the colour and the consistency.

Beeza. The BSA (*Birmingham Small Arms*) motorcycle (in production 1906–71), and hence the BSA light motorcar or cyclecar: motorcyclists' and motorists': since ca. 1920, or perhaps earlier. (Dunford; Carter.) Also spelled *Beezer*.

beeze. Penis: low joc. In 'Trooper'—a ballad in Page, 1976.—2. See:-

beeze up. To polish; to apply 'bull' to: Army: WW2. 'Medals all beezed up and a-glitter' (*Punch*, 15 Nov. 1978). As *beeze* = bullshit, it occurs in the poem 'Alamein, October 23, 1942' by Hamish Henderson, quoted in *Oasis*. Perhaps ex beeswax, used in polish. (P.B.)

beezer, n. 'Chap'; fellow: Public Schoolboys': since ca. 1920. (Blake, 1935.) Prob. ex *bugger* + *geezer*.—2. See **Beeza**.—3.

A nose: since late 1920s: poss. orig. US. (*COD*, 1934 Sup.) Perhaps ex *boco* + *sneezer*.

beezer, adj. Excellent: most attractive: since ca. 1935. Ex *bonzer*?

beg yours! I beg your pardon: Aus. coll.: since ca. 1920. (B.P.) As (usu.) *I beg yours*, Brit. coll. since 1940 at latest; also S. African, to judge by the title of a book, 1979, *Aw Big Yaws*.

beggar for work, a. A constant hard worker: coll.: late C.19–20. Also *he* (or *she*) *deserves a medal*: c.p.: since ca. 1915.

beggar my neighbour, on the. On the Labour (Exchange)—drawing unemployment benefit therefrom: r.s.: since ca. 1925. (Franklyn.) Cf. later C.20 **jam roll**.

beggar's lagging. A three-month sentence of imprisonment: c. Tempest.

behind the behind. A semi-coll., semi-c.p., ref. to sodomy: since ca. 1930.

behind the eight-ball. In an extremely difficult position; at a grave disadvantage: Can.: adopted, ca. 1945, from US. Ex pool. By 1960, also English. Wallace Reyburn, article in colour section of *Sunday Times*, 8 July 1962.

belay. To cancel, as in 'Belay that last order!': RN. Granville.

believe. In *you wouldn't believe*, you would not, or you would hardly, believe it: low coll.: mid-C. 19–20. Sayers, *Murder Must Advertise*, 1932, 'The edges of the steps get that polished you wouldn't believe.'

Belinda. 'A frequent nickname for a barrage balloon' (P-G-R): Services', esp. Army: WW2.

belker. To weep noisily: market-traders'. (*M.T.*) Partly echoic, partly a ref. to a bell. Perhaps cf. dial. *belker*, to belch.

bell. In *give* (one) *a bell*, to telephone. (Daniells, BJP, 23 July 1982.) Hence, simple v., to *bell*, to 'phone.

Bell and Horns. 'Brompton Road cab-shelter is the "Bell and Horns" and Kensington High Street shelter "All Nations" . . . I think named after forgotten pubs' (Hodge, 1939): taxicab drivers': since ca. 1920.

bell-ringers. Fingers: r.s. Wright.

bellowers. 'Football supporters or railway enthusiasts who *window hang* (lean out of windows) and shout (mainly abuse) at passengers on stations (or at the world in general).' (Watts, 1988.)

bellows. In *give* (someone) *the bellows* or *the blow-out*, to rid oneself of him: market-traders': C.20, perhaps a generation earlier. (*M.T.*) Semantics: the former, to fan a fire under his tail; the latter, to spit him out.

bells. Bell-bottomed trousers: RN lowerdeck coll. P-G-R.

Bell's palsy. The result of too much whisky drunk at one go: public houses' pun on the disease so named and a proprietary brandname. (Bishop, 1987.)

belly. Underside of the fuselage of an aircraft: RAF: since ca. 1918; by 1940, coll. and by 1945, j. Here the 'plane is soft, least protected, most vulnerable.—2. 'Wool shorn from a sheep's belly' (B., 1959): Aus. rural coll.: late C.19–20.—3. As *the Belly*: the Portobello Road, the famous London street market for antiques: later C.20. Gash, 1983.

belly flop (or flopper or flapper). A dive wherein one falls on one's belly: coll.: since ca. 1870, is, 2, the still-slang var. (since ca. 1930) of **belly landing**. Partridge, 1945.

belly-go-round. A belt: St Bees: 1915+. Marples, 'Suggested by merry-go-round'.

belly-grunting. A severe stomach-ache: Aus.: since ca. 1920. B., 1943.

belly landing. 'A landing with the under-carriage up, when it is impossible to get the wheels of the 'plane down' (H. & P.): RAF: since ca. 1918; by 1945, official j. Ex *belly-flopping*.

belly like a poisoned pup's, have a. To be pot-bellied. (T. Washington-Metcalf, 1932.)

belly muster. Medical inspection: RN, surgeons' as well as all ranks'. 'Taffrail', 1916, 2.

belly rubbing. 'Dancing. Not used in mixed company.' (Powis, 1977): low.

belly-side up, usu. shortened to **belly-up.** Dying, dead; whence, bankrupt, hence, to die, go bankrupt: Can.: since ca. 1960. Leech supplied these examples in 1975: 'He was found belly-side up'; 'He'll belly-up shortly'; 'The company went belly-up'. In all, the context indicates the sense: in the first, 'dying' or 'dead'; in the second, 'to die' (or 'go bankrupt'); in the third, 'bankrupt'. Ex quadrupeds, which so often die 'belly-side up'—on their backs.

belong. To 'be rightly a member of (club, coterie, household, grade of society, etc.)': US coll., partly anglicised by 1935. *COD*, 1934 Sup.

below. Of temperature, below 0°C. or 32°F.: gen. coll., verging on j. in specialisation. *Punch*, 17 Oct. 1917: 'I hauled Hank out of a snow-drift—it was maybe thirty "below" '. (P.B.)

below the waist. Too bad; esp. *nothing below the waist*, good or shrewd: tailors'. *Tailor and Cutter*, 29 Nov. 1928.

Belsen. A military camp, if discipline were strict: Services': 1945+. Ex the notorious death-camp run by the Nazis until their defeat in 1945.

belt, n. A copulation: low: late C.19–20. L.A. adds, 1974, 'The girl who thought an endless belt was a night out with an airman was a byword [in WW2]. RAF preoccupation with technicalities even in non-technical context is characteristic and noteworthy.'—2. Hence, a prostitute: low Aus.: since ca. 1925. (B., 1959.) P.B.: but in low Eng., any woman regarded purely as sex-object, as 'I bet she'd be a great little belt.'—3. In *give a belt*, to thrash; to overcome, defeat: Aus.: since ca. 1910. Cusack, 1953, 'Must have given eighty a belt' (be past his 80th year). Cf.—4. In *give (someone) the belt*, to dismiss or reject: low: from ca. 1925. (*Gilt Kid.*) Its complement is *get the belt*, to be jilted.—5. In *(have) under the* (or one's) *belt*, to have to one's credit: Aus., since ca. 1930 (B.P.); Brit. from perhaps a little later. Ex a good meal eaten. P.B. adds an example, heard from an Intelligence Corps Colonel in the late 1960s, 'Get a couple of languages under your belt in this Corps and you can't go wrong.'—6. In *at full belt*, at full speed: since ca. 1960 the perhaps commoner synon. of **full bore,** q.v.

belt, v. (Of the male) to coït with: low: mid-C.19–20. Cf. synon. **bang.**—2. Impersonal, as in 'It's belting' and 'It belted'. It is, or was, raining hard, e.g., 'We went for a drive and it belted all the way'. Ex the synon. *belt down*: late C.19–20.—3. See **belt up!,** 1.—4. To rush, hurry. See:-

belt along. To rush along; to travel very fast: mostly teenagers': since ca. 1945. Perhaps cf. **belting,** Hence also *belt through*, to do anything very fast, as in 'The vicar fairly belted through evensong tonight' or 'He belted through Slough at a fair old rate of knots'—he went through very fast.

belt(-)and(-)braces, n., adj., adv. (With) great care and thoroughness; the double-check ensured: coll.: since late 1940s. (P.B.)

belt (one's) batter. To coït with a woman: low: earlier C.20.—2. To masturbate: id. Cf. **pull (one's) pud.**

belt down. To rain very hard. See **belt,** v., 2.—2. To drink at one gulp: Aus. low coll.: later C.20. McNeil.

belt out. To sing a song or play music loudly and vigorously. Hence **belter,** 3, 'a song that the singer can let rip' (L.A.): since ca. 1940.

belt up! Shut up!: RAF: since ca. 1937. After ca. 1950, also office- and shop-girls'. (Gilderdale.) Ex tightening one's belt. By 1960 a fairly, and by late 1966 an entirely, gen. phrase. Sometimes shortened simply to *belt!*—2. To thrash with a belt; hence, to 'beat up' (someone): Aus.: since ca. 1925. Dick.

belter. 'A belt-driven motorcycle: current 1920s and again late 1970s' (Dunford).—2. An admirable, exciting, thrilling, etc., event or circumstance' (Green, 2): later C.20.—3. See **belt out.**

belting. A busy period: busmen's from ca. 1930. (*Daily Herald*, 5 Aug. 1936.) Opp. **convalescence,** q.v.

Bems, the. See **B.E.M.s.**

bend, n. An appointment; a rendezvous: Anglo-Irish. 'He has a bend with a filly'; 'I must make a bend with the doctor.' Ex the slight bow made at the meeting.—2. A drunken bout. Joyce, 'I was with Bob Doran, he's on one of his periodical bends.' Cf. *on a* or *the bend*, on a (drinking) spree: adopted, ex US, ca. 1890. (Kipling, 1891: *OED*.)—3. In the command *put a bend on!*, get a move on, hurry!: Tonbridge Sch.: ca. 1920. (M. Beale, 1984.)—4. See **take a bend out of.**

bend, v. To damage, e.g. an aircraft or road vehicle: airmen's > gen.: WW2 and since. De Bunsen.—2. To deflect a result from the straight by deliberately losing a match: Association footballers': since ca. 1950. In the English popular newspapers of October 1960 there was much talk of players '*bending* matches' and of 'matches being *bent*'. And see **bent,** adj., 2, 5.

bend an ear! Listen to this!; pay attention: RAF: 1939+. Punning on *lend an ear*.

bend (one's) back. To work hard: Aus. coll. Palmer, 1931.

bend over backwards. To try very hard, as in 'You needn't bend over backwards to please the children': since the late 1920s.

bended knees. Cheese: r.s., mainly theatrical. Franklyn.

bender. 'A bout of riotous drinking, often lasting several days and including random acts of excess, violence, etc.' (Green, 2): orig. US, adopted in UK late C.19. Hence *go on a bender*, to go on a drinking spree.—2. A tent, shelter, made from cloth or sheet plastic over a frame of bowed sticks: orig. gypsies' and vagrants', then in early 1980s popularised by 'Peace campers', e.g. at Greenham Common. (P.B.)—3. A lazy tramp: Aus. B., 1942.—4. A cigarette: RAF: since ca. 1938. Ex the frequently crumpled packets.—5. Such a squad instructor as gave his squad a hard time: Army: WW2. P-G-R.—6. A passive male homosexual: low: since the 1930s. Newman, 1977.—7. A suspended sentence: prisons'. (Green.)—8. A drug orgy: drugs c. (Stockley, 1986.) US since–1953 (Spears). Clearly ex sense 1.

benders. In *on (one's) benders*, 'Weary, not picking one's feet up' (Jackson, 1945): RAF, since ca. 1930 >, by 1950, more gen. Lit., on one's knees.

bending. See **catch bending.**—2. A severe parade conducted by an NCO to tire out the men: Services': from ca. 1920. Also a *sweating*.

bending drill. 'Defecation in the open': Army in North Africa: 1940–3. (Sanders, 1967.) 'Also "going for a walk with a spade".'

bends, the. Divers' paralysis or, more accurately, cramp: orig., perhaps, pearl fishers', then divers' generally. Cf:—2. 'The "bends" and acute alcoholism are very much alike in effect . . . [The former comes] from working in a tunnel under terrific air pressure. "Bends" are one of the snags compressed air workers—or "sand hogs"—encounter' (*Answers*, 10 Feb. 1940).

Bengal Lancers. Toughs armed with razor-blades and addicted to assault with robbery: Aus.: since ca. 1930. (B., 1942.) See *Underworld.*

Bengal Tigers, the. The Royal Leicestershire Regiment, pre-1881 the 17th of Foot: Army: since ca. 1825. Ex 'badge of a royal tiger, granted for services in India from 1804–23' (F. & H.). In spite of amalgamation into the Royal Anglian Regiment, they are still (1970s) known proudly in Leicestershire simply as 'The Tigers'.

Benghazi. A lavatory: r.s. on *carsey*. 'From the Libyan seaport, and prob. armed forces' slang from the WW2 desert campaign' (Hillman, 1974).

Benghazi cooker; occ. **duke's stove.** Sand saturated with oil, a paste of sand and oil, within a tin or can or metal drum; used as a field cooker in North Africa: 1940–3.

Benghazi Handicap, the. 'The confusion that was the retreat to Tobruk in 1941—we always called it the Benghazi Handicap—has rarely been equalled' (*Rats*): 7th Aus. Inf. Division's name for it: 1941+. Back from Benghazi, Glassop refers, Ibid., to it as also *The Benghazi Derby*. The forward movements were known as *Benghazi Stakes*. P-G-R.

benjo. See **squat loo** and PRISONER-OF-WAR SLANG, 7, in Appx.

Benny. As *benny*, benzedrine, esp. when taken as a drug: mostly teenagers' and addicts': adopted, ca. 1950, ex US. It is a dangerous stimulant and fairly cheap.—2. 'An overcoat used to mask the goods one is engaged in shoplifting' (Green): c. A survival of C.19 s. (since ca. 1815) *benjamin*, a coat, whence *upper benjamin*, a greatcoat.—3. 'When parents (or whoever) are really "in a bait" [= very angry: school s. since mid-C.19 and still current], they have a "mega-benny" and "crack up" ' (Simmonds, 1985): teenagers'. See also **mega**.—4. Usu. pl. *Bennies*. 'The troops call them "Bennies", after the half-wit in [the TV serial] "Crossroads", but Falklanders are cannier than their natural reserve makes them seem' (*Sunday Express* mag., 26 Feb. 1984): Brit. Forces in Falkland Is.: since 1982. A subsequent joke went that the Islanders were also called 'stills', because the derogatory 'Bennies' was forbidden by order. So why 'stills'? Because they're *still* Bennies. See also **Bubs** and **wenneyes**.

bent, n. A male pervert: low: since ca. 1945. Wilson, 1957.

bent, adj. Broken (esp. if fig.). Either dysphemistic ex such phrases as (e.g. I) *bend but do not break* or evolutionary ex any bent object, esp. a coin. B. & P.—2. (Of a person) crooked, criminal; (of a thing) stolen: c.: since ca. 1905.—3. Hence, '(of a person, his character or nature) out of line with what is generally considered normal; (of a subject) not what is generally socially acceptable: since ca. 1940' (L.A.). E.g., addicted to drugs (Stockley, 1986).—4. Hence, homosexual or otherwise deviant (e.g., flagellation): prostitutes', then fringe underworld: since ca. 1945, if not a decade or more earlier. Norman, 1959, 2.—5. (Of a police officer) open to bribery: c., since ca. 1930; by late 1930s, also police s.: Ibid. A specialisation of sense 2.—6. Suffering from 'the bends', q.v. at sense 1 of **bends**: divers' (pearl or skin or other): since ca. 1945. 'He is bent, poor bugger!'—7. In *go bent*, to turn criminal; (of things) to get stolen: c.: since ca. 1910.—8. Hence, (esp. of a girl) to become faithless: prison c.: since ca. 1920. Norman.—9. See **flatter**.

bent as a butcher's hook, (as). An intensification of **bent**, adj., 2. (Powis, 1977.)

berk. A fool: c. > low: from ca. 1930. (*Gilt Kid*.) By abbr. ex next, 1, or, as Barltrop, 1981, suggests from first-hand knowledge, ex 2: 'I would guess [that E.P.] did not fully appreciate that "tit" and its synonyms are used for ninny or milksop. [Berk] was scarcely used before [the BBC TV comedy series] 'Steptoe & Son' took it up [in the early 1960s]' (letter to P.B.).

Berkeley. The *pudendum muliebre*. Abbr. r.s. *Berkeley Hunt*, a cunt.—2. In the pl, and from ca. 1875—never, obviously, with *Hunt*—it denotes a woman's breasts; F. & H. adduce Romany *berk* (or *burk*), breast, pl *berkia*.

berker. A brothel: Army in N. Africa: WW2. Ex the ill-famed street of Cairo: the Sharia el Berker. P-G-R.

Berkshire Hunt. The female pudend: r.s.: ?mid-C.19-20. Franklyn believes it to form the orig. of the synon. *Berkeley Hunt* and the **Berkeley** form to be accidental.

Bernice. Cocaine: drugs c. (Stockley, 1986.) US since–1933 (Spears).

berries. Testicles. Vernacular-poetic.

berry. (Gen. pl.) £1 (note): from ca. 1931. (Browne, 1934.) Prob. ex US monetary sense.—2. In *get the berry*, (of an action) to be hissed: theatrical. (Collinson.) Like synon. *get the rasp*, it obviously derives ex *get the raspberry*.

Bert. 'The great bulk of mankind are mere "berts" (as in Bert-'n'Ada [i.e. Everyman and his wife]), people whose only interest in getting on a train is to arrive at a particular destination' (Allison, 1986): haulage-bashers' (q.v.).

Bertie. See **do a Bertie; breezy Bertie.**

Bescot tar sprayer. 'L.N.W.R. Super "D" Freight Loco. Bescot was the name of a Birmingham depot whose men special-

ised in this type of locomotive' (McKenna, 1970): railwaymen's: earlier C.20.

bespattered. A coll. euph., ca. 1918–30, of *bloody*. Manchon.

best. In *one of the best*, a 'good fellow', i.e. a good companion: Society: from ca. 1920.—2. In *–of the best*, (of £1 notes); thus, *five of the best*, £5. (Collinson.) P.B.: but among schoolboys *six of the best* = 6 strokes on the buttocks with a cane, on the hand with tawse, etc.

best blue or **best B.D.** The better of an airman's or a soldier's two issued uniforms (B.D. = battle dress), the one worn for 'walking-out' or for 'bullshit' parades: WW2 and the period of National Service following, say ca. 1939–1962. The Services seem to manage to have a best of two, something that led to apocryphal stories of fierce sergeant-majors asking highly-educated recruits 'Is that your best B.D., lad?' and being answered, 'No, Sir. It's my *better* B.D.' (L.A.; P.B.)

best girl(, one's). The girl to whom one is engaged, or wishful to be; the fancy of the moment: coll.: adopted, ca. 1890, ex US. Cf. **girl**, 1.

best mog. The cat-skin or coney fur worn by a bookie's wife when he has been very successful: racing c.

bester. A fraudulent bookmaker: Aus.: since ca. 1910. B., 1943.

bestest, adj. Best: sol. (and dial.): C.19–20. (*EDD*.) Cf. *betterer*. P.B.: in C.20, occ. used joc. or as endearment.

bestial. 'Beastly', objectionable, disappointing: earlier C.20. Raymond, 1929.

bet a pound to a pinch of shit (or, occ., **poop**), **I'll.** This positive 'bet', assuring something with complete confidence, has, since the 1940s, largely replaced the earlier, negative *I wouldn't bet . . .*, current since late C.19. The rather euph. *poop* prob. dates from mid-C.20, and the 'bet' is really 'chicken-feed' when compared with *bet you a million . . .* (L.A.; P.B.)

bet both ways. To back a horse for a win, also for a place in the first three: turf s. >, by 1920, coll.; now j. Hence *both ways* is used as adj. and adv. of such a bet.

bet (one's) eyes. To watch a contest without laying a wager: Aus. sporting. B., 1942.

bet London to a brick, as in '*I'll bet . . .*': to lay long odds; to be sure: Aus.: since (?) mid-1940s. Hardy, 1967.

bet on top. A bogus bet laid, *pour encourager les autres*, by a pal of the bookie. The bookie's clerk places the bet 'on top', not in the body of the betting book. Often abbr. to *on top*. Racing c.

bet on the blue, with r. var. **bet on the Mary Lou.** To bet 'on the nod', i.e. on credit: Aus. racing: since ca. 1920 and ca. 1930. (Glassop, 1949.) Claiborne suggests, 1976, that the derivation is ex *blue*, v., to pawn or pledge, still extant in this sense ca. 1920.

bet on the coat. To lodge a dummy bet with a bookmaker as an inducement for others to bet: Aus. sporting: since ca. 1925. (Glassop, 1949.) Cf. **bet on top.**

bethel. 'A nonconformist chapel of no set denomination' (Butcher, 1979): nautical.

betters-off. 'Our betters': the well-to-do: coll.: since ca. 1925. Ruck, 1940.

betting on the black. See **black marketeer.**

Betty Lea (or **Lee**). Tea: r.s.: a var. of later C.19 (Rosie or) *Rosy Lea* (or Lee). Lardner, 1949.

between-agers. Children aged 10–12: coll.: since ca. 1962. After *teenagers*.

between hell and high water. In great difficulty: nautical coll. (McFee, 1935). A deviation from S.E. *between the devil and the deep (blue) sea*.

bev. A shortening of **bevvy**; cf. **bevali**. All three occur on p. 8 of Lester.

bevali is an occ. var. (from ca. 1885) of **bevie**, n., 2.

Beveridge. The social insurance scheme of Sir William Beveridge: coll.: 1945–ca. 1955.

Bevin. 'A jocular term for a shift spent at home through a mechanical breakdown: Derived from name of Ernest Bevin'

(Forster, 1970): miners'. E.B. (1881–1951), 'The Dockers' KC', statesman, and creator of the Transport & General Workers' Union.

bevry. A var. of next, 1.

bevvy (earlier, **bevie**), n. A public house: mid-C.19–20: Parlyaree. Seago, 1933.—2. Beer; loosely, any drink: military; theatrical; market traders': late C.19–20. (F. & G.) Whence, among market-traders, *bevvy-ken*, a beer-house, and *bevvy-merchant*, a heavy drinker (*M.T.*). Either ex sense 1 or ex *beverage*. Hence:-

bevvy (earlier, **bevie**), v. To drink: Parlyaree, esp. among grafters: late C.19–20; also Army, mid-C.20. Ex prec. Hence **bevvied**, drunk: Army.

bevvy (or **bevie**) **casey.** A public house: mid-C.19–20. (*News of the World*, 28 Aug. 1938.) Lit., a beer-house; therefore cf. **bevvy**, n.

bevvy- (or **bevie-**)**homey.** Any drunkard: grafters'. P. Allingham (*bevvy omee*).—2. Hence, by specialisation, a drunken actor: theatrical.

bevvy-up. To 'drink' considerably: Cockney: C.20, but common only since late 1940s. Naughton, 1970. Cf. prec. entries.

bewer. A girl: c. (—1845): rare and ob. See '*No. 747*', p. 416. It derives, says Leland, ex Shelta.—2. Hence, a tramp's woman: tramps' c.:—1935. The word provoked a correspondence in *TLS*, late 1982–early 1983. A.R. Breeze, letter pub. 11 Feb. 1983, attests it currency among factory workers in Newark, Notts, and adds: 'the context is usually one of sexual attractiveness, whether requited or otherwise. The buer's male counterpart is the "chevvie" or "chavvie".' See also *Underworld*; *Chavo* or *chavi* is Romany for 'child' (?hence, 'A chap' or 'kiddie') which suggests a Romany orig. also for *buer/bewer*.

Bexley Heath. Teeth: r.s.: late C.19–20. (Lester.) Sometimes shortened to *Bexleys*. Cf. **Hampstead Heath**.

beyonek. An occ. form of **bianc**.

bezazz. Glamour, sparkle: entertainment world: adopted, ex US, early 1970s. 'Hats off to British technical wizards who are responsible for the glitter, bezazz and stylishness of this British studio production' (Millar, 1980).

bezzer; bezzie. 'An ex-RN friend constantly says "bezzie" for best, e.g. "I've heard a bezzer story . . . " or "The bezzie one yet was . . . " He tells me that it is in common usage currently in the RN' (Knight, 1985).

bi, n. and adj. Biology; also attributively, as in *bi lab*: medical students'.—2. (One) attracted by both sexes, usu. applied to men: since ca. 1955. Reid, 1970: 'Raphael was bi. Or perhaps it was us [two girls] who had lured him over [from homosexuality] to the other side of the fence'. B.P., 1974, drew attention to its Aus. use.

bianc. A shilling: c. and Parlyaree: mid-C.19–20. It. *bianco*, white.

biargered. See **beargered**.

bib. In *push* or *put* or *stick* (one's) *bib in*, to busybody, to interfere: Aus.: since late 1940s. B., 1959. Cf. **sticky-beak**.

bibby. A later spelling and pron. of Hindustani *bibi*, used by C.19 Anglo-Indians for a native woman or girl. (Allen, 1975.) Still in Army and RAF usage until 1965 at least. (P.B.)

bibe. A bringer of bad luck: Anglo-Irish:—1935. Corruption of an Irish word.

bible. As *the Bible*, a Service manual: RN. Granville.—2. Hence, *the Bible*, 'the "book of words" about any particular subject' (Granville): RN: since ca. 1925. Also the *Child's Guide*.—3. As *the Bible*, the Railway Rule Book: railwaymen's. *Railway*.—4. With 2 and 3 cf. '*Glass's Guide to Used Car Prices*, the motor dealers' bible' (Graham-Ranger, 1981): car dealers'. Also known as *the book* or *the bottle*.

Bible bosun, the. A ship's chaplain, or even the Chaplain of the Fleet: RN: since ca. 1910. (Winton, 1967.) Cf. **sin bosun**.

Bible-puncher. A chaplain: Army and RN (C.20) >, ca. 1935, also RAF.—2. Hence, a pious airman: RAF: since ca. 1930.

(Jackson, 1945.) Cf. **Bible-thumper**. Both senses ex the gen. used next entry:-

Bible-punching. A sermon; religious talk. (Harrison, 1935.) Cf.:-

Bible-thumper. A pious seaman: nautical coll.: mid.-C.19–20. Bowen.—2. One who, door to door, sells a Bible that 'belonged to me dear old mum, God rest her soul' and, to each new customer, implies that the preceding had generously returned it to him: market-traders': prob. late C.19–20. *M.T.*

Biblical neckline. A low neckline: Aus. raffish: since ca. 1946; by 1965, ob. 'Lo and behold!' (B.P.)

biblio. A bibliographical note (usu. on the reverse of the title-page) in a book: book-world coll.: since ca. 1920.

bicarb. Bicarbonate of soda: coll.: late C.19–20.

biccy or **bikky.** Biscuit: nursery and domestic coll.: from ca. 1870. (Blaker.) An early example occurs in Jerome, 1886, where a little girl states: 'Unkie says me dood dirl me dot to have two bikkies', footnoted thus: 'Early English for biscuits'. P.B.: still current a century later.

bice or **byce.** £2: c. and low. Cf. Fr. *bis*, twice, and:-

bice and a roht or **a half.** Odds of $2\frac{1}{2}$, i.e. 5 to 2: racing c.

bicycle. A prostitute: low, esp. teenagers': since ca. 1940. Something often 'ridden': cf. synon. **town bike** and **camp bicycle**.

bicycle bum. A seasonal worker that cycles from job to job: Aus. since ca. 1920. B., 1942.

bicycle(-)face. A strained expression caused by nervous tension in traffic: coll., esp. among motorists and cyclists: since ca. 1942. *Cycling*, 11 Sep. 1946.

bid. Shortened form of **biddy**, an elderly woman, and usu. qualified by *old*, as in 'poor little old bid', 'tough old bid': coll.: since mid-C.20 at latest. (P.B.)

bidding movements. Disposal of female partner's limbs for intercourse: since ca. 1930. (L.A.) ?Orig. among bridge-players.

biddy. Any woman: C.19, as in Holmes, 1869.—2. Hence by specialisation, a (female) schoolteacher: Aus. children's: since ca. 1925. Baker.

bidey-in. A mistress who lives in with her lover: Scots coll. (Barbara Baker, 1983.)

Bidgee, the. The Murrumbidgee River—or region: Aus. coll.: since ca. 1860.—2. Hence(?), *bidgee*, a drink consisting mainly of methylated spirits: Aus. low: since ca. 1920. Baker.

biff. A blow; (?orig. US, anglicised) ca. 1895. Prob. an abbr. and emaciated form of *buffet* (W.).—2. Slightly earlier as v., gen. v.t.: to hit resoundingly, sharply, abruptly, or crisply. E.g., 'I'll biff him one if he's not careful.' Echoic or as in sense 1.—3. Gen. *biff round*, to go round: from ca. 1930. (Scott, 1934.) Also *biff off*, go off, depart. (Hay, 1934.) n. and v.—4. Friend, mate: since ca. 1945. Perhaps ex C.19 synon. *biffin*.—5. In *a bit of a biff*, a little hard play: Aus. Rugby League footballers': since ca. 1930. Buzo, 1971, 'a bit of biff against a player who turns in a blinder'. Cf. 1.

biff-up. Smartness on parade: Services', esp. Army: ca. 1925–45. P-G-R.

biffing. See **boffing**, 2.

biffs. A caning or a strapping: Aus. schoolboys': since ca. 1920. (B., 1942.) Ex **biff**, 1.

biffy, n. A water-closet, esp. if a backyard privy: Can. Leechman suggested, 1968, 'Could this be an infant's version of bathroom?'

biffy, adj. Drunk. Perhaps a perverted blend of *tipsy*, or of *bosky*, + *squiffy*.

big A, the. AIDS (Acquired Immune Deficiency Syndrome). *Observer*, 23 Feb. 1986.

big bad wolf. A threatening or sinister person: coll.: since ca. 1935. Ex a popular song.

big(-)ballocks. A self-important man: low:—1954.

Big Ben. Orig. and still, strictly, the bell in the tower of the Houses of Parliament, Westminster; but as a loose derivative from this, the clock: coll.:—1869. Ex Sir Benjamin Hall,

B

under whose Commissionership of Works it was constructed in 1856–7.—2. Ten: r.s.—3. Hence, esp. the sum of £10. Franklyn.

big Bertha. Any one of several German long-range guns: WW1.—2. 'Banking engine at Lickey Incline. Now withdrawn' (*Railway*, 2nd): railwaymen's: ?ca. 1950–64.

big blow. A hurricane: Aus. fishermen's and sailors' coll. Devanney, 1944.

big bottle. See **bottle**, n., 8.

big brain, the. 'The Railway control office, responsible for arranging and organising the passage of trains' (McKenna, 1970): railwaymen's: mid-C.20.

big C. Cocaine: drugs c. (Stockley, 1986.) Cf. **C**, 3. US since–1959 (Spears).

big cats, the. Lions or tigers or leopards. See **cat**, 3.

big cheese, the. 'The boss': Can.: earlier C.20. (Leechman.) Some UK use also.

Big City, the. Berlin: RAF Bomber Command: 1941–5. Ex the English coll. sense 'London'.

big dig. A reprimand made by a commanding officer: Army coll.: since ca. 1920. P.B. notes: now (1970s) a 'reprimand' is usu. simply *a dig*; a 'Severe reprimand', *a severe dig*.

big dipper. See **dipping**.

big dish, the. A big win: Aus. race-tracks' and two-up players': since ca. 1930. Glassop, 1949.

big E. Elbow: see **give the elbow**.

big eats. A good meal: Services': since ca. 1925. H. & P.—2. See PRISONER-OF-WAR-SLANG, para. 1, in Appx.

big end; big-end bearing. The human posterior: Aus.: esp. mechanics': since ca. 1930. (B.P.)

big front. (A fellow with) new or good clothes: Can. carnivals: since ca. 1910.

big gee, the. Flattery, esp. flattering treatment; very high praise: market-traders': since ca. 1920. (*M.T.*) See **gee**, n.

big getter. A 'teller of the tale' in a grand and genteel manner: c. 'Stuart Wood', 1932.

big gun. A large surf-board, for use in heavy surf: Aus. surfers': since ca. 1960. (B.P.)

big H, the. Heroin: drug addicts': since ca. 1960. (Bournemouth *Echo*, 3 Oct. 1967.) Also simply **H.**, q.v.

big hammer. See **hammer**, n., 5.

big Harry. Heroin: drugs c. (Stockley, 1986.) US since–1975 (Spears).

big head. A conceited person: since ca. 1940. Cf. the US coll. sense, 'conceit; egotism'. Also in the vocative (*you*) *big head!*

big hit. To defecate: Aus. r.s., on *shit*: since ca. 1920. Franklyn.

big hour, the. 'This was the name that [London] dockers gave to an hour's overtime, mainly the 5 o'clock to 6 o'clock [stint]' (Ash): mid-C.20.

big house, the. Penitentiary or prison: Can.: adopted, ca. 1925, ex US; also in UK since ca. 1935. Cf.:—2 'Kenyon was due to give evidence . . . at the Central Criminal Court, more commonly known to the public as the Old Bailey, and to the police as "The Big House" ' (Crisp, 1978).—3. A mental hospital: since ca. 1950. (Petch.) It has become, indeed, a gen. term for any large, impersonal, threatening institution.

big jobs, do. To defecate: domestic and nursery. Bygraves, 1976.

big John. The police: drugs c. (Stockley, 1986.) US since–1967 (Spears). Cf. **John**, 1.

big licks. See **give what for**.

Big Lizzie. HMS *Queen Elizabeth*: RN. (Bowen.) Also *Lizzie.*

big locker, put in the. Dumped over the ship's side: MN: since 1940s. (Peppitt.) *Davy Jones's locker*, of course.

big M. A million ('pounds sterling' understood): financiers' and other big businessmen's: since (?)1950. Smith, 1978.

big man. A drug supplier: drugs c. (Stockley, 1986.) US since–1936 (Spears).

big mouth. A tale-teller; an informer: low Glasgow:—1934.— 2. One who talks often, much, loudly, and tending to indiscretion: adopted, ca. 1945, ex US. Often in self-accusation, as, after a *faux pas*: 'Oops! Me and my big mouth!'

big mover. One who is, either consistently or on a specific occasion, highly successful, e.g., a male with a female: Aus.: since ca. 1945. Buzo, 1969:
> 'GARY: So you're a big mover with Diane, are you?
> BENTLEY: Practically home and hosed.
> GARY: . . . Big mover with Diane! You mullet! [fool].'

Big Navy, the. 'Life in the "Big Navy" [the 'big ships'] is very different from that lived by the officers and men who serve in destroyers, light cruisers, and submarines' (Carr, 1939): RN coll.

big noise. An important person: orig. ca. 1907 in US, adopted in Britain WW1.—2. Hence, by extension, *the big noise* = 'the boss': Can.,—1910, then British English,—1918. Leechman.—3. A 4,000-lb bomb: RAF: late 1941–42.

big-note. To speak highly of; to exaggerate the worth of: Aus.: since ca. 1935. (Cf. the quot'n at **bust**, n.)

Big O, the. HMCS *Ontario* (scrapped in 1959): R Can. N: since (?)ca. 1939. Leechman.—2. As *big O*. An *orgasm*: Aus.: since ca. 1960.

big on(, esp. very). (Very) keen on: Aus.: since ca. 1940. (B.P.)

big one or 'un. A considerable lie: coll. Cf. *whopper*. (P.B.)

big P. 'Release on licence' (Home Office): Borstals' and detention centres': 1970s. *Parole.*

big penny, the. 'Overtime or mileage payments. "grabbing the big penny"—making overtime" (McKenna, 1970): railwaymen's, esp. footplatemen: since mid-C.20.

big pussy (or **Big Pussy**). The P. & M. 'Panther' motorcycle: motorcyclists': since early 1950s. (Dunford.)

big shot. A gang-leader; a notorious gangster: US, anglicised as coll. in C.20. It has, since 1935 in England, been, as from much earlier in US, applied also to a person successful in any big way. Prob. on *big gun* and *big noise*.

Big Smoke (or **B.S.**)**, the.** Earlier simply *The Smoke*, London.—2. Hence, also Sydney: Aus., esp. NSW: since ca. 1919. Niland, 1959.

big spit, the. 'Calling for Herb, see, that's one of the many euphemisms for vomit, others include spue, burp, hurl, the big spit, the long spit, throw, the whip o'will, the technicolor laugh and, in Queensland, the chuckle' (Hardy, 1967): Aus.: since (?)ca. 1930, except *the technicolor laugh*, since ca. 1955. The first, *calling for Herb*, is—for *Herb*—echoic of a man 'spewing his guts out'; *spue*, mere var. of S.E. *spew*; *burp*, not so much illiterate as echoic; *hurl*, prompted by S.E. *heave*; the two *spit* terms, entirely Aus.; *throw*, short for *throw up* (n. and v.); *whip o'will*, r.s. for *spill* (one's guts); *chuckle*, ironic. Of all these terms, some are clearly nouns only, others are both nouns and verbs. Add *chunder*, which occurs in the sentence preceding the quot'n above, thus: 'Well, you've heard a bloke having a good chunder, saying "Herb . . . Heeeerb . . . Heeeerb!" ' See also the entry at **calling for Bill** for the Brit. variants.

big stuff. Heavy shells: military coll.: late 1914–18, and after. F. & G.—2. Heavy vehicles, e.g. tanks: Army: since ca. 1930. P-G-R.—3. In the Navy, a battleship or an aircraft carrier; collectively: since ca. 1939 (Ibid.).—4. In the RAF, heavy bombs: since ca. 1941 (Ibid.).—5. In all three Services, Very Important Persons: since ca. 1944 (Ibid.).

big time, in the. Operating on a large scale: Aus., adopted, ca. 1945, ex US. (B.P.) 'In the old days of vaudeville, "big time" meant the more important circuits . . . Others, less important, were "small time" ' (Leechman): Can. and US.—2. In *to get big-time*, to put on airs, to assume a 'posh' accent. A Midlands professional man, in a BBC Radio 4 programme on class-distinction, 4 Feb. 1980. (P.B.)

big truck. A nickname for a man generously sexed: Liverpool.

big twist. 'An outstanding success, an occasion for the expression of pleasure' (B., 1959). Cf. **curl the mo**.

big un. See **big one**.

big way, in a. Very much: coll.: since ca. 1935. 'I've had him in a big way'—I can no longer stand him, I've no more use for him. P-G-R.

big wheel. A large-scale 'operator'; a gang boss. See **wheel**, 2. R.C. 1976, 'i.e., that which drives the smaller wheels, as on an old-fashioned stationary engine.'

big white chief, the. One's boss: mostly in offices, and Services': coll., often joc.: since 1930s. Ultimately ex US.

biggie, -y. A big one of anything; an important person, e.g. a well-known and successful author, as in 'the biggies are going to do pretty well at the expense of those PLR [Public Lending Rights Bill] is there to protect' (Chancellor, 1982): later C.20.

biggy, as in '*Biggy Smith*' (Smith major), is a Christ's Hospital (School) term. Marples.

bike, n. Abbr. *bicycle*: from ca. 1890; since WW1, coll. Cf. *trike*.—2. Short for **town bike**, q.v., or its variants, *office bike*, *camp bike*, etc. According to *Harpers & Queen*, April 1979, a certain woman stockbroker is known simply as *The Bike*.—3. A ship's wheel: trawlermen's. Mitford, 1969.—4. In *get off* (one's) *bike*, to become annoyed; angry: Aus.: since ca. 1930. Glassop, 1944.

bike, v., or **bike it.** To cycle: coll. Franklin, 1931.

bike spanner. Pre-decimal sixpence, i.e. a *tanner*: r.s. Barnes, 1976.

biker. One who rides a bicycle; in later C.20, esp. a motorcyclist: coll., among the fraternity. Cf. Alex Stuart's novel-title, 1971, *The Bikers*. The female of the species is a *birdie biker*. 'Gangs of mods and their rivals, the rockers, who these days call themselves "greasers" or "bikers" ' (*Loughborough Echo*, 28 Sep. 1979). (P.B.) The Aus. version is *bikie* (Barnhart, 2).

bilge, n. Nonsense; empty talk: Public Schools' (from ca. 1906) >, in 1919, gen. Coke, 1908, 'Let's go . . . This is awful bilge'; Blaker, 1934, referring to 1920, ' "Bilge" was the polite word, current in those days for the later "tripe".' Ex *bilge-water*.

bilge, v.i. To talk nonsense: from ca. 1921; ob.

bilge artist. A pointless chatterer or airy-nothinger: Aus.: since ca. 1920. Baker.

bilingual. A joc. coll., used since ca. 1944, thus: 'He's bilingual—speaks both English and American.'

bilious. Bad, 'rotten', as e.g. 'in bilious form': Society: 1930s. Shepard, 1934.

biliously. The corresponding adv.: id.: id. (Ibid.)

Bill. As *the bill*, ' "The Bill" is the Metropolitan Police cab-driver's licence, as distinct from the ordinary County Council driving licence . . . It is also called the "brief" and the "kite"; but the "bill" is the more common name. It is a large red piece of foolscap (hence "the kite"), well bespattered with legal phrases (hence, I suppose, "the brief")' (Hodge, 1939): taxi-drivers': since ca. 1910.—2. As *the Bill* or *b-*, the police. Gen. as **Old Bill**, q.v.; see also **Bill from the Hill**.

Bill Adams. Euph. for *bugger all*, nothing or extremely little: military: WW1. (B. & P.) Cf. **Fanny Adams**, to whom *Bill* is, of course, no relation. Colonel Archie White, VC, in a letter, 1970, wrote 'There used to be, in some Victorian books of recitation, a monologue, "How Bill Adams won the battle of Waterloo", and Bill Adams became known as the garrulous and bragging old soldier'.

Bill Brown. 'Within the Brigade of Guards a Grenadier is invariably known as a "Bill Brown" although this was originally accorded to men of the 3rd Battalion' (Carew). See also **Billy Browns**.

Bill from the Hill, a. 'Specifically, a Notting Hill police officer (once a very busy and active police station) and generally a very energetic policeman' (Powis, 1977). See **Old Bill**.

Bill Harris. The disease bilharzia, now, better, schistosomiasis: orig. Aus. Army, early WW1; later, medical circles generally; by late 1970s, ob. By Hobson-Jobson.

bill-o! A note of warning, whether physical or moral: Cockney schoolboys'. 'Probably a perversion of *below!*, a cry of warning used in the Navy (and the rigging yards) when men aloft were about to drop something onto the deck—sometimes *below, there!*' (Franklyn, letter, 1962.) Noted also by Powis, who suggests a connection with *Bill*, the police.

Bill shop. A police station (Powis, 1977.) Ex **Bill**, 2.

billabonger. A tramp keeping to the outback, esp. the Northern Territory: Aus. coll. Ronan, 1954.

billed. Detailed (esp. in orders) for a piece of work; briefed: RAF: 1939+ . (Jackson, 1945.) Ex the theatrical *billed* (*to appear*).

billikin. A small tin can used as a kettle: coll.: 1926 (*OED* Sup.). Ex *billy-can*.

Billy Bluegum. A native bear (koala): Aus. coll.

Billy Browns, the. The Grenadier Guards: Regular Army. The name carries a scurrilous imputation. They were also known as *Tom Browns*, as in 'those Tom Browns—they'll do any bloody thing for ten bob!', a by-word in the army of the 1950s. See also **Bill Brown**. (P.B.)

Billy Bunter. A shunter. See HAULIERS' SLANG, in Appx.

billy cart. 'A child's vehicle, often little more than a box on wheels' (Buzo, 1971): Aus. coll.: since the 1930s. P.B.: but I have heard this term used in England also.

billy-ho. See **billy-o**.

Billy Muggins. A mainly Aus. elab. of **muggins**. B., 1942.

Billy Noodle. A fellow that imagines all the girls to be in love with him: Aus.: since ca. 1920. Baker.

billy-o (or **oh**) or occ. **billy-ho, like.** With great vigour or speed: mid-C.19–20. *The Referee*, 9 Aug. 1885, 'It'll rain like *billy-ho*!' Perhaps ex the name used euph. for *the devil*.—2. In *I will—like Billy-o*, a mild synon. for *Like hell I will*, I certainly won't: earlier C.20. Cf.:—3. In *go to billy-o!*, go to the devil: Aus. coll.

billy pot. A bowler hat: ca. 1890–1940; esp. in Lancashire. Roberts, 1971.

Billy Prescott. A waistcoat: r.s. A var. of the C.19 synon. *Charley Prescott*. Franklyn, 2.

Billy Ricky. The casual ward at *Billericay* in Essex: tramps' c. Gape, 1936.

Billy Whizz. Amphetamine group of stimulant drugs: addicts': later C.20. Cutland, 1985.

bim, n. The buttocks: Scottish Public Schools' coll. (Miller, 1935.) A thinning of *bum*.—2. Hence, bottom of the class or in an examination: Scottish schools': since ca. 1910. Marshall, 1934.

bim, v. To cane, properly on the bottom: English preparatory schools': since ca. 1920 (R.S., 1967.) Cf. prec., 1.

bimble. 'When the Marines moved at a slower pace [than a forced march at speed] they were "bimbling" ' (*Don't Cry*): RM: Falklands War, 1982. Perhaps a thinning of *bumbling*. Cf. **tab**, v., 2, and **yomp**.

bimbo. A fellow, chap, 'guy': adopted by 1938 (Curtis) from US as c.; by 1945, low s. Ex It. *bimbo*, short for *bambino*, 'a child'.—2. The female posterior: since ca. 1950. Ex **bim**, n., 1.—3. '1. blonde of limited talent and limitless ambition. 2. someone who lusts after fame and fortune' (*Sunday Express Mag.*, 20 Dec. 1987): prob. journalistic and ephemeral. Source also gave some punning derivatives, and *bimboid*, adj.

bimmers. Swimming trunks: Tonbridge (and prob. other Public Schools): current by late 1940s. (P.B.)

bimp. A shilling: vagrants' c.

bin, n. A trousers-pocket: c. and low: since ca. 1920. (*Gilt Kid*.) One dips thereinto.—2. 'Living quarters in which the rooms are very small' (H. & P.): Services': ca. 1920–45.—3. 'In a Naval mess, a space curtained off' (P-G-R): RN.—4. A straw boater; a woman's large straw hat: mostly hairdressers': since ca. 1950. (Bournemouth *Echo*, 20 June 1968.) Used by 'Mr Teazy-Weazy', Peter Raymond, the hairdresser Derby Winner.—5. A (police or prison) cell (Powis, 1977): police and underworld: since (?)ca. 1950.—6. As *the Bin*, the Headmaster: Rossall. Marples.—7. As *the bin*, a lunatic asylum, as in 'He'll have to go into the bin': since ca. 1920. (Waugh, 1936.) Short for *the loony bin*.

B

bin, adj. 'He's bin (or he's had it) means he's finished–frequently used to indicate that the individual is killed' (Forbes): RAF, esp. 66 Sqn.: earlier WW2.

bin mounger. See **binner.**

binco. A light; a paraffin flare; hence, occ., a magnesium flare: nuances 1, 2 (Seago, 1934), late C.19–20; nuance 3, since ca. 1920. A corruption of It. *bianco*, white: from the whiteness of the illumination they afford: cf., therefore, *bianc.*

bind, n. A depressing or very dull person, task or duty: RAF: from ca. 1920. (Cf. **binder,** 4.) Ex:-

bind, v. To weary, bore a person: RAF: from ca. 1920. Cf. **binder,** 4. 'Jack? Oh, he binds me solid!' 'Bind must be the most used of all Air Force slang expressions' (H. & P., 1943); see esp. Partridge, 1945. Whence *bind* (someone) *rigid:* use before 1939: also, though little used after 1940, *bind stiff.* Perhaps ex the ill temper arising from being *bound* or constipated, but prob. ex garage 'It's binding somewhere'—as applied to an engine vaguely out of order.—2. Hence, of persons or things: to be tedious, to be a nuisance; to complain and grumble overmuch ('He binds all day'): since ca. 1925.—3. (Ex 1 and 2.) (Of a person) to be, with sickening frequency, 'in the know': since ca. 1930. Partridge, 1945.—4. To work; esp. hard at one's studies: RAF (mostly officers'): since ca. 1935. Hence, as n., a tour of duty.

binder. An egg: late C.19–20 c. >, by 1910, low. (Ware.) Cf. the † S.E. medical sense of *binder:* anything causing constipation.—2. A meal, esp. a good, satisfying one: NZ. Hence, *go a binder,* to eat a meal: NZ, esp. tramps':—1932.—3. See **titley and binder,** whence, also a drink, as in Binstead, 1899. Cf. **swing o' the door.**—4. A bore (person): RAF: since ca. 1920. Ex *bind,* v., 1. Cf. **bind,** n.—5. One who grumbles and moans more than is held permissible: RAF: since ca. 1925. Partridge, 1945.—6. A last drink at a party: RN: since ca. 1920: Granville. Cf. *one for the gangway.*—7. See **toe-biter.**

binders. Brakes: RAF: since ca. 1925. Jackson, 1945.

binding. Given to 'moaning': RAF: since 1925. (Partridge, 1945.) Ex **bind,** v., 2, above.—2. Boring; tedious: RAF: since ca. 1920. Ex **bind,** v., 1.

binding tubes. 'The means of communication between instructor and student [in a De Havilland Tiger Moth training aircraft] in 1943 consisted of a system of speaking tubes . . . They were called, officially, "Gosport tubes", and, unofficially, "Binding tubes" ' (Mead, 1967).

bindle. A blanket-roll or swag: Can.; adopted, ca. 1890, ex US. (Niven.) A thinning of S.E. *bundle.*—2. 'Small quantity of drugs, usually narcotics, prepared for sale and wrapped in a specially folded square of paper or card' (Green, 1): later C.20. US since—1934 (Spears).

bindle stiff. A hobo: Can. c.: since ca. 1910. Ex US.

bine. (A smoking of) a cigarette: Army: earlier C.20. Short for *Woodbine,* used generically for any brand of cigarette. Tute, 1975.

bing up. To brighten, to polish (furniture, metal etc.): furniture and curio-dealers'. Vachell, 1914.

binged. Very eccentric; mad: Charterhouse School: 1920s. Ex *binged,* drunk.

binghi. Stomach, belly: Aus. (Webster, 1926). The (Sydney) *Bulletin,* keeping closer to the Aboriginal, spells it *binghi,* and *The Drum,* 1959, *binjey—* which seems to indicate that the *g* may be either hard or soft.

bingle. A skirmish: Aus. Forces': WW2. B., 1953.—2. (?)Hence, a car crash: Aus. surfers', ex *bingle,* a dent or fracture in a surfboard (Ibid.): later C.20. Wilkes.

bingling. A combination, barberly and verbal, of *bobbing* and *shingling:* coll.: mid-1920s. Collinson.

bingo. In *like bingo,* very quickly: low. (Allingham, 1933.) Ex *like billy-o,* confused with *like winking.* See TOMBOLA.

bingo'd or **bingoed.** Drunk: Society and undergraduates': since late 1920s. Ex late C.17 c. > s. *bingo* = brandy.

binjey. See **binghi.**

binner. 'One who examines the contents of rubbish skips for items of value or of use' (Knight, 1984): Portsmouth Dock-

yard: later C.20. Patterson gives synon. *bin-mounger,* perhaps ex dial. term for, inter alia, to eat by stealth. Cf. **ashboxing.**

Binnie Hale. A tale: r.s.: since ca. 1940; by 1959, slightly ob. Ex the famous entertainer. Franklyn.

binns; bins. Glasses = spectacles; *dark binns,* dark glasses: c. >, by ca. 1930, s. (Cook, 1962.) Perhaps ex *bin*oculars influenced by *binn*acles.—2. Binoculars, esp. on a racecourse: since 1930s. (Bolt, 1967.)—3. Trousers: later C.20. (Green.) Perhaps by extension ex **bin,** 1.

binocs. Binoculars: NZ and elsewhere: since ca. 1945. Murray, 1965.

bint, n. A girl or woman; a prostitute,—in which role the female was often called *saïda* [sah-eeda] *bint,* lit. 'a "Goodday!" girl': among soldiers in Egypt: late C.19–20, but esp. in and since WW1; ob. by 1960. Direct ex Arabic.—2. One's girl friend, e.g. *lush bint,* a very attractive girl (H. & P.): since ca. 1920, but esp. in WW2 and afterwards, among servicemen. (*New Statesman,* 30 Aug. 1941.) An elevation into generalisation of sense 1. Nevertheless, even in WW2, and current, usage, it was, and is, often pej. In Arabic *bint* has no lit. meaning other than 'daughter'.

bint, v. Mostly in *go binting,* to seek a female companion, esp. as a bedmate: Regular Army in Egypt. Ex **bint,** n.

bio. A biography: orig. and mostly journalists': coll. since the 1930s(?). 'There was a bio to be written. Also one on his famous father. Oh boy!' (Davidson, 1978.)

bioscope. (A drink of) brandy: ca. 1910–14. The more a man drinks, the more 'moving picutres' he sees.

Bip, the. The Bishop: aristocratic and upper-middle class: since ca. 1920. (Allingham, 1955.) By conflation.

Birchington Hunt. An occ. var. of *Berkshire* (or *Berkeley*) *Hunt,* cunt.

bird, n. Prison: shortened r.s., *bird-lime*: c. Rare except as *do bird,* to 'do time', and *in bird,* in prison: since ca. 1940, generic for a prison-sentence. Wallace, 1925.—2. Hence, collectively, previous convictions: c.:—1935. (Hume). Again *bird-lime* = time (served).—3. A troublesome seaman: nautical: since early C.19. Glascock, 1829; Green, 1984.—4. (*A*) *bird,* a girl: since ca. 1880; a sweetheart: military: since ca. 1890; a harlot: since ca. 1900 (but now ob. in this nuance). The last two nuances may represent a survival ex early S.E., but more probably they have arisen independently. The sense sweetheart, or simply girl, had, by 1920, become fairly gen., although still uncultured. Since then it has worked its way up the social scale to arrive near the top, in the late 1960s, in the term *dolly-bird,* q.v.—5. A turkey, as in 'we're going to have a bird for Christmas': domestic coll., mostly lower-middle class: late C.19–20.—6. A certainty, esp. (*make a) dead bird of,* a complete certainty, make quite sure of something: Aus.: since ca. 1910. B., 1943.—7. 'I did not want my "bird" (crook who is not known but suspected) to get any idea that the police were on his track' (Neil, 1932): police s.—8. In *go like a bird,* of, e.g. a motorcar, to 'fly along': coll.: since ca. 1945. (B.P.)—9. An aircraft. See quot'n at **troubleshooter.**

bird, v. To watch and study birds. See BIRD-WATCHERS, in the Appx.

bird bath. See **elephant's trunk.**

bird cage. The position and situation of the huntsmen when they find themselves encircled by wired fences and hedges and can escape only by retreat or by crowding the gateways: hunting. Thomas, 1936.—2. The Wrens' quarters at a Naval establishment: RN: since ca. 1939. P-G-R.—3. A 'signal box built up in girders or gantry'; also, a 'wire-trellised road vehicle' (*Railway*): railwaymen's.—4. 'The air pipe compartment on a diesel locomotive. The open arrangement of the pipes resembling a bird cage' (McKenna, 1970): railwaymen's: later C.20.

bird-dog on the trail, like a. In relentless pursuit of a person or thing. 'Oh, Jack will find one. He's like a . . .' (Leechman): Can. coll.: since ca. 1930.

B

bird-lime. Time: r.s.:—1857 ('Ducange Anglicus', 1st ed.). See **bird**, senses 1 and 2, for a specialised sense of time spent in prison, and hence prison itself.—2. In *come off the bird-lime!*, 'tell that to the Marines!': low:—1923 (Manchon).

bird-man. An aviator: coll.: ca. 1908–18. (*OED* Sup.) In later RAF joc. or ironic, the term survives as *intrepid bird-man* (P.B.).

Bird Sanctuary, the. The WRNS (Wrens) Headquarters: RN: WW2. Formerly they occupied Sanctuary Buildings, Westminster.

bird-seed. Sweets; chocolates: military: earlier C.20. F. & G., 'Something nice for the "Bird" ': see **bird**, n., 4, 2nd nuance.—2. See PRISONER-OF-WAR SLANG, §4, in Appx.

bird-watcher and **-watching.** One given to the practice—the practice itself—of watching the girls, orig. in a park: joc.: since late 1940s. Ex **bird**, n., 4.—2. For the slang of BIRD-WATCHERS—in the S.E. sense—see Appx.

birder. A bird-watcher. See BIRD-WATCHERS' SLANG, in Appx.

birdie. A seaplane: RN: current already by, or in, 1914. Carr, 1939.—2. Time. Ex **bird-lime**, q.v.—3. A hole done in one under the bogey figure: golfing coll.: since ca. 1920. (*OED* Sup.) Cf. **eagle**.—4. An aircraft: Aus. army (in Korea): ca. 1951–3. Harris, 1958.—5. See:-

birdie biker. A girl motorcyclist: motorcyclists'. (Dunford.) Since ca. 1960.

birds. Amytal: drugs c. Stockley, 1986.

birds' nest. A Wren's cabin in the 'Wrennery' at a naval establishment: RN: since ca. 1940.—2. The human chest, esp. if hairy: homosexuals': current 1970. Adopted, ca. 1955, ex r.s.—3. In *I must go and look for a bird's nest*, an earlier C.20 euph. for 'I must go and make water', used out of doors.—4. 'The crepe wool used to construct false beards' (Green): theatre.

birdseed; birdsong. See PRISONER-OF-WAR SLANG, §4, in Appx.

birl. An Aus. variant of **burl**. Niland, 1955, 'I'm going to give Eucla a birl.' [Eucla is a town on the southern border of W. Aus. and S. Aus.] Perhaps suggested by *whirl* rather than by *hurl*: cf. the Can. *take a whirl at* (something), to attempt it, current since ca. 1925. A blend of *bash* (attempt) + *whirl*?

Birmingham, the; esp. *going up the Birmingham*, travelling up the M.1: motorists': since ca. 1960. ITV, 13 Aug. 1963.

birp. A var. spelling of **burp**.

birth control engines. ' . . . were huge locomotives which could burn up to five tons of coal per shift. Firing them in the early hours of the morning was said to make a man impotent for weeks' (McKenna, 1970; in a letter, 1981, to P.B., Mr McKenna attributes this term, and the next, to Mr Bill Handy): railwaymen's: mid-C.20. Cf.:-

birth control hours. 'Work which starts between midnight and 5 a.m. A high percentage of footplatemen's work is done during "birth control hours", as much as two weeks out of every three' (Ibid.): id. See prec.

birthday occurs in the late C.19–20 fair-ground or Sunday-market patter, 'Look here, it's my birthday, I'll give you a treat and sell it cheap.'—2. In *give* (something) *a birthday*, to clean thoroughly, e.g. a room: London women's.

birthday suit, in one's. Naked. (Smollett, 1771.) Increasingly less used in C.20 owing to the supremacy of *in the altogether*. Prob. suggested by Swift's *birthday gear*, 1731. Still widely understood in UK, and it has, in Can., remained far more gen. than *in the altogether*; very common still in Aus. also. (Leechman; B.P.)

bis. Pron. *bice*, q.v.

biscuit. A brown mattress or palliasse: Army coll. > j.: ca. 1900–60. (Collinson; B. & P.) Ex shape, colour, and hardness. Earlier, occ. *dog-biscuit*.—2. As the *Biscuit*, the 10.30 p.m. express goods-train carrying biscuits from Reading to London: railwaymen's: earlier C.20. (*Daily Telegraph*, 15 Aug. 1936.) Cf. **the Bacca**.

biscuit box. A class 'Q' freight locomotive. See **spam can**, 2.

biscuit cough. A cough caused by mere irritation in the throat, as 'Are you getting a cold?'—'No, that was only a biscuit cough'. Ex Milne, 1928: ' "you were coughing this morning" . . . "It was a biscuit cough," said Roo, "not one you tell about" ' (D. Beale).

Biscuit Factory, the. The Reading Gaol (closed down a few years ago): early C.20 c. (It adjoined Huntley & Palmer's factory.) Cf.:-

Biscuit Men, the. See ASSOCIATION FOOTBALL, in Appx.

biscuits and cheese. Knees: r.s.: esp. in RAF, 1939–40, and as *biscuits*. Franklyn, 2nd.

bish, n. A bishop: rare before WW1.—2. A mistake: Preparatory Schools' and similar establishments: mid-C.20. Also as v., to blunder.—3. A chaplain: RN: since ca. 1930. (Granville.) Ex sense 1; cf. **bishop**, 1, and **bish**, v., 2.

bish, v. To throw: Aus.: since ca. 1920. (B., 1942.) Cf. **biff**.—2. To officiate in the absence of the chaplain: Services': since ca. 1939. P-G-R.

bishop. A chaplain: Services': since ca. 1925. (Jackson.) Mainly joc.—2. A broken-down sign-post: mostly East Anglian: (?)mid-C.19–20. Because—cf. *parson*—it neither points the way nor travels it.—3. (In big business) a private detective: since ca. 1955. McCabe, 1972.—4. In *flog* (or ex army) *bash the bishop*, to masturbate: since late C.19. Ex resemblance of *glans penis* either to episcopal mitre or, more prob., to chess bishop.

Bishops, the. Archbishop's Park, Lambeth Road, London: Cockney's. Also *the Arty Bishops*.—2. See ASSOCIATION FOOTBALL, in Appx.

Bishopsgate–Cripplegate–the Workhouse. Three London clubs: The Athenæum—the Senior Services—the Union: taxicab drivers': since the 1920s. ('Peterborough' in *Daily Telegraph*, 13 Dec. 1949.) The first has many bishops; the second, many aged Service dignitaries; the third puns on modern *union* for *workhouse*.

bit. A girl, a young woman, esp. regarded sexually: low coll.: C.19–20. See the entries recorded at **bit of** . . . —2. A jemmy: Aus. c. B., 1942.—3. The sum of 12½ cents: Can. coll.: mid-C.19–20. Adopted ex US. (Leechman.) Claiborne adds, 'From the Spanish piece of eight, a coin equivalent to one dollar, which (in some versions) could be literally broken into eight bits, each therefore worth 12½ cents.'—4. Copulation from the male angle, as in 'If you're in need of a bit, you might find her attractive' (Naughton, 1970): C.19–20. 'He just lived it up. Booze, bits. A simple soul' (Hunter, 1969).—5. An activity, one's job, a hobby or a craze, esp. if specialised, e.g., 'the jazz bit'—copulation—drug addiction: adopted, ca. 1967, ex US (Wolfe, 1968). The Hippies had, by 1974 at latest, become one of the minor marginalia of social history.—6. See **do** (one's) **bit**.

bit-and-bit, n. and v. The practice whereby each rider in a *bunch* or a *breakaway* takes a turn at the front, so sheltering and setting the pace to those behind: racing cyclists': since about 1920.

bit hot, that's a. That's unreasonable, unfair, unjust: Aus.: since ca. 1910. Baker.

bit lit, a. Slightly drunk: since ca. 1925. A catchy elab. of *lit* or *lit up*.

bit much, a. Elliptical for *a bit too much*, a meiosis for *too much* in its nuances 'exaggerated, excessive; too demanding; arrogant; (very) objectionable', as in 'Oh, I *say!* That's a bit much!' It > gen. only ca. 1950, but it existed as early as the 1930s; prob. of Cockney origin.

bit of . . . occurs frequently in s. terms for 'girl, woman' regarded sexually, hence for 'copulation': cf. *bit of crumb* or *cuff* or *cunt* or *fluff* or *homework* or *jam* or *muslin* or *raspberry* or *share* or *skirt* or *soap* or *spare* or *stuff* or *tail* or *tickle* or *tit*, some of which were C.19, and the many others that will arise.

bit of a brama. See **brama**.

bit of a lad, esp. **he's a.** He is one who actively pursues sensual enjoyment: he's always after the girls, 'likes his drop [of alcohol]', and games of chance; in short, 'a live wire': in gen. coll. use since ca. 1950.

bit of all right, a (little). Something excellent, esp. an unexpected treat or stroke of good luck: coll. Macdonald, 1907, ' "That's a bit of all right," said the guard, cutting off a piece of the stem and putting it into his mouth.' Also used of situations and positions and conditions, as in 'Taffrail', 1917, 'The Germans, considerably outnumbered . . . sought safety in flight. "This", exclaimed the skipper . . . , "is going to be a little bit of all right." ' And, of course, it can be used of a pretty or an obliging female. Cf. **bit of 'tout droit'.**

bit of barney. A fight. See **barney.**

bit of black velvet. A coloured woman. See **black velvet.**

bit of Braille. A racing tip: Aus. sporting: since ca. 1930. B., 1953.—2. Hence, a tip-off: Aus. c.: since ca. 1935. After ca. 1945, usu. simply *Braille.* Ibid.—3. Feel, n. and v.t., in its sexual sense; grope: low Aus.: since the late 1930s. (B.P.)

bit o(f) bum. (Of men) homosexual gratification: low. (L.A.)

bit of cush. A light, or an easy, job or duty: Army: since ca. 1925. Ex *cushy.* P-G-R.

bit o(f) dirt. A hill: tramps' c.:—1935.

bit of dough (or **putty**) **for the troops.** 'A (fellow service-)man said to be complaisant, esp. among servicemen abroad, where women, taboo because of religion or disease, are not accessible: WW2, possibly even WW1' (L.A., 1974).

bit of fluff. See **bit of . . . ;** this example recorded by 'Taffrail', 1916.

bit of homework, often prec. by **a nice little.** A girl or woman regarded, usu. but not inevitably, sexually, for affection may be implied: military, then gen.: since ca. 1895.

bit of how's-your-father, sometimes **bit of the old . . .** Sexual 'goings-on', anything from a spot of 'slap-and-tickle' to copulation: since mid-C.20. See **how's your father.**

bit of mess. 'Prostitute's male lover who is neither her ponce nor a paying client. A completely non-commercial relationship, but not the same as a "tin soldier" [q.v.].' (Powis, 1977): since ca. 1950(?): low.

bit of no good. See **no good.**

bit of nonsense. A (temporary) mistress: Society. A. Waugh, 1936.—2. ' "A nice bit of nonsense," commented Louis, meaning a piece of villainy that had all the makings of a walk-over' (Barlow, 1968): c.: since ca. 1950.

bit of spare. Mistress of a married—or, indeed, of an engaged—man, but also the lover of a wife or fiancée: since ca. 1935: low coll.—2. Hence, loosely, anyone providing sexual favours, either on a short term or occasional basis. Busby, 1978, 'I always got the impression that Maurice was down here [at an inn] on the look-out for a bit of spare'. Hence, also *to have a bit of spare,* to commit adultery (Powis, 1977). Synon. is *get* or *have a bit on the side.*

bit of tail. 'Sodomy (public schools); also coition *a retro*' (L.A., 1974): low.—2. Normal sexual intercourse, as in 'He's off out after a bit of tail': Services': since ca. 1950. (P.B.)

bit of the other, a. Sexual intercourse: low: since ca. 1930. L.A., 1974, comments, 'the right true end of love, esp. as desirable after an evening of platonic courtship.' Contrast *the other* (q.v. at **other**), homosexuality, when it was a criminal offence.

bit of tickle. A girl or woman regarded sexually: hence, copulation: low: since ca. 1925. Perhaps ex *slap-and-tickle.*

bit of tit. Id.: id.: since ca. 1920.

bit of 'tout droit', a. A 'bit of all right', q.v.: joc.:—1923 (Manchon); ob. by ca. 1935. Ex WW1 military macaronic Fr. *un petit morceau de tout droit,* strictly *a little bit . . .*

bit of under. Sexual intercourse: c.: C.19–20.

bit off, a. (Slightly) crazy. (Collinson.) Abbr. *a bit off his head.*—2. Unfair; not quite 'the done thing'; descriptive of an unfriendly or inconsiderate action: coll.: since ca. 1950. As, 'Oh, I say! That really is a bit off!' Cf. **not on.** (P.B.)—3.

In *have a bit off* (*with*), to copulate (with): Cockney, then gen. Cf. **bit,** 4.

bit on the cuff, a. Rather 'thick'—rather excessive, severe, etc.: Aus. and NZ.: since ca. 1930.

bit on the side, a. See **bit of spare.**

bit(-) player. A stage actor with a part in pictures: theatrical and cinematic coll.: since ca. 1930.

bit previous, a. 'In poor taste, uncalled for (cf. *out of order)*' (Green): non-U: later C.20.

bit slow upstairs. Dull-witted: since ca. 1950. *Radio Times,* 5 Jan. 1967. (Petch.)

bitch, n. A male harlot: c. *Gilt Kid.*—2. Perhaps the commonest C.20 epithet for a thoroughly unpleasant, but not necessarily lewd, woman; usu. qualified, according to the speaker's social standing, as 'a real . . . , a right . . . , a proper bitch'. (P.B.)—3. A toady to a master; one who makes up to another boy: Charterhouse: from ca. 1910. Hence the vbl n., *bitching-up.*

bitch, v. To complain in a bitchy manner: Can.; hence Brit. since (?)ca. 1925. Leechman.

bitch of, make a. To spoil or bungle: low.

bitch up. An intensive of *bitch of . . . :* late C.19–20.

bitching, adj. A violent pej.: Aus.: mid-C.19–20. Ronan, 1956, ' "Wouldn't that be a bitchin' joke?" ' Perhaps orig. euph.

bitching, adv. Another violent pej.: Aus.: mid-C.19–20. Ronan, Ibid., 'But he'd manage it somehow. He bitchin' well had to.'

bitching week. 'Third week of a four-week tour on station: Atlantic weather ships': 1960s. Drummond, 1963.' (Peppitt.) Tempers are at their shortest then; cf. **bitch,** v.

bitch's bastard. 'A severe, possibly violent warder' (Green): prisoners'. Cf. **pig's bastard.**

bitchy. (Properly of women.) Spiteful; slanderous: coll.: since ca. 1910. Wilson, 1957.

bite, n. A lot of money: Aus. low. B., 1942.—2. A confidence trick; any easy-money racket: Aus. c.: since ca. 1920. B., 1953.—3. A simpleton; a dupe: Aus. c.: since ca. 1930. B., 1953.—4. In *put the bite on* (someone), to ask (shamelessly) for a loan: Aus. low coll., since WW1.

bite, v. (Of a book, a MS.) to impress or appeal to: publishers': from 1935. Thus a publisher might say to his 'reader': 'So it didn't bite you, after all?'—2. To ask for a loan: Aus. low coll.: since ca. 1930. Wilkes.

bite (one's) head off. See **head off.**

bite (someone's) name. To eat a meal paid for by another: Aus.: since ca. 1925. Also *sign* (one's) *hand* or *name.* (B.P.) Cf. **bite,** v.

bite one off. To take, have, a drink of strong liquor: public-houses': since ca. 1910.

biter. See **def.**

bitey, often spelt **bightie.** Anything that either bites or stings, e.g. a mosquito or even a chicken, or cuts or otherwise injures, e.g. broken glass or electricity. Aus. nursery coll.: since ca. 1910 (?earlier). 'Keep away from that plug. Bitey!' (B.P.)

bits. Pleasant or pretty 'pieces' of scenery: photographers' and artists' coll.—2. A male baby's genitals: domestic, esp. feminine, coll.: prob. throughout C.19–20. Lewis, 1976, of a young mother of her first child, brought to her soon after birth, ' "Got all his bits, has he?" she asked the two doctors doubtfully.'

bits and bats. Knick-knacks: r.s. Perhaps suggested by '*bits and pieces*'.—2. Hence, esp. in the underworld, small pieces of jewellery: since ca. 1910.

bits and bobs. Midlands coll. for *bits and pieces,* poss. orig. dial.: still, late C.20, very much in use. Occ. used as v., as in 'I were bittin' and bobbin' about, the whole morning.' (P.B.)

bits of. See **bit of.**

bitser. Anything made of 'bits and pieces': hence a mongrel (e.g. dog): Aus.: since ca. 1910. B., 1942.—2. A motorcycle made up of 'cannibalised' parts from other machines: motorcyclists' (Dunford): since ca. 1950, or perhaps earlier. Cf. **summer soup**.

bitter weed. 'An acidulous, grumbling type' (Granville): naval: since ca. 1925.

bitty. In bits and pieces; not in flowing narrative, but in imperfectly connected incidents: coll.: since ca. 1920. Coward, 1923, 'She is rather fat . . . , her dress is extremely "bitty", with rose-buds and small bows wherever they are humanly possible.'

bitumen blonde. 'An aboriginal girl or woman' (B., 1943): Aus.: since ca. 1930.

bivvy, n. A small, i.e. a one or two-man, tent: Army: since ca. 1940. Short for *bivouac tent*.

bivvy, v. To halt for the night: Army: from ca. 1910. Since ca. 1950 (?earlier), more generally *bivvy up*. Short for *bivouac*.

biz. Equipment for injecting: drugs c. (Stockley, 1986.) Abbr. *business*, 1. US since–1938 (Spears).

bizzo. Business: Aus. teenagers', esp. surfers': since ca. 1950. (B.P.) Ordinary s. *bizz* + ubiquitous Aus. suffix *-o* (adopted ex Cockneys).

blabber-mouth (or one word). One who cannot keep a secret; but also, one who talks too much: coll.: adopted ca. 1944 (earlier in Can.) ex US.

black, n. A blackmailer: c.—2. 'A black mark for doing something badly' (H. & P.): Services': since ca. 1935. 'A glaring error is a "black", "I have put up a black" they will say' (Bolitho, 1941). The phrase *put up a black* is RAF officers', the RAF other ranks saying, 'I've boobed' (Jackson, 1943). 'Prob. derived from the Naval custom of putting up two black balls at the masthead when the ship is out of control' (Osmond, 1948).—3. A black-currant: fruit-growers' coll.: mid-C.19–20.—4. As *the black* it also means 'the black market': since ca. 1942. Whence *on the black*, engaged in black-market activities: since ca. 1943.—5. In *in the black*, financially solvent. See **red**, n. 3.—6. A photocopy: newspaper offices': 'pre hi-tech, but still used by old-timers' (Cropper, 1987).—7. See **fast black**.

black, v. In c., to blackmail. Whence *the black*, blackmail; *at the black*, on the blackmail 'lay'; *put the black on*, to blackmail; *pay black*, to pay blackmail; and *blacking*, vbl n., blackmail(ing): Wallace, *passim*. Hunter, 1964, has *a bit of black*.

black and tam. An Oxford woman undergraduate: Oxford University: late 1921–ca. 1925. Ex the *black* gown and the *tam* o'shanter affected at that period, with a pun on the **Black and Tans** (q.v.). W.

black and tan. Porter (or stout) mixed equally with ale: from ca. 1850: c. (vagrants') >, by 1900, gen. low s. Ex resp. colours.—2. That coastal trade in Aus. which consists in conveying coal from Newcastle, NSW, to Whyalla and iron ore from Whyalla to Newcastle: MN: 1940s onwards. (Peppitt.)—3. 'Amphetamine ("Durophet M")' (Home Office): drug addicts': current in 1970s.

Black and Tans. The men who, in 1921, assisted the Royal Irish Constabulary. Ex their khaki coats and black caps, the nickname coming the more readily that, near Limerick, is the famous Black and Tan hunt. Weekley.

black and white. As in *a pennyworth of b. and w.*, of tea and sugar: Glasgow lower classes': from ca. 1920. MacArthur.—2. 'Amphetamine ("Durophet") 12.5 mgm capsule' (Home Office): drug addicts': current in 1970s.—3. In *in black and white*, written or printed; hence, binding. Late C.16–20, coll. Cf. *black on white*, which, C.19–20, only very rarely applies to writing and tends to denote the printing of illustrations, hence printed illustrations. Green, 1974, notes *black and whites* as police s. for official paperwork, warrants, receipts, notes, etc.

black and white duck. A magpie: Aus. joc. B., 1943.

black and white minstrel. Fuller version of **black and white**, 2.

black army, the. The female underworld: low:—1923 (Manchon).

black as a bag, (as). Very dark, as applied to the weather conditions, esp. the light: Midlands (and poss. more gen.) coll.: since early C.20, perhaps much earlier. Presumably the effect of putting one's head inside one is meant. (P.B.)

black as a sweep's arse. Very black: rural coll. Mays, 1969, where the author is writing of Essex ca. 1920.

black as the ace of spades, (as). Utterly black or dark: coll.: late C.19–20. P.B. adds, 1976: 'Nowadays, I think, applied more often to Negroes and other dark-skinned people than to, say, weather conditions.'

black as Toby's arse. Pitch-black, usually of a dark night: Can.: since ca. 1910.

black beauties. Durophet: drugs c. (Stockley, 1986.) US since –1967 (Spears).

black-beetle. A priest: lower classes': C.20. Also, Raab adds, used by English-speaking Roman Catholic seminarians. Ex black clothes.

black bomber. 'Amphetamine ("Durophet") 20 mgm capsule' (Home Office): drug addicts': adopted ex US late 1950s. (*Groupie*, 1968). Perhaps prompted by the fame of the Negro heavyweight boxing champion, Joe Louis, who was thus nicknamed.

black bourse. 'In the Service it covers the out-of-hours' sale of cigarettes for example' (H. & P.): early WW2. Lit., black *market*.

black box. Instrument that enables navigator to see through or in the dark: RAF: since ca. 1942. (Radar.) Partridge, 1945.—2. A hocus-pocus apparatus or piece of an apparatus: since ca. 1945.—3. Hence, a transistorised ignition system on a motorcycle: motorcyclists' (Dunford): since ca. 1970. As in sense 1, it works 'by magic'.

Black Button Mob, the. Any Rifle Regiment: Army. A feature of any rifle regiment's dark green uniform is the lack of telltale glinting brass; it would have been 'a dead give-away' for the original (Peninsular War) sharp-shooters.

black cat with its throat cut. Female pudend: low. (Hayes, 1970.) Var. of **cat's head cut open**.

black chums. African native troops: Army: 1940–5. Also *old black man*.

black (or scab) coal. 'Coal imported from abroad or dug by blacklegs during the stoppage' caused by the General Strike of May 1926: Trade Unions' coll., often revived. Collinson.

black coat. A waiter: Aus.: since ca. 1920. B., 1943.

black-coated workers. Prunes, with a pun on *work*: gen. Midlands s.: since ca. 1910. L.A. notes, 1974, that, as *black-coated workmen*, the term was given wider currency by Lord Hill in his WW2 broadcasts as 'The Radio Doctor'.

black-enamelled. (Of races, people) dark-skinned: Army joc., esp. in Canal Zone: ca. 1945-55. A term of humorous abuse, as in 'C'm'ere, Ali, you black-enamelled bastard, iggri [hurry up]!' (P.B.)

black five. 'An L.M.S. Mixed Traffic Locomotive, Class 5' (McKenna, 1970): railwaymen's: ?ca. 1930-50.

Black Friday. In Labour Party circles, *Black Friday* is the day on which the General Strike of 1926 broke up. Now, late C.20, historical.

black gang, the. 'The "black gang"—that small army of "slags" and "mobsmen" who prey particularly on the grafter [one who 'works a line' at fair or market: a cheapjack, fortune-teller, and so forth] and the bookmaker. It was the first of the hurdles I had to overcome' (Ludlow, 1938): c.: since ca. 1910. Ex *black(mail)*: they levy it, or, on its not being paid, beat up the refuser.—2. A ship's engineers and, esp., stokers: RN: prob. since ca. 1890. (Carr, 1939.) Hence also R Aus. N: since ca. 1910. Cusack, 1953.—3. Occ. used of clergymen, joc., among themselves: mid-C.20. (P.B.)

black horror. A coal- or coke-fired stove used for heating offices, barrack-rooms, etc., extremely difficult to light and keep clean: RAF: 1920s–30s. Adkin, 1983.

black light. 'Signal light, not burning' (McKenna, 1970): railwaymen's ironic.

B

black magic. The orig. form of **black box**, 1. P-G-R.

black man kissed her. Sister: r.s. But not at all gen. Franklyn.

black marketeer. An illegal bookmaker quoting his own prices: Aus. sportsmen's: since ca. 1946. (B., 1953.) His customer is said to be *betting on the black*.

Black Monday. See **Meltdown Monday**.

black-out, n., and **black out,** v. (To experience) 'a temporary loss of consciousness before pulling out of a power dive' (H. & P.): RAF coll. > by 1943, j. Ex the blackness that affects one's sight and that into which the pilot lapses. The term has, since the late 1940s, widened to mean simply 'to faint' and been extended far beyond the fighting Services. It has given rise also to the term *red out*, experienced at the top of an outside loop, when the blood rushes to the brain, instead of being drained away from it.—2. Censorship; a complete denial by the authorities of all news on a certain topic, often as 'a news black-out has been imposed on . . . ': s. or j. soon > coll.: later C.20.

black-out gong, the. The WW2 Defence Medal: since 1945; by 1970s nostalgic. It was awarded to all who had served in civilian home defence organisations, e.g. fire-watchers, Royal Observer Corps, ARP, etc., as well as to members of the armed forces.

black-outs. A Waaf's winter-weight knickers: WAAF: WW2. (Jackson.) Of navy blue: cf. **twilights**.—2. In the Navy, a Wren's ditto: since ca. 1918. Granville.

black pan. Remains of cabin food, 'in certain steamers regarded as the perquisite of the firemen who come off watch at 8 p.m.': nautical. (Bowen.) Because gathered together into a large black pan.

black peter. A solitary-detention cell: Aus. c.: since ca. 1920. Hence to *black-peter*, to put into one. Tennant, 1953.

black princes. 'Locomotive cleaners' (*Railway*, 2nd): railwaymen's: since ca. 1950(?). They get so dirty that they look like the Black Prince in his armour—or like Negro princes—or, as likely as not, like both.

black scene, the. The situation of "coloureds", esp. West Indians, in relation to whites: London West Indians': since ca. 1965. Weightman, 1977.

black show. An 'unfortunate business', a 'discreditable performance': RAF officers': since ca. 1936. (Jackson, 1945.) Cf. **black**, n., 2.

black-strapped. (Of a ship or a boat) 'carried back into an awkward position by the tide and held there' (Bowen): nautical coll.: mid-C.19–20. Peppitt convincingly derives the term from ships that, becalmed at Black Strap Bay, put into nearby Gibraltar to re-store.

black-top. 'Engineers call the topping [used in reconstructing motorways] bitumen-bound material; the men laying it know it as black-top' (*Observer*, 20 Dec. 1981).

Black Troops. Dominions Air Forces personnel: self-named and ironic: WW1; revived in WW2. 'Blake', 1941.

black varnish. Canteen stout: RN: since ca. 1920. (Granville.) Cf. **Nigerian lager**.

black velvet. Stout and champagne mixed: public-house s., mostly Anglo-Irish. Ex its colour and its smoothness.—2. In *a bit of black velvet*, coïtus with a coloured woman: military: late C.19–20. Hence, *black velvet*, such a coloured woman: gen.: C.20.

Black Watch, the. The Royal Highlanders: military: by 1881 S.E. Ex their dark tartan.—2. Hence, by an ironic double pun, stokers: RN. Granville.

blackers. 'He opened bottles and began mixing stout and champagne in a deep jug. "Blackers"? They had always drunk this sour and invigorating draught' (Waugh, 1942): orig., University of Oxford: since ca. 1910. Ex its colour; by process of the OXFORD -ER. Cf. the synon. **black velvet**, 1.

blacketeer. A *black*-market racketeer: journalists' coll.: from 1945; soon ob.

Blackfellows' (or **the Dog**) **Act.** A government order that can, by publicans, be invoked against drunkards: Aus. public-house 'society': since ca. 1920. B., 1953.

blackfellows' delight. Rum: Aus. B., 1959.

Blackfriars Buccaneers. 'The London division of the Royal Naval Volunteer Reserve, whose headquarters have been at Blackfriars for many years past' (Bowen, 1929): RN.

blackie (-y). A blackbird: coll.: mid-C.19–20.—2. A blacksmith: RN coll. Knock.—3. A black duck: Aus. Stivens, 1953.

blackie (or **-y**)**-white.** ' "I'm an Anglo-Indian—a half-chat, a chillicracker, a blackie-white—the first is the polite term—the others are what they [the full whites] call us behind our backs" ' (Mather, 1977). In short, a half-caste.

blacks. Bold type: printers' and journalists'. (Petch.)

Blackwall navy (or **N.**). Ships of the Union Castle Line: late C.19–20: nautical. (Bowen.) Ex London as base and the ships' grey hulls.

blackwash. To blacken (someone's character): since ca. 1925; ob. Prompted by S.E. *whitewash*. Cf. **bad-mouth**.

blad. A sheaf of specimen pages or other illustrative matter: booksellers' and publishers':—1933 (*Slang*, p. 181). Ex S.E. *blad*, a fragment.

bladder. 'The local newspaper, a bag of wind; a description which emanates from the Southern Railway' (McKenna, 1970): mid-C.20. Cf. prec.—2. See **bladder of lard**, 2.

bladder of fat. A hat: r.s.: early C.20; ob. by 1920. Supplanted by the more popular *tit-fer*.

bladder of lard. A playing card: r.s. Franklyn.—2. As *the Bladder of Lard*; often shortened to *Bladder*, New Scotland Yard: since ca. 1925: orig. c.; by ca. 1935, gen. Cockney r.s. Gosling, 1959.

blag, n. A watch-, or a bag-snatching: c.: since ca. 1920. (Norman.)—2. A North Country grammar schools' term of abuse: since ca. 1955. (*New Society*, 22 Aug. 1963.) Ex *blackguard*, pron. *blaggard*?—3. A piece of bluff; a tall story: since ca. 1945: c. >, by 1960, s. Ex the Fr. *blague*, as in *sans blague*. Hence, v., to bluff, to 'con'. Both n. and v. occur in Cook, 1962.—4. A wages snatch, in transit, from the carrier: c.: since late 1930s. (Norman, 1959.) Cf. sense 1.—5. Hence, a robbery, esp. of a bank or post office (Newman, 1970): c. and police s.: since ca. 1950.

blag, v. To snatch a watch-chain right off: c. (Leach.) Perhaps ex Yorkshire dial. *blag*, to gather blackberries, itself ex Yorkshire *blag*, a blackberry. Cf. **blag**, n., 1.—2. To wheedle; persuade into spending money: low, esp. among grafters.—3. To scrounge, cadge: later C.20. See Seabrook quot'n at **mump**, 2.—4. ' "Blagging" was a Paras' [see **para**, 3] term for acquiring something, usually in a less than hundred per cent honest way' (*Don't Cry*): Falklands War, 1982. Hence, among young people, a merging of this sense and sense 2, as in 'blag some beer; blag some cash' (James Williamson, 1985). Cf n., 4 and 5.—5. To waste, fritter away: young peoples': mid-1980s. (Williamson, 1985.)

blag-merchant. A pay-roll bandit: c. and police s. since ca. 1950. (Hall, 1974.) Cf. **blag**, n., 4.

blagger. In the underworld, one (usu. a youngster) who snatches a woman's handbag and runs off with it; but it was also, early in C.20, Liverpool street arabs' s.—witness *Arab*. See *Underworld*, and cf. **blag**, v., 1.—2. 'It is the job of the Blagger to invite, persuade or trap people into the [Bingo] parlour' (Holliday, 1963): bingo organisers', hence players': since ca. 1954. Ex the underworld sense, 'he who, in a "team", does the talking', a thieves' 'con man', dating since ca. 1930. Bournemouth *Evening Echo*, 20 Apr. 1966. Cf. the Fr. *blagueur*.—3. ' "They're blaggers—they rob banks." A couple of weeks ago I would have been grateful for the gloss . . . appended in Troy Kennedy's script for the second spin-off from that tough TV series about the Flying Squad [i.e. *The Sweeney*]' (Coleman, 1978). Cf. **blag**, n., 5. Tempest, 1950, writes, 'Used very occasionally to refer to men who resort to violence, particularly when operating in superior numbers. Probably an abbreviation of "blackguard".'

blah, n. Nonsense; silly or empty talk; 'window-dressing' matter: adopted, ex US, ca. 1927: publishers' and journalists'. Cf. **blurb.** L.A. notes, 1974, that, since the late 1930s, and esp. in 'the official blah', it comes near to the meaning of **guff,** q.v. Perhaps ex Fr. *blague*, but more prob. ex Ger. s. *Blech*, nonsense, there being millions of Germans in the US. Another poss. derivation is ex Scot. and Irish *blaflum*, nonsense, idle talk; Ulster has the var. *blah flah*. Or, of course, merely echoic.

blah, adj. Deliberately wordy and insincere: ex prec.—2. Mad. (Mason, 1928.) By confusion of *gaga* and sense 1; but see **go blah.**—3. Blind drunk: since ca. 1930. (Maugham, 1941.) Pron. *blàs*, as if Fr.—4. Blandly non-committal, an extension of sense 1: since ca. 1960: coll. (P.B.)

blah-blah. A occ. form of *blah*, n. Sometimes even tripled, as in 'and so he goes on [in the essay, document, etc.] blah-blah-blah . . . ' Here, simply echoic. (P.B.)

blame. Fault, responsibility: proletarian coll.: mid-C.19–20. Heyer, 1938: 'It isn't my blame'.

blandander. To tempt blandishingly; to cajole: coll.: Kipling, 1888, puts it into the mouth of his Irish soldier Mulvaney; ob. By rhyming reduplication on the stem of *blandish*. *OED* Sup.—2. To blether; talk nonsense: low: since ca. 1930. (*Gilt Kid.*) Etym. either as sense 1, or perhaps ex *blather* and *blarney*, which would do as well for sense 1.

blank. There exists a quartet of linked nuances, 'to ignore, turn a deaf ear to' someone—'to reject' a plan, proposal, suggestion—'to refuse to see or acknowledge' someone—'to miss, not to take part in' a crime, which is also an underworld nuance: a group not peculiar to, yet commonest among, police officers, esp. if high-ranking; and existing since ca. 1930. All four occur in one of G.F. Newman's 'police procedurals' (*romans policiers*): *The Guvnor*, 1977. Thus, 'He turned, blanking him, and resumed pacing'; 'He next blanked Scotch Pat's next suggestion, about culling a couple of girls'; and 'He didn't blank his erstwhile performers out of hand when they called [telephoned] him'; the fourth, used by a professional criminal. The basic sense is to *blank out*, to erase, rub out, etc.

blanket. See **on the blanket.**

blanket drill. An afternoon siesta; later, sleep generally: Army, late C.19–20; RAF, since ca. 1930: esp. 'get in some blanket drill'. B. & P.; Jackson.—2. Hence, copulation; masturbation: since ca. 1935.

blanket stiff. A tramp that never utilises the casual wards: c. ?ex US.

blanks. Drugs of poor quality: drugs c. (Stockley, 1986.) US since—1967 (Spears).

blast, n. 'To receive a blast is much the same as "stopping a bottle", a good "ticking-off" ' (Granville): orig. RN, earlier C.20; by 1950, fairly gen.—2. A party: teenagers': ca. 1961–5. (*Sunday Times*, 8 Sep. 1963, letters columns.)—3. A thrill: Can., adopted ca. 1960 ex US. Schroeder, 1976, ' "I bet you'd be a blast to get stoned with", he said.' (Leechman.)

blast, v. To 'tell off', to reprimand. Cf. the n., sense 1.—2. To go raving mad: beatniks': since ca. 1959. Anderson, 1965.—3. To take narcotics: addicts': since late 1950s. (Janssen, 1968.) Cf. sense 2, and the n., sense 3.

blast off. (Of a car, esp. if a racing car) to start: Aus.: since ca. 1960. (B.P.) 'Ex the launching of a space rocket' (Leechman).

blasted. Intoxicated with drugs: addicts': since ca. 1968. (Wyatt, 1973.) Ex **blast,** v., 3.

blatter. (Gen. in passive.) To strike, assault: Glasgow. Prob. ex dial. *blatter* (gen. *blather*), to splash or befoul.

bleachers, the. The cheap covered seats at a stadium: Aus.: since ca. 1945. (B.P.) Adapted ex US sense, 'the cheap uncovered seats at a baseball stadium', which Claiborne,

1976, explains as 'seats in which one's clothes bleach in the sun.'

blear. To stroll; to wander slowly yet purposefully: Cambridge undergraduates': 1920s. 'Let's blear down to the Festival.' Perhaps cf. Yorkshire dial. *blear*, to go about in the cold.—2. When lost, to fly about in search of a landmark: Aus. airmen's: WW2. B., 1943.

bleat, n. A (usu. feeble) grumble: orig. RN, from late C.19; by ca. 1930, also Army, and still current (1970s), as in 'What's *his* bleat, then?'—what's *he* so peevish about? (Bowen; P.B.)—2. 'A Petition to the Home Secretary. "The new geezer put in a bleat the day he arrived" ' (Tempest): prisons' s.: mid-C.20. Both senses ex:-

bleat, v. To complain, grumble; to lay information: from ca. 1560. This pej. implies either feebleness or cowardice or an unpleasant readiness to blab.

bleed. To let out water: nautical: late C.19–20. F. & H. rev.—2. Hence, to let (cask, etc., of e.g. wine) fall in order to steal the escaping liquor: c. Manchon.—3. 'To apply blow-lamps to resinous knots to cause resin to flow. This helps to prevent blistering' (a master builder, 1953): builders': late C.19–20. Prob. ex sense 1.

bleed like a pig. To bleed much: coll.: C.17–20. Dekker & Webster, 1607, 'He bleeds like a pig, for his crown's cracked.' In C.17–18, occ. *stuck pig*. P.B. and B.P. note that the longer form is current—and the more usual—in Brit. and in Aus. in the mid–late C.20.

bleed (one's) **lizard** or **turkey.** (Of men) to urinate: Can.: since ca. 1925. Not common. The *lizard* version is a later C.20 one; Leech, 1985: 'I'll go see if the lizard needs bleeding'.

bleeder. A bloody fool, ca. 1880–1914. Hence (owing to the influence of *silly bleeder*), a fellow, a man: from ca. 1880; mainly Cockney. (Rook.) It often connotes detestation or contempt; also it occ. refers to a woman, as in Naughton, 1970: 'The woman was a proper aunt and what a busy bleeder she was.' (L.A.)—2. A person whose blood does not coagulate properly: medical coll. (As a person suffering from haemophilia, *bleeder* is S.E.)

bleeding. A low coll. intensive adj. of little meaning: its import is emotional, not mental. (Rarely used as a euph. for *bloody*.) From ca. 1857 (*OED* Sup.) Hence also in adverbial use.

bleeper. A small radio-activated warning device, carried in the pocket by people who may be instantly summoned in an emergency, as nurses, firemen, duty rescue crews, etc.: among such people: late 1970s. From the 'bleeping' sounds that the device emits when activated. (P.B.)

Blenburgher. A Blenheim bomber aircraft: RAF: 1940+. (Jackson.) A blend of *Blenheim* and (ex the resemblance to a gigantic sausage) *hamburger*.

blew. See **blow,** v., 6.

blig. A town boy: schoolboys'. Ex Northern dial. *blig,* a blackguard, a cad. *EDD.*

blighted. Euph. for *bloody*: coll. Manchon.

blighter. A contemptible person (rarely of a woman): from ca. 1896. A euph. (perhaps on *blithering*) for *bugger* (W.). But, adds P.B., it need *not* be a euph., for one who does in fact cast a blight on his surroundings and company.—2. A chap, fellow: ex joc. use of primary sense.

Blighty. England; home: military: recorded by *OED* Sup. for 1915, but in use in India for at least five years earlier. Ex Hindustani *bilayati* (Arabic *wilayati*), foreign, esp. European.—2. Hence, a wound taking one home: military: from 1915. Occ. *blighty boy* (1916).—3. Adj., as in *Blighty leave*, furlough to England: military: from 1916. See esp. *OED* Sup., B. & P., and Y. & B. (at *blatty*, an early form).

blim(e)y, occ. **blymy!** Abbr. *Gorblimy* (God blind me)!: at first mostly Cockney: late C.19–20. B. & L.

blimey, adj. Sentimental; (likewise esp. of songs) sentimental and popular: theatrical, music halls': from ca. 1920. Lincoln, 1933.

B

blimp. 'A small non-rigid dirigible airship': 1915: military s. rapidly > coll., then j. Invented by Horace Shortt (*OED* Sup.; B. & P.); Shortt prob. 'telescoped' it ex '*B*-type airship *limp*'. P.B.: but Wolman, 1977, denies that any designation 'B-type, limp' ever existed, and suggests rather an onomatopoeic orig. in the sound of a thumb snapped against the craft's fabric envelope. Whence:—2. *Blimp*, a retrograde, moronic Army officer (hence, civilian), pompous and inelastic: since ca. 1938. Aided and imm. generated by David Low's cartoon type, Colonel Blimp.

blind, n. A (very) drunken bout: from ca. 1912. Ex *blind drunk*.—2. 'A grenade that did not explode and had to be disposed of by other means' (P-G-R.): Army coll.: 1939–45. 'Prob. a direct borrowing from standard military Ger. *Blindganger*—a "dud" shell' (H.R. Spencer).—3. 'A sudden all-out effort on a club run' (*Fellowship*, 1984): cyclists': since late 1920s. Cf. the v. Also known as a *tear-up* (Ibid.: id).

blind, v. To go heedlessly, esp. of a motorist recklessly speeding: 1923 (*OED* Sup.).

blind, adj. In liquor; tipsy: C.17–18 c. (Cf. the S.E. *blind-drunk*.) The c. term has, in C.20, > s., popularised during WW1.—2. Pej., as in ' "I don't want a blind word out of either of you" ' (Curtis, 1938).—3. (Cf. prec. sense.) Complete; utter: Anglo-Irish coll.: late C.19–20. O'Neill, 1959, ' "I never thought to see the day when a blind stranger wud turn a gun on me in me own mountains".'

blind along. To drive very fast and recklessly: since ca. 1925. Ex **blind,** v.

blind baggage. On a train it is a baggage car, as in the quot'n: Can. tramps'. 'At each end of the coach,' says Gape, 1936, 'is a curtained-off part which is used for passing from one coach to another on a corridor train. This is known as the "Blind". The "Blind" facing the back end of the engine is unused, and so provides a small space which affords a good foothold and good protection from the wind.' See esp. *Underworld*.—2. A purse or wallet: pickpockets': since ca. 1950. Weightman, 1977.

blind bit of notice (of), not to take a. To be oblivious; to disregard utterly: coll.

blind Bob. See **old blind Bob.**

blind date. An arrangement to meet an unknown member of the opposite sex: adopted, ca. 1942, ex US: by 1960, coll.

blind dragon. A chaperon: middle and upper classes':—1923 (Manchon); ob. by late 1930s.

blind inches. The longitudinal difference between *penis erectus* and *penis quiescens*: raffish: late C.19–20. Cf. **old blind Bob.**

Blind O'Reilly! A coll. expletive: mostly Army: C.20. Kersh, 1942, 'The moment the place opens, in they dash. Blind O'Reilly! it's like a gold rush.' Ex some legendary figure, some obscure piece of folklore. 'He was, they say, a Liverpool docker trade-unionist ca. 1910' (Shaw).

blind out. To obliterate with paint or distemper: builders' coll. Hence, *bug-blinding*, a rough distempering of cellars or slum property: builders'. (A master builder, 1953.)

blind pig. A speakeasy: Can. (from US): since ca. 1921: c. until ca. 1929, then s.—as in Westbury, 1930. In Aus., 'a house or shop where liquor may be bought after hours' (B., 1942).

blind stabbing. Blind flying: Aus. airmen's: WW2. (B., 1943.) Cf. **stab,** 1.

blind staggers. Excessive tipsiness: Aus. Baker.

blind white cripples. Supply officers: RN: 1960s. 'The Supply & Secretariat Branch used to have white distinguishing lace between their gold stripes' (Peppitt).

blind with science. To explain away an offence, etc., by talking at length and very technically, in the hope that one's interlocutor may be so bemused that he will not pursue the matter: Army: since ca. 1940. Cf. the term's late C.19 use in boxing.

blinder. A cyclist who does not go in for flirting: opp. of **poodler,** q.v.—2. (Mostly in pl.) A bad cigar; a rank cigarette, esp. a 'Wild Woodbine': Cockneys': earlier C.20.—3. 'A dazzling display of skill, especially in sport' (Buzo, 1973):

Aus., since ca. 1935; also British, since 1940s at latest: as in 'Cor! You should've seen him—he really played a blinder' (P.B.).

blinders, adj. and n. Blind drunk; a being very drunk indeed: Oxford undergraduates': since ca. 1930. Marples, 2.

blindman's buff. 'Snuff. A pinch of the blindman's' (Daniells, 1980): r.s.: later C.20.

blindo. Drunk: military: earlier C.20. F. & G.—2. A sixpenny piece: earlier C.20 vagrants' c. Cf. **broad.**

blink. A cigarette-stump: military: earlier C.20; also Aus., since ca. 1918. (F. & G.) It caused one to do so in smoking it.—2. In *like a blink*, immediately; in but a moment: coll.: earlier C.20. Oppenheim, 1935, 'Must have died like a blink.' Prob. on *like winking* or *in a flash*.—3. In *on the blink*, acting as a look-out man in, e.g., a burglary: Aus. c.: since ca. 1920. B., 1943.—4. In *on the blink*, out of order; esp. applied to mechanism: RN: WW1. 'On the 26th [June, 1915] the trawler's L.P. cylinder went on the blink and it was necessary to stop again' (Carr, 1930). Thence to RAF in WW2, and soon > gen.—5. In *on the blink*, masturbating: prisoners': later C.20. Clayton, 1970.

blink-pickings. Cigarette butts picked up from the gutter or pavement: Aus. low. (B., 1942.) Cf. **blink,** 1.

blinker. A chap, fellow: late C.19–20 dial. > earlier C.20 s. Cf. **blighter, bleeder,** and *blinking*, prob. its effective origin.

blip, n. 'The projection of light seen in a cathode-ray tube' (Bebbington): electricians' (since ca. 1930), hence RAF (since ca. 1939). Related to the echoic *bleep*, the sound made by Asdic; both senses were, by 1960, common among civilian flying personnel.—2. A snub: schools', esp. girls': 1930s. (Thirkell, 1937.) Perhaps ex A.A. Milne's Bad Sir Brian Botany, who 'went among the villagers and blipped them on the head', in *When We Were Very Young*, 1924 (P.B.).

blip, v. 'To switch an aeroplane engine on and off': RFC/RAF: from 1915. (F. & G.) Blend ex *blink up*; or a perversion of *flip*.—2. To tap: see quot'n at **blip,** n., 2, which gave rise to some gen. usage.

blister, n. 'The anti-torpedo bulge in a man-of-war': RN. Bowen.—2. An objectionable person: Public Schools': C.20. (Hay, 1914.) Prob. ex Northern Ireland, where it has been in use from before 1898 (*EDD*). Semantically it is to be compared with **blistering,** q.v.—3. Flat protuberance which, on an aircraft, lies above and below the fuselage and encloses a gun position: RAF: since ca. 1925: coll. >, by 1942, j. H. & P.—4. A police-court summons: c. (—1903) >, by 1944, low s. It stings an objectionable's pride. (See *Underworld*.)—5. A mortgage: Aus. Palmer, 1937.—6. Sister: Aus. r.s.: since ca. 1920. 'Not very common' (B.P.); a rare form of r.s., since usu. two or more words are used, cf. the Cockney *black man kissed her* and C.19 *skin and blister*.—7. 'Official request to driver for information regarding a train which had come in late . . . If the train was more than two minutes late at the terminus, the driver would be issued with a form asking the reason for the late arrival' (McKenna, 1970): railwaymen's: since (?)mid-C.19. Also known as a *skin*. Cf.:-

blister, v. To thrash: early C.20. Dawson.

blistering. A euph. for *bloody*: coll. Manchon.

blithered. Tipsy: Aus.: since ca. 1916. Prichard, 1921.

blitherer. A silly fool: coll. (Wodehouse, 1909.) Ex earlier synon. *blithering idiot*.

blithero. Tipsy: RN var. of *blithered*. 'Taffrail', 1933.

blitz. A bombing by aircraft; hence, v., to bomb (a place): 1940, esp. in *the London blitz* (Sept. 1940–May 1941). 'The word that has received the greatest currency at home and abroad is *blitz*, as noun and verb' (Berrey, 1940). Ex Ger. *Blitz*, lightning, and *Blitzkrieg*, that lightning warfare which Germany conducted in April-June 1940.—2. Derivatively, a severe reprimand, to reprimand severely: 1941, orig. military.—3. 'The spring-clean which takes place when important officials are expected' (H. & P.): Services': since late 1941.—4. Hence, the brief, thorough, intensive campaign, as by the police, to enforce a law or a regulation: since ca. 1945.—5. Hence, also, a concentration of maximum effort, as in 'The C.O. has ordered a blitz on weapon training this month': Services': since ca. 1945. (P.B.)—6. In *a solid lump of blitz*, 'A large close-flying formation of enemy aircraft' (Partridge, 1945): RAF: WW2. Ex sense 1.—7. See TIDDLYWINKS, in Appx.

blitz buggy. An ambulance; but also any *fast* transport vehicle: orig. RAF: 1941–5. (H. & P.) By 1944 its 'ambulance' sense was, in the RAF, almost official. As 'a fast utility truck or lorry', it reached Aus. ca. 1944. Marshall, 1962: 'The drivers often found it hard to get their big blitz-buggies between the trees and the termite hills.'—2. Any automobile. See CANADIAN ADOLESCENTS', in Appx.

blitz flu. Influenza caused by, or arising during, 'the Blitz': 1940. (Berrey.) See **blitz**.

blitz-ridden. 'Damaged beyond repair' (H. & P.): since 1941: ob. by 1946. See **blitz**.

blitz wag(g)on. An Aus. var. of **blitz buggy**, 1, in its secondary sense: since ca. 1941. Tennant, 1956, where also in elliptical form *blitz* (since ca. 1945).

blivet; blivit. Defined in Brit. and US Armies as '10lbs of shit in a 5lb bag': joc.: 1950s–60s. (Elting; P.B.)

bloater. In *mild bloater*, a little dandy, a dandy of no account: low: early C.20. Manchon.

blob, n. (Usu. in pl.) A mine-net float: naval: WW2. P-G-R.—2. A gonorrhoeal ulcer: low. Cf. **blob, v.**—3. The indicative verb, esp. as used in advertising: since ca. 1930.—4. A jellyfish: nautical. Butcher, 1980.—5. In *be on blob*, (of men) to be much excited, sexually: low.—6. 'A drink of sweet Australian white wine, hot water, and sugar' (Gosling, 1982): N. Country.

blob, v. Often *be blobbing*, i.e. dripping, to suffer from a venereal disease: perhaps mostly Services': ca. 1930–60. Cf. **blob, n., 2.**

blob-stick. 'A stick with paper- or cloth-covered end used by the instructor to show where shots fell on the ground during miniature-range practice. The practice itself' (P-G-R): Royal Artillery coll.

block, n. The head: C.17–20. (Shirley, ca. 1637.) By 1970s ob., except in the cliché threat 'to knock someone's block off'. In Aus. and NZ, to *use* (one's) *block* = to use one's common sense; to act sensibly, hence to act intelligently. Sargeson, 1940. (Cf. Eng. *use* (one's) *loaf*.) Contrast *lose* or *do in* (one's or) *the block*, or *do* (one's) *block*, to become angry, excited, diffident: Aus.—1916 (Dennis, who has also *keep the block*, to remain dispassionate); by 1918 also NZ (Slatter). Cf. the later synon. *do* (one's) *nut*, and *keep* (one's) *cool*. F. & G. list *off* (one's) *block*, panicky; crazy; occ., angry: late C.19–early 20.—2. 'The young lady of fine shape who in the mantle department tries on for the judgment of the lady customer' (Ware): linen-drapers' coll.: early C.20.—3. 'Black market term for ounce of hashish (resin)' (Home Office): drugs' world, current 1970s.—4. In *put the block on*; *the block goes on*, to put a stop to (something); something is stopped, or comes to an end: low: since ca. 1920. (Norman.) Tempest has *blocks* in this sense.

block, v. To coït with a woman: low: since ca. 1890.—2. To get the better of; to fool: Aus.: since ca. 1930. Durack, 1955. ' "Take this boy Job—look at his features, and smart—you can't block him! Smartest race in the world, the Jews." '—3. See **block it**.

block and fall. Irritably drunk: Anglo-Irish: earlier C.20.

block-buster. A heavy bomb 'powerful enough to flatten a city block' (Claiborne): RAF and journalistic coll.: since ca. 1942. Jackson.—2. Hence, usu. written solid, n. and adj., anything that makes a considerable impact; e.g., 'a blockbuster novel' or 'this film is a blockbuster': since late 1940s, and, by 1960, coll. (P.B.)

block it. To get 'stoned' (intoxicated) on drugs: addicts': since mid-1960s. (Groupie, 1968.) Cf. **blocked**.

block of ice. (Of a bookmaker) to abscond: low r.s. (Franklyn). On s. *shice*, to abscond. Hence:-

block of ice mob. Welshers': c. (Sharpe, 1938.) Rhyming *shice mob*: see **shice, the**.

blocked. Much-exhilarated by drugs: drug addicts', esp. teenagers': since ca. 1950. Cf. **block it**. P.B.: 'Blowsers [gluesniffers] often use the 1960s pillhead word "blocked" to describe being high on glue—and that is literally its effect: it blocks out everything' (*Time Out*, 8 Jan. 1872, p. 15).

blocker. A bowler hat: mainly stores' and hatters'. Brophy, 1934.—2. (Usu. in pl.) Barbiturates: drugs c. Stockley, 1986.—3. See **stuffer**.

blocker-man. A foreman: Liverpool, esp. dockers'. Ex **blocker**, 1, his badge of office. (Shaw.)

blocks. ' "I'm just about two-blocks, Jack" is as much as to say, "I'm fed up to the teeth." When two blocks of a purchase are drawn together, they cannot move any further' (Granville): RN: since ca. 1930. Cf. **chocker**.

blog, n. A servant-boy in one of the houses: Rugby Schoolboys': from ca. 1860. A perversion of *bloke*.—2. Hence, a common boy of the town: id.: C.20. Cf.:-

blog, v. To defeat: Rugby Schoolboys'.

bloke. Occ. contemptuous; occ. a term of address among sailors. A man; a chap, fellow (—1839). Until ca. 1860, low; until ca. 1900, low. The word continues, in the late 1970s, to have a very wide currency, akin to the US *guy*.—2. A lover ('Sally and her bloke', Ware): from ca. 1880. Hence, perhaps:—3. The passive male in a homosexual partnership: RN.—4. A book-grubber; swot; an 'outsider': universities': late C.19–early 20. Ware.—5. As *the bloke*, the commander of one's ship: RN: late C.19–20. (*Musings*, ca. 1912.) The word in every sense is perhaps ex Dutch *blok*, a fool, or (via Romany) ex Hindustani, *loke*, a man; Weekley thinks that it derives ex Shelta (Irish tinkers' c.).

bloke out (of) the Warwicks. 'Old whatsisname'. See **Warwicks**, 2.

blokery. 'The male sex in general and bachelors in particular' (B., 1941): NZ and Aus. See **bloke**.

blonde. 'Two-kilowatt television lamps are yellow at the back and known as "blondes"; the smaller lamps are red at the back and called "redheads" ' (May, 1986): television workers'.

blonde job. 'A fair-haired member of the W.A.A.F.' (H. & P.): RAF: since 1940.

Blondie or **Blondy.** The inseparable nickname of any fair-haired man: RN: since ca. 1925. P-G-R.—2. As *blondie, -y*. A blonde girl: non-aristocratic and non-cultured coll.: since ca. 1925.

blonk on, have a. To be wearing a dull, stupid look: since ca. 1930.

blooch. See **bloosh**.

blood, n. A passenger favourably regarded: ships' stewards'. (Bowen.) Ex much earlier s. *blood* = a wealthy, fashionable, handsome spender. But on those freighters which carry only a few passengers, the passengers are, by officers and crew alike, called *the bloods*, 'short for bloody nuisances' (Gielgud, 1969): since ca. (?)1950.—2. 'Penny dreadfuls, or "bloods", as the sailor-boys call them . . . ' (Goodenough, 1901): prob. goes back to ca. 1880.—3. Hence, any 'thriller': gen. public: from ca. 1918.

blood, v. To cause to bleed: Aus. Mann, 1939, 'He heard the elder Galton boy say to Willy Sigbi, "I'll blood yer snout" . . . ' See **blood nose**.

blood and snot. The Spanish flag, red over yellow over red: MN: since ca. 1940. (Peppitt.)

blood back, get (one's). To avenge a relative, a friend, by shooting down the enemy aircraft responsible for his death: RAF: WW2. H. & P.

blood brothers. Two pals that have been on active service together: coll.: WW2; †.

blood chit. 'A ransom note supplied to pilots flying over possible hostile territory in the East . . . Sometimes called "gooly chit" [q.v.]' (Jackson): RAF: since ca. 1920; by 1944, j.—2. Hence, since ca. 1925, 'any written authorisation sup-

41

plied to any individual to cover him' (Jackson). Lit., a chit or note that saves his blood or life. P.B.: or his insurance money.

blood nose. ' "Blood nose" is Australian for bleeding nose' (Courtier, 1960): coll.: from ca. 1930. Cf. **blood**, v.

blood-stained. A (mainly post-WW1) facetious alternative, rarely euph., for *bloody*, adj. P.B.: also occ. *blood-smeared*.

blood ticket. That 'chit' from a (usu. civilian) doctor which testifies to a rating's illness that has caused him to overstay his leave: RN: since ca. 1930. P-G-R.

blood-tub. A theatre 'specialising in the worst forms of blood- and thunder melodrama, and generally gives two shows a night': Londoners': from ca. 1885; still extant ca. 1935. Applied orig. to a popular theatre in NW London.—2. A var. (RAF) cited by Jackson ('flying or earthbound') of:-

blood wag(g)on. An ambulance: orig. and mainly RAF: since ca. 1939. H. & P.

bloodhouse. A public house notorious for brawls: Aus.: since ca. 1910. Cusack, 1953; Tennant, 1956.

bloody, adj. A low coll. intensive, orig., and still often, connoting detestation: from late C.17. Ex and cf.:-

bloody, adv. Also a low coll. intensive; = very. C.17-20, but respectable till ca. 1750. From ca. 1750, neutral ethically and socially, but (until ca. 1920, at least) objectionable æsthetically. Only since WW1 has it, in post-1800 days, been at all gen. written in full. There is no need for ingenious etymologies: the idea of blood suffices.—2. It is often inserted, as in *abso-bloody-lutely, hoo-bloody-rah, not bloody likely.* Manchon.—3. Elliptical for *bloody well*, itself eligible as an intensive stop-gap adv. dating from late (?mid-) C.19: lowermiddle and lower classes'. 'I don't care what you think! I won't bloody do it!'—'If he doesn't want a ride, he can bloody walk!'

Bloody Mary. Queen Mary of England (d. 1558). Ex the persecutions she allowed.—2. Tomato juice and vodka: pubs' and clubs': since ca. 1944.

bloody-minded. Obstructive, deliberately 'difficult', pigheaded, vindictive: coll. since 1930.—2. Hence (?) 'rebellious in consequence of some injustice' (Granville): RN: since ca. 1930. The noun, *bloody-mindedness*, has existed since the early 1930s

Bloody Pirates. A good-natured South-Seas nickname for *Burns, Philp & Co.*, the big steamship firm of the Pacific: earlier C.20. Punning *B.P.s*, as they are also called.

bloody shovel. Generic for unnecessarily coarse speech. Ex the chestnut of the bishop who, to a workman asserting that he always called a spade a spade, replied that that was all right but that he thought the workman usually called it a bloody shovel.

bloodywell. (Cf. **bloody**, adv., 3) Has merited, in Aus. at least, elevation from hyphenation to 'solidity'. In 1969, B.P. wrote memorably thus: 'The great Australian adverb. Unfortunately this is the only adverb used by many Australians. I stepped [recently] into the bottle department of a suburban [Sydney] hotel to buy some beer and overheard a loud voice from the public bar—"I don't bloodywell swear and any fucking cunt who says I do is a bloody liar".' No comment.

bloodying. Cursing and swearing: mostly Services': mid-C.20. P-G-R.

bloomer. A mistake: Aus. and English:—1889. (B. & L.) Perhaps a 'blend' of *blooming error*, but cf. the more recent US *blooper* for a verbal error likely to cause embarrassment (Green).—2. A town where business is (very) poor: circusmen's. 'It's a "bloomer" to be there.'—3. A 'McConnell 2-2-2 locomotive with 7 ft. driving wheels (LNWR)': railwaymen's: since ca. 1950(?). *Railway*, 2nd.

blooming. (Occ. euph.—cf. **bleeding**—for *bloody*.) A mild intensive adj. and adv. The *SOD* dates the earliest instance at 1882, and it is still almost as popular a century later.

bloosh or **blooch.** To win a trick against someone, to 'get one over' on him; to 'diddle': Leics.: later C.20. (Tony Burt, 1984.)

blot, the. The anus: low Aus.: since ca. 1930. 'He gave me a kick up the blot'. (Dick.) Cf. synon. **freckle.**

blot (one's) **copy book.** A coll.: to make a mistake, a *faux pas*, a bad impression; to spoil one's record. Ex elementary school.

blotch. Blotting-paper: Public Schools': late C.19-20. (Miller, 1935.) Also in Yorkshire dial.—2. A term of abuse: from ca. 1925. Hay, 1936.—3. Food: Anglo-Irish: since ca. 1945. Fitzgerald, 1958, 'Let's all go out and eat. You know even the smell of a cork makes me woozy and I must have blotch.'

blotto. Drunk: from ca. 1905. Wodehouse, of a drunken man, 'He was oiled, boiled, fried, plastered, whiffled, sozzled, and blotto.'

blouse or **blousy suit.** A singleton: card-players'. 'He holds only a blouse (or a blousy suit).' Perhaps *blouse* derives from the other, and that other = *bloody lousy* suit.

blouse suit. See **green suit.**

bloused. 'I had only the King (or any other card) bloused' = I had only a singleton king: Aus. card-players'. (Sutherland, 1941.) Ex prec.

blousy suit. See **blouse.**

blow, n. A copulation: from the man's standpoint.—2. A warning; secret information: c.:—1926 (*OED* Sup.).—3. (Also *cold blow* if esp. windy.) A taxi-cab rank: taxi-drivers': from ca. 1925. Ex the food or the rest one can get there.—4. A smoke; esp., a cigarette: c.: from ca. 1920. *Gilt Kid.*—5. A stroke with the hand shears: Aus. shearers': since ca. 1920. B., 1943.—6. A crater caused by demolition charges in a road; the corresponding v. *blow* = 'to blow up': Army coll.: since ca. 1940. P-G-R.—7. Exaggeration, boasting: later C.20. 'Like kids boast how much beer they can drink and how many girls they have been with. Mostly blow' (Hebden, 1974).—8. Marijuana: drugs c.: later C.20. (Cutland, 1985.) Cf. v., 5.—9. As in 'This night watchman had invited him [a policeman] inside for a blow . . . A blow is a little while somewhere in the warm, off the streets and out of the sight of prowling eagle-eyed duty officers' (Seabrook, 1987): a police specialisation of the C.19-20 coll. term for a breathing-space.

blow, v. To depart, quietly and quickly, esp. to abscond on bail: c. Since ca. 1943, *blow*, to depart, has been ordinary s.—2. Also, v.i., to 'blow the gaff' (v.t. with *to*): c. (Wallace.)—3. To supercharge (car or aero engine); ppl adj., *blown*: since ca. 1925. Cf. **blower,** 7.—4. To masturbate: Borstals' and detention centres': 1970s. (Home Office.)—5. To smoke marijuana: drug addicts': 1970s (Home Office). Adopted ex US.—6. To fail in an enterprise, esp. by one's own bungling ineptitude: 'How'd the driving test go?' 'Oh, I blew it: backed into the examiner's own car . . . ': common in UK only since the early 1980s, but in US since ca. 1920 (W. & F.). Perhaps a rationalisation of C.19 s. *blew*, to spend or waste (usu., money), and **blue,** v., 1, 2.

blow! Go away!: lower classes' (—1935). Ex **blow,** v., 1.

blow a job. 'If [a docker] wanted to break continuity by not turning up at the job he was on, especially when this could mean that he could shape for a job he was regular on. This would be followed up with a certificate to say he wasn't well that day or that he had overdone it, i.e. was late' (Ash): London dockers'. mid-C.20.

blow a reed. To have (too) much to say: Army: earlier C.20. Poss. originated among bandsmen.

blow a stick. To smoke cannabis: drugs c. (Stockley 1986.) US since —1967 (Spears).

blow a tank. To dynamite a safe: NZ c.: post WW1.

blow (one's) **bags.** To boast: Aus., ?mostly W.A. (Ronan, 1961.) Ex *bagpipes*. Cf. S.E. *blow one's own trumpet*.

blow (one's) **cap.** A beatnik var. of *blow* (one's) *top*: 1959+. Also *blow* (one's) *lump*.

blow cold. Usu. *be blowing cold*, to be cooling off in sexual ardour: coll.: since ca. 1910.

blow (one's) **cool.** To become nervous, (over-)excited; very angry; teenagers', addicts', drop-outs', etc.: 1955–65, then fairly gen. (Janssen, 1976.) Cf. the always more gen. **lose** (one's) **cool.**

blow down (someone's) **ear.** To whisper to him: low. Sharpe, 1938; Powis, 1977.

blow (one's) **dust.** (Of male) to ejaculate semen: raffish. (L.A., 1978.)

blow-hole. A very talkative person: Aus.: since ca. 1920. B., 1943.

blow-in, n. A newcomer, esp. one still unaccepted: Aus. (B., 1942.) Ex the v.—2. A chance, or casual, visitor: Aus. (B., 1943; Kelly, 1955.) One who has 'blown in'.

blow in, v. To arrive; enter (v.i.); come; *blow in on* (a person), to visit. Coll. From US.

blow it out your ear! 'A very definite, derisive refusal, as in "No way! Go blow it out your ear!", said very contemptuously. A rare usage now, but widespread in West N. Am. since the 1960s' (Leech, 1986).

blow job. The woman of a pair engaged in 'soixante-neuf' would be 'doing a blow job': low: C.20.—2. A jet aircraft, as opposed to a *piston job*: RAF: since ca. 1960.—3. Fellatio (male and female): homosexuals': current ca. 1970. Ex 1.

blow (one's) **mind.** To have a hallucinogenic experience: drug addicts': since ca. 1962. It occurs in 'A Day in the Life', a song included in the Beatles' album 'Sgt. Pepper's Lonely Hearts Club Band', released 1 June 1967. (Paul Janssen.)— 2. Hence, to lose one's self-control: since ca. 1963. (Ibid.) Also used fig. in exaggeration, as in Reid, 1970, ' "Wait till they see you," Hardy chortled. "They'll really blow their minds." ' Both senses give rise to the adj. **mind-blowing** = amazing, astounding: media usage: 1970s.

blow off. To break wind: perhaps orig. RN but common also as a euph. among women and children.

blow (someone) **one out.** See quot'n at **cut off a slice of cake,** 1.

blow-out, n. A lengthening of the odds: Aus. racing: since ca. 1925. B., 1953.—2. A puncture: cyclists' (and later, motorists') coll.: adopted, ca. 1930, ex US.—3. In *give* (someone) *the blow-out,* to get rid of that person. See **bellows.**

blow out, v. 'To have no more to do with a proposition' (Home Office): Borstals' and detention centres': later C.20.—2. To spoil an injection: drugs c. Stockley, 1986.

blow the lid off (a dubious plan, a secret, etc.).To divulge something to the public, usu. in a more spectacular way than by mere 'leakage': coll.: since ca. 1930. (Petch, 1969.)

blow the whistle (on someone). To lay information, usu. to the authorities, about illegal or secret activities; to 'grass': since (?)ca. 1960. (Based on Chambers' *C.20 Dict.*, 1977 Sup.) Ex the referee's whistle. Hence the agent, *whistle-blower,* and the action, *whistle-blowing.*

blow three horns and a bugle. 'It's going to blow three horns and a bugle to-night, if I'm any judge of weather, and we may have to beat out to sea for shelter': Aus. nautical. Palmer, 1923.

blow-through, n. A wagon that, lacking brakes, has pipes to ensure a braking system: railwaymen's: *Railway.*—2. As *have a blow-through,* to coït (of a man): low. Ex:-

blow through, v. (Of a man) to coït: low: C.19–20.—2. To depart, esp. hurriedly: Aus.: since ca. 1920. 'It's six o'clock. I'll blow through.' (Dick; B.P.) Cf. **shoot through** and **blow,** v., 1.

blow (one's) **top.** To explode with anger: adopted, ca. 1943, ex US servicemen.

blow up. (Of an aircraft) to crash-land and catch fire: RAF: since ca. 1930. (Rhodes, 1942.)—2. To exaggerate the importance of, e.g., a news item; mostly in the ppl adj. *blown up,* and in the phrase 'blown up out of all proportion': since ca. 1960. Ex photographic enlargement.

blow (one's) **wig.** See JIVE, in Appx.

blowbag. A boastful windbag: Aus.: since ca. 1925. (Herbert, 1939.) A blend of *blow hard* and *windbag.* Cf. **blow** (one's) **bags** and **blowhard.**

blower. A telephone; orig. esp. a telephone or telegraph for the transmission of racing news (—1935); hence in gen. Forces' use by 1939 (H. & P.) and in gen. civilian use by 1946 at latest. In WW2 applied also to a broadcast system, e.g., the Tannoy. Hence, in *take a job off the blower,* to receive a telephoned order for cab: taxi-drivers' (Hodge, 1939).—2. An aircraft-engine supercharger: RAF: since ca. 1935. (Jackson.) Current since ca. 1925 in motor-garage s.—3. An air-raid siren: mostly ARP workers': 1940–5. *New Statesman,* 30 Aug. 1941.—4. A deserter from the Armed Forces: ca. 1941–6. (London) *Star,* 25 Jan. 1945. Ex **blow,** v., 1.—5. As in 'When Lord Hewart asked, "What is a blower?", he was told he was a man who "blew money back to the course" and saved bookmakers from heavy losses' (London *Evening News,* 12 July 1939): racecourse s.: since ca. 1930.—6. A broken-winded horse: Aus. and English coll.: late C.19–20. *Punch,* late C.19, *passim*; B., 1953.—7. A whale or porpoise: driftermen's. Butcher, 1979.

blowhard. A boaster: Aus., since 1880; since ca. 1950, also Brit.—perhaps ex sense 2. In US (1855; ob.), an adj., whence prob. the n.—2. Whence, a blustering officer, of no use with his fists: sailing-ship seamen's: from ca. 1885. Bowen.

blowie or **blowy.** A blowfly: Aus.: since ca. 1910. Casey, 1945, ' "What d'y mean, the flies found it?" . . . "There was clouds o' blowies." '

blowing bubbles. The curses uttered by the victims of wildcat schemes and shady company-promotions: since ca. 1930. In short, *frothing at the mouth* with rage.

blowing for a tug. Out of breath: MN: 1950s. (Malin, 1980.)

blown. Of a motor, esp. a racing car: supercharged: (racing) motorists': since early 1950s. Cf. **blower,** 2.

blown(-)in. (Of a car) partially re-sprayed: secondhand-car dealers': since ca. 1950. *Woman's Own,* 28 Feb. 1968.

blown out, to have. To have missed the last chance of a fare: cabmens'. See **left sucking** . . .

blown up. See **blow up,** v., 2.

blowpiped. Sent to another job: London docks: since ca. 1945. *New Statesman,* 31 Dec. 1965, article by R.C. Hall.

blowse, v., hence **blowsing.** Glue-sniffing, 'solvent abuse': addicts'. 'Black youth, comfortable with its spliffs, disdains glue-sniffing . . . or "blowsing" as it is often called by glue-sniffers among themselves' (*Time Out,* 8 Jan. 1982, p.14). Hence *blowser,* an addict; and *blowsed-up,* thus intoxicated. (P.B.)

bludgasite. A 'bludger': Aus.: 1939–45. (B., 1943.) A blend of *bludger + parasite.*

bludge, n. An easy job: Aus.: since ca. 1920. Cleary, 1949, 'He was happy in his job, it was a good bludge.' Ex senses 3 and 4 of the v.—2. See **come the bludge on.**—3. An easy life; a period of loafing: Aus.: since ca. 1920 (Dick). For all 3 senses, cf. **bludgeoner.**

bludge, v. To use a bludgeon. In Galsworthy, 1924. Ob.—2. To be a harlot's bully: Aus. (Mann, 1937.) Ex sense 1.—3. Hence, to ask for, to 'scrounge': Aus. low: since ca. 1910. *Rats,* 1944, 'Probably a Free Frenchman bludging a lift.'—4. (Ex 2.) To *bludge on,* to impose or sponge on: Aus.: since ca. 1910. (Dick.)—5. To have an easy life; to loaf for a while: Aus.: since ca. 1920. (Dick.) Cf. prec., 3.

bludgeoner. A harlot's bully; a bawdy-house chucker-out: c. (—1852); ob. Also, in late C.19–20, *bludger.*

bludger. A sponger: Aus. low s. B., 1942. Ex **bludge,** v., 4.—2. Hence 'often used without precise reference as a general term of abuse' (Buzo, 1973): Aus.: since ca. 1910.

bludget. A female thief that lures her victims: Aus. ephemeral: ca. 1925–39. B., 1943.

bludging. The vbl n. of **bludge,** v., esp. in senses 3 and 4.

blue, n. Maltese beer: mostly RN: mid-C.20. Ex the blue label of the most general make.—2. A summons: Aus. (B., 1942.) Ex colour of paper.—3. A mistake; a loss: Aus.: since ca. 1920. Cf. **blue,** v., 1.—4. Var. of **bluey,** 3 and 5, esp. as mode of address: Aus.—5. A brawl: Aus. low. *Rats.*—6. As *the*

B

blue, it = the desert or wilderness. Perhaps orig. Anglo-Indian, as in Lorimer, 1939: 'Sahibs ride into the blue'; but, esp. as the desert, it was popularised by the army in N. Africa, 1940–3. (P-G-R.) Cf. the cliché *wide, blue yonder*, from which this may well derive (Raab).—7. The Royal Navy's Long Service and Good Conduct medal: The ribbon is a broad blue stripe between two narrow white ones. See **blue peter**. (P.B.)—8. An amphetamine tablet: drug addicts': since ca. 1955. (*Bournemouth Echo*, 17 July 1968.) Glossed in Cutland, 1985, 'Blues. Drinamyl (blue tablets), an amphetamine previously known as *purple hearts*'.—9. A 'binge'; a riotous night out with all the trimmings, during which all one's money is 'blue'd': coll.: early C.20. Hatton, 1930.—10. In *get into a blue*, to become involved in a blue; *turn on a blue*, to start one: Aus.: since ca. 1920. (Culotta.) Extensions of sense 5.—11. See **bet on the blue; in the blue; into the blue**.

blue, v. To miscalculate; bungle; ruin: 1880 (*OED*). See also **blow**, v., 6.—2. Cf. the racing c. use of *blue* as v.i. to mean: lose on a race. The bookie's clerk accordingly marks the book B. (Morris.) Cf. **cop**.—3. To fight or attack (someone): Aus.: since ca. 1920. (B., 1942.) Cf. n., 5 and 10.

blue, adj. Drunk: Aus.: from ca. 1920. Perhaps ex the resultant 'blue devils'.—2. Euph. for bloody, as in 'I haven't a blue bean'—stony-broke: since ca. 1910; by 1975, †. (R.S.)

blue, adv. See **drive blue**.

blue balls. Aching scrotum or testicles, caused by unfulfilled sexual excitement; known also as *lover's nuts* and *stone-ache*: Anglo-American: since (?)ca. 1930, but not recorded before ca. 1965. In, e.g., Landy, and Hollander.

Blue Bits. The blue-backed periodical *Chemistry and Industry*: since ca. 1946. Pun on 'Tit *Bits*'.

blue bird. The police 'paddy-wagon': Aus.: mid-C.20. Ex colour. Wilkes.

blue bottle. A beadle, a policeman: coll.: 1597 (Shakespeare). Little used in late C.17–18, but repopularised ca. 1840. Reynolds, 1846. Considerable use also in mid-C.20.—2. A Ministry of Defence uniformed warden: since ca. 1960 at latest. (R.S., 1969.) Cf. sense 1.

Blue Caps, the. Service police: from ca. 1930. (H. & P.) But Military Police wear red-topped caps; blue-topped caps are a feature of the Military Prison staffs' uniform. (P.B., 1979.)

blue-chin. An actor: Aus.: (B., 1942.) As he shaves towards evening, so, during the day, he's unshaven.

blue devils. Blue capsules that, containing a barbiturate, are used by addicts: adopted, ex US, late 1960s. *DCCU*, 1971.

blue duck. 'Anything which does not come up to expectations; a dud, a "write-off" ' (Wilkes): Aus.: since late C.19.

blue-eye. A favourite of authority: RAF: mid-C.20. Ex:–

blue-eyed boy. A pet, a favourite: coll.: (—1914) >, by 1930, S.E. (F. & G.) The allusion is to innocence: cf. (*mother's*) *white-haired boy*.

blue eyes. 'Schoolboy, pupil, favoured by teacher: 1970s var. of prec. entry.' (L.A., 1974.)

blue eyes and golden ballocks (or **bollocks**). 'A Merchant Navy version of the shore term "blue eyes" for one specially favoured: since late 1940s' (Peppitt). In Army and RAF usage the phrase is shortened to **golden ballocks**, q.v. (P.B.)

blue fever. Venereal disease: nautical lowerdeck: since ca. 1945.

blue flash. A '25,000 volt A.C. electric locomotive' (*Railway*, 2nd): railwaymen's: since ca. 1955.

Blue Flue Boats. Ships of the Blue Funnel Line: HMS *Conway*. (Granville.) Also *The Blue Flue Line*, for the Line itself: more widespread, used, e.g., in Hong Kong, one of the company's major ports of call. (P.B.)

blue foot. 'Prostitute (used in hippy communes and probably of West Indian origin)' (Powis, 1977).

Blue-Funneller (or **b.-f.**). An Alfred Holt steamer: nautical coll. (Bowen.) See also **Blue Flue . . .**

blue glasses, see through. 'To see things from a wrong—generally depressed—point of view': coll.: early C.20 (Lyell). Contrast the informal S.E. *see things through rose-tinted spectacles*.

blue heaven. Amytal, Drinamyl: drug c. (Stockley, 1986.) US since—1954 (Spears).

blue in the face, until. With the utmost energy and effort: coll.: prob. at least as early as 1850. (Prompted by a Leechman note.) 'You can try until you're blue in the face but you still won't make them understand.'

blue job. Any man in a blue uniform, e.g., RN, RAF, Police, etc.: WW2. (H. & P.) Cf. **brown job**, a man in khaki, and **blue stockinged**.

blue light. An order for money (during a temporary shortage) on the NAAFI issued by a military unit: from 1924 or 1925. (With thanks to Maj.-Gen. A.P. Wavell, CMG.)—2. A Warrant Gunner: RN: since ca. 1920.—3. A wild rumour: Army in N. Africa: 1940–3. Douglas, 1947: 'Fantastic rumours, called blue lights, began to circulate.' Perhaps from 'St Elmo's fire', or marsh lights.

blue-light clinic. A VD clinic: Aus. coll.

blue-light outfit. Anti-VD kit supplied to armed services: Aus. coll., since ca. 1930. (B.P.)

blue lights. See **shit blue lights**.

blue-liner. A navy issue cigarette of post-WW2: RN and WRNS. Specially made with a thin blue line running the length of the cigarette, presumably to prevent any black marketing of 'duty-frees'. I recall seeing them in the early 1950s. (P.B., 1978; Wood.)

blue murder (orig. -s). Cries of terror or alarm; a great noise, horrible din: from late 1850s; coll. (H., 1st ed.) Gen. as *cry b. m.* P.B.: in C.20, not only *cry*, but also *howl*, *scream*, *yell*, etc., *blue m.*—2. In *like blue murder*, with great rapidity, esp. if hastily or in a panic: 1914 (*OED* Sup.); ob. by 1950.

blue-nose certificate. That entry on a rating's Service Certificate which states that he has served north of the Arctic Circle: RN: WW2. P-G-R.

blue-nosed. Puritanical; censorious: coll.: later C.20. Daniells, 1980, 'It's going to take more than a day or two for this green and pleasant [sc. land = England] to get over Queen Victoria and her blue-nosed disciples.' (P.B.)

blue one or **'un.** A green signal light: railwaymen's. *Railway*.

Blue Orchid. 'A member of the RAAF in WW2, considered to have a more glamorous uniform than the other services' (Wilkes): Aus. The term was applied also to RAF aircrew training in S. Africa, 1941. See **College Boys**.

blue pencil. Used as euph. in place of an unprintable word or phrase: coll.: ca. 1920–50. Ex editors' use of blue pencil for corrections and deletions, e.g. 'Not blue pencil likely!' P.B.: but still current, later C.20, as v., to censor out obscenity.

blue peter. The RN Long Service and Good Conduct Medal: RN. (Granville.) Ex the blue and white of the ribbon and of the 'blue Peter' flag. Cf. **blue**, n., 7. Ex the name given to the blue and white flag flown by any ship to indicate imminent departure from port.

blue-shirt. An owner; a manager: Aus. rural: since ca. 1920.—2. Hence, a slacker: since 1925. B., 1953.

Blue Sisters, the. Members of the Little Company of St Mary: Aus. Catholics' coll. (B.P.)

blue stink. 'Concocted fuel with an alcohol base' (Dunford): motor-cyclists': since ca. 1950. Cf. **brew**, 2.

blue-stockinged white-topped slotted jobs. WRNS officers: RN: 1940s. An officers' elab. of the lowerdeck **slotted job**, a woman. (Peppitt.) Cf. **blue job**.

blue streak. 'Blue Pullman de luxe' (*Railway*, 2nd): railwaymen's: ca. 1920–40.

blue ticket, get the. To be compulsorily retired from the RN: RN. 'Taffrail', 1933, 'the notices of dismissal were not blue, but were duplicated on ordinary official paper with the name filled in in ink.'

blue-tongue. A station roustabout: Aus.: since ca. 1920. (B., 1943.) Wilkes, 'from (*blue-tongue*) lizard'.

Blue Train, the. 'The train from "Alex" into the desert, eventually . . . as far as Tobruk. There was probably a greater concentration of hangovers on this train than anywhere else on earth' (Sanders, 1967): Army in N. Africa: 1940–3. Ex **blue**, n., 6.

blue tit. 'As in "Blue Tit and Brass Monkey Club"—said to have been used of winter swimmers (RAF and Icelanders) in hot pools near Reykjavik 1941–5.' (French.) Cf. the WW2 pun, '6 wrens (WRNS) went into the sea, and 12 bluetits came out' (P.B.).

Blue Un, The. *The Winning Post*: sporting: early C.20. (Ware.) Ex its colour, adopted to distinguish it from *The Pink Un*: s.—2. See **comics**, 2.

blue velvet. 'Paregoric and an antihistamine' (Home Office): drug addicts': 1970s.

Bluebell or rather, **bluebell.** 'Metal polish, regardless of any brand name' (Granville): RN (and other Services': P.B.) coll.: since ca. 1910. Ex the the brand name *Bluebell*.

Bluebell Line, the. The part of the Lewes–East Grinstead line, Southern Railway, which is noted for the bluebells visible from the trains: railwaymen's and users' coll. (*Railway*, 2nd.) P.B.: prob. better known now, 1982, than in earlier C.20, for it is one of the better known of the 56 conserved, preserved steam-lines operating 'for fun'.

bluebird. A (pretty) 'Waaf': RAF: WW2. (Partridge.) Ex Maeterlinck's *The Bluebird* of happiness.—2. A wave that has not broken (a 'greenie'): Aus. surfers': since ca. 1960. (B.P.)

bluebottle. See **blue bottle**.

bluer. One who 'blues' his money: market-traders'. (*M.T.*)—2. A racehorse that loses: id. (Ibid.) Cf. **blue**, v., 2.

blues. Coll. var. of *best blues* or walking out uniform of blue serge: RN: late C.19–20. P-G-R.—2. 'An illegal drinking house (shebeen), especially one where amplified dance music is also provided' (Powis, 1977): police and underworld: since (?)ca 1960.

bluey. A summons: Aus. and NZ c., a familiarisation of **blue**, n., 2. Kelly, 1958.—2. A nickname for a red-headed man: from ca. 1890, esp. in Aus. and NZ.—3. A man who drinks methylated spirits: c., tramps'.—4. (Usu. in pl.) The drug drinamyl (*blueys* or *blueies*).—5. As *B-*, the Near East—Egypt, Palestine, etc.: Army: 1940–5. Ex 'the *blue* Mediterranean'; cf. the *Shin(e)y* for the East, esp. India, an old Regular Army term.—6. A 'portable gas stove' (Hawke): RM, in N. Ireland: 1970s. ?ex the blue flame.—7. A £5 note: later C.20. ' "Drop him a bluey," he said . . . a fiver changed hands' (*Sunday Express* mag., 31 Jan. 1982, 'How the Rich Live', p. 15). Cf. **greenie**, q.v.

bluff the rats. To spread panic: low:—1923 (Manchon). I.e., to trick the rats into leaving the proverbial sinking ship.

blunderbuss. A baby-carriage: Can.: since ca. 1925(?). A pun on *blunder* and *bus*. (Leechman.)

blunderturd. A Thunderbird motorcycle: motor-cyclists' joc.: since ca. 1950. (Dunford.)

blunjie, -y. Yielding, as a rubber mattress or a waterbed: coll.: since ca. 1930. Prob. a var. of *bungy* or *bunjie*, to do with india-rubber. Given some currency in the 1950s by Peter Sellers as 'Bluebottle' (an 'awful boy') in the radio surrealist-comedy 'Goon Show' series, using it as an exclamation to parody the sound of impact or explosion, e.g., in mock stage directions: 'Fires pistol. Blunjie! Trousers fall down.' (P.B.)

blunk. Half drug-exhilarated, half drunk, hence totally stuporous: drug addicts': ca. 1960–75. A blend of *blind* + *drunk*.

blunt end, the. 'Landlubber's term for the stern of the ship. See **sharp end**,' Granville.

blurb. A publishers' recommendation of a book: on the jacket, or in the front, of the book itself. Term invented by the American humorist Frank Gelett Burgess (Holt, 1936.) It was anglicised in 1924. Coll.; after 1933, S.E., but rarely heard beyond the world of books.

blurry. A slurring, gen. euph., of *bloody*: from not later than 1910. B. & P.

blurt. To let or cause an escape of anal wind: low coll.

bly. 'A burglar's oxy-acetylene blow lamp': c.:—1933 (Orwell). By telescoping *blow* and *oxy*.

bo. A tramp: Aus.: since ca. 1930. Marshall, 1946: 'I pulled up a bo.' Perhaps abbr. *hobo*, or even *abo*.—2. 'Wardroom mode of address for the Bosun' (Granville): RN: since ca. 1910.

bo-chuffed. Delighted. See **chuffed**.

Bo Joe. A variant of **bo**, 1: since early 1930s. Either by elab. of *bo* or by r. s. on **hobo**. (B.P.) Also *bo-jo*, and prob. a corruption of **bozo**, as B.P. tells me, 1966.

bo-peep. A look: NZ and Aus.: since ca. 1920. Glassop, 1949.

board, n. A picture sold in the streets: vagrants' c.—2. See **take on board**.

board, v. To put (an item of equipment) before a board to decide its fitness for continuing service, or whether it should be 'written off' (discarded): Army, esp. quartermaster's staff. Similarly, usu. in passive, of servicemen: 'He was boarded' = he was sent before a board of medical officers who would decide his future employment. Both uses are coll., perhaps j.: since ca. 1950, if not earlier. Cf. the RAF's **cat board**. (P.B.) The medical sense earlier in Aus. (*Rats*).

board job. A sandwich-man's job: c. Ex the board he carries.

Board of Trade. A 'bench seat in Hyde Park, from the amorous activity for which the locality is notorious. (Noted 26 July 1960)': since the 1940s. Cf. **trade**, 2.

Board of Trade duff. Tinned pudding: MN: later C.20. (Malin, 1979.) Cf.:-

Board of Trade sports. 'The weekly life-boat drill held every Sunday at sea': MN: 1940s [and after]' (Peppitt). Malin notes var. *Board of Trade games*.

board shorts. Shorts descending almost to knees: Aus. surfers' coll.: since ca. 1955. (Sydney) *Bulletin*, 30 Mar. 1963.

boarding-house reach. An inelegant stretch across the table: Can. joc. coll. (Leechman.)

boards. Playing cards: c. Wallace, 1927.

boat. A builder's cradle: builders' joc.—2. (Usu. pl.) A submarine: RN: since ca. 1920. Granville.—3. A motor-car used for races: motor-racers': from ca. 1928. Punning *motor-boat*.—4. In *be on the boat*, to have been drafted overseas (but *not* yet on the troopship): Forces', esp. RAF, coll.: WW2.—5. In later C.20. the usu. shortening of *boat-race*, r.s. on *face*. A con-man, talking about bank fraud: 'Cos you can tell by the faces. You can see a teller and say, "Shitnitto".' 'Cos you know by the boat, understand?' (Taylor, 1982).—6. See **miss the boat; push the boat out**.

boat-happy. Excited—often so as to become distrait—at the idea of going back home on a demobilisation ship: Army: 1945–6.

boat hook. An 8-foot pole with spitted end, used by the London Fire Brigade.

boat race. Face: r.s.: since ca. 1946. Often shortened to *boat*. (Both are in Norman.)—2. A drinking contest between two teams: each man in turn 'knocks back' a pint of beer as fast as he can, to determine which team is the hardest-drinking crew: usu. the final event in an inter-mess 'games night': Services'. (P.B.)

Boats. The Boats Officer: RN wardroom coll. (P-G-R.) Cf. **guns, torps.**—2. As *b-*, boots, esp. if (very) large: middle-class joc.—3. As *the boats*, destroyers: RN: perhaps coll. rather than s.: ca. 1900–30. (Brock, 1977.) Cf. **boat**, n., 2.

Boatsville. The Admiralty building in Whitehall, London: orig., and mainly, FAA: mid-C.20.

boatswell. An admiral: RN lowerdeck: since ca. 1930. (Granville, letter, 1962.) ?Boat 'swell'.

bob, n. A shilling: since late C.18; ob. since the decimalisation of currency in 1971, but lingering in such phrases as *queer as a three* (or *nine*) *bob watch*; *two bob* as a rough estimate of a smallish sum of money, and in **worth a bob or two**, q.v.

bob, v. To strike, slap, push sharply, punch. Kersh, 1942, 'I bob him in the stomach and he fell flat.' Cf. **bonk**.—2. To be

B

subservient to authority; to be punctilious (and often a shade anxious) in observation of the regulations; hence *bobber*, one who is this or who does this, and *bob on*, to be very respectful towards one's superior: Army, esp. in the Guards regiments. See, e.g., Grinstead, 1943. Ex the Guards' sense of 'to be named for duty'. Graham, 1919, has: 'frequently a man who "bobs on it" [guard duty at Buckingham Palace], as the saying is, gets a comrade to do it for a few shillings'. Perhaps from S.E. *bob*, to curtsey.—3. Hence, to dither: WW2. (P-G-R.) Services' coll.: perhaps, also, akin to the Midlands dial. *to be bitting and bobbing*, ex *bits and bobs* (= *pieces*), to fidget about, or 'faff'. (P.B.)

bob-a-day gunner or **guns.** A temporary gunnery-officer: RN: earlier C.20. (F. & G.; Bowen.) He drew an additional shilling a day.

Bob and Dick. Sick: r.s. (D.H., 1974).—2. Prick (= penis): id.: (Ibid.). A later var. of the synon. *Bob* (or *Tom*), *Harry and Dick* for sick, and *Uncle Dick* for both senses.

bob and sock, the game of. Boxing: boxing journalists': 1930s. Ex *bob*, to duck one's head, and *sock* to punch hard.

bob groin. A racecourse betting-ring. See **groin.**

Bob, Harry and Dick. Sick, esp. after drink: r.s.:—1868 (Ware). Now, late C.20, shortened to **Bob and Dick,** q.v.

bob(-)hole door. A 'wagon door constructed to half open' (*Railway*, 2nd): railwaymen's. So that an employee may 'bob in or out'?

Bob Hope. A flying bomb: July–Oct. 1944. *Daily Express*, 14 Aug. 1944, ' "When you hear them coming," I was told, "you bob, hope for the best." ' A pun on the name of the famous American comedian.

bob-in. A voluntary subscription: Aus. coll.: late c.19–20. (B., 1943.) A shilling a head into the kitty.

bob on. See **bob,** v., 2.

Bob Squash. A wash, to wash (oneself): r.s.—2. Hence, the lavatory division of a public convenience: since ca. 1930. 'A pickpocket is said to be "working the Bob" when he specializes in removing wallets from the jackets of people washing their hands' (Franklyn, 2nd).

bob-tack. Cleaning-wherewithal; brass polish: Army: earlier C.20. (F. & G.)

bob to a gussie. 'To ingratiate oneself with an officer' (Jackson): Services': mid-C.20. See **bobbing.**

bob under. To sing small: Services': earlier C.20. P-G-R.

bob up. To appear; to return, as in 'he's always bobbing up': coll.

bobber. A filleter of fish: fishing trade s. It now verges on coll. (The Regional wireless programme of 23 Nov. 1936.) Ex S.E. *bob*, to tap. Cf.:—2. An unloader of fish from trawlers: coll. >, by ca. 1920, j. 'Said to originate from the days when such hands were paid one shilling [see **bob,** n., 1] per day' (*OED* Sup.).—3. Always pl., in:-

bobbers. Female breasts: N. Country: since ca. 1945. Wainwright, 1968.

bobbie. See **bobby.**

bobbin. See **screw the bobbin.**

bobbing. An attempt to curry favour with a superior: Services': earlier C.20. (H. & P.) Ex curtseying.—2. In *she's a-bobbing!*, a warning, to a signalman, of an emergency: RN lowerdeck: late C.19–20. Carr, 1939.

bobbing-bastard. A disappearing-'man' target: marksmen's. Cf.:-

bobbing-drill. Target practice: military. (F. & G.) Orig. and esp. at a disappearing target.

bobbing on. Anticipating, expecting (something unpleasant): military: earlier C.20. (F. & G.) E.g. 'He's bobbing on a court martial'.

bobbins. In, e.g., 'This watch must be running on bobbins', i.e. it is not running properly or accurately: Midlands. (J. Crowther, 1986.) Perhaps ex the idea that bobbins re smooth, and so of course will not mesh as cogs. (P.B.)—2. See **stopped for bobbins.**

bobble. A tassel or pom-pom, as in 'a woolly hat with a bobble on it', or of, e.g., a bolt of raw silk, 'it's covered in [with] tiny bobbles': domestic coll. (P.B.)

bobbly. (Esp. of trousers) 'loose and undulating'; baggy: coll.:—1921 (*OED* Sup.).—2. Adj. ex **bobble.** Covered with *bobbles.*

bobby, n. a policeman: since early 1840s. Ex Mr, later Sir, *Robert Peel* (cf. *peeler*), mainly responsible for the Metropolitan Police Act of 1828.—2. A signalman: railwaymen's. (*Railway*.) Ex sense 1. '[It] goes right back to the days of the constable-signalman' (McKenna, 1970):—i.e. when, in the 1830s–40s, signalmen acted also as the railway police.

bobby, v. To serve, to be, to be occupied as, a policeman: police force coll.: since the 1930s. Hence the n., *bobbying.* Both occur in Wainwright, 1967. Ex *bobby*, a policeman. Cf. **copper,** v., 2.

bobby-dangler. Penis: Can.: since the 1930s. Perhaps a blend of *bobby*-dazzler and dingle-*dangle*. (R.S., 1971.)

bobby-dazzler. 'A top much longer and narrower than the ordinary kind': Midlands'. (Thompson, 1935.) A s. elab. of *bobby dazzler*, a dazzling thing or person: dial. (—1866; *EDD.*) In this sense, by 1890, s. in Britain; by 1900, s. in Aus., where usu. *a real bobby-dazzler*. (B.P.)—2. 'In the heyday of Cycling Clubs the police would lie in wait for their dusk return. Those without lights got in the middle, those with the new-fangled very bright acetylene lamps rode on the outside, their lamps were the Bobby Dazzlers' (Yates, 1966): a pun on *Bobby, bobby*, a policeman. *Se non è vero è ben trovato.*

bobby-dodger(s). Clip-brakes: 'Originally used when all [motor-]bikes had front brakes of dubious effectiveness (push-bike type mainly) which were required by law. Had to be used with great care—if at all' (Partridge, 1979): motorcyclists': early C.20. Clipped on to satisfy the law, personified by a *bobby*. Similarly:—2. 'A clip-on horn or lamp' (Dunford.); id.: id.

bobby-soxer. A teenage girl rigidly adhering to teenage conventions: adopted, ca. 1959, ex US: by 1965, coll. Ex *bobby socks*, white cotton socks. Cf. quot'n at **greatest, the.**

bobby's helmet. The *glans penis*: since the 1930s. Ex shape.

Boche. N., then also adj.: German, esp. a German soldier: from 1914; not much used by the British soldiers. Direct ex Fr. slang, where the word (from ca. 1870) is of uncertain origin: see esp. *Words!*, p. 221.

bocker (or **bokker**). A bowler hat: Aus.: since ca. 1920. B., 1942.

bockety. Distorted or deformed: Anglo-Irish, esp. Dubliners'. (Dr H.W. Dalton.)

boco, boko. The nose. Orig. (ca. 1820) pugilistic, but gen. by 1873. Prob. ex *beak*; but if *coconut* (also, in US, simply *coco* or, erroneously, *cocoa*) existed some years before its earliest record, then perhaps *boco* derives ex *beak* + *coco*. Ware thinks that it may derive ex Grimaldi's tapping his nose and exclaiming *c'est beaucoup*: cf. sense 3.—2. Blind in one eye. See **boko.**—3. The head: schoolboys', perhaps ex misapprehension, or extension, of sense 1: mid-C.20. (P.B.)

bod. A body, i.e. a real person, a person actually available: RAF: since ca. 1935. (Jackson.) Note *odd bod*, unattached or 'spare' man: orig. Services'; then gen. s.—2. The human body; figure: orig. middle-class feminine: since mid-1930s. 'When she saw him looking at her, she was glad that, as she put it to herself, she had "a good bod".' By 1970s, also in 'gay' vocabulary. (P.B.)—3. Sexual intercourse: mostly lower and lower-middle class: since ca. 1920. Powell, 1970, where a woman calls to her husband, 'Hey, Willie, do you want a bit of bod?' [i.e., body].—4. A passenger in an airliner: airline crews': 1950s. See quot'n at **round the houses,** 2.—5. As *the Bod*, the Bodleian Library: Oxford undergraduates'. Marples, 2.—6. See **hawk** (one's) **bod.**

bodge. Paper: Christ's Hospital (School). (Marples.) Ex *bumf*?—2. A bodgie: Aus. non-bodgies': since early 1950s. (Dick.)

bodge spanner. Pliers or grips: motorcyclists' s. (Dunford): since ca. 1950. Cf. **screw-driver**, 1.

Bodger. As *Mr Bodger*, it means a confused or inefficient man: Aus.: the 1950s. B., 1953.—2. Anything worthless. See **bodgie**, 2.

Bodger or **Bidge, the.** The Headmaster: Rugby: late C. 19–20. (Marples.) *Bodger* corrupts *boss*, and *bidge* thins and shortens *bodger*. 'First applied to Dr James, headmaster 1895–1909' (Marples). 'The latter is no longer used' (Wharton, 1965).

bodgers' chrome. 'Silver paint used on once plated fittings to imitate chrome- or nickel-plating' (Dunford): motorcyclists': later C.20.

bodgie, -ey, -y. 'The Australian equivalent of the Teddy boy' (Wilkes): Aus.: from ca. 1950; by 1970, ob. Cf. **widgie**. The word app. comes from US teenage s. for a young male jitterbug wearing his hair long and curly, and a sports jacket too large for him: W. & F. record it for 1952 and say that it was, by 1960, archaic, but they don't essay an etym. My guess is that it doesn't come from Eng. Lakeland dial. *bodgy*, fat, puffy, but is a back-formation from *bodgies*, itself a distortion of 'the *boys*' or, more prob., *boysies* (cf. **boysie**). Another guess: **widgie** ex *widgies*, an analogous distortion of 'the *wimmen*' (women)—prompted by *bodgies*—2. 'Anything worthless, such as a fake receipt' (B., 1953): Aus. c.: since ca. 1950. Also **bodger**. Prob. ex Eng. dial. *bodge*, to cobble or patch clumsily. (P.B.)—3. (Gen. in pl.) Any misfit or unclassifiable person: Aus.: since ca. 1952 (B., 1953): ex sense 1.

bodice ripper. A romantic, often historical novel, aimed at female readers, and containing a judicious admixture of titillating by violent, and often explicitly described, sex: publishers' and bookish circles: later C.20. (Raab, 1987.) Green notes the synon. *sweet savagery* and *hysterical historicals*.

body. A person to be framed for a crime: police: since ca. 1950. Newman, 1970.

body(-)and(-)soul lashing. 'A piece of rope tied belt-wise round an oilskin which a messmate can grab if a man is in danger of falling overboard' (Granville): RN. But also, in the old sailing-ship days, to keep water out of legs and sleeves of oilskins.

body-basher or **panel-beater.** A garage owner, or the garage itself: Aus. motorists': since ca. 1950. (B.P.)

body-line work. Unfair or dishonest work or play: coll.: 1933. Ex the body-line cricket controversy, which began in Dec. 1932. See esp. *Slang*, p. 234.

body-snatcher. A stretcher-bearer: Army, since early C.20 (F. & G.), and RAF since ca. 1939 (H. & P.): ob. if not †. Also, in pl., the Royal Army Medical Corps: ob. by 1950 at latest.—2. A surgeon addicted to operating on seamen: R Aus. N: WW2. B., 1943.

boff. Short for **boffin**, 3.—2. In *have a boff*, to hit out: cricketers': since ca. 1955. *Sunday Times*, 9 July 1961, Ian Peebles, 'May, with a raincloud at his back and victory just round the corner, had a boff'. Echoic. Cf. **biff**.

boff (up). To make a mistake; to do something wrong: Loughborough Grammar School: since ca. 1975. (Reed, 1977.) Prob. rather more gen. Also (not at LGS), *make a boff*, to make a mistake.

boffer. See **boffing**.

boffin. Usually *the boffins*, the inventors working for the advancement of aviation: RAF. Dating since before WW2, it > gen. in the Services only in 1944 (McDouall, 1945). It owes something to Dickens, *Our Mutual Friend*, 1864–5, where a conscientious Mr Boffin is 'a very odd-looking old fellow indeed'—and to William Morris, *News from Nowhere*, 1891, where another Mr Boffin was a dustman interested in mathematics. (Foster, 1968.) R.S. adds: 'So perhaps the origin is purely literary'. For 'perhaps' I'd substitute 'probably'—it's that sort of word.—2. In RN, any officer over 40 years of age: since ca. 1940. Granville.—3. A 'swot', a diligent student: comprehensive schoolchildren's: early 1980s. (M. Birkett, 1982.)

boffing; boffer. Masturbation; one who indulges in a specific instance: low: since ca. 1930.—2. 'A term for sexual intercourse' (Powis): low: since mid-C.20. 'Sloane [Ranger, q.v.] slang for shooting pheasants is "biffing"; Sloane slang for *indoor* sports with birds is "boffing" ' (Howard, 1987).

boffinologist. 'Derogatory term, the reversal of the affectionate, respectful "boffin", but referring to [the] same persons' (Peppitt, 1976): MN: since ca. 1970. It implies a medical *boffinology*, technology, science.

boffo. Popular; successful: Can., adopted, ca. 1970, ex US (see W. & F.). As in *Maclean's* (magazine), Aug. 1976: 'Judith Guest's . . . novel, *Ordinary People* . . . film sale to boffo book-buyer, Robert Redford'. Echoic; cf. S.E. *striking*; and s. **socko-boffo**.

bog, n. (Often *the bogs*.) Abbr. **bog-house**, q.v., a privy: since early C.19 (in *Spy*, 1825); orig. Oxford University s., > C.20 coll. Also, by ca. 1945, Aus. (Buzo, 1973). Hence *do* or *have a bog*: low.—2. Abbr. **bog-wheel**, a bicycle: Marlborough College.—3. In *make a bog of*, to muddle, to make a thorough mess of: later C.20. Ex **bog up**, influenced by synon. **make a balls** or **box of**. (P.B.)

bog, v. To defecate: from ca. 1870: s. >, ca. 1920, low coll., including Public Schools'. (Baumann; P.B.) Ex prec. 1.—2. To work hard at a manual job: Aus.: since ca. 1915. Casey, 1947, 'Bogging underground on the goldfields'. Cf. **bog in**, the more common form.

bog brush upside down. A short official haircut: RN lowerdeck: 1970s (and, I think, earlier). (Peppitt.) I.e. a lavatory brush.

bog bumf. Lavatory paper: low. Tautologous, but necessary to distinguish from the extended senses of **bumf**, q.v. (P.B.)

bog-eyed. Heavy-eyed or squinting from, e.g., too much drink, or lack of sleep: since late C.19. (P.B.)

bog-eyed drive. A derailleur gear mechanism: Lancashire cyclists'. Ex the staggering, wandering effect of being *bog-eyed*: 'Cyclists, seeing the non-aligned chain for the first time would refer to it as bog-eyed' (*Fellowship*).

bog-house. A privy: from ca. 1670: low coll. Ex the ca. 1550–1660 S.E. *boggard*. P.B.: Bishop has drawn my attention to: 'Camden Council has just received a planning application from Lincoln's Inn asking for permission to build a new screen wall . . . at the Boghouse, Base Court, Star Yard, WC2 . . . This is not, I find, any historic building, but a series of lavatories for the law' (PHS, *The Times* Diary, 4 June 1982, paragraph headed: 'All cisterns go').

bog-in, n. A hearty meal: Aus. (Cleary, 1954.) Ex the v., 1.

bog in, v.i. To eat (heartily); to work energetically: Aus.: late C.19–20. (B., 1942.) See **two, four, . . .**—2. To get started: Aus.: since ca. 1910. (Culotta.) Cf. **bog, v.**, 2.

bog man. A term of abuse in the Army, esp. in the Guards: since ca. 1930. Cf. **shit, n.**, 2.

bog off. To depart; to take off: RAF: since ca. 1937. (Graves, 1943.) P.B.: later > more gen.

bog-rat. English term of contempt for any Irishman. Cf. **Bog-Trotter**.

bog-standard. Standard, straight from a factory, with no refinement or modification: orig. applied mainly to motorcycles, since mid-1950s; by 1980s > gen. engineering, with wider application. Prob. ex **bog-wheel**. (Bishop; Hanley, 1988.)

Bog-Trotter. 'Any Irishman whatsoever' (B.E.): since late C.17. Ex the numerous bogs of Ireland. Cf. earlier *Boglander*.—2. (**b.-t.**) One who goes often to 'the bogs' = privy: joc. Manchon.—3. 'So good were the BVs, the Volvo tracked vehicles that had already proved to be adept at crossing the boggy terrain, [that] their crews and others . . . conferred on them the not inaccurate nickname of "The Bog Trotters" ' (*Don't Cry*): Services in the Falklands War, 1982.

bog up. To make a mess of; to do incompetently; hence the n. *bog-up*: Services': since 1939. (P-G-R.) Perhaps ex *bugger up*, but just as likely from **bog**. v., 1. Cf. **bog**, n., 3.

B

bog(-)wheel. A bicycle: Cambridge undergraduates': earlier C.20. (Keynes, 1981, quoting his diary for 1907.) Its wheels are—like the gap in a water-closet seat—round. Cf. **bog**, n., 1.—2. Hence, a motorcycle: Army: WW2. (L.S. Beale.)

bogey, bogie, bogy. A detective or a policeman: c. > low s. Leach.—2. A stove for heating: early C.20.—3. 'One who spoils one's game or interferes with one's pitch': grafters' and market-traders'. (*Cheapjack*; *M.T.*) Also known as a *nark*.—4. Hence, a government official, esp. a tax-man: market-traders': since ca. 1910 (*M.T.*)—5. A curse; bad luck, as in 'He put the bogy on me': market-traders'. (Ibid.) Derived ultimately, perhaps, ex *Bogy* = the Devil, but cf. senses 4 and 5 and *put the mockers on*.—6. 'Nickname given to a man with . . . unusually scooped open nostrils': early C.20. (L.A.)—7. A lump of mucus or slime or dirt in the nostril or eye-corner. (P.B.)—8. An aircraft suspected to be hostile: RAF s. > j.: WW2. P-G-R.—9. A dissatisfied customer: mock-auction s. Cf. sense 3.—10. In *go bog(e)y*, to become prophetic; be or become gifted with second sight: actors' and music-hall performers'. E.g. Jope-Slade, 1934.

bogey call. See TOMBOLA, in Appx.

bogey man (or one word). Fisheries patrol vessel: nautical. Butcher, 1980. Cf. **bogey**, 1, 3.

bogey men. 'The bogie men were men who worked in the carriage repair shop. Footplatemen rarely came into contact with them' (McKenna, 1970): railwaymen's: mid-C.20. A pun on *bogie wheels* and *bogey*, an old name for the devil.

bogie. See **bogey**.

bogle. Women, girls; particularly in 'nabbling the bogle', successfully chasing girls: RAF, esp. 66 Sqn.: earlier WW2. Forbes, 1942.

bogs. See **bog**, n.

bogus, n. One who is detected in a pretence, a bluff, a sham: Services': since ca. 1935. (H. & P.) Ex the adj.

bogus, adj. Sham; spurious; illicit. Orig. (—1840) US and = counterfeit (ex instrument, thus named, for the uttering of base coin). Acclimatised ca. 1860 in England, where it > coll. ca. 1900, S.E. ca. 1930.—2. Hence, unpleasant; dull; silly: Society: from ca. 1929. Waugh, 1930, ' "Oh, dear," she said, "this really is all too bogus." '

bogy. See **bogey**.

Bohunk (or **b-**). 'As a Polish or Slavic labourer [it] was a familiar to me in 1910 in British Columbia' (Leechman): Can. Prob. adopted from US: Mathews records it for 1903 and explains it as a modified blend of *Boh*emian + *Hung*arian.

boil. A teenager whose sex is not immediately discernible, because of long hair and clothing so much alike: ca. 1962; ephemeral. Ex '*boy* and *girl*'—with a pun on 'pain in the neck'.

boil up a storm. To play as an instrumentalist in a hot jazz session: 'pop' devotees': since ca. 1970. In a BBC radio interview, 8 Feb. 1973. (R.S.)

boiled over, ppl adj. (Of a market) that has been good but has had a set-back: Stock Exchange. Ex a kettle that has boiled over.

boiled shirt. A dress-suit shirt: coll. Ex US, where it orig. (—1854) signified any white linen shirt. (Uncultured Americans rather like the pronunciation, and spelling, *biled*.)

boiler. 'A well-used woman of forty or over' (Cook, 1962): since ca. 1925: c. >, by 1960, low s.

boiler-buster. A boiler-maker: RN.

boiler-clean. A boiler-cleaning: RN coll.

boiler-creepers. Dungarees: RN. Worn by engineers and stokers in the engine-room. Cf. **brothel-creepers**.

boiler-maker. A mixture, half of draught mild and half of bottled brown ale: public houses': since ca. 1920. It is worthwhile noting that, in US, the meaning is 'whiskey with a beer chaser—sometimes called a "boiler-maker and his helper" ' (Claiborne, 1976).

boiler-plate. Matter already set, on stereotyped plates, for filling up pages of a newspaper: Can. printers'.

boing! This imitation of the noise made by a suddenly released spring, became, ca. 1955, a Can. c.p., used on any occasion, no matter how inappropriate. (Leechman.) By 1950, also British, with var. *boink*. Cf. **kerdoying**.

boko. Blind in one eye: Aus. (B., 1942.) Wilkes, however, adducing citations from very early C.20—and none later—specifies 'a horse with one eye'.

Boley or **Boly.** A Bolingbroke light-bomber aircraft: RCAF: 1940–5. The Canadian form of the Blenheim.

Bolivian marching powder. Cocaine: 'because it makes you want to get up and go, not relax after a hard day' ('An observer of the London drug scene', quoted in *The Times*, 31 May 1988).

bollick(s) or **bollock(s),** other forms, compounds and phrases. See **ballock(s)** *et seq.*

Bolo. A Bolshevist: military (N. Russian campaign, 1918). ?Partly on *Bolo* Pasha, shot in April 1918, for carrying out, in France (bold fellow!), 'pacifist propaganda financed from Germany' (W.). Cf.:—2. A spy: id., id. Same origin. F. & G.—3. (As *bolo*) 'Friend or mate (a hippy term)' (Powis): since mid-1960s.

bolo, adj. ' "What's Bolo?" "Cock-eyed; anything not correct in the Coldstream Guards is Bolo" '. (Kersh, 1941.) Prob. ex **Bolo** = *bolshie*.

boloney; incorrectly **baloney.** Nonsense; 'eyewash'. Of this US word, anglicised by 1931 (thanks to the 'talkies'), Dr Jean Bordeaux—in a private letter—writes thus: 'Used since at least 1900 in U.S.A., especially around New York, to mean "buncombe" or "a poppycock story". It appears in songs of 1900, and [the word *boloney* as a corruption of *Bologna sausage*] probably dates back twenty years earlier because there was a music-hall song, "I Ate the Boloney" popular in the late 70's, early 80's . . . There is much to uphold belief that the sausage origin has merit, on analogy that it's a mixture of ground-up meat and then you *stuff* the casing. Hence, mix up a tale and stuff the auditor.' Yet, at the risk of appearing too sceptical, I must declare my disbelief in that origin and my opinion that 'It's (*or* that's) all boloney'—the usual form—is exactly synon. with 'That's all balls,' the etym. of *boloney* being the Gipsy *peloné*, testicles: cf. the US *nerts!* and **ballocks** (q.v.), and see **balls.**

Bolshie, Bolshy. (All senses are coll.) A Bolshevik: 1920. Any revolutionary: 1933. Joc. of an unconventional person: 1924 or 1925. Also adj.: same dates for the corresponding senses. The word *Bolshevik* (a majority socialist) seems to have been first used in 1903. See the *SOD* for an admirable summary. Cf. **Bolo.**—2. Hence, since ca. 1930 and usu. small *b*'d, a synon. with **bloody-minded;** pig-headed; obstructive and deliberately difficult; esp. in the Forces: since 1939. Without political significance.—3. In a *load of bolshie(-y)*, Communist propaganda: late 1940s–60s, then archaic. Cf. **bulsh.**

bolshies and **yellow perils.** Agents concerned mainly with Russia—and with China: espionage: since ca. 1950. Le Carré 1977.

Bolt-Hole, the. The Channel Islands, where the income-tax is low: political coll.: from ca. 1920. (Collinson.) Ex a rabbit's bolt-hole.

bolter. 'An outsider (applied more recently [i.e. later C.20] to one who wins or succeeds)' (Wilkes): Aus. sporting: since ca. 1920. Orig. esp. in *hasn't the bolter's*, 'Used of a person or race-horse that has no chance at all in a contest or situation' (B., 1941), with which cf. *Buckley's chance*—none.

Boly. A Bolingbroke aircraft. See **Boley.**

bomb, n. In address, a bombardier (the Royal Artillery rank equivalent to corporal): Army (esp. RA): since ca. 1920. H. & P.—2. 'An old car or motorcycle' (B., 1953): Aus. since ca. 1945; Brit. since, perhaps, a little later. In *The Drum*, 1959, Baker defines it as 'any old car, but esp. a car made in the 1930s'; 20 years later, in Britain, as no doubt, in Australia, for '1930s' read '1950s'—and even later when the vehicle has been uncared for but driven to the limit. (P.B.)—3. A lot of money, as in the phrases **cost a bomb** and **make a bomb**, qq.v.—4. See **drop a bomb; go like a bomb; time bomb.**

bomb, v. To dope (a horse): Aus. sporting: since ca. 1945. B., 1953—2. V.i. To drive fast, and prob. dangerously, in a motor vehicle, as in: 'There we were, bombing down the motorway, doing bloody near the ton, when out pops the fuzz': coll.: since ca. 1950. (P.B.)—3. V.i. To go anywhere informally; e.g., an assistant in a girls' dress-shop, about a fairly ordinary dress: 'Oh, it'd do to bomb around in': since ca. 1975. Perhaps ex *bum around*, influenced by sense 2. (P.B.)—3. V.i. To fail, esp. of an entertainment, performance: adopted, ex US, early 1970s.—4. 'Masters of graffiti art refer to "bombing a station" ' (R. Kerridge, in *New Society*, 4 July 1986): i.e. using aerosol 'bombs' secretly and illegally to paint intricate designs on public walls.

Bomb Alley. The Straits of Messina: RN and MN from mid-1940 to mid-1943, then only historical.—2. The enemy-held strip of coast between Tobruk and the British lines in Egypt: 1941–3.—3. On the home front in WW2, the paths taken to their targets (principally London) by the German Air Force, 1940–2, and, in 1944, by the 'doodlebug' (V1s) and V2 rockets. (P.B.)

bomb-happy. With nerves gone, through exposure to bombing: Army: 1940+. (*Rats*, 1944; McDouall, 1945.) Contrast the RAF **flak-happy**. Also, as n., a person with bomb-shattered nerves.

bomb-head (or written solid). An Ordnance Branch rating: FAA: since 1930s. (Wood.)—2. A term of genial abuse, usu. vocative: Army: 1950s–60s. Used also of someone slightly crazy or happy-go-lucky. (P.B.)

bomb out. To fail to appear as expected: media coll.: late 1970s. Leitch, 1979, ' "I gather [the minister]'s bombed out." "Not at all, . . . The Cabinet's simply not over yet." '

bomb-proof. With an impregnable excuse to prevent one being named for an unpleasant duty, as in: 'They can't touch me—I'm bomb-proof' (dangerous hubris!): Services': since ca. 1950, or perhaps much earlier, for cf. next. (P.B.)

bomb-proof job. A safe job, i.e. one at the Base: military: 1916–18. (B & P.) Hence, *bomb-proofer*, a man holding such a job. Cf. US *bomb-proof*, a Southerner who did not join the Confederate Army (Thornton).

bomb-proofer. 'A man given to scheming methods of evading duty on dangerous occasions': military: 1916–18, hence as a survival. F. & G.

Bomb Shop, the. The (formerly Hendersons') very interesting bookshop at 66, Charing Cross Road, London, WC2: it offers a notable display of advanced belles-lettres and, esp., political writings. (Bosworth's, 1932.) I myself first heard it so described by the proprietor early in 1928, but it has enjoyed this distinction since ca. 1924. (E.P. note for the 1st ed. of this Dict.) Even though the shop was bought by Collet's in 1934, the nickname remains, in some people's memories, as an association with the previous proprietor's 'anarchist' tendencies. (Raab.) Cf. **Colletburo.**

bomb-sight buglet. A bright-eyed gremlin, addicted to dazzling the bomb-aimer: RAF: 1940–5. P-G-R. See GREMLINS, in Appx.

bomb-site (or **bombsite**). Any small derelict area in city or town, such as results from demolition for slum-clearance: coll.: since 1945. (P.B.)

bomb the chat, gen. as vbl n. To practise trickery or plausible deception; to 'tell the tale'; to exaggerate: military. (F. & G.) Origin? Prob. supplied by the var. *bum the chat* (B. & P.). Also *bum one's load*.

bomb-up. 'To load an aircraft with bombs' (Jackson): RAF coll.: since 1939; at latest by 1944, j.

Bombay bowler. A service-issue topee: RAF: since ca. 1925. (Emanuel, 1945.) Alliterative—and, well, Bombay *is* hot. The Sergeant, however, says, 'Because usually jettisoned at Bombay, port of entry into India, by reason of its uncomfortable weight.'

Bombay Buccaneers or **Marines, the.** 'The Naval Service of the Honourable East India Company (C.19)—carried over to the Royal Indian Navy and again to the Indian Navy of today' (Peppitt, 1976).

Bombay fornicator. A type of chair (capacious and comfortable): RAF: since ca. 1925; ob. by 1950.

Bombay milk-cart. Waste-disposal wagon: Indian army (other ranks'): late C.19–1947. Allen, 1977.

Bombay runner. A large cockroach often encountered in the lands and islands of the Indian Ocean: nautical, esp. RN: late C.19-20. (Granville.)

Bombay Welsh. The English spoken by Indians and Anglo-Indians, ex its sing-song quality. Hence, a *Bombay Welshman*. An accent that was made familiar to many by the inimitable Mr Peter Sellers. Mostly Services': since the 1940s; by late 1970s, prob. ob. (P.B.)

bombed. Extremely drunk; hence, among addicts, drug-exhilarated: adopted, ca. 1955 and ca. 1962, ex US (Janssen, 1968). Often extended to . . . *out of one's mind* or *skull*.

bomber. A newspaper: journalistic: 1930s—2. 'A sixteen ton oil carrying wagon' (McKenna, 1970): railwaymen's: since mid-C.20.—3. A large cannabis cigarette: drugs c. (Stockley, 1986.) US since—1952 (Spears).

bomber boy. Any member (though esp. the pilot) of a bomber crew: RAF coll.: since 1939. Jackson.

bombido. Amphetamine in injectable form: drugs c. (Stockley, 1986.) US since—1967(Spears).

bombie. See **bommie.**

bombing the chat. See **bomb the chat**.

bombo. Whisky: Aus. (B., 1942).—2. Cheap wine, esp. if much fortified: Aus.: since ca.1919. (B., 1943.) Since ca. 1930, any wine. (B.P.) Cf. the rise of the synon. **plonk**, q.v., in the social scale.

bombshell. A surprise, esp. if unpleasant and/or painful, as in 'the announcement of the treasurer's embezzlement came as a bombshell': journalistic and gen. coll.: since ca. 1960 in gen. use, but isolated earlier examples have been found. It is hard to see why this almost meaningless, tautologous word should have replaced the shorter, sharper *bomb*. (P.B.)

Bomfog. 'The Brotherhood of Man, Fatherhood of God': believers': later C.20. As Roberts points out, 1984, 'Its use is clearly limited by the FOG, and many *Bommers* are not also *Foggers*.'

bommie, orig. **bombie.** A bombora, i.e. a 'submerged reef beyond the beach breakers' (*Bulletin*, 30 Mar. 1963): Aus. surfers': since late 1950s.

bomp on. To get one's unemployment-card stamped: dockers': from ca. 1930. (*Daily Herald*, late July and early Aug. 1936.) Prob. echoic: *bomp* = bump.

bomper. The stamp on dockers' Dock Labour Board cards: Merseyside and London Docks: since the mid-1940s. (*Picture Post*, 3 Dec. 1949.) Ex prec.

bompi. Grandfather, in childish address. Perhaps ex Fr. *bon-papa*. (R.S.)

bona, adj. Good; pleasant, agreeable: theatre and circus s., from ca. 1850. (Frost, 1875, and Seago, 1933.) Cf. **bono.**—2. Beautiful: prostitutes', esp. London. Ex sense 1.

bona, adv. Very: Parlyaree: since ca. 1860. (Emerson, 1893.) Ex the adj.

bond. '(Abbr.) bondage: any pornography that features men or women tied, chained or otherwise restrained for sexual purposes' (Green): later C.20. Cf. **fladge**.

bond-hook or **bondhook.** Var. of *bundhook*, a rifle. This old word is often, in late C.20, pron. *bon-dook*. (P.B.)

Bondi (tram), go through – or **travel** – **like a.** To travel very fast; hence, to decamp hastily; hence, 'to leave a task or obligation on a sudden whim' (B., 1959): Aus., esp. NSW. Cf. **go through** and **shoot through.**

bondu. Wilderness. Var. spelling of **bundoo**, q.v.

bone, n. A dollar: Can.: since ca. 1960, ex US. (Dempsey, 1975.).

B

bone, v. To interrogate (a suspect): police and fringe-of-underworld. (Bournemouth *Evening Echo*, 20 Apr. 1966).—2. To bring bad luck to, to jinx: Aus. Ex S.E. *point a bone*, an Aboriginal practice. B., 1959.

bone boots. To get a patent-leather finish on one's Service boots: Regular Army coll. A flat bone surface, such as a knife-handle, was used to flatten the new leather preparatory to the application of methylated spirits and polish (P.B.).

bone dome. A protective helmet, esp. in aviation and among motorcyclists: the former, since ca. 1935; the latter post-WW2.

bone-head. See bonehead.

bone-orchard. A cemetery: lower classes'. (B. & P.) Cf. **bone-yard**, and the US *marble-orchard* (M. Priebe).

bone out. To survey (a stretch of rail) in order to adjust the level; hence, *boning rods*, survey (or siting) boards: railwaymen's. *Railway*.

bone up on (a subject). To study, because the information will soon be needed: Can., adopted ex US ca. 1910; and in UK by ca. 1950. Either ex *bone* used for polishing shoes or ex the *Bohn* translations of the Classics.

bone-yard. A cemetery: Brit. and Can.: late C.19–20. (B. & P.) Cf. synon. **bone-orchard**.—2. 'White water in front of a wave' (*Pix*, 28 Sep. 1963): Aus. surfers': since ca. 1960.

boned. Tipsy: Society, from ca. 1937; Service officers', 1939+. (Fitt, 1949.) Wits *boned* (stolen) away (E.P.); or filleted—cf. **legless** (P.B.).—2. 'Hit on the head hard' (Powis): police and low coll.

bonehead (or *bone-head*). A boxer: RAF: since ca. 1935. (Jackson.) He needs it or he wouldn't be one.—2. 'There's [sic] been rumours of hordes of East End skinheads—mods [q.v.] call them "boneheads"—coming down [to Brighton]' (Walker, 1981).

boner. A bad mistake. (*The Passing Show*, 9 Dec. 1933, 'Poor Carol . . . She made a boner to-night . . . Ronnie was simply livid.') It occurs esp. in *pull a boner*, to commit a serious error. Claiborne suggests derivation from *bone-headed*, stupid—solid bone instead of brains.

bones. The examination in osteology: medical students':—1923 (Manchon).—2. In *be on* (one's) *bones*, to be (almost) destitute: non-aristocratic: earlier C.20. Galsworthy, 1924, 'Give us a chance, constable; I'm right on my bones.' 'One winter, in the desperate group and on the bones of my backside . . .' (Rolling, 1971). Ex emaciation. Cf. synon. *on the ribs*.—3. See **ground bones**.

bonjer. A 'duck': cricketers': 1934, 'Patsy' Hendren, *Big Cricket*, 'If I had landed a bonjer'. Perhaps ex *bon jour!*—but prob. not. (*Notes & Queries*, 13 Oct. 1934.)

bonk, n. A short, steep hill: circus s.: ca. 1840–1940. (Hindley, 1876.) Adopted from dial. (In S.E., † form.)—2. As *the bonk*, the state of being devoid of energy: cyclists': since 1930s. (P.B.: ex having encountered sense 1?) Hence *bonk-bag*, a small food-bag, containing sweets, etc., to combat *the bonk* (Bramley). Cf. **(hunger-)knock, sag**.—3. As exclam., bang!: coll., mostly Cockneys'. Echoic. Hence the v.—4. The n. ex. v. since ca. 1920.

bonk, v. To hit resoundingly (v.t.): Public Schools': since ca. 1919; fairly soon more widespread.—2. To copulate: suddenly a vogue word, in 1987. Ex sense 1, a v. of violence like so many other s. terms for the act.

bonker. See stone-wall bonker.

bonkers. Slightly drunk, light-headed: RN: since ca. 1920. (Granville.)—2. Hence, eccentric; crazy: RN since ca. 1925; by ca. 1946, fairly gen. Often in the intensive form, *stone fucking bonkers*. 'Since "that speech" by Mr Quintin Hogg, in Oct. 1964, now usually "stark staring bonkers" = "quite mad" ' (Sanders, mid-1965).

bonny Dundee. A flea: theatrical r.s. Franklyn.

bono. Good: Parlyaree: from ca. 1840. Via Lingua Franca. Cf. **bona**.

bono(h)omee (or *ommy*). Husband: Parlyaree: mid-C.19–20. (*John o' London's Weekly*, 4 Feb. 1949.) For the elements,

see **bono**, good, + *omee*, a man: cf. archaic S.E. *goodman*, husband.

bonser. See bonza.

bontoger, bontogeriro, bontoser, bonzarina, bonzerino, bonziorie. Elabb. of *bonza*: earlier C.20. (B., 1942; Stivens, 1955.) Almost nonce-words, says Wilkes.

bonza, bonzer; occ. **bonser** and, loosely **bonzo** (see also **bontoger . . .**), n. and adj. Anything excellent, delightful: Aus.: by 1950, ob. (B., 1959). Perhaps ex *bonanza*.

boo. Marijuana: adopted, mid-1960s, ex US. (Janssen, 1968.)

boo-boo. The human bottom: children's: late C.19–20. Blake, 1964, 'No use sitting around on your boo-boo, brooding.' Reduplication of *bottom*. Cf. **boo-hoo**.—2. A blunder. See **booboo**.

boo boys, the. 'Those who are ever ready to deride esp. athletes', boxers', achievements', style' (L.A., 1976): since ca. 1965. (*The Times*, 13 Oct. 1976.)—2. Hence, denigrators generally: since ca. 1970.

boo-hoo. The human bottom. 'One of my chaps got a bit of mortar [shell] in the boo-hoo . . . he was the sort of chap to whom a bit of shrapnel in the boo-hoo would be the funniest thing in the world' (Raikes, 1943). Cf. **boo-boo**, 1.

booai or **booay** (pron. *boo-eye*). Remote rural districts: NZ. 'On uncertain evidence, [the word] has been derived from Puhoi, an early settlement of Bohemians, 30 miles from Auckland (1862)'—a settlement 'which went through extremely hard times in the early days.' (Gray 1969.) But it may also be a pej. from Maori *puhoi*, slow, dull, phlegmatic. Also, since ca. 1910, Aus. for 'the open bush', as in Niland, 1955, where it is written *boo-eye*. Of the NZ use, Griffiths says, 'Heard very frequently out here in such expressions as "(way) out in the boo-ay" (far from the towns—in the back-blocks) and also "(all) up the boo-ay" (completely off the track—especially with knowledge, an opinion, etc.)' (letter, 1959). The fig. *up the booai*, lost, utterly wrong, has been common since the late 1940s (Slatter). Cf. **woop woop**.

boob, n. A booby, a fool, a 'soft' fellow; hence loosely, a fellow: US (—1912), anglicised in 1918. Collinson; *OED Sup*.—2. (*the boob*) A detention-cell; prison: military: WW1+; by 1920, also gen. Aus. (Marshall, 1962.) Ex *booby-hutch*.—3. A blunder; a *faux-pas*: since ca. 1935. Ex the v.—4. The natural singular of **boobs**, q.v.

boob, v. To blunder. Army and RAF: since ca. 1930. (Tredrey, 1939.): cf.—and see—**black**, n., 2. Usu. v.i., but occ. v.t., as in the RAF *boob a landing*, to land clumsily. P.B.: in later C.20 > widespread and gen. coll.

boob head. A prisoners' boss, i.e. a warder in charge of a division: Aus. c.: since ca. 1950. Grindley, 1977. Cf. **boob**, n., 2.

boob tube. A woman's strapless suntop of stretchable material, e.g., jersey: fashion: mid–later 1970s.

boobies. A woman's breasts: since ca. 1920. (Miller, 1934.) Ex C.17 S.E. synon. *bubbies*. See also **boobs**.

boobies' hutch. More gen. **booby-hutch**, q.v.

booboo (or *boo-boo*); esp. in *make a booboo*. A blunder: Aus. and Brit.: adopted, ca. 1959, ex US. Prob. a softening of **boob**, n., 3; but perhaps influenced by a baby's cry of pain or frustration. Atkinson, 1961.

boobs, the (or one's). The female breasts: predominantly feminine: since ca. 1960. '*The Observer* of Feb. 11, 1968, interviewing a girl emerging from Fortnums, on the subject of "see-through blouses", quoted her as saying that she wouldn't put her boobs on show for anyone' (R.S.). The singular followed naturally when needed, e.g.: 'A hairy hand crept round from behind and grasped her left boob.' As *bubbies* > *boobies*, so *bubs* > *boobs*.

booby-hatch. A lunatic asylum: Can. and (occ.) Brit. Adopted ex US.

booby-hutch. A police station; a cell: c. and low: late C.19–early 20. In later C.20 reduced to *the boob* (Clayton, 1970).—2. The 'shop' of a 'Jewing firm' aboard a ship: lower-deck: ca. 1890–1935. Knock.

bood. A bedroom; a sleeping-cubicle: girls' Public Schools': earlier C.20. (Hutchinson, 1932.) Ex *boudoir*.

booed and hissed. Drunk: r.s. on *pissed*: later C.20. (Simmonds, 1980.) Cf. synon. **Brahms 'n' Liszt.**

booey or **bouie.** A piece of nasal mucus: non-cultured Aus. domestic: since ca. 1920. (B.P.) P.B.: E.P. suggests orig. in Fr. *boue*, mud, filth; but cf. synon. Eng. *bogey*.

boof. To top up a container of liquid: Aus.: later C.20. McNeil.

boofhead. A fool; a very gullible person: Aus.: since ca. 1930. (B., 1943.) The corresponding adj. is *boofheaded*, as in Lower, 1945. Cf. synon. C. 17 s. > S.E. *buffle-head*.

boogie. The 'in' word, among the fashionable, for 'to make love': Dempster, 1979. Ex 'to enjoy oneself, have a party, a good time' (Green, 2, gives a 1975 citation), itself ex US Black 'to dance'.

boogie box. A transistor radio: mid-1980s. Contrast **ghetto blaster.**

boogie-pack. A miniature cassette-player with lightweight headphones, for listening while one is on the move: youngsters': since ca. 1981. De Lisle, 1982.

book, n. In (*be*) *with book*, (to be) engaged in writing a book: authors': since ca. 1930. On (*be*) *with child*, pregnant.—2. In *by* (*the*) *book*, in set phrases: late C.16-20; orig. coll. but soon S.E. Shakespeare, 'You kisse by th' booke.' P.B.: hence, in C.20 Services' and police coll., strictly according to the rules and regulations. Hunter, 1964.—3. In *on the book*, in the prompt corner; on duty as prompter: theatrical coll. (Gray, 1964.) The 'book of words'—the text of the play. —4. In *on the book*, on credit, as 'he let me have a couple of bottles on the book': coll. (P.B.)—5. In *in my book*, in my opinion, coll.: since ca. 1950. (P.B.)

book, v. To catch (a person) wrong-doing: Public Schools': from ca. 1895. (Wodehouse, 1902.) Hence in later C.20, police coll. for 'to arrest, thus write down in a police charge book' (Green, 2).—2. To realise; to see and understand, as in 'the man immediately booked what they [detectives] were'. Newman, 1970. —3. To assume, as in: 'I'm booking it that he'll collect it on his way to work' (Ibid.). Both 2 and 3 are police s., dating from the 1930s.

book of rig-ups (also **rig-up book**). 'Fictitious book supposed to contain all the rig-ups that a driller would require. If asked about a certain way the driller had rigged his machine, [the answer might be], "Ah! Well, that's No. 45 in the rig-up book" ' (Patterson): Portsmouth dockers'.

book of words, the. Any set of printed or typewritten instructions. Deeping, 1944.

book (one's) **seat.** To pad one's trousers with newspapers or a book before going to be caned: schoolboys': mid-C.20.

booked. In for trouble: coll. Lyell, 'Third time you've been late this week. *You're booked* all right, my boy, when the Manager comes in.' Cf. **book,** v., 1.

booked for kingdom come. Facing certain death; on one's death-bed: coll.: orig. railwaymen's.

bookends. 'The first and last episodes of a TV drama series' (Green): television circles': later C.20.

books. In *get* (one's) *books* or *cards*, to be paid off: Public Works' coll.: from ca. 1924. On being paid off, a workman, until mid-1970s, received his insurance-card. —2. As *the books*, works of reference: coll.: earlier C.20. 'Oh, look it up in the books.'

boom-boom. A soldier: children's, esp. Cockneys': from ca. 1916. Echoic. Moreover, 2, *boom boom* is a Pidgin term (Pacific Islanders', Thailanders', Koreans' and what have you) for rifle fire, cannon fire; a rifle, a cannon; fighting or to fight, war. For instance in prisoner-of-war camps in the Far East, 1942-5, *boom boom yashe* means 'a rifle rest'—see PRISONER-OF-WAR SLANG, §7, in Appx. So widely is *boom boom* accepted as echoically precise that little children all over the world use it.

boom off. To fight off; scare away: RN: 1934-5. Echoic of heavy gunfire. P.B.: but in Marryat, 1840, *boom off* = to push off with a pole.

boom the census. To get a woman with child: joc. coll.: early C.20.

boomer. A propagandist: coll. One who booms an enterprise: coll., from ca. 1890. Orig. US (—1885).

boomerang. 'Something, esp. a book, that one would like to receive back' (B.P.): Aus.: since ca. 1930.—2. A return ticket: railwaymen's: mid-C.20. McKenna, 1970.

boomeranging, n. and adj. Returning to prison: c. and prison officers', esp. in S. Africa: since ca. 1950 or much earlier. Ross, 1974.

boondock. See TIDDLYWINKS, in Appx. Ex:-

boondocks, esp. **out in the.** (In) the jungle or wilds or outback: adopted, ca. 1944, ex US soldiers. W. & F. derive it ex Tagalog *bundok*, mountain. Cf. **bundoo.**

boong. An Australian Aboriginal: Aus. Recorded by B., 1942. With occ. var. *bong*, both words being borrowed from Aboriginal. *Bo(o)ng* is also employed as adj.—2. Hence, 'any dark-skinned person' (B., 1959), or even, as in Page, 1973, where *the boong* signifies 'the Japanese [soldiers]'. The word prob. first came to widespread notice in UK with the pub., in 1950, of Neville Shute's famous novel, later filmed, *A Town Like Alice*, in which the hero, an Australian soldier, addresses the heroine, an English girl first seen by him when she is wearing Malay dress and is very sunburnt, as 'Mrs Boong'. (P.B., 1979.)—3. See PRISONER-OF-WAR SLANG, §8, in Appx.

boong-moll. A coloured, esp. a Negro, pathic: Aus. low or c.: since ca. 1930. Cusack, 1951.—2. A prostitute favouring dark-skinned men: Aus. c.: since ca. 1935. B., 1953.

boop, v.; usually as vbl n., *booping*, making a fuss about a trifle: Services': ca. 1935—45. (H. & P.) A blend of echoic *boo* + *weep.*

boost. A supercharging; additional pressure: RAF coll.: since ca. 1925. Jackson, 'I gave him [an aircraft] all the boost I had'; he cites the corresponding v.—2. In *be in high* or *low boost*, (of persons) to be in good or bad form: RN Coastal Forces': WW2. In ref. to engines.

boot, n. Money; an advance on wages: tailors' and shoemakers': late C.19-20. Ware, *Tailor and Cutter*, 29 Nov. 1928.—2. (Gen. pl.) The float of a sea-plane: aviators': from 1933. (*Daily Telegraph*, 19 Feb. 1935.)—3. An excessively compliant female: low: since ca. 1950. Cf. **old boot.**—4. In *give* or *get the boot*, to dismiss; to be dismissed: s. (1888: Rider Haggard) >, by 1920, coll. (*OED* Sup.) An early C.20 s., by 1930 coll. elab. is *give* or *get the order of the boot.*—5. See **boots; old boot; put the boot in** (includes *put in the boot*); **sock a boot into.**

boot, v.i. and t, to borrow (money) on account: tailors': earlier C.20. Ex **boot,** n., 1.—2. Elliptical for **put the boot in,** q.v.

boot, adj. Short form of **boot-faced.**

boot-brush.—1927 (Collinson). A rough beard: joc.:

boot-faced. Wearing a miserable, down-hearted, thwarted, or stony-faced expression: orig. RAF s.: since ca. 1930; thence to the other Services and into the wider world. Ex the appearance of an old boot with sole parting from the upper. Whence, by the 'OXFORD -ER', the var. *booters*, with elab. *Harry booters.* Cf. **po-faced.**

Boot Hill. A graveyard: Can. miners'. Ex one of the most famous cemeteries of the US Frontier West.

boot in. See **put the boot in.**

boot is on the other leg (or **foot**), **the.** The case is altered; the responsibility is another's; the reverse is true: coll.: C.19-20. The *boot* went from the *leg* to the *foot* as knee-boots became ankle-boots; and in early 1970s there emerged the joc. var. *the wellie is on the other foot.*

boot-leg; -ger. See **bootleg.**

boot-neck. A Royal Marine: RN: mid-C.19-20. F. & G., 'From the tab closing the tunic collar.' In later C.20, written *bootneck*: 'As [the Senior Naval Officer] puts it, [the helicopters' task is to provide] instant airlifts for the ordinary bootneck, in his boots, in the field' (Winton, 1979).

B

booter. A devotee of, or trader at, car-boot sales: 'Thousands of public [sic] and booters every time' (advert. in the *Loughborough Echo*, 10 June 1988, for a forthcoming sale). The idea of such informal markets was enthusiastically adopted ex US in mid-1980s.

booters. See **boot-faced.**

booth. As a *Booth*, a member of the Salvation Army: prison c.: mid-C.20. (Tempest, 1950.) Ex General Booth, the Army's founder.

Booth and blimey. See **soaking glass . . .**

bootie (or **-y**). A Royal Marine. (Bishop, 1982.) A shortening of **boot-neck,** q.v.

bootlace. Thin twist tobacco: orig., c.; by 1940, s. Merrow Smith, 1962.—2. A cod-fish's shrunken liver in the early spring: 'a fibrous, rubbery scrap of tissue known as a "bootlace" ' (Piper, 1974): trawlermen's.

bootleg, n. An unofficial, i.e. illicit, production and release of a phonograph record: since ca. 1960. (*Beatles*, 1975.) A Beatles 'bootleg' was for a few years called a 'Beatleg'—a good example of ephemeral 'pop music' s., recorded Ibid.

bootleg, v. By late C.20, the informal S.E. v. ex:-

bootlegger (orig. hyphenated). A dealer in and distributor of contraband liquor in the US; orig. (—1919) US, anglicised ca. 1927 as coll.; 1932+, S.E. From the old days when spirits, in flat bottles, were carried on the leg to the Red Indians: in this connexion, the word appears in US as early as 1890 (*OED* Sup.). Whence *boot-legging*, the sale and distribution of illicit liquor in the US. See, e.g., Spenser, 1933, and Irwin, 1931.

bootneck. See **boot-neck.**

boots. The floats of a seaplane. See **boot,** n., 2.—2. 'The junior ship in a formation, i.e. the ship commanded by the least senior officer' (Peppitt): since ca. 1918. (Arnold-Foster, 1931.) Ex older sense, the youngest officer in a mess.—3. In *blood* (or, more often, *sand*) *in the(ir) boots*, 'Used derisively of Desert types who threw their weight about in non-combat areas or, more gallingly, in non-desert operational areas' (Gadd, 1949): Army: 1943 onwards; after 1945, only historical. The ref.—made mostly by officers about officers—is to 'veterans' of N. Africa.—4. Tyres, as in 'She [a car]'s had a new set of boots': car-dealers'. Graham-Ranger, 1981. Cf. **shoe,** 1.—5. See **go to bed with** (one's) **boots on; hang up** (one's) **boots; put the boot in.** See also **bossy-boots.**

boots and all. Thoroughly; utterly: Aus. coll.: from mid-C.20; soon also NZ. Cusack, 1953, 'When you do a thing you go into it boots and all' (Wilkes). As adj. and adv., sometimes hyphenated.

bootsy. A 'boots' at a large, the porter at a small, hotel: since ca. 1950. (Petch, 1966.)

booze artist. A heavy drinker; a drunkard: Aus.: since ca. 1920. (Brockman, 1940.) Perhaps adopted ex Can., where current since ca. 1905. (Leechman.) Cf. **piss artist.**

booze(-)bag, esp. **get the.** To be forced to undergo the test of the breathalyser bag for the detection of excessive liquor in one's breath: motorists': since latish 1960s. (Petch, 1969.)

booze Naffy. Such a NAAFI issue as included beer and spirits: Army: WW2.

booze-wine. 'Drink—usually beer' (Forbes, 1942): RAF, esp. 66 Sqn.: WW2.

boozelier. A fusilier: Army: earlier C.20. A blend of *booze* and *fusilier.*

boozer. A public-house: English c. and low s. since late C.19; Aus. and NZ since before WW1. Leach, 1933, gives this example of contemporary s.: 'Guv'nor, the "diddikayes" are "ramping" a "tit" in the "spruce" there; they're "three-handed"; a "nose" told me in the "boozer"; there's nobody "screwing", as they don't think the "busies" are "wise"; come along quick with the "mittens".'

boozle. Sexual intercourse: mid-C.20. (Coward, 1960.) Cf. synon. **boogie.**

boozorium. A (hotel) bar-room: Can.: since ca. 1965 (Dempsey, 1975). On analogy with vomit*orium*, etc.

boozy. A drunkard: Anglo-Irish: since ca. 1920. (Kenyon, 1977.) The pl is spelt *bowsies*. See **bowsie man.**

bop, n. A blow, a punch: Aus.: adopted ex US ca. 1945. Culotta, 1960.—2. A dance: later C.20. Orig., *bop* 'was the most modern and popular jazz style ca. 1946 — ca. 1953' (W & F). See **couth.**

bop, v. To hit (usu. a person), as 'bopped him one on the nut (= head) with a rolled-up newspaper': coll.: since mid-C.20. Ex the prec. entry; echoic. (P.B.)

boracic. ' "You boracic?" she asked.—She meant boracic lint—skint' (Hobson, 1959)—that is, very short of money: r.s.: since ca. 1945. Often pron. *brassic*.—2. ' "Don't give me the old boracic" = don't tell me tall yarns, don't try to get round me with smooth words. Also *ackamaraka*' (Tempest): prisons' and low s.: mid-C.20. Prob. ex smoothness of boracic ointment.

borax. Cheap furniture: Can. salesmen's: since ca. 1920. (Leechman.)

bore the pants off (someone). To bore him to desperation: since the latish 1940s. Hence, since ca. 1950, the low, predominantly male, var. *bore the balls off*. (Petch, 1974.)

bore to tears. The polite version of the prec. entry, had >, by latish C.20, informal S.E., as 'Honestly, I was bored to tears.' Occ., *. . . to distraction*; often *. . . rigid* or *stiff*. (P.B., 1979.)

bore war, the. Concerning Nov. 1939, Clarke, 1948, writes: 'The "phoney war" was giving way to the "bore war", and at the War Office we started to resign ourselves to a long winter at our desks': Nov. 1939–April 1940, then merely historical. Punning on *boring*, tedious, and *the Boer War*. Also *the Great Bore War*, as in Waugh, 1942.

borehole. A rumour. See PRISONER-OF-WAR SLANG, 3, in Appx.

borrow. To steal: joc. coll.: from ca. 1880 and still current, 1980.—2. A palliative for *take*, in small, unlikely to be returned demands, e.g., 'Can I borrow some Sellotape?', 'May I borrow a scrap of paper?', etc.: later C.20. (P.B.)—3. In *on the borrow*, cadging, 'on the scrounge': coll.

borrow and beg. An egg: r.s.: late C.19–20. Franklyn.

Bosch(e). See **Boche,** for which these two forms are erroneous.

Bosey. See **bosie, Bosie.**

bosh. Such a game between two houses as does not count towards a cup: Rugby School. 'They are usually of low quality' (Wharton).

bosh-faker. A violin-player: vagrants' c., from ca. 1850; fairground and circus s., C.20. (Lester.) In Romany, *bosh* is a violin.

bosh lines, the. (The) marionettes: showmen's: from ca. 1855. (B. & L.) Lit., violin strings. According to Green, still current for puppet-strings.

bosie, Bosie; bosey (or **B.**). A 'googly' (ball or bowler): Aus. cricketers' coll.: 1912—ca. 1921. Ex B.J.T. Bosanquet, who demonstrated the googly in Australia early in 1903 (W.J. Lewis), in which year *googlie* (or *-y*) first occurs: s. >, by 1910, coll. >, by 1930, S.E.—2. A single bomb dropped from the air: Aus. airmen's: ca. 1914-5. (B., 1943.) Cf. sense 1.

bosko absoluto. 'Dead drunk. In, e.g., Kipling's "The Janeites", a short story published [in 1924]; but I would guess written considerably earlier . . . Clearly the superlative (with pseudo-Spanish *-o*) of bosky' (R.C., 1976). 'The Janeites' told how, in WW1, two young Infantry officers made friends because of their shared love of Jane Austen's novels. The term was † by ca. 1940. *Bosky* was s., from early C.18 onwards, meaning dazed or fuddled, mildly drunk.

bosom. A bosom friend: early C.20. Lyons, 1914.—2. The female breast: since ca. 1930: orig. euph. In 1973 a girl of 18 told me that 'only mothers have breasts'. Comparable: *bosomy*, large-breasted.

bosom clasper. A very emotional cinematic film: since ca. 1935. J. Agate in *Daily Express*, 14 Aug. 1943.

boss. An officer, esp. a commodore, commanding a group, a flotilla, of ships: RN (?)late C.19–mid-20. 'Taffrail',

B

1916.—2. As *the boss*, joc. for one's wife: Aus., since ca. 1920; some Brit. usage. 'I was hoping you'd ring. The boss has been on my back about it.' (B.P.)—3. A prison officer: Borstals' and detention centres': 1970s: Home Office.

boss-eyed. With one eye injured; with a squint: from ca. 1860. Hence, in C.20, lopsided; crooked. *COD*, 1934 Sup.

boss-hostler. Superintendent of livestock: circusmen's.

bosso. A look or glance: low. (Allingham, 1931.) Perhaps orig. a squint; if so, then prob. ex *boss-eyed* on *dekko*.

bossy-boots. A young girls' term for someone (usu. female and co-eval) over-officious and self-willed. Cf. the earlier s. use of *boots* as 'fellow' in e.g. *lazy-*, or *sly-*, or *smooth-boots*.

bosun, bo'sun. There are several compounds, e.g. **sin bosun, custard bosun**, qq.v., ship's chaplain and warrant cook, respectively.

bosun's nightmare, the. The experimental sweep used against magnetic mines: RN: late 1939–early 1940. P-G-R.

bot, n. See **bot-fly.**—2. A germ: NZ medical: from ca. 1928. Perhaps ex the *bot(-fly)*, which, in horses, lays eggs that are said to penetrate the animal's skin when they hatch.—3. Hence, a tubercular patient: id.: from ca.1929.—4. A man ever on the move and, like the rolling stone, unable to gather moss: Aus.: since ca. 1920. Ex sense 1.—5. (One's) bottom: mostly domestic: late C.19-20.—6. A sponger: Aus.: since ca. 1920. (B., 1943.) Ex sense 2.—7. In *have the bot*, to feel unwell; to be moody; querulous: NZ and Aus. (B., 1941; 1943.) Ex sense 2.—8. In *work* (one's) *bot*, to coït: low. 'Is she working?'—'Yes, her bot.' Ex 5.

bot, v. To borrow money; (usu. *bot on*) to sponge or impose on (others): Aus. and NZ: since ca. 1925. (B., 1941.) Ex n., 6.

bot about. To move restlessly from one place to another: Aus.: since ca. 1920. Cf. **bot**, n., 4.

bot-fly. A troublesome, interfering person: Aus. In WW1, and since, often abbr. to *bot*. See **bot**, n., 2.—2. A sponger or scrounger: id. B., 1942.

both sides of the street(, walk). To be bi-sexual: 'indeed he had enjoyed what Damian archly called transports of delight on both sides of the street' (Kavanagh, 1987). US has *work both sides* . . . , to take two contrary positions at once (*New DAS*).

Botties. The Royal Botanical Gardens: Aus.: later C.20. (Humphries, 1982.) P.B.: the botanical gardens in Hong Kong were known to servicemen there, 1960s, as *the botty gardens*.

bottle, n. The money taken, after a 'turn' by showmen and other entertainers: since late C.19. ' "What's the bottle, cull?" . . . "How much have we taken, pal?" ' (Lester.) Emerson, 1893, defines it as 'a share of the money'.—2. A reprimand, a 'dressing-down'; esp. *get a bottle*, to be reprimanded: RN: from ca. 1920. (H. & P.) Granville, 'Short for "a bottle of acid".'—3. A wireless valve, cathode-ray tube: RAF: from ca. 1935. (Emanuel, 1945.) Ex shape.—4. Short for *bottle and glass*, arse: low. (Cook, 1962.) Esp. in the later C.20 sense, 'Spirits, guts, courage . . . It's the worst that could be said about you, that you'd lost your bottle' (Park, 1965): Teddy boys' and teenage gangsters'.—5. As *the bottle*, the hip pocket: 1938 (Sharpe). Mostly in *off the bottle*, pickpockets' c. for '(removed) from a rear trouser pocket' (Franklyn, 2nd); cf. primary meaning of sense 4. Hence *the bottle*, pickpocketing, and *on the bottle*, engaged in pickpocketing.—6. In *no bottle(s)*, no good; not 'classy': since ca. 1920. Short for *no bottle and glass*, no 'class', itself current throughout C.20. (Gosling, 1959.) But see also **bottle top**, and cf. *turn out no bottle*, to fail: sporting: later C.19 (Baumann, 1887). ob. by 1930. Cf. also:—7. In *not much bottle*, not much good: grafters': from ca. 1920. *Cheapjack*.—8. Two pounds: Londoners': later C.20. Hence *big bottle*, £200. (Tyler, 1987.)—9. See **full bottle**; **bible**, 4.

bottle, v.i. To collect money for, or as a 'chanter': vagrants' c.—2. V.t., to fail: Public Schools'. Waugh, 1922.—3. To attack with a (usu. broken) bottle: low. Cf. **glass**.—4. To smell; stink: as in 'some of them slinks and slags in the bev-

vyken don't half bottle': market traders'. (*M.T.*)—5. To bugger (a woman). See **rim**.—6. To coït with (a woman); to impregnate: low.—7. 'To approach (someone) for a contribution' (Lester): showmen's and other entertainers'. Cf. sense 1.—8. To kiss the anus of: homosexuals': current ca. 1970.

bottle and glass. The buttocks: low rhyming, on *arse*. (B. & P.) See **bottle**, n., 4.

bottle and stopper. Policeman: r.s., on *copper*: since ca. 1950. Haden-Guest, 1972.

bottle-bottoms. Very thick-lensed spectacles; hence '(old) bottle-bottoms', anyone wearing them: Northern children's. (Bowater, 1978.)

bottle fallen out?; e.g., *has your* . . . , Are you afraid?: low: since ca. 1940. Cf. **bottle**, n., 4.

bottle o(f) beer. Ear: r.s.: Franklyn, 2nd.

bottle of cheese. A drink of Guinness: public houses':—1935.

bottle of cola. A bowler hat: r.s.: earlier C.20.

bottle of fizz, the. Pickpocketing: r.s. See **whiz**, n., 2, and **bottle**, n., 5.

bottle of sauce. A horse: r.s.: late C.19–20.

bottle of Scotch. A watch: r.s.: since ca. 1910.

bottle of water. A daughter: r.s.:—1931.

Bottle of Whisky, the. The Polish destroyer *Blyskawika*: RN Hobson-Jobson: ca. 1940–2.

bottle out. 'This is the big crime, for [the underworld]: if they are informers or if they don't have the courage to do a crime. They, as they say, "bottle out" ' (McVicar in *Listener*, 8 Mar. 1979). Cf. **bottle**, n., 4, and **bottle fallen out**, of which this is evidently a contraction. (P.B.) Cf. '[Mrs Thatcher] has never been one to back down or bottle out and I don't expect her to . . . bottle out with us either' (a prison officer, quoted in *Financial Times*, 3 May 1986, after strikes in the prison service).

bottle the field. Odds of 2 to 1: racing, esp. bookmakers'. *Sunday Telegraph*, 7 May 1967.

bottle the tot. To pour one's daily tot of rum into a bottle and save it up for special occasions: RN: WW2.

bottle top, n. and v. Cop: r.s. As n., it means 'a gain or catch. To say something/someone is "not much bottle (or bottle top)" means not much cop which implies it/he/she is a doubtful or useless asset.' Cop, as v., means 'to catch or take in, " 'e's gorn an' bottled (or bottle topped) [caught, taken] the 'oppin' pot!" or, " 'oo sed yew could bottle me linen nen!" ' (Hillman.) See, however, **bottle**, n., 6, 7.

Bottle-Trekker, 'ex *Voor-trekker*, was a usual name for a Dutchman, owing to their habit of taking a bottle of water to the latrine with them instead of toilet paper' (R.H. Panting): see PRISONER-OF-WAR SLANG, §9, in Appx.

bottled. Tipsy: Society: since ca. 1930. Traill, 1936.

bottled belly-ache. Cheap beer: tramps' c. Contrast:-

bottled sunshine. 'Scottish service (esp. Army) name for beer' (H. & P.): since ca. 1930.

bottleneck. The use of a bottle's neck (or metal bar) pressed against the strings to obtain, in guitar-playing, a glissando effect. Recorded in US in 1973 and, in Britain, 1975 (*Beatles*).

bottler, n. A collector of money for a band, a singer, an instrumentalist on the street: tramps' c.:—1935. The agent of **bottle**, v., 1.—2. Expression of high praise or deep delight: NZ, and perhaps slightly later, Aus. youngsters. B., 1941 (NZ) and 1943 (Aus.). Var. *bottling* is recorded in B., 1943.—3. A sodomite: low: since ca. 1930. Cf. **bottle**, v., 5.— 4. A non-seller (motor car): secondhand-car dealers': since ca. 1950. Cowdy, 1965.—5. Esp., *bloody bottler*, a 'real hard case': NZ: since ca. 1945. Cf. sense 2.—6. 'A coward, someone who bottles out' (Green, 2). See **bottle out**.

bottler, adj.; also **bottling**. Superlatively good: Aus.: since ca. 1920. (B., 1959.) Ex **bottler**, 2.

bottling. Persuading onlookers to put money in the hat: showmen's. Allingham, 1934. Cf. **bottle**, v., 1, and **bottler**, n., 1.

B

bottom. To clean thoroughly, not merely to dab over the top surfaces: domestic: ' "Ruby cleaned the bathroom and kitchen for me"—"Well, I hope she bottomed it!" ' (Rodgers, 1981.)—2. To solve, to get to the *bottom* of a problem: later C.20. Clark, 1982.

bottom drawer(, get together one's**).** Of a girl, (to prepare) her trousseau: coll. Mais, 1918.

bottom line, the. The 'crunch'; the crux, crisis, testing-point; as in 'When you reach the bottom line . . . ': adopted, ex US, late 1970s. (Raab.) Silverlight, 1982, explains: 'Literally the bottom line of a company's annual statement: the amount of profit, after tax, available for distribution among shareholders.'

bottom road, the. A road leading (esp. from London) to the south coast of England: tramps' c. Gape, 1936.

bottom-scratchers. A break-off group from a diving club: skin divers': since the late 1950s. 'Interested only in spear fishing (crabs, lobsters, etc.), they *scratch* the sea's bottom' (Granville, letter, 1964).

bottoms up! Empty your glass after each toast!: prob., orig., RN officers'. In later C.20, sometimes simply a friendly 'predrinking noise', akin to **cheers!,** or an invitation to finish the present drink so that another may be provided.

boulder(-)holder, occ. prec. by *over-shoulder.* A brassière: Aus. raffish: since ca. 1955. 'Used by the same people who use **flopper stopper,** q.v.' (B.P.)

bouman. A companion or friend, a 'pal'; also as term of address: Dublin lower classes': from ca. 1910.

bounce, n. Dismissal; esp. *get* or *give the bounce:* mostly military: from ca. 1910. (F. & G.) By 1940, > gen., esp. as *the grand bounce,* = (as well as dismissal) the rejection of a manuscript: perhaps a re-borrowing ex US.—2. In *put* (someone) *in the bounce,* to accost, esp. for a loan of money: Aus.: since ca. 1930. Niland, 1955.—3. 'The illegal altering of invoices, order forms, receipts, price tags, etc. so as to disguise the theft of goods by employees or by accomplices, not actually employed by the firm, who do the stealing for them' (Green): business usage. Prob. ex earlier *bounce,* or *bunce,* perquisite(s), illicit surplus.

bounce, v. (Of a cheque) to be returned, as worthless, by the bank on which it has been drawn: adopted ca. 1938 from US.—2. To attack (suddenly, unexpectedly): RAF: 1939+. Brickhill, 1946, 'About 12,000 feet they were bounced from above by three 109's.'—3. To dismiss (a person), reject (a play): adopted, ca. 1940, from US; but cf. **bounce,** n., 1.

bounce it. See **bounce the ball**.

bounce the ball. To test public opinion or sentiment; test the stock market: NZ political coll.: since ca. 1920. (B., 1941.) Ex the preliminaries usual among footballers. (E.P.) Soon after WW2, it had gained a far wider currency and acquired the var. *bounce it,* with v.t. *off* (an organisation), esp. in advertising. (P.B., 1975.)

bouncers. Female breasts: orig. low; by ca. 1960, joc. (Leech, 1972.)

bouncing Betty. 'The deadly *Schützenmine* 35, which caused so many casualties in N. Africa. A small powder charge launched it between three and five feet in the air before it exploded, scattering some 350 pellets and having a killing radius of nearly a hundred yards. Its commonest nickname was "Bouncing Betty" ' (Drage, 1963): Army: 1941–3.

bound rigid. Bored stiff: see **bind**.

bouquet. A payment in pesos: white-slavers' c. (Argentine). Londres, 1928, 'A "bouquet" always means pesos.'

Bovril. 'A few years ago most young men here [in Sydney] said "Bovril" whenever they found anything unimpressive, and University students certainly made good use of the song, "It all sounds like Bovril to me" ' (Oliver, 1937). Prob. a euph. for *ballocks* or *balls* used exclamatorily; prompted by **bullshit.** (Bovril is the tradename of a beef extract.)—2. 'I'm not having my house turned into a Bovril' (the house being a 'public'): since ca. 1930. Mais, 1948.

bovrilise. To omit all inessential matter from an advertisement: copywriters' coll.: since ca. 1935. Ex *Bovril,* 'the best of the meat', an advertising slogan for the famous meat-extract's brand-name.

bovver boots. Heavy, steel-studded boots affected by the 'bovver boys' [see next]; designed for use as weapons of offence: mostly London teenage gangsters': since 1969.

bovver boy, usu. in pl. Member(s) of a gang of louts, 'yobs', and skinheads [qq.v.], addicted to senseless violence and general hooliganism: 1968 onwards, but seldom mentioned in books or the Press until mid-1969. Ex *bovver,* a Cockney pron. of the *bother* they delight in causing.

Bovvy. Bovington Camp, Dorset, depot of the Royal Armoured Corps: Army: since WW2; prob. earlier.

bow. In *on the bow,* without paying, as 'I got in on the bow': C.20: c. >, by 1945, low s. (Sharpe, 1938.) Powis, 1977, notes *on the bow* as a var. of *on the elbow,* scrounging.

bow and arrow. A sparrow: r.s.: late C.19–20. (B. & P.)—2. A barrow: r.s. (L.A., 1969.)

Bow and Arrow War, the. See **Farmers' Strike**.

bow and quiver. Liver (the bodily organ): r.s. Cf. **cheerful giver**.

Bow Street. The orderly room: military: from ca. 1910. (B. & P.) Ex the famous London police station.

bow the crumpet or **duck the scone** or **nod the nut.** To plead guilty in a law-court: Aus. c.: since ca. 1930. B., 1959.

bow wave. A tyro sailor: R Can. N: since ca. 1920. H. & P.—2. In RN, a cap with a bow-wave effect; esp. at the RNC, Dartmouth. Granville.

bow-wow. *The Bow-wow* = the Brigade Ordnance Warrant Officer (BOWO)—the Royal Army Ordnance Corps representative at Brigade HQ: Army: since 1939. With an acronym like that, what else could he be? (P.B.)—2. In *on the bow-wow,* Aus. version of **bow**.

bower. A prison: Aus. c. >, by 1940, low s. (B., 1942.) Ironic.

bower bird. A petty thief: Aus. (B., 1943). Ex the habits of the bower bird, which hoards useless objects, as B.P. has pointed out. Cf.:-

bower-birdin(g). Picking up odds-and-ends for one's own camp or use: N.T., Aus.: since ca. 1925. B., 1953.

bowler (1882); **bowler-hat** (1861); occ. **boler** (—1890)**.** A stiff felt hat; fairly low in the crown and gen. black: coll. In its etym. it was long regarded as a *bowl*-shaped hat, but it almost certainly derives ex the name of a London hatter (W.: *Words and Names*). Dates: OED.—2. Hence, *to be given a bowler* (hat), to be sent home or 'sacked': Army: 1915–18. (B. & P.) With the coming of peace in 1918, *to be given* (one's) *bowler* > to be demobilised (F. & G.); i.e. a civilian bowler in exchange for one's 'battle-bowler'. The RN var. of the orig. nuance was *get a bowler hat,* and by 1918, all three Services were using the elliptical *(be) bowler-hatted.* In almost all cases, the phrase refers to an officer, joining or re-joining civilian professional or managerial life. In the late 1950s there arose the phrase *to get,* or *be given, a* (or *the*) *golden bowler,* to accept an offer of premature retirement: ex the very favourable terms offered by the War Office at the time when it drastically reduced the number of its officers. Cf. a retiring company director's **golden handshake** (Sanders). Cf.:-

bowler hat, v.t. ' "Gentleman Jim" Cassels will preside at a policy meeting . . . drink beer in a Sergeants' Mess, "bowler hat" a major-general . . . all with the same unfailing Edwardian courtesy and charm' (Carew, 1967): Services': since ca. 1950. The active end of the WW1 *be given a bowler hat.* Cf. prec.

bowler(-)hat boys, the. 'They were always very well dressed and visited houses of old people living alone and by posing as officials from banks, rating authorities, police departments and so on, gained access. They worked in teams of three or four' (Bournemouth *Evening Echo,* 20 Apr. 1966): c. and police s.: since ca. 1963. Cf. **prop game**.

B

bowler hat brigade. 'Railway inspectors. The bowler hat is still an emblem of authority on British Railways today [1970]. Footplate inspectors, foremen, and inspectors of all grades wore bowler hats' (McKenna, 1970): railwaymen's.

bowler-hatted. See **bowler**, 2.

bowler's double. 100 wickets + 100 runs in a season: cricketers': since ca. 1930. Humorous, on S.E. *cricketer's double*, 100 wickets + 1,000 runs in a season.

bowling green. A fast line: railwaymen's. (*Railway*, 2nd.) The 'going' is smooth.

bows down. Be quiet; esp. stop talking: RN: since ca. 1925. H. & P.

bowser king. An NCO in charge of a bowser (towed petrol tanker): RAF: since ca. 1930. (Jackson.) See **king**.

bowsie man. 'a familiar figure in rural Ireland; he perhaps owns an acre or so of his own, does odd jobs for other people, is normally dressed in clothes that someone gave him, and is pretty wild to look at. Bowsie . . . derives from bouzy = boozy = prone to drink, and this may or may not be the case' (Tracy, 1975). Since early C.19—perhaps later C.19. Cf.:-

bowsy. A low guttersnipe: Anglo-Irish. Apparently a var. of **boozy**, n. See also **bowsie man**.

bowyang or **boyang**; by corruption, **boang**. A labourer; workman: Aus. (Tennant, 1941.) Ex *bowyangs*, bands worn about the trousers—above the knee.

box, n. 'A safe of the old-fashioned kind': c.: late C.19–20. Spenser, 1934, 'It is easy to rip off the back.'—2. An abdominal [i.e., genitals] protector: sporting s., perhaps orig. Public Schools', or Universities'.—3. A man's room: Dalton Hall, Manchester: since ca. 1919. *The Daltonian*, Dec. 1946.—4. (*the box*) Short for **black box**, 2, q.v., a piece of radar equipment.—5. A 'mess' (*make a box of*): Aus.: since ca. 1920. (B., 1943.) ?euph. for *ballocks*.—6. Female genitals: low English and Aus. elliptical for 'a *box* of tricks'. Hence, also US. W. & F. record it for 1954.—7. A guitar (Powis): underworld: since (?)early 1960s. Hollis, however, glosses it as street entertainers' s. for an accordion or concertina.—8. A room, in a prison, for a 'closed visit': Borstals' and detention centres': 1970s. (Home Office.) A 'strong box'= special cell, quiet room. Ibid.—9. A submarine's main battery: RN Submariners': mid-C.20. (Malin, 1979.)—10. As *the box*, an aircraft cockpit simulator: RAF coll.: later C.20. *Phantom*.—11. As *the box*, abbr. 'witness box', as in *jump in the box*, to give Queen's evidence: Aus. c.: later C.20. McNeil.—12. In *be in a box*, to be cornered; in a fix: coll.: C.19—early 20. Surviving in military j., where *boxed in* is still used of 'a tight corner'. —13. In *be in a box*, in a state of confusion: NZ. B., 1941.—14. In *on the box*, on strike and receiving strike pay: workmen's, mainly in N. England: later C.19–early 20.—15. Hence, *on the box*, drawing Friendly Society benefits: *go on the box*, to have recourse to them. (Young, 1938.) I.e. the box containing the Society's funds.—16. In *on the box*, appearing on the television screen, as in 'Did you see the Chancellor on the box last night?': coll.: since late 1950s.

box, v. Elliptical for **box clever**, [q.v.]: since ca. 1930. (L.A.) Cf. Tempest, 1950, on *to box*, 'Something cleverly done. Something which requires brains and/or cunning to accomplish. "He boxed that fiddle okay" = he organised that bit of business very well. A "fiddle", incidentally, need not need brains or cunning.'—2. To make a mistake; muddle things: Aus. and NZ: since mid-C.20. Wilkes.

box along with (someone); **box with**. To 'get along with even would-be awkward person on give-and-take terms' (L.A., 1977): the former since ca. 1960; the latter several decades earlier.

box clever. To use one's head, be a 'shrewdy': since ca. 1925. *Gilt Kid*.

box egg. A 'bad egg'; one who doesn't amount to much: since ca. 1930.

box-getter, -getting. A stealer, stealing, from tills: c. Leach.

box-it. 'Drinking schools mix wine and cider to make a cheap heady drink called box-it' (*New Society*, 2 Sep. 1982, p. 378).

box of birds, a. Fighting-fit: NZ Services': WW2. (Fullarton, 1943.) Singing with health and happiness.—2. Hence, general as *box of birds* and in nuance 'fit and very happy': 1945+. (Marsh, 1949.) In Aus., *feel like a box of birds*, very happy. B., 1953.—3. '[Lt Cdr] Doug Taylor had seen the first Harrier ['jump-jet' aircraft] fly off a ski-jump . . . "I was not especially excited," he says. "I had always been confident that it would be a box of birds" ' (*Telegraph* Sunday mag., 6 May 1979).

box of sharks. A phrase 'indicative of vast surprise. "She nearly gave birth to a box of sharks!" Cf. **have a baby** and **having kittens**' (Leechman): Can.: since ca. 1955.

box of toys. Noise: r.s.: late C.19–20. Ortzen, 1938.

box of tricks. A tool box, or any similar receptacle: Aus. and Brit.: since (?)ca. 1910. (B.P.; Petch.) Cf. **bag of tricks** and *the whole bag of tricks*; box may be substituted for *bag* in the latter also.—2. Euston Station: taxi-drivers': 13 Sep. 1941, *Weekly Telegraph*. Ex its shape.

box office. (Of an actor) a success: theatrical and cinematic coll.: since ca. 1925. 'Now, at last, she's box office.'

box on. To keep fighting; hence to continue doing anything important or strenuous: Aus.

box on with. To punch; to fight with: Aus.: since ca. 1920. (Niland, 1958.) Cf. prec.

box-up. A mix-up; confusion; muddle: mostly military. (Rogerson, 1933.) Perhaps on *mix-up*, more prob. on *ballocks-up*; but see **box**, v., 2.

box-up. V. from prec.: Aus. Baker.

box-wallah. A native pedlar, gen. itinerant: Anglo-Indian coll.: from ca. 1820.—2. Hence, pej., a European commercial man: Anglo-Indian:—1934 (*COD*, 1934 Sup.).

boxed-up. In prison; gaoled: NZ. In UK drugs c., simply *boxed* (Stockley, 1986).—2. Thoroughly confused: Aus.: since ca. 1930. (B.P.) Cf. **box-up**, n. and v.

boy. Heroin: drugs world: 1970s (Home Office): adopted ex US, where current since –1955 (Spears). Cf. **girl**.—2. (Gen. in pl.) A prisoner: c. Cf. **boys**.

boy friend, the; the girl friend. Orig. and still used to imply an illicit sex relationship (whether hetero or not): mostly Londoners': from ca. 1920. Ex US. (Cf. S.E. *gentleman friend* and *lady friend*.)—2. Hence, without any pej. implication: orig. and mainly Londoners': from ca. 1925.

boy in a (or **the**) **boat.** Clitoris: low: late C.19–20.

boy (or **boy's**) **racer.** 'The model 7R A.J.S. racing motorcycle, designed to be bought "over the counter" by the general public, rather than a "works" bike': motorcycling enthusiasts': since 1948. (Carter, 1979.)

Boy Scout's leave. A brief shore-leave: R Aus. N: WW2. B., 1943.

boys. 'The boys, as all stage hands are called, regardless of age' (Gray, 1964): theatrical coll.

boy's favourite. See TOMBOLA, in Appx.

boys on ice. Lice: r.s.: late C.19–20. Franklyn.

boy's racer. See **boy racer**.

boysie. A term of address to a boy or, rarely by father, to son of any age whatsoever: coll., mostly Aus. Cameron, 1929; Stead, 1934.

bozo. A fellow: Can. (ex US) since ca. 1918; Aus. since ca. 1935. (Devanney, 1944.) Leechman, for Can., cites the *Daily Colonist* (Victoria, BC), 18 July 1926; R.S. adds 'Spanish bozo, man, fellow, orig. "facial down indicative of puberty"; presumably from Mexican Spanish.' Leech, 1985, stresses that the later C.20 Can. nuance is 'a strong man, with more strength than brains, often of low class, or no class at all'. Used in middle-class setting in a 'Biff' cartoon, *Guardian*, 11 July 1987; early sign of adoption ex N. Am.

bra. A brassiere: feminine: common since ca. 1934 and, ca. 1940, superseding *bras*. Since ca. 1950, coll.

Brab. A Brabazon aircraft: aircraft industry. Named after Lord Brabazon of Tara, it was the largest aircraft to have been

B

built up till that time, the late 1940s. It had a brief life as a 'flying test-bed', ca. 1950: since then, the name is merely historical.

brace and bits. Nipples; loosely, breasts: low r.s., little used in Britain. Mostly American. (Franklyn.) Also Aus.: in *Rats*.

braced. Hearty; in excellent spirits: Marlborough College coll.: since ca. 1920. Ex S.E. 'braced up'.

bracket. A vague, unspecified part of the body, prob. the nose: it occurs in threat, e.g., 'If he doesn't do it, he'll get a punch up the bracket'; 'You're asking for a punch up the bracket', etc.: popularised by the BBC radio-comedy programme 'Hancock's Half-hour' of the the 1950s. (P.B.)

bradbury, occ. abbr. to **brad.** A Treasury note; esp. a £1 note: from 1915; † by mid-C.20. (These notes, by the way, were hardly artistic.) Ex Sir John Bradbury, the Secretary of the Treasury, which circulated the 10s. and £1 notes from late 1914 until November 1928, when the nation's note issue was consolidated in the Bank of England; the Treasury's notes ceased to be legal tender on 31 July 1933. See the third leader and the City Editor's note, *Daily Telegraph*, 1 Aug. 1933. Cf. **Fisher.** Contrast C.19 **brads**, copper coins.

bradshaw, v., hence **bradshawing**, vbl n. 'Cross-country flying, using railway lines for navigation.' (Peppitt): RAF and FAA coll.: since before WW2, if not earlier. (Phelps, 1946.) Ex the publisher of the first complete UK rail timetable.

brag rags. Medal ribbons: RN: since ca. 1920. Granville.

Brahma. 'Something good. Also a flashily dressed girl': Regular Army: late C.19–20; by 1970, slightly ob. (F. & G.) Ex *Brahma*, the Hindu deity, the idols being often bejewelled. Hence **brama**, q.v.

Brahms. A frequent shortening of:-

Brahms 'n' Liszt. Tipsy: r.s. on synon. s. *pissed*: since ca. 1920.

brain basil (or Basil). A clever boy: Oxford schoolboys': Morris, 1965.

brain bosun or bos'n. A RN Instructor Officer: RN: since ca. 1925. (Parsons, 1973.) Cf. **custard bosun** and **sin bosun.**

brain child. A new idea one's proud of; one's own invention: since ca. 1945: s. >, by 1960, coll.

brain(-)drain, the. Emigration by those with able minds, from UK to places, esp. USA, where the rewards are thought to be greater, and the opportunities more untrammelled: coll.: since early 1960s; *OED* earliest citation is 1963. Similarly, ref. to people moving from university to industry, etc. (P.B.)—2. Forensic chemists: police s. See **whizz kids.**

brain-smasher. Occ. var. of **brain-teaser,** q.v. *Punch*, 17 Oct. 1917, 'This sugar [= claim] form . . . is a regular brain-smasher.' (P.B.)

brain-teaser. A puzzler, a conundrum: coll. (P.B.)

brain-wave. A sudden, esp. if a brilliant, idea: from ca. 1914; since ca. 1933, coll. Ex telepathy.

brains, the. 'The boss': Can.: ca. 1905–40. (Leechman.) Since ca. 1935, *the brain*.—2. Traffic Control: railwaymen's: from ca. 1930. (*Railway*.) Cf. **big brain**.—3. 'Ironic term for the C.I.D.' (Powis): police and underworld: later C.20.

brains on ice, have (one's). 'To be very cool-headed and collected' (Lyell): coll.:—1931; ob. by 1950.

Brains Trust, the. The Central Trades Test Board: RAF: since ca. 1938. (E.P. 1942.) Unlike the BBC's Brains Trust they ask, not answer, questions.—2. Such specialists as range-finders and surveyors: Royal Artillery: 1939+.—3. Mid-C.20 railwaymen's var. of *brains*, q.v. McKenna, 1970.)

brainstrains. 'Oxford to Cambridge via Bletchley line' (*Railway*, 2nd): railwaymen's: since late 1940s.

brake. A tutor: Public Schoolboys':—1933. Perhaps suggested by *coach*.

brake-block. 'West of England [footplate-]men relied [for sustenance] upon a pasty known by its shape and texture as a brake-block—history is silent on its taste' (McKenna, 2, p. 194): railwaymen's: earlier C.20.

brama. A pretty girl: c.: from ca. 1922. (*Gilt Kid*.) Ex *Brahma*.—2. In *a bit of a brama*, a 'good chap', though a trifle wild and unintelligent: Army: 1940s.

branch out. To become very fat: Aus.: since ca. 1925. Park, 1953.

branches everywhere. Jam containing string (or twigs) and, on the tin, the manufacturers' confession, *branches everywhere*: joc., mostly domestic: since ca. 1930.

bras. A brassiere: feminine: since ca. 1910; by 1950, †. (Ferguson, 1936.) Always, of course, pron. *brah*. Replaced by *bra*, q.v.

brass, n. Money. In late C.16–17, S.E.; in C.18, coll.; thereafter, s.—2. A confidence-trick betting-system: c. Leach, 1933.—3. Abbr. of **brass-nail**, a prostitute: since ca. 1920. *Cheapjack*.—4. '*Brass*: the officers, also *Gold Braid*', Granville: RN lowerdeck. Cf. *brass-hat* and **top brass**. The latter is sometimes, since ca. 1955, referred to as 'the brass'. Hence also *carry brass*, to hold an important rank: Army: WW2. P-G-R.

brass, adj. Fashionable; smart: raffish London: since ca. 1950. 'Some of them were speaking in French because it was the brass thing to do' (Barlow, 1968). Ex 'the *brass*', the 'heads'.

brass along. To go gaily and/or impudently ahead: from ca. 1918. (Blaker, 1934.)

brass balls. 'Something severe or testing, "a brassballs job", or someone tough and unyieldingly masculine' (Powis): police and underworld: later C.20.

brass band. Occ. r.s. for 'hand'. Cf. earlier synon. *German band(s)*.

brass it out. To brazen it out: since ca. 1950, if not rather earlier: Petch cites its use in the popular police series 'Z Cars' on TV, 10 Feb. 1969. Coll., not s. Cf. *brass*, impudence: since C.17.

brass man. A confidence trickster: Aus. c.: since ca. 1930. B., 1953.

brass monkey weather. Bitterly cold weather: Aus. (?orig.) and Brit: since ca. 1920.

brass-nail. A prostitute: c.: r.s. on *tail*.

brass-neck. Impudent: military. F. & G., 'A brass-neck lie'. Also as n., impudence: see **neck**, n., 1.

brass off. To reprimand severely: Services': WW2. H. & P.

brass-plater. 'A man of the merchant class': from ca. 1920. (*OED* Sup.)—2. As *brass-* or *door-plater*, a doctor. (Manchon.) Ex the brass name-plate at his door.

brass-pounder. A telegrapher-agent: Can. railwaymen's: since ca. 1925. (Leechman.)

brass tacks, get down to. To come to, to face, realities; to consider the practical aspect: coll.: US (1903), anglicised by 1910: *OED* Sup. (In US, there is the var. . . . *brass nails*.) I suspect, however, that *brass tacks* may have arisen before C.20 and be r.s. for *facts*.

brass up. To pay (up), gen. v.i. An early instance is in Pugh (2), 1906. The term is more gen. in the North and the Midlands than in the South.—2. 'To shell; from the brass shell casings that are ejected after firing the projectile' (Green): military.

brassed. Has, since 1944, often been used in abbr. of the next, as *cheesed* can be used for *cheesed off*. But one cannot use *browned* for *browned off*.

brassed off. Disgruntled, fed up: Services', orig. (?)RN since ca. 1927; gen. since ca. 1939. (*Observer*, 14 Oct. 1942; H. & P.) Sometimes a synonym of *browned off*; sometimes regarded as a shade milder. Cf. *brass off*: perhaps from brass-polishing in ships. For *brassed off*, *browned off* and *cheesed off*, see esp. Partridge, 1945, or *Forces' Slang*, ed. Partridge, 1948. P.B.: but Roberts, 1985, notes that the elab. *brassed* (or *cheesed*) *off to the tit ends* was 'heard in South London in the 1930s', so its spread from the Services was evidently earlier than E.P. allowed.

brassic. See **boracic.**

brassy. A friend or close companion: RN: since ca. 1920. (H. & P.)

brat. A boy soldier or airman, whether apprentice, junior leader, or any other form of 'pre-man's service'. Hence, *ex-brat*, a soldier or airman on regular man's service who has previously served thus. Army and RAF coll. (P.B.; Adkin.)

brats. Collective for a deep-sea trawler's crew below skipper and mate: deep-sea trawlers'. Luard, 1933, and 1935.

Braunhaus. 'British Rail Headquarters' (*Railway*, 2nd): railwaymen's: since *ca.* 1955(?). A pun on 'Brown' and 'brown', perhaps; or, as R.S. has suggested, joc. ex *das braune Haus*, the Nazi Party's national HQ. British Rail was established in 1948.

brave and bold. Cold: r.s.: late C.19–early 20: a var. of *taters in the mould* and *soldiers bold*. Hillman writes, 1974, 'According to my grandfather, "Brave, ain't it!" was, in the 1890s, in as common use as "Taters, ain't it!" among Cockneys.'

bread. 'In sailor parlance biscuit is "bread" . . . ; bread of the ordinary description is "Soft tack" ' (Goodenough, 1901): RN: (?)mid-C.19–early 20.—2. Money: mostly Teddy boys', drug-addicts', teenagers': as such, adopted *ca.* 1955, ex US; but, basically, the shortening of **bread and honey**, and therefore, orig., English, not US, (Ball 1962.) Also used by hippies and Flower People (Fryer, 1967); and now, in the 1970s, more and more widely used and gen. understood, popularised by novels like, e.g., Reid, 1970. Cf. also the earlier idea of money = bread in *out of bread*, out of work: coll.: mid-C.18–early 19 (Grose, 3rd ed.).

bread and boo. Bread-and-scrape: nursery coll.:—1923 (Manchon).

bread and bread. Applied to a homosexual couple: coll.: later C.20.—2. Applied more gen. to any dull combination of two similar things, or as 'six of one and half a dozen of the other' of two dull, similar things: coll.: since late 1970s. I.e., no jam. (P.B.)

bread and butter days. 'Days when a docker would pick up a job that paid very little—just enough to "put butter on the bread" ' (Ash): London dockers': mid-C.20.

bread and butter job. 'A [bicycle] assembled from anything you could find or scrounge about like about the early *Hercules* effort (£3.19s.9d, in the late 1920s); another term was "rubbish heap special" ' (*Fellowship*, 1984): club cyclists': earlier C.20.

bread and butter letter. A letter thanking one's recent hostess: Society: anglicised, as a coll., *ca.* 1905 ex US. Occ. abbr. to *bread and butter*: from *ca.* 1925.

bread and honey. Money: r.s. Much less common than **bees and honey**. Franklyn 2nd.

bread and jam. A tram: r.s. B. & P.

bread and lard, adj. Hard: r.s. Franklyn 2nd adduces 'Gorblimey! ain't that bread an' lard, eh?'

bread and point. 'The idea behind this was that [my mother] could only afford to buy, e.g. one chop or kipper for my father's tea and he had to be fed since he was the head of the house. So we [children] were issued with a piece of bread and margarine and as we took bites from the bread we were to point at my father's kipper, hence bread and point' (Lord Willis, 1986): London East End: earlier C.20. Cf.:-

bread and pullet. Just bread: joc.:—1913 (Dawson). With pun on *pull it*, an answer to, e.g. 'What's for tea?'

bread and salt, take. To curse and swear: early C.20. Manchon.

bread and solitary confinement. prisoners' coll.: late C.19–20. (Phelan, 1943.) I.e. bread and water.

bread bins. 'Eastern Region locomotives. Origin unknown' (McKenna, 1): railwaymen's: mid-C.20.

bread hooks. Fingers; loosely, hands: Can.: since *ca.* 1955 (or rather earlier). The *Daily Colonist*, Victoria, BC, 1 July 1973: ' . . . he won't take any action until he gets the money "in his bread hooks" ' (Leechman, 1973).

break, n. (Gen. *bad break*.) A mistake, blunder, *faux pas*. Coll. Ex US. By itself, *break*, esp. in US (—1827), usu. means a piece of good luck: cf., however, Thornton. In UK *a bad break* has come to mean, since *ca.* 1950 at the latest, an unforeseen stroke of bad luck, or run of misfortunes.—2. Esp. in *give* (someone) *a break*, to give him a chance, an opportunity, a slight advantage: Can. (ex US) coll.: since the late 1920s. (Leechman.)—3. In **make a break**, q.v., to

attempt to escape.—4. A break-in, or illicit entry into, a building: burglars' c.: since *ca.* 1930. Norman, 1959.

break, v. To leave the employment of (a person); to discharge (an employee): tailors'. *Tailor and Cutter*, 29 Nov. 1928, both senses.—2. (Usu. in the present perfect tense; applied only to events that are exciting or important;) To happen: journalists' coll.: adopted *ca.* 1930 ex US. Bush, 1936, ' "Anything broken?" Tuke said. "Nothing much," Ribbold told him. "Everything still slack as hell." '—3. V.i., to cost: v.t., *break for*, to cost someone so much: Aus. B., 1942.—4. V.t., to change a coin or a bank or currency note: since *ca.* 1920.—5. In *do a break*, to depart hastily: Aus.:—1916 (Dennis). Cf. **make a break**, and the S.E. *break-away*.—6. Usu. in imperative, a shortening of **break it up!**, 1, q.v., or ex the boxing j.: theatrical: (to) pause in, or at end of, rehearsal; or as in, e.g., 'the cast broke for tea'.

break a bit off. To defecate: Public Schools' joc.: since *ca.* 1920. The ref. is to a hard stool. Contrast:—2. In *break a bit off with* (a woman), of the male, to copulate: low and raffish. Occ., as a generalisation, without *with*, as 'I've got an awful lot of dirty water on my chest. It's time I broke a bit off.' (P.B.; L.A.)

break into pictures. To get on the cinematic screen: coll.: since 1925. Hence, also, to *break into* other forms of entertainment, TV, the 'pop scene', radio, etc.

break it big. To win a lot of money, esp. at gambling: Aus. Ronan, 1954.

break (e.g. **it**) **down to.** To tell (a person) something: tailors'. *Tailor and Cutter*, 29 Nov. 1928.

break loose. 'When the show breaks loose' = when the battle begins: Army: 1940+; ob. (P-G-R.) Cf. the coll. phrase 'All Hell broke loose'—all was confusion and pandemonium.

break (one's) **neck.** To long to make water: coll.: since *ca.* 1918. 'Don't know about *you*, but *I'm* breaking my neck!' Not orig. euph.; it shortens *be breaking one's neck for a piss*.

break out again. To do again something that is unpleasant or ridiculous: coll. Perhaps a development ex:-

break out in a fresh place. To commence a new undertaking; assume (lit. or fig.) a different position: ?orig. US and anglicised *ca.* 1905.

break (someone's) **rice-bowl.** To deprive that person of his livelihood, by automation, usurpation, destruction, etc.: common in the coll. in the Far East, esp. in Hong Kong:—1960. Perhaps from a Chinese phrase. (P.B.)

break surface. To wake from sleep: RN: since *ca.* 1925. Granville, 'From the submarine service'.

break the sound barrier. To break wind: orig. (*ca.* 1960) and mostly Can. 'Neat and almost inevitable' (Leechman).

break van. A van (Naafi or YMCA) driven around a Station at 'break' or recess period of a quarter of an hour, morning and afternoon: RAF (hence also WAAF) coll.: since *ca.* 1935. Jackson.

breakaway, the. Those competitors who have established a substantial lead: racing cyclists' coll.: since *ca.* 1925. Contrast **bunch**, n., 2.—2. A person broken up, whether physically or mentally: Aus. coll.: since *ca.* 1910. Prichard, 1929.

breaker. 'In Citizens' Band radio usage, a formal request by one broadcaster to employ the channel. By extension, [in pl.] those who use CB' (Green): since *ca.* 1975, adopted ex US.

breast work. The caressing of a woman's breasts: somewhat pedantic and seldom heard. Punning *breastwork*, a defensive fieldwork breast-high.

breathe down (someone's) **neck.** To be very close to someone, as in 'The cops were breathing down my neck': joc. coll.: since *ca.* 1930. (Cf. the allusive title of John Pudney's delightful collection of short stories titled *It Breathed Down My Neck*, 1946.)—2. Hence, to 'keep after' someone for, e.g., the completion of a job: since late 1940s.

breathed on. (Of a car or its engine), 'converted, often by professionals, to give greater power and speed' (Mann, 1963): since middle 1950s. Cf. **souped up.**

B

B

breather. A breathing-space; a short rest: coll., now verging on S.E.

breathing licence. 'Station card—an identity card held by all ratings, deprival of which meant loss of leave and limitation of leisure activities' (Bassett): RN: WW2. Cf. later C.20 police and security forces' use of, e.g. 'Arrest [them, her, etc.] under the breathing laws', i.e. on suspicion, or even without strictly legal cause. (P.B.)

breed. A half-breed: Can. coll.: mid-C.19–20. Dyker, 1934.

breeding-wagon. A caravan: Midlands (s., not dial.): since ca. 1930. Cf. **passion-wagon.**

breeks. Orig. dial. (esp. Scottish) form of *breeches*.—2. In *have the breeks torn off* (one), euph. for *have* (one's) *balls chewed off*, to be severely reprimanded: since ca. 1950. (L.A., 1977.)

breeze. In *it's a breeze*, it's easy: coll.: since ca. 1960; orig. Aus. (Raab.) Cf. **pushover,** and **breeze through.**—2. In *have the breeze up* (or *vertical*), to 'have the wind up', which it deliberately varies: from 1916: orig. and mainly Services'. F. & G.

breeze (along). To move or go quickly: from ca. 1920. Cf.:-

breeze in. To arrive unexpectedly: from ca. 1920. On *blow in.*

breeze through (a task). To do it quickly and unfalteringly: Aus.: since late 1940s. (B.P.) P.B.: in later C.20 also Brit.; cf. **breeze,** n., 1.

breezer. A fart: Aus. juvenile: later C.20. Wilkes.

breezy. Afraid: c.: from ca. 1918. (Leach.) Ex WW1 soldiers' s.—2. Short-tempered: s., verging on coll.:—1931 (Lyell); ob. by 1940. Apt to 'blow up'.

breezy Bertie. A brash, self-confident, thick-skinned young man: early C.20. (Deeping, 1927.) Cf. **hooray Henry.**

brekker. Breakfast. From late 1880s. By elision of *fast* and collision of *break* and the 'OXFORD *-ER*', though—admittedly—it looks rather like a child's slurring of *breakfast*. By mid-C.20, also *brekkers.*

brew. In the Services of late C.19–20: tea. Cf. the R Aus. N *the brew's wet* or *she's wet*, the tea has been made (Roberts, 1951). Cf. also **brew up,** 1.—2. 'Concocted fuel with alcohol base' (Dunford): motorcyclists': since ca. 1950. Cf. **blue stink.**—3. See **buro.**

brew-can. Army tin used for making tea: Army: since ca. 1925. Ex prec., 1.

brew-up, n. Corresponding to next.—2. Hence, a meal, including a drink of tea: since ca. 1960. Leechman.

brew up, v.i. To make tea: Army: since ca. 1925.—2. Hence, to catch fire: Army: 1940–5. 'Tank brewed up and his driver's killed' (Douglas, 1947).

brewed. Drunk, intoxicated: 'Hell's Angels' ', q.v., and their adherents': 1980s. 'We do what we want. We all get brewed and then a little later we get balled [see **ball,** v.]' (young woman at a motorcycling rally, quoted in *New Society,* 19 July 1985).

brewer's asthma. Shortness of breath: Aus. drinking s.: since ca. 1925. B., 1953.

brewer's droop. 'A large belly brought on by beer, and by extension a reference to alleged impotence in a male. Can be a most insulting phrase to use to a man in this latter meaning as it impugns his virility. Not to be used in jest.' Thus Powis, in 1977; but in the army of the 1950s, it *was* used in jest; though not so funny, perhaps, to the drunken soldier trying to 'get his end away'. E.P. dates it (?mid-C.19–)C.20, and adds 'Have often heard and seen it, yet possess no record earlier than P.B., 1974.'

brewer's goitre. A large paunch: Aus. drinking s.: ca. 1925. B., 1953.

brewer's jockey. A brewer's van-driver's self-appointed assistant: Aus. Baker.

Brian O'Lynn, occ. **O'Linn.** Gin: r.s.:—1857 ('Ducange Anglicus'); in C.20 often **Brian O'Flynn,** and abbr. *Brian,* sometimes even *Bri.* Franklyn, 1.

brick, n. A loyal, dependable person (orig. only of men); 'a good fellow': poss. dates back to early C.19, and still current among the older generation, later C.20.—2. A shell: RN since ca. 1924; Army since ca. 1930. 'That gun throws a pretty hefty brick.' P-G-R.—3. The sum of £10: Aus. sporting: since ca. 1920. (Glassop, 1949.) Poss. a decade earlier: see Wilkes.—4. 'The Brickmakers Arms is the name that cynics give to our local Transport Club. "Making brick" is slang for the various ways in which some [bus-]drivers and conductors defraud the Passenger Transport Executive' (Harris, 1979). Cf. v., 3, and **bunce,** an older synon.—5. A kilogram of cannabis: drugs c. (Stockley, 1986.) US since —1959 (Spears).

brick, v. Gen. *that's bricked it,* that's spoilt it, that's the end of it:—1923 (Manchon); ob. by 1930.—2. To push, 'barge into' (a person): Charterhouse: early C.20.—3. To cheat or defraud: market-traders': since (?)ca. 1920. 'He was bricking me, so I gave him the bellows [= got rid of him]' (*M.T.*). Hence *bricker,* a cheat or defrauder (Ibid.). See **brick,** n., 4, and **bricker.**

brick it, esp. as *bricking it*. A euph. abbr. of **shit bricks,** 2: students at Bath University (and prob. elsewhere): much used 1985–6. (Mitchell, 1986.)

bricked. 'Having an unsigned [police] statement used [against one] in court': Aus. c.: since ca. 1950. Grindley, 1977.

bricker. To steal; to filch: hippies' and 'counter-culture': since early 1960s. Reid, 1970: 'When I left London I didn't bother to bring much gear [i.e., clothing, etc.] with me—you can always bricker a dress from a shop if you need one', and 'We brickered a few false carnations.' See also **brick,** n., 4, and v., 3.

Brickie. Brixham smack or fisherman: nautical. Butcher, 1980.

Bricks and Mortar. (Often simply *Bricks.*) The Air Ministry Works and Buildings Dept.: RAF: from ca. 1930. (H. & P.) P.B.: the Army's equivalent organisation is sometimes referred to as *the Bricks and Sticks,* having also some responsibility for furnishings: since ca. 1950, at latest. Cf. **Works and Bricks.**—2. A daughter: r.s.—3. Houses; house property; esp. as in 'his money's in bricks and mortar': coll.: from ca. 1905.

Bricks and Sticks. See prec., 1, and **Works and Bricks.**

Brid. Bridlington, a Yorkshire holiday resort.

bride. A prostitute: London c.: since late C.19. (Samuel, 1981.) See quot'n at **string** (someone) **up.**—2. Hence, 'a girl', 'a young woman' (esp. to make love to): not c. but low s., mostly Londoners': from ca. 1920 (Ingram, 1935) and, by 1940, Forces'. Cf. **wife.**

bride and groom. A broom: r.s.: late C.19–20. B. & P.—2. A room: id. Franklyn 2nd declares both senses † by 1960.

bridge, n. In NZ post-WW1 c., a look, a glance.—2. An introduction, a form of approach: Aus.: since ca. 1925. (B., 1943.) It bridges a gap.—3. Hence, a plausible excuse or story: Aus.: since ca. 1930. B., 1959.

bridge, v. 'A compositor is said to have "bridged" if he fails to appear at the appointed time without subsequent excuse' (Rowles, 1948): printers'.—2. See TIDDLYWINKS, in Appx.

bridge widow; bridge widower. A wife, or a husband, often left alone by a bridge-fiendish partner: since early 1920s. On analogy of **golf widow.**

bridger. A bridge-player: mostly Society: since ca. 1925.

brief. A bank- or currency-note: bank-clerks', mostly Anglo-Irish.—2. Hence(?), a cheque: c.:—1933 (Ingram).—3. A fig. bias: c.:—1933 (Ibid.).—4. A London cab-driver's licence. See **bill,** 1.—5. 'A warrant to arrest or search, a police warrant card (or any other identity document)' (Powis): c. and police s.: since (?)ca. 1965. Cf. **W.**—6. 'Generally, any lawyer; specifically, a barrister' (Ibid.): police and the underworld-fringe: since ca. 1930. One who is briefed for a case.—7. In *hand in* (one's) *brief,* to give notice to one's employer: domestic servants': early C.20. Horne, 1923.

briefs. Very short women's knickers: feminine coll.: from 1932 or 1933. In *Books of To-Day,* Nov. 1934, C.G.T. writes feelingly, in the poem entitled 'Too Much of Too Little': 'I'm bored to tears with "scanties",/I'm sick to death of "briefs",/

Of specialists in "panties",/And combination chiefs.' Cf. **neathie-set**. It has, since ca. 1950, been applied also to men's underpants, and as underpants, for either sex, has > by late C.20. informal S.E. (P.B.)

briffen(-fin). Bread and dripping: Liverpool street arabs', and tramps' c.: since ca. 1900. (*Arab*; Cown, 1937.) Perhaps a 'near' blend of S.E. *bread* and sol. *drippen*.—2. Hence, a girl: likewise tramps' c.: from ca. 1920. (Ibid.) Regarded as 'a necessity of life'? or cf. **crumpet**.

brig, the. One's or the Brigadier-General, from late C.19; since the abolition of this rank, the Brigadier: Army s. > coll. As in *the brig's po-juggler*, Aus. Army contemptuous, WW1, for a brigade orderly officer.

brigade. A loose verbal grouping of any body of similar individuals, e.g. **the grey mac brigade**, q.v.: coll., usu. joc. (P.B.)

Brigg's (or **Briggs'**) **Rest**; esp., **Brig's rest**. A vest: r.s., esp. among convicts. C.20. (Franklyn 2nd.) Perhaps a pun on *the brig*, RN s. since mid-C.19 for a punishment cell.

bright as a button(, as). Highly intelligent; clever and alert, as in 'Oh, she's as bright as a button, that kid. Doesn't miss a trick!': coll. (P.B.)

bright bastard. A 'smart Alec': Aus.: since ca. 1910. Used in ironic disparagement.

bright boy. A post-WW2 Army var. of **wide boy**, q.v.

bright spark. A lively person; a 'life-and-soul-of-the-party' type: coll. But also used ironically, 'a real bright spark, he is'.

bright-work juice. Liquid metal-polish: *Conway* cadets': from ca. 1895. (Masefield, 1933.) Granville, 'brightwork. Any part of ship that needs to be polished daily with brass rags.' P.B.: in later C.20, used also in the motor industry for chromed bumpers, etc.

brighten (one's) **outlook.** To have one's windows cleaned; to clean the lenses of one's glasses: joc. coll.: since ca. 1920.

brightener. A dash of gin or brandy added to a soft drink: public-houses'. Robey, 1922.

Brighton Pier. Strange; ill: r.s., on *queer*: mid-C.19–20.—2. Hence, since ca. 1940, homosexual.

Brighton sands. Hands: r.s. 'Seldom heard' (Franklyn 2nd).

brill. 'Bad mood' (Butcher, 1980): nautical.—2. See:-

brilliant. Replaced *epic* and *magic* as the teenagers' vogue-word for excellent: very early 1979 (P.B.). In Liverpool, at least, it was soon shortened to *brill* (Ann Irving, May 1979); this spread to the Midlands by late 1979, and to Sloane Rangers, q.v., in the early 1980s. Anson, Christmas 1985, testified to the popularity of the expression 'ok yah, brill!' at Wadhurst Ladies' College.

bring-'em-back-alive (So-and-so). A big-game hunter that caters for zoos.

bring home the bacon. To succeed in a given undertaking: 1924 (Wodehouse: *OED* Sup.).

bring in a cooler. ' "bringing in a cooler", which meant switching the whole pack, after shuffling and cutting, for another in which the order of the cards had been specially arranged' (Drage, 1954): Can. card-sharps': early C.20. (P.B.)

bring it away. To effect an abortion: coll.

bring off. (Of a girl) to induce an orgasm in (a man); less often, (of a man) in a girl: coll.: probably since C.16. In C.20, to be classified as (familiar) S.E., even though the expression is completely ignored by the standard dictionaries: cf. the next, which it complements.

bring on. To excite sexually: coll.: prob. since C.16. (In C.20, familiar S.E.—yet unrecorded by the standard dictionaries.)—2. Hence, to delight, to please (someone) very much: Korean front: ca. 1954–5. Cf. **bring off**. P.B.: usu. in negative, as (of an objectionable person), 'I can't stand him. He doesn't bring me on one little fucking bit.'

bring on the (or one's) **china.** To effect the orgasm: low: earlier C.20. An elab. of **bring on**, 1.

brinkmanship. The practice of seeing just how far one can go in a situation already hazardous: adopted, ca. 1961, ex US: coll. >, by 1964, S.E. On the very *brink* of the precipice.—2.

Hence, the ability to win an advantage over a business, or other, competitor, esp. a position leaving this unfortunate with no genuine option: coll.: since ca. 1966; by 1975, S.E.

briny, the. See **briney**.

brisby. A coll. form (1923) of *brise-bise*, a net or lace curtain for the lower part of a window. *OED* Sup.

briskets. Female breasts: market-traders': since ca. 1925. (*M.T.*) Prob. by a pun, borrowed from butchers, for Chambers' *C.20 Dict.*, 1977, defines brisket as 'The part of the breast next to the ribs.' (P.B.)

bristler; gen. pl. A (better-class) of motor-car commandeered, in that Spanish civil war which commenced in July 1936, by the combatants, who therein rush about the streets and shoot indiscriminately all such persons as come within range: among the English colony in Spain (*The Times*, 6 Aug. 1936): ephemeral.

Bristol. See TIDDLYWINKS, in Appx.

Bristols. The female breasts: r.s., *Bristol Cities* on *titties*. P.B.: ex Bristol City 'Soccer' Club (as opp. Bristol Rovers), and prob. influenced by *breasts*—otherwise why not one of the other 'City' football teams, e.g. Leicester? See, however, **Manchester City.**

Brit. A Briton: coll. in widespread use, esp. outside the UK.— 2. A member of the British Israelite sect: coll. Usu. in pl.

Britcom, adj. *Brit*ish *Com*monwealth of Nations: among the United Nations forces in Korea: ca. 1951–5. It hovers between j. and coll.

British Brainwashing Corporation, The. The British Broadcasting Corporation: since the late 1950s. A ref. to veiled propaganda programmes.

British Standard Handfuls. See **B.S.Hs.**

British warm. A short, thick overcoat worn at first by senior, later by all, officers: Army coll. > j.

Brits. See **Brit**, 2.—2. In *have the brits up*, to be alarmed, afraid: Aus. (B., 1942.): r.s., on *shits*.

Brixton briefcase or **handbag.** Synon. for **ghetto blaster**, q.v., prob. inspired by the Brixton (London) riots of 1981. *Briefcase* in a letter in *The Times*, 22 July 1986; *handbag*: Watts, 1987, cites a recent 'Lenny Henry Show', a TV comedy series.

Brixton shuffle, the. 'Old lags . . . walk with a curious clipped gait . . . known as "The Brixton shuffle". It is a product of the prison exercise yard, where prisoners . . . had to avoid treading on the heels of the man in front' (Gosling, 1959): police s.: since ca. 1920.

bro. Brother: perhaps orig. Public Schools', then wider usage, esp. among boys: 'my bro'. Cf. the Yorkshire and Lancashire *broo*.

broach, on the. 'Stocking the bars with wines, spirits, and barrels of beer' (Marlowe, 1937): ships' stewards'. Ex the broaching of casks.

broad. A light giving flat, overall lighting. See MOVING-PICTURE SLANG, §3, in Appx. ' "Hit that broad" and "hot that broad" are orders to light up and to focus a floodlight' (*Evening News*, 7 Nov. 1939): cinema, since ca. 1930; TV, later C.20 (Green).—2. A girl, esp. one readily available: Can.: adopted, ca. 1925, ex US. Tempest, 1950, '*broad*. Popular Americanism for "half-brass". Used by those who affect Americanisms. A "broad" is a girl or woman of easy virtue who does not take money.'—3. Backside: Aus.: since ca. 1940. Harris, 1958, 'What about the blokes sitting on their broads in Seoul?' This, and sense 3, perhaps ex *broad in the beam*.—4. See **broads**.

broad brush, n. and adj. (In) general outline, without details, as 'Let me just give you the broad brush picture': Army officers' coll.: since late 1960s. (P.B., 1974.)

broad-man. A card-sharper: c. (Wallace, 1929.) Ex **broads-man.**

broad mob, the. 'Broadsmen': c.: since late C.19. Powis, 1977.

broads. Playing cards: c. from ca. 1780. Whence *broadsman*.— 2. Money in coin: c. or low:—1923 (Manchon).—3. 'Identity

B

cards. Any papers of identification, such as ration cards, insurance book, etc.' (Tempest, 1950); Powis, 1977, adds 'and recently, credit cards': c. Ex sense 1.

broadsman. A card-sharper: from ca. 1850: c. (H., 2nd ed., Leach.) Ex *broads*, q.v. Cf. **broad-man.**—2. Hence, specifically, an exponent of the three-card trick: c.: since ca. 1920. Jackson, 1946.

Brock's benefit. Very lights, star-shells, etc., over the front line: military: WW1. F. & G., 'From the annual firework display at the Crystal Palace [staged by Messrs Brock, the justly famous makers of fireworks]'. Hence, in RN since 1939, 'any pyrotechnic display of gunfire' (Granville); esp. WW2. 'Bomber slang for a particularly large display of enemy searchlights, flares, and ack-ack fire' (H. & P., 1943); in 1940–1, the spectacular aspect of a heavy German air raid: E.P., 1942.

broke. Bankrupt; very short of money. Often *dead*, *stone* or *stony broke*. Coll.: from ca. 1820. (In S.E., C.15–18.) A form of *broken* now † in S.E. but gen. enough as a sol.

broke for. In need of, esp. *broke for a feed*, hungry: Aus. coll. B., 1942.

broke to the wide. Penniless: coll.: since ca. 1910. Var. of next entry, prompted by S.E. *the wide, wide world*.

broke to the world. Penniless: coll.: since ca. 1915. A var. of prec.; both are elab. on **broke**, 1.

broken glass. See smell of broken glass.

brokko. A lowerdeck name or nickname for a spotty-faced messmate: RN: since ca. 1920. P-G-R.

brolly. An umbrella: from ca. 1873; in C.20, coll. F. & H.: 'First used at Winchester, being subsequently adopted at both Oxford and Cambridge Universities'.—2. A parachute: RAF, esp. pilots': since ca. 1930. (Beard, 1940.) Derivatively:-

brolly-hop. A parachute jump: RAF:—1932 (*Slang*, p. 259). Also as v., with frequent vbl n., *brolly-hopping* (*Daily Express*, 27 June 1934): *brolly* and *brolly-hop* ob. by mid-C.20.

bromide. A commonplace person or saying; a cliché: US, 1906 ('coined' by Gelett Burgess, who truly did coin *blurb*), anglicised by 1909; by 1930, coll. Roberts, 1934, 'Bassett occasionally put in a booming bromide.' Ex bromide, 'a dose of bromide of potassium taken as a sedative' (*OED* Sup.).

bromidic. Of the nature of a 'bromide' (q.v.): US (1906), anglicised ca. 1910; now coll. (Ibid.)

bronch. See quot'n at **bag**, v., 4.

bronza or **bronzer** is the predominantly post-1950 form of *bronzo*, ex *bronze*, anus.—2. Hence, backside: low Aus.: since ca. 1925. Niland, 1959.

bronze. A penny: Aus.: since ca. 1920. Baker.—2. Anus: Aus.: since ca. 1920. Hence the var. *bronzo*, since ca. 1935. B., 1953.

bronzer. See bronza.

bronzie (usu. in pl.). Australians. See PRISONER-OF-WAR SLANG, §8, in Appx.

bronzo. See bronze.

broody. Very thoughtful and taciturn; sullenly silent, with the implication of hatching a plan; in the Army, lethargic, slack, sleepy: coll. (F. & G.) Ex fowls inclined to sit, a C.16–20 S.E. sense. (Earlier in dial.)—2. (Of women) full of maternal feeling, as 'When I saw Sue's new baby, I came over all broody—almost wanted another of my own'. Ex the S.E. (P.B.)

Brooklands can. 'A form of silencer compulsory on racing machines at Brooklands from about 1920 until the circuit closed in 1939' (Dunford): motorcyclists'.

broom. In *get a broom!*, cancel it!: RAF: ca. 1935–45. (Jackson.) I.e. 'sweep it away!'; ex **scrub**, 1, and familiar S.E. *wash out*, 'to cancel'.

brooming-off. 'The unscrupulous or "sharp" cab driver's practice, when he is at the head of a cab rank (at the "pin position"), of refusing an unprofitable hiring and passing the intended hirer back along the cab line to a driver who will take the hiring. A practice often causing extreme bad feeling between cab drivers.' (Powis, 1977.)

Broomstick Army, the. The Local Defence Volunteers, later the Home Guard, of WW2: civilian—only very rarely Servicemen's during the war and not since—almost entirely since 1945, as in the BBC TV comedy series 'Dad's Army', ca. 1968 and later: coll. rather than s. (Petch.) Ex the broomsticks with which the early members drilled before rifles became available.

broth. See lunatic soup.

brothel(-)creepers. Suède shoes: Army (mostly officers') and Navy: 1939+. Cf. **creepers.**—2. Hence, since 1940 in Army and RAF, those short, suède, desert boots made with rubber soles made from old 'run-flat' tyres and manufactured in Egypt for use in the desert. (Sanders, who adds 'Completely silent'.)

Brothels. Brussels: Army: late 1944–5. Prebble, 1947.

brother! A mild exclamation, esp. of surprise at something unpleasant: Aus.: adopted, ca. 1943, ex US. (B.P.) Also much used by West Indian immigrants to the UK: during the 1960s, and later. (R.S., 1970.)

brother on (one's) **back, have a** (or **one's**). To be round-shouldered: RAF: since ca. 1925; †. (Emanuel, 1945.)

brought down. 'To be elated (from drugs) and then suddenly unexpectedly depressed' (Home Office): addicts': current in 1970s.

brow, the. The gangway: RN coll.: C.19–20. P-G-R.

brown, n. An error or blunder: RAF: since ca. 1935. (Partridge, 1945.) Also *brown show*. Less discreditable than a *black*.—2. Often *a bit of brown*, an act of sodomy, *brown* or *the brown* being generic: ?mid-C.19–20. Ex:—3. The anus: low: mid-C.19–20.

brown, v. To bugger: low. Cf. n., 2, and synon. low *do a brown*.

brown arm. Var. of **brown-nose**. (Watts, 1988.)

brown-back. A 10-shilling currency note. The first such notes, issued 1914–28, were red, or red and green. 'Brown-backs' were in circulation 1928–40 and 1948–70; the 1940–8 issue were mauve. Contrast **green-back**, 2, q.v. The term was rendered † by the 50-pence coin, sometimes called, nostalgically, a 'ten-bob piece (or bit)' for a few years after decimalisation in 1971.

brown bag, n.; brown-bag, v., whence **brown-bagger.** Hard work, with no social or sporting life; to live this sort of life; one who does it: Imperial College, London (—1940). Ex the little brown bags these students are reputed to carry. Marples, 2.—2. In the Army, 1950s and 60s, *brown-bagger*, a married soldier coming to barracks every day from his married quarter, carrying his lunch in a briefcase. (P.B.)

brown bomber. A car warden: Aus.: since ca. 1935. 'They wear a brown uniform. I believe that Joe Louis—"the Brown Bomber"—was top boxer at the time these policemen were introduced' (B.P.). P.B.: Harris, in the Sydney *Bulletin*, 2 Mar. 1982, p. 34, notes that this is strictly a Sydneyism; in S. Aus. a traffic warden is a *sticker licker*.

brown boots and no breakfast is applied to those who think themselves a cut above others, but without material justification for their snobbery: Leicester (?and more widespread): earlier C.20. (BBC Radio Leicester, 20 June 1984.) Cf. *fur coat* or *red hat and no knickers* or *drawers*, used to characterise a sluttish woman who is surface-smart. (P.B.)

brown bread. Dead: r.s.: later C.20. Barker, 1979.

brown creatures. Bronchitis: lower classes':—1923 (Manchon). Cf. *Bill Harris* and *Corporal Forbes*, resp. bilharzia and cholera morbus.

brown food. Beer: Services', but rarely RAF and mostly in the Navy: since ca. 1925. (H. & P.) Ex colour and (former) substantiality of beer.

brown-hatter. A male homosexual: RN: since ca. 1910. (Baxter, 1951.) By 1945, at latest, common in the other Services and, by 1950, among civilians. Also *brownie*. Powis, 1977, notes 'specifically, one of wealth or position.'

brown job. See **job**, 5.

Brown Job, the. The Army; a *brown job*, a soldier: RAF since ca. 1920 (H. & P.) and RN since 1939 (Granville). From the colour of the uniform; see **job**, 8.

brown-nose, n. and v. (To be) a toady, a sycophant: low. Cf. **brown tongue**.

Brown Nurses, the. Our Lady's Nurses: Aus. Catholics' coll. (Б.P.)

brown off, v.t. To cause a man to be **browned off**, q.v.: Army since ca. 1920; RAF since ca. 1928. H. & P.—2. V.i. To become tired of: RAF: from ca. 1920; ob.—3. V.t. To treat brusquely, send about one's business; to warn for a duty ('I'm browned off for guard duty to-night') former nuance (Army) since ca. 1930; latter (Army and RN) since ca. 1938 (Granville). Curtis, 1937; a Service example occurs in Kersh, 1941.

brown one. See **back stick**.

brown-out Romeo. A man given to molesting females in darkened streets: Aus.: 1941–5. (B., 1943.) Ex *brown-out*, a partial black-out.

brown paper. Caper (= 'game' or trick): r.s. Hillman, 1974, writes 'always used in full, as in "Wass yaw bran paper nen, mate?" '

brown show. A fairly minor blunder. See **brown**, n., 1.

brown tongue. Sycophant, toady. Mann, 1987, ' "Brown tongue" for *arse-licker* is more visible.' Cf. **brown-nose**.

brown type. An army officer: RAF: since ca. 1938. (H. & P.) Cf. **brown job** and see **type**, 2.

brown Windsor. Soap—any soap whatsoever: RAF: since ca. 1935. (Jackson.) Windsor soap issued to RAF is brown. *Daily Mail*, 7 Sep. 1940.

browncoat. 'Junior examiner at the (taxi) Police Public Carriage Office' (Powis, 1977).

browned off. (Extremely) disgruntled; depressed; disgusted: Army since ca. 1915; adopted by the RAF ca. 1929. (H. & P.) Prob. ex cookery: see Partridge, 1945, or *Forces' Slang*, ed. Partridge, 1948. Cf. **brassed off** and **cheesed off**, and note Bottrall, 1945, 'Girls browned off in Roedean' (the first appearance in true literature). But *browned off* could have been suggested by *brassed off*. A well-known, extremely well-informed RAF officer writes: 'I rather think the references are to brass buttons, which, if left uncleaned, first develop a harsh yellow or brassy effect and later go brown. I remember hearing a Regular R.A.F. N.C.O. complain that an airman's buttons were "browned off". It was obvious that for him this was the *mot juste* and far from being a joke' (letter of 1949). Nevertheless, the predominant Army opinion, from at least as early as 1940, is that the phrase was originally sodomitic.

browned up. Despondent: Cockney. (Jacobs, 1937.) Cf. prec.

brownie, -ny. A trout: anglers' coll.: from ca. 1925. *OED* Sup.—2. A male homosexual. See **brown-hatter**.—3. A cake or other confection: Can. coll., adopted ex US.—4. A bad mark: Canadian Pacific Railwaymen's: since ca. 1908. Introduced by one *Brown*. (Leechman.) In the early 1980s there were many journalistic references to synon. *brownie points*, for which the provenance was assumed to be US. However, by confusion with the Brownies, the junior Girl Guides, the sense was often altered to or assumed to mean *good* marks.

brownie box. A superintendent's carriage: Can. railroadmen's. So called because that's where 'brownies' are issued: see prec., 4. (Leechman.)

brownie points. See **brownie**, 4.

browning. Sodomy: low: late C.19–20.

browns. Uniform for civil prisoners: Borstals' and detention centres': 1970s. (Home Office.) Ex earlier *brown coat* (Tempest, 1950).

browsing and sluicing. Eating and drinking: ca. 1920–40. (Wodehouse.)

Broy Harriers. 'Men recruited into the Irish Free State Special Branch (1933–4) by the Fianna Fáil government for use in politically sensitive duties: from Eamonn *Broy* (Command-

ing IFS Police, 1933–8) and the *Bray Harriers*, a well-known hunting pack. Cf. **Black & Tans**' (Hawkins, 1987).

broy hounds. Irish Free State special tax-collecting police: Eire: from ca. 1925. On *bloodhounds*, ex the name of their first Chief.

brudge. 'Mate, friend; derived from "brother" ' (Forster, 1970): miners'.

Brummagem. Bergen, Norway: Army: 1940–1. By Hobson-Jobson.

Brummagem, adj. Counterfeit; cheap and pretentious: coll.; 1637, 'Bromedgham blades' = inferior swords. Ca. 1690, B.E., 'Bromigham-conscience, very bad [one], *Bromigham-protestants*, Dissenters or Whiggs [see *OED*], *Bromigham-wine*, Balderdash, Sophisticate Taplash.' The C.20 connotation is that of shoddiness or of showy inferiority: as such, it is coll. Ex the City of Birmingham, via local pron.

Brummagem screwdriver. A hammer: Midlands. (Merry.) The same jibe has been transferred to other places, great and small, e.g. Liverpool; and Shepshed, Leics. (P.B.)

Brummagem socialism. 'My father used to say that the political philosophy of the Chamberlain family in the 1930s was derided from within their own party as "Brummagem Socialism". (They were responsible for, among other things, founding the Birmingham Bank, the only municipal bank in the UK)' (Sayers, 1985). See **Brummagem,** adj., esp *Bromigham Protestants*.

Brummy boy. A youth or man from Birmingham: esp. Regular Army. (Kersh, 1941.)

brung. Brought: joc. use of sol. Cf. *thunk* = thought.

brush. A generic term for women: Aus. c.:—1935. Ex the pubic hair. Also, *a bit of brush*, coïtion—hence, a girl: low: mid-C.20. Dick.—2. See **broad brush; live over the brush.**

brush-off. A snub; *give* (someone) *the brush-off*, to snub: adopted, ca. 1943, ex US. As if brushing dust from one's clothes.

brush-up. To revive one's knowledge of: coll.: by 1933, thanks to the 'Brush Up Your' (e.g.) 'French' series of books, S.E.

Brussel sprout. A Boy Scout: r.s.: since ca. 1910. (Franklyn.)—2. (Often simply *Brussel*.) A racecourse tout (a watcher of horses in training): racing r.s. The famous Racing Correspondent known as 'The Scout' is, in racing circles, called 'The Brussel': Franklyn 2nd.

Brussels. A var. (from ca. 1920) of, and ex, **carpet**, n. (I.e. Brussels carpet.)—2. Elliptical for Brussels sprouts: domestic.

brute. 'A huge, self-feeding arc lamp probably named for its size—though that's too logical to have much chance of being right . . . film studio jargon' (Daniells, 1980).

Bryant and May. (Mostly in pl.) A light ale: public-houses': from ca. 1920. Via *light* from Bryant & May's matches.

Bryant and Mays. Stays: r.s.: early C.20. (B. & P.)

Brylcreem Boys, the. The RAF: Army (since ca. 1939: H. & P.) and RN lowerdeck (since ca. 1940). Granville, 'From the advertisement which depicts an airman with immaculately Brylcreemed hair.' Cf. **Crabfats**.

bubble, n. Short for **bubble and squeak,** n., 2, a Greek. (Cook, 1962.)—2. Wife: since ca. 1930. See **old bubble.**—3. See **put the bubble in; double-bubble.**

bubble, v. The short form of 'to put the *bubble* in for' someone (q.v.), or of **bubble and squeak,** v. 2, to cause him trouble by informing: since ca. 1920. (P.B., 1974.) See **no jet.**

bubble and squeak, n. Cold meat fried with potatoes and greens, or with cabbage alone. Coll. From ca. 1770. Ex the sound emitted by this dish when cooking.—2. A Greek: r.s.: from ca. 1870.—3. A magistrate: r.s. (on *beak*): late C.19–20.—4. A week: id: later C.20. Barker, 1979.

bubble and squeak, v. To speak: r.s.: (?)mid-C.19–20. *Everyman*, 26 Mar. 1931.—2. To inform to the police: underworld r.s. on the synon. 'to squeak'. (Franklyn 2nd.) Or, more prob., a specialisation of sense 1.

bubble(-)dancing. 'Pot washing in the cook-house' (H. & P.): Services': since ca. 1920.—2. Hence, washing one's irons and, at some stations, also one's plate: RAF: WW2. A pun on *bubble-dancing*, a form of strip-tease.

Bubbles and Squeaks. Greeks and Cypriots collectively: Teddy boys': since ca. 1949. (*Observer*, 1 Mar. 1959.) So many of them own or manage or man restaurants. Cf. **bubble and squeak**, n., 2—the immediate source.

bubbly, often **the bubbly.** Champagne: from ca. 1895. Also *bubbly water.*—2. Grog: RN. (Bowen.) 'Taffrail' defines it as 'rum'.—3. A look-out posted by those playing crown-and-anchor (etc.): RN. (Bowen.)—4. In ' "All bubbly?", meaning "Is everything all right?" ' (Patterson): Portsmouth dockers'.

bubbly bosun. 'That rating who serves the mess tots of rum from the "fanny", usually a different member of the mess every day' (Granville): RN: since ca. 1910. Cf. **bubbly**, 2.

bubbly water. See **bubbly.**

Bubs. Falkland Islanders: Services': 1983+. 'As the months drag on [since the 1982 War], the mocking endearments [see **benny**, 5] have changed to openly hostile ones. The new name is now "Bubs"—this is an acronym for "bloody ungrateful bastards" ' (*Observer*, 18 Dec. 1983). Cf. **wenneyes.**

Bucc. A Buccaneer aircraft: RAF coll.: later C.20. Cf. synon. **Banana Bomber.**

buck, n. Conversation: 1895 (Mrs Croker). Ex Hindustani *bak.* Also *bukh* (*OED* Sup.).—2. Hence, tall talk, boasting, excessive talk: military. F. & G.—3. Hence, impertinence, impudence: Bootham School:—1925 (*Bootham*). And, by late 1930s, in wider circulation as 'That's enough of your old buck'—which could apply equally to this and the prec. sense. (P.B.)—4. A dollar: Can.: late C.19–20; adopted ex US. By transference then to other countries using the dollar as a unit of currency, e.g. Hong Kong.—5. A rough fellow; a criminal: Liverpool: since the 1920s. Cf. the US *buck mate.*—6. In 'a load of old buck' and 'it's all a bit of buck', Army in Cyprus, late 1950s, it was short for *buckshee*, something worthless.—7. In *give it a buck* or *have a buck at* (something), to make an attempt: Aus.: since ca. 1920. (Baker.) Ex the language of the rodeo.

buck, v. In c., to fight against, withstand. Perhaps ex S.E. *buck off.* In later C.20, esp in *buck the system*, where 'the system' = any controlling organisation, whether Town Hall, the Inland Revenue, or one's employers (P.B.).—2. To boast: esp. Services': earlier C.20. Connell, 1969, quoting Sandy Reid Scott's diary, ref. a VIPs' plane-crash in 1941: 'the generals seemed disappointed at not having to swim [for their lives]—my hat, they would never have stopped bucking if they had' (P.B.).

buck for (*promotion, honours, etc.*). To make every effort to ensure recognition of oneself: often as (*be*) *bucking for*, as in 'In *Who's Who*, are you?! Be bucking for your KBE next, I suppose?' (Simmonds, 1979): orig. Services'; > gen.: since ca. 1960, perhaps earlier. (P.B.) Perhaps ex **buck**, v., 2.

Buck Guard. Guard duty at Buckingham Palace: Army. Cf. **Jimmy guard.**

Buck House. Buckingham Palace: Society. *Listener.* 10 Mar. 1937. P.B.: in RN use by 1940s, and ever since: Services'. Hawke.

buck jumper. A 'Great Eastern Tank Engine. Six-wheel coupled' (*Railway*, 2nd): railwaymen's: (?)ca. 1945–60.

buck-passing. The 1946-and-after form of *passing the buck.* Ex **pass the buck**, 2.

buck sergeant. A full sergeant: Army: WW2. P-G-R.

buck the horse. To make trouble in prison by resisting warders, etc.: c.

buckeroo. 'Anyone, among men, with whom you are friends. As in, "OK, buckeroos, let's get going!" A folky western movie or TV type actor might address children as buckeroos, all in the effort to make them feel at one with him' (Leech, 1985): Can. Orig. a cowboy in Western US, late C.19—early 20, from Mexican-Sp. *vaquero*; the orig. coll. nuance of *buckeroo* was 'more along the lines of an independent, non-conformist, outdoor-type man' (Ibid.).

bucket. As *passive bucket*, a patient listener: early C.20. (Manchon.) Making no complaint as bilge and slush are poured into it. P.B.: still in joc. or ironic use, 1980s.

bucket about. To oscillate: coll.:—1923 (Manchon). Prob. ex rowing j.—2. To 'make a splash' in one's actions and acts: Anglo-Irish: since (?)ca. 1910. See quotation at **cock-robin.**

bucket and pail. A gaol (jail): r.s. Mostly London's dockland: Franklyn 2nd.

bucket down. To rain hard: coll. Elliptical for to *rain bucketsful.* (P.B.)

bucket gaff; bucket job. A 'fraudulent company': police and underworld usage. (Powis.) Perhaps ex **bucket shop.**

bucket of beer. A pint of beer: public-house s., mostly Anglo-Irish.

bucket shop. An unauthorised office for the sale of stocks: orig. (?1881) US, anglicised ca. 1887; Ware prob. errs when he dates its English use as early as 1870. In C.19, coll.; C.20, S.E., usu. in connexion with airline ticket sales. Ex *bucket*, 'the vessel in which water is drawn out of a well' (Johnson) or ex *bucket*, to swindle, or ex the bucket into which falls the recording-tape or 'ticker'.

buckish. (Of persons) in good spirits, in excellent fettle: from ca. 1912. Ex *buckish*, (of horses) inclined to buck. *OED* Sup.

buckle. Shortened form of **buckle-my-shoe:** a Jew: r.s. B. & P.—2. See **TOMBOLA**, in Appx.

buckle-my-shoe. See prec.

Bucklebury. Euph. (—1923) for *buggery.* (Manchon.) Ex the Berkshire locality.

bucks. Short for **buckshee**, q.v. at **bakshee:** mostly Army:—1929; by ca. 1955 replaced by *buck*, if shortened at all.

Bucks hussar. A cigar: r.s.: mainly theatrical: late C.19–20. Franklyn.

buckshee has long supplanted, in spelling and pron., **bakshee**, q.v. P.B., 1974, noted that 'As a noun, it is now often pluralised: e.g., to a clerk [in the army], one might say "Can I have a spot of that bumf?"—"Sure, it's buckshees—be my guest." '

buckshee bombardier. A local NCO, i.e. with rank but no additional commensurate pay: Aus. Army: WW2. B., 1942.

bud. A débutante: Society:—1913 (Dawson); † by 1930.

Buddha sticks. '[They] went into the business of picking up drops [= caches] of Thai sticks, also known as Buddha sticks, dried and compressed cannabis from the Golden Triangle of South-East Asia' (*Guardian*, 14 July 1981, p. 14): drugs world.

buddly. See **budli.**

buddy. An American term of address (lit., brother): mid-C.19–20; partially anglicised by 1914.—2. A chum; a recruit: military: from ca. 1914. (F. & G.) See sense 1. Hence:-

buddy-buddy. Very friendly: often used disparagingly by those outside the relationship, as, e.g., 'Oh, they're all very buddy-buddy just now—but it won't last, you just wait and see': since ca. 1965, adopted ex US. (P.B.)

buddy seat. A motorcycle pillion-seat: motorcyclists': adopted ex US, 1950s. (Dunford, 2.)

budge. A promotion: Sherborne School: mid-C.19–20. A. Waugh, 1917, 'I think I had better get a "budge" this term.' Also at Harrow School (Lunn).

budgets (rare in singular). Bottled commodities, esp. toilet articles and patent medicines: fair-grounds'. Buchanan-Taylor, 1943.

budgie (or **-y**). A budgerigar: Aus. and Brit. coll.: late C.19–20. Baker.—2. 'A talkative man, especially of small stature, also used as a nickname; can be used by police to refer to a minor informer—one who has details of only "gas meter jobs" (unimportant local cases)' (Powis, 1977): since (?)ca. 1960.—3. A woman bus conductor: bus drivers': since ca. 1960. 'So called because the drivers hear them "twittering" on the platforms.' (Petch.) Cf. the RN phrase for a garrulous member of the WRNS: 'twittering like a three-badge budgie', i.e. a budgerigar with 3 long-service and good-conduct stripes.—4. In **paraffin budgie**, q.v., a helicopter. Senses 2–4 all ex sense

1.—5. ' "What's the budgie?" means "What's the time?";
very recent and used only since the introduction of Pakistani
labour. "Budgie" is a corruption of "Baje", a transliteration
from the Urdu' (Forster, 1970): coal-miners'.—6. 'Twin-
engined Hawker-Siddeley 748 [aircraft], the so-called "bud-
gies" ' (Cowan, 1982): British Airways'.

budli-bag (or perhaps *buddly-*). A kitty, or pool of cash, held
individually or in common, against 'a rainy day': RN, e.g.,
on HMS *Queen Elizabeth*: WW1. (Hardy, 1979.) ?Etym. as
next.

budli-budli, or **-ly**. Sodomy: low, esp. in India. Ex Urdu *badli*
(usu. pron. *budly*), 'change'.—2. In the late 1950s, in the
Army, it had come to mean simple exchange on a mutually
helpful basis. It had also attracted an allusive *for*, e.g., 'I'll
do your duty Sunday if you'll do mine Saturday—budli for
budli, OK?' In this instance it was unwittingly accurate, for
Y. & B. give 'Hindustani *badli*, a . . . locum tenens'. **Buggly**,
q.v., is prob. a mishearing for this.

Buenos Aires. In *go* or *take the road to Buenos Aires*, to become
a prostitute, esp. by way of a procurer's offices: coll. rather
than merely euph.: earlier C.20. Ex the Fr.

buer. Spelling used by Graham Greene in *Brighton Rock*, 1938,
for **bewer**, q.v. Also occ. to be found spelt *buor*. (P.B.)

buff. A corporal: RAF: since ca. 1919. (Jackson.) Adopted
from the Army, where, however, *orderly buff* used to mean
Orderly Sergeant: in the RAF *orderly buff* = Orderly Corporal. Cf. **buffer**, 1, perhaps the orig., via the RNAS.—2. A
stoker; esp. a *second-class buff*, second-class stoker: RN.
Granville.—3. One who, protesting that he has been swindled, threatens to go to the police: Can. carnivals'.—4. An
anal escape of wind: Oundle School. Echoic. 'Has now
reached Rugby School' (Wharton, 1965).—5. An enthusiast
of, or for, e.g. football or fires or Ned Kelly: adopted ex US
by Can., since ca. 1940; Aus., ca. 1944; and UK, since late
1940s.

buffalo. To out-bluff or out-wit, to circumvent; to overawe:
Can.: since ca. 1920; by ca. 1945, coll. Ex US, where it orig.
denoted 'to hunt buffalo'.

buffer. A boatswain's mate: RN: mid-C.19–20. (H., 3rd ed.) It
was he who, in the old days, administered the 'cat'.—2. A
petty officer: RN. (*Weekly Telegraph*, 25 Oct. 1941.) He acts
as a buffer between officers and men.—3. A boatswain,
whence *buffer's mate* and *chief buffer's mate*: RN: late
C.19–20. Ex sense 1.

buffy. To polish (esp. one's buttons): RAF: from ca. 1930; by
ca. 1950, †. P-G-R.

bug, n. A morse-key operated from side to side, instead of vertically: telegraphists' and wireless operators': since ca. 1910,
Can. and Aus.; in Brit. usage, in later C.20, often *bug-key*,
and > j.—2. An old car, rebuilt and remodelled, racing-car
fashion: Can.: ca. 1919–39. (Leechman.)—3. As *Bug*, a
Bugatti car: motorists': since ca. 1920.—4. An imperfection
in a mechanical device or invention: Can.: adopted, ca. 1945,
ex US; by 1960, at latest, Brit. also.—5. Hence, a fault, or a
delay, on a new enterprise: Aus., since late 1940s; hence also
Brit.—6. Short for **buggery**, n., q.v., in phrases such as 'daft
as bug' and 'going like bug'. (P.B.)—7. As *the Bug*, the
Natural History Museum: Rugby Schoolboys': ca.
1880–1910. 'Now any library, e.g. *the Temple Bug* = the
Temple Reading Room' (Wharton, 1965).—8. As, e.g.,
stamp bug, a collector, a 'buff': coll.: later C.20.

bug, v. To obtain shadily from: c. or low. Brandon, 1931, 'Sup-
posin' some of them [harlots] bugs a bloke for a few Brads in
a taxi'. Semantics as *sting* as an insect does.—2. To fit a building or a room with hidden microphones or transistors:
adopted, 1962, ex US.—3. To get on (someone's) nerves:
adopted, in late 1950s, ex US. Blake, 1964.—4. In **bug-out**,
q.v.

bug and flea. Tea: r.s.: esp. Army in WW1; by 1940, †. Franklyn 2nd.

bug box. A 'small four-wheeled passenger carriage' (*Railway*,
2nd): railwaymen's.

bug(-)dust. Small coal: railwaymen's: since ca. 1920. (*Railway*.)

bug-eyed monsters. See **B.E.M.s**.

bug fat. Fly repellent: market traders'. (Barnass.)

bug house. A second-rate cinema: S. Africa: since ca. 1920.
(Smith, letter, 1946.) Cf. **flea pit**, 3.

bug-house. Mad; very eccentric: anglicised, as rather low s., by
late 1936. For its usage in US, see Irwin. Adopted by Canada
in early C.20. (Niven.)

bug hut, the. See **flea pit**.

bug-hutch. 'A small hut or sleeping place' (F. & G.): Army:
WW1. Hatton, 1930, writing of 1915: '[In Egypt] we had
native beds, a framework made of palm sticks—"bug
hutches" we called them'. Later applied to any 'tatty, run-
down, dirty cinema' (Green, 2). Cf. prec.

bug-juice. Treacle: at the Borstal Institution at Portland: early
C.20.—2. Whisky: Can. (and US). (Beames.) By later C.20.,
alcohol generally. Also as *bugjuice* (Dempsey, 1975).

bug-letter. A letter in stereotyped form: typists':—1935. Perhaps orig. in the story of the man who wrote to a US railroad
company to complain about having suffered the insect-life in
their sleeping cars. He received a very polite written apology, with a promise to look into the matter, but the effect
was spoilt by someone's failure to erase the pencilled instruction, 'Send this guy the usual bug-letter.'

bug (or **bugg**) **off!** Orig. euph., then joc., for *bugger off!*, 'Run
away, stop bothering me': since ca. 1965. 'Heard on and off
on TV' (Petch, 1976).

bug-out. To protrude, as of eyes: adopted ex US, early C.20.
Mark Twain, 'Jim's eyes bugged out [with surprise].'
(P.B.)—2. To evacuate, retreat hastily: Army in Korea:
adopted ex US soldiers, 1950. See quot'n at **swan**. Also as n.
App. still in RM use (*Mail on Sunday*, 8 Nov. 1987).

bug rake. A hair comb: Aus. and Brit. juvenile: since ca. 1930
(?earlier).

bug rum. Bay rum (hair-dressing): RN lowerdeck. P-G-R.
Cf.:–

bug run. 'A parting in the hair—a gun-room phrase' (Laffin,
Jack Tar, 1969; P-G-R): RN. Implying nits in the hair. Cf.
bug rum, and **bug-walk**.

bug-trap. A small vessel; a bunk: nautical: from ca. 1890.
Because easily overrun with cockroaches. (*OED* Sup.)
Hence, in WW2 RN s., a Naval Auxiliary vessel, or any
tramp steamer. P-G-R.

bug-walk. A hair-parting: low: ca. 1890–1914. Cf. **bug run**.

bug wash. Hair oil: Felsted (and other schools): since ca. 1925.
(Marples.) Cf. **bug run**.

bug(-)whiskers. 'The result of an abortive attempt to grow a
"set",' Granville: RN: since ca. 1925. Ex Cockney s.

bugged. 'Covered with sores and abscesses from septic injection of a narcotic' (Home Office): drug addicts': current in
1970s.—2. Cf. **bug**, v., 2.

bugger, n. A man; fellow; chap: low coll.: 1719, D'Urfey. In
S.E. (C.16–20), a sodomite. In low coll. and in dial., as in the
US, the word has no offensive connotation whatsoever: cf.
the gradual and complete decolorisation of **bastard**, q.v., and
of Fr. *bougre*, as in C.19–20 *un bon bougre*, a good chap. But
also as a pej.: disagreeable person of either sex; an unpleasant, very difficult, or dangerous thing, project, episode, circumstance, as in WW1, 'It's a bugger making a raid on a wet
night.' In 1929, still an actionable word if printed (Norah
James: *Sleeveless Errand*); in 1934, no longer so (R. Blaker:
Night-Shift; Geoffrey Dennis: *Bloody Mary's*). Ex L. *Bulgar-
us*, a Bulgarian: the Albigensian heretics were often perverts. *OED*; *EDD*; and the introduction to B. & P.—2. A
person (usually male) very energetic or very skilful; esp. in *a
bugger to work—drive—drink*—what have you: Can.: since
ca. 1925. (Leechman.) Cf. the Eng. *beggar for work*, which
has presumably influenced the Eng. var. *bugger for
work*; . . . *for the women*; etc.: since ca. 1950, at latest.
(P.B.)—3. A form of rugger. See PUBLIC . . . SCHOOL SLANG,
in Appx.—4. 'An "Inquiry Agent", or a spy, who instals and

B

uses electronic listening devices (*bugs*) to acquire information surreptitiously' (*Daily Telegraph*, 7 June 1973): since ca. 1970. (R.S.) Ex **bug**, v., 2.—5. In *not a bugger*, not at all, as in *not care*, or *give, a bugger*: low coll. Dennis, 1934.

bugger, v. To spoil; ruin; check or change drastically: as a curse, since late C.18, as in *Sessions*, Dec. 1793, p. 86, 'She said, b★★st and b–gg–r your eyes, I have got none of your money'. In 1914+, *buggered* = badly wounded, done for. In WW1—and in all subsequent conflicts—the British Tommy and his Colonial peers were often heard to say, 'Well, *that's* buggered it.' Doubtless a development from the S.E. sense, to commit sodomy with. The past ppl passive, *buggered*, occurs in expletive phrases, e.g. 'Well, I'm buggered!', damned; 'you be buggered!' (cf. 'bugger you!'), go to the devil!—2. See **bugger about,** and **k.b.o.**

bugger! A strong expletive: latish C.19–20. Manchon.

bugger about. Potter about; fuss; act ineffectually; waste time on a thing, with a person. Hence, *bugger about with*, to caress intimately; interfere with (person or thing). Coll. rather than s.; in Aus. more than in Brit. Also 'to play the fool': cf. *let's play silly buggers*.—2. V.t. To stall; to be unhelpful to (someone): since ca. 1905 or, maybe, a decade earlier. (Petch cites its use in the Hansard 'The Growth of Democracy' on 7 Apr. 1968.)—3. See **bugger around.**

bugger all. Nothing. A low var. of **damn all,** q.v.; and *fuck all.* See also **Gaba.**

bugger around (on). 'To be unfaithful, usually a man unfaithful to his wife. This phrase is in common usage [in Edmonton]. Even the phrase "bugger about" is used in this connotation here in the Prairies and, I think, most of Canada' (Leech, 1980).

bugger-bafflers. Side vents at the bottom rear of a man's jacket: tailors': late 1950s. Cohn, 1971.

bugger it!; bugger me! Variants on *bugger!* used as expletive: since C.19. Chappell, 1981, article on the lower middle class, quotes: ' "Bugger me!" says a lad with a shark's tooth on a chain round his neck. "Oooh Duckie—I didn't know you cared," crows his mate [jokingly taking the order literally]'. An Aus. intensive, since ca. 1940, to express surprise, is *bugger me dead!*; the Brit. var., since ca. 1950: *bugger me gently!*

bugger off. To depart, to decamp: low: late C.19–20. Cf. **fuck off** and **piss off.** By late 1950s—e.g., Mitford, 1960—no longer low. Also, in Aus., a denial. 'An Australian friend, in the early 1960s, would gently contradict his wife's extravagant statements with, "Oh, bugger off, sweetie! You know very well . . ." ' (P.B., 1974).

buggeration factor. RAF var. of **embuggerance factor,** q.v. *Fighter Pilot*, 1981.

buggered. See **bugger,** v., 1, latter part.

buggered for (something). Lacking the wherewithal to get on with a job: low coll.: later C.20. 'Why aren't you making bricks?'—'we're buggered for straw!'

buggered if I know!, (I'm). Sorry, I just don't know: Aus. and Brit.

buggerising (or **connivering**) **about.** Aimlessly wandering or pottering: Aus.: since ca. 1935. B., 1953.

buggerlugs. A not necessarily offensive term of address: orig. mainly nautical: late C.19–20. (Brophy, 1934.) P.B.: I first heard it from a Cumbrian, during RAF National Service, early 1950s, describing the Station Warrant Officer as 'Old Buggerlugs'. Cf. the Aus. *fuck-knuckle*.—2. Those little tufts of hair which are sometimes seen on men's cheekbones: RN. Cf. **bugger's grips**.

buggeroo. An admiring description of a 'card' or 'character': non-aristocratic: since ca. 1945. The US suffix *-eroo* has been blended with *bugger*.

bugger's grips. The short whiskers on the cheeks of Old Salts: RN (lowerdeck). Also *bugger grips*. 'Tufts of biscuit coloured hair grew on his cheeks in what were called the Service "bugger's grips" ' (Winton, 1967).

buggers' muddle (often prec. by *a real* or *a right*). A shocking muddle or mess-up, 'a bloody shambles'; very common in the 'Other Ranks' of the Army during WW2, but prob. going back to ca. 1920.

buggers' opera, the. See **sod's opera.**

buggery. (In S.E., sodomy: like *bugger* and *to bugger*, it is the correct legal term: see *OED* and *SOD*.) In C.20 unconventional English, it occurs in several strong and violent phrases, often of rejection, e.g., (*all*) *to buggery*, completely, destructively, ruinously. In WW1, 'Our batteries shelled poor old Jerry to buggery' (Manchon); (*Oh*), *go to buggery!*, even stronger (in intention) than 'Go to Hell!'; also as *get to buggery!*—'Go away!'. As strong and disapproving denial: 'Did he do the decent thing? Did he buggery!'—No, indeed he did not. 'Will he do it? Like buggery he will!'—No, there is no chance that he will. *Like buggery*, used adverbially, always implies that the action is being done vigorously, but also, often, cruelly or vindictively.

buggie. A bugbear; a bogy: joc. when not merely illiterate: since ca. 1925.

Buggins Principle, the. See **next in line for admiral.** Many of these imaginary principles and laws have arisen in the wake of *Parkinson's Law*, but *Buggins's* is perhaps an older, Civil Service, var.

buggly. To exchange, to swap: Army: earlier C.20. (F. & G.) Perhaps a mis-hearing of **budli,** q.v.

buggy. A motor-car: since ca. 1945. (Creasey, 1949.) Cf. **blood-waggon.**

bugjuice. Alcohol. See **bug-juice,** 2.

bugle. Nose: Can. Cf. **hooter,** 2.—2. In *on the bugle*, malodorous: Aus.: since ca. 1930.

bugle bag. 'The in-flight sick bags provided for relief of queasy passengers' (Green): airline crews'.

Bugs. Synonym of **Bats,** 2: RN: the deck-landing officer on an aircraft-carrier: since ca. 1939. (Granville.) With a pun on **bats,** adj.

bugs, n. Bacteria; bacteriology: medical students':—1933 (*Slang*, p. 191).—2. Biology: schools': since ca. 1935. (*New Society*, 22 Aug. 1963.) Cf. sense 1, and *stinks*, chemistry.

bugs, adj. Mad, crazy, eccentric: orig. US, > by 1925, Can. Ex either a 'conflation' of *bug-house* or *crazy as a bed-bug*. Spread to UK via the popular film-cartoon 'character' 'Bugs Bunny'.

build. To stack a pack of cards. See **milk,** 3.

build up, n. & v. 'To describe most favourably in advance of an appearance. "He gave her a terrific build-up." Movie personalities are "built up" for their audiences in many and strange ways.' (Leechman.) Since ca. 1925: a coll. that, by 1955 at latest, was familiar S.E.

built for comfort. (Of a man) stout; (of a woman) agreeably plump.

built-in obsolescence. Old age, applied to people: esp. in early 1950s, but not yet (1976) †. (E.P.) Applied to things like motor-cars, it is mere j. for an immoral and wasteful practice. (P.B.)

bukra. Tomorrow: Army: since ca. 1880; but esp. among British and Dominion troops in the Middle East in the two World Wars. (*Rats*.) Ex Arabic for 'tomorrow'.

bulge. 'Bilge', q.v.: from ca. 1922. (Manchon.) Cf. Austin Reed's clever advertisement, 1935, of a waistcoat that doesn't bunch up (*Talking bulge*). Prob. of joc. origin via nautical j.

bull, n. An elephant: circusmen's. Short for '*bull* elephant'.—2. A policeman; esp. a detective: c., adopted ex US.—3. 'A wharf labourer unfairly favoured for employment' (Wilkes): Aus. dockers' coll.: later C.20.—4. Short for **bullshit,** q.v., in all its senses: perhaps Aus. before Brit.: since early C.20. Hence the Can. *peddle the bull* and *bull-peddler*, to talk nonsense, and one who does this: since ca. 1945; earlier Can., since ca. 1919, was *shoot the bull*, with derivative *bull-session*.

bull, v.i. To toil; to struggle: Can., esp. lumbermen's. Beames.—2. To brag; talk nonsense: Aus.: since ca. 1925. (B.) Like n., 4, ex **bullshit.** Hence, a *bull-artist,* one given to these failings. Cf.:—3. To put something across (one's superior officer): Army: WW2.—4. To polish, esp. one's boots; to apply any form of cleaning to uniform, equipment or quarters: Services': since 1950 certainly, prob. much earlier. Often as *bull up,* v.t. and i. Ex **bullshit,** n. and v.

bull and boloney. Idle talk; hot air: Guards Division: since ca. 1938. See the elements.—2. Hence, spit and polish *plus* window dressing: Army: WW2.

bull-ants. Trousers: Aus. r.s., on pants: since ca. 1930. Franklyn 2nd.—2. In *feel as if* (or *though*) one *will* (or *would*) *give birth to bull-ants,* to feel much out of sorts, ill: Aus. B., 1942.

bull artist, bullshit artist. Synonyms of **bullshitter,** than which, by 1960, they were commoner; since ca. 1916. All three, Aus.; the 1st, also NZ, also with derivative sense, a smooth talker, esp. of a travelling salesman, as in Slatter.

bull-dogging. A rodeo method of throwing a steer by grasping one horn and the muzzle and twisting the neck: Can.: ca. 1910–45. The term was replaced by *steer-decorating.*

bull-dust or **-fodder,** n. Nonsense: Aus.: since ca. 1919. (B., 1943.) By ca. 1940, also English. Euph. for *bullshit.*

bull-dust, v. To talk nonsense; esp., to 'kid': Aus.: since ca. 1920. ' "Fairdinkum?" said Ritchie. "Or are yuh bull-dustin'?" ' (Dick.) Ex the n.

bull fiddle. A bass viol: Can. (Leechman.) Also Brit. *New Society,* 14 Jan. 1982, p. 46, quotes an anecdote of Sir John Barbirolli talking of 'the "bull" fiddle', by which the famous conductor seems to mean the double bass. (P.B.)

bull-fuck. Custard: Can. railroad-construction crews': since ca. 1910.

bull it through. To accomplish something—esp. an outdoor task—by sheer strength rather than by skill and planning: Can. coll. (Leechman.) Cf. **bull,** v., 1.

bull-juice. Condensed milk: mostly nautical: since ca. 1920. Harbinson, 1961.

bull-night. An evening during which recruits and trainees are confined to barracks in order to prepare for inspection by CO or adjutant the next day: Services': since ca. 1945, but esp. during the period of National Service (ended 1962).

bull-trap. A crook impersonating a policeman in order to extort money from amorous couples: Aus. c.: since ca. 1930. B., 1942.

bull up. See **bull,** v., 4.

bull week. 'Local name for the week before the annual shutdown and holiday in Midland factories—"That's when we all work like bulls" ' (*Time Out,* 25 Apr. 1980). Since earlier C.19, when *bull-week* was the week before Christmas, and *calf-* and *cow-week* the two before that.

bulldoze, (orig. hyphenated). To flog severely; hence coerce by violent methods, esp. in politics. Orig. US, anglicised ca. 1880 as a coll. Hence *bulldozer,* an applier of violent coercion. Lit., to give a dose strong enough for a bull: W., however, thinks there may be some connexion with † Dutch *doesen,* to strike violently and resoundingly.—2. Hence, to ride roughshod over (someone); to force; to cow, to bully; to force a way through for a course of action: adopted, ca. 1959, ex US. Ex the S.E. term for a heavy caterpillar vehicle fitted with a broad steel blade in front used for removing obstacles and clearing land.

bulldozer. A 'locomotive for shunting coaches and taking them to termini for outgoing trains' (*Railway*): railwaymen's: since ca. 1945.—2. A 'battle-axe'; occ., a virago: since latish 1940s. (Petch, 1969.)

bulldozing around. An aimless wandering or prowling around: Aus. (at first, Army): since ca. 1940. B., 1953.

bulled(-)up. Dressed as if for parade: Army: since ca. 1943. (Thomas, 1966.) Ex *bull,* spit-and-polish: see **bullshit,** n., 2.—2. Hence, 'tarted up' or ostentatiously embellished: since ca. 1945. Deighton, 1968.

bullet. (Gen. pl.) A hard, round sweet: schoolchildren's coll. From dial. and ex hardness.—2. (Always pl.) peas: Services'. P-G-R.—3. A capsule: drugs c. (Stockley, 1986.) US since mid-1960s (Spears).

bullivant. A large, clumsy person: Cockney: since ca. 1880: by 1940, slightly ob. A blend of *bull* + *elephant.* (L.H. Perraton, letter, 1938.)

bullock's (or **bullocks') blood.** 'Strong ale and rum—extremely costive' (Gilbert, 1949): public-houses': since ca. 1920. He-man stuff.

bulls. Counterfeit coin: low or perhaps c.:—1923 (Manchon).—2. *The bulls,* the police: Aus., adopted ca. 1944 ex US. (Dick.) See also **bull,** n., 4.—3. Nonsense, rubbish; 'bullshit': Aus.: since ca. 1940. Buzo, 1969.

bull's foot. See **B from a bull's foot** under KNOW, in Appx.

bullsh. See next.

bullshit (earlier **bull-shit**), n. Nonsense; empty talk; humbug-(ging): mostly Aus., ?ex US. Often abbr. *bullsh* or *bulsh* (mostly Aus. and NZ) and *bull:* RN: early C.20 (Bowen); and, perhaps a little later, the other Services also.—2. Hence (also in forms *bulsh* and esp. *bull*), 'excessive spit and polish' or attention to detail; regimentalism: Services': since ca. 1916. Hence *bullshit morning,* that morning on which the CO's inspection takes place: Services': since ca. 1920. Cf. *bull-night,* its necessary prelude.

bullshit, v.t. and i. To deceive a person, or to 'pull his leg'. 'Are you bullshitting me?' could be the indignant enquiry of the victim: esp. Forces': since ca. 1925.—2. To prepare, in the Services, for an inspection of one's person or quarters: since WW2. Often as *bullshit up:* e.g., 'We've got to get this place bullshitted up—the CO's round tomorrow morning'; occ. joc. *bullshat,* 'Don't touch that, it's just been bullshat!' (P.B.)

bullshit and bang-me-arse. Excessive regimentalism + a little Patton-like showmanship: Army in NW Europe: 1944–5.

Bullshit Towers. 'The flying control tower, because Flying Wing HQ was usually therein; RAF, 1941–3' (French).

bullshitter. A boaster; one addicted to empty talk: since ca. 1915, esp. Aus. In mid-C.20, there were even cards printed for handing to such a one as he held forth; they read: 'I'm a bit of a bullshitter myself, but do carry on . . .' (P.B.)—2. In youth gangs, esp. at soccer matches, 'The major characteristic of this role is pretending to be someone else' (Marsh, 1976)—and, of course, exaggerating and boasting: a sense current since ca. 1960. But it has been in very gen. use since the late 1930s as a natural development of sense 1.

bullshot. 'A drink my grandfather drank while at sea some sixty years ago. It was simply two shots of vodka, one spoonful of Bovril [meat extract] and a quarter pint of hot water. The whole mess was called "bullshot" . . . Needless to say, we still drink it' (Power, 1976).

bully-beef. A chief (esp. warder): low r.s., esp. in prisons: since ca. 1919. Norman.—2. adj. Deaf: Scottish r.s. (on pron. *deef*): since ca. 1945. Franklyn 2nd.—3. See **corned beef.**

bully-splog. 'A desert dish—a ragoût of bully beef and crushed biscuits' (Sanders, 1967): Army in N. Africa: 1940–3.

bulsh. See **bullshit.**

bum, n. The buttocks: dating from M.E.; not abbr. *bottom,* which, in this sense, dates only from C.18; prob. echoic: cf. It. *bum,* the sound of an explosion. This good English word began to lose caste ca. 1790, and ca. 1840 it > a vulg. and has been eschewed.—2. A beggar; a cadger: ex US. See **hobo;** cf. v., 1.—3. In *have a bit of bum,* to coït with a woman: low: late C.19–20. P.B.: but in later C.20, more likely to mean sodomy.—4. In *on the bum,* a-begging. Ex 2.—5. In *on the bum,* broken: Can. See **on the fritz.**—6. See **airing.**

bum, v. To beg (v.t. and i.), esp. as a tramp: low coll.: ex US. This sense prob. derives as much from Ger. *Bummler,* a happy-go-lucky vagabond, as from *bum,* n., 1.—2. To boast: low (esp. in Glasgow). Cf. **bum the chat,** lit. to boast about the thing.—3. To loaf about, as a tramp does; to wander idly: Aus.: since ca. 1920. Lindsay, 1933, ' "Know what you are?" he said sternly. "A stinkin' young skite. Come bummin' in here skitin' about knockin' girls you get a hidin'." '—4. To cadge: since ca. 1944. 'Can I bum a fag off you?' A milder use of sense 1.

bum, adj. Inferior, bad; reprehensible: WW1 s. >, by 1930, coll.; orig. US, in its sense of a tramp or loafer.

bum-boy. A catamite: low coll.: late (?mid-)C.19–20.—2. One who gets the dirty jobs to do.—3. A sycophant. ' "A lot of bum-boys attached to the staff of some bloody general" ' (Manning, 1930).

bum-drops. Hen's eggs: since ca. 1930. (Parsons, 1973.) ?A pun on *gum-drops*; cf. **hen-fruit** and **cackle-berry.**

bum-face. A low derogatory form of address. (Leech, 1972.)

bum flapper. A split **mini-skirt,** q.v. at **mini:** teenagers', esp. Punks': ca. 1980. Reid, 1980.

bum-freezer. An Eton jacket: C.19–20, low.—2. Hence a Midshipman's round jacket: RN. Granville records the var. **arse-perisher.**—3. The short white jacket worn by doctors in hospitals: medical.—4. Any mess-jacket cut on the lines of an Eton jacket: Services'. (P.B.)

bum-fuck. Digital massage of prostate via anus and rectum, as diagnostic and therapeutic procedure in treatment of gonorrhœa: low.

bum-fucker; corn-holer; gooser. A pederast: low Can.

bum-hole, n. Anus: low, orig. proletarian: prob. mid-C.19–20.

bum hole, adj. Occ. var. of **piss-hole,** q.v., bad, inferior: mid-C.20.

Bum Island (or **Blanket Bay**), **in the lee of.** Lying in bed with one's random 'lay', beloved or, esp., wife: mostly MN: late C.19–20. (H.P. Mann, 1972.)

bum-licker. A toady: low coll.

bum (one's) **load.** To lounge in the canteen while one waits for a comrade to come and pay for one's drink: Army:—1923 (Manchon).—2. To boast: Anglo-Irish, and Guardsmen's: since ca. 1930. Also, in RAF, *bum one's chat* (L.A.): since 1939.

bum numb. With buttocks partially paralysed from sitting on a hard seat or too long in one position: Public Schoolboys'.

bum-numbing. The effect of having to endure frustrating circumstances, e.g., a job, 'until after the spirit revolts' (L.A., 1976). Ex the prec., literal, entry.

bum-robber. An active male homosexual: low: perhaps since ca. 1880. (Leech, 1972.) Cf. **turd-burglar.**

bum-starver. A short coat: from ca. 1920. Onions, 1930.

bum steer: esp. *give* (someone) *a bum steer*, to give bad advice or information or directions: Can.: since ca. 1925. Also Aus. and Brit. since ca. 1944. See **steer.**

bum-tags. 'Deposits of faecal matter in the hair about the anus': low. Cf. synon. *clinkers* since ca. 1830.

bum the chat. See **bomb the chat** and **bum,** v., 2.

bum trip. A bad *trip* or experience of a psychedelic drug: since ca. 1965. (Scaduto, 1974.) Var. of **bummer,** 1.

bum up. To compliment (a person): military: since ca. 1925.

bum-waggle. To perform in the sport of road-walking; hence *bum-waggler, -ling:* sporting: (?mainly Aus.) sporting. I heard, 'I'm a bum-waggler—I've walked all round Singapore Island', from an Australian Warrant Officer, ca. 1969. Ex the exaggerated motion of the posterior. (P.B.)

bumbershoot. An umbrella: Can.: since (?)ca. 1930. (Leechman, 1970.)

bumble-jar. Orig. a harmonium, but, as these instruments became rarer and were superseded by gramophones, the term was transferred to the latter: since early C.20; by ca. 1930, predominantly 'gramophone'. Bowen; Granville.

bumble (someone) **rumble.** To have a traffic accident. See **rumble** (someone) **bumble.**

bumblebug. An early (?the orig.) nickname for the flying bomb; soon superseded by **doodle-bug:** mid-1944.

bumblebus. 'Wildcat' aircraft of the Fleet Air Arm: RN: WW2.

bumf, n. A schoolboys' and soldiers' abbr. of *bum-fodder*, which since mid-C.17 has meant toilet paper: mid-C.19–20. Hence, from ca. 1870, any paper. In WW1+, chiefly among officers: 'orders, instructions, memoranda, etc., especially if of a routine nature, e.g. "snowed under with bumf from the Division" ' (B. & P.). The RN used pink bumf for 'a confidential signal pad' (Granville): from ca. 1920.—2. Hence, any collection of papers in which one is not interested: since ca. 1945.—3. At Rugby School, any piece of paper, e.g. a test paper (cf. **topos bumf**): late C.19–20. *The bumfs* = the daily Press. (Wharton, 1965.)

bumf, v.i. and t. To listen to or butt in on the conversation of others: Charterhouse.—2. (Ex sense 3 of the n.) To give a test: Rugby School. (Wharton, 1965.)

bumfleteer. See **bumphleteer.**

bummer. A *bum trip* or bad experience of a drug: orig. addicts', then the world of entertainment: adopted, late 1960s, ex US.—2. Hence, any bad, luckless, very unpleasant situation: adopted, ca. 1969, ex US. *Jagger* (Janssen); Stuart, 1971, 'This entire situation is one ultimate bummer'.—3. A rank failure, as a film or as a radio or TV programme: world of entertainment: since ca. 1970. R.S. cites the *Observer*, 7 Dec. 1975.—4. A sodomite: low. Noted in a graffito, 1967. L.A. adds, 1974, the RN var. *bummer-boy*, ?a pun on drummer boy.—5. See **John Selwyn.**

bumming. Loafing, sponging: from ca. 1895, orig. US. Often, in later C.20, *bumming around*, as 'he spent the whole summer just bumming around.'

bumming the chat. Var. of *bombing the chat*, q.v. at **bomb . . .** F. & G.

bump, n. An uneven landing; bumpy flying: RAF coll.: since ca. 1919; by 1940, almost j. H. & P.—2. Hence any landing of an aircraft: coll.: since ca. 1930. (Jackson.) See **three months' bumps.**—3. A 'bumping-off', a planned killing, an assassination: near-c. and espionage. Hall, 1966: 'the death of Primero, and it was Zotta who did the bump'. Cf. the v., 2.—4. See **feel** (someone's) **bump.**

bump, v. A c. var. (from ca. 1915) of US *bump off*, to murder (1910: *OED* Sup.). Wallace.—2. To polish a wooden or linoleumed floor with a 'bumper': Services: since ca. 1925. P-G-R.—3. To fight successfully: Aus.: WW2. B., 1942.

bump off. To kill, destroy, criminally: underworld, then more gen. Adopted ex US. Cf. **bump,** n., 3, and v., 1.—2. Hence, to dismiss (someone) from employment: since ca. 1940; ob.

bumped or **pipped, get.** To be torpedoed by U-boat or even by E-boat (German high-speed motor torpedo boat): RN: WW2.—2. Of NCOs, to get reduced in rank: Army: since 1939. By 1950s, often with *down*, as 'Did you hear about Staff-sergeant X. Bumped down to corporal, he was—something to do with the mess accounts.' (P.B.)

bumper, n. A cigarette end: Aus.: since ca. 1920. (B., 1942.) Ex '*bu*tt' + 'stu*mp*' + *er*. Hence, *not worth a bumper*, utterly worthless: Aus.: since ca. 1930.—2. An amateur rider in steeplechases: racing: since ca. 1930. His hindquarters tend to *bump*.

bumper, adj. Excellent: coll. Now (1970s) chiefly in the terms *bumper harvest* (almost S.E., certainly cliché) and the joc. *bumper fun-book*. (P.B.)

bumper hat. A safey helmet: Portsmouth dockers'. Patterson.

bumper-shooter. A picker-up of cigarette-ends: Aus.: since ca. 1940. B., 1953.

bumper-sniping. The task of picking up cigarette butts: Aus. Army: WW2. B., 1943.

bumper-up. A dockyard labourer.—2. A pickpocket's assistant: Aus. c.: since ca. 1920. B., 1943.—3. A prostitute's handyman: Aus. c.: since ca. 1925. Also *bumper-upper* or *candy-bag*. B., 1953.—4. 'A fifth horn to bolster a horn quartet, known in orchestral circles as "the bumper-up" ' (Jack Brymer on BBC Radio 3, 28 Aug. 1976).

bumpers. Female breasts: Aus. motorists': since ca. 1950; by 1960, at latest, also in UK. (Cuddon, 1967.) Cf. *buffers.*—2.

In *ride bumpers*, to ride in steeplechases: racing: since ca. 1925. (Welcome, 1965.) Cf. **bumper, n.**, 2.—3. Undergraduates' drinking ritual at Cambridge University: undergraduates': later C.20. Ex S.E. *bumper*, a full glass.

bumph is an occ. var. of **bumf.**

bumphleteer. An aircraft (or its crew or a member thereof) engaged in pamphlet-dropping: RAF: Sep. 1939–Apr. 1940, and then the scene was changed, the war ceasing to be either 'phoney' or funny. Jackson.

bumping. Delaying or obstructing a bill: Parliamentary: since ca. 1920. Herbert, 1936.

bumping-off. A murder: c.: from ca. 1932. (Brandon, 1936.) From US and ex **bump off,** 1.

bumping on the bottom. (Of market prices that have reached their lowest level: Stock Exchange:—1935. Ex boating.

bum's rush, get or **give the.** To be kicked out, or to kick out; more precisely, by that method of forcible ejection which consists in the application of one hand to the seat (often a grasping of trouser-slack), the other to the neck, and the ensuing propulsion. Common to bar-tenders and police. It occurs in O'Flaherty, 1925. Prob. adopted, early C.20, ex US.

bun. Synonym for *tart*, a young woman, recorded by B. & L. in 1889. At that time, a *tart* was not necessarily 'fast' or loose, as, except in dial., e.g. Birmingham, it had become by ca. 1920. However, *bun*, at least in Glasgow by 1934, did come to mean a harlot.—2. In *get a bun on*, to become intoxicated: lower class: early C.20. George, 1914.—3. In *have a bun in the oven*, to be pregnant: low: C.19–20.

bun-beat or **-fight.** A tea-party: late C.19–early 20: coll. Cf. *crumpet-scramble*, *muffin-worry*.

bun-house. See **over the bun-house.**

bun shop. A Lyons Corner House: London taxi-drivers': 1909–1950s. Hodge, 1939.

bun(-)trap. The mouth: low—or, at any rate, strictly non-U. Cf. **cake-hole.**

bunce (the predominant C.19–20 spelling), **bunse, bunt(s), n.** Money: C.18–early 19. In mid-C.19–20 it = (costermongers') perquisites; profit; commission. Cf. later synon. **brick.** In C.20, almost coll. and still = profit, but more esp. and gen. an unexpected profit or commission or receipt of money. Mayhew pertinently proposes derivation ex sham L. *bonus*, q.v.—2. Money earned by working overtime: workmen's: C.19–20.—3. Sheer, or almost sheer, profit; something for nothing: since ca. 1920. Ex sense 1 in its C.20 nuances. Common, after ca. 1930, in Aus. B., 1953.

bunce, v. To overcharge someone, esp. if obviously rich or eager: market traders'. *M.T.*

buncer. The agent corresponding to the v. of prec. entry: market traders'. *M.T.*

bunch. A group or gang of persons: from ca. 1905: s. >, by 1936, coll. *COD*, 1934 Sup.—2. The main group in a race, apart from *the breakaway*: racing cyclists' coll.: since ca. 1925.—3. In *the best of the bunch*, the best of them all. But usu., since mid-C.20, slightly derogatory, as in the set phrase 'the best of a bad bunch' (P.B.).—4. See **thanks a bunch.**

bunch (or **bundle**) **of bastards.** 'A hopelessly tangled jumble of rope' (Peppitt): RN lowerdeck: since ca. 1946, perhaps pre-WW2, and still current in the early 1960s.

bunch of charms. A girl, esp. if attractive: coll.

bunch of fives. The hand; fist: pugilistic, then gen. low. An early occurrence is in *Boxiana*, III, 1821. *Punch*, 1882, has 'his dexter bunch of fives'.

bunch of snarls. A disagreeable man: tailors'. *Tailor and Cutter*, 29 Nov. 1928.

buncing, vbl n. corr. to **bunce, v.**—2. Putting a ½p on selected lines, thus implying a concession: supermarket usage: since ca. 1970. (L.A., 1976.)

bunco. 'Fraud generally; sometimes false and flattering "chat" by a man to a woman. Originally exclusively an American expression, brought into use by "hippy" persons and by West Indians who have previously lived in the USA: "Don't give me that, man—I've been buncoed by experts!" means "Don't try to deceive me!" ' (Powis): underworld and its fringes. Ex **bunko,** the earlier preferred spelling, meaning 'fraud'.

bund. A wall or barbed-wire fence marking the perimeter of a Station: RAF: since ca. 1925. (Jackson.) From Persia and India, prob. ex word for 'dam' or 'dyke'.

bundle, n. A considerable sum of money: racing coll. Cf. *packet*. *OED* Sup.—2. A fight: workmen's (—1935) and criminals (—1936).—3. Hence, specifically, a gang fight: teenage gangsters' and hooligans': since early 1950s. Cf. **rumble**; see the v.—4. See **go a bundle (on)**; **go the bundle.**

bundle, v.i. To fight with one's fists: low. Behan, 1958, ' "Oh, so you want to bundle, you Irish bastard?" said Hanson. "Come on, then." ' Cf. synon. *bundle up*, C.19 s. for 'to attack (someone) in force'.

bundle of bastards. Hopelessly tangled rope. See **bunch of bastards.**

bundle of socks. The head: Aus. r.s., on 'think-*box*': late C.19–20. Baker, 1945.

bundle of ten. Army blankets, because rolled in tens: military: late C.19–20. F. & G.—2. A packet of ten cigarettes: id. Ibid.—3. The tens in a pack of cards: id. Ibid.

bundoo, bondu, bundu. Wilderness, desert; the bush, the jungle; the countryside, e.g. in N. Ireland; usu. *out*, or *off*, *in the bundoo*: Army, since mid-1950s; by later C.20, also other Services', as in 'out in the frozen "bundu", at surrounding temperatures of 30° below freezing' (Winton, 1979). Prob. ex the synon. S. African (Bantu) word *bundu* (*OED* Sup.), perhaps adopted during the campaign against the Mau-Mau in the early 1950s, but perhaps influenced by synon. **boondocks,** q.v. Also as adj., e.g. in the RAF coll. *bundu boots*: 1970s. (Wilson; P.B.)

bundook; occ. **bandook** or **barndook;** even, says Manchon, **bundoop.** A rifle; earlier, a musket; earlier still, cross-bow. Ultimately ex the Arabic *banadik*, Venice, where cross-bows were made. (Native Egyptians still call Venice *Bundookia*.) The Army stationed in India used the term as early as C.18, and in WW1 it became fairly common throughout the army; by 1920, it was popular also with the RAF (Jackson); in the 1970s it was still quite common in army usage. According to Bowen, it signified a big gun in the earlier C.20 RN. The etym. is set out at length in Y. & B. but has been disputed.

bundu. See **bundoo.**

bung, n. Cheese: military. Ex its costiveness. Also *bung-hole* and *bungy*. F. & G.—2. A poke, blow, punch: low: late C.19–20. Lyons, 1902, 'Only yesterday, said he, I got another bung in the eye'. Echoic: cf. sense 3 of the v.—3. A bungalow: since ca. 1920.—4. A bribe, esp. to the police: low: since ca. 1930. Norman.

bung, v. Often as *bung over*, to pass, hand (over), give; (not before C.20) to send (a person, e.g. into the RN; or a thing, e.g. a letter to the post): coll. Shakespeare, Beaumont & Fletcher.—2. To pay protection money to (someone): low: since ca. 1925. 'Sergeant Connor. He's one of them slime-sniffers [the Vice Squad]. Every girl in Bayswater bungs to him if she wants to stay on the game' (Turner, 1968).—3. Hence, to tip (someone, with money): since ca. 1950. Naughton, 1970, 'Bakey was nervous of bunging him, although the blagging [wheedling] came over dead strong'. (L.A.) Cf. **bung-ons.**—4. Applied also to large-scale bribery: cf. (cf. 2, 3): (mainly Cockney) coll.: later C.20. 'When bribery in high places is in the news, Cockneys agree that it encompasses lots of politicians and business men: "They all get bunged, don't they?" ' (*Muvver*). Contrast *drop*, small-scale bribery.

bung, adj. and **adv.** Precisely, absolutely: coll. Manchon, 'He's bung in the fairway.'—2. Spurious, illegal; grossly inadequate: Aus.: since ca. 1925. B., 1943.

bung (someone) **a toffee.** To do him a favour, esp. if considerable: London's East End: since ca. 1947 (Herd).

B

bung-full. Full right up; 'chockablock'; full, in fact, right up to the bung or stopper: coll. (P.B.)

bung-ho! Au revoir!; occ., good-bye!: from ca. 1925. (Sayers, 1933, 'Cheerio, Mary dear. Bung-ho, Peter.') Perhaps on *cheer-ho*.—2. Also as an upper-class toast: 1928 (Sayers). Perhaps with a ref. to the bung of liquor casks. In both senses, sometimes as *bung-ho, troops!* (P.B.)

bung(-)hole. Cheese. See bung, n., 1. Both *bung* and *bung hole* are also RN. Granville.—2. Hence (via *bread and cheese*), bread: military: since ca. 1925. (H. & P.) Constipating.—3. A bungalow: middle-class coll.: since ca. 1930. An elab. of an abbr.—see **bung**, n., 3. (P.B.)—4. The anus: low: C.18–20.

bung in it!, put a. Shut up!; shut the door!

bung it in; often shortened to *bung it*. Gin (the drink): r.s.: since ca. 1920. (Harrison, 1947.)

bung off. To depart; to die: from ca. 1905. Brandon, 1931, 'He . . . bunged off, respected by everyone.'

bung on. To dress oneself, as in 'Just hang on while I bung on a coat and some boots . . .': coll.—2. To organise, put on, as, e.g., a party or a show: 'considering the celebration had to be bunged on at the last moment . . .'. Cf.:-

bung on an act. 'To swear luridly, give way to temper, complain at length' (B., 1959): Aus.: since ca. 1920.

bung on side. To put on 'side', to show off: low Aus. coll.: since ca. 1910. (Tennant, 1953.) Cf.:-

bung on the bull. 'To put on airs, to behave pretentiously' (Buzo, 1973): Aus.: since mid-1945. See **bullshit.**

bung one on (someone). To hit him, as in 'He was getting a bit stroppy so I bunged one on him [*or* I bunged him one on]': low: since ca. 1950, poss. earlier. (P.B.)

bung one up. To salute: Services': mid-C.20. 'Well, there was this major just standing there, so I bunged him one up . . .'

bung-ons. Gifts: mock-auctions': since ca. 1930.

bung up and bung free. Everything aboard in excellent order: nautical: late C.19 s., > by 1920 coll.; by 1930, j. Ex the proper storing of barrels.—2. Hence, of a sailor enjoying a rest or sleep: RN: since ca. 1910. Granville.—3. A RN c.p. (late C.19–20) for *femina in coitu*. Ex the description of the correct position for a rum cask.

bungaloid. Infested with bungalows; esp, in *bungaloid growth* after *fungoid growth*. Coll. quickly promoted to S.E.; from ca. 1926.

bungalow, top of the bleeding. See TOMBOLA, in Appx.

bungie, bungy. (Orig. *injie-* (or *inja-*) *bungie*, pron. *bunjie*.) A typist's eraser: typists':—1935. *Injie*, ref. to ink, and with *inja*, sol. for the *India* of india-rubber; *bungie*, from the feel of it; but cf. the dial. *bungy*, anything short and thick. (E.P.; P.B.) Cf. **bunjie.**

bungs. Dutch half-castes (a var. spelling of **boongs**, q.v.). See PRISONER-OF-WAR SLANG, §8, in Appx.

bunjie or **-jee.** A physical training instructor: RN. (F. & G.) Orig., according to Bowen, where spelt *bungie*, or *bungy*, the term was *bungie man*. Granville notes that after ca. 1925, it was shortened, and often to just *bunjie*.—2. An elastic strap with a hook at either end, used for securing, e.g. luggage to a pillion: motorcyclists': later C.20. (Bishop, 1984.)

bunk, n. Nonsense: abbr. **bunkum**, q.v. Ex US.—2. 'A small Corporals' Barrack Room usually just outside the Men's Barrack Room. It contains their bunks or beds; the Corporals *bunk down* (or "kip" or sleep) there,' Partridge, 1945: RAF coll. (since ca. 1925) >, by 1944, j. Also, and perhaps earlier, in the Army, where it is, in later C.20, applied (as j.) also to single bedrooms in the sergeants' mess. (P.B.)—3. 'Freight or passenger train on Wallingford or Abingdon branches' (*Railway*, 2nd): railwaymen's: ?ca. 1920–50.—4. A Can. term of disapproval for anything disliked or unwanted: since ca. 1920. Ex sense 1.—5. As *the Bunk*, Head Office: London busmen's: 1930s. (*Daily Herald*, 5 Aug. 1936.) A comfortable billet.

bunk, v. To decamp: from early 1890s: orig. low; in C.20, near-coll. *The Referee*, 16 Feb. 1885.—2. Hence, to absent oneself from, to play truant: from ca. 1890. Mottram, 1934, 'I'll bunk my class and take you for a walk.' See **bunk off**, 2.—3. A synon. of **double-dink**, q.v., to carry a second person on the top bar of a bicycle. B., 1959.

bunk off. Aus. var. of **bunk**, v., 1. B., 1942.—2. Brit. var. of **bunk**, v., 2. 'He [a 12-year-old boy] bunks off full time from education these days' (*Time Out*, 8 Jan. 1982, p. 15).

bunk-up, n.; less gen. **bunk up,** v.t. Assistance, to assist, in climbing: Cockneys'. Barltrop, 1981, 'To bend forward and allow the climber to stand or kneel on one's back, then heave upwards.' ' "Can you give us a bunk-up?" "Yus, I'll bunk you up, Bill." '—2. To *have a bunk up*, to have casual sexual intercourse: Forces': since ca. 1939; by 1950, gen.

bunk-wife. A landlady: St Andrews University students'.

bunker. A flat used by a criminal gang as a base from which to conduct violent robberies: c.: early 1980s. BBC, 'Review of the Sunday Papers', 1 Aug. 1982.

bunker-plate with spanner. A tin of sardines with patent opener: RN. F. & G.

bunko. Fraud. A swindling card-game or lottery. See **bunco.** the preferred later spelling, and cf. **bunko artist.**

bunko artist. A confidence trickster: Can.: since ca. 1950; adopted ex US. (Dempsey, 1975.) Ex US later C.19 *bunko-steerer*, card-sharp.

bunkum or **buncombe.** In England from ca. 1856; ex US (—1827). In C.19, coll.; in C.20, S.E. and rarely spelt *buncombe*. Talk, empty or 'tall'; humbug; claptrap; insincere eloquence. Ex *Buncombe* County, N. Carolina.

bunny, n. A rabbit: in C.17 s., then coll.—2. One who stupidly talks too much: Teddy-boys': since ca. 1954. (Gilderdale, 2.)—3. A talk, a chat: low: since ca. 1945. (Norman.) Ex the verb.—4. Someone not fully alert (not 'with it'): Aus.: since ca. 1925. Hence, *the bunny*, 'Mr Muggins' or the willing horse. (B.P.)—5. A sanitary towel: women's: since ca. 1920.—6. A pilotman: railwaymen's: since ca. 1945. *Railway*, 2nd.—7. A waitress at a Playboy Club: raffish: since late 1950s. She is costumed like a rabbit.—8. A girl, as in **beach bunny**, q.v., and *dumb bunny*, a stupid girl: since ca. 1960. Perhaps ex sense 7; *dumb bunny* is prob. ex US.

bunny, v. To talk, to chat: low: since ca. 1945. (Norman.) Ex **rabbit,** v., 3. Daniells, 1980, quotes a Lambeth carpenter saying of his wife, 'She's always bunnying to her mates on the dog and bone [telephone] but she won't bleedin' rabbit to me about nothin' serious.'

bunny suit. A thick Acrilan overall worn by RAF aircrew over their anti-gravity suits. (Tilsley, 1978.) Ex the children's overall garment, sometimes decorated for fun with a tail and ears; *not* ex the costume of a *bunny girl*, q.v. at **bunny**, n., 7. (P.B.)

bunting. A signalman or signaller using flags: RN: since early C.19, but rare by 1950. Goodenough, 1901—but I've failed to record much earlier refs. Variants were *bunting-tosser* or *bunts*. Ware explained, 'Signals are small flags made of bunting.' Both were still current in WW2, *teste Weekly Telegraph*, 25 Oct. 1941.

Bunty. The inevitable nickname of any short man: military: late C.19–20. (F. & G.) Powis, 1977, adds 'affectionate term for a small person, especially a small woman of middle age'. Ex dial. (and US) *bunty*, short and stout.

buoy, go round the. (To have) two helpings from a dish: nautical.

bupper; buppie(s); bups; bupsie. Bread and butter in gen., or a slice thereof in particular: children's, whence (says E.P.) lower-classes'—but *buppies* is also middle classes', as in, e.g., O'Donnell, 1978. By 'infantile reduction', says Ware.

Burdett Coutts, often shortened to *Burdetts*. Boots: r.s.: since ca. 1925. Ex the name of the well-known bankers.

burg. A town; a city: coll.: US, partly anglicised (thanks to the 'talkies'), by 1932. *COD*, 1934 Sup. Ex Ger.

burg(h)er. A Hamburg(h)er: adopted in 1942 from the US.

burglar. A warder expert in searching a cell: prison c.: later C.20. (McConville, 1980.) Cf. **scratcher**.

burgle up. To put words in someone's mouth, as in 'the police burgled people up': c.: later C.20. BBC Radio 4, 1 May 1983.

burk(e). A misspelling of *berk*. Kersh, 1944: *burke*.

burl; esp. in *give it a burl*. To give something a chance; make an attempt: low Aus. (Tennant, 1939.) Perversion of *hurl*? By 1950, no longer low—if, indeed, it ever was! (B.P.) Max Harris, 1985, writes of *give it a burl*, 'It connotes something more than giving it a try or a go. It implies the application of all one's ingenuity and resourcefulness to a task.' He fears the phrase is ob. Cf. the Can. and Eng. *give it a whirl*. Wilkes derives it ex dial. *birl*, a rapid twist or turn (*EDD*). But cf.:-

burley. Nonsense, humbug: Aus. (Baker.) Origin? B.P. thinks that the orig. form was *berley*; so does Webster's 3rd edition—which defines the term as 'ground bait'. Therefore **burl** above, as in 'give it a *burl*', is prob. a var. of *berl*, itself short for *berley*. If a fisherman uses *berley*, he is, after all, trying to catch a fish.

Burlington Bertie. A fop, a dude: since ca. 1909; ob. by 1940, † by 1960. Ex Vesta Tilley's famous song. 'Burlington Bertie from Bow', ca. 1908.—2. Hence, since ca. 1912, any young fellow who dresses up in his leisure or even at work; by 1960, †.

Burlington Hunt. A faulty, not very common, deformation of **Berkshire** (or **Berkeley**) **Hunt**. Franklyn.

Burma. See LOVERS' ACRONYMS, in Appx.

Burma Road. Rice: Army in the Far East: 1942+. Rice is the staple Burmese food.—2. Hence, in 1943–5, in Service messes in Iraq and Persia, 'as an exclamation at frequent rice'. (L.A.)—3. *The Burma Road*. 'The principal lowerdeck fore-and-aft passage on an aircraft carrier: RN: 1950s' [and later]. (Peppitt.) 'Also in V and W class frigates in the 1950s' (Sayers, 1985). All 3 senses derive from the famous highway driven, at great cost in lives and courage, through jungle and mountain, to keep China supplied 'through the back door', via the south-west, during WW2.

burn, n. A 'showing-off' burst of fast driving: Aus. motorists': since late 1940s. A motorist 'burns' his tyres. (B.P.) Cf. **burn off** and **burn-up**.—2. A thrill, as in 'We came up by car for a burn' (Dick): Aus. teenagers': since ca. 1950.—3. In *have a burn*, to have a smoke: RN. (Granville.) By 1950, also fairly gen. low s., as in ' "Bung me a burn" = give me a smoke' (Tempest). Hence *twist a burn*, to roll a cigarette: R Aus. N: since ca. 1918. B., 1943.

burn, v. To cheat, swindle: c.: C.17–18 (extant early C.20 in dial.).—2. To smoke (tobacco): late C.19–20. Hence also 'a solitary minor smoking of marijuana' (Home Office): current 1970s.—3. 'To take someone else's narcotics and not return it' (Home Office): drugs' world: 1970s. Or 'to cheat someone out of . . . drugs money' (Stockley, 1986). Cf. **beat**. US since —1967 (Spears).

burn bad powder. To break wind: euph. coll.: early C.20. Manchon.

burn before reading! By a joc. inversion of the usu. serious injunction to burn a confidential missive as soon as it has been read: a warning to keep secret the contents of a letter or other document: since ca. 1955. Poss. from the BBC radio comedy series 'The Goon Show', and influenced by spy-thrillers. (P.B.)

burn off. To drive very fast, esp. if 'showing off': Aus. motorists': since late 1940s. (B.P.)

burn-up, n., esp. *have a burn-up*, to race in a car or on a motor-cycle: mostly teenagers': since ca. 1955. They 'burn up' the road.—2. A marked blush: Rugby School: since late 1950s. (Wharton.)—3. As *the burn-up*, 'One of the most ingenious of confidence tricks' (Gosling, 1959), involving a gang of three or four: adopted, ca. 1946, ex US.—4. 'A group dash down the road' (Roberts, 1984): cyclists': later C.20.

burn up, v. To blush; to become very much embarrassed: Rugby School: since late 1950s. (Wharton.)—2. (Esp. in the

imperative.) To fall silent; to stop talking: Aus.: since ca. 1955. (Barlow, 1971.) Cf. synon. **dry up**.

burned, be or **get.** To receive bad drugs: drugs c. (Stockley, 1986.) US since—1966 (Spears).

burned out. 'Recovering from drug dependence' (Home Office): drugs world: 1970s.

burner. Short for 'afterburner': RAF coll. > j.: later C.20. *Phantom*.—2. In *go off* (one's) *burner*, to go mad, late C.19–early 20. Pain, 1902.—3. See **back burner**; **def**.

burning, vbl n. 'Opening a safe with oxyacetylene' (Tempest): c.: mid-C.20.

burning, adj. A coll. euph. for *bloody*:—1923 (Manchon); ob. by 1930.

burning and turning. '[The air-sea rescue crew] climb in the naval Wessex helicopter . . . soon the engine is running and the huge rotor blades begin to swing round faster and faster—"burning and turning" as they say' (Winton, 1978): FAA.

burnt cinder. A window: r.s.: (—1914) on *winder*.

buro, buroo or **brew.** An employment-exchange: workmen's coll.: from ca. 1921. Hence, *on the buro*, out of work and drawing dole; esp. in Glasgow (MacArthur). I.e., *bureau*; or perhaps, *on the buro = on the Borough*. 'I can remember [from ca. 1923] hearing the unemployed . . . saying they were "on the buroo". This was in Plumstead, London, SE18 (Gilbert, letter in the *Listener*, 9 June 1983, where also Kathleen Newell recalled a Glasgow lullaby of ca. 1961, 'Fayther's signin' on the broo').

burp. Esp. of a baby, to eructate; also v.t., to cause (a baby) to belch: late C.19–20 (?very much earlier): coll. >, by 1920 at latest, S.E. Hence, *burp at both ends*, to pass wind from throat and anus simultaneously: Aus. s.: since ca. 1930. (B.P.) Oddly, this word didn't reach the dictionaries until the 1930s. Echoic—cf. **gurk**, and see also **big spit**. Also, derivatively, n. Both v. and n. have alternative spelling *birp*. Early in 1967, Dr R.L. Mackey, M.D., resident for some forty years, remarks that, 'in Wolverhampton, *birp* is used in the conversation of the uppermost classes, *rift* by the middle class, and *belch* by the remainder, which may include some public schoolboys'. Note that whereas *belch* is, of course, S.E., *rift* was—and is—a very widespread Northern and Midland dial. term.

burp a rainbow. To vomit: Aus.: since ca. 1930. (Buzo, 1973.) Cf. **technicolour spit** or **yawn**.

burp(-)gun. A sub-machine-gun: Army: adopted, ex US, ca. 1950. Echoic.

Burrifs, the. The Burma Rifles: WW2. Cf. **Rajrifs**, Rajputana Rifles.

burrower. 'A researcher of some sort, in the jargon a "burrower" ' (Le Carré, 1977): espionage and security circles': prob. since ca. 1950.

burst. A succession of bullets fired by a machine-gun: coll. >, by 1941, j. Jackson.—2. Hence, *give (someone) a burst*, to complain; to remind vigorously: since late 1940s. (P.B.)

Burton. 'When dockers were loading down into the ship's hold in pairs, if one of them wanted to place an item in a direction that was opposite to the way they were working, he would say to his partner, "Put this one on the Burton" ' (Ash): London dockers': mid-C.20.—2. See:-

Burton-on-Trent. The rent one pays: r.s.: from ca. 1880. (P.P., 1932.) Often abbr. to *Burton*.

bury old Fagin. (Of a man) to copulate: low, raffish.

burying the baby. A c.p. indicative of profit made out of the knowledge of a discreditable or even a guilty secret: from ca. 1910. Ex 'A knows where B buried the baby' and profits accordingly. *TLS*, 20 Mar. 1937.

bus, n. An aeroplane: early s. (*OED* has 1913) which soon > démodé; it was however still heard occ. in early WW2: 'Used very rarely now', Jackson, 1943.—2. Large rowing boat (18 oars): RN: ca. 1890–1930. Goodenough, 1901. Hence—3. Any (slow) ship, or an antiquated one: RN: late C.19–

B

earlyish 20. 'Taffrail', 1916.—4. A motor-car (or even a motor-cycle: Lyell): not among mechanics, says Blaker: from ca. 1920; ob. Ex sense 2, as is:—5. An omnibus volume: book-world: since ca. 1940. E.g., *the Birmingham bus*—a book of stories by George A. Birmingham. Orig. joc.—6. See **miss the bus.**

bus, v.t. To send by bus, as children from one area of a town to a school in another area: adopted, ex US, ca. 1972: coll., becoming S.E. (P.B., 1979.)

bus and tram. Jam: r.s. (L.A., 1978.)

bus-boy. 'One whose duty is to clear tables in a restaurant' (Leechman): Can.: adopted, ca. 1935, ex US. Perhaps ex Fr. s. *omnibus*, a kind of apprentice in the restaurant business.

bus-conductor. A sub-conductor, RAOC (a technical WO1): Army: since ca. 1947.

bus(-)driver. A bomber pilot: RAF: since early 1940. 'So called because he is usually on a well-beaten route' (H. & P.). And influenced, no doubt, by **bus,** n., 1.

bush. Cannabis: drugs c. (Stockley, 1986.) US since—1946 (Spears).

bush artillery. Men not normally considered as fighting men (cooks, clerks, etc.) who manned all sorts of guns during the siege of Tobruk: Aus. Ex the coll. Aus. use of *bush*, all the country that is neither city nor farmland, as an adj. meaning 'rough and ready; unskilled, as one who can ply a trade with the minimum of tools, etc.', e.g. a *bush carpenter*, *bush mechanic*. 'Captured Italian guns manned by odds and sods in the siege of Tobruk' (Sanders, 1967): Army in North Africa: WW2.

bush bunny. A simpleton; a dupe: Aus. c.: since ca. 1920. B., 1953.

bush(-)league. Second-rate: Can., adopted, ca. 1930, ex US. Ex the leagues of minor baseball teams. (Leechman.)

bush radio or **bush wireless** are post-1930 forms of *bush telegraph*. B., 1943.

bush-tail. Cunning: Aus. coll. Baker.

bush telegram or **telegraph.** Unfounded report or rumour: Aus. coll. Idriss, 1935.

bushed. 'Suffering from mild or serious mental derangement caused by long solitude in the bush. Once a very common and serious trouble, especially among trappers and prairie farmers' wives. Now much mitigated by the wireless which provides human contact even if only mechanically. "Harry's been alone for a couple of years now. He must be pretty well bushed." '—A Can. coll.: (?)late C.19–20. (Leechman.)—2. To be physically exhausted, as 'I had to run all the way to the station and I was completely bushed when I finally got on the train': coll.: mid-C.20. (P.B.)—3. Since ca. 1920, the predominant Aus. sense has been 'to have lost one's bearings'. (B.P.)

bushel of coke. A 'bloke': r.s. Franklyn.

bushfire blonde. A redhead: Aus.: since ca. 1925. B., 1943.

bushwa. A polite Can. var. of **bullshit:** since ca. 1916.

bushy. See PUBLIC . . . SCHOOL SLANG, in Appx.

business. 'Apparatus for injection of a drug': drug addicts': later C.20. Home Office.—2. In *on the business*, engaged in prostitution. See **business girl.**—3. Anything particularly good: teenagers': early 1980s. (James Williamson, 1982.) ' "They did the business" was about the highest praise you could get from fellow hooligans' for a really spectacular display of violence, such as that by the Millwall 'fans' at Luton, Spring 1985. Armstrong, 1985.

business girl, a. Prostitutes' favourite description of themselves: from ca. 1921. Likewise, *on the business* is favourable, whereas *on the bash, batter, game*, are pej. for 'engaged in prostitution, esp. at the moment'.

busker. A man that sings or performs in public-houses: c.:—1859. (H., 1st ed.) In C.20, at first among tramps, and by mid-C.20 at latest, as gen. coll., it came to mean a man who plays a musical instrument in the street; esp. one who entertains a cinema or theatre queue. P.B.: by later C.20 verging on S.E., and applied to young persons of either sex who sing

or play for a living to the public at large, esp. in the pedestrian ways of the London Underground.

busnapper. A policeman: Aus. c. (Baker). A napper or capturer of those who are engaged in 'the buzz', C.19 Brit. c. for pickpocketing.

buso, go. To turn septic. See PRISONER-OF-WAR SLANG, §6, in Appx.

buss. Only: Army: earlier C.20. Thus, 'He had his coat on, buss'—he was wearing only his coat. Perhaps ex *bus*, Anglo-Indian, 'Enough!'

bussie or **bussy.** A bus-worker: coll.: since ca. 1940. *Reynolds*, 18 Nov. 1945.

bust, n. A burglary: c.: in England, ca. 1850-1910; but in Aus. extant until 1977 at least (Grindley). Tennant, 1953: ' "Mortman the bustman!" ' Rene sneered. "Listen to him big-note himself. He's going to do a bust".'—2. A police search or raid: drug addicts', hippies': adopted, late 1950s, ex US. *Observer* colour sup., 3 Dec. 1967.

bust, v. To inform to the police: c.: C.19–20. By late 1970s it had come to mean 'to inform (especially about illicit drugs)' (Home Office). Hence the vbl n., *busting.*—2. To degrade an NCO: military coll.: late C.19–20. Either, simply, 'He was busted', or with *down*, as 'Sergeant X was busted down to corporal'.—3. To arrest, e.g., a drug addict: adopted, ca. 1955, ex US. (Wyatt, 1973.) Common also in Can. Cf. **bust,** n., 2.—4. (Cf. 1.) To inform on a fellow prisoner: prison c.: later C.20. McConville, 1980.

bust! Dash it! NZ and UK: early C.20. Also *bust it!* Cf. *bust me!*

bust a frog! 'Well, I'm damned!': Cockneys': mid-C19–early 20.

bust a gut. To make an intense effort; usu. negative as 'Well, I'm not going to bust a gut trying to finish it tonight—it can ruddy well wait': coll. (P.B.) Hence, *gut-buster*, a steep hill: club cyclists'. *Fellowship.*

bust (a policeman's) beat. To commit a crime on it: police: since ca. 1910. *The Free-Lance Writer*, April 1948.

bust the rut. To blaze a trail: Northern Territory, Aus.: since ca. 1925. (Hill, 1951.) Baker, 1959, prefers *bust a rut*. Cf. earlier US and Can. synon. *sod-buster, -busting.*

Buster. 'A name for anybody whose real name may or may not be known to the speaker. Usually but not necessarily pejorative. "Now listen here, Buster, this means trouble!" ' (Leechman): Can.: adopted, ca. 1920, ex US. Perhaps from the inoffensive, 'dead-pan' film comedian, Buster Keaton, of silent-movie fame.

buster. A piece of bread and butter: schoolboys'. Gen. in pl.— 2. A shoplifter: Can.: since ca. 1950. (Leechman.)—3. A hard roll of bread: trawlermen's. (Mitford, 1969.)

bustle. In *on the bustle*, cadging; engaged in the sly acquisition of small objects: Aus. c.: since ca. 1920. B., 1943.

bustle-punching. 'The practice, not uncommon in dense crowds, of a male rubbing his penis against the buttocks of females. The penis may or may not be exposed' (Powis): police s.: current in 1970s.

busty. (Of a girl, woman) generously breasted: low coll. > gen.: since mid-C.20. Ex S.E. *bust*, 'bosom'. (P.B.)

busy. A detective, a CID officer: c. Leeson, 1934, implies its use ca. 1908, and Powis attests its continued use into the 1970s. Earlier, occ. *busy fellow.*

busy, get. To become active: coll.: US (1905), anglicised by 1910. *OED* Sup.

busy as a bee in a treacle-pot. Very busy: coll.:—1923 (Manchon).

busy bee. PCP (Phencyclidine): drugs c. (Stockley, 1986.) US in 1970s (Spears).

Butch. A nickname given to boys by fathers proud of their own muscles and virility and desirous of the same qualities in their offspring: Can. coll.: adopted, ca. 1920, ex US. Ex S.E. *butcher.* (Leechman.)

butch. An obviously active, as opposed to a passive, male homosexual: American, adopted, ca. 1950, by English-speaking homosexuals everywhere. Waugh, 1957.—2.

Hence, a Lesbian; loosely, a masculine sort of woman: homosexuals' (both sexes'): since ca. 1945. Cf. **dike**.

butch and **camp**, 'seem to have acquired additional meanings [or nuances]—"butch " being the dominant and "camp" the submissive partner in a [indeed in any] homosexual relationship' (Wykes, 1977): since ca. 1973.

butcher's. As *a butcher's*, the more usu. later C.20 form of **butcher's hook**, a look, q.v. Often as 'Take a butcher's!'

butcher's apron. The ribbon of the United Nations medal for active service in Korea. Ex the narrow vertical white stripes and the washed-out blue. 'The nickname was already current in 1954' (P.B.).

butcher's canary. A blowfly: Aus.: since ca. 1925. (Baker.) It infests butchers' shops and buzzes loudly.

butcher's (hook). A look: r.s.: late C.19–20. B. & P.—2. (Adj.) Angry: Aus. r.s. On *crook* and gen., as sense 1, in abbr. form.

butcher's overall. A surgeon's white operating overall: RN: since ca. 1940. Clark, 1964.

bute. Coll. abbr. of *Butazoladin*, a pain-killing medicine: showjumpers' and horse world: later C.20. Broom, 1981.

butler's revenge. A particularly noisome but inaudible fart: current at Tonbridge School in mid-C.20, but prob. much more widespread, at least among Public Schools. (P.B.)

buts. Halibuts: trawlermen's coll. Butcher, 1980.

butt. Arse, as in 'working his butt off to find a solution' (*Guardian*, 23 June 1982): increasing Brit. use being made of this Americanism since ca. 1980. There is also some recent use of the synon. US *ass*. Cf. C.15–17 S.E. *butt* = buttocks.

butter. Marijuana: drugs c. (Stockley, 1986.) US since —1971 (Spears, who gives *butter flower*).

butter-basher. A taxi-cabman employed during the 1913 taxi-cab strike: taxicab drivers': 1913. Hodge, 1939, 'These new drivers, it was rumoured, were mostly unemployed shop assistants drawn mainly from the "grocery and provision" trade.'

butter-boy (usu. in pl.). A sailor: Army: 1945+.—2. A novice taxi-driver: taxi-drivers': 'coined during the 1913 cab strike' (Hodge). Cf. **butter-basher.**—3. 'A very young policeman' (Powis): underworld: current in 1970s.

butter-patter. A grocery or dairy shop assistant: earlier C.20. Often contemptuous. Cf. **butter-basher.**

buttered scone. See TOMBOLA, in Appx.

butter-snout. 'An epithet hurled at people cursed with a nose oily in appearance': ca. 1890–1920. (Leechman, 'I first heard it at Gravesend in 1905'.)

butter the fish. To win at cards: from ca. 1920. Manchon.

butterboy. See **butter-boy**.

butterflies in the (or one's) **stomach** (occ. **tummy**), **feel** (or **have**). To experience tremors, either of excitement or of apprehension—or of both: aircrews': 1940+; by 1948, fairly gen.

butterfly. A pawnbroker's ticket: lower-classes' euph.: Lancashire: early C.20. 'A pretty euphemism' (Roberts, 1976).

butterfly boy. A fickle man that 'flits' from girl to girl: Services', in Hong Kong, 1960s. A term picked up from the Chinese bar-girls. (P.B.)

butterfly cabman. A taxi-driver working only in the summer: taxi-drivers': since ca. 1910. Hodge, 1939.

buttie, butty. A comrade, a mate: coll. and dial.: from ca. 1850. Either from mining, where *butty* = a middleman, or from Romany *booty-pal*, a fellow workman, or, most prob., ex Warwickshire *butty*, a fellow servant or labourer. Perhaps cf. the US *buddy*. See also **butty-boat.**—2. Buttered bread; a sandwich, e.g. 'a jam butty': orig. Northern, esp. Liverpool, dial., since late C.19, the term later spread under the influence of Liverpool comedians such as Ken Dodd, to >, by 1970s, widespread and gen. s. for a sandwich.

buttinski. An inquisitive person: Aus. (—1924) and English (—1933). Doone. Ex US pun on *butt in*.—2. Hence, also as *buttinsky*, 'the one-piece telephone used by P.M.G. linesmen' (B.P.): since ca. 1930.

buttle. To act or serve as a *butler*: coll.

button, n. See **on the button; start off the button**.

button B. Penniless; very short of money: since ca. 1938. I.e. *pushed for money* as, until the 1960s, you pressed Button B in a telephone-booth when you wanted your money back after a failed call.

button (one's) **lip.** See **button your lip!**

button lurk, the. The 'dodge' whereby a plausible man removes from his coat a button to serve as a contraceptive pessary when a girl insists on protected coïtion: Aus. since ca. 1915. Prob., as a correspondent has suggested, a Serviceman's trick.

button mob, the. 'Uniformed police officers, especially in large numbers, e.g., at a political demonstration' (Powis): those affected: current in 1970s.

button-tosser. A radio telegraphist: R Aus. N: since ca. 1925. (B., 1943.) Cf. **bunting**.

button (up) your lip! Stop talking (now)!; say nothing (later)!: Can. c.p., adopted, ca. 1935, ex US. By ca. 1945, gen. throughout British Commonwealth. P.B.: but in another entry, E.P. had *button* (one's) *lip*: gen. in imperative: C.19–20: s. verging on coll.; once (—1868) common among schoolboys. Cf.:-

button your flap! Be quiet!—stop talking!: RN: since ca. 1920. (H. & P.) In ref. to fly of male trousers: cf. **keep** (one's) **lip buttoned.**

buttoned has, since ca. 1940, often been used for sense 1 of:-

buttoned up. (Of a situation, a plan, a job) well in hand, all prepared: Services': since ca. 1935. (Bolitho, 1941.) Admitting neither wind nor water. Cf. **lay on** and **tee up.**—2. 'Silent, refusing to answer questions' (Petch, 1959): since ca. 1950. Obeying the injunction to *button up your lip!*—3. (Of persons) alert, well-prepared: since ca. 1960. (Bournemouth *Evening Echo*, 11 Aug. 1967.) Ex sense 1.

buttons. In *get* (one's) *buttons*, to be promoted from Leading Hand to Petty Officer: Wrens' coll.: since ca. 1939. Granville, 'Given a set of brass buttons to replace the black ones on her uniform.'—2. In *put* (one's) *buttons on*, to 'bet one's shirt' on; hence, to trust absolutely in: Army:—1923 (Manchon).—3. As *the buttons*, the Police, as in 'Call in the buttons' (Moody, 1985). Prob. a shortening of *the button mob*.

butty. See **buttie**.

butty-boat. A boat working in company with another; esp. a boat towed by a motor-boat: canal-men's. (Rolt, 1944.) See **buttie, 1**.

buturakie. To jump on a person and either rob him or beat him up: 'used in Fiji and understood in Auckland and Sydney along the waterfront where it was picked up from Fijian or part-Fijian sailors. The equivalent of the Australian *put the boot in*. From Fijian *buturaka*' (Morrisby, 1958).

buy. A purchase; an opportunity to purchase: Stock Exchange coll.: from ca. 1925. In *Time and Tide*, 8 Sep. 1934, 'Securitas' writes thus: '[Anglo-Dutch rubber] looks . . . one of the soundest of the solid buys, as opposed to the exciting gambles, in the market.'—2. In *on the buy*, actively buying: commercial coll.: adopted ex US ca. 1929. *OED*.—3. Specifically, 'Purchase of drugs by an undercover police officer' (Stockley, 1986): drugs c.

buy and sell. To be far too clever for (a person): coll.—2. In *able to buy and sell* (a person), to be much superior (orig. financially) to: coll.: since ca. 1920. Cf. **own**, v.

buy it. Orig. in *I'll buy it!*, tell me the answer or catch: from ca. 1905. Cf. ' "Oh, no! I won't buy that!" I'll not accept that as an excuse or an argument' (Leechman): since ca. 1930. Cf. also *I'll bite*. P.B.: in later C.20, if not before, also with other persons, as 'That sounds rather a dicey idea. D'you think they'll buy it?'—2. To become a casualty, usu. but not always, fatally: WW1 and 2: more in RN and RFC/RAF than Army. Cf. *He bought it* (or *He bought a packet*), he was shot down: RAF: 1939+. H. & P., both forms; Brickhill, 1946, the shorter.

B

buy money. To bet heavily on a favourite: racecourse coll.: since ca. 1930 (*OED* Sup.). *Weekend*, 11 Oct. 1967: 'Ways of "buying money"—betting on so-called "good things" at odds-on.'

buy on the never tick. To buy 'on tick': lower classes':—1923 (Manchon). A blend of *never-never*, q.v. at **never, on the**, and much older *tick*, credit (since C.17).

buyer. A 'fence', a receiver: c. Leach.

buz(z), n. A rumour: orig. RN, from late C.19 (Bowen); adopted, ca. 1937, by the RAF (H. & P.) and then Services generally. Ex ob. S.E. *buzz*, a busy or persistent rumour.—2. Hence, news: RN:—1940 (Michie).—3. A thrill, a 'kick': drug addicts': since late 1940s. (Bournemouth *Echo*, 28 Nov. 1968.) 'Methadone linctus—a drug which . . . offers neither the pleasure of shooting up, nor the same buzz as a shot of smack' (*Time Out*, 15 Feb. 1980). Hence:—4. A thrill from experiences other than drugs: '[The officer] . . . says he got "a real buzz" from the warfare on Mount Harriet' (*Sun. Times* mag., 3 Apr. 1983); 'Snooker beats sex for Steve! . . . A battle on the baize gives him a bigger buzz than bed' (*Star* newspaper, quoted in the *Listener*, 28 Apr. 1983).—5. A telephone call, as 'Give us a buzz Monday, then, all right?': coll., since ca. 1950. (P.B.)—6. See **gender-buzz**.

buzz, v.i. and t., to pick pockets: from ca. 1800: c., then—ca. 1860—low.—2. Often *buzz off*. To depart; esp. to depart quickly: from ca. 1905. Pugh, 1914. (An occ. var. is *buzz away*.) See also **buzz off!**—3. (Of music) to become lively and energetic: 'pop'-music executants' and audiences': adopted, early 1970s, ex US. *Melody Maker*, 8 July 1972: 'The Gells band really began to buzz after their third number' (Janssen).

buzz about, or **around, like a blue-arsed fly**. To be—or appear to be—excessively or officiously busy: late C.19–20: Cockneys', and then, during and since WW2, Services'. Often as *buzzing about* . . .

buzz-bomb. 'The German V1 flying bomb: civilians' ' (R.S.): latish 1944-earlyish 1945. Superseded and supplanted by the more widely popular term *doodlebug*.

buzz-box. A motor-car: 1930s. (*Passing Show*, 12 May 1934.) Esp., a noisy taxicab: Hodge, 1939.

buzz-off! An imperative dismissal to a troublesome person or child; in some instances (but not necessarily) a euph. for *bugger off!* See also **buzz**, v., 2.

buzz-wag(g)on. A motor-car: 1923, Manchon. By mid-C.20, †.

buzz(-)word (or written solid). Any resounding but hackneyed, and by misuse almost meaningless, word, borrowed from the jargons of the professions or technology to enhance the utterances of the ignorant: adopted, ca. 1970, ex US. Hence *buzz-word generator*, three columns of such words, placed side by side; a great number of utterly empty yet impressive combinations may be formed by taking a word at random from each column in turn and stringing the three words together. See Swift, *Gulliver's Travels*, Part III, Ch. 5, for the prototype. (P.B.)

buzzer. A signaller by Morse: military coll.: from ca. 1910; † by 1950, if not some time earlier. F. & G.—2. A wireless rating: RN: from ca. 1922. Bowen.—3. A telephone, esp. on a house telephone system: Services': since ca. 1939. H. & P.—4. That workman who 'puts wet yarn or cloth under hydro-extracting machines' (*Evening News*, 28 Sep. 1955): industrial. Also coll. *slinger* or *swisser* or *whizzer* or *wuzzer*. All are echoic; all, originally, were s. (or dial. > s.); ever since ca. 1940, they have been semi- or entirely official.

buzzing. Pocket-picking: c.:—1812 (Vaux). See **buzz**, v., 1. Powis, 1977, 'A near-archaic term . . . nevertheless, still used by old East Londoners.'—2. In *be buzzing*, esp. of a criminal activity, to be happening: since mid-1940s. Norman, 1959.—3. 'Circulating, as in a crowded public house' (Powis): low coll.: later C.20.

buzzing about like a blue-arsed fly. See **buzz about** . . .

buzzword. See **buzz-word**.

by hand, adj. (In the predicate), as in *church by hand*, improvised: RN: since ca. 1910.

by injection. See **injection**.

by the book. See **book**, n.,2.

by the (bloody, or other adj.) **centre** or **left!** Emphatic exclamations: military. E.g., from a senior NCO, early 1950s: 'By the centre! Stuff me, standin' load! *You're* a bit pushed, ain't yer, soldier.' = 'My word, you *are* in trouble!' When a long line of soldiers is to advance in review order, the command is given '[Dressing] by the centre—slow march!' In Hunter, 1971, it is used by a detective constable: ' "In fact, it'd fit pretty well, sir," he said. "A man she might see a lot of—and Creke's wife can't be a lot of good to him." "By the centre," Bayfield said. "That's an angle, sir." '

bye-lo. A bed; to sleep: children's. A var. of *bye-byes*. ?Ex Li-Lo, an airbed: mid-1930s+ . . .

'byes! Good-bye!: Society: ca. 1920-30. (Coward, 1928.) It gave rise to the girlish var., still current in the 1970s, *byesie-bye!* (P.B.)

byoki. Sick. See PRISONER-OF-WAR SLANG, §7, in Appx.

C

C. or c. Abbr. of racing cant **cop**, v., q.v., written in 'the book' when the 'bookie' wins on a race.—2. But *with the c* is put against that horse of which, besides the favourite, bookies should be *careful*.—3. Cocaine: addicts': adopted, ca. 1950, ex US.

C or K or M or O. One's, or the, *C*.B.E.—*K*nighthood—*M*.B.E.—*O*.B.E.: Civil Servants', hence clubmen's. Cf. **C.M.G.**

C. and E. Such Church of England (*C. of E.*) members as go to church only at *C*hristmas *and E*aster: joc. since ca. 1945. (Petch, 1966.)

C.B. A confinement to barracks: military j.: > also coll. Ex *C*onfined to *B*arracks.

c.d.f. Common sense: RN lowerdeck: since ca. 1930. For naval '*common dry fuck*', common sense.

C.G.I. or **Corticene-Grabber's itch.** A strong desire to throw oneself upon the ship's deck during a dive-bombing attack: R Aus. N: 1940–5. (B., 1943.) A cork floor-covering.

C.M.G. '*Call Me Go*d', a pun on the initials of a Commander of the Order of St Michael and St George. The higher ranks, K.C.M.G. and G.C.M.G., are 'translated' as 'Kindly call me God' and 'God calls me God'. See E.P.'s note at **M.B.E.** (P.B.)

C.O. bloke. A Public *C*arriage *O*fficer: taxi-drivers': since ca. 1918. (Hodge, 1939.) Hence, simply *COs*, 'Taxi drivers' term for police officers engaged in enforcing the laws affecting cabs and the prosecuting of illegal or dishonest cab practices' (Powis): current in 1970s.

CO lot, that. 'The Special Patrol Group (the letters "CO" meaning "Commissioner's Office" are on these officers' shoulder straps). The [SPG] is a squad of experienced, uniformed officers, skilled in thief taking, deployed tactically to deal with outbreaks of street crime. Often operating in plain clothes' (Powis): current in 1970s.

cab. A motor-car: RN: since ca. 1920. P-G-R.—2. A lavatory: Felixstowe Ladies' College: since ca. 1925. Perhaps ex *cabin* or *caboose*.—3. 'A destroyer commanding officer's affectionate term for his ship; e.g., "I was driving my cab up the Channel when . . . " ' (Parsons, 1977): RN: WW2 and after. Cf. **cab-rank.**—4. A helicopter (usu. anti-submarine): RN: later C.20. (Knight, 1985.)

cab-happy. Very keen on driving motor vehicles: Army: since ca. 1950. Sometimes contracted to *cabby*. Cf. the other adjectival formations with suffix *-happy*, e.g., **bomb-, wire-happy**.

cab-horse knees. The effect produced by the wrinkling at the knees of a ballet dancer's tights when on: ballet dancers'. Gray, 1952.

cab-rank. 'A destroyer "trot" or a line of motor launches, motor torpedo boats, etc.' (P-G-R.): RN: since ca. 1925.—2. An American: r.s. on *Yank*. Hollis, 1983.

cab-rank technique. 'A number of aircraft raiding in line, one after the other' (P-G-R.): RAF coll., verging on j.: 1940+.

cab-ranker. A cheap cigar. (Frankau, 1920.) Prompted by **cab-bagio perfumo** and punning on *rank*, evil-smelling.

cab-talk. Taxi-cabmen's cab-shelter gossip, sometimes contemptuously called *cabology*: taxi-drivers' coll.: resp., since ca. 1910, 1925. Hodge uses both, 1939.

cabbage. A bomb: RAF: WW2. Jackson, 'Thus, "and then we sowed our cabbages". (See "egg", "cookie", "groceries".)'—2. Paper money: Can. c. >, ca. 1950, (low) Can. s. Also, occ., Brit.: of banknotes, 'the green stuff'.—3. The 'brain-dead' victim of a stroke or other catastrophe. *Cabbage* is also the medical acronym for Coronary Artery Bypass Surgery, and the suggestion is that too many of these operations go wrong so the patients end up as vegetables. The intensive care unit where these patients are taken after the operation is thus known as the *Cabbage Patch* (esp. appropriate as this is where patients on life support machines wait to become transplant donors). These wards are known to the doctors as *expensive scare units* (Hamblin, 1988).

Cabbage Gardens, the or **Cabbage Garden Patch.** The State of Victoria, Aus.: Aus. nickname. Hence *cabbage-gardener* or *-patcher*, a Victorian. (B., 1943.) In 1959, B. noted the derivative *The Cabbage Patch*.

cabbage hat. 'Royal Marine (green beret)' (Hawke): Services': 1960s–70s.

Cabbage Patch, the. 'That little triangle of grass behind the Admiralty Arch which they call the Cabbage Patch': London vagrants'. *Gilt Kid.*—2. See **Cabbage Gardens.**—3. See **cabbage**, 3.

cabbage perfumo; flor di cabbagio. A cheap, rank cigar; joc.: late C.19–20. Ex *cabbage* + the Sp. suffix *-o*.

cabbie, cabby. A cab-driver: coll.: from ca. 1850.—2. Hence, in C.20, a taxicab driver. Usu. as *cabby*.—3. A ride in a motor vehicle: Army: since late 1940s. (P.B., 1974.) Hence:-

cabbie, cabby, v.i. To drive a motor vehicle; occ., to be driven in one: id.: Ibid.

cabbie, cabby, adj. Addicted to the joys of motoring: id. (Ibid.) A contraction of the more usu. *cab-happy*.

cabin-boy's breeches, the. Southern nautical, esp. around Chatham and Rochester, from ca. 1870, as in Bell, 1936, ' "Dog's nose with a squirt of rum," Delfontaine replied; "called round here the cabin boy's breeches and up in the north Devil's rot-gut." ' *Dog's nose* is defined as 'gin and beer mixed'.

C

cabin fever. 'To go squirrely [q.v.], go crazy because of isolation; usu. in winter in remote locations: widespread Can. usage: since (?)late C.19 and the Yukon Gold Rush' (Leech, 1986).

cabology. See **cab-talk**.

caboose. A kitchen: tramps' c.: mid-C.19–20. Ex *caboose*, a ship's galley.—2. An office; a small cabin or compartment: RN. Cf. sense 1.—3. 'Brake van. Used especially of uncomfortable box tacked on back of liner train for ornamental purposes only (W[estern] R[egion])': railwaymen's: since late 1940s. *Railway*, 2nd.—4. A motorcycle sidecar: motorcyclists' s.: since ca. 1950. (Dunford.) Perhaps influenced by sense 3.—5. 'Unofficial hut used [to store] tools or [for] meal breaks' (Patterson): Portsmouth dockers'.

caboosh. RN lowerdeck var. of prec., 2. *Heart*, 1962.

cache. A private store or reserve, esp. of under-the-counter goods: coll.: since ca. 1910; by 1950, S.E. 'Undoubtedly Canadian (Fr. *cacher*, to hide), from the *caches* (two syllables) left by *voyageurs* on their fur-trading journeys, i.e., of supplies, etc., left for later use.' (R.C., 1976.)

cack. n. and (rare) v. (To void) excrement. Orig. S.E.; in late C.19–20 dial. and low coll. Among children, often as a semi-interjection, *cacky*. Ex L. *cacare*; prob. echoic.

cack-handed. Left-handed; hence, clumsy: orig. London and Home Counties dial., in C.20 > gen. s., perhaps through influence of Service life. For this, and the many other dial. terms for left-handedness, see Orton & Wright, *Word Geography of England*, 1974, maps 119 and 119A.

cack school. A kindergarten or infants' school 'which needs facilities for relief of nature constantly and instantly at hand' (L.A.): educational circles': since ca. 1945.

cack street. An occ. C.20 Brit. var. of **Shit Street**, q.v. 'To be up (or in) cack street' = to be in trouble.

cacked. Completely eliminated from a game or competition: Leicester board-gamers': mid-1980s. (Poole, 1986.) Cf. *pubbed*.

cackle-berry. (Gen. pl.) An egg: Can., late C.19–20; Aus., since ca. 1943; both ex US. Also coll. joc. Brit. Cf. **hen fruit**.

cackle the dice. 'To pretend to shake up the dice when actually they are held in a special grip that stops their free movement within the hand' (Green): gamblers'.

cacklebladder. 'A means—usu. chicken blood . . . —of bloodying up the body of someone whom an opposition target has been forced to shoot. [For blackmail, photographic evidence]' (Green): espionage.

cackle (one's) **fat.** 'To brag; to express self-opinionated, esp. if contradictory, point of view' (L.A., 1960): low: since late 1940s.

cacks. Children's shoes: c.:—1923 (Manchon). Ex dial.: *EDD* cites its use in Cumberland in 1880, and also, no date, but—1897, in Hampshire.—2. or *kacks*. Trousers: teenagers': early 1980s. (James Williamson, 1982.) Var. of synon. *kex*.

cad. Cadmium: coll.: since (?)ca. 1930. Smith, 1978.

Cadborosaurus (affectionately, **Caddie**) is 'a mythical(?) sea monster . . . often reported near Victoria, B.C. Named after a local bay—Cadboro Bay, where it was first reported. Cf. *Ogopogo*' (Leechman): Can. Cf. also *Nessie*, the Loch Ness monster.

caddish. Offensively ill-bred: from ca. 1860 (recorded, 1868): coll. In C.20 it tends to mean glaringly deficient in moral and/ or aesthetic delicacy. Old-fashioned by later C.20, although still extant in joc. usage (P.B.).

Cadogan Light Horse, the. 'The Special Constables mounted on the horses from Smith's riding school in Cadogan Square, London, during the general strike of 1926. Ex a cavalry officer on leave from India at that time who was specially enrolled for this "force" ' (Peter Sanders): 1926; then historical.

Cads' Bar. The junior officers' corner in any favourite 'pub': RN: since ca. 1914. P-G-R. Cf.:-

Cads' Corner. That corner of the wardroom in which the junior officers gather: RN: since ca. 1914. P-G-R.

cad's (or **cads'**) **crawlers.** Suède shoes: since ca. 1930. Cf. **brothel-creepers**.

Caesar. A Caesarian section or operation: medical coll.

cafe, occ. written *kayf*. A café, a small restaurant: low, esp. London: since ca. 1920. Simply *café* without the accent.

café au lait, adj. or n. (A half-caste) with a touch of colour: since ca. 1920.

caff. A café: low: since ca. 1920. Morse-Boycott, 1931.

Cafishio. An Argentine that is a professional pimp. See **Créolo.**

cag, n. A quarrelsome argument; gossip: nautical: from ca. 1870, slightly ob. (Bowen; F. & G.) Granville records the term as *kagg*, and defines it as 'a conference' but also as 'a naval argument in which everybody speaks and nobody listens', adding 'A "branch-kagg" means talking shop.' Presumably this nautical usage is ex **cag, v.**—2. Short for **caggie**, q.v., a cagoule.

cag, v. 'To "argue the toss" ': RN. Granville spells it *kagg*. *Musings*, 1912, p. 178.

cage. In C.16–17, S.E. (as in Shakespeare) and = a prison. In C.17–19, low if not indeed c., in C.20 low and ob., for a lock-up. In WW1, esp. as *bird-cage*, a compound for prisoners; in WW2, and after, a prisoner-of-war camp was simply a *cage*, and *in the cage* synon. with *in the bag*.—2. Goal-net: ice-hockey players': since ca. 1938.

cagey. 'Up-stage'; conceited: from ca. 1935; this meaning was supplanted by—2. Cautious; suspicious; unforthcoming; reserved: since ca. 1940; by 1946, coll. Ex animals in cages.—3. 'Keeping a look-out': prisoners' (Home Office): current in 1970s. A specialisation, perhaps, of sense 2.

caggie (or **kaggie**). A cagoule or kagool, defined in Chambers's *C.20th Dict.*, 1977 Supp., as 'a lightweight weather-proof anorak, often kneelength (Fr. *cagoule*, a monk's hood)': domestic coll.: since ca. 1978.

cagmag. A 'do-gooder': in Clark, 1982, it is used of a social worker.

cahoots. *In cahoots (with)*: 'they are in cahoots together over this'; *go into cahoots with*: in collaboration or co-operation, often with some suggestion of conspiracy or exclusiveness: coll.: adopted, ex US, ca. 1945. (P.B.)

Cain. Short for *Cain and Abel*, C.19 r.s. for 'table'.

cake. A pile of currency or bank-notes: (low) Cockney. Cf. **wad**, 1.—2. A prostitute: low Aus.: since ca. 1910. Baker, 'Whence "cake-shop", a brothel'. Euph., for *cat*, etc., but prob. suggested by **tart**.—3. In *in the cake*, in the army. Hill, 1978: 'So? When we capture Bennett maybe we'll find that he's been in the cake, will that make you happy?' (context refers to query whether Bennett has ever been in the army). P.B. adds: in 20 years in the army I never heard the term; perhaps it is a mishearing of *Kate*, short for *Kate Carney*, imperfect r.s. for army.

cake(-)eater. 'A guy in the 1920s who wore sideburns and flapping pants was called a "cake eater".' *Daily Colonist* (Victoria, BC), 6 Feb. 1971. (Leechman.)

cake-hole. The mouth: RAF: since ca. 1936. (H. & P.) Adopted ex Yorkshire s., where current at least as early as 1914. P.B.: in later C.20 much more widespread, and esp. in the phrase 'Shut your cake-hole!', popularised by such comedians as the late Tony Hancock.

cake-shop. A brothel. See **cake**, 2.

cake-walk. Money very easily obtained: Glasgow coll.:—1934. Ex that easy-motioned pre-WW1 dance, whence also:—2. Any project or obstacle that is easily overcome, e.g., a *viva voce* examination that has proved much less difficult than expected. 'It will be a c.w.' is hubris; 'It was a c.w.' is sheer relief—or boasting: coll.: since ca. 1919. (P.B.)

caked up. Well provided with money: low: since ca. 1940. (Norman.) See **cake**, 1.

cakes. Female breasts: raffish: early 1970s. (*Observer*, TV review, 13 Jan. 1974: R.S.) Ex **cheesecake**, q.v.

cakey. Cake: domestic, esp. children's, coll. (P.B.)—2. (As adj.) Half-witted: Glasgow:—1934. Ex Northern and Midland dial. (—1897: *EDD*).

cakey bar. An excuse; a 'tale'. See **bar**, 2.—2. Used in a Guards' regiment for a 'soapy' type—difficult to swallow, i.e. 'take' or tolerate: (?1920s—) 1930s. (Raab, 1977.)

Calathumpian. One who claims an imaginary religion: joc.: since ca. 1920. Perhaps cf. the US *callithump*, a boisterous, or a burlesque, parade or serenade, hence *callithumpian*, a practitioner, or a supporter, of such goings-on.

Calcutta Home Guard, the. 'A battalion of the Royal Warwickshire Fusiliers, victims of some incalculable military permutation, spent the whole of the Second World War on garrison duties in Calcutta and achieved [this] unenviable sobriquet' (Carew).

calf. 'Ten shillings. (R.s. for "half". A "cow" is one pound sterling. "Cow and calf" is, therefore, thirty shillings.)' (Tempest): mid-C.20. Since 1971, 50 pence.

calf dozer. A small *bull*-dozer (earth-shifter): WW2.

calf-licked. (Of human hair) hanging in a quiff: North Country coll. Hesling, 1954.

Calies, the. See ASSOCIATION FOOTBALL, in Appx.

call. To blame: lower classes' coll.: late C.19–20. 'Don't call me, sir, if I'm a bit clumsy at first.' Ex *call down*, or *call names*. P.B.: prob. the latter, for in East Midlands dial., where still very much current, 1980s, it = to abuse, reprimand.

call a cab. 'A jockey is said to "*call a cab*" when he waves one arm to balance himself crossing a fence' (Lawrence, 1961): racing: since late 1940s.

call-bird. In the *Observer*, 5 Jan. 1958, the writer of 'Call-Bird at the Sales' explains the term as the name shopkeepers 'give to extraordinary bargains as lures for the sale-minded': East-End Londoners': late C.19–20. Ex Ger. *Lockvogel*, a decoy-bird, prob. via Yiddish. (L.A.)

call (one's) bluff. To challenge a person, with implication of showing up his weakness: coll. Ex US.

call for a damper. To break wind: RN.

call for Bill; . . . Herb; . . . Hughie. See **calling for . . .**

call (one) for everything under the sun. To abuse thoroughly, vilify vigorously: coll.: late C.19–20. Cf. the C.17–early 19 (then dial.) **call**, q.v., to abuse, vilify. P.B.: in later C.20 the same meaning is usu. expressed in the version *call* (someone) *all the names* (or *every name*) *under the sun*.

call-girl. A prostitute, esp. one who advertises by shop-window announcement of services as so-called model: since ca. 1945. Adopted from the American—hence, by 1944 at latest, also Aus.: a prostitute available only by telephone-*call*; a use that, by 1950, > coll.

call it a day. To state one's decision to go no further, do no more; rest content, e.g. with one's gain or loss. Occ. *call it a night*, if *night* lends point to the locution, as in Spenser, 1934, 'There were at least sixty pounds [£60] there, and I quickly collared the lot and called it a night.' Coll. Perhaps ex low *call a go*, to change one's stand, alter one's tactics, give in: mid-C.19–20. H., 1st ed.: itself prob. ex cribbage. *Call a go* has in C.20, perhaps influenced by *call it a day*, > more usually *call it a go*.

call it 'it'. To say that a job is done, as in 'I'll just write this last little bit in here, see, and then we'll call it "it", OK?': mostly domestic: since ca. 1950. A shortening of *call it a day* or *a go*.

call of the great outdoors. 'The "call of nature" and reponse, in a trip to the "gents".' L.A. cites Leitch, 1965.

call over the coals. To call to task; to reprimand; address severely: coll.: C.19–20. Ex the treatment once meted out to heretics. The orig. form was *fetch over . . .*

call up. To speak to, over radio or telephone: coll.: adopted ex US by ca. 1940, at latest. 'A pilot's wife has called up [the aerodrome] to say he is sick' (Phelps, 1946).

Callao ship. 'One in which the discipline is free and easy', Granville: RN. At Callao, the principal seaport of Peru, things seem, to a naval rating, to be free and easy. Hence, *Callao routine*, one that is free and easy. P-G-R.

calliante-stroke, the. A rather clumsy method of boat-pulling that, adopted from the Italian Navy, results in many broken oars: RN: since ca. 1918. P-G-R.

calling for Bill or **. . . Hughie**, adj. and n. Vomiting, as a result of drinking too much alcohol; the former of a hiccuping, the latter of a violent, retching nature: army: 1960s. (P.B., 1974.) The *Sunday Express* supp., 11 Oct. 1982, noted that *calling for Hughie* was currently in use among **Sloane Rangers**, q.v.

calling for Herb. Aus. var. of prec. See **big spit, the.**

Cally, the: Cally Market. The Caledonian Market: Londoners': late C.19–20.

cally dosh. Money: Glasgow. (Munro, 1988.) See **dosh**—but why *cally*?

Callythumpian. Lower Wye Valley var. of **Calathumpian** (Waters, 1973).

calonkus. A stupid person: Irish-Aus.: late C.19–20. (Park, 1950.) Arbitrary.

cam. A camisole. Also *cami*, *cammy*. Cf. **com**, 1.

cambra. A dog: Shelta: C.18–20. (B. & L.) Cash, 1977, who learnt the language as a child, prefers the spelling *komra*; he recalls his grandmother saying 'that glork's komra's kanyed in the keyna'—that man's dog's made a mess in the house.

Camcreek. Cambridge: undergraduates': since ca. 1920.

Camden Town. Orig. a halfpenny: r.s. on 'brown':—1859 (H., 1st ed.); since ca. 1920 also a penny. Used mostly by buskers. Franklyn.

Camel to Consumer. 'C. to C.' (Cape to Cairo) cigarettes, sent to the troops in North Africa by kindly S. Africans: ca. 1940–3. P-G-R.

cameo part. A minor role in a play or film, but one in which the actor can make effective use of his or her talents: theatre- and film-goers' coll.: since early C.20. (Raab, 1982.)

Camerer Cuss. A bus: London r.s.: since ca. 1925. (Gardner, 1932.) P.B.: Ex the name of the watch makers, Camerer Kuss & Co., 56 New Oxford St. The firm was founded in 1788, and the Kuss family, members of which are still in it (though the shop has moved), changed their spelling to Cuss early in WW1. (With thanks to my uncle, Max C.L. Beale, who also gave me a Camerer Kuss watch.)

cami. Abbr. *camisole*: from ca. 1900; shop and women's. Also *cammy* and *cam*. Cf.:-

cami-knicks. Abbr. *cami-knickers* (1915): from ca. 1917; shop and women's.

camouflage. Disguise; pretence, 'eye-wash': ex military j., itself ex Parisian s. *camoufle*, a person's description by the police (i.e. standard-French *signalement*), and *camoufler*, to disguise. Also as v. 'Naturalised with amazing rapidity early in 1917' (W.). G.B. Shaw, 'I was in khaki by way of camouflage' (*Daily Chronicle*, 5 Mar. 1917: W.). For its military senses, see, e.g., B. & P.

camp, n. A station with or without an airfield—a unit's or a detachment's location—a training school—a depot—a landing ground; even if it (any of them) is situated in a town: RAF coll. (since ca. 1920) >, by 1943, j. (Jackson.) The ubiquity of *Camp Commandant* and the versatility of *camp commandants* have been operative.—2. Whether in ref. or in address, Camp Commandant: Army coll. late C.19–20. 'Oh, you had better ask Camp; he deals with such things.'—3. Effeminate, esp. homosexual, mannerisms of speech and gesture: mostly Society: since ca. 1945. 'The momentary absence of the customary "camp" once again calmed Elizabeth's hostility' (Wilson, 1952).—4. Hence, a male homosexual: since ca. 1950. Reid, 1970: 'There's a lot of camps in Tangier, especially English ones.' Cf. the adj., 4., and the v. For all homosexual senses of *camp*, see esp. Rodgers, 1972. See also entry at **butch**, and **camp**, adj.—5. In *high* and *low camp*, both n. and adj., extravagance of gesture, style, form, esp. if inappropriate; if used consciously, deliberately, it is *high camp*, but if unselfconsciously, ignorantly, unskilfully, it is *low camp*: since early 1960s in US, whence adopted by 1965 at latest. Recorded by the *Random House Dictionary*,

C

1966, and occurring in *Jagger*, 1974. Both *camp* and *high camp* have, since ca. 1965, also been non-pej. and even indicative of praise: Brit., Aus., and doubtless elsewhere. 'I have many examples' (B.P., who in 1969 reminded me of this unexpected, although perhaps not unexpectable, sense development).

camp, v. To be a male, or a female, homosexual: theatrical: since ca. 1945. Ex the adj., senses 3 and 4.—2. To act in a characteristically (male or female) homosexual manner, esp. if showily: since the late 1930s. Cf. senses 3 and 4 of the adj. *The Lavender Lexicon*, 1965.—3. Covering such other shades, v.i. and v.t. (as *camp it up*), of the adj. and n., as have not been indicated here.

camp, adj. Addicted to 'actions and gestures of exaggerated emphasis . . . Prob. from the Fr.' (Ware); pleasantly ostentatious or, in manner, affected: London proletarian (—1909) >, by 1920, gen. coll. Perhaps rather ex the C.19–20 dial. *camp* or *kemp*, uncouth, rough: see esp. the *EDD*.—2. Whence, objectionable; (slightly) disreputable; bogus: Society: from ca. 1930.—3. Effeminate: theatrical (—1935) and Society. (Lincoln, 1933.)—4. Homosexual; Lesbian: orig. theatrical (cf. 3): since ca. 1920; by 1945, fairly gen.—5. Hence, characteristic of homosexuals, as in 'camp words, phraseology, signs, greetings'. See n., 3.

camp about. 'To pirouette and gesture eloquently' (Cook, 1962): since ca. 1945. Cf. **camp it up**, 1.

camp bicycle. A Servicewoman readily available on camp, or any notorious harlot living near the camp: Services': since ca. 1940. Cf. **town bike**.

camp comedian. A Camp Commandant: army and RAF: since ca. 1930. Jackson.

camp dollies. The cinema on camp: FAA: since late 1940s. 'What's on at camp dollies tonight?' (Wood, 1978.)

camp it up. To render unnecessarily effeminate the part one is playing: theatrical: since ca. 1935. Ex **camp**, adj., 3.—2. To have a homosexual affair; to spend a 'queer' week-end together: homosexuals': since ca. 1945. Cf. **camp**, v., 2.—3. To exaggerate something to the point where it becomes almost too ridiculous. In, e.g., an article about the film *Superman*, 1978, in *New Society*, 1 Feb. 1979: 'Avoiding what must have been a very grave temptation to camp things up, in the manner of the old *Batman* TV show' (P.B.).

campery. That quality of 'camp' talent which is shown by, e.g., a musician with flair and wit: since ca. 1970. (L.A., 1976.)

campness. 'Degree of homosexual (camp) inclination': L.A. cites a review of the film *Some of My Best Friends* . . . in *The Times*, 24 Dec. 1971: 'The sensitive [male] lover of the married man (heavy blue eye shadow to establish sensitivity rather than campness, I think)'.

campy. Adj. corresponding to and deriving from **camp**, adj., and **camp**, n., 5: since ca. 1970. *Jagger*: 'He never looked campy with make-up' (Janssen).

can, n. A lock-up or prison: Aus.: adopted ca. 1964 ex US. Dick.—2. 'A racing silencer for a motorcycle' (Dunford): motorcyclists': since ca. 1920. Cf. **Brooklands can**.—3. As *the can*, the w.c., esp. and orig. 'an outdoor privy with a *can* or other receptacle under the seat' (Leechman): Can.—4. A pint of beer: RAF officers': early WW2. Hence also, *half-can*, a half-pint. 'Blake', 1941.—5. 'A measure of approx. 8 oz marijuana' (Green): drugs c.: later C.20.

can, v. To decide not to use an article or pamphlet: Public Relations Directorate, the Air Ministry: since ca. 1943. I.e. to put into the swill-can. Cf. *spike*.—2. Usu. *be canned*, to be taken out of service: Can. railroadmen's:—1931. But *can*, to discharge (an employee), existed in British Columbia at least as early as 1910. (Leechman.)

can it! Be quiet! Stop talking: from ca. 1918; ex US.

Canack. See **Canuck**, a Canadian.

canal boat, the. The 'tote' (racecourse totalisator): r.s.

canaries. Bananas: since ca. 1930. Ex Canary Island bananas.—2. Squeaks in the bodywork of one's motorcar: motorists': since ca. 1950. Cf. **flatter**.

Canaries, the. See ASSOCIATION FOOTBALL, in Appx.

Canary. A girl singer with an orchestra: Can. (and US): since ca. 1945.—2. 'A mouse is a young lady. (So is a *slick chick*, *duck*, *canary*, *pig*, *beast*, *head*, *sun* or *sunflower*, or *doll*.)': Beatnik s., dating from the late 1950s. (Anderson.) But also Aus.—since ca. 1930. (Glassop, 1949.)

canary ward, the. The VD ward in a RN hospital: lowerdeck. Ex its predominant colour. P-G-R.

cancer stick. A cigarette: grim humour: later C.20. Hoggart, in a *Guardian* article on the language of businessmen in pubs, noted that 'they always smoke "coffin nails" or "cancer sticks" ', i.e. that is what the businessmen call them.

candle. Short for **candle-sconce**, q.v., a ponce. Franklyn 2nd.—2. Short for *Roman candle*, q.v. at **Roman-candle landing**. Also for the faulty parachute itself. Page, 1973.—3. (Usu. in pl.) Sparking plugs, as in 'She's had a new set of candles': car-dealers'. Graham-Ranger, 1981.

candle-basher. A spinster: low: since C.19–20. Outmoded by 1967. The connotation is of masturbation.

candle money. Fire-insurance paid out: police and underworld. (Proctor, 1958.) Ex candle purposely left burning.

candle-sconce. A prostitute's protector: low r.s. (on *ponce*): since ca. 1920. Phelan, 1943.

candy. A sugar cube of the drug LSD: addicts': adopted, ca. 1965, ex US. (Janssen, 1968.) Stockley, 1986, defines 'candy' as barbiturates or cocaine, a usage current in US since 1930s (Spears).

candy-boy. A prostitute's handy-man. See **bumper-up**, 3.

candy-slinger. A vendor of toffee that he has pulled into wisps: grafters'. *Cheapjack*.

cane, n. A thieves' 'jemmy', q.v.: c. Leach, 1981.

cane, v. (Gen. in passive.) To punish, e.g., by confinement to barracks: army: WW1. F. & G.—2. To damage considerably, to shell heavily: id.: Ibid.—3. Hence, to treat badly, e.g. a motorcar: from 1918.—4. To defeat, esp. as vbl. n. *caning*: 'a beating, a defeat': since ca. 1918. With senses 1–4 cf. the perhaps later 'give it stick', to punish.—5. To coït with (a woman). Cf. *bang, belt*, and other rough terms that imply a hitting or striking.

canker. Usu. *kanker*, a var. of *kanga[roo]*, r.s. for a Jew.

canned. Tipsy: c. and low s.: since ca. 1910, adopted ex US. A WW1 army var. was *canned up*. (Leach; F. & G.) Cf. *tanked*.—2. As *to be canned*, it = to be arrested: drugs c. Stockley, 1986.

canned music. Music from phonograph or gramophone: adopted, ca. 1925, from US.

cannon. A pickpocket: c.: from ca. 1920. (*Evening News*, 9 Dec. 1936.) Hence *cannon mob*, a team of pickpockets.

cannon fodder. 'Those soldiers whose destiny was to do or die, not to reason why. A newspaper or political agitator's phrase occasionally used by the troops' (P-G-R.): derisive: 1939–45. 'Cf. the Ger. coll. *Kanonenfutter*' (R.S.).

cannot (gen. **can't**) **seem to.** Seem (to be) unable to; be apparently unable to; cannot, apparently: coll. (and catachresis). Norris, 1933, 'I must be nervous this afternoon. I can't seem to settle down to anything.' Careless thinking, perhaps via *I cannot, it seems, do* (something or other) and *I don't seem to be able to*.

canny Newcassel. Newcastle-upon-Tyne: North Country: late C.19–20. Newcastletonians also call it 'The Pride of the North'.

canoe inspection. Service women's weekly inspection for VD: Can. army: WW2.

canov. Short for late C.19–20 r.s. *can of oil*, a boil. Franklyn 2nd quotes ' 'E's gotta lovely canov on 'e's nick, ain' 'e?'

cans. Earphones used by operators and technicians of radio and TV: Can. since ca. 1950; Brit. perhaps a little later: s. > j. (Leechman; P.B.)

canteen. 'Goods purchased against earnings credited, or cash: prisons' and penal establishments' (Home Office): current in 1970s.

canteen boat. 'Rear ship in a minesweeping formation: R.N.: 1950s' (Peppitt)—and later.

canteen cowboy. A ladies' man: RAF: since 1940. Jackson, 'The origin is in the American expression, "drug-store cowboy" . . . (See "Naafi Romeo" and "Poodle-faker").'—2. Hence, orderly corporal on duty in a Station Institute, Naafi or Junior Ranks' Club: since 1941; still current early 1970s. (L.A.; P.B.)—3. 'Footplatemen taking a cup of tea in the messroom or shed while awaiting the foreman's instructions. Canteen cowboys were either maintenance men on shed duties, taking a rest between the shunting of locomotives and trains, or drivers and their mates who had signed on in a spare capacity and were there awaiting foreman's orders' (McKenna, 1970): railwaymen's: since WW2.

canteen damager. Naafi canteen manager. See **damager**.

canteen letters. 'Extra two [letters] per week if inmate pays for stamps': prisons' and penal establishments' (Home Office): current in 1970s.

Canterbury Bell(e). An 'unmarried wife' receiving an allowance from a Fighting Service. 'When conscription was introduced in April 1939, it was decided that such women could qualify for a wife's allowance. The story goes that the Archbishop of Canterbury objected to "unmarried wife" and so it was changed to "unmarried dependent living as wife" or popularly "Canterbury Belle" ' (Sanders): Forces': mid-1939, ephemeral. A pun on the flower named *Canterbury bell* and (Archbishop of) *Canterbury*, as well as on *belle*, a pretty girl, and *Belle*, a girl's name.

cantilever bust. Large female breasts seeming to defy the laws of gravity: Aus.: since ca. 1950. They do so, but only with the help of well-constructed foundation garments, sometimes referred to as *structural engineering*.

canty. (Of persons) disagreeable; irritable: Aus.: since ca. 1920. B., 1942, 'From cantankerous'. P.B.: this is the exact opposite of the North British dial. *canty*, which means 'merry, brisk and lively', as in Robert Burns' 'John Anderson, My Jo': ' . . . monie a canty day, John, We've had wi' ane anither.'

Canuck, occ. **Canack, K(a)nuck.** A Canadian: in England, from ca. 1915. Orig. (1855) a Can. and American term for a French Canadian, which, inside Canada, it still means. Etym. obscure: perhaps *Can*ada + *uc* (*uq*), the Algonquin n.-ending; W., however, proposes, I think rightly, ex *Canada* after *Chinook*.

cap. (Gen. in pl.) A capsule of drug, e.g., LSD or heroin: addicts': adopted, ca. 1965, ex US and Can. (Janssen, 1968; Home Office).

cap-badge. A 25-pounder gun; a 3.7 gun: medium gunners' (army): ca. 1940–5. Ex the gun in the Royal Artillery cap-badge. The gun was also called, satirically, a *flit-gun*; ex 'Flit', a pesticide, discharged from a syringe known as a 'gun'.

cap-tally. A sailor's cap-ribbon bearing the name of his ship: RN coll.

cap-tally drink and **collar-band pint.** A short measure pint: resp. RN and civilian. P-G-R.

cap up. 'To divide any powdered drugs—opiates, tranquillisers, amphetamines, etc.—into capsules prior to selling them. The dealer may well cut [= adulterate] his wares before capping them' (Green): drugs c.: later C.20. See **cap**.

Cape of Good Hope. Soap: r.s.:—1914. (F. & G.) Soon abbr. *cape*.

Cape Turk. In *not to have rounded C.T.*, still to regard a woman solely as an instrument of pleasure: coll.:—1923 (Manchon). Ex the Turks' reputation in sexual matters.

caped. 'Train cancelled through lack of traffic, or bad weather conditions. From Kaput' (McKenna, 1970): railwaymen's: mid-C.20.

caper. A dodge, device, performance: coll., orig. (—1851) low. *London Herald*, 23 Mar. 1867, ' ' He'll get five years penal for this little caper," said the policeman.' Ex the S.E. senses.—2. Trick or 'game', as in 'You can shove *that* caper!'

(Slatter): widespread in Brit. Commonwealth: since ca. 1920.—3. 'A large-scale crime (once exclusively an American term, now quite common)' (Powis): underworld: current in 1970s. Both senses 2 and 3 derive from sense 1.

capping. Flying on *CAP*, combat air patrol: RAF: later C.20. *Phantom*.

Captain Cook. A book: r.s.: late C.19–20. B. & P.—2. A cook: Aus. r.s. B., 1942.—3. A look: Aus. r.s.: since ca. 1948. (B.P.) Culotta, 1960, 'Let's have a Captain Cook.' But see also **cook**, and synon. Brit. rhyming *butcher's hook*.

Captain Grimes. *The Times*: Londoners' r.s.: later C.20. Patrick Glass, in a letter to that paper, pub. 10 June 1982, records hearing this, and *Currant Bun* for the *Sun*, in a Wimbledon hospital, at the time of writing.

captain's blue-eyed boy. 'The officer most in favour at the moment' (Granville): RN coll.

captain's cloak, the. The 36th Article of War: RN. (Bowen.) It relates to powers of punishment. Granville has 29th Article.

capurtle, n. Females as providers of sexual solace to males: r.s. on *myrtle*: since ca. 1950. Clark, 1975, 'So you spent the morning gizzing at bits of capurtle in flouncy dresses'. Here, *gizz*, to gaze, blends *gaze* + *quiz*: since ca. 1945. But see also **kerpurtle**, which may be connected.

caput. (Also *kaput, kapout*.) Finished; no more: military: 1915: ob. by the mid-1930s, but given fresh impetus by WW2 and subsequently by the British Army of the Rhine. Ex Ger. *kaputt*, done for, ruined, insolvent.

car-ringing. Putting a stolen car onto the road with a wrecked car's log-book (*Motor Trader*, 12 Jan. 1977): since ca. 1950. See **ringer**, 4.

Carab. An occ. form of **Carib**. P-G-R.

carb. Carburettor: motorists' coll.: since ca. 1910. The Aus. version is *carbie,-y*.

carbolic naked is a punning, not very common, var. of **starbolic naked**.

carbolic soap opera. 'A soap opera [q.v.] based in a hospital' (Green): TV: later C.20.

carbon. A carbon copy (opp. to *the top*) of a typewritten MS or sheet thereof: coll: authors' and typists'.

card, n. See **go through the card; mark** (someone's) **card.**

cardboard box. The pox: r.s.: later C.20. (Daniells, 1980.)

cardboard foc'sle. 'The peak on the cap worn by officers and petty officers (and "men not dressed as seamen")': RN lowerdeck: since ca. 1930. 'Just because you wear a cardboard foc'sle, don't think you can come in with the troops!' (Granville, letter, 1963.)

cardi. Var. spelling of **cardy**, a cardigan.

cards. In *get* or *be given* (one's) *cards*, to be dismissed: since ca. 1925: coll., perhaps orig. busmen's, but in later C.20, very common and widespread among workers. I.e., in *Gilt Kid*, 1936, one's employment card; but by 1970s this had become one's National Insurance card (—1974–5) and several other bureaucratic impedimenta. Cf. *ask for one's cards*, to leave a job voluntarily, or, at least, request to do so; and see **books**, 1. (P.B.)—2. In *off the cards*, working unofficially and informally, without disclosing one's income, as in 'He could get £40 a day as a brickie [= bricklayer; s. since –1880 (Barrett)] "off the cards", black economy and all that' (*Sunday Times*, 8 May 1988). Cf. **ghost**, n., 3.

cardy. A cardigan: domestic coll. (P.B.)

care a pin; damn; fig, not to, and all similar phrases of dismissal. See **not care a . . .**

careen is, in Can. (imitating the US), misused for 'to career', to go wildly and rapidly, esp. of a motor-car: in Can., frequent only since ca. 1935. In later C.20, also Brit.

career boy. One who, in a combatant Service, puts self-success before the public, esp. the nation's, welfare: RAF s. (1942) >, by 1944, all three Services' coll. Cf. **back-room boy**.

careless talk. (A stick of) chalk: mostly darts-players': since ca. 1945; but soon ob., if not †, as the memory of the WW2 admonition 'Careless talk costs lives', which prompted it, faded from the national consciousness. Franklyn.

cargo brand. Pilfered cargo: MN: since late 1930s. (Peppitt.)

Carib (or **c-**). A member of the *Carab*inieri: prisoners-of-war in Italy: 1942–4, then historical. (Gilbert, 1952.) Influenced (*C*-) by *Carib*, one of a Caribbean tribe and (*c*-) by *cannibal*. Cf. **Carab**.

Carl Rosa. 'A poser. Someone who is not what he seems. The name refers to a well-known operatic society. Fraud or deceit is sometimes referred to as "the old Carl Rosa" '(Powis): r.s.: current in 1970s. Raab: the Carl Rosa ceased performing in 1958.

carn. A carnation: flower-sellers': late C.19–20. Llewellyn, 1943.

carnal flu. A gonorrheal infection, 'a dose of clap': Can., poss. ex US WW2; ob. (Leech, 1986.)

carnapper. One who habitually, rather than incidentally, steals—or 'borrows'—motor-cars: since ca. 1955. On pattern of *kidnapper*; cf. **hijacker**, as a neat formation.

carney; carny, n. Seductive flattery; suave hypocrisy: coll.: 1818 (*The London Guide*). Perhaps more common as v.i. and t.; and in C.20, esp. in *come the (old) carney*.—2. Hence, a hypocrite: RN. C.20. Granville. —3. A *carnival* show; hence, a man employed there, a *carney* (or *carni*) *guy*: Can.: adopted ex US ca. 1930; not unknown in UK.

carney, adj. Sly; cunning, artful: low and military:—1914 (F. & G.). ' "Carney" . . . means cunning, but not in the subtle snake-in-the-grass way: "a carney sod" is a coarse and untrustworthy fellow' (*Muvver*).

carni. Carnival. See **carney**, n., 3.

carnovsky. See TIDDLYWINKS, in Appx.

carny. Alternative spelling of **carney**.

carol singer. Police car with loud-speaker: Brisbane, Aus.: since ca. 1930. B., 1942.

carpark. A 'nark' (informer): r.s.: later C.20. Haden-Guest, 1972. Also *Noah's ark*.

carpet, n. A prison sentence or term of three months: abbr. of *carpet-bag*, r.s. on synon. *drag*: c. (Leach; *Slang*.) Tempest, however, writes, 'In days gone by it was calculated that it took a man three months to make a certain kind of carpet produced in the shops [i.e. prison workshops].' Hence, other things involving the number 3, e.g.:—2. The sum of £3: spivs' c.: since ca. 1942. *Picture Post*, Jan. 1954.—3. Odds of 3 to 1: racing, esp. bookmakers': C.20. *Sunday Telegraph*, 7 May 1967.—4. The sum of £300: secondhand-car dealers': since early 1950s. *Woman's Own*, 28 Feb. 1968. Contrast sense 2—inflation at work!—5. In *on the carpet*, at—or very near—ground level: RAF: 1918—ca. 1939. Perhaps it survived a little longer, but in my RAF service days, 1942–5, I never once heard it. (Owed to *OED* Sup., 1972.)—8. See **sweep** (includes *push*) **under the carpet**.

carpet, v. To reprimand: coll.: recorded in 1840. Ex earlier synon. *walk the carpet*; P.B.: C.20 Services' coll., as in 'He was carpeted for some minor offence', i.e. marched in and stood on the CO's office rug.

carpet-biter; carpet-biting. One (usu. male) who gets into a fearful rage, a visibly very angry man; a distressing exhibition of uncontrollable rage: coll. since ca. 1940. Ex the stories of Hitler biting carpets in his insane rages, and ob. as the memory faded after 1945. Cf. that great US fighting general, 'Vinegar Joe' Stilwell's phrase, 'I felt like biting the radiator'. (*Stilwell Papers*, 1949.)

carpet joint. 'A well-appointed gambling venue with carpets on the floor. Also *rug joint*' (Green): gamblers'.

carpurtle. See **kerpurtle**.

carpy. 'To be locked in the cell at the end of the day (from *carpe diem*)' (Tempest): prisons': mid-C.20.

carrie. See **carry**, 2.

carrier. A Bren-gun carrier: army coll. since 1940, soon > j. These vehicles were 'phased out' soon after WW2 and term transferred, as an abbr., to other 'carriers' such as the APC,

armoured personnel-carrier. (P.B.)—2. Abbr. aircraft-carrier, and occ. for commando-carrier: military coll./j.: since ca. 1950. (P.B.)

carrot-cruncher. 'A country visitor to London' (Powis): Cockneys': since mid-C.20, if not considerably earlier.

carrots! Run away!, or slangily, *piss off!*: RN lowerdeck: since ca. 1960. (Peppitt.) Origin unknown.

carry. 'A load of drugs' (Home Office): addicts' s.: current in 1970s.—2. In Stockley, 1986, *carrie* = cocaine, which Spears has as US since 1975: drugs c.

carry a (or **some**) **clout.** See **clout**, n., 2.

carry a (or **the**) **torch for** (someone). 'To be devoted to someone' (Leechman), but often with the implication of unrequited passion, love unconsummated because of impossible circumstances, or uninterest by the one for whom the torch is carried: Can., adopted ca. 1945 ex US; soon afterwards some use in Britain too. (P.B.) Perhaps ex US torch-light processions in honour of a political, or a local-government, candidate. (Leechman.)

carry (someone) **around** or, usu., **round.** 'To do a man's job for him until he knows the routine' (P-G-R.): Services' coll.: since ca. 1910.

carry ballast. To hold one's drinks well: RN. (Granville.) Moe cites the var. *carry lots of ballast*, from Carr, 1937, ref. to the year 1914.

carry both ends of the log. To do all the work, esp. in a complementary pair: Aus. coll. 'Rann Daly' in 1924.

carry both sheets aft. To walk around with both hands in trouser pockets: RN. (Granville.) By a technical pun.

carry dog. To put on 'side'. See **put on dog**.

carry on. To endure hardship; show quiet and constant fortitude: a C.20 coll. popularised by WW1. An imperative, orig. a military order, then (1917) = go ahead!, continue!, esp. continue as you are now doing.

carry-over. A 'hang-over' in which one is still slightly tipsy: coll.: since ca. 1912. Priestley.

carry the banner. To tramp the road; to be homeless; be a tramp: vagrants' c.: 1903 (London).—2. (usu. with *for*.) 'To support or praise some movement, often one of the not so popular type' (Petch): coll.: since ca. 1950. Ex *banner-carrying* at protest meetings or on protest marches.

carry the can. To be reprimanded: RN: late C.19–early 20. (Bowen.) The RAF form, later common to all Services, and current ca. 1920–45, *carry the can back*, meant to be made the scapegoat; to do the dirty work while another person gets the credit; to accept the blame for one's own or another's error; to be landed with (usu. unwanted) responsibility for an unpleasant task. 'Blake', 1941, writing of late 1939, has ' "What is a [Fighter-]Controller?", MacMurray went on questioning. "The man who carries the can", Placket told him.' Bolitho, 1941, noted *the can-back king*, one who was very good at it. Since ca. 1945 the phrase has reverted to the shorter, orig. form yet still, 1980, carries all the senses listed above. See also **left carrying the can** and **take the can back**. (P.B.)

carry the knot . To 'hump a bluey' or go on tramp: Aus.: since ca. 1930. B., 1943.

carry the mail. To stand drinks: Aus. Baker.

carry the torch for. See **carry a torch** . . .

carrying all before her. (Of girl or woman) having a well-developed bust, or being obviously pregnant: raffish joc.: since ca. 1920.

carrying three red lights. Drunk: nautical. Bowen, 'From the "Not under Control" signal'.

carrying weight. 'Loaded with depression' (Anderson): beatniks': since ca. 1959. A burden.

carsey, carzey. A place: grafters'. Allingham.—2. A privy: low Cockney: since ca. 1870. Cf. earlier synon. *case*. This is now, late 1970s, the commonest sense of the term, and has produced quite a number of var. spellings from writers unaware of its *Lingua Franca* derivation, e.g., *kharsie, khazi*, perhaps indicating also variations in pron. (P.B.)—3. See **kahsi**, a poss. var.

cart, n. A bed: army: mid-C.19–early 20. (F. & G.) Cf. synon. **chariot.**—2. Hence, a bunk: ships' stewards': from ca. 1919.

cart, v.t. To arrest: low Glasgow:—1934 (MacArthur). Gen. in the passive.

cart-grease. Bad butter, then any butter: from ca. 1875. Cf. *cow-grease.* In C.20, applied to margarine: Cockneys' (*Muvver*).

cartoon. A technical drawing or blueprint: motorcyclists': since ca. 1950. (Dunford.) It is curious that this s. term, derived from the idea of newspaper or film cartoons, should in fact be a return to one of the orig. meanings of the word.

cartwheel. An amphetamine sulphate tablet: drugs c. (Stockley, 1986.) Spears notes US since 1967: 'the X of the scoring represents the spokes'.

carve. To slash (a person) with a razor: c., and low (esp. Cockneys').

carve (oneself) **a slice.** To copulate (from the male point of view): Cockney. Cf. **cut off the joint, a.**

carve-up, n. A fight or even a war: mostly Cockney: since ca. 1905.—2. A swindle: lower classes':—1935.—3. The amount of money left by a will. Harrison, 1935.—4. See v., 4.

carve up, v. To spoil the chances of (a person) in business: London commercial and taxi-drivers': since ca. 1910.—2. To swindle an accomplice out of his share: c. Leach.—3. To beat up and esp. to slash with a knife: orig. c.; by 1940, fairly gen. s. Cf. **carve,** and the quot'n at **duff up.**—4. (Of a driver) to cut in sharply after overtaking another vehicle; to commit similar acts of bad driving: coll.: since late 1970s. Hence, as n., *carve-up*, an instance of this. (Sykes.)

carved out of wood. Stupid. See **cedar.**

carving knife. A wife: military r.s.:—1914 (F. & G.) Much more gen. is *trouble and strife.*

Cas, the. The *C*hief of *A*ir *S*taff: Air Ministry, and the higher RAF formations: since ca. 1930. Jackson.

casant. (Usu. pl.) Chrysanthemum: a slovening of the word. Cf. **'mum** and **chrissie.** (P.B.)

case, n. That which is, in the circumstances, to be expected: coll.:—1924 (*OED* Sup.).—2. (As n. and v.) An adulterous relationship; in such phrases as 'a bit of case', 'I'm going case', 'she's case': S. London criminals'. 'It can even mean taking up with a woman in a semi-legitimate way' (Powis, 1979). Prob. ex and elliptical from **cased up with,** q.v. Tempest, 1950, has ' "to go case with" = to sleep with. "I went case with a tart at the gaff" = I slept with a woman at (my) home.' Cf. the C.18–20 *case* = brothel, and *cased up.* See **caseo.**

case, v. In c., to report (a prisoner) for slackness; punish with solitary confinement.—2. To spoil; delay inevitably: c. Spenser, 1934, 'Well, this cases things for a while. We'll have to lie low.'—3. To weep: Marlborough Coll.: since ca. 1920.—4. Short for, and synon. with, *case a joint,* q.v.: Aus. police: adopted, ca. 1918, ex US. (Kelly, 1955.) Also Eng. low by 1950 (Tempest, who has 'The job [prospective burglary] has been well cased').

case a (or **the**) **joint.** To make a reconnaissance of, before robbing, a house or other building: Can., since ca. 1925; Eng. by 1930, as in Blake, 1954. P.B.: hence, by ca. 1950, loosely, to reconnoitre any building, as 'What's this pub like?' 'Dunno. Let's go in and case the joint', i.e. 'Let's go in and find out'.

case-ranging. An inspection of houses with a view to robbery: c.:—1923 (Manchon). Cf. **case a joint.**

cased. 'Charged with an offence' (Tempest): prison coll. or j.: mid-C.20. See **case,** v., 1.

cased-up, be. To be in a brothel: low. (Hodge, 1939.) Cf.:-

cased up with, be. To live with (a woman, esp. one's mistress): c. *Gilt Kid*, 1936.

caseo. A var., in c., of *casa,* n., the C.18 orig. form of *case,* brothel. *Gilt Kid*, 1936.—2. A full night in bed with a prostitute: low: since ca. 1930. *New Statesman*, 10 May 1947.

caser. A crown-piece; the sum of five shillings: Aus. and Brit. c. or low: late C.19–20; ob. as the currencies were decimalised, in 1966 and 1971 respectively. In C.20 in Britain the term was associated with 'low life' on the race-courses. Ex Yiddish.—2. One who 'cases' buildings, houses, etc., for burglars: c.: since ca. 1950; adopted ex US. I.e. the agent of *case,* v., 4; *case a joint.*—3. 'Nickname for an officer with a reputation for "casing" or putting people on report. A strict disciplinarian' (Tempest): prisons': mid-C.20. See **case,** v., 1.

cases. Boots: military (esp. the Guards): earlier C.20. (*John o' London's Weekly*, 3 Nov. 1939.) Cf. later C.19 synon. *trotter-cases.*—2. In *get down to cases,* to 'get down to brass tacks'; talk seriously: lower classes'. *Gilt Kid*, 1936.

Casey's Court or **Donnelly's Hotel** (or **the hotel; the cottage; the villa; the drum**). The sailors' (the ratings' or lowerdeck) mess: RN: late C.19–(?)mid-20. (Sidney Knock, *via* Moe.) Kept scrupulously clean. *Casey's Court* was the title of a music hall sketch by the London comedian Lew Lake, 1920s, set in an East End courtyard (Barltrop).

Cash. An accountant officer on duty: RN. (Bowen.) Cf. **Akkas.**

cash and carry. Generic for any large, wholesale supermarket: coll.: since early 1970s. 'Have you got the [recognised retailer's] card—I'm just going up [= to] the cash and carry.' (D. Beale, 1981.)

cash in. To succeed, esp. financially: coll.: from ca. 1920. Ex *cash in,* to clear accounts, terminate a matter.—2. To die: coll. Ex:-

cash in (one's) **checks.** To die: adopted ex US ca. 1875. *Checks* = counters in the game of poker. Also *hand in . . .* or *pass in . . .* Cf.:-

cash (or **throw**) **in** (one's) **chips.** Var. of prec. To die: Can., adopted, ex US, ca. 1880; common usage in UK, C.20, perhaps earlier. As prec. ex the S.E. sense, to stop gambling, esp. at cards, notably poker.

cash up. To earn or make money; often as *get cashed up,* to earn and save money: Aus. coll. Niland, 1958, 'But I thought the idea would be to work on here for a bit longer . . . Get cashed up a bit, then move'.

casher. 'A "good casher" is a driver whose average taxi-meter money is high; a "bad casher", one whose average is low' (Hodge, 1939): taxicab owners' and drivers' coll.: since ca. 1910.—2. A front trouser pocket: pickpockets' c.: since ca. 1930 (Palmer, 1974). Because that is where a person often carries coins.

caso. A prostitute that takes a man for the night: c.—2. A brothel: since ca. 1910. (Hodge, 1939.) Var. of **caseo,** itself dissyllabic.—3. See **go caso.**

cast-iron or **bullet-proof.** Irrefutable: Services', resp. coll. and s.: since the 1920s. H. & P.

cast-iron (or **stone-wall**) **horrors, in the.** Suffering from *delirium tremens*: Anglo-Irish.

cast nasturtiums. To cast aspersions: joc., mostly lower-middle class. By a kind of Hobson-Jobson process.

caster. A broadcaster or newscaster: Can. coll., adopted, ca. 1960, ex US.

casting couch. A divan in a casting-director's office: coll.: adopted, ca. 1955, ex US (Mencken, 1948; *OED* Sup., 1972). Ex the widespread impression that many female minor parts are assigned on a basis of bedworthiness.

castle, the. The stumps: cricketers': since ca. 1925. (Peebles, 1959.) The batsman defends them.

castrating, (very). A pun on *frustrating.* Tracy, 1973: '[The predicament of the book's hero] is all, in the current speech, very castrating'. Esp. if the frustration is caused by dominant women?

casual. 'A casual payment of "something on account " to an officer or rating whose pay documents are still in his last ship' (Granville): perhaps orig. RN, but also army and RAF: coll. > j.—2. A London youngster whose chief interest is fashion, and who wishes always to wear the latest style, as in 'the multi-racial group . . . who wear £60 tracksuits. [These

C

people] are called "Casuals " ' (Gaffin, 1984): London schoolchildren's.

Cat. St Catherine's Street, Oxford. See **Cat Street.**—2. A Catalina long-range amphibious aircraft: Services': WW2, and the few years they remained in service afterwards.

cat. Abbr. **cat and mouse,** q.v., a theatrical house.—2. A gossiping woman: upper-middle class: since ca. 1927. (Wilson, 1950.) A back-formation from S.E. *catty,* spiteful.—3. (Usu. in pl.) A lion or a tiger or a leopard: circusmen's. Also, *the big cats,* all of these collectively.—4. A catamaran: boating coll.: since ca. 1955.—5. A *cat*erpillar tractor: orig., Can.: since early 1930s.—6. A hydraulic catapult on an aircraft carrier: FAA: since late 1930s. Winton, 1967.—7. A *cat*egory, either medical or, esp. in RAF, of flying ability: Services' coll.: since ca. 1945, (?)earlier. (P.B.)—8. 'Hippy term for any male within the hippy world or the drug scene. "He's a cool cat" would mean "He is a self-assured, 'knowing' man who is one of us" '(Powis): adopted, ex US, in the late 1950s.—9. Hence, a 'fan' or devotee: adopted, ca. 1965, ex US (*Jagger*). A specialisation of sense 8.

cat and class. *Cat*aloguing and *class*ification: librarians' coll.

cat and mouse. A house: r.s. (—1857); ob. 'Ducange Anglicus', 1st ed.

Cat and Mouse Act. 'The Prisoners (Temporary Discharge for Ill-health) Act of 1913 to enable hunger-strikers to be released temporarily' (*Punch,* 23 July 1913). *OED* Sup.

cat board. A board of officers convened to decide a man's medical *cat*egory, and to judge his ability to continue flying duties: Services' coll.: since ca. 1945 (?earlier). Hence, as a v., *to be cat-boarded,* to be considered by such a board. Ex **cat,** 7. (P.B.)

cat-burglar. A burglar that nimbly enters houses from the roof: from ca. 1919: coll.; S.E. by 1933.

cat crept into the crypt – crapped – and crept out again, the. A mock tongue-twister, popular in the Services: ca. 1950–70. (P.B.)

cat-fart about, mostly as vbl n. *cat-farting about.* Fussy actions, irritating in their effect: low coll.: since ca. 1950. (L.A.) Cf. synon. **faff about.**

cat house. A brothel: Can.: adopted, ca. 1925, ex US. Cf. *cat,* which has been used for 'prostitute' since C.15.

cat in hell's chance. Orig., ca. 1930, only a very slight chance; but very soon only in the neg., *not a cat . . . :* no chance whatever. (L.A.; P.B.) Orig., C.18, *. . . without claws.*

cat-skinner. Driver of a caterpillar tractor: Can. lumbermen's: since ca. 1930. A blend of *cat*erpillar + mule-*skinner.* 'No longer restricted to lumbering. Any man who drives a "cat" ' (Leechman, 1947).

cat-stabber. An army clasp-knife; a bayonet: army: early C.20. F. & G.; B. & P.

Cat Street. St Catherine's Street: Oxford undergraduates': late C.19–20. (Collinson.) Orig. *Cat.*

cat-walk. A 'brick-paved pathway, usually one brick (nine inches) wide, laid down across farm fields in Flanders': army: WW1. F. & G.—2. A horizontal 'ladder' whereby the crew of a zeppelin or large rigid dirigible could move from one gondola to another, inside the envelope of the airship. R.S. cites the caption of an illustration in *The Wonder Book of Aircraft,* 1919.—3. Hence, 'The long plank on bomber aircraft stretching between cockpit and tail' (H. & P.): RAF: since ca. 1938. In this sense, occ. *cat's walk;* but as *cat-walk,* post WW2, and with other applications, e.g., a means of walking across a fragile roof, or a gangway at theatrical and mannequin shows, it >, by 1960 at latest, S.E. (P.B.)

cat-whipper. One who 'cries over spilt milk': Aus.: since ca. 1916. (B., 1953.)

catch. To eat a snack or have a drink, hurriedly, between other activities; e.g. 'I just had time to catch a sandwich before rushing off': coll.: later C.20. (P.B.)

catch a cold. 'To get oneself into trouble by being too impetuous' (H. & P.): Services': since ca. 1930. Cf. *catch cold;*

prob. ex the earlier.—2. To 'get the wind up' (become or feel afraid): army: WW1. Ex that chilly feeling.

catch a horse; or **go and catch . . .** To urinate: Aus. (B., 1942.) Cf. *water one's nag.*

catch bending. To catch (a person) at a disadvantage: joc. coll. (Wodehouse, 1910.) Esp. in a c.p., *don't let me catch you bending* (ob.). A person bending is in a favourable position to be kicked.

catch (one) flatfooted. To catch at a disadvantage: coll.: mid-C.20. Farmer, 1945, 'We were again caught flatfooted, this time by a real bomber. There was no cover'.

catch hand. A 'casual workman who moves from job to job, esp. at commencement of new jobs, to get more favourable rates and conditions, and who has no intention of staying on one job until the end' (L.A., 1967): urban labourers' coll.: since ca. 1950.

catch on the fly. To board a train while it is moving: Can., orig. hoboes': Niven, 1927.

catch on the rebound. To get engaged to (a person) after he or she has been refused by another: coll.: from ca. 1908. Ex lawn tennis. (Collinson.) Hence *to be caught on the rebound,* of the jilted or bereaved person, thus to become engaged.

catch the boat up. To get VD: RN: since ca. 1930.

catch the zig. To get 'done'; 'buy a pup': racing c.

catch (a girl) under the pinny. To coït with her: raffish: early C.20. Cf. **under,** n.

catch up. 'To withdraw from drugs' (Stockley, 1986): addicts'. US since—1938 (Spears).

catch (someone) with his trousers down. See **caught with . . .**

caterpillar. 'A person who is scared of flying' (Green): airlines' staff: later C.20.

cath. A catheter: medical coll. See quot'n at **bag,** v., 4.

catheter. In *pass the catheter,* a joc. pedantic form of **take the piss,** q.v.

cats. As *the Cats,* the Canadian Auxiliary Territorial Service: mostly Can.: WW2.

cat's arse or **miaow, the.** Can. var. of **cat's pyjamas.**

cat's breakfast. A very common Scottish and N. Country var. since ca. 1920—of **dog's breakfast,** a mess.

cat's eyes. Usu. in pl., *cats' eyes,* 'the pilots to our nightfighter squadrons' (H. & P., 1943). Orig. a journalistic term, it was jocularly adopted by RAF flying-crews; by Jan. 1945, however, it was already ob.—2. (Or hyphenated). Marbles thus coloured: children's coll.: late C.19–20.

cat's face. A 'worker wanted' notice in the window: tailors'. *Tailor and Cutter,* 29 Nov. 1928.—2. Ace (in cards): r.s.: since mid-C.20. Hillman.

cat's head cut open. Pudendum muliebre: low.

cat's pyjamas, the. Anything very good, attractive, etc.: American (—1920) anglicised by 1923; ob. in UK by ca. 1939, but still, in 1965 anyway, 'far from dead in Australia' (B.P.). Cf. **the bee's knees.**

cat's walk. See **cat-walk,** 3.

cat's whisker. A thin wire for establishing contact on a crystal (wireless) set: from ca. 1920; ob.

cat's whiskers, the. A var. of *the cat's pyjamas* (see above): 1927 (Sayers); by 1970s poss. ob., but by no means quite dead. B.P.'s comment re *cat's pyjamas,* that in 1965 it was 'far from dead in Australia' applies here too.

cattie or **catty.** A catapult: schoolchildren's: late C.19–20.

cattle, v. To coït with: low Cockney. Ex **cattle truck,** v.

cattle(-)banger. A cattle-station hand; a milker: Aus.: since ca. 1910. (B., 1942.) Cf. **stockbanger.**

cattle truck, n. A one-man, i.e. driver only, bus. (Heard on radio, on 23 Nov. 1973. L.A.)

cattle truck, v.; since ca. 1945, always shortened to *cattle.* To copulate with, also fig.: (esp. racing): r.s. (Franklyn 2nd.) On *fuck.* 'The favourite was well cattled when he fell at the last fence.'

catty. Agile, smart; skilfully careful: Can. (esp. lumbermen's) coll. Beames.

caught short. Experiencing the onset of menstruation when no pads or tampons are available: feminine coll., esp. in Aus.: since middle 1930s. On analogy of *taken short*, but also of being embarrassed by untimely lack of, e.g., money (esp., formerly, 'a shilling for the gas-meter'), candles, contraceptives, petrol, tea-bags . . .

caught with (one's) **trousers down.** Taken unawares; unready: Services': since ca. 1920; gen. since ca. 1940; since ca. 1930, more commonly with the ex US var. . . . *pants down*. To the sense of 'totally unprepared' has been added the nuance 'caught in an undignified position and without excuse'. The var. gave rise to the WW2 abbr. *caught p.d.* (H. & P.; L.A., 1976). Cf. **stand on one leg.**

Cauldron, the. 'a notorious journalistic mistranslation of standard Ger. "Kesselschlacht", a battle of encirclement; although . . . "Kessel" *does* mean a cauldron, in hunting "Kesseltreiben" means driving game into an enclosed killing-ground' (R.S., 1967): the term was applied to part of the N. African WW2 battlefield known as Knightsbridge.

cauliflower. A goods-engine drawing wagons laden with cauliflowers and other greenstuff that had come from the Channel Islands: railwaymen's: late C.19–early 20.—2. A locomotive with a crested front: railwaymen's: since ca. 1910. *Railway.*—3. Short for *cauliflower ear*: coll.: from ca. 1925.

Cauliflower Alley; Tin-Ear Alley. The boxing world: boxing journalists': since ca. 1935.

cauliflowered and mashed. A c.p. description of a boxer's face: since the 1930s. Cauliflower ears and mashed nose.

cauliflower top. An upper deck full of passengers: busmen's (esp. London): since ca. 1935.

caulk up. To stamp, with one's spiked boots, on (a man): among Can. lumbermen (playful little fellows).

caulks to (someone), **put the.** To stamp on his face with spiked boots. See prec. and **logger's smallpox.**

cause it. To cause trouble to, to damage something, as, e.g., drilling a hole in the kitchen wall, hitting the cable and putting all the lights out: 'O Lor'! That's caused it!': since late 1940s. (P.B., 1974.)

caustic. An acoustic mine: RN: WW2. 'It exploded when the ship's engines synchronised with the beat of the mine's clock' (Granville). By Hobson-Jobson, but also perhaps ex:—2 (*Old*) *Caustic*: 'Nickname for a surly or querulous type of man' (Ibid.): RN.

Cav and **Pag.** *Radio Times*, 16 Apr. 1976, ' "Cav" was first performed in 1890, and "Pag" two years later', *Cav* being the opera *Cavalleria Rusticana* and *Pag, Pagliacci*: musical circles'.

Cavalier; Roundhead. (Usu. in pl.) A male uncircumcised; circumcised: schoolboys' and RN: C.20—and prob. earlier. L.A. notes that Katharine Whitehorn was prob. the first to get it into reputable print.

cavity gremlin. A mole-like gremlin that digs large holes just before and where the pilot is about to land: RAF: 1940–5. (P-G-R.) See GREMLINS, in Appx.

CB. Abbr. of *Citizen's Band.*

Cecil. Cocaine: drugs c. (Stockley, 1986.) US since—1938 (Spears). Ex initial; cf. **Charley,** 9.

cedar. A simpleton, a dupe: Aus.: since ca. 1930. B., 1953, adduces the synon. *log* and *mahogany* and (someone) *carved out of wood.*

ceiling. 'The bottom of a ship was called the ceiling, and when unloading if you heard the cry "I can see the ceiling" then you knew that the hold was nearly [emptied]' (Ash): London dockers': earlier C.20.

celeb. '[The company] boasts such celeb clients as Prince Edward . . . ' (*Sunday Express* mag., 4 Aug. 1985). Abbr. *celebrated*, or, with journalists' love of n. for adj., *celebrity.*

celebrate. To drink in honour of an event or celebration; hence, to drink joyously: coll. Ex S.E. *celebrate* (e.g. *an occasion*).

cell W. Illicit cell wireless: prisoners'. Clayton, 1970.

cellar-flap. To borrow: r.s. on *tap*, and often shortened to *cellar.*

celly. Cell-mate: prisoners'. Clement, 1977.

cement. Kaolin mixture, or any other cure for diarrhoea: (?mainly) Aus.: later C.20. (Raab, 1982.)—2. 'Wholesale illicit narcotics' (Green): drugs' c.

cement-mixer; esp., *have a cement-mixer,* 'to have a ball or dance' (Anderson): beatniks': since ca. 1959.

cements. Stock Exchange shares: since ca. 1935. 'Often jocularly, as "Cements are hardening" ' (Petch, 1946). Stock Exchange j. 'to *harden*' originated the term.

Centre, the. Orig. half j., half c., it has, since ca. 1925, been j. for the organisation that sent girls and women out to the Argentine to become courtesans or prostitutes. Londres, 1928.

Cert or **Certif, the Higher** (**School**) and **the School.** The Higher School Certificate; the (lower) School Certificate: rendered ob., in 1951, by the introduction of 'O' and 'A' (*O*rdinary and *A*dvanced) levels to replace them: *Cert*, mostly Public Schools'; *Certif* mostly other schools', and teachers'.

certified. Certified as insane: coll. rather than euph. Ironically as a virtual c.p., *time you were certified,* to a person acting the fool or having been exceptionally stupid.

Ces, the. The Cesarewitch, run in mid-October: sporting coll.: late C.19–20.

cess. 'Extreme rails of track' (*Railway*, 2nd): railwaymen's: since ca. 1930(?). Origin? Perhaps ex*cess.*

Chad. 'The British Services' counterpart of Kilroy . . . is known variously as Chad, Flywheel, Clem, Private Snoops, the Jeep, or just Phoo. His chalked-up picture is always accompanied by the theme song: "What no . . . ?" ' (a newspaper cutting, 17 Nov. 1945). The 'picture', a rudimentary cartoon, showed the semicircular top of a head above the top of a brick wall, its single strand of hair in the form of a question mark, its eyes mere crosses, and a nose drooping over the edge of the wall-top; sometimes a hand clutched the wall-top on each side of the 'head'. (*Mr*) *Chad* was mostly RAF and civilian usage; in the army he was *Private Snoops* and, in the RN, *The Watcher.* (P.B.)

chaff. Money: low Aus. Tennant, 1939, 'He'—a barrowman— 'gave money its rightful designation of "chaff", "sugar" or "hay".'

chain and crank. A (financial) bank: r.s. Cf. **rattle and clank.**

chain and locket. Pocket: r.s.: early C.20. Eagar, 1922.

chain-breaker. An under-vest or singlet: military: from ca. 1920. Formerly, those men taking part, as principals, in a strong-man act, who wore only a vest and shorts.

chain-gang, the. 'A special set of stewards to help cope with a spate of passengers': nautical. (Bowen.) Punning a convicts' chain-gang.—2. Those waiters who, not on saloon duty, perform the odd jobs: passenger ships'. Marlowe, 1937.—3. The Lord Mayor and Mayoress of London: late C.19–20. Ex their chains of office. (L.A., 1976.)—4. Married men: joc., in, e.g., public houses: prob. since ca. 1920. I first heard it during the 1930s.—5. A bus-running inspector: busmen's, esp. London: since ca. 1930.—6. Aircrafthands, General Duties: RAF: since ca. 1930. Partridge, 1945: 'the RAF's maids of all work'.

chain-smoke. To smoke (esp. cigarettes) incessantly: C.20: coll. >, by 1935, S.E. Ex S.E. *chain-smoker.*

chain up! 'Shut up!': low:—1923 (Manchon). Ex *chain up that dog!* Cf. **belt up!**

chain up a pup. To get drinks on credit from a hotel: Aus. See **tie up a dog.**

chair. A motorcycle sidecar: motorcyclists': since ca. 1950. (Dunford.)—2. As *the chair,* electric chair (for criminals): coll.: US, anglicised by 1931. *COD*, 1934 Sup.—3. In, e.g. 'Are you in the chair?', a broad hint that the person addressed should buy the drinks, it is his turn or 'shout': later C.20. (Scott, 1979.) In early C.19 *to call a chair* was 'to appoint a president at a tavern-party, when discussion ensues'. Cf. **saddle.**

chair-borne divisions, the. Those members of the Services who work in offices: mostly RAF: since 1942. Ironically, ex *Airborne Divisions*. Also called *chair-borne types* or *forces*.

chair-marking. To write, not figure, the date in, or heavily to endorse, a cab-driver's licence, as a hint of the holder's undesirability: cab-owners': from ca. 1885. (*Pall Mall Gazette*, 15 Sep. 1890.) Later, among taxi-drivers, an illicit marking of their licences by their employers. Hodge, 1939.

chair-warmer. A physically attractive woman 'who does nothing on the stage beyond helping to fill it' (Ware): theatrical: earlier C.20. Later the term was applied, usu. in pl., to an unresponsive audience (Green).

Chalfonts, the. Haemorrhoids: abbr. r.s., on *Chalfont St Giles* = piles: later C.20. (Daniells, 1980.) Cf. synon. **Farmer Giles; Seven Dials.**

chalk. A body of troops being transported by air: military coll. > j.: since WW2. Orig. from the use of blackboard and chalked numbers to list the various parties and their aircraft, hence *chalk number*, and *chalk commander*, the officer in charge of a party or the whole body.—2. Later C.20 shortening of **Chalk Farm** (Powis, 1977).

chalk and talk; also chalk-and-talker. A school-teacher: Aus.: since ca. 1920. (B., 1942.) In UK, in the 1970s, the phrase had come to be slightly derogatory, '*mere* chalk-and-talk', of 'old-fashioned' teaching methods, i.e. those not using visual aids, language laboratories and all the rest of the 'educational technology'. (P.B.)

chalk eaters. 'Horse race punters who bet only on favourites. From their following the bookie as he writes (in chalk) the current odds' (Green): racing. Also *chalk players*.

Chalk Farm. An arm: r.s.:—1857; by late 1920s, ob., and by 1960, virtually †. ('Ducange Anglicus', 1st ed.) In WW1, the Tommies preferred *false alarm*. But see **chalk, 2.**

chalkie. A schoolteacher: Aus.: since ca. 1930. (B., 1953.) P.B., 1979: and British too: *vide* Giles's famous cartoon schoolmaster 'Old Chalky', who, with the perhaps even better known 'Grandma', has been delighting readers of the Beaverbrook newspapers for over thirty years.

chamfer up. To tidy up, make things tidy: RN. (Granville.) Ex the stonemasonry and carpentry senses.

champ. A champion: coll.: from ca. 1915.—2. 'A drug user who will not reveal his source' (Stockley, 1986). US since—1967 (Spears).

champagne-glass. A Hampden (or less frequently a Hereford) aircraft in the plan view: RAF: ca. 1940–3, then ob. (Partridge, 1945.) Resemblance.

champers. Champagne: since ca. 1920: Oxford undergraduates': the 'OXFORD -ER(s)'; hence, since ca. 1950, also among the smart young set. (Gilderdale, 2.)

chancellor of the exchequer. Joc. coll.: the one who holds the purse-strings.

chancer. 'One who tries it on by *telling the tale*; or one who just takes chances' (H. & P.): Services': since the 1920s.—2. Hence, one not too smart in appearance or at drill: Army: since ca. 1930.—3. An expensive motor-car, oldish and of unusual make: motor trade: since ca. 1920. The dealer 'takes a chance' when he buys it.—4. A bluffer: Anglo-Irish: O'Neill, 1959.—5. A trimmer; one with 'an eye to the main chance': coll. 'Chancer may smack of the [19] twenties or thirties' (Harry Whewell: see quot'n at **hack, n., 2**).

Channel crossing. Bread-and-butter pudding: Marlborough Coll.: since ca. 1920. Resemblance to vomit.

Channel-fever. Homesickness: nautical: mid-C.19–20. (Bowen.) I.e. the English Channel. L.A., 1967, however, gives a more likely definition of the term: 'the nervous state that overcomes some sailors as their ship nears home after long absence or relatively long abstinence'. Cf. the **gate-fever** of time-expired prisoners, those nearing completion of sentence. In either sense, adds Peppitt, the term was obsolete by 1948.

Channel fleet. A street: Irish r.s. Franklyn.

chant. In vagrants' c. as in Gape, 1936, 'To "chant" this town', i.e., to sing in it for alms.

chap, n. A 'customer', a fellow. From ca. 1715; coll. In C.20, rarely (unless prefaced by *old*) of an old or 'oldish' man. (Abbr. *chapman*; ex the C.16–early 18 sense, extant in dial., a buyer, a customer. But cf. Romany *chav* in this sense, q.v. at quot'n under **bewer.**) In post-WW1 days, often used by and of girls among themselves. Cf. **customer,** and the Scottish *callant*. P.B.: Raab has percipiently pointed out, 1978, that in C.20 and esp. in Public Schools' usage—though the term is by no means confined to that class—it has come to mean, nearly always, a fellow who is 'one of us'. 'We' are 'chaps'; the rest, the outsiders, are 'oicks', 'yobboes', or whatever the current pej. may be.—2. 'Top of the pecking order—a champion': Borstals' and detention centres': current in 1970s (Home Office). Contrast **div.**

chap, v.t. To chaperon: from ca. 1921. Murray, 1933, 'Mrs. M. would chap. us if you're so fussy.'

Chapel. The C.20 abbr. of the next. 'Oh, them! They're chapel, so of *course* they sing much louder.' (P.B.)

chapel-folk. Nonconformists as opp. to Episcopalians (esp. Anglicans): a snobbish coll.; from ca. 1830.

chapter herald. A *Hell's angel*, [q.v.]: motorcyclists' (Dunford): since (?)ca. 1960. Hell's angels are grouped into 'chapters' (cf. the printing trades' unions); *herald* ex the famous Wesley carol, 'Hark! The herald angels sing . . .'

char. Tea: in late C.19–early 20, army coll.; post WW1, vagrants' c.; by mid-C.20, widespread and gen., esp. in *a cuppa char* and *char and wads*, though the latter, meaning 'tea and buns', was ob. by ca. 1960 and had always, perhaps, been confined to Forces' canteens. Ex *cha*, a S.E. form of C.16–19.

char-wallah. A teetotaller: army: early C.20. (Richards, 1933.) Ex *char*, and *wallah*. Cf. **wad-scoffer.**—2. 'In India this is a native servant who brings the early morning tea. In Gibraltar, a dining-hall waiter' (H. & P.): Services': since ca. 1930. (Emanuel, 1945.) Also used as an adj.; e.g. *charwallah squadron*, an Air Force squadron consisting of Indian personnel. P.B.: when the British Army left India in 1947, the faithful char-wallahs followed it overseas and set up their little shops, to complement the official canteens by providing 'char', Horlicks, cocoa, cold soft drinks, and banjos (sandwiches or filled rolls) of all sorts. They were in Malaya during the Emergency, 1948–60; in Cyprus from the mid–1950s; and by the 1970s had even reached the Army camps in Northern Ireland. The spirit of Gunga Din yet lives!

chara. A lower classes' abbr. (1927, F.E. Baily: *OED* Sup.) of *char-à-banc*. Also *charrie*, -*y* (1926: Ibid.). Cf.:—

charabang (*ch-* pron. *tch*). Sol., from ca. 1835, for *char-à-banc* (since 1918 gen. spelt *charabanc*). Occ. *charrybong* (*ch-* pron. *sh*). The Fr. is *char à bancs*. P.B.: the term was ob. by ca. 1970, being replaced by the S.E. [motor-] *coach*. In 1930s–40s usu. pron. *sharrabang*.

character. Whereas the RAF speaks of *types* and the RN and the Army imitate, the RN speaks of *characters* and the other two services imitate: since ca. 1925. Indeed, since ca. 1945, the term has become increasingly popular everywhere and now means simply 'fellows' or 'guys'.—2. The Southern English coll. form of the next: since (?)late C.19. (P.B.)

characters. One's references, as regards employment: Midland and N. Country coll. Vickers, 1955.

charas. Cannabis grown in India: drugs c.: later C.20. (McConville, 1980.) US since—1957 (Spears).

charge. A prisoner brought up for trial on a charge or accusation: from late 1850s. (Sala.) As 'A person arrested and held in charge' (Newman, 1970), still police coll.—2. In hospitals, *the charge* is a Charge Nurse (esp. if male), i.e. one in charge of a ward or set of wards: coll.—3. Marijuana: c.: since ca. 1943. It contains a 'charge'—produces a 'kick'. US since—1929 (Spears).—4. 'Cocaine (US)' (Home Office): drug-users' s.: current in 1970s.

charged up. 'Under influence of drugs' (Stockley, 1986): drugs c. US since—1922 (Spears).

chariot. (Also *wanking chariot*.) A bed: Army: since ca. 1940.—2. A motor car: joc.: since ca. 1945.

charity dame or **for-free.** A prostitute undercutting the prices; an 'enthusiastic amateur': Aus. c., esp. prostitutes': resp. since ca. 1930 and ca. 1944 (US influence). B., 1953. Wilkes lists later C.20 var. *charity moll.* Cf.:-

charity goods. 'A homosexual prostitute who is persuaded to give his services free' (Green): later C.20. Cf. prec.

charlady. Joc. coll. for a charwoman: since the 1890s. (E.P.) But since mid-C.20, there is no jocularity implied, and this flattering contradiction in terms is the only socially acceptable name for a charwoman. Cf. *tea-lady, cleaning-lady*, and similar functionaries. (P.B.)

Charles de Gaulle. The gall-bladder: proletarian joc. or euph.: later C.20. Ross, 1978.

Charles William. The dummy man in life-boat exercises: Dartmouth RN College. Bowen.

charley, charlie, n; or with capitals. Reveille: RN. Granville, 'The bugle call, to which the Navy has given these words: "Charley! Charley! Get up and wash yourself!/Charley! Charley! Lash up and stow!" '—2. Short for **Charley Ronce,** q.v., a ponce: low: mid-C.19–20. *New Statesman*, 29 Nov. 1941.—3. A male homosexual: since ca. 1945.—4. A chamber-pot: domestic coll.: C.20, perhaps earlier. (P.B.)—5. A fool, a 'softie': C.20 among Cockneys, but only since late 1940s at all gen.; by ca. 1960, however, very common and widespread (influence of radio and TV), esp. in such phrases as *a proper* or *a right charley*, a complete fool. Short for **Charley Hunt,** q.v.—6. Esp. in 'your Charlie', your girl: Aus., esp. Sydney: since ca. 1945. (Glassop, 1949.) Short for **Charley Wheeler,** q.v.—7. By specialisation, a prostitute: low Aus.: since late 1940s. B., 1953.—8. A bottle or glass of Carlsberg beer: army in Germany: 1950s–60s. (P.B., 1974)—9. 'Cocaine (US)' (Home Office): drug-users' s.: current in 1970s. US since ca. 1920 (Spears). Cf. *Cecil.*—10. See **Charley Oboe.**

charley, charlie, adj. Afraid; 'windy': low: since ca. 1930. 'I was dead charlie' (Norman). Hence *to turn charlie*, to turn coward or become frightened.—2. 'Cheap attempt at style, flashy, non-U' (*Sunday Express* mag., 11 Oct. 1982): Sloane Rangers', q.v.

Charley Brady. A hat: r.s. (on *cady*): late C.19–mid-20. Franklyn.

Charley (or **Charlie**) **Chaplin.** A, usu. prison, chaplain: mostly S. African: since 1930s. (Hall, 1974.) But also a RN ship's chaplain: WW2. Bassett.

Charley Coke. Cocaine: drugs c. (Stockley, 1986.) US since mid-C.20 (Spears). Cf. **Charley, 9.**

Charley Dilke. Milk: ca. 1880–1940. Franklyn.

Charley Howard. A coward: r.s. Curtis, 1936.

Charley (or **Charlie**) **Hunt;** often in C.20 shortened to *Charley* (*Charlie*). The female pudend: r.s.: since ca. 1890. A var. of **Joe Hunt**—cf. **Berkeley** (**Hunt**).—2. Hence, a 'softy', a fool: C.20; in gen. use only since the late 1940s and increasingly in the shortened form, for which see **charley, 5.**

Charley-in-Charley. 'Phonetic for C in C, itself a contraction of Commander in Chief' (Sayers, 1985): RN: mid-C.20. See Appx.

Charley (or **Charlie**) **Oboe.** Often merely *Charley*. The Commanding Officer: Army and RAF: from 1942, when, in the signals phonetic alphabet, 'Oboe' replaced 'Orange' for O. Charlie for *C* has remained constant since 1927; 'Orange' lasted 1938–41, and 'Oboe' was replaced by 'Oscar' in 1956. See Appx for the evolution of the phonetic alphabet. *Charlie Orange* was used for CO in the RAF, 1939–41 (McDouall, 1945).

Charley (or **-ie**) **Ronce.** A souteneur or prostitute's bully: late C.19–20: r.s. on *ponce*. Often shortened to *Charley* which, derivatively, = very smart, 'one of the boys'.

Charley Sheard. A beard: r.s. (Daniells, 1980.)

Charley Smirke. A berk, q.v.: r.s., perhaps 'twice removed': later C.20. 'Too many flatties understood "berk" ' (Daniells, 1980). Charley Smirke, one of the leading jockeys of earlier C.20, enjoyed a chequered career, 1922–53; he rode the Derby winner in 1934, 1936, and in 1952, on Tulyar, he won both the Derby and the St Leger. (P.B.)

Charley Wheeler. A girl: Aus. r.s., on *sheila*: 1945 (Baker). McNeil.

Charley Wiggins. Lodgings: mainly theatrical r.s., on *diggings* pron. *diggins*: late C.19–20. Franklyn.

charleys, charlies. Testicles: low.—2. (Mostly *Charlies.*) Sailors in general: R Aus. N: since ca. 1925. B., 1943.

Charley's coat. A Carley float: Aus. r.s.: mostly R Aus. N and RAAF: 1942–5. B., 1943.

Charlie(s). See **Charley(s).**

charmer. One's girl friend: Services': ca. 1935–45. H. & P.

charming! —with, among the less squeamish and never among the decent-speaking, the elab., *charming, fucking charming!* 'Was, for a short period in the early 1970s, a stock response to an unpleasant situation or remark. Said with heavy emphasis on the first syllable. E.g., teller of tale: "So she screams across the pub at him, 'You're nothing but a big, fat, idle swine!' " Interested listener, encouragingly: "Charming!" Still part of some people's speech pattern.' (P.B., 1976.) I have to add only that I first heard it in late 1968 and that, although much less common now (Apr. 1977) than at its peak in 1970–5, it is far from being dated; much less, outmoded. The reason for its very wide currency is that it presents irony at its best and disarmingly understates and gently implies a social animadversion.

charp. A bed: army and, since ca. 1920, RAF: late C.19–20. Jackson, 'From the Hindustani, charpoy'. P.B.: hence, also as a v., to sleep. Cf.:-

charpoy-bashing. Sleeping; sleep: RAF: since ca. 1920. (Emanuel, 1945.) See prec., and cf. **square-bashing.**

Charps and Dils, the. The Bedfordshire and Hertfordshire Regt.: 'In India between the wars they were sometimes known as "The Charps and Dils"—from the Hindustani, *charpoy* meaning bed and *dil* meaning heart' (Carew).

Chart and Evans. Knees: RN. (Granville.) A rationalised form of *chart an' 'eavens*, itself incorrect for *chart in 'eavens*. The semantic key is supplied by s. *benders*, knees—what you get down upon to say the Lord's Prayer, 'Our Father, which *art in Heaven*'—and strengthened by the second verb in the predominant construction and usage, 'Get down on your chart 'n 'eavens and *holy*stone the deck.'

chart-buster (s.) and **chart-topper** (coll.). A very successful song or record; the former term, the stronger, for it means 'a smash hit': both since ca. 1955. ' "Please, Please Me" was the first of an unbroken chain of 'chart-toppers' (*Beatles*).

charver. A sexual embrace: theatrical (orig. Parlyaree): late C.19–20.—2. Hence, a girl, a woman, esp. as sexual partner: market-traders': late C.19–20. (*M.T.*) Also spelt *charva*, as in *bona palone for a charva*, a good-time girl. (*John o'London's Weekly*, 4 Feb. 1949.)

chase. 'To stand over and keep urging (someone) to do and get on with a piece of work': Services' coll.: since ca. 1920. H. & P.—2. Short for **chase the dragon**, as in 'Whether snorted, chased . . . or injected, heroin will have the same impact' (*New Statesman*, 7 Mar. 1986): drugs c.

chase a fart through a bag of nails. 'In "like chasing . . . ", applied to something very hard or difficult to do: Newfoundland and Saskatchewan: since ca. 1940 at latest. Also used in ref. to a person's appearance: "You look like you've been chasing . . . " ' (Leech; Dyke, 1986).

chase-me-Charley. 'A radio-controlled glider-bomb used by the Germans': RN: ca. 1940–5. (Granville.) Ex a c.p. of the 'Naughty Nineties' and Edwardian days which survived until mid-C.20 as a harmless, mild exclam.

chase the dragon. 'Heroin users horrified by the idea of injection might also "chase the dragon", burning the drug on a piece of tinfoil and inhaling the fumes [through a straw or other thin tube]' (Denselow, 1983); 'The liquefied heroin runs along the foil, thus "the chase" ' (Green): adopted, prob. ex US, early 1980s. Spears gives earliest US record as 1969, and notes that a 1973 US source labels the expression 'Hong Kong'. Certainly in Hong Kong, 1969, when the song 'Puff the Magic Dragon' was popular, there were some who thought the words were aimed more at drug-addicts than at the children for whom it was ostensibly sung. (P.B.) Leech, 1986, notes a recent US derivative use, 'not yet heard in Canada': 'A hot and heavy sexual event or orgy, as in "We chased the dragon all night"'.

chase the hares; usu. as n. or participle, *chasing the hares*. To run after women. A pun on *hairs*.

chase-up. A race; a speedy driving: since late 1940s. Crookston, 1967, 'There were ten of us and we each stole a car from a car-park to have a bit of a chase-up'.

chase x. See **x-chaser**.

chaser. A drink taken immediately after another: coll. Esp. a 'tot of spirit taken after coffee [or a pint of beer: P.B.]; small quantity of water taken after drinking neat spirits (also fig.)' (*COD*, 1934 Sup.).—2. A woman-chaser: Can. coll.: adopted, ca. 1935, ex US.—3. A message sent after another: military coll.: WW2 and after. Connell, 1969, 'Wavell's signal to Churchill left the strategic directors of the war little or no choice. [Signal quoted]. A "chaser", sent off early the following morning, amplified this instruction.' Also means a signal demanding to know what action has been taken on the sender's previous message. (P.B.)—4. Short for *progress-chaser*, one who, in industry, ensures that work is being processed quickly and efficiently: coll. > j.: since mid-C.20. (P.B.)

chasing, vbl n. Ex **chase the dragon**, q.v.

chasp (pron. with short *a*). A joc. corruption of *chap*, voc. and usu. pl, as 'Morning, chasps!' in general greeting to assembled (male) company; occ., perhaps by back-formation, singular, 'I say, old chasp . . .': first heard by me, in Services, 1970. (P.B.)

chassis, in a terrible state of. Extremely 'plastered' (drunk); profoundly perturbed, and showing it: Anglo-Irish. (O'Casey, 1924.) (Thanks to librarian John O'Riordan, who vouched for its extancy in the 1970s.) The original quot'n refers to 'the world', so the phrase can describe any state of disorder, or chaos.

chastity belt. 'By the 1970s this S.E. [term] had started in some "intellectual circles" to be applied to the car safety-belt' (R.S., 1972). A fairly short-lived pedantic pun.

chat, n. 'The gift of the gab': low: since late 1940s. Barlow, 1968.—2. Language; way of speaking or writing; terminology: since ca. 1950. Henderson, 1968, ' "Says he's a nice fellow, likes hurting people, knocks girls about, sticks knives in people. An emotional pauper."—"How much?"—"That's college chat for a right bastard." '—3. 'An old man, usually a vagrant, deadbeat and alcoholic. The term connotes poor hygiene and general slovenliness' (McNeil): Aus. low coll.: later C.20. Prob. ex early C.19 *chatty*, lousy.—4. See **bomb the chat**; **full chat**.

chat, v. To talk to or with (someone): since ca. 1920. 'Chatting a bogy' (*Gilt Kid*, 1936).

chat marks. Quotation marks: mostly authors'. Ruck, 1935.

chat-show. A radio or TV programme in which a person of some fame, or none, is invited to converse informally with the show's 'host': coll.: since ca. 1960.

chat-state, in. Filthy: army: since ca. 1950. 'His bunk [room] was left in chat-state'. Perhaps better spelt *chatt*, since it prob. derives from C.19 *chatt*, a louse; influenced also by 'in shit state'. (P.B.) See **chatty**, adj.

chat up, n. Corresponds to next:-

chat up, v. To bluff; to 'con': since ca. 1925. Cook, 1962.—2. (Of a male) to talk to a girl, a woman, persistently and persuasively, esp. with a view to sexual dalliance: since ca. 1936.

chateaued. Intoxicated on wine: Sloane Rangers', q.v.: early 1980s. (*Sunday Express* mag., 11 Oct. 1982.) Ex the 'Cha-

teau' that appears in the *appellation* of so many wines—and its use in parody, e.g. 'Chateau Sainsburys', 'Chateau Naafi du Pop', etc. (P.B.)

Chats. The RN Barracks and Divisional HQ at Chatham: RN: late C.19–20.—2. As *chats*, articles of clothing: Glasgow:—1934.

chatsby. Anything the name of which one has forgotten: theatrical—1935; RAF, WW2. Perhaps ex C.19 *chat*, a thing, but cf.:-

chattamaranta. Any large object not immediately identifiable; a thing: market-traders'. (*M.T.*) Poss. a fanciful extension of *chat* (see prec.), itself poss. a var. on earlier *cheat*, thing.

chatterbox. A machine-gun: RAF aircrews': adopted in mid-1940 from the American Eagle Squadron; ob. by 1946. (*Reader's Digest*, Feb. 1941.) Also Aus. (B., 1942) The genuinely English form is *chatter-gun* (or one word), as in Brickhill, 1946, 'The chatter-guns opened up'.

chatty, n. A pot, esp. if porous, for water: Anglo-Indian coll.: since mid-C.18. P.B.: the term spread to other British colonies and was still in use in, e.g., Malaya and Cyprus in the 1950s. Y. & B. define it as spheroidal, but in Malaya and Cyprus it was amphora-shaped.

chatty, adj. Lousy: low until WW1: from ca. 1810. (Vaux, 1812.) A WW1 jest ran: 'He's a nice chatty little fellow.' Ex *chatt*, a louse, since C.17. P.B.: by mid-C.20, esp. in Services, it meant merely 'filthy'; cf. **chat-state**, and:-

chatty but happy. (Of a ship) 'not very smart in appearance': RN c.p. (F. & G.) See prec.

chauff. To act as chauffeur to: since ca. 1925. Holt, 1936, 'Sorry, I'm chauffing Cynthia'.—2. To drive: since ca. 1925. Adams, 1931, 'Not fit to chauff a dust-cart'.

cheapie. Anything very cheap: later C.20. *Private Eye*, 16 Mar. 1979, 'We rang British Leyland and asked if they had provided a car for [a public figure]. They said, "He got a cheapie, all right!" ' [i.e. with considerable discount, in this instance]. (P.B.) Cf.:-

cheapo. Cheap; perhaps implying 'cheap and nasty', but still an unnecessary elab.: coll.: since mid-1970s. 'The first fanzine was *Sniffin' Glue* (1976). The style is cheapo, spontaneous . . .' (York, 1977); 'the purveyors of cheapo home accessories' (Lyall, 1981). May also, like prec., be used as n. (P.B.)

cheaps, the. A cheap edition, as of a 7*s.* 6*d.* novel re-issued at 3*s.* 6*d.* Publishers', booksellers', and bookbinders': from ca. 1910; since ca. 1930, coll.

cheapskate. A stingy fellow given to cheating: adopted, ca. 1944, ex US, where, by 1960, 'standard' (W. & F.).

cheat-sheet. An instructor's aide-mémoire: RAAF: since (?)ca. 1960; I heard it in the late 1960s. (P.B.)

cheaters. Close-fitting (male) pants, esp. if with elastic leg-bands: from ca. 1910; †. Cf. **draughters**, the female version.—2. Spectacles (glasses): Can. s.: adopted, by 1930 at latest, ex US, where it was certainly gen. s. (orig. underworld) by ca. 1920.—3. Foam-plastic bust-forms ('falsies'): Aus.: since ca. 1945. Glassop, 1949, ' "Cheaters," said Mrs Shendon, as if instructing a class of dull children, "make mountains out of molehills." ' Cf. **falsies**.—4. 'Eyes. Sometimes spectacles or sunglasses' (Powis): underworld: current in 1970s. Cf. sense 2, which prob. referred also to dark glasses.

cheaty-wop. A middle-class feminine softening, prob. orig. for nursery use, of the bald assertion 'cheat!'. (P.B.)

check. 'To reprimand, to take to task, during the exercise of one's duty' (Partridge, 1945). Proleptic: it should check the recipient's evil ways.—2. The Artillery's *Check!* (As you were) came, in the Army and then in the other Services, to serve for 'I have checked', all is now well, all right, O.K.: coll.: since 1940. By 1950, *check!*, O.K., had become fairly common, and by 1955 very common, among civilians; but this civilian use was aided by adoption of American *check!*, O.K.

check up on. To eye amorously: since ca. 1936. To assess a woman's sexual charms.—2. A synonym of **keep tabs on**: adopted, ca. 1960, ex Can., where current since ca. 1920.

checker. An inspector: busmen's coll.: from ca. 1925. *Daily Herald*, 5 Aug. 1936.—2. A homing pigeon. Triston, 1938.

chee-chee. Of mixed European and Indian parentage: Indian Army and Anglo-Indian coll.: in Army usage, and esp. in first half of C.20 (after which, ob.) it meant half caste, usu. applied to a girl. Ex Hindi exclam. = fie! Late C.19–20 spelling usu. *chi-chi.*—2. As a n., the minced English of Eurasians; the half-breeds as a class (cf. **Bombay Welsh**). Both n. and adj. date from mid-late C.18. Y. & B.

cheeks. The buttocks: coll., from ca. 1750. (Grose, by implication.) Cf. *blind cheeks*. When, in 1928–30, dresses were the soul of wit, London club-men heard, prob. ex the Stock Exchange, the rhyme, 'If skirts get any shorter,' said the flapper with a sob,/'There'll be two more cheeks to powder, a lot more hair to bob', sometimes known as 'The Flapper's Lament'.

cheer!, what. See **what cheer**!

cheer-chaser, -chasing; chase cheers. The agent, the verbal noun, the verb, for 'curry favour with the mob': Aus. coll.: since ca. 1930. B., 1943.

cheerful giver. Liver (bodily organ): r.s. An allusion, not a designation; the designation is *bow and quiver*. Franklyn 2nd.

cheeribye! Good-bye, or au revoir: 1942+. A blend of *cheerio* + *goodbye*. Cf. **cheerioski**.

cheerio!; cheero! A parting word of encouragement, an informal 'Goodbye!'; in drinking, a toast: coll.: resp. 1915 and ca. 1910. The first is rather more familiar, less aristocratic, esp. after WW1 (although B. & P. attribute the development of *cheerio* out of *cheero* to the officers). While *cheerio* is perhaps the commoner in later C.20 usage, both forms are still (1980s) heard, though perhaps > slightly ob. There was until ca. 1960, when it was replaced by a Hilton Hotel, an Other Ranks' club in Hong Kong called 'The Cheero Club'; *Punch* cartoons of WW1 tend to use *cheero*. Cf. **cheers!** and **cheery-ho!** (E.P.; P.B.)—2. Hence, adj. (from ca. 1919), mostly upper-class in use, as in Sayers, 1926, ' "He seemed particularly cheerio . . . ", said the Hon. Freddy . . . The Hon. Freddy, appealed to, said he thought it meant more than just cheerful, more merry and bright, you know.' Ob.

cheerioski. 'Cheerio!' ca. 1925–38. Macdonald, 1930.

cheers! Often *three cheers!* A coll. expression of deep satisfaction or friendly approval: from ca. 1905.—2. Since ca. 1945, replacing *cheerio*, a drinking toast; by 1950, and still, mid–1980s, perhaps the commonest salutation on raising the glass. It has become, since ca. 1960, much commoner than *cheerio* as a farewell also, and is often used, moreover, since ca. 1970, as 'Thanks!', as an acknowledgment or for a small favour. All usages coll. (P.B.)

cheery-ho! A post-WW1 var. of *cheerio*!

cheese, n. Smegma: low: mid–C.19–20.—2. A round disc used in such games as skittles: sporting: since ca. 1950. (*Merriam-Webster's Sports Dictionary*, 1976.) Ex circular flat cheeses.

cheese, v. To study hard: Bradfield Coll.: since ca. 1917. Marples.—2. To smile (esp., broadly): Oundle School: since ca. 1918. (Ibid.) E.P. suggested 'ex *grin like a Cheshire cat*', but a derivation from the photographers' persuasive 'Say cheese!' seems much more prob. (P.B.)—3. To hurry, to stride out: Lancing Coll.: since mid-1930s. Ibid.

cheese (or **cheeses**) **and kisses.** Wife: r.s., on *missus*: late C.19–20. E.P. gives –1931 as date for the pl. form; Franklyn, records: 'Has more currency in Australia (where it is generally reduced to cheese) than in England.'

cheese down. 'To coil rope into neat spirals for a harbour stow' (P-G-R): RN coll.: late C.19–20; by 1940, perhaps rather j. So to coil the rope that it assumes the shape of a large cheese.—2. Hence, 'to laugh uncontrollably' (*Mail on Sunday*, 8 Nov. 1987): RM. Cf. **fall about.**

Cheese-head; mostly in pl. A Dutchman: nautical. ' "The cheese-heads have one [tug] lying handy." Probably *Witterzee* or one of the other big Dutch tugs, Nicholas thought swiftly' (Smith, 1978).

cheesecake. 'A display, esp. pictorial, of feminine beauty and physical charm: adopted, ca. 1944, ex US. The display is of as much anatomy as the law will allow.' [Thus E.P., writing ca. 1950, before the onslaught of the 'permissive society.'] R.C. suggested, 1976, that 'the ultimate source is the "girlie" photographer's injunction to his subject, "Say *cheese*", which produces an attractive, if spurious, smile.' However, the quot'n below antedates any photography by a couple of centuries, and it may be that *cheesecake* is simply synon. with, but richer than, any *tart*. (P.B.) *Rump: or an Exact Collection of the Poems and Songs relating to the Late Times*, 1662, contains a lament on the occasion of Oliver Cromwell's rusticating the ladies of the town. It contains this couplet: 'But, ah, it goes against our hearts/To lose our cheesecake and our tarts'—upon which find E.P. commented, 'certainly relevant semantically and may even be relevant lexically'. Cf. derivative **beefcake.**

cheesed. Has, since 1941, been often used for the next. Jackson, 1943.

cheesed(-)off. Disgruntled: Liverpool boys' (—1914); Liverpool troops' (1914–18); common in all Services since ca. 1935; but since 1940, esp. RAF; and, since ca. 1950, gen. (Finn-Smith, 1942; H. & P., 1943; Partridge, 1945.) Perhaps suggested by **browned off**, q.v., via the *brown* rind of *cheese*. Hamer derives it ex the Liverpool boys' *cheese off!*, run away and don't be a nuisance, itself current since ca. 1890.

cheeser. 'One who is, or whose feet are, smelly is known as a smelly cheeser': since ca. 1965. (Thomas, 1976.)

cheeses. 'The Utility sign; called in its day [WW2] "the cheeses", this was two capital Cs, standing for civilian clothing, plus 41 for the year 1941' (*Illustrated London News*, Oct. 1974, p. 28).

cheeses and kisses. See **cheese and kisses.**

cheesing rows(, three). (Three) rousing cheers. A deliberate Spoonerism.

cheesy-feet. A derogatory term of address: proletarian. (F. Leech, 1972.) Malodorous.

cheild (pron. *che-īld*). A derisively coll. C.20 pron., esp. with *my*, of *child*: in ridicule of the agonies of the transpontine drama. Infrequent before WW1, common in military fun, fairly gen. since.

Cheltenham (cold). Cold: r.s.: late C.19–20. This is an intensive var. of *Cheltenham bold*. (Franklyn.) P.B.: this does not make much sense as it stands. I suggest a mishearing of *Cheltenham Gold*, ex the famous 'Cheltenham Gold Cup' horse-race.

chem, n. and adj. Chemistry, esp. as a subject of study; in or of chemistry: Aus. students': since ca. 1910. (B.P.) Not only in Aus. Even pupils in the Anglo-Chinese schools in Hong Kong talk of *chem*—and *math*, *geog*, *phiz*, etc. (P.B.)

chemise-lifter. 'A female invert or daphne (ob.)' (Humphries, 1982): Aus.

chemist, the. A medical officer: RN and Army: 1920s. F. & G.—See **mangy cat.**

chemmy (pron. *shemmy*). The game of *chemin de fer*: coll. from ca. 1920.—2. (Pron. *kemmy*). Chemistry as a subject in school. Cf.:-

chemmy lab. Chemistry laboratory: schools'. Hatton, 1930.

cherries, the. 'The dogs' (greyhound racing), and their racing track. See **cherry-hog** and **cherry oggs**, 2.—2. See ASSOCIATION FOOTBALL, in Appx.

cherry. The hymen: late C.19–20. Cf. **cherry-popping.**—2. Hence, a girl's virginity.—3. Hence, a young man's (physical) virginity: Can. and Brit.—4. Hence, a virgin boy or youth: adopted, late 1960s, ex US. 'Both of his sons were cherries' (Hollander).—5. In *take the cherry*, to take the new ball: Aus. cricketers': since ca. 1950. (*Observer*, 21 June 1953.) Ex the ball's redness.

cherry ace. A face: r.s.: only ca. 1940–55. Franklyn.

Cherry B. HMS *Charybdis*: RN: since 1969. (Knight, 1984.) Influenced by the tradename of the boot polish 'Cherry Blossom'.

cherry berry. See **cherryberry**.

cherry-bounce. A charabanc: late C.19–earlier 20. By perversion ex *char à banc*. *Cherry-bounce* was an old term for cherry brandy.

cherry-hog. A dog: r.s.: mid-C.19–20. In greyhound racing, *the cherries* = the dogs. Cf. **cherry oggs**, 2.

cherry nobs. (Very rare in singular.) Military policemen: military: earlier C.20. F. & G., 'From their red cap covers'. More gen. **red caps**.

cherry oggs. A game played with cherry-stones on the pavement: London children's since ca. 1880.—2. Greyhound racing: r.s., on *dogs*: since ca. 1920. Often shortened to *the cherries*. See **ogg**, 2.

cherry-picker. A pathic, catamite: RN.—2. A crane-like vehicle, whether grab or lifter or both: builders'. *Illustrated Carpenter and Builder*, 24 Feb. 1967.—3. £1: r.s. on *nicker*. (Hillman, 1974.)

cherry-pie. Extra money earned by a performer doubling two roles, as, e.g., a clown acting as a ticket-collector: Can. circus s.: adopted, late 1950s, ex US. (Leechman, 1973.)

cherry-popping. Defloration: low and raffish: adopted, mid-1960s, ex US. (Hollander.) Hence, also, *pop the cherry*, to deflower. Prompted by **cherry**, 1. Leech, 1986, notes that in Can. the form is always as in, e.g. 'I popped her cherry last night', and that there it dates back to the 1940s.

Cherry Ripe. Centuripe, in Sicily: Army: 1944–5. By the process of Hobson-Jobson. P-G-R.

cherry-ripe. Nonsense: r.s. (on *tripe*).

cherry-tree class; or **the cherry trees.** HMS *Rodney* and HMS *Nelson* British battleships, because they were erroneously supposed to have had their tonnage reduced by the Treaty of Washington, the US capital: RN (wardroom): 1930s—very early 1940s. Bowen, 'Because they were cut down by Washington', the cherry-tree hero of the truth.

cherryberry. '(Red beret of) Parachute Regiment soldier' (Hawke): RM: 1970s. Contrast **crap-hat**.

Chesby or **c-.** A good-natured fellow: RAF: WW2. P-G-R.

chest stooge. A junior detailed to keep a Cadet Captain's sea-chest tidy for him: RNC, Dartmouth: since 1939. Granville.

chestnuts. The female breasts: since (I'd guess) ca. 1960. Lindsay Mackie mentions it, in reviewing a book by Miss Joy Parkinson, in the *Guardian*, 5 Apr. 1976. Not very gen.; at least I hadn't heard it.

chesty. Weak in the chest; of tuberculosis or pneumonia: coll. *OED* Sup.—2. Hence (of a patient), coughing: hospital nurses' coll.: late C.19–20.

Chev; Chevvy (pron. *Shev*). A Chevrolet motor-car: motorists' coll.: adopted, with the vehicle, ex US, ca. 1925.—2. Specifically, a Chevrolet truck: Forces': WW2. P-G-R.

chew, n. Fellatio: RN lowerdeck: mid-C.20. 'When I was pissed I wouldn't refuse anything, slut, beef, chews, anything' (*Heart*, 1962: P.B.).

chew (someone's) **ballocks off.** To rebuke or reprimand severely: Services', esp. the Army. A var. of *chew the balls off*.

chew (someone) **out.** To reprimand severely: Can. (Leechman.)

chew the balls off (someone). To reprimand severely: military.

chew the fat or **rag;** in C.20, occ. **chew the grease** (Manchon). To grumble; resuscitate an old grievance: military: from ca. 1880. (Patterson, 1885.) In WW1 there was a tendency to distinguish, thus: *chew the fat*, 'to sulk, be resentful'; *chew the rag*, 'to argue endlessly or without hope of a definite agreement' (B. & P.). Moreover, in the C.20 RN, *chew the fat* additionally = 'to spin a yarn' (Bowen), and 'Taffrail' has *chew* (one's) *fat*, to argue. With the *rag* version, cf. older s. *rag*, the tongue.

chew the mop. To argue on and on: military.

chew the rag. See **chew the fat**, and note that, since ca. 1920, it has predominantly signified 'to talk, to chat, to yarn'—with no undertone of grumbling, sulking, or brooding.

chew up. (Gen. in passive.) To reprimand, to 'tell off': mostly military: earlier C.20. F. & G.—2. To savage; to mangle (the body of). Devanney, 1951.—3. See **chewed up**.

chewed rag or **string.** See **feel like a boiled rag**, to feel excessively limp.

chewed to loon shit. Ground up, hence ruined: Can.: since ca. 1930. Leech, 1974, applies it to, e.g., a road.

chewed up, be. To be very nervous and/or off colour: from ca. 1920. Heyer, 1933.—2. See **chew up**.

chewey; chewies; chewy. Chewing gum: Aus. juvenile: since ca. 1944. (B., 1953.) Ex the habit rendered even more popular by the multiple and ubiquitous presence of US servicemen in Aus. in late 1942–5.—2. As *chewies*, Tuinal: drugs c. (Stockley, 1986.)

chi. Heroin: drugs c. (Stockley, 1986.) Perhaps abbr. *Chinese H*.

chi-chi, n. For Anglo-Indian and half-caste senses see **cheechee**.—2. Unnecessary fuss; affected protests or manners: Society coll. Adopted ex Fr. coll. Perhaps ex preceding term, but prob. an arbitrary formation.—3. Hence, excessive red-tape: Army officers': since ca. 1939. P-G-R.

chi-chi, adj. Affected, particularly in manners. Ex the n., 2.

chib, n. A weapon, particularly a razor: Glasgow teenage gangsters': since ca. 1930. (*Observer*, 4 Feb. 1973, cited by R.S.) Probably a deformation of synon. **chiv**.

chib, v. To stab. Ex the n., same usage and date.

chicadee. A flighty person, usu. female: Can.: later C.20. (Leech, 1985.)

Chicago piano (or hyphenated). A multiple pom-pom gun: RN and MN: WW2, from ca. 1940. (Michie, 1941.) As R.C. pointed out, 1976, 'The ultimate reference must be to the sub-machine-guns used by American gangsters in 1920s, perhaps esp. in Chicago' (itself perhaps named from the rattle of the nickleodeon, or other mechanical producer of 'music'. P.B.). Cf:-

Chicago typewriter. A 4-barrelled US-made ·5 in. pom-pom: RN: WW2. (Peppitt.) Var. of prec.

Chicargot. Americanism in speech: RN (wardroom): ca. 1940. (Granville.) A blend of 'Chicago' and 'argot'. Mostly in to 'talk Chicargot', to affect American expressions; it has the air of a fairly ephemeral pun.

chick. One's girl friend: dance-fanatics' and Teddy-boys': adopted, ca. 1940, ex US. This is a specialisation of US s. *chick*, a girl.—2. A male prostitute: prostitutes' and homosexuals': since ca. 1945.

chickee. A girl. See **chickie**.

chicken, n. C.17–18 coll., 'a feeble, little creature, of mean spirit' (B.E.). —2. A child (C.18–20, coll.), *chick* being more usual.—3. A boy homosexual: c. and low. Cf. senses 1 and 2.—4. 'A young runaway schoolboy, likely to be preyed upon by homosexuals. The male equivalent of a "mystery" [q.v.]' (Powis): police and underworld: current in 1970s. An extension of sense 3.—5. In *that's your chicken*, a var. of *that's your pigeon* (properly *pidgin*) = that's your concern:—1931 (Lyell).

chicken!, exclam. Coward!: 'a derisive cry hurled at one who shows signs of cowardice, or even of commendable prudence': Can. teenagers': since ca. 1950. (Leechman.) P.B.: also Brit. juvenile, and joc. adults': since ca. 1955. See also **chicken out** and **play chicken**.

chicken, adj. Cowardly: adopted, ex Can., ca. 1946 in Britain. Cf. **chicken!**—2. Petty, insignificant; pettily cheating: Can.: ca. 1910–40. The origin of sense 1. (Priestley.)

chicken-berries. Hen's eggs: RN lowerdeck. (P-G-R.) Cf. **cackle-berry**.

chicken-feed. Small change: Can. (and US), C.20; by 1937, also English. Beames, 1932.—2. Hence, a mere pittance (financial), or, less common, a bare minimum of food: coll.: since ca. 1941.

chicken-fruit. Hen's eggs: RN. (Granville.) Cf. **chicken-berries.**

chicken out. To retire from fight, risk, adventure: Aus.: adopted, ca. 1943, ex US. Cf. **chicken!** (B.P.) Current in RAF since ca. 1950, and general Eng. s. since late 1950s. The RAF usage has var. *go chicken*. Cf. **chicken**, exclam. and adj.

chicken-picker. A one-finger typist: Aus. joc.: since ca. 1930. Ex plucking a chicken.

chicken-run, the. The goal-mouth (a netted area) in Association Football: sporting: little used since ca. 1960. It occurs in, e.g., Frank Richards's school stories. (Petch.)

chicken-shit. Information from a superior: Can.: since ca. 1920. But Can. *have chicken-shit in one's blood* (since ca. 1930) = to be a coward.—2. Adj. Petty, insignificant; pettily cheating: Can.: ca. 1910–30. The orig. of **chicken**, adj., 2.—3. As exclam., = 'rubbish!'; gen. contemptuous. Adopted ex Can./US, current in 1970s.

chickie (also spelt *chickee, -ey, -y*). A serviceman's girl-friend or sweetheart: Aus. soldiers': WW2. (B., 1943.) Cf. the US *chick*, a girl.—2. Hence, any young girl: Aus. teenagers': since ca. 1945. (Dick.)

chicko, chico, n. and adj. (A) very young (person, esp. a soldier): army. (B. & P.) E.P. suggested, for this sense, 'i.e., a mere chicken', but cf.:—2. 'Used on RAF Irak stations, ca. 1925–45, for 1, a bearer, a personal servant (esp. *bungalow chico*); 2, a child, a baby. Prob. ex Sp. *chico*, "small boy: lad: dear fellow".' (L.A.) P.B.: the term, used for a child, was still current in the Army in the 1960s–early 70s.

Chidley Dyke. The line between Cheltenham and Southampton Docks: railwaymen's: earlier C.20. Known to the passengers as *the Pig and Whistle Line*. Cf. **Tiddley Dyke.**

chief (the chief). The Chief Engineer, or, loosely, the First Mate: nautical coll.: mid-C.19–20.—2. A chief inspector: police coll.: late C.19–20.—3. A Petty Officer: RN: C.20. Bowen.—4. A—gen. joc.—form of address: coll.: since ca. 1880. Esp. in *OK, chief!* (post-WW1). See **OK.**—5. A Flight-Sergeant, RAF. See **chiefie.**

Chief Con, the. The Chief Constable, head of an English county police force: policemen's by ca. 1930, at latest, also journalists'. (Petch, 1969.)

chief cook and bottle-washer. The most important 'dogs-body' in an organisation, often used in self-deprecation, 'Oh, I'm the . . . around here': coll. (P.B.)

chief housemaid, the. A 1st Lieutenant, RN. He is 'responsible for the cleanliness and good order of the ship' (Bowen).

chief pricker. Regulating petty officer; stoker: RN: since ca. 1910. (Granville.) Cf. **chief stoker.**

chief scribe, the. Chief Petty Officer, Writer: RN: since ca. 1910. Granville.

chief stoker. 'A seagull said to be the incarnation of one' (Granville): RN: late C.19–20.

chiefie. A Flight-Sergeant: RAF: since April 1918. (Rhodes, 1942.) Ex the days when in the RN Air Service the corresponding man held the rank of *Chief* Petty Officer (3rd Class). Also, in more formal address, simply *chief*.

Child's Guide. See **bible.**

chiller. A 'thriller' that chills the blood: book world: since late 1950s. On the back of the jacket of Alistair Maclean's *Fear Is the Key*, 1961, his *Night without End* is described as 'A "chiller" by Alistair Maclean'. Elliptical for *spine-chiller*.

chilli-cracker (or written solid). 'Anyone of mixed White and Indian parentage or ancestry, a half-caste or Eurasian; presumably from the Indians' love of hot spiced dishes. I heard it used in Malaya, among Service people, in the mid-1950s' (P.B., 1974): after ca. 1970, nostalgic. See quot'n at **blackie-white.**

chime. The even firing of a multi-cylinder engine: motorcyclists' coll. (Dunford.) since ca. 1950.

chin. An actor: Aus.: since ca. 1920. B., 1942, 'Cf. "blue-chin".'—2. In *up to the chin*, deeply involved; extremely

busy: coll.: from ca. 1860. P.B.: in later C.20 more usu. *up to the ears* or *eyes* (*in it*).

chin-food. A bore's conversation: Army and RAF: since the 1920s. H. & P.—2. In RN: idle prattle (Granville): since ca. 1920.

chin-strap. The buttocks: low Cockney: from ca. 1918. Derisive. See:-

chin-straps, be on (one's). To be utterly exhausted: Army: since ca. 1920. Ex *come in on* (one's) *chin-strap*.

china, chiner. A pal, a mate, a friend, of either sex: abbr. earlier *china plate*, r.s.: since ca. 1890; in C.20, esp. in WW1, and in later C.20 it occurs most often in joc. address: 'Me (or my) old china!' In later C.20 also Aus. (McNeil).

China-bird. A naval man serving on the China station: RN: earlier C.20 (Bowen). Granville observes, esp. 'one whose conversation is interlarded with "Chop Chops" and "Can do's".'

china plate. With *the*, the First Mate: MN. Franklyn 2nd.—2. See **china.**

China-side. The China station: RN coll.: earlier C.20. (Granville.) Ex pidgin.

Chinaman. A left-hand bowler's leg-break: cricketers': from ca. 1905. Ex the manner of Chinese script, right to left, or perhaps, simply, damnably devious.—2. An Irishman: English, esp. Londoners': late C.19–20. Behan, 1958.

Chinaman's copy. An exact copy, including mistakes and emendations: typists' coll.:—1935.

China's cow. The soya bean, abounding in the Far East, and very nutritious: journalistic.

Chincha dung-boat. A sailing ship engaged in the guano trade from the Chincha islands: nautical coll. Bowen.

chiner. See **china.**

Chinese. A Chinese restaurant: coll.: since later 1970s. *Time Out*, 22 Feb. 1980, 'pubs, a few pints and a Chinese before home' (P.B.).—2. 'Non-National Health heroin that is usually a yellow powder. So called because the first supplies came from the Far East' (Cutland, 1985).

Chinese attack. 'A lot of noise and activity to delude the enemy that an attack was brewing in that spot, and to distract his attention from the real one' (P-G-R): Army, mostly officers', coll.: WW2.

Chinese burn. 'Cruelty perpetrated by grabbing someone's arm with both fists close together and twisting in opposite directions' (B.P.): Aus. and Brit. schoolchildren's: since ca. 1930. (B.P.) Var.: *Chinese burner*, as in Dick. P.B.: in Eng. applied also to nipping short hairs at the nape and pulling with a small circular motion: schoolboys': mid-C.20.

Chinese consumption. The possession of only one effective lung; hence also the so-called 'smokers' cough': Aus.: since ca. 1935. A pun on *Wun Bung Lung*, one defective lung. (B.P.)

Chinese dominoes. A load of bricks. See HAULIERS' SLANG, in Appx.

Chinese drive. A snick through the slips (cricket). See **French drive.**

Chinese fashion. The sexual act performed with the partners lying on their side: Forces in the Far East, 1939–45. 'The Chinese fashion of writing at right angles to ours led the Far Eastern troops to assume that other things were at right angles to normal. Hence the female pudend was assumed to be transverse externally' (anon., 1961).

Chinese fours. 'B.R. standard 4 freight locomotives' (*Railway*, 2nd): railwaymen's: since ca. 1945.

Chinese gunpowder. Cement. See HAULIERS' SLANG, in Appx.

Chinese H. Heroin: drugs c. Stockley, 1986.

Chinese landing. A landing made with one wing lower than it should be: Can. airmen's: since ca. 1917. A pun on *Wun Wing Low*. Dr Leechman heard it in WW1.

Chinese National Anthem. A loud expectoration: RN. Granville.

Chinese parliament. A form of collusion in which 'everyone makes a decision but no one is responsible for it', e.g. in a cover-up operation. Stalker, 1988, records its use among the Royal Ulster Constabulary. Cf. the condemnation of rule by committee, 'No heart to appeal to and no arse to kick'.

Chinese screwdriver. A hammer: Aus.: since ca. 1950. 'Ex the folk belief that the Chinese, like sloppy Australian handymen, use a hammer to drive and extract screws' (B.P., 1974). Cf. **Brummagem screwdriver.**

Chinese wedding-cake. Rice pudding: RN, thence to the other Services. (*Sunday Chronicle*, 1 Mar. 1942.) Ex rice as the staple food of S. China.

ching bag. 'Street quantity of heroin, sold in folded paper' (Stockley, 1986): drugs c.

ching! ching! ching! and **whop! whop! whop!** Exclamations descriptive of 'events happening quickly in succession': since ca. 1955. (P.B., 1974.) The former, evocative of bells ringing, the latter of heavy impacts.

chinger. To grumble; scold; complain; hence, to deter a prospective customer: market traders'. Hence, *chingerer*, one who does this. (*M.T.*) Cf. **chunter**, and see **get the chingerers.**

Chinkie, -ky, n. A Chinese: Aus. from ca. 1880. (Morris.) By perversion of *Chinaman* [or from 'slit-eyes'?, P.B.]. Cf. synon. *chink.*—2. 'A rating who is always reminiscing about the good old days on China-side' (Granville): RN: earlier C.20.—3. A Chinese restaurant: gen. coll.: late 1970s. E.g., a young commercial traveller, a 'rep', complaining: 'A flat in London? *No* chance! Everlastin' bed'n'breakfast. King of the chip-shops and chinkies, me!' (P.B.)

Chinkie, -ky, adj. Chinese: rare before ca. 1950. (P.B., 1977.)

Chinki-chonks. A patronising English term for all Asians dwelling East of India. 'We could fill the school with candidates with four A-levels if we took all the little chinki-chonks who flood the public schools' (the Dean of a London medical school, quoted in the *Guardian*, 18 Dec. 1978). Cf. **nig-nogs.**

Chinky-toe-rot. A foot-complaint prevalent in the East (and in other tropics): RN. Granville.

chinless wonder. Applied to any young male of the upper classes that, because of a receding chin, gives the appearance of dull-wittedness or lack of resolution: gen. coll. derogatory: since mid-C.20. Cf. **titless wonder.** (P.B.)

chip, n. In racing c., a shilling—the coin or its value. Cockney, in the late 1930s (*Muvver*). Hence *half a chip*, sixpence (Tempest).—2. See **chips.**—3. A quarrel: Aus. 'We had a bit of a chip over one thing and another' (Tennant, 1947).—4. In *have (got) a chip*, short for **chip on** (one's) **shoulder**: coll.: since ca. 1960. (Petch.)

chip, v. To chaff, in any way whatsoever. Dent, 1917: 'Most nervous patients are reassured by "chipping", for chipping is the language they [wounded soldiers] understand.' Cf:-

chip at. As *have a chip at*, to make fun of, to chaff: coll.:—1923 (Manchon).

chip back. To rebate, to discount; to reduce (a price) by a stated sum, as in 'I'd want some change out of that. Can't you chip me a tenner back?': secondhand-car dealers', esp. in London: since ca. 1945. Cowdy, 1965.

chip on (one's) **shoulder, have (got) a** (or **to carry a**). To bear a grudge against the world, often for some specific and individual reason, as 'Oh, him! He's got a chip on his shoulder the size of a blooming wood-yard. And all just because . . . ': coll.: US, since ca. 1880; Can. since ca. 1890; Eng., only since 1942, Aus. and NZ since 1943 or 1944, all introduced by US servicemen. Priestley, 1965, 'It comes from the American boy's method of challenge to a fight —putting a chip on his shoulder and daring the other to knock it off . . . There are chips in the yard of every American farm where they burn wood. To go round with a chip on your shoulder is to be looking for a fight, constantly challenging all comers, and this is what the expression means in America.'

chip one off. To salute a superior officer: RN: since ca. 1930. Granville.

chipe. (Usu. of a woman) to talk in a high-pitched voice, often persistently, with a suggestion of complaint; as in, 'Oh, turn it [the radio] off! It's only that Maggie woman chiping on again . . . ': South Country coll., poss ex dial., though not in *EDD*. Perhaps a blend of *cheep + whine*; certainly echoic. (P.B.)

chipper. 'A prison tinder-box' (Tempest): prisons' coll.: mid-C.20.

chippery. 'Chipping'; (an exchange of) banter: Cockneys': early C.20. Pugh, 'She hadn't 'alf got over that bit of chippery with the rozzer in the station.' Cf. **chip,** v.

chipping. The action of giving a tip. (Manchon.) Prob. ex *chips*, C.19 s. for 'money'.

chippy, n. A var. of the much older *chips*, 'carpenter': Services': since ca. 1918. (H. & P.) But also builders' s., for either a carpenter or a joiner.—2. A fish-and-chip shop: orig. Merseyside, from early C.20; by mid-C.20, with a currency far more widespread. Cf. **chinkie,** n., 3.—3. Hence, since late 1940s, the owner of such a shop.—4. A semiprofessional prostitute: Aus. and Can.: adopted, ex US, ca. 1942. B., 1943.—5. Hence, since ca. 1950, any girl: Aus. low. B., 1953.

chippy, adj. Cheap: Can.:—1949.—2. Resentfully envious; with a 'chip on one's shoulder', q.v.: coll.: 1970s. Amis, 1977.

chippy rigger. A carpenter rigger: RAF: 1930s–40s. (Jackson.) See **chippy,** n. 1.

chips. Knees; esp. *on* (one's) *chips*, exhausted: RAF: from ca. 1930.—2. Chipolata sausages, the small, thin sausages, as opposed to traditional large, fat English 'bangers': lower and lower-middle classes': since ca. 1950. (Burgess, 1967.) Anglicised spelling of It. *cipollata*.—3. As *the Chips*, a train by which people working in Sydney commute to the towns in the Blue Mountains: Aus., esp. NSW: since late 1940s. Prompted by similar **the Fish,** whose journeys start later. (B.P.)—4. In *to have had* (sometimes *got*, one's) *chips*, to have died, to be dead: since 1917. Adopted ex US *pass in* (one's) *chips*, itself from the game of poker. See also **cash in . . .**—5. Hence, though more usu. *get* (one's) *chips*, to be dismissed or discharged from one's job: since ca. 1960. (Petch, 1969.)—6. In *give* (someone) *full chips*; (*his*) *chips are high*, both of which signify approval: R Indian N: WW2. Here *chip* = rupee. P-G-R.

chirrup and titter. A bitter (beer): mostly theatrical r.s.: late C.19–20. Franklyn.

chit. A letter or a note: used by Purchas in 1608, while its orig., *chitty* (still in use), is not recorded before 1673: Anglo-Indian coll.; since WW1, virtually S.E., usu. as = note, written authorisation, pass, an invoice.—2. Hence, an order or a signature for drinks in clubs, aboard ship, etc.: Society, ex India: from ca. 1875; coll.—3. A pill: showmen's: late C.19–20. (*Night and Day*, 22 July 1937.) Hence, *chitworker*, a fellow who sells pills on the markets. 'A "crocus" would say, "I'm grafting chits" ' (Allingham, 1937).—4. *Have a good chit* and *give a good* (or *bad*) *chit*. See at **have . . .** and **give . . . .**

chit-shy. Applied to one who avoids paying for his round of drinks: British in Asia: earlier C.20. (Allen, 1983.) Ex *chit*, 2.

chit-up. To seek (someone) through the head of his department: RN officers': since ca. 1940. (P-G-R.) Ex *chit*, 1.

chitari. Cannabis: drugs c. Stockley, 1986.

chiv, chive, n. (pron. also *shiv*). A knife, a file, a saw: Romany and c.: C.17–20; in C.20, applied esp. to a razor-blade set in a piece of wood and used as a weapon in the underworld. See also **ochive.**

chiv, chive, v. 'To cut with a knife' (Dalton, 1728): c.: C.18–20. As in the threat 'I'll chive him' (Ibid.).—2. Hence, to smash a glass in someone's face, or to use the weapons in **chiv,** n.: c. Vbl n., *chivving*. Leach, 1933.

chiv-man. A criminal that is a professional knifer: c. (Brandon, 1936.) Cf.:-

chivver. A professional knifer, a var. of prec.: since ca. 1920. (Gosling, 1959.)

chivvy. A moustache: London, mostly low, but not c.: since ca. 1940. Hobson, 1959.

chizzer. A 'chiseller': (preparatory) schoolboys', i.e. a cheat: Blake, 1935.

choagy. See chogey.

choc. (Often in pl.) Abbr. *chocolate*: C.20; since 1934, almost coll. Cf. choccy.—2. A militiaman (also *choco* and *chocolate soldier*): Aus.: WW2. B., 1943.

choc-absorber. 'A girl or woman who can consume all the chocolates some fool of a man can supply her with. Derived from S.E. *shock-absorber*' (Petch, 1966): since ca. 1955.

choccy (or chocky), n. and adj. Familiar term for chocolate: domestic, nursery coll. become widespread, middle-class. 'Have another choccy!'; 'Would you like some choccy cake?'; 'My God, the price of those choccies!' Cf. choc. (P.B.)

chocker. Disgruntled, 'fed up': RN lowerdeck: since ca. 1920. (H. & P.) Ex *chock(-)full* (which *SOD* dates to C.18, and shows as a var. of C.17 choke-full). Earlier (?ca. 1900), chock-full was the orig. sense. A WW1 var., *chokka*, occurs in Bennett, 1919. In the 'disgruntled' sense it corresponds to the army's *browned off*. A WW2 RN var. was *at chocker stations*. The simple *chocker* reached the RAF by 1943 at the latest. 'When used in the Service [RN] it . . . is frequently accompanied by the raising of the right hand, palm down, to chin height, and the addition of the words " . . . up to here". It seems possible that this expression joined the R.A.F. via the R.N.A.S. over sixty years ago' (Graham, 1980).

chockers. Feet: market-traders': late C.19–20. (*M.T.*) Origin?

chockhead. An Air Frames and Engines Branch rating: FAA: since ca. 1950. (Wood.)

chocks, pull the. To depart. See pull the chocks.

choco. A conscientious objector: Aus.: 1939+. *Rats*, 1944.—2. See choc, 2.

chocolate. Abbr. chocolate frog, q.v. McNeil.—2. See bar of chocolate.—3. The word occurs in certain arbitrarily varied phrases implying sycophancy: Services' (esp. RAF): since ca. 1930. The semantic clue lies in brown-nose and brown-tongue.

chocolate bobbies. See hobby-bobby.

chocolate boy. A half-caste, a dark-skinned man: army: since (?)ca. 1935. E.g., an elderly sergeant discussing a common acquaintance, a man of mixed parentage, father English, mother Indian: 'Yus, I remember 'im. Black as the ace o'spades—proper chocolate boy, 'e was.' [It was a gross exaggeration!] (P.B.) Cf. chocolate drop, 2.

chocolate box. 'Time was when "chocolate box" was a term of artistic reproach; nowadays we invite the flower of our art schools to apply their talents and training to chocolate box decoration' (*The Times* art critic, writing in 1924; quoted in Lewis, 1978). I.e., what was later known as *kitsch*.

chocolate drop. An under-the-age-of-consent girl in the habit of 'sleeping with' seamen: since ca. 1960. (Peppitt, who refers to a *Daily Telegraph* report, published in 1971.)—2. Name given by white primary-school children to coloured immigrant children: usu. pej. or provocative: 1970s. (Harré, 1979.) Contrast ice-cream, q.v.

chocolate frog. An informer: Aus. r.s., on dog, 6: later C.20. McNeil.

chocolate soldier. See choc, 2.

Chocolate Staircase, the. A road with forty hairpin bends, N. of Tiddim, Burma: army: 1941–5. P-G-R.

chogey, n. and adj. (A) Chinese: army in Hong Kong: 1960s. 'The place was swarming with chogeys'; 'Fancy coming out for some chogey nosh [a Chinese meal]?' The spelling is arbitrary, as I have never seen the term in writing; it replaced tids and was in turn supplanted by slope or slopehead. (P.B.)—2. A Pakistani char-wallah (q.v.) in N. Ireland: army: 1970s. *New Society*, 24 Apr. 1980, spelling it *choghi*.

choke, n. Usu. in pl: *chokes*, Jerusalem artichokes: greengrocers': late C.19–20.—2. A nervous shock; something grievous: low: since ca. 1945. (Cunliffe, 1965.) Ex sense 2 of:-

choke, v. A synon. of strangle, 2.: racing: since ca. 1920. Francis, 1962, 'He said if I wanted a lesson in how to choke a horse I'd better watch him on Bolingbroke.'—2. To jolt or shock; to disgust: since ca. 1930.

choke-off. An admonishment: military and prison officers': since ca. 1914. Merrow-Smith, 1962.

choked, adj., predicative only, as in 'I was, *or* I felt, real *or* proper choked'—disgusted; 'fed-up' or 'browned off', disgruntled: since ca. 1945. Cf. double-choked, and:-

choked off. 'I'm frustrated with cars, cheesed off with buses, and choked off in tubes' (*Time Out*, 4 Jan. 1980). See prec.

choker. A child: later C.20. (Clark, 1982.) Perhaps viewed as 'a tie'?

chokey, choky; rarely cho(a)kee or chauki. A lock-up; a prison. In Anglo-Indian form C.17, adopted in England ca. 1850. Ex Hindustani *chauki*, lit. a four-sided place or building (Y. & B.).—2. 'Serving time in punishment block': prisoners' (Home Office): a specialisation of the derivative sense, imprisonment: since mid-C.20. Tempest.

Chokie. Var. of chogey. Gareth Parry reporting on life on board a Royal Fleet Auxiliary vessel during the recent Falkland Is. campaign, in *Guardian*, 2 July 1982, ref. Hong Kong Chinese crew members.—2. As *choki* or *chokie*, var. of chokey.

chokker. Var. spelling of chocker.

cholly. Cocaine: drugs c. (Stockley, 1986.) A var. of Charley, 9; US since—1975 (Spears).

chony bars, fifteen, with an appropriate v. To beat (someone) up, not to kill: Can. marginal c.: since ca. 1950. (Schroeder, 1976.) *Chony* seems to be a deliberate alteration of *chocolate*.

chooch hat. 'A soft hat of the Homburg type with a dent in it. From an indelicate Maltese word' (Granville): RN, and Army (esp. in India): since 1920s; by 1960 ob. Cf. the even more obviously indelicate cunt hat.

choof (off). To go, depart: Aus., esp NSW: since, at latest, 1945. Hardy, 1967, 'Soon as my mate gave her the housekeeping money, off she choof to the club'. Echoic? Perhaps cf. childish *chuff-chuff*, a train.

chook. A chicken; collectively, chickens: Aus. and NZ coll.: mid-C.19–20. Ex E. and Irish dialect.—2. A woman, esp. if an older one: Aus. pej.: since ca. 1935 (Culotta).

choosey. Fastidious; given to picking and choosing: coll. *Gilt Kid*, 1936.

chop, n. A blow with the fist: boxing s.: mid-C.18–early 19. (Grose, 3rd ed.) This use revived since mid-C.20, with the interest taken in Oriental martial sports; cf., e.g., a 'karate chop'.—2. See get the chop.

chop, v. 'To hang, probably dates from the days of the executioner's axe' (Tempest): prisons' c.: mid-C.20. Cf. the more common top in this sense.—2. To fail (someone) from a course: Services': since late 1940s. Ex get the chop, 2. Cf. chop-board, chop-ride. (P.B.)—3. 'To alter a motorcycle to produce a *chopper* [sense 5]' (Bishop, 1984): motorcyclists': later C.20.

chop-board. A board of officers and/or NCOs that sits to decide the fate of those doing badly on a training course: Services': since late 1940s. Ex get the chop, 2, perhaps infl. by S.E. *chopping-board*. Also, by extension, *chop-test*, a crucial examination on a training course. Cf. chop, v., 1, 2.

chop-chop, n. A meal: UN troops in Korean War, 1950–3. Ex *chop suey*, a pseudo-Chinese dish, equivalent of Western hash, but perhaps infl. by C.19 chop, v., to eat.—2. 'The green top [of sugar-cane] isn't trash. That's chop-chop—horse feed—when it's chopped up' (Devanney, 1944): Aus. cane-cutters': since ca. 1910.

chop-chop, v. To make haste. Ex:-

chop-chop! Quickly! Hurry!; immediately: since early C.19: pidgin, ex an ob. Cantonese phrase for 'Hurry up!'—but it must have found a ready acceptance by early sailors in the China Sea already familiar with C.18 v. *chop*, to do quickly. Still, 1970s, popular in the Services and, as L.A. notes, it is a 'senior's, foreman's "friendly" exhortation to speed up work.' (P.B.)

chop-ride. Test flight to examine a pilot's suitability to continue flying: RAF: later C.20. (*Phantom*.) See **chop**, v., 2.

chop sticks. See TOMBOLA, in Appx.

chop to pieces. In fisticuffs or boxing, to defeat severely: Aus. sporting coll.: late C.19–20. (B., 1943.) P.B.: also Brit. military for more serious mayhem, e.g., 'We lure the enemy into the killing zone and there we simply chop him [i.e. them] to pieces'. With the Aus. sense, cf. **chop**, n., 1.

Chopburg. Hamburg: RAF (operational): 1941. (McDouall, 1945.) Obviously *ham* prompted *chop*. Another operational officer writes, in late 1961, thus, 'I always felt that Chopburg referred to the possibility of "getting the chop" over Hamburg rather than to any link between ham and a pork chop.' Both of these 'causes' were, I suspect, at work.

chopped. Killed, esp. by machine-gun fire: army and RAF: WW2. Perhaps cf. the US underworld *chopper*, a machine-gun, but see also **get the chop**.—2. To have failed a military training course: Services': since ca. 1950. 'The camp was a miserable place, full of chopped aircrew trainees, all chopped for one reason or another'. (P.B., who was one of them in 1953.) Ex **chop**, v., 2.

chopped hay. Knowledge imperfectly assimilated: coll.:—1923 (Manchon). Ex the stables.

chopper, n. A tail: mostly Cockneys': late C.19–20. 'Pleased as a dog with two choppers, 'e was, silly little bleeder' (Baron, 1950). Perhaps euph. for:—2. Penis: low. P.B.: a serviceman with a particularly large one is liable to be known as *whopper chopper*.—3. A helicopter: FAA since ca. 1955; by 1975 > gen. coll. Prob. ex US. Ex the chopping motion and sound of the rotor blades.—4. A car taken in part exchange: second-hand car dealers': since ca. 1955. (Cowdy, 1965.) Cf. S.E. 'chop and change'.—5. 'A motorcycle that has been extensively modified, with frame altered and forks extended' (Dunford): motorcyclists': current in 1970s.—6. 'A bicycle' (Powis): underworld: current in 1970s. Perhaps ex sense 5, or from the trade name of a children's bicycle.—7. Railwaymen's nickname for the class 20 locomotive: mid-C.20. (Marsh, 1986.) Poss. ex the shape. See also HAULAGE, in Appx.—8. See **choppery**.

chopper, v. To go, or to convey, by helicopter: orig. and mainly flying s.: since ca. 1960. (Walker, 1968.) Ex **chopper**, n., 3.

choppers. Teeth; *china choppers* = false teeth: Can. s.,—1949; Brit., since ca. 1950, e.g., in *National choppers*, provided by the National Health Service.

choppery. 'A companion is choppery when he is surly and unapproachable and therefore looks hatchet-faced: hence having a chopper on' (Rowles, 1948): printers' (compositors'): from ca. 1850 (*chopper* [bad mood] *on*): ob. by 1960s.

Chopping. Chopin, as in 'Oh, just something by Chopin'— 'Um! Thought it was chopping.' Lower-middle and lower class joc.: late C.19–20.

choppy. (Of a temperature chart) uneven, esp. of a fever patient: hospital nurses': since the 1920s. If even, it is *flat*.

chordy. Stolen, as in 'chordy gear' = stolen goods: market-traders'. (*M.T.*). Ex:-

chore. To thieve; hence *chorer*, a thief: market-traders'. (*M.T.*). Ex Romany *čor*, to steal.

choss up. To wreck, esp. a vehicle: army: since ca. 1946. Prob. ex the widespread deliberate pron. of *chaos* as *choss*.

chots. Potatoes: Cotton College. In C.19, the form was *chotties*: ex *teotties*, the latter being a deliberate(?) var. of *taties* or *taters*. (Roberts, 1938.) Raab: 'or a var. of *OED* dial. *chat*, a small, poor potato? My Mother, 'Pat' Betbeder, would throw out those *chats* from her potato crop that were not worth cooking.'

chow! An Anglo-Italian coll. (esp. in London) salutation: mid-C.19–early 20. After going out of gen. use, it suddenly, in the late 1950s, became common in the Espresso bars of Britain, Aus. and elsewhere. This resurgence prompted a letter to E.P. from Nicholas Bentley, 1961, noting its popularity as form both of salutation and goodbye, and particularly at the Royal College of Art. Ex It. *ciáo* (coll. for *schiavo*), at your service.

chow line, the. A food queue in RN Barracks: lowerdeck: since ca. 1925. (P-G-R.) Ex China Coast pidgin, *chow*, food.

chow miaow. 'A generic term (punning) for Chinese food': Aus.: since ca. 1945. (Morrisby, 1958.) See prec.

Chowringhee star. The 1939–45 Service medal. See **Firpo star**.

Chriggie, -y, n. and adj. Var. of **Chrissie**, 2, Christmas: coll.: heard early 1970s. (P.B.)

Chrisake! Usu. as oath 'Oh, for (or fer) Chrisake!' and occ. spelt *Chrissake*: slovenly: C.19–20.

chrissie. A chrysanthemum.—2. *Chrissie*, n. and adj. Christmas: domestic coll. (P.B.)

Christ Almighty wonder. One who thinks very highly of himself; one who 'really has something', an exceedingly able person; some thing or event that is astounding or extremely surprising: late C.19–20. 'He's a C.A.w. with cars'; 'It's a C.A.w. he's not run over twice nightly.'

Christchurch, by. A euph. oath, current since ca. 1945 (?earlier) in NZ and UK. From Christchurch, Canterbury Province, NZ; and Dorset.

Christer. An exclamation mark: authors' and typists'. Ex exclamatory *Christ!*

Christmas card. A guard: mostly theatrical r.s. Franklyn.

Christmas crackers. Knackers (= testicles): r.s. 'Less commonly heard than its derivative *Christmas crackered* for knackered (physically [or mentally] exhausted)' (Hillman, 1974).

Christmas Eve. To believe: r.s. (P.P., 1932.) Less gen. than *Adam and Eve*.

Christmas hold. 'A hold applied by grabbing an opponent's testicles (a "handful of nuts")' (B., 1953): Aus. prison s.: mid-C.20.

Christmas log(s). Dog(s): r.s.: occ. var. of *Yuletide log(s)*. (Hillman, 1974.)

Christmas tree. 'An aeroplane which had been grounded for a long period by major unserviceability, and from which items had been cannibalised to service another aeroplane quickly' (Adkin): RAF: 1920s–30s.—2. 'RAF Intruder pilots' slang [WW2] for the Luftwaffe's airfield system: flare-paths, boundary-lights and, in particular, the "visual Lorenz" approach-path lights, which from the air looked like a stylised pine-tree.' (R.S., 1967.)—3. 'The complex arrangement of pipes and valves at the head of an oil well to control the flow of oil' (Leechman): Can. oilmen's: since ca. 1950. Haggard, 1958.—4. 'Colour [?coloured] light multiple aspect gantry' (*Railway*, 2nd): railwaymen's: since ca. 1950.—5. An effect seen on an airborne radar screen used in interception by all-weather fighter aircraft: RAF coll. > j.: late 1940s–early 50s. (P.B.)—6. 'Drinamyl; Spansules (US): drugs users' slang' (Home Office): current in 1970s.

chro. Short for next: since 1930. (B.P.)

chromo. A prostitute: Aus.: since ca. 1925. (B., 1942.) Ex gay-coloured dresses.

chronic. Unpleasant; objectionable; unfair; 'rotten'. (Rarely of persons: in same senses; hence, formidable, excellent. Manchon.) Late C.19–20, ex the S.E. sense, acute (pain), inveterate (*c. complaint*.) Whence *something chronic*, badly, severely, most objectionably: lower classes'.

chronometer. A watch, however small: coll., either joc. or pretentious.

chrysant. A chrysanthemum: coll.: from ca. 1890. (Mottram, 1934.) Also *chrysanth* (C.20), as in *The Passing Show*, 20 Jan. 1934. Cf. **'mum**.

chubb. 'To lock. To chubb a man in is to lock him in. "Unchubb" = unlock. From the well-known make of lock.

[Hence] *chubbed in.* Locked in cell' (Tempest): prison c.: mid-C.20.

chubby or **dumpy.** A short, squat umbrella: coll.: 1925. Collinson.

Chuck. Charles: Can. (and US): mid-C.19–20.

chuck, n. A coll. endearment: C.16–20, but ob. by 1800.?Ex *chick.* P.B.: still current as a N. Country affectionate vocative, later C.20. (The admirable Pattie Coldwell, on BBC Radio 4's 'You and Yours', *passim.*)

chuck, v. As to toss, to throw with little arm-action, it has always been S.E., but as throw in any other sense, it is low coll. of C.19–20. E.g., 'We chucked everything we had at them' (shelled them heavily): army: WW2. P-G-R.—2. To vomit: Aus.: since mid-1940s (if not a decade or more earlier). (Buzo, 1968.) A shortening of the older *chuck up.*—3. To throw a case out of court: police s.: since ca. 1920. Newman, 1970.—4. 'To eat excessively when being withdrawn [from drug dependence]: drug addicts' s.' (Home Office): current in 1970s. Perhaps a re-emergence and specialisation of C.19 senses, food and eat.—5. '*Chucked.* Acquitted. "Of three men on trial two were weighed off and one got chucked" = two men were sentenced and the third was acquitted' (Tempest): c.: since mid-C.19.

chuck a charley. To have a fit: Aus. B., 1942.

chuck a chest. To 'tell the tale': vagrants' c. Prob. ex:—2. 'To throw forward the chest, as though prepared to meet the world': streets': late C.19–20. Ware.—3. Whence, 'to attempt to exercise undue authority', 'throw one's weight about': earlier C.20. (F. & G.) Cf. **chuck out** (one's) **chest.** The RN equivalent was to **cock** (one's) *chest.*

chuck (or **throw**) **a willy.** To have a fit: Aus. (Baker.) Cf. US *whing-ding.*

chuck (one's) **hand in.** To die: gen. coll.: late C.19–20. 'Taffrail', 1916.—2. To refuse to do, or stop doing, something: orig., military. C.20.—3. Hence, a specialised use, 'To refuse duty in order to state a "case" at the defaulter's table' (Granville): RN. All 3 senses ex cards.

chuck it! Stop it! Drop it! Leave off!: coll. G.K. Chesterton's poem 'Antichrist', satirising the pontificating of F.E. Smith on the Welsh Disestablishment Bill, ends bluntly: 'Chuck it, Smith!' (P.B.)

chuck one up. To salute, as 'There was the general, so I chucked him one up, but he never even saw me': army. An elab. of **chuck-up,** q.v. (P.B.)

chuck-out, n. Closing-time at a public house: since ca. 1920. Abbr. *chucking-out time,* itself ob.:-

chuck out, v. To eject forcibly (—1880); to discard (thing or plan), from ca. 1910. Coll.—2. Hence, joc., to cause to leave: from ca. 1915.

chuck out (one's) **chest.** To pull oneself together; stand firm: coll.: later C.19. The C.20 sense (likewise coll.) is to make oneself appear manly, to show confidence. An occ. var., *throw a chest.*

chuck the gab. To talk fluently or well; to 'tell the tale': low. Jennings, 1932.

chuck-up. A salute: army, other ranks': from not later than 1915; by mid-C.20 had > v., as *chuck* (him) *one up,* 'him' being the officer. 'From the act of throwing up the hand to the forehead in saluting'. (F. & G.)—2. Timely encouragement; a cheer (occ. ironical): RN: earlier C.20. 'Taffrail', 1916; Granville.—3. 'Term used of a buyer refusing to accept a catch of herring' (Butcher, 1979): nautical.—4. In *give* (something) *the chuck-up,* to abandon it, to send it 'to the devil': low coll.:—1923 (Manchon). Ex *chuck up* as at *chuck up the sponge.*

chuck (one's) **weight about.** To 'show off' in an unpleasantly domineering way: orig. Services':—1909 (Ware). Var. of **throw** (one's) **weight** . . . , q.v.

chucking cabbage. (A bunch of) paper currency of low denomination: Aus. journalists': adopted in 1942 or 1943 from US. Ex the predominant green of the notes or bills.

chuckle. Vomit. See **big spit.**

chuddie, -y. Chewing-gum: teenagers' (D. & R. McPheely): since ca. 1975 in UK, prob. adopted ex Aus.; cf. **chutty.** (P.B.)

chuff, n. Food: Services', esp. Army: ca. 1930–45. (H. & P.) Ex later C.19 pidgin *chow,* food: *chow > chough > chuff.*—2. Stimulation of male member by lumbar thrust in coïtion: low: late C.19–20. In Durham dial., *chuff* = to cuff.—3. Hence, *chuff chums,* male homosexual associates, a *chuff* being a catamite; and *chuff-box, pudendum muliebre.*—4. Anus: Aus. Also, since ca. 1945, English.—5. Bottom, backside: NZ. Hence, *sit on one's chuff,* to sit back and do nothing, as used by 'P.M.' Holyoake on 30 July 1967 (*Christchurch Star,* the next day). P.B.: also Brit., as in 'And that's the fellow [motorist] you get driving up your "chuff" ' (a police officer, quoted in an article about the M1 motorway, in *Observer* colour sup., 20 Dec. 1981, p. 31).

chuff, adj. Impudent: low coll.: from (?)late C.19–early 20. (Lyons, 1908.) Ex dial. *chuff,* happy.

chuff adder. 'Sodomite, "bum-chaser" ': jocular on *puff adder'* (L.A., 1969). Cf. **chuff,** n., 3.

chuff chum. A companion or 'pal', without, necessarily, any suggestion of homosexuality (cf. **chuff,** n., 3): Services' from 1930; † by 1950.

chuff-nuts. Faecal nodules on anal hair: RN. Cf. **chuff,** n., 4.

chuff piece. 'I got to wash a shift every night—if I don't want to feel like an old cow's chuff piece that is' (*Heart*): RN: mid-C.20. See **chuff,** n., 3.

chuffed. Pleased, delighted; but also, displeased, disgruntled: army. If one needed to distinguish, one used *chuffed to fuck* or *chuffed to arseholes* or *chuffed pink* or *bo-chuffed,* in the former, *dead chuffed* in the latter sense. Cf. **chuff,** adj. P.B.: in the 1950s–60s, *chuffed pink* and *bo-chuffed* were †, replaced by *chuffed to* (*little*) *naffy* [NAAFI]-*breaks,* or occ., *oil-bombs,* while the reverse became *dischuffed.*—2. Flattered: teenagers', esp. jazz-lovers': since ca. 1955. 'Janet Murray says: "I'd be chuffed" (current 'Cat' word for flattered). "It's nice to think someone fancies you" ' (*Woman's Own,* 1959). Both of the main senses derive ex English dialect *chuff,* which perhaps has two entirely different origins.—3. Hence, *real chuffed,* excited: since late 1950s.

chug-a-lug! An Aus. drinking-toast, esp. in Sydney: since the 1950s. Bonhomously echoic. Perhaps cf. **buggerlugs.** (It became the chorus of a popular song in the early 1950s. P.B.)

chummie, -y, n. A prisoner: joc. euph. police term: since ca. 1925. *Free-Lance Writer,* April 1948.—2. Hence, the prime suspect; the perpetrator of the crime under investigation: police s.: since ca. 1950 (?earlier). Hunter, 1962.—3. See next.

chummy, adj. (Of a motor-car) affording comfort and space for three or four persons: coll.: 1922; ob. by 1940. *OED* Sup.

chunder, n. and v. (To) vomit: Aus.: since ca. 1925. (B.P.) The term was given a new lease of life, and branded as 'typically Australian', by Barry Humphries in the late 1960s and 1970s. Cf. English dial. *chounter, chunter* or *chunder,* an echoic word meaning to grumble. Wilkes, however, comments, 'variously explained as an abbreviation of [nautical] "watch under" [= look out below!] and as rhyming slang *Chunder Loo = spew* from Chunder Loo of Akin Foo, a cartoon figure in a long-running series of advertisements for Cobra bootpolish in the *Bulletin* from 8 Apr. 1909'.

Chunkies, the. The Royal Pioneer Corps: Army: WW2 (?since mid-WW1). 'Ex the legend that they are all so tough they can open tins of pineapple chunks by crunching them between their ballocks' (P.B., 1974).

chunter. To grumble; to go on talking at length, esp. in a disgruntled way, or occ., merely tediously: orig. N. dial. >, since ca. 1950, gen. coll. 'He went chuntering on for hours about how ghastly the government was . . . ' Cf. dial. *chounter,* of which *chunter* is perhaps the S.E. pron. (P.B.)

chup. Silence; mostly in *keep chup,* to keep quiet: Army: late C.19–20. Ex Hindustani. P-G-R.

Church of Turkey. A non-existent religious denomination; any 'fancy religion': RN.

Churchill. A meal: taxi-drivers': late 1920s. Winston Churchill gave the taximan the right to refuse a fare while having a meal (newspaper cutting, 11 June 1945).

chut. Short for **chutty**, q.v., chewing-gum.—2. A var. of **chuff**, n., 2 and 3, and hence 'homosexual practices between men' (L.A., 1977).

chute (or **'chute**). A parachute: RAF coll.: since ca. 1930. Partridge, 1945.

chutney. Sodomy. See **Navy cake** and cf. **chut, 2.**

chutty. Chewing-gum: Aus.: since ca. 1925. 'Whence "chutto", masticate easily and pleasantly' (B., 1942). Ex *chew it*. Cf. **chuddie.**

chutzpah. See **chuzpah.**

chuvvy. A flea; hence, *chuvvied up*, infested with fleas: market traders'. (*M.T.*) Perhaps ex E. Anglian dial. *chovy*, a small, chestnut-coloured beetle. *EDD.*

chuzpah (pron. *khootspa*, and often written in the 'phonetic' form *chutzpah*). Tremendous self-confidence; sheer barefaced effrontery or impudence; selfish action, esp. tricky; unlooked-for resource, that secures advantage at any cost: US Yiddish, adopted in Britain ca. 1974. (L.A.)

ciáo! A greeting. See **chow!**

cigar. A Woodbine or Player's Weight or any other similar cigarette, small but wholesome: from ca. 1930 and mostly Cockneys'.

cigar-box. A violin. See **fish-horn** for related terms.

cigarette swag. 'A small swag carried by a tramp when he comes into a city' (B., 1943): Aus.: since ca. 1930. Ex shape and relative size.

cigga. A cigarette: Aus. coll.: later C.20. McNeil.

cig(g)aboo. A cigarette: Aus., esp. Sydney-siders': since ca. 1948. (Edwin Morrisby, 1958.)

ciggie, -y. A cigarette: later C.20. 'At least five cartons of ciggies' (O'Hanlon, 1984).

Cigs. Chief of the Imperial General Staff: Service officers': 1939–45. Ex the initials *C.I.G.S.* P-G-R.

cinch. As v., = 'corner', get a grip on, put pressure on: orig. (1875) US, anglicised ca. 1900, though never gen. *It's a cinch!* = 'the screw is on!', it's as good as a certainty, did catch on during WW1 (F. & G.); since ca. 1930 the predominant sense has been 'something (very) easy to do'. (E.P.; B.P.; P.B.) See **-ville.**

cinder. A window: thieves' r.s. (*Gilt Kid*, 1936.) Shortening earlier *burnt cinder*.

cinder-shifter. A motorcycle speedway rider: Aus.: since ca. 1924 (B., 1942). Ex cinder-track. Cf. **shale-shifter.**

Cinderella's coach; glass coach. A District Engineer's coach: railwaymen's: since ca. 1920. *Railway.*

cine. (Pronounced *sinny*.) In compounds, it = *cinema, cinematographic*: 1928 (*OED*): coll. >, by 1935, S.E. owing to its frequency as a trade abbr.

cinema. Cinematograph, -graphic: coll. (1910) >, by 1920, S.E. (*OED* Sup.) Cf. prec.

Cinema slang. See MOVING-PICTURE SLANG, in Appx.

Cipher Queen. See **Cypher Queen.**

circuit, the. 'The worn track round the compound . . . which kriegies "pounded" or "bashed" (walked) . . . to get away from their own thoughts' (Brickhill, 1946): prisoners of war in Germany, 1940–5.

circuit and bumps. 'Exercise flights consisting of repeated take-offs and landings' (E.P., 1942): since ca. 1925.

circuit-and-bumps boy: usu. in pl. A flying pupil: RAF: since ca. 1930. (Jackson.) Ex prec.

circus. Any temporary group of persons housed together, working at the same task, e.g. at an encyclopædia (for the masses rather than the classes): coll.: 1932.—2. The Security Intelligence Service; its operatives: civil servants': since ca. 1945. Willis, 1975, and the novels of Le Carré, *passim.*

cistern. A motorcycle fuel-tank: motorcyclists' s.: since ca. 1950. (Dunford.)

city slicker. A smart, smooth fellow from the city: Aus.: adopted, ca. 1944, ex US servicemen.—2. Hence, loosely, any city chap: since ca. 1950. (Cleary, 1959.) See **slicker.**

City's Light Horse, the. Female secretaries that have become their bosses' mistresses: the 1930s. (L.A., 1976.) A pun on horses easy to mount, and on *light-hearted.*

civies. See **civvies,** now, since ca. 1945 at latest, the usu. spelling.

civvie. See **civvy,** n. and adj.

civvies (formerly spelt, logically but unphonetically, *civies*). Civilian clothes: Services': mid-C.19–20. B. & L.; F. & G. (The army officers' word is S.E. *mufti*.)

civvy, civy, n. (As with *civies*, the former *i* is, in either spelling, short.) A civilian: coll.: orig. (1895), military.—2. Hence, a recruit waiting to be issued with a uniform: Services': ca. 1920–40. H. & P.—3. 'Anyone who is not a prisoner or member of the uniformed Prison Service' (Tempest): prisons', mid-C.20.—4. 'A proprietary branded cigarette, as opposed to a "roll-up" ' (Green): prisons': later C.20. Cf. synon. **straight** or **tailor-made.**

civvy, adj. Civilian, esp. with *clothes, life,* and *street*: military coll. Cf. the famous WW1 (and still going strong 50 years later) song, to the tune 'What a Friend (we have in Jesus)': 'When I get my civvy clothes on,/Oh, how happy I shall be . . . '

Civvy Street. The condition and status of a civilian. 'What did you do in Civvy Street?' was often heard, WW2, in the Services, where its use persists. (H. & P.) On the analogy of *Easy Street*, it was first used in ca. 1917 by the army. See **civvy.**

clacker. Pie crust: RN. Granville, ' "Any gash clacker loafing?" means "Any more pie?" ' Echoic (but Granville derives it from dial. *clag*, to stick, adhere.)—2. Hence, a collective for young women; individually, 'a nice piece (or bit) of clacker': RN, thence to other Services: since ca. 1950. (P.B.)

clackers; or **jam clacker.** 'Pastry, "duff", spread over with currants (or jam), prepared (by the ratings) on a small dish and which would be cooked in the galley' (L.A., 1967): RN.

clackometer. An imaginary instrument for measuring female attractiveness, as 'What does *she* read on your clackometer?': RN and army in Cyprus, late 1950s—perhaps more widespread, perhaps merely what E.P. dubbed an 'ephemeral parochialism'. (P.B.)

clag. Cloud; a cloud: RAF: since (?)mid-1930s. Ex dial. *clag*, clay, and *clag to*, stick to. Hence, *clagged in*, conditions too cloudy or foggy for aircraft to take off (before the advent of sophisticated blind-flying techniques). 'Ten-tenths clag', completely overcast with low cloud. (E.P.; P.B.)

claggy. (Of clothes) wet, from weather or sweat, and clinging, as in 'all claggy round the crutch': low coll.: since mid-C.20. Ex dial. (P.B.)

claim, n. Brutal physical attack: prisons'. Clayton, 1970.

claim, v. As to arrest (gen. in passive) it was current in the 1930s. (David Hume); but in the sense of simply 'catch hold of, seize, grasp (a person)' it occurs in *Sessions*, 19 Nov. 1902; 'Tyler jumped out at the window—I claimed him and tustled [sic] with him.'

claimed. Under arrest. See prec.

clam. One who says extremely little or is excessively secretive: coll. (The US sense is a close-fisted person.)

clamber aboard. 'Physical address to a woman for sexual intercourse' (L.A., 1974); low and raffish: perhaps esp. Services': WW2 and after. (P.B.)

clammers. Grappling-irons: used fig. in 'Get the clammers on him' = 'Don't let him get away [without buying anything]': market-traders'. (*M.T.*) *EDD* glosses *clammers* as (Cumbrian) 'a yoke for the neck of a cow, to prevent her from leaping hedges'.

clamp. To assume very close formation: RAF: later C.20. 'Boss calls, "By the IP [instructor pilot] chaps, tighten up!" That is the signal to "clamp" ' (*Phantom*). Cf. **hang in.**

clamp down on (e.g. delinquents or malefactors). To apply the full severity of the law or the regulations: since mid-1940s: coll. >, by ca. 1960, S.E.

clamped down is an RAF brevity for 'The cloud is now very low, or visibility bad' (Hinde, 1945): since ca. 1925. Cf. *clamp down*, v.i. to become foggy: RAF: since ca. 1930. Lewis, 1943.

clampers, often elab. to **Harry Clampers.** 'It's (Harry) Clampers' = It's non-flying weather: RAF: since ca. 1930. Prob. ex **clamped down.**

clampy. A flat-footed person: RN: since ca. 1925. (Granville.) Echoic; app. reminiscent both of *clatter* and *stamp* (about).

clang. To commit a *faux pas*: not common before late 1960s, and clearly a back-formation ex *clanger*, as in *drop a clanger*, e.g., 'I realised I'd clanged as soon as . . .', and in the abbreviatory exclam. *clang!*, applied usu. to one's own stupidity, uttered with some gesture of contrition such as clapping a hand to the forehead. (Based on a note from P.B., 1975.)

clanger. An error, a *faux pas*, a hideously obvious mistake; usu. in phrase **drop a clanger,** q.v., but occ. *make a clanger* (prob. influenced by *make a boo-boo*): coll., orig. Services', now (1970s) widespread: since (?)WW2, poss earlier. Either a synon. for testicle, cf. **clappers,** or merely echoic—bad blunders do resound. (P.B.)—2. A coward: Aus.: since ca. 1940. B., 1953.—3. Diminutive of **double clanger,** q.v., a gear-change on a bicycle.

clangeroo. A memorably bad misjudgment: mainly theatrical: since late 1940s. Rattigan, 1957, 'Not just a floater but a real old-fashioned clangeroo'. Ex **clanger,** 1, intensified by the *-oo* from the American suffix *-eroo.*

clanky. An engineer: RN. 'Term first heard by informant early 1970s, first applied to a shipwright with steel pins in his legs, but later to Engine Room Branch in some [other] ships; now gaining in popularity' (Knight, 1984).

clap. Gonorrhœa: late C.16–20; S.E. until ca. 1840, then low coll. Ex Old Fr. *clapoir.*

clap hands Charley (or **Charlie**), **do a.** To fly an aircraft in such a way as to cause the wings—or the rotor blades of a helicopter—to meet overhead: RAF: since ca. 1945. (With thanks to an operational RAF officer) P.B.: ex the refrain of a popular song, 'Clap hands, here comes Charlie . . .'

clap-trap. Much talk; idle chatter; nonsense and windbaggery: perhaps orig. Londoners'. Perhaps ex S.E. sense of 'language designed to win applause'.—2. Mouth: low, esp. Londoners': from ca. 1910. Perhaps ex sense 1, or shortening of much older *clapper* (= tongue)-*trap.*

clapped, adj. Utterly exhausted: coll.: later C.20. (Tracy, 1976.) A shortening of sense 2 of:–

clapped out. (Of aircraft) unserviceable, worn out: orig. RAF, and at first esp. in Far East: since 1942. Post-WW2 it was applied derivatively, esp. among racing drivers, to car engines; whence, by the 1970s, widespread and gen. coll. in phrases 'a clapped-out old banger', an old car in the last stages before being sent for scrap. But Les Winton, in *Fellowship News*, 1984, recalls the term's use among London club cyclists as early as ca. 1922.—2. Hence, (of persons) exhausted, no longer effective: since ca. 1946: esp. among teenagers since ca. 1955 (Gilderdale): ob. in this sense. (E.P.; P.B.) Claiborne suggests: 'both senses [prob.] derive from the images of a person sexually incapacitated by [the] clap.'

clapper. A sandwich-board man: street s.: since ca. 1910. Morse-Boycott, 1931.—2. Hence, a sandwich-man's boards: c.: ob. by 1932.

clappers. Testicles: mostly servicemen's: since ca. 1930. Winton, 1959, 'Don't let me hear you making another report like that again or I'll have your clappers for a necktie'. Cf. **clanger,** 1.—2. See **like the clappers.**

clappy. Strictly, infected with 'clap'; loosely, with either gonorrhœa or syphilis: Anglo-Irish. Blake, 1968, 'You son of a clappy whore.'

clar. In piece-work, to earn as much as possible: factory-workers': 1932.

Clara and **Mona.** 'Mona and Clara, the air-raid and all-clear signals . . . the moaning of the warning sirens and a contraction of the welcome "all-clear" ' (Berrey, 1940): WW2, on the Home Front.

Clarence. Like, though less than, *Cuthbert*, apt to be used as a joc. coll. See my *Name This Child*, 1936. P.B.: a *Punch* cartoon of 2 Feb. 1916 may be relevant; it shows an officer and a sergeant discussing a distant sentry: 'Officer. "Why do you think he wouldn't make a good corporal?"—Sergeant (indicating sentry). " 'Im a corporal! Lor Lumme! Why, 'is name's Clarence!" '

claret. Blood: from ca. 1600. From ca. 1770, mostly in boxing 'circles'. Ex the colour. The term is still, 1970s, current, 'especially common in South London' (Powis).

clarts. Trouble, often in (*drop*) *in the clarts*: euph. for 'shit' in this sense: used extensively in Clement, 1977. Ex dial. *clarty*, viscous. (P.B.)

clash. A set battle, planned and announced, between two gangs of hooligans and/or near-criminals: Glasgow c. and lower-class s.: from ca. 1920. (MacArthur.) It differs from a *rammy*, which is unarranged and may take place between two quite small groups. Cf. **rumble,** n., 2.

class man. A 'prisoner who has passed out of the first stage' (Ingram, 1933): c.

clatter, n. 'He has just finished a "clatter", fourteen days in the compound' (Grinstead, 1946): Guardsmen's: since ca. 1925. Echoic.

clatter, v. To smack; to hit: market-traders'. 'I clattered him'; 'clatter on to the chavvy [child]': these examples appear in *M.T.* Echoic. Hence, *clatters*, a smacking.

Clean, Mr or **Miss,** etc. One who, in politics, show-business, sport, etc., maintains an image of virtue as a selling point: adopted ca. 1980 ex US. 'I'm fed up with playing little Miss Clean. I'd like to take on a really naughty role.' (P.B.)

clean, adj. Cleared by the security vetting services: coll. > j. of those governed by the Official Secrets Act: since ca. 1950 (?earlier). (P.B.)—2. Carrying no drugs: addicts': adopted, ca. 1955, ex US. Cutland, 1985, however, glosses it 'no longer taking drugs'. US since—1959 (Spears).—3. See **come clean.**

clean gone. Quite 'cracked'; mad: coll. Manchon.

clean round the bend. An intensification of **round the bend,** q.v., crazy.

clean the fish. To 'skin' (= lead on) the victim: Can. carnival s.: since ca. 1920. Also *feed the fish*. See **fish,** 1.

clean-up, n. A victory; a rout: Aus.: since ca. 1920. (B., 1942.) Ex sense 2 of:-

clean up, v. To acquire (something) as profit or gain: coll. US, anglicised by 1910. *OED* Sup.—2. To defeat: Aus., since ca. 1915, NZ since ca. 1916. (Slatter.) Perhaps short for:-

clean up on. To get the better of, e.g., in a brawl: RN: ca. 1905–40. (Carr, 1939.)

clean wheels. 'A motor vehicle to be used in crime that has never been previously stolen or come under prior police suspicion in any way' (Powis): underworld: 1970s.

cleaners, get (or **be) taken to the.** To be cheated or swindled very badly. See **take to the . . .**

cleanie. One's best girl: military: 1920s. Perhaps a blend of *clean + clinah.*

clear. In *in the clear*, with no evidence against one; innocent, or app. so: c. *The Passing Show*, 26 May 1934.

clear decks. To clear the table after a meal: nautical coll.: mid-C.19–20. (Bowen.) P.B.: as *clear the decks*, it is still, 1970s, common to clear a space in order to work or play, and is not restricted to the orig. sense given here. Also used fig. and metaphorically.

clear up. To withdraw from drugs: addicts'. (Stockley, 1986.) US since—1967 (Spears).

C

cleavage. The gap between a woman's breasts, esp. when revealed by a low-cut dress: coll.: since ca. 1965. Chambers' *C.20 Dict.*, 1972.

cleek. 'A wet blanket (at a party)': beatniks': since ca. 1959. (Anderson.) Adopted ex American jazz s. for 'a sad or melancholy person' (W. & F.). Cf. **party-pooper.**

Clem. See **Chad.**

clem. To starve: vagrants' c., ex dial.—2. In circus s. (perhaps ex US), a fight.

clerk, the. A hospital registrar's amanuensis. See **Firm, the.**

clever. 'Nice'; generally likeable or pleasant: coll.: from ca. 1730; ob. by 1930. P.B.: not ob.—or perhaps revived: on 5 Feb. 1983 the forecaster on BBC Radio Leicester announced that the East Midlands' weather for the weekend would be 'not very clever'. He was right!

clever boots. Gen. as a comment: a clever, occ. a sly, person. Perhaps ex **clever shins,** q.v., and see also **bossy-boots,** for other examples of this usage.

clever boys, the. Servicemen (or others) with only theoretical knowledge: Services': since 1940. Derisively: *the really clever boys*, 'people with positively academic knowledge' (H. & P.).

clever clogs. A N. Country var. of **clever boots.** C.19–20 (*EDD*). Petch, 1974, notes that it occurred in, e.g., 'Our Kid'—an ITV comedy series—on 20 May 1973. P.B. adds: it was neatly used in a British Island Airways' advertising slogan, mid-1970s, 'Clever clogs fly BIA to Amsterdam'.

clever creeps. Forensic chemists. See **whiz(z) kids, the.**

clever Dick. A clever, rather, too clever, person: used derisively or sarcastically: Baumann records it as 'London schools'' in 1887, but it is still in much more widespread—use in the 1970s, although with a slightly old-fashioned ring to it. Stewart, 1961, uses var. *cleverdick*. It is also occ. used as adj. Cf. **smart Alec,** and **clever boots, shins,** etc.

clever Mike. A bicycle: r.s., on *bike.*

clever shins. A person sly to no, or little, purpose: schools': ca. 1870–1910. (Baumann.) Cf. **sly-boots.**—2. Hence, more gen., an early C.20 coll. var. of *clever boots.* Manchon.

clever sides. Another var. of **clever boots**; cf:-

clever sticks. Synon. with *clever boots, clogs, Dick, shins*: a juvenile taunt: since early 1940s (?much earlier). (P.B.)

clew-up. To finish a job: RN: since ca. 1920. Granville, 'The original meaning was to draw the clews of the sail to the yard-arm for furling.'—2. To meet an old messmate: RN: since ca. 1930. Granville, 'I clewed up with old Dusty Miller in the Smoke.'—3. For sense 'holed up', of a person in hiding, see quot'n at **up the line.**

click, n. A clique; a 'push' (Aus. senses): Aus. since—1914 (C.J. Dennis); as a somewhat pej. term for a group or set, also Brit. since ca. 1925.—2. A successful meeting with an unknown member of the opposite sex: WW1+. Much rarer than the corresponding nuance at the v., 1.—3. Hence, a girl; a sweetheart: Glasgow:—1934.—4. A kilometre: since ca. 1960 (?earlier). Thanks to Miss Barbara Martin, who heard the term while serving, late 1960s, at the 'Project Concern' Hospital in Vietnam. (P.B.)—5. As *the Click, The Clique*, the advertising journal of the antiquarian and secondhand book trade: booksellers' illiteracy; hence, educated booksellers' joc. coll.

click, v. To be successful; to have a piece of very good luck, as in *click a Blighty*, to get a 'Blighty' wound (F. & G.): 1914+. See also **click with** and **click for.**—2. (Of a woman) to become pregnant.—3. To understand suddenly; as in 'Ah, *now* it's clicked' = I see: since ca. 1930. Ex lock tumblers, or other small mechanical device, falling into place; or perhaps ex a light coming on. (P.B.)

click for. To be put down for, e.g., a fatigue or duty: army: since WW1. Perhaps ex the idea of 'to do a drill movement with a click' (Collinson).

click with. To have a successful encounter with a hitherto unknown member of the opposite sex: coll.: since ca. 1910. Cf. Scots *cleek in* (or *up*) *with*, to take up with a person (*EDD*); chiefly, however, ex the interlocking of mechanical devices, as when a key is turned. Absolutely, as 'they clicked', they took to each other at once: see **click, v., 1.**

clicker. One who, once or, esp., often, meets successfully with an unknown person of the opposite sex: WW1; ob. by 1940. See **click with.**

clickety click. See TOMBOLA, in Appx.

clicket(t)y-clicks. R.s. on *knicks* = (female) *knickers*. It occurs in one of Neil Bell's short stories—?*A Proper Beano.*

clicking. Success; 'getting off' with a girl: from ca. 1915; ob. See **click with.** Cf. P.G. Wodehouse's *The Clicking of Cuthbert*, 1922.

clicky. Cliquey: coll. Cf. **click, n., 1.**

client. A person, a fellow or chap: army: from ca. 1912; still, 1970s, heard occ. (F. & G.) Suggested by *customer.*

cliffhanger. 'A (silent) film shown in weekly serials; from the precarious predicaments in which the heroine was left at the end of each part. Dates probably from before 1914 but has been revived to describe similar T.V. serials and extended to anything exciting and drawn out, e.g. a suspense novel'. (Sanders, 1965.) By 1980s, familiar S.E.

clifty, to steal; *cliftying,* stealing, act(s) of theft: Services': also known in NZ (*Iddiwah*, July 1953). Ex Arabic *klefti*, a thief. Hence:-

clifty wallah. A thief; by extension and dilution, a too smart man: army: WW2+. Ex Arabic *klefti* + the all-purpose *wallah*, which the British Army in India took to mean simply chap, fellow, bloke, from the Hindustani or Urdu.

climb. In *on the climb*, adj. and adv., by cat-burglary: c. *Gilt Kid*, 1936.

climb the golden stairs. 'At Rugby, the lodge was connected to the engine shed by a short staircase; trainmen lodging there were invited by the foreman to "climb the golden stairs"— local slang for lodging' (McKenna, 1980): railwaymen's.

climbing Mary. A woman window-cleaner: WW2. See **whistler, 4.**

climbs (up) like a fart in a bath. 'Said of an aircraft with a high rate of climb' (French): RAF: WW2.

clinch, n. A prolonged and passionate embrace: adopted, ca. 1945, ex US.

clinch, v. To identify a rare bird. See BIRD-WATCHERS' SLANG, in Appx.

clinic. A public-house: office- and shop-girls': ca. 1955–60. (Gilderdale.) There one finds exactly what the doctor prescribed.

clinker. A failure, as in 'Before "10" [a film] was released in America, its producers were so certain it was a clinker that they unceremoniously tore up the contracts for two other Blake Edwards pictures' (*Time Out*, 8 Feb. 1980): media circles.

clinker link. A lower-grade employee, engaged in furnace-cleaning: railwaymen's: since ca. 1920. *Railway.*

clinkers. Bed bugs: homosexuals': current ca. 1970.

clip-joint. A night-club, or a restaurant, where the prices are high and the patrons are fleeced: Can.: adopted, ca. 1930, ex US. Ex sheep-shearing. P.B.: by 1950 at latest, also Brit.

clip-ons. 'Short handlebars which are clipped on low down the fork legs' (Dunford): motorcyclists': current in 1970s.—2. Dark glasses that can be clipped on to ordinary spectacles: coll.: later C.20. (Raab.)

clipped corner, the. The mark, on a discharge-paper, of a thoroughly bad character: RN coll. Also called a *blanker.*

clipper. ' "clippers", the police term for the professional store thieves' (Winn, 1965). Ex *clip*, to rob.

clippie, -y. A girl conductor on bus or train: since 1939. (*New Statesman*, 30 Aug. 1941; H. & P.) Ex clipping tickets. R.S. suggested, 1967, 'perhaps influenced by Messrs Lyons' waitresses, advertised by their employers in the 1920s and 1930s as "Nippies".'

clipping. 'Posing as a prostitute and knocking the client out with sleeping pills' (and then robbing him): mostly London and esp. among West Indians: since ca. 1960. Weightman, 1977.

clit (gen.) and its diminutive, **clitty.** The clitoris: low. The latter perhaps mostly Aus. B.P. cites David Hare, *Slag*, 1971, 'The fingers of the nation sidling for the clit.'

cloak and dagger. Phrase used by Service officers in WW2, and after, for 'secret service' (work, etc.). *In the cloak and dagger club* was prisoner-of-war s. for having access, via radio or other means, to outside information. See PRISONER-OF-WAR SLANG, 4, in Appx.

clobber; occ. clober, n. Clothes: from ca. 1850; at first, old clothes but from ca. 1870 also new; among soldiers in WW1, one's (full) equipment. Chiefly Jewish, Cockney and C.20 Aus. Prob. ex Yiddish (*klbr*). P.B.: in later C.20, gen. coll., not only for clothes, but for any impedimenta.

clobber, v. To punch or strike; to assault: since ca. 1910: orig. low; by ca. 1945, fairly gen. Echoic. A *Guardian* article, 21 July 1982, used the term metaphorically: 'the British Treasury's predilection for clobbering the poor.'

clobber out. An occ. early C.20 var. (Manchon) of:-

clobber up. To dress smartly, v.t. and reflexive: from ca. 1860. Also, occ. (gen. in passive), *clobber*: not before ca. 1880. P.B.: a common var. is *to be clobbered about with*, e.g., motorcycling gear, or any other similar encumbrance that is uncomfortable and hampers one's movements: coll. Occ. synon. with *lumbered with*.

clobber with. To impose an onerous duty or unwelcome burden on (someone). 'I got clobbered with finishing the weeding.' Cf. **lumber, land with.**

clobbered by. (Always in this form.) Applied to the victim of the imposition in prec., as in 'I was clobbered by the adjutant for (or *with*) an extra duty'; 'He was clobbered by the police for speeding'; 'She was clobbered by her boy-friend—he put her in the pudden club', etc.: coll.: later C.20.

Clobberer. HM Submarine *Conqueror* 'was called "Clobberer" after her sinking of the [Argentine flag-ship] *General Belgrano*' (*Don't Cry*, 1983): Services': Falklands War.

clobbering. A heavy bombing: RAF: 1941–5. Echoic. Ex **clobber,** v.

clock, n. A taxi-meter: taxi-drivers': since early C.20; by 1930, coll. 'It has other names: the "ticker", the "kettle", "Mary Ann", and the "hickory". "Hickory" seems abstruse until you remember the nursery rhyme and add "dickory dock" ' (Hodge, 1939). See also **clock and a half.**—2. Hence, an airspeed indicator: RAF: 1930s. Jackson.—3. A speedometer: coll.: since ca. 1920.—4. By extension, any instrument with a dial face, e.g., an altimeter, as in the famous RAF pilots' 'line-shoot': 'There I was, upside down in cloud, nothing on the clock—and climbing hard': fliers': since the 1930s (?earlier). Cf. **clock-basher.** (P.B.)

clock, v.t. To punch, to strike (with one's fist): Aus.: since ca. 1925 (Baker); by ca. 1930 also Brit., in such phrases as 'I could have clocked him' or 'clocked him one'. Perhaps orig. 'to strike on the face.'—2. To watch (someone) patiently: since ca. 1930. Norman.—3. To catch sight of, to notice: c., mostly prisons': since ca. 1935. Norman, 1959.—4. 'To "clock" someone is to follow someone and see what he backs. This is sometimes expressed as "Get on his daily" [i.e. tail; r.s. on *Daily Mail*]' (*Sunday Telegraph*, 7 May 1967, anon. article on bookies' s.): racing: since ca. 1930. Cf. sense 2, and **clock and house.**—5. To register on the speedometer; to attain a speed of (so many miles/kilometres per hour): since ca. 1925. Ex **clock,** n., 4.—6. To turn back a speedometer [i.e. mileometer] to make the mileage registered appear to be much less than it is: secondhand-car dealers': since ca. 1945. (*Woman's Own*, 28 Feb. 1968.) Hence, vbl n., *clocking*.—7. To observe closely, in an intimidating way: complaints that defendants' supporters were 'clocking' the jurors were made at a trial of football hooligans in Leeds. *Sunday Times*, 5 June 1988: 'Villains call it clocking in Leeds, eyeballing in Manchester and screwing in London's East End.' Cf. sense 3, and **clock and house.**

clock and a half, guvnor? 'Unscrupulous cab-drivers' term for the metered fare plus an extra half. Unknowing or foreign fares are sometimes duped into paying this unlawful excess' (Powis): current in 1970s. See **clock,** n., 1.

clock and house. 'Slang terms meaning to see and remember [suspects'] faces, and then to follow [the suspects] to their home' (Powis): police s.: current in 1970s. Cf. senses 2–4 of **clock,** v.

clock(-)basher or **watch(-)basher.** An instrument maker or repairer, as an RAF 'trade': RAF: since ca. 1937. Jackson. See **basher,** 6.

clock captain. A captain that alters the bowling, not by a tactical but by a chronological calculation: cricketers' coll.

clock in (or **on**), **off** (or **out**). To sign the time book on arrival or departure: from ca. 1905; coll. >, by 1930, S.E. Factory and office phrases.

clock-in a beef. To make a 'regulation' complaint or a big fuss: Wrens': since ca. 1939. Cf. S.E. *put in a complaint* and prec.

clock up zeds. See **zeds.**

clock-watcher. A lazy, uninterested employee, who spends most of his hours at work waiting for 'knocking-off time': coll. (Raab.)

clocking. Vbl n. from **clock,** v., 6, q.v., the fraudulent alteration of a vehicle's mileometer.

clockwork mice. 'Aircraft and aircrew engaged on continuous dummy deck-landing to train deck-landing officers or to test mirror landing sights: FAA: 1950s' (Peppitt).

clockwork orange. 'A male homosexual: "He's as queer as a clockwork orange" ' (Powis).

clod. (Gen. pl.) A copper coin: r.s., abbr. *clodhopper*: since ca. 1870. Among Cockneys, a penny (*Evening News*, 20 Jan. 1936); also among grafters (*Cheapjack*, 1934); still current among market-traders (*M.T.*).

clodhopper. A street dancer: c.:—1933 (Orwell).—2. A penny. See prec.

clog; cloggie. A clog-dancer: coll.: since ca. 1880. (Flynt, 1900.) The 2nd form popularised, since the late 1960s, by the serial cartoons of Bill Tidy, 'The Cloggies', concerning the antics of a clog-dancing team.—2. The Dutch language; also, occ., a Dutchman. See **cloggy,** 1.—3. (*Cloggies, the.*) By specialisation, the Royal Netherlands Marines: RM. (Knight, 1984.)

Clog and Knocker (Railway), the. The old Great Central Railway running from Marylebone to Manchester: railwaymen's: earlier C.20; after ca. 1950, merely historical. (*Railway.*) Ex the clogs formerly much worn by Lancashire women. The *Knocker* element prob. derives ex 'that other Lancashire institution the knocker-up, who in pre-alarm-clock days used to do the rounds of the mill-hands' homes, waking them in time for work by knocking on bedroom windows with the pole which he carried' (R.S.).

clog down. Driving very fast; accelerating, as in 'Right! You know the ambush drill: anything happens—it's clog down, and away!', i.e. in the event of an emergency, get the vehicle away fast: army: since ca. 1950, at latest. Cf. *put (one's) foot on the floor.* (P.B.)

cloggy. Dutch (language), as 'Hey, Bill, what's cloggy for "a dozen eggs"?': among those Servicemen who were detached from the British Army of the Rhine to duty in Holland: since ca. 1945. Ex the extensive use made of clogs there. (P.B.).—2. Deaf: perhaps dial., though not in *EDD*; I heard it from Northerners in the early 1960s. Poss. a corruption of *cloddish* or **cloth ears,** q.v. (P.B.).—3. See **clog.**

clonked (out). Of, e.g. a mechanical device, not working: teenagers': early 1980s. (Joanna Williamson, 1982.) Var. of **conked,** q.v.

close mouth. A disreputable establishment or resort: Scottish c.

close-poling. Two (trolley) buses running very close together: busmen's coll. (prob. j.): mid-C.20. Ex the trolley-poles.

close to (a person), **be.** To enjoy the act of love, as 'I was close to her last night': WW2. (L.A., 1978.)

closet. As n. and adj., this term has been extended from the next entry since later 1970s, and applied as 'secret': e.g.

'[Commercial] sponsors [of sporting events] are bringing their motives out of the closet. Not everyone is quite so upfront . . . ' (*Time Out*, 30 May 1980); and, 'Am I wrong, or are there millions of closet workers all over the country waiting to come out . . . '(Wood, 1980), i.e. are they against the apparently prevailing mood of 'strike over anything and everything'? In the latter quot'n, *come out* = to stand revealed, is also borrowed from 'gay' coll. (P.B.)

closet queen. A crypto-homosexual (male, passive): Can. 'gay': since ca. 1950. The *Daily Colonist* (Victoria, BC), 24 Feb. 1972, 'I'm 24, have a good job, I enjoy good health and am a happy homosexual. I'm what is known as a closet queen'. It may have migrated to Can. ex US (W. & F., not in 1st ed.), but I believe it to have been adopted from the UK, esp. Eng., notably London, for from several highly accredited sources I've been informed that it has existed in Eng. since the late 1940s and perhaps earlier.—2. A male transvestite. Landy, 1971.

clot. A fool, a 'stupid'; an incompetent: since ca. 1920: at first, upper-middle class. Chamberlain, 'The man's a bigger clot than I took him for.' By a pun on equivalent S.E. *clod*.

cloth-capper. A veteran motorcyclist: motorcyclists' s. (Dunford): current in 1970s. I.e., one from the days before it became compulsory to wear a safety helmet when riding.

cloth ears. In the (orig. Cockney) phrase 'he's got cloth ears', it is applied to one who doesn't wish to hear, and has spread in this sense during C.20 to other parts, witness Pilkington, 1985, writing of the Lancashire-set TV serial 'Coronation Street': 'The sound of Bet Lynch bellowing at closing time, "What's up? 'Ave you lot got cloth ears?" ' Occ. used of or to someone who appears stupidly unresponsive, or who simply has not heard, 'Gawd! Has he/have you got cloth ears?' Perhaps ex caps with ear-flaps.—2. Increasingly, in 1980s, used to mean unappreciative of what is heard, music, say, or poetry, as in 'Anyone who hears this line (or the poem as a whole) as "bawled" is cloth-eared' (Karlin, 1986). In this sense, occ. *tin-eared* or (*has*) *got tin ears* or *a tin ear*.

cloth job. In *do a cloth job*, to rob a church: c. Gash, 1983.

clothes-peg. An egg: r.s.

clothing-crusher. A 'ship's policeman superintending the mustering of kits': RN. (Bowen.) See **crusher.**

cloud-creep, mostly **be cloud-creeping.** To keep under cloud cover: RFC–RAF: 1916–18, and again in WW2. 'Trying to get into position to attack some Huns that were cloud-creeping' (Yeates, 1934).

cloud nine. In to *ride*, or *be riding around on*, or simply *on*, *cloud nine*, to be in a state of euphoria, mental or physical, or of felicitous fantasy; 'up-to-date version of "have one's head in the clouds" ' (L.A., 1976): adopted, ca. 1972, ex US—at least, the *on cloud nine* part was. Green, 1976, 'Dr Motzkin will pump you so full of pain-killers you'll be on cloud nine.' Cf. **over the moon.**

cloud on the deck. 'A cloud base coincident with a sea or land surface' (E.P., 1942). See **deck,** 2, and cf. **clag** and **clampers.**

Cloudy Joe. Nickname for a meteorological officer: RAF: 1940–5.

clout, n. A heavy blow: M.E. onwards. S.E. until ca. 1850, when it > low coll. and dial.; indeed it was far from literary after ca. 1770.—2. Power or influence: coll.: since ca. 1960. Ex the physical sense; the threat of violence is (usu. fig.) there to enforce the wielder's will. Hence the phrase *carry a* (or *some*) *clout*, to command considerable influence.

clout, v. To palm cards dishonestly; often as n. *clouting*: Aus. card-players': since ca. 1940. B., 1953.

clouting. In c., the carrying, by a woman shop-thief, of rolls of silk or cloth between her legs. Leach.

club. A propeller: RAF: ca. 1925–45. (H. & P.) Ex shape.—2. In (*she's*) *in the club*, she is pregnant; short for **the pudding club,** q.v.; to make a woman pregnant is to *put her in the club*: raffish coll.: since ca. 1940. Harrison, 1943, for *put* . . .

club number. 'Street [Police] officers . . . say of a man with a criminal record that "he's got a club number" ' (Seabrook, 1987). Ex the criminal's numbered docket at the National Identification Bureau, formerly the Central Criminal Records Office, at Scotland Yard.

club run, the. A routine convoy trip in wartime: RN (mostly officers'): WW2.

clubbability. The possession of qualities fitting a person to be a member of a club: coll.: from ca. 1875. P.B.: hence, *unclubbable*, used by social workers in the 1960s and 1970s, of individuals who refuse to fit into schemes designed for their own benefit.

Clubs. Nickname for physical training instructor: RN (lowerdeck): since ca. 1910. Ex Indian clubs.

clucky. Pregnant. Aus. low. (B., 1942.) Ex hens. Wilkes notes 'used by women only'.

clue, have no; have you a clue? To be ignorant, have no information; have you heard anything, do you know anything?: mostly Army: 1942+. Ex *clueless.*

clue up. To 'put (someone) in the picture', to brief, inform, instruct: since the middle 1940s. Cf. **gen up.**

clued(-)up. Well-informed; alert: since ca. 1941. (B.P.) Cf. **clue up** and contrast **clueless.** Intensified, in the Services, to, inevitably, *clued-up to fuck* = very well informed.

clueless. Ignorant; esp. in *clueless type* (opposite of *gen wallah*) and, in answer to a question, 'I'm clueless': RAF, since ca. 1939; hence Army, since ca. 1941. (Jackson.) Ex crime-detection.

cluey, adj. and n. (One who is) well-informed or alert: Aus.: since ca. 1945. Ex **clued-up.** B.P. quotes 'He should be on T.V.; he's a real cluey' and 'Ask Bert, he's pretty cluey', and it also occurs in Buzo, 1968.

clumper. A thick walking boot: coll., from ca. 1875. Ex *clump*, an additional half-sole. Cf. 'Cut-down, worn-out thigh-boots of ankle height known as "clumpers" ' (Piper, 1974): trawlermen's. Prob. echoic, as is the v. (P.B.).

clumping. Occ. var. of *thumping*, adj., to describe something both large and clumsy, as 'clumping great thing—I wouldn't give it house-room!': coll. (P.B.)

clunk. A man; a chap: Aus. low, esp. Sydney. (Park, 1948.) Echoic.—2. Hence, since ca. 1950, predominantly a simple fellow, or even a fool. (B., 1953.)—3. An ill-bred or ill-mannered person: Can.: since late 1950s. (Leechman.) Perhaps semantically 'a lump': cf. the *clunk, clunk-*, words in the *EDD*.

clunk!: intensively **ker-lunk!** Echoic of sounds deeper than those expressed by *boink* and *doink*: late C.19–20, but perhaps going back for centuries.

clunker. An old motorcar: Can.: since ca. 1965. Echoic; cf. **banger.**

clunky. Ill-bred or ill-mannered: Can.: since late 1950s. (Leechman.) Ex **clunk,** 3.

clut. Coll. abbr. of *clutter*, as in 'oh, the room looks tidy enough now, but usually it's absolutely bung-full of clut': middle-class: later C.20. (Haacke, 1987.)

clutch, put in (one's). To fall silent: motorists' (ca. 1920) > gen. by 1928, Galsworthy, *Swan Song*. Ex motoring.

clutz. A stupid and worthless person—a clot (Janssen, citing McCabe, 1972, adds: var. of US *klutz*, n. and adj.): adopted, ex US, ca. 1960. W. & F. derive it ex Yiddish.

co. *Co.*, or *coy* so pronounced, is a sol. for company: since early C.19. Esp. . . . *and Co.*, the rest of them [people]. For 'the rest of [the things]', see **and Co.**

co-ed. Co-educational, i.e. educating girls and boys together: coll.: from ca. 1920, when the practice was not common. Hence, as n., a girl (never a boy) at a co-educational institution, esp. a college or university: coll.: in this sense adopted, ca. 1950, ex US, where it has long been regarded as Standard.

co-Joe. The second pilot of a two-pilot aircraft: RAF: 1945+. Cf. **second dicky.**

co-op; co-op store. A co-operative store: the longer form, early 1870s; the shorter, early 1880s. Also a co-operative society: from early 1890s. *OED* Sup. P.B.: since mid-C.20, at latest, the local branch shop of the Co-operative Wholesale Society (or, 1982: Co-operative Retail Services Ltd.) has been known as *the Co-op*.

co-pilot. A 'soft' drug: mostly addicts': since ca. 1960.

co-pilots. Amphetamine: drugs c. (Stockley, 1986.) US since mid-1960s (Spears).

co-re. A co-respondent: Society: since ca. 1921. Burt, 1942.

co-respondent's shoes. Brown-and-white sports shoes: since ca. 1925. P.B.: by 1945 the term had > *co-respondent shoes*; by late 1970s, it was ob.

coal. A penny: grafters'. (Horsley, 1912.) Prob. ex lost r.s. *coal-heaver*, a 'stever', q.v. at **stiver.**—2. Petrol: army drivers': WW2. P-G-R.—3. See **pour on more coals; put the coals on**.

coal and coke. Penniless: r.s., on *broke*. See also **coals and coke**.

coal-scuttle. A Japanese heavy-mortar bomb: army in Far East: 1942–5. (P-G-R.) Ex the heavy smoke.

coals (and coke). Penniless: r.s. on *broke*: late C.19–20. Emphatically, it >, ca. 1930, *stone coals and coke* (Wolveridge, 1978); cf. *stony broke*. A later var. is *coal and coke*.

coast. Esp. as vbl n. 'Coasting. Walking near people in crowds' (Webb, 1945): Black Market: 1943+.

coast-crawling. Cruising along the coast of N. Africa: RN: 1940–5. P-G-R.

coasting. Under the influence of drugs: drugs c. (Stockley, 1986.) US since—1936 (Spears).

coat. To reprimand, esp. of a warder reprimanding a prisoner: c.—2. To arrest (a person): c.: from ca. 1910. Gen. as ppl adj., *coated*.—3. 'To ostracise. The unfavoured one is indicated to others by a tug on the lapel as he passes by' (McNeil): Aus. prison s.: later C.20.

coat and badge. To cadge: r.s.: mid-C.19–20. (B. & P.; Ortzen, 1938.) Franklyn records 'sometimes given in full as Doggett's . . .'; Doggett's were Thames watermen. He goes on: 'The term is still [1960] in use, and is generally prefixed with "on the"—"He's on the C. and B. again!" '

coat of arms. The rank badge of Warrant Officers, Class 1: Army: since ca. 1920. H. & P., 'When a man is promoted to this majestic rank he is said to "have his coat of arms up".' Humorous; the badge is in fact the Royal coat of arms. Cf. the later synon. **fighting cats** and **Tate and Lyle**.

Coathanger, the. The Sydney Harbour Bridge: Melbourne, Aus.: since 1932, when the bridge reached completion. (B.P.; Sayers, 1985.)

coating. Giving a prisoner's history: c.:—1935 (Hume). I.e. fitting him up nicely. Cf. **coat**, 1.—2. Hence(?), a thrashing: Army (esp. in the Guards): 1939+. Kersh, 1941, and 1942.

Coats an' 'Ats. Messrs C. & A., Ltd, the London outfitters: since ca. 1950.

cob. (Usu. pl.) A testicle: low: C.19–20. Behan, 1958, 'Now, no knee and nut stuff and no catching by the cobs.' Ex dial. (*EDD*).—2. In *have* or *get a cob on*, to be annoyed: MN,—1935; since ca. 1939, also RN. Prob. ex dial. *cob*, a piece, esp. a large piece. Cf. **Sweat cobs**. Hence, gen. Liverpool (K. Lewis, 1985).

cob o' coal. Unemployment relief: workmen's r.s., on *dole*: ca. 1925–60. (*John o' London's Weekly*, 9 June 1934.) Cf. later synon. **jam-roll**.

cobblers. Human testicles: low. (*Gilt Kid*, 1936.) A shortening of **cobbler's awls** or **stalls**.—2. Hence, nonsense, rubbish; as an exclam., but esp. in the scornful phrase 'A load of old cobblers': widespread and popular, and used in all innocence by those unaware of its derivation: since ca. 1960. (P.B.)—3. See ASSOCIATION FOOTBALL, in Appx.

cobbler's awls or **stalls**. Testicles: low r.s., on *balls*: late C.19–20. (Franklyn.) Cf. **orchestra stalls**.

cobblers to you! '*Balls* to you!': since latish 1960s; slightly ob. by 1975. It may have begun as a semi-euph. 'Heard fairly often on TV' (Petch, 1974). See **cobblers**, 1 and 2.

cobbling. 'The forging of passports' (*Daily Telegraph*, 22 Feb. 1988): espionage: adopted ex US (W. & F., 1975, 'recent').

cobbly-wobbly. In *boots, cobbly-wobbly*, a parody of the quartermaster's official 'boots, CWW [cold, wet weather, for protection against]', i.e. those with directly moulded soles: army: later C.20. (P.B.)

Cock. Cockfosters: London Transport Board employees': since ca. 1930.—2. See NICKNAMES, in Appx.

cock, n. 'A man who buys more than his share of drinks in a public house or club so as to have company pleasing to him. A man easy to sponge upon' (Powis): underworld: current in 1970s.—2. Short for *poppycock*, nonsense: since ca. 1938. 'You're just talking a lot of cock, and you know it!' But cf. also **ballocks** in this sense, and **all to cock**.—3. Cheek, impudence: Oundle School: since late 1920s. (Marples.) Ex *cocky*.—4. A cockle: mostly Welsh fishermen's. (Granville, 1967.)

cock, v. To copulate: raffish coll.: C.19–20; at first gen. in the passive, but in later C.20, also v.t., of the male. Whence vbl n., *cocking*, and cf. (*with*) *a cock in her eye*: sexually desirous. Naughton, 1970.

cock, adj. Male: beatniks': since late 1950s. (Anderson.) Contrast **hen**, adj.

cock a (or one's) **chest**. To preen oneself; to put on 'side'; to brag: RN. (Granville.) Cf. **chuck a chest**, 2 and 3.

cock and hen. A £10 note: thieves' and low r.s.: from ca. 1870. (*Slang*, p. 243.) Hence half a crown, £5. (Tempest.)—2. Hence, ten. B. & P.—3. (Gen. *cockernen*.) A pen: r.s., esp. grafters'. *Cheapjack*, 1934.—4. A man and wife (together): taxi-drivers': since ca. 1910. Hodge, 1939.—5. Odds of 10 to 1: racing, esp. bookmakers'. (*Daily Telegraph*, 7 May 1967) Ex sense 2.

cock-broth. Nutritious soup: tramps' c. Esp. at the Brighton casual ward: Gape, 1936.

cock-eyed. Tipsy: since ca. 1930. Lincoln, 1933.

cock-happy. Over-confident: Services': mid-C.20. 'We won, but remember, it might not be so easy another time, so don't get cock-happy about it' (Moran, 1959).

cock it over (a person). To 'boss', to impose on: coll.: —1923 (Manchon).

cock it up. To make a complete mess of a job, as in 'All he had to do was fit this bit into there; and *now* look at it: he's gone and cocked it all up something rotten!': low coll. Cf. *make a cock-up*, and see **cock-up**, n., 2, and v., 2. (P.B.)—2. 'Used of a woman offering herself sexually' (Wilkes): Aus.: since mid-C.20. Wilkes quotes Herbert, 1961, 'that nervous that if you cocked it up to him he'd put his hat over it and run.'

cock on; usually as *cock it on*. To charge excessively; to exaggerate: since ca. 1910; by 1960, slightly ob. Perhaps ex hay-making.

cock-robin. Penis: (?)mostly Anglo-Irish. 'I hope no one's seriously suggesting we've more than one artist bucketing about with a knife in one hand and his cock robin in the other' (Kenyon, 1977). An elab. of *cock*, S.E. for penis since early C.17.

cock-sparrow. A barrow: r.s.: late C.19–20. Phillips, 1931.—2. (As *cock-sparrer*.) Mad: Aus. r.s., on **yarra**, q.v.: later C.20. McNeil.

cock-sucking bastard. An epithet of extreme disgust: adopted, ca. 1944, ex US troops. 'The imputation of fellatio [is] a deep down pejorative' (L.A., 1974).

cock-tails, the. Diarrhœa: Aus.: since ca. 1925. B., 1942.

cock-tax. Alimony: Aus.: since ca. 1950. Fleming, 1964.

cock-tease. To excite sexually: low coll. (Wilson, 1957.) Whence *cock-teaser*, a female who does this; often, as Manchon notes, 1923, abbr. *c-t*. Cf. earlier synon. s. *cock-chafer*. See also **prick-tease**.

C

cock-up, n. A blunder; an utter mismanagement of the task in hand: perhaps orig. Services': since ca. 1925. Usu. as *make a cock-up*, or as in 'The whole affair was a monumental cock-up from start to finish!' Cf. **balls-up** and **fuck-up,** n. and v., for which this may be a slightly less offensive euph. Or it may be quite 'innocent', as in a discussion in the correspondence columns of the *Guardian*, early Nov. 1981, in which a number of other, older(?) origins for this term were suggested, among them book-keeping (amendments written at an angle), ale-barrels (cock = spigot), and poaching (an evasive woodcock). (P.B.)

cock up, v. To cane (a boy): Charterhouse (ca. 1870–1925) and St Bees (1915+). Whence vbl n. *cocking-up*. Marples.—2. To make a mess of. Ex n.; cf. **cock it up**.—3. P.B.: my father, from years as a Territorial 'Gunner' officer, would recall orders such as 'Elevation: plus five degrees' being translated by gun-crews as 'Cock 'er up a bit, Charlie!': Army: earlier C.20.

cocked-hat. An error in reckoning: RN, and hence RAF, navigators' coll., verging on j. Granville, 'When pencilling a course on a chart, instead of the [three, or more] lines meeting, they cross and make a "cocked-hat".'—2. In *knock into a cocked hat*, to damage very considerably (things, persons, and fig.): coll.; from ca. 1850. Orig. (1833: Thornton), US. An officer's cocked hat could be doubled up and carried flat. By late C.20, other violent verbs could occ. be substituted for *knock*: e.g., *beat, smash, trounce*, etc.

cocker. A cockroach: Aus.: late C.19–20. (Park, 1953.) But also widespread nautical, as in Trevor, 1956.

cockerel. A var. (Barnes, 1976) of:-

cockernen. See **cock and hen**, 3.

cockers-p. A cocktail party: middle-class young women: early 1980s. (Hoggart, 1983.) Yet another revival of the 'OXFORD -ERS'.

cocking a chest like a half-pay admiral. Putting on 'side': RN: late C.19–20. Bowen. Cf. **cock a chest.**

cocking-up. See **cock-up.**

cockle. Short for:-

cockle-and-hen. A deformation (conscious?) of **cock and hen**, 1–3.

cockle to a penny, a. 10 to 1 the field: racing: since ca. 1920. *Cockle = cock (and hen)*, 10; and *penny = penny bun*, 1: r.s.

cockney or **Cockney,** n. and adj. 'Western Region staff name for Midland Region lines and trains, in South Wales. Also Eastern Region term for North London train crews' (*Railway*, 2nd): railwaymen's.

cockroach. A motor coach: r.s.: since ca. 1946. Franklyn.

cockroach-crusher. A policeman, or RN police: var. of **crusher.**

cocktail route, be on the. To be drinking excessively: Society: ca. 1934–40. Vachell, 1938.

cockwood. 'Firewood "stolen" from work. Scots use pussywood' (Forster, 1970): coal miners'.

coco-nut. See **coconut.**

cocoa, n. Semen. See **come** (one's) **cocoa**, also used fig.

cocoa, v. To say; say so: r.s.: orig. prob. as in *Gilt Kid*; by ca. 1945 no longer so, and by 1965, very common, esp. in the derisive '*I should cocoa!*' See **coffee and cocoa.**

Cocoa Press, the. The *Daily News*, and other newspapers owned by Messrs Cadbury (chocolate manufacturers): journalists': early C.20. (Ward, *G.K. Chesterton*, 1944.) P.B.: this *may* have been Chesterton's own coining: in his 'Song of Right and Wrong' are the splendidly prejudiced lines 'Cocoa is a cad and a coward,/Cocoa is a vulgar beast,/ Cocoa is a dull, disloyal,/Lying, crawling cad and clown . . .'

cocoa-tin. Sturmey-Archer gear on a bicycle: club cyclists'. (*Fellowship*, 1984.) Cf. **milk-tin gear.**

coconut. 'Coconut is the Southall term for Uncle Tom [q.v.]: coconuts are brown outside, white inside' (Walker, 1981): London coloured people, (?)esp. Sikh youngsters.—2. See **swing coconuts at.**

coconut wireless. Fiji version of the **grapevine**, q.v. (*Observer*, 4 Oct. 1987.) Cf. **jungle wireless** and **bush telegram.**

cod. Burlesque; esp. *cod acting*, as in acting a Victorian melodrama as though it were a post-1918 farce or burlesque: actors': from ca. 1890. Since ca. 1965, it has been used coll. for 'pretence, or mock', e.g., *cod German, cod Russian*. (L.A., 1976.) Both nuances ex the older s. sense of the v., to hoax, play the fool.

cod and six. Fish and chips: since late 1950s. Cod is a commonly sold fish, and, once upon a time, one could get a generous helping of chips for *six*pence (2½ new pence).

cod-heids. Boots (or shoes) burst at the toes: Glasgow proletarian:—1934.

Cod War, the. A journalistic term for the considerable friction between Brit. and Icelandic fishermen over fishing rights off Iceland in the 1970s; RN vessels were involved, on protection duties. The solution to the problem gave journalists the opportunity to use the punning *cod-peace*.

code two. An escape from prison: Can. c.: since ca. 1950. Schroeder, 1976.

codgell. Produce cadged from the old Covent Garden fruit and vegetable market: Metropolitan Police, later C.20. 'One would say, as one sallied forth from one's toast and tea at six in the morning, "I'm just off to get some codgell" ' (Seabrook, 1987). Perhaps cf. Midland dial., *codgel*, to contrive, manage, economise (*EDD*).

Codi. A codeine tablet: since late 1950s. Jeffries, 1968.

codology. The practice of chaffing and humbugging: Anglo-Irish: since ca. 1910. Alan Smith, letter, 1939.

cods' eyes and bath-water. Tapioca pudding: Charterhouse.

cod's opera. A smoking concert: tailors'. Perhaps a euph. for **sods' opera**, q.v. although a derivation from **cod**, adj., is equally likely.

cod's roe. Money: r.s., on *dough*: later C.20. Green, 2.

cod's(-)wallop. Drivel, utter nonsense: orig. low, but by 1930 gen. With the phrase *a load of (old) cod's wallop*, a lot of nonsense, compare the synon. *a load of (old) cobblers*, a lot of utter nonsense (*balls*). The testicular parallel of *cods* and *balls* may, of course, be accidental: but *is* it? Note also that there is a derivative var., as in 'It's all cods' wallops', as if it were euph. for *cod's ballocks*. In S.E. *cod* = scrotum, and, loosely, *cods* = testicles: *cods* therefore may have suggested ballocks, with *cods-wallops* a tautologism, hence *cod's* (or *cods'*) *wallop*. [Thus E.P.; cf, however] 'Carbonated (or mineral) water gave a new word to the popular vocabulary, "codswallop". This was derived in part from the name of the inventor of the widely used "Codd" bottle with a glass marble closure. Hiram Codd was a London soda water manufacturer in the Caledonian Road' (Schwitzer, 1985).

coey. A thing; any object: market-traders'. (*M.T.*)

coffee and cocoa; often reduced to *cocoa*. To say so: r.s. The longer form is occ. varied to *tea and cocoa*. (Franklyn.) See also **cocoa.**

coffee-bar Casanova. A dashing frequenter of coffee bars, one who seeks stimulation in coffee, dialectic, *amour*: since ca. 1955. Epton, 1960.

coffee-pot. One of the former small tank-engines of the Midland Railway: railwaymen's: late C.19–20; ob.—2. 'That part of a barrage balloon winch from which the cable emerges' (Jackson): Balloon Barrage s.: WW2. Ex its shape.

coffee stall. A landing-craft kitchen, supplying meals to small craft off the Normandy beaches: nautical: 1944.

coffee stalls. Testicles: r.s., on *balls*, and much less used than *orchestra stalls* or *orchestras*. Franklyn 2nd.

coffee swindle, See **swindle.**

coffin. That posture in surf-board riding which consists in the surfer's lying flat on his back, with arms folded on chest: Aus. surfers': since ca. 1960. (*Pix*, 28 Sep. 1963.) Like a corpse in its coffin.—2. Hence, by extension, the same posture in skateboarding: late 1970s. (P.B.)—3. As *the coffin*, a large box wherein, under a tarpaulin, an outcast may sleep: gen. price, fourpence: c.: post-WW1. Orwell.—4. See HAUL-AGE, in Appx.

coffin-nail. A cigarette: from ca. 1885; in WW1 and after, occ. *nail.* Often in form of c.p., *another nail in one's coffin.* Cf. **gasper.**

cog. As *cog up* (or *down*), to change gear: motorcyclists' coll.: since ca. 1950. (Dunford.)

cog box, the gear box; **cog swapper,** the gear-change pedal or lever; and **cog stick,** 'as in "knock (or kick) out the cog stick", to 'coast in neutral gear', are all motorcyclists' coll. since mid-C.20 (?earlier). (Dunford, 1979.)

coiler. A dead-beat that sleeps in parks and on wharves: low Aus. (B., 1942.) He just coils up and goes off to sleep.

coin it (in). To make money, esp. quickly, as 'They had a stall in Cutler Street—fairly coining it in, they were!': coll. Ex earlier synon. *coin money.*

coke. Cocaine: c. and low: orig. US (ca. 1910), anglicised ca. 1920. Esp. in Edgar Wallace's novels. Hence, *cokey,* a cocaine-addict: anglicised, as c., ca. 1920. Brandon, 1934.—2. (A drink of) *Coca*-Cola: adopted, ca. 1930, ex US: s. until ca. 1950, then coll.—3. Hence any soft drink: soft drinks in gen.: Can.: since ca. 1935. *Evening News,* 9 Jan. 1940.

cokes. An eating-house: Liverpool: late C.19–20. Ex *cocoa.* (Frank Shaw.)

cokey. See **coke.**

cold. Ignorant: from ca. 1920. Scott, 1934, 'You don't want to start cold.' Ex the disadvantage implied in *have (got) someone cold,* to have him at one's mercy or badly beaten: prob. ex US. P.B.: since mid-C.20 *start cold* implies an internal combustion or other engine; out of context, E.P.'s chosen quot'n may well refer to that.

cold biting. 'A straight-out request by a tramp or dead-beat for money' (B., 1941.) Aus. and NZ c.: since ca. 1920. *Cold* here = cool = cheeky; cf. **cold-pigging.** But cf. **cold-canvass.**

cold blow. A taxi-rank, esp. in windy weather. Specifically, *the Cold Blow* is Euston: taxi-drivers'. (*Evening News,* 20 Jan. 1936.) But cf. **Rat's Hole,** where *the Cold Blow* is given as St Pancras.

cold-canvass. 'Breaking in with just your visiting-card. Best thing to do is to use your intros. first, and leave the cold-canvass until you've found your feet' (Harrison, 1935): insurance s. verging on coll. Cf. **cold biting.**

cold-meat job. A case involving a corpse: police: late C.19–20. *Free-Lance Writer,* April 1948.

cold-pigging. 'The practice of hawking goods from door to door' (B., 1942): Aus. and NZ. Cf. **cold biting.**

cold pot. Cold storage depots: London dockers': earlier C.20. Ash.

cold potato (pron. *potater*). A waiter: theatrical r.s. Franklyn.

cold steel. A bayonet: Army: since ca. 1930. (H. & P.) With ironic humour ex journalistic *to use cold steel,* make a bayonet charge.

cold storage. Cells; prison: low and military. B. & P.

cold turkey. Door-to-door selling: travelling salesmen's, mostly Can.: since ca. 1930. Ex a probably apocryphal story. (Leechman.) Cf. **cold-pigging.**—2. Intense withdrawal discomfort and pains resulting from cessation of drugs; the treatment involved: adopted, late 1950s, ex US, where current since—1936 (Spears). Sometimes used joc. of someone trying to give up any habit, e.g., eating sweets, or smoking.

Coleys, the. The Coldstream Guards. 'The band on the forage cap is white, providing one of the regiment's nicknames—'The Lilywhites', although this one is rarely used within the Brigade of Guards, to whom they are inevitably "Coleys" ' (Carew).

collabo, n. and adj. A collaborator, esp. of French with Germans; in, e.g., 'collabo money': ca. 1940–5. Drummond, 1969.

collar. In *have* (one's) *collar felt* or *touched,* to be arrested or stopped by the police: low (but also police s.):—1950 (Tempest); still current 1979 (Cracknell). Tempest, 'From the

police habit of touching a man on the collar, or shoulder, when it is wished to interrogate him.'—2. See:-

collar and cuff. An effeminate: c., and—esp. among grafters—low: from ca. 1920. (*Cheapjack.*) R.s. on *puff,* n., 1. Often abbr. to *collar.*

collar and tie. A lie: r.s. Not very common. Franklyn.

collar-band pint. A short-measure pint. See **cap-tally drink.**

collar felt. See **collar.**

collarology. The discussion, by tailors, of coat-collars: tailors' joc. coll.: 1928 (*Tailor and Cutter,* 29 Nov.) Cf. *shouldology, sleeveology.*

collect. To call for a person and then proceed with him: coll. 'I'll collect you at Selfridge's and we'll tea at the Corner House'.—2. To receive one's salary or wages: coll.: from ca. 1920.—3. 'To shoot down an aircraft. Thus "He was a sitting bird, I gave him a burst [of gun-fire] and collected" ' (Jackson): RAF: WW2.

collect a gong. To be awarded a decoration: Army and RAF officers': since ca. 1925. Partridge, 1945.

College Boys, the. 'With the departure of the RAF from South Africa, it is now nearly forgotten that they were christened "The Blue Orchids" (1941) and "The College Boys" (1942)' (Mackie, 1946): *blue:* uniform; *orchids:* good looks: *College:* so many had recently left University or Public School.—2. 'The customs plainclothes investigation teams . . . who admit to being secretly proud of the nickname "the college boys" given them by the police' (Denselow, 1983): later C.20.

Colletburo, the. 'Collet's International bookshop in Charing Cross Road, unkindly known as the "Colletburo" because of its Soviet affiliations . . . ' (*Time Out,* 20 July 1979). By a pun on *Politburo.* (P.B.) See also **Bomb Shop.**

Collie, -y. The Military Corrective Establishment at Colchester; detention therein, as 'and 'fore he knew where he was, he'd landed six months' Collie': army: since late 1940s. (P.B., 1974.)—2. As *colly,* a written var. of *cauli*[flower].

Collie Knox. The pox: r.s.: mid-C.20. (Daniells, 1980.) Cf. synon. **Nervo and Knox,** and **Reverend Ronald Knox.**

colney. A match: r.s. on 'Colney Hatch' [the old lunatic asylum for London]. Curtis, 1937.

Colonel. A joc. form of address: Aus.: since ca. 1945. (B.P.)—2. As *the Colonel,* abbr. **Colonel Bogey,** q.v.: coll.—3. See **Colonel Prescott.**

Colonel Barker; Colonel Barker's Own. A woman masquerading as a man; the Middlesex Regiment (a fighting term, so 'watch it'): since early 1930s. Ex the assumed name of a woman masquerader once prominent in the news.

Colonel Bogey; the Colonel. 'The number of strokes a good player may be reckoned to need for the course or for a hole' (*OED* Sup.): resp. golfers' s. (1893) >, by 1920, coll. >, by 1935, j.; and, hence, golfers' s. (1900) >, by 1925, coll. The former term is a personification of *bogey,* bugbear (of golfers).

Colonel Prescott; often shortened to *Colonel.* A waistcoat: r.s.: since ca. 1930. The Colonel was a well-known sporting character.

column of muck-up (or **fuck-up**). Column of route: army. (Hastings, 1947.) On a long march it tends to tangle.

column snake. Single file: Army in Burma: 1942–5. 'An old Standard Ger. word (C.16, perhaps earlier) for an army on the march was "das Heerwurm"—lit., army-worm (or snake)' (R.S., 1967).

com. (*com* or *comb,* more gen. *com(b)s,* and esp. *combies,* q.v. at **combie.**) A woman's combination[-garment], (in C.20, combinations). Baker, 1931.—2. (Also *Com,* and with later var. *Comm.*) A Communist: perhaps orig. Aus., ca. 1925, but by late C.20, spread to the UK and the rest of the Commonwealth of Nations. In, e.g., Grey, 1976, and earlier, Mann, 1942. Its later spread may well be due to the inevitable use of abbreviation in official documents, where, e.g., *Chinese Communist Forces* becomes *Chicom Forces.* Cf. **commie.** (E.P.; P.B.)

C

comb out, n. and v. Much used in the latter half of WW1, when every available man was 'combed out' and pressed into the fighting forces: coll. >, very soon, informal S.E. See *Punch*, *passim*, for those years. (P.B.)—2. 'To sweep over in formation, attacking ground targets with gun-fire. Thus, "We're combing out the North of France this afternoon" ' (Jackson): RAF coll. (1939) >, by 1944, j. Ex the military sense.—3. To 'sort out' or bring someone to order, to 'put him in his place': since ca. 1960. (L.A., 1976.)

combie. A woman's combination(s): from ca. 1870: women's, nursery, and shop. Since early C.20, always *coms* or *combies*. See also **com**, 1. The garment is a *combination* of vest and knickers. Cf. **drawers drac.**

combine harvester. 'Class 9 goods locomotive' (*Railway*, 2nd): railwaymen's: mid-C.20.

combined chat. A bed-sitting room: theatrical:—1935.

combined operations. Marriage, with esp. ref. to sexual aspect: Services': since ca. 1942; ob. Cf. **cooperation.** See next, 2.

combined ops. Combined operations (i.e., with two or more Services taking part in an action): Services' coll.: since 1940. P-G-R.—2. Hence, a much more usu. var. of prec.

combo. A small jazz band: adopted, in late 1950s, ex US. Ex com**bin**ation.

combs. See **com**, 1.

come. The low n., noted by Manchon (1923); corresponding to, and ex, sense 1 of the v.—2. Hence, semen: low. (P.B.)

come, v. (Occ. **come off.**) 'To experience the sexual spasm' (F. & H.): low coll.: C.19–20. Considered coarse, but it was orig. a euph. and, in C.20, how, if the fact is to be expressed non-euphemistically, could one express it otherwise with such terse simplicity?—2. To yield to bribery or corruption: police s.: since late 1940s. (Newman, 1970.) Cf. S.E. *come to hand.*

come a clover. To tumble over: r.s.: ca. 1910–30. Franklyn 2nd.

come a gutser. 'To come off a motorcycle accidentally' (Dunford): motorcyclists': since ca. 1950. Cf. **drop the pilot.**

come across. To meet accidentally: mid-C.19–20: coll., > S.E., not literary, in C.20.—2. To be agreeable, compliant; v.t. with *with*, to agree to; give, yield; lend: since ca. 1919. Hence the command *come across (with it)!*, Confess!, speak out!; Hand it over! Adopted, imm. post-WW1, ex US—the influence of the cinema.

come again(!, or, more often, ?). Repeat, please!, or Please explain! As question, What do you mean?: coll.: since ca. 1919.

come all over (someone). To thrash; defeat utterly: Aus. B., 1942.—2. With adj., as *come all over* (e.g.) *queer*, with var. *come over all queer*: to feel suddenly physically indisposed, or emotionally upset: coll. Prob. ex dial. usage. Also as the passive voice of *make* (one) *go all unnecessary*, q.v.: *come over all unnecessary*. E.P. notes *come-all-over-queer* as a n., a *je ne sais quoi* of discomfort: late C.19–20. (P.B.)

come-all-ye. Irish folk-songs and music; 'an old country song': Anglo-Irish: since ca. 1890. (Joyce, 1910.) Ex the type that begins: 'Oh, come all ye maidens and listen to me . . . '

come apart at the seams. To lose one's composure; fig., to break up: since ca. 1945.

come at. To agree to (something); to agree to do (it): Aus.: s. >, by 1950, coll. Drake-Brockman, 1938; Casey, 1947; Niland, 1958.—2. To try (to do) something: Aus.: since ca. 1930; by 1960, coll. 'I wouldn't come at that if I were you'; 'I wouldn't come at eating frogs' legs'; 'I couldn't come at a prostitute'. (B.P.)

come-back, n. A successful return, after a long break, to the scene of former success; esp. in phrase *make* (or *stage*) *a come-back*: orig. sporting coll.: since ca. 1920.

come back, v. To take back: perhaps orig. Aus., since ca. 1920, but by 1950s widespread also in UK. Esp. in the apologetic phrase, meant to cancel the effect of one's previous remark, because either wrong or hurtful: 'Now I've put my foot in it—skin deep. *Come back all I said*' (Palmer, 1957). [Italics mine: P.B.]

come back to the field. To return to earth; to cease being fanciful or romantic: Aus.: since ca. 1910. (*Rats*, 1944.) Ex straying animals.

come clean. To tell, or confess, everything; to give no trouble to the police when one is arrested: orig. c., adopted ex US ca. 1920; by 1939, s. An early example is in Sayers, 1931, 'I'll come clean, as they say. I'd better do it at once, or they'll think I know more than I do.'

come (one's) **cocoa.** (Of men) to experience an orgasm: low. See **come**, v.,1.—2. 'To make a complete confession of guilt' (Powis): police and underworld: current in 1970s.

come copper. To inform the police: c. (Leach.) Cf. **copper**, v., **turn copper**, and **come grass.**

come-down, n. In (*to be*) *on a come-down*, to be suffering from the diminishing effects of a drug: mostly teenagers': since ca. 1955. See:-

come down, v. 'To lose drug-induced exhilaration as it wears off' (Home Office): drug users': adopted, ex US, late 1960s, as v. ex n. Recorded as US usage in W. & F., 1975, and exemplified in Hollander.

come (one's) **fat.** 'To make a complete confession of guilt' (Powis): police and underworld: current in 1970s. Cf. **come** (one's) **cocoa**, 2; the semantics here are likewise ex the male orgasm.

come-from. Place of birth: lower-middle class: since. ca. 1920.

come good. To make money; be in credit or in form; to be succeeding: Aus.: since ca. 1930. Devanney, 1944; Niland, 1955.—2. Also, to 'turn up trumps', as in Cleary, 1954, 'I did a bit of smoodging to the wife of the pub owner in town, and she came good.'—3. Hence, to accede to a request for, e.g., a loan: Aus.: since ca. 1940. (B.P.)

come grass. To 'turn copper', i.e. to become an informer, or to involve a confederate in trouble: c. (Hume.) Ex *grass*, a policeman. Since mid-C.20, at latest, the form is predominantly the simple v., *to grass*. See **grass**, v.

come (one's) **guts.** To 'spill' information: low Aus.: since ca. 1920. (Tennant, 1953.) Also, since ca. 1930, Brit. c. *Gilt Kid*, 1936.

come-hither girl; come-hither look. A 'good time', money-seeking type of girl, a 'gold-digger'; a girl's inviting glance: resp., s., since ca. 1920; and coll. of C.20.

come-in. The 'glad eye'; esp. in *give the come-in*, 'To give the eye': since ca. 1945. (Petch, 1969.) Cf. **come-on**, n., 2.

come-it-over man. A dominating, domineering man that rides roughshod over people's feelings to get his own way: coll. (Walton, FLA.) Ex C.19 s. *come it over*, to get the better of.

come-love tea. Weak tea; esp. tea made with leaves already used: Aus.: since ca. 1930. (B., 1943.) Ex the mildness of 'Come, love'.

come(-)on, n. Swindler's 'bait' to dupe: Aus. c.: since ca. 1925. (B., 1942.) Adopted from US. See *Underworld*. By 1945 no longer c. By mid-C.20 also Brit.—2. A look, a gesture, of sexual invitation from a girl: since ca. 1910.

come on, v. An extension of **come**, v., 1: since ca. 1945.—2. To start to menstruate: feminine coll.

come-on guy. He who gets hold of the 'mug' for a gang of 'con men' (confidence-tricksters): c.: from ca. 1920. *Gilt Kid*, 1936.

come-out, n. Exodus of the audience after the show: circusmen's coll.

come out, v. 'Openly to declare oneself as homosexual' (Chambers' *C.20 Dict.*, 1977 sup.): homosexuals', and hence, via the media, into wider usage: since ca. 1970 (?earlier). See also **closet.**

come round on the paint. (Of a racehorse) to take the turn on the inside: Aus. sporting: since ca. 1935. B., 1953.

come the . . . as 'to perform, practise, or act the part of' occurs in many slang and coll. phrases, a number of which follow here. It should be noted that a very frequent var. of nearly all of them is the insertion of *old*, prob. influenced by *come the*

old *soldier*, itself perhaps the very origin of this popular phrase-form. (P.B.)

come the (often **old**) **acid.** To exaggerate; exaggerate one's authority; make oneself unpleasant; try to shift one's duty onto another: military: from ca. 1910. F. & G.—2. To wax sarcastic: orig. Cockneys', then much more widespread. *Evening News*, 7 Mar. 1938.

come the bag. To 'try it on', to bluff; to attempt something irregular: army and low: C.20 (Manchon). Ex horse's nosebag. Rare without the inserted *old*.

come the bat. To mention the price: grafters':—1934 (Allingham). See **bat for.**

come the bludge on. To sponge upon (someone): Aus.: since ca. 1925. Niland, 1958, 'What's the big idea, coming the bludge on us?' Cf. **bludge,** n.

come the carney. To act or speak flatteringly: low:—1923 (Manchon). See **carney,** n., 1.

come the cunt. To be particularly obstreperous or unpleasant; usu. in the neg. imperative: 'Don't you come the old cunt with *me*, mate!' uttered as a threat: low. (P.B.)

come the old soldier, v.t., *over*. To wheedle; impose on: coll.: C.19–20. An early occurrence is in Burton, 1818. Scott, 1825: 'He has scarce the impudence . . . [Otherwise,] curse me but I should think he was coming the old soldier over me.' The idea is adumbrated in Shadwell's *Humours of the Army*: 'The Devil a farthing he owes me—but however, I'll put the old soldier on him.'—2. To hector and domineer, by virtue of (self-)supposed greater knowledge, as, quite literally, the oldest-serving private soldier in barracks might do to recruits; hence, fig. in this sense: army version of *come it over*: since mid-C.20, at latest. (P.B.) See also **come the tin man.**

come the raw prawn (with). To impose, or try to impose, upon someone: Aus. coll. Wilkes says it was Service s., arising ca. 1942, which is the date of his earliest citation. A var. is *try the raw prawn act* (on someone).

come the rubber pig. To be recalcitrant, 'stroppy' and 'bloody-minded': heard among Irish labourers on a Lancashire construction site: late 1970s; poss. earlier and more widespread. (John Davies, 1979.)

come the tin man. To bluff; to 'flannel'; make oneself a nuisance: RN (Granville); also popular in Glasgow in the 1950s, esp. in the horrifying threat, 'Don't ye come the little tin man wi' *me*, laddie, or I'll *melt* ye!' (With thanks to Mrs Dorothy Birkett.) Powis notes *don't come the old tin soldier with me!*, don't be impertinent, or obstructive.

come to a sticky end. To die murdered; to go to gaol: coll.: since ca. 1915. See **sticky,** adj., 2.—2. To masturbate: a rather neat, low Aus. pun.

come to bat for. Tautological var. of **bat for,** to set a price on. Perhaps due to a conflation with *come the bat*.

come-to-bed eyes. A girl's eyes considered as particularly sexually attractive: raffish: 1960s. Cf. **come-hither look** and the **glad-eye.** (P.B.)

come to hand like a pint pot. An extension of the S.E. *come to hand*: coll. Hunter, 1964, of a blackmailer's victim: 'She'd be a wide-open touch for [the blackmailer] . . . She'd come to hand like a pint pot.'

come-to-Jesus collar. A full-dress collar: Can. Because affected by revivalist preachers.

come to that! In point of fact!, since you mention it!: lower classes' coll.:—1923 (Manchon); by mid-C.20, gen. 'Come to that, it was nothing special!'

come unbuttoned. To meet with disaster; be greatly perturbed, esp. if visibly: a Society joc. coll.: from ca. 1926. Yates, 1930, ' "I don't want her to come unbuttoned," said Roger musingly.' Cf. S.E. *burst with excitement*, and *come apart at the seams*.—2. Of a good racing tip or of any reasonable expectation: to fail: sporting: from ca. 1910. Prob. orig. of sense 1. Cf.:-

come undone, unput, unstuck. To fall to pieces, lit. and fig.; to experience disaster: coll., orig. Services': since start of WW1.—2. As a persuasive command, 'Come unstuck!' = 'come on, please tell me what I want to know', as in Tey, 1936. (P.B.)

come-up, n. No. 11 punishment: RN: since ca. 1930. The sufferers come up on deck to eat their meals.

come up, v. (Of favourites) to win: racing c.

come up on. To succeed at or with, e.g., the football pools: coll.: since ca. 1950. (Petch.) Cf. **come up,** v.

come up smelling of violets. To emerge from trouble unharmed, or even with one's situation improved; allusive, to *if* (e.g. *he*) *were to fall in the cess-pit* (*shit*, etc.), *he'd only come up smelling of violets* (occ. *roses*), an almost proverbial c.p. applied to somebody consistently and remarkably lucky.

come-uppance, get (formally **receive**) (one's). To receive one's due rebuke or deserts, punishment or retribution: adopted, ca. 1944, ex US, where orig.—ca. 1850—dial., I'd guess. Perhaps ex a pupil coming up to teacher for a caning.

comedian, the. Short for *the camp comedian*, the camp commandant, usu. of such establishments as transit camps and stores depots: RAF, hence army: since ca. 1930. H. & P.

comfort for the troops. A catamite: Services': since ca. 1925. Ex the pl, *comforts for the troops*: 'According to [the] Tommy, these included W.A.A.C.s, nurses, and anything seen in skirts on active service' (Petch): WW1.

comic. A music-hall comedian: coll.: from ca. 1920.

comic cuts. A comical fellow, esp. one who overdoes the funny stuff: since ca. 1920; ob. by 1950.—2. The confidential reports written on ratings' ability and conduct by divisional officers: RN: since ca. 1945. Granville.—3. Guts. See **comics.** 1.

comical Chris. A urination: r.s. on *piss*. (Daniells, 1980.)

comics. Belly: short for comic cuts, r.s. on *guts*: Aus. underworld: since early C.20.—2. As *the comics*, 'the weekly motorcycle newspapers and magazines' (Dunford): motorcyclists': current in 1970s. 'The terms *The Green'un* and *The Blue'un* were affectionately applied to the two popular motorcycle magazines through the vintage period [ca. 1920–40], *The Motorcycle* and *Motorcycling*. They alluded to the colour of the covers' (Partridge, 1979).

coming and going. (Of an aircraft) fitted with radio: RAF: ca. 1938–43. H. & P.

comma-hound. A proof-reader: publishers' and authors': from ca. 1930.

commando tickle. A forceful pinching of the thigh between thumb and forefinger: Services': 1941+.

commencer. 'Kickstart mechanism on a motorcycle' (Dunford): motorcyclists' joc. pedantic: since ca. 1950.

commercial traveller. A person with bags under his eyes: 1930s. Ex a music-hall joke.—2. A swagman: Aus. joc.: since ca. 1920. B., 1943.

commie, n. and adj. (A) Communist: coll.: since ca. 1943. Perhaps adopted ex US. See also **com,** 2, and cf. **commo.**

commissionaire. A better-class harlot in the Argentine: white-slavers' c.: earlier C.20. Londres.

commo. A Communist: coll.: since ca. 1918; also Aus. usage, since ca. 1925. B., 1942; *Daily Express*, 20 Dec. 1946.

common. Common sense: lower classes. *Gilt Kid*, 1936, 'Use a bit of common'. Cf.:-

common dog. Common sense: RM: later C.20. Hawke.

communionist. A Communist: joc.: since ca. 1919; by 1950, ob.; by 1960, †.

communist. Ca. 1916 it > coll. for any lawless person; from ca. 1926–41 it took a very secondary place to *bolshie*. In ca. 1941 it returned to 'favour' for a few more years, but since then *bolshie* has been the preferred use, though since ca. 1960 the latter has implied usu. simply aggressive non-co-operation. Cf. the early C.20 use of *anarchist* for a lawless person; in, e.g., Tey, 1927.

comp. A newspaper competition: since ca. 1925—a use preserved yet (1980s) by the *New Statesman*, with its mysterious, cliquish 'comp complex'. (P.B.)—2. A complimentary ticket: orig. and mainly theatrical. (Bingham, 1968.) Cf.:-

comp list. Complimentary list (for free tickets): Aus.: since ca. 1905. Stivens, 1951.

comp number. See **compo**, 4.

Company. As *the C-*, the Central Intelligence Agency of the US, usu. referred to as the CIA. An American coll. that, in appropriate circles, was adopted, in the mid-1970s, by the UK. Ross, 1978.

compass-buster. An RAF instrument-mechanic. See **basher**, 3.

compassionate. A coll. shortening of *compassionate leave*: Services': WW2 and ever since. Sometimes, of course, referred to punningly as *passionate leave*. (P.B.)

compete; gen. I'll compete. I'm available; I'll do it if you like: schoolgirls': from ca. 1920; ob. by 1940.

complete and utter. Elliptical for 'complete and utter bastard': Aus.: since late 1940s. 'You'll have trouble with him. He's a complete and utter.' (B.P.)

complex. An obsession, esp. in *inferiority complex* (excessive modesty): from 1910 but not at all gen. till ca. 1919: orig. coll., but by 1936 verging on S.E. Ex Jung's—not Freud's—psychology, the term properly meaning 'a group of ideas associated with a particular subject' (*SOD*).

compo. Compounding (e.g. an annuity for a cash payment): insurance.—2. A busman holding a licence both as conductor and as driver: busmen's: since ca. 1920.—3. Compensation: Aus. workers': since the 1920s. (Cusack, 1953.) Hence, of workmen, *on the compo*, in receipt of compensation (B., 1943); since ca. 1950, usu. *on compo* (B.P.).—4. Compensation allowance—in lieu of rations—to men ashore: RN: 'Such a job is a *comp number*.—5. A further shortening of **compo rations**, q.v.: Services' coll.: since WW2.

compo king. One who, to get workers' compensation, injures himself or malingers: NZ and Aus.: since ca. 1925. (B., 1941.) See **compo**, 3.

compo rations. A *compo*sition pack of one day's rations for fourteen men: Services' (mostly Army) coll.: WW2 and ever since. Usu. shortened to *compo*, as in 'At the Suez do we lived on compo for a week or so, until the NAAFI got really organised' (P.B.).

comprehensively. Thoroughly, or indisputably, in a very big and a delightfully humorous way: cricketers' coll., prob. orig. either at Lord's or at Oxford or Cambridge, ca. 1960; taken up by journalists and duly by the sporting public. 'He was comprehensively bowled', i.e. middle wicket, either without a stroke offered or with a stroke ludicrously inadequate or wild. (Not, I notice, in *OED* Sup.) By 1976, very close to achieving '(informal) S.E.'.

compty. Deficient, as in 'What are you, compty?': Army: late C.19–20. (Ex Hindustani?)—2. Hence, mentally deficient: Army: since ca. 1920. Cf. **diffy**.

coms. A combination-garment. See **combie**.

con, n. A con*vict*: low:—1909 (Ware); by ca. 1920, also Aus. (Buzo, 1973).—2. A lavatory attendant: c., and low.—3. A con*sultation*; a con*ference*: lawyers': late C.19–20. Brooks, 1951.—4. As *the con*, it = confidence-trickery: Can. Niven, 'I ain't a shark . . . trying to throw the con into you fellows'. But also as *a con*, a tale intended to deceive (Hunter, 1977). See **v.**, 1, 2; and **con-game**.—5. Con*densation*- or vapour-trail: aviation: later C.20. Cf. earlier **smoke-trail**.—6. See **Chief Con**.

con, v. To subject to a confidence trick: c., > coll.—2. Hence, by dilution, to persuade someone to do something, usu., though not necessarily, against his natural inclination, and usu. with *into*, as 'I don't suppose old George'll be very keen—but see if you can con him into lending a hand, eh?': coll.: since mid-C.20. (P.B.)

Con Club, the. 'That ambiguous [see **con**, **v.**, 1] abbreviation for every provincial headquarters of the Conservative and Unionist Association' (*Sunday Times* mag., 20 Aug. 1978).

con course. A conversion course: RAF: since ca. 1935. (H. & P.) For men remustering from one trade to another.—2. Hence, substitution of one type of armament for another on an aircraft: since ca. 1940. Partridge, 1945.

con into; out of. For first, see **con**, **v.**, 2. The second, to persuade someone to part with, or cease doing, anything, as 'I conned him out of his favourite magazine' or 'I conned it out of him', but 'I conned him into lending it to me'; and 'We think we've conned old George out of going quite so early': coll.: since mid-C.20. (P.B.)

con-game, -man. A confidence trick, trickster: ex US: c. >, by 1910, low. The English *locus classicus* is Percy J. Smith, *Con Man*, 1938.

concentric bird. A mythical bird 'that flies round and round, in ever-decreasing circles, until at last it disappears up its own arsehole, from which safe but insanitary refuge it hurls shit and abuse at all its pursuers' (Services' traditional monologue). Also known as the **oozlum bird**, q.v. (P.B.)

conchie, -y; occ. *conshie*, *-y*. (Pron. *kónshĕe*.) Abbr. *conscientious objector*, i.e. to military service: 1917. See esp. George Baker's arresting, yet delicate, autobiography, *The Soul of a Skunk*, 1930.

Concordski. The Russian Tu 144 airliner: journalistic, Brit. and Aus.: since late 1973. 'It is similar in appearance to the Concorde' (B.P., 1974); *-ski*, a frequent Russian suffix.

concrete, the. The track: racing motorists' coll.: since ca. 1910. Hence, *take the concrete*, to go on to the racing track, whether in a race or for a practice run.

condemn. To curse, swear at: earlier C.20. Ex the euph. *condemn it!*, damn it!

condenseritis. Leaking condensers (esp. in old destroyers): RN officers': since ca. 1925. (Granville.) Caused by old age. 'You get salt water in the closed feed system: Condenseritis, it's called. Keeps Senior Engineers awake at nights' (Winton, 1959).

condom. The preferred modern spelling of *cundum*, a sheath contraceptive.

condys, the. Advice: Aus.: since ca. 1920. (*Rats*, 1944.) Ex the curative *Condy's fluid*.

coner. A pickpocket who gets a prospective victim 'set up' by dropping an ice-cream cone on his feet: since ca. 1950. (Moynahan, 1969.) Cf. **gum-worker**.

conference, in. Engaged, busy: 'In use in Fighter Command [RAF] in 1942–3 . . . We quickly adopted it, in the jocular coll. sense [for *any* close co-operation] from our allies [the Americans], who appeared to use it so seriously' (R.S., 1971): its use spread after WW2, because of the continuing pretentious use of *conference* for any discussion or meeting, however trivial.

confessional, the. 'Coppers [policemen] have their own pet names for interview rooms. "The Confessional", "The Sweat Box", "The Truth Chamber". They are flamboyant names—slightly exaggerated no doubt—but they convey a little of the atmosphere of these official booths of candour' (Wainwright, 1971): police s., dating ca. 1950, if not a decade or two earlier.

confetti. Machine-gun bullets: adopted in 1940 ex American airmen. *The Reader's Digest*, Feb. 1941.—2. In *cowyard*, *farmyard*, or *Flemington c-*, 'bullshit', q.v.: Aus. joc.: since 1930s. Flemington = a well-known stockyard. Wilkes.

confi (or *-y*). Confidential: among the lower echelons of law and commerce: since ca. 1950. (Petch, 1974.)

confiscate the macaroon. An elab. (ca. 1918–24) of *take the cake*. W.

conflab. A fairly frequent C.20 corruption of much older *confab*, discussion or familiar talk together. The intrusive l perhaps results from an awareness of the term's shortening from *confabulation*, but cf. also *conflabberation*, later C.19 s. for 'a confused wrangle'.

confused operations. Combined Operations: RN officers': ca. 1941–3. (Granville.) Ex the viewpoint of the more conservative, the 100 per cent service-minded officers: yet even they relented.

confusion. 'A street fight (West Indian origin)' (Powis): current in 1970s.

Cong. A Congregational chapel; (usu. in pl) a Congregationalist. Also as adj., e.g., the sect's hymnary, *The Book of Congregational Praise*, was known as *Cong Praise*. R.S. noted, 1971, 'At Bishop's Stortford College (1930s) the local Congregationalist chapel was known as "The Conger".' The Congregational Church merged with the Presbyterian Church of England in 1972 to form the United Reformed Church, whose members quite soon became, in church circles, termed *Urks*.

congenital. Abbr. *congenital idiot*: coll. (Not among 'the masses'.)

congraggers. Var. of next. Murray.

congratters. Congratulations, gen. as an exclam. By 'OXFORD -ER'.

conjugals. Conjugal rights: cultured s. >, by 1930, coll.

conk. gen. *conk out*. To fail, break down, esp. of an engine, a machine; to die: aviation s., 1918, >, by 1921, gen. coll. The Aus. version, dating from the same period, is *go conk*, to fail in the sense of to cease gradually, to peter out. (Baker.) Cf.:-

conked, (be). Dead, to die; (of an engine) to stop, be stopped: aviation s., 1917, >, by 1920 gen. coll. Perhaps echoic, from the last few thumps of a failing motor.

conker. 'Internal user motor. Motor not licensed for road' (*Railway*): railwaymen's: current in mid-C.20.—2. '[A trog, i.e. a slow, careful, trundling, driver] can establish behind him what we call a "conker" (up to 50 other road users' (Gardner, 1972): motorists'. Presumably ex a string of horse-chestnuts. Note that *conkers*, the name of the game, is S.E.

conker-nut. A red-haired person, esp. if young: schoolchildren's. (Petch.)

Conkers. 'Concorde is known familiarly as Conkers to those of us who have been taken for a ride even once [aboard the supersonic airliner]' (James, 1986).

conk(e)y, -kie. A nose: market-traders'. (*M.T.*) Dim. of *conk*, s. for nose since early C.19.

Connaught Rangers. See TOMBOLA, in Appx.

connect. To understand. Ex telephones.—2. 'To make a buy' (*Hearings*, 1955) of narcotics: drug traffic: since ca. 1920. Cf. **connection**, one's contact.

connect with. In boxing, from ca. 1920, to hit. *John o' London's*, 4 Feb. 1933.

connection. A trafficker in drugs, it *can* = 'peddler'; usu., however, of a supplier; also as in 'The French connection', that organisation as a whole: orig. a euph.; by the late 1960s, coll.; adopted ex US, where current since—1936 (Spears); by late 1970s virtually S.E.

conner. Food: army: late C.19–20; ob. (B. & P.) Ex Hindustani.—2. Tinned food: army: since 1939; ob. (H. & P.) P.B.: E.P. noted 'Ex Maconochie [q.v.], the manufacturer's name, rather than sense 1'; I feel however that both had an influence. I last heard the term in the early 1970s, and then only among the longest-serving senior non-commissioned ranks.

Connie. A Constellation airliner: 1950s. ob. Culotta, 1960.—2. The Royal Enfield 'Constellation' motorcycle: motorcyclists': since the early 1950s. (Dunford.)

conning'. Generic for the confidence trick: c. >, by 1930, also police s. Ex *con*, v., 1.

connivering about. Aimlessly wandering or pottering: Aus.: since ca. 1935. Cf. **buggerising about**. B., 1953.

conny-onny. *Con*densed milk: Merseyside: since ca. 1920. A reduplication.

conrod. *Con*necting *rod* to piston: engineers' and mechanics'.

conservatory (roof). The transparent, streamlined roof fitted over the cockpit of a high-speed aeroplane: aviation: from 1934. (*Daily Telegraph*, 9 Feb. 1935.) Cf. synon. **greenhouse**.

conshie, -y. Less correct var. of **conchie, -y**, q.v., a conscientious objector.

constable, the. An unwanted companion; a burr that *will* stick: Services': 1930s. H. & P.

consti. Abbr. constipated: young women's: early 1980s. (Joanna Williamson, 1982.)

constipated. Slow to part with money: from ca. 1925.

contact. An acquaintance(ship); a connexion: both with a view to business or self-interest: coll., from ca. 1930, ex commercial j. (—1925); prob. ex US, where the v. is frequent. Fast verging on S.E., at least the near-S.E. of trade.

contacts. Contact lenses: since very soon after the widespread use of these aids, mid-1960s: coll., perhaps adopted ex US.

contour-chasing, n. and adj. (Of an aircraft) 'flying very low, and as it were following the slopes and rises of the ground' (F. & G.): RFC > RAF: since ca. 1915. Cf. *hedge-hopping*.

contours. The curves of a woman's body: joc. coll. Ex *contour* as in the *SOD*'s quot'n from Scott: 'The whole contour of her form . . . resembled that of Minerva.'

contract. A professional killer's engagement to kill someone: adopted, ca. 1960, by British underworld, espionage and, later, police, ex US. In, e.g., TV's 'The Untouchables' on 16 Dec. 1967. (Petch, 1974.)

convalescence. A slack period: busmen's: from ca. 1930. (*Daily Herald*, 5 Aug. 1936.) Opp. *belting*.

convalescent home. A place of work where conditions are 'good'—i.e. easy: joc. coll.: since ca. 1905.

conversion job, as in the threat, 'If you don't knuckle under, someone will do a conversion job on you', i.e. a severe bashing about the head, or a razor-slashing of the face: thugs' and police: since late 1940s. 'Heard on TV in crime plays' (Petch, 1969). Ex, e.g., the remodelling of a motorcar.

convincing. Effective; notable: journalistic s. > j. In literary and art criticism, it was displaced, ca. 1929, by *significant*.

cook. In *give* or *have* or *take a cook*, to take a look: r.s.: since ca. 1946. Ex Yiddish *guck*. (Franklyn.) The Yiddish v.i. itself derives from the coll. Ger. v.i. *gucken*, to look, to peep, inquisitively. But see also **Captain Cook, 3**.

cook-off, n., and **cook off,** v. (To effect) a premature or accidental discharge of a firearm or a cannon: common during WW2, esp. in the Army. Ex the too-high temperature of the barrel. Pawle, 1956.

cook – esp. **be cooking** – **on all four.** To be very busily employed: Can.: adopted, ca. 1945, ex US, which seems now to prefer *cook with gas* (*on the front burner*), using all elements, in a slightly different nuance. (Leechman.)

cook up. To falsify (e.g. accounts): late C.19–20.—2. Hence, *to cook up a story*, to produce a plausible, and by implication untruthful, account of, e.g., an incident or affair: coll. (P.B.)—3. 'To prepare an injection (dissolving heroin in spoon)' (Home Office): drug addicts'. US since mid-C.20 (Spears).

cookem fry. Hell: RN: since ca. 1870. (Granville.) Presumably ex 'to cook and fry (in hell)'; however, in Laffin, 1969, it is r.s. for 'to die'.

cookery. 'Many modern painters affect to despise the technique of their art, and deprecate attention to what they irreverently term "cookery" ' (Bodkin, 1945): artists': since ca. 1920.

cookery nook. A ship's galley; a shore station cookhouse: RN: since ca. 1926. (H. & P.) Prob. ex *Rookery Nook*, the title of one of the best-known Aldwych farces.

cookie, – y. A harlot: Glasgow s.:—1934.—2. A heavy bomb: RAF: 1940–5 (Jackson). Cf. **groceries**. 'In 1943–45, the 4,000 and then the 8,000 lb. bomb' (Partridge, 1945).

cooking-fuel. Low-octane petrol: motorcyclists' s.: since ca. 1950. (Dunford.)

cook's galley yarn. A (wildly improbable) rumour: the RN equivalent of the army *cook-house official*. (Bowen.) Cf. **latrine rumour**.

cook's last hope. 'A heavy steamed duff' (B., 1943): R Aus. N: WW2.

cool, n. 'Hippy expression for confidence or self-assuredness' (Powis). Ex the adj., 7. See also **keep** (one's) **cool**.—2. '[A] look (back s., "take a cool at that")' (Powis). First recorded in 'Ducange Anglicus', 1857.

cool, adj. (Of jazz) good and modern: jazz-lovers': since ca. 1945. (*The Observer*, 16 Sept. 1956.)—2. (Of a singer) slow and husky: since ca. 1948. (Ibid.)—3. Very pleasing or attractive or satisfactory: Can. (esp. teenagers'): adopted, ca. 1955, from US. All these senses came from US: 1 and 2 were adopted at least 5, perhaps 10, years earlier in Can. than in UK. 'Cool became a word of praise when *hot* ceased to be one; that is, when hot jazz went out of fashion, to be displaced by bop or bebop, a later—a "progressive" or "modern jazz" ' (Priestley, 1959).—4. Self-possessed; *real cool*, devilishly self-possessed: jazz, beatnik, teenage: since ca. 1950. Cf.—in S.E.—'a *cool* hand' and '*cool*-headed'. Dempster, 1979, noted that the term 'cool' was now démodé among 'the smart set'.—5. Retaining complete control—or so the addict believes—while 'turned on' (drug-exhilarated): since late 1960s. Wyatt, 1973. An extension of sense 4.—6. 'Not carrying illegal drugs' (Fryer, 1967): addicts': since early 1960s.—7. Good; acceptable; functioning: Aus. 'Heard recently, of battery in a camera' (Sayers, 1987).

cool as a virgin. Relaxed and self-possessed: RN: WW2. (Bolster, 1945.) Cf. the earlier 'Yet the troops keep as cool as lambs' (Milne, 1902).

cool cat. An addict of modern jazz: jazz-lovers': since ca. 1945. (*Observer*, 16 Sept. 1956.)—2. A rock-and-roller: adopted, 1956, from US.—3. (Ex.1.) A fine fellow: Can.: since ca. 1956.

cool out. As in 'Most kids use [glue-sniffing] to cool out from pressure—pressures from jobs, from school . . . ' (*Time Out*, 8 Jan. 1982, p.15).

cooler. A prison: orig. (—1884) US; anglicised, in c., ca. 1890; generalised, esp. as a detention cell, to s. in WW1, and used thus in the Services ever since.—2. A chilly glance: Aus. B., 1942.—3. See **bring in a cooler**.

coolie. 'A locomotive fireman. [Among] the hardest physical tasks in industry [is] firing on a steam locomotive' (McKenna, 1970): railwaymen's.

cooloo, the (whole). 'The whole lot' of whatever it is: since ca. 1935. Perhaps ex US *the whole caboodle*. But prob. from Arabic *cooloo*, all: cf. **a cooloo**.

coon. A Negro: ex US (—1870), anglicised ca. 1890. Ex *racoon*. (Thornton.) See quot'n at **scrote**.—2. Hence, in Aus. coll., an Aboriginal: since ca. 1920. (Devanney, 1944.) Cf. **boong**.—3. As in ' . . . or I'm a coon' = a highly unlikely alternative: earlier C.20 (Mitchell, 1930). Cf. synon. (*or*) *I'm a Dutchman*. (Raab.)

cooper. In vagrants' c., a casual ward to be avoided.—2. A bungling, or something bungled; a mistake: on borders between tramps' and Romany s.

cooperation. Sexual play and intercourse with no implication of marriage: searchlight crews': 1939–early 40; in short, during 'the phoney war'—'before Combined Operations had become a Staff concept' (H. R. Spencer). Contrast **combined operations**. See also **co-op**.

coopered. Tipsy: late C.19–early 20. It occurs in a letter written by Kipling to Rider Haggard on 5 May 1925, where he refers to a famous man being 'richly coopered' at a banquet: in Cohen, 1965.

cooper's droop. Used 'of a woman whose nipples point to the ground. Old, worn out. West N. America at least, and it must go back to the 50s' (Leech, 1986): Can. Contrast **brewer's droop**.

Cooper's Snoopers. Social-survey investigators: 1940, then ob. Investigators proposed by the Rt. Hon. Duff Cooper.

coopy (pron. with *oo* short). A hen: proletarian: late C.19–mid-20. That which lives in a coop. (P.B.)

cootie. A body-louse: nautical >, by 1915, at latest, military. Ex Malayan for a dog-tick. Moreover, *kutu* is common throughout Polynesia for any kind of louse: see, e.g. Tregear's *Mangareva Dict.* Occ. form *coota*, and may be shortened to *coot*.

cooty. Lousy: army (ex RN). Ex *cootie*.

cop, n. A policeman (—1859); abbr. *copper*. H., 1st ed.—2. The sighting of a 'wanted' locomotive number: train spotters': mid-C.20. Clifford, 1970. Ex:-

cop, v. Catch, capture: from ca. 1700, *SOD* recording at 1704.—2. Hence, to steal: low: mid-C.19–20. *EDD*—3. In mid-C.19–20, it also = take, receive, be forced to endure, as in *cop it* (*hot*), (occ. simply as *cop*), to be scolded, to get into trouble,—*cop the bullet*, get the sack,—*cop the needle*, become angry. The C.20 *cop out* is a var. of *cop it hot*. In WW1, *cop it* = to die, while *cop a packet* = to be wounded, gen. severely.—4. As = arrest, imprison, perhaps as = steal, it was orig. (C.19) c.; in C.20, low.—5. To catch on to; to notice, to detect: Aus., since ca. 1930 (Cusack, 1951); also Brit., as in, e.g., one young man, eyeing a girl, to another, 'Cop a load of *that* lot!'—in admiration or, sometimes, derision.—6. 'To receive corrupt payments: "Did he cop?" means "Did he receive a gratuity (or bribe)?" ' (Powis): police and underworld: current in 1970s. The word derives 1—prob. ex L. *capere*. 2—via the Old Fr. *caper*, to seize. 3—whence the C.17 S.E. *cap*, to arrest: *cap* to *cop* is a normal argotic change. Whence **copper**, q.v.

cop a deaf 'un. To pretend not to hear or not to have heard: (c. and) low: since ca. 1920. Powis, 1977, has *cock a deaf 'un*.

cop a feel. 'To make a quick "feel" on a person. If a woman, then she makes a quick grab on his privates; if a man, then he makes a quick grab–feel of her breasts: widespread N. Am., at least back to 1950's' (Leech, 1986): Can.

cop a flower-pot. A Cockney synon. (by r.s.) of *cop it hot* (see **cop,** v., 3). A news-vendor, in late Sep. 1935, said of Mussolini: 'He will cop a flower-pot if he goes on like this' (*New Statesman and Nation*, 28 Sep. 1935).

cop a packet. To be severely wounded: army: WW1. See **cop,** v., 3.—2. Hence, of a place, to be badly bombed or shelled: gen. coll.: WW2. 'I hear Southampton didn't half cop a packet in the raids last night.' (P.B.)—3. '*Copped a packet*. Given a sentence of preventive detention' (Tempest): c.: mid-C.20.

cop a plea. ' "We went to the magistrates and copped a plea (pleaded guilty to a much reduced charge) and got a two hundred and fifty fine." "A trade?" asked John McVicar. "Cost us two gee (£2,000)" ' (Taylor, 1982): c.: later C.20. And see **cop,** v.

cop it. To become pregnant: Aus. feminine (low): since ca. 1920. (Trist, 1944.) Some Brit. usage also. Ex the nuance 'get into trouble' at **cop,** v., 3.

cop out. To evade an ethical issue; to make a cowardly denial of one's beliefs; to compromise, take the easy way out; to go back on one's word; to withdraw from a project, programme, etc.: adopted, ca. 1960, ex US, where used, since ca. 1920, for 'to plead guilty'. Hence also as n., the action from any of these meanings. (P.B.)

cop-shop. Police station: Aus. c. (B., 1942); by mid-C.20, common in Brit. also.

cop the drop. (Of a policeman.) To accept bribes: c.: from ca. 1910. Cf. **drop,** n., 4, and **dropsy**. See also **take the drop**.

cop the tale. To swallow a confidence-trick story: c.: from ca. 1919.

copasetic. All safe, wholly safe; all clear; excellent, most attractive: Can. adaptation, ca. 1925, of US *copesettic* (Berrey and Van den Bark). Ex 'Chinook jargon, developed as a trading pidgin by the water-borne tribes of western Washington [State] and British Columbia. The original is copasenee, meaning "everything is satisfactory" ' (Dr D. L. Martin).

cope. 'To do one's duty satisfactorily' (Finn-Smith, 1942): Services' (esp. Army officers') coll.: since 1935; adopted from Society s. (from ca. 1933), as in du Maurier, 1938. Short for *cope with things, cope with it*, etc. 'Can you cope?' is perhaps the most frequent form. Cf. **hack,** v., 2.

copper, n. A policeman, i.e. one who 'cops' or captures, arrests: orig. theatrical: from early 1840s. *Sessions*, 16 May

1846.—2. An informer to the police: c. Cf. sense 1.—3. Hence, also, a prison informer: c. Triston, 1938.

copper, v. To inform against; cause to be arrested: c. Wallace, 1924.—2. To be a 'copper' or policeman: mostly police: since the 1940s. In, e.g., John Wainwright's novels.

copper-arse. 'A cabman who works long hours, that is, one who is able to sit in his cab longer than most. It is also applied to a man who is always cruising' (Hodge, 1939). Cf. the nautical S.E. *copper-bottomed.*

copper bolts. Excrement: low (?orig. artisans').

copper-bottom. 'A lorry driver who breaks the law by driving more than 11 hours in 24 to undercut other drivers. Also *day-and-night merchant* (Sanders): since late 1940s. (*Daily Telegraph*, 26 Jan. 1964.) The legal maximum hours, since 1982, are eight. Cf. **copper-arse.**

copper-house. A police-station: c. (*Gilt Kid*, 1936.) Ex *copper*, a policeman. Cf. the later and more succinct **cop-shop.**

copper(-)knocker. A metal worker; in pl, the metal-workers' shop on an airfield: RAF: since ca. 1925. H. & P.

copper-shop. A police station: police: since ca. 1910. Cf. **copper-house**, and the later and more succinct **cop-shop.**

Coppers in Disguise. Members of the Criminal Investigation Department: joc.

coppist. A boy—or even a man—that, at level crossings, takes the plate numbers of railway engines: since ca. 1930. (*Daily Mirror*, 19 Sep. 1946.) Ex *cop*, 'to catch; to take'. See **cop, n.**

copter. A helicopter: aviation: 1944+. Superseded by **chopper**, q.v.

copy(-)cat. A child given to copying others' work: elementary schools'.—2. Also a person annoyingly given to repeating or imitating others. Both coll.

cordite jaunty. 'Chief Gunner's Mate responsible for regulating duties at a Naval Gunnery School' (Granville): RN: since ca. 1920.

corduroy brigade. The workmen, plumbers, bricklayers employed by **Bricks**: since ca. 1930. H. & P.

corey or **corie.** Penis: circus hands' and Cockney (and Kentish dial.). Perhaps sadistic: cf. **coring mush.** More prob. ex Romany *kori*, a thorn, the penis. Barltrop, 1981, notes 'established, though not often used'.

Corgi and Bess. 'Commercial TV nickname for the Queen's annual Christmas TV broadcast' (Green). A pun on the opera *Porgy and Bess*, music by George Gershwin, based on Du Bose Heyward's novel of negro life, *Porgy*, 1925. And the Queen's well-known delight in the breed of dogs.

Corine; Corrine. Cocaine: drugs c. (Stockley, 1986.) US since—1967 (Spears).

coring mush. A boxer; a fighter: c. (*Gilt Kid*, 1936.) Ex Romany *koor*, to strike; to fight: The Romany *kooromengro* is, lit., a fight-man. For the second element, see **mush**, 4.

cork! 'Code!', as an order: RN: since ca. 1920. Occ. used in other grammatical moods. 'Decode!' was, naturally, *uncork!* Granville.

cork eye (at someone), **have a.** To look hard and disapprovingly: Aus.: since ca. 1930. Vickers, 1955.

cork head. Person who lives on the Isle of Wight: Portsmouth dockers': later C.20. (Patterson.) Also *corker.*

corked. Very drunk: earlier C.20. Lyell.

corker. Something, usu. some person, particularly estimable, or, in the instance of a girl, attractive: coll.: earlyish C.20. Ex *corking*. Cf. **brick** for good-will, *stunner* for good looks. (P.B.)—2. An explosive mine: RAF: 1942+ (H.W.).—3. 'Motorcyclists' crash helmet. Made of compressed cork. Current 1950s, and official headgear for Police motorcyclists during that period' (Dunford).—4. See **cork head.**

corks! A lower classes' coll. interj.: not recorded before 1926, but heard by the writer in late 1921. Either a corruption, prob. euph., of *cock's* as in *cock's* (God's) *body* (*OED* Sup.), or an abbr., as I think, of *corkscrew!*, an evasion of *God's truth.*

corkscrew, n. A funnel on the early ships of the General Steam Navigation Company: nautical: late C.19–early 20. (Bowen.)

Ex the black and white bands painted spirally. Hence *the Corkscrews*, the ships of that line. Cf. **Blue Flue Boats.**

corn. Hackneyed or old-fashioned, esp. of entertainment. Noun ex **corny**, 2, q.v., and cf. **corn off the cob.**

corn-holer. A pederast: low Can.

corn off the cob, as in 'Don't give me that—it's corn off the cob'—i.e. 'corny' (see **corny**, 2): Aus.: adopted, ca. 1944, ex US. (B.P.)

corn-yak. Corned beef: Merseyside: since ca. 1930.

corned beef. Thief: r.s. Hence the var. *bully beef.*—2. A Chief Officer in a British prison: r.s.: orig. and still esp. in prisons. Tempest.—3. Deaf: Glasgow r.s., on *deaf*. Sometimes shortened to *corny*. Munro, 1985.

Corned Beef Island. A Corporation housing-estate: urban: from ca. 1925. 'Like bully-beef tins' (Laing).

corned dog. Bully beef: military. F. & G.

Cornel Wilder. A hair-fashion (hair worn long) among Aus. urban, esp. Sydney, youths: Aus.: ca. 1950–9. (B., 1953.) Ex the American film star, Cornel Wilde (hair *not* excessively long).

corner. In *on the corner*, out of work; on the dole: coll.: since late 1920s. Ommanney, 1939: 'When he gets too old for a job, he is "on the corner", one of a sad little crowd.' The natural urban focal-point for those with nothing to do; cf.:-

corner-ender (mostly in pl.). A loafer: since late 1920s. Cf. euph. *free*, 'out of a job'.

corner like a postman. (Of a cyclist) to round a corner gingerly and sedately, rather than 'leaning into it': racing cyclists': later C.20. (P.B.)

Cornish (or **Sussex**) **half.** 'A top-up for a pint, ordered and paid for as a half-pint, but more than a half-pint is supplied: RN, 1870s; Army, 1920s' (Peppitt). A coll., rather than s.; and I suspect a much longer currency for both Services.

corny. Trivial: unimportant: Services': since ca. 1941. (H. & P.) Ex American *corny*, hackneyed, out of fashion.—2. Old-fashioned, hackneyed; sentimental, esp. in an outmoded way: adopted, ca. 1942, ex US. It was current among Can. musicians as early as 1930. 'It implied old-fashioned and rural; belonging to the Corn Belt [of the US] rather than to the city; also applied to jokes and humour' (Priestley).—3. See **corned beef**, 3.

coronation. A caning; esp., *cop a c.*, to receive a caning: Aus. schoolboys': ca. 1910–40. (McLean, 1954.) Cf. **crown, v.**, 3.

corp. (Very rare as non-vocative.) Corporal: military coll. (B. & P.) Cf. **sarge.**

Corporal Cookie. The larger bomb mentioned at **cookie**: RAF: 1944–5. P-G-R.

corporation cocktail. 'Coal gas bubbled through milk' (Home Office): drug addicts': current in 1970s. Contrast:-

corporation pop. Water: N. Country ironic. (Richards, 1983.) *Corporation* here and in prec. = municipal authorities.

corpse, n. A stage gaffe. See **corpser** and **corpse, v.**—2. As *the Corpse*, a party of Marines: RN. (Granville.) Perversion of the *Corps* of RM.

corpse, v. To blunder (whether unintentionally or not), and thus confuse other actors or spoil a scene; the blunderer is said to be 'corpsed': theatrical: from ca. 1855; ob. (H., 1st ed.) Brett, 1978: 'And how typical of The Backstagers [an amateur dramatic society] that they should have all the theatrical slang. A "corpse" was a breakdown into laughter on stage.' Also, to forget one's lines: drama school: since ca. 1950 (?revived): hence smart young set: 1956+. Gilderdale, 2.

corpse-reviver. Any powerful, refreshing drink: ex a specific US mixed drink.

corpser. A blunder on stage: theatrical: from ca. 1850 (B. & L.); superseded, (?)mid-C.20, by **corpse**. See **corpse, v.**, 1.

Corpy. Belonging to, or concerning, the Corporation of the City: Liverpool.

corral, n. A pimp's 'stable' (by which, prob., it was prompted): US before it became, not very widely, Brit. (Landy, 1971.)

C

corral, v. To obtain, to acquire, as in 'I'll try to corral a few drinks': Can., esp. mid-West: since ca. 1920. (Leechman.) Ex cattle-herding. Cf. **round up.**

Corridor, the. The '2 p.m. train from Euston, pioneer of corridor trains' (*Railway*, 2nd): railwaymen's: ?late C.19–early 20.

Corticene-Grabber's itch. See **C.G.I.**

corvette, a. A Wren addicted to Sub-Lieutenants. As the corvette (ship) chases 'subs', so does the 'corvette' (Wren).

cory. See **corey.**

cosh-me-gosh. A (?later) var. of *oos-me-goosh*, q.v., sliced beef and vegetables: RN lowerdeck. P-G-R.

coshes. Physical punishment: market-traders'. (*M.T.*) Ex *cosh*, the weapon.

cosmic. Adj. of high approval: teenagers': later 1970s. 'The holiday was better than lovely—it was cosmic!' (N. Hardy, 1977.)

cossie (pron. *cozzie*). A swimming costume: Aus., from ca. 1919; ob. by 1960 (B.P.); also Mersey-siders', (?)earlier—and still extant, late 1970s. Ex *cos*tume; cf. *pressie* (pron. *prezzie*), a present.

cost. To be expensive: coll.: from ca. 1916. Hoult, 1933, 'Them things cost these times.' Abbr. *cost a lot of money*.

cost a bomb (or **a packet**). To be very, or unexpectedly, expensive: since ca. 1960: coll. E.g., 'God knows where they get the money—that car must've cost a bomb (*or* a packet).' Cf. **make a bomb.**

cost an arm and a leg. Var. of prec.: coll., ex US. I first heard the phrase 1974, from a friend returned from USA. It appeared later, allusively, in a cartoon concerning London Transport fares, on cover of *Time Out*, 19 Mar. 1982. (P.B.)

Costa del Sludge. The Spanish Riviera: 'old Spanish hands', those who have long holidayed there. A bitter ref. to pollution. Moorhouse, 1980.

Costa Geriatrica. The S. Coast of England, to which so many elderly people retire: orig. medical joc., > gen. coll.: since early 1970s. (P.B.)

Costly Farces. 'Self description of "Coastal Forces" ' (Granville): WW2.

cosy. All very snug and profitable; remarkably convenient: coll.: since ca. 1940. It attains its peak in the catch-word *cosy!*, that's very pleasant, that promises some very pleasant opportunities; esp., since ca. 1950, in Can.

cot case. 'Someone incapacitated, esp. by drink: joc. (from hospital term for patient needing to be confined to bed)' (Wilkes): Aus.: mid-C.20.

cotics. Narcotics: drugs s. (Stockley, 1986.) US since—1936 (Spears).

cottage. A urinal: euph. coll.: since ca. 1900. Ware.—2. Hence, any lavatory: theatrical: from ca. 1910.—3. Hence, a public lavatory used for homosexual encounters: since ca. 1920.

cottages. Men's trousers so made as to constrict the crutch: tailors' and men's outfitters': since ca. 1920. An informal shape of *cottage trousers*, a witty piece of trade j.: 'no *ball*room'.

Cottagers, the. See ASSOCIATION FOOTBALL, in Appx.

cottaging. Going down to one's 'cottage'—often quite a largish house—in the country for the week-end: the 'two-house world': since ca. 1960.—2. The practice of homosexuality: since ca. 1970. Ex **cottage, 3.**

cotton horse. 'A feminine pad; sanitary towel: Can. low: poss. since 1940s' (Leech, 1986). Sometimes *cotton saddle*.

cotton on, v.i.; v.t. with **to.** To form, or have, a liking or fancy (for a thing, plan, person): coll. *OED* Sup.—2. To understand: from ca. 1910. *COD* 1934 Sup.

cotton-wool. Cloud: RAF: earlier WW2. Forbes, 1942.

couch potato. A passive, almost 'vegetable', compulsive watcher of television, satirised by a potato-shaped doll in US, later 1980s. '[He] is the "licensed fool" of the alternative comedy scene. He performs to yuppies and couch potatoes' (David Mayer, quoted in *New Society*, 20 May 1988).

cough, n. A piece of genuine information or of trustworthy evidence: policemen's, esp. detectives': prob. since ca. 1920.

Busby, 1978: a senior detective speaking, 'I've had a cough on less than this, before they [suspects] collect their wits.' Ex **cough up,** 1.

cough, v.i., as in 'Did he cough?' To confess: policemen's: since ca. 1910. (Henderson, 1968.) Ex gen. s. *cough it up*, to admit to something, to confess. Also cf. **cough it.**

cough! Said humorously while making a feint jab at another man's genitals: Services': since ca. 1950. Ex medical officer's inspection.

cough and a spit, a. A role in a play or film where the actor has merely a few words to speak: theatrical coll.: since early C.20. Cf. synon. **oyster part.** (Raab, with acknowledgment to Mr Marc Sinden.)

cough and stutter. Butter: r.s. (L.A., 1978.)

cough in (one's) **rompers.** To fart: raffish joc. (Watts, 1988.)

cough it. To confess: c.: adopted, ca. 1945, ex US. Bournemouth *Evening Echo*, 20 Apr. 1966, a crook *loquitur*, 'They have told me that the others have coughed it. That is their pigeon.'

cough off! Go away!: later C.20. (Moody, 1985.) Perhaps disguised/euph. back s.

cough slum. Cough lozenges: grafters'. (*Cheapjack*, 1934.) See **slum.**

cough-to-coffin. A 'cough-to-coffin cigarette', familiar to Forces serving in the Near, the Middle, the Far East in WW2. Cf. **Camel to Consumer.**

cough up. To disclose: from C.14, now ob. (not, as the *SOD* says, †): S.E. in C.14–17; coll. in C.19–20.—2. To produce, hand over: perhaps orig. US. See quot'n at **dub up.**

council-houses. Trousers: r.s.: from ca. 1925. (Harrison, 1934.) Cf. **round the houses.**

count deckhead rivets. To sleep: RN submariners': later C.20. (Martin, 1983.) Cf. **Egyptian PT.**

counter. An occasion of sexual intercourse (from the angle of the prostitute): prostitutes' and white-slavers' c.: earlier C.20. Londres.

country cousin. A dozen: r.s.:—1909 (Ware).—2. In pl., monthly courses: euph.:—1923 (Manchon). See **relations . . . .**

coup (pron. *coop*). A coupon, e.g. for clothes: mostly women's: ca. 1940–5, then historical. Dickens, 1946.

coupla. Couple of: US, anglicised ca. 1905: (low) coll. Sayers, 1934, 'He'd had nothing to eat . . . for a coupla days.'—2. Two coins that, tossed, fall 'heads': Aus.: late C.19–20. Baker.—3. 'A generality for several drinks, not necessarily two' (B., 1943): Aus. P.B.: British also! Consider Harry Lauder's famous 'When I've had a couple o'drinks on a Saturday, Glasgow belongs to me'.

couple of bob. A damp swab: darts-players' r.s.: since ca. 1945. Franklyn.—2. A non-specific sum of money, as in 'I bet that suit cost a couple of bob': Cockneys': later C.20. (Muvver.) The term has survived decimalisation by at least a decade. *Bob*, the old shilling. (P.B.)

couple o(f) doorsteps. A sandwich: low. (F. & G.) Ex later C.19 *doorstep*, a thick slice of bread.

couple of ducks. See TOMBOLA, in Appx.

coupon. (Political.) A party leader's recommendation to an electoral candidtate: 1918. (Collinson.) The term soon passed from s. to j.; thence, ca. 1930, to S.E. *The coupon election* was that of 1918 (Great Britain).—2. See **fill in** (someone's) **coupon.**

course a-grunt or **a-pig.** A bricklayers' term for the error that arises if two men start building a wall from opposite ends; one man thinks there should be, say, 24 courses of bricks, and the other, 25. The result is also known as *a pig in the wall*. (Jack Stearn, building instructor, 1978.)

court a cat. To take a girl out: RN: since ca. 1925. (H. & P.) By 1940 also RAF—via the FAA. Not in the least uncomplimentary.

court(-)short. A police-court paragraph (i.e. *short* news item): journalistic coll.: since ca. 1920. No doubt orig. a pun on **caught short,** q.v.

Courtesy Cops. That section of the mobile police which on 2 Apr. 1938, began, in England, to remonstrate politely with inconsiderate, and to instruct ignorant, motorists: motorists': 1938 (*Observer*, 3 Apr.; *The Times*, 4 Apr.).

Courts, the. Steamers of the Ropner Line: nautical coll.: since ca. 1920. The ships bear such names as *Errington* or *Wellington Court*. Cf. the *Castle boats*, of the Union-Castle Mail S.S. Co.

cousin Sis. Piss (= drink). See **go on the Cousin Sis.**

Cousins, the. 'Their American sister service, whom they [political agents] called in their own strange jargon "the Cousins" ' (Le Carré, 1978): orig. a rather transparent cover-name, ca. 1950, soon > j. Ex pedantic 'Our transatlantic cousins'.

couth. '[The soldiers of the Falklands garrison] couth a shirt in readiness for a Saturday night bop [see **bop**, n., 2] with the Bennies [q.v.]' (C. Smith, 1985), i.e. to launder, iron, make neat and tidy.

cover for. ' "Will you cover for me tonight?" meaning "Will you take my turn of duty?" Hospital internes and resident doctors' (Leechman): Can. (ex US): since ca. 1945; adopted, ca. 1950, in Britain, and soon used for anyone substituting for the 'official' person on duty, not only in the medical profession.

cow. A woman: in C.18–20, low coll. Earlier, hardly opprobrious; Howell, in 1659, speaks of that proverb which, originating *temp.* Henry IV, runs, 'He that bulls the cow must keep the calf.' P.B.: in mid-C.20 and later, the bald noun is usu. qualified; it is normally used derisively, but with a tinge of pity or regret, as *stupid cow, fat cow, lying cow,* or, as in the title of Nell Dunn's novel, 1967, *Poor Cow.* One exception to this generalisation is that Society sense, of the 1920s, which is glossed by Maurice, *I, Said the Sparrow*, 1925, thus: 'You might also explain that the word "cow" is much used in Mayfair these days and that the beautiful maidens of our circle don't mind it being applied to them in the least, provided that it is done by a friend and in a friendly spirit.' See **moo.**—2. Milk: perhaps orig. Can., late C.19–20 (B. & P.); soon also Aus. (Idriess, 1931); and, since ca. 1920, RN lowerdeck.—3. (Always either *a cow* or, more strongly, *a fair cow.*) A (very) despicable or objectionable person—even a man can be a *fair cow*; a (most) unworthy act; an obnoxious thing: Aus., hence NZ, coll. Dennis.—4. A female member of the chorus: theatrical:—1923 (Manchon). A specialisation of sense 1.—5. A tramp's woman: tramps' c.:—1935. Cf. sense 2.—6. 'One pound sterling. "Cow and calf" = thirty shillings [= £1.50]' (Tempest): c.: mid-C.20. See **calf.**

cow and calf. A half: r.s.: mostly racing men's. (Franklyn.) Cf. **cow's calf.**

Cow Cart Brigade, the. 'The Ossewa Brandwag (lit.: Ox-Wagon Sentinel), the Afrikaans Nationalist organisation against whose activities British troops were warned' in WW2: 1940–5. (Sanders.)

cow confetti. 'Bullshit': Aus.: since ca. 1930. (Tennant, 1956.) B., 1942, has the less usual *cowyard confetti.*

cow-feed. Salad; raw vegetables: Services'. F. & G.

cow-gun. A heavy naval gun: RN s. (from ca. 1900) >, by 1915, coll. (*OED* Sup.) Granville notes that these guns were manufactured at the Coventry Ordnance Works.—2. 'A 1½-pounder automatic gun fitted to the bows of a large RAF flying boat, from ca. 1935' (Sanders). Perhaps so named by ex-RNAS airmen.

cow-horns. Handlebars: club cyclists': earlier C.20. (*Fellowship*, 1984.) Dunford notes its transfer: 'High raised handlebars as used on early touring motorcycles: current 1920s–30s, revived late 1970s when the fashion came back on some American and Japanese machines.' Cf. **ape hangers.**

cow-pat. The single dropping of a cow or bull, as in 'Watch where you're stepping! The field's full of cow-pats': domestic coll. Prob. echoic; poss. influenced by butter-pat; or, perhaps, it is simply easier to say than *cow-plat*, a var. recorded in *OED* and *EDD.* (P.B.)

cow-shot. A flat, scooping leg-stroke made by a batsman down on one knee and hitting against the flight of the ball: cricketers' s. (1904) >, by 1930, coll. (Lewis.) A more clumsy shot, made by a standing batsman, is termed an *agricultural* one: coll.: from ca. 1930. See **agricultural stroke.**

cowabunga! 'Shouted as one makes down the face of a king wave' (*Pix*, 28 Sep. 1963): Aus. surfers': since ca. 1961. Cf. *yabbadabba doo!*

cowboy. A bow-legged man: since ca. 1950. Ex so much riding.—2. A minor criminal given to violence and tending to 'come out shooting': mostly police (contrast **cowboys,** 2): since ca. 1960 or a few years earlier. (Newman, 1977.) Prompted by 'Westerns'—films and novels.—3. 'A flash fellow; a know-all' (Home Office): prisons': current in 1970s.—4. Young and inexperienced, or irresponsible, driver. See **cowboys,** 3.—5. Any tradesman, e.g. plumber, electrician, mechanic, etc., unqualified and irresponsible; the sort to make quick money by undercutting regular, trained craftsmen on a 'one-off job': coll.: since later 1970s. (P.B.)

cowboys. Baked beans: RN: since ca. 1920. Supposed to be the staple diet of cowboys. Cf. **prairie rash** and **yippee beans.**—2. Policemen, the Police: Teddy-boys' and youthful gangsters': since ca. 1955. *Observer,* 15 May 1960.—3. The feckless and reckless among the international lorry-drivers on the UK–Middle East routes, who flog themselves and their vehicles to 'make a fast buck', as described by Hilary Wilce in *New Society,* 10 Feb. 1977: since late 1960s. (P.B.)

cowhide. Aware ('I'm cowhide to it'): Irish r.s., on *wide.* Franklyn.

cowie. A Western film: cinema-goers': since ca. 1955. Ex 'cowboy film'. Cf. **oater.**

cowing. Gen. pej. adj.: Services': since ca. 1950. 'Tell the driver to start sending the kit down, we'll be here all cowing night else' (*Heart*). Cf. **swining,** and of course *fucking.*

cow's. Ten shillings: shortened from **cow's calf,** q.v. *New Statesman,* 29 Nov. 1941.

cow's breakfast. A farmer's large straw hat: Can.

cow's calf. Ten shillings, in coin, currency note or value; after Feb. 1971, fifty pence: racing c. R.s. on, earlier, *half (a sov[ereign]),* later, on *half a nicker.* It complements **cow's licker** (Hillman). See also **cow,** 6.

cow's lick. Prison: r.s. on *nick:* since ca. 1962. Haden-Guest.

cow's licker. £1: r.s. on **nicker,** 1: since 1930s. (Hillman.) See also **cow's calf.**

cow's udder. 'PVC sleeve for twin connections' (*Railway,* 2nd): railwaymen's: since ca. 1965.

cowson. A var. of 'son of a bitch'; applied also to things: c., and low. (*Gilt Kid,* 1936.) Prob. ex *cow,* C.19 s. for a harlot. If so, cf. informal, archaic S.E. *whoreson* (P.B.).

cowyard cake. A cake, or a bun, containing a few sultanas: Aus.: since ca. 1925. B., 1953.

cowyard confetti. Empty talk; nonsense: Aus.: since ca. 1920. (B., 1959.) Cf. **bull-dust.**

coxswain of the pram. A seaman's first-born: RN (lowerdeck) joc.: earlier C.20. A *pram* is a small rowing boat, as well as an abbr. of *perambulator.*

coy or **Coy.** See **co,** company.

cozzer. A policeman: barrow-boys': since ca. 1930. Hence **the cozzer,** the police, the Law. Ex anglicised Hebrew *chazar,* a pig; see, therefore, **pig,** n., 1.

crab, n. The Avro 504K elementary training aircraft: RAF: 1920+. Because it was slow, and esp. because of its well-splayed and much-braced undercarriage.—2. A horse very unlikely to win a race: Aus.: since late 1940s. (Culotta.) Cf. **goat,** n., 1.—3. A member of the RAF: RN and Army: later C.20. (*Phantom.*) Short for **crab-fat,** 2, q.v.; see quot'n at **pinger.**—4. (Or *krab.*) A karabiner: mountaineers': later C.20. (Knight, 1984.)

crab, v. (Usu. as vbl n., *crabbing.*) 'Flying close to the ground or water' (Jackson), RAF: since ca. 1925. Ex the habits of a

C

crab: cf. also **crab**, n., 1. Hinde, 1945, 'Orig., to fly with a large amount of drift; hence, to fly low because drift is more apparent near the ground—aircraft appear to fly diagonally'. Also *crab along*.

crab, adj. Perverse: short for *crabby*, ill-tempered. (L.A.)

Crab and Winkle Railway (or **Line**). Two extinct branch lines on the coast of East Anglia, the Halesworth–Southwold, in Suffolk, and the Kelvedon–Tollesbury in Essex, appear to have shared this seaside soubriquet: railwaymen's: ob., except in affectionate memory. The Southwold Rly operated 1879–1929, and the Kelvedon, Tiptree & Tollesbury Pier Light Rly 1904–62.

crab-fat. Admiralty grey paint: RN: since ca. 1910. (Granville.) Ex colour of the ointment issued to be smeared on as an anti-dote to *crabs*, body-lice.—2. An airman: RN and army being mildly contemptuous: since ca. 1925, when RAF personnel served aboard RN aircraft carriers; orig. *crabfat soldier* (Adkin, 1983). Hence 'The Crab-fats', the RAF as a whole, and also *crab-fat* as adj., pertaining to the RAF. Ex the resemblance in colour between the RAF uniform and the ointment in sense 1. (L.A.; P.B.) See **crab**, n., 3.

crab on the rocks. Itching testicles: a low pun: late C.19–20.

crab station. A verminous, unpleasant camp or station: RAF: since ca. 1925. (L.A.) Ex *crab*(*-louse*), but perhaps influenced by Urdu *khrab*, bad.

crab the act. To spoil a performance: Can.; adopted, ca. 1930, ex US theatre. (Leechman.)

crabber. A fault-finder: coll. (Tey, 1936.) Ex *crab*, C.19 s., to criticise adversely.

crabs. A certain type (Fowler 5M.T.) of tender-engines: rail-waymen's: since ca. 1920. (*Railway.*)

crack, n. Esp., *have a crack at it*. An attempt: since ca. 1925. App. it was orig. a Service term. (H. & P.) Cf. 'have a *shot* at something'.—2. Short for *wisecrack*, a witticism: coll.: since late 1920s.—3. (As *the crack*.) The latest news, gossip, anec-dote, as in 'What's the latest crack?', and 'Just thought I'd drop in for the crack': Anglo-Irish; heard on a major civil-engineering construction site in Lancashire: since ca. 1976. (Davies, 1979.) Cf. Scot. *crack*, a friendly chat. (Chambers' *C.20 Dict.*, 1977.)—4. 'A form of cocaine which is used for smoking' (Stockley, 1986): drugs c.

crack, v. To change (money): used, by seamen, of cashing advance notes: mostly a Liverpool word. P.B.: since mid-C.20 > gen., as in 'Can you crack a quid?' = Can you change a pound-note for me?—2. To quip, to joke or speak in a jok-ing manner: coll.; prob. more frequent in the written form: prob. adopted ex US. Prob. ex S.E. *crack a joke*. (P.B.)

crack a fat. (Of a male) to achieve an erection: Aus. low: since ca. 1940. Wilkes.

crack about. To act vigorously and aggressively: coll. F.-M. Montgomery spoke of his army, after it had crossed the Rhine in 1945, having the chance to 'crack about on the plains of North Germany.' (Walton.)

crack an egg. 'To play with just sufficient weight to move a bowl or jack an inch or two': S. African bowls-players': since ca. 1930. (A.C. Partridge, 1968.) Ob. in UK.

crack down. To shoot down (an enemy 'plane): RAF: since 1940. H. & P.

crack down on. To suppress (lawless persons or acts); to repri-mand: Services': since ca. 1935. H. & P.—2. Seize or make off with (something): Aus.

crack down on the deck. To force-land on airfield or elsewhere on the ground: RAF: since ca. 1930. H. & P.

crack (one's) **face.** To smile broadly; to laugh: since ca. 1945. Mostly of a very serious person. (Petch, 1966.)

crack it. (Of a male) to succeed, amorously: Aus.: since ca. 1920.—2. Hence, to succeed in general: Aus., since ca. 1930; some use in Brit. Services since ca. 1960. Cf. the informal S.E. *crack a code*, applied also to other, e.g. crossword, puz-zles. Brit. usage also *get it cracked*. (E.P.; P.B.)

crack it for a quid. To prostitute oneself: Aus. low coll.: later C.20. McNeil.

crack nix! Don't say a word!: market-traders'. (*M.T.*)

crack off. To start, v.i., usu. implying 'briskly', as in 'This morning we cracked off in the old Tutor [training aircraft] again' (Tredrey, 1939): mostly Services': mid-C.20.

crack on. To pretend; esp. pretend to be ill or hurt: ?orig. mili-tary: from the 1880s, if not earlier. Cf. the current Cheshire dial. *crack on daft*, to pretend to be more stupid than one actually is (Richards, 1983). Cf. 'If [the secondhand-car salesman] cracks on it's the original paintwork, why is there overspray on the doorseals?' (*You*, 10 July 1983).

crack-pot. (or written solid). (Of ideas, schemes) crazy, unworkable, fantastic: coll. (P.B.)

Crack Regiment, the. The Women's Royal Army Corps, and prob. its forerunners, though I did not hear this indelicate physiological pun (see **crackling**) until ca. 1970: army joc. (P.B.)

crack-up, n. 'An accident causing damage that can be repaired', Jackson: RAF coll.: since ca. 1925.—2. A mental breakdown: coll. Ex the v., 2. 'He can't go on working at this pressure—he's heading for a crack-up, if he's not careful.' (P.B.)

crack up, v. To praise highly: coll.; from ca. 1840. Often, in C.20, in the disappointed negative: of, e.g., a lavishly adver-tised book, 'It's not all it's cracked up to be.'—2. V.i., to be exhausted; break down, whether physically or mentally: from ca. 1850; coll.—3. To be highly amused, to 'die laugh-ing': teenagers': earlier 1980s. (James Williamson, 1982; R. Walton, 1986.) Cf. synon. **crease** (one)**self**, and **fall about.**

cracked. To be in need of 99 points: dart-players': since ca. 1930. Cf. **split.**

cracker. In c., and gen. in pl., prisoners that are insane or epi-leptic or suicidal or injured in head and spine.—2. (Nearly always pl.) A hair-curler: Cockneys'. Esp. of one's hair in *crackers*.—3. A fog-warning detonator: railwaymen's.—4. (Mostly in pl.) A tooth: since (?)ca. 1930. ' "He's at the den-tist's," Castle said . . . "It's odd," Percival said, "When I saw Davis the other day his crackers seemed to be in good shape . . . no sign even of tartar" ' (Greene, 1978).—5. As in, 'Janet? Oh, she's a right little cracker!', in admiration (not necessarily MCP) of a smart, brisk and attractive young woman: later C.20. (P.B.)

crackers. Crazy; mad: lower classes'. Ex:—2. *get the crackers*, to go mad: id.: late C.19–20. F. & G.

cracking. See **get cracking.**

cracking. Term of high approbation, as in 'I'm sure you'll like her—she really is a cracking good sort': coll.: earlyish C.20. (P.B.)

crackle. 'Bank notes. Five pounds and upwards' (Tempest): c.: mid-C.20. Ex crisp sound of new ones, esp. the former, large, black and white issue.

crackling. Usu. *bit of crackling*, a girl: since ca. 1890. See also a number of synonyms listed at **bit of . . .** Hence, (young) women generally, as in 'Been to the dance, have you? Much crackling there?' Prob. a blend of the pleasures derived from roast pork and from *crack*, the female pudend.

-cracy. -rule, -power, -government. Often, in C.19–20, used in humorous or sarcastic coll.: as, e.g. in *beerocracy*, *cartocracy*, *dollarocracy*, *mobocracy*, *squattocracy*.

cradle-snatching, n. Marriage to a person much younger than oneself: (usu.) joc. coll.: since ca. 1935. Cf. **baby-snatcher** and *kidnapping*. Hence, also v. *cradle-snatch* and agent *-snatcher*.

crafty. Skilful, clever, well judged, well planned, well timed, sly ('Just time for a crafty'—a drink; or 'he's round the cor-ner, having a crafty drag'—a smoke): RAF, since ca. 1920, whence to the other Services and wider, civilian, coll. Par-tridge, 1945; P.B.

crafty Alice touch, she's got the. 'A sour assessment of a woman's wiles: Lancashire' (L.A., 1969.).

cramp (one's) **style.** To prevent one from doing, or being at, one's best; to handicap or check one: upper-class, then more widespread, coll.: since—1916. (F. & G.; Lyell.) Ex athletics or racing.

cramper. An inferior bicycle, as in 'When I rode with the Glendale [Cycling Club] they didn't bring a decent bike on a dirty or rough run, they came on their Cramper[s]' (a Birmingham correspondent in *Fellowship*, 1984).

crank. A term popular with RAF aircrews: 1970s. Meaning 'to turn', 'to start', as in these quot'ns from *Phantom*: 'He has yo-yoed up into the cloud and now he drops back again and I can imagine him coaxing his gunsight down to bear on my tailpipe. I am having none of that and with full afterburners lit I crank hard into him'; 'Timing is critical . . . and so right on the button we crank engines'; 'We crank up the turbines and . . . stream off into the damp air.' Joc. ex use of cranking-handle to start old-fashioned motor.

crank file. Inventions department: mainly journalistic. Office file kept for cranks' suggestions.

crank up. 'To inject a narcotic' (Home Office): drug addicts': current in 1970s. Ex setting an internal-combustion engine going. McConville, 1980, 'He cranked up with a deck of heroin.'

crap, n. A defecation: low coll.: mid-C.19–20. Esp. *do* or *have a crap*. See **crap, v.**—2. Hence, rubbish; esp. 'it's crap', it's worthless: low: since ca. 1910. Also 'utter nonsense', esp. 'It's a load of crap': adopted, ca. 1944, ex US.—3. See **get the crap on**.

crap, v. To defecate, evacuate: low coll: mid-C.18–20.?Cf. *crop*, v.i., to take in the harvest.

crap barge. An ill-disciplined ship: RN. See **shit barge**.

crap-happy pappy. 'Young father who takes incidentals of fatherhood in world-view stride' (L.A.): since late 1940s; prob. ex US. P.B.: it also forms part of one of a series of low rhyming puns, popular in the Forces, early 1950s. '*Q*: Describe a feckless Nipponese whose father has diarrhoea. *A*: A slap-happy Jappy chappy with a crap-happy pappy.' Others were 'A dwarf Eskimo with an erection' (a frigid midget with a rigid digit) and 'A giant eunuch' (a massive vassal with a passive tassel).

crap-hat. 'The Paras [see **para**, 3] . . . called every serviceman not with a red beret [i.e., their own distinctive headgear] a crap-hat' (*Don't Cry*, 1983): Falklands War, 1982. Perhaps influenced in sound by *crab-fat*. Contrast **cherryberry**.

crap on. To 'go on talking nonsense' (Buzo, 1973): Aus. low: since late 1940s. Cf. **crap, n.,** 2.

crapper and **crappus.** A privy; a w.c.: low and orig. c. or, at best, fringe of underworld: on evidence of next entry, they prob. go back to C.18. The former comes straight from **crap, v.;** the latter is a slovening of *crap-house*. *Crapper*, is, in C.20, slightly the more used; *crappus* persists mainly because of the extremely common *shit-house*, which has > coll. There has existed, since ca. 1920, among market-traders, the occ. used var. *crappereena* (*M.T.*).

crappers. 'Very drunk' (Mail on Sunday, 8 Nov. 1987): RM. By RN '*-ers*'; cf. synon. **arseholed**, and **shit-faced**.

crappy. Afraid: low Glasgow: since ca. 1920. MacArthur.—2. Of very poor quality: since ca. 1925; perhaps orig. Sc., but now, 1970s, widespread low coll. (England, 1963.) Cf. **shitty**.

crash, n. See 'It's your crash!' at **crash the ash**; it's your turn to hand out cigarettes.

crash, v. (Of an aeroplane) to come (bring) down, gen. violently, out of control: Bolitho, 1941, 'It was first used by Paymaster Lieutenant Lidderdale in 1914': at first coll., but almost imm. S.E. Prob. also soon applied also to earth-bound vehicles. Its fig. use is coll.:—1931 (Lyell). 'He . . . slipped up on a piece of orange peel and crashed.'—2. A shortening of **crash** (one's) **swede**, q.v.—3. To pass, give out, as 'Crash the sugar, yoof': Leicestershire (?wider spread) teenagers': ca. 1977. (D. & R. McPheely.) An extension of **crash the ash**, q.v.—4. 'To write off or cancel inquiries into an unsubstantiated complaint or allegation of crime, e.g., "The Smith housebreaking has been crashed" ' (Powis): police s.: current in 1970s.—5. To break down; fail: computer workers': later C.20. 'The computers were working so heavily in the

hot weather [that] some overheated and "crashed" ' (*New Society*, 8 Sep. 1983).

crash a party. To join one, uninvited, by guile or by force: coll: since ca. 1928. Perhaps a back-formation ex **gate-crasher**.

crash-box. A non-synchromesh gear box: motorists': since ca. 1950. (B.P.) Ex informal S.E. *crash the gears*, to fail, noisily, to change gear efficiently on such a box; or to jam into gear.

crash(-)course. A short, intensive course on a particular subject, e.g. a language: prob. orig. Services', WW2; now, 1970s, more gen. coll., verging on j. (P.B.)

crash-dive. 'The sudden submersion of a submarine on being surprised, or in imminent danger of being rammed': RN coll. soon > S.E.: since ca. 1915. (F. & G.) Cf. **crash, v.,** 1.

crash down. Slightly later, shortened var. of:-

crash down the (or one's) **swede.** See **crash the swede**.

crash-draft. A sudden posting to another ship or station: R. (?only Aus.) N coll.: since ca. 1930. P.B.: the Brit. Services', at least army and RAF, version is *crash-posting*: since late 1940s (?earlier), but RN still called it *crash-draft* in late 1950s (Sayers, 1985).

crash-hot. Very good; 'marvellous': Aus.: since ca. 1950. Cf. **shit-hot**.

crash into print. (Of a tyro writer) to get something published: since ca. 1920.

crash landing. A forced landing; a landing with undercarriage up: RAF coll. (since ca. 1915) >, by 1940, j. Cf. **crash-dive, crash, v.,** 1, and:-

crash lob. To make a forced landing: RAF s.: since ca. 1930. A var. is **force lob;** both occur in Brickhill, 1946. Here *lob* (ex cricket) = to arrive, to land; see **lob, v.,** 1.

crash-o! A Cockney term expressive of surprise, or wondering disgust, at a long bill to pay; used after the event: from ca. 1918. E.g. 'I had to pay a deaner; blimey, crash-o!' Cf. **thump!**

crash pad. A bed, a shelter, for one night: among addicts and 'drop-outs': adopted, late 1960s, ex US. Wolfe, 1968.

crash-posting. See **crash-draft**.

crash the ash, usu. as a demand: hand out the cigarette(s): army and RAF: since ca. 1954; ob. Hence, 'It's your crash!' = it's your turn to share out your cigarettes with me (or the rest of us). Cf **lob the snout**. Occ. also *flash the ash*. (L.A.; P.B.)

crash the (or one's) **swede.** To get one's head down on the pillow: RN, lowerdeck: since ca. 1920. (*Weekly Telegraph*, 25 Oct. 1944.) By ca. 1950, widespread in all Services, and still current early 1970s. A more violent version of the earlier Army *set the swede down*; cf. also the later **crash down**, and the simple **crash**.

crasher. A person or thing exceptional in size, merit or, esp., beauty: coll.: from ca. 1908. Mason, 1908, 'Miss Lois . . . is considered . . . rather a crasher . . . Not what I should call homey, but a crasher.'—2. A crashing bore: since ca. 1945. (Coward, 1960.) The 'OXFORD *-ER*'

crashing bore. A very tedious or tiresome person or, occ., thing: coll.: from ca. 1915. Berkeley, 1934, 'It's a crashing bore . . . to think of those dim cads knocking us for six like this, but . . . it's no use getting strenuous about it.' Ex aviation.

-crat, -ocrat. The same remark as at **-cracy**.

crat (usu. in pl.) A bureaucrat: since ca. 1939; ob. by ca. 1950.

crate. An aeroplane: RFC/RAF s.: since 1914. (B. & P.) By dysphemism.—2. Hence, an obsolescent aircraft: RAF: since late 1917. (Jackson.) Cf. **kite**.—3. A motorcar: mid-C.20. (Bailey, 1937.) Largely superseded by *banger*.

Crawfie. 'To "do a Crawfie" has come to mean betraying the trust of your employers by revealing intimate titbits about their private lives for the gratification of the gossips. And a "Crawfieism" is the name applied to the sort of unctuous drivel which characterises so much of what is written about the Royal Family' (*Daily Telegraph*, 18 Feb. 1988). *Crawfie* was the nickname of Marion Crawford, governess to the Royal Family, 1932–50, who later published such memoirs.

109

C

crawl. To behave in a disgustingly sycophant way; to toady in order to obtain a favour, promotion, etc.: low coll., Brit. and Aus. Shortening of *arse(-hole)-crawl*. Also as *do a crawl*, to cringe or grovel. (P.B.)

crawl out of the woodwork. See **woodwork**.

crawl under a snake (or **a snake's belly**), **be able to.** To be, morally, the lowest of the low: orig. Aus. (?or US), since early C.20; Brit. by ca. 1940 at latest. I clearly remember hearing the longer form in 1915; the shorter hardly anteceding 1930. P.B.: there was a mid-C.20 elab., . . . *under a snake's belly with a top-hat on*; and in Buzo's *The Roy Murphy Show* (prod. 1971), Roy says: 'To pick on a bloke for a thing like that [a speech defect], well, you could crawl under a snake in a top hat and stilts.'

crawl with (esp. *be crawling with*). To be alive, or filled with: Services' coll. (1915) >, by 1920, gen. coll. (F. & G.; Lyell). E.g. 'The whole place was absolutely crawling with trippers.' Ex **lousy with**.

crawling. Sycophantic. Short for *arse(-hole)-crawling*, as 'that crawling bastard! Wait till I get my hands on him!': low coll. (P.B.) Ex *crawl*, from C.19 *crawler*, a contemptible toady.

crawling with it. Very rich: orig. Cockneys', then gen. coll.: since ca. 1918. Often qualified by *absolutely* . . . Cf. **lousy with**.

crazy, n. An insane person; one who is extremely eccentric, esp. if unpredictable or destructive: adopted, late 1960s, ex US. (Landy, 1971.) 'The streets and subways are peopled by derelicts, crazies and strolling musicians' (*Listener* review of a British film, 21 Jan. 1988): still a vogue word borrowed ex US Yiddish grammatical usage.

crazy, adj. Good; esp., very good: dance-fanatics': adopted, 1956, ex US. 'It's crazy—the most' = It's good—the best; 'the real crazy crew' = the really good musicians. This sense had, by 1960, > gen. s. among drug addicts, hippies, Flower People. (Fryer, 1967.)—2. Hence, extraordinarily interesting; fascinating: Can. dance-fanatics': since 1957. Victoria *Daily Colonist*, 16 Apr. 1959, article 'Basic Beatnik'.—3. Alert; progressive; 'with it': esp. among beatniks: since late 1950s. Anderson.—4. In *like crazy*, adv., 'like anything', of human actions and reactions, to the utmost: adopted ex US early 1970s. Prob. ex US Yiddish. (P.B.)

crazy as a bed-bug. Extremely eccentric or crazy: mostly Can.: since ca. 1920(?); by 1977, ob. But why a bed-bug? Poss. because bed-bugs tend to make one 'itch like crazy'?

crazy mixed-up kid. A youth with psychological problems, esp. if unable to distinguish the good from the bad: adopted, in late 1940s, ex US.

Crazyman's Creek, the; often simply **the Creek.** The Straits of Messina: RN: 1941–4.

cream. (Of a woman) to become sexually excited: raffish: since ca. 1950. Hence the male boast 'I'm the one she creams her knicks [= pants] for, me!' (P.B.)—2. To beat up (someone): adopted, ex US, ca. 1975. See **creamed**.—3. See **creaming**.

cream-crackered. Exhausted; frustrated in an enterprise: r.s. on synon. *knackered*: later C.20. (A Nottingham City LGO, 1983.)

cream in. 'To enter harbour "at the rate of knots" ' (Granville): RN coll. Ex the creamy backwash.

cream puff. The huff: Glasgow r.s., 'Aw don't take the cream puff' (Munro, 1985).

creamed. Smashed to pulp, whether lit. or fig.: since ca. 1975. A slight sense-alteration, ex US s. *cream*, to beat (someone) up or injure him very severely (W. & F., 1975).

creamer. 'Someone who is over-excited or scared; by implication, not in control of his emotions or his affairs' (Buzo, 1973): Aus.: since ca. 1950. Perhaps connected with **cream**, v., 1.

creamie, -y. 'Outstanding student creamed off after advanced flying training to become a flying instructor' (*Fighter Pilot*, 1981): RAF: later C.20.—2. 'An attractive

and sexually malleable female' (Green, citing Bleasdale, 1983): Liverpool.

creaming. 'Stealing from an employer in such a way as not to be obvious. Similar to "weeding" [q.v.]' (Powis): c.: current in 1970s. See **mark-up**.

creamy do. A very special piece of luck: since ca. 1950. (L.A.)

crease. To kill (a person): c. (*Gilt Kid.*) Proleptic.—2. See **creasing**.

crease (**oneself**). To laugh immoderately; e.g., 'Sorry, but when I told 'em about you getting locked in like that, they absolutely creased themselves': low: since late 1940s; by mid-1970s, ob. ?A combination of **creased**, 2, and 'bent double with laughter'. Cf. the later **fall about**. (P.B.)

creased. Fainted; knocked unconscious: army: earlier C.20. (F. & G.) Prob. ex S.E. *crease*, to stun a horse by shooting it in ridge of neck.—2. Hence, exhausted: Services': since ca. 1930.—3. Hence, disgruntled, 'fed up': since ca. 1938. H. & P.

creasing. See PUBLIC . . . SCHOOL SLANG, in Appx.

create. To make a fuss, a 'row': from ca. 1910 (frequent among soldiers in WW1). Ex *create a disturbance* or *fuss*. Hence:-

create fuck. In protesting, to display annoyance or anger: low: since ca. 1920.

cred. See **street cred**.

creep, n. An objectionable or unpleasant person; a dull, insignificant, unwanted person: adopted, ca. 1944, ex US. Cf. *creeper*, 1. In Can. universities, a girl not voted into a sorority: ca. 1945–60.—2. Hence, a 'square': Can.: 1957+.

creep, v. To escape; to be let off with a fine rather than imprisonment: c.: since ca. 1930; ob. *Gilt Kid*, 1936.—2. The v. corresponding to **creeper**, 1, to toady: coll.—3. Only in *creep!*, go away!: office- and shop-girls': late 1950s. Gilderdale.—4. 'To burgle when there's someone in the house' (Crookston, 1967); 'I was doing a lot of creeping . . . Offices round the back of Oxford Street . . . Just walk in, stroll around and do the wallets in coats, bags, petty-cash tins' (Dovkants): c. Hence *at* or *on the creep*, doing this.—5. To dance, as in 'Come creeping with me': youngsters'—not necessarily beatniks', etc.: late 1950s. There was a form of dance known as 'the Creep'.—6. As in 'I go creeping. That means, you walk into little firms, one of you asks for a job and keeps the gaffer [foreman, manager] talking, the other sneaks around and grabs the cash box' (Harrison, 1983): c.

creeper. A cringer; a toadying lick-spittle, who tries to curry favour for himself: coll.: C.17–20. In C.20, often thought of as short for *arse(-hole)-creeper*.—2. 'A night burglar breaking into a house while the occupants are asleep' (*Now!*, 10 Apr. 1981): c. See **creep**, v., 4, 6.

creepers. 'Gym' shoes: RN: since ca. 1920. Cf. the US *sneakers*.—2. 'Boots with thick rubber soles, worn by night-patrols in the desert': army in N. Africa: 1940–3. P-G-R.—3. Short for **brothel-creepers**, q.v., the civilian fashion modelled on the boots in sense 2.—4. Occ. shortening of **jeepers creepers!**, q.v., a minced oath.

creeping. The action of **creeper**, 1, as 'We'll have to watch him! They say he's a bugger for creeping': low coll. See also **creep**, v. 4 and 6.

creeping and weeping. The recovery of an errant torpedo during trials: RN: since ca. 1910. Ship's boats 'creep' over—laboriously search—the potential area; if unsuccessful, the boats pull back—'weep'—and start again. (Granville, letter, 1947.)

Creeping Copulator, the. The last express train down from London. Var. of the **Flying Fornicator**, q.v.

creeping Jesus. At billiards, a long losing hazard played slowly: ca. 1920–40.

creepy-crawly. An insect; a spider: mostly domestic and juvenile: mid-C.19–20.

creepy weepy. 'A genre of popular fiction combining gothic horror with romantic melodrama' (Green): publishers': later C.20. Cf. **bodice ripper**.

crem. A crematorium: undertakers', and people living near one: since ca. 1920, if not earlier. We were certainly calling the one just down the road *the crem* in the late 1940s, as soon as it was operating. (P.B.) The Aus. var. is *cremmie* (Humphries, 1982).

crenk. To offend; to irritate or annoy, as in 'It really crenked me!': mostly teenagers': early 1950s. Ex Ger. *kränken* (pron. *krenken*), to hurt someone's feelings. 'Which is, of course, the same root as *krank*, ill' (R.S.).

Créolo. An Argentine that is a professional pimp: c. of the white-slavers. (Londres.) He is also *canfinflero* (more familiarly *cafishio*); also, among the French, *le compadre*.

crew-cut hair, hence 'a *crew-cut*'. A man's hair cut short and *en brosse*, popular especially among athletes and the would-be manly: Can.: adopted, ca. 1951, ex US. (Leechman.) By 1952, fairly common, and already coll., in Brit. and Aus. Perhaps because orig. affected by 'rowing types' at Harvard and Yale Universities. P.B.: or the entire US Navy?

crew up. To form, put into, an aircrew: RAF coll., > j.: since 1939.

crib, n. A literal translation illicitly used by students or pupils: coll.: from ca. 1825. Hence, in C.20, any form of written aid to cheating in examinations, etc., e.g., formulae, mnemonics, etc.—2. A grumble; a cause of grumbling: Services': since ca. 1920. (H. & P.) Ex **crib,** v.—3. A holiday cottage: NZ, esp. South Island: later C.20. (M. Moore, 1980.) See also **bach,** 3.

crib, v. To grumble: Army, C.19–20 (F. & G.); hence, also, RAF, 1919+. Prob. a back-formation ex **crib-biter.** The v.t. form is *crib at*, 'grumble or complain about' (something)—also *crib about*.

crib-biter. A persistent grumbler: coll.; from late 1850s; ob. (H., 2nd ed.) Ex the S.E. sense of a horse that, suffering from a bad digestion, bites its crib, i.e. manger.

cribbage-peg. (Gen. pl.) A leg: r.s.:—1923 (Manchon).

cricket; usu. in pl. A German night-fighter plane: RAF: 1940–4. (H. & P.) Lively at night.—2. Both *the cricket* and *the football*, cricket news and football news, are coll.

cricket team. A (very) sparse moustache: Aus.: since late 1940s. Eleven a side: eleven hairs on each side of the mid-lip dimple. (B.P.) The Brit. version of this sad little phenomenon is *football team*.

crickets, a cup of. A strong, fresh, cup of tea: domestic coll.: 1930s–40s. My Father, 'Julo' Betbeder, was very fond of this phrase. Poss. the association of a cricket and chirpiness, cheerfulness. (Raab.)

Cricklewitch. See **Abrahampstead.**

Cricklewood. Crich el Oued, Tunisia: army in N. Africa: WW2. P-G-R.

crim. A criminal: Aus.: since ca. 1925. (Tennant, 1953; Kelly, 1958.) A professional criminal: Aus.: since ca. 1945. (Dick.)

crimson dawn. Cheap red wine. See **red Biddy.**

cringe!, or **oh, cringe!** 'I'm abjectly sorry', a vocalisation of acute embarrassment, often with action suited to word; also, in sympathy with another's recounted embarrassment: perhaps mainly fem.: since ca. 1950. (P.B.) Cf. **grovel, grovel!**

crinkle. Paper money: spivs' c.: since ca. 1942. (*Picture Post*, Jan. 1954.) It easily creases. Cf. **crackle** in this sense.

cripple-cock (or solid). Cider: Dorset s.: since mid-C.20, prob. earlier. (J.B. Smith, 1979.) Cf., perhaps, **brewer's droop.**—2. A gen. low pej.: later C.20. McConville, 1980.

Cripplegate. The Senior Services Club. See **Bishopsgate.**

crippler. See **slip a crippler.**

crippler, crippling, adj. See BIRD WATCHERS, in Appx.

crisp, v. To murder by arson: c.: later C.20. Gash, 1983.

crisp, adj. New, interesting: ca. 1920–35. Manchon.—2. In *talk crisp*, to say disagreeable things: coll.:—1923 (Manchon).

criss-cross. A crossword puzzle; crosswords in general: since ca. 1935.

crit. A published criticism, a review, of a concert, play, book, etc. (Noble, 1978.)—2. Hence, as n. and v., (to make) an oral or a written critical report upon a fellow-student's work: training colleges'. Tey, 1946.

crit sheet. That printed form which is attached to a report and on which the reader indicates the accuracy and value of the report: Services' and Civil Service coll.: since ca. 1945. Cf. prec.

critical. Dangerously ill or injured: coll., orig. and still mainly journalists': since ca. 1930. Ex 'be in a critical state'.

cro. A prostitute: low Aus.: since the 1920s. (Tennant, 1953.) Loose for **chro.**—2. A *c.r.o.* or cathode-ray oscilloscope: esp. in Aus.: since ca. 1940. (B.P.)

croak, in c., means both to die and to kill; also (ob.) a 'last dying' speech: C.19–20. Vaux (to die); Egan, 1823 (to hang); H., 1st ed., the n. sense: hardly before ca. 1850. Ex the death-rattle.

croaker. A dying person, a doctor, a corpse: the second being c. and low s., the first low coll., and the third (H., 2nd ed.) low s.: mid-C.19–20.—2. 'A doctor who provides narcotics for an addict. (Can., US)' (Home Office): drug addicts': current in 1970s. A specialisation of sense 1. See also **crocus.**

croaker joint. A hospital: drugs c. (Stockley, 1986.) Cf. prec.

croakus. See **crocus.**

croc. 'Short for *Crocodile* [q.v.], a British flame-throwing tank': army: ca. 1941–5. P-G-R.

Crocket(t)'s Folly. The Olympia cab-rank: London taxi-drivers': since ca. 1910. Hodge, 1939.

crocks. Crockery, even fine chinaware; esp. in 'do the crocks', wash the dishes after a meal: domestic coll. Cf. dial. usage for, usu., coarse earthenware (*EDD*). (P.B.)

crockus. Var. of **crocus.**

crocodile. (Both n. and v.) Applied to 'paint which has contracted during drying. . . . Resembling a crocodile's skin' (a master builder, 1953): builders' and house-painters'.—2. A horse: Aus.: since ca. 1930. B., 1943.—3. 'The long-range flame-thrower version of the Mark VII Churchill tank, of which the British Army had a whole regiment in the later stages of WW2, and subsequently' (R.S., 1973). Prob. a codename. See **croc.**

crocus, n. (In full: *crocus metallorum*, and in C.19–20 occ. **croakus**). A surgeon or a doctor (esp. a quack): low (— 1785); ob. (Grose, 1st ed.; Mayhew.) Prob. ex *croak* after *hocus-pocus*, though the *OED* mentions a Dr Helkiah *Crooke* and Coles has *crocus Martis*, a chemical preparation of iron, and *crocus veneris*, one of copper. Cf. **croaker,** by which also the old scientific term *crocus* was prob. suggested in this sense. At first, naval and military.—2. (Always *crocus*.) Among grafters, it bears the above-mentioned senses; also, a herbalist, a miracle-worker. *Cheapjack*, 1934.—3. 'A fair-weather trader who appears for a while when Winter is over' (*M.T.*): market-traders'.

crocus, v. To practice itinerant quackery: c.: since mid-C.19.— 2. Hence, neutrally and widely, to sell medicines and toilet preparations to (the gathered customers): fairgrounds'. (Buchanan-Taylor, 1943.) Cf. **crocus,** n., 2.

croker. See **croaker.**

crokus. See **crocus.**

croggie, -y. A ride on the cross-bar of another's bicycle; less often, a ride on the saddle while another pedals: East Midland and Yorkshire children's:—1960 (Bowater, 1979). Cf. **saddler,** another term for the latter mode. Ex *cross*; cf. *Chriggy* = Christmas.

cronky. 'Wonky' or unsound; inferior; not well: since ca. 1920. It has re-surfaced as a gen. adj. of disapprobation among Leicestershire schoolchildren (and prob. more widely): 1983. (R. Walton, 1983.)

crook. A very characteristic Aus. term meaning generally inferior, and specifically: ill; spurious (B., 1942); (of, e.g., eggs) bad, rotten: ca. 1905 (Casey, 1942); (of persons) objectionable: since ca. 1910 (Casey, 1945); (of land) poor, infertile: id. (Stivens, 1953).—2. In *go crook*, to give way to anger; to express annoyance: Aus.: from ca. 1905.

C

crook and butcher. Cook & Butcher (a 'trade'): RAF: since ca. 1935. Jackson, 'It is commonly believed that his sins go so often unpunished.'

crop the field. To win easily: horse-racing: ca. 1870–1930. A double pun.

cross (someone's) **bows.** To offend a senior officer: RN. Granville, 'It is a flagrant breach of manners for a junior ship to cross the bows of a senior ship.'

cross (someone) **off** (one's) **visiting list;** usu. *to have crossed* . . . 'This is sometimes used jocularly, mainly by working-class people who do not keep Books of Engagements' (Petch, 1966): since ca. 1930.

cross, or **go over, the Alps.** To go to Dartmoor Prison: earlier C.20 c.

Crosse and Blackwell's Regiment. The General Service Corps: Army; since late 1930s. Ex the similarity of its cap badge to Messrs Crosse & Blackwell's trademark. (Waugh, 1942.) Cf. **Tate & Lyle.**

crossed killicks. A petty officer's badge (crossed anchors: *killich,* in Erse = a wooden anchor): RN lowerdeck. Granville.

crossers. Crossword puzzles in gen., or one in particular: since ca. 1930. Ex *cross*word by the 'OXFORD -*ER*'.

crossword spanner. A pencil: RN engineers': since ca. 1950. (Granville, letter, 1962.) Cf. *bee*r *spanner,* a bottle-opener.

crot. Excrement; usu. as *soft crot,* a loose stool: schoolboys': ca. 1935. (Jones, 1957.) Cf. **noggies.**

crotch(-)rot. 'A form of skin fungus that attacks the area between the buttocks and around the groin. Extremely common affliction. One doctor told me "Everybody and his dog has it" ' (Leechman): coll., mostly Can.

crouch. See **shampoo attitude**.

crow, n. A rating who's always getting into trouble: RN: since ca. 1920. (Granville.) Prompted by **bird,** n., 3.—2. An undertaker; an undertaker's employee, a mute: (Allingham, 1947.) Ex black clothing. (Claiborne.)—3. 'The bowler [hat] was most often referred to by working-class people as a "crow" or a "pot hat" ' (Brooker, 1988): ca. 1920. Because almost invariably black?

crow, v. To bend (rails) for the 2 ft or 4 ft 8 in. light-railway tracks: Public Works': 1935. ?Ex use of a *crow*-bar.

crow-hopping. 'Hopping with bended knees, usually up an incline and holding a rifle overhead. Probably discarded now but certainly common in the fifties in Training Establishments' (Malin, 1979): RN.

crow in working rig. A seagull: RN: since ca. 1930. P-G-R.

crow-pee, at. At dawn: British army in N. Africa: 1941–3. 'English imitation of Australian slang, Western Desert' (Sanders). R.S. notes: 'A substitution for *at sparrow-fart*—there are no sparrows in the desert!' P.B.: but Lord Willis told me, 1987, that he had recently heard of an elderly Kentish woman declaring that she was always up and about 'before the crows piddle or the sparrows fart'.

crowd. To verge on: Can. coll.: adopted, ca. 1935, ex US. 'He must be crowding forty.' (Leechman.)

crowded space. Suitcase: since ca. 1930: orig. c.; by 1940, low s. Franklyn 2nd.

crowie. An old woman: market-traders'. (*M.T.*) Ex common resemblance in garb and voice.

crown, n. (Always as *the crown*) the sergeant-major: army coll.: earlier C.20. (F. & G.) Ex the badge of a crown upon his lower sleeve. Cf. *put* (one's) *crown up,* to be promoted to Company (or Battery) Sergeant-major; also applied to colour- and staff-sergeants (Army) and flight-sergeants (RAF), who wear a smaller crown above their three chevrons: 'he's got his crown (up)'.—2. The mons Veneris, hence female pubic hair: low and raffish: latish C.19–20, but perhaps much earlier. Prob. short for older synon. low s. *crown and feathers.*

crown, v. To put a chamber-pot on a man's head: Aus. universities'.—2. To hit (a person) on the *crown*: low: Ingram,

1933.—3. To cane: Aus. schoolboys': ca. 1910–40. (McLean, 1954.) See also **coronation**, a caning.

crown, adj. Very large: Aus. coll.: since ca. 1920. Palmer, 1955, 'If it's a crown fire we're gone a million'. Prompted by the *crowning* of, e.g., 'crowning glory'.

Crown and Anchor. See Appx.

Crown Prince (or *c- p-*). In address; in ref., *the crown prince*: 'The oldest or only son of a man [sur]named *King*': since ca. 1910. (Petch, 1969.)

crow's nest. Female pubic hair: orig. and mainly nautical: (?)mid-C.19–20.

crucial. A vogue-word among teenagers, 1988, started by the TV comedian Lenny Henry. 'My children use it all the time, for anything' (H. Owen, Mar. 1988).

crud. 'Equals turd as an expression of contempt for another person. "What a silly little crud Harry is!" ' (Leechman): Can.: since ca. 1930. Ex Can. (and US) dial., itself ex English dial., *crud,* a survival from late Middle English *crudde.* Also, since late 1930s, common in Aus. (B.P.); and in Brit. Forces, esp. in 1950s. (P.B.) Theological colleges were using it in the 1960s for 'second-rate, inferior, spoiled' (Towler, 1979).—2. Dried, spilt semen: low: adopted, ex US, mid-C.20. (P.B.)

crudget. The head: Aus. since ca. 1920. Prob. a corruption of **crumpet,** 1, the head.

cruiser. 'A taxi-cab that cruises the streets in search of fares' (Leechman): Can. coll.: since ca. 1935; by 1960, S.E. Cf. the US *cruiser,* a squad, or prowl, car.

crumb act, put on the. 'To impose on another person' (B., 1959): Aus. low.

crumb-hunting. Housework. See CANADIAN . . . , in Appx.

crumble. 'A disparaging term for geriatric patients admitted as emergencies to acute medical wards in the 1960s. The usual expression is "A load of crumble"; the implication was that they had only social problems and not interesting medical ones' (Hamblin, 1988).

crumblies. Grown-ups, esp. one's own, or one's friends', parents: youngsters': current in early 1970s. Either because the parents are *crumbling* with age, or because—less likely—there's a misapprehension of *grumblies.* R.S., 1976, who drew attention to the term's occurrence in *The Times,* compares Fr. s. of the early 1950s: *lézardé,* cracked (of walls), hence the over-30s; *croulant,* crumbling, the over-50s; and *ruiné* for the over-70s.

crumbs. Small change: mostly teenagers': 1950s. Cf. **bread,** money.

crummy, adj. Lousy: from ca. 1840: perhaps orig. c., then Cockney (see H.), then low and military (certainly very common in WW1); then, ex the army, among tramps. (Jennings, 1932.) Hence, the c. *crummy doss,* a lice-infested bed. ?Ex a louse's vague resemblance to a small crumb. P.B.: or from its vague resemblance to a cow's head with in-turned horns, dial. *crummie* (*EDD*): cf. *crab-louse,* with its appearance of having in-turned horns.—2. Hence, dirty, untidy: nautical: mid-C.19–20. (Bowen.) Cf. **chatty,** lousy.—3. Hence, inferior; dull, as in *crummy joint,* a dull disco: since ca. 1946.

crummy! A low var. of *criminy* (*crikey*)! Cf. **crums,** 2.

Crump Dump, the. The Ruhr: RAF: late 1940–early 1945. (E.P., 1942.) Ex the numerous bombs the RAF dumped there.

crump(-)hole. A bomb-caused crater: 1940, Berrey. Cf. prec.

crumper. A heavy crash, as in 'The Wimpey [Wellington bomber-aircraft] came a proper crumper' (Jackson): RAF: since ca. 1925.

crumpet. The head: late C.19–20; ob. by 1930 in UK (E.P.), but extant in Aus., later C.20 (McNeil). Cf. synon. *onion,* and *turnip.* Esp. *barmy* (or *dotty*) *in the crumpet,* crazy, mad: Manchon.—2. Woman as sex; women viewed collectively as instruments of sexual pleasure: low: from ca. 1880. (*Gilt Kid,* 1936.) Cf. **crackling.**—3. A 'softy' or a 'mug'; a dupe; a fool: Aus.: since ca. 1920. (Glassop, 1944.) A crumpet is soft.—4. A female undergraduate: Durham male undergraduates':

1940 (Marples, 2).—5. In *get a crumpet*, (of a man) to copulate in a specific instance: c. (*Gilt Kid*, 1936.) Ex sense 2.

crumpet man. 'A womaniser' (Powis): low: current in 1970s, and prob. throughout C.20. Cf. **crumpet**, 2, and:-

crumpet run. Taking one's vehicle through town simply to ogle the girls, e.g. a milk tanker, which is forbidden to go through town anyway, or an off-duty fire-engine on an unofficial run: their drivers': later C.20. (Jane Littmoden cites a tanker-driver, 1984.)

crums, occ. **crumbs.** (Extremely rare in singular.) Lice: low:—1923 (Manchon). App. a back-formation ex **crummy**, 3.—2. As an exclam., it is synon. with *crummy!*: mostly boys'. Scott, 1934, 'Crumbs, mater, shove a sock in it! What tripe!'

crunch, the. The most severe—'the *real*'—test (of, e.g., strength, courage, nerve, skill, etc.): since ca. 1940. 'The crunch'll come when you have to go out and earn your living' (any irate father to teenage son); 'When it came to the crunch, his courage failed'; Bournemouth *Evening Echo*, 3 Apr. 1966. Of sporting origin, I think: prob. rugby; perhaps boxing or all-in wrestling. 'It was a favourite word . . . of Sir Winston Churchill . . . In, e.g., his letter to President Roosevelt on Lend-Lease (8 Dec. 1940)' (R.S.). Always coll. rather than s. Hence as adj., in e.g.:-

crunch-test. A test or examination which decides whether or not a student shall continue on a course of instruction: army: early 1970s. (P.B.)

crush. A large social gathering, esp. if crowded: from ca. 1830: coll.—2. Hence (in the Army) a military unit: late C.19–early 20. Cf. *crowd*, **mob**, *push*.—3. Hence, a set, a group: coll.: from ca. 1919. E.g. *Shakespeare—and That Crush*, by Dark & Derrick, 1931.—4. An infatuation; a strong liking or 'fancy' for a person: US (—1903), anglicised in mid-1920s. Clapin, 1903, 'In college slang, a liking for a person.' Prob. ex earlier Society s. *crushed on*, infatuated with. Cf. **pash**, n., 1.

crusher. A policeman: from ca. 1840.—2 A ship's corporal: RN:—1901 (Goodenough). The *Globe and Laurel* (Royal Marines journal), Sep.–Oct. 1976, remarks, in article 'Customs . . . and Terms in the Royal Navy', of the ship's corporal that he was 'assumed like all policemen to have had large feet . . . Despite his stealth he could be heard coming as he crushed cockroaches underfoot in the dark and these made a popping noise' (Whitlock).—3. By extension, a regulating petty officer (equivalent to a warrant officer in Military or Service Police): RN: since ca. 1920. H. & P.

crust. The head: from ca. 1870. Occ. *upper crust*. Hence, *off* (one's) *crust*, crazy, insane: later C.20 coll.—2. Impudence, 'cheek': since early 1920s; ob. (Wodehouse, 1924: *OED* Sup.) ?Ex hard as a crust. The term may have been adopted ex Can., where it was current from ca. 1910. (Leechman.)—3. A vagrancy charge: Aus. c. (and police s.): since ca. 1935. B., 1953.

crust of bread. The head: r.s. Usu. shortened to *crust*—but see also **crust**, 1. (Franklyn.) Cf. **loaf o(f) bread.**

crutch. An experienced skater supporting a learner: skating rinks': since ca. 1935.—2. 'Two matches, a split match used to completely smoke a marijuana (cannabis) cigarette' (Home Office): drug-users': current in 1970s.—3. see TOM-BOLA, in Appx.

crypto. A 'secret' Communist; a sympathiser with Communism: Parliamentary: 1945+. (Driberg 1946.) Gr. *kruptos*, hidden. Hence also as a prefix, in such formations as *crypto-pinko*, a hitherto unsuspected and unlikely supporter of mild socialism.

crystal. Methedrine: drugs c. (Stockley, 1986.) US since –1967 (Spears).

cu, cue. A cucumber: Covent Garden coll. (*Daily Telegraph*, 7 June 1935.) Pl: *cues*.—2. Cumulus cloud(s): RAF (orig. meteorological) coll.: since ca. 1925. (H. & P.) Also, via RAF Met. Officers on Divisional, Corps, and Army H.Q. Staffs, among Army officers since at least as early as 1940. Ex the official abbr.

cubby, short for *cubby-house*. A child's playhouse in the backyard: Aus. coll.: since ca. 1925. (B.P.)

cube. A cubicle: certain Public Schools', e.g., Charterhouse. See also **cubie.** 1.—2. A complete conformist, 'the squarest of the square': 1960s. (Correspondence columns of *Sunday Times*, 8 Sep. 1963.) Ex **square**, n., 2.—3. A cube of morphine: drugs c. (Stockley, 1986.) US since –1936 (Spears).

cubie. A cubicle: Public Schools', e.g. Tonbridge. See also **cube**, 1. (P.B.)—2. (Usu. in pl.) 'People living or sleeping in cubicles in homes [for the aged *et al.*] or doss-houses' (Petch, 1969): since ca. 1920.

cubic. A Cubist painting: art coll.: from ca. 1921. See quot'n at **Prime, the.**

cuckoo. Mad, senseless, distraught: US, anglicised in early 1920s. Ex *cuckoo*, n., s. since late C.16 for a fool.

cuckoo farm. A mental hospital: later C.20. 'The zealots who saw truth as indivisible ended up in . . . the cuckoo farm' (Kavanagh, 1980). Cf. prec., and synon. **funny farm.**

Cuckoo Line, the. The Eridge Junction to Polegate section of the London (Victoria) to Eastbourne, Southern Region line: railwaymen's: earlier C.20; the line closed in the 1960s. The halfway station was Heathfield, where every year, on 14 April, 'the old woman lets the cuckoo out of her basket' at 'Hefful Cuckoo Fair'. (P.B.)

cuddle. A rendezvous of boy and girl: low London: since ca. 1920. (Ingram, 1935.) Ex the v.; cf.:-

cuddle and kiss. A girl: Cockneys'. (Ortzen, 1938.) Rhyming on *miss*.

cuddle-cook. A policeman: early C.20: mostly, lower classes'.

cuddle-seat. One of the double seats provided in some cinemas for courting (or amorous) couples: Aus. coll.: since ca. 1955. Perhaps ex the *cuddleseat*—a sling devised for baby-carrying. (B.P.)

cuddleable. Cuddlesome: coll.: from mid-1920s. *OED* Sup.

cuds, in the. In the hills: RAF in NW India: ca. 1925–45. (Jackson.) Ex Hindustani *khud*, a steep hill-side.

cue-bite. To speak too soon on one's cues: theatrical:—1935.

cufflink. A Chinese: r.s. on synon. *Chink*. (Hollis, 1983.)

cufuffle. Any sort of disturbance. Var. of *gefuffle* or **kerfuffle**, q.v.

cuke. A cucumber: domestic coll. Leechman notes its use among Can. greengrocers since ca. 1910. Cf. **cu**, 1.

cully. A marble: Lancashire children's. (Richards, 1984.) Poss. ex. *coloured*.

cultch. Culture: joc.: later C.20. Moody, 1984, 'Soak up a bit of cultch'. Cf.:-

culture vulture. A person avid for culture; esp. one who haunts exhibitions and lectures: adopted, in late 1950s, ex US. Of the same sort of US r.s. as *eager beaver* or *legal eagle*.

cum. A late C.20 var. spelling of **come**, n., 2: gay c.

cunning as a shit-house rat, as. Very cunning indeed: Aus. (Slater, 1957.) Sense is pej., tinged with reluctant admiration. Ob. by 1980s.

cunning as a (whole) wagon-load of monkeys, as. Very cunning, with a considerable admixture of mischievousness to go with it: coll., mostly domestic. (P.B.)

cunny. As *the cunny*, it = the countryside: Merseyside. Ex *country*; cf. *cossie* from *costume*, etc.

cunt hat. A trilby, or other felt hat: low:—1923 (Manchon). There is a double pun: see **old hat** and note 'felt'. Cf. **chooch hat.**

cunt hooks. Fingers: low. 'Keep your cunt hooks off my belongings!'—2. An occ. name for the insulting gesture that consists of jerking up the first two fingers, the back of the hand towards the person insulted: low.—3. A low form of address: Services': mid-C.20.

cup. Short for **cup of tea**, 2: since the late 1930s. Wilson, 1952, 'Anyway, none of it would be your cup, darling.' P.B., 1979: the full phrase is still by far the more common.—2. As *the*

C

Cup, Football Association League trophy; esp. in describing provincial teams' supporters flocking to Wembley to watch the final: they are 'up for the cup': sporting, then gen., coll. (P.B.)

cup o(f) tea. A consolation: proletarian, gen. ironic: earlier C.20. Ware, 'Probably suggested by a cup of tea being "so very refreshing".'—2. (One's) *cup of tea* = what truly suits one; even one's ideal, one's mate: coll.: since ca. 1910. Since ca. 1940 perhaps just as often, if not more commonly, in the negative, as a polite rejection of someone else's proposal, demand, plea for help, etc., as 'I'm afraid that's not really my cup of tea', or 'Not quite everybody's cup of tea, do you think?' It has proved stronger than the synon. **ticket**, q.v. (E.P.; L.A.)

cupboard, n. As *the c-*, the sea: nautical: late C.19–20. (Bowen.) Ex *Davy Jones's locker*. P.B.: but cf. also the descriptions of the sea as *the biggest ashtray* or *gash-bucket in the world*.

cupboard, adj. (Of the prospects of a house) no good, close-fisted: tramps' and Romanies' s. (R. Dawson.) The inmates *keep* the food there.

cupcake. A male homosexual: later C.20. (Price, 1982.) Janssen notes its appearance in E. Deak, *Dictionnaire d'Américanismes*, 1966, 'Garçon éfféminé, mignon'; Green, 2, defines it as 'an attractive (young) female'.

curl. An Aus. term of address: 1960s. Short for *Curly*—though not necessarily addressed to a bald man, or perhaps same as **kurl**, q.v. (P.B.)

curl-a-mo; curl the mo. Excellent; to do very well. See **kurl**.

Curly. 'Inevitable' nickname of men with curly hair: coll.:— 1851 (Mayhew).—2. But, just as 'inevitably', used ironically for men almost entirely bald: since ca. 1910. Cf. *Tiny*, and *Lofty*.

curly, n. A story, an account: Cockneys': since ca. 1910. (Allingham, 1945.) Poss. some connection with later C.19 *chuck a curly*, to 'swing the lead', malinger.

curly, adj. Difficult, as in 'That's a curly one'—a question hard to answer: (?mostly) Aus.: since ca. 1950. (Sydney *Sunday Mirror*, 27 Oct. 1963.) Perhaps ex googly bowling in cricket, or, less prob., ex 'throwing a *curve*' in baseball. Cf. *get curly*, C.19 tailors' coll. for 'to become troublesome'.—2. But in NZ, e.g. as 'That was extra curly' (Slatter), it seems to mean 'excellent' or 'attractive' and to date since ca. 1935.

curp. (Properly *kcirp*.) Penis: London back s.; rather an in-group term than gen. (Daniells; Barltrop, 1981.)

currant bun. *On the currant bun*, on the run from the police: since ca. 1920: r.s.—orig. underworld >, by ca. 1945, also police s. Often shortened to *on the currant*. Gosling, 1959.— 2. A son: r.s.: not recorded before 1962. Haden-Guest.—3. As *C- B-*, also applied, by Londoners, to the *Sun* newspaper. See **Captain Grimes**.

currant-cakey. Shaky: r.s. P.P., 1932.

curse. One's swag or 'bluey': Aus. swagmen's. (Idriess, 1934.) Hence *hump* or *carry the curse*, to go on the tramp. B., 1959.—2. As *the curse*, the menses: fem. euph., or in *the curse is upon me*, a joc. coll. intimation, formal and deliberately archaic. A shortening of the earlier *the curse of Eve*.

curse rag. A sanitary towel: Wrens': 1939+.

curtain climber. A young child: widespread Can. and US: since ca. 1960. Leech, 1986, notes also synon *ankle-biter, rug rat* and *yard ape*.

curtains. 'Paint running down surface and setting in drape-like pattern' (master builder, 1953): builders' and house-painters'.—2. Mostly in 'It's curtains for him', implying death or dismissal or 'the end': adopted, ca. 1944, from US servicemen. Of theatrical origin.

cush. The cushion of a billiard table: players' coll.—2. Something easy to do or to endure: Army: since ca. 1918. (Kersh, 1941.) Ex **cushy**.—3. Female genitalia: among servicemen with Near East experience. Ex Arabic. P.B.: in later C.20 remembered chiefly in the 'soldiers' Arabic' phrase *shufti cush*, let's see, or show, the *cush*. Cf. **zubrick**.

cushty. A market-traders' derivation from *cushy*, adj., with the senses 'good; of good quality; enjoyable' (*M.T.*): since ca. 1917.

cushy. Easy, safe: of a job, task, or post. Not dangerous: of a wound. *SOD* records this military s. at 1915, but, to judge both from its possibly Hindustani origin (*khush*, pleasure) or its, to me, more prob. Romany one (*kushto*, good), and from report, it was used in the Indian Army some years before WW1. (It is not impossibly a slurring of *cushiony* or an extension of dial. *cushie*, soft, flabby.) Tempest, 1950, 'Familiar old word which distinguishes an "easy" prison from a "bastard nick".'

custard and jelly. 'Telly', i.e. television: r.s.: since ca. 1960. (Hillman.)

custard bosun. A Warrant Cook: RN joc. coll.: since ca. 1925. Granville.

custards. Pimples: Aus.: since ca. 1925. (B., 1942.) Ex colour. Cf. **shag-spots**.

customer. An enemy aircraft: RAF: WW2. Gibson, 1946.—2. (Usu. in pl.) 'Do-gooders who visit patients in hospitals, or elderly people in their homes, sometimes call them "customers" ' (Petch, 1966): since ca. 1950. P.B.: the 'in' word in the late 1970s is *client*.

cut, n. A phonograph record, or a special part of one: 'pop' music lovers' coll.: adopted, ca. 1955, ex US. *Beatles*, 1975.—2. As *the cut*, 'Any district where goods are bought and sold with a minimum of questions asked. Petticoat Lane, for example. Probably from "short cut" or "short way", a back alley or street' (Tempest): c.

cut, v. 'To adulterate [drugs]' (Home Office): drug addicts': current in 1970s. US since—1938 (Spears).

cut! Stop cameras and action: cinematic s., since ca. 1910; by 1930, coll. Hence, esp. in Can., 'used on other occasions and in other occupations' (Leechman): since ca. 1945.

cut a rug. To 'jive' or 'jitterbug': dance addicts': adopted from US soldiers in 1943. *John Bull*, 2 Feb. 1946.

cut about. To move smartly: Guardsmen's: since ca. 1930. (Grinstead, 1946.) Cf. **get cracking**.

cut and carried. (Of a woman) married: r.s. Franklyn.

cut and shut, adj. and, often hyphenated, n. 'The most dangerous of all [secondhand cars]. Two severely damaged cars are cut in half and the best [sic] part of one welded to the best part of the other. This technique is also used to disguise stolen cars' (*Woman's Own*, 28 Feb. 1968): shady car-dealers': since ca. 1930.

cut down to size. To bring (someone) sharply back to earth in his estimate of his own worth; to reduce to a realistic opinion of (himself): coll.: adopted, ca. 1960, ex US. *Woman's Own*, 4 Sep. 1965, an advice-to-wives article headed 'Never Cut Him Down to Size . . . You may find there is nothing left but the pieces.' Elliptical for *cut down to true size*.

cut fine. To be very near to breaking the law, or actually doing so undetected, as in 'He's running that car without an M.O.T. That's cutting it a bit fine; pushing his luck, I'd say.' (P.B.)

cut-glass accent. Middle-class, esp. upper-middle: coll.: rare before ca. 1950. Naughton, 1970: 'This Abby with her nice little overall and her cut-glass accent'. And on the very same day I dealt with this reference, I turned to a set of notes supplied by P.B., 1977, and found this: 'cut-glass accent, the clear, piercing accent of the British (female) upper classes— goes with the twin-set and pearls, sheepskin jacket and large dog, Fortnum & Mason "image".'

cut-in, n., ex:-

cut in, v. 'An automatic switch, such as a thermostat, is said to *cut in* when it makes a contact and *cut out* when it breaks it' (Leechman): electricians' coll. > j.: since late 1940s.

cut it fine. See **cut fine**.

cut off a slice. A ref. to sexual intercourse, as in 'There's plenty never gets to see any [girls], you know, let alone cut themselves off a slice' (Daniells, 1980): low and raffish: later C.20. Cf. **cut off the joint**.

cut (someone) **off a slice of cake.** To make a rude noise at him: Services': early C.20. 'The tone of his voice struck the troopers as so affected, that they promptly gave him the "bird", "blew him one out", "cut him off a slice of cake", or "gave him a raspberry"—whichever expression you prefer' (Hatton, 1930).—2. (?Hence, ironically) to salute a superior officer: RN: since ca. 1930. (Granville.) Cf. **chip one off** and **cut one off.**

cut off the joint, a. (From the male angle) copulation; esp., *have a* . . .

cut off the nut, a. 'Used jocularly with regard to vegetarian menu, or to the lack of meat when dining out, as "I'll have a cut off the nut" ' (Petch, 1946): since ca. 1942 for the latter, since ca. 1930 for the former nuance.

cut (someone) **one off.** To salute one's superior: police: since ca. 1919. *Free-Lance Writer*, Apr. 1948.

cut out. To cease; come to an end: Aus. miners' coll.: late C.19–20. Idriess, 1934, 'The gold was finished. It had "cut out".' This sense soon > widespread Aus. coll.: cf. Ronan, 1954, 'I'll hang around until this job cuts out.'—2. To depart: Can. dance-fanatics': adopted, ca. 1957, ex US. (Victoria *Daily Colonist*, May 1958, 'Basic Beatnik'.)—3. To break (electrical) contact. See **cut in**, v.

cut out to be a gentleman. Circumcised. A neat, if inexact, pun.

cut snake . . . See **mad as a cut snake**, very angry.

cut the corners. 'To cut down the work or not conform to all duties of any undertaking and yet reap the same or more plentiful fruits; to see anew and reform process or practice with increased effect (the feeling of this phrase can be compared with that of "Separates the men from the boys")' (L.A., 1969): coll.: since ca. 1950.

cut the flash. To show, make a display: Aus. low. B., 1942.

cut the mustard. 'To succeed in performing or accomplishing'; hence, 'to be of importance'; both, 'almost always used with a qualifying negative. It dates back at least to 1904, when the phrase *up to mustard*, up to standard or up to the mark was also used' (Janssen, 1976). 'All four Beatles cut the mustard as panellists on BBC-TV's "Juke Box Jury" ' (*Beatles*).—2. To enjoy copulation. 'A lady from New Zealand expressed dismay at the sight of a pair [of lovers] energetically cutting

the mustard in broad daylight' (Frater, 1977). The following quot'n, from a review by Rhoda Koenig of the film *Coming Home*, in the *Spectator*, 10 June 1978, date-lined New York, could be either ambiguous, or a *double entendre* on both senses: 'It . . . puts its ideological point with admirable concision: pacifists are good in bed; militarists can't cut the mustard.' (P.B.)

cut the rough (stuff). To cease doing or saying something obnoxious to another: Aus. and NZ (lower classes', then military) coll. Also in the imperative: 'Stop it!' (Baker).

cut to waste. 'To cut up sheets of paper in such a way that some is wasted, either inevitably or intentionally' (Leechman): a widespread printers' coll.

cut-up, n. 'A share-out of the spoils': Aus. c.: since ca. 1920. B., 1942.

cut up, v. To conduct (a contest) dishonestly: sporting: from ca. 1920. (*OED* Sup.) 'When someone suspects corruption or dishonesty in a lottery, vote, or apportionment of rewards he may say "It's a cut-up" ' (Munro, 1985): Glasgow.

cutie; occ. **cutey.** A smart girl; loosely, any (young) girl: US (—1921), partly anglicised ca. 1930 owing to the 'talkies'. *OED* Sup.

cutie-pie. 'A girl rich in (calculated) sexual attraction': ca. 1971–5. (*Daily Telegraph*, 23 Apr. 1973.) 'Inspired by sweetiepie?' Hence, as adj. (R.S., 1973.)

Cutlers, the. See ASSOCIATION FOOTBALL, in Appx.

cutter. 'To *run the cutter* is to act as a bookie's runner or simply to take another person's line to the betting-shop for him' (Munro, 1985): Glasgow.

cutting gear. 'Oxyacetylene apparatus when used to break into safes' (Powis): c., hence also police: current in 1970s.

cutting the job up. Working too hard, *making it bad for the other people*: Services': since ca. 1930. H. & P.

cylinder. Vagina: Aus., esp. mechanics': since ca. 1930.

Cyp (pron. *sip*). A Cypriot: British Forces serving in Cyprus; and Londoners affected by immigrants from the island: since mid-C.20 at latest. Also used as adj. (P.B.)

Cypher Queen. A WRNS officer engaged in cypher duties ashore: RN: since ca. 1940. Granville.

cysto. Cystoscopy: medical coll.: since late 1950s. (Leechman.)

D

d or **dee.** Short for *Captain D*, officer commanding a destroyer flotilla: RN coll.: since ca. 1920. (Granville.) 'Now [1945] also loosely used for the senior officer of a formation of destroyers or even destroyers and frigates mixed' (Bolster, 1945).

d.a. A 'duck's *arse*' hair-cut, a term used to describe a male style that was very popular, esp. among Teddy-boys, in the early 1950s. The hair was tapered and curled on the nape of the neck like the feathers of a drake's tail. Occ. euph. expanded to 'duck's anatomy'. (P.B.)—2. Var. of **d.a.s.**, q.v.

d.a.l. 'Dog *at* large'—a humorous notation put on letters that cannot be delivered: postmen's: since ca. 1920.

d.a.s. The menstrual flux: ca. 1870–1930. Abbr. *domestic afflictions*.

d.c.M. 'Don't come Monday. One day's suspension' (*Railway*, 2nd): railwaymen's. P.B.: prob. punning *district court martial*—it would hardly be *Distinguished Conduct Medal*. In later C.20 more widely used to cover a general attitude to wage-earning work. Cf. **t.g.i.f.**

D-Day Dodgers, the. The army in Italy: mostly among men of that army: June 1944–5. (D-Day, 6 June; Rome captured, 4 June.) Ex a widespread rumour that Lady Astor had called them that in a speech; subsequently denied, but not before a song had been composed, to the tune of *Lili Marlene*. One stanza goes:-

We fought 'em on the mountains, we fought 'em on the plain.
We fought 'em in the sunshine, we fought 'em in the rain.
We didn't want to go and fight
In all the mud and all the shite,
We are the D-Day Dodgers, in sunny Italy.

d.f.s. Duty-free goods: RN coll. Granville.

d.f.m. Short for *dog-fucked mutton*, scraps of food, mutton hash: mostly Forces': since ca. 1920. A pun on the *Distinguished Flying Medal*.

d.i.y. (or capitals). A coll. abbr. of 'do-it-yourself' (methods, handbooks, etc.): since the late 1960s; whence, by early 1970s, a *D-I-Y-er*, an exponent of the creed. (P.B.)

d.j. Disc-jockey, n. and v.: entertainment circles': since ca. 1970. See **disc-jockey.** (P.B.)—2. As *DJ*, dinner jacket, i.e. formal evening suit: coll.: later C.20. (Chappell, 1982.) Cf. synon. **penguin-suit.**

d.s.o. Dick [= penis] *shot off*: a Services' c.p. of WW1; rare in WW2. Punning on the *Distinguished Service Order* decoration.

D.X. (properly **dx;** cf. *wx* = weather) **hound.** A 'dial-twister'; a 'station-hunter'; i.e. one who, in a restless, senseless manner, tries station after station on the radio: wireless (radio)

s.: since ca. 1927. (Connington, 1931.) 'The essential point about D.X. is that it is the radio hound's abbreviation for "distance". In the early days of radio, hams tried for the most distant stations, at the antipodes if possible, and confirmed their triumphs by postcards to the sending stations' (Leechman, 1967).

dab. In *on the dab*, being disciplined for a minor infringement of regulations: police: later C.20. 'Anyone who [got caught] and went on the dab for whatever it was received considerable sympathy from the rest of us [police constables]' (Seabrook, 1987).

dab(-)dab; dab(-)toe. A seaman: RN stokers'. (Granville.) The seamen have so often to 'dab' about the deck in their bare feet.

dab in the dook. A tip (lit., a pat on the hand): low and military: earlier C.20. B. & P.

dabble. Stolen property: c. Samuel, 1981.

dabbler. A black marketeer in furniture: furniture trade: mid-1940s. (*John Bull*, 1 Apr. 1944.) Another term was *bubber*.—2. See **little dabbler.**

dabs. (Extremely rare in the singular.) Fingerprints: c.,—1935 (Hume); by 1940, at latest, also police s. Hence, *Dabs* (without *the*), the Fingerprint Department of New Scotland Yard (Marsh, 1940).

dachsie, -sy. A dachshund: domestic coll. Strictly, a diminutive of the more widely distributed *dachs*.

dad. A term of address to anyone ten-or-so years older than oneself, esp. in Aus.: coll.: since ca. 1945. (B.P.)

Dad and Dave. To shave; a shave: Aus. r.s.: since ca. 1930, when, approximately, the radio serial 'Dad and Dave' began to pleasure Australians. Franklyn, *Rhyming*.

daddio. Var. spelling of the prob. more common **daddy-o**, q.v.

daddle. To practise tribadism: low: C.19–20. Also spelt *dadle*.

daddler, dadler. A farthing: low, esp. Cockneys'. Horsley, 1912, has *dadla*. Perhaps a corruption of *diddler*. See also, **little dabbler.**

daddy. A 'Forceful personality' (Home Office): prisoners': current in 1970s.—2. 'A lovely ship' (Butcher, 1980): trawlermen's.

daddy of them all, the. The most notable; (of things) the largest: Aus. coll. (B., 1942). Since ca. 1970, current also in UK.

daddy-o (with var. spelling *daddio*). A teenagers' var. of *dad*: Aus.: since ca. 1950. (B.P.)—2. 'One of the most frequent words in early beatnik'—the 1950s. 'A title often conferred on the leader of a little beatnik coterie' (Leechman, 1967).

dadla, dadler. A farthing. See **daddler.**

dadle. See **daddle.**

Dad's Army. Affectionately in 1940–5, then reminiscently, as in Aird, 1970, ' "What," asked Sloan cautiously, "was Dad's Army?" . . . "The Home Guard, man. The People who came after the Local Defence Volunteers. LDVs they were known as at first." He chuckled sardonically. "The Look, Duck and Vanish brigade we called them at the time." ' Cf. the very popular comedy series on BBC-TV, 'Dad's Army', 1970+.

daff. To wash: taxi-drivers': since ca. 1910. 'Furtively "daffing" the wheels with a mixture of water and paraffin ("Willy", he calls it)' (Hodge, 1939). Ex *daffy*, C.19 s. for gin.

daffies. Strong liquor: market-traders'. (*M.T.*). Same etym. as prec.

daffodil. An effeminate and precious young man: since ca. 1945. Bason, 1952.—2. Synon. with **crocus**, 3. (Irwin, 1986.)

Daffy. A Defiant fighter aircraft: 1941; by 1944, ob. (Jackson.) By Hobson-Jobson. Also *Deffy*.

daffy. A large number of telegrams for delivery: Post Office telegraph-messengers':—1935.

daffy-down-dilly. Silly: r.s., mainly theatrical. (Franklyn.) P.B.: or it may be an elab. of synon. *daffy*, adj.

daffy-headed. Feather-brained. See quot'n at **dimmo**, 2.

daft and barmy. Army: r.s.: later C.20. Barker, 1979.

daft as a brush(, as). Extremely stupid; very silly: orig. N. Country rural, since ?mid-C.19, it > by mid-C.20, due to the mixing influence of the Armed Forces and the picturesque aptness of the phrase, very much more widely known and used. Cf. **wet as a scrubber.** (P.B.) Rees, 1980, attributes *daft as* . . . to the comedian Ken Platt, who adopted it in the early 1940s from Northern *soft as a brush*.

daft-man. To refuse (a person) peremptorily or vigorously or to take no notice of him: tailors': 1928 (*Tailor and Cutter*, 29 Nov.). Lit., to render daft.

dag up. To smarten oneself for guard or parade: Army: earlier C.20. (F. & G.) Poss. ex *dagging* sheep, that is, removing lumps of dried excreta from their rear ends; or poss. a corruption of *dog up*.

Dagenham dustbin. 'Ford motorcars in general and the Ford *Escort* specifically. Cf. **Hedge-hopper** for the Ford *Sierra*; it was alleged that the series had a tendency to do this, because of bad aerodynamic design, when cornering at high speed' (Watts, 1988): motorists'. P.B.: this sort of insult is not new: cf. **tin Lizzie.**

dagger. A jockey's general helper: Aus. sporting: since ca. 1925. B., 1953.—2. Abbr. **dagger E**, etc.

Dagger Div, the. The 14th Indian Division: Army: WW2. Ex its divisional flash. P-G-R.

dagger E; dagger G; dagger N. An officer with high specialist qualifications in engineering—gunnery—navigation: RN officers': since ca. 1925. Granville, 'In the Navy List a dagger appears against the names of such officers'; *E, G, N* are traditional abbreviations. Also a *dagger gunner*, a Gunner (W.O.) that has passed the advanced course in Gunnery.

dags. Cigarettes: military: earlier C.20. (F. & G.) Perhaps ex dial. *dag*, the stem-end of a branch, the big end of a faggot (*EDD*): cf. **fag** ex fag-end.

dailies. See MOVING-PICTURE SLANG, §6, in Appx.

daily. A daily maid-servant: from ca. 1920: coll., verging on S.E. *OED* Sup.—2. Daily bread, or the money to buy it: coll.: since ca. 1925, 'Well, I must go and earn the daily'. Ex the Lord's Prayer.—3. One's daily bet with a 'bookie': coll.—4. A tail. Short for **Daily Mail**, 1. It has, since ca. 1930, meant 'rectum, arse', as in Newman, 1970. In 1977, Newman has 'He found another car up his daily'—which could mean either sense.

daily body. A daily help (servant): coll.: since ca. 1918. Mac-Donald, 1932.

daily-bread. A wage-earner; the working head of the house: from ca. 1890. Cf.:-

daily-breader. A C.20 var. of **daily-bread**: coll. Ruck, 1940.

daily dozen, (one's or) **the.** Physical exercises, on rising in the morning: coll.: from ca. 1924.

Daily Exaggerator or **Daily Suppress.** *Daily Express*: joc.: since ca. 1912; ob. by mid-C.20.

Daily Liar, The. *The Daily Mail*: joc. (not slanderous): earlier C.20. Perhaps ex Cockney *Dily Mile*.

Daily Mail. 'Buttocks (tail): "He fell on his Daily Mail"; also bail, "Guvnor, what's the chances of the old Daily Mail?"; also tale, "He spun me a Daily (Mail) I just couldn't believe"; also sexual proclivity, e.g., "She's Daily Mail all right" (she is accommodating in the sexual sense)' (Powis): all are r.s.: all have been current throughout most of C.20; the 'bail' sense since ca. 1920, the others earlier still. Franklyn records two other senses: 'ale', ob. by 1950 (*Rhyming*); and 'nail' (Franklyn 2nd): carpenters' and joiners'. The 'tail' sense can also be used for the rear of a car, as 'He would keep driving right up my Daily, all the bloody way.' A somewhat overworked piece of slang, definitely demanding context for clarity. (P.B.)

Daily-Tell-the-Tale. *Daily Mail*: joc. r.s.: since ca. 1920. Cf. prec.!

Daily Wail (occ. **Whale**), **The.** *Daily Mail*: joc.: from ca. 1910.

dainty digger. A member of the Women's Land Army. See **whistler**, 4.

dairy. In *get the dairy on*, to see; notice (a person): low s., perhaps orig. c.: from ca. 1910. (Leach, 1933.) Var. of **darry**.

dairy arrangements. The female breasts: low:—1923 (Manchon).

dairy Dot. A female milk 'roundsman'. See **whistler**, 4.

daisies occurs, as a gen. term for 'plants', in several phrases for 'dying' and 'dead (and buried)'. The best known in the later C.20 is prob. *push* (or *pushing*) *up the d.*; hence *daisy-pusher, -ing*; *under the d.*, *kick up d.* and *grin at the daisy-roots*; earlier there was *turn up* (one's) *toes to the d.*

daisy. A male homosexual: since ca. 1950 (?much earlier). Often ex daisy chain, 3, or the forerunner of 3.

daisy chain. 'We used a device christened the "daisy chain", made from gun-cotton primers threaded on a five-foot length of prima cord . . . . Five primers went to each daisy chain spaced out and held in place by knots in the cord' (Peniakoff, 1950): military (N. Africa): 1941–3, and afterwards elsewhere. Ex its appearance.—2. Collective cunnilingus, whether heterosexual or lesbian, but usu. the former: low: since ca. 1920.—3. A circle of homosexuals engaged in collective sodomy: widespread homosexual term: since ca. 1950.

daisy-cutter. A perfect landing: RAF: since ca. 1930. Jackson.

Daisy Dormer. Warmer (adj.): theatrical r.s. Ex the famous music-hall artist. Franklyn.

daisy roots. Boots: r.s.:—1874 (H., 5th ed.). I have never heard the singular used. Often abbr. to *daisies*.—2. Hence, shoes: mostly grafters'. P. Allingham.

daiture. Ten: Parlyaree: mid-C.19–20. An arbitrary spelling based on a Lingua Franca '*deca*.' See quot'n at **dewey**, and PARLYAREE, in Appx.

Dak. A Douglas DC-3 *Dakota* transport aircraft: Services': since 1943; ob. The aircraft first entered commercial service in 1933, and in 1987 there are still a few left flying.

dakes. Marbles: Aus. schoolchildren's. B., 1942.

Dalmatian pudding. That kind of boiled currant-pudding which since mid-C.19 has been known as *spotted dog*: RN. (Granville.) A Dalmatian dog has black or blackish-brown spots on its white coat.

dam. In *be on the dam*, (of a policeman) to be in trouble: police: since ca. 1920. *Free-Lance Writer*, Apr. 1948.

damager. A manager: theatrical, since ca. 1880; boxing, C.20; of a Services' canteen, since ca. 1925. Either by sarcastic perversion, by Hobson-Jobson, or orig. r.s., as Franklyn proposes.

dame. A girl; a sweetheart: Glasgow: from ca. 1932. Ex US, via the 'talkies'; nevertheless, the US prob. derived this usage

D

from Scots, where *dame*, a girl, appears as early as 1790 (Shirrefs, *Poems*): *EDD*. P.B.: much more widespread 1940s–50s.

dammit. In (*as*) *quick* or *soon as d-*, exceedingly quick, soon: coll. I.e., as saying *damn it!* Cf.:—2. In (*as*) *near as d-*, very near indeed: coll. (Grierson, 1931.) I.e., as near as *damn it!* is to 'real' swearing.

damn all. Nothing: coll.: from ca. 1915. A bowdlerisation of *fuck all.* B. & P.

damp, n. An umbrella: joc. and not very common: since ca. 1950. A pun on the synon. *gamp.* (Petch, 1966.)

damp, adj. Soft-headed, stupid, foolish: late C.19–early 20 (Knock). Cf. later **wet.**

damsel. A girl, any girl: as employed in Society and in the universities, post-WW1, the term has a facetious and coll. flavour.

Dan. A man in charge of a male public convenience: since ca. 1920. (Bell, 1954.) Ex the children's trad. taunt: 'Dan, Dan, dirty old man/washed his face in the lavatory pan' (P.B.).—2. 'A nickname for a Roman Catholic: "Are you a Billy or a Dan?" ' (Munro, 1985): Glasgow.

Dan Leno. ' . . . bobbins, known as the "Dan Lenos" (a seaman's corruption of the name of the Frenchman who developed them), are the ultimate parts of the [trawl] trap's width' (Piper, 1974). See also **danner.**

dance the stairs. To break into a flat or an office; do a quick 'job': c. Leach.

dancers. Stairs; a flight of steps: from ca. 1670; until ca. 1840, c.; then low s. or archaic c. (Head; B.E.; Grose; Lytton.) The term, occ. heard in WW1 and since, is ob. Because one 'dances' down them. P.B.: but not ob. in Leicester, at least, later C.20. (BBC Radio Leicester, 20 June 1984.)—2. As in, 'He had it on his dancers: he ran away' (Powis): c.: current in 1970s.

dancing. 'Locomotive wheels slipping on rail' (McKenna, 1970): footplatemen's.

dancing about. 'Then the "dancing about" and "verbals" began. In such confrontations [between supporters of rival football teams], fans invite each other to "come on then", "when you're ready". Some bounce up and down on the balls of their feet, others stand relatively still' (Armstrong, 1985).

dancing-master. A boxer continually 'dancing about': pugilistic:—1923 (Manchon).

danger. 'Chance or likelihood, used ironically when something expected or desirable is not forthcoming: "Any danger of you getting a round in?" . . . *No danger* is an emphatic phrase meaning "certainly, that is a certainty, etc." "Will ye be there the night?" "Aye, no danger!" ' (Munro, 1985): Glasgow. Some Army use since mid-C.20 (P.B.).

danger light; danger signal. A red nose: mostly Cockneys'.

dangle from. To coït with a woman: low: since ca. 1910. Esp. in 1970s, in the low comment between males admiring a female, 'Cor! I could dangle from *that!*' Cf. **hang out of.**

dangler. An emotional friendship between two boys: schoolboys'. A var. is *dangling.*—2. See HAULIERS' SLANG, in Appx.

dangling the Dunlops. 'Lowering the undercarriage on a jet airliner: aircrews' ' (Green, 1984). I.e. the *Dunlop* tyres.

dank. Inferior; inefficient: FAA: since ca. 1945. See **ace,** adj.

danner. A *dan*-laying vessel: nautical coll.: late C.19–20. A *dan* is a small spar-buoy carrying a flag. (P-G-R.) See **Dan Leno.**

danny. 'A "plain-clothes" CID car for surveillance use' (Green, 1985): police.

dap. To pick up; to steal, esp. luggage: c. Perhaps ex S.E. *dab*, v., or *do up.*—2. To go; to potter: RAF, esp. in Iraq: ca. 1935–45. Esp. in *dap about—across—over.* (L.A.) Perhaps cf. Persian *dav*, 'a stroke at play; a wager'. P.B.: more likely, a thinning of *dab*: cf. **dab-dab,** or ex *daps.*

darbies. Fingerprints: c.:—1950 (Tempest). Perhaps a var. of synon. **dabs.**

Darby and Joan. A telephone: r.s.: very late C.19–20.—2. Inseparable companions, with connotation of possible homosexuality: Army in India: ca. 1880–1947. Pl. *Darby and Joans.* Allen, 1975.—3. In *on* (one's) *Darby and Joan*, alone: r.s.: earlier C.20. (Kersh, 1942.) Cf. the, in later C.20, commoner *on one's Tod*, q.v. at **Tod.**

dark and dirty. Rum and coke [Coca-Cola]: RM: later C.20. Hawke.

dark as the inside of a cow. (Of a night) pitch-black: nautical: from ca. 1880. In Can., where the phrase is not merely nautical, it has the C.20 extension *tail down and eyes shut.* (Leechman.)

dark brown voice. A voice that is low, well-modulated, and sexually attractive: at first perhaps mainly feminine usage, then more gen.: since (?)ca. 1950. The phrase was used to describe the BBC Radio 3 announcer Patricia Hughes's voice in the *Listener*, 14 June 1979, and in an unrelated article in the magazine *In Britain*, July 1979. Perhaps from the idea in '[She] spoke seldom, but when she did it was in a voice like dark brown velvet and no one interrupted her' (Tey, 1946). Cf. the Jamaican use of 'red voice', for one high-pitched with anger. (P.B.)

dark money; dark time. 'Extra wages paid for night work' (McKenna, *Glossary*): railwaymen's: mid-C.20.

dark 'un. See **dark horse.**—2. A 24-hour shift: Aus. dockers' coll.: since mid-C.20. (Wilkes.) Cf.:—3. In *cop a dark 'un*, to be put on overtime in the winter: dockers': from ca. 1920. *Daily Herald*, late July or early Aug. 1936.

Darky Cox. A box: r.s. A theatrical box. 'Rarely used' (Franklyn 2nd).

darl. (Only in address and endearment.) Darling: Aus. coll.: not gen. before ca. 1920. Prichard, 1930; Cleary, 1952.

darling in post-WW1 Society use as a term of address for even a comparative stranger is rightly considered s., though by 1933 it had > j.—P.B., 1979: in East Midlands dial. it is used in address as indiscriminately as the Londoners' 'Love' or Durham 'Flower'.

darling, adj. Charming; 'sweet': orig. Society feminine: since ca. 1900. Benson, 1910, 'But indeed I want neither pictures nor a carpet, though it is darling of you to offer me them.'

darlings, the. The prostitutes of the King's Cross (Sydney) area: taxi-drivers', and the local residents': since ca. 1930. (B.P.)

Darlo. Darlinghurst, Sydney: Sydneyites': from ca. 1920. See **-o,** coll. and s. suffix.—2. Darlington, Co. Durham: Army, esp. troops stationed at Barnard Castle: current in 1970s.

darry. 'Look. "Let's have a darry at your reader" = let me have a look at your book' (Tempest): prisons': mid-C.20. See also **dairy.**

dart. 'A very quick try or last-minute effort' (H. & P.): Services': mid-C.20. Cf. **have a stab at something.**—2. 'Abbr. Dartmouth: [hence] an RN officer trained at Royal Naval College, Dartmouth' (Green, 1984): RN: since early C.20. Contrast **Pubs.**

dartboard. See **secondhand dartboard.**

dash. An attempt, esp. in *have a dash at*: coll.:—1931. (Lyell.) Cf. *have a cut* or *smack at.*—2. Dashboard of a motor-car: motorists' coll.: since ca. 1916.—3. In *do* (one's) *dash*, 'To reach one's Waterloo' (Dennis): Aus.:—1916.—4. In *s'elp me Dash!*, a rather illiterate euph. coll. var. (Manchon, 1923) of *s'elp me God!*—5. Worthington dark beer: nicknamed thus in the Swansea area. Glover, 1985.

dash on to. See **dashes.**

dash up the channel. A coïtion: English coastal fishermen's. Mostly in the south, the English Channel being implied.

dashes. A smacking, as in 'Give the chavvy [child] his dashes': market-traders'. (*M.T.*) Hence also *dash on to* = to chastise; cf. **dell.**

date. An appointment, esp. with a member of the opposite sex: coll.: adopted, ex US, ca. 1905.—2. Hence, the person with whom one has a 'date': adopted, ca. 1944, ex US.—3. The anus: Aus. low: late C.19–20. Cf.:—4. The buttocks: market-traders': since ca. 1919. (*M.T.*) It doesn't *have* to derive from sense 3.—5. A 'soft' and silly person, a 'twit', esp. in the phrase *soppy date*: coll.: since late 1940s. Perhaps ex sense 3 or 4. Cf. the phrase *you date!* = 'Well, you are an odd sort': proletarian:—1923 (Manchon). See also **daty**.

date up. (Gen. in passive.) To fill the time of (a person) with appointments: from ca. 1930; orig. US. Ex **date**, 1.

dateless. (Usu. of a girl) silly; foolish; 'slow': coll.: since ca. 1938. Ex dial. (Knocked) unconscious, stupefied; foolish; crazy (*EDD*). Perhaps influenced by the fact that such a dim-witted wench might lack 'dates' with boys. Cf.:-

daty. Soft-headed; sun-struck: military: early C.20. (F. & G.) By perversion ex the dial. *dateless* (knocked) unconscious.

daw-daw; daw-yaw. Slow-witted: coll.: since ca. 1950. Ex a supposed yokelish stammer.

Davy Crockett. A pocket: theatrical r.s.: 1956+. (Franklyn.) In the mid–1950s there was a (completely commercially-inspired) burst of interest in the American folk-hero, and every little boy suddenly wanted a coon-skin cap. The name is still potent in the children's 'hall of fame', giving rise to such riddles as 'How many ears has Davy Crockett?' 'Three: a left ear, a right ear, and a wild front ear', thus commemorating the song about the 'King of the Wild Frontier'. (P.B.)

Davy Large. A barge: r.s.: late C.19–20.

dawn hopper. An enemy raider 'plane using the uncertain light at dawn to slip away and get home: RAF: 1940–5, then merely historical. H & P.

day and night. Light ale: late C.19–20. Rhyming on *light*.

day-and-night merchant. See **copper-bottom**, a driver who exceeds the regulation number of hours at the wheel.

day-on. 'Duty Boy' or officer-of-the-day: RN: since ca. 1925.

day-tripper. A heartbreaker, esp. one who pretends to be serious, so that he may get his sexual way: 1966+. 'Obviously from the Beatles' song 'Day Tripper', released on 3 Dec. 1965' (Janssen).

day's dawning. Morning: r.s. Superior form: *day's a-dawning*. Franklyn.

days to do. The overriding obsession of the National Servicemen, 1947–62: how many more days of their 2-year stint had they still to undergo.

dazzle(-)dust. Face-powder. See CANADIAN . . . , in Appx.

dazzle with science. To out-box; fig., to defeat by sheer brains: coll.: since ca. 1940 at latest superseded by the now (late 1970s) widespread **blind with science**, q.v.

dead, n. An empty house: c.: later C.20. *Now!*, 10 Apr. 1981.

dead, as an adv., has, since ca. 1940, been increasingly popular, esp. among teenagers, in the nuances 'extremely', e.g. 'He's dead nice', and 'completely', e.g. 'Don't be dead stupid'. These usages apparently spring immediately ex such phrases as '*dead* tired' and 'to stop *dead*', as a very intelligent teenager has suggested in a letter, 1965.

dead air-gunner. Spam (a kind of tinned meat-loaf): RAF: 1940 +. (L.A.)

dead baby. See **baby's head**.

dead centre. A cemetery: joc.: since ca. 1940.

dead chocker. Utterly bored: Services' coll., ca. 1950–70; adopted by the coffee-bar set of teenagers ca. 1955–9. (Gilderdale.) (P.B.)

dead chuffed. Highly delighted: details as prec.

dead-copper. An informer to the police: low Aus.: since ca. 1920 (B., 1943). By the 1970s, at latest, in Aus. prison s., it had become simply *copper*. (McNeil.)

dead easy is a Cockneys' coll. phrase to describe any such woman (other than a prostitute) as is ready to go home and sleep with a man.

Dead End Kids. Self-description of RNVR Lieutenants despairful of becoming Lieutenant-Commanders: 1942–5. (Granville.) Cf. **Abbeville Kids**.—2. '[Some American ferry-pilots] made a habit of flying through the most appalling weather. We [British ATA pilots] nicknamed them the "Deadend Kids" . . . To this day the term "Dead-ending" persists to

describe flying through unusually bad weather' (Phelps, 1946).

dead-end street. The female pudend: Can.: since ca. 1930.

dead fall. A Western stunt rider in motion pictures: cinematic: since ca. 1925.

dead from the neck up. Brainless; habitually tongue-tied: since ca. 1920. Mais, 1948.

dead hand. An expert: Aus.: since ca. 1925. Baker.

dead handsome. 'Said of a circumstance that is fortunate and that turns, by whatever means, to one's advantage' (L.A., 1959): since ca. 1955.

dead head. A useless person, 'dead-beat' or 'no-hoper': since ca. 1950. (P.B.) Hibbert, 1983, defines it as 'A person of low intellect; a bore'.

dead horse. Sauce: Aus. r.s. Baker.

dead in the water. 'Helpless: widespread in Can. and US in ref. to an antagonist, as, "I got him now. He can't move. He's dead in the water." ' (Leech, 1986.) Noted in UK journalese a year later: 'Mr John Leese, editor of both the [London] Standard and the Evening News [said], "This obviously means that Mr Maxwell's [rival] paper is dead in the water" ' (*Guardian*, 2 Mar. 1987).

dead legs. A lazy or stupid or useless person: Army and RAF; mildly abusive: since ca. 1950. (P.B., 1974.)

dead loss. A person, place or thing that is decidedly 'dud' (dull; inefficient; without amenities): RAF, since ca. 1940; hence, post-WW2, gen. coll. Orig. cited by McDouall, 1945: ex a plane no longer serviceable.—2. Hence, of a job, or a course of action, lacking prospects; unpromising: since ca. 1946.

dead man's effects. False teeth: Services': since ca. 1939. (H. & P.) Often the only thing he has to leave.

dead matter. Type that has been run and could now be 'dissed': Can. printers' coll.—2. Hence, anything that, used or finished, can now be either returned to its place or discarded: Can. coll.: since ca. 1920. (Leechman.)

Dead Men's Shoes Department, the. 'That section of Air Ministry Personnel Branch [that was] responsible for returning to the next-of-kin the personal effects of casualties: WW2' (R.S., 1971).

dead nuts on. A C.20 intensification of later C.19 s. *nuts on*, delighted with, enthusiastic about, obsessed with.

dead on. A var. of **dead steady**, q.v.—2. Absolutely right: since ca. 1945. Ex the RAF sense of 'right on the target'. (Behan, 1958.) Hence, an affirmative response, 'Correct!'.

dead-pan (expression). Expressionless; impassive: adopted, ca. 1944, ex US servicemen. Ex US s. *dead pan*, an expressionless 'pan' or face (cf. the Eng. s. *dial*)—orig., theatrical.

dead pony gaff. A bad site: showmen's, esp. grafters'.

dead ring – or **spit – of, the.** Exactly, or almost, like; 'a remarkable likeness' (Dennis): Aus. *Ring* ex next; *spit* perhaps ex *spitting image*, and also Brit.

dead ringer of (or **for**). A 'spitting image': esp. Aus.; also Can., and perhaps later, Brit. 'The valet dressed in black (played by Eric Adjani, brother of Isabelle, and a dead ringer for her) is probably an illegitimate son of Don Giovanni' (*Guardian*, 24 Jan. 1979). Cf. prec. (Raab.) Cf. also **ringer**, 4, in the sense 'any genuine-appearing fake' (P.B.).

dead spit and image, the. The exact facsimile: Can. coll.: since ca. 1910. (Leechman.) In Brit. Eng. often appears, later C.20, as *the spitten image*. (P.B.)

dead spotted ling of. Very much like, strikingly similar to: Aus.: since ca. 1910. (B., 1942.) Rhyming on **dead ring of**.

dead steady or **dead on.** Applies to 'a good fellow': Guardsmen's: since ca. 1920. Grinstead, 1946.

dead stick is applied to the controls of an engine that has stopped: RAF: since ca. 1925. (Jackson.) Hence in phrases like 'a dead-stick landing' (R.C.).

dead to the world. Utterly drunk: s. verging on coll. P.B.: in later C.20 its use often implies simply 'very deeply asleep'.

dead trouble, be in. Mostly in the Services: 'to have flouted regulation or discipline, wittingly or not, in such a way that condign punishment is inescapable' (L.A., 1976): since ca.

1930. This use of *dead* seems, in such contexts, to be for *deadly*, but in many—as, e.g., 'That's dead easy'—it is clearly an adv. meaning 'extremely'.

deadend kids. See **Dead-End Kids.**

deadener. A bully; one who, strong and quarrelsome, tends to resort to his fists: Aus. Russell, 1936.

deado. A corpse: since ca. 1950. Craig, 1976.

deads. Dead drunk; fast asleep (*dead to the world*): RN: since ca. 1920. (P-G-R.)

Deaf and Dumb, the. The Ministry of Information: taxi-drivers': ca. 1940–5. *Weekly Telegraph*, 13 Sep. 1941.

deal. 'I had a deal last night'—a successful crime: c. Sharpe, 1938.—2. 'Small amount of cannabis. May refer to an ounce of hashish' (Home Office): drug-users': current in 1970s.

Dean and Dawson was Stalag Luft III's prisoner-of-war-in-Germany s. for their forgery department: 1942–5. (Brickhill, 1946.) Ex the fact that it handled passports, identity cards and other 'papers'; in short, a compliment to the well-known firm of travel agents.

deaner, occ. **denar, deener,** or **dener.** A shilling: from ca. 1835; orig. tramps' c.; in C.20, racing and low.—2. One penny: c.: mid-C.20. (Tempest.) Perhaps confused with *dee*.

dear John. A girl's letter telling a man in the Armed Forces that she no longer loves him. Orig. US, since 1942, >, by 1945, Can., by ca. 1950, Brit. In the very early 1950s there was a 'pop' song, of which one stanza ran 'Dear John, Oh, how I hate to write!/Dear John, I must let you know tonight/That my love for you has gone/Like the dew upon the lawn/and I'm to wed another, dear John.' (P.B.)

dear-stalker. A wealthy idler addicted to ogling and following pretty shop or office girls: earlier C.20. (Vachell, 1914.) Pun on *dear, deer.*

death. In *in the death*, finally; at last: since ca. 1945. (Norman.) Perhaps ex S.E. *in at the death*.

death adder. Machine-gun: Aus. soldiers': 1940+. B., 1942.— 2. (Mostly in pl.) A gossip; a cynic, esp. if old: Northern Territory (Aus.): since ca. 1930. Hill, 1951.

death adder man. An eccentric solitary, more often called a *hatter*: mostly northern Aus.: since ca. 1920. 'Some of them go under the name of death adder men, for it is reckoned they will bite your head off if spoken to before noon' (Marshall, 1962).

death chamber. 'The high tension cubicle of a diesel [locomotive]' (McKenna, 1970): railwaymen's, esp. diesel drivers', s.: since mid-C.20.

death drop. Butyl chloride, a very powerful drug: c.

death or glory lads, the. The Commandos: Army: 1942–5.

death seat, the. The front seat, next to the driver: Aus. motorists' coll.: since ca. 1945. The occupant is the most likely to be killed in an accident. (B.P.) Cf. **ride shotgun**.

death-tally. An identity disc: RN. P-G-R.

death watch. Attendance upon a man condemned to death: prison officers'. Tempest, 1950.

deb. A *débutante* in Society: coll. from ca. 1919; prob. ex US. Harrison, 1934, 'The usual dreary deb-parades they have in the country.'

deb chick. A *débutante* beatnik: mostly beatniks': late 1950s. (Anderson.) Punning S.E. *dab chick*.

debag (orig. usu. *de-bag*). An Oxford and (less) Cambridge term, from ca. 1890: to remove the 'bags' or trousers of (an objectionable fellow student). By early C.20, much more widespread usage. Cf.:-

debagged. Struck off the rolls: since ca. 1920. 'Sapper', 1935. Ex **debag**.

debbery. The state of being, the occasion of being presented as, a *débutante*—a practice that ceased in 1958: since the 1920s; by 1970, slightly ob.

debollicker. A small British mine that, trodden upon, fired a bullet upwards: Army: 1941+. (P-G-R.) The *de-* connotes 'removal'; for the main element, cf. **ballock**, testicle.

deb's delight, a. A 'highly-eligible [for marriage] chinless wonder', with plenty of money and little brain-power—the plebeian view of the upper-class young man: since ca. 1960 (?earlier). (P.B.)

debtor's colic. 'Any feigned illness whereby a man can get into hospital or remain sick in his cell, in order to avoid meeting his creditors. Every prison has its bad payers and when these report sick word goes round that "so-and-so has debtor's colic" ' (Tempest): prison s.: mid-C.20.

debug. To rectify mechanical, electrical, etc. faults: motorcyclists'. (Dunford.) Used also of computers and computer programmes: coll., verging on j.: adopted, ex US, ca. 1955. (P.B.)

debuggerable. Disreputable: 1930s.

decarb. To decarbonise: motorists' coll.: since ca. 1915. See **decoke**.

dece (pron. *deece*). Exceptionally good; 'wonderful': Can.: since ca. 1975. (Raab, 1977.) Cf. 'It's awfully *decent* of you' and the later **fab(ulous)**.

decider. (Gen. **the d.**) The winning set from even, i.e., the 3rd or 5th: lawn tennis coll.: from ca. 1925. Occ. in other games, e.g. cards. Ex racing, when a *decider* is a heat run off after a dead heat (*OED*).

decimal bosun. A Warrant Schoolmaster: RN: since ca. 1930. (Granville.) Ex mathematics.

deck. A landing-ground: RNAS/RAF: since ca. 1915.—2. Hence, 'the ground' in gen.: orig. RAF, since ca. 1925 (Jackson); by 1945, gen. s.—3. Floor: RN: late C.19–20. Carr, 1939. The orig. of sense 1.—4. 'Shot, injection, e.g., A deck of horse, an injection of heroin (Canadian, US)' (Home Office): drug addicts': current in 1970s. Stockley defines it, in UK usage 1986, as 'a small packet of drugs'. Used concerning quantities of drugs in US since—1936 (Spears).—5. In *on the deck*, penniless; destitute: c.: since ca. 1925. (*Gilt Kid*, 1936.) Prob. suggested by equivalent *on the floor*.

deck ape. A seaman: RN: later C.20. (Knight, 1985.) Cf. **fish-heads**, 2.

decker. A hat: Aus. (Baker.) Ex 'top deck'.—2. A peaked cap: Liverpool: ca. 1900–50.—3. A glance, a look: Aus. var. of *dekko*. Stivens, 1951.—4. A double-decker bus: Aus. omnibus users': since ca. 1935. (B.P.) Also among Brit. bus-drivers, later C.20. (L. Burt, 1987.)

decker-out. 'One who kept "cave" during any (card-)games of "banker" played in the streets of Belfast: 1930s. Ex Romany/Hindi *dekko*, to look' (Gardner, 1978). Cf. **decker**, 3.

deckie. A deck-hand: coll.: from ca. 1910. (*OED* Sup.) ?Esp. trawlermen's: Piper, 1974; Lyndon, 1980. Hence *decky learner*, an apprentice deck-hand (Piper).

decks. Trousers: young men's: later C.20. (Hibbert, 1983.) P.B.: perhaps ex *Daks*, a tradename.

decoke has, since ca. 1945, everywhere superseded **decarb-** (onise) engine cylinders.

decorate the mahogany. To put down—on the bar—money for drinks: Can.: earlier C.20. (Leechman.) This sort of jocularly verbose and pompous slang belongs chiefly to the years ca. 1890–1914 (July).—2. (Of a man) to lay the housekeeping money on the table: mostly lower-middle class: 1930s.

dedigitate. Joc. pedantic form of *take your finger out*, hurry.

dee. See **d.**

deejay. See **disc jockey**.

Deek. A D.K.W. [*Das Kleine Wunder*] motorcycle, in production since 1919: motorcyclists'. (Dunford.)

deener. See **deaner**.

deep end. See **off the deep end**.

deep freezer. 'A girl or woman of the prim or keep-off-me type' (Petch, 1969): since ca. 1960. Obviously an allusion to the 'deep freeze' part of a refrigerator.

deep-noser. A pot of beer: Aus.: since ca. 1920. (Upfield, 1937.) As the beer sinks, so does the drinker's nose into the pot.

deep-sea beef. Haddock: RN lowerdeck. P-G-R.

deep-sea diver. £5: r.s., on *fiver*: later C.20. Advertisement in *Amateur Photographer*, 6 Dec. 1980.

deep-sea fisherman. A card-sharper on an ocean-liner: c. Leach.

deep-sea tot. A short measure of rum, the shortness (supposedly) caused by the roll of the ship: RN. P-G-R.

deep six, the. The grave (burial): Can.: since ca. 1920. (Leechman, 1970.)—2. Behind and below: RAF j. > coll.: later C.20. 'I [a fighter pilot] try sneaking up on [the enemy aircraft], hiding low in the trees in their "deep six" ' (*Phantom*).

deer-stalking. Running after women: joc.:—1923 (Manchon). By pun on *dear*. See also **dear-stalker**.

def. 'When Danny [a young graffiti artist in N. London] speaks approvingly of certain lettering he says it is "def". A great piece is a "burner". Poor work is "toy". Someone who copies another's style is a "biter" ' (*Guardian*, 14 Oct. 1987). Perhaps elliptical for '*definitely* (good, etc.)'; a *burner* is US black s. for a superlative performer (Chapman, 1986).

defective. A detective (not the fictional detective): joc.: since ca. 1925.

deff out. 'If a young woman started to go out with a fairly regular boyfriend, she usually lost touch with most of her girlfriends, often at the boy's insistence. This is *deffing out*. Mandy and Sandra [two working class girls] knew how easily deffing out could break up groups of friends . . . "We always said . . . that we wouldn't deff each other out if we went out with fellas, but she always does in the end" [said Sandra]' (Griffin, 1985): Birmingham.

Deffy. A Boulton and Paul *Defiant* two-seater fighter plane. See **Daffy**.

deficient. A person mentally deficient; also adj. Much less common than *mental* as adj.

degomble. 'Fids [q.v.] are a strange race, often with their own language. "Degombling" means to shake the snow off one's clothes: there is an affinity with a word like yomping [q.v. at **yomp**]' (a review of Sir Vivian Fuchs, *Of Ice and Men*, 1982); British Antarctic Survey members': later C.20.

dehydrate. 'Let's have a drink, all this talking dries me—dehydrates me, to use the modern slang' (Coles, 1946): since 1942, when dehydrated foods became fairly common.

deke out. 'To back out, shirking or failing in one's duties; to let others down: Can. and US: since 1950s. "Because Joe deked out on us, we can't do any more work" ' (Leech, 1986).

dekko, n. (esp. **take** or **have a dekko**) and v. An earlier var. was **dekho**. To see; to, or a, glance. Vagrants' (—1865), ex Romany *dik*, to look, to see (Sampson). In Army, common since ca. 1890, via Hindustani.

dekkoscope was, among soldiers in India in WW2, a var. of **shuftiscope**. The short, thick variety (*dekkoscope, mark one*) was also known as a *pile-driver*; the long, thin variety as *dekkoscope, mark two*.

delegate. A person seeking an advance: bank-clerks' (esp. Anglo-Irish): from ca. 1923.

Delhi Belly. Indian variety of the illness known as **Gippy Tummy**, q.v.

deli. A delicatessen: Aus.: adopted, ca. 1944, ex US soldiers. In later C.20, ?since ca. 1960, the term has followed the appearance of similar establishments in UK. (*Observer* mag., 4 Apr. 1982.) Cf. **chippy** and **chinkie**.

delicatessen. See **meat shop**.

dell. To chastise; to beat with one's fists; as in 'Dell on to him' (*M.T.*). Origin so obscure that the v. could come from '*dealt* with', or even '*deliver* a blow'. ?Romany.

delo. 'Delegate, in trade union parlance' (Wilkes): Aus.: since mid-C.20.

delouse. 'His squadron was "delousing" Fortresses as they came back home out of Holland . . . liquidating such enemy fighters as still persisted in pestering the bombers' (Brickhill, 1946): RAF: 1940+.—2. To remove mines and booby traps from (a terrain): Army: since ca. 1941.—3. To clear (a room) of secret listening devices: since ca. 1965. (Petch, 1969.) A pun on the US, hence almost imm. Brit., *debug*, which has always been coll., verging on informal S.E. in this sense.

Deluge. A Delage car: Cambridge: ca. 1925–39. By a pun.

delushious or **delushus.** (Esp. of a fruit dish) delicious: since the late 1940s. *Delicious* + *luscious*.

dem, n. and v. A demonstration; to demonstrate, esp. of how an article works: sales representatives', fairgrounds, etc.: since ca. 1925. (Butterworth, 1968.) Cf. **demo**.—2. See **dems**.

demmick. A soldier on the sick list; an article become unserviceable: Army: earlier C.20. H. & P., 'The derivation is probably "epi-demic-ked"; probably. P.B.: the second sense is still very much alive at, e.g. the Crich Tram Museum, for a broken down vehicle (Irwin, 1986).

demmy. A demonstrator: University of Leeds undergraduates': since ca. 1930. (Marples, 2.) Ex the official abbr., *dem*.

demo. A (political) demonstration: political: from ca. 1930. *Gilt Kid*, 1936.—2. A demonstration of *how* something is to be done: Army: since mid-1930s.—3. A lowering of one's place in class; also a v.t., esp. in passive: Charterhouse: from ca. 1919. Cf. **promo**.—4. Demolition, as in 'big baskets like you see demo boys filling up with stuff when they're knocking a dump down' (Draper, 1970): since ca. 1945.

demob, n. Demobilisation; hence *demob leave*, leave awarded on, and immediately following, demobilisation: Services': since 1945. Cf.:-

demob, v. To demobilise: since 1918. Gen. in passive.

demobitis. Among Servicemen, restlessness and excitement at approaching demobilisation: 1945+. See also **funnel fever**.

demon, n. and adj. applied to 'a super-excellent adept'. Coll.; from ca. 1882.

demon tweak. 'A motorcycle enthusiast who does his own tuning at home, in order to get more speed from his machine' (Dunford): motorcyclists': current in 1970s.

demon vino. Cheap Italian wine: Army in Italy: 1944–5. (P-G-R.) A pun on S.E. (revivalists') *the demon rum*.

Dempsey Press, the. The Kemsley Press: joc.: later 1930s. Ex its purchase of local newspapers and Jack Dempsey's heavyweight-boxing fame.

dems. 'All Naval personnel connected with "Defensively equipped merchant ships" ': RN: WW2. (Granville.) Also Army, because the army had sometimes to supply the ammunition.

Den, the. New Cross, London: earlier C.20.

dena; denar, dener. Var. spellings of **deaner**, a shilling.

denari. Since ca. 1910, the predominant form of C.19 Parlyaree *denarly* or *dinarlee* money. Noted by Pugh, 1914, and the only form adduced by Lester.

Denim Light Infantry, the. The 2nd Corps Reinforcement Unit in Tunisia: Army in N. Africa: 1943. (P-G-R.) A pun on the Durham Light Infantry, fighting in Tunisia at the same time.

dennyaiser. A mighty punch. See **Dinny Hayes**.

dental. Abbr. dental student: university coll.: from ca. 1905.—2. In the Services, to *go dental* is abbr. for 'to report sick with dental trouble'. (P.B.)

dented. Damaged; wounded. See **dinted**.

dentures. Gear wheels: motorcyclists' (Dunford): since ca. 1950.

Denver boot, the. 'The wheel clamp [to trap parking offenders], known variously as the Denver Boot or Jock's trap (after Assistant Commissioner Jock Wilson, who ordered the clamps)' (*You*, 20 Nov. 1983).

deolali tap. See **doolally tap**. Also *deolalic tap*.

dep. A deputy-governor of a prison, esp. at Dartmoor.—2. A department (e.g. Physics): Imperial College, London: since ca. 1930. Marples, 2.

Department of Stealth and Total Obscurity, the. Joc. (or, sometimes, bitter) ref. to the Dept. of Health and Social Security: earlier 1980s. (Barbara Huston, 1984.)

depot stanchion. 'A rating who has been an unconscionable time in barracks or Shore Establishment' (Granville): RN: since ca. 1930. Sarcastic. Cf. synon. **barrack stanchion**.

depresh, the. The Great Depression, the financial crisis that began in US in late 1929 and hit England in Jan. 1930: orig. (1931) US; anglicised in 1933; †.

depressed area. The abdomen: joc.: since ca. 1930. (Houghton, 1946.) Ex the sociological sense.

depth charge; but nearly always in pl., *depth charges*, figs: RN: since 1939. (H. & P.) By ca. 1941, RAF for prunes (Jackson). Both are mild laxatives. P-G-R.—2. *Emissio in coitu*: low joc.: since ca. 1942, orig.—like **combined operations**—a Services' witticism.—3. 'Prison "duff" . . . Anything heavy or stodgy, such as dumplings' (Tempest): since ca. 1941; orig., prison c.; by ca. 1955, also (low) s.

Derby. A railwaymen's coll. for the Midland Region: since ca. 1950. *Railway*, 2nd.—2. In *be in the Derby*, to be competing in the race for promotion, whether in the wardroom or on the lower deck: RN: since ca. 1940. P-G-R.

Derby Kelly. Belly: r.s.:—1900. (B. & P.) Gen. abbr. to *Derby Kell*, as in the pre-WW1 ditty, 'Boiled beef and carrots [twice]:/That's the stuff for your Derby kell,/Makes you fat and keeps you well . . . ' (L.A.).

dermo. Any skin affection: Services' and gen.: since ca. 1939. Ex dermatitis.—2. In Aus. Army, 1942–5, specifically a New Guinea skin disease. Cleary, 1954.

dero. 'A derelict, i.e. someone unemployed and destitute' (Wilkes): Aus.: since early 1970s.

derry. 'Derelict house' (Home Office): prisoners' s.: current in 1970s. Also 'used by homeless drunks' (Clayton, 1970).

Derry and Toms. Bombs: r.s.: WW2+. The ref. is not only to the former famous London store, but doubles on the *derry* of **derry on**, q.v. Franklyn.

Derry-Down-Derry (or *d.-d.-d.*). Sherry: theatrical r.s. Franklyn.

derry on, have a. To have a 'down' on: Londoners' and Aus. coll.: since ca. 1895. (Franklyn; Morris.) Morris derives ex the comic-song refrain *hey derry down derry*; but also operative is the dial. *deray*, uproar, disorder, itself ex Old Fr. *desroi, derroi*, confusion, destruction (*EDD*).

derv. Oil for diesel engines: Army coll., from 1940; soon > j. and gen. Ex *D*iesel-*e*ngined *r*oad *v*ehicle (fuel).—2. Hence, such a vehicle: coll./j.: since ca. 1950.

desert chicken. Bully beef: Army in N. Africa: 1940–3. P-G-R.

desert drivers. 'Men who worried excessively about reserves of sand and water' (McKenna): railwaymen's: since mid-1940s. An allusion to WW2 service in N. Africa.

desert lily. A circular or box-shaped funnel, adjustable—according to direction of wind—to a urine receptacle: RAF, esp. in N. Africa: 1940+. (L.A.) Cf. **desert rose.**

desert loneliness. Horseplay, or suggestive chaffing, in the desert: coll.: RAF in N. Africa: 1940–4. Atkinson.

Desert Rats, the. The Seventh Armoured Division in N. Africa: self-bestowed: 1941–3. Ex Mussolini's 'despicable desert rats'. (P-G-R.) The divisional flash worn on shoulder and shown on vehicles was the jerboa or desert rat.

desert rose. A urination-can let into the sand: Army in N. Africa: 1940+. Ironic. Cf. **desert lily.**

designer jury. A jury of predominantly young people, who may be intimidated or 'nobbled' (q.v., sense 8) by supporters of defendants facing charges of, e.g. hooliganism. Such a jury may be chosen ('designed') by defending lawyers' judicious use of challenges. *Daily Telegraph*, 3 June 1988.

desink. To de-synchronise (one's motors): RAF aircrews': since ca. 1938. Michie, 1940.

Desmond, a. A lower second-class degree: universities' joc.: mid-1980s. Ex coll. *two-two* [see **two-one**] and the S. African bishop, Desmond Tutu.

desk. See **fly a desk.**

despatch (one's) **cargo.** To defecate: euph., yet rather objectionable: low:—1923 (Manchon).

destat. To get rid of the *stat*utory tenants from (a property): since ca. 1954. Cf. the quot'n at **schwarz.**

destiny. One's fiancé (rarely fiancée): from ca. 1910: middle-class coll.

destroying. Serving, or a serving, in destroyers: RN coll.: since ca. 1939.

det. A detonator: Services' coll., since ca. 1910; since ca. 1945, gen. Draper, 1970.

detox. Detoxification: coll.: later C.20. (P.B.)

detrimental. A male homosexual: coll.: earlier C.20.

deuce. The sum of two pounds (£2): London's East End: since ca. 1947. (Herd, 1957.)

deucer. A double shift; double time: Aus. (industrial) workers': since ca. 1910. Cusack, 1953.—2. One who can shear 200 sheep in a day: Aus. rural: Wilkes.—3. The second steward in a liner: nautical: earlier C.20. (Bowen.) Like senses 1 and 2, ex deuce = two (since mid-C.17).

devastating has, from ca. 1924, been Society s., as in 'Quite too devastating, darling.' Benson, 1933, 'The banal epithets of priceless and devastating just fitted her.'

Deviation Dick. A compass-adjustor: RAF: ca. 1940–5. (Hinde, 1945.) By personification, by alliteration and by ref. to the correction of compass deviation.

deviator; deviation. A crook; a crime: since ca. 1950: c. >, by 1965, s. (Cook, 1962.) Ex euph. S.E. *devious*, 'shady' or crooked. P.B.: or from sociological j.

devil me arse! An expletive: Anglo-Irish: Leechman.

devil nobody, that. Applied to the person causing an accident, or responsible for an error, when no one admits culpability.

dew-drop. 'I am going to knock off that "dew-drop", meaning the lock of the gas meter' (*Sessions*, 17 Oct. 1910): low.—2. 'Right in the nose of a rigid airship is a large metal coupling known as the "dewdrop", for making fast to the mooring mast, when on the landing ground' (*Airship*, III, no. 10, 1936): aviation coll.: since ca. 1933; by 1946, merely historical.—3. Drop of transparent liquid on the end of a person's nose: coll. (P.B.)—4. A compliment: 'much used by Society young ladies in the early C.20; they were avid for dew-drops. See, e.g., Lady Cynthia Asquith's *Letters*' (Carrick, 1985).

dew on, (have) got a. (To be) sweating: miners'. *Daily Herald*, 11 Aug. 1936.

dewey. Two: Parlyaree: mid-C.19–20. Lester, 1937, ' "What's the bottle, cull?"—"Dewey funt, tray *bionk*, daiture soldi medza, so the divvi is otta bionk nobba peroon, and tray medzas back in the aris (Aristotle)", which in plain English would read: "How much have we taken, pal?"—"Two pounds, three shillings and tenpence halfpenny, so we get eight shillings and ninepence each and put three-halfpence back in the box (bottle)".' See PARLYAREE, in Appx.

dex; dexo (pl. *dexes, dexies*). A dexamphetamine sulphate tablet: drug-users': since mid-1940s. The *dexo* form is Aus.

dhobi, dhoby; sometimes anglicised as *dhobey; dobie; dobey; dobee.* A native washerman: Anglo-Indian coll.: C.19—mid-20. Ex Hindustani *dhōb*, washing.—2. Hence, the laundry: Servicemen in Middle and Far East: since ca. 1945 at latest. 'Is it today sheets go to the dhobi?' (P.B.)—3. Hence, one's laundry: Services': since ca. 1945. 'What'll I do with my dhobi?'—'Take it up the QM's [Quartermaster's stores]'. See also **flying dhobi.**

dhobi, v. To wash one's clothes; often in form *dhobi-ing*: nautical (Bowen), then all Services: since mid-C.19. Sayers adds a chant from later 1950s RN: 'Dhobi, dhobi, dhobi, never go ashore./Never have to muster at the sick-bay door': i.e. stay on board and wash clothes and you will be safe from VD.

dhobi day. Washing day: RN: late C.19–20. H. & P.

dhobi dust. Any washing-powder; any of the advertised detergents: RN lowerdeck: since late 1940s.

dhobi itch. Skin-irritation, esp. ringworm: Army in India: latish C.19–mid-20. (Allen, 1977.) In C.20, also *dhobi rash.*

dhobi wallah. A washerman. Var. of **dhobi**, n. 1.

dhobi-ing firm. A partnership of ratings who—quite unofficially—do their messmates' laundry: RN. (Granville.) Also *dhobi firm.*

di-da, di-da, di-da. 'Mocking burden to drawn-out explanation or, esp., complaint. Frequent in Geoffrey Cotterell, *Then a Soldier*, 1941' (L.A.): since ca. 1930.

diabolical. 'In the late 1960s this S.E. [word] has suddenly attained wide popularity as a coll. intensive of dislike, [as in] "It's diabolical, the way the rates keep going up" ' (R.S., 1969). P.B.: 'diabolical liberty' seems to have become, later 1970s, a tied phrase, as in 'They're taking a diabolical liberty if they think they can. . . .' Cf. *horrendous*.

Diana dip. A swim naked: girls' schools': late C.19–earlier 20. Ruck, 1935.

Diana Dors. See TOMBOLA, in Appx.

diarrhoea. In 'I've got the diarrhoea' = I've got the idea: South London: 1930s. (Roberts, 1985.) A deliberate mangling for joc. effect.

diary, the. Diarrhoea. See PRISONER-OF-WAR SLANG, §12, in Appx.

dib. A partly-smoked cigarette, cached for future use: National Servicemen's coll.: early 1950s. Perhaps ex the action of stubbing it out. (P.B.)

dib-dabs, the. A frequent var. of the **abdabs**, q.v.

dibs and dabs. Body lice: r.s. on *crabs*. Franklyn 2nd.

dic. A dictionary: coll.: late C.19–20. In Murray, 1977, with a chapter headed 'The Dic and the Little Dics'. So prob. first used by Sir James Murray (1837–1915) and his family. Also *dick* and *dicker*.

dice. To ride strenuously: Army mechanical transport: WW2. See **dicing** for derivation.—2. To get rid of: Aus.: since ca. 1920. *Rats*, 1944, 'It's me name, but it's too cissy, so I dices it and picks up "Mick".' Ex *discard*, proposes E.P.; but Wilkes suggests the more likely 'lose by playing at dice'.

dicer. A pilot undertaking a 'dicey' operation: RAF: ca. 1940–5.—2. The sortie itself: RAF: 1941–5. Ex **dicing**, 1. (Sanders.)

dicey. Risky; dangerous: RAF: 1940+; by 1946, common among civilians: cf. next entry.—2. Hence, esp. in 'It's a bit dicey', chancy and tricky: since early 1950s. (L.A., 1960.)

dicey on the ubble. 'Going thin on the top': Teddy boys': ca. 1955–60. (Gilderdale, 2.)

dicing. Flying; properly, operational flying: RAF: 1940+. Cynically and refreshingly joc., in derision of the journalistic *dicing with death* (so often heard in May.–Oct. 1940). 'In a letter to *The Daily Telegraph* of 22 June '68, Mr W.A.H. Watts of Sunbury says that "dicing with death" was commonly used by motor racing enthusiasts long before 1939 and attributes it to the motor racing correspondent of one of the motoring journals of that era' (R.S.).—2. Hence, a 'duel' between two drivers: car racing drivers' and the commentators': since ca. 1955.

dick, n. The penis: military, from ca. 1880. The term had, by ca. 1960, acquired the generic sense of the female need for sexual intercourse, as in 'She was crazy for dick' (Thomas, 1976). Prob. by personification; cf. **John Thomas**.—2. A perambulator: early C.20. Lyon, 1916.—3. A detective: C.20. Owes something to the 'Deadwood *Dick*' stories and to the '*Dick* Tracy' comic strip?—4. A look, a glance: market-traders': late C.19–20. (*M.T.*) Ex the v.—5. In *have had the dick*, to be 'all washed-up' or finished, esp. financially or in one's career: Aus.: since ca. 1920. (B.P.)—6. See **clever dick** and **thick dick**.—7. (Usu. pl.) 'Lice, vermin' (Tempest): low or c.: mid-C.20.

dick, v.t. and i. To look, peer; watch: N. Country c.: from ca. 1850. (H., 3rd ed.) Ex Romany: cf. **dekko**. Current, 1970s, in market-traders' *argot*, as in 'Dick at the gorger's conkie' (*M.T.*).

Dick Dunn. Sun: r.s. Lester derives it ex 'a famous book-maker'.

Dick Turpin. 13: darts players': r.s. *Evening News*, 2 July 1937.

dicker. 'In its intelligence gathering, the IRA uses a wide network of "dickers", or spotters, to study security force movements' (*Daily Telegraph*, 17 June 1988). Agent of **dick** v.

dickey, dicky, n. A word; shortened r.s. See **dickey-bird**, 1.—2. The sailor's blue 'jean' collar: RN.—3. A windscreen on a motorcycle: motorcyclists': since ca. 1950. (Dunford.) Ex S.E., a detachable shirt-front.

dickey, dicky, adj. In bad health, feeling very ill; inferior, sorry; insecure; queer: from ca. 1790; hence, in C.20, of plans or things: tricky, risky, 'dicey': coll.

dickey-, gen. dicky-bird. A word: r.s.: late C.19–20. In full in such contexts as 'What you lookin' at me like *that* for?—I never said a dicky-bird, did I!'; but in Harrison, 1943, shortened: 'I give yer me dicky.'—2. See PRISONER-OF-WAR SLANG, §4, in Appx.—3. The penis: Can. schoolboys': since (?)ca. 1950. (D.J. Barr, 1968.) An extension of **dick**, n., 1.—4. A clock: London c., *dickory dock* shortened. Barnes, 1976.

dick(e)y diddle. To urinate; a urination: Cockney juvenile r.s. on *piddle*. Cf. **Jimmy Riddle**. Franklyn.

dick(e)y dido. The female pudend: low and raffish: C.20; ob. by ca. 1950, except where embalmed in the chorus of a ribald song, to the tune of 'The Ash Grove': 'I've felt it, I've seen it; I've been in be-bloody-tween it—and the hairs of her dicky dido hung down to her knees!' (P.B.)

dickey pilot. A pilot flying with an experienced pilot for instructional purposes: RAF: since ca. 1930. He occupied the *dickey seat*. See also **second dickey**, 2.

dickhead An idiot; stupid fool: later C.20. Hibbert, 1983.

Dickie's. Dr Barnardo's Home at Kingston, Surrey: boys' and old boys': since ca. 1950. (*Woman's Own*, 2 Oct. 1965.)

dickory dock. A clock: r.s.: from ca. 1870. Ex the nursery rhyme.—2. Penis: r.s. on *cock*. Franklyn 2nd.

did. Short for *didikai, didekei, diddikoi*, etc., all var. spellings of the term for a near-gypsy: S. England rural coll. (P.B.) See **didekei** and **diddy**.

did I buggery – or **fuck** – or **hell!** A violent negation. See **like fuck!**

diddle. To digitate sexually and successfully: Can. Cf. **daddle**.

diddlum. Dishonest; illicitly manipulated: low, esp. grafters'. *Cheapjack*, 1934, ' "It's these ruddy diddlum machines wot's done it," he said.' I.e. *diddle 'em*.

diddly-donks. 'Main engines, diesel' (Malin, 1979): RN Submariners': mid-C.20. See **donk**, 4.

diddly-dum, esp. *it's all diddly-dum*. Everything's fine: 'A term of approval among drop-outs at a "free" pop festival on Exmoor' (*Observer*, 13 June 1976: R.S.). A transient expression, worth recording not for its value in the vocabulary of youth, but for its apparently irresponsible origination.

diddy, n. 'A mild insult meaning idiot' (Munro, 1985): Glasgow. Ex widespread dial. for a woman's breast or nipple; cf. synon. insulting use of *tit*. Munro also notes *diddy around* or *about*, to act like a fool, mess about.

diddy, adj. Little: nursery (C.19–20) >, by ca. 1930, gen. coll.; by 1970s widespread, perhaps influenced by the comedian Ken Dodd and his references to the 'Diddy-men'. Cf. the Cornish *didgy* = small, tiny (*EDD*). (P.B.)

didee, the. The water-closet: Aus. (Hardy, 1967.) Perhaps orig. euph. for *dunnaken* or its derivative *dunny*.

didek(e)i. A gipsy: c. (Orwell, 1933.) Ex Romany *didakeis*, half-bred gipsies (Smart & Crofton). There are several var. spellings, e.g. *didakai, diddikoi*.

didgy. A dustbin: Glasgow. Munro, 1985.—2. 'Short for digital: "Err's yer didgy watches, three fur a pound!" ' (Ibid.): id.

didn't ought. Port (wine): r.s.: late C.19–earlier 20. (Franklyn.) Ex 'Oo! I didn't ought to.'

didn't oughter. Water: r.s.: ca. 1890–1920. Franklyn 2nd.—2. 'Daughter' (Powis): r.s.: current in 1970s.

dido. 'To steal from carts in the street' (B., 1942): Aus. c.

die the death. (Of a performer) to meet with a complete lack of response from the audience: theatrical, but esp. Variety, chiefly among comedians: since ca. 1940. Since ca. 1950, usually shortened to *die*, as in 'My gags didn't mean a thing (to the audience). I died!' (Merry).

123

diet pills. Amphetamine: drugs c. (Stockley, 1986.) US since—1972 (Spears).

diet sheet. A Mess menu: Service officers' (esp. RAF): since 1941. Jackson.

diff. A differential: since ca. 1920. Casey, 1942.

different. Special, unusual, recherché: 1912 (Canfield) >, by 1935, coll. (*OED* Sup.) P.B.: in 1960s and 70s used as a polite escape formula, similar to *interesting*, by those called upon to admire something which, in all sincerity, they cannot: 'Well, it's—er—different!'

differs. Difference: Anglo-Irish. O'Neill, 1959, ' "I don't suppose it'll make any differs, but," he said.' Perhaps via '*difference*'.

diffy. Deficient, as in 'He was diffy a hussif at the inspection yesterday': Army: since ca. 1939.—2. Difficult: Society: mid-C.20. Marsh, 1949.

dig, n. Loss of privileges: Guards': since ca. 1930.—2. A reprimand as an officially recorded punishment, 'sentenced to be reprimanded . . .': Army and RAF: since ca. 1925. Hence, a 'severe reprimand' is a *severe dig*. These punishments may involve loss of privileges, and be tied to loss of seniority. (P.B.)—3. An injection: medical: since ca. 1910. (Deeping, 1944.) Cf. **jab.**—4. In cricket, a turn at batting: Aus. schoolboys': since ca. 1930. (B.P.) An opportunity to 'dig in'?—5. A fisherman's stretch of water or other definite 'area': Aus. fishers' and anglers': since ca. 1920. Culotta, 1963.

dig, v. To irritate or annoy: Aus.: since ca. 1920. 'The man was taken aback. "What's digging you?" he blustered.' Niland, 1958. Semantically cf. 'What's got into you?'—2. To become aware of; look at and enjoy; to enjoy; to look at and understand; to understand and enjoy: jazz-musicians', hence also dance-fanatics': adopted, in Brit. ca. 1945, in Can. ca. 1938, ex US. (*Observer*, 16 Sep. 1956.) 'To get into and under the melody' (Priestley); ultimately from S.E. *dig into*, to investigate, to examine very closely. 'Now [among teenagers] means only "to enjoy or appreciate".' (Greenwood, 1965.) As a schoolboys' word, it had, by mid-1963, reached the 7–10 age group: *New Society*, 22 Aug. 1963.—3. Among beatniks, 'to *dig* is to like, admire, understand or be at one with' (Anderson): since ca. 1957. Ex sense 2.

dig out. To work cheerfully and with a will: RN lowerdeck: since (?)late C.19 (Goodenough, 1901). Granville quotes the WW2 'If anyone can do any better, let him ruddy well dig out, I'm chocker with the job.' R.C. suggests 'perhaps from digging out in swimming or rowing'.—2. To tidy (a hut, etc.): Army in France, 1915–18, and again in WW2. Kersh, 1941.

dig the drape. To buy a new dress. See CANADIAN . . . , in Appx.

dig up. To look for, to obtain, both with connotation of effort and/or difficulty: US (late C.19) >, ca. 1910, anglicised. Ex mining.—2. 'To annoy or deliberately provoke a clash with someone . . . "Are you digging me up?" is roughly equivalent to "Are you looking for trouble?" ' (Munro, 1986): Glasgow.

digger. The guard-room: Army:—1909 (Ware); ob. W. glosses 'short for "Damned guard-room".'—2. Hence, a prison: c. MacGill, 1920.—3. A common form of address—orig. on the goldfields—in Aus. and NZ since ca. 1855, and esp. common in WW1+.—4. An Aus.-style widebrimmed hat: hippies': ca. 1962–74.—5. (Often *D—*.) 'Idealist hippies undermining capitalist economies by giving away free clothes, washing machines to needy' (Fryer, 1967): hippies'. Probably the same sect as those defined in *Groupie*, 1968: 'the Diggers (those who have dropped out into rural bliss)': since latish 1950s. R.C. remarks: 'Presumably a reference to the [mid-]C.17 English radical movement of that name'. E.P.'s final comment: *Il faut cultiver son jardin*.

diggy. 'Inclined to give sly digs': coll. *OED* Sup.—2. Adj. of approbation: Leicestershire (?more widely) schoolgirls': ca. 1983. (C. Williams.)

dike, dyke. (Usu. *dyke*.) A lesbian: adopted, ca. 1935, ex US. Rodgers, 1972, defines the term: '1. the mannish, swaggering, cigar-puffing lesbian. 2. (pejorative) any gay woman'. —2. Diconal, a pain-killing drug: drugs c.: later C.20. *New Society*, 11 Aug. 1983.

dikey or **dykey.** Lesbian: since the late 1930s. Ex prec., 1.

dil. See **dill,** 2.

dill. *Dist*illed water: pharmaceutical chemists':—1909 (Ware).—2. At first recording, in B., 1942, *dil*, but thereafter *dill*. A simpleton; a fool: Aus.: earlier C.20 (*Lance-Corporal Cobber*, 1918). Cf. **dill,** 2.—2. An admiring substantive for a pretty, attractive girl, 'She's a real dilly': young men's: 1950s–60s. ?Ex the adj., sense 1. (P.B.)—3. As *the D-*, Piccadilly (the London street): c. (*Gilt Kid*, 1936.) Among prostitutes, *on the Dilly*, working that area.

dilly, adj. *Del*ightful: ca. 1905–25. *OED* Sup.—2. Foolish; half-witted: Aus. (Dennis.) Cf. **dilly,** n., 1, and **dill,** 2; but consider also Somerset dial. *dilly*, queer, cranky, recorded in *EDD* for 1873.

dillypot. See **dill-pot.**

dim, n. Someone blind, or almost so: Royal Nat. College for the Blind, Hereford, students': later C.20. Hence *dim-game*, a game organised for those so handicapped. (Scott, 1984.)

dim, adj. Unimportant, undistinguished; colourless, insipid. (Persons only.) Oxford University: ca. 1927–34. [Thus the orig. gloss; but the term, in this sense, has since become widespread gen. coll., and is applied to all sorts of things, affairs, places. P.B.] Waugh, 'Who's that dear, dim, drunk little man?' Suggested by **subfusc,** q.v.—2. Hence, dull, silly, stupid: Society: 1931; like sense 1, this has > widespread gen. coll. (Milne, 1931, in sense: dull, boring.) See quot'n at **crashing bore.** Cf. early C.19 s. synon. *opaque,* and **dim type.**

dim bulb. A very dull person; adj. very dull: Can.: ca. 1918–40. (Priestley.)

dim sim. A duplicating var. of **sim,** 1, a con-man's dupe, a simpleton: Aus. c. and low: since ca. 1950. (B.P.) *Dim sim* (or *sum*) is Cantonese for a snack, and appears thus in Chinese restaurant menus. (P.B.)

dim type. A stupid fellow (or girl): RAF (hence, WAAF): since ca. 1936. (Jackson.) See **type.**

dim view. See **take a dim view of,** to regard with disapproval.

dim-wit (occ. written solid). One who is slow to understand what is going on: since ca. 1935. A natural consequence of **dim,** 2.

dimbo. Var. of **Dimmo,** 2.

dimmer. A cigarette-end: Cardiff: since ca. 1930. (Shaw, 1952.) Cf. **dimp** and **nicker,** 2.—2. An insignificant person, or one out of favour: Public Schools': late 1940s. Poss. more gen., and later, usage. Ex **dim,** 2, by the 'OXFORD -ER'. (P.B.) Cf. **grimmer.**

Dimmo or **Dimo.** (Only in the vocative.) A Greek: Cockney. Ex *Demo*, short for *Demosthenes*, a very common given-name among the Greeks. Usu. pron. *Jimmo*. (Franklyn.)—2. A blockhead; stupid person: 'Move it [= hurry!], you dumbheads, you dimmos, you jerks' (Claire Villiers, reporting the words of a spoilt Canadian 'brat', in the overseas *Guardian*, 4 Sep. 1977); if not already Eng. in late 1970s, then soon > so: 'The daffy-headed dimmo who worries about glove compartments doesn't exist' (Jean Denton, re women buying their own cars, in *Sunday Express* mag., 25 Oct. 1981, p. 7). Also spelt *dimbo*.

dimp. A cigarette-end: Army: 1939+. (*Daily Mail*, 7 Sep. 1940.) As vagrants' coll. for 'the still-smokable stub of a cigarette' (Wilson, 1980). Cf. **dimmer.**

din-din. Dinner; hence, any meal; food: nursery coll.: late C.19–20. Hence, > adult joc. Has var. *din-dins.*

dine at the Y. To indulge in cunnilingus: Aus.: since the 1940s. *Y* is both the fork of the body and short for the *YWCA.*

diner. The racing c. form of **deaner,** q.v.

Ding. An Italian: Aus.: since ca. 1930. (B., 1942.) Also, a Greek: since ca. 1940. (Wilkes.)

ding, n. 'A shortening of *wing-ding,* a party: Aus.: since ca. 1958' (P.B. 1974). Echoic of noisy boisterousness; cf. **ding-dong,** 2.—2. The bottom of anything, esp. either the buttocks or a surf-board's base: Aus.: since late 1950s. (B.P.) Cf. **dinger,** 3.—3. 'A hole in the fibreglass sheath of the board' (*Pix,* 28 Sep. 1963): Aus. surfers': since late 1950s. Ex sense 2, which may also mean 'anus'.

ding, v.t. To name for a duty or responsibility: Army: late 1960s. Usu. in passive, as 'I've just been dinged for mess committee.' (P.B.)

ding-dong. A song: r.s.:—1859 (H., 1st ed.).—2. Hence, a domestic sing-song. In his *Cockney Ding-Dong,* 1975, Keeping begins his preface thus: 'All the songs in this book were sung at family parties (or "ding-dongs", as most Londoners would call them)': since ca. 1880 or a decade earlier. Extended, C.20, to a party: music-hall and theatrical.—3. A quarrel; set-to; fight: 'They were having a right old ding-dong'. Presumably ex the altercation, as of bells, or, cf. **barney,** 1, from a noisy party. (P.B.)—4. As an exclam. = 'That rings a bell' [stirs a memory]: semi-c.p.: since ca. 1960. (Petch, 1969.) Occ. also as a meaningless exclam. of surprise or pleasure.—5. See quot'n at **winkle-trip.**

ding dong bell. Hell, as in 'What the ding dong bell does he think he's playing at?': r.s.: esp. in RAF, WW2. Franklyn 2nd.

dingaling. An eccentric or 'oddball': Can., adopted, ca. 1965, ex US. *Daily Colonist* (Victoria, BC), 8 Oct. 1976. (Leechman.)

dingbat. A thingummy: Can.: since ca. 1920. (Leechman.)—2. A Chinese: Aus.: since ca. 1925. B., 1943.—3. A crank; an eccentric: Aus.: since ca. 1930. (Culotta.) Ex **dingbats,** 1.—4. A daredevil motorcyclist: motorcyclists': since ca. 1950. (Dunford.) Cf.:—5. In *go like a dingbat,* to travel very fast, esp. of aircraft: RAF: since ca. 1920. Perhaps ex the idea of a mad bat: cf.:–

dingbats. Eccentric; mad, gen. slightly: Aus. Army, ?—1914; since ca. 1925, gen. and common. (B.P.) Prob. ex *the dingbats,* delirium tremens: Aus. and NZ. Hence, madness: id. In later C.20, sometimes shortened to *dings* (Wilkes). Perhaps also influenced by *bats* or *batty,* crazy, and the longer synon. *bats in the belfry.* (Raab.)

dinge. Black (colour); generic for Negroes: from ca. 1930. (Harrison, 1934.) Ex *dinginess.*—2. A Negro: low s., adopted ca. 1944 ex US. (Cook, 1962.) The American term derives ex S.E. *dingy.* P.B.: by 1960s it had come to mean any member of a dark-skinned race: still low s.—3. As *the dinge.* The black-out: RAF bombing crews': 1939+.

dinged (pron. *dingh'd*). Concussed; in a state of concussion—hence in a confused mental state: sporting. It occurs in an article in the *Lancet,* 25 Apr. 1970. Ex the now informal S.E., and the dial., *ding.*—2. See **ding,** v.

dinger (pron. *dingh'r*). A telephone; a bell-system: since early 1930s. (H. & P.) Echoic.—2. Short for *humdinger,* 'anything excellent': Aus.: since ca. 1920. B., 1942.—3. Anus: (low) Aus.: since ca. 1935. 'Don't forget that he'll get more than a gentle tap up the dinger if something really goes wrong' (Harris, 1958, but dealing with Australians in Korea, 1953).—4. In *do a dinger,* to dodge work: RN lowerdeck.

dinghy. A sidecar: motorcyclists': since ca. 1950. (Dunford.) Cf. **caboose** and **chair.**

dingle-berries. Female breasts: low and raffish: later C.20. (Daniells, 1980.) See quot'n at **jujubes.**

dingo, n. An armoured scout car: Army: 1940–55. The term soon > coll. and then, by 1945, j.—2. A coward; a mean-spirited person; a human jackal: Aus. (rather allusive coll. than s.). Palmer, 1948.—3. Hence, a treacherous person: since ca. 1900. (B., 1953.) Ex **dingo on.**—4. A batman: Aus. soldiers' (esp. in New Guinea): 1942–5.

dingo, v. To shirk; to quit, back out of: Aus. coll.: since ca. 1910. Cleary, 1952, 'I don't think he's dingoing the race'.

dingo on. To betray (someone); to fail (him): Aus.: since ca. 1910. B., 1942.

Dink. A Chinese: Aus.: since ca. 1920. Baker in *Observer,* 13 Nov. 1938. Perversion of *Chink* on **dinge.** Franklyn 2nd holds it to be r.s. on *Chink.*

dink. Riding two on a bicycle meant for one. See **double-dink.**—2. Penis: Can.:—1949.—3. Hence (cf. synon. **prick**), 'A fool; a twit; a drippy person. Used thus in California in 1947' (Leech, 1985): Can.

dinkied up. Smartened up, made lively, 'tarted up': '[Northamptonshire] has few places dinkied up for the coach trade' (Purser, 1981). See **dinky,** adj.

dinkum Aussie. A native Australian: Aus.: late C.19–20. B., 1943.

dinkum oil, the. The truth: Aus.: from ca. 1910. (Dennis.) Ex *dinkum,* adj., honest, genuine.

dinky, n. As *the dinky,* the truth: Aus.: since ca. 1920. (Baker.) Short for *dinky-die.*—2. A 'big car, say, BMW' (York, 1980): upper-middle-class s.: later 1970s. Prob. by meiosis, on the brand name of a very popular make of model or toy cars. (P.B.)

dinky, adj. Up to the minute; lively, e.g. of pop music: since ca. 1970, or a year or two earlier. Naipaul, 1976: ' "Time for a little music," the first black publican says. "Reggae?," I ask innocently. He glares. "No," he says, calming himself. "Something really dinky." The music of Bert Kaempfert oozes from the speakers.' BK = large popular danceband, playing quite 'middle-of-the-road' music. (P.B.)

dinky-die. A var. (—1914) of *dinkum.* (Doone.) 'An intensive form,' says Wilkes, 'usually with nationalistic overtones.'

dinky doo. See TOMBOLA, in Appx. The number 22 in the game of House: military r.s. F & G.—2. 'Thingummy'.

Dinny Hayes, let loose a; Dinny Hayes-er. To punch; a punch, esp. a mighty punch: Aus. Ex a noted pugilist. Wilkes, in four citations spread from 1907 to 1949, has the var. spellings *dennyaiser, dinnyaiser, dinnyazer, dinnyhayser.* E.P.'s own source was Brandon, 1931 (for both forms used as key word).—2. Hence, something notable: Aus.: since ca. 1910. B., 1943.

dinted, occ. **dented.** Damaged; wounded, injured; greatly diminished: of persons, reputations, or fortunes: facetious coll.; from ca. 1910.

dinting. 'Digging out old ballast' (*Railway,* 2nd): Southern Region railwaymen's. Ex N. Country dial. *dinting,* 'the taking up of the bottom of a colliery road, in order to enlarge the road' (*EDD*).

dip, n. A hit at, esp. a continuous hard hitting of, the bowling: cricketers': earlier C.20. Cardus, 1934.—2. Diphtheria; a patient suffering from diphtheria; a case of diphtheria: medical, esp. nurses': 'We had three dips in this morning'; 'It's dip, you know'.—3. A simpleton: Aus. (known also in UK and US): since ca. 1925. (B., 1943.) Ex **dippy.**—4. A member of the Diplomatic Service: esp. in the Civil Service: since ca. 1945. Le Carré, 1968.—5. (Of a male) a short copulation: low and raffish: since ca. 1950. (Thomas, 1976.) Cf. **dip** (one's) **wick.**—6. 'A smaller lamp [than a **brute,** q.v.] movable by one man; its name goes back to the theatre where dips were plugged into outlets down small traps in the stage' (Daniells, 1980): photographers'.—7. As in 'Giz [give us, i.e. me] a dip', 'May I have some of your glue, please?': Northumberland teenage glue-sniffers': early 1980s. (Blyth Ridley, 1984.) Cf. **blowse.**—8. See **Dip, the.**

D

dip, v. See AUSTRALIAN . . . , in Appx., and **dipping.**

dip, adj. Diplomatic; of the Diplomatic Service: Civil Service and Police. (Benton, 1973.) Cf. **dip,** n., 4.

Dip, the. 'That part of Piccadilly (the thoroughfare) adjoining St James's Park, where male prostitutes once importuned wealthy homosexuals. A term known to many homosexuals throughout the UK and even abroad' (Powis).—2. As *the dip*. The assistant purser: nautical, esp. ships' stewards. Marlowe, 1937.

dip-boss, the. The senior officer in charge of a flight of anti-submarine helicopters: RN: later C.20. (Wingate, 1981.) Ex dipping sonar.

dip chick. A diver: RN. Granville, 'Corruption of Dabchick, or Little Grebe, a small diving bird'.—2. An evolution by an M-class submarine, in which it dives on approaching its target, bobs up, fires its 12-inch gun, and dives again: RN: 1930s. Edwards, 1939.

dip in. See BIRD-WATCHERS', in Appx.

dip (one's) **killick.** (Of a Leading Hand) to be disrated: RN. Granville, '[Killick is] the anchor which symbolised his rate'—cf. the RAF **props.**

dip out. To be unsuccessful in spotting a rare bird. See BIRD-WATCHERS', in Appx. This is a specialisation of:—2. To be unlucky when favours are being shared out, as 'Only a quarter of us were allowed away that weekend, and I dipped out': Services': since mid-C.20. Perhaps ex the idea of a bran-tub dip. (P.B.)—3. To 'duck out', e.g. of going on an outing, attending a mess function, etc.: Services': since mid-C.20. (P.B.) Aus. has *dip out on*, 'to renege, withdraw' (Wilkes).

dip south. To put one's hand in one's pocket for money, esp. if the money is running low: Aus. and NZ. B., 1959.

dip squad, the. Detectives operating against pickpockets: c., hence s., including police: since late 1940s. (Weightman, 1977.) Ex *dip*, C.19 s. n. and v., pickpocket.

dip the clutch. To de-clutch at the wrong moment, or, later, to de-clutch when, e.g., going down-hill, to conserve fuel: orig. Army mechanical transport drivers', then motorists' gen.: since ca. 1939. (P. Chamberlain, 1942.)

dip (one's) **wick.** (Of the male) to copulate: low: since ca. 1880. See **Hampton,** and **get on** (one's) **wick.**

dipping. 'The funnelling off by [airline] stewards of liquor from the free bottles of liquor that are available to first class passengers. This stolen drink is then decanted into empty miniature bottles and either taken home or more usually sold to regular cabin class passengers at the regular price, all of which is pocketed by the stewards. Thus big dipper = a jumbo jet on which such illicit profits are commensurately massive' (Green, 1984).

dippy. Extremely eccentric or foolish; mad: from ca. 1910. Not impossibly ex Romany *divio*, mad, a madman (Sampson); cf., however, **dipso.**—2. Delirious: medical students':—1933 (*Slang*, p. 191).

dipso. Abbr. *dipsomaniac*, a confirmed drunkard: cultured s. >, by 1930, coll.

dipstick. Term of abuse, heard directed at an ice-hockey referee, who wears a white top and black trousers—but there is a *double entendre* on *prick*: Can.: late 1960s–early 70s. (Pearsall, 1980.)—2. (or hyphen.) A stupid person: teenagers': early 1980s. (Joanna Williamson, 1982.) Prob. coinage independent from sense 1. Cf. synon. **thick dick.**

dire. Objectionable; (very) unpleasant: from ca. 1920: non-proletarian. (Heyer, 1933.) Cf. **ghastly.**

direct O. A wireless *o*perator employed directly by the ship-owners: nautical: from ca. 1924. Bowen.

dirt. Anti-aircraft fire: RAF: WW2. H.& P.—2. Bad weather: RAF Coastal Command: 1940 +. Hinde, 1945.—3. Scandal: adopted, ca. 1930, ex US. Ex *cast, fling* or *throw dirt* (or *mud*), v.t. with *at*, to be vituperative, malicious: from ca. 1640: coll. till ca. 1800, then S.E.—4. A trump card, esp. if unexpected ('He's put a bit of dirt on it'): card-players': since ca. 1945.—5. In *in the dirt*, in trouble: mostly RAF: since ca.

1925. (P-G-R.) Euph. for *in the shit*.—6. In *in the dirt*, derailed: railwaymen's. (*Railway*, 2nd.) McKenna, 1, has *hitting dirt*, to become derailed.

dirt-box. Rectum; hence *up your dirt-box!*, a vulg. c.p., defiant or merely provocative: low, esp. Army. Cf. next and **dung-funnel.** (P.B.)

dirt-chute or **-shoot.** The anus: Can.

dirts, the. 'The dirty', a mean trick: from ca. 1926. (Weymouth, 1936.) On *bats* and *pots*.

dirty, adj. Is—in low, and in semi-literate, English—often used as a mere intensive, not in the least pej.: since ca. 1910 (perhaps from a decade earlier). 'He [Dante] meets another geezer down there called Virgil or something, and they make dirty great speeches at each other' (Norman). Cf. **dirty big** and **dirty great.**—2. 'With it all hanging down', i.e. (of aircraft) with undercarriage, flaps, etc., all down, in order to fly as slowly as possible, as 'He's coming past dirty now': aviation circles': heard at Leicester air show, Aug. 1979. (P.B.)

dirty! 'When, after a fire, bombing raid, etc., a notice appeared saying "Business as usual", some cynic would surely add "Dirty".' (Petch, 1969): 1940–5.

dirty big. A var. of **dirty great:** mostly Services': since ca. 1910. Among Australians, it has, since ca. 1920, tended to synonymise *bloody*: B., 1943.

dirty daughter. Water: r.s. (Franklyn 2nd.) Perhaps suggested by the words of a popular song: ' . . . water,/In which you wash(ed) your dirty daughter.'

dirty end, get – or **be handed – the.** To come off the worse in a deal or an encounter: coll. 'Sapper', 1924, has the second form.

dirty great. A strong pej.: Services': since ca. 1910. E.g. 'That dirty great bastard'. Cf. **dirty big** and **dirty,** adj., 1.

dirty hands. Practical computer-operating, as opp. to the theory, systems-analysis, etc., side of it: computer people's: since late 1970s. (P.B.)

dirty mac. Generic term for sexually perverted males, a grubby old grey macintosh being recognised as the 'uniform' of the voyeur, exhibitionist, etc.: since early 1970s. Daniells, 1980, 'That little newsagent round the corner's got so many bum and tit mags [magazines] on display you feel like one of the dirty mac outfit just going in for an evening paper.' Another version is the *grey mac(intosh) brigade*. (P.B.)

dirty money. Extra pay for very dirty work: labour coll.

dirty night at sea. 'A nocturnal drinking bout' (Baker): Aus.

dirty old Jew, and **dirty 'ore.** See TOMBOLA, in Appx. In the game of House, it means 'two': r.s. Franklyn.

dirty pool. Dirty tricks; unfair tactics: Can.: adopted, ca. 1970, ex US. Ex the game of *pool*. (Leechman.)

dirty sacks. Bedding: London Fire Brigade. Ex sleeping bags?

dirty up. To render a show (radio, TV, film) more sexually titillating: since late 1960s. 'Used by a [film] reviewer in his "Universe" column, 1 Dec. 1974' (Petch).

dirty water off (one's) **chest, get the.** (Of men) to obtain sexual relief by emission: low.

dirty week-end. A week-end spent with one's mistress; joc., with one's wife but without the children: perhaps orig. Aus., since ca. 1930 (B.P.), but very common in the UK since late 1930s, esp. during WW2.

dis. Disconnected: signallers': since ca. 1910. See also **dissed.**—2. Hence, *go dis*, to go crazy: since ca. 1919. Lyell.—3. Unserviceable or out of order: Army: since ca. 1950, at latest. Ex previous senses. (P.B.)

Disappointments Board, the. The University Appointments Board: undergraduates' (esp. Oxford and Cambridge): since ca. 1950.

disaster. A piastre: Aus. and NZ soldiers in the Middle East theatre, 1915–18; renewed by troops in N. Africa, 1940–3. By rhyme and pun—the coin being of low value.

disaster area. See **walking disaster area.**

disc (or **disk**) **jockey.** A radio man whose job it is to play records and comment on them: adopted, ca. 1955, ex US; by 1965, coll., and by 1970s frequently abbr. *DJ*, which can be used also as v. The latter is also sometimes spelt *deejay*, and the activity *deejaying*.

dischuffed. See **chuffed.**

discip. Abbr. disciplinary, as in 'discip sergeant', 'Discip Branch': RAF: since ca. 1940.

disco. A repository for gramophone discs, i.e. a *discothèque*: music-lovers': since ca. 1955.—2. Hence, 'a club where music is provided by disc or tape as apart from a live = performing group' (*Woman's Own*, 31 July 1965): since ca. 1960.—3. Hence, by later 1970s, any occasion at which dancing, flashing lights, and very loud 'canned' music form the entertainment. 'We're having a party for Sharon's coming-of-age—a bit of a disco'; 'Gary runs a disco every Wednesday afternoon for the teenagers, at the Social Centre': coll., verging on informal S.E. (P.B.)

discuss. A discussion: girls' Public Schools': since ca. 1925. Spain, 1949.

disease. Weather erosion or chemical-fumes deterioration of statues or buildings: since ca. 1940. Ex the leprous appearance they assume.

disembark. Disembarkation leave: Services', esp. Army: since 1939. As in 'After a Far East tour I got 28 days' disembark, plus another 14 days' priv that I'd accumulated'. See **priv,** 2.

disenchanted. Dissatisfied (often with *with*); bored; 'fed-up': mostly middle-class, a loose coll.: later C.20. 'I'm getting bloody disenchanted with his whole attitude.' Prob. ex US, esp. the cartoons of James Thurber. (P.B.)

disguddy blusting. A transposition of *bloody disgusting*: schoolgirls': ca. 1935–50.

disgusting. Unpleasant; silly: Society: from ca. 1920. Mackail, 1925, ' "You can have a Russian bath—if you know what that is." "Don't be disgusting," said Felicity—just to be on the safe side.' Cf. **filthy, foul.**—2. A term of approbation: middle-class youngsters': late 1970s. Prob. ex such phrases as 'You're looking disgustingly fit' (= very well) and 'Isn't she disgustingly brown' (= well sun-tanned), where *disgustingly* is used ironically. (P.B.)

dish. A girl; (young) woman: adopted since ca. 1936 from US. (Curtis, 1938.) For semantics, cf. **crackling,** and **crumpet.** Shakespeare adumbrates the term.—2. Hence, among Teddy boys, an attractive girl: since ca. 1953. Also *doll* or *tart*.—3. Buttocks, posterior: homosexual: since ca. 1954. Ex senses 1 and 2.—4. Any attractive person, of either sex: since ca. 1955. Ex senses 2 and 3. 'Screen dishes can be dark, fair, tall or tiny, but *never* tubby' (*Woman*, 23 Oct. 1965).

dish it out. To be either physically or verbally severe towards others: since ca. 1925. Cf. the c.p. 'he can dish it out, but he can't take it' and **dish out.**—2. To hand out punishment, information or, indeed, anything else, with ease and rapidity: Can., since ca. 1926; Eng., since ca. 1940. (Leechman.)

dish out. To distribute (food) equally or decorations indiscriminately: military col.: since 1914. B. & P.

dish up. To wash up: RN (cook's galley): since ca. 1920. P-G-R.

dish-wrestler. A dish-washer: low from ca. 1925. *Gilt Kid*, 1936.

dishy. Attractive: since ca. 1960. Rathbone, 1968, 'Dishy, I call him.' Ex **dish,** 4.

disinfectant. Sauce; condiments or other garnish: joc.: later C.20. Cf. **varnish.** (P.B.)

disinfo. Disinformation: espionage: coll., verging on j.: since (?)ca. 1950. 'A disinfo tool doesn't always survive' (Hall, 1976). Cf. **info.**

dismants. 'Workshop for dismantling GPO equipment' (Clayton, 1970): prisoners'. Hence the old bits of electrical equipment themselves.

dissed. Disconnected: wireless s.: from ca. 1930; ob. *Wireless World*, 26 Feb. 1937, 'There's no warning whistle to tell [the radio listener] the speaker is "dissed".' See **dis,** 1, which is still the preferred term.

distant relation. 'Jocular use for a relative who is either snobbishly "distant" or . . . one has quarrelled with' (Petch, 1969): since ca. 1950.

district, on the. (Of a student) doing his midwifery course, which involves the care of the parturient poor in his hospital's district: London medical students':—1933 (*Slang*).

dit. See **spin dits.**

ditch, v. To land (an aircraft) on the sea: RAF: since ca. 1939.—2. To discard (something no longer useful): since ca. 1942: orig. RAF, then Services' and gen. coll. Ex C.19 nautical s. for 'throw overboard'.

Ditch, the. The Fleet Street taxicab rank: taxi-drivers': since ca. 1910. (Hodge, 1939.) Ex that brook, the Fleet Ditch, which formerly ran, above ground, to join the River Thames south of Fleet Street.—2. *the ditch,* the sea; *the Ditch,* the Atlantic: coll.: from ca. 1860. Also, by later specialisation, the English Channel, esp. in WW1: 'We had a beautiful journey across the ditch . . . ' (letter quoted in Dent, 1917); and in WW2 RAF.

ditched, be. To get into trouble, be abandoned: Can. and Eng. c. (mainly vagrants'). Orig. US; ex being thrown into a ditch from a moving train.—2. Also as *get ditched.* (Of aircraft and aircrews) to come down in the sea: RAF: since ca. 1938; by 1943, j. After 1940 usu. v.i.; as, e.g., in 'We had to ditch soon after we left the French coast.' Cf. **Ditch, the,** 2, and **ditch,** v.

ditty. (Gen. in pl.) A fib; a long circumstantial story or excuse: coll. (mostly Aus. and NZ): late C.19–20. Ex dial. (*EDD*).

div. A division (military): Army. E.g., 'The Iron Div'. —2. 'Lowest in the pecking order: Borstals' and detention centres' ' (Home Office): current in 1970s. 'Work? . . . Berk, more like. What a div!' (Matthew, 1983). Here, it means merely 'a dim-witted fool', and, among middle-class young women, as Hoggart notes, 1983, 'they agree that "the dreaded Roger" is a bit of a creep (or sometimes, these days, a "wally" or a "div").'

divebombing. 'Picking up dog ends [q.v.] from the pavement' (Wilson, 1980): vagrants': 1970s.

dividers. Divided knickers (female): ca. 1910–40. Ex *divided,* by the 'OXFORD -*ER*(s)'. Not being sewn, i.e. closed, along the crutch, they offer free access.

divine. Pleasant; 'nice': Society: from ca. 1920. (Waugh, 1928.) Cf. **marvellous.**

diving suit. A condom: industrial Aus., esp. NSW: since ca. 1945. A raffish pun. Cf. **willie wellie.**

divorced, be. To lose one's girl; (of a girl) to lose one's boy: Aus. joc., esp. teenagers': since ca. 1950. 'You'd better take her out more often, or you'll be divorced.' (B.P.) Some Brit. use also.

divvies. Divination: since ca. 1920. (Allingham, 1947.) Cf. the later C.20 use in sing., as in Gash, 1978: 'Divvie? Maybe from the old word "diviner", as in water, but who knows? It's slang for anybody who can guess right about a thing without actually knowing. Some people have it for gems or paintings . . . a precious knack that goes separate from any learning. I'm an antiques divvie.'

divvified. Daft: an elab. of **divvy,** adj.

divvy, v.i. and t. To divide: coll.: from ca. 1880. In C.20 has attracted prepositions, as *divvy up,* and, also as noun, *divvy out:* 'There's a good lot here—let's have a divvy-out': since late 1940s.

divvy, adj. Daft: market-traders'. (*M.T.*) Cf. **dippy** and **divvified.**

divvy-hunter. One who joins a co-operative society merely to share in the dividends: since ca. 1910.

dizz. RN var. of **zizz,** n. and v., sleep. Bolster, 1945.

dizzy, adj. Scatter-brained; wild; foolish: since ca. 1930. See **get dizzy.**

dizzy blonde. 'A highly conspicuous blonde, both in appearance and in behaviour' (Leechman): Can.: adopted, ca. 1935, ex US; by 1956, fairly common in England. Cf. **dizzy,** adj., and **dumb blonde.**

dizzy limit, the. Mostly Aus. var. of the *giddy limit*: the utmost: since ca. 1930, predominantly 'the final touch, the last straw' (B., 1943).

dlinkie. 'Facetious and pseudo-juvenile and pidgin for *drink*' (Leechman): Can.: since ca. 1920, and, one hopes, soon ob.

do, n. An entertainment, a social function. In *New Statesman and Nation*, 23 Sep. 1933, we read of 'a famous West Indies cricketer, who speaks perfect English' (Constantine, no doubt) being puzzled by the phrase, *a slap-up do*, applied to a tea. The puzzlement was admittedly caused more by the *slap-up* than by the *do*, though the juxtaposition may also have been partly the cause. In this sense *do* obtained in dial. as early as 1820.—2. A gang fight: teenage gangsters': since ca. 1955.—3. In pl., a share: esp. **fair doo's** (or **do's**), q.v.—4 See **doggie doo**.

do, v. Like *chuck, come, cop, get, give,* etc., *do* is, as F. & H. have it, 'a verb-of-all-work, and is used in every possible or impossible connection': this shows very clearly in the following set of phrases—a mere selection—where the status is s. or coll. according to the nature of the n. For others, not listed here, please see entry at the operative noun. Many of the *do a . . .* phrases simply duplicate the appropriate v. as a n., e.g., *perish* = do a perish, etc.

do, v. To arrest, prosecute: c. (*Gilt Kid*, 1936.) See **done**, 1.—2. To coït (with a girl): low.—3. Hence, to perpetrate sodomy upon: low.—4. With prec. senses, cf. coll. use of *do* for 'punish' or 'get one's revenge upon', as in 'If you don't do as I say this very minute, I'll flippin' well *do* you!' Usu. joc., but not always. Prob. a shortening of **do for**, or **do in**, qq.v. (P.B.)

do a beer, a bitter, a drink, a drop, a wet. To take a drink of something stronger than milk or water, the domestic trio (coffee, cocoa, tea), or soft drinks. *Do* here = drink; it dates from ca. 1850. All, orig. s., are, except *do a wet*, coll. in C.20. Cf. *do a meal*, to eat a meal: same period and status. Occ. heard in invitation to alcoholic drink: 'Can you do one?' In later C.20 applied—of course—to drugs.

do a Bertie. 'Doing a Bertie: giving evidence against accomplices in a criminal trial; turning "Queen's evidence"' (Powis): c.: current in 1970s. Ex one Bertie Smalls, 'so infamous among London's robbers for becoming a supergrass' (*Bullion*, 1988).

do a bust. To break into a place: c. Leach.

do a four-o-six (406). To make a routine inspection on a vehicle: Army: since 1939; if at first coll., then soon > j. Ex the form number of the relevant army 'book'.

do a Garbo, a Gaynor. See MOVING-PICTURE SLANG, §§10 and 9, in Appx.

do a good turn to. To afford (a woman) sexual satisfaction: male coll., mostly joc. Usu. as a raffish aside, between two men admiring the same girl: 'Cor, I could certainly do *her* a good turn!'

do a job. To defecate: Eng. and Aus.: late C.19–20. (B., 1942.) Among children, sometimes *do a jobbie*.—2. To render a woman pregnant: Aus. Baker.

do a job for (one)**self.** To defecate. Cf. prec., 1.

do a knock – or do a knock line – with. To be amorously interested in—and involved with—a member of the opposite sex: Aus.: low. (Baker.) Cf. **knocking-shop**.

do a line with. To walk out with (a girl): orig. and mostly Anglo-Irish.

do a moody. To behave suspiciously: prison c.: later C.20. McConville, 1980.

do a Nelson. To withstand danger, or extreme difficulty, in a confident spirit: mostly Cockney: late C.19–20. 'Knowing that whatever may befall, as upon Nelson on his column in Trafalgar Square, one will, like him, "be there" to-morrow' (L.A. 1948).—2. Hence, to be in irrepressibly good spirits: a 'London Blitz' word among Civil Defence on duty: late 1940–mid-1941, then at intervals until 1945.

do a Penang. To run away; to retreat ingloriously: Aus. airmen's: 1942–5. (B., 1943.) Ex the Brit. and Aus. retreat down Malaya.

do a perish. Almost to die for lack of a drink: Aus.: since ca. 1920. Baker.

do a runner. 'A few students (from different parts of the country) suggested *to do a runner* for the German Zechprellerei [begehen], which Collins translates "failure to pay the bill for drink or food consumed at a restaurant, bar, etc."' (John B. Smith, Bath University, 1981). Munro, 1985, notes Glasgow var. *do a run-out*.—2. To attempt, or to make good, one's escape, as in 'These two lads were just being brought into court, and one of 'em tried to do a runner, didn't 'e': s.: 1980s. Has var. *take a runner*. (P.B., 1986.)

do a snatch. To indulge in a hasty, illicit or mercenary copulation. See **snatch**, n., 1.

do a starry. To sleep in the open: c.

do as you like. A bicycle: r.s., on *bike*: late C.19–20.

do-badder. An actively bad person: coll.: since ca. 1960. Prompted by **do-gooder**, 2.

do (one's) **bit.** In WW1 and 2, to serve in Armed Forces: ex the late C.19–20 coll., do one's share, to help a general cause. In the Boer War, a soldier wrote of his fellows, 'They all do "their bit" well' (Milne, 1902).

do business with. 'Has the innocent meaning but also means to have corrupt transactions with' (Powis): c.: current in 1970s.

do (one's) **cash.** To spend, to lose one's money: Aus. Baker.

do (one's) **crunch.** To become enraged: Army: since ca. 1955. 'You shoulda seen 'im when 'e found it—done 'is crunch, 'e did.' (P.B.)

do (someone) **dirt.** To play him a mean trick: mainly Aus. A var., from ca. 1920, is *do dirt on*. Cf. **do the dirty on.**

do-do (pron. *doo-doo*). To excrete; excreta: school-children's: late C.19–20. Hence, *do-do noise*, a fart. Cf. **doggie do.**

do (one's) **dough.** To lose one's money: mostly Aus.: since ca. 1925.

do for. To kill: c., since earlier C.18; in C.20, low.

do (one's) **fruit.** To go mad: s.: since early 1970s. (Slater, 1978.) Prob. suggested by synon. *bananas*. Cf. **do** (one's) **nut**, 2.

do-gooder. Among Liverpool street arabs of late C.19–earlyish 20, 'misguided folk' (ignorant of the true needs of the poor). *Arab*.—2. An inveterate busybody, intent on reforming everybody's soul but his own: Can. coll.: since ca. 1946. (Leechman.)—3. Gen. in pl., a re-emergence of sense 1, applied to people who interest themselves in social work: English coll., became widespread only ca. 1957. (*Evening Echo* (Bournemouth), 7 July 1959.) Hence, since ca. 1960, the occ. *do-goodery* and adj. *do-gooding*.

do-hickey. A 'thingummy-jig', a gadget. See **hickey**, 1 and cf. **gilhicky**.

do in. To kill: late C.19–20. Cf. **do for**.—2. To despatch, dispose of; to spoil completely; to cancel: joc., to eat, to drink: from ca. 1920.

do it. To coït: when not merely euph., it is coll.: C.18–20.—2. Hence, usu. in the question 'Does she do it?', to be gen. ready to indulge in sexual intercourse: status id.: C.19–20.

do-it-yourself. Masturbation: since ca. 1950. Monsarrat, 1960.

do it yourself kit. 'Steam locomotives' (*Railway*, 2nd): railwaymen's: since ca. 1950. Ironic, in the age of the diesel ease. McKenna attributes the term to his driver-colleague Mr Bill Handy.

do me good. A *Wood*bine cigarette: r.s: late C.19–20.—2. Timber: carpenters' and other workmen's r.s. on *wood*: late C.19–20. Franklyn 2nd.

do (one's) **nut.** To lose one's head: lower classes' and military: earlier C.20 in this sense. F. & G.—2. To explode with anger: coll.: since ca. 1945. Cf. **blow** (one's) **top.**

do one for the King (or **Queen**). To be on a 24-hour guard: Army: since ca. 1950. P.B.: the phrase was still current in the early 1970s, in such forms as 'Well, that's another one for the Queen!' at the conclusion of, e.g., a 24-hour duty as orderly sergeant.

do over. In C.19 c., to search the pockets of; c. *frisk*. Raab: in C.20 coll., this sense expanded: 'The Customs at Heathrow did me over, but they never found the other 400 ciggies.'—2. To *do the rank over* is to take position in a taxicab park other than one's usual; taxi-drivers': since ca. 1912. (Hodge, 1939.) But *do a man over* is to take a fare rightfully another driver's: Hodge.

do-re-mi (pron. *dough-ray-me*). Money, esp. cash: Aus., adopted—ca. 1945—ex US; but since late 1930s in Can. An elab. of *dough* = money, and a pun on the tonic sol-fa.

do right by our Nell, to. 'Do right in the letter and the spirit of an undertaking. Ex C.19 romances in which the squire has got innocent maid with child and must honour paternal responsibility' (L.A., 1974).

do some good for (oneself). (Of the male) to be amorously successful: Aus. B., 1942.

do (one's) **tank.** To become enraged: Army: since ca. 1955. Cf. **do** (one's) **crunch, nut,** etc. (P.B.)

do the chalks. To write the score at darts, esp. at match-games: dart-players': since ca. 1945. With chalk on a board.

do the decent thing. When used joc. and in trivial context it is coll.; e.g., in persuading someone it is his turn to buy a round of drinks, 'Come on then, sport, do the decent thing for once!': since mid-C.20. (P.B.)

do the dirty (on). To play a mean trick (on someone): coll., from ca. 1912; by ca. 1935, verging on informal S.E. (*OED*). Here *dirty* = dirty trick.—2. Esp. *do the dirty on* a girl, to seduce her and then abandon her: since ca. 1913.

do the (e.g. *religious*) **dodge** (over). 'To pretend to be religious and so seek to obtain some favour' (from a person): coll.:—1931 (Lyell).

do the honours. To assume responsibility for pouring drinks, whether alcoholic, soft, or hot, as in 'Shall I do the honours, then?': coll.: since (?)ca. 1950. Cf. **be mother,** which usu. applies only to tea or coffee from a pot. (P.B.)

do the lot. To lose all one's money: coll.

do the tap. To win a game of cards; mostly as vbl n., *doing the tap*: Army: earlier C.20.

do the ton. Of motorcycle, car, to reach 100 m.p.h.: since ca. 1945. See **ton,** and **one ton.**

do (one's, *or* one's own) **thing.** To express oneself in one's life; do what one wants to do, from mere gratification, to profession, to ideal: Can. hippies' (soon, much more gen.): adopted, ca. 1965, ex US; reached Britain ca. 1969 and there became gen. ca. 1971.

do things to (one). To excite, esp. sexually; to arouse either passion or a mere momentary 'letch': since ca. 1930. 'That girl does things to me, I don't know why.' A var. is *do things for*, though this may be to excite one's interest mentally as well as physically. The implications are functional; cf. synon. phrase: 'He makes me come over all unnecessary.'

do what the steer did. To, at the least, try: Can.: since ca. 1920. 'From the observed efforts of these underprivileged animals to lead a normal love-life' (Leechman).

doat. 'A "doat", usually spelt so in Ireland, is someone or something fit to be doted on' (Tracy, 1975): Anglo-Irish.

dob. A small lump or 'dollop', usu. applied to butter, jam, cream, etc.: orig. widespread dial. (*EDD*), in C.20 > domestic coll. (P.B.)

dob in. To inform on (someone): Aus., esp. teenage gangsters': since ca. 1930. 'He wouldn't dob me in, I knew that' (Dick). Ex the widespread English dial. *dob*, to put down heavily, to throw down.

dobash. A pal or a girl-friend: RN lowerdeck: since ca. 1925. (Granville.) Cf. *wingsy-bash*, q.v. at **winger.**

dobbin. A rum-container: Army in the East: 1942–5. (Rolo, 1944.) Ex the S.E. *dobbin*, a small drinking-vessel.

dobee, dobey, dobie, doby. Laundry. See **dhobi.**

doc. In RN wardrooms, the usu. address to the ship's surgeon. (Granville.) But, on the lower deck, *doc* always, in address, means a sick-berth attendant, the doctor himself being, in ref., *the quack*. See **doctor**, 3. Also, in Army from at least as early as 1939, a medical orderly.

dock. In *in dock* of motor cars, being serviced or repaired: motorists': since ca. 1920.

dock asthma. 'Pretended gasps of surprise by accused persons when incriminating evidence is given against them. Used generally to describe the reaction to any unpleasant surprise, whether in court or not' (Powis): c. and police s.: current in 1970s.

docker. A large sum of money; *go a docker*, spend much money: Aus.: since ca. 1925. (B., 1942.) Origin?—2. A partially smoked cigarette, extinguished for use later: Northern coll. (Nuttall, 1979.) Cf. **dib** and see **dog-end.**

docker's hankie. 'The rude peasant cheerfully discharging his snot on to the ground, first through one nostril and then through the other (sometimes called a "docker's hankie") . . . ' (Thompson, 1979). *Hankie* = handkerchief. (P.B.) Cf.:-

dockyard oyster. Elab. of *oyster*, since C.18 and still current, low s. for a gob of phlegm. (Cropper, 1987.)

docs. Documents, in the sense of a soldier's, sailor's, airman's official papers (attestation form, medical rating, classification, etc., etc., etc.): Services' coll. (Jackson.) Hence, in civilian, e.g. police, usage: prob. via ex-servicemen.

doctor. Occ. shortening of **magic doctors,** q.v., RAF ground engineers.—2. A journeyman in collar and tie: tailors'.—3. A sick-berth attendant: RN lowerdeck: late C.19–mid-20. Goodenough, 1901.—4. Nickname given to 7th child of 7th child: C.19–20. 'Supposed to bring good luck' (Petch, 1974).—5. See TOMBOLA in Appx.

Doctor Cotton. Rotten: r.s. (P.P., 1932.) Also *Dolly Cotton* and *John(ny) Cotton.*

Doctor Crippen. Dripping (the culinary n.): r.s.: early C.20.

Doctor Foster; doctor's chum or **favourite** or **orders** or **shop.** See TOMBOLA, in Appx.

doddering Dick. A Maxim gun; hence, any machine-gun: RN: WW2. P-G-R.

doddle, n. Money very easily obtained: Glasgow (—1934). By 1940, fairly gen., but low. (Norman.)—2. A 'walk-over': racing, since ca. 1920; by mid-1940s, gen. s., as in 'Pity you didn't come last night. It was a doddle' (Progl, 1964). Ex *dawdle*, or ex *toddle*?—3. Hence, esp., 'It's a doddle' = it's easy, simple: Services', since ca. 1945; by 1955, widespread.

doddle, v. To 'walk it' or win very easily: racing: since ca. 1925. Winton, 1963, (of a filly) 'I think she started at even money but anyway she doddled it.' Ex sense 2 of the n.—unless it was the other way about.

doddy. 'A term said to have originated from Granville [colliery] but not general in Leicestershire. The period of time which has to be worked to claim $\frac{1}{4}$ shift overtime' (Forster, 1970): coal-miners'.

dodge. In *on the dodge*, engaged in something dishonest: coll. *OED Sup.*

dodge Pompey. To steal grass: Aus.: from ca. 1920. *Pompey* personifies the Law. Ex:—2. To avoid work on shipboard: RN (pre-WW1) >, by 1918 at latest, gen. nautical. Bowen.—3. 'To work on a sheep station' (Wilkes): Aus.: late C.19–early 20.

dodge the draft. See **draft-dodger.**

dodgeman (rather than *dodge man*). A trickster, a 'fly boy': secondhand-car dealers': since mid-1940s. (*Woman's Own*, 28 Feb. 1968.) Cf. **dodge.**

dodger, n. In early C.20 c., a half-sovereign. Ex its elusiveness.—2. A Good-Conduct Badge: Army. Ironic; cf. *canteen medal.* F. & G.—3. A sandwich: Army:—1914 (F. & G.). Because the meat therein dodges the consumer.—4. Hence(?), bread; food: Aus., since ca. 1918 (Baker); also, in the sense of bread only, in Brit. Army, replacing sense 3. (P.B.)—5. 'A printed sheet, usually on coloured paper, and on one side only, for distribution door to door, advertising something or other' (Leechman, 1967): Can. printers' and journalists': since ca. 1910, also Aus. coll.—6. 'A canvas screen on the bridge of small craft as protection against the weather' (P-G-R): RN coll.—7. A shunting truck: railwaymen's, mostly Western Region. *Railway*, 2nd.

dodger, adj. First-class, excellent, fine: Aus.: since late 1930s. B., 1943; Stivens, 1953.

dodgy. Difficult or complicated or tricky; risky; likely to become dangerous, esp. of a situation, a transaction, a concerted action: since ca. 1943. In, e.g., the film *Seven Days to Noon*, 1950; Norman. But foreshadowed in G.B. Shaw, *Mrs Warren's Profession*, 1894.—2. Hence, stolen; esp. in *dodgy gear*, stolen property; since ca. 1955.—3. As an exclam. it >, early 1960s, a one-word 'c.p.', popularised by the comedian Norman Vaughan. Like sense 1, it conveyed a vague disapprobation, and its opposite was *swingin'!* N.V. accompanied *dodgy!* with a thumb-down gesture. (P.B.)

Doe. A Dornier 'plane: RAF: 1939+. (Partridge, 1945.) Ex the official abbr., *Do*.

does she? Euph. for 'Does she copulate?'—to which a frequent answer is, 'You know what': since at least as early as 1920, and prob. going back to 'the Naughty Nineties'.

dog. A cigarette-end: c. (Harrison, 1935.) Cf. the, in later C.20, more usu. var., *dog-end*.—2. Hence, a beggar-searcher for cigarette-ends: c. Harrison, 1934.—3. A type of mild dysentery. See **Malta dog**.—4. A plain-clothes railway detective: Aus. c. B., 1942.—5. A police 'shadow': Aus. police: since 1920s. (Kelly, 1955.) Ex the S.E. *dog*, v., to track?—6. Hence, 'one who assists, or has at some time assisted, the authorities to make an arrest' (McNeil): Aus. coll.: current in early 1970s. See also **tuckerbox**.—7. Food: Aus. rural. (B., 1942.) Cf. **dogs**, 1, and **corned dog**.—8. A drinking debt: Aus. urban (Ibid.). See **tie up a dog**.—9. 'A "dog" is punting poison—a horse that will really only race when it feels like it': turf: since late 1940s. (*Weekend*, 11 Oct. 1967.) Cf. the fig. use of **bitch**.—10. Something worthless: Can.: since ca. 1960. (Leechman, 1976.) Adopted ex US.—11. An unpleasant girl, a 'slag': teenagers': early 1980s. (Joanna Williamson, 1982.) Ex US.

Dog Act, the. See **Blackfellows' Act**.—2. Any such Act, or part of an Act, of Parliament as enables people to follow a profession even though they are not academically qualified to do so: Aus.: since ca. 1955. (B.P.)

dog along. To fare tolerably, passably: Can. coll. Beames.

dog and basket. The lion and crown as parts of the Royal Marines' badge: since (?)earlier C.20. (Knight, 1984.)

dog and bone. Telephone (mostly n.): r.s.: since ca. 1945. (Franklyn 2nd.) See quot'n at **bunny**, v.

dog-box. A passenger carriage on rural railway services: Aus. (B., 1942.) 'Refers only to carriages without corridors. Each compartment has its own door to the platform and its own w.c.' (B.P.)

dog-clutch. 'A disconnectable coupling' (H. & P.): RAF: from ca. 1930. P.B.: *SOD*, 1977, notes the use of *dog* in many terms for gripping-devices; this RAF use is therefore prob. j. rather than s. or coll.

dog(-)dancing. 'Useless and exaggerated activity, such as a dog indulges in, capering with glee at the return of his master' (Leechman, 1967): orig. and mostly Can.: since late 1966 or early 1967.

dog driver. 'Policeman, used in an insulting or contemptuous context (West Indian)' (Powis): current in 1970s.

dog-end. A cigarette-end: low Cockney; since late 1920s, fairly gen., though still low. (*Evening News* (London), 21 Dec. 1936.) It is prob. a corruption of *docked end*: a cigarette that is kept for another smoke has first been quenched or docked.

dog-fashion, have it. To coït *a posteriori*: low coll. Cf. *dogways*. Another var. is *doggy-fashion*.

dog-fight. An RAF coll. (1915) >, by 1930, S.E., as defined, implicatively, Wren, 1934, 'But best sport of all was a dog-fight, an all-on-to-all scrap between a flight of British Bristol Scouts and a bigger flight of Fokkers, everybody shooting-up everybody, a wild and whirling mêlée from which every now and then someone went hurtling down to death in a blaze of smoke and fire.'—2. A regimental sergeant-major's badge: Army: since ca. 1930; ob. Cf. **fighting cats** or **dogs**, and **Tate and Lyle**. The badge is the Royal Arms: 'The lion and the unicorn were fighting for the crown . . . ' (P.B.)

dog-fight buttons. Buttons worn by those on the army's General Service list: Army: mid-C.20. The badge on them is the Royal Arms; see **dog-fight**, 2.

dog-house. A bass viol. See **fish-horn**.—2. In *in the dog-house*, in disgrace or bad odour: since ca. 1954. 'A man fallen out with his wife may say, 'I'm in the dog-house.' Ex dogs banished from house to kennel. Prob. ex US.

dog(-)leg, n. A good-conduct chevron: Services': since ca. 1925. (H. & P.) Ex the shape.

dog-leg, v. To make an angled detour, e.g. around a 'forbidden zone': air navigators' coll. > j.: since early days of aviation. (P.B.)

dog licence. 'A Certificate of Exemption to allow an aboriginal to buy a drink in a hotel' (B., 1959): since late 1940s.

dog list, be on the. To be debarred from drinking: Aus.: since ca. 1920. B., 1942.

dog-napping. (The practice of) stealing pets: low.

dog out. To keep watch: low: since ca. 1945. Procter, 1966, 'You can have Harry to dog out for you' and 'Higgs left Wayman dogging out at the corner'.

dog-robber. A servant or aide of a high officer, who to 'supply his master with food and liquor suitable to his rank, will "rob even the goddam dogs" ' (R.C., citing Huie, 1960). Brit. ex US, Services': ?since ca. 1943 for Brit. usage.

dog-robbers. Civilian clothes (usu. tweeds) worn by officers on shore leave: RN: since ca. 1900. (Granville.) By 1950, RAF officers' also (P.B.).

dog-rough. Very unpleasant, hard: Services': since ca. 1920. (P-G-R.) Rough—even for a dog.—2. Hence, very ill: mainly Services': since ca. 1920. (Raper, 1973.)—3. See **doggo**, adj.

dog-shelf. The floor, as, sarcastically to a child dropping something, 'That's right, hang it up on the dog-shelf!': Northern coll.: (prob. mid-C.19)—20. (Dilke-Wing, 1980.)

dog-stiffener. A professional dingo-killer: Aus. B., 1942.—2. Usu. in pl., *dog-stiffeners*, leather leggings: Aus.: since ca. 1910. Baker.

dog-tag. A metal or other indestructible identity disc: Army and Aus.: WW2 onwards. (P.B; B.P.)

dog-walloper. A stick; a cudgel; a policeman's baton: Aus. Baker.—2. A cheap metal tyre-pump: club cyclists': earlier C.20. *Fellowship*, 1984.

dog(-)watch; esp. *on the dog-watch*, on night duty: Services': since ca. 1920. (H. & P.) Ex nautical j.—2. 'To say of a man that he hasn't been in the Service "half a dog-watch" is to imply that he is still in the green New Entry stage' (Granville).

dog-whipper. 'Superintends work of pony drivers and leaders in metal mines' (*Evening News*, 28 Sep. 1953): industrial.

dogged-up, (all). In one's smartest clothes: since ca. 1925; ob. Cf. **doggy**, adj., and **doll up**. (P.B.)

dogger. One who practises *dogging*, the collecting, cleaning and selling of dog-end tobacco: low: since 1941.—2. One who practises acrobatic skiing; short for *hot-dogger*, q.v. at **hot-dogging**.

Dogger Bank Dragoons, the. The Royal Marines, esp. the commandos: RN: from ca. 1914. (Spenser, 1948.) Superseded by:-

Dogger Bank Hussars or **Light Infantry.** Variants of prec.: RN: 1970s. (Peppitt.)

doggers. 'Multi-coloured swim shorts' (*Pix*, 28 Sep. 1963): Aus. surfers': since ca. 1960. Ex 'putting on *dog*' or 'side'? Or ex *hot-dogging*, q.v. at **hot dog**.

Dogget coat and badge. Full version of the r.s. *coat and badge*, to cadge. Franklyn.

doggie, -y. An officer assisting an admiral at his work; 'a midshipman regularly attending a captain or flag officer': RN: from ca. 1910. Ex faithfulness to duty. *OED* Sup; 'Taffrail'.—2. A 'hot dog': Aus.: since ca. 1944. Park, 1950.—3.

'Platelayer. (Eastern Region)': railwaymen's. (*Railway*, 2nd.) Poss. of mining origin, but more likely humorous.

Doggie (or **-y**) **Day.** New Year's Day: Post Office officials'. Ex the dog-licences renewable then.

doggie (or **-y**) **do(o).** Dog turds: later C.20 euph. ' "Eat crap!" barked the [film] director. And suddenly Divi was up to his dentures in doggy doo' (*Time Out*, 6 June 1985). Prob. ex US; a NY friend tells me, 1986, of a young woman exclaiming, 'Ah, shit! I got doggie doo all over my shoes!' (P.B.)

doggin (mostly in pl.). A cigarette-butt: NZ: since ca. 1930. An adaptation—?rather a slovening—of **dog-end.** Henderson, 1945.

dogging. See **dogger.**

Doggo. Nickname for a plain-featured person: RN. (Granville.) See **doggo party.**

doggo, adj. (Of a car) 'Rough inside, particularly upholstery' (Graham-Ranger, 1981): car-dealers'. Also **dog-rough,** q.v.

doggo party. An unattractive female: RN. 'I didn't feel like it by then, after all the screech we'd put away, but Ted did . . . he sorted himself out a doggo party of about sixty and disappeared with her for half an hour' (*Heart*, 1962).

doggy, n. See **doggie.**

doggy, adj. Stylish; smart, whether of appearance or of action: from ca. 1885. Ex a *sad dog, a bit of a dog.* Now, 'just a little too gay and dashing' (Mackail, 1934).

dogman. That workman who travels with the load of a crane: Aus.: since ca. 1930. Clark, 1962.

dogs. (Always pl.) Sausages: low: from ca. 1860; post-1925, it tends to mean 'hot cooked sausages' (short for *hot dogs*). The former sense is ex reputed origin; an early occurrence of the latter is in Vivian, 1933.—2. Feet: low coll.: adopted, ex US, ca. 1935. But *dogs that bite* seems to be an English elab., since ca. 1944, for sore feet; and, since ca. 1950 (?earlier) there has been the var. *me* [*my*] *dogs are barking*, my feet are sore.—3. The position achieved in mine-sweeping when two ships open out and finish stern to stern: R Aus. N: WW2. Ex two dogs breaking off relations.—4. As *the dogs*, the dog watches: RN: since ca. 1910. P-G-R.—5. As *the dogs*, greyhound race-meeting: coll.: since 1929. (The Dog-Racing Bill was of 1928.) *OED* Sup.

dog's ballocks. The typographical colon-dash (:—). See **dog's prick.**—2. Esp. in the phrase 'It sticks out like a dog's ballocks', said of something that the speaker considers is patently obvious: low: since ca. 1920.

dog's body. (Usu. *dogsbody.*) Any junior officer, RN; esp. a midshipman; hence, pej., of any male: RN (>, by 1920, gen.): late C.19–20. L.A. notes, 1976, 'In its general use, it applies notably to the junior or, e.g., superannuated man, esp. of office staffs, upon whom the wearisome errands and unwelcome jobs devolve; he who gets slapped.'

dog's bottom. A facetious term of address: 1930s.—2. In *is he* (or *it*, etc.) *any dog's bottom?*, is he any good?: Aus.: from ca. 1930. B., 1942.

dog's breakfast. A mess; confusion; turmoil: low coll., perhaps orig. Glasgow; also Aus.: since early 1930s. B., 1943.

dog's cock (or **diddy**). An unwieldy back splice; hence 'an unholy mess': training ships'. (Peppitt.)

dog's dinner. A shilling: Aus. r.s. (B., 1945.) On *deaner*.—2. Pej., as in 'Something-or-other was a dog's dinner'—bungled, messy, no good: since ca. 1945. Cf. the earlier **dog's breakfast.**

dog's disease. Influenza: Aus.: since ca. 1930. (B.P.) B., 1953, notes it as WW2 Aus. s. for malaria.

dog's licence. Seven shillings and sixpence: from ca. 1930. Ex the cost of that licence. P.B.: but not used for the equivalent 37½p, which it still cost over half a century later.

dog's prick. An exclamation mark: authors' and journalists'.

dogsbody. See **dog's body.**

dohickey. A mechanical whatnot. See **doohickey.**

doing a moody. 'Doing something suspicious' (Home Office): prisoners': current in 1970s.

doing the party. 'A ploy in three-card trick where a confederate of a card sharp pretends to be a winning player so as to encourage "mugs" to stake heavily and, of course, to lose' (Powis): c.: current in 1970s.

doings, the. The thing (*any* thing); esp. what is at the moment needed or otherwise relevant: from ca. 1912. Perhaps ex the US usage, the materials for a meal (1838): Thornton. Cf. **gadget, ooja-ka-piv.**—2. Hence, one's possessions or equipment: Aus.: since ca. 1919. (Devanney, 1944.) P.B.: some Brit. usage in this sense also.—3. Excrement, human or animal: domestic coll. 'There's a lump of bird's doings on the windowsill.' (P.B.)—4. In *in the doings*, in the guardroom: Army: from ca. 1914. (F. & G.) Ex 1 and prob. 3; cf. *in the shit*.—5. Esp. as *Old Doings*, a ref. to someone whose name the speaker has momentarily forgotten, 'Old Whatsit, old Doings . . . *you* know': perhaps mainly Army Officers': since WW2, perhaps earlier. (My father, Capt. L.S. Beale, TD, 1940s; Judd, 1981.) An extension of sense 1. (P.B.)

dole. In *go on the dole*, to receive unemployment benefit: s. (ca. 1925) >, by 1930, coll. P.B.: *SOD*, 1977, dates *the dole* in this sense back to 1919: to *go on the dole* had, by mid-C.20, > informal S.E. Cf.—2. As *the dole*, food handed out at a station to a tramp: Aus.: since ca. 1925. B., 1942.

doley or **dolee.** A person on the dole: Aus. coll.: since ca. 1930. *Caddie*, 1953.—2. A soldier in an employment platoon: Aus.: since ca. 1940. (B., 1943.)

doll. Any very attractive person of either sex: Can. juveniles': adopted, ca. 1935, ex US. (Leechman.)—2. As in *a doll of a . . .*, an attractive (e.g. house, gown): since mid-1950s.—3. 'Any drug in pill form' (Landy, 1971): adopted by Brit. addicts ca. 1972.—4. See **dish,** 2; **napper.**

doll up, v.i. and reflexive. To dress oneself very smartly. Whence *dolled-up*, dressed 'to death'.

dollar bosun. A warrant writer in charge of pay accounts: RN: since ca. 1925. Granville.

dollars to doughnuts. Long odds: low coll.: from ca. 1920. *Gilt Kid*, 1936.

dollops of. 'Heaps' of; 'lots' of: coll.:—1923 (Manchon). P.B.: in later C.20 sometimes intensified to 'great dollops of . . .'

dolly, n. A small shunting-engine: railwaymen's: since ca. 1920. *Railway*. Cf.—2. A camera-trolley. See MOVING-PICTURE SLANG, §4, in Appx.—3. 'Dwarf Ground Signal (London Midland Region)': railwaymen's: since ca. 1930. *Railway*, 2nd.—4. A secondhand car in perfect condition: dealers': since ca. 1955. (*Woman's Own*, 28 Feb. 1968.) Cf.—5. A girl, esp. an attractive girl: since ca. 1955. Cf. **dolly-bird.**

dolly, v. See AUSTRALIAN UNDERWORLD, in Appx.

dolly, adj. Excellent; very attractive; very pleasant, as in 'Isn't that dolly?'; 'darling': an article published in *Daily Telegraph*, colour sup., 10 Mar. 1967; note the title of Alan Diment's novel, *The Dolly Dolly Spy*, 1967. Cf. **dolly,** n., 5.—2. Hence, 'as used by, e.g., Diment, it has the additional connotation of "mod" or "hip" or "with-it" ' (R.C., 1976): since latish 1960s.

dolly-bird. A sexually attractive, usu. young and pretty, girl; often in flocks as, e.g., 'secretaries' or clerks: since early 1960s, but not gen. before ca. 1967. Cf. **dolly,** n., 5, and adj., and **bird,** n., 4. The term belongs particularly to the brief era of the mini-skirt. (P.B.)

dolly mixture. 'Sets made up of various items' (Ash): London dockers': earlier C.20. A *set(t)* = a crane-load of cargo. Ex the name of a children's sweet.—2. The pictures (cinema): r.s. (Hollis.) Cf. **camp dollies.**

Dolly Varden. A garden: r.s.: late C.19–20.

dollypot. A simpleton: Aus.: since ca. 1925. (B., 1942.) Cf. **dill-pot.**

dolphin. See **swing the dolphin.**

dominoes. 'Durophet 12·5 mgm spansules' (Home Office): drug addicts': current in 1970s. And see **doms.**

Dommie. A Norton 'Dominator' motorcycle: motorcyclists'. (Dunford.)

Doms, the. Members of the Order of Preachers (*Dom*inicans): Aus. Catholics'. (B.P.)—2. As *doms*. Dominoes, as in 'King of the "Doms" ' (*Loughborough Echo*, 4 June 1982, p. 2).

don. 'A top skipper': driftermen's. Butcher, 1979.

Don Freddie. Euph., using the PHONETIC ALPHABET (see Appx.), for **dutch fuck**, q.v., the lighting of one cigarette from another: Army: WW2.

Don R. A dispatch rider: Services': since the 1920s. (H. & P.) From the early PHONETIC ALPHABET: see Appx.

Donald Duck. Luck: r.s.: later C.20. (Barker, 1979; Munro, 1985.) Ex the famous Walt Disney cartoon 'character'.

done. 'Arrested; caught, having committed some offence' (Tempest): c. > coll. P.B.: also, being subsequently penalised, as in 'He was done for speeding in a built-up area.' See also **drum**, n., 1.—2. 'Beaten up. "So and so got done last night" ' (Tempest): low. This may be a shortening from **do over**, 1, q.v., in its nuance 'knocked down'. (P.B.)—3. Baptised. (Petch, 1974.)—4. See **do**, v., 1; **done thing**.

done thing, the. Whatever is considered to be 'good form', as opposed to those things that 'simply are not done, you know': upper classes', officers', Public Schools'. Also, whatever is the current fad; e.g., referring to July 1914, Ewart wrote, 1921, 'Very young ladies were fond of calling young gentlemen by their Christian names—it was rather "done" in their current idiotic phrase.'

dong, n. A blow, a punch: Aus. Ex the v.—2. Penis: Brit. and Can.: since mid-C.20. Slightly less vulgar than *prick*. P.B.: perhaps a shortening of late C.19 low *a donkey's*, a penis.

dong, v. To strike; to punch: Aus. and NZ; in later C.20, also Brit. Perhaps echoic, ex the *dong* emitted by a bell when struck; perhaps a blend of *ding* + *dot*.—2. To charge (someone) with a crime; often in the passive: Army: since late 1940s. (P.B., 1974.)

donk. A donkey: mostly Aus.—2. Hence, a simpleton: mostly Aus.: since ca. 1910. B., 1942.—3. Carrying a second person on the top bar of a bicycle. See **double-dink**, and cf. **croggie**.—4. A ship's engine: RN Submariners': 1950s (?and later). Peppitt compares j. *donkey-boiler*, 'providing steam for auxiliary machinery'—but why not straight from *donkey-engine*? See also **donkshop** and cf. **diddly-donks**.

donkey. A '350 h.p. shunting locomotive' (*Railway*, 2nd): railwaymen's: since ca. 1955. It does the '*donkey* work'.—2. A sewing-machine: RN lowerdeck: since ca. 1890. (Goodenough, 1901; Knock.) The pl. *donkeys* tends to mean 'sewing-machines, mechanics' tools, sea-chests' (Knock).

donkey box. 'Small wooden tool-box for the stowing of tea-makings, best hat and coat, and going home boots' (Patterson): Portsmouth dockers'. Cf. mid-C.19 *donkey*, a sailor's clothes-chest.

donkey-drops and custard. Prunes and custard: Marlborough College: since early 1920s.

donkey-lick. To defeat easily, esp. in a horse race: Aus. sporting: since ca. 1920. B., 1953.

donkey vote. 'A vote where the votes are numbered straight down the voting card. In Australia the voter has to number the candidates in order of preference'—esp. when there are many candidates: Aus. coll.: since ca. 1960. (B.P., 1974.)

donkey stone. In *give a donkey stone*, to give the real value when buying an antique: dealers': later C.20. Gash, 1983.

donkey's ages. A very long time; var. of **donkey's years**: since ca. 1940 (?earlier). (P.B.)

donkey's breakfast. A straw mattress: Services' coll.; orig. nautical, by WW1, Army, and by ca. 1925, RAF. Bowen; Jackson.

donkey's ears. A var., dating from just before WW1, of *donkey's years*.

donkey's eggs. Sugared almonds: mostly juvenile: since ca. 1920; by 1975, rare. (P.B., 1974.)

donkey's years. A long time: suggested by the sound of *donkey's ears*, when illiterately pronounced *donkey's years*, and the length of a donkey's ears: from ca. 1900.

donkshop. Engine room; hence *donkshop horse*, 'Senior Engine Room Artificer in the engine room, but not the chief E.R.A.': RN Submariners': mid-C.20. (Malin, 1979.) See **donk**, 4, and **donkey**, 2.

Donnelly's Hotel. RN lowerdeck mess. See **Casey's Court**.

donnybrook. A fracas: Aus. (esp. among soldiers): since ca. 1920. Ex *Donnybrook* Fair, famous for its free-for-alls.

Dons, the. See ASSOCIATION FOOTBALL, in Appx.

don't make a fuss. A bus: r.s., chiefly theatrical. Franklyn.

doo. See **doggie doo**; **pea doo**.

doo-da or **dooda(h),** all of a. Excited: from late 1914. Ex the echoic refrain *doo-da, doo-da, doo-da day*, prob. on *all of a dither*.

doo-flicker; doo-hickey. See **dooflicker; doohickey**.

doob. Penis: Aus. schoolboys': since ca. 1950. Perhaps ex *dood*, or ex older (since mid-C.18) synon. *doodle*.—2. (Usu. pl.) Amphetamine tablets: Cambridge: late 1960s–early 70s. (Cropper, 1987.)

doobri; doobri-firkin (occ., **macfirkin**). An elab. of **doofah**, 2, a gadget, a 'whatchermacallit'; may also be applied to persons, as usu., 'Old Doobri-firkin—old whatsisname': Army: 1950s. (Jones, 1979.)

dooby. Dowdy; old-fashioned: Aus., mostly feminine: since ca. 1950. (Campbell, 1964.) Either a distortion of *dowdy* or an imperfect blend of *dowdy* + b*ooby*.

dood. A pipe. Aus.: since ca. 1910. (B., 1942) ?Ex Aboriginal.

doodad. A thingummy: Can.: adopted ca. 1930, ex US—A word of fanciful formation.

doodah. A thingummy: since ca. 1910. 'Pass me the doodah'. Ex **ooja-ka-piv.**—2. An air-raid siren: WW2. Ex the alternating note of the wail.—3. A duodenal ulcer: since ca. 1945. Partly ex sense 1 and party ex *duo*denal.—4. Wholly ex sense 1 is its 'use as a euphemism, in such ways as "Where's the doodah?" When somebody wants to know where the w.c. is' (Petch, 1966): since late 1940s.

doodie, -y. Excellent, superlative: Oxford undergraduates'. 'He worked out a doodie route to Scotland' (Bartlett, 1988).

doodle, n. Short for **doodlebug**, 3: since Aug. or Sep. 1944.—2. Corresponding to, and deriving from:—

doodle, v. To write or draw aimlessly while one is listening to others at, e.g., a conference: since ca. 1930: coll. >, by 1950, S.E. Perhaps an arbitrary formation, but prob. ex dial. *doodle*, to waste time, to trifle.

doodle-ally; doodally. Mentally deficient: since ca. 1940. Prob. a misapprehension of **doolally**, q.v.

doodle-bug (or **doodlebug**). A small, cheap car: motorists':—1935.—2. Hence, 'utility truck, or light motor van, as used by the Army' (H. & P., 1943).—3. A German flying-bomb (V.1): since mid-June 1944; for the duration of the weapon's onslaught, then historical. P.B.: E.P. derives this from sense 1, and sense 1 from **doodle**, v.; I have a strong feeling, however, that the term *doodle-bug* is South Eastern counties' dial. (not in *EDD*, but I was brought up in rural East Sussex) for the booming cockchafer, or June-bug: the noise and shape fit sense 1, and the blundering flight, sense 3.—4. A gremlin: FAA: ca. 1940–5.—5. 'A new-style locomotive' [i.e. diesel-engined] (*Railway*): railwaymen's: ca. 1945–60.

dooee, occ. **dooe; doee; douie; duey.** Two, as in *dooee salter*, two pence: Parlyaree: mid-C.19–20. The sum of £200: second-hand-car dealers': since late 1940s. (*Woman's Own*, 28 Feb. 1968.) With both senses, cf. **deuce.**

dooey, doey. Always *large do(o)ey*, a large cup of tea: orig., and mainly, carmen's: from ca. 1920. Ex the notice: *tea 1d., large do., 2d.* But clearly influenced also by prec.

doof. To strike; punch: Northumberland teenagers': later C.20. (Blyth Ridley, 1984.) Cf. synon. **duff**; both are ex dial.

doofah, doofer. A partly smoked cigarette, extinguished so as to *do for* another smoke: orig. workmen's,—1935; much used in Services, WW2; by latish 1930s also Aus. (Raab, 1977).—2. A gadget; anything not specifically named, any 'box of tricks': Forces', esp. RAF: since ca. 1936. Something that will '*do for* the time being'. Cf. **gubbins.**—3. A humorist, a wag: 1944+. (Dunn, 1946.) Ex 'You'll *do for* me!'—i.e. I'll die laughing at you; or, as H.R. Spencer pointed out, this sense might perhaps have derived from Ger. s. *doof* = daft, crazy.

dooflicker (or *doo-flicker*). 'Any mechanical tool, instrument, or gadget': Can. Army: 1915+. (B. & P.) Cf. the later **doofah, 2,** and **doohickey.**

dooflop. Anything for which the proper name is momentarily forgotten, as 'the whatsitsname, er, thingummy, dooflop . . .': since mid-C.20. (P.B.)

doohickey, dohickey (or *doo-hickey*). 'An airman's term for any small, detachable fitting' (F. & G.): since 1915. The term spread throughout the Eng.-speaking world; Can. is said to have adopted it ex US ca. 1930, and it was becoming common in NZ ca. 1939; the RN used it, in WW2, for any gadget one can't find a name for. Of fanciful origin; cf. **dooflicker, doofah, 2** and **gilhickey.**

dook. To give: Aus.: since ca. 1910. (Niland, 1955.) Ex C.19 s. *duke/dook*, a hand. Cf.:-

dook on it, have (one's). To seal a bargain with a handshake: Aus. Baker.

doolally (or **doolali**). (Orig., and still, very occ. among old soldiers, the full form was/is **doolally tap.**) Off one's head; mad; 'he's gone doolally': orig., late C.19–mid-20, Army s.; since then, much more widespread, and > gen. coll.; the abbr. *doolally* dates from ca. 1920; the occ. corrupt variants *doodle-ally* or *doodally* have crept in since ca. 1940. The prob. derivation is ex *Deolali*, a military sanatorium in Bombay, and Hindustani *tap*, fever.—2. Hence, exceedingly drunk: Army: from ca. 1930; by ca. 1950, ob. if not †. H. & P.—3. Of a machine, e.g. a vehicle, out of action, broken down: heard from a London bus conductor, 1983. (Raab.) Loosely ex sense 1.

doolan. A policeman: Aus. (Niland, 1959.) Prob. ex the Irish surname Doolan, there being so many Irishmen in the police force.

doolander. 'A heavy blow: "He gave him a doolander on the nut" ' (Munro, 1985): Glasgow. Cf prec., **Dinny Hayes,** and **Larry Dooley.**

dooley. See **Larry Dooley.**

Doomie. An RAF nickname for the character adorning the 'What no —?' drawings: 1944+. See **Chad.**—2. As *d-*, 'Bodgie or widgie with criminal tendencies' (*Sunday Chronicle*, 6 Feb. 1952): Aus.: ca. 1950–60. All three terms are urban, raffish and confined mostly to Sydney.

doomy. Very depressed and discouraged; dismal: since ca. 1960. (*Groupie*, 1968.) A blend of *doom*-laden and gloomy. 'It took me two doomy weeks to get myself together.'

door-plater. See **brass-plater.**

door to door. Four; occ., where the context is clear, 24 or 34 or 44 or . . . : r.s. Franklyn.

Doorknob. 'A Belgian ("Doorknob" in Grimbarian) beam trawler' (Sweeney, 1984): Grimsby fishermen's.

doors. 'The lock gates on a canal' (Granville, 1949). By humorous meiosis.

doorstep. To intercept someone face-to-face, for a story, interview, etc.: journalists': later C.20. Parry-Jones, 1981.

door-stepping. Waiting around before a newsworthy event, e.g. a royal wedding: journalists': later C.20. Edmonds, 1986.

doo's. See **fair doo's,** fair shares or behaviour.

dooser (or **D.), the.** The Second Steward: ships' stewards'. (Marlowe, 1937.) I.e. *deucer*.

doover. Aus. military var. of **doofah, 2,** q.v., any object whatsoever: WW2. (Baker.) In *Rats*, 1944, it refers specifically to a dug-out.

dooverlackey; occ. **dooverwock(e)y.** An elab. — since ca. 1945 – of prec. (B.P.)

doovers. See PRISONER-OF-WAR SLANG, §10, in Appx.

doozer. 'Anything very large or outstanding; here [Dowell, 1975] a drunk', (esp. an alcoholic): Can.: since ca. 1955. Very prob. ex the synon. US *doozy*; cf. US *lollapaloozer*.

dope, n. A drug: 1889. Also, in C.20, an anæsthetic: medical students'.—2. Drugging: from ca. 1900.—3. Adulterated liquor: Aus.:—1964.—4. Fraudulent information: 1901. —Hence, 5, any information: from ca. 1910. All coll. ex US, where orig. of any thick lubricant or absorbent (*SOD*); itself ex Dutch *doopen*, to dip: W.—Whence, 6, a fool, a bungler: military: 1915 (F. & G.), though perhaps ex Cumberland dial. (1867: *EDD*), and, 7, 'news bulletin sent by wireless' (Bowen): nautical: from ca. 1925.—8. A heavy drinker: Aus.: from ca. 1912. Ex sense 3.—9. In the S. African underworld, it = dagga (*Cannabis indica*). (J.B. Fisher, letter, 1946.) A specialisation of sense 1. By later C.20 also UK (Stockley, 1986).—10. Petrol (esp., if specially treated): since ca. 1930.—11. One's work: copywriters': since ca. 1930.

dope, v. To smear: garage hands': since ca. 1905. Hodge, 1928, 'I soon acquired the knack, learning to "dope" the cylinders with petrol.'

dope out. To discover, ascertain, comprehend: US (1906, O. Henry), anglicised ca. 1917. Cf. **dope,** n., 5.—2. 'To work out; get hold of': US (1906), partly anglicised by 1934 owing to the 'talkies'. *OED* Sup. Cf. synon. **suss out.**

dope up. To check (an aircraft's engines): RAF: since ca. 1938. P-G-R.—2. Esp. *dope it up*, to take drugs: drug addicts' (and their like): since ca. 1965. 'How did the police know they'd been doping it up all day?' (*Jagger*).

doped off. As in 'I could easily go in there relaxed, carefree, "doped off", "thumb in bum, mind in neutral" ' (*Phantom*): RAF: later C.20.

dopey. A drug-addict: c. and low: from ca. 1920. Brandon, 1934.—2. A very dull or slow fellow; a fool: Army in WW1, then gen. Ex **dope,** n., 6, and the adj.

dopo. A sycophantic colleague or employee or friend: mostly police: since late 1940s. (Newman, 1970.) Ex **dope,** n., 6.

dopy. Dull, lethargic, half asleep (lit. and fig.). Ex **dope,** n., 1.—2. Stupefying: 1925, Wallace (*OED* Sup.).

Dora. The *Defence Of the Realm Act*: 1914. Orig. s., soon coll.; by 1920, S.E. and considered as officialdom's equivalent of Mrs Grundy.

Dora (Gray). A threepenny piece: Aus. r.s. on *tray*, Parlyaree = three.

Dorchester. An armoured command vehicle: WW2. Ex the famous London hotel. See **gin palace, 2.**

Doris. A drophead model Morris Minor: aficionados': later C.20. (*Sunday Telegraph Mag.*, 8 Mar. 1987.) Cf. **Moggie.**

dork. A 'doorstep' (q.v.) of bread and butter: lower classes': since ca. 1895. Still in use at the Duke of York's Royal Military School, Dover, in the late 1940s (Paine, 1978). By 'telescoping' or conflation.—2. A harmless fool: later 1970s. 'Sid Vicious chain-whipping this hippy . . . [giving] this poor dork a going over' (York, 1980). Ex US s. = penis (W. & F., 1975).

dorrick. To tell fortunes, whence *dorricker*, a fortune-teller: market-traders'. (*M.T.*) ?Romany.

do's, fair. See **fair doo's.**

dose. To shell: Army: WW2. Hence, *dosing*, a shelling. P-G-R.

dose of salts, like a. Very quickly and effectively; esp. *go through* (something) *like* . . . : coll., albeit low. In a letter to P.B., 1976, Mr G. Briggs-Smith, a gallant veteran of WW1, used the var. ' . . . the attack on Messines Ridge in June 1917 . . . went through like a dose of salts through a weak Chinaman'; and E.P. noted the Can. var., since ca. 1930, . . . *through a serpent girl*, to which he added the comment, 'a very picturesque elaboration'. Wilkes notes the later C.20 Aus. var. *packet of salts*.

dosh. Money, esp. cash: Aus. juvenile: since ca. 1944. (B., 1953.) Perhaps a blend of *do*llars + *cash*.—2. '*I dig dosh.* Can you lend me a fiver?' is the Andersons' very free paraphrase: beatniks': since ca. 1950. I suspect that *dosh*, as in

D

Eng. dial., is a var. of *doss* and that the speaker is hinting that he needs money for bed and lodging. Increasing s. use in UK since later 1970s. (Joanna Williamson, 1980; BBC Radio 4 serial 'The Archers', broadcast 17 June 1988.)

doss. A, and to, sleep; lodging, to lodge; a bed. All implying extreme cheapness and/or roughness: late C.18–20: vagrants': c. > ca. 1890, gen. s. Presumably imm. ex † *dorse, doss*, back; ultimately ex L. *dorsum*, the back.—2. Hence, to 'hang the time out', to loaf: telegraph-messengers' (1935). Still in use among young Londoners in the late 1970s: Walker, 1979, reports a teenage football-supporter as saying, 'We never usually go out anyway during the week, just doss around.' P.B.: gen. teenage s., late 1980s.

doss down. To sleep very rough: low, from ca. 1880; by mid-C.20, gen. s., as in 'Can I doss down at your place tonight?', meaning 'Can you provide me with a proper bed, or, failing that, may I sleep on the floor, settee, etc.?'

dosser. A frequenter of doss-houses: low: from ca. 1865. Whence (h)*appy dosser*, a homeless vagrant creeping in to sleep on chairs, or in passages or cellars: low:—1880 (Sims). Presumably ex *happy* but just possibly ex *haphazard*.—2. A regular old tramp: tramps' c.—3. Hence, the late 1940s, any single, homeless person, usu. a man.—4. The 50 ring, which counts as a double, there being no 25-ring double: dart-players': since ca. 1930.—5. As in 'Boys are still anxious not to be swots [q.v.]. They prefer to be known as "dossers", who "mess about" in lessons' (Turner, 1983). Cf. **doss,** 2.

dossers' hotel. A casual ward: tramps' c. Jennings, 1932.

dossy. Soft; daft: low. ' "Don't know what she ever saw in that dossy bastard" ' (Behan, 1958). Perhaps cf. N. Country dial. *dossy*, soft, dull.

dot. Anus: low Aus. Niland, 1959, 'Shove it up your black dot' — said to a Negro.—2. See **on the dot.**

dot(-)and(-)dash. Cash: r.s. (Cook, 1962.)

dots. Sheet-music, as in 'you can switch repertoire at a moment's notice, which you can't if you're tied to "dots" — music — and the backing' (Foster-Carter, 1982): club entertainers'. Dr Kemp Fowler, of Sydney, remembers that, in Brit. in the 1950s, some folk musicians were very scornful of others who could 'read the dots' and who, therefore, did not extend their repertoire in the truly 'authentic' way, by oral tradition only. (Raab.)—2. See **put dots on.**

dotted line. See **sign on the dotted line.**

doub, occ. written **dubb.** A double, e.g. two crows with one shot: Aus.: since ca. 1920. Devanney, 1951.

double. In c. a street-turning: from ca. 1870. Powis records the sense of 'a street' as still current a century later.—2. A pornographic picture of a man's and a woman's genitals: raffish coll.: since ca. 1920.—3. In *on the double*, (of doors, gates) double-locked: c. Ingram, 1933.

double-ace poker. See **kangaroo poker.**

double act, do the. To get married, be married: low:—1923 (Manchon). Prob. ex *run in double harness.*

double-bagger. See **single-bagger.**

double-bank, n. and v. See **double-banking.**—2. See **double-dink.**—3. (Of a novice or trainee) to share an experienced man's job with him, in order to learn it; of, e.g., radio operators: Army: since early 1940s. Hence, a *double-banker*, one who does this. (P.B.)—4. 'To have two strings to one's bow': coll.: since late 1940s; by ca. 1960, S.E.

double-banking, n. (The fact of) two lines of vehicles going in the same direction: Army coll. (1940) >, by 1945, j.

double bass. A motorcycle with twin exhaust pipes: motorcyclists': later C.20. (Dunford.)

double-blue. 'Amphetamine/barbiturate' (Home Office): drug addicts': current in 1970s.

double bubble. 'The [film camera] crew will be on double bubble to achieve the [tight] schedule. In this case bubble is not Greek, but overtime—"A nice little earner" ' (*You*, 9 June 1985): London. The 'Greek' ref. is to r.s. *bubble and squeak.*

double-bubble. 'Short-hand money was paid to workers standing in for colleagues absent through illness . . . Then there were the double-bubble payments: overtime paid if the ship arrived within one hour later than scheduled' (*Times*, 2 May 1988): cross-Channel ferry crews'.

double carpet. Odds of 33 to 1: racing, esp. bookmakers'. (*Sunday Telegraph*, 7 May 1967.) Ex **carpet,** n., 3.

double-choked. Extremely disappointed or disgruntled; utterly disgusted: since ca. 1950. Cunliffe, 1965, 'The bogies knew he had had it away but just couldn't pin the job on him. Which meant he was laughing and they were double-choked.' Cf. **choked.**

double clanger. The double chainwheel on a (racing) bicycle: cyclists': since ca. 1920. Ex 'the noise made by the chain shifting from one wheel to the other' (W. Woodman).

double-dink, v. and derivative n. 'To carry a second person on the top bar of a bicycle. It is also a noun. Exchangeable terms are "*dink*", "*donk*", and "*double-bank*", both as verbs and nouns,' B., 1942: Aus.: since ca. 1925. Prob. the orig. term is *double-bank*, and *dink* and *donk* are echoic variations. Cf. **croggie.**

double event. A glass of whisky and a glass of beer: public-houses' (esp. in Glasgow).

double fair! Goes one better than *fair enough!*: mid-C.20. (L.A.)

double figures, go into. To have 10 children at the least: lower classes' coll.:—1923 (Manchon).

double home turn. 'Train crew lodging over-night at terminus and returning next day' (*Railway*, 2nd): railwaymen's coll.: since ca. 1945(?).

Double Hunts, the. 'New type of Hunt-Class Destroyers, twice the size of the old type' (Granville): RN: since ca. 1940.

double in brass. 'Originally vaudeville, [applied to] one who could perform his own act and also play in the orchestra; later, . . . do more than one thing' (Leechman): Can., adopted ca. 1950 ex US, where orig. circus (W. & F.).

double knocker. Twin camshafts: motorcyclists': since ca. 1950. (Dunford.)

double-take; esp. *do a . . .* A second look, taken because one doesn't credit the first: since ca. 1948. Orig., film-producers' j.

double talk. Such speech, hence such writing, as deliberately misleads, orig. with the interpolation of meaningless syllables; hence, deliberately ambiguous and tendentious political matter: adopted, ca. 1959, ex US: coll. >, by 1966, S.E.

double top. A good shot: RAF: WW2. (Forbes, 1942.) Ex darts-scoring.

double trouble. Tuinal: drugs c. (Stockley, 1986.) US since −1968 (Spears).

double u. Var. of *w*, short for *the w.c.*

doubled over like a dog fucking a football. Doubled right over: Can. soldiers': WW2.

doubleton. See TIDDLYWINKS, in Appx.

Douche Can Alley. Palmer Street, Sydney, Aus., formerly a brothel district: Sydneyites': ca. 1910–60. A douche can is, in Aus., popularly supposed to be used only—or, at the least, mainly—by prostitutes.

dough-nut. (Gen. pl.) A Carley life-saving float: nautical. Bowen.—2. See **golden doughnut.**

Doughboy. An American infantryman: US coll. (—1846), adopted in UK ca. 1917.—2. (**d-**) A punch in the face: low: from ca. 1919. Ingram, 1933, has it in its usual form: *give* (a person) *a doughboy*.

doughy. Dull, stupid: Aus. Tennant, 1947.

Dougie. A Douglas motorcycle (in production 1907–56): motorcyclists'. (Dunford.)

down, n. A prejudice against, hostility towards: Aus. coll.: from ca. 1850. P.B.: in later C.20, Brit. also, esp. in such phrases as 'He's got a down on me, always has had, for no good reason that I can think of'. Also *downer*.—2. Inside information: market-traders'. (*M.T.*) Ex *low-down*.—3. Also *downer, downy*. A barbiturate: adopted, ca. 1965, ex

US. In Bronsteen, 1967, *downs* were described thus: 'the beautiful thing about downies is that there's no come down . . . you just go to sleep.'

down, v. 'To drink down, as in "I couldn't half down a pint" ' (Petch, 1969): coll.: since ca. 1910. Cf. **drop a pint**.

down by the head. Overloaded with work: MN: by 1960 at latest—but surely since a generation earlier? 'An overloaded vessel tends to be deeper in the water forward' (Peppitt).

down in. Surrounded by hills and (usu.) trees; of a house in a valley: 'Yes, it's very nice, but it's a bit down in, don't you think?': coll. (P.B.)

down like flies. Always with pl. subject, and v. *go*, to succumb to epidemic or other adversity: coll. Presumably ex the effect of cold weather on flies that, paradoxically, thrive on the conditions in, e.g., 'The natives went down like flies to the effects of heat and fever'. (P.B.)

down on. In *get down on*, to remove; appropriate; steal: Aus. low s. B., 1942.

down on his knees and at it! A male 'facetious exclamation at [the sight of] a man kneeling down to do a job of work' (L.A., 1974); hence a joc. ref. to a man performing a marital duty: since the 1920s.

down on (someone, something) **like a ton o(f) bricks, be** or **come.** To be very angry with someone, or some fault, as in 'The old man's mustard on safety precautions. If he catches you parked like that by the fire-doors, he'll be down on you like a ton o' bricks': coll.

down on the hooks. See **hooks**.

down the block. In punishment cells: prisoners' (Home Office): 1970s.

down the chute. In prison: Aus.: since ca. 1920. Baker.

down the line. See **all down** . . .

down the mine. 'Buried' by a heavy wave that collapses suddenly and violently: Aus. surfers': since middle 1950s. (Culotta.) Perhaps ex the famous song, 'Don't Go Down the Mine, Daddy.'

down the nick. (Of a locomotive) short of steam: railwaymen's: mid-C.20. *Railway*.

down the pan. Too far behind; done-for: motor-racers': from ca. 1922. (Chamberlain.)—2. A Cockney equivalent of the older *down the drain*, ruined with no chances left: since the 1930s. (Franklyn.) The pan is that of the water-closet, with perhaps a glance at *up the spout*.

down the plug. (Of a tender) running short of water: railwaymen's: mid-C.20. (*Railway*, 2nd.) Short for . . . *plug hole*.

down the sink. Lost, wasted; squandered, misspent. Cf. *down the drain* and . . . *the pan*.

down the slot. (Of a slow train) diverted onto a side-line to allow faster trains to pass: railwaymen's: since ca. 1910. *Railway*.

down to it, get. See **get down to it**.

down to Larkin. 'Free: "Who's paying for this round?" "Shush! It's down to Larkin" ' (Powis): 1970s. See **larking**.

downer. A heavy fall: the turf:—1923 (Manchon).—2. A bed: tramps' c.:—1935. Either ex *down* (cf. synon. **feather**) or ex *get down to it*.—3. A small unofficial strike: workmen's: since the early 1960s. *Sunday Citizen*, 4 July 1965: a news feature, 'He defends "downers".' Ex 'to *down* tools'.—4. Var. of **down**, n., 1, a prejudice or hostility, in its Brit. usage.—5. Var. of **down**, n., 3, a barbiturate tranquilliser or sedative: since ca. 1962 (addicts'); by 1965, gen. teenagers'. (Wolfe, 1968; Janssen, 1968.) Cf. **uppers**, 2.

Downing Street. See TOMBOLA, in Appx.

downright, the. Begging, esp. as a tramp: tramps' c. Whence *on the downright*, on the tramp, 'on the road': tramps' c.:—1932 (Jennings). Earlier, engaged in straight, unashamed begging: id. (Davies, 1908.) Still current late 1970s (*Toby*, 1979).

downrighter. A destitute person that, quite openly, goes in for begging: c. (Davies, 1933.) Ex prec.

downstairs. At low altitude (of aircraft). See **upstairs**, adv.

downy. See **down**, n., 3.

downy earwig. A sympathetic person: c.:—1932 (Jennings).

D'Oyly Carte. (A) fart: r.s. (Daniells, 1980.) Often simply *D'Oyly*, which, as R.D. points out, is confusible with paper table-mats.

'dozer or **dozer.** A bulldozer: Aus.: since late 1950s; orig., construction workers', but soon in gen. use. (B.P.)

dozy. Lazy; inefficient: orig. Guards' Regts' coll., later spread to the rest of the army. Lit., 'sleepy'. Often in the imprecation, to a dull recruit. 'You're an idle, dozy man!'—2. As a gen. coll., it means '(mentally) somnolent'.

d'rac, drac. (Gen. in pl.) A card: back s. in c. (Leach, 1933.) Also *derac(k)*.

drack, n. A very plain female, esp. if lacking in personality: Aus.: since ca. 1950. Perhaps ex the adj. and certainly at least influenced by it, but prob. = *Drac(ula)*: cf. **Dracula**, 2.

drack, adj. Inferior; (of person) uninteresting, plain-looking: low Aus.: since ca. 1930. (Park, 1950.) Yiddish? Cf. the Ger. *Dreck*, dung, muck (lit. and fig.). A *drack sort* is an unattractive person, opposite to *good* (superlative *extra*) *sort*. Cf. **drawers drac(k)**, and **drecky**.

Dracula. A pathologist: hospitals': since ca. 1920. Ex the blood samples he takes. (Sanders.)—2. A plain, esp. if uninteresting, girl: Aus.: since ca. 1950. Ex the legend of Dracula. (B.P.)

draft-dodger. A Serviceman who 'dodges the draft'—avoids being sent overseas: Services': WW2. (P-G-R.) Contrast the US sense, 'one who avoids conscription'.

drag, n. Three months' imprisonment: c.:—1851 (Mayhew; Leach). Now rather *three moon*. This sense current in Aus. late C.19–mid-20, at least. (Wilkes.)—2. 'Petticoat or skirt used by actors when playing female parts. Derived from the drag of the dress, as distinct from the non-dragginess of the trouser' (Ware): theatrical:—1887. Also as adj. Since ca. 1910, this sense has predominantly signified 'female clothing as worn by men', esp. among homosexuals.—3. An arrest that the criminal considers is unjustified: c.:—1935 (Hume).—4. A motor-car: c.: since ca. 1920. Ex earlier s., horse-drawn vehicle.—5. A quick draw at a cigarette: Cockneys' and Services' since ca. 1920. H. & P.—6. 'Pull'—influence with the right people: Can.: since ca. 1910.—7. Ex sense 5. A cigarette: mostly Services': since ca. 1925.—8. Anything or anyone boring or tedious: Can. and Brit. since ca. 1950, adopted ex US; orig. mostly beatniks' and young peoples' usage. Esp. in 'It's a drag!' or 'What a drag!'—9. 'A marijuana cigarette, (inhalation of its smoke)' (Home Office): Aus. since ca. 1955; Brit. drug-users' in 1970s. ?Earlier. Ex senses 5 and 7.—10. Any act that requires a special effort: coll. Cf. sense 8.—11. A dance or ball: Can., ca. 1925–30; since ca. 1950, Aus. and Brit. teenagers'. (B.P.)—12. A particular kind of dance, as in the number entitled 'Doin' the Varsity Drag': Can. and Brit.: since ca. 1930. (Priestley.)—13. A casual female companion, as opposed to one's girl-friend: Aus. teenagers': since late 1950s.—14. That portion of winnings which one reserves for further play: Aus., esp. two-up, gamblers'. Ex *drag*, v., 2. Ronan, 1954. 'By the time I gave you the kip I had a few quid out of drags and showers'.—15. An invitation to race, and—16, the race itself: Aus. teenage motorists': since late 1950s. Ex *drag*, v., 3, q.v.—17. In *on the drag*, (of Flying Squad cars) on patrol: c.: from ca. 1927.

drag, v. To arrest: c. (Wallace, *passim*.) Cf. **pull**, v., 1.—2. V.i and t., to take a portion of the stakes in a gambling game as a reserve for future play: Aus. and NZ. Cf. **drag**, n., 14.—3. To challenge to, or to oppose in, a speed duel with cars: Aus. teenagers' (esp. surfers'): since late 1950s. Cf. **drag strip**.

drag (one's) **feet.** To be mean or 'stingy', as in paying for a round of drinks: since ca. 1950. In Aus., commoner than *have a snake in one's pocket*. (Raab.) Cf.:-

drag (one's) **heels.** To be either reluctant, or intentionally very slow, to co-operate or to do one's duty, and yet finally do so if encouraged: coll.: since ca. 1940. Ex a person trying to 'dig in' his heels as he is being hurried, or dragged, away. (A reminder, 1976, from L.A.)

135

drag on. (Of a man) *drag on a woman*, to marry her: Aus.: since ca. 1910. B., 1942.—2. To undertake (a task): Aus. coll.: since ca. 1910. B., 1943.

drag queen. A male homosexual addicted to transvestism: since ca. 1930.

drag-race A contest, between drivers of specially built vehicles, to achieve fastest acceleration over a very short distance: poss. at first coll., but soon, by early 1970s, > informal S.E. Hence also as v., and vbl n. *drag-racing*. Cf. **drag strip**, and:-

drag slicks. Racing-car wheels: Aus.: esp. Sydney, motor mechanics': since ca. 1950. (B.P.)

drag strip. A short stretch (say a mile) of *road* on which teenagers try out or, esp., race their motorcycles or cars: Aus. teenagers': since late 1950s. (Westerway, 1963.) Cf. **drag**, n., 15.

drag the chain. To be at the rear in a race or in a game (of, e.g., cribbage): NZ. Niall Alexander, letter, 1939, 'The ploughman's term to designate his slow horse that does not keep its chains tight'. Also Aus. (B., 1943). Often of a slow drinker. (Slatter.)

dragged, be. To be returned to a convict prison to serve the rest of one's sentence: c. Wallace, 1925.

dragging (one's) **arse along the ground** (**so's you could cut washers off it**). Utterly exhausted: Can. Army: 1914+. P.B.: not completely †; I heard the phrase on occasion, 1950–70, in the Brit. army.

dragging lark. The practice of stealing from motor-cars: c.: from ca. 1910. (*Gilt Kid*, 1936.) Cf. the earlier *drag-lay*, the same from horse-drawn vehicles.

draggy. Of persons, boring; of things and incidents, tedious: mostly teenagers': since ca. 1955. 'A lot of draggy housework' and 'Right draggy the whole thing was' (Francis, 1968). Ex **drag**, n., 8.

dragon. An old prostitute: low: since ca. 1959.—2. Heroin: drugs c. (Stockley, 1986.) Cf. **chase the dragon**.

dragons' teeth. A form of anti-tank obstacle, lines of small concrete truncated pyramids: WW2, then merely historical. H. & P.

drain. A melancholy, affectionate cadger of bed and board: beatniks': since ca. 1958. (Anderson.) A drain on one's provender and patience.—2. As *the Drain*, the 'Waterloo & City Underground Railway under the Thames' (*Railway*, 2nd): railwaymen's: since ca. 1920.—3. See **main drain . . .**

Drain(-)pipe. RN nickname for an excessively thin man. Also *Snak(e)y*. Granville.

drain-pipes. Short for *drain-pipe trousers*, particularly narrow-cut and tight-fitting trousers, part of the 'Teddy-boy uniform', worn with a long draped jacket: since ca. 1950. (P.B.)

drain (one's) **radiator.** (Of men) to urinate: Can. and Brit., an occ. joc. since ca. 1940. Cf. **bleed** (one's) **turkey**, an occ. earlier synon., as also is *drain* (one's) *snake*.

draining down all over. RN Submariners' synon. for *dripping*, complaining. Martin, 1983.

drape. A 'suit of clothes: prisoners' ' (Home Office): 1970s, adopted ex US. See **drapes**.

draped. Somewhat tipsy: Services officers': since 1939. (H. & P.) Draped about a friend or a lamp-post.

drapes; set of drapes. A man's suit of clothes: beatniks': since ca. 1958. (Anderson.) Adopted—and adapted—ex synon. American *drape*.

draughters. Close-fitting, undivided knickers, the female counterpart of the male *cheaters*: since ca. 1920? They keep out the draught. Contrast *dividers*.

draughty. Nervous; (vaguely) afraid: military (1918) >, by 1920, gen.; ob. (Lyell.) Cf. **windy** in the same sense.

draw, n. An inhalation from a cigarette, as in 'Just skiving off for a mo', I'll be round the back—must have a quick draw'; often in the (?now ob.) phrase 'a spit and a draw'.—2. Hence, marijuana, and, as v. in e.g. 'let's draw', 'let's smoke marijuana'. (Turner, 1986.) 'Plenty of [prison] officers smoke [marijuana] too. I know some who'll have a search for draw and

then pocket it' (A prison officer, quoted in *Guardian*, 5 Sep. 1987).

draw, v. In *do you draw*, do you take your daily tot of rum?: RN coll. Granville.

draw-back (or solid). Something withheld; an assurance, a promise reneged. (Leech, 1972.)—2. Deliberate inhalation of cigarette smoke: smokers' coll.: since ca. 1930. In part a pun. Cf. **draw**, n.

draw the crow. To experience (an outstanding piece of) bad luck: Aus.: since ca. 1910. (*Rats*, 1944.) Contrast a *regular crow*, a great success.

drawers drac(k). Underpants of the official issue pattern, healthy, but uncomfortable, to wear: Army: since ca. 1960. Ex *Dracula*, and mocking the standard army j.

drawing a pint. Using the controls of an aircraft: RAF: since ca. 1939. H. & P., 'An action similar to that employed behind the public bars.' Cf. **beer-lever**.

drawing up the verbals. 'Det. Williams said it meant completely misinterpreting what a person said' (*Evening Standard*, 30 Jan. 1962): police: since ca. 1930. Ex the preparation of '*verbal* reports'? See **verbals**.

dread. 'A Jamaican teenager with dark glasses and a big woolly hat' (*Daily Telegraph*, 6 Jan. 1977): since early 1970s. Cf. **tea-cosy mob**, and **dreadlocks**. Hebdige, 1979, ' ' "Dread" is a polysemantic term. It seems to encompass righteousness, Biblical "wrath" and the fear inspired by that wrath.'

dreaded lurgi, the. 'Any malaise or minor ailment. A straight quotation from "The Goon Show" . . . I feel that there is certainly room for a learned monograph . . . on "The Influence of the Goon Show on the English Language", for the influence has indeed been widespread and lasting. "Dreaded" is also often applied, humorously and affectionately, to people, as in, on his perhaps unexpected appearance, "Why!, it's the dreaded Jim Bigam!" ' (P.B., 1974.) This programme was promoted by Michael Standing, BBC's Director of Variety, 1945–53. The Goons—orig. *Crazy People*—included, during the opening period, Peter Sellers, Harry Secombe, Michael Bentine, and Spike Milligan; by the 2nd series it was 'The Goon Show'. It 'stood the supposedly real world on its head'; 'under [Peter] Eton it prospered'. Spike Milligan scripted many numbers, but the show 'came to an end because Milligan had become fed up with it' (Took, 1976). It ended very early in 1960.

dreadlocks. 'The long, plaited hair worn by some Rastafarians was originally intended to reproduce the "ethnic" look of some East African tribes' (Hebdige, 1979): orig., the wearers' > by later 1970s, gen. (P.B.)

dreadnought. A condom: low: early C.20.—2. A very high, stiff corset: low: early C.20.—3. A heavy, clumsy, strong pedal bicycle: club cyclists' earlier C.20. (Roberts, 1984.) Cf. **sit up and beg**.

dreadnoughts. (Like the prec., ex the battleship.) Close-fitting (gen. thick) woollen or flannel female drawers: from 1908; low. Later, 1940+, an ATS and QAIMNS synon. of the Wrens' E.T.B.s (*Elastic Top* and *Bottom*).

Dreado. HMS *Dreadnought*: RN: early C.20. ('Taffrail'; Bowen.) *Nought* = 0.

dream, a. A very delightful or agreeably odd person: coll., chiefly among either the nation's youth and girlhood or romantic women. (As applied to things, even lovely dresses, it is S.E.)—2. Six months in prison: Aus. c.: since ca. 1920. B., 1942.

dream-boat. An attractive young man: girls' and young women's: adopted ex US late 1950s; ob.

dreamer. Morphine: drugs c. (Stockley, 1986.) US since—1969 (Spears).

dreamy. (Of a man) very attractive: girls' and young women's: since ca. 1965. Cf. **dream**, 1 and **dreamboat**.

dreamy REME. See **Reemy**.

drecky. Rosten, *Joys of Yiddish*, 1968, defines *dreck*, 'of grossly inferior quality', ex Ger. for 'shit(ty)'. Carter, 1979, 'I can only conclude that she penned her sniggering memoirs

in order to give her drecky movies . . . an extra touch of notoriety.' Cf. **drack.**

dreg. One of the lowest of the low: Public Schools'. By back-formation ex S.E. *dregs.* Hence adj., *dreggy.*

dress-fencer. (A tramp or peddlar that is) a seller of lace: c. 'Stuart Wood', 1932.

dress the nuts off. To reprimand (someone) severely: prob. orig. Army: since ca. 1910. Cf. **chew the balls off.**

dressed up like a dog's dinner, (all). Wearing one's best uniform: Services', esp. Army: since ca. 1925. P-G-R.

dressed up like a sore finger. Too elaborately dressed: Aus.: from ca. 1912.

drift. As in ' "just off for an afternoon's drift" (He meant an afternoon of making love)' (Piper, 1974): trawlermen's.—2. In *on the drift*, on the tramp: Aus. coll. B., 1942.—3. See **get** (one's) **drift.**

drill, the; occ., *the right drill.* The correct way to do anything: Army—by 1942, also RAF—coll. (mostly officers'): since ca. 1910. (H. & P.; Jackson.) A man that knows his drill *must* be good.—2. Hence, the appropriate course of action, as 'Right!, What's the drill now, then?': Services': WW2 and after. (P.B.)

drill – fill – and bill. 'That is the way we [dentists] 're taught, that is the way we're paid: "Drill, Fill and Bill", as the saying goes' ('A Practising Dentist', in *Green Light*, Loughboro', Oct. 1986).

drill pig. A drill instructor: orig. Guards' Regts', since ca. 1910; by the time of National Service, 1948–62, the term had spread throughout the army and to the RAF. Applied esp. to those NCO instructors who are excessively officious and 'regimental'. Kersh, 1941. (P.B.)

drink. 'Euphemism for blackmail payment or money bribe. "There's a drink in it for you" may mean there will be such payments; "Does he drink?" may mean "Is he willing to be bribed?" ' (Powis): c.: since (?)ca. 1950. Read, 1978, defines *drink* as 'Reward for services rendered by police, solicitors, witnesses or criminals. Usually not less than £50, but because of the vast sums involved in the Train Robbery [of 1963], a drink escalated to £20,000.' 'A "big drink" can be £20,000 or more; a "soppy drink" between £20 and £50, depending on the size of the original theft' (Hoggart, 1982). Cf. the same basic idea in the Chinese *chaqian*, lit. tea-money, = a bribe, and the Fr. *pourboire*, a tip in this sense. (P.B.)—2. As *the Drink*, the sea: RAF: orig., from ca. 1925, the English Channel; in WW2 and since, the ocean generally. (H. & P.; P-G-R.) Cf. **(the) Ditch.**—3. As *the drink*, water: London Fire Brigade. Also London dockers': 'Term for water in the docks; similarly the "beach" would denote the dock or quay' (Ash): mid-C.20.

drink out of a nigger's clog. To be intemperate: Liverpool: since ca. 1945.

drink with the flies, n. and v. (A) drink by oneself: Aus. coll. Cf. **Jimmy Woodser.**

drinker. 'Unlicensed drinking premises or "drinkers" (less commonly but still referred to as "shebeens" or "blues")' (Powis): police and frequenters': 1970s.

drinkies. A drinking party: middle-class young women's: early 1980s. (Hoggart, 1983.) Ex the nursery usage.

drinks. Medicine: hospital nurses':—1933 (*Slang*, p.191).

drinks on, have the. To have (a person) at a disadvantage: lower classes':—1923 (Manchon).

drip, n. Nonsense: Public Schools', then, from ca. 1920, gen. For semantics, cf. **bilge** and S.E. *drivel.*—2. Hence, a simpleton, a 'stupid', a 'wet', a bore: coll.: since ca. 1920.—3. A complaint: RN: since ca. 1910. Winton, 1967.—4. 'Sloppy' sentiment; a person 'sloppily' sentimental: since ca. 1930. Gray, 1946.—5. In *on the drip*, engaged in hire-purchase: retail commercial world, perhaps orig. among secondhand-car dealers: since ca. 1950. (*Woman's Own*, 28 Feb. 1968.) Cf. **on the knock** and **on the never-never.**

drip, v. To talk nonsense: Public Schools'; by ca. 1925, gen. coll.—2. To complain, to 'grouse': RN: since ca. 1910. Gran-

ville.—3. To be stupid, to be a bore, to be 'wet': Public Schools': since late C.19. See quot'n at **wet dream,** 2.

drip-pan. Var. of **dripper,** 2, a 'grouser': RN. Granville.

dripper. 'Old prostitute past her best (and no longer controller of her emissions)' (Newman, 1970): low: since ca. 1930.—2. A bore or an inveterate 'grouser': RN: since ca. 1930. H. & P.

dripping for it. (Of a woman) inflamed with lust: low: since ca. 1910.

dripping tight. Completely drunk: low classes':—1923 (Manchon). I.e. 'soused'; an intensive of C.19 s. *tight*, drunk.

drive. To irritate (someone) intensely: Aus. teenagers': since ca. 1950. (Dick.) Perhaps elliptical for '*drive* mad' or '*drive* crazy' or '*drive* up the wall'.

drive at (or **on**) **the limit.** 'Driving [a racing-car] as close as possible to the car's optimum performance is called "driving at (or on) the limit" ' (*Now!*, 2 Nov. 1979).

drive blue. To drive 'all out': motor racers': from ca. 1920.

drive the train. 'To lead a number of squadrons' (Jackson): RAF: since ca. 1938. Cf. **traindriver.**

drive (someone) **up the wall.** To send him mad (well, almost): since the mid-1940s.

driver. A pilot: RAF: since ca. 1929. (Rhodes, 1942.) 'Taken over from the RNAS' (Partridge, 1945): Jackson points out that it is an old Navy custom to refer to the captain of a ship as *the Driver*; McDouall, 1945: ' "Drivers, airframe" is what pilots are called by navigators.' P.B.: this last piece of humour lasted until at least the early 1950s.

drizzle. See **sling** (one's) **drizzle.**

droggy or **drogy,** a hydrographic officer; **Droggy,** the Hydrographer of the RN; also as a nickname: RN: since ca. 1910. The 2nd is in Winton, 1964. A conflation of '*hydrographer*'.

dromestoners. 'The men who clear the aerodromes before runways are laid down' (H. & P.): RAF: since ca. 1930.

drone. A rear-gunner: RAF: 1939+. (Jackson.) Except (what an except) during an attack he sits and sits.

drong. A shortening of **drongo,** 2: Aus.: since the late 1930s. (B.P.)

drongo. A new recruit: Aus. airmen's—1943. Immediately ex:—2. An ugly fellow; a 'bastard': low Aus., esp. Sydneyites': since ca. 1925. (Park, 1950.) Sydney's *Sunday Herald*, 28 June 1953, defined him as 'a lazy and usually undesirable human being'. 'Perhaps from a racehorse called Drongo, whose performances on the track were disappointing' (Baker); the horse got its name from the Australian bird called the *drongo*. Since ca. 1950, a widely used term of dislike. 'In Australian slang a drongo is a bit of a galah, a goat or a no-hoper . . . Drongo . . . raced on Melbourne tracks from 1924 to 1926. Drongo was a good galloper, but . . . second-rate . . . Any who arouses the contemptuous disapproval of an Australian is apt to be described as a bloody drongo' (Marshall, 1962).

droob. A dull person: low Aus.: since ca. 1944. (Park, 1950.) A blend of *dr*ip + *b*oob. Occ. spelt *drube*. Hence adj., *drooby* (Wilkes).

droog. A hooligan imitating, in costume and violence, the hooligans of *A Clockwork Orange*, the film based, early 1970s, on Anthony Burgess's strange and moving novel (1962). Ex the Russian-based argot of the book; the word enjoyed a certain popularity during the period in which the film was being shown.

drool, v. Often as vbl n., *drooling.* To loiter; to waste time: Aus.: since ca. 1930. (B., 1942.) Ex S.E. *drool*, 'to dribble at the mouth'.

droolin' with schoolin'. See CANADIAN . . . , in Appx.

droop-snoot, the. 'There was in the late 1950s an experimental delta-wing supersonic aircraft flying at RAE Farnborough, which, because its nose could be lowered at an angle to improve the pilot's field of view when landing, was known as "the droop-snoot"—and very odd it looked.' (R.S., 1967).—2. The sobriquet was later applied to the Anglo-French supersonic airliner Concorde, which can lower its nose.—3.

As *droopy snoot*, it refers to the handlebar fairing and screen on a streamlined motorcycle: motorcyclists': 1970s. (Dunford.)

droopers. Sagging breasts: Aus.: since ca. 1930.

droops, the. A sinking or droopy feeling; lassitude: coll.: from ca. 1912. A London underground-railway advertisement of 1935 ran: 'Down those mid-morning "droops" with tea. You'll be better for a cup at 11 a.m.'

droopy drawers. 'A girl . . . who habitually looks undecided in tackling day-to-day living, [a tendency] often reflected . . . in dress' (L.A.): orig. and mostly lower-middle class.

drop, or rather **the drop,** n. A receiver of stolen goods: c. (—1915). *OED* Sup.—2. A tip to a docker: nautical: early C.20. Bowen.—3. Hence, a tip: transport-workers' (—1935) and underworld's (—1936), the latter in *Gilt Kid*. P.B.: see esp. *Muvver*, p. 21, for a thorough analysis of all the term's monetary nuances. '4. A 'backhander' or 'rake off' given by civilian victuallers to RN stores personnel: prob. since late 1940s. *The Times*, 14 Nov. 1972, contained a report on RN catering frauds. (Peppitt.)—5. 'Place at which a letter carrier has to deliver mail' (Leechman): Can. post-office employees': since ca. 1960. Semantically, not ex US, but perhaps ex:—6. Worldwide c. for 'a covert address or place where messages or money can be left for a third person' (Powis): since (?)ca. 1950.—7. See **cop the drop; take the drop; fabulous drop.**—8. In *get* or *have the drop on*, to forestall, gain advantage over, orig. and esp. by covering with a revolver: (US and) Aus. since late C.19; some UK use in later C.20.

drop, v. To get rid of (a person): Aus. and NZ c., >, by 1940, s. in both countries.—2. To get into trouble: Army: WW2 and after. Short for *drop in(to) the shit*.—3. To leave (a competitor) far behind: racing cyclists': since ca. 1945.—4. To knock (someone) down: coll., esp. in Aus.: since ca. 1945. Culotta.—5. To give illicitly, to get rid of surreptitiously, e.g., a stolen cheque: since late 1940s.—6. To tip; to bribe: as in "He tried to drop the mingra [policeman]", "I dropped him a flim": Cockney and market-traders'. (*M.T.*) Cf. **drop,** n., 3 and 4, **dropsy,** 3, and **cop the drop.**—7. To take a drug, esp. by swallowing, as in 'I dropped my first acid in Paris'. Bronsteen, 1967: adopted, late 1960s, ex US.

drop a ballock – banger – clanger – goolie. To blunder badly: Services', since ca. 1930; the *clanger* version has, since ca. 1970, had much more widespread and gen. use. All are, in this sense, synonyms of 'testicle', and the phrase prob. derives from the inoffensive *drop a brick*, itself now almost informal S.E.

drop a ballock for (someone). To let someone down; to fail him: Army: since ca. 1935. Kersh, 1942.

drop a bomb. To cause a very unpleasant or painful surprise: coll.: since ca. 1919. Ex bomb-dropping, first practised on a large scale in WW1. Cf. **bombshell.**

drop a pint. To drink ale or beer: public-house frequenters': since ca. 1930. (Petch, 1969.)

drop a tab. Make a mistake: RAF: WW2. Passim in the series 'Letters to a Conscript Father' in *Punch*, 1942.

drop acid. To take LSD. See **drop,** v., 7.

drop across. To scold severely: from ca. 1925. (Lyell.) Perhaps by confusion of S.E. *drop across*, to meet casually, and *drop on*, to scold or accuse.

drop-dead. A drop-head convertible: secondhand-car dealers': since ca. 1955. *Woman's Own*, 28 Feb. 1968.

drop 'em. See **drop them.**

drop (one's) **guts.** To break wind: low.

drop heavy. 'To tip well is to "drop heavy" ' (Hodge, 1939): taxi-drivers': since ca. 1915.

drop in the clarts or **shit.** To get into trouble. See **clarts.**

drop (one's) **leg.** (Of a woman) to curtsey: lower classes':—1923 (Manchon). Prob. suggested by *make a leg*. See also **drop the leg.**

drop lullaby. A hanging: Aus. low. B., 1942.

drop of gens, a. *Gen*eral leave: RN: earlier C.20. Bowen.

drop of the hard (stuff), a. A drink of spirits: proletarian: since ca. 1930. Cf. **hard stuff,** (P.B.)

drop off. 'To desist from hectoring or otherwise pressuring someone, to ease the pressure' (McNeil): Aus. coll.: later C.20.

drop on (one) **from a (very) great height.** To reprimand very severely; to land in dire trouble: orig. Services', WW2; by ca. 1970 much more widespread. In, e.g., Hunter, 1974, a hippie-type speaking: 'Yet somehow I'm feeling that the fuzz [police] have got a trap here. Like I just take another step forward and I shall be dropped on from a great height.' The Services' var., from same date, is *shit upon from* . . . , sometimes perverted to **shat on** . . . , q.v. (E.P.; P.B.)

drop one. To perpetrate an inaudible but pungent fart: low. (Turner, 1986.)

drop-out, n. 'One who opts out of society' (Fryer, 1967): drug addicts', hippies', Flower People's: since ca. 1960. P.B.: by ca. 1970 in gen. use and often, esp. among conformists, pej.

drop out, v. To become a *drop-out*. See prec.—2. To resolve itself; of, e.g., a mathematical problem, 'This one dropped out quite easily': coll.: later C.20. (P.B.)

drop the bucket (on). 'To throw responsibility for an offence on to someone else' (B., 1959): Aus. c.

drop the leg. To decamp: lower classes':—1923 (Manchon).—2. To make a leg, to bow or curtsey: rural coll.(—1923) and dial. Ibid.

drop the pilot. To come off one's motorcycle accidentally: motorcyclists'. (Dunford.) Since (?)ca. 1950.

drop them. (Of a woman) to be sexually accommodating: low coll.: since mid-C.20. *Them* = her knickers, panties, as 'Her? She's not fussy—she'll drop 'em for anyone.' (P.B.)

dropped. Arrested: drugs c. (Stockley, 1986.) US since—1959 (Spears).

dropped magnets. Flat feet (?rather fallen arches): London busmen's: since ca. 1940.

dropped on. Astounded, thunderstruck, as in 'Well, when I asked her if she'd like an egg for her tea, she looked quite dropped on': East Midlands coll.(P.B.).

dropped right in it, (I, he, etc.**).** 'I (he, etc.) got into serious trouble—made an appalling *faux-pas*—was in an awkward spot': low: since ca. 1910. The *it* is gen. understood as *the shit*. (Petch, 1971.)

dropper. A passer of counterfeit, esp. paper money: c. Rhodes.

dropperman. A police informer: Aus. c.: since ca. 1940. B., 1945.

dropping. Bribery: c. Wallace, 1924.

drops. Dropped handlebars, the two outer parts being below the rest: cyclists': since ca. 1930. Hence, to *ride on the drops*.

drops his slacks. A roughly joc. imputation of passive homosexuality: Services': WW2 and after. (L.A., 1978.)

dropstick. Pickpocketing: London West Indian c.: since ca. 1955. See **sticksing.**

dropsy. A request to pay what is owed (esp. in money): low:—1935.—2. Salary: theatrical:—1935.—3. Bribery, in gen. or as a single bribe: grafters' and market-traders'. *Cheapjack*, 1934; *M.T.*—4. Hence, specifically, hush-money:—5. 'Tips are dropsy' (Hodge, 1939): taxi-drivers': since ca. 1910.—6. The habit of dropping things accidentally, of being 'butter-fingered': Aus. and Brit.: since ca. 1950. (B.P.) R.C. notes, 'Almost certainly adopted ex US, where current much earlier'. Like all the other senses it is a pun, using the name of the disease to signify the appropriate meaning of the s., coll. or S.E. *drop*.

Drover's Guide, The. An imaginary periodical quoted as the source of a rumour: Aus.: since ca. 1920. (B., 1959.) Cf. **The Bagman's Gazette.**

drown. To put too much water into whisky or brandy: joc. coll. 'Don't drown it!'

drube. Var. spelling of **droob:** B., 1953.

drug-store cowboy. (Gen. in pl.) A tyro cowboy, esp. one of those who carry a revolver dangling from a loose belt to somewhere near the knee: South American white men's derisive coll.: from ca. 1910 (Craig, 1935).—2. Any lout that hangs about a corner drug-store, talks tough, gives the girls 'the glad eye': Can. coll.: adopted, ca. 1935, ex US. (Leechman.) Cf. **canteen cowboy, cowboy**, 2–4, and **cowboys**, 3, all derisive.

drug up. Deliberately illiterate form of *dragged up*, in the query 'Where was you drug up, then?' = where were you brought up (sc. that your manners are so uncouth)?: since ca. 1940, ?earlier. (P.B.)

druggie, -y. A drug addict: adopted, ex US, by ca. 1970 at latest. (Kenyon, 1978.) Cf. **junkie**.

druid. See HAULAGE, in Appx.

drum, n. A building, house, lodging, or (in C.20) a flat: c. and low (—1859). H., 1st ed.; Leach. Hence, *have* (one's) *drum done*, to have one's house searched by detectives: c.—2. A tin for making tea, etc.: tramps' c.: since ca. 1890; in C.20, also railwaymen's.—3. A racecourse tip: Aus. sporting: (B., 1942.) Hence, any *tip* or *warning*.—4. Hence, information; 'the score' or true state of things: Aus.: since ca. 1912. Niland, 1955, 'If it's a fair question, what's the drum?'—5. See **Casey's Court**.—6. In *run a drum*, in a race, esp. of horses or dogs, to win a place: Aus. sporting: since ca. 1940, ?earlier. Wilkes, who glosses, 'to perform as tipped'. Ex 3.

drum, v. In c., *drum (a place)* is to ring or knock to ascertain if it is occupied. (Leach.) Hence a *drummer* is a woman that does this, or that gets a job as a servant in a house some months before her man robs it; *drumming*, robbery by these means. P.B.: in later C.20 c., *drumming* has come to mean simply 'breaking into a house' (cf. **drum**, n., 1), as in *Now!*, 10 Apr. 1981.—2. To inform, tell; to 'put wise', to warn, tip off: Aus. low: since ca. 1910. (*Rats*, 1944.) Also *drum (a person) up* (Wilkes). Ex n., 3.—3. To drive fast in a vehicle, as in 'Can you imagine drumming along the M1 and some clown does a U-turn ahead of you?' (policeman, quoted in *Observer* colour sup., 20 Dec. 1981).

drum and fife. A knife: r.s. Franklyn.

drum around. To prowl, as a thief does: police: from ca. 1910. Cf. **drum**, v., 1.

drum-up, n. A drink of tea; the making of tea: tramps'; and troops' in WW1. (Jennings, 1932.) Ex v., 1.—2. 'Effort to obtain results' (Powis): c.: 1970s.

drum up, v. To make tea, esp. by the roadside: tramps' c. (—1864) > also, by 1914, military s. '*No. 747*'; B.&P. Loosely, in C.20, to cook a meal. Ex Romany *drom*, the highway, or **drum**, n., 2.

drummer. A commercial traveller: adopted in Aus., ca. 1920, ex US. (Baker.) Ex S.E. *drum up*, to solicit trade.—2. Anyone notorious for boring his companions: Army: late 1940s.—3. See **drum**, v., 1, and with it cf.: 'He chose the screwsman'—burglar—'best fitted for the particular job. He sent with him a "drummer"—a man who had to make sure the coast was clear and help the screwsman with unskilled jobs, such as carrying the ladder' (Gosling, 1959): c.: since ca. 1910.—4. But cf. 'Burglars are called "drummers" because they screw drums (steal from houses), not because they drum on doors' (*Time Out*, 11 Feb. 1983).

drummer-up; drumming-up. The agential and the vbl n. of **drum up**, 1; esp. among labourers on public works, the man that makes tea for the gang; the making of tea.

Drummond and Roce. *Drummond* = *drum and* = *drum and fife*, a knife; *Roce* = *roce* = *roast* = *roast pork*, a fork. Harrison, 1943.

drunk, adj. Mad; crazy: London teenagers': mid-1980s. (Simmonds, 1986.)

drunk-up. A drinking bout: Aus. coll. (Baker.) Cf. **beer-up, punch-up**.

Drunken Duchesses. 'We sailed from Liverpool on Christmas Eve, 1936. Our ship was the *Duchess of Bedford*, one of the small sturdy Canadian Pacific liners which were known as "Drunken Duchesses" for their lively performance in heavy seas' (Buchan, 1982).

drunkery. A saloon: Can. s.: 1960. Dempsey, 1975, 'the countless drunkeries which, for single men, form the centre of social life . . .'

drunok. Tipsy: from ca. 1930. A perversion of *drunk*.

dry, n. A 'drying-up' or being at a complete loss for one's lines: theatrical. Hence, *dries*, instances of such loss. Ex 'to *dry up*' or forget one's lines. Holt, 1950.—2. As *the Dry*, desert; semi-desert; waterless country: Aus. coll.: late C.19–20. (Cable, 1938.) Cf. English dial. *dry*, a long period of rainless weather.—3. Also *the Dry*, the dry season (winter) in N and NW Aus.: coll.: late C.19–20. B., 1942; Devanney, 1944.

dry, adj. (With the low nn. of coïtion) rape and homosexual intercourse: Aus.: since ca. 1950.

dry as a basket. Very thirsty: since ca. 1930. (L.A.)

dry as a sun-struck bone, extremely dry; **dry up like a sun-struck billabong**, to become so. 'Both similes are also used figuratively; "dry" suggesting irony, and "dry up" meaning to become silent or run out of words' (B., 1959): Aus. coll.

dry bath. 'A search [of a prisoner] when stripped': c. Ingram, 1933.

dry-blower. A gold-miner (s.), esp. one who dry-blows gold instead of sluicing it (coll.): Aus.

dry dock (or hyphenated or one word); esp. *go into dry dock*, to stay for a long time in hospital: Services': since ca. 1925. Hence, *in dry dock*.—2. Out of work: coll.: from ca. 1927. *OED* Sup.

dry glasses without using a cloth. To 'booze': joc.

dry-hump. To simulate copulation with: since ca. 1960. *Observer*, TV review, 7 Dec. 1975. Cf. **hump**.

dry list. Officers listed for shore service only, as opp. to the *wet list*, listed for sea appointments: RN. (Granville, 1967.)

dry old stick. An elderly person (esp. male) either boring or possessed of a very dry sense of humour: coll.: late C.19–20.

dry out. To take a course of treatment to cure oneself of alcoholism. Also v.t.: coll. (Chambers' *C.20th Dict.*, 1977). Hence, vbl n. *drying out*, undergoing this treatment; applied also to a 'slow withdrawal from narcotics' (Home Office).

dry run. A dummy run, q.v., but with much wider connotation of 'experimental rehearsal' (Dr Leechman's phrase): Services': since ca. 1950 at latest. Perhaps adopted ex Can., where coll. usage since ca. 1925, or perhaps orig. RN.

dry scrub; scrubber. A marker's signalling of a 'magpie', the disk being rapidly moved up and down in front of the target: Army (not officers'): from ca. 1920.

dry-shave. To deceive, befool, humbug (a person): lower classes':—1923 (Manchon). Prob. on *drub* reputed = *dry rub*.

dry ship. One whose wardroom has a poor drinking reputation: RN. Contrast **wet ship**. Granville.

dry swim. A ground operational exercise: RAF: since ca. 1936. Cf. **grope**, 1.

dry up. To anger or exasperate beyond words, as in 'It dries me up when I think of the terms he offered for the part': theatrical, an allusion to 'drying up' on stage. (Granville.)

dry-wipe. To win two legs straight off from (an opponent): dart-players': since ca. 1930. Cf. **whitewash**, 2.

dryknacking or **drynacking**, as in 'a spot of dryknacking', a little music-copying: Guards' Regiment musicians': since ca. 1920. It's *dry* work but rapidity therein is a *knack*.

dual. 'Dual-flying instruction' (Jackson); i.e. flying dual-engined aircraft: RAF: since 1939.

dub. To open: mid-C.16–18; (by confusion with *dup*), to close, gen. in form **dub up** (Vaux): early C.19 c. Prob. ex Walloon *adouber*, to strike; tap. W.—2. To make (e.g.) Brit. nationals appear, by means of a fresh sound-track, to speak (e.g.) French in films being shown in (e.g.) France: cinematic: since ca. 1935: by 1946, j.

dub up. To pay out money: s. (—1823, Bee) >, by C.20, coll. Developed from **dub**. On its later C.20 Cockney use, *Muvver* has, 'Calling on someone to disgorge cash, the phrase is "dub up" or "dub out"; "cough up" and "fork out"

are middle-class schoolboys' expressions. "Hand over" has a certain appeal because it makes a comic-book bad joke—"The Highwayman, by Ann Dover".' —2. See **dub**, 1, which apparently 'went underground'—existed without being recorded—for it is extant, 'Everybody in the nick had already been dubbed up'—locked in his cell—'for the night' (Norman). It occurs also in, e.g., Gosling, 1959.

dubby, the. The water-closet: children's: C.20—perhaps late C.19–20. Ex '*double*-u cee': *W.C.* (Yates.)

Dublin University graduate. 'A particularly dense person, or a person unable to read or write. Intended to be humorously ironic' (Powis): police and underworld: 1970s.

dubs. Marbles played in a ring: Aus. schoolchildren's. B., 1942.—2. Hence(?), nipples of a girl's breasts: Aus. (Blunden, 1935.) Current among Southampton schoolboys before 1920, occ. in the form *dubbies* which suggests a deformation of *bubbies*. On the other hand, *dubs* may have been influenced by S.E. *dugs* (in its 'nipples' sense).

ducer, the. See **deucer.**

duchess. 'To treat anyone "as a duchess", esp. applied to the courtesies extended by overseas governments to visiting Australian politicians, as though imposing on their naivety' (Wilkes): Aus.: since mid-1960s.

duchesses. Female counter clerks in post-offices: mostly lower-middle class: since ca. 1948. Ex the airs so many of them give themselves.

duck, n. A type of large amphibious troop-carrying vehicle: Services', esp. Army: from 1942; by 1944, at least semi-official. Ex the factory serial initials *DUKW*, usu. written thus, but always pron. *duck*.—2. A young lady; a girl: beatniks': 1959+. Cf. **hen**, and see the list at **canary**, 2.—3. An instance of copulation: shortened r.s., from *goose and duck*.—4. 'Coll. for "Cold Duck", a sparkling red wine' (B.P., 1977): since ca. 1970.

duck, v. To avoid; to neglect to attend (e.g. a meeting): coll. (Shanks, 1933.) See also **duck out.**

duck and dive. To hide: r.s. 'Good semantics, but poor phonetics' (Franklyn). *Muvver*, however, explains the phrase as rhyming on **skive**, q.v., and meaning 'to dodge work', which seems more likely to be correct.

duck (or goose) bumps. Gooseflesh; goose pimples: mostly Can., the latter sense joc. (Leechman.)

duck-disease; duck's disease. 'Shortness of leg' (*OED* Sup.); the army explained it differently; a nickname (*Duck's Disease*) for any very short man: (low) coll.: from ca. 1910.

duck dive (or hyphenated). A period of bad mistakes—of laxity—in operations: espionage: since ca. 1950. Le Carré, 1977.—2. A sudden escape: id.: Ibid.

duck eggs. Coal ovoids: railwaymen's: mid-C.20. *Railway.*

duck-house, n. In *one up against* (someone's) *d-*, (something) that baffles, outwits, defeats, delays: Aus.: ca. 1910–70. 'I admit that this is one up against my duck-house.' Ex a game-score chalked on a duck-house roof or wall.—2. In *upset* (one's) *duck-house*, to upset someone's plan or calculations: Aus.: since ca. 1920. (Franklin, 1931.) Cf. *mind one's own duck-house*, to mind one's own business: Ibid. See **lead from the duck-house.**

duck-house, v. To baffle, outwit, score a point in some way against: Aus.: ca. 1925–70. (B., 1942.) Ex n., 1.

duck (one's) nut. To put one's head down for safety. Here, *nut* obviously = head.—2. Hence, to disappear: Can.: since ca. 1955. Dempsey, 1975.—3. See **duck the nut.**

duck out (of). To avoid responsibility, fail to attend a meeting: 'Did you go last night?' 'No, I ducked out' or 'No. I ducked out of it': coll.: later C.20. An elab. of **duck**, v. (P.B.) Cf. **chicken out.**

duck-pond. The Atlantic Ocean: WW2 and after (earlier?): Services', then gen., coll. (M. Manoukian.)

duck-shovelling. 'Passing the buck': RAF: since ca. 1960. (Farley, 1967.) Prob. a var. of sense 2 of:-

duck-shover, -shoving. A cabman who is guilty of breaking the rank and thus unfairly touting for custom; this extremely reprehensible practice: Melbourne: ca. 1869–95. Morris.—2. (*d.-shoving.*) Hence(?), an evasion of duty: military: late C.19–20. F. & G.—3. (Ex 1.) One who is over-sharp in business; unfair business methods: Aus. B., 1942.

duck the nut. Synon. with next: Brit. c.: *New Society*, 23 Dec. 1982, p. 501.

duck the scone. To plead guilty in a law-court: Aus. c.: since ca. 1930. B., 1959. Cf. **bow the crumpet** and **nod the nut.**

duck weather. Very wet weather: Aus.: since ca. 1920. Ex *fine weather for ducks*. (B.P.)

ducks. A mainly London and Home Counties var. of the older endearment *duckie*, mostly in address.—2. See TOMBOLA, in Appx.

duck's breakfast. A drink of water with nothing to eat: esp. NZ. Cf. *Irishman's dinner*, and the Aus. synon. *duck's dinner.*

duck's disease. See **duck-disease.**

ducky, duckie. Expressive of admiration: coll.: since ca. 1930. Often, in Aus., used sarcastically or joc. by men: since early C.20. 'She was wearing a ducky little pair of shorts.' (B.P.)

dud. Worthless: coll.: since ca. 1895. *Sessions*, Feb. 1898, 'I have it, it is a *dud* lot' (watch and chain).—2. Useless, poor, unattractive; e.g., 'a dud show', a poor entertainment: orig. Army, from ca. 1916; thence to RAF, ca. 1918, 'dud weather', unsuitable for flying (H. & P.); and then into gen. civilian use, an expressive, almost echoic, word, 'demobbed' with the Forces in 1919.

dud up. To arrange (things) illicitly: serve short measure to (someone): Aus. c.: since ca. 1925. (Tennant, 1939.) See prec. Also 'Deliberately to misinform or mislead (someone). Whence, *dudder* and *dudder-upper*' (B. 1959).

dude. A swell, fop: orig. (1883) US and almost imm. anglicised: coll. till ca. 1918, when it > S.E.—2. Light; a light: either low s. or tramps' c.:—1923 (Manchon). Ex Romany.—3. 'A serious, usually rather older, bird-watcher'. See BIRD-WATCHERS, in Appx.—4. Almost any male person, as *guy, fella*, etc.: later C.20. Hibbert, 1983.

Dudley. A water bottle: railwaymen's (E.R.): since ca. 1950(?). *Railway*, 2nd.

dues, fair. See **fair doo's.**

duff, n. A tin in which pudding is served: prison s. (not c.). Triston, 1938.—2. Tobacco: Aus. c.: since ca. 1945. (Grindley.)—3. 'Sometimes we trawled up a bag of "duffs", globes of compacted weed, a grey oatmeal sort of colour, which looked like big puddings' (Piper, 1974): trawlermen's.—4. In *up the duff* (of a woman), pregnant: Brit. and Aus. low. 'He put (or got) her up the duff.' (B., 1942.) Cf. **pudden club**, which prob. suggested it.—5. A British Rail Class 47, 'the common all-purpose BR workhorse' (Allison, 1986): railway enthusiasts'.

duff, v. To render unusable; to ruin; to destroy: RAF: since ca. 1935. (Jackson.) See also **duff up.**

duff, adj. No good; inferior: Glasgow, late C.19–20; in WW2 and after it enjoyed very widespread use in the army and RAF (e.g. 'duff weather', cf. the earlier *dud weather*, and *duff gen*); later it spread to the world of entertainment. L.A. cites the *Observer*, 27 Jan. 1974, where a 'duff script' is used to describe a very loosely constructed, at times pointless, film script. Cf. the v.

duff-bag. 'Formed in the sailor's black "silk" when the bight is tied in by the tapes of his jumper forming a loop just wide enough to hold two fingers' (Granville): RN: since ca. 1910.

Duff-Choker. Nickname for a Yarmouth fisherman: drifter-men's. Butcher, 1979.

duff gen. Unconfirmed and improbable report; unreliable news: RAF since ca. 1930. See **duff**, adj., and **gen**. Partridge, 1945.

duff up. To wreck; to bungle badly: since 1940s. Ex **duff**, v. as is:—2. To beat up or assault (a person): since ca. 1950. 'He was duffed up pretty badly by a crowd of young louts . . . ' (P.B.)

duffie. A duffel jacket or coat: Aus. teenagers', esp. surfers': since the late 1950s. *Pix*, 28 Sep. 1963.

Duffoes. Ratings of the Plymouth Division: RN. (P-G-R.) Perhaps ex *duff*, older nautical s. for food; cf. **Guzzle**. Bowen records *duffo* as also a Devonport ship.

duffy, n. In *have a duffy*, to have a look: RAF: since ca. 1920. Poss. a corrupt var. of *dekko*. Contrast:—2. *Have a duffy at*, have a try at: Services': since ca. 1935. P-G-R.

duffy, v. To polish (e.g. one's buttons): RAF: 1930s–WW2.

dugger-dugger-dugger, often prec. by *a little bit of*. An attack by jet multi-role combat aircraft against a ground target, using cannon rather than bombs: since mid-1970s. (Grey, 1977.) Obviously ex small boys' imitation of machine-gun fire.

duggies. Market-traders' dim. of:-

dugs, of a woman's breasts or nipples, has, since ca. 1880, been a vulg., though it is permissible in S.E. if used as a strong pej.

Duke. Cf. **Duke of Kent.**—2. A *Duc*ati motorcycle; in production since 1950: motorcyclists'. (Dunford.)

Duke of Kent. Rent: r.s. (P.P., 1932.) Often shortened to *duke*.

Duke of York. Chalk: r.s. Ortzen, 1938.

Duke of Yorks. Forks: r.s.:—1874 (H., 5th ed.; Jones, 1971). —2. Hence, fingers; hence hands; hence **dukes**, q.v.

dukes, often, esp. in C.20, pron. *dooks*. Hands; fists: low:— 1874. Ex *Duke of Yorks*, 2. Another theory holds the term to be ex the rules of the Duke of Queensberry. P.B.: but *he*, 1844–1900, was a marquess; so I advance yet another theory: could the term stem from the Romany *dukker*, to tell fortunes (?palmistry)?

dukes stove. A field cooker used in N. Africa, 1940–3. See **Benghazi cooker.**

Dukie. (Gen. pl.) A boy of the *Duke* of York's Royal Military School: coll. *OED* Sup.

dullsville. Anything dull and boring. One of the more widely-used of the terms formed with the suffix **-ville**, q.v., adopted ex US ca. 1960.

dum-dum. See **dumb-dumb.**

dumb blonde. An extremely pretty, but very stupid, girl, blonde by nature or by artifice; the sort portrayed to perfection by Marilyn Monroe in the film *The Seven-Year Itch*: coll.: adopted, ex US, ca. 1940. Cf. **dizzy blonde**. (P.B.)

dumb cluck; dumbcluck. A stupid, foolish or dull person: coll.: adopted ex US by mid-C.20; now (late 1980s) ob.

dumb-dumb, dum-dum. 'Suddenly, within the last few months, this rather unpleasant epithet has erupted among us, army and civilians alike. Presumably'—factually, indeed—'from the US and therefore prob. imported via TV and radio. "She's a stupid cow—a right dumb-dumb!" ' (P.B., 1974).

dumb-waiter. An elevator: r.s., mostly workmen's: from ca. 1920. *John o' London's Weekly*, 9 July 1934.

dumbhead. See quot'n at **dimmo.**

Dumbo. Nickname for an at least app. slow-witted fellow: prob. popularised by Walt Disney's famous 'full-length' cartoon of that name, 1941.

dummy. In c., a pocket-book: from ca. 1810. (Vaux.) In C.20, it has the specific sense 'wallet'.—2. 'Ground disc' (*Railway*). I.e. a subsidiary signal, set at ground level, and used in shunting work.—3. Poor quality drugs: drugs c. (Stockley, 1986.) US since—1967 (Spears).

dummy chucker. A goods shunter: railwaymen's: since ca. 1945. (*Railway*, 2nd.) See **dummy, 2.**

dummy engineer. An engineer midshipman: RN: since ca. 1920. P-G-R.

dummy run. A practice evolution: RN coll. Bowen.—2. Hence, a rehearsal: RN: since ca. 1910. R.S., ' "Bartimeus" uses it, *à propos* preparations for a marriage service, in *Naval Occasions* (1914).' The army and RAF had annexed it by ca. 1943; by 1950, it > fairly gen. civilian; by 1955, coll.; by 1960, among scientists and technicians, j.

dummy up. 'To keep silent. Sometimes used as a command to an over-talkative accessory in dangerous company: "Dummy up!" ' (Powis): c.: 1970s.

dummy week. Non-payment week: RN. The ratings are paid fortnightly. It is often called also *blank week*: RN coll.: since ca. 1939. (Granville, 1962.)

dump, n. A place: orig. Army, since ca. 1915, soon > gen. and widespread; usu. pej., except when used in jest. Ex the j. sense, a place where war material, old or salvaged, is stored, for the most part in the open, hence a refuse heap, itself ex S.E. **dump**, v. —2. Hence, a hotel: tramps' c.:—1923 (Manchon).

dump, v. To throw or set down heavily; let fall heavily: ex US (—1830), anglicised ca. 1870 as a coll. that, ca. 1900, > S.E. —2. Hence, esp. in WW1 and after, to put, set, place, no matter how. An earlier instance occurs in George, 1911.—3. Hence, to abandon (e.g. stores): Services', from 1940; by 1945 in gen. civilian use, by which time even people could be *dumped* in this sense.—4. To defecate: later C.20. Ex either prec. senses, or via computer j. ex sense 3.

dumper. A heavy wave on a surfing beach: Aus. coll.: since ca. 1920. (B., 1942.) It picks one up and dumps one down.—2. A cigarette-end: Aus.: since ca. 1925. (B., 1943.) An object one 'dumps'. Hence a *dumper-dasher*, one who picks up cigarette-ends off the street and smokes them (B.). This sense specialises the gen. English sense 'cigarette', which seems to have existed since late C.19, to judge by Peppitt's proof (J.R. West, 1909).—3. 'A very tiresome experience or event' (Hibbert, 1983): later C.20. Ex prec., 4; cf. **bummer**.

dunch. To *dine* at *lunch*-time: cultured middle class's: late 1920s. Maugham, 1930, 'Verbs that you only know the meaning of if you live in the right set (like "dunch")'.

dung. To defecate; when used of animals it is S.E.: of humans, it is not: upper classes': late C.19–early 20.

dung-hunter. The De Haviland D.H. 6 aircraft: Aus. airmen's: 1920s–30s. (B. Huston.) Prob. a pun on the initials.

Dungheap. A Dunelt motorcycle: motorcyclists' nickname: 1920s. (Dunford.)

dunhead. An undesirable character: Aus.: since ca. 1930. Niland, 1955.

dunker. The observer aboard an anti-submarine helicopter: RN: later C.20. Ex the dipping or *dunking* of the sonar. (Knight, 1985.)

dunkie. A girl: mostly Londoners': since ca. 1965. Short for *Dunkin' Donuts*, a sort of crumpet, a pun on *crumpet*, a girl regarded sexually.

dunkle. 'Anything bad, e.g. weather' (Wilson, 1979): RAF: 1970s. Prob. ex Ger. *dunkel*, dark, familiar to RAF in Germany from *Dunkelbier*, dark ale.

Dunlop. See **dangling** . . .

Dunlop brackets. 'Rubber bands cut from old inner tyre tubes' (Dunford): motorcyclists': 1970s.

Dunlop tyre (often shortened to *Dunlop*). A liar: r.s.: since 1905. Cf. earlier synon. *holy friar*.

Dunn's three-and-ninepenny. Generic term for men's cheap headgear.

dunny. A privy: Aus.: since ca. 1880. Ex earlier *dunnaken*. Cleary, 1959.

duo. A *duo*denal ulcer: medical students': from ca. 1920.

dup (pron. *doop*, often in pl.), n. A *dup*licate copy of a document, key, etc.: Services', since ca. 1950 (?earlier); whence, esp. for documents, office typists', secretaries', etc., by ca. 1955. Cf. *trips* = triplicates, *quads* = quadruplicates. (P.B.)

dupey-dupe. A slow-witted police constable, esp. one likely to be returned from detection to uniformed duty: police s.: since ca. 1950. Newman, 1970.

durry. A cigarette butt: low Aus. (B., 1942.) Ex Romany *duria*, fire?—2. Hence, since ca. 1910, a cigarette: id. B., 1943.

dust, n. Semen; as in the phrase 'blow one's dust', to ejaculate: low: later C.20. (L.A., 1978.)—2. 'Cocaine or PCP' (Stockley, 1986): drugs c. US since—1942 (Spears).

D

dust, v. To blind (fig.); befool, as in *dust the public*: Stock Exchange: from ca. 1814; ob. by 1930. Abbr. the S.E. *dust the eyes of.*—2. *dust* or *dust off* (or *out*), v. To depart hurriedly: in C.17 S.E.; in C.19 US s., whence C.20 English s.—3. To discipline (someone) severely: Army, esp. the Guards: since ca. 1920. Hence, *get a dust*, to receive severe disciplinary treatment. P-G-R.

dust-bin. Gun position on the underside of an aircraft: RAF: ca. 1939–49. (H. & P.) It receives the *dirt*; also, some types of pre-WW2 bomber had a belly-turret shaped like a dust-bin. (Hinde, 1945.)—2. Bridge in a motor torpedo (or gun) boat: RN: since ca. 1938. Ex the shape and appearance. Granville.—3. Mark VII depth charge: RN: WW2. Johnson, 1978.

dust-bin lid (usu. pl.). Child: r.s. on *kid*: Franklyn 2nd.—2. A Jew: r.s. on *Yid*: later C.20. Barker, 1979.—3. (Usu. pl.) A type of car wheel with a solid-looking disc cover that became fashionable ca. 1983: motorists'. Cf. **barrow-wheels**. (P.B.)

dust-bin seven. An old, cheap, small car: ca. 1925–50. App. suggested by *Austin Seven*, the famous small family car of the period.

dust-bin totting. Unauthorised removal of refuse from dust-bins. (*The Times*, 25 Apr. 1940.) Also *d-b tatting*.

dust parade. 'Morning fatigue party for cleaning up' (H. & P.): Army: since ca. 1920.

dusted, adj. Beaten; worn out: Aus.: since ca. 1930. Cusack, 1953.

dusters. Testicles: Army: ob. by 1948. But extant in RN and among Cockneys. Perhaps joc., ex dust accumulated by shorts-wearers, esp. in India or in desert country. P.B.: or boastful—they hang so low as to dust the deck?

dustman's hat. A slouch-hat of much the same shape as a dustman's: coll.: early C.20. Collinson.

dutch. In *in dutch*, in trouble; under suspicion: Can., adopted ex US ca. 1925, with additional nuance 'in disfavour' (Leechman); Aus. since ca. 1935 (B., 1942).—2. See **go Dutch**.

Dutch cap. A type of female pessary: orig. Londoners' and Services', since ca. 1925; by ca. 1950 far more widespread. Ex the shape.

Dutch cheese. The divisional sign of the 4th British Infantry Division: Army: WW2. (P-G-R.) Ex the shape, a circle with one quarter 'sliced' and slightly protruding. (P.B.)

Dutch fuck. Lighting one cigarette from another: Forces': 1940 +. Prob. ex Territorial Army, where current from or before 1938. Also called *Don Freddie*, the Signalese for D.F. See PHONETIC ALPHABET, in Appx.

Dutch kiss, n.; **Dutch-kiss,** v.i. Low coll., as in Auden, 1935, 'The boots and the slavey dutch-kissing on the stairs', it seems to mean indulgence, or to indulge, in sexual intimacies. Cf. synon. **French kiss**.

Dutch oven. The olfactory state of the bedclothes after one has broken wind in bed: low: since ca. 1910, esp. in the Army. ob.—2. The mouth: boxers':—1923 (Manchon).

Dutch pegs. Legs: r.s.:—1923 (Manchon). Cf. *Scotch pegs*.

Dutchie. In Aus., any Central European: coll. Baker.

Dutchman. (Gen. pl.) The 'mark' made by a drop of rain on still water: children's:—1923 (Manchon).

Dutchman's fart. A sea-urchin: trawlermen's. Butcher, 1980.

duties. Duty-free goods, esp. cigarettes: RN: since ca. 1940. Short for *duty-frees*, itself coll.

dutt (or **dut**). A hat: North Country: earlier C.20. Ex a hatter named Dutton?

duty beauty. A WRNS duty officer: RN (mostly wardroom): WW2.

duty boy. The officer of the day or of the watch: RN officers': since ca. 1920. P-G-R.

duty dog. Duty Officer; loosely, Orderly Officer: Services': since ca. 1920. (H. & P.) Cf. **dog-watch**.

duty stooge. A duty corporal or airman: RAF: since ca. 1938. (Emanuel, 1945.)

duty-sub, the. 'The duty sub-division of the watch, to be called upon to relieve pressure when needed' (Granville): RN coll.

dwang, in the. In grave trouble, 'in the shit': Services', esp. RAF, mostly in the Middle and Far East: since late 1930s. (Jones, 1974.) Still current in 1970s. (Wilson, 1979.)

dwarf. 'A [type of] signal' (*Railway*, 2nd): railwaymen's: current in 1950s.—2. See **poison dwarf**.

dwell on. To like very much, to long for (someone): Aus. coll.: since ca. 1930. (Campion.)—2. 'Eagerly to await another's decision of action' (B., 1959): Aus.: since ca. 1930.

dwell the box. To be patient; to wait: low: since ca. 1930. Norman.

dyke; dykey. See **dike; dikey**.

dynamite, n. Baking powder: Aus.: since ca. 1920. (B., 1942.) It causes cakes, scones, etc., to rise during cooking—to 'blow up'.—2. Mixture of cocaine and morphine: drugs c. (Stockley, 1986.) US since—1937 (Spears).

dynamite, adj. (Of persons) violent, brutal, drastic, autocratic, powerful, expert—all or each to an alarming degree; (of things) extremely dangerous or sudden. Coll., from ca. 1914.

dynamiter. Cocaine addict: drugs c. (Stockley, 1986.) US since—1950 (Spears).

E

E. See **give the big E.**

e.b.p. 'This means Every Bloody Penny—the wages due to you that you elect to draw before going ashore in a decent foreign port' (Tredrey, 1939): MN: earlier C.20.

E-Boat Alley. 'Quite a sizable fleet . . . entered the World Channel, to which the war had given the name E-Boat Alley' (Jordan, 1946): nautical: WW2. (Off the Yorkshire coast.) —2. Granville defines it as 'the stretch of coast between Great Yarmouth and Cromer and The Wash'. 'E-boats' were fast German torpedo-boats; E = enemy.

e.g.b. and its source, *expected gentlemanly behaviour*. 'In fairly general use in the defence industry as a term of sarcastic abuse' (Peppitt): since ca. 1960. (Calder, 1967.) Ex Services' j.

e.t.b.'s. Issue knickers: WRNS: since ca. 1940. I.e., *elastic top* and *bottom*. Granville.

eager beaver. 'One who pitches right in, sometimes to the dismay of less highly geared colleagues, and sometimes none too intelligently' (Leechman): Can., adopted ca. 1940 ex US; in Brit. use since ca. 1955, perhaps earlier. By imperfect reduplication: perhaps suggested by the US (*as*) *busy*, or *industrious, as a beaver*. The term has prob. contributed to the popularity of the phrase *to beaver away at* (a task), q.v. at **beaver,** v.

eagle. A hole done in two strokes under bogey: golfers' s., adopted ca. 1922 ex US; by 1930 > j. Prob. suggested by golfers' *birdie*.—2. Chicken: RN College, Dartmouth: Bowen.—3. A German Stuka dive-bomber: RAAF: ca. 1940–5. B., 1943.

ear. A policeman: urban S. African: low: since ca. 1940(?). Driscoll, 1973: ' "The ears. The jacks. The *tokoloshes*. The police," Slack explained.' He listens—esp. if he's a detective. P.B.: cf. the Malay *mata mata*, eyes [everywhere], police.—2. In *on* (one's) *ear*, in disgrace: adopted ex US ca. 1909. Ware.—3. In *on* (one's) *ear*, tipsy: Aus.: since ca. 1910. Prichard, 1930.—4. Hence, *get on one's ear*, to get drunk. (Prichard, 1921.)—5. *On one's ear* also means '(of a task or undertaking) easily accomplished' (B., 1959). Aus.: since ca. 1920. As R.C. points out, 1976, 'One can do it lying down.'

ear-bash. A talk: Aus.: since ca. 1925. Cf. next. Cleary, 1952.

ear-basher. One who is a bore: Aus.: since ca. 1945. (*The Times*, 27 Dec. 1963.) Cf. prec. and:–

ear-bashing, n., v., and occ. as adj. Conversation; talking, esp. fluently and at length: Aus. soldiers': 1939+. *Rats*, 1944, ' "You musta thought me a queer sorta feller with me French plays and me Bach fugues—ya know them things he's often ear-bashing about." '

ear-flip. A sketchy salute: Services': since ca. 1930. H. & P.

ear-guards. Small side-whiskers: Aus. Baker.

ear-(h)ole; lad, lobe, n. 'The lads are the non-conformists'— esp. the boys of 15–16 years—'in a school. Conformists are called "Ear'oles" or, more succinctly, "Lobes" ' (Willis, 1976): as a group and separately, state school pupils': since ca. 1965 (?since ca. 1960). An *ear'ole* or 'ear-hole' is so called because he's a listener, and compliant, lobe is short for S.E. ear lobe and loosely, inaccurately, var. of ear-hole. See also **lads.**—2. In *on the ear-(h)ole*, cadging (esp. money): orig., early C.20, Army (F. & G.); by 1919, low s. (Curtis, 1937.)

ear-(h)ole, v. To take a corner at an acute angle: motorcyclists': since ca. 1925.—2. To eavesdrop, to listen in to someone's conversation: low: since ca. 1930. (Norman.)

ear-lugger. A persistent borrower; a 'scrounger': Aus. (Baker.) Cf. **ear-swinger,** and **ear-hole,** n., 2.

ear'ole. See **ear-(h)ole.**

ear phones. Women's hair-style, with hair drawn to the side and clamped over the ears: since ca. 1930.

ear-swinger. An unemployed docker dunning his working mates for a loan: nautical. (Bowen.) Cf. C.19 synon. *ear-biter*, and **ear-lugger.**

ear to the ground(, usu. **keep an,** or one's). Be alert to what is going on, and to what is likely to happen: coll.: since (?)ca. 1950. (P.B.)

early bath. In ref. to an unexpectedly early departure or retirement: ex soccer j. 'He was sent for an early bath' = the referee ordered the player off the field *or* another player was substituted: mid-1980s. Hence fig., as in Redhead, 1987, 'the tragic cases of [star footballers] Best and Greaves driven into a very early bath when their careers should have been peaking.'

Early Bird, the. An express goods-train carrying provisions, through the night, to London: railwaymen's: from ca. 1920. (*Daily Telegraph*, 15 Aug. 1936.) Cf. **the Early Riser.**

Early Pullman. 'An imaginary architectural style marked by over-elaborate decoration like the first Pullman cars on North American railways' (Leechman): Can. (ex US): since ca. 1945. Cf. **North Oxford Gothic** and **Stockbrokers' Tudor.**

early riser. Blanket carried by a tramp: Aus. B., 1942.—2. As *the Early Riser*, a fast freight train running to London: from ca. 1920. (It arrives early in the morning.) *Daily Telegraph*, 15 Aug. 1936.

earn, n. See AUSTRALIAN UNDERWORLD, in Appx.

earn, v. 'To make corrupt or dishonest profit. A thief might say about a proposed fraud or illegal scheme: "We can all *really earn* on this one!" ' (Powis): c.: 1970s.

E

earner; earners. The former is glossed by Newman, 1970, 'Money earned, esp. illicitly'. The latter occurs in Yuill, 1974, 'Your earners is coppers' language for pay-off money . . . Minty had always believed I was on the take'. Police s., prob. since the 1930s. Cf. **earn**, n. and v.—2. (As *earner*) 'Any circumstances that thieves can turn to corrupt or dishonest advantage: "We are on to an earner here!" ' (Powis): c.: 1970s. Cf. **earnings**.

earnings. Proceeds from robbery or other crime: c.: prob. since 1930s. Hall, 1974.

ears. 'Those little frames on either side of the title of the paper which journalists call "ears" or "ear-tabs" ' (Ralph, 1901): journalists' and copy-writers' s. >, by 1930, coll.—2. In *have* or *keep* (one's) *ears flapping*, to listen, esp. if closely; to make an effort to keep track of events: coll.: since ca. 1950. Cf. **ear to the ground**.

earth-chasers. The Torpedo Officer's electric-light party; seamen torpedomen: RN: since ca. 1920. (Granville.) *Earth* in its electricity sense.

earwig, n. (Mostly in pl.) Recruits in Training: Army NCOs': since late 1940s. (P.B.)—2. 'An eavesdropper. Generally, one who uses information, overheard by eavesdropping, to curry favour with the authorities' (Tempest): c.: mid-C.20. Cf. **earwigger**.

earwig, v. To detect; to understand: r.s. on *twig*.—2. To eavesdrop: proletarian, perhaps esp. common among market-traders. (M.T.) Cf. n., 2.—3. Hence, to listen in on radio telephone at sea: trawlers' and drifters': since ca. 1930. Granville.

earwig, go! 'Small comedy, esp. of marching recruits, wending their unwanted way through small seaside towns' (L.A., 1976): late 1940s. P.B.: prompted, prob., by the children's pun, ' " 'ere we go!", as the earwig said when he fell over the cliff.'

earwigger. An eavesdropper; a conversational interloper: Services': adopted, in 1940, from US. H. & P.—2. In pl., headphones: Services': since ca. 1941. H. & P.

ease it. 'Let up on it; go easy. In the case of "fiddling" getting too dangerous, it is given as advice to lie low for a while' (Tempest): c.: mid-C.20.

ease off. To urinate: midway between s. and euph. Naughton, 1970, 'I slowly got out of bed to ease off and tidy up.'

ease up! Steady!: coll.:—1923 (Manchon). Lit., slacken your pace!

easel. Motorcycle prop stand: motorcyclists': since ca. 1950. (Dunford.)

east and west. Breast: r.s.:—1923 (Manchon).

East Country. See **West Country**.

Easter knees. To *suffer from*, or *have, Easter knees* = to be out of training: club cyclists': earlier C.20. *Fellowship*, 1984.

easy, n. Spare money; ready cash: late C.19–20. *Green Envelopes*, 1929, p.37. (Petch.)

easy, adj. Esp. in 'I'm easy'—I don't mind one way or the other: orig., late 1930s, RAF coll.; whence to the other Services and thus into much wider use by ca. 1950.—2. Easily imposed upon: Can. coll. (Leechman.)

easy a bit! Don't hurry!: coll.:—1923 (Manchon).

easy as apple-pie, as. Very easy indeed: Aus. coll.: since ca. 1920. (B.P.) Cf. **easy as pie**. The West Can. version, from about the same time, poss. earlier, is *easy as duck soup* (Leech, 1986).

easy as pie, (as). Very easy indeed to solve, do, etc.: children's and coll. Cf. prec., of which this is perhaps a shortening. Could it have orig. in the old abecedarian mnemonic 'A is for apple-pie . . .', which, once mastered by the child, was *easy*? (P.B.)

easy as taking money (or **toffee**) **from a child**; gen. preceded by **as.** Very easy (to do): coll.: late C.19–20. The Can. (and US) version is . . . *candy from a kid*. (Leechman.) P.B.: in the same vein is the mid–later C.20 . . . *pennies from a blind man*.

easy as winking(, it's as). With (consummate) ease: coll.

easy mark. A girl easy to persuade into sexual intercourse: since ca. 1920. See **mark**, n.

easy meat. 'She's easy meat'—of a not invincible chastity: since ca. 1920.—2. (Of a thing) easy to obtain; (of a plan) easy to effect: since ca. 1925. 'Oh, that's easy meat!'

easy on! Steady!: Aus. coll. (B., 1942.) Short for *go easy on it!*

easy-peasy. 'Easy', but with an undertone of contempt or diminution, as in 'the computer-till, which sounds as if it should be easy-peasy' (J. Nisbet, on serving behind a modernised pub-bar, in *Sunday Express*, 1 June 1986). There is perhaps an echo of low s. *piss-easy*.

easy rider. A man living off a prostitute's earnings: since late 1960s in Brit., where prob. popularised by the film so titled and starring Peter Fonda.

easy to look at; easy on the eye. (Esp. of women) good-looking: the former, anglicised, ex US, by 1930; the latter, derivatively ex the earlier, first heard by the editor [E.P.] in 1936. By meiosis.

eat. To enjoy enthusiastically: theatrical. Merrick, 1911, 'They ate the piece'; Brandon, 1934, 'The audience were, in theatrical parlance, literally eating this scene.'—2. To worry; sorely puzzle: from ca. 1919. MacDonald, 1933, 'But I don't *think* that's what's eating you.' Cf. dial. *eat oneself*, to be very vexed (*EDD*).

eat crap. Later C.20 version, prob. ex US, of S.E. *eat dirt*, to submit to spoken insult, degrading treatment. An ex-banker, of a City firm, 'I was there for two years and I had to *eat crap*. If you weren't from Eton or Rugby, no-one talked to you' (*Sunday Telegraph*, 17 May 1987). But cf. the quot'n at **doggie do**, where the meaning is literal. US also has *eat shit*.

eat (someone) **out.** To reprimand severely: Can.: since ca. 1930. (Leechman.) A var. of synon. **chew out**.—2. 'Muff dive, cunnilingus (a male on a female, not vice versa). As in, "I ate out Mary last night." Widespread and common all over N. America: since mid-50s or early 60s' (Leech, 1986, who adds that he has never heard the term used as in sense 1). Cf. **chew out**.

eat (oneself) **stiff.** To eat a hearty meal; to gorge: schoolboys'. Weymouth, 1937.

eating irons. Knife, fork, and spoon: Services' coll.: since ca. 1920. (H. & P.) Weapons (cf. **shooting-irons**) with which to attack the meal.

eats. Food: coll. Cf. *eat*, M.E., a meal, and C.11–early 17, food, both S.E.

eau (pron. *ooh*)-**clobber.** Waterproof clothing: motorcyclists': since ca. 1950. (Dunford.)

eau-de-Cologne, often shortened to **eau(-)de.** Telephone: r.s. 'Give me a blow on the eau de.' (Franklyn 2nd.)—2. A girl or woman: itinerant entertainers' r.s. on the earlier Parlyaree *palone*: late C.19–20. (Lester.) Sometimes shortened to *eau-de*.

'eck-as-like. In such phrases as 'did he/she 'eck-as-like!', 'would they 'eck-as-like do it for us', certainly not, 'it is highly unlikely': since mid-C.19, if not earlier—and still very much current in N. Country coll. (*EDD*, 1898, at *eck* and *heck*; Bowater, 1979.)

Ecks. See **Ekes**.

ecnop. A prostitute's bully: back s. on *ponce*: low.

eco nut. 'A pejorative term for [one] excessively concerned about the protection of the environment' (B.P.): prob. orig. US; Aus. and Brit. since ca. 1970. Ex *ecology* + *nut*, n., 4. A similar formation, dating from perhaps slightly later, is *eco-freak*; again, ex *ecology*, + *freak*, n. The meaning is the same.

ecstasy. Amphetamine-type drug with hallucinogenic effects: drugs c. (Stockley, 1986.) Ex US: Spears notes it as new, 1985.

ed. Editor: only in compounds, as *city-ed*: journalistic. Cf.:-

ed (or **ed.**), **the.** The editor: journalists' and authors' coll. Bell, 1934.

Edgar Wallace. 'Man who confuses an argument to win it' (Clayton, 1970): prisoners'. Ex this author's profusion of baffling thrillers, some 150 titles (see bibliog. for a mere handful) in a short, hectic life (1875–1932).

edge. Antagonism; tension arising from mutual dislike: coll.: since mid-C.20. 'It was a peaceful discussion until *she* came in, and then of course there was bags of edge had to be involved.' (P.B.) Phillips, 1979, 'There is a little bit of regional edge to all this. The "Redhill Crowd" are just a bit miffed about being beaten by the "Midlands Mafia".'—2. In *have the edge on*, to have a slight advantage over: Can. coll., adopted ex US. (Beames.) The phrase has been in coll. use in Brit. since mid-C.20 at latest, esp. in sporting language. (P.B.)—3. For *noise the edge*, see MOCK AUCTION, in Appx.—4. See **outside edge; over the edge.**—5. Crowd; audience: street entertainers': London. (Hollis.) Cf.:–

edge 'em. To commence drawing a crowd: market-traders' (e.g., Petticoat Lane).

edge fever. 'A condition of mental tension produced by prolonged drug indulgence' (Hibbert, 1983): drugs c.

edge it! Be quiet! Stop it!: Aus. Herbert, 1939, 'Hey—edge it, Mum!'

edge of nothing. Nowhere to sit.

edge up. (Gen. in imperative.) To move quickly: Glasgow:—1934.

edgy. Irritable; nervous: coll. Ex *nerves on edge*.

Edie. A cheap prostitute: Londoners', esp. police: since ca. 1945. 'From the point of view of the police, the best of the street-walkers, or "Toms" as they were called, was the Mayfair professional, and the worst the Edies of the East End, Piccadilly and the railway stations' (Gosling 1960).

Edna. In *on* (*my, your*, etc.) *Edna May*, on one's way: r.s.: C.20; since ca. 1930, predominantly theatrical. Ex the famous music-hall entertainer. Franklyn.

educated. 'Wide'—experienced and intelligent, but 'bent': police: since late 1940s. Newman, 1970.

Educated Evans. 'The man who dispels lore with information. In the silence that ensues someone will sum *him* up: Educated Evans!': workshops, etç. (L.A., 1974.) *Educated Evans* was the title of an Edgar Wallace thriller, 1924.

educated ignorant. A term used by 'ordinary people' to describe one who, though highly educated and full of 'book-learning', is woefully lacking in common sense, and quite incompetent at those everyday tasks that the 'ordinary people' perform through practice forced on them by necessity: since ca. 1950, at latest. (P.B.)

Edwardian. A Teddy-boy: joc.: ca. 1956–64. Cf. **Teddy-boy.**

Edwards. King Edward potatoes (a very popular kind): growers' and sellers' coll.: since ca. 1910.

eek. Face; perhaps orig., the cheek: since ca. 1960. Shortened back s. *e-caf* (Ashley). 'Round The Horne'. See also **eke.**

eekcher. Cheek: central s.: from ca. 1880. Ware.

eekies. 'Equal, all square, or the same: "You give me a pound and that's us eekies." "It's eekies to me whether I go or not" ' (Munro, 1985): Glasgow.

eelerspee. A confidence trickster: Aus. c.: since ca. 1910. (B., 1943.) Via *eeler sp*(*ee*), centre-s. of *speeler* or *spieler*, 1.

Eemers. 'Familiar reference to EMERS, the compendious *Electrical and Mechanical Engineering Regulations* of the Army, which goes to it when it wants to carry out, cost, or time any mechanical job' (P.B., 1974): Army: since ca. 1950.

eff, v.; **effing,** vbl n. and ppl. adj. To say *fuck*; foul-mouthed (swearing). Harrison, 1943, 'They'd eff and blind till your ear-'oles started to frizzle." ' At first euph., it soon > joc. allusive also.

eff off! Orig., obviously, euph. for 'Fuck off!' But soon—by, say, 1935—establishing an independent identity; neutrally, *eff off* = to depart; *eff off!* = 'Oh, run away!'—' "No" to that offer or proposal, it's either contemptible or unworthy of consideration.' (L.A., 1976.)

effing and blinding, be. To be using bad language. Cf. **eff,** v.

Effluent Society, the. A bitter pun on 'The Affluent Society', title of the 1958 analytical, historical study of economics by

J.K. Galbraith. The anger is directed against all that is worst in our selfish, materialistic, wasteful Western society. (P.B.)

effort. 'Something accomplished involving concentration or special activity': from ca. 1870: S.E. >, by 1930, coll., esp. in *that's a pretty good effort* (C.20).—2. A 'thingummy'; an interjection: Bootham School:—1925. (*Bootham*, 1925.) P.B.: in the sense of 'thingummy', a whatnot, it was in much wider use than is implied here. It had spread to other Public Schools by 1945 at latest, and was in earlier, WW2, use by the Services: see, e.g., PRISONER-OF-WAR SLANG, §10, in Appx.

Egg. Nickname for a bald-headed messmate: RN. (Granville.) Cf. **skating rink.**

egg-beater. An affectionate term for an oldish motorcar, perhaps less powerful than a 'banger', q.v.: coll.: later C.20. (Raab, 1981.)

egg-boiler. A bowler hat: Aus.: since ca. 1920. (B., 1943.) Not because one could boil eggs in it but because, in torrid weather, one's own 'egg' (head) boils in it.

egg-bound. Slow-witted: RN. Eggs are very constipating; constipation renders 'heavy'.

egg-head, n. and adj. A scholar; an erudite person; anyone interested in intellectual matters; pertaining to persons or matters intellectual, as, e.g., *the egghead press* = the 'serious' newspapers: orig. US, adopted in Can. ca. 1953, in Britain in the late 1950s. Ex the high brow and the general shape of the scholar's head—in the popular misconception.

egg-head brigade, the. See **whiz.**

egg-laying. Dropping the second ball just behind the serving line when the first service has actually been 'in': lawn tennis: since ca. 1930. *Daily Telegraph*, 7 Aug. 1937.

Egg-Market, the. The Falkland Islands: whalers': ca. 1830–1910. Ex swarming sea-fowl. Bowen.

egg on, mostly in imperative. To get a move on, to hurry: low Aus.: since the 1920s. (Tennant, 1953.) Probably ex S.E. *egg on*, to incite.

egg on (one's) **face, get.** To come out of an affair, esp. political or commercial, badly, and thus to suffer loss, humiliation and embarrassment; to make a fool of oneself through presumption or lack of judgment: adopted, ca. 1974, ex US. E.g., Mr (later Sir) Freddie Laker was quoted by the BBC in May 1974, on his challenge to British Airways that he could run Concorde aircraft at a profit, 'Some people are going to end up with a lot of egg on their faces over this one.' (R.S.; P.B.) In the *Guardian*, 27 Feb. 1986, was a ref. to 'his face is eggless'.

egg-shell blonde. Any bald person: Aus.: since ca. 1945. B., 1953.

Egg-Shells. HMS *Achilles*: RN: earlier C.20. (Bowen.) By Hobson-Jobson.

egg-timer. See HAULAGE, in Appx.

egg(-)whisk. An autogyro: RAF: since ca. 1938. (H. & P.) Ex its rotatory motion. Cf. **windmill.**—2. A helicopter: RN: since ca. 1948. Ex its appearance. Cf. **chopper** and **whirlybird.**

Egg Wiped. Egypt: Army: 1940–55. A rudimentary pun on *Eg-ypt*. P-G-R.

egged. A bus: Army in Palestine: ca. 1942–5. Ex the name of a Palestinian proprietor of a fleet of buses. P-G-R.

egged off, be. To be pelted off stage or platform with eggs, preferably rotten: coll.: since 1930s. (Petch, 1974.) By a pun on S.E. *egg on*.

eggs. 'Ovoid briquettes, made of coal dust and cement dust, used during coal shortage' (McKenna, 1970): railwaymen's: mid-C.20.—2. See **lay eggs; off** (one's) **eggs.**

eggy. Irritated; excited: Liverpool: since mid-C.20, at latest. Ex dial. *egg*, to tease; to irritate. Simmonds, 1985, 'Have heard this alot recently, meaning *well bad* [= very bad], but also meaning "in a bait" [= angry]—"Dad was well eggy this morning"; also "feeling eggy", i.e. not quite 100%': teenagers'. James Williamson, 1985, glosses it as 'disagreeable; very bad; a gen. denigratory adj.'

ego(-)trip. A total absorption in one's career: the underground: since ca. 1965. (*Groupie*, 1968.)—2. Used cynically, derisively, or pej. of any activity, usu. public, that may appear self-indulgent and gratifying to the performer, as 'Oh, that [political] campaign of his—it's all just one big ego-trip!': coll. and journalistic: later 1970s. (P.B.) See **trip, n.,** 4.

Egypt. Bread: Army: early C.20. (F. & G.) Perhaps ex *corn in Egypt.*—2. See LOVERS', in Appx.

Egyptian AFOs. 'Pornographic books as sold at Port Said: RN: since early 1950s. A ref. to Admiralty Fleet Orders' (Peppitt). Cf. **Hong Kong bibles.**

Egyptian PT. Sleeping in the daytime, esp. in the afternoon: Services', orig. perhaps, since ca. 1925, Army officers'—but soon also other ranks'—and, by ca. 1945, RN. PT = *physical training.* (Granville; P.B.) Cf. synon. **Maori PT.**

eighteen bob in the pound, often prec. by *only.* (Of persons) not very bright: Aus.: earlier C.20. Culotta, 1963.

Eighteen Imperturbables, the. A formation of eighteen Desert Air Force planes: Eighth Army officers': 1942–3.

eighteenpence. Common sense: r.s.: *Gilt Kid,* 1936, 'He did not know Maisie had all that eighteenpence.' Also in P.P., 1932.—2. A receiver of stolen goods: r.s. on *fence.* Barnes, 1976.

Eighth, the. The Eighth Army: coll. (mostly Army): 1942–5, then historical.

Eights. The Oxford boat-races held in Eights Week, in June: coll.

eighty-eight, the. Piano. See **fish-horn.**—2. See **thirty.**

Einstein's mate. 'A dense person, especially in relation to faulty calculations' (Powis): low, ironic: 1970s.

Eisenhower Platz. Grosvenor Square (London), while it contained the American H.Q.: 1942–5.

ek dum. At once; straightaway: Army: earlier C.20. Ex Hindustani, 'one, two'; see *ak dum.* Blaker, 1935.

eke. Make-up (cosmetic beautification); hence, a room for it: homosexuals': current ca. 1970. See also **eek.**

Ekes (or **Ecks**), **School of.** London School of Economics.

ekka. An exhibition, e.g., the annual agricultural and pastoral held at Brisbane: Aus.: since ca. 1965. (Lovett, 1978.)

elbow, the. A long attack of nervousness and even of 'nerves': (lawn) tennis-players': since ca. 1965. Many refs in the Press during the 1969 Wimbledon Championships. Ex S.E. *tennis elbow,* severe strain on the elbow and forearm from hard play over-long sustained.—2. In *on the elbow,* 'on the scrounge' (Powis): low: later C.20. Cf. **ear-hole, n.,** 2.—3. See **give the elbow.**

elders. A woman's breasts: Aus.: since ca. 1920. (B., 1942.) Either in ref. to an elder tree in full growth and leaf, or with an allusion to the story of Susanna and the Elders.

electric. 'Efficient, weird, sudden or marvellous' (Powis): proletarian coll.: 1970s.

electric cow. A machine for the conversion of milk-powder and water into 'milk': RN: since ca. 1940. Granville.

electric soup. 'A fortified wine called Eldorado—known locally as "electric soup" ' (*New Society,* 10 Mar. 1983, p.365): Scots. Munro, 1985, glosses it as Glaswegian for 'a mixture of meths and red biddy [q.v.] as drunk by alcoholic down-and-outs'; Eldorado he notes as *EID* or *L.D.*

Electric Whiskers. Bergonzoli, an Italian general in N. Africa: Army: ca. 1941–3. Ex It. *Barba Elettrica.* P-G-R.

electricial [sic] **string.** Electric cable: RN: since late 1960s. (Peppitt.)

elegant sufficiency, an. Joc. indication, mocking lower-middle-class gentility, that one has had enough to eat and drink, as 'I've had an elegant sufficiency, ta!': since ca. 1950, ?earlier. (P.B.)

elements embrocation. (Exposure to) rough weather that makes one's face red: since ca. 1925; †. With a pun on *Elliman's Embrocation.*

elephant. Heroin: drugs c. (Stockley, 1986.) But see **elephant tranquilliser.**—2. In *cop the elephant,* to be tipsy: a shorten-

ing of C.19 r.s. *elephant('s) trunk,* drunk:—1923 (Manchon).—3. A shortening of late C.19 r.s. *Elephant and Castle,* anus, on illiterate ars'le. Powis, 1977.

Elephant and Castle. Hell, as in 'How the Elephant and Castle!': r.s. (*castle* being pronounced *caste'll*).—2. A parcel: r.s.: since ca. 1920. Often shortened to *Elephant.* Gosling, 1959.

elephant houses. Old forts at Dunkirk: Services': 1940: ob. H. & P.

elephant hut. A Nissen hut: Services': since ca. 1919; † by 1950. (H. & P.)

elephant on the casing. 'Called or piped soon after "Finished with main motors and steering. Fall out Harbour Stations below". The rum that had been bottled day by day was then disposed of. Peculiar to HM Submarine *Astute,* 1964–6; just a phrase that happened, and stuck' (Malin, 1979).

elephant tranquilliser. PCP: drugs c. (Stockley, 1986.) US since—1969 (Spears, who explains: 'a veterinary anesthetic').

elephant's. See **elephant, 2.**

elephants' burial ground, the (or with capitals). Petersfield, Hampshire, 'The home of vast legions of retired admirals': RN: since late 1940s. Jones, 1970.

elephant's trunk and **bird bath.** 'Canvas trunk fitted around the control room ladder [of a submarine] with a flap for getting in and out. The ladder stands in a canvas bath secured to the trunk. Water coming in is contained and pumped out' (Malin, 1979): RN Submariners': 1960s.

elevator. See next:–

elevenpence ha'penny in the bob. Slightly 'cracked'; apparently not quite sane: pre-1971 (decimalisation of currency), but lingering still among the older generation. (Cross, 1984.) Cf. the Can. 'his elevator doesn't go to the top floor' (Leech, 1986).

elevenses. Mid-morning drink of tea, coffee, etc., and perhaps a bite to eat: C.20 coll. ex C.19–20 dial.; dial. also *elevener.* I.e., at eleven o'clock. Wodehouse; Sayers.

eleventh commandment, the. 'Thou shalt not be found out'— when breaking any of the other ten: a cynicism of the C.20. *Punch,* 31 July 1918. (P.B.)

eliminate. To kill (a person): joc. coll.: from ca. 1915. P.B.: after two world wars and numerous dictatorships, still extant—but no longer jocular.

'Ell of a Mess. The LMS: London, Midland and Scottish Railway (1922–48): railwaymen's nickname. *Railway,* 2nd.

Ellen Terry. A chamberpot: r.s., on C.19–20 s. *jerry:* mostly theatrical. Franklyn.

Elly and Castle. The Elephant and Castle itself, or its immediate neighbourhood: Londoners', esp. Cockneys' coll. (L.A., 1976.)

Elmer. See HAULAGE, in Appx.

Elsan Eddy (loosely **Eddie**). A latrine-cleaner ('sanitary wallah'): RAF: WW2. A blend of *Elsan,* a proprietary name, and, by a pun, *Nelson Eddy,* the famous singer.

Elsan gen. Unreliable news: RAF: since 1939. (H. & P.) Ex the excellent make of chemical lavatories on bombers.

Elsie. *East London College:* London University undergraduates': ob. since 1934, when renamed Queen Mary College.—2. 'A special searchlight adapted for use in the Maunsell Forts in the Thames Estuary': Londoners' (Services and Port of London Authority): 1939(?)–45. Ex *L.C.,* Light Control. P-G-R.

emag. Game; trick; dodge: back s.:—1873. Ware dates it 1870. Powis, 1977: 'usually in the sense of disgust: "What a bleeding emag this is!" '

embalming fluid. PCP: drugs c. (Stockley, 1986.) US since—1984 (Spears). Cf. **elephant tranquilliser.**

embark. Abbr. *embarkation*; at first usu. in combination, as 'go on embark leave'; later, used alone to mean the same, 'I only got 7 days' embark—should've had at least 14': Services' coll.: since 1939. (Jackson; P.B.) Cf. **disembark.**

E

embuggerance factor. A natural or artificial hazard that complicates any proposed course of action: Army: since ca. 1950. An elab. of the simple term *embuggerance*, as in 'They threw in every form of embuggerance they knew how, to try to stop me getting here'. (P.B.) Cf. **F.A.F.**

emcee, n. and v. (To act as) *m*aster of *c*eremonies. See **M.C.**

emmet. 'In Cornwall the derisive word for a holiday-maker is "emmet"—there are even T-shirts on sale locally saying "I am not an Emmet" ' (Winton, May 1978): *emmet* is dial., = ant. Holiday-makers swarm. (P.B.)

emmies. Shares in the *E*lectrical and *M*usical company: Stock Exchange: from ca. 1930. *Daily Telegraph*, 18 Nov. 1933.

emoh ruo. Suburbia; esp. in its smugness: Aus. journalists' and publicists', hence others': since ca. 1950. The back-s. form of *our home*. Its use as a house-name—cf. *our home* itself and *chez nous*—led to its becoming generalised. (B.P.)

emote. To be or become emotional; to show excessive emotion: adopted, ca. 1950, ex US, where orig. theatrical: s. >, by 1960, coll. 'He is incapable of rational behaviour. He just reacts and emotes.' A back-formation ex *emotion*. (B.P.)

empire. A large, esp. if unnecessarily large, department, usu. administrative: Services', prob. orig. RAF: since ca. 1944. (P-G-R.) Cf.:–

empire-builder. One who, as head of a department, manages—or tries—to extend his responsibilities and increase his staff as to appear to merit promotion to a rank concomitant with the size and 'importance' of his empire: orig. Services', ca. 1944; since WW2 > gen. coll., and widespread. Hence vbl n. *empire-building*. Ex the S.E. term applied to such Victorian heroes as Cecil Rhodes. (P.B.)

empire-builders. 'White tropical shorts that always reached the knees and beyond' (Malin, 1979): RN: since—1936.

empties back (or **coming back**) **from Manchester.** Threatening clouds that don't rain: joc. (Huston, 1981.)

emshee. An occ. corruption of *imshee*, q.v., go away!

Emsib. The *E*astern *M*editerranean *S*pecial *S*ervice *I*ntelligence *B*ureau: military coll.: 1915–18. P.B.: clearly an early example of the military acronym of which WW2 spawned so many—and retained in this work as such.

emu. A member of the ground staff: RAAF: WW2. (B., 1943.) Cf. **penguin,** 1.

emu-bobber. 'Someone employed to pick up after clearing [trees] or burning-off in the bush' (Wilkes): Aus. coll.:—1920. Hence the activity, *emu-bobbing.*

emu-bobbing. Picking up cigarette-ends and other litter: Aus. soldiers': WW2. (B., 1943.) To do it, one bobs one's head as an emu does. Hence also *emuing*, and *emu parade*, 'In the army, a parade to clean up an area by "emu-bobbing" ' (Wilkes): WW2. Ex prec.

encore, get an. To have a second erection at one 'session' of love-making: raffish.

end. The glans penis; mostly in compounds: *bell-end, blunt end, red end*: esp. Services'. Hence to *have* or *get* (one's) *end away*, to achieve sexual intercourse (usu., but not exclusively, of the male): raffish: since ca. 1910. Often joc.; e.g., of one's own ill-humour, 'Too much dirty water on the chest; it's time I had me end away again', or 'Bit of a blow to the Stud's reputation—been here 3 days already, and *still* hasn't got his end away!' (P.B.) In Aus., later C.20, to *get* (one's) *end in* (Wilkes).

end-bit dobber. A tramp, or a beggar, collecting cigarette-ends from gutters: Cambridge Town (*not* University): from ca. 1910.

end of the line, the. As in 'Well, I'm afraid that's the end of the line for him', he is finished physically, socially, professionally, etc.: coll.: since ca. 1960; ?ex US. From the end of the railway- or tram-line.—2. The end of, e.g., an affair of the heart, 'It's the end of the line for us': id. (P.B.)

end of the pier. Pornographic: media circles'. The recorded telephone-'message was a three minute tape in what is known in the trade as the "end of the pier" range' (*Daily Telegraph*, 20 Feb. 1988); a harking-back to the old 'what the butler saw'

mechanical peepshow machines, or to 'naughty' seaside post-cards.

end to end. *In coitu*: low. (L.A., 1974.) Cf. **ends away.**

ender. 'A dan buoy with a flag indicating a line of fishing nets or pots' (Granville): deep-sea fishermen's coll.

endless belt. A prostitute: Aus.: since ca. 1925. (B., 1942.) Cf. **belt.** A pun on the engineering term.

ends away. In copulation, as, 'they were ends away almost before he'd put his kit-bag down'; as exclam., a 'gloat' by one who has just, or hopes shortly to have, achieved sexual intercourse: Army: 1960s. (P.B.)

endy. 'A car with worn big-*end* bearings' (*Woman's Own*, 28 Feb. 1968): secondhand-car dealers': since ca. 1950. Also as adj.: 'Endy engines sound like diesels' (*You*, 10 July 1983).

engine. A sewing-machine: tailors'. (*Tailor and Cutter*, 29 Nov. 1928.) Contrast **sewing-machines.**

engineer and stoker. (Gen. pl.) A broker: r.s. Philips, 1931.

engineering pie. A special sort of pie served at lunch in the RN Engineering Shop at Dartmouth: RN: since ca. 1930.

engineer's spanner. Sixpence: apparently at first, and perhaps still mainly, nautical, esp. RN: since ca. 1920. R.s. on *tanner*, sixpence. P.B.: But, as Ashley points out, it is used for other coins: the r.s. is coincidental; the coin is used to lever open a bottle or tin.

Engines. *E*ngineering (or Technical) Officer: RAF coll.: since ca. 1925. Jackson.

England's umbrella. Ireland: joc. coll.:—1923 (Manchon).

english. Spin on a ball, whether, as orig. and usu., in billiards or in baseball: Can.: since ca. 1918. Cameron, 1937, explained the stages of the origination thus:—'1. Language ekes out its own deficiency by gesture, hence, gesture equals "body English".'

'2. By direct transference, any gesture or contortion (as in trying to do a difficult physical task) becomes "body English".'

'3. In a game (e.g. billiards), effect of effort on the ball becomes "body English" on the ball.'

'4. By natural contraction, this becomes "English" on the ball or "spin". . . . Can be written with little "e".'

Mr Cameron adds that those who say *side English*, instead of *english* or *spin*, are merely being anti-English. Whereas *english* >, ca. 1945, a technicality and part of the Standard language, *side English* has remained s., but was, by 1945, ob. Then there's *bottom-english*, back english plus side spin.

English Channel, the. The National Health Service: r.s., on *panel* (of doctors): since ca. 1955. Haden-Guest.

enob. Bone: back s.: late C.19–20. Ware.—2. Hence, in later C.20, an erection: gay c. (Ashley, 1987.)

Enoch. (Gen pl.) White primary-school children's nickname for coloured immigrant children: 1970s. (Harré, 1979.) By ironic transference from Enoch Powell, a noted opponent of immigration into the UK. Name used alongside *Blackie, Nig-nog*; contrast **ice-cream.** (P.B.)

Enoch Arden. A garden: ?orig. (1942) among prisoners-of-war in the Far East; hence, since (but ?earlier), among civilians. B., 1953, quotes from (Sydney) *Sun* of 22 Sep. 1945.

Eno's. He knows: derisive: earlier C.20. Punning *Eno's Fruit Salt*. Also *'e knows*.

enough on (one's) **plate, have** (**got**)**.** To have as much work as one can manage, or as much as one can do: Services', 1939 +, and then into gen. use; still current mid-1980s. Ex lit. domestic sense. An East Midlands var. is 'I've got (enough/too much) on my wheel already.' (E.P.; P.B.)

entry. 'This job came in that I thought would be right up your entry' (Daniells, 1980). A var. of *right up* (one's) *alley* or *street*.

epic. Adj. of high approbation: teenagers': ca. 1977. (D. & R. McPheely.) Cf. **cosmic.**

eppi. See **take a heebie.**

-er. Coll. when agential as in *pea-souper*, fog: C.19–mid-20. Also when, among children playing 'conkers', one speaks of e.g. a *niner*, a chestnut that has smashed nine others.—2. See 'OXFORD -ER', in Appx.

'er indoors. A joc. ref. to a wife: used by the character Arthur Daley (played by George Cole) for his never-seen wife in the TV Cockney comedy series 'Minder', early 1980s, and soon generally known. 'It is as difficult to imagine what [Auberon Waugh's] wife might be like as it is to conjure up the precise appearance of Arthur Daley's 'Er Indoors' (Sandilands, 1984).

'Erb. A wag; also in address to a person of name unknown to the speaker: Cockney and military. (F. & G.) I.e., **Herbert**, q.v.

erdies (sing. *erdy, erdie*, rare; often with capital *E*). Those who are earth-bound, earthy; unimaginative and conventional; 'square': since early 1970s. Ex Ger. *Erde*, earth, the Earth, ground. Scaduto, 1974: ' "Bunch of Erdies," Jagger moaned . . . Erdies denoting all those faceless and mindless men who weren't hip, who were trapped in jobs and careers and prisons of the mind.'

erk. A lower-deck rating: nautical: late C.19–20. (Bowen.) Perhaps ex dial. *irk*, to grow weary, or from officers' impatient 'They irk me, these— —!' See also **irk.**—2. Hence(?), a recruit, an AC2 [Aircraftman, 2nd class; AC1 = 1st cl.] (the lowest of the low: I was one for 2 years 9 months, so *experto crede!*); occ. applied (Jackson, 1943) also to, but much resented by, an AC1: RAF: since 1918. Prob. ex 'aircraftman'. Heading, 'The term "Erk" was first used in the R.A.F. Depot, Uxbridge, in 1920. The origination . . . was brought about when I wrote the song "One of the Aircs", Aircs being an abbreviation of aircraftsmen. Through frequent use the term came to be pronounced Erk and I have no knowledge of the term being used in the R.F.C., R.N.A.S. or R.A.F. before the year 1920'; 'To me Air Mechanics of the R.A.F. were always known as Ack Emmas'. The weight of the evidence, however, shows that the song reinforced and hastened the growth of a term that was, in fact, already current.

Ernie, the electronic brain that selects the numbers of the winners of Premium Savings Bonds, was never lower than coll. and very soon became the accepted name: since Oct. 1956, the month before the first bonds were issued. Ex the initials of the full technical and official name of the instrument—*Electronic Random Number Indicator Equipment*.

Ernie Marsh. Grass: r.s.

Errol. See:-

Errol Flynn; esp. *on the . . .* , on the chin: r.s.: ca. 1938–60. (Franklyn 2nd.) Ex the swashbuckling film-actor.

ertia. Opp. of S.E. *inertia*: Aus. joc.: since late 1950s. (B.P.)

-ery is a frequent suffix in s. and coll., esp. at schools and universities.

esclop. A policeman: back s. It occurs in Mayhew, I, 1851, and Powis, 1977, records its continuing use in the underworld. The *c* is never pronounced, the *e* gen. omitted: hence the well-known *slop*.

esma! Listen!: Services' in the Middle East, 1915–18 (F. & G.) and again in WW2. Directly ex Arabic. 'Used as a means of summoning waiters in Egypt, whence arose the popular belief that the word meant "fellow" ' (P-G-R).

essence. An excessive profit, as in *put the essence on* (someone), to overcharge him: market-traders': since ca. 1920. *M.T.*—2. Anything of the very best: Services', other ranks': the National Service era, 1948–62. (P.B.) Perhaps borrowed from:—3. A good-looking, desirable sailor or Wren: RN, WRNS, FAA: WW2 and after. (Wood.) Prob. a shortening of:-

essence of pig-shit, the. A luscious girl: RN lowerdeck: since ca. 1925, but never very gen. Satirical of names for scents; but also allusive to *as happy as pigs in shit*. Cf. prec.

Esso. This acronym trade-name for the fuels and lubricants marketed by *Standard Oil* was re-interpreted, among garage-hands in the late 1930s–1940s, as *Every Saturday and Sunday Off*. (P.B.)

Eten Halen. Nickname for a Dutchman. See PRISONER-OF-WAR SLANG, §9, in Appx.

ethno. An ethnic or 'member of an ethnic group or minority' (*APOD*, 1976): Aus.: since the early 1970s. Thanks to B.P. for the s. term: the ubiquitous Aus. suffix *-o*.—2. Hence, any immigrant: Aus. schoolchildren's since ca. 1976. (Wilkes.)

etsi-ketsi. Rather feeble and indecisive, 'wet': from ca. 1946. Ex modern Greek. (E.P.). By the later 1950s it was in very common use among the Army and RAF in Cyprus, where it was pron. more as *itsi-gitsi*, and was taken to mean 'so-so, fair-to-middling'—usu. in answer to 'How's it going?' (P.B.)

ettie or **etty.** A girl: low London: since ca. 1950. Gloag, 1962, 'Jimmy's no good to etties, see? Can't give what they take' and 'Leader Lad going for this cute ettie'. Ex *Ettie, Etty*, a girl's name.

Evans. See **Educated Evans.**

evasive action, take. 'To keep away from trouble' (Jackson, 1943): see **take evasive action.**

even-handed. (Of a transaction) fair; honest. As adv., fairly, honestly, equitably. L.A., 1976, dates both as arising late 1974–early 1975.

even Stephen (or **Steven**). Share and share alike: Can. and Aus., C.20; Brit. since mid-C.20 at latest. By reduplication of *even*; and *Stephen* was earlier C.19 s. for money. Perhaps an adoption ex US. L.A., 1974, notes the Brit. var. *even(s) Stevens* and Leech, 1986, adds: '*Even-Stephen* (trade): to trade across with nothing else involved in the deal, "I'll trade you even-Stephen my knife for your watch!" West Can., since 1930s at latest.'

even terms. (To work) merely for one's keep: Aus. coll.: since ca. 1910. Baker.

Evening, The. *The Evening News*: coll.

evens. In *do evens*, to go at 20 miles per hour: cyclists' coll.

evensnog. Evensong in the Anglican Church: 1970s, poss. earlier. By a pun; cf. **matings**, matins. (Rev. D. Paterson.) See **snog.**

event, quite an. Something important, significant, or unusual: coll.

ever. An intensive coll. usage, adopted by non-cultured Can. ca. 1940 ex US. 'In the Yukon, ca. 1950, I heard "Well, did Hard-Rock MacDonald ever tie one on!" ' (Leechman.)—2. In *the best, worst, greatest*, etc., *ever*, the best, etc., that has ever been: coll.: adopted ca. 1930 ex US.

ever so. Ever so much, as in *thanks ever so!*: mostly proletarian: from ca. 1895. Pugh, 1898, ' "But I like you ever so," she faltered.' P.B.: 'Ta ever so!' or, worse, 'Ever so ta!', for 'Thank you!', is sometimes used facetiously by those who ought to know better. (1979.)

everlastings. Bare feet: Aus.: ca. 1910–50. Ex *everlasting shoes*, C.19 coll. for feet.

every fart's end, at. With tedious or obsessed repetition, applied esp. to 'repeated demand or interruption by unsure, or unconcerned, person' (L.A., 1977).

every which way. In every manner or direction: joc. coll., orig. (1840) US; anglicised ca. 1910. Perhaps ex confusion caused by *every way (in) which*. Often as *every which way but* (the correct one), in every direction except the right one.

evo. Evening: Aus. (Baker.) Cf. **afto, arvo.**

evolution, make an. 'To do anything with the maximum of fuss' (P-G-R): RN officers': since ca. 1918.

ex, n. Ex-wife or ex-husband: Society: since ca. 1920. Christie, 1944, 'Leonard's new wife and his Ex'.

ex, v. To excise by crossing out: Aus. coll.: since ca. 1930. (Niland, 1958.) To put an X through.

ex-brat. A soldier who started his military career as a 'boy-soldier', junior leader or apprentice: Army coll.: later C.20. (P.B.)

ex-con. 'A former prisoner' (Home Office): former prisoners': 1970.

exam weather. That perfect weather that seems so often to occur at the time of the university, college and school summer examinations, to taunt the poor candidates—and their invigilators: educational establishments': 1970s. (P.B.)

excremental. Joc. pej., as 'What an excremental bastard the bloke is!': Services': later C.20. Cf. the more down-to-earth **shitty.** (P.B.)

excuse me, the. The w.c.: r.s.: since ca. 1930.

exec. Short for *executive* committee, esp. in *exec meeting*: since late 1950s.—2. A business executive: business world. Chappell, 1982.

execution. A very large crowd drawn by a 'grafter': grafters'. *News of the World*, 28 Aug. 1938.—2. Hence, a large crowd around a market man: street market vendors': since ca. 1930. (Franklyn, 1962.)

exercise P.U. A drinking-session, or *piss-up*; joc. use of the military '*exercise* + codename' formula: RN officers': WW2. P-G-R.

exes (or **exis**) **to fere.** Odds of 6 to 4: racing c. *exis* is C.19 back s.; *fere* is *four* corrupted.

exhibish, the. Any notable exhibition: RN.—2. *exhibish*, or *exhibeesh*. Any exhibition containing sexual display, from a strip-tease show to a public copulation: orig. Services', then wider usage: 'I heard it in Cairo in 1943 with ref. to a brothel-show at Alexandria conflated (?) with ATS quarters at Sidi Bish outside that city: the inference was obvious' (Bishop, 1984). Ex the native tout's importuning of passing servicemen; cf. **feelthy pictures.** (P.B.)

expat. An expatriate; applied esp. to a white man electing to earn his living in an Asian or East Indian or African state: since the late 1940s.

expendable. Servicemen whose loss is 'anticipated (and accepted) as the price of success': coll.: Services': WW2, and subsequent conflicts. 'Ex store-keeping accounts' (R.S., 1971).

expensive. Wealthy, sumptuous; exceedingly or distinctively stylish: from ca. 1920: s. >, by 1930, coll.

expensive scare unit. See **cabbage**, 3.

experience. 'LSD or Mescaline experience' (Home Office): drug addicts': 1970s.

export trade, the. The procuring of women and shipping them to the Argentine: white-slavers' c.: from ca. 1890. Londres, 1928.

extern. An external examiner: University: late C.19–20.

extra. Dull, boring: 1929; †. Milne, 1931.

extra-curricular activities. Adulterous sexual play and intercourse: cultured coll.: since late 1940s.

extra ducks. Additional waiters employed to serve at banquets: caterers': since ca. 1920. Ex their waddling gait. Mars, 1984, has it as *extra duck*.

extra early. First rate, very good, excellent: NZ: since ca. 1945.

extra grouse. Exceptionally well or attractive or meritorious: Aus. (B., 1959.) Cf. **grouse, the.**

extra sort (superlative to the positive *good sort*) is a person exceedingly attractive to the opposite sex; contrast *drack sort*: Aus.: since ca. 1945. B., 1953.

extract the Michael. To make fun of (someone); to jeer at; joc. pedantic for *take the mike* (or *mickey*) *out of*: since ca. 1950, perhaps earlier. A polite version of:–

extract the urine (from). See prec. This version is 'euphemistic' for *take the piss out of*: Services': since 1939. P-G-R.

eye. A look-out man: c.: from ca. 1925.

eye! eye! 'A call for vigilance' (Phelan, 1953): c.: since ca. 1920. A pun on the nautical *aye aye!*

eye in a sling, have an or **get** (one's), or **with** (one's). (To be) crushed or defeated; to get into trouble: proletarian coll. (Ware.) *Arse* has sometimes replaced *eye*, since ca. 1930. (Trevor, 1967.) Cf. **ass in a sling.**

eye(-)lotion. Wine in small quantity: Services' officers' since ca. 1925. (H. & P.)

eye-opener. Amphetamine: drugs c. (Stockley, 1986.) US since—1970 (Spears).

eye-out. Someone keeping watch: c.: later C.20. Clement, 1977.

eye-picker. 'One who "picks the eyes out" of a grazing district by taking up the best land' (B., 1943): Aus. Cf. earlier synon. *peacocking*.

eyeball, n. See **mark-one eyeball.**

eyeball, v. To fly very low, by flair and intuition rather than by intricate gadgetry: RAF: 1970s, and prob. earlier. *Daily Telegraph*, Sep. 1975.—2. As v.t., to see, physically; to meet face to face: beatniks' and CB: later C.20.—3. See **clock**, v., 8. This sense prob. ex CB radio j., ultimately ex US black s.

eyeball to eyeball. (Orig. journalistic) descriptive of very close, usu. hostile, confrontations: since ca. 1960.

eyeballs out. Sustained effort: club cyclists'. (*Fellowship*, 1984.) Also defined as 'a communal sprint to be first at the tea-place, the top of a hill, or wherever' (ibid.).

eyeful. An attractive girl or young woman: coll. She takes the eye.—2. An accidental but fortunate glimpse of even the partial nakedness of a member of the opposite sex.

eyelid inspection. Sleep: RN Submariners': later C.20. (Martin, 1983.) Cf. **count deckhead rivets.**

eyes for, have. To crave (a thing), be amorous (of a person): adopted ex US, perhaps helped by the popular song by Henry Warren, composed for the film *Dames*, 1935, 'I only have eyes for you'. Revived among beatniks, 1950s, as 'John's sure got eyes for that bottle!' (Leechman.)

eyes front. (You) cunt!: r.s.: not anatomical, but applied derisively, in full, to a fool. (Hillman, 1974.) Ex the military command.

eyes like a bulldog's (sc. *ballocks*). Protuberant eyes: low.

eyes like a shit-house rat, usu. prec. by **with** or **he has.** Having shifty eyes and keen eyesight: since ca. 1910. (H.P. Mann, 1972.)

eyes like chapel hat-pegs. See **eyes stick out . . .**

eyes like cod's ballocks, have. To be pop-eyed: low. Cf. **eyes like a bulldog's.**

eyes sewed (or **sewn**) **up with red thread(, have** one's**).** (With) eyes bloodshot from weariness or from alcoholic or other excess: Army in Hong Kong, 1960s; perhaps more widespread, or perhaps ex Chinese idiom. (P.B.)

eyes stick out like chapel hat-pegs or **like organ stops,** e.g. **his;** the tense is adjustable. His eyes are (fig.) protuberant: coll.: since ca. 1910. Applied, e.g., to one wide-eyed with astonishment, or to a young man watching a pretty girl.

Eyetie. An Italian (usu. pl.): orig. Army in WW1 (F. & G.); later spread into civilian life, and then much used in WW2; also as adj., in, e.g., *an Eyetie*, an Italian aircraft (Jackson). Ex the sol. pron. *Eye-talian*. Cf. **Raddie, Wop**. An Aus. var. is *Eyeto*.

F

F.A. or **sweet F.A.** or **sweet f.a.** See **fuck all**.

F.A.F. 'The thing I go least on of all [in the Army] is what we call the FAF—that's the "Fuck About Factor", all the bull-shitting and the hanging around which you get, and general pissing around' (a Private, quoted in Parker, 1985). Cf. **embuggerance factor**.

f.a.q. *Fair Average Quality*: Aus.: orig. wheat merchants', earlier C.20, > gen. and widespread by later C.20. Wilkes.

f.u. A grave muddle or 'fuck-up': low. It had considerable vogue among servicemen in WW2, itself an extreme example of the **m.f.u.**, q.v.

f.u.J. *Fuck you Jack!* (sc. I'm all right); also as predicative, as in 'Oh, he's f.u.J.': indifferent to others' misfortunes: Services': WW2.

f.y.f.a.s. A provocative conversational opener. See **fyfas**.

fa. Father: upper classes' coll. Mitford, 1945.

fab. Very good; successful: teenagers': since late 1950s. Shortening of:-

fabulous. A verbal counter, meaning 'very—or merely—agreeable' or 'unusual' or '(very) interesting' or '(very) large' or 'distinguished' or . . . : coll.: since ca. 1945. After being theatrical s. of ca. 1945–50, it > gen. s. and, by 1962, something of a vogue word. Cf **fab**, and **fantabulous**.

fabulous drop, a. A very attractive girl: Aus.: since late 1940s. (Culotta.) Cf. the Aus. *not a bad drop*, a good alcoholic drink.

face. Personal appearance: Aus.: since ca. 1925. (B., 1942.) Cf. American *front*.—2. A person, esp. if well known: since late 1950s, mostly in underground society. (*Groupie*, 1968.) See quot'n at **faces**.

face-ache. At first, an ironically joc. term of address, but by ca. 1960 often used 'straight', as in ' "He is a face-ache"—his presence is very unpleasant and undesirable' (Thomas, 1976).

face at half-past eight, with one's. Mournful; wry-mouthed.

face in a knot, get or **tie** (one's). To become angry—or agitated—or bewilderingly excited: Aus. Baker.

face-lifter. An uppercut to the jaw: pugilistic: since ca. 1925. Ex beauty-parlour treatment.

face like a bagful of spanners, a. A face hard and rough, applied mostly to women. Coren, 1975, refers to a man thus describing his mother-in-law.

face like a coastguard station, have a. To look stony and grim: since ca. 1940. (L.A., 1967.)

face like a milkman's round, a. I.e., long: urban: since ca. 1950. (L.A., 1976.)

face like a mountain goat('s), have a. To be an Irish, Scottish or Welsh dupe: c.

face like a scrubbed hammock, (have) a. To have a pale sour-looking face: RN: since ca. 1920. (Granville.)

face like a yard of pump-water. A 'long'—i.e. miserable or glum—face: coll. A var. is . . . *like three yards of tripe* (Roger Richards, 1983).

face like the back of a bus, have a; occ. **face that would stop a bus** or **a clock**, or **like the side of a house**. Of girls or women: to be very plain-looking: since late 1940s. A more brutal var. is . . . *like the rear end of a cow*. P.B.: in 1940s there was still the var. . . . *back of a tram*.

face the music. To cope bravely with an unexpected emergency: adopted, ex US, ca. 1880: coll., >, by ca. 1920, S.E. A later, C.20 meaning is to go through an ordeal, e.g., the possibility of a severe reprimand or other punishment, as 'I know they don't like what I've done, but I suppose I'd better go back and face the music'; or simply 'to do a job of work, esp. Edwardian wives' and mothers' flattering menfolk of the family who had to "go to the City" or whatever business.'

face-ticket. A season ticket: among those who travel by train or 'tube': coll.: from ca. 1920.

faces. 'A term for notorious cab drivers (fortunately few in number) who quite unscrupulously make their own rules and take only profitable hirings or those where they can more easily extort from fares, e.g., "airport faces", "hotel faces", "abortion faces". Also used in general sense for known criminals' (Powis): police and underworld: 1970s. See **face**, 2.

factor, as in *the chuff factor*, the degree of a soldier's acceptance, contentment, eagerness, and in **embuggerance factor**, q.v., a risk: Army, perhaps mainly officers': WW2 and after: j. > s. (P.B., 1974.) The *embuggerance factor* later came to mean rather 'to what extent one's plans or actions could be "buggered-up" by forces beyond one's control' (P.B., 1981).

Factory, the. 'Specifically, a large Metropolitan police station of severe appearance (the Old Commercial Street "nick", for example); generally, any police station. Not now so common an expression as it once was, perhaps because police stations are not now quite as stark and forbidding as they once were' (Powis, 1977). In the c. of ca. 1860–90 it signified Old Scotland Yard, as in '*No. 747*'.—2. 'The model agricultural colony at Carroceto (Anzio bridgehead), a prominent landmark': Army: early 1944+. P-G-R.

factory. Equipment for injecting drugs: drugs c. (Stockley, 1986.) US since C-1937 (Spears). Cf. **artillery**.

fade, n. In *do a fade*, to disappear without paying the rent: Can. carnival workers'.—2. In *on the fade*, (by/in) evading justice, dodging the police: Aus. c.: since ca. 1920. B., 1942.

fade, v. To depart; to disappear (of persons): gen. s.: since ca. 1950. Hunter, 1957, 'it's pretty obvious that this geezer and her were planning to fade together . . .' Cf. prec.

faded, have got (someone). To have someone at a disadvantage: Can.: since ca. 1940. Esp. in relation to the dice game of craps. Ex US, where 'I've got him faded' = 'I can match any trick or threat of his with one just as potent' (R.C.).

faff; usu. **faff about.** To mess about, restlessly and ineffectually, wasting time, often while something quite urgent needs attention; 'Oh, do come *on*! Stop faffing about! We shall *never* get there at this rate!': since ca. 1930. Used as euph. for synon. *fuck about* or *fart about*, but in fact ex Yorkshire dial. (*EDD*'s example, 1874).

fag. An inferior cigarette, from ca. 1887; by late 1890s, in Services, any cigarette, and this usage >, by ca. 1915, gen. Abbr. *fag-end* (late C.17 s. for 'the part nearest the end').— 2. A male homosexuality, esp. if a pathic, a 'female' partner in male homosexuality: adopted, ca. 1960, ex US; Powis notes, 1977, 'now not uncommon in West London'. Very prob. a shortening of **faggot**, 2.

fag-ash. Cigarette-ash: low coll. Hence, *Fag-ash Lil*, a nickname for a girl or woman who is a heavy smoker. (P.B.)

fag-end. 'To have only a partial or muddled understanding of something that has been said' (Bentley, 1961): since ca. 1955.

fag-end man. A collector—for a living—of cigarette-ends: lower classes':—1923 (Manchon).

fag-hag. A girl who smokes. See CANADIAN ADOLESCENTS', in Appx., and cf. a Brit. equivalent, *Fag-ash Lil*. [—2. The N. Am. sense, a girl or woman who habitually consorts with male homosexuals, has not yet (1987) made much, if any, impact in UK.]

fag-hole. The mouth: contemptuous: since ca. 1945. Semantically, cf. **cake-hole**.

fag it. To smoke cigarettes, as in 'faggin' it in the loos' (smoking, illicitly, in the lavatories): schoolchildrens': early 1980s. (C. Williams, 1983.)

Fagan (or **Fagin**). The penis: in such expressions as 'Have you introduced her to Fagan?' (joc.: = 'Have you achieved sexual intimacy with your girl?'), and 'to bury old Fagin' (= of a man, to coït): 1950s. (L.A.; P.B.)

faggeroon. A cigarette: fanciful embellishment of bald **fag**, 1. Simmonds, 1983.

fag(g)ot. A 'baggage'; a pej. applied to a woman (—1600), also—gen. prec. by *little*—to a child (—1859): low coll., the former in C.20 being dial.—2. A homosexual male: low coll.: since ca. 1960, ?earlier. Prob. ex sense 1. (P.B.)

faggy. Homosexual, esp. if passive: since ca. 1965. (Scaduto, 1974.) See **fag**, 2.

faintest, the. The least idea; as in 'I haven't the faintest': coll.: since ca. 1910. I.e. *the faintest* (remotest) *idea*.

fainting fits, often shortened to *faintings*. Female breasts: r.s. on *tits*: since ca. 1950. (Haden-Guest.) See **Bristols**.

fair. Undoubted, complete, thorough: dial. (1872) >, by ca. 1885, s. (*OED* Sup.). See, e.g., **cow**, 3. P.B.: in later C.20, it has much coll. use as an intensive adj. and adv.: 'That's a fair ol' drop' could mean either 'It's a long way from the top to the bottom [of cliff, well, etc.]' or 'I'm enjoying this drink.'

fair ball. 'Legal; acceptable; agreeable. As in, "If they want to do that, it's fair ball by me." Widespread N. Am., prob. orig. US: poss. since 1920s or 30s' (Leech, 1986).

fair cow, a. See **cow**, 3.

fair crack of the whip, a. 'North Country for "fair play"' (Petch, 1971). 'To give someone a fair crack of the whip' = to deal fairly with that person: Aus. (B., 1959) and Brit. L.A., 1974, 'Hence the form of complaint that someone is "not getting a fair . . . ", when he is over/under-burdened with work, responsibility, etc.', which has been RAF usage since ca. 1936, and soon spread to the army.

fair doo's or **doos** or **does** or **do's** or **dues.** The last is the orig. form, as in C.T. Clarkson & J. Hall Richardson, *Police*,

1889, 'Now then, fair dues; let everybody be searched, I have no money about me'. A fair deal; justice; just proportion: coll., ex Yorkshire dial. (1865: *EDD*). From ca. 1930 often as *fair do's all round*. P.B.: by mid-C.20, spelt and thought of as *fair do's*, on analogy with such phrases as *dicey do's* and *shaky do's*.

fair few, a. A considerable number: Aus. coll.: late C.19–20. 'I have a fair few sheep in this paddock.' (B.P.) P.B.: Brit. usage also in C.20, and prob. as long as in Aus.

fair skint. Very short of money or even entirely 'broke': mainly North Country.

fair-weather drink. 'Small celebration with intimates before some enterprise or holiday' (Powis): coll.: 1970s.

fair wind, give (something) **a.** To pass (e.g. the salt): nautical: late C.19–20. (Bowen.) P.B.: applied in the Services, esp. among officers, to such things as a request for posting, an application to attend a course, etc.; i.e. to give it favourable attention: I heard it used thus in late 1960s+.

fairy, n. A catamite: adopted ex US ca. 1924. Irwin, 1931; *OED* Sup.

fairy, adj. Used of someone who apparently never needs to visit the w.c.: Nottingham schoolgirls': 1930s.

fairy cycle. A child's bicycle, roughly half the size of an adult's: coll.: 1930s–50s. Poss. ex a brand name. (P.B.)

fairy glen. A lavatory: railwaymen's: since (?)ca. 1945. (*Railway*, 2nd.) R.C. suggests 'perhaps a reference to homosexual activities in public lavatories'; cf. **fairy**, n.

fairy powder. A mixture of potassium chlorate and sulphur: Aus. schoolboys': since ca. 1930. 'Struck with a hammer, it makes a noise quite unlike a fairy (*lucus a non lucendo*)' (B.P.).

fairy story or **tale.** A 'hard luck' tale: low s. verging on tramps' c.; any unlikely tale, often euph. for a downright lie: coll.

fairyland. 'Colour light multiple aspect gantry' (*Railway*, 2nd): railwaymen's: current in 1960s.

Faith, Hope and Charity. The three WW1 campaign medals, better known as *Pip, Squeak and Wilfred*: since 1919 or 1920.—2. Names given to the three Gladiator biplane fighters that in June 1940 defended Malta against the Italian air force. *The Air Battle of Malta*, HMSO, 1944. (P.B.)

faithful as a hunk of shit. 'Said of a person or pet, meaning that they are completely unfaithful or disloyal, as in, "Judy? She's as faithful . . ." W. & N. Can.: mid-1950s. Not heard elsewhere' (Leech, 1986).

fake and fakers. In the Army, latish (?mid-)C.19–20, cleaning 'tackle' has included *fake*, 'the various polishes, blancoes, pipeclays and ochres'—and *fakers*, 'brushes and polishing cloths. Even the brushes had strange names, "putters on" and "shiners off" ' (Mays, 1975), the last two being coll. rather than s. Cf. the sense of *fake* as theatrical make-up.

fake, v. To hit: Parlyaree: Seago, 1933.—2. V.i. To hurt, as in 'It fakes like hell!': low s. or c.:—1923 (Manchon). Prob. ex C.19 v.t.—3. To improvise; to play by ear: Can. dance-bands': ca. 1920–36. P.B.: prob. far more widespread in place and time: cf. the old two-liner about the bar-room pianist, 'Say, do you know your monkey's pissing in my beer!'—'No, but you hum it, and I'll fake it.' The v. was much used in C.19 theatrical and artistic s.—4. To receive (a gratuity) illegally; knowingly to accept (a bribe): late C.19–20, esp. among market traders, as in 'Fake the dropsy and crack nix' (*M.T.*).

fake (or **work**) **the broads.** To issue counterfeit coin: c.:—1923 (Manchon).

fake the marks. 'They're faking the marks'—footnoted 'the shares were changing hands at fictitious prices' (Kitchin, 1949): stockbrokers'.

fakems. Quack medicines.—2. Pinchbeck.—3. Counterfeit goods.—4. Disguised trash.—5. Cosmetics. All 5 senses are market-traders' usage. Hence *put* (or *get*) *the fakems on*, to offer trash for sale as valuable merchandise; to disguise defects; to apply cosmetics. Thus 'She's got the fakems on' may mean either 'She is selling disguised trash' or 'She has plenty of make-up on'. All in *M.T.*

fall. To conceive a child: coll.: C.19–20. In later C.20, usu. **fall for**, q.v.—2. To be arrested: c.:—1883. Noted by Stockley, 1986, as drugs c.—3. Hence, to go to prison; e.g. *fall for three years*: c. 'Stuart Wood', 1932.—4. (Prob. also ex sense 2.) To fail: c. and low s.: from ca. 1910. *Gilt Kid*, 1936.—5. To arrive; esp. of 'the law', suddenly. See AUSTRALIAN UNDERWORLD, in Appx.

fall about (sc. with laughter). To laugh immoderately, as in 'I go in with a tale like that, why, they'll fall about [i.e. laugh their disbelief]': often used fig.: gen.: since mid-1970s. Cf. **crease oneself.** Clement, 1977; P.B.

fall down (on). To make a bad mistake or error (in or at): s. >, ca. 1935, coll.: US (ca. 1870), anglicised ca. 1910. Often with *on*. (*OED* Sup.) Esp. in Services, before and during WW2, and gen. since, *fall down on the job*, to fail very badly, or inexcusably, at it.

fall for. To be greatly attracted by (esp. a member of the other sex): US (ca. 1910), anglicised ca. 1920; by 1935, coll.—2. To conceive a child. Ex **fall**, 1. Army corporal's wife, 1968, 'She'd been married only a couple of months and she fell for it'; Pahl, 1978, quotes a 16-year-old girl's essay about her likely future life: 'I kept my job for about 3 years after we were married, that is until I fell for our first child.' Cf. **fallen heavy** and **fallen on.**

fall guy. The person who is made to suffer; the scapegoat: coll.: 1970s. 'The [quality] inspectors are the fall guys—it's them that has to carry the can for management, *and* they get stick from the blokes on the shop floor'. An adaptation of the US c., a victim, hence a specially set up scapegoat. (P.B.)

fall off. As in ' "It's falling off the air" ', used when a programme is being broadcast, means "It's a failure" ' (May, 1985): television workers'.

fall-out, n. 'Jocularly used regarding the danger of pieces falling out of an old car' (B.P.): Aus.: since ca. 1955. Ex atomic *fall-out*.—2. The risk of breasts falling out of a scanty bra or a bikini swimsuit: Aus.: since ca. 1960.

fall out, v. To lose consciousness from over-indulgence in drugs: drugs c.: late 1960s+.

fall out of bed. 'This refers to anyone who thought he was on to a good thing and it turns out to be otherwise' (Ash): London dockers'. ?The end of a pleasant dream.

fall out of the boat. To become unpopular in a naval mess: RN. P-G-R.

fall over (oneself). See **falling over . . .**

fall over backwards. To go 'above and beyond' what is apparently necessary. See **lean over backwards.**

fall to pieces. (Of a woman) to be confined; to give birth to a child: Aus. lower-middle-class. (B., 1942.) Cf. synon. *explode.*

fallen heavy. The Newcastle-Upon-Tyne var. of the next. (Dr I. Beale, 1984.)

fallen on. Pregnant: (mostly lower and lower-middle class) women's: since ca. 1930. Chamberlain, 1976, 'As soon as a woman realised she had "fallen on", or "got caught", she would take action [to obtain an abortion].' Cf. **fall,** 1, **fall for,** 2, and prec.

fallie, -y (pron. with short *a*; usu. pl.). A flower: feminine, domestic. Ex childish pron. (P.B.)

falling over (one)**self** (to do something). Very eager: coll.: since ca. 1920. In other tenses also, as 'He really fell over himself trying to be helpful'.

false. To tell dishonest lies: (orig. low) Aus.: since ca. 1930. Glassop, 1949, ' "Perce," said "Lucky" earnestly. "You knew me well in Sydney. Have you ever caught me falsin'?" '

false flap. A bad cheque: N.T., Aus.: since ca. 1930. Hill 1951.

falsies. Imitation breasts, breasts artificially aggrandised: adopted, ca. 1944, from US servicemen.

fam trip. 'Familiarisation flight (in a new aircraft)' (*Fighter Pilot*, 1981): RAF: later C.20.

family jewels, the. A man's sexual apparatus: both domestic and, between man and man (men), joc. and often bonhomously ironic. 'I heard it during RAF service, 1941–5' (L.A., 1976)—but, within my own memory, it goes back to the 1920s; what's more, it smacks of educated Edwardian raffishness. Still current, 1970s, among RM (Hawke). Cf. **wedding kit.**

family prayers. Var. of *morning prayers*, the daily staff conference at HQ: Army: WW2 and decades afterwards.

family tree, the. The lavatory: r.s.: mostly Services': since ca. 1930. (P-G-R.) By 1960, †. (Franklyn 2nd.)

famous crimes. 'Any man with a scowling face, reminiscent of the pictures of famous criminals in the now defunct *Police Gazette* . . . This journal was immensely popular on the lower deck of HM ships. It specialised in detailed and illustrated reports of murders' (Granville).

fan, n. An enthusiast, orig. of sport: ex US:—1889, anglicised ca. 1914; by 1930, coll. Abbr. *fanatic.*—2. An aircraft propeller: RFC/RAF: from ca. 1916 (H. & P.); by ca. 1950, †, except when mimicking the Americans, who also used the term, with such phrases as 'four-fan bombardment ship' (= 4-engined bomber). (P.B.)—3. A ship's propeller: RN: since ca. 1918. Cf. **whizzer.**—4. Short for *fanny*, female pudend, as in 'her old fan': low: since ca. 1950.

fan, v. In c., to search a person, or his clothes: from ca. 1850. (Mayhew.) Powis notes its continued currency in the 1970s. Cf. **frisk.**—2. Esp. to search illicitly (a man) for watch or wallet: c. Leach.

fan belt. See **puss pelmet.**

fan in fin. 'An Aerospatiale/Westland Gazelle [helicopter]'s . . . 13 tail rotors which, since they are shrouded, are known as "fan in fin" ' (*Sunday Times* mag., 25 Nov. 1979): RN. Cf. **fan,** n., 3.

fan-mail. Letters received from unknown admirers, esp. by a film star: adopted, ca. 1925, ex US; by 1936, it had > coll. Ex **fan,** n., 1.

fanad. None, nothing: Army: since the 1920s; by 1950, †. (H. & P.) Short for 'Sweet Fanny Adams'.

fancy, n. A 'best girl': lower classes':—1923 (Manchon). Abbr. *fancy piece* or *-woman.*—2. 'His father took a great deal to the fancy . . . it meant dealing in birds, and dogs, and rabbits' (Greenwood, 1884): poor Londoners' coll.: from ca. 1860. (B. & L.) P.B.: still current in later C.20, perhaps with particular ref. to racing pigeons; now considered to be S.E. (*OED* Sup., 1973).

fancy, v. To desire sexually: mostly (though not necessarily) feminine: coll.: latish C.19–20, but esp. common since ca. 1950, as in 'I could fancy him!' Implied in *fancy man.*

fancy (one's) **chance(s).** Var. of **fancy** (one's) **weight,** with implication that the (usu.) man in question will rely upon his charm or skill to see him through, in one specific instance, or through life: coll. 'Aylen he [the NCO] saw as a skiving bastard who fancied his chance, so he was out to needle him whenever he could' (*Heart*). (P.B.)

fancy pants. Any male, esp. a child, 'dressed to the nines': Can.: since ca. 1925. (Leechman.) Adopted in Britain, mid-C.20, and applied loosely to any member of either sex who is 'all dressed up'. (P.B.)

Fancy Tart, the. HMS *Vansittart*: RN (lowerdeck): 1920s and 1930s. A Hobson-Jobson.

fancy waistcoats. See **speak fancy . . .**

fancy (one's own) **weight.** To have an unduly high estimation of one's own importance; hence, to act in a conceited and arrogant manner: mostly Services': earlier C.20. (Hatton, 1930.) Hence, by extension, 'He's a bit of a weight-fancier, but not a bad chap at heart, really.' (P.B.)

fancy work. Genitals, including the pubic hair, usu. of the male parts: feminine euph. s. 'He must be a sexual maniac; he persists in showing his fancy work.'

fang. 'To drive a car fast and in an aggressive manner' (Buzo, 1973): Aus.: since the 1950s. 'Let's hop in the B and fang up to the beach.' (Buzo, 1969).

fang bo'sun. Dentist: R Aus. N: since ca. 1910. An Aus. Army var. is *fang(-)carpenter.*

fang(-)farrier. A dentist: Army. (H. & P.) Known also in Aus.; cf. prec. A further var. is *fang-snatcher.*

fangs in, put the; v.t. **into.** To borrow money: Aus. (Baker.) Cf. **put the bite on.**

Fannies, -ys. The *First Aid Nursing Yeomanry.* See next, 2.

fanny, n. The female *pudenda*; the pudend: low: from ca. 1860 (perhaps much earlier).—2. (*Fanny.*) A member of the (Women's) *First Aid Nursing Yeomanry* (FANY); founded 1909, it became in 1933 the Women's Transport Service, and in WW2 some of its members did gallant service in Nazi-occupied Europe.—3. Talk; eloquence: c.: from ca. 1910. See **right fanny** and sense 7.—4. Esp. a grafter's sales-talk: grafters': from ca. 1920. Allingham. See v.—5. A large mess-kettle: RN: since ca. 1925.—6. The backside: adopted, ca. 1930, ex US. (Coward, 1930.) P.B.: this usage is still regarded, 1970s, as predominantly US, sense 1 proving powerful enough to withstand American adulteration.—7. A story: Guards Regiments'. A specialisation of senses 3 and 4. Kersh, 1942.—8. The knuckle-duster used by Commandos: Army: 1942–5.—9. In *put up the fanny,* 'To explain the working of a job to other criminals to induce them to come in' (Hume): c.: from ca. 1930. Perhaps ex sense 3; perhaps ex sense 1,—for semantics, cf. **bullshit.**

fanny, v.i. To 'tell the tale': market traders' (e.g. Petticoat Lane). Cf. *fanny a pitch,* to 'spiel'—talk glibly, hand out 'the patter'—until enough people have gathered: showmen's: late C.19–20. *John o' London's Weekly,* 4 Mar. 1949.

fanny about. To proceed, or perform, ineffectually; to 'potter' or 'faff' about: later C20. 'We spent all afternoon watching that [player's name] fannying about' (Burn, quoting a Northerner's comment, 1983). Ex **fanny,** 1; perhaps a 'polite' version of *fuck about.*

Fanny Adams. Tinned mutton,—1889 (B. & L.); from ca. 1910 predominantly stew (Granville): RN >, ca. 1900, also Army (B. & P.). P.B.: ex the brutal and maniacal murder, on 24 Aug. 1867, of 8-year-old Fanny Adams, at Alton in Hampshire.—2. Hence, *Fanny Adams* (and, for emphasis, *sweet Fanny Adams*) > euph. expansion of the initials *F.A.* = *fuck all* = nothing at all: Army, hence other Services': since ca. 1914. B. & P.

Fanny Barnett. A Francis Barnett motorcycle, in production 1919–64: motorcyclists' nickname. (Carter, 1979.) Cf. the affectionate dim. of *Frances* to *Fanny,* common until mid-C.20, and see also **Frantic Bee.**

fanny hat. A trilby: low: since ca. 1930. Ex, of course, the dent in the crown. Cf. **chooch,** or **cunt, hat.**

fanny rag. A sanitary pad: low Aus.: since ca. 1945. Ex **fanny,** n., 1.

Fannys, the. See **fanny,** n., 2.

fantabulous. A blend of *fantastic* and *fabulous:* ca. 1961–4. (Winton, 1963.) A var., *fantabulosa,* theatrical and mock-Parlyaree, was used in 'Round the Horne', in the later 1960s.

fantastic. Very good, or even merely good; excellent or almost so; attractive, unusual, esp. unusual and either good or attractive or both: since late 1940s.

fare. A male professional homosexual's client: homosexuals': since ca. 1930. Norman, 1959.

Farewell Jetty. 'Officially they call it South Railway Jetty, but all Portsmouth and the Navy's nearest and dearest have know it for decades as Farewell Jetty. It is down at the seaward end of the dockyard where warships lie their last night or two before leaving for abroad' (*The Times,* 15 June 1964): coll.: late C.19–20.

farm. See **funny farm.**

Farmer Giles. Haemorrhoids: Aus. r.s. (on *piles*). Durack, 1955, 'This form of rhyming slang is . . . commonly used in the outback.' P.B.: not unknown in Britain. Daniells, 1980, 'The late Monsewer Eddie Gray, in drag as a gipsy clairvoyant, used to invite questions from the audience . . . more accurately, planted Moulin Rouges—stooges—and to the

query "How would you help the farmers?" he replied, "I'm a fortune-teller, not a chemist." '

Farmers, the. The Tank Corps: Aus. Army: WW2. B., 1942.—2. See **Farmer Giles.**

Farmer's Bible, the. The mail-order catalogue of the T. Eaton Co.: Can.: since ca. 1918.

Farmer's Boy, the. An express goods-train carrying provisions to London: railwaymen's: from ca. 1920. (*Daily Telegraph,* 15 Aug. 1936.) Cf. **the Feeder.**

Farmers' Strike, the. 'The Boer War was referred to as this, when comparing it to the 1914–18 War': WW1, esp. among soldiers. The latter war was, in turn, called the Bow and Arrow War when WW2 got under way—of course, only by those who had had no experience of the first one': ca. 1940–5. (Petch, 1966.)

farmyard nuggets. Eggs: RN (lowerdeck). Granville.

fart. In *like a fart in a gale* or *wind-storm,* puny; ineffective; incommensurate: low: for most of C.20. In later C.20, however, for someone or -thing much more offensively useless, *like a fart in a space-suit* (Burt, 1984).—2. See **chase a fart . . . .**

fart about. To dawdle; to waste time; play about: low coll., late C.19–20. Ex dial.

fart-arse about (or **around**). Same as prec.: C.20. The orig. of **fartarsing about,** q.v. Cf.:-

fart-arsed mechanic. A clumsy person: Londoners': from ca. 1925.

fart-catcher. A homosexual: low: since ca. 1930. Gardner, 1967, 'Oh, bleeding hell . . . manager's a flaming pouve. A fart catcher.'

fartarsing about or **around.** 'Moving (in a motor vehicle) without definite knowledge of one's exact location. Army from ca. 1940. There is a subtle difference between this and *swanning around.* If one was swanning around the **blue** (sense 6) one still *thought* one knew where one was.' (Sanders.) Cf. **fart about.**

farting. A pej.: low. Wilson, 1956, 'Or some other farting nonsense.'

farting shot. A vulgar way of showing contempt for the company (whether sing. or pl.) one is leaving, esp. after a quarrel: since ca. 1940. A pun on *parting shot.*

fast. (Mostly of animals.) Engaged in coïtion: earlier C.20. 'She would blush if she saw two dogs fast.' I.e., fastened together.

fast black. A taxi: RN: 'A corruption of fast back, the sales jargon for a car with a sloping rear window. In BBC TV 'Warship', 10 Dec. 1974' (Peppitt). York, 1980, notes the term as upper-middle-class s. of late 1970s.

fast(-)buck artist. A person, usu. male, eager to make a lot of money—and *fast:* Can.: since ca. 1950. (Robertson, 1973.) P.B.: such pej. phrases as *they're only out to make a* (or *out for the*) *fast buck* have been Brit. coll. since ca. 1960, if not earlier.

fast one. 'A remark giving rise for thought' (H. & P.): Services': since ca. 1935; ob. by 1946. Ex Larwood fast-bowling at cricket.—2. Hence (or independently ex same origin), esp. in *pull a fast one,* to 'do the dirty', to malinger, to wangle something one is not entitled to, to evade a duty: Services': since ca. 1938. H. & P.

fast talker. A confidence trickster or 'con man': since ca. 1930. Ex S.E. sense, 'a glib talker'.

fat, n. Good luck: Army: late C.19–20. By ca. 1930, gen. lower-class s. Branch, 1951.—2. An erection of the penis: Aus. Armed Forces', WW2; > gen. low. See **crack a fat** and **fatty.**—3. Semen: low. Esp. in phrase *come one's fat,* to ejaculate, and hence, also, to confess or inform. Cf. **cocoa.** Powis.

fat, adj. Rich; esp. with *cull:* c.: late C.17-early 19. Ex C.16 S.E. Revived in later C.20, esp. in phrase **fat cats,** q.v.—2. Good: Aus. coll.:—1890. Also used by FAA, 1960s: see **ace.** A revival of the C.17 S.E. usage; cf. sense 1.—3. Out-dated, esp. in sense 'square': teenagers': late 1970s. ' "Hippies are fat," said one 16 year old I spoke to last week' (Kettle, 1980).

fat-arse around. To waste time; to dawdle: NZ shape of **fat-arse about**, q.v.

fat as a match. (Esp. of a person) very thin indeed: Aus.: since late 1940s. (B., 1959.) Cf. *like a match with the wood shaved off*: Brit. coll.: later C.20. (P.B.)

fat cats, (the). The ostentatiously wealthy in any place or of any profession or class: since ca. 1955; by 1975, coll. P.B.: it was much used of the Hong Kong tycoons during the 1960s; L.A. cites the *Observer*, 22 Sep. 1974, for its application to, e.g., sleek stockbrokers.

fat chance. No chance at all: ironical coll. The NZ var. is *fat show*. Cf.:-

fat lot, a. Always in actual or virtual negative, which = nothing; very little: coll.: 1899, Cutcliffe Hyne, 'Shows what a fat lot of influence . . . Congo has got' (*OED* Sup.); now verging on S.E.

father. An admiral commanding a squadron: RN. Bowen.—2. The captain: RN: since ca. 1954. 'Seems to be used mainly by pussers, but is coming into general use very fast' (Granville, 1962).

Father Bunloaf. A Catholic priest: Belfast. Pej.

Father Christmas. A venerable old man: coll.

father (something) **on** (someone). To blame someone for something he did not do; to impute responsibility where it does not rest: coll.: since ca. 1910. Ex fathering an illegitimate child upon the wrong man.

fati gu'ed. A joc. pron. of *fatigued*; *fati-gu'e* is less gen. Occ. *fattygew(ed)*. Perhaps orig. derisive of dial. pron.

Fatso. Common nickname for any fat person, esp. a fat youth: Can., since ca. 1945 (Leechman); Brit., since ca. 1950, adopted ex US.

fatter than a shithouse rat. Really fat; obese: W. Can.: since 1940s. (Leech, 1986.)

fav., the (pron. *fayve*). The favourite: racing coll.: 1950s. 'The Clonmel fellas is puttin' one in to knock over the fav., and if you're quick about it there'll be all the hundred to seven . . . you can lay your hand on' (Campbell, 1960).

fave. Favourite: later C.20. 'Kipper Williams' collection of your fave drippy strips, "The Lady and the Wimp" ' (*Time Out*, 24 Sep. 1986); earlier in *The Tube's Mark Miwurdz*, 1984, p. 50. Cf.:-

fave-rave. 'Favourite [musical] group, gramophone record, etc.; anything that is superb, excellent' (Hibbert, 1983): teenagers': mid-1960s.

favourite. Excellent; the best; esp. in *This is* (or *that's* or *that'd be*) *favourite*: Services': since ca. 1930. (H. & P.) P.B., 1974, adds: 'Later, 1950s, often pluralised, with the *a* sound drawn out. Thus . . . appreciatively of the first beer of the session, "Fa-a-a-vourites bevvy!", before taking a deep swig.'

favvers. The army shape of 'favours' (*Daily Mail*, 7 Sep. 1940); † by 1950.

fazz. Grease: Post Office telegraph-messengers' (esp. in London); from before 1935. P.B.: prob. a corruption of *fat*; see **−z**.

Fearful. 'The twin assault ships *Fearless* and *Intrepid* were dubbed respectively, "Fearful" and "Insipid" ' (*Don't Cry*, 1983): Services': Falklands War.

fearnought. A condom: RN: earlier C.20. Cf. synon. **dreadnought**. Perhaps ex:-

fearnoughts. 'White loose-fitting trousers made of a good thick blanket material with seamen's flaps instead of fly buttons' (Piper, 1974): trawlermen's coll. Perhaps ex a brand name. Butcher, 1980, has *fear-nots*. Cf. synon. **dreadnoughts**.

feat. An exclusive piece of news: journalistic: adopted, early 1930s, ex US. Abbr. (*special*) *feature*.

feather. A bed: tramps' c. (Davies, 1918.) Abbr. *feather and flip*, the same: r.s. on *kip*: late C.19–20. (*Cheapjack*, 1934.)

feather-bed. To make things easy for someone or for a group; v. of next. As adj., attrib. of one that benefits; often enviously pej., as in the sporadic outcry against, e.g., 'the feather-bed farmers', thought to be receiving large government subsidies.

feather-bedding. The practice of making things very easy for an elderly or indisposed member of a gang, e.g., dockers: industrial: s. >, by 1940, coll.—2. In Can. (adopted ex US), 'to take on extra and unnecessary help, as in hiring 10 men to do a job that could be done by 3' (Leech, 1986): since (?)1920s.

feather-plucker. An objectionable fellow: City of London businessmen's euph., sometimes only mildly pej.: since ca. 1945: r.s. on *fucker*. Cf. **pheasant-plucker**, a deliberate spoonerism.

feathered arsehole. 'The old RAF Observers' brevet, an O with a single wing growing out of it to the right, superseded by the navigators' badge early in WW2' (P.B., 1974): RAF: since latish WW1; from ca. 1942, merely nostalgic. Cf. **flying arsehole**.

feature, n. and v., in newspapers and films, is s. (>, by 1925, cinematic coll.) if simply = either a part, or to present (prominently). US (ca. 1897), anglicised ca. 1905. (*OED* Sup.) P.B.: in later C.20 *feature*, n. and v., > accepted part of media j., verging on informal S.E.

feature with. 'To achieve sexual intercourse with [given currency by the Barry McKenzie comic strip]' (Wilkes: brackets his): Aus.: later C.20.

features. A satirical term of address: ca. 1900–14 in Britain (Ware); still in use in Aus. Army in the 1960s (?a revival), understood as short for, e.g., *penis-features*. (P.B.)

feaze, feeze. To harm; to trouble: Can. Ex Eng. dial. P.B.: prob. more strongly influenced by US *faze*, to perturb, a var. of the same.

Feb. February: coll. Ex the abbr. The only other months thus treated (so far!) are January, as *Jăn*, and, rarely, August, as *Aug* (org). P.B.: that *so far!* was E.P.'s note, 1937; other months have now, mid-1980s, long succumbed.

fed to the back teeth. An intensive var., dating from ca. 1910, of the next. Occ. *fed up . . .* or *fed to the wide*. Manchon.

fed-up. Bored; disgusted; (*with*) tired of: orig. military, possibly ex the Boers (witness Pettman): from ca. 1899.

Feds, the. 'Employees of the US Federal Bureau of Investigation, hence, in UK, police in general' (Hibbert, 1983): counter-culture.

feed (one's) **face.** To eat: contemptuous or, at least, depreciatory.

feed (a person) **meat.** To supply with very rich and nutritious food: 1920 (Wodehouse: *OED* Sup.). Here, *meat* is opp. *milk*, the food of infancy.

feed of jeelyreek. A whiff of gelignite fumes: Scottish miners'.

feed the chicks. To carry out air-to-air refuelling, by a large tanker aircraft, of the smaller, fighter aircraft of RAF Strike Command: RAF: since mid-1960s. Petch, 1971.

feed the fish. To 'skin' (lead on) the victim: Can. carnival s.: since ca. 1920. Also *clean the fish*. See **fish**, 1.

Feeder, the. A GWR express goods-train connecting 'several important services' carrying provisions to London: railwaymen's: from ca. 1919. (*Daily Telegraph*, 15 Aug. 1936.) Cf. **the Bacca**. [GWR = Great Western Railway, until incorporation into British Rail.]

feel (someone's) **bump.** To know what he is thinking: coll.:— 1923 (Manchon). Contrast *feel* (or *read*) someone's *bumps*, to practise phrenology on that person.

feel like a baby at a wedding. To feel very much unwanted or out of place: since ca. 1930. (Hemingway, 1944.) Alignable with such anomalies as 'whore at a christening' and 'spare prick at a wedding'; but little used since ca. 1950.

feel like a boiled rag. 'To feel excessively limp', or unwell: coll. (Lyell.) Variants are . . . *like a piece of chewed rag* or *string*.

feel like death warmed up. To feel very ill—half dead, in fact: (until ca. 1940 proletarian) coll. 'For hours and hours he had to stick to the controls [of his aircraft], feeling like death warmed up' (Brickhill, 1946). The earliest recording I've seen occurs in the anon. little *The Soldiers' War Slang Dictionary,* published on 28 Nov. 1939.

feel like nothing on earth. To feel wretched or ill: coll. (—1927) >, by 1933, S.E. (Collinson.) Also as *look like* . . .

feel like shit. A coarse var. of the prec.: Services': since ca. 1950. (P.B.)

feel no pain. To be (very) drunk: since ca. 1945, esp. in Can. (Leechman.) Perhaps ex the old song, 'I feel no pain, dear Mother, now . . . ' (P.B.)

feel (one's) oats. To get bumptious or very high-spirited: orig. (ca. 1840) US >, ca. 1905, anglicised as coll.; by mid–1930s verging on S.E. Ex a horse feeding on oats.

feel (one's) own man (usu. **again**). To feel (quite) oneself, i.e. fit, normal and recovered from indisposition: coll.: since ca. 1910.

feel rough. To feel unwell, indisposed, esp. after 'the night before': rather low: from ca. 1917.

feel the draught. To be gravely inconvenienced; esp., to be hard put to it financially: 1925 (*OED* Sup.).

feel up. To caress sexually: coll.: prob. throughout C.20. I heard it in Aus., ca. 1919—and as early as 1914 the ribald feminine witticism, 'A fellow feeling makes us wondrous kind'. R.C. attests its US currency as being at least as early as 1930; he also records it as extant in UK in Diment, 1968. I suspect that it goes well back into C.19 and that, by 1940 at the very latest, it was already 'familiar S.E.'

feele. A girl; a daughter; loosely, a child (H., 1st ed.). In pl., occ. = mother and daughter. Low Cockney: from ca. 1840. Ex It. *figlia*, via Lingua Franca. In Parlyaree, often *feelier* (Seago, 1933). Hollis, 1983, lists *feelyfake* = pregnant; *fake* was very widespread C.19 s. for 'make' or 'do', or an action.

feelies, the. The next stage of cinema, following on *movies*, *talkies* and *smellies*: projected in Aldous Huxley's satirical *Brave New World*, 1932. (R.S.) Hence, since ca. 1945, an occ. term, ?esp. in Aus., for any cinema—ex the mutual petting in the darkness.

feelthy pictures (or **pitchers**). Pornographic postcards, etc.: joc. and allusive: since ca. 1920. Ex the pictures offered by native vendors to troops and tourists in the Near and Middle East.

feet muddy, get (one's). To be in trouble, especially with the criminal law, e.g., "He got his feet muddy before he had straight work" ' (Powis): police and underworld: 1970s.

feet under the table. On very friendly visiting terms with a family, esp. if one is courting a female member of the household: RN, since ca. 1925; soon spread to other Services: coll. rather than s. (Peppitt; P.B.)

feet-up artist. A motorcycle trials rider: motorcyclists': later C.20. 'So called because in competition trials a rider is penalised every time he uses a foot to steady himself, thus the aim is to keep feet on footrests—"pegs" ' (Dunford).

feetesick wallah. A male prostitute: Services' (esp. Army): earlier C.20. A mixture of Arabic (*feetesick*) and Hindustani (*wallah*). Also *gunga wallah*.

feisty. App. = spirited, lively: entertainment world: late 1970s +, prob. ex US. 'A feisty battle of wits' (*Now!*, 8 Aug. 1980); 'True to its tacky little roots, [the film] rips off all sorts of nice genre items with shameless abandon. There's a feisty talking computer . . . ' (*Time Out*, 20 Feb. 1981).

feke. Methylated spirits: c. Also *finish* and *finish-drinker*.

feke-drinker. A drinker of methylated spirits in either water or beer: c.: from ca. 1920. (Mackenzie, 1932.) Presumably *feke* = *fake*, faked.

fella(h), feller. A coll. pron., the former somewhat affected and aristocratic, and form of *fellow*: resp. C.20 and from ca. 1870. Esp. *young fella(h)*—or *feller—me lad*, joc. vocative: C.20. (*OED* Sup.)—2. Simply, male, as in 'That chimpanzee's a fella' (Ross, 1978): proletarian coll.: later C.20. A slovening of *fellow*. See quot'n at **deff out**.

feloosh. Money: coll. among soldiers with service where Arabic is spoken: earlier C.20. Direct ex Arabic. Other approx. phonetic spellings are *felooss*, *felous*, and *valoose*. See also **mafeesh!**

female belongings. Female relations: (orig. joc.) coll. 'Taffrail', 1917.

female Hornblower. 'A nautical-minded woman, often a WRNS officer, esp. a senior and [notably] a "fire-eater". After Forester [in the Hornblower novels, late 1930s]: RN: 1970s' (Peppitt)—but surely since ca. 1955.

femlin. See **beach bunny**.

Fenland Polytechnic, the. Cambridge University: other universities' derog.: since mid-C.20. Cf. **Sleaford Tech**.

fenookering. 'A sort of underhand slap-and-tickle, behind other people's backs' ('Crosstalk', 1984): Lancashire: earlier C.20.

Ferdinand. Nickname for a German self-propelled assault gun: adopted ca. 1942, by the Brit. Army from the Russians. P-G-R.—2. A bull: mostly Aus.: since ca. 1938. Ex a famous book, *Ferdinand the Bull*, 1936.

ferk!; ferking. Mincings of *fuck!*; *fucking*. See **furk!**

ferret. 'German security guard, usually in blue overalls' (Brickhill, 1946): prisoners-of-war in Germany: 1940–5. Ex his sharp eyes and the colour of his overalls. P.B.: and, of course, his spying activities.—2. A veteran Norton motorcycle, in production from ca. 1908 to ca. 1920: motorcycling enthusiasts'. (Partridge, 1979.)—3. (Also *ferreter*) A customs officer ferreting in cargo or cabins for smuggled goods: MN: 1940s esp., but also later. (Peppitt.)—4. An electronic sweeper—a man engaged on 'debugging' duties: espionage: (?)since ca. 1950. Le Carré, 1977.—5. See **trouser-ferret**.

ferry. A prostitute: Aus. B., 1942. She carries numerous men. Cf. synon. **bike**.—2. (*The Ferry*.) The Atlantic Ocean: nautical. Jackson, 1931.

ferv, n. and v. Divinity, as subject of study; chaplain;—to be religious: Cranbrook School: early C.20. Ex. 'religious *fervour*'.

festering, adj. and adv. An intensive, as in 'You festering toerag' and 'It's festering hot': Glasgow: since ca. 1920. Euph.—2. To be 'out on the town, or, at least, out at the College bar': St Catherine's College, Oxford. (Apt, 1978.)

fetch up. To vomit: coll., orig. and mainly N. Country.

few pence short in the shilling, a. 'Silly': half-witted; (slightly) mad: earlier C.20. † with the introduction of decimal coinage.

few snags short of a barbie, a. 'Is a recently made popular phrase in Sydney. It is used as a description for someone who has less than perfect mental facilities' (*Australasian Express*, 6 July 1982). *Snags* here = sausages; *barbie*, a barbecue. (Raab.)

fiasco. A fiancé; occ., a fiancée: joc. coll.: from ca. 1920. Cf. *finance*.

fiddle, n. An exasperating task or job: lower classes' coll.:— 1923 (Manchon). Ex *fiddling job*.—2. A swindle: low (since ca. 1920) > by 1939, Services'; since WW2. gen. coll. and widespread in later C.20, almost any form of dishonesty can be termed a *fiddle*, from 'working a tax fiddle' to petty pilfering of 'perks'. Hence to be *on the fiddle*. A late C.19–early 20 version was *get at the fiddle*. Cf. several senses of the v.—3. A theodolite: surveyors'. (Knight, 1984.)

fiddle, v. To cheat: C.17–20; S.E. until ca. 1800, revived by the underworld ca. 1840. Mayhew.—2. 'To purloin or obtain by a wangle'. Thus *fiddler*, one who is expert in *fiddling*', H. & P.: Services': since ca. 1910.—3. V.i and v.t., to cheat, swindle, be a swindler; to sell secretly or illicitly: low (since ca. 1912) >, by 1925, Services', and then, by 1945, common civilian s., esp. among 'spivs'.—4. Hence, by specialisation, 'to falsify, as a statement of expenses. Diment uses "expense-fiddling" in *The Bang Bang Birds*, 1968' (R.C. 1976): since ca. 1945. Esp. in the phrase *to fiddle the books*.

fiddle-arse about. To 'mess about'; to waste time: low Aus.: since ca. 1920. (B., 1943.) Some occ. Brit. use also; cf. **fart-arse**.

fiddler. A sharper or a cheat: low C.19–20. Ex **fiddle**, v., all senses, hence:—2. A 'wangler', a constant schemer or contriver: c. (Anon., *Dartmoor from Within*, 1932.) In Labour s.

(since ca. 1925), thus ' "Fiddler" (earns money on the quiet without telling labour exchange)' (Massingham, 1936). By 1939, at latest, also Services' s.

fiddley. A £1 note: Aus.: since ca. 1920. (Baker.) In the pl., (?)*fiddleys* or *fiddlies,* it is generic for money. (*Rats.*) Apparently short for *fiddley did,* Aus. r.s. on *quid.* B., 1945.

Fids. 'The book is about FIDS, which came to mean not only the Falklands Islands Dependence Survey . . . , but also the men who worked for that organisation. The men were known as Fids, and the name stuck even when their organisation changed titles and became the British Antarctic Survey' (a review of Sir Vivian Fuchs, *Of Ice and Men,* 1982).

field. To be a bookmaker operating on the course: Aus. racing: since ca. 1910. Glassop, 1949. ' "Well, boys," he said. "On Thursday I'll be fielding at Nerridale. I'm a licensed bookmaker now." '

fierce. Objectionable, unpleasant; difficult, very inconvenient: current in S. Africa at least as early as 1908 and perhaps late C.19; in Brit. since ca. 1920. The second nuance is very ob.; the first is still current, late 1970s.—2. Exceptional in some way: US, anglicised ca. 1910. Mason, 1930, ' "Such a one!" "A regular comic." "Fierce, I call him." '—3. As in, 'Once, the ultimate accolade was "sharp". It turned into "brill" and then "triff" [qq.v.]. Now it's changed again and a girl's wardrobe [i.e. its contents] has got to be "fierce" to be worth anything' (*Daily Mail,* 3 Oct. 1985).

fif(f). Fifteen, of time: coll. Benson, 1924, ' "Where and when?" "Two fiff. Our ground".'

fifas or **FIFAS.** See **fyfas.**

fife and drum. The buttocks: r.s., on *bum.* Franklyn.

fifinella. See GREMLINS, in Appx.

fifteen-two. A Jew: r.s.: an English adaptation, ca. 1945, of the American *fifteen-and-two.* Ex the cribbage score.

fifteen years (of) undetected crime. (Applied to) the long service and good-conduct medal: RN: since ca. 1895. (Bowen.) The army have to serve 18 years 'undetected' for their 'long-distance' medal, but they share the same idea.

fifth business man. 'A [Can.] theatrical term that describes a character who is neither hero nor villain, but is nevertheless essential to the unfolding of the plot' (Leechman, 1971). Ex US.

fifth pricker. 'One who signs on for a further five years' service after twenty years in the Royal Navy. He has, as it were, a "stab" at a fifth five' (Granville, 1962).

fifth wheel. (Applied to) 'the very, very rich, e.g. the Duke of Westminster. In use among the Gloucestershire horsey set' (Mann, 1985). Conspicuous consumption, the height of useless luxury.

fifty-fifty, adv. Equally; adj., equal: coll., orig. US; anglicised resp. ca. 1914, 1920. I.e., on a basis of 50%. (*OED* Sup.) In later C.20, most often in the phrase 'a fifty-fifty chance'.

Fifty-First State, the. 'Missile control room of British Polaris submarines': RN: since late 1960s. (Winton, 1971.) A bitter jibe at US control.

fifty-one A.R. A liar: schoolchildren's. London: earlier C.20. I.e. LI=*ar.*

fifty up, have. To copulate: RN lowerdeck: since ca. 1920. (Parsons, 1977.) Cf. a *nifty fifty,* masturbation.

fig. A numerical *figure:* lower-middle class: late C.19–20. Bell, 1946.

fig and post. Toast (bread): Army r.s.: WW2. Franklyn, who suggests a corruption of synon. *pig and roast.*

fight like a threshing machine. To fight, esp. with the fists, very vigorously: Aus.: since ca. 1925. B., 1959.

fighter boy. Any operational member—but esp. a pilot—of Fighter Command: RAF coll.: 1939+. Jackson.

fighter type. Synon. of prec.: RAF: WW2+. Brophy, 1944.

fighting cats. The coat of arms on a warrant officer's lower sleeve: Army: since ca. 1920. (H. & P.) A later var. is *fighting dogs.* Cf. **Tate and Lyle.** (P.B.)

fighting cobra(, old). Penis: RN joc., esp. HM Submarine *Astute:* mid-1960s. (Malin, 1979.)

Fighting Cocks, the. No. 43 (Fighter) Squadron, RAF: ex the squadron badge. Tilsley, 1978.

fighting dogs. Var. of **fighting cats.**

Fighting Eighth, the. The RN's coll. for 'The 8th Destroyer Flotilla, which deservedly earned the sobriquet in the war of 1939–45' (Granville).

fighting irons. Army issue cutlery: WW2. J.B. Mindel, of Lower Galilee, recalls the term from his service with 4th (Durham) Survey Regt, RA. Cf. the more usu. **eating irons.**

figlia. A child: *figlia homey,* a male child; *figlia polone* (or *poloney*), a female child: Parlyaree: late C.19–20. (Lester.) In the older Parlyaree, *figlia* is strictly a girl: cf. **feele.** In Italian, the m. form is *figlio.*

figure, n. See **take a figure . . . .**

figure, v. In *it* or *that figures,* lit. 'that works out correctly as a sum'; but often used ironically for 'that's just what one would expect': adopted, ex US, ca. 1955. (P.B.)

file 13. The office waste-paper basket, esp. when used for the disposal of either nonsense or insolubles: since ca. 1950.

fill. An artificial pneumo-thorax ('A.P.'): medical coll.: since the 1930s. Cusack, 1951.

fill in. To render (a woman) pregnant: low Aus. s. Ronan, 1956.—2. To thrash, beat or 'duff up': orig., since ca. 1925, RN lowerdeck; since ca. 1950, fairly gen. among the less literate. 'Next time he says that to me, I'll fill him in' (P-G-R).—3. To inform or instruct (someone): coll.: since early 1940s. 'Can you fill me in on the drill' = please tell me how things are done here.

fill in (someone's) coupon. To attack a person's face with the jagged end of a smashed bottle: low Glasgow: late C.20. (Stone, 1980.) Ex football coupons.

fill the bill. To fill a need: applicable in almost any circumstance, of the right thing at the right time in the right place: coll.: since ca. 1950 at latest. (P.B.) A var. is *fit the bill.*

filled. 'Repaired with glass fibre' (*Woman's Own,* 28 Feb. 1968): secondhand-car dealers': since ca. 1955. Implying cheap, or makeshift, repair.

filler. That 'member of the editorial staff of a newspaper who provides fill-up matter written by himself or supplied by agencies' (Petch, 1974): journalistic coll.: since ca. 1910. Cf.:-

fillers. Fill-up matter: journalistic. (Leechman.)

fillet of cod. Sod, as a mildish pej.: r.s.: later C.20. 'Cheeky little fillet (of cod)' (Barker, 1979).

filter. A synon. (—1927; very ob.) of **trickle,** q.v. (Collinson.) Cf. **ooze.**

filth, the. The police, members of the police force: c. (among the bosses of crime) and low s.: since ca. 1950. Barlow, 1968.—2. Esp. the Criminal Investigation Department: c., since mid-1950s; but by 1960, s. (Newman, 1970.) Powis, 1977: 'Filth: specifically, dishonest policemen; generally, any police. Used only by confirmed and embittered criminals. Any extreme hypocrite, not necessarily in the police sense, might be so referred to.'

filthily. Very. (Heyer, 1935, 'He was filthily offensive.') Ex:-

filthy. A coll., pej. and intensive adj., applied e.g. to an entertainment, holiday, present, etc., etc. (Hay, 1907; Collinson.) Cf. **foul.** It occurs in Devonshire dial. as early as 1733 (*EDD*) in the sense: excessive. Cf. the Oxfordshire 'I be in a filthy temper' (*EDD* Sup.; 1905). P.B.: in later C.20, prob. most often in non-pej.—though envious—phrase, 'Of course, he's filthy rich', i.e. very wealthy; cf. *stinking rich.* Poss. influenced by *the filthy,* abbr., since ca. 1875, of *filthy lucre.*

fin. 'A *fin* is a five-dollar bill, ex the large V (five) which marks it and looks like a fin. A ten-dollar bill is a *sawbuck,* from the X it bears' (Leechman.): Can. But, as R.C. points out, it is just as likely to be derived from **finnif,** q.v., of which it is an abbr. anyway.

final. The latest newspaper-edition on any given day: from ca. 1920, coll.: by mid-1930s > S.E. (*COD,* 1934 Sup.)—2. The fourth round in a pub drinking-session. See **swing o' the door.**

final gallop, the. An orgasm. See **anchors**, 3.

finals. (Orig. at Oxford.) The last of a series of examinations, esp. for bachelors' degrees: coll.: from ca. 1894. Grant Allen (*SOD*).

finance. A fiancé, esp. if rich: joc. cultured; also Society s.: from ca. 1905.?Ex US. Cf. **fiasco**.

financial. In funds: Aus. Doone, *to be a financial member*, to have paid one's due subscription. Hence the query 'Are you financial?' = 'Have you got any cash?': since late 1940s. (Raab.) 'If you have friends whose membership [of the Federation] has lapsed, please urge them to . . . become re-financial as soon as possible' (*W. Aus. Folk Federation Mag.*, Mar. 1986).

find, n. A person worth knowing (e.g., of a 'daily help', 'She was a real find, a treasure'), a thing worth having: coll.

find, v. To steal: Services': WW1 and ever since. 'To "pick up" something which is needed by your section. Finding is generally less selfish than fiddling, and more silent than scrounging' (H. & P.). Cf. *earn, win*; also *make*. Perhaps reminiscent of the C.16–18 proverbial *find things before they are lost*. Cf. Ger. *finden* in military s.; note, too, that Cæsar uses *invenire* thus in his *Gallic Wars*.

find a pie. To find a person willing to make a small loan or to offer a drink: theatrical.

find it. To back a winner: turf c.

find something. To obtain a job: coll.: mid-C.19–20. 'Found anything yet?'

fine and dandy. Brandy: later C.20. Jones, 1971.

fine ham-an'-haddie! All nonsense: Glasgow: earlier C.20.

fine print, n. and adj. The details; detailed: coll.: later C.20. 'But the fine print became inescapable when the question of the Charter and Statutes arose yet again' (*Loughborough University of Technology Gazette*, Apr. 1979, report on Council and Senate activities). Ex the fine print, the footnotes and appendices printed in small type, which contain the company's escape clauses in, e.g., insurance contracts. (P.B.)

fine-tune. To modify (sometimes, by meiosis, drastically), as in 'The first draft of the essay is OK, but of course it'll need fine-tuning' (a theological college tutor, 1987); heard also in the field of 'creative accounting' [euph. for **fiddle**, v., 4]. 'Self-defence, in the end, is what all euphemisms come back to . . . "It needs a lot of fine-tuning" is often a very satisfactory way of saying "I've done nothing about it yet" ' (May, 1986). Ex tinkering with internal combustion engines, with perhaps a glance at radio/TV sets. (P.B., 1988.) ' "We've learned some things [from an amphibious landing exercise, Nov. 1987]; we'll fine-tune existing procedures. In the main, we find they work" ' (McLeod, 1988).

finger, n. A 'term of contempt for man or woman': c.:—1933 (Ingram). Cf. *finger of scorn*, a contemptible fellow (*EDD*). —2. An official: busmen's: from ca. 1930. *Daily Herald*, 5 Aug. 1936. —3. See **give the finger**.

finger, v. By a specialisation of the S.E. *finger*, to point at: to nominate a person for a job: coll.: since ca. 1965; prob. ex US, an extension of **finger on, put the**, q.v. (P.B.)

finger and thumb. A companion or 'mate': r.s., on *chum*: since ca. 1930.

finger bowl. An outdoor cinema: Can.: since ca. 1960. 'Ex U.S. sports arenas, the Rose Bowl, the Orange Bowl, etc.' (Leechman.)

finger-fuck, v.i. (Of women only) to masturbate: low coll.: C.19-20.—2. V.t. To caress a woman intimately or, homosexually, a man: low. Vbl n. in *-ing*.

finger on, put the. To point (a wanted man) out to the police: c. Adopted ex US. [To have the] *finger on* = to be accused: prisoners': 1970s. (Home Office.)

finger-tight, adj. and adv., as in 'Just make the nuts finger-tight and I'll follow you around with the spanner': coll. (B.P.) As tightly as possible with the fingers.

finger trouble; esp. in 'He has'—or 'He's suffering from'—'finger trouble': he's lazy; he is given to procrastination: RAF: since ca. 1935. (Emanuel, 1945.) Ex the widespread Services, mid-C.20 imperative *get, pull* or *take your finger out!* (sc. of your female companion's private parts). I.e. Get a move on!

finger up (or **well in**), **have the.** Synon. of prec.: mostly Army: 1940+.

Fingers. Nickname for a pickpocket: c.: by 1930, at latest, also police s. Gosling, 1959.

fingers! 'Hurry up, get a move on!'; abbr. of *take your finger out*, (see **finger trouble**): Army: WW2+. (P.B.)

finick. A finicky person: Aus. coll.: since ca. 1925. (P.B.) Ex synon. Eng. dial. *fin(n)ick*.

finickerty. Finicky: Aus.: since ca. 1935. (B.P.) A blend of *finicky* + *pernickety*.

finicky Dick. A finicky person: Aus.: since late 1930s. (B.P.)

finif, finip. See **finnif** and **finith**.

finish. Methylated spirits: c.:—1932. Perhaps because drinking it leads to, and is, death. Hence, a *finish-drinker*, one who drinks methylated spirits. See also **feke**.

finished, be. To have finished (v.t. or absolute): loose coll.

finith or **finif.** Five; e.g. *finith to fere*, (odds of) 5 to 4: racing c. Of same origin as **finnif**, q.v.

finito! Exclam. of completion: Aus.: since ca. 1950. The It. *finito*, finished. Also occ. use in UK.

fink. An unpleasant, esp. if felt to be untrustworthy, person: Can.: adopted, ca. 1965, ex US. (Leechman.) In drugs c., *fink* = an informant (Stockley, 1986). See *fink* in *Underworld*. May be intensified to *ratfink*.

finn. See **finnif**.

fin(n)if, -ip, -uf(f), -up; occ. derivatively **finny, finn, fin;** in C.20, occ. **finnio** (Leach). A £5 note, hence *double finnif* (etc.) = a £10 note, and *ready finnif* (etc.) = ready money. B. & L. defines *finnup ready* as 'a five-pound note'. C.: from ca. 1835; in C.20, often heard in low racing s. Brandon (1839). Ex Ger. *fünf*, five, via Yiddish.

Finsbury Park, often shortened to *Finsbury*. An *arc* light: cinematic technicians' r.s.: since ca. 1945. 'Cut the Finsburies!'

finuf or **finup.** See **finnif**.

fire-alarms. Arms: r.s. B. & P.

Fire Brigade, the. A brigade held in reserve in the UK, in a high state of readiness, to be sent anywhere in the world at very short notice to combat 'brush-fire wars': Army coll. > j.: since late 1940s. (P.B.)

fire-eater. Esp. during and after WW1, an excessively belligerent person, esp. if under no necessity to fight: coll. Cf. the S.E. and the US usages, the orig. sense being that of a juggler that 'eats fire'. Hence adj., *fire-eating*.

fire place. A denture: railwaymen's joc.: mid-C.20. McKenna.

fire-proof. Invulnerable; esp. in *fuck you, Jack, I'm fire-proof*, RAF c.p.: since ca. 1930. Cf. the RAF pun on the RAF motto (*Per ardua ad astra*): 'Per ardua ad asbestos'. (Partridge, 1945.) An adaptation of the century-old RN *fuck you, Jack, I'm all right*. Fire-proof soon spread to the army. Cf. **bomb-proof.** —2. Hence, unimpeachable when trouble threatens: since ca. 1937.

fire up. To start the engine: motorcyclists'. (Dunford, 2.) Cf. next.

fire's gone out, the. The engine has stopped: FAA: 1940+. P-G-R.

fireside and featherbed. 'Derogatory for a shore billet' (Peppitt): RN: since ca. 1950.

fireworks. Severe anti-aircraft fire: RAF, esp. among bomber crews: since 1939. Berrey, 1940; H. & P. —2. A copious dropping of flares: RAF: since 1940. Partridge, 1945.

firkin. A thingummy, a 'doofer': orig. RAF, since ca. 1925; by 1950 well known also in the Army. (Emanuel, 1945; P.B., 1979.) Ex the frequency with which one hears 'the fucking thing!' or, euph., 'the firking thing!' Cf. **doobri-firkin.**

firm. A criminal gang, of e.g., burglars: c.: since ca. 1950. Crookston, 1967, 'I blew a couple of peters for our firm.'—2.

Powis notes sense 1 and adds, 'also humorously used to describe a particular squad of detective officers, especially a closely knit and comradely band': police: 1970s.—3. A criminal set-up, e.g. between CID man (or men) and a gang: c., and police s.: since early 1950s. Newman, 1970.—4. A gang following a leader, among young, violence-prone, football supporters: late 1970s. Walker, 1979.—5. See **go firm**.

Firm, the. The registrar, the house physician and the house surgeon, with an attendant junior taking notes (and known as 'the clerk'); medical, esp. hospitals': since ca. 1930.

Firpo – or **Chowringhee** – **Star.** The 1939-45 Star: servicemen's (esp. RAF), mostly among those with long service in India: 1945+. 'Chowringhee is Calcutta's Regent Street, Piccadilly and Leicester Square; it houses Firpo's Restaurant' (RAF correspondent).

first, a. A first-class degree: (?mid-)C.19-20. Likewise *second*, *third*, *fourth*. See also **two-one**.

first and first. First Class for leave and for conduct: RN coll.: since ca. 1920. P-G-R.

first cab on the rank, be (the). To be the prime suspect: Aus.: since ca. 1950. (B.P.)

first-class rock. Naval Boy, 1st Class: RN: since ca. 1920. Granville.

first-classer. A person, thing, of the first class: coll.: 1925. *OED* Sup.

first cracks or **dibs.** 'First chance at doing something, as in "I get first dibs": Can. Ex children's marble games' (Leech, 1985).

fish. One who plays a game where he has no chance of winning: Can. carnival s.: since ca. 1920. Ex US c. for 'newcomer' (in a prison): see *Underworld*.—2. Short for **tin fish**, torpedo: RN: since ca. 1918. Harling, 1946.—3. As *the Fish*, this well-known Aus. train serves the commuters between Sydney and the towns and townships of the Blue Mountains to the west: since the early 1920s. Two or three of the first crew had 'fish' surnames. Its journeys start earlier than those of **the Chips,** q.v. (B.P.; Raab.)

fish-and-chip van. Old Sentinel steam coach: railwaymen's: ca. 1890-1940. *Railway*, 2nd.

fish and chips. An oil lamp: club cyclists': earlier C.20. (*Fellowship*, 1984.) Cf. **gasworks**.

Fish-Head Hall. At the RN Engineering College, at Manadon, Plymouth, a wing in which officers specialising in Marine Engineering are accommodated: RN: since ca. 1946. Granville.

fish-head sailor. A salt-water fisherman: the Can. Maritime Provinces': since (?)ca. 1920. Leechman, 1961.

fish-heads. 'Salthorse' officers—'those who go down to the sea in ships as opposed to going up in the air': FAA: (Granville): since ca. 1944. In later C.20 applied not only to officers but to seamen and stokers as well (Gell, 1985).—2. The Navy to the other two Services; the Seaman Branch to the Technical Branches of the RN: since ca. 1950. Stock, rarely bitter, insults; cf. **crab-fat**, **pongo**.

fish-horn. A soprano saxophone: Can. musicians': since late 1930s. To the same group, place, period, belong *African harp*, a banjo; *bed springs* or *git-box*, a guitar; *cigar-box*, a violin; *dog-house*, a bass viol; *gob-stick*, a clarinet; *grunt-horn*, bass horn, or tuba—coll., rather than s.; *horn*, trumpet or cornet—not s. but coll.; *the ivories* or *the 88*, the piano; *slip-horn* or *slush-pump* or *tram*, a trombone; *wood-pile*, a xylophone. Priestley, 1949, 'All these are current in a limited and jocular way among musicians in jazz bands; originally used by U.S. musicians ca. 1925; revised, extended and popularised in late 1930s, when swing became popular'. In 1965, he noted further: '*Horn* includes saxophones as well as trumpet and cornet. Among modern jazz players, "blow" means to play any instrument, as "He blows nice piano".'

Fisher. 'Treasury note signed by *Sir Warren Fisher*, replacing (Oct., 1919) the earlier *Bradbury*' (W.). At first s., it soon > coll. and, at its withdrawal from circulation on 31 July 1933,

it was almost S.E. (*Daily Telegraph*, 1 Aug. 1933.) Cf. **bradbury**.

fisherman. 'A trawler, drifter or other fishing craft' (Granville): RN coll.

fisherman's. Shortening of later C.19 r.s. *fisherman's daughter*, water. P.P., 1932.

fishing expedition; esp. **on a . . .** Applied to one who is spying or 'pumping' others for information: joc. coll.: since ca. 1930. Ex Japanese fishing boats going into foreign waters in order to obtain information. This English nuance may well be independent of the American senses, even though the latter precede it.

fishing-fleet. 'The wives and families of naval officers spending the season at Malta': RN: from ca. 1890. Bowen.—2. Hence, 'women who frequent the Ladies' Lounge at the Union Club, Malta' (Granville): RN: since ca. 1920. On the look-out for eligible Navy men. See **Snake-Pit**, 2, and cf. the earlier:—3. Eligible girls going, during the UK winter, to India to stay for 2–4 months and to meet eligible young men: among Army officers in India: ca. 1900-40. Those girls who failed returned in the (UK) spring—and 'were known as the Returned Empties' (Allen, 1977). See also **herring fleet**.

fishy. Morally or financially dubious; equivocal, unsound: from ca. 1844: s. >, by 1880, coll.—2. Hence, gen. suspicious, often with criminal implications, as 'I don't like it; there's something fishy going on, somehow': coll.: since mid-C.20 at latest. (P.B.)

fit, n. Sufficient evidence to convict (a wrongdoer): Aus. and NZ c.: since ca. 1930. For Brit. equivalent, see **fit up**, n.

fit, v., corresponds to n.: Aus. and NZ c.: since ca. 1930. McNeil, 1973, defines it 'to convict, with a suggestion of manipulation; to fit the facts to the indictment', and classes it coll. Cf. **fit up**.

fit, adj. 'Used mainly by males to describe females who are very attractive sexually; used less by females to describe men. E.g. "God, she's *fit*!", "She's as fit as fuck." Popular usage in N. England, esp. Greater Manchester and Liverpool' (Turner, 1986).

fit as a buck rat(, as). Very fit and well: NZ.

fit as a butcher's dog(, as). In very good health: Lancashire.

fit to be tied. Furiously angry, 'hopping mad': Can.: adopted, ca. 1908, ex US. (Leechman.) Cf. Aus. *ropeable*.

fit(-)up. Also **fit**, n. [q.v.] or **fitting**; synons., *put-up* and *stuck-up*. All describe the situation existing 'When the police find an innocent person (a body) and make the crime in hand fit him' (Newman, 1970)—in short, a 'frame-up' or 'framing'. Orig. c., then also police s.: since 1930s. All five nn. mentioned are also used as verbs.—2. By extension from 1, a planned piece of criminal deception, a deliberately planted lie: police: since (?)ca. 1955.

fitba. ' . . . is the Glesgy [Glasgow] pronunciation of football. It is often aped by non-Glaswegians as a demonstration that they are braw lads like the rest of us' (Howard, 1978). 'Fitba Crazy' is the title of a Glasgow children's street song.

fitting. (Of a patient) having a fit: hospital nurses': since ca. 1935.

Fitzroy cocktail. An improvised drink with basis of methylated spirits: Aus.: since ca. 1925. (Baker.) Ironic.

Fitzroy Yank. A Melbourne youth who apes the Americans: Aus., esp. Melbourne: since ca. 1942. (B., 1953.) Cf. *Woolloomooloo Yank*, the Sydney version.

five, n. As *the five*, 'The five pounds weight allowed to apprentice jockeys': turf: from ca. 1920; now verging on coll. *OED* Sup.—2. A five-eighth: Rugby football: from ca. 1910. Cf. *three*, a three-quarter.—3. Fifteen (in scoring): lawn tennis players': from ca. 1920. Cf. **fif**.—4. A Jew: since ca. 1930. (Kersh, 1941.) Ex *five by two*.—5. A five-years' prison sentence: police and criminal coll.: late C.19–20. (Norman.)—6. A sum of five pounds sterling: coll.: late C.19–20.—7. See **black five**.

five, v. To tout: drapery trade. Perhaps ex **five-to-twos** (below), via Jewish shoe-shops.

five and (a) half, the, usu. **five 'n 'arf, the.** See **where the five 'n'arf . . . ?**

five and nine. Esp. *put on* (one's) . . . , a juvenile make-up: theatrical: ca. 1870–1930. (Warwick, 1968.) Raab: the numbers 5 and 9 denote shades of make-up.

five and nine: the Brighton line. See TOMBOLA, in Appx.

five-barred gates. The method of keeping written count by fives, using 4 down strokes and a 5th to cross them through: coll. (P.B.)

five by five; often Mr Five by Five. A very short, fat man: Can.: since ca. 1930. Leechman: 'Presumably 5 feet tall and 5 feet wide'.

five by two. A Jew: r.s.: since ca. 1925. (P.P., 1932.) See **five, 5,** and **four by two;** cf. **five to two** and **buckle-my-shoe.**

five-eight. 'The phrase *just a common five-eight* is an expression used to describe an ordinary person with no airs or pretensions' (Munro, 1985): Glasgow. P.B.: perhaps ex average height; but cf. WW1 Army use of *five-eight(h)* for a lance corporal—that much of a 'full' corporal.

five finger(ed) sandwich (or sarnie). A punch in the mouth: Army other ranks': since late 1940s. (P.B., 1974.)

five finger spread. To vomit: RN: 1950s. (Malin, 1980.)

five-letter woman. A 'bitch': since ca. 1925. Prompted by **four-letter man,** q.v.

five-minute jerk. A very short taxi-ride: London taxi-drivers': earlier C.20.

five-oner; five ones man. One who gets a first class certificate in each of his five examinations for lieutenant: RN: earlier C.20. Bowen.

five-spot. A five-pound note: low coll.: later C.20. Hence *ten-spot, twenty-spot.* Perhaps orig. ex dominoes, but adopted imm. ex N. America, where Can., from US, since ca. 1905: a five- or ten-spot, etc. = a five-, ten-dollar bill. Bickersteth, 1912, has 'five-spot'. See also **spotter,** 3.

five to two. A not very gen. r.s. term for 'Jew'. Cf. **five by two.** Contrast:-

five-to-twos. Shoes: r.s. Ortzen, 1938.

fiver. A fifth-columnist: WW2+. Stuart, 1942.—2. Five thousand pounds, as in 'This house is worth a fiver': since ca. 1930.

fix, n. The taking of a narcotic drug, esp. by injection: adopted, late 1950s, ex US. By late 1960s, widely known—and used.—2. A well-thought-out plan. See AUSTRALIAN UNDERWORLD, in Appx.—3. In *get a fix,* to obtain the ship's or aircraft's position: RN; RAF: from ca. 1939; by 1945, > j. (Granville.) From a remote-navigation-aid station, *get a fix on* (aircraft, etc.).

fix, v. To dog (very) cunningly an enemy aircraft: RAF s. 1940; >, by 1944, coll. (Partridge, 1945.) Cf.—2. To 'settle a person's hash': coll.: since ca. 1920. 'I'll fix him!' is a frequent threat.—3. To bribe (someone): adopted, ca. 1939, from US: c. > by 1946, low s. Hence *fixer,* e.g. a lawyer, a political 'boss', that bribes, e.g., officials: still c.—4. To prepare or plan: to arrange: Can. (ex US) coll.: since ca. 1910. 'I'm leery of Bill. He's fixing to shoot me!' (Leechman.)—5. To inject a drug—usually into blood vessel' (Home Office): drug addicts': adopted, since ca. 1965, ex US.

fix (someone's) **clock.** To settle his hash: Can.: since ca. 1940. (Leechman.) Here, *clock* perhaps = face.

fix (someone's) **duff.** Synon. with the 'prompter', *settle his hash:* Army: since ca. 1930. (P-G-R.) Cf. **duff up.**

fix (someone's) **little red fire-engine.** To settle someone's hash: adopted in 1965 or, at latest, 1966 ex US. (R.S.) R.C., 1976, 'The US phrase (rare) elaborates the earlier "fix one's wagon".' P.B.: the Brit. usage, however, carries an air of mock childishness, a ref. to breaking another child's toy. Cf. *I hope your rabbits die!* and:-

fix (someone's) **wagon.** (Cf. prec.) 'This term is still widely used in Can., in the sense of stopping someone, so that he cannot continue doing something. E.g.: "Mummy, Tom's going to town." "Oh, he is, is he? Well, I'll just fix his wagon for him!" ' (Leech, 1986).

fix the old gum tree. (Of a 'rolling stone') to settle down at last: Aus. B., 1942.

fix (someone) **up.** To provide him with lodgings or other quarters: coll.: from ca. 1888. P.B.: by mid-C.20 at latest, to provide with other necessities, e.g., money, clothing, weapons, or even a female companion (for a male, of course): coll.—2. To murder: Anglo-Irish: since ca. 1930. Kenyon, 1977, a 'rapee' speaking, 'He said he would baste me and trounce me and fix me up.' P.B.: 'To murder' is E.P.'s interpretation, but *fix up* may also be synon., in English, with *baste* and *trounce*: later C.20 low coll.

fixed, be. ' "Well!" said Iggy . . . "How are we fixed, then?" This, in lags' [convicts'] parlance, meant simply, "What are you going to do for an old pal last night?" ' (Roberts, 1976), the time ref. being to the late 1950s: c.—2. Hence, in wider, more licit circles, 'How are you fixed? Can you lend me a fiver?' or 'How are you fixed for lending me a fiver?': perhaps from the S.E. *fixed* in the sense of 'prepared': later C.20 coll. (P.B.)—3. Under the influence of drugs: drugs c. (Stockley, 1986.) US since 1930s (Spears).

fixer. An agent, esp. one who makes arrangements for 'pop' musicians: since ca. 1950.

fixit. 'She said you operated a fixit . . . you know, stolen cars repainted and given bastardised parts and a new licence number!' (Allen, 1972).—2. As a title, *Mr Fixit,* one who is known to be able to 'fix' things, whether politically, or by technical knowledge, as in 'do-it-yourself'; often pej., by the envious, 'Oh, proper little Mr Fixit, he is!': later C.20. (P.B.)

fizz, n. Synon. with its source: **fizz-gig,** 2: Aus. c. and police s.: since ca. 1953. B., 1953.

fizz, v. A var. of *fizz out.* Drake-Brockman, 1940, 'Fizzed on you, didn't she? They're all the same.'

fizz around. To 'buzz around'; move speedily and busily: from ca. 1930. 'Ganpat', 1933.

fiz(z)-gig. From such S.E. senses as a squib, a whirligig, a silly pastime, the word has come, in C.20, to approximate, in its meaning, to *gadget.* Coll.—2. An informer to the police: c. of Sydney, NSW: from ca. 1930. Also, in the same milieu, merely a busybody. Var. *phizgig,* in Kelly, 1955, where also as v., to act as an informer. See AUSTRALIAN UNDERWORLD, in Appx.

fizz out, n.; **fizz out on,** v. (To be) a thoroughly unreliable person (in respect of someone): Aus.: since ca. 1919. Baker.

fizzer. A failure, esp. in *it's a fizzer,* 'the traditional c.p. when a mechanical device being demonstrated fails to work' (B.P.): Aus.: since ca. 1920. Perhaps a slovening of *fizzler,* something that 'fizzles out'.—2. (Also as *fizza.*) A charge, or charge-sheet, esp. in *put* (*him*) *on a* (or *the*) *fizzer,* to put someone's name on to a charge-sheet: Army, since ca. WW1, RAF since ca. 1925; ob. Hence, loosely, *fizzer* may = guard-room, detention cell; or even 'parade ground'. Perhaps, ultimately, the term then derives ex *defaulters on fizza,* doing pack-drill on the parade ground. *Daily Mail,* 7 Sep. 1940; H. & P.—3. Hence, an adverse report against an employee: busmen's: since ca. 1925.

Fizzie. The FS1E model Yamaha 50 cc motorcycle: motorcyclists' (?esp. Southampton): later C.20. (Bishop, 1984.) A pun on the initials and on the noise of the machine itself.

flab. Flabbiness, obesity: since ca. 1935: s., rapidly > coll., prob. orig. among slimmers. Either a back-formation from *flabby,* or simply an abbr. of *flabbiness.*

flabby(-)knackers. A term of genial, friendly abuse: low coll.: since ca. 1950. Cf. *horror-bollocks,* **fuck-knuckle,** etc. The 'daddy' of the group is **buggerlugs.** (P.B.)

flack. Mis-spelling of **flak:** noted 1979, in a journal that should have known better. (P.B.)—2. A publicity person: adopted ex US. 'A flustered flack at [the] publishers was remarkably reticient [sic]' (*Observer* mag., 6 Dec. 1987).

fladge, also written *flage.* Flagellation; one who resorts to it in order to induce an orgasm, as *a fladge-merchant:* prostitutes': since ca. 1920. Norman, 1959, has the compound; there is also *fladge-fiend*, a masochist. Ex *flage*llation. P.B.: in a shop selling pornography, 'Got any fladge, guv?' = have you any works in which the emphasis is on flagellation?

flag day. Menstruation: since ca. 1918. Flag days were introduced in the latter part of WW1: from that, via older (since mid-C.19) s. *flag*, a sanitary pad, was but a small quick step to the pun.

flag-flying. Overbidding (occ., a tendency to overbid) at bridge: from ca. 1915: s. >, by 1930, coll. Hence *flag-flier*, one who does this. *OED* Sup.

flag-Jack. The officer in charge of signallers, 'chief bunting-tosser', on board ship: RN: C.20. *Musings*, 1912; Gell, 1981.

flaggers, in. See **in flaggers**, 'red-handed'. Cf.:-

flagrant delight. A (mainly legal) joc. Englishing of *in flagrante delicto*. Mackenzie, 1933, 'To-night's the night for flagrant delight.'

flak. German anti-aircraft fire: from 1939: prob. always j.; certainly so by 1942. Ex the initials in *Flug*A*bwehr*K*anone*, Ger. A.A. guns.—2. Hence, adverse criticism; back-talk, verbal impudence: since mid-1940s in US and late 1940s in UK, though not widespread in Britain till ca. 1975. Janssen cites *Beatles*, 'John was . . . riddled with media flak by surly and cynical public commentators'. The derivation had been so forgotten by 1979 as to produce the mis-spelt *flack*.

flak-happy. Not caring; reckless: RAF: 1941: †. (McDouall, 1945.) Prob. an analogy of *slap-happy*; contrast the Army **bomb-happy**, q.v.

flake, n. Cocaine: drugs c. (Stockley, 1986.) US since –1922 (Spears).

flake, or, in full, **flake out,** v. To go to bed, or merely to take a nap: Can.: since ca. 1940. (Leechman.) But see also entry at **Harry Flakers,** at HARRY in Appx., which suggests a much earlier dating.—2. Hence, to fall asleep from sheer exhaustion or drunkenness, or, later, from the effects of narcotic drugs: perhaps, in this sense, orig. Aus., since ca. 1945 (B.P.), but, by 1950, common throughout the Brit. Commonwealth.—3. Hence, also, to faint: orig. Services', WW2 and ever since. Cunliffe, 1965.

flaked out. Orig. merely tired, listless, or 'hungover' with the after-effects of too much alcohol; later, asleep, as, 'There he was flaked out on his pit—I hadn't the heart to wake him': Services', orig. RN, since late WW1. Cf. **worn to a frazzle**, and:-

flakers. See **Harry Flakers,** at HARRY in Appx.—2. (Always *flakers*.) Half-drunk; mildly tipsy: Aus.: since ca. 1945. Lambert, 1951.

flakey, -y. Apparently crazy or eccentric in behaviour: since late 1960s. Poss. ex **flake**, n., and ex US.—2. Of poor or uneven quality: media persons'. Hibbert, 1983.

flame! or **flaming hell!** Expletive *hell*: C.20, the latter; since ca. 1925, the former.

flame-out. A record that achieves instant popularity, and then just as quickly loses it: 'pop' industry: later C.20. Hibbert, 1983.

flamer. A person, incident, or thing very conspicuous, unusual, or vigorous: since ca. 1805. It has, since ca. 1900, been esp. applied—prob. under the influence of the 'OXFORD *-ER*'—to 'a flaming row' or quarrel, as in Act II of Rattigan, *The Deep Blue Sea*, 1952.—2. An aircraft coming down in flames: RFC/RAF: since 1916. Wren, 1934.—3. Hence, a target—esp. an aircraft or vehicle—set on fire by the RAF: RAF: WW2. P-G-R.

flaming arsehole. A large red circle painted on side of Japanese aircraft: Aus. airmen's: 1942–5. (B., 1943.) P.B.: the circle is the Jap. military 'cockade' and represents the rising sun.

flaming onion. A German anti-aircraft projectile (some ten fireballs on a chain): Services': WW1. (F. & G.) Ex the strings of onions sold by hawkers. In WW2, 'tracer fire from the ground' (H. & P.). Not all tracer fire, but only such as justifies this pertinently descriptive term. Cf. **scarlet slugs**.

Flamingo. (Gen. pl.) An inhabitant of Flanders: from ca. 1910. (Raymond, 1931.) By sound-suggestion ex Fr. *Flamand*, as if = 'flaming'.

flamp. To flatter; to wheedle: RAF: since ca. 1937. (L.A.)

flan. Red tape: RN. (Bowen.) Ex *red flannel* on *red tape*.

flange. *Corona glandis*. Ex S.E. sense.

flanker. In *do* or *play* or *pull* or *work a flanker*, to deceive; trick; outwit; give the slip; 'pass the buck': the first, lower classes',—1923 (Manchon); the second, RAF, since ca. 1925 (Jackson); the two last, gen. but esp. Army, since ca. 1925. The sense 'pass the buck' emerged in Army usage, WW2.—2. Among club cyclists, 'refers to sneaking up on the blind side in a "tear-up" [q.v.]' (*Fellowship*, 1984).

flannel or **flannels,** n. Derisive coll.: flannel drawers (women's). Var.: *red flannel(s)*.—2. Sweet things or small gifts to one's superiors in order to ask favours later on; flattery: Services', esp. RAF: since ca. 1935. *New Statesman*, 30 Aug. 1941; H. & P.—3. Always *flannel*. 'Waffle', empty and pretentious talk, 'hot air' to disguise ignorance, bluff: Services': since ca. 1920.

flannel, v. Corresponds to prec., 2 and 3. Hence, *flanneller* and *flannelling*, the corresponding agential and verbal nouns. Granville notes RN var. *flannel through*.

flannel flappers. Baked beans: RN training ships': since ca. 1945. Fart-inducing. (Peppitt.)

flannel-jacket. 'Merchant Navy Class 4-6-2 S[outhern] R[egion]. Probably based on Cockney r.s. for the first locomotive of the class "Channel Packet" ' (*Railway*): late 1940s–1950s. Perhaps influenced also by the 'wrapped-around', high-sided boxed-in appearance of these locomotives. (P.B.)

flannel-mouth, n. and adj. (A) well-spoken (person, esp. if a man): Can. I.e. *soft-spoken*. P.B.: but no doubt influenced by senses 2–3 of **flannel**, n., and the v.

flannel through. See **flannel**, v.

flannelette. 'The sailor's soft answer which occasionally succeeds in turning away wrath' (Granville): RN: since ca. 1936.

flap, n. 'Any evolution on board or movement of warships': RN: late C.19–20. (Bowen.) Applied esp. to the bustle ensuing on an emergency order (F. & G.).—2. Hence, great excitement; panic: Services': prob. arose in 1916. 'Taffrail', 1917. Also, since ca. 1930, *have a*, or *there is a, flap on* (H. & P.). Whence *flapping*, undue or uncontrolled excitement (Ibid.). The term reached its height with *the Flap*, 'That great retreat from the battle of Sidi Rezegh (N. Africa) which ended at Alamein' (P-G-R): Army: middle of WW2.—3. A cheque: c.

flap, v. To talk (always with *about*): from ca. 1925: ob. Ex *flap one's mouth* (gen. *about*), the same: 1910, Wells (*OED* Sup.); ob.—2. Verb corresponding with **flap**, n. To panic, dither, be in a state of great excitement, unable to think 'straight': Services': since ca. 1950 at latest. Intensified, *to flap like a cunt*. (P.B)

flap around. To rush about aimlessly, to dither: Services', esp. RN: since ca. 1920. (Granville.) Ex **flap**, n.

flap shot. 'In film or still pictures, a close up of the labia and the vagina' (Green, 1984): pornographers': later C.20. Poss. a pun on labia and the older coll. *snapshot*. Cf. **beaver**, n., 3.

flap (one's) mouth. See **flap**, v., 1.

flapper. In Society s. of early C.20, 'a very immoral young girl in her early "teens" ' (Ware)—a sense surviving in the US; in England, however, WW1 firmly established the meaning (already pretty gen. by 1905), *any* young girl with her hair not yet put up (or, in the late 1920s and the 30s, not yet cut short).

flapper-bracket, -seat. A (mostly, motor-)bicycle pillion, esp. used to carry a girlfriend: resp. s. (from ca. 1915) and coll. (from ca. 1918; ob.) Cf. the later **peach-perch**.

flapper vote, the. The 'franchise granted in 1928 to women of 21 years and over': coll.: 1928. *COD*, 1934 Sup.

flappers. A sandwich-man's boards: tramps' c.: the 1920s. (The transition term between *clappers* and *wings*.) Jennings, 1932.

flapping; occ. **flapper.** Racing not subject to either Jockey Club or National Hunt Regulations: turf: 1910. (*OED* Sup.) Ex lack of dignity.—2. Hence, from ca. 1915, as adj.

flapping track. 'Small (and unlicensed) dog[-racing] track' (Powis): c.: 1970s. Cf. prec., 1.

flaps. 'Ears. Often a nickname for a man with large ears' (Powis): low coll.: later C.20.

flare-path. A petrol cigarette-lighter: RAF: from ca. 1935; †. *New Statesman*, 30 Aug. 1941.

flared. Tipsy: Can.: since (?)ca. 1960. Wylie, 1965, 'When I take enough liquor to reach the point you're talking about, I know I'm flared.'

flares. Trousers that are flared out over the ankles: coll. The fashion was popular mid-1970s. (P.B.)

flarty is obscure; ?an outsider. It is grafters' s. *Cheapjack*, 1934, ' "I'm a flarty too," she told me in confidence. "I don't really belong to the fair." ' Origin?

flash, n. As *the flash*, the banner or other name-displaying cloth or card-device of a bookmaker's stand: racing c. Abbr. *the flash part*. Analogous is the grafters' sense: 'A grafter's display. Anything to attract the crowd' (Allingham).—2. Priority given, by news-agencies, to sports' results: journalists':—1935.—3. An electric torch: c.: from ca. 1910. *Gilt Kid*, 1936.—4. The electrical officer: RN: since ca. 1940. Granville.—5. Embroidered badge worn on the very top of the uniform sleeve, denoting regiment, division, etc., as 'He was wearing I Corps flashes on his B.D.' = the soldier wore the title 'Intelligence Corps' on the shoulders of his battledress: Army; if at first coll., soon > j.: WW1 and after. Cf. sense 1.—6. 'Effect of cocaine, and to a lesser extent of methedrine' (Home Office): drug addicts': 1970s.—7. A 'know-all': Borstals' and detention centres': 1970s. Home Office.—8. A token attempt at independence. See **show of flash.**—9. Illicitly distilled liquor: Brit. expatriates', in Saudi Arabia: since latish 1970s. (J.B. Smith, 1981.)

flash, v.i., with var. *flash it*, to make a display, show off: ca. 1770–1830. In later C.20 applied esp. to ostentatious use of money. The term derives ex *flash* in the sense, 'show as in a flash, hence, brilliantly' (see esp. **flash, n. and adj.,** qq.v.—2. A specialisation of 1 is a v.i., with elab. (rather, orig.) *flash it*, q.v., which means 'to expose, suddenly and briefly, one's genitals in public'; hence, *flasher*, one who does this, *flashing*, the habit.

flash, adj. Fashionably flash: Aus. and NZ: late C.19–20. '[The girls] think it's flash' to take strong drink (Devanney, 1930). This sense is used also in UK, since mid-C.20 at latest. (P.B.)—2. Cheeky. See **show of flash,** and quot'n at **strong, v.**—3. 'Loud, striking and technically impressive' (Hibbert), usu. applied to an 'ace' guitarist: fans': later C.20.

flash Alf (usu. in pl.). Men in the swim of the smart world: ?since ca. 1900; not entirely ob. by 1970. Lees-Milne, 1975. Cf. **flash Harry.**

flash as a Chinky's horse, as. (Very) high-spirited: Aus.: since ca. 1930. Baker, 1959.

flash-back. 'Recurrence of effects of hallucinogenic "trip", which can be months after last taking of LSD' (Home Office): coll.: since ca. 1960. Cf. **flash, n.,** 6. Ex cinema j.

flash gear. Showy, yet superior, goods. See MOCK AUCTION, in Appx.

flash Harry. The UK version of, and prob. earlier than, **flash Jack,** a showy fellow, glossed below as Aus. But this is in occ. British use also. Perhaps the best known *Flash Harry* of C.20 was Sir Malcolm Sargent (1895–1967), the conductor, noted for his elegance and showmanship.

flash it or **flash (one's) meat.** (Gen. of men) to expose the person: low: from ca. 1840. See also **flash, v.,** 2.

flash Jack. A showy fellow; a boaster: Aus. (Russell, 1934); but the term is known and used in Brit. also. Cf. **flash Harry.**

flash lot. A smart new taxicab: taxi-drivers': since ca. 1920. Hodge, 1939.

flash (one's) meat. See **flash it.**

flash pack. 'A product displaying a reduced price on the package' (Barnhart, 2): retailers': since ca. 1970. See **flash, n.,** 1.

flash the ash! 'Produce, and give me, a cigarette (*or*, us, cigarettes)!': Army: 1950s. Cf. **crash the ash.** (P.B.)

flash the upright grin. (Of a woman) to expose her private parts: low: ca. 1860–1930, but re-emerged in US as 'vertical grin' (L.A.). Cf. *flash* (one's) *meat*, of men, at **flash it.**

flashed-up. Dressed stylishly or in one's best: c., and low. (*Gilt Kid*, 1936.) Cf. *dolled-up*, q.v. at **doll up.**

flasher. A synon. of **quickie** (q.v.): Glasgow:—1934.—2. In Glasgow c. (—1934), a 'dud' bank-note.—3. A stall-holder at a fair: market-traders'. Ex **flash, n.,** 1.—4. A sexual exhibitionist, esp. male, one who 'flashes it'. See **flash, v.,** 2.

flashing, n. Signalling; also *flash*, v.i., to signal: RN coll., > j. Ex use of Aldis lamp or heliograph.

flat, n. A greenhorn; a fool; an easy 'gull' or dupe: from ca. 1760. Cf. the C.20 story of the girl that refused to live either with or in one. By contrast with *sharp*.—2. An abbr. of *flattie*, late C.19 s. for a uniformed policeman: c. Hume.—3. See **flats.**—4. As *the Flat*, the season of flat horse-racing: sporting coll.: from ca. 1910.—5. 'Worn part on wheel tyre due to skidding, or, in London Transport, due to excessive braking' (*Railway*, 2nd): transport workers' coll.: since late 1940s.—6. Coll. shortening of 'a flat tyre': later C.20, ?ex US. (P.B.)—7. In *do* or *have a bit of flat*, to copulate: low: mid-C.19–20.—8. A working man: London. (Hollis, 1983.) ?Ex sense 1.

flat, adj. Penniless; short of money: low: since ca. 1925. Short for *flat broke.*—2. Conventional: London. (Hollis, 1983.) Cf. **n.,** 8.—3. See **choppy.**

flat, adv.; **flat out.** At top speed; 'all out': motor-racers': resp. s., from ca. 1928, an abbr. of the second term; from ca. 1910, s. >, by 1930, coll. and now verging on S.E.: prob. ex a horse's pose at the gallop, but see also **flat to the boards.**

flat a-back. 'Naval rating's cap worn on the back of his head as a sign of bravado ashore. . . . Naval patrols can charge the wearer with being improperly dressed.' The Aus. spelling (B., 1943) is *flatterback*.—2. 'Be taken by surprise, taken a-back' (Granville): RN.

flat-backing. Copulation, from the female angle: groupies' [q.v.]: later C.20. (Hibbert, 1983.) Cf. **flat, n.,** 7. Whence *flat-backer*, a prostitute (Ibid.).

flat feet. In *go on* (one's *or its*) *own flat feet*, 'A man walking or a tank moving invariably went "on their own flat feet" ' (P-G-R): Army: WW2. Cf. **merry men.**

flat foot. A policeman: lower classes':—1935.

flat head or **flat-head** or **flathead.** A simpleton: Aus.: since ca. 1910. (B., 1942.) Elab. of **flat, n.,** 1, perhaps influenced by synon. *fathead*.

flat out. See **flat, adv.**

flat out for. Strongly in favour of: RAF: since ca. 1938. Jackson, 'I'm flat out for him having some leave.' Ex prec.

flat out like a lizard (1) *drinking* or (2) *on a log*. To lie on one's belly; but also, to work at great speed: Aus. Wilkes cites Devanney, 1944, for 'a rat running flat out like a lizard drinking', and later examples of working flat out.

flat spin, in a. 'In 1916, to spin was a highly dangerous manoeuvre . . . The expression "in a flat spin", invented in those days, denoted that whoever was in it had reached the absolute limit of anger, nerves, fright, or whatever it might be' (Lewis, 1936). Hence, **go into a flat spin,** q.v.

flat to the boards. Synon. with, and prob. the origin of, **flat (out):** since early C.20. 'From the early days of motoring, when cars had wooden floor-boards. The car was at its maximum performance when the accelerator was pressed flat against the floor-boards' (B.P.).—2. Hence, fully extended; extremely busy: Aus.: since ca. 1925. 'Can't you see that I'm flat to the boards?' (B.P.)

flat top. An aircraft carrier: RN since ca. 1935. Granville.—2. Hence, a haircut similar to the crew cut but flat on the top: Aus.: since ca. 1945. (B.P.) Prob. ex US; known also in UK: there was, in the 1950s, a song about 'My boy flat-top'. (P.B.)

flatch. A half: back s., with the rigid *flah* modified: since late 1840s; still current, late 1970s.

flatite. A dweller in a flat: Aus. coll.: since ca. 1925. B., 1959.

flats. (Very rare sing.) Long, thin envelopes: among sorters on mail trains. *Daily Herald*, 5 Aug. 1936.—2. 'Credit cards' (Powis): underworld and its fringes: since ca. 1970. Perhaps a revival, in new sense, of the C.19 s. *flats*, playing cards.

flatter. 'The private motorist . . . knows that the squeaks in his bodywork are caused by "canaries" and that the tremendous speed he attains is due to "flatter" in his speedometer. When he "runs out of road", he gets severely "bent" ' (Dennis, 1961): motorists' terms: resp. since ca. 1950, ca. 1950, ca. 1945, ca. 1930.

flatters, n. A calm sea: RN (mostly wardroom): since ca. 1920. By the 'OXFORD -ER(s)'. See also **Harry flatters**, at HARRY in Appx.

flatters, adj. Penniless, *flat* broke: since ca. (?)1950. By the 'OXFORD -ER(s)'. Wilbur Smith, 1977.

flattie, -y. A member of the audience: circus-workers' s. (Seago, 1933.) To showmen in gen., it means an outsider.—2. Anyone, usu. male, not a market trader: market-traders': late C.19–20. (*M.T.*) Cf. sense 1.

flatties. Flat-heeled, as opp. to high-heeled, shoes: feminine coll.: since ca. 1945. (Boswell, 1959.) Cf. **wedgies**.

flavour of the month. Anything suddenly very popular, though (usu.) the popularity is recognised as ephemeral: 1980s. Adopted ex US, where the orig. ref. is to ice-cream advertising. Later also negative, as in, 'I realised I was *not* [or no longer] the flavour of the month, when the boss called me in . . . ' (Hemming, 1986).

flea-bag. A bed: low: ca. 1835–1915.—2. Hence, (an officer's) sleeping-bag: from ca. 1909. Collinson.—3. Hence, a seaman's hammock: RN: since ca. 1920.—4. A dog; less gen., a cat: Aus. (B., 1942) and Brit.

flea box. 'A guard's brake van on a goods train. Scottish term. The old guard's brake was very small and cramped' (McKenna, 1970): railwaymen's.

flea-chariot. A flea-ridden palliasse: Anglo-Irish: since ca. 1920. Doncaster, 1947.

flea-circus. A cheap cinema: Aus.: since ca. 1925. (Baker.) Cf. **flea-pit**, 2.

flea-market. A street-market, and, hence, any market, trading chiefly in trinkets, bric-à-brac, and cheap 'antiques': *OED Sup.*, 1977, records as s., but by 1980 it had > coll., the term being used widely in advertisements for these events. Cf. Fr. *marché aux puces* in Paris (*OED*).

flea-pit. A flat (apartment): from ca. 1919. (Brandon, 1934.) On *flea-bag* with joc. allusion to S.E. *cubby-hole*.—2. A second-rate, dirty cinema: since ca. 1918: 'In every town at one time earlier C.20 there was a cinema known as the Bug Hut or the Scratch or Flea Pit' (*Listener*, 23 Dec. 1982). Cf. **bug-house**.

flea powder. Poor quality drugs: drugs c. (Stockley, 1986.) US since—1955 (Spears).

fleas(-)and(-)itchers, the. The cinema: Aus. r.s. (on *pictures*): since ca. 1946. (B., 1953.) Probably influenced by **flea-pit**, 2.

Fleet Air Arm Wallah. See **matelot**, 2.

Flemington confetti. Rubbish, nonsense, 'tripe', 'bulsh': Aus.: since ca. 1920. (B., 1942.) Ex the appearance of Flemington racecourse at the close of a big meeting: paper everywhere. Cf. **Flemo**. 'More likely to be from the Flemington Saleyards in Sydney or Melbourne' (B.P.).

Flemo. Flemington district (a north-west suburb of Melbourne) and racecourse: Aus. Baker.

fleshy. A flesh wound: Aus. soldiers': 1940+. *Rats*, 1944, ' "Just a couple of fleshies. Be back again in a few weeks, dealing it out to old Jerry again." '

flick, n. A moving picture; the performance at a cinema: 1926 (Wallace: *OED* Sup.). E.P. orig., 1937, noted: '† by 1936'. But the term did not die, and has been revived in the 1970s, esp. in *skinflick*, a film depicting nudes, and explicitly erotic. (P.B.)—2. A flick-knife: coll.: since ca. 1955.

flick, v. Gen. *flick along*. To cause (e.g. a motor-car) to move rapidly: from ca. 1915: s. now verging on coll. Galsworthy, 1924.

flicker. A flycatcher. See BIRD-WATCHERS, in Appx.

flickergraph. Cinema: early C.20. 'All our flickergraph halls . . . ' (Denby, 1911).

flickers. A fainting: tramps' c.: from the early 1920s. (Jennings, 1932.) Ex US c. *flicker*, in the same sense.—2. A var. of **flicks**, first noted in Collinson, 1927.

flicking. A corruption (from ca. 1910), orig. perhaps euph., of **fricking**.

flicks, the. The films; the moving pictures; (*go to the flicks*) a cinema: since—1927 (Collinson); slightly ob. by 1983, very common in UK, 1940s, and in Aus., still in 1966. (P.B.; B.P.) Ex **flick**, n., 1.—2. Searchlights: RAF: WW2. Jackson.

flid. A schoolchildren's pej.: late 1970s. 'One fourth-year boy referred to another as a "flid" . . . [he explained] "It's short for flidomide [i.e. thalidomide]" ' (*New Society*, 31 Jan. 1980). Cf. **mongie; spag**.

fidget-sergeant. A flight-sergeant: RAF: since ca. 1933. (L.A.) An attempted phonetic pron. of *flight*.

fliers. Bands of striking miners, 'flying pickets' who travelled to other pits to try to persuade non-strikers to join the dispute: the coalminers' strike, 1984–5. Also known as *Arthur's fliers* (Arthur Scargill, President of the Nat. Union of Mineworkers); the activity as *going flying*. (*Enemy*, 1986.)

Flight. In address (rarely otherwise): Flight-Sergeant: RAF coll.: since ca. 1919. (Jackson.) It has never—at least by the other ranks—been so widely used as **chiefie**.

flight deck. Female breasts: raffish: later C.20. 'Lovely flight deck she's got!' (Simmonds, 1981).

flight looie or **louie.** A flight-lieutenant: RAF: since ca. 1930. (Jackson.) Ex US *lootenant* for 'lieutenant'.

flight magician. A flight mechanic: RAF: ca. 1925–40. Ibid.

flights. Hangars: RAF: since ca. 1937. Jackson, 'Thus, "Down in the flights" ': from the hangars the aircraft are moved preparatory to flying.

flim. Abbr. **flimsy,** n., esp. in sense of a £5 note: among grafters, spivs, market traders and the like, particularly of the old, large white, thin banknotes. (Allingham; *Picture Post*, 2 Jan. 1954; *M.T.*) Hence, the sum of £5 (Tempest).—2. 'A sentence of five years' penal servitude' (Tempest): c.: mid-C.20.

flimping. A 'rigging' of the weights on a pair of scales: barrow-boys': since ca. 1920.

flimsy. A banknote: from ca. 1810: low. Occ. abbr. *flim* (—1870).—2. An important message written on rice paper, which, if one is captured, can be swallowed without ill effects: Services': since 1939. H. & P.—3. A cheque: Aus. (B., 1942.) Ex 1.—4. 'A four-gallon petrol can of tinplate (later ternplate) made in Egypt and used throughout the "Middle East". Egyptian industry was not capable of making a more substantial can. The ordinary British two-gallon can was an engineering marvel by comparison' (Sanders): Army: ca. 1940–3.

fling one up. To salute an officer: RAF: since ca. 1930. (Jackson.) Cf. synon. **chuck** or **throw one up**.

flinking. Employed by youths to impress their friends that they are still 'he -men', not 'cissies', usually if women or strangers might overhear them: since ca. 1940. Ex S.W.-English dial. *flink*, 'to *fling* or toss', whence *flinker*, 'a proud woman'.

flip, n. (A short) flight or trip in an aircraft, esp. in an aeroplane: aviators' (1914) >, by 1920, gen. (*OED* Sup.) By ca. 1935 the term was applied also to a trip in a motor-car (H. & P.), but this latter nuance was ephemeral. The orig. sense, a trip in an aeroplane, may now, 1983, be ob. but is by no means †. (P.B.)—2. (A taking of) a dose of heroin: drug addicts': since ca. 1950. (Norman, 1959.) Adopted ex US.—3. Short for **flip side**: since late 1950s.

flip, v. To fly in an aircraft: aviators' (1915) >, by 1920, gen.—but much less gen. than the corresponding n., whence it derives. F. & G.—2. To approve wildly, to become deliriously elated: Can. dance-lovers' and jazz musicians': adopted, 1957, ex US (where orig. *flip one's wig*).—3. To go literally mad: Can. jazz musicians' and lovers': since 1956 or 1957. Cf. the US *blow one's top*.—4. To masturbate: Aus.

male: late C.19–20. Also *flip oneself off*.—5. To arouse enthusiasm: drug addicts', hippies', Flower People's: since ca. 1966. Fryer, 1967.—6. (Also *flip out*.) To have a mental breakdown, esp. if drug induced: adopted, orig. by addicts, in Brit. in late 1960s. Ex US, and senses 2 and 3 above.

flip, adj. Flippant: US s., adopted ca. 1918 in Can., ca. 1945 in Aus. (Park, 1961); late 1940s in NZ; ca. 1950 in UK.

flip-flaps. See **flip-flops,** 1.

flip-flop. 'Soixante-neuf': since ca. 1950. Landy, 1971.

flip-flops. (Or *-flaps*.) Bouncing breasts: Aus.: since ca. 1920.—2. Hence, girls with bouncing breasts, as in 'standing in Martin Place [Sydney] and watching the flip-flops go by': Aus.: since early 1920s.—3. Those sandals that are simply a rubber sole, with a thong over or between the toes: orig. Army in the Far East, by 1954 at latest; then, ca. 1976, when the style was introduced into UK, widespread and > coll. Echoic. (P.B.)

flip (one's) **lid.** To go to the extreme of any emotion; to go crazy: later C.20. Cf. **flip** (one's) **top** or **wig,** and **flip,** v., 6.

flip (oneself) **off.** See **flip,** v., 4. Used as v.t., and Brit., C.20.

flip side. The reverse side of a record disc: teenagers', ex disc jockeys': adopted, ex US (R.C.), late 1950s.—2. From early 1980s used fig., for the reverse of anything; as in 'she fell victim to the flip side of La Dolce Vita, took a drug overdose' (*Observer* mag., 21 Mar. 1982), and 'the flip side of this argument is . . . ' (*Guardian*, 2 July 1982), the reverse, or converse.

flip (one's) **top.** To become extremely angry or excited, almost crazy: Aus.: adopted, ca. 1950, ex US. (B.P.)

flip (one's) **wig.** To become highly elated: some teenage use in UK in early 1960s. See **flip,** v., 2.

flip-wreck. Vaguely pej. for a man: Aus.: since ca. 1910. Ex *flip,* to masturbate, with a pun on 'ship-wreck'. Cf. the 1970s Brit. use of *wanker*.

flipped. Crazy: Aus.: since early 1950s. (B.P.). Ex *flip* (one's) *top* or *wig*.

flipper. 'A top-spinner delivered by the bowler with an extra flip of the fingers' (Sanders): cricketers': since ca. 1920.—2. Friend: since ca. 1960. 'And somehow that was the moment she became my best flipper. From that time on I truly loved her . . . Oh . . . don't think we were lesbians' (Reid, 1970).

flipping. A pej., usu. intensive, adj. and adv.: proletarian: since ca. 1920. 'I sha'n't do the flipping thing'—'I don't flipping well know.' (The film, *Seven Days to Noon*.) Orig. euph. In Mais, 1948, we find: ' "No flipping Bovril about the Barley Mow, Aggie," said Lomax. "And I'll trouble you not to swear, Mr Lomax. There's ladies present." ' Since ca. 1940 the commonest of all euphs. for *fucking*, adj., as in the common exclam. of disgust 'Flippin' 'eck!' = *Fucking Hell!*, so often used unwittingly and in all innocence.

flit. A male homosexual: pej.: 1950s. Hibbert, 1983.—2. Adulterated amphetamine powder: drugs c.: later C.20. (Hibbert, 1983.) Ex the brand name of a well known fly-killer.—3. In *do a flit,* to run away with another's share: c.:—1933 (Leach). See also **moonlighter.**

flit commode. A flight commander (not a rank but a function): RAF: since ca. 1935. (Jackson.) Cf. **air commode.**

flit-gun. A 25-pounder gun: Army medium gunners': WW2. See **cap-badge.**

flivver. A cheap and/or small motor-car (1920) or aeroplane (ca. 1925). (*OED* Sup.) (P.B.: the aeroplane sense is long since †; the term is now, 1983, chiefly assoc. with the early model Ford cars, and has thus > historical.) The *OED*'s dates are for Britain, but as 'a small, cheap motorcar' it was current in Can. by 1910 at latest (Leechman).

float, n. A till; the contents thereof: c.:—1935. Hume.—2. That cash in the till which is there for ordinary trading: coll.: since the 1930s. (Mogridge, 1950.) Perhaps ex 1, and by later C.20, S.E.

float, v. To die, 'give up the ghost': Aus.:—1916 (Dennis).—2. To make a mistake: perhaps, orig.,—1919 at Eton (Marples); Manchon, 1923, records some more widespread use.—

3. To go: from ca. 1910. Cf. **float up.** To sail as a seaman: MN. Piper, 1974, 'I have never floated in the big crack ships . . . '—5. To eat a meal after drinking heavily: the sort of people who would: later C.20. Hibbert, 1983.

float around. To fly near by 'in a leisurely fashion for the fun of it or to kill time' (Jackson): RAF: since ca. 1930.—2. Hence (or ex?), of a person, to loaf about aimlessly, as 'I just happened to be floating around (or about) town, and thought I'd drop in on you': coll. (P.B.)

float up. To stroll up to a person or a group; to arrive unexpectedly: NZ coll. Hence, > n.

floater. A mistake, a faux pas; a moment of embarrassment: university s. (ca. 1910) >, by 1929 (Wodehouse), gen. to the upper and middle classes. Lunn, 1913; Knox, 1934, 'It produced . . . in the original and highly esoteric sense of that term, a "floater".' Perhaps because it cannot be recalled, though perhaps suggested by *faux pas* slurred to *fōper*; cf., however, **float,** v., 2.—2. Esp. in *floaters and mash*, sausages and mashed potatoes: RAF: since ca. 1920. Jackson.—3. A departmental file that circulates for the information of the branch: Army officers': since ca. 1920.—4. A meat pie in a plate of peas or gravy: Aus.: later C.20. Wilkes.—5. See:-

floaters. Spots before the eyes: since ca. 1950 or a decade earlier. (*Weekend*, 21 May 1969.) Also known as **flying flies.**

floaters in the snow. Sausages and mashed potatoes: RN (lowerdeck): since ca. 1920. Cf. **floater,** 2. P.B.: perhaps ex turds left floating in a lavatory bowl; cf. the 1920s Army c.p., 'Don't pull the plug, Dad, I like to see them floating!'

floating. Intoxicated, whether with liquor or, hence, drugs: adopted, ca. 1950, ex US. (Wyatt, 1973.) Richard McKenna, in *The Sand Pebbles*, 1962, a novel about the US Navy in China in the mid-1920s, writes of an enjoyable weekend-long bout of intoxication as 'a floating drunk'. (P.B.)

floating coach-and-four, the. The Isle of Man paddle-ship *Ben-My-Chree*, after being re-boilered and fitted with four funnels: nautical: later C.20. Bowen.

floating one. Passing a worthless cheque or arranging a loan without definite security: Services', esp. among officers: since ca. 1930. H. & P.

flob. To spit: esp. among early-teenage boys: since the 1930s. (Weightman, 1977.) Prob. echoic, influenced by *gob,* a lump of phlegm. Hence, *flobbing* = spitting. (P.B.)

flock. A bed: tramps' c. Ex the flock in a mattress.

flog. In late C.19–20 military, to sell illicitly, esp. Army stores; and, in post-WW1 c., to sell 'swag' to others than receivers. F. & G.; B. & P.—2. Hence(?), to exchange or barter: c.: from ca. 1920. *Dartmoor*, 1932.—3. (Ex 1.) 'To offer for sale (especially when financially embarrassed)' (H. & P.): Services': since ca. 1935. By ca. 1950 the term had broadened to mean simply 'to sell', gen. and widespread low coll., as 'They're flogging apples at ten pee a pound down the supermarket' (P.B., 1979).—4. To 'borrow without permission': Services': since ca. 1937. H. & P.—5. To masturbate: Aus. low.—6. In *on the flog,* which may refer to any of senses 1–4, but usu. with an implication of some dishonesty. (P.B.)

flog (one's) **chops.** To wear oneself out: Aus.: since ca. 1940. Buzo, 1968.

flog the cat. To vent one's bad temper on someone: RN: since ca. 1925. Granville.

flog the clock. To quit one's job before the due time; to knock off early: RN: since ca. 1920. (Laffin, 1969.)

floggin' the oggin. Sailing the seas: RN: later C.20. See **oggin,** sea; this term is an 'inevitable' rhyme.

flogging, adj. and adv. Objectionable; vaguely, yet strongly, pej.: Aus.: since ca. 1920. Ex **flog,** 5; semantically cf. the equivalent **flipping.** Atkinson, 1961, ' "Down they come like the floggin' wool prices" and "They might land in the floggin' desert" '.

floor, n. In *on the floor,* penniless: orig. c.:—1933 (Leach) >, by 1939, low s. Cf. familiar S.E. *down and out,* and *on the deck,* a var. of this entry. Prob. ex boxing.—2. In *on the* *floor*, adj. and adv., derailed: railwaymen's. (*Railway*, 2nd.) Cf. *on the dirt*.

floor fuck. Copulation on the carpet, 'having a naughty on the rug': Aus. low: since ca. 1910.

floor polish. To prove (someone) to be utterly wrong; a severe defeat, in argument or in a contest: since ca. 1942. (*John Bull*, 2 Dec. 1944.) Ex 'to *wipe the floor* with someone'.

floorman, the; the top man. Drawing upon Messrs William Hill Ltd's diary for 1953, *Sunday Dispatch* of 14 Dec. 1952 writes: 'Tic-tac is used chiefly to liaise between the big operators and the little bookmakers in the minor ring. The liaison man is usually to be found perched precariously in the main stand, and for that reason is called "The Top Man". He relays information to his partner, "The Floor Man", who stands down below on the rails.' The latter passes it on to the small bookmakers themselves. These terms go back at least as far as 1930.

floorman pitch-getter. One of those assistants at a mock or rigged auction who entice crowds into the auction room: mock-auction world: since ca. 1945. (*Sunday Chronicle*, 28 June 1953.) Strictly, only *pitch-getter* is slang and, in this 'world', very much commoner than the full expression.

floosie (or -y). A girl (as companion): RN: since ca. 1940. Granville; *John Bull*, 6 Apr. 1946. Adopted ex US s.—2. In more widespread, and post-WW2, use, it = a 'good-time girl', a tart, an 'enthusiastic amateur', or even a prostitute.

flop, n. 'A house or garage where escaping thieves can safely offload weapons, implements or stolen property, thus leaving their own homes free of incriminating articles' (Powis): c.: 1970s, and prob. two or three decades earlier.—2. In *do a flop*, to faint: current, esp. among VADs, in WW1; still extant mid-C.20.

flop, v. To sleep: tramps' c. (Gape, 1936.) Ex S.E. *flop down*.

flopper. A weak or 'floppy' person: coll.:—1923 (Manchon).—2. A road-sweeper: Liverpool street arabs': late C.19–mid-20.

flopper-stopper. A brassière: Aus. teenagers': since ca. 1955. Cf. **flip-flops,** 1.

flopperoo. A spectacular 'flop' or failure: adopted, ca. 1960, ex US.

flossy or **flossy up.** To dress up (oneself); to furbish: Aus.: since ca. 1935. (B., 1953.) Ex the S.E. adj. Cf. *tart up*.

flounder. A shortening of C.19 r.s. *flounder and dab*, a cab.

flounder-spearing. Conducting an orchestra. See **spear flounders.**

flour-mixer. A Gentile girl: esp. Jewish Cockneys': r.s. on Yiddish *shiksa*. (Franklyn 2nd.) Powis defines it as 'girl domestic or shop assistant'.—2. 'An inoffensive man, particularly a clerk' (Powis): underworld: 1970s.

flow. A 'travelling the bees' sojourn at a place where blossoms abound: Aus. coll.: since ca. 1945. Tennant, 1956.—2. 'Cash, as in money. Contraction of [business j.] *cash flow*: W. Can.: mid-1980s. Poss. ex the drug cults. "How's the flow?", or "How much flow have you got?" ' (Leech, 1985). A synon., in same milieu, is *bone*.

Flower pot, the. Covent Garden (Market): London taxi-drivers': since ca. 1905. (Hodge, 1939.) Ex the Flower Market there until the mid-1970s.

Flower power. 'Revolutionary philosophy akin to ideas of Young Liberals, e.g. Make Love Not War' (Fryer, 1967): hippies', Flower People's: since early 1967. Ex 'the Flower (or Beautiful) People'. P.B.: historical within a decade, as the ideals became swamped by hard materialist realism.

flower-power suit. Camouflaged combat-suit, of natural colours in a random pattern: Army: early 1970s. Ex prec. Cf. **ginger suit,** khaki battle-dress or formal uniform. (P.B.)

flowers. Orders, decorations, honours or degrees, indicated by letters after name: Services': WW2. They look pretty. (L.A.)

flowers and frolics. Testicles: Anglo-Irish r.s., on *bollocks* or *bollicks*. Franklyn.

flowery. Short for next, and hence, also, = a cubicle: low: since ca. 1920. Behan, 1958.

flowery dell. A prison-cell: r.s. (P.P., 1932; Home Office, 1978.) Hence the nuance 'imprisonment', as, at least twice, in MacGill, 1920.

flue. The rectum or anal passage: raffish. (Thomas, 1976, where erroneously spelt *flu*.) Mostly in the insulting and derisive *up your flue!*, often abbr. *up yours!* Ex a chimney flue.—2. '*Flue.* (Rarely used.) Prison officer. R.s. for "screw" ' (Tempest): prisons': mid-C.20.

fluence (or **'fluence), the.** Delicate or subtle influence: Aus. and NZ, since ca. 1930; some Brit. use also, in this sense. Cardus, 1934, 'Grimmett's fingers are always light and wonderfully tactile; when he passes the salt at dinner he imparts the "fluence"'.

fluey. Characteristic of, or characterised by, influenza, as '*fluey* weather': coll.: since ca. 1930. (Petch, 1966.)

fluff, n. Nonsense, esp. 'That's all fluff!': Aus.: ca. 1935–40. (Oliver, 1937.) Ex earlier synon. *bum-fluff*.—2. A railway ticket: Aus. low: since ca. 1920. B., 1942.—3. 'A spoonerism or other verbal misadventure on the radio' (Leechman): Can.: since ca. 1945.—4. Girl(s), esp. in *a* (*little*) *bit of fluff*: poss. orig. Aus. (Dennis, 1916, has it, but *OED* records it for 1903). Prob. ex S.E. *fluffy*, soft and downy; Tempest, 1950, qualifies thus, 'Any woman who tries to look younger than she really is and who overdoes it.'—5. The police: Can. (St Pierre, 1970.) Cf. **the fuzz.**

fluff, v. (Of porters), when off duty, to hang about in the hope of tips: railwaymen's:—1923 (Manchon). Ex later C.19 railway s., *fluff*, to give short change.—2. To boast; to tell lies: military: earlier C.20. F. & G.—3. To suspect; to understand; to guess or detect: Army, esp. the Guards: since ca. 1910. (Graham, 1919; Kersh, 1941.) Also *fluff to* (someone): to 'tumble to' him. Prob. ex sense 2.—4. Break wind: Aus.: since ca. 1919. (B., 1942.) P.B.: some Brit. use also.

fluffer. A woman who cleans greasy machinery beneath escalators: London Underground Transport Workers'. *Times*, 4 May 1988.

fluffing; fluffings. 'Selection of rich passengers by off-duty employees' (*Railway*, 2nd): railwaymen's. Cf. **fluff,** v., 1.

fluffy suit. WRNS no. 2 suit, worn for work; made of a coarser material than the no. 1, 'best' suit: WRNS in basic training: 1960s. 'Usually discarded after a year or so because it advertises one's newness to the Service' (Wood, 1977).

fluk(e)y; gen. **flukie.** A whale: nautical coll.: from ca. 1920. (*OED* Sup.) Ex a whale's *flukes*.

flumdiddle. A coll. var. (—1923) of *flummery*, S.E. for flattery, polite nonsense. (Manchon.) I.e. *flummery* influenced by *diddle*. Cf.:-

flumdoodle. To humbug (someone): Aus. (Baker.) Cf. prec.

flummoxed. Silenced; disappointed, outwitted; spoilt; ruined; drunk; sent to or sure of a month in prison (c. only): from the 1850s. Ppl adj. ex *flummox*, v. P.B.: by mid-C.20, it had gained the additional meaning of 'confused in mind, often by an unexpected turn of events, and uncertain what course to take'.

flunk. To fail in an examination: Can. universities: late C.19–20. Adopted from US; of unknown origin. Some Brit. use also, C.20.—2. Occ. used, perhaps influenced by *funk*, for to shirk, fight shy of, balk at, as, 'at the last moment, he flunked going to the police, for fear that . . . ': coll. (P.B.)

fluo tube. A fluorescent-lighting tube: Aus. coll.: since ca. 1955. (P.B.)

flush, n. 'Those [convicts] with Army and Navy experience use the Maltese word for money, i.e. "flush",' (Wicks, 1938).—2. A fellow with plenty of money, esp. if a free spender: Can. carnival s.: since ca. 1910. Ex the older s. adj.

flush, v. 'To draw blood back into syringe' (Home Office): drug addicts': 1970. Hence vbl n. *flushing*.

flute. A, to, whistle: police and prison warders'. The n. in Bracey, 1934; n. and v. in Phelan, 1941.—2. A jockey's whip: Aus. sporting s.: since ca. 1910. B., 1942.

fluter. A tail wind: club cyclists': earlier C.20. Also *tail puff*. *Fellowship*, 1984.

fly. A shunting truck; hence *fly shunt*, 'uncoupled wagons diverted after engine has passed the points' (*Railway*): railwaymen's.—2. In *on the fly*, shrewdly, cunningly, secretly: low:—1923 (Manchon).

fly a desk. Of an aircrew member: to be grounded and doing an office job: RAF: 1940–5. (Brickhill, 1951.) Cf. **chairborne . . . .**

fly a (or the) kite. To raise money by means of accommodation bills: from ca. 1808.—2. Merely to raise money (—1880). In Anglo-Irish banks, it = to cash a cheque against non-existent funds. Also *cash a dog*, and since ca. 1945, *fly a dodgy kite* (Cook, 1962); c. >, by ca. 1950, low s. See **kite**, n.,1.—3. To test public opinion by tentative measures: copy-writers' coll.: from ca. 1926.—4. 'To tell a tall story' (Baker): Aus.

fly-balance; shotter; sighter. A column of figures added correctly at the first attempt: bank-clerks': resp. coll., now verging on j.; s.; s. Obviously *shotter* derives ex *at the first shot*; *sighter* ex rifle-shooting. 'One bank today also employs *flyer*, the particular cry of joy being "a flyer to a penny!" However, in North-East England, the fortunate cashiers borrow the local dialect term *plump out* (= unequivocally) and say that they have got a *plumpo* or have simply *plumped*' (Taylor, 1986).

fly-blow. A flying-boat: RAF: since ca. 1935. (Jackson.) By a pun on S.E. *by-blow*.

fly-bog. Jam: Aus.: ca. 1930–50, but never very gen. B., 1943.—2. More gen. is the sense occurring in 'Sometimes you take a tin of fly-bog (treacle) with you as a luxury' (Devanney, 1944); since ca. 1920.

fly-boy. A FAA pilot or observer: among other branches of the RN and mostly officers': since ca. 1950; after 1965, only historical. (Granville.) Occ. used also by Army officers, joc. pej. for the RAF (P.B.). A pun on *fly*, artful, and on S.E. '*flying*', adj.—2. A 'wide boy': since ca. 1950. In, e.g., the Automobile Assn's magazine *Drive*, spring 1975. (P.B.)

fly-buttons. See **talk through** (one's) **fly-buttons**, to talk nonsense, or smut.

fly-by-night. Tipsy: r.s.: † by 1960. On synon. *tight*. (Franklyn 2nd.) Cf.:-

fly-by (pron. *be*)**-nights.** Tights (stockings): r.s.: later C.20. Barker, 1979.

fly by the seat of (one's) **pants.** To fly by instinct rather than by instruments: airmen's: since ca. 1930, perhaps earlier. Ex the days before such things as turn-and-bank indicators, when the tightness of an aircraft's turn could be judged only by the feeling of centrifugal force against the pilot's seat.—2. Hence, to essay a task (not necessarily aeronautical) and, although one is unfamiliar with it, to improve as one continues: orig. (1942) and still (1960) mainly RAF. (L.A.)

fly cemetery. A current pudding: certain schools': since ca. 1945. *New Society*, 22 Aug. 1963.

fly-gatherer. That workman who 'sweeps up and bags waste and "fly" (fibre dust) in spinning rooms' (*Evening News*, 28 Sep. 1955): textile employees': late C.19–20.

fly gay. Intelligent dupe of a confidence trickster: Aus. c.: since ca. 1920. (Baker.) On analogy of *fly flat*. See **gay**.

fly man. A cunning man: 1816 (Rammohun Roy, *Translation of an Abridgement of the Vedant*: as *flymen*, translating pl of Sanskrit *kitava*, gambler, cheat).—2. An expert thief: c. Wallace, 1927.—3. A professional criminal: Glasgow c.: from ca. 1919. (MacArthur.) Still current in Glasgow, 1985, in sense 1 (Munro).

fly over the hills. A fly-button undone and showing: Essex schoolchildren's: 1979. (Raab.)

fly-paper, be on the. To be justiciable under the Prevention of Crimes Act: c.: from ca. 1912. (*Gilt Kid*, 1936.) Ex:-

Fly Paper Act, the. The Prevention of Crimes Act (1909): c.: 1910. (Leach.)

fly-pitch; fly-pitcher. A cheapjack's 'pitch'; a cheapjack selling

from a pitch: showmen's. Allingham, 1934. Esp. of 'a casual spot' (Buchanan-Taylor, 1943).

Fly Speck, the. Tasmania: continental Aus. (B., 1943.)

fly-swisher stew. Oxtail stew: Aus. rural: since ca. 1910. (B., 1959.) Cattle swish their tails to keep the flies away. Cf. the earlier, more genteel *fly-disperser soup*.

fly the kite. See **fly a kite**.

fly-walk, the. The ridge on a loaf of bread: domestic.

flyer, flier. Someone thought to be destined to get on fast, with quick promotion ahead of him, as 'Watch that young man, I feel he's going to be a flyer': coll. (P.B.)—2. A very fast start in a foot race: athletics coll.—3. A smart, lively, very attractive person, esp. a pretty girl: coll.: 1930, Temple Thurston (*OED* Sup.).—4. See **fly-balance**.

Flyers, the. The (police) Flying Squad: c.: 1920s–30s. Wallace, 1928.

flying. Under the influence of drugs: drugs c. (Stockley, 1986.) US since—1942 (Spears).—2. For *going flying* see **fliers**.

Flying Angel (Club), the. The Mission to Seamen('s Club): seamen's. 'From the flying angel on the blue ground of the Mission's flag, from Rev., 14, 6, "And I saw another angel fly in the midst of heaven . . . " ' (L.A., 1967). Peppitt records that, in the 1940s, the Mission was known to the MN as *the Flying Ashbag*, 'their flag has a flying angel carrying a harp (lyre?), rather bag-like in shape'.

flying arsehole. An observer's badge: RFC/RAF: since 1915 (B. & P.). The badge consisted of an **O** with the representation of a wing; it was superseded early in WW2 by the navigators' brevet. Cf. **feathered arsehole**.—2. Hence, in RAAF, early WW2, the observer himself. B., 1943.

Flying Banana, (the). A Wooler motorcycle, ceased production 1955; 'This particular name really only applied to one model which had a very long tank and was painted yellow. First appeared in the T.T. ca. 1920' (Partridge, 1979).—2. A Vertol H.21 helicopter: RCAF: since ca. 1955 or/1956. *Whig-Standard* (Kingston, Ont.), 8 Mar. 1957.—3. Any of British Rail's Intercity '125' trains, which have a pointed, yellow power-unit at either end: later C.20.

flying bedstead. The 'flying testbed', a square frame not unlike a bedstead, used for testing engines designed for vertical take-off and landing: Royal Aircraft Establishment and journalistic: late 1950s. (P.B.)

flying boxcar. 'The new Junkers freight plane "Ju-52", "flying boxcar", belonging to Canadian Airways Limited, aroused a great deal of interest' (the *Beaver*, a magazine, Mar. 1932): Can.: 1930s. 'Also applied to the C.119 [transport aircraft]' (Leechman, 1968).

flying cigar, (the). The Vickers Wellington bomber (viewed laterally): RAF: 1940+. (H. & P.) It was more commonly and widely known as a **Wimpey**, q.v., and was in service 1938–52.

flying coffin, (the). The Vengeance dive-bomber: RAF: 1944–5.

flying dhobi. A native washerman giving quick service: Army in India, late C.19—mid-20, and, in later C.20, Services' in other countries, e.g., Malaya and Singapore. Cf. 'the mysterious Arab who would turn up at every camp . . . however far from civilisation, to provide a one-day laundry service' (Sanders, 1967): Army in N. Africa: 1940–3.

flying duck. A section insulator: railwaymen's: since ca. 1950. *Railway*, 2nd.

flying dustbin. 'The bomb thrown by an A.V.R.E. (Armoured Vehicle, Royal Engineers) for demolishing defences. ". . . a 12″ spigot mortar, the Petard, which could throw a 25-lb. H.E. charge (known as the 'Flying Dustbin') up to a distance of eighty yards" (Hart, 1959). Probably not widely used until 1944, as these vehicles were a secret weapon for the landings in Normandy.' (Sanders.)

flying elephant. (Usu. in pl.) Barrage balloon: 1939+. Berrey, 1940.

flying flies. Spots before the eyes: since ca. 1950 or a decade earlier. (*Weekend*, 21 May 1969.) Also known as **floaters**.

Flying Fornicator, the. The last express train home from London: in many English provincial towns, esp. Oxford and Cambridge: earlier C.20. Also **the Fornicator**.

flying fuse-box. 'Any electrical rating or officer holding an aircrew qualification as well, esp. if he is the Electrical Officer of a squadron: Fleet Air Arm: 1950s' (Peppitt).

flying gas-main. A V2 rocket: 1944–5. (Gordon, 1950.) The rockets arrived at such speed that there was no warning of their approach; when the first few went off in London it was thought that gas-mains had exploded. See also **gasometer.**

flying handicap, the. An attack of diarrhœa: Aus. sporting. (B., 1942.) Cf. **Sheffield handicap**.

flying horse. A Gloster Gladiator fighter aircraft of the FAA: RN: early WW2. Granville.

flying pencil. The Dornier 17 bomber: RAF: WW2. It had a noticeably thin fuselage.

Flying Pig, (the). A fast freight train bringing bacon to London: railwaymen's: from ca. 1920. (*Daily Telegraph*, 15 Aug. 1936.) Cf. the **Farmer's Boy**.

flying pig. An aerial torpedo, ex its appearance in the air: 1940 (Berrey).—2. A Vickers Vulcan aircraft of Imperial Airways: 1920s. McIntosh, 1963. Cf.:—3. A Vickers Varsity aircraft, a development of the Valetta but with a row of astrodomes—resembling teats—along its spine, used for training batches of navigators: RAF: 1950s. (P.B.)

flying plumber. 'Engineer officer attached to the Naval Air Branch' (Granville): RN: WW2 +.

flying saucers. Morning glory seeds: drugs c. (Stockley, 1986.) US since—1969 (Spears).

flying sixty-nine. Var. of **soixante-neuf**, q.v.

flying speed, get up. 'To consume a few quick drinks before a social or official gathering, especially when late (in order to achieve parity with those already present and well under way)' (Parsons, 1973): RN officers': since early 1920s.

flying spitkid. 'Sixteen-foot motor dinghy. A spitkid is a spittoon' (Granville): RN.

flying suitcase; flying tadpole. Both nicknames were applied to the Handley-Page Hampden and the shorter-lived Hereford bombers: RAF: late 1930s—early WW2. (H. & P.; Jackson.) The aircraft were very similar; the narrow fuselage was disproportionately deep in the forward section. (P.B.)

flying tin-opener. The Hawker Hurricane fighter in its role as tank-destroyer: RAF: 1941+. (H. & P.)

flying without a licence. Of a male, forgetfully leaving his fly-buttons or zip undone: comprehensive schools': heard in Leicestershire and Sussex, 1977. Elab.: *flying low without* . . . Cf. **fly over the hills**.

Flywheel. See Chad.

foaming at the mouth. Exceedingly angry: coll.: since ca. 1910.

fob. 'A hiding-place, usually for tools underground. To hide— "to make a fob" ' (Forster, 1970): coal miners'.

fodded. Of an '[engine] damaged by foreign object', ex *FOD*, 'Foreign object damage. A noun, screw, nut, etc. that gets into [aircraft] engine or control system' (*Fighter Pilot*, 1981): RAF: later C.20.

fog-bound. Tipsy: earlier C.20. Herbert, 1934, ' "Was I a bit tiddly last night?" "Tiddly?" "Tiddly. Skew-whiff. Fog-bound" ' Cf. *fogged*, its C.19 equivalent.

fog factory. 'A locality where fogs are plentiful' (Berrey): RAF: WW2.

fogey. Old-fashioned or unusual; 'freaky': Leicestershire (and prob. further afield) teenagers'; as, 'Oh Mum, what a fogey pair of shoes!' (= last year's fashion): ca. 1977. (D. & R. McPheely.)

fold. Elliptical for sense 2 of next.

fold up. (Of an aircraft) to crash: (of a person) to go sick unexpectedly or without warning: Services', esp. RAF: since 1939. (H. & P.) Ex the 'to collapse' sense of the S.E. term; adopted from US; perhaps, semantically, ex the 'action' of a defective parachute.—2. Hence, of a policy or a plan, of a

business or a periodical: to fail, to collapse; to cease: since ca. 1945. Usu. shortened to *fold*, as in 'This magazine is expected to fold before long'.

folkies. Devotees of folksong and folk music: later C.20. (*New Society*, 18 Aug. 1983.) Cf. **foodie, trekkie**, etc.

follow the waterworks. To travel about the country on reservoir jobs: navvies': since ca. 1920.

follow through, v.; whence, **follow-through**, n. To ejaculate twice without withdrawal in the sex act. Ex sporting j.

fonfen. 'The spurious stories of fraudsmen (common Yiddish word) in the world of commercial fraud or near-fraud' (Powis): 1970s.

foo. A favourite gremlin: RAAF: ca. 1941–5. Arbitrary, though perhaps with a pun on *FOO*, a Forward Observation Officer. Baker, 1943, less precisely writes: 'A fictitious person to whom all lapses and bungling are attributed' and classifies it as general war slang: whence *fooism*, a saying, or an exploit, attributed to *Foo*. Or, perhaps, ex a popular US cartoon strip called 'Smokey Storer': there, the 'hero' used it as a stop-gap name for anything for which he couldn't be bothered to find the correct word. And see GREMLINS, in Appx.

foo-foo barge. A sewage boat on the Yangtze River: RN: earlier C.20. Granville.

foo-foo (powder). 'Talcum powder, used a great deal by sailors in the tropics' (Granville): RN lowerdeck: since ca. 1930. Cf. prec.

foo-foo valve. 'A mythical "gadget" that's always blamed for any mechanical break-down' (Granville, letter, 1947): RN since ca. 1910.

food inspector. A tramp: Aus. (B., 1942.) He goes about the country sampling food wherever he can get a 'hand-out'. By 1959, †: teste B., 1959.

foodie. Someone obsessed by food, a connoisseur and gourmet: earlier 1980s. Barber, 1984.

foot-and-mouth disease. The tendency of golfers to talk at night of the day's exploits: joc. coll.: from 1923 or 1924: cultured. (Ware, 1909, records that, in Lancashire, the phrase indicates 'swearing followed by kicking'.)

foot-back it. To go on foot, carrying one's pack: Aus. coll. (Russell, 1934.) And see **footback.**

foot-in-arse. The little grebe: Isle of Man s., or perhaps dial. (Van Dulken.) Cf. † *arse-foot*, a penguin.

foot-in-the-door bloke. 'A canvasser or door-to-door salesman. Used in "Dr Finlay's Casebook", BBC TV, 12 March 1967' (Petch): since ca. 1955. Ex a trick practised to ensure at least some attention.

foot on the floor, put (one's)**; with** (one's)**.** To accelerate; by accelerating: motorists': since ca. 1920. Cf. the later **clog down**, and **turn up the wick**.

foot-rotting. 'Kicking one's heels in idleness' (B., 1943): Aus.: since ca. 1930.

foot-slogger. An infantryman: military coll.: from early 1890s.—2. Hence, occ., a pedestrian: coll. The v., *foot-slog*, though likewise coll. (C.20), is seldom used.—3. A policeman on his beat: Aus.: from ca. 1920.

foot-walk (it). To travel on foot: Aus. coll.:—1935.

footback or **on footback.** On foot: Aus.: since ca. 1920. (Russell, 1934 (*footback*); B, 1943 (*on f-*)). Punning *horseback*.

football, the. Football news: coll.

football feet, have. (Of an aircraft pilot) to make excessive use of the rudder: RAF: since ca. 1930. H. & P.

footie, -y. See **play footie**.

footle around, usu. as vbl n., *footling around*, 'continuously circling over an area in search of a target or a landing-ground' (E.P., 1942). Cf. **stooge**, v.

footlight favourite. A chorister that thrusts herself forward: theatrical coll.:—1935. Ironic use of a standard cliché.

footprints, pair of. A pipe-wrench: Aus.: since ca. 1930. 'Apparently so named because, when open, they are wide at the ends and narrow in the middle like a [human] footprint' (B.P.).

footsies. See **play footies.**

footy. Futile: Society: later 1930s. Allingham, 1938.—2. As in '*footy* match', football match: Aus.: since ca. 1920. Farrell, 1963.

foozle about (with). To fool about (with): coll. Cole, 1930.

for crying out loud! A London phrase, from ca. 1930, used in the place of—and with more effect than—*for Christ's sake.* Prob. ex US, where euph.

for ever and a day. An intensification of 'for ever', as an indefinite, but considerable, length of time: coll.: since mid-C.20. (P.B.)

for-free. A cut-price prostitute. See **charity dame.**

for free. Free: coll.: adopted, ca. 1954, ex US 'I got it for free'. Tautology. Cf. *free, gratis and for nothing* and **freebie.**

for fuck's sake! (usu. pron. *fucksake.*) In later C.20 the main low, esp. Services', all-purpose expletive and intensifier; used sometimes in resignation, most often in anger, as simple exclam., 'Oh, for fuck's sake!', or to emphasise a (usu.) rhetorical question: 'Well, for fuck's sake, why don't they . . . ?' An oath in its own right, obviously, but perhaps also a 'euphemism' for *For Christ's sake.* (P.B.)

for it, be. To be due for punishment; hence, imm., in trouble: military s. (1915: ?late 1914) >, by 1919, gen. coll. The *it* = punishment. F. & G.

for Pete's sake! Used emphatically, as a mild oath, prob. ex *for pity's sake*: coll. (P.B.)

for real, adj. and adv. Real(ly); true, truly: coll.: adopted, ca. 1965, ex US. (Petch, 1969.)

for starters. For a start; to begin with, as of a meal: coll.: since ca. 1960. Perhaps on analogy of *afters*, the dessert course. As in: 'What's wrong?'—'Well, for starters, I'd like to know why . . . ' (P.B.)

for sure! 'A confirmation, a term meaning, "Yes, I will", or "Yes, that's right." Past 5–10 years; widespread Can. and US' (Leech, 1986). A cartoon by Dan Piraro in *Edmonton Jnl.*, 2 Jan. 1986, has *fer sure.*

for the love of Mike! For goodness' sake!: (low) coll.: mid-C.19–20: Anglo-Irish > gen., and, as L.A. points out, 1974, 'As a safe bet "For the love of Christ!" but without blasphemy, prob. orig. Roman Catholic.'

for your information . . . Sarcastic reply to an over-inquisitive or impertinent busybody: since ca. 1955. With ironic allusion to the legitimate queries of commerce—and bureaucracy.

force-lob, n. and v. (To make) a crash landing in an aircraft: RAF coll.: var. of **crash lob,** q.v. See also **lob,** v.

fore and aft (or hyphenated), n. 'Horizontally opposed twin-cylinder engine, set along the [motorcycle] frame rather than transversely. Used on early Douglas and A.B.C. machines, for instance: early C.20 motorcyclists' ' (Partridge, 1979).—2. 'Field service cap, as distinct from dress service or peaked cap' (Jackson): RAF, since ca. 1925: in later C.20, also Army. I.e. a forage cap.

fore and aft. 'Descriptive of a sailor's clothes, cut on the generous lines known to all' (H. & P.): Services', esp. RN. I.e. with plenty of freedom both in front and behind.

forecastle wireless. A rumour; rumours: nautical: from ca. 1925. Bowen.

Foreign Legion, the. 'Men on loan' (*Railway*, 2nd): railwaymen's: since late 1940s. McKenna, *Glossary*, 1970, clarifies, 'During busy railway periods, men from slack depots would be lent to depots suffering from staff shortages.' Cf.:–

foreign line. Any line other than that on which the speaker is employed: railwaymen's coll.:–1909 (Ware).

foreign order. An Aus. synon. of **foreigner:** since early 1940s. (B.P.)

foreigner. An article made in the Service's time and with its materials: RAF: since ca. 1941. (H. & P.) Adopted from civilian workers, who had used the term since at least as early as 1939. Still current among Midlands factory workers (Hedges,

1982). Cf:—2. An extra fake banknote, painting, etc., made by a forger for himself, beyond the 'order' given him: c. Gash, 1983.

Forest, the. 'Short for **Sherwood Forest** [q.v.], which, because of its adoption by journalists and film producers, has become non-U in the Navy' (Peppitt).

Forever Amber or **f– a–.** A fixed distant signal: railwaymen's: since late 1940s. (*Railway*, 2nd.) Ex the title of Kathleen Winsor's famous popular novel, published in Britain in 1945—and the film two years later.

forget it! Don't worry any more about it; it's not worth worrying, or even thinking, about: lowish coll.: since ca. 1950.—2. Sometimes used in irritation at someone who, through inattention or dull-wittedness, has failed to catch what the speaker has said, and when the matter is too trivial, or even too complicated, to be worth repeating: like sense 1, adopted ex US, ca. 1950.

forggy, n. and adj. A dim-wit; (also *forggified*) dim-witted: market traders': since ca. 1910. *M.T.*

fork. ' "On the left fork" means to the left, and "on the right fork" means to the right' (Marks, 1977): Cockneys': mid-C.20.

fork and knife. A wife: r.s. (Lester.) Far less common than synon. *trouble and strife.*

fork lifts. The two striped cushions placed in the rear window of a car: Aus. raffish: since late 1950s. 'This is a status symbol, in that people with small cars or old cars with a small rear window have no room for the cushions' (B.P.). These cushions are reputed to facilitate rear-seat copulation, and there is a pun on the *fork* of the human body. In S.E., a *fork-lift* is 'a kind of industrial carrier that lifts goods by inserting a fork beneath a pallet stacked with goods'.

form. A prison record, esp. if serious or recidivist: since ca. 1925. Norman, 'You can get at least a fiver and maybe even a neves for getting captured with a shooter especially if you've got a bit of form behind you.' Also Aus. prison s. (McNeil, 1973.) See also sense 3.—2. Situation, position, as in 'What's the form?' or 'It took me a couple of days to find out the form at H.Q.'—to ascertain how things were done and what the people were like: Services officers': since ca. 1930. 'What's the form?' became, later, ca. 1950, synon. with 'What's the drill?' = How do I/we go about this matter? Orig., however, the question was a Society usage, from the mid-1920s, and meant simply 'What's it like (at, e.g., a party-house)?' Waugh, 1934, of a household, ' "What's the form?" "Very quiet and enjoyable." '—3. In *with form*, having a police record: c. (and police s.): since ca. 1925. Crookston, 1967, 'They [the police] might check on everyone with form living within easy reach of the crime.' Ex 1.

form up (about it). To make a formal request or complaint to a superior officer: Army, mostly officers': WW2. (P-G-R.) Ex the formal parading of a soldier before his officer for interview of any sort.

-former, e.g. **fourth-former.** A pupil in the (e.g. 4th) form: Public Schools' coll.

Formy. HMS *Formidable*: RN: since ca. 1930. Granville.

fornicating, adj. Lying; humbugging ('You fornicating sod!').

fornicating the poodle. Irritating and senseless occupation. Var. of **fucking the dog,** q.v.

fornicator. See **Flying Fornicator.**

Forsyte Saga. Lager: r.s.: later C.20 (Barker, 1979.) John Galsworthy's famous series of novels was given new popularity by dramatisation for television in the 1970s.

Fort. Familiar name for the Boeing B-17 Flying *Fort*ress bomber: RAF; journalists'; aeroplane-spotters': 1941–5.

Fort Bushy. The female pudend: Can.

Forth Bridge Job. Anything needing constant amendment or renewal or updating: coll.: later C.20. E.g., editing a dictionary—like keeping the Forth Bridge repainted: the painters are reputed to start again at one end as soon as they have reached the other. (With thanks to James G. Ollé, MA, FLA.)

F

fortie. Var. (B., 1942) of **forty.**

fortune cookies. 'Gold diggers'—girls looking for a 'sugar daddy', an elderly or an old man with money: Can.: since late 1960s. P.B.: adopted ex US; a pun on the standard term.

forty. A sharper: Aus.: from ca. 1925. (The *OED* Sup. records it at 1927.) Perhaps suggested by *the forty thieves.*

forty-eight. A 48-hours' pass or leave: Services' coll.: since ca. 1914. Cf. a *thirty-six*(-hours' pass).

forty-four. Door to door: r.s. Franklyn.

forty-watt. Applied to a person not very bright, intellectually dim: later C.20. (Hamblin, 1988.) Ex low power light bulbs; cf. **dim bulb.**

foss. Generic for patent medicines and toilet preparations: fairgrounds'. (Buchanan-Taylor, 1943.) Perhaps on *phosphorus?*

foul. In C.20 (mainly post-WW1) hyperbolical use is fairly to be described as s. > coll. of the *awful* and *terrible* kind. Cf. **filthy.** Coke, 1911, 'A foul row'; Delafield, 1933, 'He's terribly foul, isn't he?'—2. 'If the rank is full, and he "puts on" the tail end in the hope that the first cab will "get off" before a policeman catches him, he "puts on foul". When he has done so, *he* is "foul" ' (Hodge, 1939): taxi-drivers': since ca. 1910. Ex the *foul* of sport, as in 'to play *foul*'.

found a nail. Round the tail: NZ sheep-shearers' r.s. B., 1941.

Foundling, the. The Harmsworth Memorial Playground at Coram's Fields: Cockneys': from (?)ca. 1930. Ex the Foundling Hospital, the long-established Foundation on that site.

four-and-two. A sandwich. (Bell, 1931.) Cf. **four-by-two.**

four-by-three. Small; insignificant (rarely of persons): from ca. 1924. Sayers, 1932, 'An adjectival four-by-three wateringplace like Wilvercombe'.

four by (usu. merely **b'**) **two.** An army biscuit: Army: from ca. 1912. (F. & G.) Ex the size, in inches, of the piece of flannelette that, threaded through a loop on the end of a cord (the pull-through), is used to clean the inside of a rifle-barrel.—2. A Jew: r.s.: orig. Cockney soldiers', from 1914 (B. & P.), but by 1920 fairly common among users of r.s.

four F method, the. This is the lowerdeck's allusive synon. of its sexual motto, *Find, feel, fuck and forget,* itself current since ca. 1890.

four-flusher. A braggart, a cheat: Army coll.: from not later than 1918. (F. & G.) Ex US senses, a pretender, a humbug, themselves ex poker j.

four(-)foot. '4 ft 8½ in. gauge' (*Railway*, 2nd): railwaymen's coll.

four Johnny boys or **ladies** or **monarchs of the glen.** Quatorzes in picquet. (Ross.)

four-letter man. A very objectionable fellow: rather low:— 1923; heard among army officers as early as 1917. (Manchon; B. & P.) I.e., a *s-h-i-t.*—2. A *homo*(sexual): id.: from ca. 1930.

four-letter word. A 'rude word' of four letters: since 1929 (1st edition of *Lady Chatterley's Lover*: 1928): coll. >, by late 1950s, S.E.

four-ringed captain. 'A Captain R.N. as distinct from the captain of a ship who holds a junior rank' (Granville): RN coll.: late C.19–20.

four-wheeled kip. A taxi-cab: Dublin taxi-drivers': from ca. 1910. A ref. to fornication therein.

four-wheeler. A Catholic who goes to church only for baptisms, marriages, funerals. (*Universe*, 28 Feb. 1969.) Petch, 1976 'It is now used in other churches. It implies that a person has been to church only by pram to be christened, by car to be married, and in a hearse to be buried.' P.B.: also heard as a 'four-wheel Christian'.

fourble, adj. and—mostly in pl.—n. Quadruple: Aus. juveniles': since ca. 1930. B., 1953.

fourpenny one. A cuff; clip on the ear: r.s. on *hit* (presumably, orig. *fourpenny bit* or *pit*). (*Evening News* (London), 29 Feb. 1936.) Hence to *get a fourpenny one,* to receive a thrashing, get a hiding: since ca. 1910. In RAF s., 1940+, to *get a fourpenny one* = to be shot down.

fourteen penn'orth (**of it**). An award of fourteen days in the cells: RN. Granville.

Fourth of July. A tie: r.s. B. & P.

fowl-roost, start a. To assume a hyphenated surname: Aus. B., 1942.

fox, n. Member of a drinking 'school' who dodges his obligation to 'shout' (to pay for his round when it comes to his turn): Aus. drinkers': later C.20. Hornadge, 1980.

fox, v. To puzzle (a person)—e.g. with a flow of technicalities or of other erudition: Services' coll.: since 1939. (H. & P.)— 2. 'To follow an enemy aircraft cunningly' (Jackson): RAF: 1939+.—3. To field (a cricket ball): Aus.: since ca. 1925. Mann, 1942, 'You bowled it, you fox it.' To run to earth.

foxer. An apparatus used for foxing the *gnat* (German acoustic torpedo): RN: ca. 1941–5.

fox's wedding. An earlier C.20 var. of the S. African (?and Brit.) *monkey's wedding*: rain or drizzle while the sun shines. (Bishop, 1986.)

foxy. 'Seductive, sexually attractive. Usually of a female' (Hibbert, 1983): orig. Black US, adopted later 1970s in UK mainly by CB radio users, who took so much from US.

frack. A noisy quarrel; an assault: Soho, London: since ca. 1920. (Oliver, 1948.) Ex *fracas.*

fragile. (Of girls) exported under age to the Argentine: whiteslavers' c. Londres, 1928.

frame, n. In *in the frame*, 'Suspected, with some good reason, of being concerned in a serious crime; "Well in the frame" is even stronger' (Powis); 'Scotland Yard works on informers, and if you go in the frame for something, you get picked up and fitted up, as they say . . . ' (McVicar, 1979).—2. See **frame,** v., 2.

frame, v. To work up and present an unjustified case or serious complaint against (someone): coll.: adopted, ex US, ca. 1924. See Irwin.—2. To effect a pre-arranged conspiracy, a faked result: id. (Irwin; *OED* Sup.) Also n. This sense has been overborne by sense 1 since mid-C.20 at latest.—3. To get the 'John' or 'mark' (the proposed victim) into a posture that facilitates the theft: pickpockets' c.: since ca. 1950. Palmer, 1974.

frame-up. The result of the machinations defined in **frame,** v., 1 and 2, as 'The whole thing was just a frame-up: he was completely innocent': c. > coll.: adopted, ex US, by ca. 1940 at latest.

franchucha. A French prostitute in the Argentine: white-slave c.: late C.19–20. (Londres, 1928.) In Argentina, a *Franchucha* was orig. 'Frenchwoman', but, as R.C. points out, 1976, it is 'A possible portmanteauing of [Spanish] *Francesa* (Frenchwoman) and *chucha* or *chocha,* low Sp. for cunt.'

frangine. Brother: Can. (F. & G.) Ex Fr.-Can.

frank. Obscene or tending to obscenity: book-world s. or j.: from ca. 1926. Whence *frankness.* Cf. Pope's usage: unchaste.

frank and fearless. A discussion, no matter how trivial: Sloane Rangers' [q.v.]: early 1980s. (*Sunday Express* supp., 11 Oct. 1982.) A parody of the political cliché.

Franklin teeth. Projecting teeth: Can.: adopted, ca. 1920, ex US; by 1935, †. Projecting, hence 'air-cooled': ex 'the air-cooled engine of the Franklin car. Became obsolete with the disappearance of the car in the Depression' (Priestley).

Frans, the. Members of the Friars Minor (*Franciscans*): Aus. Catholics'. (B.P.)

frantic. 'Awful', 'terrible'; coll.: 1908 (*OED* Sup.). E.g. 'a frantic hurry' or 'muddle'. Ex:—2. Notable; well-known; confirmed: Public Schools' coll.: 1902, Wodehouse, 'Who's that frantic blood who owns all the land?'—3. (Of a party) gay, lively: smart young set (esp. girls'): ca. 1955–60. (Gilderdale, 2.) Perhaps ex sense 2. Also (as in 'It's frantic' or good fun or exciting) Aus. surfers', esp. teenagers': since late 1950s; by 1966, slightly ob. (*Pix,* 28 Sep. 1963.) Proleptic.

Frantic Bee. A Francis Barnett motorcycle, in production 1919–64: motorcyclists'. (Dunford.) Cf. **Fanny Barnett.**

frantically. Adv. corresponding to **frantic,** 1.

frap(ping). 'A substitute for *fuck(ing)*, for use in emphasis or as an intensifier: W. US and Can.' (Leech, 1985): later C.20. Cf. **flip(ping).**

frarny (or **F-**). Rain: taxi-drivers': since ca. 1915. See **instalment mixture**. A very rare type of shortening from older r.s.: *France and Spain*. Influenced by *parny* (see **parnee**).

frat, n. Same as *fratter* in next entry: ca. 1945–50. *John Bull*, 8 June 1946.

frat, v. To fraternise (with people that had lately been the enemy, chiefly Germans and Austrians, and esp. with the younger women and girls): Services': from May 1945; ob. by ca. 1950. By back formation. Hence, *fratter*, a fraterniser. (North of the Brenner, the Allied Forces in 1945 referred to Austrian girls as *frats*.) 'In the British Army an army-issue cheese or corned beef sandwich—a proven way to a hungry Fraulein's heart—was known as a "frat sandwich". There was even a "frat" song, set to the tune of "Lilli Marlene", which went: "Underneath the bushes,/You take your piece of frat,/You first take off your gas-cape/And then remove your hat . . . " ' (*Sunday Telegraph*, 12 May 1985).

frat rat. 'A fraternity member (on a university campus)' (Leech, 1985): Can.

fratchy. Bad-tempered, irritable from inter-personal friction, as in 'Luckily, we both like laughing quite a bit and that got us through the fratchy bits' (Howard, in *Sunday Telegraph* mag., 17 May 1987, on collaborating in writing a book). Cf. synon. **fricky.**

fraught. Risky or dangerous: smart set: since early 1960s. Garve, 1968, ' "Almost [no risks] in the early stages . . . The end could be a bit fraught." ' Elliptical for 'fraught with danger'.—2. Very anxious or worried; perturbed: coll.: since early 1960s. 'I saw Wendy today, having her first driving-lesson. She looked distinctly fraught.' Ex the riskiness of the situation, and influenced, perhaps, by *distraught*. (P.B.)

Frazer-Nash. 'Slash (urine). [R.s.]. Although *slash* is a verb and a noun its rhyming complement may only be used as a noun. One has (or goes for) a Frazer-Nash/**pie and mash**. Frazer-Nash manufactured sports cars prior to WW2' (Hillman, 1974).

frazzle, n. (Always *to a f–*.) Very badly; absolutely, utterly: adopted, ex US, ca. 1905. Hence *faded to a frazzle*, completely exhausted: ca. 1908–14; in later C.20, occ. *beaten*, more often *done*, usu. *worn, to a frazzle*, all = utterly 'done up', defeated or exhausted. Ex Southern US *frazzle*, a frayed-out end: cf. East Anglian *frazzle*, to fray out. Thornton; *EDD*.

frazzle, v. To rob: Aus. B., 1942.

freak, n. 'Trying to ring in a freak . . . A double-header' (Palmer, 1948): Aus. two-up-players': since ca. 1910.—2. A devotee, an enthusiast, a 'buff': adopted, early 1960s, ex US. P.B.: may be used as a suffix, e.g., in *eco(-)freak*, one whom others consider to be slightly unbalanced or 'fanatical' on the subject of conservation of the *ecology*; or *phone(-)freak*, one who gets his thrills in abusing the telephone system, by, e.g., telephoning his own number by routing the call around the world.

freak, v. To 'arouse or share collective enthusiasm (freak-out)': hippies' and then Flower People's: since late 1966 or very early 1967. Fryer, 1967. Cf. the next two entries.

freak-out, n. ' . . . These curious way-out events, simulating drug ecstasies, which are known as "freak-outs", in which girls writhe and shriek and young men roll themselves naked in paint or jelly' (Pitman, 1967): since late 1966. Ex:—2. Often applied to a bad 'trip': adopted, mid-1960s, ex US. Recorded by *The Living Webster*, 1970.

freak out, v. To suffer a 'freak-out', a bad 'trip' on drugs; to become temporarily (occ. permanently) insane from the effects of LSD—its victims act freakishly: Can. drug addicts', since ca. 1965; > Brit., ca. 1966. (Leechman; R.C.) Perhaps ultimately ex the S.E. adj. *freaked*, 'vivid with contrasting streaks of colour occurring capriciously' (Webster), but more likely ex a *freak*, or *sport*, of nature.—2. To scare

(someone): since late 1960s. (Jagger.) Also simply *freak*.—3. To snap under intolerable pressure: sporting coll.: late 1970s. '[The 3 racing-drivers] have all punched marshals at one time or another, which Hunt calls "freaking-out" ' (*Now!*, 2 Nov. 1979).

freaky, n. One who has 'freaked out' (sense 1); var. of simple *freak*: ca. 1970. Barnhart cites *Punch*, 22 Oct. 1969.

freaky, adj. Exhibiting the characteristics of a drug-addict; not merely confined to those who 'freak out': since late 1960s. Landy, 1971.—2. 'Sexually deviant' (Powis): later 1970s. Cf. **kinky.**

freckle. The anus: Aus. low. 'I'm going to shove your flaming teeth so far down your flaming throat that you'll have to shove your toothbrush up your freckle to clean them' (West, 1985).

Fred. 'The ordinary, unimaginative Australian; the average consumer' (Wilkes): Aus.: from early 1970s.

Fred Karno. 'A train made up of goods and passenger stock. In use among the L.M.S. employees ca. 1930. (As Fred Karno has not appeared on the halls for many years it is probably earlier)' (Boycott, 1938).

Fred Karno's Army. The 'New Army': military: WW1. (F. & G.) Ex 'the popular comedian, Fred Karno, noted for his troupe of whimsical oddities and caricaturists'.—2. Hence, in WW2, 'the Army on Home Service, and particularly the specialist branches regarded with a satirical eye' (H. & P.). But Aldiss, 1978, is nearer the mark when he says 'it was still popularly used in WW2 of any platoon or section which was *shit-or-bust*, careless or inept'; and the term was still being used in this sense well into the early 1970s, 'a proper Fred Karno('s) outfit'. (P.B.)

Fred Karno's Navy. The Dover patrol: RN: WW1. (Bowen.) Granville notes that the term was revived in WW2 for the Auxiliary Patrols made up of trawlers, drifters, armed yachts and the like. Cf. *Harry Tate's navy.*

Freddie, -y. 'Ephedrine tablet' (Home Office): drug-users': 1970s.—2. See **Old Freddies.**

Fred's. Fortnum & Mason's: Londoners': since ca. 1945. Still in use among Sloane Rangers [q.v.], early 1980s. (*Sunday Express* supp., 11 Oct. 1982.)

free-and-blowing. 'Sailor's "square rig" with its blue jean collar that blows round his neck and the bell-bottomed trousers that flap round his ankles in a breeze' (Granville): RN.

free chewing-gum. A chin-strap: Aus. soldiers': 1939+. B., 1942.

free issue. A condom: RN: since ca. 1920.

free-loader. See **freeloader.**

free of sense as a frog of feathers, as; or . . . **from . . . from.** Complete fool: Aus. Baker.

freebasing. Smoking pure cocaine: drugs c. (Stockley, 1986.) US since—1980 (Spears).

freebie, -y, n. and adj. '(Something) obtained free of charge; something gratis' (Barnhart); esp. in connexion with advertising 'give-aways'; occ., perquisites: adopted, ex US, later 1970s. 'The freebie magazines keep on coming . . . Freebies have never looked back' (*Time Out*, 28 Mar. 1980).

Freedom Corner. Marble Arch (but inside Hyde Park)—a spot famous for its orators.

freeloader. 'One who crashes in on cocktail parties, luncheons, and other such affairs that are part of a publicity campaign, or otherwise accessible. The sin he commits is "freeloading" ' (Leechman); the v., to *freeload*, is less common. Can., adopted, ca. 1955, ex US; by 1960, fairly common in UK. An early occurrence in Brit. print is in Campbell, 1960, 'this free-loading, literary bee [party]'.

Freeman, Hardy and Willis. The three campaign medals awarded for service in WW1; their ribbons on a man's chest: RAF: ca. 1921–41. (Jackson.) Ex the well-known chain of shoe-shops. The medals were much more commonly known as *Pip, Squeak and Wilfred.*

F

freewheeling. Such a treatment of a stage play, or of a film, as possesses a technical pattern allowing freedom of character and plot: since ca. 1955. (L.A., 1976.)

freeze, n. As *the freeze*, a wife's deliberate withholding of sexual intercourse: Aus.: since ca. 1930. 'Wives know that "the freeze" is their most potent weapon' (B.P.). Cf. v., 3. Ex:—2. In *do a freeze*, to be ignored, neglected, overlooked: Aus.: since ca. 1910. B., 1942.

freeze, v. To send (someone) to Coventry: Service officers': since ca. 1925. H. & P.—2. To stand stock still, e.g. when an enemy flare lights up the surroundings: coll. Idriess, 1932: Diary entry of 30 May 1915, 'When a blasted shell comes screaming . . . I don't move at all, just lie perfectly still and "freeze", waiting.'—3. (Usu. of the wife.) To confine one's spouse to 'the dog-house': Aus.: since ca. 1925. (B.P.)

freezer. A Salvation Army term. 'General Bramwell Booth was in the habit of putting too energetic officers into what was called the "freezer"—that is, sending them to remote and unexciting posts where their ardour would soon cool' (Muggeridge, 1940). William Bramwell Booth became the Salvation Army's chief organiser at the age of 26, in 1882; in 1912, he became its General.—2. A prison: Aus. low. (B., 1942.) Cf. **cooler**, 1.

French. To perform an act of fellation upon: low. 'She thought he was asleep, and Frenched him' (in a novel published ca. 1965). Cf. *French tricks*, since mid-C.19, for oral-genital sex.

French blue. 'Amphetamine/barbiturate pill. New type Drinamyl' (Home Office): drug-users': since late 1960s.

French by injection. See injection.

French Consular Guard, the. French prostitutes (Franchuchas) plying around the French Consulate at Buenos Aires: c., esp. white-slavers'. Londres, 1928.

French drive and **Chinese Drive.** A snick through the slips: cricket s., the former Eng., the latter Aus.: since late 1940s. The former exemplifies 'the British tendency to ascribe anything irregular to the French' (Sanders), the latter the Aus. tendency to attribute anything odd to the Chinese.

French kiss. A deep, heavy kiss, with much use of the tongue: coll.:—1923 (Manchon).

French (rarely **American, Italian** or **Spanish**) **letter.** A condom: low coll.: from ca. 1870; by ca. 1950, familiar S.E. Cf. Fr. *capote anglaise*.—2. A wind-sock, or wind-indicator: RAF: since ca. 1925. Ex shape.—3. A 'lightest track tubular [tyre]' (*Fellowship*, 1984): racing cyclists'.

French letter on the prick of progress. A shackle or shackling; anything that slows down an activity: Army officers': early 1970s. (P.B.)

French loaf. £4: r.s. on the back s. *ruof*, pron. *roaf*. (Hillman, 1974.)

French safe. Can. synon. for *French letter*, a condom: since ca. 1910. (Leechman.) See **safe**, n.

French seventy-five (written **75**). A 'Tom Collins' mixed with champagne: since ca. 1918: ob. (Waugh, 1936.) Ex the powerful French gun.

Frenchie, -y. A condom: low coll.: since ca. 1910. Ex *French letter*.—2. (In pl.) French knickers: feminine coll. Moore, 1983.

fresh out of. Being short of; having no: Can. coll., esp. among shopkeepers: adopted, ca. 1910, ex US. 'Sorry, sir, but we're fresh out of bacon.' (Leechman.)

fresh w(h)ack. 'Further Borstal sentence' (Home Office): Borstals' and detention centres': 1970s.

fresher. A refreshment room, or a set of refreshment rooms: railwaymen's. *Railway*.—2. A trawler with fish packed in ice, therefore with a refrigerator: trawlermen's: since ca. 1955. Peppitt, 1973.

freshers. Fresh air: RN. By the 'ʘᴏxꜰᴏʀᴅ -ᴇʀ(s)'.

fretkidney (or hyphenated). One who worries, and who pesters others, about trifles and inevitables: C.19–20. Ex *fret* (one's) *kidneys*, and fretting others, as in 'What a fretkidney that child is, really!' (P.B.)

friar's balls. Friar's Balsam (a patent medicine): Aus. low joc.: since ca. 1930.

fricking. A s. euph. for *fucking*, adj. On or ex *frigging*, adj.

fricky. (Of persons) nervously irritated or on edge: coll.: since (?)1940. Perhaps ex the *friction* generated in people under pressure. (L. S. Beale.) Cf. **fratchy**.

Friday (afternoon) car (or **job**). A car that is constantly going wrong, as if made by workers skimping on the last shift of the week and anxious to be off: since early 1970s. Hence, may be fig., e.g., of a person with abnormally short fingers, who feels 'unfinished', as in Dickinson, 1979. (P.B.)

fridge; frig or **frige** (all pron. *fridge*). A refrigerator: perhaps orig., as the first large-scale users, cafés' and restaurants', since ca. 1925; by 1950, at latest, gen. domestic coll. The first spelling has, since mid-1930s, been the predominant one in the British Commonwealth. (Prob. ex Frigidaire, the trade-name of one of the earliest makes; Raab.) Brooks, 1935.—2. Prison: Aus. Low: since ca. 1910. Cf. **freezer**, 2.

fried. Drunk: office-girls': late 1950s. See **honkers**.

fried egg. A company sergeant-major's badge: Army: ca. 1930–50.

fried eggs. Legs: Aus r.s. (A.A. Martin, letter, 1937.)—2. Underdeveloped female breasts: Aus. male: since ca. 1930.

friendly hostile. An enemy aircraft that doesn't attack: RN: WW2. P-G-R.

frig, n. 'Any military operation, from an exercise to a battle. "What time does the frig start?" ' (P-G-R): Army: WW2. Prob. ex *frig about*.—2. See **fridge**.

frig, v.t., i., refl. To masturbate: from ca. 1590: low coll. The imperative with *it* is late C.19–20, occ. an exclam.: cf. *fuck it!* Ex L. *fricare*, to rub.—2. Hence, loosely, to copulate with: mid-C.19–20.—3. Hence, in RAF (since ca. 1935), to fix; e.g. fuses could be so 'frigged' that they would never blow.

friggypoo. Pretentious nonsense; a big, ill-based piece of boasting: since ca. 1950. (Granville, 1974.) A blend of the contemptuous *pooh* and *friggy*, suggesting *fuck-all*, nothing.

frighten the living daylights (or **the shit**) **out of** (someone). To scare badly: coll. and low: C.19–20. Var. *scare the . . .* : id. (P.B.)

frightener. A scare: since ca. 1930. 'I'd been terrified . . . , but once I'd got over the first frightener I sort of liked it' (Cunliffe, 1965). Cf.:-

frighteners on, put the. To scare (someone): low: since ca. 1930. Norman.

frightening powder. A stern warning: police: since ca. 1930. Fabian, 1954, describes it as 'private police slang'. Cf. prec.

frightfully fright, (just too). Applied to someone absolutely bursting with conceit, or overwhelmingly upper-class and 'county'; also occ. of tasteless decorations overdone: coll.: mid-C.20. (P.B.)

frill. A girl; a woman: from ca. 1933; by 1950, †. Brandon, 1934, 'The hen, the frill—the skirt!'

frilled lizard. 'A man with a whisker-framed face' (B., 1942): Aus. Family likeness.

fringer. One who wears side-whiskers only, or moustache and side-whiskers: beatniks': since ca. 1959. Anderson.

frippet; usu. *a bit of frippet*. A young lady: military (officers'): from ca. 1933. Origin? Also among Leeds undergraduates for a townsman (or -woman): since ca. 1940. (Marples, 2.) 'Might this be a conflation of Lancashire *frip* ['anything worthless or trifling': *EDD*]—cf. **fripping**—and **snippet**?' (R.S.)

fripping. Bickering; a more or less continuous irritation, petty quarrelling, esp. between husband and wife: Society and middle-class: since ca. 1919. (Maugham, 1921.) Perhaps 'tearing things to tatters'.

frisk for. To take from (the person): c. Cowan, 1937, 'You have to keep your eye open for some cop who'll frisk you for a quid or threaten to take you up.'

frisking. Preliminary petting: Aus.: since ca. 1930.

fritter. Bacon-rind and/or bacon-fat wrapped up in rag to serve as a fire-lighter: tramps' c.

frivols. Frivolities: since ca. 1920.

friz, frizz. A female member of a show or carnival: Can. carnival s.: since ca. 1920. Ex frizzed hair.—2. (Always *frizz*.) A 'flap', a panic: mostly theatrical: since ca. 1930. Coward, 1952.

frock. A man wearing a frock-coat, i.e., a civilian in authority: coll.: earlier C.20; ob. with the decline of widespread use of the garment. Hart, 1970. (P.B.)

frog. A Frenchman (also *Froggy*): from ca. 1790.—2. Hence, the French language: since (?)ca. 1940. In Thomas, 1978 (an espionage novel): minor agent to a major one: 'You're the only one whose Frog is good enough for this, sir.'—3. Abbr. earlier r.s. *frog and toad*, road: tramps' c., then gen. among users of r.s.—4. A £1 note: Aus.: since ca. 1910. (Palmer, 1931; B., 1942.) A shortening of the Aus. r.s. *frog-skin = sovrin* = £1: late C. 19–early 20.—5. A condom: mainly Aus.: since ca. 1925. E.P. noted 'prompted by **Frenchy**, 1', but more prob. merely an abbr. of *frog-skin*, a condom. (P.B.)

frog in the throat. A boat: r.s. (B. & P.) Ex:—In *have a frog in* (one's or) *the throat*, to have phlegm in the throat; hoarseness: coll.: (?)mid-C.19–20.

frog-skin. £1: Aus. See **frog**, 4.—2. A condom: orig. mainly Aus., since ca. 1925; Brit. by ca. 1950, at latest. (B., 1943; P.B.)

frog-spawn. Tapioca: Public Schoolboys': since ca. 1890. Spencer Chapman, 1949.

Froggie, -y. A 'French letter', a condom: RN: since ca. 1910.

frog's eyes. Boiled sago: Aus.: since ca. 1910. B., 1953.

from here on in. Brit. var., and more immediate than:-

from there on in. From this, or that, point forward: coll., perhaps mostly Can., but not unknown elsewhere: since ca. 1925. 'I'll get the thing set up for you, and you can play it from there on in.' (Leechman.)

front, n. Bearing, deportment; style: coll.:—1923 (Manchon); also, since ca. 1930, Aus. (B., 1942.) Cf. S.E. *front*, self-confidence, effrontery; and see AUSTRALIAN UNDERWORLD, in Appx.—2. The scene of a thief's operations: c.: anglicised ca. 1929 from US. (Franklyn, 1934.) Ex shop-*fronts*. P.B.:?or from the various *front*-lines of the then recent Great War.—3. A large diamond tie-pin or ring (usu. genuine) worn by vaudevillians to indicate prosperity: Can.: since ca. 1930.—4. The seemingly legitimate or respectable façade of actually criminal or radical organisations: Can., ex US, hence also Brit.: since late 1940s.—5. As *the front*, it = the main road or street of a Teddy-boy gang's district: Teddy boys': late 1940s and 1950s. *Observer*, 1 Mar. 1959.—6. As *the Front*, Piccadilly: male prostitutes' and homosexuals': since ca. 1945. (Sharpley, 1964.) Cf. **the Dilly**.—7. Also *the Front*, Oxford Street, London: later C.20. Powis.—8. In *at the front*, 'When one drug is taken before another' (Home Office): drug addicts': 1970s.

front, v. To cover the operations of an associate pickpocket: c.:—1879; ob. in Brit., but still extant in Aus., mid-1940s (B., letter, 1946).—2. V.i. and t., to break in by the *front* door: c.:—1933. (Leach.) Vbl n., *fronting*.—3. To go in front of (someone), to be reprimanded (by him): Aus. coll.: since ca. 1930. Tennant, 1953.—4. (V.i.) To appear in public, esp. if conspicuously; to turn up: Aus. teenagers': since late 1940s. *Pix*, 28 Sep. 1963.—5. To *front* a band, esp. in the big-band era of the 1930s, is—'often with little skill, but with a winning personality'—to be, or to be made, leader of a band: Can. jazz-men's: since the late 1920s. (Priestley.)—6. See **front**, n., 4: to serve as, to operate, such a façade: since ca. 1950. Often to *front as* (whatever the cover chosen). Cf. sense 1.

front man. A go-between, e.g. one who deals with a job-lot buyer for the principal in a **long firm** *fraud* [q.v.]: c. and police s.: since ca. 1930. *Underworld*; Powis.—2. He who lures the victim into a crooked game of cards: Aus. c.: since ca. 1935. (B., 1953.) Also, by ca. 1940, Eng. c. and, by 1950, police s. (Gosling, 1959.) Also known as a *psyche man*—he needs to use psychology. Cf. **front up**.

front money. 'Money in advance to pay for drugs' (Stockley, 1986): drugs c. US since—1969 (Spears).

front stuff. A smart appearance designed esp. to impress either prospective dupes or one's companions: low: since ca. 1930. See **front**, n., 1.

front suspension. A brassière: Aus., esp. mechanics': since ca. 1930.

front the bull. To face a charge: Aus. Army: WW2. (B., 1943.) Cf. **front**, v., 3.

front up. (Usu. with *to* or *before*.) To appear, on interview or 'orders', before one's officer commanding: Army: later C.20. (P.B.)—2. See MOCK AUCTION in Appx.

front-wheel skid. A Jew: r.s., on *Yid*: not very gen.: since ca. 1920. (Franklyn, 2.) Hence, 'front-wheeler' (Powis, 1977). The term is 'intentionally more offensive than five-to-two' (Daniells, 1980).

frontsman. See MOCK AUCTION, in Appx.

frosty-faced. Scowling, sour-faced: coll.

frosty Friday. 'A most unusual day. "What? Go out with him? That'll be a frosty Friday!" ' (Leechman): Can.: since ca. 1940. R.C., 1976, suggests, 'Prob. an elaboration of the US "It'll be a mighty cold day before I'll . . . "—meaning, essentially, never.'

frot. To rub against another person for sexual stimulation, often surreptitiously, e.g. in a dense crowd: literate low. *Observer*, 11 Feb. 1973, film review: 'These transvestites, nymphos, junkies are in hell. They frot and turn on—take drugs—to give them[selves] the illusion of living, the shadow of happiness'. P.B.: I first heard the term in Hong Kong in mid-1960s; it may have arrived ex US. Ex Fr. (*se*) *frotter*, and the agent *frotteur*. (Partly R.S.) See also **bustle-punching**.

froth bugle. A condom: RN: since ca. 1920.

frothblower. A certain type (Fowler Class 5 M.T.) of tender-engine: railwaymen's: since ca. 1925(?). *Railway*.

frozen limit, the. The utter limit of the obnoxious or the intolerable: coll.: from ca. 1915. ('Taffrail', 1916.) Cf. **the dizzy**, or *giddy*, **limit**. See **limit, the**.

frozen mit (or **mitt**), **get** or **give the.** To receive or apply the 'cold shoulder': coll.: adopted ex US early C.20. *Punch*, 7 July 1915: 'Begging for leave to do [their] bit/And getting for [their] pains the frozen mit.' F. & G. has **mitt**.

frozen on the stick. Paralysed with fear: airmen's from ca. 1925. (*Daily Herald*, 1 Aug 1936; Jackson.) Prob. the 'joy-stick' of an aeroplane is implied.

fruit. An obviously homosexual (passive) male: orig. c., adopted ca. 1937 ex US; >, by ca. 1960, gen. low coll.—2. A term of address among Teddy boys: since ca. 1954. Gilderdale, 2: 'Anyone may be a fruit, though it often denotes class. One Ted told me: "To a City chap—all stuck with his umbrella—we call out " 'ello, me ol' lemon." ' See **old fruit**.

fruit machine. An anti-aircraft predictor: AA crews': WW2. (H. & P.) Ex its appearance, akin to the coin-operated gambling machine, as is:—2. An electrical calculator used in radar: RAF: 1942–6. Hence also:—3. Any prediction device: RN, esp. among submariners: WW2. Jenkins, 1959.—4. See **gooseberries**.

fruit salad. 'A large collection of medal ribbons which runs to three or more rows' (H. & P.): Services', esp. the RAF: since ca. 1919. As worn on the left breast, where they made a colourful display. P.B.: by 1950, Services' gen. of any largish display of medal ribbons, not necessarily as many as three rows.

fruitie, -y, n. Port (wine). Bennett, 1919.—2. A desirable girl; one's girl: 'heard among infantry officers, Hong Kong, mid-1960s' (P.B., 1974): characteristic of that decade; cf. the earlier **popsie**.

fruity, adj. Amorous: raffish: since ca. 1955. Thomas, 1976.

fruppencies. Female breasts: r.s., *threepenny bits* on *tits*: later C.20. Daniells, 1980.

fry. 'If the "mike" should begin "frying" or picking up camera noises, "Sound" in his "ice box" (so called because it is usually very hot inside the glass-fronted booth) would soon protest to the "slinger" (or microphone operator)' (*Evening News*, 7 Nov. 1939): cinema: since ca. 1930.

fu-fu. See entries at **foo-foo . . .**

fuck, n. An act of sexual connexion: from ca. 1800. (Ex the v.)—2. A person (rarely of the male) viewed in terms of coïtion, as in 'She's a good f.': C.19–20. These two senses are excellent examples of vulgarism, being actually S.E.—3. The seminal fluid, esp. if viewed as providing the requisite strength (*full of fuck*, potently amorous): low coll.: C.19–20.—4. In such intensive phrases as 'Get to fuck out of here!', *fuck* is apparently a n.: low: late C.19–20.—5. See **create fuck**, to make a considerable fuss, usu. in protest at something.—6. Cf. *like fuck!*, 'certainly not!'; see also **is it fuck!**

fuck, v.t. and i. To have sexual connection (with): v.i. of either sex, v.t. only of the male: a vulg., C.16–20.—2. See **fuck off**, and **fuck you!**

fuck about factor. See **F.A.F.**

fuck all. A low var. of *damn all*: nothing: late C.19–20. Sometimes, sarcastically, *sweet fuck all*.

fuck arse. A low term of contempt.

fuck-dust. Term of (usu.) genial abuse: barrack-room and factory-floor: since early 1930s. Cf. **spunk-dust**. (P.B.)

fuck-in-a-fog. A low, joc. var. of the flower name love-in-a-mist. (P.B.)

fuck-knuckle. An Aus. coarse ref., often not unkind—though usu. implying stupidity, by one man of another: heard early 1960s. (P.B.)

fuck like a mink. (Of a woman, 'she fucks . . . ') amorous and promiscuous: Can.: since ca. 1920. Cf.:-

fuck like a rattlesnake. (Of the male) to coït vigorously: low Aus.: from ca. 1895. As there are no rattlesnakes in Aus., the phrase would seem to be of N. Am. orig. Cf. **mad as a cut snake**, q.v. The Brit. version, since mid-C.20, is *shag like a . . .* Cf.:-

fuck like a stoat. Synon. with the prec., but Eng. in origin and UK in distribution. Raper, 1973, remarked, à propos WW2, 'Both of these phrases were used to describe the sexual activities of women rather than men'; in Aus., however, the *rattlesnake* var. was, during WW1 anyway, applied more commonly to men.

fuck me! An often wry or semi-humorous expletive, common—in all senses: since late C.19. Since ca. 1950, it has often evoked the responses *not now* or *later* or *no thanks!*

fuck me and the baby's yours! Elab. of prec.: 'exclam. of astonishment, surprise, disbelief' (L.A.): low: since ca. 1930.

fuck me gently or **pink!** Exclamations of surprise or wonderment: since ca. 1920, 1910, resp.

fuck my luck! Oh, what a pity!: Services': since ca. 1940.

fuck off. To depart, make off: low: late C.19–20. Cf. **bugger off, piss off**.—2. Esp. in the imperative: id.

fuck-pump. A married man; envy felt by unmarried men: low and joc.: since ca. 1950. (L.A., 1976.)

fuck up, v.i.; hence **fuck up**, n. To fail dismally: low: since ca. 1930. N. in *make a fuck-up of*, to fail miserably at, or to spoil utterly. Cf. **make a balls(-up) of**.

fuck-wit (or written solid). 'A general-purpose pej.; a "nitwit" ' (B.P., 1977): Aus. low: since late 1940s. Poss. a blend of *fuck all*, nothing, + *nitwit*.

fuck you! The natural correlative of *fuck that!*, applied to a person: since (?)latish C.19. The strongest of low condemnations, and never meant lit., it = *confound*, or *damn, you!*, and may of course be applied to *him, her*, a person's name—and *fuck 'em all*.

fucked in the car and **fucked without getting kissed**; both connote that 'someone has done something to you that you did not deserve': Can.: since ca. 1950, if not rather earlier.

fucking arseholes!; fucking hell! Exclamations of incredulous, dismayed, surprise or anger: low. Often reduced to *'kin' arse'oles!* and *'kin' 'ell!* (L.A.; P.B.)

fucking the dog; occ. elab. to *fornicating the poodle*. Irritating and senseless occupation: Can. soldiers'.—2. Hence, the avoidance of work by appearing to be busy at a useless task: Can.: since ca. 1920.

fuddy-duddy, esp. 'an old . . . '; **fuddy-dud**. A fussy, old-fashioned, narrow-minded person; an 'old woman': coll.: adopted, ca. 1944, ex US.—The latter term, mostly Aus., arose derivatively ca. 1955. *Fuddy-duddy* may blend *fussy* + *fogey*, influenced by s. *dud*, an insufficient person; or it may be an altered reduplication of that *dud*.

fudge. 'Late News' column: journalists': since ca. 1920. (Hume, 1942.) 'The source, I suggest, is the journalists' jargon *fudge-box*, found on the front pages of afternoon papers at least as late as 1930s. This was an area printed solid black . . . into which the latest [sporting] results could be stamped with a punch—thereby avoiding the remaking of the entire page' (R.C., 1976).

fuff. 'Fake snow for wintertime effects' (Green, 1984): television s.

fug box. 'A saloon car: motorcyclists' derogatory' (Dunford): since (?)ca. 1930.

fug pants. Thick winter underwear: RN: since ca. 1925, or perhaps earlier. Granville.

fugleman. The strong-arm man of a gang or of a racket; a petty gangster: Aus. c.: since ca. 1945. (B., 1953.) Perhaps ex old s., to cheat, trick; or ex † S.E. *fugleman*, that soldier from whom the others take their time in drill movements. (R.S.)

Führer's boys, the. The German armed forces: RN officers': WW2.

Fujiama. Telegraphese for 'Fuck (or, more politely, flip) U Jack I am all right'. Mays, 1971, writing of the late 1930s Post Office.

full. 'Full of drugs' (Home Office): addicts': 1970s.

full as, (as). Some synon. for drunk: *as full as a boot* (Aus.: since ca. 1925. Niland, 1955); . . . *a bull* (NZ. Slatter); . . . *an egg* (Aus.: since ca. 1925); . . . *a fiddler's fart* (Aus.: 1950s. Slater); . . . *a goog* (Aus.: since ca. 1925. Baker. *Goog* = egg); . . . *a tick* (Aus. and Brit.: since ca. 1890. Joyce, 1922). Replete with food (and usu. drink as well): *as full as an egg*. (Brit.: coll. rather than s.)

full bang. Esp. *go . . .* , (to go) at full speed or as quickly as possible: coll.:—1923 (Manchon).

full belt, at. At full volume or speed: coll.: since ca. 1960. Cf. **full bore** and **full bottle**.

full blast, at or **in.** Very active; highly successful; (hard) at work: coll.:—1859. Orig. North Country and ex the engine-room, esp. furnaces. P.B.: in later C.20, of, e.g., broadcasting equipment, usu. *at full blast*, or simply *going full blast*. Cf. **full bottle**, 2.

full bore. At full speed: RAF coll.: since ca. 1925. Jackson, 'Thus, "I went after him full bore" '; Brickhill, 1946. Ex motoring coll. (dating from ca. 1918).

full bottle. Expert; of reliable authority: Aus. coll.: since ca. 1950. 'He's a full bottle on the neddies.' (Raab.)—2. In *at full bottle*, at full volume or speed: Cockneys': since ca. 1950. 'Screeching away at full bottle' (Daniells, 1977).

full chat, at. At full speed: racing motorists': since ca. 1950.

full colonel. A colonel, or that rank, as opp. to 'half-colonel'(= lieutenant-colonel): Army: later C.20. On analogy with *full corporal*, as opp. to *lance-corporal*. (P.B.)

full deck, in *not to have a*, or *not playing from a*. To be of less than average intelligence: Can.: later C.20. (Leech, 1986.)

full hand, a. Syphilis and gonorrhœa simultaneously: Aus. B., 1942.—2. A life sentence: low Aus.: since ca. 1920. Tennant, 1953.

full house. A busy time: coll.: from ca. 1925. (Blaker, 1934, 'Sunday nights were, perhaps, the fullest house.') Ex *full*

house notices at places of indoor entertainment.—2. A mixed grill (dish): RN: since ca. 1930. Granville.—3. 'A double dose of V.D., syphilis and gonorrhœa together: Merchant (and, I think, Royal) Navy: since ca. 1930' (Peppitt)—if not a decade, even a generation, earlier, and usage not confined to mariners. Cf. **full hand.** Of senses 2 and 3, Peppitt remarks, 1976, 'A general RN and MN term for a complete set of anything [either] particularly pleasant or particularly unpleasant.'—4. To sense 3, Powis adds: 'To have more than one form of body infestation with parasites, e.g., both head and body lice': low: later C.20.

full moon. Bare or displayed buttocks: raffish. (Leech, 1972.) Cf. **moon,** v.

full of beans. Vigorous; energetic; in high spirits: from ca. 1870. (H., 5th ed.) Cf. *beany,* synon. but, by mid-C.20, †, whereas *full of beans* is still going strong, 1988.

full of piss and vinegar. Robust in health, and full of energy: low Can. In Can., as in US, *vinegar* has a sexual connotation.

full quid. Having all one's faculties: Aus.: since ca. 1920 until change to decimal currency. B., 1959, adds: 'A person . . . *ten bob in the quid* or any smaller sum down to *tuppence in the quid,* is held to be stupid.' Also, since ca. 1925, NZ, esp. in 'He's *not the full quid*', mentally defective. (Griffiths.)

full sail. Whiskers and beard, the 'full set': RN. *Evening News* (London), 25 Feb. 1936.

full to the guards. Dead drunk: nautical. (McFee, 1930.) Ex nautical j.: lit., full to the top of a vessel.

full up. Dead: taxi-drivers':—1935. Ex taxi-driving.

full up to (the) dolly's wax. Replete with food: Aus. (?esp. Tasmania). Perhaps from the days when little girls' dolls had head and shoulders made of wax, surmounting bodies of cloth and stuffing.

fullies. Women's drawers that are very full: feminine coll.: from 1933. See quot'n at **neathie-set.**

Fuming Freddie. Fiumefreddo, a Sicilian township, a Calabrian village: Army in Sicily and Italy: 1943–5.

fumtu. *F*ouled, *F*rigged or *F*ucked *u*p *m*ore *t*han *u*sual: Army: 1940–5. P-G-R.

fun, adj. Amusing; interesting; of anything that would be fun to do, or see, or wear, etc., e.g. 'a fun dress', 'having a fun time': coll.: since ca. 1975. ?Ex US. (P.B.)

fun and frolics. Testicles. See **flowers and . . .**

fun and games. A (very) agreeable time: middle-class coll.: since ca. 1921.—2. Hence, 'any sort of brush with the enemy at sea' (P-G-R): RN officers': WW2. *Fun and games* is often used in this ironic sense in later C.20. Contrast:—3. Love-making, esp. intercourse: since ca. 1925. A specialisation of sense 1.

Fun City. 'Bletchley, Bucks—a town based on a railway shed and marshalling yard' (McKenna, 1970): railwaymen's ironic.

fun of Cork, the. A very 'good time': Aus. (B., 1942.) Adopted from Irish immigrants.

fundy (or **Fundy**), n. and adj. A Fundamentalist, a believer in the literal truth of the Bible; the adj. therefrom: used by several of the other intolerant sects that form the Christian church. (P.B.)

fungus(-)features. 'A man with a heavy beard' (Leech, 1972): since ca. 1950. Cf. **features.**

funk. With derivative adj. *funky;* the same as *funky music,* 'having an earthy, unsophisticated style and feeling; esp., having the style and feeling of the blues, a melancholy kind of song and music (of American Negro origin)': the n., at first among Negro jazz musicians mid-1950s; adopted in Britain ca. 1960. The adj., since ca. 1958 in US and since early 1960s in Britain, yet not at all gen. until 1964. (*Beatles;* Janssen, 1976; W. & F.) 'The first time I saw [the 'Talking Heads'] was . . . in November of 1977 . . . They were making sounds that were tuneful . . . The music was—I had to reach back three or four years to find the correct usage—it was . . . by Christ! It was *funky!*' (Dadomo, 1979).

Funk Express, the. 'Used during WW2 for the train carrying well-off dodgers from bombed areas to places like Devon and Cornwall' (Petch, 1974).

funk(-)stick. In gen. coll., a person cowardly or very timorous; in Servicemen's usage, a malingerer, a shirker: early C.20. (Mason, 1930; Crozier, 1937.) Ex **funksticks,** q.v.

funk 'um. A bag of lavender carried by a beggar more as pretence than as merchandise: c. (Harrison, 1935.) Ex C.18 *funk,* v., to stink; *'um = 'em,* them.—2. Hence, any perfume as merchandise: grafters': from ca. 1910. *Cheapjack,* 1934.—3. Hence, ironically, a fart. Often in pl., as in 'Who's made the funkums?' or 'Who's done the funkums?': market-traders'. *M.T.*

funksticks. One who fears the fences (*sticks*): hunting: 1889. *OED.*

funky. Horribly smelly; stinking. Hence n., a smelly man, often elab. to *funky Willie.* Both: market-traders'. (*M.T.*)—2. Pertaining to *funk,* or *funky music.* See **funk.**—3. Hence, alert, 'with it' or 'groovy', fashionable: adopted ex US ca. 1974, mostly by teenagers, addicts, 'drop-outs', *et hoc genus omne.*

funnel fever is the demobitis (1945+)—or restlessness—of soldiers overseas: Army: perhaps not before 1946. The funnels of the homebound troopship. P.B.: troopships were superseded by aircraft in the late 1950s—but 'plane fever' still continued to afflict Servicemen nearing the end of an overseas tour. Cf. the **gate fever** of a prisoner nearing the end of his sentence.

funnies, the. 'Armoured vehicles used for purposes which had hitherto been unorthodox' (P-G-R): Army: ca. 1942–5.—2. See **funny,** n., 2.

funny, n. In filmland, the comic man is called *the funny:* since ca. 1910. McCabe, 1937.—2. A comic (magazine or newspaper): Can.: since ca. 1920. (*Evening News* (London), 9 Jan. 1940.) Usu. as *the funnies,* which in UK, since ca. 1946, = the comic strips in a newspaper.—3. A joke; a funny story: Aus., since ca. 1950; Brit., since perhaps a little later. Hamilton, 1967, ' "What makes you say that?" "Nothing. Just trying to make a funny." '—4. (Usu. pl.) An intelligence officer: 'Most senior British policemen are not of the generation to use too much American slang. In their parlance, intelligence officers are not spooks, they are funnies. The funnies are funny because they are not officially supposed to exist' (*Observer,* 17 Jan. 1988).

funny, adj. In *get* or *turn funny,* to feel—esp. to show that one feels—offended: coll. Cf. **nasty.**

funny as a piece of string(, as). Very humorous, esp. of a situation or an incident: NZ: since ca. 1930. (Griffiths, 1970.) Often ironic.

funny business. A shady transaction, dubious dealing; monkeying about: s. >, ca. 1930, coll.: from ca. 1890. Ex a clown's *funny business.* Cf. the US *phoney business.*

funny-face. A joc. term of address: coll.: late C.19–20. Cf. **face-ache.**

funny farm. A mental hospital or institution: since ca. 1970. (R.S.) Cf. *loony bin.*

funny fellows (or **-ers**). Policemen, esp. the college-trained ones: London, esp. children's: since ca. 1935. (Langford, 1941.)

funny(-)money. See **mad money,** 2.—2. Counterfeit money, esp. notes: since ca. 1960 or a little earlier.—3. Hence, derogatorily, any foreign notes or coins, even Scottish notes, Channel Islands' coinage, etc. Cf. **mickey mouse money.**—4. 'A reference to the theories of the Social Credit Party' (B.P., 1974): Aus.: since ca. 1955.

furfie, -y. A rumour. See **furphy.**

Furibox. The aircraft carrier *Furious:* RN: WW2. Granville.

furk!; furking. Euph. var. (—1923) of *fuck (it)!* and *fucking.* Manchon.

furph. A shortening, since ca. 1925 (B., 1943) of:–

furphy; incorrectly **furphie, furfie** or **-y.** A false report, an absurd story: Aus. military: from early 1915. Ex *Furphy*, the contractor supplying rubbish-carts to the camps at Melbourne. (Dennis, 1916; B. & P.) Or perhaps rather ex the tall stories told by Joseph Furphy (1843–1913), the 'Tom Collins' who wrote *Such Is Life*, 1903.

further behind than Walla Walla. 'Delayed, at a disadvantage (from place-name, with implication of remoteness)' (Wilkes): Aus. coll.

fusilier. Penis: Army: earlier C.20. Cf. **Skin-Back Fusiliers**. (L.A., 1977.)—2. See **McAlpine Fusilier**.

fuss-box. A post-1910, mostly upper-class var. of older *fuss-pot* (*OED* Sup.). Cf. US *fuss-budget*, popularised by Charles Schulz in his 'Peanuts' cartoon-strips (P.B.).

fuzz, (the). The police: adopted, in Can., by late 1950s, and in Brit. by ca. 1964, ex US. Perhaps ex the *fuzzy* or very hairy faces of old-style policemen; but more prob. from certain furry growths of parasitic mould.

fuzz-ball. (Or written solid.) A fart, as in 'someone's dropped a fuzz-ball'; often in pl., 'Who's made the fuzz-balls?': market-traders'. *M.T.*

fuzz jar. A police car: motorcylists': since late 1960s. (Dunford.) Ex *fuzz*, and abbr. *jam-jar*, r.s. = car.

fuzz-spotter. Rear-view mirror: id.: Ibid.

Fuzzgug, Mr or **Mrs.** John or Jane Doe, the ordinary citizen: Aus.: since ca. 1930. (B.P.) Arbitrary.

Fuzzy-Wuzzy. A Papuan: Aus: since ca. 1918. Cf.:–

Fuzzy-Wuzzy Angels. New Guinea men carrying Allied wounded to safety over the Owen Stanley Mountains: mostly Aus.: 1942–5.

fyfas, often, erroneously, written **fifas;** or with capital letters. *Fuck Yourself For A Start* (or *Starter*): orig. in a certain Brit. unit, during the latter half of WW2. Later it enjoyed more widespread use in the Services, mostly, of course, as a conversational 'opener'.

G

G. Abbr. **grand**, 2: £1000. Cf. **K.** in this sense.

G.A.B.A See **Gaba**.

g. and d. *G*uts (courage) and *d*etermination: professional tennis-players' coll.: since ca. 1970. *The Times*, 8 Nov. 1975, 'his stock of "G" and "D" (the trade abbreviation . . .)'.

g.b.c. A *g*old-*b*raid *c*haser, i.e. a 'Wren' (WRNS) rating who dates only RN officers: since ca. 1950 (Peppitt)—but I think, since early 1940s. Perhaps suggested by *GCB*, the sailors' Good Conduct Badge, as Peppitt suggests—or by ironic allusion to another interpretation, (Knight of the) Grand Cross of the Bath, as I propose.

G.B.P. The *G*reat *B*ritish *P*ublic: often used ironically: since ca. 1950, or perhaps earlier. Cf. **B.P.** (P.B.)

G.C.M. '[The director] used to call me Stratford [Theatre]'s Head Boy and I was always the GCM, Good Company Man, leading the team out to bat in whatever was in the repertoire that season' (Holm, 1981): theatrical: later C.20.

G.C.M.G. See **C.M.G.**

G five. 'A beard cut to resemble that of King George V' (Granville): RN: since very soon after date (1910) of his accession to the throne; by 1950, ob.

G.G., the. The *G*overnor-*G*eneral: Aus. and NZ coll.: late C.19–20. B., 1941.

G.I. An American soldier (not an officer): adopted in 1943 from US. R.C., 1976: '*could* be '*G*overnment *I*ssue''—but *not*, as I've seen reputably proposed, *g*alvanised *i*ron, as in garbage can.'

g.i.b. *G*ood *i*n *b*ed. See **good-oh**, adj.

g.m.f.u. 'Major organisational disaster' (*Sunday Express* mag., 11 Oct. 1982): Sloane Rangers' [q.v.]. Ex **I.M.F.U.**, q.v.; here *g* prob. = 'grand *or* greatest'

g.m.t. *G*ood *m*issionary *t*raining; e.g., eating unappetising meals cheerfully, as a good preparation for what a missionary might be called upon to stomach 'in heathen lands afar'—or, more politely, among Christians of other cultures: students', at Selly Oak (Birmingham) theological colleges: early 1960s. (D. Beale.) A pun on rather better known *G*reenwich *m*ean *t*ime.

g.o.F. *G*ood *o*ld *F*riday: schoolteachers': earlier C.20. Cf. *t.G.i.F.*, the 'Thank God it's Friday', so popular in the 1970s.

G.P.; the Street. *G*reat *P*ortland Street, London; esp., the car-mart there: motor-trade s., now (mid-1930s) verging on coll.: from ca. 1928. Blaker, 1934, 'Great Portland Street—"The Street" one and only and unmistakable; "G.P."—the street of perdition.'

G.P.I. Eccentricity; (extreme) folly: medical students': earlier C.20. Ex its lit. sense, *G*eneral *P*aralysis of the *I*nsane.

g.p. on, have a. To be much in love with (someone): ca. 1905–40. I.e. *grande passion*.

g.r.f. *G*ood *r*ough *f*ucking. 'Based on estate agents' *g.r.s.* (good rough shooting) and applied to any enthusiastic but [maladroit] girl viewed as a sexual partner. First heard in 1942' (R.S., 1973).

G.S. Keen; esp., excessively keen: Army: WW2+. Ex the '*G*eneral *S*ervice' so beloved of the army vocabulary, as 'caps, G.S., 1', and even, the GSM[edal].

G-string. See PRISONER-OF-WAR SLANG, 13, in Appx.—2. *Frenulum preputii*: low.

G.W.R. 'So strong is the affection [the Great Western Railway] engendered that [its] initials have been interpreted . . . as standing for . . . "Gone With Regret" ' (Aaron, 1982).

gab. Gaberdine: London clothes-dealers'. McShane, 1960.

gab-fest. A long conversation, e.g. an evening of talk (and drink): adopted, ca. 1955, ex US. Ex Ger. *Fest*, a feast.

Gaba. 'We fly over hundreds of miles of bush, scrubby gum-trees, dry paddocks, and salt flats. "That's it, mate," says [the pilot]. "GABA—Great Australian Bugger All" ' (Harding, 1981).

gaberdine! Excellent!: Londoners': since ca. 1918. It is prob. a pun on Fr. *très bien!*

gaberdine swine. 'Staff officers in Cairo, so christened by forward troops in the Western Desert' (P-G-R): ca. 1941–3. With a pun on Biblical *Gadarene swine*.

gad. A shirt: tramps' c.:—1923 (Manchon). Ex Romany.

gaff. A fair: c. of ca. 1750–1845. (*The Discoveries of John Poulter*, 1753.) Then grafters' s.: *Cheapjack*, 1934.—2. A house that is being 'drummed' (see **drum**, v., 1): c. (Hume.) Cf.:—3. The place or scene of the crime concerned: c. *Gilt Kid*, 1936.—4. An affair; a criminal enterprise: c.: from ca. 1920. Ibid.—5. Synon. with **gaffer**, 1. Can. carnival s.—6. A brothel: c. and low s.: since ca. 1920. *New Statesman*, 10 May 1947.—7. Home: c.: since ca. 1920. 'The most common prison word for a dwelling-place, house, or room. "They did him in his gaff" = they arrested him at home. "He screwed a gaff" = he robbed a house' (Tempest, 1950). Cf. sense 2.—8. A market: market-traders': late C.19–20. (*M.T.*) Ex the grafters' nuance of sense 1.

gaff joint. A game of chance where there is no chance of winning: Can. carnival. Contrast **legit joint**.

Gaff Street. Theatreland; more generally, the West End: London taxi-drivers': since ca. 1920. Hodge, 1938, where also: 'Before the theatres broke—or, as we say: the "gaffs burst"'.'

gaffer. The man who runs a gambling game or device: Can. carnival s.: earlier C.20.—2. Hence, the brake with which he stops the wheel, etc., at any desired number: id.—3. (As *the*

175

gaffer.) The officer commanding an HM ship: since the 1920s. Cf. much older sense, master or employer.—4. 'In the motion picture industry, the foreman electrician. This has long been US and Can., but prob. also UK' (R.C., 1976).

gag. To beg: tramps' c. Gape, 1936.

gag me with a spoon. Disgusting, no good: 'may refer to an object or a person, e.g. "Oh, you gag . . . "; usu. in ref. to personality, looks, etc.: strictly adolescents', adopted ex Californian teenager "Valley Girls": ephemeral, early 1980s' (Leech, 1986): Can.

gaga; incorrectly *ga-ga*. Evincing senile decay; stupidly dull, fatuous; 'soft', 'dotty'. Kipling used it twice, with the hyphen, in a letter dated 1 Dec. 1917 to Stanley Baldwin, quoted in Birkenhead, 1978. Adopted ex Fr. s. Often in the phrase, *go gaga*.—2. Galsworthy, 1926, uses it for 'strait-laced'.—3. Childish for *grandfather*. *Daily Telegraph* obituary, 7 Jan. 1974.

gage. A greengage plum: lower classes' coll.:—1923 (Manchon).—2. '(As in greengage). Cannabis. (US)' (Home Office): drug addicts': 1970s. US since —1944 (Spears).

gagger. To tell the pitiful tale: tramps' c.:—1932 (Jennings). Cf. **gag**, and:-

gagging lark. Unconcealed begging in the streets: c. (*Gilt Kid*, 1936.)

gaggle. A number of aircraft, e.g. 'a gaggle of Jerries': RN: WW2. Ex 'a *gaggle* of geese'.

gain. To obtain deviously or questionably: Leeds undergraduates':—1940 (Marples, 2). Cf. synon. s. use of *win*, **organise, liberate,** etc.

gaiters or **gaters.** Leg shields on a motorcycle: motorcyclists': since ca. 1950. (Dunford.)

gajo. An outsider: Parlyaree:—1933 (Seago). Ex Romany *gaujo*, a stranger.

galabieh. See **tighten** (one's) **galabieh**.

galah. A chap, fellow, 'bird': Aus. Drake-Brockman, 1940; *Rats*, 1944.—2. A simpleton, a fool: Aus.: since ca. 1930. (B., 1953.) It prob. derives 'from the old bush saying, "As mad as a treeful of galahs" ' (Marshall, 1962). A galah is 'a big pink-and-grey cockatoo' (Ibid.). Wilkes notes an app. more common version of the saying, 'mad as a gumtree full of galahs'.

galah session. 'An interval on the Flying Doctor radio network when anyone may come on to the air to exchange gossip' (Wilkes): Aus.: since mid-C.20.

gale fruit. Baked beans: RN: since ca. 1950. They cause farting. (Peppitt.) Only one of several such s. names for baked beans.

galley-slave. (Usu. in pl.) 'Cockroaches in the Sunday plum-duff; they turn white when cooked, and are not unpalatable' (R.S., 1967): MN.

galley-wireless. News of destination, etc.: nautical: from ca. 1925. Bowen remarks that it 'reaches the men from the officers by way of the stewards'.

gallop. See **raise a gallop** . . . , to have an erection.

gallop (one's) **antelope** or **maggot.** To masturbate: low; the first Cockneys', C.20, the second, gen., mid-C.19–20, and perhaps prompted by the older *get cockroaches*. Cf. synon. *jerk* (one's) *mutton* or *gherkin, pull* (one's) *pud(ding)* or *wire*. *Gallop* (one's) *antelope* occurs in Curtis, 1938.

gallopers. An occ. term for a respirator case: RAF: WW2. Cf. **goon-bag**.

galloping horses. The coat of arms on a warrant officer's lower sleeve: RAF: since ca. 1920. H. & P.—2. Hence, the WO himself: since ca. 1930. (Rhodes, 1942.) Cf. **fighting cats** and **Tate and Lyle**.

galloping irons. Spurs for riding: Can. joc.: since ca. 1930.

galloping knob-rot, (a touch of the). A phallic itch; a phrase often used 'in palliation of attempted alleviation' (a correspondent, 1967, who gave its milieu as RAF in Malta, since ca. 1955). The phrase was, in fact, quite widespread in the army also, over the same period. (P.B.)

galvo. Galvanised iron: Aus.: later C.20. (Wilkes.) By the Cockney > Aus. suffix *-o*.

gam. Abbr. *gamaroosh*: mostly Services', and taken by them world-wide. For instance, I heard a prostitute in Malaya, 1954, on being asked her charge, say, 'I no fuck. I holiday. But, I give you gam for ten bucks'. (P.B.) Roberts, 1983, notes that it now refers also to cunnilingus.—2. A sanitary tampon or pad: Aus. girls': since ca. 1950.

gamaroosh, -ruche, n. and, hence, v. (Of women.) (To practise) penilingism: late C.19–20 low. Ex Fr. (?ex Arabic).

game as a piss-ant(, as). 'Very brave or angry (Wilkes): Aus. coll.: since early C.20. By 1975 (Wilkes quotes Richard Beilby, *The Brown Land Crying*) elliptically, as in ' "Ho! Real piss-ant, ain't 'e," Bamma jeered. "I like ya, boy. Ya got guts." '

game as Ned Kelly(, as). Extremely brave; willing to tackle heavy odds: Aus.: late C.19–20. (B., 1942.) Ex the famous bushranger (1854–80), who held out against the police for two years.

game ball, adj. (predicatively). In good health or spirits or form: Anglo-Irish: since ca. 1940.

game sewn up, have the. To be in a position where one cannot lose; to have a monopoly; to be on a 'good thing': mostly Aus.: since ca. 1925. Ex games in which one side can hardly lose. 'Anyone who does not know this one is not an Australian' (B.P.).

gammon rasher. A 'smasher' = anything superlative: r.s. Hillman, 1974, notes, ' "Ennit a gammon rasher!" is used in appreciation of almost anything.'

gammy. False, spurious; forged: c.:—1839 (Brandon). Hence:—2. Of low quality, as in *gammy gear*, inferior goods: market-traders': late C.19–20. *M.T.*

gamo or, phonetically, **gammo.** Var. of *gamaroosh*: since ca. 1915.

gander. A look through the mail, or over another's shoulder at a letter or a newspaper: Services', esp. (orig.) RAF: since 1941 (H. & P.). In post-war years, e.g., *let's have a gander* meant 'let's have a look at' anything, not necessarily a document; by analogy with *a butcher's* or *a dekko*. The term and phrase are now, 1983, ob. Adopted ex US: cf. US *rubberneck*—the gander is a long-necked bird. (E.P.; P.B.)

Gandhi's revenge. Matches that, made in India, would, when struck, either ignite explosively or lose their heads: RAF: ca. 1935–48. The Mahatma Gandhi (1869–1948) preached a passive resistance.—2. Synon. with **ring-burn,** q.v.: later C.20. (Seabrook, 1986.) Prob. analogous with, e.g. *Montezuma's revenge*. May also be used in ref. to the curry itself, e.g. 'the prawn vindaloo's a Gandhi's revenge job!' (Turner, 1986). Soon generalised to cover any 'incapacitating stomach upset caused by food poisoning [abroad]' (*Times*, 12 May 1988).

gandy dancer. 'A section hand on the railway; the "gandy dance" is the vigorous exercise indulged in when tamping ties—that is tamping ballast under the sleepers with a spade or shovel. US and Can. railwaymen's: 1908+.' (Leechman.) Ex US c., of unknown origin. Adopted by Brit. railwaymen, mid-C.20 (McKenna).

gang, v.t. from the next entry. L.A. cites Richard Allen, *Boot Boys*, 1972, where a multiple rape is threatened as revenge on, or punishment of, a girl, by a group of teenage louts: 'We'll . . . gang her . . . '

gang-bang or **-fuck** or **-shag.** One girl serving many males in succession: the first Brit., the second mostly Can.; first and third Aus.: mostly teenage gangsters' and mentally retardeds': since ca. 1950, 1st and 3rd; 2nd perhaps two or three decades earlier. *Gang-bang* occurs in *New Society*, 2 July 1963. Cf. **back-up,** 1, and **pig-party**.—2. Powis, 1977, defines *gang-bang*: 'Depraved sexual orgy between several pairs, or a violent multi-rape of one female: also in a humorous ironic sense of, say, a garden party or a vicarage fete—"a real gang-bang".'

gang up on (someone). (Of a group of people) to make a 'dead set' at (someone), esp. in opposition: coll.: since late 1940s. Chambers' *C.20th Dict.*, 1972 ed.

ganja, ganga, gunja. Cannabis: orig. Anglo-Indian drug addicts': since ca. 1920. Ex Hindi. By 1970s, the Home Office could ascribe it to West Indians, using the 2nd spelling; Powis uses 1st and 3rd. (P.B.)

gannet. Orig. nautical coll. for a greedy seaman, mid-C.19–20 (Bowen), the term had, by mid-C.20 at latest, spread to the other Services, and from them into occ. gen. usage. (P.B.) Ex the bird of voracious habits.

gantry. 'The area behind the bar where spirit bottles are displayed or mounted on optics. The term is also applied to the range of spirits, especially malt whiskies, available in a particular pub: "The wee Vicky Bar's got a crackin gantry" ' (Munro, 1985): Glasgow.

gaol-bait, (usu. **jail**). A girl under sixteen (the age of consent): Can., adopted ex US ca. 1940; by ca. 1950, known and used in Britain also.

gap, n. The cleavage between the female breasts: Aus. motor mechanics' and car fanatics': since ca. 1945. Ex the gap of a spark plug.—2. In *take the gap*, earlier, to leave a party early while the going is good; later to emigrate from Zimbabwe/Rhodesia to S. Africa, esp. after the election which brought Mr Mugabe to power in Mar. 1980. Also *gap it*. The *Listener*, 6 Mar. 1980. John Cartwright, of Cape Town, suggests ex a Rugby football term.

gap, v. To make gaps in (wire obstacles): Army coll. > j.: WW2. P-G-R.

gap it. See **gap**, n., 2.

garage band. 'A musical group whose enthusiasm far outweighs their technical ability. [Ex] domestic garage for car storage, a popular rehearsal location for young, amateur groups' (Hibbert, 1983): suffering audiences'.

Garbo. In *do a Garbo*, to avoid Press reporters and photographers and other publicity: journalists' and publicity men's, also film-world's: since ca. 1925; ob. See also MOVING-PICTURE SLANG, § 10, in Appx.—2. As *garbo*. A garbage man, a dustman, a rubbish-collector: Aus.: since ca. 1930. B., 1953.

garden-gate. A First Officer: MN occ. r.s. (on *mate*). Franklyn 2nd.—2. Eight: (mostly underworld) r.s. Ibid.—3. 'A Norton motorcycle with plunger type rear springing: current late 1930s–40s. Used still [early 1980s] to describe the marque by Vintage motorcyclists' (Dunford, 2).

garden gates. Rates (and taxes): r.s. Franklyn.

garden-hop. To betray (a confederate): c.: from ca. 1920. (Wallace, 1923.) By r.s. on c. *shop*.

garden lint. 'Herring nets so badly damaged as to be no use for anything else' (Butcher, 1979). Here *lint* = the meshes of a net (Ibid.).

garden-party. Those prisoners who, suffering from phthisis, do their time in the open-air and sleep in special wards: c.:—1932 (Mackenzie, 1932).

gardening. Mine-dropping from aircraft: RAF Bomber Command: 1940–5.—2. 'As in "to go gardening", to run off the road' (Dunford): motorcyclists': since ca. 1950.

garry, gharry. A (gen. light) carriage: Anglo-Indian coll.: from ca. 1800. P.B.: still in use, in early 1960s in the army, for any vehicle, but usu. a lorry. Ex Hindi *gari*, a cart, a carriage; see Y. & B.

garters. 'The streamers jumped by the lady rider' (Seago, 1934): circus: late C.19–20.

gas. ' "Gas" is a very Irish term of approval; "Ah, you're gas!" means "You're a great one, you are" in the sense of being amusing and good company' (Tracy, 1975): Anglo-Irish: since ca. 1935. Ex *'laughing* gas'? Cf. the English:—2. A joke, a jest; a very amusing situation: since ca. 1945. 'That's spy stuff, isn't it? What a gas!' (Blake, 1964).—3. Petrol. See **step on the gas**.—4. In *taking the gas*, (of a patient) having a pneumothorax treatment: hospital nurses': since ca. 1935. *Nursing Mirror*, 7 May 1949.—5. As *the gas* (or *the Gas*), a person representing the Gas Company: coll. Frome, 1933.—

—6. 'Steam—to "gas-up"—to make steam' (McKenna, 1970): railwaymen's.—7. 'A pleasurable and exciting thing, event or experience' (Hibbert, 1983): 1950s. Cf. senses 1 and 2, and **gasser**, 2.

gas-boat. 'A motor fishing vessel in the Grand Banks': nautical. (Bowen.) Here, *gas* = gasolene.—2. Any small boat driven by gasoline: Can. coll.: since ca. 1920. (Leechman.)

gas-cape stew. See PRISONER-OF-WAR SLANG, §10, in Appx.

gas man, the. 'Used jocularly in reference to insurance men and canvassers who waste the time of housewives. From the gas-meter reader or collector' (Petch, 1966): since 1940s.

gas-meter bandit. 'Ironic term of contempt for a small-time thief. Stealing from gas meters [is] considered a petty crime' (Powis): c. and police s.: since late 1940s. See **bandit**, 1.

gash, n. The female pudend: C.18–20: low coll.—2. ' "Is there any gash around?" Are there any willing girls in the vicinity? Early C.20 and current' (Leechman, 1967). Ex sense 1. P.B.: that is the logical etym., but I have a strong feeling that a more likely derivation is ex:—3. (Often *the gash*.) Waste food; an over-issue: anything surplus: Services', orig. RN: since ca. 1910; since ca. 1939, also Aus. (B., 1943; H.& P.). See **gashion**.

gash, adj. From the n., 3: spare; available: Services', orig. RN: since ca. 1915. (Harling, 1946.) *Gash* occurs in several, mainly RN, terms, e.g.: *gash-boat*, a stand-by duty boat; *gash-hand*, a rating, or other serviceman, temporarily idle; and, in the sense of 'waste, refuse, rubbish', in *gash-barge*, *-bin*, *-bucket* (even a waste-paper basket may be called a 'gash-bucket'), and *-shoot*, a refuse-shoot. The first two, and last, in Granville; the 3rd in Winton, 1959, 4th and 5th, P.B. See:-

gashion. Additional; free; often in pl. as n., 'extra of anything', esp. rations: RN: late C.19–early 20; superseded by the shortened **gash**, n. and adj. (Bowen; F. & G.; Granville.) Cf. **buckshee(s)**. Prob. ex dial. *gaishen* (*gation*), an obstacle in one's way, perhaps via *additional*.

gaslight. 'To create an illusion for the purpose of spooking or deceiving someone: Can., ex US: since early 1970s' (Leech, 1986).

gasometer. 'Just before Christmas, 1944, when we had all more or less got used to life accompanied by flying-bombs at intervals, and when the V-2s were no longer being referred to as "gasometers" and we in London were trying to get used to this new and more frightful [than V-1s, see **doodlebug**] weapon . . . ' (Worsley, 1948): mostly Londoners': later half of 1944. Ex the rumours, after the first few rockets had landed, that the gas-mains had exploded, there being no preliminary warning as there had been with the 'buzzbombs'. Cf. **flying gas-main**. (P.B.)

gasp and grunt. Var. of **grumble and grunt**, q.v. Franklyn 2nd.

gasper. An inferior cigarette: from ca. 1912: orig. military; popularised during WW1; by 1930, coll. Ex its effect on one's 'wind', i.e. staying powers.—2. Hence, any cigarette: from ca. 1914. ('Taffrail', 1917.) Cf. **fag**.

gasping. Over-anxious: Glasgow:—1934. Ex excited panting.

gassed. Tipsy: orig. military: not, I think, before 1917. (F. & G.) Ex the stupefying effects of gas. A later example is in Campbell, 1960.

gasser. A cigarette: Aus., esp. Sydney: since ca. 1945. Perhaps a slovening of the synon. **gasper**.—2. Something wonderful, very exceptional, extraordinarily successful: Can., adopted ex US, early 1950s; by ca. 1955 also Aus. Perhaps ex US *gasser*, a gas-propelled oil-well that needs no pumping. (B.P.) Cf. **gas**, n., 7.—3. Hence, something quite breathtaking: adopted by jazz-lovers, ca. 1960, ex US; ob.

gassy. A gas-meter: Midlands and Northern: since ca. 1950.

gastro. Gastro-enteritis: medical coll. > gen. ca. 1940. Throughout the British Commonwealth. B., 1953.

gasworks. An acetylene bicycle-lamp: club cyclists': earlier C.20. (*Fellowship*, 1984.) Cf. **fish and chips**.

gat. A revolver: Can. (—1914), orig. US. (Ex *gatling gun*.) Since ca. 1924, thanks to gangster novels and films, the word has > fairly well known in Britain.—2. Hence, a machine-gun: RAF: late 1930s. Jackson.

gate. The mouth: NZ: from ca. 1910; esp. soldiers' in WW1. Also RN lowerdeck: Granville lists *Gate* as a 'nickname for anyone inclined to loquacity.'—2. A form of greeting. See JAZZ TERMS, in Appx.—3. In *on the gate*, (of a prisoner who is) in an observation-cell: c.:—1933 (Ingram). The door is left open.—4. On the danger list at a hospital: lower classes': from ca. 1925. P.B.: Muvver states, authoritatively, that this sense of *on the gate* 'refers to pre[-WW2] arrangements, when visits and enquiries outside a twice-a-weekly routine were allowed only for critical cases and the gatekeeper had a list of them. "On the special" was another term for the same thing.'

gate and gaiters. 'Gunnery instructor, from *gate*, meaning a loud mouth, and the gaiters worn by instructors and instructed. The phrase means excessive squad drill. Also known as *gas and gaiters* (Granville): RN. The phrase 'originated at Whale Island, the Naval Gunnery School and hot-bed of discipline'. (Ibid.)

gate-crasher, -crashing. One who attends, attendance at, a private party or entertainment without invitation: coll.: US, anglicised in late 1926. The v., *gate-crash*, orig. rare, hardly—in Eng., at least—antedates 1930. Ex forcing one's way through a gate to attend an out-door sport.

gate(-)fever. That restlessness which affects long-term prisoners due to be released fairly soon: prisons': since ca. 1920. (Norman.) Home Office, 1978, lists this as current, with synon. *gate-happy*. Cf. **funnel fever** and **wire-happy**.

gaters. 'Leg shields on a motorcycle' (Dunford). Var. of **gaiters.**

gates of Rome. Home: r.s. An off-shoot from the older *Pope o' Rome.* Franklyn.

Gateshead. 'To *get off at Redfern* [q.v. at **Redfern**] . . . is dull and unoriginal. Since the nineteenth century, natives of Newcastle-upon-Tyne have described the procedure [*coitus interruptus*] alliteratively as getting out at Gateshead' (*TLS*, 4 Dec. 1970, quoted by Wilkes). Cf. **get off at Hillgate.**

Gateway to the South. 'Ironic term for the Balham district of S. London' (Powis). Ex a satirical 'travelogue', a monologue recorded by Peter Sellers ca. 1960, in which, in a mock-American accent, he describes the 'glories' of 'Bal-ham'.

gatey. Suffering from **gate-fever,** q.v.: convicts' c. and warders' s.: since ca. 1930, or even 1920. (Norman, 1959.)

gather. (Usu. as *be gathered*) to be arrested. See AUSTRALIAN UNDERWORLD, in Appx.

gathering the mush, n. Potato-picking: tramps' and Romanies'. (Dawson.)

gauch (pron. *gowch*) **out.** Usu. *gauched*, or *gauching*; the *out* may be omitted. To fall asleep, or pass out, from weariness or through intoxication: teenagers', ex US drugs' c.: early 1980s. (James Williamson, 1982.) Perhaps from the image of the S. American peasant asleep under his tilted sombrero.

gaucho; usually in pl. 'When the Ashkenazim (Jews from North and Central Europe) are discussing the Sephardim (Jews from Spain and Portugal) they sometimes refer to them as the *Gauchos* (Franklyn, letter 1946): since ca. 1936. *Gaucho*, a cowboy of the pampas and a notable horseman, is of mixed Spanish and Indian descent: the Spaniards used to be notable horsemen (caballeros); *gaucho* prob. derives ex Araucan *cauchu*, 'wanderer' (Webster's); the Sephardim came from *Sepharad*, credibly identified with Spain (*OED*).

gaudy. Very: lower classes'. Galsworthy, 1924, 'Ah! It's a gaudy long wait.' Prob., like *ruddy*, a euph. for *bloody*.

Gawdsaker. 'Marjorie cried: "What is a Gawdsaker?" "Oh," said Trafford, "haven't you heard that before? He's the person who gets excited by a deliberate discussion and gets up . . . screaming, 'For Gawd's sake, let's do something now!' I think they used it first for Pethick Lawrence" ' (Wells, 1912). Arising ca. 1905, it was † by ca. 1950.

gay, n. A dupe: Aus. c. (esp. prostitutes' and confidence-tricksters'). Tennant, 1939.—2. A homosexual person, of

either sex: orig. homosexuals', > gen. and widespread: later C.20. Ex:-

gay, adj. Homosexual, of either sex, but at first usu. of the male: common in US since 1945, and, since ca. 1955, in Britain.

gay boy. A homosexual: Aus. (Lambert, 1951.) Cf. prec.

gay cat. A tramp that hangs about for women: Can. low and Brit. tramps' c. Adopted ex US.

gay deceivers. 'Falsies' or foam-plastic bust-forms: raffish: since ca. 1950.

gay girl; gay woman. A prostitute: proletarian: mid-C.19–20; †. 'Killed' by **gay,** adj. Orig. sense recorded in B. & L. In later C.20 this term = a lesbian.

gazer. 'A pedlar who walks about a fair or market selling as he goes': grafters'. *Cheapjack*, 1934.

gazelle, in a. 'Feeling good'. See CANADIAN . . . , in Appx.

gazinta. See **guzinter.**

gazump. (This is, 1970s, the gen. accepted spelling; among earlier variants are: *gazoomph, gazumph, gezump, gezumph, guzzump*.) To swindle: grafters'. (*Cheapjack*, 1934.) Hence, *gazumper*, the agent, and *gazumping*, the action. Allingham used the *gezumph* version; *News of the World*, 28 Aug. 1938, *gazumph*.—2. To give (someone) short change: barrow-boys': since ca. 1935.—3. By a specialisation of sense 1, and also as n., 'to subject, the subjecting of, the buyer of a house to demands for a higher price after the purchase has been arranged' (Barnhart): the term has been widespread since this immoral practice became common during the great forced rise in house-prices in 1972. Although it sounds Yiddish, it does not appear in Rosten; nor can well-informed Hebrew-speakers in Israel suggest a likely etym. (Mindel, 1987). P.B.: perhaps an elision of *goes* + another garbled element; cf. **guzunder.**

gazunda. See **guzunder.**

gear, n. ' "Got a load of gear (stolen property) for you, John," he'd say' (Gosling, 1959): c.: since ca. 1930. See also the similar, though wider, sense noted at AUSTRALIAN UNDERWORLD, in Appx.—2. Any narcotic, but esp. marijuana: (mostly teenage) drug addicts': since the late 1940s. In later 1980s, esp. heroin (Dovkants, 1988).—3. 'Belongings, including supplies of drugs, syringes, etc.' (Home Office): drug-users': 1970s.—4. As *the gear*, always predicatively: very good: low, but also Liverpool ordinary: late C.19–20. Popularized by the Beatles, to mean 'something that is unique and extra good' (*News of the World*, 19 Nov. 1963).—5. Clothes: in common, mostly teenagers', usage since ca. 1950. (A correspondent to *Woman's Own*, 25 Feb. 1967, claims to have seen it in a novel pub. 1888, but unfortunately doesn't say whose or which.)

gear, adj. Homosexual: since ca. 1930. Poss. r.s. on *queer* (Franklyn 2nd), but more prob. a var. of synon. **jere,** 2 and 3, q.v.—2. Excellent; attractive: orig. Merseyside teenagers', then much more widespread: since 1955 at latest; ob. by 1965. See **gear,** n., 4. (P.B.)

gear-box. The vagina: East Anglia, esp. Suffolk: since late 1940s. (Leech, 1972.) A survival, and technological updating, of late C.16–19 S.E. > s. *gear*, the human genitals.—2. 'In Can. and US, a homosexual: in Can. since ca. 1970. I presume the gay community in US started this one [but not in Rodgers, 1972], as it is so much more widespread in US' (Leech, 1985). Cf. prec., 1.

gear lever. An erect penis: Servicmen's: mid-C.20. Johnson, 1973.

geared up. Dressed up, as in 'She was all geared up like a dog's dinner': market-traders'. (*M.T.*) Also used of, e.g., motor-cyclists in full travelling rig. Cf.:–

geary. Fashionably stylish, as in 'Picture Flora in her geary shades [her elegant sunglasses]': later C.20. Var. of **gear,** adj., 2.

Geddes axe. See **axe,** 1.

gee, n. Grafters' s.: 'A grafters' accomplice or assistant who mingles with the crowd. Note: To give a grafter a gee is to buy something off him to encourage the crowd' (*Cheapjack*, 1934). Cf. 'A *gee* is a *rick* (stooge) who stands among the audience (*hedge*) and *slings gees*—praising the goods and saying audibly how satisfied he is' (Buchanan-Taylor, 1943). See MOCK AUCTION in Appx., and **rick**.—2. Bluff; empty talk or 'fanny': c.: from ca. 1920. (*Gilt Kid*, 1936.) Hence *put in the gee*, to blarney, to tell a plausible tale (cf. sense 1): Ibid. Contrast *put on the gee*, to 'swank'; act or talk pretentiously: c.: from ca. 1925. Ibid. See also **get at the gee**.—3. In *on the gee*, annoyed, irritated: proletarian:—1923 (Manchon). Perhaps ex *on* (one's) *high horse*.—4. Derived from and synon. with *gen box*, a complicated instrument [a navigational radar]: RAF: since ca. 1942. (McDouall, 1945.) P.B.: by 1950 at latest, *gee* in this sense > j. See **gen**, n.

gee, v. To encourage, incite; delude: c.:—1932 (*Dartmoor*, 1932). Esp. to do this as a grafter's assistant: showmen's. See *put in the gee* at **gee**, n., 2, and **gee-man**.—2. 'To put in the "G". To exert pressure . . . To give information to the authorities about a fellow-prisoner' (Tempest, 1950): prison c. A development of sense 1. See **gee-er**.—3. 'To gee is to be a stalking horse or *agent provocateur*, often in relation to sexual offences' (Crick, 1980): 1930s.

gee! By mid-C.20 the usu. spelling of *Jee!*, an orig. euph., now mostly US coll. corruption of *Jesus!*, as oath or exclam.: mid-C.19–20.

gee, adj.; esp. a *gee fight*, a catchpenny bout that is not a true contest: boxing: since ca. 1930. See **gee**, n., 2.

gee-er. 'One who puts in the "G". A trouble-maker. One who tells lies about another in order to provoke a fight. In this sense "gee-er" is in common use' (Tempest, 1950): prison c.: mid-C.20. See **gee**, n., 2 and v., 2.

gee-man. Aus. showmen's var. and synon. of **gee**, n., Tennant, 1941, 'In the show world a "gee-man" or "micky finn" was socially on the level of a duck's feet.'

gee-up, n. A spree; a jollification: Aus., esp. Sydney: since ca. 1920. Park, 1948.

gee up, v. As *gee up*, to pull someone's leg: c.: since ca. 1940. (Norman.) Var. of **gee**, v., 1.—2. As v.t. To annoy, upset by 'playing up': schoolchildren's: later C.20. 'Truanting is an extension of their bolshy behaviour at school—"geeing up" the teachers' (*New Society*, 23 Sep. 1982). Also in wider usage (Hibbert, 1983). Cf. **wind up**, v.

gee whillikens!; gee whiskers!; gee whiz(z)! The first two are occ. var. of the 3rd: juvenile exclamations, orig. euph. for *Jesus Christ!* The 3rd, late C.19–20; the 1st, earlier C.20; the 2nd, an earlier C.20 NZ facetious var. All are elab. of **gee!**, q.v.

geek. A (long) look: Aus.: since WW1. 'Gis'—give us—'a geek at that book.' B.P. derives it ex German *gucken*, to peep or peek; perhaps influenced by Cornish dial. *geek*, to look intently at.—2. 'The fair-ground monster who bites off chickens' heads and eats any filth customers deposit in his begging-cup'; (*Observer*, 2 Jan. 1977): fairground and allied. On the other hand, a *Daily Telegraph* book reviewer had, on 23 Oct. 1975, described a geek as the lowest form of carnival performer, perhaps one who is merely stared at. Both may be right. The origin could well be the same as for sense 1. R.S., to whom I owe sense 2, thinks that the orig. may lie rather in the Ger. dial. and s. form *kieken* than in *gucken*, for both forms have the same meaning. The term has come from US: see W. & F., 1960.

geeze. Injection of narcotics: drugs c. (Stockley, 1986.) US since 1967 at latest (Spears).

geezer or **geeser** (rare); occ. **geyser** (incorrectly); esp. *old geezer*. A person: in the 1890s, gen. of women; in C.20, gen. of men (cf. *old buffer*). Low coll.: 1885 (*OED*). Perhaps ex † *guiser*, a mummer, via dial.; but note that Wellington's soldiers may, ca. 1811, have picked up Basque *giza*, man, fellow, and changed it to *geezer*. (Hugh Morrison, Perth, W. Aus.)—2. Hence, occ., *my* (or *the*) *old geezer*, my 'old

woman' (wife): lower classes':—1923 (Manchon).—3. A fellow prisoner: c.: since ca. 1930. (Norman.)—4. A 'mug'; an easy dupe: since ca. 1945. Rather by specialisation of sense 1 than—as Norman proposes, 1959—by way of S.E. *geyser*, as a pun on *steamer* (*steam-tug*), a 'mug'.

gefuffle. See **kerfuffle**.

geggie. A 'penny gaff'; a cheap vaudeville show: showmen's. Ex *gag*? Also spelt *geggy*.

geg(g)s. Spectacles: W. Midlands'. (Scott, 1984.) Sounds dial., but not in *EDD*; cf. C.19 synon. s. *gig-lamps*.

gelly. An occ. var. of **jelly**, gelignite. Because of the spelling; cf. **genny**, generator.

gelp. C.20 market-traders' var. (*M.T.*) of much older (in C.16, S.E.) *gelt*, money.

gen, n. (Often as *the gen*.) Information: *gen* may be classed as *pukka*, trustworthy, *duff*, incorrect, or (WW2 only) *phoney*, doubtful and unreliable: RAF: since ca. 1929, but widely used only since 1939; in WW2 it spread also to the army, though not widely. Michie, 1940, 'Operations room where I got my Gen (RAF slang for information, instruction)'; and esp. in Partridge, 1945. Ex the consecrated phrase 'for the general information of all ranks' or ' . . . of all concerned'. *Pukka* is Hindustani, whereas *duff* and *phoney* are from the underworld.—2. Hence, notes on procedure; notes for a test; notes taken during a course: RAF: since 1938. Partridge, 1945.

gen, adj. 'Genuine', trustworthy: not an abbr. of *genuine*, but either ex the n., 1, or more prob., ex the combination *pukka gen*: Services': since ca. 1941. Partridge, 1945.

gen book. A note-book (for useful scraps of information): RAF: since early 1930s. (Jackson.) See **gen**, n.

gen box. See **gee**, n., 4.

gen file. A general file (general to a particular department: policy, procedure, etc.): RAF clerical: since ca. 1939. Partridge, 1945.

gen kiddy. A thoroughly good chap: RAF aircrew trainees': early 1950s. 'Who's your flight commander? . . . Oh, he's a real gen kiddy, you'll be OK with *him*.' (P.B.)

gen king. One who is well supplied with trustworthy information: RAF: since ca. 1939. H. & P.

gen man has, since 1938, been rather more usual than its synon. *gen wallah*. Davison, 1942; Brickhill 1946.—2. An Intelligence Officer: RAF: 1939+. P-G-R.

gen up, v.i. and v.t. To learn (esp., quickly), to swot, to study: RAF: since ca. 1933. (Jackson.) P.B.: as v.t., to inform or brief, *gen* (someone) *up on* (subject); and in 'to swot', 'I must gen up on (subject)'. Ex **gen**, n., 1.

gen(-)wallah. Anyone conversant with Service procedure or with Service 'occurrences' (postings, promotions), esp. an Orderly Room Sergeant or Corporal: RAF: since ca. 1935. (Jackson.) See **gen**, n., 1.

gender-buzz. 'It's the hottest little game around, this gender-buzzing . . . "But David, are you out to fool the fellas into thinking you're a girl?" "God, no . . . I'm after the exact opposite sort of buzz: to get people to appreciate how much like a girl I *can* look but to *recognise* me as a boy . . . Hey, it's only a game" ' (Martin, 1984).

General, the. A general post-office: coll.—2. 'The imaginary presiding genius of General Motors-Holden's' (Wilkes): Aus. journalistic: 1970s.

General Schools. General School Leaving Examination: schools' coll.: from ca. 1920; †. (Cowan, 1937.) Replaced after 1950 by the GCE 'O' Level exam.

genned(-)up. Well supplied with information: RAF: since ca. 1934. (Partridge, 1945.) Ex **gen up**.

genny. A generator: mechanics' > gen.: since ca. 1916. Deighton, 1970; Hunter, 1956, spells it *jenny*.

gens; occ. **a drop of gens**. *Gen*eral leave: RN. Bowen.—2. 'Also used for General Quarters' (Granville): RN.

gentleman's (or **gent's**) **gent**. A 'gentleman's gentleman' or valet: earlier C.20. Both forms in Brandon, 1931.

gents', the. A men's convenience: coll.

gent's gent. See **gentleman's gent.**

genuwine (often spelled *Genoowine*) **Bedoowine Ayrab.** 'A Bedouin Arab. A joc. elaboration of the American pronunciation of Arab' (Sanders, 1967): Brit. soldiers', in N. Africa, 1940–3. P.B.: but the phrase lingered on, well known in the army, for at least three decades after the N. Africa campaign. *Genoowine Bedoowine* was occ. used to mean 'the true, the real thing'.

geo. A geophysical report: oil industry coll.: later C.20. St Clair, 1976.

geographically impossible. A girl rendered, by the distance of her home from Sydney, inconvenient to see for long, esp. in the evening and, above all, to take home: Sydneysiders': since ca. 1945. (B.P.)

geography. Female genitals: cultured: from ca. 1920. Isherwood, 1933, 'He'll get a bit of geography with luck. She's only a teaser.' I.e. to the *exploring* hand.

Geological Survey, the. A stony stare: RN officers': since ca. 1930. Granville.

Geordie, geordie. A pitman; any Northumbrian: N. Country coll.: from ca. 1760. Prob. ex the Christian name there so pronounced.—2. Hence, a N.E. Railway employee: railwaymen's: C.20, after ca. 1950, any employee in that region. (*Railway.*)

George, george. An automatic pilot on an aircraft: airmen's: since ca. 1928. H. & P., 'The saying "Let George do it" may well have suggested the name'; but 'I think the auto-pilot was worked on, if not developed, by a man called *George* Lloyd. He was a crazy pilot and do-it-yourself enthusiast. He had no house but lived in a motor-caravan, in which he travelled from job to job. Unfortunately electrocuted' (Bishop, 1986).—2. A common vocative to a Negro whose name is unknown: Can.: since ca. 1920; by 1960, ob., and prob. considered offensively patronising, for it 'was customarily applied to the porters (stewards) on Pullman [railway restaurant] cars, who were invariably Negro. The custom, along with the cars, is obsolescent' (R.C., 1976).—3. Defecation: RN. Winton, 1959: 'Bowles, I'm going to have my Morning George now . . . Bowles, always have your George in the *morning*' (Captain to midshipman). Personification.

George Bohee. Tea (the beverage): r.s.: ealier C.20. Ex the name of 'a famous Banjoist', says Lester; but obviously influenced by the Chinese tea named *Bohea* (pron. *Bohee*) *tea.* Cf. earlier synon. r.s. *Rosie Lee.*

George Gerrard. A gross exaggeration: Aus. (B., 1942.) Ex an Aus. 'character'.

George Raft. Draught: r.s.: since mid-1930s. 'Not the kind one pours down one's neck but that which sends shivers down it! I once heard a Cockney apprentice complain of a 'bleedin' George Raft' that was blowing right up his "Khyber". Name of an American film star popular in the 'thirties for his gangster roles' (Hillman).

George Robey; esp. **on the George Robey.** The road, or tramping; on the road, or a-tramping: tramps' r.c. (on old synon. s. *toby*): from ca. 1910. On Sir George Robey (1869–1954), music-hall comedian and actor.

George the Third. A var. of **Richard the Third,** a bird, in both lit. and theatrical senses. Franklyn 2nd.

Gert and Daisy. Two Messerschmitts familiar to troops in the Green Hill area of Tunisia: ca. 1942–3. Ex the music-hall comediennes, 'Gert and Daisy' (Doris and Elsie Waters).

Gertie. A woman van-driver: WW2. See **whistler,** 4.

Gertie Gitana. Banana: r.s.: earlier C.20. Ex a music-hall star of Edwardian days. Franklyn.

Gertie Lee. See TOMBOLA, in Appx.

Gertrude. See MOVING-PICTURE SLANG, §4, in Appx.

gessein. To dupe, to 'con': c.: mid-C.20. Tempest.

gesseiner. 'Valuables. Possessions. Belongings' (Tempest): c.: mid-C.20.—2. 'In the Merchant Navy this means a garbage can' (Ibid.).

Gestapo, the. The Service (later RAF) Police: RAF: since ca. 1938. Rhodes, 1942, 'Service police are "Gestapo" much more often than "snoops".' But also RN (Bassett) and Army (Kersh, 1941). Humorous on the name of the German Secret Police of the Third Reich.—2. Hence, the police; even such others in 'a little, brief authority', e.g. bus inspectors: since late 1940s. (Petch, 1969.)

gesture. An action for the sake of show, good or bad: when used trivially, it is coll.: from ca. 1925. (As S.E.: 1916, says the *OED* Sup.)

get, n. A chump, a fool: Army: since ca. 1930. *Daily Mail*, 7 Sep. 1940. Usu., in later C.20, qualified by 'stupid', 'silly', etc. Ex S.E., sense, 'bastard'. See also **git.**

get, v. To annoy or worry: coll., orig. (ca. 1880) US, anglicised ca. 1920. P.B.: later C.20, usu. with *about*, as in 'What gets me about him is his confounded complacency', which is perhaps elliptical for the quot'n in:—2. To render, succeed in rendering: coll., orig. (ca. 1890) US, anglicised ca. 1910. E.g. 'He gets me wild,' he makes me angry. *OED* Sup.—3. To impress, move, attract: coll.: from ca. 1915. E.g. 'That play, Romance, got me properly.' (*OED* Sup.) Prob. ex sense 1 influenced by sense 2.—3. As v.i., used for *get (oneself) here* or *there*, where previously the full phrase was customary: coll.: since late 1970s. 'It's at my place tonight. Can you get, or do you want picking up?' (P.B.)

get a heave on (someone). To treat severely or unpleasantly: Army: ca. 1930–50. P-G-R.

get a knob. To catch a venereal disease: low, ?esp. Army. (Thomas, 1966.)

get a load on. To become tipsy: Aus. (Palmer, 1948.) The *load* comes ex Can. where current since late C.19. (Niven.)

get a marked tray. To catch a venereal disease: Can. hospitals' (perhaps orig. a euph.): since ca. 1910.

get a pick on (a person). To pick on, ill-temperedly mark out, quarrel with: Can. (Beames.)

get a squeak. (Of police) to become suspicious: police: since ca. 1910. (*Free-Lance Writer*, Apr. 1948.) Cf. **squeak,** n., 1.

get a wiggle on. (Mostly in imperative.) To get a move on; to look lively: RN. P-G-R.

get aboard (someone). To reprimand that person severely; to hound him: Army: 1950s–60s. 'The RSM really got aboard old Smudger' (P.B.).

get across; get it across. To succeed; esp. to make oneself fully understood or suitably appreciated: resp. ca. 1915 and in 1913: coll. >, by 1933, familiar S.E. Ex US *get it across the footlights. OED* Sup.—2. In *get across* (*her* or, more brutally, *it*), to copulate (with a woman): low coll.: since late C.19.

get (one's) act together. To take concerted and effective action, as in 'If only the heads of departments'd get their act together, this college could really go places': adopted ex US, later C.20.—2. Hence, of an individual, to organise one's talents and abilities: 'You won't impress any potential employer unless you can get your act together a sight better than you come over now': since late 1970s. See also **get it together.**

get among it. To be making a lot of money: Aus.: since ca. 1910.—2. To 'have a woman' from time to time: Aus.: since ca. 1915. Stivens, 1951.

get (someone) at – intensively, **right at – it.** To make fun of, to jeer at; to make a fool of: low: since ca. 1940. (Norman.)

get at the gee. To 'spoof' (v.i.): c.:—1933 (Leach). See **gee,** n., 1 and 2.

get away with it. To succeed beyond expectation and/or contrary to the full rights of the case: coll.: from ca. 1918: ex US (—1912). (F. & G.; *OED* Sup.) In a phrase such as 'You're not going to let him get away with it, are you?', it has the nuance of 'to take advantage of' or 'gain an advantage over'.—2. Hence, 'just to scrape through a difficulty': coll.:—1931 (Lyell).

get by, v.i. To escape notice, esp. when that notice is feared or inopportune. V.t., *get by with*, gen. followed by *it*. Coll., ex US. Cf. **get past.**—2. To make barely enough money to live on, often with connotation of great care and the active use of common-sense and intelligence: coll.: since ca. 1925. P.B.: often, however, since ca. 1945 used ironically for 'to make a comfortable living', as in 'Oh, he gets by, you know. Got his two cars and his "little place in the country".'

get cracking – get mobile – get skates on – get stuck into it – get weaving. To respond (immediately) to an order; to get a move on: Services' (the 2nd, 3rd, 4th, gen.; the 1st, orig. Army and then gen.; the 5th, RAF—see separately at **weaving**): since ca. 1925, except *stuck* (ca. 1916) and the last, q.v. All usu. in the imperative. Origins: whip-cracking at the mustering of cattle: *mobile* and *skates*, obvious refs. to speed (cf. a *mobile* column); *stuck*, perhaps ex dough-kneading but prob. ex ditch-digging, road-making, mining; see **weaving**.— 2. Hence, to think or plan seriously; to take the steps necessary to achieve an end: since 1940. Cf. **organised.**

get dizzy. To get angry: RN: from ca. 1920. ('Taffrail'.)

get down on. To appropriate illicitly; to steal: Aus. and NZ. E.P.; B., 1942.

get down to it. To begin to work seriously: coll.: ?ex US.—2. To go to sleep: military coll.: from ca. 1910. F. & G.—3. To coït: coll.

get (one's, or the) drift. 'To understand, follow; as in "If you do that again, I'll flatten you. Get the drift?": widespread in N. Am.: since (?)early 1950s; still current, but ob.' (Leech, 1986). Current in UK later C.20, often vaguely minatory.

get egg on (one's) **face.** See **egg on . . .**

get (one's) end away. (Of a man) to copulate: low and raffish: since ca. 1960. Tinniswood, 1969. Cf.:-

get (one's) end in. (Of the male) to achieve copulation, to copulate: low: since ca. 1910. Thomas, 1966, 'It was the place in the town for getting one's end in, they said, and it was naturally very crowded.'

get (one's) head down. To lie down and go to sleep: Services' coll.: since ca. 1920. (Emanuel, 1945.)—2. To plead guilty in court. See AUSTRALIAN UNDERWORLD, in Appx.

get his. To receive a wound, an injury, esp. a fatal one: Army: since ca. 1914. (Knox, 1937; Kersh, 1942.) P.B.: the pronominal adj. may, or course, be varied: 'I got mine in Malaya. Where did you cop yours?'

get (someone) in. To put a story over on, to deceive with a story: Aus.: since ca. 1925. Niland, 1958, 'Old Ted Proctor . . . the greatest liar God ever put breath in—even he could get you in.'

get in bad. To make (someone) disliked; as v.i., to cause oneself to be disliked: adopted ex US, —1928 (*OED* Sup.). This usage supplanted by *get in bad with* . . . , q.v. at **bad with.**

get in for it. To establish oneself firmly: proletarian:—1923 (Manchon); ob. by ca. 1940.

get in (one's) hair. To annoy or irritate: adopted, ca. 1936, ex US. 'Like grit embedded in the hair', suggests L.A., while W. & F. gloss 'to irritate as lice in the hair would irritate.' Also as in 'I want to get him out of my hair', often shortened to 'I want him out of my hair.'

get in wrong. To incur the dislike of another person: adopted ex US ca. 1932 (*COD*, 1934 Sup.). Cf. **put in wrong with**, and **get in bad.**

get into. To come to know; hence, to know: the underground: since early 1960s. *Groupie*, 1968: 'The more I got into Davey, the more I felt I loved him and depended on him.' See also **into.**

get into bed with. To 'merge with, become a partner of, start a venture with': big businessmen's and financiers': since late 1960s. 'At a recent board meeting where such a venture was discussed, no other phrase was used' (Playfair, 1977).

get it cracked. A verbose colloquialisation of S.E. *crack*, to solve a difficulty, a code, a puzzle: uncommon before ca. 1950. See **crack it, 2.**

get it off (one's) **chest.** 'To deliver a speech; express one's feelings' (Dennis): perhaps, orig., Aus. s., from early C.20; by 1930, gen. coll. In later C.20, usu. in sense 'to confess'.

get it off with (a female). (Of a man) to copulate: low coll.: later C.20. (P.B.) In Can., since ca. 1970, var. *get it on with* (Leech, 1986).

get it on the whisper. 'To buy on hire purchase (because at one time you didn't tell the neighbours you couldn't afford to pay cash)': lower and lower-middle class: since ca. 1920. (Gosling, 1959.)

get it together. To gain control of oneself, to become organised: the underground: since early 1960s, adopted ex US. (*Groupie*, 1968.) Hence, in slightly different social register, to acquire social poise. (*Observer* mag., 15 Aug. 1971.) Ob. by ca. 1980; the US *get it all together* never 'caught on'. By 1982, sometimes shortened to *get it on*. (Armitage). See also **get (one's) act together.**

get it up. To achieve, rather than merely experience, an erection: US coll., adopted in Britain mid-1940s. But *get it up her*, to achieve coïtion (from the male point of view).

get joined; get (k)nicked; get knotted. As angry, exasperated, or derisory dismissives, prob. orig. euph. for *get fucked!*: orig. Services', later widespread: 1st (ob. by 1980) and 3rd since ca. 1930, the 2nd since ca. 1970. But, as *New Society*, 22 Aug. 1963, noted of *get knackered* [q.v. at **knackered**] and *get knotted*, they 'have come to mean, innocently enough, "go to hell".' Always as imperatives, or as in 'No! they can't have 'em. Tell 'em to go and get knotted.' (P.B.)

get knocked. To be punched, or knocked out: Aus. sporting coll.: later C.19–20. Baker.—2. Hence, to suffer a set-back: Aus. coll.: since ca. 1930.

get knotted! See **get joined!**

get (one's) lines, but usu. **wires, crossed.** See **wires crossed.**

get mobile. See **get cracking.**

get nicked! See **get joined . . .**

get no change out of. To receive no satisfaction from; fail to learn from: coll.

get nowhere fast. To try very hard but to achieve little; perhaps through unintelligent action, but usu. because frustrated by, e.g., bureaucratic delays: coll.: since ca. 1950.

get off. In *get off it*, to stop talking, befooling or chaffing a person, playing the fool, exaggerating, etc.: mostly in imperative: coll.:—1923 (Manchon). In later C.20, superseded by *come off it!*—2. To cease being obnoxious, presumptuous, or meddlesome: anglicised (ex US coll.) ca. 1929: verging on coll. Esp. in, e.g. 'I told them where to get off' or 'She told him where he could get off': the person was told to cease being a nuisance. Ex a conductor's or ticket-collector's or guard's telling a person where he gets off the tram, etc.—3. (Of a taxi-driver) to pick up a fare: taxi-drivers': from ca. 1919.

get off at Hillgate. To practice, to exercise, *coitus interruptus*: coll.: later C.20. Chamberlain, 1976: 'Coitus interruptus (variously termed "pulling out", "being careful" and "getting off at Hillgate"—the bus-stop before the one for home) . . . ' Clearly there was orig. a pun on gates, which can be closed, and the *mons Veneris* or female pelvic mound. Cf. synon. . . . **Gateshead,** and . . . **Redfern.**

get off (one's) bike. To get angry. See **bike.**

get off it! See **get off, 1.**

get off on. To derive pleasure and enjoyment from, as in 'He gets off on classical music': N. Am.: since mid-1960s. (Leech, 1986.) Some UK use, later 1970s (Hibbert, 1983).

get off with. To make friends with one of the opposite sex, esp. with a view to 'a good time': coll., orig. (1914 or early 1915) military >, by 1918, gen. F. & G.—2. Hence, to have a good time together, including sexual play and intercourse: since the late 1930s, esp. among teenagers. Also as *get it off with*.

get on (someone's) daily. To follow him. See **clock, v.,** 4.

get on it; n., getting on it. To go on a drinking bout; such a bout: Aus.: since ca. 1920. Cusack, 1951.

get on (one's) tit(s). To annoy or irritate: low Aus. and Brit. (Norman, 1959; B., 1959.) Cf. **get on (one's) wick:** both phrases are used regardless of the sex of the speaker.

G

get on to. To suspect; find out about: coll.: late C.19–20. (Spenser, 1934.)—2. To question or reprimand (somebody), usu. in a somewhat aggressive way, as 'Well, if they haven't done anything by Friday, I should get on to them about it': coll. (P.B.)

get on (someone's) **tripe.** To get on his nerves: Aus.: since ca. 1930. (Vickers, 1955.) Cf.:-

get on (one's) **wick.** To exasperate, irritate, annoy: low: since ca. 1920. *Wick = Hampton Wick = prick*, but is still used, in all innocence, by some ignorant women—cf., in reverse, **get on** (one's) **tits** used by men, and:-

get on (one's) **works.** To annoy—even to infuriate: Aus.: since ca. 1925. (B., 1942.) ?Euph. for prec.

get (one's) **one.** To be promoted from aircraftman 2nd class to 1st class: RAF coll.: from ca. 1925. (Emanuel, 1945.)

get organised. See **organised, get.**

get-out. An evasion: coll. (Spenser, 1934.) An earlier example, though in the nuance 'an escape from a difficult or dangerous position', occurs in E.H. Hornung, *Raffles*, 1899. The term now verges on S.E. See also **get out of**, from which this n. is formed.—2. In *as* (e.g. *crowded*) *as all get out*, to the utmost, extremely (crowded): adopted ex US (W. & F. dates back to 1884) as occ. Brit. use, C.20.

get out and walk. To use one's parachute: aviators' and Airborne Divisions': 1939+.

get out (one's) **mad.** To become (very) angry: Aus.: since ca. 1920. B., 1943.

get out of. To escape the consequences of one's folly or mistake: be excused punishment or duty: coll.: from ca. 1880; in C.20, S.E. Cf. **get off** and **get-out.**

get out of it! A dismissive, usu. loud and offensive, directed at animals, trespassers, etc.; often represented phonetically as *gerrahtavit*, or similar: coll. (P.B.)

get out of the shine! Get out of the light!: ca. 1925–40.

get past, get past with (gen. **it**). To escape detection; hence to succeed against odds or justified (moral) expectation: coll.: from ca. 1915: ?orig. military. Cf. **get by.**

get pilled up. See **block it.**

get rooted! or **go and . . . !** (Go and) get fucked!: low Aus.: late C.19–20. B., 1953.

get roused on. Var. of *rouse on*, q.v. at **rouse**, 1: since ca. 1920. B., 1943.

get shit of. Low var. of *get shot*, or *shut of*, to become rid or free of.

get (one's) **shit together.** Var. of **get it together**: Can., adopted ex US: 1960s. (Leech, 1986.)

get (one's) **skates on.** To 'get a move on', hurry. See **skates** and **get cracking.**

get slopped out. To empty one's slops: prison coll.: late C.19–20. Norman.

get some flying hours in. 'To get some sleep' (Jackson): RAF: since ca. 1935. Cf.:-

get some straight and level in. To obtain some sleep: RAF: since ca. 1939. (Hinde, 1945.)

get stuck in. As absolute, 'Right, let's get stuck in!', to start work hard and seriously: coll.: later C.20. Ex *get stuck into* (something), q.v. at **get cracking**, and next entry.—2. Hence, to tuck into one's food: low coll.: later C.20. (P.B.)

get stuck into. To 'get stuck into someone' is to fight him with one's fists: Aus. Baker.—2. Hence, to abuse verbally: id. B., 1959.—3. To copulate with a woman: workmen's.

get that way. (Gen. *how do* or *did you get that way*?) 'To get into the condition implied': coll., orig. (—1922) US, anglicised by 1930. *OED* Sup.

get the chingerers on. To grumble, complain, scold; as in 'she's got the chingerers on': market traders' *M.T.*

get the chop. To be killed, to 'go for a Burton': RAF aircrews': since 1940. (McDouall, 1945.) Applied to aircraft, it meant to lose them on a raid. See **chopped.**—2. Hence, in the Services, post-WW2 and still, 1980s, current, to be removed from a course of training for any reason, usu. incapability or disciplinary. (P.B.)—3. The term has spread into civilian life

since the late 1940s, with much the same sense as 2: to be dismissed from one's job or, in the case of, e.g., a politician, from a privileged position.

get the crap on. To be afraid, 'get the wind up': low Glasgow: from ca. 1919. (MacArthur.) Ex that loosening of the bowels which often results from fear.

get the drift. See **get** (one's) **drift.**

get the drop on (someone). To assume or achieve a superior status to, often by questionable means: later C.20; adopted ex US. Perhaps cf. **shit on from a great height**; though poss. orig. ex one gun-fighter surprising another.

get the goods on (someone). To learn the truth about, the 'lowdown' on him: adopted, ca. 1943, ex US. (*DCCU.*) Cf. *pin the goods on*, q.v. at **pin on.**

get the gooner. See **gooner.**

get the hell out (of here). To depart quickly; merely an intensification of 'get out': adopted, ca. 1950, ex US. Also *get to hell out*, and occ. even shorter, as in Hunter, 1964. 'He belted across to the garage, got in the car, got to hell.'

get the message. See JAZZ TERMS, at *message*, in Appx.

get the papers. To be indicted as an habitual criminal: c.:—1935 (Hume). Mostly as vbl n.

get the rag out. 'To get a move on, get busy: W. Can.: since ca. 1950. Ex pulling out the tampon, or taking off the sanitary pad, so that intercourse can take place' (Leech, 1986).

get through. 'To obtain drugs (US term)' (Home Office): drug addicts': 1970s.

get through to (someone). To succeed in getting a (dimwitted) person to understand something: coll.: prob. since the 1930s, but little heard before late 1940s. Perhaps ex telephone communication.

get to fuck. Go away, usu. in expanded form, 'Let's . . . ' or 'Why don't you'—'get to fuck out of here (?)'; an elab. of *get fucked!*, with, in the first example, an assumption that it might have been applied to oneself: low: later C.20. Perhaps influenced by Scot (*get*) *awa' tae fuck!* An intensification of the phrase, adopted ex US, *get to hell out of here*. See **get the hell . . .** (P.B.)

get-together. A (usu. informal) meeting or assembly: coll.: since ca. 1925. (Moseley, 1952.) Ex:-

get together. To help each other, one another: coll.: from ca. 1920. Ex S.E. sense, to meet, assemble (late C.17–20): cf. the US sense, to meet in amicable conference, to come to terms.

get tonked. To be punched; to be defeated: Aus.: since ca. 1920. (Baker.)

get tore! Get a move on!: Services': since ca. 1930; † by 1950.

get tossed. To lose money on a horse-race: Aus. sporting. Glassop, 1949.

get under (someone's) **neck.** To beat or outwit or circumvent (someone): Aus.: since ca. 1930. (B., 1953.) Lit., to get in front of him; ex horse-racing.

get-up. A 'framing', a 'frame-up' (a trumped-up case): c.: since mid 1940s. Crookston, 1967, 'I can't really get annoyed when the police have a get-up against Harry.' Ex coll. *get up a case*, to prepare one.—2. Any criminal or, at the least, illegal dodge or play, a 'ramp': since ca. 1960. Newman, 1970.

get up and go. A person's energy, initiative, courage; a car's acceleration, a lawn-mower's reliability, etc.: coll.: adopted ex US, perhaps first in Aus.; by 1950, fairly common in Brit., esp. of a person. By ca. 1980, slightly ob., but preserved in the pun, 'My get up and go just got up and went.' (B.P.; P.B.)

get up (one's) **back.** To exasperate, to infuriate, one: coll.: later C.20. (Cole, 1980.) Cf. synon. *get up* (one's) *nose*, and the much earlier *get* (one's) *back up*.

get (a girl) **up the stick.** To render her pregnant: universities' and Public Schools': since ca. 1945, at latest. (Stewart, 1976.) Cf. **up the spout** and **up stick.**

get up to, as in 'What's he getting up to?'—What mischief is he doing or planning?: coll.: late C.19–20.

get weaving. See **weaving**.

get with it. See JAZZ TERMS, in Appx., and **with it, be**.

get worked! A low Aus. expletive. (Stivens, 1951.) Synon with *get rooted!* See **work it** . . .

getaway man. (coll., become semi-official); or *lucky Charlie* (s.). On a patrol, that man who, keeping in the rear, was detailed, in an emergency, to escape and report: Army coll.: 1940–5.

getting off or **out**, with ref. to coïtus interruptus. See **get off at Hillgate; Gateshead; Redfern**.

Gezira Box, the. Base troops at Cairo: Army in N. Africa: 1941–3. (P-G-R.) Ex the 'boxes' that formed the defence plan in the desert fighting. Cf. **Groppi's Light Horse**.

gezump(h); gezumpher. See **gazump**.

Ghan, the. 'The fortnightly train running between Adelaide and Alice Springs' (B., 1942); 'since the 1950s the service is weekly' (Raab): Aus.: since ca. 1930. Short for *Afghan*: from those camel-trains which were so often conducted by the Afghan cameleers, as in 'One old Ghan cameleer . . . had ridden from Alice Springs to Oodnadatta . . . 355 miles away without undue fatigue' (Russell, 1934): there *Ghan* is a coll., dating since ca. 1890.

Ghardimaou Yeomanry, the. The 2nd Corps Reinforcement Unit, mobilised as infantry at the time of the German threat at Kasserine: Army in N. Africa: WW2. This unit was stationed at Ghardimaou in Tunisia. P-G-R.

gharry. See **garry**.

ghastly. A vaguely pej. or a merely intensive adj.: coll.: from ca. 1860. Thackeray, 'A ghastly farce'; Mackail, 1924, ' "Ghastly," said Peter, "Filthy," answered James' (of the weather). In C.20, a frequent injunction is 'Don't be a ghastly idiot!,' as in Grierson, 1931. Cf. *awful*, **bloody, filthy, foul**.

ghee factory. Any unit of the Royal Indian Army Service Corps: WW2. Because of their predilection for *ghee* (Indian clarified butter). See also **Rice Corps**.

ghee-guts. A fat man: Army in Far East: 1950s–60s. (P.B.)

gherkin. Penis: Aus. low coll.; not unknown in UK, as in *jerkin'* (one's) *gherkin*, masturbation, influenced by both rhyme and shape: since ca. 1950. (McNeil; P.B.)

ghetto blaster. A portable stereo radio/cassette player, esp. when used at full volume out of doors: since early 1980s. *New Society*, 8 Sep. 1983.

ghost, n. A radio officer: Services': WW2. H. & P.—2. An intrusive secondary image on a TV screen: since ca. 1950: television coll. >, by 1965, S.E.—3. '[Black Economy] Units investigate areas where people are ghosts—that is, there are no tax records on them at all—and they seek out moonlighters, those who have an undeclared part-time job as well as a job with taxed salary' (*Times*, 30 Apr. 1988): Inland Revenue coll.

ghost, v. See **ghosting**.

ghost gun. A machine-gun operated from a distance by cable: Army in Italy: 1943–4.

ghost in goloshes, the. The BBC time-signal: since ca. 1938; †.

ghost story. A 'bad luck' story: tramps' c.:—1932 (Jennings). Ex US: see Irwin.

ghost train. (See **ghosting**.) 'From train compartments with windows obscured with brown paper when carrying prisoners identified as trouble-makers from one prison to another. Used chiefly in 1930s' (Clayton, 1970): prisons'.

ghoster. A full night's work preceded by a full day's work: builders'. (A master builder, 1953.)—2. Term for a Portsmouth docker 'working late in the evening to just past midnight, and then claiming a full night's nightshift [pay]' (Patterson).

ghosting. Transferring an inmate from one prison to another for disciplinary reasons: prisons': 1970s. (BBC Radio 3, 25 July 1978.) See also **ghost train**.

gibby. A spoon: RN:—1901 (Goodenough). Perhaps ex dial. *gibby* (stick), a hooked stick.—2. 'A round cap worn by new entries in a training ship' (Granville): RN: since ca. 1930.

gibs. 'Guys in the Back Seat (Navigators)' (Wilson, 1979): RAF aircrews': 1970s. Cf. **gifs**.

giddy aunt!, my. A trivial, senseless exclam.: coll.: 1919 (W.N.P. Barbellion: *OED* Sup.). An elab. of *my aunt!*.

giddy goat. The totalisator or 'tote': Aus. r.s.: since ca. 1925. B., 1945.

giever. A life-saving jacket sold by Messrs *Gieves*, the naval outfitters: RN wardroom: since ca. 1946.

gifs. 'Guys in the Front Seat (Pilots)' (Wilson): RAF aircrews': 1970s. Cf. **gibs**.

gifted. (Usu. of men) homosexual, as in 'Is he gifted?': ?orig. Can.: since ca. 1925. 'Presumably because so many of them are' (Leechman).

gig, n. An engagement to play at a party for one evening: dance bands': since ca. 1935. (Jackson, 1946.) Ex S.E. *gig*, a dance. This sense was, ca. 1966, adopted by hippies and, in 1967, by the Flower People. Fryer, 1967.—2. A young lady: Aus.: since the 1920s. Perhaps ex *giggle*. Tennant, 1953.—3. A simpleton, a dupe: Aus.: since ca. 1930. (B., 1953.) Whence 'to *gig*' or lure simpletons: B., 1953.—4. A shortened form of **fizz-gig**, 2: Aus. c.: since ca. 1935. Hence the r.s. *Moreton Bay fig*, itself often shortened to *Moreton Bay*. B., 1953.—5. A detective: Aus.: since ca. 1935. (B., 1959.) Hence, *any* 'person of intrusive curiosity' (McNeil, 1973).—6. One's hobby, talent, ambition, current craze; what affords one the greatest pleasure: adopted, late 1960s, ex US.—7. An entertainment, e.g., a 'pop', jazz, folk band: performers' and fans' > coll.: since early 1960s. (*Groupie*, 1969.) Ex sense 1.

gig, v. To tease, make fun of (someone): since ca. 1945. B., 1953.—2. So to toss a coin that it does not spin: Aus. two-up-players': since ca. 1910. Also 'to *butterfly*' or 'to *float*'. B., 1953.—3. To stare (at someone): Aus.: since late 1930s. (B., 1959.) Cf. synon. **geek**.—4. To perform before an audience at a **gig** [n., 7], as in 'They shortly began gigging at the famous Cavern Club' (*Beatles*). W. & F. date this sense mid-1950s in US usage.

giggle. A group or 'bunch', or crowd of girls: orig. as a n. of assembly, it had, by ca. 1935, become a cultured coll. Ruck, 1940, 'Picked her out of a giggle of society debutantes.' Ex *giggling*, as in 'a lot of giggling girls'.—2. 'When the show or party is fun—it's a giggle, or it's a screech' (Gilderdale, 2): smart young set (esp. girls): ca. 1955–60. But also low s.: since ca. 1945, as in Norman. Cf. **no giggle**.

giggle and titter. A bitter (beer): r.s., mainly theatrical. Franklyn.

giggle-hat. Worn with a **giggle-suit**: Aus. soldiers': WW2. B., 1943.

giggle-house. A lunatic asylum: Aus.: since ca. 1925. Niland, 1958, 'Unless something's done he'll end up in the giggle-house. And that'll finish her.'

giggle-smoke. Marijuana: the term was used by Fritz Spiegel in the *Listener*, 4 Jan. 1979, in a list of synon. for the drug. Orig. US; Barnhart cites a quot'n from 1970. (P.B.)

giggle-stick. The penis: low. Cf. **joy-stick**, 2, and **giggling-pin**.—2. A stick, a spoon, used to stir a cocktail or other mixed alcoholic drink: Aus.: since ca. 1920. (B., 1942.) A perversion of *swizzle-stick*.

giggle-suit. Working dress; overalls: Aus. soldiers': 1939+. (*Rats*, 1944.) Cf. a comic appearance.—2. Hence, prison clothes: Aus.: c.: since ca. 1945. B., 1959.

giggle-water. Champagne: since ca. 1910. Ex its effect. Granville, 1962, notes caustically: 'Sarcastic allusion to the "unseamanlike" drinks popular with young officers of today. Over-indulgence in cocktails makes their girl friends giggle, hence the old-timers' jibe at effeminacy.'

giggling-pin. A var. of **giggle-stick** (penis).

giggy. Anus: low Can. Hence, *up your giggy!*, a low c.p. of contemptuous rejection: id.

gilded ballocks, have. To be extremely lucky: Army: since ca. 1936. Cf. **golden ballocks**.

gilhickie, -y. Anything whose name has slipped the memory: mainly nautical: since ca. 1930. A blend of earlier synon. *gilguy*, and *doohickie*.

Gillie Potters. 'Trotters. I think possibly both pig's and people's' (Daniells, 1980): r.s.: mid-C.20. G.P., a radio comedian very popular in 1940s–early 50s.

Gillpots, Mr Gillpots. Sobriquets for a drunkard: market-traders'. *M.T.*

gilly. One of the audience: (circus) Parlyaree:—1933 (Seago). Ex:—2. A man, a fellow: market traders': late C.19–20. A dim. of early C.19 s. *gill*, a chap.

gilt, n. A gilt-edged security: financial: since ca. 1915. Ferguson, 1936.

gilt, adj. Having golden or very fair hair: c.: from ca. 1920. *Gilt Kid*, 1936.

gimlet. A half-glass of whiskey: (mostly Anglo-Irish) public-houses':—1935.—2. A gin and lime: RN. A 'drink suggested by Sir T.O. Gimlette, a naval surgeon from 1879 to 1917. It was considered that the drinking of neat gin was bad for naval officers' health, and Sir T.O. Gimlette introduced the dilution of the gin with limejuice' (Granville).

gimmer. A female gossip: market-traders'. (*M.T.*) In Pennines dial., an old sheep.

gimmick. A conjurer's trick: magicians': adopted, ca. 1930, ex US.—2. Hence, any device or plan or trick calculated to ensure success: since mid-1930s in Can.; since ca. 1946 in Brit. In later C.20 esp. assoc. with advertising and sales-draw.—3. The brake on a gambling wheel: Can. carnival s.: since ca. 1920. Poss. echoic, or poss. from same orig. as senses 1 and 2.—4. (In pl.) Equipment for injecting drugs: drugs c. (Stockley, 1986.) US since –1967 (Spears).

gimmies. Gifts of clothing, equipment, etc., made to sportsmen by their sponsors: later C.20. (Edmonds, 1986.) I.e. *gimmes*, a slovening of 'give me(s)'. Cf. **freebies.**

gimp. A simpleton; a fool: Aus.: since ca. 1925. (B., 1942.) A corruption of American *gink*, 'chap, fellow'?

gimpy. Lame in the leg: Can.: adopted, ca. 1930, ex US. The adj. of c. *gimp*, a lame leg, hence a lame person. (Priestley.)

gin and it. Gin and *I*talian vermouth. Cf. *gin and French*, coll. abbr. for gin and French vermouth.

gin and Jaguar belt, the. 'The upper-class districts of [esp.] Surrey, and a fruitful area for worth-while housebreaking' (Powis): since ca. 1955. The *Jaguar* refers to the expensive motorcar highly favoured as a status symbol in the expensive residential area around London. Cf.:-

gin and Jaguar bird. 'A wealthy (usually married) woman from this [see prec.] area and in some senses likely to be "racy", "with it" or sexually accommodating' (Powis): 1970s.

gin burglar. Synon. with **gin-jockey:** Aus.: Wilkes' earliest quot'n is from Harney, 1947.

gin-jockey. A white man habitually consorting with Aboriginal women (*gins*): Aus. rural, esp. in the North: since ca. 1920. Henry, 1960.

Gin Palace, gen. **the.** Any RN vessel named *Agincourt*: RN: C.19–20. ('Taffrail'; Bowen.) A pun.—2. As *gin palace*. 'Armoured Command vehicle or "Dorchester" ' . . . 'The nerve centre of the armoured brigades' (H. & P.): military: since 1940. Cf.:—3. 'Any impressive interior, such as that of a static A.A. Command Post' (H. & P.): since 1941. Ex the elaborateness and the apparent comfort.—4. 'Staff car. Any luxurious vehicle for the use of a superior officer' (Frank Roberts, letter, 1946): Army: 1942. P.B.: occ. as *gin wagon*. Sense 2, for any large radio, or command, vehicle, was current until at least 1970.

gin pennant. A green-and-white flag run up by a ship as an invitation to all officers to come aboard for a drink.

gin shepherd. 'Someone seeking to protect Aboriginal women from white men: derogatory' (Wilkes—cf. **gin burglar**—cites the same source). See also **gin-jockey.**

gin up. 'To consume hard liquor'—esp. spirits—'before a party' (Jackson): Service officers': since ca. 1930. Cf. **ginned-up.**

gin up, however, means—not to get drunk but merely to induce the party-spirit.

ginch. Elegance, smartness, esp. of skill or manner or clothing, or an instance of any of these exhibitions: adj., *ginchy*: Aus. teenagers' (esp. surfboard riders'): since ca. 1960. *Pix*, 28 Sep. 1963.

ginchy. See prec.—2. Hence(?), excellent, first-class: in the lower forms of Merseyside schools: ca. 1960–4.

ging. A catapult: Aus. children's. (B., 1942.) Echoic.

ginger, n. (With hard *g*.) A catapult: Aus. juvenile: since ca. 1945. (B., 1953.) A var. of *ging*.—2. Elliptical for **ginger-beer,** 3.—3. In **knock down ginger,** q.v., to knock at a door and run away.—4. 'A general term for all varieties of fizzy soft drinks: "Gie's a boatle a ginger, missis"—"What kinna ginger, son?"—"Lemonade." ' (Munro, 1985): Glasgow.—5. See next:-

ginger, v., **gingering,** n. To rob; robbery: Aus. c. (prostitutes'): since ca. 1930. Tennant, 1953, ' "gingering", or robbing prospective clients, was considered low taste, but after all, the man was a copper'. Hence the n., *ginger*, a prostitute that does this; also called a *ginger girl* or a *gingerer*; B., 1953. Hence also *work a ginger*.

ginger-beer. An engineer: nautical r.s.—2. Hence, *the Ginger Beers*, the Engineering Corps in the Aus. Army: Aus. military: WW2. B., 1942.—3. A homosexual male: r.s. on *queer*: since ca. 1920. Draper, 1970.

ginger group. 'Politicians actively impatient with their own party' (Laing): political: 1934. By later C.20, > informal S.E.

ginger-knocker. See **knocking-down . . .**

ginger one. A distant signal: railwaymen's. See **back stick.**

ginger string. 'Rope unlaid into its separate yarns has a variety of uses about ships. It is the original ginger string: RN: 1980s' (Peppitt)—and later; coll. rather than s. Ex the colour, says Granville.—2. Hence, 'flag lieutenants' goldwire aiguillettes: RN: 1970s' (Peppitt)—but surely rather earlier?

ginger suit. 'Army uniform: first the old battle-dress, and now the khaki no. 2 dress uniform; used to differentiate from the camouflaged combat jacket and trousers or *flower-power suit*' (P.B., 1974).

gink. A fellow: always pej.: US (ca. 1910), partly anglicised by Wodehouse in 1920 (*OED* Sup.) and (in NZ as a stupid fellow) thoroughly naturalised, owing to the talkies, by 1934. Possibly derived ex *gink*, a trick, whence Scots *ginkie*, a term of reproach applied to a woman: Irwin.—2. The senior member of a gang of engine-cleaner boys: railwaymen's. McKenna, 2.—3. A look, esp. in *get* or *have a gink at*: Aus.: since mid-C.20. Wilkes.

ginned-up. Tipsy: from ca. 1920. (Sayers, 1933.) Cf. **gin up.**

Ginnie, -y. A Vickers *Virginia* aircraft: RAF: 1920s–30s. Adkin, 1983.

ginning-up. A reprimand: Can.: since ca. 1960. Dempsey, 1975.

ginny. Addicted to gin: coll. Wilson, 1957.

ginormous (pron. *jyenormous*). Very large: orig. RN and RAF, WW2 (Granville; McDouall): in post-war years more widespread, esp. among teenagers. Reid, 1970: 'The prices were ginormous'. A blend of *gigantic* + *enormous*.

gin's flop. A jumping into water with hands clasped around knees: Aus. children's. Cf. **honey-pot,** 2. B., 1943.

Gip. *G*arden *I*sland *P*rison: R Aus. N: WW2. B., 1943.

gip (var. *gyp*). To cheat (someone); to swindle: Can., ex US; adopted in UK ca. 1930 (*OED* Sup.). Usu. with *of*, as in 'I was gipped of a day's pay'.—2. Hence, to steal: mostly Services'. B.P. notes, 'common also in Australia'. Either ex *gipsy*, or from service in Egypt and experience of lower-class Egyptians.

gip artist. A confidence trickster: Aus.: since ca. 1925. B., 1942.

gippa, -er, -o, -y, gypoo (all with soft *g*). Grease; gravy; butter: nautical, since ca. 1850, then all Services', C.20. *Gippy* mainly RAF, since ca. 1928; *gypoo* an old form, from ca.

1912. Hence, *gipoo* = a cook and *master gippo* = head cook: Army: since ca. 1918. Directly ex C.19 nautical s. *jipper*, n., gravy, meat-juice, and v., to baste (*EDD*).

gippo, n. A gipsy: coll.—2. See prec.—3. An Egyptian: Services': late C.19–20. The pl., also spelt *gyppos*, very soon in WW1 denoted Egyptians in general and in WW2 came to be loosely employed for Arabs, a sense common enough, post-WW2, in Aus., e.g. in Buzo, 1968.

gippo, adj. Corresponding with n., 1 and 3.

gippy (or **gyppy**), n. A gipsy: coll. *OED* Sup.—2. See **gippa**.

gippy (or **Gippy, Gyppy**) **tummy**. Stomach-trouble (specifically, diarrhoea) in *Egypt* (hence also in Libya): orig. Army, since late C.19; by mid-C.20, gen. Also in var. *gippo tummy*. Known in India as *Delhi belly* (influence of rhyme) and in Malta as *Malta dog*; both latish C.19–20.

gipsy's ginger. Human excrement found out of doors: joc. Ex characteristic colour; cf. **baby's yellow**. (P.B.)

gipsy's (or **gypsy's**) **kiss**. A urination: r.s. on *piss*: 1970s. 'I need a gipsy's' (Jack Dash, ex London docker, 1979).

gipsy's warning. Morning: r.s.: mid-C.19–20. Franklyn notes that 'this term is not so popular as *day's a-dawning*'.

girl. A male harlot: c.: from ca. 1920. *Gilt Kid*, 1936.—2. 'Cocaine (US)' (Home Office): drug-users': 1970s. US since –1953 (Spears). Cf. **white girl**.

Girl Friday. A girl very useful to have about the place as one's 'right hand': since ca. 1955; coll. > by 1975, familiar S.E. (Chambers, ed. of 1973). Ex Defoe's tale of Robinson Crusoe and his *Man Friday*.

girlie bar. A drinking place at which 'hostesses' are available: later C.20. (*New Society*, 17 Jan. 1980.) Cf.:-

girlie magazine. A magazine containing many pictures of female nudes or provocative semi-nudes: Aus., esp. teenagers', coll.: adopted, in late 1950s, ex US. (B.P.) Adopted also in Brit., about the same time.'[The potential assassin] will consume gun magazines in the same way as many men consume girlie magazines' (*Illustrated London News*, July 1973).

Giro technician. ' "I'm gonna be a Giro technician, me" (go on the dole). Afro-Caribbean fifth formers' (RKP academic Spring, 1985). Bitterly ironic; dole, or 'unemployment benefit' is paid through the Post Office Giro system.

gism or **gissum**, or **gizm, gizzum**, or **jiz(zu)m**. Semen: low: adopted, ca. 1970, ex US, perhaps under the influence of Philip Roth's *Portnoy's Complaint*, 1967. ?Ex Yiddish.

gismo. See **gizmo**.

git. A fool; a useless fellow: mostly Cockney: since ca. 1920. An illit. pron. of *get*, in the sense of 'bastard'. In the Services, since ca. 1950, if not much earlier, often as *spawny git*, one who is undeservedly lucky.

git-box. A guitar. See **fish-horn**.

give. 'In the case of bullion robberies criminals usually rely on inside information—or "gives" as they are known' (*Now!*, 3 Apr. 1980): c.: later C.20.

give (someone) **a chalk**. To beat, defeat, or swindle that person: low:—1923 (Manchon). Cf. **give** (someone) **chalks on**.

give (a person) **a double broad**. 'To hit with a piece of marginal wood-furniture 4 picas wide': printers':—1933 (*Slang*).

give (someone) – or **get – a dusty answer**. To give, or get, 'the rough side of someone's tongue', a bad-tempered, unco-operative reply: coll. 'If he comes that old flannel with *me*, he'll jolly soon get a dusty answer, I can tell you!' (P.B.)

give (someone) **a go**. To give him a run for his money, to give 'something to think about'; Aus. coll.: since ca. 1910. (H. Drake Brockman, 1947.) And see **give it a go**.

give (someone) **a good** – or **bad – chit**. To speak well or badly of someone: Army. See also **have a good chit**. *Chit* ex Anglo-Indian, a note of commendation.

give (something) **a miss**. To avoid doing something or seeing some person or thing; cease doing something: coll.: from ca. 1912. Ex billiards, *give a miss in balk* ('avoid hitting the object ball', *SOD*), itself often used in the same way. Wodehouse, 1907, 'And James . . . is giving this miss in baulk!'

give a monkey's fuck, not to. Not to care a damn: low. In later C.20 often shortened, as in 'he couldn't give a monkey's'. See **not care a . . .**

give a peg. See AUSTRALIAN UNDERWORLD, in Appx.

give a rap, not to. Not to care a damn: coll.: mid-C.20. See also **not care a . . .**

give a rolling. An elab. of *roll*, to assault, molest, as in *rolling ginger-beers*, attacking male homosexuals, 'queer-bashing': low: later C.20. 'There was this queer, see, so we give [i.e., gave] him a rolling, duffed him up proper.' (P.B.)

give a shout. To call (another station): wireless (orig. nautical wireless): from ca. 1925. Bowen.

give (a girl) **a thrill**. To coït: coll.: since ca. 1920.

give (someone) **a touch of 'em** (or **them**). To irritate intensely: to get badly on the nerves; to disgust: Aus. low: since ca. 1925. (*Rats*, 1944.) Them = 'the shits'.

give air. See **give the ball air**.

give away. 'To abandon, give up, cease operations' (Wilkes, whose earliest quot'n is from 1948): Aus. coll. Usu. as *give it away*, but a specific person or thing may be the object, as with Eng. *give* (it) *up*.

give (someone) **Bondi**. To 'give him hell': Aus. (Stivens, 1951.) Bondi beach: a lively place.

give (someone) **chalks on**. To be (much) superior to: late C.19–20. Richards, 1933, 'We all admired the Adjutant very much: he could give us all chalks on at swearing.'

give (someone) **fits**. To scold thoroughly: Can. (Leechman.)—2. To frighten or upset someone: coll.

give (someone) **gip** (**gyp, jip**). To cause pain to (someone), esp. a sudden pain: coll.: since ca. 1905. 'My back's giving me gip again this evening' (P.B.).

give head. To fellate: low: adopted ex US, later C.20. 'He/she gives great head', s/he performs the act well. See **head job**. Cf. the later 1980s 'fast set' phrase, 'you give great phone': you have a charming telephone manner. (P.B.)

give her the gun. See **give the gun**.

give it (to a woman). To copulate with (her): low. Naughton, 1970: 'I gave it her'.

give it a go. To make an attempt at something; to experiment, as in 'I've no idea what it'll be like, but let's give it a go anyway': mainly Aus.; used also in UK: since early C.20.

give it all that. 'To brag, to show off' (Powis): low coll.: 1970s.

give it away. (Of women) as 'she'd give' or 'she just gives it away': she is ready to offer herself at the slightest, or on no, provocation: low coll.

give it big licks. See **give what for**.

give it nanti, or . . . **rice**. See **give what for**.

give it stick. See **give stick**, 3.

give out. See JAZZ TERMS, in Appx.

give out calendars. To issue unemployment cards prior to dismissing employees: workmen's: 1930s.

give over! Stop! (that activity that is annoying the speaker): coll. Ex dial. Cf. **lay off!**; **pack it in!**

give (someone) **something for** (his) **corner**. To make him 'sit up', to punish: N. Country. Ex boxing.

give stick. In *give some stick*, to encourage punters to bet freely on (a certain horse, esp. the favourite): racing c.:—1933. Ex the use of the jockey's whip.—2. In *give* (someone) *stick*, (lit., to punish), to inflict physical damage, e.g., in a fist-fight, or by bombardment: Army: later C.20.—3. In *give it stick*, to do something, to enjoy something, to the utmost, and noisily, as in 'the lads are all down the Naafi—they're really giving it stick tonight': Army: 1950s–60s. Ex sense 2. (P.B.) Cf. **stick**, 9.

give (someone) **the air**. To dismiss: adopted, ex US, early 1930s; ob. (*COD*, 1934 Sup.)

give (someone, or -thing) **the arse**. See **arse**, n., 4.

give the ball air. 'To bowl the (slow) ball with a high trajectory': cricketers' coll.: 1919. Lewis cites E.R. Wilson, that nigh the most wonderful of all slow bowlers, as using the phrase in 1920.

give the big E or . . . **the elbow**. See **give** (someone) **the elbow**.

G

give the book. See AUSTRALIAN UNDERWORLD, in Appx.

give (someone) **the brush-off.** To dismiss; to snub: Can. (ex US): since ca. 1925. Hence, Eng. and Aus., since ca. 1943.

give (someone) **the business.** To inflict punishment, whether physical or mental, upon: Can.: adopted, ca. 1945, ex US.

give (someone) **the elbow.** To dismiss, jilt, or otherwise get rid of by ignoring: coll.: since late 1970s. (Burchill, 1978.) Hence, the slightly later var., *give it* (or someone) *the big E* (Raab, 1980), and to be *on* (one's) *elbow list*, to be among those one dislikes (Hibbert, 1983).

give (someone) **the finger.** To 'goose' by sign or even verbally or metaphorically: adopted, ca. 1965, ex US. 'To make a thrusting motion with the extended middle finger, meaning . . . "fuck you" ' (*DCCU*); McCabe, 1972, 'The Apple staff give her the finger behind her back and mutter "bitch".'

give (someone) **the freedom of the world.** To sack him.

give the game away. 'To abandon interest in any activity or pursuit' (B., 1953): Aus.: since ca. 1939. An elab. of *give away*.

give the go-ahead. See **go-ahead**.

give the goo. See CANADIAN, in Appx.

give (someone) **the gooner.** See **gooner**.

give (usu. **her**) **the gun.** To open the throttle (of one's aircraft): orig. RAF and aircraft engineers', since ca. 1920; hence, more widespread, applied to automobiles; ob. *Gun* = accelerator.

give the heat. To murder with a firearm: c.: anglicised, ca. 1932, ex US usage (see Irwin). Brandon, 1936.

give (someone) **the length of one's tongue.** To reprove severely, to 'dress down': Londoners'.

give the miss in ba(u)lk. See **give** (something) **a miss.**

give (someone or something) **the old heave-ho.** Basically, to eject; hence, to dismiss, jilt, expel: light-heartedly cynical. Cf. **give the elbow.**

give (a person) **the ram's challenge.** To nod to: tailors'. *Tailor & Cutter*, 29 Nov. 1928.

give (a person) **the road.** To avoid (him): Can.: from ca. 1910. Beames.

give (one) **the shits.** To get on a person's nerves: low, esp. Londoners'. P.B.: this may orig. have been 'esp. Londoners', but by mid-C.20, and prob. by WW2, > widely used throughout the Eng.-speaking world, though still 'low'.

give the tug. See **tug**, v., at AUSTRALIAN UNDERWORLD, in Appx.

give us a touch (usu. with vocative *tosh*). Let me light my cigarette from yours, or from your pipe: National Servicemen's: since ca. 1947; † by mid-1950s.

give what for; occ. **what's what.** (With dative.) To beat, thrash: scold, reprimand: coll., the former C.19–20, the latter C.20 and gen. joc. P.B., 1974, noted 'There are many, many Service variations, all with the same meanings. Here are a few:—1. *give it nanti*: Malaya, mid-1950s. *Nanti* is Malay for "wait"; I suppose we just liked the sound of it, or maybe it was a hark-back to *niente*.—2. *give it big licks*. Emphasis on *big*. Somewhat later.—3. *give it whoomperta* or *whompo*. Both mid-50s.—4. *give it rice*. Current.—5. *give it stick*. Current. In each case, a noun or pronoun can be substituted for *it*, to give the meaning "to reprimand or punish". With *it*, the meaning may also be "to have a high old time", e.g., "The lads are down the Naafi really giving it rice", possibly smashing the place up as well as enjoying themselves any other way.' See also **what for**.

giz. 'To read a pal's letter to his girl friend' (H. & P.): Services': WW2. Perhaps ex 'gi's a look-see, then', or from:—2. To stare at (lustfully). See quot'n at **capurtle**.

gizmo, gismo. A gadget; an appliance; adopted, ex US, late 1960s. *Daily Telegraph* mag., 18 July 1969: 'The fuzz-box is an electronic gismo for making a guitar sound like a bagpipe' (R.S.). But earlier, and still, synon. with **gimmick**, 2.

gizzit. 'Looted items were known as "gizzits", short for "give us it" ' (Witherow, 1982): Services': Falkland Is. campaign, 1982.

Glad. A Gloster *Glad*iator fighter aircraft: RAF coll.: 1939–42. Aldridge, 1942.—2. (*glad.*) A gladiolus: flower-sellers': late

C.19–20. (Llewellyn, 1943.) Cf. *carn*, *casant*, *gyp*, etc., and **gladdie**.—3. In *give the glad*, elliptical for (give the) **glad eye**, q.v.: prob. since WW1. (Wilson, 1956.) Petch cites *Sappers's War Stories* for the complementary *get the glad*.—4. See **serve** (someone) **glad!**

glad-and-sorry system, the. Hire-purchase, since ca. 1910. Sava, 1945.

glad eye, the. A come-hither look (gen. from female to male). Esp. in *give* or *get the glad eye*. C.20: s. >, by 1930, coll. *Roussilon Gazette*, Jan. 1913. Ex † sense of *glad* = bright (Ware).

glad rags. One's best clothes, as in: 'Let's get our glad rags on, darling; we're going to be late for dinner': coll. Adopted ex US ca. 1906; ob. by ca. 1950. *OED* Sup.

gladdie. A gladiolus: Aus.: coll. since ca. 1960s. Made memorable by the ritual finale of performances by Barry Humphries as 'Dame Edna Everage'—'I watched him throw his "gladdies" to his audience and persuade them to wave them back at him' (Osborne, 1978).

gladi, usu. in pl. *gladis*. A gladiolus: Aus.: since ca. 1925. (B.P.) Cf. **glad**, 2, and prec.

glam, n. Glamour: film-world hangers-on: since ca. 1940.

glam, adj. Glamorous: mostly feminine: since ca. 1950. Winton, 1964, 'Her name's Maxine. She's rather glam, isn't she?'

glammed up. Made up and 'all dressed up', esp. for a party or a 'date': mostly feminine: since ca. 1955. (Petch, 1974.)

glamour. Hair-cream: Army: ca. 1939–49. (P-G-R.) Ex next.

Glamour Boys, the. The RAF: Army and RN: since 1937; ob. (E.P., 1942, 'Glamour Boys—RAF, especially flying crews'.)

glamour gown. A khaki full-dress uniform: Aus. Army: WW2. (B., 1943.) Cf. **ginger suit**.

glamour-pants. An attractive girl: since the late 1930s. (Montsarrat, 1951.) Cf. **smarty-pants**.

Glasgow Rangers; often shortened to **Glasgows**. (I spy) strangers: r.s.: since ca. 1920. Not, by the way, in Parliament, but at mock-auctions and other shady gatherings. Ex the football team, which itself is known in Glasgow as the Gers (Munro, 1985).

glass. To hit with a tumbler or a wine-glass, esp. to cut a person with one: low: since ca. 1910. (Benney, 1936.) In Aus., since ca. 1920, it has borne the nuance, 'to slash a person with a piece of broken glass' (B., 1942). Also in Brit., later C.20. To attack with broken bottle or other jagged glass edge: '[The game of pool] is all tattooed arms and people who'll glass you as soon as look at you' (*New Society*, 5 Aug. 1982). Cf. **bottle**, v., 3.

glass back. 'A fireman who did not relish main-line duties. Many men objected to the heavy physical work involved . . .' (McKenna, 1970); railwaymen's ironic: earlier C.20 (pre-diesel-engine era).

glass coach. 'District Engineer's coach' (*Railway*): railwaymen's: mid-C.20. Cf. the synon. and ironical **Cinderella's coach**.

glass house. A guard-room: esp. detention-barracks or cells for long-term prisoners: Army: from ca. 1905. (B. & P.) Ex:—2. As *the Glass House*, the military prison at North Camp, Aldershot. So called 'presumably because it has a glass roof. It is known to, and dreaded for its severity by, every soldier . . . , just as the Naval Prisons at Chatham and Portsmouth are known and dreaded by every sailor in the Navy,' ('Wood', who 'served' there in 1902, 1932).

glaze-ons. Nickname for one who wears spectacles. Herbert, 1969.

glider. A children's makeshift vehicle of soap-box and pram-wheels. See **guider**.

glider pilot. 'A driver or fireman who was required to ride on a "dead" locomotive when it was hauled back to the depot' (McKenna, 1): railwaymen's: 1945+.

gliding angle of a brick, usu. prec. by **it has the** or **it's got the.** The aircraft glides badly or hardly at all: RAF: since ca. 1950. (An RAF Officer, 1963.) Cf. 'she flies like a brick-built shithouse'.

glim, glym, n. A thief's dark lantern: late C.17-early 19 c. (B.E.) Perhaps abbr. *glimmer* (of light). In C.20, esp. 'an electric torch with the bulb covered over with paper except for a very small aperture' (Hume).—2. A match: either c. or low s.:—1923 (Manchon).—3. Eyesight: c. of ca. 1820–60. As simple 'eye', *glim* survives in C.20 market-traders' usage. *M.T.*—4. In *on the glim*, adj. and adv., a-begging: c., mostly tramps'. Cf. **glimmer,** 1.

glim, v. To look (*for* a taxicab): London taxi-drivers': since ca. 1905. (Hodge, 1939.) Ex sense 3 of the n.

glim dropper. Headlamp dip-switch: motorcyclists'. (Dunford.)

glimmer. A beggar: c. Leach, 1933.—2. ?Hence, a teller of hard-luck stories: c.: since ca. 1920. Jackson, 1946.—3. A match-seller (in the street): police s. (Bradhurst, 1937.) Ex **glim,** n., 1.—4. See next, and **not a glimmer.**

glimmers. The eyes (pl. only): low: since ca. 1814; ob., except in market-traders' usage (*M.T.*). Cf. **glim,** n., 3.

glimmie glide, usu. prec. by *far* or *other*. Side (of, e.g., the dog-track or street, etc.): Anglo-Irish r.s. Franklyn.

glitch. A malfunction in a spacecraft; a space 'gremlin': adopted, ex US, ca. 1964. (BBC1 TV, 20 Oct. 1965.) Ex Yiddish for 'slip'. 'Originally glitch meant a small voltage surge in an electrical line which affected sensitive devices powered by the line' (Turnill, 1970). (P.B.)—2. Hence, 'Glitching is a term to describe the loss of control the [radio-controlled model aircraft] flier suffers if another signal interferes with his signal' (Weightman, 1979): aero-modellers': 1970s.

glitterati, the. The more flashily publicity-conscious successful, mainly in the fields of creative art, where they are judged to have attained the cliché'd 'glittering prizes': a journalistic pun: since early 1980s. Cf.:-

glitzy. Glamorous, glittering and ritzy: 'the introduction of competitive and populist elements into the new [literary] awards has been a conscious step . . . to make the prize "a bit more glitzy" ' (*Bookseller*, 20 July 1985): adopted ex N.Am., early 1980s. Barnhart, 2, cites US and Can. usage, 1977–8.

gloak. To tell a piteous tale: tramps' c.:—1932 (Jennings). Perhaps a corruption of *croak*.

Glockenspiel! '(Used for) a "toast" when one lifts one's glass: "smart", late 1950s–early 1960s. One or two of the officers . . . used it when I went for a time to [RAF] Reunions . . . I would respond with "Cheers" limply from outer non-smart darkness' (L.A., 1974). P.B.: there *may* be some ref. to the cheerful sound of bells, but it is a good 'toast-sounding' word as it stands, not unlike 'Good luck!'

gloik. A simpleton; a fool: Aus.: since ca. 1910. (B., 1953.) Ex Irish *gloichd*, an idiot.

glom onto. To grab; to steal: Can.: since ca. 1920. (Leech, 1974.) Via US, ex Scots dial. *glam, glaum*, to clutch.

glooms, the. A mood, a fit, of depression; gloominess, despondency: Anglo-Irish: late C.19–20. Joyce, 1922, 'I'm not going to think myself into the glooms about that any more.'

glop, n. An underwater explosion: depth-charge; mine; near-miss explosion: RN: 1939+. Echoic.—2. Any viscous substance, e.g., blancmange, baby-food or wallpaper paste: domestic coll.: later C.20. Echoic, influenced by *slop*. Cf. **goo** and **gunge.** (P.B.)

glop, v. 'To slump [q.v.] or drink hurriedly' (*Mail on Sunday*, 8 Nov. 1987): RM. Echoic: see the n., 2. Hence, *glophead*, 'a drunkard' (*Ibid.*): id. Cf. synon. **piss-head.**

Glorious Glosters, the. Sobriquet and honorific gained by the Gloucestershire Regiment through their gallant and stubborn stand in Korea, at the Battle of the Imjin, 1951.

glory-hole. Any room or cupboard where oddments are stored: domestic coll. (P.B.)

glossies. Glossy-paper magazines: adopted, ca. 1945, ex US; by 1950, coll. Cf. the Can. *slicks*.—2. 'The driver's Weekly Notices. Published each week and issued to every [loco-motive] driver [advising] him of speed restrictions, signal

alterations and other important information' (McKenna 1, 1970): railwaymen's: ironic on sense 1.

glow clobber. A brightly coloured suit for motorcycle riding: motorcyclists' since ca. 1965. (Dunford.) Prob. ex *Day-glo*, a trade-name for the luminescent material from which some such suits are made. (P.B.) Cf. *eau-clobber*, waterproofs.

glue, n. A glue-sniffer: teenagers': early 1980s. Also *glue-ie* or *-y*, and *glue'd up*, 'high' on glue. (T. Williams, 1983.)

glue, v.i. To sniff glue: addicts': since late 1970s. (*Time Out*, 8 Jan. 1982, p. 15.) See **blowse,** v.

Glue-Pot, the. London: showmen's: earlier C.20. P. Allingham, 1934.

glued on. Being paced, in a cycle race: club cyclists'. Also known as *back wheel*. *Fellowship*, 1984.

gnaff or **n'aff.** A low, irritating, no-account fellow, not averse to petty theft or informing to the police: low Glasgow: mid-C.19/20. Cf. Parisian s. *gniaffe*, a term of abuse for a man. See also **naff,** n., 1.

gnat. A type of German acoustic torpedo, countered by an apparatus known as the *foxer*: RN s. > j.: ca. 1941–5.

gnat's. See **tight as a gnat's arse; within a gnat's.**

gnat's blood. 'Tea purchased [by railway staff] from railway canteen or refreshment bar. Railwaymen believe that freshly made tea in the driver's or fireman's tea can was very much superior' (McKenna, 1): railwaymen's.

gnat's piss. A weak beverage, e.g. beer, tea, **swilge** (q.v.), etc. Cf. **weasel pee.**—2. In *have blood like gnat's piss*, to feel (very much) afraid: low: earlier C.20.

gnaw-gut. Cider: Dorset s.: since mid-C.20, or earlier. (J.B. Smith, 1980.) Cf. **cripple-cock.**

gnomes of Zurich, the. International—orig. and properly, Swiss—bankers and financiers: coll., mostly journalistic: later C.20. 'George Brown [Minister of the Economy, later Lord George-Brown] came out of a meeting and snapped: "The gnomes of Zurich are at work again" ' (Fehrenbach, 1966, writing of Nov. 1964).

gnoming. Staying in college and working; the opp. of **festering,** q.v.: St Catherine's College, Oxford. (Apt, 1978): since (?)ca. 1970.

gnosh. To eat: Services'. This is the F.&G., 1925, version of **nosh,** q.v.

go, n. A bout, an attack, of sickness or illness: coll. *OED* Sup. —2. A chance; esp. in *give* (a person) *a fair go*: perhaps orig. Aus. and NZ coll., from ca. 1910; in later C.20, informal S.E. in Brit. also. McNeil, 1973, defines *a fair go*: 'an equitable chance to put one's point of view or take one's part'.—3. An argument, discussion; quarrel; as in 'She had a bit of a go with him, and wouldn't speak to him for a week': coll. (P.B.)—4. The news; what is going on: Aus.: later C.20. 'I asked him what the go was.' (Raab, 1980.)

go, v. To deal with; to find acceptable: English (?mostly Cockney) s., since ca. 1910; by ca. 1925, also Aus. ' "I'll bet you could go a cup of tea, Sonny," I asked' (Caddie, 1953).—2. To say; in reporting speech: 'He goes "I don't want to", so she goes, "Well, if that's it, then . . . ", etc.' I heard this usage in the Channel Islands, mid-1970s, and later, in England, among teenagers; judging by a Charles M. Schulz 'Peanuts' cartoon of 1979, it is current also among US youngsters. (P.B.)—3. In asking a child if he/she needs to relieve him/herself: 'Do you want to *go*?', it is a euph.

go a bundle on. This phrase has, since ca. 1930, been the predominant var. of the earlier *go the bundle on* = to support, approve, or think highly of. E.g., in the disparaging 'Can't say I go a bundle on him'. See also under JAZZ TERMS, in Appx. Cf. the late C.19–20 solo whist term *go a bundle*, to bid *abundance*. (P.B.)

go-ahead. In *give* (*it* or *someone* or *-thing*) *the go-ahead*, to order or to allow an action or agent to proceed: perhaps mainly journalistic, as in, e.g., 'Government gives go-ahead to plan for . . . ': later C.20. (P.B.)

go all out on. To trust completely; to make the most of (a person): coll.: 1933 (Compton Mackenzie). Ex athletics.

187

go all the way. (Of a girl) to permit copulation as well as just 'petting': coll., perhaps orig. Can.: since ca. 1920.

go all unnecessary. See make go all . . .

go and piss up your kilt! Rudely synon. with 'No!': mostly Forces': since ca. 1939.

go ape. See ape.

go(-)back. A reply; a retort: Aus.: since ca. 1921. Glassop, 1944, ' "You had a go-back?" I asked, "You didn't let him get away with it?" '

go back at it. To return to crime, after having served a prison sentence: prisoners'. Clayton, 1970.

go bananas. See bananas.

go big; go over big. (Of a play, a book) to be very successful: both US and both anglicised in 1928. The latter was, in US, the earlier; *go big* derives from it. *OED* Sup.

go blah. See blah, adj. Prob. ex:—2. To have one's mind go blank: from ca. 1907: Parliamentary >, by 1930, gen. Mason, 1930, in ref. to the year 1908 and to a prospective speaker in Parliament, 'If only his mind didn't go blank. Minds often did, even the best minds. Darkness descends on them, inextricable . . . These seizures . . . always chose ruinous moments. There was a slang phrase which described them—horribly graphic, too, like most slang phrases. To go blah. Well, there it was! He, Mark Thewless, would go blah this afternoon.' Perhaps *blah* represents a perversion of *blank.*

go by the book. To keep strictly—even if unreasonably so—to the rules and regulations: Services'; police; bureaucrats': since ca. 1920; coll. >, by 1970, informal S.E.

go case with. To go to bed with: since ca. 1910: c. that, by 1940, had > low s. (Norman.) Cf.:-

go caso. To take a room or a flat and become a genteel prostitute: c. >, by 1935, low s. 'He only married her for her money, and she got it going caso' (Kersh, 1938). See caso.

go chicken. See chicken out.

go cold at. To reprove, blame, reprimand: Aus.: since ca. 1925. B., 1943.

go cold on. To lose one's initial enthusiasm for (an idea, a plan, etc.): coll.: since ca. 1920.

go crook. To speak angrily: Aus.: from ca. 1910. See crook.

go dental. To report on sick parade to see the dentist: Services' coll.: later C.20. Cf. go sick. (P.B.)

go dis. See dis (disconnected) and cf. gone dis.

go down. To be sentenced, imprisoned: c. > low s. (Wallace, 1927.) Often as go (*went*) *down for* (so many) *months* or *years.*—2. To give birth to a child. Jones, 1926, 'The girls who were with me waiting to go down.'

go down a bomb. To be very well received, either by an audience, or of the individual recipient of a gift, as in 'I sent her flowers on the anniversary, and they went down a bomb': show-biz > gen., later C.20. Contrast opp. bomb, v., 3, and cf. go like a bomb.

go down on (one's) **bended.** To pray (on one's knees): coll.: since ca. 1925.

go down south on. To practise either fellatio or cunnilingus on: low. In later C.20, simply *go down on.*

go Dutch. To join in a 'Dutch treat' (the term is S.E., ex US: *SOD*, 1977), i.e. to pay one's own share instead of being treated, to drinks, food, etc.: coll.: since (?)mid-C.20. 'My girl and I always go Dutch when we go out.' (P.B.)

go firm (on). To come to a definite decision and to abide by it: Services': since 1960s. 'Brigade agreed to go firm on that one, and the operation began next day' (P.B.).

go for a quick one. See quick one.

go for broke. To 'try to crash through the soup' (*Pix,* 28 Sep. 1963): Aus. surfers': since ca. 1960. R.C.: ex the much earlier (—1930) US meaning, orig. in gambling, to risk all at one throw or on one bet.

go for it. (Of a girl) to be extremely eager for sexual intercourse: Aus.: since ca. 1925.

go for (one's) **quoits.** To run, to work, at one's fastest and best: Aus.: since ca. 1925. (B., 1943.) Perhaps ultimately ex *quoit* or *coit*, buttocks, arse.

go for (one's) **tea.** To die: underworld: 1970s. Powis, 1977.

go for the doctor. To ride (a horse) fast: Aus. rural: since ca. 1910; by 1960, slightly ob. B., 1953.—2. To bet heavily on a horse in the expectation (?hope) of winning a lot of money: Aus. sporting: since ca. 1930. Glassop, 1949.

go foreign. To go on an overseas commission: RN officers': since ca. 1925. P-G-R.

go gardening. To run off the road: motorcyclists': later C.20. (Dunford.)

go-getter. A very active, enterprising person; a pusher: coll.: adopted, ex US, ca. 1925. (*OED* Sup.) Ex *go* (and) *get what one wants.*

go-go. See gogo girl.

go grunts. To defecate. See grunts.

go-in. A difference of opinion, a row: low Aus.: since ca. 1920. Tennant, 1953.—2. An agreement, a partnership: Aus.: since ca. 1930. B., 1943.—3. A run of bad luck, necessitating recourse to the central pool: Aus. domino players'. B., 1953.

go into a flat spin. To become muddled: airmen's and aircraft engineers': since 1920s. See flat spin.—2. Hence, (also as *get into . . .*) to know not which way to turn, to become flustered: esp. in Services and chiefly RAF: since ca. 1937. *English Digest*, Feb. 1941; H. & P.—3. More intensively, to panic: Services': since ca. 1942.

go into smoke. To go into hiding: Aus. c.

go like a bomb. Orig., RAF in WW2: 'Modern version of *goes like a train*, i.e. with precision' (H.W., 1942). Civilianised and, by 1950s, used for cars with a fine turn of speed and a very rapid acceleration; by early in the 1960s it was being applied to expeditions, visits, parties, love affairs, what have you. See also go down a bomb.

go like a rabbit. As *he* or *she goes* . . . : approvingly, of a sexual partner: later C.20. (Reynolds, 1979.) Cf. fuck, or shag, like a rattlesnake.

go like the clappers; . . . the hammers. See like the clappers, and hammers of hell.

go much on. (Usu. in negative, except in question.) 'Do you go much on him?'; 'I don't go much on her/it, myself': to like, to care for: perhaps orig. NZ and Aus., but soon also Brit. coll. Devanney, 1926.

go mulga. To take to the bush; hence, to decamp, to seek solitude: Aus. B., 1959.

go muzzy. To bid *misère* in solo whist: esp. Merseyside.

go native. To assimilate oneself with the local population, adopting their customs and way of living, used esp. of expatriate British settling in tropical countries; as in the rueful, mocking comment of a soldier, in, say, Hong Kong: 'Can't leave us here too long, can they? After all, might marry one of the local beauties. Can't have the chaps going native, what!'—a parody of the upper-class empire-builders' attitude to their colonial subjects: coll. It might also be applied to a Londoner settling contentedly in the provinces. (P.B.) See also gone native.

go off. A hotel, a club, raided by the police for serving liquor after hours is said to 'go off': Aus. urban: since ca. 1925. Baker.—2. To experience orgasm: coll.—3. To *go off* to prison, be sent to gaol: Aus.: since ca. 1910. Casey, 1945.—4. Hence, merely to be fined, esp. for gambling. Glassop, 1949.—5. To cease to be attracted (not necessarily sexually) by someone, or to gain pleasure from some thing or interest: coll.: since ca. 1950. As in the (usu.) joc. remark, made *at* someone, 'You can go off some people, you know!' used as a retort. (P.B.)

go off (one's) **brain.** To rave, be ecstatic, about something: Aus.: since latish 1940s. (Buzo, 1969.) Cf. the informal S.E. *go off* (one's) *head*, to go mad.

G

go off (one's) **burner.** See **burner**, 2.

go off (one's) **face.** To burst out laughing: Aus.: since ca. 1945. Buzo, 1969.

go off the boil. Of a pregnant woman: to cease, temporarily, to feel the contractions and pangs of childbirth: medical students': since ca. 1910.—2. Of a woman: to lose, temporarily or momentarily, the desire for intercourse: raffish and mainly Aus.: since ca. 1920.

go on the Cousin Sis. To drink heavily: low, since ca. 1925. (Kersh, 1942.) R.s. on **go on the piss.**

go on the knocker. See **knocker**, 7.

go on the oil. See **oil**, 4.

go on the piss. See **piss** 4.

go on the sharpo. To rob from buildings: tramps' c.:—1932 (Jennings).

go out like a light. Suddenly to lose consciousness. See **out like a light.**

go over. To become a sexual pervert: Aus.: since ca. 1910. B., 1942.

go over big. See **go big.**

go over the side. To commit a first offence: police: since ca. 1918. Cf. **over the side.**

go over the top. To leave one's own trench and join in the attack on the enemy: Army coll.: from 1916. The *top* is both the top of the trench and the open ground between the trenches. (B. & P.) See also **over the top.**—2. Hence, to do something dangerous and/or notable (e.g. getting married): from 1919; †. Collinson; Lyell.

go places. To travel extensively, or merely to gad about: coll.: adopted ca. 1938 from US. Often *go places and see things*.—2. To become truly effective; to succeed in one's ambitions; 'places' in this sense = upwards, 'to the top of the ladder': 'He'd got a bit of money behind him now, and he was really going places': coll.: since mid-C.20. (P.B.)

go round the corner. To visit the privy: euph. coll.: since ca. 1890.

go sick. To malinger: Services' coll.: WW1. Collinson.—2. Later, by WW2, in Services' coll., it became simply elliptical for 'to go on sick parade', to report for medical diagnosis and/or treatment, with no suggestion of malingering. By later C.20 > j.; cf. **go dental.**

go slumming. To mix with one's inferiors: joc. coll.: since ca. 1905. Bartlett, 1940.

go spare. To become distraught, esp. 'mad', with anger: Forces': since ca. 1935. (L.A.) By 1950, also fairly gen. civilian, as in Norman.

go steady. (Of juveniles) to be constantly together as boy-and-girl companions; to be a courting couple or one member thereof: coll.: Can.: since ca. 1945. (Leechman.) By 1955, a common expression in England.

go steady with (one's) **right hand.** (Of either sex, but usu. male) to masturbate: adopted, prob. via Can., mid-C.20. Ex *go steady with*—see prec.—which Hollander uses to mean 'to keep potentially sexual company with', without the implication of fidelity.

go the bundle on. To support strongly; plump for; be enthusiastic concerning: RN: earlier C.20. Lit., go the whole lot on, stake one's all on; perhaps cf. *go nap on*, but prob. cf. **bundle**, n., 1. An early example occurs in 'Bartimeus', 1915. See also **go a bundle on.**

go (or **last**) **the full distance.** To last the scheduled number of rounds in a contest: boxers' coll.: from ca. 1910; by 1940, S.E. *The Times*, 24 Nov. 1936.

go the knock on. To steal (something): low Aus.: since ca. 1910. Niland, 1959.

go the knuckle. To fight—esp. if well—with one's fists: Aus.: since ca. 1920. (Devanney, 1944; Niland, 1955.) See also **knuckle**, n., 2.

go the limit. In courting or love-making, to achieve or permit coïtion: coll.: since ca. 1916.

go through. To abscond on bail: Aus. c.—2. To give up, cease, desist: Aus.: since ca. 1925. Devanney, 1944.—3. To desert (from the Forces): Aus.: since 1939. B., 1943; Cleary, 1949.

go through for. ' "He's going through for law": Can. and US. Means he is taking a course of study in law (or medicine, or what else). Ex going through the university' (Leechman): coll., not s.; since ca. 1935.

go through like a dose of salts. See **dose of salts.**

go through on. To leave; give the slip to; see no more of (a person): Aus.: since ca. 1920. *Rats*, 1944: 'We'll go through on them two milk-bar sorts.'

go through the card. 'To cover comprehensively, or to have everything that is on offer (on a menu, for example); originally meant to back every winning horse at a meeting' (Powis): low coll.: later C.20.

go through the gate. To let the throttle full out, strictly in an emergency, with the use of *emergency* power: RAF: since ca. 1937. E.P., 1942; Hinde, 1945, 'This means literally to push the throttle through a small projection on the side of the groove in which it operates. Sometimes the gate takes the form of a breakable wire. Used only for emergency power, not synonymous with *turn up the wick*.'

go through the motions. To give the appearance of doing something, without actually doing it, or without doing it wholeheartedly; to conform, whether in spirit or, esp., only in the letter, e.g. at church: orig. Services', from ca. 1920 at latest, ex a squad doing rifle drill, when not every man has a rifle, and the NCO's order: 'Them without weapons, go through the motions'; since ca. 1950, in gen. coll. usage. (Petch, 1966; P.B.)—2. Hence, as Petch cites from the BBC TV series 'Dixon of Dock Green', about the police force, programme of 13 Jan. 1968, 'to make the usual routine enquiries; to observe routine'.

go through the roof. Suddenly to be extremely angry; to fly into a rage: coll.: since ca. 1960. A logical extension of **hit the roof**, q.v. (P.B.)

go to a hundred feet. To sleep (very) deeply: submariners': since ca. 1939. (Hackforth-Jones, 1943.) Ex a submarine's submersion.

go to bed with (one's) **boots on**, usu. **not to.** (Of the male) to deliberately omit to use a contraceptive: since ca. 1950. Cuddon, 1967. ' "Yes", said Vera, "You can't make them wear something. I tried to tell Reggie once . . . 'No fear,' he said, 'I don't go to bed with my boots on!' " '

go to market. To kick up a fuss; cut a dash, let off steam: Aus. coll. Pritchard, 1926: of a spirited stallion not yet fully trained to the saddle. Cf. **go to town.**

go to the bank. To go to the Labour Exchange: workmen's: from ca. 1924.

go to the country. To go to prison; cf. *in the country*, in prison, esp. at Dartmoor: c. (Wallace, 1927.) P.B.: perhaps also a pun on the political j., to hold a general election.

go to the movies. To go into action: RAF: WW2; adopted 1940 from US airmen. *Reader's Digest*, Feb. 1941.

go to town. 'To enjoy things in a big way' (Granville, 1969); to tackle with zest, actively, fiercely, etc., as 'The CO really went to town on those blokes who were caught out of bounds', i.e. he punished them severely; it has also the senses of the Aus. **go to market**, q.v.: adopted, prob. via US servicemen in Brit., ca. 1943, by which date it was already in use in Can.

go uncling. To run after a married woman: RAF: from ca. 1920. Her children call him 'Uncle'.

go up a gully. (Of a person) to vanish; get out of the way, make oneself scarce: Northern Territory, Aus.: since ca. 1920. Hill, 1951.

go up the Noo. To go on leave to Edinburgh—or to Scotland in general: RN. (Granville.) Prob. ex Scots pron. of *now*.

go up the Smoke. To go on leave to London: id. (Ibid.)

Go When Ready. A railwaymen's nickname for the Great Western Railway: earlier C.20. (*Railway*, 2nd.) Cf. **God's Wonderful Railway.**

G

go while the going's good. See **going's good.**

goalee; gen. **goalie.** A goal-keeper: Association football coll. (ca. 1920) now verging on S.E. (*OED* Sup.) Also in ice-hockey: Can.: since ca. 1910.

goat. A horse having no chance of winning: Aus. sporting: since late 1940s. (Culotta.) Cf. **crab,** n., 2.—2. In the phrase *get* (someone's) *goat,* to annoy him: adopted, ex US, ca. 1916; s. >, by late 1930s, coll. (*OED* Sup.) Perhaps ex Fr. *prendre la chèvre,* to take the milch-goat, often the poor man's sole source of milk.

goat's toe, be the. To be pre-eminent: Anglo-Irish: since ca. 1920. Applied, e.g., to James Stephens soon after his death in 1951. On the analogy of *the cat's whiskers* and with special ref. to a mountain goat's sure-footedness.

gob, n. A coastguard. Stimson, 1946, 'The English also [?as well as the Americans] call any coastguard a gob'. Short for later C.19 s. *gobby.*—2. An American sailor: adopted, ex Can., 1940.—3. As *the gob,* theft from a man as he is washing at a public lavatory: c. Ex v.: the thief spits on the back of a man's coat, steers him to a lavatory, helps him remove his coat and robs him of his wallet.

gob, v. To spit, esp. copiously: C.19–20 low coll.

gob and rub. (Of males) to masturbate. Callow, 1969.

gob-iron. A harmonica: since ca. 1950. (BBC2 programme 'Folk on Sunday', 13 Feb. 1972.) Cf. **gob-stick,** 1.

gob-shite. A fool; an easy dupe: Services'; market-traders'.

gob-smacked. Rendered speechless by astonishment, anger, etc.: ex NW Eng. dial., 'popularised' by Liverpool politicians, mid-1980s. (Watts, 1988.)

gob-stick. A clarinet: musicians'. (Baker.) See **fish-horn.**—2. 'A valve-grinding tool consisting of a stick to which was attached a rubber suction pad that needed wetting, usually done with spittle: since 1920s' (Dunford, 2): motorcyclists'.

gob-stopper. ' "gob-stoppers" . . . is becoming a general term for "any sweet difficult to chew", as humbugs, large aniseed balls, and fruit drops. (The true, colour-changing gob-stopper was for long unobtainable during and after [WW2]' (Opie, 1959): children's: prob. since late C.19, for the orig. in the quot'n.

gobber. Var. of (orig. dial.) *gob,* the mouth: since ca. 1920. (L.A.) Perhaps that with which one *gobs,* or spits. (P.B.) Hence also, one who spits.

gobbie. See **gobby.**

gobbified. Stupid: an elab. of **gobby,** adj. *M.T.*

gobble, n. An act of fellatio: low: C.19–20.

gobble, v. To work overtime—esp., excessive overtime: printers'. Hence *gobbling,* n., (excessive) overtime.—2. To commit fellatio: low: C.18–20. Cf. **gobbler,** 2.

gobbledygook. Coined, 1944, by Maury Maverick in US for pompous, long-winded, vague speech or writing, heavily laced with jargon. There, it caught on almost immediately; well-known in Britain by ca. 1951 – defined and copiously exemplified in my *Chamber of Horrors,* 1952. Ex the fussy, self-important gobbling sound made by a turkeycock. Never s.; began as coll.; by 1960, at latest, informal S.E.

gobbler. 'An Eastern Region tank engine 2–4–2' (*Railway,* 2nd): railwaymen's: post-WW2.—2. A fellator or penilingist: low, and homosexual: C.19–20. Ex **gobble,** v., 2.—3. Hence, a woman who prefers oral sex, both actively and passively: since ca. 1920 at the latest, perhaps since late C.18.

gobbling irons. Knife, fork, and spoon: trawlermen's. (Mitford, 1969.) Cf. **eating irons** and **fighting irons.**

gobby, or **gobbie,** n. A coastguardsman: nautical: later C.19–early 20. *OED* Sup.; Bowen.—2. A stupid fellow: market-traders'. A var. of *gob-shite.* (M.T.) Prob. ex dial. *gawby, gobby,* the Northern pron. of *gaby* (*EDD*). Cf. adj.—3. 'Civilian employee in an [RN] establishment, usually a Naval pensioner' (Malin, 1979): RN: later C.20.

gobby, adj. Stupid. See n., 2.

goby. A criminal 'fixer' or arranger; an intermediary in nefarious dealings: since ca. 1945. (Newman, 1970.) Ex *go-between.*

God-awful. A stressing of *awful* in its coll. sense: (low) coll. Cf. **God's own.**

God-botherer. A parson: RAF, from ca. 1920; later, to the other Services, and into civilian usage, prob. by the late 1930s. Cf. **God-pesterer.**

God in the box. A radio set: since ca. 1939. (Armstrong, 1941.) Ex authoritarian news-announcements. P.B.: surely this was ephemeral.

God love her. Mother: r.s. on the Cockney pron. *luvver* for *muvver.* (Hillman, 1974.)

God-pesterer. A bishop: RAF: 1920s–30s. Cf. **God-botherer.**

God rep, the. The college chaplain: orig. New College, Oxford, 1950s and 1960s; later in other universities. Ex *rep,* a commercial traveller or representative.

God save. (Pl. **God saves.**) The national anthem: from ca. 1910.

God slot. A religious programme on radio or TV, anything from a 90-second 'Thought for the Day' to something much longer: broadcasters'. Among those taking part, perhaps a conscious parody of jargon.

God's own. A great . . . ; esp. *God's own fuss,* a 'terrible' fuss: expletive coll.:—1923 (Manchon). Cf. **hell's own.**

God's Wonderful Railway. The *Great Western Railway:* railwaymen's ironic. (*Railway,* 2nd.) Cf. **Go When Ready.**

goer. A horse being honestly ridden to win: Aus. sporting: since ca. 1910. Glassop, 1949.—2. A member of the gang; 'one of the boys': Teddy boys': since ca. 1947. Sigal, 1959.—3. One (of either sex) who enthusiastically seeks sexual satisfaction: since late 1940s.—4. Something, esp. a plan, likely to prosper or succeed—or is, in fact, doing so: since ca. 1955. Ross, 1977.—5. Someone always active and keen, willing to 'have to go'; not necessarily—contrast sense 1—adept, but an 'enthusiastic amateur': coll. P.B.: it was used in this sense by my grandmother, b. ca. 1880.

gofer. One who runs errands for others, the 'office dogsbody' who is told to 'go for' this or that: adopted ex US (where current since ca. 1970: Barnhart, 1) ca. 1980. 'There was a time when women were the gofers of the publishing industry' (Miller, 1984). D. Mann notes, 1984, that in 'political, bureaucratic context, [it =] an intermediary and fixer for the Big Man'. The orig. US perhaps influenced by *gopher,* the busy burrowing ground-squirrel (P.B.). Note, however, that Patterson writes of *gof-fa,* as used by gangs of fitters in Portsmouth Royal Dockyard, mid-C.20, 'used . . . [for] a man nominated, or who volunteers, to collect stores or equipment for the rest of the gang: '' 'ere, Fred, gof-fa a tin o'grease, will yer?'' '

goffer. (Gen. pl.) A mineral water: nautical, esp. RN. (Bowen.) Ex a trade name *Goffa.*—2. Hence, 'a man selling mineral water or lemonade on board ship': RN: from ca. 1910. (F. & G.) Knock records *goffer firm* as the lowerdeck term for a ship's 'firm' selling lemonade. See:-

goffer wallah. 'Asian national selling confectionery, etc., to troops' (Hawke): RM in Northern Ireland (and, no doubt, everywhere else in the world): early 1970s. An extension of **goffer,** n., 1, to which it is fitting that the RM should have added the predominantly army term *wallah;* it is interesting that both terms have survived well into later C.20. (P.B.)

gog-eye. A catapult: Aus. children's. B., 1942.

goggle. Occ. abbr. of **goggle-box:** an instance, from 1970, cited in Barnhart.

goggle-box (or written solid). A television set: since ca. 1958. Hence, *goggler,* a persistent viewer, and *goggling,* n., persistent viewing. Cf. **idiot box** and **idiot's lantern.**

goggled goblin; usu. in pl. A British night fighter: RAF joc.: since ca. Oct. 1940; † by 1945. (H. & P.) Cf. **cat's eyes.**

goggling. See **goggle-box.**

Goggo. A Goggomobil car: Aus.: ca. 1955–70. (B.P.)

gogo girl. A performer of lewd dances in strip-tease clubs: since ca. 1970. (BBC radio interview, Aug. 1973.) Cf. Fr. s., *à gogo,* whatever you want; ad lib; galore.

gogs. A motorcyclist's goggles: since ca. 1940. Jeffries, 1958, but dealing with the year 1948.—2. Spectacles: coll. A shortening of older s. *goggles*. Hence, *gogs-case*, a spectacles-case.

going and coming. 'The two-way radio telephonic system. Thus, "Had a word with him on the going and coming" ' (Jackson): RAF: since ca. 1935; ob. by ca. 1950.

going for. In phrases such as 'he's got a lot—not much—nothing—going for him': he has considerable—few—no—advantages on his side, in a specific enterprise, or in life generally: coll.: since ca. 1970. (P.B.)

going for a walk with a spade. Defecation in the open. See **bending drill.**

going home. Of an elderly person 'well on the way down the hill of life': coll. (not necessarily euph.): since ca. 1910. (Petch.) Ware records it, 1909, simply as 'a-dying', which E.P. glossed in 1930s as 'proletarian: slightly ob.'—2. Of clothes, machinery, etc., wearing out, in the last stage of usefulness: coll. (P.B.)

going on a kick. 'An intensive period of drug-taking' (Home Office): drug-users' s.: 1970s.

going-over. As in, e.g., 'They gave him a thorough going-over', which may refer to any process, usu. disagreeable, applied to a person: a medical examination, an interrogation, robbery with violence, etc.: coll. Cf. later C.19 c. *go over*, to search and rob.

going recce, a. A reconnaissance made to determine 'the going' in the country ahead: Army: since ca. 1940. (P-G-R.) Cf. **recce.** Also, esp. in N. Africa, *going shufty*. (Sanders, 1967.)

going spare. Available and easily obtainable or even stolen, esp. of things not strictly private property and even for unattached girls: since ca. 1940. 'She is not going spare': engaged and therefore not fair game. (Petch.)—2. See **go spare.**

going to pay the water bill. (Of men) going off to urinate: low. Clement, 1978.

going's good!, (go) while the. The English version of the US (*beat it*) *while the beating's good* and Scots *go while the play is good*: coll.: in Eng. from ca. 1912; slightly earlier in Aus. Lyell.

goitre. 'A large number of banknotes, usually kept in fob pocket of trousers' (Powis): c.: 1970s.

gold braid. (Collective n.) The principal warders: prisoners' c.: from ca. 1920. Ingram, 1933.—2. 'Lowerdeck collective noun for officers; cf. **brass**' (Granville): RN.

gold brick. A fraud, a swindle; a sham; an app. chance of making a lot of money: US (ca. 1888), partly anglicised by Wodehouse in 1915; Spenser, 1934. Ex the US *gold-brick swindle*, a particular form of fraud. *OED* Sup.

Gold Coast, the. 'Nickname for the New Fresh Wharf just below London Bridge on the north side. Men would earn fantastic wages when working on the tomato boats' (Ash): London dockers': earlier C.20. A pun on the pre–1957 name of the former British colony, Ghana.

gold-digger. A female attaching herself to a man for (her) self and pelf: US (ca. 1925); anglicised by 1930. Ex the lit. S.E. sense.—2. Also *gold-digging*, the corresponding (not too) abstract n.

Gold Dust. Tobacco, when supplies are short: nautical: late C.19–20. (Bowen.) P.B.: it may well apply to any sort of commodity in short supply, particularly when, as in 1970s–80s, panic-buying sets in on, e.g., sugar, lavatory-paper, etc. Specifically, to:—2. Cocaine: drugs c. (Stockley, 1986.) US since—1931 (Spears). Cf. synon. *gold star* (Ibid.).

gold watch. Scotch (whisky): r.s.: later C.20. (Hillman, 1974.)

Goldbergs Green. See **Abrahampstead.**

golden. Much used in financial circles, later C.20: Howard, 1987, notes 'Golden Hello (a large signing-on fee to bribe an employee to join a company); Golden Parachute (a contractual guarantee of compensation [on redundancy or demotion]). They joined the existing Golden Handcuffs (a large bribe paid to persuade an employee not to defect to the opposition).'

golden balls. Horse dung: Army: early C.20. Hatton, 1930.

golden ballocks. Applied to a man lucky in 'love' and at cards: Forces': since ca. 1935. Contrast **grey ballocks.**

golden bog-seat time. In those establishments, e.g. local government, where short-sighted policy insists that book-keeping is conducted as though the end of the financial year were the end of the world, and where money cannot be carried from one year to the next, but must be spent or lost, that time when unspent cash is suddenly 'discovered', only to be frittered away on small, comparatively unnecessary trimmings instead of being accumulated for something larger and far more worthwhile. A *bog-seat* = lavatory cover. (D. Williams, 1987, the term; P.B., the explanation.)

golden bowler. See **bowler hat.**

golden doughnut. The female pudend: Aus.: since ca. 1970. Wilkes quotes Williamson, 1972, 'We'll be in like Flynn there tomorrow night. We'll thread the eye of the old golden doughnut—no worries.'

golden duck = king duck. A batsman so unfortunate as to get out, first ball, in both innings of a cricket match: the former, schoolboys' s.—since ca. 1960; the latter, cricket commentators'—since early 1950s. (Sanders, 1965.)

Golden Eagle shits on Friday, the. Friday is pay-day: Army and RAF: since ca. 1941; slightly ob. by 1970, with the introduction by then of payment to bank accounts for all ranks. Friday was the normal day for the weekly pay parade. The phrase was adapted from the US Army's *the eagle shits on pay-day*; the eagle concerned is that which figures on the US dollar. P.B.: prob. earlier. T.E. Lawrence, *The Mint*, concerning the RAF of early 1920s, has the euph. *the golden eagle moults today*. Hence, in the Army, from ca. 1946, *the golden eagle* was the paying officer himself (Bishop, 1985).

golden handshake. A large gift of money to a departing director or important employee: coll.: since ca. 1950. A *richly gilded* farewell handshake. Cf. the **golden bowler** for redundant Service officers. P.B.: by late 1970s a *golden handshake* had > gen. for any lump-sum payment to any employee being made 'redundant'. See also **golden**, and cf. late C.18–19 coll. *golden grease*, a bribe. Cf. The more lowly **redundo.**

golden oldie. (Usu. in pl.) A 'hit' tune that has lasted well and is still popular: disc-jockeys', particularly in the 'nostalgia boom' of the mid/late-1970s, when a 'hit' of only two years before could qualify for the description. (P.B.)

golden rivet, the. What a sky-hook is to an airman, *the golden rivet* is to the seaman (RN); the latter, however, concerns an unrepeatable piece of folk-lore. It prob. goes back to ca. 1860.—2. Hence, *penis erectus*: RN: since ca. 1910. Cf. **Navy cake.**—3. A 'Dockers' term for the bottom of the ship's hold. When you reached the bottom of the ship the cry would be "I've found the golden rivet" ' (Ash): London dockers'.

golden stairs. See **climb the golden . . .**

Golden Triangle, the. The opium-poppy-growing area of South East Asia: drugs c.: later C.20. *Time Out*, 15 Feb. 1980.—2. The area between the M3 and M4 motorways as they converge WSW of London, where commerce and industry were booming in the late 1980s: 'land prices in the so called golden triangle are already high, up to £1.5m an acre . . . ' (*Daily Telegraph*, 17 May 1988).

goldfish. A chorister who opens her mouth but does not sing: theatrical:—1935.—2. ' "Termorrer," said Eddie, "we oughter have some goldfish." Goldfish were herrings' (*Rats*, 1944): Aus. soldiers': 1941–2 at Tobruk.—3. Hence, tinned fish: Aus.: since ca. 1943. B., 1953.

Goldfish Gang, the. The Fleet Air Arm: RN: since ca. 1937. Cf. **fish-heads,** the FAA's counter-insult.

Goldie. A BSA 'Gold Star' motorcycle: motorcyclists': later C.20. (Dunford.)

golf-ball. Protective, pressurised dome housing a ground radar installation: RAF: later C.20. Ex colour, and shape seen from a distance. (P.B.)

golf widow. A wife isolated by her husband's zeal for golf: joc. coll.: from ca. 1920. On *grass widow*.

gollion. 'A gob of phlegm' (B., 1942): Aus. Perhaps *golly 'un*: see **golly**, v.

golliwog. A caterpillar: Aus.: since ca. 1920. (B., 1942.) In ref. to the numerous very hairy caterpillars found in Aus. and ex their resemblance to a golliwog doll.—2. A 'fence' or receiver of stolen goods: low (verging on c.): since ca. 1930.

golliwogs (or **gollywogs**), **the.** Greyhound racing: since ca. 1910. Rhyming on *the dogs*.

gollock. An issue machete: RM: since (?)earlier C.20. (Knight, 1984.)

Golly. 'For the average Tommy, black or white, any local, be he Arab, Indian, or Somali, is a "Golly"—a marginally less insulting retread of the old-fashioned "Wog" ' (Jorre, 1967): since ca. 1950. See **wog**, 1, and cf.:—2. A Negro: low raffish London: since ca. 1960. Both short for *golliwog*, thick black crinkly hair and all, and perhaps ex *golly!*, common—or once common—among Negroes. Fairborn, 1976.

golly, v. and n. To spit: Aus. juvenile: since 1930s. (Wilkes.) It gives rise to *golly* (*gum*), chewing-gum: since ca. 1944; and *golly pot*, a spittoon: id. B., 1953.

gonce. Money: Aus. s.: late C.19–mid-20. Wilkes, who notes '?Yiddish'. B., 1941, spells it *gons*.

gone. Jazz-ecstatic: adopted, ca. 1948, ex US.—2. Hence, excellent: Merseyside teenagers': ca. 1960–5.—3. Hopelessly drug-addicted (on the 'hard stuff'; e.g., heroin): since ca. 1950. (Norman, 1959.) Cf. sense 1.

gone a million. 'In a hopeless state; utterly disadvantaged or beaten' (Wilkes): Aus.:—1916 (Dennis). Wilkes cites Sir Paul Hasluck, in the *Sun-Herald,* 24 Aug. 1969, attributing the phrase to John Scaddan, prime minister of W. Australia (1911–16), who app. lavish with State finances.

gone an' dunnit. A man's hat: Glasgow r.s. on *bunnit* = bonnet (the old-fashioned man's flat cap). Munro, 1985.

gone-by. One who belongs to a recently gone-by period, a 'has-been': coll.

gone dis. Mentally deficient; crazy, crazed: Services': since ca. 1915. (F. & G.) Ex the signallers' *gone dis* (of wires) having had a breakdown (disconnected): since 1914.—2. Hence, any piece of machinery or equipment that has gone wrong or will not work may be described as *gone dis*: Army: still current early 1970s.

gone for six. Missing; killed: RAF: ca. 1930–50. (Jackson.) Ex *hit for six.*

gone native. A man that has gone native: coll.: from ca. 1920. A. Waugh, 1932, 'He seemed equally at ease with Mexican half-castes, niggers from the Southern States, and "gone natives" from God knew where.' See also **go native.**

gone on tour with (any notable actor recently deceased). Dead: theatrical and homosexuals': later C.20. (D. Mann, 1984.)

gone out. (Often *look(ing)* so or *right* or *proper* or *all . . . gone out.*) Stupefied by surprise; vacuous; 'gormless': coll.: later C.20. 'Well, don't just stand there looking gone out—bloody well get and *do* something!' Cf. synon. **dropped on.** (P.B.)

gone to Moscow. Pawned: Aus.: since ca. 1918. (B., 1942.) With a pun on C.19 s. *mosk* or *moskeneer*, 'to pawn'.

gone with the wind. Disappeared, e.g. money or spouse: since late 1930s. Ex the world-famous novel and film.

gong, n. A medal; loosely, a decoration: orig. Army, later all Services': since late C.19. (F. & G.) E.g., **Naffy gong**, q.v.—2. A bell: busmen's: from ca. 1925. *Daily Herald,* 5 Aug. 1936.—3. As *the Gong,* Wollongong, nr Sydney, Aus.: mainly Sydneysiders': since ca. 1925. (B.P.)

gong, v. (Of the mobile police) to strike a gong in order to stop a motorist: since ca. 1925. Notably as *be gonged,* (of a motorist) to be stopped by the police, and have one's name taken: since the late 1920s. MacKail, 1937.

gong girl. A girl 'picked up' by a motorist for dalliance in a lonely spot: 1930s. (London *Evening News,* 19 Aug. 1937.) ?Some connection with **gong**, v.

gong-ridden. Heavily be-medalled: RAF: WW2. Ex **gong,** n., 1.

gong team. 'A Fleet Air Arm Albacore [aircraft] with both pilot and observer D.F.C.s' (P-G-R): RN: ca. 1940–4.

gonga. Anus: Services': earlier C.20. Origin? (P-G-R.) Short for *gonga-pooch*. It sounds like an army perversion of some Hindustani word. Cf. **gunga wallah**, a male prostitute.—2. In *up the gonga,* mad: Brit. Army in India: late C.19–earlier 20. Ex Hindustani *ganga* (cf. the Ganges): 'supposedly because lunatic asylums were up-river' (Allen, 1977).

gongers, the. A police patrol in cars: since ca. 1935. Llewellyn, 1943, ' "Gongers up," he says. "Right behind us." ' Cf. **gongster.**

gongoozler. An idle, inquisitive person that stands staring for prolonged periods at anything unusual: canal-men's: late C.19–20. (Rolt, 1944.) Lakeland word (see *EDD*): arbitrary: cf. **goon,** 2.

gongster. A man on police speed-limit motor-patrol: motorists': from April 1935. On *gangster* and ex the warning *gong.*

gonio. A goniometer—a device used in radar: RAF: WW2.

gonk, n. 'A prostitute's contemptuous term for a client' (Powis): later C.20. Perhaps ex:—2. A sleep, as in *having a gonk.* See v.—3. Arbitrary name given to a small, furry, toy animal/homunculus grotesque, a fad of the late 1960s. (P.B.)

gonk, v. To sleep, esp. during the day: Army and RAF: since ca. 1950 at latest. Echoic. (P.B.) Cf. **slonk.**

goo, n. The mouth: low or perhaps orig. c.:—1923 (Manchon). I.e. *gob* perverted.—2. Any semi-liquid or viscous stuff: Can., adopted ex US ca. 1912 (Leechman), in later C.20 also gen. in UK. Mathews, *Americanisms,* has suggested a derivation ex older s., for stew, *burgoo*. B.P. notes 'common in Australia, since ca. 1930'.—3. See **goo-wallahs.**

goo, v. (also *goob.*) 'To spit a gob of phlegm' (B., 1942): Aus.

goo-wallahs, the. A sanitary squad: Army: earlier C.20. (F. & G.) Ex low *goo,* an excremental 'button'; but see also **goo,** n., 2.

good and . . . Properly; in such phrases as 'She'll come when she's good and ready—and not before!': coll.

good chit. See **have a good chit.**

good Christmas! A euph. blasphemy: since ca. 1925.

good eating. (Of a girl, a woman) very attractive: Aus.: since ca. 1921. Baker, 'Darling I could *eat* you!'

good egg. That's fortunate!: early C.20. ('Taffrail', 1917.) Ex its application to 'a good chap'.

good for a giggle, it's (and other tenses). . . . even if for nothing else!; as a 'persuader', or as a mock-reluctant acceptance of a suggested course of action: 'Come on, it's good . . .', or 'Oh, I suppose it's good . . . '; a gen. stop-gap reply: since late 1940s. (L.A., P.B.)

good for him (or **you**)! Excellent work! Splendid news! Coll.: from ca. 1910. Cf. **good on you!**

good for the parts. 'Said as if of the digestion but, allusively, of the sexual parts. Excuse for eating more, or for tippling. Public school or upper crust' (L.A., 1974).

good guts, the. The true facts: Aus.: since ca. 1930. 'That just about gives you the good guts of our end of the street' (Dick).

good iron. (Of things) good; agreeable, desirable: Aus. (Baker.) Not just 'any old iron'.

good line. A smart or unusual remark: theatrical: from ca. 1920. Herbert, 1934.

good looker. A pretty girl (woman) or handsome fellow: coll., orig. (ca. 1890) US, anglicised ca. 1920. (*OED* Sup.) Also with hyphen.

good – or bad – marble, have a. (Of racehorse). To have a good, or a bad, position at the starting barrier: Aus. racing: earlier C.20. *Sydney Morning Herald,* 8 Aug. 1964.—2. Hence, of a person, to be (dis)advantageously placed: since ca. 1920; by 1960, ob. (B.P.)

good murder, a. A detective novel with a strong murder-plot: circulating library subscribers' coll.: since ca. 1925. Raab: with the demise of these libraries, later C.20, the term is used by 'murder-novel' fans'.

192

good-o(h)! Excellent!: Aus. coll. Also, since mid-C.20, Eng. Cf. **whackoh!** Hence also adv.: well.

good-oh, adj. Excellent: Aus.

good oil. A var. of **good guts**, q.v.: reliable news.

good on the fang (or **tooth**). Applied to one who is a good trencherman: Aus.: since ca. 1945. Culotta.

good on you! (emphatic *on*). Good for you; excellent!: Aus. coll. P.B.: I have even heard it shortened to 'on yer!'; the phrase, although acknowledged to be quintessentially Australian, may well have been borrowed from Cockney: 'Good on 'em!' = good for them, well done!, appears in the caption of a *Punch* cartoon 10 Oct. 1917.

good shade. A good 'type' or fellow: Gordonstoun School. *Woman's Own*, 2 Mar. 1968, ref. to the Duke of Edinburgh.

good show. See **show**, n., 1.

good skin. A decent fellow: ?mainly Liverpool.

good sort. A beautiful girl: low: from ca. 1920. Esp. of one not remarkably reluctant.—2. As a person attractive to the opposite sex, it is the opposite of *drack sort* and has the superlative *extra sort*: these are Australianisms current since ca. 1939 but gen. throughout Aus. only since ca. 1945.

good thing. As a *bon mot*, as something worth having, and as a successful speculation, it is hardly eligible, but as a presumed certainty it is racing s. (—1884), whence, in C.20, a gen. coll. applied to a business, an investment, etc. P.B.: in later C.20, esp. in phrase (*be*) *on to a good thing*, to stumble on, or to be pursuing, something advantageous or profitable; it may even be used in ref. to the pursuit, by a male, of a particularly attractive, or willing, girl.—2. (Of a person) easy to exploit or swindle: Aus.: since ca. 1910. Baker.

good(-)time Charley. 'A man whose sole interest in life and especially in women is to have a "good time", often at no expense to himself' (Leechman). Cf. **handsome Harry.**

good value. Worth having, esp. of people: Aus. and NZ coll., since ca. 1920; in later C.20, also Brit. Fullarton, 1943, 'Wavell's pretty good value'. P.B.: Wavell: FM Viscount W. (1883–1950), penultimate Viceroy of India—and contributor to Partridge's *Dict. of Slang*, 1st ed., 1937.

good wicket. A profitable transaction or venture: Aus.: since ca. 1919. (Baker.) The phrase reflects the Aus. passion for cricket. Always in (*be*) *on a good wicket*. (B.P.) P.B.: not unknown in Brit. also.

good-willer. A person of good will: since ca. 1930. (Moseley, 1952.) Cf. **do-gooder.**

goodies and **baddies.** In films, the good and the bad people: adopted, ex US, late 1950s, perhaps earlier. Hence, by extension, in other fields, as in a 'war-game': 'In this scenario, Fantasian armies are the goodies, Amnesian the baddies'. Of cowboy films, 'You can always tell the goodies, because they wear white hats.' (P.B.).

goodness me, it's no. 3. See TOMBOLA, in Appx.

gooey, n. 'A gob of phlegm' (B., 1942): Aus. low. Cf. **gollion.**

gooey, adj. Viscous or semi-viscous: since mid-1930s. Ex **goo**, n., 2.—2. Hence, excessively sentimental; fatuous, 'drippy'; infatuated: coll., Services' (esp. RN) by 1936 and civilians' by 1944. Granville, 'He's gooey over the dame'; Binyon, 1983, 'the tone oscillates oddly between the brutally tough and the gooeyly sentimental'.

goof, n. A person that is silly, 'soft', or stupid; hence adj. *goofy*: 1923, Wodehouse (*OED* Sup.), but certainly in use in 1922. Ex dial. *goof, goff*, a fool.—2. Hence, a man ever running after women: RAF: from ca. 1925; † by 1950.

goof, v. To run after (a woman): see n., 2.—2. To watch enemy aircraft, or aircraft taking off and landing, esp. on aircraft carriers: RN: WW2 and since. See **goofer**, 2, 3.—3. To watch TV intently: Aus.: since late 1950s. (B.P.)—4. To blunder: since ca. 1950. Ex n., 1.—5. By specialisation of 4, 'Give oneself away to the police' (Home Office): prisoners' c.: later C.20.—6. 'To spoil an injection of a narcotic, either when making it up or when injecting it' (Home Office): drug-users' s.: later C.20. Specialisation of 4.

goof balls (rare in singular). Drugs that, in pill or tablet form and whether taken alone or in a drink, produce exhilaration; some are dangerous: Can., adopted, ex US, ca. 1945. (Leechman.) In Brit. the term applies, 1970s, to barbiturates. (Home Office.)

goof box. A television set: Aus.: since late 1950s. (B.P.) See **goof**, v., 3, and cf. Brit. **goggle-box.**

goof off. 'To play the fool: mainly US, and now in use in Can. Prob. US armed forces', WW2 (Leech, 1985).

goofa. RAF version, later 1920s–1930s, of **goofer**, 1; esp. in *on the goofa*, 'on the boat' (for home or overseas). (Jackson.) Perhaps ex *go for.*

goofed up. 'Intoxicated with barbiturates' (Home Office): drug-users': later C.20.

goofer. A bumboat: RN: since ca. 1925. (Granville.) Cf. **goofa.**—2. One who, in WW2, gaped at enemy bombers instead of taking shelter: RN.—3. 'The after end of the superstructure on an aircraft carrier has a gallery reserved, by tradition, where any off-duty officer or rating can watch deck landings. Both the place and the watcher are "goofers", the place [being] differentiated by always having "the" prefixing it: RN' (Peppitt): WW2 and after. Ex v., 2., to stare like an idiot, or *goof*.—4. Hence, by extension, any idle gawper: 'Often the [cliff-]edge rescue is hindered by . . . onlookers who simply will not keep out of the way. The sight of a helicopter at once attracts spectators—called "goofers" by the Fleet Air Arm' (*Illustrated London News*, May 1978).

goofers' gallery, the or **goofers, the.** The gallery in **goofer**, 3.

goofy, n. A surfer riding with his right (*not* left) foot forward: Aus. surfers', esp. teenagers': since ca. 1960. (*Sun-Herald*, 22 Sep. 1963.) In full, *goofy-footer*. 'Goofy' was the name of a crazy dog-like creature in Walt Disney's 'Mickey Mouse' cartoons.

goofy, adj. Stupid; dull-witted and almost crazy; wildly crazy; excessively sentimental; (*goofy about*) infatuated with: since ca. 1935. Ex **goof**, 1 and 2. Since ca. 1950, as L.A. notes, 1976, the nuance has been more 'awkward, diffident, and given to unintentional *faux-pas.*'

goog (pron. short *oo*, 'gwg', like good). An egg: Aus. B., 1942. 'A dozen googs, mate' would be an acceptable request in the appropriate shop. Also *googie-eggs*. (Barclay, 1982.)—2. A simpleton; a fool: Aus.: since ca. 1943. B., 1953.

googlie, -y, n. 'A slow ball, pitched fairly high, which may break either way and often upsets the batsman's conjecture' (E.V. Lucas). See **bosie**.—2. Hence, an awkward question: Aus.: since ca. 1925. (B., 1943.) Cf. **curly.**—3. A single bomb dropped from an aircraft: Aus. airmen's: WW2. (Ibid.) Cf. **bosie**, 2.

googlie(-y) merchant. A bowler of 'googlies': cricketers': 1924 (H.C. Maclaren; Lewis).

googly, adj. Sentimental. Williams, 1932, 'Henry and I would lean over the side of our honeymoon liner and hear your voice coming to us over the sea in the evening, and have . . . *heimweh*, and be all googly.' Perhaps ex *goo-goo* eyes.

Gook. A Japanese: Aus.: since ca. 1942. Cusack, 1951.—2. A Korean (cf. **Noggies**): United Nations troops': ca. 1951–5 in Korea. Perhaps influenced by **goon**, but probably derived from Korean *Kuk* (pron. *kook*), 'used to convey the idea of nationality; e.g., in *Popkuk*, France, *Chungkuk*, China, etc.' (*Iddiwah*, July 1953).—3. During the Korean War (1950–3), it was applied also to Formosans. Note that sense 1 is rare, † by 1960, possibly catachrestic. Note also that orig. *Gook* was American s.—derived from the *Gugus* of the Filipino Insurrection of 1899—for a Filipino and that, during WW2, the Americans applied it also to other friendly peoples of the Pacific. (B.P.) The word was given new impetus by the US involvement in Vietnam, and spread even to the Government Force in Rhodesia, late 1970s, being applied to the guerrillas. The Rhodesian campaign borrowed some of the language of death from S.E. Asia. (P.B.) The argot of the Falklands garrison, 1982 onwards, 'is all interlarded with zapping, gooks, and remfs' (C. Smith, 1985). —4. As *gook*, a tramp: low. (Lyons, 1914.) Ex dial. var. of *gowk*.

goolie, -y. A testicle: orig. Army in India: since late C.19. Ex Hindi *gooli*, a pellet, e.g. *Beecham Sahib's goolis* = Beecham's pills; cf. *pills*, testicles. Hence, *drop a goolie = drop a ballock*, to make a mistake.—2. 'A stone of suitable size for throwing' (Wilkes): Aus. juvenile. *Gull* and *gully* are terms used in the game of marbles: they may be the source of this sense, or all may derive as sense 1, via Romany; *gully* however may refer to a dip into which an opponent's marble must be forced.

goolie(-y) chit. A ransom note carried by the members of aircrews flying over hostile or doubtful territory in the Middle East: RAF: since ca. 1920. Ex **goolie**, 1: a common form of native torture consists in the excision of a man's testicles. See also **blood chit**. Jackson; Partridge, 1945.

goon. A recruit: Services', esp. in the west of England: since 1940. (H. & P., 1943.) In Flying Training Command, RAF: a pupil: 1941+. Not a dial. word; prob. ex:—2. A gaper; a very stupid fellow: since 1938 or 1939. Perhaps it blends *goof* and *loon*; US orig.—3. Hence, a German prison-camp guard: prisoner-of war s.: WW2. (McDouall, 1945.) 'The goon', a large and stupid character in Elzie Segar's comic strip, *Popeye the Sailor*, ca. 1935–8, popularised the word, as W. & F., 1960, tells us. *Goon* was also used, ca. 1938 and esp. in US s., for a thug used to terrorise workers (*SOD*, 1977). Mr R.C. Hope informs me that a character called 'Alice the Goon' first appeared in the comic strip *Thimble Theatre* in 1919 and, after several American etymologists, suggests a prob. orig. in Eng. dial. *gooney*, a simpleton; and *gooney* may be akin to M.E. *gonen*, to gape, from O.E. *ganian*, to gape, to yawn. Cf. the S.E. *yawn*.—4. A person with a peculiar wild, surrealist and zany sense of humour: ex 'The Goon Show', the BBC radio comedy series of the 1950s, starring Spike Milligan, Peter Sellers and Harry Secombe, which exemplified, *par excellence*, this form of humour. Allingham, 1963: 'Mr Campion . . . was very easy to talk to with those long clown lines in his pale face, a natural goon, born rather too early [the young woman] suspected.' (P.B.) From this sense come *goonery*, *goonish* and *goonishness*.

goon bag. A respirator case: RAF: WW2. Ex **goon**, 1.

goon crystal. PCP (Phencyclidine): drugs c. Stockley, 1986.

goon-stick. An officer's swagger cane: Aus. soldiers': WW2. B., 1943.

goon suit. A flak apron: R Can. N: WW2.—2. 'Naval officers' specialised flying suit, designed for protection in the event of ditching in the sea; rather similar to a "wet suit", but baggy and with waterproof neck, wrist and ankle seals: RN: 1950s' (Peppitt): and later, and in RAF usage. By association with 'The Goons', whose show (see **goon**, 4) was orig. called 'Crazy People'; it was re-titled 'The Goon Show' on 9 July 1951. Therefore *goon suit* prob. originated either in late 1951 or early 1952. (Took, 1976.) But see also **goonskin**.—3. 'Clothing to protect [servicemen] against nuclear, biological or chemical attack' (*Times*, 7 Mar. 1984). Cf. **noddy suit**.

gooner, give(, or get) the. To dismiss; be dismissed: low: since ca. 1925. (Curtis, 1937.) ?Ex *go on*!

goonery; goonish. See **goon**, 4.

gooney bird. A Douglas DC-3 transport aircraft, the Dakota: Aus., adopted ex US: 1943–5. Ex the blackfooted albatross, which has an exceptional flight-range (B.P.; W.&F.).

goonskin. 'Observer's flying suit and parachute harness made in one piece' (Jackson): RAF: since ca. 1939. Prob. ex **goon**, 2, + *skin*.—2. Battledress: Army: 1940+. (Sanders.)

goop; goopy. A fool, fatuous person; foolish, fatuous: from ca. 1917. (*OED* Sup.) Prob. a corruption of *goof*; cf. **looby, loopy**.

goose. To jab a finger up a person's anus, or between the legs from the rear, in order to surprise or to annoy: Can., since ca. 1910; adopted, ca. 1944, in Brit. and Aus.—2. To accelerate, as in 'he goosed the gas pedal': Can.: since ca. 1945. (Leech, 1974.)

Goose and Dickie Line, the. 'The branch railway line from North Walsham to Yarmouth, now discontinued. The train used to carry farm produce and cattle, hence geese and dickies (donkeys) on occasion' (Granville, 1970): mostly East Anglian, and railwaymen's: earlier C.20

goose and duck. A truck: r. s.

goose girl. A lesbian: since ca. 1918. Ex the synon. Fr. s. *gousse*. Mackenzie, 1967.

gooseberries. Also known as *fruit machine*: 'old freighters sunk end to end off the Normandy beaches to provide artificial shelter for small boats' (Holman, 1944): RN: 1944–5. If not a code-name, prob. suggested by **mulberry**, q.v.

gooser. A pederast: low Can. See **goose**, 1.

goose's neck. A cheque: r.s.: app. not before 1950. (Franklyn 2nd.) See **sausage**, v.—2. A bottle to urinate into: nursing coll.:—WW2. (Raab, 1982.)

gopher. Granville's spelling of **goffer**, 1. See also **gofer**.

gorblim(e)y; gawlim(e)y! A corruption of *God blind me!*: orig. and mainly Cockneys: 1870, says Ware for the latter form; 1890, for the former.—2. 'Colloquial for what was considered loud dress; until the late 1950s applied to men's wide cap, with big projecting peak and vivid, often check, pattern' (L.A., 1967); the term received a boost in the late 1950s from a popular song sung by Lonnie Donnegan, noted skiffle-musician, 'My old man's a dustman . . . he wears gorblimey trousers . . . ' (P.B.).

gorby. 'A tourist, esp. an American one, driving about in a large Winnebago-type van, with wife, kids, etc. inside, and bikes and other junk festooning the outside: W. Can.: since early 1980s' (Leech, 1986). Cf. **grockle**.

Gordon and Gotch. A watch: r.s. 'An old-established firm of book exporters' (Franklyn).

Gordon Bennett! A mild expletive: coll. It is sufficiently 'explosive' to be a useful euph. for, e.g., *Gawd a' mighty!* James Gordon Bennett (1795–1892) founded and edited the *New York Herald*; his son of the same name (1841–1918) succeeded him, and was responsible for, among other things, sending Stanley to Africa in search of Livingstone.

Gordon Thailanders. See PRISONER-OF-WAR SLANG, §15, in Appx.

gorger. A large enamel jug: driftermen's. (Butcher, 1979.) Cf. *gotch*, C.18 term for a large round jug.

gorgonzola, n. The Africa Star: Army: 1943+. The ribbon of this campaign star is sand-coloured, with thin red, yellow and blue streaks.

gorgonzola, adj. (Very) good: Aus.: since ca. 1920. (B., 1942.) A very rich cheese.

gorm; gawm, n. Tobacco for chewing: tramps' c.:—1932 (Jennings).

gorm, v. To stare, gape, look long (and greedily) *at*, e.g., second-hand books: since ca. 1910. (Berkley, 1929.) Ex dial., *gaum*, to stare idly, vacantly or stupidly.

gormalised (or -ized). Stupid: market-traders': since ca. 1920. (*M.T.*) Cf. **gormless**.

gormless. Stupid; slow-witted and lacking in common sense: adopted, ca. 1935, ex dial., the predominant dial. form *gaumless* being adapted.

goss. A hat; at first a 'four-and-nine': coll.: 1848 (*OED*). Ex. *gossamer hat*, a light felt fashionable in the late 1830s.—2. A naval peaked cap, peculiar to artificer apprentices: RN: since ca. 1940. (Peppitt.)

gossage. A barrage balloon: RAF: 1940+. *New Statesman*, 30 Aug. 1941; Jackson, 1943, 'Named after Air Marshal Sir Leslie Gossage, KCB, CVO, MC, Air Officer Commanding Balloon Command': Partridge, 1945, 'With a pun on *sausage*' (ex the shape).

got on. In *to have got* (something) *on* (somebody), to have in evidence against that person: coll.: late C.19–20. Cole, 1928, 'That's the gist of what we've got on [the arrested man], and it's my belief he'll find it a hard job to answer.'

got you! I understand—and will comply: since ca. 1940. Sometimes rendered as *gotcher*.

G

got your ladder. See PRISONER-OF-WAR SLANG, §14, in Appx.

gotcha. 'Snatch raid in which air-crew are taken for unannounced survival training' (*Fighter Pilot*, 1981): RAF: later C.20. Ex *got you*. The word became notorious as the newspaper *Sun*'s gloating headline when the Argentine cruiser *Admiral Belgrano* was torpedoed and sunk with the loss of at least 368 lives on 2 May 1982, during the Falkland Islands campaign.

Gottfordommer (pl. in *-s*). A Dutchman. See PRISONER-OF-WAR SLANG, §9, in Appx. (Also with one *t*.)

gouch out. See gauch out.

gouge; gouger. To seek (for opal); an opal miner or seeker: Aus. coll.: late C.19–20. (Russell, 1936.) Ex manner of extraction.

goulash. 'Savoury stew (also solid steamed pudding)' (Home Office): prisoners': 1970s.

governor. An acknowledged expert: low coll.: late 1970s. Daniells, 1980, 'Artistic dirty pictures . . . Time was, you used to be the governor at tasteful nudity without whiskers.'

govvy. Government(-run or -sponsored), as in an article about young people in N.E. England: 'half of them are unemployed, while the other half are best described as having moved in and out of "shit" jobs and "govvy" schemes. (Their words.)' (*New Society*, 2 June 1983). See guvvie.

Goyle. See HAULAGE, in Appx.

gozz. 'A good long gossip on the telephone' (Hoggart, 1983): middle-class young women's: early 1980s.—2. A look, a glance, esp. *have a gozz* (*at*): Nottingham. (Walton, 1984.) Perhaps, like synon. *gleg*, dial.—but not in *EDD*.

gozzie, n. A gooseberry: Aus.: late C.19–20. (B.P.)

gozzie, adj. Insultingly applied to the partially-sighted: special schools'. (P. Scott, 1984.)

grab, n. An observer's or air gunner's brevet: RAF: WW2. H.W., 1942.

grab, v. See altitude.

grab (oneself) **a ball.** See JAZZ TERMS, in Appx.

grab hooks. Fingers: RN, lowerdeck: since ca. 1910. (Granville.) Cf. grabbling irons.

grab leather. 'A cowboy who takes hold of the saddle horn while riding a bucking horse is said to grab leather; this disqualifies him if he is in competition' (Leechman): Can.,?ex US: since ca. 1925.

grabbling irons. Knife, fork and spoon: Army. (P-G-R.) P.B.: by ca. 1950, more commonly *eating irons*.

Grable-bodied seaman. 'Wren member of a trot boat's [q.v.] crew. After Betty Grable, the curvaceous film star of the 1930s. The term was current during [WW2] when Wrens ran picket and despatch boats' (Granville). A pun on *able-bodied seaman*, the RN rank AB.

grabs. See up for grabs, available.

graceful degradation. 'An anglicised form of the Americanism, "fail soft": electronics industry: 1970s' (Peppitt).

Gracie Fields. 'Rochdale to Manchester parcels train' (*Railway*, 2nd): railwaymen's: mid-C.20. Miss Fields (1898–1979), the famous singer and variety-actress, was born at Rochdale.

gracing; occ. greycing. A telescoping of *greyhound racing*: sporting: 1927. *OED* Sup.

grackle. A var., perhaps the orig., of grockle, q.v.; does not extend to derivative phrases.

grad. A graduate: rare, except at University of Durham: late C.19–20. (Marples.) After *undergrad*.—2. 'Among Cambridge landladies, ca. 1925, it was used (mostly in the plural) to denote *undergraduates*' (H.R. Spencer).

grade. See make the grade, to be able to do a thing.

graft, n. Work, labour: coll.: from ca. 1870. Esp. in *hard graft*, (hard) work: in C.20, mostly in the Army and in Aus. and NZ.—2. Hence, any kind of work, esp. if illicit: low coll.:— 1874 (H., 5th ed.). Cf. the US (orig. s.) sense, illicit profit or commission (mainly in politics), which, adopted into S.E. ca. 1900, prob. derives ex the Eng. term, as, ultimately, does its corresponding v.—3. Hence, the line one takes in a crime;

one's role therein: c. *Gilt Kid.*—4. 'Food and lodging. Thus *good graft*—comfortable living' (H.&P.): Services': since 1939. Ironically ex sense 1.

graft, v. To be actively a criminal: c.: from ca. 1910. Wallace, 1924.—2. To be or work as a grafter (see grafter): grafters' coll. *Cheapjack*, 1934.—3. As a grafter (see grafter) to sell (something): fairgrounds'. 'He had grafted the tubed stickem for years' (Buchanan-Taylor, 1943).

grafter. One who is actively a criminal: c.: from ca. 1912. Ex graft, v., 1.—2. 'One who works a line in a fair or market: as fortune-teller, quack doctor, mock-auctioneer, etc.': late C.19–20. (*Cheapjack*, 1934.) Also, a man skilled in extracting money from a difficult 'audience' at a mock or rigged auction: mock-auction world: since ca. 1945. (*Sunday Chronicle*, 28 June 1953.) At these auctions, the 'trick' is to sell inferior goods at top prices: cf. top man. See also GRAFTERS', in Appx.—3. Among market traders, a market trader: C.20, if not 10–20 years earlier. (*M.T.*) Often called, in full, *market-grafter.*—4. 'A man who looks for opportunities for other thieves' (Read, 1978): c.

gram. As *the Gram*, the local grammar school: schoolboys': late C.19–earlier 20. (Hamilton, 1946.) Cf. the Tech, the Poly.—2. A gramophone.—3. A gramophone record: since ca. 1930; ob. by ca. 1950 at latest, supplanted by *disc.*—4. A radiogram: since ca. 1955. (Petch.)

grammargogs. Grammar school boys: other secondary school boys': mid-C.20. Walker, 1982.

gramo studio. A gramophone studio: filmland: since ca. 1910. McCabe, 1937.

gramophone record. A canteen bloater: RN: late C.19–20. (Bowen.) Because out of a tin. P.B.: or ex thickness?

gramp. Grandfather: hypocoristic, perhaps mostly Southern English: mid-C.19–20. I.e., 'grandpapa' slurred. Sometimes as *gramps*, or *grampa*. Cf.:-

gran. A grandmother; esp. in address: dial. and nursery coll.: late C.19–20. Cf. *granny*.

grand. 1,000 feet: RAF: since 1940. (Jackson.) Ex US c., where it = $1,000.—2. Hence, also adopted ex US, £1,000: since ca. 1940. (Hoby, 1946.) Hence to *do a grand*, to lose £1,000: sporting: later C.20. Lipsey, 1979.

grand slam. Complete or spectacular success: coll.: from ca. 1910. Ex the game of bridge.

Grand (or **Ground**) **Walloper, the.** 'King of all the *gremlins*—their director of operations' (H. & P.): RAF: 1940+. See GREMLINS, in Appx.

gran(d-)daddy. Grandfather: familiar coll. In later C.20 the phrase *the grand-daddy of them all* is sometimes applied to one, e.g. a jazz-musician, pre-eminent and long in his field—as being, of course, greater than the daddy of them all, q.v.

grandma. An affectionate abbr. (C.19–20) of *grandmother*: coll.—2. Hence, 'A mixed pint [of ale], either old and mild or else (Midlands) sweet stout and old' (Glover, 1985): public houses'. Cf. mother-in-law.

grandstand, v. Esp. as vbl. n. *grandstanding*, playing to the crowd: Aus.: adopted ex US ca. 1944. (B.P.)

Granite Jug, the. Dartmoor Prison: since ca. 1930 (*Reynolds News*, 16 Aug. 1953). With a pun on *jug*, c. and s. for prison since early C.19.

Granny. *Sydney Morning Herald*: Aus. (B., 1942.) Long established, very respectable; also known as *The Old Girl.*—2. A Granny Smith apple: mainly Aus.: since ca. 1920. 'Australia's most popular apple' (B.P.)

granny. A pretext; a 'blind' or 'front': market-traders': late C.19–20. *M.T.*—2. 'A legitimate business used as a cover for nefarious activities, particularly that of fence' (Tempest): c.

granny's ear'oles. Dried apricots: Cumbrian children's: 1940s. (Haines, 1962.)

Grant Road. See TOMBOLA, in Appx.

grape. In *have a grape on*, to be ill-disposed towards: Aus.: since ca. 1925. (Marshall, 1946.) Perhaps ex sour grapes. Its opp. is *have a toby on.*

grape on the business, a. (Of a person that is) a 'wet blanket' on cheerful company; a bluestocking: a 'wallflower': Aus.: since ca. 1925. B., 1942.

grapevine, the. A secret means employed by the chiefs of the underworld to ensure rapid and trustworthy transmission of important news: c.: adopted ca. 1920 from US, where orig. in form *the grapevine telegraph* and not c.—2. Hence, the mysterious source of rumours: Services': WW2. 'I heard it on the grapevine.' P-G-R.—3. That haphazard network of rumour-mongers in the Services, in factories, in offices, which through Unit or Staff, transmits advance knowledge—often not inaccurate—of policy and of administrative decisions: since ca. 1945: s. that, by 1955, had > coll. Also, in this sense, *the bush telegraph*, a term that has radiated from Aus., where current since ca. 1890. P.B.: by 1970s S.E. to the extent that a weekly publication devoted to advertisement of vacancies in the educational world could be so titled.

grappling hooks. 'Making a big effort, we . . . "We threw out the grappling hooks and reached for height"—we climbed at maximum speed' (Forbes, 1942): RAF, esp. 66 Sqdn.: WW2. Cf. **altitude,** 1.

grasp and grunt. An occ. var. of **grumble and grunt.** Franklyn, 2nd.

grass, n. A policeman: abbr. r.s. **grasshopper,** q.v.: low coll.: earlier C.20. Hodge, 1939.—2. Hence, an informer: c.,—1933 (Leach); by 1970, coll. Cf. **super-grass.**—3. '*Grass* was the normal "picture" seen on certain types of radar cathode-ray tube, as distinct from the signals produced by aircraft, etc. It looked like waving grass' (correspondent): RAF coll. > j.: WW2 and after.—4. *Cannabis indica*, marijuana: orig. c., adopted ex US ca. 1965. McCabe, 1972, 'grass was virtually unheard of in England at this time [1964]', but by 1971 the (London) *Evening News* could use the term, without gloss, in reporting the case of a 14-year-old boy 'pusher' (distributor).

grass, v. To inform on: c.: from ca. 1930. *Gilt Kid*, 1936, 'Anyhow it was a dirty trick grassing his pals.' Ex **grass, n.,** 2.

grass chamber. 'Grosdek entered the cabinet . . . reluctantly. Criminals had named it by their epithet for an informer, as the grass chamber' (Barnett, 1978): a very narrow telephone-box for statements or confessions.

grass-cutting. As in 'to go grass-cutting' = to run off the road: motorcyclists': later C.20. (Dunford.) Cf. **go gardening.**

grass-fighter. A slugger, a brawler, a bruiser; a fighter not a boxer: Aus.: since ca. 1930. (Niland, 1958.) One who, in a field, fights to the finish.

grass-hopping. Low flying, in order to beat ground-fire: RAAF. 1940–5. (B., 1943.) Aus. var. of *hedge-hopping*—in a country where hedges are infrequent.

grass in the park. An informer to the police: r.s. on *nark*. (Franklyn 2nd.) Very prob. suggested by **grass, n.,** 1, 2: a characteristic elab.

grass line. 'Coir rope which floats on the surface of the water' (Granville): RN coll.

grass park. A shortening of **grass in the park** above: since ca. 1930. Franklyn 2nd.

grass up. To inform upon, as in ' . . . expedition of revenge, to pay off someone who has grassed up a friend' (J. Seabrook, 1984). An elab. of **grass, v.**

grasser. An informer to the police: London's East End: since ca. 1945. (Richard Herd, 1957.) Var. of **grass, n.,** 2.

grasshopper. A policeman: r.s., on **copper:**—1893. See **grass, n.,** 1 and 2, and v.—2. Hence, an informer. Bruce, 1974, ' "What do you think we are? Bleeding grass-hoppers? . . . Shoppers", said Des. So that's the origin of "grass". I thought it was "snake in the grass".' Clayton, 1970: 'Informant who is used both by police and prison authorities, also by prisoners': prisoners'. Cf. **grass, n.,** 2.—3. An Italian one-man torpedo: RN: 1940+.—4. A 'customer who inspects one line of goods after another without buying anything' (*M.T.*): market-traders'.—5. '90 XX Class locomotive. Tendency to slip. (Western Region)' (*Railway*): 1950s–60s.

grassy. Var. of **grass, n.,**1, a policeman: c.:—1935 (Hume).

grauncher. An inept and unskilled mechanic: motorcyclists': later C.20. (Dunford.) Cf.:-

graunching stick. A reamer or large round file: motorcyclists'. (Dunford, 2.) P.B.: *graunch* is dial. for 'to grind the teeth', and a var. of *crunch* (*EDD*); prob. partly echoic. Cf. **groinch.**

Grauniad, the. 'Among [the satirical magazine *Private Eye*'s] services was the enlargement of the vocabulary . . . the . . . *Guardian* newspaper, celebrated for its lousy typesetting, can henceforth never escape being "The Grauniad" ' (Cameron, 1979): the nickname became gen. usage, among the papers' readers, ca. 1976. (P.B.)

gravel(-)basher; gravel(-)bashing. (One who has to participate in) *square-bashing* or marching, esp. as a recruit at squad drill, on the parade ground: Services', esp. RAF: since ca. 1936; by ca. 1950 ob., *square-bash(ing)* being the predominant term. (H. & P.) Contrast **swede(-)basher.**

gravel-crusher. A soldier at defaulters' drill: Army: ca. 1880–1900. B. & L.—2. Then, but † by ca. 1930, any infantryman: mostly cavalrymen's. Cf. *beetle-crusher*. Also *gravel-crushing*, n. and adj.—3. The term was revived in WW2, all Services', for a drill instructor, and, as H. & P. note, for a physical training instructor [but this latter seems unlikely. P.B.].—4. Hence, a recruit, the drill instructor's victim: WW2.—5. Farmers' strong and heavy boots: Anglo-Irish.—6. A tramp: Anglo-Irish: late C.19–20. Campbell, 1916.

gravel-grinder. (Usu. in pl.) A gunner's mate: RN. (Granville.) He takes the squad drill, hence, *gravel-grinding*. Cf. **gravel-crusher.**

gravel-grinding. See prec.—2. 'We crawled all round the park in bottom gear—"gravel-grinding", as we call it' (Hodge, 1939): taxi-drivers': since ca. 1915.

graves. (Extremely rare in the singular.) Long, dirty finger-nails: lower classes':—1923 (Manchon).

graveyard flying. Dangerously low flying: RAF coll.: WW2.

graveyard shift. A night shift: shipbuilders' and munition workers': since ca. 1915. (*John o' London's*, 18 June 1943.) Cf.:-

graveyard watch. The middle watch (from midnight to 4 a.m.): RN.

Gravy, the. The Atlantic: RAF aircrew, esp. of Coastal Command: WW2. Cf. synon. *Pond; Ditch; Duck-pond.*

gravy. Fuel for aircraft or automobile: RAF: mid-C.20. Partridge, 1945.—2. Perquisites: adopted ex US ca. 1943. See **gravy-train.** For the term's use as 'money' see sense 7.—3. Any tinned food: Aus., esp NSW, children's: since ca. 1947. Ex the cartoons of Emile Mercier. B., 1953.—4. Sexual innuendo; bawdiness: since ca. 1970. R.S. cites a BBC radio programme, 13 Sep. 1973, 'Put some gravy in it—make it saucy!' A pun on *sauce*.—5. In *going down for the gravy*, as vbl n. Fellatio or cunnilingus: low: since ca. 1950. (Slater, 1978.)—6. 'During Quarter Sessions or Assizes, when a Judge is giving heavy sentences, he is spoken of as "dishing out the gravy (or porridge)" ' (Tempest): c.: mid-C.20.—7. Money: s.: later C.20. 'Assuming that the Ministry [Dept. of Transport] comes up with the gravy . . . ' (*Observer* colour sup., 20 Dec. 1981). Orig. US: see JIVE, in Appx. (P.B.).

gravy(-)train, the. Easy money, esp. from a well-paid but undemanding task in political life or with a large commercial or industrial company: frequently in *to ride the gravy train*: orig. US (*OED*: 1910); known in Britain, but not widely adopted until mid-1970s. (P.B.)

gray. See **grey.**

grazer. 'Are you a "grazer" (hip advertising jargon for someone who eats small amounts often)?' (*Telegraph* Sunday mag., 7 Feb. 1988).

grease. See **shit, n.,** 3, quot'n.

grease her on. To make a smooth landing, *her* being the aircraft: RAF: WW2. Hemingway, 1944. See **greaser,** 5.

grease monkey. A mechanic: (non-Civil) engineers': from ca. 1910. Common also in Aus. (B.P.)

G

grease (one's) skates. To get ready to go—and go, promptly and speedily: Aus.: since ca. 1920. Durack, 1955.

greaser. An objectionable or disgusting fellow: lower classes':—1923. Manchon: '*Un sale type*'.—2. An engineering student: Aus. universities'. (B.P.)—3. 'One who angles for time off' (H. & P.): Services': WW2.—4. A teenage rowdy, esp. a member of the young, aggressive motorcycling fraternity: since early 1960s. Ex long hair, heavily oiled. Cf. **rocker,** and see quot'n at **biker.**—5. 'The undercarriage structure was intact and . . . the plane could make a "greaser", a light landing to avoid further damage' (Nelson, 1980): RAF coll.: later C.20. Ex **grease her on,** q.v.

greasy, n. A butcher: Aus. B., 1942.—2. A sheep-shearer: Aus.: since ca. 1920. Vickers, 1955, 'When those five greasies get moving they'll shear a lot of sheep.' Ex the greasy wool.—3. 'An outback cook; any cook for a collection of men' (Wilkes): Aus.: since later C.19. This sense perhaps includes sense 1.

greasy, adj. Pomaded: lower classes' coll.:—1923 (Manchon).—2. Dirty, as in 'a greasy chap': Public Schools'.

greasy pig. 'A bet laid on tails after a long run of heads, or vice versa' (B., 1953): Aus. two-up players': since ca. 1925.

greasy spoon. A railroad eating-house: Can.:—1931. Adopted ex US.—2. Hence, almost immediately any small, dirty restaurant: Can. (Leechman.) Ex the state of the cutlery.—3. A public house serving food: upper-middle-class s.: later C.20. York, 1980.

great; great-great. An ancestor or a descendant in the 'great(-great)' degree: coll. *OED* Sup.—2. As *great*, a great, or a (very) famous, person: coll.: since late 1940s. Elliptical for '*great* man' or '*great* woman'. P.B.: cf. the later C.20 media phrase 'one of the all-time greats of (e.g.) jazz'.

Great Bore War, the. See **bore war.**

Great Brown Bomber. A Lockheed *Hudson*: RAAF: ca. 1942–5. (B., 1943.) Cf. nickname of the great Negro boxer, Joe Louis.

great divide (or capitals), **the.** The cleavage between the female breasts as revealed by a low décolletage: Aus.: since ca. 1930. Ex the Great Divide, the Blue Mountains, of eastern Australia. (B.P.) P.B.: prob. influenced by the earlier 'Ballad of Eskimo Nell', where that lady's private parts are likened to 'The Great Divide'; there it is the Rocky Mountains of N. America that provide the ref. One would think that the Grand Canyon might be more appropriate—but it didn't rhyme.

great-great. See **great.**

great guns. An intensive adv.: RN: late C.18–early 20.—2. In *go(ing) great guns,* an extant and gen. usage of sense 1, as in 'Jo? *Last* time I saw her, she was going great guns with Richard—but of course that was *then* . . . ', i.e., getting along extremely well: later C.20. (P.B.)

Great Silent, the. The Royal Navy: derisive, occ. self-name: WW2. Ex journalistic 'the Silent Service'. P-G-R.

great smoke, the. London: orig.,—1874, c.; in C.20, s. (H., 5th ed.) In later C.20, usu. *the big smoke,* or more often simply *the smoke.*

great stuff. Excellent, whatever it may be; also as n.: coll. E.g. *Evening News,* 11 Sep. 1934, 'Great stuff, sweeps—that is, when you find one, see one, and speak to one!'

great unwashed, the. The proletariat: at first (late C.18), derisively joc. S.E.; but since Scott popularised it, (non-proletarian) coll.—and rather snobbish.—2. In the late 1960–70s, it was applied to hippies of both sexes and all sorts. (Powis.)

Great White Chief, the. A head of department: Civil Service: since ca. 1910. P.B.: in later C.20 applied joc., or ironically, to the head of any establishment, organisation, etc.

Great White Whale, the. The SS *Canberra,* the P. & O. cruise liner, when used as a troopship for the Falklands War, 1982: Services'. (Knight, 1984.) An allusion to Melville's classic, *Moby Dick,* 1851; the ship is startlingly white.

greatest, the. The best; adopted, ca. 1961, ex US. Wallace Reyburn, 1965, 'The Americans snigger at the British when they use words and phrases like these: *bobby-soxer, in the groove, aw shucks, jive, baloney, you can say that again, what's cooking, the greatest.* To American ears they are all so dated.' Given impetus by the proclamation of the Negro boxer Cassius Clay, alias Mohamed Ali, 'I am the greatest.'

greb. A North Country schoolboys' term of abuse: since ca. 1930. (*New Society,* 22 Aug. 1963.) Origin?

Greco. A Greek: Army in N. Africa: 1940–3. Adopted from the Italians.

greedy pigs. 'Contemptuous term used by card-sharps for the public they cheat' (Powis): later C.20. Ex children's term for a glutton.

greefa or **grefa.** A marijuana cigarette: beatniks': adopted, ca. 1958, ex US drug addicts. (Anderson.) US since—1931 (Spears). Ex Sp. c.

green, n. Stage: theatrical: abbr. r.s. *greengage:*—1935.—2. A supporter of the Ecology Party and of conservation generally: coll.: since ca. 1981. *New Society,* 22 July 1982.

green, adj. '[Irish] Republican/Catholic in sympathy' (Hawke, 1979): Northern Ireland: C. 20.

green acres. See **greenacre.**

green and blacks. 'Librium capsules' (Home Office): drug-users': 1970s.

green-back (or written solid). A dollar bill (i.e, note): Can.: adopted ex US ca. 1905; the colour.—2. A £1 note: low coll. or joc. Green £1 notes were first issued by the Bank of England on 1 Feb. 1917, and have remained this colour, despite diminishing size and value, ever since, except for the period 1940–8, when they were blue. Cf. **brown-back,** and see also **greenie,** 5.

green boats. 'Passenger boats as against the freight boats, and in spite of the fact that all the hulls are now orange' (Malin, 1979): Townsend Thoresen ferries' crews': later C.20.

green boys. 'Variant of *green stripers,* the officers of the Special Branch of the R.N.V.R. in W.W. II. Ex the coloured bands of green between the gold stripes of rank' (Granville, 1967).

green cart, the. That mythical vehicle in which people are conveyed to a lunatic asylum: Aus. juvenile: since ca. 1920. (B.P.) Cf. **grey van.**

green coat, wear the. 'To act the innocent—a ruse tried by new entries who plead ignorance' (Granville): RN: since ca. 1910. *Greenness* = inexperience.

Green Death. 'Affectionate service slang for the elite unit [Special Boat Squadron, RM] who wore jungle-camouflaged fatigues' (Parry, 1982): Falklands War.

green fingers, have. To be a successful gardener: to succeed, as an amateur, with one's flowers and vegetables: coll.: since ca. 1925. Coined by the late Mr Middleton, BBC broadcaster and newspaper writer on gardening. Less usual: *a green thumb.* Perhaps the phrase was merely popularised by Mr Middleton, for various trustworthy correspondents place it at ca. 1910, at latest, but probably a generation earlier. 'I think the original was "a green thumb", probably by analogy with the miller's "golden thumb" (as in Chaucer)' (Priestley, 1965).

green grocer job. A job that has been done badly: Portsmouth dockers': mid-C.20. Patterson.

green lizards. Civilians in the Control Commission for Germany: Army: ca. 1945–8. Ex the green epaulets they used to wear.

Green Man, the. A urinal: pub-frequenters'. Ex urinals' often being painted green and ex *the Green Man* as a fairly common name for a public house.

green pastures. 'High earnings. Overtime. Bonus payments' (McKenna, 1): railwaymen's: mid-C.20.

green rub, (get) a. To be reprimanded for another's fault: RN: since ca. 1910. (Granville.) Ex the centuries-old metaphor, 'the rub of the green'. Malin, 1979, defines *a green rub* as 'any raw deal or misfortune'.

green shielder. A graduate cadet-entrant to RAF College, Cranwell, on commissioned officer's pay: RAF: later C.20.

G

G

(*Telegraph Sunday Mag.*, 27 July 1980.) Prob. a ref. to the 'Green Shield' trading stamps so popular in earlier 1970s.

green-striper. See **green boys**.

green suit or **blouse suit**. A suit of which one has no cards in a hand at bridge: Aus.: since ca. 1925. (B., 1942.) An 'ungrown' suit.

green thumb. See **green fingers**.

Green Un, the. The *Motorcycle* magazine. See **comics**, 2.

green wellie brigade. At first, 'the County Set', since early 1980s when traditionally black gumboots suddenly glared forth in other colours (see **yellow wellie**); by later 1980s 'also derog. for arriviste *yuppies* [q.v.] who have moved to the country and become aspirants to membership of the country set' (Watts, 1988).

green yoke. A young inexperienced horse: steeplechase jockeys'. Oaksey, 1977.

greenacre. 'The falling of a set of goods out of the sling': dockers': mid-C.19–20. (*OED* Sup.) Perhaps ex Greenacre, a murderer (who buried the victim in sections in various parts of London) hanged at Newgate in 1837: the rope broke. As *green acres*, still current among London dockers mid-C.20 (Ash). Perhaps cf. railwaymen's **green pastures**, rich pickings.

greenback. See **green-back**.

Greenfields. In *Mrs Greenfields*, a 'bed' or a shelter in the open fields. Gape, 1936, 'Their lousy "kips" . . . I'd sooner have "Mrs Ashtip" or "Mrs Greenfields" any day.' 'Mrs Ashtip' = a shelter near a lime-kiln or a furnace: both tramps' joc. c. Also *Greenfields Mission*, as in *Toby*, 1979. Cf. **sleep with Mrs Green**, and:—2. In *sit under* [i.e. listen to a sermon by] *Dr Greenfields*, 'To go for a rural walk rather than attend divine worship. In use among the older Nonconformists' (Boycott, 1938).

greenfinch. 'UDR [Ulster Defence Regt] women soldiers—known as Greenfinches from their original codename . . . ' (*Now!*, 11 Apr. 1980).

greenfly. Collective for Intelligence Corps personnel since their adoption, mid-1970s, of a bright green beret: Army nickname. (P.B.)

greengage. Stage: theatrical r.s.: from ca. 1880. (London *Evening Standard*, 19 Aug. 1931.) Later shortened to *green*.

greenhouse. Applied to the cockpits of WW2+ Service aircraft that were conspicuous for their amount of perspex 'window', e.g. the Bristol Brigand fighter-bomber, late 1940s–early 50s. (H. & P., 1943; Partridge, 1945.) Cf. **conservatory**.

greenie, -y. A doping pill for a greyhound: Aus. (esp. Sydney) c., > low, esp. sporting s.: since ca. 1946. Glassop, 1949.—2. A smooth, unbroken wave: Aus. surfers': since ca. 1950. (B.P.)—3. A Radio Electrical Branch rating: RN, esp. FAA: since ca. 1950.—4. 'A supporter of the "green bans" on . . . projects considered contrary to principles of "conservation"; a trendy conservationist' (Wilkes): Aus.: since early 1970s.—5. Var. of **greenback**, 2, a £1 note, as in 'a brutal lunge at the greenies in your wallet' (*Time Out*, 9 May 1980).

gregory. A shortening of all senses of:-

Gregory Peck. The neck: r.s.: Londoners' and low Aus.: later C.20. Ex the well-known film actor.—2. A cheque: r.s. The abbr. *Gregory* was a Society 'in' word (Dempster, 1984). Opp. **Nelson** (Eddy), ready cash.—3. (In pl.) Spectacles: Glasgow r.s. on *specs*. May be shortened to *Gregories*. Munro, 1985.

grem. A person not good at skateboarding; a maladroit generally: teenagers': late 1978+. (C. Paterson.) Short for **gremlin**, q.v. at senses 3 and 4 for evidence of the term's derivation from surfers' s.

gremlin. A mischievous sprite that, haunting aircraft, deludes pilots: airmen's: since late 1920s. E.P. maintained, despite the word's appearance in H. & P. and Jackson (both 1943), that it is now S.E. Watson, 1979, refutes Roald Dahl's claim to have invented the term, and cites its appearance 'several times' in a poem that appeared in the journal the *Aeroplane*, 10 Apr. 1929. Mr Watson remembers that gremlins could

even be helpful on occasion; they were 'responsible for *all* unaccountable happenings—good or bad'. (Thanks to Mrs C. Raab for drawing the letter to my attention. P.B.) See Appendix for further discourse.—2. A surfer lacking a board and sponging on his mates: Aus. surfers': since ca. 1955. (B.P.)—3. (Also *gremmie*.) A boy of 12 or 13 aping his elders: Aus. teenage surfers': since ca. 1960.—4. (Also *gremmie*.) 'A young and exuberant surfer, who is learning but still shows off' (*Pix*, 28 Sep. 1963): Aus. surfers': since ca. 1960.

gremmie. The pet-form of **gremlin**, 3 and 4. Sydney *Bulletin*, 30 Mar. 1963.

grey. A 'middle-aged, conventionally dressed/minded person' (Fryer, 1967): hippies' (1965 or 66) and Flower People's (1967). Adopted ex US Negro derogatory s. for 'a white person'.

grey ballocks. Applied to a sour-tempered or sober-sided man: Forces': mid-C.20. Contrast **golden ballocks**.

Grey Funnel Line, the. The Royal Navy: mostly RN. By a pun on Alfred Holt & Co.—the Blue Funnel Line, of Liverpool. RN ships are *grey-funnel liners*.

grey ghost. 'A N.S.W. parking policeman, successor to the "brown bomber" [q.v.]: from colour of uniform' (Wilkes): Aus.: 1970s. Cf. **grey meanie**.

grey mac(intosh) brigade. See **dirty mac**.

grey man. Black s. for a white man. See **pinkie**, 2, and cf. **grey**.—2. A dull, boring undergraduate: Oxford and Cambridge students' pej. coll.: mid-C.20.

grey mare. One's or the fare: r.s. P.P., 1932.

grey meanie. 'A parking policeman in Victoria: from colour of uniform' (Wilkes): Aus.: 1970s. See **meanie**, 2.

grey (or **blue**) **van.** 'The legendary vehicle in which the insane are said to be taken away to be locked up: "The big grey van'll be comin for him any day now" ' (Munro, 1985): Glasgow. Cf. **green cart**.

greycing. Greyhound racing. See **gracing**.

greyers. Grey flannel trousers and other-coloured coat: mostly undergraduates': from ca. 1925. By the '*OXFORD -ER(s)*'.

gribble. The action of sheep on moorland, 'gribbling across the hillside': shooting coll.: later C.20. ?A blend of *graze* + *nibble*. (P.B.)

grice or **gricer.** An engine-spotter: railway enthusiasts': since late 1960s. Also as v., *to grice*, to watch locomotives. (*Railway World*, Dec. 1969.) Hence *undergricer*, one whose enthusiasm is for the London Transport Underground railways (Watts, 1988).

grid. A bicycle. *OED* Sup. cites D.H. Lawrence, 1924. Ex *grid*, a grid-iron. See **gridiron**, 1.—2. In to *have* (someone) *on the grid*, to have someone awaiting trial: police s.: since ca. 1930. (Gosling, 1959.) ?Ex the start of a motor-race; or perhaps from **gridiron**, 2, q.v.

gridiron. A bicycle: Aus. and Brit.: since early C.20. (B., 1942.) Cf. **grid**, 1.—2. In *on the gridiron* (either absolute, C.19–20, or with defining circumstances, C.16–18), harassed; in a bad way: coll.: late C.16–20; ob., but see **grid**, 2.

grief. Rejected film cut from the day's take. See MOVING-PICTURE SLANG, §6, in Appx.

griff. In RN (*the*) *griff* = news, information. (H. & P.) Cf. **gen**, n. In the MN, since ca. 1939, it has the specialised sense of inside information (Peppitt), and in Aus. since ca. 1930, it is trustworthy information (B., 1943). L.A. notes, 1976, that phrases like 'What's the griff?' and 'Give me the griff on . . . ' had, by 1950, come into gen. use in Brit.: by 1980, slightly ob. Abbr. later C.19 synon. *griffin*, a signal or warning.—2. As in *griff sense*, a pickpocket's ability to size up an intended victim's psychology: since late 1940s. Moynahan, 1969.

griller. See AUSTRALIAN UNDERWORLD, in Appx., at **bake**, n.

grim, n. In *on the grim*, 'on the North-West Frontier of India. I believe Rudyard Kipling used the phrase' (Jackson): RAF: 1919+. It is, indeed, a grim place.

grim, adj. Unpleasant: a C.20 (rare before 1918) middle- and upper-class coll. intensive. Waugh, 1928, 'Marriage is rather a grim thought'. Cf. *awful* and **ghastly,** and contrast *nice.*

grim show. A (very) exhausting ordeal: RAF: since ca. 1939. A not unnatural sense-development of *grim;* see **show,** n., 2.

grimbo. 'Yesterday's "wimps" and "nerds" [qq.v.] are, for no reason, this morning's "squids" and "grimbos" but tomorrow they'll both be "dexter" ' (*Daily Mail,* 3 Oct. 1985).

grimmer. An unpleasant person: Public Schools': since mid-1930s. Ex *grim,* by the 'OXFORD *-ER*'.

grimmy. A middle-aged woman: since ca. 1960, ?earlier. Winsor, 1972, 'you'd see them at the Mecca . . . going for the "old women", as he says. What he means is, the grimmies are grateful'. Ex *grim*-faced.

grimpeur. A good hill-climber: cyclists': since ca. 1945. Sense-adapted ex Fr.

grin on the other side of (one's) **face,** esp. in some such minatory context as 'You'll be grinning on the other side of your face when I have finished with you': coll.: late C.19–20. (Petch, 1966.)

grind, n. The sexual act: late C.16–20: low coll. (Florio; D.H. Lawrence). Esp. in *do a grind* (rarely of a woman), to coït: C.19–20. Hence, a girl or woman regarded as a sex object, as in 'She's a great little grind'; in lesser nuances, the sexual titillation of a woman, or mere masturbation: the first, low and raffish, later C.20; the two latter, teenagers' of the later 1930s. Cf.:—2. (Of a woman) difficult to copulate with. Thomas, 1976.

grind, v. To copulate: low coll.:—1811 (*Lex. Bal.*). Less gen. than *do a grind,* but still, 1983, current; *have a grind* is now much more usu. than *do a grind* (L.A., 1974). Cf. the n.—2. To titillate a woman sexually, v.i. and t.: teenagers': late 1930s.—3. To masturbate: id.

Gringo. An Englishman: used by Englishmen (and, of course, by the natives) in S. America. (Alexander, 1939.) An American Spanish name, ex Sp. *gringo,* 'gibberish': to the Spaniards and to the Mexicans, the Englishman appears to speak gibberish.

grinning through. 'When undercoat or any previous coat is partly visible after finishing coat of paint has been applied' (master builder, 1953): builders' and house-painters': late C.19–20. P.B.: I have heard the phrase applied also to underclothing showing through, e.g., a rent in one's trousers; this perhaps prompted the decorators' usage.

grip, n. Abbr. *gripsack,* a traveller's handbag: E.P. noted that, in the 1930s, both forms (orig. US) were occ. used in the British Empire as coll.: since ca. 1950, at latest, the short form has been very common, the longer rare.—2. Occupation, employment: Aus.: early C.20. Dennis.—3. Any knowledge, skill, privilege or possession which enables one to boast or practice oneupmanship: Army: since ca. 1950. Cf. v., 1, from the victim's point of view. (P.B.)

grip, v. To bore (someone); hence *gripper,* a bore, and *the big grip,* one's military autobiography: Army, esp. officers': since ca. 1939. Perhaps suggested by the RAF's *bind;* cf. also the n., 3.—2. See **grip off** at BIRDWATCHERS', in Appx.

grip (one's) **shit.** In such phrases as 'He grips my shit' or 'What really grips *my* shit about it all is . . . ', to annoy, irritate, anger: RAF: early 1970s. (P.B.)

gripe. To complain, as in 'What are you griping about?': coll.: since ca. 1910, within my own knowledge; but probably late C.19–20. Ex the pains of colic. Hence, although much less common, n., as in 'What's the, or your, gripe now?': since ca. 1915.

gripped at the knickers. Nervously tense: mid-1970s. (BBC Radio 4 discussion, 26 Feb. 1975.) Prompted by *get* (one's) *knickers in a twist,* and *get a grip of your knickers.*

gripped off. Angrily disappointed. See BIRD-WATCHERS', in Appx, and cf. **grip,** n., 3.

gripping. Mean; miserly: Glasgow:—1934. Cf. **gripe.**

grippo. (Usu. in pl. *grippos.*) A free entertainment of any kind: RN. Hence, a *grippo run,* 'Free treat and entertainment ashore. A public entertainment for a ship's company which happens to be in a port or seaside resort' (Granville, who derives it from O.E. *gripe,* to grasp or take anything that's going).

grips or **gripps.** A scene-shifter: filmland: since ca. 1920. McCabe, 1937.

Grips, the. The Hongkong Hotel, Hong Kong: Far East: earlier C.20. Archer, 1946.

grit. Food: Army, esp. Royal Artillery: since ca. 1930. H. & P.

gritty. Penniless: lower classes': since ca. 1870. (B. & L.)—2. Hence, in difficult, 'rugged', straitened circumstances or position, characterised by hardship and sociological handicap: since the late 1950s. Lejeune, 1967, 'The Prime Minister's sheep words range from "gritty" (meaning—well, what does it mean?) to the statesmanlike exhortation "Belt up".'—3. (Of a person) in a bad humour or mood: since ca. 1955. (Petch, 1969.) I.e. abrasive, like sandpaper.

gritty whiskers. A day's, or a few days', growth of beard: domestic coll. (P.B.)

grizzle. To sing, esp. in the streets for a living: c.:—1926 (Jennings). Perhaps by pun ex *griddle,* and:-

grizzle-guts, occ. **-pot.** A tearfully or whiningly ill-tempered or melancholy person: low coll.: from ca. 1875. The *grizzle-pot* form has, since ca. 1920 been common also in Aus., where (since ca. 1944—under American influence) *grizzle-puss* has > even commoner. (B.P.)

groan and grunt. Copulation. An occ. var. of **grumble and grunt,** q.v. Franklyn 2nd.—2. In *the groan and grunt game,* professional wrestling: sporting: since ca. 1950. (Leechman.)

groanies. Adults. See **grownies.**

grobbly. 'A farewell booze-up, financed by voluntary contributions from mess members' RN: 1970s' (Peppitt).

grocer. An Equipment Officer: RAF: since ca. 1925. Jackson, 'The suggestion that he has a nasty commercial attitude towards life.' Ex:—2. A Victualling Warrant Officer: RN. P-G-R.

groceries. Bombs: RAF: since ca. 1930. 'Thus, "We delivered the groceries" ' (Jackson). Cf. **cabbage, cookie** and **gardening,** all euph. for bombs and bombing.

Grocer's Express, the. A train running four times a week from London to Aberdeen with margarine, tea, coffee, cocoa: railwaymen's: 1920s and 30s.

grocer's hitch. 'A nondescript knot that won't come undone' (Granville): RN. Landlubberly.

grocer's shop. An Italian: r.s., on *wop:* later C.20. Barker, 1979.

grockle. A regular visitor to the Torbay area: 1962, when used in a film (*The System*) scripted by Peter Draper. Mr Draper didn't invent the term, which arose from a remark that the hordes of visitors resembled clowns, *Grocks,* whence *Grockles,* little Grocks, the ref. being, obviously, to the famous clown. It has attracted some attention in the national press. Writing to me, 1977, Mr Draper adds that, in near-by Dartmouth, the word has been changed to *grackle.* I don't pretend to know; but it does seem that it's a spontaneous-combustion word. P.B.: as *grockle* it had, by 1978, widespread currency throughout the South-West and the Channel Islands. And at the FAA Search and Rescue helicopter squadron at Culdrose, Cornwall, 'rescuing is "grockle-grappling". The SAR crews talk ironically of "good grockling weather", that is weather in which holiday-makers are likely to get into difficulties . . . ' (Winton, 1978). Derivatives include *grockle bait,* cheap arcades; *grockle cans,* motor coaches full of visitors, and *grockle fodder,* fish and chips.—2. 'An outsider, an oik, a weed' (*Sunday Express* supp., 11 Oct. 1982): Sloane Rangers' (q.v.).

grog. 'To spit. A *grog* is a lump of spittle: "Which wan a you ratbags grogged on ma jaikit?" ' (Munro, 1985): Glasgow. Cf. **gob.**—2. See **grog on.**

grog-blossom. A pimple caused by strong drink: low:—1791: ob. Grose, 3rd ed.—2. Hence, the red nose itself, esp. if

199

bulbous, whether caused by strong drink or not: coll.: C.19–20. (L.A., 1974.)

grog on. To drink heavily over a long period: Aus. coll.: since ca. 1940. Hence, since ca. 1945, *grog-on*, n., a heavy drinking party. (B.P.) The verb was current among United Nations troops in Korea, ca. 1952–5, where Australian Forces, as usual, distinguished themselves, and thence it gained some later usage among British servicemen. (P.B.)

groggy. In poor health. Cf. Aus. *crook*.

groin. A (race-course) betting ring: c. Esp. among pickpockets and race-course thieves, who frequently refer to the betting rings as *the bob* (shilling) *groin* and *the dollar* (five-shilling) *groin*. (Hume.) Prob. by a pun on:—2. A finger ring: c. Sharpe, 1938.—3. Hence, a diamond: c.: since ca. 1940. (Gosling, 1959.) Cf. **groiny.**

groinch. To carve away great scoopfuls of rock and soil, as a mechanical digger does; whence *groincher*, such a machine, a bulldozer, grader, etc.: later C.20. (J.F. Beale.) Cf. **grauncher.**

groiny. (also pron. *griny*). A ring; a diamond—or other precious stone—when in a ring: c., and grafters' s. (Allingham, 1931.) A diminutive of **groin.**

groise, n. Grease: Haileybury. (Marples.) At Tonbridge School, esp. hair-oil: mid-C.20. (P.B.) By form perversion.—2. At Uppingham, it = one who is over-efficient, one who curries favour by showing his efficiency: since the late 1920s. Cf. the Cheltenham *groise*, to curry favour; hence, *groiser*, one who does so: since ca. 1925. Marples.

groise, v.i. To work hard; hence n., a 'swot': Harrow School: late C.19–20. Lunn.—2. See **groise**, n. 2.—3. To 'fiddle'; to cheat in a petty way: Charterhouse: since ca. 1930. (Sanders.)—4. See **groyze.**

groiser. A toady: Tonbridge School: mid-C.20. Cf. **groise**, n., 2. (P.B.)

groisy. Oily, as in 'Who's that groisy oick?', that swarthy youth using overmuch hair-oil; also, contemptuously, 'sycophantic': Tonbridge School: late 1940s. (P.B.)

grommet. Var. spelling of **grummet**, coïtion, hence, the female sex.

gronk. 'A very ugly lady friend' (Knight, 1984): RN: later C.20. P.B.: just poss. connected with the dinosaur, whose only utterance this is, in the strip cartoon 'B.C.' by the American cartoonist Johnny Hart, pub'd worldwide since late 1950s.

grool. A sinister person: since ca. 1950. A back-formation ex:-

grooly. Sinister: from ca. 1920; now almost coll. Knox, 1934, 'Dashed cowardly of me, but . . . It's just the tiniest bit grooly, isn't it?' A blend of *gruesome* + *grisly*.

groove, n. A profound pleasure, a true joy, whether a thing, an act, or a person: beatniks', hippies', and among their like and their descendants: since ca. 1960. As in 'It was a real groove, being with Hardy', and, of a delightful youth, 'He's a groove', both in Reid, 1970.—2. See **groovy**, 2, for *in the groove*. Cf.:—3. As in 'I am back in the groove', I am working properly again after a momentary lapse of concentration, co-ordination, etc.: RAF: later C.20. 'I feel comfortable and in the groove' (*Phantom*).

groove, v. To 'make good progress, co-operate' (Fryer, 1967): jazz- and drug-addicts' and hippies': since ca. 1960.—2. To be relaxed and happy: id.: since early 1960s. Reid, 1970.—3. V.t. To please (a person): adopted, ca. 1972, ex US. (It has been admitted by *COD*, 1976.)

groovy. Also *in the groove*. Lost in jazz (swing music) ecstasy: adopted, ca. 1940, ex US. (*Observer*, 16 Sep. 1956.) 'Like most jazz expressions, referred first to players, and only later to "fans". When the player suddenly hit his real stride, so that he improvised brilliantly and effortlessly, he was "in the groove".' (Priestley.) See also JAZZ TERMS, in Appx.—2. Excellent: Aus. teenage surfers' (*Pix*, 28 Sep. 1963); in later 1960s, also Can. and Brit. teenagers', adopted ex US (Leechman; Reid, 1970); ob. by 1975. Ex:—3. Notably alert, progressive, well-informed, esp. in jazz music: beatniks': since ca. 1959. (Anderson.) By 1967, widely used by teenagers.—

4. Sexually attractive: jazz- and drug-addicts', and hippies': since early 1960s. Fryer, as at **groove**, v., 1.—5. Used, by addicts, to describe the effect of amphetamine: 1970s. Home Office.

grope. A *ground operational exercise*: RAF: since ca. 1935. (Jackson.) Cf. **dry swim** and **tewt.**—2. See **group grope.**

Groper. A Western Australian: Aus. (Doone, 1926.) Abbr. **sandgroper**, q.v. Hence also, since ca. 1925, *Groperland*, W.A.

Gropework, the. The Gourock Ropework Co. Ltd.: Scottish: † by 1960.

gropper. A grasshopper warbler. See BIRD-WATCHERS', in Appx.

Groppi gong. See **Naffy medal.**

Groppi's Light Horse; Short Range Desert (or **Shepheard's**) **Group.** Combatant soldiers' names for Base troops at Cairo: Army: 1940–3. Sarcastic ref. to a famous tea-shop and a famous hotel in that city; the latter refers also to the Long Range Desert Group, a forerunner of the Special Air Service of post-war years. Also sometimes *Groppi's Hussars*. Sanders, 1967.

gross. All-purpose adj. of disapprobation: teenagers': mid-1980s.

Grosvenor Highlanders, the. The Gordon Highlanders: Army (mostly officers'): earlier C.20. Envious.

grot. A mess(-room): RN. (Bowen.) I.e. a grotto.—2. A hideout: Aus. c. B., 1942.—3. One's home, house, other residence or accommodation: RN; RM: since ca. 1930. Winton, 1960 (RN); Hawke, 1979 (RM). Ex sense 1.—4. Dirt, filth, 'gunge': Services': 1960s. A back-formation from **grotty**, 2 and 3. 'It was no palace. There was grot in the corner for one thing, and it stank' (*Heart*).

grotch, n. and v. (To) vomit: Services', esp. Army: since ca. 1950. (P.B.)

Grotsend-on-Sea. Any unprepossessing township, as in 'Oh, it was absolute Grotsend-on-Sea, but there *were* a couple of good bookshops there': since mid-1970s. (Huston, 1980.) Ex **grotty**, 2.

grotty. New, or newfangled, but useless; esp. in 'dead *grotty*': since ca. 1961. Ex '*grotesque*'.—2. (Very) inferior, bad—'crummy' or, in longer-established s., 'lousy': Liverpool s. Popularised by the Beatles and, by 1962, fairly gen. among teenagers. It occurs notably in *Hansard*, 25 June 1968 (Petch).—3. (Of things) very disagreeable; (of persons) very irritable. D.B. Gardner notes that it was in use at New College, Oxford, by 1957. Reid, 1970, 'The weather turned grotty in the mountains'.

ground. In (*to be*) *put on the ground*, to be made an insurance inspector: insurance s. (Harrison, 1935.) He spends much time visiting prospective clients.

ground-bait. 'Small gift, such as stockings or cosmetics, given to female acquaintance, with ulterior motive' (Bassett): RN: WW2, and ever since (Knight, 1985).

ground bones. Artificial, powdered milk: academic joc. (Estevé-Coll, 1985.) Cf. *plastic milk*, q.v. at **plastic.**

ground floor. As *the ground floor*, the inside, lower deck, of a double-decker bus: busmen's: from ca. 1931. *Daily Herald*, 5 Aug. 1936.—2. In *let* (someone, or people) *in on the ground floor*, (of the promoters) to allow to share in a financial or commercial speculation on equal terms: adopted ex US ca. 1900: mainly Stock Exchange and commerce. From the opp. angle, *get*, or *be let*, *in* . . . —3. Hence, to *be in on the ground floor*, to be in on the early stages of, e.g., a trend or technical development: coll.: later C.20. (L.A., 1974.)

ground(-)loop. 'Aircraft crash' (Gerald Emanuel, 1945): RAF: 1940+. The last looping of the loop. 'An aircraft bursting a tyre on landing would swing (perhaps if the undercarriage collapsed) through 180°. This is referred to as a ground loop' (RAF officer, late 1961), and is j.

ground-pounders. Air-to-ground attack crews: RAF: 1970s. (Wilson, 1979.) Cf. **mud-mover,** and the earlier **ground-strafer.**

ground-strafer; agent corresponding to next (both senses). Partridge, 1945.

ground-strafing. A low-flying attack on, e.g., transport: RAF: since 1939. (H. & P.) See **strafe.**—2. Hence, 'careless driving by servicemen' (H. & P.): 1940+.

ground wallah. Any RAF member working only on the ground: Air Force coll.: 1915. (F. & G.) The term continued in use until WW2 (Jackson), but was † by ca. 1950.

Ground Walloper. That fat little gremlin who is in charge of flying: RAF: 1941+. Perhaps a perversion of *Grand Walloper*, the gremlin king. See GREMLINS, in Appx.

grounded. Deprived of alcoholic and amorous adventure; applied esp. to a newly married man: RAF: since ca. 1940. (Partridge, 1945.) Ex the technical sense, '(temporarily) affected to ground duties': he can no longer be a *fly-by-night*.—2. 'Stranded for lack of petrol' (Sanders, 1967): Army in N. Africa: 1940–3.

grounders. 'Your "oppo's" entire tot of rum given to you as a very exceptional favour' (Granville): RN: since ca. 1910. 'Ground and all', by the 'OXFORD -ER(S)'.

groundhog. A meteorologist: Can.: since ca. 1969. 'Based . . . on the traditional appearance of the groundhog on Feb. 2 to determine weather prospects'. (Leechman, 1971.) On that day, called Groundhog Day, this North American marmot comes out of hibernation: if it's sunny and he can therefore see his shadow, he prudently returns to hibernation for six more weeks because he then presumes the weather will be wintry. (Can. and US folklore.)

groundies. Ground crews: RAF: WW2. (Mindel, 1980.) Cf. **rouseabout.**

group grope. Originally, 'heavy petting only' (W. & F., 1975), but soon 'a sexual orgy', as in 'At group gropes . . . , you can get anything you want' (Hollander): adopted, ex US, ca. 1971. Cf. **gang-bang.**—2. 'In the 1960s the United States saw the growth of a number of group-therapy cults which introduced into their procedures various rituals of mass-touching. These "group-gropes", as they were called . . . ' (Morris, 1977). By ca. 1974 the term was being applied, in UK, to the use of group-working in psychotherapy, where the mutual 'groping' is mental rather than physical. (P.B.)

group-happy. Unreliable as soldier, because his release (according to age-group) is near: Army: 1945–6.

grouper. 'An Officer on a Group Headquarters Staff' (Jackson): RAF coll.: since ca. 1925.

groupie, -y. Group Captain: RAF coll.: since before 1930. H. & P.—2. 'A teenage camp-follower of pop-groups' (*TLS*, 16 Oct. 1970); 'a girl who associates with musicians for social and sexual purposes. An English book, *Groupie*, by Jenny Fabian [1968] is devoted to this subculture' (B.P., 1974). *OED*'s earliest citation: 1967. In fact, used in Brit. since ca. 1965. P.B.: also in joc. usage, as 'After two productions at the National Theatre ("I [Maria Aitken]'m a Peter Hall groupie") the parts are more important that the place . . . ' (*Telegraph* Sunday mag., 1 July 1979).

grouse, n. A grumble: orig. (ca. 1890) soldiers' s.; since WW1, gen. coll. Ex the v.—2. As *the grouse*, the very best of anything: Aus. c. > gen. coll. McNeil, '*Go for the grouse*, seek what is worthwhile': later C.20.—3. 'Most commonly used in reference to "outside" tobacco: [Aus.] prison slang' (McNeil): later C.20.

grouse; occ., but not after 1914, **grouce,** v. To grumble: dial., from ca. 1850 (see W.), >, by ca. 1880, soldiers' s. that, ca. 1919, > gen. coll.

grouse (or **grouce**), adj. First-class (e.g. hotel); excellent: Aus.: since ca. 1920. (B., 1942.) Cf. the n., 2 and 3. *Grouse sort:* agreeable person, the opp. of *drack sort*: since ca. 1940. B., 1953.

Grove, the. 'West Indian slang for Notting Hill, W. London (possibly from Ladbroke or Westbourne Grove)' (Powis): 1970s.

grovel, grovel! Expression of abject apology for, e.g., arriving late at a meeting with a friend: joc. coll., often fem.: later C.20. Cf. **cringe!** (Raab, 1983.)

groves, the. The latrines: Lancing: since ca. 1920. (Marples.) Cf. Marlborough's *woods*.

growing pains. The difficulties and anxieties of getting settled down in life when one is young: coll. Ex the lit. *growing pains*.

growing up. 'Doctors' desk-side synonym for growing old' (L.A., 1969).

growler. 'A low-lying mass of ice, frequently not showing up white like an iceberg, in the night-time not distinguishable from the surrounding sea' (and usually small): mostly nautical: since ca. 1910. Jackson,1931.—2. A sausage: RAF Other Ranks': 1920s–30s. (Adkin, 1983.) Var. of **dogs,** 1.

growly. Subject, temperamentally or incidentally, to moroseness or ill temper expressed in growls: coll.: from ca. 1920.

grownies. 'Grown-ups', esp. one's own, hence also one's friends', parents: teenagers': 1970s. Often spelt, where the pun is intentional, *groanies*. Synonyms are *crumblies, oldies, wrinklies*: witness 'The Times Diary' in *The Times*, 6 Sep. 1976, where *grownies* is mentioned.

groyze. To spit: Conway cadets':—1891; ob. (Masefield, 1933.) Perhaps cf. dial. *growze* (etc.), to have a chill before a cold.—2. Or as *groyse*: var. spellings of **groise,** q.v.

grozzle, n. and v. 'This takes place at well-conducted tea-parties' (*Daltonian*, Dec. 1946): Dalton Hall, Manchester: since ca. 1920. Perhaps a blend of *grub* +*guzzle*.

grub-stake. To give (an author) money to keep him going while he writes a book: publishers', hence also authors', coll.: from ca. 1920. The term derives from the Western Can. (and South-Western US) practice whereby someone with capital provides a gold-prospector with food and, if necessary, equipment. It prob. goes back to 1849 in California, and it could have reached Can. by 1851 or so. It had reached Aus. by 1900 at latest; Macdonald, 1907, 'The hotel-keepers "grubstake" men to work for them.'

grub up! Food's ready: s. > coll. (Raab, 1976.)

grubber. A workhouse: tramps' and market-traders' c.: since late C.19. *EDD; M.T.*—2. Hence, a casual ward: tramps' c.:—1932 ('Stuart Wood').

grubber-dock. A workhouse infirmary: tramps' c.:—1931 (Stamper).

grue. Morbid; nervously upset or afraid; since ca. 1924; orig., Society. ' "Well, I don't want to go all grue," said Woody, somewhat abashed' (Brand, 1945). Ex S.E. *gruesome*.

gruesome twosome. 'Two young girls who are inseparable' (B.P.): Aus.: adopted, ca. 1943, ex US.

grumble and grunt. Female genitals. (Benny, 1938.) R.s. on *cunt*: less usual than *Berkeley Hunt*.—2. Hence, coïtion. Franklyn.—3. Hence, 'Specifically, "grumble and grunt" means women who are sexually available so long as one is not too fastidious: the female equivalent of "a bit of rough" ' (Barltrop, 1981).

grumblie, -y. RAF nickname for the Hercules C-130 heavy transport aircraft: late 1960s–early 70s. Ex engine noise. (P.B.)

grummet (or **grommet, -it**). The female pudend: low: nautical, since mid-C.19, > low gen. Ex *grummet-hole*, itself ex *grummet*, a little ring used merely to tie gaskets (Manwayring, *Seaman's Dict.*, 1644—cited by W.).—2. Hence, coïtion: nautical and low: since mid-C.19.—3. Hence, girls and women, regarded as sexual objects: raffish, low and joc.: since ca. 1950, ?earlier. Campbell, 1960, 'two lovely bits of grummet'. Also Aus. (B.P.)

grungy. Dirty, unwashed and smelly; squalid: orig. pop music world, early 1970s, > more gen. (Hibbert, 1983.) Paul, 1982, 'She walked into the clubhouse feeling grungy and uncomfortable [having just woken up on a golfcourse, without knowing how she got there]'. Perhaps a blend of *grotty* and *gungey*; cf. **scungey.**

G

grunt. In low coll., to *make* (a girl) *grunt*, to copulate with her.

grunt-horn. Bass-horn or tuba. See **fish-horn.**

grunter. 'Any type of wireless spark transmitter other than quenched gap, or high frequency': RN: from ca. 1922. Bowen.—2. A motor-car: lower classes':—1923 (Manchon); ob. by 1933.—3. 'A baked suet roll to contain strips of pork or bacon' (Wilson, 1957): domestic: mid-C.19–20. Ex much older s. for pig.—4. A sunken iceberg: trawlermen's. (Mitford, 1969.) Cf. **growler,** 1.—5. 'A promiscuous girl' (Buzo, 1973): Aus. 'lowish': since ca. 1940. *In coitu* she grunts (cf. **grunt.**)—contrast a 'moaner' (E.P.). P.B.: could also be a pun on this sense of *pig*.

grunts. In *go grunts,* to defecate. Burland, 1968, 'He wanted to go grunts too but he did not dare to take his pants down.'

gryer. A horse: market-traders'. (*M.T.*) Ex Romany *gry.*

guaranteed parachute (usu. pl.). 'If they fail to open, you get another for nothing' (Petch, 1969): since ca. 1942.

guard. A conductor on an omnibus: busmen's: late 1920s–30s. (*Daily Herald,* 5 Aug. 1936.) Ex railway j.—2. *The Old Guard* and *the Young Guard.* A team consisting of the masters and one consisting of younger boys; the former also = the masters, in any connexion: Rugby School. (Wharton, 1965.)

guard-mounter. An article kept solely for guard-duty: military: from ca. 1925. The best-dressed man is excused guard.

guard-rail critic. One who tenders overmuch advice and no assistance: RN: since ca. 1920. (Granville.) He leans back against the rail while *you* work.

guard the ace. To form 'a destroyer screen round big warships at sea': RN: 1914. (Bowen.) Ex bridge. The phrase was revived in WW2 (P-G-R).

guard's bedroom. A brake van: railwaymen's. (*Railway,* 2nd.) Affording the opportunity for a quiet rest.

gubbins. Rubbish, trash: coll.: late C.19–20. Ex S.E. sense, fish-offal.—2. Hence, 'thingummybob'; anything one is too lazy or too forgetful to name: Services', esp. RAF: since ca. 1918. (Emanuel, 1945.) The transition from 1 is eased by the fact that in 1914–18 *gubbins* predominantly signified 'stores' or 'one's personal belongings'.—3. Also ex 1, 'trimmings, e.g., "steak with all the gubbins", i.e. parsley, fried potatoes, vegetables, etc.; also in gen. use for trimmings, odds and ends, not necessarily rubbish' (L.A.): since ca. 1919. The latter nuance is merely a civilian adoption of the WW1 usage in sense 2.

gucky. Nauseating; disgusting: Sloane Rangers' (q.v.): early 1980s. (*Sunday Express,* 11 Oct. 1982.) Cf. *yucky,* at **yuck,** perhaps here punned on Gucci, Italian fashion designer.

guessing-box. A pocket, transistor-operated, calculator: coll.: since ca. 1965. (P.B.) Cf.:–

guessing-stick. A slide-rule: coll.: since ca. 1950, ?earlier.

gues(s)timate, n. and v. To calculate approximately; a rough calculation: orig. s., adopted ex US by 1950; >, by 1960, coll. A blend of *guess* + *estimate.*

guff, n. Official, or other genuine and precise, information, esp. concerning the formal rules or the Service's regulations; mostly in *give* (someone) *the guff on* whatever the problem, etc., may be: chiefly in the Services: since ca. 1945. (L.A.)

guff, v. 'To romance, to humbug, to pitch yarns' (Jackson): RAF: since ca. 1930.

gugnunc. *Gug* and *nunc* were the only noises made by Wilfred, of **Pip, Squeak and Wilfred,** q.v. It became a 'one-word catchphrase' in 1920s, and there was even a 'Gugnunc Club'. Horn, 1976: 'Old Gugnuncs still greet each other with their secret password "Ick-ick! Pah-boo!" ' (P.B.)

gugu (or **gu-gu**). Tapioca gruel. See PRISONER-OF-WAR SLANG, §11, in Appx.

guide. 'Someone familiar with a drug and relatively sober while others try it for the first time' (Home Office): drug addicts': 1970s.

guider. Makeshift vehicle of 'soap-box and pram-wheels', for racing down-hill: Yorkshire (and more widespread?) children's:—1960. (Bowater, 1979.) Known also as a *glider.*

guinea-pig. An evacuated Civil Servant: 1939+. (*New Statesman,* 30 Aug. 1941.) This included BBC personnel to whom the Government paid one guinea a week towards their board and lodging.—2. One upon whom an experiment—or anything new—is tried: since ca. 1930: coll. >, by 1945, S.E. Ex guinea-pigs used in medical experiments.

Guinness(-)label. Tax disc: motorcyclists': 'dates from when the tax disc looked like a beerbottle- —or Guinness- —label, when these could be used in the holder to fake a tax disc. Probably originated in Ireland' (Dunford).

guintzer. Fellow: Aus. (urban). Yiddish? Stivens, 1951, 'I wanted to ask the old guintzer where all his bright boys were.'

guiver. Flattery; artfulness: theatrical: from ca. 1880. L.A. adds, 1974, 'Persuasive patter, to persuade another to accept a given idea . . . It was always used as "Jewish guiver" by my mother, who was born and lived into womanhood in the East End among Jews whom she knew and liked as neighbours.' Powis, 1977, glosses *put on the guiver,* 'To pretend gentility or affect a "well-bred" voice.'—2. Whence, in Aus., C.20, it is gen. s., with additional sense of fooling, nonsense, esp. if plausible; make-believe. 'Guyver: Make-believe, still used in Anglo-Jewish slang. It is Hebrew for pride but has now come to mean pretence and is synonymous with . . . swank' (Abrahams, 1938).

gully, the. The fielding-position between point and slips: cricketers' coll. (—1920) >, by 1934, j. Lewis.—2. 'Any geographical indentation from a fair-sized drain to a grand canyon' (B., 1942): Aus. coll.

gulpers. 'A levy for a major service, made against a seaman's tot [by the one doing the service]. Small levies for minor services were sippers: RN: 1950s' (Peppitt, 1976): prob. from some 50 years earlier.

gum. Opium: drugs c. (Stockley, 1986.) US since —1936 (Spears).

gum(-)chum. An American soldier: 1942+. Ex the constant request '(Got) any gum chum?'

gum-sucking. A low var. (—1923) of *French kiss.* (Manchon.) P.B.: used loosely, in low joc., for any kissing.

gum up the works. To spoil or upset things: since ca. 1918, when adopted from US. Heyer, 1938, 'That North dame's story gums up the works.'

gum-worker. A pickpocket whose trick is to put chewing-gum on next seat in bus or train and then, while courteously helping the victim to get clean, cleans out the victim's pockets as well: c.: since ca. 1950. (*Sunday Times,* 11 May 1969.) A var. of the **coner,** q.v.

gummers. Gumboots, 'wellies': domestic coll.: later C.20.

gummie, -y. A shark: Aus.: from ca. 1925. Ex the lavish display of teeth.

gump. Common sense. Mitchell, 1945, ' "Show a bit of gump!" ' 'Now current schoolchildren's slang' (Sanders, 1965). Short for *gumption,* synon. coll. since early C.18.

gun, n. A syringe: drugs c.: adopted ex US, later C.20. (Home Office.) Cf. **artillery,** 2.—2. In *get* (one's) *gun,* to be promoted from lance-sergeant to full sergeant: Royal Artillery. H. & P., 'On being promoted . . . an artillery-man wears a gun above his three stripes.' Cf. **get** (one's) **crown,** on promotion to staff-sergeant (Army) or flight-sergeant (RAF).—3. See **give the gun; in the gun; under the gun.**

gun, v. To accelerate an automobile: coll.: since ca. 1935 has supplanted *give* (*her*) *the gun.* (Hunter, passim.) R.C. notes that the term was not necessarily adopted ex US.

gun-buster. An artificer (or *tiffy*) of the Royal Army Ordnance Corps: since ca. 1920. H. & P.

gun-fire. Early morning tea (or cup of tea): Army: prob. since ca. 1890. (Burrow, 1912.) Rogerson, 1933, 'Very brown, very sticky, but very stimulating.' By ca. 1950, at latest, it had come to mean esp. the early morning mug of tea liberally spliced with rum, in the army's ritual of the senior ranks serving the junior ranks with this drink in bed on Christmas morning; hence, the ritual itself: Army coll. > j. (P.B.)

gun-fodder. Shells: artillerymen's: 1940+. Contrast *cannon-fodder*, the victims at whom the shells are fired.

gun for, esp. **be gunning for,** someone. To seek someone in order to cause him very serious trouble: adopted, ca. 1944, ex US. Ex hunting for, and shooting at, game.

gun-man (or **gunman**). A lawless man likely to carry a fire-arm: adopted, ex US, ca. 1925; orig. coll. >, by ca. 1935, S.E.

gun moll. A female gangster, criminal, thief: Can., adopted, ex US, ca. 1930.

gun speaker. A practised, proficient mob-orator: Aus. political: since ca. 1920. (B., 1942.) Loud and rapid.

gung-ho. A US term, coined mid-WW2, adopted by Brit. journalists esp. during the Falklands War to mean 'actively, militaristically jingoistic'; it may also mean 'with aggressive esprit de corps'. Orig. used as a rallying call for his battalion of the US Marine Corps by Brig. Evans Carlson, who had misunderstood it during previous service in China. The two elements are from the Chinese title of the Chinese Industrial Co-operatives Society, and Carlson assumed they meant 'Work together'; in fact, to a Chinese, *gung-ho* would make about as much sense as *co soc* (thus abbr.) does to an English-speaker. But of course, once a useful word has entered the language, it will continue to be used regardless of logic or correctness. (P.B.)

Gunga Din. Gin (the drink): Aus. r.s. Mostly in *Gunga din and squatter's daughter*, gin and water. Franklyn.

gunga wallah. A male prostitute: Army: earlier C.20. Ex Hindustani. Cf. **gonga**, and **feetesick wallah.**

gunge. Grease; oily dirt: engineers, since ca. 1940; in later C.20, gen. coll., and applied to all kinds of filth; e.g. (of cows' horns obtained straight from a slaughter-house) 'they are in a fairly disgusting state . . . we have to boil them to take off all the membranes and gunge' (*Observer* mag., 4 Nov. 1979). Hence v. *gunge*, usu. with *up*, to make dirty; *gung(e)y* or *gunged up*, the adj. Towler, 1979, notes that *gungey* = 'second-rate, inferior, spoiled' was current in theological colleges, 1960s. Cf. **gunk.** (Wharton, 1965; P.B.)

gungineer. An *engineer* officer turned over to *gun*-mounting: RN (wardroom): since ca. 1930.

gungoo. Genuine; complete, entire: RN: earlier C.20. (F. & G.) ?A perversion of *damn' good.*

gunja. Marijuana. See **ganja.**

gunk. 'Chemical compounds, especially those which provide solid fuel for space rockets' (Leechman): Can.: 1958+. A composite word? Now has a much wider application (1965), and is known in UK, where used as a tradename for a chemical cleanser. Cf. **gunge.**—2. Non-physical rubbish, trash; e.g. of a radio or TV broadcast, matter deficient either technically or artistically, also vulgar and lacking in moral responsibility: since late 1960s. *The Times*, 30 Nov. 1976.

Gunners, the. See ASSOCIATION FOOTBALL, in Appx.

guns. A gunnery-lieutenant: RN: since ca. 1910. (F. & G.; Bowen.) Also as a nickname; virtually the vocative of earlier *gunnery Jack* ('Taffrail'). See quot'n at **pilot.**

Gunter's perms, or **jeeps.** 'These were the men that came into the docks after decasualisation took place [late 1960s]—the minister [responsible] was Ray Gunter' (Ash): London dockers'. *Perms* = those men on permanent appointment; *jeeps* = ?

guntz, the. The whole lot, the whole way, etc., esp. in *go the guntz*: low. Ex Yiddish; cf. Ger. *das Ganze*, all of it.

gup. Gossip, scandal: coll.: Anglo-Indian, with stress on its idleness: C.19.—2. From ca. 1920, however, the sense of the term has, in Eng., been much influenced by *gush* and *tosh* or *tush*; and even by 1883 (*OED* Sup.) it represented, also, silly talk.—3. Hence, information: Army: ca. 1930–50. (P-G-R.) See also **guff,** n.—4. (Also *guppy*.) A fool: Aus.: since ca. 1925. (B., 1942.) Perhaps ex sense 2.

guppy. See **gup,** 4.—2. Hence, adj., foolish, stupid, silly: since ca. 1930. Baker.

gurk, v.i. and (occ.) n. (To) belch: coll.:—1923 (Manchon). Echoic; or ex *gurgle*, itself echoic.—2. In Aus., to fart. B., 1942.

gussie. An affected and/or effeminate man: Aus.: since ca. 1890.—2. One of the army's nicknames for the officers is (ex sense 1) *the gussies*: since ca. 1930. (H. & P.) By ca. 1940 also, occ., in RAF (Jackson). Partridge, 1945. 'Familiar for Augustus, a "tony" name.'

Gussies. *G*reat *U*niversal *S*tores; stocks and shares thereof: commercial: since ca. 1940.—2. (Also *gussies*.) Women's lace panties: 1954+. Ex 'Gorgeous Gussie' Moran, a picturesquely dressed American lawn tennis star.

gust-guesser. A meteorological officer of Imperial Airways: 1920s. (McIntosh, 1963.) Gusts of wind, obviously!

gut. In *put* (or *get*) *a gut on*, to put on—gain in—weight: Aus. (Culotta), since ca. 1920; also Brit.—2. As *the Gut*, 'Strait Street, Valetta [Malta], (notorious red light district)' (Hawke, 1979): Services', esp. RN.

gut-buster. See **bust a gut.**

gut-rot. 'Unhealthy-looking food or strong drink' (B., 1942): Aus. Cf. *rot-gut.*

gut-spiller. A Ghurka soldier: Aus. servicemen's: WW2. (B., 1943.) For *guts-spiller.*

gutbash. A bellyful of food; hence, a resultant bellyache: Services', esp. RN: since ca. 1925. P-G-R.

gutbucket 'is the most "dirty" or "low-down" sort of playing, with deliberately distorted tonalities, "growl" effects, and so on. The term [came into use] before 1930' (Priestley, 1965): jazz: ca. 1948–56.

gutkas. Trousers: Cockney: 1920s–30s. Ex Yiddish. *Muvver.*

gutless. Cowardly: coll. Cf. *guts*, courage.—2. (Of automobiles) under-powered: coll.: since ca. 1945. (B.P.)

guts. To eat; to eat greedily: Aus.: since ca. 1890. Tennant, 1943, ' "Gutsing again, Briscoe?" she reproved.' In later C.20, also some Brit. use.

guts-ache. A contemptible person: Aus. (B., 1942.) Cf. 'She's a pain in the bum', she's a nuisance.

gutser (occ. **gutzer**). A heavy fall: low: from ca. 1905. Esp. *come a gutser*, to come a 'cropper'. Fig. from ca. 1914, but in WW1 applied esp. to a fall from an aeroplane and to a sharp rebuff or disappointment (F. & G.).—2. Four cards retained in the hope of making a straight: Aus. poker-players': since ca. 1920. B., 1953.

gutser. To come a 'gutser' (see n., 1), fail badly: Aus. Niland, 1959, 'You had your chance and you gutsered.'

gutsful. In *have had a gutsful of*, a var., perhaps esp. NZ, of *have had a belly-full of*, to have had too much of something: since ca. 1920. (Slatter.)

gutsful of grunts. A disagreeable person: Aus.: since ca. 1910. (B., 1942.) Cf. **guts-ache.**

gutsy. Courageous: coll.—2. Greedy; or merely very hungry: RAF, since ca. 1920 (Jackson); later, also Army.—3. Utterly sincere; deeply felt; esp. of songs, music: world of entertainment: since ca. 1965. (*Jagger*.) Perhaps a Brit. adaptation of synon. US *gutty.*

Gutta-Percha. 'A bird on a station roof' (McKenna, 1): railwaymen's pun; mid-C.20.

gutted. Disgusted, 'fed-up', chagrined: footballers': early 1980s. Barnes, 1983.

gutter. Esp. *in the gutter*, (of an advertisement) occupying an inside position, next to the fold (*gutter*) in the paper: copywriters' coll.: from ca. 1920. The term *gutter* is common among printers and publishers.

gutter-crawler (hence **g.-crawling**). One of that flower of modern youth which specialises in driving its cars slowly along by the kerb in the expectation that some girl will allow herself to be 'picked up': since ca. 1920. Cf. synon. **kerb-crawl.**

gutter-crawling. Route-marching through streets: Army: earlier C.20. (F. & G.)—2. See prec.

gutter-gripper. 'A motorist who drives with one arm out of the car window gripping the "gutter" on the roof' (Wilkes): Aus.: 1970s.

guttered. 'A popular term for drunk' (Munro, 1985): Glasgow. Cf. mid-C.19 s. *lap the gutter*, to be extremely drunk, and early C.19 *gatter*, beer.

gutty. Dirty and disagreeable, esp. of a task: since ca. 1950. Ex intestines. (P.B.)

gutzer. See **gutser**.

guv'nor, the. The head of a Teddy-boys' gang: Teddy boys': ca. 1950. (*Observer*, 1 Mar. 1959.) A slovening of 'governor'.

guvvie. School-leavers 'go on a "guvvie" (a government [-sponsored] training scheme) for twelve months' (Gofton, 1984): N.E. England. See also **govvy**.

guy. A man, fellow, chap: adopted, ex US, by 1903 (Binstead). Until mid-C.20 still felt to have a US tinge, it became, in 1960s–70s, esp. popular among army officers, and Munro, 1985, notes particularly heavy use in Glasgow. E.P. favoured a derivation ex Yiddish *goy*, a Gentile.—2. The manager, the boss: circus s. or coll.:—1923 (Manchon). ? Ex *guy-rope*.

guy-a-whack. Incompetent; hence, n., a defaulting bookmaker: Aus. low. B., 1942.

guyver. See **guiver**.

guyvo. A smart fellow; a dandy: RN: earlier C.20. (F. & G.) Granville, 'it means any unorthodox rig. Contrary to regulations or Admiralty's pattern: e.g., a sailor's "tiddlies" [see **tiddley**, 4] with too generously cut bell-bottomed trousers.' Ex later C.19 s. *guiver lad*, a dandy.

Guz. See **Guzzle**, Devonport, of which it is the usu. C.20 form.

guzinter. A division sum in arithmetic: elementary schoolchildren's. Ex a slovenly pron. of *goes into*. Also known as *share-by's*.—2. Hence, in Aus., a schoolteacher (Wilkes): mid-C.20.

guzinters. An animal's entrails: Aus. rural: since ca. 1910. (Baker.) What *goes into* it to make up its 'innards'. Cf.:–

guzunder. A chamber-pot: domestic coll., Aus. and Brit. It *guzunder* the bed.—2. 'A inspection cradle which is lowered by crane, and then swung underneath a bridge for purposes of inspecting the brickwork' (McKenna, 1, where spelt *gozunda*): railwaymen's: mid-C.20.

Guzzle. Devonport: RN: late C.19–20. (*Musings*, 1912.) Beckett refers it to the heavy-eating habits of West Country men; Peppitt, who cites this explanation, implies that this may not be true, and notes that he cannot find the shortened form *Guz* before the naval use of radio communication—adding that the Devonport W/T callsign is GUZ.

guzzump. Var. of **gazump**, q.v.

gwennie (-y), or **G,** n. A high-angle, anti-aircraft gun on board ship (cf. **archie**): RN: earlier C.20. (F. & G.; Bowen.) Ex *Gwendolen*, an aristocratic name.—2. Hence, the gunner: RN: from ca. 1918. *Weekly Telegraph*, 25 Jan. 1941.—3. In WW2, any gun: a not very gen. RN usage. P-G-R.

gwenny, adj. Old-fashioned: Leicestershire girls': 1970s.

gyke. A gynæcologist: among middle-class women, esp. in hospital: since ca. 1950. Cf.:–

gynae. Gynæcology; also attributively, as in 'the famous gynæman': medical: late C.19–20.

gynie or **gyno.** Aus. variants of prec., but also for a gynæcologist: since ca. 1920 and esp. among medical students.

gyvo. Humbug: Aus.: since ca. 1935. (B., 1953.) Var. of **guiver**.

G

H

H. Heroin: drug addicts' and purveyors': adopted, ca. 1945, ex US, where current since –1930. (Norman, 1959.) Hence, *H. & C.*, heroin and cocaine taken together: id.: since ca. 1965. (Wyatt, 1973.) A pun on *h*(ot) *and c*(old) water. Cf. **Henry,** 2.

h.b.s. Human beings: joc.: since ca. 1930.

H.E. An 'H.E.' is a severe reprimand: Services': since late 1940. (H. & P.) Ex the abbr. of 'high explosive': cf. synon. *blowing up.*—2. A coll.—in ref. only—for *H*is Excellency (ambassador; Governor-General): late C.19–20.

h.m.g. ' "Home-made gents"—one of the many obsolescent phrases here lovingly resurrected' (Ferdinand Mount, in *TLS*, reviewing Ingrams & Wells, *Dear Bill*, 1981). A pun on HMG, Her Majesty's Government. Cf. the idea behind **temporary gentleman.**

h.s. 'Hot stuff', esp. in the sexual sense: from ca. 1930. Mackenzie, 1933. 'She's h.s. all right.'

H. Samuel Never Right. A slander on H. Samuel's inexpensive watches, brandnamed 'Ever Right', in such phrases as 'What's the time by your H. Samuel?', 'The time by my H . . .': parodies of the firm's advertising: mid-C.20; ob. by 1980. But any publicity is perhaps better than none! (P.B.)

Hab. The RAF station in Iraq, formerly Dhibban and renamed Habbaniya on 25 Mar. 1938. (Moyes, 1964.) RAF withdrew from Iraq mid-1950s.

hab-dabs (occ. **habs-dabs**). (Often, *the screaming hab-dabs.*) Var. of **ab-dabs**, q.v., nervous irritation: mostly RAF: since ca. 1937. (L.A.) Cf. **heebie-jeebies.**

habit. '(*a*) Addiction to drugs with physical dependence (US). (*b*) Dosage commonly taken' (Home Office): 1970s. US usage throughout C.20 (Spears).

haby. A *haber*dashery department (in a store): trade: earlier C.20. Punshon, 1933.

hachi. See **never hachi!**

hack, n. As used in Public Schools for a kick, blow, punch, it verges on s. Benson, 1916, has 'A juicy hack'. Also as v. A. Waugh, 1917.—2. In the Oxford of today, a hack is 'Someone who seeks to make his way by joining all the right groups, attending the best parties, and being elected or appointed to the most prestigious posts. In short he is what I would call a chancer' (Harry Whewell, *Guardian*, 23 Apr. 1980): Oxford undergraduates'. See **chancer,** 5.

hack, v., often *hack down*. To shoot (*out* of the sky); to shoot *down*: RAF: 1939+. Brickhill, 1946, 'A couple of [the] 109's hacked two Hurricanes down near Montreuil on the 10th of June, 1940, and Eric jumped from his pranged kite and ran for it.' Prob. ex Rugby j. (for hearty work by the forwards): cf. **hack,** n., 1.—2. To achieve, cope with and surmount a (usu. difficult) task, as in 'It's a pretty tall order—do you reckon you can hack it?': Services': since late 1950s. (P.B.)—3. Hence, to endure boredom, danger, privation, etc., e.g., 'It'll only be for a couple of months or so, we can hack it that long, can't we—or can't we?': id. (P.B.) Cf. **hacked off.**—4. See **hacker**: to use a computer thus.

hack pilot, hack pusher. A taxi-driver: Aus.: since ca. 1944. (B., 1953.) Suggested by and perhaps confused with the US s. synons. *hackie* and *taxi-pusher.*

hacked off. Utterly bored; irritated; angry: Services': since late 1950s. Cf. **brassed off, cheesed off,** etc. (P.B., 1974.)

hackems. Hostilities; conflicts: Aus. coll.: later C.20. McNeil.

hacker. 'Unauthorised interloper who breaks into a computer network. Often a child just trying to prove the true potential of a home computer' (*Telegraph* Sun. mag., 10 June 1984): since early 1980s.—2. Hence, any computer enthusiast: addicts': Schofield, 1984.

hackette. A female journalist: journalists' joc.: later 1970s. (Arnold, 1980.) *Hack*, a literary drudge, since 1700 (*SOD*).

Hackney Gurkhas, the. 'The army has already trained engine drivers, signalmen and platelayers in the Royal Corps of Transport. "Hackney Gurkhas" as the railwaymen call them' (*New Society*, 1 July 1982). Revival of an early C.20 nickname for the 10th County of London Battalion of the London Regt.

Hackney Marsh. Glass (of liquor): s.: late C.19–mid-20. Franklyn 2nd.

had it. See **have had it.**

haddock. 'Haddock is the English version of the Latin *ad hoc*. (Cf. Rt. Hon. J. H. Thomas.)', editorial footnote to editorial entitled 'Haddock Intervention', in *Week-End Review*, 7 Oct. 1933: cultured s.: late 1933–4.

hæmatoid. A cultured euph. for unconventional *bloody*: ca. 1920–6. Manchon.

haggis-basher. A Scot: RAF joc.: since mid-1930s. (L.A.) *Haggis*, one of the toothsome national dishes of Scotland; see **basher,** 3, 4.

hags, the. The nuns: Catholic priests' joc. Not, of course, ex the S.E. *hag* (although, naturally, there's an allusion), but from Greek *hag*iai, holy women.

hag's bush. Synon. of **Sikh's beard,** q.v. at PRISONER-OF-WAR SLANG, §5, in Appx., a coarse, local Singapore tobacco. Here *bush* prob. = pubic hair.

hail and rain. A train: r.s.:—1923 (Manchon).

hail smiling morn. An erection: r.s., on *horn*. (Daniells, 1980.) Cf. synon. **September morn** and *Colleen Bawn.*

hair. See **within a hair.**

hair curl. See **make** (one's) **hair curl,** to frighten or astonish.

hair-cut. Barber's coll. for a customer wanting his hair cut.—2. 'Any very short term of imprisonment. In a local prison, one or two months or weeks. In a convict prison, three to five years' (Tempest): c.: mid-C.20.

hair-do. Having one's hair dressed in a fashionable style: feminine coll.: since ca. 1920.—2. Hence, a style of coiffure: (feminine) coll.: since ca. 1925.

hair down. See let (one's) **hair down.**

hair-drier. The device used in a police radar speed trap: motorcyclists'. *BMF Motorcycle Rider*, Sep. 1984.

hair of the dog that bit (one). A drink taken to counteract drunkenness; usu. of the same liquor that caused the state, e.g., the previous night: coll.:—1546. By C.20, frequently shortened to 'hair of the dog'. 'The allusion is to an ancient notion that the burnt hair of a dog is an antidote to its bite' (*Brewer's Dict. of Phrase and Fable*, 1956 ed.).

hair-raiser. An exciting adventure-story: coll.: from ca. 1910.

haircut with a hole in it. 'Jocular for barbering of bald man's tonsure' (L.A.).

hairing, adj. Tearing; furious: Scottish Public Schools'. Miller, 1935, 'It was not worth risking a hairing great row.'

hairless. Very perturbed and/or angry: Army, since ca. 1955; by ca. 1970, fairly gen. 'Cor, you should've seen him: he went *hairless!*' (P.B.)

hairy, n. *The hairy,* as in the following quot'n, hence, sing., *a hairy*; 'She was "one of the hairy"—a hatless slum girl conscious of her station in life'; Glasgow slum girls collectively: lower class Glasgow: late C.19–20. 'In Glasgow, as in Rome, the hat is the badge of feminine quality' (MacArthur). Still in use, 1985 (Munro): 'A contemptuous term for a sluttish girl'.—2. A lineman of the Royal Corps of Signals: Army, esp. in R. Sigs: WW2 and after. They need to be, and are, tough for their often hazardous outside work. (P.B.)—3. (Usu. in pl.) 'Unkempt and bearded proponent of self-expression' (*Observer*, 13 June 1976): since ca. 1970.—4. 'Former NCO, generally an old sweat, training to become an officer' (*Fighter Pilot*, 1981): RAF: later C.20.—5. An enthusiast keen to photograph anything slightly unusual: derogatory, among transport and traction enthusiasts. (C. Irwin, 1986.) Also known, more locally, as *festoon*, because hung about with camera equipment.

hairy, adj. Unpleasant; rough; Army: since ca. 1935. 'We had a hairy time on patrol last night.'—2. Hence, dangerous, exciting: since ca. 1945. 'Applied esp. to wild, reckless driving in a race—to the limits of the car and safety' (Mann, 1963). R.C., 1975. 'Some influence, perhaps, from small-boat sailing, in which "bald spots" (calms) on the water are contrasted with "hairy patches"—i.e., where the wind is gusting perhaps dangerously.'

hairy-arsed. Mature and hirsute and virile: RN: since ca. 1947. A young servicemen's term of the 1950s for a 'type' of rugged masculinity and maturity; esp. in the gen. Services' phrase 'a hairy-arsed mat'lo'.

hairy-bottomed tromp. A term of abuse: Cambridge undergraduates': early 1930s. I.e. tramp with a joc. 'Dutch' twist.

hairy canary. 'Unlikely eventuality/hypothesis. Used by a doctor of my acquaintance in June 1979 in discussing the (unlikely) possibility that someone was suffering from a particular illness' (John B. Smith, 1979). JBS adds, 1981: 'Cf. *Don't look for the canaries, look for the sparrows first.* This, or variants, is used as a warning to medical students not to assume the existence of some comparatively rare disease . . . where a commoner one might be possible.'

hairy devil. A flying fox: Aus.: late C.19–20. B., 1942.

hairy dive. A dive made into a (very) fast and dirty current and with the diver hanging on to an anchor line: skin divers': since ca. 1950. Cf. **hairy,** adj., 2.

hairy fairy. (Of a man) displaying feminine traits of personality: a pun on *airy-fairy*, adj.: later C.20. (L.A., 1978.)

hairy goat, run like a. (Of a horse) to perform badly in a race: Aus. Baker.

hairy-heeled. Ill-bred; bad-mannered: ca. 1930. Ex late 1890s+ *hairy at* (or *about*) *the fetlocks* or *heels*, a metaphor from the stables.

hairy mary (or **Mary**). 'The prickles that cover the cane' (Devanney, 1944): Aus. cane-cutters'.—2. A tangle of rope: RN lowerdeck: since ca. 1950. (Peppitt.) Partly anatomical, partly alliterative.

Hal, the. The Hallé orchestra: music-lovers': since ca. 1920.

hale and hearty. A party: r.s. Hillman noted, 1974, that it has superseded *gay and hearty*. P.B.: presumably because of the devaluation and degradation of *gay*.

half. A half-holiday: schools' coll. Mais, 1918.—2. A child travelling half fare: coll.—3. See **not half bad,** much, very.—4. See **half seven,** for use in time-telling.—5. In . . . *and a half,* used as an intensive: coll.: since (?)ca. 1930. 'This turned out to be a wedding and a half' (Mays, 1971). Cf. *he's a cunt and a half,* he's an extraordinarily obnoxious person.

half a (pint, mile, hour, million, etc.), a. Half a (pint, etc.): Can. sol. >, by 1955, non-educated coll. (Leechman.) P.B.: but for how many years have British children been chanting 'Half a pound of tuppency rice, half a pound of treacle . . . '?

half a bar. Ten shillings: Cockneys > gen. low. (George, 1911.) Powis notes that, since decimalisation of currency in 1971, it has been applied to 50 pence. Has var. *half bar.*

half a cock. 'Five pounds (from r.s. cock and hen—ten)' (Tempest): c.: mid-C.20.

half a crack. Half-a-crown: earlier C.20. Knox, 1933.

half a crown. See TOMBOLA, in Appx.

half a cup of tea. Tea and whisky mixed: Covent Garden. Partly r.s.

half a mo. Half a moment: coll.: late C.19–20.—2. A cigarette: Cockneys' and soldiers': ca. 1910–40. B. & P.

half a nicker. Vicar: r.s.: later C.20. (Hillman.) Ex:—2. Ten shillings or 50 pence: low coll.: 1895 (*EDD*). In mid- and later C.20, more usu. than var. *half-nicker.* See **nicker,** 3.

half a sheet. Punishment incurred by prison warders, mostly a fine: prisons', both warders' and prisoners': since ca. 1930. Norman, 1959.

half a stretch. Six months in prison: c.:—1859 (H., 1st ed.); still current 1977 (Powis). See **stretch.**—2. Hence, odds of 6 to 1: racing, esp. bookmakers'.

half a ton. £50. See **ton,** 2.

half an hour. Flour: Aus. r.s.: late C.19–20. B., 1942.

half-and-half. As in 'Give me a half-and-half', a man's request to a prostitute to copulate and to practise fellatio: prostitutes'. Landy.

half bar. Ten shillings. See **half a bar.**

half brass. 'A girl or woman who associates freely with men but does not accept money in return for her favours' (Tempest): low: mid-C.20. See **brass,** n., 3.

half bubble off level, a. Of below average intelligence: N. Am.: since later 1970s. (Leech, 1986.)

half-can. A half-pint tankard of beer: RAF officers': since early 1930s. Tredrey, 1939.

half-canned. Half drunk: since ca. 1925.

half-chat. An Indian Army term dating from ca. 1880, thus in Richards: 'Half-caste, or "half-chat" as the troops in my time [ca. 1901–9] contemptuously called them.' Also, C.20, an Aus. and Pacific Island term. (Parkman, 1946.) P.B.: the term was still in use, among Brit. soldiers in the East, in the 1950s.

half-colonel. A lieutenant-colonel: Army, orig. officers'; by mid-C.20, all ranks'.

Half-Dirties. 'Willesden men on dual steam and electric duties' (*Railway*, 2nd): railwaymen's: 1950s.

half-hard. (Of the penis) semi-erect; hence, not very intelligent: (L.A.) low. A var. **lazy lob.** See **half-mast.**

half-inch. To steal: r.s., on *pinch*: c. and low s.:—1914 (Leach).

half-iron. 'One who associates with homosexuals but who is not [one] himself' (Tempest): low: mid-C.20. See **iron hoof.**

half 'itch. Portsmouth dockers' version of **half-inch.** (Knight, 1984.) The nautical knot, half-hitch.

half-mast. See **half-hard.**

half-nelson. Partly drunk: low:—1923 (Manchon). Ex the wrestling-hold.

half-nicker. Ten shillings: Brit., Aus., NZ: until decimalisation in resp. countries. In UK often **half a nicker,** q.v. Cf. **half-bar/half a bar,** and:-

half-note. A ten-shilling note; hence its value: mostly Aus. On the other hand, *half a note* = the sum of ten shillings. (B.P.)

half-past two. A Jew: r.s. Franklyn.

half-pie. Insincere; little respected; (rather contemptible): Aus. and NZ. Cf. **pie at.**—2. Hence, worthless: Aus.: since ca. 1925. (B., 1959.) McNeil, 1973, glosses *half-pie(d)* as 'half-baked, dilettante'.

half-pie farm. 'A small nondescript holding' (Griffiths): NZ: since ca. 1930. (Slatter.)

half-pint; Half-Pint. (Very) short; an often complimentary nickname for a short man: since ca. 1925. (*News Chronicle,* 13 July 1954.) Also 'a term of endearment applied to a very small woman. Heard in 1938' (Leechman).

half-pint hero. A boaster, a swaggerer: RAF: since ca. 1930. (Jackson.) The implication being that a half-pint of beer or ale will make him 'shoot a line'.

half-pissed. Mildly tipsy: low.

half-ringer. A pilot officer. See **ringer.**

half-rinsed. Tipsy: Aus. and NZ: since ca. 1912; perhaps a little later in Aus. B., 1959.

half round the bend. Not mad, but often doing very silly things: RN: late C.19–20. (Bowen.) See also **round the bend.**

half section, (one's, usu. *my*). One's particular friend: Services': earlier C.20. Sometimes applied, usu. joc., to one's wife.

half seven (one, four etc.), **(at).** At half-past seven, etc.: orig. Army, prob. throughout C.20; by mid-C.20, gen. proletarian. Perhaps ex the military method of indicating direction, e.g., 'At three o'clock from the bushy-topped tree . . .'; cf. the German and Dutch way of telling the half-hours, which is, however, an hour ahead of this Brit. usage. (E.P.; P.B.)

half-sharp. 'Dialect, e.g. Sussex dial., or mock dialect: said of one who lacks understanding of his (or the) circumstances. " 'E be 'arf sharp 'e be" ' (L.A., 1978).

half-squarie. A prostitute: Aus. low: since ca. 1920. (B., 1942.) Ironic.

half-stamp. A tramp (the person): r.s., orig. underworld.

half-timer. A kipper: nautical. (Bowen.) So small on a dish.

half-wheeling. 'That irritating habit of a companion always slightly ahead of you, alongside' (*Fellowship,* 1984): club cyclists'. Hence *half-wheeler;* the habit 'often led to hotting-up the pace'.

Halibag, Halibasher, Hallie, -y. A Handley-Page *Halifax* bomber aircraft; RAF: 1941–6. The first by analogy with *Stringbag,* a Swordfish or Albacore of the FAA, WW2.

hallelujah-hawking. Religious speaking; evangelism; esp., city-mission work: Aus.: since ca. 1910. B., 1942.

hallelujah hell-sniffle of a(n). A truly 'awful' (something or other): Can.:—1932 (Beames).

Hallie (or **-y**). See **Halibag.**

halt, tomatoes, turds! An army parody of the sentry's command to halt, used in Cyprus, 1950s–60s, where the Greek = *Stamata!* and the Turkish = *Dur!*: all three words had to be uttered. A modern example of military Hobson-Jobson.

ham, n. An amateur wireless transmitter: wireless s. adopted in late Sep. 1936 ex US. (*Daily Herald,* 19 Sep. 1936.) Hence in combination, *ham-radio, ham-station,* etc. Ex C.19 *hambone* or *ham-fat(ter):* an inexpert actor or musician. Green, 1, derives it ex 'those second rate, and thus poor actors who in earlier days were forced to rub hamrind over their faces as the base for powder rather than being able to afford the more sweet-smelling and expensive oils'.—2. 'Overtime. "Fatty ham", excessive overtime' (McKenna, 1): railwaymen's.

ham, v. To be an inferior actor: esp., to act badly: adopted, ca. 1939, from US. See prec., 1. Also adj.: 'inferior': adopted ca. 1930. See also **ham it up.**

ham, adj. Short for *ham-fisted* or *-handed,* as in 'ham use of the [engine-]primer could mean nil compression, and ham use of the throttle . . . could result in a burst surge valve.' (Adkin, 1983): RAF: WW2.

ham(-)and(-)beef. A chief warder: prison r.s. Phelan, 1941.

ham(-)and(-)egg shift, the. A shift from 10 a.m. to 6 p.m.: Brit. miners': late C.19–20. 'Derived from former days—the ham was eaten before the shift began and the eggs in the evening at its finish' (*Toronto Globe,* 6 Jan. 1950).

ham-bone. See **ham,** n., 1.—2. A sextant: RN. (Granville.) Ex the shape.—3. A *Hampden* bomber: RAF: earlier WW2. (Jackson.) Ex name, influenced by shape-resemblance. See also **flying suitcase.**—4. (Usu. printed solid.) A male strip-tease (act); a nude dance: Aus.: since ca. 1960. (B.P.)

ham-fisted. Clumsy, maladroit: orig. RAF, esp. of pilot or mechanic, since mid-1930s (Tredrey, 1939); since WW2 much more widespread in distribution. Cf. **ham,** adj., **ham-handed, ham pilot,** and **mutton-fisted.**

ham-frill. A pair of female running shorts: (University) girls': from ca. 1925. (Stanners, 1937.) Cf. early C.20 *ham-bags,* female drawers.

ham-handed is the RN's form of **ham-fisted:** since early C.20. (*Musings,* ca. 1912, p. 62.) 'Hands like hams' are usually clumsy—or look it.—2. Hence, almost imm., fig., 'of clumsy people and those who lack tact' (L.A., 1976). This applies also to **ham-fisted.**

ham-handle. 'To handle ham-fistedly' (gloss to WW1 song, 'R.F.C. Alliterations', in C.H. Ward-Jackson, *Airman's Song Book,* 1945, containing the line 'See how heavy-handed Hans ham-handles handy Halberstadts!').

ham it up. To act a part extravagantly; hence, to wreck (something) by ill-advised conduct: Can. (ex US): since ca. 1930; by 1945, Eng.

ham pilot. A clumsy pilot and/or one rough on his machine: RAF: adopted, ca. 1932, ex US. Perhaps ultimately ex *ham-bone,* influenced by *ham-handed.*

Ham Shank. See **Hamshank.**

hambone. See **ham-bone.**

hammer, n. Penis: Can. low:—1949.—2. In (*right*) *on* (one's) *hammer:* (right) on one's tail; immediately behind: Aus.: since ca. 1920. (*Rats,* 1944.) Also *flat on* (one's or its) *hammer,* as in Devanney, 1951. Prob. ex **hammer and tack** or **hammer and nail,** qq.v.—3. Hard wear and tear; rough usage of, e.g., machines: coll.: since ca. 1960. 'The photocopier certainly taken some hammer this week' (P.B.).—4. A ham sandwich: since ca. 1930. (Drummond, 1967.) By the 'OXFORD *-ER*' on *ham.*—5. In *putting in the big hammer,* working to rule: railwaymen's: since mid-C.20. (McKenna, 2.) Cf. *put a spanner in the works.* (P.B.)—6. In *get the hammer,* 'to be mined or torpedoed' (Granville): RN: WW2. Cf. v., 1.—7. 'To *give* (something) *the hammer* is to stop it or switch it off: "Give that telly the hammer, will ye?" ' (Munro, 1985): Glasgow.

hammer, v. To shell heavily; to defeat severely: Army: since ca. 1940. P-G-R.—2. See:-

hammer(-)and(-)nail. To follow (someone, as a detective would): r.s. (on *tail*), orig., and still in 1966, mainly underworld. (Franklyn 2nd.) Often shortened to *hammer.*

hammer and tack. A track, e.g. a metalled road: Aus. r.s.: since ca. 1920. (Baker.)—2. The human back: id.: later C.20. (McNeil.) Cf. *right on* (one's) *hammer,* at **hammer,** n., 2.

hammer-chewer. An amateur: ca. 1910–40. (Petch, 1969.) A somewhat clumsy would-be jocularity.

hammer into. To fight and defeat: coll.:—1931. Lyell, 'One of the boys lost his temper and fairly hammered into him.' Cf. **pitch into.**

hammered. Married: metal workers': since ca. 1880. (Ware.) P.B.: in C.20 some wider use, perhaps with a side-glance at the Gretna Green blacksmith.—2. Tipsy: Can.: since ca.

1960. *Islander* (Victoria, BC), 30 May 1976, 'All it took was a case of beer to get hammered to the eyeballs'.

hammering. The transmission of wireless messages: nautical: from ca. 1924. Bowen.

Hammers, the. See ASSOCIATION FOOTBALL, in Appx.

hammers of hell, go like the. To move very fast. (Parsons, 1973.) Var. of **bat out of hell**, q.v.

hammock. The dip in TV audience viewing produced by, e.g., a dull, factual programme set between two more 'attractive' programmes; hence *hammocking*, as 'It's to do with the technique of hammocking—in which you put a thing like *Coronation Street* before and a strong situation comedy after it' (*Listener*, 17 Jan. 1980). An attempt to counter the 'sag' by 'anchoring' the dull feature to two strong ones.

hammy. A hamster: domestic: since ca. 1925.

Hampden roar. Score: Glasgow r.s., as in 'what's the Hampden roar?' = 'What's going on?' Ex the long famous noise 'made by the assembled celebrants at times of excitement', esp. at international matches at Hampden Park, home ground of the Queen's Park F.C. Munro, 1985.

Hamps. Teeth. Short for *Hampstead Heath*, via *Hampsteads*. (*New Statesman*, 29 Nov. 1941.) Jones 1971, 'Like me new 'amps?'

Hampstead Heath. The teeth: r.s.: from ca. 1880. (*Referee*, 7 Nov. 1887.) Cf. synon. earlier *Hounslow Heath*. It is, in C.20, often abbr. to *Hampsteads* (*Daily Express*, 25 Jan. 1932).

Hampton Wick, often abbr. to **Hampton.** The penis: r.s.: late C.19–20. (B & P.) On *prick*. See also *Wolver*.—2. Hence, a fool; 'He's a right Hampton' (Powis): low: later C.20.

Hamshank, or hyphenated. An American: r.s. on *Yank*: since ca. 1944. McShane, 1960.

hand-in, give (someone) **a.** To help: Aus. coll. (B., 1942.) As into tram or train.

hand in (one's) **checks** or **chips.** Mostly US var. (cf. **cash in** (one's) **checks**) of:-

hand in (one's) **dinner pail.** To die: since ca. 1920. (Wodehouse.) Perhaps suggested by *kick the bucket*. Cf. later C.19 US *pass in* (one's) *checks*.

hand it to (someone). To admit the superiority of, to give credit to: coll.: adopted, ex US, by 1914. (Carr; Moe.) In later C.20 usu. in . . . *must* (or *got to*) *hand it to* . . .

hand-jive. 'System of rhythmic hand-movements in time to music where floor is too crowded to allow people present to jive (dance), esp. as in coffee bars' (L.A.): jazz-lovers': since ca. 1950.

hand job. Masturbation: low, raffish: later C.20. 'She gave me a hand job' (Turner, 1986).

hand like a foot. In *have a hand like a foot*, to have a very bad hand of cards: card-players': by 1950, ob., except in Can. (Ross, 1956.) Sometimes intensified to . . . *like a club-foot* (Slater, 1978).

hand-me-downs. Ready-made clothes: coll.

hand-out. A meal handed out to the indigent; hence, a gift of money to the needy: Can. by late C.19 (Niven); adopted, ex N. America, ca. 1920. Harrison, 1935.

hand out the slack. To cheek a superior, to be rude to a colleague: Services' (esp. RN): since ca. 1925. (H. & P.)

hand over the baby. 'To pass on a responsibility no one particularly desires' (*Daily Express*, 5 Apr. 1937): coll.

hand-rag. 'An underling, e.g. a clerk uninstructed in profession, etc.; assistant to a skilled senior' (L.A., 1974): coll.: since ca. 1930.

hand-reared. Phallically well-endowed: low. A ref. to masturbation.

hand (someone) **the cold and frosty.** To snub; to treat coldly: since ca. 1920.

hand-to-hand. Hand-to-hand fighting: Army coll. Kersh, 1942, 'We done a bit of the good old hand-to-hand with the good old Wogs.'

hand-warmers. Female breasts: Aus. raffish: since late 1920s. Cf. synon. *British standard handfuls*, at **B.S.H.s.**

handbag. Money: male homosexuals': current ca. 1970. Simply because that's where a woman usually keeps it.

handcuffed. 'Description of an audience who will not applaud' (Green, 1): actors'.

handful. Five: racing c. Cf. **bunch of fives.** Hence, *win by a couple of handfuls*, by ten lengths, i.e. easily.—2. Hence, £5: c.—3. Odds of 5 to 1: racing, esp. bookmakers'. Ex sense 1.—4. A prison sentence of 5 years: since ca. 1940: c. >, by 1960, s. Norman, 1959.—5. 'Troublesome person, usually a young person' (Powis): gen. coll., also domestic, as in 'Oh, Baby's a right handful, I can tell you'.—6. See **B.S.H.s.**—7. In *to have a handful*, 'To fondle a woman's bosom or other sexual parts (taboo expression)' (Powis): low coll.—8. In *take a handful*, 'to open the throttle wide with the twistgrip' (Dunford, 2): motorcyclists': later C.20.

handies. 'A fondling of hands between lovers' (Dennis): Aus. Esp. in *play at handies*, or *play handies*, to fondle thus, or merely to hold hands: joc. coll., Brit. also. An English var. is *play at handy* (Manchon, 1923). Cf. **play footie.**

handle, n. 'The name by which someone is known' (Hibbert, 1983): pop coll.: later C.20. Cf. older *handle to* (one's) *name*, a title, as Dr, Mr, etc.—2. In *have a handle on* (something), to have it under control, to understand it, as in 'The police have a handle on the mob problem': Can.: since mid-C.20. (Leech, 1986.) Cf.:-

handle, v. To control, cope with: coll.: later C.20. 'His problem is, he just can't handle drink', or 'When she blows her top [loses her temper], I can't handle it any more'. (P.B.)

handlebars. Moustaches resembling bicycle handlebars: since ca. 1910.

Handley Page. A stage: r.s.: since ca. 1920. 'Mainly theatrical' (Franklyn 2nd). Ex the famous firm of aircraft designers and manufacturers.

hands to fishing-stations. The picking-up of dead fish after a depth-charge has been dropped at a test: RN: since ca. 1938. P-G-R.

handshake. A 'backhander'—a tip, or a bribe, handed surreptitiously: since ca. 1930. See also **golden handshake.**

Handsome Harry. A 'gay Lothario' or exponent of the love-'em-and-leave-'em technique: feminine, esp. shop-girls' and office-girls': since ca. 1930.

handwriting. 'Habits of technique' (Le Carré, 1977): perhaps orig. espionage and police, but by 1970s, gen. coll., as in 'It's got his handwriting all over it': since late 1940s. Cf. the now ob. cliché *fine Italian hand*.

handy Billy. A housewife (pron. *hussif* or *hussuf*), a small sewing holdall (needles, thread, etc.): RN: since ca. 1940, says Peppitt, but I think since ca. 1930.

handy-man. A man unable to 'bring off' his female partner and therefore obliged to resort to manual caresses to 'finish her off': since ca. 1950, if not a decade earlier. (Hollander.) A pun on the S.E. term for a man of all work.

hang a monkey. To buy a suit: proletarian (?mostly Liverpool).

hang about! Always in the imperative, a demand to 'wait a moment!': gen. coll.: since ca. 1960. 'Teacher requires a swift answer from a boy in class; the response may well be "Hang about, Miss! Ain't got me book open yet"—this to my wife, 1973' (P.B., 1974).

hang dog Charlie. 'The pilot in a formation of four who comes up below and behind the leader, in a diamond-shaped formation' (H.W., 1942): RAF. Cf. **tail-end Charlie.**

hang five – hang ten; hang eleven. To hang with one foot (five toes)—with both feet—over the *nose* or front of the board; 'ten toes and rider over nose of board': Aus. surfers', esp. teenagers': since ca. 1960. (*Pix*, 28 Sep. 1963.) Hence also, skateboarders': late 1970s.

hang in. (Of aircraft) to maintain formation, as in 'I close up on my leader's wing and wedge my wing-tip solidly behind his and hang in' (*Phantom*): RAF aircrews': 1970. Opp. **hang loose.**

hang it out. To delay a matter: coll. P.B.: E.P. considered this Aus., and cited 'Rolf Boldrewood' (1890); but in C.20, at any rate, certainly Brit., as 'the unions hung it out, hoping for a settlement'.

hang loose. See **hang in.**

hang on. To wait: coll.: Perhaps ex telephoning; as 'I'll just hang on (for you) until you come, then.'—2. Hence, as imperative, *hang on!*, 'Don't be so hasty!', or 'Oh, come! Be reasonable!': coll. P.B.: E.P. dates this usage 'mid-C.19–20', so it may, in fact, have given rise to sense 1, with the telephone influence as a reinforcement. Cf. **hang about!**

hang on by the (or one's) **eyelashes** (**-lids, -brows**). To be near to ruin, death, or defeat, *eyebrows* being much preferred in this sense. A var. of both senses is the likewise coll., though Biblical (*Job*), *hang on by the skin of* (one's) *teeth*.

hang on the slack! Don't be in a hurry!: RN. (Malin, 1979.) Perhaps an elab. of **hang on.**

hang one on. To get (very) drunk: Can.: adopted, ex US, ca. 1935. Also *tie one on.*—2. To strike (someone), esp. in the eye: adopted, late 1960s, ex US. In, e.g., a *Sunday Express* cartoon, 28 Sep. 1969. (R.S.)

hang out of. To coït with (a woman): RN lowerdeck. Cf. **dangle from.**—2. Hence, to commit sodomy: id.: since ca. 1920.

hang-over. A 'morning after the night before' feeling: from ca. 1910. Since ca. 1945 the preferred form has been *hangover.*

hang-up, n. Delay; frustration: Can. jazz-lovers': since ca. 1956. Victoria *Daily Colonist,* 16 Apr. 1959, 'Man—Omnibus salutation extended to men, women, domestic animals—saves cool cat hangup of remembering names.' The distribution, prob. owing to the rapidly increasing use in US, covered, by ca. 1970, the entire English-speaking world; along with it, a widening of the sense to 'any problem, emotional, psychological, professional' and 'any considerable difficulty, esp. if irritating': cf. 'Ringo [Starr], while the least creative, had no hangups about not being the equal of [the other Beatles]' (McCabe, 1972). Also in Reid, 1970, in the nuance 'embarrassment; a grave nuisance'. The adj. for a person with a hangup, or hangups, is *hung up.*

hang up, v. To withdraw from drugs: theatre c. (Stockley, 1986.) US since—1967 (Spears).—2. *Hanging it up,* cruising or dawdling near a given spot: taxi-drivers': since ca. 1910. (Hodge, 1939.) See **hanging-up.**—3. To end a tic-tac message. See **phone,** 3.

hang up (one's) **boots.** To be forced by age, ill-health, etc., to stop playing football: sporting. By analogy, applied in other circumstances, as *hang up* (one's) *tits,* of a female impersonator, to leave the music-halls after one's career has ended. Ex either the phrase made familiar by 'Western' films, of the aged gun-fighter 'hanging up his guns', or the older (from mid-C.19) s. *hang up* (one's) *hat,* to die.

hangashun or **hangava.** Very: Aus. children's: since ca. 1920. (B., 1942.) E.g., ' "hangashun good", very good, excellent. Cf. **helluva.**'

hangers. Female breasts: Aus. raffish: since ca. 1930.

hanging on the slack. 'Waiting for something to happen' (Granville): RN coll. See **hang on** . . .

hanging-up. 'Unscrupulous cab driver's illegal practice of deliberately failing to move up on an official (or unofficial) cab rank and not taking hiring in rotation. Done to enable obtaining more favourable hirings. Causes of disputes and bad feeling between cab drivers' (Powis). See **brooming-off** and **hang up,** v., 2.

hangover. See **hang-over.**

hangup. See **hang-up,** n.

hanky-panky. Legerdemain; hence, almost imm., trickery, double or underhand work: 1841 (*Punch*).—2. Hence, sexual caressing or intercourse, esp. in infidelity.

hanky worker. One who gets out of strait jackets: showmen's:—1934 (Allingham). Cf. *hanky-panky bloke,* later C.19 s. for a conjuror.

Hannah. A Wren serving with the Royal Marines: 1939+. 'From the famous Hannah Snell who, disguised as a man, fought with the Marines on land and sea in the eighteenth century' (M.o.I.'s *News-Clip,* 16 Feb. 1944).

hap. Happy: upper-class feminine: 1920s–30s. (Mosley, 1982.) Opp. **mis,** q.v.

ha'penny (mainly pron. *haypny,* at least in C.20). A coll. form, since C.16, of halfpenny. *OED.*—2. The female pudend; sometimes as 'little ha'penny': feminine.

ha'penny dip. A ship: Dockland r.s.: Franklyn 2nd.—2. A bed: 'Kip, "Steaming in his ha'penny when he ought to be doing a bit of George Raft (graft, work)" ' (Daniells, 1980): r.s.: later C.20. The orig. *ha'penny dip* was a very cheap candle.

ha'p'orth. A term of contempt for someone considered silly, a 'poor doer'; always qualified, often as *soppy* (h)*a'p'orth,* or *daft . . .* Ex the centuries' old contraction of *halfpenny-worth.*

ha'p'orth (or, less common, **pen'orth**) **of.** Contemptible of either small cost or, usu., potency (or efficacy) of a measure, as 'She gave me a haporth of gin to soothe my toothache' (L.A., 1976), or as in 'Such an effective controlled revelation marred by a ha'porth of sensationalism' (Morrison, 1976). P.B.: often in 'It won't make a ha'porth of difference whether . . .'

happen. To achieve success: prob., *not* certainly, ex US: current among jazz musicians and their public since the early 1960s or perhaps even as early as mid-1950s. 'They're not happening and I think they were finished as Beatles the day Brian [Epstein, their manager] died. I don't think the Beatles would have happened at all if Brian had been motivated exclusively by money' (McCabe, 1972).

happen for (someone) **with** (something). ' "I hope it may happen for her with this one" (meaning "I hope this one may be a success")' (Lejeune, 1967): since ca. 1965. Cf. **happen.**

happening. A 'spontaneous eruption of feeling or display' (Fryer, 1967): jazz and drug addicts', and hippies': since ca. 1966.

happy. As suffix, in, e.g. *bomb-happy, flak-happy,* with nerves shattered by exposure to imminent death or mutilation; or, as in *demob-happy,* reckless by reason of impending escape from present circumstances: WW2 and after: orig. Services', > gen. coll. (P.B.)

happy as a boxing kangaroo in fog time. Thoroughly discontented: Aus. coll. (B., 1942.) Cf. the variants cited by Wilkes: *happy* or *lucky* or *miserable as a bastard on Father's Day.*

happy as a nun weeding the asparagus. Exceedingly happy: ?mostly Can.: since ca. 1910. 'Uncommon but not rare' (Leechman). Erotic.

happy as Larry, (as). Very happy; delighted at the way things have turned out: Brit. and Aus. coll.: late C.19–20. Prob. ex Northern dial.

happy cyclist. 'Description of an epicyclic gearbox on motorcycle or car—noteworthy example, the Ford Model "T" car' (Dunford, 2): motorcyclists': earlier C.20. By Hobson-Jobson.

happy days. Strong ale and beer mixed: public-houses' (esp. at Glasgow); from ca. 1920.

happy dust. Cocaine: drugs c. (Stockley, 1986.) US since—1922 (Spears).

happy-ender. A story with a happy end: coll. (esp. in the book-world): late C.19–20. Ruck, 1935.

happy hour. A period early in the evening, when a pub or bar may offer drinks at less than normal price, to boost trade, and to encourage those who have taken advantage to stay: ex US. I first heard the term in Hong Kong, early 1960s, but not in UK until a decade later. (P.B.)

Happy Valley. Any city or locality, area, region, that is being (very) heavily bombed; esp. the Ruhr: RAF, esp. Bomber Command: 1941+. H. & P.—2. A valley between Taungmaw and the Mankat Pass in Burma: Army: 1942–5.—3. (Usu. lower-case.) Female genitals: C.20.

harbour light. All right: r.s.: late C.19–20; since ca. 1920 'nearly always reduced to *all harbour . . .* as an expression of satisfaction and well-being' (Franklyn 2nd.).

harch off. 'To abandon or leave' (B., 1953): Aus. (orig. Services'): since ca. 1940.

hard-arse. A wooden chair: cf. *T.S.R. arse*, the effect of the hard chairs in Temple Speech Room: Rugby School: resp. since ca. 1910 and since ca. 1945. (Wharton.)

hard as a goat's knees. Extremely hard: Aus. B., 1959.

hardcase. 'A Hardcase—or Aggro leader—commands the greatest respect of all within the Rowdies' group. He is the person who will lead attacks against rival fans . . . In achieving his position, the Hardcase must convincingly demonstrate his masculinity through acts of courage and fearlessness' (Marsh, 1976): youth gangs', esp. soccer rowdies': later C.20.

hard doer. A wag; an irrepressible, devil-may-care, dryly amusing person; a 'sport': Aus.: s. >, by 1930, coll. Cf. US *hard doings*, hard work, rough fare. Occ., from ca. 1910, abbr. *doer*.

Hard-Faced Parliament, The. The one elected in 1919: coll.: ca. 1919–22, then merely historical. It contained many war-made millionaires. (Lawson, 1932.)

hard-hat man. An inspector: railwaymen's. *Railway*.

hard head. A 'hard case' in an earlier sense, a person morally tough but not necessarily incorrigible: Aus.: since ca. 1910. Caddie, 1953.—2. A top operator in crime; a real professional: Aus. c.: since ca. 1950. (Grindley, 1977.)

hard hit. Defecation: r.s. on *shit*; as in 'go for a hard hit'. (Slater, 1978.)

hard (-)hitter. A bowler hat: Aus.: earlier C.20. Doone.

hard-liner. A wicked, greedy and unscrupulous person, e.g. a professional and confirmed shop-thief: 'When you arrest these "hard-liners" with adequate evidence . . . you may think it all over bar the formalities' (Powis): later C.20.—2. One who takes an inflexible, rigid, line in politics, etc. See **hard man**, 2.

hard man. Term used in the Services to describe a 'hard case' (See **hard head**, 1): since ca. 1950. Usu. with some disparagement implied, 'Oh, *him*! Fancies himself as a bit of a hard man—take no notice!' (P.B.)—2. A strong, rigid man, a hard-liner of the trades unions—and of politics in general: political coll.: since ca. 1960. (Forsyth, 1976.) A var. is *hard boy*.—3. A professional thug or hit-man: c.: since late 1960s. Maclean, 1977.

hard-mouthed, wilful, is S.E., but as = coarse-spoken it is coll. of ca. 1860–1910. Ex the stables.

hard neck. Extreme impudence: low coll.: late C.19–20. ' "You had the hard neck to pass the time of day with him" ' (Behan, 1958). Cf. **neck**, n.—2. Hence, a very impudent or brazen person; occ. as adj.: esp. in Glasgow.

hard-nosed. Stubborn: adopted, as coll. rather than s., ex US, late 1960s. R.C. defines its US sense as 'Unyielding, often unscrupulously so, hence likely to prevail in a "nose-to-nose" confrontation'. L.A. reports hearing on BBC Radio, Nov. 1973, this very phrase, 'hard-nosed confrontation', of a situation in which neither, esp. political, party will give way.—2. Full of commonsense, as in 'there are good, hard-nosed practical reasons for the carrying out of mini road-blocks . . . in minor streets' (Powis): coll.: 1970s.

hard O'Brien, the. A complimentary remark: Anglo-Irish: since ca. 1925. Perhaps ex some famous Irish flatterer surnamed O'Brien.

hard on. As in ' "He's got a hard on for me" means either he doesn't like me, or he's going to try to beat me up (fight)' (Leech, 1981): Can.: later C.20.

hard-skinned. (Of vehicles) armoured: Army: since 1940; by 1944, coll. > j. P-G-R.

hard stuff. Whisky: low coll. Gen. as *the hard stuff*.—2. Morphine: drugs' c. (Stockley, 1986.) US since—1955 (Spears).

hard-up. A cigarette-end: low: 1923 (Manchon)—but prob. dating from ca. 1870.—2. Hence, a cigarette made from fag-ends: c. and low: from ca. 1924. (Harrison, 1934.) Also known as *kerbside Virginia* and *pavement twist*.—3. Tobacco

from picked-up stumps of cigarettes: c., mostly vagrants': from ca. 1920. Ex sense 2.

hard word on, put the. To ask (a person) for something, esp. a loan: Aus. (—1914: Jice Doone) and NZ (Crump, 1961). Cf. **put the nips in** and **sting**.—2. Of a man urging a woman to lie with him: Aus. (B., 1942.) The phrase has, in Aus., long been applied to any request or approach difficult or unpleasant to make. (B.P.)

hardened tea-drinker. A person as fond of tea as a drunkard of his liquor: joc. coll.: since ca. 1910.

hardware. 'The mechanical, electrical, or structural components of a computer or other automatic machine' (Barnhart): adopted, ex US, ca. 1960: orig. s.; very soon > j. and by mid-1970s, S.E.

hare. To run very fast: Shrewsbury School coll.: late C.19–20. (Coke, 1908.) By 1920, fairly gen. S.E.—2. Hence, to fly at full speed: RAF: ca. 1925–45. (Jackson.) See also **hary**.

harem, the. The living-quarters of the Waafs or the Wrens (Waffery or Wrennery): Forces', mostly RAF and esp. in the Near or the Middle East: WW2.

harness. Parachute straps: RAF: perhaps orig., ca. 1935, s., but very soon > j.—2. Foundation garments: feminine coll., mostly Aus.: since ca. 1930.

harness bull. A uniformed policeman: low Can.: adopted, 1930s, ex US, where orig. underworld.

Harold Lloyd, often shortened to **Harold.** Celluloid, 'an instrument of housebreaking' (cf. **loid**, q.v.): r.s., dating from ca. 1917; orig., underworld; by 1940, also police s. (Gosling, 1959.) Ex the deservedly famous American cinematic comedian, whose heyday was ca. 1914–35.

harp. A harmonica: 'pop' musicians' and their public: adopted, early 1960s, ex US. *Melody Maker*, 8 July 1972.

harpic. Mad, crazy; bomb-shocked: orig. RAF, since early 1930s, then by ca. 1945, gen.; ob. A pun on the claim of the makers of Harpic, the famous lavatory cleanser, that it will *clean round the bend*. See **round the bend**.

Harriet the Chariot. In Aus., any *Harriet* has, since ca. 1930, tended to be thus nicknamed. The nickname is derogatory—with *chariot*, semantically cf. **town-bike**. '*Myrtle the Turtle* and *Harriet the Chariot* are so well known that any Australian male would veto the choice of such a name for his daughter. I have never heard of a Harriet, no matter how virtuous, who was not called *Harriet the Chariot*' (B.P.).

Harris. See **play Harris**.

Harris tweed. 'Speed' (amphetamines): drugs c., r.s.: mid-1980s.

Harry. Heroin: drugs c. (Stockley, 1986.) US since—1954 (Spears). An elab. of initial H.—2. See HARRY, in Appx.

Harry hoof. A male homosexual: Glasgow r.s. on *poof*: since 1960s. Munro, 1988, 'It was well known in its shortened form, as in "Beat it, ya harry!", and no-one [at school, late 1960s] would have dared to use the expression "hoof it" of walking. The name of one of Glasgow Celtic F.C.'s star players, Harry Hood, may have had some influence here'. P.B.: but cf. **hairy-heeled**, and HARRY, in Appx., with synon. **iron hoof**.

Harry James. Nose; nostrils: low: since ca. 1940. 'There is plenty of dust floating about . . . which gets in your north and south and up your Harry James' (Norman). Prob. ex the idea of 'trumpet' as nose (cf. **hooter**) connected with Harry James the famous trumpet-player and band-leader.

Harry Lauder. Order: Aus. r.s.: later C.20. (McNeil.) Sir Harry Lauder (1870–1950), Scot. comedian and singer. Cf.:-

Harry Lauders. 'Contrary to popular opinion, the use of "rhyming slang" is not exclusively a product of London, and the Border Regiment sometimes referred to themselves as "The Harry Lauders" ' (Carew).

Harry Lime. Time (of day): r.s.: late C.20. (Haden-Guest.) Ex the villain, played by Orson Welles, in the film *The Third Man*, 1950. 'The Harry Lime Theme', played on the zither, swept the country.

Harry Randall (loosely **Randle**). A handle; also, a candle: r.s.: early C.20. (B. & P.) Ex a comedian, famous ca. 1900. Cf. *Jack Randall*.

Harry Tate. A free-and-easy rating: RN lowerdeck: ca. 1905–30. (Knock.) Ex the great comedian and performer († 1940).—2. Late: r.s.: ca. 1905–15. Franklyn.—3. First Officer: MN r.s., on *mate*: since ca. 1910. Franklyn 2nd.—4. A plate: r.s.: from ca. 1910. B. & P.—5. State: r.s.: from ca. 1920. (P.P., 1932.) Cf. **two-and-eight.**—6. (Usu. pl.) Player's *Weights*, the brand-name of small, once-cheap cigarettes, competitors of the perhaps more famous *Woodbines*: r.s.: later C.20. (Hillman, 1974.)

Harry Taters. 'A job that has not been done right' (Patterson): Portsmouth dockers'. Cf. prec., 1.—2. Cold: Services': mid-later C.20. See HARRY, in Appx., and **taters**.

Harry, Tom and Dick. Unwell: r.s. Cf. **Tom, Harry and Dick.**

Harry Wragg. A cigarette: r.s. on synon. *fag*: since ca. 1930. Ex the famous ex-jockey and racehorse-trainer.

Harvest Moon. A racial term used, since ca. 1945, in the London docks. (*New Statesman*, 31 Dec. 1965.) R.s. on *coon*.

Harvey. An abbr. of the next. P.P., 1932.

Harvey Nichol. Trouble, predicament: r.s. on *pickle*. (P.P., 1932.) Ex the well-known London West End linen-drapers and furnishers. Pl.: *Harvey Nichols*, the orig. form; and in this form it usu. denotes 'pickles', condiments. Franklyn.

Harvey Smith sign. The 'V' sign made with the fingers, back of hand to viewer: gen. coll.: since 15 Aug. 1971, when the show-jumper Harvey Smith was seen by the spectators at Hickstead, the British show-jumping Derby, and by the many watchers of the event on TV, to make this defiant and derogatory gesture at the judges. The term is still in occ. use 1980, with its var. *doing a Harvey Smith*. (P.B.) See also **touch of the . . .**

hary. 'You make one hary dash as soon as you land, and rush down to the mess to change and get away on Friday' (Tredrey, 1939, writing in 1935): RAF. Prob. adj. ex *hare*, 2; but cf. also **hairy**, adj.

has-beens. Greens: r.s., orig. and still (ca. 1950) mainly underworld.

hash. Hashish: teenage drug addicts': since early 1950s. By 1960, all addicts', as in Diment, 1963.—2. 'A usage . . . peculiar to those concerned with computers. In their jargon . . . *hash* refers to the "field mark", which indicates the end of a section or "data field". The word in this context is presumably a corruption of *hatch* as it occurs in "cross-hatching" [#]. So I regard it not as a technical term but as slang' (Mainprice, 1975): since ca. 1970.

hash-me-gandy. Station stew: NZ and Aus. rural: since ca. 1920. B., 1942, suggests: ex Mahatma Gandhi's frugal meals. An elab. of *hash*. 'Could the form of this word be based on S.E. *salmagundi*' (R.S.)—a spiced dish of minced meat and eggs, hence a medley? It does indeed sound a plausible suggestion. P.B.: cf. the form of synon. **oos-me-goosh.**

hash-slinger. A cook: Services': earlier C.20.

hash tea. 'Concoction of herbs (containing cannabis)' (Home Office): drug addicts': later C.20.

hash up. To spoil, ruin (a chance, an entertainment, etc.): coll. Spenser, 1934.

hassle, n. A fuss, a disagreement, a row; a hullabaloo: Can., adopted ex US ca. 1860 (Leechman); by ca. 1975, increasingly common in UK (P.B.). Perhaps a blend word, from, e.g. *haggle* + tu*ssle*; or ex Cumbrian dial., to hack at with a blunt knife (*EDD*). Hart-Davis, 1972, ' "Aggro"? Big trouble . . . Opposite of "hassle", which is small.' Dempster noted, 1979, that the term was 'on its way out' among smart society.

hassle, v.t. To harrass, annoy: adopted, ex US, ca. 1970. Ex the n. 'They're being hassled . . . by [his] old friend . . . Chief Inspector Molt' (Stuart, 1971).

haste! 'Look out! Mainly used in criminal jargon. Whence *haste it!*, to cease some activity, equivalent of Stop it! Synonymous is *ace it!*' (B., 1959): Aus. c.: since ca. 1935.

haste, adv. Quickly; immediately: Aus.: since ca. 1930. Tennant, 1953, 'So hand over the two quid and give it haste.' Probably ex S.E. *post-haste*.

hat. As exclam. *my hat!*: mild, coll. Cf., e.g., *my aunt!*, *my stars!*—2. In *need a new hat*, to have become conceited; the implication: 'swollen-headed': earlier C.20.—3. As the *Hat*, Medicine Hat, Alberta: Can.: since ca. 1920. (Leechman.)—4. See **wear more than one hat.**

hat off. In *with his hat off*, (of a soldier) charged with a 'crime': Army: from ca. 1920; † by 1950. A soldier must remove his hat when he is being tried for an offence. Cf. **hat on.**—2. In, e.g., *I take my hat off to him* or *take off my hat to him*, I compliment him, I praise him (sometimes with the nuance 'for tackling something I couldn't, or wouldn't, do myself'). Carr, 1939. Sometimes absolute, as in 'So hats off to . . .', let us compliment . . .

hat on. Formally dressed for (esp. disciplinary) interview with a senior officer: RAF officers': late C.20. ' "See the Boss pronto—with hat on!" ' (*Phantom*). Contrast prec.

hat rack. Thin, scraggy horse or ox: Aus. B., 1942.

hatchet job. A 'murderous' undertaking: policemen's and, thence, politicians': since (?)ca. 1960; orig. s., but soon coll. and, by 1978, virtually S.E. 'I have heard that there were a few hatchet jobs taking place along the corridors of police power, but isn't this [the murder, by decapitation, of the Commissioner] going a bit far?' (Barnett, 1978). Cf. the fig. *stab in the back*, and:-

hatchet man. That executive in a business, an institution, who is chosen to tell employees when they're no longer wanted: adopted, ca. 1974, ex US. (*DCCU.*) Ex US underworld sense, the appointed killer in a gang or mob. Cf. **hit-man.**

hate. To dislike: Society coll.: from ca. 1919. Mackail, 1925, 'I should hate it, of course, but I shouldn't mind it.'

hate (someone's) **guts.** To hate someone intensely: adopted, ca. 1937, from US. Christie, 1944.

hate oneself, as in 'You do hate yourself, don't you': ironic coll., applied to a person with a fine conceit of himself: since ca. 1938.

Hathern band. In *don't give me Hathern band!*, don't keep on repeating yourself!: N. Leicestershire s. Ex the village band of Hathern, alleged at one time to know only one tune, and to keep on playing it. (Clarke, 1980.) A good example of local s. that is *not* dial., but allusion.—2. Everyone 'doing his own thing': id. (Oldham, 1980.)

hatless brigade, the. Those men who do not wear hats: early C.20: coll. >, by 1930, familiar S.E. (Collinson.) Cf. also *no hat brigade*.

hatted; in hatted order. Used randomly, in a systematically unsystematic order, as e.g. radio callsigns changed to obscure a station's identity: Services', esp. cypher clerks', coll. > j.: WW2 and since. Ex 'put in a hat and drawn out like, e.g., raffle tickets.' (P.B.)

hatter. A pal, a mate, usu. in a homosexual sense. Cf. **brown-hatter.**

Hatters, the. See ASSOCIATION FOOTBALL, in Appx.

haul arse. To go off or away, often quickly: Can.: since ca. 1930. 'Come on, Jack! Let's haul arse out of here.' (Leechman.)

haul (ones) **ashes.** To coït: Can. low: late C.19–20.

haul (someone) **one off.** To strike someone hard with one's fist: low coll.: later C.20. (P.B.)

HAULAGE-BASHER. See Appx.

HAULIERS' SLANG of mid-C.20. See Appx.

hava no and **hava yes.** (Mostly of persons, occasionally of events) to be ineligible or unattractive or inferior; to be very eligible or attractive; hence also n. and adj.: United Nations troops (in Korea): ca. 1951–5. (*Iddiwah*, July 1953.) As it were, the 'have-nots' and the 'haves'; ex pidgin *hava*, to have.

have a baby. See **have kittens.**

have a ball. To have a good time: among teenagers, since ca. 1945; among beatniks, since ca. 1957. In 1960s–70s, as an encouragement to enjoyment: 'Have yourself a ball!'

have a bash. To have a determined try at something: coll.: since ca. 1935.

have a beat. To try; in cricket, to bat vigorously: since ca. 1925.

have a beat on. To have an erection: low and schoolboys'.

have a bit. A shortening of:-

have a bit off (with). To copulate with: Cockney, then gen.

have a cob on. To be annoyed. See **cob**, 2.

have a cook. Have a look: r.s.

have a crack (at it). See **crack**, n., 1.

have a down on. See **down**, n., 1.

have a go. To coït: late C.19–20. Very gen.—2. To try to prevent a crime, esp. to apprehend a criminal: coll.: since early C.20.

have a good chit. To be well spoken, or thought, of: Army officers': since ca. 1930. Ex **chit**, 1 and 2.

have a heart. To suffer from a weak heart: coll.: late C.19–20. 'Auntie can't go far, you know. She has a heart.'

have a quick one or **a quickie.** Have a, e.g., drink, urination, copulation: coll.: late C.19–20.

have a roll! (usu. prec. by *go and*). Go to the devil!: Aus.: since ca. 1925. B., 1943.

have a stab (at). See **stab**, n., 1.

have a tickle. See **tickle**, n., 2.

have (one's) **brains on ice.** 'To be very cool-headed and collected' (Lyell): coll.:—1931; ob.

have down the banks and **have high-ding-dong.** To have a 'row', a fight: Liverpool: late C.19–20. '*High-ding-dong* suggests a noisy fight; *the banks* refers to Canal banks, where fights often took place' (Shaw, 1952).

have fifty (or **a hundred**) **up.** To coït with a girl: sporting. Ex billiards. P.B.: or cf. **nifty fifty**.

have for breakfast; occ. **before breakfast** (as a rare appetiser). A humorous way of implying that a thing is easy to do, (gen.) a man easy to beat. E.g. 'Why! I have one like him every day before breakfast' or 'I could wash or do with six like him for breakfast.' For task or feat, the *before breakfast*, often with *do* or *have*, is preferred. Coll.: perhaps orig. mostly Aus. and NZ. Cf. the quot'n at **nine ways . . .**

have had it. Esp. in *You've had it,* You won't get it, you're too late, etc.: RAF: since 1938 or 1939; current in Army since late 1940 or early 1941; >, 1944, fairly gen. civilian. (*New Statesman*, 30 Aug. 1941; Jackson.) Ironic—perhaps short for 'Somebody else has (or, may have) had it, but you certainly won't.'—2. ' "He's had it" and "He's gone for a Burton" indicate that he's been killed' (Rhodes, 1942): RAF: since late 1939. I.e. 'copped' it. Marshall, 1962, '[this sense] originated in the Gulf Country of northern Queensland, where one of us heard it as early as 1929. Oddly enough, the phrase was never current in the populous south before the war. It was taken to Europe by Queensland troops or airmen and there, where lots of chaps were having it, so to speak, it came into general currency. It was circuitously from Europe, and not directly from the north, that the expression reached the southern parts of Australia.' R.S. adds, 1971, 'This usage is rooted in the sands of the Roman circus; of a stricken gladiator it was said (or shouted): "Habet" or "Hoc habet"—he has it (his death wound). Virgil *et al.* Kipling uses it of a death wound in "The Church That Was at Antioch", one of his last stories, *Limits and Renewals*, 1932—but he had a classical education. The Australo-English use of the perfect tense makes for even more graphic finality.'—3. To have had more than enough, be 'sick and tired' of it: by 1950, at latest.

have had it in a big way. To have no chance whatever of that hope being fulfilled: since ca. 1944. An extension of prec., 1.

have had it up to here, (usu. I). With a gesture at the throat or top of head, to indicate the depth to which one is 'fed up'; an extension of **have had it**, 3: since 1950s.

have (someone) **in.** To make a fool of: Aus.: since ca. 1940. (Culotta, 1960.) A var. of earlier synon. *have on.*

have it away. To escape: prison c.: since ca. 1940. (Norman.) See quot'n at **over the wall**, 2.—2. A shortening of *have it away together* or *get* (one's) *end away,* to copulate: since mid-1950s. Cf. also **have it away with,** 2.

have it away on the hurry-up. To depart, to leave, smartly or hurriedly: since ca. 1945: c. >, by ca. 1955, low s. (Cook, 1962.) An extension of prec., 1.

have it away together. To copulate: mostly teenagers': since ca. 1950. Cf. sense 2 of:-

have it away with (something). To steal it: since ca. 1925. Cook, 1962.—2. As *have it away with* (someone, of either sex), to copulate with: mostly upper and middle classes': since late 1940s. (*The Times*, 26 Aug. 1975.) Semantics less obvious than appears, 'it' being, I think, 'sexual urge' and *have away* 'to get rid of'. Also of homosexual acts between men, as in Mortimer, 1971.

have it off. To engage successfully in a criminal undertaking, esp. by oneself: c.: from ca. 1925. (*Gilt Kid*, 1936.) It is the c. equivalent of *pull it off.* 'It is also used by a punter who has had a successful bet or by a man that has contrived to seduce a girl' (Curtis, letter to E.P., 1937).—2. Hence, simply to copulate: low: since ca. 1940. (Cook, 1962.) See quot'n at **nine ways . . .**

have it on (one's) **dancers.** A later C.20 elab. of the next. (Powis.)

have it on (one's) **toes.** To run away; 'escape from legal custody' (Home Office): prison c.: since ca. 1940. (Norman.) Cf. the S.E. *heel and toe it,* to walk in a race.

have kittens. To become nervous, agitated, 'all hot and bothered': coll.: since ca. 1933. In, e.g., *The Times*, 15 Feb. 1937, in the form *having kittens;* in later C.20, in phrases like, 'You should've seen him—he nearly had kittens'. Ex a cat's perturbation during this crisis. Since ca. 1938, also *have (having) a baby,* or worse, *triplets,* and, among RAF officers, ca. 1940–5, *having a set of metal jugs.* In each phrase *have* = to give birth to.

have on. *To have someone on* is to be prepared, or actually, to fight: Aus. B., 1942.

have one for the worms. To take a drink of liquor: ca. 1880–1940. (Connington, 1938.) Ex joc. pretext of medicinal use. 'Compare Spanish *matar el gusano*—to kill the worm—applied to the first drink of the day, particularly if spirituous' (H.R. Spencer).

have one on the house. '(Of men) to take opportunity to make water before leaving a friend's house rather than need public facilities at a possibly inopportune moment' (L.A., 1976): joc. coll.: since late 1940s. 'From pub landlord's complimentary drink to good customer.'

have (someone) **over.** 'To outwit that person; or, if the person had over be a woman, to seduce her' (Powis): c.: later C.20.

have (someone) **over a barrel.** To have him at a grave disadvantage: adopted, ca. 1950 (earlier in Can.), ex US. Actively, *get* (someone) *over a barrel,* 'We've got them over a barrel on this one'.

have (one's) **packet.** To incur disaster, as by bombing: since ca. 1940. (Allingham, 1947.) Cf. **cop a packet.**

have the bird. To be sent about one's business: non-cultured: from ca. 1910. Wallace, 1926, 'In the vulgar language of the masses, I have had the bird.' Ex *get the bird,* to be hissed while on stage.

have the dead needle. See **have the needle.**

have the dirt on (someone, -thing). To know some scandal about that person or affair; since ca. 1930. Later, merely to know about the person or affair, to have the news on. See **dirt**, 3.

have the edge on. See **edge**, 2.

have the goods on. To have abundant evidence for the conviction of a person: NZ c.,—1932; by 1935 also Aus., and by 1940, > s. B., 1943.

have the needle – intensively, **dead needle** – **to** (someone). To be (extremely) angry with: since ca. 1925; c. >, by 1940, low s.

have to. To be sure to, as in 'They have to know more than they've been saying' (Hunter, 1969), where no compulsion other than historical circumstance is implied; also much used in sporting commentaries, as 'This just has (got) to be the greatest match of the season', said not before, but in subsequently reporting, the game: coll., prob. influenced by US usage: since mid-1960s. Ex S.E., e.g., 'I have to go now' = I must go. (P.B.)

have triplets. See **have kittens.**

have (someone) **well under the cosh.** To have someone completely in one's power: since ca. 1935.

have words. See **words.**

having a baby or **kittens.** See **have kittens.**

hawk (one's or *the*) **bod.** To sell one's body, to prostitute oneself: Aus. low coll.: later C.20. (McNeil.) Cf.:-

hawk (one's) **brawn.** To be a male prostitute (i.e. a man offering his 'charms' to women); to be a passive homosexual for money: low (esp. Cockneys').

hawk (one's) **pearly.** (Of a woman) to be promiscuous, to 'put herself about': low raffish: early 1970s. (Sharpe, 1976.) Cf. older (from mid-C.19) synon. s. *hawk* (one's) *mutton*. Perhaps a shortened blend of *pearly ace* (q.v. at **ace**, adj.) and *red ace.*

hawker's gag. Boot-laces carried as an excuse for begging: tramps' c.:—1932 (Jennings).

Hawkesbury Rivers. The shivers: Aus. r.s. Hence *Hawkesburies*. B., 1942.

hawkish. Descriptive of one who adopts a hard, warlike line: political j. > gen. coll., and, by 1983, informal S.E.: adopted ex US, where current since ca. 1962 (the Cuban missile crisis), late 1970s. Ex *hawk*, such a person; opp. is *dove*. See esp. Barnhart.

Hawkshaw. 'CID officer. A derisive term, originally exclusively US, but used by West Indians' (Powis): 1970s. The orig. 'Hawkshaw the detective' was a character in the English dramatist Tom Taylor's melodrama, *The Ticket-of-Leave-Man*, 1863.

hay. Money: see **chaff**, n.—2. Cannabis: drugs c. (Stockley, 1986.) US since ca. 1920 (Spears).—3. See **hit the hay.**

Hay Lee. A rare var. of r.s. *Rosie Lee*, tea. Lardner, 1951.

hay-tit or **haytit.** A woman (*tit*) given to sleeping under haystacks; hence, a tramp prostitute: c., mostly tramps'. Cowan, 1937.

hay-wire, gen. **haywire.** In wild, or utter, disorder; chaotic: adopted, ex US, just before WW1; used in this sense by the RN in 1914 (Carr, 1939).—2. Hence, to be beside oneself with anger; crazy, very eccentric: adopted, ex US, 1936. (Weekley, 1937.) Hence, *to go haywire*, to go crazy; of mechanisms, to get (completely) out of order.

haymaker. A jolly sort of fellow: tailors': earlier C.20. Ex *make hay while the sun shines*.—2. A swinging blow: boxers': from ca. 1920. (*OED* Sup.) Cf. **cow-shot** and **agricultural.**

haze. 'Slang term for violent bullying of a homosexual, combined with insulting banter and ridicule' (Powis): later C.20.

he. By particular personification, the penis: euph. > coll.: prob. almost immemorial. Naughton, 1970, 'Abby puts her hand under the table, then gives him a squeeze', exemplifying *him* for *it*; therefore also *his* for *its*.

He, Me and You. 'Familiar German types (of aircraft) are summarised in the technical joke, "*He*, *Me*, and *You*", the Heinkel, Messerschmitt, Junkers' (E.P., 1942); earliest printed record, however, is a terse paragraph in the *Daily Express*, 3 July 1940.

head. A long-term prisoner: Aus. c. (B., 1942.) Looked up to by his fellow convicts.—2. A girl, a young woman: beatniks': late 1950s–early 60s. (Anderson.)—3. Habitual user of a drug, as in *acid-head, hop-head*: adopted, ex US, late 1960s. P.B.: but no doubt influenced by *piss-head*, a habitual heavy drinker: since ca. 1930 in NZ (E.P.) and in Services since ca. 1960 at latest; cf. also **shit-head**, an objectionable

person.—4. The mind, or brain, as in *get* (one's) *head together*, to concentrate thought, and *out of* (one's) *head*, rendered incapable by drugs: pop and drugs c.: later C.20. Hibbert, 1983.—5. See **bite** (one's) **head off**; **head job.**

head-banger. See **headbanger.**

head hag. Headmistress: schoolgirls'. Brophy, 1937.

head (or **skull**) **job.** Cunnilingus; fellatio. *Head jockey*, a practitioner of cunnilingus: since ca. 1950 (?much earlier). (Landy, 1971; Hollander, 1972.) Also **give head**, q.v., to engage in 'soixante-neuf' (Hollander). Also abbr., as in Stuart, 1972 (heavily influenced by US), 'treated to as expert a spot of head as ever he's experienced.'

head off. To begin a journey: Aus.: since ca. 1925. 'Supposing that we get everything squared away, when'll you be ready to head off?' (Harris, 1958). Ex cattle-droving?

head out. The N. Am. version of **head off**: prob. since WW2. (Leechman, 1986.)

head office. 'Prison department of Home Office' (Home Office): prisoners' s.: later C.20.

head picket. Defecation; the faeces: RN training ships': recorded for 1946, but prob. earlier. A ref. to RN j. *heads*, privy. (Peppitt.)

head-serang. An overseer, master; one in authority or a 'bigwig': Bengali English coll. and nautical s. (—1864) >, ca. 1900, gen. s. In Portsmouth Docks, mid-C.20, pron. *sherang* (Patterson). Ex Persian *sarhang*, an overseer, a commander.

head-shrinker. A psychiatrist, esp. if a psychoanalyst; in prison s., also a psychotherapist (Home Office): adopted, ex US, late 1950s. Dickens, 1964, 'Deliver me from the head shrinkers, I have prayed.' An allusion to the shrinking of corpses' heads practised by certain South American tribes. P.B.: by ca. 1970, at latest, the (orig. US) abbr. *shrink* had become gen. coll. in UK.

headache. A problem; a worry ('That's *your* headache!'): since ca. 1920: coll. >, by 1947, familiar S.E.

headbanger (or hyphenated). A moronic teenager given to shaking his head very violently in time to very loud music, instead of dancing: from late 1970s. 'Headbangers—the zombies' revenge' (York, 1980). Earlier, in *Harpers & Queen*, Dec. 1977, P.Y. wrote, 'The music . . . was boring. Its appeal was to the acidheads . . . banging their heads on the bass speakers.'—2. Hence, loosely for a teenage 'hard case' or 'nutter' (qq.v.): Fife secondary school pupils', hence staffs': early 1980s. (Harold Hindle, 1981.) Munro, 1985, of its Glasgow usage, suggests an earlier coinage, poss. ex 'the idea of a violent lunatic banging his head on the wall', and notes var. *header*, with which, again, cf. synon. **nutter.**

headcase. A crazy person, a lunatic: Glasgow version of the perhaps more gen. **nut case**: since mid-C.20. Munro, 1985.

headlights. Spectacles: Aus.: since ca. 1905. B., 1942.—2. Female breasts: Aus.: since ca. 1910. Baker.

headlines. In *make the headlines*, to get one's name into the headlines or on to the front page: journalistic coll.: since ca. 1925. P.B.: in later C.20, just as often in the negative, as in the derogatory 'Huh! That'll never make headlines!'

heady. Very ingenious (things) or shrewd (ideas, plans, actions): coll.: mostly Aus. and NZ.—2. Biliously headachy: mostly aviators' coll.: 1934 (Nov.), *Air Review.*

health, for (one's). (Always in negative or interrogative.) For nothing, the implication that one *is* there, doing this, etc., for money, i.e. for profit: coll.: orig. (1904), US, Thornton citing 'I'm not in politics for my health'—nor, presumably, for the body politic's: anglicised ca. 1912.

healthy. Large; excellent: coll.: from ca. 1920. E.g. 'a healthy cheque'.

heap. A person, a section, a detachment that is very slack and slovenly: Army: 1940+. (H. & P.) Cf. **shower.**—2. An old car, esp. if owned by youths: Can.: since ca. 1939. Ex '*heap* of old iron'. (Priestley, 1949, 'Displaces *jaloppy*, which barely survives, though still heard.') P.B.: since mid-C.20, also Brit. (Hunter, 1960).—3. *In the heap*, (of a horse) losing: Glasgow racing:—1934. It is in the ruck.

heap big. Joc. use of term used by Indians in 'Western' films; applied not only to objects, but also to persons, e.g., of the head of an organisation 'Him heap big man': earlier and mid-C.20. (P.B.)

heap of pot. A quantity—5 pounds in weight—of marijuana: drug addicts': since ca. 1960. *The Times*, 19 Feb. 1964.

hear (one's) **belly knocking against** (one's) **backbone.** To be near starvation. Hayes, 1968.

hear say or **tell, to.** Hear it said, related (that . . .): in C.20, 'considered vulgar' (W., 1920), i.e. low coll. Orig. S.E. with ellipsis of *people, persons, someone*, etc., before the second v. P.B.: in C.20 often, at least in Sussex dial., 'I did hear tell as how . . . ' E.P. noted: 'C.13–20: S.E. until mid–C.19, then coll. and dial.; absolutely, as in "So I've heard tell", so I've heard.'

hear (oneself) **think.** Always neg., and with ref. to excessive noise, in such complaints as 'Turn that damn radio down, I can't hear myself think even' or 'the disco was so deafening she could hardly hear herself think': coll.: since ca. 1916. (E.P.; P.B.)

hearse. An enemy submarine: RN and RAF on Western Approaches: 1941+. Derogatory rather than macabre.

Heart-Break Corner. A store-room for postal matter wrongly or insufficiently addressed or too loosely tied: post office workers': since ca. 1935.

heart-throb. A glamorous film-star (either sex): mid-C.20, usu. joc.

heart-to-heart. A heart-to-heart talk: coll.

heart-trouble. Euph. for 'fear' or 'cowardliness': 1940+.

hearth rug. A dupe, a simpleton: r.s.: since ca. 1910. On *mug*.—2. (Usu. in pl.) A bug, esp. a bed-bug: r.s. Both senses, ob. by 1960. 'Never was so popular as steam tug' [q.v.] (Franklyn 2nd.).

hearty. (Gen. *a hearty*.) A person enjoying boisterous health and few brains, esp. if a devotee of outdoor games and sport: from ca. 1910: coll., orig. undergraduates', >, by 1935, S.E. Partly in opp. to *arty*.—2. Hence, adj., sporting; occupied in sport or in strenuous exercise: mostly, as orig., university coll. Not, it would seem, before 1924 or 1925. E.g. 'I've just had a very hearty week-end.'—3. (Slightly) tipsy: Anglo-Irish: late C.19–20. (Joyce, 1910.) Cf. synon. coll. *happy*.

heat. A being wanted by the police: adopted, ca. 1936, from US, ('The bleeding heat's on here for me', Curtis, 1938) and >, by 1946, low s.—2. Hence, the police themselves: low: later C.20. 'I had you sussed for the heat . . . I thought, here's another of them comic camouflaged coppers come to give us business girls a hard time' (Daniells, 1980).—3. As '*heat*, short for 're-heat'; afterburner: RAF: later C.20. 'In the land of 'heat, hundreds of knots appear from nowhere in seconds' (*Phantom*).

heater. 'Revolver. This word is the English equivalent of "gat" or "rod", expressions used by those who affect Americanisms' (Tempest): c.: mid-C.20. P.B.: but *heater* too smacks of the US gangster film.

heave, n. An effort; display of energy: Guardsmen's: since ca. 1925. 'To tell us "to get a powerful heave" on our kits and lay them out neatly' (Grinstead, 1946). But *to get a heave on* a person is to treat him unpleasantly or severely.—2. A bouncer or chucker-out: Sydneyites': since ca. 1943. (London *Evening News*, 16 Feb. 1949.)

heave, v.t. To discard; to throw away: mostly Aus.: since ca. 1920; more use in UK in later C.20. Elliptical for *heave out* or *overboard*. Cf.:-

heave-ho. See **give the old heave-ho.**

heaven. '*Seven* or *Eleven*. A good example of a one-word rhyme. It is used by dice-gamblers only—the score is possible with not less than a two-dice throw' (Franklyn 2nd).

Heaven(-)Born, the. The members of the Indian Civil Service, esp. its higher echelons: late C.19–earlier 20. ?Ex an Indian honorific. (P.B.) Applied also to the Malayan Civil Service: id. Allen, 1983.

heavens above. Love: r.s. Franklyn 2nd.

heaver. A coin of low value; a penny: earlier C.20. (Coppard, 1921.) 'A shortening of synon. *coal-heaver*, r.s. on C.18–19 *stiver*' (Franklyn.)

heavies, the. 'Group of prison officers coping with incident/riot' (Home Office): prison c. A shortening of **the heavy mob**, q.v.

heavy, n. A heavy bomber or large bomb: RAF coll.: 1940+. (Jackson.)—2. A serious actor: film world: since ca. 1915. McCabe, 1937.—3. A girl: Aus. teenage surfers': 1960+. *Pix*, 28 Sep. 1963.—4. As *the heavy*, R.C. notes, 1966, 'In recounting the incident, he made me the heavy (= he made me the villain of the piece)'. Prob. ex sense 2.—5. 'A couple who were "at the heavy" (i.e., robbers)' (Taylor, 1982).—6. A bodyguard: c.: later C.20. (Hollis, 1983.) Cf. **heavy**, in AUSTRALIAN UNDERWORLD, in Appx.—7. See **heavy metal**.

heavy, v. To 'beat up'; to slash; to disfigure (a person): c. and low s.: since ca. 1955. Barlow, 1968.—2. See **heavy metal**.

heavy, adj. 'Hard' or 'killer', as applied to drugs: since ca. 1960. (R.S., 1969.)—2. Important; prominent; esp. in popular entertainment: adopted, late 1960s, ex US. Scaduto, 1974.—3. Wonderful; 'marvellous' = fine or excellent, and adjacent nuances: adopted, ca. 1971, ex US. *Melody Maker*, 8 July 1972: 'Just the funkiest, heaviest set of girls . . . and complete with outstanding new back-up band.' See also **heavy metal**.—4. Sexually aroused: prostitutes': later C.20. 'He was getting heavy, and I'm trying to get myself together to split from this car . . . ' (*Time Out*, 30 May 1980).

heavy-duty. Seriously and ardently committed (and apt to emphasise the fact), as in 'It was quite a good party—for Golders Green—but too many heavy-duty Jews' (Raab, 1985, quoting a young 'City-type'), and 'I hate that pub, it's always full of heavy-duty feminists' (Simmonds, 1986): mid–1980s. Ex, e.g., heavy-duty tyres, clothing, etc.

heavy-handed. 'Said of one who makes his drinks, and those of others, too strong' (Leechman), e.g. 'Don't be so heavy-handed with the gin!' (R.S., 1971): coll., in Britain since 1930s, in Can. since ca. 1955. Ultimately ex the S.E. sense, 'clumsy'.

heavy lurker. A 'teller of the piteous tale' in a large way: c. Wood, 1932.

heavy metal, n., whence **heavy-metal,** adj. and v.; often shortened to *heavy*, n., and to *metal*, n., and v.i. (= to play 'heavy metal'). The full n. means 'a type of very loud [and] dense blues music that uses electronic instruments, drums, and many amplifiers' (W. & F., 1975, but giving no date). There is even *metallurgist*, a player of 'heavy metal', included, as is *metal*, n. and v., by W. & F. *Heavy metal* apparently orig. in the adj. *heavy* (of music), 'important', thence 'loud, forceful'. *Heavy-metal*, adj., is used in *Beatles*, 1975.—2. Powerful, military jet fighter and bomber aircraft, as opp. to 'real' aeroplanes: vintage aircraft enthusiasts' joc., punning sense 1: since late 1970s. (Huston, 1980.) I have seen it applied also to battleships: same period. (P.B.)

heavy mob, the. The prison police: prison c.: since ca. 1944. (Norman.)—2. 'Any gang that specialises in warehouse-breaking. Gangs which go in for big-scale robberies. (Particularly the former)' (Tempest): c.: mid-C.20.

heavy petting. 'Petting' that is very passionate and stopping just short of coition: mostly teenagers': adopted, in late 1940s, ex US.

heavy stuff. Unsympathetic and over-paternal advice or moralising: coll. Ult. ex the theatrical sense, serious, esp. sombre or tragic (1826).—2. 'Motorised police who follow up a raid on club or "gaff". Reinforcements to a police raid, often using the Black Maria for transport' (Tempest): c.: mid-C.20.

heavy sugar, the. 'The big money': low: since ca. 1925. Kersh, 1938.

heavy worker. A safe-breaker: c. Because most safes are heavy.

hectic. Exciting, esp. with tendency to dissipation or to excessive activity (as in *a hectic time*); (of a book) sensational in theme, luridly indelicate in language, or both: coll., esp. since WW1.

hedge. A market stall: market-traders' and showmen's. A shortening of *hedge and ditch.*—2. Hence, the people gathered round a stall or a stand: fair-grounds'. Buchanan-Taylor, 1943.

hedge and ditch. A market or street stall or stand: r.s. on *pitch*: late C.19–20. Often abbr. to *hedge.*—2. Hence, since ca. 1910, a football, or a cricket, pitch. Franklyn.

hedge-hopper. See **Dagenham dustbin.**

hedgehog. An anti-submarine weapon: RN coll.: WW2.

Heeb. A Jew: adopted, mid–1970s, ex US. Abbr. *Hebrew.* The film *The Life of Brian*, 1979. (P.B.)

heebee. See **take a heebee.**

heebs, the. A post-1930 var.—and derivation—of:-

heebie (or **-y**)**-jeebies, the.** A fit of depression or irritation: US (1927) >, by 1928, anglicised. Ex a dance that, so named, resembled the *Blues* (*OED* Sup.); perhaps a reduplicated perversion of S.E. *creepy* or *the creeps*: cf. the Scottish adv., *heepie-creep*, 'in a creeping, sneaking manner' (1873: *EDD*).

heel. 'A fellow who seeks your company for the sake of a free drink' (H. & P.): Services', esp. among officers: since 1940. Adopted from US airmen, ex the US sense, 'hanger-on'. 'Thus *heeling*, paying a heel for something' (H. & P., 1943).—2. Ex US, ca. 1938, the sense 'objectionable fellow'—esp., 'one who is untrustworthy or treacherous'. You can't usually see your heel.—3. Apparently it was at first a polite short form of *shit-heel*.

heel and toe. To apply accelerator and then brake in rapid succession, a jerky means of progress: motorists': since late 1940s. (B.P.) A pun on heel-and-toe dancing.

heel up. To follow behind a person: Glasgow:—1934.

heeled. In possession of drugs or a weapon: drugs c. (Stockley, 1986.) US since—1968 (Spears). Cf. coll. *well-heeled*, wealthy.

Heffer, the. 'A desk diary published by W. Heffer & Sons [the famous booksellers]' (Wharton, 1965): University of Cambridge: since ca. 1950.

heifer-dust. Airy or meaningless talk: Aus.: since ca. 1930. (B., 1942.) Prob. adopted ex US; certainly it was, at first, euph. for *bullshit*; also Can., but not common. Aus. has synon. *bull-dust* (Niland, 1955).—2. 'A dry, artificial coffee-creamer' (Leech, 1985): Can. Derog.; cf. **ground bones** and **plastic**.

Heine, Heinie; occ. **Hiney.** The Can. (and later the US) soldiers' name for 'Fritz' or 'Jerry': WW1 (and after). Ex *Heinrich*, an extremely common Ger. first name. (F. & G.) In WW2 used by the Brit. Army in Italy, 1943–5 (*Oasis*, 1984).

Heinz; (one of) the 57 varieties. A mongrel dog: since ca. 1925. A ref. to the 57 varieties of tinned edibles and potables manufactured by Messrs Heinz, the American food-product manufacturers.—2. *Heinz varieties* = 57, in Bingo: since ca. 1955; earlier in Services' tombola.—3. 'Six selections in every combination of doubles, trebles, fourfolds, fivefolds and sixfolds. A total of 57 bets. So named after a famous canned food firm's 57 varieties' (Evans, 1983): the turf: later C.20.

heist. Robbery, theft, and the originating v.: c. >, ca. 1965, low s. Adopted ex US. Ex **hoist**, perhaps via Yiddish—cf. Ger. *er heisst*, he hoists (R.S.).

heli. Helicopter: journalistic: 1970s. *Sunday Times* mag., 25 Nov. 1979.

helicopter. A ski-ing manoeuvre. See **hot dog.**

hell. In *the hell*: 'To hell and *the hell* are often confused in the US and Canada. Apparently the abbreviated *Go t' hell* has been misapprehended, resulting in the ridiculous "Get the hell out of here!" ' (Leechman): coll.: since ca. 1930.—2. In such emphatic expressions as, e.g. 'Will I hell!' = no, I most certainly will not!: coll.: later C.20. (P.B.)

hell and high water, between. In a great difficulty: nautical coll. (McFee, 1935). A deviation from S.E. *between the devil and the deep sea*, perhaps influenced by the cliché *come hell and/or high water*, come what may.

hell and spots. A var. (s. >, by 1934, coll.) of the next. Blaker, 1934, 'Another sort of woman could have knocked hell and spots off of you.'

hell and tommy, esp. in *play h. and t.* and, in C.20, *like h. and t.* A picturesque intensive (s. > coll.): by ca. 1930 slightly ob.; by 1980, † in UK (but see below). An early occurrence: Gardner, 1831. MacDonald, 1933, has var.: 'Where the devil and Tommy did I put that corkscrew?', with which cf. prec. Genesis obscure; *and tommy* is a tag added to (*play*) *hell*, precisely as *and Betty Martin* is tagged to (*all*) *my eye*. Ware, who does support *Hal and Tommy* (Henry VIII and Thomas Cromwell playing havoc with Church property), proposes *hell and torment* (by corruption or perversion), than which I have not heard, nor can I think, of a likelier origin. In Northumberland dial. (1894: *EDD* Sup.), *play hell and tommy with* = 'to set utterly at variance'. The phrase is (1950s) very much alive as an oath (*hell and Tommy!*) in Aus.: witness, e.g., Niland, 1958.

hell-bending. Preaching: esp., fervid preaching: Can.: from ca. 1910. Beames.

Hell-Fire is short for *Hell-Fire Pass*, which is soldiers' Hobson-Jobson for Halfaya Pass in N. Africa: 1940–3, then merely reminiscent. See quot'n at **basinful**, 1.

Hell-Fire Corner. The Dover area, subject to shelling from German guns across the Channel, 1941–4; earlier (Aug.–Sep. 1940), S.E. England, conspicuous in the Battle of Britain.

hell week. A husband's or boy-friend's term for the older, fem. coll. *bad week*, the week of a woman's period.

hellishun. Very: Aus. children's: since ca. 1920. (B., 1942.) Cf. **hangashun**, obviously a euph. for adv. *hellish* or *hellishly*.

hellova, helluva, heluva. Hell of a: coll. slurring, as in Milne, 1931, 'Making a heluva bad job of it'. It can also = 'hellishly', i.e. extremely—or (no more than) very: low, esp. Glaswegian: from ca. (?earlier than) 1919. MacArthur, 'They're looking hellova well too, aren't they?'

hell's angel. (Usu. in pl.) One of an intimidating gang of young men on powerful motorcycles, characterised particularly by the wearing of black leather jackets decorated with metal studs, and other eccentricities of dress, a fashion popularised by the US film *The Wild Ones*, 1954. The motorcycle gang movement developed until it became organised into 'chapters'; hence the name *chaper herald* for a *hell's angel* (from Wesley's familiar Christmas Hymn, 'Hark, the herald angels sing . . . '). Also known as *leather Jacks*—cf. the S.E. term for the grub of the cranefly—and *coffee-bar cowboys*. (Dunford; P.B.) *Hell's Angels* was orig. the title of a film, 1930, about the air war over the Western Front, WW1.

hell's bells! Hell!: coll.: late C.19–20; orig. Colonial. By rhyme: cf. *here's cheers!* Also in construction as in 'Regular hell's bells of a fuss' (Bailey, 1932). P.B.: sometimes elab. (usu. mock-)ferociously to *hell's bells and buckets of blood!*: mid–C.20.

hell's own, adj. and adv. Intense(ly), as in 'hell's own busy': since ca. 1930. Prob. of Public Schools' orig. (P.B.)

hell's teeth! A mild exclam. that can be made to sound quite vicious: since late C.19. (P.B.)

Helluva (or **Hell of a**) **Bellow Chorus, the.** The Hallelujah Chorus in Handel's *Messiah*. Derisive among the unmusical. (Petch, 1974.) I [E.P.] knew it as the 'Hullabaloo Chorus'. See **hellova.**

helmet. A (uniformed) policeman. Cody, 1985.

help in. To join in (a gang fight): Teddy boys' coll.: late 1940s–early 50s. *Observer*, 1 Mar. 1959.

helter-skelter. An air-raid shelter: (mostly Londoners') r.s.: 1939+. *New Statesman*, 30 Aug. 1941.

hemp. Marijuana: (mostly teenage) drug addicts': since ca. 1955. US since ca. 1930 (Spears). This drug is extracted from a plant resembling hemp, and the term is merely an ellipsis for American s. *Indian hemp*.

Hempire, the. The British Commonwealth of Nations: sometimes joc.; sometimes disparaging.

hen, n. Its use as a mode of address, or as an endearment, is, unless joc., dial. (P.B.)—2. As *Hen*, a (German) Henschel aircraft: RAF: 1940+. (Partridge, 1945.) Cf. **He, Me and You**.

hen, adj. Female: beatniks': late 1950s–early 1960s. Anderson.

hen-cackle. A mountain easy to climb: NZ mountaineers'. (B., 1941.) Difficult enough to cause a cackle among the women. Cf.:—2. In *a mere hen cackle*, a trifle: NZ. B., 1941.

hen-fruit. Eggs, collectively: Can. (Beames.) Cf. **hen's fruit** and **cackle-berry**.

hen-peck (or **henpeck**). A hen-pecked husband: domestic coll.: since ca. 1920.

Henry. Occ. used as a mock-solemnity for HARRY, q.v. in Appx.—2. Heroin: drugs world. (*Observer*, 24 Apr. 1983.) Prob. an extension of **H.**

Henry Nash. Cash: r.s.

hen's fruit and hog's body. Bacon and egg(s): RN stewards': from ca. 1925. *Sunday Chronicle*, 1 Mar. 1942.

hens' teeth, as scarce as. Very scarce indeed: mostly Aus. and Can.: late C.19–20. (B.P.; Leech.) John Smith, 1981, notes the Eng. var. *as rare as hens' teeth*.

hep. In the know; having good taste: Brit. jazz-lovers', since ca. 1945; ex Can. jazz-musicians' and -lovers', who adopted it, ca. 1925, ex US. Cf. **hep cat** and **hip**. Ultimately ex the ploughman's, or the driver's, *hep!* to his team of horses ('Get up!'); the horses 'get *hep*'—lively, alert. In US, hence Can. rural dial. of late C.19–20, 'He's mighty hep' = he's very shrewd.—2. Hence, alert and progressive and well-informed: beatniks' (as in 'hep doll') and others', esp. teenagers': late 1950s–early 60s. Anderson.

hep! 'Left!' in military commands, as being so much easier to pronounce explosively.

hep cat. See JIVE, in Appx. A jazz 'fiend' (swing music): adopted in Can. ca. 1925, in Brit. ca. 1935, ex US; ob. by 1950. (*Observer*, 16 Sep. 1956.) Superseded by *hipster*.

herb. Cannabis: drug-users': later C.20. Home Office.

Herbert. A chap, a fellow, a guy: mildly pej. Usu. pron '*Erbert* and sometimes shortened to '**Erb**, q.v.

herbs. Oats: Aus. racing: earlier C.20. 'When a horse became sluggish, it was given more "herbs" ' (B.P.).—2. Hence, power of engine or motor: Aus. motorists': since ca. 1930.

here and there. Hair: Aus. r.s. (Martin, 1937.)

Hereford Hooligans, the. The SAS (Special Air Service): RN: later C.20. Also *the hooligans from Hereford*: id. (Knight, 1984.) The Regimental depot is at Hereford.

Herefords. 'Used at Birch Coppice and Desford [S. Midlands collieries] to denote the oncoming shift; a reference to their white faces. Also known as the *others*' (Forster, 1970). Ex the distinctive breed of cattle.

Herman Finck. Ink: theatrical r.s. Franklyn.

hermaphy. A hermaphrodite: joc. diminutive, used in medical circles: earlier C.20.

Herpes. HMS *Hermes*: Services': Falklands War. (*Don't Cry*, 1983.) Herpes: a form of venereal infection that received some public notoriety in the early 1980s.

herring fleet, the. 'The flock of wives and marriageable girls who followed the Fleet from home waters to Malta on its summer cruise': RN officers': late C.19–mid-20. 'Double pun on *fleet* and *her ring* (anatomical)'. Hackforth-Jones, 1948. See also **fishing fleet**.

herrings in. A coll. ellipsis for ' . . . tomato sauce': RN: since ca. 1940. (Peppitt.)—2. Hence, 'a query when offering a cup of tea or coffee': *herrings in?* = with or without sugar': RN: since ca. 1965. (Peppitt.) For usage, cf. the Fr. *café avec*, with *du rhum* understood.

het. A shortening of **hetero**. Phillips, 1976.

het-up; often **all het-up.** Excited; 'in a state': adopted (as a coll.), ca. 1935, from US. I.e. heated up.

hetero, adj. and n.Heterosexual: coll.: since late 1940s. 'All kinds of fun and games, hetero and homo.' Cf.:-

heters. Heterosexuals: s.: mid-C.20. Larkin, 1980.

hex (esp. *put a hex on*). To lay a spell upon a person or, e.g., a machine: Aus. (and occ. Brit.): adopted, ca. 1950, ex US. 'Directly from German [*Hexe*, a witch], via the Pennsylvania Dutch (i.e., Deutsch) dialect. Barns in East Pennsylvania still are occasionally painted with "hex signs" (to ward off witchcraft) and as late as 1930s there were occasional "hex murders"—i.e. of supposed witches' (R.C., 1976).

hi! Of Can. coll. usage, Leechman, 1959, remarked: 'This is becoming almost the universal informal greeting. Juveniles use it, even when first introduced, and babes in arms will answer "Hi!" when spoken to.'

hi-de-hi, greeting, answered by **ho-de-ho** (Kersh, 1941). *Hi there!: ho* (or *hullo*) *there!*

hi- (or **'i-**)**diddle-diddle.** The middle, as 'right in the i-diddle-diddle': r.s. (Rogers, 1980.)

hi-diddler. A violin player: Glasgow r.s. on *fiddler*. Munro. 1985.

hi-fi. Of a gramophone recording, tape recorders, etc.: having *high fidelity* in tone and pitch: since the middle 1950s: coll. >, by 1960, S.E.

hi-jack (in later C.20, usu. **hijack**). (Of one criminal) forcibly to deprive (another criminal) of booty: c.: adopted ca. 1931 ex US, where orig. and mostly of one bootlegger's robbing another on the highway. Brandon, 1936.—2. To seize ('kidnap') an aeroplane: since early 1970s. The derivative *skyjack* is rather journalistic j. than true s.

hi-jacker. One who acts as in prec., 1: c.: adopted, ca. 1932, ex US.

hi, Rube! 'The signal given to circus people that rubes (townies [q.v.]) are causing trouble': Can. circus s., adopted, ca. 1925, ex US. Irwin, 1931; *Islander* (Victoria, BC), 19 Dec. 1971.

hiccup. A fault in administration: Service officers': since ca. 1965. (P.B., 1974.)

hickety. Rough: trawlermen's. Butcher, 1980.

hickey. (Often elab. to *do-hickey*.) A 'thingummy, what-cher-macallit': NZ: late C.19–20. (B., 1941.) Perhaps influenced by a Maori word, but the form *do-hickey* has long been common in the mid-west US.—2. An unsophisticated person: Aus.: since ca. 1943. Park, 1950.—3. A long, hard, 'suction' kiss that raises a blister; hence the blister so caused; a 'love-bite': Can.: since ca. 1930(?). Origin?

hickey(-)hockey. A jockey: Aus. sporting r.s.: since ca. 1920. Glassop, 1949.

hidden treasure. A landlady's husband that, rarely seen, does much work below stairs: joc.

Hide, the. The Covered Market: Caledonian Market pitch-holders'. Brown, 1946.

hide. Impudence; excessive self-assurance: Aus. Doone.—2. A hide-out: coll. > j. of, e.g., bird-watchers: since ca. 1910. Revival of M.E. sense (*SOD*). In WW2, esp. a hide-out for vehicles—against enemy aircraft (P-G-R).

hide-up, n. A 'hide-out' (hiding-place): Aus.: since ca. 1920. B., 1942.

hide up, v. (Of police or other authorities) to defend or shield (a wrongdoer): c.: from ca. 1920. Wallace, 1928.

hideously. Very: mostly Society: from ca. 1920. Mackail, 1925, 'It was so hideously awkward.' Cf. *fearfully*.

hidey (or **highdy** or **hidy**)**!** How are you?: Aus. and elsewhere: since ca. 1935. (B., 1942.) Adopted from US, it < *how d'ye do*; cf. **hi-de-hi.**

high, n. A peak or record in, e.g., production or sales, the opposite being *low*: coll.: since 1940.—2. Drug exhilaration: adopted, ca. 1960, ex US. (Scaduto, 1974.) Ex the corresponding adj.—3. Hence, any period of exhilaration, however produced or inspired: since early 1970s.

high, adj. Intoxicated: 1627, May in his *Lucan* (*OED*): from ca. 1880, mostly US.—2. Under the influence of an exhilarating drug: Can. since ca. 1925, Eng. since ca. 1930.—3. 'The bird'—girl—'might be high (high principled) in which case he would get no dice or merely "a bit of bazooka"—petting' (correspondence columns in *Sunday Times*, 8 Sep. 1963): since ca. 1960.—4. Over-excited, abnormally bright, e.g. from relief, or before the onset of depression or migraine; ex sense 2, but no alcohol or drugs are involved: coll.: since mid-1970s. (P.B.)

high as a kite, (as). Extremely drunk: since ca. 1944. Perhaps adopted ex US. Occ. *higher than a kite.*—2. An intensive of **high**, adj., 2 and 4: coll.: since early and mid-1970s, respectively. Home Office; P.B.

high-ball. A signal to go: Can. railwaymen's: since ca. 1910. Hence, in gen. s. (since ca. 1925), *give* (someone) *the high-ball*, to approve, to sanction; hence also *high-balling*, n. and adj., travelling fast, succeeding.—2. See **highball.**

high boost. See **boost,** 2.

high-brow. See **highbrow.**

high camp. See **camp,** n., 4.

high-grading. Stealing—or dealing in stolen—processed gold ore; illegal trading in gold from a mine: Can. miners': since ca. 1918. (Priestley.)

high-hat, v. To treat (a person) superciliously: an American coll. partly anglicised by 1930. P.B.: it was never fully adopted as v., but as adj., see next, is still extant, 1983.

high-hat, adj. 'Superior'; supercilious: since ca. 1930. (Kersh, 1938.) P.B.: also as adv., e.g., 'She was acting very high-hat and à la; thought no end of herself, she did.'

high jump. In *be* (later C.20: *up* or *in*) *for the high jump* (orig., occ. *jumps*), to be about, or obliged, to face a difficult or a very unpleasant task: military: since ca. 1912. Esp., to be on the crime-sheet, hence due for trial (F. & G.), who note WW1 var. *be up for the long jump*). L.A., 1974, noting the phrase's widespread use in later C.20, writes 'esp. to have a decisive interview, surgical operation, test or examination in prospect at fixed date'. Ex steeplechasing.—2. In *take the high jump*, to be hanged: police: late C.19–20. *Free-Lance Writer*, Apr. 1948.

high kick. A thrill obtained by taking a drug: drug addicts': since ca. 1940. Gosling 1960.

high-kicker. 'A girl who is over fond of "a good time", somewhat fast' (Lyell): coll.: earlier C.20.

high octane. High quality and powerful: a joc. metaphor ex fuel rating: later C.20. Arnold, 1986, 'She used to work for ICI Paints in Slough and whilst there attended a high octane two-day advanced management course offered only to rising executives in blue-chip companies'.

high-roller. A big gambler, orig. with dice, then on the race-track: Can.: adopted, ca. 1960, ex US. Robertson, 1973.

high spot. (Often pl.) The outstanding part or feature of something; e.g. 'the high spot of the evening's entertainment', 'the high spots of the recording': coll.: adopted, ex US, ca. 1925. *OED* Sup.—2. See **hit the high spots.**

high-stepper. Pepper: r.s.: earlier C.20. F.&G.

High Street, China. Any remote place beyond one's ken: mostly RAF: since 1938. 'The underlying sense is that it is too remote to be taken seriously' (L.A.). But this 'address' was Cockney humour much earlier: either in this sense, or as a 'mind your own business' answer to 'Where do you live?' *Muvver.*

high-tail. To make off speedily without looking behind; to bolt; e.g. 'We high-tailed out of there': Can. coll., adopted ex US. Ex the stiffly upright tails of bolting cattle. (F. & G.) P.B.: some Brit. use in later C.20, sometimes with *it*, as 'We high-tailed it out . . .'

high-up. (Usu. pl.) Persons with high rank; politicians enjoying their brief authority 'on top of the world': coll.: since ca. 1937. An occ. var. is *higher-ups*, i.e. those not quite 'at the top of the pile', as in, e.g., *John Bull*, 28 Aug. 1943.

high, wide and handsome. Going all out—swimmingly—very successfully: Can. coll. (Leechman.) Also in the London Fire Brigade, of a building well alight.

highball. A drink of whisky served in a tall glass: s., 1899 (*SOD*); by 1930, coll., orig., and still (1983) mostly US. See

high-ball.—2. 'A mixture of heroin with either cocaine or amphetamine' (Cutland, 1985): drugs c.

highbrow. A person affecting intellectual superiority: coll., orig. (1911), US; anglicised ca. 1917. Cf. **lowbrow.**—2. Hence, as adj., anglicised at about the same time. (Mencken.)

higher prostitution, the. The writing of books sponsored by great firms, corporations, institutions (e.g. universities): humorously among the authors thereof: since the late 1940s. I first heard it from that delightful man, the late David Keir, in 1954 or 55. Such writers jocularly implying that they are comparable with the great *demi-mondaines*. The prostitution is of their talent.

Higher Schools. A var. of **Highers,** q.v.

higher than a giraffe's toupet. Very 'high' on drugs: beatniks': ca. 1959–62. (Anderson.) P.B.: the more gen. phrase is *higher than a kite*; see **high as . . .**

Highers. Higher School (or leaving) Certificate: schools': ca. 1920–50, when superseded by General Certificate of Education, Advanced level (GCE 'A' levels).

Highland fling. King (playing cards): r.s.: later C.20. (Hillman.)

highway surfer. One who 'rides highways with board on top of car but never surfs' (*Pix*, 28 Sep. 1963): Aus. surfers': since ca. 1961.

hijack; hijacker. See **hi-jack.**

hike, n. A long walk, esp. for exercise and (?)pleasure: dial. and US, > Eng. coll. ca. 1926. Ex the v.—2. A sharp lift, esp. a rise in pay; 'Miners seek pay hike' (any tabloid newspaper): journalistic: adopted, ex US, mid-1970s. Prob. influenced, in UK, by *hoick*. (P.B.)

hike, v., orig. (1809) dial., = to tramp (from 1927, for pleasure and/or exercise); *hike off*, orig. (—1728) c., = to run away. (Grose, 2nd ed.) Becoming, except in dial., disused in England, *hike* went to US, whence it returned, to gen. coll. usage in Eng., ca. 1926. In late C.19–20 also Can. coll. (Niven.) P.B.: in later C.20, informal S.E.

hiker; hiking. One who 'hikes' (**hike,** v., q.v.); n. and adj. (connected with, characteristic of) the going for long walks. Both coll.: 1927. P.B.: like the v., it has become, in later C.20, informal S.E. See also **hitch-hike.**

Hill, the. Among Londoners, is a coll. for the Notting Hill district: late C.19–20. (Blake, 1954.) Cf. **Bill from the Hill.**—3. See **over the hill.**

hill and dale. 'The tale' as practised by 'con men' and their like: orig., and still mainly, underworld r.s. Phelan, 1953.

Hill (or hill) captain. A military officer that spent his summer leave in India in a Hill station in preference to spending it in some more manly way, e.g. in shooting: military, esp. Indian Army's: ca. 1890–1947. It implied undue addiction to feminine society.

hillbilly. Chilly: Glasgow r.s. Munro. 1985.

Hillgate. See **get off at Hillgate.**

Hiney. See **Heine.**

hing aff. Get off!: Glasgow:—1934. Lit., 'hang off!' Cf.:-

hing-on, a. A walking arm-in-arm: Glasgow coll.:—1934.

hinting gear. See MOCK-AUCTION, in Appx., q.v. also for **hinton.**

hip. 'Equipped with enough wisdom, philosophy and courage to be self-sufficient, independent of society; able to swing on any scene' (Victoria, BC, *Daily Colonist*, 16 Apr. 1959): Can. jazz-lovers' and musicians': adopted, 1956, ex US. A boppers' alteration of *hep*, which, in 1958, began to regain its virtue and its potency (Hinton, 1958). By 1961 (Anderson), it was old-fashioned among beatniks—cf., however, **hip duck.**—2. Hence, aware, realistic, worldly: coll.: since early 1960s. Hunter, 1969, a 'tough cop' interrogating a Black suspect: 'I do think so . . . And if you're hip you'll think so too, because you're up to here in trouble'.

hip(-)disease. The habit of carrying a hip flask: Aus.: since ca. 1925. B., 1942.

hip duck. A nice girl, i.e. an attractive or sympathetic one: beatniks': since ca. 1959. Anderson.

hip flask. A revolver: RAF: 1939+. (*Reader's Digest*, Feb. 1941; E.P., 1942.) Ex the position in which it is worn and its appearance in the case.

hip-hip-hurrahs. Engine-room artificers: RN (lowerdeck): since ca. 1920. (Granville.) Ex the initials *ERA*.

hip-hop. Hoppingly: coll.: ca. 1670–1920. (Villiers, in *The Rehearsal*; Congreve.) Reduplication of *hop*. The *OED*, perhaps rightly, considers it S.E.—at least after ca. 1700.

hippy, hippie. 'The hippies, latter-day beatniks, along with the younger "teeny boppers", met in Stanley Park' (*Daily Colonist*, Victoria, BC, 28 Mar. 1967): Can.: since 1966 or perhaps 1965. By 1967, also Brit. Fryer, 1967, defines a hippy as a 'product of Haight-Ashbury district of San Francisco. Anarchic successors to Beat generation. Essential beliefs: protest, legalised drugs, opting out. Not to be confused with *plastic* hippies, conventional youth who like to dress up at week-end.' P.B.: hence *hippy* (adj.), *hippiedom, hippyism*. Ultimately ex **hip**, 1.

hipster. A jazz 'fiend' (modern jazz): adopted, ca. 1950, ex US. (*Observer*, 16 Sep. 1956.) Cf. **hep cat**, its predecessor.

Hipsy hoy. A boy: r.s.: earlier C.20. B. & P.

hire it done. To hire someone to do something: Can. coll.: since ca. 1930. 'I never mow my own lawn. I hire it done' (Leechman).

his dibs. Applied, punningly to a wealthy man (on the C.19 *his nibs*, slightly mocking 'title' for the person mentioned): ca. 1925–40.

His Ex. His Excellency (the Governor-General): Aus. and NZ. B., 1941.

His Master's Voice. 'The assistant [engine-shed] foreman was known to all as "His Master's Voice" or "the foreman's half-back" ' (McKenna, 2): railwaymen's.—2. A sycophant, a 'crawler': id. (Ibid.) Both are puns on the well-known gramophone record company's name. (P.B.)

hit, n. A killing by gangsters; hence by spies: orig. c.; by early 1970s, also police: adopted, ca. 1965, ex US [?earlier: cf. **hit-man**].—2 The taking of a drug, as in 'musicians getting a quick hit while [the police] are out of the way' (Stuart, 1972): a borrowing ex US. Applied even to the sniffing of glue, as in '[They] take dope, practised hits from a white, plastic supermarket bag' (*Time Out*, 8 Jan. 1982).

hit, v. To go to and then travel along or work or play at or rest in, as in *hit the road* or *trail*, *the high spots*, *the haystack*, was orig. and still US: these usages can hardly be said to be fully anglicised; but they prob. will be—very soon too! [Note in 1st ed., 1937. E.P. made no entry for *hit the haystack*, but **hit the hay** is presumably a shortening of it.]—2. To buy drugs: drugs c. (Stockley, 1986.) US since—1936 (Spears).

Hit and Miss. Hitler and Mussolini: since mid-1940; ob. by 1947.—2. *hit and miss*, r.s. for both 'kiss' and 'piss': later C.20. (Jones, 1971.) Franklyn records both as US, but notes that *piss* is 'of Australian antecedence', and that the meaning *kiss* occurs in Orwell, 1933. Var. *hit or miss*, since late C.19.

hit dirt. To become de-railed: railwaymen's. McKenna, 1.

hit (someone) for six. To rout decisively in argument or business or other battle of wits: since ca. 1920. Ex cricket.

hit it a crack. 'To create a considerable disturbance, whether over an enemy town or in one of our own; to adopt a vigorous offensive' (H.W., 1942): RAF: WW2. Cf. **hit it up** and **crack about**.

hit it in the head with a heavy hammer, but mostly with the four aspirates abandoned, is either a genuine or a mock Cockney expression to indicate a threat used as a means to persuade. (L.A., 1976.)

hit it up; orig. **hit things up.** 'To behave strenuously; riotously' (Dennis): Aus.

hit it with (someone). To get along well with: Aus. B., 1942.

hit-man. One who will, for hire, kill or maim a specified victim: underworld, whether central or peripheral: adopted, ca. 1955, ex US; by 1970s journalistic, and more widespread; occ. used fig. Cf. *hit-squad*, in quot'n at **taxing**, and **hatchet man**.

hit (the) pay-dirt. The strike it rich; to so manage an enterprise that it becomes suddenly financially rewarding: coll.: adopted, ca. 1975, ex US. Also used fig., e.g. in research. Ex prospecting for minerals, where 'pay-dirt' is S.E.

hit that broad. See **broad**, 1.

hit the deck. To land: RAF: since ca. 1925. (Jackson.) See **deck**.—2. Hence, to crash-land: RAF: since ca. 1940.—3. 'To sleep, cf. **hit the hay** ' (Hinde, 1945).—4. To fall prone: Services': later C.20. Perhaps ex US; may be used as imperative.

hit the hay. To go to bed: Can., by 1900; anglicised in 1929 by Conan Doyle (*OED* Sup.); prob. orig. US tramps'. See **hit, v.**

hit the high spots. To go to excess (of dissipation or merry-making); to attain a very high level: coll.: adopted, ca. 1927, ex US.—2. 'To do something superficially' (Leechman): Can.: since ca. 1925.—3. To 'have a night out on the town'; i.e. to visit some of the best places of entertainment, restaurants, etc., in a city or town: coll.: later C.20. (P.B.)

hit the jackpot. See **jackpot**.

hit the kellicks. To apply the brakes: Aus. motorists': since ca. 1940. Cf. the synon. **anchors**; *kellick* is an Aus. form of S.E. *killick*. (B.P.)

hit the rhubarb. 'Run off the road [in a vehicle] into the bushes (by accident); go off the tracks' (Leech, 1985): Can.: later C.20.

hit the road. See **hit, v.**, 1. An interesting parallel is the Norfolk dial. *hit the road*, to walk fast, as in Emerson, 1893.

hit the roof. To flare up, be or become extremely angry: coll. Cf. S.E. *fly into a rage*. A later C.20 intensive is *go through the roof*.

hit the sack. 'To go to bed . . . In New Zealand, probably used before 1900, and certainly since' (Gray, 1969). 'In early Colonial days, people in rural areas sometimes slept on a bag of chaff, or used sacks nailed to a wooden frame.' *Not* of US origin. P.B.: some Brit. use in, e.g., Army s., where perhaps it *is* of US orig.; but cf. C.19 nautical s. *sack* = a hammock.

hit the taps. To open the throttle: RAF: 1939+. Graves, 1943.

hit the ties. To 'tramp the ties' or walk along the railway track: Can. (?ex US): since ca. 1905; by 1959 somewhat ob. (Leechman.) Here, *ties* = (transverse) railway sleepers.

hit the toe. To go: Aus. r.s., esp. surfboard riders': since ca. 1958. (B.P.)

hit the wall. To reach the point of exhaustion: athletes', esp. long-distance runners': later C.20. (Newport, 1982.) Cf. the cyclists' synon. **bonk**.

hit the white. To succeed: Aus. sporting. (Baker.) Ex games j.

hit their hobbles. (Of horses) to gallop despite their hobble chains: Aus. coll. Buzo, 1973.—2. (Of persons, esp. in sports) to make a glorious comeback: Aus.: since ca. 1950, as in Buzo, 1971.

hit things up. See **hit it up**.

hit (a person) up for (something). To ask (a person) for: Colonial and South-American-English s. Craig, 1935, 'I . . . hit him up for a job, and here I am.'—2. Hence, to charge (someone) unreasonably for a purchase, etc.: Aus. Baker.

hit where (one) lives. To mean much to, make a great impression on, a person: 1907, Wodehouse, 'This is just the sort of thing to get right at them. It'll hit them where they live.' Ex US: Artemus Ward (1834–67) uses it.

hitch, n. A term of enlistment: Can. Services': adopted, ca. 1935, ex US.

hitch, v. A coll. shortening of **hitch-hike**, n. and v.: later C.20. 'He got there by a series of hitches, by truck, aircraft, anything going' (P.B.)

hitch-hike. To obtain a free ride on a walking tour, or, esp., to obtain a series of free rides, going on, or returning from, leave, vacation, etc.: adopted, ca. 1936, ex US; orig. coll. >, in later C.20, S.E. (*SOD*). Hence *hitch-hiker, -hiking*; also as n.

Hitler. See **little Hitler.**

Hitler's War. WW2, to distinguish from the **Kaiser's War,** 1914–18: later C.20.

hitsville. Success, as opp. *squaresville*, failure: early 1960s. (BBC Light Programme, 30 June 1963.) See **-ville** and **square,** n., 1.

hive off. To depart: Aus.: since ca. 1910. B., 1942. Ex bees. P.B.: some use still, 1983, in UK. In the sense 'to form a separate group' it is S.E. (*SOD*, 1977.)

ho-de-ho. See **hi-de-hi.**

hobble. Come, or go: joc. coll.: late 1970s. A lady editor recounting, on the BBC Radio 4 programme, 'Quote, Unquote', 7 Aug. 1979, a *faux pas* she had recently made: 'I rang this writer up and invited him to hobble over and see me sometime. He turned up in a wheel-chair!' An American popular song, ca. 1950, had the refrain, 'hobble off and hit the hay' = go to bed. (P.B.)

hobby-bobby. 'Derisive terms used on several occasions to describe community [police-]officers were "hobby-bobbies" and "chocolate bobbies" ' (*The Times*, 16 July 1981): among police lower ranks. *Hobby-bobby* is applied also, by the regulars, to the part-time, voluntary special constable, of whom the Force has over 16,000 (*Daily Telegraph*, 14 Apr. 1988).

hobdayed. Applied to 'a horse that has been operated on to improve its breathing. Its vocal chords are cut and it cannot afterwards neigh' (Evans, 1983): the turf: later C.20.

hobo, pl. **hoboes.** A tramp; esp. one who works. Orig. (—1891, Flynt), US; anglicised ca. 1905. The v. has not 'caught on' in England. 'Americanism rarely heard in English prisons' (Tempest, 1950).—2. In NZ and Aus., in post-WW1 days, it was often applied to a rough-and-ready fellow. The etym. remains a puzzle: see esp. Irwin, who quotes a tramp's C.20 distinction: 'Bums loafs and sits. Tramps loafs and walks. But a hobo moves and works, and he's clean.'

Hobson's choice. A voice: theatrical r.s.: late C.19–20; now gen. abbr. to *Hobson's*, as in 'I've lost my Hobson's' (Warwick, 1968).

hock, n. An active male homosexual: r.s. on *cock*: c. Franklyn 2nd.

hock, v. To pawn: orig. s. >, in later C.20, coll. Hence the sense of *in hock*, in pawn.

hockey. See **hoggins.**

hockey stick. 'The hoist used for loading an aircraft with bombs' (Jackson): RAF: WW2. Ex the shape.

hocking. Var. of *houghing*, see **hough.**

hocum. See **hokum.**

hod. A bookmaker's money-bag: turf c. *Slang*, 1935.—2. A *bit of hod*, a fast girl, a prostitute: teenagers': since late 1950s.

hodad. A 'non-surfing beach bum' (*Pix*, 28 Sep. 1963) or, alternatively, 'a surfer not loyal to one beach' (B.P.) or ephemerally (ca. 1962–4) 'a youth who has a surfie haircut and a rocker's clothes' (B.P.): Aus. surfers', esp. if teenage: since ca. 1961. Perhaps, as Leechman suggests, a mock Black Am. pron. of 'Who's that?' W. & F., 1975, give US use since 1961, but offer no etym.

hoddie. A hod-carrier, one who carries bricks: Aus.: since ca. 1920. (B., 1953.) Brit. in later C.20, perhaps earlier.

hoe into (a task). To work hard and diligently at (something): Aus.: since ca. 1920. Agricultural metaphor. (B.P.)

hog, n. A locomotive; hence *hogger* or *hog-head*, a locomotive engineer: Can. railroadmen's:—1931. Ex US.—2. A home-built motorcycle: motorcyclists': later C.20. (Dunford.) Adopted ex US. Hibbert, 1983, however states that it is used for a Harley-Davison, esp. one ridden by a Hell's Angel [q.v.]; he notes further the usu. pron. *hawg*. ?Hence:—3. A large American car: fans': later C.20. (Hibbert.) A 'gas-guzzler' built for show.—4. PCP: drugs c. (Stockley, 1986.) US since 1967 (Spears). Cf. synon. **elephant.**

hog, v. To appropriate, esp. appropriate and eat or drink, greedily: orig. (1887), US; anglicised ca. 1912; > coll. ca.

1930.—2. As *hog it*, to sleep soundly, esp. snoringly: coll.:—1923 (Manchon).—3. To behave like, a road-hog: coll.: 1925. (*OED* Sup.) Also *hog it*.

hog-fat. (Of a person) a nuisance, useful-for-nothing, a parasite: Aus. Prichard, 1930.

hog-wash. See **oggin** and **ogwash.**

hog-whimpering. Elliptical for orig. *h-w drunk*: extremely, and incoherently, intoxicated: Sloane Rangers', yuppies' [qq.v.]: since early 1980s.

hoggers. 'Day dreaming. (Perhaps not unconnected with the after-effects of Hogmanay?)' (H. & P., 1943): Services': since ca. 1930. Rather, I think, a sense-development ex **hog,** v., 2.

hoggin. See **oggin.**

hoggins or **oggins.** A due share, esp. in pleasure—e.g. sexual, i.e. 'hoggish', pleasures: low. 'Cf. *hoggins line* at darts' (L.A.). *The (h)oggins line*, the line or position at which one stands to make the throw, has, since 1957 or 1958, been predominantly *the (h)ockey*.

hog's wash of the fo'c'stle head. The deck-hands on a merchant ship: nautical: earlier C.20.

hoi (Rossall and Haileybury), the lowest team, set, or game at Rugby football: **oips** (Haileybury) and **hoips** (Christ's Hospital), beginners at football; *hoy* (Bishop's Stortford), a townsman, a 'cad'; *polloi* (Cheltenham: since ca. 1925), the lowest football team or set: all these terms come from the Greek *hoi polloi*, lit. 'the many', hence, 'the multitude, the masses, the common people'. Marples.

hoick, n. A jerk as one's stroke begins or ends: rowing coll.:—1898 (*OED* Sup.).—2. Hence, any swift, jerking movement, as 'Is it caught? give it a hoick': coll. (P.B.)

hoick, v. To climb steeply, jerk oneself up (and *out of*): coll.: from ca. 1925 (*OED* Sup.).—2. To spit (mostly as v.i.): gen., and Aus. (Baker.) In phrase, e.g., 'he hoicked and spat', where it represents a blend of *hawk + hoick*, in earlier sense, to raise with a jerk. (P.B.)

hoick off. To become airborne: RAF: since ca. 1925. (H. & P.) An elab. of **hoick,** v., 1.—2. Hence, to depart, to begin a journey, to be on one's 'way to somewhere' (H. & P.): since ca. 1930; † by 1950.

hoips. See **hoi.**

hoist. To drink, v.i.: (low) coll.: ca. 1860–1920. P.B.: still extant, later C.20, in such joc. phrases as 'let's go and hoist the odd jar', let's go for a drink.—2. To strike (someone) with one's fist: Aus. low. (B., 1942.) Cf. **lift,** n.—3. To discard: Aus.: since ca. 1930. (B.P.) Cf. **heave,** v.—4. To steal: Aus.: mid-C.19–20. B., 1959.

hoist a cock. 'To win a regatta and display a silver or tin cut-out of a cock in the rigging of a winning ship' (Granville, letter, 1962): RN coll.

hoist in. To endure, tolerate; to accept: RN: since ca. 1945. 'I put it to the Commander but he wouldn't hoist it in' (Granville). Cf. later 1980s synon. **take on board.**

hokum, occ. **hocum.** Anything designed to make a melodramatic or a sentimental appeal; bunkum: US (ca. 1920), anglicised by 1926. Prob. ex *hocus(-pocus)* on *bunkum. OED* Sup.

hol. See **hols.**

hold. See **put on hold.**

hold a spear. 'To take a very minor non-speaking part' (P.B.): Aus. theatrical: since 1950; by 1965, coll. Cf. Brit. **spear-carrier.**

hold a tangi. See **tangi.**

hold (one's) **corner.** To hold one's own against others: coll., esp. Lancashire: (?)mid-C.19–20. (Roberts, 1976.) Perhaps ex boxing.

hold down (e.g. a job). To overcome the difficulties of; hence to do satisfactorily, with the connotation of keeping abreast of the 'snags' and problems of a difficult job: coll., orig. (ca. 1890) US, anglicised ca. 1910.

hold it. (As imperative.) Stay in precisely that position!: painters' s. (from ca. 1895) > coll. ca. 1910 in the theatrical, and ca. 1925 in the cinematographic world.—2. Hence, **Wait! In later C.20 has var. *hold everything*. Cf. **hang about!** (P.B.)

hold no brief for. Not to support, defend, actively sympathise with (a person): coll.: since ca. 1910. *OED* Sup.

hold out on. To keep something (esp. money or important information) back from (a person): adopted, ex US, ca. 1924.

hold the bag. To be duped: c.: from ca. 1920. By 1940, at latest, it was gen. s., usu. in the form *be left holding the bag*. Can. has, since ca. 1950, used also an extended form: *(be) holding the nose bag*, 'left in a ridiculous position after somebody has stolen the horse' (Leechman). 'Rather, I suggest, from the "snipe hunt", a practical joke current (among hunters, cowboys, etc.) in 1900 or earlier, in which the victim (usually a "greenhorn") is literally left holding the bag. Cf. under "snipe hunt" in Bernard Botkin, *A Treasury of American Folklore*' (R.C., 1966).

hold the fort. To mind the shop for someone while he's away (e.g. urinating): coll. Hence to deputise or substitute temporarily in all sorts of posts.

hold the phone! 'Wait, stop, don't go!: as in "Hold the phone while I just . . . ". Widespread N. Am., prob. since earlier C.20 when telephones became common' (Leech, 1986).

hold tight! Stop!; don't move!; Steady!: coll.: since ca. 1910. Ex bus-conductor's adjuration.

hold-up. A highway robbery; any robbery in which a person is held up at firearm-point: orig. US; anglicised ca. 1905 as a coll.; by ca. 1933, S.E.

holding. In funds: Aus. and NZ: s. > coll. Esp. *how are you holding?*, how much money have you? Cf. **financial**.

Hole, the. The Severn Tunnel: railwaymen's: late C.19–20. (*Railway*.) A specialisation of railwaymen's gen. s. *hole*, any tunnel; from mid-C.19.—2. The underground Operations Room at Fighter Command Headquarters, Bentley Priory, 1940–5: RAF: after 1945, merely historical. (R.S.)

hole, n. (Gen. in pl.) A shilling: tramps' c.:—1935. Also grafters' s.:—1934 (*Cheapjack*).

hole, or **hole out, in one.** To become pregnant as the result of one's first amour: Aus.: since ca. 1910. (B., 1942.) Ex golf.—2. Often used at male parties just before the marriage of the guest of honour, in relation to first-night intercourse. 'A man who "does it the first night" is a "man". One who does not is a "mouse" and one who has already done it is a "rat" ' (a valued correspondent): Aus.: since ca. 1920.

hole-in-the-wall employer. A small employer of sweated labour: Labour coll. (almost j.). Sells, 1923.

hole up, v.; **hole-up**, n. To hide; a hiding place: Aus. c. (B., 1942), adopted, ca. 1930, ex US; in later C.20, also occ. Brit. coll. In N. Africa, 1940–2, Aus. troops used *hole up* for 'to lie hidden'; later Brit. usage seems to prefer, e.g., 'I was holed up in this dreadful hotel . . . '

holiday. A transfer from a position to an easier one: c.

Holland. See LOVERS' ACRONYMS, in Appx.

holler wagon. 'The police radio car ("holler" = to shout)' (Tempest): c.: mid-C.20.

hollow-legs. Applied to a thin person, usu. male, who habitually eats a great deal; often in the potential, never quite realised, c.p., *he's* (occ. *she's*) *got hollow legs*, and sometimes also as a nickname. As 'Mr Hollowlegs' it appears in Hildick, 1976. The term goes back to C.19—I first heard it ca. 1904.—2. Hence anyone, again usu. male, who habitually drinks a considerable quantity of beer: heard in Service messes, post WW2. (P.B.)

Hollow Tooth, the. 'Ironic and disgruntled term for New Scotland Yard, used by some police, and thus by certain knowledgeable criminals. Very much an "in" term' (Powis, 1977).

Holloway's Unfinished Symphonies. The Maunsell forts erected in the estuary of the Thames: WW2. Ex the contractor's name? P-G-R.

hols. (Rarely *hol*, a single day's holiday; and in *half-hol*, a half day's holiday.) Holidays: orig. and mainly schools'. The *OED* Sup. dates at 1906, but the term was in use at least five

years earlier. The term is often treated as a singular. Thus Lunn, 1919, 'Where are you going this hols?'; 'Did you have a good hols?'

Holstein. A police car: Can.: since the mid-1950s. The black and white cars are likened to the black and white cattle. (Leechman, 1968.)

Holy City, the. St Albans: railwaymen's. *Railway*, 2nd.—2. Married quarters at the RN submarine base at Faslane, Holy Loch: RN: later C.20. (Winton, 1971.) Prob. ex *Holy* Loch, with a pun on *hole*, vagina.

Holy Communion. 'Rum collected by the Coxswain in a bottle and drunk quite illegally by the Chiefs' and Petty Officers' messes on Sundays, especially in small ships' (Osmond, 1948): RN.

Holy Ghost. The winning post: turf r.s. P.P., 1932.—2. Toast (bread): orig. WW2 Army r.s. (Franklyn); the term soon > gen., and still is so; I heard it casually uttered in June 1976.

holy ground. Those parts of a ship prohibited to the lower deck. Knock.—2. Used joc. and gen. for any area of restricted access. E.g., in the Army: 'You mustn't walk on the drill square! My God, that's the RSM's holy ground!' (P.B.)—3. As *the Holy Ground*, Ireland, in traditional ballads; *the boys of the Holy Ground*: coll. (Raab.)

holy Joe. 'The shallow, circular-crowned hat worn by clergymen' (*Slang*): ecclesiastical.—2. Hence, any, esp. ostentatiously, pious man: coll.: late C.19–20. (B. & L.) In Aus., a narrow-minded 'goody-goody'. B., 1942.

holy mackerel! A mild oath, imported, ca. 1944, ex US. 'Probably euphemistic for "Holy Michael!" but perhaps with a hidden dig at [US] "mackerel snappers"—Roman Catholics, who were (then) supposed to eat fish on Fridays' (R.C., 1976).

holy nail. Bail (legal): mostly c.: late C.19–20. *Underworld*, 1961.

Holy Rollers, the. Roman Catholics: since ca. 1920.

holy water. Water 'laced' with whiskey.

home. As *H-*, Great Britain and Ireland; esp., and gen., England: Colonial: prob. first in US (by 1912 very ob., says Thornton) in C.18. In C.20, mostly Aus. and NZ; esp. as *at Home*, *go Home*. A coll. usage bordering on—indeed, by *OED* considered as—S.E.—2. As *the Home*, the preventive-detention part of Camp Hill prison: c.: from ca. 1925. Cf.—3. A convict prison: c.:—1932 ('Wood').—4. In *go home*, (of clothes) to begin wearing out; to wear out: lower classes':—1923 (Manchon). B., 1941, notes this also as NZ: 'When an article of clothing, etc., ceases to be of service it is said *to have gone home*', and relates it to visiting *Home*, i.e. Britain, in old age; more likely ex earlier sense of *go home*, to die, and taken out by emigrants from UK.

Home and Colonial. 'One would think that [since its foundation in 1537] the Honourable Artillery Company would have acquired a multitude of nicknames, but only one is recorded—the homely and domestic sobriquet "Home and Colonial" ' (Carew). After the famous chain of food-stores.—2. 'The London-based Regional Crime Squad office, comprising Metropolitan detectives ("Home") and provincial officers ("Colonial")' (Powis): police nickname. Etym. as sense 1.

home-bird. Someone who, perhaps unadventurous, prefers the comforts of his own home: coll. (P.B.)

Home for Lost Frogs, The. London; or England or even Britain: joc.: since ca. 1930. Punning *home for lost dogs*; and, as R.C. points out, with ref. to the British climate. A var., noted by Petch, is *The Home for Lost Fogs*.

homers. A 'home from home' in a port not one's own; a homely, comfortable place: RN since ca. 1925. By the 'OXFORD -*ER*'. See **up homers**.—2. Homework: Public and Grammar schoolchildren's: since ca. 1930. The 'OXFORD -*ER*'.

homework. Girls in gen.; one's girl in particular: RAF since ca. 1935, RN since ca. 1940, Army since 1940 or 1941. (Jackson.) Also *piece* (or *bit*) *of homework* (Partridge, 1945). Cf. **knitting**—2. In *do* (one's) *homework*, to do all the preliminary work necessary for the successful completion of any job, e.g., prepare a lecture, write a book, etc.: coll. from ca. 1955; by early 1970s, S.E. Often negative, in condemnation, 'Unfortunately, the speaker hadn't done his homework.'

homey, n. An Englishman: Aus. and NZ. (B., 1941, 1942.) Ex *Home,* 1. For NZ use, cf. Devanney, 1927, and Mulgan, 1939.—2. Theatrical and grafters' var. of *omee,* a man. *Cheapjack,* 1934.

homey, adj., and **hominess.** See **homy.**

homo, n. A (usu.) male homosexual: since ca. 1925. (Mackenzie, 1933.) Cf.:–

homo, adj. Homosexual: since ca. 1925. 'Mr Arkham's thinkin' very serious abaht the 'omo stuff' (Harrison, 1939). Ex the n.; both n. and adj. were superseded, 1970s, by **gay,** q.v.

homo sap. A derisive alteration, implying that man (*homo*) is more of a 'sap' or fool than a wise man (*sapiens*): since ca. 1930; by 1965, ob.

homy, occ. **homey.** Affable; friendly: coll. See quot'n at **crasher.**

Hon. An Honourable: upper classes' coll.: late C.19–20. Mitford, 1945.

hon. 'Honey' (endearment): Aus. coll.: adopted, ca. 1920, ex US. (Cleary, 1949.) Cf. Aus. use of 'Darl' = darling.

honcho. The person in charge; chief; boss: Aus.: adopted ex US, where orig. Services' s. > gen. s. later 1960s. The *Australian,* 17 Mar. 1986, '[the firm] have scoured the world for a head honcho'. Ex Jap. *hanchō,* group leader (Barnhart, 1).

honest John. An honest citizen: coll.: adopted, ca. 1943, ex US; ob. since its adoption, 1950s, as the name of a short-range ballistic missile.

honest(-)to(-)dinkum. Aus. var. of:–

honest-to-God or **-goodness,** adj. and adv. Real(ly), genuine(ly), thorough(ly): coll., orig. (—1916) US, anglicised by Galsworthy in 1921. *OED* Sup.

honestly! (Often prec. by *Oh!* or *Well!*) An expression of disgust, exasperation, unpleasant surprise. (Petch, 1966.) In later C.20, usu. a middle-class feminine usage.

honey. Abbr. *pot o' honey,* money: r.s.:—1923 (Manchon).—2. An American Stuart tank: Army: 1943–5. P-G-R.—3. 'A shot you are pleased with is a "honey" or a "peach" or an "eagle"' (London *Evening News,* 7 Nov. 1939): cinema: since ca. 1920.—4. Anything choice or excellent: Can., since ca. 1945; Brit. from soon after. Prob. ex US. 'Have you seen Jane's new hair-do? It's a honey!' (Leechman).

honey-bucket. A latrine-receptacle for excreta: Can. military: from 1914. (B. & P.) P.B.: prob. earlier, and certainly later, e.g. in the Far East, esp. in Hong Kong, where the night-soil was still, 1980, removed from older dwellings by municipally-employed 'honey-bucket women'. See also **honey-wagon.**

honey-bun or **bunch.** An attractive girl; also an endearment to one: adopted, ca. 1943, ex US servicemen; also in Aus.

honey-do day. A man's odd, or unexpected, day off from his work, a day his wife will seize upon to urge him to 'Please *do* this, *honey*—please *do* that, *honey*': adopted, 1966, ex US. *Daily Telegraph,* 8 Oct. 1966.

honey-pot. A jumping into water with hands clasped around the knees: Aus. children's. B., 1942.

honey-star. One's sexual mistress: since ca. 1925.

honey thighs. A Can. endearment to a girl: since ca. 1945.

honey-wag(g)on. A night-cart (only in outback towns): Can. In Can., WW1, the corresponding truck was called the *honey-cart.* Cf. **honey-bucket.**

honeymoon cystitis. 'Jocular medical term for inflammation caused by frequent sexual activity in women who have recently lost their virginity' (B.P., 1974): esp. in Aus.: since ca. 1950. *Cystitis*: an inflammation of the female urinary bladder.

honeymoon salad. Lettuce: joc. '*Let us* alone!'

Hong Kong bibles. Small, locally produced, usu. badly printed volumes of pornography, available in Hong Kong: Services': 1960s. (P.B.)

Hong Kong dog. A tropical fever: RN. ('Taffrail'.) Cf. **Malta dog.**

honk, n. A bad smell: Aus.: since ca. 1925. B., 1953, suggests origin in Maori *haunga,* ill-smelling.—2. The nose: Aus. (Niland, 1959.) Echoic. Cf. **honker**—3. A wild party, with much drinking: Eng.: since ca. 1945. (*Daily Express,* 23 July 1959.) Ex **honking.**

honk, v. To vomit: Services', esp. RAF: since ca. 1940 (Farley, 1967); in later C.20, common Glasgow (Munro, 1985). Echoic.—2. To stink: Aus.: since ca. 1925. (B., 1959.) Ex **honk,** n., 1. P.B.: also Brit: low coll.: later C.20. Prob. ex **honk,** n., 2.—3. To grumble or gripe incessantly: Services': later C.20. Dickens, 1983, about the Borneo campaign, 1962–6.—4. See **honking.**

honk like a gaggle of geese. To stink very much indeed: Aus.: since ca. 1930. (B., 1959.) An elab of **honk,** v., 2.

honk (one's) ring up. To vomit violently: Army and RAF: since ca. 1950. An elab. of **honk,** v., 1. Here, *ring* = anus. (Farley; P.B.) Cf.:-

honk up (one's) tank (or **no. 6 tank**). To vomit after a 'beer-up': RAF: WW2.

honked. Drunk: Services': since ca. 1950. (Winton, 1959.) Ex drunken vomiting; cf. **honk,** v., 1.

honker. A (large) nose: Aus., esp. Sydney: since ca. 1910. (Park, 1948.) Ex the *honk* of a motor horn. Cf. **hooter.**

Honkers. Hong Kong: Services', esp. officers'. By the 'Oxford/RN *-er(s)*'; cf. *Singers,* Singapore. (P.B.) Hence, also, *the Honkers and Shankers,* the Hong Kong and Shanghai Banking Corpn. (Granville.)

honkers, like **fried, jugged, sloshed,** is 'drunk' among office- and shop-girls—and presumably their companions—of ca. 1955–60, with one or two of these terms likely to last for another few years. (Gilderdale, 1958.) With **honkers,** cf. **honk,** n., 3, and **honking;** with *jugged,* cf. **jug,** n. and v.; and see **sloshed.** *Honkers* was orig. (ca. 1950) and is still, 1975, Services' s. for 'very drunk'. Farley attests its currency in the RAF, 1967.

Honkie, -y. 'Racist negro expression (unpleasant) for a white person (usually male)' (Powis): since (?)mid-1960s in UK. ?Cf. **honker.**

honking. 'A drinking session' (Granville): RN: since ca. 1940.—2. As adj., drunk: synon with **honked.** (P.B.) Cf. *minging* q.v. at **ming.**—3. Out of the saddle, standing on the pedals for extra power when going uphill: cyclists'. (*Fellowship,* 1984.) London club cyclists, ca. 1930, used *small tea egg and a slice* as descriptive of the rhythm required.

honkoe. A loafer; a seedy punter: Aus.: since ca. 1930. (Dick.) Origin? Perhaps ex Aus. s. *honk,* a bad smell. Wilkes, 1977, notes 'rare'.

honky-tonk (or one word). Jangling piano music; noisy jazz: adopted—?rather adapted—ca. 1950 ex US, where it predominantly means ' a low place of amusement, or a low burlesque show, esp. where strong drink is available'. Origin un known. Perhaps either a rhyming reduplication of *honk,* to make a honking noise (cf. **honk,** n., 3, and **honking**), or related to N.W. England dial. *honk,* to idle about. Also as adj.

honour mods. Honour moderations: Oxford University coll.: earlier C.20. *OED* Sup.

honours (are) easy or **even!** We (etc.) are level: coll. Ex bridge.

hoo. A fuss; perturbation: later 1930s. (March, 1939.) A shortening of the still, 1983, more common *hoo-ha.*

Hoo Flung Dung. A Chinaman: joc. mock-Chinese. (In fact, 'flung' is a syllable/sound non-existent in native Chinese speech. P.B.) Cf. **One Hung Low.**

hoo-ha. An argument; a 'row' or fuss: coll. See **hoohah,** for further observations.—2. 'Twaddle. (A term revived by Margaret Whitlam)' (Humphries, 1982): Aus.

hoo-jahs, the. *Delirium tremens:* Aus.: since ca. 1930. Upfield, 1956.

hooa. See **hoor.**

hooch, hootch. Alcoholic liquor, esp. spirits: coll.: adopted, during WW1, ex US. Ex Alaska *Hoochino*, a very strong drink, made by Alaskan natives. F. & G.; Irwin; *OED* Sup.

hooch in quarters. '*Hooching in quarters*. Holding a party in one's room' (H. & P.): Services': since ca. 1940; ob. by 1950. Ex prec.

hoochie or **hoochy.** A temporary shelter serving as living-quarters: among United Nations troops in Korea: ca. 1951–5. Ex Japanese *uchi*, a house. *Iddiwah*, July 1953.

hood. A hoodlum: Can.,—1949; in Brit. Eng., since ca. 1965, a (usu. petty) gangster: adopted ex US.

hoodoo. Such an adverse charm as the evil eye; any person or thing causing bad luck (cf. *Jonah*): orig. (—1885), 1881 resp., US; anglicised, as a coll., ca. 1910, but common in Aus. several years earlier. Prob. *voodoo* corrupted; *voodoo* being a Dahomey native word.—2. Hence, adj.: unlucky: anglicised ca. 1920.—3. A useless hand shanghaied by a crimp as an AB: nautical: from ca. 1910. Bowen.

hooer. See **hoor.**

hooey. Nonsense; 'eyewash': adopted, ca. 1937, ex US. Short for *ballyhooey*.—2. A (loud) disturbance: 1940s. (Allingham, 1947.) Like **hoo**, q.v, prob. ex *hoo-ha*.

hoof, n. In *get the hoof*, to be dismissed or turned out: proletarian. (George, 1914.)—2. See **Harry hoof**.

hoof, v. i.; also *hoof it*. To dance: from mid-1920s. *OED* Sup.

hoof-and-mouth disease. Boasting, esp. at night to one's wife, of one's exploits at golf: joc. coll.: from ca. 1923. Also **foot-and-mouth-disease**, q.v.

hoofer. A dancer: Can.: since ca. 1925. Ex **hoof**, v.—2. A chorus girl: Aus.: adopted, ca. 1930, ex US. Cleary, 1954.

hoohah (or **hoo-ha**). A water-closet: since ca. 1920: domestic coll. Brand, 1941, spells it *huhhah*. R.S. suggests its orig., perhaps not entirely seriously, as 'the grunting *hoo!* of effort, followed by the *ha!* of satisfaction.' But see 3.—2. A two-tone warning horn, as on an ambulance: since ca. 1955. Petch cites the Bournemouth *Evening Echo*, 21 Apr. 1966.—3. But earlier is the group of nuances noted at **hoo-ha**: 'argument' or 'a row', a noisy fuss, which are extant, indeed, active, during the 1980s and they look like being with us for some time, as in *make a (big) hoohah* or fuss over something. Of this subgroup, R.C. wrote in 1976: ' "Hoo, hah!" is a not uncommon Yiddish exclamation, meaning approximately "What's all this?" Hence also the n. meaning fuss'—which is decidedly relevant to the origin of the term. Cf. Fr. *brouhaha*.

hook, n. That member of a confidence-trick gang whose job it is to introduce the prospective victim: c.:—1935 (Hume).—2. A shop-lifter: c.—3. An anchor: nautical: since ca. 1890. Hence, an anchor badge: RN.—4. A chevron, NCO's badge, usu. in pl *hooks*: Aus. Army, since ca. 1910; also occ. in Brit. Army. B., 1943; P.B.—5. A '7': Aus. poker players': since ca. 1920. (B., 1953.) Cf. *crutch*, a 7 at Tombola.—6. *On the hook*, in HAULIERS' s. (see Appx.) = on tow: since ca. 1920.—7. *Off the hook* has two senses: Aus., since ca. 1920, of a married man 'out with the boys' (B.P.); and Can., since ca. 1945, hence also Brit., 'out of a difficult or embarrassing situation: often as *get (one) off the hook*.' (Leechman; P.B.)

hook, v. To punch (someone): Aus.: since ca. 1925. (Dick.) Ex boxing: the punch known as *the hook*.—2. See **hooking.**

hook! Run away!: 1908, Hutchinson, ' "Hook!" said Bob. David asked: "What's hook?" "Run away." ' Ex much older synon. *hook it*.

hook in. See **tuck in.**

hook-pot. The 'lower regions' of a warship, or even the ship itself regarded adversely: RN lowerdeck: (?)ca. 1890–1940. (Knock.)

hook-up (a horse) is applied to a jockey that prevents it from winning, usually by strong-arm tactics: Aus. sporting: since ca. 1930. (Glassop, 1949.) By 1940, also Brit., as in 'The occasional horse will be "*stopped*" or "*hooked up*" ' (Lawrence, 1961).

hook-up party. 'Men who, for some reason, avoid Divisions' (Granville): RN.

hook up with. To join forces with; occ. merely 'to encounter': coll., also Can.: since ca. 1910. (Leechman.)

hooked. (Hopelessly) addicted to drugs: orig. US, adopted in Can., ca. 1925; by 1945 also Brit. and Aus.: esp. among drug addicts. *The Times*, 19 Feb. 1964.—2. Hence, in later C.20, used fig. of addiction to anything, from a girl, to golf, to chocolates: coll. Usu. as *hooked on*. (P.B.)

hooked on. (Of a woman) casually 'picked up': Aus. B., 1942. Cf. sense 2 of:-

hooked up. Dead: low:—1923 (Manchon); ob.—2. Provided with a sweetheart or a temporary girl: low. Hyder, 1934.

hooker. A shunter: railwaymen's. *Railway*, 2nd.—2. A drink of strong liquor: Can.: since ca. 1930. (Leechman, 1976.)—3. 'Transatlantic term for a prostitute becoming current [in UK], probably because of American hippy influence' (Powis, 1977). Well enough naturalised to appear in the *New Statesman* leader, 13 May 1983: '[Mrs Thatcher] alone appeared not to know that Ms [Maggie] May was a celebrated Merseyside hooker'—a ref. to the Prime Minister's nickname *Maggie* in the press, and the old ballad about 'Maggie May, they have taken her away . . .' (P.B.)

hooking. 'A dishonest informer attempting to entangle public officials or police officers in a proposed crime, for his own benefit' (Powis): c., and police s.: later C.20.

hooks. Brakes: motorcyclists' s.: later C.20. (Dunford.) Cf. **anchors** used in this sense, and **hook**, n., 3.—2. *Get* (or *got*) *her hooks into* (a man), (of a woman) to have him in tow, or engaged, or married: since ca. 1920.—3. In *down on the hooks*, holding the lowest point of the dropped handlebars: cyclists'. *Fellowship*, 1984.—4. See **put the hooks on.**

hookum. A regulation; the hookum, 'the correct thing': Army coll.: late C.19–early 20. (F. & G.) Ex Hindustani *hukam*.—2. Hence, true information: Army: ca. 1920–40.

hooky, n. A Leading Seaman: RN: since ca. 1900. (H. & P.) 'Ex the anchor he wears as a badge of office' (Granville).

hooler hoop. The ringed keel of a nuclear submarine of the Dreadnought type: RN and dockyards': early 1960s, when the *hula hoop* craze raged briefly (Granville).

hooley or **hoolie.** A spree; later (by 1970), simply a party: orig. Anglo-Irish, perhaps from the Irish Guards. In Glasgow, a wild party (Munro, 1985). Perhaps a var. of the Gaelic *ceilidh*, pron. *kaley* (Raab).—2. A storm, esp. with a lot of wind: Liverpool. (K. Irwin, 1985.) Knight, 1984, notes gen. nautical *blowin' a hoolie*, strong winds. Cf. next, 3.

hooligan. A lively rough, not necessarily nor usually criminal: from ca. 1895: s. till ca. 1910, then coll.; in later C.20, S.E. Most prob. ex Irish surname Ó hUallacháin, which normally appears in anglicised form as 'Houlihan, Hoolohan' (Quin).—2. An Oerlikon gun: RN: WW2. By a pun. Granville.—3. ' "Holligan" is the half-fearful, half-respectful term for the kind of blizzard that lashed Southern Cornwall in December 1981' (Bhatia, 1983): a local specialisation of sense 1.—4. See **Hereford Hooligans.**

hooly van. 'A van for photographic surveillance of football crowds which is also likely to be used to watch demonstrations and riots . . . [is] known unofficially as the hooly van' (*Guardian*, 9 May 1985): police. A pun on the prec.

hoon, whence the rhyming *silver spoon*, a procurer of prostitutes: Aus. c.: since ca. 1935. (B., 1953.) Herbert, 1939, ' "You flash hoon," he went on, "Kiddin you're white, eh?" ' Perhaps of immigrant origin, as R.S. has suggested; he suspects German.

hoop. A jockey: Aus. sporting: since ca. 1920. (B., 1942.) E.P. has 'with a pun on race-course *ring*': I suggest ex the jockey's colours (P.B.).—2. *Go through the hoop*, as in circus tricks, was C.19 s. for to pass through the Insolvent Debtors' court. Hence, in C.20 coll., to have a bad time of it; and, as military specialisation, to be up for punishment (F. & G.): ca. 1910–50.—3. Hence, *put through the hoop*, to give a bad time to, to punish: coll. Hence, to reprimand, or question closely: from ca. 1912.

hoopy (**?whoopy**). Superlatively good; excellent: teenagers': early 1980s. (James Williamson, 1982.) Cf. synon. **smeary**.

hoor, hooer, hooa or **hua**. A sol. pronunciation of *whore*: C.19–20. Sometimes used joc., in mock-Scot, 'Ye dirty wee hoor'; but may be used fig., to a man, with serious intent to insult or abuse. Also NZ and Aus., as in Niland, 1955: 'Get out of here, you drunken hooer.'

hooray, n. Good news, as in 'the other bit of hooray that the truck fraternity had been telling me . . . ' (a reporter on BBC Radio 4 News, 14 Apr. 1983).

hooray! This coll. form of *hurrah*, *hurray* is half-way between dignity and impudence: C.18–20.—2. Good-bye!: Aus. and NZ: since ca. 1930. Leonard Mann, *Mountain Flat*, 1939, ' "Good-bye, Jim, good-bye, Lottie." "Hooray, George," Jim answered.' Cf. **hooroo!**

Hooray Henry. An upper-middle class (or would-be upper-middle class), 'wahwah' (q.v.)-speaking male, often affecting a heartiness that appears bogus to ill-disposed observers: journalistic: from late 1970s. 'A gang of Hooray Henrys from Sotheby's travel round the country crying "Bring out your junk" ' (Barnes, 1979). The term was invented by Jim Godbolt (see bibliog.), who drew my attention, 1985, to the journalistic *hooray Henrietta*, used for the female of the species.

hooroo! Goodbye!: Aus.: since early C.20. B., 1942, who lists also *aroo*. Perhaps ex *au revoir*.—2. C.20 var. of **hooray!**, 1.

hoosegow. A jail: US s.; some joc. use in UK: since early C.20. Ex 'S. Amer. or Mex. Sp. *juzgao* = *juzgado*, tribunal' (*OED*).

hoosh. A thick soup with plenty of body: 1905 (Scott).—2. 'Hoosh—corned beef prepared as a hash with potatoes' (*Daily Colonist*, Victoria, BC, 19 June 1960): R Can. N: ca. 1900–25. Cf. the RN **spud-oosh**, 'Kind of stew in which rather sodden potatoes predominate' (Granville), and **oos-me-goosh**.

hoosh out. To force (water) out:—1923 (Manchon). E.P. proposes derivation ex Irish dial. *hoosh*, to heave or raise; more prob. merely echoic (P.B.). Also in form **oosh**, q.v.

hooshgoo. A cook: Can. Cf. **hoosh**.

hooshing. Landing at high speed: RAF: 1938+. (H. & P.) Echoic.

hoosie Frazer. Razor: Glasgow r.s., on *House of Frazer*, the vast retailing organization. Sometimes shortened to *hoosie*. Munro. 1985.

hoot, n. A cause for laughter; nearly always in such exclamation as 'That's a hoot!' (sarcastic) or 'What a hoot!', that *is* funny (not necessarily kindly meant): coll.: since ca. 1940. Ex the sound, to *hoot* with laughter. (P.B.)

hoot, v. To stink: Aus. low: since ca. 1920. (B., 1942.) Cf. **honk**, v.

hooter. A wooden trumpet designed to make a horrible noise: coll. >, by 1930, S.E.—2. (?)Hence, the nose: low joc.: since ca. 1940.

hootin' Annie. A var., partly joc. and partly folk-etym., of the American *hootenanny*, an informal variety show held around a so-called camp fire: Aus. surfers' coll., adopted ca. 1962. (*Pix*, 28 Sep. 1963.) *Hootenanny* is of obscure origin and, in 1963, was still mainly dialectal. At first, as in 'I don't give a hootenanny, I don't care a damn.'

Hoover. See HAULAGE, in Appx.

hoover. 'A Hovercraft, or to fly in a hovercraft, as in "We're hoovering across the Channel" ' (Watts. 1988). Contrast:–

hoovering. 'The now famous "sweeps" by Fighter Command over Northern France. They get into all the corners!' (H. & P., 1943): RAF. Ex the Hoover vacuum-cleaner.—2. 'In use among Cockneys during the 1940 blitz: applied to the undulating note of the unsynchronized engines of the German Heinkel 111 bomber' (H.R. Spencer).

hop, n. (*hop* or *Hop*). A policeman: low Aus.:—1935. Perhaps suggested by synon. *cop*. Cf. **John Hop**.—2. A stage (the flying done in one day, or at a stretch: e.g. 'We did it in two hops') of a long journey by air: RAF coll.: since ca. 1925.

Jackson.—3. Opium: drugs c. (Stockley, 1986.) US throughout C.20 (Spears).

hop, v. To get a lift on (a vehicle), as in 'I'll hop a lorry'; whence *lorry-hopping*: Services' (orig. Army): since ca. 1918; by 1946, civilian. (P-G-R.) Elliptical for *hop on to*.—2. Hence, simply to board, as *hop a tram* or *a bus*: coll.: since ca. 1945.

hop Harry. A bowler hat: Aus.: since ca. 1920. (B., 1942.) It'll just *bowl* along.

hop it. To depart quickly: coll., orig. Cockney: from ca. 1912. In the form *'op it!*, it is (when not illiterate) joc. *John o' London's Weekly*, 23 Mar. 1935.

hop on. (Of men) to coït: low. Ingram, 1935.

hop-out, n. A definite challenge to fight: mostly Aus.: from ca. 1908. Ex:-

hop out, v. To challenge (a person) to fight: lower classes' and military: earlier C.20. F. & G.

hophead. A wild fellow; a rash, foolish one: NZ: since ca. 1943. (Slatter.) Ex:—2. A drug addict: orig. US, an opium addict, early C.20 (*Underworld*); in later C.20, adopted ex US, usu. of a marijuana-user.

hopped up. Under the influence of an exhilarating drug: Can.: adopted, ex US, ca. 1935; by ca. 1945, s. Cf. **hophead**, 2.

hopper. A bus inspector: Londoners': since ca. 1935. He keeps hopping on and off buses.

hoppies. Fleas: Cockneys'. *Muvver*.

hops. To be *on the hops* is to be on a drinking bout: c.: ca. 1920–50. I.e. *on the beer*.—2. Hence, (to have) *got* (one's) *hops in*: to be tipsy: c.:—1933 (Leach).—3. As exclam., (acclamation for) a winning throw: darts-players': since ca. 1930. 'A double thirteen achieved this. If you get a single, you are said to be *split* or *cracked*, with two darts left and thirteen to make' (Granville).—4. *The hops*: the school lavatories: Mills G.S., Framlingham, Suffolk: 1960s. (P. Kirkland, 1986.)

Horace. 'A jocular form of address, often used by men to boys in offices, etc.' (Petch, 1946): coll.: earlier C.20.

horizontal. Tipsy—very tipsy: Service officers': since ca. 1935. H. & P.

horizontal champion. 'One with an infinite capacity for sleep' (Granville): RN: since ca. 1930. Ironic. Ex boxing.

horizontal exercise. Sexual intercourse: RN (?Aus. only): since ca. 1930.—2. Merely, sleep: Services' joc. coll.: mid-C.20.

horizontal relaxation. Sexual intercourse: Aus. and NZ low joc.: since late 1940s. (Slater, 1978.)

Horlicks. In *make a* (*right*) *Horlicks of* (anything), to make a complete mess of it: euph. for *ballocks* in this sense/usage: early 1980s. (*Sunday Express* supp., 11 Oct. 1982.) Ex the well known brand of soporific beverage.

horn. As a drink, almost wholly US since C.18. In later C.20, at latest, it appears to have been adopted in Can., to judge from Dempsey, 1975, 'Take down flask from shelf and pour stiff horn down your throat'.

horn in (**on**). To interfere; to intrude upon: Aus., late C.19–20; Brit. since earlyish C.20. Sayers, 'Glaisher might not like this horning in on his province.' Ex cattle.

horn-pills. Aphrodisiacs: low: since ca. 1910. Ex *horn*, an erection: s. since C.18.

horn sticks. Celery: Cockneys'. *Muvver*.

Hornet's Nest, the. Heligoland Bight: RAF Bomber Command: 1939–41. Ex multitudes of German fighters based near by.

horns. Cattle: Aus. coll.: late C.19–20. Russell, 1934, 'A mob of "horns" for the markets of the south.'

hornswoggle. Nonsense, humbug: ca. 1860–1905. Ex US *hornswoggle*, to cheat, deceive (1852). 'Believed to be of *American* origin' (H., 1864; Thornton). P.B.: both n. and v. have appeared in English print in 1980, used resp. in *New Statesman*, 25 Jan. and in *The Times*, 5 Mar.

horny, n. A bull, steer, cow: Aus.

horny, adj. With rising *membrum*; disposed for carnal woman: C.19–20 low coll. Esp. in *feel horny*.—2. Hence, sexually exciting or stimulating, as, e.g., a pornographic book or picture: low coll.: since ca. 1950. (P.B.)—3. To *sleep horny*, to go to bed naked and be sensually aware of it: later C.20. Callow, 1968.

horny-steerer. A bullock driver: Aus.: ca. 1920–50. B., 1943.

Horrible. HMAS *Melbourne*: RAN: ca. 1950–80. 'Living conditions [aboard] . . . were by and large abysmal and, noting that the original name of [HMAS] Sydney had been HMS Terrible, the sailors were quick to dub the two carriers HMAS Terrible and HMAS Horrible' (Robertson, 1985).

horrible, n. A larrikin: Aus.: ca. 1925–55. B., 1943.

horrible man. 'Sergeant's sarcastic mode of address' (H. & P.): Army, mostly in recruit training, as, 'Come 'ere, you 'orrible little man, you!': since ca. 1930.

horrors. '(*a*) Acute psychosis caused by amphetamines. (*b*) Depression after stopping amphetamines. (*c*) Heroin withdrawal symptoms' (Home Office): drug addicts': later C.20. Cf. C.19–20 use of the term for *delirium tremens*.—2. Menstruation: schoolgirls': later C.20. Clark, 1980.

horrorscope. A frightening horoscope-reading: since ca. 1930.

hors d'œuvre book. An order book: Aus. joc.: since ca. 1950.

horse. A vocative to a man whose name isn't known: RN: since ca. 1917; some later use in other Services. Often, *old horse*.—2. A practical joke: University of Alberta: 1930s. Prob. ex S.E. *horse-play*.—3. A prostitute: RN since late 1940s. Ex the pl. *whores*.—4. Hence, 'a casual girlfriend, as opposed to a *party*, who is a more steady acquaintance' (Granville, 1962): since ca. 1950.—5. Heroin: drug addicts'; hence, very soon, police: adopted, ca. 1945, ex US, where orig. c. 'Because it has more "kick" than the softer drugs' (R.S., 1969).

horse-and-buggy. Old-fashioned; antiquated: Can. (prob. ex US) coll.: since ca. 1925; by 1955, S.E.

Horse and Cart, the. The 'Wolverhampton to Willesden parcels train' (*Railway*, 2nd): railwaymen's:—1966.

horse and cart. '*Fart*.' ' 'orsed' and ' 'orsin' give the past and present participles of the verb. The term is not generally used for the verb's infinitive' (Hillman, 1974): r.s.: later C.20.—2. 'A locomotive and guard's brake van' (McKenna, 1): railwaymen's: mid-C.20.

horse and horse. 'When shaking dice, best two out of three, if the first two throws result in a tie, the players have *a horse apiece*, or are *horse and horse*' (Leechman): Can. See also **horse on one.**

horse and trap. To defecate: r.s., on *crap*. Franklyn.

horse bandages. Puttees: RAF: 1930s. Tredrey, 1939.

horse-box. 'Control station in the engine room containing the engine controls, switchboard, alarms, etc.' (Malin, 1979): Townsend Thoresen ferry-crews'.

horse-doctor. A medical officer: occ. Forces' usage in WW2.

horse it. To work hard: coll.

horse on one, have a. When rolling best of three, to be one down: Can. dice-players': since ca. 1925. See also **horse and horse.**

horse-painting. The disguising of racehorses: racing-world coll. Lane, 1938.

horse(-)pug. A horse-driver on a labouring job: Aus.: since ca. 1910. (B., 1942.) Rough on the horse's mouth.

horse with the green tail. See **showing the girls . . .**

horsed. Exhilarated with heroin: drug addicts': since ca. 1950. (Cook, 1962.) See **horse,** 5.

horses. Short for *galloping horses*, q.v.: RAF: since ca. 1930. 'He's got his horses' = he's been promoted to Warrant Officer. (Bebbington.)—2. See **horse's hoof.**—3. For *water* (one's) *horses* see **water** (one's) **nag,** to urinate.

horses and carts. (The game of) darts: mostly theatrical. (Franklyn.) Contrast **horse and cart,** q.v.

horse's arse or **hoss's ass** is contemptuous for a person disliked and distrusted: Can. (esp. soliders). Joc. elab.: (*the*) *north end of a horse going south*,—or (*the*) *east end of a horse heading west*. Cf.:–

horse's hang-down. Var. of prec.: Can.: later C.20.

---

horse's hoof; often shortened to *horses*. A male homosexual: r.s. on *poof*: since ca. 1910. Cf. the commoner **iron (hoof).**

horse's neck. A drink of ginger ale and brandy: Public Schools' and RN: since ca. 1925. Granville; *Daily Telegraph*, 14 Aug. 1956.—2. A polite form of *horse's ass*: Can.: since ca. 1920.

horsing around. The playing of practical jokes: Can. Servicemen's: since not later than 1939. (H. & P.) Cf. S.E. *horseplay*.

hose or **hosepipe.** To spray liquid fire from a flame-thrower: Army: 1941+. P-G-R.

hose job. A deception; cheating, a swindle, as in 'I gave him a real hose job when he bought that old car': W. Can.: mid-C.20, now ob., except in smaller communities. (Leech, 1986.)

hosepipes. 'Cheap tubulars [= tyres] used by the impecunious' (*Fellowship*, 1984): club cyclists': earlier C.20.

hoser. 'A guy, a person, usu. implying contempt. Poss. Ontario orig., also now used in Maritimes, and to a lesser degree in W. Can.: since ca. 1970. Reported heard for a prostitute (Calgary usage), but I have never heard it so used' (Leech, 1986).

hosing. 'Failure meant a beating with a length of rubber pipe. Even that had its special euphemism; it was called a hosing or siphoning' (Sinclair, 1977): Eton: mid-C.20.

hospital bum. 'A young doctor who, having completed his medical training, cannot persuade himself to leave the hospital and enter general practice. This psychological block is so well known to the profession that those afflicted by it have become known as "hospital bums". I first heard it in October 1961' (Leechman). Can. medical: since late 1950s.

hosteller. A 'scrounger' and/or adventurer frequenting Work Aid Homes and such places: vagrants' c.: from ca. 1920. Gape, 1936.

hostie. An airline hostess: Aus.: since ca. 1955. Culotta, 1960, ' "That hostie's a slashin' line," Dennis said.'

hostile. 'Inimical, esp. to hoboes' (Niven): Can. tramps': late C.19–20; adopted ex US.—2. (Often pron. *horstile*.) Angry, annoyed; esp. *go hostile*: Aus. and NZ military: WW1+. In later C.20 > Aus. gen.

hostile ord. An ordinary seaman enlisted for 'hostilities only' (q.v.): RN: WW1, and revived in 1939. *OED* Sup. 1976.

Hostile Territory. Eastern Region: railwaymen's: since mid-1940s. *Railway*, 2nd.

hostilities (only). Those who joined the Navy for 'the duration of hostilities only': RN: WW1. Bowen.

hot, v. To reprimand severely: coll.: 1920s. (*OED* Sup.) Ex *give it hot*, in the same sense.

hot, adj. (Of a horse, in C.20 also of persons) much betted-on. Esp. in *hot favourite*. Orig. (1894) racing, from ca. 1905, gen. sporting s. Esp., in C.20, regarded as likely to win, e.g. of a candidate in an election.—2. Exceedingly skilful. Cf. **hot on** and **hot stuff.** Collinson.—3. In insurance s., applied to a very likely insurer, a promising 'prospect', q.v. Ex *hot* in children's games.—4. Excessive, extreme: from ca. 1910. Dennis.—5. (Of a Treasury bill) newly issued: coll.: 1928. (*OED* Sup.) Cf.:–6. Novel, new: orig. Bootham School, 1925 (Bootham); by 1933, gen. This anticipated the sense 'recent or fresh' as applied to information, as in **hot gen,** q.v. P.B.: and presumably a shortening of *hot from the* [news-] *press*.—7. Stinking; (e.g. of fish) stale: Aus. traders': since ca. 1930. B., 1953.—8. Stolen: Can. (ex US) since ca. 1925; Brit. and Aus., since ca. 1935. Orig. c.; by 1945, at latest, s. Cf. **hotstuff,** v.—9. Hence, smuggled: Aus.: since late 1930s. (B.P.)—10. As a term of 'all purpose praise', it was noted as 'in' (= vogue) by Dempster, 1979.—11. In *make it hot*, to ask too much; exaggerate grossly; in short, to behave as if one were ignorant of the limits and limitations imposed by the commonest decency: s. >, by 1930, coll. Esp. in *don't make it too hot!* Prob. ex S.E. *make it hot*, i.e. uncomfortable, *for*.—12. *Not so hot*, bad; unattractive; inefficient; ineffective: adopted, ca. 1930, ex US. In fact, the forerunning negative of sense 10.

hot air. Boastful or exaggerated talk; talk for the sake of effect: from ca. 1910. Ex US, where used by George Ade in 1899.—2. Hence, *hot-air merchant*, rare in England, and *hot-air artist*, a person indulging in this sort of thing: anglicised ca. 1913. *OED* Sup.—3. For *hot-air round*, see **round**, n., 2.

hot and bothered, all. See **all hot and bothered.**

hot and cold. Gold: r.s. Franklyn 2nd.

hot as a fire-cracker. Sexually hot-blooded and promiscuous: Can.: since ca. 1910.

hot at. See **hot on.**

hot-bot. A highly sexed or over-sexed girl; often *Miss Hotbot* or *Lady Hotbot*: non-aristocratic, non-cultured: since ca. 1920.

hot cack. Good; very good: Aus. low. (B., 1942.) With a low pun on *go like hot cakes*. B.P. doubts the pun and thinks *hot cack* a semi-euph. for **shit-hot.**

hot cock. (Utter) nonsense: Aus.: since ca. 1940. (B., 1959.) Cf. synon. *a lot of cock.* Not to be confused with:—2. *Give* (usu. a female) (usu. *six*) *inches of hot cock*, to copulate with: low, raffish: since mid-C.20. (L.A., 1974.)

hot cross bun. On the run (from the police): r.s. Franklyn.

hot dog. A Malibu board, i.e. a wide, not very large, board, made of 'foam' and sheathed with fibreglass: Aus. surfers': adopted, ca. 1960, ex Hawaii. Hence, *hot-dogging* (n. and adj.), making 'fast turns and fancy stunts on waves' (*Pix*, 28 Sep. 1963): since ca. 1961.—2. Hence, 'a bit of fancy skiing' (*LAM*, 4 Feb. 1986): skiers': later C.20.

hot drop, the latest. The latest fad or fashion; the latest craze of any kind: Aus.: since ca. 1950. (B.P.)

hot fog. Steam: RN (engineers'): since ca. 1930.

hot foot. To hasten; walk very quickly, to run; to decamp speedily: adopted ca. 1917 from US. But mostly *hot foot it*. As adv. it is, despite F. & H., S.E.

hot gen. Up-to-the-minute information: RAF: 1939+. See also **hot**, adj., 6.

hot joint. 'A [taxicab] rank is a "mark", and the first position is the "point" or "hot joint" ' (Hodge, 1939): taxi-drivers': since ca. 1920. Cf. the Army's **sweat on the top line.**

hot line. A telephone line without a switchboard: coll., orig. political: since ca. 1960.

hot load. An overdose of drugs, which may be fatal: drugs c. (Stockley, 1986.) Hibbert, 1983, has var. *hot shot*, current in 1950s.

hot money. Stolen notes of numbers known: c.: from ca. 1930. Ex US. Cf. **hot**, adj., 5 and 8.

hot on. Extremely severe towards or in respect of: s. > coll.—2. Unusually good or skilful at: from ca. 1895: coll. Var., *hot at*. Cf. **hot stuff.**

hot pants. In *have hot pants* (for someone): esp. of women: to be very much in love: adopted, ca. 1938, from US. Cheyney, *passim*. P.B.: as absolute, e.g., 'She's got hot pants, that one' or 'She's a hot-panted one', it is synon. with the earlier *hot-arsed*, extremely lascivious; later C.20.—2. Tight-fitting female short trousers, a form of *lederhosen* in other materials, designed to indicate, or even to emphasise, the vulval crease: a short-lived fashion of ca. 1970–1. Cf. **mini.**

hot-plater. 'A person who drives a car that is painted to look like a taxi and operates mainly at night to avoid detection' (B., 1953): since ca. 1945. Also called a *flea*. P.B.: prob. a ref. to the vehicle's number-plate, as in Hong Kong Cantonese *baak pai* (= white plate, where taxi plates are red), for an illegal taxi.

hot poop. Latest information: RAF: 1970s. (*Fighter Pilot*, 1981.) Presumably *shit-hot*. Hibbert, 1983, notes its use among young people generally.

hot pot. An 'engine emitting steam from safety valves' (*Railway*, 2nd): earlier C.20.

hot potato. A political, or a sociological, problem too hot to handle comfortably: adopted, ca. 1954, ex US; by 1965, coll. Ex:—2. *Drop like a hot potato*, to abandon with—often callous or unseemly—alacrity: (orig. low) coll. >, ca. 1920, S.E.: from before 1893. F. & H.

hot prot. An enthusiastically committed Protestant: church circles': ca. 1980. See **Prot.** (P.B.)

hot rod. A very fast motor-car: Can. motorists': adopted, ex US, ca. 1948; by ca. 1950, also Aus. and Brit. Cf. **jet job.**

hot scone. A policeman or detective: Aus. r.s. on synon. s. *John*: since 1920s. Also *scone*.

hot seat – Irishman – second horse – split ace; all prec. by **the.** The confidence trick: c.: the 1st and 4th from ca. 1919; the others from ca. 1905; the 1st, orig. US. *Hot seat* occurs in Leach, 1933; its extension, *hot seat mob*, confidence tricksters, in Sharpe, 1938.—2. (To be in) *the hot seat*, (to be in) a very difficult, or even a dangerous, position, esp. of responsibility; (to be in) grave trouble: adopted, ca. 1950, ex US. Ex:—3. *The hot seat* or *hot squat*, the electric chair: adopted, ca. 1935, ex US—but as allusive s. not as c.

hot session. Coïtion: low coll.: ca. 1920–50.

hot shot. See **hot load.**

hot spot; esp. *be in a . . .* Trouble: c.: anglicised, ca. 1928, ex US; by 1945, s. Cf. **hot seat**, 2.

hot spud. *Drop like a hot spud* was a Services' var. of *. . . hot potato*, 2. Recorded by Knock.

hot squat. A Terry bicycle-saddle: club cyclists': earlier C.20. *Fellowship.*—2. See **hot seat**, 3.

hot stuff, n. A person out of the ordinary in degree,—dangerous,—(mostly of women) sexually hot or lax: coll. Collinson.—2. A thing that is remarkable, behaviour that is either remarkable or censurable, a striking action: coll.—3. 'Stolen property that is liable to be traced with comparative ease' (Tempest): c.: mid-C.20. Cf. **hot**, adj., 8, and:—

hot-stuff, v. To requisition, take without permission, steal: Services', perhaps orig. RN:—1914. (Carr, 1939.) Perhaps the fore-runner of **hot**, adj. 8, stolen.

hot stuff, adj. or admiring exclam. of gen. approbation: coll.: from ca. 1910; ob. by mid-C.20, except perhaps for pornography.

hot, sweet and filthy. See PRISONER-OF-WAR SLANG, §11, in Appx. With a pun on the prescription, 'Coffee should be as *hot* as hell, as *sweet* as love, and as *black* as night.'

hot-tailed. (Of women) to be of passionately amorous nature: later C.20 version of *hot-arsed*, low coll.

hot that broad. See MOVING-PICTURE SLANG, in Appx.

hot to trot. Ready and eager to be away: Aus.: heard late 1960s, prob. current since 1950s. The influence of rhyme. (P.B.)—2. Of a nuclear reactor heated enough to start a submarine: adopted by RN, ca. 1960, ex USN. Jenkins, 1966.

hot under the collar, get or **grow.** To become annoyed or angry: since ca. 1920.

hot up, v.i. and v.t. To become lively or esp. exciting; to render so, to enliven: (I remember the v.i. during WW1): s. >, by 1930, coll. A reminder of the v.t.: Weightman, 1977.

hot wire, n. and v. 'Apparatus used to bypass ignition systems. Once entry has been gained, a skilled motorcar thief can "hot wire" the older style in less than two minutes' (Powis): c.: later C.20. Cf. **jumper lead.**

hotel barber. A thief that lives in a hotel to rob it: Aus. c. (B., 1942.) Ex:–

hotel-barbering. Bilking: lodging at hotels and departing without paying the bill: low: 1892; † by 1930. *Daily Chronicle*, 28 Mar. 1892.

Hotel Crowbar. A gaol: Can.: since ca. 1920. 'Only one guest had occupied Hotel Crowbar overnight' (St Pierre, 1970).

Hotel Tropicana. 'The staff and patients at the London Hospital for Tropical Diseases have nicknamed it "Hotel Tropicana" ' (*Observer* mag., 26 Nov. 1978).

hots, the. In, e.g. *have the hots for*, to lust after: later C.20. Simmonds, 1981.

hotters. Hot water: RN: since ca. 1920. By the 'OXFORD *-ER(s)*'.

hottie. A very tall story: Aus. Baker.—2. A hot-water bottle: domestic. (Petch, 1974.) Cf.:–

hotty-watty bottles (or **b's**). Hot-water bottles: upper-middle class domestic s.: since ca. 1945.

Houdini, do a. To escape, esp. from a seemingly inextricable position: mostly Aus.: since ca. 1920. Ex the feats of the late Harry Houdini. (B.P.)

hough; occ., erroneously, **hok.** To kick; act roughly towards: Hampton Grammar School:—1935. Ex:—2. To hack, in Rugby football: Ibid.: from ca. 1920. Whence *houghing*, rough or 'dirty' play, and *dirty hougher*, a term of contempt: Ibid.

hound. Applied pej. to a man, it is S.E., whence *dirty dog*. But when = person, as in *drinkhound*, a drunkard (Waugh, 1930) and *gloom-hound*, a gloomy person (Brandon, 1934), it is s., verging on coll., of the upper and upper-middle classes, and it dates from ca. 1919. Cf. the use of *wallah*.—2. Orderly officer: Army: from ca. 1925. Suggested by **orderly dog** q.v.

house-keeper. A paramour servant: low: since ca. 1850. E.P. glossed the term 'ob.' in mid-1930s, but Petch, 1974, notes the use of *housekeeper* as 'a kept mistress', since (?)mid-C.20. Cf. earlier synon. *house-bit* or *-piece*.

house lighter. A lighter (boat) fitted with a cabin: canalmen's (esp. Fenland) coll. (Rolt, 1944.) On S.E. *house-boat*.

House of Corruption, the. 'The Glasgow Municipal Buildings were commonly known [among the city's slummies] as the "Chamber of Horrors" or the "House of Corruption" ': earlier C.20. MacArthur.

House of Lords, the. A urinal: Glasgow schoolboys'.

house tic-tac. A 'tic-tac man' that acts for a group of small, subscribing 'bookies': race-course s. Westerby, 1937.

house to let. A bet: r.s.: late C.19–20. Sharpe, 1938.

housekeeper. See **house-keeper.**

housekeeping. Housekeeping money: lower and lower-middle class coll. (Kersh, 1946.) P.B.: usu., within the home, *the housekeeping*.

housemaid's knee. Sea: r.s.: later C.20. Barker, 1979.

hovel. Any vessel abandoned on the high seas: trawlermen's. Mitford, 1969.

how, n. A patrol flight(?): RAF: ca. 1939–41. Aldridge, 1942, ' "We're going on a how. Eleven hours," Hickey said.'

how! A coll. Aus. salutation, adopted, ca. 1944, ex US. 'Often with right hand raised, palm forwards, and with an expressionless face. Ex Amerindian greeting.' (B.P.) Not unknown in UK; the influence of 'Western' films.

how. Interrogatively, *as how?* = in what way?: coll. Knox, 1934, ' "I think he's too stupid . . . " "As how?" "Oo, I mean about why he ran away . . . " ' A blend, or perhaps a confusion, of *as for instance* and *how*.

how are you diddlin(g)? A joc. var. of, e.g., *How are you?*: coll.: heard late 1970s. (J. Riddles.)

how come? How does that come about? or Why is that?: adopted, ca. 1943, ex US Servicemen.

how-do-you-do, how-d'ye-do. A source—or an instance—of trouble; a quarrel, a brawl: since ca. 1910; by ca. 1960, coll. 'A nice—*or* what a—how-d'you-do!' Burgess, 1961.

how goes? How goes it? Sayers, 1932.

how in hell's name . . . ? A common intensifier of *how the hell?*, itself an intensifier of *how?*: coll. (P.B.)

how is . . . See **how's . . .**

howl. Something very amusing: earlier C.20; since mid-C.20, *hoot* has been the common synon. (Sayers, 1933.) Ex *howlingly funny*, or ex *howler*, an amusing blunder.

howler. A child: upper-middle-class s.: later C.20. 'The ideal deb . . . will raise a few children (howlers or kiddi-winks)' (York, 1980).

howling-box. A gas chamber: RAAF: WW2. B., 1943. P.B.: Perhaps a decompression chamber is meant.

how's your father? as n., hyphenated, or written *howsyerfather*, used, esp. in Services, for 'Whatsisname' ('where's old howsyerfather got to now, then?') or, more gen., as ribald 'thingummy', sexual dalliance, as in 'a spot of the old howsyerfather behind the haystack'.

hoy, n. The game of TOMBOLA (q.v. in Appx.) or bingo: Aus., esp. Queensland: later C.20. Wilkes.

hoy, v. To haul: Aus. (?coll. rather than s.): since ca. 1920. (Devanney, 1944.) Perhaps a blend of *hoist* and *haul*.—2. Hence, to take, as in 'I had to hoy myself down to Bega': Aus.: since ca. 1920.—3. To discard: Aus.: since ca. 1930. (B.P.) Cf. **hoist,** 3.

huddle, go into a. To go into secret or private conference; (of several people) to 'put their heads together': joc. coll.: since ca. 1930.

Hue and Cry, the. The *Police Gazette*: mostly journalistic:—1923 (Manchon). Ex the *wanted*'s.

Huey. The (Melbourne) *Police Gazette*: Aus.: late C.19–20. (B., 1942.) A shortening of prec.

huff – duff. HF – DF, high-frequency direction-finding device, by phoneticised initials. '[It] was in use in the R.N. in 1943 . . . When [it] started to play an important part in winning the Battle of the Atlantic' (R.S., 1973). See also **shuff-duff.**

huffy. A Service girl that refuses one's invitation: Servicemen's: 1940 †. (H. & P.) Cf. **toffee-nosed.** Perhaps ex the S.E. adj.

hug-me-tight. A jersey, a jumper, a pull-over: Glasgow:—1934. Cf. **huggers.**

hug the limelight, often as vbl n. *hugging*. To try to become the outstanding player in a scene: theatrical: late C.19–mid-20. (Gilbert, 1968.) Also used fig., of a constant 'show-off'. (P.B.)

Huggers or **St Huggers.** St Hugh's College: Oxford undergraduates':—1922 (Marples, 2).

huggers. Stockings: Glasgow lower classes':—1934. They cling.

huhhah. See **hoohah.**

hula hoop. See **hooler hoop.**

hulk. A severely damaged aircraft: RAF coll.: since ca. 1925. H. & P.

hull down, or **turret down,** under cover, hidden, occurs esp. in *get . . .* , to take cover: Army: since ca. 1940; by 1960, slightly ob. Ex tank j. P-G-R.

Hullabaloo Chorus, the. The Hallelujah Chorus. See **Helluva Bellow .**

human sausage-machine. A woman having a baby every twelve months: Aus. coll.: since ca. 1930. (B.P.)

humbug. 'A sham, a concocted insect with the head of one species, the prothorax of another, and the remainder of a third: since early C.20, at latest: widespread in N. Am. biological circles. Such a creation cannot be run through a key, and is used to humble "know-it-alls" in, e.g. a university entomology dept.' (Leech, 1986). A pun on the orig. *humbug* = sham, impostor or imposture, s. since mid-C.18.

humdinger. A fast aircraft or vehicle; a smooth-running engine: Services', but mostly RAF: adopted in mid-1940 from American airmen. US s.: echoic: *hum* (speed) + *dinger* (something forceful).—2. Anything superlatively good: Aus.: adopted, ca. 1945, ex US. (B.P.) Also Brit. in this sense, applied even to an attractive girl, 'She's a real . . . ' (P.B.)

humid. Stupid: RN: since ca. 1939. 'A pun on synonymous *wet*' (P-G-R). Cf. **saturated.**

hummerskew. A Can. joc. perversion of *humoresque*: since ca. 1950. (Leechman.) The preferred Brit. version is *humorous queue*. (P.B.)

Hump, the. The mountain range, rising to peaks of 15,000 ft, over which supplies had to be flown from Assam to Kunming for the relief and support of China in WW2; an extraordinarily hazardous route, and esp. for the unpressurised aircraft of the time. (In memory of my gallant cousin, Flt Lt Rodney Millard, RAF, † 1980, one of the Dakota pilots on that route. P.B.)

hump. To have sexual intercourse: ca. 1760–1800, Grose in 1785 remarking: 'Once a fashionable word'. It was transported to the US, where it survived in c. (Irwin, 1931) and resurfaced in UK in later C.20 (Allen, 1972). Cf. also its use in **dry-hump,** simulated sexual intercourse.

hump it. To die: lower classes': —1923 (Manchon). Ex:—2. To depart: Cockney: late C.19–20. Lyons, 1908.

humped off. Noted for punishment by the captain: RN.

humpsy-di. As in 'These [homosexual] fellows need help—especially the bisexual ones. I keep hearing of cases where a man will be carrying on humpsy-di in the bedroom and his wife can't get to sleep in her bedroom because the whole house is vibrating' (Rusbridger, 1985).

humpty-dumpty. A stretch of desert road that, with tarmac laid straight on to the sand, follows every ridge and hollow: Army in N. Africa: ca. 1940–3.—2. A rank or disastrous failure; a fiasco: c.: ca. 1920–40 (*Gilt Kid*, 1936). Ex 'Humpty-Dumpty had a great fall' in the nursery rhyme.

Hun. Joc., or pej. for a very objectionable person: coll.: in WW1 applied to the Germans. E.P. noted 'from 1914 to ca. 1920 strongly; virtually † by 1929', but WW2 revived the term in full force, if anything more strongly yet; often collectively as *the Hun. Hun* was the main pej. for the enemy in WW2, as *Boche* had been in WW1. For pre-coll. history, see Ware. (P.B.)—2. A German aircraft: RFC/RAF: WW1 and 2. Partridge, 1945.

hunch. A suspicion; an intuition or premonition: orig., and in 1930s still considered mainly to be, US (—1904); adopted, via Can. army, by 1916. In later C.20, verging on informal S.E. In phrase *play* (one's or) *a hunch*, to act according to a suspicion or intuition, as a gambler might.

hundred-per-center. A thoroughly good fellow (or girl); one whole-heartedly devoted to a cause: coll.: since ca. 1930.

hundred to eight. Rhyming on **plate**, therefore r.s. on r.s.: later C.20. (Howard, 1984.)

hundred to thirty. Dirty: r.s.: later C.20. 'An alternative to *two thirty* no longer confined to racing-men and used in the manner outlined for the latter term [i.e. grimy]' (Hillman, 1974).

hundred-year wave, the. *In re* 'The Cape of Storms': 'This was the breeding ground of the freak wave, the one that mariners called the "hundred-year wave", because statistically that was how often it should occur' (W. Smith, 1978).

hung. A shortened form of **hung up**, 2: since early 1960s. Beatles' song album 'Strawberry Fields Forever', 1967.

hung on. Very fond of and, to some degree, dependent on (another person): teenagers' and other young people's raffish s.: since ca. 1955. Sherwood, 1961, defines it as 'emotionally dependent on'.

hung over (or solid). Suffering from a **hang-over**, q.v.

hung up, (to be). To be (foolishly) involved or entangled; to be stalled or frustrated: Can. jazz-lovers': since ca. 1956. The Victoria, BC, *Daily Colonist*, 16 Apr. 1959.—2. Hence, annoyed; irritated, irritable; tense and under nervous strain, because of delay, difficulty or dilemma: Brit. jazz-lovers', hippies': since ca. 1960, when adopted by Can. and UK almost simultaneously, ex US. (W. & F. Sup. of 1975.) Cf. **hang-up.** Which came first? R.C., 1976, notes 'Surely derives from, or is a variant of the US form . . . *hung up on*.'—3. Addicted to, obsessed by, e.g. ambition, revenge: adopted, ca. 1965, ex US. Scaduto, 1974.—4. 'Unable to get drugs, depressed, let down, disappointed' (Home Office): drug addicts' specialisation of sense 2: 1970s.

hunger-knock. Exhaustion: since ca. 1945 a cyclists' synon. of the **bonk**, q.v.

Hungry, the. The Hungarian Restaurant: London taxi-drivers': since ca. 1920. Hodge, 1939.

hungry. Close-fisted; selfish: Aus.: later C.19–20. (Wilkes.)—2. Greedy: Aus.: since ca. 1925. Mann, 1942.—3. Determined to win, to overcome all opposition: some adoption, late 1960s–early 70s, ex US, where applied to, e.g. football teams. '[He] is hungry and ambitious. He's pulled himself all the way from his childhood in the dole-ridden North-East to Conservative M.P. And he doesn't intend to stop there' (Stuart, 1971). In US, pron. *hongry*. (P.B.)

Hungry Forties, the. The years 1940–5, when food was short: since ca. 1946; by 1951, merely historical. Ex Ireland's famine years, the 1840s.

hunk. A steward in the 3rd class: nautical. (Bowen.) Perhaps ex Scots *hunk*, a slut, or, more prob., ex the older s. verb, to clean or polish.—2. A big man: Aus.: since ca. 1920. (Baker.) Ex *hunk of beef*.—3. An attractive boy, not necessarily large or muscular: teenage girls': 1982. (H. Burt.) Cf. **slice**.

hunk of dodger, a. A slice of bread: Aus., since ca. 1920 (Culotta); also Brit. Army, C.20. (P.B.) See **dodger**, n., 3, 4.

hunks or **hunky-dory**; esp. **everything's hunky-dory.** Predicatively, as in 'That's hunky-dory'—fine, just the thing: adopted ca. 1938 from US.

hunky. Good: since ca. 1945. Ex prec.

Hunland. The country behind *any* enemy lines occupied, wholly or in part, by German soldiers: RFC/RAF coll.: 1915. (F. & G.) Some revival of the term in WW2. (P.B.)

Huns. Cricklewood men (i.e., employees): London transport men's: since ca. 1920(?). *Railway*, 2nd. Why?

Hunts, the. The Hunt Class destroyers (named after famous packs, as Pytchley, Quorn, etc.): RN coll.: 'These ships did splendid service in both World Wars' (Granville).

hurrah. In Aus. labour s. *on the hurrah* = with hustling and shouting: since ca. 1930. B., 1942, 'The boss works us on the hurrah'.

hurrah boy. (Gen. pl.) A college student: 1928+. *OED* Sup.

hurrah cruise. 'A naval cruise to attract popular attention': RN: from ca. 1920. (Bowen.) 'So called because of the cheering which usually greeted the ships [as they dropped anchor off British popular seaside resorts]' (Granville). Cf.:–

hurrah party. 'Naval men going ashore for a spree' (Bowen): RN. Cf. *banzai party*, an earlier synon.

hurriboys. Pilots and ground crews operating Hawker Hurricane fighters and 'tank-busters' ('Hurribombers'): RAF: 1940–5. See also **Hurry**.

hurricane buttie. 'The little hand-carried oil lamps, issued to all army units and known as "hurricane butties" . . . ' (Mead, 1967). A blend of *hurricane* lamp + *buttie, y*, a friend, mate. (P.B.)

hurricane deck. Neck: theatrical r.s. Franklyn.

Hurry, Hurribird, Hurribox, Hurry-back/Hurryback, Hurribuster. A Hawker *Hurricane* fighter (as *Hurribuster*, in fighter-bomber form): RAF: WW2. The first, and the commonest, was noted by E.P. in *New Statesman*, 19 Sep. 1942; it, and the rest, are recorded by Jackson, 1943.

Hurry Boys. See **hurriboys** and **Hurry**.

Hurry-buster. A *Hurricane* aircraft employed as a tank-buster: RAF and Army: ca. 1940–5. (P-G-R.) See **Hurry**.

hurry-up. A hastener, esp. a shell or two fired to make the enemy hurry: Army coll.: since ca. 1941.—2. A police car: since late 1940s: orig. c.; by 1960s, s. (Norman, 1959.) Cf. **hurry-up van**.—3. *On the hurry up*, 'Very quickly, perhaps taking action before there was time to prepare' (Powis): low coll.: later C.20.

hurry-up van. '[Police] vans, sometimes known to older members of the public as "Black Marias" or "Hurry-up vans", were in those days [later 1950s] the cornerstone of the force transport' (Cole, 1980). Cf.:-

hurry-up wag(g)on. A 'black Maria': Can.: since ca. 1945. (Leechman.) Also Brit. c.: mid-C.20. Tempest.

husband. Active member of a homosexual partnership: late C.19–20. Cf. **wife**, 2.

hush. Silence: coll. when used, as in Hall, 1976: 'He was keeping strict hush'; but cf. S.E. 'There's a breathless hush in the Close tonight . . . ': since (?)ca. 1945. P.B.: often as in 'All right, all right! Let's 'ave a bit of 'ush, then!' Cf. **shoosh**.

hush-hush. Secret; not to be divulged: orig. Service s., WW1 >, in WW2, widespread gen. coll. 'Of course, it's all very hush-hush still, so don't breathe a word to a soul!'

hush puppies. 'German made gateway supports; a corruption of the trade-name "usspuiwies" ' (*Pit-Talk*, 1970, ed. W. Forster): S. Midlands' coal-miners'.—2. 'Silencing equipment on a diesel rail car' (McKenna, 1): railwaymen's. Both senses

227

later C.20, and punning or Hobson-Jobson on the brand-name of a popular make of shoe, which, as Sue Arnold explains in *Observer* mag., 13 June 1982, derives in turn ex the name orig. given by US hunters to the small corn fritters thrown to their dogs to keep them quiet. (P.B.)

hustle. To cadge, as a beggar: coll.: adopted, ex US, late 1970s. Walker, 1980: 'He hustles a deutschmark off the G.I.s, then disappears to the bar.'—2. To work a confidence trick; esp., in later C.20, to lure inexperienced players into losing money at billiards, pool, etc.: adopted ex US, and popularised by the film *The Hustler*, 1961. The orig. sense was US since later C.19.

hustler. An employee whose duty is to hurry people on to 'Tube' (q.v.) trains in London: 1920: s. > j. > coll. (W.)—2. A pedlar of peanuts, etc., at a fair: Can. carnival s.—3. A prostitute: low coll.: adopted, ex US, in Can. ca. 1925, in UK ca. 1970. Powis records the UK usage.—4. One who *hustles*, as in the v., 2.

hustling. Prostitution: low coll. (Powis.) Cf. prec.

hutchy. (Of atmosphere) stale, frowsty, as the inside of a, e.g. rabbit-, hutch: coll. (P.B.)

Hyde Park. An actor's mark: r.s.: the film world: since ca. 1950. Haden-Guest.

hydraulic (jack). 'Nickname for anyone with the habit of "lifting" things, i.e. a thief, esp. on the waterfront' (Wilkes): Aus.: later 1970s.

hydro. A hydroplane: coll.: 1930s.

hype, n. Something intended to stimulate sales, etc.; a publicity stunt; the person or thing promoted by such a stunt: s. > coll.: adopted, early 1970s, ex US. (Chambers' *C.20th Dict.*, 1977 Sup.) 'Most PR [public relations] hypes are crass, and the Poor Little Rich Girl hype is the crassest of the lot' (Carter, 1979). Barnhart derives the term ex the US s. for a 'hypodermic injection (especially of a narcotic drug)'.—2. 'Addict (from hypodermic) US' (Home Office): drugs world: 1970s.

hype, v. To stimulate by publicity stunts. (Stuart, 1971.) Ex the n. Also *hype up*.—2. 'He fabricated—or, as journalists prefer it, *hyped*—a "dawn interview" with a disconsolate and fictitious bar-girl' (Le Carré, 1977): since ca. 1960(?). Ex US, where current since the latish 1940s.

hyper. A promoter or publicist: s.: since latish 1960s. Ex **hype,** n. and v. Barnhart quotes *Sunday Times*, 11 Aug. 1968.

hyper- (as prefix). Extremely: coll. when used in such compounds as 'hyper-filthy', 'hyper-interesting': teenagers': ca. 1980. (R. Paterson.) Perhaps suggested by 'hyper-market'. (P.B.) E.g. ' "We go into hyperflap on Saturdays in Summer" ' (Allison, 1986), i.e. 'that is when we are particularly excited'.

hypo. A hypochondriac; a valetudinarian; one who is both: Aus.: since late 1930s. (B.P.)

hysterical historical. See **bodice ripper**.

I

I.B.A. *I*gnorant *b*loody *a*ircrafthand: RAF: since ca. 1930. Jackson, 'Aircrafthands are the jacks-of-all-trades of the R.A.F. . . . Officially, they are unskilled.' On the analogy of the IRA and the **P.B.I.**, q.v. Cf. **Ibach**.

I.C., the. The officer, NCO or senior man in charge of a squad, a detachment, a barrack-room, a hut, etc.: Service (esp. RAF) coll.: since ca. 1930. Partridge, 1945, 'I must ask the I.C. about that; he's sure to know.' P.B.: in Army col., sometimes joc. extended (wrongly) to *O.C. i/c*, the 'Officer Commanding in charge'.

I.I.s. *I*llegal immigrants: Army in Hong Kong: from later 1970s. (*Weekly Guardian*, 14 Sep. 1980.) Prob. coll. ex official abbr., > almost imm. j.

I.M.F.U. or **imfu.** An *I*mperial *m*ilitary *f*uck-*u*p: Services', esp. Army: WW2. (P-G-R.) Cf. **s.a.m.f.u.**, etc.

I.T.A. See **Irish toothache**, 2.

I beg your garden! I beg your pardon: r.s., or simply a joc. malapropism: not at all gen.: ca. 1920-45. Harrison, 1943.

I-sup. A shortening of the next, 1: Lester (1937) has 'She's got . . . a terrific I-sup (she has a beautiful nose).'

I suppose. The nose: r.s.:—1859 ('Ducange Anglicus').—2. I suppose so: coll.: rare before C.20 and not, even now, very widespread. E.g. ' "Will you be coming to town next month?" "Yes, I suppose." '

Ibach (short *i*, stressed; indeterminate *a* = ĕ). *I*gnorant *b*astard *a*ircraft *h*and: RAF: since ca. 1939. Also *fibach*, when *f* = *fucking*.

Ibsenity. A characteristic, or the chief characteristics, of Ibsen (d. 1908), esp. of his plays: ca. 1905–14: joc. coll., coined by *Punch* on *obscenity*. (W.)

ice. Diamonds; loosely, gems: c.: anglicised ca. 1925 ex US. (Brandon, 1936.) Ex the icy sheen of diamonds. Tempest, 1950, 'This word has completely supplanted the old word "rocks".'—2. Impudence, effrontery: Society: from ca. 1927. (West, 1936.) Cf. **cool**, impudent.—3. Cocaine: drugs c. (Stockley, 1986.) US since—1974 (Spears).—4. In *on ice*, in prison: drugs c. (Stockley, 1986.) Cf.:-

ice-box. A solitary cell: Aus. c.: adopted, ca. 1920, ex US. (B., 1942.) See *Underworld*, and cf. **cooler**, 1. Hence, not only in Aus., *put him on ice* = put the man in solitary confinement for a while, to 'soften him up' before interrogation.—2. See **fry**, v.

ice-cream, short for **ice-cream freezer**. A person, usu. male; a fellow: since ca. 1920; c. >, by 1960, also low s. (Cook, 1962.) R.s. on *geezer*.—2. (Gen. pl.) Nickname given by coloured immigrant primary-school children to the white children; used as a 'defence', a retort against *Blackie*, *Nig-Nog*, *Enoch*: 1970s. Harré, 1979.

ice-cream freezer. See **ice-cream**, 1.

ice-cream habit. Irregular drug habit: drugs c. (Stockley, 1986.) US since—1936 (Spears, who notes that it may be the prelude to complete addiction). Cf. **weekend habit.**

ice-cream ship, the. The Cunard liner *Antonia*: nautical: 1920s. Bowen.

ice-cream suit. Except at Port Darwin and in the York Peninsula, ironic for the white tropical clothes worn by newcomers: Aus. (Baker.) Probably adopted from US, where it isn't ironic and where it denotes 'men's summer garb, light in weight, cream or white in color' (Alexander McQueen), as also in Can. (Leechman.)

ice-creamer. An Italian: since ca. 1955. A var. of — and obviously a derivative from — the prec.: 1916, 'A Post-Mortem' — a University of Sydney song written in 1916 (and reprinted in *The Company Song Book*, 1918) and therefore presumably current from a few years earlier. (B.P.) P.B.: but the derivation may equally well be ex the traditional Italian immigrant trade of ice-cream vending.

ice-Jack. An ice-cream seller: coll.:—1923 (Manchon); †.

ice-o. An iceman: Aus.: since ca. 1920. Niland, 1959.

iceberg. One who always goes swimming, no matter how cold the water: Aus.: since ca. 1925. B., 1943.

ickle. Little: child's attempt at pron., occ. 'borrowed' by adult females, e.g., 'ickle me': in the nursery, prob. for centuries; as coll., since (?)ca. 1930. (March, 1934.) Cf. var. *lickell*.

Icky, pronoun. I; me: often in conjunction with **Joe Soap** or **muggins,** qq.v., as 'So who gets lumbered? Icky, Muggins again!': Services', perhaps esp. Army in Germany: since ca. 1945. Ex Ger. *Ich*. (P.B.)

icky, adj. Overly sentimental, 'corny': orig. US jazz musicians', ca. 1935 (W. & F., 1960). Used, perhaps as var. of *yucky* (q.v. at **yuck!**) by Coleman, 1980, film review: 'Ms Streep . . . is no mess, in an extremely icky role as a none-too-motivated runaway parent.' Perhaps ex *sticky*, either 'gooey' or difficult. (P.B.)

Iddy-Umpties, the. The Royal Corps of Signals: Army: ca. 1920-40. See next,

iddy (or **itty**) **umpty.** A signaller: Army: late C.19–earlier 20. (F. & G.) Ex a phrase used in India for teaching morse to native troops.

idea. Exclam. *the idea!*; often *the very idea!*: what an idea!, always disapprovingly: (usu. feminine) coll. Manchon.

ident. An identification, as in 'Did you make a positive ident?': Services' coll. > j.: since ca. 1955.—2. A signature tune: musicians' and entertainment world: since ca. 1960. McLaughlin, 1976.

idiot board. A teleprompter or similar device used out of camera range to prompt persons appearing on television: world of TV: since ca. 1970. (B.P.) Cf.:-

idiot box and **idiot's lantern.** A television receiving set: since ca. 1955: the former (cf. **goggle box**) is fairly gen.; the latter also Can. (Leechman.) See **box**, n., 16.

idiot broth. Cider: West Country s.: later C.20. Cf. **jumble-juice.** (Patten, 1979.)

idiot pills. 'Street name for barbiturates' (*Time Out*, 19 Sep. 1985).

idle. Careless, slovenly ('an *idle* salute'—'*Idle* on parade'); dirty ('an *idle* cap-badge'): Guards Regiments': C.20; hence, since ca. 1939, RAF. By ca. 1955, verging on j.—2. Hence, slow, as applied to, e.g., a batsman in a cricket match: since ca. 1960.

idle-itis. Laziness: joc. coll. Cf. synon. **lazyitis.** (P.B.)

if and and. A band (of instrumentalists): r.s.: since ca. 1945. Franklyn 2nd.

if God permits. White Horse whisky: public-houses': late C.19–20. This whisky has on its label the old coaching notice, 'If God permits'.

if your face fits. If you're in favour with the authorities: Services': since ca. 1930. P-G-R.

iffy (incorrectly *iffey*). Uncertain: unsound, risky: coll., esp. in Aus.: since ca. 1920. B., 1942.—2. Addicted to excessive *ifs* in conversation: coll.: since ca. 1925.—3. 'Doubtful or dishonest. An "iffy brief" would mean a dishonest lawyer, an "iffy motor" would mean a (probably) stolen car' (Powis): underworld: later C.20.

ifs. (Rare in sing.) Spavins, etc.: horse-dealers'. They lead to doubts and queries.

igaretsay. A cigarette: Aus. (urban): adopted, ca. 1944, ex US servicemen. (Morrisby, 1958.) An example of 'Pig Latin, which as you no doubt know is one of the most venerable of children's secret languages. *Ixnay* (= nix) is one of the few PL terms that penetrated the adult world'. (R.C., 1966; he states that even *ixnay* is ob.)

iggerance or **igorance; iggerant.** Ignorance; ignorant: coll. when used joc. to reinforce the rebuke, e.g., 'ooh, you aren't 'alf iggerant!'

ignorant. Ill-mannered; unaware of the proper or conventional way to act in any given situation: Services' and proletarian: since ca. 1950 (prob. earlier). 'Proper ignorant, that was, bawling out the corporal in front of the whole platoon like that'—'Well, he always was an ignorant bastard'. A specialisation of the S.E. sense, 'lacking in knowledge'. (P.B.)—2. In *make ignorant*, 'make angry (South London)' (Powis): later C.20.

ignorant as pig's muck. Extremely ignorant, with an implication of comparable illiteracy: late C.19–20. (Naughton, 1966.) Cf. synon. **pig-ignorant.**

igorance. See **iggerance.**

ikeys. Ice-cream: joc. childishness sometimes affected by adults: later C.20. (P.B.)

I'll be there. A chair: orig., and still mainly, underworld, esp. convicts', r.s. Franklyn 2nd.

I'll put my kudos on the . . . To back, to place one's bets on, the object: Can.: 1970s. (Robin Leech, 1978.)

illegit. Illegitimate, n. and adj.: schoolboys'. Lunn, ' "Was he a blooming illegit?" asked Kendal.'

illegitimate glow-worm. A 'bright bastard' (= a 'smart Alec'): Aus. pedantic: since ca. 1950. (B.P.)

illywhacker. A trickster, esp. a confidence man: Aus. c.: since ca. 1930. (B., 1943.) Cf. *whack the illy*, to trick or swindle someone: id. (Ibid.) ?*illy* = 'silly'.

I'm a. An (over)coat: abbr. C.19 r.s. *I'm afloat*. Lester writes it *I'm-a.*

I'm so. Whisky; short for orig. *I'm so frisky*: r.s. Lester, 1937, 'A tumbler of hot I'm-so.'

I'm sure! Certainly; certainly it is (or was or will be, etc.): lower-class coll.: from ca. 1870. Pugh, 1895, ' "Ah, that was a funeral!" "I'm sure! Marsh Street ain't likely to see another

for many a, etc." ' P.B.: also used for emphasis, as in 'Oh, beg pardon, I'm sure!', where the speaker is taking umbrage against what (usu. she) feels is an unjustified rebuke: proletarian, and occ. middle-class joc.: mid-C.20.

I'm willing. A shilling: r.s. Lester.

ima(d)ge. Imagination: ca. 1905–20. Lyons, 1914.

imaginitis. A tendency to imagine things: coll.: since the late 1940s.

imbars bidbib. An Army 'motto', current in WW2 and composed of the initial letters of *I may be a rotten sod, but I don't believe in bullshit.*

imbo. A simpleton; a dupe: Aus. c.: since ca. 1935. (B., 1953.) Prob. ex shortening of *imbecile* + Aus. gen.-purpose suffix -*o*.

Immelmann. To have or to get one's own back: aircraft engineers': ca. 1917–37. (*Daily Telegraph*, 1 Aug. 1936.) Ex the name of a well-known fighter pilot—one of the three greatest German WW1 'aces', whose name is commemorated in the aerobatic manoeuvre he perfected, the 'Immelmann turn', by which he 'turned the tables' on a pursuing aircraft.

imperial. See **I.M.F.U.**

imperial raspberry or **rocket.** A severe or very severe reprimand. See **raspberry** and **rocket.**

impixlocated. Tipsy: mid-1930s. A blend of *intoxicated* and **pixilated,** q.v.

implement. Fulfil (a promise). Ca. 1927–33 this term was so abused that it might, for that period, be fairly considered as cultured, even pedantic, s.

imposs or **impos.** Impossible: coll.: from early 1920s. *OED* Sup.

imprac. Impracticable: coll.:—1923 (Manchon).

improve, on the. Improving: coll., mostly Aus.: from ca. 1925.

Imps or **imps.** Imperial Tobacco Company shares: Stock Exchange: from ca. 1919.

imps file. A file or dossier on important persons: journalistic: since ca. 1975. Gardner, 1976.

Impuritans. People anything but puritanical: since ca. 1950. Ex *impurity* on *Puritan.*

imshee, imshi, imshy! Go away!: WW1–mid-C.20; orig. military. Ex Arabic. (Also, intensively, *imshee yaller!*)

in, n. Elliptical for 'a way, a means, of getting inside'; lit. and fig.: coll.: later C.20. 'If only we could think of some way of getting an in into the organisation . . . ' = how can we get in? (P.B.)—2. *Have an in*, 'To have a contact in a place to be robbed or in a place where secret negotiations would be advantageous' (Powis): underworld: later C.20. Cf. sense 1.

in, adj.: esp. *be in*, to be accepted by, and a welcome member of, a group or a place: coll.: esp. Aus.: since ca. 1920. 'Always written within inverted commas' (B.P.)—2. As in *in-joke* and *in-thing*, was orig., ca. 1960, coll. Chambers' *C.20th Dict.*, 1972 ed., has the former; P.B. uses it, early 1974, as a term long familiar to him. Such idiomatic terms as these are the most difficult to pin-point: implying intimacy, they are themselves so intimate, so unconsciously employed, that one doesn't think to record them. Prob. elliptical for *in fashion.*

in, adv. In to London: tramps' c. Cowan, 1937, 'Will you give us a lift in?'—2. In *and a bit in*, with a little extra; with a tip in addition: coll.:—1923 (Manchon).

in, preposition: all phrases not found here—and only a few are listed here—must be sought at the dominant n. or pronoun.

In-and-Out, the. The Naval & Military Club, London: 'From the words "In" and "Out", painted on the pillars of the approach to the courtyard in front' (F. & G.): C.20, among RN and military officers; but Franklyn thinks the nickname originated years earlier among the cab-drivers. In full, *the In-and-Out Club.*

in and out job. A passenger that returns to his point of departure: taxi-drivers': since ca. 1915. Hodge, 1939.

in-and-out man. An opportunist thief: London's East End: since ca. 1945. (Herd, 1957.) Quickly in and soon, or furtively, out.

in-and-out shop. 'A shop through which one can walk in and out along a passage, where the goods are hung up for inspection' (*OED* Sup.): coll., orig. and mainly Londoners'.

in dead trouble. Synon. with *in stook*, q.v. at **stook**, 2.

in flaggers. *In flagrante delicto* (caught in the crime): in ca. 1920 in Brit., and ca. 1950 in Aus. (Buzo, 1973.) By the 'OXFORD -ER(S)'.

in for (one's) **chop**, (be). Engaged solely for one's share; esp. for more, if poss.: NZ, since ca. 1920; Aus. since 1940s. 'From the best cut of the carcase' (Buzo, 1973). Cf. Aus. s. *chop*, a share.

in for it. (Of a woman), pregnant: lower classes':—1923 (Manchon).

in *my* book. In my opinion: coll.: since ca. 1950. (P.B.)

in on. Participating in, admitted to a share of, some thing or some affair of unusual interest or importance: coll.: from ca. 1919. 'Am I to be in on this?'

in stitches. Highly amused, 'in tucks': coll. Perhaps ex the 'stitch' brought on by shortage of breath. (P.B.)

in the blue. Gone astray, gone wrong; having failed, a failure: Army: early C.20. (F. & G.) Perhaps = 'gone off into the blue haze of the horizon'.—2. Hence, in a 'deserted place far away and difficult of access': coll.:—1931 (Lyell). See also **blue**, n., 6.—3. In debt; in a 'fix': Aus.: since ca. 1927.—4. Out of control: Aus.: since late 1920s. (B., 1942.) Cf. senses 1 and 3.—5. Being a policeman. Allingham, 1942.

in the death. Finally: since ca. 1945; by 1960, also s. (Cook, 1962.) Perhaps a blend of 'in the end' and 'at the *death*'.

in the gun. (Of a person) about to be dismissed from job: Melbourne: ca. 1910–30. I.e. about to be *fired*.—2. Hence, in trouble: gen. Aus.: since ca. 1920. (Cusack, 1951.) Palmer, 1924, has *get* (someone) *in the gun*.

in the lurch. Church: Aus. r.s. 'Left in the lurch, waiting at the church.'

in the mood. Desirous of sexual intimacies: euph. coll., mostly feminine ('I'm not in the mood'): late C.19–20.

in the nude (pron. as Cockney, *nood*). Food: r.s.: later C.20. Barker, 1979.

in the picture. Aware of what is going on, either immediately, or in a wider context: orig. Services', WW2, it soon > gen. coll., as in 'Is he in the picture about what we're doing tonight?' See **picture**, 4 and 5.

in the pipeline. Already in train; waiting to be produced; (of measures, things) prepared in anticipation: coll., almost j.; in widespread use: since ca. 1965. (P.B.) Cf.:-

in the works. 'In preparation; being effected. "Your two weeks' leave? Oh, yes, it's in the works now. Come back for it at three." ' (Leechman.) Can.: since the middle 1940s.

in tucks. Highly amused, 'creased with laughter': coll. (D. Beale, 1982.) Cf. synon. **in stitches** and the more modern **fall about**; also **crack up**.

in waiting. On duty: Guards Regiments'. Ex performance of Palace guards. With a pun on *lady-in-waiting*. P-G-R.

inboard. 'A motor permanently installed inside the hull [of a small boat]' (Leechman). Can. coll.: since ca. 1935. See also **kicker**.—2. Ashore: RN Submariners': later C.20. Martin, 1983.

inch stick. A measuring instrument, e.g. a ruler: motorcyclists': later C.20. (Dunford, 2.)

incident. An illegitimate child: Society: adopted, before 1909 (Ware), ex US; ob. by 1930.—2. 'There are no occasions, occurrences, or events in an airman's life. Anything that happens to him is an "incident" . . . why, nobody knows' (H. & P.): coll.: since 1938.

income-tax. Those periodical fines to which they are subject for soliciting: prostitutes': since ca. 1930. *New Statesman*, 10 May 1947.

increase. Another baby: bourgeois joc.—I.e. in (or of) the family.

Incubator, the. HMS *King Alfred* (a shore establishment), 'where embryo R.N.V.R. officers are trained': RN: since ca. 1939. Granville.

incy, pron. *insy*. An *inc*endiary bomb: Services': 1940–5. (H. & P.) Prob. ex abbr. in written reports (P.B.).

India. 'Cannabis' (Home Office): drug-users': 1970s.

India-rubber man. A physical training instructor. See **bunjie**.

indigragger. Indignation: Aldenham School: earlier C.20. (Marples.) See **-agger** and cf.:-

indijaggers. Indigestion: Oxford undergraduates' and Public Schools': from ca. 1908. In, e.g., Sayers, 1930 (used by Lord Peter Wimsey); Spain, 1949; and used to good satirical effect by Simmonds in her admirably observant weekly cartoon-strip in the *Guardian*, late 1970s. (E.P.; P.B.)

Indo. Indonesia; Indonesian, adj. and n.: Aus. journalistic coll.: since late 1950s. (B.P.) Cf.:-

Indon, n. and adj. Indonesian: Services', esp. during the period of 'Confrontation' against Sukarno's Indonesian forces in Borneo, 1962–6. Influenced by commonly used abbr. in written reports. (P.B.)

indulge, as in 'He doesn't indulge'. To take strong drink, whether habitually or incidentally: late C.19–20; by 1930, coll.—2. To have sexual intercourse: Aus.: joc. rather than euph.: since ca. 1930. (B.P.)—3. 'Take free, non-duty passage in RAF transport aircraft' (*Fighter Pilot*, 1981). Ex the j. 'indulgence flight', Service term since early 1950s, poss. earlier.

industrial dungeon. Engine room: RN, esp. HM submarine *Astute*: mid-1960s. (Malin, 1979.)

infanteer. An infantry man: Army joc.; orig. Royal Artillery, but in later C.20 used by any non-infantry arm or branch. On analogy with *musketeer*, *carbineer*, etc. (E.P.; P.B.)

infantile. Infantile paralysis: coll.: since ca. 1910; orig. medical; only since ca. 1945 at all gen. P.B.: by ca. 1950, the term *polio*, short for poliomyelitis, had > more gen.

Infinitely More So. A pun on the initials I.M.S., the Indian Medical Service: earlier C.20. (Carew.) Cf. **The Heaven-born**, the Indian Civil Service.

influ. An occ. var., early C.20, of *flu*, short for influenza. Manchon, 1923.

info. Information: perhaps orig. Aus., mostly low and esp. among racing touts, since ca. 1930 (E.P.); but it had, by 1940, > very widely known—and coll. Moreover, by 1955, it was, in the Services, also used as v., 'to inform'; this usage ex the 'copy to' lists appended to signals and letters, '[for] info[rmation of]'. (P.B.) Cf.:-

infor. Information: convicts' c. until ca. 1940, then gen. prison s. Phelan, 1940.

ingie-bungie. See **bunjie**.

injection. A bullet: c.: since ca. 1960. Petch cites a report, June 1968, of the Kray brothers' trial.—2. In *by Dutch* (or *French* or *German*, etc.) *injection*, a Londoners' term dating from ca. 1925 and applied to a woman living, as wife or as mistress, with a foreigner. Punning *by extraction* (or birth) and the act of copulation; cf. **meat-injection**.

injury. Euph. for 'rupture', in the (usu. joc.) c.p. *don't do yourself an injury!*, to someone about to lift something heavy: since ca. 1950, at latest. Noted by Ross, 1978.

ink in (one's) **pen.** Since ca. 1910, an occ. var. of **lead in** (one's) **pencil**, q.v., sexual vigour.

Ink-Line, The. Fleet Street: London taxidrivers': from ca. 1905. (*Evening News*, 20 Jan. 1936.) Cf. **cold blow, Pill Avenue, Spion Kop**, 2.

inky. See MOVING-PICTURE SLANG, §3, in Appx.

inky blue. ' "A touch of the inky blue" means flu [influenza]' (*Muvver*): r.s.: later C.20.

inky fingers. The Accountant staff; one of them: RN: since ca. 1920. P-G-R.

inland navy and **waterborne** were applied, by the Army, to Brit. and Can. troops using Ducks and Buffaloes for fighting in the flooded areas between Nijmegen and Cleve: 1944–5. (P-G-R.) P.B.: code names for amphibious vehicles.

innards. The internal mechanism of any mechanical or electronic appliance: coll. (B.P.)

inner, the. 'The enclosure of a racecourse' (Baker): Aus. sporting coll.: since ca. 1910.

inoc. An inoculation: Services' coll.: since ca. 1930. (Partridge, 1945.) Cf. **jab**, n.

inquest. A joc. var., esp. among players at whist drives, of *post mortem*: since ca. 1946.

insanitary suspecter. A sanitary inspector: joc.:—1935. P.B.: *Punch* was making fun of the illiterate housemaid with 'Please, ma'am, it's the insanitary spectre' very early in C.20.

insects. See HAULAGE, in Appx., and:–

insects and ants, often simply *insects*. Trousers; knickers: r.s., on *pants*.

inside. In the innermost circle of the underworld: c.: from ca. 1910. Brandon, 1936, 'A man's got to be right on the "inside" before he'll get as much as a breath over the "grapevine".'

Inside, the. Central Aus.: Aus. coll.: late C.19–20. Ex coll. *inside*, in the interior. Hence, *Insider*, one either born or long resident in this region. Ronan, 1954 and 1956, uses all three terms.

inside job. A crime, esp. a burglary, a theft, committed by, or with the help (e.g., vital information, door left unlocked and unbolted) of someone inside the house or the business premises (e.g. a bank): orig., ca. 1920, c. and police s., both US and within the Commonwealth; by 1935, at latest, used more generally.

inside the mark. Moderate: coll.: adopted, ex US,—1909 (Ware); ob. by 1940.

insinuendo. Usu. in pl. (*-oes*). A coll. blend of *insinuation* + *innuendo*. Adams, 1940.

Insipid. See **Fearful**.

-insky. A comic suffix added to almost any word; often abbr. to *-sky*, as in *buttinsky*, one who butts in. Prob. ex US.—2. Also in imitation of Russian, as is *offsky*.

inspector of manholes. A sanitary inspector: since ca. 1920.—2. A male homosexual: low: since ca. 1930. P.B.: but see also entries at **manhole**.

instalment mixture. 'Rain is "Instalment Mixture"—at least, to owner-drivers. The owner-driver is a "mush", and when still buying his cab, a "starving mush". Rain is sometimes referred to by journeyman drivers, therefore, as "Mush's Lotion". Otherwise it is simply "Frarny" (France and Spain)' (Hodge, 1939): taxi-drivers' terms: since ca. 1910.

instant. Powdered coffee, as in 'a big tin of instant'. See:-

instant mum. A foster mother: since ca. 1960. 'From the common use of "instant" [as applied] to certain food products [esp. coffee]' (Petch, 1969).

instrument-basher. An instrument-mechanic: Services'. See **basher**, 3.

insult, the. One's pay: RN (lowerdeck): since ca. 1925. (Granville.) P.B.: i.e., not long before the Invergordon Mutiny.

insy. See **incy**.

intense. Serious; soulful: coll.: ca. 1878–1920.—2. Hence, excited; excitable: Society coll.: from ca. 1920. Waugh, 1930, ' "Darling, I *am* so glad about our getting married." "So am I. But don't let's get intense about it." '

Inter. Esp. *the Third Inter*, the Third International: Socialist coll.: post-WW1. Cleugh, 1934.

inter-uni. Inter-university: Aus. coll. B., 1942.

intercom. Inter-communication telephonic system of an aircraft, ship, etc.: orig., ca. 1936, RAF coll.; by 1939, all-Services' j. Michie, 1940.—2. Hence, of a factory, a school, a business, a post office, etc.: coll.: since ca. 1946.

intercoursed. Exhausted, 'done up': joc. pedantic for *fucked*. Dempster, 1979, notes it as a new 'in' word, with the example: ' "How was the office, darling?"—"I feel utterly intercoursed".'

interflora. Love-making: among the Flower Boy and Girl 'hippies', esp. in London: 1967. *Inter*course between 'Flowers', with a pun on Interflora, the large firm of florists.

international milk thief (or **gas-meter screwsman**). 'Ironic terms for a petty thief' (Powis): police s.: 1970s.

interrogative QRN. 'An offer of sexual dalliance. QRN, preceded by the interrogative prefix in Morse = 'Are you being interfered with?' It arose, ca. 1950, among Royal Navy communicators' (Peppitt). P.B.: *pace* Lt Cdr Peppitt, but *QRM* seems more likely, since that signifies 'man-made interference' (other signals) as opp. *QRN* which means 'natural interference' (static from electrical storms, etc.). The joke has helped for many years to lighten the rigours of learning morse and the 'Q' code.

interrupter. An interpreter: joc. Can. mispronunciation (Civil Service): since ca. 1910. (Leechman.) Powis, 1977, notes it as 'A court interpreter' (sc. court of law).

into. *Be into* (something), to be very interested, involved in, and hence enthusiastic about that thing: a vogue usage, adopted ex US, current in 1970s. Charles M. Schulz, the famous American cartoonist, 'sent up' the usage, 1978, in his strip 'Peanuts', by depicting the dog-character Snoopy 'saying' of his little bird friend: 'Woodstock is into macramé. He's also into running, and he's into poetry. He's into meditation and he's into genealogy. Actually, he's into "into"!' (P.B.)

into the blue. With no horizon whatsoever: Mediterranean skin-divers': since ca. 1955. (Granville, letter, 1964.)—2. See **blue**, n., 6.

introduce Charley (or **-ie**). Of the male: to coït. The penis is frequently personified.

Invisible. HMS *Invincible*: RN. Commissioned in 1977, the aircraft-carrier received this nickname during the Falklands War, 1982. (Knight, 1984.)

invisibles. Invisible exports: economic and financial circles' coll.: since ca. 1956.

Iodines, the. The Australian Army Medical Corps: Aus. soldiers': 1939+. (B., 1942.) Cf. **poultice-wallopers**.

ira. Hair: homosexuals': current ca. 1970. Centre s.

Irish. A wig: show business r.s., on *Irish jig*. (Daniells, 1980.) Cf. synon. **syrup**.

Irish confetti. Brickbats. Kersh, 1939.

Irish jig. See **Irish**.

Irish Mail. Potatoes: nautical, esp. RN. (H. & P.) So many potatoes are shipped from Ireland to Britain.

Irish rose. Nose: r.s. Franklyn 2nd.

Irish toothache. Pregnancy: lower classes':—1909 (Ware). Also *I.T.A.*—2. 'The sexual frustration suffered by young men whose fiancées or girl-friends kept on saying "No" ' (Nowell, 1983): late 1940s.

irk. A troublesome seaman: nautical: late C.19–20. (Bowen.) Abbr. *irksome*. Also *bird* and *fowl*. Cf. **erk,** which is prob. a derivative.—2. An early (WW1) spelling of *erk*, an aircraftsman. B. & P.

iron, n. A male harlot: shortening of *iron hoof*, q.v. *Gilt Kid*, 1936.—2. A bicycle: cyclists': mid-C.20. Cf. synon. **grid-iron**.—3. See **good iron; iron horse; irons**.

iron, v. To kill: low: late C.19–20. Branch, 1951.—2. Hence, to attack or fight (someone) successfully: Aus. (B., 1953.) See also **iron out**, 2.—3. See **iron horse**.

iron bomb. 'Conventional' aerial bomb, as opp. guided missile: RN; Falkland Is. campaign, 1982. Parry, 1982.

iron-fighter. A constructional engineer: master-builders' and engineers': since ca. 1930.

iron hoof. A male homosexual: r.s. on *poof*: c. > low coll. In later C.20, shortened to *iron*. Cf. **nigh enough** and **collar and cuff**, which both rhyme on var. *puff*; a further var. is **horse's hoof**.

iron horse, n. A racecourse: r.s. Franklyn.—2. (Of coins) a toss. Sometimes abbr. *the iron* or *ironing*. See next:–

iron horse, v. To toss (a coin): r.s., on Cockney pron. *torse*: late C.19–20. (P.P., 1932.) Sharpe, 1938, has 'I'll iron you for it', and notes the abbrev. in prec., 2.

iron lung. A Nissen hut: Barrage Balloon personnel's: WW2. H. & P.—2. A shelter in the deeper Tube stations: Londoners': 1940–5.—3. As *The Iron Lung*: 'The new Underground line, running from Shoreditch to Essex, known to the criminal classes as the "iron lung" ' (*New Statesman*, Nov. 1950): c.: 1950s.—4. A '2–8–0 ex W.D. locomotive' (*Railway*, 2nd): railwaymen's: ?ca. 1940–50.—5. 'Old-fashioned street urinal with iron fixtures' (Powis): low coll.: later C.20.—6. A tip, gratuity: Glasgow r.s., on **bung**, n., 4. Munro, 1985.

iron man. A £1 note: Aus.: sense-adapted, ca. 1944, ex US *iron man*, a dollar.—2. 'At the heart of all trawling operations is the winch known as the "iron man" ' (Piper, 1974): trawlermen's.

iron (something) **out.** To put (it) right: perhaps orig. Aus.: since ca. 1930. (Robyns, 1949.) Ex the removal of creases by ironing.—2. *Iron* (someone) *out*, to attack or fight (a person) and hence to flatten him: Aus.: since mid-C.20. B., 1953.

iron tank. A bank (for money): r.s.: since ca. 1918. Franklyn.

ironmongery. Arms, from small arms (hand-guns) to cannon to bombs, aerial or other: WW1 and WW2 and since: orig. Services', but by 1940, esp. in London, also civilian. (Petch's note on the term, 1971, reminded me that I heard it—not inappropriately—on the Somme in 1916.)

ironmongery department, the; His or **Her Majesty's School for Heavy Needlework.** Prison: cultured: since ca. 1945.

irons. As a coll. shortening of **eating irons**, knife, fork, and spoon: since ca. 1925. H. & P.

is all. That is all: Can. coll.: adopted, ca. 1947, ex US. 'I'm tired, is all' (Leechman). Some Brit. use in later C.20, but with awareness of its trans-Atlantic origin.

is it fuck! (or **buggery!**) Emphatic negative: low. L.A. cites Frederic Raphael, [n.d.]: 'Is that being truly adult? Is it fuck!'

is it? – or is it? Tacked onto a question, and relegating the first *is it?* to the status of mere verbal question-mark, means 'or perhaps you don't agree with me', as in, 'It's not really quite like that, is it?–or is it?': coll. (P.B.)

I'se. I am; occ., I shall: dial. and sol.: C.18–20. Included here for its (usu. feminine) C.20 joc. usage.

Ish. Ismailia, in the Suez Canal Zone: Army: late C.19–mid-20.—2. As *ish*, short for **issue**, q.v.

-ish. When attached to cardinal numbers, esp. when indicative of the time (as in *fourish*, at about four o'clock), it is decidedly coll. 'Now, in coll. use, possible with nearly all monosyllabic adjj., and some others' (*SOD*).

Island, the. Camp Hill, the prison on the Isle of Wight: police and criminal coll.—2. 'Cockatoo Island Gaol (until 1919)' (Wilkes): Aus.—3. The Isle of Man: motorcyclists'—they associate it with the famous Tourist Trophy races. (Partridge, 1979.)—4. See:–

island, the. A battleship's, but esp. an aircraft carrier's, superstructure: RN: since late 1930s (?earlier). Winton, 1967, 'The flight deck and the island were scenes of continuous activity'.

island-hopping, n. The capture of one island after another: Allies in the Pacific: 1945. P-G-R.

Isle of Wight. Right: r.s. Franklyn.

issue, the (**whole**). 'The complete set, number, amount; the lot': military: from 1915. Ex an *issue* or distribution of, e.g., cigarettes. (B. & P.) By 1919, also civilian; soon shortened, perhaps mainly in Services, to *the ish*.

it. 'Coll. use of *it* for the consummate is [orig.] U.S.' (W.): from ca. 1910 in England. E.g. 'He thinks he's it' or 'just it'.—2. Sexual appeal: from ca. 1920. Now joc. coll. Ex the novels of 'Victoria Cross' and Elinor M. Glyn. Adumbrated by Rudyard Kipling when, in his story of 'Mrs Bathurst', 1904, he wrote: ' 'Tisn't beauty, so to speak, nor good talk necessarily. It's just it.'—3. In *gin and it*, it = Italian vermouth: coll.: since ca. 1910. Cf. *gin and French* (vermouth).

it just goes to show. A conventional stop-gap of vague comment: since the 1920s.

it just isn't true. Used as intensifier, with *so* or *such*, as in 'He's such a fool it just isn't true': coll.: later C.20. (Ross, 1978.) Var.: quot'n from James Galway, in *Sunday Express* mag., 3 Jan. 1982, 'I just wanted to play the flute like you wouldn't believe it.'

it takes you! It's your turn to, e.g., hand round the cigarettes, buy the drinks, perform a duty, etc.: Army: mid-C.20. See **take**, v., 2.

Italy. See LOVERS' ACRONYMS, in Appx.

itch pitch. 'Cells reserved for cases of scabies' (Tempest): prison s.: mid-C.20.

itchy back, have an. (Of women) to desire intercourse: Aus.: since ca. 1920. 'Women in bed with dozing husbands reputedly ask them to scratch their backs. The resulting propinquity often has the desired effect' (Anon.). Perhaps cf. the English *a bitch with an itch*, a lascivious woman.

itchy feet. Attributed to 'potential absconder/inmate thought to be unsettled' (Home Office): prison staffs': later C.20. A specialisation of the coll. *to have itchy feet*, to be restless, as 'After 20 years of moving on every two or three years, we're starting to get itchy feet even though there's no reason to go', the ex-regular serviceman's reaction to settling down in 'civvy street'. (P.B.)

Ite. An Italian; 1940–5. (P-G-R.) Ex *Ities*, var. spelling of *Eyeties*.

Ities. Var. spelling of **Eyeties**, q.v., Italians. Michie, 1941.

-itis. A suffix indicating—or facetiously imputing—a disease: often a joc. coll. in late C.19–20. E.g. *jazzitis* (1919). W.

its. 'When modern youths and girls look so much alike . . . some [people] refer to them as "its" ' (Petch, 1969): ca. 1965–75. Ex calling a baby *it*, before its sex is known.

itsi-gitsi. So-so. See **etsi-ketsi.**

itty umpty. See **iddy umpty.**

Ivan. A Russian private soldier: military coll.: 1914; † by 1920. (B. & P.) Cf. *Tommy*. P.B.: revived in WW2 and current ever since; sometimes *Ivans* for Russians in general.

Ivanhoe. Home-distilled liquor: Can.: since ca. 1950. Leechman cites the (Victoria, BC) *Islander*, 13 June 1976. Origin?

ivy-leaf. (Usu. in pl.) Small plaice: trawlermen's. (Butcher, 1980.) Cf. **penny stamps.**

J

j. Abbr. **joint**, 2. Hibbert, 1983.

J. Arthur Rank. A bank (financial): r.s.: since late 1940s. 'Evolved when Mr Rank was making both films and news' (Franklyn 2nd). Mostly shortened to *Jay Arthur*.—2. 'Wank. Usually in the sense "not worth a . . . " rather than masturbation' (Daniells, 1980): r.s.: mid-C.20. Cf. synon. **Yorkshire Penny Bank; tiger tank.**

J.B. Johore Bahru. See **K.L.**—2. See **Joe Baxey**.

J.C.'s area representatives (or **reps**). Dignitaries of the Church: RAF, but not very gen.: since ca. 1950. Cf. **God rep**.

J. Carroll Naish. A urination: r.s. on **slash**, q.v.: later C.20. Barker, 1979.

J.P., the. Husband: at mothers' unions and meetings: since ca. 1935. (*People*, 14 Oct. 1945.) I.e. junior partner.

J.T. A euph. for *John Thomas*, the penis:—1923 (Manchon).

Jaapies, the. 'These are Afrikaners,/The burly Jaapies, the Saray Marays', glossed thus, ' "Jaapies" was a slang name for the South Africans, also known as "Saray Marays" from the title of the Afrikaans song they sang' (Henderson, 1967). P.B.: pron. *yawpys*; *Jaapie* is, in later C.20, sometimes used loosely as an adj. = S. African generally, not confined to Afrikaner.

jab, n. An inoculation: Services': since 1914. (H.& P.) Hence, *get a jab*, to be inoculated: Services' coll. >, in later C.20, also civilian, as 'Going abroad? Had (*or* got) your jabs yet?'

jab, v. To inoculate or vaccinate: Services': since 1939. (P-G.R.) More usu. in passive, as, 'I've been jabbed that many times, me, I'm like a bleedin' pin-cushion' (P.B.).—2. Hence, to inject drugs: drugs c. (Stockley, 1986.) US since mid-1920s (Spears).

Jabo Club, the. 'Any airman Just About Browned Off automatically qualifies' (Jackson): RAF since ca. 1934. In India, in the 1930s, often *J.A.F.B.O.*, 'just about feeling (or fucking) browned off' (W/Cdr A.J. Wild, 1945).

jack, n. (The capital is fairly gen. where a person is designated; otherwise the initial letter is in lower case.) The c. sense is a policeman (ca. 1865)—this last > gen. Aus. s. ca. 1910. (Ware.) This, one of the main senses of *Jack*, has remained current both in UK, and in Aus., where it also = a police informer, a 'dog' (McNeil). Nally, 1979: 'A barman in a [Leeds] shebeen [says], "I don't care what the jacks say . . . He may not be a blackie, but we've had the lot round here".'—2. Money: low: adopted, ex US, 1937.—3. Syphilis: Aus. low: C.20. Also Brit. Abbr. later C.19 r.s. *jack in a box*, pox.—4. Short for *black-jack*, a bludgeon: Aus. coll. Stivens, 1951.—5. A double-headed penny: Aus. B., 1943.—6. Methylated spirit taken as an intoxicant: low: since ca. 1930. Lyall, 1961.—7. Arse; anus: low: C.19–20. Notably in *up your*

jack!, either defiant or derisive, or both. Cf. **jacksie**, 1.—8. Copulation: raffish: since ca. 1950.—9. 'A treatment of one tablet [of a drug, e.g., heroin] dissolved in water' (Bournemouth *Echo*, 19 Aug. 1967): since ca. 1955. Home Office glosses specifically 'a heroin tablet'. Cf. **jack up**, 3, q.v.—10. *On* (one's) *Jack*, alone; short for **Jack Jones**, q.v. *Gilt Kid*, 1936.—11. The sum of £5, in the 'rhyme' 'nicker, bottle, jack, cockle' [= £1, 2, 5, and 10]: Cockneys': later C.20. (Tyler, 1987.) Abbr. r.s. **Jack's alive**, q.v

jack, adj. Mentally or morally tired or sick, esp. as *get jack of*, occurring both in Henry, 1960, and in 'I'm getting jack of these holidays' (Dick): Aus.: since ca. 1920.

Jack and Jill. A (small) hill: r.s. *John o' London's Weekly*, 9 June 1934.—2. A fool: Aus. r.s., on **dill**, q.v.: later C.20. NcNeil.

jack-bit. Food: Army: 1939 †. *Daily Mail*, 7 Sep. 1940.

Jack Club, the. See PRISONER-OF-WAR SLANG, §14, in Appx.

Jack Horner. A corner: r.s. (B. & P.) See also the more usu. **Johnny Horner.**

jack (it) in. To abandon, v.t.; to give up, v.i.: proletarian: since ca. 1910; by ca. 1930 sometimes reduced, as v.t., simply to *jack*, as in Baron, 'Jacked me for a civvy'. The v.i. sense, as in 'Here, I've had enough of this! I'm jacking (it) in', derives perhaps from *jack it*, to die, recorded by Ware, 1909; a later var. is **jag (it) in**, q.v. See also **jack up**. (E.P.; P.B.)

jack it. To die: low:—1909 (Ware). See also **jack (it) in**.

Jack Jones, (usu. **on** one's). Alone: (imperfect) r.s., orig. Services'. (F. & G.) Among Servicemen in WW2, and since, it has often implied a feeling of being abandoned: 'There I was, all on me Jack Jones . . . ' Frequently abbr. to *Jack*. Cf. the rarer **Jack Malone**, and the equally common *Tod Sloan*, q.v. at **Tod**, both of which provide better rhymes. (L.A.; P.B.)

Jack Malone. See prec.

Jack-my(or **me)-hearty.** 'Boisterous "Jack's the boy" type of rating who makes himself a nuisance ashore' (Granville): RN: since ca. 1895. Cf. **Jack Strop**.

jack of. Weary of or bored with: Aus.: since ca. 1890. Dyson, 1901, 'Oh, well, Twitter's jack of it, an' I don't think it's much fun.' Cf. **jack in** and **jack up**.

jack off. (Of males) to masturbate: adopted, mid-1940s, ex US. Cf. C.19 low s. *jack*, the penis, and an erection thereof.

Jack policy, or **Jack System, the.** An attitude—the habitual expression of—utter selfishness: Aus.: since ca. 1945. (B., 1953.) 'Spontaneously combusted' ex *fuck you, Jack, I'm all right* (RN, hence Army, hence gen.)—the peculiarly RN . . . *I'm inboard*—and the specifically RAF . . . *I'm fire-proof.* Cf. also **the Jack Club**, at PRISONER-OF-WAR SLANG, §14, in Appx.

Jack Shalloo. A braggart: RN: ca. 1850–1900. Bowen.—2. Whence 'a happy-go-lucky careless officer, and hence a slack ship is called a Jack Shalloo ship' (Bowen): RN: earlier C.20.

Jack Smithers. A drink taken by a man alone: Aus.: ca. 1900–30. B., 1943.—2. Hence, a man drinking alone: Aus.: since ca. 1930. (B., 1959.) Cf. **Jimmy Woodser**, 1.

Jack Strop. 'A truculent "Jack-my-hearty" [q.v.]' (Granville): RN. 'The mess-deck sobriquet for a conceited man who fancies himself a dashing buccaneer, but is better at boasting than acting' (Laffin, 1969); R.C. notes the spoonerism on *jock strap*, while Granville derives the term 'from the lower deck ob*strop*ulous for obstreperous, hence the adjective **stroppy** [q.v.]'. Hence *Jack Strop's old woman*, a dogmatic know-all (Knock): late C.19–20.

Jack tar. A bar (for drinks): r.s., mainly theatrical. Franklyn.

Jack the biscuit. A var. of **Jack the lad**, q.v.: perhaps an elision of that with much older *take the biscuit*, to be supremely remarkable. See **street credibility**.

jack the contract. To leave a job, esp. if difficult: Aus.: since ca. 1910. (B., 1943.) A specialisation of **jack in**, v.t.

Jack the lad. 'I was always Jack the Lad—the one everyone liked but nobody wanted to know' (*New Society*, 4 June 1981); since mid-1970s applied to the most conspicuous member of any gang of young men of the 'larky', trouble-making sort, though not necessarily vicious. (P.B.)

Jack-trap. Railway points. See **man-trap**.

jack up. To reprimand for slackness: Can.: since ca. 1920. 'Harry's not doing his job. He needs jacking up.' (Leechman.)—2. To arrange: NZ: since ca. 1930. 'I'll get an early start tomorrow—I've jacked up a lift into town' (Murray, 1965). Ex 'to *jack up* a car'. —B.P.: used in this sense in Brit. Army, later C.20.—3. 'Take an injection of a narcotic' (Home Office): drug-users': 1970s. Cf. **jack**, n., 9.

jackall. 'An expression used for a job that failed to produce a tip' (O'Neill, 1988, writing of the 1940s–50s): furniture removal men's.

Jackanory. A glib excuse: r.s. on *story*: entertainment world: since ca. 1970. Ex the title of a very popular TV show for children. Haden-Guest, 1972.

jackdaw. 'To acquire dockyard paint or other materials with which to beautify your ship' (Granville): RN. Ex the jackdaw's acquisitiveness.

jackdaw and rook. A theatrical '*book* of words': r.s. (theatrical). Franklyn.

Jacket and Vest, the. The West End of London: r.s.: since ca. 1910. Prior, 1937.

jacket job. A good job (e.g., a barman's) in the steward's department: nautical. Bowen, 'From the distinctive uniform.'

jacketing. A policeman's (very) severe report on a prisoner in the dock: police, and legal: since ca. 1920. Wensley, 1931, 'After I left the box the prosecuting counsel beckoned to me, "That was a pretty fierce 'jacketing'," he said. "I don't think you should have rubbed it in so hard." ' Ex C.19 s. for a thrashing, or severe reprimand.

jackey, -ie. See **jacky**.

Jackies. American sailors: 1942+.—2. (Also *jackies*.) Aborigines in general: Aus.: since ca. 1930. (B., 1953.) Cf. **jacky**, 1.

Jacko. A shunting engine, esp. in spoken ref.: railwaymen's. *Railway*.

jackpot. In *crack, hit* or *strike, the jackpot*, to meet with exceptionally good luck: adopted, ex US servicemen, 1943 in Brit., which favours *hit* . . . , and 1944 in NZ, and Aus. where *crack* . . . is the preferred form, as B.P. notes. Orig. ex the game of poker, but, as R.C. writes, 1976, 'more directly from slot- (or fruit-) machines, which at (very long) intervals will disgorge a "jackpot" of accumulated coins. Current in this sense [in US] at least since 1930s'.—2. A dangerous situation; a grave difficulty: Can.: since ca. 1965. (Dempsey, 1975.) Adopted ex US.

Jack's alive. The number 5, esp. in the game of House: military r.s.: earlier C.20. B. & P.—2. Hence, £5 note: low. (Sharpe, 1938.) Rhyming *five*. Often shortened to *Jack's* (or *Jacks*), as in 'I'll bet you a Jacks' (Norman). See **jack**, n., 11.

Jack's come home. A slap-dash hotel or boarding house: theatrical. Marsh, 1938.

jacksie,-y. The buttocks; later, the anus, as in 'Up your jacksie!': Services': late C.19–20. (H. & P.) Cf. **jaxy**.—2. Hence, a brothel: Aus. low. B., 1942.

jacky. A male Aboriginal, esp. in address (*Jacky*): Aus. coll.: mid-C.19–20.—2. A kookaburra: Aus. (B., 1943; Devanney, 1944.) Ex 'laughing *jack*ass'.—3. In *sit up like Jacky*, to sit up straight; to be on one's best behaviour: Aus. s. >, by 1930, coll. (B., 1942.) Like a monkey on a barrel-organ, Jacky or Jacko being a common nickname for a monkey. B., 1959, however, derives it ex sense 1. Wilkes, '[sitting up] almost cheekily'.

Jacob's join. What is sometimes called a 'faith supper' in church circles, i.e. the eating equivalent of a bottle party, each participant making a contribution to the communal meal: NE Lancashire. Margaret Pilkington, of Accrington, Lancashire, from whom I first heard the term, writes 'evidently belonging to a quite limited region. But no one could suggest an origin for it, though all say it should be Biblical' (P.B., 1976). Such terms are difficult to provide with an etym.; for one thing, some of them are far more widely distributed than one has suspected.

jade. A long prison-sentence: Aus. c. (B., 1942.) There is prob. an obscure pun on S.E. *sorry jade*.

Jafbo Club. See **Jabo Club**.

Jaffas. 'Large chunks of coal, too big to put into fire box without first breaking up with coal pick' (McKenna, 1, 1970): railwaymen's: earlier C.20. Ex *Jaffa* oranges.

Jag. A Jaguar motor-car: coll.: since ca. 1946.

jag. An injection: medical: adopted, ca. 1905, from US. Cognate with *jab*; Munro, 1985, notes its use esp. in Glasgow.—2. In Aus., 'a dose of a narcotic administered for purposes of addiction' and 'in any way whatsoever' and therefore having nothing to do with *jab*: since ca. 1945. (B.P.)—3. An 'organic solvent inhaled from a handkerchief' (B.P.): Eng.: since ca. 1955. 'The child becomes dependent upon a regular "jag" ' (*New Society*, 20 June 1963).

jag-cure, the. Treatment for alcoholics: Can.: since ca. 1950. (Leechman.)

jag it in. To give up: RN: since ca. 1945. Winton, 1967, 'The messdeck dodger got discouraged and just jagged it in.' A slurring of *jack it in*, q.v. at **jack in**.

Jagger. A Cornish rating: RN (lowerdeck). An *-er* adaptation of the common Cornish surname *Jago*. (P-G-R.) Cf. **Janner**, q.v. at **Jan**, 2.

jagging, go. To make social visits, esp. in order to gossip: NZ: C.20. B., 1941, who recalls *gad* and *on the jag*. Also, since ca. 1920, Aus. (B., 1959.)

Jago. A victualling paymaster: RN (lowerdeck). Granville, 'After the officer who introduced improved messing and victualling conditions in R.N. barracks'. Hence, *going to Jago's*, 'Feeding, pre-canteen-messing in the Royal Navy: ca. 1920s: used only in Plymouth Command' (Peppitt, 1977). Cf.:-

Jago's Mansion. Royal Naval Barracks, Devonport: RN.

jags. Self: itinerant entertainers'. Always in combination, as *my jags*, I or me: *your jags*, you; *his* or *her jags*, he or she, him or her. 'Mind that your *jags* (self) keeps this book in your *skyrocket* (pocket) until you have mastered the lingo' (Lester). Perhaps an imperfect blend of *jills* and *nabs* used similarly.

jailer; loosely jailor. A policeman: Glasgow:—1934. Not ex the current S.E. sense, but coined anew from *jail*.

jainormous. See **ginormous**.

jaisy. An effeminate and polite man: Midlands. The Merseyside shape is *jessy*. Cf. **Jessie**.

jake. Methylated spirits: c., mostly tramps': from ca. 1920. Gape, 1936.

J

jake, adj. Honest, upright; equitable, correct; 'O.K.', excellent: Colonial and US. (I cannot adduce an early example, but *jake* was certainly used, in these senses, at least as early as 1910.) In Aus., *we're jake* = we're all right; *she's jake* [or *she'll be jake*] = it's jake, all is well. (Culotta.) Often elab. to *jake-a-loo* or *jakerloo*, occ. to *jake-a-bon* or *tray jake*, i.e. *très* (very) *jake*. A Can. superlative, from ca. 1920: *jake with the lever up*, excellent; extremely satisfactory or pleasant.

jake, adv. Well, profitably; honestly, genuinely: Colonial: from ca. 1905. Ex prec.

jake-drinker. An addict to methylated spirits: c. (Gape, 1936.) Cf. **feke-drinker**. Also *jake-wallahs*, as in *Toby*, 1979, where spelt *wallers*.

jakealoo, jakerloo. See **jake,** adj.

jakes. Var. of **jake-drinker**. Clayton, 1970.

jaloppy, jalopy. A cheap, or an old, motor-car: adopted, ca. 1950, ex US. The term always implies some degree of dilapidation.

jam. A difficulty, awkward 'mess': coll.: from ca. 1920. Ex sense, crowd, crush. Esp. in *get into a jam.*—2. A joy, a great pleasure: preparatory schools'. Benson, 1916, 'It had been "jam" to see the Head stamp on that yellow-covered book.'—3. Affectation: Aus.: since ca. 1905. (B., 1942.) Remembered by E.P., ca. 1910–14. Hence, *put on jam*, to put on 'side' (Wilkes).—4. See **jam-jar.**

jam bosun. A victualling officer: RN: since ca. 1920. Granville.

jam butty car. 'Police road or motorway patrol car, white with prominent red stripe along sides' (C. Turner, 1986): Merseyside. See **buttie**, 2; and cf. **jam sandwich.**

jam clacker. See **clackers**, pastry with currants on.

jam-jar. A tram-car: r.s.: early C.20. B. & P.—2. A motor-car: id.: since ca. 1925. (*Cheapjack*, 1934.) Often abbr. *jam.*—3. Hence, an armoured car: Army and RAF: since 1938. Jackson.

jam on it. An (agreeable) surplus or addition: Services': since ca. 1920. 'D'you want jam on it?' = Aren't you satisfied? or haven't you already got enough? (P-G-R.)

jam-packed. (Usu. of a crowd) 'jammed together, closely packed' (L.A., 1976): coll.: since ca. 1950.

jam-pot. 'A rear-suspension system shaped like a jam-pot, used during the 1950s on A.J.S. and Matchless motorcycles. Indeed there is [1979] a "Jam-pot Club" whose members use these machines' (Dunford).

jam roll. Parole: prison r.s.: later C.20. Green, 2.—2. Social Security payment: r.s. on *dole*. (James Williamson, 1984.)

jam-sampler. Motorcyclist turned car-driver: motorcyclists': later C.20. (Dunford.) Ex **jam-jar**, 2.

jam sandwich. A police car: 'Three big jam sandwiches, lights flashing, roared into the village' (*Guardian*, 12 May 1988). A var. of **jam butty car**, q.v.

jam-strangling bastard. 'A man whose phenomenal luck suggests a degree of manoeuvring to ensure it, esp. R.N. sailor lucky in time and place of duties, privileges, etc.' (L.A.): Services': current by ca. 1950. Later shortened, sometimes, to *jammy bastard*, though the latter's luck may be really pure luck. (P.B.) See **strangle**, 1.

jam tart. Heart: r.s. Cf. synon. **strawberry tart**.—2. Fart: r.s.: later C.20. 'I first heard the expression "a pound to a jamtart" from an Australian professor ca. 1975' (Hamblin, 1988). With the 'bet' cf. the synon. *a pound to a pinch of shit.*

jamas. Pyjamas: Aus. Humphries, 1982.

jamberoo. A 'good time'; esp. a drinking-bout: Aus.:—1935. A perversion of orig. s. meaning of *jamboree*, a spree, frolic.

James the First. The First Lieutenant in an HM ship: RN (officers') joc.: since ca. 1920. Prompted by *Jimmy the One.*

jammies. (Also pron. *jahmies*.) Pyjamas: middle classes'. Ex nursery. (P.B.) Occ. spelt *jarmies* (Humphries, 1980).

jammy. Unwashed: Aus. low coll.: later C.20. McNeil.

jammy bastard. See **jam-strangling bastard**, and cf. **spawny git.**

Jampans, the. The Japanese: among East African soldiers in Burma: ca. 1943–5. P-G-R.

Jan. See **Feb.**—2. Frequent nickname of ratings with a Devon burr: RN. Hence, *Janner*, a West Countryman: id.: since ca. 1910. Granville.

Janc, the. The *J*unior *A*rmy and *N*avy *C*lub: RN and Army officers': earlier C.20. F. & G.

jane, n. A woman; a girl: Aus.:—1916 (Dennis); by ca. 1918, also Can. ?Ex US. Cf. synon s. **judy**, and **sheila**. Brit. in this sense by 1933 (Sayers).—2. Hence, by specialisation, a sweetheart or girlfriend: coll.: mid-1920s. Tey, 1927.—3. See **straight Jane . . .**

Jane, adj. Glasgow c., from ca. 1925, as in MacArthur, 'Isobel was clearly a real "Jane bit o' stuff"—a girl of quality who wore a hat, without affectation, because she was accustomed to it.' Ex *jane*, a girl. Contrast **hairy**, n., 1, q.v.

Jane Shaw. See:-

Jane Shore. Tinned meat: RN: C.20. (Bowen.) Suggested by *Harriet Lane* and *Fanny Adams*, for they too were decapitated. Since ca. 1940, more commonly spelt *Shaw.*

jank, janky. Impudence; impudent: Oundle: since mid-1920s. (Marples.) Perhaps *jank* is a back-formation ex *janky*, and *janky* may be a perversion of *jaunty.*

janker(-)wallah; rarely jankers wallah. An airman undergoing punishment: RAF: since ca. 1920. (Jackson.) See:-

jankers. Defaulters; their punishment; punishment cells; defaulters' bugle-call: since early C.20. There is doubt about whether the term was orig. Army, as Granville suggests, or RN, as E.P. maintains, following Bowen. Echoic: prob. ex *janglers* or *jangles*. The term was ob. by mid-1960s, when the form of punishment was largely superseded by fines, but to thousands of national servicemen (1939–62), to be *on jankers* meant parading at all sorts of awkward hours, in various modes of uniform, being confined to barracks, and performing menial, usu. very dirty, and often pointless, tasks. The defaulter, a *jankers man*, was at the whim and mercy of the *jankers king*, the provost sergeant: both terms in F. & G., and dating from (prob.) early WW1. 'Well, what did you get? [i.e. what punishment]'—'Worse than I thought: ten days effing jankers!' (E.P.; P.B.) Support for E.P. comes from Goodenough, 1901, who records the RN var. *jenker*, a defaulter.

Janner. See **Jan**, 2.

jannock, jonnick, jonnock, jonnuk. Honest, loyal, equitable; proper, customary; conclusive: s. since ca. 1820, > in 1914, fairly gen. coll. In Aus., where it dates ca. 1880–1960, it is gen. pron. *jonnuk*. In RN usage, since ca. 1925, it has meant 'in accordance with Service etiquette' (Granville).

janusmug. An intermediary, esp. in shady arrangements or transactions: Aus. c.: since ca. 1915. (B., 1942.) I.e. *Janus* (facing two ways) + *mug* (not necessarily a fool: merely small-town, insignificant).

Jap-happy, often contracted to *Jappy*. Unduly afraid of, or subservient to, the Japanese: prisoners-of-war in Far East: 1942–5. (Rivett, 1946.) **Jap-happies**. See PRISONER-OF-WAR SLANG, §13, in Appx.

japanned. (Of a criminal) converted by a prison chaplain: Aus. c. (B., 1942.) Ex C.18–19 s., to ordain a priest.

japper. 'In theory, discipline [in the engine-cleaning sheds] was very strict . . . However, the "japper" fights, messy affairs of throwing clods of oily waste at each other, still went on' (McKenna, 2): railwaymen's.

jar. A pint or 'handle' of beer: Aus.: since ca. 1920. Baker.—2. A glass of beer: since ca. 1950. Recorded as Lincolnshire dial. in *EDD* Sup., 1905.—3. Imitation jewellery so skilfully made that it seems real; to *do a jar up* is to sell it to a 'mug' or 'sucker' and the *jar* comes when the trickery is discovered: c.: since mid-1940s. (Norman, 1959.) Tempest, 1950, has, 'faked diamonds. "Phoney" diamonds = Schnide [see **snide**, adj.] jars (from jam jar—glass).' But Taylor, 1982, defines it as a replica jewel used in shoplifting jewellery, and offers yet another etym.: 'so called because, nine times out of ten, the stone would be made of jargon, a derivative of the relatively valueless zircon.'—4. A stoneware hot-water bottle: Anglo-

Irish gen. coll.: C.20 or earlier; less used with the arrival of the modern rubber/plastic 'hottie'. (Raab.) Perhaps to be considered dial., but this sense not recorded in *EDD*.

jar-up. See **jar**, 3.

jargoon. To show (a person) a real diamond and sell him a paste: c. Ex the S.E. n. Cf. **jar**, 3.

jarms, jarmies. See **jammies**.

jarrah-jerker. A W. Aus. timber-getter: Aus.: since ca. 1920. (B., 1943.) The *jarrah* is an Aus. hardwood.

jarred off. Depressed (and disgusted); 'fed up': Services' (mostly Army): since ca. 1930. Kersh, 1942; H. & P., 1943.

jarring. A reprimand: Public Works':—1935. Ex *give a person a jar* (jolt) or else ex *jar on one's nerves*.

jaspers. Cockroaches: MN: since ca. 1930. (Peppitt.) Origin?

java (or **Java**). Coffee (only rarely, and not since ca. 1920, tea): Can. (B. & P.); it is noted in RM (and hence, prob. RN) use in later C.20, in Hawke, 1979.

jaw-box, the. Journalism. Munro, 1931.—2. The kitchen sink, with the constant chatter over the washing-up: Glasgow domestic: C.19–20; somewhat ob. by 1970. Duncan, 1960.

jaw-jaw. Talking; discussion. Harold Macmillan gave the term wide currency when, speaking at Canberra on 30 Jan. 1958, he declared: 'Jaw-jaw is better than war-war', prob. consciously echoing Churchill's dictum of 1954, 'Talking jaw to jaw is better than going to war.' Singer, 1980, on Barlinnie Special Unit, Glasgow, used the headline 'The prison where "jaw-jaw" replaced "war-war" '. (P.B.)

jawbone. To urge, as by political, trades union, leaders, etc., to comply with government policy: adopted, ex US, early 1970s. (Barnhart; Chambers, 1977.) Hence n., *jawboning*.

jawl. To decamp: market-traders'. (*M.T.*) Adopted and adapted ex Romany.

jaxy and **joxy.** Female pudend: prostitutes' (notably Liverpool). Cf. **jacksie**, 1, the buttocks.

jay-walker. (Hence, *jay-walking*.) One who crosses a street to the peril of the traffic: 1925: s. (ex US) >, ca. 1934, coll., and, by 1960, S.E. Ex US *jay*, a provincial 'loon'.

jaybird. 'A housewife who does her housework in the nude. An American term often used in Australian newspapers' (B.P., 1974): potentially Aus. since 1973.

Jays, the. Members of the Society of Jesus: gen. Catholic coll.: C.19–20. *The Jays* merely phoneticises 'the Js'.

jazz. Nonsense, 'baloney': adopted, ex US, 1960, but heard occ. in UK as early as 1957. In *Sunday Times*, 26 Nov. 1961, with var. *razzmataz(z)*.—2. In *get a jazz on*, (to) get a move on, esp. in imperative: mostly Army: WW2. P-G-R.—3. See JAZZ TERMS, in Appx.

jazz trains. '1920 suburban stock with coloured strips over doors denoting class of compartment (GWR)': railwaymen's: 1920s. *Railway*, 2nd.

jazz up. 'To modernize; to add decorative touches to; (jocularly of a book) to revise and augment' (B.P.): since ca. 1950. To enliven; esp., to convert classical music into 'pop': since ca. 1945.

jazzer. A 'K3 N.E.R. locomotive' (*Railway*): railwaymen's: ?ca. 1940–50.

jazzing. 'The rapid shooting and hauling of nets in the path of the incoming salmon' (Granville): trawlermen's: since ca. 1945.

jazzy. Loud-coloured; 'flashy': since ca. 1935. Harrison, 1943, 'He wore a blue jumper of that inarticulate boisterousness called "jazzy".'

Jeanie boy is the North Country's equivalent of **Nancy boy**.

jee. A var. of grafters' **gee** (q.v.). Orwell, 1933.

jeed. Slightly derogatory term, used by technical and specialist soldiers in a signals regt. in Cyprus, late 1950s, for one of those vitally necessary members of the unit who had no special 'trade' and who did all the hard manual work. Used also as adj. Ex G.D. = general duties; cf. next, 2. (P.B.)

jeep. A member of the R Can. NVR: ca. 1938+. (H. & P.) Prob. ex Eugene the *Jeep*, name of an animal in the US comic strip 'Popeye the Sailor-man' by E.C. Segar.—2. A

utility, orig. military, small truck: adopted, ex US, by the Canadians in 1939, by the Brit. army in 1941 and by the RAF early in 1942 (H. & P., 1943); since mid-C.20, S.E. Ex *G.P.* (= general purposes) vehicle.—3. Hence, late 1942+, Services' term for a girl friend.—4. A junior production- (or programme-) engineer: BBC: since ca. 1944. Worsley, 1948, 'These Junior Programme Engineers, known in the B.B.C. as "Jeeps", are very important people'. A vocalisation of *j—p*.—5. *The Jeep*. See **Chad**.—6. See **Gunter's perms**.

jeepable. (Of roads or tracks) usable by jeeps (see **jeep**, 2): Army coll. > j.: since ca. 1944. P-G-R.

jeepers creepers, occ. merely **jeepers!** An exclam. adopted, ca. 1944, ex US servicemen; ob. by ca. 1970. Euph. ex *Jesus Christ!*

Jeese or **Jeez!** Jesus!, as exclam. or oath: low. Ex US.

jeezly. The discovery of gremlins 'is credited to a certain pilot of No. 55(B) Squadron, one Flying Officer Bain or possibly Baynes, known as Jeezle, from his invention of the word *jeezly*, which "covered almost everything miserable or rotten—septic, unfortunate, low-grade or inferior, dull, ill-conceived, etc." . . . proof of [the word's] existence comes from Malcolm Lowry . . . , who has it [in] his novel *October Ferry to Gabriola* [1964]—"some jeezly fool" ' (quoted in Edwards, 1974).

Jekyll and Hyde. Crooked; spurious, counterfeit: since ca. 1920; orig. and still mainly underworld, but, by 1940 at latest, also police. It rhymes on **snide**, q.v., and, esp. in the underworld, is often shortened to *Jekyll* (Gosling, 1959). A neat pun on R.L. Stevenson's characters.

jel. Jealous: girls' Public Schools': since ca. 1920. Spain, 1949.

jell, n. A coward: Aus.: since ca. 1950. (Dick.) Cf. the S.E. 'to tremble like a *jelly*', and **jelly-belly**.—2. See sense 2 of:-

jell, v.i. (Of ideas, plans) to take full shape, to fall into place, to become settled: adopted, ca. 1945, ex US; by 1955, coll.; by 1975 perhaps, by 1977 certainly, familiar S.E. Ex a jelly's cooling and setting. (Dick.) See **jell**, n.—2. As *jell it*, to act like a coward: Aus. (Dick.)

jelly. Gelignite: poss. orig. Aus., since ca. 1918 (B., 1942); by 1925, gen. Brit. s.—2. A gelatine diffuser. See **put a jelly** . . . .

jelly baby. A gelignite expert: since late 1940s. (Clayton, 1970.) Ex prec., 1, and the children's jelly sweet in the shape of a baby.

jelly beans. Amphetamines: drugs c. (Stockley, 1986.) US since—1971 (Spears).

jelly-belly. A coward: Aus.: since ca. 1930. (B.P.) Hence the adj. *jelly-bellied*: since ca. 1935. Cf. **jell**.

jelly-legged. (Of a boxer) groggy: sporting coll. L.A., 1960.

jellymould. A Morris Minor saloon car: later C.20. *Telegraph Sunday Mag.*, 8 Mar. 1987.

jemimas. Elastic-sided boots: coll.

Jenny. See **Jenny Wren**.

jenny. A var., e.g. in the police novels of Alan Hunter, of **genny**, q.v., a generator.

Jenny Lea or **Lee.** Tea: r.s.: late C.19–20. Also *Rosy Lee* and *you and me*.—2. A flea: id.:—1923 (Manchon). P.P., 1932, differentiates thus: *Jenny Lea*, tea; *Jenny Lees*, fleas.—3. A key: id.

Jenny Scribe. A member of the WRNS with Writer rating: RN: since ca. 1940. Cf. **Jenny Wren**.

Jenny Willocks. A very effeminate male; a hermaphrodite: Glasgow:—1934.

Jenny Wren. A member of the WRNS, a 'Wren': since 1939. (H. & P.) Ex the centuries old folk-name for the wren. Cf. **Jill Tar**.

jere or **jeer.** A turd: c.: since C.17. This sense survives in market-traders' s., e.g. 'He's gone for a jeer' = he is at stool (*M.T.*).—2. Hence(?), one's backside: low; esp. showmen's: C.19–20. Bell, 1936, and (an Aus. example) Park, 1950.—3. A male homosexual: Franklyn records this sense as deliberate r.s.—4. In *off the jeer*, it = 'off the rear', 'mid-20 C. pickpockets' slang for a wallet removed from the victim's rear trousers pocket' (Franklyn 2nd).

J

jerecase or **jeercase**. The buttocks; arse: market-traders'. As in, e.g., 'I'm not going to lick his jeercase' (*M.T.*). An extension of prec., q.v.; cf. *arse-piece*, at **-piece.**

Jeremiah. A fire: r.s., esp. urban labourers': *John o' London's Weekly*, 9 June 1934.

jerk, n. A musculo-tendinous reflex (action): medical students':—1933 (*Slang*). E.g. a 'knee-jerk'.—2. A chap, fellow, 'guy'; usu. with pej. tinge: adopted, 1943, ex US servicemen. Webb, 1945.—3. Custard: Aus. Army: WW2. (B., 1943.) ?Ex *jerk off*.—4. In *had a jerk in*, 'Mileometer turned back (now illegal)' (Graham-Ranger, 1981): car dealers': later C.20.—5. See **jerks,** 2; **jerk in it.**

jerk, v. Elliptical for **jerk off,** q.v., to masturbate.

jerk in (to) it, put a. To act smartly or vigorously; hurry: from ca. 1912. Ex physical training and prob. suggested by *jump to it*. (B. & P.) —2. See **jerk,** n., 4.

jerk of the cirk (or **sirk**). Clerk of the motorcycle competition course, at racetrack, rally, etc.: motorcyclists': ca. 1930s. Prob. ex 'Clerk of the Circuit'. (Dunford, 2.) Cf. **shufti jerk.**

jerk off, v.i. and v. reflexive. To masturbate: low coll.: C.18–20. An ob. low s. var. is *jerk* (one's) *jelly* or *juice*. Other, extant, variants are *jerk* (one's) *mutton* or *turkey*. *Jerkin'* (one's) *gherkin* (low: later C.20) is obviously ex the shape, but is heavily influenced by rhyme, as in 'Perkin was furkin' jerkin' his gherkin' (Forwood, 1962). Cf. **gallop** . . . and **pull** . . . in this sense, which may, like *jerk*, also be v.t. (E.P.; P.B.)

jerks. Physical training: from ca. 1905: perhaps orig. naval or military. Abbr. *physical jerks*.—2. Elliptical for *fly-jerks*, 'small pieces of cork suspended from the brim of a tramp's hat to ward off flies' (B., 1943): Aus. coll.

jerrican. A petrol can captured from the Germans (*Jerries*); then any petrol can of similar type: Army in N. Africa: 1940–3. (P-G-R.) Extant and, since ca. 1945, S.E.

Jerry; occ. **Gerry.** N. and adj., *German*; esp. (of) a German soldier: 1914+; ob. From mid-1916, more gen. than *Fritz(y)*. Often half-affectionately, as in 'Poor old Jerry's copping it hot from our heavies.' (B. & P.) There is much to be said for derivation from *jerry*, C.19–20 s., a chamber-pot: the German soldier's large steel helmet did, in fact, look rather like a chamber-pot.—2. Hence, 'a German aircraft': since ca. 1915 and current again in 1939–45; in 1940–1, frequently used by civilians (Berrey, 1940).—3. The inevitable nickname for anyone surnamed Dawson. (*John o' London's Weekly*, 12 Dec. 1936.) Why?

jerry, adj. Mostly in *be full jerry to* (someone), to be fully aware of his tricks or schemes or ulterior purpose: since ca. 1930. (Griffiths, 1960.)

jerry(-)diddle, or one word. 'A drink on the house' (B., 1942): Aus. Cf. **Jimmy Riddle.**—2. (Also *Jerry Diddle*.) A violin: r.s.: late C.19–20. Franklyn.

Jerry O'Gorman. A Mormon: r.s.

Jerry's Backyard. The Skagerrak and Kattegat: RAF Coastal Command: 1943–5. (Noble, 1945.)

Jerusalem (or **Jews'**) **letters.** Tattooing: nautical:—1923 (Manchon).

Jerusalem parrot. A flea: low:—1923 (Manchon).

Jerusalem screw. 'A strict disciplinarian. The term refers to a base Provost unit which earned displeasure at Tel Aviv in 1941 during World War II' (McNeil): Aus. coll.

Jes (pron. *Jěz*). A Jesuit: Catholics': C.19–20.

Jessie. An effeminate man: Glasgow:—1934. Cf. **Nancy** and **pansy.**

Jesus boots. 'Used in reference to any requirement to cross water barriers: e.g. "You'll need Jesus boots for that" ' (F.J. French): RAF: WW2.—2. Sandals: teenagers', and thence Army (where sandals are part of WRAC tropical kit): since early 1960s. (P.B.) R.S. suggested, 1972, 'A by-product of the contemporary . . . Jesus-cult?'

Jesus factor. 'The extra safety-margin allowed for imponderables' (Peppitt): RN: since ca. 1940. (Jenkins, 1966.) Cf.:-

Jesus nut. '[The helicopter] depends on the "Jesus nut", the nut that keeps the main blades on . . . ' (*Sunday Times* mag., 25 Nov. 1979): RN helicopter crews'.

Jesus wept! A low exclam. expressive of commiseration or disgust or annoyance. See John 11. 35.

jet, n. A jet-propelled aircraft: RAF (and aircraft engineers') coll.: mid-1944; by ca. 1960, S.E.

jet. To travel by a jet aircraft: coll.: since ca. 1960.

jet job. An extremely fast racing car: Can. motorists': 1948+.

jet jockey. 'A fighter pilot' (Wilson, 1979): RAF: later C.20.

jet set, the. The very rich socialites flying by 'jet' from one 'in' capital or resort to another: since early 1960s: at first, coll., but by 1975, S.E. Hence *jet-setter*, one who belongs to this society and way of life: since late 1960s.

jetty. Having the supposed glamour of the **jet set;** characteristic of them. 'For Pubbing: Thomas à Becket, the "local" on Old Kent Road [London]. Noisy and musical, and not at all jetty' (Everly, 1966).

Jew chums. Jewish refugees from Germany and Central Europe: Aus.: since ca. 1936. (B., 1942.) With a pun on *new-chums*: cf. US *refujews*.

jewer. A rating who, for money (or rum or tobacco), will make another man's uniform for him: RN lowerdeck: late C.19–20. (Carr, 1939.) Ex older nautical *jew*, a ship's tailor, whence *jewing*, tailoring.

Jewie. A Jew: Anglo-Irish coll.: late C.19–20. (Joyce, 1922.) Cf. **Jewy.**—2. As *j-*, a jewfish; a jew lizard: Aus. coll. B., 1953.

jewing-firm. 'A tailoring concern run by one or more of the ship's company' (Granville): RN.

Jewish forest. Three threes: poker-players'. Ex the pron. *t'ree t'rees*. (A. Ross.)

Jewish Joanna. 'Ironic term for a cash register' (Powis): low coll.: later C.20. *Joanna* = piano (r.s.).

Jewish Oxo. Money: Londoners' joc.: later C.20. (Dures, 1982.) *Oxo* is a famous beef extract.

Jewish piano or **pianola.** 'Ironic term for a cash register' (Powis): low coll. The 2nd form is Aus., recorded by Baker, 1943.—2. 'Although taximeters were not made compulsory until later in 1907, the General Cab Co. Ltd were adamant that they were not running cabs without them, and they had been steadily recruiting drivers pledged to take out cabs with the "jewish pianos" or "zeigers", as they called them' (Warren, 1976).

Jew's Bentley. Var. of **Jew's Rolls-Royce.**

Jew's letters. Tattooing. See **Jerusalem letters.**

Jew's Rolls-Royce. A Jaguar motor-car: since ca. 1938. Much chromium plating 'and all that'.

Jew's typewriter. 'Ironic term for a cash register' (Powis): low coll. Cf. **Jewish Joanna** or . . . **piano.**

Jewtocracy. The art of hatching or developing mysteries: cultured: since ca. 1930. On *plutocracy*.

jewy. Var. of **jewie.** (Mann, 1945.)

jez. Sonar sweep by aircraft or ships: RN: later C.20. Ex codeword 'Jezebel'. Knight cites Wingate.

jib show. A show featuring only girls: Can. carnival s.: since ca. 1920.

jigger. A man; esp., *silly jigger*: since ca. 1918. Orig. euph. for non-opprobrious *bugger*.—2. An entry; a passage between terrace-house backyards: Merseyside: late C.19–20.

jigger-rabbit. A cat: Merseyside. Ex prec., 2. (Hughes, 1984.)

jiggers. Stairs: market-traders'. (*M.T.*) Prob. simply ex S.E. *jig*, v., to move jerkily.

jiggle and jog. A Frenchman: r.s., on *Frog*: later C.20. Barker, 1979.

jiggle juice. Special fuel for racing cars: racing motorists': adopted, ex US, ca. 1955. *Autocar*, 8 June 1962.

jiggler. 'Skeleton key for pin tumbler lock' (Powis): c. Poss. ex US: *Underworld* records its use in the American car-stealing racket, late 1920s.

jiggly. Of a woman, inclined to copulation: low.

jiggy. A jigsaw puzzle: domestic coll. *Sunday Times* mag., 27 Sep. 1981.

jildi, jildy, jildo; occ. **jeldi(-y).** Adj. and adv., 'lively'; as imperative, 'Look sharp!'; as v., to be quick, move quickly or promptly; also used as n., in *on the jildi, get a jildi on*: Army: late C.19–20; ob. by 1975. Blaker (ex-Indian-Army sergeant speaking): 'Come on. We'll catch 'im if we jildi'. The n. uses, esp. *get a jildi on*, are WW2+, as is *do a jildi move*, to retreat hastily or, among tank men, to take evasive action (P-G-R). Ex Hindustani n. *jildi*, quickness. Cf. Romany *jido, jidilo*, lively; and **jillo,** q.v.

Jill, hence also **jill.** A girl: since ca. 1945; not very common. Probably ex 'Every Jack has his *Jill*'.

Jill Tar or **Jiltar.** A member of the WRNS: 1939+. (H. & P.) Prob. a journalistic coinage; never much used, and soon supplanted by **Jenny (Wren),** q.v. Cf.:-

Jillaroo or **j-.** A land girl: Aus.: WW2. (B., 1943.) A joc. feminine of *jackaroo*.

jillo! Hurry up!; look lively!: Army: late C.19–mid-20. Ex Hindustani *chalo*, move off!, get going!, imperative of *chalna*, to move off. Influenced by **jildi,** q.v.

jillpots, his or **her.** He, she—him, her; that person: itinerant entertainers'. Often shortened to *his*, or *her, jills*. Lester.

Jim. The sum of £1: Aus.: earlier C.20. (B., 1943; Wilkes.) Ex older *Jimmy o'Goblin*, a sovereign.—2. (Or *jimmie, -y.*) 'Wherever prostitutes congregate with their clients . . . there will be other loiterers—the "jims", the "men in raincoats" [see **dirty mac**], who watch the transactions and purchased intimacies in a morbid and unhealthy silence' (Powis): c. and police s.: later C.20.—3. 'Sparks is just the universal word for a working electrician—though in the film studios usually preceded by Jim: Jim Chippy [carpenter], Jim Rigger, Jim Sparks . . . Never Jim Producer, though' (Daniells, 1980).

Jim Crow. An aircraft on reconnaissance flight: RAF: WW2. Forbes, 1942.—2. A roof spotter of aircraft: civilian Services': 1939+. H. & P.—3. Hence, one who keeps watch while, e.g., gambling is in progress: combatant Services': since ca. 1940. H.&P.—4. A plate-layer: railwaymen's: since ca. 1945. (*Railway,* 2nd.) He needs to keep a look-out for oncoming trains. Cf. senses 2 and 3.—5. Racial prejudice, esp. against Negroes: since ca. 1955. Cf. the song 'Jim Crow Blues' sung by the American Negro folk-singer Huddie Ledbetter ('Leadbelly'), ca. 1870?–1949.—6. A professional actor: r.s. on *pro*: itinerant entertainers'. Lester.

jim(-)jams, the. The fidgets; nervousness; the 'creeps'; low spirits: coll. (Hutchinson, 1908; Galsworthy, 1926.) Also *the jimmies*: coll.: from ca. 1920. *OED* Sup.—2. As *jim-jams*, pyjamas: domestic coll. Humphries, 1982.

Jim Skinner. Dinner: r.s. Ortzen, 1938.

Jiminy (or **Jimininy**) **Crickets!** A widespread Can. (ex US) expletive: since ca. 1920. W. & F. suggest that it stands for *Jesu Domine*; Leechman and I, that it is a euph. for *Jesus Christ*.

Jimmie's. See **Jimmy's;** also, short for **Jimmy Britts.**—*The jimmies*. See **jim-jams,** 1.

Jimmies' Union. The First Lieutenants in a flotilla of destroyers, an informal association presided over by the senior 'Jimmy': RN officers': since the 1920s. Cf. **watchkeepers' union.**

Jimmy or **jimmy** (capital where appropriate), n. St. James's Palace, London: mostly Regular Army, esp. Guards': late C.19–20. This, and **Jimmy guard,** q.v., occur in, e.g., Kersh, 1941.—2. 'Piece of metal illicitly placed in blast pipe causing [= to cause] greater draught on fire and better steaming. Used in 1890–1930 period when drivers were paid a bonus for saving coal and oil and Railway Companies bought cheap coal' (*Railway*): railwaymen's, esp. among drivers and their mates.—3. The figure of Mercury in the badge of the Royal Corps of Signals: Royal Signals': prob. since soon after the Corps' formation, 1920. (P.B.) Cf. **Jimmy on a rock cake.**—

4. 'An injection of a narcotic. (Canadian)' (Home Office): drug addicts': later C.20.—5. See **Jim,** 2; **Jimmy the One.**

jimmy, v. Powis glosses *jimmying* as, '(a) Obtaining entry into cinemas, theatres, dog tracks and enclosures at race meetings by subterfuge and without paying. (b) Urinating.': (a) is c., (b) low coll. For (b) see **Jimmy Riddle.**

Jimmy Britts, often shortened to *Jimmies* and always preceded by *the*. Diarrhœa: Aus. r.s., on *the shits*.—2. Hence, fig., 'a fit of nerves; a state of anger' (Wilkes): Aus.: B., 1941, lists *have the Brits up*, to be afraid, and Hungerford, 1952, uses the var. 'a touch of the Jim-brits'.

Jimmy Green. As in *I was Jimmy Green on that*, I let myself be taken in or duped about that: coll. (L.A.) A personification of *green*, naive, gullible.

Jimmy guard. Ceremonial guard duty at St James's Palace: Army, esp. Guards'. See **Jimmy,** 1, and cf. **Buck guard,** duty at Buckingham Palace.

Jimmy on a rock cake. Joc. description of the Royal Corps of Signals' badge, the figure of Mercury, one foot resting on a tiny globe: Army, esp. RCS: since early 1920s. (Mays, 1969.) In later C.20 usu. abbr. **Jimmy.** Cf. **a pansy resting on its laurels,** the Intelligence Corps' badge. (P.B.)

Jimmy Prescott. Waistcoat: r.s. Lester.

Jimmy Riddle, n. and v. A urination; to urinate: r.s., on *piddle*: late C.19–20. (B. & P.) In later C.20 usu. *have a Jimmy Riddle*. Cf. rarer and, in later C.20, ob. var., *Jerry Riddle*. See **jimmy,** v. Occ., facetiously, a *James R*.

Jimmy Rollocks. Testicles: r.s., on *bollocks*: low. An earlier var. was *Tommy Rollocks*. Franklyn 2nd.

Jimmy Skinner. A dinner. See **Jim Skinner.**

Jimmy the One. 'The first lieutenant (a lieutenant-commander as he usually is in these days [1916]) is "Jimmy the One" ' ('Taffrail'): RN. Often simply *Jimmy* (Granville). See **Jimmies' Union.**

Jimmy Woodser. A person who drinks alone; a drink by oneself: Aus.: late C.19–20. Wilkes cites Acland, 1933, who derives it ex an actual 'loner', one Jim Woods; one drinking alone was said to be 'doing a Jimmy Woodser'. Cf. **drink with the flies.**—2. Hence, a person alone, esp. an orphan: Aus.: since ca. 1935. Niland, 1958.

Jimmy Woods-ing. Solitary drinking: NZ, esp. miners'. (Devanney, 1928.) Ex prec., 1.

jimpie,-y. The Argentine troops 'were doomed the moment the commandos set up their "jimpies" (general-purpose machine-guns) on Wireless Ridge' (Wain, 1982): Services': later C.20.

jingle. Money: Aus. and NZ: since ca. 1925. (B., 1942.) Echoic.

jingled. Tipsy: ca. 1910–30. Muir, 1917.

jink, v.; **jinking; jinks.** Resp., 'To turn quickly and skilfully in the air to avoid enemy action; the activity or the practice of making these turns; the turns themselves. Also *jink away*, noun and verb' (Partridge, 1945); 1943, H. & P., the 2nd and 3rd; *Reader's Digest*, Feb. 1941, the first, which dates from at least as early as 1937 in the RAF, whose use thereof is merely an application of S.E. (mainly Scottish) *jink*, 'to make a quick elusive turn' (*OED*): since ca. 1920. Tennant, 1939.—2. To swindle (someone): Aus.: since ca. 1920. Tennant, 1939.

jinker. A bringer of bad luck: Newfoundland: since ca. 1920. A back-formation ex *jinx* (apprehended as *jinks*). English, 1955.

Jinties; the sing. *Jinty* is rare. 'Class 3 0–6–0 tank engines (MR)': railwaymen's: ?ca. 1940. *Railway*.

jinx, n. A bringer, a causer, of bad luck: adopted, ca. 1936, from US. Greenwood, 1938, 'Lay off the dames, Mario, they're all jinxes'. Cognate with **jink,** the implication being that 'they are all twisters'. Hence, bad luck, as in 'That's put a jinx on it.' More precisely: something that, midway between a devil *in* a thing and a curse *on* it, causes it to go repeatedly wrong, as in, 'This machine—this undertaking—has a jinx on it.' P.B.: in later C.20, verging on S.E. *SOD* proposes deriv. ex *jynx*, a spell or charm.

J

jinx, v., corresponds to both senses of the n. and follows within a year or two; likewise adopted from US.

jitter-bug. A very nervous or 'jittery' person: adopted, ex US, 1938; by 1945 superseded by:—2. A dancer to hot rhythm music: adopted, ex US, early 1940s. Hence *jitterbuggery* or *jitterbugging*, this style of dancing. See **jitters.**

jitter party. A party of Japanese sneaking around a camp's perimeter and trying to cause alarm by making noises and throwing grenades: Burmese front: 1942+.

jitters, the. A feeling, a bout, of (extreme) nervousness or of irritation, annoyance: from ca. 1930. (*Passing Show*, 15 July 1933.) Cf. **jim-jams.** Perhaps a perversion of S.E. *twitter*, a trembling.

jittery. On edge; very nervous: adopted in 1935 or 1936 from US. Maugham, 1937, 'For two or three weeks she was very jittery'. Ex prec.

jive, n. and v. (A form of) dance: orig. devotees' of the form, late 1940s, then gen.; ob. with change of fashion, by late 1950s. 'In the palais [de danse] you don't dance. It is—care to jive, or, get terpsichorical (Terpsichore was the Greek muse of dancing)' (Gilderdale, 2). Ex the n., itself probably of Negro origin (perhaps synon. with *jazz*). See JIVE, in Appx.—2. To talk: a talk: jazz fanatics': since ca. 1948. (*Observer*, 16 Sep. 1956.)—3. Hence, in *don't give me that jive!*: don't talk such (utter) nonsense!: jazz addicts': early 1950s. Fordyce, 1956.

Jixi, occ. **-y.** A two-seat 'taxi' licensed in 1926: coll.: 1926–7. Sir Wm Joynson-Hicks was then Home Secretary. On *taxi.* (*OED* Sup.) The H.S.'s nickname was *Jix.*

jizz. 'The distinctive character and style of [a] bird which makes it different from every other species': birdwatchers': later C.20. Carmichael, 1983, applies it fig. to stereotypes of people, e.g. drunks, punks, policemen, etc.

jizzer-rizzer. Gravy; meat juice: prob. fanciful var. of older *jipper.* (Clark, 1976.) Cf.:-

jizzup. Var. of older synon *jossop*, gravy, etc.: Birmingham s.: late C.19–20. (Onions, 1939.)

jo. A banjo (the musical instrument): mostly Can. Beames.

jo-bag. A condom: mostly Servicemen's: mid-C.20.

joag. A shilling: market-traders': mid-C.19–20. (*M.T.*) The modern form of C.19 *jogue.*

Joan of Arcs. Sharks: Aus r.s.:—1945 (Baker).

Joanna; occ. **Johanna** or **-ner.** A piano: r.s., on *pianner.* (Lyons, 1912.) Often *the old joanna.*

job. A robbery: C.18–20, c. >, ca. 1850, low. Hence, in later C.20 police coll., any crime. McClure, 1980.—2. A clock: c.:—1923 (Manchon). Why?—3. A passenger: taxi-drivers': since ca. 1910. (Hodge, 1939.) A specialisation of the S.E.—4. An aircraft: RAF: since ca. 1939. (Jackson.) Ex a *job of work.*—5. Hence, fig. as in *blonde job, blue job, brown job.* ' "I saw a wizard job in the village this morning." ' ... He had seen a beautiful girl' (Bolitho, 1941); Jackson, 1943, 'Thus, "She's a blonde job" '; *et* (how many?) *alii.*—6. A drunk: Aus.: since ca. 1939 at least. B., 1943.—7. An inferior worker; a fool; 'a bit of a mess': Aus.: since ca. 1930. Casey, 1945.—8. Always as *the job,* (working in) the Police: policemen's: later C.20. (M. Seabrook, 1986.) A specialisation of S.E.—9. A surgical operation done for cosmetic reasons, e.g. 'a nose job', a shortening or straightening of the nose, 'a boob job', an operation to render a woman's breasts more shapely: coll.: later C.20.—10. See **on the job.**

jobber. Defecation: RAF: 1970s. (Wilson, 1979.) By the 'OXFORD -ER', on earlier s. *do a job for oneself.*

jobsworth. Any very petty (in all senses) factotum or official who delights in intoning, 'It's more than my job's worth to let you ...': jazz musicians', > more gen.: since early 1950s. (Godbolt, 1985.)

jock, n. Any athlete: Can., adopted ex US: since ca. 1975. (Leech, 1985.) A physical education student (the orig. US meaning): Brit. since early 1980s at, e.g. Loughborough University. Ex S.E. *jockstrap*, an 'athletic support garment'.—2. Food, as in *jock tin*, a food container: railwaymen's. *Railway.*

Jock, adj. Scottish: Services': later C.20.

Jock columns. Highly mobile bodies of troops in the Western Desert: Army coll.: 1942–3. Ex Brigadier *Jock* Campbell. P-G-R.

Jock Guards. See **Jocks.**

jocked off, be. (Of a jockey) to be deprived of an agreed mount: racing: since ca. 1930. Francis, 1964, 'I discovered that two of my three prospective mounts were mine no longer. I had been, in the expressive phrase, jocked off.'

jocker. Athletes' 'jock-strap' [see **jock,** n.]: Public Schools'.

jockey. The piece of bread added to a 'toke' (small loaf) to make up the correct weight: prison c. Spenser, 1934.—2. A bus-driver: busmen's: from ca. 1920. (*Daily Herald*, 5 Aug. 1936.) The driver of any heavy-load vehicle: hauliers' s.: from ca. 1925.—3. A policeman: c.: mid-C.20. Gosling, 1959.—4. A pilot: RAF: since ca. 1950. Esp. *jet-jockey*, a fighter-pilot. Cf. sense 2.—5. 'Wherever prostitutes congregate with their clients, or "jockeys" as they contemptuously call them' (Powis): later C.20.—6. 'Early English thieves' cant ... which is occasionally used today [ca. 1950], particularly by gipsies and "didikais". "Hullo, Jockey, how are you?" ' (Tempest).

jockey-stick. The thin piece of wood with which the 'jockey' (see 1) is attached to the 'toke': prison c. Spenser, 1934.

jockey up. To ride pillion: since late 1940s. Willis, 1976.

jockey's whip (occ. **jockeys**). A bed; (a) sleep: r.s., on *kip*: ca. 1940–60. Franklyn.—2. (In pl.) Potato chips: trawlermen's r.s. Mitford, 1969.

Jocks. Esp. *the Jocks,* the Scots Guards; in full, *the Jock Guards:* Army: late C.19–20. Kersh, 1941, cites also *the Micks* and *the Taffs,* the Irish and the Welsh Guards.

Jodrell Bank. A worn-out old whore: since ca. 1965: r.s. on synon. *tank.* Haden-Guest.—2. (An act of) masturbation: N. Country r.s., on *wank:* later C.20. (Buchan, 1986.) Cf. synon. **J. Arthur** (Rank).

joe (and **Joe**). 'A name for anyone in the Service' (Jackson): RAF: since ca. 1920.—2. Short for **Joe Soap** (Emanuel, 1945), and **Joe Blake,** qq.v.—3. In such phrases as 'a good Joe', a good fellow, 'an honest Joe', an honest man, 'the ordinary Joe', 'the ordinary man-jack, esp. RN' (L.A.), it was, ca. 1944, adopted ex US.—4. 'Weak person, easily imposed on' (Home Office): prisoners' c.: later C.20. See **div,** 2, and cf. **Joe Soap.**

Joe Baxey. A taxi: Merseyside r.s., as 'Let's get a JB', 'Let's get a Baxey', etc.: later C.20. (C. Turner, 1986.)

Joe Blake. A cake: r.s.: late C.19–20. B. & P.—2. A snake: Aus. r.s.—3. Beefsteak: r.s.—1933.

Joe Blakes, the. Delirium tremens: Aus. r.s., on *snakes.* Marshall, 1946.

Joe boy, Joe job. One who is detailed for an unpleasant job (a 'Joe job'): Can. Army: since ca. 1940.

Joe Buck. Coïtion: low Aus. r.s.; not very common: since ca. 1930. (B.P.)

Joe Cardboard. A synon. of *Joe Soap,* a softie, a constant dupe: mostly Services': early 1950s.

Joe Cunt. The man who gets all the dirty work to do; the one who lets himself be imposed upon: Services': since ca. 1920. *Joe Hunt* is the rhyming euph.: id.

Joe Erk. 'A peculiar and ingenious combination of "Joe" (Canadian abbreviation of "Joe Soap"), "erk" (British) and "jerk", American for a dull-witted fellow' (Blair, 1947): RCAF: 1939+. Perhaps r.s. on US, hence Can., s. *jerk.* Franklyn.

Joe Goss. Boss: Aus.r.s.: since ca. 1910. Franklyn.

Joe Gurr. Prison: c.: since ca. 1930. (Sharpe, 1938.) Rhyming on C.19 s. *stir.*

Joe Hook. (A) crook: r.s. P.P., 1932.—2. A book: r.s.: since ca. 1930. Cf. **Joe Rook.**

Joe Hunt. See **Joe Cunt.** Hence, a fool. Franklyn.

Joe job. See **Joe boy.**

Joe Marks. Sharks: Aus. r.s.:—1945 (Baker). Cf. **Joan of Arcs.**

Joe Morgan. Aus. var. of *Molly O'Morgan*, an organ:—1945 (Baker).

Joe Muggins. Elab. of **muggins,** 1.

Joe Rocks. Socks: r.s. Suggested by **almond rocks,** q.v.

Joe (occ. **Jo**) **Ronce.** A harlot's bully: r.s., on *ponce.* Hence, *the Jo(e) Roncing stakes,* 'poncing'. *Gilt Kid,* 1936.

Joe Rook. Same as **Joe Hook.** Cf.:-

Joe Rooks (singular very rare). Bookmakers, esp. those who ply on the course: racing r.s., on synon. *books.* Franklyn 2nd.

Joe Rourke. A thief, esp. a pickpocket: c.: mid-C.19–20. (Sharpe, 1938.) Rhyming on older s. synon. *fork.*

Joe Shmo. Everyman, as in 'Every Joe Shmo on the street will say . . .' (Walker, 1981): US influence.

Joe Soap. An unintelligent fellow that is 'over-willing' and therefore made a 'willing horse': Services', esp. RAF: since ca. 1930. (H. & P.) R.s., on **dope,** n., 6. Also as v.: 'Thus, "Yes, I'm always Joe Soaping for somebody" ' (Jackson). P.B.: in later C.20 usage has > gen. and widespread; the origin prob. now, 1983, almost obscured. Hence:-

Joe'd, in *be Joe'd.* To be given the dirty work, or to be left 'carrying the can': RAF, then other Services' and gen.: since ca. 1945. Ex prec.

joes, the. Melancholy thoughts: (low) Aus.:—1915 (Dennis). Perhaps ex **the Joe Blakes,** q.v.—2. Hence, (a state of) nerves: Aus.: since ca. 1925. Palmer, 1957, 'What I saw in the sugar country gave me the joes'.

Joey or **joey** (capital where appropriate). A hermaphrodite: a sodomite; an effeminate or foppish young man neither hermaphrodite nor sodomite: Aus. low. (B., 1942.)—2. An evasion; a small lie: Aus. B., 1943.—3. A worthless cheque: Aus. (low; police): since ca. 1910. Ibid.—4. Hence, a fake: Aus. servicemen's: WW2. B., 1953.—5. The senior RM officer in the wardroom: RN officers'. P-G-R.—6. As in 'I'm having my Joey' or menstrual period: middle- and upper-middle-class feminine.—7. In *it's Joey,* a call at knocking-off time: Midlands collieries': *Manchester Guardian,* 19 Aug. 1954.—8. A familiar form of *Joe Hunt* or **Joe Cunt,** q.v. Franklyn.—9. 'A small double-ended canal boat without sleeping berths' (Gladwin, 1923): canalmen's: late C.19–20. Perhaps mere personification.—10. 'Illegal parcel sent into— or out of—prison' (Tempest): prison c.: mid-C.20.

jogari (h)omey or **polone(y); joggering omee.** Any instrumentalist or singer, esp. if itinerant, resp. male (homey) or female (polone): Parlyaree: late (?mid-)C.19–20. The first form in Lester, 1937. Ex It. *giocare,* to play.

jogue. A shilling: c. from ca. 1810; in C.20 market-traders' argot (as *joag*). Vaux; *M.T.*

Johanna, -ner. See **Joanna.**

John. A policeman: mostly Aus. *OED* Sup. cites *Westminster Gazette,* 18 Sep. 1901; Dennis, 1916. Poss. abbr. **John Hop,** q.v., but cf. **jack,** n., 1. It has, since ca. 1910, been common also in Can.—'I think, in this case, from John Darm (*gendarme*)': Priestley. Cf. **big John.**—2. An arrest: since ca. 1945: c. >, by ca. 1965, also low s. Short for *John Bull,* r.s. on *pull,* an or to arrest.—3. A 'mark' or the victim (whether potential or actual) of a theft, esp. pickpocketry: c.: since ca. 1945.—4. 'Prostitutes' contemptuous term for a client. A ponce might say to a prostitute: "Don't you treat me like a john or I'll mark your face" ' (Powis, 1977).—5. 'Prostitutes' contemptuous term for a sheath contraceptive' (Ibid.). A shortening of **Johnnie,** 6.—6. As *the john,* the privy: earlier C.20 upper and middle class; in mid-C.20 predominantly US, returning to more gen. UK usage in later 1970s.

John Audley; occ. **Orderly!** Abridge the performance!: theatrical: from ca. 1810.—2. Also occ. as a v. Also, to depart: circus s. (Seago, 1933.) Hollis, 1983, glosses it 'run away', and spells it *Johnalderley.*

John Bluebottle. A policeman: Cf. **blue bottle,** 1, and **John Hop.**

John Bull. In *Toby,* 1979, simply 'a policeman' in tramps' c. See **John,** 2.

John Davis. Money: c.:—1926 (Jennings).

John Dillon. A shilling: NZ r.s.: since ca. 1930. 'From the name of a famous racehorse' (Franklyn 2nd).

John Dunn; usu. pl., *John Dunns,* policemen: Aus.: since ca. 1920. (B., 1942.) For origin see **johndarm.**

John Henry. The penis: late C.19–mid-20. Cf. older, commoner synon. **John Thomas.** Naughton, 1966.

John Hop. A policeman: r.s. on *cop:* Brit., Aus., NZ: earlier C.20. (P.P., 1932.) Aus. var. *Johnnie Hopper.*

John L.s. 'Long underpants, after the old-style boxing gear worn by John L. Sullivan: Merchant Navy and Royal Navy: 1940s' (Peppitt)—but I suspect since later 1880s, Sullivan being at his height in 1882–92. Also known as *long Johns* or *longjohns.*

John Orderly. See **John Audley.**

John Selwyn. A failure, a dud, a **bummer,** q.v.: r.s. on J.S. Gummer, leader of the Conservative party: ephemeral. Barltrop heard it only a fortnight after J.S.G's appointment to that post, 1984, but Steve Bell, the *Guardian* cartoonist had already used it in 1983.

John Thomas. See **John Henry.**

John Willie. Synon. of **John Henry:** since ca. 1930.

johndarm (or **J-**). A policeman: London taxi-drivers': since ca. 1917. (Hodge, 1939.) Ex Fr. (*gens d'armes* >) *gendarme.*

Johnnie, Johnny. A Chinese: Aus.: since ca. 1905. (B., 1942.) Ex C.19 *John Chinaman.*—2. As *the Johnny,* the water-closet. (Archer, 1946.) Ex **john,** 6.—3. An Arab: Army: WW2. P-G-R.—4. Penis: mostly feminine: late C.19–20. Cf. **John Henry,** a personification, and **dick.**—5. A kookaburra: Aus. (Prichard, 1930.)—6. A condom: Services': since early 1940s. Cf. **John,** 5, and **rubber Johnny.**—7. A sanitary pad: polite feminine s. of the 1930s.—8. A threepenny piece: Yorkshire: earlier C.20. (Measures, 1985.)

Johnnies and **Sallies.** Kinds of 'Kaffirs', the former being specifically shares in the Johannesburg Consolidated Investment Company (*Continental Daily Mail,* 29 Aug. 1933): Stock Exchange: C.20. *Evening Standard,* 5 Feb. 1935.

Johnny Armstrong. Manual work, hand-power: joc. nautical: from ca. 1920. (*OED* Sup.) Cf. *elbow-grease,* and 'the elementary motive power known as "handraulic" ' (Granville): RN.

johnny bait (or one word). A sexually attractive girl. See **bait,** n., 2.

Johnny Bliss. (A) urination: Aus. r.s., on *piss:* later C.20. (Buzo, 1973.) Cf. **Mickey Bliss,** the Brit. form.

Johnny-come-lately. 'A nickname for a farm hand recently arrived from England.' (B., 1942): NZ rural: since ca. 1910.—2. In Aus., any newcomer. (B., 1942.) Cf. late C.18–19 *Johnny Newcome.*

Johnny Cotton. Rotten: r.s. *Everyman,* 26 Mar. 1931.

Johnny Gallacher (or **Gallagher**). A uniformed policeman: tramps' c.:—1935. Cf. the synon. **John.**

Johnny Gaucho. An Argentinian: Services': Falklands War, 1982. Cf. WW1 *J. Squarehead,* a German, and *J. Turk.*

Johnny go home! A coll. phrase applied, since early 1970s, to those children or adolescents who flock to London (or other great cities) in search of excitement or jobs and, failing to find them, become a problem for the authorities. Symons, 1976.

Johnny Gurk or (more politely) **Gurkha.** A Gurkha soldier: Army: since ca. 1915.

Johnny Hopper. A policeman: Aus. r.s., on *copper:* since ca. 1920. (B.P.) Cf. **John Hop.**

Johnny Horner. Round the corner; i.e. to at, a 'pub': r.s.:—1909 (Ware). P.B.: but in mid-late C.20 often in 'round the Johnny 'Orner'.—2. See **Jack Horner.**

Johnny in the middle. One 'who can see both sides, and more clearly than the contending parties' (L.A., 1976): coll.: later C.20.

J

Johnny pocket. A long narrow pocket, close to the flybuttons, in battledress trousers: Army: WW2+. (?Mythically) for contraceptives. (Johnson, 1973.) Cf. **johnnie**, 6.

Johnny Rollocks. Var. of **Tommy Rollocks**, testicles.

Johnny Ronce. Var. of **Joe Ronce**, ponce. Kersh, 1938.

Johnny Russell. A bustle: Aus. r.s. B., 1942.

Johnny Rutter. Butter: r.s.: since ca. 1880. P.P., 1932.

Johnny Skinner. Var. of **Jim** or **Joe, Skinner**, dinner. Franklyn.

Johnny Warder. A lone drinker: Aus.: ca. 1910–40. (B., 1959.) Cf. **Jimmy Woodser**.

Johnny Woodser. Aus. and NZ var. of **Jimmy Woodser**, q.v.

Johnny's. A doss-house: Aus. servicemen's: WW2. B., 1943.

Johnson. A prostitute's bully, esp. if a black: c., and low: from ca. 1910.—2. A US merchant seaman: London dockers': later C.20. (Ash.) Prob. ex President Lyndon B. Johnson, or perhaps ex the C.19 RN synon. *Jonathan*.

join a brick wall. To crash into a wall: since ca. 1925. In 1939–45, young fellows thinking of volunteering for the Forces were sometimes told that they would do better to join a brick wall.

joined. In *get joined!*, an occ. var. of *get knotted!*, *get stuffed!*, etc., exclam. of contemptuous dismissal: low: later C.20.

joint. In grafters' and market-traders' s. of late C.19–20: a tent; a stall; any stand from which, or object with which, a grafter provides amusement. *Cheapjack*, 1934; *M.T.*—2. A 'reefer'. To *roll a joint* is to make up a marijuana cigarette. This is the commonest synon. in current use among young people (1968).—3. The penis: low, 'pop' world. Hibbert, 3.—4. See **cut off the joint.**

joke. See **no joke.**

joke damper. 'Inefficient suspension or springing' (Dunford): motorcyclists': later C.20.

joke over! may be used by one in authority, e.g., a schoolteacher or group-leader, to recall wandering attention after any sort of disruptive incident: since (?)ca. 1940.

jokey. Funny: teenagers': from ca. 1955. Blake, 1964, ' "Leake," I said, "your mind's as jokey as your clothes".'

jole. To hit or strike (esp. a person): market-traders': ?late C.19–20. (*M.T.*) Var. of **joll**, itself a var. of † S.E. *jowl*, to jolt, shake, strike, now very widely distributed dial.

jollies. In, e.g., *get* (one's) *jollies*, get one's pleasure or one's special thrills from (something); e.g. 'He gets all his jollies from watching soccer on TV': since ca. 1950. By mid-1970s had acquired a rather derogatory or patronising tone, and often a sexual innuendo: 'getting his jollies squalidly, like one of the dirty mac brigade'. Prob. ex US: W. & F. cite a quot'n, 1965.

jollo. A festive occasion; a party: Aus.: since ca. 1925. (B., 1942.) Ex *jollification*. Aus. s. is fond of the jolly terminal -*o*.

jollop. 'Strong liquor, especially whisky' (B., 1942): Aus. Ex:—2. A laxative, a purgative: Aus. coll.: late C.19–20. A corruption of S.E. *jalap*.

jolly. Abbr. *jollification*: coll.; prob. orig. Public Schools': since ca. 1910. Sassoon, 1930, has 'a bit of jolly' in quot'n marks.—2. Hence, a pleasant excursion: Army: 1960s. 'We're off on a jolly down to Fama-G [Famagusta], are you coming?' or 'Some big nebby from the War Box out here [Cyprus] on a jolly'. (P.B.)

jolly beans. 'Benzedrine (US)' (Home Office): drug addicts' s.: later C.20.

jolly boat, take the. To break out of barracks: RN lowerdeck: since ca. 1920. P-G-R.

jolly d. 'Jolly decent', i.e. very good: girls' Public Schools'. 'I say, that's jolly d of you' (Spain, 1949).

jolly Jack. Sailors' term for the civilian conception of (and illusions about) the seaman in the Navy: RN coll.: since ca. 1920.

jolly-up. A 'beano'; a drinking-bout: lower-middle class: early C.20. A. Waugh, 1934.—2. Hence, a 'good time': middle class: since the early 1920s; by 1960, ob. Waugh, 1942, 'One

gives a jolly-up to a girl in a shop. She goes her way, he goes his.'

Jolson Story. The penis: r.s. on synon. *cory*. (Daniells, 1980.) Ex the title of a popular film, made in 1946, based on the life of the American Al Jolson, the singer.

jolt, n. A drink, esp. of brandy and whisky: Aus.: since ca. 1920. Blunden, 1935. ' "Take another jolt, sport," said Clarrie with a grin.' Adopted ex Can., where current since ca. 1900. (Niven.)—2. In *pass* (someone) *a jolt*, 'to deliver a short sharp blow': Aus.:—1916 (Dennis).

jolt, v. To stike (someone): Aus.: since ca. 1920. (B., 1942.) Cf. **jole**, and prec., 2.—2. To inject drugs into a vein: drugs' c. (Stockley, 1986.) US since ca. 1916 (Spears). Cf. **mainline.**

Jones. See **keep up with the Joneses.**

Joneses' disease. Synon. with 'keeping up with the Joneses', q.v. at **keep up . . .** Mellar, 1966.

jonna, jonnop. Aus. var. of **John Hop**, q.v., a policeman. (Campion, 1942; Herbert, 1939.) In W. Aus., since WW2, pron. *jonnup*.

jonnick, jonnock, jonnuk. See **jannock.**

jonto. A fellow, a chap: East End of London: recorded in the London *Evening News*, 27 Nov. 1947.

jorrie. A girl: low Glasgow: late C.19–20. (MacArthur, 1934.) Perhaps ex gipsy—ultimately Syrian gipsy—*djúry*, a woman.

José. A canteen attendant: RN: 'Enough to employ all the Joseys for three days lookin' for the cheese that 'e swore 'ad escaped from the canteen' (*Musings*, 1912). Bowen, 'A relic of the days when the Maltese did a lot of this business.'—2. Any Maltese, usu. *Josie*—or *Malts*: RN: prob. since late C.19. (Knock.) 'José [is] a very common Maltese Christian name' (Granville).

josh. To banter; indulge in banter: US (1880s), anglicised by 1935, thanks to the 'talkies'. (*OED* and Sup.) Perhaps ex Northern dial. and Scottish *joss*, to jostle, push against: possibly influenced by 'Josh Billings', that humorist whose writings were, ca. 1866–95, a household name in the USA. An early English occurrence is in Tey, 1927, ' "Look here . . . all joshing apart—do you *believe* the man didn't do it?" '

josh about or **around.** To move clumsily or carelessly: Brandon, 1931.

josher. A boat belonging to Messrs Fellows, Morton & Clayton, Ltd, canal carriers: canal-men's. (Rolt, 1944.) The late Mr Fellows' name being Joshua.

Josie. Var. of **José**, q.v.

joskin. A country bumpkin: low: since ca. 1810; still extant among market traders, who, I'd guess, have used it since mid-C.19. (*Lex. Bal.*; *M.T.*) Prob. ex dial. *joss*, to bump, after *bumpkin* itself (*OED*).—2. Hence, 'a green hand under sail': nautical: early C.19–early 20. (Bowen.) In Evans, 1970, it has the nuance 'farm-labourer casual-fishing in Winter'.—3. Hence, a recruit: Army. Particularly popular among National Servicemen in the late 1940s–early 50s (P.B.).

joss. An idol: Anglo-Chinese 'pidgin': C.18–20. Ex Portuguese *Deos*, God.—2. Hence, luck: nautical: late C.19–20. Bowen.—3. As *the joss*, a master-at-arms: RN. Whitlock, 1976, derives it ex sense 2, 'from the burning of joss-sticks to ward off evil spirits'; cf. var. *josh man*, recorded earlier by Knock.

joss man. 'Measure of Plymouth gin; from the picture of a monk on the label' (Granville): RN wardroom. Ex prec.

joss piece. A talisman or mascot: RN. P-G-R.

jostled about like turds in a piss-pot. Applied to ships crowded together: MN. (H.P. Mann, 1972.)

jotter. A pad on which to take or make notes (*jotting pad*): secretaries' and typists' coll.: since late 1930s. James, 1963, 'Let's have a look at that jotter.'—2. (Usu. pl.) 'The same as cards, in the sense of a worker's employment documents held by his employer. Thus to *get your jotters* means to get the sack' (Munro, 1985): Glasgow.

journey. A term in prison: c.:—1932 ('Wood'). (?)Ex:-

J

journey's end. Prison: low: 1929+. Ex R.C. Sherriff's famous play of that title, first performed in that year.

journo. A journalist: Aus.: since ca. 1940. (B.P.) The almost ubiquitous Aus. *-o*, taken over—in part, at least—from Cockney immigrants. Often used by Philip Howard in *The Times*, 1980s, *passim*.

jousey or **jowsey.** Lucky: Leicestershire schoolboys': 1982. (J. Burt.) Cf. **jammy.** Perhaps a var. of *juicy*.

jow out. To get someone away, to prise loose, 'winkle out', from a place or situation, e.g., from a drinking session at the mess bar: Army. By 1970s, mostly among older soldiers. (P.B.) Ex Hindustani.

joxy. See **jaxy.**

joy. Satisfaction; luck; success: mostly in 'Any joy?' and 'No joy!': RAF, since ca. 1930; RN by ca. 1935, and Army soon after. (Partridge, 1945; Granville.) Brickhill, 1946, 'At 9.15 the workers had been down [the escape tunnel] nearly forty minutes and still "no joy".'—2. Hence, effective operation, as in 'Is the W/T giving any joy?'—'Is the radio working?': RAF: since ca. 1930. (Emanuel; Hinde, 1945.)—3. As *the Joy*, Mountjoy Prison, Dublin: Anglo-Irish: late C.19–20. O'Neill, 1959.—4. Heroin: drugs c. (Stockley, 1986.) US since—1973 (Spears). Abbr. *joy powder*.—5. A theatre review or critical article: newspaper offices': 1980s. (Cropper, 1987.)

joy-bag. A condom: mostly RAF: 1950s. Cf. **jo-bag,** and **joy-stick,** 2.

joy boy. A male homosexual: undergraduates': earlier C.20.

joy pop, v. and n. To inject, and injection of, a drug under the skin, as opp. to 'main-lining' into a vein: addicts': adopted, ex US, ca. 1966. Wyatt, 1973.

joy powder. Heroin or cocaine: drugs c. (Stockley, 1986.) US since—1922 (Spears).

joy-prong. Penis: adolescents' coy or facetious: since ca. 1920. Cf. **mutton dagger, pork sword** and **joy-stick,** 2.

joy-ride. A ride at high speed, esp. in a motorcar: orig. (1909), US; anglicised ca. 1912 as a coll.—2. Hence, v.i. and *joy-rider, -riding*.

joy-stick. The control-lever of an aeroplane: 1915: s. > by 1925, coll.; now verging on S.E. 'Phallic symbolism' ex:—2. The penis: low: late C.19–20.—3. Either of the two levers by which the steering of tanks and certain other tracked vehicles was controlled: Army: since ca. 1925. (P-G-R.) Ex 1 and 2.

joy-wheeler. A girl given to pleasure, esp. 'joy-rides': 1934 (Vachell).

Joynson Hicks. Six: theatrical r.s.: since ca. 1927. Ex a famous Home Secretary. (Franklyn.) See **jixi.**

jubber. An iron bar used by a burglar to force a door: c. (Samuel, 1981.) ?Var. of *jabber* or *jobber*.

jubilee track. A 2-foot gauge track used mostly by petrol-locomotives and wagons: Public Works': 1935. Cf.:–

jubilee wagon. A 2-foot gauge skip: id.

juck, with diminutive **juckle.** A dog; hence, disparagingly, of a man, as in 'the old *juck*' (*M.T.*): market traders': perhaps since mid-C.19. Directly ex Romany *jook*, a dog.

juck's, or **juckle's, lips.** A personification of a quarrelsome or otherwise vocally disagreeable man: market traders'. *M.T.*

judder, n. and v.i. Engine noise; to shake convulsively: orig. RAF: from ca. 1925; by 1950, coll. A blend of *jar* + sh*udder*. P-G-R.

Judge Davis. Three tens: poker-players'. Ex a judge who mostly awarded '*thirty* days'.

Judy or **judy** (as appropriate). A girl, a woman of ridiculous appearance, but also, in low s., any woman.—2. A policewoman: RN lowerdeck: since ca. 1930. Granville.—3. A Palestine Jew: Army, both in 1914–18 and in 1939–45. Ex Arabic *Yehudi*, 'a Jew'.—4. A duodenal ulcer: since ca. 1930. Ex '*duodenal*'. (Sanders.)

judy scuffer. A policewoman: Liverpool s.: later C.20. (Rev. John Walker, 1981.) Cf. **Judy,** 1, 2, and see **scuffer.**

Jug. A Jugoslav: since 1919 (the Peace Conference): orig., Civil Service; in 1940–5, Army (Gielgud, 1949).

jug, n. A can of beer: RAF officers': since ca. 1930. (McDouall, 1945.) P.B.: also used in 'hearty' bar talk elsewhere; cf. **jar,** and **jug,** v.—2. A female baby: see **teapot,** 1.

jug, v. To drink: RAF since ca. 1930. (Jackson.) Ex the holding of a jug to one's mouth and drinking therefrom, also ex the idea of jugs of beer: cf. sense 1 of the n. P.B.: in later C.20, also Army usage, esp. in *jug on*, to keep on drinking. Cf. **jug up,** and the much earlier *jug-bitten*, tipsy.

jug and pail. Prison: r.s. on *jail*. Franklyn 2nd.

jug-handle; jug lug (both usu. pl.). Prominent ears. (Petch, 1969.) Cf. **Wing-nut.**

jug troupe. A 'highly efficient team [of pickpockets], specialising in banks' (Moynahan, 1969). Ex *jug*, s. for a bank since ca. 1860.

jug up or **scupper up.** To drink liquor, esp. beer: office- and shop-girls': ca. 1955–60. (Gilderdale.) P.B.: *jug up* had a wider and longer usage than E.P. allows here; also *jug on*, to keep on drinking, hard. Cf. **jug,** v.

jugged. Arrested; imprisoned: in later C.20, esp. drugs c. (Stockley, 1986), but cf. C.19 c. *jug*, a prison, to imprison.—2. Drunk. See **honkers.**

juggle with Jesus. 'To fly dangerously' (French, 1979): RAF: WW2. P.B.: the idea, if not the exact wording, is almost as old as Service flying itself: Boyle, 1962, has an account of Gordon Bell, a pioneer pilot, complaining that another man was 'jaunting with Jesus in my craft'.

juggler. An addict selling drugs to finance his own habit: drugs c. (Stockley, 1986.) US since—1969 (Spears).

juggo. In the punishment-cell; hence, out of action, ill: military: from ca. 1910. (F. & G.); † by 1950. Ex **jugged,** 1.

Jugland. Jugoslavia: coll.: since WW2. Cf. **Jug.** (P.B.)

jugs. Female breasts: low Aus.: since ca. 1920. Ex 'milk-*jugs*'. Also Brit., later C.20. See quot'n at **jujubes.**

Juice, the. The North Sea: RAF aircrews': WW2. (H. & P.) Contrast **the Gravy.**

juice. Petrol: 1909. Hence, from ca. 1918, *step on the juice*, to accelerate. *OED* Sup.—2. Electricity; electrical current: electricians' s. (1903) >, ca. 1920, gen. s. *OED* Sup.—3. Hence, *on the juice*, 'Running on electrified lines' (*Railway*): railwaymen's (esp. London Underground): since ca. 1955.—4. See **take the piss.**

juice joint. A stand where refreshments are sold: Can. carnival s.

juice money. Extra money paid for working on an electrified line: railwaymen's: since ca. 1920. Ex **juice,** 2.

juiced. Drunk. Var. of **juicy,** 2. Hunter, 1955.

juicer. See MOVING-PICTURE SLANG, §5, in Appx.

juicily. Excellently; 'splendidly': 1916 (Benson).

juicy, n. 'Telegraphist' (Granville): RN. Ex **juice,** 2. Cf. **sparks,** 1.

juicy, adj. Excellent: 1916: Benson (*OED* Sup.). Cf. **juicily.**—2. Drunk: Glasgow:—1934. But it was being used in this sense at least two centuries earlier: in Franklyn, 1737.—3. (Of stocks and shares) attractive in price: Stock Exchange: from ca. 1920. *Time and Tide*, 8 Sep. 1934, 'But still, with this juicy price in prospect, the shrewd professionals are hesitant.'—4. (Of targets) either easy or profitable: artillerymen's: WW2. (P-G-R.) A specialisation of the S.E., as in, e.g., 'a nice, fat, juicy steak'.

juicy about. Aware of: Aus.: since ca. 1925. B., 1942.

jujubes. A woman's breasts: low and raffish: later C.20. Daniells, 1980: 'Daddy says tits. Daddy says knockers and jugs and bazooms and dingleberries and jujubes. And then he laughs and goes "wuff! wuff!" '

juke-box (or written solid). An automatic, coin-operated, gramophone-record player: adopted, ca. 1945, ex US; by ca. 1970, familiar S.E. See also **jute box.**

jumble. A jumble-sale, or articles therefor: coll.: from ca. 1930. *OED* Sup.

jumble-juice. Cider: Dorset s.: later C.20. (J.B. Smith, Bath, 1979.) Perhaps a conflation of *jungle-juice* with *jumbling* effect of powerful liquor on the brain. (P.B.)

J

jumblie, -y. A jumble sale: domestic coll.: later C.20. Winterborn, 1977.

Jumbo or **jumbo** (as appropriate). A clumsy, heavy fellow: from ca. 1820: coll. >, ca. 1900, S.E.—2. A big goods-train engine: railwaymen's: from late C.19. *Railway.*—3. The backside: NZ: since ca. 1945. Kay, 1968, 'Parry for the high kick, or you'll land flat on your jumbo sir.' In many persons, the largest part.—4. A heavy-lift derrick; a mobile crane: MN: since ca. 1940. (Peppitt.)—5. A half-wit, slow-wit, fool: detectives' term for uniformed constable: since late 1940s. (Newman, 1970.)—6. A Boeing 747 airliner, which, on its introduction in the late 1960s, was the largest aircraft in operation with civil airlines: coll., verging, within a decade, on familiar S.E. Abbr. *jumbo-jet.* Senses 2–6 prob. all via *Jumbo,* name given, ex 1, to a famous elephant († 1885) at the London Zoo.

jumbo-size. Very large, or, in commercial coll., slightly larger than normal for whatever 'line' is being 'plugged': since ca. 1950. 'Notably in advertisements' (R.S., 1967). Cf. **king-size.** Cf. prec., 6.

jump, n. An act of sexual intercourse: coll.: since C.17. Esp. *have,* or *get, a jump;* or e.g., *a good jump,* (of a girl) sexually compliant or readily available: C.20. Occ. var., mid-C.20, *jumpies.*—2. A bar in a public house: W. Aus.: since ca. 1970. E.g., 'up at the jump' or 'go to the jump and get a beer.' (Slater, 1978.)—3. 'An unexpected attack' (Home Office): prisoners' c.: later C.20. Cf. v., 2.

jump, v. To get a free ride on (train, lorry, etc.): Services' coll. Short for *jump on to.* Cf. WW1 synon. *lorry hop.*—2. To attack suddenly in the air: RAF: since ca. 1940. Short for *jump on.* (P-G-R.) Hence, to attack (a person); cf. n., 3.—3. To understand, deduce: Aus.: since ca. 1910. B., 1943.—4. To forestall. Short for *jump the gun.*

jump in the box. To give Queen's evidence: Aus. c.: later C.20. McNeil.

jump off the dock. (Of a man) to get married: RN. Granville. Suicidal.

jump on the bandwagon. See **bandwagon** . . .

jump on the binders. To apply one's brakes: Can. (and US) Services': since 1939. H. & P.—2. Hence, to brake hard: RAF: since ca. 1940; † by 1950. P-G-R.

jump-out, the. The beginning: Aus. (B., 1942.) Ex sport.

jump out (of) the window(s). To make a parachute descent from an aircraft: RAF: WW2. Michie, 1941 (*jump out the windows*); E.P., 1942 (. . . *window*).

jump-rope, n. and v. A skipping-rope; to use one: Can. coll.: adopted, ca. 1950, ex US. (Leechman.)

jump ship. To desert: nautical.

jump the gun. To be premature, act—esp., to publish 'news'—prematurely: journalistic: since ca. 1920. Ex athletics.—2. Hence, 'to have [had] sexual intercourse or to have a baby "on the way" before marriage' (L.A., 1974): coll.: since ca. 1943.

jump the queue. To get ahead of one's turn: coll.: since ca. 1943. Ex:—2. To cheat for a place in a queue: coll.: since 1940.

jump through. To assault by kicking, to 'put the boot in': skinheads', q.v. Hibbert, 1983, with a 1969 citation.

jump to it. To bestir oneself; often as imperative: Services', esp. NCOs': since ca. 1912. (B. & P.)

jump-up lark, the. 'The practice of stealing commercial travellers' cars loaded with samples, and then driving to an agreed rendezvous to meet a van, transferring the stolen goods and then driving off . . . described in an article by John Tiley in *Reynold's News,* 6 May 1951' (Petch); but applies also to any other van or lorry containing liquor, or other goods, e.g. a van left driverless outside a 'pub' or a café: orig. c. since ca. 1930; then soon police s. Hence *jump-up man,* 'lorry hijacker' (Powis).

jumper lead (or **wire**). 'Thieves . . . steal the car of their choice by shorting the ignition with a "jumper" wire' (Powis): since

(?)ca. 1940. *Wire* is underworld, but *lead* is more gen. usage, even j. Cf. **hot wire.**

jumpies. Copulation: mostly Services': mid-1950s–60s. Ex **jump,** n., 1. (P.B.)

jumping, adj. Lively. See JAZZ TERMS, in Appx. But by ca. 1960, also fairly gen. s., as in Progl, 1964, 'By the time I arrived the place was jumping.' Often, by alliteration, *the joint is* (or *was*) *jumping.*

jumping Jinny. A mechanical stamper used in road-repairs: workmen's: from ca. 1920. The London *Evening News,* 7 Dec. 1936.

jumpy as a bag of fleas. Extremely nervous; 'windy': Services' coll.: from 1915. Richards, 1933.

Junction, the. 'Clapham area of South London' (Powis): Londoners': later C.20.

Jungle, the. The Salvation Army Hostel in Blackfriars Bridge Road: c.: from ca. 1920. Harrison, 1934; Gape, 1936.

jungle, adj. Wild, untamed; hence, rarely, angry: Army in Burma and India: 1942–5. See esp. PRISONER-OF-WAR SLANG, §10, in Appx.

jungle-bashing. Forcing one's way into and through the jungle and, esp., fighting there: Services', in Malaya, 1948–60 ('The Emergency'), and wherever campaigns or training have taken soldiers into the jungle during and since that time. Hence *jungle-bashers,* troops so engaged. (P.B.)

jungle(-)bunny. 'Patronising and unpleasant racist expression for a Negro, never used in black company' (Powis). One might add 'except with intent to insult'. But it is applied not only to people of African origin; schoolchildren in an East Midlands market town were using it of Asian fellow-pupils in 1971: since late 1960s in the Services. (P.B.)

jungle-bunny outfit. 'Camouflaged combat kit, known officially as disruptive-pattern clothing and unofficially as jungle-bunny outfits' (*Fighter Pilot,* 1981): RAF Officer Cadets': later C.20. Cf. synon. **flower-power suit.**

Jungle Jim. A Roman Catholic: Glasgow r.s., on synon. *Tim.* (Munro, 1985.) Cf. **wine grape.**

jungle(-)juice. African rum: Liverpool: since ca. 1920.—2. Hence, any cheap, strong liquor: Services': WW2 and since.—3. Cider: West Country s.: later C.20. (Patten, 1979.) A specialisation of 2.

jungle telegraph, the. The way in which gossip and rumours are disseminated by men and women in public-houses: disparaging and joc.: since late 1940s. (Petch, 1966.) Ex:-

jungle wireless. Inside information; a rumour: Army: 1940+. Also *jungle telephone.* (P-G-R.) Cf. **bush telegram,** and **grapevine.**

jungli. Uncouth; unrefined: Anglo-Indian coll.:—1927 (*OED* Sup.). Ex Urdu; *jungli* means, lit., 'belonging to jungle', hence uncouth or uncultured.

jungly, n. A commando officer or marine: Services' s.: late 1970s. See quot'n at **pinger.** Trained in 'jungle-bashing'.

jungly, adj. Disorganised, unsmart: Sloane Rangers', q.v.: early 1980s. (*Sunday Express* supp., 11 Oct. 1982.) Cf. earlier, more 'correct' **jungli.**

junior Nelson. A Lieutenant-Commander: RN lowerdeck. Granville.

junior wolf. See CANADIAN . . . , in Appx.

junk. Liquor; dregs: Aus. (and US) nautical. Bowen.—2. Perique tobacco: RN. *Weekly Telegraph,* 13 Sep. 1941.—3. Opium: Can. drug addicts': adopted ex US ca. 1925; by 1930, also Eng.—4. Hence, any narcotic; narcotics in gen.: addicts': adopted, ca. 1945, ex US.—5. Short for *junkie,* a drug addict: Aus. c.: since late 1950s.

junker. 'A [orig.] low four-wheeled vehicle used for transporting logs' (B., 1942): Aus. coll. Ex *junk,* unvaluable stuff. The usu. later C.20 form is *jinker* (Raab).—2. A heroin addict: drugs c. (Stockley, 1986.) US since ca. 1922 (Spears).

junket around. To waste time, play the fool: Aus. coll. Baker.

junket bosun. A ship's steward: RN: since ca. 1910. (Granville.) Cf. **custard bosun,** a cook.

J

junkie, -y, n. A drug addict: orig. teenage drug addicts', adopted ca. 1955 ex US; by ca. 1970, gen. coll. Ex **junk**, 3, 4.

junky, adj. Pertaining to narcotics: drug addicts': since ca. 1950. Ex **junk**, 4.

jury. As in 'I'll have to jury this pair of socks, the others are at the laundry'—to wear them upside down: ?orig. nautical, for the usage clearly stems from 'a jury mast', a makeshift mast. (Barr, 1976.)

just. Quite, very, truly, as in 'It's just splendid!': coll.: from ca. 1905.

just as I feared. A beard: theatrical r.s. (Franklyn.) Prob. influenced by Edward Lear's limerick about 'There was an old man with a beard,/Who cried "It is just as I feared . . ." '

just come up. Inexperienced, stupid. 'Don't come that old caper on me. I ain't just come up' (Curtis, 1937). Ex plants very recently come up above the ground: *green*. But, among Londoners, it means 'just come up from the country for the day'.

just hold one! Wait just a moment while, e.g., I look for someone, or something: Servicemen's coll.: since ca. 1955. Cf. the commoner **wait one!**

just nicely. Tipsy: euph.: from ca. 1930. (Heyer, 1935.) Abbr. S.E. *just nicely drunk*.

just the hammer. Synon. with next: since ca. 1950. (P.B.)

just the job. Precisely what I need or wish: Services': since ca. 1935. H. & P.

just the shiner. Precisely what was, is, needed: Aus.: since ca. 1920. Baker.

just the shining. Perfect; a synon. of, and commoner than, the prec. B., 1943.

just the shot. Exactly what is needed: Aus.: since ca. 1918. Cleary, 1959.

jute box or **jukebox.** A player-piano or pianola: RN: since ca. 1916. (Granville.) The first is perhaps a mishearing of the second; see also **juke-box.**

juve. Juvenile; hence, a juvenile part or act: theatrical and music-halls': late C.19–20. 'Trev's accustomed to leading child-juves', Marsh, 1967. Cf:-

juvenile John. An actor of juvenile parts: theatrical. (Granville, 1948.)

jyro. Horse-play; rough treatment: Cockneys': early C.20. Pugh, ' "I'll prong yer!" she says. Then I give her a bit of jyro, till she squealed and bash'd me 'at in.' Perhaps cognate with dial. *jart*, to whip, or S.E. *jar*, a quarrel.

J

K

K or k (as appropriate). A kilometre: orig. (late 1940s) Services'; by 1965, gen.—2. Coll. abbr. for knighthood of any British Order, a shortening of the initials *KBE*, *KCVO*, etc., as in 'I see old Buggins has got his K at last. Well, he's worked hard enough for it!': among those in the running for such honours. (P.B.) Richard Usborne writes: 'I understand that there is a phrase in the upper echelons of Whitehall known as Knight-starvation: used derogatorily by the already gazetted about lesser beings hungry for their K's' (book review, *Guardian*, 23 Sep. 1982): a pun on 'night-starvation', a term used by the advertisers of Horlicks.

K.A. is a coll. shortening of HMS *King Alfred*. (Granville.) See **Incubator.**—2. A 'know-all': Aus.: since ca. 1950. (B.P.)

K.b.b. See **K.h.b.**

k.b.o. 'Keep buggering on', as in Winston Churchill's comment, recorded in Gilbert's *Churchill*, vol. VI, *Finest Hour*, p. 1273, ' "We must just KBO" ', i.e. 'we must keep plugging on, struggling against adversity'. The phrase, and the abbr., have an earlier C.20, upper-class, ring to them; contrast the far more common *bugger off*, and cf. the politer **keep on keeping on**. (I am grateful to Mr Conrad Dehn for the ref., 1983: P.B.)

k-bar. 'United States Marine Corps survival knife' (Hawke, 1979): RM: 1970s.

K Block. A building, a wing, a ward set aside for the (temporarily) insane: RN: since ca. 1935. (H. & P.) I.e. for the *knuts* in the **nuthouse**.

K.C.M.G. See **C.M.G.**

K.G. Common Jew: 'used by "better-class" Jews. I first heard it ca. 1933' (Franklyn). A pun on *K*night of the *G*arter.

K.G. Five; K.G. Vee; Kay Gee 5, or **vee.** HMS *King George V*: RN coll.: 1912–mid-1950s. F. & G.; P.B.

K.h.b. A 'King's hard bargain', more gen. 'King's bad bargain'; an undesirable serviceman: Services' coll. 'Taffrail', 1925. (*OED* Sup.) The term, as *Queen's* . . . , remains, but usu. in full. (P.B., 1975.)

K.L. Kuala Lumpur: Europeans in Malaya/Malaysia. Towns in the Malay Peninsula lend themselves to this treatment, e.g.: *K.K.B.*, Kuala Kubu Bahru, and *J.B.*, Johore Bahru. Apart from their use by colonial administrators, planters, etc., they became particularly well known among Servicemen, 1948–60, 'The Emergency'. (P.B.)

k.o.; occ. **kayoe.** V. and occ. n. Knock-out. Also *give one the k.o.* Orig. and mostly pugilists': ex US.

K.P. A common prostitute: Aus. low: since ca. 1945. B., 1953.

kafuffle. Var.of **kerfuffle.**

kag. Tank crew's equipment and rations stored on the side of a tank: Army in Burma: 1943+.

kaggie. See **caggie.**

kahsi. Rectum; esp. in *up your kahsi!*, a gratuitous, usu. humorous c.p., mostly on meeting or parting: Services': 1940s. P.B.: prob. a var. of **carsey**, 2, q.v., a privy.

kaifa. Var. of **khyfer**, q.v., woman.

kailed up, get. To become drunk: late 1920s–30s. As though alcoholised. Perhaps cf. **canned**; note also **alc,** q.v. P.B.: was this a var. of synon. **ka(y)lied?**

Kaiser's War, the. The war of 1914–18: coll.: since ca. 1945. An avoidance of such question-begging labels as 'The Great War' and 'The First World War'. Often used to distinguish the first great conflict from *Hitler's War*, the second.

kali-water. Champagne: later C.20. (Clark, 1981.) Ex *kali'ed* drunk, q.v. at **kaylied.**

kanakas. Testicles: low Aus. A pun on **knackers,** and *Kanakas,* who formerly used to do the hard work on the sugarcane fields.

kanga. Money: Aus. s.: later C.20. Wilkes, who suggests perhaps ex r.s. *kangaroo = screw.*—2. As abbr. for *kangaroo,* the animal: Aus. coll.: since ca. 1890.—3. Hence, abbr. **kangaroo,** 1, 2, 3.

kangaroo, n. 'Harry was a Jew. In his own phrase: a "tin lid". Otherwise, a "four-by-two", a "kangaroo", or a "five-to-two" ' (Harrison, 1974): r.s.: since ca. 1930. *The Leader,* Jan. 1939.—2. A prison warder: r.s. (on *screw*), orig. and still mainly c.: since ca. 1920. Often shortened to *kanga.* (*Underworld,* 2nd ed., 1961.) Also Aus. c. (B., 1953).—3. A pneumatic drill: labourers': since ca. 1935. It was soon shortened to *kanga,* which, indeed, has been predominant since ca. 1950. It's always jumping.—4. Mostly in pl. *kangaroos,* wild young cattle: Aus. rural: since ca. 1920. (B., 1943.) They're always rushing and leaping.

kangaroo, v. 'To move jerkily (used of a car when the engine is warming up)' (Wilkes): Aus. and Brit. s.: later C.20. Cf. **kangaroo juice** and **. . . start.**

Kangaroo Gulch. A var. of **Kangaroo Valley.**

kangaroo it. To have a **kangaroo shit,** q.v.: Aus.: since ca. 1920.—2. To **kangaroo,** v., q.v.: Aus. s.: since ca. 1946. See next, and **kangaroo start.**

kangaroo juice. 'A driver making an awkward, jerky start may be asked, "What are you using? Kangaroo juice?" (instead of petrol). Services'.' (P.B., 1974): later C.20. Cf. **kangaroo,** v., and **. . . start.**

kangaroo (or Anzac) poker; also **double-ace poker.** A gambling game played by confidence-tricksters: c., and police s.: from ca. 1916. (Leach, 1933.) Prob. introduced by Aus. soldiers in 1915, when hundreds of them were evacuated, wounded, from Gallipoli to England.

kangaroo shit. A defecation from the haunch sitting position: Aus. B., 1942.

kangaroo start. 'A *kangaroo start* is caused by a faulty clutch or bad technique. The car shudders and moves off jerkily' (B.P.): Aus. s.: since late 1930s.

Kangaroo Valley. Earl's Court (London), an area popular among Aus. expatriates: since ca. 1950. 'There is a Kangaroo Valley in N.S.W., but the term was probably coined by a newspaper.' (B.P.)

kangarooster. An eccentric—or very amusing—fellow: Aus.: since ca. 1920. Baker.

kango. An Australian: since ca. 1945. (F. Leech, 1972.) Ex *kangaroo*.

Kansas cocoa. 'Coca Cola' (Powis): London low: later C.20.

Karno. See **Fred Karno** . . .

karzy. Var. of **carsey**, 2, a privy.

Kate Carney or **Karney.** The Army: defective r.s., orig., Army: late 1890s–early C.20; then gen., esp. among WW2 soldiers, shortened to *Kate*, as in 'He's in the Kate' (Franklyn 2nd). Occurs in phrase 'The Kate and Andrew', the Army and the Navy (P.B.). In the 1890s there was a very popular comedienne named Kate Carney.

kath or **Kath.** An indefinitely long term of imprisonment: Aus. and NZ c.:—1914. Cf. **Kathleen Mavourneen.**

Kathleen Maroon. A three-year prison-sentence: Aus. c. (Baker.) A corruption of sense 2 of:-

Kathleen Mavourneen. A non-paying debtor: commercial:—1909 (Ware); ob. by 1930. Ex the title of the song, by Louisa Macartney Crawford, in which occur the words 'It may be for years, and it may be for ever'. An occ. var. was *Eiley Mavourneen*.—2. An indeterminate gaol-sentence: Aus. and NZ. (B., 1943.) Cf. **kath**.—3. (Often corrupted to *Mavoureen*.) A habitual criminal: Aus. c.: since ca. 1910.—4. Morning: defective r.s. Lester.

Kathleen Mavourneen system. The hire-purchase system: Anglo-Irish:—1932. See prec., 1.

Kay Gee 5. See **K.G. Five.**

kaylied. Drunk: perhaps mainly N. Country: spelt thus in Gash, 1978, but poss. better *kali'ed*, if, as I surmise, it derives ex *kali*, a N. Country children's sweet of sherbet, wrapped in a triangular bag and sucked through a liquorice straw. Cf. the use of **pop** for alcoholic liquor, chiefly beer, and **kailed up**, q.v. (P.B.)—2. Overcome (not necessarily by drink); crazy. Clark, 1982.

kayoe. See **k.o.**

keaster. Occ. var. of **keester**, backside.

keck or **kek.** A specially heavy mail: Post Office telegraph-messengers' (esp. in London): from ca. 1920. Perhaps ex dial. *keck*, a jolt, a blow.

kecks is the Liverpool shape (C.19–20) of *kicks*, trousers. Hence the 'camp' *punch up the kecks*; C.20.

keel the goods. 'To code consigned goods for loading' (*Railway*, 2nd): railwaymen's. Ex Scot. dial. *keel*, to mark with ruddle (*EDD*).

keen. Excellent; highly desirable: Can., esp. teenagers': adopted, ca. 1955, ex US. 'Seen Tom's new girl? Boy, is she ever keen!' (Leechman).

keeno. Among schoolchildren, a 'swot'; among adults, any enthusiast: mid-1970s. (P.B.)

keep (one's) **cool.** To retain one's self-possession: coll.: adopted, ex US, ca. 1960; and in Aus. ca. 1967 (B.P.). Opp. *lose* one's *cool*. Cf. **cool**, adj., 4. Distinguish this s. > coll. usage from familiar S.E. *keep cool*.

keep down. To retain, hold (a job) against difficulties: Aus. coll. (B., 1942.) Var. of the S.E. *hold down*.

keep (one's) **fingers crossed.** To 'pray' for success or merely to avert defeat, failure, or bad luck: coll.: uncommon before ca. 1925. A layman's modification of the ecclesiastical sign of the Cross. Cf. *touch wood*.

keep (one) **guessing.** To keep one uncertain or 'in the dark': coll.: adopted, ca. 1910, ex US. *OED* Sup.

keep it. To pay heed: coll. (Jordan, 1937.) Ex *keep it in mind*.

keep it out! Mind your own business!: low coll.: later C.20. The 'it' is the nose, 'sticky beak' or 'cherry-picking shonk'.

keep (one's) **lip buttoned.** To maintain silence; to tell nothing: Cockney: since ca. 1910. Kersh, 1938, 'Pay, and I'll keep my lip buttoned.'

keep nit. To keep watch; to be on the 'qui-vive': Aus.: late C.19–20. Dyson, 1901.

keep (one's) **nose clean.** To avoid drink: Army:—1909 (Ware). Usu. in imperative.—2. Hence, a c.p. addressed, usu. on parting, to a person one is warning to keep out of trouble: since ca. 1925.—3. To mind one's own business: id.

Keep Off Young Ladies' Insides and, by reversion, **I Love You Only, Kid.** Punning nicknames of the *K*ing's *O*wn *Y*orkshire *L*ight *I*nfantry: Army: ca. 1910–60.

keep on keeping on. To persevere in the face of all discouragement or misfortune: a Salvation Army exhortation.

keep stumm (pron. *shtumm*)! Keep quiet!: underworld: since ca. 1950. See **shtoom.**

keep tabs on. To observe (someone) long and closely, in order to see what he's up to or how he's getting on: coll.: adopted, ex US, early C.20. (Sayers, 1934.) The US phrase orig. meant to keep a (tabulated) list of, e.g., winnings and losses, cards in and out, etc. In Aus. usage, *keep tab of*, 'for any record, esp. the bill at restaurants . . . for taxation purposes' (B.P., 1963). Also Aus. is the var. *tab* (*up*) *on*, to note the doings of a person (Casey, 1945).

keep (one's) **tail clear.** (Of a pilot or his plane) to stay out of the sights of an enemy aircraft: RAF: since 1939. Berrey.—2. Hence(?), to prevent a rear attack: 1940+. Partridge, 1945. Cf. *watch* (one's) *six o'clock*, at **six o'clock.**

keep the ball rolling. To keep things going: coll.: since ca. 1910. Ex Association football.

keep the obs (or **obbs**) **on** (someone). To keep under observation: since ca. 1945: c. >, by ca. 1950, also police s. Cf. **obbo.**

keep (something) **under** (one's) **hat.** (Esp. in imperative.) To say nothing about: coll.: late C.19–20.

keep up (one's) **frock.** To keep (information, plan, etc.) secret: mostly Services' (esp. Army): since ca. 1930. P-G-R.

keep up with the Joneses. To hold one's own in 'the rat race' of survival at a decent level: coll.: since ca. 1950. As R.C. notes, 1976, it refers 'rather to conspicuous consumption than to mere survival'. Cf. **Joneses' disease**, the compulsion to do this.

keep (one's) **wig cool.** To remain calm: orig. legal, but soon gen.: from ca. 1910. Cf. **flip** (one's) **wig**, to lose one's self-control.

keep yow. To keep watch: low Aus.: since ca. 1925. (B., 1943.) Perhaps ex *yowlie*, an ob. term for a night-watchman.—2. Hence, to act as an observer: RAAF: WW2. Ibid.

keeper of overdrafts, the. The manager: bank-clerks'. Joc. on the titles of museum-officials.

keester. Human backside: Can.: adopted and adapted, ca. 1930, ex US, where, orig. c., predominantly spelt and pron. *keister*. (Leech, 1974.)

keifer. F. & H. var. of **khyfer**, q.v., woman as sex object.

Kelly. A crow: Aus. B., 1942.—2. As: Aus. Baker, ' "On the kelly", engaged in axe work'. '*Kelly* is reputed to be from the name of a manufacturer of axes' (B.P.).—3. A ticket inspector on the buses: Aus.: since ca. 1945. Perhaps 'because often Irish' (B.P.).—4. See **Ned Kelly.**

kelly bow. Money: Glasgow r.s., on *dough*. Munro, 1985; in 1988, he wrote to P.B., 'of obscure origin, but cf. synon. **cally dosh**'.

Kelly's eye, legs. See TOMBOLA, in Appx.

Kelper. A Falkland Islander: nickname that received wide publicity during the crisis of 1982.

Kennington Lane. Pain: r.s. Franklyn 2nd.

Kensington Gore. Artificial blood, e.g. tomato juice, as used on the stage: theatrical: since the 1920s. (Petch, 1974.) A pun on the fashionable London area so named—and obviously on S.E. *gore*, spilt blood.

Kensington High (School). The University of New South Wales in the days when its name was the NSW University of Technology (founded in 1949): Sydneysiders', esp. University of Sydney undergraduates'. See also **Kenso**, 2.

Kenso. Kensington racecourse, Sydney: Aus. sporting. B., 1942.—2. 'The University of NSW' (Wilkes). See prec.

Kentish Town. A pre-decimal halfpenny or penny: occ. var. of **Camden Town**, q.v. Franklyn 2nd.

kerb boy. A vendor of combs, elastic and other such things: London-street coll.

kerb-crawling, n. and adj. Looking out for a street prostitute: since ca. 1925. In later C.20, esp. from a slowly-moving vehicle.

Kerb Market, the. Very frequent for **Street**, 2, q.v.

kerb-walker. A singer on the pavement-edge: Glasgow:—1934.

kerbside Virginia. A cigarette made from fag-ends. See **hard-up**, 2, and cf. **kerbstone mixture**.

kerbstone jockey. A street, or other unreliable tipster: Aus. B., 1942.

kerbstone mixture (or with capitals). Such tobacco for pipe or cigarettes as has been made up from fag-ends. For sale among the very poor. Cf. **O.P.B.**, and **kerbside Virginia**.

kerdoying, -doing, -doink, or **ger-**. Echoic of impact, as *crash!*, *wallop!*, etc.: perhaps orig. RAF: since ca. 1939. 'He was cruising along, when—gerdoying!—he suddenly crashed.' (Bates, 1945.) [E.P. and H.E. Bates worked together at the Air Ministry during the latter part of WW2, E.P., 'the oldest soldier', as junior clerk. P.B.] Emanuel, 1945, noted the phonetic var.—the more exact form—*kerdoink* and defined the term 'interjection to indicate crash of aircraft, etc.' Cf.:-

kerdumf! Exclam. of surprise, amazement, etc.: RAF: since ca. 1938. Jackson, 'Its origin is the crump of a crash-landed aircraft. Sometimes used as a verb, meaning to crash into.' Cf. **prang**, v., q.v. P.B.: this 'noise' has not lasted, whereas the prec. became more gen. and is still, early 1980s, extant.

kerfuffle; gefuffle; cufuffle. An amorous embrace: Anglo-Irish: late C.19–20.—2. A row, a brawl, a disturbance: since ca. 1930. (Leechman.)—3. Hence(?), a to-do, a fuss; a 'flap': RAF, since 1939, then other Services' and gen. (McDouall, 1945.) Partly echoic and prob. reminiscent of such terms as *fluster* and *waffle*. The immediate origin lies in Scots *curfuffle*, n., ex *curfuffle*, v., based on Scot. *fuffle*, to throw into disorder, whence the n. *fuffle*, violent effort, fuss. The *cur-* may, as *OED* suggests, be Gaelic *car*, to bend or twist or turn about. (With thanks to Mr R.W. Burchfield.) The modern s. usage arises, naturally enough, in the dialectal, and the *cu(r)-*, *ge(r)-*, *ke(r)-* element has been influenced—perhaps even superseded—by the echoic *ge-* or *ke(r)-* indicative of effort or noise (cf. **kerdoying**, **kerdumf**, and esp. **kersplosh** for an earlier use.) So widespread is this use of the prefix that the American cartoonist Charles Schulz could even, for comic effect, use 'ker-leaf' to represent the sound of a falling leaf landing (ca. 1970).

kerfuffle valve. 'An imaginary valve . . . supposed to be at risk when one lifts heavy weights' (B.P., 1977): Aus.: later C.20.

kero. Kerosene: Aus.: since ca. 1920. (B.P.) P.B.: and Brit., where the stuff (paraffin) is used: e.g. *kero-tin*, a container for kerosene.—2. Beer: Aus. joc.: since ca. 1930. Herbert, 1939.

kerplonk, kerplunk. Slap-bang; also an exclam., cf. **kerdoying**: adopted, ca. 1944, ex US. Echoic. See **kerfuffle**, 3.

kerpurtle. Esp. in 'it won't kerpurtle', work, function, act: RAF: ca. 1940-4. An arbitrary formation; see **kerfuffle**, 3, and cf. synon. **ackle**.—2. See **capurtle**.

kerried. Broken: abbr. r.s., *knackered*, on Kerry Packer[ed]. (Keating, 1981.) K.P., the Aus. cricket sponsor.

kersplosh! Splash!: Aus.:—1916 (C.J. Dennis). See **kerfuffle**, 3.

ketchup. Beer: Aus. (Baker.) Ex colour.

kettle. In c., a watch. A *red kettle* is a gold watch; a *white*, a silver one. Mid-C.19–20.—2. Hence, a wrist-watch: since ca. 1920: c. >, by 1930, fairground s. (Cook, 1962.)—3. A locomotive: Can. railroadmen's:—1931. See HAULAGE, in Appx.

kettled. Tipsy: mostly Midlands and lower North: late C.19–20. Roberts, 1976.

key, n. A habitual criminal: Aus. c. (B., 1942.) To the police he is a 'key' suspect.—2. Detention under the Habitual Criminals Act (1905); hence, *key(-)man*, a prisoner under this Act: Aus. c.: since ca. 1910. B., 1959.

key, v.t. So to word (an advertisement) that one can check its selling-appeal: publicity men's and publishers': from ca. 1920: s. > j. >, by 1934, S.E.

key-basher. A wireless-telegraphy operator: Army: 1939+.

key of the door. See TOMBOLA, in Appx.

keyholing. A singing, and a playing of musical instruments, at public-house doors: since ca. 1950. L.A. notes having heard it in 1961.

khaki. Pease-pudding: low: early C.20. (Ware.) Ex colour.

khaki brains, get or **have; khaki-brained.** To become, to be, excessively military-minded: Army: since late 1960s. Cf. **action man**. (P.B., 1974.)

Khaki Marines, the. The Royal Marine Commandos: RN: 1940-5. P-G-R.

khaloss. Exhausted; finished; dead: Aus. soldiers in Palestine and N. Africa: 1940-2. (*Rats*, 1944.) Arabic.

khazi. Later C.20 spelling var. of **carsey**, 2, q.v., a privy. Hibbert, 1983; Bell, *passim*.

khyfer. (Prob. the 'proper' spelling of the term variously rendered as *kaifa*, *keifer*, or *kyfer*.) The female as sexual partner; woman in general regarded sexually, as in 'What's the place like? Any good khyfer?', or 'a bit of khyfer', = 'a bit of skirt': orig. Army, from latish C.19, then all Services', and still extant 1975. Hence the term *khyfer-mashing*, vbl n.: courting a girl: still current in 1940, but † by 1950. This spelling in Allen, 1977. (P.B.) R.S., 1973, suggests a prob. distortion of Arabic *kèyif*, solace, esp. 'the amiable beauty of a fair woman' (C.M. Doughty, *Arabia Deserta*, 1888). Powis, 1977, notes the vbl n. *kifering*, 'Act of sexual intercourse, sometimes specifically an act of adultery'. Ware, 1909, notes *kypher*, v.i. and t., to dress (of a woman).

ki. 'Cocoa or prison chocolate' (Tempest, 'medium usage'): prison s.: mid-C.20. See **kye**.

kibitz. Corresponding to **kibitzer**: adopted ca. 1962 ex US. 'The Yiddish word "kibitz" is a valuable import because it has no equivalent in English' (Lejeune, 1967).

kibitzer. A watcher, esp. if inquisitive or interfering, rather than a participant; e.g. one who plays your game of patience, or does your crossword puzzle for you, over your shoulder: adopted, ca. 1960, ex US, but not as gen. as its usefulness warrants. Ex Ger. *Kiebitz*, the peewit,—'the little bird very much an onlooker in life' (Reyburn, 1962).

kibosh, n. and v. See this entry in Appx.

kick, n. A thrill: coll.: adopted, ca. 1943, ex US servicemen. Perhaps ex (?or the orig. of) the c.p. *just for kicks*.—2. A trick; a 'line' or 'stunt': low: since ca. 1945. (Norman.)—3. A half-knot: RN. ('Taffrail', 1917.) Granville defines it as 'a fraction of a nautical knot', and derives it ex older s., where it = sixpence = half a shilling. Cf. **onion**, 1.—4. Intensive drug-taking, as in **going on a kick**, q.v.: later C.20.

kick, v. To dismiss (a man from a job): Aus.: since ca. 1925. (Vickers, 1955.)—2. To reject, overcome or forswear, as in *kick it*, where 'it' = the habit. See **kick the habit**.

kick a gong. To start a quarrel: RN: since ca. 1910. (Granville.) Cf. synon. **open a tin**. Prob. ex boxing.

kick-back. A *sub rosa* payment, esp. as commission on a more or less shady deal: adopted, ca. 1944, ex US. (B.P.)—2. That portion of a fee which, in the unethical practice of fee-splitting, is returned (or not collected): adopted, in late 1940s, ex US, perhaps via Can.

kick her into a manœuvre. To take evasive action: RAF: 1940-2. (Berrey.) Adopted from American airmen.

kick-in, n. 'A doing-over and putting the boot in': police: since latish 1960s. Petch cites 'Dixon of Dock Green', BBC TV, 6 Jan. 1969.

kick in, v. To subscribe to a kitty or pool, charity collection, etc.: later C.20. 'Yes, I'll kick in, but I haven't any change on me just now' (P.B.)

kick in the pants, a. Applied fig. to any grave disappointment or set-back: coll.

kick off. To die: Aus. B., 1959.

kick on. 'To carry on, with just enough funds for the purpose' (Wilkes): Aus. coll.: mid-C.20.

kick out of, get a. To find that something is exciting or absorbing: coll.: since ca. 1925. Adopted from drug addicts? Cf. *just for kicks.*

kick the arse out of it. Var. of **tear the arse . . .** , to take something to an unnecessary extreme; to exaggerate.

kick the habit. To cease, intentionally, an addiction (whether, as orig., drugs, or else smoking, alcohol, etc.): drug addicts' s. > gen. coll.: ca. 1955, ex US.

kick the tin. To make a financial contribution: Aus. coll.: since early 1960s. (Wilkes, who suggests '?from the rattling of collection box'.) Cf. **kick in,** v.

kick up. Elliptical for 'kick up a breeze, dust, fuss, shindy, trouble, etc.', to cause trouble: coll.: since late 1940s. *Kick up a fuss,* coll., prob. dates from ca. 1880.

kick up a dido (or **Dido**). To 'kick up a row': Cockneys': earlier C.20. 'Used solely for kids . . . adults [would say] to grizzling children "It's no use you kicking up a Dido! You ain't getting your own way" ' (Wolveridge, 1978).

kick up (one's) heels. To enjoy 'a high old time': coll. Ex dancing, or perhaps suggested by cattle released into a field after being penned up for a while. (P.B.) Contrast C.16–19 meaning, to die.

kick up the backside. One jeep pushing another out of the mud: Army in Burma: 1942–5. Hanley, 1946.

kick with the left foot. As in *he* (*she, they,* etc.) *kick(s)* . . . , he (etc.) is a Catholic; an elab. of **left-footer,** q.v.: Services': later C.20. (P.B.)

kicker. An auxiliary motor fitted into a sailing ship: Can. (and US) nautical coll.: from ca. 1890; ob. (Bowen.) Ex its action on the ship. 'Now applied to portable outboard motors for small boats. An "inboard" is . . . a motor permanently installed inside the hull' (Leechman, 1959).

kickers. A fit of nervousness, or of nerves: 1930s. Mottram, 1934 (concerning aviation), 'I won't go if it gives you the kickers.' Cf. **jitters,** which it may 'folk-etymologise'.

kid brother or **sister.** One's (however slightly) younger brother or sister: coll.: adopted from US ca. 1925. Cf. Cockney 'one's *kid*'—'brother' or 'sister' understood.

kid gloves, use (on someone) or **handle** (someone or -thing) **with.** To treat gently and with circumspection; handle in such a way as to avoid upsetting things: coll. (P.B.)

kid-stuff (or **kids'-**). Any activity (from games to reading) characteristic of, or suitable for, children: adopted, ca. 1945, ex US. (Petch, 1976.) P.B.: usu. derogatory, for something one has (perhaps only recently) 'grown out of'.

kidder. A person employed by a (usu. hawker-)tradesman to "buy" and therefore to stimulate genuine sales: tramps' c.:—1932 (Jennings).

kiddo. A chap, a fellow; also as term of address to a young man: low coll.: mid-C.20. Hunter, 1969, 'He's a bright kiddo'. Both senses by the Cockney/Aus. suffix *-o,* on *kid,* n., a child. (P.B.)

kiddology. Humbug: pseudo-scientific: later C.20. A BBC Radio 4 programme on class distinctions, 4 Feb. 1980.

kiddy. A man, youth, boy: low coll.: an early occurrence is in Lewis, 1816. P.B.: in the 1st ed. of *DSUE* E.P. noted that this sense was '† by 1920'; but in RAF, early 1950s, I heard a first-rate officer described as 'a gen kiddy', and this phrase was quite popular among aircrew under training.

kiddy (or **-ie**) **lit** (or one word). Books for young children: librarians' coll.: since ca. 1970. Hannabuss, 1976.

kiddywinks (**kiddiwinks**); **kiddliwinks** (**kiddlywinks**). Sometimes affectionate, but more often disparaging, term for children: schoolteachers' and domestic: since ca. 1930. Elab. of

kiddies, influenced by older *kiddleywink.* (P.B.) See quot'n at **howler.**

kidger. A cadger: low Aus.: late C.19–20. (Park, 1950.) P.B.: prob. Aus. rendering of Cockney form *kedger.*

kidney punch. A, to, lunch: theatrical r.s. Franklyn.

kidney-wiper. Penis: low. Ex a ribald song. Also *kidney-scraper. More Rugby Songs,* 1968.

kids. The study of children's diseases; 'the children's department in a hospital': medical students':—1933 (*Slang*).

kidstakes (or hyphenated). Pretence; nonsense; both, esp. in *cut the kidstakes!,* stop beating round the bush, or stop talking nonsense: Aus. Dennis, 1916; B., 1959.

kie. A var. of **kye.**

kie show. A wild-man or wild-beast show: grafters'. (*Cheapjack,* 1934.) Origin?

kief. 'Cannabis (N. Africa)' (Home Office): drug-users': later C.20. Var. *kif* (McConville, 1980). 'An Arabic word meaning tranquillity and applied to cannabis' (*Time Out,* 19 Sep. 1985).

kif. See prec.

kifer. Woman as sex object. See **khyfer.**

kike. A Jew: adopted, ca. 1935, ex US: low, and usu. offensively derogatory (cf. **sheeny**). An early Eng. occurrence is in Postgate, 1940. Rosten, 1967, convincingly derives it ex Yiddish *kikel* (pron. *ky-kel*), a circle: illiterate Jewish immigrants to the USA would sign their names with a circle, never with the cross.—2. A cheque: c.: since ca. 1950. (Bournemouth *Evening Echo,* 20 Apr. 1966.) P.B.: a mishearing of **kite,** n., 1? I have seen *cake* for *Kate,* where 'The Army' was meant.

kiko. To say so: low. Llewellyn, 1943. ' "I should bloody kiko," says Slush . . . "He's the Smasher, he is." ' Rhyming on *sye* (Cockney for 'say') *so.* It is a Cockney alternative spelling of **cocoa,** v., q.v. Franklyn.

Kilburn. 'Diary, especially a plain clothes officer's official diary (which may be examined in court)' (Powis): r.s., shortening *Kilburn Priory:* London policemen's: later C.20.

Kildare, the. 'A major operation, with full outfit, masks, white overalls, etc. "Will it be a major op?"—"Yes, at 19.30 tomorrow; the full Kildare." ' Ex the T.V. programme 'Dr Kildare', a glamourised, American version, in serial form, of a surgeon's life: mid-1960s. (Granville, 1967.)

kiley. A two-up 'kip': Aus.: since ca. 1920. (B., 1943.) Ex the Aboriginal *kiley,* a boomerang.

kill, n. In *make a kill* (or *killing*): to win substantially from the bookmakers, or on the stock market: Aus. sporting, since ca. 1919 (Baker); also Brit.

kill, v. As *'kill* a story', to suppress or discard it: journalistic: since ca. 1910; by 1940, coll.—2. To get rid of, as **kill that baby,** q.v.: cinema: since ca. 1930. In later C.20, more gen. coll., verging on informal S.E., for 'to douse a light', switch or turn off anything inanimate, e.g. an engine (Keene, 1980).—3. To destroy (aircraft or tanks); hence as n.: Army and RAF coll.: WW2. P-G-R.—4. To consume (usu., drink) with some urgency: joc.: later C.20. As in, 'I could kill a coke [coca-cola drink]', which I heard a well-spoken teenage girl declare to an uncomprehending great-aunt, 1984. (P.B.)

kill a snake. To 'see a man about a dog': Aus. (B., 1942.) With a pun on *penis erectus.*

kill that baby! Turn out the spot-light: film-industry: from ca. 1930. A *baby* because it is only a small light. See MOVING-PICTURE SLANG, §3, in Appx., and **kill,** v., 2.

kill the widow. 'As young journalists, we were horrified on being told to: "Kill that widow in column three." (Don't be frightened—it merely meant "Alter the spacing so that there isn't a word all by itself in one line")' (*Woman,* 19 Dec. 1964): journalistic s. Cf. **kill,** v., 1 and 2.

Killarney. Synon. more gen. as n. (madman) than as adj., of **lakes,** q.v., and likewise an abbr. of *lakes of Killarney,* imperfect r.s. = barmy. Allingham, 1936.

killer. A 'lady-killer', as in 'He was a killer with the sheilas' (Dick): Aus.: since ca. 1925.—2. (Also *whispering death.*) 'A

Diesel unit' (*Railway*): railwaymen's: since ca. 1955. Ex its stealthy approach.—3. 'The final action or argument which means the end to whatever hopes have been held' (B., 1959): Aus.: since ca. 1945. P.B.: this sense is also Brit. in later C.20.

killerdiller. A wildly good time: beatniks' and teenagers': adopted and adapted, ca. 1959, ex US s. *killerdiller*, any remarkable or attractive or successful thing or person or occasion (W. & F.). A reduplication of *killer*. P.B.: in later C.20, some use in Brit. and Aus. of the US sense.

killing match. A fierce battle: Army: 1940–5. P-G-R.

kilted brickie (or **-y**). A woman employed in the building trade: WW2. See **whistler**, 4.

kindy. A kindergarten school: Aus. coll.: since ca. 1950.

kinell! An exclam.; short for *fuckin' 'ell!*, i.e. *fucking hell!*, very low but, in late C.19–20, very common; it occurs in Prebble, 1947, in the sensible form, *'kinell.'*

King, the. The National Anthem: coll., prob. orig. Brit. Armed Forces officers'; 'We always stand for "The King".' Since 1952, of course, *the Queen*.

king, n. The man in charge of anything: e.g., a steward on a liner may be *the liner king, the crockery king, the silver king* (Bowen); also, in the Services, *the jankers king* (see **jankers**), *prodder king*, even *the latrine king*. Hinde, for the RAF, 1945, 'Someone who is good at a particular thing, e.g. Met[eorology] king, Navigation king'. With *latrine king*, cf. the Aus. and NZ **compo king**, equally ironic. These uses arose at the beginning of, or fairly early in C.20. Aus. usage app. began earlier: Wilkes cites several late C.19 examples of *cattle king, sheep king, wool king*, for powerful men owning large stocks. (Brit. Eng. might substitute *baron*, as *tobacco baron, cotton baron*, for leaders of those industries.) In these examples the epithet is given in admiration, however grudging, for the man's achievements; not so, perhaps, in the obviously ironic *squatter king*, although the *Australian Journal*, July 1869, equates '*Wool King*, a squatter'. (See esp. Wilkes.) Also Aus. is the use of *king* for the leader of a *push* (or gang) of larrikins: ca. 1890–1940 (B., 1953), perhaps here abbr. of **king-pin**, q.v. Among Can. railroadmen,—1931, the title was accorded to a freight-train conductor, or, occ., to a yardmaster. *EDD* records the use of *king* as 'adept' in dial., 1865. Cf. **queen**. (E.P.; P.B.)—2. Abbr. **king hit, n.**—3. See **kings**, 2.

king, v. Abbr. **king-hit, v.**, q.v.

king, adj. Super-eminent or excellent: coll. See several phrases below.

king Canute. The crane-fly or 'daddy-long-legs': Midland children's: mid-C.20. (Harrison, 1962.)

King Dick. A leader, boss, overseer: Aus. B., 1942.

King Dicky. A bricklayer: builders' r.s. (on *bricky*). Franklyn 2nd.

king hit, n. A knock-out blow: Aus. sporting coll.: since ca. 1920. Baker.—2. 'A surprise punch, probably unfair' (Wilkes): Aus. coll.: since ca. 1940.

king-hit, v. From both senses of prec.: Aus.: datings similar.

king-hit merchant or **artist.** A brawler; a bully; one who employs unfair tactics: Aus.: since ca. 1935. *Rats*, 1944; B., 1959.

king kong. A drink of methylated spirits mixed with lavender water: beatniks': since ca. 1959. (Anderson.) Deadly; ex the film *King Kong*.

King Lear. Homosexual: r.s. on *queer*: since ca. 1940. Franklyn.

King Parnee. Rain: late C.19–20 showmen's var. of **parnee**, 1, q.v. *John o' London's Weekly*, 19 Mar. 1937.

king-pin(, the). The leader; most important person: Aus.,—1916 (Dennis); also some Brit. metaphorical use. Cf. S.E. mechanical *king-bolt*, itself prob. influenced by much earlier architectural *king-post*.—2. Hence, the airman in charge of a ground-crew gang: RAF: WW2. Cf.:-

king pippin. An important, usu. the most important, person: since ca. 1910. Cf. prec.

king-size(d). Very large; relatively large (esp. in advertising, e.g. cigarettes, where the difference between that and 'normal' may be very slight indeed): Aus., since ca. 1920; Can. (?ex US), since ca. 1930; Eng. since ca. 1945: by 1950, coll. In later C.20, taken over by advertising copy-writers, and so used by 'ordinary' people only ironically. There exists *queen-size(d)*, e.g. of beds, a little smaller than *king-size*.

King Street Run, the. A tie awarded to those who successfully drink a pint of beer in each of the eight public-houses in King Street, without any form of physical relief and within two hours; a competition held twice a term and supposed to have been instituted by Ted Dexter; present record (Wharton, 1965), 28 minutes: Cambridge undergraduates': since early 1950s.

kingdom come. Rum (the drink): r.s. Lester.—2. Bum (the buttocks): id.: later C.20. Barker, 1979.

kinger (with hard *g*). 'A good customer, especially at the end of an otherwise bad day' (*M.T.*): market-traders'. The king among the day's customers.

kings or **kings and crosses.** Children's cry for truce, the first in E. and N.E. England, the second in E. Anglia, where also occurs *exes*. The Can. equivalent combines both in *king's ex!* (Opie, 1959.)—2. *Kings* (rare in sing.). Drivers: railwaymen's ironic: since ca. 1945. *Railway*, 2nd.

King's (or **Queen's) bad bargain.** A worthless soldier or sailor. See **bad bargain** and **K.h.b.**

Kings on the roof; kings up. A pair of kings and a lower pair: Aus. poker-players'. B., 1953.

King's Silly Little Idiots, the. 'The King's Shropshire Light Infantry, the KSLI, known irreverently as the King's Silly Little Idiots, or, reversing the initials, "I Love Soldiers' Kisses" ' (Critchley, 1981): Army: 1881–1958.

kinifee. ' "Yeah," said Ritchie, "they could get three months for carrying a kinifee." This was our bodgie slang word for a knife' (Dick): since early 1950s; by 1966, ob.

kink. A fig., esp. a technical, 'wrinkle'; a smart idea: Aus.: since ca. 1930. (B.P.)—2. An odd, an eccentric, person: since ca. 1960. (Petch.) Cf. **kinky**, adj., 2.

kinker. (Usu. in pl.) A contortionist: circus and variety.

kinky, n. A homosexual, whether male or female: semi-medical: from ca. 1920. (Bell, 1950.) Cf.:-

kinky, adj. As in 'the surface is a bit kinky—it has rucks and kinks in it' (Thomas, 1976); crinkled or wrinkled: coll. This, ex dial., is prob. the orig., the prototype, of all the following senses and of the n.—2. Eccentric; mentally twisted: coll. Ex S.E.—3. Homosexual: from mid-1920s. Cf. the n.—4. ?Hence, addicted to unusual or abnormal sexual practices: coll.: since ca. 1930.—5. Hence, anything, esp. clothes (see **kinky boots**) so contrived as to excite sexuality in the opposite sex: coll.: since ca. 1935. A revival of this meaning in the 1960s prompted Menkés, 1967, to write, 'For the past few months, the word "psychedelic" has been used by certain sections of the press and public much as "way out" or "kinky" was once employed.'

kinky (or **-ey) boots.** Tight-fitting calf- to thigh-length boots with very high, spiky heels; usu. black, and worn for display rather than practicability by fashionable women: ca. 1963–early 1970s. From later 1960s, applied joc. and loosely to similar boots of more moderate, practical pattern.

kip, n. Sleep: perhaps it arose in WW1, when it was much used by Brit. soldiers.—2. 'A small chip used for tossing pennies in the occult game of two-up' (Dennis): late C.19–20: s. >, by 1920, coll. >, by 1930, j. Perhaps a corruption or a perversion of *chip*.—3. A job (employment): Anglo-Irish: late C.19–20. Joyce, 1922, 'I get paid this morning, Stephen said.—The school kip? Buck Mulligan said.'

kip, v. To lodge; sleep: c., from ca. 1880 (B. & L.); > in C.20, via n., 1, gen. s. or low coll. Cf. **doss**, and:-

kip down. To go to bed; dispose oneself for, go to, sleep: a mainly Services' var. of **kip**, v. B. & P.

kip in, v. To 'shut up': low: late C.19–20. (Behan, 1958.) Ex *kip*, to go to bed (and sleep).

kip-in, adj. Easy: 'It's only right that they should get the kip-in jobs when they're here longer than anyone else' (Behan, 1958). Ex *kip*, to go to bed.

Kipper. Occ. nickname for a man habitually sleeping in doss-houses. (Petch, 1966.) P.B.: and, indeed, for any man given to sleeping a lot: mostly Services'. Ex *kip*, v.

kipper, n. (Esp. *giddy* (*young*) *kipper*.) A person; a child. (*OED* Sup.)—2. A tailoress help: tailors':—1933.—3. A serviceman, esp. a soldier, from Britain: Aus. servicemen's, esp. soldiers': 1940–5.—4. 'I evaluate its firing power as eighteen torpedoes—I think Kipper is a distressing piece of naval slang—in thirty minutes' (Jenkins, 1959): since ca. 1930. Suggested by *fish*, 2.—5. Of an English person, usu. male, visiting Aus., being very nice about everything while he is there, and then, back in Eng., writing 'nasty little things that he failed to mention while among the people whose hospitality he accepted. This unlovable trait has led to the application of the expression *kipper* to a certain type of Englishman. A kipper, by virtue of the processing, has become two-faced with no guts' (Marshall, 1962). This sense, deriving ex sense 3, arose ca. 1945.—6. A doss-house, a bed, or indeed anywhere to sleep: down-and-outs'.—7. The female pudend. A Cockney fellow-soldier, on reading of the birth of Siamese twins, exclaimed pityingly of the mother, 'Poor cow! I bet that split 'er old kipper'. (P.B.)—8. Coll. term for 'the kipper-shaped tie with a broad, pointed blade as much as five or six inches wide introduced in the mid 1960s in a striking range of new designs and bold colours' (Byrde, 1979): as ephemeral as the fashion. (P.B.)—9. In *not*, or *only*, *as far through as a kipper*: of anything or person, very thin; of a village, wood, etc., very small: Lancashire coll. (Pilkington, 1980).

kipper, v. To ruin the chances of (a person): from ca. 1920. Prob. ex *scupper* influenced by *cook* (one's) *hash*.

kipper and bloater. Motor: r.s.: later C.20. Daniells, 1979.

kipper kites. 'Aircraft engaged on convoy escort duties over the North Sea and casually giving protection to the fishing vessels' (H. & P.): esp., Coastal Command RAF: since 1940. See *kite*, n., 3.—2. Hence, Coastal Command aircraft in general: RAF: WW2+.

kipper season, the. The period from Christmas to Easter: costermongers': late C.19–20. 'No trade—the customers are kipping' (sleeping): Franklyn.

kipper trip. An anglers' special train: railwaymen's. *Railway.*

kipping(-)house (often pron. *kippin' ahse*) is a low s. var. of *kipper*, 6. Jervis, 1925.

kipps. Bed; sleep. (Harrison, 1943.) On *kip*, n.

kipsey. A house; the home: low Aus.:—1916 (Dennis).—2. (Also *kipsie*.) A cheap lodging-house: Aus.: since ca. 1910. Ronan, 1954.

kirk. To break into a house while its occupiers are at church: c.:—1933 (Leach).

kiss. (Gen. pl.) A full-stop: shorthand-typists':—1935.

kiss (one's) **aircraft goodbye.** To bale out: RAF aircrews': WW2. H. & P.

kiss of death, the. A fatal, or at the least a very dangerous, contact: coll.: since ca. 1950. Ex Judas' kissing of Jesus, thence to any other callous betrayal; perhaps with a famous US thriller of that title intervening. Foster, 1968, defines it as 'an apparently advantageous action which in reality will bring trouble or destruction' and adds that it 'seems to be a fairly new expression, current in speech for some time before it was met with in writing. A recent instance from the *Observer* supplement clearly illustrates the meaning. "Allying with Churchill was regarded as the political kiss of death even in 1939" (Sep. 18, 1966).'

kiss of life, the. 'Used jocularly of the usual type of kiss between lovers' (Petch, 1966): since ca. 1964. Ex mouth-to-mouth resuscitation, and, like that, in contradistinction to the prec.

kiss the cross (?Cross). To be knocked out; in, e.g., boxing: Aus.: since ca. 1925. B., 1943.

kisser. A baby: Romanies' and tramps' s.: since ca. 1920. So many women kiss it.

kissing bug. A (young) man intent on kissing: Can.: early C.20. 'Fifty years ago Canadian girls on a picnic might cry the warning, "There's a kissing bug about!" ' (Leechman, 1959). With a pun on the true *kissing bug*, a blood-sucking insect of N. America.

kisswosh, kisswosty. A thingummy: Army: late C.19–mid-20. Perhaps ex a (?)Hindi word.

kit. Drug addict's equipment or paraphernalia: drugs c. (Stockley, 1986.) US since—1959 (Spears).

kit-check, have a. To vomit, usu. as a result of over-drinking: Army: since late 1940s. Var. of *lay out* (one's) *kit*.

kitch. Kitchen: mostly lower and lower-middle class: since ca. 1920. (Norman.)

kitchema. A public house: market traders'. (*M.T.*) Ex Romany.

kitchen, the. That part of Monte Carlo casino which 'caters' for small-stakes habitués. Lowndes, 1937.—2. 'I knew him to be the second percussion player—one of the "Kitchen", in orchestral slang' (Wood, 1936).—3. A sharp knife: c.: later C.20. Tyler, 1982.

kitchen range. Change (of scene or costume): theatrical. Franklyn.

kitchen stoves (singular rare). Cloves: Aus. r.s. Franklyn 2nd.

kite, n. An accommodation bill; a bill of exchange, esp. if worthless: commercial: 1805 (*SOD*). Hence *fly a kite*, to 'raise the wind' by such bills.—2. Hence, a cheque; esp. a blank or a worthless cheque: c. (Wallace, 1928.) See also **kite-lark** and *fly a kite*, 2.—3. Any type of aircraft: RAF: from ca. 1919; ob. by ca. 1950, but still, 1983, occ. heard ironically, as in the exclam. by an anonymous voice in a BBC Radio programme about the 'Red Arrows' formation aerobatics team, 'To the kites, chaps!' 'In the earliest days of aviation, aeroplanes looked like, and were called, box-kites. Early in the Great War (1914–18) design changed, and "box" was dropped. But kite was not generally used by the Royal Flying Corps till 1917–18, when "crate" came to be confined to obsolescent or obsolete types, "kite" taking its place. It has since been the most generally used slang-word for "an aircraft" ' (Jackson).—4. A ship's sail: nautical. Parkman, 1946.—5. A newspaper: Aus. low: later C.20. McNeil.—6. An omnibus. See **barrow**, 2.—7. See **Bill**, 1.

kite, v. See **kiter** and **kiting.**

kite blue. A worthless cheque: Aus. c. See AUSTRALIAN UNDERWORLD, in Appx., and **kite,** n., 2.

kite-dropper. An issuer of worthless cheques: since ca. 1945. (Sanders.) Cf. **kite,** n., 2.

kite-flyer. A passer of worthless cheques: c.:—1935 (Hume). See **kite,** n., 2.

kite-lark. 'Stealing letters in transit, removing any cheques they may contain, and, after suitable manipulation, cashing them at the banks': c. A gang that operates this 'racket' is known as a *kite mob*. (Leach, 1933.) See **kite,** n., 2.

kite-man. A crook specialising in cheques and bills of exchange: from ca. 1920. (See **kite,** n., 2.) Wallace, 1928.

kite-mob. See **kite-lark.**

kiter; kiting. An issuer, or the issuing, of worthless cheques: c.: since ca. 1930. (Newman, 1970.) See **kite,** n., 2, and **kite-flyer.**

kites. The practice of forging cheques, and/or issuing cheques against a merely nominal bank-balance: c. (*Gilt Kid*, 1936.) Ex **kite,** n., 2.

kiting. 'The illegal alteration of a prescription to increase the number of pills or other drugs written down by the doctor' (Green, 1984): medical. Cf. prec.

kitsch. Rubbish or trash: in any of the arts, such work as is inferior or pretentious or in poor or dubious taste: since the late 1960s: s. rapidly > coll. >, in literary or artistic or musical circles, j. Chambers' *C.20th Dict.*, 1972 ed.—whose definition I paraphrase—gives it as S.E., without modification or comment; so also the *COD* of 1976. Not Yiddish but Ger., it

251

comes from *kitschen*, to throw together, esp. if hastily; hence the n., a work devoid of aesthetic value. Imported from the US.

kittens. Esp. in *having kittens*, nervous, agitated; 'all hot and bothered': from ca. 1933. (*The Times*, 15 Feb. 1937.) Ex a cat's perturbation during this crisis. Since ca. 1938, also *having a baby* and, among RAF officers of ca. 1940–5, *having a set of metal jugs*. P.B.: in later C.20, as frequent in the form, e.g., 'I nearly had kittens'.—2. In *like kittens in a basket*, (of two girls that are) very friendly to each other: WAAF: ca. 1942–5. H. & P.

Kitty. A Kittyhawk fighter aircraft (1941–2): RAF coll. Brickhill, 1946.

kitty, the. The important part: RAF: WW2. H.W., 1942.—2. In *in the kitty*, in the ammunition trays; in the bag (sense **bag**, n., 5): id. Ibid.—3. The jack at bowls: London and Southern bowls-players': current in 1970s. (Butcher, 1979.) The Midland version is synon. *the pot*.

kitz. See **put on the kitz.**

Kiwi, kiwi. 'A man on ground duty and not qualified for flying service' (F. & G.): RFC/RAF: from ca. 1917; superseded, by WW2 at latest, by *penguin*—another flightless bird.—2. A New Zealander: orig. Aus., then gen. Eng. coll. (B., 1942.), 'New Zealanders have retained their national title from World War II and are widely known to other soldiers as "Kiwis"': *Iddiwah*, July 1953: UN troops': ca. 1951–5. And Brit. Services' ever since.

klondyke. Money easily obtained: Glasgow:—1934.

klondyking. 'Catching herring on Dogger Bank, salting, barrelling at sea, sailing to Russia to sell it' (Peppitt): North Sea fishing trade s.: from ca. 1890; in the 1930s applied to taking fish to Germany. Hence *klondyker*, a North Sea captain (or owner) who does this. With a pun on Klondyke mines and 'gold-fever'. Butcher, 1980, notes *klondyke herring* for the fish thus exported to Germany.

klootch, an Indian woman of the Canadian Pacific Coast, is short for the synon. *klootchman*, a Chinook jargon word ex Nootka Indian: Can. (Leechman.)

kludge. 'An improvised do-it-yourself lashup that may well work.—2. A factory made computer that still has some (endearingly) odd characteristics' (Green, 1984): computer engineers'. *Weekend Australian Mag.*, 1–2 Feb. 1986, defined it as 'a convoluted, jury-rigged design that is clumsy to use and grossly inefficient.'

klutz. A stupid lout: adopted, ca. 1970, ex US. (An *Observer* TV review, 17 June 1973.) Via Yiddish ex the coll. Ger. *Klotz*, blockhead, lout. (R.S., 1973.)

kn-. Common to the Teutonic languages, but, in S.E., silent since C.17. In C.20 'there has been a s. tendency to re-introduce the *k*-sound in *knut, Knightsbridge*' (W.) Cf. the joc. pron. (connotative also of emphasis) of *twenty* as *ter-wenty*.

knacked. Contraction of **knackered**, q.v.: teenagers': early 1980s. (Joanna Williamson, 1982.) Also Glasgow (Munro, 1985.) Cf. **knick-knacked.**

knacker, v. (Rare except as *knackered*, ppl. adj.) To rob (a person) of something: *Conway* cadets':—1891 (Masefield, 1933). Still in use, later C.20, in W. Midlands industries (Jefferson, 1983).

knacker crusher. A rough road or a pothole: motorcyclists': since mid-C.20. (Dunford.) Ex **knackers**, 1.

knackered. See **knacker, v.**—2. Thwarted; in a predicament: low. Ex **knackers**, 1; cf. **balls-up.**—3. (Usu. physically) exhausted. Occ., as adj., *knackering*, as in 'that new assault course is absolutely bloody knackering'. Both, Services': since ca. 1950 (?much earlier). (P.B.) Jefferson, 1983, notes 'I'm knackered up' = I am as good as dead; 'it's knackered up' = It is absolutely worn out and beyond repair: W. Midlands industries.

knackers. The testicles, occ. of animals: low: C.19–20. Prob. ex dial. *knacker*, a castanet or other 'striker'. P.B.: hence, also, as exclam. = nonsense!, or in a dismissive, e.g., 'knackers to

you, mate!': cf. identical use of synon. **balls** and **ballocks**. A retort to *knackers!* is, sometimes, *yours or mine?*

knee. Short for *knee him in the balls*: low coll. Euph. variants: *hit him where he'll feel it* and *hit him where it hurts him most*, both dating from ca. 1930.

kneecap. To shoot a victim, e.g. an informer, through the kneecaps, a 'punishment' that cripples without actually killing, practised esp. in Ireland: later C.20. (Green, 2.) Some later fig. use, applied to the crippling of an argument.

knees. *On* (one's) *knees*, exhausted physically, as after a route-march, or a long day's grinding housework: since ca. 1920.

knees-up. A jovial evening, esp. with some kind of dance: mostly Londoners': since ca. 1945. Ex the song (and dance) 'Knees up, Mother Brown'. (Jones, 1978.)

knick-knacked. Euph. for *knackered*, ruined (sense ex the slaughter of, e.g. horses), when the derivation has become confused with that of *knackers*: coll.: mid-1970s.

knicker-nicker. A C.20 version of the various names for stealers of clothes from clothes-lines (Petch). A ca. 1960 var. is *knicker-spong'er*, but he is one who specialises in 'lifting' women's knickers. (P.B.) Cf. **knickers bandit.**

knicker-sticker. Woman traffic warden: motorcyclists': 1970s. (Dunford.)

knicker-twisting. From **knickers in a twist**, q.v., esp. senses 2 and 3.

knickers and stockings. A term of penal servitude: c.:—1932 (Wood).

knickers are (or **were**) **on fire, as if her.** In a state of flustered fear and excitement: since ca. 1960. Petch, 'Used in the "Coronation Street" episode of 27 Jan. 1975.' (A long running TV serial of working-class life.)

knickers bandit. 'A petty thief stealing from clothes lines' (Powis): police s.: later C.20. See **bandit.**

knickers in a twist. *Don't get your . . .* , don't become cantankerous or contentiously touchy: both among men (implying femininity) and from men to women: since ca. 1950. (L.A., 1976.)—2. *Get* (one's) *knickers in a twist*, to get flustered, to panic: coll.: since ca. 1960 at latest. [A petty officer speaking:] 'Just pay attention to what I say and then we'll have nobody adrift or roundabout mid-forenoon getting his knickers in a twist' (*Heart*).—3. To be under a misapprehension, or muddled, about something, as ' 'fraid he's got his knickers in a twist on *that* one': since late 1960s: coll. Cf. *get* (one's) *wires crossed*, or *have a leg over*. This nuance perhaps influenced by the earlier synon. *get* (one's) *knitting twisted*. (P.B.)

knicks. Women's drawers. Abbr. *knickers.*

Knife and Fork, the. The Master Cutler, the express train running between Sheffield and London: railwaymen's. McKenna, 1970.

knife-and-fork course. Course for servicemen commissioned from the ranks: Services', esp. RN lowerdeck: WW2. (Rendell, 1980.) Supposedly to teach course-members manners acceptable to an officers' mess. (P.B.)

knife-edge. A sand-dune ridge in the N. African desert: Aus. Army: 1940–2. B., 1943.

knifey. (Of a person, esp. a customer) that cuts things painfully fine when dealing in the money-market: stock-brokers':—1935.

knit it! Stop!; 'shut up!': Glasgow:—1934. Cf. **keep nit.**

knits. Knitted comforts, esp. garments, for Service men and women: feminine coll.: WW2. Superseded, in later C.20, by *knitteds*, applied to knitted garments in general.

knitting. Girls generally or one girl particularly: RAF: since ca. 1930. (Jackson.) Also *piece of knitting* (Partridge, 1945). It belongs to the **homework** genus of metaphor, and was used by RN and Army also, in WW2.

knitting twisted, get (one's), as in 'You've got your . . . ', you're wrongly informed; you're getting one fact or incident or statement confused with another: since ca. 1950. (L.A., 1976.) Cf. *get* (one's) *wires crossed* and *get* (one's) *knickers in a twist*, q.v. at **knickers in a twist**, 3.

knob-end; -head. Strong pej. for an irritatingly foolish person: later 1980s. With ref. to the *glans penis*; cf. synon. **dickhead.** (Tyler, 1987.)

knobber-up; knobbing-up, n. A shunter operating points in a marshalling yard; the operation: railwaymen's: ca. 1910. *Railway.*

knobsticked, be. To be beaten: railwaymen's: since ca. 1920. *Railway.*

knock, n. A copulation: low coll.: C.16–17. The term prob. 'went underground', for it recurs in low Aus. s. of C.20. 'I had caused him to miss out on a knock . . . with Elaine' (Dick).—2. An innings: cricketers' coll.: from ca. 1919. Palmer, 1934.—3. A synon. of the *bonk*: cyclists': since ca. 1945. Short for *hunger-knock*.—4. A promiscuous, easy girl: low Aus.: since ca. 1910. (Dick.)—5. Stolen goods: policemen's (mostly, N.E. England), also fringe of the underworld: since ca. 1950. (Wainwright, 1975.) Ex *knock off*, steal.—6. 'Used by anglers for a bite [by a fish]' (Petch, 1969).—7. *On the knock*, shortening of *on the knocker*, on credit. Prob. influenced by *on tick*. Later C.20.—8. *On the knock*. 'Calling at houses, as canvassers, market researchers, etc.' (Petch, 1969): coll.: since late 1940s.—9. *On the knock*, engaged in hire-purchase: since ca. 1950. (*Woman's Own*, 28 Feb. 1968.)—10. *On the knock*. Practising prostitution. Roberts, citing Hebden, 1983, comments that it was 'only slightly less common usage than "on the game" in 1920s–30s'.

knock, v. To welsh: racing c.:—1932.—2. To be unable to make a move in a game, e.g. dominoes, when it is one's turn to do so: players'. '(I'm) knocking' or 'Knock, knock!', prob. ex the signal of tapping the table to indicate the same thing.—3. To kill: Aus. Palmer, 1937.—4. To wound; esp. *knocked*, wounded: Aus. Army: WW1 and 2. *Rats*, 1944.—5. To disparage: adopted ex US, ca. 1943 in UK, ca. 1944 in Aus.—6. To sell (a car) at a loss: secondhand dealers': since ca. 1950. (*Sunday Times*, 24 Oct. 1965.) Cf. **knock down**, v., 1.—7. To 'date' or to flirt with (a girl): Aus.: since ca. 1920. Lindsay, 1933—see quot'n at **bum**, v., 3.—8. 'To get an article or meal on credit and not pay, or pay by bad check' (Cook, 1962): since ca. 1945.

knock, as an intensive adv. 'Will you lend me some money?'—'No, will I knock!' North Country grammar-school s.: since ca. 1955. Cf. synon. use of *heck* and *thump*: both may be euph. for *fuck!* used in this emphatic way.

knock along. (Often with *together*.) To get on (with a person): coll.: since ca. 1910.—2. To get through life, as 'Oh, we'll knock along all right', i.e. without *too* much difficulty, though perhaps in reduced circumstances: coll.: later C.20.

knock around with. To keep company with, as 'Who's she knocking around with now, then?' or 'He generally knocks around with his mates from the club': lowish coll. (P.B.)

knock(-)back, n. A refusal; a grave disappointment: coll. A specialisation is 'a bad result re adjudication/petition/parole' (Home Office, 1978): prisoners'. The broader meaning is common also in Aus. and NZ.—2. A participation in a 'back-up': Aus. gangsters': since ca. 1945. (Dick.)

knock back, v. To cost a person so-much: coll. 'That knocked him back a fiver.'—2. Hence, to fine: Cockney: since ca. 1910.—3. To refuse; to reject: mostly Aus. (Kylie Tennant, 1939), and Glasgow (Munro, 1985). Cf. the n., 1.—4. To consume, usu. drink, less commonly, to eat. Cf. **knock it back.** Variants are *knock over* or just *knock*: B., 1942, records all three; the *Eastbourne Herald* (England), 6 May 1939: *knockback*.

knock cold. To render (someone) unconscious by striking him; hence, to astound, to flabbergast: Aus. (Baker.) Cf. **knock 'em cold.**

knock commission out of, e.g., a vehicle. To damage, by either misuse or over-use: Aus.: since late 1940s. (B.P.)

knock-down, n. An introduction: Aus. (Dennis.) Adopted ex US; cf. the v., 1.—2. A loan: Aus. Stivens, 1951.

knock down, v. To introduce (one person to another): Aus., adopted ex US. But Wilkes notes the gen. form *give the knockdown*. Cf. the n., 1.—2. To shirk, to idle: Can.: since ca. 1950. Dempsey, 1975: 'and the boss thinks you are knocking down.'

knock down ginger, n. and v. The 'game' of knocking at doors and running away; to knock on a door and run away: South London schoolchildren's.—2. See **knocking down ginger.**

knock 'em. To 'make a hit' or achieve success. Vachell, 1913.

knock 'em cold. To amaze 'them': to have a sensational success: since ca. 1920. Ex boxing.

knock for a (or **the**) **loop.** To astound: s. > coll.: since ca. 1910 or earlier (Leechman).

knock (someone's) **hat off.** To astound: mostly Cockneys': since ca. 1940. 'It would knock your hat off if I told you.' As a result of a heavy blow on the head.

knock hell out of. To damage severely; to trounce: mostly Aus.: late C.19–20. (B., 1943.) P.B.: in later C.20, common also in Brit.

knock into. To fight with (someone): Aus.: since ca. 1910. Baker.

knock it back (invariable). To eat; occ. to drink: mostly military: from ca. 1912. (B. & P.) In later C.20, more widespread, and usu. referring to drinking, as in 'he knocked back his pint quicker than that, and rushed out' (P.B.).

knock it off! Stop talking! (or whatever else is being done to annoy the complainer): coll.: since late 1930s. Cf. **pack it in!**

knock it on the head! Shut up!: Aus.: since ca. 1920. (Dick.) Ex killing a snake.

knock-knock (usually in pl—*knock-knocks*). An acoustic mine: RN: 1941+. (Granville.) Echoic.

knock me silly; usually shortened to *knock me*. A billy can: Aus. r.s. B., 1945.

knock-off, n. Time to leave off work: coll. Abbr. *knock(ing)-off time*.—2. Something that has been 'knocked off', stolen: low: mid-C.20. See the v., 1, and:—3. *On the knock-off* (adj. and adv.), a-thieving in any way: c.: from ca. 1925. *Gilt Kid*, 1936.—4. A cheap copy of a fashionable item or best selling line, in e.g. clothing, cutlery, etc.: commercial and industrial: later C.20. (Green, 1984; *Caterer*, 27 Mar. 1980.)—5. Hence, 'Quick hack productions that echo a best seller—usually non-fiction and tied into a major event, e.g. the Falklands War—to cash in on the public appetite for such material' (Green, 1984): publishers'.

knock off, v. To steal: nautical > military in 1915. (Bowen.) Cf. S.E. sense, to deduct.—2. To do, commit, esp. in *knock off a job*, to commit a crime: c.:—1932 (*Dartmoor*).—3. To arrest (a person): c.:—1933 (Leach).—4. As in 'I could knock off a pint': since ca. 1920. Var. of **knock back**, v., 4.—5. To kill: Army: WW2 and since. P-G-R.—6. To seduce: low Aus.: since ca. 1910. ' "Remember the time old Ethel tried to knock off Terry?" they would start' (Dick).—7. To coït with (a girl): perhaps orig. mostly Aus., since ca. 1930 (B.P.), but by ca. 1960 at latest, common in Brit., often with implication of marital infidelity or mere sexual gratification. Carter, 1971, 'knocking off this chick', and 'I've been knocking off one of my fifth form . . . '

knock-off bag. 'Pilferable items [are] usually considered as part of normal and expected earnings in many restaurants. Hence "knock-off bag"—the kind of capacious shopping bag carried by women staff—often used jocularly' (Mars, 1984): hotel and catering industry. Cf. **knock-off**, n., 2.

knock-on effect. The effect that an event has upon subsequent events, e.g., in multiple vehicle 'pile-ups'; the effects of a strike being complicated by later strikes; etc.: coll., verging on j.: late 1970s. BBC Radio 4 News, 24 June 1979.

knock one off the perch. As in, e.g., 'He's knocked one . . . ', he is a prospective father: Midlands': since 1930s. Cf. synon. *he's rung the bell.* (Fearon, 1984.)

knock out, n. A knock-out competition (one in which a single defeat entails elimination): since ca. 1925: coll. >, by 1965, S.E.

knock out, v. To fascinate; to impress profoundly; to 'enthuse': mostly teenagers': since earlyish 1960s. In, e.g., the Beatles' song. 'Back in the U.S.S.R.', in their 'White Album', released in Nov. 1968 (Janssen).—2. 'To knock out a place is to burgle it thoroughly, leaving it cleaned out of anything of value' (Tempest): c.: mid-C.20.

knock-out drops. A liquid drug—gen. butyl-chloride—'put in liquor to facilitate robbing': US (1876), anglicised ca. 1904: low. (*OED* Sup.) Bailey, 1933, ' "Chloral hydrate" . . . "That stuff! Knock-out drops. The common thieves' dope for putting a man to sleep". '—2. In Aus., 'drugged or impure liquor': from ca. 1910. Dennis.—3. A soothing syrup (containing either opium or laudanum) for babies: late C.19–20. Roberts, 1971.

knock-over, n. A considerable, esp. if surprising, success: Aus.: since ca. 1920. (Baker.) Cf. **pushover.**

knock over, v. To kill (man or beast): Aus. (Niland, 1958.) Cf. **knock off,** v., 5.

knock over a doll. 'To incur the consequences entailed in any activity (?from the contest of throwing at dolls at a sideshow)' (Wilkes): Aus.: since mid-C.20.

knock (someone) **rotten.** To trounce; to defeat heavily: Aus. B., 1942.

knock-up, n. 'An unpleasant device by which dealers conspire to rig the bidding at antique auctions' (*Evening Echo*, Bournemouth, 17 Apr. 1966): antique dealers'.

knock up, v. 'To impregnate intentionally, as in "I'll knock up the old lady [my wife] one of these days": widespread in Can., ex US, 1950s' (Leech, 1985).

knock up a catcher. Gen. *to have knocked up* . . . , to be put on an easy job: dockers': *Daily Herald*, 1936.

knock with, do a. To arrange a meeting with (one of the opposite sex): Aus.: since ca. 1920. (Lindsay, 1933.) See **knock-down,** n., 1.

knocked to the wide. Utterly exhausted: Army: since ca. 1940. P-G-R.

knocker. A person given to discouraging or fault-finding: coll.: adopted, ex US, in Aus. by ca. 1920 (Wilkes), in Brit. by ca. 1930.—2. A person taken by the police: tramps' c.:—1932 (Jennings).—3. A person who contracts debts without the intention to repay them: Army: since late C.19. In later C.20, more gen. for 'a hire-purchase defaulter' (*Woman's Own*, 28 Feb. 1968).—4. Hence, a welshing bookmaker: Aus. sporting: since ca. 1925. (B., 1943.) Hence *take the knack on*, to welsh his clients: since ca. 1930. (Glassop, 1949.) In later C.20, Brit. prisoners' c. for 'person who welshes on a bet' (Home Office).—5. A 'Class E freight train (Midland Region)' (*Railway*): railwaymen's: mid-C.20.—6. Camshaft: motorcyclists'. Hence, *double knocker*, twin camshafts. (Dunford.)—7. *On the knocker*: applied to one who sells things by going from door to door (i.e., constantly using the knocker): orig. low s., esp. grafters' (*Cheapjack*, 1934); >, by ca. 1965, coll., as used by the *Financial Times*, 16 Nov. 1973, in *go on the knocker*, to be a door-to-door canvasser.—8. *On the knocker*: on credit: Londoners': from ca. 1930. (London *Evening News*, 11 Dec. 1936.) In later C.20 sometimes shortened to *on the knock*, and more gen. Cf. **knock,** n., 7.—9. *On the knocker*, 'Promptly, on demand, esp. in the expression "cash on the knocker" ' (Wilkes): Aus. coll.: later C.20.

knocker-off. A thief specialising in motorcars: c.: from ca. 1920. Ex **knock off,** v., 1. Wallace, 1926.

knocker-worker. A door-to-door pedlar: low s., esp. grafters'. (Allingham.) See **knocker,** 7, for which this is the n.

knockers. Female breasts: low Aus. By late 1950s, also English, as in Kennaway, 1967, 'She was slight . . . but with great little knockers—breasts being for mothers.' Cf. also quot'n at **jujubes.**

knocking. See **knock,** v., 2.—2. 'Pretending to be an antique dealer, knocking on doors' (*Now!*, 10 Apr. 1981): c.

knocking company. A hire-purchase company: since late 1940s. (Cook, 1962.) See **knock,** n., 9.

knocking-down ginger is a London street-boys' coll. for the game of follow-my-leader, during which boards and loose goods outside shops are thrown down. The practice is also called *ginger-knocking*; a practitioner, *ginger-knocker*. See also **knock down ginger.**

knocking-joint. A brothel: c. >, by 1915, low s. Cf. C.19 synon. *knocking-shop.*—2. The stand of a bookmaker that intends, if unlucky, to welsh: racing c.:—1932.

knocking on (a bit). Growing middle-aged—or elderly; or merely being older than the speaker: low coll.: since ca. 1930.

knocking-shop. See **knocking-joint.**

knot-flashing. Heterosexual self-exposure by men: police s. Fraser, 1968.

knots. 'The status mark of the surfer—lumps on knees and top of foot from knee paddling' (*Pix*, 28 Sep. 1963): Aus. (teenage) surfers': since ca. 1961.

knotted. As in 'Do you think that Passmore who goes chasing arse every time he's ashore has got much self-respect left? Or Harvey? Or Hatch? They're all knotted in some way' (*Heart*, 1962, a Naval NCO speaking); i.e. with problems. Cf. (*all*) *bitter and twisted*, and the **hung-up** ex 'suffering from a hang-up'. (P.B.)

Knotty, the. The North Staffordshire railway: railwaymen's: ca. 1890-1940. *Railway*.

know all the answers. Applied to a person smart in repartee or in circumventing the cunning; often ironic or exasperated: adopted ca. 1939 ex US. Ultimately ex Ger. *Bescheid wissen*, 'reaching the US with German immigrants' (R.S.). It becomes ironically apposite when the answerer, not necessarily a young know-all, doesn't even understand the questions.

know-how. Skill; the knack of doing something: coll., adopted, ca. 1943, ex US; >, by ca. 1955, S.E. Short for the '*know how* to do it'.

Know-it of Know-all Park. A know-all: coll.: from ca. 1910. Mackenzie, 1933.

know the ins and outs of a duck's bum. 'To know the "trick" of mechanism or formula, to be familiar with complicated process, or obscure facts' (L.A., 1974). Cf. (she) *wants to know all the ins and outs of a cat's arse*, (she) is very inquisitive.

know the score. To know the risks involved, mostly in personal relationships and esp. in amorous ones: coll. Perhaps ex cricket or billiards.

knowledge, the. 'In London, on a small scooter, you [a policeman] can make yourself look exactly like a probationary taxi-driver learning "the knowledge" (of London streets) for the Public Carriage Office written examination' (Powis): taxi-drivers' coll. > almost j.

Knubs. German soldiers: 1939+. Perhaps ex Ger. *Knabe*, a youth.

knuckle. A fistfight: low: since ca. 1930. Norman.—2. In *go the knuckle*, to punch, fight: Aus. In earlier C.20, with *on*, which carries the nuance rather 'to cheat, defraud, take down' (B., 1959). Wilkes cites Niland, 1959, and later authors, for the shorter, 'fighting' form.

knuckle-bone, down on the. Penniless: c.: from ca. 1880 (Baumann). Wolveridge, 1978, expands it to 'down on the knuckle-bone of [one's] arse', and implies that, by the 1930s, it was in gen. Cockney use.

knuckle(-)boy. A bare-fisted fighter: Aus. (Dick.) See **knuckle.**

knuckle-head. 'A fool or [a] thick-head' (Petch, 1969): adopted, ca. 1944, ex US servicemen.

knuckle pie. See **slice of** , and cf.:-

knuckle sandwich. A punch on the mouth or the jaw: since ca. 1920, esp. in the North; then, post-WW2, more widely used, perhaps, as Petch suggests, thanks to the long-running Independent TV serial 'Coronation Street', where used, e.g., on 22 May 1974. In later C.20, also Aus. (Buzo, 1973). Cf. the C.16–17 *eat fist-meat*; and prec.

knuckle-up. A fight, esp. with bare fists: NZ: since late 1940s. (Griffiths, 1970.) Cf. Brit. **punch-up.**

knuckles on the ground (or **deck**), (**with his**). Applied to a youth or (usu.) young man of low intellect and primitive appearance: coll.: since ca. 1930 or perhaps a decade earlier. Forester, 1975, reports a recruiting sergeant as saying, 'sometimes you get a right thickie, with his knuckles on the ground [i.e., ape-like], who wants to be a brain surgeon.' (P.B.)

koala. A motorist—e.g., a diplomat—immune from being booked for parking offences: Aus.: since ca. 1945. (B., 1953.) A koala is a protected creature.

koala bear. A militiaman: Aus., mostly servicemen's: WW2. B., 1943.

Kockler. A Model MP5A3 submachinegun: Army, esp. SAS: later C.20. A compounding of Heckler & Koch, the guns' manufacturers. (Knight, 1984.)

kone; hence **koniacker.** Counterfeit money; counterfeiter: Aus. c. (B., 1942.) Adopted from US.

kooferred, be. To be killed: naval (African Squadron): ca. 1860–1910. Bowen, 'Borrowed from the Swahili.'—2. 'Now considerably watered down to merely "exhausted" rather than "quite dead" ' (P.B., 1974): Army: since 1950, at latest.

kook. A clown; a simpleton: Aus. (teenage) surfers': since ca. 1961. (*Pix*, 28 Sep. 1963.) Ex American *kook*, an odd person, a simpleton, in short anyone the speaker dislikes. Ex *cuckoo*, as in 'you silly cuckoo!'

kooloo. Var. spelling of **cooloo.**

Kop, the. 'A bank of terracing for the supporters of the home team, esp. the one at Liverpool FC' (Green, 1984): Soccer fans'. Orig. *Spion Kop*, after the battle in the S. African War, 1900.

Kosbies, the. 'Throughout the British Army they are known as "The Kosbies", although if you were to ask an officer of the Regiment about the Kosbies he would curtly inform you that he had never heard of them and presume that you referred to The King's Own Scottish Borderers' (Carew). Ex the initials, of course: cf. **Wasbees** and **Wosby.**

krab. See **crab**, n., 4.

Kraut. A German, esp. a German soldier: Army, mostly in Italy in 1944–5. 'It is the only building left standing in the vil-

lage. The Krauts blew up the rest'; 'The Kraut will have to fall back' (Scott, 1946). Ex that favourite dish of the Germans: *sauerkraut*. P.B.: owing more to US influence than to 'the D-Day Dodgers', the term has, in later C.20, > much more widespread and is applied, not necessarily disparagingly, to Germans in general. Also used as adj., as in:-

Kraut carrier. A Volkswagen 'Beetle' car: later C.20. (Turner, 1986.) Cf., as insulting, **Rice-Burner.**

Krautrock. 'What the music press called Krautrock, the generic name for the work of the rather highbrow German pop bands who developed after 1967, playing synthesised electronic music' (York, 1977).

kree. Short for *kreegy*, q.v. at **kriegy.**

Kremlin, the. The headquarters of British Railways: railwaymen's: since ca. 1950. *Railway.*—2. New Scotland Yard: later C.20. Powis.—3. May be applied, joc. or ironic, to any imposing, important building in Service camp, barracks, or other similar establishment: later C.20. (P.B.)

kriegy. 'A prisoner of war (from the German "Kriegsgefangener"). *Kriegydom*: the world of kriegies, or, as the Germans put it so succinctly, "Kriegsgefangenschaft" ' (Brickhill, 1946); 31 Aug. 1944, *World's Press News* (only *kriegy*): prisoners-of-war in Germany: 1940-5. Var. *kreegy*; shortening, *kree.*

kurl or **kurl-a-mo.** Excellent: Aus.: since ca. 1920. (B., 1942.) Fanciful.—2. Hence, *kurl the mo*, to succeed brilliantly or far beyond expectation; to win 'in a big way': since ca. 1925. B., 1943.

kushy. See **cushy.**

kweis(s); occ. **kway-ess** or **quis.** Usu. as exclam.: 'Good!', 'Capital!', 'O.K.!': Army and RAF: earlier C.20. Directly ex Arabic. See **quiess kateer.**

kybo. A privy; a w.c.: low. Ex *Khyber Pass*, C.19 r.s., on *arse*.

kye. Ship's cocoa of a rich and delicious consistency served during the Middle Watch (midnight to 4 a.m.): RN. (H. & P.) Granville, 'The origin of the word is dialectal, from the adjective kyish, muddy-looking, brown . . . ' See **kye-boy,** and **ki.**—2. Hence, chocolate: RAN. B., 1943.

kye-boy; often simply **kye.** That member of the watch whose turn it is to make cocoa: since ca. 1910. Ex prec.

kyfer. See **khyfer.**

L

l.b.d. The 'little black dress' suitable for almost any social or official occasion: feminine: mid-C.20. (D. Beale, who recalls its use at Leicester University, late 1950s.)

l.b.w. See **leg before wicket**.

l.f. gear. 'The proceeds of a long firm [q.v.] fraud often offered at very low prices; often, too, quite honestly obtained property of low quality is falsely described as "LF gear" to explain cheapness and stimulate customer interest' (Powis): c.: later C.20.

l.i. The offence known as '*l*oitering with *i*ntent': spivs' coll. and police j.: since late 1940s. *Picture Post*, 2 Jan. 1954.

l.i.l. 'Live-in Lover', one's unmarried partner for the time being: coll.: later C.20. (Mindel, 1981.)

L.K., short for **L.K. Clark.** Mark: racing and underworld r.s. 'We get off the L.K. at nine' (o'clock): Franklyn 2nd.

l. of c. swine. Lines-of-communication troops: front-line troops': 1940–5. P-G-R.

L.P.C. Army boots, 'Leather Personnel Carriers—in fond memory of the APCs, the armoured personnel carriers' (*Sunday Express* mag., 13 Mar. 1983, p.19): Services': Falkland Is. campaign, 1982.

la. A *l*avatory, a public convenience: Aus.: since ca. 1945. Hesling, 1963.

la! An exclam.: C.16–20: polite till ca. 1850, then low coll. and dial. Cf. *la, la!*.—2. (Often pronounced *law*): in C.17–20, a low coll. euph. for *Lord!*, this sense merging with the prec. Cf. *lor', lawk!*.

la-di-da, lah-di-dah, lardy-dah. Very stylish; affectedly smart of costume, voice, manners: from ca. 1860: coll.—2. A tramcar or motorcar: r.s. (Gardner, 1932.) Cf. **jam-jar.**—3. 'Cigar (sometimes just "lardy")' (Powis): r.s.: later C.20.

La Lin. La Linea, street of bars, etc., just over the Spanish border from Gibraltar: Services' in Gibraltar. *Heart*, 1962.

lab. Laboratory: school and university s. >, by 1910, coll.: late C.19–20. Masterman, 1933.

labbie. A Labrador dog: coll. (P.B.)

Labour, the; gen. *on the Labour*, on unemployment-relief: working classes' coll.: from ca. 1921. Harrison, 1935.—2. The, or a, Labour Exchange: working-class coll.: since early 1920s. Still used, for the local office of the DHSS, later C.20 (*New Society*, 23 July 1981).

lace curtain. Foreskin: raffish; homosexual.—2. Beer: r.s. on *Burton*, hence any beer: since ca. 1930. Usu. shortened to *lace*.

lace into. A coll. var. of S.E. *lace*, to thrash. Lyell.

lace-ups. Laced-up boots: coll.:—1887 (Baumann). P.B.: in mid- and later C.20 applied to laced-up shoes, as opp. to sandals, 'slip-ons', etc.

lacks or **lax.** Lacrosse: schoolgirls': since ca. 1950. (Sanders, 1965.)

lacky. (Poss. *lackie* or *-ey*.) 'The vocabulary of the school [an industrial, i.e. reform, school near London, 1920s] allowed but two classes in the community: the "cocks" and the "lackies". Relatively to each boy, the lackies comprised all those boys whom he could bully without fear of reprisal, and the cocks all who could bully him on the same terms' (Benney, 1936).

laddio. A fellow, a chap: Anglo-Irish. 'By the time you've finished with them laddios you'll have the back teeth out of their heads. I wouldn't cod you' (Campbell, 1960).

ladidah. See **la-di-da**.

ladies', the. Women's lavatories: coll. Dickens, 1946.

ladies' dingdong night. See **winkle-trip**.

lads, the. 'The men of a familiar group; in the team, drinking companions, in pub or NAAFI; men without notable rank, as distinct from commissioned officers [or managerial class]; a company of convivial men on equal terms: coll., among Servicemen, sportsmen, shop-floor, etc.: ex North Country use of "lad" for grown man' (L.A., 1974). 'I believe he holds quite a high position, but at weekends, down here in the village, he likes to think he's "just one of the lads"—you know the sort!' (P.B.).—2. See **ear-(h)ole**.

lady-bird, ladybird. A WAAF officer: RAF: 1941+. (Jackson.) Cf. **blue bird.**

lady from Bristol. A pistol: r.s. *This Week*, 10 Mar. 1968.

Lady Godiva. A note or sum of £5 sterling: r.s., on *fiver*.

lady-in-waiting. A woman visibly pregnant: ?orig. and mainly Can.: since early 1960s. (Leechman.) Adopted in Brit. by 1965 at latest; it occurs in the Bournemouth *Evening Echo*, 24 Feb. 1966.

Lady Lavery. (Gen. in pl.) An Irish Free State legal-tender note: Anglo-Irish, esp. among bank-clerks: from ca. 1925. Obviously ex her notability.

Lady Magger Hagger. Lady Margaret Hall: Oxford undergraduates':—1922 (Marples, 2).

lady marm. An affected, pretentious woman: lower classes' coll.:—1923 (Manchon). Var.: *stuck-up marm.*

Lady Muck. The female complement, a further var. of the prec.: low coll.: since the 1890s. 'Stuck-up pair—think they're Lord and Lady Muck, don't they just!' (P.B.).

lady penguins. Nuns in general: Aus. Catholics'. (B.P.) Ex their black-and-white habits.

lady's waist. A waisted glass in which beer is served; hence, the beer itself: Aus.: since ca. 1920. B., 1942.

lag, n. (Also *lage*). Water: c.: ca. 1560–1870. Harman.—2. A sentence of transportation: c.: C.19. Hence (also *lagging*) a term of penal servitude: c.: from ca. 1850.—3. Hence, a prison-term of 3 years: Aus. and Brit. c. (B., 1942; Tempest, 1950, specifies 'three years penal servitude'.) A *lagging* is, in Aus., a sentence of more than 2 years.—4. A urination, as in 'I'm going for a lag': market-traders' (*M.T.*): a survival into later C.20 of the v., 1. Ex sense 1.

lag, v. To urinate: c. and low coll.: ca. 1560–1860. But see prec., 4.—2. To send to penal servitude: c.: from ca. 1850. Wallace, *passim*.—3. V.i., to serve as a convict: c.: C.20. Ex sense 2.—4. To inform on (a person) to the police, to 'shop': c.: from ca. 1870. As 'to give up to the authorities; to convict' (McNeil), current in Aus., later C.20.

lagger. An informer to the police: from ca. 1870: c. Ex **lag**, v., 4. Current in Aus., later C.20. (McNeil.)—2. A water-closet: market-traders': late C.19–20. By extension, *laggereena*: cf. **crappereena**. *M.T.*—3. Hence, a commode or a chamber-pot: id. (Ibid.) Senses 2 and 3 ex **lag**, n., 1 and 4, and v., 1.

lagging. The vbl n. corresponding to **lag**, v., 2 and 3, qq.v. Esp. as a penal term of three years: c.:—1932 (*Dartmoor*). To be *lagging* is a c. var. of **lag**, v., 3. Wallace, 1927.

lagging-station. 'Provincial security prison for long termers' (Clayton, 1970): c.

laggy band. An elastic band: E. Midlands schoolchildren's: later C.20. Often abbr., as in (children to teacher who has confiscated 'weapons') 'Please miss, can us 'ave us laggies back?' (P.B., 1987.)

lagi. See PRISONER-OF-WAR SLANG, §9, in Appx.

lahdee or **lahdie**. Smart (clothes); fashionable (hotels, resorts, etc.): Cockneys': since ca. 1930. (Barling, 1973.) Ex **la-di-da**, q.v.

laid back. 'Being relaxed in style and character; easy-going, unhurried' (*6000 Words*, 1976): adopted, ex US, ca. 1977. (*Listener*, 19 Oct. 1978, once with ref. to an American concert audience, once to West African music.) ' "Laid back" can mean anything from "uninterested" to "lazy slob", and it is used usually by people who don't want to do anything' (Berry, 1979).

laid on. See **lay on**, to arrange.

lair. 'A flashily-dressed man. "Dead Lair": one who overdoes this vulgar dressing—*lair-up*: to dress, esp. to don one's best clothes for a festive occasion. [Esp. *all laired-up*.]—*lairy*: vulgar, flashily or showily dressed' (B., 1942). See also the var. **lare**. Brockman, 1940, has 'a regular lare' (synon. with 'dead lair') and 'lare around' (synon. with 'lare up'). —2. Hence a larrikin or young hoodlum, esp. if flashily dressed: since ca. 1935. Hence, since ca. 1946, such compounds as *mug lair*, *two-bob lair*, *ten-cent lair*, all pej. B., 1953.

lairise. To behave flashily; 'to act or dress as a lair' (B., 1953): Aus. low: since ca. 1940. (Tennant, 1953.) Ex prec.

lairy. Conceited: Teddy-boys': mid-1950s. (Gilderdale, 2.)—2. See **lair**.

lakes, abbr.; **Lakes of Killarney**. Mad: r.s. (on *barmy*), esp. among grafters. (*Cheapjack*, 1934.) O'Shaughnessy (*M.T.*, 1979) glosses *lakes*, and var. *lakesy*, simply as 'stupid'.

laking, n. and adj. (The) being out of work: N. Country, esp. Yorkshire: since ca. 1920. Ex dial. *lake*, to play. (Hillaby, 1950.) Cf. **playing**.

Lal Brough. Snuff: r.s., perhaps mostly feminine usage. Pre-WW1 *Lal* or *Lally*, a Cockney dim. of Alice, was a gen. nickname for an old woman: 'the inference was that elderly women were snuff-takers' (Franklyn 2nd).

laldie, give (something). To enjoy it greatly: Glasgow:—1934. Ex dial. *give laldie*, to punish. Still current, 1985 (Munro).

lallies. Legs: 1960s–early 1970s. Popularised by Hugh Paddick and Kenneth Williams in their 'camp' dialogues for the BBC radio comedy series 'Round the Horne', mid-1960s. Davies, 1970, 'strip off naked and flash yourself to the viewers. "What do you think, sexy?" Jake shouted to the make-up man. "Are you in the mood to see my lallies?" '

lally. Var. of **Lal Brough**, esp. in Holloway (women's) prison. Franklyn, 2nd.

lam. In *on the lam*, on the run from justice, or as a deserter from the Armed Forces: in UK adopted ca. 1944 ex US servicemen; in Can., ca. 1935.

lamb. Short for *lamb chop*, r.s. on *pop*, 'An injection of a narcotic' (Home Office): drugs c.: later C.20.

lame-brain(ed). (One) feeble of intellect; silly, daft: coll. verging on informal S.E. Prob. adopted ex US. Nuttall, 1979, 'the minions, the also-rans, the lame-brained underlings'. Sometimes used where *lame* alone would suffice, as 'a lame-brained excuse'; prob. influenced by, e.g., *a lame-brained idea*, a bad or useless one. (P.B.)

Lamington. A Homburg hat: Aus.: from ca. 1910. B., 1942.—2. A small sponge cake covered with desiccated coconut: Aus. coll. (Raab.)

lamp. To see, to espy; to gaze at, to stare: some Brit. use in c. since ca. 1920 (Greene, 1938), adopted ex US; Aus. c. and low s. since ca. 1944 (Tennant, 1953; McNeil).—2. 'To lamp a bloke is to attack him with your bunch of fives [fists] or knives or razors. To job 'im means the same thing. A street-corner fight is a bundle or a tole' (Gilderdale, 2): Teddy-boys': mid-1950s. Current, 1985 (Munro) in Glasgow: '*Lamp* can mean to strike ("He lamped him wan") or to throw ("Lamp that oot the windy").' P.B.: perhaps a C.20 version of C.16 *lam(b)*, *lamme*, to beat, thrash.

lamp-post navigation. Going from buoy to buoy: RN. (Irving, 1946.) Perhaps, as R.C. suggests, a ref. to 'a "drunk" tacking from lamp-post to lamp-post'.

lamps trimmed. In *have* or *get* (one's) *lamps trimmed*, to 'suffer injury or punishment in fight or brawl' (Bassett): RN: WW2.

Lanc or **Lank**. An Avro *Lanc*aster bomber aircraft: RAF coll.: 1942–6. Partridge, 1945.

Lancashire lasses. Spectacles: Manchester: r.s., on (*eye*)*glasses*. (Jaffe, 1959.)

lance-comical. Lance-corporal: Army: since ca. 1946.

Lance-Corporal Towrope. A driver mechanic: Army: since ca. 1939. 'These "driver mecs" were not usually highly trained, and the tow-rope was the tool they used most to get a broken-down truck to workshops. Not complimentary' (Sanders).

lance-jack. A lance-corporal: Army coll.: late C.19–20. F. & G.

lancey. See BIRD-WATCHERS, in Appx.

Lancs (pron. *lanks*)**, the**. The Lancashire regts: Army coll. (Young, 1930.) As in, e.g., 'The Yorks and Lancs'.

Lancy or **Lanky**. A Lancashire—hence, loosely, also a Yorkshire—employee: railwaymen's. *Railway*.—2. An Avro *Lanc*aster bomber aircraft: mostly Can.: WW2. Spelt *Lanky*, 'under the influence of a very popular radio serial entitled "L for Lanky" ' (Leechman). Cf. **Lanc**.

land and sea. 'Last night, near Shepherd's Bush, I caught an airman, not from this Depot, eating "land and sea" (fish and chips)' (Lawrence, 1955, but dealing with the year 1922): airmen's: ca. 1918–40.

land crab. A sailor who forsakes the sea: nautical, esp. RN. Karlsson, 1966.—2. The super-express engine of the London, Midland & Scottish: railwaymen's: ca. 1930–50. Ex the abundance of outside machinery.—3. See **Matelots**.

Land of Hope. Soap: r.s. (Franklyn 2nd.) Var. *Cape of Good Hope*.

Land of No Future. The Ruhr: RAF, esp. Bomber Command: 1941–3. (Pudney, 1945.) Cf. **Happy Valley**, 2.

land office. An on-shore police station: Metropolitan River Police term, midway between j. and coll.: later C.20. London *Evening News*, 29 June 1972.

land squatters. (Very rare in singular.) Those tramps who, in their begging, do not specialise in either themes or localities: tramps' c.:—1932 (Jennings).

land with. To impose an onerous duty or unwelcome burden on (someone): coll. Cf. synon. **clobber with** and **lumber**, v., 2.

lander. A blow or punch that reaches its mark: pugilistic:—1923 (Manchon).

Languisher and Yawner, the. The Lancashire & Yorkshire Railway: railwaymen's: ca. 1890–1925. (*Railway,* 2nd.) Also known as *the Lanky and York.* Cf. **Lancy.**

Lank. See **Lanc.**

Lanky, the. The London & North-Western Railway: railwaymen's: earlier C.20. (McKenna, 2.) Cf. synon. **Lean and Narrow-Waisted**; **Wessy**; and see **Languisher . . .**

lantern. In *hold the lantern,* 'to relax while someone else does the work' (B.P.): mostly Aus. Ex the song, 'I hold the lantern while my mother chops the wood'.

lanterne Rouge. The last man home in a cycle race: racing cyclists' facetious Fr. (*Fellowship,* 1984.) Cf. the 'French' of **eau-clobber.**

lap-gunner. 'The member of a (Sherman tank) crew seated in the hull alongside the driver and firing a machine-gun' (Hart, 1959): Army: ca. 1943–5.

lap it up. To enjoy the fictions of novelists and film-producers: coll.: since ca. 1920. Ruck, 1935.—2. To be susceptible to flattery. See **lap up.**—3. (Usu. as *lapping it up.*) To have a safe, or easy, time; to be aware of this advantage and to be actively appreciative of it: orig. Guardsmen's, from 1939 (Grinstead, 1946); later, widespread coll. throughout the Army, and applied to the enjoyment of anything (P.B.).

lap up. To flatter (a person): c. (Sharpe, 1938.) Ironically ex *lap it up,* to swallow flattery as a cat does cream: coll.

lard head. A fool; a very simple fellow: Aus. B., 1942.

lare. A loud-voiced, flashily dressed man: c. Cf.:–

lare up, n. A smart, shrewd fellow: Aus. low. (Tennant, 1941.) See **lair,** and cf.:–

lare up, v.i. To boast: c. Origin? Prob. ex:—2. To dress flashily: see entry at **lair.**

larking. Theft: c., and police s.: since ca. 1920. Norman.—2. In *down to larking,* wrongly convicted: c., hence low plebeian s.: since ca. 1945. Cf. **down to larkin,** which Powis, 1977, glosses as 'free', as of 'a free drink'; this may be connected with sense 1.

Larry Dooley. Esp. in *give* (someone) *L- D-,* 'To administer punishment, give a hiding (unexplained, although a connection has been claimed with the pugilist Larry Foley)' (Wilkes): Aus.: since mid-C.20.

larstin(g)s. Elastic-sided boots: Aus. low: since ca. 1910. Baker; Campion, 1942.

lary. Cheeky; 'cock-a-hoop': low. (Gardner, 1923.) Cf. **lare,** and *lairy,* q.v. at **lair.**

laser. See HAULAGE, in Appx.

lash. Violence: Aus.:—1916 (Dennis). Perhaps ex *lash out at.*—2. A trick: Aus.: since ca. 1920. B., 1942.—3. In *have a lash* (*at*), to try (v.i.); to attempt (v.t.): Aus. (B., 1942.) Cf. *have a bash at,* and similar phrases.

lash-up. A break-down; a failure, a fiasco or 'mess-up': RN (late C.19–early 20) >, by 1915, Army. F. & G.—2. Hence, a turmoil: nautical:—1935.—3. Anything makeshift: RN coll. (late C.19–20) > widespread gen. 'Taffrail', 1936, 'The boat . . . was what a blue-jacket would have called a "lash-up", a thing of bits and pieces.' I.e. lashed together.—4. Hence, an informal social occasion, esp. an informal party: since ca. 1950. Bagley, 1968.

lash-up repairs. Rough-and-ready repairs: RAF coll.: 1939+.

last. ' "To last", derived from lashing a boat, meant that the man who actually got the money or cheque defrauded them of some part of their share' (Bournemouth *Evening Echo,* 20 Apr. 1966): c.: since ca. 1930.

last card in the pack. A snack: theatrical r.s. Franklyn.

last knocking, the. The late(st) fares: taxi-drivers': since ca. 1920. Hodge, 1939.—2. *Be on the last knockings,* to be nearing the end of a job or an undertaking: since ca. 1925.—3. (In pl.) 'Last calls for drinks near pub closing time, and comparable last calls' (L.A., 1978): coll.

last the full distance. See **go the full distance.**

last three(, one's). The last three figures of a serviceman's or -woman's number: Services' j. rather than coll.; and certainly not s. The last three figures are often used instead of the full

number. Esp. useful in the Welsh regts, with their paucity of surnames. (E.P., who thought it was used only in the RAF; amended by P.B., formerly 697 Pte Beale, P.C.)

laster. A large piece of toffee, designed to last a long time: Lancing: ca. 1890–1935. Marples.

lastins. Var. of **larstins.**

lat or **lat-house.** A latrine: military. (B. & P.) Occ. *the lats.*

latch-key kid. A child whose parents are away at work all day, and who must therefore let himself into the home after school, etc.: coll. verging on informal S.E.: later C.20. (D. Beale.)

latch lifter. 'The first drink of the evening. An aperitif' (McKenna, 1): railwaymen's. Cf. 'Some on 'em used to call it a *sneck-lifter,* a latch-lifter—get a few pence just to get inside the pub' (Evans, 1975): E. Anglian: later C.19–earlier 20. *Sneck* is dial.; cf. **latch-opener.**

latch on, usu. intransitive, as in 'He didn't latch on'. To understand: since ca. 1919. Ex dial *latch,* to catch, to seize, to grasp.

latch-opener. The 'price' of a drink (cf. *entrance-fee*): military: early C.20. (B. & P.) Cf. **latch lifter.**

Late and Never Early, the. The London & North-Eastern Railway: railwaymen's: 1923–47. (*Railway,* 2nd.) Cf. **Lean and Narrow-Waisted.**

Late Arrivals Club, the. Those aircrews who had, in the desert, been forced to walk back to their lines: RAF in N. Africa: WW2. (P-G-R.) Cf. *the Resurrectionists* of the Crimean War, soldiers believed killed or missing, who later returned to their units.

late night final. 'That last drink before the wardroom bar closes' (Granville): RN officers' joc.: mid-C.20. With ref. to the last edition of an evening newspaper.

lates. 'Drinks sold after permitted hours of opening' (Glover, 1985): public houses'.

latrine rumour. False news: a wild story; a baseless prediction: military: 1915. Ex the fact that latrines were recognised gossiping places. Cf. synon. *cook-house official* or *rumour, ration-dump r.* or *yarn,* and *transport r.* or *tale.* B. & P.

latrine wireless, the or **a.** Rumour in gen.; a particular rumour: Aus. Army coll.: WW2. *Rats,* 1944, 'Time was so short, the latrine wireless insisted that we would sail any day.' Adaptation of prec.

latrino. A short form (1940+) of:–

latrinogram. Army officers' (1939+) var. of **latrine rumour.**

lats. See **lat.**

laugh and joke. A smoke: r.s.: later C.19–20. Barrett, 1880; Davis, 1939. In C.20 often shortened to *laugh.* (Phelan, 1954.)

laugh like a Chief Stoker. To laugh a raucous 'belly laugh': RN. Granville, 'Ex the harsh cackle of a seagull, which is said to possess the soul of a departed Chief Stoker.'

laugh like a drain. To chuckle heartily: orig. RN ward-rooms'. (Granville.) Water gurgles down a drain-pipe: babies gurgle with pleasure and a similar noise. The phrase has an intensive: *laugh like a row of drains* ('a jovial display of dentures, symbolised by the common iron grille over a kerbside drain, brings about this phrase' (RAF officer, 1962): since ca. 1950, and esp. in the RAF.

laugh of (someone), **have the.** To outdo, outwit someone: coll.

laughing(, be). To be 'comfortable, safe, fortunate': Services' coll.: WW1; revived in WW2, and still, 1983, extant. Hence, more gen., to be winning. B. & P., 'He's got a job at Brigade Headquarters, so he's laughing'. Ex one's laugh at such good luck.

laughing academy. Joc. var. of **funny farm,** q.v., a mental hospital. Dures, 1982.

laughing all the way to the bank, be. To have, financially, been very successful, esp. in a *coup,* and in the face of long odds or disapproval: since ca. 1965. Adopted ex US; attributed to the popular and successful pianist Liberace.

laughing boy. 'Saturnine or gloomy-looking people are disliked by Cockneys . . . Often the person is dubbed "Smiler" or "Laughing Boy" ' (*Muvver*): also Services'.

laughing-side. An elastic-sided boot or shoe: Aus.: since ca. 1920. (Park, 1948.) It stretches in, as it were, a grin.

laughs. A make-up: theatrical:—1935. I.e., putting on one's laughs.—2. In *for laughs*, often as *only* or *just for* . . . , as a joke; for the fun of it: coll.: since ca. 1950.

laughy. A farce: filmland: since ca. 1925. McCabe, 1937.

launching pad. A water-closet seat in a (moving) train: railwaymen's: since ca. 1962. (*Railway*, 2nd.) Evacuation into outer space.

launder; laundering. To whitewash, as a sepulchre; the concealment by states and governments of their own hypocrisy: political coll. > j.: since ca. 1975. 'Special long-range shells and artillery were shipped last year to South Africa by way of Antigua, the . . . Caribbean island for whose foreign affairs and defence Britain is responsible. This allegation of "laundered" arms traffic in defiance of the U.N. embargo is being shown tonight in the BBC Television programme *Panorama*' (*The Times*, 6 Nov. 1978: P.B.). Cf.: [presumably?]-

launderer, be a. To commit a Stock Exchange 'washing' (itself j., not s.): Stock Exchange: from ca. 1930. London *Evening Standard*, 26 Jan. 1934.

Lauras. Chocolates: Can.: since ca. 1930. (London *Evening News*, 9 Jan. 1940.) 'Made by the firm "Laura Secord" [a name commemorating] a Canadian heroine of the war of 1812' (Leechman).

lav. Lavatory: coll. (Sayers, 1932.) Dempster, 1979, noted *lav* as an 'in-word', supplanting *loo*.

lavatory (or **lavatorial**) **bombing.** 'The dropping of bombs from a great height. Army, World War II, generally referring to the Italian Air Force, which preferred staying out of the range of A.A. guns to accuracy. Cf. **pull the plug,** which is probably connected' (Sanders).

lavatory brush. 'Description of a certain cut of beard peculiar to Submariners in WW2' (Granville): RN.

lavish. Bacon fat; the fat on 'shackles' (stew): mostly military: early C.20. Semantics: 'rich'.

lavo. Lavatory: Aus.: since ca. 1920. B., 1942.

lavvy. A Scottish, esp. children's, easing of *lavatory*.

lavvy-diver. 'A disparaging term for a plumber' (Munro, 1985): Glasgow. Ex prec.

law, n. (Usu. *the law.*) The police; a policeman: London's East End: coll.: since ca. 1945. (Herd, 1957; Norman, 1958.) Cf. the US *John Law.* Also as in 'Two law came up to me and grabbed hold of me' (Norman). Cf. **Lily Law.**

law, v. 'The villainy [of posing as a policeman] became so widespread that the crooks' word for it went into their argot. They began to talk of "Law-ing" a man—robbing him in the guise of a policeman' (Gosling, 1959): c.: since late 1945.

lawner. Refreshment served on the lawn to a hunt: middle and upper classes': from ca. 1925. (E. Waugh, 1934.) By the 'OXFORD *-ER*', as is:—2. Lawn tennis: earlier C.20. (E. Waugh, 1936.) Cf.:-

lawners and **royallers.** Lawn tennis and royal tennis: Oxford and Cambridge undergraduates': earlier C.20.

lax. Lacrosse. See **lacks.**

lay, n. A seaman's wages: MN. ' "Give your mate my lay, will you. That's it, that one there." The money in its envelope was passed through the hatch' (Piper, 1974).—2. Borrowed money: Army: ca. 1925–40. See v., 1.—3. A girl, a woman, regarded as copulatory partner: adopted ex US, in Can., ca. 1945, by ca. 1955 also in Brit. As in 'an easy lay', 'a good (*or* a great little) lay'. See v., 2.

lay, v. To borrow (money): Army: ca. 1920–40.—2. To coït with, usu. of a man with a woman: low: adopted, ca. 1944, ex American servicemen. 'But a dame's only a dame, Charlie-boy, you lay 'em and leave 'em' (Warner, 1961).

lay-about (later, **layabout**). A man that lives by cadging from thieves: c.: from ca. 1919. I.e. 'lie-about'.—2. Hence, a professional loafer: c.:—1932 (Pearson).—3. Hence, as in

'There are always "layabouts"—out-of-works—hanging around [law] court buildings': police s. since ca. 1935; by ca. 1960, gen. s. Gosling, 1959.

lay an egg. To make a great fuss; esp. 'Don't lay an egg!'—stop worrying: Aus.: since ca. 1920. Niland, 1958.—2. 'In show biz in Canada and US, to "lay an egg" is to put on a performance that fails to please the audience. This applies to a single actor or to the show as a whole' (Leechman): since ca. 1910 in Can. The implication is that it's a *bad egg*.

lay-by, n. and v. 'To secure an item for sale by making a deposit and paying instalments until the full price is paid, without interest charges, the goods being taken only when payment is complete' (Wilkes): Aus. coll.: since ca. 1925. Ex money *laid* aside, esp. from 'the housekeeping'.—2. Hence, *on the lay-by*, on the 'never-never' (hire-purchase): Aus. coll. >, by 1960, S.E. *Heinemann Dict. of Aus. English*.

lay-down. A rest; a sleep: sol.: C.19–20.—2. Hence, a (fortnight's) remand: c. (Sharpe, 1938.) Also as v., 'to remand in custody' (Powis).

lay down tracks. To put songs on records: pop music practitioners' and devotees': since mid-1960s. Scaduto, 1974.

lay eggs. 'To lay mines; *not* to drop bombs' (H. & P.): RN and RNAS/RAF: since 1915 at latest. (Carr, 1939.) Cf. **gardening,** 1.

lay it down. To come off a motorcycle accidentally: motorcyclists': later C.20. 'I laid it down' (Dunford).

lay it on the line. To explain thoroughly, with the implication that the hearer must act accordingly: coll.: since 1950s. Campbell, 1960.—2. An elab. of *lay on*, q.v., to organise. Ibid.

lay me in the gutter. Butter: r.s.:—1923 (Manchon).

lay off! Stop! (the activity that is annoying the speaker): coll. Ex dial., to *take a rest.* Cf. **give over!; pack it in!**—2. As *the lay-off*, 'the off-season when the seasonal jobs are over' (Petch, 1969): Aus. coll.: since ca. 1930.

lay off to (someone). To try to impress (him): lower classes' coll.:—1923 (Manchon). Perhaps ex nautical j.

lay off with. To lie with—copulate with (women): Aus. *Rats*, 1944, ' "Eddie," I said, "You like laying off with girls better than anything else in the world, don't you?" '

lay on; esp. in 'It's all laid on'—planned, arranged, assured: Army: since ca. 1930. (E.P., 1942.) Adopted by the RAF, where it tends to be restricted to availability (Jackson, 1943). Also by the Navy (Granville). Ex plumbing. Cf. the Army's synon. **tee up** and RAF's **organise.**

lay on air. To arrange for, obtain, provide, air support: Services': 1940+. Hodson, 1945.

lay on to be. To pretend to be: lower classes, esp. Cockneys': 1914, Lyons, 'I don't lay on to be a saint'. Cf. **crack on.**

lay-out. A confidence-trickster's plan of action: Aus. c.: adopted, ex US, ca. 1925.

lay out (one's) **kit.** To vomit, usu. as a result of drunkenness: Army: later C.20. (P.B.)

lay the dust. To take a drink of beer, spirits, etc.: since ca. 1910.

lay the leg. To copulate: Can.: since ca. 1930. Dempster, 1975, 'She could not very well have her admirers know that she was laying the leg with Old Horny.'

lay-up. A period in prison: c. Orwell, 1933.

layabout was orig. hyphenated: see **lay-about.**

laze-off. A rest from work: coll.: 1924 (Galsworthy).

lazy. Applied to person or thing 'serving no particular purpose at the moment' (Granville): RN. Cf. the Army use of **idle.**

lazy-bed cooking. Cooking in the ashes of a camp-fire: Aus. coll. (B., 1943.) Practised by, and copied from, the Aborigines.

Lazy K. Long Kesh, HM prison, N.Ireland: Services', in N.Ireland: since ca. 1970. Hawke, 1979.

lazy lob. A semi-erection of the penis: low coll. (P.B.) Cf. **lob,** n., 2.

lazyitis. Mere laziness, used as a pretext for shirking: since ca. 1945. Joc. use of the medical suffix *-itis,* disease. Cf. synon. **idle-itis.**

lead. In *strike the lead* (metal), to be successful: Aus. coll. (B., 1942.) Ex gold-mining.

lead from the duckhouse. To lead from lowest card of suit: Aus. card-players': since ca. 1910. (B., 1953.) Perhaps cf. the entries at **duck-house.**

lead in (one's) **arse.** Laziness; torpor: Can., esp. labourers': since ca. 1945. 'Shake (*or* get) the lead out of your arse!'

lead in (one's) **pencil.** Sexual vigour: raffish, > gen. Hence, esp. of, e.g., a drink of strong liquor, 'Here, that'll put lead in your pencil!' Cf. 'That'll put hairs on your chest!', in the same context. Also used, derivatively, of women.

lead off. To lose one's temper, be angry: orig. Services', from ca. 1910 (F. & G.); by ca. 1930, fairly gen. (Vickers, 1949.) Perhaps ex boxing.

lead-pipe cinch. An absolute certainty: Can.: since ca. 1945. (Leechman.) Ex the effectiveness of a short length of lead-pipe as a weapon.

lead-swinger. A loafer, schemer, malingerer: military. (B. & P.) Ex **swing the lead,** q.v., and cf. synon. *leg-swinger.*

lead (someone) **up the garden(-path).** To blarney (a person), humbug, entice, mislead: since early 1920s. Ex gently suasive courtship.

leader. As *the leader,* the commanding officer; *the grand leader,* the senior general or other officer commanding a garrison: semi-joc. Army (officers'): ca. 1933+. Ex newspaper accounts of Adolf Hitler (*der Führer*). Cf.:—2. A leading seaman; esp. in address: RN coll.: from ca. 1934. C.S. Forester, *The Ship,* 1943.

leaf. Furlough: RN lowerdeck (late C.19–early 20) >, by 1914, Army. (F. & G.) Almost † by 1950 (P.B.). A perversion of *leave,* ?influenced by Welsh pron.—2. Cocaine: drugs c. (Stockley, 1986.) US since –1959 (Spears).

leak. A police informer: Aus.: since ca. 1925. Kelly, 1955.—2. A trick, a dodge: Aus.: since ca. 1930. Marshall, 1946, ' "I use Eno's Fruit Salts instead of baking powder," he said. "I know all the leaks." ' (B.P.)

leak-house; leakery. A urinal: Aus., mostly juvenile: since late 1940s. (B.P.) Cf. *leak,* urination, low coll. since mid–C.19.

leaky. Tearful, apt to weep: lower classes':—1923 (Manchon).

lean and hungry. The markings on the ships' funnels of the Lampert & Holt Line: ca. 1900–40. The conditions have long since been improved.

Lean and Narrow-Waisted, the. A railwaymen's pun on the initials of the London & North-Western Rly: early C.20. (McKenna, 2.) Cf. **Lanky** and **Wessy.**

lean on. Of a ganster, to use force in order to persuade or convince: underworld: since ca. 1940. Of a policeman, esp. a detective, to threaten, to manhandle a known or suspected criminal, for the same reason: since late 1940s. Crisp, 1978.—2. Hence, in more gen. coll., the use of power, veiled or naked, in 'bringing pressure to bear on' a person, body, or even state: later C.20. (P.B.)

lean trot. A bad or hard time: Aus. coll.: later C.20. 'He had a lean trot for a couple of years.' (Raab, 1980.) See **trot,** n., 1.

lean over backwards. Later C.20 predominant form of *fall over backwards* (since ca. 1945), to go beyond the normal and the expected in order to show how honourably disinterested or how honest or upright one is: coll. 'We leant over backwards to try and help these people, and what happened? . . . ' (P.B.)

leap. 'I have been to Germany many times before on Phantom [aircraft] "leaps", the nickname given to those weekend forays from the UK to sample [all the good things there]' (*Phantom*): RAF: later C.20.

leaper. A stimulating or keep-awake pill, the opposite of a *sleeper:* drug-users': mid–1960s. *Groupie,* 1968.

Leaping Lena. The train running between Darwin and Birdum: Aus. (esp. NT): since ca. 1930. (B. 1953.) Also known as *the Abortion Express* (Marshall, 1962). *Leaping Lena* is recorded as US (W. & F.) s. for an automobile: ca. 1915.

leary, leery. 'Flash'; showy of dress and manners: low: ca. 1850–75.—2. (Of personal appearance) somewhat wild: from ca. 1850.—3. In Aus. (—1916), low, vulgar. (Dennis.) See also **lair,** with which cf. senses 1–3.—4. *Leery:* 'Bad-tempered, disagreeable, and cheeky' (Powis): low: later C.20.

leather. A wallet: c. Sharpe, 1938, 'An inveterate pickpocket is sometimes called "A Leather Merchant".'—2. As *the leather,* a kick with a booted foot: c. (*Gilt Kid,* 1936.) Cf. later C.20 **put the boot in.**

leather-bottom; usu. in pl. A Civil Servant tied to his desk. Mackenzie, 1956, 'It's worse than ever with these Colonial Office leather-bottoms'. Cf. **arse-polishing.**

leather-jacket. Another name for a **rocker,** 2, q.v., a young motorcyclist of rough appearance and behaviour, whose distinctive form of dress is a leather jacket: coll.: later C.20. Poss. also influenced by S.E. *leather-jacket,* the grub of the crane-fly. (P.B.)

leave a monkey. To pay one's (weekly) bill only in part: Midlands and Lancashire: ca. 1880–1940. Roberts, 1976.

leave (one) **cold.** To fail to impress or convince or please: coll. 'My dear fellow, your offer leaves me cold.' Cf. the Fr. *cela me laisse froid.* (F. & G.)

leave (one) **for dead.** To be vastly superior to (a person): perhaps mainly Aus., but with some Brit. use; ?adopted ex US: since ca. 1930. Ex horse-racing. (B.P.; P.B.) Cf. **left, be,** q.v., of which this may be an elab.

leave in the air. To leave without support: Army coll.: since ca. 1940. P-G-R.—2. To promise, warn, inform someone of an intended action, and then to tell him nothing further, as in 'They practically promised to do it about a month ago, but since then we've heard nothing, so we're left rather in the air': coll.: later C.20. (P.B.)

leave it out! Shut up!; stop it!; leave off!: c. > lowish coll.: early 1980s. (Dures, 1982.) 'Now very "in" ' (Barltrop, 1982).

leave it with me. 'Leave it to me': coll.: later C.20. Noted by Ross, 1978, as 'non-U'.

leave the lickings of a dog, not. 'Give a sound rating and leave one without a reputation. Often used in the North Country when there has been a row and one of those involved has had his past raked up' (Petch, 1946): late C.19–20.

leave visiting cards. To bomb a locality: RAF: WW2. Berrey, 1940, records *leave calling cards,* a var. among the Americans in the RAF.

leaver. A racehorse that won't eat enough: racing coll.: late C.19–20. (Winton, 1963.) Obviously because it leaves its food.

leaves. Money: beatniks': 1959+. (Anderson.) Ex 'lettuce leaves'.—2. Dungarees: beatniks': 1960+. Ibid.

lech. A sexual attraction towards, or urge for, someone: since early C.20. 'She has what is vulgarly known as a "lech" for *The Times* Peking correspondent' (G.E. Morrison, diary, 1910, quoted in Pearl, 1967: M. refers to himself). A back formation ex *lechery.* See also **letch.**

lechy. Lecherous: since ca. 1950, prob. orig. underground. *Groupie,* 1968.

lecky or **leccy.** An electric tram: Liverpool: earlier C.20.—2. As adj., electric, as in *lecky blanket, kettle,* etc.: domestic coll.: later C.20. (P.B.)—3. An electrical officer: MN: later C.20. (Malin, 1984.)

ledger bosun or **dollar bosun.** A Warrant Writer in charge of pay accounts: RN: since ca. 1925. Granville.

Leek, the. A fast goods-train running to Llanelli, S. Wales: railwaymen's: ca. 1910–40. (*Daily Telegraph,* 15 Aug. 1936.) Cf. **the Bacca,** the train up from Bristol.

left. Revolutionary; socialist(ic); communistic: coll. (?before 1918); in 1930s verging on S.E. 'In Kiel, where the revolution started, matters appear to be going "left" with a vengeance' (*Daily Chronicle,* 2 Dec. 1918).

left, be or **get.** To fail; to be outdistanced metaphorically; be placed in a difficult position: coll.: adopted, ex US, ca. 1895. Abbr. *be* or *get left in the lurch* (Ware). Cf. **leave for dead**.

left and right. Fight: r.s.: late C.19–20. (Franklyn 2nd.) Cf. C.19 synon. *read and write*.

left-breast technique, the. 'A technique for seducing women, the first step of which consists in caressing the left breast. Fairly common' (Raper, 1973): raffish coll.

left carrying the can, (to be). To be made the scapegoat, or to be burdened with (usu. unwanted) responsibility, or both, as in 'Wavell was appointed supreme commander in the Far East just as everything was crumbling under the apparently invincible Japanese onslaught, and there he was—left carrying the can': coll.: since mid-C.20. Cf. (left) *holding the baby*, and see **carry the can**. (P.B.)

left-footer. A Catholic: orig. N. Ireland Protestants'; common in the Armed Forces. 'Orig. in the different styles (Protestant/Catholic) of turf-cutting in Ulster. Catholics used spades with the lug on the left side, Protestants those with the lug on the right' (Green, 1984). Cf. **kick with the left foot**, a Services' elab. of this term.

left-handed bricklayer. A Freemason: Army: since ca. 1950 (?earlier). Perhaps cf. **left-footer**. (Bigam, 1975.)

left-handed spanner. An imaginary tool which an apprentice may be sent to fetch: workshops'.

left hook. An attack delivered from the left flank: Army coll.: 1941–5. Ex boxing. P-G-R.

left in the lurch. (A) church: r.s.: since ca. 1880.

left, right, and centre. (Of bombs) dropped accurately upon the target: RAF: 1939+. H. & P.—2. Hence, as an injunction, 'Put your cap on straight!': RAF: 1940+. 'In fact, to get everything just right' (Ibid.): id. (Not a v., but an adj. or an adv.)—3. Hence, in post-WW2 civilian use, but esp. among ex-servicemen, 'how retribution will strike: "Wait until the 'old man' gets back, then you'll cop it, left, right, and centre"' (L.A., 1974).

left roasting. 'Term used to denote that you were the only person on a call that had not been taken on for [casual] work' (Ash): London dockers': earlier C.20.

left some groceries in the supermarket, he/she's. 'Applied to a person of less than average intelligence: since mid-1970s' (Leech, 1986): Can.

left sucking the mop, be; or **to have blown out.** 'When a cabman puts on a theatre or restaurant rank, and gets first just as the lights go out and the door shuts, he has "blown out" and is "left sucking the mop"' (Hodge, 1939): taxi-drivers': since ca. 1920. The lights have 'blown out', the driver is like a servant-girl out of a job, left with nothing to do but 'suck the mop'.

Lefty. A socialist or a communist: coll.: from 1936. In *Phœnix News-Progress*, Spring, 1937, we find the caption, 'COUNTERBLAST TO LEFTIES'. Ex S.E. *left wing*. In later C.20, often in sneer *trendy lefties!*

leg. 'A stage between landings on a long-distance flight' (Jackson): RAF coll. > j.: since ca. 1925. Prob. ex the tack of a sailing ship.—2. Hence, a stage—a portion—of a journey; hence, of an undertaking: coll., since ca. 1930; by 1960, S.E. In *have a leg*, (of a horse) to have an injured leg: racing, esp. steeplechase, coll. (Lawrence, 1961.) Cf. **have a heart**, of a person suffering from heart-disease.—4. In *make a leg*, (of a woman) to display ler leg(s): proletarian coll.:—1923 (Manchon). Contrast *make* (one's) *leg*, to feather one's nest: id.: Ibid.—5. See **push some leg**.

leg-bail, give. To hoodwink (someone) or catch unawares: Aus.: since ca. 1910. B., 1943.

leg before wicket, occ. **L.B.W.** A ticket: r.s. Note esp. 'That's the l.b.w.'—That's good. Franklyn 2nd.

leg in. As *get a leg in*, to win on the first horse of a 'double': Aus. sporting. B., 1942.

leg-opener. A strong drink, esp. gin: raffish: since ca. 1945. Hayes, 1973, 'Did you make my gin as strong as this on purpose? I know what you men call it . . . Leg-opener.' On the assumption that 'liquor is quicker' (L.A., 1976). Also Aus. (Wilkes).

leg over. As in 'He's got a leg over', he is under a misapprehension: Army, esp. officers' (at first, particularly Royal Artillery). Ex a horse getting a leg over the traces.—2. In *a bit of leg over*, (of a woman) *give*, or (of a man) *have*, to copulate: raffish: later C.20. Tinniswood, 1969.

leg-over and chips. A good night out: RAF: since ca. 1950. (Reynolds, 1979.) See prec., 2.

leg-pull. A good-natured, innocuous hoax or deception: coll. Ex later C.19 *leg*, *pull* (someone's) *leg*, to befool.

leg-rope on, put the. To tame or master a recalcitrant person: Aus. coll. (B., 1943.) Ex leg-roping cattle.

leg-up, esp. **give** (someone) **a leg-up,** to assist him: coll., esp. Aus.: late C.19–20. B, 1942.

legal. A passenger that pays only the legal fare: taxi-drivers' coll.: since ca. 1910. (Hodge, 1939.) Ex:—2. *The legal*, abbr. 'the legal fare': proletarian coll.:—1923 (Manchon).

legal beagle. A lawyer more than averagely keen, with a sharp nose for errors and omissions: Can., mostly journalistic: since ca. 1950. (Leechman.) Ex:-

legal eagle. A lawyer: adopted, in late 1940s, ex US. This sort of rhyming is very common in post-WW2 US s.: see esp. W. & F.'s Appx.

leggner. 'Sometimes used instead of "stretch" when referring to one year's imprisonment' (Tempest, who notes 'rare usage'): c.: mid-C.20. ?Cognate with *lag* (P.B.).

leggy, n. See PRISONER-OF-WAR SLANG, §6, in Appx.—2. Adj. ex **legs,** 1.

legit, the. A theatrical abbr. of *legitimate drama*. See **legitimate, the.**

legit, adj. and, derivatively, adv. Legitimate(ly): low s., verging, at least orig., on c. ' "I get my maggot [money] legit these days" ' (Straker, 1968).

legit joint. A game of chance where the genuine player has a chance of winning: Can. carnival s. Contrast **gaff joint**.

legitimate, the. Legitimate drama, i.e. good (mainly Shakespearian) drama, as opp. to burlesque: theatrical:—1887.

legless. Drunk: low coll.: since ca. 1965. (P.B.)—2. See **legs,** 1.

Legoland. 'British Fleet HQs at Northwood, Middx.; ex a make of plastic building bricks for children, referring thus to the architecture of the building and possibly to the fantasies created inside' (Green, 1984): RN: later C.20. Cf. **Lenin's Tomb.**

legs. 'Any film that shows staying power at the box office [is said to *have legs*] . . . thus *legless*: a flop' (Green, 1984): cinema and TV. Applied also in publishing, to best-selling books, with var. *page-turners* (Ibid.).—2. In *get* (occ. *rear*) *on one's hind legs*, to fall into a rage: earlier C.20. Ex a horse rearing.—3. A ship's main engines: MN, esp. Townsend Ferries: later C.20. (Malin, 1979.) Cf. synon. **sewing machines**.

lel or **lell.** To take, seize, arrest: low London s. verging on c.: from ca. 1860. (B. & L.) Ex Romany.—2. Hence, to summons or prosecute (someone): market-traders': late C.19–20. *M.T.*

lemon. Something undesirable: coll.: since ca. 1920. *OED* Sup. cites 'Middlesbrough seem to have picked a lemon, for the draw gives them South Shields as opponents' from *Daily Express*, 13 Dec. 1927.—2. An unattractive female, esp. if a girl: adopted, ex US, ca. 1932. *COD*, 1934.—3. A Rugby football: sporting: from ca. 1895. Wells, 1911, 'Naylor . . . negotiated the lemon safely home'.—4. A car that is hard to sell: motor trade: since early C.20.—5. A car that has many defects, discovered one after another: Can. car-owners': since ca. 1945. (Leechman.)—6. A woman's *pubes*; hence, loosely, the female pudend: low. The raffish will remember a well-known parody to the tune of 'Men of Harlech' (L.A., 1976).—7. In *hand* (someone) *a lemon*, to swindle, esp. in a business deal: commercial: since early 1920s.—8. Poor quality drugs: drugs c. (Stockley, 1986.) US since—1967 (Spears).

261

lemon and dash; often shortened to **lemon**. A *wash*-place (public lavatory): since ca. 1950: orig. and still mainly underworld. (Franklyn 2nd.) Cf.:–

Lemon and Balkan States. ' "Wash and grease" up, greasing the hair being an important part of the "spiv's" toilet. (Greece—grease. Lemon squash being the r.s. for wash.)' (Tempest): prison c.: mid-C.20.

Lemon Avenue. Spiritual home of 'wowsers': Aus.: since ca. 1920. B., 1943.

lemon squash, n. and v. Wash: r.s. See **Lemon and Balkan . . .**

lemon-squeezer. A peaked hat worn by NZ soldiers: NZ Army, WW2; adopted, ca. 1940, by Aus. Army. (B., 1953.) Ex the shape.—2. A fellow, chap, bloke: r.s., on **geezer**, q.v.: later C.20. Barker, 1979.

lemon tea. A urination: r.s., on *pee*. (Daniells, 1980.)

lemon time. A break for rest and light refreshment: railway shunters'. McKenna, 1970.

lemonade. Var. of **lemon**, 8. Stockley, 1986.

lemonade turn, the. The shift from 2 to 10 p.m.: railwaymen's: since ca. 1920. (*Railway*, 2nd.) The shift on which it is easiest to obtain refreshments.

lemonhead. A surfer whose hair has been bleached by the sun: Aus. Qantas advert., 1987.

lemony. Disgruntled, irritated, angry: Aus. B., 1942, 'go lemony at', to become angry, express anger towards someone'. A lemon is *sour*.

lend. A person to whom one lends money: Aus.: since ca. 1930. 'He was a safe lend all right' (Dick).—2. In *take a lend* (or *loan*) *of*, to impose on (someone); treat as a fool or a 'softie': coll.: since ca. 1910. Also *have a lend of*.

Lenin's tomb. That part of the Admiralty building—officially 'the Citadel'—which faces St James's Park and which, built during WW2, was regarded as impregnable: RN officers': since ca. 1943. (Granville.) Cf. **Kremlin** and **Legoland**.

lens louse. 'Bane of the news-reel cameraman is what he calls a "lens louse". They come in male and female species, publicity-hunters who never miss a chance of getting in front of a newsreel camera and hogging the scene as long as they can. Then there are the "anglers" . . . who have learned at which angle they photograph best, and always try to present that angle to the camera' (Hall, 1950): since ca. 1945.

leopard's crawl. An allegedly noiseless approach towards sentries to be overpowered: Army (prob. orig. in the East): coll., since 1941; >, by 1950, j., and gen. *leopard-crawl*, n. and v. P-G-R; P.B.

lepper. A dog (esp. as runner): dog-racing: since ca. 1925. (Westerby, 1937.) Ex dial. *lepper*, lit. 'leaper'.

leprosy. Cabbage: Aus. B., 1942.

Les. A Lesbian: Society, from ca. 1930; by ca. 1950, fairly gen. In Aus., since ca. 1935, *lesbo* or *leso/lezo*; an Aus. var. since ca. 1945 is *Leslie* (B., 1953).

let down (a person's) **blind.** To indicate that he is dead: coll.:—1923 (Manchon). Ex old custom of closing curtains of a house where a death has just occurred.

let go a razzo. To break wind: low raffish, or merely rather low: C.19–20. Hence, in C.20, simply *let one off* or *go*. (F. Leech, 1972.) *Razzo, rarzer* and *rarzo* are all var. abbr. of *raspberry* (*tart*), r.s. = fart.

let (one's) **hair down, let down** (one's) **hair.** To let oneself go; to enjoy oneself thoroughly; to be very friendly, intimate; to be (perhaps uncharacteristically) uninhibited: coll.: since ca. 1925, but not very common in UK before ca. 1950. Ex a number of girls talking together, esp. late at night. Also *take* (one's *back*) *hair down* and *unpin* (one's) *back hair*, prob. the orig. form. 'Although strictly applicable to women only, the phrases have, even in short-hair days, been used by men of themselves, or by either sex of men' (L.A., 1967).

let her roll! Let's have it!'; 'on with the dance!': Can. lumbermen's. (Beames.) Ex logging.

let (one) **in on** (a secret, a project, etc.). To tell about (the affair) in confidence: coll.: since ca. 1940. (Petch, 1974.)

let it slide! Let it go!; don't trouble!: coll. Merrick, 1911.

Let Me Sleep. Railwaymen's pun on the initials of the London, Midland & Scottish Railway Co.: 1923–48. *Railway*, 2nd.

let off steam. To give vent to pent-up exuberance, or, occ., anger: coll.

let one off. See **let go a razzo**.

let-out, n. Exoneration; alibi: coll.: since ca. 1920. Ex v., 1.—2. 'A spree, an entertainment' (Joyce, 1910): Anglo-Irish: late C.19–20.

let out, v. To exonerate, vindicate, clear from all suspicion of guilt: coll. Adopted, ca. 1918, from US, where employed before 1909 (Ware). 'This new piece of evidence certainly lets him out.' See almost any post-WW1 detective novel.—2. v.i. To sing heartily: coll. Horne, 1923.

let out at. To aim a blow at: Aus. coll. B., 1943.

letari. Var. of **lettary**, a lodging. Knight, 1936.

letch, n. and v. (To have) an amorous feeling: s. > coll.: since early 1900s. Ex *lechery*. See also **lech**.—2. Hence, as v. (usu. with *at*) to look, not necessarily amorously, at women: orig. Services', since ca. 1940 (P-G-R); post-WW2, more widespread. 'Sitting in the window of a caff, having a mild letch at the birds as they stroll self-consciously by in pairs' (P.B.).

letching-piece. A loose woman: low.

lets. Bed-and-breakfast visitors: landladies' coll. Vosper, 1929.

lettary. A lodging; lodgings: grafters': late C.19–20. (*Cheapjack*, 1934.) A var. of **letty**, q.v.

letter-box. An accommodation address or the person(s) operating it for a spy-ring: since ca. 1950.

letter-man. One who has been in prison an indicated number of years: prison c.:—1933 (Leach). Each year an alphabetical letter is assigned by the prison authorities to indicate the current year of a sentence.

letters. Degree-letters after one's name: coll.: mid-C.19–20. (E.P.) In C.20, if not earlier, applied also to abbrev. of awards for gallantry, and other honours; the phrase is often used in full, as 'he's got a load of letters after his name' (P.B.).

lettuce. Money: adopted, ca. 1945, ex US. Prompted by Am. *green stuff*, paper—hence any—money. Hence:-

lettuce leaves. Money in cash, orig., £1 notes: since ca. 1960. In, e.g., the ITV serial 'Coronation Street', episode broadcast 21 Sep. 1966.

letty. A bed; a lodging. Also v.i., to lodge. Parlyaree:—1859; in C.20, mainly theatrical. Ex It. *letto*, a bed, via Lingua Franca. (H., 1st ed.; Seago, 1933.) Also occ. *latty*.

leuc (or *leuk* or even *luke* or *Luke*), as in 'He's had a leuc', a leucotomy operation: doctors' and nurses': since ca. 1935.

level. To speak or act honestly and frankly: Can. coll.: adopted, ca. 1950, ex US. (Leechman.) In later C.20 Brit. usage, occ. *level with*, to speak frankly, as 'Look, I'll level with you. It's like this . . . ' (P.B.).

level money. ' "Level money" means the most appropriate exact multiple of £100' (Cowdy, 1965): secondhand-car dealers' coll.: since ca. 1945.

levels on the splonk. Evens, as betting odds: racing, esp. bookies'. *Sunday Telegraph*, 7 May 1967.

Levy and Frank. (An instance of) male masturbation: low r.s., on *wank*: from ca. 1880: often shortened to *Levy*: C.20. Franklyn, 'the name of a well-known firm of public-house and restaurant proprietors, Levy and Franks.' Cf. **J. Arthur Rank**, 2.

Lew Lake. Crazy: earlier C.20. (Cross, 1984.) Ex the Cockney music hall comedian and sketch-writer. Cf. synon. **Fred Karno**.

lewd infusion. Coïtion: low joc.: since ca. 1925.

Lewis and Witties. Breasts or nipples: Aus. r.s.: since ca. 1890. (B., 1945.) Ex a now defunct trading house in Melbourne. Cf. **Bristols**.

Lezo. See **Les**.

liaise. To get into touch (*with* someone); hence, to co-operate (*with*), confer (*with*): Army officers': 1938+; by 1941 coll.; by mid-1943 j. (E.P., 1942.) Ex *liaison* (as in Liaison Officer).

lib. A *Liberator* bomber aircraft: RAF: 1943–6. (Emanuel, 1945.)—2. In the 1970s Lib or lib referred only (when not abbr. 'Liberal') to the women's liberation movement directed against sexism and male domination, usu. in the term 'women's lib', n. and adj.: *OED* Sup., 1976, notes it as coll. abbr., and dates its derivatives *libber* and *libby* to 1970 and 1971. (P.B.)

Lib Lab. Any one of the Liberal–Labour alliances (ca. 1915–22) professing Radical principles: political: 1916+; by 1925, merely historical. P.B.: revived, late 1970s, in 'the Lib-Lab pact' against the Conservative opposition.

libber. Usu. *women's libber*, a member or supporter of the women's liberation movement. See **lib**, 2.

libby. 'Giving up that strident "women's libby thing" in order to blossom into Real Women' (Tweedie, 1980). See **lib**, 2.

liberate. To gain illicitly or deviously; to steal: Army: 1944 (Italy) and 1945 (Germany). By humorous euph.

liberating. Stealing, e.g. shoplifting: since late 1940s, mostly among the lawless. Ex prec.

liberty boat; liberty bus. Boat taking leave-personnel ashore; free vehicular transport for men on leave: Can. (1940), hence Eng. (1941); adopted from US Navy and Army: j., not coll.—much less, s.

liberty kit. 'Outfit for discharge. Borstals' and Detention centres' ' (Home Office): later C.20.

library. A book borrowed from a lending library: coll.—2. A theatre-ticket agency: theatrical. Mackail, 1921, 'In the Christmas holidays people will go to any show that the libraries tell 'em to go to.'

licker. An ice-cream cornet: mostly children's: since ca. 1910.—2. One who 'creeps' for favours; a toady: Loughborough Grammar School: late 1970s. (Roger Willson.) Ex *lickspittle* or *arse-licker*.

lickerish all sorts. Strongly sexed: since ca. 1925. 'It takes *all sorts* to make a world.'—'Yes; and some are lickerish' (lecherous). Ex the well-known brand of confectionery, Liquorice All Sorts.

lickety-split. At full speed; in a tearing hurry: (mostly) juvenile: adopted ca. 1918 from US.

licks. (With *my, your, his* etc.) A thrashing: late C.18–early 20. (Burns.) The sense of putting all one's effort into, i.e. fig. thrashing, survives in *give* (something) *big licks*, adapted, ca. 1950, in the Services—'You should've seen him bulling up his kit for guard. Really giving it big licks, he was'—from the Glasgow nuance, earlier C.20, of 'to enjoy greatly'. This latter meaning has the mid-C.20 var. *go big licks on*, or, as in Moran, 1959, 'Asians go great licks on Roy' (i.e. Roy Rogers, the popular cowboy filmstar of the 1940s). In these phrases *licks* is always on *big*. *Big licks*, by itself, was Aus., from ca. 1888 ('Rolf Boldrewood') for 'hard work'; also adv., by hard work, 'great guns', in, e.g., *going it big licks*. (E.P.; P.B.)

lid. Submarine hatch cover: RN Submariners': later C.20. (Malin, 1979.)

lie down on a, or **the, job.** To loaf: Aus.: since ca. 1925. (Stivens, 1958.) P.B.: in later C.20, also in Brit. Eng., with the implication not only of loafing, but of actual inefficiency.

lie in state. To sleep protected by mosquito nets: Services': 1939+.

lie like a bastard. To tell bare-faced lies, shamelessly: low: later C.20. (P.B.)

lie like a pig. To tell clever lies: Aus. (B., 1942.) Cf. **lying hound**.

lie-off. An afternoon siesta, which was 'a word that soon gave way in the newcomer's vocabulary to the curiously nautical "lie-off", used throughout the Far East' (Allen, 1983): (?)late C.19–mid-20.

life of Reilly (or **Riley**), **the;** esp. *live the* . . . , (to live) a carefree and comfortable life: poss. orig. Anglo-Irish. P.B.: in later C.20, it carries a strong suggestion of luxury.

lifer. See BIRD-WATCHERS, in Appx.

Liffey water. Porter (the drink): r.s.: late C.19–20: before 1914, mostly Anglo-Irish. (Franklyn 2nd.) P.B.: but Guinness stout is sometimes joc. called *the waters of the Liffey*: since ca. 1950, at latest.

lift, n. A punch: lower classes' coll.:—1923 (Manchon).

lift, v. To arrest: low Glasgow: 1934: also Northern Ireland, later C.20 (Hawke, 1979). Hence, *lifted*, under arrest.—2. To move stock overland from one place to another far away: Aus.: late C.19–20. Russell, 1936. —3. To punch or strike (someone): Aus. (B., 1942.) Cf. the n. and the S.E. *raise one's hand to* (a person).—4. (Of the penis) to become erect: coll., orig. low. Lawrence, 1922, eventually pub'd 1955, 'Golly, I didn't half want it: she [the organ] fair lifted'.

lift a rope. To be in employment: since ca. 1950(?). (Seymour, 1966.) Presumably ex nautical coll.

lift arse on (or **over**). '(Of a man) to engage in an act of extramarital sexual intercourse (with)' (L.A.): low coll.

lifted, be. See **lift**, v., 1.

lifters. Hands: since ca. 1930: c. >, by ca. 1955, low s. (Cook, 1962). Ex *lift*, C.16 s., steal; cf. C.17 synon. *pickers and stealers.*—2. The arms: since ca. 1960. (Petch, 1974.)

lifting lines, vbl n.; rare as v.i. 'A young man earning a fairly good weekly wage by "lifting lines"—or acting as runner—to a baker in Bridgeton' (MacArthur). Low Glasgow s.

lifty. A liftman: mostly Aus.: since ca. 1930. Hesling, 1963.

lig, n. and v. A freeloader, freeloading (*ligger, ligging*); one who takes, taking, the advantage of free drinks: 'pop' music, media, journalistic: since earlier 1980s. (John Ryle.)

light, n. A light ale: coll.

light, adj. In or of silver: c.:—1923 (Manchon).—2. Rather short of money: coll. Gen. as *very light*.—3. Also *light of*, which it shortens. Short of (something); 'I'm light a haversack': (mostly Forces') coll. since ca. 1925. Cf. **diffy**, 1.

light ale bandit. 'A beer scrounger' (Powis): police s.: later C.20.

light and dark. A park: late C.19–20. P.P., 1932.

light-house, lighthouse. A tramp acquainted with the police or with their methods: tramps' c.:—1932 (Jennings).—2. A salt- or pepper-castor: RN: since late C.19 (pepper prob. before salt, according to written refs). 'Pepper' in Goodenough, 1901; 'salt' in M. Brown, *Scapa Flow*, 1968. Ex shape, usu. conical.—3. See **play lighthouses**.

light of. Lacking. See **light**, adj., 3.

light o(f) love, the. The Prison Governor: prisoners' r.s., on *guv*: mid-C.20. Tempest.

light on. Aus. var. of **light**, 2, q.v. *Rats*, 1944, ' "You're a bit light on too, aren't you?"—"Purely a temporary state of poverty" '.

light on (one's) **feet, (to be).** To be (male) homosexual: later C.20. (Thomas, 1983.) Prob. ex 'like a fairy'.

light pastry hand, a. One who is able to handle, lightly and easily and tactfully, any relationship or situation or negotiation, either with an adroit bonhomie or, diplomatically, as if no difficulty existed: since ca. 1970. (L.A., 1976.)

light the re-heat. 'More or less synonymous with **turn up the wick**. To light the afterburner of a jet engine: a phrase which obviously started as S.E. but is now used to denote rapid acceleration of any form of mechanical transport' (Sanders): RAF: since ca. 1960. Cf. **burner**, 1.

light up. To give (a person) a dose of cocaine: c.: from ca. 1920. Wallace, 1928.—2. (V.i.) To reach—to experience—an orgasm: mostly teenagers': from ca. 1945.

lighter. An animal's *lights*: low Cockney and tramps' c.:—1932 (Pearson).

lighters. 'The merest wetting of the lips in your pal's tot of rum' (Granville): RN: since ca. 1905. Ex '*light* drinking'; by the 'OXFORD -ER(s)'; cf. **sippers**.

lightning-conductors. Naval officers' full-dress trousers: RN: since late C.19. They have broad gold stripes down the seams. Cf. the synon. *lightning-conductor pants*, recorded by Goodenough, 1901. Also pre-WW2 RAF (prob. via RNAS): 'If we're good boys we go up to the giddy rank of flight

L

lieutenant and get "lightning conductors" down the side of our mess kit pants' (Tredrey, 1939).

lightning jerker (or **squirter.**). A telegraph operator: Aus.: since ca. 1910. (B., 1942.) Among Can. railroadmen the term is *lightning slinger*.

lights. As in 'if the family catch her [a second wife] slipping, it'll be lights for Lady Laura' (Hunter, 1964): low coll.: mid-C.20. Elliptical for 'lights out' = the end. (P.B.)

lights on – no one home. Of below average intelligence: N. Am.: since later 1970s. (Leech, 1986.)

like, adv., at the end of a phrase or a sentence. Somewhat, not altogether; as it were, in a way; in short, expressive of vagueness or after-thoughted modification: (dial. and) low coll.: 1801, 'Of a sudden like' (Scott: *OED*). Cf.:-

like. '*Man* and *like* have'—'no actual meanings. They are code-signs, as in Morse or Semaphore, to show that communication has begun and ended' (Anderson): adopted, ex US, ca. 1955. The American satirical musician Stan Freberg (fl. 1950s), in his parody of 'The Banana-boat Song', had a tremulous-voiced drummer say 'Oh man! Like I don't dig spiders'. W. & F., 'Prob. to avoid making a definite, forthright statement, part of the beat philosophy; reinforced by Yiddish speech patterns.' Cf. prec. (P.B.)

like a baby's fist (or **arm**) **holding an orange.** Proverbial, low description of a particularly large male organ. (P.B.)

like a cat in a tripeshop – overjoyed. Self-explanatory Lancashire phrase of fairly recent origin. (Jack Slater, 1978.)

like a dose of salts. See **dose of salts.**

like a fart in a bottle. See **pea in a colander.**

like a pea on a drum. Applied to a small hat on a large head, e.g. a cap that a schoolboy has long since grown out of, but persists in wearing: coll. (P.B.)

like a pig, as in the common *sweat like a pig*, is a very frequent Aus. coll. intensive. (B.P.) Cf. **lie like a pig.**

like a pimple on a cow's (or **bull's**) **arse,** or **. . . on a pig's bum.** Synon. with **like a pea on a drum**; but also used to express insignificance: low coll., rural in orig. (L.A.; P.B.)

like all get out. 'Like anything'; vigorously; thoroughly; very fast or hastily: since ca. 1930s. 'In the 1930s . . . I occasionally heard "like all get out" ' (R.S., 1969); a dating that long prec. its American use (as recorded by W. & F., 1960)—yet during WW2, esp. from 1943 onwards, its currency accelerated because of US servicemen's presence in Great Britain.

like bats out of (1) **Hell** or (2) **a cave.** In great haste, or with alacrity, esp. of departure: (1) mainly Eng.; (2) mainly Can. (Leechman.) Since middle 1930s.

like Brown's cows. In (*we're*) *all together like . . .* , (we're) alone: Anglo-Irish. The anecdotal Brown possessed only one cow.—2. Hence, 'In single file, in a straggling manner' (Buzo, 1973): Aus.: since ca. 1920.

like hell. Very badly: coll.—2. Certainly not! Not at all!; as, e.g., 'Did you go?'—'Like hell (I did)!': s. > coll. Hence, since early 1920s, *like hell I* (or *he, you,* etc.) *will!*, I (you, etc.) certainly won't do anything of the sort.

like nobes. An ephemeral shortening of the next. Bolitho, 1941.

like nobody's business. An adverbial intensive: since ca. 1939.

like shaking hands with a pair of gloves on. A coll. phrase 'deprecating diminished ardour from use of contraceptive device' (a condom): since ca. 1930. (L.A., 1976.)

like shit through a goose. Very fast: low Can. Cf *like a dose of salts*, at **dose of . . .**

like taking pennies from a dead man's eyes. Easy; unimpeded: coll.: C.19–20. (L.A., 1969.) Unscrupulously taking advantage of easy pickings; cf. **easy as taking money from a child** or *. . . pennies from a blind man.*

like the clappers. 'Very fast, or very hard (e.g. "run like the clappers"; or "the clappers of hell")' (Emanuel, 1945): coll. E.P. noted, 'As *clapper* suggests *bell,* so *hell* rhymes on *bell;* and *go like hell* is to run very hard indeed'; but an equally common low intensive is *like the clappers of fuck.* (P.B.)

like trying to open an oyster with a bus-ticket. Hopelessly ineffectually: RN. (Peppitt.)

like two of eels. Nonplussed; at a loss: Londoners': late C.19–20. L.A.

likely story, a. Always used ironically, as an expression of profound disbelief: coll. 'Come home with your knickers torn, and say you found a shilling? A likely story!' (P.B.)

likeness, take a. To take a criminal's measurements and record physical characteristics, almost solely of the face: c. of ca. 1810–1910. (*Lex. Bal.*) Ex *likeness,* a portrait. In C.20, often a joc. invitation at the taking of photographs: 'Come here and have your likeness took' (P.B.)

likewise. I agree; I share the sentiment. Thus: 'Mr A. "Well, we must be off. We've had a wonderful time. Thank you so much!" Mrs A. "Likewise." ' Can.: since ca. 1965. (Leechman.) P.B.: in Brit. 'genteel' usage long before 1965, esp. in reciprocating a compliment, and in joc. parody, often with *I'm sure* added.

lilac. Effeminately homosexual: c. or low coll.: later C.20. Clement, 1978.

lilac wonder. A day-return ticket: railwaymen's: ?ca. 1920–50. (*Railway*). Ex its gay colour.

Lilian Gish. A fish: theatrical r.s.: since ca. 1920. Ex the famous film actress. Franklyn.

lilies. Floating runways for aircraft: FAA: WW2. Irving, 1946.

Lilley and Skinner. Dinner: London r.s.: from ca. 1910. Ex the well-known boot- and shoe-makers and retailers; the firm was established in 1835.—2. A beginner: retail trade r.s. Franklyn 2nd.

lily. An ear-trumpet; also fig., as in ' "Get your lily at the keyhole" = "Eavesdrop" ' (*M.T.*): market-traders'. A shape-resemblance.

Lily Law (and Inspector Beastly). The police; the fuller form is intensive: London barrow-boys': since ca. 1930. Prob. of 'camp' origin.

lily-pond, the; or **sweet-pea ward;** or **male gynae ward.** A ward set aside for male pelvic-organs and prostate-gland patients: hospital nurses'. *Nursing Mirror,* 7 May 1949.

lily-white, n. A young pathic: late C.19–early 20. Cf.:—2. But 'the lily-white boys' signifies a complementary pair of not necessarily youthful male lovers: since ca. 1920. Jones, 1937.

lily-white, adj. Cowardly: Aus. (teenage) surfers': from ca. 1960. (Sydney *Bulletin,* 30 Mar. 1963.) Perhaps suggested by a lack of sun-tan, and influenced by S.E. *lily-livered.*

limb. Elliptical for *limb of the law* in its Aus. sense 'a policeman': Aus.: since ca. 1930. 'Carefully searching among the straw, the limb found nothing': *Hay, Hell and Booligal,* Melbourne, 1961. (B.P.)—2. In *out on a limb,* in a dangerous situation; hence, at a grave disadvantage: adopted, ca. 1945, ex US. Implying a precarious branch high up.

lime, in the. Popular; much publicised: Aus.: since ca. 1925. (Baker.) I.e. 'in the limelight'.

lime slime. See PRISONER-OF-WAR SLANG, §11, in Appx.

Lime Tank, the. The RN Hospital, Haslar: RN: since ca. 1920. Granville.

limers. Limejuice: RN: since ca. 1930. Winton, 1959.

limes. Limelight: theatrical. Cf. **lime, in the.** Electric footlights are, of course, included.

limey, Limey. An Englishman. US >, in 1933, partly anglicised, thanks to Spenser's *Limey,* a notable book on the US underworld. Ex *lime-juicer,* the US (–1881 but †) term for a Brit. ship or sailor, lime juice being served on Brit. ships as an antiscorbutic. Adopted in Aus., ca. 1943, ex US servicemen.—2. Hence, esp., a Can. name for a Brit. seaman: since ca. 1925 (H. & P.).

limit. Esp. in *that's the* (usu. qualified) *limit,* a person, act, or thing that is the extreme (or beyond) of what one can bear; gen. in joc. use, although qualification may be suited to degree of exasperation caused: coll.: adopted, ex US, ca. 1908 (*OED* Sup.). It may be the *dizzy* or *giddy* or *frozen* or *outside limit,* or even *just about the fucking limit.*

limo (pron. *limmo*), n. A *limo*usine car: motorists': since ca. 1960. (Martin, 1975.) Hence, in later 1980s, *stretch limo,* a particularly long one.

limo, adj. Luxurious, as a limousine car: early 1980s. '[She] may have taken to the limo treatment accorded to hot cinema property, but . . .' (*Sunday Express* mag., 30 May 1982). Ex n.

limo-limo. See PRISONER-OF-WAR SLANG, §11, in Appx.

limp wrist. A male homosexual, hence *Limp Wrist society*, homosexual society: Can., ex US: later C.20. Leech, 1985, 'Prob. ex movie depictions of homos holding their hands limply at the end of a horizontally held forearm. Usage is usu. derog., and not in common, though in widespread, use.'

limping Annie. See Annie, 1.

Lincolnshire gremlin. A sharp-toothed gremlin, fond of biting the control wires: RAF: 1940–5. See GREMLINS, in Appx.

line. As *the line*, the line of bookmakers on a race-course: racing-men's s. verging on c.—2. A large amount of stock; a large number of shares: stockbrokers' coll.:—1935. (Cf. the technical sense in insurance: see *OED* Sup.)—3. A customer that has purchased heavily is known to drapers, hosiers, and their like as *a good line*: ex *a good line* of drapery-stock: a sense that is S.E.—4. A printed form: Public Works':—1935.—5. A girl or a young woman, e.g. *nice line*, (not so) *good line*: Aus.: since ca. 1920. B., 1942; Glassop, 1944. Since ca. 1950, esp. *a slashing line*, a very attractive girl (Culotta).—6. A special verbal approach, esp. from male to female: coll.: since ca. 1920. Ex the S.E. '*line* of goods (for sale)'. Cf. **shoot a line**, to boast.—7. 'A measure of powdered drugs laid out in a narrow strip upon a mirror or similar glass surface for easy nasal access' (Hibbert, 1983); Stockley, 1986, specifies amphetamine or cocaine: drugs c. US since—1979 (Spears).—8. In *go (for a trip) up the line*, to go to prison. (Young, 1934.) Contrast:—9. *Up the line*, on leave: RN. (Granville.) Up the railway from a Service port.—10. In *have in line*, to have the measure of (a person): Army: earlier C.20. Richards, 1933, 'Even the young soldiers . . . had him in line.' Cf. *have* (a person) *taped*.—11. In *get a line on*, to get information about, or a clue to (either identity or meaning): coll.: adopted, ex US, not later than 1925. (*OED* Sup.) Ex marksmanship.—12. As exclam., short for '(That's a) line-shoot!': Forces': 1940+. *Observer*, 4 Oct. 1942.—13. In *on the line*, in jeopardy, as in 'Our stripes [NCOs' badges] will be on the line for this' (Petch, 1968).

line book. See lines book.

line of country. One's vocation, profession, or particular interest, hobby, etc.: Service officers'. ' "What's your line of country in civvy street?" asked [a Yeomanry major, 1937]' (Verney, 1955). 'Not quite my line of country, old boy. Better see the Adj. [= adjutant] on that one'. (P.B.)

line on. See **line**, 11.

line-shoot. A tall story; boasting: RAF: since 1940. (*Observer*, 4 Oct. 1942.) Ex **shoot a line**, q.v. Hence, *line-shooter*, one who specialises in, or is addicted to, 'line-shoots' (Jackson); and *line-shooting*, the corresponding vbl n.

line the pencil. 'Make a bee-line for anywhere, especially the beach' (Granville): RN. Ex a device, invented by Adml Sir Percy Scott (1852–1914), to facilitate accuracy in firing; it included a pencilled line of dots, and was known as a 'dotter'.

line up. To approach (v.i.); as v.t., with *to*; to accost: Aus.:—1916 (Dennis).—2. In the Services, to form up before an interview with the commanding officer, usu. as a defaulter, for disciplinary action. Hence, to *be lined up*, to stand thus. (Granville.)—3. To arrange: since ca. 1920. Ex setting things or persons in an orderly line: 'Not to worry, old boy! I've got it all lined up.' Cf. **lay on**, in sense of 'to organise'.

linen. Shortened form of C.19 r.s. *linen-draper*, paper. Hence, newspapers collectively: since ca. 1945 (Clayton, 1970.) But also pl., as in 'I'm just poppin' out for the linens'.

lines book. A book kept in the Mess for the recording of exaggerations by its members. 'Sometimes called a "Shooting Gallery". From the early 1920s' (Jackson). In the *Observer*, 4 Oct. 1942, John Moore uses the occ. var., *line book*. Cf. **line-shoot** and **shoot a line**.

ling. A stink: Aus.: since ca. 1920. B., 1942.

linguist. A practitioner of cunnilingism: Aus.: since ca. 1950.

linguistic exercise(s). Kissing: since ca. 1925.

liniment. Alcoholic liquor: joc. coll. (McKenna, 1.) Cf. **oil**, 4; **tincture**, 2.

linings. 'In the North of England, underpants were [late C.19–mid-20] called linings, because originally workingmen's trousers were lined' (Petch, 1969).

link. A group of porters working under a foreman: railway porters': since ca. 1940. (*Radio Times*, 21 Jan. 1965.) A link—often somewhat tenuous—between staff and public.

links of love. Sausages: RN: since ca. 1925. (*Weekly Telegraph*, Nov. 1942; Granville.) Phallic symbolism. Note that simple *links* = sausages is not s. but dial. Because linked together.

lino. A coll. abbr., from ca. 1880, of *linoleum* (1863).—2. In C.20, among printers and journalists, a coll. abbr. of *linotype* (1888), itself contracting *line of type*.—3. A cheap bicycle-tyre: club cyclists': earlier C.20. (*Fellowship*, 1984.) Ex sense 1.

lion. To intimidate: Aus.: since ca. 1930. B., 1942.

lion-tamer, adj. As in ' "lion-tamer" rig-out', the full dress uniform, with frogging on the tunic, of cavalry regts: Army: early C.20. (Hatton, 1930.) Ex the fanciful dress affected by circus-folk. (P.B.)

Lionel Blair. Chair: r.s.: later C.20. (Barker, 1979.) Ex the well-known dancer.

lip read. ' "Lip" or kiss features or physiognomy in amorous dalliance' (L.A., 1974): teenagers': later C.20. Cf.:-

lip service. By a pun on S.E. *lip service*, it has, in s., come to mean 'female penilingism': adopted, mid-1960s, ex US. Hollander.

lippy. Lipstick: Aus.: since ca. 1930. 'Not heard from women under forty' (B.P., 1963).

liquid sunshine. Rain: railwaymen's joc. ironic: mid-C.20. (McKenna, 1.) Parodying advertisements for alcohol. (P.B.)

liquorice legs. 'Naval officers' black gaiters for ceremonial parades, and also the Gunnery officers who wear them: RN: 1970s' (Peppitt)—and rather earlier, I think.—2. As a taunt, a schoolboys' cry directed at a schoolgirl wearing black stockings: Aus.: 1950s. (B.P.) Obviously ex the colour in both senses.

liquorice stick. A clarinet: dance bands' (whether jazz or not): since ca. 1945. 'Obviously because (*a*) it is of black wood; and (*b*) it is sucked vertically to the lips' (Merry).

lister. An enthusiastic bird-watcher. See BIRD-WATCHERS' SLANG, in Appx.

lit (slightly), gen. *well lit* (quite), tipsy: from ca. 1920. Cf. **lighthouse**. Also *lit up*, slightly drunk (Lyell).

lit up. Under the influence of drugs: drugs c. (Stockley, 1986.) US since—1938 (Spears). Ex prec.

Little Arthur. The ARP (Air Raid Precautions) wardens' pet name (1939–45), then (1941–5) used by the RAF, for arsenic gas. (H. & P.) By personification and by phonetic approximation.

little Audrey. The bull's-eye in the game of darts. The term bears sexual implications. (Slater, 1978.)

little black book. The notebook in which bachelors are reputed to keep girls' telephone numbers: mostly Aus.: since ca. 1930. (B.P.)—2. In Brit., applied to the (prob. non-existent) list of anyone suspected of 'keeping tabs on' people for any reason, as in, e.g., 'You want to watch him. He'll have you down in his little black book': coll. Influenced by *black list*. (P.B.)

little boys' (or **little girls'**) **room, the.** The men's—the women's—lavatory: euph.: adopted, ca. 1944, ex US servicemen. The former occurs in, e.g., Wilson, 1957.

Little Brown Men. A var. of *Little* (*Yellow*) *Men*: B., 1943.

little dabbler. 'The decimal halfpenny . . . derived from Cockney children's "daddler" for the old farthing before the first world war' (*Muvver*): 1970s.

little devils. Three '2' cards: Aus. poker-players': since ca. 1920. (B., 1953.) A ref. to children of two years—with which cf. **little horrors.**

Little 'F'. The Lieutenant-Commander (Flying) in charge of flying details: FAA: later C.20. Wingate, 1981.

little finger. The male member: female euph.

little friend, (one's). The menses: Can. (a feminine euph.): since ca. 1920. But also Aus.; deriving mainly ex the fact that the menses are often welcome as a sign of *non*-pregnancy.

little Hitler. Opprobrious sobriquet for any minor jack-in-office, throwing his weight about and abusing his tiny power, one rung up from the bottom; may also apply to a female: since WW2. (P.B.)

little horrors; little monsters. Young children: mothers': perhaps orig. among those women who cook and serve primary-school dinners: since the late 1940s. Leechman notes that the 2nd term is also Can., esp. (in sing.) if the child is objectionable: since ca. 1950.

little man. Upper and middle-class females' (sometimes quite unconsciously) patronising term for a tradesman, artisan, etc., as in 'I have a little man deliver from the village twice a week'. (P.B.) Cf. **little woman round the corner.**

Little men, the. (Often *the little brown*, or *yellow, men*.) The Japanese: coll., mostly in the Army: 1942–6.

little men with (their bloody) hammers, the or **those.** Rueful ref. to a (usu. drink-caused) headache: coll.: later C.20. Allen, 1972.

little monster. See little horrors.

Little Moscow. Chopwell, County Durham: during the General Strike, 1926. It was the strikers' HQ.—2. Mardy, a town in S. Wales: *Daily Worker*, 16 Nov. 1949.

Little Muddy. 'The River Yarra, Victoria (from colour of water. *Big Muddy* is the Missouri)' (Wilkes): Aus.

little number, (one's). What one wants: since ca. 1940. Wilson, 1952.—2. (Without the possessive.) Any object, gadget, as in 'I bought this little number [a metal detector] for Nigel at Christmas . . . ' (*Private Eye*, 16 Mar. 1979); or a dress, 'a slinky little number': would-be smart coll.: later C.20. Perhaps ex its use to describe a song, as radio music-hall comedians of the 1940s would finish their acts with 'a little number here, written specially for *you* . . . ' (P.B.) As dress, recorded in US in 1928, and therefore US. orig. (R.C.).—3. A girl, young woman, mostly as regarded sexually, as in 'a hot little number': since ca. 1945. Cf. **number**, 2.

Little Rome. Liverpool (England): coll. Ex the large number of Catholics there. (Petch, 1966.)

little smack. A half-sovereign: c.:—1926 (Jennings).

little something, a. A dash of spirits: coll. 'Would you like a little something in it?'—2. A snack, a bite, between meals: domestic coll. Popularised, or given fresh impetus, by Milne's *Winnie-the-Pooh*, 1926, who was always on the look-out for 'a little something'. (P.B.)

little terror or **Toby** or **Turk.** An extremely mischievous child: domestic coll.: later C.19–20. Cf. **little horrors.** (P.B.)

little visitor, have a. To be undergoing one's period: feminine, esp. in suburbia, and notably in the 1920s–1930s.

Little Willie, -y. A (small) boy's penis: primary schoolchildren's (esp. girls) and teachers': heard in 1920s, but not very common before ca. 1945. A euph. at once playful and sensible. *Willie* by itself is recorded in *EDD* as North-Western s. for the same thing, 1905; and L.A. notes that the term may be elab., as in Hill, 1934, to *Little Willie Winkle*, a conflation of *Wee Willie Winkie* of the nursery rhyme and *winkle*, another children's term for the penis.

little woman, the. 'This revoltingly coy way of referring to one's wife . . . Cf. the Chinese husband's "my inside person" ' (P.B., 1975): coll.: prob. since mid-C.19. Ex male condescension, sometimes at least half-affectionate. Cf. **little man.**

little woman round the corner, (often my). One's dressmaker or sewing-woman: middle-class feminine patronising coll. Cf. **little man.** (P.B.)

littler, littlest. Smaller, -est; younger, -est. C.19–20: unintentional, they are sol. or dial.; deliberate, they (though rarely *littler*) are joc. coll., as in *the littlest ones* (the youngest children). *Observer*, 1932, Christmas number.

littlies. 'Heard recently among younger mothers as a general term for the smaller children. "Sorry, no, I can't then. Katy's just started at the littlies' ballet class and I've got to take her" ' (P.B., 1976): coll.: also Aus.: since ca. 1965. These diminutive nn. have become very common since the late 1940s: notably *the baddies* and *the goodies* of films, *the meanies*, etc. They help to reduce people and things to a comfortable and friendly size.

live in (one's) **boxes.** Lacking a fixed abode, to move from place to place: coll. (Hay, 1917.) Cf. **live in** (one's) **trunks.**

live in (someone's) **pocket.** To be constantly accessible and instantly available to him: since 1930s: coll. >, by 1960, informal S.E. (P.B. cites a coll. usage, 1956; *COD*, 1976, adjudges it S.E.)

live in (one's) **trunks.** To be at a place for so short a time that it is not worth while to unpack; to live in a confined space, esp. a ship's cabin: coll.:—1931 (Lyell). Cf. in later C.20 more gen. *live out of* (one's) *suitcase*.

live it up. To lead a gay extravagant life: coll.: since ca. 1960. P.B.: E.P. is here using 'gay' in its orig. sense, happy.

live off the land. To live the life of a tramp: Aus. coll.: late C.19–20. (B., 1942.) The tramp is non-productive.

live on the smell of an oil-rag. 'To subsist on very little' (B.P.): Aus. coll.: since ca. 1920. (Cusack, 1951.) Adopted ex Anglo-Irish usage of late C.19–20. 'A penurious miserable creature who starves himself to hoard up:—He could live on the smell of an oil-rag' (Joyce, 1910).

live out of (one's) **suitcase. See live in** (one's) **trunks.**

live over the brush. (Of man and woman) to cohabit, unmarried: N.W. Eng. coll. (Mrs P.M.C. Pearsall, 1980.) Cf. older *live tally*, and *jump* or *leap over the brush* or *broomstick*, to go through a secular, mock, wedding ceremony.

live over the shop, when lit. is S.E., but merely living near one's work, as say a university lecturer living on campus, it is coll.: since the late 1940s. Dickinson, 1975.

live rabbit. The penis: low: C.19–early 20. Whence *skin the live rabbit* or *have a bit of rabbit-pie*, to coït. Cf. dial. *rabbit*, 'to coït'—as in Masefield, 1919, ' ' "I'll larn 'ee rabbit in my shed!" ' '

live square. To be an honest citizen: Aus. c. and low s.: since ca. 1950. See AUSTRALIAN UNDERWORLD, in Appx.

live stock. House bugs: domestic. Orig., and still mainly, euph.

live with. In *can*, or *able to*, *live with*, to be able to play (a person) on level terms: sporting: from ca. 1928.—2. In *live with it*, to accept, endure, task or difficulty, esp. of small things and with preceding *can* or *will*, as in 'Oh, we'll manage to . . . ': since late 1940s. Haggard, 1964.

live wire. An indefatigable but not necessarily reliable news-gatherer: journalistic coll. Ex the familiar S.E. sense.

liver and grapes. 'Fried liver and bacon for the wardroom breakfast': RN. (Bowen.) Why *grapes*?—unless it = *grape-shot*.

livid. Furiously angry; very much annoyed: since ca. 1920. Short for *livid with rage*.

living daylights. See frighten the living . . . Also in *belt, smash, thump* (and other vv. of violence) *the living daylights out of*, thoroughly to physically damage someone: coll. (P.B.)

living end, the. The very end, 'the last straw': Aus. ('not common' B.P.): since ca. 1950. Either *living* is ironic or it's an intensive.—2. 'Perfection, the ultimate, the ideal. "But, Daddy, you should meet Harry! He's the living end!" ' (Leechman): Can.: since ca. 1955.

livener. A drink; alcoholic liquor: market-traders'. (M.T.) ?A deliberate mispronunciation of *livener*.

Liz. Abbr. **Lizzie**, 1, and 4. The 2nd, E.P., 1942.

lizard. See bleed (one's) **lizard.**

Lizzie. A (cheap) motor-car, orig. and mainly a 'Ford': 1921. By personification. Also *tin Lizzie*. Occ., from ca. 1924,

Liz.—2. (Also *l-*.) Cheap *Lis*bon red wine: c. and low: from ca. 1920. *Gilt Kid*, 1936.—3. HMS *Queen Elizabeth*: RN. ('Taffrail'.) Also *Big Lizzie*.—4. A Lysander reconnaissance and liaison aircraft: RAF: WW2. (P-G-R.) Partly ex *Lys*(ander), partly an allusion to sense 1.—5. A Lesbian: since ca. 1928. (Wilson, 1949.) Ex *Lesbian*; cf. *Les*.—6. A London, Midland & Scottish Pacific class locomotive: railwaymen's: mid-C.20. *Railway*, 2nd.

Lloyd. See **Harold Lloyd** and **loid**.

load. An idler or 'loafer'; a lazy person: coll.: earlier C.20. He is a *load* on those who have to 'carry' him.—2. Fabricated evidence: Aus. c.: since ca. 1930.—3. 'Stock of illegal drugs' (Home Office): drug-users': later C.20.—4. In *get a load of*, to see, to perceive; to understand: adopted, mid-WW2, ex US.—5. See **get a load on.**

load bummer. A 1941–5 var. of *line-shooter*, a boaster. (Partridge, 1945.) See **bum** (one's) **load,** 2.

load of cods. A shortening of *a load of codswallop*. See **cod's wallop**; cf. next 2 entries, and **load of old cobblers.**

load of crap. A lot of, or all, nonsense: a US synon. of *load of old cobblers*, etc.: fully adopted by late 1960s, but first used in Brit., by Britons, in 1943.

load of guff. 'A lot of humbug or nonsense' (Jackson): RAF (mostly officers'): since ca. 1937.

load of old cobblers, a, esp. in 'That's a load . . . '—that's rubbish or nonsense: since ca. 1960. Often used by people ignorant of its origin in C.19 r.s. *cobbler's awls*, testicular nonsense. A comparison with **cod's wallop** is unavoidable. Cf. also:-

load of old wank. See **wank,** n., 2.

load of rough. A bus-load of pass-holders: London busmen's: since ca. 1930.

load of wind. A light load. See HAULIERS', in Appx.

load (or **weight**) **off** (one's) **behind.** A defecation: low: since ca. 1925. Parodying:-

load (but usu. **weight**) **off** (one's) **mind.** A haircut: mostly in working-class barber-shops: since ca. 1920. Especially if the 'crop' is heavy.—2. Also (cf. prec.) a defecation, the pun rather than parody (cf. **shit-head**): low: later C.20. (P.B.)

loaded. Well off; having plenty of money: coll.: since ca. 1945.—2. Tipsy: adopted, ca. 1958, ex US, and used esp. by beatniks.—3. Hence, 'full of drugs' (Home Office): drug-users': later C.20. Cf. **load,** 3.—4. 'Having all the extras, as in "Man, this car's loaded". Widespread N. Am., and dating from early 1960s' (Leach, 1986).

loaded with it. Elab. of **loaded,** 1: since ca. 1950.—2. Over-sexed: beatniks': since ca. 1959. (Anderson.)

Loadsamoney. The comedian 'Harry Enfield created a monstrous character, Loadsamoney, to represent the grotesque side of Thatcherite acquisitiveness' for Independent TV Channel 4, early 1988: the c.p./name quickly > a vogue word, to the extent that the Leader of the Opposition could, in the House of Commons, 20 May, accuse the Government of creating a 'Loadsamoney economy'. (*New Society*, 20 May; *Daily Telegraph*, 21 May 1988.) The character would end his ranting about his material wealth by brandishing high-denomination banknotes and 'squawking his catchphrase'. Cf. the earlier *lovely money*.

loaf. In later C.20 the usu. form of **loaf of bread.**

loaf o(f) bread. The head; predominantly in the sense of brains, thought, and, in the very common phrase 'Use your loaf', a certain amount of cunning is implied: r.s., used by a very wide register of speakers: since late C.19. B. & P.; Franklyn.

loafing. (Of gear) left lying about: RN. (Granville.) Cf. **lazy.**

loafing number. 'A nice easy job in depot' (Granville): RN. Ex prec.: cf. next.

loafing stations. Shore stations where men await drafting to ships: RN.

Loamshire dialect. Faulty dialect as used by ignorant writers: authors' coll. There being no such county, there is no such dialect. Cf. synon. **Mummerset.**

loather. A cad: Rugby: since early 1920s. Ex *loathsome* by the 'OXFORD -ER'.

lob, n. A haul of money: Aus. c. B., 1942.—2. A partial erection of the penis: low coll.: since C.18. Cf. **lazy lob.**—3. One's turn to 'lob out'—distribute or pay for—cigarettes and drinks at a convivial gathering: mostly Services': since ca. 1930. (L.A.)—4. As *the lob* it also means 'the w.c.': Londoners'.—5. In *crash lob* or *force lob* as nn., crash- or forced-landings. See **lob,** v.—6. 'Pay. The weekly pay received by prisoners. "Gash lob" = spare money. [See **gash.**]' (Tempest): prison c.: mid-C.20.

lob, v. In *crash lob, force lob,* (of pilot or aircraft) to land, crash-land; force-land: RAF: WW2+. (Brickhill, 1946.) Also as *lob in*, to land. Cf. **lob in,** 1. P.B.: Tredrey, 1939, has *lob down*, to land, as pre-WW2 RAF usage.—2. To distribute. See n., 3, and **lob out.**

lob in. To arrive; to call at a place: Aus. Wilkes cites Dennis, 1915, 'lob along', and Brady, 1924, 'A man who would insist on telling things lobbed in'.—2. Hence, to intromit the penis: low. Also, derivatively, *lop in*. P.B.: but this is also ex S.E., 'to chuck'.—3. See **lob,** v.,1.

lob onto. To obtain or discover by a stroke of luck: Aus.: since ca. 1925. B., 1943.

lob out. See **lob,** n., 3. Hence applied to anything that must be distributed: pay, issues from stores, rations, etc.: Services': later C.20. (P.B.)

lob the snout. Usu. as a demand: 'Hand out your cigarettes!: Army and RAF: since early 1950s; ob. Hence 'It's your lob!' = it's your turn to give me (or us) a cigarette; or 'Is it my lob?' Cf. **crash the ash,** and **lob,** n., 3. (L.A.; P.B.)

lobber. A till robber: London c. (Barnes, 1976.) A survival ex the early C.18 c. *lob*, a till.

lobe. A conforming schoolboy. See **ear-(h)ole.**

local. A public house in one's own district: coll. London *Evening News*, 11 Sep. 1934.—2. A local newspaper: coll.: since ca. 1910.

local yokel. Slightly contemptuous term for an indigenous inhabitant of the area where one is stationed: Army and RAF: since ca. 1950. As in 'stationed in some God-forsaken spot the other end of nowhere. Organised a darts match against the local yokels. They thrashed us, of course—but it was a great evening.' (P.B.) In later C.20, > also civilian, usu. joc.

Lochinvar, (do) the. To catch, the catching of, Aboriginal women (lubras) to work cattle and perform other rough services: NT, Aus. Hill, 1951.

lock on with. To fight: Aus. juvenile. (Wilkes cites Hamilton, 1959.) Hence *locked on*, fighting.

lock up. 'To have an engine or transmission seize up' (Dunford): motorcyclists': later C.20.

lock wheeling, n. and adj. 'Cycling between locks on a canal, to open and close locks'; and thus to ensure 'a faster passage than if the "wheeler" travelled with the boat': coll. Cove-Smith, 1970.

locket. A pocket: Aus. r.s. (Baker.) One might expect *Lucy* (P.B.).

loco. Insane; crazy; 'daft': adopted, ex US, in Can. ca. 1930; by the MN (Granville); and into Brit. coll. by mid-C.20. (Hunter, 1964.) Ex the effects of the loco weed. The weed itself derives its name ex the Spanish *loco*, mad, which 'presumably reached N. America with the Jesuit missionaries in California, etc., in C.17–18' (H.R. Spencer).

loco da poco. 'Fanciful elaboration of the preceding' (Granville): MN, adopted from the US Merchant Marine.

loco weed. Cannabis: drugs c. (Stockley, 1986.) US since ca. 1931 (Spears).

lodge and comp. Lodging-and-provision allowance granted to officers and men living ashore: RN. (Granville.) Short for 'Lodging and Compensation' Allowance.

log. Abbr. *logarithm*, coll.: C.19–20: universities'; since ca. 1920, common also in schools. Equally frequent in pl.—2. An energetic afternoon's exercise: RNC Dartmouth. (Granville.) Cf. nautical j. *a day's log*.—3. A person without brains or ability or energy: Aus.: since early 1930s. (B., 1959.) See also **cedar**.—4. In *go up a log*, to hide: Aus.: since ca. 1910. (B., 1942.) As snake or lizard does.

logged. Utterly drunk: from ca. 1920. (Knox, 1934.) Ex *water-logged*.

logger's smallpox is those markings on a man's face which are caused by a man's stamping on it with his spiked boots, an activity known as *putting the caulks to* (a man): Can. loggers'. Kersh, 1939.

logic bomb. See **time bomb.**

logo. A logotype, in its commercial/advertising, rather than its typographical sense: advertisers' coll.: since mid-1960s, >, by mid-1970s, S.E. (B.P.; P.B.)

logs. Turds: teenagers': early 1980s. Cf. the ribald song 'In Mobile', in which occur the lines, 'There's no paper in the bogs, so they wait until it clogs, then they saw it off in logs, in Mobile'. (P.B.)—2. See **log**, 1.

loid. Celluloid: since ca. 1910. Hence, *the loid*, the art of using a piece of celluloid to slip open the latch of a door: mostly police: since ca. 1920. (Procter, 1958.) See also **Harold Lloyd.**

loiner. A townsman: Leeds undergraduates':—1940 (Marples, 2). Perhaps cf. dial. *lointer*, to loiter.

lollied. See **lolly**, v.

lollipop, lollypop, n. A policeman: r.s., on *slop* or *cop*. Franklyn.—2. A 'shafted tool with iron ball for testing sleepers' (*Railway*): railwaymen's. Ex shape.—3. One's girl friend: RAF: WW2. (R.S.) She is *sweet*.—4. Acronym: *Lots of local leave in place of Python* (military code-name given to leave due at end of overseas service): Army: 1944–5.—5. A 'sugar-daddy': shopgirls' and typists': ca. 1955–60. Contrast sense 3.—6. Anything specially good, e.g. the pride of one's collection: coll.: since ca. 1965. In, e.g., BBC Radio 4 programme 'The Living World', 24 Apr. 1975. Perhaps influenced by the famous conductor Sir Henry Wood, who used the term for his favourite pieces of music. (P.B.)—7. A (money) tip: r.s., on *drop*. Franklyn.—8. See **lolly**, n., 1, and cf.:-

lollipop, v. To inform (on someone): r.s., on *shop*. Franklyn.

lollipop lady or **man.** A traffic warden specially recruited to shepherd children at street-crossings, esp. near primary schools: orig. coll. >, by 1980, informal S.E.: later C.20. Ex shape of sign, a disc on top of a pole, used to signal traffic to stop.

Lollos. Female breasts, esp. if impressive and shapely: Aus.: since ca. 1955. 'Not common. Probably originally journalistic. Ex the famous Italian film star, Gina Lollobrigida' (B.P.).

lolly, n. A shop: short for *lollipop* (cf. the v.): grafters'. *Cheapjack*, 1934.—2. Money: orig. Cockney (Franklyn derives it ex **lollipop**, n., 7) >, in later C.20 gen. low coll. Harrison, 1943, 'Touches the Guv'ment for a nice drop of lolly'—which is almost tautologous.—3. Anything easy: Aus. Baker.—4. An easy catch: cricketers': earlier C.20. de Sélincourt, 1924.—5. A trickster's (easy) victim: Aus.: since ca. 1910. B., 1943.—6. A criminal either timid or half-hearted, esp. towards a coup: Aus. c.: since ca. 1920.—7. In *do* (one's or) *the lolly*, to get very angry: Aus.: since ca. 1950. (Dick.)—8. Shortening of **lollipop**, n., 1. Tempest.

lolly, v.t. To give (a fellow crook) away to the police: c.:—1933 (Leach). See **lollipop**, v. Still extant in 1970s: 'He was lollied' (Powis).

lolly(-)water (in later C.20, written solid). 'Soft drink, esp, if coloured' (Wilkes, whose earliest quot'n is B., 1945): Aus. Esp. among those who prefer something stronger.

lolly-worker. 'A swindler who starts a shop and immediately sells the alleged goodwill' (*Cheapjack*, 1934): grafters'. Cf. **lolly**, n., 1.

lollypop. See **lollipop.**

London Blizzard. Leighton Buzzard: railwaymen's: from ca. 1920. (*Daily Herald*, 5 Aug. 1936.) By rhyming equivalence.

London Closet-Cleaners. London County Council: Londoners'. By pun on the initials of the body which came into existence in 1888 and was replaced by the Greater London Council in 1965.

London-super-Mare. Brighton: since ca. 1955. Brown, 1968.

lone wolf. 'Fighter pilot who leaves formation' (McDouall, 1945): RAF: mid-1940+. Ex wild-life woodlore. Cf.:-

loner. One who prefers solitude or independence, or both, to 'running with the herd': coll.: adopted, ca. 1945, ex US; by early 1970s, S.E. (*COD*, 1976). Cf. **lone wolf**, of which it is perhaps a shortening.

lonesome pine. 'A person with unusual ideas or views' (McKenna, 1): railwaymen's: mid-C.20.

long as (one's) **arm(, as).** Very long, as in 'He's got a record sheet [of petty crimes] as long as your arm': coll.: since late C.19.

long bacon. The derisive gesture of thumb to nose, with fingers extended and waggling: juvenile. The action is *make* or, occ., *pull, long bacon.* Cf. older *cock snooks at*; *(Queen) Anne's fan.* (P.B.) Also *make a long nose.*

long barrow. See **barrow**, 5.

long-distance. 'Long service. Thus, a long-distance medal' (Jackson): RAF: since ca. 1930. Esp., also, *long-distance type*, a long-service airman (Partridge, 1945). P.B.: in the Army, since 1950 at latest, *long-distance gong* is common for the long-service medal. Granville notes it as RN usage also.

long drag, the. The 'uphill run from Carlisle to Settle' (*Railway*): railwaymen's.

long drop, the. Familiar term for the DTL (deep trench latrine, or earth closet): Army. I met it in Cyprus, later 1950s, but the name was prob. in wider usage—wherever such a primitive arrangement was needed. (P.B.)

long firm. A swindling group of phantom capitalists: commercial coll. An early occurrence is in *Orchestra*, 2 Jan. 1869. Powis defines a long firm fraud as 'a type of fraud where a great deal of property is ordered on credit through legitimate channels and then sold at "knock-down" prices. Suppliers are not paid and fraudsmen abscond.' In C.20 usu. abbr. *l.f.*

long-G. 'Long gunnery course at Whale Island Gunnery School, Portsmouth' (Granville). RN.

long glass. 'General nautical colloquialism for a telescope' (Granville): C.20; prob. earlier.

long grass, the. The Provinces: theatrical. (L.A., 1967.) Cf. *the sticks*, q.v. at **sticks**, 3.

long-hair. An intellectual; a highbrow: Aus.: adopted, ca. 1944, ex US. (Cusack, 1951.) P.B.: some Brit. use also, usu. contemptuous, 'long haired intellectuals' being a cliché, until the advent of 'The Beatles' in the early 1960s set the fashion for long hair on males for a couple of decades.

long hand, the. Pickpocketry: c.:—1923 (Manchon). Therein, a long, thin hand is useful.

long-handled underwear. Men's 'extra-warm winter woollen underclothes, with long legs and sleeves' (Leechman): Can.: since ca. 1950. Also *long Johns.* Cf.:-

long hangers. Long knitted woollen underpants supplied to seamen on the convoys to Russia: WW2.

long-head. A 'shrewd-head' or very shrewd or cunning person: proletarian coll.:—1923 (Manchon). Prob. back-formation ex S.E. *long-headed*, shrewd.

long in the tooth. Elderly: from ca. 1910: (low) coll. >, by 1930, S.E.

long Johns. Long-legged underpants. Also written *longjohns* (*Phantom*, 1979). See **John L.s** and cf. **long-handled** . . .

long jump, the. A being hanged: c.: from ca. 1921. Also *take the* . . . , to be hanged.

long neck. A camel: Aus.: late C.19–20. Russell, 1934, 'He is the despised "humpie", the "filthy camel", the "stinking old long neck", that "mangy brute" of the traveller; but he is also . . . the great utility animal of the Inland.'

long nose. See **long bacon.**

long paddock, the. The open road: NZ and Aus. coll. B., 1941 and 1942.

long-playing record. 'A non-stop gossiper; a very talkative woman' (Petch): proletarian coll: since ca. 1960.

long-plummer. 'Engineer officer who has taken the long-E (the old engineering scheme, which was abolished in 1948—the course seemed endless)' (Granville): RN: earlier C.20. Should this perhaps be *-plumber*? (P.B.)

long slab. A tall, very thin woman: Londoners': early C.20.

long-stopper. A look-out man: Aus. c. (B., 1959.) Ex cricket.

long strokes, the. Intromission in coïtion: raffish. (L.A., 1974.) Cf. **short strokes.**

long-tailed beggar. In c. (—1923: Manchon), the same as:–

long-tailed finnip or **'un.** A bank-note of high denomination: c.: from ca. 1835. (Brandon; Snowden's *Magistrate's Assistant.*) *Long-tailed 'un* is still extant, 1970s: Powis records its use for £10 and £20 notes.

long Tom. A 'paintbrush lashed to the end of a 4-foot stick: M N: 1940s' (Peppitt)—and after.—2. A 'riding crop used by racecourse starter. ITV Racing Commentary, 16 Jan. 1975' (Ibid.)—and for at least a generation earlier.—3. (Usu. written *long tom*.) A camera with long-distance lenses: photographers':—1945 (Farmer).—4. See:-

long Toms. 'Yorkshire coal, delivered in long, jagged pieces' (McKenna, 1970): railwaymen's: earlier C.20.

long underwear. Highbrow music: beatniks': ca. 1959+. (Anderson.) Adopted ex US, where applied also to other forms of music, e.g. sweet, 'corny' jazz (W. & F.). 'The implication is that highbrow music, like long underwear, is old-fashioned' (R.C., 1976). But *can* it ever become so?

longer and linger. Finger: r.s.

longjohns. See **long Johns.**

Lonsdale (Belt), give (someone) the. To dismiss, get rid of: low: since ca. 1940. (Norman.) An elab. of *give the belt.*

loo. Usu. *the loo*, the water closet; late C.19–20, but esp. gen. in later C.20. (Wilson, 1949.) See note in Appx. on suggested derivation.

loo'd, or **looed, be.** To be very short of money: nautical:—1923 (Manchon). I.e. to be to leeward. Imm. ex:—*loo'd*, 'beaten, defeated' (B. & L.): coll.: mid-1880s—ca. 1930. Ex the game of loo (EDD).

Look Duck and Vanish Brigade, the. The *Local Defence Volunteers*: late 1939–early 1940. See quot'n at **Dad's Army.**

look for Henry. (Of a confidence-trickster) to look for a victim: c.: from ca. 1920.

look-in, n. A chance of success: sporting. (*Bell's Life*, 12 Feb. 1870.) P.B.: in later C.20 usu. doubtful or negative, as 'Do you think he has a look-in?' or 'She never even had a look-in'.

look in, v.i. 'To use a wireless receiver adapted for television': coll.: Aug. 1928. *OED* Sup.

look like a wet week. To look miserable or wretched: coll.

look like death warmed up. To look seriously indisposed or even gravely ill: perhaps orig. Aus., but by ca. 1940 also Brit. coll. (B.P.) Cf. **feel like death . . .**

look like nothing on earth. To look wretched, ill; or, eccentric, ludicrous: coll. (—1927) >, by 1933, informal S.E. (Collinson.) Also as *feel like . . .*

look like the wrath of God. See **wrath of God.**

look out for. 'To take over a shipmate's watch for a spell. "Look out for me for ten minutes, there's a good chap" ' (Granville): RN coll.

look to be. To seem (as if); to look as though (it) will; as, e.g., a sports commentator about an approaching success, 'Oh, and it looks to be a good one . . . Yes! He's scored!'; hence, also, in political comment, 'The Prime Minister looks to be set for a clash with . . .': in sporting circles since ca. 1976; extensions since ca. 1979. Perhaps ex the ideolect or dial. usage of some individual commentator. (P.B.)

looker. A pretty girl: coll.: since ca. 1920. Short for *good looker.* 'I say, she's a real looker—oh, boy! what a smasher!'

looker-out. A cab-rank attendant: taxi-drivers' coll.: since ca. 1905. Hodge, 1939.

looking as if he'd left the room too late. I.e. as if he had been taken short: partly joc. and partly euph.: since ca. 1950. (Petch, 1970.)

looking-stick. 'Binoculars (rather surprisingly not telescope): RN: 1970s' (Peppitt). A pun on S.E. *walking-stick.* P.B.: in late C.19, however, a *look stick* did = telescope in RN s.

looks good, (it). It looks very promising (to me): coll.: adopted, ex US, ca. 1918. (*OED* Sup.) P.B.: also as in sports jargon, 'things are looking good for this top player now'.

loon. To fool about, like a *lunatic*: the underground, since early 1960s; by 1970, more gen. (*Groupie*, 1968.) P.B.: E.P. emphasises *lunatic*, but there is prob. influence from the Scot. and dial. n. *loon* and, since the term is adopted ex US, from the bird-name. 'The hippy penchant for play survives in the way sisters [in the Women's Lib movement] enjoy "bopping" and "looning" together, that is, dancing and clowning around for fun' (Carter, 1980). Cf.:-

loon about. Extension of prec., as in ' "OK, girls, just loon about and sign a few autographs," said the producer for Radio Orwell . . . ' (Duncan, 1979).

loon shit. 'The mud or muck on the bottom of a pond' (Leech, 1974): (mainly Eastern) Can. Its technical name is *gyttja.*

loop. A fool; a simpleton: Aus. low: since ca. 1920. B., 1942.—2. Short for **loop-the-loop,** 1.

loop-liner. A short pint, sold at about three-quarters of the price of a full pint: Anglo-Irish, esp. Dubliners': ca. 1920–50. A play on *porter*, the short pint being invariably of this beverage: the Loop Line, running through the centre of the city of Dublin, is an accommodation line linking two systems; similarly a *loop-liner* is an accommodation *porter* that lacks the dignity of a full pint.

loop-the-loop. Soup: r.s., Aus. and Brit. 'Gimme some more loopers' (Jones, 1971).—2. (Also written *loop-de-loop.*) 'Soixante-neuf': since late 1950s. Landy, 1971.

loopy. Slightly mad: s. (or coll.): late C.19–20. ?Ex *looby*, influenced by ironic allusion to Scots *loupy*, crafty. Occ. *looby.*—2. In *go loopy*, to become very excited, very angry, to 'get mad': schoolgirls': later C.20. (Brigid Irwin, 1980.)

loose. *On the loose*, on a drinking bout: Aus. (B., 1942.) Hence, by diminution, merely 'on a quite innocent spree': coll.:—2. In *let loose*, to express one's anger or other emotion freely, to 'let fly': coll.:—1939. Stivens, 1946.

loose off. To fire a machine-gun or rounds therefrom: RAF: since ca. 1938. (Jackson.) Of US orig.

loosies. 'Cigarettes bought "individually" are called loosies because they are bought loose, or at least [they] were when I was not much younger' (Holt, 1978).

loot. 'Scottish slang for money received on pay day' (H. & P.): adopted by the Services, ca. 1925; in later C.20, gen. and widespread, usu. joc., as 'hard earned loot' (*Time Out*, 30 May 1980). 'The money in the "game" or business: since late 1940s' (L.A., 1976).—2. Wedding presents, esp. those garnered collectively: Aus. joc.: since late 1940s. (B.P.)

lop it out. To expose one's penis for medical inspection: low: since ca. 1930.

loppy. Louse-infested; infected: Services': ca. 1930–45. (H. & P.) Ex Yorkshire dial. *loppy*, 'flea-ridden'.

lord and master, my or **the.** Husband, as in 'My lord and master will soon be home—and hungry': feminine joc. coll.: since ca. 1910. (B.P.)

Lord love a duck! A mild, mostly proletarian expletive. 'Taffrail', 1917.

Lord's My Shepherd, the. A pun on the initials of the *London, Midland & Scottish Railway*: railwaymen's: 1923–48 was the period of the company's existence. *Railway*, 2nd.

Lord's Own, the. HMS *Vengeance*: RN. Bowen, 'Vengeance is Mine, saith the Lord'. An old naval pun, re-applied to the aircraft-carrier *Vengeance*, 1944–56. (Knight, 1984.)

lorry. Motoring enthusiasts' pej. term for a dull car: later C.20. 'I do not share his enthusiasm for the MGC [sports car]—

which we all consider a sluggish lorry . . . ' (Editor, *Motor*, 18 Apr. 1981: P.B.).

lose. To be much superior to; overcome, defeat easily: coll.

lose a meal. To vomit: Aus., joc. euph. B., 1942.

lose (one's) **bottle.** See **bottle**, n, 4.

lose (one's) **cool.** To lose one's self-possession; to become nervous, (over-)excited, very angry: adopted, ex US, ca. 1955; in Aus., (?)a decade, later: hippy s. > gen. coll. Opp. *keep* (one's) *cool*. Cf. **cool**, adj., 4.

lose (one's) **hair.** To lose one's temper: orig. s. >, early 1930s, coll. Opp. *keep* (one's) *hair on*. Cf. synon. *lose* (one's) *wool*; *keep* (one's) *wool on*.

lose (one's) **hook.** To be demoted from Leading Seaman: RN. (*Heart*, 1962.) I.e. the anchor badge of rank. (P.B.)

lose it. To come off one's motorcycle accidentally: motorcyclists': later C.20. (Dunford.)

lose (one's) **name** or (earlier) **number** or **monnicker.** To be 'crimed', charged with a Service 'crime': Army: the *name* form since ca. 1920. The latter perhaps from the inspecting officer's formula to the accompanying NCO, 'Take his name, Sergeant!', when charging a man in the ranks with, e.g., having an 'idle' (i.e. dirty) bayonet. (B. & P.; P.B.)

lose out, v.i. To lose; be swindled or merely fooled: coll.: Aus.: late C.19-20. *SOD* records it in sense of 'to fail' as US, 1889. In later C.20 also Brit., and, as v.t., *lose out on*.

lose (one's) **rag.** To lose one's temper: Glasgow,—1934, > more gen. widespread. Ex *get* (one's) *rag out*, to bluster or grow angry.

lose the run of (one)**self.** To lose one's self-control; to 'run amok': Anglo-Irish. Gardner notes hearing, 9 Nov. 1978, the phrase 'Don't lose the run of yourself' used facetiously on an RTE phone-in programme, to a quiz-contestant who had just won a small sum of money.

loser. A handicap, obstacle, disappointment: low: from ca. 1920. *Gilt Kid*, 1936, 'It was a bit of a loser, feeling bored before the trial had started.'

loss-leader. Something displayed prominently, and at cut-price rate, to encourage further buying of other stock: Can. (Leechman.) Prob. ex US (*SOD*); by early 1970s Brit. commercial j. (P.B.)

lot. A group of associated persons, or of things of the same kind: from ca. 1570: S.E. until ca. 1875, then (except for merchandise and livestock) coll. P.B.: in mid- and later C.20 much favoured by Service NCOs for such orders as 'Right, you lot! Outside—on the double!' A useful group-vocative.—2. Independently, as in 'I know the *lot* you mean, I was there' (*Sessions*, 17 Feb. 1902), or (ironically/sarcastically) 'Yes, I was in the Suez do of '56—nice little lot *that* was!' (P.B.): coll.—3. In *red lot* and *white lot*, resp. a gold and a silver watch: c.:—1933 (Leach). Tempest, 1950, lists 'the lot. Watch and chain together'.—4. A taxicab: taxidrivers': since ca. 1915. (Hodge, 1939.) Ex the auction-room sense.—5. In *do the lot*, to lose all one's money: coll.

loud-mouth. One, usu. male, who speaks loudly, excessively and either boastfully or bullying or very indiscreetly: coll.: adopted, ca. 1944, ex US.

loud pedal. The accelerator: Aus. motorists': since ca. 1940.

louie (pron. *looee*). A lieutenant: Forces': adopted ca. 1939 from US.

Louis. A harlot's bully: low: adopted,—1935, ex US. Cf. Fr. *Alphonse*.

lounge. A lounge suit: tailors' coll., now verging on S.E. *Tailor and Cutter*, 29 Nov. 1928.—2. 'The prisoner's box in a criminal court' (B., 1942): Aus. c. Ironic.

lounge-lice. An Aus. var. (pl.) of the next: since ca. 1930. Baker.

lounge-lizard. A sleek adventurer frequenting lounges in the expectation of women, their money and caresses: US s. (1923), anglicised by 1925; by 1935, coll.

lounge Lizzie. A (usu. female) writer of gossip for a newspaper: journalistic, mainly: since ca. 1925. (Horler, 1938.) Ex prec.

louse-bag. A term of opprobrium or deep scorn for a person. Kersh, 1942.

louse-bound. 'Lousy' as a disparaging adj.: since ca. 1920. (Raper, 1973.)

louse-ladder. 'A stitch fallen in a stocking' (Grose, 1st ed.): ca. 1780–1840. Extant in dial.—2. A run in a woman's stocking: since ca. 1935. Ex sense 1: either a revival or a subterranean survival. (These words which go underground for a generation or a century or even longer provide one of the prettiest puzzles in the whole network of a language.)

louse-ladders. Side-whiskers: since ca. 1920. Contrast prec. and cf. synon. *louse-traps*, from later C.20.

louse up. To ruin an opportunity, a plan, an operation; in short, to spoil *anything*: since ca. 1919. Ex the Tommy's vivid memories of WW1. Often as *louse it up*.

louser. An objectionable person: Anglo-Irish: since ca. 1920. Blake, 1968, ref. the year 1939.

lousy as a bandicoot, (as). Extremely lousy (lit. sense): Aus. coll.: since ca. 1916. (B., 1943.) Cf.:-

lousy as a cuckoo, (as). Brit. Army var. of prec.: since ca. 1915. (B. & P.) Cf. the Yorkshire phrase *as scabbed as a cuckoo* (*EDD*).

Lousy Brown, the. The Rose and Crown (tavern or inn): r.s., esp. Londoners'. (Franklyn.) *Brown* here = brown ale.

lousy with. Full of: 1915: orig. military, as in 'lousy with guns'; esp. in 'lousy with money'. Ex the prevalence of lice.

love a duck! (Usu. prec. *Cor*, *Lor(d)* or *Gawd*, and occ. spelt *luvvaduck*.) A mild proletarian expletive. The var. spelling by, e.g., Scott, 1934.

love-bubbles. Female breasts of a pleasing contour: Army (not very common): since ca. 1930.

love-in. 'A gathering associated with groovy scene' (Fryer, 1967): beatniks' and then hippies': since early 1960s. On analogy of the prototypal -*in* compounds *sit-in* and *teach-in*. Cf. **think-in.**

love in a punt. Very weak beer; orig. and specifically 'a brew sold in the Portsmouth area (mid-1950s)': RN lowerdeck. 'That is, fucking-near-water', as a correspondent told me in 1973. A double pun and prob. an allusion to *cunt*.

love-letter. (Gen. in pl.) A bill of exchange: bank-clerks':—1935. Ironic.

love-truck. A 'small covered-in lorry' (*New Statesman*, 30 Aug. 1941): Services': WW2. Cf. **passion-waggon**, 2.

love-up, n. Intimate caresses; love-making: Aus. low coll. Caddie, 1953. ' "Come on, what about a little bit of a love-up?" he went on.' Ex:-

love up, v. To caress intimately, make love to: Aus.: low coll. Prichard, 1932.

love weed. Cannabis: drugs c. (Stockley, 1986.) US since—1938 (Spears).

lovely, n. A very pretty girl: from ca. 1930. Ex:—2. (Gen. pl.) A débutante; a young married woman in Society: from ca. 1926; ob. by 1939.

lovely, adj. Attractive, delightful; excellent: coll.: C.17-20.—2. Hence: well; fitting; satisfactory; as in 'How are you, then?'—'I'm lovely, ta'; or 'Here's your change, dear'— 'Lovely!'. In the latter = almost 'thank you' in itself: coll.: since late 1970s. (P.B.)

lovely money. Good money; esp. plenty of money: Londoners': from ca. 1931. cf. **Loadsamoney.**

lover, in address, was adopted, ca. 1965, ex US: coll., not s. Often it connotes little, or indeed nothing, more than 'man', as in Hill, 1973, '[The landlord] grinned and fetched me a drink over. "Have that one on me, me lover," he said'. (L.A., 1976.) P.B.: but this could be West Country dial.

lover boy. 'Man of age and appearance to be disposed to love: sometimes mock-affectionate or contemptuous' (L.A., 1967); 'A would-be Romeo or one of the Casanova type' (Petch, 1969): coll. rather than s.: adopted, ca. 1960, ex US.

lover under the lap. A Lesbian: Aus. Not very gen.

loverly. A late C.19-20 sol., also an ironically joc. s. form of **lovely** (q.v.), due partly to mis-pron., partly to S.E. *loverly*, like or in the manner of a lover. See also **luvly.** Given impetus in later C.20 by Eliza Doolittle's song, 'Oh, wouldn't it be loverly' in the musical *My Fair Lady*, based on Shaw's *Pygmalion.*

lover's leap. 'The first early-morning train from London to Portsmouth' (Granville): RN wardrooms'.

lover's nuts. See **blue balls.**

lovey-dovey stuff. 'Sentimental fiction published for the servant-girl type' (Petch, 1946): book-world coll.: since ca. 1925.

low. Opp. of **high,** n., in all senses: the very depths of depression, whether mental, physical, or of market or fortune generally: coll.: later C.20.

low as . . . (, as). 'There's no way we're flying out of here today, the clouds are as low as a penguin's backside . . . ' (Harding, 1981, reporting an observation by an Aus. pilot).

low-brow (or solid), n. and adj. One who is not, occ. one who does not claim to be, intellectual: orig. (1913), US; anglicised (both n. and adj.) ca. 1923, as s.; by 1932, coll.; now almost S.E. (*OED* Sup.; Mencken's *The American Language.*) Opp. **highbrow,** q.v.

low-down, the. A mean trick, as 'They did the low-down on him': s. >, by ca. 1935, coll.—2. Information, esp. incriminating or scandalous: adopted, ex US, ca. 1930 as s.; by 1950, coll. Browne, 1934, 'He will lurk for days in the most unlikely places . . . to get the low-down on the home-life and marital customs of the pink-chested buzzard or the mottled wattle-rat.'

low flying. 'No speed limits enforced now [during the guerrilla war], so you put your foot down and hope for the best. The Rhodesians call it "low flying" ' (*Listener*, 9 Nov. 1978); travelling along the roads as fast as possible to avoid being shot: pre-Zimbabwe Rhodesia.

low-heel. A prostitute: Aus. B., 1942.—2. A dead-beat: Aus.: since ca. 1920.

Low Road, the. The 'Glasgow line via Dalry' (*Railway*, 2nd): mid-C.20. Prob. ex the famous Scot. song. 'Ye take the high road, and I'll take the low road . . . '

lower the boom on. 'To stop; prevent from doing, as in "If I lower the boom on him, he'll not do it again." Western N. Am., poss. from ship or logging industry. First heard by me mid-1950s, but prob. much older' (Leech, 1986).

lowerdeck wireless. 'The grapevine': RN: ca. 1910–40. (Bennett, 1919.) A naval shape of *bush telegram.*

lowerdeckese. The slang used by the lowerdeck (non-commissioned officers and men): RN officers' coll. (since ca. 1900) >, by 1945, S.E. (Granville.)

lowest form of animal life, the. A reporter: journalistic: since ca. 1925.—2. An Aircraftman, 2nd Class: RAF: since ca. 1935.—3. Hence, joc. for apprentices, trainees, office boys *et hoc genus omne*: since ca. 1945.

lowie. A prostitute: low Aus.: since ca. 1930. Cf. **low-heel,** 1. Tennant, 1953.

lubber. A black-marketeer in furniture: furniture trade: mid-1940s. (*John Bull*, 1 Apr. 1944.) Cf. synon. **dabbler.**

lube. Lubrication, as in 'a *lube* job': motorists': since ca. 1920; by 1950, coll.—2. 'A drink, esp. of beer' (B., 1959): Aus.: since late 1940s. *Lubrication* of the throat.

luck of a fat priest or **of a pox doctor, the.** 'Both said of one consistently and uncannily fortunate, esp. in gambling' (Cdr C. Parsons, RN, ret., 1973). Both go back to (I'd guess) mid-C.19; and both are semi-proverbial coll.

luck out. 'To strike it lucky, as in "He sure lucked out on that one!" But I also hear it being used to mean the exact opposite, as in "Boy, you really lucked out that time!" (said sarcastically): to run *out* of luck. Since late 1970s: N. Am.' (Leech, 1986).

lucky. A recruit: Army: WW2. (Cobb, 1975.) In a letter to P.B., 1981, Prof. Cobb amplifies: '[Luckies] was certainly the word in use in 1941–2 for new recruits. When we reached the entrance to Chepstow . . . initial training camp, we were greeted with "Come on you luckies" and of course . . . we called our successors "luckies".' Prob. ex NCOs' ironic summons 'Come along, my lucky lads—let's be 'avin' you!'

lucky dip. 'The practice of aircraft loaders who snatch suitcases, bags or packages at random, on the off-chance that they might contain something worth stealing: air crews' ' (Green, 1984).

lucky for some. See TOMBOLA, in Appx.

lucky lads, the. Those who were too young for WW1 and too old for WW2: coll., mainly during the latter. (Petch, 1969.)

Lucy. LSD: drugs c. 'From *Lucy in the Sky with Diamonds*, Beatles song of 1967 widely assumed to be about LSD' (Hibbert, 1983).

Lucy Locket. Pocket: r.s.: later C.20. (Jones, 1971.) Ex the well-known nursery rhyme.

luff. 'To do someone's work as well as your own [in order] to allow a workmate an early relief: Thames watermen: 1970s' (Peppitt)—and considerably earlier, I think. A pun on the S.E. nautical sense, (of ship) to turn against the wind or, of a seaman, so to turn it.

lug. In *on the lug*, 'on the borrow' or 'ear-biting' (seeking a loan): N. Country.

lug around (a person). 'To have an unpleasant person in one's company because of orders received for a sale to be made' (Powis): low coll.: later C.20.

lug (one's) **ear.** To ask for, to borrow, money from: Aus. low. (B., 1942.) Cf. **lug.**

lug-(h)ole. Ear-hole; 'much used by certain comedians in the 1940s and '50s . . . Less often heard in the 1960s' (R.S., 1968). An affectation of proletarianism? The term has been common throughout C.20 and prob. since mid-C.19.

lugger. A sponger; defaulter; 'one who drinks with others but never buys a round' (*M.T.*): market-traders'. Perhaps ex Midlands dial. *lugger*, a burden; more prob., cf. **lug.**

lulu. A very good show-place, where much money is made: Can. carnival s.: since ca. 1925. Ex US s. *lulu*, anything very attractive—or profitable.—2. The US sense was adopted in Aus. ca. 1944 (B.P.), and in UK, esp. with ref. to a dizzy, pretty girl, 'she's a real lulu', mid-C.20 (P.B.).—3. Hence, *it's a lulu*, 'It's a good one, it's a winner, of wrestling hold; noted from TV, but no doubt with applications in other sports' (L.A., 1969).—4. As *the lulu* (or *Lulu*), a water-closet: upper classes': since ca. 1925. (Coward, 1939.) An elab. of *loo.*

lumber, n. 'Hide-out for stolen property' (Sharpe, 1938). A shortening of *lumber-house*, c. synon. first recorded 1811.—2. Trouble: low: since ca. 1935. Crookston, 1967, 'One night I got into a bit of lumber because I started giggling at the efforts of a fat lady who was a terrible singer.' Often *in dead lumber.*

lumber (as v.i.; but usu. in form *lumbering*). To court a girl: Teddy-boys': since ca. 1954. 'Lumbering, mate. You know—courting. Going steady with a chick.'—2. As v.t.: to land a person with an unwelcome burden, an onerous or thankless task, etc.: gen. coll.: later C.20. Cf. **clobber with** or *for*, and see **lumbered.** Ex either S.E., 'to encumber'; or to land *in lumber* (see n., 2); or a back-formation ex *to be* or to *get lumbered.* (P.B.)—3. 'Biddy the Chiver [see **chiv**] would have a go at anything "lumbering" a man and all the rest of it—i.e. luring him into some dark alley and then stripping him' (Samuel, 1981). See quot'n at **string up,** 2, and cf. **lumberer,** 2.

lumber gaff. A prostitute's professional bedroom or 'bedsitter': prostitutes': since ca. 1930. (Norman, 1959.) Soon > more gen. Cf. prec., 3.

lumber out. To eject (a person): Aus. B., 1942.

lumbered. Arrested; in prison: c.:—1812 (Vaux). Re-emerged(?) in Aus., earlier C.20. See AUSTRALIAN UNDERWORLD, in Appx.—2. Short of cash; financially embarrassed: London's East End: since ca. 1946. (Herd, 1957.)—3. In any sort of trouble: see **lumber,** v., 2, which gives, as passive, to *be* or *get lumbered*: coll.: since ca. 1950. At first, esp. in sense 'landed with an onerous task, an unwelcome burden'; by ca. 1970, often used more loosely.

lumberer. A confidence man: c.:—1933 (Leach).—2. A brothel tout; one who lures men down alleys in order that others may rob them: Aus. c.: since ca. 1920. See **lumber, v.,** 3.

lump, the. 'The highly organised pool of labour in the building trade' (R.S., 1968); non-union, mobile labour: orig. building industry, then esp. in the media. Early in 1967 BBC 1 produced a TV play so titled. Ex the j. *lump labour*?

lump, v. To carry: Aus. Prob. influenced by *hump* in the same sense. P.B.: also Brit., usu. of heavy or cumbersome load: *lump* (it) *about*.

lump of lead. (Loaf of) bread: Aus. r.s.

lumpectomy. The surgical removal of an unspecified tumour: doctors'. 'LIBIDO means "lump in breast one day only". I coined this myself in 1968 and was surprised to see it still in current use for day case "lumpectomies" ' (Hamblin, 1988).

Lumpers, the. The Household Cavalry: Army: C.19–20. (F. & G.) 'Because of the tremendous weight their horses have to carry' (Carew).

lumps. In *get* or *take* (one's) *lumps*, to be given, or to receive, punishment or other unpleasantness, either physically or by reprimand; loosely, to be badly treated: orig. and mainly US, but some Brit. usage late 1960s–early '70s. See esp. W. & F. (P.B.)

Lumpy Gravy, the. The Royal Navy: RAF r.s.: 1970s, says Peppitt; yet I think it arose late in, or very soon after, WW1.

lunatic hat. A (very) wide-brimmed hat: Aus.: since ca. 1930. B., 1943.

lunatic soup. Strong drink: NZ. B., 1941, 'Lack of vigour or colour could not . . . be a charge levelled against such terms for strong drink as *lunatic soup, Africa speaks, plonk, steam, red Ned*, or *sheep wash*.' In Aus. it specifically = 'cheap, red wine' (B., 1942). Elsewhere (Harrison, 1943) we find the var. *lunatic's broth*; and earlier, *Daily Telegraph*, 20 June 1902, has *in lunatic's broth* = drunk. Cf. Aus. *madman's broth*, brandy.

lunch. A paper sold at lunchtime, esp. one giving the cricket scores: newsvendors' coll.: 1921.—2. Any meal other than breakfast; a term used for food taken at almost any time of the day, 'used in the older sense of a "lump", especially if it is, in some way, out of the usual run of events' (Leechman, 1959): Can. coll.:—1932. Ex dial. (*EDD*).—3. 'What you become after a wipe out' (*Pix*, 28 Sep. 1963): Aus. teenage surfers': 1961+. Prob. ex US s. *lunch*, = 'a fool' (W. & F., 1975).—4. See **out to lunch.**

lung. The female bosom, as in 'Get a load of that doll! She's got plenty of lung' (prominent breasts): Aus. low: since ca. 1955. 'Ex proximity of breasts to lungs?' (B.P.) Hibbert, 1983, notes synon. *lungs* as later C.20 Brit.

lung-disturber. Penis: low. Ex the same ribald song as **kidney-wiper.**

lungs. See **lung.**

luppers. Fingers: Parlyaree. (K. Williams, 1980.)

lurid limit, the. The very limit: Aus.: since ca. 1925. (Baker.) Cf. English *the ruddy limit*.

lurk, n. 'A dodge, scheme, stratagem' (Wilkes): since ca. 1940: Aus. low > coll. Hence *up to all lurks*, wide-awake, alert; and *a good lurk*, a smart plan, a good idea. (B.P.)—2. A hanger-on; an eavesdropper; a sneak: Aus. low. Baker.

lurk, v. In *be lurked*, 'To be ordered to do some unpleasant job without a chance of avoiding it' (Bowen): nautical: mid-C.19–20. *Musings*, 'Always being lurked for other people's watches.' Later also RAF, prob. via RNAS (Tredrey, 1939). Cf. (?ex) the † S.E. *lurk*, to shirk work.—2. V.i., to sell, on the move, to an occasional customer: grafters'. (Allingham.)—3. As v.t., 'to impose on another's kindness: RN' (Knight, 1984, says 'still current'). An extension of sense 1.

lurker. A petty crook: Aus. low. B., 1953.—2. 'A new breed of market stallholders, known to veterans of the trade as "lurkers", has arrived with a new breed of market' (*Radio Times*, 30 July 1983); i.e. traders not 'born to the job', and operating in private, weekend or one day a week flea-markets. Prob. ex **lurk, v.,** 2.

lurkie, -y. A very wide-awake person, 'up to' all the 'lurks' or tricks: Aus.: since ca. 1940. (B.P.)

lurkman. A petty criminal: Aus.: later C.19–early 20. Cf. **lurker,** 1.—2. Hence, one who cheats at cards; a cardsharp: Aus. B., 1953.—3. A racketeer or a 'shady' schemer. Also *lurk artist*: Aus.

lurkmanship. The art and practice of the **lurk, n.,** 1 and 3. B., 1959.

lurn. Scrotum: since ca. 1910. Origin? R.S. tentatively suggests Fr. *luron*, 'a strapping fellow, one of the boys'.

lush, n. Beer: RN lowerdeck. (Granville.) *Lush* has meant strong drink since late C.18.—2. Hence, in C.19, it > a very heavy drinker, a sense that in later C.20 has been adopted back from US where its use is widespread. Also used fig., in such expressions as 'the car was a lush for petrol'—it consumed much more than the average car: coll.: later C.20. (P.B.)

lush, adj. (Of a girl) extremely attractive: since ca. 1915. Esp. 'a lush bint', which dates from WW1, and was still in Service use in 1960s. Granville, 'Rivals "smashing" in popularity on the lower deck.' Granville derives it ex *luscious* and he may be right. I propose, however, an extension of *lush* as in S.E. 'lush grass', where it = 'fresh and juicy': cf. *zoftig*.—2. (Of creature comforts) rich; appetising; plentiful: Services': since 1939. Ex 1.

lush puppy. 'A young inebriate. [Ex **lush, n.,** 2 +] Hush Puppy, a proprietary brand of suede shoe' (Hibbert, 1983).

lush-roller. A pickpocket operating on drunkards, half-wits, paralytics: c. (Lodge, 1936.) See **lush, n.,** 2.

lush (someone) up. To stand someone a treat (of strong liquor); as v.i., *lush up*, to drink heavily: since ca. 1930. Granville derives the v.t., in its RN lowerdeck usage, ex **lush, n.,** 1.

luvly. 'With this spelling it takes on a Cockney pronunciation or a Cockney setting . . . In the musical version of Shaw's *Pygmalion*, "My Fair Lady", it was used for an extra beat [see **loverly**], but without authority from either Shaw or Cockney' (L.A., 1976). 'Mandrake', 1975, has 'Everything luvly in the Garden' (Covent).

Lyceum Charley. A (young) male entrant in, and for, the 'Mecca dancing' contests at the Lyceum Ballroom (formerly the Lyceum Theatre); or any youth in full evening dress, whether he intends to dance or not: Cockneys': since ca. 1960.

lying hound; lying fuck-pig. Bitter denunciation of someone who has lied, esp. when the lie has been detrimental to the plaintiff: low: since mid-C.20, prob. earlier. (P.B.)

M

M. Morphine: drugs c. (Stockley, 1986.) US throughout C.20.—2. See entries at 'C or **K . . .**'; **M.B.E.**

M.B.; suffer from M.B. Tipsy; to be tipsy: Aus.: since ca. 1930. Ex the well-known brand of beer, Melbourne Bitter. B., 1953.

M.B.E. ' "My [own] Bloody Efforts"—as opposed to *O.B.E.*, "Other Buggers' Efforts". Compare the Order of St Michael and St George [q.v. at **C.M.G.**]' (P.B., 1975). Also, since mid-C.20, *M*akes a *B*alls of *E*verything (Bishop, 1984). This irreverent set of ribald and adverse comments [E.P. refers here also to *C.M.G.*, etc.] seems to have originated among Army officers [P.B.: and the Diplomatic Corps] during the disillusioned period, 1946–60, when the Brit. possessions were being gaily surrendered, yet the Army had still to operate in Malaya, Cyprus, Aden, and other troubled areas. See also **old boiled egg**.

M.C. or **m.c.,** n. and v. (Sometimes *emcee*.) Master of ceremonies, and to act as one: provincial journalists' and function-organisers': the v. since ca. 1950, the n. very much earlier. 'The dance was ably emcee'd by . . . ' (P.B.)

M.C.P. 'Male chauvinist pig' (common usage among 'women's libbers'): Aus. since early 1970s (B.P.); and Brit. since late 1970s: adopted ex US.

M.F.U. 'Military fuck-up' or muddle: Services', mostly Army: WW2.

M.O.T.d. (Of a motor vehicle) officially tested: coll., hence occ. joc. of things other than vehicles, e.g. a wife of some years' standing: since latish 1960s. (P.B.) Ex the Ministry of Transport (test).

M 1. 'A hovercraft saved a woman's life after a difficult birth in a midnight dash up the "M1"—the great Rejang river that is the only highway in an anarchy of peaks and jungle completely devoid of road or rail in central Sarawak' (Bloodworth, 1975): Brit. troops in the Borneo Campaign, 1962–5. (P.B.)

M.Y.O.B. Mind your own business. Also *M.Y.O.B.B.* (. . . bloody business).

ma'alish, maalish, maaleesh. See **maleesh**.

mabsoot or **mabsut.** Happy: Services': WW1 & 2. Ex Arabic.

Mac; m-. McMaster University, Hamilton, Ontario: Can. coll.—2. A non-cultured Can. (?ex US) form of address to a man whose name is unknown to the speaker: since ca. 1930; and so to UK in the mid-1960s, via the hippy movement.—3. Abbr. of *tarmac* (lit. and fig. senses): RAF: 1930s.—4. (Also *mack.*) Coll. abbr. of a *mac(k)intosh*: late C.20.

Mac. – Paps., the. The Canadian Mackenzie-Papineau Battalion of the XV International Brigade in Spain, 1936–8.

McAlpine Fusilier. 'Irish labourer employed in the construction business (from the name of the famous building firm)' (Powis): joc. coll.: later C.20.

macaroni. An Italian: somewhat low: C.19–20. Also, esp. in 1940–4, an Italian aircraft (Jackson). Ex the national dish; also, two leading makes of Italian warplanes were Macchi and Caproni (P.B.).—2. £25 – a 'pony': r.s.—3. Lengths of electric flex: cinematographic: since ca. 1925. Meynell, 1937.—4. Nonsense; folly: Aus.: since ca. 1930. B., 1943.—5. (Also as v.) Excrete, excreta: prison s.: later C.20. McVicar, 1974.

Macaroni Boats or **Liners, the.** The Norddeutscher Lloyd vessels: nautical: ca. 1890–1914. They carried many emigrants from Italy to US. Cf. prec., 1.

macaroon. A new recruit: RAN: WW2. B., 1943.—2. In *confiscate the macaroon*, an elab. (ca. 1918–24) of *take the biscuit*. (Ware.) B. & L. note var. *monopolise the . . .*

Macdonald. The rigid, two piece iron bed used in RAF barrack rooms, 'because they, like the supposed characteristic of the Scots, had no give in them' (Adkin, 1983): RAF: 1920s–30s.—2. In *do a MacDonald*, to desert one's party: Labour leaders': since ca. 1930. Like most political gibes, this one is unfair. Long since superseded by the names of subsequent defectors.

mace, n. In *on (the) mace*: on credit: c.:—1893 (Emerson). Still, 1983, current among market-traders (*M.T.*).—2. In *on the mace*, on the 'mace' racket: c.: C.19–20. Vaux, 1812; *Yorkshire Post*, late May 1937, has *getting stuff on the mace*, obtaining goods by false pretences.

mace, v.t., occ. v.i. To swindle, defraud: from ca. 1790: c. Still current, later C.20, among market-traders (*M.T.*).—2. Hence, to owe (money) to (someone): market-traders': late C.19–20. 'He maces me a flim [£5]' (*M.T.*).—3. Powis, 1977, glosses *macing*, 'Stealing or cheating (especially at the three-card trick)': c.

macer. A welsher: c.:—1874 (H., 5th ed.). Powis, a century later, glosses the term, 'Thief or cheat'.

MacGimp. A pimp: low r.s.: adopted, ca. 1930, ex US. Franklyn 2nd, 'It is rarely used in Britain.'

MacGinnis (or **McGinnis** or **Maginnis**) **on, put the.** To render an opponent *hors-de-combat*: Aus. (B., 1942.) Ex wrestling?—2. Hence, to put pressure on: since ca. 1910.

machine gun. A syringe: drugs world: later C.20. (McConville, 1980.) Also shortened to *machine*; cf. **artillery**, and:-

machinery. Equipment for injecting: drugs c. (Stockley, 1986.) US since—1937 (Spears).

macho, n. and adj. 'Male bravado' (Leechman): Can., adopted, via US, ex Mexican Sp., since ca. 1972; the term

273

crossed the Atlantic soon afterwards, 'We don't have to bother with the strutting, the cockiness, the macho routines' (Schroeder, 1976). Ex the Continental, hence American, Sp. *Machismo*, belief in male supremacy, and the need to demonstrate virility; Sp. *macho* = male.

Mack. See **mac.**

Mack Sennett. See MOVING-PICTURE SLANG, §8, in Appx. Coll., not s.

macker. A familiar Aus. form of **macaroni**, 2, but as horse, not £25. B., 1945.

Mackie. A bottle, or a drink, of Mackeson's stout: public houses' and spirits–wine–beer merchants': since ca. 1945—or even much earlier.

mackintosh trade, the. 'The less flamboyant, the less well dressed or smart, patrons of music-halls and theatres' (L.A., 1976): coll.: since late 1940s.

macky. Make-up: theatrical and TV. (Green, 1984.) Ex Fr. *maquillage*.

mad, app. as n., in *get out* (one's) *mad*. To become angry: Aus.: since ca. 1920. B., 1959.

mad as a cut snake. Very mad; exceedingly angry: Aus.: from ca. 1890. Here, *cut* = castrated. Other Aus. similes are *mad as a beetle—a Chinaman—a dingbat—a goanna—a gum-tree full of galahs—a meat-axe—a snake* (B., 1942). Also *silly as a curlew—a two-bob watch—a wet hen.* B., 1959.

mad as a maggot, with or without prec. *as.* Extremely eccentric: hence, egregiously foolish: NZ. (Slatter.)

mad as a meat-axe. Extremely angry; dangerously crazy: Aus.: since the 1920s. (Culotta, 1960.) Cf. **mad as a cut snake.**

mad as a wet hen. Intensely annoyed: Can. (Leechman.) Cf. **mad as a cut snake.** Leech, 1981, adds *madder than* . . .

mad as mud. Exceedingly angry: from ca. 1925. Keverne, 1928, 'Joan will be as mad as mud with me for telling.'

mad dog. 'An account which the debtor refuses to pay' (B., 1942): Aus. See **tie up a dog.**—2. 'An unpaid score at a public house' (Baker): Aus.

mad haddock. A very eccentric, a crazy, or a very foolish person: Aus. Baker.

mad major, the. 'Any very eccentric or excessively daring officer, especially if . . . of that rank' (B. & P.): military coll.: 1914–18. Ex a legend about a foolhardy and bloodthirsty officer. P.B.: the legend lingers: one of my schoolmasters, late 1940s, was so nicknamed; and I met the sobriquet several times during my army service, 1953–75.

mad Mick. A pick: Aus. r.s.: since late C.19. (B., 1942.) Hence *mad Mick and banjo*, a pick and shovel: Aus., esp. Army.—2. Penis: Aus. r.s., on *prick*: since ca. 1910. Franklyn.

mad mile, the. That part of the Perth–Fremantle road which runs through Claremont: W. Aus.: since ca. 1920. Baker.—2. Hence(?), the round made by a man either on draft, in or out of a depot, or in being demobilised: R. Aus. N: WW2.—3. Any such stretch of a road as was continually being shelled by the enemy: Army: WW2.—4. A straight, flat stretch of road where cars are likely to speed unchecked; heard with ref. to a realigned length of road south of Chichester: coll.: ca. 1970. (Raab.)

mad minute. Bayonet drill, esp. in its finale: Aus. Army: WW2. B., 1943.

mad money. A girl's return fare, carried lest her soldier friend got 'mad', i.e. too amorous for her: NZ soldiers': 1916–18. Mostly a legend, and concerning only English girls. The term has, since ca. 1918, meant money that a girl carries as a precaution against any such quarrel with her boy friend as might leave her monetarily stranded, and been widely used also in Aus. and Can.—2. Money saved up for 'splurging' while on holiday, or on some other special occasion; 'as long as me mad money lasts, I'm going to have a good time': coll.: since ca. 1950. (P.B.)

mad nurse. A teacher, usu. female, in a school for mentally handicapped children: mostly primary schoolteachers': since ca. 1920.

madam, n. Nonsense; line of talk: c.: from ca. 1930. (*Gilt Kid*, 1936.) Hence, *it's* or *that's all madam*, it's all nonsense or bunkum or 'eye-wash': since ca. 1935: orig. low, but by 1940 gen. Cf. **Madame de Luce.**

madam, v. To tell a tall story; 'pitch the tale': c.: from ca. 1930. (Sharpe, 1938.) Ex prec.

Madame de Luce. Deceptive talk: r.s., on *spruce*: late C.19–20. (Franklyn.) Since ca. 1930, usu. **madam,** q.v. Cf.:–

Madame Misharty. 'The personification of sales-talk, exaggerated claims, wild predictions, blarney, flattery and claptrap. "Don't give me the Madame Misharty" ' (*M.T.*): market-traders'. Perhaps ex an actual fortune-teller. Cf. prec.

madder than . . . May be applied to many of the **mad as . . .** entries as an intensive.

made. Lucky: tramps' c.:—1933 (*Week-End Review*, 18 Nov.). Hence, perhaps, as in 'We've got it made', everything is satisfactory; often conditional, as 'Once he's done *that*, well, then he's got it made': coll.: later C.20. (P.B.)

made up. Promoted: Services'. 'He was made up to corporal one day, and busted straight back down again the next' (P.B.).

made up strong. Heavily yet effectively painted and powdered: (low) coll.

madhouse! The call for three (one *plus* double one): darts players': since ca. 1930.

Madhouse, the. The Public Relations Office at Algiers: Army officers': 1943–4. P-G-R.—2. Granville glosses it as 'The Admiralty, Whitehall, London', but it is frequently applied to any headquarters, administrative office, or even one's own establishment ('Welcome to the madhouse!'): coll.: later C.20. (P.B.)

madman's broth. Brandy: Aus. (Durack, 1955.) Cf. **lunatic soup.**

Mae West. A life-jacket worn by aircrews: RAF: since 1937 or 1938. 'A pilot "goes to the movies" . . . wearing a "Mae West" – a life-jacket which bulges in the right places – in case he lands in the water' (Michie, 1941); Jackson, 1943, 'The film actress Mae West being especially notable for her buxom bosom thereby assuring for herself a place in the dictionary. Now used officially.'—2. Hence, a lifebelt issued to troops at sea: Army: 1940–5.—3. A breast: r.s.: ca. 1930–50. Franklyn.

mafeesh! Finished; done with; dead: Eastern Front military in WW1. (B. & P.) Ex Arabic. P.B.: the term continued in Army use until well into later C.20, esp. in *mafeesh feloos*, no money!, or, occ., 'free'.

mafia. Occ. joc. use: see e.g. quot'n at **edge,** n.

mafish is an occ. var. of *mafeesh*.

mag, n. A magneto: motorists' coll.: 1919.—2. The magazine of a rifle or machine-gun: Services'. As in the joc. parody of the 'immediate actions to be performed' when a bren-gun jammed: 'Mag. off, butt off, fuck off!' (P.B.)

mag, v. To talk to or at: Aus. 'You magged the poor boy into a daze. You and your silly stories' (Williamson, 1959). A survival from C.18–19 Eng. coll.

Magger of Bagger, the. The Master of Balliol: Oxford undergraduates':—1920 (Marples, 2). Cf.:–

Maggers' Memugger, the. The Martyrs' Memorial: Oxford Undergraduates': from late 1890s. (Ware.) The 'OXFORD -ER'.

maggie, n. A magnetic detector: wireless operators': from ca. 1925. (Bowen.) Cf. **mag,** n., 1.—2. As *M-*, HMS *Magnificent*; the White Star liner *Majestic*: resp. RN (C.20) and nautical (late C.19–20). Bowen.—3. A Miles Magister elementary training aircraft: RAF: since ca. 1938. (E.P., 1942.) I.e. '*Magister*'.—4. A *magnetic mine*: RN: 1939 +.—5. A machine-gun nest: Army: 1940–5. (P-G-R.) *Maggie* is the diminutive of *Mag*: here we have *mag*, derived thus: *machine*-gun nest.—6. Mostly in pl. *Maggies*, matrons at Borstal institutions: since ca. 1930. Home Office.—7. A magpie: Aus. coll. Cf. *cocky*, a cockatoo.—8. 'The nickname

"Maggie" was given to the pound coin in a House of Lords debate shortly after its issue [June 1983], on the grounds that it was "hard, rough at the edges and pretending to be a sovereign" ' (*Guardian*, 2 Feb. 1984); the pound coin is called Maggie 'because it is thick, it is brassy and it thinks it is a sovereign' (Holliday, 1984): an (ephemeral?) political squib, a punning jibe at the then Prime Minister, Mrs Margaret Thatcher. (Raab.)

Maggie, adj. Pertaining to Newcastle United Football Club: sporting: later C.20. Corrigan, 1979, quotes a local teenager describing his leisure activities: 'We find a few Maggie supporters and kick them in', and glosses ' "Maggies" are Newcastle United supporters: the team's black and white are supposed to make them look like magpies'. Cf. *Magpies*, the team's nickname in sporting circles.

Maggie Ann. Margarine: from ca. 1910: military >, by 1919, gen. (B. & P.) Cf. **marge**.

Maggie Moores, often shortened to *maggies*, is Aus. r.s. for (women's) drawers. B., 1942.

Maggies, the. The French *Maquis*: Army in France: 1944–5. P-G-R.

maggot. Money: low s. and c. See quot'n at **legit**, adj. Perhaps ex the idea of bait.—2. 'A non-specific term of abuse' (McNeil): Aus. coll.

maggoty. Very drunk: Anglo-Irish, esp. public-house s. Cf. **mouldy**, adj., 1.—2. 'Angry, irritable, "snooty" ' (Baker): Aus.: since ca. 1915.

magic. Excellent; first-rate; adj. of gen. approbation: popularised by the TV 'Selwyn Froggit Show' character created by the actor Bill Maynard, 1975: in later 1970s, gen. and widespread among the younger generation. Opp. is *tragic*, for the sake of rhyme, in taunts like 'Leicester City [Football Club] are magic, Nottingham Forest are tragic'. (P.B.)

Magic Carpet, the. A fast goods-train 'not from Arabia, but Kidderminster, bringing fine weaves to London's floors': railwaymen's: from ca. 1920. (*Daily Telegraph*, 15 Aug. 1936.) Cf. **the Biscuit** and **the Bacca** (q.v.).

magic circle, the. 'The area within a quarter-mile radius of Piccadilly Circus' (Hodge, 1938): London taxi-drivers': since ca. 1920. Plenty of 'jobs'.

magic doctors. Ground-staff engineers: RAF: ca. 1930–42, then ob. *Weekly Telegraph*, 25 Jan. 1941.

magic mushrooms. Mushrooms that cause hallucinations: drugs c. (Stockley, 1986.) Cf. **paper mushrooms**.

magic wand, the. That effectual peacemaker, the penis: joc. rather then euph.: since mid-1960s (?occ., very much earlier). *Observer*, 29 June 1969.

magnolia, a piece of. A piece of 'tail', sexual intercourse: Can.: since ca. 1960. (Barr.)

magpie. The 'blue naval uniform with white trousers for semi-tropical service': RN. Bowen.—2. A *Magpie*, a South Australian. Baker.—3. An official who leaves State papers in a car or taxi: since ca. 1938.

magpie rig. 'The distinguishing, degrading uniform worn by non-swimmers—white duck trousers and blue jumpers' (Summers, 1966). Cf. **magpie**, 1.

magsman; occ. **megsman.** A street swindler; a confidence trickster: 1838 (*The Town*, 27 Jan.); Powis, 1977, notes 'Petty thieves and cheats, in a small way of business, and used contemptuously.'—2. A talkative person, a chatterer: Aus.: since ca. 1925. (Niland, 1958.) Cf. **mag**, v., 1.

mahogany. In *on the mahogany*, (of locomotive crews) 'Returning to home depot as a passenger after working a special train. Also known as returning "on the cushions" ' (McKenna, 1): railwaymen's. Ex C.19 s. *mahogany* = furniture. Cf.:-

mahogany bomber. The desk which an office-bound pilot 'flies': RAF: later C.20. *Fighter Pilot*, 1981.

maid. To act as maid to: theatrical coll. Maugham, 1937, ' "I'm young enough to dress 'er. And maid 'er." '

Maid tends, in Aus., to be prefixed to any girl named Marion. Ex the *Maid Marion* of the Robin Hood legend. (B.P.)

maiden. Probationary nurse who is paid less and works more: Norland nurses': since ca. 1920.

mail run, the. Regular air-raids on Benghazi: RAF in N. Africa: 1941–3. Cf. **milk round**, 1.

main drain on the wallet. 'A heavy expense, usually female. After one of the large bore pipes' (Malin, 1979): RN, esp. HM Submarine *Astute*: mid-1960s.

main-drain rangers. 'Fish of an indeterminate species served at dinner in the wardroom. A pej. term' (Granville): RN officers'. Cf. prec. Also *main-drain loungers*.

main-line. 'To inject [a narcotic drug] intravenously' (Home Office): drugs world: adopted, ex US, ca. 1950 (?earlier). Hence, *main-liner*, 'Confirmed "hard" drug addict who injects drugs directly into a vein' (Powis), and *main-lining*, the practice: id.

main vein, the. The female pudend: to *stab in the m.v.*, to coït with (a woman): low, esp. among drug addicts: since ca. 1950.

major in. To take (e.g. Latin) as a major subject: from ca. 1925: coll. >, by 1933, S.E. Ex *major subject(s)* or perhaps direct ex US *major*, a major subject.

Major Loder. Soda: r.s. 'From Major Eustace Loder (b. 1867), owner of the famous racehorse Pretty Polly' (Franklyn 2nd). Chiefly in 'whisky and soda'. Cf. **Rosy Loader**.

major operation. Cutting a person *dead*: since ca. 1935.

Major Stevens. Evens (in betting): r.s.

make, n. In *on the make*, (of either sex) seeking sexual adventures: Can.: since ca. 1920. Cf. **make**, v., 2.—2. *On the make*, (of either sex) engaged in winning affection: Aus.: since ca. 1925. B., 1943.

make, v. To catch (a train, boat, etc.): from ca. 1885: in 1930s, verging on coll. Ex the C.17–20 S.E. sense, orig. nautical, 'arrive at'.—2. Hence, to coït with (a girl): Can.: adopted ca. 1918 ex US; Aus. since ca. 1944; and, by ca. 1955, Brit.—3. As in, 'Nor did they [suspects] "make me" ' (i.e., identify me for what I was [a plain-clothes policeman]), as I went sloping past in my filthy jeans' (Seabrook, 1987): police: later C.20.

make a balls (of). To make a thorough mess (of a job). See **balls**, 3, and cf. **make a box of**.

make a big feller (occ. **fellow**) **of** (one)**self.** 'To give the impression that one is magnanimous' (B.P.): Aus.: since ca. 1945.

make a bog of. See **bog**, n., 3.

make a bomb. To become rich, to 'make a packet': low: since ca. 1945. (Norman.) 'Sold the house just at the right moment, luckily—made a bomb on it, too'.

make a box of. To muddle: Aus. (B., 1942.) Cf. **make a balls of**; prob. euph. for *ballocks*.

make a break. To run away from the police: Aus. and NZ c.,—1932, >, by 1940, s. The Eng. is usu. *make a break for it*; used by prisoners of war, WW2.

make a come-back. To succeed again after a (long) retirement: orig. sporting coll.: since ca. 1920. (*Punch*, 11 Apr. 1934.) Var. *stage a comeback*.

make a (good, poor, etc.) **fist at** (or **of**) **it.** To do, or attempt to do, a thing, with a good, bad, etc., result: US, perhaps orig. Brit.: since early C.19: coll. By mid-C.20 'poor' or 'bad' could be merely implied, as in 'He began to pack his belongings. He made such a fist of it that I joined in to help' (Moran, 1959).

make a go of (it). To succeed: since ca. 1920.

make a meal of (what normally needs only one swallow). To go on and on about some matter; to wallow in it: coll.: since ca. 1925.—2. To be over-conscientious, looking for problems: publishers' coll.: later 1970s. 'There's no need to make such a meal of those straightforward proofs.' (Raab.)

make a meet. To meet the immediate seller of the drug (the connection): drug addicts': since ca. 1930, if not a decade earlier. *Hearings*, 1955.

make-a-million-quick merchants. 'The modern get-rich-quick types' (Petch, 1974): since late 1940s.

make a monkey of. To make someone look ridiculous: adopted, ex US, ca. 1930. Cf.:-

make a monkey out of; be made a monkey of. To use, be used, as a dupe, esp. as a cat's-paw: adopted, ca. 1943, ex US Servicemen.

make a noise and **make a noise like a . . .** See **noise**.

make a pass at. To attempt (a person's) virtue; to try to caress: adopted ex US ca. 1930. Cf. Dorothy Parker's famous couplet: 'Men seldom make passes/At girls who wear glasses.' (Usu. of the male) to suggest sexual intimacies to: the nuance predominant in Brit. since ca. 1945.

make a sale. To vomit: NZ and Aus. low. B., 1941.

make an ascension. 'To forget one's lines or one's business; they simply "fly into the air" ' (Green, 1984): theatrical.

make an honest woman of. To marry: joc. coll. Ex lit. sense, to marry a woman one has seduced or lived with. Collinson.

make and mend. The naval half-holiday on Thursday, nominally for attending to one's clothes: RN:—1899 (*Navy and Army Illustrated*, 14 Oct.).—2. Hence, off-duty hours: since ca. 1930. Cf.:-

make and mend pudding. 'Baked jam roll, a heavy helping of which induces sleep on a sailor's half-holiday' (Granville): RN.

make brick. See **making brick**.

make (one's) expenses. To gamble in the train: cardsharpers' c.: late C.19–20.

make free with the land. To hug the shore: nautical coll. Bowen.

make (someone) go all unnecessary. To excite, esp. sexually; to arouse passion or a mere momentary 'letch': since ca. 1930. 'She made him go all unnecessary, the hussy.' Also 'He makes me come over all unnecessary.' Var. *do things to*. The implications are functional.

make good. To succeed: coll.: adopted, ex US, ca. 1913. P.B.: in later C.20, esp. in phrase 'Local boy makes good', often used ironically or mockingly, parodying cliché headline in provincial newspaper.

make (one's) hair curl. To cause one to shudder, to frighten: coll.:—1931 (Lyell). 'Quite frequently heard during WW2 when a particularly potent drink was being offered, "This'll make your hair curl"—i.e. do you good' (R.S., 1971). Low variants are *make* (one's) *liver* (C.19–20) or *teeth* (mid-C.20) *curl*. Cf. 'put hairs on your chest' or 'put lead in your pencil', and contrast *curl* (one's) *hair*.

make it. To succeed; to become prosperous: coll.: adopted ex US ca. 1933. Ex **make**, v., 1.—2. To cope with anything: Can. (hence Brit.): adopted ex US ca. 1942. Hence the punning slogan, ca. 1951, 'Britain can make it!' Cf. **hack**, v., 2, 3.

make it a welter. See **welter**.

make it bad for other people. To set too good an example in one's work: Services': since ca. 1925.

make it stick. To assert or plead convincingly: coll.: since ca. 1940. (Petch, 1969.) P.B.: ex police or lawyers' coll. of 'making a charge stick' on a criminal it is hoped to convict.

make it, usu. **be making it, together.** To copulate: mostly teenagers': since late 1940s. Cf. **make**, v., 2.

make like . . . To act like; e.g., *make like a bird*, go away; *like an oyster*, make no noise; *like a rich guy*, pretend to be rich: Can.: mid-C.20, adopted ex US. 'From the Yiddish "mach wie . . . " ' (Leechman, 1967). *Make like a boid*, in CANADIAN ADOLESCENTS' SLANG in Appx., is the US form. Cf. **make with . . .**

make (one's) marble good. To improve one's position or status: Aus.: since ca. 1925. (Tennant, 1956.) Ex the game of marbles.

make (one's) mouth go. To talk too much: since ca. 1960. Applied esp. to a gossiping mischief-maker. (Petch, 1969.)

make no never mind. To be either unimportant or of no importance whatever, as in 'That makes no never mind'; the palliative or the consolatory 'Never mind!' doesn't apply: Can. coll.: adopted, ca. 1930, ex US, where prob. orig. dial. (Leechman.)

make noises about. To talk about, to discuss, not necessarily in public; often with implication of being concerned about, or

pressing for, something, as in, 'They're making noises about wanting to take it to higher authority': coll.: since early 1970s. (P.B.) Cf. **make the right noises.**

make (one's) numbers. To make oneself known: RN. (Bowen.) Ex 'a ship showing her pennant numbers when entering harbour' (Granville, who glosses it further, 'to report for duty in a new ship'). Adopted, ca. 1930, and still current 1970s, among army officers, as *make* (one's) *number*, and in the sense 'to get oneself acquainted in the right quarter'. E.P., 1942; P.B.

make on. To make-believe, to 'pretend': children's. 'Let's make on!'

make one, as in 'The Jerries are making us one', the Germans are making fools of us: Army: since ca. 1930. P-G-R.—2. 'Make (or attempt to) escape, make a demonstration, riot' (McVicar, 1974): prison s.: later C.20.—3. In *make one with* (another person), to partner him in a robbery or other crime: c.: since ca. 1940. Newman, 1977.

make passes at. See **make a pass at.**

make shuffling mutes like a cardsharp. To play the trumpet with muted or muffled notes with exceptional skill: entertainers' (in 'pop' music and among their devotees): since ca. 1960. *The Times*, 2 Oct. 1973. (L.A.)

make strange. (Of a child) to behave shyly: Can. coll. 'See the nice lady? Don't make strange now!'

make (a machine) talk. To design, or to use, it with extraordinary skill: coll.: since ca. 1920.

make the county. To become an accepted member of County society: since ca. 1945. Wilson, 1957.

make the grade. (Gen. in negative or interrogative.) To be able to do a thing; to meet a standard, 'come up to scratch': US (late C.19) adopted in Brit. ca. 1930. Ex railway j.

make the right noises. (Often *all the right . . .*) To use unexceptionable platitudes, as, e.g., Civil Servants often do; to keep to the letter of the party line, as politicians are wont; or simply, in general, to be polite and politic in circumstances where courtesy demands: coll.: since ca. 1950. (L.A., 1976.) Cf. **make noises about.**

make the scene. Paul Janssen, 1968, quotes Miss Needham, an American authority, as defining it thus: 'To become part of a social, artistic, or political movement. Loosely . . . to go "someplace" and . . . indulge in a specific activity.' He then quotes Mr Peter Stansill: 'The expression . . . is (in England at least) a rather loose phrase. Essentially . . . to get involved with something. For example, "to make the country scene" means quite simply "to go to the country". In publicity . . . "Glamour, the lipstick that makes the scene" . . . just implies that it is the lipstick that gives your lips the grooviest (best) look . . . It is a rather flexible, loose and vague expression that is slowly becoming more widely used in Standard English'—well, hardly that! Let's say that, even by 1977, let alone 1968, it was—and still is—becoming widely used in gen. Brit. s. P.B.: by 1983, it felt 'dated'.

make the turn. To withdraw from drugs: drugs c. (Stockley, 1986.) US has *turn around*: since—1967 (Spears).

make waves. To upset established or accepted routine or procedure: Civil Service, politicians', businessmen's: since ca. 1972. (Playfair, 1972.) In short, to 'rock the boat'.—2. Hence, to stir up (usu. unnecessary) trouble. In Clement, 1977, a prisoner says of himself: 'Only eight months to do if I keep my nose clean. Why make waves, eh?' (P.B.)

make with. To make: adopted, ca. 1959, ex US. ' "Has he tried to blackmail you?" "Well, not exactly. But he sort of makes with sinister hints, you know" ' (Blake, 1964). There are other nuances, esp. 'to use', the others more or less deriving therefrom. Of Can. usage, Leechman, 1967, noted that ' "Now, Fritz. Make with the fiddle!" and similar expressions are often heard. "Make with the accelerator!" "Make with the beer!" From the Yiddish "mach mit der . . . " '

make yes of it. To agree; to accept: lower classes' coll.:—1923 (Manchon).

M

make your hair (or **liver**, or **teeth**) **curl, this'll.** See **make** (one's) **hair** . . .

makee-learn. A new-hand, a beginner: RN. ('Taffrail', *Stand By!*, 1916.) Ex (prob. China Stations') pidgin.—2. Hence, in the Army, a young officer: earlier C.20. (F. & G.) In later C.20, may be applied, in the Services, to anyone learning a job, on the job; for euphony or greater effect, *makee-learnee*, which applies also to the actual activity of learning. Cf. the fishing fleet's *decky learner*, an apprentice deck-hand. (P.B.)

-making; as, and esp., in **shy-making** and **sick-making**. An adjectival 'suffix' fathered, perhaps in derision of the German love of compounds, by Evelyn Waugh: the fashion (not yet quite extinct) raged in 1930–3. See esp. Evelyn Waugh's *Vile Bodies*, 1930. Rather s. than coll. and restricted almost wholly to the educated and/or the cultured, esp. in Society and near-Society; never very gen. outside of London. P.B.: so wrote E.P. in mid-1930s. The form 'caught on' and is still, 1983, in use in much the same circles: Dempster, 1979, noted that '-making, e.g., blush-making' was an 'in' term in Society. It is a usage subject to the waves of fashion, like, e.g., the prefix 'HARRY' or the 'OXFORD -ER(s)'.

making brick. Defrauding the public and the Passenger Transport Executive: busmen's s.: late 1970s. See quot'n at **brick**, n., 4.

makings. 'Cigarette papers and tobacco, the materials for a roll-your-own cigarette': coll. Also Aus. (McNeil).

malad. A 'maladjusted' child: social workers': later C.20. *New Society*, 20 Nov. 1980.

malarkey. Nonsense; risible exaggeration; stuff and nonsense; 'bull': Can., adopted, early 1940s, ex US, where current since the early 1930s in s., and prob. since the mid-1920s in the underworld. Perhaps ex modern Greek *malakia*. The term made only an entirely negligible impact on Britain. P.B.: I feel E.P. errs here; the impact has been far from negligible. The term is still extant, and the phrase 'come the old malarkey', to pitch a tall story, has an almost Cockney ring to it. Cf. **Madame Misharty**.

Malayan madness. 'Bloody-mindedness': Aus. Servicemen's: 1942–5. (B., 1943.) Ex the bitter campaign waged against the Japanese invaders, Dec. 1941–Feb. 1942, in which Australian Forces were notably and heavily involved.

Malawi grass. Cannabis: drugs c. Stockley, 1986.

Malcolm Scott. Hot: theatrical r.s. Franklyn.

male gynae ward. See **lily-pond**.

maleesh, malish; or, properly, **ma'alish** (pron. *marleesh*), v. To be completely indifferent to or about; to ignore; to consign to the waste-paper basket: Army and RAF since ca. 1925. As injunction, 'maleesh!' or 'maleesh it!', Never mind!, Forget it! ex:-

maleesh (and variants as prec.), adj. Indifferent; even, fatalistic; 'easy'; esp. 'I'm maleesh', I don't mind, either way: I'm agreeable: among Brit. troops in Egypt since late C.19; given fresh impetus, and wider service usage, in the Middle Eastern campaigns of WW1, and again in WW2. Ex Arabic.

malky. Any weapon neither firearm nor bomb: Glasgow teen-age gangsters': since ca. 1960. (*Observer*, 4 Feb. 1973.) Munro, 1985: it 'is a safety razor used as a weapon. To *malky* someone is to cut him with a razor. To *get malkied in* is to set about someone or something with a will.' Munro suggests an orig. in r.s. *Malcolm Fraser* = razor. But who was *M.F.*?

mallee root. A prostitute: Aus. r.s. (B., 1942.) With a pun on *root*, to coit with a woman. '*The mallee* [is] equivalent to "the scrub" in expressions like "take to the mallee" (from the mallee scrub in Victoria)' (Wilkes).

mallet. To smash or defeat: SAS, in the Falkland Is.: 1982. (Fox, 1982.) Cf. synon. Paratroopers' **banjo**, v., and RM **wellie**, v.

malleted. Reprimanded (by an officer): Gibraltar servicemen's (since c. 1930) >, ca. 1940, gen. servicemen's. (H. & P.) Forcible.

mallum, malum. To understand (gen. v.t.): Army: since late C.19. (F. & G.) Hence, 'Yes, mallum' = Yes, fair enough (or, that's good); interrogatively, *mallum* = Got that?; 'Use your mallum' = Use your common sense. 'A blank cheque of a word' (John Bebbington): Forces' (in the East): 1939–45. P.B.: and, among older sailors, for two decades or so longer, esp. in the sense 'common sense'—'Oh, come *on*! Use a bit o' mallum!'

Malt. A Maltese: mostly nautical: late C.19–20. (Davies, 1961.) Cf. **José**.

Malta dog; often simply *dog*. Diarrhœa; mild dysentery: RN: late C.19–20. Cf. the all-Services **gippy tummy**. Winton, 1959, 'There's a very awkward and unpleasant disease which people catch in the Mediterranean. It's a form of dysentery and it's known as the Malta Dog. Some people catch it because they're not used to the water . . . You can catch it from shellfish or from meat that's a bit too old . . . or from greens that have not been washed.'

Maltese lace. 'Frayed edges of well-worn bell-bottomed trousers (RN); frayed shirt-cuffs, etc. (RN & MN)': since ca. 1905. (Granville.) Also *Spanish pennants*.

Maltese shuffle. 'Shambling gait that is supposed to pass for a quick march in the Navy' (Granville): RN.

Maltese style. 'Any lackadaisical manner of doing a job. The reverse of smart and orderly, "any old how" ' (Granville): RN lowerdeck.

Malteser. A Maltese: joc. coll.: mid-C.20. Ex a popular brand of chocolate sweets. (P.B.)

malum. See **mallum**.

mam. A Lesbian: low London: since ca. 1945. Gloag, 1962, 'You're more than half a Lizzie, aren't you? I've met lady mams before: one of 'em kept a girl I wanted. It was easy for her: she had the lolly.'

mama. 'A (real) mama: a promiscuous female' (Powis): low coll.: later C.20.

mammoth. Huge: coll.: from ca. 1920. The reviewer of the 1st ed. of *DSUE*, in *TLS*, 20 Mar. 1937, 'If "demon" is an adjective, why not "mammoth"?' Ex circus- and show-men's hyperbole. Cf. later C.20 posters advertising, e.g., 'Mammoth flea market'. —2. Hence, excellent: RN: mid-C.20.

mammy mine. Wine: Glasgow r.s. Munro, 1985.

man. A coll.: 'an exclamatory form of address in common use all over South Africa, employed often enough quite irrespective of either the age or the sex of the person addressed' (Pettman). Cf.:—2. In English Public Schools, as in Wodehouse, 1909, 'Awfully sorry, you know, man.' Cf. See also note at **like**. The beatniks adopted the vocative *man* (cf. 1) ex jazzmen's usage, itself taken from the very numerous Negro jazzmen.—3. A pimp: white-slavers' c.: late C.19–20. Londres.—4. 'Service of drugs supply, a dealer': drugs c. (Stockley, 1986.) US since—1942 (Spears).—5. As *the man*, 'the police; anyone in authority; anyone with [conventional] middle-class values': counter-culture: 1960s. Hibbert, 1983.

man fat. 'Semen virile' (L.A., 1974): low coll.

man help. 'Paintbrush lashed to a 4-foot pole' (Peppitt): MN: since 1940s. Cf. synon. **long Tom**.

man in the box, the. The announcer of weather forecasts over the radio telephone: deep-sea fishermen's: since ca. 1946. Granville.

man-killer. The cumbersome, very heavy tank-engine of the LMS: railwaymen's coll.: first decade, C.20.—2. 'A piece of machinery geared to run so fast as to tire the men who feed it': Can.: since ca. 1925. (Leechman.)

man-mad. Of a girl or a woman: extremely sexy: since the early 1920s: coll. >, by 1955, S.E.

man outside Hoyt's, the. 'A mythical person alleged to create rumours' (B., 1959): Aus.: since late 1940s. Cf. **furphy**. Wilkes, 'The commissionaire outside Hoyt's Theatre in Melbourne in the 1930s, so elaborately dressed as to seem a person of consequence.'

man-sized job. A difficult task: since ca. 1925: coll. >, by 1945, familiar S.E.

man-trap. 'Catch points to prevent unauthorised entry from siding' (*Railway*): railwaymen's: since ca. 1920. Also *Jack*(-)*trap*.

man with no hands, like a, adj. and adv. Miserly; in a miserly manner, esp. in *throw money around like a . . .* : Aus.: since ca. 1945. B., 1959.

manage it. To 'get off' with a fellow; to get married: feminine coll.

management (or **M–**), **the.** The officers, esp. the senior ones of a unit: Territorial Army's: from ca. 1925. Cf.:-

manager. The head of one's department at a H.Q.: Army officers': since ca. 1934. Ex:-

managing director, the. The commanding officer: Army officers': from ca. 1933. Prob. ex **leader**, q.v.

manany. 'A sailor who is always putting off a job of work': nautical. (Bowen.) Ex Sp. *mañana*, tomorrow.

Manc. A native of Manchester; a pupil at Manchester Grammar School: Manchester: late C.19–20. Ex *Manc*unian.

Manchester City. A var. of *Bristol City*, q.v. at **Bristols**; mostly in pl. and shortened to *Manchesters*. (Franklyn 2nd.) I.e. female breasts.

mandarin (or **M.**). A politician; a Government official, esp. if pompous: coll.: 1916. (F. & G.) Ex S.E. *mandarin*, a very important or a great man.

mandies. '*Mandrax*. Methaqualone, a sleeping pill' (Cutland, 1985): drugs c.

mandrake. (Usu. in pl.) A waterproof cape worn in the tropics: Aus. Army: 1942–5. (B., 1943.) P.B.: perhaps ex the cape costume worn by the hero of the American comic-strip, 'Mandrake the Magician', started by Lee Falk and Phil Davis in 1934, and still, 1980, going strong.

mangle. A bicycle: Aus. juvenile: earlier C.20.—2. A mangel-wurzel: farm labourers': late C.19–20. Via *mangol*, slovenly for orig. *mangold*.—3. A manual drilling-machine: railwaymen's: since ca. 1945. (*Railway*, 2nd.) A pun both on *manual* and on the effect it has on the nerves.

mangle (one's) **meat.** Of males, to masturbate: 'I bet you've mangled your meat many a time over pictures of lasses skinnier than Sandra' (Hill, 1978): low. Cf. synon. at **gallop . . .**

mangy cat. ' "The mangy cat" is the man who's told to go to a distant dock a bus-ride away and says, "I 'aven't got de fur''; the "chemist" is the one who loads up a truck and says " 'Ere's more f'yer (morphia)'' ' (*New Society*, 18 Sep. 1980): Liverpool dockers' s.: later C.20. ' . . . dockers' nickname slang—the Scouse equivalent of Cockney r.s.' (Ibid.).

manhole cover. A sanitary pad: Aus. low male: since ca. 1950.

manhole covers with custard. Bread and pudding: perhaps mostly lower-middle classes': since ca. 1945. (Petch, 1974.)

mankie, -(e)y. Rotten; very inferior: orig. Cockneys': esp. popular among National Servicemen mid-C.20 in sense of 'dirty'. Largely supplanted in this by 'gungey'. Prob. ex Fr. *manqué*. (E.P.; P.B.)

mannigant. 'A conceited person' (*M.T.*): market-traders' ?A blend of '*managing*' (sort of person) + '*arrogant*'.

manny. A strong sleeping pill: since early 1960s. (*Groupie*, 1968.) Var. of **mandies**, q.v.

manor. A police-district: orig. c., from ca. 1920 (Wallace, 1928); by 1940 police s. for a police Division or area, 'He's Superintendent of this manor' (Powis, 1977). But Seabrook, 1987, writes, 'Bow Street [police station]'s ground (as police call their territory – the word "patch" is used rarely, and "manor" I never heard once [early 1970s] used by a real policeman).' Cf. **midden; patch**.—2. Hence, 'The area where one lives and is known' (Cook, 1962): Londoners': since late 1940s.—3. The district where a 'Teddy-boy' gang lives and operates. See **team**.

manual exercises. (Mostly male) masturbation: low.

Maori P.T. 'Taking it as easily as possible, i.e. resting when one should be undertaking physical training' (W. Colgan): NZ Servicemen's: WW2. Cf. synon. **Egyptian P.T.**

map. Face, head, skull: military and lower classes': earlier C.20. (B. & P.) Cf. the Scottish sense: a portrait.

map of England (occasionally **Ireland**). A stain on bed-linen: Forces', esp. RAF: since ca. 1918. The latter in Lawrence, 1955.—2. In, e.g., *he has the map of Ireland written all over his face,* he is unmistakably Irish: since ca. 1930. (Petch, 1967.)

marble. In *make* (one's) *marble good*, 'To make the grade, confirm or improve one's status or prospects (Wilkes): Aus.: since mid-C.20.

Marble Arch. The Arco Philaenorum near El Agheila, N. Africa: Army: 1943.

marble orchard. A cemetery: Can.: since ca. 1920.

marbles. Money, cash; salary: mostly Londoners', esp. theatrical: since ca. 1950. 'The big marbles are not earned at the Festival Theatres or the Old Vic.'—2. In *have lost some of* (one's) *marbles,* to be not quite sane: Can.: adopted, ex US, ca. 1930. (Leechman.)—3. Hence *to have all* (one's) *marbles,* to be no fool; lit., 'to be all there': since ca. 1950.

marbles for old men. The game of bowls: joc.: since ca. 1930.

marched, get. To make a formal complaint to the CO: Army coll., esp. among regulars: earlier C.20. One is marched in by an NCO. (CO = Commanding Officer.)

marching in marmalade, n. and adj. Working hard but getting nowhere; struggling to achieve a useful purpose while being hampered and obstructed by red tape or one's superiors: Army (mostly officers'): WW2+.

marching money. Travelling expenses: Aus.: since 1918–19. (Baker.) Also, since ca. 1945, English, as in Cook's (1962) definition, 'small change to get from place A to B'. Influenced by the WW2 army.

Marconi. Generic nickname for telephone operator in the foreman's office of an engine shed: railwaymen's: McKenna, 2.

Marconi mast. 'The tall racing yacht's mast in which the top-mast is socketed instead of being fiddled. First seen in *Istria*, whose owner was facetiously said to have fitted it to wireless for more whisky when supplies ran out': nautical: from ca. 1925. Bowen.

mare. 'Unpleasant and bad-tempered woman. "Bitch" connotes contrariness in addition to slight bad temper; "cow" the next degree of unpleasantness. "Mare" is easily the worst and most insulting' (Powis, 1977): low coll. In *Underworld*, E.P. notes its use, 1930s and '40s, for 'prostitute'; see also his remark at **moo**. Cf. **stallion**.

Maren or **marinette.** A *Mari*ne *Wren*: RN: 1941+. Granville, 'Employed at a Royal Marine Barracks . . . distinguished from their sisters by the Marine badge on their caps in place of the H.M.S. ribbon'.

marge. Margarine: from ca. 1905. (*Margarine* itself, 1873: *OED*.) An early example is in Jones, 1926. Also *marg*.

mari. A marijuana cigarette: since late 1920s: c. until ca. 1935, then s. Cf. **Mary Jane**.

Marie Corelli. Television: r.s., on *telly*: later C.20. (Jones, 1971.) Powis notes that it is usu. shortened to *Marie*. M.C. was the pen-name of Mary Mackay (1855–1924), English romantic novelist sensationally popular around the end of C.19.

Mariners, the. See ASSOCIATION . . . , in Appx.

Marine's breakfast. See TOMBOLA, in Appx.

marinette. See **Maren**.

maritimes. Men of the Royal Artillery Marine Regiment, serving as AA gunners in merchant ships: RN: WW2. P-G-R.

Marjie. Marijuana: Aus. c. (since ca. 1943) >, by 1950, low s. (B. 1953.) Cf. **Mary Jane**.

mark, n. A victim, esp. a prospective victim (cf. the v.): c.:— 1885. Since WW1, among pickpockets, it has tended to mean the person already robbed (Moynahan, 1969).—2. A newcomer, esp. if she is ingenuous, among prostitutes: prostitutes' c.:—1923 (Manchon).—3. A good giver: tramps' c.:— 1935.—4. A taxi-cab rank: taxi-drivers': since ca. 1910. Hodge, 1939.—5. In *get a mark*, (of a publican) to be fined for illicit practice: Aus. (Baker.) Short for *get a black*

mark.—6. In *off* (one's) *mark,* having run away: Glasgow:— 1934. Ex foot-racing.

mark, v. To watch; pick out a victim: c.: from ca. 1860; perhaps, however, implied in Brandon, 1839, '*Marking*—watching, observing'. Perhaps the orig. of the n., 1.—2. To realise; to see and understand: low coll.: later C.20. (Newman, 1970.) Cf. synon. **book,** v., 2.

mark (someone's) **card.** To give him the information he needs; to put him right: barrow-boys': since ca. 1945. Ex the racecourse.—2. 'To tell or warn him', with wider connotation and distribution: since late 1940s. (Cook.) Tempest, ' "A" marks "B's" card when he tells "C" that "B" is planning to do him, "C", an injury. A tip-off.' Also, 'When you [a gangster chief]'ve got just yes-man [in your gang], you're in danger. You'll never get your cards marked' (Taylor, 1983)—i.e., you do not receive the information or warnings that you need.—3. To bear someone in mind for, e.g. a particular job of work: business world: later C.20. (Franklin, 1982.) Cf. synon. **to slate.**

Mark Foy. Boy: Aus. r.s.: since ca. 1910. (B., 1943.) 'The term is clearly of Cockney origin, being based on the name of a firm of cartage contractors who functioned in the London area in late C.19 to early C.20.' (Franklyn.) Perhaps later reinforced by the name of the Aus. department store? (Raab.)

mark-off or **tick-off** or **tick-down.** The process of checking the entries in one set of bank account-books with those in another set: bank-clerks': s. verging on coll.

mark-one eyeball. The human eye, as opp. to electronic vision: RAF: later C.20. *Fighter Pilot,* 1981.

mark time on. To wait for: Army: WW2. Ex the drill movement.

mark-up. 'At the mark-up: secretly taking more than your "rightful" share of a bribe or blackmail payment. Often done by the middleman or stakeholder who actually receives the total money from the briber or victim, or their agent . . . Also referred to as "creaming" ' (Powis): c.: later C.20.

markers steady, be on. To be quite sober and without a tremor, esp. after a drinking-bout: Army: since ca. 1930. Ex the order 'Markers steady!' given to the NCOs (or others) acting as markers to the platoon or squads before a parade.

market. *Go to market,* to become angry or complain bitterly: Aus. B., 1942.—2. In *in the market,* having plenty of money: c.:—1935 (Hume). Opp. *on the floor.*

market ranger. 'Fish-wharf thief: a "spiv" of the fisheries' (Granville): nautical: mid-C.20.

Marks. A Marks & Spencer store: coll.: since ca. 1925. Cf. **Timothy's** and **Woolies.**

Marks and Sparks. An elab. of prec.: since late 1940s. *Sunday Times,* 5 Apr. 1964.

marmalade. The gold braid worn on the cap-peak by officers of Group Captain and higher ranks: RAF: early WW2. (H. & P.) Cf. the commoner synon. **scrambled eggs.**—2. See **marching in marmalade.**

marmalade boat. 'Thames sewage barge' (Granville): nautical. Cf. **honey-bucket.**

Marmalade Country, the. Scotland: music-halls' coll.: ca. 1905–14. (Ware.) Ex the marmalade that is a staple industry of Scotland.

maroon, n. In ' "what a maroon!"—what a dolt, what a dummy!' (Leech, 1981): Can.: later C.20. P.B.: ?a perversion of *moron*—or of *macaroon*; hardly ex the firework.

Maroon Machine, the. An occ., mostly journalistic, sobriquet for the Parachute Regiment. (Carew.) Ex the colour of their berets; cf. **cherryberry.**

Marquess of Lorn. An erection: r.s., on **horn**: rare. Franklyn.

marquis. A shortened var. of the prec., as in 'a prolonged attack of the marquis' (Naughton, 1970).

married man's friend, the. The war-time black-out: WW2. It enabled him to take out other women without fear of being seen by 'friendly' neighbours.

married man's side. 'The left-hand half of the dart board, presumably because the "doubles" are found there' (Granville): darts players': since ca. 1950.

married man's trade. 'Ships of the Port Nolloth copper ore trade, so called because the crews were seldom able to get ashore and spend money' (MacFee, 1947).

married pads. Married men in the Armed Forces: usu. their bachelor fellows', but may be applied also to the married men by themselves. In, e.g., a single mess-member's complaint, 'You pads come down here and scoff all our breakfast . . .' Often reduced, allusively, to (*the*) *pads.* From late C.19 *pads* = (in Army s.) wives.

married patch, the. Married quarters in permanent barracks: Army. (P-G-R.) In later C.20 also RAF (*Phantom*). Cf. prec.

marrieds, esp. *young marrieds.* Married couples: Aus. coll.; since ca. 1925; Brit., perhaps rather later. Niland, 1958.

marry up. An expression often used by auctioneers, it means 'to put one lot with another'; often an article of little value that would be difficult to get a bid for by itself is 'married up' with something for which there is likely to be a good demand and the two articles sold as one lot: coll.—2. 'To add additional (sheets of) notes to filed papers; collate new information or additional facts with original notes' (L.A., 1974): coll.: later C.20.

marrying, vbl n.; **marry,** v.t. Stockbrokers's. (—1935), thus:—'When a broker receives simultaneous orders to buy and sell the same security, he can marry the deal. I.e. he puts one bargain against the other.'

Mars bar. A scar: Glasgow r.s. (Munro, 1985.) On the famous confectionery.

marts. Fingers: homosexuals': current ca. 1970. A shortening of later C.19 *martins,* hands, prob. itself a shortening of r.s. (*St*) *Martin-('s)-Le-Grand,* the famous City of London church.

marv. Marvellous: teenagers': since late 1950s. Cf. the much more popular **fab**(ulous), **brill, triff** and:-

marvelious. (*mar-veé-lĭ-us*). A joc. intensive of *marvellous:* since ca. 1925; virtually † by 1960.

marvellous as used in Society since ca. 1920 is s. for 'pleasant', 'nice'; a mere counter of a word! See, e.g., 'Slang Words', in *Daily Mirror,* 1 Nov. 1933, and Ibid., 26 Oct. 1933 (*too, too marvellous*); Linchon, 1933, 'If you forbade that girl to say "marvellous", then stopped her from saying "definitely", she couldn't speak at all.'

Mary. '*Marys* . . . Post war suburban units' (*Railway,* 2nd): railwaymen's: mid-C.20. I.e. locomotives.—2. The liner *Mauretania:* nautical: ca. 1912–40. Cf. *Lucy,* the *Lusitania.*—3. A Glenn-Martin *Mary*land bomber: airmen's: WW2.—4. Cannabis: drugs c. (Stockley, 1986.) US since—1952 (Spears). Shortening *Mary Jane.*

Mary Ellen. 'If you are in Liverpool, stroll in the evening up the Scotland Road, and talk to the fascinating people you meet there, such as the "Mary Ellens"—the picturesque women who wear shawls over their heads, carry babies in their arms, work in the markets all day, and always have a good "tip"for tomorrow's race' (Lynd, 1945): Liverpool: since ca. 1910.

Mary Jane or **mary jane.** Marijuana: drugs c.: since ca. 1950. Maclaren-Ross, 1954.—2. Durophet, a long-lasting amphetamine: id. Stockley, 1986.

Mary Lou. See **bet on the blue.**

Mary Warner. Marijuana: prison c.: mid-C.20. Tempest.

maryanning. 'Cleaning, sweeping, polishing' (*Radio Times,* 21 Jan. 1965): railway porters': since ca. 1930. Ex *Mary Ann,* a type-name for a housemaid or a charwoman. Cf. 'To wash up the dishes and tidy the table, a duty known in the [Wormwood] Scrubs as "Mary Ann" ' (Harvey, 1936).

marzipan. 'Filler used on bodywork after accident or corrosion' (Graham-Ranger, 1981): car-dealers'. Cf. **pudden,** n.

masby. A motor *anti*-submarine boat (with an affectionate *y* added for euphony): RN: since ca. 1940. Granville.

mash, n. Mashed potatoes: orig. 'lower classes' coll. verging on sol.; but by mid-C.20, in dishes such as 'sausage and mash', gen. and widespread. *Mashed*, in this sense, is also coll. (Manchon).—2. Sentimental nonsense: Aus.: since ca. 1920. B., 1942.

mash, v. To study very hard: Aus. RMC, Duntroon: since (?)ca. 1920. B., 1953.

mash-note. A love letter: Can.: since ca. 1920.

mashed. See **mash,** n.

mashing. 'A little screw of paper containing tea and sugar mixed': lower classes': late C.19–20. Gape, 1936.

Massey-Harris. Cheese: Can.; by contacts made in WW1, also Aus. (B. & P.; B., 1953.) Ex the Massey-Harris self-binder (a forerunner of the combined harvester) + the costiveness of cheese.

mast. A pin (in golf): trawlermen's: since ca. 1920. (*Daily Mail*, 16 Aug. 1939.) Humorous.

master. A master-at-arms: RN coll.

Master Gyppo, the. 'In the Household Cavalry and the Foot Guards the senior NCO of the cookhouse was inevitably known as "The Master Gyppo". Anything hot or liquid, custard, soup, stew, was "gyppo" ' (Carew); late C.19–20.

Master of ceremonies. That 'plane which hovers high over the target to direct a bombing raid: RAF: 1941+.

mat. A matinée: theatrical coll.: 1914 (*OED* Sup.).

mat-boy. A professional wrestler: Aus.: since ca. 1946. Kelly, 1958.

mataby. Cannabis grown in Zaire: drugs world: later C.20. McConville, 1980.

Matapan hammer tapper. 'Anyone who favoured the hammer [as opp. to any more delicate tool]' (Malin, 1979): RN, esp. HM Submarine *Astute*: mid-1960s. A ref. to the battle of Cape Matapan, 28 Mar. 1941, in which the Brit. Mediterranean Fleet decisively defeated the Italian fleet with no loss to itself. A mortal blow indeed! (P.B.)

Matapan stew. A stew made of odds-and-ends: R Aus. N: 1942–5. (B., 1943.) Cf. prec.

matchbox (or hyphenated). A troop-carrying glider: RAF and Army: 1941–5. P-G-R.—2. A *Matchless* motorcycle: motorcyclists': since 1930s. (Dunford.)—3. A 57 XX locomotive: Western Region railwaymen's: mid-C.20. Ex its small pannier tank. (*Railway*.) Like the comparable nickname *spam-can*, the term was applied to several types of locomotive.

matelot, mateloe, matlo(w). ('Taffrail' has pl. *matloes*.) 'Self-adopted nickname of all blue jackets' (Granville): RN >, by 1939 at latest, more widespread: E.P. gives ca. 1880 for *matlo(w)*, *SOD* 1909 for *matelot*.—2. (Esp. *matlow*.) Hence, like *Fleet Air Arm wallah*, a member of the FAA: Services', esp. RAF: since ca. 1918. (Partridge, 1945.) Ex Fr. *matelot*, a sailor; cf.:-

Matelots, the. The London River Police: esp. among the other branches of the Metropolitan Police: since ca. 1945. The River Police return the compliment with *the Land Crabs*, all the other Metropolitan policemen: in, e.g., BBC TV programme 'No Hiding Place', 24 Sep. 1963.

Maternity Home, the. 'The war-time nickname for the Liverpool Naval Base, whose headquarters were in the Liver Buildings, which had two storks or "livers" on the roof'(P-G-R): RN: 1939–45.

mat(e)y. (Gen. in pl. and as *maties*.) A dockyard labourer: nautical. ('Taffrail'.) In later C.20 often in full as *dockyard matey*: occ., as a worker at an airfield, *airyard matey*: RN. (P.B.)

matings and **evensnog.** Joc. perversion of *matins* and *evensong*: later C.20. (Paterson, 1975.)

matloe, matlo(w). See **matelot.**

mats. Matrimonial cases: probation officers', hence local government: since ca. 1960. (Parkinson, 1969.) By ca. 1975, coll. Perhaps a blend, both phonetic and semantic, of *matrimonial* + *matters*.

mattress. 'When underworld figures want to go "in the mattress" until the heat dies down, they go to Essex' (Burn, 1987): c. I.e., into hiding.

Mau Mau, the. RAF Air Traffic Control officers: RAF Fighter Command aircrew officers': early 1950s. Ex the terrorist organisation waging guerrilla warfare in Kenya at the time. (P.B.) Cf.:-

Mau Mau dancing. Scottish country dancing (e.g. reels)—a wardroom fad: RN: 1950s. (Peppitt.) Cf. prec.

Maud. A male prostitute: prostitutes' and homosexuals': since ca. 1940.

Maud and Ruth. Truth: r.s. Clement, 1977.

maul. 'Since ca. 1950, a coll. increasingly used by radio and press commentators to mean a wrestle for the ball in any part of the field. One even hears of "a loose maul", and a scrum has become "a set scrum" ' (H.R. Spencer, 1963): Rugby football.

mauley; occ. **mawley** or **morley.** A fist, the hand: low: 1781.—2. Hence, handwriting, 'a fist'; a signature: low: from ca. 1850. (Mayhew, 1851; Powis, 1977.) The term derives ex *maul*; or is perhaps 'a transposition of Gaelic *lamh*, hand, used in tinkers' s. or Shelta', W., 'in form *malya*'; the Romany s. is *mylier*.

max. Coll. shortening of *maximum*, as in 'involving max effort from masses of aeroplanes' (*Phantom*): Services': later C.20. Influenced by technological j.; taken from written abbreviations such as 'max revs' (maximum revolutions) or 'max temp' (m. temperature). (P.B.)

maxi. A full-length skirt; reaction to the 'mini': mostly feminine: since Sep. 1967: by Jan. 1968, coll. See **mini.**

mazuma. Money; esp. cash: orig. US, adopted in Can.—1914 (B. & P.), and Aus. ca. 1944 (via US servicemen), esp. in sporting circles (Glassop, 1949); not unknown in Brit., but never common. Ex Yiddish.

Me. A Messerschmitt fighter 'plane: 1940 (Berrey). See **He, Me and You** and cf. **Mess** and **Messer.**

me and you. A menu: from ca. 1910. P.P., 1932.

meadow mayonnaise. Airy talk; worthless assurances: Aus.: since ca. 1930. (B., 1942.) With a pun on *bull-shit* (found in meadows). Cf. **confetti,** 2.

meal ticket. 'Wren's boy friend' (Granville): RN: WW2+.—2. More seriously, a person regarded as one's (often sole) financial support: coll.: in this sense, adopted ex US mid-1970s. Brook, 1979, 'He was using her as a meal-ticket [he was unemployed and on drugs, while she earned the money to support the two of them]. Or, of a woman in pursuit of alimony, 'She was trying to secure a meal-ticket for herself.' (Raab.) 'Their names never became household words synonymous with "Punk Rock", but all four [bands] consoled themselves with hooking a meal-ticket from a major label [= recording company]' (Burchill).

mean. So good as to be unfair (*mean*): Can. coll.: adopted, ca. 1910, ex US. 'He swings a mean bat!'—in baseball. (Leechman.) P.B.: this sense has never been truly anglicised, though in the earlier 1980s *mean* = 'superlatively good' had some vogue among teenagers, perhaps via the BMX (cycle) craze.—2. Sly; crafty: Aus.: adopted, ca. 1944, ex US coll. senses. 'This job usually takes an hour, but I know a few mean tricks.' (B.P.)

mean a thing. (Always in negative or interrogative sentences.) To mean, to signify, anything; be of importance: coll.: from ca. 1927. 'He doesn't mean a thing in my young life.'

meanie or **-y.** A person reluctant to pay his share: Services': since ca. 1930. (H. & P., 1943.) Diminutive of *mean*. Ex the more usual sense, a mean person: lower-middle class coll.—2. A spoilsport; one disobliging and petty: coll.: since mid-C.20. The Beatles, in the cartoon film, *The Yellow Submarine*, 1968, popularised the term 'the blue meanies' as an intensification for those that cast a blight on joyfulness; cf. Aus. *grey meanies*, traffic wardens. (P.B.)

measles. Syphilis: medical students' ironic:—1933 (*Slang*).

meat, in many of its various sexual connotations, dates from late C.16.—2. 'The thickest part of the blade of a bat': cricketers' coll.: 1925 (D.J. Knight).—3. Tissues for microscopical examination: medical students':—1933 (*Slang*).

meat and two veg. A man's sexual organs: low.

meat-axe, savage or **mad as a(, as).** Extremely angry: coll.: the 1st, adopted, ex US, ca. 1905 (Thornton), and † by mid-C.20; the 2nd, an Aus. var., since early 1940s, and denoting also 'insane'.

meat-box. The Gloster Meteor, the first operational British jet-fighter (in action, 1944): RAF: mid-C.20. (Glynn, 1972.) By affectionate perversion.

meat-head. 'Derogatory term for a member of the Royal Military Police. Current [since mid-1940s]. Usage: the rest of the Army!' (P.B., 1974): adopted ex US. Implication: stupidity.

meat-injection, give (her) **a.** To coït with a woman: Services': since late 1940s. (P.B.)

meat rack, the. 'Pavement beside railings under the colonnade of the County Fire Office, Piccadilly Circus, where male prostitutes gather' (Powis): 1970s. Adopted ex US generic term for such gathering-places (Rodgers, 1972).

meat-safe. That oblong box-pew (gauze-fronted and curtain-sided) in which, at divine service, the condemned murderer sits in the prison chapel: c.:—1932 ('Stuart Wood').

meat shop. A rendezvous, such as a nightclub, where unattached men and women go to find one another, usu. for sexual purposes. 'The meat shops are the run-of-the-mill places. Then there are "delicatessens", where the customers are most discriminating. Widespread N. Am. usage, poss. going back to 1940s. *Delicatessen* is a newer term which I have heard of in West USA and BC' (Leech, 1986).

meat-tag. An identity disc: Services', esp. Aus.: WW2. Cf.:–

meat-ticket. An identity-tag: WW1.—2. 'A small, rectangular voucher showing the amount of cash paid in by a designated customer' (Taylor, 1986): bank clerks'. Perhaps ex sense 1; both ultimately ex butcher's price-tag on his wares.

meat wag(g)on. An ambulance: Services', esp. RAF (Jackson), and low coll. (Home Office): since ca. 1925. In RAF, also a flying ambulance.—2. A 'black Maria': policemen's and prisons': since ca. 1930. Norman; Home Office.

meaters. A dissection class; dissection as part of a medical course: medical students': from ca. 1910. Ex *meat* by the 'OXFORD -ER(s)'.—2. Hence, esp. at Cambridge, the laboratory in which it is conducted: since ca. 1910. (R.S.)

meaty. Obscene: book-world coll.

mech. Mechanic; esp. in the old *air mech* (see **erk**) of the RFC, and the later *flight mech* of the RAF: coll.: since ca. 1912. Also as adj., in, e.g. *mech enge*, the mechanical engineering department of an establishment for technical education. Cf. **tech.** (E.P.; P.B.)

mechanic. A dishonest card-player; a card-sharp: Aus. (B., 1953) and Can., adopted ex US where orig. c. (Leechman): since (?)ca. 1940.

mechanical man, the. The chief parade-ground instructor at the Gunnery School, Whale Island: RN: 1940s. (Peppitt.) I suspect: for longer—and elsewhere.

Med, the. The Mediterranean. (Llewellyn, 1943.) Hence *Med* as adjective, as in *a Med*, a bird-watchers'.s. abbr. of 'a Mediterranean bird' (cf. BIRD-WATCHERS', in Appx.).

med lab. Medical laboratory: medical students' coll.:—1933 (*Slang*).

Meddy, the. 'The Navy's alternative for *Med*' (P-G-R): since ca. 1910.—2. See:–

medi (pron. *meddy*). Medicine: nursery, as 'Come on, now, drink your medi like a good girl' (P.B.).—2. Hence, a joc. euph. for alcoholic drink, as in ' "He had an awful lot of meddy too," ' . . . Phil indicated that it was the kind of medicine taken in a glass' (Sims, 1984). Cf. synon. **tincture**. *Medicine* = 'liquor' dates from mid-C.19.

medic. See **Medics**.

medical. An examination by a Medical Board: since ca. 1914: coll. >, by 1940, S.E.

Medics, the. The Royal Army Medical Corps: Army coll.: orig., WW1, not very gen. (F. & G.), but by ca. 1950 at latest, the commonest informal term for the RAMC. Hence such j. compounds as *para-medics*, members of the RAMC trained as parachutists. (P.B.)

meet. An assignation: Aus. coll.,—1916 (Dennis); by 1919 also Eng. proletarian coll. See **make a meet** for drug-world specialisation.

meet (one)**self coming back.** Applied, since ca. 1945, to a slow or dilatory person, as in 'Hurry up or you'll meet yourself coming back!' (Petch, 1976).

meg. A megaphone: cinematic: since ca. 1912. (McCabe, 1937.) Cf. **megger**, 1.

mega. Used as prefix to form a superlative: teenagers': adopted ex US 1983. 'Oh, Dad! You are mega inconsiderate, playing my hi-fi at full blast like that' (Miss Deborah Cracknell). Prob. ex its evil use in, e.g. *mega-death*, rather than from electrical j. (P.B.) See **benny**, 3, and cf.:–

mega-bucks. A vast sum of money. *Australian*, 17 Mar. 1986.

mega(-)keggery. 'Derogatory term for the huge processed-beer factories built by the national brewers' (Glover, 1985): public houses'.

mega-mardy. In **throw a mega-mardy** (*at*): to be angry (with): Midlands teenagers': mid-1980s. (Nicola Tate, 1986.) A pleasant humanising of 'hi-tech' *mega* by conjunction with old dial. *mardy*, spoilt (of a child), hence petulant. Cf. **benny**, 3.

megatick. A very rare bird; the sighting of one. See BIRD-WATCHERS', in Appx.

megger (properly, *mega*). A megaphone: coll. abbr.: since ca. 1920. Cf. **meg**.—2. A reversed cone exhaust extractor: motorcyclists'. Used particularly on racing machines, for 'the lack of baffles would be—to say the last—frowned upon by the law' (Dunford): since mid-C.20. Ex the shape; cf. sense 1.

megs. Spectacles: market-traders'. *M.T.*

megsmen. 'North Country term for cardsharpers' (Sharpe, 1938): c.: late C.19–20. Phonetic var. of **magsman**, q.v.

meh-meh-meh . . . 'The bleat, repeated ad nauseam, of troops queuing for breakfast, dinner, tea and supper, for clothing, supplies, inoculation; flocking here and shepherded there. A World War II contribution by the ordinary man in uniform to philosophy and language' (L.A.): Services': WW2 and since.

mein gamp. 'Had a passing use in reference to Neville Chamberlain and his famous umbrella, carried when he visited Hitler' (Petch). There were, in fact, two meetings, the earlier at Berchtesgaden and then with Hitler, Mussolini and Daladier, 29–30 Sep. 1938, at Munich. A double pun on s. *gamp*, umbrella, and Hitler's *Mein Kampf*, 'My Struggle', an inflammatory political manifesto.

Melba. '*To do a Melba*: to make a habit of returning from retirement, in a number of "farewell" performances (from Dame Nellie Melba 1861–1931)' (Wilkes): Aus. coll.: later C.20.

Melbourne Pier. Ear: Aus. r.s.: since ca. 1930. B., 1945.

Meltdown Monday. 'On the Monday [19 Oct. 1987]—Black or Meltdown Monday as is was soon called—Wall Street crashed, the result of a sudden and frightening loss of confidence' (*Illustrated London News*, Jan. 1988). Mann noted it as *Meltdown*, Nov. 1987, and its derivation ex nuclear physics. It was only the latest of a long series of ill-starred 'Black Mondays': an early example of this phrase is in Fielding's *Tom Jones*, 1749.

men dress as Jesus. 'Bearded: Royal Navy: 1950s' (Peppitt). Mock pidgin.

menace. A person that is a bore or a general nuisance: coll.: since early 1930s.

mendic. Sick, ill: Aus.: since ca. 1925. (B., 1942.) Ex '*mendicant*'? Many beggars look sick, many are ill.

meno, n. Menopause; hence adj., experiencing the menopause: domestic, esp. conjugal; educated and cultured: since the 1920s. Llewellyn, 1968, 'I saw, then, that she hadn't been meno at all.' Perhaps on the analogy of the mainly Brit. *nympho* and the mainly US *psycho*—or rather, their prototype.

mentioned in despatches. To have one's name appear in a newspaper, a parish magazine, or even on a notice-board: joc.: 1940+.

Merc or **Merce.** A *Merc*edes motor-car: orig. Society, from ca. 1920; by ca. 1950, at latest, gen. and widespread, and always pron. *merk*. Lincoln, 1933.—2. (Pron. *merk*.) A professional mercenary soldier, hiring himself out to (almost) any country: since ca. 1960. Forsyth, 1974.

Merchant, the. Elliptical for the Merchant Navy: nautical coll.: since late 1920s.

Merchy. Merchiston: Scottish Public Schools': late C.19–20. Miller, 1935.

mercy blow-through. A WW1 soldiers' Hobson-Jobson of Fr. *merci beaucoup*, many thanks. (Manning, 1930.) P.B.: still occ. used in the army, 1960s. Cf.:-

mercy bucket (or **buttercup**). Aus. var. of prec. (B.P.)

mercy buckets. Thank you: middle-class young women's: later C.20 use of schoolchildren's Hobson-Jobson. (Hoggart, 1983.) Cf. prec.

mercy launch. An air-sea-rescue launch: RAF: WW2.

mere. Foolish; inept; ridiculous: mostly Society: since ca. 1939. Perhaps ex '*merely* ridiculous'.

mermaid. 'Department of Main Roads weighbridge inspectors . . . are called "mermaids" . . . because they have scales' (Wilkes, quoting the *Sun*, 28 May 1976): Aus. Prob. an ephemeral pun.

merry men, (name) **and his.** Phrase much used in army sergeants' messes, 1950s–60s, when informal working parties were detailed by the RSM or mess president, as in 'Right then: the Foz and his merry men will be responsible for setting up the tannoy', i.e. the Foreman of Signals and his helpers were to arrange a loud-speaker system. Ex the legend of Robin Hood *and his merry men*. (P.B.)

merry-merry. Intoxicating liquor of dubious origin, esp. in Gibraltar: RN. ?A pun on *beri-beri*.

Merry Widow, the. Champagne: since ca. 1906. Punning both the champagne '*Veuve* Clicquot' and Franz Lehár's light opera *The Merry Widow* (1905).

Mersey Funnel, the. 'The Catholic Cathedral in Liverpool, from its shape' (Petch, 1969): Lancashire: since ca. 1960. An article in the *Universe*, 21 Apr. 1967, was thus titled. A pun on the Mersey Tunnel.

meshuga. (Tolerantly humorous in application.) Crazy: Jewish coll.: mid-C.19–20. Ex Yiddish; cf. Hebrew *meshuga*, error (whence the Yiddish word and sense). Joyce, 1922, 'Meshuggah. Off his chump.'—2. 'There's a further nuance. A Jew might say "I never look at the moon through glass. That's my meshuga"—my personal idiosyncrasy. I heard a Jewish comedian say it only a few weeks ago' (Leechman, 1967). In this sense properly *mishegoss* (Rosten, 1968).—3. Genuinely mentally deficient: Cockneys'. *Muvver*.

Mespot. Mesopotamia: Services'; at first, officers': 1915–ca. 1960. (F. & G.) Also, occ. *Mess-pot*, *Mesop* and *Mess-up*.—2. Hence, 'letter from wife or sweetheart announcing unfaithfulness or break with husband or sweetheart serving in Forces overseas, esp. RAF Iraq and Middle East' (L.A., 1959): since ca. 1919.—3. Hence, but usu. *Mespot piss-up*, 'ritual of group execration of unfaithful wife or sweetheart, at which beer was drunk. On this occasion a letter was written to the woman; of which each of the injured man's hutmates wrote his unhampered part. The woman's offending letter, pinned to the floor, was treated to gestures of contempt. RAF Habbaniya, and current throughout Iraq 1940–5 and no doubt earlier' (Ibid.): app. since ca. 1925; by 1960, ob., RAF links with Iraq virtually ceasing in 1959.

Mess; Messer. A Messerschmitt (German fighter aircraft): RAF: since 1939. (Jackson, 1943 (*Messers*); Partridge, 1945.) Cf. **He, Me and You.**

mess, n. Applied to a person either objectionable or pitiably ineffectual: since ca. 1921. Priestley, 1936.—2. Euph. for

excrement, as 'a lump of bird's mess landed on her hat'. (P.B.)—3. See **bit of mess.**

mess, v. (Of a married person) to go (sexually) with someone else: low: from ca. 1915.

mess-deck Peggy. Elab. of **peggy,** 1, q.v., the odd-job man who cleans the mess-deck: RN: WW2. (Tom Gamble, 1979.)

mess of, make a. To defeat utterly, overcome easily or signally: from ca. 1910.

Mess-Pot. See **Mespot.**

mess-up. See **Mespot.**

message. In *do a message*, to run an errand: N. Country coll.: late (?mid) C.19–20. 'Heard as "I want you to do a message for me", when somebody wanted a child to get something from a shop, etc.' (Petch, 1966).—2. ' "The message," he said impatiently, "you know, the news. He was passing on the news. If we had a fancied runner, he would tip off a professional backer" ' (Francis, 1964): racing: since ca. 1920.—3. In *get the message*, to understand; to 'catch on': widespread s.: since late 1940s.

message by wireless. See **wireless,** earlier C.20 s. for 'a rumour'.

messer. A 'near' prostitute; an amateur not above taking money or a present: prostitutes' c.: from ca. 1915. Low also, though little used by harlots, is **whore's robber,** dating from ca. 1916.—2. A man, or a woman, that does not keep to one lover: low: from ca. 1916.—3. 'One who puts the stall-holder to a great deal of trouble without buying anything' (*M.T.*): market-traders': prob. since ca. 1920.—4. See **Mess.**

Messerschmitt Alley. Any road subject to attention from German aircraft; esp. the long, straight stretch from Ghardimaou to Souk el Arba in Tunisia: Army in N. Africa: WW2. P-G-R.

messman's horror. A hungry man: RN. (Bowen.) The messman thus loses his 'perks'.

Met, the. The Metropolitan Railway: London coll.: late C.19–20.—2. The Meteorological Office: Services': since ca. 1925. Hence, *Met man* or *Mets*, Meteorological Officer: Services': since ca. 1920. (E.P., 1942.) Also *met*, a weather report: RAF: 1939+, > gen.—3. Enemy vehicles (not tanks nor guns): Eighth Army: 1941–5. (H. & P.) Ex *M.T.*, 'mechanical transport'.—4. Always *the Mets*, the Metropolitan Police: police-officers'. (Hume, 1944.) In later C.20, usu. *The Met.*—5. *Mets*, 'trains, usually freight, operating over Metropolitan widened lines section from King's Cross to Southern Region' (*Railway*): London railwaymen's: since late 1940s.

Met man. See prec., 2.

metal. See **heavy metal.**

meter maid. A female traffic-warden: since ca. 1970; orig. coll., but very soon S.E. Janssen cites *Beatles*. Also US: from later 1950s.

meter thief. 'Term of contempt for a petty thief' (Powis): police s.: later C.20. Cf. **gas-meter bandit.**

meth. Methylated spirit: abbr. (Marshall, 1933.) P.B.: since ca. 1940, at latest, the usu. form has been *meths*.—2. Methadrine ('Speed'): drugs world: adopted, ca. 1970, ex US. *DCCU.*

metho. Methylated spirits, esp. as drunk by 'down-and-outers':—1935. Hence, from slightly later, an addict of 'metho'; also *metho artist* (B., 1959): Aus. By the Cockney/Aus. suffix *-o*.—2. A Methodist: Aus.: since ca. 1920. B., 1942.

meths. Methylated spirits: coll.: since earlyish C.20.

methy. Synon. with **meth, metho,** 1, and **meths.**

metro, the. The underground-train system of Paris; hence occ. that of London. Fr. (*le*) *métro* (abbr. *Métropolitain*), itself often loosely used.

Metrollops, the (great). London; a perversion of metropolis: joc. Cf. *the Metrollope*, any hotel with *Metropole* in its name: id. (P.B.)

Mets, mets. See **Met, the.**

Mexican credit card. 'Stealing gas [= petrol] by syphon from another's car or truck. Central Alberta only. Dates back to

1950s or earlier. Mostly small community usage' (Leech, 1986).

Mexican drag-line. A shovel: Can.: since ca. 1930. Leechman cites St Pierre, 1970, and adds, ' "Irish harp" is another facetious [Can.] name for it'.

Mexican two-step. Var. of **Aztec two-step**: N. Am.: since ca. 1960. (Leech, 1985.) Cf. **Montezuma's revenge.**

mezzo brow. Middle-brow (of taste): cultured coll.: since the late 1930s; by 1947, slightly ob.

mhutti. Muck, dirt, shit: RAF in Iraq: ca. 1920–55. One of the RAF's most famous songs, 'Those Shaibah Blues', begins, 'A little piece of mhutti fell from out the sky one day' (Jackson, 1945). Ex local Arabic.

mice. Synon. with pl. of **widgie**, q.v.: Aus.: early 1950s. B., 1953.

Mick or **mick.** An Irishman: orig. (—1869), US; adopted ca. 1890 but, at first, more gen. in the old Dominions. Ex common Irish name *Michael*.—2. Hence, a Roman Catholic: Aus. low coll., since late C.19; in Brit. not common until later C.20. (Wilkes; P.B.) See **Micks,** 2.—3. 'A car used for several years in Ireland, then imported and re-registered in England. The log book gives the impression of a much newer car' (*Woman's Own*, 28 Feb. 1968): car dealers': since late 1940s. Ex sense 1.—4. 'Short for 'ammick: lower deck for hammock' (Granville): RN.—5. See **soft mick.**

mick, adj. Corresponding to prec., senses 1 and 2, i.e. Irish or Roman Catholic.

Mick Jagger. A lager: Glasgow r.s., as in 'Three heavies [standard draught beer] an' a Mick Jagger' (Munro, 1985).

Mick O'Dwyer. A fire: r.s.: late C.19–20. Much less usual than *Anna Maria*.

Mick-takers, the. Scotland Yard's anti-IRA Intelligence Unit: police: ca. 1974. (*Daily Telegraph*, 30 Nov. 1974.) Ex **Mick,** 1, via S.E. *thief-takers*, and *take the mickey*.

Mickey, Micky; or **m–.** A pint flask of whisky or other 'hard' liquor: Can. (and US): since ca. 1920. (Leechman.) Ex '*Irish whiskey*'.—2. In *chuck a micky*, 'To throw a fit; panic' (Wilkes): Aus.: mid-C.20.

Mickey Bliss. Var. of **Mike Bliss,** q.v., piss. (Franklyn 2nd.) Chiefly (shortened) in phrase **take the mick(e)y.**

Mickey Finn. A drink drugged with, e.g., chloral hydrate; a liquid knock-out: orig. US (W. & F. note that it was first,— 1930, applied only to a laxative pill made for horses); adopted in Brit. ca. 1943. Perhaps ex a trade-name. Allingham, 1947; the American author Elliot Paul wrote a satirical detective story, pub. 1939, titled *The Mysterious Mickey Finn*. Later, an ostensibly harmless drink 'spiked' with a stronger, 'hard' liquor, used as a practical joke. (R.C.; P.B.)—2. See quot'n at **gee-man.**

Mickey Mouse. 'The bomb-dropping mechanism on some types of bomber aircraft is so called because it strongly resembles the intricate machinery portrayed by Walt Disney's [Mickey Mouse] cartoons' (H. & P.): RAF: 1939+. Walt Disney began to produce Mickey Mouse cartoon films in 1928.—2. A motor mechanic: RN: since early WW2. (Granville.) He does such very odd things, and there may be influence by *motor mech*.—3. A house, in its theatrical senses: r.s.: since ca. 1930. Franklyn.—4. A small, inshore minesweeper used during WW2: RN: ca. 1940–6. (Granville.)

Mickey Mouse Airlines. Airlines of Western Australia: 'Its widely used nickname . . . is a gently critical comment based on the company's original name [MMA: MacRobertson Miller Airlines Ltd.] and has always been a term of affection rather than derision' (Dunn, 1984).

mickey-mouse book-keeping. 'Fiddling' the books for the company to outwit the Inland Revenue authorities: Aus.: later C.20. (Bruce Irwin, 1978.) Cf.:–

mickey-mouse money. Any unfamiliar currency, e.g. Scottish pound notes, the 20p coin when first introduced in 1982: Eng. parochial joc.: adopted ex US, later C.20. (P.B.)

Mickey Mouse movies. Films so called, 'because they show lots of pubic hair but little else, the trade [in 'exploitation-of-sex'] contemptuously dubs [them thus]' (White, 1976).

mick(e)y off. To decamp, run away: St Bees: since ca. 1910. (Marples.) At St Bees, *do a mike* is to break bounds; the N. Country has *do a micky*.

Mickey Rooney. Macaroni: Londoners': mid–C.20. (Barnes, 1976.) By Hobson-Jobson on name of a popular US filmstar.

Micks, the. The Irish Guards: military. (F. & G.) In later C.20 often the *Mick Guards*. Cf. **Mick,** 1.—2. The Teaching (or Christian) Brothers: Catholic Aus. schoolchildren's: late C.19–20. 'The Brothers formerly came from Ireland' (B.P.). In general s., *the Micks* = all Catholics whatsoever.—3. In *at the mick's* (or *mix*), 'Causing trouble' (Powis): low coll.: later C.20. Munro, 1985: 'To *put the mix in* is to deliberately stir up trouble between others': Glasgow. Cf. **mix it,** 1, and **mixer,** 2.

Mickser. An *émigré* Irishman: since ca. 1950. (Campbell, 1964.) Ex *Mick*, an Irishman.

Micky or **micky.** All senses and phrases: see **Mickey** . . .

mid-day, a. Bread and cheese: tramps' c.: from ca. 1920. When he leaves a casual ward in the morning, a tramp receives an issue of bread and cheese.

mid-Vic. A mid-Victorian: cultured s.: 1932+. The adj. was rare.

midden. A district, a 'patch', q.v.: police coll. Hebden, 1974.

midder. A midwifery case, i.e. a childbirth attended by a doctor; physicians': late C.19–20. Lyons, 1909, 'We get about seven "midders" every day.'—2. A midwife: since ca. 1925. By the 'OXFORD *-ER*'.—3. Midwifery: medical students':— 1933 (*Slang*).

middie. See **middy.**

middle for diddle. The method of deciding who shall start a darts game: darts players': since ca. 1920. Each side throws a single 'arrow'—and the side landing the dart nearest to the centre has first throw.

middle name, (something or other) **is his, my,** etc. Indicates that some quality or tendency forms a marked characteristic, as 'Gossiping is her middle name'. (I first heard it in 1920, but I'm sure it's much older—perhaps going back to ca. 1870.) 'One year, when I was doing field work in the Yukon, an entomologist appeared in Whitehorse. He was a nice lad and much admired for his intimate knowledge of the "bugs" he studied. As one incredulous old-timer said, "He knows every damn bug by his middle name" ' (Leechman, 1967).

middle-page spread. 'Matter printed over the centre of pages, not uncommon since paper shortage' (Petch, 1946): journalistic: 1941+. Punning on *middle-age spread*.

middle stump. Penis: cricketers'.

middy. 'A measure of beer: in N.S.W., 10 oz; in W. [Aus.], 7 oz' (Wilkes): Aus.: since ca. 1930. O'Grady, 1972, 'Because it's midway between nothing and a pint'.

midties. '[In Cyprus, late 1950s] we worked 24 hours, and doing the midnight to early morning shift was always called "going (or being) on midties" ' (P.B., 1974): Royal Signals'. A pluralised elision of '*midnight to* . . .'

midwaaf or **midwaf.** A 'Waaf' NCO 'very officious with her girls' (H. & P.): WAAF and RAF: 1940+. Punning *mid-WAAF* and *midwife*.

midwife's friend, the. Quinine contraceptive pessaries: since ca. 1925. Ex their unreliability. *Lancet*, 1935, p. 1133.

mike or **Mike,** n. A microphone: coll. abbr.: since ca. 1927.—2. A microscope: medical students':—1933 (*Slang*).—3. A cup of tea: low Aus.: earlier C.20. (Park, 1949.) Wilkes notes 'rare'.—4. A 'shunting yard engine (Eastern Region)': railwaymen's. (*Railway*, 2nd.)—5. A microgramme of LSD: drugs world: since early 1960s. (Janssen, 1968.)—6. *Take a* (or *the*) *Mike out of* is a var. of **take the mickey** . . . , q.v., but *take a mike at* = to have a look (at): low. Brandon, 1933.—7. A casual ward: tramps' c.: late C.19–20. Either r.s. on C.19 synon. *spike*, or ex:–

mike, v. To 'hang about', either expectantly or idly: low: 1859 (H., 1st ed.).—2. To cause to decamp, i.e. to steal: earlier C.20. Mitchell, 1930, a workman speaking: 'Somebody miked a . . . Flemish Giant off me.'

Mike and George. A decoration of the Order of St *Michael* and St *George*: military: 1915; ob. by ca. 1935. F. & G.

Mike Bliss, n. and v. Piss: r.s.: late C.19–20. Often shortened to *Mike*; a var. of *Mickey Bliss*. See **take the mick(e)y.**

mike boom; mike slinger. 'To follow the players about, the "mike" [microphone] is moved across the floor on a long arm called a "mike boom", and its operator is a "mike slinger" ' (London *Evening News*, 7 Nov. 1939).

mike fright. (Extreme) nervousness in front of television, or news-reel, camera: radio and television operators': since ca. 1934. *Daily Mail*, 24 May 1950.

mike up. To take accurate measurement with a micrometer: engineers': prob. since the process of 'miking up' began. Cf. **mike,** n., 1 and 2, 'microphone' and 'microscope'. (P.B.)

mild as maiden's water(, as). 'Proverbial and alliterative phrase, expressing degree of mildness [of liquor or language], and perhaps innocuousness' (L.A., 1976): coll.: since early C.20.

mileage. Something extra; that which may be extended: as in 'Paradoxically the fact that there is no "mileage" in [*The Barnhart Dictionary of New English*] contributes to the feeling that there is plenty of mileage in it for future reviewers' (Nixon, 1975), and 'although [the playwright] wrings some dramatic mileage out of keeping us guessing . . . ' (*Time Out*, 29 Feb. 1980); also negatively, as in Nixon's word play: coll.: since early 1970s. Ex motorists' j., estimates of how many more miles, or *mileage*, a vehicle is capable of being run. (P.B.)

mileage yard. 'Station siding yard (Western Region)' (*Railway*, 2nd): railwaymen's coll.

miles away, be. To be either day-dreaming or lost in thought: coll.: since ca. 1910.

milestone-inspector. A professional tramp: tramps' c.:—1932 (Jennings).

milestones. Heavy seas breaking inboard when one is homeward-bound: RN. (Irving, 1946.) 'Like milestones on country roads they seem to make the journey longer and harder, and one's progress slower in consequence' (Granville).

milk. To withdraw part of one's winnings before a session is finished: gamblers': from not later than 1923. (*OED* Sup.) Ex the S.E. sense in 'That cow milks well.'—2. Hence(?), to remove spot-lamps, extra clocks, spare plugs, from second-hand cars and, 'on the quiet', sell them as accessories: motor trade: since ca. 1920. Often as vbl n., *milking*.—3. To stack a pack of cards: Aus. card-players': since ca. 1920. (B., 1953.) Also 'to *build*'. The nn. *building* and *milking* are common.—4. To steal the petrol from (a car) by syphoning: ca. 1940–50, while petrol was short.—5. Hence, to syphon petrol (from tank of car) for legitimate purposes: since late 1940s. These two senses esp. common in Aus. (B.P.)

milk-bar. Since mid-C.20, occ. low var. of ob. *milk-shop*, the female breasts.

milk-jug. A simpleton, a dupe: Aus. c.: since ca. 1920. (B., 1953.) As 'dupe' it is also Brit. and, of course, it rhymes on s. *mug* (Franklyn 2nd). Aus. has var. *milkie*.

milk round. 'A run made fairly regularly by a squadron or a Force, if it returns to its station or base in the early morning' (Partridge, 1945): RAF: 1940+. Cf. **milk train,** and var. *milk run*, used by US and, slightly less, Brit. airmen. R.C. notes, 1976, that it is applied esp. to raids supposed to be as safe and regular as delivering the milk, and cites Michener, 'The Milk Run', 1947.—2. The sending of recruiting teams from industry, the Civil Service, banking, etc., to the universities: since ca. 1960: s. > coll. >, by 1980, informal S.E. or j., as the Post Office advertised in *The Times*, 9 Jan. 1980, 'Our Milk Round Programme' of visits to Universities, in search of graduate recruits. ?'Creaming off the talent'. (P.B.)

milk run. See prec., 1.

milk the cow with a spanner. Open a tin of milk: RN lowerdeck joc. Granville.

milk-tin gear. A three-speed hub on a pedal bicycle: club cyclists': earlier C.20. (*Fellowship*, 1984.) Cf. **cocoa-tin.**

milk train. The early-morning reconnaissance flight(s): RAF: 1940+. (H. & P.) Cf. **milk round,** 1, and **mail run.**

Milk Tray order. Dressed in black jumpsuit: attrib. to SAS in Beevor, 1983. Ex a series of advertisements for this brand of chocolates, each ad. showing a young man thus attired, in the midst of some act of derring-do, captioned 'and all because the lady loves Milk Tray'.

milking. The 'robbing' of a closely following bus of passengers: busmen's. P.B.: presumably from early C.20 when rival bus companies were struggling for traffic, which practice, with the deregulation of road passenger traffic, has re-started, 1987.

milky. Cowardly; *turn milky*, to become afraid: c. (*Gilt Kid*, 1936.) Ex fear-caused pallor.

mill around. (Of aircraft) to fly in and out, at high speed, crossing paths; or to fly 'in a defensive circle, with the nose of one aircraft a few yards from the tail of another' (Jackson): RAF: 1940+. Adopted ex US airmen; ex 'to *mill (around)*, a cowboy term for corralled cattle going round in an ever-tightening circle' (Leechman).—2. Hence, (of tanks) to move about, either looking for targets or merely creating a dust: Army in N. Africa: 1942–3.—3. Applied also to people in crowds, as 'all these intense-looking women, milling around in front of the shop, waiting for the sale to start': coll.: since 1940s. (P.B.)

Millibar Mike. A meteorological officer: RAF, esp. officers': ca. 1940–5. (Hinde, 1945.) By alliterative personification and by ref. to millimetric readings. Specifically to the *millibar*, 2nd) a unit of atmospheric pressure.

million, a. A safe bet, a certainty (to, e.g., succeed); 'It's a million' (a plan), 'You're a million' (for promotion): police, then gen.: since ca. 1950. (Newman, 1970.) Prob. ex the odds 'a million to one'.

milly. A shirt: market-traders': C.20—perhaps since ca. 1880. (*M.T.*) Prob. ex C.18 *melthog*, Shelta for shirt.

mim! Excuse me laughing!; you make me laugh!: telegraphists'. Ex code.

Mimi Lau's. See PRISONER-OF-WAR SLANG, in Appx.

mimmies, used as a pl., generically for strong liquor: market-traders': since ca. 1930. (*M.T.*) Perhaps ex *screaming mee-mies*, US s. for excessive tantrums or esp., hysteria, itself adopted in gen. Brit. s. during the 1930s.

min. A *Mini* car; orig. Austin and Morris > BMC > British Leyland: motorists': since (?)late 1960s. As in ' 'fraid the tin termites are getting at my old min'. (P.B.)—2. Occ. abbr. of minute (of time): coll. Cf. earlier *sec*, a second.

Min. of Ag., the. The Ministry of Agriculture: since ca. 1930. (Dickens, 1946.) It was superseded by *Ag and Fish*, but was still loosely known as *the Min. of Ag.* until 1980, if not longer.

minces. Short for earlier r.s. *mince-pies*, eyes: late C.19–20. A C.20 var. is *mincers*. Franklyn 2nd.

mincing machine, the. 'The marshalling area mechanism . . . must break up units and provide mixed loads for the various forms of sea transport' (Holman, 1944): RN.

Mincing Lane. 'Alleyway in a ship where the purser's staff have their being; after the tea district of London' (Granville): RN.

mind. To be at hand to help (a crook): c. (Wallace, 1924.) Cf. **minder.**

mind-bender. A knotty problem; something that potently changes one's thinking, as, e.g., drugs: adopted, 1974, ex US. (*DCCU.*) Also the adj. and n., *mind-bending*, much more gen. than the next, and almost = *brain-washing*.—2. 'The advent of diesel trains meant that many thousands of footplatemen required training in the [new] forms of traction. Many of the tutors were drivers from the ranks of footplatemen who offered to pass their knowledge on. Because the tutors had come from their own ranks the footplatemen gave them the name of mind-benders' (McKenna, 1): railwaymen's: mid-C.20.

mind-blower. A hallucinant drug: adopted, ca. 1971, ex US. Ex *blow* (one's) *mind* (and cf. next). Hollander, 1975, 'I'm talking about drugs and alcohol and their use and abuse as mindblowers and leg-openers'. (Barnhart, 1973; W. & F., 1975.) Cf. prec.

mind-blowing. 'Ecstasy-producing' (Fryer, 1967): jazz and drug addicts', and hippies': since ca. 1966.—2. Hence, amazing; almost unbelievable: media and advertising usage: 1970s. (P.B.)

mind boggles!, the. A c.p. comment on any marked absurdity: since late 1950s. (P.B.) Hence adj. *mind-boggling*, astounding: 'popularised by BBC Radio series "Hitch-Hikers' Guide to the Galaxy", later 1970s' (Bishop, 1984.).

mind-fuck. 'Any experience that challenges previously held convictions' (Hibbert, 1983); a more emphatic var. of *mind-bending* in its brain-washing sense. Hence as v.t., and adj. *mind-fucking* (Roberts, 1983). Ex US (W & F, 1975).

mind the Dianas! Mind the doors!: bus and underground train conductors': ca. 1950–70. Ex Diana Dors, the stage and film actress.

minder. A pickpocket's assistant; one who 'minds' as in **mind,** q.v.: c. Wallace, resp. 1928 and 1924.—2. Hence, a 'con' man's assistant, who keeps the victim happy and unconscious: c.—3. 'Occasionally he acted as "minder" to one of the top-class "stable" girls (that is, he was paid to keep an eye on the harlots to make sure that they were not molested by clients or rivals)': the world of prostitution. Gosling, 1960.—4. A bouncer in a club or dance-hall or . . . : low: since late 1940s. Barlow, 1968.—5. Powis, 1977, defines the current meanings, 'A man used as an "enforcer", or to extract money from persons making regular extortion payments; a person who "minds" or looks after stolen property and, less commonly, a milder term for a ponce.'

mine-layers. 'Men who drop cigarette-ends from their hammocks. If they are seen there is an explosion from Authority' (Granville): RN lowerdeck.

miners' friends (or capitals). 'Royal Scots locomotives' (*Railway*, 2nd): railwaymen's: since ca. 1925(?). P.B. presumably, they used a lot of coal.

mine's. Mine is: coll.: C.19–20. E.g. 'Mine's a gin.' P.B.: and the mid-C.20 slogan advertising a brand of small cigarettes, 'Ten minutes to wait—mine's a Minor'.—2. *Mine's up!* See PRISONER-OF-WAR SLANG, in Appx.

ming. To stink; hence, mainly in *minging*, 'stinking', > by ellipsis, '(stinking) drunk': Army (Other Ranks'): early 1970s. Perhaps ex dial., though not recorded in *EDD*. (P.B.) Munro, 1985, notes it as Glasgow.

minge, n. Female society: military: 1915–18. (F. & G.) Ex:—2. In c., the female pudend: late C.19–20. (*Gilt Kid*, 1936.) Ex Romany. Also Services' usage: 'Booze and minge, that's what got most blokes inside [gaol]. Men's eternal downfalls' (A prison officer, ex-RM, quoted in *Guardian*, 5 Sep. 1987).

minge, v.; minger; mingy. To prowl about in order to discover misdemeanours; one who does this; addicted thereto: St Bees: early C.20. (Marples.) Cf. dial. *minch*, to move stealthily, and the generally mean (see **mingy**) attitude of one who does this.

mingra. A policeman, as in 'Nanty! The mingra's screwing you!' (*M.T.*); market-traders'. Orig. obscure; neither dial. nor Romany. P.B.: cf. n. *minger* at **minge, v.**

mingy. Miserly, mean; hence (from not later than 1915) disappointingly small: coll. Thinned ex *mangy* (W.) and prob. influenced by *stingy*. App. first 'lexicographed' by W., 1920, but (as 'mean') definitely remembered by the author at least as early as 1910.

mini. A mini(-)skirt: early, although not common until late, 1967, with multitudinous references, spoken and written, throughout 1967: coll.; by 1968, S.E. Hence, since (ca. Sep.) 1967, an adj., as in 'She was wearing the miniest of minis': s.

The term *mini(-)skirt* stands for *minimum* (rather than *minimal*) skirt, ensuring the minimum of decency: you can't see her panties until the girl sits down or offers a rear view as she bends down. One of the most revolutionary fashions ever to enhance the gaiety of nations during a period when gaiety is rarer than gold. Usually, however, *mini* is short for the adjectival use of *miniature*. Cf. **pussy-pelmet** and **bum-flapper.** Also known as a *fan-belt*.

minions of the moon. 'Our night fighters and bombers' (H. & P.): journalistic, it was jocularly taken up by the RAF in 1941–3. Ex the S.E. sense, 'moonlight-utilisers'.

Ministry of Fish and Chips, the. The Ministry of Agriculture and Fisheries: joc. political: since the 1930s.

Minnie. As *Minnie*, the *Mini*stry of Information: WW2.—2. Also as *Minnie*, the mini-car; briefly, at the time of the vehicle's appearance, ca. 1960. Thereafter, simply *mini*. Edwards, 1961.

minnow. (Usu. in pl.) A torpedo: RN: 1937+. Cf. synon. **mouldy.**

mint. Absolutely as new; clean and with leaves uncut: esp. in *a mint copy*: booksellers' s. (—1927) >, ca. 1932, j.

miraculous. (Very) drunk: Scottish:—1870. Perhaps abbr. *in miraculous high spirits*. (*EDD*.) Munro, 1985, notes its continued use in Glasgow, 'usually, who knows why, pronounced "marockgoolus" . . . "Maroc" is sometimes heard as a shortened form of this.'

mis. Disorientated; 'lost' or bewildered: theatrical: since ca. 1960. (Morice, 1977.) Perhaps ex '*mis*laid' and influenced by '*amiss*'.—2. (Pron. *miz*.) *Mis*erable: (mostly domestic) coll. 'This maranta's looking very mis. Have you watered it lately?' (P.B.)

miser rate. 'A minimum bonus payment. Miser rate comes from the advertisements presented by the South Eastern Gas Board who produced a gas cooker which allegedly was so economical that its trade mark was "The Miser"' (McKenna, 1): railwaymen's.

miss a trick. Always negative, in such phrases as 'He's a crafty so-and-so, he never misses a trick', i.e. he never misses a chance, an opening, or whatever 'he' is watching for: coll.: since mid-C.20. Ex card games. (P.B.)

Miss Emma. Morphine: drugs c. (Stockley, 1986.) US since—1938 (Spears). Cf. **M.,** 1.

Miss Fist. In *make* (or, usu., *making*) *love to Miss Fist*, male masturbation: Services': mid-C.20. Cf. synon. *five-fingered widow.*

Miss Fitch. A *bitchy* girl or woman: r.s. Franklyn 2nd.

miss (one's) guess. To be mistaken: Can. coll. (Beames.) Ex US.

miss out on. To miss; lose an, or the, opportunity for: coll.: adopted, mid-1940s, ex US. Naughton, 1970, 'Though I miss out on many a piece of tail where another bloke would grab it.' Also, absolutely, *miss out*.

miss stays. 'To be slow to "register"; to miss the purport of a signal, or fail to see the point of an argument or a wardroom story' (Granville): RN coll. Ex a sailing-ships' technicality.

miss the boat. To be too late: nautical coll. > widespread and gen.—2. 'Not to catch the point; to be "clueless": W. Can.: since ca. 1950. As in, "Boy, you sure missed the boat that time. Let me rephrase it more simply"' (Leech, 1986). Cf.:-

miss the bus. To lose an, or the, opportunity: coll.: since ca. 1915. (Dennis.) 'One thing is certain: [Hitler] missed the bus' (Neville Chamberlain, the Prime Minister, in a speech, 4 Apr. 1940).

mission, off the, adj. and adv. Applied to a lapsed priest: Aus. Catholic priests': since ca. 1960. (B.P., 1969.)

missionary's or **missionaries' downfall, the.** A light rum; or—esp. Demerara—rum diluted: since ca. 1930. *Trader Vic's Book of Food and Drink*, 1946, p. 36, 'Don the Beachcomber of Hollywood and Chicago, the originator of such outstanding drinks as the Zombie and Missionary's Downfall': therefore perhaps of US origin.

mist. See **Scotch mist.**

Mister Charlie. A white man. See **pinkie, 3.**

Mister Middleton's Light Horse. 'A flotilla of flower-named corvettes. (After the late Mr Middleton, the B.B.C. gardening expert)': RN, esp. officers': 1939+. Granville.

Mister (or **Mr**) **Muggins.** Oneself regarded, esp. by oneself, as a dupe, a simpleton: Aus.: late C.19–20. (B.P.) Cf. **muggins.**

mistressing. Acting as a concubine: early 1980s. E.g. in *LAM*, 12 Oct. 1982, two advertisers, each describing himself as a 'businessman', offered free accommodation in return for 'part-time mistressing'.

mit. See **mitt.**—2. As preposition: see **with or without,** with which cf.:-

mit a. With a grain of salt—i.e. sceptically—as in 'I'd take that story mit a': Aus.: since ca. 1950. This is the Ger. *mit*, with; 'possibly due to New Australian influence' (Morrisby, 1958).

mitney, mitni. A policeman: c.:—1923 (Manchon). Prob. ex either Romany or Shelta.

mitt; occ. mit. (Gen. *the mitt.*) Handwork, work by hand: tailors': earlier C.20.—2. Hand: low coll.: adopted, ca. 1918, ex US. 'We heard much of . . . Turkey and Austria, both having "thrown in their mits" as the current jargon phrased it' (Graham, 1919), i.e. part of the surrender of the Central Powers, 1918.—3. See **frozen mitt.**

mittens. (Very rare in sing.) Handcuffs: c.:—1933 (Leach).

mix. See **Micks, 3.**

mix it. To fight vigorously: Aus. (—1916) >, by 1918, gen. and, by 1936, coll. (Dennis.) Cf. US *mix-in*, a fight.—2. *Mix it for*, to inform against (someone) to the police: low. (Benney, 1940.) Cf. **Micks, 3.**

mix the red and the black, whence the synon. *play roulette.* To assault an officer when brought before him on a charge: Army: since ca. 1925. (Wild, 1943.) † by 1950.

mix-up. A fight, esp. a general scrimmage. Cf. **mix it.**

mixer; good mixer. A sociable person; one who gets on well with others: US (resp. early C.20 and late C.19), anglicised ca. 1924: coll. >, by 1933, S.E. Maugham, 1925, *good mixer*. (The opp. is *bad mixer*.) *OED* Sup.—2. One who makes mischief, esp. one given to mischief-making: Cockneys': from ca. 1912. E.g. 'He's a reg'lar mixer! He mixed it up for me with Joe, and he tried to mix it with Tom.' See **Micks, 3.**

miz. See **mis, 2.**

mizzle. To complain: Aus. (Baker.) Perhaps an elision of *miserable.*

mningi. 'A great number' (Wilson, 1979): RAF: 1970s. Orig. ex Swahili.

moan. To complain, grumble; to do so habitually: RN > Services' generally: since 1915 at latest. (F. & G.) Ex dial.

moaner. A pessimist: Services' coll.: since ca. 1914.

moaning Minnie. An occ. var. of *Mona*, the air-raid warning siren: see **Clara.**—2. A German multi-barrelled mortar: Army: 1940+. Echoic.

mob. In late C.19–20, esp. in WW1 and 2, a military unit, esp. a battalion or a battery. (Not disrespectful.) S. rapidly > coll. (B. & P.; F. & G.) Later, *this mob* or *the mob*: 'I've been with this mob for three years now' (this particular unit), but 'I've been in the mob . . . ' = the army as a whole. (L.A.: P.B.)

mob-handed. In a 'mob'; in a group: grafters'. (*Cheapjack*, 1934.) *M.T.*, 'The bogy came mob-handed', the police arrived in force.

mobile, n. A traymobile, i.e. a dinner wagon on castors or wheels: Aus. coll.: since late 1940s. (B.P.)

mobile, adj. In *get mobile*: see **get cracking,** move quickly.

mobile dandruff. Body-lice, 'crabs': Services': since ca. 1955. (P.B.)

mobile knee-trembler. An early motorised scooter on which a saddle was an optional extra; in production 1919–20. (Dunford, 2.)

mobs of. A large number, even a large quantity, of; e.g. *mobs of stones—birds—water*: Aus. coll.: late C.19–20.

mocassin (or **moccasin**) **telegraph, the.** A frequent Can. 'shape' of the **bush telegram** and the **grapevine:** since ca. 1910 at latest. (Leechman.)

mock. A halfpenny: Aus. B., 1942.—2. (Or *mocks*.) A mock or trial-run examination: schools' coll.: since ca. 1955. 'Yes, the exam's not till next term, but we're holding the mocks in February'. (D. Beale, 1974.)—3. See **mock on . . .**

mock auction. For slang associated, see this entry in Appx.

mock on. In *put the mock* or *mocks* or *mocker* or *mockers* or *moz(z) on* (someone or something): 'to frustrate someone's plans; to put a [jinx or] hoodoo on someone, destroy his luck' (Wilkes, who cites Aus. examples of *mock*, 1911, 1965; 'I've got a mocker hung on me', 1923; *mocks*, 1938; *mockers*, 1974). Wilkes and E.P. imply a predominantly Aus. usage, but Franklyn suggests that all variants stem from Yiddish 'wish the *mockers* on (someone)'—to wish him very bad luck, itself ex Hebrew (one of the Ten Plagues). The phrase has certainly had very wide Eng. use since mid-C.20 at latest, in the form *put the mockers on* (a person, event, machine, etc.); O'Shaughnessy records it as market-traders' argot, which might poss. indicate continuity from C.19 London Jewish traders. See also **mozzle,** v. (P.B.) See also **mogador.**

mock up. To improvise; as n. (*mock-up*), a large- or a full-scale, although not usu. a working, model: Services' coll. (1939), became, by 1942, j.

mocker. 'Clothes in general' (B., 1953): low Aus.: since ca. 1920.—2. Hence, a woman's dress: NZ: since ca. 1935. Slatter, 'Have you seen that trot in the blue mocker?' See also **mockered up.**—3. See **mock on.**

mockered up. Dressed in one's best: low: late C.19–20. Ironically ex *mockered* on *molled up*. ?The orig. of **mocker,** 1 and 2, q.v.

mockers on. See **mock on.**

mocking bird. A word: theatrical r.s. (Franklyn.) Cf. synon. **dickey-bird, 1.**

mocks on. See **mock on.**

mod. A mechanical improvement or change in an aircraft: RAF coll.: since ca. 1920. (Jackson.) Short for '*modification*'.—2. A teenager unable to afford a motorcycle, and doing his damnedest with a scooter: 1963(+), partly in opposition to **rocker,** n., 2, q.v. Short for *modern.*

mod con. (Usu. in pl, *all mod cons.*) Modern convenience: joc.: since ca. 1945. Derisive of estate agents' jargon.

model, n. Working-men's hotel or lodging-house: Glasgow: from ca. 1920. (MacArthur.) Presumably ex some 'model' establishment of this sort; cf.:—2. *The Model*, Pentonville Prison: low: mid-C.19–early 20. Ex *model prison.*

model, v. To pose as a model; to act as a mannequin: artists' and models' coll., since early C.20; by mid-C.20, at latest, familiar S.E.

modern girl, 'from a proprietary brand of Chinese cigarette, was a common name for the particularly odorous dried fish we sometimes obtained in the rations': among Far East prisoners of war: 1942–5. (The aspersion is directed at the cigarette, not at the girl.)

modest quencher. A small drink: from ca. 1860; ob.: coll. H., 3rd ed.—2. Hence, in C.20, 'an expensive drink or simply a drink of any kind' (Lyell).

modified. Applied to a car that has been in an accident; also known as *had a set*: car-dealers'. (Graham-Ranger, 1981.) Cf. **mod,** 1.

mog. A cat: mainly schoolboys'. (Collinson.) Perhaps ex dial. *moggy*, applied to various animals.—2. Hence, a cat's-skin tippet or other fur: racing s. or c.:—1932. (*Slang.*)

mogador. (Of persons) confused; depressed; all at sea: Cockneys': since ca. 1910. (Franklyn, 1939.) Also *mogadored*, prob. the orig. form and therefore perhaps a perversion of *moidered*. The police have, since ca. 1940, used *mogadored* of a suspect that, at an interrogation, is 'broken' to the state of giving facts (L.A., 1948). Franklyn, however, thinks *mogadored*, (fig.) floored, is r.s.; but cf.: 'The word comes from the Romany *mokardi* or *mokodo*, which has also produced "put the mockers on" [q.v. at **mock on**] something = to jinx it. It refers to gypsy taboos: the *mokardi* article is tainted and has to be destroyed' (*Muvver*).

mogger. A cat: low. Cf:-

Moggie, -y; or **m-.** A cat: Cockneys' (and dial.): late C.19–20. Cf. **mog**, 1.—2. A Morgan cycle-car (a light car with a motorcycle engine): devotees': since the 1930s. (Partridge, 1979.)—3. A Consolidated *Catalina* long-range amphibious aircraft: RN: WW2. Silverlight, 1984.—4. (Usu. pl.) Mogadon, a proprietary brand of sleeping pill: drugs c. Stockley, 1986.

Moggy Thousand. Morris Minor 1000cc saloon car: later C.20. (P.B.)

Mohammed Ali. A regimental institute: coll. among regular soldiers in India: ca. 1920–40. Such institutes are often supplied by a merchant so, or analogously, named.

moist round the edges. Very slightly tipsy: rare: earlier C.20.

mojo! A yell of approval or of excitement: rhythm-and-blues fans', esp. teenagers': ca. 1964–6. Ex an American Negro s. term of vague meaning (e.g. a spell, power).—But in American drug addicts' s. it = 'any narcotic': prob. a different word. R.S. suggests, 1972, that the latter sense may derive ex Sp. *mojo*, a condiment or seasoning.

mole. The penis (whence *mole-catcher*, the female pudend): low: C.19–earlier 20.—2. A secondary nuance, rather than a well-differentiated sense, is 'A girl who will have sexual intercourse with anybody who asks. The term seems to be used as a pejorative by those who will [do so] with almost anyone. The word could be an altered form of *moll*, or the animal' (B.P., 1969). Aus. and, by late 1970s, NZ.—3. An agent of penetration and subversion: orig. espionage, since late 1940s; in later 1970s, more gen., as various 'moles' were 'uncovered' in the Civil Service, trades unions and other high positions of trust. See also **sleeper**, 3. (P.B.)

molegrip size. 'Name given to a bastard size nut or bolt. A molegrip is an adjustable wrench' (Dunford, 2): motorcyclists': later C.20.

moll, n. A harlot: C.17–20: c. >, ca. 1890, low. P.B.: in later C.20, ob. in Brit., but still current in Aus.: McNeil defines thus, 'Woman of easy virtue and low social status, a prostitute'. Ex the familiar form of *Mary*.

moll, adj. Ugly: Northumberland teenagers'. (Blyth, 1984.)

molly-dooker; whence **molly-dook.** A left-handed person, whence (the adj.) left-handed: Aus.: since ca. 1930. (B., 1943.) Wilkes lists var. *molly-duked*.

Molly Malone. Telephone: r.s.: later C.20. Jones, 1971; Powis, who indicates, 1977, a usu. shortening to *Molly*. Ex the heroine of the trad. ballad 'Cockles and Mussels'.

Molotov bread-basket. 'A bunch of incendiaries which blow out in a group as they drop to the ground' (H. & P.): 1940+. Cf.:-

Molotov cocktail. An anti-tank missile consisting of a bottle containing flammable material and fitted with a fuse: 1939–45. (H. & P.) Like prec., ex the name of the Russian statesman. Adopted from Finnish usage. Still in use in late 1970s, and S.E.: BBC News, 4 Feb. 1979, reported the Iranian Prime Minister as saying that he would 'answer Molotov cocktail for Molotov cocktail'.

momma. 'The "Hell's Angel's" [q.v.] girl passenger: motorcyclists': ca. 1950s' (Dunford, 2).

Mona. A nickname for a female given to complaining, unless by chance it is her Christian name: Londoners': from ca. 1919. Punning *moaner*. From 1947 often elab. to *Mona Lott*, after the famous depressed washerwoman in the BBC radio comedy series 'Itma'; her drearily uttered 'It's being so cheerful as keeps me going' became an extremely popular c.p.—2. The air-raid warning siren: civilians': WW2. See also **Clara** and **Wailing Winnie.**

Monday. A very large hammer that can be effectually used by fit men only: railwaymen's: since ca. 1920. (*Railway*, 2nd.) Men free of a week-end hangover.

Mondayish. As in 'The class were very Mondayish', i.e. they were inattentive, not 'with it', gen. suffering from the effects of resuming study after the weekend: teachers': later C.20. (P.B.)

money. In *in the money*, receiving good wages or a large salary: coll.: since ca. 1934. P.B.: also, occ., to be enjoying the proceeds of a large win.

money-box. A 'Royal Mail train' (Railway, 2nd): railwaymen's.

money to burn, have. To have plenty to spend; to be rich: coll.

mong. A *mongrel* dog: Aus.: since ca. 1910. B., 1912.—2. Hence, pej. for any dog, even of the best pedigree: Aus. since ca. 1940. 'Get that bloody mong out of my yard!' (B.P.)—3. Children's pej. term, short for *mongoloid*: later 1970s. (*New Society*, 31 Jan. 1980.) Cf. **mongie.**

mongie (hard *g*). Dull, stupid: teenagers': since ca. 1975. (D. & R. McPheely.) Also *mongish* (*New Society*, 31 Jan. 1980). Ex *mongoloid*. (P.B.)—2. Dirty, fusty, evil-smelling; nasty: Leicestershire children's: 1970s. (P.B.)

monk. In *out the monk*, no longer available or serviceable, e.g. water or trucks: Army: WW2. Page, 2, with ref. to the Royal Army Service Corps in Italy, 1944.

monkey. £500 (in US $500): 1856, *The Druid*; Whyte Melville. (The *OED* cites an 1832 text in which, prob. erroneously, it = £50.) Among stockbrokers, however, *monkey* (in C.20) = £50,000 of stock, i.e. 500 shares of £100. Note that Tempest, 1950, lists *monkey* as prison c. for £50.—2. Morphine: drugs c. (Stockley, 1986.) US since—1971 (Spears); perhaps ex **monkey on** (one's) **back**, q.v.

monkey and the nut, a or **the.** 'The Cunard houseflag with its lion and globe': nautical: earlier C.20. Bowen.

monkey(-)bite. A mark left—often on the shoulder—by amorous biting: Can.: since ca. 1930.

monkey-boat. 'In the plural, ships of the Elder Dempster Line, which carry nut kernels in their cargoes' (Granville): nautical: earlier C.20.

monkey-cage. The steel structure of a modern building: mostly Cockney's.

monkey(-)crouch. An American 'seat in the saddle', introduced to Eng. jockeys by a Negro jockey named Sims: racing coll.: since ca. 1925. Sarl, 1938.

monkey dirt. 'Heavy sand from Huddersfield, used as packing between wood and iron in shipbuilding' (Seymour, 1966).

monkey-dodger. A sheep-station hand: Aus. Wilkes quotes Tait, 1912, 'Behold in me chief serang, head monkey dodger to the high and holy Hungry Harris.' Ex *monkey*, Aus. C.19 s. for sheep.

monkey-farting, n. and adj. Applied to useless employment, waste of time, silly behaviour: Can. (esp. soldiers').

Monkey House, the. The Admiralty: RN: since ca. 1890. Cf. **Madhouse**, 2.

monkey hunt. A beach-party (esp. at Trincomalee, Ceylon/Sri Lanka); a run ashore: since (?)C.19: nautical. Orig. literal, but by 1960s, simply 'a good time'. (Clive Hardy, 1979.)

monkey oboe. A medical officer: Army: early WW2. Ex the signals PHONETIC ALPHABET, q.v. in Appx., for *M.O.* P-G-R.

monkey on a gridiron. A cyclist: Cockneys': late C.19–20. (Horsley, 1912.) Hence *sit like a monkey on a gridiron*, to be a bad, or very ungraceful, horseman: coll.:—1923 (Manchon).

monkey on a stick. 'Term used to describe the riding position adopted on early veteran motorcycles. Because of the high seat, and particularly alluding to the very long handlebars which came back to almost level with the saddle' (Partridge, 1979): motorcyclists': earlier C.20. Ex a C.19 toy.

monkey on (one's) **back(, have a).** (To be ridden by) the drug habit: Can.: adopted, ca. 1945, ex US; by 1950, police and low s. (Leechman.)

monkey suit. Uniform provided by carnival proprietor: Can. carnival s.

monkey tail. A 'handle for opening doors on mineral wagons' (*Railway*, 2nd): railwaymen's.

monkey-traps. Female finery, to 'catch' men: since ca. 1930.

monkey(-)tricks. Sexual liberties: proletarian coll.: from ca. 1890. George, 1914.—2. Hence, any annoying action: since ca. 1920. Sayers, 1937.

monkey's, a. Short for *a monkey's fuck* or *toss*, q.v. at **not care a . . .**

monkey's breakfast. 'Any untidy piece of work is said to look like a "monkey's breakfast" ' (Granville): nautical.

monkey's wedding. 'Lowerdeck term used to describe an unpleasant smell' (Granville): RN.

monnisher. Young woman: market-traders'. (*M.T.*) Cf. C.19 synon. *mollesher* or *mollisher*; all prob. ex Romany *monoshi*, a woman, perhaps influenced by *moll*.

mono. A monotype machine or process: printers' s. (—1910) >, ca. 1925, coll.—2. A monochrome car, radio or TV set, or whatever: coll.: since late 1940s. (McClure, 1977.) P.B.: by late 1970s applied to anything *mono-*, opp. *multi-* or *stereo-*: j.

mons. As *da mons*, one of many motor-trade s. terms for 'money' (others being, *bees and honey, gelt, kite, oats for the donkey, smash*): since ca. 1920. Joc. on It. pron. of *money*.

Monte. Monte Carlo: a coll. used mostly by those who have never been there. 'Quill', 1936.—2. Hence, the Monte Carlo Rally: motorists': since late 1940s.—3. (Also *monty*.) A certainty, 'a sure thing': Aus.: since late C.19. Wilkes, who derives it ex the US card game (Mathews, 1841); *SOD* says Spanish or Mexican, 1850, for the game.—4. (?)Hence, a lie: Aus.: since ca. 1935. B., 1959.—5. 'The three-card trick' (Powis): c.: later C.20. See sense 3.

Montezuma's revenge. A severe attack of diarrhœa, 'the screaming shits': perhaps orig. Services'; I heard it in Cyprus, late 1950s; later, more widespread. (P.B., 1974.) Adopted ex US, where orig. 'used by tourists in Mexico' (W. & F.). The Aztec emperor Montezuma II was defeated, 1519–20, by the Conquistadores. Cf. **Aztec two-step.**

montygram. A signal written by F.-M. Montgomery: Army officers': later WW2. (P-G-R.) He was known to all as 'Monty'.

Monty(s) moonlight. 'Artficial light provided by search-lights set a short way behind the front . . . , thus enabling men and vehicles to move [at night] in comparative safety without lights' (P-G-R.): Army: later WW2. Cf.:-

Monty's Own. Minesweepers clearing the fairway along the N. African coast for the 8th Army: Services': 1943. P-G-R.

moo. *Old—silly—silly old moo*; *old—silly—silly old mare. Moo*, which shortens nursery *moo-cow* and is euph. for **cow**, q.v., is virtually synon. with *mare* as a mild Cockney pej. of late C.19–20. (But see **mare** for later C.20 usage.) Whereas *old mare* and *old moo* are neutral and often affectionate, *silly mare* and *silly moo* connote silliness; more common than either of those pairs (Franklyn, 1967) are *silly old mare* and *silly old moo*; the last is the commonest of all and has moved out of the merely Cockney region to the social atmosphere wherein a young husband can, without fear of instant divorce, address his wife as *silly (old) moo*. Granville recalls that, in the old Caledonian Market (see **Stones**, 2), he often heard such admonitions as 'you silly moo, that was worth five bob more that you let him have it for', and has, then as since, heard it 'applied to kids returning from errands. "You stupid little mare, you've forgotten the tea"'. Addressed to females only, of course.

mooch. A dupe, esp. in respect of stocks and shares; *mooch man*, a good canvasser for the sale of (dud) shares; *mooch manna*, a (rich) business man too proud to admit that he has been victimised by share-pushers: commercial (under)world: since ca. 1925. (*John Bull*, 21 Jan. 1939.) The first, at least, has been adopted from US—see *Underworld*.

moocher, moucher. A customer owing money to the bank: Anglo-Irish bank-clerks'.

moochers' mile. 'The Mecca of the suburbanites . . . along Piccadilly, through Piccadilly-circus to Leicester Square' (*Daily Express*, 12 June 1944): since ca. 1930. Ex the sauntering.

moody, n. 'Gentle persuasion, blarney, flattery': grafters'. (*Cheapjack*, 1934.) Perhaps ex sense 4.—2. As *the (old) moody*, a psychiatrist's man-to-man, or even genial, approach to a prisoner: prison c.: since ca. 1945. (Norman.) A special application of sense 1.—3. (*Old*) *moody*, 'Lies, a deceit and, in another sense, something that goes wrong. "What he said was just a load of old moody" means it was deceitful and false, and "It went moody on us" would mean that the expected successful result did not materialise' (Powis): c.: later C.20.—4. Short for *Moody and Sankey* (now always *Moody*, hence *moody*)—r.s. on *hanky-panky*, itself perhaps an elab. of *hanky*, handkerchief, that 'with which the conjurer employing the quick hand deceives an observing eye' (Franklyn 2nd).—5. A period of (extreme) moodiness: since ca. 1965. *Groupie*, 1968.

moody, v. 'Put into good humour by means of ingratiating talk; wheedle; flatter; humour' (*M.T.*): grafters'. (*Cheapjack*, 1934.) Cf. n., 1. Hence, *do a moody*, to treat someone thus.

moody, adj. Simulated, faked, as in 'a moody ruck' or faked quarrel: prison c.: since ca. 1945. (Norman.) By ca. 1950 it had > police s., as in ' "I don't have to tell you," Kenyon went on, "how easy it is to plant moody information about a copper" ' (Crisp, 1978). 'What we market-traders call "a moody ruck" . . . an argument two stall-holders pretend to start to get attention, draw a crowd' (*New Society*, 23 Apr. 1981).

moody-merchant. 'One who can "tell the tale"; smooth-tongued fellow; flatterer' (*M.T.*): market-traders'.

moody ruck. See **moody**, adj.

moola(h). Money, esp. ready money: Can. (Leechman), adopted ex US, where 'not in common use until ca. 1935' (W. & F.); by mid-C.20 also Brit. raffish; ob. by ca. 1970. Campbell, 1960.

moon, n. A month's imprisonment: c.: 1830, Moncrieff, 'They've lumbered him for a few moons, that's all.' Hence, *long moon*, a calendar month. Cf. **drag**, n., 1. *Moon* = month recorded by Powis, 1977, as current c. See quot'n at **strong,** v.—2. (Illicit) home-brewed whisky: Can., adopted late 1960s ex US (Leechman.) Abbr. *moonshine* (W. & F.).

moon, v. To display one's naked buttocks: adopted ex US, where orig. student s. (W & F, 1975), late 1970s. A coarse and barbaric gesture of defiance or derision. Vbl. n. *mooning*; cf. **moon job.** It was reported that during the First Opium War, ca. 1839, Chinese sailors lined the decks of their war junks and thus exposed themselves to scare off the invading British forces—and were peppered with grapeshot for their efforts.

Moon City. 'The [RN] officers [at Clyde Submarine Base] live on [a] site with its own angular charm, perfectly nick-named "Moon City" ' (Winton, 1976).

moon job. 'He had intended to hurtle down the runway [aboard a home-bound aircraft] exposing his backside at the Falklands [Islands] in the time-honoured manner known as "doing a moon job" ' (*Don't Cry*, 1983).

moonie, -y. 'A new arrival in a tropical country, distinguished by the fact that his face is pale and hence, presumably, "moon-like" ' (Reynolds): RAF overseas: 1950s–60s.—2. (Also *Moonie*, and usu. pl.) Member of the Unification Church, a sect founded in S. Korea, 1954, by the Rev. Sun Myung Moon. In 1959 it spread to USA, and by early 1977 its missionaries had reached London. US 'Moonies' were referred to in print in the *Economist*, 9 Apr. 1977, and, in an Eng. context, in *New Statesman*, 24 June 1977.

moonlighter. One who holds two paid positions at the same time; hence, *moonlighting*, the practice involved, and *moonlight*, v.: Can. (Leechman) and Brit. coll.: adopted, mid-C.20, ex US, where popular during and since WW2 (W. & F.). Most such jobs involve evening work. See also **ghost**, n., 3.

moony. Romantic: coll.: since early C.20.

Moor, the. (The prison on) Dartmoor: c. Wallace, passim (e.g. *The Squeaker*).

moose. 'An eligible female of Japan or Korea is known as a "moose" . . . from the Japanese word "musume"—girl' (*Iddiwah*, July 1953): UN troops' in Korea: ca. 1951–5.—2. (Also *regular moose* and *bull-moose*.) A huge, powerful fellow: Can. coll. 'A moose of a man'.

moose milk. 'Any of various home brews concocted in the Yukon. One consists of Eagle Brand condensed milk laced liberally with rum': NW Can.: since ca.1920. (Leechman.)

moosh. Var. of some senses of **mush**.

mop. A horse-whip: Aus. sporting: since ca. 1920. B., 1959.— 2. (*Mop*.) 'A jocular form of *Ma* or *Mum*, used to rhyme with *Pop*' (Petch): since mid-C.20, perhaps earlier.

mop down. To empty a glass, etc.: a var. of earlier *mop up*, v. Gen. in form *mop it down*, to drink freely.

mop-top. One, usu. a youth or a young man, who wears his hair mop-shaped; applied notably to the Beatles "pop" group: 1960s. (Petch, 1969.)

mopey as a wet hen. Glum: NZ and Aus. coll. B., 1941, 1942.

mopper. See **wine-mopper**.

Mopper-Up, the. A fast goods-train travelling to London with food-supplies: railwaymen's: from ca. 1920. *Daily Telegraph*, 15 Aug. 1936.

moppie or **-y.** One of a cleaning-up party: Services': since ca. 1925. Ex the mop he wields so vigorously.

mopping up the miles. Speeding: motorists' coll.—1935.

more about (him, her) **than most, have.** As in 'She has more about her than most girls of her age and position', more ability, intelligence, sense: since ca. 1945, in my memory; a coll. that, by 1977, was familiar S.E. Cf. 'He has much more to him than most'.

more like, preposition. Nearer: coll. Headlam, 1902, ' . . . 4 . . . I gladly adopted more like 12.' *OED*.—2. Abbr. *more like it*, better, more acceptable or reasonable or sensible: coll.

more (adj.) **than soft Mick.** An intensification of the adj.: Army: 1950s. Cf. *drunk as soft Mick*. (P.B.) See **soft mick**.

morf. Morphine: drugs c. (Stockley, 1986.) US since—1933 (Spears).

Morgan's orchard. In cribbage, 4: players'. Priestley points out, 4 contains two pairs (pears). Cf.:—2. In the game of poker, it is 9. Anecdotally ex Morgan, a poker-player famous at end of C.19 as being a character and as having a speech defect; he used to say 'tree trees' for 'three threes'. Hence, 9 = three trees. (I do not guarantee the authenticity of this.)

Morgue, the. Obituary press-cuttings; obituaries kept ready for notabilities likely to die shortly: journalistic. This 'department' also contains all the necessary information about anyone likely, for any reason at all, to become news.

morguey manor. 'A district dangerous for "screwing" jobs [= burglaries]. A well-policed district' (Tempest): c.: mid-C.20.

morning glory. 'Sexual intercourse before getting dressed in the morning' (B.P., 1974): Aus.: later C.20. Ex the flower-name.

morning prayers. See **prayers**.

Morocco (gold). Cannabis (resin): drugs c. Stockley, 1986.

moron. A half-wit: orig. (ca. 1922), US; anglicised in 1929 as a coll. (James, 1929.) Ex the technical sense, 'one of the highest type of feeble-minded' (US: 1910), itself ex Gr. μωρός, foolishly stupid.

Morris, the. 'The Cowley works [of British Leyland > Austin Rover, at Oxford], which gave its name to William Morris's first successful [car] model in 1915, is still known locally as "the Morris" ' (*New Society*, 22 July 1982).

Morrison mousetrap. A Morrison table air-raid shelter, a prefabricated metal affair for erection inside the home: 1941+. Ex the sides of wire-work. (*New Statesman*, 30 Aug. 1941.) Cf.:-

Morrison time. Double British Summer time: coll.: 1940–5 (Minister of Home Security: the Rt Hon. Herbert Morrison).

mort. A woman: c.: since ca. 1530–1890. Awdelay; B.E., 'a Wife, Woman, or Wench'; Disraeli. As 'older woman', 'wife' it remains current in market-traders' argot, later C.20.

(*M.T.*)—2. An honest, old-fashioned person: Aus.: since early 1960s. Ex Fr. *mort*, dead. (B.P.) Presumably a youngster's view of a 'square'.

Mort's Dock. Penis: MN: 1960s–70s. Peppitt, 1976, writes: 'Sydney dockers threaten to grab you by/in a mythical part of the port's complex, Mort's Dock. It is rhyming slang for cock. Unique to Sydney in my experience'. Therefore classifiable as Sydney dockers'.

mortuary. The fish storage room of a trawler: trawlermen's. Piper, 1974: 'I climbed down into . . . the quiet and chilly atmosphere of what was known as the mortuary.'

Moscow, n. A pawnshop: Aus. (B., 1943.) Hence *gone to*, or *in*, *Moscow*, in pawn. (Caddie, 1953.) See:-

Moscow, v. To pawn: Aus. (B., 1943.) A folk-etymological alteration of later C.19 synon. *moskeneer*, to pawn (a Yiddish corruption of modern Hebrew *mishken*, to pawn).

Moscow mule. 'Just add two ounces of vodka to a lager, and a couple of cubes of ice . . . It should have a splash of lime juice as well' (York, 1967): bar-rooms': since ca. 1950. *Moscow* refers to the vodka, *mule* to the 'kick'.

mosey. Often with adv., *about*, *along*, *around*, *off*, *over*, etc.: to jog along (*OED* quotes Kipling, 1891, 'I'll mosey along somehow'); in C.20, even less active than 'jog', more 'to stroll idly, perhaps lingering vaguely in the hope that some circumstance, pleasant or of interest, may develop out of it' (L.A., 1974), as 'I think perhaps I'll just mosey over to the NAAFI—anyone coming?' (P.B.). Orig. US (—1836).

mosk. To pawn: perhaps orig. c. A shortening of *moskeneer*, q.v. at **Moscow**, v.

moskeen. Broke, without money: RAF in Iraq: ca. 1920–55. Jackson, 1945.

mosker (occ. **mosca**). A professional pledger of 'fired' sapphires, paste diamonds, and the like who sells his pawn-tickets at a profit.

mosking. Ex **mosk**, q.v.: low (?orig. c.): 1902, the *Standard*, June 5 (*OED*), 'The practice of obtaining a living by professional pawning—known as "mosking",' which word has almost superseded *moskeneering*. See **Moscow**, v.

Moslem broker is a folk-etymological var., since ca. 1930, of *mozzle and brocha*. Franklyn.

Moss Bross. Messrs Moss Brothers, Ltd, the firm from which so many people hire their formal (masculine) clothes: esp. Londoners': since ca. 1920. Ex conventional abbr. *bros*, brothers.

mossie. As 'mosquito', see **mozzy**.

mossing. Depositing things in pawn: mostly among Londoners. (Davis, 1941.) A corruption of **mosk**.

mossy. (Of persons) hairy.

mossy agate. 'If something was "just the thing" my Father used to say "It's just the mossy agate". He was from the Sheffield–Grimsby area' (Chambers, 1980): early C.20. Presumably ex the S.E. moss-agate, perhaps applied to a marble; cf. synon. *just my alley-marble*. (P.B.)

most, the. The best, superlatively good, extremely attractive, as in 'He's the most': teenagers' and office- and shop-girls': since ca. 1957. (Gilderdale.) Adopted ex Can., where current since ca. 1955. (Leechman.)

mostest, with the, adv. and adj. With—or having—every attraction: adopted, ca. 1959, ex US: esp. among jazz-addicts and beatniks. Outside the US, best known as 'the hostess with the mostest', from the musical *Call Me Madam* (Irving Berlin, 'book' by R. Crouse and H. Linday), prod., New York, 1950.—2. Also used, in later C.20, as a joc. superlative, as in 'Let's see then who can get there fastest with the mostest'. (P.B.)

mot, mott. The female pudend: Army: mid-C.20. 'Her great big, hairy mott', in a mock-Irish accent, was a pun on the insect *moth*. (P.B.)

mothball. To set on one side, against poss. future use, as in, e.g., 'After being "mothballed" for two years because of lack of support, a brief meeting of the committee was held recently' (*Library Association Record*, Feb. 1979): committee-men's coll. > j.: later C.20. (P.B.) Ex:-

mothball fleet. A reserve fleet: RN coll. > j.: since ca. 1945. It is chemically 'cocooned'; as R.C. notes, 1976, 'because the ships have been stored away, like woollens in mothballs'.

mothballer. A ship recalled to service, as during the Suez crisis of 1956, from the *mothball fleet* (see prec.): RN: since ca. 1946. (P.B.)

mothballs. Tracer bullets: Aus. Servicemen's: WW2. B., 1943.

mother. A seagull: trawlermen's. Mitford, 1969.—2. 'One very senior secretary—in the jargon, these ladies were known as "mothers" ' (Le Carré, 1977): espionage: later C.20.—3. A low term of abuse: adopted, later 1970s, ex US pej. **motherfucker**, q.v. *Phantom*, 1979.

mother and daughter. A *quarter* post: r.s. 'Used by Thames watermen with reference to the posts along London's river frontage at which a tug, a lighter, or other craft may be tied up' (Franklyn 2nd).

mother-fucker. A very low term of abuse: adopted, ex US, earlyish 1970s. See also **mother,** 3, and **Remf.**

Mother Hen, the. See **Argie-nought.**

mother-in-law. A mixture of *stout* and *bitter*: Aus. and Brit. public-houses': since ca. 1945. B., 1953.

mother-judge (of pricks). A brothel proprietress: mostly, RN officers'. (A Naval correspondent, 1973.)

motherless. 'Used as an intensive, esp. in the phrase "motherless broke" ' (Wilkes): Aus. low: late C.19–20. Sorensen, 1925, 'That leaves me stony, motherless broke again' (Wilkes).

mother's. Gin (the spirit): mostly Londoners', esp. Cockneys. Elliptical for:-

mother's (or -s') ruin. Gin: late C.19–20; in later C.20, usu. joc. 'Perhaps it is r.s.', suggested E.P.; a poor rhyme—more likely literal. (P.B.)

motor, n. A motorcar: coll.: since ca. 1920.

motor, v. To set going the motor (of boat or car): motorists' coll.: from ca. 1928. Chamberlain, 'They'd started to motor the damn thing.'—2. To go very well indeed, to proceed satisfactorily, as in ' "We really are motoring," executives are telling one another' (*Observer*, 20 Mar. 1983): coll.: later C.20. Ex sense 1, which had, by mid-C.20, come to imply 'to travel at speed'—in all sorts of vehicle.

motor mech. Motor mechanic: RN coll. Granville.

motsa or **motser.** A large sum of money ('He made a motsa'): Aus.: since ca. 1920. Yiddish. (B., 1943; Morrisby, 1958.) The Yiddish *motsa* is an outsize biscuit, about a foot in diameter.—2. Hence, in later C.20, 'a "certainty" that would ensure a [large gambling] win' (Wilkes, citing Beilby, 1970).

mott, n. See **mot.**

mott, v. To look hard—or to stare—at (someone): Aus. low, verging on c.: since ca. 1920. B., 1953.

mottled. Dull, boring; disgusting: from ca. 1929; ephemeral. Milne, 1931 (quot'n at **throw up**).

motto. Drunk: tramps' c.:—1923 (Manchon). Ex Romany.

mouldering ruin. (Used predicatively.) Prehistoric; or merely very old: several Brit. preparatory schools': since late 1940s.

mouldies. Copper coins, perhaps ex tendency to go green if unused: London low: since mid-C.19. Also *moulies.* Later, any money, esp. loose change (Hollies, 1983). D. Roberts, 1984, and Hardy, 1985, both recall particularly, as London boys in early 1920s, calling to coach loads of returning racegoers, 'Chuck us your mouldies!', evidently a tradition.

mouldy, n. A torpedo: RN: ca. 1910–25; adopted, via the RNAS, by the RAF in 1918 (Partridge, 1945). Hence, *squirt a mouldy*, to fire a torpedo (F. & G.). Brock, 1969, 'I suspect that [it] was due to a feeling that it was an unethical and lousy, or at least unsporting, weapon'.

mouldy, adj. Very drunk: Anglo-Irish (esp. public-houses'). Cf. **maggoty.**—2. 'Miserable . . . "two blocks chocker" ' (Granville): RN.

mouldy fig. A person even duller and more boring than a 'wet blanket': beatniks': since ca. 1959. (Anderson.) Ex the following sense.—2. 'Applied by the young supporters of the "new jazz", or "cool" or "progressive" jazz, to those who remained loyal to the old, "traditional", "New Orleans", or "hot" jazz. This was during the strong revival of hot jazz in the 1950s. The term, which had a limited circulation, became virtually obsolete by 1960' (Priestley, 1967).

moulies. See **mouldies.**

Moulin Rouge. A 'stooge': theatrical r.s. (Daniells, 1980.) See 2nd quot'n at **Farmer Giles.**

Mount, mount, n. Any machine; *on a mount*, driving a derrick, etc., etc.: Public Works':—1935. Ex S.E. *mount*, the mounting of a machine. Cf.:—2. '*The Mount*. One's bicycle' (H. & P.): Services' joc.: since ca. 1930.—3. *The Mount*: Montreal: Can. tramps' c., hence gen. low s. Gape, 1936. 'Because one of its most notable topographical features, right in the city, is Mount Royal, or Mont Royal, an extinct volcanic peak, one of a number in that part of Quebec Province' (Leechman).—4. In *do a mount*, to give evidence (B., 1942), a var. of **mount the box**, q.v.

mount, v. To read the record of the previous convictions of (a criminal): c.:—1933 (Leach).

Mount Misery. The upper bridge; 'Monkey Island [q.v.], from its coldness in bad weather' (Bowen): nautical: late C.19–20. 'Last night, when the fog kept you up on Mount Misery' (Shaw, 1932). Granville, however, defines the term as 'the crow's nest'.

mount the box. To give evidence in court, from the witness-box: Aus. c. (and police s.): since ca. 1930. (B., 1953.) Cf. *do a mount*, at **mount,** n., 4.

mountain passes. Spectacles: r.s., on *glasses*: earlier C.20. Franklyn.

Mountains, the. The Yorkshire moors: transport drivers': since ca. 1945.

Mountains of Mourne. Ash heaps: railwaymen's. (*Railway*, 2nd.) Ironic.

Mountbatten pink. That shade of pink paint which was used on invasion craft: Services': 1943–5. 'Suggested by Lord Louis Mountbatten when he was Chief of Combined Operations' (Granville).

Mounties, the. The Royal Canadian Mounted Police (first organised, 1873, as the Northwest Mounted Police): from ca. 1890: Can. s. >, ca. 1930, coll., and via the cinema, well known overseas, esp. in the slogan 'The Mounties always get their man'. Occ., in singular, a member of that force.—2. Hence, the Camel Corps in Egypt: coll.: 1920s–30s. *OED* Sup.

mouse. A man who does not consummate his marriage on the first night: see quot'n at **hole in one,** 2.—2. A young woman; a girl: beatniks': late 1950s. Anderson.

mouse-trap. A submarine: RAF: since early 1940. (*Reader's Digest*, Feb. 1941.) For the crew, that's what it is when caught on the surface by an aircraft.—2. Cheese: esp. 'ordinary', unnamed cheese: Services', perhaps orig. RN lower-deck. Because it's the sort that traps are baited with. Granville; P.B.

mous(e)y. (Of a car) having rust holes: secondhand dealers': since ca. 1950. (*Woman's Own*, 28 Feb. 1968.) Cf. **tin termites.**

mouth like a cow's cunt, (have) a. (To be) excessively talkative: low, mostly Cockney: late C.19–20. (Franklyn, 1976.)

mouth like a vulture's crutch, (have) a. (To have) a 'mouth' after drinking: prob. mainly Services': since late 1940s. A var. of:-

mouth like the bottom of a bird-cage or (Manchon) **parrot-cage, have a;** or (one's) **mouth feels like the bottom,** etc. Earlier (since ca. 1920) versions of prec. Further variants are the Services', esp. RAF, . . . *of a baby's pram—all shit and biscuits,* itself ex the older (?Northern dial.) . . . *of a crow's nest—all shit and twigs,* used to describe a confused mess (Haines, 1962); and . . . *like the inside of a Turkish wrestler's jockstrap*: low: since the late 1940s (L.A., 1974).

mouth music. 'A taboo and gross expression meaning the practice of cunnilingus. Never used in mixed or family company' (Powis): later C.20.

mouth-organ. See **play the mouth-organ.**

mouth-wash. A drink of liquor: since ca. 1930.

mouthy. Given to 'running off at the mouth'; 'gabby'; loquacious: uncultured, esp. Londoners': since ca. 1930. Barling, 1973.

move. A motion picture: s.: mid-1930s. Prob. short for **movies.**

movement at the station(, there's). 'Expression for hurried activity, esp. portending some imminent event (from the opening line of A.B. Paterson's "The Man from Snowy River", 1895)': Aus.: since mid-C.20. (Wilkes).

movie, rarely **movy**. Of the cinema: from ca. 1914: coll. Esp. in *a movie star.* Ex:—2. A moving picture: coll., orig. (1906 or 1907) US, anglicised ca. 1913. Much less gen. than the derivative *movies.* P.B.: thus E.P. in 1935, but in later C.20 'a movie' is common for a film, while *movies* = cinema, as in 'we're off to the movies tonight'. Occ. *catch a movie,* to see a film; prob. ex US.

movies. Moving pictures; the cinema: US (—1913), anglicised as a coll. ca. 1917. W., 'Current [1920] use of *movies* (U.S.) is curiously like that of Tudor *motions* for a puppet-play.'

mow the grass. To smoke cannabis: drugs c. (Stockley, 1986.) See **grass,** n, 4.

mowat. A woman: c.: from ca. 1910. Of North Country origin. Perhaps ex dial.: cf. N.E. and E. Anglian *mawther,* a big, lumbering girl. (R.S.)

mowing the lawn, n. and ppl. Shaving with an electric razor: Aus.: since ca. 1955. 'Hang on a jiffy, I'm mowing the lawn.' (B.P.)

moz or **mozz.** Since ca. 1920 the commoner form of **mozzle,** n. and v. See also **mock on.**—2. Also as *Mozzy, Mos* (pron. *moss*) or *Mossy:* a De Haviland *Mos*quito all-wooden fighter-bomber, reconnaissance aircraft: RAF: from 1943. Partridge, 1945, the *s* forms; McDouall, 1945, the *z* forms.

Mozart and Liszt, usu. shortened to *Mozart.* Tipsy: r.s., mostly racing: since ca. 1945. On s. *pissed.* (Franklyn 2nd.) Cf. the perhaps commoner synon. **Brahms 'n' Liszt,** likewise usu. shortened, to *Brahms.*

mozzle, n. Esp. as in ' "My mozzle is out, Collins?" he said with an effort' ('Tom Collins', *Such is Life,* 1903), i.e. my luck has run out: Aus.: ca. 1870–1920. Wilkes quotes (Sydney) *Bulletin,* 17 Dec. 1898, Red Page: '*Mozzle* is luck . . . *Good mozzle* = good luck; *Kronk mozzle* = bad luck.' Ex Yiddish.

mozzle, v.; also shortened to **moz.** To hinder, to interrupt (someone); esp. to 'jinx' (someone): Aus.: since ca. 1920. See esp. **put the moz on,** (at **mock on**), of which *moz*(*z*), v.t., is a shortening. Prob. ex prec., 'jinx' being 'bad luck', rather than E.P.'s suggestion of 'ex *muzzle*' (P.B.).

mozzle and brocha. A door-to-door salesman or canvasser. May be r.s., on *on the knocker,* but perhaps, as R.S. suggests, 1968, from the Yiddish 'Mazel and broche', 'Good luck and a blessing', which could well be a Jewish salesman's greeting, like the Irish tinker's sales-greeting, 'Yer goin' to be lucky.' R.C. points out that both *mazel* and *broche* are badly needed by canvassers.

mozzy. A mosquito; *mozzy net,* a mosquito net: Aus. (late C.19–20) and Services', esp. Army and RAF (since ca. 1925). B., 1942; Emanuel, 1945. Hence, see also **moz,** 2.

Mr. This abbr. occurs in many combinations; see the following entries: **Mister . . . ; Clean;** *Mr Cochran's young ladies* are at **awful people; five by five; fixit,** 2; **Fuzzgug; wood,** 2.

Mr Big. The head of a criminal gang: police, hence journalistic: adopted ex US ca. 1930.

Mrs. An occ. written form of *missis; missus.*

Mrs Ashtip. See **Greenfields.**

Mrs Chant. Aunt: r.s. P.P., 1932.—2. Hence, the w.c., for which *aunt* is a euph.: later C.20. (Jones, 1971.) Cf. **Mrs Murray.**

Mrs Ducket(t). A bucket: r.s. P.P., 1932.—2. As an expletive, 'Fuck it!': low. r.s. Franklyn.

Mrs Gafoops. Any woman not specifically named: Aus.: since ca. 1930. 'Are you going to make that dress yourself, or will you get Mrs Gafoops to run it up for you?' (B.P.)

Mrs Green. See **sleep with Mrs Green; Greenfields,** 1.

Mrs Mop(p). A woman cleaner, i.e. one who uses a mop: coll.: since ca. 1944. Ex the famous *Mrs Mopp* of Tommy Handley's radio-comedy series 'Itma' during its WW2 days.

Mrs Murray, see. To go to the water-closet: Aus.: late C19–20. (B., 1942.) With a pun on the Murray, the greatest river in Australia. The ref. is esp. to a privy. Cf. **Mrs Chant.**

Mrs Thing. See **thing,** 2.

much! Short for the ironic *not much!*; Services' (esp. RAF) coll.: 1940+. Partridge, 1945, ' "He never goes out with Waafs"—"Much!" ' (He very often does.)

muck, n. Anti-aircraft fire: RAF: 1940. Michie: 'I climbed to 12,000 feet, circling along the outside of the searchlights and all the muck [gunfire] that was coming up'.—2. (Very) dirty weather: RAF pilots' and Army officers': since ca. 1938. (H. & P.) Also *shit.*—3. In *as muck,* exceedingly; as much as is possible: coll.: from ca. 1910. Esp. *sick as muck,* thoroughly disgusted or disgruntled or displeased, as in Masterman, 1935, of a cricket match: 'He would be out any ball and poor old George would be as sick as muck.' Also *rich as muck,* 'filthy rich'. Cf. **mad as mud.**

muck!, mucker, mucking, have from ca. 1915 represented *fuck!,* etc. Except when used joc., these are mere printers' words; and even when joc., they derive from these letter-equivalences of the actual vulgarisms and are deliberate. Frequent in war books of 1929–30, and since. A century hence, some curious errors will arise in respect of *muck* = *fuck,* etc.]

muck about. To play the fool, esp. in an aggravating way, which may produce the response 'Oh, come on now—don't muck (*or* keep mucking) about': coll.: since mid-C.20 at the latest. (P.B.)

muck-arsing about. Larking about, esp. amorously: low.

muck-bird. 'Dirty oil waste' (*Railway*): railwaymen's: since ca. 1930.

muck in, v.i. To share rations, sleeping quarters and certain duties; an informal method and group, this social unit of the Army was arranged by the men themselves and respected by NCOs; it protected and furthered its own interests. The system was obviously known in the pre-WW1 RN: Knock records the term as lowerdeck usage, before the army started using it, ca. 1915. See esp., though *passim,* Manning, 1930; and B. & P. at *mucking-in* (3rd ed., p. 141).—2. Hence, v.t., *muck in with.* (F. & G.) Also, *the mucking-in spirit,* the feeling among Servicemen in adversity that makes the whole thing possible (P.B.).

muck (someone's) orange. Spitefully to spoil someone's policy or project: journalistic and political, but presumably of school-playground origin: later C.20. *The Times Educational Supplement* (3rd leader), 2 Apr. 1976. (P.B.)

muck out. To clean out (the place)—to be a servant, esp. *for* someone: miners'. Ex cleaning out the stables down in the mines.

muck slinging. Slander: var. of *mud-slinging.*

Muck, Sludge and Lightning, the. The Manchester, Sheffield and Lincolnshire railway: railwaymen's: ca. 1890–1925. *Railway,* 2nd.

muck(-)stick (or **solid**). 'Inversion of musket, a rifle, hence *muckstick drill,* rifle drill on the parade ground of a Naval barracks' (Granville): RN.

mucker. (See the **muck!, mucker, mucking** entry.)—2. A friend, mate, pal: Army: since ca. 1917. Ex **muck in,** q.v.; cf. **mucking-in spud.** York, 1980, notes some use among civilian young 'hearties', 1970s. J.B. Smith, 1985, notes Ger. s. *Macker,* which dates back to early C.20 and = 'mate, pal', and the equivalent Dutch *makker.* Both are pron. as Eng. *mucker*: could there have been an influence?

mucking-in spud. One's chief friend or companion: Army and RAF: since ca. 1930 (H. & P.); virtually † by 1950. H. & P., ' "Spud" is used in camps to denote "pal".' See **muck in.** *Mucker* continued in use for a 'pal' until at least 1970, though perhaps ob. by then (P.B.).

mucky duck. Yorkshire var. of next, 1: earlier C.20. (Measures, 1985.)

mucky pup. A joc. var. on the theme 'dirty dog', a raffish, or a sexually promiscuous fellow. I heard it in Australia in 1912.—2. In Brit., however, it has > a term of disapproval or dismay at a particularly dirty or untidy child, 'Oh, you *mucky little pup!*', or of contempt for an adult. (Petch; L.A.)

mud. Wet concrete: Aus. builders' and similars': since ca. 1920. (Culotta.)—2. Hence, thick, muddy coffee: Aus.: since ca. 1930. Ibid.—3. 'Mate of the upper deck—the seaman Petty Officer charged with cleaning the upper deck: Royal Navy: 1950s' (Peppitt). ?And later.

mud and blood. A mild and bitter: public-houses'.

mud-fat. Exceedingly fat: Aus.: since ca. 1925. (B., 1942.) Ex the Aus. *as fat as mud.*

mud-hook. An anchor: nautical:—1884 ('H. Collingwood': *OED*).—2. Hence, the anchor in the game of Crown and Anchor: Services'. Also, since ca. 1910, for the board itself: Services'. H. & P.—3. A hand: NZ and Aus.: since ca. 1915. B., 1941, 1942.—4. A foot: Aus.: since ca. 1920. Baker.—5. A finger; usu. in pl.: Can. (Leechman, 1968.) Not in cultured circles.

Mud Island. Southend: East London's nickname: ca. 1900–14. (Ware.) Ex its muddy beach. Granville notes that Canvey Island was also thus known.

mud map. 'A sketch drawn by a bushman on the ground, to give directions' (Wilkes): Aus.

mud(-)mover (usu. pl.). Member of an air-to-ground attack crew; air-to-ground attack aircraft, e.g. a Jaguar: RAF: since early 1970s. (Wilson, 1979.)

mud-pads. The feet: lower classes':—1923 (Manchon).

mud-plug. 'A cross-country or off-road motorcycle trial' (Dunford): motorcyclists': later C.20.

mud pup. An agricultural student, esp. if working on a farm: since ca. 1950. (Granville.)

mud-walloper. One who is used to, or has to work in, mud: Army in Burma: 1942–5.

mudder. A horse that goes well on a wet track: Can. sporting coll.: since ca. 1925. Cf. *mud-lark*, the Aus. synon.

muddie. One of the 'labourers engaged to dig clay from Essex marshes to load on sailing barges grounded . . . between tides. Used on Thames barges in the 1920s [?and later]' (Peppitt, 1976).—2. 'A Queensland mudcrab' (Wilkes): Aus.

Muddle Ages, the. A facetious ref. to the historical Middle Ages: students'. Cf. **Muddle East.**

Muddle and Go Nowhere, the. A pun on the initials of 'the old Midland and Great Northern Railway, which meandered across North Norfolk from Norwich to Peterborough' (R.S., 1967): early C.20.

Muddle East. An all-Services' name: 1941–4: for the Middle East.

muff-diver. A cunnilingist: low, also Can. In, e.g., the verse of Gavin Ewart (review in *the TLS*, 11 July 1980). Hence, *muff-diving*, the action (Powis). *Muff* has = the female pudend since late C.17, though now perhaps † except in this term.

mug, n. A fool; an easy dupe: 1857 ('Ducange Anglicus'); Mayhew. I.e. something into which one can pour anything. Hence, in C.20, 'Anyone not of the Underworld' (Sharpe, 1938): i.e. from the viewpoint, the angle, the 'slant' of the underworld itself. Cf. the American c. use of 'honest John' (see *Underworld*). 'There is a whole range of talk which cannot be understood by the "mug", a word which describes *all* members of the public who attend fairs' (Buchanan-Taylor, 1943).—2. A police photograph of a criminal: police: since ca. 1950. Short for **mug-shot**, q.v., itself ex *mug* = a face, s. since early C.18.

mug, v. To rob (esp. by the garrotte): low: from ca. 1860; ob. by ca. 1900. (Mayhew.) Note that, in C.20, the sense narrowed to 'to garrotte', and the word was current, mid-C.20, in Can. and US. R.C. wrote, 1976, that this sense 'has now broadened again to mean almost any street robbery with violence', and indeed, in this sense the word returned to Britain in the early 1970s. Hall, 1978, records that the word, in its 'new' sense, was first used in the *Daily Mirror*, 17 Aug. 1972. Hence, *mugger*, the agent; *mugging*, the crime.—2. ' "Are you going to 'mug' us?" . . . 'What does 'mug us' mean?" . . . "Are you going to stand me a drink?" ' (*Daily Mirror*, 14 Mar. 1939).—3. To loaf: Aus.: since ca. 1930. Palmer, 1957.

mug alec(k). Aus. synon. of **smart Alec**: since ca. 1930. *Rats*, 1944.

mug book, the. 'Police photographs of criminals, generally bound in book form' (Petch, 1969): orig. and mainly police; hence, journalists'.

mug chop. A dealer pretending to be an ordinary customer in order to sell someone a 'dud': secondhand-car dealers': since late 1940s. *Woman's Own*, 28 Feb. 1968.

mug cop, mug copper. Variants of *mug John*: Aus. B., 1959; 1942.

mug-faker. A camera: grafters': from ca. 1920. *Cheapjack*, 1934.

mug in together. A lower classes' post-WW1 corruption of **muck in,** 1.

mug John. A policeman: Aus. c.:—1935. Ex **mug,** n., + **John,** 1.

mug list. 'Police photographic files; *to be on someone's mug list* means by extension to be classified by him as a mug (a fool) or personal enemy' (McNeil): Aus. low coll.: later C.20. Cf. **shit-list** and **mug book.**

mug punters. 'Gullible fools. Contemptuous term used by fraudsmen and card sharps for the persons they cheat' (Powis): later C.20 c. See **punter.**

mug-shot. A head (and shoulders) photograph of a prisoner or of a suspected criminal: police and professional crooks': adopted, ca. 1955, ex US. (Clayton, 1970.) Ex *mug*, the face. Hence, gen. photographers' s. for a portrait photograph, as in 'The first time I met him I was up at his gaff in Hampstead to do a mug shot' (Daniells, 1978).

mug-up. Lunch; a snack: 'A common expression in the [Canadian] far North, especially among fur-trade men and trappers: 1934 and earlier' (Leechman).

mugger. Orig. euph., then joc., for *bugger*: since ca. 1945. (Shute, 1951.) Cf. **muck, naff,** as euphemisms.—2. One who, in the street, robs with violence: adopted, ex US, early 1970s; by 1980, verging on familiar S.E. See **mug,** v., 1.

muggins. A simpleton, 'juggins' (q.v.), fool: adopted, ex US, ca. 1880. Ex **mug,** n., 1, suggested by the surname *Muggins*. A C.20 elab. is *Billy Muggins*, and later C.20, *Joe Muggins*. P.B.: if applied to oneself, in Army coll. of 1950s–60s, it sometimes, ex influence of service in Germany, became *Icky muggins*, as 'and who got lumbered for coping with it? Why, Icky muggins here.' Ger. *Ich* = I.

muggles. Marijuana: drugs world: later C.20, adopted ex US. Home Office; W. & F.

muggo. A tea break: London dockers': since ca. 1950. (BBC TV 1, 15 July 1965.) I.e. a 'mug o' tea'; cf. *cuppa.*

mugs' alley. That bar along the edge of a rink along which learner-skaters feel their way: ice and roller skaters', esp. at Wembley: since ca. 1930.

mugs away! The call which means that the loser(s) of one round of a game, e.g. darts, billiards, dominoes, etc., shall have first throw, stroke, etc., in the next round: orig. Services', in recreation halls, junior messes: since late 1940s.

mug's ticker. A counterfeit Swiss watch: c.: later C.20. (Powis.) See **patacca.**

mugsnatcher. 'Photographer operating at a fairground, in the street, or at the seaside' (*M.T.*): market-traders': since (?)ca. 1930. Cf. **mug-shot.**

mulberry; usually in pl. A prefabricated harbour: Services': 1944, then ob. Ex *Operation Mulberry*, the erection of the two prefabricated harbours on the coast of Normandy in June 1944.

mule. A drug-carrier or -smuggler: underground: adopted, ex US, later 1970s. 'Some [Westerners] have brought drugs back to Europe to sell . . . Some . . . may be used as "mules" by dealers' (*Time Out*, 15 Feb. 1980).

mulga. Short for **mulga wire(s)**, q.v. Ex:—2. 'A species of acacia: colloquially "the mulga" may refer to uninhabited or inhospitable regions generally' (Wilkes): Aus.—3. See **go mulga**.

mulga madness. 'The "queerness" sometimes developed in lone bushmen or fossickers' (B., 1943): Aus. coll. Ex prec., 2.

mulga wire(s). A (sometimes) unfounded report, often incorrect; var. of 'bush telegram', 'grapevine': Aus.: since late C.19. Wilkes quotes Quinn, 1899, ' "How do you hear it, Micky?" "Mulga wires, missus, mulga wires".' Often shortened to **mulga**, q.v., as in Prichard, 1950, 'The troops've had it all by mulga' (Wilkes).

mullarkey. Aus. adaptation, from ca. 1944, of orig. US *mal-(l)arkey*, 'blarney'. Niland, 1955.

Muller. A German: Guards regts': 1939–45. Ex the common German surname *Müller*. P-G-R.

mullet. See **prawn-headed mullet; stunned mullet**.

mulliga stew. A soupy sort of stew: Aus. tramps': since ca. 1925. (B., 1942.) Ex US *mulligan* (see *Underworld*), or, perhaps, from *mulligatawny* soup.

mulligans. Playing cards: Aus.: C.20. (B., 1942.) Why?

multi-coloured yawn. A vomiting; vomit: Aus. 'educated' joc.: early 1970s. 'From Barry Humphries' shows and records' (Raab, 1977). Cf. synon. **technicolour yawn**.

multiples. Company shops, chain stores: commercial coll.: since ca. 1920; by 1946, S.E.

mum. 'One's wife or long-established mistress, and *not* one's mother, unless it is plainly made to sound so by the addition of such words as "my dear old mum" ' (Powis): low coll.: later C.20.—2. A chrysanthemum: flower-growers' and -sellers'. Cf. synon. **casant**.

mummerset. 'Derogatory for actors' "dialect" speech, approximating to West Country' (L.A.): since earlyish C.20; coll. > S.E. A punning blend of *mummer*, a contemptuous term for an actor, + *Somerset*.

mummery and millinery. 'Religious ritualism, mainly by those who do not approve of it or think that it is overdone' (Petch, 1966): coll.

mump. To obtain by begging: from ca. 1680; ob. Spence.—2. To call at (a house) on a begging round: from ca. 1865: c. >, ca. 1890, low s.; ob. (For these two senses) *OED*. Powis, 1977, records *'mump*, to scrounge or beg' as extant, and Seabrook, 1987, writing of early 1970s police life, has 'I come out [of the pub] . . . with some cans [of beer] I've blagged (i.e., "mumped", ponced, scrounged, cadged).' Orig. ex C.17 Dutch *mompen*, to cheat.

mumper. A beggar: from ca. 1670; ob.: c. >, by 1720, low s.—2. Hence, a sponger: ca. 1720–1830. Macaulay, 1849, 'A Lincoln's Inn mumper was a proverb.' Powis, 1977, records *'mumper*, a beggar or scrounger' as extant.—3. A half-bred gipsy: later C.19 gipsies' c. (Hindley); C.20, a 'low-grade' gipsy, one who has no van.—4. A tramp (person): c. (Cowan, *Loud Report*, 1937.) Mumpers' talk is tramps' c.

mums-and-toddlers. A group activity organised at, e.g. local community or social centre, for mothers with very young children, affording a chance and a reason to get out of the house and meet others; as in 'Tuesday afternoons it's mums-and-toddlers': social workers' coll. verging on j.: later C.20 (D. Beale, 1980.)

mumsie. Motherly: mostly lower-middle class. Naughton, 1970.

munch. To eat heavily; 'stuff': proletarian coll.:—1923 (Manchon). Cf. **Munching House, 2**.

muncher. 'A Nimrod anti-submarine reconnaissance aircraft, so nicknamed for the allegedly lavish meals that their crews take with them for their 10-hour missions: RAF.' (Green, 1984.)

muncher boy. A fellator: mostly RN: since ca. 1950 (?earlier). Cf. **gobbler**, 2, and a low, Army c.p. current in the Far East, early 1960s, *munch my bunch!*

munchies. In '(e.g. I've) got the munchies', (I'm) hungry: teenagers': early 1980s. (James Williamson, 1982.)

Munching House. Mansion House (London): City:—1885; ob. Ware, 'From the lusty feeding going on there'.—2. Hence (*m.-h.*), a cheap restaurant: lower classes: early C.20. Manchon.

mung, n. A look, a glance, a brief search. (Westerman, 1927.) Perhaps cf.:-

mung, v. To beg, gen. v.i.: tramps' c.: from ca. 1810; ob. Ex Romany *mong*, request, beg (*mongamengro*, a beggar). Cf. **mump**.—2. Hence, specifically, to ask, to 'tap', for a loan; 'Mung him for a flim [£5]': market-traders'. *M.T.*—3. To ask or request, as in 'Mung the messer to scarper' (*M.T.*): id. Senses 2 and 3 also spelt *mang*.

mungaree. Begging, 'working as a tramp': tramps' c. (gen. as *mongaree* or *-gery*).

mungaree stuck. Penniless, esp. if temporarily: showmen's and grafters'. I.e. 'stuck for'—short of— *mungaree*, food (since mid-C.19).

mungaria. Food: Army in N. Africa: 1940–5. The prec. word influenced by Arabic? P-G-R.

mungas or **munja.** Food; a meal, esp. lunch: NZ: since ca. 1919. Perhaps the Services' *mungey* given a Maori shape.—2. Also, among NZ soldiers in WW2, rations, as in 'the munja party' (Slatter).

mung(e)y. Food: Services': since ca. 1860. (Bowen.) Either ex Fr. *manger*, to eat ['borrowed' from French allies in the Crimean War? P.B.], or a re-shaping of C.19 synon. **mungaree**, q.v. P.B.: *mungeys* was an RAF version in the later 1950s.

murder bag. A bag made of hide and containing all such equipment as is necessary in the investigation of a murder: Scotland Yard coll. *The murder bags are out*, 'a murder is being investigated'. Crofts, 1942.

murder-house. Pun on the initials of *m*ilitary *h*ospital: Army, other ranks': ca. 1920–39.

murder on the mountain. Semolina pudding, (esp. if mound-shaped) splotched with (red) jam: schoolgirls': since ca. 1945.

murder suit. 'Get hold of a "murder suit". That's a long pair of overalls with deep pockets for carrying grenades, wire-cutters, and ammo. Nothing will shine if you wear that' (*Rats*, 1944): Aus. Army at Tobruk 1940+.

murg. A telegram: Post Office telegraph-messengers':—1935. P.B.: Perhaps orig. a perverted back s. of '*gram*, but more directly ex *murginger*.

murgatroyd. See TIDDLYWINKS, in Appx.

murginger. A telegraph-boy: Post Office: from ca. 1920. A perversion of *messenger*.

murky, n. An Aborigine: Aus. (B., 1942.) Suggested by *darky*.

murky, adj. Containing secrets, 'shady'; sinister, discreditable: esp. in (e.g. *his*) *murky past*: from ca. 1920: joc. coll. Ex the late C.18–20 senses, very dark (of colour) and dirty, grimy. Keverne, 1930, 'I felt pretty sure she was terribly worried . . . But, by Gad! I'd no idea things were quite as murky as they are.'

Murky Navy, the. The Merchant Navy: nautical: since ca. 1940. (TV, 1 July 1964; Cunliffe, 1965.) A pun on '*Mer*chant'.

Murphy. As in 'The pilot's worst enemy is the incompetent "Murphy" in the hangar' (*Phantom*): RAF: 1970s. ?Ex 'potato-head' for a dull-wit, or perhaps the Murphy of *Murphy's Law*. (P.B.)

Murphy's law. US version of *Sod's law*, q.v. ('If something can go wrong, it will—and even if it can't, it still might'): adopted in Brit., as a euph., ca. 1975. See esp. Paul Dickson, *The*

Official Rules, 1978, pub. in UK 1980. Cf. synon. **Spode's law.**

Murray. See **Mrs Murray.**

Murray cod, on the. 'On the nod, i.e. on credit' (Wilkes): Aus. r.s.: later C.20.

muscateer. An addict of (very cheap) muscat wine: Aus.: since ca. 1930. (B., 1943.) A pun on *musketeer.*

muscle. See **on the muscle.**

muscle bo'sun. A physical-training officer; RN. (Bowen.) A synon. of *india-rubber man.*

muscle factory. A gymnasium: mostly Army and esp. the Guards. Kersh, 1941.

muscle in. To intrude, by violence, on another's 'racket': US c. anglicised ca. 1928 and, by 1935, > gen. s. = to poach, fig., on another's preserves. (*COD*, 1934 Sup.) Abbr. *muscle one's way in.* P.B.: later, usu. with *on*, as in 'He tried to muscle his way in on the act, but we weren't having any [sc. of that sort of behaviour]'. An early example is in Weymouth, 1937.—2. Hence, to profit by another's advantage of good luck: Services': 1940s. Partridge, 1945.

muscle merchant. A physical-training instructor: RAF: since ca. 1940. Jackson.

Muscles. Polite, informal vocative to a physical-training instructor: Services'. (P.B.)

mush. (Pron. *moosh*, or to rhyme with *push*.) The mouth: boxing, then low: mid-C.19–20. Prob. orig. US. (Matsell, Walford.) Also Aus. (Niland, 1955).—2. The face: NZ low. Ex the softness of mush, and ex 1.—3. Short for **mush man**, q.v., a cab-driver. See quot'n at **instalment mixture.**—4. A man: c. and market-traders': late C.19–20. (*Gilt Kid*, 1936; *M.T.*) Often in combination: see **coring mush** and **rye mort.** Pron. to rhyme with *push*, and ex Romany *moosh*, a man.—5. Hence, by specialisation, a man from somewhere else, e.g. a newcomer from Liverpool to Southampton: seamen's: since ca. 1910.—6. A companion, mate, pal: low, perhaps esp. Services'; often as (not necessarily friendly) vocative. Powis notes its use among South Country thieves: ' "Hello, my old mush" would be a friendly greeting.' Also spelt *moosh.* Ex sense 4. Cf. **tosh.** 1.—7. A prostitute's client: Liverpool. *Observer*, 28 Feb. 1988.

mush man. 'A driver who mounts his own cab': cabmen's: ca. 1880–1910. His passenger was sheltered, it were, by a *mush* or umbrella. From ca. 1890, abbr. *mush*; sometimes as *little mush.* Also known as a *musher*: cab-trade: late C.19–early 20. (*Globe*, 22 Apr. 1887: *OED*.) Powis, 1977, records variants *mushie* and *mushter* for a 'taxi driver who owns his cab'.

mushed(-)up. Well-dressed: c.:—1933 (Leach).

musher. A mushroom: market-gardeners' and greengrocers': late C.19–20. (Bournemouth *Echo*, 29 June 1944.) A shortening of the dial. pron. *musheroom.*—2. See **mush man.**

mushie. See **mush man.**

mushroom. 'A market-trader who appears only occasionally or spasmodically. Regular stall-holders tend to view him with suspicion' (O'Shaughnessy, 1979): market-traders': current in 1970s. Cf. **crocus**, n., 3.—2. 'The Royal Fleet Auxiliary crew considered themselves "mushrooms"—they were kept in the dark about almost everything.' (Parry, 1982.) Ex the US witticism current during the 1970s, 'I feel like a mushroom: everyone keeps me in the dark and is always feeding me bullshit' (Krzymowski, 1978); the saying had reached UK by 1979, when I saw it used as a slogan on a T-shirt. (P.B.)

mushroom factory. 'Compartment under a nuclear submarine's missile room, with mushroom-shaped compressed-air flasks for missile launching': RN, esp. Submariners': since ca. 1960. Jenkins, 1966.

mush's lotion. See quot'n at **instalment mixture.**

mushter. See **mush man.**

music. A car-radio: car dealers'. Graham-Ranger, 1981.

musical bathtub. 'A motor-car, especially a small one, looked upon with little favour by professional drivers' (Leechman): mostly Can.: since ca. 1960.

musical chair. 'A latrine consisting of a pole set over a trench' (P-G-R): Army: 1940–5.

musical comedy smile, a. 'Eyes, tits and teeth, as they say in the (theatrical) profession' (Hayes, 1970).

musical fruit. Any fruit or vegetables, e.g. beans, brussels sprouts, that produce flatulence: domestic. (P.B.) Cf. **wind-pills.**

muskra. A policeman: market-traders'. (*M.T.*) A corruption of Romany *mo(o)s(h)kero*, a constable. Cf. **mingra** and *mork*, synons.

must, n. Something that must be done, seen, heard, read, bought, etc., esp. if one is to keep up to date: coll.: since early 1950s, but not very gen. until late 1950s. P.B.: occ. used negatively, as in the line from a 'pop' song of the mid-1960s, 'She's a must to avoid'. Hence, also as adj.: 'I recognised [Orwell] as absolutely a must author for me to publish' (Warburg, 1970).

Mustafa (or **Mustapha**) **Crap.** Punning (on *must have a*) on the need to defecate: mostly Services', perhaps orig. in the Middle East: since (?)1930s.

mustard (at), be. To be excellent (at anything); (of a woman) *be mustard*, to be sexually 'hot stuff': from late 1920s. Lyell. Ex *hot stuff + keen as mustard*.—2. In *be mustard on*, elliptical for 'be as *keen as mustard* on'—or esp. 'against'—something: coll.: since ca. 1950. 'This society is mustard on contamination offences' (*Guardian*, 26 Feb. 1979). (P.B.)—3. See **cut the mustard.**

mute. The vagina. Noted in Rodgers, 1972, as 'British gay slang'. Cf. the *mouth that says no words.* (P.B.)

mute as a maggot. Excessively silent: proletarian coll.:—1923 (Manchon).

mutt. A 'stupid', a fool, a gawk: US (1910), anglicised in France in 1918. Ex earlier synon. *mutton-head* (*OED* Sup.).—2. An affectionately disparaging term for a dog: coll.: since mid-C.20, ?earlier, perhaps ex US. Certainly ex sense 1. (P.B.)

Mutt and Jeff. The British War Medal and Victory Medal: military: 1918. (B. & P.) Ex the famous pair of comic figures. Cf. **Pip, Squeak and Wilfred**, these two medals, or their ribbons on a uniformed chest, plus the Mons Star.—2. Deaf: theatrical r.s. (Franklyn.) Also, by 1945 at the latest, gen. Cockney s.

mutt(-)eyes. Corn as food: Aus.: since ca. 1935. B., 1953.

mutt(-)house. One's former school; preparatory school: Royal Naval College, Dartmouth. Granville.

mutter and stutter. Butter (n. and v.): r.s.

mutton boats. M-class submarines: RN: 1920s. Edwards, 1939.

mutton dagger. Penis: see **pork sword.**

mutton-eye. 'One of the rather cruel nicknames for someone with a squint' (*Muvver*): Cockneys'.

mutton-fed. Big, fat, and red-faced: coll.:—1923. Manchon, 'A mutton-fed policeman'.

mutton-fisted. (Of a pilot) heavy on the controls of an aircraft: RFC/RAF: since 1914. In later C.20, much more gen. and widespread coll.; 'Having hands figuratively as large and clumsy as legs of mutton' (R.C. 1976). Cf. **ham-fisted.**

Mutton Flaps. 'Japs' (the Japanese): prisoners-of-war in the Far East, 1942–5; then, to a limited extent, among civilians, mostly in Aus. B., 1953.

muttons. In such phrases as 'to the muttons again' (Hatton, 1930) or the more gen. 'Let us return to our muttons': let us get back to the subject under discussion: joc. coll. (E.P. considered it S.E.) Ex the Fr. *Retournons à nos moutons*, where *moutons* = sheep. (P.B.)—2. 'When we speak of something being *our muttons* or *a person's muttons* we mean that we regard it with particular favour, that we like it especially well' (B., 1941): NZ and Aus. Ex the excellence of NZ mutton.

muzzle; occ. **muzzle.** A charm; *work the muzzle* (or *-el*), to sell charms: grafters'. (*Cheapjack*, 1934.) Prob. ex Yiddish *mazel*; cf. entries at **mozzle.**

muzzle velocity. 'Tinned meat and vegetables, from the initials M & V' (Bassett): RN: WW2.

my foot! As suffix, a direct denial of a statement, suggestion, point just made, as 'You're sorry? Sorry, my foot! You couldn't give a damn, and you know it!': coll. Prob. a bowdlerisation of the much older, more vulgar *my arse!*; cf. also the later *nothing!* used in this way. An occ. var. is *pig's foot!* or, for extra emphasis, *my left foot!*

my goodness. A drink of Guinness: mid-C.20. Ex the variously illustrated slogan, 'My goodness, my Guinness!'

my granny! Nonsense!: coll. Stephens, 1912.

my left foot or **knacker** or **tit.** Emphatic variants, the two latter low, of **my foot!,** q.v.

my mother's away. The other day: Aus. r.s.: since ca. 1890. B., 1945.

my sainted aunt! A mild exclam.: coll.: since ca. 1920; ob. by 1970. *OED* Sup.

my spies. My sources of information: Army and RAF officers' joc.: since ca. 1939. ' "Have you any news about yourself?"—"My spies tell me . . . that I may be posted to a squadron very soon" ' ('Blake', 1941). Cf. **agents.** (P.B.)

my very word! Exclamatory or emphatic form of 'my word!' (affirmative 'certainly'): Aus.: since ca. 1945. ' "Did he come good?"—"My very word!" ' (B.P.)

myrtle. Sexual intercourse: Aus. (Baker.) Why? It can hardly refer to that Myrtle who, in a famous limerick, failed to realize that 'the turtle was fertile', yet it's very odd that both *myrtle* and the synon. **nurtle** (q.v.) should rhyme with *fertile.* Also cf. **turtle** and **capurtle.**

Myrtle the Turtle. Aus. nickname of any girl named Myrtle: since ca. 1910. (B.P.) Cf. **Harriet the Chariot,** and prec.

mystall crikey! Christ almighty!: Aus. (Stivens, 1951.) Both a truncated spoonerism (> gen.) and a sort of back s., with words in reverse order and *mystall* (mĭstall) a partial form. Cf. *myst all critey!*, the form recorded by Baker.

mystery. 'An adolescent female absent from her home, approved school or Borstal and "floating" around the streets. "Chicken" is the male equivalent' (Powis): mostly London, fringe-of-the-underworld raffish: since late 1940s. Tempest, 1950, 'A stranger (female) to the district. "A mystery in the manor" = a new girl in the locality . . . . It can also refer to a girl who is "down and out" in London and looking for a job.'

mystery mad; mystery punter. 'A ("girl crazy") man who spends time obsessively on the look-out for such young girls [see prec., 2], so that he can live with them for a short period' (Powis); underworld: later C.20.

myxo. Myxomatosis: Aus.: since ca. 1945. (B., 1953.) But, since ca. 1950, also current in Brit.

mzuri! All right!: Army in Burma: 1943+. (Swahili word, adopted from African troops serving in Burma.) 'Everything mzuri, chum?' (Hanley, 1946).

295

N

n.a.f.f. See **naff,** adj.

n.b. Penniless; temporarily without money: earlier C.20. I.e.'*not a bean*'; with a pun on *nota bene* (N.B.), note well.

n.b.g. or, as in the other 'initial'-words, more gen. with capitals. *No bloody good*: coll.

N.I. (often written *N/I*). *Not interested*: RAF: 1938+. (Jackson.) On the analogy of the official abbr., *N.A.* (or *N/A*), 'not available' or 'not applicable'.

n.i.h. 'Not invented here': 'In UK and US industry the *NIH factor* is sometimes blamed for rejection of the best option (design, production method, materials, etc.) in favour of a local (maybe in-house) choice' (Fearon, 1984).

n.i.m.b.y. As initials or as acronym: 'Not in *my* back yard'. Applied to a project acknowledged as (perhaps) necessary, but 'please build it, dump it, etc., somewhere else'; e.g. a third London airport, or dumps for nuclear or noxious waste. Ex US, since early 1980s. A homegrown UK version would be *n.i.m.b.g.*, *g* = garden, for which Americans use yard. (P.B.) 'The Nimby syndrome' (*Guardian*, leader, 23 Aug. 1986).

n.o.c. ' "N.O.C., dear" was a remark by a physiotherapist at St Thomas's Hospital, London, about other girls: Not our class, dear' (Max Beale, 1985): mid-C.20.

Naafi. See **Naffy.**

Nab Nelsons. Those members of the Royal Yacht Squadron who make only short cruises in the Solent, i.e. no further than Nab Tower, and in fine weather; hence, all fairweather or 'armchair'-sailors: yachtsmen's. (Peppitt.) Partly alliterative; partly an ironic ref. to Nelson.

nabble. To catch or get: RAF, esp. 66 Sqn.: earlier WW2. (Forbes, 1942.) A prob. deliberate var. of synon. dial. *nobble*, or older c. *nab*; see **bogle.**

nach. See **natch.**

nadgers, the. Synon. with *the mockers*, q.v. at **mock on**; esp. in *put the nadgers on*, 'applied to a co-worker supposed to exercise, or to be exercising, an evil influence on equipment' (L.A., 1960): perhaps orig. RAF, early 1940s; in the 1950s given much wider currency by the radio comedy series 'The Goon Show', as an all-purpose nonsense-word in such remarks as 'I've got a touch of the dreaded nadgers', joc. for 'I don't feel very well'. (P.B.)—2. 'Any small problem in equipment': TV men's' (Green, 1984).

nadgery. 'A difficult section in a motorcycle trial, usually a steep, twisty and rough-surfaced area' (Dunford, 2): competitors': later C.20.

naf(f), n. The female pudend: ?back s. on *fan*, abbr. **fanny,** n., q.v.: from ca. 1845. If not obscure dial. of independent origin

—ex or cognate with *naf(f)*, the navel (—1866), or with *naf(f)*, the hub of a wheel (—1796), *EDD*—then this is perhaps the earliest of back-s. terms. (Halliwell.) See also **gnaff.**—2. Nothing: prostitutes': since ca. 1940. Origin? A shrewd and learnèd correspondent asks, 'Might the origin just possibly be "rien à faire"? Or perhaps "not a fuck"?' The latter is the more probable, yet far from a certainty. P.B.: or perhaps ex sense 1; cf.:—3. Euph. substitute for *fuck* as oath, expletive, etc., making it slightly less obvious than *eff*; in *naff all*, nothing (cf. sense 2); *naff off!*, go away!; and *naffing*. All are used extensively in Clement & La Frenais, *A Further Stir of Porridge* 1977 (stories of prison life, from a TV series). Elkan Allan, writing about euphemisms and moral standards in *Now!*, 15 Feb. 1980, has 'A newly-invented double standard from Porridge, where the language—"why don't you naff off?"—was made up by the writers.'

naff, adj. Vulgar, common; despicable; 'A theatre critic (*Observer*, 24 Sep. 1978) discusses a performer who "has a mania for the lowest kind of show business, for things which are tacky, and, to use the old trouper's term, 'naff' " ' (R.S.): theatrical: C.20.—2. Hence, generally contemptible; Kenneth Williams, writing to P.B., 1980, of 'camp' dialogue in the 1960s, defines it, 'Unlovely; a gay denigration of someone was *naff omi*, dreary man'. Its use, in 1970s, spread beyond the world of homosexuals, even to the children of Service families stationed in Germany (Miss J. Jones, 1979); Dempster, in *Telegraph Sunday Mag.*, 11 Mar. 1979, noted that the term was by then 'out' in Society usage. It had come, by early 1980s, to imply the same condemnation as the 'Non-U' of the 1950s. Mortimer, 1985, recalled *naff* as a WW2 RN officers' acronym for 'Not available for fucking; deeply ghastly, in other words'; according to John Ryle, 1983, this interpretation had recently been resurrected by the 'gay' jet-set.

naff it up. 'Now some people have naffed it up by putting out too much power [and] the Tunbridge Wells breakers resent anything that naffs it up for them locally' (White, article on CB radio, 1981).

naff off! 'Why don't you just naff off?' was alleged to have been said to importunate pressmen by Princess Anne at the Badminton Horse Trials, 1982. Dempster, 1984, noted that this was still one of Society's 'in' words.

Naffy or **Nafy;** properly **Naafi;** loosely **Narfy** (though pron. thus by Indian Army officers). The canteen: Services': from ca. 1930. Ex the 'Navy, Army, and Air Force Institute'. See:-

Naffy, used as a pej. adj., connotes 'shirking': Services': since ca. 1940. Cf. the RN's *Naffy rating*, a shirker. Here, the initials *NAAFI* are interpreted as standing for 'No aim, ambition or *fucking initiative*'. P.B.: a var. of this interpretation, since ca. 1950 or earlier, is '*No ambition and fuck-all interest*'; both are a completely undeserved slander on a fine organisation.

Naffy break. The army equivalent of **Naffy time,** and mostly applied to the mid-morning break: since (?)late 1940s; ob. by 1970. (P.B.)

Naffy gong. The 1939–45 star: Services'. Partridge, 1945, 'For the semantics, cf. *rooty medal.* It is also called the *spam medal.*' Ex the resemblance of NAAFI shoulder-strap colours to the ribbon colours, i.e. dark blue, light blue, red, symbolising the three Services. See next, 2.

Naffy medal; Groppi gong. Both mean 'the Africa Star', but the former belongs to the 1st Army, the latter (from the famous Cairo confectioners) to the 8th Army: 1943+.—2. Post-WW2, *Naffy medal* (or *gong*) was more often applied to the WW2 Service Medal (red, white and blue ribbon), said to have been awarded for '28 days' service in NAAFI queues': Services'. Cf. prec. (P.B.)

Naffy Romeo. A ladies' man: RAF: since 1940. Jackson.

Naffy rumour. A baseless report: Forces: 1939+.

Naffy sandwich, deal a. To deal a hand of 2 cards + one card + 2 cards: Services poker-players': since ca. 1930. Ex relative thickness.—2. See TOMBOLA, in Appx.

Naffy time (or hyphen or as one word). The morning break: RAF coll.: 1939+. H. & P.

nag. A Diesel shunting engine of 350 h.p.: railwaymen's: since ca. 1955. (*Railway,* 2nd.) A pun on *nag,* a horse.

nag (one) **narrow.** Esp. in *she'll nag you narrow,* her continual criticism will destroy your health: Midlands': since 1930s. (Fearon, 1984.)

Nagger Staggers. The *New Statesman* mag.: joc., among its readers: mid-later C.20. (Raab, 1982.)

nags, the. Horse-racing; the races themselves: racing coll., mostly Aus. (B.P.) Cf. **neddies.**

nail. A valve: motorcycle racers': from ca. 1927. P. Chamberlain.—2. A vehicle whose engine is particularly unreliable and inefficient: Leicester busmen's. (Burt, 1986.)—3. A needle for a hypodermic syringe: drugs c. Stockley, 1986.

nail-can. A top hat: Aus. (B., 1942.) Ex shape.

nailers. (Very rare in the singular.) A hold on prospective buyers: grafters'. *Cheapjack,* 1934, ' "He's got his nailers out . . . " I enquired what he meant by "nailers" . . . "Well, you see," he explained "he's got their shillings and he hasn't given them anything yet. So he's sort of nailed them down. They can't walk away. He can hold them as long as he likes." '—2. See MOCK AUCTION SLANG in Appx.

nailing the kipper. Touring actors' retaliation against rapacious landladies: latish C.19–early 20. 'A kipper or bloater was nailed under the dining-room table and the annihilating stench went undiscovered often for many days' (the source, not the stench, presumably): Warwick, 1968.

Nalgo. The NALGO, or National and Local Government Officers' Association: coll.: since ca. 1935. P.B.: by 1970s at latest, > informal S.E. (used in BBC news broadcasts) or j. Perhaps, strictly, it no longer belongs in this dictionary, but it stands as an example of many other acronyms of similar organisations. A noteworthy exception from this treatment—?by common consent—is the *National Union of Teachers.*

name. Esp. in *get a name,* to get a (very) bad name: coll. Mackail, 1925, 'If they weren't jolly careful, their beloved house would be getting what is known as "a name".'

nana. (pron. *nahna* or *narna*). A banana: nursery coll.: late C.19–20.—2. ?Hence, 'the head, in such expressions as "off one's nana", "do one's nana" ' (Wilkes): Aus.: later C.20.—3. A fool; an ass; esp. in *a right nana,* a real softy: low: since ca. 1930; in later C.20, altho' still low, in very widespread use. Cf. **banana,** 3.

nana (hair-)cut. A womanlike hair-cut, the back of the head being shaved clean: Aus.: since ca. 1920. (B., 1942.) Short for *banana . . .* ?

nance; earlier C.20, **Nance.** Var. of next, 1 and 2. Hoult, 1933 (the capital form).

Nancy, Miss Nancy, Nancy boy. A catamite: (low) coll.: C.19–20. Also as adj. Walpole, *Vanessa,* 1933, 'But he isn't one of those, you know. Not a bit nancy.'—2. Also, an effeminate man: C.19–20.

Nancy Lee. A occ. var. of *Rosy Lee,* tea.

nannie, -y. The tote: see **nanny-goat,** 1.—2. 'Lieutenant-Cdr in charge of midshipmen' (Granville): RN. Ex informal S.E., a nursemaid.

nannik. App. current only in pres. ppl., *nanniking,* fooling or larking, but also showing off ('nanniking off'): market-traders'. (*M.T.*) Ex E. Anglian dial. *nannick,* to play the fool.

nanny-goat. Usu. *the nanny.* Totalisator: racing r.s., on *tote:* since ca. 1925.—2. A boat: since ca. 1930; by 1960, slightly ob. Franklyn.—3. A coat: r.s.: later C.20. Jones, 1971; Hillman, 1974.

Nansen passports. Passports given by the League of Nations after WW1 to persons without nationality. Ex the famous Norwegian explorer and philanthropist Fridtjof Nansen (1861–1930) who was in 1921 appointed the first League of Nations Commissioner for Refugees. (R.C.)

nantee, nanti (rare), **nanty.** No; not, or nor, any. Also absolutely: I have none; 'shut up!'; stop! (e.g. 'Nanty that whistling!'): from ca. 1850: Parlyaree and c. > also, by 1900, gen. theatrical. (Mayhew.) Among grafters: beware! (*Cheapjack,* 1934.) In C.20, usu. written *nanty,* as in 'Nanty, my jills, I'm whacked' = No, my friend, I'm exhausted. (Lester.) Ex It. *niente,* nothing, via Lingua Franca.—2. In *give it nanti,* to put all one's effort into something, work or play: Army Other Ranks' in Malaya: mid-1950s. Imm. ex Malay *nanti,* to wait, but prob. influenced by sense 1. See **give what for.** (P.B.)

nantee; adj. See **nanty.**

nants. A var. of **nantee,** as in Cockney and theatrical *nants for the dook,* no money for the rent (r.s., *Duke of Kent*). Fry, 1950.

nantwas. Nothing: prostitutes': since ca. 1930. Perhaps a filling out of **nants.**

nanty. Silent; reticent; as in ' "He kept nanty about it" = "He kept quiet about it" ' (*M.T.*): market-traders'. Ex the injunction: see **nantee.**

nap and double. Trouble (n.): r.s. Allingham, 1930.

nap and crabs. 'V.D. and crabs' (Malin, 1979): RN. The Army's use is 'Syphilis and gonorrhoea, twice' (Mays, 1969): late C.19–20. Ex the card game, *nap,* but *nap* was also late C.17–18 c. for these diseases.

napoo; rarely **napooh.** Finished (esp., empty), gone; non-existent; dead; 'nothing doing!'; 'it's no use arguing any longer', '(it's) no good': orig. and mainly military: WW1+. Ex Fr. *il n'y en a plus,* there is none left, in reply to enquiries for drink.

napper. Rolph, 1954, notes the following chimneysweeps' terms: (*napper*) ' "That's the brush you screw on the doll. Oh, the doll's what we call the set of rods . . . " . . . A chummy is an ordinary sweep.' Ex s. and dial. sense, since C.18, the head.

narc; narcs. A drug-traffic detective; narcotics: adopted, ca. 1970, ex US. Scaduto, 1974, 'the narcs from the Chelsea drug squad'. Also spelt *nark(s),* as in:—2. *The narks, a dose of the narks:* that stupor which has been poetically described as 'the rapture of the depths' and is medically known as 'nitrogen *narc*osis': skin divers': since late 1940s. (Granville, 1964.)

nark, n. A police spy; a common informer: c.:—1864 ('*No. 747*'). Often *copper's nak,* i.e. 'nose' (q.v.). Ex Romany *nak,* the nose. Cf. **nark,** v.—2. Hence, in C.20 low s. a spoil-sport; a spiteful or nagging person. (Dennis.) B.P. noted that, by

1963, the term was 'no longer low slang in Australia', and McNeil, 1973, writes 'the British slang usage, meaning a police informer . . . is irrelevant here'. Cf. the v., 3.—3. Hence, rancour; a spite (*against* a person); umbrage, as in 'He took nark' (*M.T.*): low. Manchon.—4. 'A man eager to curry favour by running about and doing odd jobs for a superior' (F. & G.): Army: early C.20.—5. A person on inquiry from head office: London clerks', managers', etc.: from before 1935.—6. Hence, 'A visiting senior officer on a tour of inspection' (P-G-R): RAF: 1939+. Cf.:—7. 'An expert; e.g. explosives nark' (McDouall, 1945): RAF: 1937 +. Cf. also sense 2.—8. 'An awkward customer; one with no intention of buying' (*M.T.*): market-traders'.—9. In *put the nark on*, 'discourage; put a stop to; as in "That put the nark on his gazump" ' (*M.T.*): market-traders'. Cf. **nark it!** and contrast **narkies**.—10. A policeman: prison c.: mid-C.20. (Tempest.) An extension of sense 1.—11. Var. spelling of **narc**.

nark, v. To watch; occ., look after: c.:—1859 (H., 1st ed.). Ex the n., 1.—2. V.i., to act the informer: Morrison, 1896, 'It was the sole commandment that ran there: "Thou shalt not nark" ' (*OED*).—3. To annoy, exasperate: low s. ex dial. (—1888) slightly influenced by the c. senses. EDD.

nark it! 'Shut up!'; 'Be quiet!': low: from ca. 1912. (F. & G.) A specialised use of:—2. 'Stop it!': low: since ca. 1910; > by ca. 1935 fairly gen.

narked. 'Peeved; angry' (Wilkes): Aus. and Brit. low s. >, in later C.20, coll.: late C.19–20. Ex v., 3. Cf. **narky**, 2.

narkies, esp. *get the narkies on*. 'Get bossy; get on one's "high horse"; take umbrage' (*M.T.*): market-traders'. Cf. **nark**, v., 3, n., 9, and **narky**, 2.

narky. Sarcastic: Cockney. (Harrison, 1943.) Cf. **nark**, v., 3; but perhaps, in part at least, r.s. on *sarky*.—2. Ill-tempered; irritable: Aus.: since ca. 1910. (B., 1942.) Cf. **narked** and **narkies**.

nashie, the. National Assistance (the dole): NE England: later C.20. (Gofton, 1984.) Cf.:-

nasho (strictly, **natio**). A National Service trainee: Aus.: since ca. 1950. Dick; B.P.—2. National Service training: Aus.: since ca. 1945. 'Compulsory military training [was] abolished in 1972' (Wilkes).—3. *The Nasho*, the National—later the Royal National—Park, near Sydney: Aus.: mostly Sydneyites': since late 1940s. Hence, *a pash show at Nasho*, violent love-making at National Park. (B.P.)

Nasties; gen. **the N-.** Nazis: from 1934; ob. by 1946. By Hobson-Jobson.—2. Hence the Germans generally: mid-1940+.

nasturtiums. See cast nasturtiums.

nasty, n. All-purpose term for something bad, something 'nasty'; e.g., an unexploded bomb, a difficult question, a traffic accident, or unspecific, as in 'You assume it's Frankenstein's monster come to do you a nasty' (BBC radio programme on class distinction, 20 Jan. 1980): coll. In 1983, esp. in term *video nasties*, video-tapes full of violence, pornographic or otherwise distasteful. (P.B.)

nasty, adj., ill-tempered, disagreeable, dangerous, unpleasant in its results, is S.E. verging on coll. (the *OED* gives it, rightly no doubt, as S.E., and the *EDD* as coll.), except when used by children to mean 'naughty' (coll.: late C.19–20); *nasty* [= *jar*] (—1902) is also S.E.; *nasty one in the eye*, a set-back, an affront, is, however, definitely coll. (—1902). P.B.: E.P.'s remarks mean that he prob. dismissed *get* or *turn nasty*, to become threatening, dangerous, and gen. unpleasant, as S.E., but it has, in later C.20, still a distinctly coll. flavour.

nasty piece of work. An objectionable person: coll. Occ. *nasty bit.*

Nat, nat. In politics, a Nationalist: since the mid-1950s (?earlier), a Scottish, a Welsh, etc., Nationalist. Unfortunately my earliest printed record occurs only on 28 July 1977, when the *Daily Telegraph* included an article headed 'Welsh Nats Are Sceptical over Devolution Bill.'—2. In *in* (*all*) (one's) *nat*, in (one's) life: Cockney: early C.20. (Pugh.) Abbr. *in all* (one's) *natural* [sc. life].

natch! Of course! E.P. glossed this as 'Canadian: adopted, ca. 1945, ex US', with Dr Leechman as his authority; but I am fairly certain that we were already using it, as children round about that time. (P.B.) Ex *naturally*—natch! Occ. var. *nach.*

nater (pron.—prob.—*natter*). An international player: sporting:—1923 (Manchon); ob. by 1933. By the 'OXFORD -ER' on *nat.*

National, the. National Assistance: coll.: since ca. 1946. 'He is doing well now—on the National.' Cf. **nashie.**—2. Abbr. 'the Grand National', the great steeplechase run annually at Aintree, Liverpool: sporting > gen. coll.: since mid-C.20 at latest. (P.B.)

National Debt. A bet: theatrical r.s. Franklyn.

national indoor game (or **sport**), **the** (**great**). Sexual intercourse: late C.19–20: low coll. Contrast *Australia's national game*, two-up: Aus. coll.: since early C.20. Wilkes.

Nationals, the. The so-called 'National' daily newspapers: coll.: mainly journalistic: since ca. 1920.

native leave. Leave granted to men whose homes are in, or near, the port at which a ship is lying: RN coll. P-G-R.

natter, n. A chat, a conversation: coll.: since latish 1930s. (L.A.) Ex the v. A Northern dial. word that has come to have a much wider usage: *EDD* treats it at length under *gnatter.*

natter, v. To talk aimlessly, endlessly, irritatingly; to talk when speech is forbidden. Services', esp. RAF: since ca. 1938. (H. & P.) Partridge, 1945, 'Hence the frequent vbl n., *nattering*.' P.B.: since WW2, in very widespread coll. use.—2. Hence, in WW2, esp. in RAF coll., 'to grumble in a minor way' (Jackson). Directly ex dial.: see prec.

natter can. A person, esp. a 'Waaf', prone to excessive speech: RAF: 1941+. (Partridge, 1945.) Ex prec.

natter party. 'A conference which leads nowhere' (H. & P.): RAF: 1939+. Ex **natter**, v., 1. RN version: *nattering match* (Bolster, 1945).

nattum. Sexual intercourse: Aus. low. (B., 1942.) Arbitrary? Perhaps ex 'do the *naughty*'.

natural. One who has an inborn gift, whether musician or painter or writer or games-player 'or whatever'; a thing eminently suitable or adaptable (e.g. of a book: 'a natural for a film'): coll.: adopted, early 1950s, ex US.—2. Mostly in plural *naturals*, 'non-hip people', 'squares': beatniks', then hippies': since early 1960s; ob. by 1975. Fryer, 1967.—3. In *for* (or *in*) *all* (one's) (gen. *my*) *natural*, for or in all one's life; ever: s. >, by 1930, coll. As in the next sense, sc. *life* after *natural*; as also there, perhaps an allusion is understood to *for the term of his natural life*.—4. Hence *not on* (or *never in*) *your natural!*, certainly not!

nature calls (usu., politely, **excuse me, but**). I must go and relieve myself: joc. coll. (P.B.)

nature of the beast, the. Eligible only when applied to things, not to animal life: coll.: since ca. 1910. 'This car tends to oversteer when cornered fast. It's the nature of the beast.' (B.P.)

nature run. A short leave ashore at night: R Aus. N: since ca. 1920.

Naughton and Gold. Cold (in the head): r.s.: since ca. 1945. Ex the famous music-hall pair. (Franklyn 2nd.) They formed part of the 'Crazy Gang'; another equally famous pair were **Nervo and Knox,** q.v.

naughty, n. A copulation: Aus.: late C.19–20. Niland, 1959.—2. Occ. used as synon. with **nasty,** n., in such instances as 'Careful how you lift that—you could do yourself a naughty', where *naughty* = a rupture or other injury: coll.: later C.20. (P.B.)

naughty, adj. (Of an actor, actress) inferior: theatrical: late C.19–20. Marsh, 1938.—2. ' "Naughty" is the term used in the [antique furniture dealers'] trade for [an antique] piece that has been converted . . . or tampered with, without the alterations being declared' (Crawley, 1971).—3. *Naughty* is often used, in later C.20, in senses that were S.E. in C.16–18, but which now, 1983, have an archaic, joc., or coll. flavour;

e.g., of a piece of machinery that fails to work because of faulty construction, it might be said 'Oh, that's naughty!' (P.B.)

naughty, v. To coït with: Aus. 'He naughties her'. Ex n., 1.

nause, n. (pron. *nawze*). Trouble; a disgusted complaint or plaint: c.: since ca. 1950. ' "He don't do as he's told—that's the fucking nause" ' (Newman, 1977). Abbr. **nausea**, q.v. The abbr. usage was very popular in all the Services in late 1960s, early 1970s, in the senses given at *nausea*, and also for 'trouble' in the sense of nuisance, inconvenience, e.g. 'but that means going all the way over to the depot, and that's such a nause' (P.B.). Cf:-

nause, v. To spoil, as in 'it went against the grain for all of them to "nause" such a bit of [criminal] business' (Read, 1978): c.: later C.20. Cf. prec., and:-

nausea. A fuss; trouble: Royal Naval College, Dartmouth: since ca. 1950. Winton, 1959, 'I'd forgotten about the cap. I knew there'd be a nausea about it.' P.B.: in spite of the remarks at **nause**, n., the unabbr. form was still in RN/RM use in the early 1970s, as in 'making it necessary for pilots to check constantly against drifting into Irish air space with the immense subsequent nausea' (Hawke, 1979).

nauseate. To reprimand; to make life difficult for (someone): RN: since ca. 1950. Winton, 1959, ' "Have you tried the cable deck?" asked Michael. "He sometimes goes up there to nauseate the foc's'le men." ' Cf. prec.

Naussie. A New Australian (esp. a recent migrant from Europe): Aus.: since ca. 1950. (B., 1959.) A blend of *New* + *Aussie*.

Nautics, the. The Royal Navy: RAF: WW2. Slightly derogatory. (Brickhill, 1951.) But in later, non-RAF, use, only very slightly if, indeed, at all derogatory.

nauze. See **nause**.

nav. A navigator: RN and RAF: since ca. 1920. Commoner than **navvy**, 1. P.B.: by ca. 1950, in the RAF, it had > j.: I trained, unsuccessfully, in 1952 to be a 'navrad', i.e. a navigator (radar), to operate as an electronic gun-layer on a night-fighter.

Nav House, the. 'The Navigation School situated in HM Dockyard, Portsmouth' (Cdr John A. Poland): RN.

naval bank holiday. A day spent in coaling the ship: RN: since ca. 1925. (P-G-R.) An ironic pun on *banking*, or heaping up, coal.

naval engagement. Sexual intercourse: Can. naval officers', hence more gen.: since ca. 1940. Navel to navel.

navel exhibition (or **show**). Belly-dancing: raffish: since ca. 1945. A pun on *naval*.

Navigators' Union, the. 'A select, most unofficial body which met in pubs anywhere near a Bomber Station.' (John Bebbington): RAF: ca. 1940–5.

navvy. The navigating officer: nautical: late C.19–20. (Bowen.) Also, derivatively, an RAF or an RN navigating officer: since ca. 1920. Jackson (at *G.R. navvy*), 1943; Partridge, 1945; Granville.—2. (Gen. pl.) 'General Steam Navigation's ships' (Bowen): nautical: late C.19–20. To London dockers they were *Navvy boats* (Ash).

navvy's (or **navvies'**) **piano.** A pneumatic drill: roadmakers' and builders': since ca. 1925.

navvy's (or **navvies'**) **wedding-cake.** Bread pudding: Services', esp. the RAF; railwaymen's: since ca. 1925. H. & P.; Jackson; McKenna.

Navy cake and the commoner **Navy cut** (ex *Navy Cut* tobacco), like *chutney* and *port-hole duff*, are synon. with *back-scuttle*; all are low RN terms for sodomy. Hence, to *have a bit of Navy cake*, to indulge in sodomy: Army and RAF: since ca. 1918. An unmerited aspersion. Cf. **golden rivet**.—2. Collective masturbation: RN training ships': since (?)ca. 1920.

Navy chicken. Corned beef: RN: since ca. 1917. In WW2, it also designated spam.

Navy fish, n. and adv. A Naval beard, a beard worn in the Naval fashion: since ca. 1930.

Navy House. The Sailor's Rest, Chatham: RN. Granville.

Nazi Goering. Hobson-Jobson on Malay for 'fried rice': see PRISONER-OF-WAR SLANG, §6, in Appx.

Nazi-scrammer. An actor or actress that, because of Jewish blood, has left Germany to perform, permanently, in another country: theatrical: mid-1930s. (*Daily Express*, 20 Sep. 1935.) See **scram!**

near-. Approximating to, incomplete(ly); ostensible; a substitute for, hence artificial (things); superficial: coll.: from ca. 1925 in England; ex (—1919) US: see esp. Mencken. In such phrases as *near-silk*, artificial silk; *near-thinker*, almost or ostensibly a thinker. By 1937, knocking at the S.E. gates.

near and far. A car: r.s.: later C.20. Jones, 1971.

near as dammit is to swearing, as; hence the usu. shortened (*as*) *near as dammit*. Very near indeed; usu. in the slightly weaker sense 'near enough'. I don't remember hearing it before 1921, but it goes back, I believe, another 10 or 20 years.

neat. (Ironically) rare; fine: ca. 1825–1915; ob. by 1890. Cf. the Can. teenagers' non-ironic use for 'very pleasing or attractive' (Leechman): adopted, ex Standard US, mid-1950s. Some use among Brit. youngsters in the 1970s (P.B.).

neaters. Undiluted rum or any strong drink taken neat; rum before it is made into grog: RN, orig. officers'. (Bowen; Granville.) By the 'OXFORD *-ER*(*s*)'.

neathie-set. A woman's term for a set of feminine underclothes: mid-1930s. C.G.T., 1934, 'I'm weary of their "woollies", Their "step-ins" and their "pullies",/Their "tighties" and their "fullies",/Their darling "neathie-sets".' (Cf. the quotations at **briefs** and **undies**.) Ex *underneath*.

neb. A nebelwerfer (the German six-barrelled mortar): Army: 1940(?1939)–45. (P-G-R.) The German *Nebelwerfer*, lit. 'fog-thrower', has 'two distinct meanings: 1, a smoke-bomb mortar; 2, a cover-name (cf. "tank" as orig. used in English) for the multiple rocket-launcher (*not* a mortar), nicknamed "Moaning Minnie" by our Army, and similar to the Russian weapon called by them "Anooshka", and by the Germans "Stalin's organ" ' (H.R. Spencer).

nebbish. Pitifully unfortunate: Barnhart quotes *The Times*, 6 Apr. 1968: 'The central character is so nebbish he has not even a name', and derives it ex 'the Yiddish interjection *nebekh* ', which Rosten derives ex Czech *neboky*.

nebby. A VIP, e.g., an inspecting general (a 'big nebby'), or a politician 'on a swan': Army in Cyprus, later 1950s: perhaps more widespread. (P.B.)

necessaries, the (*or* one's). The male genitals: raffish: since ca. 1940. Jefferies, 1962.

neck, n. Impudence; very great assurance: coll. Ex Northern dial. (*EDD*). Hence, *have a neck*, to be impudent, to make an outrageous request (Baker records the phrase as Aus.). Perhaps the term's most famous occurrence is in Winston Churchill's speech to the Can. Senate, 30 Dec. 1941, when, deriding the Nazi threat that 'in three weeks England will have her neck wrung like a chicken', he retorted: 'Some chicken! Some neck!' A frequent var. is *brass-neck*; cf. **cheek** and **lip**.—2. In *give* (one's) *neck*, to give up; to become apathetic: Eng. Midlands s. (F.B. Vickers, 1955.)

neck, v. To make love: chiefly in **necking**, q.v.

neck-warmer. The frill at the lower end of a nightdress: Aus.: since the late 1940s. That's where—if still being worn at all— it tends to be found at the conclusion of conjugal love-making.

necker. A heavy fall: Aus.: since ca. 1910. (B., 1942.) Liable to break one's neck.

necking, vbl n. and ppl adj. Love-making. Orig. and mainly US; partly adopted in Eng. ca. 1928, esp. in *necking* (cf. **petting**) *parties*. Lit., hugging each other around the neck, and ultimately ex Scots. P.B.: by mid-C.20 thoroughly anglicised, as in 'Couples necking all over the shop', and 'going in for a spot of necking'; gen. taken to mean no more than 'kissing and cuddling'.—2. Committing suicide by hanging oneself: Aus. c.: since ca. 1945. (Grindley, 1977.)

necktie. In c., a *necktie-party* was a hanging: 1932 ('Stuart Wood').

ned. Head: Aus.: since ca. 1910. (Park, 1950.) Perhaps rhyming, perhaps a dim. of *noddle*.—2. 'A young Scots hooligan, a member of a Glasgow gang of roughs, not necessarily criminals (used slightly contemptuously)' (Powis): later C.20. Cf. **Ted,** 2.

Ned Kelly. 'Any person of buccaneering business habits' (B., 1942): Aus. coll. Ex the famous bushranger: whence also *Kelly Gang*, an unscrupulous firm or a tax-grabbing government: since ca. 1910. The actual Kelly Gang numbered four persons.—2. The belly: Aus. r.s.: since ca. 1920. Franklyn.—3. A story of the 'Deadwood Dick' kind: Aus.: since ca. 1925. B., 1943.—4. A poker machine: Aus.: since ca. 1930. Ibid.—5. Television: r.s., on *telly*: later C.20. Barker, 1979.

neddies, the. Racehorses; (almost) horse-racing in general: Aus. (Dick.)

need (something) **like a hole in the head.** To need it not at all: adopted, ca. 1950, ex US. 'Originally, I think, Yiddish: "Like a loch in kop" ' (R.C., 1976). Rosten, 1968, confirms it.

needle, n. A hypodermic injection: Aus. (and, slightly later, Brit.) coll.: since ca. 1918. (Cleary, 1959.) Cf. **jab,** n.—2. 'An awkward customer, with no intention of buying' (*M.T.*): market-traders'. Cf. synon. **nark,** n., 8.—3. 'Resentment: "It's plain he's got the needle to me" ' (Powis): proletarian coll.—4. In *be on the needle*, to be addicted to drugs requiring an injection: (esp. teenage) drug addicts': since ca. 1950. 'Implies a step from the theoretically non-addictive drugs to the more dangerous ones' (Greenwood). Cf. sense 1.

needle, v. To 'winkle' or prise information from someone: journalistic: since ca. 1940. ' "Needled" from him by reporters' (*New Statesman*, 12 Jan. 1946). P.B.: some provocation is prob. implied, 'stinging' the victim to retort.

needle-fight. 'A boxing match in which the combatants have a personal feeling or grudge against each other': sporting coll.:—1931 (Lyell). Cf. **needle,** n., 3.

needle-match. A dispute: Glasgow:—1934. Ex the *needle-match* (a very important one) of sporting j., on **needle-fight,** q.v.

needle-noses. 'The railway auditors who make periodical visits to the depots and examine the drivers' and guards' sheets and way-bills in order to discover any unproductive time' (McKenna, 1): railwaymen's: mid-C.20.

needled. 'Inoculated before overseas service' (H. & P.): Services': since ca. 1930. Cf. **needle,** n., 1.

neg. A negative: photographers' coll.

neg driving. Negligent driving: (mostly Aus.) motorists' coll.: since the late 1940s. (B.P.)

negateef! No!: RAF, hence other, personnel: since ca. 1955. A joc. alteration—prob. influenced by Fr. *négatif*—of *negative*. 'It's not uncommon for persons connected with flying to use "affirmative" and "negative" for "yes" and "no", this being R/T [radio telephone] procedure. Monotony is broken, and a feeling of "not on your Nellie" is implied by using "negateef" ': an RAF officer, late in 1961. Granville notes RN coll. use in, e.g., 'I'll have apple tart, negative custard'.

neither lilac nor sawdust time. Neither one thing nor the other; var. *neither breakfast time nor Wednesday* and *neither arm'ole* [euph. = arsehole] *nor watercress*: Leicestershire: earlier C.20. *Crosstalk,* 10 Oct. 1984.

neither use nor ornament. Contemptuous description of a useless person or thing: (perhaps mainly North Country) coll. (Dilke-Wing, 1978.) In *Musings,* 1912, an officer says to the wardroom steward, 'Waiter! I'm not here for ornament or amusement!' (P.B.) 'The pupils [in the London suburban dancing-class] didn't appear to me to be either useful or ornamental performers' (Ferguson, 1942).

Nellie, -y. Any cheap wine: Aus.: since ca. 1920. B., 1942.—2. (also *nelly*.) 'An effeminate, affected homosexual who makes public display of his homosexuality' (*Lavender Lexicon,* 1965): US: partially adopted, ca. 1945, in Brit.—3. See **nervous Nellies.**

Nellie Bligh. An eye: Eng. and Aus. r.s.—2. A fly; in this sense usu. *Nellie Bly* and mostly in pl.: Aus. r.s.: since ca. 1910. Durack, 1955, 'Thanks, Stan. I never was one for drinking with the Nelly Blys.' Franklyn notes that this is used by London children, 'their elders tend to use terms more robust'. P.B.: Nellie Bligh was the 'other woman' in the American ballad 'Frankie and Johnny were lovers'.

Nellie's death. Cheap red wine: Aus.: since ca. 1930. (Stivens, 1953.) Cf. **Nellie,** 1.

Nelly. See **Nellie.**—2. As adj., 'denoted all that was favoured by the commonalty' (Williams, 1980, concerning 'camp' dialogue of the 1960s).—3. As exclam. of disgust or contempt: effeminate men's: mid-1950s. (P.B.)

Nelson. One pound, one shilling and one penny: bank cashiers': late C.19-20. Folklore derives it ex 'Nelson's one eye, one arm and one anus'.—2. Hence, a score of 111 in e.g. cricket, or darts. Green, 1984.—3. Ready money: truncated r.s., on Nelson Eddy, the actor/singer (fl. 1930s–40s). One of Society's 'in' words in early 1980s (Dempster, 1984). Contrast **Gregory** (**Peck**), a cheque.—4. Stella [Artois] beer: London r.s., on Nelson Mandela, the Black S. African leader. (Tyler, 1987.)

Nelson stock. 'Driver's window on one side and an indicator board on the other (Southern Region)': railwaymen's. (*Railway,* 2nd.) An allusion to Lord Nelson's lost eye.

Nelson's Column. See TOMBOLA, in Appx.

nembies; nemies; nems. 'Nembutal. Yellow capsules of pentobarbitone' (Cutland, 1985, the first; Stockley, 1986, the others): drugs c. US since—1950 (Spears).

neo-barrack. A joc., disparaging adj. applied to 'the barrack-like architecture so common today' (Petch, 1966): since ca. 1950. Cf. **North Oxford Gothic** and **Stockbrokers' Tudor.**

Nepalese (**black**). Cannabis (resin): drugs c. Stockley, 1986.

nerd (or **nurd**). A foolish person, a 'twit': adopted, ex US, late 1970s. *New Statesman,* competition, 4 Aug. 1979.

nerk (or **nurk**). An unpleasant or objectionable or foolish person: low coll.: since mid-1950s. Hawke, 1979, has an RM corporal talking of N. Ireland, 1972, 'The poor bloody squaddies carry the can, both from the nerks on the street and the nobbers in their own lot'. Perhaps orig. a euph. for *berk*, by those who know the latter's derivation, or merely a blend of *nit* (wit)+*berk*. (P.B.)

nerts! Nonsense!: low, though not always apprehended as low: adopted ca. 1935 ex US, where it is polite for *nuts* = **balls,** q.v.

nerve war, a. The making of constant complaints in order to get things done: Aus. Army: 1940–5. B., 1943.

Nervo and Knox. Socks: (mainly theatrical) r.s.: since ca. 1940. Ex the well-known pair of entertainers who formed part of the popular 'Crazy Gang'; cf. **Naughton and Gold.** This leaves only Flanagan and Allen 'unaccounted for'.—2. 'Syphilis (pox). "A dose of the old Nervo" ' (Powis): low: later C.20.—3. Television: r.s., on *the* (*goggle-*)*box*: later C.20. Jones, 1971.

nervous Nellies. American isolationists: 1939-41. Perhaps ex *Nervous Nelly,* 'Nickname of US Secretary of State Kellogg, who gave his name to the 1928 Pact outlawing war' (R.S., 1967).—2. Hence, in sing., a naturally timid, even a cowardly, person: adopted, ca. 1970, ex US (*DCCU*).

Nessie. The Loch Ness monster, often revived during 'the silly season'' on Loch Ness, hence journalists': since late 1933. (It was on 2 May 1933 that the newspapers announced that a giant marine creature had been seen in Loch Ness.)

nest. A 'stick' of aerial bombs: RAF: 1939+. (H. & P.) Ex *egg*, WW1+ s. for an aerial bomb.—2. An aerodrome: R Aus. AF: WW2. (B., 1943.) To which all the little aircraft fly home.—3. In *be on the nest*, to enjoy the gratification of the marriage (or, since ca. 1945, any other) bed: low coll.: C.19-20. *L.L.G.,* 20 Dec. 1823.

nesting-box. (Usu. in pl.) A Wren's (WRNS) cabin: RN: 1939+. Granville.

Neurope, n. and adj. New Europe: philatelists': Ware cites the *Daily Chronicle*, 13 Nov. 1919. For formation, cf. **Naussie**, a New Australian.

never, on the. On credit; by wangling: military (1915) >, by 1919, gen. (B. & P.) From ca. 1925, often *on the never-never*. Prob. abbr. *on the never-pay system*.

never get enough. Esp. in 'he (or she) can never get enough': an observation on the insatiability of a person's sexual appetite. (L.A., 1974.)

never hachi. Nonsense; 'it never happened (or never will happen)': United Nations troops in Korean theatre, ca. 1951-5; in the 1960s, sometimes heard in Hong Kong. By Hobson-Jobson ex Japanese *abu hachi*, a proverbial phrase meaning 'nonsense'. (P.B.)

never had it! '(Said of an unmarried woman) never to have had the felicity of a good or able man; taunting call to girl by "yobs", 1930s-40s' (L.A., 1978).

never in a pig's ear. Never: r.s., on *year*: later C.20. Powis.

never-never, the. Marriage, 'it being a case of *7s. 6d.* [pre-decimalisation price of a marriage licence] down, and the weekly payments ever after. The "down" payment is probably more now' (Petch, 1969): joc.: since ca. 1920.—2. For *on the never-never*, hire-purchase, see **never, on the.**

never-never policy, the. 'The late Mr. Cook's . . . much-parodied . . . slogan, *Not a penny off the pay, not a minute on the day*. (The General Strike, May 1926)': political coll.; now only historical. Collinson.

new bit, the. The new fashion or vogue: since ca. 1970. (*Observer*, 26 May 1974.) Cf. **bit**, 5. P.B.: there is, naturally, 'the same old bit', the current fashion.

new boy. A new member of a ship's wardroom: RN officers': WW2. (P-G-R.) Ex school, the phrase can be, and is, applied in many other circles, for a new arrival. (P.B.)

new growth. A (gen. cancerous) tumour: medical coll.:—1933 (*Slang*, p. 192).

new jacks. Junior players in a football club: since ca. 1925.

Newington Butts. The stomach; (fig.) guts: r.s.: since late C.19. (P.P., 1932; Jones, 1971.) Usu., if not always, shortened to *Newingtons*. Ex a thoroughfare in S. London. (Franklyn.) Powis notes, 1977, that the term is now 'not used to mean courage, [but] especially a large corporation'.

Newk. Newcastle: Durham and Newcastle undergraduates'. (Marples, 2.) Cf. **Newy**, and:-

Newky(, the). Newcastle-upon-Tyne: local teenagers': late 1970s. Corrigan, 1979.—2. 'Newcastle Brown Ale': an appreciative dim. of the trade name: later C.20. (P.B.)

newly wed. A sergeant recently promoted to a lieutenancy: Aus. soldiers': 1939+. B., 1942.

news. To work as a news-journalist: journalists': mid-C.20. Hunter, 1964, (of a man who has left a press agency) 'He hasn't been newsing for anyone since.'

news(-)hawk or **news(-)hound.** A reporter: journalistic: adopted, ca. 1925, from US; by 1938, coll.

News of the World. A very long letter, containing nothing of note, from a woman: joc.: since ca. 1930.

newsie (or **-sy**). A newspaper-seller: mostly Aus. B., 1953.

newspaper. 'A thirty-day jail sentence; supposedly the time it would take an illiterate to read one' (Green, 1984): prison c.

newt. In (*as*) *drunk* or *tight* or *pissed as a newt*, very drunk indeed: Services', prob. orig. Army officers'. Perhaps more often, at first, *tight*, but since WW2 usu. *pissed* . . . The newt is an amphibious reptile, with a tight-fitting skin. Cf. **tight as a drum**. P.B.: I have heard, mid-1970s, the derivative term *newted*, drunk; and cf. 'They would never be sick in the flower bed like a newtish Sloane [see **Sloane Rangers**]' (Barr, 1983).

Newton Heath. Teeth: Manchester r.s. (Jaffe, 1959.) Ex the industrial suburb so named. Cf. **Hampstead Heath.**

Newy. Newcastle, NSW: Aus.: since ca. 1910. (B., 1953.) Cf. **Newk.**—2. *Newy.* A new one; a newcomer: Aus. coll. Drake-Brockman, 1940; Cusack, 1951.—3. (Also *newie.*) A new trick, as in 'That's a newy on me!': Aus.: since ca. 1925.—4.

A new story: Aus.: since ca. 1930. (B.P.) In fact it could prob. be applied to anything new, in coll. Aus. (P.B.)

next in line for admiral, be. To be the first due for promotion (to *any* rank): orig. RN, since (?)ca. 1940; by 1950 also used, joc., in the Army. Often in 'Who's next . . . ?' It is to be hoped that the promotion, when it does come, will not necessarily be on 'the Buggins principle' of mere length of service, hence seniority. (P.B.)

Niagara Falls. Testicles: r.s., on *balls*. (Harrison, 1943.) Usu. shortened to *Niagaras*, and predominant over:—2. Stalls (of a theatre): theatrical r.s. (London *Evening Standard*, 19 Aug. 1931.) Cf. the use of **orchestra stalls** for testicles.

nib (off). To run away; depart quickly: Leicestershire teenagers': mid-1970s. (McPheely, 1978.) Prob. cognate with synon. *nip.*

nibble, n. An as yet non-committal approach by a buyer, as in 'I see your house is up for sale. Had any nibbles yet?': coll. Ex S.E. sense of fish trying a bait. (P.B.)

nibble, v. 'To fine as a punishment for being absent over leave . . .The accountant officer takes a nibble at the defaulter's pay' (Granville): RN: late C.19–20. (Knock.) Cf.:-

nibbler. 'Leave-breaker to a small extent who nibbles a bit of extra time from his allowance of leave' (Granville): RN. Cf. prec.

nibbling. Taking out a girl fairly regularly, fairly often; courting: Services': since ca. 1925. H. & P.

niblick. A kind of cocktail: ca. 1910-40. In Harwood, 1927, 'Or a cocktail—what about a niblick?'

nice as pie(, as). (Of persons) very polite, very sweet and agreeable: coll.: since ca. 1910. P.B.: in later C.20, often qualified by reservation, as 'Oh, everything went as nice as pie until I mentioned *that*, but then . . . !', or 'We went not knowing quite what to expect, but actually, she was as nice as pie.'

nice drop of. A coll. formula, dating since ca. 1935; e.g., *nice drop of work—sock—tie—jacket*, etc.; 'plurals are never employed in this phrase' (L.A.). A common var. is *lovely drop*; cf. **fabulous drop.**

nice going! An exclam. of approval, approbation, congratulations: adopted ex US ca. 1920. Orig. ex athletics, it soon came to be applied to artistic performance also.

nice life! 'Sarcastic congratulations on a foolish move: Can.: early 1980s' (Leech, 1985, who compares ironic use of prec., 'Nice going, buddy!').

nice little chap. A (very) inferior car: dealers': since ca. 1950. (*Woman's Own*, 28 Feb. 1968.) Ironic euph.

nicely, thank you!, used as adj. for 'mildly exhilarated with liquor', as in 'He's nicely, thank you': Society: since –1923 (Manchon: *thanks*); by 1960 ob. Marsh, 1938.

nick, n. In *do a nick*, to decamp: Aus. (B., 1959.) Cf. v., 1.—2. In *down the nick*, (of a locomotive) short of steam: railwaymen's. *Railway*.—3. In *in good nick*, physically fit (of persons); in good condition and working (of machinery): coll. Very common in NZ.—4. As *the nick*, a prison ('Stuart Wood', 1932); a police-station (Leach, 1933): c. (from 1919). Ex military s. (from ca. 1910), the guard-room, detention-cells (F. & G.). Tempest, 1950, notes 'The most commonly used slang word for any prison', while Powis, 1977, glosses it 'Police station or, less commonly, prison.' In either case, it's where one is sent after getting 'nicked', arrested.—5. In *go down the nick*, to become unprofitable because obsolete: businessmen's: since ca. 1965. (Playfair, 1977.) Perhaps cf. sense 2.

nick, v. To depart, esp. if promptly or speedily: Aus.: late C.19–20. (B., 1942.) Cf. n., 1. Also **nick off**, q.v.—2. 'To place on report' (Home Office): Borstals' and detention centres': later C.20.

nick off. To play truant; to 'skive': teenagers': early 1980s. Esp. in '(e.g. he was) nicking off'. (Joanna Williamson, 1982.) Cf. **bunk off**, and **nick**, v., 1.

nickels. Leaflets dropped: RAF: 1939-40.

nicker. A pound sterling; a sovereign; a £1 note: perhaps orig. c. or racing s., since early C.20; soon > gen. low s. > coll.; also Aus. (B., 1942) and NZ. ('Stuart Wood', 1932; P. Allingham, 1934; Powis, 1977.) The pl. is *nicker: Gilt Kid*, 1936 (and is still, 1983).—2. A cigarette-end: Liverpool: since ca. 1930. 'You nick it out on a wall.' (Shaw, 1952; he compares the synon. Cardiff *dimmer*.)

niff, n. A sniff: Cockney: late C.19–20. Lyons, 1908.—2. An unpleasant odour. Prob. ex:-

niff, v.i. To smell unpleasantly: Dulwich College: from late 1890s. (Collinson.) Back-formation ex *niffy*. P.B.: by mid-C.20, gen. low coll.

niff-naff; esp. in *Don't niff-naff*, 'stop fussing and get cracking' (Jackson): RAF: since ca. 1930. Raphaely, 1987, 'The flip side of airforce life, the nifnaf, as the jolly chaps I met at 229 Operational Conversion Unit call the tedious paperwork that plagues them.' A var. reduplication of *niff*, which seems to combine *niggle* and *fuss*. Cf. **faff.**

niffy. Smelly: Sussex dial. >, ca. 1890, low s. Ex dial. n. and v., *niff*, smell; stink.

nifty. Agile, speedy; nimble; usu. something small is implied, but also as in 'He may look big and clumsy, but he can be really pretty nifty when he gets going': coll.: since ca. 1950, at latest. (P.B.)

nifty fifty, a. An act of masturbation: mainly Services': since late 1940s. (P.B.)

nig. A new soldier, either recruit, or just out of recruit training: Army: since mid-C.20. (Lodge, 1962; still current: *Time Out*, 25 July 1980.) Abbr. **nignog,** 2.

nig-nog. See **nignog.**

nig pig. A native (of a 'coloured', i.e. not-white, race): RAF: since ca. 1925. (Jackson.) Ex *nigger pig*?

Nigerian lager. 'Guinness stout' (Powis): public-houses' joc.: later C.20.

nigger. A member of a clique: Dalton Hall, Manchester: from ca. 1925. Hence *niggery*, cliqueyness. *Daltonian*, Dec. 1946.—2. See MOVING-PICTURE SLANG,§3, in Appx.

niggers' knackers. Prunes: RAF: since ca. 1925.

nigger's lips. (Potato-)chips: r.s.: later C.20. Daniells, 1980.

niggle, v.t. and i., in the variety of its pettifogging, over-meticulous, 'finicky', nagging (of which it is, prob., ultimately a dim. or thinning: cf. dial. *(g)naggle*) senses, has a coll. flavour but is, in C.20, S.E. (*SOD*, 1977): ex dial. (*EDD*). Its derivatives (see below), however, do seem still to be coll. (P.B.)

niggled, ppl adj. Cross; irritated, esp. by disappointment or the pettiness of others: coll.: since ca. 1950. 'They cancelled my 48[-hour pass] at the very last moment. I was just a *leetle* bit niggled!' Ex **niggle,** v. Cf. **niggly.** (P.B.)

niggling. As adj., (of any person) irritating because of over-attention to detail; (of a thing) irritating because of the amount of minor detail and precision required, as 'having to fill in all these stupid, niggling forms': coll.: since mid-C.20. Ex **niggle,** v. (P.B.) Cf.:-

niggly. Bad-tempered; apt. about trifles: coll.: since ca. 1910. 'Oh, don't be so bloody niggly!'

niggly(-)gouger. A finicky, tiresome fellow: RN: since ca. 1930. (Irving, 1946.) Ex prec.

nigh enough (or **enuff**). A passive homosexual; esp. a male harlot: c.: from ca. 1920. (*Gilt Kid*, 1936.) Like synon. *collar and cuff*, it is r.s. on *puff*.

night(-)bind. A turn of night duty: RAF (esp. NCOs): since ca. 1930. (Emanuel, 1945.) See **bind,** n.

night hawk. A thief; a prostitute: Aus. B., 1942.—2. In later C.20 merely one that, habitually, keeps very late hours: coll. (P.B.) Cf. **night owl.**

night ops. Night-operations; orig. in manœuvres, later, in action: Services' coll.: since early WW1.—2. Medical operations performed at night: medical s. > coll.: since early C.20.

night owl. One who keeps late hours; one who works through the night: Aus. coll.: since ca. 1920. (B.P.) Cf. **night hawk,** 2.

night starvation. Sexual deprivation, lack of sexual intimacy: since ca. 1938. By a pun on the advertisements that urge us to take a drink of this or that 'delicious beverage' before we go to bed.

night watchman. A (usu. second-rate) batsman sent in to 'hold up an end' until the close of play: cricketers' s., soon > j.: since ca. 1946. An early printed instance in a report by Swanton, 1946.—2. Hence, the batsman left at close of one day's play, who will re-open the batting the next day: id.: later C.20. (P.B.)

nightie(-y) night! Good night!: nursery—and joc.—coll.: since late C.19, perhaps earlier. P.B.: my grandfather, b. 1873, bade us children good night with the phrase *nightie nightie pobberjee-wig!*, but whether the addition was his own invention or a late Victorian piece of nonsense, there was no telling.

nignog, nig-nog. A fool: Army: late C.19–20. Perhaps ex C.17–18 synon. *nigmenog*.—2. Hence, a raw recruit: Army: since ca. 1925. See also **nig,** and **pinkie,** 8.—3. Hence, 'usually taken as a mildly contemptuous but good-humoured name . . . on the railways and elsewhere . . . for an unskilled man or novice' (*The Times*, 30. Nov. 1967). The quoted report concerned a charge of colour prejudice among engine drivers, who were objecting that they did not want 'these nig-nogs' (i.e. guards) in the locomotive cab. The misunderstanding arose because of:—4. 'A younger generation has begun referring to coloured immigrants as "nig-nogs", but Aslef [the Assoc. of Locomotive Engineers and Firemen] deny even knowing this practice' (Ibid.): pej. coll., low: the use had > widespread by the mid-1970s, perhaps sooner. This usage has arisen from confusion of senses 1 and 2 with *nigger*. (P.B.)

nik, 'as a suffix is common in Yiddish slang. It refers to a person of not much account and may follow a Yiddish word or its English equivalent, as in "He's a boozernik—or gamblernik—or spielernik". It is as old as all other Yiddishisms' (Franklyn, 1962). Cf. **Beatnik.**

nimby. See **n.i.m.b.y.**

nine. 'A nine-gallon keg of beer' (Culotta): Aus. coll.: since ca. 1920. See **niner,** 2.

nine-acre smile. A very broad grin, indicating supreme satisfaction: Can. coll.: since ca. 1930. (Leechman.)

nine ways from breakfast. In all sorts of different ways: low coll.: later C.20. Daniells, 1980, 'some athletic geezer half my age, hung like a young colt and having it off nine ways from breakfast.'

nine yards. 'Everything ("the whole nine yards")' (Wilson, 1979): RAF: late 1970s, adopted ex US.

niner. A woman nine months pregnant: Aus.: since ca. 1930. Stivens, 1951.—2. A nine-gallon keg: Aus. coll.: since mid-C.20. (Buzo, 1973.) Cf. **nine.**

nineteen. In games, a score of nothing (nought): public houses'. At cribbage one cannot score 19.

nineteen canteen. A long time ago: since (?)ca. 1940. (Clayton, 1970.) Prob. ex the years nineteen thir*teen* to nine*teen*: cf.:-

nineteen oh (or **ought** or **nought**) **dot** or **plonk** (or similar**), since the year.** From a very long time ago: coll.: since mid-C.20. See **nought-,** and cf. prec. (P.B.)

nineteener. A swindler, sharper; an opportunist loafer: Aus. c. (B., 1942.) A plausible talker 'nineteen to the dozen'.

nineteenth hole, the. The bar-room of a golf club-house: golfers': from not later than 1927. (*OED* Sup.) A golf-course has 18 holes.

ninety bender. A torpedo fitted with a device set to turn it through 90° after leaving the firing tube: RN Submariners': WW2. Bryant, 1958.

ninety days' wonder. A newly commissioned second lieutenant: Army: 1946+. Perhaps an adaptation of the US *ninety-day wonder* (hence . . . *blunder*), applied during WW2 to second lieutenants obtaining their position by passing a 90-day course after being selected from 'other ranks', as R.C. suggests. Raab: surely an intensification of S.E. *nine days' wonder?*

ning-nong. A nincompoop, a naturally foolish person: Aus.: since ca. 1930; by 1963 (B.P.), ob. An assimilation of *nincom-*(poop) and a var. of *ningnog*, itself a var. of *nignog*; perhaps influenced by N. Brit. dial. *ning-nang*. See also **nong.**

ninnified. Foolish: coll. (Spenser, 1934.) Ex S.E. *ninny* + *-fied*, made.

nip, n. A child: Aus.: since ca. 1920. (Cusack, 1951.) Short for synon. *nipper.*—2. In *make a nip for it*, to try to escape at a run; e.g. from a train: Forces', but esp. prisoner-of-war: 1940–5. (Morgan, 1945.) Cf. the civilian coll. *nip along*, to make haste.—3. See **Nips.**

nip, adj. Cheeky, impudent: Marlborough College: since ca. 1920. His speech nips.

nip in or **nip in smartly** or **nip smartly in.** To take advantage of an opportunity: Services': WW2; hence gen. Ex a drill formula.

nipper. That junior member of any gang who 'fags' for the others: railwaymen's. *Railway.*

nippers. 'Sound yarn taken from condemned cordage and marled together' (Granville): RN. Pinched or 'nipped' together.

nippy, n. A waitress in Lyons' restaurants and tea-shops: from 1924: j. >, by 1930, coll., indeed by 1935 almost s. Sayers, 1927, ' "Nippy" found dead on Wandsworth Common.' 'The word is a registered trade mark of the company' (*OED* Sup.). 'The nippies got their name in the 1930s when Lyons sent 1200 waitresses to serve 7500 Freemasons at a banquet at Olympia and somebody said: "They're not waitresses— they're too nippy" ' (*Financial Times*, 10 Jan. 1981). Ex *nippy*, lively.—2. Hence, any waitress, esp. in a cheap establishment: from ca. 1930.

nippy, adj. Well-dressed; smartly fashionable: lower classes':— 1923 (Manchon). Just possibly influenced by Fr. *nippé*, 'togged up' (Kastner & Marks).

nippy with the weight. (Of a shopkeeper) giving short weight or, grudgingly, the bare weight: since ca. 1920.

Nips. Japanese: adopted, ca. 1941, ex US. Ex *Nipponese.*—2. In *put the nips in* (*to*), to ask a loan (from someone): Aus. and NZ: from ca. 1908.

nishte. Nothing: low s.: since ca. 1918. (Cook, 1962.) Via Yiddish ex Ger. *nichts.*

nit, n. A simpleton, a moron, a fool: Aus., since ca. 1925 (Baker); from ca. 1950, a common, low, widespread UK abusive term for a fool, esp. 'stupid nit'. Either short for *nitwit*, or more prob., directly pej., ex S.E. head-louse. Powis; P.B.—2. See **keep nit**, with which cf. **nit-keep.**

nit, v. As in ' "Nit the jorrie (Leave the girl alone)!" he yelled. "Nark it! Nark it!" ' (MacArthur). Prob. ex *nix.*—2. To decamp: Aus. low. (Baker.) Perhaps a corruption of **nick**, v., 1, influenced by the *nit* of *keep nit.*

nit-keep, v. and n. To keep watch; one who does this: Aus. c. (B., 1959.) Also *nit-keeper* (B., 1942). See also synon. **keep nit**, and:-

nit nit! 'Stop talking—someone's listening!': prisons' c.: since ca. 1930 or a little earlier. Lit. 'nothing, nothing!', *nit* being a var. of C.18–20 *nix*. Cf. **nitto!**

nit-picking, n. and adj. Petty, cavilling, fault-finding, as by critics of the arts: coll.: since ca. 1960, but not very common before ca. 1970. (Canonised in *COD*, 1976.) Hence the v., *nit-pick*, and the agent, *nit-picker*. Ex picking nits from a child's hair. R.S. compares coll. Ger. *Flöheknacker*, lit. 'flea-crusher', i.e. 'one who finds futile fault'.

Nitchie. A Prairies Indian: Can.: since ca. 1910.

niterie. A night-club or -spot: advertisers' and journalistic: adopted, ex US, ca. 1975. '[The film] set against the sex, drugs, and chicken-in-the-basket ambience of London's niteries . . . ' (*Time Out*, 9 May 1980). Ex a corrupt spelling of *night*. (P.B.)

nitrate. 'Time-and-a-quarter [pay] for night work' (McKenna): railwaymen's pun: mid-C.20.

nits on a gnat's nuts. Reputedly the smallest things in the world: joc. low: from ca. 1920. (P.B.) Cf. **within a gnat's.**

nitsky. A var. of *nix*, nothing. Hyder, 1934.

nitto! 'Stop!' or 'Be quiet!': c.: since ca. 1940. (Gosling, 1959.) The Cockney *-o* on **nit nit!**, q.v. See also **shitnitto.**

nitty. Idiotic: since late 1950s. Moyes, 1967, 'If the girl was nitty enough to contemplate marrying him, she was only getting what she deserved.' Ex *nit*, short for *nit-wit*. P.B.: but see also **nit**, n., 1.

nitty-clitty, get down to the. To practise, or to perform, cunnilingism: low: latish 1960s. (Hollander.) A (prob.) ephemeral pun on *clitty*, diminutive of *clit*, the clitoris, and:-

nitty-gritty, the. 'The very core of something, the fundamental truth about it' (Holland, 1968): adopted, 1967, ex US, where current at least as early as 1963. Often in phrase '(Let's) get down to the nitty-gritty'. W. & F., 1975, define it as 'the . . . essentials of any situation, predicament, etc., esp. the hard unvarnished facts . . . or harsh realities'. 'And slang like "hip" and "trendy" and "nitty-gritty" ' (*Daily Mail*, 2 Nov. 1968). Holland adds, 'The thing that fascinates me about the expression is that it is one of the very few pieces of *original* pop music slang ("grotty" is another) and is not derived . . . from the scene'. W. & F. state that, in the US, it was, orig., Negro use.

nix fish-tins. 'I don't understand': see PRISONER-OF-WAR SLANG, §1, in Appx.

nix on it! Stop that!: Aus. low. (B., 1942.) Cf. **nit**, v.

nix(e)y! No!: circus-workers':—1887 (Baumann). Ex *nix* and *nix!*—2. Besides the first sense, the interj. conveys 'It's rubbish—it's not worth bothering about': market-traders'. *M.T.*

nixies. A female's drawers: from 1933. Not ex S.E. *knickers* but ex *nix*, nothing, as an advance on *scanties.*

no bottle, as in 'It's no bottle'. No good: Services'. Also, graduated, 'not much bottle', not much good or use. See **bottle**, n., 6, 7.

no-can-go-ist. 'Lowerdeck for non-conformists who are excused Church parade' (Granville): RN. Has var. *non-can-go-ist.*

no giggle. No fun; no joke; (very) unpleasant: low coll.: from ca. 1920. *Gilt Kid*, 1936, 'It's no giggle being in the nick [in gaol], I can tell you.'

no-go area. An area temporarily out of use; strictly, as in N. Ireland, where the term app. originated, an area in which the residents refuse to recognise the state's authority: since ca. 1970 (*OED* New Sup.); by 1977, S.E. But its transferred usage, applied to, e.g., a bathroom or a water-closet, remains coll. (Playfair, 1977).

no good. Esp. in *do* (someone) *a bit of no good*, actively to do him some harm: ironic coll.: since ca. 1910. Also, as in 'I fell off halfway round, and o' course that did me a lot of no good': rueful joc.—2. In such expressions as 'As I thought, the cat was up to no good in the larder again', it is S.E., but the equal stress on 'no' and 'good', as if hyphenated and a n., give it a coll. flavour. (P.B.)

no-gooder. A selfish, or a cynical, person given to adverse criticism of the 'do-gooders' and, indeed, all good-workers: coll.: since the late 1950s.

no guts! A derisive exhortation—a 'dare'—to do something dangerous: Londoners': since ca. 1920. Hence also, since ca. 1940, Forces'. *Guts* = courage, spirit.

no hass! 'It will be no trouble': teenagers': mid-1980s. Abbr. **hassle**, q.v.

no holds barred. Without legal, moral, etc., constraint; 'anything goes': coll.: later C.20. Ex all-in wrestling. (P.B.)

no-hoper. A hopeless case: Aus. coll.: since ca. 1915. *Rats*, 1944, ' "Is he bad?" I asked.—"A no-hoper, Mick. Copped two in the guts." '—2. An outsider, a horse with little, or no, chance: Aus. racing s.: since ca. 1919. Glassop, 1949.—3. Hence, a person lacking in drive, ambition, or any attribute likely to bring success: coll.: later C.20. Some currency outside Aus.

no-hoping. Hopeless: Aus.: since ca. 1920. 'Argles's youngest brother was a no-hoping ratbag . . . He was a true bludger' (Dick). Cf. prec., 3.

no jet. ' "Won't listen." (See **bubble** [v.]. "To put the bubble in the tube" = to put in a "squeal", to tell tales. If there is "no jet", then it means that the person told will not listen or will not take any action.)' (Tempest): prisons' c.: mid-C.20.

no joke, it's. It is far from being a joking matter: coll.

no joy. See **joy**, 1.

no-no. A boring fiasco: world of entertainment, esp. theatrical: since ca. 1960. Brett, 1975, ' "Whole thing"—a midnight matinée (sic)—"will probably be a ghastly no-no, but everyone will be there".' Ex '*No, no!* Not my cuppa—scene—bag.'—2. Anything impossible; forbidden: later 1970s–80s. Ex sense 1 apprehended as 'No, no, you mustn't/can't do that!' (P.B.)

no object. E.g. 'distance no object' and, esp., 'money no object'; a mis-use of n. *object* when = 'no obstacle' or 'not an objection': coll.: mid-C.19–20. The correct sense 'not a thing aimed at or considered important' has been vitiated by confusion with *no objection*.

Noah's ark. Dark: r.s. esp. among urban labourers. *John o' London's Weekly*, 9 June 1934.—2. A park: r.s. Jones, 1971.—3. A very dull, stupid person: Aus. r.s., on **nark**, n., 2: since ca. 1920. B., 1942.—4. 'One who accompanies a customer but deters him or her from buying' (*M.T.*): market-traders' r.s., on **nark**, n., 8. Jones notes its use also for **nark**, n., 1, an informer.

nobber. 'Pompous, important person' (Hawke): RM: later C.20. Cf. **nebby**.

Nobbie, -y. 'Used when name of colleague is not known' (*Evening News*, 27 Apr. 1954): busmen's: since ca. 1940.

nobble. To tamper with, by attempting to bribe or otherwise, a person, esp. a juryman: coll.: later C.20. 'Jurors screened in nobbling scare' (headline in *Observer*, 12 Sep. 1982), and on BBC Radio news, 4 Mar. 1983, a High Court judge was quoted concerning 'the nobbling of juries'. Ex C.19 sense of tampering with race horses.

nobes. See **like nobes**.

noble. A mainly girlish, chiefly school-girlish, coll. of approbation for persons or things, esp. in *that's* (*very*) *noble of you*. Ex aristocratic connotation.

nod, n. A very junior second lieutenant, Royal Marines, straight out of officer training school: RM: late 1970s. 'We had to go on an exercise with this nod, but we soon put him right' (an experienced RM Private, 1978). Short for **noddy**, 1, q.v.—2. 'Pass *on the nod*', used e.g. of Borough Council, committee, or even Parliamentary business, where items on an agenda may be passed without even comment, each page or item receiving merely a nod of assent from all present: committee-men's.—3. In *on the nod*, under the influence of drugs: drugs c. Stockley, 1986.

nod, adj. Naked: (?mostly Leicestershire) teenagers': ca. 1977. (McPheely, 1977.) A var. is *in the nod*. A perversion of *nude*; cf. **nuddy**.

nod the nut. To plead guilty in a law-court: Aus. c.: since ca. 1930. (B., 1959.) Cf. synon. **bow the crumpet** and **duck the scone**.

nodding donkey. Morgan, 1977: 'Initially the oil will be forced to the surface by the natural pressure in the reservoir. But when this declines, pumps about 20 feet high, known as "nodding donkeys" because of their shape, will be needed to maintain production': oilmen's s. > j.: later C.20. (P.B.)

noddy. The old S.E. sense of 'a fool, simpleton, noodle' (*SOD*) received an impetus towards coll., and gave rise to several coll. or s. derivatives (see below), in mid-C.20: ex a series of very popular stories for young children, by Enid Blyton; they had as 'hero' a rather stupid elf called 'Noddy', who possessed, e.g., a 'noddy-car'.—2. Hence(?), a '100 h.p. diesel shunter 0-4-0' (*Railway*, 2nd): railwaymen's: since later 1950s. (P.B.)—3. 'Cutaways, which is the technical term for brief shots of faces, inserted in a recorded discussion to give an

impression of the give and take of the participants' reactions . . . are known as "noddies" ' (May, 1985): television cameramen's. Cf. **talking head**.

noddy approach, make (or **use**) **the.** Lit., 'the simpleton approach' to a subject 'taught' to informed students, merely to be thorough in one's teaching, and as an aid to revision: coll. rather than s.: I first heard it at the RAF School of Education, Upwood, in 1972. (P.B.) Cf. **noddy guide**.

noddy-bike. The L.E. Velocette light motorcycle used by the police for general use before the introduction of 'panda cars': 1950s. (Partridge, 1979.) Police s. > j. Ex **noddy**, 1.

noddy-boat. A canal-using pleasure-boat—not the conventional canal narrow-boat: since ca. 1950. (Gagg, 1972.) Ex **noddy**, 1.

noddy cap. 'A protective cap that covers the sensitive nose of a missile; from the pointed cap worn by a popular children's comic character: RAF' (Green, 1984).

noddy('s) guide. '[WW1 fighter pilots'] rules of thumb ("Beware the Hun in the sun"), those ancient noddy's guides ("Good gunnery is the key to success")' (*Phantom*): Services': 1970s. Ex **noddy**, 1. 'A var. was "Noddy meets . . . "; thus "Noddy meets Claude Bernard" was the affectionate name for Samson Wright's rather simplistic textbook of physiology' (Hamblin, 1988).

noddy suit. Protective clothing to be worn under conditions of NBC (nuclear, biological, and chemical) warfare: Services': since late 1960s. *British Army Review*, Dec. 1972. See **noddy**, 1.

Noggies. Koreans: United Nations troops': ca. 1951–5 in Korea. (*Iddiwah*, July 1953.) Fanciful? Also *Nogs*: B., 1953.—2. As *noggies*, turds; esp. in *do* (or *have* one's) *noggies*, to defecate: English preparatory schools': 1930s. (P.J.E. Jones, 1957.) Prob. of nursery orig.; just poss. the orig. of sense 1.

noise. In *make a noise like a(n)* . . . , to pretend to be a (thing); (momentarily) to suppose oneself to be an (animal; occ. a person): from ca. 1908. Baden Powell, in his *Scouting for Boys*, instructed scouts in danger of detection to take cover and make a noise like a (say) thrush; Wodehouse brought out, with humorous illustrations, a skit on this particular piece of scout-craft, and the phrase took the public fancy. The phrase is ob., 1983, but a good example is in Sayers, 1927, 'And now we'll just make a noise like a hoop and roll away.'

noise the edge. See MOCK-AUCTION SLANG, in Appx.

nolified and **noly,** the latter also n. (the *o* is long, as in *holy*). Simple-minded: market-traders'. (*M.T.*) Most prob. ex Lincolnshire dial. *knohl* (at knoll (2), 4, in *EDD*), a knock, esp. a blow, on the side of the head. (P.B.)

non-can-go-ists. See **no-can-go-ist**.

non-car(e)ish. Insouciant: coll.: early C.20. Manchon.

non-flam (film). Non-flammable: filmland: since ca. 1915. McCabe, 1937.

non-frat. Order(s) forbidding fraternisation: Army: 1944–6 (?later). (P-G-R.) See **frat**, v.

Non-skid. A Jew: r.s., on *Yid*: since (?)ca. 1920. (Llewellyn, 1943.) Cf. **tea-pot lid**, n.

non-speaks. 'What other people called *sending to Coventry*, we called *non-speaks*' (Sinclair, 1977): Eton College: mid-C.20.

nonce. A sexual deviant or pervert, esp. one that assaults children: c. and underworld: later C.20. (Home Office; *Community Care*, 2 Nov. 1977.) Elliot, 1988, has var. *noncer*. Perhaps a shortening of *nonsense*? (P.B.)—2. 'A stupid chap' (Home Office); a lunatic or 'nut-case': id.

nonch. Completely at one's ease; utterly relaxed ('dead nonch'): since late 1930s, perhaps earlier; Gilderdale, 2, notes its use among Teddy-boys in the later 1950s. Ex *nonchalant*.

nong; nong-nong. A fool: Aus.: since ca. 1945. 'The word *nong* probably Aboriginal; the reduplicated form has been influenced by Aboriginal names and such expressions as *woop-woop*' (Morrisby, 1958). B.P., however, states that *nong* is short for *nong compos*, an Aus. assimilation of L. *non compos* and is no more an Aboriginal word than, say, the *Nullarbor* (L. *null' arbor*, no tree, hence, 'treeless') Plain. Wilkes compares it with *nigmenog*, q.v. at **nignog**; see also **ning-nong**.

nonsense. A fiasco: since ca. 1938. Cheyney, 1943.—2. A piece of nonsense; an absurdity, e.g. a charmingly outrageous toque or hat; *make a nonsense*, to make nonsense, to make no sense, to mean nothing sensible: since early 1950s.

Noo, the. Scotland: see **go up the Noo**.

nook. A penny: c., esp. vagrants': earlier C.20. (Manchon; *Gilt Kid*, 1936.) Origin?

nookie, -y. Sexual intercourse: middle-class and almost polite; certainly a kind of baby-talk: late C.19–20. Perhaps ex S.E. *nooky*, resembling a nook, characterized by nooks, but probably related to older synon. *nug*, v, and *nugging*.—2. Hence, a girl, a woman regarded sexually: since ca. 1920. To which Peppitt added, 1976, 'Rather broader than you mention. It is anything female in the sexual sense—ranging from women who do, through what they do, to what they do it with.' P.B.: since ca. 1965 often pluralised, as in *to get* (one's) *nookies*.

nooner. 'Sex at and during noon time. As in "You look tired this afternoon—what did you do, go home for a nooner?": since mid-C.20, poss. earlier: widespread N. Am.' (Leech, 1986). P.B.: cf. Brit. synon. punning *grub-screw*.

nooves. A s. shortening of *nouveaux riches*: early 1980s. 'The Nooves were named by kids at Queens Gate School in Kensington, who have a sharp eye for social nuances' (Barr, 1983). P.B.: attention was prob. distracted from the term by the arrival of the *yuppies*.

nope. This US pron. of *no*, the semi-exclamatory adv., has, esp. since 1918 and as a low coll., gained ground in the British Empire. 'Ganpat', 1933.

norgies (mostly a feminine usage); *norgs* and rare *norkers* (both mostly masculine). Female breasts: Aus. low: since ca. 1950. The *-g-* forms derive ex *norkers*, itself deriving ex those advertisements for *Norco* butter which show a copiously uddered cow. (B.P.) Wilkes lists only the var. *norks*, quoting several examples from 1962 onwards.

Normanton cocktail. Wilkes quotes Cantwell, 1963: ' "Give us a Normanton cocktail, darl—a gin and two blankets," one of the cutters said.' *Gin* = Aboriginal woman.

north. 'There is much talk of money among young City people—talk of prices going "north" and "south" (up or down), [and] of being "in a spread" (making money)' (Taylor, 1987).

North Oxford Gothic. Bogus Gothic architecture: since late 1940s; by 1960, coll.; by 1966, almost S.E. Cf. **Stockbrokers' Tudor**.

Northern, the. King's Cross railway station: London taxi-drivers' coll.: since ca. 1905. (Hodge, 1939.) The most important of the lines serving the North; also, it is in N. London. Cf. **Western, the**, Paddington station: id.: ibid.

Norwegian (or **Scandinavian**) **steam.** Synon. with *handraulic power*, q.v. at **Johnny Armstrong**. Common in the MN: since ca. 1920, if not the 1890s. (H.P. Mann, 1972.)

nose, n. One who supplies information to criminals: c. (Wallace, 1923.) Ex s. or c. sense, since C.18, an informer.—2. A Jew (usu. male): esp. Lancashire proletarian: latish C.19–earlyish 20. Ex tendency to large noses.—3. As *the nose*, the front of a surfing-board: Aus. surfers' coll.: since ca. 1950.—4. 'In the late 1970s a "genteel" amelioration of *arse*: media and gen. "If he complains any more about his (e.g. skateboard), I'll stuff it up his nose." Cf. also the declaration of a witness in a notorious kidnapping case, who asserted herself ready to "ski naked down Mt Everest with a chrysanthemum up [her] nose" ' (R.S., 1978). Perhaps influenced by:—5. *Get up* (one's) *nose*, to disgust, irritate, anger, render 'touchy': since ca. 1935 (E.P.). but in really widespread use only since ca. 1970. Prob. orig. euph. for such phrases as 'It gets on my wick', 'What gets on my tits

is . . . '; *nose* here (cf. 4) may also be euph. for *arsehole*. In Aug. 1980 there appeared a poster with the coarsely punned slogan: 'If the Tories get up your nose—picket', a consequence of the newly-introduced amendment to the law on strike picketing. (P.B.)

nose, v. To spy on, keep under police observation; to watch (a building): c. Wallace, *passim*.

nose and chin. A win (on, e.g., the horses): bookmakers' r.s. Franklyn.

nose candy. Cocaine: drugs c. (Stockley, 1986.) US since—1934 (Spears).

nose-dive. A snatch, a swoop, an attempt, as in ' 'E makes a nose-dive at me eats, but I donged 'im': Aus.: from ca. 1919. Ex the nose-dive made by an aeroplane.

nose on. To give information to the police about (a person): c. Wallace, *passim*.

nose picker. 'Salesman's derogatory description of a potential client who cannot make up his/her mind and has no power of decision-making within the firm: commercial' (Green, 1984).

nose-scratch. A very sketchy salute: Services': ca. 1938–48. (H. & P.) Cf. synon. **peek-a-boo**.

nosey (or **nosy**), n., esp. in *take a nosey around*, to take a look around, as a detective does at the scene of a crime: since ca. 1950. Ex **nosey**, adj.; perhaps influenced by **mosey**.—2. 'The prison censor' (Tempest): prisoners' c.: mid-C.20. Ex:-

nosey, adj. Inquisitive: coll.: since mid-C.19.

Nosey O'Grady. An inquisitive person, usu. female: Can.: later C.20. (Leech, 1981.)

nosh, n. See the next. Among beatniks, this sense arose ca. 1958. (Anderson.) Orig., in Yiddish, of food eaten between meals. P.B.: Mr Maurice Butcher, orig. of Fulham, told me, 1979, that in WW2 Londoners were already saying, e.g. 'Let's slip along to the coffee-house for a nosh.'

nosh, v. To acquire furtively: children's: C.19–20. (L.A.) Origin? Perhaps ex Ger. *naschen*, to eat on the sly, to nibble secretly; cf. Ger. *Nascherei*, a nibbling of dainties on the sly. Also spelt *nash*.—Hence, *nosher*, one who samples food before buying; a greedy person: mid-C.19–20. If ex German, it comes via Yiddish; 'In the 1960s this verb seems to have come to mean "to eat heartily and quite openly". I have frequently heard it used in this sense by radio comedians. As a noun, it seems now to mean just "food", "a meal" ' (Spencer, 1975). Deghy, 1957, declares that *nosh* is properly 'to sample desirable food voluptuously, surreptitiously . . . One eats breakfast or lunch, but one noshes in between.' He also notes the frequent use of *noshing* as n. P.B.: that F. & G., 1925, list the Services' use of *gnosh* simply as 'to eat'—ex Yiddish, or from service in Palestine? It was certainly current in this sense among troops in Palestine during WW2 (Bishop, 1978). Hence:-

nosh down. To eat a meal: beatniks': 1959+. (Anderson.) Cf. prec. and:-

nosh-up. A bout of eating; a banquet: coll.: since late 1950s. Ex **nosh**, v.

not. As in *it (just) isn't* or *wasn't* (e.g. *her*, name, etc.), it doesn't—or didn't—truly suit her (etc.); it isn't or wasn't in character: since ca. 1956. Apparently it originated in the smart fashion shops of Society.

not a bone in the truck, as in 'Ten o' clock, and not a bone in the truck', expressive of time-wasting during working hours: ?Aus. and ?factories'.

not a dicky bird. Lit., 'not a word' (r.s.), it has come to mean 'nothing', as in 'What's going on in there? Can you see anything?'—'Not a dicky bird!' (P.B., 1975). Prob. since ca. 1920 or considerably earlier; I did not happen to hear it before the 1920s. Cf. **not a sausage**.

not a glimmer. Not (or none) at all: coll.: from ca. 1925. Only in answer to some such question as 'Have (had) you any idea how to do this, *or* that this would happen?' Abbr. *not the glimmer of an idea*.

not a hope in hell! There's no hope at all: coll.: from ca. 1910. (Onions, 1923.) Cf. **not a snowball's**.

not a sausage. Not a plane in the sky; no luck: RAF: since 1940. (H. & P.) Ex **sausage,** n., 3. P.B.: since mid-C.20, at latest, much more gen. than implied here, for 'nothing at all'; cf. **not a dicky-bird.**

not a snowball's. Elliptical for 'he (it, etc.) hasn't as much chance as a snowball in hell', i.e. no chance whatsoever: since ca. 1950. Clement, 1977.

not backward in coming forward. Not shy; 'eager-beaverish': coll.: late C.19–20. (P.B.)

not bothered. Unconcerned, as in 'Well, which shall I do?'—'I'm not bothered—suit yourself': coll. Cf. Brit. use of **not fussy.** (P.B.)

not care (or give) a. P.B.: The later C.20 form is usu. (e.g. *he) couldn't care* (or *give*) *a . . .* , or *he didn't care*, etc. As with *not worth a . . .* , there are so many phrases of dismissal, rejection, and uninterest, that no list could hope to be exhaustive. Some of the better known C.20 versions are: . . . *two hoots in hell*, later shortened to . . . *two hoots*, at first mainly Services', then > gen.; . . . *a button*; *a brass farthing*; *a fart*; *a hang*; *a tuppenny damn* (all gen.); *a chip*; *a cent* (mostly US); . . . *two tin fucks* (and, of course, . . . *a fuck*); and the, perhaps orig. RN, . . . *a monkey's fuck* or *toss*, which, later, and in the other Services also, > simply 'couldn't care (*or* give) a monkey's.' In Kavanagh, 1980, occurs 'they didn't give a wine waiter's cork about it'; and in Clement, 1978, 'Don't give a rat's, me!'

not fucking likely! A low, emphatic negative: an intensification of the form in, e.g., see **absoballylutely.**

not fussy. Not particularly keen: Can. coll.: since ca. 1920. 'Wear your evening things tonight, Harry.'—'All right. But I'm not fussy about it.' (Leechman.)—2. Unconcerned; indifferent: coll.: since ca. 1950, at latest. 'What dress shall I wear?'—'I'm not fussy, love; wear whatever's comfortable' (the reply of any unhelpful husband. (Mrs P.B.)

not go much on (something). Not to like, not to be very keen on, it: coll.: since ca. 1920.

not half bad. Really quite good: coll.: from late 1890s. Ex *not half.* 'There's a photo of my girl-friend. What do you reckon?'—'Hmm, not half bad—lucky you!' (P.B.)

not know from a bar of soap. Var. of next: Aus.: from—1918 (Pearl, 1967); still current 1970s.

not know from a crow. To have no idea what a person looks like: Aus.: since ca. 1870. B., 1942.

not lost for it. 'Not at a disadvantage for lack of objective cheek. If Jack borrows Tony's bike without asking, he's *not lost for it*' (Franklyn): Cockney: since late 1940s.

not of this world. 'Superlative in either direction, of both people and things. About 15 years ago [say 1947–48] it was *the* thing to say; now [1962] it is used with restraint' (Franklyn). It forms the orig. of *out of this world*, q.v. at JAZZ, in Appx.

not off. 'A given horse was not intended to win [cf. *not meant*] on a given occasion. When you hear that so and so [a horse] is or was "*not off*", "*not fancied*", "*on the arm*", "*having an easy*", or simply "*strong*" . . . ' (Lawrence, 1961): racing: prob. since ca. 1920.

not on. Not permissible; not practicable: coll.: since ca. 1940. Prob. ex military j., as of an operation being 'on'. P.B.: increasingly, in later C.20, with nuance 'contrary to accepted social and moral behaviour'; what in later C.19–earlier 20 was termed '(Simply) not done'.

not quite. Mentally deficient: mostly Aus.: since ca. 1920. For '*not quite* all there'. (B.P.)

not short of a bob or two. Relatively wealthy, usu. in comparison with the speaker; with sufficient funds: still in use, over fifteen years after decimalisation of Brit. currency (Feb. 1971). (P.B.)

not so dusty. Informal, semi-joc. reply to 'How are you?' (i.e. in health, or getting on). Occ. elab. by . . . *I don't need brushing down.* (P.B.)

not taking a blind bit of notice. To be (sometimes deliberately) completely oblivious of something: (low) coll. Also 'unheed-ing', as in 'There you go again—not taking a blind bit of notice of what I'm saying!' (P.B.)

not the foggiest. No idea at all: cf.:-

not the ghost of. Not the slightest idea: Society: mid-1930s. Delafield, 1935: ' "Who's that marvellous woman" "Darling, don't you know?" "Darling, I haven't the ghost of." ' Cf.:-

not the ghost of a chance. No chance at all: coll.; 1857 (*OED*).

not to speak to. Not to see or know at close quarters: joc. coll.: from ca. 1925. Blaker, 1934, of a motor-car, 'I've never seen one like this before—not to speak to.'

not up. Inferior; bad, very poor in quality: Aus.: since ca. 1930. (B., 1943.) 'Not up to standard.'

not very how. Feeling somewhat indisposed, poss. with some vague malaise; more seriously, not very well: coll. Ex Milne, 1926, ' "And how are you?" said Winnie-the-Pooh. Eeyore shook his head from side to side. "Not very how," he said. "I don't seem to have felt at all how for a long time." ' Raab notes the phrase's use in later C.20 Aus.

not very sweating. Decidedly cold: low coll.: since ca. 1940, ?earlier. (P.B.)

notch. A pocket: Aus. low. B., 1942.

note. A state of affairs; a happening: since ca. 1925. Curtis, 1937, 'It would be a hell of a note if he was to be knocked off [i.e. arrested] to-night.' Ex music.

nothing. Used as a suffix, in direct denial of a statement, suggestion, point just made, as 'Dictionary of Slang? Dictionary, nothing! It's just an excuse for a load of academic porn!': coll.: adopted, ex US, not later than 1910. Perhaps orig.,—1888, an American-Yiddish construction.

nothing but. Nothing else; *anything else but*, anything but, any-thing except; the former is coll., the latter catachrestic. Brandon, 1934, 'As far as that poor devil's concerned . . . it's accident and nothing but,' i.e. nothing but an accident.

nothing on its feet, have. (Of a racehorse) to be either shoeless or to wear only light plates: Aus. sporting coll.: since ca. 1925. B., 1953.

nothing on the clock. Of an aircraft that is out of control: RAF: since ca. 1938. P.B.: strictly speaking, it means an indication of 'nought feet', or little more, on the altimeter, as in the famous 'line-shoot', 'There I was, upside down, nothing on the clock, and climbing hard!'

nothing startling, adj. (predicative only). Unimpressive: coll. 'Oh, it's nothing startling.'

notice. A contract to do a job; a commission, esp. if illegal, on that job: police: since late 1940s. Newman, 1970.

noticing. Given to noticing everything; observant (and censorious): non-cultured coll. Postgate, 1940.

Notty. A familiar and affectionate name for Nottingham, used by, e.g., its university students. (P.B.)

nought–. (In) the year nineteen hundred and (any figure from 1 to 9 inclusive): coll.: from 1902 or perhaps 1903. 'Taffrail', 'The little 3000-ton Britisher, built in "nought five", carried only twelve 4-inch quickfirers.' See also **nineteen oh . . .**

nought feet, at. (Of flying) very low: RAF coll.: WW2 and since. Cf. **nothing on the clock.**

November, the. The Manchester November Handicap: racing coll.

nozzer. 'New entry boy at the training establishment, HMS *Ganges*, Shotley, near Harwich. These boys have been called nozzers, and their mess Nozzer's Lane, since the establish-ment opened, because the petty officer in charge was nick-named "Nosey" ' (Granville): RN: earlier C.20.

nuddy, in the. Naked: Aus., since ca. 1945 (B., 1953); by ca. 1960, at latest, common coll. also in Britain. Ex 'in the *nude*'. Cf. **nod,** adj.

nudged. '(Of a ship) slightly damaged by bomb shell or tor-pedo' (B., 1943): R Aus. N: 1940–5. By meiosis. 'In *The Dam Busters* (1951), Brickhill quotes W/Cdr Tait (CO 617 Squadron) as saying, when returning from the raid that finally sank the *Tirpitz*: "We gave her a hell of a nudge, anyway" ' (H.R. Spencer).

nudger (gen. *little nudger*). The penis: raffish joc.: heard late 1960s. Prob. ex a nursery term. (P.B.)

nudie, n. 'A film featuring nudity as its main attraction' (*Observer* film review, 30 June 1974): since ca. 1970. Hence, adj., as in 'I want to get rid of the nudie image so we can be taken as a serious singing group' (Duncan, 1979).

nuffer. A handkerchief: childish coll.: later C.20. (Clark, 1981.) ?Ex childish pron. of *snuffle*.

nugget. A very attractive girl, of whom it is hoped that she is not 'as good as gold': Aus.: since ca. 1925. B., 1943.

nuggets. Crystals of cocaine: drugs c. Stockley, 1986.

nuke, n. A *nuclear* missile: since ca. 1960 or earlier: military s. > j.: prob. ex US. (Deighton, 1975.) Hence, also *anti-nuke*, n. and adj., (one who is) opposed to the use of nuclear weapons or energy (*Time Out*, 9 May 1980).—2. A nuclear-powered submarine: RN: later C.20. 'Could he handle the clockwork in a nuke?' = operate the engineering/electronics in such a vessel.—3. See **Newk**.

nuke, v. To attack with a nuclear weapon: id. *Daily Telegraph* mag., 13 Apr. 1973.

nukky. An occ., mostly Cockney, var. of **nookie, -y**. Naughton, 1970.

number. A bedroom in hotel or large boarding-house: coll. (*OED* Sup.) Ex the fact that it has one.—2. A person: adopted, ca. 1944, from US servicemen; ob. (Marsh, 1949.) But as, specifically, a girl, it was already in use by 1940 (Ritchie).—3. A job, a post, employment: orig., mostly Services', perhaps esp. Army: since early C.20. 'Quite a nice, cushy (little) number, really'. (P.B.) See **square number**.—4. In *have* (someone's) *number*, to have someone sized up or potentially mastered: since ca. 1910. Ex telephony.—5. As in 'Too many people were using the "so bad it's good" number as a way of avoiding making any judgments about quality at all' (York, 1980). Perhaps ex *number* as a song or music-hall turn. (P.B.)

number-catcher. A checker of goods wagons: railwaymen's: since ca. 1920. (*Railway*.) Cf. **number-snatcher**.

number-crunching. 'The latest number-crunching machines can make sixteen billion calculations a second. (Number-crunching is computer jargon for the sort of monstrous calculation that would take X men Y years.)' (Large, 1984). Also *number-cruncher*, such a machine (Green, 1984).

number eight hat. 'A highly intelligent, usually intellectual, individual' (R.C.): since late 1940s; ob. Ex the superstition that a large head connotes a large brain.

number one. 'No. 1 diet, with close confinement' (Ingram, 1933): prisoners' c.: from ca. 1920.—2. A boat owned by the boatman that works it: canal-men's: late C.19–20. Rolt, 1944.

number one – ten – ninety-nine. 'The various degrees in the state of a soldier's feelings in Korea are seldom expressed in the well-worn favourites of World War II. He is rarely "browned off", "cheesed" or "brassed". No, sir. He's just "number one" to "number ten" and occasionally he may be "number ninety-nine" or "number hava no" ' (*Iddiwah*, July 1953): United Nations troops fighting in the Korean War of the early 1950s. For *hava no*, see that entry.

number one boy. The Chinese chief steward of a Service mess, or similar establishment, regardless of his age: orig. China coast; since 1949 only Hong Kong. (P.B.)

number seventeens. 'Any unofficial rig [clothing] of the day, for dirty work (Patrol Service slang)' (Granville): RN: 1940+. Ironic, in ref. to the numbers designating the various official 'rigs' for sailors.

number(-)snatcher. A 'checker of goods wagons' (*Railway*, 2nd). Cf. **number-catcher**.

number three. Sexual relief, whether normal or self-induced: low. A development ex the nursery *number one*, urination, and *number two*, defecation: since later C.19.

numbers game, the. In argument, the use of statistics instead of principles: Civil Servants', politicians', businessmen's: since early 1970s. Ex US *numbers game*, a form of betting. (Playfair, 1977.) See **play the numbers game**.

nun in a knocking-shop, like a. Incongruous, inappropriate, and utterly out-of-place: Lancashire: late C.19–early 20. (Roberts, 1976.) Cf. synon. *like a whore at a christening*; *like a pork chop in a synagogue*.

nunky (occ. **nunkey**); **nunks**. Coll. forms of † S.E. *nuncle*, an uncle: resp. late C.18–20.—2. A Jew more or less a moneylender: lower classes':—1923 (Manchon). Cf. **uncle**.—3. Also, a pawnbroker, whether Jewish or not: mostly Cockneys'.

nurdle. See TIDDLYWINKS, in Appx.

nurk. Alternative spelling of **nerk**, q.v.

nurry, n. The head: market-traders'. (*M.T.*) Perhaps derived ex *nurral*, E. Anglian dial. for 'the neck' (*EDD*). Cf.:-

nurry, v. 'To hit on the head, as in "She nurried the Noah's Ark" ' (*M.T.*): id.

nursemaid. 'A long-distance escort for bombers' (Jackson): RAF: 1939+.

nursery. A training station for flying personnel: RAF coll.: since ca. 1935; ob. by 1945. (H. & P.) Ex cricket nurseries.—2. As *the Nursery*, the Intelligence's, esp. the political agents' (the men in the field) training school: espionage: later C.20. Le Carré, 1977.

nursery slopes, 'the easy targets allotted to beginners on bombing tests' (H. & P.). Ex skiing.—2. Hence (the singular is used in both 1 and 2), any easy target: like sense 1, RAF: since ca. 1939.

nursie stories. Sentimental and romantic pulp-fiction in which the heroines are hospital nurses: coll., mainly book-trade, derogatory: later C.20. Cf. **lovey-dovey stuff**. (P.B.)

nursing. An exceptionally slow collecting of fares: London busmen's: since ca. 1920.

nursing it. (Of a pregnant woman) holding her arms folded over her belly: lower-classes' coll.

nurtle. Sexual intercourse: Aus. low. (B., 1942.) Cf. **myrtle**.

nut, n. The head: 1858, Mayhew, 'Jack got a cracker [a heavy punch] on his nut.' In mid- and later C.20, usu. in violent action to do with the head, as in the Mayhew quot'n; *give* (someone) *the nut*: ' "That's right, Paddy, give him the nut!" I was trying to pull his head back by the hair to hit him in the face with my head' (Behan, 1958—where occurs also the var. *give* (him) *the loaf of bread*): Anglo-Irish. Cf. the v., 1. A var. of *give . . . is put the nut on*: since ca. 1910 (Petch.)—2. Rent for stall or sideshow or stand at a fair: Can. carnival s. Adopted ex US. McQueen's explanation is, 'because rent is a nut to be cracked (paid) before reaching kernel (income).'—3. A 'nut case' (q.v.), a mental case: s. > coll.: adopted ex US ca. 1944; W. & F. record its use for 'an eccentric' as early as 1914. In 1960s and 70s popular phrases, adopted ex US, were 'what do you think I am *or* what do you take me for—some kind of nut?' = do you think I'm crazy, or stupid, enough to do (whatever it is)?, and 'what are you—some kind of nut or something?' = (loosely) your suggestion is absurd.—4. A fan, a devotee, one who is 'nutty' or 'nuts' about something, esp. concerning a particular sport or hobby: later C.20.

nut, v. To butt (someone) with the head: low: since ca. 1920. (London *Evening News*, 22 Nov. 1946.) See **nut**, n. 1.—2. To think, to 'use one's nut': Aus. Stivens, 1951, 'I did a bit of hard nutting.' Cf. **nut out**.

nut case. A mental case or patient (a 'nut'): adopted, ca. 1959, ex US. Field, 1963, 'I'm not a nut case.' Cf. **nutter**.

nut-house. A hospital, a wing, a ward set aside for the (temporarily) insane; an asylum for the insane: adopted, ca. 1925, from US. 'They're *nuts*!' Lindsay, 1933, ' "Whose old Aunt Beadle had to go to the nut-house?" roared Bill.'—2. As *the Nuthouse*, the RN auxiliary hospital at Barrow Gurney: RN: WW2. P.B.: many establishments have been awarded this sobriquet—and some were not necessarily mental hospitals! Sense 2 is therefore merely an example.

nut out. To consider; work out; devise: Services': from ca. 1908; by late 1930s (?earlier) also Aus. F. & G., 'I've got to nut it out'; Niland, 1955.

nut-rock, adj. and n. (A) bald (person): lower classes':—1935. A 'nut' bare as a rock.

nut-rule. An en rule: printers'. (Gardner, 1971.)

nut screws washers and bolts. A mainly s. pun, popular among low-minded youths, mid-C.20; said to be the headline over a newspaper story of the sex-maniac who fled after raping some laundresses. (P.B.)

nuts, n. The human testicles: since C.18. Whence, '*get by the nuts*, to hold securely. As in "I got him by the nuts. He ain't goin' nowhere" (lit., or fig.). In the legal sense, to have all the facts against, in the sense of an iron-clad, open-and-shut case. Widespread western US and Can.: since pre-WW2' (Leech, 1986).

nuts, adj. Crazy: orig. (ca. 1905), US; anglicised, thanks mainly to 'the talkies', in 1929. Ex older synon. *off* (one's) *nut*.

nuts! Nonsense: Can. adopted ca. 1940, ex US; by ca. 1945, also Brit.—2. Also as *nuts to* (name or pronoun)!, exclam. of defiance, as 'Well, nuts to them and their orders—I'm going anyway!': low coll.: since mid-C.20: ex sense 1. Both senses ex **nuts**, n.; cf. **balls** (= testicles) in this sense. (P.B.)

nuts and bolts; nuts and bolts with awning. Resp., a stew; a meat pie: RN. Granville.

nuts and bolts man. One who has admirable practical skills: coll.: since ca. 1960s. 'We'll leave the actual planning to old Smudger. He's a good nuts and bolts man.' (P.B.)

nutter. A crazy person: low: since ca. 1945. (Norman.) 'Off one's *nut*' or head. Since ca. 1961, no longer low, but merely an alternative to **nut case**. Morever, the 'low' tone of the word prob. arose from the London *milieu* to which it filtered from the Merseyside school children and teenagers. (See, e.g., *Woman*, 28 Aug. 1965.) In a youth gang, the licensed jester, tolerated precisely because he *is*, or acts, 'nutty'—and is therefore entertaining: since ca. 1960 or a little earlier (Marsh, 1976).

nutters, adj. Crazy; wildly mad: teenagers': since ca. 1980. Dickinson, 1982, 'She looked absolutely nutters'. The OXFORD *-ERS'* form supplanting the older synon. *nutty.*

nutty. 'Chocolate, whether or not it contains nuts' (Granville): RN: since ca. 1930.—2. Hence, candied sweets in general, as in 'the nutty ration': RN: since ca. 1935.

nutty as a fruitcake. Insane; hence, loosely, crazy: Can: (prob. ex US), since the 1930s; since ca. 1943 also Eng., partly via US servicemen. An elab. of older *nutty*, crazy.

nutty-nutty. See PRISONER-OF-WAR SLANG, §11, in Appx.

nymph. Short for nymphomaniac: since mid-C.20. (Haggard, 1964.) Cf.:-

nympho. A nymphomaniac: since ca. 1910.

O

O. See **C** or **K** or **M** or **O**.—2. Opium: drugs c. (Stockley, 1986.) US since—1933 (Spears).

O.B.E. See **M.B.E.; old boiled egg.**

O.C. i/c. Lit. 'Officer Commanding in charge'; an Army 'dig' at the plethora of initials and abbreviations amid which it lives; a blend of *O.C.* + the j. *NCO i/c* (a particular section, billet, etc.): Army: 1950s–60s.

O.D. An *ord*inary seaman: nautical. ('Taffrail'.) Granville explains, 'Naval colloquialism . . . *OS* or *Ord* is the official abbreviation, and *OD* is never permitted on documents but is used by officers and men alike when referring to new entries.' Cf. **odds and sods**.—2. As v., to take an *over*dose of a drug, leading to mental derangement or to wilful or accidental suicide: drugs c. Evans, 1983, 'Last I'd heard, she'd OD'd'. Hence:—3. 'To indulge in some activity to excess, to "go over the top" ': counter-culture: later C.20. Hibberd, 1983.

o eight (less frequently, **nine**) **dubbs.** Time: 0800 (or 0900); 'almost always used to refer to an early start after a heavy night's drinking': RN: 1970s' (Peppitt)—but surely since late 1940s. *Dubbs* = double(s), the double nought; cf. the Services' j., *o eight hundred hours*, and **oh Christ double o.**

O.K. is a coll. tag when appended to such a statement as 'X is innocent, OK', or 'Spurs rule, OK'—sometimes enunciated as an app. mild interrogative disguising a strong affirmative, 'Well, *isn't* he?! . . . , *don't* they?!' (E.P.). Rees, 1979, 'The addition of "OK" to slogans first became noticeable in Northern Ireland during the early 1970s, as in "Provo Rule, OK" referring to the Provisional IRA. This was adopted by graffitists in England for such pronouncements as "Man U Rule" [Manchester United Association Football Club] and "Notts Forest rule OK" [Nottingham Forest AFC], and lasted during mid–late 1970s.'

O.K. yah. A 'Sloane Ranger', q.v., agreeing noise: mid-1980s. Victoria Anson, 1985, testified to its popularity at Wadhurst Ladies' College; then the (London) *Standard* wrote of the show 'The Sloane Ranger Revue', 'OK Yah, that's brill!' (quoted in *Harpers & Queen*, Jan. 1986).

O levels, have (one's). 'Used amongst the present sex "swinging" generation to indicate either fellatio or cunnilingus' (Slater, 1978). A pun on the General Certificate of Education, Ordinary level examinations.

O.P. Other people's: joc. coll. Esp. a borrowed cigarette (B., 1959). Often in pl.: 'Do you smoke?'—'Only O.P.'s!' (P.B.) Cf. **O.P.T.,** and:-

O.P.B. Choice cigarette-ends: Aus.: since ca. 1920. B., 1942, 'Old Picked Bumpers'. See **bumper**, 1. But also 'other people's *b*utts' or cigarette-butts garnered from ashtrays: since ca. 1910. Cf. **kerbstone mixture**.

O.P.T. *O*ther *p*eople's *t*obacco, a favourite 'brand'; esp. *smoke O.P.T.*: joc. coll. See also **O.P.**

o.s. or **O.S.** Very large; '*outsize*': from ca. 1930. Ex drapers' j. Joseph, 1934, of an imagined performance of *La Bohème*: 'An O.S. Mimi loved by a C.3 Rudolph'.

O.T. and E. 'Over-tired and emotional', i.e. drunk: Sloane Rangers', q.v.: early 1980s. (*Sunday Express* Supp., 11 Oct. 1982.) Ex the journalistic cliché, (?)orig. in *Private Eye*: *tired and emotional*, used of intoxicated politicians.

O.T.T. 'Over the top', q.v., sense 3; 'usually "absolutely" or "totally O.T.T." ' (*Sunday Express*, 11 Oct. 1982): as prec. Moody, 1985.

oak and ash. Cash: theatrical r.s. Franklyn.

oars in the water. See **all** (one's) **oars . . .**

oater. A 'Western', cowboy film: 1970s. Jenkinson, 1976–7, *passim*. The cowboys' horses would eat oats. Cf. synon. **cowie** and **shitkicker**. (P.B.) Ex US: W. & F. date it from 1950.

oats for the donkey. Money: motor trade: since ca. 1910.

ob. An objection: policemen's. Dickson, 1937.—2. An observation car, esp. on the Transcontinental: Aus.: since ca. 1945. (North, 1960.) Cf. **obbo**.

Obadiah. A fire: r.s. Rare. Cf. older *Anna Maria*; **Jeremiah**.

obbo. Observation-work: policemen's: from ca. 1919. (Leach, 1933.) Has var. *obo*.—2. Hence, also, a police observation post. Crisp, 1976.

obie man. 'The obie man read obituaries. (The funeral will be at Wood Green on Tuesday and the house will be empty [and so vulnerable to burglary])' (Barlow, 1968): c. and low s.: since ca. 1920. P.B.: was there a pun on *obi-man*, a witch-doctor?

oblige. (Of a woman) to make herself sexually available to: coll. 'She soon found that she'd never get promoted unless she were willing to oblige her boss.' (B.P.)

obo. Var. of **obbo**, 1. Duffy, 1978.

obscene. Objectionable: upper classes': from ca. 1933. Blake, 1936, '[At Christmastide] the shop windows are piled with that diversity of obscene knick-knacks'—actually of impeccable respectability—'which nothing but the spirit of universal goodwill could surely tolerate.'

observatory. The astrodome of an aircraft: RAF: since ca. 1938. Jackson, 'Through which the navigator takes the observations of the stars'.

obstets. Obstetrics: nurses' and medical students'.

Occupied Territory, the. That part of West Hampstead (London) which contains numerous Germans, whether residents or lodgers: since late 1930s, by which time many Germans had removed themselves from a 'Hitlerised' Germany they deplored; † by 1950.—2. Bayswater (London): taxi-drivers': 1947–9. Ex the large number of foreigners there, and the familiar wartime phrase 'enemy occupied territory'. (London *Evening News*, 19 Mar. 1948.) Cf. **Resistance**.

ocean-going grocers. 'Members of the NAAFI staffs in HM ships' (Granville): RN: 1939+.

ocean rambler. A herring; a sardine: proletarian.

ocean wave. A shave: r.s. *John o' London's Weekly*, 9 June 1934.

Ocker, ocker. A constant disparager, whose assurance matches his ignorance and prejudice; 'the uncultivated Australian' (Wilkes): Aus.: since early 1970s. Ex such a character so named, in an Aus. TV series. Prob. orig. from *Ocker* or *Okker*, a pet-name for Oscar (Barnhart, 2). Hence *Ockerdom*; *ockerism*. See OCKER in Appx. for further discussion and another etym.

ockier. A liar: market-traders'. (*M.T.*) Also *ocky*, a lie; *ockying*, lying. Ex N. Country dial. (*EDD*).

ockle-cockle box. 'Disturbing a REME [Royal Electrical & Mechanical Engineers] fitter corporal on some secret gadget: "What you on there, Corp?"—"Making an ockle-cockle box. Now sod off!"—"What's one of them, then?"—"It's about this long and this wide, with holes in, and when you chuck it over the side of the ship, it sinks, going 'ockle-cockle-cockle' all the way down to the bottom. *Now* sod off, will you!" ' (P.B., 1974, with thanks to WO2 'Scottie' Parker-Wade, WRAC).

octu (pron. *octyew*). An *O*fficer *C*adet *T*raining *U*nit: Services' coll.: since 1939. Partridge, 1945.

octy. An octopus: Aus.: since ca. 1925. B., 1953.

odd. A police detective: c.: since ca. 1935. Hence, *odd(-)lot*, a police car. (Both in Norman.) The *Observer*, 1 Mar. 1959, using spelling *ods*, noted its use among Teddy-boys.—2. A police station: c.: since ca. 1935. (Norman.)

odd-ball, n., hence also adj. (An) eccentric: adopted, ca. 1950, ex US. Ex certain games, ?esp. golf.—2. (Often written *oddball*.) A—usu. male—homosexual: since ca. 1955.

odd bod. An odd-man-out: Services': WW2, and later. (L.A.) Cf. **odds and sods**, and:-

odd bods and sods. Miscellaneous persons: Aus. var., since ca. 1945, of **odds and sods**. (B.P.)

odds, n. In *above* (Aus.) or *over* (Eng.) *the odds*, outside the pale; exorbitant: s. >, by ca. 1930, coll. (Dennis.) Ex horse-racing.

odds, v. To try to avoid; to avoid, as in 'I can't odds being mixed up in crime. By listening in the right places I get results' (Newman, 1970): c. and low: since ca. 1945. Perhaps ex 'to bet against the odds'. Norman, 1959, has *odds it*.

odds and sods. ' "Details" attached to Battalion Headquarters for miscellaneous offices: batmen, sanitary men, professional footballers and boxers on nominal duties, etc.' (B. & P.): Army: since ca. 1915. Hence, civilianised in 1919, hangers-on, miscellaneous persons. Perhaps ex the phrase as used to cover those Service personnel falling outside any main group or classification, esp. in the field of 'religion', i.e. those who are neither C. of E., nor R.C., but *O.D.s*, Other Denominations. In RN use it covers ' "Hoi polloi"—the rank and file' (Granville); here it is perhaps influenced by **O.D.**, q.v.

odds-on. An odds-on favourite: Aus. racecourse coll. B., 1942.

Oedipus Rex. Sex: later C.20. Barker, 1979.

of omitted. A Can. coll., gen. only since ca. 1945. 'Here, it's never "a new type of engine" but "a new type engine." "He's just bought a new type lawn-mower" ' (Leechman). The second example shows how the usage may have originated. 'Prob. U.S.—Jewish origin. "A nice type feller" and "A piece candy" are typical immigrant Jewish locutions, some of which . . . have passed into American speech (chiefly) through Jews in the entertainment industry' (R.C.,

1966). P.B.: the omission, esp. with 'type', 'style', etc., has been common in English since the 1950s.

ofay. 'The word . . . is former Black slang for a white person (early Black Power days [in USA]). It is meant to derive from "foe" turned back to front' (Melly, Feb. 1979): understood, though not much used, in Brit., since late 1960s.

off, n. Start of a horse-race: sporting coll.: late C.19–20. 'You can bet, on the course, right up to the off.' Ex the cry 'They're *off*'. P.B.: hence the coll. 'Are you (we, etc.) ready for the off?', Are you ready to go (to move off)?: since mid-C.20.

off, v.t. To kill: adopted, ex US, late 1970s. 'We know now that the lad . . . offed himself by blowing out his brains in a kinky suicide pact with his teenaged mistress' (Johnson, 1980).

off-beat. Unconventional, but not unique nor unaccepted; (slightly) macabre: adopted, orig. by highbrows, ca. 1960 ex US. Cf. quot'n at **shoe-string**, 2. Ex music.

off-colour. 'Used of jokes that are blue around the edges' (Aldiss, 1978), i.e. impolite or indecent: coll.: since mid-C.20. Hence occ., fig., of an action, distasteful. Ex either the S.E. term for an unhealthy paleness, or from 'blueness'.

off (one's) **eggs.** Straying; hence, wide of the mark: Midlands. (Mackay, 1967.)

off like a long-dog. Departing very swiftly: Sussex dial. > coll. A *long-dog* = greyhound, lurcher. (P.B.)

off net. 'I'm a bit off net' = I don't quite get what you're trying to say: Army: 1941–5. The technical *off net* was applied to a wireless set not attuned to the collective needs of a unit.(P-G-R.)

off pat, (have) got it (all). To have learnt the lesson, recitation, etc., as by rote: schoolchildren's. (P.B.)

off-put. An 'off-putting' (repellent) characteristic. (Roberts, *A Ragged Schooling*, 1976, writing of ca. 1914.) *SOD* lists *off-putting* as a coll., 1941.

off the back. A synon. of *dropped* handlebars: cyclists': since ca. 1945.—2. Said of a cyclist when he is 'dropped from the group' (*Fellowship*, 1984): club cyclists'.

off the beam. See **beam**.

off the cuff. (Of a statement) spontaneous; unsupported by evidence: coll.: since 1920s. Ex note scribbled on stiff shirt-cuff.—2. Hence, (of an action) in immediate response, a 'one-off job', as in 'If you're not too busy could you do something off the cuff for me?' (Tey, 1952): coll.: since mid-C.20. (P.B.)

off the deep end, go (in). To get very excited, angry or passionate: Services' (F.& G.),—1918 >, post WW1, gen. *TLS*, 22 Dec. 1921, 'He never, to use the slang of the moment, "went in off the deep end" ' (*OED* Sup.)—by ca. 1930, verging on coll. Ex leaping from a diving-board into the water at the deep end of a swimming-pool. An occ. var., influenced by synon. *fly off the handle*, is *fly off the deep end*. See quot'n at **take a toss**, 2.

off the hook. Relieved of responsibilities: Can.: since 1920s, if not earlier. (Leech, 1987.)—2. 'Used often, esp. in ref. to someone charged, then released by the courts' (Leech, 1987): id. As a fish escaping. P.B.: hence also, to escape from life itself: Blythe, 1979, reports hearing an apparently contented octogenarian say to another, 'But how does one get off the hook?'

off the wall. 'Unusual, not normal. As in "I don't like that. It's pretty off the wall." N. Am., widespread, younger generation: since 1960s. Prob. ex California and the drugs cult' (Leech, 1986). '[His] success does not stop people thinking [Glen Baxter] odd. "They say to me 'Your work is off the wall' or 'so weird'," he said in an interview' (Wise, in International Herald Tribune, 18–19 Jan. 1986; the accompanying photograph shows one of Baxter's pictures firmly *on the* wall).

offbeam. An elision of *off the beam*, q.v. at **beam**. 'While not all police transactions with the public are so offbeam . . . ' (Tyler, 1986).

office. An aeroplane cockpit: RFC/RAF: from 1915. (F. & G.) Ex its speaking-tube and writing-pad. Still in use, as, e.g., in *Their Finest Hour*, 1940, and Jackson, 1943, although Rhodes, 1942, remarks, 'This seems to be dying'. But it is still in use among commercial airline crews, later C.20 (Green, 1984).—2. As *the Office*, the Marble Arch public convenience: a correspondent (1946) writes, 'Hyde Park orators, who are not allowed to take collections, sometimes say: "If anyone would like to speak to me after the meeting, they can see me at my office." ' Cf.:—3. 'The area, usually some part of a street, where a homosexual hustler establishes his pitch and meets his clients' (Green, 1984).

office boy. A Pay Lieutenant acting as Assistant Secretary in the Captain's office: RN: since ca. 1947.

office copy, the. 'The other half; the second drink to match the first' (H.W., 1942): RAF: WW2.

office manager. 'In motor rallying, the co-driver who takes care of navigation, checkpoints, documents and similar tasks outside that of driving the car' (Green, 1984): sporting. Cf. sense 1 of **office**.

officers' groundsheets. Members of the Women's Military Services, including the Nursing Services: Services', esp. Other Ranks', scurrilous: since mid-C.20. (P.B.) Cf.:-

officers' mess. 'Any female working in officers' quarters, or any female companion of officers': military: from ca. 1910. B. & P.

offsider. An assistant, e.g. 'a cook's offsider': Aus. and NZ coll.: later C.19–20. Ex 'The assistant to a bullock-driver, walking on the offside of the team, [hence] a helper of any kind, in a subordinate position; an understudy' (Wilkes). Hence, also, a mere hanger-on: since ca. 1925.—2. A friend, 'pal': Aus.: from ca. 1919.

'og-wash. See ogwash.

ogg or **og.** A shilling: Cockney (Wolveridge, 1977), hence market-traders' (*M.T.*), Aus. and NZ. A corruption of older *hog*, a shilling. Cf. **ten-ogg**.

oggin, the; occ., **hoggin.** The sea: RN (lowerdeck). (Granville.) The origin is obscure: perhaps a shortening of S.E. *noggin*, with a prompting by (**the**) **drink**; if *oggin* merely = unaspirated *hoggin*, then the semantics may be that, as hogs wallow, so do some ships. P.B.: but Granville contends that it is merely 'A perversion of 'og-wash'. *Floggin'the oggin* = sailing the seas.—2. Hence, a canal: spivs': late 1940s–early 50s. See quot'n at **peep**, n., 2.

oggy. See tiddy oggy.

Oggyland. Cornwall: RN. 'The home of the *tiddy oggy*, beloved of the Janners in depot at Guzz' (Granville, 1962). See tiddy oggy.

Ogopogo. 'A mythical lake-dwelling monster (cf. Loch Ness) believed(?) to inhabit Okanagan Lake in the southern interior of British Columbia' (Leechman): Can. coll. or rather, folk-lore: late C.19–20. The name is fanciful: cf. **Cadborosaurus**.

ogo-pogoing. 'Looking for unidentified aircraft' (H. & P.): RAF: 1942–3, then ob. Fanciful, perhaps ex prec. entry: there were many Canadians in the RAF. (P.B.)

ogwash, i.e. **hogwash.** A var. of **oggin**, the sea, the ocean: RN (lowerdeck). Recorded by *Weekly Telegraph*, Nov. 1942. Also—prob. via the FAA—RAF: since ca. 1945. Wilson notes its continued RAF use, 1979.

ogyalglazers. Spectacles. Hollis, 1983, lists this as 'parlyaree'. If true, it represents a remarkable, though tautologous, survival of earlier c.: *ogles*, since mid-C.17, and *glaziers*, since mid-C.16, both = eyes. (P.B.)

oh Christ double o. 'We [in the Household Cavalry] rose at the impossible hour of five forty a.m. (known as oh Christ double o), but the horses had a lie-in until six o'clock' (Carew): ca. 1940. A pun on the Services' 24-hour day, in which the small hours are written, e.g. 0500, said 'o five double o'. (P.B.)

oh, my dear. Beer: r.s.: earlier C.20. (Franklyn.) Cf. older, but still common, later C.20, *pig's ear*.

oh-slow. Oslo: Army: 1940–1. By Hobson-Jobson.

oil. As *the oil*, news, information: Aus. and NZ. Ex prospecting for oil. In *the dinkum*, or—more common in later C.20—*the good, oil*, the truth, reliable information.—2. Pretentiousness; presumption; 'side': Public Schools'. (Coke, 1910.) Cf. **groise**.—3. Tea: Army: since ca. 1930; ob. 'Due to the fat which often appears on top' (H. & P.)—or simply due to its lubricant qualities? (P.B.)—4. In *on the oil*, on a drinking bout: Army: earlier C.20. Hence, of course, *go on the oil*, which McKenna, 2, notes as 'the Great Western term for alcoholic excess'.

oil-boiler. 'A motorcycle fitted with oil-cooled engine designed by Bradshaw—in use from 1922' (Partridge, 1979): motorcyclists': the inter-war years, and then nostalgically.

oil down. See oil up, 3.

oil of angels. Money: beggars' and tramps' c. (Jennings, 1926.) Cf. its late C.16–17 c. meaning, a gift or a bribe.

oil out. To slip out or away: preparatory-schoolboys': from ca. 1920. Blake, 1935.

oil-rag. A fitter's mate: engineering trades': from ca. 1910.—2. A cigarette: earlier C.20 var. of *oily rag*, q.v. P.P., 1932.—3. In *live on the smell of an oil-rag* or *oily rag*, 'Metaphor for the ability to survive on minimum food or income' (Wilkes): Aus.: since late C.19. Ex Anglo-Irish.

oil-spoiler (usu. in pl.). A stoker (in a turbine ship): RN: since ca. 1925. (Granville.) Cf. *grub-spoiler*, a cook.

oil up. To advise; to 'tip off': Aus.: since ca. 1920. (B., 1942.) Ex **oil**, n., 1.—2. To enliven (a bullock) with blow or stroke: Aus. bullock-drivers'. Prichard, 1926.—3. With *oil down*, 'Cyclists' calls as a motor vehicle approaches from behind or in front' (*Fellowship*, 1984); club cyclists': earlier C.20.

oil up to. To attempt to bribe (a person): 1934 (*The Passing Show*, 1934).

oiled. Drunk: s. or coll.: since early C.18 (Franklin, 1737). In C.20, gen. as *well-oiled*. Cf. C.17 *oil of barley*, beer, and *the oiled, oiled story*, a mid-C.20 c.p. ref. the drivel of the tipsy—an ephemeral pun on 'the old, old story'.

oiler. A person (gen. male) addicted to drink: 1916. Prob. ex prec.

oily. An oilskin coat: 1926 (Richard Keverne).—2. 'Any legal visitor, often a solicitor's clerk or his assistant; the main solicitor himself becomes an "oily" since he, in fact, is an assistant to the barrister' (Green): prisons': later C.20. P.B.: perhaps cf. **oil-rag**, 1, and the insulting 'put-down', 'I'm talking to the engine-driver, not to his oil-rag', i.e. I won't deal with underlings.—3. See **oily rag**.

oily-boy. Expatriate employee of a Near Eastern oil-company: Service officers': WW2+. (P.B.)

oily lamp. A tramp: r.s. Hollis, 1983.

oily rag. A cigarette: r.s., on *fag*. Often shortened to *oily*; cf. **oil-rag**, 2.

oink! oink! 'Imitation of pig's grunt, used as comment' (L.A., 1976): since mid-C.20.

oke! 'O.K.', adj., q.v.; yes!: C.20 US >, ca. 1930, anglicised, thanks(?) mainly to the cinema.

okey-doke or **-poke; okey-pokey.** Perversions of **O.K.**: resp. 1934, 1935, 1936. The first occurs, e.g., in Harrison, 1936.—2. (*okey-doke*.) A wallet: (orig. and still mainly underworld) r.s.: since the late 1930s. (Franklyn 2nd.) On older synon. *poke*. Often shortened to *okey*.

Okeydoke Pass. 'There is a track across the Nayu range [north of Akyab, Burma], which it crosses by the Ngakyedauk Pass, known to British troops as the Okeydoke Pass' (Mason, 1974): 1943+. A good example of the Brit. soldier's irrepressible determination to Hobson-Jobson every unfamiliar or difficult place-name. (P.B.)

old age, the. The old age pension; hence, a pensioners' club or other organisation; as 'I've been down the Post Office to get my old age' or 'We went to Bristol on a trip with the Old Age': coll.: since mid-C.20, perhaps earlier. (P.B.)

old age pension. See TOMBOLA, in Appx.

O

old and bitter. A mother-in-law: proletarian:—1935. A pun on the brews of ale.

Old and Bolds, the. 'Naval officers brought back into the Service from the Retired List in time of war' (Granville): 1938+.

old battle-axe. An old, or an elderly, woman that is resentful and vociferous, thoroughly unpleasant, usually arrogant, and no beauty: since the early 1920s, if not, indeed, since ca. 1910. Cf:-

old battleship or **old battle-cruiser.** A woman of the humorous mother-in-law type; a broad-shouldered, or stout, aggressive-looking woman: joc. coll.: since ca. 1914.

old bean. A term of address: perhaps orig. RN, from 1914 (Carr) >, by 1917, gen.; ob. by ca. 1935, except joc. Collinson.

Old Ben. Newsagents' *Ben*evolent Association Fund: journalists': since ca. 1920.

Old Bill. A veteran; any old soldier, esp. if with heavy, drooping whiskers: military coll., mostly officers': 1915; very ob. by 1930. (F. & G.) Ex Capt. Bruce Bairnsfather's WW1 cartoon character.—2. 'An extraordinarily profitable fare' (Hodge, 1939): taxi-drivers': since ca. 1917. Ex same source: 'Old Bill' usually wore a fairly benevolent expression.—3. A rank outsider (horse): racecourse: since early 1920s. (Betts, 1967.) Prob. ex same source as senses 1 and 2.—4. A policeman: c. and fringe-of-the-underworld s.: since late 1950s, perhaps earlier. (Cook, 1962.)—5. Hence, the Police Force in general, the Law personified, as in 'the Old Bill knew about him' (Scott, 1977): since ca. 1965. Has var. *Uncle Bill*, and, in the 1970s, simply *the Bill*. P.B.: in the absence of any known etym., I tentatively suggest an association with the pre-WW2 London police, many of them WW1 veterans with 'Old Bill' moustaches. Arthur Moyse, of W. Kensington, comments, 1983, 'I cannot imagine working-class people using a term like "Old Bill" for the police for it sounds too sentimental; the Bairnsfather drawings were strictly for a middle-class readership as a view of the lovable Kipling type of private soldier'. He then proposes a very possible etym.: a blend, by the popular song 'Won't You Come Home, Bill Bailey?' out of 'The Old Bailey'. This may sound rather far-fetched, but there are many stranger derivations in this *Dict*.

old blind Bob. Penis: low and raffish. (L.A., 1974.) Cf. the **blind inches.**

old boat. 'A house, usually in an untidy state, where old people live' (Bournemouth *Evening Echo*, 20 Apr. 1966): c.: since ca. 1930.

old boiled egg. An O.B.E.: since ca. 1925. A. Waugh, 1959, 'He was not grumbling at a C.M.G.; the best he'd hoped for when he started was the old boiled egg they'd given him in the Middle East.' See also **M.B.E.**

old boot. Derogatory for a sluttish, promiscuous—and not necessarily physically old—woman: low: since mid-C.20.

old boy net, the. Since mid-1950s, at latest, a shortening or var. of:-

old boy (or **Old Boy**) **network, the.** That social and, esp. business, connection between *old* (former) Public School *boys* which, the envious assume, operates from reciprocal advantage in the professions and which is, by outsiders, regarded as social bias—as if the same sort of thing didn't operate in the trades and in all social classes! It is, at all levels, at least based upon old and trusted standards. Not, of course, s. but coll. and dating from the early 1950s. L.A. noted overhearing, 1959, the remark, 'The old boy network helps in getting jobs.' P.B.: by 1970, the Public School aspect had, at least in the Services, receded, and 'the net' had become merely a matter of 'knowing a chap', whether it be the commanding officer of one unit knowing that of another, or of coöperation among quartermasters who had helped each other in the past; i.e. men familiar enough to address each other as 'old boy'. Perhaps lower in the social register comes the synon. *old pals' act*, a mythical 'Act of Parliament' whereby friends are bounden to one another.

Old Brown Cow. Any 'difficult' aircraft: airmen's: since ca. 1930. Ex a popular song so entitled.

Old Brown Windsor. The anus: Aus.: since ca. 1920. (B., 1942.) Ex the soap thus named.

old bubble. One's wife: r.s., on the already rhymed *trouble* (*and strife*): since ca. 1930. Wyndham-Lewis, 1968.

old buck. Impudence; back-answering: Services' and low: since early C.20. H. & P.

old buzzard. Contemptuous for elderly or old man: coll.: since ca. 1910. Orig., euph. for *old bastard*.

old China hand. One who has spent many years in China in commercial or civil service or as a missionary: coll.: since ca. 1910. By 1945, few of them remained, except in Hong Kong: and the term will necessarily become less and less a matter of usage, more and more a relic of history.

old clanking irons. A constant grumbler: RN. P-G-R.

old cock. Frequently for **cock**, n., nonsense, as 'Oh, that's just a load of old cock!': since mid-C.20 at latest. Cf. synon. *old cobblers*.

old daddy. A Cockney 'prefix', as in *old daddy beer tonky—old daddy grumps—old daddy puddin'—old daddy tea-pot* (examples furnished by Franklyn, 1962): prob. since ca. 1870. Moreover, *old mother* is used in the same way.

Old Dart, the. England, esp. London: Aus. and NZ. An early occurrence is in Kennedy, 1902. Wilkes cites Egan, 1832, 'News has been received from London, of this extraordinary match, which excited exceeding interest amongst the sporting fraternity in the *Old Dart*.' Etym.?

old egg. A very familiar term of address (rarely to women): coll.: ca. 1918–28. *OED* Sup.

old-fashioned look. A look, a glance, of quizzical disapproval: since ca. 1930.

Old Freddies, the. (The consortium of) merchant banks: financial world: since late 1940s. *Observer*, 28 June 1959, 'The Old Freddies quietly partition the City's vast business among themselves—which is why the City can put over a huge money deal in half the time it takes Wall Street—and the world is presented with a united front.' Cf. the **old boy network.**

Old Frizzle. The ace of spades ('Old Mossy-face'): card-players': late C.19–20. *Country Life*, 17 Jan. 1963.

old fruit(, my). A joc. term of address: since early C.20. Cf. *my pippin* and **old bean, egg,** etc.

Old Fruit and Nut. King *Tut*ankhamun: r.s.: British Museum guards' and attendants': during the Treasures of Tutankhamun Exhibition, Mar.–Sep. 1972.

old fucky-off to Q.E. What's-his-name: RN: since ca. 1950. The *Q.E.* is, of course, the *Queen Elizabeth*.

old hat. Old-fashioned; out-of-date: coll.: since ca. 1945. Hence:—2. 'Old stuff, well understood, as in "Hell, that's old hat. Anyone can do it." Also has the meaning of plain familiar' (Leech, 1986): Can.: later C.20.

old haybag. Disparaging for a woman: low: since ca. 1910.

old heave-ho. See **give** (someone or -thing) **the old heave-ho.**

old henwife. Var. of **old haybag.**

Old Home Town, the. Cairo: Eighth Army: 1942–3. P-G-R.

old iron. 'Small pilferings of any sort of material entrusted to workmen on a job': South Lancashire s. (—1905) rather than dial. *EDD* Sup.—2. A bicycle; bicycles: since ca. 1925. H. & P.—3. 'Any copper coins which an airman will risk in a card game or raffle' (H. & P.): RAF: since ca. 1930.

Old Kent Road, the. A long alleyway running, between decks, from bow to stern of HMS *Kent*, the guided-missile destroyer, commissioned in 1963: RN: 1963 +. (Granville, 1963.)

old King Cole. The dole: r.s.: since the late 1920s. (Franklyn.) Since ca. 1950, the *old* has often been displaced by *Nat*, in deference to *Nat King Cole*, the American entertainer; since ca. 1955, usu. *Nat*, as in 'on the Nat'. (Franklyn 2nd.) Influenced by *National*?

old kohai. 'One who has long been out East and knows the ropes' (Jackson): RAF: ca. 1925–45. Ex *qui-hi*, old term for an Anglo-Indian.

Old Lady Five Fingers. Masturbation: low; mostly Can.

old lag. See **lag**, n., 3. 'A recidivist. A convict who has served several sentences of penal servitude' (Tempest, 1950).

old lug. A term of abuse or of reproach: Army: ca. 1930–45. P-G-R.

old man. Any chief, captain, employer, prison governor, head-master, etc.: coll. All the 'commander' senses become crys-tallised and pinnacled in the very English coll. use of *the old man* for the head of a Service—a Ministry—a great institu-tion—a profession, even the head of the State (e.g. the Prime Minister), the country.—2. 'That part of a beer-engine in which the surplus beer collects' (Dalton, 1951): Anglo-Irish.

old mark, the. One's favourite taxicab rank: taxi-drivers': since ca. 1910. Hodge, 1939.

Old Mick. Nauseated: r.s., on *sick*: late C.19–20. In an inter-view published in *Cinema*, early in Dec. 1967, Tommy Steele, 'Blimey, after you've got abaht twelve spoonfuls down yer, on top o'Christmas dinner, yer don't half feel Old Mick.'

old moo. See **moo**.

old mother. See **old daddy.**

Old Oak. London: locomotive 'spotters': mid-C.20. Clifford, 1970, 'told me that No. 6000 "King George V". . . . had just been. . . . slanderously called a "crate" because, being an "Old Oak" (London) engine it was seen too frequently.' Prob. r.s., on *the Smoke*, London. (P.B.)

old one-two, the. Copulation: low: since early C.20. 'I gave her the old one-two one-two' (Raper, 1973). Ex boxing, swift punches.—2. Male masturbation: low, mostly Cockneys': late C.19–20.

old pals' act. See **old boy network**.

old pip. An upper-classes' coll. term of address: from ca. 1930. (Brandon, 1933.) Cf. **old fruit**, and later C.19 synon. *old pippin*.

old pit, the. See **pit**, n., 2.

old rabbit. 'Nonsense, [the term is] usually applied to official statements' (Clayton, 1970): prisons'. See **rabbit and pork**.

old rope. (Very) strong or rank tobacco: Services': since ca. 1925. (H. & P.; Granville.) In the Navy, it specifies perique (*Weekly Telegraph*, 13 Sep. 1941).

old sherbet, the. A drink, as in 'a drop of the old sherbet': ca. 1890–1975. (Petch, 1969.) As a drink—an effervescent fruit-juice—it was, in Edwardian days, fashionable. Since ca. 1950, it has predominantly meant a variety of water-ice. P.B.: in later C.20 (perhaps always?) it has been joc. euph. for any form of alcoholic drink; cf. synon. use of **pop**.

old so-and-so, that or the. A figurative bastard: joc. euph. coll.: though heard ca. 1930, not gen. until ca. 1938.

old socks. A term of address: Can. Radcliffe, 1934, 'Hey, Mor-rison, old socks. How's things?' Also in the sing., as in 'If, in 1933,/you had said to me/Virginia, old sock, I see it all planned . . .' (V.G., 1942).

old squirt. An elderly passenger: (London) taxi-drivers': since ca. 1912. Hodge, 1939, 'An affectionate term'.

old thing. A familiar term of address, to a person of either sex, or of ref. as 'She's a funny old thing . . .': coll. Galsworthy, 1913, 'My dear old thing' (*OED* Sup.).

old thirds. Three men working on the one job or together: tailors':—1935.

old Tom. A var. of **tom**, a harlot; in C.20, not necessarily of masculine appearance (the orig. implication).

old trot. Ironically: a likely story, as in 'What was all that old trot about your mother never loving you?': since late 1940s. Often *a load of old trot*. Perhaps ex a story *trotted out* to suit the occasion. (P.B.)

old tub. 'The old tub, as she [a ship] was ironically, but fondly called' (B. Hall, 1831): nautical, esp. naval: (prob.) late

C.18–20.—2. By extension, other forms of transport, e.g., a car or aircraft: coll.: earlier C.20. (P.B.)

old unspeakables, the. The silent films of the cinema: cultured; not at all gen.: mostly or, at the least, orig. Can.: since ca. 1945; by 1960, slightly ob. (Leechman.)

old vet. 'Pensioner called back to the R.N. with the Fleet Reserve' (Granville): 1939+. I.e. 'old veteran'.

Old Whittle. The Armstrong-Whitworth *Whitley* bomber air-craft: RAF: 1940–3. The *old* is affectionate: the aircraft did much good work. (Noble, 1945.)

Old Worser and Worser. 'The Oxford, Worcester and Wolver-hampton railway before 1923 amalgamation' (*Railway*): ca. 1890–1923, then historical. A pun on *Worce*stershire. P.B.: rather, on the initials. See RAILWAYMEN's in Appx.

oldie, -y. An old trick or an old story; hence, an old film or play: coll.: since ca. 1925. Haggard, 1958 (first nuance).—2. As old, or comparatively old, person: coll. See next.—3. An old song: coll.: since ca. 1945. Ex sense 1. See also **golden oldie**.

oldies(, the). One's parents; hence also one's friends' parents: childrens': since ca. 1955. Cf. **grownies.**

Oliver; occ. **oliver.** A fist: abbr. (—1909) of r.s. *Oliver Twist*. (Ware.) Hollis, 1983, prefers 'wrist'.—2. To *put the Oliver on it* is to handle or work something dishonestly: c.: since ca. 1910. (Sharpe, 1938.) Short for *Oliver Twist*, 'the Twist' (a dishonest practice).—3. In *do you Oliver?*, do you under-stand?: abbr. r.s., *Oliver Cromwell* on *tumble* (pron. *tum-bell*), to understand. (W.) Raab: or var. pron. *Crummle* on (pron.) *tummle*?

Oliver Twist. See **Oliver**, 1.

olo piecee. Anything shabby, e.g. a cap: RN officers': since ca. 1905. At first, genuinely China-side; since ca. 1946, either derisive or sentimental. Pidgin for *old piece*.

Olympic pool. A drive-in cinema: Aus. feminine: since ca. 1960. Ex the petting, esp. the breast-stroking, that goes on there. Cf. **passion pit.**

om-tiddly-om-pom. A w.c. or 'loo': ca. 1910–40. See quot'n at **umpty-poo**, 2.

omelette, make an. To blunder; commit a *faux pas*: since the late 1920s. *On ne fait pas d'omelette sans casser des œufs*; cf. *make a mess of it*.

omipalone. A (passive) male homosexual: Parlyaree. (Took, 1974.) I.e., man-woman: both elements, *omi* and *palone*, ex C.19 c.

omnibus. An omnibus volume: since ca. 1920: book-world coll. >, by 1945, S.E.

omo-boys. London bus-drivers' term for taxi-drivers, i.e. *one man* operators: since ca. 1960. (L.A. 1974.) Prob. a pun sug-gested by the 'Omo' brand of washing-powder.

on, adj. Possible; feasible: billiard and snooker players' coll.: from ca. 1930. Lindrum, 1935, 'The majority of amateur [snooker] players . . . wildly attempt shots that are not "on".' Lit., on the table: cf. *on the cards*, possible or almost probable.—2. 'Used in crime circles [and promptly by the police also], meaning that a well-planned crime operation has started' (Petch, 1969): since at least as early as 1945, if ex military j., and as 1930, if ex horse-racing.

on, preposition. To be paid for by: coll. Esp. in 'The lunch is on me.' (*OED* Sup.)—2. To the detriment, or the disadvantage, or the ruin, or the circumventing, of. 'It got away on me' and 'He did it on me' are Can. examples; sometimes, to one's loss, as in 'Our old dog went and died on us'. Wall, 1939, sug-gests an origin in Erse idiom.

on him (or **her** or **you**, etc.), **be.** Culotta defines as an 'excla-mation, equivalent to "Just listen to him!" i.e. "He's talking nonsense" '.

on ice. See **ice.**

on it. On the liquor; drinking hard: Aus. coll. Wilkes, whose first citation is from 1938.

on the backs – down. Asleep: Army: since ca. 1930. On analogy of P.T. 'evolution' *on the hands—down*.

O

on the blanket. 'The morale of the men on the blanket [refusing to wear prison uniform]—is very high' (*Guardian*, 27 Apr. 1979): the men are self-styled political prisoners in the Maze Prison, N. Ireland: late 1970s. (P.B.)

on the bricks. Released from prison: drugs c. (Stockley, 1986.) Cf. **on the grass**, 2.

on the bum. See **on the fritz**.

on the button. A later C.20 var., ex US, of **spot on**, q.v.

on the coach. 'If two compositors fall out . . . they avoid each other . . . and the word goes round: "Bill's got Jasper on the coach".' Ex travelling inside, and on top of, a stage-coach. Rowles, 1948.

on the cuff. On credit: since ca. 1925: low >, ca. 1940, fairly respectable. (Sharpe, 1938.) Ex pencilling the debt on one's cuff. Contrast **off the cuff**, q.v., extempore, the widespread use of which has, in later C.20, obscured the use of *on the cuff*.

on the dot. At exactly the right time: coll. (Eng. and Can.); since ca. 1920. 'On the dot of nine.'—2. As *be on the dot*, on the spot: Can.: from ca. 1920. (Beames.)

on the drip. Engaged in hire-purchase. See **drip**, n., 5.

on the elbow. On the scrounge: low: later C.20. Powis.

on the floor. Poor: r.s.: late C.19–20. (Franklyn.) See also **floor**, n.

on the fritz; on the bum. Broken; out of order: since ca. 1934. 'Both expressions are quite widely acceptable in refined circles' (Priestley, 1949). These Canadianisms have been adopted ex US.

on the grass. (Of a horse that has) fallen: turf coll.:—1923 (Manchon).—2. (Of a criminal) free; at large: Aus. c.: since ca. 1925. (B., 1943.) Cf. **on the bricks**.

on the job, adv., hence also adj. (Engaged) in copulation; *be on the job*, to be copulating; *get on with the job*, to lose no time in beginning to copulate: coll. (Burgess, 1966.)

on the muscle. 'On the square—not cheating' (Drage, 1954): Can. gamblers': early C.20. See quot'n at **producer**.

on the never(-never). Hire-purchase: see **never, on the**.

on the nod. See **nod**, n., 2 and 3.

on the nose. Objectionable; no good: Aus. (B., 1942.) Ex *have a nose on*, to dislike, bear a grudge against (someone): Aus.: ca. 1860–1920.—2. Smelly: Aus.: since ca. 1910. Tennant, 1947; B., 1953.—3. (Often as exclam.) That's exactly it!; a bull's-eye: adopted, ex US, early 1970s. (L.A., 1974.)—4. 'She's on the nose,' she is a prostitute: earlier C.20. Cross-talk, 13 Feb. 1985.

on the ooze. Drinking: r.s., on *on the booze*: since ca. 1920. (Franklyn.) P.B.: should this be *on the Ouse*, as, e.g. the village of Linton on the Ouse?

on the out. 'When not in custody' (Home Office): prisons' c.: later C.20.

on the pension. 'A person receiving regular bribes or blackmail payments, acting as a "leech"' (Powis): underworld: later C.20.

on the pig's back. In luck's way: Anglo-Irish (—1903) >, by 1914, gen. (*EDD*). A translation of the old Erse saying *ar mhuin na muice* (Skehan, 1941). In gen. coll., sometimes *riding on the pig's back*, as in Hatton, 1930.

on the roof. 'On the surface. (Submariners)' (Granville): RN.

on the sheep's back. Dependent on wool; 'A phrase often applied to the Australian economy' (B., 1959): Aus. coll. Contrast **on the pig's back**, q.v.

on the side. See quot'n at **screw**, v., 3.

on the stop. 'With throttle full open' (Dunford): motorcyclists': since mid-C.20.

on the town. Applied to one who has gone into town in search of sexual or other entertainment: Can.: since ca. 1920.

on (one's) tod. See **tod**.

on top. 'About to happen' (Home Office): prisons': late C.20.—2. In *be on top*, to be discovered committing a crime or engaged in illegal activities; to be arrested: c. and police

s.: since ca. 1955. (Newman, 1970.) To have become exposed—conspicuous—vulnerable.—3. See **rick**, adj.

once. A quick, shrewd glance: since ca. 1920. Wallace, 1928, 'You rumbles me. I saw you giving me the "once".' Short for **once-over**.—2. One pound sterling: c.: since ca. 1935. (Norman.) Perhaps a slovening of **oncer**, 1; but cf. **ounce**.

once a week. 'Cheek' (n. and v.): r.s.:—1914 (F. & G.); perhaps much earlier. Still current (Clement, 1977).

once a year. In *she takes it once a year*, a low, raffish pun on annually/anally, in ref. to anal sex: later C.20. (C. Turner, 1986.)

once-over. A quick, penetrating glance: coll. adopted, in 1919, ex US. (British soldiers had heard it in France often enough in 1918.) P.B.: usu. in *give (someone or -thing) a (quick) once-over*.

oncer (pron. *wun-cer*). A £1 note, and later, coin: c. > s.: since earlyish C.20. Leach, 1933; Powis, 1977.—2. Impudence: Cockneys'. Ex *once a week*.—3. Something available, or occurring, only once; mostly Aus.: since ca. 1925. (B.P.) Cf.:—4. As in a discussion about a murder, Hunter, 1974, a policeman speaking: 'I don't see that it matters that Walling doesn't have form. There are professional killers and there are oncers . . . [This is] just the sort of thing a oncer would pull if he didn't know about violence.'

ondleton (pron. *wundletun*). At bridge, a singleton: Aus.: since ca. 1925. Baker.

one, n. In *on a one*, under open arrest: Army, esp. Other Ranks': ca. 1925–45. The *one* is the charge-sheet on which the soldier's name appears.—2. Short for **one and t'other**. Birmingham *Evening Despatch*, 19 July 1937.—3. Short for the RN *number one*, since late C.19, a ship's first lieutenant (cf. **Jimmy the One**): since ca. 1930. P-G-R.—4. See **get (one's) one**.

one, v. To score two heads on a throw of the two coins: Aus. two-up players': since ca. 1910. 'Joe, peering through the smoke . . . , called "And he's—one'd 'em!"' (Glassop, 1949).

one-acter. A (short) play in one act: theatrical coll.: from ca. 1910. Ex *one-act play* by the 'OXFORD *-ER*'.

one and a half. A prison-sentence or -term of 18 months (1½ years): London's East End: since ca. 1945.

one and eight. A plate: r.s. Uncommon. (Franklyn 2nd.) Contrast **two-and-eight** and **six-and-eight**, qq.v.

one and ninepence in the florin (occ. **the two shillings** or **the two bob**). A little weak in the head: coll.: from ca. 1910; † with decimalisation of currency, 1971. TV serial 'Market in Money Lane', 1 May 1967.

one-and-one. Fish and chips; esp. a portion enough for one person: Anglo-Irish, notably in Dublin. Recorded by Brendan Behan in 1963, but dating at least 10–15 years earlier. 'Said to go back to the days when Dublin was well supplied with Italian immigrants who set up in the fish-and-chip business and (many of them) knew little English, so that it became the custom for the natives to order fish and chips by holding up one finger for fish and another finger for a portion of chips. There is a folk-song called "Down by the Liffeyside" with the lines "Ah, John, come along for a one-and-one/Down by the Liffeyside"' (Gardner, 1977).

one and t'other. Brother: r.s.: late C.19–20. B. & P.—2. Mother: id. P.P., 1932.

one another. Occ. var. of prec. Ortzen, 1938.

one-armed bandit. A fruit machine, a slot machine: adopted in late 1950s, ex US. Ex the main lever, resembling an arm, and ex the odds against the user.—2. 'Cab equipment for automatic warning system' (McKenna, 1): railwaymen's, esp. diesel-engine drivers': later C.20. Suggested by sense 1.

one-armed lady. 'Pump on board a fishing smack' (Granville): nautical.

one away! 'The cry that goes round the prison when a prisoner has escaped . . . [a pun] on the cry of officer . . . collecting a man from a working party, . . . "One away", meaning, one off the roll' (Tempest, 1950).

one-badge nothing. 'Derogatory term for a sailor who has served four years without being rated a leading hand' (Wood, 1978): RN, WRNS, FAA: later C.20. All he has to show is a good-conduct badge.

one brick shy of a load; one card short of a deck. Both these phrases 'smack of less than average intelligence' (Leech, 1986): Can. Cf. **one and ninepence** . . .

one-er, one-r. The sum of £100: orig. (?ca. 1930) c.; by 1960, gen. Cockney s. Norman, 1959.—2. In *do* (one's) *oner*, to die; get killed: Aus.: since ca. 1918. (*Rats*, 1944.) The one 'turn' one has.

one-eyed occurs in several low joc. terms for the penis, e.g. *one-eyed Bob* and . . . *guardsman*: since earlier C.20 (L.A.); *one-eyed milkman*: RN; and . . . *trouser-snake*: perhaps orig. an Aus. coinage of the mid-1960s (B.P.), but also favoured by the RN, later 1960s (Malin, 1980).—2. (Of a person) narrow in outlook, almost obsessive: coll.: *OED* Sup. gives 1863 as the earliest date. ?Poss. ex earlier *one-ideaed*. 'They were so one-eyed about these "health foods" that they would not even taste a leaf of parsley from my own "non-organic" garden'. (Raab.)

One-Eyed City, the. Birkenhead. (Brophy, 1934.) Mostly among 'Liverpudlians'. In full, *the one-eyed city of undiscovered crime*: while the city was very rapidly expanding, the city's police force was constantly inadequate.

one fat lady. See TOMBOLA, in Appx.

one-finger exercise. Typing with one finger: joc.: since ca. 1925. Ex pianoforte lessons.—2. Digital stimulation of the clitoris: raffish: since ca. 1920.

one for (something), **a.** 'A devotee, admirer, or champion of (anything)' (*OED* Sup.): coll.: since ca. 1930. 'He's certainly a one for his Sunday morning golf!'

one for his nob. A point in cribbage for holding the knave of trumps: 1870 (*OED*).—2. A shilling: street traders' r.s., on *bob*: † with decimalisation of currency, 1971. Franklyn 2nd.

one for the King (or **Queen**). An 'extra' year of military service, as in 'He had done his "pontoon", and "one for the King", and to the layman this period of time amounts to twenty-two years' (Carew, 1967): Army: earlier C.20; ob. by ca. 1955, by which time the regular long service of 22 years was an accepted fact, and the **pontoon**, q.v., a thing of the past. (P.B.)—2. As *another one for the Queen* the phrase survived into at least the mid-1970s; it was said at the completion of, e.g., a day of duty as orderly sergeant, or simply at the end of the working day: Army Other Ranks'. Also, *one more for the Queen*. (P.B.)

one-gun salute, get a. To be court-martialled: RN coll. (F. & G.) The ship on which the Court is to be held fires one gun at 8 a.m.

One Hung Low. Joc. name for a Chinaman: low. Cf. **Hoo Flung Dung.** (P.B.)

one in the oven, have. To be pregnant: orig., proletarian; by 1960, much more gen. Cf. older synon. *one in the box*. Ex synon. *have a bun in the oven*. (Petch.)

one Labour gain. 'A yellow light at a colour signal' (*Railway*, 2nd): railwaymen's: since ca. 1945.

one lung-er. A single-cylinder motorcycle: motorcyclists'. (Partridge, 1979.)

one-man band. A person that takes rather too much on himself: coll.: slightly ob., as is *l'homme orchestre* supplying the origin.

one mother too many(, have). (To be) illegitimate: mostly lower-middle class. Implying 'the child shouldn't have been born'.

one-night stand. A night with a prostitute: since ca. 1930. Ex the j. of theatrical touring companies.

one O. A First Officer, WRNS: RN: 1941+. (Granville.) I.e. 1st Officer.

one of the best. A 'good fellow', i.e. a good companion: Society: from ca. 1920.

one of the bones. A member of a '*skeleton* staff': Can. Civil Service: since ca. 1930. (Leechman.)

one of the boys. Var. of *one of the lads*, q.v. at **lads.**

one of those. A catamite; any homosexual: euph. Cf. the rhyme, 'Pretty little fellow, wears his sister's clothes,/Don't know what to call him, but I think he's one of those', and see quot'n at **Nancy,** 1.

one-off (job). 'A large Scot who had such a unique personality that it quite baffles description—definitely what an engineer would call a "one-off job" ' (Phelps, 1946). In later C.20 often used to describe something happening, or likely to happen, once only; e.g., the police spokesman *re* the attempted kidnapping of Princess Anne, 1974, 'We reckon it was a one-off job'; or 'We'll do it on a one-off basis', a circumlocution for 'We'll try it once': coll.; by late 1970s, familiar S.E. (P.B.)

one off the wrist. A ref. to male masturbation: Cockney s.: later C.20. Leitch, 1973.

one on! 'Train! Beware!' (*Railway*, 2nd): railwaymen's coll. On the line.

one-out fight. A fist fight between two (usu. selected) individual members of rival gangs: Aus. teenage coll.: since ca. 1925. (Dick.)

one-out man. A 'lone wolf' cardsharp: Aus. c.: since ca. 1920. B., 1953.

one out of the bag. An unexpectedly good thing, occ. person: ?mostly Aus.: since the 1930s. (Raab, 1977.) Cf. *one out of the box*, at **out of the box.**

one over the eight. One drink too many; hence, slightly drunk: Services',—1914 (F. & G.); by ca. 1925, gen. coll. (Lyell). Eight beers being considered permissible. A slightly later var. is *one over the odds*.

one-pause-two course. An officer's initial-training course: RAF: 1939+. Jackson, 'From the left and right turn instruction . . . , when the instructor times the movement by saying, "one-pause-two." '

one-piece overcoat. A condom or 'French letter': since ca. 1950.

one-pot screamer. Someone who becomes drunk twice as easily as a **two-pot screamer** (q.v.): Aus. coll.: later C.20. (Raab, 1983.)

one them. See **one,** v.

one ton. 100: darts-players'. Impressive number: impressive weight. (London *Evening News*, 2 July 1937.) See also **ton.**

one up on. In *be one up on* (someone), to have scored an advantage over that person: coll. *Punch*, 11 July 1933.

one up the spout. See **up the spout.**

onedleton. Var. of **ondleton.**

ones, the. 'Ground floor cells' (Home Office): prisons'.

oneth (or **onth**) **of the month** (pron. *wunth*, to rhyme). A facetious way of saying 'the first (day) of the month': used regularly by an announcer on the then Rhodesian Radio, 1960s (Philip Symes, 1983). P.B.: I have also heard similar use of *two'th* and *three'th*, for 2nd and 3rd.

ongcus or **-cuss, onkiss;** esp., **oncus,** or **onkus.** (Of food) good; (of a place) passable: N.Z.: from ca. 1914, chiefly among the soldiers.—2. (Ex the second nuance.) Inferior or bad; unjust: Aus.: from ca. 1914. It is, however, possible that sense 2 is the earlier and that the origin is the US *ornery*.—3. Hence, crooked; out of order: Aus.: since ca. 1925.

onion. 'Part of a knot speed' (Bowen): nautical. 'Taffrail', '[The British cruiser] could not be relied upon to steam more than "twenty-one and an onion", as her own engineer lieutenant-commander expressed it.' Joc. on *fraction*.—2. A fool, a 'mug', spare man, 'Joe Soap': Army, WW1, and later in civilian life. ' "I clicked for beds and sister's told me off now," I heard him informing the orderly. "I'll cut the bread if you like. I seem to be the onion this afternoon." "You the onion!" laughs the orderly. "I like that, don't come it over me with that yarn. It's gassed, sonny, gassed. It's tanked" ' (Dent, 1917).—3. Abbr. **flaming onion,** q.v. Hence, occ. among civilians as pl., it = any anti-aircraft fire or shells: 1940 +. Berrey.—4. A person no good at skateboarding:

teenagers': 1978+. 'It makes you cry to watch' (C. Paterson, 1978).—5. In *feel much of an onion*, to feel very bored: proletarian:—1923 (Manchon).

onish. (Pron. *onnish*.) Rather late: e.g. 'It's getting onish.' Coll.

onka. Short for:–

onkaparinga. A finger: Aus. c., r.s. Rare, says Wilkes; a place-name.

onkey. Stinking; (e.g. of fish) stale: Aus.: since ca. 1925. (B., 1953.) See **ongcus**, 2, and cf. *honk*, to stink.

onkeypoo. Crooked; out of order: Aus.: since ca. 1925. Cf. prec.

onkiss; onkus. See **ongcus**.

only two speeds, or, in full, *have only two speeds: dead slow and stop*. To be very slow in one's movements; esp. to refuse to be hurried or flurried: since ca. 1910. In, e.g, a cartoon in *Punch*, 14 Mar. 1917: 'I've only got two . . .' (P.B.).

oo-er, occ. written solid. A children's exclam. of either surprise or disgust, or of both. An intensification of *oo!* or *ooh!*, itself a var. of *oh!* 'I remember this from 1907. It was long drawn-out and marked by an extreme affectation of femininity or foppishness' (Leechman). Cf. *coo-er*.

oo-er bird. Aus. equivalent of the **oozlum bird**, q.v. (Raab, 1982.)

oo-la-la. Esp. *a bit of the (old) oo-la-la*, an example of supposed typically French 'naughtiness'; unnamed erotic excitement, as 'Going to Paris, eh? For a bit of the old oo-la-la, I'll bet!', where even the speaker is prob. not very sure what he is implying: coll. See **oolala**.

oobyjiver. A what's-it, a thingammy: N. Country grammar schools: since ca. 1945. Cf. **ooja-ka-piv**.

oodery. 'A new term, coined at HMS *Northwood* in 1973. It refers to the work or role of the O.O.D., the Officer of the Day' (Peppitt).

ooey-gooey! A rhyming reduplication of **gooey**, q.v., but used as a juvenile exclam. of disgust, esp. at something viscous: Aus.: since ca. 1920. (B.P.)

oofle dust. 'The "secret magic powder" used on "fakes" or "gimmicks" that are not too new' (Hickey, 1945): magicians' (i.e. conjurers'). An arbitrary, fanciful word, *oofle*: ?ex *spoof*. *Dust* in the eyes. Perhaps influenced by, or even derived ex, the now ob. US Negro *goofer dust*, a magic powder alleged to be an aphrodisiac, as R.C. has suggested.

ooja. See **oojah**.

ooja-ka-piv or **ooja-ka** (or **cum**)-**pivvy,** the latter being the original corruption, is prob. a corruption of the nautical *hook-me-dinghy* (as Manchon says); military, earlier C.20, it means a 'gadget'—anything with a name that one cannot at the moment recall. Further corruptions were *ooja-cum-spiff* and, later still, *oojiboo*, with which cf. the Can. *hooza-ma-kloo*. (B. & P.) P.B.: my uncle, Max Beale, recalls learning shearing in 1922: 'I was trying to clip a ewe in 4 minutes. Had her sitting between my legs, had cleaned off the belly and was going up the inside of the legs, when the shepherd said, "Ooh, sir, you nearly got her oojakapiv—and if you had she wouldn't have been able to pour out." '—2. Hence, *the old oojah*, the Colonel: military: from ca. 1905. (Manchon.) P.B.: and, without *the*, still occ. heard (late 1980s) as a somewhat dated ref., usu. affectionate, to a person or animal. In my own household my wife's dog Tom is a.k.a. Old Oojah, having been thus 'christened' by our expert painter-and-decorator, John Green.

oojah. Sauce; custard: Services': ca. 1938–48. (H. & P.) Ex prec.—2. An air-raid siren: WW2.—3. Always the *ooja(h)*, the w.c. or 'loo': ca. 1916–40. (Rattigan, 1950: see quot'n at **umpty-poo**, 2.) A shortening of prec.—4. See prec., 2, and:–

ooja(h)-pips. A woman's breasts: Public-School-men's: since ca. 1920. Hardy, 1985, 'the model . . . took off her blouse and revealed a beautiful pair of oojahs.'

oolala. (Of a girl; a woman) readily accessible; amorous: Services': since ca. Oct. 1939. I.e. the Fr. *ô la! la!* (expressive of sexual delight). See also **oo-la-la**.

'Ooligan. An Oerlikon gun: RN (lowerdeck): ca. 1941–6. By the honourable process of Hobson-Jobson.

ooloo. See **ulu**.

oomph. Sex-appeal: adopted, ex US, ca. 1941. Echoic: ex a bull's mating bellow. Hence *oomph-girl*, a young woman exuding considerable sex-appeal: mostly US usage. *Oomph* had a wonderful Press on 16 Oct. 1946. Cf. earlier **it**, 2.—2. Hence, impetus, power; esp. in, e.g., a sports-car, fighter-aircraft, etc., 'She's a powerful beast—plenty of oomph in that engine!': coll.: early-1940s; ob. by ca. 1960. Cf. synon. **urge**. (P.B.)

oont. Pej. for 'fellow', 'chap'; a fool: low: since ca. 1920. Llewellyn, 1943, 'What's the matter with you, you big-headed oont, you?' Cf. dial. *oonty* (empty) and the at least cognate *vont* or *hoont* (to want, to lack); paralleled by 'mental *deficient*'.—2. A camel: Aus. (Baker.) Ex Hindustani.

oony. Seasick: Aus. (Baker.) Arbitrary formation, vaguely echoic of sufferer's groans.

oops! 'An exclamation of apology when two persons collide or when one accidentally enters a room where someone is dressing': since ca. 1930. (B.P.)

oos-me-goosh. 'Meat cut into squares, [with] vegetables, and baked' (Knock): RN lowerdeck: late C.19–20. Origin? Cf.:–

oosh, n. Seagull stew: RN: WW2, and nostalgically later. (Brown, 1968.) Cf. **hoosh**.

oosh, v.t. To drive off or out, as in 'Oosh that wretched dog off my chair!', or 'oosh Joy out until we're ready with her surprise': coll.: later C.20. Perhaps echoic of noises to drive animals, or a version of *shoo*, or ex *usher*; but cf. also **hoosh out**. (P.B.)

oot. Money: Aus. low.: since ca. 1920. *Rats*, 1944: ' "Smash?" asked Clive. "What's that?" "The most important thing in the world. Smash, dough, fiddlies, coin, tin, hay, oot, shekels, mazooma, sponduliks, cash." ' Prob. unaspirated *hoot*, or perhaps a var. of *loot*.

Ooty. Ootacamund: Anglo-Indian: late C.19–20. (Gosse, 1934.) P.B.: in C.20—since 1947, nostalgically—*Snooty Ooty*. Cf.:–

Ooty Snooty Club, the. The Ootacamund Club (in the Nilgiri Hills), to which RN officers serving in India were sent for recuperation or for leave: RN: ca. 1940–5. 'Junior officers found the "Poona" element a little over-powering' (P-G-R).

ooze. To depart: from ca. 1920. Mackail, 1930, 'I've got some work this afternoon. Shall we ooze?' Cf. *filter* and **trickle**.—2. See **on the ooze**.

oozle. To obtain illicitly or schemingly: NZ soldiers, from ca. 1915 (E.P.); Aus., since ca. 1920 (Baker, 1942); ob. Perhaps ex *oojah* + *wangle*.—2. 'To search for, capture, ambush, shoot or otherwise harry (bandits, rebels or other disturbers of the peace in Palestine): British Army in Palestine [1938 +]. E.g., "D Company will send an oozling party." Ex Arabic *oozlebast* ("brigand"), in brief glossary of Arabic terms issued to "the troops".' (Letter, 1939, from Earl Wavell.)

oozlum (or **oozlelem**) **bird.** 'A bird whose species you cannot recognise on sight' (Granville): RN. Granville compares the RAF's *concentric bird*. P.B.: G.'s comparison shows that he was aware of his bowdlerisation. For one version of the bird's attributes, see B. & P., at the monologue titled 'The Showman'; another, perhaps better-known, version describes the bird as flying 'round and round, in ever-decreasing circles, until finally he disappears up his own arsehole, from which safe but insanitary refuge he hurls shit and abuse at all his pursuers.' Perhaps ex prec., 1: *oozle 'em*—this would accord with the B. & P. bird; it made off with maidens, and evil intent.

op. Any surgical operation: medical, hence also patients', coll.: since ca. 1900.—2. Any military operation: Services'.—3. An operator; esp., *wireless op*: orig. nautical, since ca. 1922; soon spread to the other Services.

opcar. A policeman: Aus. c.: since the 1920s. (Tennant, 1953.) A modified centre s. on *copper*.

open. An open golf-championship, as the *British open*: sports coll.: from ca. 1920.

open a can of worms. 'To introduce an unsavoury subject into the conversation': Can.: since ca. 1955. (Leechman, who qualified it as 'rare'.) Such a tin of worms as is purchased by a week-end fisherman.—2. 'To loose a perhaps insoluble complication of unwanted subjects' (Bernstein, 1971): adopted, ca. 1971, ex US; by 1978 quite common, esp. in political commentaries: 'The minister's refusal to . . . has opened a whole new can of worms . . . ' (P.B.)

open a tin. To start a quarrel: RN: since ca. 1910. (Granville.) Cf. synon. **kick a gong.**

open for business. Start of the day's routine, when the flag is 'made': RN: later C.20. (Malin, 1979.)

open slather. Free for all; 'anything goes'; 'open house': Aus.: since early C.20. (Wilkes quotes Marshall, 1919.) Perhaps ex Irish *slighe*, craft; a way; access.

open the door. See TOMBOLA, in Appx.

opener. Any case, bag, package, etc., opened by customs officials: customs' s. (ca. 1908) >, by 1930, coll. (*OED* Sup.)

operation. 'Note to sub-editors and others: please co-operate in killing . . . the most overworked of current clichés—the whimsical application to a variety of topics of the military locution "Operation—" ' (Driberg, 1946): coll.: late 1945+.

Operation Park. Bondi Esplanade Park Sydney: Sydneyites': since ca. 1925. (Baker.) Erotic.

oppo. 'My oppo' is my chum, pal, usual companion: RN, RM,—1914; Army and RAF in WW2; all 3 Services since. Ex *opposite number* (Granville).—2. Hence, sweetheart (H. & P.) or even one's wife (Jackson): Services' joc.: WW2.—3. Senior officers in mess: RN lowerdeck: since ca. 1920. Ex *operational*.

opposite number, (one's). 'The *opposite number* to a Brigade Intelligence Officer, for instance, is the Battalion Intelligence Officer on the one hand, the Divisional Intelligence Officer on the other' (E.P., 1942): Army: since ca. 1936: by 1942, it was j.—2. 'One who carries the duties of another in a different watch' (Knight, 1984): RN.

ops. Operations (activities): Services': since ca. 1915.—2. In RAF, Operations Room: Operations Officer: since ca. 1938. Partridge, 1945.

opsh. Something optional; e.g., a ball where fancy dress is optional; esp. in *without the opsh*, no choice: prob. since late C.19. MacGill, 1920.

or three. 'Used, for emphasis, instead of "or two", as in "Looks to me as if you're going to need another bookcase or three" ' (P.B., 1976): I first heard it ca. 1950, but think it goes back to the early 1930s.

or what-have-you. A tag, indicative not of doubt but of a refusal to go into a catalogue: orig. (ca. 1942) and still (1960) a mainly cultured coll. It 'provides for any reasonable conceivable possibility appropriate to the context . . . For want of example, or as opening the sluice-gates of possibility' (L.A., 1948). P.B.: since ca. 1970, if not earlier, usu. *or whatever*.

orange peel. 'The orange colour jacket worn by platelayers to warn drivers that they are working on the line' (McKenna, 1, 1970): railwaymen's: later C.20.

orange pip. A Japanese: r.s., on *nip*: later C.20. Barker, 1979.

oranges. Dexedrine tablets: drugs c. (Stockley, 1986.) US since—1967 (Spears).

orbit. To circle: Fighter Command: WW2. It became official: cf. **angels.** Ex astronomy.—2. Hence, to *go*, or *get, into orbit*, to go, get, into a lively circle; when used by women, it implies an escape from housework and a too quiet evening: since ca. 1946. (Petch.) P.B.: but E.P. has here, I think, not moved with the times; Petch's reminder must have come after the first sputnik, space-satellite, was shot into orbit in 1957. The phrase, as in, e.g., 'he's gone into orbit', soon came to mean 'he is in a "flap", a panic', or 'he is very angry': Services'. Cf. **go through the roof.**

orchestra stalls. Testicles: r.s., on *balls*: later C.19–20. 'The term is always reduced to "orchestras", and is employed as a

euphemism at several social levels' (Franklyn). Cf. **cobblers.**—2. Prison cells: police joc.: from ca. 1920. Cf. the Fr. C.19–20 s. *violon*, gaol.

orchestras. See prec., 1.

orchids and turnips. People important and insignificant: joc. coll.:—1923 (Manchon). Cf. the Fr. s. phrase, *les grosses et les petites légumes*.

ord. An Ordinary Seaman: RN lowerdeck. ('Taffrail'; Bowen.) Cf. the more gen. **O.D.**, and **hostile ord.**

order. 'A portion or helping of a dish or article of food served in a restaurant': coll.: US (—1906) anglicised by 1920. *OED* Sup.

orderly dog. Orig., in Army s., an orderly corporal, but soon, in Army and RAF, applied to the orderly officer, sergeant, corporal, or even to a canteen orderly. (Tredrey, 1939; P.B.) At first, for the lower ranks, it may have implied 'the orderly [i.e. duty] officer's dog'. Var. were *orderly pig* (Army and RAF), *poodle* (RAF), and *stooge* (Army), all earlier C.20, WW2.

ordinary. A bicycle: earlier C.20. (Manchon.) Ex *an ordinary bicycle*, opp. to a motorcycle.

orft. A deliberately illiterate pron. of *off*, for joc. effect; in, e.g., 'Well, I'm orft then' and 'Orft we jolly well go!': later C.20. Rees, 1980, attributes the latter phrase to the disc-jockey Jimmy Young.

organise. To 'wangle' something; to get something deviously or illicitly; to obtain or arrange something (very) cleverly but not necessarily illicitly: RAF: since ca. 1938. Jackson, 'Thus, "Leave it to me to organise some beer." ' Hinde, 1945, 'Used particularly in the sense "I must get organised with a girl in Town" or "with the C.O." ' Cf. Ger. military s. *organisi(e)ren*, 'to **liberate** something'.—2. To avoid (an unpleasant duty), as 'I organised that fatigue all right': Army: WW2. P-G-R.

organised, get. 'To arrange one's kit or the work to be done in order before starting the day' (H. & P.): RAF coll.: since ca. 1930.—2. Hence, to so arrange work, or a plan, as to achieve one's purpose; he who has done this *is*, or *has got, organised*: since 1939. Partridge, 1945.

orgy. A party: mostly teenagers': since the late 1950s; by 1966, slightly ob.

orifice. Joc. perversion of *office* (place of work): later C.20.

orkneyitis or **scapathy.** That mental and moral depression which tends to ensue after one has been stationed for some time in the Orkneys: RAF: WW2. (H. & P.) *Scapathy* deftly blends '*Scapa* Flow' and 'apa*thy*'.

orks. Short for *orchestras*, itself short for *orchestra stalls*, r.s. on *balls*, testicles: since ca. 1925.

orphan. 'Any discontinued model of a car: second-hand motor traders' ' (Green): later C.20.

'orrible 'ole, the. The gun-room, 'home' of the midshipmen: RN officers': since ca. 1925. (P-G-R.) Derivative of a typical Petty Officer's characteristic scorn.

Oscar, n. An annual award to the best film actor or actress of the past 12 months: cinematic: since ca. 1940. (*John Bull*, 24 Aug. 1946.) Ex the inaugurator's given name.—2. A Japanese Army aircraft: RAF in Far East: 1942+. (Sutton, 1946.) P.B.: this is an example of the codenames given to Japanese aircraft with unpronounceable, or undistinguished letter or figure, designations; cf. the famous Zero fighter.—3. Money, esp. coin: Aus. r.s. on *cash*. Ex Oscar Asche, the Aus. actor (1871–1936).—4. 'A large shovel; relatively recent and based on a humorous reference to the presentation of an Oscar film award [sense 1, now familiar S.E.] to the miner using the shovel' (Forster, 1970): S. Midlands coalminers'.

Oscar (or **o.**), v.t. To bugger: lower class. Ex Oscar Wilde.

Oscar Slater. Later: Glasgow r.s., as in 'See you Oscar Slater'. 'The man in question was involved in a famous Glasgow murder case' (Munro, 1985).

Oscar-Wildeing. Active homosexuality: lower class: earlier C.20. Cf. **Oscar,** v.t., and:-

Oscarise. To be (an active) homosexual: earlier C.20.

O

ostrich farm, the. 'The White and Gold Room at Buckingham Palace, in which ladies sit in rows before passing into the Throne Room to curtsy to Their Majesties, is irreverently referred to, on Court nights, by junior members of the household as "the ostrich farm" ' (*Daily Colonist*, Victoria, BC, 16 July 1926): Court circles'.

other, the. Homosexuality as a criminal offence: c.: from ca. 1925. (*Gilt Kid*, 1936.) As opp. to prostitution.—2. See **bit of the other**, heterosexual copulation.

other half, the. 'The return drink in the wardroom, all naval drinks being traditionally a half-measure': RN coll. (Bowen.) See also **swing o' the door**.

other side, the. Mail travelling in the opposite direction: rail-waymen's, esp. on mail trains: from ca. 1920. *Daily Herald*, 5 Aug. 1936.

ouds, the. The *Oxford University Dramatic Society*: Oxford University s. (from ca. 1890) >, by 1920, coll.

ounce. £1 sterling: spivs' c.: mid-C.20. (*Picture Post*, 2 Jan. 1954.) Cf. **once**, 2.

our –. A familiar way of referring to that thing or, more gen., person: C.19–20. Sayers, 1933, 'I've an idea our Mr. Willis was a bit smitten in that direction at one time.' Prob. a development of the practice, noted by Petch, 1946, 'In the North of England and Scotland [but also among Cockneys], mainly working-class, "our" is nearly always used in referring to a member of the family, as "Our Billy" or "Our Mary Ann".' Cf. the following:-

our kid. The eldest boy in the family: northern coll.: C.20 (prob. earlier). Contrast, e.g. *kid sister*, a younger sister; and see prec.

out, n. A walking-out together: lower-middle and lower class: since ca. 1920. Ruck, 1940.—2. An excuse; an alibi: adopted, ca. 1942, from US. Cf. **outers**.—3. See **on the out**.

out, v. To dismiss from employment: late C.19–20. Lyons, 1902, 'Yes, I shall be outed.' I.e. *to put outside*.—2. Hence, to eject from a meeting: Aus. B., 1942.—3. To suspend (a jockey or a professional games-player): Aus. sporting: since late 1940s. (B.P.)

out, adj. Esp. in 'That's *out*!': Petch, 1969, 'heard today when people don't want something or they cannot afford it'; (of a plan, a theory) (utterly) impracticable: since late 1940s: orig. s. >, by 1960 at latest, coll.

out for the count. (Often prec. by *put*.) Ruined; dead: since ca. 1880. Ex boxing.—2. Hence, utterly tired out; fast asleep: coll.: since ca. 1920.

out front. Straightforward; honest: coll.: adopted, early 1970s, ex US. (Powis.) Cf. synon. **up front**.

out in the blue. Isolated—esp. in the desert: RAF: from 1930s. (Jackson.) See **blue**, n., 6.

out like a light(, be or **go** or **put).** Unconscious; to become, or to render, unconscious, from or by excessive liquor, fatigue, drugs, or any other cause, very suddenly and deeply: coll., ex boxing s.: since ca. 1930. Frequent in *Rats*, 1944; Hunter, 1964, 'the jab [injection] put her out like a light.'

out of (one's) box. Crazy; mad: coll.: later C.20. (*New Society*, 12 Mar. 1981.) See also **out of the box**.

out of commission. Out of order; not running: coll.: since ca. 1920. 'We can't take the car; she's out of commission.' Ex ships lying idle.

out of curl. Indisposed; vaguely ill at ease: coll.: mid-C.19–earlier 20. Ex the hair. Hence, *go out of curl*, to collapse, as in Galsworthy, 1924.

out of it. Oblivious to one's surroundings, by reason of intoxication from drugs or alcohol: later C.20. Elliptical for synon. *out of* (one's) *box, head, gourd*, etc. Hibbert, 1983.

out of sight. 'May be given as a reply to an inquiry as to the state of one's health, suggesting that the person is in such good form he could leap up into the clouds, out of sight' (Sandilands, 1913): W. Can.—2. (?Hence:) excellent; delightful; surprising: counter-culture > more gen. s.: adopted ex US mid-1960s. (Janssen, both senses.) The latter may be spelled *outtasight, outasite*, etc.

out of synch (pron. *sink*). Out of synchronisation; fig., incompatible: coll., ex j.: later C.20. 'She laughed curiously out of synch with what was being said' (Walker, 1982).

out of the blue. Something that happens (to a person) quite unexpectedly, pleasant or unpleasant; as a windfall or thunderbolt: coll. 'What a week! Monday the eldest boy turns up out of the blue, plus scruffy girl-friend, demanding fifty nicker; then on the Wednesday, also completely out of the blue, she was offered this fantastic film contract.' (Raab.) Contrast **out in the blue**, q.v.

out of the box. Unusual: Aus., mostly rural: since ca. 1920. Devanney, 1951, 'But you mustn't run away with the notion that I'm anything out of the box in back-country conditions.'—2. Hence, very special; exceptional; unusually favourable: Aus., since ca. 1920; NZ, since ca. 1930. Courtier, 1964; Slatter. *One out of the box*, derived from this, for something very special, has the var. *one out of the bag* (Raab, 1978). See also **out of** (one's) **box**.

out of this world. See JAZZ, in Appx., and cf. **out of sight**, 2.

out of (one's) tree. 'Crazy, stupid; wrong: "Man, are you out of your tree?": Can., adopted ex US mid-1970s' (Leech, 1986). Noted in a UK advertisement for cider, late 1987; the advertisement was soon withdrawn, because of complaints that *out of* one's *tree* is Aus. s. for drunk (London *Star*, 16 Mar. 1988).

out of whack. See **whack**, n., 4.

out on (one's) ear. An intensive of *out*, as in 'thrown out on his ear': since ca. 1920. Has Aus. var. *out on* (one's) *pink ear* (B.P.).

out on (one's) own. Peerless; a very good sort (of fellow): coll.

out on its own – like a country shit-house. Excellent; unique: NZ: since ca. 1910. An elab. of prec.

out [of] the window. 'Ridiculous; out of the question; usually applied to a rejected idea or proposition' (Hibbert, 1983, gives a 1981 citation): show business. Cf.:-

out to lunch. 'Not with it, inaccurate; "That answer's way out to lunch." At least since 1960s, widespread in N. Am.' (Leech, 1986).—2. Crazy; plain mad: adopted ex US late 1970s. (Adams, 1978.) 'Dostoevsky notwithstanding, it's not always a good idea to have a central character [in a crime novel] who's out to lunch most of the time' (*TLS*, 30 Dec. 1983, p. 1462). Hibbert, 1983, attributes the state mainly to intoxication by drugs and/or alcohol.

outdoor plumbing. An outdoor privy: (US and) Can. 'ironic, since there is no plumbing' (Priestley).

outed. Dismissed from employment: Aus.: since ca. 1925. (B., 1943.) See **out**, v., 1.

outer. A betting-place, in the open, overlooking a racecourse: low Aus.: from ca. 1920. Hence, and much more usu., '(of a racecourse) the section outside the enclosure' (B., 1942).—2. (*the outer.*) Outside coat pocket: c.: late C.19–20.—3. In *on the outer*, penniless: Aus.: from ca. 1920. (Doone.) I.e. on the outer edge of prosperity; ex running on the outside track.

outer edge, the. See **outside edge**.

outers. 'What thieves call "outers"; in other words, a pat explanation if things go wrong'; to *give outers* is to allow 'a way of escape or a way of avoiding responsibility. E.g.: "Give me outers, guv'nor, and I'll tell you where the gear is" ' (Powis): c.: later C.20. Cf. **out**, n., 2.

outfit. 'The paraphernalia used for an escape. "He's got his outfit" = he has all the necessary impedimenta for an attempt to get over the wall and is awaiting a favourable opportunity' (Tempest, 1950): prison c.—2. In *the whole outfit*, the whole thing or collection of things: coll.: from ca. 1910.—3. Hence, by specialisation, 'Drug addict's equipment or paraphernalia' (Stockley, 1986): drugs c. US since –1937 (Spears).

outro. A finale: 'pop' music circles: since ca. 1960. (*Beatles*.) As opp. *intro*, short for *introduction*.

outs. Out-patient department of a hospital: medical:—1933 (*Slang*).—2. A *run of outs* is a succession of racing losses: Aus. sporting: since ca. 1920. Glassop, 1949.—3. In *on the* *outs*, 'on the outside; shunned; unwelcome' (Hibbert gives a citation for 1974): world of 'pop' culture.

outside. In civilian life: RN coll. Granville, ' "I don't care what you were 'outside'; you're in the Andrew now, so don't forget it, or you'll be in the rattle," Petty Officer to recalcitrant New Entry.' Cf. the very much older coll. Can. sense, 'in, or into, civilized parts'—as opposed to the backwoods. 'Trappers will spend the winter in the bush and then come "outside" to sell their catch. My earliest example is 1827' (Leechman, 1959).

outside edge, the. 'The limit'. (Lyell.) App. first recorded by Hay, 1907. Orig. a skating var. of *the limit*. Also *the outer edge* (Collinson).

outside man. 'Lookout man for criminals but particularly for a "firm" of card sharps engaged in the three-card trick. Such lookout men may be posted as far as 200 yds away from the venue of the "action" ' (Powis): c.: later C.20.

outside tiffy; outside wrecker. An RN artificer working 'outside': RN: since ca. 1925. (Granville.) Strictly a submariners' term for 'an artificer working outside the hull or engine-room of a submarine' (Granville, 1967). 'Most of the machinery outside the engineroom was maintained by the man who was known by the traditional submarine title of the outside wrecker' (Winton, 1961).

outside view. A view of the target seen from the air: RAF: 1939 +. H. & P.

outsider. A homeless person: Glasgow:—1934. Pregnantly ex the lit. sense.—2. 'A person living in the *outback*' (B., 1959): Aus.

outy. An outing, esp. for a pet animal: domestic. Kitchin, 1949.

ouya. You: back s., mostly Cockneys': since ca. 1900. Exemplifies the C.20 -a, or vocalising, var. of 'straight' back s. Norman, 1959, 'I saw ouya the theroa ightna up the hpeilersa' (I saw you the other night up the spieler).

over and under. 'A combination of stimulant and depressant drugs' (Stockley, 1986): drugs c. US since—1973 (Spears).

over-baked. Disappointed; 'fed up': RN. Cf. **browned off**. P-G-R.

over my dead body! A declaration of strongest will to resist: coll., sometimes joc. (dependent on context). (P.B.)

over-'omer. That kind of Englishman who talks constantly of how much better things are done 'over 'ome': Can. Naturally, he's much resented.

over the air. By radio: orig. (mostly nautical) coll., from ca. 1925; since WW2, familiar S.E.

over the Alps. In Dartmoor prison; loosely, in any prison: c.: from ca. 1920. Wallace *passim*.

over the bun-house. On public assistance: dockers': from ca. 1930. (*Daily Herald*, 1936.) As if getting food from the bakery.

over the edge. Unreasonable; excessive; improper: Aus. (B., 1942) and Brit. coll.: earlier C.20. Esp. in situations where 'just about the limit' would be an understatement, e.g. 'in WW1 the "Tommy" would describe the shelling of hospitals as "over the edge" ' (Petch). P.B.: since early 1980s, *over the top*, adj.

over the falls. Applied to a surfer 'trying to pull out of a wave too late' (*Pix*, 28 Sep. 1963): Aus. surfers'.

over the fence. (Of a person) unashamed; scandalous; greedy; very unreasonable: NZ coll. var., late C.19–20, and Aus. since ca. 1910 (B., 1942), of S.E. *beyond the pale*. Perhaps ex local rules for cricket.

over the hill. Esp. *go over the hill*, to desert (the Armed Forces): Services': later C.20. (P.B.) Cf. **over the side**.—2. (Of persons, also of machines, animals, etc.) middle-aged, 'getting on (in years)', long in the tooth: rueful coll. 'Poor old Polly; until a few weeks ago he would drive us mad with his talking, but now he's so quiet that he must be getting over the hill.' (Raab.)

over the moon. Wildly excited or delighted; 'in seventh heaven of happiness': coll.: since early 1970s. *Daily Telegraph*, 29 July 1974, 'I think it is fantastic. I am over the moon and

really pleased about it.' 'Diaries of May, Lady Cavendish, (pub'd in 1927) entry dated February 7, 1857, where she describes breaking the news of her youngest brother's birth to the rest of his siblings: "I had told the little ones who were at first utterly incredulous and then over the moon" ' (Rodgers, 1983).

over the side. Absent without leave: RN. (F. & G.) I.e. of the ship. Hence, 'Absent from place of duty, or home' (Powis): low coll. Cf. **over the hill**, 1.

over the top. 'Flying above the clouds or above the bad weather' (Jackson): RAF coll.: since ca. 1939. Cf. the lit. S.E. *fly above the roof-tops*.—2. 'Used by trans-Atlantic flyers to designate the Northern route by way of Greenland and Iceland' (P-G-R): RAF: since 1940; by 1946, also civilian.—3. Highly exaggerated: early 1980s. 'At first some of the stories [of criminal violence] seemed so nasty that I assumed the teller was going over the top—that he was revealing some unfortunate pathological obsession' (Taylor, 1983). Also without *go*: 'That's a bit over the top, innit?'

over the wall. 'In the guard-room, confined to camp. Thus, "9*d*. over the wall" means, "Nine days C.C." ' (Jackson). The phrase has been adopted from American c. (see *Underworld*): Services': since ca. 1935. Contrast:—2. 'An escape. In the event of a rumoured or actual escape, one man may ask another what has happened. The reply might be "So-and-so's gone over the wall" or "He's had it away over the wall" ' (Tempest, 1950): prison c.—3. In *go over the wall*, to go mad, become insane: coll.: later C.20.

overbroke. Too much, too heavily; esp. *bet overbroke*, applied to a bookmaker: the turf.

overgots book. 'Book showing credits in hand for which official debit not available. NER usage' (*Railway*, 2nd): coll.

overlanded. Of goods 'arriving without invoice' (*Railway*, 2nd).

overs. Any food or rum left over from the 'official' issue: Army: WW1. Elliptical for 'left-overs'.—2. 'Shells and bullets that passed over their targets' (P-G-R): Army coll.: WW2+.—3. 'Surplus of property or money after a theft that can itself be stolen by trusted persons' (Powis): c.: later C.20. Cf. sense 1.

overseas. 'Half seas over' or half-drunk: since ca. 1930. By a reversal and a pun.

overtakement. The state of being smitten with love: usu. 'to suffer from an . . . ': perhaps idiolect, in Ferguson, 1942, writing of earlier C.20.

'Ow dare she. HMS *Audacious*: RN: since ca. 1930. (Granville.) By Hobson-Jobson.

Owen Nares. Chairs: theatrical r.s.: since ca. 1910. (Franklyn.) Ex a very popular actor.

owl. An ATS wireless operator: ATS: 1940–5. Ex the initials of *O*perator, *W*ireless and *L*ine; ATS = Auxiliary Territorial Service (1938–49), the predecessor of the Women's Royal Army Corps.—2. As *the Owl*, the night train from Paddington to Penzance: railwaymen's: earlier C.20. (*Railway*, 2nd.) A night bird for night birds.

Owlsville. Late-night London: 'with it' revellers': early 1960s. (London *Evening Standard*, 17 Mar. 1964.) See **-ville**.

own. In lawn tennis, since the early 1970s, it means that one player consistently dominates another, even though their world ranking may be very close, as, e.g., 'Borg owns Vilas', which I saw in print a few days before Wimbledon 1978 began. P.B.: E.P. was always a keen sports fan, esp. of cricket and tennis; in the 1930s he 'made a bit on the side' by reporting Wimbledon for the *Manchester Guardian*.

own(-)goal. A terrorist—or, collectively, terrorists—killed by their own faulty, or prematurely detonated, bombs: since ca. 1974: the British Army in N. Ireland, 'borrowing with grim humour from footballers' jargon for a defender inadvertently putting the ball into his own side's goal' (R.S., 1977). P.B.: hence, soon > more gen., e.g. among bankers (Mann, 1985, who compares *shoot* one*self in the foot*), and applied to any self-damaging blunders and errors of judgment. George, 1986, 'You are absolutely right about own-goals. For Nirex

O

[the nuclear waste disposal agency] to embark on a new programme of trial borings when [the] Chernobyl [nuclear plant explosion] is still fresh in everybody's mind shows an insensitivity that almost passes belief.'

owner. 'The captain of a ship [RN] is invariably "the owner", "old man" or "skipper", while . . . the second in command is "the bloke" ' ('Taffrail'): RN: late C.19–20.—2. A visitor from on shore, come to look over the ship: id. (F. & G.) Cf. **Owners.**—3. The captain of an aircraft; *the Owner* is also the Commanding Officer: RAF: since 1918. (Jackson.) P.B.: no doubt taken into the newly-formed RAF by its RNAS co-founders.

owneress, the. 'Jocular reference to the wife of the captain of a merchant ship who sails with her husband' (Granville).

Owners, the. The British public: RN: since ca. 1925. (Granville.) The B.P. owns it.

owner's scribe. The Commanding Officer's confidential clerk: RAF: since ca. 1930. (Jackson.) Cf. **owner**, 3.—2. Hence, a Personal Assistant to an Air Marshal or an Air Chief Marshal: since ca. 1940. Partridge, 1945.

ownsome, on (one's). By oneself: lower-middle-class coll.: since ca. 1920. (Harrison, 1939.) Ex *on one's own* = lonesome. Cf.:-

owny-o, on (one's). Same as prec.: joc. By fanciful Italianisation; cf., e.g. the name *Antonio*. Joyce, 1922, spells it *ownio*.

Ox and Cow, the. The Oxford and County Secretarial College: upper-middle-class nickname: later 1970s. York, 1980.

Ox-Wag(g)on. An *Oxford* aircraft: airmen's, esp. in S. Africa, where this craft was extensively used in training: WW2.

Oxbridge. 'Coined by Thackeray in *Pendennis* [1848–50] and revived by Virginia Woolf in 1928, but not popularised until the 1950s' (Foster, 1968). It was not wholly forgotten in the interval, however, for it occurs in the caption of a Gerald du Maurier boat-race cartoon in *Punch*, 1883 (P.B.). Since ca. 1955 it has been journalistic coll. for Oxford and Cambridge as = the older English universities, and as adj., of that which is characteristic of them both.

oxford, Oxford. A crown piece: low: ca. 1885–1914. Hence *half-oxford*, a half-crown piece: ob. It is an abbr. of **Oxford scholar**, q.v. P.B.: as a crown, five shillings, and even,

among the older generation, 25 pence, it survived into the 1970s. Jones, 1971.

Oxford bleat. From ca. 1925 (coll.), as in Brown, 1934, where he speaks of an exaggerated form of the Oxford or Public School accent: 'Surely it is permissible to suggest what [outsiders] rudely call the Oxford Bleat by writing down the direction given me the other day as "past a whaite house, between the water-tah and the pah station" '.

Oxford scholar. Five shillings (piece or sum): r.s., on *dollar*: since later C.19. In C.20 nearly always abbr. *Oxford*, as in *half an Oxford*, half-a-crown. See **Oxford.**—2. Shirt collar: r.s., not very gen.: earlier C.20. Franklyn.

oxo. Nothing: c.: late C.19–20. Ex '*0 × 0* (nought multiplied by nought) = *0*', an old schoolboys' joke, but prob. influenced by the popularity of *Oxo*, the beef-extract. *Gilt Kid*, 1936.—2. See **Jewish Oxo.**

Oxo cube. The London Underground (Railway): r.s., on *tube*. See prec.

oxometer. An apocryphal instrument for the measurement of '*bull*shit': RN lowerdeck: 1939+. Granville.

oy! A call for attention, as in 'Oy! Come (h)ere, you!', 'Oy! Mind your backs!', or of remonstrance, 'Oy! You can't do that there 'ere!'; in fact a most useful, all-purpose, noise of protest: mostly low: C.20, prob. earlier. A slovening of the (?)much older *hoy!*, perhaps influenced by the East End Jewry's Yiddish. Rees, 1980, notes that the famous 'Crazy Gang' comedian Bud Flanagan used it to round out his jokes or routines with his partner Chesney Allen. (P.B.)

oyster. A gob of phlegm: low coll.: late C.18–20. Grose, 1st ed. Cf. C.20 elab. **dockyard oyster.**

oyster part. A part in which one speaks but a sentence: theatrical coll.:—1923 (Manchon).

Oz, n. and adj. A mere phonetic var. of the abbr. *Aus* = Australian. The n. is used esp. to mean 'the Australian language': later C.20.

Ozzy. Phonetic var. of **Aussie**, as in the sense 'an Australian'. I first noticed it, in England, in *The Times*, 24 Mar. 1977—a review of the late Grahame Johnston's *The Australian Pocket Oxford Dictionary*.

ozzletwizzle. See **uppard twizzle.**

P

p. or **P.** A ponce: mostly Londoners'. Kersh, 1938.—2. Standard abbr. for a penny, or pence, in decimal coinage; but see **pee,** n.

p.d. or **P.D.** Esp. in *caught P.D.*, 'caught with one's pants down', i.e. at a disadvantage: since ca. 1935.

P.G. or **p.g.** A paying guest: joc. coll.: from ca. 1910.

p.h. See **purple heart.**

p.j.s or **P.J.s.** Physical exercises: coll.: from ca. 1925. (Sayers, 1933.) I.e. 'physical jerks'.

P.O. or **p.o.** is the shorter and probably the original form of **p.o.q.** Mackenzie, 1913-14, 'You can give me dinner and then I'll P.O.'—2. A coal wagon: railwaymen's: since ca. 1920. (*Railway*, 2nd.)

p.o.e.t.s. See **poets.**

P.O. Prune. See **Prune, P/O.**

p.o.q.! or **P.O.Q.!** Push (or *p*iss) off *q*uick(ly): Services' coll.: WW1+. (F. & G.) Modelled on older *p.d.q.*, pretty damn(ed) quick.

p. (or **P.**) **off!** Euph. for 'piss off!'—i.e. 'Oh, go away!': since ca. 1960. Petch, 1967. Cf. prec., and **P.O.**

p.p. Piss-proud, i.e. having, esp. on waking up, an erection because of a distended bladder: since ca. 1920. (F. Leech, 1972.)

p.s. Penal *s*ervitude: c. or low s.:—1923 (Manchon).

p.S.a. A recreational afternoon organised by a Bible society: ironic coll. (—1923) by abbr. Ex *pleasant Sunday afternoon.* Manchon.

P.T. Physical Training: orig. Services' coll., from ca. 1910 (F. & G.); by ca. 1945, if not much earlier, gen. in schools, colleges, etc., and > j.—2. A desirable female: (low) urban, esp. London. Ex **prick-teaser**, q.v.

p.v. A professional virgin or 'prick-teaser', q.v.; a 'wren' after an officer for a husband: RN: since late 1940s. (Peppitt.)

p.y.o. Pick-your-own, applied to soft fruit, and vegetables: initialised first in the summer of 1982. Influenced by **d.i.y.**, q.v. *New Society*, 19 Aug. 1982, as PYO.

P.Z.s. Tactical exercises: RN: from ca. 1920. Bowen, 'From the two code flags hoisted as an order'.

pack, n. In *go to the pack*, to go to pieces (fig.); lose a leading position; 'to deteriorate, to fall into disrepute' (Wilkes): Aus. and NZ s. > coll.: since early C.20. In NZ, it has a secondary sense: to fail persistently (Crump, 1960). Perhaps ex a trained or a domestic animal going wild, or ex a dog falling back into the pack. Perhaps cf.:—2. In *send to the pack*, 'to relegate to obscurity' (Dennis, 1916): Aus.

pack, v. To be ruined or spoilt; to become useless: motor-racers': from ca. 1920. Chamberlain, 'Back-axles will pack before half distance anyway.' Ex **pack up**, 2, q.v.—2. To 'pack up', to desist, give up: cyclists': since ca. 1945. 'Where did you come?'—'Oh, I packed after fifty miles.' By 1960, fairly gen. Diment, 1967.—3. To beat: to be superior to, or more enjoyable than: Aus.: since ca. 1920. Lindsay, 1963, ' "Fun o' the world, goin' with girls," said Peter, "By jings, you oughter try it on . . . By jings, it packs football easy!" ' And ' "Oh, I'm pretty good," he said. "It takes a bit to pack me once I get goin'." '

pack a punch. To be powerful, as a motorcycle or car; also of ballistic weapons; it may even refer to a sermon: coll.: later C.20. Ex boxing, of a strong punch. (P.B.)

pack 'em. See **packing 'em.**

pack (one's) **hand.** See **pack up,** 1.

pack heat. To carry personal firearms: c.: later C.20, adopted ex US. Moody, 1985.

pack in. Synon. with **pack up,** v., 2. (McDouall, 1945.) Cf.:-

pack it in; pack it up. To stop talking; to cease fooling or some foolish practice: Services' (from Cockneys?): since ca. 1925. (H. & P.) Ex *pack the game in* and *pack up.*—2. Since the late 1940s, commoner than *pack it up*, to give up one's job: mostly manual workers', as in 'I'm packing it in; too much like hard work!' Cf. synon. **jack (it) in.**

pack the game in. To desist; esp. abandon a way of life: lower classes'. (*Cheapjack*, 1934.) Cf. **pack up.**

pack-up, n. Corresponds to next, 2: RAF: since ca. 1937. (McDouall, 1945.)

pack up, v. To retire; stop working or trying; to die: Services' coll., WW1 (F. & G.) >, by 1920, gen. Prob. ex *pack (up)* one's *kit(-bag)*. Var. *pack* (one's) *hand (in)*, prob. ex cards. Opp. *carry on.*—2. Hence, (of an aircraft) to cease to function: RAF: since ca. 1937. (Partridge, 1945.) P.B.: very soon applied, widely, to any machine, mechanical or electrical, that has failed; likewise, to animals: in later C.20 verging on familiar S.E., as is sense 1.

packer. A platelayer: railwaymen's joc. *Railway*, 2nd.

packet. A (large) sum of money lost or won in betting or speculating: from mid-1920s. *OED* Sup.—2. Any kind of ship or boat: nautical coll., gen. as an endearment. (Bowen.) See **three-op packet.**—3. A lady: nautical. Ibid.—4. In *cop*, or *stop*, *a packet*, to be wounded, esp. if fatally: Services' (mostly Army): since ca. 1915. Occ. *cop it.* Ex to catch; *packet* may be the missile. B. & P.—5. Hence *cop* (from ca. 1915) or *catch* (from ca. 1925) *a packet*, to have bad luck, meet with trouble: Services': WW1+. (F. & G.) *Catch a packet*, to be severely reprimanded: mostly Army. P-G-R.—6. In *take a packet*, to reach a point at which effort is painful: racing cyclists': since ca. 1946. Cf. sense 5.—7. (Cf. senses 4 and 5.) In *cop a packet* (by mid-C.20 usu. *get (have got) a* *packet*), to become infected with V.D.: coll.—8. For *buy a packet*, see **buy it**, 20.

packet from Paris. A baby: Aus. and NZ. Var. *parcel from* . . .

packet of salts. Occ. var. in the phrase (*go*) *through like a dose of salts*, for something happening very swiftly: earlier C.20.

packet of three. A coll., euph. ref. to a packet of condoms; a usage surfacing with the AIDS scare, 1980s. Tinniswood, 1985; Greenberg, 1986, 'The very idea of the old-fashioned "packet of three" and its furtive associations.' Long sold thus in, e.g. barbers' shops, 'Anything for the weekend, Sir?'

packie. 'The "packie" (derisive trade slang for a package tourist)' (Marling, 1984).

packing (th)em. Scared: Aus. low, orig. Services' s.: since ca. 1940. I.e. holding back nervous diarrhœa, packing *the shits*. Var. *packing death*. Cf. **sterky**. B., 1959; Wilkes.

pad, n. 'A lot, "packet" ' (Culotta): Aus.: since late 1940s.—2. Abbr. **married pad**, q.v., a married soldier or airman: since mid-C.20. From late C.19 *pads* (gen. pl.) = women, hence *married pads*, wives: Army.—3. A bed: ca. 1570-1890: low s. verging on c. Ex the S.E. sense, a bundle of straw, skins, etc., on which to lie. This sense crossed to N. America to be in use among drug addicts (W. & F.) whence it entered the vocabulary of jazz-lovers and musicians mid-C.20, to be adopted, in mid-1950s, in Can. The *Daily Colonist* (Victoria, BC), 16 Apr. 1959, defines *pad* 'Living quarters, often a bare room with a mattress on or near the floor'—cf. esp. W. & F. And in this sense it was soon taken up with, then some joc. use among the more 'respectable'. Powis, 1977, 'Hippy slang for room or bed, now becoming a commonly used term in non-hippy company'.

pad, v. To put handkerchiefs, etc., in one's trousers-seat before being caned: Public Schools' coll.

pad the hoof. To go on foot: from ca. 1790 (Grose, 3rd ed.).—2. Hence, to make off quickly: racing c.

pad the wall. To sit on a comfortable leather seat against a wall, esp. in a restaurant or a bar: coll.: 1936 (*Gilt Kid*).

Padder. Paddington terminus (Great Western Railway): Oxford undergraduates':—1899 (Ware). The 'OXFORD -ER'. Later, also *Padders* (*New Statesman*, 5 Feb. 1965). Cf. **Paddo.**

padding-can contractor. A jerry-builder: Gloucestershire. Waters, 1973.

paddler. A policeman: Aus. c.: since ca. 1945. (B., 1953.) Prob. of sadistic orig.; cf. synon. **walloper**, 3.

Paddo. Paddington, the Sydney suburb: Sydneyites': since ca. 1920. (B., 1953.) Cf. **Padder.**

paddock. L.A. noted TV commentator's use of *keep it on the paddock*, for 'keep the [rugby] football in play': 1969. Var. of *keep it on the island*.

Paddy or **paddy.** In Aus., with var. *Pat*, it = a Chinese. B., 1942, has both; *Pat* occurs also in Baker, 1938.—2. 'A colliery train from mine to railhead' (*Railway*): railwaymen's.—3. A padlock: c., mostly burglars': since ca. 1930. Norman, 1959.—4. 'The padded cell. Used for violent cases. Often men who "smash up", and who do not calm down immediately after, are given a spell in the paddy until they have cooled off' (Tempest, 1950).

paddy-boat (properly *padi-boat*). A vessel of the Henderson line from the Clyde to Burma: nautical: earlier C.20. (Bowen.) Suggested by S.E. *paddy-boat*, a ship for the carrying of rice: Burma exports much rice.

Paddy Kelly. A policeman: Liverpool dockers': late C.19-20; by 1960, slightly ob.

Paddy wag(g)on. A van for the conveyance of prisoners: Aus., adopted, ca. 1955, ex US. (B.P.) Ex the prevalence of Irishmen in the police forces of the USA? P.B.: or ex the number of Irishmen 'wheeled in'; or from *padded wagon*, for the conveyance of the insane? Cf. **paddy**, 4.

Paddy's Milestone. 'Ailsa Craig, just half-way between Greenock and Belfast on the packet route': nautical: late C.19-20. Bowen.

Paddy's taxi. A police 'Panda' (patrol)car: since latish 1960s. 'Used in "Public Eye", BBC1, 13 Aug. 1969' (Petch). Cf. **Paddy wagon.**

Paddy's watch. Employed allusively, Irish ratings being (according to themselves) never off watch: RN: since ca. 1920.

padhouse. One's bedroom or lodging: beatniks': since ca. 1958. (Anderson.) An extension of **pad**, n., 3, later nuances.

padlock. Penis: r.s., on **cock**. Haden-Guest, 1972.

pads. As (*the*) *pads*, a padded cell, or the padded cells, in a lunatic asylum: esp. the attendants': since ca. 1925. The use had spread to prisons by later C.20: 'Padded cells to prevent self-injury' (Home Office). Cf. **paddy**, 4.—2. Feet: homosexuals': current ca. 1970. Ex either S.E. sense of 'feet or footprints of foxes, wolves, etc.', or a shortening of C.19 c. *paddles*.

Pag. The opera *Pagliacci*: see **Cav and Pag.**

page. 'Where two compositors are working side by side they are known as side pages; where three are working, the one in the middle refers to his companions as "my right-hand side page" and "my left-hand side page"; if men are working back to back they are known as back pages; if frames or machines are facing each other, the men are front pages' (Rowles, 1948).

page three (or **3**) **girl.** Ref. to the photograph featured daily on page 3 of the *Sun* tabloid newspaper: each day brings a different, very attractive, scantily-clad or nude girl. The series has become well enough known in the late 1970s for allusions, e.g.: 'if we saw such associations in an image together with a page 3 girl [in an advertisement, etc.] we would suspect a satirical intention' (book review in *Brit. Jnl of Photography*, 10 Aug. 1979). (P.B.)

pagger. To break or smash; to wreck: market-traders'. 'That's paggered it!' (*M.T.*) Influenced by *bugger*, to ruin; neither Romany nor dial.

Paggers. St Peter's Hall: Oxford undergraduates': since ca. 1935. (Marples, 2.) After *Jaggers*, late C.19 University s., applied to Jesus College, Oxford.

pain. ' "The men are patronising. At first it's a bit of a pain, but you get used to it," says Karen' (*New Society*, 24 Apr. 1980): strictly speaking, S.E. = 'mental distress', but given a coll. flavour because derived ex sense 2: since ca. 1975. (P.B.)—2. In *pain in the arm—arse—back—balls—bum—neck—penis* (etc., etc.); esp. *you—he—they* (etc.) *gives(s) me a pain* . . ., I utterly disapprove of your (etc.) behaviour; I thoroughly disagree with your point of view; or, most frequently, you annoy, bore, disgust (etc.) me: (mostly low, depending on part of body) coll. *You give me a pain!* is a common abbr. for any of them; cf. synon. *you give me the balls ache!* Also used predicatively as, 'Yes, I remember her—a real pain in the bum, that one'; cf. **pain in the neck**. (E.P.; P.B.)—3. Trouble; nuisance: as in, 'I need 40p change—is that a pain?' (an art student, 1984). Ex 1.

pain in the neck. A tedious or boring or irritating person: coll.: since ca. 1910. Ex *give* (one) *a pain in the neck*, to bore intensely, to irritate. This is prob. the commonest, or, at least, most widely acceptable version of the choice at **pain**, 2, q.v. A low parody, current in the 1920s, was *a pain in the nick*, i.e. the cleft at the fold of the buttock. In later C.20 often abbr. *pain*, as in **pain**, 1.

pain in the puku. A stomach-ache: NZ coll.: late C.19-20. (B., 1941.) *Puku*: a Maori word.

paint a picture, 'vaguely to describe a situation or to outline a plan': Services': 1939–41. Rather j. than coll.: certainly not s. (H. & P.) P.B.: this piece of j. has lasted well, and has given rise to such phrases as 'I'll just give you the broad-brush picture'; cf. *put* (someone) *in the picture,* which may have been its origin, although, e.g., 'He painted a rosy picture of their future together' verges on informal S.E.

paint a job. To scorch one's work: tailors'. (*Tailor and Cutter*, 29 Nov. 1928.) Cf. **painter.**

painted edge. A coat-edge in, or of, coloured cloth: tailors'. *Tailor and Cutter*, 29 Nov. 1928.

painted lady. 'Imperfectly cured (kippered) herring which has been dyed with anatta to give the appearance of the true kipper' (Granville): nautical.

Painted People, the. 'A fugitive term for a transitory group or sub-group of opt-outs from accepted norms of behaviour: orig. US, where members of this cult . . . did actually paint their bodies: noted in the *Observer*, 13 June 1976, in ref. to a pop festival held on Exmoor during that torrid summer' (R.S., 1976).

painter. A workman that scorches his job: tailors'.

pair of Arthurs, esp. **a tidy pair** . . . Female breasts: young men's raffish: early 1980s. (James Williamson, 1984.) Poss. abbr. r.s., but on what/whom?

pair o(f) kicks. Boots; shoes: tramps' c.:—1935.

pair of kippers. A public reprimand: RN: since ca. 1939. Ex such a signal from flagship to a ship slow to respond to signals. (Peppitt.)

pair o(f) subs. A pair of shoes, boots: Glasgow lower classes':—1934. ?Ex *submarines*: cf. **boats** in this sense. Still current later C.20 (Munro, 1985, who notes *put the sub on* for synon. *put the boot in*, to kick).

pair of white gloves, a. 'Safe return of all aircraft from a bombing operation': RAF: 1939+. Jackson, 'From the ancient legal custom whereby a judge is presented with a pair of white gloves if his calendar is free from crime.'

pajamas. See **cat's pyjamas.**

Paki (illiterately **Pakki**, pron. *packy*). A Pakistani immigrant; loosely, any native of the Indian sub-continent: low, usu. derogatory or patronising: later C.20. Cf. quot'n at **scrote.**

Paki (or **Pakki**)-**bashing.** An organised hunting out and assaulting of Pakistanis—or Indian, no distinction is drawn—immigrants, mostly by gangs of white youths moved less by political prejudice or xenophobia than by a so-called need for thrills: orig. among London, esp. if delinquent, teenagers, e.g. 'skinheads', q.v.: since ca. 1965. Hence the agent, as in 'Pakistanis living in terror of the "paki-basher" mobs of skinheads' (London *Evening Standard*, 19 Apr. 1970).

Paki (black). Cannabis (resin): drugs c. Stockley, 1986.

Paki pox. Smallpox: since ca. 1960. 'As it is often the Pakistanis who bring it here' (Petch, 1969).

Pakki. See **Paki.**

pal-looral. Drunk: Glasgow:—1934. Cf. **palatic.**

Pal Police, the. The Palestine Police: since ca. 1946. Jeffries, 1958 (period concerned: 1948). The adj. is *Pal Police*, as 'a Pal Police type' (not in Jeffries). P.B.: the Force ceased to exist with the termination of the British mandate in Palestine, on 15 May 1948; the State of Israel came into being on the next day.

palat, for **Palatinate purple,** is a Durham 'blue'. Marples, 2.

palatic. Drunk: 1885 (*The Stage*): theatrical; still current a century later, esp. in NE England (Gofton, 1983). I.e. synon. *paralytic,* corrupted.

Palestine ache. Severe diarrhœa: see **wog gut.**

Pall Mall. Girl: r.s.: later C.19–early 20. 'Cockney dialect makes Paow Maow—gaow' (Franklyn).

palled-in. 'Living with a woman' (Samuel, 1981): c. Ex earlier *pal in with,* to become friendly with.

Palm Beach. A cove at Tobruk: Army in N. Africa: 1940-3. Much bathing there in quite unluxurious circumstances. The place referred to is not American but Australian; it was Aus. soldiers who so named it from a resort in NSW.

palsy-walsy. Jovially friendly: since ca. 1934. (Brand, 1949.) Reduplication of *palsy,* itself ex pally + (*to be*) *pals.* P.B.: slightly ob. by 1983; when used, gen. ironic or sarcastic, as 'Oh yes, they're all very palsy-walsy *now*, but you just wait . . . ' Cf. *lovey-dovey.*

pan. See **down the pan.**

pan, v. V.t. (gen. as p.ppl passive), to beg: tramps' c. Cowan, 1937.—2. To strike (someone) in the face: low:—1943 (H. & P.). Cf. *New Society,* 22 Aug. 1963, ' "To pan" is to punch just once, but "to ted up" or "to ted in" is to beat systematically, as in teddy boy' (or, rather, in its shortened form *Ted* or *ted*): N. Country grammar school s.—3. To criticise adversely; to disparage: Aus., adopted, ca. 1945, ex US (B.P.); soon common, mostly journalistic, in Brit. also (P.B.).

pan-flasher. A transitory meteor in the world of sport, esp. lawn tennis: sporting coll.: from 1935. Ex S.E. *flash in the pan.*

pan-handler. See **panhandler.**

Panda. 'A police patrol-car, so called from its broad white stripe resembling the markings of the giant panda. 1966. In full *panda car*' (*SOD*): coll.

panel, be or **go on the.** To 'place oneself under the care of a panel doctor': coll.: from 1927 until the advent of the National Health Service, post-WW2. 'On the panel means absent from work, having been certified unfit by a doctor. This phrase is a survivor [in Glasgow] from the former "panel" of non-paying patients treated by certain [general practitioners]' (Munro, 1985).

pangy bar. Five pounds sterling: c.: from ca. 1919. (*Gilt Kid*, 1936.) A bar is £1; *pangy* may derive ex Fr. *cinq*, but it is more prob. a corruption of Romany *pansh*, five.

Panhandle, the. The long peninsula extending to the north-east of Cyprus, ending with Cape St Andreas: British Forces stationed on the island: since (?)ca. 1950. Ex shape; cf. US geographical usage. (P.B.)

panhandler (or hyphenated). A hospital orderly: Services' coll. A pun on the US coll., a prospector panning for gold (which later > s., a beggar).

panic, n. Preparations at full speed on a ship preparing for sea: RN: WW1. F. & G.—2. Hence, in *bags of panic*, much (mostly unnecessary) rushing around in any emergency: Services': WW2 and since. (P.B.)—3. 'Shortage of drugs' (Stockley, 1986). US since –1937 (Spears).

panic, v. 'To pick up cigarette butts and small débris in an army camp' (B, 1943). Aus. Army: WW2. P.B.: ?because of impending inspection by senior officer; cf. prec.

panic bowler. A steel helmet: RAF: 1939+. Jackson, 'The R.A.F. never wear it unless there's a panic on.' Cf. **panic hat.**

panic button. Any switch or button to be operated for assistance in emergency, e.g., to restore oxygen, summon help, etc.: coll., verging on j.: later C.20. Hence, *press the panic button,* to panic; hastily demand immediate action: since late 1960s. *DCCU.*

panic hat. A steel helmet: Aus. Army: WW2. (B., 1943.) Cf. **panic bowler.**

panic merchant. A person given to panicking: Aus.: since early 1940s. *Sydney Morning Herald,* 5 Aug. 1963.

panic-party. 'The men whose job it was to leave a Decoy Ship . . . in disorder when a German submarine opened fire': RN coll. (1916) >, by 1918, j. Bowen.—2. The RN's synonym of *flap on* (see **flap,** n., 2): since ca. 1925. H. & P.—3. Any rash move: Aus. Army: WW2. B., 1943.

panicker. 'A man showing needless anxiety beforehand' (F. & G.): Army coll.: later WW1, passing afterwards into gen. usage.

pansy, n. A very effeminate youth; a homosexual: from ca. 1925. Cf. **Nancy (boy).** Also *pansy-boy:* from ca. 1930; *New Statesman and Nation,* 15 Sep. 1934, concerning the Fascist meeting in Hyde Park on 9 Sep., notes that there were, from the crowd, 'shouts about "pansy-boys" '.

pansy, adj. Ex prec.: from late 1920s. Devanney, 1929, 'a pansy voice'—occurring in NZ.

Pansy Patrol, the. Those officers who are sent by Scotland Yard to get evidence at a night club before the police raid it: mostly policemen's: from ca. 1930. They go in full evening dress and are usually chosen from the Public School members of the Force.

pansy resting on its laurels, a. Joc. (and punning—see **pansy**) description of the Intelligence Corps' badge, a rose (symbolising secrecy) surrounded by conventional laurel leaves: the Corps', its friends'—and enemies': the Corps was reformed in 1940, after a short life in WW1, and the phrase arose prob. soon after that. (P.B., Int. Corps, 1953-74.)

pansy up, v.i. and v. reflexive. (Of a man) to adorn oneself, to smarten oneself up sartorially, in an effeminate manner: since ca. 1932. Cf. synon **tart up.**

pant. See **panto.**

pantaloons. Knee-breeches, formerly worn as part of RAF uniform: since ca. 1920; by 1940 merely historical. (L.A.)

pantechnicon. Abbr. *pantechnicon van* (furniture-removing): coll., 1891 (*OED*); by 1920, at latest > S.E.—2. Hence, a Whitley bomber aircraft: RAF: 1939-41. 'At one period it was our largest, with the biggest capacity' (Jackson).—3. A large glider: RAF: 1942+, but ob. by the end of 1945.

panther-sweat. Surgical spirit and Italian vermouth mixed to form a potent drink: beatniks': since ca. 1959. (Anderson.) Adopted and adapted from American s. *panther-sweat*, raw inferior whiskey.

panther's piss. Strong liquor, esp. spirits: Aus. (B., 1942.) Cf. prec., **tiger piss** and *tiger's milk*. The term is prob. an adaptation of the US *panther piss*.

panties. Drawers (women's, children's): 1905: coll. >, by 1933, S.E. Cf. **pants, scanties** and **undies.**

panto. A coll. abbr. of *pantomime*. Ware. Occ. (—1923: Manchon), *pant*.

pantomime poisoning. Ptomaine poisoning: ca. 1925-60. Would-be joc. (Parsons, 1973.)

pants. Only in address to a pantryman: ship's stewards'. Marlowe, 1937.—2. In *got the pants*, panting, breathless: low:—1909 (Ware).—3. In *bore* (or *talk*, *bind*, etc.) *the pants off* (someone), to talk to that person on and on, garrulously and uninterestingly: later C.20. (Cole, 1980.) Cf. the earlier *scare the pants off*, to frighten badly. (P.B.)—4. A scrounger: prisons': later C.20. Green, 1984: 'He's always on the bum.'

pantsman. A notorious womaniser: Aus.: since ca. 1960. (B.P., 1977.)

panzer beetle. A large, hard-topped black beetle found in North Africa: Army: 1941-3. Ex *panzer*, Ger. 'armoured'.

Panzer Pete. A formidable liquor made by troops in New Guinea: Aus. Army: 1942-5. (B., 1943.) Cf. **panther's piss.**

pape. Newspaper, mostly in newboys' cries: late C.19-20. B., 1942.—2. 'A fairly rude name for a Roman Catholic, obviously a contraction of papist' (Munro, 1985): Glasgow.

paper. 'Cigarette paper. "Give me a paper" = give me a cigarette paper. A packet of these costs one "roll-up" [q.v.]' (Tempest, 1950): prison c.: mid-C.20.—2. Marked cards: card-sharps': Can., prob. ex US: early C.20. Drage, 1954.—3. A prescription: drugs c. (Stockley, 1986.) US since −1968 (Spears).

paper-chewing. (Official) correspondence: Anglo-Indian. Orwell, 1935.

paper doll. A woman of easy virtue: Aus. r.s., on *moll*: later C.20. McNeil.

paper end, the. 'The report, correspondence and documentary aspect of some matter as distinct from the matter itself' (Jackson): RAF coll.: since ca. 1925.

paper-hanger. A passer of worthless cheques: Aus. c.: adopted ca. 1925, from US. (Baker.) Hence, *paper-hanging*, the action; also Can.

paper mushrooms. LSD: drugs c. (Stockley, 1986.) Cf. **magic mushrooms.**

paper-tearer. A clerkly type, a 'pen-pusher' or 'admin-wallah': policemen's: later C.20. 'When [discipline] is imposed by senior officers of the kind to whom [constables] refer contemptuously as "paper-tearers", insult is added to injury. "I don't mind being stuck on, but to be stuck on by *that* paper-tearing *prat* I can't take" ' (Seabrook, 1987).

paper war. 'Army red tape' (B., 1943): Aus. Army: WW2.

para. Abbr. *paragraph*, esp. as part of a book, an article, etc.: book world. While *par*, since later C.19, is used mainly by printers and journalists, *para* is used mainly by authors; some publishers prefer *par*, some *para*.—2. A *para*plegic (a spinal-cord paralytic): Can. doctors' and nurses': since ca. 1946. (Leechman.)—3. A member of Paratroops: Services': since mid-WW2. Cf. next.—4. See **purple para.**

paraboy, usu. in pl. A member of a parachute regiment: Army: 1942-5. P-G-R.

parachute in. 'To bring in someone from outside the organisation to do a job or fill a post' (Leech, 1985): 'big business' in Can. and UK, adopted ex US.

paradise. Cocaine: drugs c. (Stockley, 1986.) US since −1971 (Spears).

paradise strokes, the. (Of a man) the culmination of a copulation: raffish. (P.B.)

paraffin. A smart appearance: lower-class Glasgow. (MacArthur.) In 1897–1900, 'the word "paraphernalia" was much used by the working classes [of Glasgow] to describe anyone who was very much "got up" or overdressed. It was pronounced "paraffinelly" . . . "There he was, dressed up wi' a' his paraffinelly" . . . My theory is that "paraffin" is simply a contraction of "paraffinelly" and is now used by a generation that knows nothing of its original meaning' (McMurdo, 1937, and doubtless correctly).—2. Hence(?), a suit of clothes: (low) Glasgow: since ca. 1920. Mackenzie, 1936.

paraffin budgie, often abbr. to **budgie.** A ship's helicopter: RN: since late 1960s. (Peppitt.) Cf. **petrol pigeons.**

Paraffin Pete. 'An Airfield Control Officer or N.C.O. . . . responsible . . . for ensuring that the flares are laid and lit at the right time and places; these forming the flare-path, guide . . . aircraft in darkness' (Jackson): RAF: since ca. 1938.

paralysed. Tipsy: s. verging on coll.: ca. 1890-1920. Ex the effect. Cf. next.—2. Joc. (or ignorantly) for analysed: earlier C.20. 'Paralysed by the public anarchist.'

paralytic. Dead drunk: from ca. 1910. Ex prec., 1. Cf. **palatic.** Still current in Glasgow (Munro, 1985).

Paras, the. The Parachute Regiment: since WW2: military > gen.

parcel. A sum (esp. if considerable) won or lost. Esp. *drop a parcel* (Wodehouse, 1923: *OED* Sup.). Cf. **packet,** 1.—2. A rolled blanket, with one's personal belongings inside: Aus. tramps' coll.: since ca. 1910. B., 1943.—3. In *blue the parcel*, to spend all one's money; lose everything on a bet: sporting: since ca. 1910. (Wallace, 1924.) Cf. sense 1.—4. 'A quantity of stolen goods being delivered to a receiver' (*Now!*, 10 Apr. 1981): c.: later C.20. A specialisation of S.E. (P.B.)—5. In *take a parcel*, synon. with **packet,** 6: club cyclists'. *Fellowship*, 1984.

parcel from Paris. See **packet from Paris.**

parcel post. 'Epithet applied to the newly arrived and inexperienced, esp. N.T.' (Wilkes): Aus. rural. *Parcel post men* or *boys* arrive on station from the cities like a parcel in the mail.

park, n. In *down the park*, (of a horse that is) losing: Glasgow sporting:—1934.

park, v. To place, gen. with implication of safety: coll.; adopted, ex US, ca. 1915. *The Times*, 1 Feb. 1918, 'A policeman "parked" [the] perambulators and mounted guard . . . while the mothers made their purchases' (W.). Ex military usage, to put in an artillery-, a car-park, via *park a gun, lorry, car*.—2. V. reflexive (of persons): to place oneself; hence, to sit: coll.: from ca. 1920. Both senses are now on the border-line of S.E.—3. To do, to effect; e.g. *park a bath, a walk*, take, go for . . . ; *park an oil*, do something (over-) smart: Oundle: since early 1920s. Marples.—4. 'To give: "oo'll park me a fag, then?": Brit. gay slang' (Rodgers, 1972). Perhaps orig. ex parlyaree *partire* > *parker*, > C.19 s., to hand out (money).—5. See **parking.**

park a custard. To vomit: RN, mostly wardroom: since ca. 1930. (Parsons.) Adopted by Sloane Rangers, q.v., early 1980s. *Sunday Express* supp., 11 Oct. 1982.

park your arse; carcass; fanny; frame; stern! (Usu. imperative) Be seated!; occ., e.g. 'Where shall I park my . . . ?', where shall I sit?: joc. coll. extensions of **park,** v., 1 and 2: resp. since ca. 1920; ca. 1955; ca. 1939, adopted ex US; ca. 1930, NZ—and elsewhere (Gray, 1969); ca. 1925, orig. nautical.

parkee, -ie, -y. A park-keeper: mostly children's: since ca. 1920. (Petch, 1969.)

Parker trouble, have. To have one's conversation listened to by an outsider: office- and shop-girls': since ca. 1945. (Gilderdale.) Ex *Nosey Parker.* The use of *trouble* in coll. phrases— e.g. *to have woman trouble*—was orig. American.

parking. The use of a parked motor vehicle for love-making: Aus., adopted ex US, since ca. 1945. (B.P.)

parking lot. The vagina: teenagers' (and among their older equivalents): since the latish 1960s; app. predominantly feminine. (Scaduto, 1974.) Ex US, a pun.

parlamaree. A 'gee' or that companion who starts a sale, or the donations, going: earlier C.20. Perhaps, as Franklyn proposes, ex a version of PARLYAREE (see Appx.); see also **gee.**

parlary. Slang: prostitutes': since ca. 1930.—2. See PARLYAREE, in Appx.

parlatic. Newcastle-upon-Tyne pron. of **palatic,** q.v.

parlour pinks. Socialists not violent (*red*) but very moderate: political: adopted, ca. 1935, from US. Since ca. 1960, usu. as var. *parlour pinkos* (L.A.).

Parlyaree. See notes at this heading in the Appx.

parnee, parn(e)y, n. Water: orig. (—1862) among strolling actors (Mayhew): by 1890, fairly gen. low s. English usage derives ex Romany *pani, paani, pauni* (Smart & Crofton), itself ultimately the Hindustani *pani.*—2. Hence, tears (in the eyes): Parlyaree.—3. Hence, also, urine, urination, as in 'I'm going for a parney' (*M.T.*): market-traders'.

parnee, v.i. To rain: showmen's and marketmen's. Ex prec.

parrot. See **pissed; sick as . . .**

parrots and monkeys. Goods and chattels; personal possessions: Army: since ca. 1930. Cf. the (1941+) c.p. addressed to recruits, *All right! Pick up your parrots and monkeys, and get mobile*; occ. *parrots and monkeys in the left hand* or *on the left shoulder . . .* Ex the returning seaman's pets or souvenirs.

parrot('s)-cage. See **mouth like the bottom . . .**

parsley. Nonsense: Cockneys': early C.20. (Pugh.) Cf. older *gammon and spinach.*

parson's collar. Froth on a glass of beer: public-houses': since mid-1940s. (Petch, 1966.)

parson's wife. Gin: orig. and properly Vickers Gin: Aus.: since ca. 1925. (B., 1953.) *Vickers: vicar's; gin:* an Aboriginal woman.

parson's yeoman, the. 'The volunteer organist at Divine Service' (Granville): RN.

partic. Particular; esp. as adj. (fastidious): trivial coll. Bell, 1935.

particulars. Panties, esp. take down one's own or have a man remove them: joc. raffish: since ca. 1920. A pun on *take down* (someone's) *particulars,* name, address, etc. Thomas, 1976.

party. A love affair: Society: ca. 1928–38. Waugh, 1938.—2. An aerial combat; a bombing raid: RAF: since early 1940. H. & P., 1943; Granville, 1945, of a commando raid or a naval operation, for it was also an RN and an Army term; Brickhill, 1946, ' ' "Oh, crumbs! Night fighter," he muttered. "What a b— party!" ' By nonchalant meiosis.—3. A very busy day: Services'; esp. RAF ground staff: since ca. 1940. (H. & P.) Ironic.—4. A girl friend: RN: since ca. 1910. Granville.

party in the attic. An elab. of **party,** 2: RAF: 1940+. Partridge, 1945, '*Attic* because the fight takes place aloft.'

party line, the. The 'official version', to be adhered to whether truthful or not; not *necessarily* a 'cover-up story', but often with that implication: since ca. 1920: orig. political, > gen. coll. Perhaps orig. ex the methods and ethics of extremist political parties, but now, sadly, right across the spectrum. Cf. **toe the line,** 2.

party piece. 'Women play a distinctly secondary role. They are accepted as wives, girlfriends, or "party pieces" ' (article on Hell's Angels [q.v.], Davenport, 1982).

party pin. A working party in an aircraft carrier: RN: 1939+. P-G-R.

party-pooper. 'One who wrecks a convivial party by "pooping" it' (Leechman): Can.: since ca. 1940, poss. earlier. 'Water over the poop? Or "pooping", defecating, are it?' P.B.: adopted ex US; a *poop* is an insignificant or stupid person (W. & F.), but Leechman's second suggestion is prob. correct.

pas devant l'enfant! Domestic 'Franglais' for 'not (to be mentioned) in front of the child': since mid-C.20. (Raab, 1977.)

pash, n. An infatuation; among schoolchildren, one for a teacher; at a few English Public Schools, a homosexual fondness for another boy. (Sayers, 1927.) Raab: also at girls' schools; younger on older girls or girls on teachers, in 1930s. Abbr. *passion.* Cf. **crush,** 4.—2. A letter: RN: since ca. 1930. H. & P., '*Number one pash* being a letter to one's best girl'. Ex sense 1.

pash, adj. Passionate; e.g. *pash pants,* non-regulation trousers affected by some officers: Can. soldiers': 1914+.

pash on; sex on. To indulge in sex, from petting to intercourse: Aus. teenagers': since ca. 1950. *Sydney Morning Herald,* 11 Sep. 1963.

pash show. A film that graphically shows love-making: Aus. teenagers': since the late 1940s.—2. Hence, ardent love-making: Aus. teenagers': since ca. 1950. (B.P.)

pash wag(g)on. A liberty bus: mostly RAF: 1940–5. (P-G-R.) Cf. **passion-waggon.**

pass, n. A transfer of drugs or drugs money: c. (Stockley, 1986.) US since—1969 (Spears).

pass, v. To fail to understand; have no concern in: coll. Ex euchre, though its post-1910 usage is mainly owing to the bridge formula. P.B.: in later C.20, ex the use of 'pass!' (= I cannot answer) in TV quiz-shows and general knowledge contests.

pass along. To send (stolen articles, *the stuff*) to a 'fence'; to conceal them: c.:—1923 (Manchon).

pass in a crowd, may – might – could – would – will. Is just average: coll. An elab. is *pass in a crowd with a push.* Sayers, 1934.

pass out. To lose consciousness through liquor: military (1916) >, by 1919, gen.—2. Hence, or ex earlier coll. sense, to die, to faint: from ca. 1920. As L.A. points out, 1974, this can be from any cause, a blow, a fall, the heat, hunger, etc.—3. Hence, weakened still further, merely to fall asleep: coll.: later C.20. (L.A., 1974.) An intensification is *pass spark out*; see **spark out.**

pass the buck. To 'tell the tale', q.v.: low: earlier C.20. Cf. *buck,* conversation.—2. To pass on something one cannot trouble oneself with: Civil Service: since ca. 1938. An Americanism. By 1950, fairly gen. The expression derives from the game of poker.—3. But, in Can., as Leechman wrote, 1959, 'again the general sense has changed. Now it means simply to evade responsibility, usually by passing the job on to someone else, but often by simply ignoring it. Used even in such senses as evading a difficult question in an argument.' P.B.: the sense of shifting responsibility on to someone else has been the predominant Brit. one since ca. 1960 at latest.

pass the can. To shift the blame, responsibility, etc., from one's own shoulders on to someone else's: Army: since ca. 1941. (P-G-R.) Cf. prec., 3, and see also **carry the can.** (P.B.)

pass the catheter. See **take the piss . . .**

passed-over; usu. in pl. A Lieutenant-Commander who has failed to become a Commander: RN coll. Granville.

P

P

passion-killers. Issue knickers, 'sensible', warm—and secure, worn by the Women's Services in WW2 and after: Services': since 1940. (Jackson; Peppitt.) See also **black-outs** and **twilights**.

passion(-)pit. Synon. with **Olympic pool**, q.v.: same usage, but 'prob. originally US' (R.C., 1976).

passion(-)wag(g)on. Transport for WAAF personnel: RAF: 1941+. (Hinde, 1945.)—2. A 'liberty truck'; unit recreational transport, arranged to take troops in to the near-by 'bright lights': Army: 1940s–50s. (P.B.)—3. A young man's car, esp. when used for courting or love-making with his girl-friend: young people's: post-WW2+. Cf. **love-truck**. (P.B.)

passionate leave. Compassionate leave: RAF: since ca. 1925. Contrast:–

passionate release. Compassionate release from WAAF because of pregnancy: RAF: since ca. 1940.

past it. To be, because of age or infirmity, no longer able or powerful enough, either to perform a specific task ('I used to be able to cycle 50 miles in a day, but I'm past it now, I'm afraid'), or gen., as in 'Poor old bugger! He's past it now' = he is no longer the man he was—and never will be again: coll. (P.B.)

past (one)self, get. To be fractious or (very) excited: coll.: from ca. 1910; ob. Cf. *get above* (one)*self*, to become over-excited, or conceited.

pasties. 'Nipple covers pasted over the nipples by showgirls' (B.P., 1974): Aus.: since ca. 1965. The sing. is either *pasty* or *pastie*. The term comes from US, where it is common in the world of theatre, variety, burlesque (W. & F., 1975).

pastry. Collective for young and pretty women: ca. 1885–1935. (B. & L.; Manchon.) Ex synon. *jam*, *jam-tart*, and *tart*. 'Hence the, perhaps later, "a tasty bit of pastry", for one of those girls in particular' (L.A., 1974).

Pat, pat. A Chinaman: Aus. and NZ c., Eng. (esp. London) low: earlier C.20. Prob. suggested by the relevant sense of *John*. See **Paddy**, 1.—2. In *on* (one's) *pat*, alone; single-handed: Aus. and NZ: since early C.20. Shortened from **Pat Malone**, q.v. Dennis, 1916.

Pat and Mick. A, or to, lick (lit. and fig.): Aus. r.s.

Pat Malone. Alone: Aus. and NZ r.s. Gen. *do a thing*, *go*, *on* (one's) *Pat Malone*. Soon reduced to *on* (one's) *pat*: see **pat**, 2. Cf. **tod**.

patacca. 'Italian slang term, pronounced "pataka", meaning worthless rubbish, but now particularly used in the dubious jewellery trade, and amongst air stewards, to describe a counterfeit Swiss watch . . . Also referred to as a "ramped watch" or "mug's ticker"' (Powis, 1977). P.B.: it may be relevant that *patacca* is the name given to a small coin used in Macao.

patch. A police area or district: Northern and Midland police-men's: since ca. 1920. 'Look, Ripley, my patch is the city. I'm not like you—a country officer. Your area is wide open' (Wainwright, 1965). One's own 'cabbage *patch*'. P.B.: by 1965, it had become common to all public services, e.g. social workers, probation officers, for either area of jurisdiction or range of official activity.—2. A Wren's bed-space: WRNS: 1960s. In RN, a sailor's *pit*. (Wood, 1978.)—3. In *on the patch*, in trouble: R Aus. N: earlier C.20. (B., 1943.) On the (patch of) carpet fronting the Commanding Officer's desk.— 4. As *Patch*, the 'inevitable nickname for anyone who has a bald patch on his head; one who is "a bit thin on top", but does not quite merit the sobriquet *eggo* or *Skating Rink*' (Granville): RN.

patch-worker. A pickpocket specialising in outside pockets other than fob-pockets: c.: from ca. 1910. (*Evening News*, 9 Dec. 1936.) Ex S.E. *patch-pocket*, defined by the *OED* Sup. as 'a pocket consisting of a piece of cloth sewn like a patch on to a garment'.

patchy. Variable in quality: C.20: coll. >, by 1930, S.E. E.g. of form in sport. Ex *patch*, a piece.

patent safety. 'My mount was a wiry nondescript animal, sober and unexcitable. It was what is known as a "safe con-veyance" or "patent safety"' : hunting s.: late C.19–20. Sassoon, 1928, concerning the pre-WW1 period.

path (pron. with short *a*). Pathology; pathological: late C.19–20: medical s., now verging on coll. E.g. *path lab*, abbr. pathology laboratory. See also **pathy**.

pathetic. Ludicrous: coll. (?orig. s.). Contrast *funny*, odd.

pathfinder. An airman either very lucky or enviably judicious in finding women: RAF: 1942–5. Ex the official sense of the term. (P-G-R.) I.e., a very highly-trained and efficient navigator, like those in the aircraft sent ahead to mark targets for the bombers.

pathy. A pathologist: police s. (Hunter, 1956.) See **path**.

patsy. A dupe, or 'fall guy', q.v.: adopted ex US, later C.20. *New Society*, editorial, 23 July 1981. Raab: prob. known in Brit. rather earlier. In ca. 1947 the Dundee Repertory Touring Theatre produced *The Patsy* by Barry Connors (pub. in US, 1925). (With thanks to the University of London American Library.)

Paul Pry. A 'giant searchlight': WW2. Berrey, 1940.

Pauper's Grave, the; the Morgue. The smaller-print, brief reviews at back of *The TLS*: the world of books: resp. since ca. 1925 and 1920. There was, ca. 1920–40, a var.: *the Paupers' burial-ground*, as in Brittain, 1933.

pavement. See **across the pavement.**—2. In *hit the pavement*, to be thrown out (of, e.g., a night-club); to be dismissed from one's job: since ca. 1936.—3. In *on the pavement*, involved in a robbery: c.: later C.20. (*Now!*, 3 Apr. 1980.) Prob. ex sense 1.

pavement artist. A 'dealer in precious stones who stands about in Hatton Garden' (Leach): c.:—1933. Ex S.E. sense.—2. An espionage agent acting as 'leg man'—surveillance and street attendance on a suspect: espionage: since ca. 1945. Le Carré, 1977.

pavement pusher. A man selling goods on the kerb or anywhere in street or street-market: mostly Londoners': since ca. 1942. (Webb, 1945.) Ex **push the pavement**.

pavement twist. See **hard-up**, n., 2.

paws off! Addressed, e.g., to 'children picking the icing off a cake' (Raab): domestic coll.

pax. 'Then the pax rang in the rumpus room—pax being jargon for "internal phone"' (Le Carré, 1977): espionage: since mid-C.20.

pay-off, n. Punishment; settlement for infringing the rules of the underworld: c. Brandon, 1934.—2. Hence, the final settlement: Services': adopted, 1943, ex US; by 1950, fairly gen. civilian s.

pay off, v. (Of plans, ventures, attempts) to prove successful: Can. since ca. 1940; Eng. and Aus. since ca. 1950. 'I put in for extended leave, but it didn't pay off' (Leechman). Ex gold-mining?

pay-off Gieves. 'It is an old Wardroom "crack" that anyone starting a sweepstake or a subscription does so in order to pay his outfitters . . . Gieves' (Granville).

pay-off line. A printed form that a man receives on being paid off; he signs it as a receipt: Public Works':—1935. See **line**, 4.

pay on. To pay cash (for a bet): turf s. verging on coll.

pay the earth. To pay excessively: coll.: since ca. 1925.

pay the price of Admiralty. See **price** . . .

payola. Money: adopted, 1961, ex US, but already by end of 1964, slightly ob. and, by 1966, virtually †. Ex *pay* + *-ola*, a common, fanciful American s. suffix of Italian and Spanish origin (W. & F.). Soon predominantly with the implication of 'dirty' money, from some racket: extortion, protection money, etc., and in this nuance perhaps still, early 1980s, not quite † (Raab).

pea-ballast. Gravel that will pass through holes of half an inch (or less): Public Works' coll. Prob. suggested by S.E. *peas*, coals of a small size.

Pea-Bellies. Nickname for Lowestoft fishermen: nautical. (Butcher, 1979.) Cf. *bean-belly*.

pea-dodger. A bowler hat: Aus.:—1935. Cf. **hard-hitter**.

pea doo. See peadoo.

pea in a colander, like a. Flustered, agitated, jumpy: Services'. H. & P., 'Running round in small circles.' Just as common in the Services, who took it from civilians, is the late C.19–20 low *like a fart in a bottle*, with which cf. *in and out like a fart in a colander* (mid-C.19–20), used to describe restless and aimless movement. A Services' var. (since ca. 1920 at latest: probably since ca. 1890): *rushing round like a fart in a colander—doesn't know which hole to come out*. It had also, early C.20, the var. *like a pea in a rattle*, whence, 'heard early 1940s, *in a state of rattle and pea*, occ. with an implied pun on *pee*, i.e. agitated to the point of incontinence' (R.S., 1976). Whereas the former has survived, the latter seems to have disappeared. (E.P., 1977.)

pea-picker. A punter investing only very small sums: bookmakers': since ca. 1972. A pun on *p* for 'pence' and *peanuts* for 'small cash'—and on *pick*, to choose.

pea pod, on (one's). Alone, on one's own: Glasgow double r.s., on synon. **tod**, q.v. Munro, 1985.

pea-shooter. A rifle: Army's joc. irony: esp. in 1914–18. Cf. sense 3.—2. A pea-shooter, says Berrey, is 'a pursuit plane' (a fighter). No; it is a machine-gun, or a light-calibred cannon on an aircraft (esp. if British): H. & P., 1943. Dating from 1939. By meiosis.—3. Also, a revolver: RAF: since mid-1940. (E.P. in *New Statesman*, 19 Sep. 1942.) But the term has existed in Aus. since ca. 1900 (Macdonald, 1907).—4. 'A Harley-Davidson speedway motorcycle of the late 1920s–early '30s. Poss. so called because of its short exhaustpipes' (Dunford, 2).

pea-soup. A French-Canadian: Can.: late C19–20. Ex the frequency of that dish on French-Canadian tables: late C.19–20. Beames.—2. Hence, *talk pea-soup*, to talk French-Canadian; loosely, French. Ibid.

Peabody. A 'block of houses built under the Peabody Bequest to the poor of London': lower-classes' coll.:—1909; ob. Ware.

peace pill. PCP, Phencyclidine: drugs c. (Stockley, 1986.) US since—1969 (Spears, who notes, 'Said to be the source of P.C.P., i.e. PeaCe Pills').

peace-time soldier. One who, in the army, does the same work as he would do in civilian life: military: since ca. 1920. H. & P.—2. But also, in the predominantly civilian army of 1939–45, a Regular soldier. (P-G-R.) Hence, *peace-time soldiering*, being in the Regular Army when there is no major war being fought (P.B.).

peach-perch. The pillion-seat of a (young) man's motorcycle, esp. when used to transport a girl-friend: motorcyclists': 1935. Ex *peach*, since 1880s s. for an attractive girl. Cf. earlier synon. **flapper-bracket**.

peachy. Very pleasant: adopted, ex US, ca. 1925. *OED* Sup.; *Daily Telegraph* mag., 14 July 1972 (R.S.).—2. See **peechy**.

Peacocks, the. See ASSOCIATION FOOTBALL, in Appx.

peadoo. Pea soup: RN lowerdeck: late C.19–mid-20. Knock; Bassett.

peaked-cap. A police inspector: coll.:—1923 (Manchon).

peaking. Any behaviour unworthy of a courageous person; e.g. a facile complaint or 'bellyaching' or yelling if you're hurt: Aus. coll.: since ca. 1920. (Tennant, 1956.) Ex the E. dial. *peak*, to squeak like a mouse; echoic.

peanut alley; p. gallery; p. row. The front row of stalls in a cinema: Aus. urban juvenile: since ca. 1945. (B., 1953.) The 1st and 2nd were adopted ex US—more prob. ca. 1944, ex American servicemen (R.C.). From a gallery, the occupants could throw peanut shells on to those of ground-floor seats; cf. WW2 *bomb alley* for any heavily bombed area.

peanuts. A (very) small sum of money; a trifle: Aus., since ca. 1930 (not necessarily ex US); Brit. since ca. 1950 (prob. ex US). (West, 1956.) Any striker, later C.20, 'I'm fed up with working for peanuts'; cf. synon. **shirt-buttons**.—2. Barbiturates: drugs c. (Stockley, 1986.) US since—1967 (Spears).

pear-shaped. Applied to something gone out of kilter, wrong, out of control, as, when thunderstorms upset the flying dis-

play at Duxford air show, 17 Jun. 1984, the commentator apologised that the programme had 'gone all pear-shaped'. (Barbara Huston.) A collapse from the perfect sphere.

pearl-diver. An assistant-pantryman in charge of the washing of the saloon crockery: Western Ocean nautical >, by 1930, fairly gen. in proletarian s. Bowen.—2. A five-pound note: Glasgow r.s., on *fiver*. Munro, 1985.

pearlies. (The singular hardly exists.) Pearl buttons, esp. on a coster's clothes: from ca. 1885: low coll. Henley.—2. Hence (fairly gen. in singular), costermongers; low coll.

pearling, adj. and n. 'Allowing the nose of the surfboard to slip under' (*Pix*, 28 Sep. 1963): Aus. surfers': since ca. 1961. Perhaps because, as R.C. points out, a surfer doing this emulates a pearl-diver; but perhaps influenced by *purler*, a heavy fall.

pearly ace. See ace, adj.

pearly gates. Morning glory seeds: drugs c. (Stockley, 1986.) US since—1971 (Spears, who adds, 'seeds of a specific color variety').

peasant. (Usu. pl.) One who is in the ranks, esp. an aircraftman: RAF and R Aus. AF joc.: WW2. B., 1943.—2. Hence, in civilian life, one of a social position lower than one's own; joc., of an equal displaying 'uncouth' qualities: since WW2. Cf.: ' "Peasants" are people whose conduct and appearance give the impression that they are not accustomed to dining out' (Mars, 1984): hotel and catering industry.

peasy. Adj. formed ex *peas*, truncated later C.19 r.s. *peas in the pot*, hot. Jones, 1971.

pebble on the beach, not the only. (Of persons) not the sole desirable or remarkable one available, accessible, potential: semi-proverbial coll. (Lyell.) Cf. the proverbial *there's plenty other* (or *there are as good*) *fish in the sea*, often used, in consolation, to one who has been unlucky in love, jilted.—2. In (*remember*) *you're not the only . . . .*: there are plenty of other people equally as deserving as yourself: id. (P.B.)

pec. A pectoral muscle: body-builders': late C.20. '[The bodybuilders] drop on to one knee and pop out their pecs' (*New Society*, 4 June 1981).

peck. 'To attack and break away quickly' (Jackson): RAF: 1939+.

peckerhead. A term of abuse, 'insult, meaning his head has as much brain as the glans of the penis. Widespread in N. Am., at least back to the mid-1950s' (Leech, 1985). Cf. synon. **dickhead**; *pecker* = penis (?a pun on *cock*) since C.19.

Peckham Rye. Tie (n. and v.): r.s. (F. & G.) In later C.20, usu. a necktie (Jones; Barker).

pecks. People: London s. (Hollis, 1983.) P.B.: ex unrecorded r.s. *Peckham Rye* = guy?

peculiar. Mentally deranged: coll. Ex S.E. sense, strange (1888, *OED*).

pedal. To send (a message) by wireless transceiver: Aus. coll.: since ca. 1936. Ex the obligatory pedalling on the generator pedals. Ronan, 1954.

pedal; get the pedal or **be pedalled.** To dismiss—to get oneself, or to be, dismissed—from a job: motor and cycle trades': since ca. 1920. Westerby, 1937.

pedal-pushers. Three-quarter length, i.e. calf-length, pants suitable for female sportswear: teenagers': adopted, ca. 1962, ex US.

peddle (her) **hips.** To be a prostitute: since ca. 1920. Valtin, 1941.

peddler; pedlar. Seller of drugs: drugs c. (Stockley, 1986.) US since—1931 (Spears).

pedigree-man. A recidivist (criminal): c.:—1923 (Manchon). The police can trace him back a long way.

pedlar's pack. Dismissal: r.s., on *sack*: later C.20. (Daniells, 1980.)

pedo. A patient with a pedicle: Aus. (Services') hospitals': ca. 1942–6. Stivens, 1946.

pee. Phoneticised *p* = penny, pence: coll.: since decimalisation of currency in Feb. 1971. E.g., *a two-pee piece* or *bit*, two-pence; 'that's fifty pee you owe me'. (P.B.)

pee-hee. To ingratiate oneself with one's superiors: 1939+; by 1946, ob. (*New Statesman*, 30 Aug. 1941.) Echoic. Cf. **tee-heeing**.

pee like a rabbit. As an intensive, 'Gawd, I want to pee like . . . ', I need very much to urinate: earlier C.20. (My father, Leslie S. Beale, 1904–81, as the need arose.)

pee – po – bum – drawers! Childish scatological, as in the chant 'Mum's out, Dad's out. Let's say rude words: pee, po . . . etc.': earlier C.20. Cf. the more 'advanced' *shit, bugger* . . .

pee (one)self laughing. To laugh very heartily and/or long: since ca. 1910. (Kersh, 1946.) Also *piss* . . . P.B.: in later C.20 often absolute, as 'I nearly pee'd myself' (sc. laughing).

pee-warmer. See **piss-warmer**.

pee-Willy. An effeminate male: Can.: since ca. 1925.

peechy; rarely **peachy.** Soon; presently: Army, coll.: late C.19–20. (F. & G.) Hindustani *pichhe*.—2. Hence, behind, both adv. and n. (backside): Army: early C.20. 'What are you doing, sitting on your peechy like a char-wallah?'—i.e. idling.—3. (Ex sense 1, and also spelt *peechi*.) Of a soldier, using a near-approaching release from the army, or at least a posting home, as an excuse for doing very little or no work; 'Can't touch [i.e., affect] me, I'm peechi!': Army, esp. in Cyprus: later 1950s. Hence *peechy-boy*, one in this situation. (P.B.)

peek, the. 'The observation cell. "He's in the peek" = he is under observation' (Tempest, 1950): prisons': mid-C.20. Also known as *the peep*.

peek-a-boo or **peek(-)a(-)bo.** A very sketchy salute: Services': ca. 1938–48. (H. & P.) Cf. synon. **nose-scratch.**—2. Any garment made from 'Swiss cotton' (*broderie anglaise*): Aus.: since ca. 1950. (B.P.)

peeko. A glance; a quick look-about: since ca. 1910. Cobb, 1949.

peel-off, n. Illicit removal of part of a common booty: low s., police s., and underworld. 'He wanted a lot more. He . . . indulged in a little "peel-off" ' (Gosling, 1959).

peel off, v. To give money; esp. as 'He peeled off one', he gave me a pound: c.: from ca. 1925. I.e. to slip a (currency) note from a wad of notes.—2. To break away, esp. in a dive, from a formation: RAF coll. (since ca. 1925) >, by 1941, j. Ex peeling off one's clothes.

peelo. A pilot: RAF: ca. 1940–55. (Jackson.) Ex the French pron. of the English *pilot*; obviously not ex Fr. *pilote* (as occ. implied).

peep. A car belonging to a Command H.Q.: Can. Army: ca. 1941–5. Suggested by *jeep*, 2.—2. A word: mostly spivs': since ca. 1945; adopted ex US (R.C.). ' "One more peep out of you, Mister, and I'll get the boys to push you and your b— stall in the oggin"—which was a nearby canal' (*Picture Post*, 2 Jan. 1954, article on young spivs).—3. 'Smaller than a hit-man, bigger than a peep' (Hall, 1976): presumably an observer: espionage: later C.20. Cf. *the peek*, q.v. at **peek.**—4. Hence, the observing itself, as in 'the other two wouldn't have been manning the peep' (Ibid.): id.

peep freak. A voyeur: adopted, ca. 1970, ex US. (Hollander.) Ex synon. S.E. *peeping Tom*.

peeping Tom. A pilot that is expert at flying in bad weather and at dodging from cloud to cloud: RAF: since 1939. (H. & P.) His prey is less exciting and much more dangerous than that of Lady Godiva's peeping Tom.

peery. (Gen. in pl. *peeries*.) A foot: c., and low.

peeve, n. Drink; alcoholic liquor: market-traders'. (*M.T.*) Cf. **peever.** Perhaps cognate with synon. **bevvy**, q.v.—2. Pee-vishness, either in gen. or a particular instance: coll.: since ca. 1930. Ex the v. Hence *pet peeve*, something especially irritating, as in 'Oh, pay no attention to his whingeing! The iniquities of the unions are his pet peeve at the moment.'

peeve, v.t. To disgruntle; to annoy: from ca. 1920: coll. By back-formation ex:–

peeved. Annoyed; cross: 1918 (*SOD*): coll. Ex *peevish*. Perhaps orig. US.

peever. A public house: market-traders'. (*M.T.*) App. neither dial. nor Romany; see also **peeve**, n., 1.

peg, n. Abbr. *peg-top*: children's coll.:—1923 (Manchon).—2. Esp. in 'It's a peg!', it's first-class or -rate: Aus.: from ca. 1930. B., 1943.—3. (Mostly in pl.) A signal: railwaymen's. *Railway*.—4. (Mostly in pl.) Footrest on a motorcycle: motorcyclists': since ca. 1950. (Dunford.)—5. A look-over; See AUSTRALIAN UNDERWORLD, in Appx.—6. A watch [?time-piece, or as 5]: Aus.: later C.20. McNeil.

peg, v. To throw: Aus. low: since ca. 1930. Baker, 'As in "peg a gooly", throw a stone.—2. To put (someone) on a charge: Army: since ca. 1910. P-G-R.—3. Hence, 'To put on report' (Home Office): Borstals' and detention centres': later C.20.

peg-house. A public house: low: from ca. 1920. (*OED* Sup.) Ex older *peg*, a drink.

peg-leg. A person with a wooden leg: (low) coll.: C.19–20. Ex S.E. sense, a wooden leg.

peg-legger. A beggar: Glasgow:—1934. Either r.s. or ex prec.—2. Var. of **peg-leg.** Bournemouth *Echo*, 28 Oct. 1943.

peg out. To have one's strength fail during some endeavour, esp. sporting, as 'He looked all set to win the mile, but then pegged out on the last lap': coll. (P.B.) Parsons notes, 1973, that according to *Pears Cyclopedia* the orig. of this usage lies in the game of croquet, where *peg out* is 'the term used for finishing a croquet round by hitting the peg.' But still crib-bage, from lower down the social scale, seems the more prob. orig.

peg up. 'I would sometimes spend the whole day "pegging up". That's an old trick of the trade. It goes back to Victorian times. You'd just put a matchstick or a little piece of wood in the doors. You go back at night and if the pegs ain't moved you'd know the house was empty and safe to rob' (Church, 1986): c.

Peggy, peggy. 'A hand . . . called upon to do all the odd jobs in a watch' (Bowen): nautical: C.19. In C.20 RN, often *mess-deck peggy*. 'From his maid-of-all-work duties', says Gran-ville; but Gamble, 1977, suggests that the term derives from the time when disabled ex-seamen, many of them 'peg-legged', were given jobs in naval barracks to keep them going and as a form of pension (P.B.).—2. Hence, 'The man who looks after the seamen's and firemen's messes in a modern liner' (Ibid.): nautical. —3. A *Pegasus* engine—used on certain RAF aircraft: RAF coll.: 1943+. Partridge, 1945.—4. See **stand** (one's) **peggy.**

peke, Peke. A coll. abbr. of *Pekin(g)ese*, sc. *dog* or *spaniel*: from ca. 1910. Rarely *Pek*; occ. *Pekin* (1920: *OED* Sup.).

pellets. Shells: Royal Artillery: WW2. A meiosis.

pelt. In *have a pelt at*, to attempt vigorously, 'have a shot at': coll.:—1923 (Manchon).

pelter. Any person, etc., going very quickly, esp. a horse: coll.

pen. A *pen*itentiary; a prison: low, almost c.: from ca. 1820; in C.20 usu. identified with US usage. Cf. **pen bait.**—2. A pris-oner-of-war cage: Army: 1941–5. (P-G-R.) 'Via Canadians; cf. sense 1', says E.P. But may it not be simply from, e.g. a sheep-*pen*? (P.B.)

pen and ink. A stink: r.s.: from ca. 1858. H., 1st ed.—2. To 'kick up a stink', i.e. to yell (with pain): Cockney: late C.19–20.—3. Hence, 'Pain or suffering, especially when inflicted as a punishment or in revenge. "He didn't half give me some pen and ink" ' (*M.T.*): market-traders'.

pen and inker. 'A person of mean habits, not to be trusted, possible a "squealer" (informer). To be "on the pen and ink", is to be under suspicion of having informed, and there-fore ostracized' (Franklyn): r.s., on *stinker*: since ca. 1945.

pen bait. An under-age girl that flirts with show boys: Can. carnival s. Cf. Brit. synon **gaol-(jail-)bait**, and see **pen**, 1.

pencil and tassel. A (little) boys's penis and scrotum: lower classes' euph. *Tassel* is often used on its own, but = penis.

penguin. 'A ground-staff, i.e. nonflying, member of the RAF' (H. & P.): from ca. 1925.—2. 'A cunning specialist who disposed of sand excavated from tunnels so that the ferrets [see **ferret**] could not find it' (Brickhill, 1946): among prisoners of war in Germany, 1940–5.

penguin party. 'Those who go ashore every night but never go to sea . . . For these men there are shouts of derision: "Penguin Party, fall in!" ' (correspondent, 1959): RN: since 1946 or 1947. Cf. prec., 1.

penguin suit. Formal evening dress, black suit and bow tie, white shirt: since late 1950s. BBC, 1 Feb. 1964. 'He has abandoned his waistcoat with "Jellybaby" embedded on the back in sequins and got more soberly "penguin-suited up" ' (Roberts, 1982).

peninsular. A very inquisitive female, often with a long neck stretched out to *see*: joc.: since ca. 1955. Sometimes called an *ostrich*, esp. if seen peering over neighbours' hedges or fences. (Petch.) Leech, 1981, glosses Can. use as '(of a woman) long, thin, and getting in where not wanted.'

pennies from heaven. Easy money: since ca. 1925: coll. >, by 1945, familiar S.E. Ruck, 1940.

pennif. A five-pound note: back slang: 1862 (*Cornhill Magazine*).—2. Hence, any bank or currency note: *single-pennif* being a £1 note: c.

penn'orth. Abbr. *pennyworth*: coll.—2. A year's imprisonment, esp. of a convict and mostly in combination: c. >, by 1930, low s. Harrison, 1934, 'Ronnie will get fourteen penn'orth . . . Fourteen years hard.'

penn'orth (or **ball**) **of chalk.** A walk: late C.19–20. Sharpe, 1938 (both); Bracey, 1934 (**ball** . . .). Often shortened to *pennorth*. Hence, *take a penn'orth* (often in the imperative), (to) go away (!): since late C.19. (Franklyn.) In later C.20 the *ball* version is commoner.

penny-a-mile. A smile: r.s. Franklyn.

penny-farthing. 'A term invented in the early 1890s by the London guttersnipes who used to call it after riders who remained faithful to the almost obsolescent high ordinary' (Roberts, 1983): therefore, orig., derisive or pej. Also known as the *high bicycle* or *high-wheeler*, having one very large wheel in front, and one very small, its resemblance to the then largest and smallest of copper coins was readily apparent. The term is now historical and informal S.E. (P.B.)

penny packet; usu. in pl. A small party of soldiers—smaller than a platoon—as seen aerially: RAF: since early 1940. (H. & P.) P.B.: also Army, for a small number, as in 'It's no use whatever sending the tanks in penny packets . . . '

penny red. 'Coloured fizzy drink sold in the canteen at Dartmouth before WW2' (Granville): RN. Cf. **goffer.** Ex the penny postage stamp that succeeded the *penny black* which was the earliest of all.

penny steamboat. A ferry: joc. coll.

penny stamps. Very small plaice: trawlermen's. (Butcher, 1980.) Cf. **ivy-leaf.**

Pensioners, the. See ASSOCIATION FOOTBALL, in Appx.

pep. Energy: spirited initiative: coll.: 1920 (*SOD*). Orig. (ca. 1914) US. Abbr *pepper*. Cf. *go* and **pep up.**—2. Peppermint.

pep pill. A stimulant (in tablet form) to the central nervous system: since the late 1940s. Cf. prec., 1.

pep talk. A talk or speech designed to improve morale: coll.: since ca. 1925. See **pep,** 1, and :-

pep up. To infuse (gen. a person, but may also apply to, e.g., a display, writing, etc.) with new life, spirit, courage: coll.: adopted, ex US, ca. 1927. (*OED* Sup.) See **pep,** 1.—2. Hence, to become lively: from ca. 1930. *Passing Show*, 15 July 1933.

Pepper Pot, the. 'The gallant *Penelope* which was so damaged by bomb splinters that she resembled one' (Granville): RN: WW2.—2. A *pepper pot* is a 'small pierced silencer fitted to some veteran bikes' (Partridge, 1978): motorcyclists'.

peppermint flavour. Favour: r.s. Petch cites TV, 14 Mar. 1967.

peppermint rocks; often **peppermints.** Socks: r.s. Cf. older *almond rocks.*

peppy. Energetic: spirited, e.g. work: from ca. 1921. Ex **pep,** q.v. Waugh, 1930; in the *Humorist*, 28 July 1934, a typical retired admiral is described as 'addressing peppy letters to the editor of *The Times*'.

per. Per hour: since ca. 1910. Chance, 1935, 'An average of eighty miles per.'—2. An inevitable abbr. of *permission*, as in 'I say, have you got per?': Public Schools' and Services'. (P.B.)

per c. 'Per cent, as in securities—"gilt-edged three per Cs" ' (R.C., 1977): money-market coll.: since ca. 1925.

perc. A (coffee) percolator: Society: since ca. 1920. (Bailey, 1934.) Hence, as v.t. or i, to percolate (of coffee). Also **perk.**

Perce. A *Perc*ival communication plane: RAF: 1942+. Partridge, 1945.—2. (Also *Percy.*) Penis; esp. in *point Perce at the porcelain*, to urinate: Aus.: since ca. 1945. 'Perce the *piercer*'?—cf. Fr. *percer*, to pierce. P.B.: prob. merely alliteration; the *Percy* version was ephemerally popular in Brit. raffish circles, ca. 1970, having been introduced by the cartoon series featuring the complete 'Ocker', Barry McKenzie, in *Private Eye*.

percentage. Profit; advantage: Army, since ca. 1940; civilian, since ca. 1945. 'There's no percentage in it'—nothing's to be gained by it. P-G-R.

percenter. One who works on a commission; one who does this and that, arranges this deal and that, for a percentage: business(-)world coll.

perch. See **peach-perch.**—2. In *on the perch*, handcuffed: police s.: since ca. 1925. 'A uniformed constable with his prisoner "on the perch" ' (Gosling, 1959).

perched on an oar like a budgerigar. 'Unable to pull the oar properly, because of small stature: Royal Navy: 1970s' (Peppitt).

percher. A 'sitter', a 'dolly' catch, a very easy catch, esp. when it's been missed: cricket writers', commentators', lovers': since the late (?middle) 1960s.—2. 'An easy arrest, or an easy victim' (Powis): police s., and c.: later C.20.

percolator. Carburettor: motorcyclists': since (?)ca. 1955. (Dunford.)—2. 'To *have a shake, rave or percolator* . . . to have a party' (Anderson): beatniks': since ca. 1959. Ex the coffee percolator that so often features at these affairs.

Percy, in the RN, has, since ca. 1925, meant an effeminate man; but since ca. 1940, also and esp. a studious, quiet, educated man as opposed to an uncouth 'tough'.—2. See **Perce,** 2.

Percy Filth. 'Sexy talk or actions, a condemnatory expression. Made briefly popular by "The Lovers" TV series, with Richard Beckinsell, in the 1960s: UK' (Fearon, 1984). Presumably a pun on *persiflage*.

perf. A perforation: stamp-collectors' coll.: late C.19–20. P.B.: this, by later C.20 > j., refers to the edges of the stamp. *Perf-in*, on the other hand, refers to letters or other devices punched through the face of the stamp.

perfect. Amusing; pleasant, delightful: Society coll.: from ca. 1910. Denis Mackail, 1925, 'But *rowing*. How perfect!'

perfect day, a. A day that one has very greatly enjoyed: coll.: 1909 (*OED* Sup.)

perfectly good . . . , a. An indubitably—or, merely, a quite—good, sound, satisfactory something or other: from ca. 1918: s. > coll. Cf. **perfect.**

perform. To swear vividly, to show a furious temper: Aus.: since ca. 1925. B., 1943.—2. 'To do a burglary. "They picked me up before I had time to perform" = I was caught before I had time to start' (Tempest, 1950).

performance, grand or **command.** 'Referred to a person supposedly good at something' (F. Leech, 1972): ephemeral; late 1950s–60s. Ex the j. of the world of entertainment.

performer. 'A sailor who makes a habit of causing trouble' (Green, 1974): RN. Ex later C.19 s. *perform*, to make a (considerable) fuss.

P

perhapser. A very risky stroke: Aus. cricketers': since ca. 1930. Stivens, 1958.

perim. Perimeter track (encircling an airfield): RAF coll.: from ca. 1937. (Jackson.) P.B.: † by 1950, superseded by j. term *peritrack*.

period! Finally; without extension or modification, palliation or repeal: orig. (ca. 1945), journalists', authors', broadcasters', perhaps typists': only since ca. 1955 has it been at all gen. 'Dead as a doornail? Just dead. Period!' P.B.: prob. ex US, where *period* is the term for 'full stop' in punctuation.

periphery. A big belly: cultured, joc. coll.:—1923 (Manchon). Prob. suggested by *circumference*.

periscope depth, at. 'Half asleep; lightly dozing, as a submarine is said to be when at periscope depth' (Granville): RN: mid-C.20.

perisher. A 'freeze', mostly in *do a perisher*, to feel extremely cold: coll.: earlier C.20. Cf. **perishing**, adv.—2. As *the perisher*, the Commanding Officers' course for submarine commanders: RN: since ca. 1940.

perishing, adj. A gen. pej., as in 'Damn the perishing thing!': coll.—2. Very cold, as in 'I didn't 'ave no coat on, an' it were perishing': Cockneys': late C.19–20. (Franklyn.) Ex:-

perishing, adv. A pej. intensive adv.: coll. Orig. and esp. (*it's*) *perishing cold*.

perk. To vomit: Aus. low. (B., 1942.) A thinning of 'to puke'.—2. To percolate as in 'Coffee won't be long—it's perking nicely': since ca. 1955. Ex *percolator* rather than ex *percolate*, and occ. spelt *perc*.

perm, n. A supposed *perm*anent wave (of the hair): coll.: from ca. 1925. By 1940, > merely a synon. for a 'hair wave': hence, since ca. 1940, *permanent perm*, q.v. for the orig. sense.—2. A *perm*utation: coll.: since mid-1920s.—3. A *perm*anent employee, esp. a typist, as opp. to a **temp**[orary]: the world of office girls and employment agencies: coll.: since ca. 1950, but common only since ca. 1960.

perm, v. To subject a person's hair to a permanent wave: coll., and gen. in passive: since ca. 1927. Ex n., 1.—2. To permute, esp. with ref. to entries in a football-pool coupon: coll. (P.B.)

perpetrate a nonsense. 'To issue an order (local A.A. Slang)' (H. & P.): earlier WW2; later the phrase > more widespread in the Services, with meaning not only 'to issue a (stupid) order', but also 'to make an administrative bungle' (P.B.).

Perry. A *Pere*grine engine: RAF ground crews': 1942+. (Partridge, 1945.) Cf. **Peggy**, 3.—2. The Manchester version of a **casual** [q.v., sense 2], 'because of . . . predilection for traditional Fred Perry shirts' (*You*, 4 Dec. 1983).

Peru window. A one-way window that, in a bedroom, enables a third party to watch coïtion: low Aus.: since ca. 1963.

peruse. A 'look round' ashore: nautical coll. Prob. on *cruise* (*ker-ruse*).

perv, n. Corresponding to the adj.: Aus.: since ca. 1930. (B.P.) In nuance 'a male homosexual', it occurs in Hesling, 1963. Buzo, 1973, '*Pervs* . . . perverts, often specifically voyeurs; often used as a pejorative term for men who like watching girls'. P.B.: the term has been in low Brit. use, perhaps mostly Services', since mid-1950s at latest.—2. 'The act of "perving" ' (Wilkes): Aus: since ca. 1960. See **perve**.

perv, adj. Erotic: Aus.: since the late 1920s. Glassop, 1944, 'Bluey brought a perv book back from Cairo with him'. I.e. a sense-perversion and shortening of *perverted*.

perv show. A strip-tease show: Aus.: since ca. 1930. (B.P.) Cf. prec.

perve. To practise perversion; mostly between women and esp. as in 'What about a spot of perving?': Aus.: since ca. 1930. (Communication, 1941, from Melbourne.)—2. Aus., since ca. 1930, as in 'Eddie was . . . doing, as the boys expressed it, "a bit of perving". He was looking at his gallery of nudes and semi-nudes and trying, as usual, to reach a decision about the one he would prefer to sleep with' (*Rats*, 1944). 'Its use here often involves no more than watching a girl or woman in admiration. Whence, *to perve at* (a girl), to extract pleasure from looking at her, esp. if she is scantily dressed as on a beach' (B., 1959).

perverted. A Society euph. for *buggered*: from ca. 1918. MacDonald, 1933, 'I'm perverted if I know!'

pervy. Synon. with **perv**: 1944 (Glassop).

pesi-pesi. See SWAHILI, in Appx.

pest. To pester: Aus.: since ca. 1930. Trist, 1944, 'It's enough to have a hangover, without you pesting me all the time.'

pester; pester-up. (V.i. and v.t., resp.) To pay; pay up: c., and market-traders'. *Gilt Kid*, 1936; *M.T.*, 'Don't pester for the gilly—he's a lugger'. Ex Romany *pesser*, to pay.

pestiferous; pestilential. Gen. pej., often joc.; usu. of children, pets, that pester or 'badger': coll. (P.B.)

pet peeve. See **peeve**, n., 2.

petal. An effeminate man: RAF: since ca. 1938. (Partridge, 1945.) Prompted by *pansy*.—2. As vocative (cf. *flower*, *ducky*, etc.): low coll.: Chappell, 1980, ' "Yes, petal—what do you want to know?" the band-leader says with determined cheerfulness'. (P.B.)

peter. To weep: market-traders'. (*M.T.*) There seems to have been an obsolete *peter*, to grumble; echoic, probably.

peter-man, peterman. 'A safe-blower, cracksman, safe specialist' (Tempest, 1950): c.: since (?)ca. 1940. Ex C.19 (poss. earlier) c. *peter*, a safe or strongroom.

peters. Luggage: taxi-drivers': since ca. 1910. (Hodge, 1938.) Ex much older, since C.17, c. > s. *peter*, a portmanteau or suitcase.

peth. Pethidine: drugs c. Stockley, 1986.

petrol booser. See GREMLINS, in Appx.

petrol pigeons. Naval aircrew: RN: since ca. 1970. (Peppitt.) Cf. **paraffin budgie**.

petting-party. A party at which much caressing is done; esp. a party held for that purpose: adopted, ex US, ca. 1925. Cf. **necking**.

phagassies. 'Those gremlins which sit on the wings and blow on the aileron and send it down' (P-G-R): RAF: 1940–5. Graves, 1943. And see GREMLINS, in Appx.

Phallic Symbol, the. The University Library: Cambridge undergraduates': since ca. 1955. Ex the shape of its tower.

phallic thimble. A sheath pessary: c. 1920–40. 'Low "educated" punning on "phallic symbol" ' (R.S.).

phantom. A fraction: law-clerks'. Pugh, 1912, ' "How much more?" inquired Uncle Algernon, wearily. "Three and a phantom," replied McGaffney.' Cf. **onion** in this sense.

Phar Lap. A derisive Aus. term of address (from 1933) for a person slow in his movements. Ex Phar Lap, a splendid Australian racehorse (its name = 'flash of lightning') that died of poison in Mexico in 1933.—2. 'They specialized in "Phar Laps", wild dog with the hair burnt off, trussed and cooked in the ashes' (Hill, 1951, quoted by Wilkes): Aus., esp Northern Territory.

Phar Lap gallop. A foxtrot: Aus.: since ca. 1932. (B., 1943.) See prec., 1.

pheasant-plucker. 'Derisive of an unpleasant person' (usu. male), i.e. ironically for 'pleasant fucker' (fellow): mostly RN officers': ca. 1920–70. (Parsons, 1973.) Clearly a contrived spoonerism. P.B.: in Army usage, always joc.

phenobarb. Phenobarbitone: coll.: since ca. 1930.

phlizz. A failure: from ca. 1925; ob. (Galsworthy, 1926.) A blend of *flop* + *fizzle*.

phon clerk. 'The noise-meter operator. In current use [early 1980s] to measure the noise (phons) at race meetings, etc.' (Dunford, 2): racing motorcyclists'. Cf.:-

phon snuffler. A silencer: motorcyclists': since ca. 1950. 'It "snuffles" the "phons" by which [exhaust] noise is measured' (Dunford).

phone, 'phone. N. and v., tele*phone*: coll.: n., 1884; v., 1900 (*OED*). From ca. 1910, gen. *phone*; now virtually S.E.—2. Hence a telephone message: coll.—3. In *go for* or *use, the* *phone*, to tic-tac: Aus. racing: since ca. 1930. (B., 1953.) To cease doing so is to *hang up* (the phone).

phone freak. 'A person who electronically and fraudulently manipulates international calls' (Powis): adopted ex US ca. 1970.

phoney or **phony**, n. Blarney: c.: from ca. 1930. (*Gilt Kid*, 1936.) Ex:–

phoney, occ. **phony**, adj. Fraudulent, 'shady', criminal: c.: US, anglicised ca. 1920. (Edgar Wallace's later works.) Ex *fawney*, late C.18–19, a ring (prob. ex Irish *fáinne*), whence elliptical for the fraudulent practice of ring-dropping: a trickster drops a fake gold ring, so that he may pick it up before a gullible witness to whom he then sells it 'cheap'.—2. Hence, unreal, make-believe, as in *the phoney war* (Sep. 1939–Mar. 1940), coined by the Americans late in 1939 and adopted by Englishmen early in 1940.—3. Applied to make-believe players in a gambling game: 7 Apr. 1946, the *People* (article by Alan Hoby).

phoney gen. See **gen**, n.

phoney war, the. See **phoney**, 2.

phonie. An ephemeral, early name for a motion-picture with a sound-track: journalistic: 1928. (BBC Radio 3, 26 Aug. 1980.) Cf. **audies, talkies**.

Phoo. See **Chad**.

phooey! An expression of utter disbelief or pronounced distaste or even, contempt. Adopted, ca. 1959, ex US. Deriving ex the Yiddish form of German *pfui* and popularised by Walter Winchell during the 1930s. Reyburn, 1962.

phosgene. The Passive Defence Office: RN: 1939. (Granville.) Anti-phosgene and all other enemy gases.

photey. A photograph; the dial. or illiterate version sometimes used for humorous effect: prob. throughout C.20. Martin, 1975.

photo finish; often reduced to *photo* (pron. *photer*). A Guinness: r.s.: since ca. 1946. Franklyn.

Photo Freddie. 'Photo reconnaissance aircraft' (Emanuel, 1945): RAF: 1942+.

photog. A photographer: coll.; rare: later C.20. Stuart, 1971.

photographic. (Of a face) easily or strikingly photographable: coll.: from ca. 1910.

phut-phut. 'A small two-stroke engine' (Dunford, 2): motorcyclists'. Echoic.

phyllis, Phyllis. *Syphilis*: medical and military euph. coll. rather than s.: from ca. 1910.

phyamps. Methadone: drugs c. Stockley, 1986.

phys. Physics: schools': late C.19–20. Cole, 1985.

physical jerks. See **jerks**.

physio. Physiotherapy: physiotherapists', their patients', students': Aus.: since ca. 1950.—2. A physiotherapist: medical, hospital, social services' coll.: since ca. 1950.

pi-squash. A prayer meeting; any similar assemblage: schools' and universities': from ca. 1910; ob. by 1935. (W.) Ex *pi*, later C.19 s. for pious, sanctimonious, and **squash**, n., q.v., which may be an abbr. of it.

piache. Mad; on *stone-mad*, often *stone-piache*: Army: late C.19–20. (B. & P.) Ex Hindustani. Cf. **pie-ackers**.

piano. A chamber-pot: workmen's: earlier C.20. Echoic.—2. Ribs of beef: Cockney's: late C.19–20. Horsley, 1912.—3. Often slovened to *piana*. A cash register: Anglo-Irish: since ca. 1920. It plays a merry tune. Cf. **Jewish piano**.—4. See **Chicago piano; play the piano**.

pianoforte legs. The legs of a bishop in ecclesiastical costume: joc.:–1923 (Manchon). Ex the former draping of the mahogany, therefore *black*, legs of a piano.

pianola. At cards, a hand that almost *plays itself*: Aus.: since ca. 1925. (B., 1942.) Hence, occ., 'an easy task'. Ex 'player piano'.

pic. A picture: artists'; photographers'. Montague, 1910.—2. See **pics**, 1.

Pic, the. The Piccadilly Restaurant and Grill Room: Gibbs, 1934.—3. See **Sunday Pic**.

Piccadilly bushman. Any wealthy Aus. who lives in the West End of London: Aus.: since ca. 1920. B., 1942.

Piccadilly commando. A London prostitute: since 1941, and orig. in the Forces; since 1946, increasingly ob. 'They certainly had the art of achieving a "kill" in the streets without creating a disturbance': the feeling comment made (in 1961) by a war-time RAF officer.

Piccadilly Cowboys, the. The Household Cavalry: 'The province of The Life Guards and The Blues was really London, and for that reason they were known derisively as "The Piccadilly Cowboys" ' (Carew): Army: earlier C.20.

Piccadilly daisy. A prostitute: ca. 1905–40. Keable, 1924.

Piccadilly Part II Orders. See **Whores' Gazette**.

Piccadilly Percy. Mercy: r.s.: later C.20. Barker, 1979.

piccolo. 'A long-stroke motorcycle engine' (Dunford): motorcyclists': since mid-C.20.

piccolos and flutes. Boots: r.s.: since ca. 1930; not very gen. Franklyn.

piccys. Pictures: coll.: since early C.20. Kipling, 1925, 'incised and painted Cromagnon piccys of bison, horse, wolf and Rhino . . . '—2. Illustrations in a book: id.—3. The cinema, as in 'going to the piccys': since late 1940s. (All 3, P.B.) Cf. **pic, pics, pix**.

pice(-)money. 'Chicken feed' (small change): Army and RAF in India: earlier C.20.

pick. To guess: lower-class Aus. coll. Niland, 1959, 'I pick it right?' Ex *pick out*, to choose.

pick and choose. Strong drink: theatrical r.s., on *booze*. Franklyn.

pick on. To gird at; annoy actively: coll. Ex dial. *pick upon*. The *OED*'s 'Now U.S. dial.' ignores the coll. Eng. usage, which undoubtedly exists, esp. as = pick a quarrel with. Cf. the v. **pick up**.—2. To find fault with: Can. and (?hence) Eng. coll.: since ca. 1910; this, since ca. 1930, has, indeed, been the predominant sense. (Leechman.) P.B.: but the use of the term by one of a number of people, concerning their superior, as, e.g. 'Why does the bastard always have to pick on *me*!', implies the *pick* of 'select in order to be unpleasant to.'

pick-out job. 'A man with a smart new cab . . . is sometimes "picked out" by a passenger from the middle of the rank. He has, therefore, got a "pick-out job". They're not much cop, as a rule' (Hodge, 1939).

pick the daisies (at – Station). To rob passengers arriving in London by the Continental boat-trains: c.: from ca. 1920.—2. Hence, *pick-up (man)*, a luggage-thief: c.:–1932 ('Stuart Wood').

pick-up, n. A recovery of form: lawn-tennis coll.: from ca. 1927. E.g. 'A wonderful pick-up! From 1–5 to 5 games all.'—2. A ride in lorry or motor-car: tramps' c.: from ca. 1910. Cowan, 1937.—3. An arrest: c.: from ca. 1919. Ex sense 2 of the v.—4. *The . . .*, theft from unattended cars: c.: since ca. 1925. (Sharpe, 1938.) See prec., 2.

pick up, v. To take (a person) up sharply: coll.—2. To arrest (a wrongdoer): c. Brandon, 1936.—3. To obtain (esp. promotion): RN: coll. Granville, 'So-and-so hopes to pick up his half stripe next year.'

pick up fag-ends. To listen to a conversation that does not concern one: Scottish Public Schools': from ca. 1910. Miller, 1935.

pick-up man. See **pick the daisies**.

pick up the tab. To pay for, stand the expense incurred by, something, e.g. a meal, an entertainment; used esp. of a sponsor who has organised an entertainment, a sporting event, as an advertisement, or in his own interest: coll.: adopted, ex US, ca. 1960. (P.B.)

picked before he was ripe. (A person) 'under-sized or rawly innocent' (B., 1959): Aus.: since ca. 1920.

pickin' a quin (pron. *kewin*). 'A teasing answer to call from someone out of sight asking "What are you doing?"': Londoners': C.19–early 20' (L.A., 1974, who speculates that *quin* might be an innocently used corruption of *quim*).

P

pics, the. The illustrations: book, etc., designers', journalists' and authors'. (Bell, 1934.) In later C.20, under US influence, occ. spelt *pix*, as in Campbell, 1960 (P.B.). See also **pic.**

picture. In *make a picture of*, to render (a person) unrecognisable: coll.: earlier C.20. Manchon.—2. In *get* (one's) *picture*, to 'get one's cards'—be dismissed from one's job: since ca. 1920. Llewellyn, 1943.—3. In *get the picture*, to understand (esp. the general idea): coll.: since ca. 1935. Cf.:—4. *Put* (someone) *in the picture*, 'To give you, as a newcomer, an idea of what is happening . . . and so enable you to play your part in it' (H. & P.): Services' coll.: since ca. 1935. Cf. **paint a picture.**—5. *Not in the picture*, not understanding, or not in a position to appreciate, what is going on; the opp. of having been 'put in the picture' (see sense 4): Services': since mid-C.20.

picture-and-blank. A game played with cigarette (or other) cards: Lancashire: late C.19–early 20. Roberts, 1976.

pictures, the. The cinema: coll.: 1915, Burke, 'Mother and Father . . . go to the pictures at the Palladium near Balham Station' (*OED* Sup.).

pictures-queue. Joc. perversion of *picturesque*: coll. Cf. *humorous-queue.*

piddle about. To make an ado about nothing much; to 'faff about'. Cf.:-

piddling. Trivial; insignificant: low coll.

pie. A prize, treat, 'easy thing': adopted, ex US, ca. 1910. Ex fruit pie. Cf. **easy as pie.**—2. 'Association of buyers at auction to buy at low prices and act as a monopoly' (B.P.): Aus. coll., esp. 'the wool *pies*': since late 1940s. Ex 'to have a finger in every *pie*'.

pie-ackers. '[The Petty Officer] shook his head: "I don't know, these National Service [sc. sailors] give me the screaming pie-ackers" ' (*Heart*, 1962); i.e. give a feeling of intense irritation and revulsion: RN: mid-C.20. Perhaps cf. **piache.** (P.B.)

pie and mash. A urination: r.s., on *slash*: later C.20. Hillman, 1974, 'An alternative to **Frazer-Nash** [q.v.], and a culinary delight for East Enders.' *Mash* = mashed potatoes.

pie and one. Son: r.s. 'Seldom heard, and probably applicable also to "sun" ' (Franklyn 2nd).

pie-ard. A term of abuse in the Army: late C.19–20. Ex Hindustani for a pariah dog. The RAF used the term, ca. 1920-45, for 'any dog' (Jackson), and the Army, WW2 and after, esp. in Middle and Far East used *pie dog* of any desert or pariah dog. Y. & B. note its use in this sense, and spell it *pye*.

pie at (or **on**), **be.** To be very good at (something): NZ and Aus. (B., 1941.) *Pie on* is prob. ex Maori *pai ana*.

pie-can. A fool; a half-wit: lower classes':—1923 (Manchon).

pie-eater. 'Someone of no importance' (B., 1959): Aus. Wilkes notes variants *pie-biter* and *pie-cruncher*. P.B.: ?ex the simile (*as*) *Australian as meat-pie*, whence 'Everyman'.

pie-eyed. Tipsy: adopted, ca. 1943, ex US, where it derives ex Standard American *pie-eyed*, having the eyes *pied*, i.e., disordered, unable to focus.

pie-face. Another version of *pie-eater.*

piece. A half-crown; gen. *two pieces*, 5s, or *three pieces*, 7s 6d: racing c.: earlier C.20. Abbr. *half-crown piece.*—2. In *on piece*, very much; very quickly: Services', other ranks': earlier 1930s. A man buying many drinks within a very short space of time is said to *get them in on piece.*—3. Container, a dose, of drugs: drugs c. (Stockley, 1986.) US since—1936 (Spears).—4. An unofficial mural: 'Cans of spray paint to do pieces (graffiti)' (Notting Hill, London, child quoted in *Guardian*, 22 May 1988).

-piece. 'As a suffix, e.g. in *arsepiece* and *crutchpiece*, applied to those portions of the anatomy: "Lovely little arsepiece on her, hasn't she!" or, as superfluous explanation by one indelicately scratching himself, "Itch in the crutchpiece!" ' (P.B., 1974): prob. mainly Services', perhaps orig. RN (see quot'n at **chuff-piece**): since ca. 1950.

piece of ass or **tail.** Woman viewed as sex object; coïtion: Can., ex US: since mid-C.20. (Leech, 1985.)

piece of cake, a. 'A thing that is easy to handle or an unmistakable opportunity' (H. & P.): RAF: since ca. 1938. 'A cakewalk, a snip' (H. & P.): or rather, perhaps, something easy to take as a portion of cake. P.B.: the phrase dated rapidly after WW2, but was still current at the time of the Berlin air-lift, 1948, when a cartoon appeared depicting a Transport Command pilot saying, 'Oh, it's a piece of Gatow, old boy!' Gatow was one of the Berlin airfields vital to the supply operation.

piece of dough for the troops. A catamite: Forces': since ca. 1910.

piece of duff, a. An occ. var. of the prec. Jackson, 1943.

piece of homework (or **of knitting**). See **homework** and **knitting.**

piece of nice. An attractive girl: RN and RAF: 1940+. (Granville; Partridge, 1945.) H.W., 1942, on RAF s., notes 'corrupted latterly to any pleasant entertainment'.

piece of piss. A 'piece of cake' (as above): RAF: 1940+. So often it turned out to be not quite so easy, not quite so pleasant as the 'It'll be a piece of cake' had led one to expect. P.B.: in later C.20, common also in the army, and applied always to something considered very easy, often contemptuously. Later, much more gen. (Hibbert, 1983).

piece of resistance (not *pièce de résistance*). Constipation: Aus.: since ca. 1930. (B., 1942.) A pun!

piece of stray. A chance complaisant woman; a married man's mistress: mostly Forces': 1939+.

piece of tail. See **piece of ass.**

piece of toffee. A 'toff': c. and low s.: since ca. 1920. Blake, 1954.

piece of work. A person: from ca. 1920. Always pej.: nearly always prec. by *nasty* ('X is a nasty piece of work'); the ref. is either to moral character or to physical appearance, esp. looks, the latter often with an ethical implication.

piece up. As in 'pieced up with her husband', broken up, finished with him: Leicestershire, perhaps dial. (Pylypiac, 1984.) Contrast dial. *piece it up*, to become reconciled.

pieces. In *do* (one's) *pieces*, to go mad: Army: ca. 1925–50. Cf. *do* (one's) *nut, crunch, tank*, etc.—2. Also in *do* (one's) *pieces*, to lose money by betting: racecourse: since ca. 1925. Betts, 1967.—3. As *the pieces*, the ship's guns: RN officers' coll. (Granville). The coll. revival of an S.E. term long obsolete, as in 'pieces of ordnance'.

pier-head jump. To *do a . . .* is 'To join a ship at the last moment' (Bowen): nautical: since early C.20. Hence a *pier-head jumper*, one who does this, and the use, in the RN, since ca. 1918, of *pier-head jump* as a term for a wholly unexpected draft-chit (P-G-R). Cf. **crash-draft.**

Piffie(-y) on a rock-bun, (sitting there like). Incongruous, useless, intrusive: prob. Lancashire: from earlier C.20. (Pinder, 1984.) Cf. synon. *standing round like a lost lemon.*

piffing. Sub-calibre firing: artillerymen's coll.: from ca. 1925. Also naval gunners', gen. as *pfiffing*: Bowen.

piffling. Trivial; feebly foolish; twaddling: s. >, ca. 1925, S.E.

pig, n. A policeman, a detective; esp. (also *grunter*) a police-runner: c. of ca. 1810–90. Vaux; H., who, in 1873, writes, 'Now almost exclusively applied by London thieves to a plain-clothes man, or a "nose".' The first two meanings, after going underground for two generations, were actively revived, throughout the British Commonwealth, by the 'counter-culture' and prob. influenced by US usage, ca. 1960, and applied even to prison guards and other law-enforcing men. See also **cozzer.**—2. A chancre: c. *Gilt Kid*, 1936.—3. An elephant: circus. Seago, 1934.—4. A naval officer or Petty Officer: see **pigs aft.** As an Other Ranks' term for an officer, *pig* was also used by the R Aus. AF in WW2.—5. A rugby football: Aus. rugby footballers'. (B., 1942.) Ex pigskin casing.—6. A prostitute: low Can.: since ca. 1930. Moore, 1960.—7. A girl; a young woman: beatniks': late 1950s+. (Anderson.)—8. A Humber 10-ton armoured personnel-carrier: Army, esp. in N. Ireland: since ca. 1969. (P.B.)—9. As *the Pig*, The Blue Boar Hotel, Trinity Street, Cambridge: University of Cambridge, mostly undergraduates'. (Wharton, 1966.)—10. In *go at it like a pig at a tater* (i.e. potato), to act 'like a bull in a china shop': late C.19–20; orig., Black Country dial.; by 1930, a gen. Midlands coll. (Richard Merry.)—11. A barrage balloon. See **pigs are up.**—12. See **flying pig.**

pig, v.t. To damage or spoil completely: tailors'. To treat as a pig would.

pig and roast. Toast (bread): Army r.s.: ca. 1939–45. Franklyn.

Pig and Whistle, the. A ship's canteen; the crew's, entertainers' recreation room and bar on passenger line: nautical. Ex popular name for esp. country or working-men's pub.

pig-fucker or, when there's company, *the P.F. man.* That man who, in a lumber camp, looks after the tools: Can. lumbermen's.

pig-ignorant. Very ignorant, esp. of social usage: coll.: since ca. 1945. Occ., joc., *pig-iggers.* Perhaps orig. Cockney: cf. **pig-sick.** (P.B.)

pig in the middle. See **piggy in the middle.**

pig in the wall. See **course a-grunt.**

pig in with. To share a home, esp. lower-middle-class deprecation of offer of temporary lodging: early C.20. (L.A., 1974.)

pig-mill. A canteen: industrial Aus.: since ca. 1920. Niland, 1958.

pig-on-bacon. A bill drawn on a branch firm not gen. known to be such: commercial: from not later than 1920. (*OED* Sup.) Its two signatures are therefore worth, or equivalent to, only one. A var. of much older financial s. > j., *pig on pork.*

pig-party. Copulation with the same girl by several males in succession: teenage gangsters' and mentally retardeds'. (*New Society,* 2 July 1963.) Cf. **gang-bang,** and **pig,** n., 6 and 7.

pig shearing time. Never: railwaymen's. McKenna.

pig-sick. Extremely irritated; annoyed and disgusted; esp., e.g., 'He makes me pig-sick the way he keeps on . . . ': mainly Londoners'. Cf. **pig-ignorant** for use of *pig* as intensive. Also *pig-sick of* (someone or -thing); an intensification of older *sick* in this sense.

pig-stick. ' "A high-powered disrupter, a standard weapon for use against devices." Bombs are never bombs, always devices' (*New Society,* 24 Apr. 1980): Army bomb-disposal experts', esp. in N. Ireland.

pig-sticking. Sodomy: low Can.: since ca. 1920.

pig-sty. RN lowerdeck term for the wardroom: since ca. 1914. See **pigs aft,** and cf. Aus. Services' use of *snake-pit* in this sense, for an officers' or NCOs' mess.—2. A stye: Aus. joc. (Park, 1950.) 'No longer jocular. It has become a solecism' (B.P., mid-1963).

pig trough. 'Defensive weapon used in merchant ships against low-flying aircraft or surface raiders; from the appearance of this secret device' (Granville): WW2.

pigeon. In 1941–2, an airman was occ., in the RAF, called *pigeon.*—2. 'A Naval nuisance and trouble-maker' (Granville): RN.

pigeon-gremlin. See GREMLINS, in Appx.

pigeon on. To drop (something) on to a person from above: Aus. B., 1942.

pigeon pair. (Human) feet of exactly the same size: shoemakers'. Perhaps j. rather than s. (L.A., 1976.) The phrase is used also of family comprising a girl and a boy.

pigeon post. 'Used facetiously for Air Mail, mostly among postal workers' (Petch, 1974): later C.20.

piggery. A room in which one does just as one wishes and which is rarely cleaned: coll. Prob. suggested by S.E. *snuggery.*

piggie. See **piggy.**

piggie turn. 'The "piggie turn" is a 360 degree wing over turn' (*Sunday Times* mag., 25 Nov. 1979): RN helicopter pilots': late 1970s.

piggies. The oppressors—anyone from bigots to racists, fascists, the police: among teenagers and their mental, moral,

cultural equivalents in their twenties: since ca. 1965. Janssen cites the song 'Piggies' in the Beatles' 'White Album', released Nov. 1968. A derivative ex **pig,** n., 1.

piggy. Pick-a-back: children's. Short for *piggy-back,* pick-a-back.—2. A rating detailed to keep tidy a Petty Officers' mess; a messman: RN lowerdeck: since ca. 1910. Mostly as a nickname. (P-G-R.) Cf. **peggy,** 1–2.

piggy-back. 'The art of tapping communication lines used by legitimate users and then using their passwords to break into their computers' (*Telegraph Sunday Mag.,* 10 June 1986): electronic fraudsters' c.

piggybacker. One who avoids paying income tax by working 'under an assumed name or for cash while still collecting unemployment or supplementary benefit' (*Telegraph Sunday Mag.,* 17 Apr. 1988): in the struggle between the Inland Revenue Service and the 'Black Economy'.

piggy bank. One's 'nest egg' or savings: joc. coll.: since ca. 1930. Often, in later C.20, as in, e.g., 'That's a bit steep! I shall have to raid the piggy bank for that!' Ex children's moneybox in this traditional shape. (P.B.)

piggy (occ. **pig**) **in the middle.** A person 'caught in the middle' of a dispute, yet obliged to make some decision: since ca. 1960. (*The Times,* 1 and 27 Sep. 1977.) Ex the game played by three in a line, in which the middle one has to intercept a ball tossed between the players on each end.

pig's bastard. A person, usu. male, much disliked; a particularly unpleasant task or thing: low coll.: since the 1930s. 'He's a right pig's bastard, that one!' Also *pig's orphan*—as a euphemism! (P.B.)

pig's ear. A 'side light colour signal' (*Railway,* 2nd): railwaymen's.—2. In *make a pig's ear,* to blunder: mostly middleclass: since ca. 1945. Hargreaves, 1954, ' "I've made a real pig's ear of it, haven't I?" said Basil, with an attempt at lightness.' (L.A., who suggests poss. r.s. on *smear.* More prob. a euph. for *pig's arse.*)—3. In *never in a pig's ear,* never: r.s., on *year:* later C.20. Powis.

pig's fry. To try: r.s. Bracey, 1934.

pig's meat. Officers' wives—or mistresses: RN lowerdeck: since ca. 1930. (Peppitt.) See **pigs aft.**—2. Hence, 'a Wren who will go out only with officers and who is constantly dated by them' (Wood, 1978): WRNS: since ca. 1950.

pig's orphan. An unpleasant, disagreeable fellow: RN: since late 1940s. (Peppitt.) See also **pig's bastard.**

pigs. Beer: elliptical for C.19 r.s. *pig's ear,* beer. (P.P., 1932.) 'Nah, not a pint of pig's' (Tommy Steele, the famous comedian, as reported in *Cinema* early in Dec. 1967).—2. Small potatoes: farmers'. P.B.: also small and worthless tomatoes: gardeners', Sussex: earlier C.20.—3. Rugby League Football forwards: Aus. sporting: since ca. 1930. Buzo, 1971.—4. Elliptical, ex **pig's ear,** 2, q.v. 'Mistakes, mess, hash—to make a pigs' (*Fighter Pilot,* 1981): RAF: later C.20.

pigs! A derisive or contemptuous exclam.: Aus.: since ca. 1930. (B., 1943.) But prob. earlier: witness Lindsay, 1933, 'Pigs to your old man.' Wilkes, 'Abbr. *in a pig's arse*'.

pigs aft. The officers regarded as drinking in the Wardroom: lower-deckese: since ca. 1910. (Harling, 1946.) In sing., usu. reduced to **pig** (see also **pig,** n., 4). Also as *Naval pigs* (officers) and *small pigs* (petty officers): lowerdeck. P-G-R.

pigs are up. 'The barrage balloons are up' (H. & P.): Services': WW2. Ex the shape, and wallowing motion.

pigs in shit; e.g., *as comfortable as . . .* The utmost comfort, utterly comfortable: low coll.: esp. in the Services: late C.19–20. P.B.: cf. the, in later C.20, more common *as happy as pigs* (or *a pig*) *in shit:* both phrases sometimes euphemised as *pigs in clover.*

pike. To indulge in sharp practice; to cheat: see **piking.** Some Brit. use since mid-C.20.

piker. A man that habitually takes more than his share: low: adopted, ca. 1931, ex US.—2. One who ventures but timidly: Can. (ex US) since ca. 1930; also Aus. (B.P., who notes that it has 'killed sense 4').—3. Hence, a shirker: adopted, ca. 1943, ex US; also NZ (Slatter).—4. A confidence trickster:

Aus.: since ca. 1935. B., 1943.—5. 'A mean, contemptible person' (Culotta): Aus.: since ca. 1944.

piking. 'Sharp practice' (Culotta): Aus.: since late 1930s. Cf. **piker**, 1 and 4, and **pike**.

pilchard. A foolish person; a 'twit': teenagers': 1983 (T. Williams).

pile, n. A large sum won: Glasgow coll.:—1934.

pile, v. See **pile into**.

pile-driver. In 'soccer', a low, fast shot keeping about a foot above the ground: sporting: from ca. 1920.

pile into. To climb; get (into a train): S.E. of a number of persons, but coll. when used of one person. Sayers, 1934, 'He found a train going to London, and he piled into it.' I.e. in a heap or mass.—2. To attack; of a single person, usu. unarmed, coll., as 'He piled into his tormentor with fists flying'; like sense 1, of a number of people, armed, or of, e.g. tanks and aircraft, informal S.E.: since mid-C.20 at latest. (P.B.)

pile-jump. See TIDDLYWINKS, in Appx.

pile on the coals. 'To accelerate rapidly, to open the throttle of car or aeroplane' (Sanders): since ca. 1950. Cf. **pour on . . .**

pile-up, n. A 'crash', orig. RAF, of aircraft: since ca. 1918. See next, esp. 2.—2. (Hence?), a crash involving several cyclists: racing cyclists' coll.: since late 1920s.—3. Hence, a motorway accident involving several cars: journalists' coll.: since ca. 1955; by 1965, fairly gen., and by 1970s informal S.E.

pile up, v.t. To run (a ship) ashore: nautical coll.: late C.19–20. Bowen.—2. Hence, to smash (a motor-car) in such a way that it buckles up into a *pile* or heap: motorists' coll.: from ca. 1915. In WW1, *pile up one's bus* was the airmen's phrase for 'to crash' (F. & G.).—3. Hence, as v.i., (of an aircraft) to crash land: RAF: since ca. 1930. The plane becomes a pile—a heap of useless material. Cf. **piled-in**.

pile up points. 'To curry favour. A person who draws attention to his [own] "excellent qualities" with a view to advancement is said to pile up points' (Granville): RN: since ca. 1925. Ex sport.

piled(-)in. (Of an aircraft) crashed: RAF: since ca. 1930; ob. by 1946. (Jackson.) Cf. **pile up**, v., 2 and 3.

pill. (Of a person) a bore: 1897, Maugham, 'Well, you are a pill!' P.B.: still extant, 1983, it is perhaps now thought of as much as a contraction of *pillock*, as being 'hard to swallow' or take.—2. A cigarette: Can.: early C.20. B. & P.—3. A 'shot' of dagga (i.e. marijuana, *Cannabis indica*): S. African c. *Cape Times*, 22 May 1946.—4. As *The Pill*, the Catholic periodical *The Tablet*: journalists', hence gen. use: since ca. 1945. (Petch, 1969.)—5. As *the pill* (or *pill*), esp. in *on the pill*, an oral contraceptive: coll.: since ca. 1960. But as Barry Prentice, a pharmacist, points out, 1974, 'there is no oral contraceptive in the form of a pill. They are tablets.'

Pill Avenue. Harley Street: taxi drivers' (*Weekly Telegraph*, 12 Sep. 1941). Later known as Pill Island (*Daily Telegraph*, 18 May 1948). See **pill-box**, 2.

pill bo'sun. A doctor: R Aus. N: since ca. 1910. Cf. *fang bo'sun*, a dentist.

pill-box. A revolver: rare. Woodward, 1929.—2. As *the Pill-Box*, Harley Street, where practise the top consultants in the medical profession: London taxi-drivers': from ca. 1910. (London *Evening News*, 20 Jan. 1936.) See **Pill Avenue**.

pill-builder. A doctor: nautical. (Bowen.) Cf. *pill-pusher*; contrast:–

pill-grinder. A pharmaceutical chemist. (Allingham, ca. 1947.) Cf. synon. **pill-roller**.

pill head. An amphetamine user: drugs c. (Stockley, 1986.) US since ca. 1965 (Spears).

Pill Island. See Pill Avenue.

pill opera. A play or film about life in hospitals: since ca. 1960. 'Television doctor, romantic Dr Kildare, [is the] grand exemplar' (L.A., 1976). Influenced by *soap opera*, q.v.

pill popper. 'One who uses drugs in pill form, usually barbiturates, amphetamines and tranquillisers' (Cutland, 1985): drugs c. Cf. **skin pop**.

pill-roller. A pharmaceutical chemist: lower classes'. *Gilt Kid*, 1936.

pillar box. A rocket-projector: RN: since ca. 1942. Ex the shape. P-G-R.

pilled-up(, get). (To get) 'stoned'—intoxicated—on drugs: drugs' world: since ca. 1965. *Groupie*, 1968.

pillers of society. Persistent black-ballers at club elections: Royal Yacht Club: since ca. 1920. (Peppitt, 1976.) Cf. C.19 s. *pill*, to reject by ballot; an obvious pun on the cliché *pillars of society*.

pil(l)icock, pil(l)cock, pillock. The penis: a vulgarism: C.14–18.—2. Hence an endearment, addressed to a boy: late C.16–17: a vulgarism.

pillionare. A female occupant of a 'peach-perch' or 'flapper-bracket': motorists'—1935. Ex *pillion + millionaire*.

pillock. 'Contemptuous expression for a man, esp. one who does not grasp manifest but unexpressed spirit of group' (L.A.,1976): low coll.: since ca. 1950, perhaps earlier. Among teenagers (and in more gen. use) simply 'an idiot, a foolish person' (McPheely, 1978).—2. See **pillicock**, and:-

pillocks; pillocky. 'He's talking pillocks' (nonsense) and 'Don't talk so pillocky' (so foolishly and nonsensically): Cockneys': late C.19–20. Blends of *pill(s)*, testicle(s), and its synon. *ballocks*, adj. *ballocky*. (Franklyn.)

pillow-biter. A male homosexual: 1979. Ephemeral, ex a contemporary scandal (Hibbert).

pills (up). To spoil, mess up, 'make a pig's ear of': teenagers': early 1980s. (James Williamson, 1982.) Var of synon. *balls up*.

pilot. 'The navigating officer of a man-of-war' (Bowen): RN. Also as a nickname, as in 'Taffrail': 'The first lieutenant . . . is "Jimmy the One": the gunnery and torpedo lieutenants, the "Gunnery Jack" and "Torpedo Jack" respectively, but, to their messmates in the wardroom, these three officers, with the officer borne for navigation duties, are usually "Number One", "Guns", "Torps", and "Pilot".'—2. A racing-car driver: sporting: later C.20. (*Time Out*, 9 May 1980.) Perhaps ex:—3. The driver of any heavy-load vehicle: hauliers' s.: since ca. 1945.

Pilot's Cockpit, the. The WAAF: RAF other ranks': later 1940s. A low pun.

Pils. (A drink of) Pilsener lager: since ca. 1925. (Le Carré, 1968.) In May 1978 an advertising slogan appeared, 'Keep (on) taking the Pils', a pun on the c.p. *Keep (on) taking the tablets*—with a poss. side-glance at **pill**, 5.

pimp, n. A police informer: Aus. low pej.: since 1930s. Wilkes quotes Herbert, 1938. Cf.:—2. A sneak, a tell-tale: Aus. and NZ (mostly juvenile) coll. B., 1942; E.P.

pimp, v. To 'tell tales': Aus. and NZ children's. (B., 1943; Park, 1955.) Cf. n., 2. Often in the form *pimp on* (B.P.), as is:—2. To inform the police or other authority: Aus. low: since ca. 1940. Wilkes quotes Casey, 1945; B., 1943 (Casey, *pimp on*; B., *pimp*).

pimp-stick. A cigarette: Can. low. (Niven.)

pimple. A hill: lower classes': from late 1890s. Hence also, as hauliers' s. for a steep hill (see HAULIERS', in Appx.), and as a shunting hump in railwaymen's s. (*Railway*, 2nd).—2. A gun-position cover 'just visible above the fuselage of a 'plane' (H. & P.): RAF: since ca. 1930.—3. A contemptible person: Marlborough College: since ca. 1930.—4. Syphilis: RN. By joc. meiosis.—5. 'Faeces incompletely contained (in indecent parody of "Comin' through the Rye" verse)' (L.A., 1974): since ca. 1930, perhaps earlier.

pimple and blotch. Whisky (strictly Scotch): r.s.

pimple on a bull's arse (or **a pig's bum**, etc., **like a**). Mainly rural comment applied to, e.g., a hat that appears to be far too small for the wearer's head: certainly C.20, prob. much older. (Haines, 1978.) The Cockney version is *a pimple on a tea-tray* (*Muvver*).

pimplie, -y. 'So who were the hits? Would you believe the adolescent pimplies, the two-tone punks, the ethnic minorities' (Daniells, on a street-photographer's main customers, 1980).

pimpsy. 'Far too easy, "the course was pimpsy" ' (*Sunday Express* supp., 11 Oct, 1982): Sloane Rangers', q.v.

pin. To make a 'dead set' at (a person): low Aus.: from ca. 1920. (Stead, 1934.) Ex S.E. *pin down.*—2. To coït with (a woman): low. Cf. *prick* = penis.

pin-head. See pinhead.

pin-money spoof. Vague, pointless amateurish writing: journalistic: since ca. 1910.

pin on. To justify an accusation against, or a suspicion of, someone; to 'make it stick': coll.: later C.20. As in 'I don't see how we can pin this one on him', or as in Noël Annan, *TLS*, 7 Dec. 1979, 'would not make a premature move against Philby [the 'Third Man' spy], until he could indisputably pin the goods on him.' Prob. ex the idea of pinning a medal, or, fig., a label, on someone. (P.B.)

pin position (or just **pin**). 'First cab on an authorised standing' (Powis): taxi-drivers'.

pin-splitter. A first-class golfer: sporting: from ca. 1925. Ex the pin bearing the flag.—2. Since ca. 1935, predominantly a golf-shot dead on the pin: golfers' coll.

pin-up, n. An attractive girl, or her likeness: coll.: adopted, 1944–5, ex US servicemen. Extended, ca. 1955, to a handsome male, similarly 'honoured' by teenage girls. Orig., ex the 'likeness' 'pinned-up' on barrack-room wall.

pin up, v. To sell (songs) in the street: lower classes':—1923. (Manchon). Ex affixing music sheets with drawing-pins.

pinard. Liquor; wine: Soho:—1935. Ex French Foreign Legion s. for cheap wine.

pineapple. The female pudend: L.A. recalls a 'yobs' chant' of ca. 1914: 'You can have it all/Up against the wall/—pineapple!'; †.—2. A male homosexual: raffish: since ca. 1960. (Thomas, 1972.) Perhaps a specialisation of the more gen. **fruit,** 1.—3. In *on the pineapple*, on parish relief: lower classes':—1935. Perhaps ex the famous Dole Pineapple Company of Hawaii (a correspondent in the *Observer*, 30 May 1971).—4. See **rough end of the pineapple.**—5. Clydeside r.s. for chapel (*New Society*, 15 Apr. 1982). Munro, 1985, notes that the stress falls on *apple.*—6. See:-

pineapple chunk. A bunk (to sleep in): merchant seamen's r.s. Often shortened to *pineapple.*

pineapple cut. A 'basin crop': Aus. (Baker.) Shaggy.

ping, n. An Asdic officer: RN wardroom name, and vocative: since ca. 1935. (Granville.) Echoic. *Asdic* is a particular type of hydrophonic device; the acronym = Anti-Submarine Detection Investigation Committee—which was set up between the two World Wars to study defence against submarines. —2. In *get a ping*, to receive a sound on the Asdic gear: RN coll. > j.: since ca. 1935. P-G-R.—3. As exclam., a synon. of **line**!, q.v., a tall story derided: RAF: WW2. Perhaps echoic of 'the line' being 'shot'. (P.B.)

ping, v. Perhaps mostly in the passive, as in 'I've been pinged for another committee' (i.e. nominated or detailed for, 'lumbered with', it): RN and RM officers': prob. since WW2. (*Globe & Laurel*, issue of July–Aug. 1977.) Prob. ex *ping on.* (P.B.)

ping jockey. 'An Asdic operator; on the analogy of *disc jockey*' (Granville): RN: since 1950s. See **ping,** n., 1.

ping on. 'Obtain an Asdic echo bearing on a submarine or submerged object' (Granville): RN: since later 1930s. See **ping,** n., 1.

pinger. An Asdic officer or rating: RN: since ca. 1936. See **ping,** n., 1.—2. Hence, as in 'They were originally "two pingers, a jungly and a crab" as Service slang describes antisubmarine, Commando and RAF pilots' (*Sunday Times* mag., 25 Nov. 1979).

pinhead. A simple fellow; a fool: Aus.: since ca. 1920. (B., 1942.) So small a head can contain but few brains.—2. A freak in a sideshow: circus s.:—1933 (Seago).—3. 'Fleet Air Arm personnel, as opposed to ship's company, in aircraft carriers' (Bassett, 1979): RN: WW2. Cf **Airy-Fairy** and

w.a.f.u., and contrast **fish-heads.**—4. Anyone with a very small head; esp., a very tall man with a head either really or apparently very small: since ca. 1945.

pink, n. 'Close-up shots of the open vagina used in hard-core pornography, either on film or in magazines' (Green, 1974): pornographers'. Cf. **flap shot** and **beaver,** n., 3.—2. In pl., Seconal: drugs c. (Stockley, 1986.) US since—1968 (Spears).

pink, adj. 'Bloody': euph.; esp. *the pink limit*:—1923 (Manchon); ob. by 1930. Cf. *ruddy.*—2. Mildly socialistic. Prompted by *red*, communistic. See **parlour pinks** and **pinko.**

pink-eye. An addict of 'pinkie', methylated spirits: Aus. Baker.

pink fit, have a. Intensive of *have a fit*, to be much perturbed or alarmed: since ca. 1935.

pink lint. Penniless: racing circles' r.s., on *skint*: since ca. 1920. Cf. *boracic.* Franklyn 2nd.

Pink Palace, the. The Leander Club; its headquarters: oarsmen's. Its colours are pink.

Pink Panther. 'Patrol *Landrover* [truck] painted in a dark pink desert camouflage finish' (Knight, 1984): SAS: later C.20.

pink tea. 'A more than usually formal tea-party' (Leechman): Can.: since ca. 1925. Leechman, 'Derisive'.

Pink 'Un, The. *The Sporting Times*: from 1880, says Ware, 'from the tint of the paper, and to distinguish it from the Brown 'un, Sportsman.'—2. *The Financial Times*, founded 1913: businessmen's. Also ex tint of the paper.

pinkers. A pink gin: RN officers': since ca. 1920. The 'OXFORD -ER(s)'.

pinkie, -y. Anything small; orig., and still, esp. the little finger: orig. Scots coll., mostly among children, C.19; in C.20, much more widespread. Lit., the little pink one. Leech, 'As in, "Come in, we'll do all your pinkies". I heard this at the Edmonton [Alberta] City Police Station on 27 Jan. [1986] in the section where fingerprinting for security clearance is done.' Can. Police joc., evidently: how many have Scottish forebears?—2. (Or *Pink*.) Inevitable nickname of any pink-eyed albino: late C.19–20. Gloag, 1962.—3. A white man or, less common, woman: black teenagers' in Britain: since late 1950s. *Observer*, 10 Sep. 1967, 'By the time they leave school, whites have become "pinky", "the grey man" or—less common—"Mr Charlie".' Powis notes 'Originally an expression for a light-coloured Negro . . . not used in polite company'.—4. Methylated spirits coloured with red wine—or with Condy's crystals: Aus. Russell, 1936.—5. Hence, an addict of methylated spirits: Aus.: since ca. 1925. B., 1943.—6. A lesbian: low: since ca. 1925. Kersh, 1938.—7. A new hand: London dockers': since ca. 1945. *New Statesman*, 31 Dec. 1965. Cf.:—8. 'In England a new recruit was called a nig-nog, but in Egypt all new arrivals were called "pinkies" ' (Johnson, 1973): Army: ca. 1948–55. Not yet sun-tanned. (P.B.)—9. In *ship's pinkie*, a ship's writer [i.e. clerk]: RN: later C.20. 'Possibly from pink forms' (Knight, 1984). Green, 1984, '*pink*. RN: secret, confidential; from the colour of the signal pads used for writing such messages'—a usage dating from WW1.

pinkler. Penis, esp of a boy and among boys: late C.19–20. (Naughton, 1966.) Perhaps a blend of *pintle + tickler.*

pinko, n. 'A person who holds wishy-washy feminist/left-wing/gay liberationist views; a *Guardian* reader' (Hibbert, 1983): opponents of such views. See **parlour pink**, and next, 2.

pinko, adj. Drunk on methylated spirits: Aus.: since ca. 1925. (B., 1943.) See **pinkie,** 4 and 5.—2. (Also as n.) (Someone) politically left wing: Public Schools', officers', etc.: since late 1940s. (Johnson, 1973.) Cf. **pink,** adj., 2, and prec.

pinky. See **pinkie.**

pinny. In *catch* (her) *under the pinny*, to coït with (a woman): low. *Pinny*, nursery form of pinafore since mid-C.19.

pint-sized. Applied to someone small-made and (very) short: coll.: since ca. 1920, if not earlier. (Petch, 1969; *COD*, 1976.) Cf. US synon. *half-pint.*

pinta (pron. with *i* long). A pint of milk: since ca. 1962. Ex the slogan *Drinka pinta milka day*. Semantically and phonetically cf. *cuppa*, a cup of tea.

pip. A star on the tunic, or jacket, sleeve or epaulet of a junior officer, army; senior police officer. F. & G., ' "He is putting up three pips"; he is now a captain'; Turner, 1982, ref. to a TV police drama, 'What do you mean, they wouldn't bring you a coffee? You've got the pips up!' Cf. **pipper**, 2.

pip in. 'To clock in, to synchronise the time in an aircraft while in flight with the time at base in order that the navigational position may be fixed by radio' (Jackson): RAF: 1936+.

pip off. To die: mid-1930s. Ex the *pip-pip* of the radio (E.P.).

pip-squeak. An insignificant person or object: 1910 (E.V. Lucas: *OED*). Among the WW1 Army other ranks it had the nuance of 'second lieutenant'—very common in the war novels and memoirs concerning that period. Echoic, but for latter nuance, cf. **pip**, n. Also as adj., as in 'pip-squeak little twit'.—2. Hence, a toady: Aus.: since ca. 1919. B., 1942.—3. A two-stroke motorcycle or moped (*motor-assisted ped*al cycle): motorists' and motorcyclists' derisive: the first from ca. 1923 (*OED* Sup.); the second since mid-C.20 (Dunford). Both ex sense 1 and echoic.—4. RAF aircrews' coll. for a particular direction-finding device: see PIP-SQUEAK, in Appx.

Pip, Squeak and Wilfred. The medals (or medal ribbons), 1914–15 Star, War Medal, Victory Medal: Services': since 1920. Ex the three eponymous characters of the children's strip cartoon created by Bertram Lamb and A.B. Payne for the *Daily Mirror*: Pip, a dog; Squeak, a female penguin; Wilfred, a baby rabbit. The three appeared in many adventures between 7 Feb. 1920 and 14 June 1940; a post-WW2 revival never really caught on. The background from *The World Encyclopedia of Comics*, ed. Maurice Horn, 1976; see also **gugnunc**. (P.B.)—2. 'The naval gun units known as Pip, Squeak, and Wilfred are being increasingly used in co-operation with the Army against the Arab rebels [in Palestine]. Pip is a two-pounder, Squeak is a three-pounder, and Wilfred is a searchlight. All are mounted on open lorries' (London *Evening News*, 2 Oct. 1936). By 1936 the three names were an inevitable nickname for any set of three; cf. the 'Shake, Rattle, and Roll' of the three tanks at Port Said twenty years later (P.B.).

pipe, n. In the rude retort **up your pipe**, q.v., always to a male, it is usu. apprehended as 'the rectum'.—2. A telephone: hauliers' s.: since ca. 1925. Cf **blower**.—3. As *the Pipe*, the Underground: London taxi-drivers': since ca. 1930. Cf. the earlier *the Rattler*.—4. In *it's a pipe*, it's a certainty: filmland: adopted, ca. 1925, ex US. McCabe, 1937. 'Perhaps contraction of "lead-pipe cinch" = dead certainty, but possibly derived rather from *pipe-dream*—orig., from the opium pipe, which makes all things seem easy' (R.C., 1966).—5. Daily information broadcast through the public address system to a ship's company; as 'the men were informed over the pipe that . . .': RN: later C.20. Cf. sense 2, the v., and the *piped muzak* of superstores and other public places. (Raab, 1983.)

pipe, v. To speak too loudly: (lowerdeck) coll. 'All right, Jack, don't pipe it. We can hear.' Ex the bosun's piping the routine calls.—2. To look at: Can. (ex US): since ca. 1930. A thinning of earlier c. sense, to watch, spy on.

pipe off. To sound or pump (a person): low:—1923 (Manchon).

pipe-spoiler. A plumber: RN lowerdeck. (P-G-R.) Cf. *grub-spoiler*, a cook.

piped up, be or **get.** To be, or become, tipsy: since ca. 1925. Holt, 1936.

pipeline. An aerial: RAF: 1939+.—2. See **in the pipeline**.

piper. 'Term used by [London] dockers for a man who was not rated or a man who was not pulling his weight' (Ash): mid-C.20.

Pipey. A pet-name for a small boy: late C.19—mid-20. 'Ex distinctive feature' (L.A., 1976).

pipped. Annoyed: s. > coll. An early occurrence: ' "How's Leverton?"—"Rather pipped, thank you," replied Miss Disney' (Lyons, 1914). Cf. **pippish**.

pipped on (or **at**) **the post, be.** To fail or be circumvented after having been within reach of success or victory or one's goal: sporting (ca. 1892) >, by 1920, gen. (*Daily Telegraph*, 16 Apr. 1937.) Also occ. *pipped on the tape*, as in Wodehouse, 1924.

pipper. Something, esp. a play, that turns out to be very successful: theatrical: since ca. 1930. Berkeley, 1937.—2. A suffix, as in *one-pipper*, a second, *two-pipper* a first or full lieutenant: Army: since early WW1. Ex **pip**, n.

pippish. Disgruntled; depressed: Cockney: early C.20. (Pugh.) Cf. **pipped**.

pippy. Aus. var. of **pipped**: since ca. 1925. B., 1942.

pipsqueak. See **pip-squeak**.

pipy. See **Pipey**.

pirate (also v.). A man that picks up casual feminine company; *on the pirate*, watchful for such company: Aus.: since ca. 1925. Baker.—2. (Gen. pl.) 'Motorised traffic police, in cars and on motorcycles; also unlicensed cab drivers' (Powis): later C.20.

Piscie. A member of the E*pisc*opalian Church: Scottish Public Schools'. (Miller, 1935.) A var. of **Piskey**.

pish. Whisky; any spirituous liquor: military: earlier C.20. (F. & G.) Origin obscure: possibly the word derives ex *piss* (the effect) on *whisky*.

Piskey or **Pisky.** Episcopalian: Scottish: (?mid-C.19)—20. Cf. **Piscie**.

piso. A miserly or stingy fellow: Army: late C.19–early 20. (F. & G.) Still in use among RM (*Mail on Sunday*, 8 Nov. 1987). Cf. the † Northern dial. *pesant*, 'a stern, hard-hearted miser' (*EDD*); cf. also older synon. *picey*, adj. ex *pice*, the smallest Indian coin.

piss. Urine: late M.E.+: S.E., but in C.19–20 a vulgarism; it has, since ca. 1960, been regaining very fair respectability. Ex the v. Hence, *do* or *have a piss*, to make water: low coll.: C.20.—2. Any drink of poor quality: since ca. 1920.—3. Beer: (low) Aus.: since ca. 1925. (B.P.)—4. In *on the piss*, drinking alcoholic liquor, usu. as in 'he's always on the piss, that bloke': low. Hence *go on the piss*, to start drinking heavily; *go out on the piss*, to go out for, e.g. an evening's or a night's hard drinking: low: since ca. 1910.—5. See **piece of piss**; **take the piss**.

piss about or **around.** To potter; fritter one's time away; to stall for time: low.—2. V.t. To befool (someone); mess about with; to boss: low: since ca. 1950. Craig, 1976.

piss and wind. Empty talk; unsubstantiated boast(s): low coll. He can urinate, not defecate. P.B.: in later C.20, usu. 'wind and piss'. Cf. **piss-artist**.

piss-ant around. 'To waste time, dawdle, "mess about" ' (B., 1959): Aus. 'For God's sake, stop piss-anting around!' Wilkes spells it *pissant*. Cf.:-

piss-arse about. To fool about, waste time: Army: since ca. 1920. (P-G-R.) An intensification of **piss about**, 1. Cf. **piss-ball about**.

piss-artist. A habitual drinker: low coll.: since late 1940s. (Parsons, 1973.) Cf. **piss-head**.—2. A pretentious, usu. pompous poseur who is incompetent, but full of 'promises'; the person is usu. perfectly sober!: coll.: later C.20. Cf. **piss and wind**. (E. Donaldson.)

piss-ball. A query to be answered: lower grades (male) of Civil Service: since ca. 1945. A 'stinker'.

piss-ball about. To act in a futile or an irritating manner: low: since ca. 1920. Cf. **piss-arse about**.

piss (broken) glass. 'Descriptive phrase referring to gonorrhœa or any other urinary infection. Also to anything particularly unpleasant. A boring conversation, possibly, or an unexpected disappointment in a sexual encounter' (Powis): low: later C.20.

piss-cutter. See **piss-warmer**.

piss-flaps. 'Labia minora. In common use, e.g. ' "Her trousers are so tight, you can see her piss-flaps" ' (Turner, 1986): low. Cf. **flap shot**.

piss hard-on, a. A matutinal erection caused by the desire, and need, to urinate; Can. low. Cf. *piss-proud*.

piss-head. A habitually heavy drinker; an alcoholic: perhaps orig. NZ, earlier C.20, > by ca. 1955, also Brit. low. Cf. **piss-artist** and, in form, **shit-head** and *acid-head*.

piss-hole (or solid), n. A urinal: low, mostly Cockneys' and Services'. Norman; P.B.

piss-hole (or solid), adj. Bad; rubbishy, e.g. of an entertainment or sporting performance: low: since (?)ca. 1945. (P.B.)

piss-hole bandit. 'A homosexual who importunes in lavatories' (Powis): police s.: later C.20.

piss in (someone's) **chips.** To put an end to his hopes or plans: low; esp in RAF: since ca. 1925; ob. by ca. 1950. Ex woodchips used as kindling. P.B.: or, as prob., potato chips; cf. **muck** (someone's) **orange.**

piss in (someone's) **pocket.** To ingratiate oneself with him: (low) Aus.: since ca. 1920. (B.P.) 'I'm not pissin' in ya pocket, mate, but ya done quite a good job there!' (as I might thank B.P., on E.P.'s behalf, for all the former's contributions to this *Dict*. P.B.)—2. Hence, 'To be in close liaison with someone' (McNeil): low Aus.: later C.20.

piss it up the wall. The C.20 allusive version of:-

piss money against the wall. To squander, waste, money, esp. in liquor: late C15–19: S.E. until C.18, then (low) coll. Grose; Baumann.

piss off, v.i. To depart, esp. to depart quickly (often as an imperative: *piss off!*, go away!): low: late C.19–20. Cf. **p.o.q.**—2. V.t. To irritate, annoy, often with connotation of either malaise or disgust: since late 1940s. Scaduto, 1974, 'And it pisses me off when Mick does that'. Hence **pissed off**, q.v.

piss on (one's) **props.** To leave the stage for ever: pej. theatrical:—1935.

piss out of. See **take the piss** . . .

piss-poor. Penniless: low: since ca. 1925.—2. Hence, (of the weather) abominable: RAF aircrews': 1939+. Here, *piss* is a mere pej. adverb.—3. Hence, and quite soon, gen. Services' coll. to describe anything bad, feeble, ineffective, disgusting, etc.: still current 1975. (P.B.) Cf. **piss-hole,** adj.

piss-pot. A drunkard: Aus.: since ca. 1920. (Buzo, 1973.) Cf. **piss-tank.**

piss-pot juggler. Chambermaid in hotel: Can.

piss-pots. In, e.g. 'He's got piss-pots full of money', he is indeed wealthy: Can.: since early C.20, poss. earlier. (Leech, 1986.)

piss-pottical. Ludicrous; stupid; 'daft', as of ideas: East Midlands' coll. (Clarke, 1980.)

piss-quick. (Also adj.) A term of contempt: Army: WW2 and after. Implying incontinence. (Raper, 1973.)

piss (one)**self laughing.** See **pee** (one)**self** . . .

piss-taking. Mockery: answers to **take the piss**, q.v.: low: since ca. 1930. Crookston, 1967.

piss-tank A drunkard: low: since early C.20. (F. Leech, 1972.)

piss through (something). To do something with ease, usu. a test of any sort; e.g. 'Oh, he's a clever bastard all right—he just pissed through his finals': low coll.: since ca. 1910. Cf. **a piece of piss**, something very easy to do.

piss-up. A drinking-bout: low. Hence (he) *couldn't organise a piss-up in a brewery*, of an ineffectual administrator.

piss up a rope! go. Go away!; stop bothering me: W. Can.: since mid-C.20. (Leech, 1986.)

piss (or **pee**)**-warmer.** A highly complimentary term for anything cordially approved: Can. Also *piss-cutter*, adopted in R. Can. N (—1952), ex US (R.C., for the source).

pissed (earlier, also **pissed-up**). (Very) drunk: low, and Services'. Many of the older similes for (*as*) *drunk as* . . . may, in C.20, have *pissed* substituted for *drunk*; a few of the common intensives are (*as*) *pissed as a fiddler's bitch*; . . . *as arseholes*; . . . *as a coot*; . . . *as a cunt*; . . . *as a newt* (perhaps the most widespread, certainly since mid-C.20); . . . *as a parrot* (Aus.: mid-1960s: Slater); . . . *as a piard* (RAF in Iraq: 1920–45: L.A.); . . . *as a rat* (Daniells, 1980).—2. Angry; furious: late 1960s–early 70s. (Stuart, 1971.) Short for:-

pissed off. Disgruntled, 'fed up'; very much displeased (*with* someone or something): since late 1940s, Services'; in 1970s very common among students. See **piss off**, 2. (P.B.)

pisser. The penis; the female pudend: low s. or coll.: C.19–20.—2. A day of heavy rain: low, esp. Cockneys': since ca. 1920. Ex the low *it's pissing down*, raining heavily, itself of late C.19–20. 'Cf. the Fr. coll. "Il pleut comme trente-six vaches qui pissent" '. (R.S.)—3. An electric pylon: since ca. 1930. (Crispin, 1977.) Phallically ex sense 1.—4. See **pull** (one's) **pisser**.

pisseroo. A ramp or a racket(?): since ca. 1955. Mitford, 1960.

pissing. A pej., as in 'I can't get the pissing car to move': low. Cf. **cowing;** *cunting*. (P.B.)

pissing to windward. Doing something stupid and futile: MN. (Mann, 1972.) A common var. is *pissing into the wind.*

pisso. A drunkard; loosely and often, any frequenter of public-house or hotel bars: low Aus.: since ca. 1930. (Dick, 1965.) Ex *pissed*, tipsy.

pissy. Drunken. Heavy drinking induces frequent urination. P.B.: but cf. also the senses of *piss* as alcoholic liquor.—2. Cocky; cheerfully or brashly confident: since ca. 1950. (F. Leech, 1972.) P.B.: cf. *all wind and piss*, and **piss-artist**, 2.

pissy-arsed. Prone to crapulous inebriation: low.

pissy pal. A public-house crony: mostly Cockney: late C.19–20. Ex their simultaneous use of the urinal for the discharge of their heavy cargo.—2. Hence, a bosom friend: Cockney commercial. Thus, 'Go and see if you can't get an order from old so-and-so, he's a pissy pal of yours.'

piston (occ. **pistons**). '*Piston*. The nickname for any Engineering Officer' (H. & P.): Services': since ca. 1920. —2. (Also *pistol-rod*.) Penis: engineers' and similars'.

piston broke. Drunk and penniless, a pun on *pissed and . . . ,* as in 'like my old car, piston broke': since ca. 1960. (P.B.)

piston job. See **blow job**, 2.

pit. A breast pocket; a fob: c.: from ca. 1810 (*Lex. Bal.*); extant in C.20 for 'inside coat-pocket' (Sharpe, 1938). Cf. **pit worker**.—2. One's bed: perhaps orig. RAF, soon spreading to RN and Army: since (?)ca. 1925. (Emanuel, 1945.) Cf. *flea-pit* in this sense; often in the form *the old pit*. 'Lazy bastard—spent all Sunday just resting in his pit!' (P.B.)

pit(-)worker. A pickpocket specialising in theft from victims' inside pockets: c.: since ca. 1930. (Moynahan, 1969.) Ex **pit**, 1.

pitch. A camp: Aus. (B., 1942.) Ex 'to pitch tents' or 'pitch camp'.—2. A plan; a 'game' or trick: Can.: since late 1940s. (Leechman.)—3. The crowd around a stall or in the auction room: see MOCK AUCTION, in Appx.

pitch a game for a gay. To arrange a crooked game of cards in order to rob an outsider: Aus. professional cardsharps': since ca. 1930. B., 1953.

pitch a woo. To commence a courtship: Services': ca. 1935–45. (H. & P.) W. & F. notes *pitch* (*the*) *woo* as US s.; 1937.

pitch and toss. The boss: Aus. gen. (B., 1945) and Eng. theatrical r.s. (Franklyn).

pitch fly. 'A person who uses another's street-selling position without permission' (Powis): later C.20. Since mid-C.19 *pitch* has = selling-place.

pitch on. To nag at, to abuse, to reprimand: Aus. (B., 1942.) A confusion or, perhaps a blend, of *pick on* and *pitch into* (a person).

pitchers. Pitch-black, very dark: since ca. 1920. By the 'OXFORD -ER(s)'. Marsh, 1968, of a night: 'It was awfully dark. Absolutely pitchers.'

pitching the plod. Greetings, talk between miners coming on and going off shift: Aus. (B., 1942.) See **plod**, 1.

pitiful object. 'Naval petty officer. A play on PO' (Granville).

pitmatic. 'The Doric or dialect of the Northern coal-mining counties' (Petch, 1969): ca. 1920–70.

pits, the. The very bottom, depths; the nadir: adopted, ex US, late 1970s. Perhaps ex arm*pits*. 'If [Diana] Dors is the very personification of the buxom backside of the other

Britain . . . then Joan Collins is the pits. Just the pits' (Carter, 1979).

pitter-patter, n. and v. An elab of *patter*, cheapjacks' oratory, s. since ca. 1780: v.t., as in 'You've got to pitter-patter the punters' (*M.T.*): market-traders'.

pivoter. A golfer that, in swinging his club, turns his body as on a pivot: golfers' coll.: from middle 1920s. *OED* Sup.

pix. Photographs, esp. for illustration or publicity: a written form, var. of pics, q.v.

pixie suit. The 1944-pattern overall for tank crew: Army: later WW2. (Knight, 1984.) Cf. **noddy suit** and **flower-power suit.**

pixilated; often **pixolated.** Tipsy: since ca. 1930. Perhaps a blend of '*pixy-le*d' and 'intoxic*ated*'. Cf. **impixlocated.** 'Came into general use with the release of the film "Mr Deedes Comes to Town" (ca. 1930); in which, however, it was used in the sense of "not right in the head" ' (H.R. Spencer).

pizz or, in full, **pizzicato.** Tipsy: since ca. 1930. (Marsh, 1935.) Pun on *pissed*.

place where you cough, the. The water-closet: coll.: since ca. 1920. Ex coughing to warn an approacher that it is occupied.

placer. A seller of stolen or forged ration coupons: 'Many times we could have picked up the "placers"—the men who actually sold the coupons—but this was no good to us' (Gosling, 1959): since ca. 1940: orig. c., but by 1945 also police s. Petch, 1969, 'By 1965, it had acquired the nuance, one who places stolen property, usually to fences.'

placky, plaggy. Plastic, esp. in *plaggy bag*: *placky* heard in Middlesbrough, early 1970s; *plaggy* in E. Midlands. A further var. is *plazzy*. (P.B.)

Plain and Gravy, the. The Navy: r.s.: late C.19–earlier 20. Var. of *Soup and Gravy*.

plain and jam. A tram: r.s.: earlier C.20. A ref. to suet roll.

plain Jane (and no nonsense). A woman who, esp. if plain-looking, is staid and capable and unassuming: coll.: late C.19–20.

plain-turkey. A professional 'bush' tramp, always on the move, rarely working, old-fashioned, secretive: Aus.: since ca. 1910. Niland, 1955.

plain-vanilla. Of conventionally organised transactions: financiers': later C.20. (Mann, 1984, who compares it with synon. sense given to *missionary position*, s. term for 'normal' copulation since mid-C.19). Elab. of **vanilla.**

planky. Dull-witted, stupid: evolved, ca. 1955, ex '(as) thick as two short planks': Services'; later, more widespread. (P.B.)

plant. (Of a horse) to stand, or remain, still: Aus. racing coll.: since ca. 1925. B., 1943.—2. To insert such an incident, etc., into a story as, although unnoticed at first reading, will eventually prove to influence the outcome: Can. authors' and free-lance journalists': since ca. 1945. (Leechman.)

plaster, n. A mortgage: Can.: from ca. 1920. Beames, 1932, 'We might put a plaster on the house'.—2. An account or bill: Aus.: since ca. 1930. Cusack, 1951.

plaster, v. Often as vbl n., *plastering*: to bomb from the air; bombing, a heavy raid: RAF: since 1918. 'Jerry is so annoyed about the plastering we've given him recently . . . ' (Michie, 1940).—2. To put (money) out on mortgage: NZ. (Mulgan, 1934.) Cf. **plaster,** n.

plastic, on the. 'Defrauding persons, banks and stores with false credit or bank cards' (Powis): c.: later C.20. Such cards are made of plastic. The use of *plastic* for credit cards soon > coll.: 'I never have problems in shops when I ask, "Do you accept plastic?"—even if I don't have a credit card in my hand' (Watts, 1988); and Howard, 1988, notes *plastic*, v., to use a credit card.

plastic. Artificial; ersatz; bogus: of people, 'plastic Teds' = those of the younger generation, late 1970s, aping the Teddy-boys of the early 1950s; of things, 'plastic milk' = powdered milk; 'a plastic smile' = one of patent insincerity: coll.: since ca. 1960, but in more gen. use in 1970s. Brit. before it became US. In, e.g., *Apple*. (E.P.; P.B.) See quot'n at **hippy.**

plat. A simpleton, fool, easy dupe: Aus.: since ca. 1925. (B., 1942.) Ex Fr. *plat* (adj.), 'flat'.

plate. To indulge in oral congress, both homo- and heterosexual: low s.: since mid-C.20. *Groupie*, 1968. Newman, 1972, and in *The Guvnor*, 1977, ' "You missed the best act, guv," Dyce shouted. "A pair of strippers; talk about form. They did everything, including plating each other".' Ex **plate of ham,** q.v.

plate of beef. Borstal r.s. for a Chief (Officer): since ca. 1920 (?earlier, the first institution—at Borstal in Kent—dating from 1902). *Daily Telegraph*, 4 June 1958.

plate of ham. often shortened to **plate.** A police term for *fellatio*: r.s., on *gam*(erouche).

plate(-)rack. A horse: r.s., on *hack*: late C.19–20. Strange, 1930.

plateful, have a; or, **have too much on** (one's) **plate.** To be desperately busy; hence, to feel 'browned off': Army: 1941+.

plates and dishes. Kisses: r.s. P.P., 1932.—2. Wife: r.s., on *missis(-us)*.

platinum blonde. A female with gold-grey hair: coll.: adopted ex US, by 1933. (*COD*, 1934 Sup.) Also as adj.

Plato to Nato(, from). 'Horribly prevalent among dimmer academics; used [as title] for a BBC programme on political thought (Radio 4) in 1984' (Parker, 1986). Cf. the academic c.p., *from Beowulf to Virginia Woolf*, the equivalent for 'Eng-Lit.'

plausy or **plauzy.** 'When a person is smooth-tongued, meek-looking, over civil, and deceitful, he is *plauzy*' (Joyce, 1910): Anglo-Irish: late C.19–20. Ex '*plausible*'.

plawt. A boot or shoe: market-traders': late C.19–20. (*M.T.*) Neither dial. nor Romany.

play, v.t. To tell (a 'mug') a story by which to get his money: c.: anglicised ex US, ca. 1910.—2. To stay unnecessarily away from work: workmen's.—3.V.i., to work in co-operation; to reciprocate; to agree: Services': since ca. 1930. (H. & P.) Short either for *play the game* (or *play fair*) or, more prob., for *play ball*.

play a hunch. To act on an intuitive idea: coll.: adopted, ca. 1945, ex US. Reyburn, 1962.

play about. To waste money.

play-actor. A humorous fellow: Glasgow coll.:—1934.

play-away. A weekend staying with someone else in the country: Sloane Rangers' [q.v.]: early 1980s. *Sunday Express* supp., 11 Oct. 1982.

play ball. To co-operate; to reciprocate; to be helpful: coll.: since ca. 1937. Ex children's ball-games.

play billy with. To play the deuce with: coll.: late C.19–earlier 20. Knox, 1933.

play chicken. Among children, esp. young teenagers, to take part in feats of daring; the most notorious and dangerous, perhaps, is trying to be the last across a road or railway, right in the path of an oncoming vehicle or train. The last to survive can then hurl the taunt 'Chicken!', q.v., at those who have gone before. Adopted, ex US, early 1950s. Michael Innes wrote a detective novel in 1956 titled *Appleby Plays Chicken*. See also **chicken out.** (P.B.)

play down. ' "I am *not* upper class . . . It's true I seldom 'play down'—but that's because I'm not a good enough actress. I'm not sure I could do a working-class woman" ' (Rigg, 1984): theatrical.

play cross-swords. (Of small boys) to stand side by side to urinate, so that the two streams cross half-way to the ground: coll.: late C.19–20. (P.B.)

play fathers and mothers, late C.19–20, coll.; **play mums and dads** or **dads and mums,** since late 1940s, s. To coït. The latter occurs in Gardner, 1967. P.B.: an adult perversion of children's game of make-believe, *playing mummies and daddies*.

play footie, -y. To play feet: (mainly lower) middle-class coll.: late C.19–20. Also *footies* or *footsie(s)*, or *footy-footy*.

play for lends. 'To gamble under agreement to return one's winnings; as opposed to playing for keeps, which is to gamble in earnest' (McNeil): Aus. coll.: later C.20.

play for time. To temporise: coll.: since early 1920s; by ca. 1945, familiar S.E. (du Maurier, 1938.) Ex such games as football and cricket.

play hard to get. (Usu. of girls) to resist amorous advances, all the while intending to acquiesce eventually: Can. (and US) coll., since ca. 1925; by 1945, also Eng. and Aus.—2. Hence, more gen. '(of person or group), to be difficult in complying with what is expected of them' (L.A.): coll.: later C.20.

play Harris. ' "Playing Harris," where the salesman says to the customer: "I have got Mr. Harris on the phone wanting to know if the car has been sold, shall I say yes?" ' (Guardian, 5 Apr. 1984): secondhand-car salesmen's 'prod'.

play it by ear (e.g. 'We'll just have to . . . '). To make adjustments as the changing circumstances demand; to cope with a situation as seems best to one: since late 1940s: s. >, by 1970, coll. (P.B.) Ex e.g. a pianist picking up a tune with no written music as guide.

play it close. See sense 2 of:–

play it close to (one's) **chest.** To hold one's cards close to one's chest so that nobody can see them: Can. (and US) poker-players' coll.: since ca. 1910.—2. Hence, to be secretive or 'cagey': Can. (and US) s.: since ca. 1925. (Leechman.) In later C.20, Brit., and sometimes shortened to *play it close*, as in Hunter, 1969. In 1977, he uses the var. *keep it close*.

play it cool. To take things calmly, or cautiously and moderately: coll.: since ca. 1955. Cf. **cool**, adj., 4.

play lighthouses. To have an erection in the bath: low coll.

play lively occurs mostly in the imperative. To 'get a move on', to bestir oneself: RN: since ca. 1925. Granville, 'See "Smack it about!" '

play long. A golf-course is said to 'play long' when, owing to heaviness of ground and/or air, one has to hit the ball much harder than usual: golfers' coll.: from ca. 1920. *The Times*, 30 Sep. 1936.

play pop (either absolute, or with **with**). To 'play the devil (with)'; to make a great fuss about something, because angry: (?mainly) N. Country coll. (P.B.)

play pussy. 'To take advantage of cloud cover, jumping from cloud to cloud to shadow a potential victim or avoid recognition' (H. & P.): RAF: since 1939 or early 1940. Cat-and-mouse.—2. From same origin, to keep someone in suspense, as in 'I turned [the captured terrorist] round and prodded him towards the bridge with the tip of my carbine. I was content now to play pussy and wait for him to unfold' (Moran, 1959).

play silly buggers. To 'mess about'; wilfully or not, to cause trouble, inconvenience; e.g. 'Well, why weren't proper arrangements been made?'—'I don't know. The people in charge here seem to have been playing silly buggers . . . ': Army: WW2 and since. (P.B.)

play smash (with). Var. of **play pop**.

play the game of dockets. To avoid giving a decision, or expressing a definite opinion, by passing on the matter to some other department: civil servants'. Cf. synon. **pass the buck**.

play the glim. To cheat at cards by using mirrors: Can. card-sharps': early C.20. Drage, 1954.

play the mouth-organ. To use a matchbox cover to 'chase the dragon', q.v.: drugs c. Stockley, 1986.

play the numbers game. A form of 'empire-building', q.v.; e.g., in a college, to get as many students as possible, regardless of their suitability, on to a given course, in order to obtain more funds: coll.: later C.20. (P.B.)

play the organ. To copulate: Aus. Prompted by the euph. *organ* (of reproduction), the penis.

play the piano. To have one's fingerprints taken: c.: from ca. 1910.—2. To release bombs from an aircraft, one by one or in irregular numbers at irregular intervals: RAF: 1939+. (Jackson.) Contrast **pull the plug**.

play tiddlywinks. To coït: partly euph., partly trivial.

play up. To be troublesome: coll.: late C.19–20. Of animals, esp. horses, and persons. P.B.: hence in C.20, of machines,

and also of illnesses, as 'My rheumatism plays up something rotten this weather'.—3. To make fun of, to annoy or tease: from early 1920s: coll. >, by 1933, S.E. (*OED* Sup.) Cf. **wind up**.

player. One who 'plays' a dupe: c.: from ca. 1931. See **play**, 1.—2. A person, esp. if female, ready for 'amorous dalliance': NZ: since ca. 1950. Griffiths, 1970, instances 'Why don't you take out that blonde? They say she's a player.' One who likes to 'play about'.

playground. A parade-ground: RAF: ca. 1925–45. Jackson.

playing, vbl n., and adj. (The) being on half- or part-time work: North Country, esp. Yorkshire: since ca. 1920. Cf. **laking** and **tromboning**. (Hillerby, 1950.)—2. 'Homosexual flirtation and involvement' (McConville, 1980): women prisoners': later C.20.

playing the harp. Drunk, and going home by the railings: Anglo-Irish. Ex the tapping on the railings, here likened to harp-strings.

plazzy bags. Plastic bags: coll.: since late 1960s. Var. *placky*, *plaggy*.

pleased as a dog with two choppers. Delighted: mostly lower-class: late C.19–20. (Baron, 1950.) P.B.: E.P. interpreted this as 'two tails', and so it may be used by the unaware; but cf. *chopper* = a penis, and L.A.'s var., noted 1974, *pleased as a dog with two cocks*—'delighted at quite improbable and unlikely good fortune'.

pleasure and pain. Rain: r.s. Franklyn.

pleasurer. A person, e.g. a journalist or other 'tourist', taken along for one trip on a trawler 'just for the ride': trawler-men's. (Piper, 1974.) I.e., one on a pleasure trip, as on a boat-trip round the harbour or lake.

pleb or **plebs.** At Westminster School, a tradesman's son: pej.: mid-C.19—earlier 20. Ex L. *plebs*, the proletariat.—2. (Only as *pleb*.) Any plebeian: 1823 ('Jon Bee'). Cf. US *plebe*, a newcomer at West Point. The term was still current in the 1980s, among middle- and upper-class schoolgirls and **Sloane Rangers**, q.v., for anyone they considered an *oik* or *oick*, another C.19 s. term for any lower-class cad or townee. (Anson, 1987.)

pleep. A German pilot that refuses combat: RAF: 1939+. (H. & P.) Ex echoic *pleep* as the sound made by, e.g., a frightened bird: cf. dial. *pleet*, a peevish cry.—2. A sleep: nursery, hence, adult joc.: Aus.: since late 1940s. (B.P.) A childish rendering of *sleep*.

plink. A shortened form, mostly Aus. (B., 1943) of:–

plink-plonk; plinkety-plonk; also **blink-blonk.** White wine: facetious military: 1915–18. (B. & P.) On Fr. *vin blanc*.

plob. 'Hourly log kept by pilots, recording weather conditions on their patrols. (Coastal Command.) From *patrol-log* observations?' (P-G-R): since ca. 1941.

plod. Story: Aus., esp. miners': since ca. 1930. Casey, 1945, ' "I suppose he told you the whole plod?" I sneered. "What plod?" Sadie wanted to know.' Wilkes, 'From *plod* a short or dull story; a lying tale. *EDD*'.—2. 'The piece of ground on which a miner is working; the work card relating to this: Western Aus.' (Wilkes): miners' coll. > j.—3. 'Two policemen hurled bricks . . . "It's the plods, chucking bricks," said a soul-boy, giggling in disbelief' (*New Society*, 16 July 1981, article on the recent riots in Brixton. Prob. ex P.C. Plod, in Enid Blyton's stories of Noddy the Elf. (P.B.) Hence also as adj. 'She was taken home in a plod car' (*Guardian*, 27 Feb. 1986).

plonk, n. Pinky, cheap port, sold by the quart: Aus. and NZ: from ca. 1926. Prob. ex **plink-plonk**, q.v.—2. Hence, any kind of wine of no matter what quality: Aus. and NZ, since ca. 1930; common also in Eng. since mid-C.20, gen. joc., and often as from a beer-drinker's point of view. The RN used the term for inferior brandy sold in Italy (Granville), and Anderson noted that beatniks were using it in the late 1950s for 'any cheap handy form of drink'. By 1975, gen. coll.—3. A woman. See quot'n at **scrote**.—4. A shortening of **plonker**, 2, penis.—5. See **A/C Plonk**.

P

plonk, v. To set, esp. in *plonk down*, to put, set, down, and *plonk out*, to set out—i.e. pay out, distribute—money: Aus. (B., 1942); also Brit. (orig. RN), since—1914 (Knock). Var. of *plank*, but also prob. echoic.—3. (Of the male) to coït: certainly current, esp. among National Servicemen, in 1950, and dating, I believe, since during WW2. Cf. the n., 4.

plonk bar. A wine bar: Aus.: since ca. 1935. Ex **plonk**, n., 2.

plonk-dot. 'A confirmed wine-bibber' (B., 1953): Aus.: since ca. 1945. Ex **plonk**, n., 2.

plonk down. See **plonk**, v., 1.

plonk up. 'To hurry up and drink' (Anderson); to drink copiously: beatniks': late 1950s+.

plonker. A (cannon) shell: Aus. Army: 1939+. Baker.—2. Penis: low: since ca. 1917. Esp. in *pull* (one's) *plonker*, to masturbate; often shortened to **plonk**.—3. A smacking kiss. Echoic (P.B.)—4. 'A single-cylinder 4-stroke motorcycle: contrast **phut-phut** [q.v.]. Usually a large capacity engine' (Dunford, 2). Cf. **thumper**.

plonkers. Feet: mostly Londoners' and esp. among policemen: since ca. 1920. (Henderson, 1968.) Ex *'plonking,* or *planking,* one's feet down'.

plonko. A drunkard addicted to **plonk** (n., 2): Aus.: since ca. 1950. (Dick.) Cf. **metho; pisso**.

plootered. Tipsy: Anglo-Irish: since ca. 1920. Ex Anglo-Irish *plouter*, to splash or wade in water or mire.

plot. 'Cardsharps' term for the venue in the street or on waste land where illegal gaming can and often does take place. A three-card trick cardsharp's pitch' (Powis).

ploy, 'ploy. To employ: dial. (late C.17–20) and, hence, coll., late C.19–20. As a n., it is used in the Public Schools for a task. P.B.: although it is, as a n., S.E., for hobby, trick, escapade, it has in later C.20 gen. carried a coll. flavour, esp. when used for a (sometimes slightly cheating) gambit in game, sport or human relations; this under the influence of Stephen Potter's 'gamesmanship', which is full of such 'ploys'.

pluck. To take out a part of one's winnings: Aus. two-up-players'. ' "You've got forty quid in the guts, Sailor," said Stan. "Want to pluck some?" ' (Glassop, 1949).

plue. Tea: RN. H. & P.; Granville, 'A cup of luscious plew.' Why? Perhaps a blend, *'pl*easant or (*pl*easing) brew'. Also used by Aus. seamen. Note *wet the plue*, to make tea. (P-G-R.) Var. spellings *plew, ploo, plu*.

plug, n. A piece of publicity, a 'boost': since ca. 1935. Ex 'to *plug*' or 'boost': since ca. 1930: orig., advertising. Perhaps ex *plug away at*, to persevere with. Cf. v., 1.—2. In *down the plug*, (of a tender) running short of water: railwaymen's: earlier C.20. (*Railway*, 2nd.) Short for . . . *plug-hole*.—3. See **pull the plug**.

plug, v. To try to popularise (a song) by dinning it into the public ear: coll.: 1927. *OED* Sup.—2. To throw (a cricket-ball): many schools'.

plug hat. A bowler hat: Aus. Baker.

plug-holed. Severely damaged, hence ruined, worthless: orig. RAF, from 1939; since ca. 1950, gen. low coll. (R.C., 1977.) Fit only to be flushed down the plug-hole (P.B.). Cf. **plug**, n. 2.

plug in. Fig., to 'switch on': jazz and drug addicts', and hippies': since ca. 1966 (Fryer, 1967). Ex **switched on**, q.v.

plug in both ways. (Of a male) to be both hetero- and homosexual: later C.20. (Kavanagh, 1980.) Cf. **AC-DC**.

plug mush. ' "Free for all" fight in the Merchant Navy. Literally, a "punch face" ' (Granville).

plug-ugly. Orig. a rowdy, a tough; hence applied to any brutal-looking, violent character, e.g. a gang-leader's bodyguard: low s. > coll.: adopted, ex US, ca. (?)1940.

plugged. (Of a bidder) silenced at once by a seller: Stock Exchange: from ca. 1919.

Pluggeries, the. The Light Repair Squadron attached to the Long Range Desert Group in N. Africa, 1942–3. A worthy unit of a fine formation. Their OC was Captain 'Plugs' Ashdown.

plugging. The interposition of advertisement 'gags' in 'turns' on the wireless: from 1933. (*Evening News*, 13 July 1934.) See **plug**, n., 1, and v., 1.

plum. 'The "plums" were red glass slides that were slid down behind the bullseye lens [of an engine lamp] to convert a white light to a red one' (McKenna, 2): railwaymen's.—2. See **plums**.

plum in the mouth. Used to describe an affected manner of speech that sounds so; either as adj. or simile: coll. (P.B.) Hence *plummy*, of a voice.

plum pud. Good: Aus. r.s. Hence, *any plum?*, (is it) any good? B., 1942.

plumb. A plumber: RN lowerdeck. P-G-R.

plumber. An armourer: RAF: since ca. 1925. (E.P., 1942.) Facetious.—2. *The Plumber* is the RAF's name (cf. coll. *Engines*) for an Engineering Officer: since ca. 1930. Jackson. Cf.:—3. 'Plumbers: Generic term for Engineroom staff' (Granville): RN: since ca. 1920.—4. Physicians' derogatory term for a surgeon: St Bartholomew's Hospital, London: mid-C.20. (Dr Ivor Beale, 1985.)

plumber's nightmare. 'A motorcycle with a mass of oil, petrol and exhaust pipes, e.g. a Vincent HRD' (Dunford, 2): motorcyclists'.

plumbing. 'The art of bugging telephones' (*Daily Telegraph*, 22 Feb. 1988): espionage. Adopted ex US, where the *plumbers* were those who 'plugged the leaks' during the Watergate scandal, 1971–2 (W. & F., 1975).

plumbum oscillans, n. and adj. 'Lead-swinging' (malingering or blatantly idling): 'Naval officers' jocular' (Parsons, 1973). Mock-Latin: *plumbum*, lead, the metal, hence a depth-sounding plummet + *oscillans*, present participle of *oscillare*, to swing.

plummy. Dull; stupid; too respectable: low Glasgow: from ca. 1920. (MacArthur.) Perhaps cf. Yorkshire *plum*, honest, straight-forward; prob. influenced by US *dumb*, slow.—2. See **plum in the mouth**.

plump (a person) **up to.** To inform him opportunely or secretly about (something): lower classes':—1923 (Manchon). Ex *plump*, to fatten.

plumper. One hundredweight: London dockers': earlier C.20. Ash.

plumping. Unusually or arrestingly large: coll.

plumpo. See **fly-balance**.

plums. A warship's engines: RN coll.: since ca. 1930. Granville.

plunder. One's equipment and personal belongings: Can.: since ca. 1905. 'O.K.—grab your plunder and come along!' (Leechman.) It prob. derives ex Ger. *Plunder*, lumber, junk, rags. (R.S., 1967.)

plunder-snatchers. See MOCK AUCTION SLANG, in Appx.

plunger. A hypodermic syringe: orig. medical: from ca. 1912. Holt, 1932.—2. ' "Plungers" is the name given to the men who clean the streets of the City [of London] with hoses and squeegees' (Jervis, 1925): London. They plunge about in the swirling waters.

plunk. To strike (someone): Aus.: since ca. 1918. B., 1942.

plunk a baby; get plunked; get trubied; get karitanied. To go into a maternity home and have one's baby there; hence, to become pregnant: NZ. B., 1941. The first (*plunked a baby*) refers to the Plunket Society, as obviously does the derivative second; the third refers to Sir Truby King, noted for sage advice upon, and sustenance for, the feeding of infants; the fourth comes ex Karitane Home.

plunk for. To plump for; support enthusiastically: coll.

plus-fours. Wide knickerbockers, orig. and esp. as worn by golfers: 1920: coll. till ca. 1925, then S.E. Ex *a plus* (e.g.) 2 *golfer*, or, more prob., ex the fact that, to get the overhang, the length is increased, on the average, by four inches. (*OED* Sup.; *COD*, 1934 Sup.)

plush. An over*plus* of grog: naval: prob. since ca. 1800.—2. Hence, a surplus of anything; 'perks': RN lowerdeck: *Mus-*

ings, 1912, a storekeeper speaking: 'Well, there ain't no chance of even makin' any rightful plush in nothin'.' Cf. **plushers.**—3. In *take plush*, to accept an inferior position or appointment: coll.: earlier C.20. (Manchon.) Perhaps ex the plush worn by footmen.

plush-bum (mostly in pl. and written *plushbums*). 'Rich folk' (*Arab*): Liverpool low: ca. 1890–1940.

plushers. Sur*plus* rum left over after the daily issue: RN lower-deck: late C.19–20. (Knock.) Granville, who uses var. *plussers*, notes 'Ironic, since the rum is poured away into the scuppers, in accordance with *Queen's Regulations*.' By the 'OXFORD (and RN) -ER(s)' on **plush**, 1. The custom of the daily issue ceased in early 1970s.

plute. A plutocrat: coll.: adopted, ex US, by 1930; † by 1940.

pneumatic bliss. See **shock-absorbers**.

pneumo. A pneumococcus: medical. Gen. in pl. (-*os*).—2. In *have a pneumo*, to have artificial-pneumothorax treatment (*have an A.P.*): coll.: TB patients': since ca. 1930.

pneumonia blouse. A girl's low-cut blouse: since ca. 1920.

Pneumonia Bridge. A certain bridge that, at Gosport, is exposed to all the winds that blow: RN. Granville.

Pneumonia Corner. The junction of Putney Bridge and Lower Richmond Road: London policemen's: since ca. 1925. Many policemen on duty there ended up by catching pneumonia.—2. The corner of Whitehall and Downing Street: Press photographers': since during the Munich crisis, Sep. 1938. Ex long, cold, wet waiting to 'snap' Ministers and other notables.

pneumonia rig. A set of tropical clothing: RN: since ca. 1925. P-G-R.

pneumonia truck. 'Open lorry without doors or hood' (*New Statesman*, 30 Aug. 1941): ARP workers': 1940–5.

P/O Prune. See **Prune**.

po. A chamber-pot: C.19–20: coll. >, ca. 1880, low coll. Ex the pron. of *pot* in Fr. *pot de chambre*.—2. In *full as a po*, extremely drunk: low: earlier C.20.

po-faced. With features as blank as the appearance of a *po* (see prec.): since ca. 1900. It was used by Terence Rattigan in *French Without Tears*, 1937, but the Lord Chamberlain (who knew it, and remembered using it as a boy) objected and *pie-faced* was substituted by the actors. (Based on a note from Sir Terence a few months before his death in 1977.) It > a fashionable term: R.S., 1967, notes 'A 1960s elastic word of disapproval, based on *po*. It seems to equate with "square", "establishmentary", but also with "hearty". Debs' and book-reviewers'. Found in literary supplements and heard on radio'; and L.A., almost simultaneously, wrote: 'Of features bland or blank; set, socially correct, immobility of expression; the term implies social supercilious mask of a face that, unreasoning, claims deference by hauteur. One of the class brick-bats of the early 1960s, used in reflection, i.e. disapproval, by and of upper classes'. Mr Quintin Hogg in the *Guardian*, 30 Mar. 1960, referred to the Honourable Mr Wilson as 'po-faced', where the connotation seems to be rather that of 'poker-faced'. The term was not heard so much after the late 1960s. Hence, *a smile like a po*, 'round , benign and full-hearted' (L.A., 1976)—i.e. bland and non-committal.

poached egg. 'A yellow-coloured "silent cop" placed in the centre of intersections as a guide to traffic' (B., 1942): Aus.: mid-C.20.—2. The Japanese national flag: Eastern Theatre of WW2: 1942–5. (Parsons, 1973.) Cf. **flaming arsehole**.

pobble. 'To ride at a leisurely pace' (Dunford): motorcyclists': since (?)ca. 1950. Imit. and echoic.

pocket-billiards(, usu. *playing*). (Of a male) palping his genitals: Public Schools' and Services' synon. of *pinch the cat*: since ca. 1910.

pod, n. The *Post Office Directory*: commercial:—1909 (Ware).—2. A marijuana cigarette; marijuana: Can. underground: late 1950s, adopted ex US. Victoria, BC, *Daily Colonist*, 16 Apr. 1958.

pod, v. To give birth: low coll.: since mid-C.20 (?earlier). Also *podding*, pregnant, as in 'Had a baby! I didn't even know she was podding!' (P.B.) Ex older *in pod* (*pod* = belly).

podged. Replete; over-full: middle-class: later C.20. 'Wow . . . that was quite a blow-out . . . I'm podged!' (party guest, in a 'Biff' cartoon, *Guardian*, 11 July 1987). Ex much older *podge*, n., and *podgy*, applied to a short, stout person.

poets. Excuse for, or action of, leaving the office early on Friday: Services': since early 1960s. Acronym ex 'Piss (*or* Push) off early—tomorrow's Saturday'. Hence *poets' day* = Friday. (Peppitt; P.J.E. Jones.) Cf. *t.G.i.F.* = Thank God it's Friday.

poggled. (Of a car) that 'has had crash damage repaired' (*Woman's Own*, 28 Feb. 1968); hence, *poggler*, such a car: car-dealers': since late 1940s, if not a decade earlier. P.B.: the term was used on BBC Radio 4 News, 3 Jan. 1977.

poggler. 'Purse, sometimes a wallet' (Powis): c.: later C.20. Cf. **pogue.**—2. See **poggled**.

pogue. 'Purse, sometimes a wallet' (Powis): c. Prob. ex older dial. *poke*, a bag, pocket.

point, n. 'Any writing implement: "Do you happen to have a point on you?" (Brit. gay slang)' (Rodgers, 1972): homosexuals'. Perhaps abbr. ball-point pen.—2. First place on a taxi-cab rank: taxi-drivers': since ca. 1910. Also *point position*; cf. **pin position.**—3. A smart, esp. a too smart, trick; an unfair advantage: Aus. (Ronan, 1954.) Ex the v.

point, v. 'To seize unfair advantage; to scheme' (Dennis): Aus.—2. Hence, to malinger: Aus.: since ca. 1910. B., 1959.

point Percy at the porcelain. See **Perce**, 2.

pointer. A schemer; one watchful for mean opportunities: Aus. (Doone.) Ex **point**, v.

pointing. Vbl n. corresponding to **point**, v. B., 1943.

pointy. Pointed: coll. Kersh, 1946, 'Where men wear pointy shoes.'—2. Terse; full of point; pithily economical. *OED*, 1909.

poison dwarf. Gen. pej. term: low coll.: later C.20. (McConville, 1980.) Prob. a direct trans. of an abusive nickname given by the inhabitants of a West German town to a certain Scottish regiment that caused havoc and unpleasantness while stationed there in the 1950s. (P.B.)

poison on armour plate. 'Ship's biscuits dipped in beef tea' (Granville): RN wardroom.

poisoner. A cook: Aus. joc. (Baker.) Cf. RN *grubspoiler*.

poisonous. A coll. intensive adj. (cf. *putrid*: from ca. 1905, according to Raymond, 1929). Pugh, 1912; Young, 1924, 'With these Perfectly Poisonous People'—very satirical; Keverne, 1930, 'He's a poisonous beast. As shifty as they make 'em'; 'Poisonous child' (Shepard, 1934). Ex S.E. fig. sense, morally corrupting or destructive, of evil influence, or that of deadly as poison.

poisonously. Very, extremely: coll.: ca. 1924–39. Barr, 1935.

poke, n. Money: circus s., or perhaps genuine Parlyaree. (Seago, 1933.) Prob. ex Fr. *poche*, a pocket. By 1940, fairly gen. s., as in 'It's a very satisfying feeling knowing you can put your finger on a bit of poke. (Which is slang for money: get it, poke, loot, poppy—any of them will do!)' (Cunliffe, 1965).—2. A purse: c.: mid-C.19–20. E.P.; Powis, 1977.—3. Horsepower: motorists': since ca. 1945. Bickers, 1965, 'With all that poke under the bonnet'. Cf. synon. **urge**.—4. A racehorse, esp. one worth betting on; hence, a bet on a horse: the turf: since ca. 1960, perhaps a decade earlier. As in 'a 2 to 1 poke' = a 2–1 'shot' or chance. (Gardner, 1977.)

poke, v. To hit (someone): mainly Aus. (Baker.) Esp. as in 'Why don't you poke him one?'

poke-bouncer. 'One who, by sleight of hand, appears to put money or valuables into a paper bag, which he then twists and offers for sale' (*M.T.*): marker-traders': late C.19–20. Ex S.E. *poke* = a bag.

poke Charley (v.t. demands *at*). To 'poke fun (at)', to be derisive—to deride: RN: since ca. 1935 (Granville); by WW2, also RAF (Forbes, 1942). Ex the given-name of some noted humorist.

P

poke through on the rails. (Of a racehorse) to come through the field on the inside: Aus. sporting: since ca. 1930. B., 1953.

poke up. To prepare the perforated paper tape by which a message may be sent by teleprinter or fed into a computer: Services' signals personnel: since ca. 1955, or earlier. (P.B.)

poker-face. 'An inscrutable face, betraying no emotion' (*SOD*): coll., since later C.19; in later C.20, verging on informal S.E. Ex such control needed to play the bluffing game of poker. Hence, adj., *poker-faced*.

pokey, -ie, -y. A poker machine: Aus. urban: since late 1930s. Hamilton, 1965.

pokey-dice. Bluff poker, played with dice: Army. (Kersh, 1942.) P.B.: since mid-C.20, usu. *pokey-die*.

pokie. See **pokey**.

pola(c)k. A Pole, Russian or Czech dealing in Polish Jewesses: white-slavers' c. (Londres.) A *Polack* is a Pole.

polaroids. Seamen of a *Polaris* missile submarine: RN: 1970s. (Peppitt.) A pun on, e.g., polaroid glasses or cameras.

pole, n. The control column of an aircraft: RAF: later C.20. (*Fighter Pilot*, 1981.) Cf. earlier **joy-stick**.—2. See **up the pole**.

pole, v. To be an expense, obligation, nuisance; to 'scrounge': Aus. (Tennant, 1939.) Also *pole on* (somebody).—2. To steal: NZ c., since ca. 1930 (McNab, 1938); Aus., since ca. 1935 (B., 1943).—3. (Of the male) to copulate, as in 'He poled the girl': Anglo-Irish. Cf. synon. **shaft**.—4. With *along*, *down*, *into*, *off*, etc., *pole* = to go (usu. with a purpose): coll.: later C.20. In contrast to *drift*, to go rather aimlessly. 'It was my nephew's christening last weekend, so we all had to go poling off down to Sussex for that', or 'damn dog got out soon as we arrived, was adrift four hours and then came poling back in, bold as brass and thirsty as hell'. (P.B.)

pole on. To sponge on (somebody): Aus. (Palmer, 1932; Caddie, 1953.) Ex **pole**, v., 1.

pole-pole. See SWAHILI, in Appx.

poled. Stolen: Aus. and NZ. (B., 1959.) See **pole**, v., 2.

poler. A scrounger: Aus.: since ca. 1930. (B., 1953.) Ex **pole**, v., 1.

policeman. A 'squeaker' or 'squealer', a betrayer of confederates to the police: c. Wallace, 1923.

policeman's helmet. The glans penis: low. Cf. **bobby's helmet**. Ex shape.

polio. *Polio*myelitis or infantile paralysis: coll., medical >, by 1958, gen.: since ca. 1930. *Leader Magazine*, 23 July 1949.

Polish Corridor, the. Cromwell Road, London, S.W.: taxi-drivers': 1945+. (*Daily Telegraph*, 18 May 1948.) Ex the many Poles resident there.—2. The passage leading from the front main hall to the Reading Room of the British Museum: B.M. habitués' and attendants': since ca. 1940, but esp. ca. 1944–8. Ex a certain visitant and entourage. P.B.: for almost forty years E.P. was himself one of those habitués: his regular seat in the Reading Room was K1.

polish off. Summarily to defeat an adversary: boxing s., 1829 (*OED*) >, ca. 1835, gen. coll. = to finish out of hand, get rid of (esp. a meal) quickly.—2. Hence, to kill secretly: c.:— 1923 (Manchon).

polish the apple. To curry favour, orig. of school-children polishing, on sleeve, an apple about to be presented to teacher: adopted, ca. 1945, ex US. Tempest, 1950, 'To curry favour with the authorities by sycophancy. To put on a show of being busy. (From the costermonger's habit of rubbing the best apple on his sleeve but selling inferior ones.)' The US derivatives *apple-polisher*, *-ing*, never really caught on in Brit.

politico. A politician either ambitious or unscrupulous or, esp., both: Aus.: adopted, ca. 1955, ex US. (B.P.)—2. Hence, any politician: Aus. coll.: since ca. 1960. Ex. S. American Spanish *político*—or merely appearing to be? P.B.: in later C.20, some Brit. use for this sense, and also applicable to any politically-minded person, e.g., one who 'plays politics' on an academic board of governors.

pollies. Politicians: Aus. abbr.: since ca. 1970. Wilkes.

polling on, ppl. or adj. phrase. Reckoning on, assuming; hence, taking advantage of: military: from ca. 1910. (F. & G.) Semantics: *counting on*; (electoral) *poll*.

Pollycon (or **p-**). *Pol*itical *Econ*omy: undergraduates'. A blend.

polone. A girl or woman: theatrical; grafters': since mid-C.19. Often used in combination as adj. 'female', as in *strill polone*, a female pianist (Lester). Var. spellings are *palone*; *palon(e)y.*—2. A pony: circus and theatrical r.s. Franklyn 2nd.

Polto. 'Petty Officer, Electrician. From when the Torpedo Branch did the electrics' (Malin, 1979): RN submariners': mid-C.20. Cf. **spo**.

Poly, the. The Polytechnic Institute: Londoners' coll. P.B.: in later C.20, any local polytechnic; or, in ref., as Leicester Poly, Oxford Poly, etc.

polybagging. The use of a stout polythene bag laid flat on snow as a makeshift toboggan: Leicestershire schoolchildren's: winter 1983–4. (Woodworth.)

pom. Short for **pommy**, q.v. Also written with a capital, as in Boyd, 1965, 'The Poms have a kink on sex.'

pom-pom. A maxim automatic quick-firing gun: 1899: echoic coll. >, by 1905, S.E.—2. A multi-barrelled anti-aircraft gun: Services', esp. RN, coll.: 1940+. P-G-R.

pombi. See SWAHILI, in Appx.

Pommie, -y; p-, n. An English immigrant; an English national: Aus.: app. since late C.19, orig. among dock-workers; by early C.20, gen. Aus., and almost always derogatory. See esp. Wilkes, who quotes, among many other relevant items, this from H.J. Rumsey, *The Pommies, or New Chums in Australia*, 1920, 'colonial boys and girls, ready to find a nickname, were fond of rhyming "Immigrant", "Jimmygrant", "Pommegrant" and called it after the new chum children. The name stuck and became abbreviated to "pommy" later on'. Often in combination, as *Pommy bastard, bloody poms, pommyland* = England, *whingeing pommy*.—2. A Petty Officer Mechanician (Engineering): RN: since ca. 1950.—3. Hence, any stoker Petty Officer: id.: since ca. 1954. (Granville, letter, 1962.)

pommies' pittance. 'Meagre wages, from the small overseas allowance paid to Royal Navy personnel on exchange with Royal Australian Navy: R Aus. N: 1950s' (Peppitt)—and later.

pommy, adj. English: Aus. Ex n., 1.

pomp. A pompous person, as in 'Oh, he's such an old pomp, and he does go on so!': middle-class coll.: since mid-C.20. (P.B.)

Pompey. 'Traditional . . . name for Portsmouth Town and Dockyard, and the naval barracks known as HMS *Victory*' (Granville): RN: since late C.19. ('Taffrail', 1916.) Perhaps ex its naval prison: cf. Yorkshire *Pompey*, a house of correction (*EDD*).—2. Hence, Portsmouth Association Football Club: sporting.—3. A temporary lid set on a cask that, in testing, is being fired: coopers':—1935. Cf. the Lancashire dial. *pompey*, a tea-kettle.

Pompey (or **Portsmouth**) **defence, the.** Lying explanation, by a man arrested for robbery, that his victim had made 'vile homosexual suggestions', and so he had hit him: 'I don't know where his money went—somebody must have stolen it after I left him lying there': so called because of its currency at one time in this large naval port. (Powis.) Police and underworld.

Pompey 'ore, rarely **whore.** See TOMBOLA, in Appx.

Pomponian. A native of Portsmouth. (*New Society*, 3 June 1982.) See **Pompey**.

ponce, n. A harlot's bully or keep: (prob. c. >) low s.: from early 1870s. Perhaps ex earlier *pouncey* (Mayhew, 1861); † by 1920. B. & L. list *po(u)nce-shicer* as a man living infamously upon an actress. H., 5th ed., 1874, 'Low-class East-end thieves even will "draw the line" at ponces, and object to their presence in the boozing-kens'; Henley, 1887, 'You ponces good at talking tall.' Prob. ex *pounce on*, though possibly influenced by Fr. *Alphonse*, a harlot's bully (W.), or, as Michael Harrison suggests in a letter to me, 1947, 'Perhaps from Fr. *pensionnaire*' (boarder, lodger), conceivably with a pun on the English *pensioner*. Cf. earlier *bouncer, fancy-cove, mack, prosser, Sunday man* or *bloke*.—2. Hence, a young and dandified subaltern: Army, esp. Royal Artillery: from ca. 1930.—3. The navigator: RN: since ca. 1940. Peppitt, 1976, comments: 'Pun on Pontius Pilate [*pilot*] (and subtle allusion to living off others' earnings?) Perhaps now obsolete.'—4. In *on the ponce*, 'homosexual touting' (Home Office): prisoners' c.: later C.20.

ponce, v. To act as, be a 'ponce': low. (Moncrieff, 1932.) Often as vbl n., *poncing*.—2. Hence, to sponge, scrounge, cadge: low: since ca. 1915. (Curtis, 1937.) A later C.20 example: '[The skinheads, q.v.] make £5 or £6 a day each on the street, "poncing" or "tapping" or "taxing", but Mutt [a leading 'skin'] prefers to just call it begging. He doesn't beg *off* someone though. He just *begs* them. *Poncing* is a big difference. "Poncing" is *part* of being a skin, "Zeb [Mutt's 'side-kick'] says. . . . A lot of poncing is reciprocal among the different gangs on the circuit. A big group of skins will ponce a mod, a group of mods will ponce a solitary punk . . . ' (Harris, 1984). See also Seabrook quot'n at **mump**, v., 2.—3. To obtain (money) by 'poncing': low: since ca. 1920. 'I don't ponce it orf 'em' (Kersh, 1938).

ponce about. To live in an idle, aimless, and luxurious way, as implied in ' "What's that boy of yours doing now, Charles?" "Doing? Nothing. Never does. Just poncing about on his mother's money" ' (Daniells, 1978): since (?)ca. 1950. Ex v., 2, and influenced by *ponce up*. (P.B.)

ponce-hole. A place where a policeman can cadge a free meal: Metropolitan Police: later C.20. 'A place carefully cultivated by an officer . . . woe betide any callow newcomer who attempted to trespass in an old hand's ponce-hole—in which he knows he is welcome to come in and ponce a breakfast' (Seabrook, 1987). Cf. **ponce**, v., 2, and **watering-hole**.

ponce on. To live on the earnings of (a prostitute): low: late C.19–20. *Gilt Kid*, 1936.

ponce up, v.i. and v. refl: usu. *ponce oneself up* or *be ponced up*. To smarten up one's dress or appearance: Army: since ca. 1925. To put on one's best, esp. if flashy, clothes: since ca. 1950. (Wainwright, 1965.) Hence, also of things, as in 'Every bloody thing that comes into the [advertising] studio has to be ponced up in some way or another before it's bloody presentable' (Daniells, 1980). Cf. **tart up**.

ponc(e)y. Flashy, ostentatious: since early C.20, raffish and fringe-of-underworld, but by late 1940s fairly gen. (Naughton, 1970.) Cf. **ponce up**.

Pond-hopper. 'An R.A.F. Transport Command flight across the Atlantic. The routine is known in the Forces as "Pond-hopping" ' (L.A.): WW2 and after.

pond water. 'Ginger beer with a dash of lime, good for hangovers' (Peppitt): RN: since ca. 1965.

Ponderosa, the. 'The Kentish Town–Barking line, so named because of the shortage of water columns between these two points' (McKenna): railwaymen's: mid-C.20. *Railway*, 2nd, says 'Also Lake District'.

pongo, n. A monkey: showmen's: mid-C.19–20. In S.E., properly 'a large anthropoid African ape'; loosely, indeed erroneously, the orang-outang, 1834. Native name. *SOD*.—2. 'Soldier, a Naval nickname dating from the time when the Navy and Army joined forces in annual manoeuvres before the First World War. The forage cap worn by soldiers resembled that worn by the pet dog *Pongo* which appeared in a Punch and Judy show.' (Granville.) Prob. influenced also by sense 1, and *pong*, (to) stink. By WW2, also RAF (H. & P.), esp. for an army officer, and derogatory.—3. Hence, a nickname for a marine: RN: WW1. Copplestone, 1916 (W.). But a later C.20 RM elab. of sense 2 is *Percy Pongo* (*Mail on Sunday*, 8 Nov. 1987).—4. An Australian infantryman: Aus.: from 1915. This Aus. usage has been influenced by the Aboriginal name for a flying squirrel.—5. An Englishman,

esp. an English serviceman: NZ: since ca. 1943. (Slatter.) Prob. ex sense 2.

pongo, adj. Pertaining to the Army: RN, RM and RAF: later C.20. Hawke, 1979; P.B.

ponies, the. Horse-racing: sporting coll.

pontoon. Vingt-(et-)un, the card-game: 1900: military coll. >, by 1910, gen. S.E. A corruption of, more prob. an approximation to, *vingt-un*. *SOD*.—2. Hence, a twenty-one months' imprisonment: London's East End: since ca. 1925. (R. Herd, 12 Nov. 1957.) But also (Norman) of 21 years: c.: since ca. 1910. The latter is also an Army usage (P-G-R). In earlier C.20 to have *done* (one's) *pontoon* was to have completed a full regular engagement with the Colours, the 21 years (P.B.).

Ponty. A local coll. (C.19–20) for any town named *Ponty*—e.g. Pontypool, Pontypridd.—2. A Pontiac car: Aus.: 1930s. (B.P.)

pony, n. Inferior goods; trash: market-traders' (e.g., Petticoat Lane): since ca. 1920.—2. A young girl's *pony-tail* hair-style: coll.: since ca. 1960.

pony, adj. Trashy: market-traders'. (*M.T.*) Presumably ex n., 1.

pony in white. A sum or value of twenty-five shillings: racing c. Ex *pony*, orig., later C.18, £25; *in white*, in silver.

pooch. A dog, esp. if small or mongrel: Can.: late C.19–20. (Leechman.) Perhaps, as R.S. suggests, cognate with Ger. *Putzi*, 'a fairly common name given to a lap-dog'. Can. usage seems to antedate US usage.—2. Hence, common for any dog: Can., since ca. 1920; Brit., since mid-C.20, prob. adopted ex US.—3. By specialisation, a greyhound: Aus. (B., 1942.) All 3 senses are ironic or joc.

pooch-flop. Dog excreta, esp. in urban areas: since late 1960s. (*Observer*, 2 Mar. 1975.) See prec.

poochie, -y. Affectionate diminutive, usu. as vocative, of **pooch**, 2: later C.20.

poochies. Insect and similar pests in Malaya: residents' and Army's. Ex Malayan?

pood. An effeminate youth or man: Aus. low: since ca. 1910. (B., 1942.) Cf. **poof**.

poodle, n. (Rare in sing.) A sausage: low: early C.20. Lyons, 1914, 'We fair busted ourselves on poodles and mashed' (Manchon).—2. 'The main [radio-]set crackles to the news of a robbery alarm . . . south of the river [Thames]. "We'll have a poodle at that," said [the Met. Police emergency squad driver] putting on the siren. A poodle is going 70 miles an hour, dodging in and out of traffic on Pall Mall' (Hearst, 1985). Ex:-

poodle, v. To go, usu. as in 'so we poodled off down to the coast for the day' or 'I think I'll just poodle over to see Jane': middle classes': since mid-C.20, if not a decade or two earlier. Has var. *pootle*, poss. a blend of *poodle* + *tootle* (q.v.), Clark, 1980 (2). Cf. synon. **toddle**, and see **poodler**, 2. (P.B.)—2. To ride easily: club cyclists'. (*Fellowship*, 1984.) But cf. **poodler**, 1.

poodle-faker. A man, esp. a Service officer, who, for the time being rather than habitually, cultivates the society of women: Anglo-Indian, hence Army, hence RN: since early C.20. 'Bartimeus', 1915, has the vbl n. *poodle-faking*; 'Taffrail', 1917, *poodle-faker*. Granville, defining the term's nuance by WW2, and after, writes, 'A payer of polite calls; a balancer of tea cups ashore'. An allusion to lapdogs. R.S. suggests a poss. connection with **dog-robbers**, q.v.

poodle parade, the. The nightly parade of dog-owners exercising their dogs: coll.: since ca. 1920.

poodler. A 'womaniser' or confirmed flirt among cyclists: cyclists': from ca. 1930. Ex *poodle-faker*.—2. A small vehicle: hauliers' s.: since ca. 1935. See HAULIERS', in Appx.

pooey. See **poohy**.

poof. A male homosexual: orig. c. and low, earlier C.20; >, by ca. 1950, gen. Also spelt *pouf, pouffe*; perhaps ex N. Country pron. of *puff*, a C.19 low term for a sodomist. 'A few words on Margeries . . . In the last few years the number of these brutes in human shape, generally called "Marger-ies", "Pooffs", etc. . . . ' (*Yokel's Preceptor*, 1851, quoted in Evans, 1979). E.P. noted: 'In Australia since ca. 1910. I defi-nitely remember both *poof* and *poofter* as being used in the A.I.F. in 1915–18.' Cf. **poofter,** and **poove**, 2. Tempest, 1950, spells the word *pouff*.

poof-rorting (or **-wroughting**). Robbing male prostitutes with violence: c.: from ca. 1920. See **poof** and **rorty**.

poofdah. Var. spelling of next. Priest, 1983.

poofter. A homosexual male: Aus.: by ca. 1970, fairly gen. also in Brit. where used by, e.g., *The Times*, 15 Mar. 1973, 'minc-ing pansy, head-shaking poofter'. Occ. spelt *pooftah*; Wilkes quotes Patrick White's use, 1965, of elab. *poofteroo*.—2. Hence, an effeminate-looking man not necessarily homosex-ual; a gen. pej. and derogatory term: Aus.: since ca. 1920. 'Move over, yer pommie poofter!' (B.P.; P.B.)—3. A loud civilian suit: RN lowerdeck: since ca. 1940. P-G-R.—4. 'A pejorative term for . . . any man with artistic or not overtly "masculine" interests' (Buzo, 1973): Aus.: since ca. 1945. A further weakening, via sense 2, of sense 1.

poofter rorter. 'One who procures for a male homosexual' (B., 1959): low Aus.: since ca. 1935. Compare and contrast **poof-rorting**.

poofy. Smelly: children's: since ca. 1945 (?much earlier). 'I'd rather have a bath. I'm poofy' (Blake, 1964). Echoic of dis-gust: cf. the Scottish and N. Country *poof!*, an exclam. of dis-gust. But perhaps imm. ex **poohy**.

pooh, n. Anything smelly or disgusting, esp. faeces: nursery and juvenile: since ca. 1930 (?earlier). B.P. notes its use in Aus.—2. Hence, *in the pooh*, in trouble: Aus., since ca. 1935 (B.P.). Lit., 'in the shit'; cf. *in the cack, clarts, dwang*, etc.

pooh, v. To defecate: domestic coll.: later C.20 (?earlier). Ex prec. (P.B.) See next, 2. 'If a cat came poohing in your yard wouldn't you chuck something at it?' (Hunter, 1963).

pooh-pooh. As n. and v., domestic coll.: later C.20. Dupli-cation of **pooh**, n., 1, and v.

poohs. A var. of **pooh**, n.

poohy, occ. written **pooey.** Lit. or fig., faecal; hence disgusting: Aus. juvenile: since ca. 1935. Ex **pooh**. (B.P.)—2. Hence, *poohy!* or *pooey!*, rubbish. Perhaps slightly influenced by US *phooey!*

pooky-acky pill. A panacea for someone out of sorts, or suffer-ing from an inexplicable depression: N. Leics, older gener-ation. 'You've got a touch of the old dog and you need a pooky-acky pill' (Hurt, 1984). Somewhere between dial. and s., *pooky-acky* itself seems to mean 'depressed, depressing, unsatisfactory', as in 'a pooky-acky day' of dull weather.

Pool, the. Liverpool: chiefly Liverpudlians'.

pool, v. To incriminate: to spoil the reputation or chances of someone *with* someone else: Aus. low: since ca. 1910. *Rats*, 1944, 'He pooled me with the Q.M. Just a top-off merchant, that's all he is'. 'By 1960, no longer low—and with a meaning less narrow'. (B.P.)

pool(-)shark. One who is, or believes himself to be, exception-ally adept in the game of pool: Can.: adopted, ca. 1925, ex US. (Leechman.) But, as R.C. cautions, 'rather a skilled player who pretends to ineptness [in order] to trap suckers [playing for money]'. Perhaps, orig., a pun on 'pool of water' and the game of *pool*.

poon. A lonely, loneliness-eccentric dweller in remote places: Aus. (B., 1942.) Ex Aboriginal?—2. Hence(?), a simpleton; a fool; a gen. pej. since ca. 1910. E.g. at Dulwich School since ca. 1930 (Marples).—3. A common shortening of **poon-tang.** Leechman.

Poona or **Poonah**, adj. Typical of the majors and colonels of the pre-1940 Regular Army: earlier C.20. 'He's very Poonah'—fiery, martinet, narrowly conservative, not excessively intelli-gent. Poona was a famous military centre in India, until the British Raj ended in 1947.

poonce. An Aus. var. of **ponce**: Buzo, 1973.

pooned up. Flashily dressed up: low Aus.: since ca. 1930. B., 1943; Arthur Chipper, 1972, notes 'often with sexual success in view' (quoted by Wilkes).

poontang. Copulation, esp. with a coloured woman: Can. Sup-posedly of Chinese origin, there being such variants as *poong tai* and *poong kai*. (Whence *poontanger*.) Common also among homosexuals for 'sexual relations' (*The Lavender Lexicon*). The nuances 'copulation' and 'sexual relations' prob. derive ex the basic sense 'female pudend'. 'One of the most mysterious of sexual words.' (R.C., 1976.) Like me, he rejects derivation ex Fr. *putain*, a prostitute; therefore despite also *Webster's Third International*, 1961, 'If I had to guess, I would say some Philipino language, via US Army ca. 1900' (R.C.); and if *I* had to do so, I'd hazard an Amerindian (N. or Central American) origin—via Pidgin.

poontanger. Penis: Can. lumbermen's.

poop, n. A foolish person: coll.: already current during WW1, as in Benstead, 1930. Benson, 1924, 'When we're young we're pifflers, and when we're old we're poops.' Cf. **poop-stick**, and (?S.E.) **poopjack**, a 'jack-in-office'; but prob. abbr. of **nincompoop**, as *COD* suggests.—2. (Also pron. with *oo* short, as in Standard Received Eng. *book*.) A defe-cation; esp. in *do* or *have a poop*: mostly children's. Ex v., 2.—3. See **hot poop**.

poop, v. To break wind: dial. and low coll.: C18–20. Ex S.E. *poop*, to make an abrupt sound; to toot. Occ. *poupe*. *OED*.—2. Hence, to defecate: (?late) C.19–20: low coll., mostly of and by children (*EDD*).—3. With senses 1 and 2, cf. the military v.i., to fire a gun, i.e. a big gun, *not* a rifle or machine-gun; (of a gun) to bang: coll.: from not later than 1916. (B. & P.) Often *poop off* (F. & G.).—4. Hence, v.t., to shoot a person: coll.: from ca. 1930. Heyer, 1933.

poop-stick. An objectionable fellow, esp. if a soldier: earlier C.20. MacDonald, 1932, ' "You make me sick!" he said. "Let a little poop-stick like that walk all over you!" ' Cf. **poop**, n., 1, and later C. 20 synon. **dipstick**.

pooper. See **party-pooper**.

poopoo. See **pooh-pooh**.

poor as piss (**and twice as nasty**). RN lowerdeck pej. (Gran-ville.) Occ. reduced to *porous*. Cf. **piss-poor**.

poor blind Nell. A girl wronged (i.e. seduced and abandoned); the everlasting victim: Aus. Ex the well-known chant: 'And did he marry poor blind Nell?' 'He did (pause) like effing hell!'

poor man's. When used to preface the name of a famous per-son, it is a coll. indication that another, referred to as e.g. (*a* or *the*) *poor man's Noël Coward*, is but a pale, and perhaps unwitting, reflection of the star. (P.B.)

poor-mouth. BBC Radio 4, 'Newstand', 17 Mar. 1979, review-ing the weekly papers' reactions to President Carter's peace mission in the Middle East: 'They seem to be pursuing a policy of poor(-)mouthing his efforts', i.e. crying down, or, at best, damning his achievements with faint praise. Adopted, late 1970s, ex US; cf. **bad-mouth**.

poor show! See **show,** n.

poor view. See **take a poor view**.

poorboy. 'Something substantial and inexpensive, such as a big bottle of cheap wine' (Victoria, BC, *Daily Colonist*, 16 Apr. 1959, 'Basic Beatnik'): Can. jazz-lovers': since ca. 1956.

pootle. See **poodle**.

poove; pooving. Food; feeding, i.e. grazing for animals: either circus s. or Parlyaree:—1933 (Seago). Prob. ex Romany *phuv*, a field. P.B.: Hillaby, 1968, notes a gipsy in Cornwall explaining that 'they had been up to their usual trick of poo-vin' the greys [horses (also. ex Rom.)]. To poove it is to put it in a field at night without permission, and retrieve it . . . next morning.'—2. A homosexual or effeminate male; also, as v.i., to act as one; hence, *pooving* (*about*): since mid-1940s. Perhaps, as R.C. suggests, a back-formation ex pl. of *poof*; also spelt *pouve*: both *poove* and *pouve* occur in Gardner,

1967. Later derivatives (since ca. 1965) are *poovery*, homosexual practices; *poovish*, and *poovishness*. All are derogatory. (E.P.; P.B.)

pop, n. A drink that fizzes from the bottle when the cork—'pop goes the cork'—is drawn; gen. ginger-beer: coll.: 1812 (Southey). In full, *soda-pop*; and, since ca. 1910, applied to all 'soft drinks'. Hence, in Army s. of early 1970s, (*to be*) *on the pop*, meant, by ironic understatement, '(to be) drinking (liquor) heavily' (P.B.).—2. Father: orig. US, as also are the later *poppa* or *popper* [but perhaps *poppums*, applied to my grandfather by his sons, born pre-WW1, is wholly English: P.B.]. All ex *papa*. Hence, in address, any old or even, to the young, any middle-aged man: adopted, ca. 1944, ex US servicemen.—3. An orgasm, usu. of the male: low coll.: perhaps from mid-C.19. Yet—my ignorance!—I hadn't seen it in print before Hollander, 1975. The corresponding v. prob. preceded the n.—4. A bet, usu. at specified odds: Aus. racing: since ca. 1920. ' "Aeolus couldn't win it," said Lucky. "It'll be a fifty to one pop" ' (Glassop, 1949).—5. An attempt, as in 'I'll have a pop at it, of course' (Priestley, 1929); in Aus. the phrase means also 'to engage (someone) in a fight' (B., 1942). The NZ var. for 'to have a try' is *give it a pop*, which also means 'to make a bet' (cf. sense 4): since ca. 1919 (McNab, 1938).—6. As *a pop*, each time, or each, as in 'What did these set you back?'—'Five quid a pop': Aus.: since ca. 1920. (B.P.)—7. A popular song: song-writers' and publishers': since ca. 1920; > by ca. 1950 'popular music, whether vocal or instrumental or both', as in 'The Capital of Pop', a sobriquet for Liverpool during the 1960s. *Pop* or *pop music* are terms widely used to cover the opposite of 'classical music.'—8. In *not a fair pop*, not a fair chance: NZ: since ca. 1925. (Slatter.) Cf. sense 5, *pop* as shot, go, try, etc.—9. In *sure pop!*, certainly!: juvenile:—1923 (Manchon).—10. In *be on the pop of*, to be about to: Anglo-Irish: late C.19–20. Joyce, 1922, 'He was on the pop of asking me to the night in the kitchen I was rolling the potato cake.'—11. To *have a pop* 'means to argue with another' (Ash): London dockers'. Cf. **play pop**.

pop, v. To do a burglary: c.: later C.20. *Now!*, 10 Apr. 1981.—2. See **skin pop**.

pop a tuck. To display surprise, anger; to react strongly: coll.: later C.20. (Hall, 1975.) Prob. ex possible effect on clothing.

pop (one's) clogs. To die: mainly Northern. Either ex *pop*, s. 'to pawn', since early C.18, or from *pop off*, to die, id.

Pop-Eye or **Popeye**. A ship's look-out man or an aircraft observer: since ca. 1938. (H. & P.) Ex 'Popeye the Sailor' in a famous series of comic cartoons (cf. **Wimpey**): anyone with such large eyes *must* have excellent eyesight.—2. The Pope: anti-papists' derogatory: since ca. 1945.

pop-eyed. Having bulging eyes, or eyes opened wide in surprise: US (ca. 1820), anglicised by ca. 1910. *OED* Sup.

pop-out. A mass-produced surfboard: Aus. (teenage) surfers'. (*Pix*, 28 Sep. 1963.) Ex the production process.

pop-pimping. The spotting of theatrical talent: since ca. 1950. *New Statesman*, 5 Feb. 1965, competition.

pop the cherry. See **cherry-popping**.

pope of Gozo. 'Occurs in expressions of exasperation, e.g. *sod the Pope of Gozo!*' (Malin, 1979): RN: mid-C.20. Gozo is the small island belonging to Malta.

Pope's telephone number, the. 'Vat 69' whisky: since ca. 1905. Punning '*Vati*can'.

Poplar finance. Maladministration of public funds, esp. by a town-council: political coll.: from ca. 1925. (Collinson.) Ex the misuse of the relief system in Poplar ca. 1920–5 and with a pun on *popular*.

popper. Loosely, any drug addict: ca. 1960–75. (Bournemouth *Echo*, 28 Aug. 1967.) See **skin pop**.

popping. In *how are you* (or *how yer*) *poppin(g)* (earlier with *up*)?, how are you getting on?: Aus. coll.: late C.19–mid-C.20. Lindsay, 1933, 'How yer poppin' s'mornin'?'

poppy, n. Money; esp., cash: Cockneys' and market-traders'. Powis; *M.T.*

poppy, v.i. and t. To pay: market-traders'. 'Try to get the lugger to do some poppying' (*M.T.*). Ex the n.

poppycock. Nonsense: US s. (1865, Artemus Ward), orig.—and throughout C.19—in sense of bombast; anglicised ca. 1905; by 1930, coll. (Thornton.) The word originates in Dutch *pappekak*, soft faeces, hence 'utter nonsense' (*Chambers*, 1972): cf. 'Don't talk shit!' or 'Don't give me that shit!' In short, *pap*, soft food for babies + *cack*, excrement, ultimately ex L. *cacare*, to defecate, itself as echoic as *piss*.

pops or **Pops**. Father: rare before 1919. (Delafield, 1933, 'Pops says that . . .' and 'My Pops says . . .') Cf. **pop**, n., 2.

Popski's Private Army. An irregular, long-range penetration and guerrilla force formed in the Middle East, late 1942, under Vladimir 'Popski' Peniakoff (later Lieutenant-Colonel, DSO, MC); after service in N. Africa, the unit saw action in Italy. See Peniakoff's autobiography thus titled, pub. 1950.

popsie, -ey, -y. A girl, not merely in address but also, and more usu., in ref.: Services' (mostly officers'): since ca. 1935. (H. & P.; Granville.) Ultimately ex S.E. *poppet*, 'a small dainty person; a term of endearment' (*SOD*) for centuries.—2. Hence, a woman conductor: busmen's: since ca. 1945.

popsie pal. Girl motorcycle-pillion rider: motorcyclists': since mid-C.20. (Dunford.)

popularity Jack. An officer given to currying favour either with the men or with the public: RN, gen. as nickname. Bowen.

porc. A porcupine: Aus. coll. Idriess, 1932.

Porcupine. 'A racing A.J.S. motorcycle of the 1950s: the cylinder fins were shaped to a point similar to quills' (Dunford, 2).

Porcupine, HMS. HMS *Penelope*: RN: 1941+. Ex holes plugged with protruding wooden pegs; also known as *the Pepper Pot*, from the number of holes inflicted on her by bombs. Granville.

Pork and Lard, the. The 'St Ives [Huntingdonshire] to Ely line (closed)' (*Railway*, 2nd): railwaymen's: earlier C.20.

pork-pie. A coll. abbr. of *pork-pie hat*, a style of men's hat popular ca. 1920–50: coll. (P.B.)—2. A lie: r.s.: since mid-1980s. (Bell, 14 Feb. 1986.) Soon elab. *porkypie*, then truncated to *porky*, pl. *porkies*, as in a poster advertising the *Sunday Express*, Dec. 1987, an article about astrology: 'Porkies or Aries?'

pork sword. Penis: Army joc.: since ca. 1950. Cf. synon. **mutton dagger**, **beef bayonet**.

porker. A policeman: low: late 1970s. A var. or elab. of **pig**, n., 1. Daniells, 1979; in 1980, he uses *porker patrol* as a gen. term for 'the police'.

porking. Sexual intercourse: low: later C.20. (Hibbert, 1983.) Prob. ex *pork sword*.

porky. See **pork-pie**, 2.

porn. Pornography: mostly photographers' and journalists': since late 1940s. Luard, 1967, 'Porn or portrait they're all available.' See also **porny**.

porn flicks. Salacious or 'blue' films: since late 1960s. (*Observer*, 15 Nov. 1970.) Cf. the slightly later synon. **skinflick**.

pornbroker. A seller of pornographic magazines and books: since ca. 1960. (*The TLS*, 19 Jan. 1967.) An 'inevitable' pun on *pawnbroker*; cf. **pornshop**.

porno. Pornography; a var. of **porn** since late 1950s, but gen. only since 1967. *Porn* is the more usu. version.

pornshop. Shop where pornography is sold. Witty pun on 'pawnshop'. Since about 1960.

porny. Bawdy (persons), smutty (talk, etc.): either direct ex *pornographic*, then prob. since early C.20; or as the -y adj. ex **porn**, therefore not much before ca. 1947. A good quot'n occurred in the *Sunday Times* article, 'Just how porny can you get?', on 29 Aug. 1971. On the same page appeared an article titled 'Longford's anti-porn money'.

porous. A mild or polite form of **poor as piss**: Services', perhaps mainly RN: since late 1930s. P-G-R; Peppitt.

porridge; esp. **a bit of porridge.** Imprisonment; a term in prison: c.: since ca. 1930. (Norman.) Perhaps suggested, in part at least, by the semantics of S.E. *stir*, by a pun on *stir*, a prison. P.B.: the term > much more widespread with the popular TV series of the earlier 1970s about prison life, called 'Porridge'. See **gravy**, 6.—2. 'Sludge removed from drains' (*Railway*): railwaymen's. Of a similar consistency.—3. Wet, sticky snow: skiers': later C.20. *LAM*, 4 Feb. 1986.

Porridge Bowl or **Box, the.** The Royal Scot express: railwaymen's: since ca. 1920(?). *Railway*, 2nd.

porridge education. 'Sometimes when a knowledgeable chap is told that he must have had a college education, he says "*No*; I had a porridge education"—meaning that he was brought up in the Scottish manner, fed on little more than porridge and "educated" by some heavy-handed village dominie' (Petch, 1966): coll.

port. A portmanteau, suitcase: Aus. and NZ s. > coll.—2. Porter, as term of address: earlier C.20.

Port and Lemon(s), the. The Port and Travel Security Sections of military counter-intelligence: Intelligence Corps', e.g. in Cyprus in late 1950s where they were deployed against arms-smuggling by sea and air. Hence, a *Port-and-Lemon*, a member of such a unit. Joc. use, suggested by the popular drink. (P.B.)

port-hole duff. Sodomy: low RN. A pun on catching the 'victim' with his head out of a port-hole; cf. **Navy cake**, 1, and earlier *back-scuttle*.

Port Said bible. Any pornographic book: RN. (Malin, 1979.) Cf. synon. **Hong Kong bible.**

Port Said garters. 'Any contraceptives worn by amorous (and prudent) soldiery': Army: ca. 1939–55.

pose, n. A puzzling question: children's:—1923. (Manchon). Ex S.E. *poser*. Cf. the † S.E. *pose*, a state of perplexity.

pose, v. To skive, q.v.: RN (perhaps mostly HM Submariners'): later C.20. (Gell, 1983.) ?Hence *posey*, as in 'all the yachties [yachtsmen] in their posey gear', quoted as RN Search and Rescue aircrew usage, in *You*, 22 May 1983, though here it may of course mean merely 'dressing for effect'.

posh, n. Money; specifically, a halfpenny or other coin of low value: c.:—1839; ob. (Brandon, 1st ed.) Ex Romany *posh*, a half, as in *posh-horri*, a halfpenny, and *posh-koorona*, a half-crown.—2. A dandy: Society s.:—1897; † by 1920. (B. & L., 2nd ed.) ?Ex sense 1; i.e. a moneyed person.—3. See ASSOCIATION FOOTBALL, in Appx.

posh, adj. Stylish, smart; (of clothes) best; splendid: military >, by 1919, gen.: 1918, says *OED*; but it appears as Cambridge University s., though as *push* or *poosh*, in 1903, when Wodehouse says of a brightly coloured waistcoat that it is 'quite the most push thing at Cambridge'. Avoided by polite society since ca. 1930. (B. & P.) Ex *posh*, n., 2; or possibly a corruption of Scottish *tosh*, clean, neat, trim. The usual educated explanation—'*port* outward bound, *starboard* home' (sun-avoiding, hence the 'best', cabins on the England–India run in hot weather)—is ingenious and plausible; but, distrusting it, I prefer this: a contraction of *polish*, itself a slovened pron. of *polished*. P.B.: a cartoon in *Punch*, 25 Sep. 1918, shows an RAF officer talking to his mother: ' "Oh, yes, Mater, we had a posh time of it down there."—"Whatever do you mean by 'posh', Gerald?"—"Don't you know? It's slang for 'swish'!" ' The word is sometimes pron., perhaps affectedly, with the *o* long.—2. Hence, free, esp. if illicitly acquired: Army: since ca. 1912 (E.P.); † by 1950 (P.B.).

posh; gen. **posh up.** (Gen. in passive—esp. *all poshed-up*.) To make smart in appearance; to clean and polish: military > gen.: from 1917 or 1918. (F. & G.; B. & P.) Ex *posh*, adj.

posso-de-luxe, possodelux. A very rich dupe, or con-man's victim: Aus. c.: since ca. 1930. Both versions from Baker: the 1st, 1953; the 2nd 1959. Ex **possum**, 2.

possum. A 'ring-in' (q.v.): low Aus.: since ca. 1925. B., 1943.—2. A simpleton; a dupe: Aus. c.: since ca. 1925. B., 1945.—3.

In *stir the possum*, 'To liven things up, create a disturbance; raise issues that others wish left dormant (?from song *Possum up a Gumtree* 1831)' (Wilkes): Aus. coll.

possy; occ. **possie, pozzy.** A *posi*tion; esp. a dug-out, or other shelter: Army, mostly Aus. and NZ: WW1, esp. from Gallipoli. B. & P.; F. & G.—2. Hence, from 1919, mostly in the Colonies, a house, a lodging, etc.; a job. (Doone.) As Wilke's quotations show, it soon came to mean, esp. in Aus., specifically one's 'drinking position' at a bar.

post. To betray: see AUSTRALIAN UNDERWORLD, in Appx.

post-and-rail. A fairy tale, esp. a lie: Aus. r.s.: since ca. 1910. (B., 1945.) Ex *post-and-rail* fences.

postman's knock. A lock: burglars' r.s. Chubb's advertisement in *Daily Telegraph*, 5 Mar. 1962.

Postman's Park. A little 'square' within the GPO block, London, EC4: Londoners': earlier C.20. Because this tiny square—the only square in the block—is nearly always filled with postmen who have come out for a breather.

pot, n. A cylinder, esp. in one of the old rotary engines: RFC/RAF: 1914–18. Hence, any aeroplane-engine cylinder: R Aus. AF: 1939–45. (B., 1943.) 'Hence, a cylinder in any internal combustion engine, as in the phrase "hitting on all pots" = firing on all cylinders. Common in the 1930s' (Sanders).—2. A potentiometer: users' coll.: since ca. 1950. (B.P.)—3. The Jack at bowls: Midlands bowls-players': current in 1970s. (Maurice Butcher, 1979.) The Southern version is *kitty*.—4. Marijuana: orig. and still mostly drug addicts': adopted ex US, ca. 1945 in Can. ca. 1947 in Brit. ca. 1950 in Aus. (B.P.) *COD*, 1976, suggests deriv. ex Mexican Sp. *potiguaya*.—5. Microphone: broadcasters': later C.20. 'He actually hissed the word "damnation", and all England gasped . . . The dangers of an open "pot" are now, no doubt, well documented' (Vaughan, 1978).

pot, v. To throw, e.g. a stone: Aus. B., 1942.—2. To put a baby on a chamber-pot: domestic coll.—3. To inform upon, lay information against: Aus. low: since ca. 1920. Caddie, 1943, 'To myself I said, "What dirty swine has potted me?" ' A shortening of **put** (someone's) **pot on**, q.v.—4. See TIDDLYWINKS in Appx.

pot and pan. One's father; usu. *old pot* . . . : r.s., on *old man*: fairly rare before 1925. Ortzen, 1938.

pot-gutted. Pot-bellied: Aus. coll. Baker.

Pot Hall. St Peter's Hall (now College), founded in 1929: Oxford undergraduates': since 1930; by late 1960s, ob. (With thanks to Dr J.I.M. Stewart, 1976.)

pot-head. (Or written solid.) A cannabis smoker: prisoners' and drugs world': later C.20. (McConville, 1980.) See **pot**, n., 4.

pot o(f) honey. Var of **bees and honey**, q.v., money. (Franklyn 2nd.) Sometimes shortened to *honey*.

pot the white. (Of a man) to coït with a woman: since ca. 1930. (Bates, 1955.) Ex billiards.

Potash and Perlmutter. Butter: r.s.: since ca. 1915; by 1960, ob. Montague Glass's play of that title 'was first produced in London at the Queen's Theatre, Shaftesbury Avenue, London, on 14 Apr. 1914. The play was a huge success and the term may have come into use even before 1915' (Franklyn 2nd).

potato-pillin' (orig., prob. **peelin'**). A shilling: r.s. (mostly workmen's). (*John o' London's Weekly*, 9 June 1934.) Cf. the more gen. *rogue and villain*.

potatoes in the mould, hence often *potatoes* whence *taters*. Cold (adj.): r.s.: late C19–20. (Franklyn, *Rhyming*.) P.B.: in later C.20 *taters* is the predominant, perhaps the only, form. Cf. **soldiers bold**.

potential. A potential officer: Army coll.: since ca. 1940. P-G-R.

pothead. See **pot-head.**

Pots. A *P*etty *O*fficer *T*elegraphist (*s* either = 'Special', since ca. 1950, or added for euphony): RN: since late 1930s. (Malin, 1979.) Also as vocative.—2. '*Chambers Twentieth Century Dictionary*, a best seller known with respect in some households as "the Pots" ' (*The Times*, 23 July 1980). A pun on *chamber-pots*. (P.B.)

pots; gen. be pots, to be mad, or extremely eccentric: from ca. 1925. (Weymouth, 1936.) Ex *potty* on **bats**, q.v.; in Cheshire, occ. elab. to *pots for rags* (Richards, 1984).

pots and dishes. Wishes: r.s.: later C.20. Barker, 1979.

potted. Exhilarated by taking marijuana: drug addicts': adopted, ca. 1956, ex US. See **pot**, n., 4, and **pot-head**.

Potteries, the. See ASSOCIATION FOOTBALL, in Appx.

potting-shed. The lavatories where young children go after a meal: day nurseries nurses': later C.20. (Roberts, 1983.) A pun on the gardener's potting-shed. Cf. **cack-school**.

potty, n. A chamber-pot, esp. a child's: nursery and domestic coll.

potty, adj. Indifferent; shaky; very unpromising (business scheme); 1860 (H.); rather ob.—2. Silly; crazy: from ca. 1910. Cf. **batty**, *dotty*, **loopy**.

potty-training. A pun on the initials of *Post-Ordination Training*: Anglican priests', in the Leicester Diocese. (Sheard, 1976.) Ex **potty**, n., and the domestic coll. 'potty-training' of infants.

pouch a gun. To carry a revolver: c.: from ca. 1920. (Wallace, 1927.) On US *pack a gat*.

pouf-wroughting. See **poof-rorting**.

pouffe. See **poof**.

poufter. See **poofter**.

poultice. A bore (person or thing): Glasgow:—1934. Cf. **pill** in this sense..—2. A mortgage: Aus. Prichard, 1932.—3. A (large) sum of money; e.g. in wages: Aus.: since ca. 1920. Niland, 1948, 'I got paid off, and it was a whacking big *poultice*.'—4. Hence, a bribe, esp. in *sling in a poultice*, to offer a bribe: Aus.: since ca. 1925. Culotta.—5. As *the Poultice*, the taxicab rank outside the Middlesex Hospital: London taxi-drivers': since ca. 1910.

poultice plasterer, the. The medical officer: RN: since ca. 1920. (H. & P.) Cf.:-

poultice-wallopers; also with capitals. Occ. **P. Wallahs.** The Royal Army Medical Corps: Army nickname: earlier C.20. Also *the Pills, the Linseed Lancers*.—2. In the sing., a sick-bay attendant or nursing orderly: late C.19–20: at first RN; later, also RAF. Bowen; Jackson.

poultry dealer. 'A homosexual pimp who specialises in young boys—"chickens" ' (Green, 1984).

pounce, n. A severe, esp. if written, criticism: book-world coll.: from ca. 1930.

pounce, v.t. 'Active part in (homo-)sexual intercourse. Jean Genet, *Querelle of Brest*, 1953, " . . . pounced by Nono" '.

pouncer. A female fire-watcher: see **whistler**, 4.

pound-not(e)ish. Stylish; aristocratic; affected of speech or manner: lower classes': from ca. 1930. *Gilt Kid*, 1936, 'Her pound-noteish voice both annoyed and amused the Gilt Kid.'

pound the beat. 'To walk the streets as a prostitute' (McNeil): Aus. low coll.: later C.20. A parody of the police usage.

pour (a person). To see a person, who has had plenty of 'farewell drinks', off, and on to his transport, as 'We poured old Nobby on to his plane about three in the morning' (P.B.), and 'it was a slightly jaded company of artists who were "poured over the side" into launches [from HMS *Anson*]' (Worsley, 1948): coll., mostly Services.

pour on more coals. To open the throttle of either a piston or a jet engine: RAF: since ca. 1950. Cf. *open the taps* at **taps**.—2. 'Also used for accelerating in a motor car' (Leechman): motorists': since ca. 1955. Also *pour on the coal, put the coals on*.

poured into. (Of a girl or woman) wearing very tight-fitting clothing to the greatest enhancement of her figure, as 'She was poured into a sky-blue uniform' (Campbell, 1960). Orig. in the simile 'she looked as if she had been poured . . . ' (P.B.)

pouve. Occ. var. of **poove**, 2.

Poverty Row (picture). See MOVING-PICTURE SLANG, §8, in Appx.

powder. (Of a horse) vigour, spirits: turf:—1923 (Manchon). Perhaps ex *gunpowder*.—2. 'Cocaine, amphetamine sulphate, or other drugs in powdered form' (Hibbert, 1983); heroin (Stockley, 1986): drugs c. As = heroin, US since ca. 1920 (Spears).—3. See **take a powder**.

powder away. To perform fine but useless deeds: coll.:—1923 (Manchon). Ex S.E. *powder*, to scatter or sprinkle like powder.

powder (one's) **nose.** To go to the lavatory: women's euph.: since ca. 1940.—2. Hence, by a pun, 'to absorb cocaine via the nasal passages' (Hibbert, 1983): drugs c. Cf. **powder**, 2.

power. To move in a powerful manner, as in '[pictures of] some of the most famous locomotives . . . powering along this famous track' (Keeley, 1985), or 'the Chelsea striker powered down the field to slam in the equaliser'.

poxed, poxt. Infected with syphilis: late C.17–20: S.E. until mid-C.18, then a vulg.

poxed-up. C.20 low coll. shape of prec., as in 'a poxed-up whore' (Raper, 1973).

poxy. (Of things) old and either inferior or in deplorable condition, as, e.g., a pair of shoes. Naughton, 1970.

poz, pozz. In *pozzing about*, 'messing' or 'faffing' about, behaving in a fussy and futile way: Leicestershire: perhaps dial., but not in *EDD*. Pylypiac, 1984.

prac. A practical test or examination: Aus. students', esp. in Science or Medicine: since ca. 1925. (B.P.) Cf.:-

pracs. Practical classes: Reading undergraduates': since ca. 1920. Marples, 2.

Practical Jokes Department, the. The Administrative branch of the Army: soldiers', esp. officers'. Goodsall, 1925.

prairie pudden. Nothing to eat, an empty plate: ' "Djou know what prairie pudden is? . . . It means the wide open spaces . . . In other words, bugger all" ' (Seabrook, 1967: concerning early C.20 Northampton).

prairie rash. Baked beans: RN lowerdeck: WW2. (*Weekly Telegraph*, 13 Sep. 1941.) Ex *cowboys*; cf. **yippee beans**.

praise with faint damns. Occ. joc. inversion of Pope's original line. (P.B.)

pram. A perambulator (for infants): (until ca. 1920, considered rather low) coll. abbr.: 1884, *Graphic* 25 Oct.—2. In *get out of* (one's) *pram*, to become very, or over-, excited; hence, very angry: since ca. 1950. (Clapperton, 1970.) Cf. *off* (one's) *trolley*.

Prancing Queers, The. Ivor Novello's show, *The Dancing Years*: theatrical: late 1940s–early 1950s.

prang, n. A crash; esp., a crash-landing: RAF: since ca. 1937. (H. & P.) Ex the v.—2. A bombing raid: 1939+. (Partridge, 1945.) Ex sense 2 of v. But Anthony Burgess, *Observer*, 18 July 1982, writes, '*Prang* still has no etymology [in *OED* Sup., vol. 3], despite its near-certain provenance in Malay *perang*, which means fighting or war (*orang perang*—fighting man).'

prang, v. To crash-land an aircraft (usu. v.t.): RAF: since ca. 1935. Rhodes, 1942; Jackson, 1943, 'To damage, destroy, wreck . . . From the sound of the impact of a metal aircraft with the ground'; Brickhill, 1946 (see quot'n at **hack**, v., 1). Reminiscent of *bang*.—2. Hence(?), to bomb (a town, a factory, etc.): since late 1939. John Moore, *Observer*, 4 Oct. 1942; Jackson, 'He pranged the target to blazes.'—3. (Ex 1 or 2—or both.) 'Sometimes applied to non-flying accidents, e.g., "Jones pranged his arm at rugger to-day" ' (H. & P., 1943).—4. To coït with (a girl): RAF: 1940+. Cf. **bang**, v., 1, and **target** . . .

prang artist. An accident-prone motorcyclist: motorcyclists' (Dunford): since ca. 1945. Ex **prang**, n., 1 and v., 1. See **artist**, esp. sense 2.

prat, pratt, n. The female pudend: low: C.19–20.—2. A girl, a young woman: low. 'The pratt's marked [i.e. spotted] us! . . . Get after her!' (Newman, 1977).—3. Also ex sense 1 is the term's use as a gen. low, virtually meaningless, pej.: 'Stupid prat—what's he think he's doing?': since mid-C.20, prob. earlier. Cf. synon. sense of *cunt*, **prick**, **twat**, etc.

P

P

prat, v. To speak, to talk, to someone: Aus. low: since ca. 1918. (B., 1942.) Cf. S.E. *prattle*.

prat(-)fall (or one word). 'A fall on one's bottom or *prat* [n., since C.15], esp. as part of stock-in-trade of a knockabout comedian' (L.A., 1974): Can., adopted ca. 1935, ex US; by ca. 1950, Brit.

prat for (someone). To act, in a specific instance, as the passive partner in a male homosexual relationship: low. Ex *prat*, buttocks, since C.15.

praught. Past tense of *preach*: deliberate sol., among the literate, for humorous effect. (P.B.)

prawn-headed mullet. A very stupid fellow: Aus.: since ca. 1930. (Culotta, 1963.) Cf. **stunned mullet.**

prawnie, -y. A catcher or a seller of prawns: Aus.: since ca. 1920. B., 1953.

pray. 'No use to protest. To squeal, or to pray as they called it, might mean worse' (Barlow, 1968): raffish London, esp. teenage addicts': since ca. 1960.

prayers. In *morning*, or *family*, *prayers*, a daily Staff Conference at HQ: Army: WW2. (E.P.) The *morning prayers* form was still in use at GHQ Hong Kong, in the later 1960s (P.B.).—2. In *know more than* (one's) *prayers*, not to be as innocent as one seems: Aus.: since ca. 1930. Wilkes.

praying-mantis. 'A tail landing, whether accidental or intentional if the undercarriage fails to work' (H. & P.): RAF: since ca. 1930. Ex that insect, *Mantis religiosa*, which holds its forelegs in a position suggestive of prayer (*OED*)

pre-fab. A pre-fabricated house: 1945+; by 1947, coll. P.B.: these cosy little 'instant dwellings' were a stop-gap measure to counter the housing shortage caused by WW2. A few are still in use, 1988. The term was enshrined in a chant, orig. in Charley Chester's radio comedy series 'Stand Easy': 'Down in the jungle, living in a tent: better than a pre-fab—no rent!' Very popular among children, later 1940s.

Pre Sci (pron. *sky*). *Pre*liminary *sci*ence examination, University of London: (mostly students') coll.: late C.19–20.

preem, n., v. 'The premiere of a film, play, show or TV programme or series; to launch a new film, play, etc.' (Green, 1984): entertainments world.

preemie. See **premie.**

preggers. Pregnant: Oxford and Cambridge graduates': since ca. 1920. By male insensitivity out of Alma Mater tribalism. Cf. the next two.

preg(g)o. Pregnant: Aus.: since the 1920s. (Cusack, 1951.) The ubiquitous Aus. suffix -*o*.

preggy. Pregnant; hence, bulging: upper and upper-middle classes': since early 1920s. Marsh, 1938, 'There was your bag, simply preggy with bank-notes, lying there on the writing-table.'

Pregnant Duck. A Hudson bomber aircraft: RAF: 1940–4. Ex appearance. (Pudney.)

prejaganint. (Too) thrustful, interfering; having the unfortunate knack of being always in the way: NZ: from ca. 1912. Perhaps a corruption of *prejudiced*.

prelim. In pl., the pre-text pages of a book, i.e. title-pages, preface, contents-page and, when there is one, the dedication: printers' and publishers'. Abbr. *preliminaries*.—2. A preliminary practice or match: sporting. *OED* Sup.

Prels. Preludin: see DRUGS, in Appx.

premie (pron. *premmie*). A *pre*maturely born child: Can. and Aus. medical world: since ca. 1925. (Leechman; B.P.) By 1930, and sometimes pron. *preemie*, common also among Brit. doctors and nurses.—2. A premature sexual ejaculation, and one subject to it: adopted, mid-1960s, ex US. Hollander.

prep. To prepare (a person; a limb; etc.) for operation: hospitals'. Bell, 1937, 'Macdonald started to prep him' and 'She had finished prep'ing the leg'.

preppy. 'Typical of the manners and attitudes of a [N. American] preparatory school boy' (W. & F., 1975, sup.): some borrowing in Brit., as in 'The Exploited [a pop group], who

make Robert de Niro in *Taxi Driver* look preppy' (Steve Bradshaw, *Listener*, 12 Nov. 1981).

Presbo. A Presbyterian: Aus.: since ca. 1925. B., 1953.

presh. Pressure (q.v.): police and c.: later C.20. Kavanagh, 1980.

Press Button. A Presbyterian: Aus., mostly Catholic. Cf. **Pressed Beef.**

press on regardless; press-on type. 'I must press on, regardless' = I have urgent work to do, I must finish this job. Ex lit., *press on*, to continue one's way towards the objective, despite damage or injury. Hence, *press-on type*, an energetic or very conscientious fellow: 1941+: often derisive. (Noble, 1945.) ' . . . the striking thing is how many [of the Battle of Britain pilots] have made good. "And why not?" says Douglas Bader. "They were all press-on chaps" ' (*Sunday Telegraph* mag., 9 Sep. 1979).

press the button. To be the person to make a definite and/or important beginning: coll.:—1931 (Lyell).

press the panic button. To panic: Aus.: since ca. 1960. (B.P., 1969.) A pun on S.E. *press the alarm.*

Pressed Beef. A Presbyterian: since ca. 1950. It occurred in, e.g., *Lucky Jim*, on TV, 6 June 1967. Cf. **Press Button.**

presser. An electric torch: one presses the switch to operate it. Tey, 1929.

Pressie, adj. and n. (A) Presbyterian: Aus. MacInnes, 1952.—2. (Usu. pron. *prezzy*.) A present: trivial coll.: later C.20, gen.; perhaps earlier, Aus. and Merseyside. Cf. **cossie.** (P.B.) 'Presents so potty that another word has to be found for them. They are not presents but "prezzies". Prezzies are fun presents. Nobody is supposed to take them seriously' (*New Society*, 23 Dec. 1982).

pressing engagement. An appointment with a girl: joc. coll. With pun on *pressing.*

pressure. Police investigation; police interrogation: Aus. c.: since ca. 1920. (B., 1942.) Ex *put pressure on.* See **presh.**

pretty. A pretty girl, a 'lovely': since ca. 1935. Ex a domestic term of address to a girl child or adolescent, whether pretty or not: coll.: late C.19–20.—2. As *the pretty* the *fair*way: golfers' coll.: 1907 (*OED* Sup.).

pretty as paint, as. Very pretty: coll.: 1922, E.V. Lucas, 'She's as pretty as paint' (Apperson). Because like a painting.

pretty (-) boy. 'An effeminate young man' (B., 1942); Aus. and low Brit. coll.

pretty-perch. A very neat landing: RAF:—1932. Opp. a *thumped-in landing.* Cf. **grease her on.**

pretty please. An intensification of 'please', often as a rather wheedling request, 'Will you do it—pretty please?': domestic.(P.B.)

pretty up. To 'make a mess of', to disfigure: Aus.: since ca. 1920. Niland, 1959, 'I'll pretty up your face, boy.'

previous. A previous conviction; collectively, previous convictions: police coll.: since ca. 1930. Newman, 1970.

prezzie. See **Pressie,** 2.

price. In *have a price*, to have a chance: sporting: since ca. 1960. ' "Rendall ran and never had a price" ' (News commentary on a cricket match, 29 July 1977). Ex the turf, where, if a horse in a race is not quoted in the odds, the bookmakers think that it either won't run or, if it does, stands not the remotest chance of getting a place, 1, 2, 3 or even 4' (Gardner, 1977).

price of pint, the. A sum sufficient to buy a pint of ale or beer: coll.: late C.19–20.

price of Admiralty. Mostly *pay the . . . ,* to be killed at sea: RN officers' sarcastic euph. (Granville.) 'The source of this is "A Song of the English", one of the poems in Rudyard Kipling's *The Seven Seas* (1896). The line "If blood be the price of admiralty" is repeated cumulatively (an additional repetition in each succeeding verse), and produces an unintentionally hysterical effect that invites sarcasm from those who may be expected to pay it' (R.S., 1967).

pric(e)y. High-priced: Aus. and NZ coll., app. since ca. 1910; Brit. since early 1940s. Drake-Brockman, 1940; *World's Press News*, 31 Aug. 1944.

prick. An offensive or contemptuous term (applied to men only), always with *silly*; gen. *you silly prick*, occ. *the s.p.*: low: late C.19–20. Since ca. 1940, usage has decreed that whereas *you silly prick* need be neither contemptuous nor even derogatory, *you prick* is both—and, indeed, very offensive. This sense-shift applies in N. America as well as in Britain. Ex formerly S.E. (till ca. 1700) *prick* = penis.—2. A pin: tramps' and beggars' c.: —1933.—3. A drugged, esp. a marijuana, cigarette: c., merging, esp. among teenagers, into drug addicts' s., notably in London: since ca. 1970. Phallic imagery.

prick-farrier. A medical officer: RAF: late 1920s–(?)late 1940s. Cf. **prick-smith** and **fang-farrier**.

prick-parade. A VD inspection: Services' coll.

prick(-)smith. Medical officer: Army: 1939+. Ex the venereal inspection he administers.

prick teaser (occ. **tease**). 'A woman who pretends an interest in sexual affairs, but deliberately does not "follow through". Often used as an insult to a woman, or a gross insult to a completely innocent and virtuous woman who has caused annoyance, when both words and not the abbreviation [see **p.t.**, 2] would be used' (Powis): low: since late C.19. Cf. synon. **bedside virgin**.

pricked, with its ears. (Of a horse winning) easily: racecourse coll.: —1932 (*Slang*, p. 243).

pricker. In *get the pricker with* (someone), to take a dislike to: NZ: since ca. 1930. Slatter, 'Got the pricker with me'. Prob. cf. *get the needle*, to get annoyed (P.B.).—2. As *chief pricker* a chief stoker: RN: since ca. 1910. Granville.

Prim. A Primitive Methodist: Nonconformists': late C.19–20.

Prime, the. The Prime Minister: from ca. 1919. Galsworthy, 1924, 'Didn't he think that the cubic called "Still Life—of the Government", too frightfully funny—especially the "old bean" representing the Prime?'

Prince of Wales. A locomotive's blowing-off of steam: railwaymen's: since ca. 1920. (*Railway*.) Perhaps r.s. on *gales* (of wind), unless it refers to King Edward VIII's refreshing outspokenness post-WW1, while, of course, he was still the Prince of Wales. P.B.: or perhaps a ref. to Prince of Wales' feathers = plumes of smoke; ob. with the demise of steampower on the railways.

prink. *The Prink* is the Principal, esp. of a women's college: girl undergraduates' and trainee teachers': since ca. 1905. Also *Prinny*.

prison-bug. A man that spends most of his time in prison: c.: from ca. 1920.

Prisoner of War. See PRISONER-OF-WAR SLANG, in Appx.

prissy. Effeminate: mostly women's: coll.: adopted, ca. 1943, ex US servicemen. (Dickens, 1946.) Perhaps a blend of *pr*im + *sissy*, as Mitford M. Mathews has suggested. Hence a noun, as in Adrian, 1958.—2. Prudish: mostly men's: Aus.: since ca. 1943. Niland, 1958.

prissy-pants. 'Elderly or middle-aged citizens of bourgeois tastes; in contrast with the "blue jeans" ' (R.S., adducing the *Daily Telegraph*, 9 June 1975, on the contemporary theatre): since ca. 1970.

priv. A privilege: Public Schools': late C.19–20. (Marples.) See also **privs**.—2. *Priv*ilege leave; the allowance of leave, excluding compassionate, sick, public holiday, and odd week-end leaves, as 'I got 7 days priv to come; they can't stop that—or can they?': Services': since ca. 1950. Cf. **embark**. (P.B.)

private eye. A private detective: adopted, ca. 1944, ex US servicemen, with the late Raymond Chandler intervening. A pun on '*priv*ate *i*nvestigator', with esp. ref. to the initial of the 2nd word.

private navy. Any detached RN unit working far from the surveillance of the Commander-in-Chief: RN joc.: since ca. 1920.

private property. An engaged girl: joc. coll.: since ca. 1920.

Private Snoops. See **Chad**.

Private Tojo. A Japanese soldier: Army in the Pacific and Indian Oceans 'theatre': 1942–5. Ex the war-mongering Japanese Premier, Tojo. P-G-R.

priver. A private school: Public Schools': earlier C.20. (Lunn, 1919.) By the 'OXFORD -ER'.

privs. In *have* (one's) *privs*, to have 'the privilege to fag and "whop" ' (Lunn). A late C.19–20 Harrow term. Also in the singular, as in Lunn: a privilege; a privileged person: 'You couldn't go into a room without finding some fag smoking. And so the privs got rather fed up. It was jolly bad for the House footer. So they make it a four-year priv.'

privy. A preparatory school: Marlborough College: late C.19–20. So many 'prep' schools are *privately* owned; cf. **priver**.

prize. Egregious; esp. 'prize idiot': coll. Ex S.E. sense, first-class.

pro. An actor: theatrical:—1859 (H., 1st ed., Intro.). I.e. one who belongs to *the* profession, i.e. acting. (N.B., *the profession* is rather j. than coll., though orig. it may possibly have been theatrical coll.)—2. Hence, any professional as opp. to an amateur: e.g. cricketer, 1867; journalist, 1886; golfer, 1887. Coll. *OED*.—3. Since WW1, esp. of a prostitute whose *profession* is body-vending: as opp. to a notoriously or very compliant 'amateur', esp. an 'amateur' that makes a little extra by sexual 'adventures'. P.B.: but also understood as a shortening of '*pro*stitute'.

pro-y. Professional; esp., of or like a professional prostitute: since ca. 1920. Curtis, 1937, 'I always think those rooms at Paddington make it seem so pro-y.' See **pro**, 3.

prob. A period of probation, esp. for a juvenile delinquent: since ca. 1930. Draper, 1970. Cf. **proby**.—2. A problem: trivial abbr.: Services': later C.20. ' "No probs," said the Para's [Parachute Regt] commanding officer' (*Don't Cry*, 1983).

proby. A probation officer: police and social services': since ca. 1955. (Petch.)

prod. A Protestant, as opp. to Catholic: var. of **Prot**. Cf. **Prod-do**, *q.v.*—2. In *on the prod*, ready to fight; in a fighting mood: Can. coll. Dempsey, 1975, 'The old man was on the prod'. Leechman, 1976, 'A battlesome cow is said to be "on the prod", i.e. ready to use her horns.'

Proddie, -y, adj. and n. Protestant: late (?mid-)C.19–20. Naughton, 1966. (L.A.) Cf. **Prot, prod**, 1, and:-

Prod(d)o. A Protestant: Aus. Catholics'. (B.P.)

produce, gen. in imperative. To pay over the money won: two-up players'. Abbr. *produce the money*.

producer. 'A sucker with an outside source of income who produces the money for the gambler to win . . . The difference between the producer and the gambler is this . . . The gambler, when he's playing "on the muscle" [*q.v.*] and finds the luck running against him, will get up and quit, while the producer will stay in the game and lose his shirt' (Drage, 1954): Can. gamblers': early C.20.

productious. Productive: book-world. Ruck, 1935.

professor. A professional: cricketers'. Gordon, 1939.—2. An Education Officer: RAF (mostly officers'): since ca. 1938. Jackson.

proff. To profit(?): RN: since ca. 1930. Winton, 1960, 'Except in a Leap Year, of course, when I proff and get no work at all.' Hawke, 1979, about the RM in N. Ireland, early 1970s, defines the term as 'To "acquire" ', cf. to **win, organise, promote**, etc. 'To acquire by less than legal means' (Fox, 1982): Parachute Regt.

prog, n. A proctor (Oxford, Cambridge): undergraduates' s. By perversion. Also *progger* and *proggins*. Cf. the v.—2. A *prog*ramme: not very gen. coll.:—1923 (Manchon). A term revived in later 1970s (Simmonds, early 1979; *Now!*, 11 Apr. 1980).—3. A Perceval *Proc*tor training aircraft: RAF: 1943+. Ex sense 1. Partridge, 1945.

prog, v.t. To proctorise: Oxford and Cambridge. Ex **prog**, n., 1.

prog, adj. *Prog*ressive, as of schools or methods: since ca. 1950. Benge, 1969.

progger. (Also **proggins.**) A proctor. Oxford, + 'OXFORD *-ER*'. Cambridge. Ex **prog**, v.

progging. A proctorial discipline: Oxford, Cambridge. Ex **prog**, v.

proggy mat. A mat, or a rug, made from cloth-cuttings, with a 'progger' (a type of prodding instrument): N. Country coll.; late C.19–20.

prole, n. Mostly *proles*, the proletariat: Aus. Labour: since ca. 1925. Cf. next. P.B.: the term has also had some joc. patronising, or sometimes pej., use among, e.g., Public Schoolboys of all ages, for members of the 'lower classes': 'He's a bit of a prole', he is noticeably uncouth in behaviour.

prole, v. To educate the *prole*tariat to become conscious of themselves as Labour: *proling*, political speaking at street-corners: Aus. Labour: since ca. 1925. B., 1942.

prole, adj. Corresponding to Brit. sense of the n. York, 1976.

promise. In *on a promise*, 'Awaiting a gift or personal services; sometimes used in anticipation of sexual favours to come' (Powis): c.: later C.20.

prommer. A member of the audience at the Henry Wood Promenade Concerts. James Loughran, in the conductor's traditional last-night-of-the-Proms speech, 11 Sep. 1982.

promo. ' "Promos", videotaped films used to promote records' (White, 1983): entertainments world. In use in US for this kind of commercial advertising since early 1960s (Barnhart, 2), but as abbr. of S.E. promotion, a rise in rank, in Tod, 1900.

promote. To borrow, or to scrounge, something; loosely, to steal: Aus. Army: WW2. (B., 1943.) Euph.: cf. **organise** and *win*. P.B.: its use is wider than E.P. allows here: US c. > gen s., since ca. 1915 (W.& F.); Brit. Services' since ca. 1950 at latest.

promotionitis. The symptoms displayed by officers potentially promotable: RN coll. Bowen.

prong. (Of a man) to copulate: a low euph., *prong* = prick, penis: later C.20. In his fine novel about the US Navy in Chinese waters, mid-1920s, *The Sand Pebbles*, 1962, Richard McKenna uses the term to represent *fuck* as a meaningless oath, 'Prong me!', etc.

prongs. The front forks on a motorcycle: motorcyclists'. (Dunford.)

pronk. A fool: ' "of all the useless, pompous pronks I've ever met . . . " ' (Cody, 1985). An arbitrary formation, influenced by synon. **prick**.

pronto. Promptly; quickly: coll.: adopted, esp. by Servicemen, ex US Services in 1918, and still current (in e.g., *Phantom*). Bowen; F. & G. Ex Sp. *pronto*, promptly.

proovy. Approved school, corrective establishment for juveniles: prisons'. Clayton, 1970.

prop. A propeller: aviators' coll.: from ca. 1915. B. & P.—2. Propaganda: journalists': 1939+.

prop game, the. The gaining of useful information about, and access to, buildings, esp. to private houses, by posing as local government inspectors or as builders and later stealing from them: since ca. 1963. In the Bournemouth *Evening Echo* of 20 Apr. 1966, a detective sergeant stated that 'the "prop game" appeared to be . . . unique to Leeds, something that has cropped up in the last two and a half years': cf. **straight prop** and **bowler-hat boys**.

prop up. 'Originally and most commonly short for "proposition". Still used in that sense but also to suggest or arrange, particularly through a third person: "we must prop up a story over this" ' (Powis): c. Cf. **proposition**, v.

proper bastard (*bugger*, etc.). Something (or someone) thoroughly unpleasant, infuriating, exasperating; as, e.g., 'Honestly! It's a proper cow the way they can just . . . ': low coll. A somewhat specialised use of older S.E. > coll. *proper*. (P.B.)

proper crowd(, one's). One's personal friends; the circle or clique to which one belongs: Aus. coll.: since 1920. B., 1942.

proper do. A very fine party or wedding-feast: working classes': since ca. 1910.

property. Any creative work; e.g. a book, play, song, not yet published: agents', book and music publishers', *et hoc genus omne*: coll. verging j., or *vice versa*: since ca. 1930.

proposition, n. A matter: coll. (orig. US); prob. soon to be S.E. 'That's quite a different proposition.' Ex the very closely allied S.E. (orig. US) sense, 'a problem, task, or undertaking . . . a person to be dealt with' (*SOD*). See, e.g., the Fowlers' *King's English*.—2. A *tough proposition* retains its US flavour.—3. See:-

proposition, v. To '*proposition*' a girl is to suggest sexual intimacy: hence the n.—cf. the c.p., or viritual c.p., 'Is this a proposal or proposition?': Can. (?ex US) since ca. 1940; Brit. and Aus. since ca. 1943. Cf. **prop up**.

propping. The encouragement of a junior by addressing her by her first name: Lady Margaret Hall, Oxford: since ca. 19.. (Marples, 2.) Ex S.E. *prop*, to support.

props. In *get one's props*, to become a Leading Aircraftman: RAF: since ca. 1930. H. & P., 'The propeller-shaped badge worn on the sleeve.'

pros. Proscenium: theatrical: since ca. 1910. Holt, 1950.

prospect. A person more or less likely to take out an insurance policy: an insurance coll. now verging on j. Ex S.E. mining sense, a spot giving prospects of, e.g., gold.

prospector. A confidence trickster: Aus. c.: since ca. 1925. (B., 1953.) For mugs' gold.

prossie. Late C.19–20 Aus. var. of earlier *pross*, a prostitute. (B., 1942.) Also Brit: Ada E. Jones, 1931. Cf.:-

prosso. A prostitute: Aus.: since ca. 1925. (Dick.) Cf. prec.

prostitute, the. The twelfth man, or a *substitute*, in a cricket match: cricketers': ca. 1870–1914. Gordon.

prostitution. See **higher prostitution**.

Prot, n. and adj. (A) Protestant: Catholics': mid-C.19–20. In N. Ireland, 'Protestant/Loyalist' (Hawke, 1979).—2. As adj. (also *protty*), Low Church: theological colleges': 1960s. (Towler, 1979.) See **hot prot**.

protected. Lucky; uncannily or very lucky: Aus. and NZ. Prob. . *protected by the gods* or *by one's superiors*.

protection. In *take* (a girl) *under* (one's) *protection*, to take care of a girl and send or accompany her out to the Argentine: (Polish) white-slavers c. Londres.

protection racket. The extortion of money, services, etc., from shopkeepers or other businessmen, as a bribe to leave them and their property unmolested: adopted, ex US, early C.20, as c.; in later C.20, S.E.

Protestant herring, a. A stale, a bad, herring; hence, any inferior provender, as in 'Oh, that butter is a Protestant herring' (Joyce, 1910): Anglo-Irish coll.: mid-C.19–20.

proverbial, the. A fall, smash; disaster: military: 1916; ob. (F. & G.) Abbr. *the proverbial fall* that comes after pride.—2. In later C.20, often used allusively for other things, e.g., 'Oh, he's the proverbial bastard', i.e. he is a most unpleasant man; or, almost meaninglessly, relying on the context for sense, as 'I think I've got a touch of the proverbials' (= e.g., *the shits* = diarrhœa): coll. (P.B.) D. Williams, 1987, adduces further examples in which it = *shit*: 'up the proverbial creek', and 'when the proverbial hits the fan'; both mean trouble.

Provie. See **Provo**, 3.

provo. A provost marshal: Aus. Army: WW2. Page, 1973.—2. A *provocateur*, not necessarily an *agent provocateur*: since ca. 1955. (Petch, 1969.)—3. But a *Provo* is a 'member of the Provisional wing of the I.R.A' (*COD*, 1976): gen. coll. since 1970 >, by 1975, S.E. Also, earlier, *Provie*.

provy. See **proovy**.

prowl car. A police patrol-vehicle: adopted, ex US, mid-C.20. They prowl about the streets on the look-out for offenders. (P.B.)

Pru, the. The *Pru*dential insurance company: insurance: late C.19–20. Collinson.

Prudential men, or **men of the Prudential.** Officers in the Special Branch of the RNVR: RN: 1939–45. With a pun on the Prudential insurance company. P-G-R.

prune is short for *Prune*, *P/O*. Moore, 1942, ' "Lost anybody?" "Some prune who thought he could beat up the searchlights" '; B., 1942.—2. 'A shrivelled-up spinster, no longer a "plum" ' (Petch, 1974): later C.20.

prune, v. To adjust or otherwise tinker with (a ship's engines): RN: since ca. 1930. P-G-R.

Prune, P/O; in speech, **Pilot Officer Prune.** 'A pilot who takes unnecessary risks, and generally loses his neck through his *prunery*' and ' "P/O Prune" is the title bestowed upon a pilot who has several "prangs" on his record' (H. & P.): RAF: since ca. 1935. He is a constant emblematic monitory figure in the pages of the *R.A.F. Journal*. Not unconnected with the impracticality of 'prunes and prisms'. Created, Jackson tells us, by S/Ldr Anthony Armstrong and LACW Hooper ('Raff').

prune-juice. Hard liquor: since ca. 1935. Gordon, 1953.

pseud, since mid-1960s, ex **pseudo,** since ca. 1955. A 'phoney', an affected, esp. if so-called intellectual, *poseur* and 'make-believer': Public Schools' > gen. coll. Popularised by regular feature in the satirical magazine *Private Eye*, 'Pseuds' Corner', which simply quotes examples of the worst current *pseudery*. The orig. Public School sense was 'One who holds pretentious or unorthodox opinions . . . a Socialist or any other non-Conservative. Mostly used pejoratively—almost the exact opposite of **staunch** [q.v.]' (Lambert 1968). See PUBLIC . . . SCHOOL SLANG, in Appx.

psych, n. A 'psychological' bet, one made on a hunch: Aus. two-up-players': since ca. 1930. Glassop, 1949.—2. A psychiatrist: coll. abbr.: since ca. 1950. Cf. **shrink,** n.

psych, v. (Earlier, *psyche*.) To subject to psychoanalysis: coll.:—1927 (Collinson).—2. (Often *psych out*.) To render uneasy; to intimidate or scare: adopted, ca. 1974, ex US. W. & F.; *6000 Words*.—3. See **psych up.**

psych up. To prepare oneself, or another, mentally for something, esp. an ordeal: 'patients have been psyched up for operations and then been told to go home' (Davies, 1982). Adopted, ca. 1973, ex US. See **psych,** v., 2.

psyche. See **psych,** v., 1.

psyche man. See **front man,** 2.

psychedelia. 'Drugs, flashing lights, sound, colour, movies, dance—usually experienced simultaneously' (Fryer, 1967): drug addicts' and hippies': since early 1967. Ex *psychedelic*, (of a drug, e.g. LSD) inducing the taker to feel 'expanded' and to reveal his soul; an imperfect form, *psychodelic* (soul-revealing) being correct.

psyching and **– out** and **– up.** The vbl n. corresponding to **psych,** v.

psycho. Psychoanalysis (1921); to psychoanalyse (1925): coll. *OED* Sup.—2. A psychopath: since ca. 1945.—3. Hence, a lunatic or a very eccentric person or merely an egregious fool: since ca. 1955.

pub-crawl; esp. **do a p.-c.** A liquorish peregrination from bar to bar: from not later than 1910. Hence *pub-crawler*, *pub-crawling*: from ca. 1910.

pub verandah push. Frequenters of the verandahs of country public houses: Aus. B., 1942.

pubbed. Completely eliminated from the game or competition: Leicester board-gamers': mid-1980s. 'A pub is the most likely place to retire to' (Poole, 1986).

pubes. (As one syllable.) The pubic hair: a deliberate mispron. among raffish literate: since ca. 1950. (P.B.)

public. One who avails himself of the personal facilities of a public library: Can. librarians': since ca. 1920. (Leechman.) He not only is a member of the general public but also makes a public convenience of the place. But also one who, although not a reader, applies to a library for assistance in a problem involving knowledge.

public convenience. A prostitute. Cf. earlier *public ledger*.

Public Enemy Number One (or **no. 1.**). Adopted in 1936, via the Press, ex US journalese not only in its correct (the literal) sense but in extended applications; thus, among English lawn-tennis players, Von Cramm and Budge were, in June 1937, described as 'Joint Public Enemies Number One'.

public-room men. 'In modern liners, the deck, smoke-room, library and lounge stewards and the like': nautical coll. Bowen.

publish-or-perish syndrome, the. 'A disease that afflicts career-minded academics—and helps to keep librarians in business' (P.B., 1975): the world of learning, and mostly derisive: since late 1960s, prob. ex US. A practice, an attitude, not prevalent at the best universities. The term is, in part, a gibe at *syndrome* itself.

Pubs. 'Naval cadets formerly entered direct from Public Schools, as opposed to those from Dartmouth ("Darts")' (Parsons, 1977): RN: ca. 1910–39.

puce. Very bad, inferior: Charterhouse: from ca. 1920. Esp. 'Absolutely puce!' Perhaps suggested by *bloody* and *putrid*.

pucka, puckah, pucker. See **pukka.**

pucker paint. See CANADIAN . . . , in Appx.

pud. 'Fleetwood term for an East Anglian fisherman' (Butcher, 1980). Cf. **Duff-Choker.**—2. See **pull** (one's) **pud.**

pudden. Metal filler: 'Watch for pudden on door sills. They're an MOT failure point and they're often toshed up with sheet Fibreglass and a can of spray paint' (*You*, 10 July 1983, p.26): car dealers': later C.20. Ex dial. pron. of *pudding*. Cf. **marzipan.**—2. See **pudding club.**

pudding. 'Join in an electric cable; from the bulge caused by the insulation tape' (Granville): RN: mid-C.20.

Pudding and Gravy, the. The Royal Navy: r.s.: since ca. 1940. Franklyn 2nd.

pudding-basin. The old style of motorcyclists' crash-helmet, shaped like half an egg: motorcyclists': since ca. 1940. (Dunford.)—2. The early issue WRNS uniform cap: WW2. (Knight, 1984.)

pudding-basin hair-cut. A hair-style that looks as though a basin had been inverted over the victim's head, and then any hair showing had been shaved or snipped off: coll. (P.B.)

pudding club. A ref. to pregnancy, esp. *join the . . .* or *be in the . . .*, to become, to be, pregnant; *(to) put in the . . .*, to render, be rendered, pregnant: low. Gardner, 1932, *join*; *Gilt Kid*, 1936, has var. *pudden*.

pudding round. 'In 1920s, dairies in UK had four daily rounds: [early] morning, pudding (11 a.m.), afternoon, evening' (Peppitt, 1976).

puddle-jumper. A small communications-aircraft: RAF: 1942+.

puddled. Very eccentric; insane: 1936 (Macarthney).

pudery. Pornographic books or prints: cultured: from ca. 1930. E.P. had suggested an orig. in L. *pudor*, shame, but R.S., 1973, queried, 'Might the immediate origin rather be the not unfamiliar S.E. *pudenda* (1634) displayed in such works than the basic but obsolete Latin emotion *pudor*? . . . Presumably the form was influenced as much by S.E. *prudery* (1709) as by 1920s s. *rudery*.'

puff, n. A sodomist: tramps' c.: from ca. 1870. Cf. **poof,** of which this is perhaps the origin.—2. A ladies' man: RAF: from ca. 1935. (Jackson.) P.B.: E.P.'s comment was, 'Prob. ex "powder-puff" ', but there may also be the effeminacy associated with sense 1.

puff, v. As in the caption to a cartoon in *Punch*, 14 May 1919, showing a prospective office-boy being interviewed: '[I've] Given up [smoking]. Find it "puffs" me for jazzin'.' (Jazz was suddenly 'all the rage'.)—2. To smoke cannabis: drugs c. (Stockley, 1986.) US since—1937 (Spears).

puff-adder. An accountant: RAF (mostly officers'): since ca. 1930. (McDouall, 1945.) Well, he *is* an adder of figures—and to some, as dangerous as that particular species of snake.—2. As a schoolboys' and Service joc., one who farts in the bath, and then counts the bubbles: mid-C.20. (P.B.)

puffler. A 'foreman or ganger' (*Railway*, 2nd): railwaymen's. Adopted ex mining.

pufo. 'In India in 1943 the end of a military exercise would be signalled on the wireless as the one word "Pufo". When speaking to a senior officer it was explained to him as an acronym for Pack Up and Fade Out. However, this is a euphemism' (Hayward, 1979). The word, pron. *pewfo*, could still be heard, in the sense 'let's push off', among older soldiers up to the early 1970s. (P.B.)

pug, n. 'Lancashire & Yorkshire [Railway] 0–4–0 clock saddle tank' (*Railway*, 2nd): railwaymen's. McKenna, *Glossary*, lists also 'Pannier type shunting locomotive from Glasgow & South-Western Railway'.

pug, v. To hide: low. Esp. of goods stolen by workmen, who 'pug it up' or 'pug it away' until they find it convenient to remove the article from the premises. Cf. Surrey dial. *pug*, 'to fill in a joint with softened clay', which seems to be a more likely origin than West Country *pug*, to thrust (*EDD*).

puggy. A Great Central Railway employee: railwaymen's: ca. 1900–25. (*Railway*.) Why?

pukka. Certain, reliable; genuine; excellent: Anglo-Indian coll.: from ca. 1770. In *pukka sahib* (in C.20, often derisive), it connotes the acme of gentlemanliness. Ex Hindi *pakka*, substantial. *OED*; Y. & B.

pukka gen. Completely reliable information: Services', esp. WW2. Ex prec. + *gen*, q.v. Opp. *duff gen*.

puku. See **pain in the puku.**

pull, n. In *give* (someone) *a* (*strong*) *pull*, to speak severely to; to reprimand: c. and low s.: since ca. 1930. (Norman.) Cf. *to pull* (someone) *up sharply.*—2. In *give it a pull* or *take a pull*, 'To desist, to discontinue' (Dennis): Aus. The first in, e.g., Drake-Brockman, 1937. In the imperative, occ. *take a pull on yourself!*

pull, v. To arrest: c.: 1811 (*Lex Bal.*). The sense is still current in later C.20, with further nuance 'to investigate, to stop (someone) for questioning, as in '[such behaviour] is definitely suspicious and "worth a pull" (worth investigating) promptly' (Powis).—2. To do; commit: US, adopted ca. 1925. Cf. *pull off*, to achieve. Heyer, 1936, 'If Rendall pulled the murder, Hyde's out of it.'—3. To 'pull off', to achieve: Army: since ca. 1920. 'It was eighteen years before I pulled sergeant.'—4. To earn (as income), to make (a sum of money, e.g., by a sale): Aus.: since ca. 1925. B., 1943.—5. As a v.i., it is the ellipsis of **pull** (one's) **wire** (and variants): (of the male) to masturbate; whence the vbl n. *pulling*: prob. since late C.19. Hollander.—6. To attract the attention, the notice, of (someone) sexually: 'It was obvious Jagger was trying to pull her . . . too shy to approach her and try to chat her up' (*Jagger*): since ca. 1955.

pull a fast one. See **fast one,** 2.

pull a flanker. See **flanker.**

pull a pint (often as vbl n., *pulling* . . .). To operate the controls of an aircraft, to do a pilot's work: RAF: since ca. 1930. (H.& P.) See **beer-lever.**

pull a stroke. 'To be faster, smarter, quicker [and more deceitful] than your opponent' (Cook, 1962): since ca. 1945: c. >, by ca. 1960, also low s. Cf. *pull a fast one*, q.v. at **fast one,** 2. Powis, 1977, quotes ' "talk about Oxford and Cambridge!" (involved allusion to the "strokes" in the University Boat Race).'—2. Hence, to commit a successful crime: c., hence police s.: since ca. 1950. Clayton, 1970.

pull(-)away. See AUSTRALIAN UNDERWORLD, in Appx.

pull down, v. To earn (money): from ca. 1920. Sayers, 1933.—2. V.i., to close up a fairground: fairground and grafters' coll. The London *Evening Standard*, 27 July 1976, concerning the murder of a fairground owner, '[His] family decided that the fair should pull down today, six days before the scheduled closing date.'

pull faces. To accost (celebrities): teenagers': later C.20. *Groupie.*

pull leather. 'A rider of a bucking horse in a rodeo is not allowed to "pull leather"—that is, to grab the saddle horn to

steady himself, an act which would disqualify him' (Leechman): Can.: since ca. 1920.

pull (one's) **leg.** To befool; to impose on: coll.,—1888; by 1940, familiar S.E. Ex tripping up. Extended, pre-WW2, to *now pull the other leg* (or, allusively, *the other one*)—*its's got bells on!* An early C.20 var. was *haul* (one's) *leg* (*Musings*, ca. 1912).

pull-off. A parachute jump from the wing of a plane: paratroops': since 1942. H. & P., 'A man opens his parachute and is then pulled off.'

pull on (a woman). To marry (one): Aus. B., 1942.—2. To tackle, contend with; hence, to test: Aus.: since ca. 1920. 'I'll pull on the Prime Minister himself if I can't get a permit for my business' (Morrisby, 30 Aug. 1958); B.,1953.—3. Elliptical for *pull a gun on*, to shoot at: ?mostly Dubliners': since ca. 1919.—4. In *pull* (something) *on*, to cite (something) as an excuse: Can. (and US). Beames.

pull one out of the bag. To make a special effort; draw on one's reserve powers: from ca. 1920. An elab. of **pull out.**

pull-ons. A pair of women's drawers that are merely pulled on without fastening: from 1923 or 1924. Coll.: by 1935, virtually S.E. Ex S.E. *pull-on*, n. and adj., (of) a garment that can be pulled on and needs no fastening or tying. Cf. **step-ins.**

pull out, v. To achieve, as in 'He pulled out a special effort'.

pull (one's) **pisser.** To 'pull his leg': Services', perhaps orig. RAF: since ca. 1930.

pull (one's) **pud, pudden** or **pudding.** (Of a male) to masturbate: low: since later C.19; the *pud* form is the more usu. in later C.20. See also **gallop** (one's) **maggot.**

pull (one's) **punches.** To exercise moderation, esp. in punishment or in blame: boxing coll. (since ca. 1930) become, ca. 1950, gen. coll. Often in negative, as 'They pulled no punches when it came to . . . '

pull rank (v.i.); with **on,** v.t. To exercise superiority of Service rank to achieve a purpose, get a job done, to wield the authority accruing from seniority: Services', since before WW2, perhaps as early as ca. 1918; by ca. 1960, in police, civilian, and quite other circumstances, e.g., to quieten someone down or get rid of him. (Petch and P.B., 1975.)

pull (one's) **Scotch** (often as vbl n.). To 'pull his leg': Services' r.s., short for *Scotch peg*, a leg: ca. 1930–50.

pull (one's) **socks up.** Often as imperative, *pull your socks up!*, or 'I do wish he'd pull his . . . ': to take heart, to try harder: since ca. 1910. Var. *pull up* (one's) *socks.*

pull strings. C.20 shape of **pull the string,** 1, as in 'He was pulling strings on my behalf I never even knew about'. (P.B.)

pull the chocks (**away**). To depart, to 'get going' (Jackson): world of aviation: since ca. 1918. Ex 'the process of removing the chocks beneath the wheels of aircraft before taxi-ing for the take-off' (Jackson).

pull the monkey. To pull a rubber disc through a cess drain in order to clean the drain: railwaymen's. *Railway.*

pull the plug. To release all the bombs simultaneously: RAF: 1939+. (Jackson.) Cf. **play the piano.**—2. 'Get, usu. quickly, from where you are. As in, "C'm on guys, let's pull the plug!" W. Can. at least, and heard from mid-1950s' (Leech, 1986).—3. 'British Telecom has pulled the plug on a telephone message company because of a saucy talk by "Nina the Nurse" ' (*Daily Telegraph*, 20 Feb. 1988): here journalistic punning on US s. sense 'to withdraw support' (W. & F.). Ex switchboard (?or lavatory).

pull the plug out. To dive a submarine: RN submariners': 1960s. (Malin, 1979.)

pull the rug out. Badly to disturb the *status quo*, as in 'Suppose he decides to pull the rug out—change his Will—set up with a fresh woman' (Hunter, 1974): since ca. 1970. Ex toppling someone by snatching the rug he's standing on. (P.B.)

pull the (or, **one's**) **stops out.** To apply all one's energy to the task in hand; often imperative, as in 'You'd better start to pull your stops out!': since ca. 1955. As of organ. (L.A., 1975.) Notably in contrast to an evident hanging-back. As *pull out all the stops*, Can. since 1930s or earlier (Leech, 1987).

pull the string. To use all one's influence: tailors' coll.: mid-C.19–20. (B. & L.) See **pull strings.** In Can. usage, *pull the strings* refers to a 'hidden power', 'as in "Joe is the guy you always hear about, but Pete's the guy who pulls the strings". Poss. orig. in puppetry. Widespread N. Am., since early C.20' (Leech, 1986).

pull the strings. To release the vacuum brake on a vehicle: railwaymen's. *Railway.*

pull the weight. 'To meet a financial emergency' (Baker): Aus.: since ca. 1910.

pull-through. A Jew: r.s. (Hillman, 1974.) See **four-by-two.**

pull (someone's) **tit.** To pull someone's leg, to make a fool of—or to fool; to delude: low Aus.: since ca. 1910. (Lindall, 1959.) Also, by ca. 1920, NZ. Slatter, 'Is he pulling my tit?'

pull up stakes. To depart; to move house: Aus. Baker; Wilkes.

pull (one's) **wire.** (Of a male) to masturbate: low. Cf. **pull** (one's) **pud** . . .

pull wires. Var. of **pull strings:** since (?)mid-C.20. (P.B.)

pullie, -y. A pullover, jumper: domestic coll.: since (?)ca. 1930. Cf. **woolly pully.**

pullies. Women's drawers that are pulled on: feminine coll.: from ca. 1932. See quot'n at **neathie-set.** Imm. ex **pull-ons,** q.v.

pulling. A challenge from a gang, or from one of its members: Teddy-boys': since ca. 1947. Sigal, 1959.

Pullman. A shunting truck: railwaymen's. (*Railway.*) Ironic. See **sidedoor Pullman.**

pulp. Nonsense; excessive sentimentality: Society: 1924 (Galsworthy).—2. A later C.20 shortening of:-

pulp magazines. The cheap, inferior (not the good) American magazines dumped on the Eng. market: coll.: since ca. 1920. Leechman, 'These were so called because they were printed on pulp paper, which is the same (approx.) as newspaper'; orig., the paper was presumably wood-pulp paper. P.B.: in later C.20, often *the pulps*, with special ref. to science fiction magazines of the 1930s–40s.

pulpit. The cockpit of any aircraft: RAF: since ca. 1935. H. & P.

Pulverizer, the. 'Nickname for the giant Stirling bomber, and very apt too' (H. & P.): RAF: 1941–3.

pump (one's) **pickle.** (Of a male) to masturbate: Can. low. Cf. **jerk off.**

pumped, be. 'To stand drinks all round': nautical. Bowen.

punce. An occ. var. of **ponce:** Brit and Aus. Baker, letter, 1946; Powis, 1977.—2. The female pudend: Aus. (B., 1942.) See also **punse.**—3. An effeminate male; a homosexual: Aus. low: since ca. 1925. (B., 1943.) Ex either 1 or 2, or both.

punch-drunk. Slap-happily crazed from the punching he's received: boxing coll.: since ca. 1925. (*Answers,* 30 Nov. 1940.) By ca. 1942 it was S.E.

punch-up. A fight with bare fists: low coll., from ca. 1920, > by 1970, gen. and widespread. Norman.

punch up the bracket. See **bracket.**

puncher. A boxer: low: since ca. 1930. Norman.

punchy. Punch-drunk: low: since ca. 1930. Norman.—2. Aggressive, looking for a fight, as in 'It is "punchy" and operational to get the formation airborne rapidly' (*Phantom*): RAF: later C.20.

punctured. Damaged, fig., as in 'a punctured reputation': coll.—2. Vaccinated: Services': ca. 1920–45. H. & P.

pungo (esp. *go pungo*). (Of a rubber tyre) to burst: coll.: earlier C.20. (Kipling, 1910; Manchon, 1923.) Partly ex *punctured,* partly echoic; cf. **blunjie.**

punish lugs. 'To talk incessantly' (McNeil): Aus. coll.: later C.20. See:-

punisher. A long-winded bore: Aus.: since ca. 1925. B., 1953.

punk, n. [Orig., a prostitute or strumpet, a harlot: ob. or rare arch.: 1596 (origin unkn.): *SOD.*]—2. Nonsense, 'bilge', twaddle: 1927, Sayers, 'We had to sit through a lot of moral punk . . . about the prevalence of jazz and the immoral

behaviour of modern girls.' Like the adj., it comes from the US.—3. A young fellow that, having just started to work for a carnival, thinks he knows everything. Can. carnival s.: since ca. 1910. Adopted from US. See *Underworld.*—4. (?)Hence, a young elephant: Can. circus s., adopted ca. 1950 (if not 20 years earlier) ex US. Leechman cites *Islander* (Victoria, BC), 19 Dec. 1971.—5. As the term for a type of music (short for *punk rock,* an apparently deliberate working-class teenage flouting of middle-class conventions and taste that was soon to be commercialised) it arose in mid-1970s and was very soon S.E. Self-derogatorily ex the adj. (P.B.)—6. See **punk and plaster.**

punk, adj. Worthless; decidedly inferior; displeasing, 'rotten': from ca. 1917, via American soldiers: low, as in US, where, via *punky* (1876), ex *punk* (touchwood), it originated in late C.19. Thornton; Irwin.

punk and plaster. Bread and margarine: tramps' c.: adopted, ex US,—1932 (Jennings).

punk grafter. A beggar: Liverpool street arabs': late C.19–early 20. *Arab.*

punkah. Engine-cooling fan on a motorcycle: motorcyclists': since (?)ca. 1950. (Dunford.) Ex S.E. use of Hindi *pankha,* a fan.

punse. The female pudend: Yiddish and low London: late C.19–20. See also **punce,** 2.

punt, n. A promotion in school: Scottish Public Schools'. (Miller, 1935.) Ex v., 3.—2. A look: since ca. 1950. (Willis, 1976.) Ex Rugby football.

punt, v. To bet upon a race, etc.: 1873, implied in *punter; Pall Mall Gazette,* 13 Sep. 1887. (*OED.*) Ex punting at faro, baccarat, etc.—2. Hence, to be a purchaser, to buy something: grafters': late C.19–20. (*Cheapjack,* 1934.) Cf. sense 4 of **punter.**—3. (V.t., gen in passive.) To promote to another form: Scottish Public Schools'. (Miller.) Ex football.

punter. 'A grafter's customer, client, or victim': grafters': late C.19–20. (Allingham.) Ex **punt,** v., 2.—2. A large mug or tankard (of beer): joc. public-house term: from ca. 1930. With a pun on older sense: 'a big mug'.—3. A pickpocket's assistant: NZ c. (B., 1941.)—4. 'The "punters" (dealer-buyers) who promenade the Street' (Warren Street, centre of the London secondhand-car dealers): the secondhand-car business: since ca. 1945. (Cowdy, 1965.)—5. 'Someone with money looking for a scheme to put it into and ignorant of the ways of the morrie world [underworld and its fringes]. An extreme case would be called "a mug punter" or "a half-wide mug" ' (Cook, 1962): since ca. 1945: c. >, by ca. 1960, also low s. Ex the racing sense.—6. As in 'Men who cruise around in cars looking for women—the punters—will be taken to police stations and interrogated' (*Bradford Telegraph & Argus,* 28 Mar. 1978). Perhaps also in this sense is the use, in *Amateur Photographer,* 19 July 1978 (article about 'glamour' photography), 'Clinical shots for the sake of a turn on for some punter are not my scene.' These senses are perhaps ex prostitutes' use of sense 1, a 'customer'. (P.B.)—7. (As specialisation of sense 4) 'Person who comes in [to the car showroom] but has no intention of buying anything' (Graham-Ranger, 1981). But by 1983 the term had come to mean loosely, and merely, a customer of any sort: s. verging on coll. (P.B.)

pup. A pupil: school and college s.: 1871 ('M. Legrand'). Joc. approximated to *pup* = a puppy. Cf. **pupe.** *OED.*—2. Hence, in RAF, a pupil pilot (Jackson); also *pups* (Graves, 1943). Cf. **pup's Bible.**—3. A paid-up policy: insurance world's.—4. A trailer: hauliers' s.: since ca. 1920. Cf. entries at HAULIERS', in Appx.—5. Mostly in *the night's (only) a pup,* it's still early: Aus., at least mainly. (Tennant, 1947.) Suggested by the (familiar) S.E. *the night's still young.*

pupe. One who, to learn acting, is attached to a company: theatrical: from ca. 1920. (*Passing Show,* 29 Apr. 1933.) Ex *pupil.*—2. A pupil pilot: RAF: WW2. (P-G-R.) Cf. **pup,** n., 2.

P

puppies, the. 'The dogs', greyhound racing or coursing: Aus.: since ca. 1946. (B.P.) Cf. synon. **the yappies.**

puppy-dog. 'In "puppydogging" a customer is given the chance of borrowing a demonstration car to take home and show his wife' (*Guardian*, 5 Apr. 1984): car salesmen's. P.B.: in the hope that she will react as to a stray puppy? 'Oh, we *must* keep it!'

puppy(-)fat. Fattiness that, acquired from eating starchy food, lacks substance: coll.: since ca. 1910. P.B.: applied to children and adolescents; by later C.20, S.E.

puppyism. Affectation or excessive care in costume or posture: Army officers' coll.:—1923 (Manchon). Cf. **doggy**, adj.

pup's Bible, the. *The Flying Training Manual*: RAF: since ca. 1925. (Jackson.) Ex **pup**, n., 2.

pure. Good quality, high purity drugs: drugs c. (Stockley, 1986.) US since—1967 (Spears). Elliptical.

purgatorial list. (Of officers) to be retired: Army officers' joc. coll.:—1923 (Manchon). Ex *purgatory* (between hell and heaven).

purge, n. 'A newly arrived batch of kriegies from . . . the Luftwaffe interrogation centre. From this, also, the passive verb, "To be purged" ' (Brickhill, 1946): prisoners of war in Germany, 1940–5. Satirical ref. to the Nazi purges and 'blood-baths'. *Kriegie* = prisoner of war.—2. 'A concentrated complaint or moan from a well-known source is called "a purge-on by So and So". A habitual grumbler is called by this name in many places' (H. & P.): Services': since 1939.

purge, v. To dismiss from employment (gen. in passive): coll.: since ca. 1930.—2. See n., 1.

purler. Something exceptionally good: Aus.: since ca. 1910. (B., 1942.) Also *purl*. P.B.: perhaps rather *pearl*?

purple emperor. 'The senior engineer of a squadron or fleet: RN: 1950s' (Peppitt). A pun on the butterfly's name. Also known as a *purplie* (Knight, 1984). See:–

purple empire. An establishment in which many of the executive officers are Engineering Officers (wearing a purple stripe between their gold bands): RN officers': since ca. 1945. 'The space between the stripes on the cuffs of these [technical] officers was to be filled with coloured velvet [from 1863], later changed to cloth . . . purple for engineers. In 1918 . . . the electrical branch was given dark green . . . In 1955 all distinguishing colours were abolished' (*Badges*, 1974).—2. Hence, FAA officers, there being numerous Engineering Officers in this branch of the Service: RN officers': since ca. 1946.

purple heart. A dexedrine pill used narcotically: teenage drug addicts': since ca. 1960. One of the minor drugs. P.B.: a 'Purple Heart' is a US decoration equivalent to the British Services' wound-stripe, a badge denoting that a man has been wounded in action. The drug term was adopted ex US. See **blue**, n., 8.

purple para. 'A brand of port; more generally a pejorative term for port' (McNeil): Aus.: later C.20.

push, v.i. To get through time which must be endured rather than enjoyed, as in 'How long to do [= serve] now?'—'Three weeks to push': National Servicemen's: 1950s. (P.B.)—2. V.t. To sell drugs: drugs c. (Stockley, 1986.) US since—1938 (Spears).

push-and-pull. A (little) motor-train that reverses at the termini: railwaymen's:—1935.

push-bike, n. A foot-propelling bicycle as opp. to a motor-cycle: coll.: resp. from ca. 1910. Cf. derivative:–

push-bike. (Gen. v.i.) To ride on a bicycle: from ca. 1910. Mais, 1918, 'I "push-biked" the eight miles into Lewes.' Ex the n.

push in the truck. Copulation: low r.s., on *fuck*: Curtis, 1938, 'I ain't had a push in the truck since I came out of the nick.'

push (one's) luck. To take a risk, to 'chance one's arm': coll.: since the 1930s. Esp., in mid-C.20 Army usage, negative, as 'Don't push your luck [with me]!' Cf. US synon. *crowd (one's) luck.*

push (one's) own barrow. To boast; to look out for oneself only: Aus. coll: since ca. 1910. Palmer, 1948.

push powder. To sell narcotics: adopted, ca. 1955, ex US.

push-pudding. A bachelor: low. A ref. to self-abuse.

push some leg. To copulate: entertainments world. Hibbert, 1983.

push the boat out. To pay for a round of drinks: orig. RN wardroom, since ca. 1924; later, also Army and RAF, and Other Ranks'. (Granville; P.B.) Perhaps ex old-fashioned wine-container, shaped like a boat—a suggestion in *Soldier Magazine*, July 1979.—2. Hence, to be generous, act generously, with money: low. Curtis, 1937.—3. Loosely, to exaggerate to extremes, to 'make a splash of', as in: 'Thames did a T.V. documentary based on Sloane Rangers and really pushed the boat out' (York, 1980).

push the brush out. (Of a convict) to attract the attention of a warder: c.:—1933 (Leach). It is occ. done in this way when the convict is in his cell.

push the chain. To depart: Can., esp. Southern Saskatchewan: later C.20. (Leech, 1974.)

push the knot. To be on tramp: Aus. B., 1942.

push the pavement. To sell goods in the street: Black Market: since ca. 1941. Webb, 1945.

push up. In *be at the push-up*, to work with a gang of pickpockets: c.:—1933 (Leach). B., 1942, records Aus. c. *push up for*, to approach, as a pickpocket his victim. Powis, 1977, defines *at the push-up*, 'Stealing by picking pockets in crowds.'

push up the scale. A rise in salary: lower classes' coll.:—1923 (Manchon).

push up Zs. To sleep: later C.20. (A *Qantas* advertisement, 3 Aug. 1986.) Ex cartoonists' convention of a string of Zs issuing from a sleeping person's mouth, representing snores. Cf. **zeds**.

pushed. Bustled: ship-stewards' coll.:—1935.—2. Late: Army: since late C.19. Ex 'pushed for time'. See quot'n at **tripe**, 4.

pusher. (Usu. pl., and often *old pushers*.) Shoe or slipper, loose from wear, that hangs on, rather than fits, the foot: domestic coll. (L.A., 1978.)—2. A scene-shifter: theatrical:—1935.—3. One who 'pushes' or sells drugs to others (rather than taking them himself): drug addicts': adopted, ca. 1955, ex the underworld. See **push**, v., 2.

pushing (such-and-such an age). 'Getting on for', as in, e.g., 'He's 59, pushing 60': coll. (Petch; L.A.) Cf. *knocking on for.*

pushover. Something easy to do; a girl easy to 'make': Aus.: adopted, ca. 1925, from US. *Rats*, 1944, 'I've got a couple of smashing lines who've come from Sydney for the Mayoral Ball. They're a couple of pushovers.' By 1945, also English.—2. A 'mug' or a 'softy': since ca. 1940; orig., Aus. (B.P.)

pushy. Pushful; thrusting: Anglo-Irish coll.: since ca. 1925. Ex *push*, energy, thrustfulness.

puss. 'Feminine type of lesbian' (Powis): low coll.: later C.20.

puss-pelmet. Var. of **pussy-pelmet.**

Pusser, pusser. Any wound, sinus, or boil that freely discharges pus: medical students':—1933 (*Slang*).—2. The late C.19–20 lowerdeck, later gen. nautical, shape of *purser*. An early occurrence is in some nautical verses dated 1 Jan. 1852, in *Punch*, 24 Jan. 1852.—3. In to *be pusser*, 'To be one hundred percent Service' (Granville), i.e. entirely Service-minded: RN.—4. *Purser* or *pusser* occurs in many combinations denoting 'Naval', or 'RN issue': those recorded in this dictionary follow below:-

pusser-built. (Of a ship) smartly turned out, whether the vessel itself or its personnel: RN: late C.19–20. (Knock.) Hence, of a person, thorough-going, as in 'a pusser-built bastard': R Aus. N lowerdeck. P-G-R lists *pusser ship*, a very smart, severely disciplined ship.

pusserised. Synon. with **pusser**, 3: see also **anchor-faced.**

pusser's, n. and adj. 'Anything [of] official pattern' (Knock): RN and RM (Hawke): late C.19–20. Cf. **pusser**, 2–4.

pusser's brown. 'Toilet paper; from the colour' (Granville): RN: mid-C.20.

pusser's cow. Tinned milk: R Aus. N: since ca. 1915. (B., 1943.) Cf. US Services' *armoured cow*, corned beef.

pusser's duck. A Supermarine *Walrus* flying-boat: RN: 1940+. Granville.

pusser's grey. Admiralty grey paint: RN coll. Granville.

pusser's halo. 'Cap grummet' (Granville): RN: mid-C.20.

pusser's hard. Naval issue soap: RN: since late 1950s. (*Heart.*) Granville, 1962, notes 'Now used exclusively in preference to the old term, *pusser's yellow* or *pusser's Vinolia.*'

pusser's lisle. Regulation black-lisle stockings issued to Wrens: WRNS: from ca. 1940.

pusser's medal. A food stain on clothing: RN. (Knight, 1984.)

pusser's packed (sc. lunch). Navy issued packed lunch, usu. in white cardboard box or brown paper bag: RN. (Knight, 1984.) Cf. **unexploded portion** . . .

pusser's planks. Skis: RM: later C.20. (Knight, 1984.)

pusser's pound. 'Fourteen instead of sixteen ounces' (Granville): RN.

pusser's red. A bicycle provided for use in RN camp or barracks: RN/WRNS: later C.20. Usu. painted red. (Wood, 1978.)

pusser's Spitfire. 'Swordfish aircraft [see **Stringbag**] which did magnificent work in WW2. It was very slow, as opposed to the Spitfire, but it was the best the Admiralty could supply to the Fleet at the time, hence the sarcasm' (Granville).

pusser's tally. A Naval patrol: RN. P-G-R.

pusser's Vinolia. Naval issue soap: RN: since ca. 1920. (P-G-R.) Ex a well-known brand. See also **pusser's hard.**

pusser's wag(g)on. A warship: R Aus. N: since ca. 1930. B., 1943.

pussies. 'When a crook speaks about "the pussies" he's talking about furs—or women. They go together. Furs, to the thieves, are the product of "cats"; and women are cats, as every crook knows' (Gosling, 1959): c. and low s.

pussies and tussies. *P*ermanent *u*nattached *s*upply *s*taff and *t*emporary *u*nattached *s*upply *s*taff, two grades of part-time supply teachers, substitutes who 'fill in' for absent schoolteachers: coll. acronyms: Leicestershire (?and other authorities') County Education Department, finance section. (Gordon, 1978.)

pussy. Woman regarded as sex-object, as in 'Is there much pussy in this town?'; cf. *puss,-y*, the female pudend, since C.17.—2. The cat-o'-nine-tails: prisons': earlier C.20. The use of this punishment was abolished in 1948. Tempest.—3. Used with any verb of action—as in 'They could gas pussy' (Montague, 1923)—to express ineffectuality or inefficiency.—4. See **pussies.**

pussy (in). To move very quietly: see AUSTRALIAN UNDERWORLD, in Appx.

pussy Nellie, -y. A male homosexual: mostly RN: since ca. 1910.

pussy pad. 'The rear half of a dual seat on a motorcycle' (Dunford): motorcyclists': since ca. 1960. Cf. **peach-perch**, and:-

pussy-(or puss-)pelmet. A very short mini-skirt: later 1960s. A neat pun on *pussy*, the female pubic hair (and pudend). P.B.: an equally neat pun was the Home Counties var. *fan belt*. (Lt Col K. Beale, 1985.)

pussy-struck. (Of a male, esp. a youth with a much older woman) infatuated: low. Although low, it is yet, in a measure, euph. for *cunt-struck*.

pussy-whipped. (Of a man) 'hen-pecked': N. Am.: later C.20. (Leech, 1986.)

pussy willow. A pillow: r.s. (*This Week*, 10 Mar. 1968.) Cf. *weeping willow.*

put a jelly on the ashcan (or **on the baby**). 'Fix a gelatine diffuser in front of an iron-cased lamp' (*Evening News*, 7 Nov. 1939): cinema: since ca. 1930.

put a knife through (the) money. To share out illicit winnings: Aus. two-up-players': since ca. 1920. B., 1953.

put a squeak in. To complain to a superior: Services': since ca. 1935. (H. & P.) Adopted from cant, where it = 'to inform to the police' (see *Underworld*).

put a streak into it. To hurry; to 'get a move on': Anglo-Irish. Blake, 1968, 'Through the pandemonium cut a megaphone voice, adjuring the laggards in some class to "put a streak into it! Numbers 3, 7 and 16, we're waiting for you." '

put a washer on. To urinate: Lancashire s.: since ca. 1955 (?much earlier). Janssen, 1976, attests its use in 1967.

put about. See **put** (one)**self about**, and **put it about.**

put across. To achieve; execute successfully: from ca. 1910: coll., now verging on S.E. Whence:-

put across a beauty. To execute a smart move: coll., mostly NZ: from ca. 1914.

put along; gen. **put her along.** To cause (a motor-car) to travel at a high speed: motorists' coll.: 1924 (Grierson).

put-and-take. Sexual intercourse: mostly Londoners' (somewhat raffish). The male puts, the female takes, it in.

put away. To bribe a jockey to lose a race. *Sporting Chronicle*, 8 Sep. 1978.

put (one's) balls in a knot. A low equivalent of S.E. *put one's nose out of joint*: Aus.: since ca. 1930. Also *put one's tits in a tangle.*

put (someone) crook with (a third party). To reduce one's standing in the eyes of someone else: NZ: since ca. 1930. 'You wouldn't put me crook with him, would you?' (Harold Griffiths, 1959.) A var. appears in 'Got a snitch on me and put me in crook with the boss' (Slatter).

put dots on (someone). To weary or bore him: Army: earlier C.20. Ex 'to dot every i'?

put-down, n. A belittling; a snub: coll.: since ca. 1960.

put down, v. To reject; to belittle (e.g. someone's playing): Can. jazz-lovers': adopted, in 1956, ex US jazz musicians. P.B.: soon also Brit., and with much wider application.

put (one's) feet up. To lie in one's hammock; to sleep: RN. (*Weekly Telegraph*, 25 Oct. 1941.) Mother does this to rest her weary feet.

put (one's) hand down. To pay; to stand one's turn.

put (one's) hands up. 'He put his hands up = He surrendered or he admitted all the crimes put to him' (Powis): police s., and c.: later C.20.

put her along. See **put along.**

put her face on. To make up (apply cosmetics): since ca. 1930. 'I'll just go upstairs and put my face on.'

put in. To '*put* somebody *in*' is to involve or embroil him; to get him into trouble: Aus.: since ca. 1925. Niland, 1958, 'Don't put me in. Don't try to hang anything on me.' See also **put in with.**

put in the leather. 'Others . . . "put in the leather" ' (Phelan, 1943): to kick: low. Cf. **put the boot in**, and **leather**, 2.

put (one) in the picture. See **picture**, 4.

put in the pudden, or **-ing, club.** See **pudding club.**

put (someone) in with (someone else). To blacken someone's name in the mind of a third party, to put him in his bad books: Aus.: since late 1920s. (Henry, 1960.) See also **put in**, v. Elliptical for:-

put in wrong with. To cause another person to incur someone's dislike: adopted, ex US, ca. 1932 (*COD*, 1934 Sup.). Cf. prec., and **get in wrong.**

put inside. In detention: Services' coll.

put it about. (Of either sex) to be sexually promiscuous: raffish: since (?)late 1940s. Brett, 1975, 'The simplest explanation was that he had just got tired of Jacqui . . . He was a man who had always put it about a bit.' See also quot'n at **slag**, n., 6 and **put** (one)**self about.**

put it across (a person). To punish, get even with, revenge oneself on: coll.: from ca. 1914. (Now verging on S.E.)—2. To deceive, delude, trick, impose on: coll., now verging on S.E.: 1915 (Edgar Wallace: *OED* Sup.).—3. See **put across.**

put it on, v.i. To overcharge: coll. Ex *put on the price*; prob. influenced by:—2. V.t. To extract money from (a person) by threats, lying or whining: low London: late C.19–20. *People*,

P

6 Jan. 1895 (Ware).—3. To 'show off'; to put on 'side' or 'airs': coll.—4. To make a suggestion—a proposition—to (someone): Aus.: since ca. 1925. *Rats*, 1944, 'I'll have a pint at the Royal tomorrow and put it on the blonde' (an invitation).

put it over (a person). See **put it across**, 1, 2: same status and period.—2. See **put over**.

put me in! Let me join you: prison c.: earlier C.20. Lit., '*Include* me!'

put-on, n. A nondescript frock for afternoon wear: women's coll.: ca. 1925–40.

put (one) **on,** v. A var. of *have* (one) *on*, to fool or impose upon one, to 'con': coll.: adopted, ex N. American, ca. 1960. Victoria, BC, *Daily Colonist*, 18 Apr. 1967. 'The mail attests that the men . . . thoroughly enjoy dressing up in women's clothes. I assure you these people are not putting me on. They are strictly for real.'

put on a smoke. To begin to smoke (tobacco): coll.: later C.19–earlier 20. Crofts, 1931, 'Dispirited, he sat down on the shore . . . , put on a pipe, and gave himself up to thought.' Cf. S.E. *put the lights on* for 'to light up'.

put on dog. To put on 'side', to show off: coll.: earlier C.20. (*OED* Sup.) Occ. var. *carry dog*. Cf. **doggy,** adj.

put on foul. See **foul,** 2.

put on hold. 'To put off for a while: common in N. Am., perhaps since the 1920s, when telephones became common. "I'll put you on hold", is operators' j.' (Leech, 1986).

put on the arse. See AUSTRALIAN UNDERWORLD, in Appx.

put on the back burner. See **back burner.**

put on the bee. See **bee,** 2 and **put the bee on.**

put on the big hammer. See **hammer,** n., 5.

put on the kitz. To put on one's best clothes: since the late 1930s. Ex Yiddish.

put on the long rank. To cruise: taxi-drivers': since ca. 1912. Hodge, 1939.

put on the rattle (or **the whizzer**). To report a policeman to his superior: police. (*Free-Lance Writer*, April 1948.) Cf. **put the acid,** or **the bubble, in.**

put one on (someone). To punch (him): Aus.: since 1930s. (Clapperton, 1976.) See **hang one on,** 2.

put one or two on the floor. To fire a few rounds: artillerymen's: WW2. P-G-R.

put out. As v.i. (of a woman) to copulate; esp., to be promiscuous: Can.: adopted, ca. 1945, ex US.

put (someone) **out to grass.** To retire him: coll.: since ca. 1955. (Petch, 1969.) As is done to old horses.

put over. To cause to be accepted; to succeed in getting a favourable reception for: orig. US; anglicised ca. 1920 as a coll., > by 1935 S.E.

put (someone's) **pot on.** 'To inform upon; to destroy someone's prospects' (Wilkes): Aus.: since later C.19.—2. To detect in a misdeed; to settle his hash: NZ: since ca. 1945. Murray, 1965.

put sand in (someone's) **Vaseline.** 'Selfish act by person which overrides show of considerate concern' (Williams, 1970). A ref. to the use of this ointment to aid sexual intercourse. Cf. **muck** (someone's) **orange.**

put (one)**self about.** To work as a prostitute; to be promiscuous; 'Glad[ys] put herself about around the King's Cross area' (Daniells, 1980): low coll.—2. To 'circulate' (Powis); to get around and be seen: coll.: later C.20.

put (one's) **snout in the trough.** To drink (beer or ale rather than wine or spirits): mainly public-houses: since ca. 1945.

put the acid (or **the squeaks**) **in.** To tell-tale; to make mischief by causing a bias against one in another's mind: orig. and mostly Cockneys': from ca. 1910, ca. 1918, resp.

put the acid on. To test (man or statement); to put a stop to: lower classes': from ca. 1908. F. & G.—2. To ask (a person) for a loan: Aus.: from ca. 1912.

put the bee on. To borrow money from: Aus.: since ca. 1935. (B., 1953.) Either 'to *sting*' or ex the next two (*bite*). See also **bee,** 2.

put the bit on. Aus. var. (Niland, 1958) of:-

put the bite on. To ask someone for a loan of money: Can.: since ca. 1910; by 1940, also Eng. (Leechman.)

put the black on. To blackmail: c.: from ca. 1920. (Wallace, *passim*.) Abbr. *blackmail*.

put the blacksmith on. To lock out, as in 'He came home late from the bevvyken and the mort put the blacksmith on him' (*M.T.*): market-traders'. From an earlier argot.

put the block. To 'mask' or cover a thief at work: c.:—1933 (Leach).

put the blocks to. To coït with (a woman): low: earlier C.20. Ca. 1900, there was a Can. lumbermen's ballad, with the pertinent lines, 'Some were fiddling, some were diddling, some were lying on the floor,/I was over in the corner putting the blocks to the Winnipeg whore' (R.C., 1966).

put the boot in. (Earlier, *put in the boot.*) To kick a prostrate foe (Dennis): orig. (?)mainly Aus.,—1916; by mid-C.20, gen. among the violent. As v.t., with *into*, which is now, since ca. 1960, the mainly Brit. form. The phrase is also, since ca. 1965, used fig., as in political or commercial infighting and betrayal. Powis, 1977, defines the shortened version, *boot*, as 'unnecessary cruelty after victory'. Cf. **sock a boot into.**

put the bubble in. To give the game away, esp. to expose a racket: dockers'. Ex bubble and squeak, v. Also *put in the bubble*.—2. Hence, to cause trouble, esp. by informing to authority: since ca. 1920. As *trouble* rhymes with *bubble*, and *sneak* with *squeak*, so *bubble and squeak* prob. combines both of these sounds and both of these senses. P.B.: but with both senses cf. **tube,** n., 7.

put the caulks to. See **logger's smallpox.**

put the cleaners through (someone). Var. of *put* (someone) *through the cleaners*, or *take to the cleaners*, to get the better of, to swindle: R Aus. AF: WW2. B., 1943.

put the coals on. To increase speed: London busmen's: from ca. 1935. See also **pour on more coals.**

put the finger on. See **finger on.**

put the hard word on. See **hard word** . . .

put the hooks on; more usu. **put** (someone) **on the hooks.** To put (someone) on a charge: RAF: since ca. 1920. Davison, 1942; Jackson, 1943.

put the lid on. To close (a hotel bar) at the legal time: Aus.: since ca. 1925. B., 1943.

put the mock or **mocker(s)** or **moz(z) on.** See **mock on.**

put the nips in. See **Nips,** 2.

put the (or, one's) **skates on.** See **skates.**

put the skids under (someone). To dismiss from a job, a course, etc.: since ca. 1940: Army, then—by 1944—gen. Forces' s.— 2. Hence, to speed or hurry (him) along: Forces': since 1945.

put the weights on. To seek a loan from or ask a favour of (someone): Aus. sporting: since ca. 1910. (B., 1942.) Ex horse-racing. Cf. **put the bit,** or **the hard word, on.**

put (one's) **tits in a tangle.** See **put** (one's) **balls** . . .

put up. To wear (of badges of rank): Services' coll.; e.g. 'He put up his second stripe (or pip)', he was promoted corporal (or lieutenant).

put up a black. See **black,** 2.

put up a squeak. To give information to the police: c.: from ca. 1920. Wallace.

put up the (or, one's) **dukes.** To prepare for fisticuffs: orig. low s.; in C.20, low coll.: later C.19–mid-20. Slater recalls hearing 'Put up your dooks!' in Aus. in 1962.

put up (one's) **third.** To put up one's third star, i.e. to become a captain: Army coll. (P-G-R.) See **put up,** v.

put-upon. 'A stooge in plays [and music-hall turns]. Used in an article in *Radio Times*, 9 Feb. 1967' (Petch). Ex 'to *put upon*', to impose upon, hence to make fun of, a person.

put (someone's) **weight up.** To declare—to disclose—his (illicit) activities; to 'pimp on': Aus. miners': since ca. 1925. Casey, 1945.

put wise. See **wise (to).**

put your skates on! Hurry up!; get a move on! See **skates**.

putrid. A pej. of the *awful* kind: s. now verging on coll. *Sporting Times*, 27 Apr. 1901, 'All beer is putrid, even when it's pure.' Prob. suggested by synon. *rotten*.

putter-down. A presenter of forged cheques or counterfeit money: c.:—1933 (Leach).

putting her in a bath. 'Used jocularly in reference to one of the plumber's jobs' (Petch, 1969): since ca. 1930(?). A pun on 'put a bath in (the house) for her.'

puzzle palace. Headquarters building: RM: later C.20. *Mail on Sunday*, 8 Nov. 1987.

pyjamas. See **cat's pyjamas**.

pyjams. Abbr. *pyjamas*: from ca. 1910: s. >, by 1935, almost coll. Never *pajams*.

pyrotechnic. A reprimand: RAF: since ca. 1938. (Jackson.) Cf. **rocket,** which suggested it.

Pythonesque. ' . . . is now common English usage on both sides of the Atlantic . . . it describes a set of events that are more than bizarre, yet less than surreal' (Iain Robinson, 'Monty Python: the Early Years', *Listener*, 28 June 1979): coll.: current in late 1970s. Ex the TV surrealist comedy series 'Monty Python's Flying Circus'. (P.B.)

P

Q

Q or **q.** A homosexual: theatrical, whence also Army: since ca. 1930; by 1950, † in Army. For **queer**, n.—2. As *the Q*, short for the quarter-master or *-bloke*: Army: since ca. 1925. (H. & P.) Since mid-C.20, usu. *the RQ* (P.B.).

Q.B.I. (Of flying condition) deplorable: aviation: ca. 1937–9. (*The Times*, 3 Mar. 1938.) Lit. *q*uite *b*loody *i*mpossible. P.B.: perhaps orig. a spoof trigraph attributed to the international radio 'Q' code; or a pun on QFI, *q*ualified *f*lying *i*nstructor.

Q bloke. See **Q**, 2.

Q boat. 'Nondescript police radio car with plain-clothes crew (named after the disguised naval vessels of the First World War)' (Powis).

quack. A pretended doctor: 1659 (*OED*): coll. till C.19, then S.E.—2. Hence, in the Services, notably at first RN, since ca. 1912 (Knock); later RAF; and also among the Aus. Forces: the medical officer. Civilianised to become (mostly male) gen. coll. for any doctor of medicine; usu. *the quack*.

quacker. A Japanese Kawasaki motorcycle: motorcyclists': since (?)late 1960s. (Dunford.) Cf. **Rice-Burner**, a Honda motorcycle.

quaint, adj., as used from ca. 1920 (the practice was on the wane by 1934) to mean amusingly old-fashioned, entertainingly unusual, even occ. as funny in an odd way, is (mostly upper-)middle- and upper-class s.

Quaker. A conscientious objector (*conchie*): military coll.: from 1916. (F. & G.) Ex the honest attitude of Friends towards war.

Quaker oat; gen. pl. and more properly, **Quaker Oats**. A coat. (P.P., 1932.) Ex the brand-name of a well-known breakfast food. Franklyn notes that it is much less common than the synon. *I'm afloat*.

Quaky Isles, the. New Zealand: Aus. coll. (B., 1943.) Earthquaky.

qualify for the pension. To be getting on in years: coll.:—1927 (Collinson).

qualities, the. The higher-class, as opp. the tabloid, newspapers: later C.20. Johnson, 1987, writing with irony, 'The *Sun* [the mostly widely looked at of all the national tabloids] could be said to be *the* judges' paper. Unlike the qualities, it has never attracted the adverse attention of the Law Lords or . . . the Attorney-General.' Cf. the C.17–20, orig. S.E., > low coll. *the quality* = the gentry.

quandong. A prostitute: Aus. c. (Tennant, 1939.) 'After the fruit: soft on the outside, a hard centre' (Baker, letter, 1946). Although blue-coloured and cherry-sized, it is also known as 'native peach'; the word is of Aus. Aboriginal origin.—2.

'Someone disreputable, living by his or her wits' (Wilkes): Aus.: later C.20.

quanger. A quince: Aus. juvenile: later C.20. Wilkes.

Quango. *Qua*si *n*on-*g*overnment *o*rganisation: coll. acronym, orig. ca. 1975; rapidly > informal S.E.; many of these agencies, arising in the early 1970s, were disbanded as an economy in 1979. (R.S., 1977; P.B.)

quarter to two. A Jew: r.s. Franklyn.

quash; quash kateer. See **quiess kateer.**

Quasimodo. 'The chapel redband. Prisoner who is responsible for cleaning the prison chapel. (From Lon Chaney's "Quasimodo" in the film *The Hunchback of Notre Dame* [1923]). Rare' (Tempest, 1950).

quaver. To dither, esp. whether to purchase: market-traders'. 'The crowie was quavering about' (*M.T.*). Hence a *quaverer*, 'a vacillating customer' (Ibid.).—2. Hence, to potter; tinker; mess about with, as in 'The gorger's quavering about with the screeve' = the man's tinkering about with his car. Ibid.

quean; incorrectly **queen**. A homosexual, esp. one with girlish manners and carriage: low: late C.19–20. Prob. ex *quean*, a harlot, influenced by *Queenie*, a girl's name, and dial. *queanish*, effeminate. Cf. **queanie**. In later C.20, this meaning still current in prison c. (Home Office); among homosexuals, it means 'an ageing passive homosexual', with adj. *queeny*, as in 'He's very queeny'.—2. A lesbian: male homosexuals': ca. 1970.

quean up; mostly as (*all*) *queaned up*, 'carefully, not necessarily effeminately, dressed': Aus.: since ca. 1920. (B., 1942.) See **quean** and cf. **doll up**. Also *queen up* (B., 1959).—2. 'To fall into homosexual company' (Rodgers, 1972): later C.20.—3. 'To assume girlish mannerisms, such as coating the face with cosmetics and fussing with the hair' (Ibid.): like 2, Brit. gay s.

queanie, n.; incorrectly **queenie**. A 'Nancy', an effeminate man: Aus.: late C.19–20. See **quean**, 1.—2. A very good looking man or boy: Army: earlier C.20.

queanie, -y, adj. Effeminate; soft: Aus.: since ca. 1910. (Baker.) Ex prec., 1.

queen. In combination, a girl: RAF: 1940+. Jackson, 'Thus, "I'm going to the flicks tonight with one of the ops room queens".' Humorous. P.B. trans.: 'I am going to the cinema this evening with a girl from the operations room'.—2. The woman in charge; e.g., among social workers 'the queen of X area' would be the top-ranking woman in that profession there: coll.: later C.20. A development ex *Queen At* and *Queen Bee*. Cf. similar use of *king*.—3. See **quean**.

Queen Anne's Mansions. 'The combined control tower and fore bridge of the *Nelson* and the *Rodney*, named after the tallest block of flats in London' (Bowen): RN: earlier C.20.

Queen At, the. 'A Chief Commander of the A.T.S.' (H. & P.): Services': ca. 1939–49. See **At** and cf.:-

Queen Bee, the. 'The Director of the Women's Auxiliary Air Force; or the senior W.A.A.F. officer on a station' (Jackson): WAAF and hence RAF: since 1940 or 1941. Cf. prec. Peppitt adds 'But also of, and among, the W.R.N.S.—the Wrens'. Similarly, since late 1940s (the ATS became WRAC in 1948), in Army usage (P.B.).—2. As *queen bee*, 'A 'plane used for anti-aircraft firing practice, having no crew and controlled by radio from the ground. (Not a new invention)' (H. & P.): 1943: RAF: since ca. 1935; by mid-1942, at latest, it was j.—3. A stranger: RN lowerdeck: mid-C.20. 'They were both anxious to impress the newcomers, the queen bees' (*Heart*, 1962).

Queen Mary. A long, low-loading, articulated vehicle for the transportation of aircraft by road: RAF: since ca. 1938. (Jackson.) An occ. synon. is *artic*. (Jackson.)—2. 'The basement under the new House of Commons where the secretaries and typists work . . . (From its appearance and general decorative scheme.) The term is in pretty general use now, I gather' (Granville, letter, 1953).—3. A very large goods brake van: railwaymen's: since the middle 1940s. Ex sense 1; in full, *Queen Mary brake van*. (*Railway*.) P.B.: all three senses ex the famous Cunard liner.

queen-size(d). An advertising term. See **king-size(d)**.

queen up. See **quean up**.

queenie. See **queanie**.

Queen's, the. 'Last tot in the bottle. A bonus, it is the last complete tot, plus the remaining part tot' (Peppitt): RN: 1960s.

Queen's Park Ranger. A stranger: r.s. Ex the famous London soccer team. 'Its use ranges from a proud father's announcement that the baby has arrived, to an underworld warning that restraint in conversation is indicated' (Franklyn 2nd).

queeny. See **quean**, 1, and **queanie**, n. and adj.

queer, n. A male homosexual: since ca. 1920. (Wilson, 1952.) Ex the adj., 2.—2. A simpleton; a fool: Aus.: since ca. 1925. (B., 1942.) Ex the adj., 1.—3. In *on the queer*, acting dishonestly or shadily: low.

queer, adj. Of strange behaviour; (slightly) mad, orig. (*a bit*) *queer in the head*: coll.: 1840 (Dickens).—2. Homosexual: rather coll. than s.: ex US. *Listener*, 10 Mar. 1937.—3. Roughly 'any', but vaguely intensive, in e.g., 'The queer thing' (thingummy) and 'old queer man' (what's-his-name): Army: late C.19–20. From several dial. uses (adj. and adv.), themselves vaguely intensive.

queer and; *queer* nearly always pronounced *quare*. An intensive of the adj. preceding, as '*quare and* hot', very hot, or '*quare and* sick', very sick; N. Ireland coil.: C.19–20. Joyce, 1910.

queer-bashing. 'Assaulting male homosexuals either for gain or for perverse pleasure' (Powis): low, esp. among the mindless thugs who do this: later C.20.

queer fella, the. The man that happens to be in command: Army: late C.19–20. P.B.: by mid-C.20, applied to anyone whose name is momentarily forgotten, 'you know, old queer-fella, whatsisname—bloke out the Warwicks . . . ' See **queer**, adj., 3, and next.

queer fellow. A vessel in the Fishery Protection Service: among those living in, or frequenting, the Western Islands: since when? I first noticed it in one of Bill Knox's brisk 'Webb Carrick' tales.

queer hawk. An eccentric person: mostly Army: 1930s. Var. of older (from C.19) *queer bird*.

queer place, the. Prison: c.: late C.19–20. *Gilt Kid*, 1936. 'In the queer place'. By euph.—2. Euph. also for 'a w.c.': coll.: since ca. 1950, at latest. (P.B.)

queer-rolling. 'Robbing male homosexuals' (Powis): c. and low: later C.20. See **queer**, n., 1, and cf. **queer-bashing**.

-queer-thing. Used as suffix, when the speaker cannot remember, or cannot pronounce, the end of a long, unfamiliar word; e.g., 'He was suffering from bilharzia—schisto, er, shitso-queer-thing. You know—Bill Harris': Services'. See **queer**, adj., 3. (P.B.)

queer-up. 'A male homosexual bout' (L.A., 1974): low coll.: since ca. 1950.

queue-barge. To insert oneself, by force—hence, by guile, into a queue; whence the n., *queue-barging*: coll.: since ca. 1940.

quick and dirty. Topically and hastily compiled (and published or used before correction): orig. computer men's coll., > more widespread: adopted, ex US, late 1960s. Barnhart, '*U.S. Slang*, a snack bar or lunch counter.' (P.B.)

quick, dead and the plumbers. A hugger-mugger of people, as in 'we got in each other's way . . . and generally created an amorphous mass of "quick, dead and the plumbers" ' (Hatton, 1930): Army: early C.20.

quick one. A drink taken quickly: coll. verging on familiar S.E.: from ca. 1910.—2. (Also a *quickie*.) A brief and brisk copulation: rather commoner among women than among men: low s.; by 1930, coll. Cf. **quickie**, 3.—3. 'Among, e.g., male office staff, intimation of brief absence to make water, "Just going for a quick one"—hence frequent response from colleague also under pressure: "Have one for me" ' (L.A.). By transference from sense 1.

quick quid has, since ca. 1925, been the Aus. answer to the American *fast buck*. (B.P.).

quick(-)shits, the. Dysentery: Army in N. Africa: 1940–3. Sanders, 1967.

quick squirt. A (sudden and) brief burst of machine-gun fire from one aircraft at another: RAF: since 1939+. H. & P.

quick sticks! Aus. domestic coll.—addressed to children—and synon. with 'Hurry up!' (B.P.).

quickie, -ee, -ey, -y. The act of backing a horse after the result of a race is known: Glasgow sporting:—1934. Perhaps ex *quick return on one's money*.—2. A fast bowler: cricketers' coll.: 1934, P.G.H. Fender in several articles (e.g. on 21 June) in the *Evening News*.—3. A rapid burst of machine-gun fire at close range: (mostly) RAF: since 1939. (H. & P.) Cf. **quick squirt**.—4. A drink, esp. 'a quick one' (q.v.: 1): orig. Service officers', esp. RAF, since ca. 1940; soon > gen. coll. (McDouall, 1945.)—5. A brief bawdy story told at the break-up of a party: since the late 1940s. 'Just time for a quickie?'—6. 'In radio panel quizzes, a final interpolated question with a short time-limit for answering: "We've just got time for a quicky." Since the 1950s' (R.S., 1973).—7. See **quick one**, 2; **quota quicky**.

quidlet. A sovereign; £1: low. (Horsley, 1912.) Diminutive of older synon. *quid*.

quids in. Applied to a state of things when one is doing well; 'I'm quids in!': Army (C.20); by 1919, it was gen. Short either for *quids in the till* or for *in, to the tune of quids* (pounds).—2. Hence, *be quids in* is to accomplish something with plenty of time, effort, etc., to spare; to do it easily or comfortably: since ca. 1935. Perhaps ex the result of a highly successful wager.

quiess kateer (also *qui-es*; *quis*; *kweis(s)*: pron. *kwyce* or *kwoyce*). How are you?: Army: late C.19–earlier 20. Arabic *kwush kethir*, very good; used in this sense by Army and RAF, ca. 1915 (Eastern Fronts)—ca. 1960. See also entry at **kweiss**. It occurs in Steevens, 1896: 'the earliest printed use [as a phrase familiar to British regular soldiers] I have seen' (R.S.); or I. P.B.: given fresh life in the Services by WW2, it lingered in the speech of the older soldiers for a decade or so after the withdrawal from Middle Eastern commitments.

quill. A matchbox cover, may be folded, used for sniffing narcotics: drugs c. (Stockley, 1986.) US since—1967 (Spears).

quilling. The carrying of (rich) passengers' luggage and getting a tip for doing so: railwaymen's, esp. porters'. Semantically = favour-currying. See also **fluffing**, 2. *Railway*, 2nd, modifies the definition by confining the practice to off-duty employees.

quince. A soft, an effeminate person; a softly stupid person: low Aus.: since ca. 1920. (B., 1942.) P.B.: prob. influenced by *quim*; cf. *cunt* in this sense, and:—2. In *get on* (one's) *quince*, to annoy, irritate, exasperate someone: low Aus.: since ca. 1920. (Baker.) Cf. 'These bloody trees are getting on me quince!' (Farrell, 1963). P.B.: prob. a euph.: cf. **get on** (one's) **wick, tits**, etc.

Quins, the. The Harlequins Rugby Football Club: sporting.—2. The Dionne quintuplets of Canada; born 28 May 1934: coll., mainly journalists'. Cf. *the Quads*, the English quadruplets born in 1935. Both terms have been applied to the offspring in similar multiple births since.

quint. 'Any one of a set of quintuplets; common in Canada since the birth of the Dionne children in 1934 in Calendar, Ontario' (Leechman). Cf. next.

Quints, the. The Can. shape of the **Quins**, 2. (Leechman.)

quirker. Any odd little thing, animate or inanimate; e.g., a small child, or a tuft on the child's head: coll.: earlier C.20. Prob. ex dial.: *quirk* = the end of a pig's tail. (*EDD*.)

quirley. A cigarette: Aus.: since ca. 1930. (B., 1953.) Cf. **twirly**.

quisling. A tell-tale, esp. one who curries favour with the CO by acting as tale-bearer: Services': since mid-1940. (H. & P.) Ex Vidkun Quisling (1889–1946), the Norwegian Army officer turned traitor. (See, esp., my *Name into Word*, 1949.)

quit, to leave off in a very lazy or a cowardly manner, and **quitter,** a shirker, are coll. ex US. Ultimately ex S.E. *quit*, to cease doing something (in US), or ex Anglo-Irish *quit*, to 'clear out'—as in Lover, 1848, 'Quit this minit', cited by *EDD*.

quite. 'Quite the thing'—somebody first-class, very well—better—or—mannered, etc.: since ca. 1920. Drake-Brockman, 1938, 'There is a polite fiction current that once he went to Oxford, and he isn't "quite", and everybody knows this, in the strange way that everybody does know these things.'

quite a while. A considerable length of time: coll. Elinor Glyn, 1905 (*OED*).

quite an event. Something important, significant, or unusual: coll.

quite quite. (Usu. in neg.) An intensification of **quite,** as 'He's really not quite quite, is he, do you think?': middle-class coll.: since (?)the 1930s. (P.B.)

quiteish, not. Indisposed: from ca. 1920. Keverne, 1926, 'You look a bit not quiteish, eh?' I.e. *not quite the thing.*

quizzy. In*qui*sitive: Aus. Niland, 1955.

quoit. A simpleton; a fool: Aus.: since ca. 1930. (B., 1943.) Perhaps ex:—2. (Also spelt *coit.*) The backside; the arse; Aus.: since (?)1925. (B., 1942.) P.B.: E.P. suggests 'Ex roundness'; but Franklyn's proposal re sense 1, 'Probably because a quoit is a hollow ring—nothing in it' forms a better explanation for this 2nd sense.—3. In *go for* (one's) *quoits,* 'to travel quickly; go for one's life' (Baker, 1941): Aus. Wilkes quotes Cleary, 1952, 'Going for the lick of his coit up the street.' Prob. connected with sense 2.

quondong. Var. of **quandong**.

quota quicky. A short British film made as quickly and cheaply as possible, and put on a cinema programme to fulfil the regulation concerning the quota of British films to be used, in Brit., in proportion to foreign (including American) films: cinema world: 1936. (It doesn't matter how short the films are; a nasty reflection on British films.)

R

r.h.i.p. ' "Rank hath its privileges": reason for juniors to "dip out" socially: US Navy, 1950s; adopted by Royal Navy, 1960s' (Peppitt). P.B.: cf. the saying 'What is rank without privilege?', an Army phrase used to justify even the slightest advantage in the struggle for 'perks': later C.20.

r.o. lollies. *R*un-*o*ut money: mock-auction world: since ca. 1945. (*Sunday Chronicle*, 28 June 1953.) See **run-out,** and cf.:-

r.o. workers. Men who 'frame' a mock-auction: showmen's. (Allingham, 1934.) See **run-out,** and cf. prec.

r.p.c. A party: RN wardroom: since ca. 1950. Ex *R.P.C.*, '*R*equest the *p*leasure of your *c*ompany'. (Peppitt.)

ra-ra skirt. A tiered 'mini-skirt', q.v., worn by teenage girls, 1982. Perhaps better spelt *rah-rah*, ex poss. derivation ex the uniform skirt of US drum-majorettes or cheer-leaders. (P.B.)

rab, the. The till: c. (Sharpe, 1938.) With a pun on *Rab*, the Scots form of *Rob*.

rabbit, n. 'Property stolen from the Royal Dockyards, most frequently used in Devonport': RN. (Bowen.) Hence, 'a rabbit is anything made with Navy material for personal use' (*Punch*, 20 Mar. 1946, p.257). See also **rabbits.**—2. A bottle of beer: Aus. B., 1942.—3. A young girl: Aus.: since ca. 1920. Baker.—4. A native-born Australian: since ca. 1925. Baker.—5. A short-journey passenger: busmen's and trammen's: since ca. 1910. Also, since ca. 1912, railwaymen's. (*Railway*.) Mostly in pl.

rabbit, v. '(In football) to collar a player by the ankles when he is running with the ball' (Baker): Aus. sporting.—2. To borrow or 'scrounge' something: R Aus. N: since ca. 1920. B., 1943.—3. See:-

rabbit and pork, n. and v. A, or to, talk: r.s. (Kersh, 1941.) Often shortened to *rabbit*, as in 'She can't arf rabbit' (Jones, 1971); see also quot'n at **bunny,** v., and **rabbit on**. Shortened to *rabbit*, it = to grumble and mumble: low. Cf. **rabbit's paw.**

rabbit-hutch. 'Crutch. Crotch. "These bleedin' rounders [i.e. *round-the-houses* = trousers] is a lot too tight in the rabbit hutch' (Daniells, 1980): r.s.

rabbit job. See **rabbits,** 2.

rabbit-killer. 'A punch on the nape of the neck, like a karate chop' (Wilkes): Aus.: since ca. 1925. Cf. **rabbit-punch.**

rabbit-meat. See **rabbit's food,** 1.

rabbit on, often as vbl n. **rabbiting on.** To ramble on over a triviality, either boringly or complainingly; to grumble and mumble: coll.: since ca. 1960. (Raab attests its use also in Aus.) An elab. of the shortened **rabbit and pork,** q.v.

rabbit-punch. A blow, usu. given from behind, on the nape of the neck: coll. Ex the blow struck with side of the hand to kill a rabbit by breaking its neck. The v. from this. Cf. **rabbit-killer.** Earlier, *rabbit's punch*, as in *Daily Telegraph*, 30 Jan. 1936, and *rabbiter*.

rabbit run. 'An excursion ashore primarily for the purpose of gift-buying' (Bassett, 1979): RN: mid-C.20. Ex **rabbits,** 3, in sense of 'gifts or souvenirs, usually purchased ashore, intended for family or friends at home' (Ibid.).

rabbiter. 'One who makes a habit of smuggling "rabbits" [q.v., sense 2] ashore' (Granville): RN.

rabbit's food. Vegetable salad: RN. (*Birmingham Mail*, 24 Feb. 1939.) Among civilians: *rabbit meat*: since ca. 1920.—2. Hence, esp., lettuce: Services': WW2 and after.

rabbit's paw; often shortened to *rabbit*. Conversation: r.s. (on *jaw*): since ca. 1930. Cf. **rabbit and pork.** Franklyn 2nd.

rabbits. A customs officer: RN: late C.19–20.—2. ' "Rabbits" are illicit goods smuggled ashore by Naval ratings going on leave. At one time the men were allowed to take food with them for consumption at home: "top pieces" of prime meat, and rabbits, which, with their entrails removed, made excellent hold-alls for, say, tobacco which the sailors were forbidden to take out of the ship' (Granville): RN. An earlier explanation: 'It is said that in the days of the [Portsmouth Royal Dockyard] extension, rabbits roamed free on the parts of Portsea Common that were enclosed by the extension wall of 1864. These could be caught and taken home by the Dockyard workers. If stopped going out the gate with a package, the cry would be "only rabbits, mate", and they would be let through. Today, anything made of government material for home, or illegal jobs on ships, are termed "rabbit jobs" ' (Patterson).—3. Hence, perquisites; anything 'buckshee': RN: since ca. 1920. As in Rendell, 1980, 'the enormous sideline in "rabbits", with endless prints of camp functions'.—4. Hence, also, *make rabbits*, to indulge one's hobby, esp. in making things, e.g. gifts for children: RN coll.—5. As *the Rabbits*, 'Leicester to Birmingham parcel trains' (*Railway*, 2nd): railwaymen's nickname: mid-C.20.

race. For *day of the race* = the important occasion, see quot'n at **ticketty-boo.**

race for the steward's basin, n. and v. (To experience) seasickness: joc. Parodying the race-course *race for the Stewards' Cup.*

race (a girl or woman) off. 'To seduce; whisk away with a view to seduction' (Wilkes): Aus. low: since ca. 1960.

racehorse. A long, slim cigarette: Aus.: since ca. 1930. Tennant, 1953.

races, be at the. To walk the streets as a prostitute: c., and low.

R

rack. In *stand the rack*, to stand the strain: low. (*Gilt Kid*, 1936.) I.e. *the racket.*—2. See **meat rack.**

rack off. 'To go missing; as an imperative, "Get lost" ' (Wilkes, who suggests it may be a var. of *nick off*, *fuck off*): Aus. low: since ca. 1975.

rad, n. A radiator: servants': from ca. 1905. Young, 1935, 'The rads are stone-cold.'—2. As *the rads*, the Police: 'heard from black teenage boy in Hackney [London], "He had some bother with the rads" ' (Rowbotham, 1988).

rad, adj. Superlatively good: teenagers': 1984 (Burt). Ex the BMX bicycle fad.

radar king, the. The senior radar officer: RN: since ca. 1940. See **king,** n., 1.

Radder, the. The Radcliffe Camera: Oxford undergraduates'. (Collinson.) By the 'OXFORD -ER'.

Raddie. An Italian: low. (Sharpe, 1938.) Ex the *raddled*-seeming complexion of many Southern Italians; but cf. **Reddy.** Powis, 1977, notes 'particularly an Anglo-Italian domiciled in London. Originally a term descriptive of Italian families in Clerkenwell.' Benney, 1936, of the early 1920s, may be relevant: 'Bookmakers from one part of the country would club together and hire bands of terrorists to secure the pitches for them. In this way there sprang up two rival organisations, the "Raddies" and the "Birmingham mob", contending for supremacy of the open race meetings.'—2. A radical in politics: since ca. 1930. Parr, 1964, 'He discovered that his acquaintance was a bit of a raddie at heart'.

raddled. (Of a face) much made-up: pej. coll.: from ca. 1920. (Collinson.) Ex *raddle*, red ochre.

radge. Silly. Prob. ex *rage* via 'mad'. Cf. Northern dial. *radgy*, mad.

radgepot. An idiot: market-traders'. Ex prec. Also ex dial. *radgy* is the market-traders' *radgified*; *radgy*, idiotic, very silly (*M.T.*).

radio. Crazy; insane: r.s. *Radio Rental* on mental. *Financial Times*, 7 June 1973.

radio actor. 'I'm what other actors refer to contemptuously as a "radio actor", which has nothing to do with whether you're on radio or not, but means that you always give a good first reading of the part and then never get any better' (Vosburgh, 1980).

Rafer. See **Raffer.**

Raff, the. The Royal Air Force: RAF coll., from 1918; soon also other Services'; by 1950, considered 'bad form' in the RAF itself. (Partridge, 1945; P.B.)

Raffer; rare in singular. A person in the RAF; not usu. applied to officers: civilian: 1939+.

Rafferty('s) rules. No rules at all, esp. as applied to boxing—'M.Q. (and Rafferty) rules' is the heading of a boxing section in the Sydney *Bulletin* of 1935—hence to a 'rough house'; *according to Rafferty rules*, without rule or restraint or, in politics, honour: Aus. coll.:—1914. Ex dial. *raffatory*, *raffertory*, *ref(f)atory*: refractory (*EDD*). The *Rafferty's* form since mid-C.20: Wilkes; Franklin, 1956.

raft. A (very) large number, as in 'A raft of people attended the meeting': NZ: since ca. 1944. (Griffiths, 1970.) Adopted ex US servicemen.—2. 'A number of wagons during shunting' (*Railway*): railwaymen's: since ca. 1945. Same source as 1.—3. See **George Raft.**

rag. In *on the rag*, menstruating: Can.: since 1950s at latest, still common. (Leech, 1986.) Var. of Brit. synon. *to have the rags on*: since mid-C.19. Cf. **rag-rider.**

rag bramah. A rag-and-bone merchant: police: since ca. 1925. *Free-Lance Writer*, Apr. 1948.

rag-dolling. See **ragging.**

rag-dragger. 'Captain of a sailing ship' (Granville): nautical: earlier C.20. Cf. **rag-wa(g)gon.**

rag-head. 'A Sikh with a turban' (Leech, 1986): Can.: since mid-C.20. Ex US (W. & F., 1960), where used also of Hindu. P.B.: I have seen it also as US expatriates' usage for Arab, n. and adj.

rag order. 'The Argentines had left [Port Stanley] in rag order' (Carty, 1983), i.e. in a disgusting mess: Army: later C.20. Cf. synon. **shit order.**

rag-rider. 'A woman during her menstrual period: low Can.: since mid-C.20' (Leech, 1986). Cf. **rag.**

rag-time. Merry: coll.: from 1901 or 1902.—2. Haphazard; carelessly happy-go-lucky; farcical: coll.: from ca. 1910. Esp. in a *rag-time army*: military coll.: since 1915. Cf. **Fred Karno's army.** (B. & P.) Cf. the RN coll., from 1915, *rag-time navy*, esp. of the auxiliary patrol during WW1. 'Taffrail', 1916.—3. Hence, free-and-easy: Services': since ca. 1920. Knock.

rag-time girl. A sweetheart; a girl with whom one has a joyous time; a harlot: all, from 1908 or 1909. Ex *rag-time (music)* = jazz. Cf. JAZZ, in Appx.

rag top. A convertible car: car-dealers': later C.20. Graham-Ranger, 1981.

rag-trade. Tailoring; dressmaking; the dry-goods trade in gen.: from ca. 1880: coll. (B. & L.) In later C.20, always the clothing trade, from *haute couture* to the meanest sweatshop (P.B.).

rag-wa(g)gon. A sailing-ship: steam or turbine, esp. if Aus. (or American): seamen's pej.: from ca. 1910. (Bowen.) I.e. *rag*, set of sails.

ragged. Unwell; tired and unwell: Aus. coll.: late C.19–20. (Niland, 1958.) Cf. **rough.** P.B.: also Brit., C.20; with suggestion of nervous exhaustion, as in 'Those bloody kids—they run the missus ragged.' Cf. the idea of 'frayed' nerves.—2. Skilful, esp. at games; as exclam., 'Ra-a-gged!' = Well played!: Black youth, London: mid-1980s. (Rowbotham, 1987.) Perhaps a deliberate reversal of C.19 coll. > S.E. *ragged*, inferior, wretched (of a game, display).

ragging. 'A younger Blade [Sheffield United AFC Supporter] told me with a smile, "We're gonna get a right raggin' " (short for *rag-dolling*, a term to describe a good kicking)' (Armstrong, 1985).

raging queer. A particularly ostentatious or importunate male homosexual: coll.: mid-C.20. (P.B.)

rags. A low-class harlot: proletarian:—1935.—2. As *the rags*, a bookmakers' term for horses that ran, esp. those which 'also ran': since ca. 1920. P.B.: a shortening of 'ragtag and bobtail' or 'the ragged remains'?

rail. Edge of a surfboard: Aus. (teenage) surfers': since late 1950s; by 1963, coll. (B.P.)

railroading. A reprimand: Public Works':—1935.

rails. 'The "Rails" are railway stations, as distinct from the Underground' (Hodge, 1939): taxi-drivers': since ca. 1919.

Railway Men, the. See ASSOCIATION FOOTBALL, in Appx.

rain(-)check. 'Any request or promise to accept an invitation at a later date' (W. & F.); hence, in Brit. usage, a postponement of any arrangement, as in, 'we'll have to take a rain-check on that one': adopted, ex US, ca. 1970. W. & F. explain the derivation ex the receipt, usu. a ticket-stub, given to spectators at a rained-off baseball match, allowing them to see another, later, game. An English example occurs in Hunter, 1977, 'I couldn't afford what [the blackmailer] wanted. I made him understand that.'—'And he settled for a rain-check?'—'No.' (P.B.)

rainbow. A post-Armistice reinforcement or recruit: military: late 1918–19. F. & G., 'As arriving after the storm was over'. Hence, in 1939–45, applied to various late-comers or those who, relatively, came late; as, e.g., by the 6th to the 7th Australian Infantry Division (*Rats*, 1944).—2. In *go up the rainbow*, 'to abandon oneself to gamut of sexual ecstasy' (Allen, 1972).—3. (Usu. in pl.) Tuinal drugs: drugs c. (Stockley, 1986.) US since—1967 (Spears).

raise. To complete (a form): Services', esp. RAF and Army coll.: since ca. 1935: by 1943, j. Jackson, 'Thus, "You want a vehicle? O.K., raise a Form 658 and push it into the Adj." ' Perhaps ex 'to *raise* all relevant points and deal with them'.

raise a gallop; esp. *unable to.* To have—esp. to be unable to have—an erection: mostly workmen's: since ca. 1930. Ex horses.

Rajrifs, the. The Rajputana Rifles: WW2. Cf. **Burrifs.**

rake, n. A (timber) train on a narrow-gauge line: Aus. (Prichard, 1926.) Probably a pun.—2. A 'complete set of coaches' (*Railway*): railwaymen's: since ca. 1910. Cf. sense 1.

rake, v.i. and t. To steal from a letter-box: c.:—1933 (Leach). Gen. as vbl n. (*raking*).

rake off. A(n unlawful) profit; a commission: orig. (1899), US; anglicised as coll. ca. 1920. (Thornton: *OED* Sup.) P.B.: ?ex gaming-tables and the croupier's rake.

Ralph Lynn. Gin: r.s.: from ca. 1925; ousted ca. 1940 by *Vera Lynn.* 'At least this pair remains in the world of popular entertainers' (Burgess, 1970). Ralph Lynn (1882-1962), actor famous for his parts in the well-known and very popular series of farces at the Aldwych Theatre; he also starred in the filmed versions.

ram, n. A confidence trickster's accomplice: Aus. c. (B., 1942.) Wilkes suggests cognate with later C.19 *ramp,* a swindle.

ram, v. To act as a confidence trickster's accomplice. See prec.

ram it! 'Stop!' or 'No!' = 'Up yours!': Can. low: since 1930s. (Leech, 1974.)

rammies. Breeches, trousers, knickers: Aus.: since early C.20. (Wilkes.) Perhaps ex mid-C.19 s., *rammers,* legs.

rammy. A sudden fight between gangs: Glasgow c. MacArthur, '[The police] knew that evidence about a rammy is always conflicting, never reliable and frequently perjured.' Ex Scottish *rammish,* violent, untamed. Contrast **clash,** q.v.—2. (*R*—), 'A Ramsgate man or a Ramsgate smack' (Butcher, 1980): nautical. Cf. *Brickie,* of Brixton.

ramp, n. A swindle: c. >, by 1905, s.: from ca. 1880. (Sims.) Hence, *on the ramp,* engaged in swindling: id. Manchon.—2. Hence, a swindle 'depending on an artificial boom in prices': 1922. *SOD.*—3. A parody; a skit: book world: 1934.—4. A counter (in a shop): c.:—1935 (Hume). One climbs over it. Cf.:—5. Hence, a public-house bar counter (Gosling, 1959), or, more generalised, a public house (*Daily Express,* 25 Mar. 1935).—6. In *on the ramp,* on a 'spree': low:—1923 (Manchon). ?Shortened *rampage.*—7. In *on the ramp,* finding fault: Glasgow:—1934.

ramp, v.t. To change the colour of (a horse): c.:—1933 (Leach).

Rams, the. See ASSOCIATION FOOTBALL, in Appx.

ram's head. The wooden rudder post of a canal-boat: canalmen's: late C.19-20. (Rolt, 1944.) Usu. bound with pipe-clayed *Turk's Head* knots.

ram's horn. One who shouts as he talks: coll.:—1923 (Manchon).

ramsammy. A celebration or similar party: Army officers', esp. Indian Army or ex-I.A.: late (?mid-)C.19-20. (In C.20, certainly by ca. 1950, also other ranks': P.B.) (Wainwright, 1975.) Of Hindi, via Hindustani, orig. *EDD,* 1905, glosses: 'Cornish dial. A noisy gathering; a family quarrel' and adds in brackets, 'not known to our correspondents'.

ranch. A cookhouse: N. Queensland (coll. rather than s.): since ca. 1910. Devanney, 1944. Hence:-

rancher. 'In North Queensland a rancher is a bloke who runs a sort of boarding house out in the bush, near a big job' (Hardy, 1967): since late 1920s. Ex prec.

rancid. Very objectionable or unpleasant: upper classes': from ca. 1910. Pain, 1912, 'Black kid gloves, the most rancid form of gloves'; Benson, 1924, 'How frightfully rancid!' Brandon, 1934. Prob. after **putrid,** q.v.—2. By complete reversal, an adj. of high approval: teenagers': 1986 (Burt).

randy. Violent; esp. sexually warm, lecherous: from ca. 1780: dial. and coll.; in C.20, mainly dial. (Burns, 1785; *Lex. Bal.,* 1811; Halliwell, 1847; *EDD*). Perhaps orig. ex *rand,* to rave, and poss., as S.H. Ward proposes, influenced by Hindustani *randi-baz,* a lecher. Sanders noted, 1965, 'Now

becoming almost respectable'; since mid-C.20 certainly coll. rather than dial. (P.B.)—2. 'Homosexual; perhaps rather rabidly or dangerously so' (Lambert, 1968): Public Schools': later C.20.

randy Andy, or simply **Randy.** (Properly the pet-form of *Randolph.*) The 'inevitable' nickname of anyone first-named *Andy* (pet-form of *Andrew*): late C.19-20. Cf. the Aus. *Merv the perv; Phil the dill;* etc.

Rangers, the. See ASSOCIATION FOOTBALL, in Appx.

rap, n. A charge; a case: c. The sense '*Rap,* Swearing against a Person' occurs in James Dalton, *A Narrative,* 1728; but the Brit. C.20 use, as in *Gilt Kid,* 1936, 'That is if they did not do [= arrest] him on this murder rap', has prob. been adopted ex US. See esp. *Underworld.*—2. In *get the rap,* to get into trouble: Aus. low: adopted, ca. 1925, ex US. (B., 1942.) Cf.:—3. In *take the rap,* to be (punished or) imprisoned, esp. for another person: adopted, ex US, ca. 1920: low s. verging on c.—4. See:-

rap, v. To talk, esp. either much or excitedly: mostly among musicians, disc-jockeys; hence teenagers': adopted, late 1960s, ex US hippie argot; ob. within 5 years. (Janssen, 1968; P.B.) Hence, n., a talk, a conversation: early 1970s. Some maintained that the term was a shortening of *rapport,* esp. when used for serious, 'soul-searching' conversation; but for its US c. or low s. use for 'to talk' in late C.19, see esp. *Underworld.* (P.B.)—2. To speak in rhythm with musical background; adopted, ca. 1950s in Brit., ex W. Indian cultural idiom—also known in US. (Raab, 1982.)

rap (one's) hand in. To give up, desist: RM in N. Ireland: 1970s. Hawke, 1979.

rap off. A conversational 'to and fro', exchanging ideas, etc. Cf. **rap,** v., 1. Drugs world, hippies'; ?ex jazz use. Adopted, ex US, 1950s. (Raab, 1982.)

rap up. To praise, speak highly of: Aus.: since ca. 1930. Niland, 1939, 'They could rap him up enough then.'

Raquel Welch, v., and occ. n. Belch: r.s.: ca. 1970+. 'Not yet widespread' (Haden-Guest, 1971). Commemorating the curvaceous film actress who became famous in *Myra Breckinridge,* 1970.

rare as rocking-horse manure, as. See **rocking-horse . . .**

rarin' to go. Eagerly impatient to get started: coll.: adopted ex US dial. Orig. of horses, *rearing to go.*

rarze(r). A 'raspberry' (sense 1): theatrical: C.20. B. & P. (at *raspberry* in 3rd ed.). By the 'OXFORD -ER'. Also spelt *ras* in its shorter form.—2. Army Other Ranks' form of **raspberry,** 2: ca. 1925-45. (E.P. 1942.) Cf.:-

rarzo (or rahzo). A red-nosed man: Cockney s.: late C.19-20. 'Whatcher, rarzo!' Ex *raspberry* colour.—2. Hence, a red nose—red from whatever cause: id. As in 'You ain't 'arf got a rarzo!' (L.A., 1976). Also spelt *razzo.*

ras. See **rarzer,** 1.

ras(-)class bastard. A first-class bastard or thoroughly objectionable fellow: among West Indian immigrants at Wolverhampton: since 1962. (Mackay, 1967.) Perhaps cf. *Ras Tafari,* the Royal title and surname of the late Emperor Haile Selassie of Ethiopia. (P.B.)

rasbs. Raspberries: greengrocers' coll. Ex the usual, careless, pron. of the full word, omitting the *p.* And cf. **strawbs.** (Raab, 1982.)

rash. A boy or young man that gets 'all over' a girl: teenage girls': ca. 1980. (R. Paterson.)

rasher and bubble. 'Double. This refers to a "double" in darts only. A rasher of bacon, served with "bubble and squeak"—left-over greens and potatoes, mashed and fried—is a square meal to many Cockneys' (Hillman, 1974): r.s.: later C.20.

rasher and fingers. A rasher of bacon and potato-chips: low eating-house. Jennings, 1932.

rasher-splasher. A mess cook: RN lowerdeck: since ca. 1925. (Granville.) Reduplicatory. Cf. *grub-spoiler.*

rasp. A shave: prisons'. Behan, 1958.

rasp away, v.i.; esp. in present participle. To make coïtal movements: Aus., esp. mechanician fitters' and turners':

since ca. 1925. Ex the movements of a *rasp* (a coarse file) being used.

raspberry. A disapproving, fart-like noise, described by F. & H. as stable s., but gen. considered to be theatrical of late C.19–20. A shortening of later C.19 r.s. *raspberry tart*, fart. Hence *get* or *give the raspberry*, to 'get the bird', to be 'hissed'; to 'hiss': theatrical: late C.19–20. Cf. **rarze(r)**.—2. Hence, a reprimand: Service officers': since ca. 1925. (E.P., 1942.) A particularly severe reprimand was, in RAF officers' s. of early WW2, an 'imperial raspberry' ('Blake', 1941). Cf. **rocket.** The opp. of a *raspberry*, that is, a commendation, is a *strawberry*.

Raspberry-Landers. Tasmanians: Aus. coll. B., 1943.

rasper. A (very) noisy breaking of wind: low. Anticipated by Swift in one of his improper poems (a bridal night).

Rasputin. 'A proper Rasputin: ironic phrase for a meek-looking and unworldly clergyman' (Powis): Londoners': later C.20.

rass. Var. of *ras*, q.v. at **rarze(r)**.

rassing. 'Acquisition by less than legal means . . . from the naval RAS—Replenishment at Sea'; also in sense merely of 'to scrounge', as in 'I was "rassing" a cup of tea, or "brew" ': Services'. Fox, 1982.

rat. A thief: c.: from ca. 1920. Wallace, 1928.—2. Short for **rat and mouse**, q.v., a louse. Sharpe, 1938.—3. 'Rats, the man who sneaked into the men's mines when they were on good stuff, and took out their opal during the night' (Prichard, 1921): Aus. opal-miners'.—4. Hence, any opal-thief, and the n. *ratting*. Cf. sense 1.—5. In *have a rat*, to be insane: Aus.: since ca. 1910. (B., 1942.) Cf. **bats in the belfry.**—6. See HAULAGE, in Appx.

rat and mouse. A louse: Army: WW1. (B. & P.) Hence, 'an occasional usage in the underworld where it has reference to a person—generally an informer' (Franklyn 2nd).

rat-arsed. Drunk, tipsy: teenagers': early 1980s. (Joanna Williamson, 1982.) Cf. **ratted.**

rat-bag. See **ratbag.**

rat-catcher (or solid). Unconventional hunting dress: hunting people's:—1930 (*OED* Sup.). Brock, 1963, 'In "The Horse Marines" (1911), Kipling writes, " . . . After he'd changed into those rat-catcher clothes . . . " Two very different people whom I have tried have both said that to them "rat-catcher" implies a rough shooting-rig, e.g. knickerbocker trousers with stockings and a Norfolk jacket, and a date considerably before 1931.—I suggest that "rat-catcher" was once used for a purpose even more plebeian and much more countrified than "dog-robbers" [q.v.], at much the same period, and was far less dressy than any hunting kit, though it may have arrived at this by 1931.'

rat fink. A '"stool pigeon" or informer to the police' (Leech, 1974): Can. c. > low s., prob. adopted ex US, earlier C.20. Orig. it = 'a strikebreaker' (Barnhart). See esp. *rat* and *fink* in *Underworld.*

Rat Hole, the. The 'Camden short tunnel' (*Railway*, 2nd): London Transport workers': since late 1940s. See also **Rat's Hole.**

rat-house. An asylum for the insane: Aus.: since ca. 1910. (B., 1942.) Cf. **rat**, 5.

rat on. To fail (someone); to betray: Aus.: adopted, ca. 1925, from US. (Baker, letter, *Observer*, 13 Nov. 1938.) Mostly, to inform to the police about (someone); also Can. (Leechman.)

rat pack. Ration pack, package of 'rats, G.S.' (= General Service): Army: later C.20. *Don't Cry*, 1983.

rat race, the. Fierce competition to make a living, esp. in the professions: coll.: since ca. 1945.

rat run. (Often in pl.) A back alley, ginnel, or jetty; a narrow way between buildings; 'It is a matter of local pride to know the "back doubles" [q.v.] and "rat runs" well' (Powis): low coll.

rat-trap. The brake on a bicycle: cyclists':—1923 (Manchon). Cf.—?ex—Fr. *rattrape-pédales.*—2. The mouth: lower

classes':—1923 (Manchon).—3. A balloon barrage: civilian: since 1939. Berrey, 1940.—4. In the RAF, a submarine: since 1939; but since ca. 1915 in the RN. (E.P., 1942.) Also *mouse-trap* (less usual). The crew being doubly *rats*.—5. 'Type of carburettor [for a motorcycle engine] made by Binks. So called because of its shape and the length of the air-intake' (Partridge, 1979): motorcyclists'.

rat up a drain pipe, like a. (Of a male) quick off the mark, esp. sexually, as in 'I can recall your impetuous youth when you'd have been round the lot of them [female models] like . . . ' (Daniells, 1980). Cf. the Aus. parody, 'like a rat up a rhododendron'.

ratbag (in earlier C.20, usu. hyphenated). An ill-disposed person: Aus. (Baker.) Since ca. 1960, also Brit., its spread perhaps helped by its use in the popular 'Perishers' strip-cartoon, written by Maurice Dodd and drawn by Dennis Collins, in the *Daily Mirror.*—2. An eccentric: Aus.: since ca. 1910. (Palmer, 1948.) Cf. *have* or *be rats*, to be eccentric.—3. A worthless person, esp. if young and with near-criminal tendencies and habits: Aus.: since ca. 1940. The *locus classicus* resides in William Dick's scarifying novel, *A Bunch of Ratbags* (1965), where he postulates an origin to which I prefer the probability that it simply = a bag in which to carry rats, hence the rats themselves, hence a single *rat* or thoroughly objectionable person.

ratbaggery. A display of eccentricity; eccentric activities: Aus.: since ca. 1930. B.P. notes, 1963, that Baker's *ratbagging* (in *Australia Speaks*, 1953) is a 'ghost word'.

rate is the rank of *the Rate*, a Leading Rate (or Leading Hand) in any branch of the Royal Navy: RN coll., esp. lowerdeck: late C.19–20. P-G-R.

rate, v.i. When used alone, as in 'Well, I mean, he just doesn't rate, does he!' = he has no qualifications and is unlikely to count for anything, it is informal S.E. verging on coll.: later C.20. (P.B.)—2. Hence the use of *rate*, v.t., disparagingly, as in 'She didn't rate him' = she thought very poorly of him, she rated him low on her personal scale. The 'rating' is app. never 'up' or 'high', but always 'down' and negative. P.B., 1987.

ratepayers' hotel. A workhouse: tramps' c.:—1935. Workhouses were maintained out of the rates and taxes.

Rather A Mixed Crowd. One of the several punning explanations of the initials of the *Royal Army Medical Corps*: WW2. (Carew.) Cf. WW1 *Run Away, Matron's Coming*, and *Rats After Mouldy Cheese.*

rather-nicers. 'A term of contempt stigmatizing ladies who pottered about sale rooms applying substantive and adverb to "gems" which they had no intention of purchasing' (Vachell, 1924): sale rooms'.

rations king. Catering Officer; a messing clerk: RAF: since ca. 1930. (Jackson.) Cf. **radar king.**

rats. Rations: Services': later C.20. Influence of official abbreviation; cf. **rat pack.**

rats and mice. Cards of '3' and '2' in one hand: Aus. poker-players': since ca. 1920. B., 1953.

rat's head. A fool: low: earlier C.20.

Rat's Hole, the. 'Victoria Station is the "Vic", King's Cross the "Northern", Paddington the "Western", St Pancras the "Cold Blow", and Charing Cross Underground the "Rat's Hole" ' (Hodge, 1939): London taxi-drivers': since ca. 1905. See also **Rat Hole.**

ratted. Drunk, tipsy: early 1980s. (Joanna Williamson, 1982.) Cf. **ashed (as a rat)**, and **rat-arsed.** An example in print: Carrott, 1982.

ratting jacket. 'Ca. 1940, I met the term "ratting-jacket", meaning one's oldest clothes, esp. if worn when [one is] doing rough or dirty jobs. Ex [S.E.] *hacking jacket*, informal wear when riding an inferior horse for exercise' (R.S., 1973). Cf. **rat-catcher,** and:-

ratting suit. Tweedy civilian clothes, 'dog robbers': RN officers': since ca. 1930. (Parsons, 1977.) Cf. prec.

rattle. 'The commander's report of defaulters' (Bowen): RN: since late C.19. Hence, *in the rattle*, under arrest, in detention; on a charge, as in 'A "bird" is a man who is always "in the rattle", i.e. defaulter' ('Taffrail'): C.20. Perhaps later is *score a rattle*, to get oneself put on the list of defaulters (Granville, who suggests a connection with warders' keys). Cf. the † S.E. *rattle*, a sharp reproof.—2. Money, esp. in *have a bit of rattle*, to be (moderately) comfortably off: late C.19–earlier 20. Manning, 1930.—3. In *have a rattle*, (of men) to coït: low.

rattle and clank. Bank (for money): r.s. (Franklyn 2nd.) Cf. rattle, 2.

rattle-blanket. A great-coat: Army: earlier C.20. (L.A.) Often used as a blanket, a greatcoat has buttons, etc., that clink. P.B.: but cf. rattle, 3, and officers' ground-sheets.

rattle (one's) cash. To 'stump up', pay out: c.:—1923 (Manchon).

rattler. A bicycle: 1924 (D.H. Lawrence: *OED* Sup.).—2. 'The Underground used to be the "Rattler" but has lately become the "Pipe" ' (Hodge, 1939): London taxi-drivers': ca. 1905–30.—3. (Of men) an assiduous amorist: since ca. 1920.

Ratty, the. Nickname of the Ravenglass & Eskdale Miniature Railway. Ex its founder, William Ratcliff.

ratty. Silly; stupid: NZ, hence also Aus.: since late C.19. (Lancaster, 1904; B., 1942.) Hence, *ratty on*, infatuated with; also *ratty over* (B., 1943). Concerning those older Australians who volunteered to fight in Korea, 1950, Carew wrote, 1967, 'These older men were the "Ratty Diggers", so called by some of Australia's young men because it was thought that having survived one major war, they would have sufficient sense to avoid another.' Cf. rat, n., 5.

raunchy. 'Earthy'; risqué; lustful; euph. for 'pornographic': 'increasingly met with in the media, mid-1970s' (R.S.)—but adopted, ex US, in Can. and Brit., ca. 1965, by 'pop' devotees and the drugs world (Janssen; Leechman); recorded by *DCCU*, 1971. I surmise: either derived from or, at least, prompted by S.E. rancid. P.B.: cf. also the West Country dial. *raunch*, raw and uncooked, of vegetables (*EDD*), and late C.19 *rorty*, 'amorous'.

rave, n. A strong liking; esp. of a warm friendship between schoolgirls: 1919 (Lunn); Tey, 1946. Cf. pash.—2. An enthusiastic notice in the Press: theatrical: since ca. 1920; in the world of books, since ca. 1945.—3. 'At a rave, blast or orgy—all synonyms for party—a guy (never a boy) meets a bit of hod, or tart (whether or not she is)'—to quote from 'Cool Culture' in the correspondence columns of the *Sunday Times*, 8 Sep. 1963: teenagers': ca. 1961–5. Also a dance.—4. Among beatniks, a bottle party: late 1950s–early 60s. See rave-up.

rave, v. See AUSTRALIAN UNDERWORLD, in Appx.

rave-up. Elab. of rave, n., 4. Still current, among the middle-aged, ca. 1980, but usu. ironically, as in 'Are you going to the rave-up at the vicarage after evensong?' (P.B.)

raver. A confirmed party-goer: beatniks': late 1950s. (Anderson.) Ex rave, n., 4; cf. ravist.—2. 'A young woman who is enthusiastically promiscuous or merely of a passionate (but not promiscuous) nature' (Powis): coll.: later C.20.—3. See AUSTRALIAN UNDERWORLD, in Appx.

ravers. Raving mad: since ca. 1925; by 1960, slightly ob. Marsh, 1938.

raving Noah. See MOCK AUCTION SLANG, in Appx.

ravist. A party-goer, esp. if habitual: office- and shop-girls': ca. 1956–9. (Gilderdale.)

raw. In *sleep in the raw*, to sleep naked: adopted ex US, ca. 1943 in Brit., ca. 1944 in Aus. P.B.: or, in later C.20, simply 'I sleep raw'.—2. In *on the raw*, adj. and adv., roughing it: Aus. coll.: since ca. 1920. Devanney, 1944.

raw deal. Harsh or bad, esp. unfair, treatment: coll.: adopted, ex US, ca. 1930. Ex card games; cf. rough spin.

raw stock. See MOVING-PICTURE SLANG, §6, in Appx.

rayed. X-rayed: hospital coll.: since ca. 1910.

raz, in the. In the nude: Aus.: since late 1940s. Joc. alteration of *in the raw*.

razoo, rahzoo. A farthing; a small coin; any very small sum: NZ; by ca. 1920, also Aus. Howard, 1934, 'Haven't got a razoo left. Gave me last two bob to the wife'; heard mainly in the negative phrases *I haven't a razoo* or . . . *a brass razoo*, for . . . no money at all (B., 1941). App. a corruption of the Maori *rahu*. Raab: *brass razoo* also known in London, ca. 1930s.

razoos. (Human) testicles: NZ.

razor, n. See razor blade.

razor, v. To slash (a person) with a razor: Glasgow lowerclass coll., obviously destined to > S.E.: from ca. 1920. MacArthur, 'There's been some hooligan who has razored poor Frank and very near done him in awthegither.'

razor-backs. 'Cattle that are lean and scraggy' (B., 1943): Aus. coll.: late C.19–20.—2. 'In the U.S. and, to a less extent, in Canada, a razor-back is a pig, semi-wild and of no ascertainable ancestry' (Leechman): late C.19–20. Both senses are occ. used in the singular.

razor blade. A Negro: r.s. on synon. spade, q.v.: since ca. 1955. (Newman, 1970.) Often shortened to *razor*.

razor gang, the. 'An investigating committee . . . who come to examine the day-to-day working of drivers and guards . . . for "unproductive time" . . . very often successful in reducing the staff complement at depots' (McKenna, 1): railwaymen's: mid-C.20. Cf. needle noses, and trappers.

Razor King, the. The Glasgow hooligans' and gangsters' name for one who, using as weapons a razor in each hand, is recognised as the head of a gang of hooligans: from ca. 1920. The 'hero' of MacArthur's damning book is a 'razor king'.

razz. A good talking-to, an harangue; esp. by a master to a boy: Eton. Ex *raspberry*. McConnell, 1967.

razz-ma-tazz, razz(a)matazz. See JIVE, in Appx. Perhaps as Franklyn has suggested, it is r.s.—2. Nonsense. See JAZZ, in Appx., and cf.:—3. 'The SDP moved in in force, had extensive media coverage and applied the full razz-ma-tazz of an American presidential campaign' (*Financial Times*, 18 July 1981).

razzle. To steal: Aus. c. (Baker.) Often shortened to *razz*. P.B.: ?a corruption of *rustle*.

re-bushed. 'Men's egotism applied to woman who is thought to be no longer of attractive physique: "She'd have to be rebushed—put a ham in and pull the bone out." Noted about 1962' (L.A., 1967): since ca. 1940, prob. orig. among artificers in the RAF.

read (someone's) palm. To tell him off: RN: since ca. 1960. (Peppitt.) Ex palmistry: to determine and describe his character.

reader. A prescription: drugs c. (Stockley, 1986.) US since—1936 (Spears).

readers. Reading-glasses: coll.: since ca. 1925.

readies. Money in bank and/or currency notes: orig. bank-clerks', –1935; by later C.20, gen. low coll. for any 'ready money'. Usu. as *the readies*, as in Daniells, 1979. Cf.:-

ready, or the ready. Money, esp. money in hand: c. until C.19, then low s. till ca. 1870; by 1930, rather ob.—2. A swindle, a conspiracy: Aus. (B., 1959.) Oftener *ready-up*. Hence, *work a ready*, to effect a swindle: id. B., 1942.

ready. To give, illicitly, a drug to (a person) in order to render temporarily innocuous: c. Wallace, 1928.

ready-eyed. 'Knowing the full story, [having an] awareness of the real "low-down" of the situation' (Powis, 1977): police and c.: later C.20. R.S. quotes the *Daily Telegraph* law report, 14 June 1975, 'Underworld for a planned crime which has been betrayed to the police and so, if carried out, will be a trap for the criminals involved.' Cf. ready-ied.

ready-ied. Made ready, prepared; also, bribed: market-traders'. *M.T.* instances 'The place was ready-ied for us', and 'He's got to be ready-ied'. Is this the same as ready-eyed?

ready-made. (Of a racehorse) likely to win: turf: since ca. 1920. (L.A., 1976.)

R

ready-up, n. A conspiracy; a swindle: Aus. low. Doone, 1926; B., 1943. Ex:-

ready up, v. To prepare, or contrive, illicitly or not honourably: Aus.: 1893, Melbourne *Age*, 25 Nov., 'A great deal has been "readied up" for the jury by the present commissioners' (Morris). Prob. ex **ready,** v.—2. Hence, to produce or procure ready money: Aus.: since ca. 1910. Baker.—3. To 'put someone wise' or 'tip off': Aus.: since ca. 1912. B., 1943.

readying, readying-up. Vbl nn. of **ready,** v., and **ready up,** qq.v.

real. 'The most basic of all basic beat-age words is *real*. This really covers everything. Whatever else they may be, all beat-agers are real. Everything they do, or think they do or not, is *real*. Everything they say is *real*' (Anderson): beatniks': since ca. 1958. Hence **really,** n.

real Air Force, the. Flying personnel: the others': 1939+. Jackson.

real cool. See **cool,** adj., 4.

real Mackay, the. The real thing, 'the goods', that which is completely authentic: coll., orig. a Scotch phrase: since later C.19. 'Tom Collins' (Joseph Furphy's) *Such is life,* 1903, contains 'There was an indescribable something . . . which made us feel that station aristocracy to be mere bourgeoisie, and ourselves the real Mackay.' The US version, *McCoy,* is a folk-etymologising, prob. via 'the pugilist, "Kid" McCoy, who was for some time at the head of his class' (Irwin). See esp. E.P.'s essay on the subject in his *From Sanskrit to Brazil,* 1952.

real money. A large sum, or large sums, of money as opposed to 'chicken feed': coll.: since ca. 1955. (Petch, 1966.)

real nervous, dad; commoner, **'way out.** Adjectively admirative: jazz-lovers': 1950s. (*Observer,* 16 Sep. 1956.) Perhaps ex 'It makes me real nervous [excited], dad' and ex ' *'way out* in front of the rest'.

real root, the. The real thing; the best or the correct thing (to do): earlier C.20. Prob. ex *the real root of the matter is . . .*

real turned on. Very 'high' (drug-exhilarated): beatniks': since ca. 1959. Anderson.

really, n. A beatnik, male or female: beatniks', hence among those on the fringe: since ca. 1959. The Andersons exemplify it four times on p. 2 of their witty and informative article. Ex **real,** adj.

really! You don't say so!; well I never! coll. tag: late C.19–20. P.B.: in C.20, an almost meaningless admonition, as in 'Well, really! Of all the stupidest things you could say!'

really really. An intensive, as 'very', 'extremely': world of 'pop', and feminine coll.: ca. 1980. 'I was, you know, really really pleased when he said that.' (P.B.)

reaper. A submarine: RN: 1940+. Ex the U-boats' 'reaping' of merchant vessels in early WW2.

rear admirals. 'Those Naval rugby experts in the stand who call for "More feet, Navy, more feet!" ' (L.A., 1976).

rear-up, n. A noisy argument; a quarrel; a 'row': lower classes'. (F. & G.) Ex:-

rear up, v. To become extremely angry: coll.: late C.19–20. Ex horses.

reast in (one's) **pit,** (usu. *reasting*). To lie abed after it's time to rise; to stay in bed for want of anything better to do: Army: since mid-C.20. Ex dial., rancid. (P.B.)

rebound. See **catch on the rebound.**

rebushed. See **re-bushed.**

rec-space, the. 'The men's recreation space for games, etc.' (Granville): RN coll.

recap, n. Recapitulation: schools' (late C.19–20) and authors' (C.20) and BBC (since ca. 1938) coll.—2. A synon. of **retread:** Aus.: since ca. 1939. (B.P.)

recap, v.i. To recapitulate: coll. Cf. prec., 1.

recce, pron. and occ. written *recky.* Reconnaissance in gen., a reconnaissance in particular: Services': since ca. 1920: orig. coll., it was, by 1941 at latest, j. In WW2 every Army division had a Recce Battalion.—2. Hence, as v.i., to go on a reconnaissance, and as v.t., to reconnoitre: since ca. 1935 in

Army and by at least as early as 1939 in the RAF: coll. >, by 1942, j.—3. A reconnaissance 'plane: since ca. 1936: RAF coll. >, by 1942, j. H. & P.

recco. A reconnaissance flight: RAF: 1939+. (Jackson.) Ex prec.

reccy. A var. spelling of **recce.**

reckon. To count as worth-while; to esteem: London's East End: since the late 1940s. Always negative, as 'I don't reckon him' = I don't think he's much good. (*Evening News,* 12 Nov. 1957; Norman.) Elliptical for '*reckon* to be worth much'.

reckon (one)self. To be conceited; to over-estimate one's own abilities: since mid-1940s. (Henderson, 1968.) A snooker hall hustler, quoted in *Sunday Express* supp., 2 Aug. 1987, 'Wherever you go, you look for the bloke who reckons himself a bit.' Cf. **think** (one)**self.**

recliner. (Usu. in pl.) A Crown issue armchair: RN officers'. (Granville.) By the 'OXFORD *-ER*' on *recline.*

Recs, the. The *Records* and Fingerprints Department: police coll.

red. Gold: orig. c.; by 1950, low s. Cf.:—2. A sovereign: c. or low:—1923 (Manchon).—3. In *in the red,* a gen. coll. phrase for 'in debt': since ca. 1920. *Red,* in book-keeping, indicates debt; its complement, *in the black,* hardly antecedes 1945. Hence, *put in the red,* bankrupt; penniless: trade and commerce. In Can. carnival s., it = having failed to make one's expenses. Contrast:—4. *In the red,* 'In the money. Money (red—gold) is coming in easily' (Tempest, 1950): prisoners' c.: mid-C.20. Cf. sense 1.—5. See **red arse; red birds; reds.**

red and blues. Tuinal: drugs c. (Stockley, 1986.) US since—1969 (Spears).

red 'Arry. A £10 note: Aus.: since ca. 1930. B., 1959.

red arse. A recruit: Guardsmen's. (Grinstead, 1946.) P.B.: by 1950, common also in the rest of the Army, esp. among National Servicemen, and shortened in the jibe *you big red!*.

red Biddy. Cheap red wine: Glasgow (where also called *crimson dawn*):—1934 (Baxter). The term soon spread: witness, e.g. Harrison, 1943.—2. Methylated spirit as a drink: c., esp. tramps': from ca. 1910. Also *jake.*

red birds. Seconal: drugs c. (Stockley, 1986.) US since—1954 (Spears).

red cap (or with capitals). A military policeman: Services' coll.: WW1 and since. (B. & P.) Ex his distinctive head-dress.—2. The penis: low: since ca. 1918.

red centre, the. The inland: Aus. coll. (Baker.) Ex the red soil: see *passim* Russell, 1934.

Red Devils, the. 'The Parachute Regiment has only one nickname. The Germans in North Africa [WW2] called them "The Red Devils"; apart from the Germans this is a name used only by journalists and never by soldiers' (Carew). Ex the maroon berets worn by the regt. P.B.: to the rest of the army they are 'The Paras', or occ. in later C.20, 'The Cherryberries'.—2. 'Midland Railway compound locomotives' (*Railway,* 2nd); 'painted red and making plenty of sparks at the chimney', adds McKenna: railwaymen's: earlier C.20.—3. As *red devils,* little tin-encased Italian hand-grenades: Army in N. Africa: 1941–3.—4. [Capsules of] Seconal: drugs c. (Stockley, 1986.) US since—1959 (Spears).

red eye. 'A flight that takes off late at night and arrives very early in the morning, its passengers [?and crew] emerging with eyes red from lack of sleep: aircrews' ' (Green, 1984).

red face (or **neck**), **have a.** To be ashamed: Glasgow:—1934. Ex blushing. An earlier, pre-WW1 var. was *take a red face to* (one)*self.*

red flannel. Collective for high-ranking officers: Army (not officers'): WW2. (Moorehead, 1944.) Ex the red bands on their hats and their red gorget patches. P-G-R.

red-head. See **blonde.**

red-headed tea and bare-footed bread. Lenten fare: Anglo-Irish. Milk in tea and butter on bread being prohibited on the fast-days.

red hot. (Of a female) sexually aroused: low coll. 'Give her a couple of gins and she's red hot, believe me!'

red-hots, the. Trotting races: Aus. r.s., on 'the *trots*': since ca. 1920. (B.P.)

red lead. Tomato juice: RN: since ca. 1925. Ex colour.—2. Herrings in tomato sauce: RN lowerdeck. Granville.

Red Light News. See **Whore's Gazette.**

red line. 'To go up to the maximum recommended revolutions on a tachometer' (Dunford): motorcyclists' coll., verging on j.: later C.20.

red Lizzie (cf. **red Biddy**). 'About once a month he used to get drunk on Red Lisbon—a deadly and incalculable wine concocted of the squeezed-out scrapings of rotted port casks and laced with methylated spirits—a terrible drink . . . , which smites the higher centres as with a sandbag. It is otherwise known as Lunatic's Broth or Red Lizzie' (Kersh, 1939): low: since ca. 1930.

Red Mike. See CANADIAN . . . , in Appx.

red neck. Nickname for a Yarmouth fisherman: nautical. (Butcher, 1979.) Cf. **Duff-Choker** and **Pea Bellies.**

red-necked. Excessively martial, chauvinistic and 'hawkish': adopted ex US ca. 1977. E.g., a report in the *Listener*, 9 Nov. 1978, on a USAF/RAF (simulated) nuclear bombing competition, described the prize-giving ceremony as taking place 'in a red-necked atmosphere'. (P.B.)

red Ned. A cheap muscatel wine: Aus., esp. Sydney, and NZ: earlier C.20. (B., 1941.) In Aus., the orig. sense has > generalised to any 'rough red wine' (Buzo, 1973).

red one. A town where the show has made a large profit: circusmen's. Contrast **bloomer**, 2.

red-penny man. See AUSTRALIAN UNDERWORLD . . . , in Appx.

red pottage of Esau. 'Lentils cooked into a porridge-like mess' (Petch, 1946): domestic. Ex the Biblical Esau's 'mess of pottage'.

red-ragger. A Communist: Aus.: since ca. 1930. (Cusack, 1953.) Ex the song 'The Red Flag'.

red recommend. 'A recommendation in red ink on a Service Certificate, much coveted by ambitious and zealous ratings' (Granville): RN lowerdeck coll.

Red Shield, the. Generic for clubs, particular for a club, conducted by the Salvation Army: Services' coll.: 1939+. (H. & P.) Ex the sign displayed.

red 'un. A red-tipped match: low eating-houses'. Jennings, 1932.

red, white and blue. A shoe: r.s.: later C.20. Haden-Guest, 1972.

Redbrick, generic for the provincial English (i.e. not **Oxbridge,** q.v.; or London) universities and university colleges, founded before WW2; also adj., as in 'the *Redbrick* universities': journalistic coll., dating from the late 1940s and, by 1955, S.E.

redders. Red wine: Oxford undergraduates', since ca. 1920; then also, since ca. 1950, among the smart young set. (Gilderdale, 2.) By the 'OXFORD -ER(s)'.

reddite. 'A jeweller. (One who handles gold)' (Tempest, 1950): c. See **red**, n., 1.

Reddy. An Italian: c., and low. Prob. ex red Italian wine; yet cf. **Raddie.**

Redfern. In *getting off at Redfern*, the practice of *coitus interruptus*: Sydneyites': since ca. 1950. Redfern is a railway station immediately before Sydney Central. (B.P.) Cf. **get off at Hillgate,** and see quot'n at **Gateshead.**

redhead. See **blonde.**

reds. Fleas: Aus. B., 1942.—2. As *the Reds*, the Redemptorists: Catholics'; esp. in Aus.; but this sense does occur in Joyce, 1922.—3. As *the Reds*, the Russians—i.e. the Russian Communists: since—1917 or 1918. In later C.20, applied to communists in general.

reduce. To take (someone) down a peg: Shrewsbury: 1938+. (Marples.) I.e. 'cut him down to size.'

redundo. Redundancy payment: Londoners'. 'And while it is true he would stand to pick up, well, he thinks it might be six or seven thousand in redundo were the [Greater London Council] to disappear . . . ' (*Guardian*, 24 Aug. 1984). Lower down the scale than a *golden handshake.*

reeb. Beer: back s.:—1859 (H., 1st ed.). This is one piece of back s. that has lasted: Powis, 1977, notes its current use in London.

reef. To steal: Aus. (*Rats*, 1944.) Cf.:-

reef it off in lumps. 'To extract large sums of money from someone' (B., 1959): Aus.: since ca. 1920. An elab. of:-

reef off. To take (money) from (a person): Aus. racing: since ca. 1910. (Glassop, 1949.) Cf. prec. and **reef.**

reefer. 'A pickpocket's accomplice' (Baker): Aus. c.: since ca. 1910. Ex **reef.**—2. A marijuana cigarette: orig. c., adopted ex US ca. 1935; by mid-C.20 widespread in drugs world, hence > gen.—3. (Or *Reefer.*) An inhabitant of—or one who is familiar with—the Great Barrier Reef: Aus. coll.: since ca. 1925. Devanney, 1951.

reeler. Esp. in *cop a reeler*, to get drunk: low: ca. 1920–40. Curtis, 1937.

reels of cotton. Rotten: r.s.: later C.20. Barker, 1979.

reely. Tipsy: coll. (—1933); not at all common. (Juniper, 1933.) Cf. **reeler.**

Reemy or **Reemee.** The Royal Electrical and Mechanical Engineers (formed in 1942): Services' (esp. Army) coll. of 1942–3, then j. Ex the initials *R.E.M.E.* Also the Royal Canadian Electrical and Mechanical Engineers: Can. coll. > j. 'In spite of the C' (Leechman). P.B.: occ., esp. at first, by an 'inevitable' rhyme, *the dreamy Reemy.*

ref, n. A *ref*eree: sporting.—2. A *ref*erence (as to ability, etc.): commercial: 1907 (Wodehouse).

ref, v. To referee (a match): coll. Ex the n., 1.

refained or **refayned.** Excessively refined and genteel: cultured coll.: since ca. 1920. Ex a 'refained' pron. of *refined.*

refec. Refectory: Birmingham undergraduates':—1940. Marples, 2.

reffo. A refugee from Europe: Aus.: 1939+. (B., 1942.) Cf. the American *refujew*, refugee Jew. (Usu. in pl.) ' . . . later called "Balts" (after Baltic States)' (Humphries, 1981, gloss.): Aus.: mid-C.20.

refill, have a. To have an inflation, in the artificial-pneumothorax treatment of TB: patients': since ca. 1930. Cf. *have a pneumo.*

reg, n. (pron. *rej*). Year of *reg*istration of a motor vehicle, shown by a letter on the registration plate, as in 'Ours is a T-reg', or 'the question of which is the most economical "reg" of car to own. (Here is an interesting effect of bureaucracy on language: "age" is now "reg")' (Allison, 1983): motorists' coll., verging on j.: later C.20. The letter suffix on the plates was introduced in 1962.

reg., adj. Regular; according to regulations: Guardsmen's: since ca. 1920.

Reggie. The *Reg*imental Sergeant Major: since ca. 1919. 'Watch it!, here comes Reggie.' Not in his hearing. Cf. later synon. *Tara.*—2. A *reg*istered customer: home front civilians': 1940+. *New Statesman*, 30 Aug. 1941.

reggie or **reggy** (hard *gs*), adj. Regimental; intensively, *dead reggie*: RAF: since ca. 1930. P.B.: also Army (with soft *g*); esp. 1950s. The term covered anything excessively military, from discipline in a training barracks, to the 'khaki-brained' attitudes of an individual soldier.

regimental. A downfall: Army: from 1916. Esp. *come a regimental*, 'to be court-martialled and reduced to the ranks' (F. & G.). Sc. *smash*. Cf. **proverbial, the.**—2. A 'mess', a 'ballsup'; a signal failure: Londoners': from 1919. 'Oh, I made a regimental of the whole bloody thing'. Short for *regimental fuck-up*. Also synon. *regulation*. Ex sense 1, via demobbed Servicemen.—3. As *the Regimental*, the Regimental as opp. to the Company Sergeant-Major: Army coll.: earlier C.20. F. & G.

regimental as a button-stick(, as). Rigidly 'regimental' (cf. **reggie,** adj.): Army. A button-stick is that brass or plastic oblong baffle, with a slit in the middle lengthways, that enabled a man to metal-polish his brass buttons without soiling the cloth of the uniform to which they were attached. (L.A., 1976.)

Reginald Denny. 'A penny. London lad made good in Hollywood, thus commemorated' (Daniells, 1980): r.s. Denny (1891–1967) acted in many films ca. 1920–50.

rego (soft *g*). Registration of a motor vehicle: Aus.: since ca. 1945. 'The rego is up [expired] next month.' (B.P.) Cf. **reg**, n.

regs. Regulations, as in *King's* or *Queen's Regs*: Services', orig. and mainly Army: since ca. 1870.

rehab. A rehabilitation ward or department in a hospital: since ca. 1945. Ex the official abbreviation *rehab*.—2. A rehabilitation loan: NZ servicemen's: since ca. 1944. Slatter, 'Rehab was the caper, you jokers'.

relations (or **country cousins**) **have come, her.** She is in her menstrual period: lower classes': mid-C.19–20. Manchon (*les Anglais ont débarqué*).

reload. 'To ensnare a "mug" by letting him think he is winning (at the three-card trick, for example) or has gained a smallish profit or advantage (in a confidence trick, for example) and then, while he is in the mood of false confidence and with his appetite whetted, to cheat him of all he possesses, or as the term has it "to send him to the cleaners" ' (Powis): c.: later C.20.

Remf. 'The base camp of a unit moving forward was known as its "echelon". Hence those who never went to the front line, but stayed with the echelon were known as "Remfs" or Rear Echelon Mother Fuckers' (*Don't Cry*, 1983): Fighting Forces': Falkland Is. campaign, 1982. The US influence is clear here.

remount, gen. pl. A woman for export as a harlot, esp. to Argentina: white-slave traffickers' c. (Londres.) Hence *on remount service*, (of a white-slaver) engaged in procuring fresh women. Ex such terms as *remount depot*, of cavalry horses.

Renee. 'Recording their new album *Rocking with the Renees* (. . . Renee is a Mod [q.v.] term for a girlfriend)' (review in *Guardian*, 28 Mar. 1983).

rent. Blackmail: since ca. 1920; by 1965, ob. Mackenzie, 1956.—2. A male always, or nearly always, charging for his homosexual services: homosexual: since ca. 1930 (?much earlier). He earns his rent in this way. Hence, and usu., and adj., as in 'Be careful of that one, he's rent' (he will ask payment). Contrast **trade**, 2, and cf. **rent boy**.

rent boy. A boy hiring himself out to homosexuals: homosexuals': since ca. 1970. (A correspondent, 1970; *Time Out*, 23 May 1980.) Cf. **rent**, 2; **rent guardsman**; **renter**.

rent guardsman. A soldier—hence, any other man—consenting to homosexual practices for money: 'gay' society: since ca. 1950.

renta-. Prefix applied first in such terms as *rentacrowd* or *rentamob*, where it = 'a crowd of people specially assembled at a political demonstration, to impress the authorities'; these people are alleged to be unlikely to be emotionally engaged, merely a hired claque: coll.: since late 1960s. Ex such commercial usages as 'Rentavan' the name of a hired, 'drive-it-yourself', van company, and 'Rentavilla', for holiday accommodation. The prefix has subsequently been attached to many other objects, as in 'The reply was just another Downing Street rentamissive' (*Guardian*, 25 June 1982), where it means that the letter was impersonal and, by implication, unhelpful. (P.B.)

renter. One who, not a prostitute (female or male), sells casual sexual or homosexual favours for money or presents: low life: since late C.19. Letter from Max Beerbohm, ca. 1895, Cecil, 1964. Cf. **rent**, 2.

reo (usu. in pl. *reos*). Reinforcements: Aus. Army: 1939+. (*Rats*, 1944.) By abridgement + the Aus. suffix *-o*.

rep, n. A repertory theatre; gen. *the Rep*, a specific theatre, or *the Reps*, the world of repertory: mainly theatrical: from ca.

1920.—2. A reprimand: Army (esp. NCOs'). (Kersh, 1941.) Cf. **severe dig** or *rep*.—3. A politician, athlete, cricketer *rep*resenting a State: Aus.: since ca. 1920. B., 1942. Cf.:—4. A trade-union representative: trade-unionists': since ca. 1920. Palmer, 1948.—5. A firm's representative, a mealy-mouthing of '(commercial) traveller': since mid-C.20; hence, since ca. 1960, a firm's trouble-shooter. Cf. universities' **the God rep**, the chaplain.—6. A crook or a convict, having status; c., hence low s.: since ca. 1950. (Clayton, 1970.) Ex C.18 *rep*utation, which has been revived in C.20 in the nuance 'a good, a great, reputation'.

rep, v. To act as a representative, esp. for a commercial firm: coll.: since mid-C.20. See n., 5.

repaint. 'Any retired Naval officer called back to the Service in time of war or national emergency' (Granville): RN: WW2. Cf. earlier **dug out**, and **retread**. P.B.: applied earlier to army officers in WW1 (Blaker).

repat, n. and adj. Repatriate, repatriation; repatriated: coll.: since ca. 1941. Brickhill, 1946, 'Typical of the repat boys was "Chuck" Lock.' Cf. **expat**.

repeaters. As in 'It give me the repeaters' (of food): Aus. coll. (Park, 1980.) Cf. the genteel 'onions do repeat so', although here the sense is often rather that their taste lingers, than that they are 'windy'.

repro. Reproduction, as in replication: '*bijou* residences with repro carriage lamps by the door' (Barker, 1988): coll. Ex catalogue j., and the language of estate agents' advertisements.

reptile. 'A creep, low-life, jerk: very insulting, as in "Shut up, you reptile!"': usu. male to male: since later 1970s' (Leech, 1986): Can., adopted ex US.

repulsive. Unpleasant; dull: Society: 1930, Waugh, 'Isn't this a repulsive party?'

res. A restaurant; as in *a British res*, one of the British Restaurants (excellent public canteens set up in the mid-1940s): later 1940s. (Bell, 1950.) Cf. **rest**, n., 1.

rescrub. To do (a job) over again: RN. Granville.

resin. 'Liquor given to musicians at a party' (B., 1942): Aus.— 2. Cannabis: drugs c. Stockley, 1986.

Resistance, the. Harley Street: taxi-drivers': 1948. Ex the medical profession's opposition to the Aneurin Bevan health-plan. On the analogy of *La Résistance*, the Resistance Movement in France (1940–4). Cf. **the Occupied Territory**, Bayswater (London): taxi-drivers': 1947–9. Ex the large number of foreigners there, and on *enemy-occupied territory*. Both terms were recorded in the London *Evening News*, 19 Mar. 1948.—2. That part of West Hampstead which contains numerous Germans, whether residents or lodgers: since late 1930s, by which time many Germans had removed themselves from a 'Hitlerised' Germany they deplored.

reso. A residential, i.e. a boarding-house for permanent guests: Aus.: since ca. 1950. (B.P.) *Residential* + the ubiquitous Aus. s. suffix *-o*.—2. A working–residential boat, with living accommodation: canalmen's: since ca. 1920. Gladwin, 1973.

rest. A restaurant: urban:—1923 (Manchon). Cf. **res**.—2. A year's imprisonment: Aus. c. (Baker.) Hence *resting*, (of a person) 'in gaol'. See **and the rest**.

rest (one's) **eyes.** To have a short sleep: semi-joc., usu. evasive, coll. A clerk surprised sleeping, 'Sorry! I was just resting my eyes' (Petch, 1966).

result. 'Favourable answer to adjudication/petition/parole' (Home Office): prisoners' coll.: later C.20. A specialisation of the S.E.—2. ' "Get a result" [is] a current term meaning to secure one's objective. It was originally footballers', a "result" being a win or a draw . . . ; then was taken up by the police for getting a conviction. From there, via TV series about the police, it has recently been generally adopted' (Barltrop, letter, about London, 1981).

results. News of sports results: journalistic coll.: from ca. 1921.

retired gremlin. See GREMLINS, in Appx.

retired to a stud. (Of a woman who has) married: Aus. joc.: since late 1940s. (B.P.)

retread (or **re-tread**). A 1914–18 soldier serving in 1939–45: Aus.: WW2. B., 1943.—2. A short-service officer on a second commission; but usu. any officer retired and then recalled to the service: FAA: 1950s. (Peppitt.) But I think since ca. 1943 or 1944.—3. A retired officer re-employed by the Army, as a civilian, in an administrative post, e.g. as adjutant of a small static unit: Army officers': since ca. 1950. (Hayward, 1979.)—4. 'An officer who's been promoted from the rank [sic]' (*New Society*, 24 Apr. 1980): Army: later C.20.—5. 'Aviator returned to flying duties after ground tour' (*Fighter Pilot*, 1981): RAF: later C.20.—6. A retired schoolteacher still teaching: Aus.: since ca. 1950. (B.P.) The orig. of all these senses lies in the car-trade j.: a used tyre given new life by the application of new treads. But there is also the pun, retired = re-tyred, in each instance. Cf. **repaint**.

Retreat from Moscow, the. The exodus from Britain to Eire, in late 1946 and throughout 1947–8, in order to escape ruinous taxation, short rations and general totalitarianism. First used in Eire in March or April 1947, it 'caught on' in Britain on or about 12 May (1947). With an allusion to Napoleon's retreat in 1812 and to Russia's bedazzlement of British socialists.

return home. (Of a convict) to be released on ticket-of-leave: police coll. Leach, 1933.

return the other cheek. Instead of 'turning the other cheek' to return—or give—the other 'cheek' or impudence: since ca. 1955. (Petch, 1966.)

reune. To hold a reunion: 1929 (E.W. Springs: *OED* Sup.).

Rev. Form of address to a clergyman: non-aristocratic, non-educated. Llewellyn, 1943.—2. (As *rev.* and usu. pl.) An engine's revolution: Air Force: 1914. (F. & G.) P.B.: but prob. engineers' j. before then.

rev, v. To pray: Cranbrook School. Prob. ex *reverence.*—2. As v.t., a shortening of:-

rev up. To increase the *revolutions* of (an engine): from ca. 1916: coll. >, by 1930, S.E. Also v.i., of the engine. *OED* Sup.

Reverend Ronald Knox. The pox: r.s.: mid-C.20. 'Or just The Reverend or the Right Reverend' (Daniells, 1980). Cf. synon. **Collie Knox**; **Nervo and Knox**. Ronald Knox (1888–1957), Catholic priest and sometime domestic prelate to the Pope, won fame as a writer—perhaps, for the layman, mainly by his detective stories.

reversed ear. That 'naval disease' which is caused by wearing 'dry' hoods, the pressure inside exceeding the pressure outside: skin divers': since ca. 1950. (Granville.)

revo. Revolution: Aus.: since ca. 1945. B., 1953.

revved(-)up, often prec. by *all.* Very much excited; very tense: since ca. 1960. The opposite of *relaxed.* (Petch, 1966.) Of machines, esp. motor cars and bicycles.

rewrite. A virtual re-writing of another person's book: publishers' coll.:—1933 (*Slang*). Ex the v.

Rhine. See **trip up the Rhine.**

rhino-arse. A large, long, tough bread roll having cheese in the middle and issued on OTC field days: Rugby School: since ca. 1910.

Rhodesian Army. For terms used during the civil conflict that preceded the establishment of Zimbabwe, see RHODESIAN, in Appx.

rhodie, -y. A Rhode Island Red fowl or chicken: coll.: late C.19–20. Roberts, 1976.—2. (Also as *rhodo.*) A rhododendron: 'nursery' and familiar coll.

Rhondda Valley, the. 'Special name for the "Burma Road" (central alleyway) on HMS *Glamorgan*, now general on missile cruisers: Royal Navy: 1970s' (Peppitt).

rhubarb. Nonsense; 'Sometimes the word is used three times thus, "Rhubarb, rhubarb, rhubarb" as emphasis. (From the muttering of actors when simulating the sound of a crowd)' (Powis): coll.: later C.20. Occ. 'That's a load of rhubarb!' (P.B.)—2. (Pron. *rhubub*.) Sub, abbr. of suburbs: r.s.: earlier C.20. Franklyn.—3. See **hit the rhubarb**; and:-

rhubarb pill. A bill (for payment): late C.19. 'The inference is that both necessitate an outpouring' (Franklyn). Often abbr. *rhubarb.*

riah. Hair: back s.: esp. in the 'gay' world: since mid-C.20 (?earlier). Took, 1974 (scripts from mid-1960s); in Rodgers, 1972, *riha* [sic] is glossed '(Brit. gay slang, a garbling) head hair.'

rib, v. To make fun of; pull someone's leg, as 'They ribbed him something rotten [= very badly]': orig. Cockney (and Can.) since ca. 1925, >, by ca. 1945 gen. Harrison, 1943.—2. To swindle: Aus. c.: since ca. 1930. B., 1942. Both senses perhaps ex late C.16–early 20 coll. rib-roast, thrash, punch.

ribbing. Vbl n. counterpart of **rib**, v., 1.

ribbons. Ropes forming the boundary; hence, loosely, any boundary: cricketers': from ca. 1920. Cardus, 1934, 'George Gunn cut it to the ribbons, as the saying goes'.

ribby. Destitute; (of places) poverty-stricken, squalid: c., from ca. 1930, > by 1939 low London s. (Ingram, 1935.) 'Short of cash' (Powis, 1977). Ex **ribs**, 2.—2. Hence, (of things) inferior; (of conditions) unsatisfactory: mostly lower-class London: since ca. 1939. 'Substandard' (Powis, 1977).—3. Worn out, depleted or vigour: id.: since mid-1940s. Naughton, 1970.

ribs. In *on the ribs*, (of horse or dog) no good at all: racing c.: from ca. 1926.—2. In *on the ribs*, destitute; down and out: c. (*Gilt Kid*, 1936.) Cf. older synon. *on one's back*, and *down on the knuckle.*—3. In HAULIERS' SLANG, q.v. in Appx., *on the ribs* = very old. Cf. sense 1.

rice. For *give it* (or someone) *rice*, see **give what for.**

rice-bowl. See **break** (someone's) **rice-bowl**, to deprive him of his livelihood.

Rice-Burner. A (Japanese-made) Honda motorcycle: motorcyclists' nickname: later C.20. (Dunford.)

rice-cake!, for. Public Schools' euph. s. for *for Christ's sake!*

Rice Corps. Royal Indian Army Service Corps: WW2. Any of its units tended to be called a *ghee factory*, because of their predilection for *ghee* (Indian butter).

Richard. In *have had the Richard*, (of persons) to have been dismissed; (of things) to have been superseded; to be 'all washed up' or finished: Aus.: since ca. 1930.—2. A shortening of the various senses of:-

Richard the Third. A bird: r.s.: late C.19–20. B. & P.—2. Hence, a bad reception, a hissing: theatrical s. on older, C.19 s. *bird*, itself ex the hissing *goose.*—3. Also ex sense 1 is the meaning 'a (or one's) girl': r.s., on synon. *bird.* Often shortened to *Richard.* Tempest, 1950.

rick, n. A 'gee' in the grafters' sense (trade accomplice): grafters'. (*Cheapjack*, 1934.) Perhaps ex *rick*, a wrench.

rick, adj. Spurious: low racing: since ca. 1950. 'If you are standing near a bookie's joint, undecided, and a merchant dashes in and places a bet, such as "Seventy pounds to forty. On top," don't take a blind bit of notice. The give-away is the "On top". It's a rick bet. It don't mean nothing. It don't even go in the book. Its sole object is to push or goad you into making your bet' (*Sunday Telegraph*, 7 May 1967, anon., 'A punter's guide to the bookie's secret lingo'). Ex the n.—2. See **take a rick view.**

rick, v. To remove one testicle of (usu. a horse): Aus. Ex Eng. N. Country synon. dial. *rig* (*EDD*). 'That horse was ricked and Sammy Hall' = It was rendered unitesticular. *Sammy Hall* is Cockney and Aus. (esp. Sydney) r.s. on *ball*, testicle, the ref. being to a song very popular in mid-C.19 and still heard occasionally 'where men are men' (Morrisby, 1958).

ricket. A mistake: low (?orig. c.): since ca. 1930. 'You've made a bit of a ricket' (Norman). Used in the BBC's account of the Great Train Robbery Trial, 23 Aug. 1963.

ricko. A ricochet: Army: WW1. (B. & P.) Since ca. 1925 the form has been *ricky* (P-G-R).

Ricky. Rickmansworth (Hertfordshire): Hertfordshiremen's: from ca. 1920.—2. See prec.—3. For *ricky-ticky*, see JIVE, in Appx.

riddle. See **Jimmy Riddle.**

369

riddle, v.i. and t. To steal by pocketing part or all of the takings, as in, 'He was riddling the till' (*M.T.*): market-traders': late C.19–20. Hence the agent *riddler*, one who steals thus, hence any dishonest assistant. P.B.: perhaps ex the S.E. *riddle*, n. and v., (to) sieve.

ride, n. (Gen. used by women.) An act of coïtion: low: C.19–20. Ex centuries older *ride*, v.—2. Hence, woman as sex object, as in the raffish male observation on an attractive girl, 'I bet she's a great little ride': since mid-C.20. (P.B.)—3. In *find a ride*, to be given a car to drive in a race: motor-racing s.: from ca. 1925. (Chamberlain.)—4. See **take for a ride.**

ride, v. To keep girding at: Can. (Beames.) Ex Lancashire dial. *ride*, to be a burden to (*EDD*.)—2. Prob. from the same origin is the sense 'to irritate; deliberately to annoy, sometimes subtly or indirectly', as in an NCO's comment on a troublesome, devious soldier, 'I'll have that bugger yet—he's been riding me all week': Services' coll.: since mid-C.20, perhaps earlier. (P.B.)

ride bumpers. See **bumpers,** 2.

ride on the cushions. 'Engine men travelling as passengers' (*Railway*): railwaymen's: since ca. 1920. Cf. Can. *ride the cushions,* q.v., at **ride plush,** and also **mahogany.**

ride out. To depart: London teenagers': late 1950s. (Gilderdale.) Prob. ex 'Western' films.

ride plush. To travel illicitly free on a train: Aus.: adopted, ca. 1920, from US. (B., 1942.) Cf. the Can. hoboes' *ride the cushions*: late C.19–20. (Leechman.)

ride shotgun. 'An extraordinary survival of the stage-coach days. When gold or other valuables were carried, or a hold-up apprehended, a man, armed with a shotgun, rode on top of the coach with the driver. In the speech of the period, this man "rode shotgun". It is still [1963] used, sometimes in the sense of "Quis custodiet . . . ?"' (Leechman). Only is the derivative sense eligible, and then as a coll. P.B.: but coll. also is its Service use, to ride as escort to a driver: esp. Army: since ca. 1950.—2. Hence, to escort in any way, as e.g., of aircraft, 'The last two Jaguars [aircraft] with Dave riding shotgun between them' (*Phantom*): RAF: 1970s.—3. To take the front seat, on a vehicle, next to the driver: joc. coll.: since ca. 1955. (P.B.) Ex sense 1.

ride (one's) stripes or **tapes.** (Of a NCO) to be over-strict or officious: Army: earlier C.20. Contrast **ride,** v., 2.

ridge. Good; valuable: Aus. c.: late C.19–20. Ex C.17–19 c. *ridge*, gold.—2. Hence, genuine: Aus. c.: since ca. 1930, > ca. 1945 low sporting s. Glassop, 1949.

ridgy-didge. Bevan, 1953: '*Ridgy Didge* (derived from "rigid digger", in its turn meaning a straight-up soldier, and hence implying integrity) means "the truth". The phrase is used invariably either as a simple question "Ridgy Didge?" or an unequivocal assurance: "Ridgy Didge!"': Aus.: mid-C.20. More prob. simply an alliterative reduplication of **ridge,** adj., 2 (P.B.). Variants are *ridgey-dig*; and also 1953, *ridgy-dite* (Tennant), the latter perhaps r.s., on *all right.*

Riff Raff, the. The RAF: 1930+. Partridge, 1945, 'A jocular—sometimes a contemptuous—elaboration of *Raff*.'

riffs. See CANADIAN . . . , in Appx.

rifle. See:-

rifle range. 'Change. As in a quick break between scene changes in the rubbedy [club], "Here's the sausage [*and mash* = cash]. Look sharp with the rifle" (Daniells, 1980): mainly theatrical r.s.

rift. Energy, speed; esp. *get a rift on*, to move or work quickly, energetically: Guards Regiments': since ca. 1920. (Kersh, 1941.) Perhaps a blend of *rush* + *shift*, or ex:-

rifting. 'Cleaning gear, harness, etc.' (F. & G.): Army: late C.19–20. Perhaps ex dial. *rift*, 'to break up grass-land with the plough' (*EDD*).—2. (?)Hence, a severe telling-off, a tongue-lashing: Army: since late 1940s, perhaps earlier. 'Sar'-major said he was idle on parade. Give him a right good rifting, he did . . . ', i.e. verbally 'took him to pieces'; only occ. used in the sense of physical assault. (P.B.)

rig. Penis: Can. (F. Leech, 1972.)—2. A large lorry or truck (orig. applied to an articulated vehicle): their drivers': since ca. 1980. Ex Citizens' Band Radio j., where the term is also applied to a CB radio set; perhaps the derivation is from the set to its setting. In the Peak District of Derbyshire, 1983, I saw a large quarry lorry prominently labelled 'Sir Jim's Rig'. (P.B.)—3. The collective equipment of a musical group: pop musicians': later C.20. Hibbert, 1983.

rigger mortis. 'A good-for-nothing airman' (Jackson): RAF: since ca. 1938. Ex the pre-1939 official *rigger* (later > flight mechanic 'A'), with a pun on *rigor mortis*: as Jackson neatly puts it, 'a dead type' (dead above the ears).

right. Safe: Aus. coll. (Kelly, 1955.)—2. Unquestionable, indisputable; thoroughgoing, as in **right bastard,** q.v.: coll.—3. In *right?*—answered by *right!*: is that correct? do you agree?—Yes!: adopted ex US, ca. 1960; by 1970, S.E. P.B.: my first meeting with this usage was in a railway compartment I once shared with a four-man USAF aircrew, early 1950s: the captain ended every statement 'Right?', and the other three duly answered in turn 'Right!'—the effect was almost theatrical.

right bastard, a. A thoroughly mean-spirited, bloody-minded man: coll., orig. mostly RN: since ca. 1925.

right fanny. 'Real, or pathetic, story or tale': c.: from ca. 1925. Ingram, 1933.

right-(h)o, right-oh, righto. Very well!; certainly!; agreed! Cf. **rightio (righty-o).**—2. Hence, 'That's enough! Break it down!' (B., 1959): Aus.: since ca. 1920.

right into (one's) barrel. Precisely what one needs or desires: Aus. B., 1942.

right oil, the. Correct information: Aus.: since ca. 1920. (Baker.) Var. of *the dinkum*, or *good, oil.*

righteous. An adj. applied, in the 1920s and early 1930s, by musicians to good jazz and to those who recognised it: Can. (ex US). 'A good hot chorus would be greeted with cries—from other members of the band—of "Righteous, brother! Righteous!"' (Priestley, 1959).

rightie, -y. A member of a right-wing political party or organisation, or even a person on the right wing of a socialist party: political and journalistic: since late 1960s. Contrast **Lefty.** (P.B.)

rightio!, righty-o!, righty-ho! All right!; certainly; gladly!: from ca. 1920. Ex *right-(h)o!* Sayers, 1927, Lord Peter Wimsey *loquitur*: 'Righty-ho! Wonder what the fair lady wants.'

righto! See **right-(h)o.**

righty-(h)o(h)! See **rightio!**

rigid. In **shook rigid,** q.v., and in **bind rigid:** see **bind,** v. Substitution for 'to (bind) *stiff*'. Whence:-

rigid bind. One who bores you stiff: RAF: since ca. 1938. H. & P.

rim. To bugger (a woman): c. Also **bottle,** likewise v.t. Both, brutally anatomical.—2. To perform anilingus: homosexuals'. Adopted ex US (Rodgers, 1972).

ring (gen. with the). Anus (also *ring-piece*): low: C.19–20.—2. An RAF officer's badge of rank: RAF: since 1919. See **ring-chaser, ringer,** 5, and **rings.**—3. In the **dead ring** (of someone), q.v., a remarkable likeness.

ring a bell. 'That rings a bell': that brings something to mind; that sounds familiar: coll.: adopted, ca. 1925, from US. P.B.: ex fairground games, the telephone—or Pavlovian experiments? See also **ring the bell; ring bells,** 2.

ring-a-ding. 'Sure-fire, as the bell that rings at success on the strength machine at fairs' (L.A.); Williams, 1970, 'A youth centre would be a ring-a-ding stamping ground for picking up boys': coll.: later C.20. Occ. *ring-a-ding-ding!*, an expression of pleasure and triumph.

ring bells. A coll. that (dating from ca. 1930) is gen. in the negative, as in Holt, 1934, 'When it comes to pets, snakes don't ring any bells in my emotional system', i.e. do not appeal to me. Ex the bell that rings when, at a shooting-gallery, a marksman hits the bull's-eye.—2. In later C.20, more often as var. of **ring a bell**, as in 'No, I'm afraid that name rings no bells with me'. (P.B.)

ring-burn. The sometimes painful after-effect of eating too much of too fierce a curry: Services', in tropical stations where such curries were available: 1960s. See **ring**, 1. *Sunday Express* supp., 11 Oct. 1982, lists synon. *ringburner* as being in use among Sloane Rangers [q.v.]. Cf. **ring-stinger**.

ring-chaser. An officer seeking promotion: RAF, mostly officers': WW2. (P-G-R.) See **ring**, 2.

ring-conscious. (Of an officer) manifestly conscious of recent promotion; also, of an officer excessively officious: RAF coll.: since ca. 1925. Cf. **rings**.

ring-dang-do. A spree: Aus.: since late 1940s. Harris, 1958 (events of 1953), 'They've earned a bit of a ring-dang-do'.

ring-in, n. A horse, a dog, etc., entered for a contest either under a false name or 'in disguise': Aus. sporting. (B., 1942.) Ex the v.—2. A stacked pack of cards: Aus.: since ca. 1910. B., 1953.

ring in, v. To insert, esp. to substitute, fraudulently: from ca. 1810: orig., perhaps c., certainly at least low s. (Vaux.) Notably in gambling. Ex earlier *ring*, to change illicitly.

ring it on (someone). To outwit, as in 'They have rung it on us' (Powis): low: later C.20.

ring o(f) roses. Venereal disease: nautical low.

ring off! Desist!; shut up!: coll.: earlier C.20. (Lyell.) Ex telephonic *ring off, please!*

ring-piece. See **ring**, 1, and **-piece**.—2. See **twittering ring-piece**.

ring-rot. As in 'Ha' ye got ring-rot?' = Have you farted?: Northumberland teenagers': later C.20. (Blyth Ridley, 1984.)

ring-snatcher, -ing. A sodomite, sodomy: low.

ring-stinger. 'Very hot curry, particularly Vindaloo, etc.' (Turner, 1986): later C.20. Cf. **ring-burn**.

ring-tail. A coward: Aus. (Baker.) Ex:-

ring (one's) **tail.** To cry quits; to give in: Aus. Baker.

ring the bell. To render a girl pregnant: since ca. 1910.—2. To bring on an orgasm in one's female partner: since ca. 1920.—3. 'To hit the target; to hit the nail on the head; to win an argument by proving one's statement' (H. & P.): Services' coll.: since ca. 1920. Ex the fairground game.

ring-twitch or **-twitter.** See **twittering ring-piece**.

ringer. A quick changer of disguises: c. Cf. Wallace's title, *The Ringer*.—2. A crowbar: railwaymen's. (*Railway*, 2nd.) Ex the ringing noise it emits on contact with metal.—3. As in 'If it were mere poison . . . I could have dosed his malted milk or slipped a ringer in his vitamin pills' (Hunter, 1964). Cf. **ring in**, v., and:—4. 'Man who steals vehicles and alters their appearance skilfully for sale here or abroad; also, such an altered vehicle. Originally meant horses or greyhounds that had been similarly disguised. Not so common in this sense now. Also used to describe any genuine-appearing fake' (Powis): c. > low s.—5. In combination, the commissioned ranks of the RN and RAF, as *half-ringer* (RAF, Pilot Officer); *one-ringer* (Sub-lieutenant or Flying Officer); *two-*; *two-and-a-half ringer* (Lt-commander or Squadron Leader); etc.: Services': C.20 (RN); since 1919 (RAF). (Granville; Jackson.) 'On the lower deck officers are known as *ringers*; in the wardroom they are known as *stripers*' (Granville). Their respective ranks are denoted by rings on the cuff, not by stripes on the arm, or by stars and what-have-you on the shoulder.—6. 'If [the street bookmakers] knew beforehand that they would be nicked [= caught] then they would get a "ringer" who for a price would take the can back for the bookie' (Ash): London dockers': earlier C.20. Cf. **ring in**, v.—7. See **dead ringer of**.

ringerangeroo (both *gs* hard). The female pudend: feminine and joc.: since ca. 1930. Prob. fanciful duplication of centuries-older synon. *ring*, + US suffix *-eroo*, the latter a usage of which W. & F. list over 100 examples.

ringerbarry. 'Customer who brings goods back for exchange or refund' (*M.T.*): market-traders': late C.19–20. A sophisticated back-slanging.

ringest. Best: Aus. teenage surfers': earlier 1960s. (B.P.)

ringmaster. A Squadron Commander (function, not rank): RAF: since ca. 1937. (Jackson.) Ex the circus ring.

rings. 'Abbreviated reference to an Officer's rank, denoted in the Navy and R.A.F. by the number of rings on his sleeve' (H. & P.): since ca. 1890 in the RN and since 1918 in the RAF: coll. >, by 1930 at latest, j. See also **ringer**, 5.

rinse a sock. Esp. in 'I must go and rinse a sock' = I need to urinate: heard in Yorkshire, but prob. more gen. (Bishop, 1978.) Cf. synon. **strain** (one's) **greens**, **squeeze the lemon**, etc.

Rio Tinto, the. The 'Glasgow to Carlisle parcels train' (*Railway*, 2nd): since ca. 1950. Presumably ex the Portuguese or the Spanish town so named.

riot. A person, an incident, or a thing that is very amusing or very laughable: upper classes': from ca. 1931. E.g. 'That girl's a riot!' An early occurrence is in Coward, 1933.

Riot Act, (to) read the. To read the Fire Arms Act to prisoners about to be discharged: prisons': since ca. 1920. Norman.

rip, n. A reproof indicated by a master's tearing up of work shown up to him: Eton. He tears the sheet or sheets of paper. McConnell, 1967, with synon. *tear-over*.

rip, v. To annoy intensely; to disgust: Aus.: since ca. 1921. *Rats*, 'Wouldn't it rip you!'

rip hell out of. To defeat severely (in a fight); to reproach, or reprove, bitterly: Aus. B., 1942.

rip into. To defeat utterly in a fight; hence, to reprimand or reprove severely or bitterly: Aus. coll.: since ca. 1910. B., 1943.

rip job. 'Anything that looks like a giant tin opener . . . is very suspicious. It is used for "rip jobs" when opening cheaper safes [i.e. cutting into the weakest side]' (Powis, 1977): c.: since ca. 1930 (*Underworld*).

rip-off, n. Corresponds to all senses of the v.:-

rip-off, v. 'To treat with contemptuous disregard; hence, to swindle' (*Observer* mag., 15 July 1973): adopted, ca. 1968, ex US. (R.S.)—2. 'To abandon, break away from' (Ibid.): id.—3. Illegally to take—and claim as one's own—something belonging to, esp., the Establishment: mostly teenagers': adopted, ex US, early 1970s.—4. To satirise; burlesque; deride: coll.: earlier 1970s. *Melody Maker*, 8 July 1972.—5. In the drug traffic, to snatch drugs from, or fail to pass on drugs bought from, someone ('to rip him off'): adopted, ca. 1974, ex US. *Daily Telegraph*, 12 Jan. 1977 (R.S.). Cf. 3.—6. To overcharge someone—commoner in passive than in active, as 'Don't try that restaurant—we were ripped off something rotten there': coll., since ca. 1970; also Aus. (Gadsdon, 1977; P.B.) Cf. sense 1, to swindle.

rip-off artist. One who excels in the *rip-off* (in all its senses), of which it is a natural extension—cf. all the other 'artists': coll.: since late 1960s. *Beatles*.

rip-rap, the; also 'to **rip-rap**'. A borrowing of, to borrow, money: r.s., on *tap*: since ca. 1935. Franklyn 2nd.

rip-snorter. Anything exceptionally good; an eccentric or very entertaining person: Aus., adopted ex US, since ca. 1910 (Baker); by ca. 1945, gen.—2. An uncontrolled breaking of wind, as 'He let go a real rip-snorter': since late 1940s. (L.A., 1976.)

rip the piss out of. ' "You have to be prepared," said Claire, "to be thrown against the filing cabinet and told to take your pants down. It's their [male members of an advertising agency] way of ripping the piss out of you. So you rip the piss out of them as well" ' (Jack, quoting a young London secretary, 1983). An intensification of **take the piss**, q.v., perhaps influenced by *rip-off*.

Rip Van Winkle money. 'Money earned whilst asleep such as returning to depot as a passenger during the night hours' (McKenna, 1): railwaymen's: mid-C.20.

ripe. Complete, thoroughgoing, unmitigated; esp. 'a *ripe bastard*': Services': since ca. 1920. P-G-R.

ripped. With fly-buttons undone. I.e. ripped open.

ripper. One who overcharges flagrantly: coll.: since mid-1970s. With -off, the agent in the other senses (1–5) of **rip-off**, v.—2. Hence, **ripper!**, Aus. exclam. occasioned by an example of **rip off**, v., 6: from late 1975. (Gadsdon, 1977.)

ripper deal. A deal 'in which the discount [-offering] dealer is inviting the purchaser to "rip him off" ' (Gadsdon, 1977): Aus. Cf. prec.

ripperty. The adj. formed on **ripper**, 1. The Times, 18 Nov. 1985.

ripple. To fire air-to-ground missiles: Services': later C.20. Thompson, 1985.

rise. An erection; esp. in get or have a rise, to experience an erection, and (of the female) give a rise, to excite a male sexually: raffish coll.: late (perhaps throughout) C.19–20. Cf. hard-on; beat, n., 3.

rise and shine. See TOMBOLA, in Appx.

rise to the occasion. To have an erection when desirable or suitable: raffish: since ca. 1920. Cf. rise.

risk. Doubt: Aus. coll.: since ca. 1920. In Buzo, 1968, Norman—an 'ocker' of the worst kind—says, 'Mind you, if a mug copper ever started pushing me around, I'd job him proper, no risk of that'.

risley. In vaudeville a risley is 'a performance in which a man lies on his back on a special couch and juggles a boy or a small person with his feet' (Leechman). Ex Richard Risley Carlisle, US acrobat, † 1974 (Green, 1984).

risy. Apt to, trying to, take a rise out of persons: Cockney. Esp. 'Don't be risy!' (Heard on 21 Aug. 1936.)

Rit, rit. Ritalin, a stimulant drug: drugs world: later C.20. New Society, 11 Aug. 1983. Also Rities (Stockley, 1986).

ritzy. Rich; stylish, fashionable: adopted ca. 1935 from US. Curtis, 1937, 'Ritzy-looking dames with dogs.' Ex the various Ritz hotels in the great capitals, esp. that in London. (See E.P.'s Name into Word.)

ritzy tart. Any upper- or middle-class woman or girl, esp. if she dresses well and speaks well: since ca. 1945. Tempest, 1950.

river. 'An accidental effect produced in a page of type, when spaces occur in succeeding lines in such a way as to lie almost above each other, thus forming long thin lines (rivers), more easily observed when the page is held nearly level: printers' and publishers': from about 1910' (Leechman).—2. In up the river, reported to the Trade Union officials for speeding: workers':—1935. Perhaps ex American c., wherein sent up the river = sent to prison.

river hog or **pig.** A lumberman specialising in river work: Can. lumbermen's. Beames.

river(-)rat. A member of London's harbour police: late C.19–early 20. Carr, 1939.

Riverina. A shilling: Aus. r.s., on synon. deaner: ca. 1920–66. B., 1943.

rivet. In on the rivet, cycling 'flat out', very fast, having moved forward to the peak of the saddle: club cyclists'. Fellowship, 1984.

riveted. Fascinated, as in 'The truth is that she is riveted by butterflies' (Kendall, 1980). Ex:-

riveting. Very exciting; fascinating: upper-class: since ca. 1955. Francis, 1970, ' "Darling," she said, "Too riveting. Nothing would stop me." ' Prob. ex S.E. 'to fasten one's attention upon'. P.B.: in more gen. media use from late 1970s. See quot'n at **Sloane Rangers**.

Ro-Ro. A Rolls-Royce motorcar: motorists': since mid-C.20. (P.B.) Cf. synon. **Roller**.—2. As ro-ro, n. and adj., roll-on/roll-off ship, 'designed to carry trailers, containers, rolling stock' (North Sea Observer, 26 Feb. 1979); the concept of operating such vessels: nautical coll., since 1960s (Madigan), prob. > j. (P.B.)

roach. The butt of a 'joint' (marijuana cigarette): drugs world: adopted, latish 1960s, ex US.—2. A cardboard filter for a hand-rolled cigarette: young peoples': early 1980s. (James Williamson, 1984.) A softening of sense 1.

road. In get the road, to be dismissed from employment: Glasgow:—1934. Cf. the Aus. coll. on the road, out of work (B., 1942).

road louse. A small car that, holding the road and proceeding, stately, at about 25 m.p.h., refuses, when hooted at, to move to the side: Cambridge undergraduates' (1930) >, by 1935, rather more gen. Prob. orig. a pun on wood-louse (P.B.).

roadie, -y. The road manager of a touring 'pop group' company of musicians: since early 1950s. (Groupie, 1968.) By 1960, broadened to:—2. 'The roadies are the hired mercenaries of the music business, a tough and self-sufficient group of men whose duties are to care for the equipment, get it arranged and set up for the concerts, and to anticipate the wishes of their masters' (Daily Telegraph mag., 17 Nov. 1972): world of entertainment. They keep the show on the road.

roadman's hammer. 'A mythical tool called for by all [coal-] miners who have difficulty in moving tubs along roadways: the cure for all their ills' (Foster, 1970). Cf. **sky-hook**.

roar up. To speak abusively to; shout at: proletarian: earlier C.20. F. & G.—2. Hence, to reprimand: Services', as in Gibson, 1946, 'the C.O. roaring someone up for not having his parachute handy [on 3 Sep. 1939]'; also Aus., mostly juvenile: since ca. 1940. B., 1953.—3. To scrounge; to find by hustling: Army: WW2. P-G-R.—4. (Of destroyers) to attack: RN coll.: WW2. P-G-R, 'Roar in, roar up, and roar out again'.

Roarer, the. The Southern Aurora, a Melbourne–Sydney train: Aus.: 1962+. (B.P.)

roaring forties; R.F. 'The degrees of latitude between 40° and 50° N—the most tempestuous part of the Atlantic' (F. & H.); occ. the corresponding zone in the South Atlantic. Nautical coll.; in C.20, S.E. From ca. 1880.—2. Hence, Lt-Cdrs between 40 and 50 years of age: since ca. 1917; esp. in 1939–45. P-G-R.

roarin' horn. An urgent erection: low Aus.: late C.19–20.

roaring horsetails. The aurora australis: Aus. B., 1942.

roast. See **bake**, at AUSTRALIAN . . . , in Appx.

roast pork. To, a, talk: r.s.: since ca. 1910. Often, as v., shortened to roast. Cf. **rabbit and pork**.—2. A table fork: r.s., since ca. 1930; esp. in the Army, 1939–45. Both: Franklyn.

roaster. A person burnt to death in a crash: RAF:—1935. Cf. roaster or boiler, applied to cooking fowl: since late 1940s.—2. A 'hot dog'.

Rob Every Poor Soldier. The Royal Engineers Postal Services: Army: 1920s–30s.

rob my pal. A girl: r.s., on gal. The modern version of C.19 Bob my pal. Franklyn.

Robert. A spell of watch below, or a short rest at any time: deep-sea trawlers'. 'I've given the brats a Robert' (Luard, 1933). P.B.: perhaps ex 'bob down'.

Robert E. Lee. A quay: London dockland r.s.

Robertson & Moffat; usu. Robertson. A profit: Aus. r.s.: since ca. 1930. B., 1945.

Robinson & Cleaver. Fever: Londoners' r.s.: earlier C.20.

Robinson Crusoe, adj.: e.g., travel . . . , to travel alone: Aus. teenagers', esp. surfers': since ca.1962. Pix, 28 Sep. 1963.

rock. To speak: tramps' c. and market-traders': late C.19–20, and still, 1976, actively current among the latter (M.T.). Abbr. **rocker**, q.v.—2. To startle (someone) with news or assertion: mostly RAF: since late 1941. H. & P., 1943, 'A new version of shake.' P.B.: since WW2, much more gen. and, esp., journalistic, as 'The City was today rocked by the news that . . . ' As L.A. notes, 1974, sometimes elab. to rock (someone) to (e.g. his) foundations, really to astound.

Rock Apes, the. Personnel of the RAF Regiment: Services'; prob. orig. RAF in Gibraltar (cf. the barbary apes kept as mascots of the garrison there): since WW2. Cf. synon. **Shitehawk Soldiers**.

rock-bottom seats. Slatted seats in the buses of war-time construction: 1941+.

Rock Cake. A Roman Catholic: since mid-C.20. (Watts, 1988.) Presumably ex initials R.C.

R

rock cake. A bore; a nuisance: RAF in India: ca. 1925–35. (Wall, 1945.) Rhyming on **bake**, n., 3.

Rock Dodgers, the. Pilots and their aircraft flying to the Western Isles: RAF Transport Command: 1944–5. They have to be! (Noble, 1945.)

Rock-happy. Suffering from acute melancholia occasioned by too long service at Gibraltar: RN: since ca. 1939. Cf. **orkneyitis**.

rock-hopper. 'A person who fishes from rocks on a sea coast' (B., 1959): Aus.: since ca. 1930.

rock in. To accelerate or intensify; esp. *rock it in!*, hurry up: Aus. B., 1942. Cf.:-

rock it in. To talk, esp. aggressively or boastfully: Aus. low. *Rats*, 1944, 'Nearly all of 'em could speak English, an' they starts to rock it in about the war.' Glassop, Ibid.: 'We rocked it back'—i.e. retorted.

rock of ages. Wages: r.s.—2. In *by the rock of ages*, relying on sight; without a measure: tailors'. *Tailor and Cutter*, 29 Nov. 1928.

rock-off. Fast asleep, as in 'Oh, he's rock-off—he'll sleep till lunchtime now, with luck' (of a baby having a nap): (?domestic) coll. (Bacon, 1986.)

rock spider. A petty thief that robs amorous couples sporting in parks or by the seashore: Aus. c.: since ca. 1939. B., 1953.

rock the boat. To disturb the *status quo*: since ca. 1920. Hence *sit down—you're rocking . . . !* and *Don't rock the boat!*, 'exhortation to someone about to disturb a comfortable situation' (Norman Franklin, 1976).

rocker, n. A devotee of rock-and-roll: since ca. 1959; by 1966, ob.—2. A youthful motor-cyclist aspiring to be a 'ton-up' boy, doing 100 miles an hour: since ca. 1960. See **Rockers**.—3. Hence, a leather-jacketed non-surfer, esp. one of the *Rockers* gang; 'a youth who would formerly have been a motor-bike fiend' (B.P.): Sydney teenagers': 'not heard before 1962'. See **Rockers** for the Brit. version.—4. A song—or the recording of one—exhibiting the characteristics of rock-and-roll: Anglo-American: since ca. 1965. *Beatles*.—5. In *off* (one's) *rocker*, (temporarily) mad: since late 1890s. Ex *rocking-chair*.

rocker (or **rokker**); v. occ. **rock**, q.v. To speak: tramps' c.: from ca. 1850; since ca. 1900, gen. low s. Ex Romany *roker* (Sampson's *raker*), to talk, speak, with variant *voker* (cf. L. *vox, vocare*); cf. Romany *roker(o)mengro*, lit. a talk-man, i.e. a lawyer. Still current, later C.20, among market-traders (*M.T.*, 1979).—2. Hence, to understand. Pugh (2), ' "An' I must have 'em to go away with. Rokker?" "Yes, Chick," she faltered.' Ex Romany.

Rockers and **Mods** (both rare in singular). 'Teenagers today are split into two fairly even factions—the Rockers and the Mods. Their difference is simple: Mods are the fashion-conscious, with-it teenagers; Rockers are the old-fashioned, ton-up kids who think more of motor-bikes than themselves. Their only link lines are pop music and the fact that they are both young' (McGowan, 1963): since ca. 1960. *Rockers* ex rock-and-roll music; the terms are still current, 1988.

rocket. A severe reprimand (stronger than **raspberry**, 2): Army officers': since ca. 1934. 'To *stop a rocket*—receive a reprimand' (*New Statesman*, 30 Aug. 1941); 'An exceptionally severe one is either an *imperial rocket* or an *outsize in rockets*' (E.P., *New Statesman*, 1 Aug. 1942); by late 1941, in fairly gen. use in the RAF also—witness Jackson; and by 1942, in the RN—witness Granville. It blows the recipient sky-high. Whence the var. **pyrotechnic**.

rockie. See **rocky**, n.

rocking horse. An 'oscillating guards van' (*Railway*): railwaymen's: late C.19–20.—2. Sauce: later C.20. Barker, 1979.

rocking-horse manure. Applied to anything extremely scarce: Aus. and Brit. use: since mid-C.20. E.g., as in 'Getting a chance to use [my] skills and put the theory into practice is like finding rocking-horse manure' (Hawke). By early 1980s, if not sooner, had evolved the simile *as rare as rocking-horse shit*.

rocks. Jewels; pearls; precious stocks: c.: from ca. 1920. Ex US *rocks*, diamonds. Tempest, 1950, has 'Diamonds. More popularly referred to as "ice" [q.v.]', and notes that the term was then rare.—2. Teeth: low.—3. Short for **rock of ages**, 1, wages.—4. In *on the rocks*, (of a strong drink) 'without water or soda, but simply poured over the rocks (lumps of ice)': Can.: adopted, ca. 1945, ex US; by 1958, also fairly gen. English. (Leechman.) P.B.: perhaps cf. quot'n at sense 1.—5. In *get* (one's) *rocks off*, of the male, to copulate: later C.20. 'Much of the average King's Cross working girl's working life would be spent in the back of the punters' cars where, by one cramped means or another, rocks could be got off as quickly as physiologically possible' (Diamant, 1982). Ex US: W. & F., 1975, define as 'ejaculate' (from 'rocks', = testicles), and date from 1973.—6. Heroin or small pure crystals of cocaine used to 'freebase': drugs c. (Stockley, 1986.) US since—1969 (Spears).

rocks in (one's) **head, have.** To be crazy, foolish, stupid: N. Am.: since 1940s, prob. earlier. 'You got rocks in your head if you think you can do that [impossible task]' (Leech, 1986). Prob. ex US Yiddish.

rocky, n. A Royal Naval Reserve or Royal Naval Volunteer Reserve rating: RN 'proper': from ca. 1890 and ca. 1914. (Bowen.) Granville, however, defines *rockies* as 'RNR, or RNVR officers' and implies that in both nuances the word was still current in 1945. He adds 'An allusion to unsteady sea legs of RNVRs when first at sea. RNRs are professional seamen.'

rocky, adj. Penniless—or almost: coll.: 1923 (Galsworthy: *OED* Sup.). Cf. *stoney broke*.—2. Pertaining to **rocky**, n., 1. Granville notes *Rocky navigator* and *Rocky scribe* (= clerk).

rod. 'Common Americanism affected by youths of a certain type when speaking of a revolver or automatic pistol' (Tempest, 1950): some use in Brit. since ca. 1931. Brandon, 1936.—2. An overcoat or macintosh: c. Sharpe, 1938; Powis, 1977. Perhaps ex C.19 *rod-a-low*, itself from Fr. *roquelaure*.

rod in pickle. A good horse that is being either reserved or nursed for a sure win: Aus. sporting: since ca. 1930. Glassop, 1949.

rodney or **R.** A S. Wales railwaymen's nickname 'for last Saturday night trains from Newport and Cardiff for valley destination' (*Railway*, 2nd).

Rodney boater. 'Careless individual keeping an untidy boat. A slum-dweller of the inland waterways' (Smith, 1982): inland waterways. In Northern and Midlands dial., *Rodney* was used for an idle fellow.

Rod's. Harro*d*'s (London): Londoners': since ca. 1945. Cf. **Fred's**.

roger, n. In *do a roger*, to depart swiftly: teenagers'. (James Williamson, 1985.)

roger (often **rodger**), v. To coït with (a woman): low coll., perhaps orig. c.: since early C.18 (?earlier); still current later C.20. Grose, 1st ed., 'From the name of Roger, frequently given to a bull'. But the penis was nicknamed *Roger* as early as mid-C.17.

roger! All right!; OK!: Services': since late 1930s. Ex radiotelephony j., the use of the letter *R* for 'Message received and understood' (see PHONETIC ALPHABETS, in Appx.). Post WW2 it was often rhyme-elaborated to *Roger-dodger*, and sometimes shortened from that to *Roger-D*; ob. by mid-1970s. (P.B.) Cf. **wilco!** and **ridgy-didge**.

Roger the Lodger. A c.p. directed at, or alluding to, a male lodger that makes love to the mistress of the house or apartment: since ca. 1925. Kersh, 1946, ' "Proper bloody Bluebeard." "Henry the Eighth," said Knocker White. "Roger the Lodger," said the Sergeant. "Breaking up homes," said the man in the next bed.' *Roger*, because it rhymes with 'lodger'; there is, moreover, a pun on **roger**, v.

Rogues' Gallery, the. 'Used disrespectfully of a collection of photographs of distinguished former officers adorning some of the public rooms, corridors, etc., of an officers' mess'

(Parsons, 1977). P.B.: and any similar collection anywhere else.

roll, n. A fight: RN: since mid-1940s.—2. In *go and have a roll!*, go to the devil!: Aus. (B., 1942.) P.B.: perhaps euph. for *go and get fucked!*; cf.: —3. In *have a roll*, to copulate: low: perhaps since ca. 1920. Prob. ex *roll in the hay*.—4. In *a roll that would choke an anteater*, a very large roll of money: Aus.: since ca. 1945. B., 1959.—5. In *on a roll*, on a winning streak, as in 'Keep him in as goalie. He's on a roll, and they can't get a goal off him.' N. Am.: since mid-1970s. (Leech, 1986.)

roll, v. 'To steal from a man bemused by drink, from an unconscious person, or from one engaged in sexual intimacies' (Powis, 1977): perhaps orig. nautical, esp. of robbing a drunken person, since early C.19. The word passed to the US and became an underworld term; it was also adopted, ca. 1920, as Aus. c. (B., 1942.)

roll call. 'When a man counts up his money he has "a roll call" ' (*Muvver*): Cockneys': later C.20.

roll 'em! Start filming: cinema: since ca. 1925. (London *Evening News*, 7 Nov. 1939.) 'They' are of course the cameras.

roll in the hay. A little love-making: orig. rural, then loosely gen.

roll it back. To decelerate; close the throttle-twistgrip: motorcyclists': later C.20. (Dunford.)

roll on! (Either alone, or prec. by an intensive, e.g. *fucking roll on!*, or followed by an object.) Let it proceed rapidly: coll.: since mid-C.20. A natural development ex the *roll on* phrases used in so many Services and prisons to invoke the end of the utterer's servitude.—2. Hence, esp. as, e.g., *fucking roll on!*, an exclam. of annoyance, surprise, disgust, etc.: low, prob. mainly Services': since mid-C.20. Cf. synon. deriv. **stroll on!** (P.B.)

roll (one's) **own.** To make extemporaneously: Aus.: since ca. 1930. Ex *roll one's own* cigarettes. (B.P.)

roll them in the aisle(s). Applied to a comedian that has his audience (*them*) roll, helpless with laughter, in the aisle(s)—or are in danger of doing so: theatrical, including music-hall: since ca. 1920.

roll-up, n. An order for a 'three-cross double' (q.v.) doubled: Glasgow public houses':—1934.—2. 'Cigarette, handmade, not from packet' (Home Office): prisoners': since—1950 (Tempest); by late 1970s > more gen., if its use in the advertisements for a certain brand of tobacco is anything to judge by (P.B.).—3. Attendance, number of persons present: coll.—4. 'The roll-ups are those [customers] who have found the genuineness of the goods and walk into the "shop" for repeats' (Buchanan-Taylor, 1943): fair-grounds': since ca. 1910.

roll up, v.i. To appear on the scene: coll. *COD*, 1934 Sup.—2. To die: low. Llewellyn, 1943.

Roller. A Rolls-Royce car: motorists'—and others': since ca. 1950. (Martin, 1975.) Cf. **Ro-Ro.**

roller skate. A small, light wagon. See HAULIERS' SLANG, in Appx.

roller skates. A tank, or tanks: RAF: 1940+. (*Reader's Digest*, Feb. 1941.) To the airmen overhead, a tank looked as if it moved on roller skates.

rollick. To make much fuss; become angry: Londoners': from ca. 1925.—2. As v.t., to 'tell off'; usu. as vbl n., *rollicking*: low: since ca. 1920. (Sharpe, 1938.) It rhymes **ballock,** v., so may prob. be considered euph.; see **rollocks!**

rollies, with the *o* either long or short. Testicles: low: since ca. 1930. Ex (*Tommy*) *Rollocks*.

rolling. Vbl n. ex **roll,** v., 1.

rollocks or **rollicks!** Nonsense!: since ca. 1960. (Thomas, 1976.) A shortening of *Tommy Rollocks*, testicles.

Rolls. A Rolls-Royce motorcar: motorists' coll.: since ca. 1925. Cf. **Roller.**

Rolls-can-hardly. An old car: Aus. youthful car-owners': since ca. 1950. 'Rolls down a hill but can hardly get up the next.' Youthful Aus. car-owners' synon.: *bomb* (ironic), *jalop(p)y*,

tin-bitser. (B.P.) Not only Aus.: heard also in Brit., usu. as *Rolls-Canardly*. On such long dead car names as Dina-Panhard (P.B.).

rolls in dry dock, she. Disparaging of a ship, esp. of a corvette: RN: WW2 and after. Cf. *a corvette would roll on wet grass*.

Rolls Royce, n. Voice, esp. a very good one: theatrical r.s. Franklyn.

Rolls Royce, adj. 'Fancy'; expecting too much: RN (esp. wardroom) coll.: since ca. 1918. 'A bit Rolls Royce in his ideas'.

Rolly. A Rolliecord or Rollieflex camera: photographers': since ca. 1945.

rom. A *r*adar *o*perator *m*echanic: RAF: 1943+. (Emanuel, 1945.) Ex the abbr., more fully *R. Op/Mech*.

Roman(-)candle landing; Roman candles. A bad landing (RAF, since ca. 1938; Jackson); a parachutist's fall to earth when his parachute has failed to open (paratroopers', since 1941; H. & P.). Ex the flare of the parachute from its pack, like an unopened umbrella (P.B.).

Roman roulette. Var. of **Vatican roulette.** Powell, 1969.

romance. A person obviously in love: from ca. 1926. Ex influence of the cinema.

romft. '(Pronounced as a word.) "Roll on, my fucking twelve!"—end of a 12-year engagement' (*Navy News*, June 1973).

romp. A little light-hearted love-making: coll.: adopted, ca. 1945, ex US. Cf. *roll in the hay*, whence the blend *romp in the hay*: since ca. 1950.

romper. A merchant ship that forges ahead of a convoy instead of keeping station, as ordered: RN: WW2. (Granville.) Synon. *runner*; opp. *straggler*.

rompered. Beaten up: Services' in N. Ireland: 1970s. Ex 'Romper Room', ITV programme in N. Ireland, 'twisted . . . to describe the facilities in which illegal "kangaroo courts" dispense their perverted brand of justice . . . (The victim usually dies of his injuries)' (freelance journalist, Belfast, 1974, quoted in Hawke).

rompworthy. (Of a woman) sexually desirable: upper- and middle-class coll.: since ca. 1935. Cf. **bedworthy.**

Ronson. A Sherman tank: Tank Corps: 1943–5. Deighton, 1971, explains, ' "The old Sherman had a terrible reputation for brewing [i.e., going up in flames]. Ronsons, they called them; automatic lighters, see?" ' Ex trade-name of a well-known brand of cigarette-lighter.—2. A 'ponce': very imperfect r.s., and showing the influence of high-powered advertising: since ca. 1954. Franklyn; Powis.

roof-spotter, usu. in pl. An observer posted on a roof to watch for enemy aircraft: an all-Services and Civil Defence coll.: WW2. P-G-R.

roofer. A wretched little theatre: proletarian:—1923 (Manchon).—2. A hat: Aus.: since ca. 1920. B., 1942.—3. (Orig., *hospitable roofer*.) A letter of thanks to one's host or hostess or both, after staying with them: mostly at the Universities of Oxford and Cambridge: since ca. 1925. By the 'OXFORD -ER' ex *roof* (over one's head).

rook, n. A recruit: Services', perhaps orig. RN: since late C.19. (Goodenough, 1901 (RN); Kersh, 1941.) A shortening of the older *rookey*.

rook, v. To grumble or complain: market-traders': late C.19–20. (*M.T.*) Perhaps ex the raucous cry of the birds.

rooker. A grumbler, esp. 'a dissatisfied customer' (*M.T.*). Ex prec.

rookette. A female recruit: Services': 1940+. (Partridge, 1945.) Never much used. Cf. **rook,** n.

rooster tail. 'Wake of a board' (*Pix*, 28 Sep. 1963): Aus. surfboarders': early 1960s.

root, n. The penis: low coll.: C.19–20. Also *man-root*; *the old root*.—2. Hence, an erection; esp. *have* or *get the root*: low: late C.19–20.—3. Hence, sexual intercourse: Aus. low: since ca. 1905.—4. Hence, the (usu. female) partner therein: low Aus., as in *week-end root*, a casual sexual partner: since ca. 1920. Buzo, 1973.

root, v.t. The great Aus. v., ex the n. corresponding in all senses, physical and fig., to Brit. 'fuck': low: since 1930s. See esp. Wilkes, p. 277. Notably in such phrases as *wouldn't it root you!*, where it = annoy, infuriate; *get rooted!*, I don't believe you!, go away!; *root my old boot!*, I am surprised, displeased—cf. Brit. *fuck my old boots!* Baker defines its fig. senses, 1959, as 'To outwit, baffle, exhaust, utterly confound (someone)'.

root about. To search, esp. by rummaging about: dial. and, by C.20, coll. Ex pigs rooting.

root for. To support ardently and esp. vocally: Aus.—adopted, ca. 1945, ex US—but not common: **root,** v. inhibits gen. use of *root for*. (B.P.) Also some use in Brit. (P.B.). Cf. *barracking*.

rootle. To go or run about the place: from ca. 1925. (Knox, 1933.) Ex *root* (*around*) + *tootle* (to go).

roots. Boots: Aus. (B., 1942.) Shortening of r.s. *daisy roots*, of which the Cockney version is *daisies*.

rooty-toot. See JIVE, in Appx.

rooty wallah. Ship's baker: MN. (Granville.) Ex mainly military Anglo-Indian: *rooty* = bread; *wallah* = a 'chap', 'merchant', 'artist', etc.

rope. A cheap lodging-house: Liverpool street arabs': late C.19–mid-20. (*Arab.*)—2. Marijuana: prison c.: later C.20. (Home Office.) Perhaps ex US, where *hemp* and *rope* were occ. synon. joc. for 'a cigar' (W. & F.).

ropey, ropy. Applied to 'paint drying out with a rope-like appearance' (a master builder, 1953): builders' and housepainters' coll. > j.: late C.19–20.—2. (Of a person) inefficient or dilatory or careless of appearance; (of an action, etc.) clumsy or inefficient; (of things, e.g. an aircraft, a meal) inferior: RAF: since ca. 1930. (H. & P.; Jackson; Partridge, 1945.) Perhaps ex sense 1, but more prob. 'from certain obsolete types of aircraft that carried an excess—or what seemed an excess—of ropes' (Partridge). Cf., however, *rope*, 'a bacterial infection of beer . . . The infective agent is an anaerobic bacterium called Zymamonas, whose action produces slimy gelatinous threads in the beer—a cask can be completely ruined in a matter of hours. "Ropey" beer has given the language the general slang expression for bad or poor quality' (Glover, 1985).—3. Hence, generally disliked; unpopular: RAAF: WW2. B., 1943.—4. 'This is in current use among beatniks and teenagers, and any smelly member of a gang is called "ropey" ' (Petch, 1966): since ca. 1960. Ex sense 2.

ropey trophy. An 'award which, if it exists at all, is usually a lavatory seat, given to the sailor who dances with or dates the girl considered to be the ugliest at the dance': FAA Station, Lossiemouth: 1960s. (Wood, 1977.)

rort, n. A dodge, trick, scheme, racket: Aus. c.: since ca. 1910. B., 1942.—2. A crowd; hence, showmen's patter: Aus. low: since ca. 1912. Baker.—3. Something exceptionally good: Aus.: since ca. 1920.—4. A wild party: Aus.: since ca. 1930. Ex senses 2 and 3. (B.P.)

rort, v. 'To be loudly argumentative' (Granville): RN.

rort at. To complain of; blame fiercely: low. (Harrison, 1935, 'It isn't you . . . that I'm rorting at.') Prob. ex prec.

rorter. A professional swindler: Aus. c.: since early C.20. (Baker.) Ex **rort,** n., 1.—2. Hence, a hawker of worthless goods; a petty confidence trickster: id.—3. Var. of **rort,** n., 3.

rorting. Confidence trickery: Aus. c.: since ca. 1910. (Baker.) Ex **rort,** n., 1.—2. Hence, sharp practice: low: since ca. 1920.

rorty. Always in trouble: Army: early C.20. F. & G. Cf.:—2. 'Noisily drunk and argumentative' (Granville): RN.

Rory or **rory.** Short for older (since mid-C.19) *Rory O'More*. Esp. *on the rory*, (1) penniless (Sharpe, 1938; Powis, 1977, lists just 'rory'); and (2) of a horse, fallen: both = *on the floor*.

ros-bif Yorkshee. A red-faced Yorkshireman: in the catering trade, esp. in Italian restaurants. Ex the fact that Yorkshire-

men expect to find roast beef and Yorkshire pudding even in Italian restaurants.

rosary, the. A variation of the confidence trick: c. Leach.

rosary-counter. A Roman Catholic: Irish Orangemen's:—1934.

roscoe. A hand gun: prisoners'. Clayton, 1970.

rose-coloured. 'Bloody' as swear-word: coll. euph.:—1923 (Manchon, who lists also synon. *roseate*).

Rose Cottage. 'Formerly where V.D. cases were isolated' (Malin, 1979): RN: earlier C.20. An ironic euph. prob. suggested by *ring-o'-roses*, nautical coll. for venereal disease. Peppitt defines it specifically as 'Mess on submarine depot ship for seamen with V.D.: 1940s'.

rose garden. 'Separate cells/Punishment block' (Home Office): prisons': later C.20.

rosella. A European working bared to the waist: Northern Aus.:—1898. 'The scorching of the skin . . . produces a colour which probably suggested a comparison with the bright scarlet of the parrakeet so named' (Morris).—2. In Aus. and NZ, since ca. 1910, has been sheep-shearing s. for 'a sheep bare of wool on the "points" (hocks, head, foreleg, etc.) and consequently very easy to shear' (Alexander, 1939).—3. A staff officer: Aus. Army: WW2. (B., 1942.) Ex his red tabs.—4. Hence, any high-ranking officer: since ca. 1942. B., 1953.—5. 'A customer whose hair is easy to cut because of his partial baldness' (B.P.): Aus. barbers': since ca. 1930. Partly ex sense 2.

roses. A woman's period: Anglo-Irish: late (?mid-)C.19–20. Joyce, 1922, 'Such a bad headache. Has her roses probably.'

rosie, -y. A (large) garbage-bin: ships' stewards. (Marlow, 1937.) Ironically ex 'A rose by any other name would smell as sweet'.

rosiner or **rosner** or **rozner.** A very stiff drink with a hell of a kick: Aus.: since ca. 1930. (Drake Brockman, 1947.) Ex older *rosin*, to indulge in strong drink.

Rossy Docks. Socks: Glasgow r.s., where *Rossy* = Rothesay. Munro, 1985.

Rosy (or **Rosie**) **Lee** (or **Lea**). A flea: r.s. Lester.

Rosy (or **Rosie**) **Loader** (or **Loder**). Whisky and soda: r.s. (Franklyn.) Cf. earlier synon. *Major Loder*.

rot-up, n. Misbehaviour, esp. excessive noise-making, by pupils: Public Schools': earlier C.20. Also as v., to be tiresomely mischievous.

rotary hoe, often shortened to **rotary.** A joc. var. of *righty-ho, rightio,* etc.: Aus.: early 1960s. (B.P.)

Rothesay Docks. See Rossy . . .

rotten. Drunk: Glasgow (—1934); Aus., often in *get rotten*, to get very drunk indeed: since ca. 1930 (B., 1942). Prob. merely short for 'rotten drunk' rather than E.P.'s explanation, 'proleptic' (P.B.)

Rotten Mess, the. That mess in which the venereals are quartered, on most ships No. 1 Mess: RN: since ca. 1910. Rotten with disease. Cf. **Rose Cottage.**

Rotters' Rest, the. Public School s., as in Lunn, 1919: 'He was assigned to "Lower Field", a game [of football] more usually known as "The Rotters' Rest".'

rotto. Rotten: Anglo-Irish. Joyce, 1922, 'The father is rotto with money'. Cf. *lousy*—or *stinking*—*with* money.

rouf. Four: back s.: since mid-C.19. Mayhew, I, 1851, where also *rouf yennep*, fourpence. Tempest, 1950, spells it—phonetically—*rofe*, in connection with:—2. Hence, a four-year prison-sentence or -term: c.: late C.19–20. (Norman.)—3. The sum of four shillings: London's East End: ca. 1945–70. (London *Evening News*, 12 Nov. 1957.) Cf.:—4. The sum of £400: car-dealers', etc.: since ca. 1945. *Woman's Own*, 28 Feb. 1968.

rough, n. Short for *rough stuff*, esp. in *cut the rough stuff!*: Aus.: since ca. 1925.

rough, v. To manhandle: Aus.: since ca. 1925. Niland, 1958, 'They grabbed Shelton and roughed him outside into the rising wind.' P.B.: later C.20 Brit. version is *rough up*.

R

rough, adj. Later C.20 shortening of *rough on*, and, like it, adopted ex US: coll. Occ., in joc. sympathy for harsh treatment or circumstance, 'Oh, that's rough! R-U-F-F, rough!' (P.B.) Cf. *a bit rough*, unfair, unreasonable; extortionate: Aus. coll. (B., 1943); since mid-C.20 also Brit.

rough as . . . occurs in several similes: some are noted here. *Rough as a bag* or *as bags*, (of a person) uncouth or objectionable: mainly Aus. and NZ; cf. . . . *a sand-bag*: Brit. Army version of prec., early C.20, meaning also '(of a story) very exaggerated' (F. & G.); . . . *as a badger's arse* or *behind*, (of skin) bristly, (of a youth's beard) coarse and straggly: orig. rural, late C.19–20 > by ca. 1930, gen. (Morgan; L.A.); . . . *as a goat's knees*, exceedingly rough, perhaps also fig.: Aus.; . . . *as guts*, 'An old Australian expression with a wealth of meaning . . . from admiration, toughness, ingenuity to slapdash and vulgar . . . It is widely used as an epithet throughout Australia' (Baglin, 1973); in Brit., esp. Services', since mid-C.20, . . . *as old guts*, applied to inanimate objects, e.g. wine, or the way a badly-tuned engine is running (P.B.); . . . *as a pig's breakfast*, (of persons) uncouth: Aus. and NZ. B., 1942.

rough end of the pineapple, the. 'Hostile or unfair treatment' (Wilkes): Aus. coll.: since mid-C.20.

rough house, n. Disorder; a quarrel; a noisy disturbance or struggle: coll.; US (1887) anglicised ca. 1910.

rough-house, v. To treat roughly: coll., orig. (ca. 1900) US; anglicised ca. 1914. (*OED* Sup.) Ex the n.—2. Hence, to act noisily or violently: coll.: 1920 ('Sapper': Ibid.).

Rough Interior. Nickname of the Brough *Superior* motorcycle, in production 1921–40: motorcyclists'. (Dunford.) A punning Hobson-Jobson.

rough neck, rough-neck, roughneck. A rough, ignorant fellow: US (1836, a rowdy), anglicised ca. 1910: coll.—2. Hence, one who, in a carnival, does the rough work: Can. carnival s.—3. An oil-rig crewman: since ca. 1920.

rough row to hoe. 'A tough time of it, difficult time, a hard time; as in "I don't know if he's gonna make it—he's got a pretty rough row to hoe": widespread in Western N. Am.: since early C.20' (Leech, 1986).

rough spin. Unfair treatment: Aus.: since ca. 1910. Ex games in which a coin is spun.

rough stuff. 'Any trawl-fish that isn't classed as prime' (Butcher, 1980): trawlermen's coll.

rough trade, the. The underworld of homosexual practices, esp. of homosexual prostitutes: low: since ca. 1950. (*Evening Standard*, 12 July 1967.) See *trade*, 2.

rough 'un. (A 'bed' in) an improvised shelter: tramps' c. Gape, 1936.

rougher. A rough-rider: coll.: early C.20. *OED*.—2. A rough time; a severe tackle at Rugby football: Scottish Public Schools': from ca. 1910. (Miller, 1935.) By the 'OXFORD -ER'; cf.:-

roughers. A rough sea; foul weather: RN, at first mainly officers': since ca. 1920. Occ. *Harry roughers*; see HARRY, in Appx.

roughie, -y. A rough man; a rough horse, etc.: Aus. coll. *What I Know*, 1928; Idriess, 1932.—2. Esp. in *put a roughy over*, to 'pull a fast one on', to impose upon, to trick: Aus. Tennant, 1941, in form *roughie*.—3. A story hard to believe: Aus.: since ca. 1920. (B.P.)

roughneck. See *rough neck*.

Roughs, the. 'The City of London Yeomanry (Rough Riders) were habitually referred to as "The Roughs" by the other London Yeomen . . . In 1960 the Rough Riders amalgamated with the Inns of Court Regiment' (Gaylor, 1977). Also in Hatton, 1930.

roughy. See *roughie*.

round, n. 'A bedside dissertation and demonstration of cases in a ward by the senior physician or surgeon to students'; if the audience consists of qualified practitioners, and if the cases are obscure, it is a *hot-air round* or *shifting dullness* (cf. the technical sense): medical students':—1933 (*Slang*). P.B.: still current 1980s; I had the misfortune to be the object of a *grand round* in 1982 (Leicester Royal Infirmary).—2. See TIDDLYWINKS, in Appx.

round, adj. (Of paint) needing to be thinned: builders' and house-painters'. Perhaps cf. Cumberland dial. *round*, coarse, thick.

round for *on* (preposition) is a characteristic of Cockney speech: coll.: mid-C.19–20. Pugh, 1912, 'If you don't gimme a bit . . . I shall punch you round the jaw.' P.B.: cf. the Sussex threat 'I'll give you a clout 'side the ear'ole'.

round box. An ephemeral var. (1957–8) of *square*, a staid, old-fashioned person: Teddy-boys'. Gilberdale, 2.

round file, the. A wastepaper basket: later C.20. (Raab, 1982.)

round heels, she has or **she's got.** She's sexually compliant: Can.: since ca. 1925. A girl with heels so round that the least push will put her on her back.

round shot. Peas: Services' (mostly Army): earlier C.20. H. & P.

round the bend. Crazy; mad: RN: since mid-C.19. (Bowen.) E.P. noted in the 1st ed. of this *Dict.*, 1937, 'ob'.—but the term was much used in the RAF, WW2 (Hinde, 1945), and has since become much more gen.; quite common, indeed, among civilians. In 1957 the intensive *round the bend—and back again* was coined. Ex *Harpic*, a water-closet cleanser, advertised to '(clean) round the bend', comes the var. *clean round the bend*. Cf. *harpic*. It has, since ca. 1957, had a second intensive: *round the bend—and half-way down the straight*, and also an occ. var., **round the twist**, q.v. P.B.: perhaps orig. ex nautical *bend*, a knot. Cf. *half round the bend*.

round the buoy. See *buoy*.

round the corner. In *be round the corner*, to get ahead of one's fellows by unfair or dishonest methods: from ca. 1960.—2. In *have* (a woman) *round . . .* , to keep a mistress; to commit adultery: later C.20. BBC Radio 4, 27 Feb. 1976. For the idea of secrecy or privacy, cf. the almost S.E. euph. *go round the corner*, to visit the w.c.

round the hay-stack. Round the back, either lit., or euph. for a visit to the w.c.: r.s. Franklyn.

round the houses. Trousers: r.s., on Cockney pron. *trousies*: since mid-C.19. Still current, later C.20, in variants *rounds*, *round me's*, *rounders*.—2. Confined to Europe, as opp. to worldwide: airline crews': 1950s. Campbell, 1960, ' "I wasn't genned up," said [the air hostess]. "I'd only been round the houses before—London, Paris, Rome, etcetera. I didn't know the [orange juice] was so concentrated that the bods [i.e. passengers] were going to use all my fresh water." '—3. 'In *go (all) round the houses*, to go by the most circuitous route, as a country bus might; or, fig., to give a very long-winded and rambling explanation of a simple point' (David Williams, 1987): coll.

round the Johnny (Horner). Round the corner; usu. 'street corner', hence to, at, a 'pub': r.s. Ware.

round the twist. A var. of—and modelled on—**round the bend**, crazy: coll.: since ca. 1957. Petch notes early 1970s var. *up the twist*, prob. influenced by synon. *up the pole*.

round up. To obtain, to acquire, as in 'I'll try and round up a few drinks', or 'let's round up the girls and go out the evening': Can., esp. mid-West, since ca. 1920 (Leechman); Aus. (B.P.); whence also Brit., by mid-C.20 at latest. Cf. *rustle up*; both ex cattle farming or droving.

rounder. A return: busmen's: since ca. 1920.

rounders. See *round the houses*, 1.

Roundhead. See *Cavalier*.

roundhouse rangers. Fish that swim about the stern of a ship at anchor: RN. (P-G-R.) Cf. **main-drain rangers**. *Round house* = Officers' lavatory in HM ships.

rouse, (pron. *rouss*). To 'grouse', to scold (v.i.), esp. if coarsely: Aus. Perhaps ex *rouse a person*, to anger him. Constructed with *on* (a person).—2. (Also *roust*.) V.t., 'to upbraid with many words' (Dennis): Aus.

rouse on; get roused on. To upbraid (someone); to reprove (him) forcibly: Aus. (B., 1959.) Cf. **rouse**.

rouseabout. A member of the ground staff: R Aus. AF: WW2. (B., 1943.) Cf. **groundies.**

rousie. A *roustabout*, or handy man at a shearing: Aus.: since ca. 1930. Vickers, 1955.

rousting. A 'going-over', as in 'Doing the selfsame job he does day in, day out, as the rozzers are well aware, and it came round to his turn to get a rousting' (Daniells, 1980): Londoners'. See also **rouse**, 2.

roust on. Var of **rouse on.**

row back from (it all). To avoid trouble, involvement, by backing out: coll. L.A., 'noted in 1974'. Cf. **row on to.**

row in. To work or enter into association (*with*): grafters' s. (*Cheapjack*, 1934.) Cf. Hatton, 1930, ' "Crimes [euph., = Christ!], chum", he [a sergeant in the NZ Mounted Rifles] shouted with enthusiasm, "that [London]'s where I'm off to, guess I'll row in with you blokes." ' They were soldiers returning from Palestine, late 1918.

row (oneself) **on to** (a person or a group). To attach oneself to: low: since ca. 1940. (Norman.) Cf. **row in.**

Roy. The "trendy" Australian, opposite to "Alf" [q.v.] (Wilkes): Aus.: since later 1950s. Prob. ex the name; but cf. **royalie.**

Royal. Abbr. Royal Marines: RM coll.: later C.20. (Hawke, 1979.) Cf. **Royal Machine.**

Royal Anglicans, the. The Royal Anglian Regiment: Army; sol. when not a deliberate pun: since soon after the Regt's formation in 1964. See also **Angle-irons.** (P.B.)

Royal Corps of Pigs (occ. **Royal Pigs**). The Royal Corps of Signals: Army, esp. the Royal Corps themselves, and ranging from affection to disparagement: since ca. 1950. (P.B.)

Royal Hearse Artillery. The gun support company of 2 Corps Reinforcement Unit: Army in N. Africa: middle of WW2. A pun on *horse.* P-G-R.

Royal Machine. A Royal Marine; often shortened to *Machine*: RN r.s. [prob. rather, a pun: P.B.]: 1970s, Peppitt says, but I'd surmise it to date from the 1930s or, at latest, 1940s.

royal mail (or capitals). Bail (legal): r.s., orig. and still mostly underworld. Franklyn 2nd.

royal order, the. Dismissal, e.g. from a job: mostly Aus.: since ca. 1925. (B.P.)

royal salute. See TOMBOLA, in Appx.

Royal Sluice. Deuce; a Jack in cards: Aus. r.s. (ex the famous Australian comedian, Harry Van der *Sluys*): since ca. 1940. B., 1945.

Royal Yachtsmen. Personnel serving in the Royal Yacht: RN (mostly officers'): since ca. 1920.

royalie (or **-y**). An effeminate; esp., a catamite: Aus.: earlier C.20. Prob. ex 'royal *quean*', with a pun on 'royal *queen*'.

Royals, the. Members of the Royal Family of Britain, or of the royal families of the Continent: since ca. 1950: orig., sophisticated and upper-middle class s.: then, by the late 1950s, journalistic coll.; then, by 1960, fairly gen. coll.

rub. 'The rub is [a] cleaner or stain-remover' (Buchanan-Taylor, 1943): fair-grounds'.

rub-a. Short for next, esp. sense 2.

rub-a-dub(-dub). (Sometimes *rub-a-di-dub*.) A 'sub', to 'sub' (advance wages): workmen's r.s. *John o' London's Weekly*, 9 June 1934.—2. A public house: r.s., on *pub*: since late C.19. See also **rubberdy.** P.P., 1932.—3. A club (social meeting): r.s. late C.19–20. (Ibid.) Hence, also a night-club.

rub about. To make a fool of: tailors'. *Tailor and Cutter*, 29 Nov. 1928, 'Took me for a josser. Nothing below the waist, me. I'm not to be rubbed about.' Ex a process in tailoring.

rub-down, n. Corresponds to v., next: c.: since late C.19. *Gilt Kid*, 1936; Home Office, 1978.—2. In *give* (one) *a good rub-down*, to thrash: coll.:—1923 (Manchon).

rub down, v. To search (a prisoner) by running the hands over his clothed body: coll.: since—1887 (*OED*). Applied also, by dockers, to London Dock Police stopping stevedores going off work, to see whether they were hiding stolen goods. (Ash.) Also, early C.20, *run the rule over*.—2. To scold, reprimand: coll.: ca. 1895–1925.

rub off on. (Esp. of money or good luck) to come one's way: since early 1950s. 'The lucky devil! Just come into a packet of money.'—'Wish some of it would rub off on *me*!'

rub out. To disbar (person or horse): Aus. coll. B., 1942.—2. To dismiss (a suggestion): Aus. coll.: since ca. 1920. Baker.

rub-up. A refresher course in a subject: RN coll. (Granville.) With corresponding v. Cf. synon. **brush-up.**

rub with a brick. In 'I need rubbing with a brick,' I am replete, or over-full (Roulstone, 1986): where it is a matter of an upset stomach, one may say 'My stomach needs rubbing . . .', or 'rub your stomach . . . ' (Huston, 1986): domestic coll.

rubbed-in. 'When a picture is commenced, it is spoken of as being "rubbed in" ' (Lobley): artists' coll.: from ca. 1910. Ex the technical sense of the phrase.

rubber, n. A condom: low coll.—2. A male homosexual: low and slightly contemptuous: prob. since early C.20. (Petch.) In French, there's a parallel term for a lesbian.

rubber, v., or **rubber at.** To gape (or stare) at: adopted, ex US, ca. 1942; soon ob. Ex **rubber-neck,** v.

rubber cheque. A worthless cheque: adopted, ca. 1935, ex US: by 1960, coll. It 'bounces'—like a rubber ball.

rubber-dick. To 'con' or entice (someone) with false promises into doing something: low: later C.20. Ex the 'falsity' of a dildo. (P.B.: heard 1973.)

rubber firm. 'Lower deck money-lending concern' (Granville): RN.

rubber heels. Hard fried eggs: Services': since ca. 1920. (H. & P.) The form *rubbers* denotes simply 'eggs' (P-G-R).—2. That department of the CID which investigates its own personnel: police, esp. CID: since ca. 1955. (Newman, 1970.) Ex the silence, the secrecy, of its methods.

rubber Johnnie, -y (or **j-**). A condom: gen. low: since mid-C.20 (?earlier). (P.B.)

rubber knackers. An impudent man: low.

Rubber(-)Lips. 'Nickname for a seaman with such big mouth and lips that he can get more than a sip from "sippers" [q.v.]' (Peppitt): RN lowerdeck.

rubber(-)neck; (-)necking. A very inquisitive person; excessive curiosity or inquisitiveness: US (—1900), partly anglicised, esp. in Aus., ca. 1905; slightly ob. Ex 'considerable craning and stretching', as though one's neck were made of rubber: as in *Pall Mall Gazette*, 8 Mar. 1902.

rubber-neck, v.i. in sense of the n. (q.v.): 1932, Sayers, 'She . . . could not waste time rubber-necking round Wilvercombe with Lord Peter [Wimsey].'

rubber pig. See **come the rubber pig.**

rubber walls. Esp. in 'I'll go rubber walls', I'll go crazy, mad: homosexuals': later C.20. (Rodgers, 1972.) Ex the padded walls of a cell.

rubberdy or **rubbity** or **rubby.** A public house: Aus. low: since ca. 1920. B., 1942, 'Rhyming slang on "rub-a-dub-dub" for "pub". ' In full, *rubberdy*—usually *rubbity*—*dub*. (Culotta.) Also Brit., *rubberdy*: later C.20. (Daniells, 1980.)

rubbish. To tease; to criticise adversely, to carp at: Aus.: since ca. 1925. Some Brit. use in 1980s. Ex 'treat as *rubbish*' and 'say *rubbish* about'.—2. Mostly in passive, as 'The fate the board rider dreads is the "wipe out". This is when he is "rubbished" or tipped violently off a wave' (*Sun-Herald*, 22 Sep. 1963), like so much rubbish: Aus. surfies', esp. teenagers': since ca. 1961.

rubbish heap special. See **bread and butter job.**

rubblechuck. Odds and ends of pastry left after pie-making, kneaded together and baked, esp. for a child's benefit: London domestic. (Mrs P. Hughes.)

rubbling or **rubling.** Generic for oils used either medicinally or cosmetically: fair-grounds'. One *rubs* them in. Buchanan-Taylor, 1943.

rubby. See next:-

rubby-dub or **dubby.** A drinker of cheap spirits or wine: low Can.: since ca. 1920. Orig. and properly, a drunkard that drinks *rubbing* alcohol. (Leechman.) Commoner than the prec.

rubby-dubber. An old fellow that follows a carnival for what he can pick up and spends most of his money on drink: Can. carnival s.: since ca. 1920.

rube; reub, reuben or **Reuben.** A country bumpkin: US (middle 1890s); anglicised, among movie-fans, by 1931. (*OED* Sup.) Cf. **hick** (ex *Richard*).—2. Something exceptionally good or desirable; also as adj., 'fine, excellent': Aus.: since ca. 1925. (B., 1942.) Ironic ex sense 1?

ruby. 'Other [Members of Parliament], though raised in middle-class suburbs, affect Cockney slang ("ruby" for curry; "tom" for jewellery) under the mistaken impression that they appear streetwise' (Hoggart, 1984): r.s., on Ruby Murray, a popular singer of the 1950s–60s.

ruby(-)dazzler or as one word. A synon. of **rube**, n., 2: since ca. 1930. (Baker.) A blend of *rube* + *bobby-dazzler*.

ruby note. A ten-shilling note: c., and low: from ca. 1920. See **brown-back**.

ruby red. The head: r.s.: early C.20. F. & G.

ruby wine. Methylated spirits serving as liquor: c., esp. among tramps. Gape, 1936.

ruck, n. A word, or a deposition, that is idiotic: c.:—1923 (Manchon). Ex the v., 1.—2. A cigarette-end: lower classes':—1923 (Ibid.). Perhaps because *rucked up* (S.E. sense).—3. A heated argument; an angry fuss: low. (Norman.) Ex the v., 2. See quot'n at **moody,** adj. 'Now fairly respectable. Used in a news item in the *Daily Telegraph*, 23 Oct. 1962. Perhaps ex US *ruckus*' (Sanders).—4. Hence, a gang fight, as in 'If there's a ruck we steam in' (Walker, 1979): violence-prone football supporters'. Hence also *ruck*, v., and *rucker*, a fighter.—5. 'Anti-authority prison demonstration' (Clayton, 1970): prisons'. Cf. sense 3.

ruck, v. To grow angry or irritated: low: ca. 1890–1940. Perhaps ex *ruck (up)*, as applied to clothes. Also as *ruck up* (Manchon).—2. Hence, to chide, nag at: low London: Ingram, 1936.—3. To masturbate: prison s.: later C.20. McVicar, 1974.—4. To 'mix it' in a gang-fight. See **ruck,** n., 4.

rucker. A gang-fighter. See **ruck,** n., 4.—2. A customer given to complaint and to 'ruckus'-making: secondhand-car dealers': since ca. 1955. *Woman's Own*, 28 Feb. 1968.

rucking. A severe 'telling off', a reprimand: mostly prisons'. (Norman.) Ex *ruction*.

rudder. A quadruped's, esp. a dog's, tail: mostly joc. (cf. *stern*, backside).

ruddy blush. As in 'in a ruddy blush', a bloody rush: joc. and euph. spoonerism: since ca. 1930. (L.A., 1976.) Cf.:-

rude. In *in the rude*, naked: mid-1930s. Ex 'in the nude'. (L.A., 1974.)

rudery. A rude remark; risky conversation; amorous gesture or behaviour: middle- and upper-class coll.: since the middle 1920s.—2. Hence, an air-raid; a surface attack: RN: WW2. Granville, 1949.

rug. A £1 note: Aus.: since ca. 1945. B., 1953.—2. A toupee, hairpiece: entertainments world. Green, 1984.

rugged. Uncomfortable, characterised by hardship, 'tough': since ca. 1935. *News Chronicle*, 30 Aug. 1946, 'The first night was a bit rugged'—there being no bed, no conveniences in the hut occupied by 'squatters'. Ex the lit. S.E. *rugged*, 'rough, craggy'.

ruggsy. Applied to 'a super-tough image involving a skinhead haircut, large boots, and a tattered T-shirt for the maximum display of muscles: Army, esp. paratroopers' (Green, 1984, who notes synon. *warry* from same milieu).

ruined. Drunk, tipsy: teenagers': early 1980s. (Joanna Williamson, 1982.) Cf. synon. **wasted**, and the much older *mother's ruin*, gin.

rule O.K. See **O.K.**

rum bosun. The man serving out the rum ration: RN: earlier C.20. (P-G-R.) Cf. **custard bosun** and **rum fiend**.

rum fiend. Such a rum-server as allows rum to drip over the brim of the measure into the 'save-all', the wastage being 'perks': RN: since ca. 1910. P-G-R.

rum rat. 'A rating very fond of his tot, and anyone else's if he can get it' (Granville, letter, 1962): RN: since late 1940s. Cf. **scrumpy rat**.

Rum Row. 'Position outside the prohibited area taken up by *rum-running* vessels': coll.: US, anglicised before 1927; ob. Collinson; *COD*, 1934 Sup.

rumble, n. The surreptitious opening of the throttle to enable one to land at the desired spot: RAF: 1930s.—2. A gang fight, often carefully planned, and esp. among teenagers: Can. and Aus. teenagers': adopted, ca. 1944, ex US. Cf. **clash**.—3. A police search or inquiry: drugs c. (Stockley, 1986.) Perhaps ex later C.19 s. *rumble*, to detect.

rumble, v. 'To steal food and drink from the air-liner's in-flight stores: air crews' ' (Green, 1984).

rumble-bumble. A shooting-up of targets on enemy coastline: Coastal Forces: 1940–4. Echoic.

rumble (someone's) bumble and the derivative **bumble (someone's) rumble** are punning elaborations of *run up (someone's) arse*, to collide with either a person or a motor-car (etc.): Cambridge undergraduates': ca. 1925–40. In the first phrase *bumble* elaborates *bum*, and *run* is rhymingly perverted to *rumble*.

rumble strip. 'The Department of Transport is experimenting with "rumble strips" where variations in road surface provide warnings and yellow stripes indicate approaching exits [on major roads]' (*Sunday Times*, 1 May 1988). Cf. **sleeping policeman**.

rumbo. Elegant, fashionable: early C.20. Manchon.—2. Successful: theatrical:—1923. (Ibid.)

rump-sprung. 'Said of a woman's dress that, through much wear and a good deal of bending, has taken a permanent bulge over the rump. Knitted dresses are especially vulnerable. Canadian coll.; since ca. 1940.' (Leechman.) 'Quoted by Joseph Mitchell, ca. 1937, in an account of festivities among B.W.I. residents of New York City' (R.C., 1976).

rumpo. A pretty girl: Cockneys': mid-C.20. (Marks, 1977.) But cf. C.19 low *rumper*, a whore.

rumpty. Excellent: Aus.: since ca. 1910. Baker. Often elab. to *rumptydooler*. Ex C.19 *rumtitum*, in fine condition.

rumpy. Coral: trawlermen's. Butcher, 1980.

run, n. In *have a run*, to get drunk; to go absent without leave: R Aus N: WW2. (B., 1943.) Cf. **run ashore**.

run, v. To charge with a 'crime': RN (Bowen) and Army: from not later than 1915. Ex *run in*.—2. Hence, to arrest: Services', esp. Army, early C.20, > by 1931, gen. s. (Lyell); † by 1950. Usu. in passive, *to be run*, 'To be placed in arrest'. (F. & G.)—3. To report (a prisoner) to the governor of a gaol: c.:—1932 (anon., *Dartmoor from Within*).—4. To go out often with (a person of the opp. sex; gen. of a man with a girl): from ca. 1910. Prob. ex the turf.—5. To let the water run into (the bath): domestic coll. Hichens, 1933, 'Without summoning his valet, [he] went to "run" the bath.' P.B.: since mid-C.20 at latest, informal S.E.—6. To desert (v.i.): RN: late C.19–20. (Granville.) Short for *run away*.

run a banker. To run high, as in 'Shanghai's Chinese Citizens behaved admirably considering national feelings were running a banker' (Farmer, 1945). See **banker,** 1.

run a drum. In a race, esp. of horses or dogs, to win a place: Aus. sporting: since ca. 1945. Culotta.

run a mile(, usu. he'd). Orig., in full, *he'd . . . rather than face* (an object of terror); later, absolute: coll. Fearon, 1984, instances 'He'd be scared of meeting the real thing, esp. a brazen offer of sex: since WW2, i.e. as opp. to merely *talking* about it. But may refer also to its opposite, as in the hyperbole which may have popularised the phrase, in Al Jolson's famous song, 'I'd run a million miles for one of your smiles, Mammy!'

run a skirt; frequent also as vbl n., *running* . . . To have a mistress. McFee, 1930.

run a tight ship. To exercise firm command; hence, to maintain one's control over a team, a mess, a committee, etc.: orig.

RN; by ca. 1950, also the other two Services'; by 1965, also civilian. Cf. **taut hand**. (P.B.)

run-around, get or **give the**. To be treated, to treat, contemptuously or so as to serve a mere whim: Aus.: since ca. 1910; by ca. 1945, coll. (B., 1953.) Some use also in Brit., since ca. 1945 at latest. (P.B.)

run around like a hoo-hum-hah. To act as if one were hysterical or crazy: smart young set (esp. girls'): ca. 1955–60. Gilderdale, 2.

run ashore, a. 'Spell of evening leave in a dockyard port or from Naval barracks, as distinct from weekend or long leave' (Granville): RN lowerdeck. Sometimes abbr., as in 'Have a good run?'

run-flat. A tyre that, if punctured, could be run-on flat for half a mile or so: Army coll., WW2 (P-G-R) >, in later C.20, motorists' j.

run-in. Concerning thefts of bulk goods, 'The normal method was to hire a van from a small lorry-owner, run the van to the warehouse, break in, load the van, take the contents to a "run-in"—usually a shed or garage in the central London area—and return the van' (Gosling, 1959): since ca. 1920: c. >, by 1940, also police s.

run off, have a. To urinate: Society and middle-class: since ca. 1930. Cf. the S.E. *to run off the bath water* and *drain off*.

run-out. Esp. *have a run-out*, to urinate. (L.A.)—2. As *the run-out* (often abbr. to *R.O.*), a faked auction: grafters'. (*Cheapjack*, 1934.) See **r.o. workers**.

run out (at). To come to; to cost: coll., mostly Aus.: since ca. 1920. 'How does this run out?'—'It runs out at six shillings a yard.' (B.P.) P.B.: fairly common also in Brit., in both versions: 'At ten p. a sheet, photocopying'll run out pretty steep.'

run out of road. A motorist's accident not involving another vehicle; e.g. skidding off into the ditch, ramming a telegraph pole, etc. To 'run out of runway', of an aircraft, would I think be a coll. var. (P.B.) See **flatter**, n.

run out on. To leave (someone) in the lurch: coll.

run-out powder, take a. To depart hastily, as in WW2 Services' 'You can take . . . ', your presence is unwelcome; by late 1940s, gen. (L.A., 1976.) Cf. **take a powder**.

run the ferret. 'In Severn tunnel, to descale the water main by inserting small propeller' (*Railway*): railwaymen's.

run the rabbit. 'To convey liquor from a public house' (Dennis, 1916); 'To obtain liquor, esp, if illicitly, after hours' (B. 1942): Aus. low.

run the (occ. **a**) **rule over**. To examine (someone) medically: coll.: since ca. 1914.—2. To interrogate (a suspect): police. *Free-Lance Writer*, April 1948.

run the show. To 'manage' an enterprise, entertainment, etc.: from ca. 1915.

run the tapes. Consider a series of items in orderly manner to pick out item(s) required, e.g. from a list of suspects. (Price, 1982.) Metaphorical use of computer or recorder j.

run up a lane. (Of a horse) to fail to get a place: Aus. sporting: since ca. 1935. (B., 1953.) Also *run up lanes*, as in Glossop, 1949.

run up (someone's) **arse**. See **rumble** (someone's) **bumble**.

run up the wall, make (someone) . . . To become bewildered or scared or crazy; to cause someone to do so: 1944+, Army; 1948+, gen. Perhaps ex a famous exercise in Commando training. '(To have someone) climbing walls is a common and by no means new U.S. expression denoting a state of extreme agitation. A cat seeking to escape from an enclosure will do this' (R.C., 1966).

runcible. (Of women) sexually attractive: since ca. 1925. 'Rhyming' on *cuntable*; cf. also S.E. *runcible spoon*.

runner. An exchange clerk: bank clerks': from ca. 1916.—2. A clerk, or a collector, for a street 'bookie': Glasgow:—1934. P.B.: by mid-C.20, gen. coll. verging on informal S.E., and usu. qualified 'bookie's runner'.—3. A platform inspector: railwaymen's. *Railway*.—4. 'A vehicle that was in running order, as opposed to one that was off the road' (P-G-R):

Army coll.: WW2.—5. 'WW2 merchantman that deliberately breaks away from a convoy' (Middlebrook, 1976). Cf. **romper**, n.—6. 'Inmate who collects dues for a baron' (Home Office): prison c.: later C.20. Cf. sense 2.—7. A deserter from the Armed Forces: since ca. 1940: orig. and still mainly c. (Gosling, 1959.) Cf.:—8. 'A person, arrested by police, likely to abscond if given bail' (Powis); 'Absconder from a Borstal or detention centre' (Home Office): c.: later C.20.—9. A hit-and-run driver: s. (Bishop, 1987.)—10. See **do a runner**.

runners. He who 'calls over' the names of the horses competing or *running* in a race: turf c.:—1932.

running around like a cut cat. Extremely angry, and acting accordingly: Aus. (Slater, 1958.) Cf. **mad as a cut snake**.

running doss; running skipper. That sleeping place which, on a damp night, a tramp obtains by kicking a cow and lying down on the warm, dry spot vacated by the animal: tramps' c. See **skipper**.

running on bobbins. See **bobbins**.

running rabbit. Any small object hauled along a horizontal wire to enable trainee predictor-layers to get practice in following a target: anti-aircraft: 1938+. (H. & P.) Ex 'the dogs'.

running shoes, give (someone) **his**. To dismiss from office: NZ political. B., 1941.

running skipper. See **running doss**.

running writing. Cursive script: Aus. schoolchildren's coll. (B.P.) Cf. S.E. *running hand*.

runny. A coll., dating from ca. 1910, and used as in Canning, 1935, 'The ices had been runny with the heat.' I.e. deliquescent.

Rupert. A young subaltern: Other Ranks' derogatory: later C.20. (Parker, 1985, quoting a sergeant-major.) Perhaps ex upper-class name, influenced by 'Rupert Bear' in the children's long-running (over 50 years) cartoon stories. Cf. earlier C.20 Services' use of *Rupert* = penis, hence, metaphorically, a 'prick'.

rush, n. A wave of drug-induced euphoria: drugs c. Hibbert, 1983.—2. Hence, any sudden pleasant feeling: 'pop' world. Ibid.—3. See MOVING-PICTURE, §6, in Appx.

rush, v.t. To cheat (gen. *rush out of*); esp. to charge extortionately: 1885, former; ca. 1895, latter. From ca. 1910, coll. *OED*, *SOD*; F. & H., 'I rushed the old girl for a quid.' The semantics being: not to give time to think.—2. Hence, to deceive: Glasgow:—1934.—3. To appropriate: Marlborough College.

rush (one's) **fences**. To be impetuous: 'County' coll. > gen. Ex the j. of hunting.

rush of blood to the crutch, a. A sudden access of amorous desire: since ca. 1930. Also . . . *crotch*.

rush of teeth to the head, a. Prominent teeth: facetious: since ca. 1925.

rush the bucket or **growler**. To send the printer's devil for a bucket of beer: Can. printers'. (Leechman.) 'From the "growling" of the beer taps'. (R.C.)

rushed job. A 'short time', i.e. a brief copulation: low.

Rusk; usu. in pl., *Rusks*. The Russians: since ca. 1945. Ex *Russki*. Mather, 1968.

Russian duck. Muck: r.s.:—1923 (Manchon); † by 1959 at the latest. (Franklyn).—2. Copulation: low r.s.: since ca. 1942. Franklyn 2nd.

Russki or **-y**, n. and adj. (A) Russian soldier: Services' WW1 and 2, and since 1919, gen. coll. for any Russian, or as adj. (B. & P.) Ex *Russian* + *ski*, a frequent Russian termination.

rust-bucket. 'A car in a dangerously rusted condition' (Wilkes, who adds 'from application to ships'): Aus.: later C.20.

rustic. A recruit: military (mostly officers'): from ca. 1925. Ex his 'greenness'.

rustle up. To obtain, 'organise'; to prepare, v.t., as in 'Try and rustle up some drinks' or 'I'll just rustle us up some supper': coll.: since ca. 1950 (?earlier). Ex US, and ultimately ex cattle-stealing.

Rusty. 'A nickname for any red- or auburn-haired man' (L.A., 1974). And some girls, too; cf. the familiar *Ginger*.

Rusty B. The aircraft-carrier > commando-carrier HMS *Bulwark*: RN: later C.20. (Knight, 1984.) She was in service 1948–80; commissioned 22 June 1948, scrapped 1984. Cf.:-

rusty guts. HMS *Restiguch*: RN: WW2.

rusty rifle, get – or **have – a.** (Of men) to catch—to have—a venereal disease, esp. syphilis: mostly Services': since ca. 1925.

rutty. In a, leading to, consisting of a metaphorical rut, e.g. *rutty jobs*: coll.: since ca. 1930. *Weekly Telegraph*, 27 Apr. 1946.

rux, n. Bad temper; (a gust of) anger, passion: Public Schools':—1934 (*COD* Sup.). Either ex Lincolnshire *ruck*, a noise, a racket, or, more prob., ex Kentish *have one's ruck up*, to be angry (*EDD*).—2. 'Noise, fuss, etc.: RN College, Dartmouth, slang' (Granville). The ultimate source of these senses is perhaps **rough-house**, n., as it is of US and Can. *ruckus*.

rux, v. To 'rag', to get up to mischief: Dartmouth Naval College. (Bowen.) See n., 2.

rye mort; rye mush. A lady; a gentleman: c. (*Gilt Kid*, 1936.) See **mush**, 4. *Mort*: centuries-old c. for a girl or woman.

R

S

's. As a; mostly in *'s matter of fact*: low coll.: late C.19–20. Bloor, 1934.—2. Does: coll.: late C.19–20. Bell, 1934, 'When's Parliament reassemble, Stephen?' Mostly after *when* but not unknown after *how*, as in 'How's he do it? It beats me!'

s.a.; S.A. Sex appeal: from ca. 1929. Christie, 1930; Sayers, 1932, 'The girl . . . exercising S.A. on a group of rather possessive-looking males.'

s.a.m.f.u. *Self-adjusting military fuck-up*: S. African Services': 1940–5.

s.b.a. Nothing: *sweet bugger all*: perhaps mainly Can. (Leech, 1974.) Cf.:-

s.f.a. or **S.F.A.** Nothing: *sweet fuck all*; politely, *sweet Fanny Adams*. (Kersh, 1942.) See **Fanny Adams**, 2, and cf. prec.

s.l.j.s. 'Silly Little *Jobs*' (Wilson): RAF officers': 1970s.

's luck! (Pron. *'sluck*; occ. written so.) Here's luck!: coll.: from ca. 1912. Grierson, 1934.

s.o.b. '*Son of a bitch*': Aus. and Can., occ. Brit.: adopted, ex US, ca. 1925. Stead, 1934, 'That s.o.b. Montagu got me the job 'ere, you know.' Of the Aus. use, B.P. says, 'It is very widely known but not very commonly used'.—2. '*Shit or bust*', q.v.: since ca. 1925.

s.o.h.f. 'Sense of humour failure. Someone not amused by Sloane antics' (*Sunday Express* supp., 11 Oct. 1982): Sloane Rangers', q.v.

s.p. Information: raffish, almost c.: since ca. 1950. (Hill, 1975; Newman, 1978.) Ex bookmakers' j. for 'starting price', as in *s. p. joint*: a starting-price betting-shop: Aus. (Baker), whence *s.p. merchant*, a starting-price bookmaker (B., 1953).

s.p.o. A cheap restaurant specialising in *sausages, potatoes* and *onions*: London: from ca. 1925.

s.p.q.r. *Small profits, quick returns*: joc. coll. (*OED* Sup.) A pun on the L. *Senatus Populusque Romanus* (the Roman Senate and People).

s.t. *Sanitary towel*: feminine coll.: since ca. 1940.

s.w.a.(l.)k. See LOVERS' ACRONYMS, in Appx.

s.y.t. A '*sweet young thing*' (girl): Aus.: since ca. 1950. (B.P.)

Sabrina. 'Prestwin silo wagon' (*Railway*, 2nd): railwaymen's: mid-C.20. Ex shape: 'Sabrina' was the stage-name of a well-known and shapely 'dumb blonde' of the 1950s.

sac. A *saccharine* tablet: coll. (domestic, and small traders'): heard in 1917, but not gen. until 1942.

sack of taters. A stick of (small) bombs, e.g. incendiaries: RAF: 1939+. (H. & P.) Humorous. Delivered like **groceries.**

sacks. Long trousers: Charterhouse. On *bags*.

Sacks and the Sinks, the. The planning staffs of the *Supreme Allied Commander, South-East Asia* (Lord Louis Mountbatten) and of the *Commanders-in-Chief* subordinate to him: Higher Command in India: ca. 1943–4. Mason, 1978.

sackwah. 'Place where drinking, usually illegal or irregular, takes place (W. Indian)' (Powis): later C.20.

sad sack. A spoil-sport or a wet-blanket: RN lowerdeck: adopted, in 1943, ex US servicemen. But in US, a *sad sack* is 'the inevitable hopeless recruit or enlisted man, always a figure of fun'. (Orig., a blundering, unlikeable youth—students' s., since ca. 1930; see W. & F.) 'In the U.S., almost a culture hero, and well-known in Canada' (Leechman).

saddle. *In the saddle* was a phrase 'often used to indicate whose turn it was to buy the teas' (Ash): London dockers'. Cf. **chair**, 3.

saddler. As in *give us* [i.e. me] *a saddler*, 'Let me ride on the saddle of your bicycle while you pedal' (Bowater, 1979): Yorkshire children's:—1960. See also **croggie**.

Sadie and Maisie. Sado-masochism; its practice: addicts'. *New Society*, Nov. 1983; Ashley, for US use, 1979.

safe. A condom: Aus.: since ca. 1925. Perhaps suggested by **safety.** Leech adds, 1980, 'In Canada we say either "safe" or "French safe" for rubber or condom. The usage is not understood in the U.S. at all . . . in use in the early 20s, so it may be a WW1 term.' Prob. influenced by *French letter.*

safety. A condom: Aus.: since ca. 1920. 'She said it was no go without a safety.' ?Orig. euph. Wilkes, 1979, 'Not peculiarly Aus.: also US'.

Saff. *South African Air Force*: 1939–45. On analogy of **Raff**.

sag, n.; esp. **have the sags,** to lack energy: racing cyclists': since ca. 1930. Cf. 'the bonk'. Hence, *sag-wagon*, a van that, following a race, picks up exhausted riders; and, among London club cyclists, early 1930s, 'Old man Saggy has got him' (*Fellowship*, 1984).

sag, v. To be illicitly absent from work: Liverpool: late C.19–20: hence:—2. To play truant: Merseyside: since ca. 1930. *Woman*, 28 Aug. 1965.

saga. 'A small job that develops into a major one' (Patterson): Portsmouth dockers'. P.B.: ex joc. use of S.E. *saga* for any tale retold at inordinate length, or as in 'the continuing, never-ending saga of the nurses' struggle for a decent, commensurate living-wage'.

sail close to the wind has in the RN (late C.19–20) a specific coll. sense: 'to take risks with Naval Law' (Granville). P.B.: hence in civilian usage, C.20, to conduct operations close to, or over, the line of illegality.

sailing a Naafi queue. 'Pretending to be a sailor' (Peppitt): RN: 1970s.

sailing like a pensioner. Of a ship sailing too close to the wind, i.e. with sails 'trembling like an old person's hands' (Peppitt): nautical: prob. mid-C.19–20.—2. Hence, in the metaphorical sense of 'corner-cutting', or sharp in business: RN: since ca. 1950. (Ibid.)

sailors. See **sailors on the sea**.

sailor's best friend, a. A hammock: RN. Granville records the pleasant tradition that, 'if properly lashed with seven regulation marline hitches', it 'will keep him afloat for twenty-four hours'.

sailor's cake. An occ. var. of **Navy cake:** Services': since ca. 1940.

sailor's farewell. A parting curse: nautical, military.—2. 'By WW2 it had come to mean the attitude of—euphemistically speaking—love 'em and leave 'em' (Bishop, 1979).

sailor's hornpipe. A Wren (member of WRNS): RN: ca. 1941+.

sailors on the sea; often shortened to *sailors*. Tea: r.s.: since ca. 1940, but not common. (Franklyn 2nd.) Cf. C.19 r.s. *Rosie Lea*.

St Louis blues. Shoes: r.s.: since mid-C.20. (Daniells, 1980.) Ex the popular American tune.—2. News: Glasgow r.s. Munro, 1985.

sainted aunt!, (oh,) my. A joc., mostly upper-class, expletive: ca. 1905–25, lingering in schoolboy usage for perhaps 20 years more. ('Taffrail', 1916.) Cf. *my giddy aunt!*

Saints. See ASSOCIATION FOOTBALL, in Appx.

Sal. In *sleep at Sal's*, to sleep at a *Sal*vation Army shelter: lower classes':—1923 (Manchon).

salaams! (My) compliments (to you, her, etc.): Anglo-Indian coll., fairly gen. in earlier C.20 and almost S.E. Ex Arabic for 'Peace (be upon *or* with you).'

salad oil. Hair-oil: lower classes':—1923 (Manchon).

salami fraud. 'So called because the crooked computer operator slices off interest due on investors' accounts one piece at a time and then pays it into his own false account. He can cream off several hundred pounds' (*Now!*, 25 Jan. 1980).

sale. In *make a sale*, to vomit: Aus. low. B., 1942.

Sale of Two Titties, A. Dickens' *A Tale of Two Cities*: an intentional spoonerism: since ca. 1925. Perhaps orig. Can. (Leechman.)

Salford Docks; sometimes merely **Salfords.** Rocks, esp. on a shore or coastline: r.s., esp. in Manchester. Salford stands on the Mersey Ship Canal.

Sallies. See **Johnnies.**—2. As *the S.*, it = the Salvation Army: Aus.: since ca. 1910. (Niland, 1958.) Cf.:-

Sally. Also as *Sally Ann*, a Salvation Army hostel or canteen. The short form occurs in Curtis, 1939. Cf. **Sal.**

Sally Bash, the. The Salvation Army: occ. low coll.: later C.20. (P.B.)

Sally Rand. HMS *St Lawrent*: RN: WW2.

Sally Thompson. A shearer's cook: Aus. rural: since ca. 1910. B., 1942.

salmon. Abbr. **salmon and trout.**

Salmon and Gluckstein. The *Scharnhorst* and *Gneisenau*, heavy German cruisers: RAF: 1941–2. By Hobson-Jobson, on the former well-known firm of tobacconists.

salmon and trout. The nose: r.s. on *snout*. (B. & P.) But Hillman amends, 1974: 'This implies snout is the nose, but to many Cockneys "snout" is slang for cigarette(s). Thus "got any salmon 'n' trout" is a request for a cigarette'.—2. A (usu. bookmaker's) tout: id. P.P., 1932.—3. Gout: id. (Ibid.) Franklyn says 'rare'. However, Daniells writes, 1980, 'There is even a Salmon Trout Club, restricted to gout sufferers. They arrange tours of breweries, distilleries, etc.'—4. Stout (the drink): id. Franklyn notes that this is now the commonest use of the term.

salmon trout. Var. of prec.

Sal's. See **Sal.**

salt. To introduce secretly into (a meeting) opponents of, or persons to oppose, the speaker: coll.:—1923 (Manchon).

salt chuck. Sea-water; *the s.c.*, the sea: Can. Amer-indian pidgin? 'Ex the Chinook jargon (*chuck*, water). Quite common in British Columbia' (Leechman).

salted. Tipsy: from before 1931, but not very gen. For semantics, cf. the synon. *corned* and *pickled*. P.B.: but cf. late C.19 r.s. *salt junk*, of which this could be a shortening.

saltie, -y. A man-eating crocodile of the coastal areas: N. Queensland coll. Devanney, 1951.

salvo. A member of the Salvation Army; *the S.*, the Salvation Army; as. adj., Salvationist: Aus.: since late C.19; the adj., since ca. 1920. Also in pl., and sometimes as *the Salvoes*, the S.A.—2. 'A "snappy come-back" which in an argument, completely floors your opponent' (Granville): RN officers': since ca. 1938. Cf. the RAF's **shoot down in flames**.

sam. 'To cheat or deceive' (Powis): c.: later C.20. Perhaps ex *sam*, C.19 s., a fool, i.e., to make a fool of.

Sam Hill. Hell, e.g. 'What the Sam Hill': Cockney euph.

same time. At the same time: i.e. nevertheless, or, 'but, mark you, . . .': coll. (mostly in dialogue). Crofts, 'Same time, if we do not learn of her elsewhere, we shall see the skipper of every lugger on the coast.'

same wavelength. See **wavelength.**

samey. Monotonous: coll.: from ca. 1920. Ex:—2. Indistinguishable; the same: schoolboys': late C.19–20. Raymond, 1929, 'The days that followed, becoming "samey" . . . , sank out of memory's sight.' Also *samish*.

Samson. 'A combined magnetic and acoustic mine; from its devastating effect' (Granville): RN: 1940+.

san. A sanatorium: coll.: from not later than 1913. Orig. Public Schoolboys': witness Hay, 1914.

san fairy Ann (may also be written as one word). It doesn't matter *or* it's all the same *or* why worry?: later WW1, then nostalgically; *the* military c.p. (B. & P.; F. & G.) Hugh Kimber ends his war novel, *San Fairy Ann*, 1927, thus: 'There is a magic charter. It runs, "San Fairy Ann".' A perversion of Fr. *ça ne fait rien* (that makes no odds). Variants: *Sally fairy Ann; san fairy Anna;* (*Aunt*) *Mary Ann*; occ. *sandbag Mary Ann*; *send for Mary Ann*. See *DCpp*.

San Mig. *San Mig*uel beer, orig. brewed in the Philippines, and later in Hong Kong: drinkers', in the Far East. (P.B.)

San Toys. Crooks: c.: r.s., on *boys*. P.P., 1932.

Sanctimoody. Sanctimonious and moody: mostly Nonconformists': earlier C.20. With a more than casual glance at the American evangelists, Ira David *Sankey* (1840–1908) and Dwight L. *Moody* (1837–99), who, at their meetings, used their own hymnals, *Sacred Songs* (1873) and *Gospel Hymns* (1875–91).

sand-happy. Odd or eccentric as a result of long service in the desert: Army: 1942–3. Cf. **bomb-happy,** and:-

sand in (one's) **hair, have.** To be accustomed to the desert: Army in N. Africa: WW2. (P-G-R.) Cf. and contrast *sand in their boots*, q.v. at **boots,** 3.

sand-scratch. 'To search for surface gold' (B., 1959): Aus. rural coll.: late C.19–20.—2. (Hence?) 'To be on the lookout for a feminine companion' (Ibid.): Aus. low: since ca. 1930.

sand-scratcher. 'Seaman rating, one of whose jobs is sanding the deck' (Granville): RN.

sandies. A shortening of **Sandy McNab(s),** 3.

Sandy. 'A cute little surfing girl' (*Pix*, 28 Sep. 1963): Aus. teen-age surfers'.—2. See next, 3.

Sandy MacNab (or **McNab**). A taxicab: r.s.: since ca. 1946. Franklyn.—2. A scab: Aus. r.s.: since ca. 1920. Devanney; B., 1953.—3. (Usu. pl.) A body louse: r.s., on *crab*: since early WW1. (Inglis, 1977.) 'A dose of the sandies. Animated dandruff' (Daniells, 1980).

Sandy Powell. Towel: r.s.: mid-C.20. S.P. was a pre-WW2 Northern comedian, on music-hall and radio. (Hillman, 1974.)

sane. The sum of ten shillings: low Aus.: since ca. 1925. (B., 1943.) Origin? 'Seems to be derived from S. German numeral "zehn" (pron. *tsane*). Could it have been brought in by German immigrants, or conceivably by repatriated Anzac ex-POWs of World War I?' (R.S.): more prob. the latter; if so, the dating should rather be 'since 1919 or 1920'.—2. The sum of one pound: Aus. low: since ca. 1925. B., 1959.—3, 4. A prison sentence of ten months; 10 ounces of tobacco: Aus.: the former, c.; the latter c. and low s.: since ca. 1930. B., 1959, adds that '10 years' jail or £10 is most commonly a *brick*'.

sanger (rhyming *banger*). A sandwich: Aus. coll.: later C.20. I first heard it in 1968 (P.B.). Cf. Brit. **sarnie**.

sanitary, the, as in 'Here comes the sanitary'. The sanitary inspector: coll.: since ca. 1946.

sanniferan. Rare for: **san fairy Ann**.

sanno. A sanitary inspector: Aus.: since ca. 1930. B., 1953.

sanny. Sanatorium: Public Schools'. Cf. synon. **san**.—2. A sanitary towel or tampon: middle-class feminine: mid-C.20. Scott, 1971.

Santa Claus. A 'sugar daddy' (rich elderly man keeping or assisting a young mistress): since ca. 1920.

sap. A fool or a simpleton: 1815 (Scott): coll. >, ca. 1900, S.E.—2. 'A weak trainee—"not very bright" ' (Home Office): Borstals' and Detention Centres': later C.20. Ex sense 1.

Sara. A *Sara*toga trunk: Aus. (Brandon, 1931.) Often personified.

Sarah Soo. A Jew: since ca. 1925: r.s., orig. underworld, >, by 1960, fairly common. Gosling, 1959.

Saray Marays, the. See **Jaapies**.

sarc. (Occ. *sark*.) Sarcasm: schools': from ca. 1920. Cf. **sarky**.

sarcky. An occ. form of **sarky**, q.v. Brophy, 1934.

sardine-tin. A Bren-gun carrier (a small, lightly-armoured, tracked vehicle): Army: WW2. (H. & P.) Humorous.—2. A torpedo-carrying aircraft: RAF: 1939+. Jackson.—3. A submarine: RN lowerdeck: 1939+. Granville.—4. A mini-car: coll.: 1960s. Bournemouth *Evening Echo*, 16 Apr. 1966.

sarga, sarge. Sergeant: military coll.; *sarga* only, *sarge* mostly, in address. (F. & G.) *Sarga* († by 1950) was orig. an Arabic pron., adopted in the Regular Army. Cf. *Corp* = corporal, *Bomb* = bombardier, and contrast the more formal *sarnt*.

Sarie Marias. Var. of **Saray Marays**, q.v. at **Jaapies**.

sarker. See MOCK AUCTION, in Appx.

sarky. *Sarcastic*: (low) coll.: late C.19–20. Cf. **sarc**.

sarm. Image: Aus.: since ca. 1945. 'He's the dead sarm of his father.' This could derive ex a dial. pron. (*sahm*) of *same*; but probably Morrisby's explanation, 1958, is correct: Chinese *san* (pronounced *sahn*), the number 3, as used in the game of fan-tan, where 3 is said to be the 'safest' number on which to bet. P.B.: 3 is, in Cantonese, pron. *sarm*.

sarnie. A sandwich: prob. orig. Army, since early C.20; in later C.20, more gen. coll. Cf. Aus. synon. **sammo**, and **sanger**.

sarse; occ. **sarspidilly.** Sarsaparilla: since ca. 1925. B., 1953.

s'arvo. This afternoon: low Aus.: since ca. 1910. (B., 1953.) This *arvo* (see **arvo**.)

sasshay (occ. **sashy**). To go; to move slowly, to promenade: mainly US, but some Brit. use, now ob., in C.20. Ex a perversion of *chassé* (in dancing); cf. *waltz* used in this sense. (P.B.)

Sasso, the. The Senior Air Staff Officer: RAF coll.: 1936+. (Partridge, 1945.) Ex the initials by which he is usu. referred to: *S.A.S.O.*

satin and silk. Milk: Glasgow r.s. Munro, 1985.

saturated. Very drunk: occ. var. of *soaked*: early C.20. Lyell, 1931.—2. 'Without personality, i.e., wet' (H.W., 1942): RAF equivalent of WW2 RN synon. *humid*.

Saturday afternoon sailors. WW2 R Aus. N version of **Saturday night sailors**. B., 1943.

Saturday afternoon soldiers. The Home Guard: Army: 1940–5. Cf.:-

Saturday night sailors. 'Lowerdeck pre-1939 view of the Royal Naval Volunteer Reserve' (Granville). But the Service are still known as *Saturday sailors* by the RN in later C.20 (Knight, 1985). Cf. the RAF's **Weekend Air Force**, and **Saturday night soldiers**.

Saturday-night security. A steady boy friend: Aus.: since ca. 1945. He ensures that she doesn't have to stay at home on Saturday nights—a condition truly to be deplored. (B.P.)

Saturday night soldiers. The Territorial Army. (Roberts, 1976.) Cf. later C.19 synon. *Saturday soldier*.

Saturday-to-Monday Station, the. The Gibraltar naval base, so near England: RN. Bowen.

sauce. In *on the sauce*, drinking (alcohol). (Kington, 1987.) Cf. *on the pop*, and similar euph.

saus, often spelt *soss*. A sausage: mostly juvenile. Frank Richards's school stories.

sausage, n. A draught-excluder placed at foot of a door: domestic coll. Ex shape.—2. A dog in heat: since ca. 1945. A pun on *hot dog*.—3. Short for *sausage and mash*, money in cash: since ca. 1870. From ca. 1927, esp. in coll. *not* (*to have*) *a sausage*, (to be) penniless, esp. temporarily (Chamberlain); whence, in much wider sense, *not to get a sausage*, not to get anything—of whatever is under discussion, as 'Have you heard anything?' 'Not a sausage!' (P.B.)—4. (Usu. in pl.) Human faeces: children's. (P.B.)—5. 'A motorcycle that has been in a crash' (Dunford): motorcyclists': later C.20. See **sausage and mash,** 2.—6. A marijuana cigarette: prisoners' c.: later C.20. Home Office.—7. See **sausage roll**.—8. A term of (usu.) joc., affectionate reproof, esp. to a child or sweetheart, e.g. 'You silly sausage!', or as in '[He] confessed to enjoying his image as a dirty old man. "As I get old, I love people saying, 'There he goes, what a character, what a lusty old sausage' " ' (*LAM*, 7 Sep. 1982): domestic. (P.B.)

sausage, v. To cash; esp. *sausage a goose's*, to cash a cheque: low: from ca. 1920. Abbr. *sausage and mash*, r.s., to cash, itself dating from ca. 1870. Moreover, *goose's* = *goose's neck*, r.s. (late C.19–20) for a cheque.

sausage and mash. See **sausage**, n., 3, and **sausage**, v.—2. A collision: r.s., on *crash* or *smash*: since the late 1950s. Franklyn 2nd.

sausage dog. A dachshund: since WW1, poss. earlier. *Punch* cartoons of WW1 years noted the ludicrous, almost hysterical animosity felt towards them—but then, *Punch* has always been quick to satirise the follies of unthinking public opinion. Also Aus., since ca. 1930 (B.P.). Ex shape, and later C.19 *sausage*, (a) German.

sausage machine, the. A synon. of **mincing machine**.

sausage roll, or capitals; often shortened to *sausage* (or *S.*). A Pole: r.s.: prob. since 1939, ex Poland's fate in WW2. Gosling, 1959; Franklyn 2nd.—2. As *the s. r.*, the dole: r.s.: since ca. 1925. (Haden-Guest, 1972.) Cf. synon. *jam roll*.

sav. A saveloy: low. *Gilt Kid*, 1936.

savage, Savage. (Gen. pl.) A member of the Savage Club: coll.: late C.19–20. *Observer*, 11 Aug. 1935.—2. A man able to claim *native leave*, granted to those whose homes are in or near the port where their ships are lying: R Aus. N: WW2.

savage as a meat-axe. See **meat-axe**.

saveloy. A boy: r.s. Franklyn 2nd.

Saveloy, the. The Savoy Hotel: London taxi-drivers': since ca. 1910. Hodge, 1939.

saw-off. 'A tie; one wins on this deal and loses on that, it's a saw-off' (Leechman): Can.: since ca. 1910.

saw off a chunk or **a piece.** To coït: Can.: since ca. 1920. Semantically cf. the synon. phrases *take a slice*, and **tear off a piece**.

saw them off. To snore; to sleep soundly: C.20 c. >, ca. 1940, low s. (Worby, 1939.) Ex the noise made with a saw clumsily handled.

sawdust lurk, the. 'Stuffing the differential of an old car with sawdust to get a better price for it' (B.P.): Aus. secondhand car dealers': since ca. 1920. Cf. **speedo lurk**.

sawed-off. Short in stature: Can., and occ. Brit., form of **sawn-off**. 'Look at that sawed-off little runt' (Leechman).

S

sawn. A softy, a 'dope': low Aus.: since ca. 1920. (Tennant, 1953.) Ex much older *sawney*, a fool.

sawn off. (Of a person) short; small; Services' (esp. RAF) coll.: since ca. 1920. (H. & P.) I.e. truncated.

sax. A saxophone: trivial: from ca. 1910. Cf. next.—2. Sixpence: Aus.: since ca.1920. (B., 1942.) Cf. **zack**.

saxa. A saxophone: Aus.: since ca. 1920. Prichard, 1930.

say. Six: Parlyaree: mid-C.19–20. (Ware.) Ex It. *sei*. Hence, e.g. *saysaltie*, sixpence (Hollis); *saltie*, or *-ee*, also ex It., *soldi*.

say 'cheese'! Command by amateur photographers taking snapshots of friends and relations, used in an effort to get at least a semblance of a smile for the picture: since (?)early C.20: always joc.; ob. by 1980. See **cheesecake**. (P.B.)

say (one's) piece. To say what one has intended to say, esp. in business or in moral duty: coll.: since ca. 1910. Ex obligatory recitation at, e.g., a party.

say-so. Authority (e.g. 'On whose say-so?'); a right, privilege; power of making decisions: latish C.19–20. Naughton, 1970, 'I let them see I had the complete say-so'.—2. Hence, a leader or chief; a boss: Aus.: from ca. 1930. B., 1942.

scab. A rupee: Army in India: earlier C.20. Cf. synon *rat*.—2. A scarab: mostly Public and Grammar Schools': since ca. 1925. Blake, 1948.

scads. Much; e.g. 'scads of money': adopted, ca. 1935, from US, esp. by would be 'slick' thriller-writers.

scag. (Uncut) heroin: drugs world: adopted, ca. 1970, ex Can., orig. US. (MacKenzie, 1976.) In *6000 Words*, 1976, it is defined simply as heroin, with alternative *skag*, and derived as prob. from earlier US s. *scag, skag* = a cigarette or its butt, of unknown orig. W. & F., 1975, define as 'heroin' among addicts.

scalded-cat raids. German air-raids of 1943 and earlier half of 1944: that period. Fearing invasion, the Germans were jumpy; they made numerous tip-and-run raids.

scale. (Also *scale off*.) To run away; depart hurriedly or furtively; to disappear of one's own motion: mostly Colonial (esp. Aus.). Possibly ex *scale in*, (of a jockey) to be weighed after a race.—2. (?)Hence, to steal (a thing), rob (a person): NZ.—3. Hence, to swindle: Aus.: since ca. 1920. B., 1942.—4. Hence(?), to ride illicitly free on train, tram, bus: Aus.: since ca. 1920. (Baker.) In later C.20 the predominant sense, according to Wilkes.

scale on. To treat (someone) sarcastically: Shrewsbury: since mid-1930s. Marples.

scaler. A thief; a fraud, a swindler; in NZ, esp. one who decamps with his mates' share of the loot: c. > gen. coll., Aus. and NZ: since ca. 1920. Ex **scale**, 1.—2. One who rides illicitly free on public transport: Aus. low > gen. coll.: since early 1920s. Ex **scale**, 4. B., 1942; B.P.

scales. 'Plain gold shoulder-straps worn by sub-lieutenants in full-dress uniform. *Scales* are less elaborate than the epaulettes worn by lieutenants and ranks above' (Granville): RN.

scallie, -y. 'In Liverpool *The End*, a fanzine run by a gang of "scallies" (or scallywags) began writing about "football culture" ' (*You*, 4 Dec. 1983); 'Local [Liverpool] slang, shortened from scallywags, scallies are today's street urchins . . . the scally mythology . . . ' (Ibid., 20 May 1984).

scallywagging. Guerrilla warfare: military: since 1940. Fleming, 1957.

scalp ticket. Return half of a train or bus ticket: Aus.: since ca. 1920. Baker.

scaly, n. A crocodile: Aus.: since ca. 1910. B., 1943.

scaly, adj. Difficult; beset with pitfalls, as in 'It is simply that buying a wedding present is one of the scaliest tasks known to man' (Heller, 1987). Cf. synon. **hairy**.

scaly-back. A Naval pensioner: RN: since ca. 1910. P-G-R.

scaly bloke. A thin man: NZ:—1935.

scam. A (risky) scheme: low coll.: later C.20. (Lindsey, 1980.) Powis defines it as 'a long-firm fraud', whence *scamming*, taking part in such a fraud. Soon > loosely used, as in 'The style of his success is a clue to the meaning of the whole "new romantic" scam' (*New Society*, 23 Apr. 1981).

Scandihoovian, Scandinoogian, Scandiwegian. A Scandinavian: W. Can. and nautical: *Scandinoogian* in McFee, 1930; the other two, Bowen. Beames has var. *Scandahoofian*. Cf. *Scowegian*.

Scans. 'Scandinavians: imported, possibly smuggled magazines, books and films of Danish and Swedish pornography, supposedly "harder" than the UK variety and concomitantly more expensive' (Green, 1984).

scanties. A pair of women's knickers: from ca. 1930. Cf. **panties, tighties**. See quot'n at **briefs**, and:-

scants. 'Scanties' (its orig.; see prec.): mostly feminine, but applied to both female and male 'briefs': since ca. 1950. *Groupie*, 1968.

scapa. An occ. var. spelling of **scarper**. (Hunter, 1964.) A folk-etymol. elab. of **scarper**, as if *Scapa Flow* = (r.s.) go: since ca. 1918.

scapali. Var. of C.19 *scaparey*, an early version of **scarper**.

scapathy. See **orkneyitis**.

scare the living daylights out of; . . . the pants off. To frighten badly: the 1st a var. of **frighten the . . .**, q.v.; the 2nd, coll., since ca. 1955 (Bournemouth *Echo*, 25 Oct. 1967). Both are prob. euph. for *scare the shit out of*: low: since late C.19. From this latter derive *scare shitless* (or euph. *spitless*) and *fartless*: see **scared . . .**

Scarecrow Patrol, the. Coastal Command's patrol by small, single-engined Hornet Moth and Tiger Moth trainer biplanes in Sep.–Dec. 1939: RAF Coastal Command: 1939+. Ex their pathetic inadequacy to the immensity of the task.

scared fartless or **shitless.** Admittedly much afraid: Can., C.20; Brit. since late 1930s, the first less common in Eng. usage. The euph. var. *scared spitless* arose ca. 1942. See **scare the living . . .**

scaredy. A timorous person; a frightened one: Anglo-Irish: since ca. 1910. (Doncaster, 1947.) P.B.: also Eng. children's, as adj., esp. in the taunt for cowards: 'Nyah! Scaredy cat, fraidy cat!'

scarlet slugs. Tracer-fire from Bofors anti-aircraft guns: Services' (esp. RAF): 1939+. H. & P., 'Apt name'. Cf. **flaming onion**.

scarper. To run away; v.t. decamp from: Parlyaree and c.; as latter, it > low Cockney ca. 1905. Selby, 1844, 'Vamoose—scarper—fly!' Ex It. *scappare* via Lingua Franca. See also **scapa**.

scarping omee; scarp. A policeman: parlyaree. (Hollis, 1983.) 'Omee', a man.

scat. Man employed to push barrows at Billingsgate Fish Market. (*Observer* mag., 17 Jan. 1982.) Rolph, 1987, writing of the early 1920s: 'Billingsgate Market [with] its pathetic population of "scats", a small army of unemployed (and probably unemployable) casuals who loitered about the market at the busy time in the hope of earning an occasional sixpence.' Not therefore to be confused with the regular fish-porters.—2. Heroin: drugs c. (Stockley, 1986.) US since –1949 (Spears). Perhaps cf. **scag**.—3. 'Police name for meths drinker picked up on vagrancy patrol' (Clayton, 1970).

scat! In the RAF (1939+), to take off in a hurry. Partridge, 1945.

scats. An occ. var. of **scatty**, as 'She drives me scats': mid-C.20. (P.B.)

scatter-gun. A shot-gun: coll.: US. (ca. 1870), anglicised ca. 1920. *Passing Show*, 24 Dec. 1932.

scatters, the. Diarrhœa; *get the scatters*, to feel very nervous: RN. (Taffrail', 1917.) Cf. synon. **skitters** and **squitters**.

scatty. Crazy, feather-brained; slightly mad: lower classes' > gen. coll. (Horsley, 1912.) In Davies, 1909, the sense appears to be rather that of 'short-tempered', but the gen. sense is perhaps ex *scatter-brained*: cf. Derbyshire *scattle* (*scattel*), easily frightened (*EDD*).

scavenge. To clean up a mess: Public Schools': from ca. 1920.—2. To cadge money, or to thieve in a petty way: Aus.: since ca. 1925. B., 1942.

scavenging party. In Society s. of 1932–34, thus in Knox, 1933, ' "A scavenging party—what on earth's that?" "Miles, dear, don't be old-fashioned. A scavenging party is when you go round in cars picking up tramps and feeding them fish and chips . . . ; or collecting sandwich-boards and doorscrapers and things like that. All the brightest young people do it." '

scawp. To hit or strike: market-traders'. (*M.T.*) Var. of Yorkshire dial. *scalp*, 'To beat about the head; to flog' (*EDD*).

scenario. An ephemeral elab. of the next: mid-1970s.

scene. 'Something that's happening or the place where it's happening' ('Basic Beatnik'): Can. jazz-lovers' and musicians': since ca. 1955. Adopted, ca. 1962, in Britain by jazz musicians and devotees, by drug addicts, by beatniks and then hippies, for the 'world' comprised by those three classes or for 'any specific part of it' (Fryer, 1967).—2. In the underworld, the scene of a crime, the set-up of a burglary or a hold-up: by 1964 at latest. Barlow, 1968.—3. Hence, the performers, the active participants: raffish London: since ca. 1964. Ibid.—4. The favoured setting or *milieu* or activity of a group of people or even of an individual: adopted, ca. 1966, ex US; ob. by 1980. Often in negative, as 'I'm afraid jolly little church parties are not my scene', 'Skiing isn't my scene'.—5. Hence, a way of life; an attitude: since ca. 1967.

sceney. Up to the minute in appearance, habits, practices: mid-late 1960s. *Groupie*, 1968, 'It was all very trendy and sceney at Theo's.' While *trendy* has remained, 1983, 'trendy'—*sceney* has not.

sch- and **sh-.** *Sch*- seems to be the gen. expected spelling in Britain for terms adopted ex Yiddish—and correctly so if directly ex German via Yiddish—and for mock-Yiddish expressions. However, because of the arbitrary and piecemeal way in which this Dictionary has grown over the past half-century, entries are almost randomly split between the two forms *sch*- and *sh*-, according to the spelling in which they were first met by the compiler. If a word of this sort is not found immediately below, please see also under **sh-**, which, it should be noted, is the spelling preferred by Leo Rosten in his highly recommendable study of Yiddish in America, *The Joys of Yiddish*, 1968.

schainer yid. 'An honest and absolutely trustworthy Jewish man (Yiddish)' (Powis): Londoners': later C.20. Rosten (see prec.) spells it *shayner*.

scheissspot. 'A person of low character' (*Muvver*): Cockneys': later C.20. Cf. more 'conventional' Eng. *shitbag*. Ex Yiddish, but cf. *shicer*.

schfatzer. A fellow, a chap: c.: since ca. 1930. (Norman.) 'Refers esp. to an old or, at the least, elderly man and is a misshapen form of the Yiddish word for "father" ' (Franklyn). R.S., on the other hand, writes, 1967: 'This appears to come from Standard German "Schwatzer"—chatter-box, bore, gas-bag, blatherskite.'

schill. See **shill.**

schimpf. To complain, to grouse: Army, esp. and orig. among troops stationed in W. Germany: prob. since 1945. Hence, *be schimpfed*, to be 'miffed', irritated, peeved. An adaptation of Ger. *schimpfen*, to revile, abuse. (P.B.)

schitz or **schiz** or **skitz** or **skiz.** A schizophrenic: since the late 1920s. (Field, 1963.) Cf.:-

schizo. A schizophrenic: psychologists', esp. psychiatrists' coll.: since ca. 1925. Balchin, 1945.

schlent, n. An impostor: c.: from ca. 1921. (Brandon, 1936.) Ex the v.i., to double-cross; to be evasive for illicit ends: c.: from ca. 1920. (Ibid.) Ex:-

schlenter. Dubious, untrustworthy; make-believe: S. African (diamond fields): from ca. 1890: c. >, by 1900, low s. The term derives ex Dutch *slenter*, a trick (*OED* Sup.). Cf. **slinter.**

schlep, shlep, v.t. and v.i. To move or travel laboriously; to carry or transport laboriously. Ex Yiddish *schlep* or *schlepen*, to drag. Also n., a clumsy or inept person. The v. is Brit.; the n. is Am., whence also Brit. (R.C., Sep. 1977.)

schlepper. Casual labour, odd-job boy taken on by a market-trader for the day: market-traders': later C.20. (H. Williamson, 1984.)

schlepper-in. A barker: orig. and mainly Jewish. Via Yiddish ex Ger. *schleppen*, to tug, haul, hence to tout for customers. (R.S.)

schlocky. Adj. derived ex *schlock* (see next entry) to mean shoddy and used, loosely, as gen. pej. as in 'A wonderful scarf . . . On one side—beautiful, witty, perfect—was a Breughel reproduced on fine wool. On the other—campy, tacky, schlocky—were Lurex stripes' (York, 1976). York also puns *schlock horror* on the media cliché *shock horror*, current since mid-1970s. (P.B.)

schlog (or **slog**) **it on.** To raise the price extortionately: Aus.: since ca. 1925. (B., 1942.) 'A literal translation of Standard Ger. *auf den Preis schlagen*—clap the price on, hence push the price up' (R.S.). However, R.C. suggests, 1966, 'Probably from *schlock* (Yiddish) = shoddy, overpriced "It's the biggest schlock house on Seventh Avenue"—J. Weidner, *I Can Get It for You Wholesale*, c. 1940'.

schmal(t)z, n. and adj. (Something) entirely satisfactory, notably if it exhibits panache and esp. of a performance, as in 'Gee, that's schmalz!': theatrical, mostly in *Variety*: adopted, ca. 1957, ex US, but drastically adapted from the orig. sense of the n., which means 'sweetly sentimental music or song or performance'—a sense current, since ca. 1955, in Brit. also. (Merry.) Ex Yiddish *schmaltz*, 'chicken fat, used for cooking, hence greasy, slick'. (W. & F.) Hence the adj. *schmal(t)z*, sweetly and excessively sentimental. Also *schmaltzy*, as adj.

schmeer. See **whole schmeer.**

Schmitter. A Messerschmitt aircraft (a German fighter): Services': WW2.

schmock. A fool: c. and low s.: since ca. 1910. 'Yiddish for "fool", is used in a particularly derogatory way, and has variant *schmuck* (Franklyn); its lit. Yiddish meaning is 'penis'—cf., therefore, the low 'you stupid prick!' Note that Yiddish *schmuck*, orig. 'jewel' or 'ornament', has been adopted from Ger. *Schmuck*. (Leonard Goldstein, 1967.)—2. Heroin: drugs world: later C.20. (*The State of the Language*, 1980.) Also spelt *shmock* (Home Office). Cf. sense 1, and synon. *smack*, prob. a var.

schmo(e). A foolish or very naïve person, hence anyone objectionable to the speaker: adopted, ca. 1959, ex US. It seems to be a contrived word; mock-Yiddish. (W. & F.) Perhaps, however, ex Yiddish: cf. prec., 1. R.S. adds, 1967, 'Ca. 1950 in the U.S., there was a comic strip featuring small, armless, pear-shaped bipeds called Schmoos. They were simple, amiable, and everlastingly "put upon" .'

schmuck. See **schmock,** 1.

schmutter. 'Clothing, or rags, or rubbish (Yiddish), but especially a suit: "That's a nice schmutter you've got" ' (Powis): London.

schnoink. 'Unpleasant and insulting term used by a non-Jew for a Jew (not a Yiddish or Hebrew word)' (Powis): low: later C.20. Cf. earlier s. *shonk*, a Jew.

schnozzle. A nose: adopted, in Brit. and Can., ex US ca. 1940. Can. also took the elab. *schnozzola*, while Brit. preferred the US abbr. *schnozz*. Popularised in UK by the famous American comedian with the very prominent nose, Jimmy 'Schnozzle' Durante, † 1980. Ex Ger. *Schnauze*, an animal's snout or muzzle (W. & F.).

school. Prison: convicts', hence crooks': late C.19–20. Perhaps esp. in *at school*, in prison, as in Manning, 1930.—2. A regular gathering of the same 'serious' drinkers: messes', pubs', etc. (P.B.)

School for Heavy Needlework, His or **Her Majesty's.** Prison: cultured joc.: mid-C.20. Cf. synon. **ironmongery department**.

School of Wind, the. The RN School of Music: RN: since ca. 1920. P-G-R.

schoolie, -y, n. An education officer: orig. Army, where coll. for official 'Army schoolmaster', since ca. 1890; thence to RN, ca. 1920 (Granville), and RAF, ca. 1930 (Partridge, 1945). During WW2 and National Service years, ca. 1939–62, applied very widely to the NCOs of the Royal Army Education Corps (P.B.).—2. A schoolteacher, of either sex: Aus. coll. Wilkes' first quot'n is dated 1907, for a girl teacher.—3. A school—as opp. to a house—prefect: Scottish Public Schools': from ca. 1880. Miller, 1935.

schoolie, v.t. To inflict a prefects' beating on (a boy): Scottish Public Schools'. (Miller, 1935.) Ex n., 3.

schooner-rigged. Destitute: sailing-ships': late C.19–early 20. Bowen.—2. Hence, not wearing a full, good set of trawler deck-hands' gear: trawlermen's coll. 'Certain hands used to go to sea "schooner-rigged"—one of the differences between a schooner and a square-rigged vessel is that the schooner needs less canvas to drive her' (Piper, 1974).

schwartz(e), schwarz, swartzer. A Negro; an Indian or Pakistani; loosely, a half-caste: since ca. 1950: low s., perhaps orig. c. (Norman, 1959, the 1st spelling; the 3rd in Newman, 1970.) Via Yiddish ex German *schwarz*, black. 'Put in the schwarzes and de-stat it'—rid the property of *stats* or statutory tenants (*Sunday Times*, 7 July 1963).

schwaya or **shwaya.** Small or insignificant; as n., a small quantity, a little: Army in N. Africa: 1940–3. 'He's a schwaya job'—'Give me a schwaya more char'. Ex the Arabic *suqair*. (P-G-R.) Also spelt *shwaiya*, and prob. in Service use, esp. Army and RAF, since ca. 1925; ob. with the withdrawal from Middle East, ca. 1955. Esp. in *stand a shwaiya, stanishwiya*, wait a moment. (L.A.; P.B.)

scissor-bill. A nagging, gossiping, and otherwise objectionable woman: low:—1931 (*OED* Sup.). Ex the bird so named.

scissor-grinder. An engine-room artificer: RN. 'Taffrail', 1916; Bowen.

scoach. 'Term used at the old Chepstow Board School. "He's scoaching me" meant "He's not allowing [me] my fair share of room on the form' (Waters, 1973).

sconce. In *do* (one's) *sconce*, to become extremely annoyed or angry: NZ servicemen's: ca. 1944+. Slatter, 'I'll do my sconce proper'. Cf. semantically **do** (one's) **nut.**

scone, n. (Pron. *skon.*) A detective: Aus., shortened s., *hot scone = John*, a policeman: since ca. 1920. B., 1942.—2. The head: Aus.: since ca. 1930. Often *go off* (one's) *scone*, as in Niland, 1958. Hence *suck your scone in!*, pull your 'scone' in!—stop talking nonsense: Aus.: since ca. 1950. (Culotta.) See also **scoper**, and:-

scone, v. To hit (someone) on the top of the head: Aus.: since ca. 1935. Ex **scone**, n., 2. (B.P.)

scone-hot, adj. and adv. An intensive, whether favourable ('He's scone-hot at cricket'), unfavourable ('unreasonable', 'extortionate'), or neutral ('Go for someone scone-hot'—vigorously): Aus.: since ca. 1925. (Baker.) Newly baked scones are both hot and delicious. P.B.: Wilkes' quot'ns at this entry, from 1944 onwards, make it clear that the phrase is *go* (someone) *scone hot*, rather than Baker's *go for* . . .

sconer. 'Any skull-threatening bumper' (Robinson, 1946): Aus. cricketers': since ca. 1925. Ex **scone**, n., 2.

scooby doo. A clue, an idea: Glasgow r.s., sometimes shortened, as in 'Ah haveny got a scooby' (Munro, 1985). Ex the name of an immensely popular cartoon dog, first shown on the US CBS TV in 1969, and soon appearing worldwide (Brasch, 1983).

scooch. Spirituous liquor(s): RN (Bowen) and, occ., Army: early C.20. A blend of *scotch + hooch*?

scoop. In singing, the attack on a commencing note 'by way of a chromatic slide from the "fourth" below': coll.:—1911 (*OED* Sup.).

scoop the pool. To make a 'killing': financial coll. Ex gambling.

scoot. 'A continued bout of drunkenness' (*Truth*, 27 Apr. 1924): Aus. Hence (*get* or *go*) *on the scoot*, (to go) on the spree, on a drinking-bout: Aus., since ca. 1930; by ca. 1940 also NZ (Slatter). Wilkes.

scooter. A single-deck bus; a one-man operated bus: busmen's: since ca. 1945. Prob. derog., ex the children's toy.

scope. A telescope; a periscope: since ca. 1910; by 1940, coll.—2. A cystoscope (used in examining the bladder): medical students':—1933 (*Slang*).—3. An oscilloscope: technicians': since ca. 1940. (B.P)

scorched earth. Destruction of everything that might be useful to an advancing enemy: 1937 (*SOD*); coll. >, by 1943, S.E.

score, n. 'The number of drinks consumed or the bill to be paid' (H. & P.): Services coll.: since ca. 1915.—2. A successful operation: c., esp. pickpockets'; hence, a likely victim: id. Both since late 1940s. Moynahan, 1969.

score, v. To buy or otherwise obtain drugs, esp. if unexpectedly: adopted, ca. 1955, ex US. Wyatt, 1973.—2. To achieve intercourse with (also as v.i., to copulate): orig., ca. 1950, the underground, e.g. the 'pop' groups, as in *Groupie*, 1968, 'Groupies like to tell other groupies who they've scored and what they're like.' The later C.20 Aus. (male) version is *score between the posts* (Buzo, 1973): ex football (Wilkes).

score a bull with (one's) **first sighter.** 'To effect conception in a single act of intercourse . . . Current among undergraduates ca. 1920, hence presumably WW1 or earlier. Army or other marksmen's' (R.S., who adds: 'In competition shooting, a preliminary non-scoring shot is allowed, to check the calibration of the rifle').

scotch. (Usu. in pl. *scotches.*) A police—esp. a CID—detective: c.: since ca. 1945; hence, also, since ca. 1950, police s. (Carr, 1956.) ?Ex Scotland Yard, or some obscure r.s.

Scotch bed, make a. To fold blankets into the form of a sleeping-bag: Forces': since ca. 1918. Economical conservation of heat. (L.A.)

Scotch by absorption. Not of Scottish extraction, yet fond of Scotch: since ca. 1930.

Scotch eggs. (Female) legs: r.s.: since ca. 1950. (Haden-Guest, 1972.) Cf. older synon. r.s. *Scotch peg*.

Scotch Mist, the. The Scottish Church canteen at Abbassia (Cairo): Army in N. Africa: ca. 1940–3. P-G-R.

Scotch mist, adj. Tipsy: racing r.s., on *pissed*: since ca. 1920. Cf. **Brahms 'n' Liszt.**

Scotch navy. The Clan line of steamers: nautical. Bowen.

Scotsman's Cinema, the. Piccadilly Circus: Londoners': from 1933. Ex the numerous electric or neon light advertisements to be seen there—without admission charge.

Scotsman's fifth. Coasting in neutral, i.e. 'fifth gear': see HAULIERS', in Appx.

scour. A cleansing; a polishing: coll. 'Give the floor a good scour' (*OED*). Ex Scots. P.B.: or ex the S.E. v., the scouring action of a fast-flowing river on its bed; whichever, S.E. in later C.20.

scours. A purge: coll.:—1923 (Manchon). Ex S.E. *scours*, diarrhœa.

scout. 'A reproachful name for a bold forward girl' (Joyce, 1910): Anglo-Irish: late (?mid) C.19–20.—2. A detective: Glasgow:—1934.—3. In *good scout*, a good, a trustworthy or helpful person: adopted, ex US, ca. 1920—no doubt reinforced by the popularity of the Scouting movement; by 1980, ob. Occ., *scout* was used independently = a fellow.

scram! Clear out! go away!: US; anglicised, among film fans, by 1930. Perhaps ex v. *scramble*: cf. South Cheshire *scramble*, 'to get away; with a notion of fear or stealth' (*EDD*). It is also short for the official *scramble*, wrongly classified in the *Reader's Digest*, Feb. 1941, as s.: (of aircraft) to take off: RAF: since 1939. (E.P., 1942.) See **amscray.**

scramble. Aerial combat, a 'dog-fight': RAF: 1939+, but rare. Berrey; Jackson.

scrambled egg (RAF: since ca. 1930) is the wearer (mentioned by Jackson), and in the RN, an unpopular wearer of:-

scrambled eggs. 'The ornate gold oak leaves on the peak of an Air Commodore's cap [in fact, on that of any officer from Group-Captain upwards] are called "scrambled eggs"' (Bolitho, 1941): RAF: since ca. 1925. P.B.: by 1950 often *s. egg*—the dish was usu. accompanied by a considerable display of **fruit salad**, q.v. According to Messrs Gieves & Hawkes, Ltd, 1982, the term has long been common to all three Fighting Services for the decoration on senior officers' caps. In the MN it is applied to similar headgear worn by master mariners of the major shipping lines.

scrape, n. and v. An act of sexual intercourse; to copulate: Aus. low: since mid-C.20. Wilkes.

scrape the bottom of the barrel. To use, or to approach in order to enlist, anyone at all to do something, esp. to fill a vacant position: coll.: since ca. 1945. After ca. 1955, often simply *scrape the barrel.*

scraper ring. 'The middle or half-ring on the cuffs of a Squadron-Leader's tunic': RAF: since ca. 1920. Jackson, 'In a piston there is a compression ring, an oil-retaining ring and a middle, or scraper, ring.'

scrapings. In *be away to scrapings*, to be doomed or done for or dead: lower classes': early C.20.

scrappo. A scrap or fight: Aus. (mostly youthful): since ca. 1925. B., 1943.

scratch, n. Generic for genuine bank- and currency-notes: c.:—1935 (Hume). In later C.20, used in drugs c. for any money (Stockley, 1986). Contrast *slush.*—2. The Captain's Secretary: RN. (Granville.) Also *Sec.* (Winton, 1959). Cf. **scratcher,** 1.

scratch, v. To go fast, travel rapidly: Aus.: since ca. 1920. (Baker.) Like a sprinter from the scratch-mark? App. † in later C.20; by 1930s supplanted by:—2. To be struggling for a living. See **scratching,** 2.

scratch-cat. A sour-tempered female: NZ feminine: ca. 1910–50. (Devanney, 1929.) P.B.: not unknown in Britain.

scratch it. To depart; make off: low:—1923 (Manchon).

scratcher. A paymaster, or his clerk: RN: late C.19–20; ob. Ware, 'From the noisy times of quill pens.'—2. A bed: low Glasgow:—1934. For the semantics, cf. **flea-bag.** P.B.: since 1939 also Services', esp. RN and RM. (Hawke, 1979.) Army in WW2; not so common later, *pit* being the usu. term.—3. A slow driver: busmen's: since ca. 1925. He 'scratches about'. Contrast **slasher,** 2.—4. Any scratching tool; also, the person operating it: fair-grounds': Buchanan-Taylor, 1943.—5. A second coxswain: RN submariners': 1960s. (Malin, 1979.) Perhaps cf. sense 1.—6. A warder expert in searching a cell: prison c.: later C.20. McConville, 1980.

scratching, be. To be in a dilemma, a quandary: Aus.: since ca. 1910. (B., 1942.) Like a hen, scratching about for food. P.B.: prob., more specifically:—2. 'To be struggling, in difficulty' (Wilkes): Aus. coll.: since 1930s, perhaps earlier. Often elab., as *scratching for a living*, or *for jobs*, or *for a crust*, etc. Cf. Brit. use in, e.g., '[RAF] Pay was still [in the 1920s] at WW1 rates and was to remain so for many years, and most airmen were scratching for money before Friday [pay-day]' (Adkin, 1983).—3. 'Searching prison establishment buildings' (Home Office): prisons' c.: later C.20. Cf. **scratcher,** 6.—4. Occ. synon. with *be sweating*, waiting for a possible, imminent, win at, e.g. tombola: Army: mid-C.20. Hence, *go scratching*, to take part in the game: id. (P.B.)

scratchings. 'Scraps of cooked potato and the broken bits of batter which had fallen from frying fish' (Roberts, 1971): coll., among the poor, esp. of Lancashire: ca. 1890–1940.

scream, n. An extremely ridiculous or funny person or thing: 1915 (*SOD*): s. >, by 1935, coll. Often *a perfect* or *absolute s.* P.B.: a cartoon by A. Wallis Mills, in *Punch,* 1 Oct. 1919, entitled 'A Proposal à la Mode', shows a dapper young man, accompanied by a fashionably dressed girl; they are passing a shop advertising bridal cakes; he says: 'Well, old scream, what about it?'—2. An uproar; a tremendous fuss, e.g. in the Press: since ca. 1925. Norman.—3. As exemplified by the

announcement, 'Police wish to interview a man in connection with . . .' (Read, 1978).

scream, v. To turn King's (Queen's) evidence: low: from the early 1920s. (*OED* Sup.) Cf. older synon. *squeal.*

scream like a wounded eagle. 'Said of one who makes a terrific fuss about something' (Leechman): Can.: since ca. 1955.

screamer. An exclamation-mark (cf. **Christer** and **shriek-mark**): from ca. 1920 and mostly among printers, authors, journalists, typists, and copy-writers. Sayers, 1933, 'Capital N, capital P, and screamer.'—2. A whistling bomb: civilians' and Services': Sep. 1940+. (H. & P.) A 'terror bomb' with a scream-producing device.—3. A man very obviously homosexual: since ca. 1950. (Gardner, 1967.) A '*roaring* queer'.—4. See **two-pot screamer.**—5. 'Persistently complaining customer' (Graham-Ranger, 1981): car-dealers'.

screamer over the target. A man that sees danger everywhere—and is constantly drawing attention to it: RAF: 1940+.

screamers, the. An intense dislike of operational flying: RAF: 1940–5. (P-G-R.) Cf. **screaming shits.**

screaming abdabs. See **abdabs,** 2, 3.

screaming Alice. Crystal Palace: r.s. Hillman, 1974, 'probably another example of railway workers usage'.

screaming downhill. 'Making a power dive in a fighter aircraft' (H. & P.): RAF: since ca. 1938. A whistling noise is caused by the wind and perhaps by the propeller. P.B.: or simply a graphic description of speed.

screaming meemies, the. Hysteria; excessive fear, noisily expressed: adopted, 1930s, ex US. Cf. **heebie-jeebies,** which may also be 'screaming' on occasion.

screaming ostrich. A 'super bird', an exceptionally marked hissing by the audience: theatrical:—1935.

screaming pie-ackers. See **pie-ackers.**

screaming shits, the. Diarrhœa: Forces': since ca. 1939.—2. Hence, *give (one) the s.s.,* to get on the nerves of: Forces': since ca. 1940.

screb. A halfpenny: Derbyshire schoolboys': 1920s. 'A clod was a penny, and a screb, a ha'penny' (Kerslake, 1985).

screech. Wine obtained by 111 Fighter Squadron, RAF, from the White Fathers at Thibar in Tunisia: 1943. Cf. earlier low use, for whisky.—2. Any hard liquor: RN lowerdeck: mid-C.20. (*Heart,* 1962.) See quot'n at **doggo party.**—3. The throat: homosexuals': current ca. 1970.—4. See **giggle,** n., 2, and cf. **scream,** n., 1, synon. with this sense.

screecher. A street singer: showmen's: Allingham, 1934.

screechers. 'Screeching' drunk; hysterical: since ca. 1930. (Brickhill, 1951.) Occ. *Harry Screechers*: see HARRY, in Appx.

screeve. A motor-car: market-traders': since ca. 1920. (*M.T.*) The etym. is not so simple as it looks: prob. ex dial. *scrieve,* to write, or ex the Dutch *schrijven*; ultimately ex L. *scribere*; whence, perhaps, the vehicle licence.

screw. To burgle; also, to keep watch for one's burglar-confederate: c. (Leach, 1933.) Ex much earlier s. *screw,* to break into a building by using a *screw,* a skeleton key.—2. To look at: grafters'. Allingham.—3. To copulate with (a female): low:—1785. (Grose, 1st ed.) P.B.: by the mid-1970s—?thanks to Women's lib.—the v. was applicable to both sexes, as in Crisp, 1976, 'Apparently she used to screw around on the side as well' (cf. **sleep around**); and '[She] . . . screwed a number of exceedingly dull men' (Carter, 1979).—4. To scrutinise (a person); to eye, accusingly, up and down: mostly teenagers'. (L.A., 1967.) Cf. sense 2, above.—5. To ruin or, at the least, spoil badly: Can.: since ca. 1965. *Maclean's,* 17 May 1976, 'I think they've screwed biology in this country for ever.' See **screwed up,** 1.—6. To swindle: since ca. 1930. Cf. sense 1.

screw-driver. A drink of vodka (or gin) and orange-juice: since late 1940s. (Wharton, 1966.) P.B.: contrast *gimlet*, gin and lime.—2. 'Principal [prison] officer': prisons' c. pun: later C.20. (Home Office.) Ex early C.19 c. > s. *screw,* a turnkey.

S

screw the arse, or **back legs, off** (a woman). To coït with, vigorously and often: low. Crookston, 1967.

screw the bobbin! (Usu. imperative.) Use your common-sense!: Army: late 1960s–early 70s. (P.B.)

screw-up, n. 'A loser; a ne'er-do-well. As in "Him? He's a real screw-up." Widespread N. Am., heard thus in early 1950s in Vancouver' (Leech, 1986).

screw up, v.i. To do something badly: low coll.: adopted ex N. Am., later C.20. 'I am not flying smoothly, accurately, conservatively. In fact, I am screwing up in a big way' (*Phantom*, 1979). See **screwed up,** 1. Also as v.t.: 'How was the exam?'—'I screwed it up' (P.B.).

screwball, adj. and n. (An) eccentric: Can., adopted, during the 1930s, ex US. Perhaps from billiards or snooker. 'More likely from baseball, in which the screwball is a recognized pitch, but heavily influenced by *screwy*' (R.C., 1966).

screwdriver. See **screw-driver.**

screwed. Broken-up with hard work: Aus. (B., 1942.) E.P. suggests 'Cf *screw*, a worn-out horse'—but cf. also **screwed up,** 1.

screwed up. (Utterly) spoilt; wrecked; fouled up: Can.: since ca. 1930. (Leechman.) Euph. for *fucked-up*. In later C.20 also Brit.; see **screw up.** (P.B.)—2. 'Shut in cell—"banged up"' (Home Office): prison c. pun: later C.20. See **screw,** v., 1, etym.—3. As in 'Studies of adults who are screwed up about mathematics' (St John-Brooks, 1981): loosely, neurotic; anxious: coll.: later C.20. (P.B.)

screwer or **screwman.** Occ. variants (Wallace has the latter; 'Stuart Wood', the former) of *screwsman*.—2. A burglary: c.: since ca. 1945. (Norman, 1959.) Ex **screw,** v., 1.

Screws of the World. See **Whore's Gazette.**

screwsman. A thief using a skeleton key: c.:—1812 (Vaux). In C.20, esp. a petty house-breaker ('Stuart Wood', 1932). But Powis, 1977, defines as 'Housebreaker of some skill'.

screwy. Crazy, mad; (very) eccentric: lower classes',—1935, but in NZ since ca. 1910 (Park, 1955). P.B.: prob. elliptical for *screw loose* (in the head), or perhaps merely 'twisted'.

scribe. Any clerical rank or rating: RN coll. Bowen.—2. A forger: c. Sharpe, 1938.

scrim up. To camouflage with scrim (open-work material, netting): Army coll.: since mid-C.20, perhaps earlier. (P.B.)

script. Prescription for drugs: drugs c. (Stockley, 1986.) US since—1936 (Spears).

scroat. See **scrote.**

Scrob. 'Danish fishermen—called Scrobs in Grimsby [fishermen's] slang' (Sweeney, 1984).

scrote. A low term of abuse. 'Being "in" or "trendy" or "hip" is to be a member of a closed community, created by an act of conscious dissociation from the wider society—whether it be the wrinklies, the proles, the scrotes or the squares' (Young, 1986); 'Thus the battle lines are drawn, not just against those on the margins—known in police canteen parlance as scrotes, slag (as in coal), yobs, punks, plonks (any woman), coons and Pakis—but junior against senior officer' (A. Tyler, 1986). Clement, 1977, spells it *scroat*. Perhaps a shortening of *scrotum*.

scrotty. Var. of **grotty,** q.v., dirty: teenagers': early 1980s. (Joanna Williamson, 1982.)

scrounge, n. Esp. in *do a scrounge*, to go looking for what one can 'find'; to take it: military: 1914 or 1915. Ex the v. P.B.: by mid-C.20 the phrase had > *on the scrounge*, usu. *be . . . ,* occ. *go . . . ,* as ' 'fraid I'm on the scrounge again! Can you lend me . . . ?'

scrounge, v.t. To hunt for; cadge, to get by wheedling; to acquire illicitly; hence, to steal; also v.i.: Services' in WW1; from ca. 1920, fairly gen. Ex dial. *scrunge*, to steal (esp. apples). The *SOD* records at 1919; W. quotes *Westminster Gazette* of Jan. 1920; but the soldiers used it from the early days of the war. See esp. B. & P.—2. In WW2 the soldiers used it to mean 'to avoid a fatigue'. P-G-R.

scrounge on. To sponge on: US (—1911) >, by 1918, anglicised. *OED* Sup.

scrounger. One who does 'scrounge' (see the v.): military: from 1915.

scrub. Esp. in *scrub it!*, cancel it!; forget it!: Services': since ca. 1910. Esp., later, RAF (H. & P.). I.e. wash it out (as e.g., with a scrubbing-brush).—2. To dismiss or give up or abandon (someone): Aus.: since ca. 1935. Niland, 1958.—3. 'To assist in a surgical operation. "Will you scrub with me tomorrow?" I.e., will you scrub your hands (for asepsis) and follow me and assist?' (Leechman): Can. surgeons': since ca. 1945.

scrub cockie. A small farmer working land mainly covered with trees, or other rough land: Aus. coll. (B., 1942.) Ex C.19 *cockatoo*, a small farmer.

scrub-happy. Suffering from nervous exhaustion resulting from service in outback regions, hence in the tropics: Aus. soldiers': 1940–5. (B., 1943.) Cf. **bomb-happy, sand-happy,** etc.

scrub her (gen. **'er**). To sponge off the big odds on one's [bookmaker's] board: turf c.:—1932. Cf. **scrubbing-brush.**

scrub out. To cease to be friends: low: from ca. 1919. I.e. to wash it (friendship) out.

scrub round. To agree to forget; to omit, to cancel, ignore: Services': since ca. 1935. (H. & P.) Elab. of **scrub,** 1. Also *scrub all round.*—2. To take evasive action: 1939+: RAF. (Jackson.) Not gen., because of confusion with sense 1. In the RN, however, the term is frequently used (Granville, 1945).

scrubber. Any Other-Ranker: Army: ca. 1920–45.—2. A low woman: orig. mostly Army, since ca. 1925; by ca. 1950 Services' gen. Ex port cities', e.g., London, Portsmouth, Liverpool, use of the term for a prostitute. Cf. C.18 synon. *scrub*. Often, in later C.20, qualified *old* or *young scrubber*, both pej.—3. Hence, a girl not at all glamorous: since ca. 1955. Via, 'An unwashed female teenager' (Cook, 1962): since ca. 1945: c. >, by ca. 1955, also low s. I.e. *young scrubbers*.—4. 'Any weedy or unpleasant person' (B., 1943): Aus.: since ca. 1925.—5. As exclam., *scrubbers!*: that's finished, exists no longer: orig. and mainly RAF: since early 1930s. (Jackson.) Ex **scrub,** 1; cf. **scrub her.**

scrubbing-brush. An 'outside' horse or dog that 'scrubs' or beats the favourites: turf c.:—1932 (*Slang*).

Scrubs, the. The convict prison at Wormwood Scrubs: c. (—1916) >, by 1923, low s. E.g. in Manchon, 1923; *Dartmoor,* 1932.

scruff. A scruffy-looking person: since ca. 1950. 'Who're that load of scruffs, then?' *Scruffy* is S.E., in gen. use since ca. 1925 (*SOD*). (P.B.)—2. As *the Scruff*: 'The Desert Airforce (a combination of *scruffy* and *R.A.F.*). Eighth Army used to think that men of the Desert Airforce were dirtier and scruffier than themselves. A debatable point' (Sanders, 1967).

scruff-bag. A 'down-and-out': police and low s.: since ca. 1930. (Barling, 1973.) P.B.: in later C.20 joc. coll. for any scruffy-looking person.

scruff order(, in). Very informally dressed: Army: later C.20. (P.B.)

scrum. Wonderful, excellent: schoolgirls': earlier C.20. Ex *scrumptious.*

scrummy. 'Scrumptious' (whence it derives): from ca. 1906, on the evidence of Collinson (p. 24); 1918 (Galsworthy: *OED* Sup.).

scrumpy rat. A habitual drunkard: RN lowerdeck: mid-C.20. (*Heart,* 1962.) Ex (mainly) W. Country dial. *scrumpy*, rough cider, itself from dial. v. *scrump*, to steal apples (*SOD,* 1977).

scrunch. Food; esp. sweets (lollies): Aus.: since ca. 1920. (Baker.) Echoic.

scrunge. See TIDDLYWINKS, in Appx.

scrutch. To scratch one's c*rutch*: Aus. joc.: since ca. 1930. B., 1943.

scud. A travelling ticket inspector: railwaymen's: since ca. 1920. (*Railway,* 2nd.) He works fast.

scuffer. A policeman: Liverpool. Ex dial. *scuff*, to strike. (Shaw.) Cf. earlier N. Country c. *scufter*. P.B.: in later C.20, more gen. s., perhaps spread by the 'Merseyside boom' of the 1960s. Hence *judy scuffer*, a policewoman.

scuffle. To 'get by' or barely manage to exist: beatniks': since ca. 1959. Anderson, 'Some scuffle on leaves and coke' (lettuce and Coca-Cola).

scuffle-hunter. One who hangs about the docks on the pretence of looking for work but actually to steal anything that 'comes his way': c. and nautical s. from ca. 1790; ob. (Colquhoun, 1796.) By mid-C.20 this had > *scuffler* (Ash).

scull about. To seek something easy to steal: c.: since ca. 1910. (*Free-Lance Writer*, Apr. 1948.) Cf. next; in WW2 *sculling about* was a var. (P-G-R).

sculling around. (Of a person) wandering aimlessly; (of a thing) left lying about: nautical. ('Taffrail', 1917.) Ex leisurely rowing. P.B.: by mid-C.20 gen. coll., and not always aimless: e.g., 'They're all sculling around looking for her.'

scum. A 'fag'; *new scum*, a new boy: Shrewsbury. Marples.

scun. To wander aimlessly or, by meiosis, purposefully: Services' (?mostly Army): WW2. Prob. a blend of *scull + swan*. (Raab.)

scungy or **-ey.** 'A pejorative currently'—June 1963—'popular in Sydney and Melbourne undergraduate circles' (B.P.). Perhaps ex Scottish and N. Irish *scunge*, to slink about, and Scottish *scunge*, a sly or vicious fellow; or, as B.P. suggests, ex Aus. *scungy*, scabby, itself perhaps s.—dating from ca. 1920. Cf. the archaic S.E. adj. *scurvy*, and s. *gungey*.

scunnered. Physically exhausted: Newcastle cyclists': later C.20. (*Fellowship*, 1984.) Cf. **shattered**, 2. Akin to, and ex, gen. N. Country dial. *scunner*, of various related meanings (*EDD*).

scupper. To spoil or ruin: coll. 'I'm afraid he scuppered his chances at the interview by looking so scruffy' (P.B.). Ex earlier s. to kill, ultimately from nautical j.

scutcher. Anything very large or, esp., very good; adj., excellent: Aus.: since ca. 1910. (B., 1942.) ?*Scotcher* something 'killing' (to *scotch* a snake).

scuttle but(t). Rumour; gossip: adopted, late 1960s, ex USN coll.; by 1972, coll. (Chambers' *C.20th Dict.*, 1972.) Ex lit. nautical sense. *Guardian*, 18 Jan. 1986, had it as one word, *scuttlebut*.

scuz bag. 'Low life; [a] jerk' (Leech, 1986): N. Am.: since ca. 1980. Cf. US *scuzzy*, dirty, filthy: since early 1970s (W. & F.).

sea-flea. 'A very fast motor boat that skips and bounces over the ocean like a flea on a sheet' (Leechman): mostly Can.: since ca. 1950. Perhaps ex the US s. *sea-flea*, an outboard motor boat (W. & F.).

seabees. RAF men serving with the RN: 1944–5. (Holman, 1944.) 'Prob. ultimately from US Seabees, Naval Construction [Battalion] workers whose emblem is a (busy) bee, whose six legs hold a hammer, wrench, saw, etc.' (R.C., 1976). Ex initials *C.B.*

seagull. 'A casual wharf labourer (from the bird's habit of waiting for and swooping on scraps)' (Wilkes): Aus. In UK, esp. Portsmouth Docks, 'One who is willing to work all hours' (Patterson).

seagull on. Synon. with *pigeon on*: Aus. B., 1942.

seamer. A medium- or a fast-medium-paced ball delivered with a skilful use of the seam: cricketers': since ca. 1948. By 1960, coll.

search. (Of a pickpocket) to rob (a person): c. Hume.

searcher. A searching question, an embarrassing problem: coll.:—1923 (Manchon).

seat, the. The hip pocket: c.: late C.19–20. I.e. in pickpocketing. Cf. **outer**, 2.—2. See **hot seat**.

seat-of-the-pants flyer. One of the pioneers of air transport over the unmapped Canadian North during the 1920s and 1930s: Can. coll.: at first, modestly among themselves; then, admiringly by journalists: since ca. 1925; after ca. 1950, mostly historical. 'They flew, with few instruments, over practically uninhabited country, to land on small lakes or rude airfields' (Priestley). See **fly by the seat** . . .

seats. Buttocks: partly humorous and partly euph.; and, in the main, middle-class dom.: since ca. 1945. 'She has prominent'—or 'a prominent pair of'—'seats'.

sec. A secretary: coll.:—1923 (Manchon). Granville, 'An Admiral's or a captain's secretary': RN.

secko. A (male) sex pervert: low Aus.: since ca. 1925. (Park, 1949.) By abbr. + Aus. *-o* (Wilkes).

second-class buff. A stoker, 2nd class: RN: earlier C.20. P-G-R.

second dickey, -ie, -y. The second mate: nautical: late C.19–20. Bowen.—2. Hence, the reserve or second pilot in an aircraft: RAF: since ca. 1938. (Jackson.) Don't give yourself away by speaking of a 'first dicky'—the term does not exist. Cf. the RAF boast of long service, 'I flew second dicky to Pontius Pilate.' Cf. **dickey pilot**.

second eleven, the. The Commander and the deputy heads of department, as opposed to the Captain and the heads of department, on board a capital ship: RN: since ca. 1940. Ex cricket.—2. 'Old frigates resuscitated from the reserve, and known somewhat unkindly as the "Second Eleven" ' (Winton, 1977): RN, esp. Fisheries Patrol.

second-hand dartboard. A promiscuous woman, as in 'characterising her with epithets new to me: *village bicycle, second-hand dartboard, lavatory door in a gale*' (Walker, 1982, writing of the late 1940s). Cf. the full derogatory phrase, 'She's had more pricks than a second-hand dartboard'.

second horse. See **hot seat**.

second looie. A second lieutenant: Army: WW2, perhaps earlier.

seconds, the. Esp. in *a touch of the seconds*, defined by Powis as 'Fear of consequences, second thoughts': police and c.: since mid-C.20. Blake, 1954; Hunter, 1964, has 'get the seconds'.

secret Harry. 'Wardroom jocular for the secretary who knows all the secrets, and, tantalisingly, divulges none' (Granville): RN: mid-C.20.

secret squirrel. 'Intelligence operative' (Hawke, 1979): Services' in N. Ireland: since ca. 1970. Ex a US TV cartoon character, 'In 1965, Hanna-Barbera created the descriptively-named Secret Squirrel, a somewhat nutty supersleuth who spent one season fighting spies and urban criminals' (Brasch, 1983).

see. To bet (a person); call his bluff: cotton-factors':—1909 (Ware). Ex the v. *see* in the game of *poker*.

see-ers-off-ers. 'R.N. drinking gradations, when drink is shared: allowed to drink the whole of (the rest of) a tot' (L.A., 1967): RN.

see further through a brick wall than most, (he/she) **can.** Phrase applied to a shrewd, percipient person: since mid-C.20, ?earlier.

see (one) home. To reprimand, to 'tell off' someone: coll.: earlier C.20. (Raymond, 1930.) Cf. **see off**, 1.

see it coming a mile off. As 'you could see . . . ' or 'we saw it . . . ', intensification of 'see it coming', of an event of any sort, good or bad; esp. in the 'I told you so!' mood: coll.: C.20, ?earlier. (P.B.)

see off. To 'tell off', reprimand, scold severely, from ca. 1912. (Raymond, 1930.) Granville adds 'Much used in the Navy'. Cf. **see home**. Prob. ex 'see off the premises'.—2. To defeat (in, e.g., a boat race): RN. (Granville.) Current among Cambridge undergraduates at least as early as 1930, as in 'I had an affair with a Buick near Reading, but as he can't corner, I saw him off through that esses bend' (passed him in his despite).––3. Hence, to outwit: RN: since ca. 1920.—4. To attend to (a task, an emergency) effectually: since ca. 1940. Cf. **see-ers-off-ers**.

see (somebody) over the side. To accompany someone to the door in saying *au revoir*: Can.: since ca. 1945. Ex the Navy. (Leechman.)

see red. To be in, fly into, a rage: coll. Ex a bull's reaction to red.

see the shine by moonlight. To take a night walk with a female companion: Aus.: since ca. 1925. (Baker.) The shine on the water of sea or river or billabong. (More poetic than most Aus. s.)

see (a newspaper) **to bed.** To set the presses in motion for the print of an edition: journalistic.

see you next Tuesday. An 'explanation' of the letters *c.u.n.t.*: Services': WW2. (Bishop, 1978.)

seeds. Hempseeds used as a drug: drugs world: since ca. 1960. Bournemouth *Evening Echo*, 21 Jan. 1971 (Petch).

seggy or **secies.** Seconal: drugs c. (Stockley, 1986.) US since late 1960s (Spears).

segs on the dooks. Work-callused hard skin, or callosities, on the hands: Services', esp. Army: since ca. 1939. H. & P., 'Very popular amongst transport drivers.' See **dukes**; *seg* or *segg* is N. Country dial., ?ex Fr. *sec*, dry.

sei-cordi box. A guitar: Parlyaree: since ca. 1945. Lit., a *six-strings* box: a guitar usu. has six strings. Like most Parlyaree terms, it comes from Italian.

sell-out, n. A contest for which all the seats are sold: sporting coll.: from ca. 1930. *Daily Mail*, 1 Dec. 1934, 'The interest in McAvoy's fight with Kid Tunero . . . is so great that . . . the match is a sure sell-out.' P.B.: soon applied also to all the other sorts of entertainment. Prob. a back-formation ex S.E. *sold out*.—2. Noun for action at synon. v. **cop out**, q.v.

sell out, v.i. To vomit: Aus. B., 1942.—2. To betray a cause, one's country, etc.: coll.: adopted, ca. 1945, ex US. Ex selling out one's business to a competitor, esp. if unexpectedly or after loud assurances to the contrary. 'Why not simply S.E. *sell*, with *out* as an intensifier implying "totally"?' (R.C., 1976). Well, at least as likely.

sell the dump to a mate. Among Aus. Rugby League players, 'to pass the ball to a team mate in order to avoid being tackled oneself; [hence] generally, to pass the trouble to someone else' (Buzo, 1973): since latish 1940s. The phrase occurs also in *Norm and Ahmed*, prod. 1968.

sell the pass. To give away an advantage to one's opponent(s): coll. Ex Rugby Football; cf. prec.

seller; sellinger. A selling race (one in which the winner must be auctioned): sporting coll.: from ca. 1921. *OED* Sup.

selling calico. To have one's shirt-tail hanging out or showing through the seat of one's pants: Midlands proletarian: later C.19–earlier 20. Roberts, 1976.

semi. A semi-detached house: suburban coll.: since ca. 1930. (Ferguson, 1939; Symons, 1958.) Also Aus., orig., as prob. in Brit., an estate-agents' term: B., 1953.—2. A semi-final: sporting, esp. Aus.: since ca. 1930; by 1965, coll. (B.P.)

send. To afford much pleasure to, as in 'His music doesn't send me': Can. (?ex US): since ca. 1935. Perhaps elliptical for 'send' into ecstasies'. (Leechman.) Also, to excite. Both nuances were, ca. 1960, adopted by Brit. s., esp. among jazz-lovers.

send down. (Usu. in passive.) To expel from university: orig. s.,—1891; by later C.20, informal S.E. Marples.—2. To send to gaol; Powis, 1977, 'Sent down. Imprisoned': low coll.: later C.20. Cf. sense 1.

send-up, n. A satire, burlesque, parody: coll.: since late 1950s. (*Guardian*, 17 Dec. 1964.) Ex v.

send up, v. (Gen. in passive.) *En masse* to scoff at and mock: upper- and middle-class coll.:—1931. Lyell, '*He was sent up* unmercifully by half the room.' Ex the Public School j., to send (a boy) to the headmaster for punishment.—2. Hence (and gen. in active), to make fun of by burlesque, to parody: since ca. 1955. Rattigan, 1958, Ron says: 'So you're very fond of me. So why are you always needling me, sending me up, taking the mickey out of me?' Often, since ca. 1970, intensified to *send up rotten*, as 'They sent him up something rotten.'

Senior. The senior Engineer Lieutenant of the engine-room: RN officers' coll. P-G-R.—2. As *the Senior*, the United Service Club in London: Service officers'. Bowen.

senior scribe, the. The NCO in charge of the Orderly Room: RAF (mostly officers'): since ca. 1930. (Jackson.) Humorous. Cf. **owner's scribe.** Ex RN usage (Granville).

sentimental. 'A man in an Australian pub will offer a *sentimental*, meaning a smoke or cigarette, though the verses of *A Sentimental Bloke* are probably now not much read' (Burgess, 1970): r.s.: ?ca. 1920–75.

separates. The period (often three months) served in a local prison by one condemned to penal servitude before he begins that servitude: c.:—1932 ('Stuart Wood').

September morn. An erection: r.s., on **horn**: later C.20. (Daniells, 1980.) Cf. synon. **hail smiling morn** and *Colleen Bawn*.

septic, n. An American: Aus. r.s., *septic tank* = *Yank*. Wilkes quotes *Cleo*, Aug. 1976: 'Even before R[est] and R[ecuper-ation], leave from the Vietnam War], Americans [in Sydney] were septics . . . Septic is now general usage.' Cf. **Sherman Tanks.**

septic, adj. Sceptic: joc. (The author first heard it in 1912.)—2. Unpleasant; objectionable: from ca. 1930. (Vachell, 1934.) Suggested by **poisonous**, q.v.

serang. See **head serang.**

serf. A fag (at school): Cranbrook School.

serge bruises. 'Marks on the limbs caused by sweat bringing out the dye from a seaman's serge uniform' (Granville): RN.

sergeant. A Commander; Head of Department in a battleship or aircraft carrier: RN wardrooms'. Ex 'the similarity of his three gold stripes to a Marine sergeant's chevron' (Bowen).

sergeant-major('s). Tea; orig., strong tea esp. if good, then tea drunk between meals: military: from ca. 1910. (B. & P.) The SM could get tea almost whenever he desired it. Also, tea laced with rum.

sergeant's (or **sergeants') run.** 'A run ashore given by the Heads of Departments (fellow Commanders—wearers of three stripes) to a departing Commander on the eve of his leaving to take up an appointment elsewhere. If [he is] a popular messmate, members of the sergeants' union give this traditional gin-up at the favourite pub in the port to which the ship is attached' (Granville, 1967). See **sergeant.**

sergeants' union. The Commanders aboard an HM ship: RN: since ca. 1920. See **sergeant**; cf. prec., **Jimmies' Union** and **watchkeepers' union.**

seriously. An almost meaningless intensive, at first applied to wealth, as in 'seriously rich': cf. 'Serious Money', title of play concerned with the workings of the post-Big-Bang 'City' world of finance, by Caryl Churchill, which opened in London in July 1987. Soon used more widely and loosely: e.g., of taking wildlife photographs, ' . . . how to stay very, very seriously still' (BBC *Wildlife* mag., Jan. 1988).

Serpentiners. Those who like(?) to bathe in the Serpentine when it is icy: from ca. 1925.

serpently. (Only in dialogue.) Certainly: joc.: since ca. 1930; ob. by 1970. Sayers, 1933.

Serps, the. The Serpentine: low London. Curtis, 1937.

servants' entrance, send (it) in by the. (Of the male) to coït with (a woman) from the rear: raffish. Hayes, 1972. 'Standing behind her . . . I held her as she was, dragged her drawers off, . . . set her legs apart, sent Sir John in by the servants' entrance.'

servants' united effort. Lemonade: RMA, Woolwich: from ca. 1920. By indelicate allusion to the colour of the fluid. Gen. abbr. to *s.u.e.* RMA Woolwich was amalgamated with RMA Sandhurst in 1946.

serve. A service in lawn tennis: coll. Ex the v.—2. (?)Hence, unjust or painful treatment; adverse criticism; an unfair reprimand: Aus. c. > coll.: later C.20. Wilkes; see also AUS-TRALIAN UNDERWORLD, in Appx. Poss., as Wilkes suggests, from the serving of a summons.

serve (someone) glad! Serve (e.g. him) right!: from ca. 1910. Sayers, 1926, ' "Serve him glad," said Lord Peter viciously.' Ex North Country dial.:—1891 (*EDD*).

serve-out. An issue (of, e.g. clothes): RN coll. Cf. *fit to bust a double ration serve-out of navy-serge*.

served with his papers. 'Being dealt with as an habitual criminal' (Sharpe, 1938): police.

service-stripes. 'Broad diamond bracelets, as collected by experienced cocottes' (*Listener*, 10 Mar. 1937): Services', hence Society: from ca. 1918. An allusion to 'long service and good conduct' badges.

sesame. A password: since ca. 1930. Ex the *open sesame!* of the Arabian tale.

sesh. Session, as in 'A "rug-cutting" sesh at the local dance-hall' (private letter, 1947): coll. Esp., in Brit. Eng., short for **session**, q.v.

sesquies, the. 'The 150th anniversary celebrations of Sydney and Parramatta . . . in 1938' (B., 1942).

session. 'A period of steady drinking in a group' (Wilkes): Aus. and Brit. drinkers' coll.: since mid-C.20. A specialisation of the orig. coll., by 1980 informal S.E. *session*, 'A period of time spent in any one activity (Chambers' *C.20th Dict.*), e.g., a session with one's dentist, girl-friend, etc. (P.B.)

set, n. An accident: taxicab-drivers': from ca. 1925. Hence car-dealers' phrase, of a car that has suffered (considerable) crash damage, 'it's been in a set', as in *Woman's Own*, 28 Feb. 1968. Cf. **set-out**, and *set-to*, a fight.—2. Full beard and moustache: RN. (Granville.) Occ., tautologically, *a full set*.—3. See **modified**.

set, adj.; gen. **all set.** Ready and willing; thoroughly prepared: coll.: perhaps orig. mostly Aus. Prob. ex S.E. sense, carefully arranged in advance.

set back. To cost (a person) so much: adopted, ex US, ca. 1932: coll. (*OED* Sup.) 'That set him back a tidy penny, I'll lay' (P.B.).

set-down. A sit-down meal: tramps' c.:—1932 (Jennings).

set of metal jugs. See **have kittens**.

set-out. A to-do or fuss: (low) coll.: late C.19–20. Sayers, 1933, 'Coo! that was a set-out, that was.'

set the swede down. To have a (short) sleep: military: from ca. 1910. (F. & G.) Ex the resemblance of a large Swede turnip to a man's head. Cf. older *couch a hogshead*, and the rather more urgent synon. **crash the swede**.

set-up, n. 'A place setting at the dining table: knife, fork, spoon, plates, etc. "How many set-ups for the Smith banquet?" "Oh, let's say a hundred and twenty." ' (Leechman.) Can. restaurateurs' and caterers' coll.: since ca. 1950.—2. 'A girl whom [a male] has readied and made an assignation with' (L.A.): raffish: since mid-C.20.—3. An arrangement; an organisation or establishment, as 'What sort of a set-up have the Yanks got over there, anyway?': coll., perhaps orig. Services', from mid-C.20; by 1980, verging on informal S.E. Cf. the v. (P.B.)

set up, v. To arrange: coll.: since ca. 1930; by 1970s, informal S.E.

set up (one's) **stall.** To settle down on an easy wicket and make a big score: since ca. 1930. 'The ball came off the turf and unhurried . . . It was par excellence the sort of pitch on which, in the cricketer's phrase, a batsman can "set up his stall" ' (Swanton, 1946).

settle-us powders. Seidlitz powders: (mostly) Aus.; partly joc. and partly folk-etymological. (B.P.)

settlement. A cemetery: Aus.: late C.19–20. B., 1942.

seven and six – was she worth it? See TOMBOLA, in Appx.

seven-bell dinner. 'Special meal served to men at seven bells in the forenoon watch (11.30 am) who are going on watch at mid-day' (Granville): RN.

seven-bell (tea). Wardroom tea at 3.30 p.m.: RN officers' coll.: since ca. 1910. Granville.

seven-beller. A 'watch-keeper's meal hours' (Knock); s. version of *seven-bell dinner*: RN lowerdeck.—2. A cup of tea: RN: since ca. 1920. H. & P.

Seven Dials. Haemorrhoids: r.s., on *piles*: later C.20. (Daniells, 1980.) Cf. **Farmer Giles**.

seven(-)pennorth; sevenpence. (Also *seven-pennyworth*.) Seven days' confinement to barracks: Army: earlier C.20. F. & G.—2. *Seven-pennorth*. A rest-day when one should be

working: London busmen's: since ca. 1930.—3. In *seven-pence over the wall*, seven days' confinement to camp: RAF: since ca. 1925. (Jackson.) Cf. sense 1 and see **over the wall**; the abbr. 7*d* for 'seven days', has been apprehended as 'seven pence'—and vice versa.

seventy-two. A 72-hours' pass or leave: Services' coll.: since ca. 1914.

severe. A severe reprimand: Army (esp. NCOs') coll. (Kersh, 1941.) P.B.: by mid-C.20, usu. as:-

severe dig or **prod.** A formal reprimand from a senior (officer): military coll.: from 1915. B. & P.—2. (Also *severe rep*.) A severe reprimand, in the military legal sense: Army coll.: since mid-C.20, at latest, by which time *prod* had > rare. (P.B.) Cf. **severe**.

sew-sew boy. A sailor undertaking to sew for his mates: RN. (Granville.) Prob. ex old China Stations' pidgin (P.B.).

sewer press, the. The gutter press (newspapers careless of morals, negligent of truth, but very, very wide-awake to profit): coll.: since ca. 1943.

sewer-rats. 'L.T.E. motormen' (*Railway*, 2nd): London Transport employees': since ca. 1945(?).

sewing machines. Main engines: MN, (?)esp. Townsend Thoresen Ferries': later C.20. (Malin, 1979.) Cf. synon. **legs**, and Granville's, 'she runs like a sewing machine. Said of an engine that runs well and true.'

sewn up. (Occ. *sewed-up*.) In the game of pool, (to have been) put into such a ball-position that it is difficult to play: Can.: since ca. 1925. (Leechman.) A specialisation of earlier s. sense, since mid-C.19, nonplussed, brought to a standstill, as is its Brit. application to almost any game in which the winning side has an overwhelming and unbeatable advantage (P.B.).—2. A var. of **buttoned up**, 1, q.v.: Services': since ca. 1936. (H. & P.) By 1946, quite common, esp. in 'Everything's sewn up' or organized, arranged, settled. Cf. **stitch up**.

sex. Sexual gratification: coll.: since mid-1940s; since ca. 1950, *have sex*, to copulate, has been common and, by 1975, is well on the way to S.E. B.P. told me, 1969, that 'Sydney [Aus.] prostitutes use the term "sex" to distinguish between sexual intercourse and other available services.'—2. The external sexual organs (usu., but not always, female): literary coll.: since ca. 1950. 'She tried to cover her naked sex with an inadequate hand' (any piece of 'classier porn', *passim*). (P.B.)

sex-appeal bombing. Air-raid(s) directed against hospitals, schools and, in short, against civilians: RAF: 1930+. (Jackson.) Ironic.

sex-appeal Pete. A semi-*a*rmour-*p*iercing shell: RN: WW2. (P-G-R.) In the 1930s–40s, the initials *S.A.* would almost inevitably be taken as = *sex appeal*.

sex-bomb. Journalistic label for any obviously sexually very attractive girl: late C.20. Cf.:-

sex-kitten. A (young) girl addicted to making the most of her sexual attractions in order to gain masculine admiration and attention: coll.: since late 1950s. It used, ca. 1960, to be very freely applied to Brigitte Bardot and, since ca. 1965, to her imitators.

sex on. See **pash on**.

sex-pot, sexpot. A very desirable female: adopted, ca. 1960, ex US. Cf. **sex-bomb**. R.C. adds, 1976, 'Not merely desirable, but (apparently) willing.'

sex(-)up. To render a manuscript (more) sexually exciting: authors' and publishers': since ca. 1945.

sexiness. Attractiveness, as in 'Political sexiness and excitement' (Pearce, 1982). Cf. **sexy**, adj.

sexing-piece. Penis: since ca. 1925. Cf. S.E. *fowling-piece*.

Sexton Blake. The provost sergeant: Army: early C.20. (F. & G.) Ex the popular fictional detective.—2. Cake: r.s.: late C.19–20. Franklyn, 'S.B. was Sherlock Holmes debased to "Penny-blood" level'.—3. A 'take', in the cinematic sense: r.s.: since mid-C.20. Haden-Guest, 1972.—4. A fake antique, work of art, etc.: r.s.: later C.20. (Raab, 1986.) Like sense 2 and 3, usu. shortened to *Sexton*.

S

sexy, -ie, n. A sexual offender, esp. against children: police coll.: from ca. 1910.—2. A Korean girl generous in her favours: United Nations troops in Korea: ca. 1952–5.

sexy, adj. Agreeably efficient; simple and neat and efficient: Aus., esp. Sydney: since the late 1950s. 'Have you seen the automatic choke in that car?'—'Yes, rather sexy, what!' (B.P.) P.B.: in Brit., also, 1960s–80s, an almost meaningless s. term of approbation, of limitless application; often used ironically. E.g., '[Journalists] believe that McKay [a public relations man] delivers the sexiest stories [about British Leyland] through selected newspapers and carefully-chosen journals' (Dunn, 1981).—3. As in 'the only reason for many companies being involved is "sheer fashion", or, in the popular marketing phrase of the moment, sponsorship is "sexy" ' (*Time Out*, 30 May 1980).

sh-. See note concerning Yiddish and allied terms beginning *sch-* and *sh-*, at **sch-**.

shack. A tramp; any vagrant: market-traders'. *M.T.*

shack off. To abuse; to reprimand: Oundle: since mid-1920s. (Marples.) Origin?

shack up. To live together although unmarried: Can.: adopted, ca. 1945, ex US. By ca. 1955, also Brit., esp. Londoners'. Also as in 'They've been shacked up for some months' (McShane, 1960). Perhaps ex 'to live together in a *shack*'.—2. Hence, loosely, *shack up with* (someone), to marry: since ca. 1960. (Barlow, 1971.) By early 1960s, both senses common also in Aus.

shackie. A white girl living with a coloured man: low London: since ca. 1950. Cf. prec.

shackle, n. and v. A, to, 'rag': Dalton Hall, Manchester: since ca. 1935. *Daltonian*, Dec. 1946.

shackle-up. A meal of stew or broth: vagrants' and tramps' c. (*Gilt Kid*, 1936.) Hence also to cook such a meal, esp. by the roadside. Cf.:-

shackles. Remnants and scrapings of meat in a butcher's shop: lower classes':—1923 (Manchon). Prob. ex *shackle*, abbr. *shackle-bone*, a knuckle-bone.—2. Stew; meat-soup: military: earlier C.20. (F. & G.) It bears, among trawlermen, the nuance 'meat, potatoes, carrots, etc., cooked in a pot' (Mitford, 1969).

shade. To be superior to or better than: Aus. coll. Semantics: 'to overshadow'. Niland, 1958. 'Her figure's no better than mine; in fact, I'd shade her a bit, I'd say.'

shade off white, a. 'A black man' (H.W., 1942): RAF: WW2.

shaded. Reduced in price: commercial and trade: since ca. 1920.

shades. Dark glasses: (?orig. c. >) rather low coll.: since 1930s, 'when dark-tinted spectacles began to be worn in place of the old-fashioned eyeshade which was like a green celluloid cappeak worn with an elastic band round the head; instead of a shade one wore a pair of shades' (Barltrop, 1981).

shadows – the singular is rare. Members of the Opposition's 'Shadow Cabinet': political and journalistic coll.: since ca. 1964. P.B.: ephemeral; perhaps influenced by a 'pop-group' in high esteem early 1960s, Cliff Richard and the Shadows.

shaft, n. An act of intercourse; a woman regarded as sex-object, 'She'd be a great shaft': low: later C20. Ex:-

shaft, v. To copulate with (a girl): low: since late 1940s. Perhaps prompted by **pole**, v., 3. Hence (cf. **fuck**), in exclam., e.g. 'Cor, shaft me!' (*Heart*, 1962).

shaftable. (Of a woman) bedworthy: low: since ca. 1950. Ex **shaft**, v.

shafti, -y. See **shufty**.

shag, n. In *it's a bit of a shag*, it's a bore, a nuisance: certain Public Schools'.—2. As *Shag*, a friendly vocative = mate, old chap: Public Schools': mid-C.20. (P.B.)—3. Someone 'rough and ready (he's a real shag)' (Wilson, 1980): RAF: late 1970s. Perhaps ex S.E. *shaggy*, hairy.

shag, adj. Exhausted, esp. after games: Marlborough College. See **shagged**.

shag-bag. A hammock: midshipmen's: latish C.19–early 20. (Parsons.) Prob. ex later C.19 public schools' s. *shag*, to mas-

turbate.—2. A whore: mostly Army: since ca. 1930. (Johnson, 1973.) Cf. late C.18–20 s. *shag*, to copulate, and *bag*, derog. for a woman.—3. An extension of **shag**, n., 2. (P.B.)—4. In pl., *shag-bags*, a dirty pair of flannel trousers: Cranbrook School: earlier C.20.

Shag-bat. See **Shagbat**.

shag labourer. A labourer (or almost) member of the beatnik clan: beatniks': ca. 1960. Anderson, 'Partial to a particularly powerful blend of shag' (tobacco).

shag like a rattlesnake. (Esp. *she shags . . .*, or, more likely, *I'll bet she . . .* '). The later C.20 low Brit. version of **fuck like . . .**, q.v. (P.B.)

shag (one's) lugs off. (Of a male) to coït vigorously and enthusiastically: RN.

shag-nasty. A name for an unpopular man, often *old s.-n.* Cf., e.g., *horror-bollocks* and *fuck-knuckle*.

shag-spots. Adolescent pimples: Tonbridge School, and prob. elsewhere: mid-C.20. Also *toss-spots*, both in allusion to later C.19 *shag*, v., to masturbate, thought to be the cause of the affliction. Occ. used as a vocative; cf. **shag**, n., 2. (P.B.) Cf. **shags-pot**.

Shagbat. Nickname for the Vickers *Walrus*, a pusher biplane reconnaissance flying boat of cumbersome appearance: RN and RAF Coastal Command: WW2. (H. & P.) Partridge, 1945, 'A bat flies; walrus whiskers are shaggy', to which R.S. adds that in WW1 there existed a Sopwith flying-boat nicknamed a *bat boat*, 'which affords the precedent for the Services' use of the bat component' or element.

shagged. Weary, exhausted: Public Schools', thence Services', WW2 and since; since ca. 1946, in gen. use. Cf. **shag**, adj. Intensified as *shagged (right) out*, and thus in use among London club cyclists ca. 1930 (*Fellowship*, 1984). Cf. also:-

shagged to a thin whisker. An intensification of prec., but referring specifically to exhaustion through sexual excess: Services' and raffish: mid-C.20. (P.B.)

shagger. A 'dud' boy: Public Schools'. Prob. ref. to masturbation.

shaggin' wag(g)on. A station wagon, a panel van, curtain-fitted and double-mattressed: Aus.: since ca. 1965. Also *sin bin*. (B.P., 1977.) Cf. *passion-wag(g)on*, and see **shag-bag**, 2.

shags-pot. A term of abuse for a man, but esp. for a fellow schoolboy: Clifton College: earlier C.20. I.e. a 'pot' (chap) that 'shags'. P.B.: but see also **shag-spots**.

Shaiba blues, the. Homesickness among airmen overseas, orig. at the RAF Station, Shaibah, on the Shatt-el-Arab in the Persian Gulf: RAF: since ca. 1925. Jackson, 1945.

shake, n. A throw of the dice to decide who is to pay for drinks: Aus. coll. B., 1942.—2. A party: beatniks': since ca. 1958. (Anderson.) Prob. rather an informal type of freestyle dance popular at the time (Hibbert, 1983).—3. As *the shake*, pick-pocketing: c.

shake, v. To stir up (the sluggards): Services', esp. RN, coll.: since ca. 1920. P-G-R.

shake(-)book. A notebook that, kept by the quartermaster of the watch, contains the names of the men to be roused during the night: RN. Granville.

shake-down or **shakedown,** n. and v. Blackmailing of bookmakers: c. In Aus., violent threats; a 'rough house' (B., 1942, as *the shakedown*). Prob ex US: *SOD*, 1977; W. & F. have 'blackmail, exaction under duress'.—2. As v.i., to get used to a job or a condition: coll.: late C.19–20. ('Taffrail', 1916.) Cf. S.E. *shake-down*, a rough bed, and nautical j. *shakedown cruise*, a fresh crew getting used to a new ship.

shake it rough, often as ppl adj. or vbl n., *shaking it rough*. To do one's prison sentence the hard way, instead of 'riding it smooth': Can.: since late 1940s. Leechman cites A. Schroeder, *Shaking It Rough*, 1976.

Shake, Rattle and Roll. The three tanks landed at Port Said in the campaign against Egypt in late 1956. Ex the title and chorus of a contemporaneous popular song. (P.B.) Cf. **Pip, Squeak and Wilfred**, 2.

shake-up. Strenuous 'gym' for a large class: Royal Naval College, Dartmouth. Granville.

Shakers, the. See ASSOCIATION FOOTBALL, in Appx.

shaking the tree, n. and ppl, either gen., or *shaking* (someone's) *tree*, particular. 'Lighting a fire on his doorstep', i.e. putting very severe moral pressure on someone: later C.20. Le Carré, 1977.

shaky. Tinned milk: MN: later C.20. (Malin, 1979.)

shaky do. A mismanaged affair, e.g. a bungled raid, work badly done, something that has—or very nearly has—serious consequences; also:—2, a risky, haphazard raid necessitated by general policy.—3, a dangerous raid, esp. a very dangerous one: RAF: the first (H. & P.,), since ca. 1935; the second, since late 1939 (Brickhill, 1946); the third, since late 1940, as in Aldridge, 1942, and in Hinde, 1945.—4. Hence, an arrangement or agreement or contract that, apparently fair, is, in the fact, one-sided: since ca. 1945. P.B.: often in pl., as in a protesting 'I say—shaky do's, old boy!' = play fair! Ob. by ca. 1960.

Shaky Isles, the. New Zealand: Aus. coll. (B., 1943.) Ex numerous earthquakes, esp. in the North Island.

shaky tot. Synon. with **deep-sea tot**, P-G-R.

shale shifter. Motorcycle speedway rider: motorcyclists': later C.20. (Dunford.)

shalloming. Doing something one wishes or likes to do: Army: since ca. 1925. Ex emphatic *shall*? 'Can Hebrew "shalom" (peace) be involved?' Dr Leechman pertinently asks. Well, it does seem possible. P.B.: from Service in Palestine? † by 1950.

shallow-water sailor. Applied occ. to someone walking with legs wide apart so that he almost appears to be drunk, but mostly as 'a term of contempt used by old seamen for men having made only one or two trips to sea [who] are trying to impress others' (Slater): heard in 1963, it goes back to the 1920s—if not a generation earlier.

Sham Berlin. The Rt Hon. Neville Chamberlain: lower and lower-middle classes': 22 Sep. 1938–3 Aug. 1939. Ex his propitiatory visits to Hitler (but he was buying time in which to produce weapons in Britain: P.B.). R.C., 1976, recalls the relevant 'Fr. expression, *M[onsieur] J'aime Berlin* [I love Berlin]'. Included as an example of punning Hobson-Jobson.

shambles. Uproar; confusion; 'mess': Services' (mostly officers'): 1939+; by 1945, also civilian. Brickhill, 1946, 'While the new camp was in the shambles of moving in and settling down' and 'Everything was in a shambles'. Ex the definition of *shambles* as, e.g., 'bloody confusion'. Hence, as in 'close up from the "loose shambles" formation [the aircraft] have been maintaining so far into a tight, professional-looking box' (*Phantom*): RAF: 1970s.

shambling. Ragging the authorities: Royal Naval College, Dartmouth: since ca. 1930. (Granville.) Creating a 'shambles'.

shambolic. 'In a shambles'; chaotic; in a mess, of place, person, equipment, etc.: Services', esp. in National Service training: since mid-WW2 (an early example in *Punch*, 15 Dec. 1943); ob. by 1980. Fancifully ex **shambles**, q.v., perhaps blended with *diabolic*. (P.B.)

shame. In *the last shame*, imprisonment; prison: euph. coll.:— 1923 (Manchon).

shamez. 'Synagogue official used as a slang word for policeman' (Yiddish)' (Powis): c.: later C.20. Cf. **shamus**.

shamfered. 'Damaged. A ship suffering damage in action was said to have been "shamfered" ' (Bassett): RN: WW2. P.B.: ex S.E. *chamfer*, to bevel; cf. similar understatement of later C.20 synon. **bent**.

shaming. Shameful; 'shy-making': Society: ca. 1929–34. E. Waugh, 1930, 'How too shaming.'

shampoo attitude or **crouch, the.** The Nonconformist practice of sitting with head bowed to pray, instead of kneeling: church circles'. (Rev. W. Green; D. Beale, 1980.) Also known as *the Free Church crouch*.

shamrock tea. Weak tea—only three leaves in it: tramps' c. *Toby*, 1979.

shamus. A private detective: adopted, ca. 1944, from US service-men. (Cf. **private eye**.) Franklyn suggests that the word may represent *the shamos*, the sexton or caretaker of a synagogue. Hence, anyone who takes care of somebody else's problems for a fee. 'Assuming this was originally c., as seems likely, it would be consistent with the incorporation of other Yiddish terms into c. (e.g., "gun-moll" from "goniff-moll")' (R.C., 1966). Cf. **shamez**.

shandy man. Electrician: circus: since ca. 1910. (Seago, 1934.) He causes things to sparkle. See also **shanty-man**: ?misprint or var., and which of which.

Shanghai'd (or **shanghaied**). Tossed from a horse: Aus. (B., 1942.) Ex Aus. *shanghai*, to shoot with a catapult.

Shanghailander. An inhabitant of the International Concession territory in Shanghai: China coast coll.: earlier C.20. Farmer, 1945.

shangie. A catapult: Aus., esp. juvenile: since ca. 1930. (B., 1953.) Ex *shanghai*.

shanker bosun. Chief sick-berth attendant: RN: 1940s. (Peppitt.) Strictly, *chancre bosun*. Cf., e.g., **custard bosun**, for joc. use of *bosun*. (P.B.)

shanky. 'Thrifty; close-fisted': Army: earlier C.20. (F. & G.) Perhaps ex one who walks when the ordinary person would ride or go by bus or train: cf. older *Shanks' pony*.

shant, n. A quart or a pot; a pot of liquor: mid-C.19–20: c. and low s. Mayhew, 1851; Emerson, 1893.—2. Hence, a particular (alcoholic) beverage, 'Thought you'd go for top-end shants—cocktails or sherry' (Gloag, 1962). Cf. **shanting**.

shant, v. To defecate: Felsted School. Ex Essex dial.

shanting. The drinking of alcoholic liquor: low London: since ca. 1910. Gloag, 1962; cf. **shant**, n., 2.

shanty-man. An electrician: circus-men's:—1932 (Seago). But see **shandy man**.

shape. To shape up to, to (offer to) fight someone: Aus. Baker.—2. To behave well: coll., esp. Lancashire: ca. 1870–1940. (Roberts, 1976.) Elliptical for *shape up well*.

shapes. 'The meat ingredient of a meal, especially breakfast: usually the same but in a different shape: rolled for sausages, in a ball for faggots, or round and flat for rissoles': Army: early C.20. (B. & P.) Cf. use of *shape* for a moulded blanc-mange. C.20. B. & P.

share. A female easily accessible, esp. in 'a bit of share' (copulation): low: since the 1920s. Shared out?

share-bys; timesing. Sums involving division; ditto multiplication: primary schools'. (D. Beale, 1975.) I.e. 'What is A's *share* of . . . if . . . ' and 'seven *times* seven'.

share-certificate. A pimp's prostitute: white-slavers' c.: from ca. 1910. Londres.

shark, n. A professional punter: bookmakers':—1932 (*Slang*).—2. A ticket inspector: railwaymen's. *Railway*, 2nd.

shark, v. To steal, 'borrow without asking': RN wardroom: early C.20. ' "Who's sharked my chair? Suggested, Mr President, that the mess committee take steps to prevent people's chairs being stolen in their absence."—"Oh! Go to Jerusalem!" ' (*Musings*). Cf. synon. **vulture**.

shark-bait. 'Pickets supplied by a military unit to a town' (Baker): Aus. Army: 1939+. Ex:—2. Var., in Prichard, 1937, of:-

shark-baiter. A too venturesome swimmer: Aus. coll.: since early C.20.

Shark Parade. Bedford Row (many solicitors' offices): taxi-drivers': since ca. 1920. Cf. **Thieves' Kitchen**, 2.

sharkerie, better **-y.** Financial sharp-dealing or shameless exploitation of others: Aus. coll.: since ca. 1925. B., 1942.

sharp. Rather too smartly dressed: Can.: since ca. 1940. A *sharp set of drapes* = a too smart suit. Hence, by ca. 1944 (?ex US servicemen), English.

sharp as a box of monkeys. See **straight off the turnips**.

S

sharp as a tennis ball. Intellectually very dull indeed: joc.: later C.20. (Gell, 1984.) Cf. later C.19 synon. *sharp as the corner of a round table*; both by opp. to S.E. *sharp as a needle*, etc.

sharp end, the. The bows of the ship: RN joc. upon landlubbers' ignorance. (Granville.) Cf. **blunt end.**—2. Hence, *at the sharp—the blunt—end*, well forward (at the front), well behind the lines: Army: 1940–5. (P-G-R.) Also as *up the sharp end*; still very common in Army usage, 1974 (P.B.).—3. *At the sharp end* has, late 1970s, found its way into 'civvy street': the *Guardian*, Jan. 1979, reported the General Secretary of the Society of Civil and Public Servants as saying that secret decision-making in Whitehall on spending was done by 'people who could not know the effect [it] would have on those "at the sharp end" ', i.e. the ordinary workers. Adam Thompson, chairman of British Caledonian Airways: 'I've been in at the sharp end of things and I know that in the end cheaper fares will come to Europe' (*Sunday Telegraph* mag., 30 Nov. 1980).

sharpen (one's) skates. Euph. for urination, as in 'I'm going to sharpen my skates': W. Can., esp. the Prairie States: 'poss. early C.20, when couples would be out skating together' (Leech, 1985).

sharpies. That band, or gang, of rivals to the bodgies which lasted only about a year: Aus., esp. Melbourne, teenagers': since mid-1950s. 'I guess you could say they were square-bodgies' (Dick). Ex their 'sharp' bodgie clothes. An Aus. version of the later Brit. *bovver boys* and *punks*.

sharpish. Almost always in understatement, by implication giving the *-ish* suffix the force of 'very' (as opp. the S.E. adj., where it = somewhat, fairly): coll. In, e.g., 'They started shooting, so we moved out a bit sharpish', or 'Sarnt-major wants you. Better get over there pretty sharpish.' (P.B.)

Sharps, the. 'The 3rd County of London Yeomanry (Sharp-shooters) were usually referred to by other London Yeomen as "The Sharps" . . . [the] unit dated from 1901 . . . [merged with the Kent Yeomanry] in 1961 . . . to become the Kent and County of London Yeomanry' (Gaylor). Also in Hatton, 1930. Cf. **Roughs.**

sharpshooter (activity: **sharpshooting**). 'A person who mingles with a crowd round a bookmaker's stand, holds out his hand, and demands a ticket for a non-existent bet' (B., 1953): Aus. sporting: since ca. 1930.

sharry. A charabanc: low coll.: 1924 (*OED* Sup.). Imm. ex *chara*.

shat, v. Joc. irreg. formation for a past tense for *shit*, as in 'The poor old Jaunty nearly shat hi'self' (*Heart*, 1962); 'he shat blue lights' = he was extremely scared; 'Who's shat?' = who has farted?: low coll.: since ca. 1920. (L.A.; P.B.) But in, e.g., *I won't be shat upon!*, I won't be squashed, it is prob. a punning blend of *sat* + *shit*.

shat or **shat-off**, adj. Very angry; very much annoyed: low Aus. since ca. 1945. (B.P.) Cf. prec., in such phrases as 'he shat himself with rage' (P.B.).

shat on from a great height. Reprimanded by someone of much higher rank: Services', esp. Can.: WW2. P.B.: since then very widespread in Service use, particularly in remarks like 'he deserves to be shat upon from a great height'.

shatter. Esp. in *out on a s.*, engaged in making a heavy raid: RAF Bomber Command: WW2. *John Bull*, 17 Apr. 1943.

shattered; shattering. Nervy, nervous; tiresome, upsetting, boring, unpleasant: Society: from ca. 1925. Christie, 1930, 'I feel shattered' and 'Life's very shattering, don't you think?'; E. Waugh, 1928, 'My dear, how too shattering for you.'—2. Utterly exhausted, physically or mentally or both, as 'Doing his finals *and* running the 1500 metres in the same week? God, he must be shattered!': coll.: since mid-C.20.—3. Completely and helplessly drunk: mostly Services': since ca. 1955. 'Then he took in the slack and went ashore three or four nights on the trot, with subs like, and got absolutely shattered every bastard time' (*Heart*, 1962).

Shaun Spadah. A car: ephemeral r.s.: 1921+. 'Winner of the Grand National [steeplechase] in that year' (Gardner).

shauri, shauria. See SWAHILI, in Appx.

shave off! An exclam. of surprise or amazement: RN: since ca. 1920. Perhaps ex *shave off!*, an order issued to those who, after a probationary period, are refused permission 'to grow' (a beard). P.B.: also of defiance, as in a naval chant I heard ca. 1950, 'I'll go to Trafalgar Square [after my demob.] and I'll say to Nelson: "Shave off, get stuffed, you fuckin' RN bastard! . . . " ' Cf.:-

shave off, v.i.; **shave off at** (someone). To deliver a severe reprimand (to someone): RN since ca. 1920. (Granville, 1962.) Winton, 1959, 'He shaved off at *me* this morning before I'd even had a chance to get a grip on things.'

shawly. A shawl-wearing working-class woman: Anglo-Irish. (Doncaster, 1947.) Cf. the Anglo-Irish *shawl*, a prostitute, as in Joyce, 1922, 'Fornicating with two shawls and a bully on guard.'

she. Penis: Londoners'. Partly euph., partly proleptic. Lawrence 1955 (of 1920s), 'Golly, I didn't half want it, she fair lifted'. The sense occurs also in the card-players' *double-entendre*, 'Up she comes and the colour's red'.—2. Used for *it* in impersonal constructions: Aus. coll., based upon a practice common in the dialects of Ireland, Scotland, the North Country: late C.19–20. Aus. examples, extant in the 1960s: **she'll be** (or **she's**) **apples—jake—right.** It's all right, or All's well. (B.P.)—3. 'Frequently used when referring to a [male] homosexual—"She's an untidy bitch" ' (Tempest, 1950): prisoners'.

she-male. A male with (very) long hair or other of what were once considered to be female external characteristics: since 1920s. Also written solid.

she was only the (someone's) **daughter – but she . . .** did something or other that, in scabrous terms appropriate to the father's profession or trade or office, meant that she sexually complied. Not strictly s., nor yet a c.p.: but a coll. usage, a speech pattern. It goes back to late C.19. (A reminder, 1974, from P.B., who instances, *inter alia*, 'She was only the carpenter's daughter—but she took a foot as a rule.')

sheary. (Of a painted surface) drying out unevenly: builders' and house-painters'. Perhaps cf. Lincolnshire dial. *sheary*, sharp, cutting, (of grass) coarse (*EDD*).

sheba. An attractive girl or woman; esp. as the counterpart of **sheikh** (sense 1): from 1926, and mostly American. Ex the Queen of Sheba, reputedly alluring.

shebo. Navy soap: RN lowerdeck. R.S. suggests a deriv. ex Sp. *jabón*, soap, via Gibraltar.

shed. A hangar: RAF coll.: since ca. 1925. (Jackson.) By humorous depreciation.—2. Chapel: St Bees: since ca. 1910. Marples.—3. A common Aus. conflation of **shit-head**, q.v., itself Aus. as well as NZ [and Brit.: P.B.]: since ca. 1925. (B.P.) Cf. **shouse.**—4. ' "I got right out of my shed", meaning drunk, and "You must be right out of your shed", meaning mad: London teenagers': current. *Shed* prob. comes from football fans' usage' (Simmonds, 1986). 'Fulham [constituency] includes . . . the Hurlingham [polo] Club and Chelsea Football Club—from sunshades to The Shed, so to speak' (Cole, 1986).

shed a tear. To urinate: since mid-C.19. Since ca. 1940, ?earlier, often elab. to *shed a tear for Nelson*: prob. at first RN, but soon spread to the other Services (P.B.).

sheebing. 'Black-market racketeering and profiteering in Germany. From the German *schieben* . . . "to push or shunt", the racketeer gangs making a practice of uncoupling a goods wagon from a train and shunting into a siding' (Petch, 1946): Brit. Army, and civilian officials', in Germany: later 1945+.

Sheeny; occ. sheeney, -ie, or **shen(e)y.** A Jew: 1816 (Lewis): in C.20, always opprobrious (Powis says 'unpleasantly racist'). Llewellyn, 1943, ' "Well, there's sheenies and Sheenies you know . . . " he says . . . "Then there's Yids and Non Skids, to say nothing of the Shonks. Then there's Three Be Twos, and Jews." '—2. Hence, a pawnbroker: mid-C19–20.—3. A

S

dark-coloured tramp: tramps' c.:—1932 (Jennings).—4. A very economical, money-careful man: military: early C.20. (F. & G.) W. risks the guess that *sheeny* may derive ex Yiddish pron. of Ger. *schön*, beautiful, used in praising wares; very tentatively, I suggest that the term arose from the *sheeny*, i.e. glossy or brightly shiny, hair of the average 'English' Jew. P.B.: Rosten, 1968, quotes heavily from this entry, dismisses the suggested derivations, and proposes instead that the term is ex Yiddish 'a miesse meshina ('An ugly fate or death'), a phrase widely used by and among Jews.'

sheep-dodger; sheep-dodging. A sheep hand; 'sheep mustering and droving' (Russell, 1936): Aus. Cf. *poddy-dodger, -ing*, calf-stealer, -ing.

sheep in wolf's clothing. A boy looking like a 'wolf', but so timid as to ask permission to kiss a girl: teenage girls': since ca. 1950.—2. 'A clergyman (not wearing his clericals) who tries to appear a man of the world' (Leechman): since ca. 1930.

Sheep-Shaggers, the. The Black Watch: Scot. military nickname: mid-C.19–20. P.B.: highly offensive, and not used—by the prudent—in the hearing of one member of the Regt, let alone a crowd; even a subdued 'baa!' could be dangerous.—2. The Coldstream Guards. 'For reasons which are mercifully lost in the mists of time, guardsmen of other regiments—men not kindly disposed towards the Coldstream—bestowed upon them the unsavoury soubriquet of "sheep shaggers" ' (Carew).

sheep-wash. Inferior liquor: Aus. and NZ. B., 1941, 1942.

sheepo. A shepherd: Aus. and NZ: Devanney, 1926.—2. As *sheepo!*, it is the call 'for the rousie (rouse about) to fill 'the catching pen' (*Straight Furrow*, 21 Feb. 1968): NZ shearers'.

sheep's back, on the. Dependent upon wool: Aus. coll.: B., 1942, 'Australia's economic existence'.

Sheer Nasty; Sheer Necessity. Sheerness: RN: late C.19–20. Bowen. (Naval men go there only when necessary.) 'Sheerness [Kent] closed down in 1960 after 300 years as a Naval depot' (Granville).

sheet. A £1 note: orig. Cockneys', 1940s (*Muvver*), > since ca. 1950, c. and drugs world. Bournemouth *Echo*, 20 Nov. 1968.—2. In *have a sheet short*, to be mentally deficient: Aus.: since ca. 1910. B., 1942, who adds 'sometimes *short of a sheet of bark*'.

sheet it home to (a person). To prove something against him: coll.:—1923 (Manchon). Perhaps ex entry of person's name on a charge-sheet.

Sheffield handicap. A defecation: prob. r.s., on *crap*.

sheikh; loosely but usu. **sheik,** n. A 'he-man': s.: adopted, ex US, ca. 1922. Edith Maude-Hull, *The Sheikh*, 1919 (UK), 1921 (US), was a best-seller of the period. See last quot'n in entry at **shoot a line.**—2. Hence, a lover, a girl's 'young man': from ca. 1926: mostly US (*OED* Sup.).—3. Hence, any attractive and/or smartly dressed young man: from ca. 1931.

sheik(h), v. Esp. *go sheik(h)ing*, to seek feminine company: Aus.: since ca. 1925. B., 1942.

sheister. See **shicer.**

shelf, n. An informer; esp. one who has himself participated in the crime: Aus. c.:—1926 (Doone).—2. A pawnshop: Aus. c.: since ca. 1930. (Baker.) Cf. *on the shelf*, in pawn: C.19–early 20. *Lex Bal.*; H., 1st ed.—3. As *the shelf*, the dress circle in a cinema: Aus. juvenile: since ca. 1945. B., 1953.

shelf, v. To inform upon: Aus.: since ca. 1920. Kelly, 1955.

shelfer. An informer to the police: Aus. and NZ c.:—1932. (Baker.) A var. of **shelf,** n., 1.—2. (Usu. in pl., as in) 'The "shelfers", those good-sized cod which in the last three days of our work we stretched out in tiers, shelved on beds of ice . . . They are the pride of the trip—for every kit of them we reckon to earn plenty of money' (Piper, 1974): trawlermen's.

she'll be apples!; . . . jake!; . . . right! Quintessentially Aus. and NZ expressions of gen. reassurance and optimism: 2nd

and 3rd, from earlier C.20, and usu. as *she's* . . . ; the 1st, since mid-C.20 (perhaps, as Wilkes suggests, ex r.s., *apples and spice*, 'nice', or from 'apple-pie order'). Sometimes combined as 'She'll be right, mate—she'll be apples!' See **she,** 2. (Wilkes; P.B.)

shell, n. A hearse: lower classes':—1923 (Manchon, '*corbillard des pauvres*').

shell, v. As in 'He shelled it', dropped a catch: cricketers': later C.20. Gardner, 1977.

shell-happy. Suffering from shell-shock: Army: WW2. (P-G-R.) Cf. **bomb-happy.**

shell-like. An ear: curiously poetic; often as '[may I have] a word in your shell-like': since mid-C.20. I first heard it in the Army, ca. 1955; a Qantas advertisement, 3 Aug. 1986, has pl., 'To tune in your shell-likes . . . ' (P.B.)

shell (a person) **out.** To pluck him at cards or dice: low:—1923 (Manchon).

shell-shock. Cocoa: c.: from ca. 1918. Harrison, 1935.—2. Casual-ward tea: tramps': from ca. 1919.—3. A drink of spirits: Aus. low: id. B., 1942.

shelve (one's) **cart.** To defecate: Kentish rural: earlier C.20. To *shelve*, dial., to empty a dung-cart. (Max Beale, 1985.)

Shepheard's Short-Range Group. 'G.H.Q., Cairo; especially when it was moved forward' (P-G-R): Army: 1940–3. Ex Shepheard's hotel; cf. **Groppi's Light Horse.**

sherbet. A taxi: abbr. r.s., *sherbet dab* (a popular sweet) = *cab*. (Watts, 1988.)

sheriff. An occ. Service term for the provost sergeant in a unit: mid-C.20. Ex 'Western' films rather than the old English office. (P.B.)

sherman. An act of masturbation: r.s. on *wank* (one of many: cf. **Barclay's Bank, J. Arthur Rank**): later C.20. (Bell, 1986.) For etym. see:-

Sherman tanks. Americans: r.s., on *Yanks*: since WW2. (Barker, 1979.) Cf. Aus. var. *septic tanks*. A *Sherman* was a US medium tank, WW2.

sherrick, v.t.; **sherrickin(g),** vbl n. To scold severely, or to show up, in public; such a scolding or showing up: low Glasgow coll. MacArthur, 'That strange and wild appeal to crowd justice and crowd sympathy which Glasgow describes as a "sherricking" '. Ex Scottish *sherra-*, *sherry-*, *shirra-* or *shirry-moor*, a tumult or 'tongue-banging' (*EDD*).

Sherwood Forest. 'The two rows of Polaris missile tubes which run along each side of a submarine's interior. They resemble the trunks of trees in a forest glade' (Granville, 1961): RN: since 1960.

shice. Nothing, as *work for shice*: c. or low s.:—1859 (H., 1st ed.). Still very common, 1979, among market traders (*M.T.*). Personified in that trade's *Shice McGregor's about today*, trade is slack.—2. As *the shice*, welshing: c. Sharpe, 1938.

shicer; occ. **schicer.** A worthless person (the predominant, and virtually the only C.20, sense); a very idle one; a mean, sponging man; a humbug: low:—1857 ('Duncange Anglicus'); H., 1st ed. Also *shyster* (H., 1874). In Aus., often uncompromisingly used for 'a crook' (B., 1942); and Powis, 1977, has 'A cheat or "welsher" ', adding var. *sheister*. This latter meaning has been Aus., esp. turf, coll., since ca. 1895 (Morris). Cf. **scheisspot.**

shick, n. A drunken person: Aus.: since ca. 1920. (B., 1943.) Ex the adj.—2. A slice, share, rake-off: the underground: since late 1950s. *Groupie*, 1968.

shick; shicked, adj. Drunk: low Aus. (Dennis; Baker.) Abbr. *shickered*.

shicker, n. Intoxicating liquor: mostly Aus. (Dennis.) Esp. in *on the shicker*, drinking (heavily). Ex:-

shicker, v.i.; occ. **shicker, shikker, shikkur.** To drink liquor; get drunk: C.20 (prob. from late 1890s: cf. next entry): mostly Aus. low. Ex:-

shicker, etc. Adj., drunk: from late 1890s. (?Ex the v.) Binstead, 1899, 'She comes over shikkur and vants to go to shleeb.' Ex the Hebrew for 'something unclean or reprehensible. The East End Cockneys got it from the early Jewish immigrants in the 80s of the last century' (Barford, letter, 1971). Rosten, spelling *shikker*, defines the Yiddish as simply 'drunk'. Cf.:-

shickered. Tipsy: Ex prec.—2. Bankrupt; very short of money: c.: since ca. 1945. Cook, 1962.

shif. Aus. c. var. of *shiv*, a knife. Grindley, 1977.

shift. To change (clothing): nautical coll. (Bowen.) Ex dial.—2. To travel speedily: Aus. coll.: late C.19–20. Of a sprinter it is often said that 'He can shift!' (B., 1942.) But also, since ca. 1919, English.

shift yer barrow! Move on!: Glasgow, mostly lower classes':—1934. Cf. *on yer bike!*

shifting backstay. 'Man who, not being very bright, is moved from job to job in the hope that he may be found a niche where he can cause the least trouble. Backstays help the shrouds to support a mast in heavy weather' (Granville): RN.

shifting dullness. See **round, n.**

shill, schill. A confidence-trickster's confederate, as in 'I became a "shill" (a stooge) for Harry the Gonof who sold purses' (Drage, 1954: General Cohen, who emigrated at 16 to Canada, on his childhood in the London East End): Can. and Aus. c.: since early C.20.—2. In Can. carnival s., also one who plays or bets in order to encourage the genuine customers. Perhaps a shortening of synon. *shillaber*; prob. ex US. Also known as a *stick*. Powis, 1977, lists the term as Brit. c., 'A decoy, particularly in fraud or the three-card trick, who lures or encourages a victim.'

shilling. 'Circular hammer-mark on wood—the sign manual of a poor carpenter' (Leechman): Can. P.B.: but surely Brit. in orig.—2. See **shine like a shilling.**

shilling emetic. 'A pleasure boat at a seaside-resort': nautical (officers'). (Bowen.) Cf. **sicker,** 1.

shillings in the pound; e.g. *eighteen* or, say, *twelve and six*, to indicate slight mental dullness or mild insanity; 'He's only twelve and six in the pound': NZ: from ca. 1925. Alexander, 1939.

shilling tabernacle. A Nonconformist tea-meeting at one shilling per head: lower classes':—1909 (Ware); ob. by 1930. Cf. *tin tabernacle.*

shimmy, n. The game of *chemin de fer*, of the first two syllables of which it is a corruption: Society: late C.19–20. Mason, 1933, 'I think we ought to play a little at the shimmy table.'

shimmy, v. To oscillate or vibrate, esp. of the front wheels of a small motor-car: Can.: ca. 1924–39. (Leechman.) Ex:-

shimmy-shake. A kind of foxtrot popular in 1920s: coll. > S.E.

shin off. To depart: mostly Cockney: from ca. 1870. Lyons, 1908.—2. Hence, to decamp in haste: Aus. Also simply *shin*, or *do a shin.* B., 1942.

shin tangles. 'Low, dense underbrush; scrub brush: Brit. Columbia: since ca. 1960' (Leech, 1986).

shindig. A dinner party; a large (and lively) party: Aus.: since ca. 1925. (*Sydney Morning Herald*, 18 Aug. 1963.) Used by Sinclair Lewis, 1922; in orig., therefore, prob. Irish-American. P.B.: in this sense, some Brit. use also, since mid-C.20.

shine. Good; likable, e.g., 'a shine chap': Aus. and NZ. Ex brightness as opp. obscurity. Dennis, 1916, spells it also *shyin'*, and defines it 'Excellent, desirable'.

shine like a shilling up a sweep's arse. To be refulgent: low coll.: earlier C.20. Mays, 1971, 'With a bit of elbow grease and some wax polish it'll shine . . . ' The var. *show like* . . . , to be extremely conspicuous, occurs in England, 1968. Seabrook, 1986, adds 'also, for the blindingly obvious, "sticks out like a shillin' on a . . . " '

shiner. A black eye: RN [P.B.: and more gen.]: since ca. 1920. Forester, 1943.—2. A French-polisher; a window-cleaner: builders': resp. coll. and s.

shiners. Jewels. Sayers, 1934.—2. A cleaning-up parade; something highly polished: Army: from ca. 1920.

shining bright. 'The phrase *that'll be right* . . . is an ironic or sometimes angry riposte meaning exactly the opposite, i.e.

there's no chance of that, you certainly will not, etc. . . . This phrase has its own equivalent in rhyming slang: "That'll be shining bright" ' (Munro, 1985): Glasgow.

Shinner. (Usu. pl.) A Sinn-Feiner: coll.: from ca. 1917. (Vachell, 1924.) Ex pron. *shin fáner.*

shiny, -ey. (Usu. pl., *shinies.*) A 'glossy' magazine: upper-middle-class coll.: late 1970s. (York, 1980.) Printed on shiny paper.

Shiny Bob. One who thinks very well of himself: Aus.: since ca. 1925. B., 1942.

shiny-bum, v.; shiny-bumming. To have a desk-job; the occupant; the occupancy: Aus.: WW2. The v. and vbl n. occur in Cusack, 1951; the n. *shiny-bum*, in Cusack, 1953.

Shiny Sheffield (or **Shef**). The destroyer HMS *Sheffield*, hit by an Argentine Exocet missile off the Falkland Is., 4 May 1982; she subsequently went down: RN: 1971–82. Because some of her components were made of Sheffield stainless steel. BBC News, 4 and 5 May 1982.

shiny ten. See TOMBOLA, in Appx.

ship, n. An aircraft (any sort—not only a flying-boat): RAF: 1939+. (Jackson.) Perhaps an adoption of US Air Force usage, where *pursuit ship* = fighter aircraft, *bombardment ship* = bomber, etc.; if so, prob. joc. (P.B.)—2. A bus: Sydney busmen's joc.: since ca. 1944.

ship, v. To turn upside down, to 'rag': Oxford undergraduates'. A. Waugh, 1934, 'Aesthetes . . . whose rooms are shipped on bump-suppers.' And 1917, as Public School s. This sense has been wittily derived from 'to shipwreck'.—2. To obtain promotion: RN: Granville, 'An A.B. who is rated Leading Seaman "ships his killick".' Ex S.E. sense, 'to take aboard'.—3. To assume (an expression): RN: since ca. 1900. Granville, ' "Unship that grin, my lad!" '

ship under sail. A begging or a confidence-trick story: r.s., on tale. Phelan, 1939.

shippie, -y. 'Shipmate, the fishermen's version of the Navy's old ship' (Granville).—2. A shipwright: id. Ibid.

ship's. Naval tobacco: RN coll.: since late C.19. (Goodenough, 1901.)—2. Naval cocoa: RN coll. Bowen.—3. Sodomy; esp. *have a bit of ship's*, to commit it: low. Cf. **Navy cake**, from which it prob. derives.

ship's pinkie. See **pinkie,** 9.

ship's price. 'Charge for food, sweetmeats, cigarettes, etc., smuggled on board and sold at double the price' (Granville): training ships'.

ships that pass in the night. 'A regular's term for wartime serving airmen and officers' (Jackson): RAF coll.: 1939+. Ex the cliché started by the famous novel so entitled. This novel, by Beatrice Harraden, published in 1893, itself drew its title from Longfellow's *Poems*, 1873.

shipwreck chorus. See **gutbucket.**

shipyard confetti. 'On many occasions, [the IRA's] terrorists surrounded explosives with bolts and nails. In Northern Ireland, the shrapnel weapon is known as "shipyard confetti" ' (*Times*, 10 Mar. 1988). Perhaps a cruel pun on *cowyard confetti.*

shirt-buttons. In *go on s.-b.*, (of clock or watch) to be erratic: since ca. 1920. (L.A.) Ex shoddy works. P.B.: cf. synon. *run on bobbins.*—2. 'Trivial counters, to categorise unworthy payment': coll.: later C.20. L.A. cites Mrs Finnegan, wife of the Olympic boxing gold-medal winner, as saying, 27 Oct. 1968, on her husband's likelihood of turning professional, 'He's not turning out for shirt-buttons'. Cf. **washers.**

shirt-front wicket. A cricket-pitch that looks glossy and is extremely hard and true: Aus. cricketers' coll. (—1920) >, by 1934, S.E. Lewis.

shirt lifter, shirtlifter. 'A male homosexual' (Wilkes quotes Baker, 1966): r.s.; hence, 'poofter': Aus. low.

shish joint. A 'shady' bookmaker and assistant: turf c.:—1932. Also *knocking-joint.*

shit, shite, n. Excrement; dung: late C.16–20 (earlier as diarrhœa, a sense † by C.15): S.E., but in C.19–20 a vulgarism. As n., *shite* is in C.19–20 comparatively rare except in dial. As excrement, prob. ex the v., common to the Teutonic languages. I.e. it is ultimately cognate with *shoot*. It has always been common in earthy speech, and seems to be particularly so in that of Can., if I judge correctly from the evidence supplied, over a period of many years, by a number of Canadians—most of them, well-educated men; all, exceptionally knowledgeable. Some general fig. uses are as follows:—2. As a term of contempt applied to a person (rarely to a woman), it has perhaps always, C.16–20, been coll.; in C.19–20, it is a vulgarism. In C.19–20, esp. *a regular shit*, in late C.19–20 *an awful s*. Cf. synon. **bog man** and **shit-house**.—3. (Gen. subjectively.) A bombardment, esp. with shrapnel: Army: WW1. (B. & P.) Still in use in the Falkland Is. campaign, 1982: 'Artillery rounds were referred to as "shit", particularly when incoming, and a target which had been wiped out with casualties had been "greased" ' (*Don't Cry*, 1983). With this use of *greased*, cf. **creamed**.—4. 'Bad weather is always invariably "shit" ' (Rhodes, 1942): RAF: since ca. 1918. Cf. synon. **dirt**.—5. Short for *bull-shit* in senses 'hot air; blarney': Can. Army: WW2. Esp. in 'Don't hand (or feed) me that shit!' = I don't believe you. Adopted by Brit. Services, since mid-C.20, usu. as 'Don't give me that shit!' (P.B.)—6. 'An over-fanciful concoction of food' (L.A.): chefs': since ca. 1945.—7. Applied to various drugs, and used by addicts and police: marijuana, since ca. 1950 (Norman, 1959)—hence, *shit-smoker* (Ibid.); heroin, since ca. 1960. Cf.:—8. Tobacco, esp. *boot shit*, prison tobacco: Aus. prison c.: later C.20. McNeil.—9. Abuse; unfair treatment: as in '[the West Indian youths] think because they've taken so much shit from the police, they're going to dole some back in court' (a solicitor, quoted in *New Society*, 24 Jan. 1980): low coll., an extension of sense 5: later C.20. (P.B.)—10. In *not to mean shit*, not to mean anything, to mean nothing: low: since ca. 1955. And in *not to mean shit to* (someone), as in 'He doesn't mean shit to her any more' = she's so used to him that she takes him for granted; not, therefore, as derogatory as it sounds: low: since ca. 1920, at latest. (L.A., 1977.)—11. See **shoot the shit**.

shit, v. To disgust, as in 'It shits me' (Dick): low Aus.: since ca. 1930. I.e. 'it gives me the shits'.

shit a brick. As exclam., an expletive of annoyance: Aus., since ca. 1925; adopted, ca. 1960, in Brit.—2. In *Yeah, you could shit a brick*, Like hell, you could: Can.: since ca. 1930.—3. See **shit bricks**.

shit a top-block. To become excited or angry or both: shipyard workers', then rather more gen. 'Get that straightened—if the boss sees it, he'll shit a top-block.' *Top-block* is a ship-building term.

shit-ass luck. Extremely bad luck: Can.

shit barge; also **crap barge**. A ship lacking efficiency and discipline, and generally known to be such: RN: the latter since ca. 1945. (Granville, letter, 1967.)

shit blue lights. To feel extremely afraid: Services': since ca. 1940. P.B.: often intensified by the elab. *. . . and rows of houses*. Cf. synon. *(in a) blue funk*, and:-

shit (esp. **be shitting**) **bricks**. To be really worried: low Can.—2. To be thoroughly frightened: Army: WW2. Cf. **shit a brick**, and **brick it**.

shit-can. To wrong (someone deserving it): Aus. low: since ca. 1950.

shit ducks. 'In W. Can. at least, pretty well any duck except a mallard, pintail, teal or gadwall. Mostly refers to diving ducks which often have a fish-like or muddy taste: post-WW2, prob. since early 1950s in Alberta, Saskatchewan and Manitoba' (Leech, 1985).

shit-eating. 'Most of us had to be sycophants ("shit-eating" we called it)' (Piper, 1974): trawler men's.

shit-eating grin. May be a sycophantic smile (cf. prec.); or may be a grimace of pure chagrin, the desperate attempt to appear 'a good loser' becoming the more horrified expression such an exercise would induce: adopted ex US early 1980s. (Van Dulken, 1988.)

shit-faced. 'Drunk, often to the point of vomiting: US and Can.: usage became common in the early 1970s' (Leech, 1985). Also, later C.20, UK (Hibbert, 1983).

shit fish. Fish caught around sewage outfalls: fishermen's.

shit for brains. 'Insult to a dimwit, as in "Ah, you got shit for brains"; or "Man, you're a real shit for brains", with the meaning that you're wrong: Can.: since 1950s' (Leech, 1986).

shit from China. As in, 'Bit like shit from China, that — far-fetched': S.W. Herts. (Seabrook, 1986.)

shit-head. An objectionable person: orig. NZ low, since ca. 1918: >, by mid-C.20, also Brit. low. In later C.20 often unhyphenated, as in 'Your detractors are shitheads, pure and simple' (a letter pub'd in *Time Out*, 19 Mar. 1982: P.B.).

shit-hole. Occ. var. of **piss-hole**, as adj. of disapproval: Services': later C.20. (P.B.)

shit-hot. Unpleasantly enthusiastic; e.g. 'He's shit-hot on spit and polish': Can. soldiers': 1914+.—2. Very skilful, cunning, knowledgeable: low: since ca. 1918. P.B.: by mid-C.20, although still 'low', always used in approbation, usu. of a performer or his performance, as 'He scored a couple of shit-hot goals'.—3. Up to the minute; extremely topical: coll.: since ca. 1950. 'A truly shit-hot story' (Davidson, 1978).

shit-house. A C.20 var. of **shit**, n., 2, as nasty person.—2. A hospital (or a hospital ward) or a home for very old people who have lost control of their natural functions: hospital staffs'.—3. Frequently used in the Services for any place not at highest state of cleanliness, as 'This room's like a shit-house!'; I have even heard it, used quite thoughtlessly, applied to a lavatory itself: since ca. 1950, prob. much earlier. Hence, also as adj.: 'What a shit-house camp!' (P.B.)

shit-house luck. Very bad luck indeed: low Can. Cf. **shit-ass luck**.

shit-kicker. See **shitkicker**.

shit-list. Esp. in, e.g. 'You're right at the top of my shit-list, brother!', I regard you with complete disfavour, and shall do all in my power to make life unpleasant for you: low: since ca. 1920. Perhaps there was orig. a pun on *short-list*, as of candidates for interview. (L.A.; P.B.)

shit-locker. Bowels: RN lowerdeck: since ca. 1910.

shit off a shovel, like. Smart, prompt, esp. of human movement: RN: since ca. 1950. It is linked with the MN's *When I say shit, jump on the shovel*, 'Do as I say (and quick about it)': same period. (Peppitt.) P.B.: both phrases were quite well known and common in Army and RAF usage, mid-C.20.

shit official, in the. In serious trouble: Army, mostly officers': 1942–5.

shit on a raft. Beans on toast: RN: since late 1940s. (Peppitt.) Cf. *shit on a shingle*, mince on toast: Army and RAF: id. Perhaps borrowed ex US. (P.B.)

shit on from a great height. (Of one who has been) landed in great trouble by others: low (esp., since ca. 1925, RAF). P.B.: often in var. **shat on from . . .**, q.v.; also as v.t., e.g. 'It's time he was shit (*or* shat) (up)on . . . '

shit or bust. *Be shit or bust*, to be given to trying desperately hard; to do a thing and damn the consequences: non-cultured coll.: since ca. 1910. 'I set out in direct disobedience of orders . . . My batman was delighted . . . "I like you, sir," he said. "You're shit or bust, you are" ' (Douglas, 1947). But 'I'm shit or bust' was, in WW2, very often used ironically, to mean 'I'm completely indifferent'.

shit order, in. Applied to a dirty barrack-room, hut, dress, equipment, etc.: Army. But, as L.A. points out, also 'of army, RAF establishment or personnel, lacking in proper standard of military order or discipline, as in "If we were fighting the desert war . . . they could work in shit order" (Hayes, 1971).' Cf. **scruff order**.

shit out (on). To miss an opportunity, or one's due: Services': since mid-C.20. 'Sorry! Last one's just gone. Looks as if you've shit out, doesn't it?' or 'The rest got one, but I shit out on it.' (P.B.)

S

shit-scared. Extremely scared, almost to the extent of nervous diarrhœa: low, perhaps orig. RAF: since ca. 1935.

shit, shot and shell. The ammunition in the anti-aircraft 'rocket' barrage, first used in the Portsmouth area: RN lowerdeck: 1942+. (Granville.) Even nails and bits of old iron were used.

Shit Street. Esp. *in Shit Street*, in extreme difficulties, in dire trouble: low: since ca. 1920.

shit through the eye of a needle. As in 'I could . . . ' or 'it'll make you . . . ' in refs to diarrhœa and its causes: low, perhaps orig. mostly London: since late C.19. An occ. elab. is . . . *without touching the sides*.

shit to a blanket. In *cling* or *stick like* or *close as* . . . , to stay, be, very close to, usu. in an unwanted way: low: since ca. 1930. (Kersh, 1956—but concerning the 1930s.) E.g. a suspected crook's exasperation at a persistent detective, 'He sticks as close to me as . . . ' Cf. the mid-C.19–20 *like shit to a shovel*, very adhesive(ly) indeed, also low coll., with which contrast **shit off a shovel**.

shit(-)wallah. A sanitary man: Army: late C.19—mid-20. P-G-R.

shite. See **shit**, n. and v.

shite(-)hawk (or written solid). A nasty person: low.—2. A vulture: Services': in India later C.19–mid-20; elsewhere in the tropics, of kites and other scavenging birds of prey, since mid-C.20. (E.P.; P.B.)—3. The badge of the 4th Indian Division: Army: 1940+.—4. (Cf. 2.) A seagull: MN. (Peppitt.)—5. 'A man who will eat anything; often used derogatively' (Patterson): Portsmouth dockers'. Cf. 2 and 4.

Shite-hawk Soldiers, the. The RAF Regiment: Army: later WW2+. For a few years after their formation, mid-WW2, they wore khaki battledress with RAF berets and the RAF blue eagle shoulder-flash; cf. prec., 2. Later they became known as *the Rock Apes*. (E.P.; P.B.)

shite-hawk's breakfast. In *feel like a* . . . , to feel absolutely dreadful, e.g. as a result of the previous night's alcoholic excesses, etc.: RN lowerdeck: mid-C.20. *Heart*, 1962.

shithead. See **shit-head**.

shitkicker. 'Western cowboy novel/film' (Hawke): RM: later C.20. Cf. synon. **oater**.

shitnitto. 'Nothing doing!': c.: later C.20. See quot'n at **boat**, n., 5.

shitpot. Second-rate: Aus. low coll.: later C.20. McNeil.

shits, the. An evident dislike of operational flying: RAF Bomber and Fighter Commands: 1940+. (S/Ldr H.E. Bates.) Ex the mid-C.19–20 coll. sense 'diarrhœa'.—2. In, e.g., 'He gives me the shits', he annoys me and I dislike him intensely: low coll.: since mid-C.20. May also be applied to things, organisations, activities, etc., as 'Politics and priests give me the shits'. (P.B.)

shitter. The rectum or anus: low. 'Shove that up your shitter!' is a vulgar retort to an unwelcome suggestion. (P.B.)

Shitting Chickens, the. The 14th/20th King's Hussars: Army: mid-C.20. Ex the shape of the eagle, or 'hawk', in the regimental badge. (P.B.)

shitty, n. See next, 2.

shitty, adj. Of poor quality; shabby and unfair of behaviour or conduct, as 'What a shitty way to treat a bloke!': Services' coll. (P.B.)—2. Angry; irritated; very resentful: Aus.: since late 1930s. Williamson, 1972, '*Ross*—about to put off meeting his girl: "She won't be as shitty if she knows I'm getting paid." ' Hence, also Aus., since ca. 1960, *have a shitty on* (someone), to be angry, or in a bad mood, with: Braddon, 1977, ' "Sorry I had a shitty on you," King murmured.'

shiv, n. and v. (To) knife (someone). Alt. spelling of older Romany *chiv(e)*.

shmee, shmock. Heroin: drugs' world: later C.20. (Home Office.) Cf. synon. **smack**. *Shmock*, see **schmock**, 2.

shnorrer. See **snorrer**.

shock. 'To cook. A dish taken to the galley would be accompanied by a request to "give it a shock" ' (Bassett): RN: WW2. Ex the electric chair.

shock-absorbers. Female breasts, the suppliers of *pneumatic bliss*, a cultured coll. of the 1960s–70s: since ca. 1950. (Petch, 1976.)

shocker. Also *complete shocker*, 'A hopeless individual or object—simply terrible' (H. & P.); a thoroughly unpleasant fellow: Services', the latter mostly officers': since ca. 1920; >, by mid-C.20, gen.—sometimes used in affectionate reproof, e.g., to a child, 'Oh, you're a right little shocker, you are!' Prob. ex *shocking*, adj.—2. A shock-absorber: motorists' and motorcyclists': since ca. 1925.

shod. 'Colloquially applied to motor vehicles. A car with good tyres is described as *well shod*' (B.P.): Aus.: since ca. 1945. Cf. **shoe**, 1.

shoddy-dropper. A seller of cheap serge: Aus. and NZ c.:—1932. B., 1942, for the Aus. usage.

shoe. A tyre, esp. of a car: garages' s.: from ca. 1920. (Blaker, 1934.) Cf. **boots**, 4.—2. A sanitary pad: Aus. feminine: since late 1940s. Ex shape.

shoe pinches him, his. Barltrop, 1981: 'throughout my lifetime in London, probably among the working class generally, the phrase has meant that the man referred to has (or prob. has) a large penis. Its origin is in myths that the size of a man's feet, or of his nose, corresponds with his sexual proportions.'

shoe-string; esp. *operate*, or do it, *on a shoe-string*. A small sum of money, esp. as working capital: coll.: adopted, in late 1950s, ex US. (See W. & F.)—2. Hence the adj. *shoe-string*, operating on a (very) small capital; 'run' very economically: coll.: since ca. 1960. 'Acting in Scruggs, an off-beat, shoe-string movie' (*Woman*, 23 Oct. 1965). P.B.: E.P. may have dated this rather late; the phrase was popularised by Laurier Lister's revue *Airs on a Shoestring*, which opened at the Royal Court Theatre in 1953.

shong. A catapult: Aus., mostly juvenile: since ca. 1925. (B., 1943.) Ex synon. *shanghai*.

shonky; shonk. A Jew: low: mid-C.19–20. Knock, 1932 (for ca. 1903–24); Matthews, 1938 (the latter). The former is the diminutive of the latter which derives (via American) ex Yiddish *shonnicker*, 'a trader in a small way, a pedlar'.—2. As *Shonky*, 'Nickname for any stingy, miserly, "close" person; one who hates paying for a round of drinks but is not averse to accepting treats from others' (Granville): RN. Ex sense 1.—3. As *shonk*, nose: Cockneys'. 'Keep your cherry-picking shonk out of it!' (George Forwood, 1962) = Mind your own business! Perhaps ex distinctive feature in sense 1. (P.B.)

shoo-in. One favoured to win, esp. to win easily: Can., ex US (W. & F. date it 1935). (Leech, 1985.)

shook, ppl (adj.), itself sol. In *that shook* (*him*, or *me*, etc.), that astonished, surprised, perturbed, perplexed, baffled, him: orig. Services', esp. RAF, since 1939; >, fairly soon, very widespread and gen. (Rhodes, 1942; H. & P.) Intensively: 'I was shaken rigid (or rotten)'.

shoosh. Silence: Aus., esp. among two-up players: since ca. 1925. Glassop, 1949, ' "Gents," he said plaintively, "a bit of shoosh, please, gents. Just a little bit of shoosh. We don't want no coppers breakin' in on us." ' P.B.: ex the very widespread injunction to be quiet, as in 'Shoosh now! Daddy's trying to read', etc.

shoot, n. Dismissal, esp. in *get*, or *give* (a person), *the shoot*: earlier C.20. Ware derives it ex a flour-mill's shoots.

shoot, v. To inject (e.g. *smack*, heroin): adopted, ca. 1965, ex US. *Daily Telegraph*, 22 Nov. 1973.—2. To give utterance to: 1929. Ex sense 1 of:-

shoot! Go ahead; speak!: from ca. 1925. Ex the cinema: in making a film, *shoot!* = use your camera now: orig. US.—2. Euph. for expletive *shit!*: Can. Current in US much earlier: 'It appears, e.g., in *Tom Sawyer* [1876], though probably *not* as a conscious euphemism' (R.C., 1966).

shoot a card. To leave one's card at a house: Society: ca. 1910–40. 'Sapper', 1924.

shoot a – rarely the – line. To talk too much, esp. to boast: RAF since ca. 1928, Army officers' since 1940. 'I don't know why, but it's a "line" in Fighting Area [= pre-WW2 Fighter Command] to wander about with [one's top] button undone . . . A line . . . is something that is shot. If you shoot a line, in effect you do or say something in order to impress the uninitiated and fail. Hence the saying "He who shoots a line rarely shoots anything else" ' (Tredrey, 1939). Jackson notes that in the 1920s the RAF used *shoot a line of bull*, which they soon shortened; the longer phrase may combine the theatrical *shoot one's lines* (declaim them vigorously), and **bulsh**, and the American *shoot off one's mouth*, as Jackson has suggested. The phrase perhaps dates from as early as 1919, for *line-shooter* occurs in a song sung at Christmas, 1925: witness Jackson, 1945. Perhaps, as Priestley has suggested, reminiscent of the fact that in the early 1920s every 'sheik' had a special verbal approach—or 'line'—with the girls. See also **line-shoot**.

shoot a man. Gen. as vbl n., *shooting a man*, the common practice of jobbers who, guessing whether a broker is a buyer or a seller, alter their prices up or down accordingly: Stock Exchange:—1935.

shoot a paper-bolt. To circulate a false or unauthenticated rumour: coll.:—1923 (Manchon).

shoot down – shoot down in flames – shoot down from a great height. 'To defeat in an argument; to be right on a question of procedure, dress, drill, etc.': RAF: resp. since ca. 1938, 1939, 1940. Finn-Smith, 1942, has the first, as has H. & P.; the latter records also the second; E.P., 1942, has the first and second; Partridge, 1945, 'The first—though far from colourless—is the weakest; the second connotes a victory that utterly routs the opponent—as does the third, with the added connotation of calm and/or great intellectual superiority in the victory.' Obviously ex aerial warfare; compare the Navy's *salvo*.—2. Only *shoot down*: '*Shot down*. Pulled up for not saluting or for being improperly dressed' (H. & P.): RAF: since ca. 1939. In gen., 'To reprimand a subordinate' (Hinde, 1945). Of same orig. as 1. See also **shot down**.

shoot-flier. The agent in next. Samuel, 1981.

shoot-fly. The snatching theft of watches: c.:—1933 (Leach).

shoot (one's) **load.** (Of the male) to experience an orgasm: low. (Raper, 1973.)

shoot (one's) **mouth off.** Var. of **shoot off** (one's) **mouth**, than which, C.20, it is commoner. (Sayers, 1933.) Also, as Wade, 1934, *shoot one's mouth*. Cf.:-

shoot (one's) **neck off.** 'To talk loudly and self-assertively' (P-G-R): mostly Services': ca. 1920–50. Ex prec.

shoot off. To depart hastily or very quickly: NZ: since ca. 1919. (Devanney, 1930.) Cf. **shoot through**.

shoot off (one's) **mouth.** To talk; esp. to talk boastfully or indiscreetly; to tell all one knows (cf. **spill the beans**): orig. (1887) US and = talk abusively; anglicised, thanks to the 'talkies', in 1930–1; in Can., by 1925. Cf. *say a mouthful*.

shoot on early. Beginning work at 6 a.m.: London labourers': from ca. 1920. *Evening News* (London), 13 Nov. 1936.

shoot (one)**self in the foot.** To make a self-defeating, counterproductive blunder: coll.: 1980s. Mann, 1985, notes its use in the world of finance, but it can apply wherever an **own goal** [q.v.] is perpetrated.

shoot the amber. (Of a motorist) to increase speed when the amber light is showing, in order to pass before the red ('stop') light comes on: motorists': from late 1935. P.B.: in later C.20 gen. *shoot the lights*; one who does so is known, perhaps mainly journalistically, as an *amber gambler*.

shoot the bones. To throw dice: gamblers': since ca. 1942. (Webb, 1945.) Also *shoot craps*, adopted from US ca. 1940.

shoot the breeze. To chatter idly; to gossip: Can., adopted ca. 1950 (if not a decade earlier), ex US. (Leechman.)—2. To raise cash: c. Moody, 1985.

shoot the lights. See **shoot the amber**.

shoot the shit. To chat; tell tall stories: Can. Army: WW2. P.B.: since ca. 1950 (?earlier) also Brit. Services', and esp. in the 2nd sense, 'boasting'.

shoot the tube. See **tube, n.**, 6.

shoot-through, n. 'Someone who fails an undertaking' (*Mail on Sunday*, 8 Nov. 1987): RM: later C.20. Perhaps cf.:-

shoot through, v. To go absent without leave: Aus.: since ca. 1940. Cusack, 1951.—2. Hence, to escape from prison: Aus. c.: since ca. 1950. Grindley, 1977.—3. Hence, simply 'to depart', as 'Well! It's four o'clock—time we were shooting through': Aus.: later C.20. (P.B.) Cf.:-

shoot through like a Bondi tram. To travel very fast (and not stop): Sydneyites': since ca. 1935. (B.P.)

shoot up. 'To dive on to' (an enemy 'plane): aviators': from 1917. (*New Statesman and Nation*, 20 Feb. 1937.) Ex the shooting that follows.—2. 'To "shoot up" a place or a person is to make a mock diving attack' (Rhodes, 1942): RAF: since late 1939. [P.B.: but cf.!] Jackson, 1943, 'The origin is American gangster slang meaning to attack with gun-fire.'—3. To inject drugs: drugs' world: adopted, mid-1960s, ex US. Wyatt, 1973.

shoot (a person) **up with.** Not to do something that someone wishes done; to do something other than what was desired: military: from ca. 1925.

shooting a ruby. A hæmotypsis, i.e. a spitting of blood: hospital nurses': since ca. 1935. *Nursing Mirror*, 7 May 1949.

shooting double-headers. 'We would use both nets, so that the whole of a large area [of water] would be encircled. This is called "shooting double headers" ' (Culotta, 1963): Aus. fishermen's: since ca. 1920. Ex the game of two-up.

shooting for, be. 'Recently, in hospital, I saw a very old man tottering about and discovered that he was 93 . . . "and shooting for 100". Aiming at, hoping to reach.' (Leechman.) Mostly Can.: since ca. 1920.

shooting gallery. 'One reason given [for the rapid spread of Aids] was "shooting galleries"—drug users sharing needles and syringes' (Guardian, 22 Feb. 1986); Stockley, 1986, 'A meeting place for addicts where they inject drugs': drugs c. US since—1952 (Spears).—2. See **lines book**.

shooting-iron. A rifle: mostly marksmen's: adopted, ca. 1918, ex US.

shooting-match. See **whole shooting-match**.

shop, n. A causing to be arrested: c.: from ca. 1920. (Wallace, 1925.) Ex the v.

shop, v. To lay information on which a person is arrested: c.: since early C.19.—2. To deliberately get (someone) into trouble: Services': since ca. 1930. Ex sense 1.—3. To shop at: Can. advertisers' and radio coll.: since ca. 1957. 'Shop Eaton's' for 'Shop at Eaton's' affords a good example. (Leechman.)

shop around. (Of housewives) to go round the shops in search of the best offers being made: since mid-1950s: coll. > informal S.E. (Petch, 1969.)—2. Hence, (mainly, though not exclusively) of women 'trying' numerous men before deciding to marry: since ca. 1960. 'Why don't you marry, Liz?'— 'Oh, I may. I'm still shopping around.' See also **shopping**.

shopper. He who causes the arrest of a malefactor: c. Wallace.

shoppie, -y. A shop-girl or, less often, -man: coll. 'Taffrail', 1916; Vachell, 1934.—2. A shoplifter: see AUSTRALIAN UNDERWORLD, in Appx., at **shoppy**.

shopping, participle, hence also n. Looking around for a wife or, *vice versa*, a husband: since late 1940s: by 1965, coll. (*Woman's Illustrated*, 2 Jan. 1960: 'Does Your Date Rate as a Mate?') See also **shop around**.

shoppy; shoppying (job). See AUSTRALIAN UNDERWORLD, in Appx.

shorders. A Cockney var. of *shorters* or drinks in short measures. Franklyn.

shore boss. 'The steward's name for the superintendent steward': nautical coll. Bowen.

shore-side. Retirement; life as a civilian: RN coll. of late C.19–20. Ex pidgin. (Granville.) Cf. **China-side**.—2. The shore or beach; ashore: RN. 'Are you coming shoreside this afternoon?' (P-G-R.)

short, n. A 'short' drink, i.e. of spirits, as opp. beer, but not necessarily absolutely undiluted; 'They were drinking shorts' might include, e.g., brandy with a dash of soda, but not a 'brandy sour', which is served in a tall glass, and is therefore 'a long drink': coll. (E.P.; P.B.)—2. A short circuit: electricians' coll.—3. A short excerpt; a short film or musical composition: coll.: from not later than 1927.

short, v. Of a selection committee: to shortlist (a candidate): esp. Civil Service: since ca. 1930.

short, adj. Not very 'bright'; stupid: Aus. B., 1942, 'Esp. "a bit short".' Ex older *have a shingle short.*

short and curlies. The short hairs, used fig., as 'Got him by the short and curlies'—caught him properly: Army: since ca. 1935. (P-G-R.) Since WW2 it has gradually and widely spread (Playfair, 1977). P.B.: in *curlies* there is perhaps a ref. to pubic hair.

short-arm inspection. An inspection 'conducted periodically . . . to detect symptoms of venereal disease': military: from ca. 1910. (B. & P.) With a pun on pistols. Occ., since 1916, abbr. *short-arm.*

short circuit. Gastro-enterotomy: medical. Ince, 1932, 'The pleasant little major operation they call . . . facetiously "a short circuit".'

Short Range Desert (or **Shepheard's**) **Group.** See **Groppi's Light Horse.**

short strokes. In *be on the . . .* , (of the male) to be approaching orgasm: humorous rather than euph. (L.A., 1977.) Cf. **paradise strokes**, and **long strokes.**

short (or **long**) **soup.** A soup with short, or one with long, noodles in it: Aus. coll.: since ca. 1920. (Morrisby, 1958.)

short-timers. An (amorous) couple hiring a room for an hour or two: low. Manchon.

short(-)weight. (Of a person) rather simple; mentally, a little defective.

shorters. Johnny Morris, in one of his amusing radio travelogues (1 Aug. 1983) spoke of 'a touch of the Harry Shorters' = a lack of money. See also HARRY, in Appx., and **touch of the . . .** ; *shorters* ex *short* + Oxford/RN *-er(s).*—2. See **shorders.**

shorts. Short-dated securities: money-market coll.: from ca. 1930. *OED* Sup.

shot, n. An extremely hard cake, tart, etc.: coll.:—1923 (Manchon).—2. Hence, something difficult to tolerate or believe: id. Ibid.—3. Money: low:—1923 (Ibid.).—4. A photograph taken with cinematograph camera: coll.: US (ca. 1923), anglicised by 1925. *OED* Sup.—5. A dram (of spirits): coll.: US, anglicised by 1932. Ibid.—6. A dose (of a drug): 1929. Ibid.—7. A stroke with cane or strap: Harrow School: late C.19–20. Lunn, 1913.—8. An injection: medical: adopted, ca. 1920, ex US.

shot (ppl adj., always *be shot*). To be exhausted: Aus.: since ca. 1920. Vickers, 1955, 'Another man turned on the water and out it gushed. But only for a minute, then it spluttered, then it dribbled. "She's shot," the man at the hose shouted.' (Cf. **she,** 2.) Also (of persons), at the end of one's tether: Wilkes supplies a quot'n from 1945, and suggests '?shoot one's bolt'.

shot-away. Drunk: nautical: late C.19–20. Bowen; *Heart*, 1962, 'Once you start worrying yourself it gets so big you can't even see the sides, and then you become so knotted everybody thinks you're either shot-away or working it' [*it* = 'your ticket', for release from the Navy].

shot down. Beaten in an argument: aircraft engineers': from ca. 1918. (*Daily Herald*, 1 Aug. 1936.) Ex planes being shot down in WW1.—2. Crossed in love: mostly RAF: WW2. (Shute, 1944.) Ex sense 2 of next.—3. Under the influence of drugs: drugs c. (Stockley, 1986.) US since—1982 (Spears). Perhaps cf. **shoot up,** 3.

shot down in flames. See **shoot down.**—2. Hence, crossed in love; jilted: RAF aircrews': 1940+. Partridge, 1945.

shot full of holes. Tipsy: NZ (1915+) and Aus. (since ca. 1918). B., 1941, 'An elaboration of shot' [in this sense].

shot-ging. A catapult: Aus., mostly juvenile: since ca. 1925. (B., 1943.) Suggested by *shanghai* + *shot* + *gun* + *sling.*

shot on a hand. Beaten by a better hand: Aus. card-players': since ca. 1918. B., 1953.

shot on the swings. A copulation: ?mainly Scot.: since late 1940s. *Daily Telegraph*, 10 Sep. 1975, in a Scottish police-court report.

shot up; shot to ribbons. Very drunk; as drunk as one can possibly be: RAF: since late 1939. (Partridge, 1945.) Ex aerial warfare. Cf. **shot full of holes.**

shot up the arse (more politely, **back**). Rendered *hors de combat* by some witticism; detected, found out: Army.—2. (Of aircraft) shot-up from the rear: RAF: WW2.

shotgun. See **ride shotgun.**

shotgun mixture. A pharmaceutical mixture containing numerous ingredients, any one of them prob. efficacious.

shotgun wedding (or **marriage**). A wedding necessitated by the bride's pregnancy (i.e., orig. at her armed father's insistence): adopted, ex US, (?)early C.20, prob. at first as coll., soon > informal S.E., esp. in fig. usage, e.g. in the commercial world, a *shotgun merger.* (P.B.)

shotter. See **fly-balance.**

shouse. A privy, a conflation of *shit-house*: Aus.: since ca. 1925. (B., 1941.) L.A. notes *shoust* as a post-WW1 Cockney var. Cf. **shed.**

shout. A summons (to duty): nautical, esp. stewards', coll. 'He'd asked me for an early shout' (Shaw, 1932).

shout and holler. A collar: r.s. (Lester.) Cf. older synon. *holler, boys, holler.*

shout the odds. To talk too much, too loudly, or boastingly: lower classes': from ca. 1910. (F. & G.) Ex the race-course. P.B.: an uncle of mine, at school in the 1920s, always remembered in later life a master whose pet phrase was 'Boy, do you think I stand up here shouting the odds for the good of my immortal soul? No! I do it for money, and so . . .'

shout up. To address vigorously by way of warning: coll.: from ca. 1930.

shove. To stop; to forget: low Aus. and NZ: since ca. 1910. Slatter, 'You can shove that caper'. Ex *shove it up your arse!*, a vulgar phrase throughout the English-speaking world; and the Brit. var. *shove it where the monkey shoves* (or *shoved*) *his nuts!*

shove along. To make one's way quietly: coll.: early C.20. Joyce, 1922; Manchon.

shove (one's) **nose in.** To interfere; interpose rudely: low coll.:—1887 (Baumann); still current, 1980. 'She's always shoving her nose in where it's not wanted, that woman.'

shove off. To depart: coll. (Ware.) Ex nautical sense, prob. on much older *push off.* Cf. **shove along.**

shove under. To kill; mostly in passive, *be shoved under*: Aus. (Russell, 1934.) Ex *shove underground*, to bury: itself a coll., dating since ca. 1870, but Eng. as well as Aus. and NZ.

shovel along. 'To move around, to go somewhere. Seems to be used by the young' (Mann, 1985). Has var. *sugar along* (Ibid.); with both, cf. **shove along**, the old gen. dial. *shog*, and *sugar!*

shovel and broom. A room: r.s.: since ca. 1910; by 1959, ob. Franklyn.

shovel and tank. A bank (for money): r.s. Franklyn 2nd.

shovel-engineer. 'An artificer engineer; an engineer-cum-stoker, which used to be a warrant rank but is now abolished' (Granville): RN coll.: earlier C.20.

shoving money upstairs. 'When a man is worrying about going bald, someone tells him banteringly it must be with "shoving money upstairs" ' (Petch, 1946): mainly North Country. Instead of putting it into a bank—where it's safer.—2. Spending money on useless 'cures': Londoners': since ca. 1920. Franklyn.

shoving shit uphill, n. Sodomy: low joc. (P.B.)

show, n. In *bad*, or *poor*, and *good show!*, phrases expressive of disapprobation and approval or praise: Services' (mostly officers'): since ca. 1925. Other qualifying adjectives may be used, e.g. *wizard*, WW2. Prob. ex:—2. A fight, an attack: WW1 military: but not, I think, before 1915. B. & P.—3.

S

Hence, in *put up a show* (gen. qualified as in sense 1), to give some, gen. good, account of oneself: orig. Services', from 1915.—4. 'During the run-up to a race, a broadcasting service gives . . . a "show" on that race . . . the prices being offered at that time on the various horses taking part' (*Ladbroke's Pocket Betting Guide*, 1976): the turf: since late 1940s. Cf.—5. In *there's another show*, a 'tic-tac' [= bookmaker's semaphore] has signalled new odds: turf c.:—1932.—6. As *the show*, signs by which three card-sharpers, who have a 'mug' in tow, tell one another how to play: c. Also known as *showing out*.—7. In *do a show*, to go to a public entertainment: coll.: since ca. 1906.—8. See **steal the show**.

show, v.i. To surrender, give up, desist: coll.: from ca. 1930. In the j. of cards, 'to show' is to throw in one's hand. *Daily Telegraph*, 16 Apr. 1937.—2. To gain a place: turf coll. Symons, 1950.

show-down. A test of the real strength and backing of two persons, parties, peoples: adopted ca. 1930 from US: coll. until ca. 1940, then S.E. Ex bluff poker.

show like a shilling up a sweep's arse. See **shine like . . .**

show of flash. A slight, an affront, to a gang's tenets of proper behaviour: Teddy-boys': since ca. 1950. Sigal, 1959.—2. Hence, any display of truculence or arrogance, e.g. by arrested youthful gangster to police: later C.20. (P.B.)

show-off. One who 'shows off': coll.: late C.19–20. Blunden, 1935, 'MacKissock's a "show-off".' Ex the much older coll. v.

show-out. 'Another cardinal rule in making contact with a snout [= informer] was that the detective never made the first move. When you entered the rendezvous and saw your man you waited for the "show-out"—a brief nod—before you joined him' (Gosling, 1959): police s.: since ca. 1920. See also **show,** n., 6.

show the flag. To put in an appearance, just to show that one is there: business and professional men's coll.: from ca. 1919.

show-up, n. An exhibition (of work): coll.: 1930. (*OED* Sup.) Prob. suggested by Fr. *exposé* and *exposition*.

show up, v. To appear. Esp. of a released convict reporting once a month to the police: c.:—1933 (Leach).—2. To report (a boy): Charterhouse. E.g., 'I'll show you up.'

showbiz. Show business: the commercial, and the professional, side of the world of entertainment; orig. of the theatre and music hall, then of films, then of radio and TV: s. at first, ?early 1930s, it had, by ca. 1960, > coll. (Chambers' *C.20th Dict.*, 1972 ed.) Those are American dates; Brit. usage followed within a couple of years. In both countries, it began as theatrical. W. & F., 1975, include it, without dates or quot'n. It hadn't been accepted by 'Webster's Second International', 1934, but it did appear in 'Webster's Third', 1961. I don't know of the printed appearance of the derivative adj. *showbizzy* earlier than in *Beatles*, 1975, although I surmise there must have been earlier ones.

showboat, n. Large 8-wheeled van. See HAULIERS' SLANG, in Appx.

showboat, v. To show off, 'swank around', as in 'We won't allow you to showboat around in your uniform. We are a very shy and retiring organisation' (a recruiting advertisement for 21 Special Air Service, pub. in London *New Standard*, and reported in *Guardian*, 11 Feb. 1981).

shower. 'A dust storm—as in *Cobar shower*, *Bedourie shower*, *Darling shower*, *Wilcannia shower*, etc.' (B., 1959): Aus. rural: late C.19–20. All are place-names.—2. See quot'n at **drag,** n., 14. A contribution from players to operators: Aus. two-up gamblers'. Ronan, 1954.—3. A large number of aircraft: RAF: WW2. 'A shower of Messerschmitts' (P-G-R).—4. Short for *shower tea*, an occasion when a bride is given small 'prezzies' by her women friends: Aus.: since ca. 1950. (B.P.; Raab) P.B.: prob. ex US. Before leaving Hong Kong, 1967, to get married, my wife was given a 'shower tea' by Aus. and US women friends, to receive a 'shower' of small gifts for her new status as housewife, tokens of larger

wedding-presents to come. Raab: Wilkes notes only *kitchen tea*, when the gifts are items specifically of kitchen equipment.—5. Short for *a shower of bastards*, *of shit*, etc.: Services': since ca. 1919. See esp. DC pp 2 at *what a shower!*

shower bath. Ten shillings: r.s. (on Cockney pron. of *half* a sovereign); usu. *shower*, esp. in pl., as *shahs to a shillin'*, odds of 10 to 1: sporting r.s. Franklyn.

shower of bastards. As a term of contempt and loathing has, in the Services since ca. 1955, largely displaced earlier *shower of shit*; by ca. 1970, often merely derisive, in a semi-affectionate, tolerant way. (P.B.)

showie or **showy.** A handkerchief worn 'for show only': Aus.: since ca. 1950. Campbell, 1964.

showing the girls the horse with the green tail. 'Twice weekly there were Other Ranks' dances at the Cavalry Club [Aldershot] . . . , where there were cavalry goings on in the straw laid down to comfort sick horses; a process known throughout cavalry history [until horses disappeared] as "showing the girls the horse with the green tail"; this was a highly popular pastime for shop girls' (Mays, 1975). Cf. the late C.16–18 *give a girl a green gown*, to 'tumble' her on the grass.

shreddies. Male underwear: coll.: since ca. 1960. Because of its usual state among bachelors; by a pun on the breakfast cereal so named. (P.B.)

shrewd. In *Picture Post*, 2 Jan. 1954, there was an article on youthful 'spivs'. It began thus: 'The word "Spiv", it seems, is out of date. The new word, we are reliably informed, is "Shrewd"—and it is used as a noun, adjective and verb. The "shrewd" is not an American by-product. He is home-bred and thoroughly English, in style and slang.' With the word itself, compare **shrewdy,** and:-

shrewd head. Aus. and NZ var. of:-

shrewdie, -y. A shrewd, esp. a cunning, person; a trickster: coll.: late C.19–20. Mostly military and Aus. F. & G.

shriek. An alarmed, surprised, or reproachful outcry: coll.: 1929 (*OED* Sup.).—2. A 'scream' (q.v.): coll.: 1930 (Bramah: Ibid.).

shriek-mark. An exclamation-mark: authors', typists' coll. Cf. **Christer.**

shriekers. Noisily, demonstratively drunk: mostly Services': since ca. 1950. The 'OXFORD -ER(S)' suffix on *shrieking* (*pissed*) or *drunk*. (P.B.)

shrimp. 'Tamping machine used for cleaning ballast and returning it to the track. The many cranks and pistons make them look like shrimps' (McKenna): railwaymen's. Also known as a *Waltzing Matilda* (Ibid.).

shrink, n. Psychiatrist: a back-formation ex **head-shrinker**: adopted, ca. 1965, ex US, where current since 1960 (W. & F.). (P.B., 1974; *COD*, 1976.) Hence, as v., to act as a psychiatrist, as in 'British Leyland's shrinking is now done by . . . a small company that enjoys talking to people' (Dunn, 1981).

shroff up; buff up. To smarten up: RN. The first, ex Urdu *shroff*, a banker (who judges the quality of coins).

Shroppie, the. The Shropshire Union Canal: canalmen's: late C.19–20. (Granville, letter, 1966.)

shrub. 'A hippie. Replaces the word *hippie*. Poss. orig.: either the bushy faces of hippie men, or the fact that they live in the bushes (shrubs): W.Can., mostly BC, and [orig.] within the past 3 years' (Leech, 1986).

shtick. Act; behaviour: adopted, mid-1970s, ex US. ' . . . why the comic Fyffe Robertson shtick?' (Daniells, 1980). Prob. ex Ger. *Stück*, bit, piece, via Yiddish. (P.B.)

shtoom (or **shtum**), **keep**; properly, *stoom* (*stum*). To keep quiet; to 'act dumb': low; mostly East End of London. Often in imperative, or as *keep shtoom*. 'Simply the anglicised phonetic spelling of S. German "stumm"—dumb, silent. Presumably it reached England through Yiddish' (R.S.). Powis, 1977, notes *stumm and crum*, 'emphatic version of "stumm" '.

shtoriku. 'Strong-arm or muscle man' (Clayton, 1970): prisoners' c.

shucks! Nonsense!; *I* don't care!: coll.: 1885 (*OED*): US partly anglicised ca. 1900. Ex *shuck*, typifying the worthless, itself orig. (and still) a husk or shell.—**2.** Hence, an exclam. of annoyance, frustration, etc.: Can., adopted ex US, ca. 1910; in mid-C.20 also Brit., esp. juvenile.

shuff-duff. Super high frequency direction-finding gear: RN: since ca. 1955. (Granville, letter, 1962.) Phoneticised initials, a natural extension of **huff–duff**, q.v.

shuffle and grunt. Less common var. of **grumble and grunt.**

shuffle-bottom. A fidgety child, often in address: domestic: since late C.19. (P.B.)

shuffler. A tramp; any vagrant: market traders': prob. since ca. 1870. (*M.T.*) App. a ref. to that shuffling gait which carries a man along economically for mile after mile.

shufti. Alternative, and more 'correct', spelling of **shufty** in the following entries.

shuftiscope. Instrument used by a doctor for research in cases of dysentery: Army: since ca. 1930.—**2.** A telescope; a periscope: mostly Army: since ca. 1935.—**3.** Hence, 'a long metal probe with a light on it used by Customs officers for probing into cars and baggage' (Sanders): since ca. 1945. *The Times*, 12 Apr. 1962, news item. All 3 senses ex:-

shufty, v. (Usu. in imperative) 'Look' or 'watch': RAF, since ca. 1925, ex stations in the Middle East; whence soon also Army. Jackson, 'The origin is Arabic'. Also *shafti* (or -*y*) or *sharfty* (McDouall, 1945). Also as a n., esp. in *have a shufty* (*at*); as 'a look' it has, since ca. 1944, been NZ Services': 'We had a good shufti' (Slatter). For *a going shufty* see **going recce;** see also **airmen of the shufty.**

shufty bint. A (Middle Eastern) woman willing to reveal her charms: orig. RAF, whence also Army: since ca. 1930. Cf. the cry *shufti cush!* (see **shufty,** and **cush,** n. 3) in a vulgar WW2 song about King Farouk of Egypt; *shufty bint* occurs in a companion ditty about his queen, Farida (Page, 1973).

shufty-hatch. 'A trap door in the cab of some trucks through which a passenger could keep a lookout for enemy aircraft' (Sanders, 1967): Army in N. Africa: 1940–3.

shufty jerk. 'The scrutineer or machine examiner at competition motorcycle meetings: ca. 1930s' (Dunford, 2). Cf. **jerk of the cirk.**

shufty-kite. A reconnaissance aircraft: RAF, esp. in N. Africa and Burma: 1940–5. P-G-R.

shufty-truck. A scout car: Army in N. Africa: 1940–3. Sanders.

shuftyscope. See **shuftiscope.**

shug, sug. Money: Aus. low: since ca. 1920. (B., 1942.) The second is pron. as first: short for *sugar*.—**2.** Domestic coll. abbr. for *sugar*, the sweetener: C.20. (P.B.)

shunt, n. A serious accident, in motor racing: racing drivers': since late 1950s, ?earlier. Moss, 1969; *Now!*, 2 Nov. 1979.

shunt, v. To shift responsibility of (a thing) on to another person: coll.:—1923 (Manchon). —**2.** To *shunt* (*a horse*) is to start it in a race 'with no intention of winning . . . , to induce the handicapper to reduce the horse's weight as if it were a bona fide loser' (Baker): Aus. racing.—**3.** Also *shunt off.* To get rid of peremptorily, to dismiss (someone): Aus.: since ca. 1910. Baker.

shushy. Chicken: market-traders'. (*M.T.*) Cf. synon. *chookie, coopy.*

shut-eye. Sleep: Services' and low coll., since late C.19; >, by 1925 at latest, gen. joc., esp. as *a spot of shut-eye*. Stockholm, 1899; (in Aus.) Prichard, 1921.—**2.** Hence, a deception, a trick, a swindle: Glasgow:—1934.

shut (one's) **lights off.** To commit suicide; whence, loosely, to die: from ca. 1929. Lyell.

shut(-)out, have (got) a. (Of the goal-keeper) to have no goals scored against one: at ice-hockey: from 1936. (*Evening Standard*, 25 Feb. 1937.) Cf. S.E. *lock-out* and s. *put up the shutters.* 'Immediately ex the jargon of baseball, where "to *shut out*" = to hold scoreless in an entire game' (R.C.).

shutter(-)bug. An amateur photographer: Aus.: adopted, ca. 1945, ex US. (B.P.) P.B.: some use in UK, later C.20.

shutters. In *put up the s. against*, to debar, or to black-list, someone: coll.: since ca. 1925. Moseley, 1935.

shwaiya, shwiya. See **schwaya.**

shy. In *have a shy for* (someone), to search for: Aus.: since ca. 1920. Baker.

shy-making. Alluded-to by Maugham, 1930, thus, 'Popular adjectives (like "divine" and "shy-making")', this adj., used lit., was nevertheless ob. by 1934. It was coined, or rather first recorded, by Evelyn Waugh. P.B.: despite E.P.'s 'ob.' here (in 1st ed. of *DSUE*, 1937), the term has persisted at least until 1982 — perhaps influenced by the popularity of E.W.'s novels — and may be compared with other similarly-formed adj., e.g. *blush-making*, and *sick-making*, q.v. at **-making.**

shypoo (occ. *shipoo*). 'Liquor of poor quality' (Wilkes); hence, as adj., inferior, cheap, worthless: Aus.: the 1st, since late C.19; the 2nd, since ca. 1920 (Baker). Ronan, 1962, suggests an orig. in 'bastard Chinese': just possibly it could come from Cantonese *sai po*, a little shop (P.B.). Occ. short for *shypoo shanty*, a 'sly-grog' shop, and:-

shypoo joint. An inferior public-house: Aus.: low: since ca. 1925. Baker.

shypoo shop. 'A place where you bought beer and wine, but nothing stronger' (Ronan, 1961): Aus.

shyster. An unprofessional, dishonest, or rapacious lawyer (1856); hence, anyone not too particular as to how he conducts business (1877); hence (—1903), a generic pej.: US, anglicised resp. ca. 1890, 1900, 1905. Either ex older *shy*, of doubtful quality, disreputable, or ex *shicer.* (Thornton, F. & H., *OED*.) Powis, 1977, notes *shicer* or *sheister* as 'a cheat or "welsher"'.

sib. 'One department [of the Special Operations Executive] did nothing but contrive "sibs"—bizarre and hair-raising rumors to be spread over the Continent' (Fussell, 1975): espionage circles': WW2.

sibe. See BIRD-WATCHERS' SLANG, in Appx.

sick. (Of a ship) 'in quarantine on suspicion of infectious disease' (Bowen): nautical coll.—**2.** Silly, stupid; extremely eccentric, (slightly) mad: Aus. (B., 1942.) Orig. euph.—**3.** As applied to humour: morbid—esp., gruesomely morbid; mentally or morally unhealthy; callous; viciously unkind; callously or sadistically unkind: but often too unreal, or even too ludicrously morbid, to carry a deadly sting: coll.: adopted, ca. 1959, ex US; by 1965, S.E. (Cf. sense 2.)—**6.** In *knock* (one) *sick*, to astound, 'flabbergast': coll.:—1923 (Manchon).—**4.** See **pig-sick.**

Sick and Tired. 'Signal and Telecommunications Department' (*Railway*, 2nd): railwaymen's: since ca. 1955(?).

sick as a cat, or **parrot.** *Sick as a cat*, in earlier C.20, had the nuance 'extremely annoyed': s. >, by late 1930s, coll. (Lyell.) cf. C.19 *sick*, disgusted. Later variants are the Aus. *sick as a blackfellow's dog* (B., 1959), and *sick as a parrot*, noted by Howard, 1980, as a (mainly footballers') cliché for 'extremely chagrined'; he traces it to scare-stories in the popular press, early 1970s, about psittacosis or parrot fever—but cf. the C.17–19 *melancholy as a parrot*. And Fearon, 1984, recalls a 'Monty Python' TV comedy sketch featuring an extremely 'poorly' parrot—in fact, it was dead. The phrase became so well-known that it could lead to: ' "Nice to see them [The Parachute Regiment] looking pissed off too," said one Marine. "Cocky buggers have had it all their own way so far. I s'pose you might say that each and every one of them is looking as sick as a Para" ' (*Don't Cry*, 1983, reporting on lowered morale, anticlimax after the Falklands fighting).

sick-bay cocktail. A dose of medicine: RN: since ca. 1925. P-G-R.

sick-bay goose, a bed-pan; hence, *gooseneck bos'un*, a Warrant Wardmaster: RN.

sick-bay loungers. Fellows that go to Sick Bay to avoid Divisions or studies: Royal Naval College, Dartmouth.

sick-bay shackle. A safety-pin: RN: since ca. 1939. *News Chronicle*, 4 Nov. 1954.

sick-bay tiffy. A medical orderly in the sick-bay: RN: since—1914 (Knock). Cf. **tiffy**, an artificer.

sick bunk. A hospital bed: Army coll. (regimental aid-posts'): 1940–5. P-G-R.

sick-list, on the. Ill: coll. Ex *s.-l.*, an official list of the sick.

sickening. Unpleasant; inconvenient; (of persons) rude: Society coll.: from ca. 1920. Mackail, 1925, ' "Just a little demonstration of two men telephoning to each other. Twenty seconds by the clock." "Don't be sickening, Ian," [said Felicity].' P.B.: usage quite soon (?by 1935) became much more widespread and gen. Cf. *sickmaking*, q.v. at **-making**.

sicker, as in *sixpenny*, or *shilling, sicker*, a seaside pleasure-boat. (Deeping, 1944.) Cf. **shilling emetic**.—2. (Usu. as *the sicker*) a sick-room, an infirmary: Public Schools': since ca. 1910. By the 'OXFORD *-ER*'. Cf. **san**.

sickie. A day off, allegedly because of sickness: Aus.: since ca. 1930. (B.P.)—2. A day of one's 'sick' leave', esp. 'to *take a sickie*'—a day of such leave of absence: Aus.: since the late 1940s. (B.P.) Hence, attributively, as in 'a *sickie* conscience' (*Sydney Morning Herald*, 8 Sep. 1963).

Sid Walker gang. A crash-landing salvage party (from a salvage and repair unit): RAF: 1939+. Jackson, 'From the Cockney comedian of that name famous for his broadcast song "Day after day, I'm on my way, Any rags, bottles or bones?" ' This philosophic fellow, who died before WW2 ended, has, by posing problems and asking, 'What would you do, chums?' generated a c.p.

side, n. In (have/having) *a bit on the side*, indulge 'in an extra-marital affair' (Powis): coll.: later C.20.—2. In *on the* (e.g. cool) *side*, rather cool: from—1923 (Anderson), coll. >, by 1933, S.E. (Collinson; *OED* Sup.)

side, v.i. To hide away: police: since ca. 1920. Proctor, 1958.

side-burns. See **sideburns**.

side door pullman. See **sidedoor Pullman**.

side-kick. A close companion; a mate, occ. an assistant, on a job: Can. and Aus.: from not later than 1914. Ex the *side-kicker* of USA, where, since 1920, *side-kick* has been the more frequent; *side-kicker* is occ. heard in England, as e.g. in MacDonald, 1932. As *side-kick* it was, WW2, common in the Brit. Army as a whole. Cf. **offsider**.

side-lever, gen. in pl. Hair growing down the cheek at the side of the ear. (Author first heard it in 1923.) Cf. the orig. US *sideburns*. P.B.: *side-burns* has since > coll. Eng., but *–levers* has not lasted.

sidebox. To surround in a menacing manner, as in 'The next day I got sideboxed by three faces [well-known criminals] in a club' (McVicar, 1982): c.: later C.20.

sideburns. Side whiskers: form-adopted, ca. 1945, ex US, and sense-adapted. A var. of *burnsides*, named after the famous General A.E. Burnside (1824–81), who affected them. Cf. earlier coll. *sideboards, -scrapers, -wings*, and see **side-levers**.

sidedoor Pullman. A box-car: Can. railroadmen's and tramps' ironic: adopted—1931 ex US. In *Toby*, 1979, spelt *side door*.

sidewalk. See **superintendent of the . . .**

sideways. Of a sum of money: split each way, i.e. winner and place: racing s. McShane, 1960, 'Saucepan, sideways, Lanternjaw' = One pound, half to win, half for a place.

sidewinder. 'An unknown, but very fast, horse; a "dark" horse' (Leechman, 1976): Can.: since ca. 1960. Ludditt, 1974, 'George had a string of packhorses, but always seemed to bring in one real "sidewinder".' Not recorded, in this sense, but their origination is doubtless correct: 'From the Western sidewinder rattlesnake, which moves by coiling from side to side.'

sidies. Side whiskers: mostly RN. Granville, 1967; *Sunday Express*, 17 Apr. 1983.

sig. A signature: Harrow School: late C.19–20. Marples.—2. A signaller: Army: WW1 and since. In the Royal Corps of Signals, a (usu. joc.) abbr., in address or ref., of Signalman, as 'Tell Sig. Smith I want to see him' (P.B.). Earlier, also in *sig-[nalling]-station*.

sighter. See **fly-balance**.

sightseers. 'Card-sharps' term for the "hedge" or crowd of members of the public around the action of a three-card trick conspiracy, each such undecided person being regarded as a potential "mug" ' (Powis, 1977).

sigma (phi). Syphilis: coll. medical euph.:—1933 (*Slang*). Ex Gr. letters written on the patient's certificate.

sign on. To become a regular serviceman or -woman, or to re-engage for a further period of service with the Armed Forces: 'What! You're never signing on *again*?' (P.B.)

sign on the dotted line. To sign: joc. coll.: from ca. 1925. Ex the instructions on legal and official documents.

signal basher, usu. in pl. A signaller: Army: since ca. 1930. P-G-R.

Signalman Jimmy. The figure of Mercury in the Royal Corps of Signals badge: RSC: since ca. 1939. (P-G-R.) In later C.20 usu. simply *Jimmy*: see **Jimmy**, 3.

significant. Attractive, esp. as being in the forefront of modernity: art s. verging on j.: from ca. 1920. A vogue-cheapening of *significant*, very expressive or suggestive, perhaps influenced by *significant*, important or notable.

Sigs, the. The Royal Corps of Signals: Army: prob. since the Corps' formation in 1920. Cf. **sig**, 2.

sikhery; Sikh's beard. See PRISONER-OF-WAR SLANG, §5, in Appx.

silent cop. A traffic dome: Aus.: adopted, in late 1920s, ex US; by 1955, coll.; by 1966, verging on S.E. 'About 100 times as common as **poached egg**' (B.P., 1963). Cf. **sleeping policeman**.

silent death. An electric train: railwaymen's: since ca. 1950. (*Railway*, 2nd.) Cf. **Whispering Death**.

silent hours, the. From 11 p.m. to 5.30 a.m. (ship's bells not sounded): RN coll.: since ca. 1910. P-G-R.

silent walkabout. 'Inability to obtain work because the trawler-owners have put the word about: Fleetwood trawlers. "A Life Apart": ITV programme, 13 Feb. 1973' (Peppitt).

silly. 'The answer to "How are you?" is often "Feeling a bit silly" (has a hangover)' (York, 1980): upper-middle-class coll.: later 1970s.

silly as a hatful of worms; . . . a bag; . . . a two-bob watch; . . . a wheel. 'Extremely silly or stupid' (B., 1959, with ref. to first two): Aus.; the 1st and 3rd also Brit.; the 3rd, and prob. the others, NZ: since ca. 1930, the 3rd perhaps a decade earlier. (H. Griffith; Dick; P.B.) Cf. **daft as a brush**, and see esp. **mad as a cut snake**.

silly buggers. See **play silly . . .**

silly cunt! A low pej. address or ref. to a person: late C.19–20. In 1914–18, the soldiers applied the term, with or without this or some other epithet, to material objects.

silly kipper. A mild term of disapproval; affectionate address to a child: non-aristocratic: earlier C.20. Cf. *giddy kipper*.

silver pheasant. A beautiful society woman: 1920s. Manchon.

silver plate! Please: joc.: since ca. 1916. A Hobson-Jobson of French *s'il vous plaît*. Holt, 1932, has the var. *silvoo play!*

silver saddle. A bed-pan made of stainless steel: since ca. 1950. ' "They call them silver saddles in the Air Force," he said' (Blight, 1952).

silver sausage. A barrage balloon: 1938+. (H. & P.) Ex its shape and, in the sun, its colour.

silver-tail (or solid). A 'swell'; 'someone affluent and socially prominent' (Wilkes): Aus. derogatory.—2. Hence, an affected person, one who puts on airs, a social climber: since ca. 1910. B., 1942.—3. A better-class prisoner in gaol: Aus. c.: since ca. 1930. Brewster, 1944.

silvery moon. A Negro: r.s., on *coon*: later C.20. Barker, 1979.

silvoo play! See **silver plate!**

sim. A confidence-trickster's dupe: Aus. c. (B., 1942.) I.e. a simpleton.—2. Coll. shortening of (aircraft cockpit) simulator: RAF: later C.20. 'Each session consists of two sim rides . . . ' (*Phantom*).

simp. A *simp*leton: coll.: adopted, ex US, ca. 1910. In use at St Bees at least as early as 1915 (Marples).

simple-lifer. One who leads 'the simple life': 1913: coll. >, by 1930, S.E. Collinson; *OED* Sup.

simply. Used as an intensive, e.g. *simply frightful*; *simply too awful for words, my dear!*; etc., it is very much a coll.: upper and middle classes': since (?)1920s. In mid-1980s it > simply, an irritating advertisers' tic, a vogue word, as in 'Simply, the best there is . . . '. (P.B.)

sin-bin. Penalty box: ice-hockey players', commentators', journalists': since ca. 1946. The penalty against an offending player is a two-minute 'rest' there. Some 'crimes', however, attract a more than two minutes' penalty. 'Prob. Canadian, almost the homeland of ice-hockey' (R.C., 1976).—2. As in 'Sin-bins or opportunity centres? Caroline St-John Brooks assesses special units for the disruptive' (headline in *New Society*, 8 Jan. 1981); in the article, the writer has '[Children disruptive in school] are sent to special units—the "sin-bins" of the newspaper headlines.' Hence, anywhere where miscreants, or the merely mischievous, may be sent to 'cool off'.—3. See **shaggin' wag(g)on**.

sin bosun, the. The ship's chaplain: RN: since ca. 1925. (Granville.) There are numerous *bosun* compounds—e.g. **custard bosun**.

sin-shifter. A Catholic priest: Aus.: since ca. 1930. (Marshall, 1962). An allusion to Confession.

sing. 'To break from evasion, or from false cover, to tell the truth' (L.A.); hence, to inform to the police: adopted, ex US underworld, ca. 1930; by 1940, police; by 1950, gen. Cf. the earlier synon. *sing out*, the prob. orig. A police elab. is *sing like a canary* (Hunter, 1969).

Singapore tummy. Diarrhœa, with extreme queasiness, contracted in Singapore: at Singapore, among expatriates. (Petch, 1969.) Regional var. of *Delhi belly, Malta dog*, etc.

singed. 'Fed-up'; tired. (Clark, 1982.) ?A var. of *browned-off*.

Singers. Singapore: orig. RN, hence other Services': since ca. 1930. (Granville, 1962.) By the 'OXFORD -ER(s)' Cf. **Honkers**, Hong Kong.

single-bagger. A cruel ref. to an unprepossessing girl: ' "A single-bagger . . . is so ugly that you have to insist she wears a paper bag over her head before going anywhere near her. A double-bagger is so unspeakably disgraceful that you have to wear a paper bag as well in case hers falls off" ' (A RM officer [but evidently not a gentleman], quoted in *Don't Cry*, 1983).

sink. To 'lower' or drink: from ca. 1926. Holt, 1932, 'Let's go out and sink a few beers. We can talk at the pub.'

sink (h)er. To intromit the penis: low (?orig. nautical). Cf. **sink the soldier**; and see **she**, 1—although the ref. could be to torpedo-ing a ship.

sink the boot in. To kick (someone) brutally: low Aus. (B., 1953.) Cf. Brit. **put the boot in**.

sink the soldier. (Of the male) to copulate: low. Cf. **dip** (one's) **wick**, and **bury old Fagin**.

sinker. A shilling: tramps' c.:—1932 (Jennings).

sinks, the. See **Sacks and the Sinks**.

siphoning. A beating with a length of rubber pipe: Eton College: mid-C.20. See quot'n at **hosing**.

sippers. 'A sip from the "tot" of each member of the mess, allowed to the Leading Hand who measures the rum' (Granville): RN: since ca. 1900. By the 'OXFORD/RN -ER(s)' on *sip*.—2. Peppitt defines the mid and later C.20 sense: 'A sip from a seaman's tot, levied by mess mates for minor services': RN. Cf. **gulpers**.

sir. One's teacher: elementary schools': earlier C.20. 'I'll tell sir.' Ex the *sir* of respectful address.

Sir Anthony. A fool, an obnoxious man: abbr. r.s. Sir A. Blunt = cunt: ephemeral, at the time of the spy scandal in which he featured. (N.Watts, 1988.)

Sir Basil Spence, the. The Household Cavalry Barracks: Cockney soldiers': since ca. 1960. Ex the famous architect—?and rhyming on S.E. *tents*.

Sir John. Penis: joc. coll.: C.19–20. Cf. **John Henry**, and see quot'n at **servants' entrance**.

Sir John and Baby John. 'A pun. Senior *surgeon*/doctor of a two-man medical team. "Doctor at Sea", ITV show, 21 Apr. 1974' (Peppitt)—from the book by Richard Gordon, 1953.

sissified. Effeminate: coll.: since ca. 1925.

sister. A term of address to any woman: (low) coll.: adopted, ex US, ca. 1925, at first chiefly among journalists; ob. by 1980.—2. As *Sister* [in charge of the] *Children's* [ward, etc.], *Sister Theatre*, etc.: medical coll. *Slang*, 1935.

sit, n. Esp. *have a sit with* (a girl, a boy): Aus., mostly teenagers': since ca. 1920. Lindsay, 1933.—2. In (*be*) *at the sit*, 'To travel by buses and trams for the purpose of picking pockets' (*The Referee*, 17 Feb. 1907: *OED*): c.

sit, v. To sit for, to take (an examination): middle-class coll. (Wilson, 1957.) P.B.: in later C.20, informal S.E.

sit-down, n. A sit-down meal: Can. (ex US) hoboes' coll.: late C.19–20. Niven. 1927.

sit down, v. To land: airmen's coll.: from ca. 1925; † by 1950. *OED* Sup.—2. To settle (at or in a place); to take up land: Aus. Baker.

sit on a draft-chit, esp. *be sitting . . .* , about to be transferred to another ship: RN lowerdeck: since ca. 1920. (P-G-R.) Granville points out that its full force is 'unable to leave until one's relief arrives.'

sit pretty. To (be very comfortable and) look pretty: coll. Orig. US. Ex fowls, esp. chickens, sitting prettily on the nest.—2. Esp. (*be*) *sitting pretty*, (to be) in a very advantageous position: coll.: since ca. 1920. I.e., as R.C. suggests, to be 'handsomely situated'.

sit up and beg. 'He can make it sit up and beg' indicates that a man has become extremely proficient in working some material, e.g. a metal: since ca. 1930. Ex teaching a dog to do so.—2. Applied to the position adopted by a rider on an early veteran motorcycle: motorcyclists'. (Partridge, 1979.)—3. Phrase used to describe elderly cars or old-fashioned bicycles: coll.: since ca. 1950. Perhaps ex 2, and ultimately ex, like 1, a dog taught to do so: the upright appearance. (P.B.)

sit with Nellie. To learn a new job, trade, occupation, etc., by sharing work, under instruction, of someone already adept at it: coll. Usu. as vbl n., *sitting . . .* (P.B.)

sitter. A regular drinker of alcoholic liquor: Aus., esp. Sydneyites': since ca. 1940. (Robyns, 1949.) He sits and sits—and drinks and drinks.—2. 'An enemy submarine on the surface' (Granville): RN: WW2. I.e., an easy target, as 'a sitting bird'.

sitting drums. One's working-trousers: tailors': early C.20.

sitting on their hands. (Of an audience) that refuses to clap: theatrical: from ca. 1930.

sitting pretty. See **sit pretty**.

Sitz, the. The 'phoney war' of late 1939–early 1940: coined, 1940, in retrospect and as a pun on the German 'blitz' invasion of N.W. and N. Europe; by 1946, ob. 'Gunbuster', 1941; P-G-R, 1948. P.B.: also *sitzkrieg*, on *Blitzkrieg*.

siwash gunner. 'Acting gunnery officer. What a siwash duck is to a real duck. (An Alaskan dog that resembles an Eskimo dog)' (Granville): RN.

six-and-eight. Honest: r.s., on *straight*: since ca. 1930. Gosling, 1959.—2. A 'state', as in 'Wasn't home till sparrow-fart and my old tiger (wife) was in a right six-and-eight' (Daniells, 1980): r.s.: later C.20. The combination of figures is prob. ex the traditional engagement fee for a solicitor or attorney: 6 shillings and 8 pence ($\frac{1}{3}$ of £1). Occ. also *two-and-eight*.

six doss in the steel. Six months' imprisonment: Aus. c. B., 1942.

six foot. '6 ft 5$\frac{1}{2}$ in. space between tracks' (*Railway*, 2nd): railwaymen's coll.

six knots and a Chinaman. Unknown speed: RN: late C.19–20. Of anecdotal orig. (Peppitt.)

six months hard. A card: r.s. Esp. in WW1 for a ticket in the game of House (tombola). Franklyn. Ex coll. *six months' hard* (labour).

six o'clock. One's rear quarter, as in ' "Watch your 6 o'clock", cover your rear/look behind you' (Hawke): Army and RAF (*Phantom*) coll. verging on j.: later C.20. Ex method of giving direction by the clock-face, e.g., 'At 3 o'clock from the bushy-topped tree'. Cf. **deep six.** (P.B.)

six o'clock swill. 'The rushed drinking before 6 p.m. in hotel bars. Mainly Victorian, since ten o'clock closing was introduced into N.S.W. some years back' (B.P.): Aus.: since ca. 1930. Also NZ, as in 'New Zealanders . . . vote today on whether to end their "six o'clock swill" ' (*Daily Mail*, 23 Sep. 1967).

six o-six; gen. written '606'. Salvarsan, a remedy for syphilis: medical, hence military coll.: from ca. 1910. B. & P.

six (-) to (-) four. A whore: r.s. (Curtis, 1939.) Ex racing odds.

six-wheeler (usu. in pl.). A draught horse: cavalrymen's: late C.19–20; by 1945, ob. Armstrong, 1937.

sixer. 'Six of the best'—six strokes of the cane: Public Schools': earlier C.20.—2. In *chuck*, or *throw, a sixer*, to be startled or completely nonplussed: Aus.: since ca. 1910. (Stivens, 1951.) Ex cricket—or dice; cf. **throw a seven.**

Sixpenny Sick. The Portsmouth—Gosport ferry: Portsmouth area: 1930s. (Peppitt.) Cf. **shilling emetic.**

sixpennyworth; ninepennyworth. A prison sentence or term of *six*, of *nine*, months: London's East End: since ca. 1945. Herd, 1957.

sixty nine! 'The shearers' code-warning that ladies or visitors are approaching and bad language is "out of order" ' (*Straight Furrow*, 21 Feb. 1968): NZ.

sixty-niner; occ. variants, **flying sixty-nine** and **swaffonder** or **swassander.** The sexual practice known in France—and in Brit. and the Dominions—as *soixante-neuf*, 69: RN ratings': since ca. 1940. See **soixante-neuf.**

sizzler. 'A restaurant steak served on a metal plate . . . so hot that the meat sizzles vigorously when it reaches the table' (Leechman): coll., mostly Can., since ca. 1945.

skads. Var. spelling of **scads.** Thomson, 1932.

skag. See **scag.**

skate, n. A troublesome rating: RN: since ca. 1920, perhaps adopted ex US, where, since ca. 1890, it has been short for *cheapskate* (W. & F.). 'A leave-breaker and "bad hat", generally. A skater on the thin ice of Naval law and discretion' (Granville). Cf. **bird** in this sense, and **skates-lurk.** L.A., 1969, adds 'But skates are out for themselves and to pull a fast one against their mates, so that I have only heard "skate" from ex R.N. men with intensive "absolute skate".' However, Mr P. Daniel, in a transcription of a lively lower-deck conversation, starts with 'Hello you skates—dripping and loafing as usual?', in which it is clearly joc.—2. See sense 2 of:-

skate, v. To 'act Jack-my-hearty; to go in search of wine, women and song' (Granville): RN: since ca. 1925.—2. (Also *skate off* or *do a skate.*) To depart hurriedly: Aus. low: since ca. 1925. B., 1942.

skate-bashing. 'Groups of civilian youths who beat up sailors call it skate-bashing, because sailors are like skate: ("two-faced and no guts")' (*New Society*, 3 June 1982, p. 381). But cf. **skate,** n., 1.

skate-lurker. See **skates-lurk.** 'Prob. the "dodge" is *skates lurk*, the impostor *skatelurker.*'

skates. In *put* or *get* (one's) *skates on*, to hurry; evade duty; desert: Army, perhaps pre-WW1; >, by 1919 and in at least the 1st sense, gen. F. & G.—2. See **sharpen** (one's) **skates.**

skates(-)lurk. 'A begging impostor dressed as a sailor' (H., 1st ed.): c.; † by 1903. Perhaps = *skate's lurk*, a fish's—hence a 'fishy'—trick! (Bowen has *skate-lurker*.) P.B.: just poss. the orig. of **skate,** n.

skating. Drug-exhilarated: raffish: since ca. 1955. 'She had nearly half a bottle—and, boy, was she skating?' 'Hardly a question, but rather an exclamation of delighted astonishment, therefore " . . . was she skating!" ' (Leechman.)

skating rink. A bald head: joc.: since ca. 1910. (Riley, 1933.) Short for *flies' skating-rink.* Granville notes it as RN lower-deck, with var. *eggo*: cf. **egg,** the head.

sked. A *sche*duled time to transmit/receive: radio operators' coll., soon > j.: since ca. 1930.

skeg, n. and v. '(Take a) look' (Hawke), as in 'Keep a skeg on the street', keep watching: RM: later C.20. Ex E. England dial. (*EDD*.)

Skeggy. The East coast seaside resort Skegness: Midlands', from which so many of its summer visitors come. (P.B.)

skein. A glass of beer: Army: early C.20. (F. & G.) 'Could this be a perversion of Ger. *Stein*, an earthenware beer-pot, in use in US from 1901?' (R.S.)

skeleton. 'A typical sentence, not to exceed sixty words; no word therein to be of more than two syllables,' as an old journalist defines it: journalists' coll.

skel(l)ington. A sol. (and a dial.) form of *skeleton*: C.19–20. (*EDD*.) In C.20 occ. used for humorous effect. Cf.:-

skelly. A skeleton: archaeologists' joc. coll. Cf. prec.

skerrick. A small fragment; particle; scrap. (Idriess, 1931; *M.T.*) Ex N. Country dial. (*EDD*.) Hence the mainy Aus. *not a skerrick*, intensifying 'nothing', as 'Did you find anything?' or 'Did they leave you anything?'

skers (pron. *scurze*). A naval rating wearing a full set (moustache and beard); often in address: RN: since ca. 1925. Abbr. whis*kers*: contrast **skin,** 3. (Granville; P.B.)

sketch. To deal with (someone) in a disciplinary way: Army: WW2.

skew. App. only *be skewed*, to be caught or punished: schools':—1923 (Manchon). Ex older s., to be failed in an examination.

ski. A taxi: Aus., esp. bodgies': since ca. 1950. (Dick.) Rather ex *taxi* than by r.s.—2. Whisky: RAF: WW2. The no. 11 (Legs Eleven) Squadron song, in Jackson, 2, p. 140, penultimate line: 'And wherever there's a bottle or a *chota* drop of "ski" . . . '—See **sky,** 2.

ski-slope. 'Series of steep ladders that progress through many decks' (Malin, 1979): MN, esp. Townsend Thoresen Ferries'.

skib. A house-painter: builders'. Cf. the Warwickshire dial. *skibbo,* a house-painter, a whitewasher. (*EDD*.) The var. *skiv* (ca. 1920+) was probably suggested by **skivvy.**

skid, v. To go; to depart: mostly joc., esp. schoolboys': early C.20. (Collinson.) Cf. synon. *scoot* and *scuttle*; see also **ski-doo.**

skid artist. 'Get-away [after a crime] car driver' (Powis): c.: later C.20.

skid kids. Boys racing, speedway fashion, on ordinary bicycles: 1945+. A factual rhyme.

skid lid. A motorcyclists' crash-helmet: since late 1950s. (Wharton, 1966.) Cf. prec., and s. *lid*, a hat.

skid marks. Faecal smears on the inside of underpants: low coll. (P.B.)

Skid Road. 'That part of town where the hopeless down-and-outs congregate. Derived from a logging term, *the skid road*, a logging road down which logs were skidded to the river or other water for driving to the mill. When a logger had blown his stake and was ready to return to work, he waited at the end of the skid road, hoping for a lift back to camp. Hence, any place where penniless men congregate. Almost invariably, and quite mistakenly, rendered as *Skid Row*' (Leechman): US and Can.: late C.19–20 and C.20 (*Row*). It isn't definitely known whether Can. or the US originated the term; it may have arisen simultaneously in the two countries. Cf.:-

Skid Row. A notoriously depressed street in a city: Aus., esp. Melbourne and Sydney: adopted, ca. 1955, ex US. (B.P.) Some use also in UK (P.B.). See prec.

skidoo, skiddoo. To make off, to depart: 1907 (*OED* Sup.). Ex *skedaddle*.

skids, as in 'The skids are under him', he has been dismissed from a job: Army: 1940+. (P-G-R.) Post-WW2, > gen.; applied to, e.g. a politician who has lost his popularity (P.B.).

Skies. Italians: Aus. r.s., on *Eyeties*: since (?)1920s. B., 1943; B.P.

skiff. To upset, to spill: Christ's Hospital (School). Marples.

skilamalink. Secret; 'shady': East London: late C.19–earlier 20. Origin? R.S. writes, 1973: 'In my early youth (ca. 1910–25) I occasionally met *skinamalink*, a derisory noun or nickname for unusually skinny and undersized individuals . . . its form is, app., based on *skilamalink*, but its meaning is that of *skilligareen*.' R.S.'s word lasted at least until late 1940s—used of me (P.B.).

Skilligareen. An extremely thin person: lower classes':—1923 (Manchon). Perhaps, by slurring, ex S.E. *skin-and-bones*, but cf. also C.19 *skilly*, gruel.

skilly. 'A stew made of a little of everything' (Carr, 1939): RN lowerdeck: late C.19–20.

skimish, skimmish. Drink; liquor: market-traders'; Romanies', tramps', and other travellers'. (Davies, 1933.) Hence as v., to 'drink alcoholic liquor', as in 'He was out skimishing', and *skimished*, drunk, tipsy (*M.T.*). Also *skim(m)isher*, 'a heavy drinker' (*M.T.*) or 'a public, an inn, esp. if rural' (Dawson). To me it sounds like a word ex Shelta.

skimmer. (Also *skimming dish.*) A fast planing motor-boat: RN: since ca. 1935. (P-G-R.) It skims along.—2. 'Submariners term for General Service ratings' (Knight, 1984): RN: later C.20.

skin, n. Women in general, girls in particular: as in 'a taut drop of skin', a shapely female: RN. A *bit of skin* is also Anglo-Irish. See comment at **skin and blister.**—2. A person: Anglo-Irish: late C.19–20. 'He was known far and wide as a decent old skin' (Behan, 1958). Cf.:—3. An RN lowerdeck vocative: since ca. 1950. Perhaps opp. **skers,** q.v. *Heart,* 1962 (P.B.)—4. An official explanation required for any discrepancy: Post Office telegraph messengers' (—1935). Among railwaymen, it = an incident report: prob. since mid-C.19 (McKenna, 2).—5. A cigarette paper: prisoners' c. and drugs world: later C.20. Wyatt, 1973; Home Office.—6. Shortened form of **skinhead,** q.v.: since ca. 1970. (Bournemouth *Echo,* 2 Jan. 1971.) 'No skins will be served', notice outside a Camden Town (N. London) bar, reported in *Time Out,* 13 June 1980; 'What is it then that provokes skins to punch, kick, nut and razor?' (Walker, 1980).—7. In *get under* (one's) *skin,* with complementary *have* (*got*) *under* (one's) *skin,* to irritate: to be constantly irritated by, aware of, someone or something, as in the famous love-lyric by Cole Porter, 1936, 'I've got you under my skin': coll.: since ca. 1925.—8. In *have a skin,* to possess (overmuch) self-assurance: RN: since ca. 1920. (Granville.) Short for *thick skin*; cf. *have a hard neck.*

skin, adj. Fresh, new: RM: later C.20. Hawke.

skin-a-guts. A proletarian var. (—1923) of S.E. *skin-and-bones,* a very thin person. (Manchon.)

skin and blister. A sister: r.s.: late C.19–20. (F. & G.) Franklyn comments, 'it is one of the few rhyming slang phrases that is never employed in a reduced form, the reason being that to refer to women and girls as "skin", or as a "bit o' skin" [see **skin,** n., 1], is highly disrespectful, implying a laxity of morals . . . '

Skin-Back Fusiliers, the. 'A satirical attribution of a Serviceman's affiliation to an imaginary regiment or unit: WW2' (L.A., 1976). Cf. **skin the live rabbit,** for the name occurs in a bawdy song in which foreskins are mentioned (P.B .).

skin dog. A male 'sexual athlete': Can. low: since ca. 1950. Cf. **skin,** n., 1.

skin(-)flick (or solid). A film in which some of the characters appear in the nude, and which usu. includes scenes of sexual

intercourse: since ca. 1972. Chambers' *C.20th Dict.,* 1977 Sup.

Skin-footer. See **Skinfooter.**

skin-game. Facial plastic surgery as practised on would-be glamorous women: since ca. 1935.

skin(-)head. See **skinhead.**

skin off your nose!(, here's to the). Your good health!: a, mostly Services', toast: earlier C.20. F & G.—2. In esp. *it's no skin off my nose* (occ. *his, your,* etc.), it makes no difference to me, because (the affair, activity, etc.) will put me at no disadvantage; a declaration of disinterest: coll.: since mid-C.20. (P.B.)

skin out. To desert: RN. Bowen.

skin pop. 'Inject narcotic drug (heroin, for example) into the skin rather than into a vein ("main-lining"): the words "skin-popper" may be used as a term of patronising contempt by a confirmed addict to one just starting' (Powis): drugs world: adopted, ex US, late 1950s. Wyatt, 1973; W. & F.

skin the live rabbit. To retract the prepuce: low: late C.19–early 20.

Skinfooter. An Icelander: Grimsby fishermen's: later C.20. 'So called because they were shod with animal skins until [WW2]' (Sweeney, 1984).

skinful. Esp. in *to have had,* or *got, a s.,* to be extremely drunk: coll.: since early C.18. Franklyn, 1737; Truck, 1825; P-G-R, 1948.—2. Hence, *to have had a skinful,* to have had more than enough of anything; to have had too much to put up with: low coll., mostly Services'. (Seton, 1935; P-G-R.) Cf. *bellyful.*

skinhead. One of a gang of teenage louts and hooligans characterised by their closely cropped or shaven heads: at first, mid-1960s, coll.; very soon > S.E. similar **bovver boys, punks, mods and rockers,** etc. Early in 1970s Richard Allen published a series of novels, *Skinhead,* 1970, and *Skinhead* elaborations. Ex the earlier (since late 1940s) *skin-head,* n. and adj., (a) bald-headed or close-cropped (man).

skinner. 'One guilty of indecent assault, esp. on children' (Schroeder, 1976): Can. c.: since ca. 1950—or earlier.—2. A very successful bet, from the bookmakers' point of view, on a horse-race: Aus.; since mid-C.19 (Wilkes) and, since ca. 1920, Brit. (*Sunday Times,* 3 Oct. 1965).—3. An appointment deliberately missed: Aus.: since ca. 1925. B., 1943.—4. Sexually 'in her': low Aus. r.s., rare: since ca. 1930.

skinny. A girl or young woman: Aus. (B., 1942.) Cf. **skin,** n., 1.

skinny dip. A swim in the nude: Aus.: adopted, ex US, ca. 1960. Also hyphenated, as v., > Brit.: *Guardian,* 17 Sep. 1981, 'The women [at the Turkish bath] talk, fantasise, bicker, skinny-dip . . . '

skinny Liz. Any elderly woman: St Bees. (Marples.) P.B.: but this is mere localisation of gen. and widespread *skinny Lizzie,* rudely applied to a thin woman of any age. It shows yet another example of the attraction of assonance in popular speech.

skinny malink. Can. var. of *skinamalink,* q.v. at **skilamalink.**

skint. Very nearly or, more usu., completely penniless: orig. joc., lower classes' and Services', > by 1945 fairly gen. (F. & G.) In Cockney, *skint stony* for emphasis: 1930s (Wolveridge, 1978). I.e. *skinned.* See also **boracic.**

skip, n. A portmanteau; a bag, a valise: grafters'. (*Cheapjack,* 1934.) P.B.: specialisation of dial./S.E. *skep* or *skip,* a basket or other container.

skip, v. In *skip* (*bail*), to abscond on bail: c. > gen. coll.

skip it! Don't trouble! Forget it!: coll.: adopted ca. 1939 from US.

skip-stop. A train that 'skips' every second station: Aus.: since ca. 1925. (B.P.)

skipper. A barn: c.: mid-C.16–19. Hence, a 'bed' out of doors: tramps' c.: late C.19–20. In later C.20, an empty house, where one can 'doss': vagrants'. (Wilson, 1980).—2. (Always *the skipper* and not *Skipper So-and-So.*) Since 1917 or 1918, the commander of an aircraft in flight: RAF coll. Ex S.E.

skipper, the master of a vessel.—3. A mode of address, as in 'What's the time, skipper?': since ca. 1920. Cf. *captain, colonel, squire*, used thus.—4. As *the skipper*, the Section Sergeant: police: later C.20. Seabrook, 1987.

skipper's doggie. A 'midshipman acting as captain's A.D.C.' (F.& G.): RN: earlier C.20.

skips. The ship's captain: RN lowerdeck: since ca. 1925. Familiar for *skipper*. P-G-R.

Skirt-Chasers, the. The Royal Army Service Corps: Army: since ca. 1940. A pun on 'R.A.S.C.' P.B.: the Corps was 'rationalised' out of existence in 1965. Cf. the older *Ally Sloper's Cavalry*.

skirt-hunting. A search, 'watch-out', for either girls or harlots: coll.: late C.19–20. (Spenser, 1934.) A Service (esp. RAF) var., WW2, was *skirt-patrol* (H. & P.).

skirt job. Formal dress for a formal occasion: female social workers': later C.20. 'Oh damn, that means changing again! In court this morning—that'll be a skirt job—and then youth club later, back to T–shirt and jeans' (D. Beale, 1988).

skit. A large number; a crowd; esp. in pl., lots (*of*): coll.: 1925 (Hutchinson: *OED* Sup.). Cf. US *scads* in same sense.—2. Used exactly as synon. *nit*, or the older *cave*, to keep watch for, and give warning of, the approach of authority: Duke of York's Army boys' school, Dover: later 1940s. Also as exclam. *skit!* = someone's coming! (Paine, 1988.)

skite. A motorcycle: 1929 (*OED* Sup.). Perhaps ex the abominable noise it makes.—2. In *on the skite*, having a terrific binge: Scottish Public Schools'. Cf.:—3. In *go on the skite*, to go drinking: Army: ca. 1920–45. P-G-R.

skits. A schizophrenic: since ca. 1930, but not common before ca. 1960. Ex **schizo.**

skitter. A person: pej.: earlier C.20. Perhaps ex mosquito.

skitterbug. A Bren-gun carrier (small, lightly-armoured, tracked vehicle): Aus. Army: WW2. (B., 1943.) Prob. ex next, with a pun on *jitter bug* (P.B.).

skitters, the. Diarrhoea: Services': since ca. 1930. (P-G-R.) Cf. synon. **squitters.**

skittle. To knock down; to kill: mostly Aus.: late C.19–20. (B., 1942.) Ex the game of skittles. P.B.: in Eng., usu. *skittle out* or *over*, mostly in 1st sense, and with implication of easiness.

skittling. The feminine practice of washing stockings, handkerchiefs and 'smalls' in the bedroom or bathroom washbasin: hotel-keepers' and hotel-staffs', esp. in Scotland: since ca. 1920.

skitz. Var. of **skits**; ex *schizo*, a schizophrenic.

skive, n. An evasion; a loafing: low: since ca. 1925. (Norman.) Ex the v.

skive, v.t. and i. To evade (a duty, a parade, etc.): Services': from 1915; the v.t. from slightly later. (F. & G.) Perhaps ex Lincolnshire *skive*, to turn up the whites of the eyes (*EDD*), or from Fr. *esquiver*, or from dial. *skive*, to skim or dart about, esp. rapidly. P.B.: by mid-C.20, very widespread and gen., and often as *skive off*, v.t. and i.

skiver. A shirker, 'schemer': orig. Army, since ca. 1915 (Kersh, 1941); by ca. 1950, gen. Ex prec. 'Some children can stop a class in its tracks. What should be done with the muckers about, the skivers, the bunkers off?' (*New Society*, 8 Jan. 1981).

skivess. A female servant: Stowe School: 1930s. (Worsthorne, 1977.) Cf.:-

skivvy, n.; occ., at first, **skivey.** A maid-servant, esp. a rough 'general': from ca. 1905. (George, 1914.) Perhaps a perversion of earlier synon. *slavey*.

skivvy, v; **skivvying,** vbl n. To perform heavy, boring, menial household chores, either in the home, or in hotel or other institution: coll.: later C.20. Ex n.

skiz. See **schitz.**

skoosh. A sweetheart: Army: early C.20. (F. & G.) Poss. cognate with dial. *scouse*, to frolic.—2. 'A general term for any soft drink . . . , also used to mean anything easily accomplished, to which an alternative form is *skoosh-case*: "Four

nuthin tae the boys — a pure skoosh-case!" To *skoosh it* means to do something easily or win by a mile' (Munro, 1985): Glasgow.

skoshi. A little (Fr. *un peu*): UN troops': ca. 1951–5 in Korea. (*Iddiwah*, July 1953.) P.B.: hence, some use among Brit. Servicemen in Far East, later 1950s–early 60s. Ex Jap. *sukoshi*, little.

skull. The head of a two-up penny: Aus.: since ca. 1910. Glassop, 1949, where the nuance is 'a two-up penny turning heads'. B., 1953.—2. In *out of* (one's) *skull*, out of one's mind; mad; crazy; drunk, as in 'slewed out his skull': adopted, ca. 1970, ex US. Wainwright, 1975.—3. A passenger in a lorry. See HAULIERS' SLANG, in Appx.

skull-dragging. 'Pulling a victim downstairs by his feet so that his head is painfully battered' (B., 1953): Aus. c.: since ca. 1930.

skull job. Fellatio or cunnilingus. See **head job.**

skul(l)duggery. Underhand practices; villainy: coll., orig. joc. An extension of the mostly American senses (malversation of public money; obscenity), spelt *skullduggery*, of the Scottish *sculduddery*, in C.19–20: also *sculduggery* (or *sk*-), itself of obscure origin.

sky, n. In *have a sky*, have a look, to glance around: ?mostly Liverpool: since ca. 1920. Matutinal meteorology.—2. Whisky: Aus.: since ca. 1950. (B.P.) Ex whi*sky*. Cf. **ski,** 2.

sky, v. (Of a horse) to throw (its rider) high into the air: Aus., mostly rural: mid-C.19–20. Ronan, 1956.

sky(-)artist. A psychiatrist: RN lowerdeck and Army: 1940+. (Granville; Michael Harrison, 1943.) By Hobson-Jobson—and wit.

sky-blue pink. Joc. for colour unknown or indeterminate: since ca. 1885. In C.20 elab. to *sky-blue pink with a finny addy* [= Finnan haddock] *border* (Richards, 1984, Cheshire); or . . . *with yellow spots/dots in* (Huston, 1984, N. Country; she adds that it = *dandy grey russet*, itself a var. of *dandy-go-russet*, which in *EDD* = worn-out, faded clothes).

sky-hacking (or one word). Back-biting; slander: Aus.: since ca. 1925. (Baker.) P.B.: ?cognate with older *chy-ack*, to chaff or cheek.

sky-hog. An airman that flies low over houses: 1945+. On *road-hog*.

sky-hook. 'A useful, but mythical, piece of apparatus which enables an airman to hover over one spot. Can also be used for any difficult job of lifting,' (Emanuel, 1945): RAF, esp. among the regulars: since 1918. But Leechman vouches for its use, in Can. (esp. among loggers), as early as 1909.

sky-rocket; occ. **skyrocket.** A pocket: r.s.: 1879 (Horsley); Powis, 1977.

sky wire. A radio aerial; an antenna: Aus. radio hams': since ca. 1955. (B.P.)

skypiece. 'Smoke trails of sky-writing' (H. & P.): RAF: since ca. 1930. Ex painting.

skyrocket. See **sky-rocket.**

slab. A slice of bread and butter: streets'. Vivian, 1933.—2. A long paragraph: journalists': since ca. 1910.—3. In *on the slab*, on the operating table: RAF aircrews': 1940+. (L.A.) The butcher's slab.—4. A sandwich. Cf. sense 1, and see CANADIAN ADOLESCENTS', in Appx.—5. See **slabs.**

slabbed and slid. 'Dead and gone. One who left prison a long time ago, and who has been forgotten, may be spoken of as "slabbed and slid", meaning that he went out long ago and that anything may have happened to him' (Tempest): prison c.: mid-C.20.

slabs. Testicles: butchers' back s. *Muvver*.—2. Plaice that have recently been spawned: trawlermen's. (Butcher, 1980.) Cf. **ivy-leaf; penny stamps.**

slack bobs. The small minority of boys excused from rowing and cricket, but allowed to play tennis: Eton. McConnell, 1967.

slack out. To go out: Public Schools'. Benson, 1916.

slack party. Punishment for defaulters: Royal Naval College, Dartmouth. (Granville.) Ironic.

Slackers. Halifax, Canada: R. Can. N: WW2. (P-G-R.) See also **Squibbley.**

slag, n. Has many senses, or nuances, all pej The earliest is from later C.18, a coward, 'one unwilling to resent an affront' (Grose, 2nd ed.). A C.20 example is in Bell, 1936, as showmen's s. Corruption of *slack-mettled*. See **slaggy.**—2. 'Cheat, villain, contemptible person' (McVicar, 1974): prison c.: since ca. 1930. See quot'n at **scrote.**—3. One who looks at the free attractions but avoids the paying shows: showmen's: since ca. 1880.—4. Hence, a layabout; a rough: market-traders': since (?)late C.19. (*M.T.*) Cf. **slink,** n., 2.—5. 'A man, never less than 35, who has often been in trouble with the police and who, more often than not, is liable to be sentenced to preventive detention when he next gets into trouble' (Roeves, 1958): low, mostly London: since ca. 1945. Cf. synon. **lag.**—6. A prostitute; but rare except in *old slag*, always contemptuous: low: since late 1950s. Cf. 'The eternal teenage sexual paradox is that boys who "put it about" are called "studs" by their admiring friends, but girls who do the same are "slags" (and nobody likes them) . . . ' (a St Paul's, London, schoolboy, quoted in *Harpers & Queen*, Aug. 1978). Cf. also:—7. Collective for 'young third-rate grafters, male or female, unwashed, useless' (Cook, 1962): since ca. 1945: c. >, by ca. 1960, also low s. Also, *ibid.*, such an individual.—8. Females collectively: low: since ca. 1950. 'Surburban slag filling in time' (Barlow, 1968).—9. Rubbish; nonsense: Aus.: earlier C.20. Palmer, 1948.—10. An insulting comment: Glasgow. (Munro, 1985.) Ex v., 3.

slag, v. To expectorate or spit (v.i.): low Aus. ' "Hell," muttered Richie, "he's slaggin' on me car!" ' (Dick.) Ex Scottish dial. *slag*, to moisten, to besmear.—2. 'To admonish in violent terms' (Powis): low: later C.20. Cf.:—3. To 'run down', to slander: low: since ca. 1945. Norman, 1959.

slag about. To come up around and about: low: late 1970s. 'Slagging about in all weathers . . . ' (Daniells, 1979). Cf. **trog,** and relevant senses of **slag,** n.

slag down or **off.** To disparage, to run down and 'bad-mouth': later C.20. Elab. of **slag,** v., 3.

slag-name. An insulting nickname, as in 'Ma right name's Archie an ma slag-name's Cokynut-heid' (Munro, 1985): Glasgow schoolchildren's.

slagger. The agent ex **slag,** v., 2 and 3. Letter, *Guardian,* 27 June 1982.

slaggy. The adj. for most senses of **slag,** n.: low. Buchanan-Taylor, 1943, 'It seemed slaggy to me. (A *slag* is a person who is not much *bottle*—not much good; a person for whom you have no respect, even if he or she is holding a *poke* (plenty of money) . . . '

slam. To strike or punch (someone): since ca. 1910. (Marlow, 1937.) Sometimes as *slam him one*.

slam hammer. 'Slide hammer. Sometimes called a "slam hammer", "slam puller", or "Yankee" . . . A tool used by car thieves to pull out the cylinder of the ignition lock; it also has a legitimate use in removing dents in wing and bodywork of cars' (Powis): later C.20.

slammer. A prison: Can. c.: adopted, ex US, ca. 1965. Cf. earlier US c. *slammer*, a door (W. & F.). P.B.: by later 1970s adopted also in UK: Hitchens, 1980, 'two charges . . . which would have carried a maximum of 14 years in the slammer'. Cf. entry **twister,** at JIVE, in Appx.

slammer shuffle. A walking peculiar to convicts. See prec., 1. Also known as *the prison waltz*.

slang-dipper; -dropper. A *slang-dipper* is 'one who gilds metal chains for the purpose of selling them as gold.' A *slang-dropper* is the man 'who disposes of them, as he usually does so by pretending to pick [one] up in the street under the nose of his victim, [whom] he immediately asks to put a value on it': c.:—1935 (Hume). Ex c. *slang*, since early C.19, a watch-chain, hence any chain.

slant. A sidelight (*on*); a different or a truly characteristic opinion (*on*) or reaction: US, anglicised ca. 1930. Via *angle* (*on*).

slap. 'A slap-up meal' (Anderson): beatniks': since ca. 1959. Anderson, 'Others have the folding-lettuce for slap.'

slap a few on the deck. To fire a few rounds: artillerymen's: WW2. P-G-R.

slap and tickle, a; esp., *have a bit of slap and tickle*. 'Necking', to 'neck'; but, since late 1950s, usu. to make love: the former, since ca. 1910, the latter since ca. 1920; since ca. 1950, both are coll. The former occurs in, e.g., Maugham, 1924.

slap-happy. Very—strictly, boisterously—happy; esp., recklessly happy: coll.: adopted in 1942 from US (see quot'n at **stream-lined**). Jackson. I.e. back-slappingly happy.—2. A synon. of *punch-drunk*: since ca. 1945. London *Evening News*, 27 Oct. 1950.—3. Hence, loosely, careless and feckless, as in 'a regrettably casual and slap-happy way of doing things': coll.: later C.20. (P.B.)

slap in. To put in a formal application to higher authority, e.g. for redress of grievance, leave, etc.: RN lowerdeck: since ca. 1930. P-G-R; *Heart,* 1962.

slash, n. A urination: c., and low. See the v., 3.—2. Hence(?), a drink: low London: since ca. 1930. (La Bern, 1950.) For the semantics, cf. **piss-up,** a drunken bout.

slash, v.i. To cut a person across the face with a razor: c.:—1933. Esp. as vbl n. (Leach.)—2. V.t. to deprive (an accomplice) of his share: c.:—1933. (Ibid.) Cf. **carve up.**—3. To urinate (usu. of males): low. (Thomas, 1976.) P.B.: rare; much more common as n., esp. in *have*, or *go, for a slash*.

slasher. A man in charge of a 'fleet' of steam or petrol locomotives: Public Works':—1935. Perhaps ex:—2. A fast driver: busmen's: since ca. 1925. Contrast **scratcher,** 3.—3. A hockey stick: Cranbrook School: since ca. 1920. Proleptic.

slasheroo. Excellent, most attractive: Aus.: since ca. 1944. (B., 1953.) The suffix *-eroo* was adopted from US servicemen; *slash*ing + *-eroo.*

slashers. Testicles: low. England, 1968.

slate. To assign (someone) for a job: Services': since mid-C.20. Usu. in passive + *for*, as 'We've got you slated for 2 i/c to Tom', or 'He's slated as Jim's replacement'. Ex putting name on a slate. (P.B.)

slated. Drunk: s. (Richards, 1983.)—2. With petticoat showing below the skirt: Cheshire. 'Crosstalk', 1984.

slather. See **open slather.**

slathered. Tipsy: Aus.: since ca. 1920. (B.P.) Prob. ex N. Country dial. *slather*, to spill, to rain, to splosh.

slats. The ribs: US, whence Aus.,—1916 (C.J. Dennis), and Can. (Beames); by ca. 1950, also Brit., esp. in a *kick*, or *punch, in the slats* (P.B.). Ex shape.

slaughter, n. A wholesale dismissal of employees: proletarian:—1935. Also a *work-out*.—2. 'Superintendent Kneff lost his temper. "If we can't catch 'em, we must find the slaughter," he decreed. (A slaughter is the quiet, secluded spot, generally a farm or a walled car park, where thieves transfer stolen goods from one vehicle to another, split consignments into easier-handled amounts, display items to receivers, and go about their unlawful occasions.)' (Scott, 1977); police s.: since 1950s. Elliptical for *slaughter yard*, used metaphorically. Recorded earlier in Clayton, 1970.

slave. An aircraftman or aircraftwoman: RAF (since ca. 1939) and WAAF (1941+). Jackson. Humorous.

slavey market. An employment bureau for domestic servants. (Horne, 1923.) A pun on S.E. *slave market*, and C.19 *slavey*, a servant.

Sleaford Tech. The RAF College at Cranwell, Lincolnshire: Services': later C.20. (Green, 1984.) Sleaford is the nearest town (cf. **Slush**); Tech. shortens 'technical college'. Cf. **Fenland Polytechnic.**

sleaze. Sleaziness: coll.: later C.20. 'Cognoscenti of trash, aficionados of sleaze' (York, 1976); 'The [play] was dripping showbiz sleaze' (Robson, 1980). Both forms of n. ex:-

sleazy. Grimy or dilapidated—or both; (cheap and) inferior: adopted, in late 1950s, ex US. A blend of *slimy* and *greasy*, or—just as prob.—ex a racial slur on Silesia.—2. Hence, in

Brit., garish and disreputable: since ca. 1959. 'Half the wardroom were in some sleazy night club that was raided' (Winton, 1960). P.B.: *SOD* dates sense 1, 1946; adj., and n. *sleaziness*, by 1983, informal S.E.

sledder. A thief: Liverpool street arabs': late C.19–mid-20. (*Arab.*) ?Origin.

sledging. 'In cricket, the taunting of a batsman by members of the opposing team in order to undermine his confidence' (Wilkes): Aus. sporting(!): 1970s.

sleep around. '(Of a woman) to be on terms of sexual familiarity with various men friends and acquaintances' (L.A., 1969): coll.: since late 1940s. P.B.: later applied also to males; perhaps not quite so undiscriminating as is implied in pej. 'promiscuous'. Prob. an extension of the euph. *sleep with*, to copulate. Cf. **sleepabout.**

sleep at Mrs Greens. See **sleep with . . .**

sleep-walker. A sneak thief: Aus. c. B., 1942.

sleep (one's) way (up). (Of a woman) to gain advantage by dispensing sexual favours, as in Hunter, 1974: '[She] is a promiscuous bitch, to my certain knowledge. She was using Adrian [a theatrical producer] to sleep her way to the big time.': later C.20, poss. ex US. (P.B.)

sleep with Mrs Green. To sleep in the open: NZ tramps' c.,— 1932; hence, also Aus. (Baker). Aus. var., in Prichard, 1932, *sleep at Mrs Green's.* I.e. on the green grass. Cf. **Greenfields**, 1, and **Star Hotel.**

sleepabout. A man that will 'sleep around', q.v.: since ca. 1975. (Keating, 1978.) A blend of '*sleep* around' and 'lay*about*.' (P.B.)

sleeper. A player too much favoured by his handicap: lawn tennis:—1923 (Manchon).—2. A delayed-action bomb: from 1940.—3. (?)Hence, as in 'Haydon who . . . was recruited by Karla the Russian as a "mole", or "sleeper", or in English, agent of penetration' (Le Carré, 1977); he remains 'asleep' until called upon to act for his masters, perhaps many years later: espionage: since ca. 1945.—4. A book, gramophone record, etc., that, after starting unsatisfactorily to sell, eventually becomes a 'hit': trade coll.: since ca. 1950. (B.P.; Wharton.) Cf.:—5. In the secondhand book trade, a book one dealer finds in another dealer's stock, and buys considerably underpriced according to the current market: 1970s. (Wakeman, 1980.) A specialisation of 4.—6. 'Second man on diesel' (*Railway*, 2nd): railwaymen's: since late 1950s.—7. A sleeping pill, or sedative drug: since late 1920s. The agential *sleeper*, a soporific.

sleeping. Slow-witted: Glasgow:—1934. Cf. **slept in.**

sleeping policeman. A ramp on a private or restricted-access road to slow down traffic: since (?)ca. 1960; by 1970, coll.; by 1977, virtually S.E. Cf. **silent cop.** (P.B.)

sleever. A drinking straw: NZ. B., 1941, compares Aus. (*long*) *sleever*, a long drink: later C.19–mid-20.

sleigh ride. Cocaine: drugs c. (Stockley, 1986.) US throughout C.20 (Spears). Cf. **snow.**

slept in (he, she, etc.**).** A Glasgow c.p. (—1934) = too late; not quick enough.

slewing a head. See **pullaway** at AUSTRALIAN, in Appx.

slice. A slice of bread and butter: coll. *Week-End Review*, 18 Nov. 1933.—2. In *take a slice*, 'To intrigue, particularly with a married woman, because a slice of [*sic*] a cut loaf is not missed' (Grose, 2nd ed.): coll.: mid-C.18–mid-19. Extant as *take* (or *help yourself to*) *a slice off the loaf*, as in Sarl, 1938, 'You could safely help yourself to . . . '; and, allusively, in Hunter, 1955, 'He'd give his arm to tumble her [and] I wouldn't mind a slice myself, if it comes to that.'—2. An attractive girl: teenage boys': 1982. (H. Burt.) Cf. **hunk,** and the synon. **tart, pastry,** etc.

Slice of Cheese, the. 'The monument erected by Mussolini west of Tobruk. It was wedgeshaped' (Sanders, 1967): Army in N. Africa: 1940–3.

slice of knuckle pie. A punch in the mouth: low. (*Heart*, 1962.) Cf. synon. **knuckle sandwich,** and contrast:-

slice of pie. Army var. of **piece of cake:** ca. 1940–6. P-G-R.

slick. Neat or smooth; attractive, desirable: Can.: adopted, ca. 1946, ex US. 'Boy, look at Jane! There's a slick chick.' (Leechman.) The term *slick chick* for a girl, esp. a young lady, was fashionable among teenagers, beatniks, etc., in the late 1950s (Anderson); cf. quot'n at **Canary, 2.**—2. See **slickee . . .**

slick as a whistle. 'Very smoothly done; well done: W. Can.: earlier C.20' (Leech, 1986). Cf. **slicker than snot.**

slicked down. (Of male head-hair) plastered down with brilliantine, etc.: coll.: adopted ca. 1930 from US.

slickee-slickee, n., and **slicky-slick,** v. Theft; to steal; not in a big way: United Nations troops in Korea: ca. 1951–55. (*Iddiwah*, July 1953.) By pidgin English out of *slick*, not-quite-honestly smart, itself adopted, ca. 1918, ex US—as coll., not s.

slicker. A city person 'who tries to out-fox the country folk; or someone who dresses "real slick" in very fancy, stylish or expensive clothing. Usu. a man. Also "city slicker" ' (Leech, 1980): Can.: later C.20, adopted ex US, as it has been in coll. English, where the term *city slicker* is, when used as e.g. political pej., bordering on informal S.E. W. & F., 1960, note 'archaic' for US, but give quot'ns ca. 1950 for both terms. The orig. is the US *Samuel Slick of Slickville, The Clockmaker* of Thomas Haliburton, 1837; *slick* ultimately ex *sleek*. (P.B.)

slicker than snot (on a doorknob). 'Really smooth. Numerous connotations: as in a job very smoothly or neatly and well done; or as in to pull off something, e.g. a movement or an action in athletics: Saskatchewan: since 1940s' (Leech, 1986).

slicks. Magazines printed on glazed stock: Can. journalists', printers', publishers', news-vendors': since ca. 1930. (Leechman.) Cf. synon. **glossies,** and **shiny.**

slide. Butter: RN lowerdeck: since ca. 1930. Hence *slide and glitter*, butter and marmalade: id. Ex greasiness.

slider. An ice-cream wafer: Glasgow:—1934 (Baxter).

Slim. 'The Navy's ironic name for a fat man' (P-G-R): since ca. 1920.

slim, adj. Tricky, artful: 1674 (*SOD*); by later C.19 coll., almost s.; by mid-C.20, ob. 'We were discussing "slim" practices and the prevalence of the basic desire to get something for nothing' (*Punch*, 15 Jan. 1919).

slim-dilly. A girl, young woman: Aus.: since ca. 1920. (B., 1942.) Cf. **skinny.**

slime, n. Semen: low: C.19–20.

slime, v. To flatter, to curry favour: Aus. low coll.: later C.20. McNeil.

slimy. Deceitful; treacherous: coll. Ex *slimy*, vile.

sling, n. A bribe: Aus. c. and low: since 1930s. Also *sling back* (Prichard, 1948: Wilkes). Ex v., 1.—2. Hence, a tip (of money): Aus.: since ca. 1935. (B., 1959.)—3. In *beat it for the sling*, fail to appear in court. See AUSTRALIAN, in Appx.

sling, v. 'To pay a bribe or gratuity, esp. as a percentage of wages or winnings' (Wilkes): Aus.: since 1930s.—2. To fire (shells): Army: WW2. P-G-R.—3. (Of a horse) to throw (its rider): Aus.: since ca. 1910. B., 1943.

sling a yarn. To relate a story: C.20: s. >, ca. 1930, coll.—2. Hence, to tell a lie: 1904, *The Strand Magazine*, March, 'Maybe you think I am just slinging you a yarn' (*OED*).

sling (one's) drizzle. To urinate, as in 'The slob shouts across the stage, "There's some bird here who wants to sling her drizzle" ' (*Sunday Telegraph* mag., 25 Oct. 1987, on teaching by negative example, at RMA Sandhurst): raffish.

sling it. To leave one's work or one's job: Aus. coll.: since ca. 1910. Prichard.

sling off. To depart; to make off: Aus.: since ca. 1925. B., 1942.

sling one up. Var., Army and RAF, of *throw* (a commissioned officer) *one up*, to salute: since 1930s. Jackson.

sling round. 'To air-test an aircraft' (Jackson): RAF, and civilian test pilots': since ca. 1930. The pilot does aerobatics.

sling (one's) service about. To boast, esp. of the length of one's service: Services': earlier C.20. F. & G.

sling the hatchet. To make off; escape: c.:—1923 (Manchon). By prob. deliberate confusion with earlier synon. *sling one's hook*.

sling to. To pay out (esp. protection) money to; to bribe: Aus.: since ca. 1920. See **sling, v.**, 1.

slingers, the. Dismissal, rejection; abandonment: low, then gen.: since ca. 1940. Norman, 1959.

slink. A sneak, skulker, cheat: dial. (—1824) >, ca. 1830, coll. *The Examiner*, 1830, 'Such a d—d slink' (*OED*).—2. Hence, in C.20, and esp. among market traders, a loafer, as in '*slinks and slags*, loafers and layabouts' (*M.T.*).—3. Meat fat; hence *slink-walloper*, someone fond of it; hence, adj., greedy, hence inferior: RN training ships': early C.20. (Peppitt.)

slinkers in for (someone), **put the.** To hint adversely to authority about (someone): L.A. notes hearing it ca. 1960. To *slink* evokes an impression of craftiness and slyness.

slinky. Sneaky, mean, sly, furtive: dial. and coll.: since late C.19. E.g., among schoolboys, *a slinky one* = a silent but pungent fart, released with malice aforethought (P.B.). Ex **slink, n.**, 1.—2. Hence, (of gait) slyly smooth; glidingly and unobtrusively sensuous or voluptuous.—3. Applied esp. to a woman's smooth and clinging dress or gown, e.g., 'a slinky little number in black, with velvet trimming': coll.: later C.20. (P.B.)

slinter. A trick, esp. if unfair; mostly in *work a slinter*, to effect a mean trick, tell a false story: Aus. low: since ca. 1920. (B., 1942.) Cf. **schlenter.**

slip. Abbr. *side-slip*, a method of losing height quickly without gaining speed: RAF coll.:—1932. Cf. **slip off.**—2. A small sum given by the operators to a loser now penniless, to enable him to get home: Aus. two-up-players': since ca. 1920. (B., 1953.) They slip it to him.

slip, v.i.; gen. **be slipping.** To weaken, physically; go downhill, fig.; lose grip, ground, status, etc.: coll. Ex one's foot slipping.

slip (her) **a crippler;** sometimes . . . **a quick crippler.** Synon. with **slip a length,** 1: low, mostly Services': since (?)ca. 1950. (P.B.) Cf.:-

slip a fatty. To copulate: low: later C.20. (Hibbert, 1983.) Cf. **crack a fat.**

slip a joey. (Of a woman) to have a miscarriage; but also, to give birth to a child: Aus. low B., 1942.

slip (her) **a length.** To coït with (a woman): low: late C19–20.—2. Hence, *slip him a length*, to reprimand: Army: since ca. 1925.—3. Of a man, to have homosexual relations with: Aus. low s.: late C.19–20. Construction: *slip a length into*. MacInnes, 1952.

slip-horn. See **fish-horn.**

slip in the gutter. (Bread and) butter: r.s. Franklyn.

slip it about (a woman). To coït with.

slip it across or **over** (a person). To hoodwink; to befool: from ca. 1912. B. & P.—2. To punch or strike: Army. Also *push* . . .

slip off (height). To fly lower esp. by rapid descent: aviators' coll.: from ca. 1925. *New Statesman and Nation*, 20 Feb. 1937.

slip-slops. Slippers: domestic coll. Also a var. of *flip-flops*, the oriental drag-slippers or sandals. (P.B.) And see **thongs.**

slip-stick. A slide-rule: Can. engineers' and architects': since ca. 1940. (Leechman.) Cf. RN *look-stick*, a telescope.

slip (one's) **trolley.** To go mad; to lose control of one's emotions: since late 1940s. Ex *slipped off* his trolley, or *lost* it? Perhaps orig. trolley-bus or tram-drivers' s., as R.S. has suggested; if so, then dating from ca. 1925 or earlier.

slip-up, n. An appointment or rendezvous intentionally failed: Aus. B., 1942.—2. An error, the n. ex v., 2: coll. verging on informal S.E.: since (?)mid-C. 20. ' 'Fraid you've made a bit of a slip-up there.' (P.B.)

slip up, v. In *slip* (a girl) *up*, to render her pregnant unexpectedly or by trickery: lower classes':—1923 (Manchon).—2.

V.i. To make a mistake, to fail: mid-C.19–20; US, anglicised ca. 1910 as a coll. var. of *make a slip*. *OED*; Lyell.

slippers on(, with or **it's got).** Said of a noiseless fart: schoolboys'. (L.A., 1978.) Cf. **slinky,** 1.

slippery, n. Forged banknotes: orig. c., then low s.: prob. throughout C.20. (Petch, 1971.) Cf. **slither, n.**

slippery, adj. Clever; (very) skilful or adroit: lower-class: since ca. 1930. Crookston, 1967, 'Some of the old blacksmiths were very slippery.' P.B.: but usu. with an implication of shrewd cunning.

slipping, be. To be dying: white-slavers' c., applied to a prostitute (working for a pimp). (Londres.) Cf. **slip, v.i.**

slips. In theatre or cinema, the sides of a gallery: Aus.: since ca. 1920. (Baker.) Wilkes, letter, 1979, comments, 'Not Aus. I had seats in the gallery slips at Covent Garden in the 1950s, and they were so advertised', to which Raab adds, 'since season 1946–7, according to C.G. archives'.

slips his braces, he. Said of a man complaisant to homosexuality: coll.

slit. Clitoris: raffish: since ca. 1920.—2. (Gen. in pl.) Women: low: since early 1920s. Ex 1.

slither. Counterfeit money: c.:—1929 (*OED* Sup.). Cf. **slippery, n.**—2. A rush, a great hurry: 1915 (Wallace: *OED*). Ex the v.—3. Short for *slither and dodge*, a lodge (e.g. of Oddfellows): r.s.: late C.19–20. *New Statesman*, 29 Nov. 1941.

slitherum. A counterfeit coin: c. (*Yorkshire Post*, latish May 1937.) Ex **slither,** 1; lit., a 'slither' one.

slithery. Sexual intercourse: c., and low.

slittie. A slit trench: Army, Other Ranks': 1940–5. P-G-R.

Sloane, n. and **adj.** Since mid-1980s, common abbr. of:-

Sloane Rangers, the. Generic nickname, coined by Peter York for his article in *Harpers & Queen*, Oct. 1975, for the distinctive upper-middle class, ex public and finishing school girl secretaries, living around Sloane Square, London, and going to their county homes at weekends. A witty pun blending the district, the cartoon character 'The Lone Ranger', and various regimental names. P.Y. writes, 'They haven't a big vocabulary, though they heighten the effect of their few adjectives by exaggeration—"the most", "utterly", "riveting", "spastic", "blissful", "draggy".' See esp. York, 1980, for a wickedly observant natural history of the genus. (P.B.) Whence also *Sloanish*, adj. See also **Soanly Ranger.**

slob. A 'softy', a fool, a (stupid) lout: (orig. low) coll. (Park, 1955.) Ex the Anglo-Irish *slob*, 'A soft fat quiet simpleminded girl or boy:—"Your little Nellie is a quiet poor slob": used as a term of endearment' (Joyce, 1910).—2. Hence, a heavily-built, slow-moving, dull-witted, meagre-principled, imperceptive man: since ca. 1920. (L.A., 1976.) Since WW2, occ. of a female. P.B.: prob. reinforced by US influence.

slobber-swing. A complete circle on the horizontal bar: circus s. verging on j.:—1933 (Seago).

slobberings. Money, esp. cash: c.:—1923 (Manchon).

slonk. To sleep, doze, or just laze: Services': since ca. 1950. Interchangeable with **gonk.** (P.B.) E.P. suggests perhaps a blend of *sleep* + either *gonk* or *honk*, both of which are echoic; but there is also a strong element of *slump*.

sloop. A neckerchief: c.:—1933 (Leach). Perhaps because '*s a loop*.

slop. A prisoner's overcoat: Dartmoor c. (Triston, 1938.) Ex *slops*, old and very cheap clothes.

slop back. To drink freely, as in Slatter, 'Sloppng back the suds': NZ: since ca. 1925.

Slop Carriers, the. The Australian Army Service Corps: Aus. Army: 1939+. (B., 1942.) Play on initials: cf. **Skirt-Chasers.**

slop chest. 'Ship's clothing store' (Granville): RN: C.19–20. Cf. **slop.**

slop-chit. A 'form made out by the Supply rating, which enables a man to buy "slops" in the stores' (Granville): RN coll. 'He's quot'n at **adrift.**—2. Hence, as in 'I can't do that job, I've enough on my slop-chit already' (cited by Granville): since ca. 1900.

Slop House, the. The House of Commons: journalistic: since ca. 1910. (Horler, 1938.) Ex the amount of 'slop' talked there.

slop-made. Disjointed: Aus.: coll.:—1909; very ob. (Ware.) Presumably ex *sloppily made*.

slop-pail. A man doing housework: low coll.:—1923 (Manchon).

Slope (usu. in pl.; also as adj.), (a) Chinese: some use among Brit. and Aus. servicemen in the Far East: from early 1960s, perhaps earlier. Ex WW2 US Service usage, orig. *Slopie*, later *Slope* (W. & F.). Also var. *Slope-head*. Cf. **Chinkie**; **tid**; **chogey**. (P.B.)

sloping billet. A comfortable job for a married naval man: RN. (Bowen.) I.e. with many opportunities to 'slope off' (s. since mid-C.19) to be ashore with one's family.

sloping shoulders, he's got. Said of a column-dodger, a shirker, or one with 'a chip on his shoulder': RN: later C.20. (Gell, 1984.) Patterson ascribes the phrase to Portsmouth dockers, with the imputation that 'a right sloping shoulders merchant' is one adept at avoiding responsibility. Graphic.

sloppy. Negligent, inefficient, careless, slack: coll.

slops. Sailors' readymade clothing: RN: C.19–20. See also **slop chest**, **slop-chit**.—2. Subjects other than classics or Mathematics: Cambridge University:—1923 (Manchon).—3. Beer: Aus.: since ca. 1920. (B.P.) Perhaps ex C.19–20 nickname for Allsopp's [London] ales.—4. The Service Police: RAF: ca. 1930–42. Ex *slop*, orig., since mid-C.19, back s. of *police*.

slosh, n. Nonsense, esp. if sentimental: from ca. 1920. (Mackail, 1933.) Ex *slush + bosh*.—2. A form of coarse billiards, 'in which all the coloured balls except red were used, and the striker of the white ball could cannon, pot or go in off. It was a game for the exuberant and not very skilful' ('Blake', 1941): RAF officers' messes': since late 1930s (?earlier). (P.B.)—3. Beer: RN lowerdeck: since ca. 1910. Echoic. Cf. **slops**, 3.—4. Boiled rice: Christ's Hospital (School): early C.20. Marples.—5. Coffee: Aus.: since ca. 1920. B., 1953.—6. A blow, as 'a slosh across the chops': coll. Ex:-

slosh, v. To hit, esp. resoundingly, and often wildly: low coll. > gen. 'I sloshed him one' (*Sessions*, 13 Dec. 1904); ' 'Im what I sloshed for readin' my letters' (Lyons, 1912). Prob. ex S.E. *slosh*, to splash about in mud.

slosh and mud. A collar stud: theatrical r.s.: late C.19–20. Franklyn.

slosh around. To strut about; take one's 'swanky' ease: proletarian:—1923 (Manchon). Cf. **slosh**, v.

sloshed. Drunk: low coll. > gen.: late C.19–20. P.B.: cf. the Chinese idiom, 'as drunk as mud'.

sloshy. Emotional, excessive in sentiment: orig. at Harrow: Lunn, 1913; Benson, 1924, ' "Positively his last appearance," said David. "Rather theatrical, but not sloshy . . ." '; 1933, *Daily Mirror*, 26 Oct. ' "Sloshy talk" '. Ex *sloppy + slushy*.—2. Very moist: preparatory schools': from ca. 1910. Benson, 1916, 'Sloshy buttered toast.' Ex dial. P.B.: dial. *sloshy* may well be the orig. of sense 1, i.e., dripping, 'wet'.

slot, n. A prison cell: Aus. c.: later C.20. (B., 1953.) Hence, gaol generally (Wilkes).—2. In *down the slot*, (of a slow train) diverted to allow faster trains to pass: railwaymen's: since ca. 1910. *Railway*.

slot (strictly **'s'lot**)! Thank you very much: Aus.: since ca. 1945. Obviously 'thanks a *lot*'. (B.P.)

slot (one) **in.** To choose (someone) to fill a vacancy, as 'We're slotting you in as 2 i/c to Tom for the time being': Services', > gen.: later C.20. Cf.:—2. To score a goal: sporting, mostly soccer, as in the commentator's 'Oh, and he's slotted that one in beautifully': later C.20. (P.B.)

Sloth Belt, the. Southern India: Army officers in India, 'a derogatory expression': late C.19–earlier 20. (Allen, 1977.) Ex heat-induced lethargy + pun on uniform 'cloth belt'.

slotted kip. A two-up 'kip' in which, to hold a two-headed penny, a slot has been cut: Aus. two-up gamblers' c. B., 1942.

slotted job. A woman: low, orig. Services': since ca. 1940; ob. by 1970. Physiological. Cf. **blue-stockinged**. . . .

sloughed. 'Euphemisms for death abound in hospitals. *Unwell* and *terminally unwell* are well used; *uprooted* I heard recently (more a witticism than established slang [see **cabbage**, 3]); *sloughed* (by analogy with the skin of a snake) is probably the commonest' (Hamblin, 1988).

Slow and Dirty, the. The Somerset & Dorset Railway: railwaymen's: 1874–ca. 1966. (Althill, 1967.) Also known, by more satisfied passengers, as the *Sweet*, or *Swift, and Delightful* (Marsh, 1986).

slow as molasses in winter(, as). Exceedingly slow: coll.: late C.19–earlier 20. (Collinson.) In winter, molasses is very stiff. Later C.20 Can. version is *slower than molasses in January* (Leech, 1981).

Slow, Easy and Comfortable, the. The South-Eastern and Chatham railway: railwaymen's: early C.20. *Railway*, 2nd.

Slow Starvation and Agony. A joc. interpretation of the initials of the Shaw Savile and Albion shipping line: since ca. 1910; by 1965, ob.

slowpoke. A dull or (e.g. socially or sexually) slow person: Aus. (Stead, 1934.) Perhaps a corruption of *slowcoach*.

sludge. Beer: office- and shop-girls': ca. 1955–60. The var. *plasma* lasted less than the year 1958. (Gilderdale.) P.B.: the term had wider currency than E.P. allows; cf. Service messes.

sludger. Member of a 'crew of Greater London Council "mud hoppers" [sludge-removers], working with dredgers': coll.: from before the GLC ever existed. London *Evening News*, 5 March, 1973.

slug, n. A heavy bill: Aus. (B., 1942.) Ex earlier s. *slug*, a setback.—2. A small shell (projectile): Army: 1940+.—3. An armour-piercing shell or shot: artillerymen's: 1940–5. P-G-R.—4. 'A horse lacking vitality': Aus. coll. (B., 1953.) Prob. not a transferred sense of S.E. *slug* but a backformation ex S.E. *sluggish*.—5. A nugget of gold: Aus. miners'. Prichard, 1932.

slug, v.t. To charge (someone) as a price: Aus.: since ca. 1920. (B.P.) 'He slugged me a quid.'

slug-up n. A 'frame-up' (fraudulent charge or victimisation) Aus. c.: since ca. 1910. B., 1942.

sluggers. 'Wardroom telescoping of *sloe gins*, gin cordials flavoured with sloe berries.—2. Heavy seas that pound a ship's hull; from the boxing sense of hard hitting' (Granville'): RN.

sluice. The female pudend: low coll.: late C.17–20; ob. by 1970. Hence, copulation: low. Naughton, 1970, 'I asked her would she like a sluice. She wasn't quite sure what I meant.'—3. Fuel pipe: motorcyclists':—1950. (Dunford.)

sluicing. Pickpocketry in public wash-places: c.: from ca. 1920. Wallace, 1924.

slum, n. Sweetmeats for coughs: market-traders' (e.g. Petticoat Lane). Also, in full, *cough-slum* (Cheapjack, 1934).

slum, v. Applied to those members of the Government who, disapproving a policy, sit among the back-benchers: Parliament: since ca. 1920.

slum-box. A (typical) house in the slums: coll.:—1923 (Manchon).

Slum(m)abad. Islamabad, the new capital of Pakistan: United Nations personnel: since 1976. (Mindel, 1977.)

slumber-suit. Pyjamas: derisive: from ca. 1924. Ex drapers' j.

Slump Alley. Carey Street, where the Bankruptcy Court is situated: mostly Londoners': since ca. 1930.

slunch. Eton pudding. Also *slunching*.

slurge. 'A very *ropey* recruit' (H. & P.); 'a studious-minded chap' (H.W., 1942): Services': earlier WW2. Perhaps a blend of *slack + snurge*. See **ropey**.

slurp. To eat, to drink, noisily, messily, in an uncouth way: coll.: adopted, ex US, ca. 1955. Echoic, and prob. influenced by such cartoon 'noises' as 'slurp, drool'. (P.B.)

S

slurpies. 'Psychedelic slurpies, forms or patterns formed by the manipulation of rays of light, and similar *passé* forms of decoration' (heard on BBC Radio 4, 17 Feb. 1975: P.B.). Prob. ex the idea of slop food or pap.

slush. Counterfeit paper money (esp. notes): c., orig. US, anglicised in 1924 by Edgar Wallace (*OED* Sup.). Ex the inferiority of slush.—2. 'To work and toil like a slave: a woman who toils hard' (Joyce, 1910): Anglo-Irish: late C.19–20.—3. As *Slush*, the town of Sleaford, Lincolnshire: RAF stationed in the area: late 1940s–50s, perhaps longer. (P.B.)—4. 'Unsolicited manuscripts which very rarely make their way into becoming actual books: publishers' ' (Green, 1984).—5. Hence 'Unsolicited demo[nstration of artistic ability] tapes received by a recording company' (Hibbert, 1983).

slush-bucket. Since ca. 1950, Aus. var. of next. (B.P.)

slush fund. A secret fund of money, prob. raised from dubious sources, kept by a large organisation, political or commercial, for bribery and other shady dealings: orig. US s., since ca. 1860, > C.20 coll. (W. & F.); adopted in Aus. ca. 1930 (B.P.), and later in UK, where given wide publicity at the time of the Leyland 'Slush fund case' in May 1977. (P.B.)

slush-pump. A trombone: musicians' (esp. in theatres). Ex saliva tending to gather in instrument. Cf. the entry at **fish-horn**.—2. A car with automatic gears: car-dealers'. 'Not used so much these days' (Graham-Ranger, 1981).

slusher. One who (prints and) circulates counterfeit paper-money: c.: 1924 (Wallace). Ex **slush**, 1.

slushy. Extremely sentimental. Ex *slushy*, washy, rubbishy. Cf. **sloppy**.

slut about. To go about working: coll., esp. at Harrow School. Lunn, 'They [the 'swots'] groise their horrid eyes off and get out of fagging in a term or two, while we poor devils [the 'hearties'] have to slut about "on boy" for three years'. P.B.: i.e. to work as a slut, in sense of *slavey* or *skivvy* or *scut*, does.

sly-bag (or solid). A cunning person: Aus.: since ca. 1930. (B., 1953.) Perhaps ex *ratbag*, or earlier *sly-boots*.

smack. Heroin: drugs c.: adopted, mid-1960s, ex US. (Stuart, 1971.) US since—1938, says Spears, who suggests orig. in Ger. *schmecken*, a taste, via Yiddish, reinforced semantically by the jolt of the drug.

smack-bang. Suddenly and violently: echoic coll.: prob. since mid-C.19. 'Commodore Keyes ran smack bang into several enemy cruisers' (Carr, 1939, RN in WW1). An elab. of S.E. *smack* in this sense, which dates from later C.18 (*SOD*).—2. As in 'smack-bang in the middle', right, exactly, in the middle: an intensification. (P.B.)

smack-head. A heroin addict: drugs c. *Observer*, 28 Feb. 1988, quoting a Liverpool prostitute.

smack in the eye. A rebuff, refusal; severe disappointment; set-back: coll., perhaps at first esp. Aus. (B., 1942.) A more graphic var. of the synon. S.E. *smack in the face* (*SOD*).—2. A pie: r.s.: earlier C.20. Barltrop, 1985.

smack (a man) **in the rattle.** To charge a rating with an offence and confine him in the brig: RN. *Globe and Laurel* (the RM magazine), Sep.-Oct. 1976.

smack on (occ. **in**). Esp. *catch smack on*, squarely, or with heavy, accurate impact. (L.A., 1977.) Cf. **smack-bang** and **bang-on**.

smacker. A peso: S. American English: late C.19–20. Craig, 1935, ' ''I will give you a thousand beautiful smackers for your church . . . '' Mac took out a thousand peso bill and handed it to me.' P.B.: prob. influenced by US s. *smacker*, a dollar, ex 'the sound of the silver dollar hitting the counter' (W. & F.), and—2. £1 sterling, note or coin: Aus. (Stead, 1934); Brit. from perhaps a few years later (P.B.). B.P. notes, of Aus. usage, 'used of large sums only; *two smackers* would not be used'—but 'a couple of smackers' is acceptable in Eng. Cf.:—3. A dollar bill (note): Can.: adopted, ca. 1925, ex US. (Leechman.)—4. A boy; a youth: Aus.: since ca. 1930. Stivens, 1951.

smackeroonie, -y. A kiss: teenagers': early 1980s. (Joanna Williamson, 1982.) A smacking kiss, hence *smacker*, given the US s. suffix *-eroo* + a 'diminutive'.

small arm, (one's or) **the.** The penis. Esp. in *small-arm inspection*, a medical inspection, among men, for venereal disease: military: from ca. 1910. Ex *small arms*, revolvers and rifles. (B. & P.) P.B.: since ca. 1950, at latest, usu. *short-arm*, and only in the context given here.

small bull's-eyes. The odds and ends, the smouldering remains, of a fire: London Fire Brigade. They glow like a bull's eyes. Or, rather, 'they are *targets* for the jet' (of water from the hose). Franklyn, a Volunteer Fireman during WW2.

small fortune, a. An extravagantly large sum paid for something, esp. for something small: coll.: since ca. 1890. Ex the largish amount implied in, e.g., 'he won a small fortune on the pools'.

small go. 'A reasonable night out with everybody happy and nobody drunk' (H. & P.): Services': since ca. 1930. P.B.: † by 1950.

small-parter. A player of small parts: theatrical coll. *Passing Show*, 24 June 1933.

small pigs (rare in the singular). Petty Officers: RN lower-deck. As opposed to *Naval pigs*; cf. the Guards Regiments' **drill pig** (Granville).

smalley or **-y.** Small, little, esp. in *smally porsh*, a small portion, esp. of food: orig. RN, since ca. 1940; hence soon Army and RAF. P.B.: a friend in an army unit, later 1950s, suffered puns about his little Porsche car.

smalls. Underclothes, men's or women's: coll. Ex S.E. *smalls*, 'small clothes, breeches'.—2. Small advertisements, esp. those in classified lists: mainly journalistic coll.: since ca. 1910.

smarm; occ. smalm. To behave with fulsome flattery or insincere politeness: coll.: from not later than 1915. Ex:—2. *smalm, smarm,* coll. (late C.19–20), to smooth down, as hair with pomade. *SOD*.

smarminess. Oily politeness: coll. The n. ex:-

smarmy. Apt to flatter fulsomely, speak toadyingly or over-politely or with courteous insincerity: coll.: from ca. 1915. Ex:—2. *smarmy*, (of hair) sleek, plastered down: coll.—3. Also as adv. in both senses, esp. 1.

smart Alec. A know-all, an offensively smart person: coll.; orig. (ca. 1870), US, anglicised by 1930. (*OED* Sup.) Also *Smart Alick*.

smart arse (or one word). An obnoxiously—not a cleverly—smart person: Aus.: since mid-1930s. Hence also as adj., sometimes *smartarsed*. (Wilkes.) Cf. **smarty-pants**.

smarten up (one's) **parade.** To work more efficiently; to make oneself smart: Army and RAF: since ca. 1925. (L.A.) † by 1950 (P.B.).

smarty. A would-be clever, cunning, or witty person: US (1880), anglicised—as a coll.—ca. 1905, chiefly as an impertinent one and esp. in Aus. and NZ. P.B.: by mid-C.20, mainly juvenile use.—2. A fashionable person; one in the swim: coll.: from ca. 1930. Benson, 1933, 'Social smarties.'

smarty-pants. A smart person, either clever or fashionably dressed; one who would be either: a coll. elab. of prec., both senses: prob. adopted ex US, perhaps first in Aus., late 1930s; in later C.20 mostly juvenile, or imitation juvenile, usu. envious or pej. Cf. **fancy-pants**, and **smart arse**. (P.B.) Cleary, 1950; Blake, 1954.

smash, n. A drink of brandy in iced water: Aus.: ca. 1920–30. B., 1942.—2. A fearsome person: Aus.: since ca. 1910. Devanney, 1938—of a man violent in drink. Proleptic.—3. Money; wages: low Aus.: since ca. 1920. Tennant, 1953, 'Giving her his smash on pay-night.' Cf. UK *smash* = loose change (cash), since mid-C.19.

smash, v. To break burglariously into (a house, etc.): c.: from ca. 1920. (Wallace, 1926.) Cf.:—2. To commit a smash-and-grab raid on (a shop, etc.): since the late 1940s. Crookston, 1967, 'When you're driving away from a jeweller's you've just smashed . . . '

smash a load. To get rid of twenty counterfeit coins: c.:—1933 (Leach).

smash-ankle. Deck hockey: RN.

smash up. To barricade one's cell: prisoners' c.: later C.20. McConville, 1980.

smashed. Tipsy: since ca. 1960. Sangster, 1968, 'Getting smashed on airline champagne.' Cf. synon. **shattered**.

smasher. Anything very large or unusually excellent: coll.: 1794 (*EDD*).—2. Hence, from the 2nd nuance, applied to persons, esp. since post-WW1, an extremely pretty girl; also, e.g., in admiration of an infant, 'Ooh, aren't you a little smasher!': coll.—3. See adj. A receiver of stolen goods: c.:— 1929 (*OED* Sup.); Leach, 1933.

smashing, adj. Excellent; the adj. corresponding to **smasher**, 1 and 2. C.19–20. It had in WW2, a phenomenal popularity in the RAF; *smashing job* might be 'a very fine aircraft; a task excellently performed; a girl exceedingly easy on the eye' (Partridge, 1945). On 4 Feb. 1850, Harry (later Sir) Burnett Lumsden said, 'When our cloth arrives we shall be the most smashing-looking regiment in India' (Cadell, 1953). The adj. caught on among post-1945 civilians; after ca. 1957, it began to lose popularity, except among school-children, teenagers, lower middle-class. This sense may have originated in boxing: cf. C.19 synon. *crushing, smacking* and *stunning*.

smashing, adv. Intensive—'very' or 'much' or 'extremely' or 'notably': Kersh, 1942, 'He'd done . . . a smashing hot job' (extremely expert and artistic piece of tattooing). Ex prec.

smashing line. A beautiful girl: low: ca. 1920–40. Cf. **smasher**, 2.

smatteract. As a matter of fact: shorthand typists'.

smawm. A var., mainly dial., of **smarm**.

smear, n. A murdered person: Aus. c.: since ca. 1925. B., 1943.—2. See **tumour**.

smear, v. To defeat heavily at fisticuffs: Aus. low: from ca. 1925. (B., 1942.) Cf. **wipe the deck with**.

smeary. Superlatively good, esp. of clothes, fashion: teenagers': early 1980s. (James Williamson, 1982.) Cf. **hoopy**.

smell like a badger's touch-(h)ole. Emit an offensive odour, either naturally or, more usu., because heavily and artificially scented: RN, influenced by W. Country: since early C.20 (?earlier). Sutcliff, 1980.

smell like a whore's boudoir or **garret** or **handbag.** To be heavily scented; esp. 'of a man using scent (or merely highly scented hair-oil, after-shave lotion, etc.)' (Parsons, 1977): resp. mainly RN; MN; MN and Army—but interchangeable of course. 'Garret' here = handbag.

smell of broken glass. A strong body-odour, e.g. in a Rugby footballers' changing-room after a game: male joc.: earlier C.20. (P.B.)

smell of the barman's apron, he's had a. Applied to one who easily gets drunk: since ca. 1920. For *smell, sniff* is occ. substituted; P.B.: and for *barman, barmaid*. Cf. the Aus. synon. **two-pot screamer**.

smellie, -y, n. A film, or a play, in which scents or sprays are used to create a realistic effect: since ca. 1958.

smelly, adj. 'Shady', dishonourable, illicit, suspicious: low and police. (Manchon, 1923; Newman, 1970.) Prob. after *fishy*.

smelt it, dealt it. Retort from one accused of farting, which may be countered by the further accusation, *said the rhyme, did the crime*: schoolboys': later C.20. Woods, 1983.

smice. To depart; make off: Aus. low: since ca. 1925. (B., 1942.) Yiddish? 'Yes; it means "to smack" ' (Franklyn).

smig. A *s*ergeant-*m*ajor *i*nstructor in *g*unnery: Army: since ca. 1920. H. & P.

smigget(t). 'Lower-deck term for a good-looking messmate' (Granville, who says 'ex Maltese'): RN: since ca. 1925.

smile. 'Bare flesh—either sex—showing between shirt, or pullover, and jeans, back and front; or, earlier, gap between silk stocking and suspender belt' (Hardman, 1977): the earlier, ca. 1910–50; the latter since ca. 1950.

smile-please run. 'A photo-reconnaissance flight' (Jackson): RAF: 1939+. Ex the photographer's stock phrase.

smite. An infatuation, a passion: Society: ca. 1932–40. (Lowndes, 1937.) Cf. **crush**, n., 4.

smitzed. See MOCK AUCTION SLANG, in Appx.

smoke, n. Short for **smoke out**: Hall, 1975.—2. In *in smoke*, in hiding; hence, *go into smoke*, go into hiding: Aus. and NZ c.: since early C.20. B., 1942.—3. Cannabis: drugs c. (Stockley, 1986.) US since ca. 1946 (Spears).

smoke, v. To perform fellatio: low.

smoke-ho; -oh; smoko. A cessation from work in order nominally to smoke, certainly to rest: coll.: 1897 (*OED*).—2. Hence, a cup of tea, orig. one drunk during a rest: Aus. coll.: since ca. 1920 (Campion).—3. Cups of tea, collectively; a pot, a billy, of tea: Aus. coll.: since ca. 1925. Trist, 1946, 'I'll just trot the men's smoko over.'

smoke-jack. An inspector of factories, esp. of their chimneys: proletarian:—1923 (Manchon).

smoke like a chimney. To smoke (tobacco, usu. cigarettes) heavily and habitually: coll. (P.B.)

smoke out. A secret, or an at least protected, departure or removal operated by someone other than the speaker(s); a 'safe house': espionage: since (?)ca. 1950. (Adam Hall's novels, *passim*.) Prob. ex idea of smoke-screen.

smoke pole. A shot-gun: Can.: since ca. 1950 (poss. a generation earlier). St Pierre, 1970. Cf. **smokestick**.

smoke-trail. Vapour- or condensation-trail left by aircraft: coll., esp. among civilians in WW2; since superseded by standard j., often abbr. *con*(-)*trail* (P.B.).

smoked haddock, the. The paddock: racecourse r.s. Franklyn 2nd.

smoked Welshman. Any dark-skinned man speaking a little English, esp. the variety known as 'Bombay Welsh': Army joc.: later C.20. (P.B.)

smoker. 'Driving home at night in his "smoker" (car that a trader is using for himself) or just whatever car is left over' (Cowdy, 1965): secondhand-car dealers': since late 1940s. Cf.:—2. A high mileage car: car dealers'. (Graham-Ranger, 1981.) Ex the exhaust emissions.

smokers. Smoked salmon: since ca. 1925. By the 'OXFORD -ER(s)'; cf. **champers**.

smoker's tickers. 'Shag tobacco; any coarse dark tobacco' (B., 1943): Aus.: since ca. 1925.

smokestick. A rifle: Aus. Army: 1939+. (B., 1942.) Cf. **smoke pole**.

smoking gun. Directly incriminating evidence: US, popularised by the Watergate scandal, 1974 (Barnhart, 2); adopted in UK by mid-1980s (*The Times*, 11 Aug. 1986). P.B.: a C.20 version of the much older 'red-handed'.

smoko. See **smoke-ho**.

Smoky Joe. 'A Fleet Class minesweeper. This type being coal-burning' (Granville): RN: WW2. P.B.: the attraction of assonance; cf. **skinny Liz**.

smooch. To caress amorously: Can. Cf. **smoodge**, **smooze**.—2. Hence(?), to flirt or (v.i.) to court: beatniks' > gen.: since ca. 1959. Anderson, 'Come smooching with me, real-ly' (cf. **really**).

smoochy. Adj. from **smooch**, esp. sense 1. 'Masters of the three-minute pop song whether it be an uptempo number or a smoochy ballad' (Orme, 1979).

smoodge. To flatter, wheedle, speak with deliberate amiability: Aus.: late C.19–20. Ex *to smoothe*.—2. Hence, to make love, pay court: Aus. Dennis (*smooge*). Hence, *smoodger*, the agent, and *smoodging*, the action. Prob. ex ob. S.E. *smudge*, v.t., to caress, and dial. *smudge*, to kiss, to yearn for, *smudge after*, to begin to pay court to: on dial. *smouch*, to kiss. But cf.: 'Smoodge: to flatter or fawn. Still used in Anglo-Jewish slang and pronounced shmooze . . . from the Hebrew's shmoo-os, meaning news or hearsay. Later came to mean gossip, flattery' (Abrahams, 1938). It 'is now used only in jocular fashion. Even when we use it in sense 2, our mind is half on sense 1. If a man is said to be smoodging with a girl, he is more likely to be trying to make amends for forgetting her birthday than planning to make an attack on her virtue. "Stop smoodging!" is said to young couples holding hands, etc.' (B.P., 1963).

smoodge up to. Var. of prec.: B., 1943.

smooth as a baby's bottom; like a b.b. See **baby's bottom**.

smooth move. A well-done job; a compliment for a clever action or piece of work, as in 'Purchasing the old Jones's place was a smooth move on his part': Can.: since mid-1950s. 'May also be used sarcastically: "Smooth move, Joe", meaning "You really fouled up on that one" ' (Leech, 1985).

smootherouter. 'Steve was a born diplomat, the greatest "smootherouter" . . . the perfect Adjutant' (Phelps, 1946): coll. I.e. *smoother-outer*.

smoothie (or **-y**), n. A ladies' man; (among non-dancers) a good dancer: RAF: since ca. 1920. (H. & P.) Ex his smooth ways and manners.—2. A smooth-spoken person, esp. if male: since ca. 1925. (Blake, 1954.) P.B.: untrustworthy plausibility and deliberate charm are always implied in this pej. term, at least in later C.20.

smoothy. Adj. corresponding to prec., 2.

smooze. NZ var. of **smoodge**, 2: Devanney, 1926.

'smorning. This morning: coll.: late C.19–20. Sayers, 1933, ' "When's he coming?" "Smorning".'

smother, n. A hiding-place for stolen goods; an overcoat folded over a pickpocket's arm to mask his movements: c.:—1933 (Leach).—2. Good stuff; material of quality; coat; overcoat (*M.T.*); *Cheapjack*, 1934, specifies 'a fur coat or overcoat'; Sharpe, 1938, a macintosh: market-traders', grafters'; common in the underworld and its fringes: perhaps orig. market people's, from ca. 1870. E.P. suggested 'prob. ex the warmth it gives', but Powis prefers a deriv. ex Yiddish **schmutter**, q.v. (P.B.)

smother, v. To cover up; to hide: Aus. and NZ c.:—1932. (B., 1942.) See quot'n at AUSTRALIAN in Appx.

smother (up). To secrete a part of (the accumulated stakes and winnings): Aus. two-up-players' and esp. operators'. Ronan, 1954, 'Darcy [the cash-holder] was too shaky with laudanum. He couldn't smother up the money. We had to leave it all in sight and just let you spin for our win.' Cf. **smother**, v.—2. To wear a mask, or a stocking over the face, during a crime: since late 1940s. Clayton, 1970.

smudge. A photograph: grafters': from ca. 1920. (*Cheapjack*, 1934.) Ex blurred effect seen in many cheap photographs.—2. Hence, esp. pornographic photographs, or magazines containing them: pornographers'. Green, 1984.

smudger. An inferior street photographer: photographers'. Cf. prec., 1. Hence, any photographer: Services'; espionage: since mid-C.20. Also elab. *smudge merchant*.—2. An engine-cleaner: railwaymen's. *Railway*.—3. A pavement portraitist: '[he] charges £5 for a pencil sketch' (*Sunday Telegraph*, 12 Jan. 1986). Cf. 1.

smurf. A youth employed, under the Youth Opportunities Scheme, by transport conservation society, e.g. Crich Tramways Museum, and the Loughborough Main Line Steam Trust: early 1980s. Ex the busy elf-like creatures of a current National Petrol advertising campaign. (Irwin, 1981.)

smut-hound. A man with a marked predilection for bawdiness: coll.

snack. A certainty; hence, a thief's or a swindler's dupe: Aus. c. B., 1942.—2. Hence, something easy to do; esp., 'it's a snack': Aus.: since ca. 1920. (B.P.)

snacker. ' "You'd make a good snacker on a Hull ship," meaning a deck boy" (Piper, 1974); also used as term of address to the deck boy/odd-job man aboard a trawler.

snag. 'A formidable opponent' (Dennis): Aus. s., prob. mainly Sydney. Ex *snag*, an obstacle. James, 1975. (AUSTRALIAN UNDERWORLD, in Appx.)—2. A jagged tooth: Aus.: since ca. 1910. Park, 1950.—3. (Usu. in pl.) A sausage: id. B., 1942 (pl.); Park, 1950 (sing.).—4. An aircraft apprentice with one small chevron (*snag*): RAF, Halton: from ca. 1939.

snagger. A proletarian: Clifton College: since ca. 1910. 'The College ran [in 1915] a *Saint Agnes* mission for poor children'

(J. Willis, letter).—2. A clumsy or inexperienced shearer; a cow-milker; a cow hard to milk: Aus. rural: since ca. 1910. B., 1943.

snake, n. A lively party: RAF: from ca. 1925; † by 1950. Jackson, 'Thus, "Out on the snake"—out on a party'. Perhaps cf. **snake-juice**, and certainly cf. **snake-charmers**.—2. A very long rag-worm used as bait: anglers'. Bournemouth *Echo*, 4 July 1968.—3. As *the snake*, the hose: London Fire Brigade.—4. A senior NCO, esp. a sergeant: Aus. Army: WW2 and after. See **Snake-Pit**, 3. Wilkes.

snake, v. 'To wriggle about in the air by constant jinking when taking evasive action' (Jackson): RAF: since ca. 1938; by 1944, j. Cf. the American *snake-* (or *snaky*) *hips*.—2. (Also *snake off*.) To go quietly; slip along quietly: Anglo-Irish. Behan, 1958, uses both terms—as exact synons. To move silently, as a snake does. P.B.: or Irish pron. of *sneak*?

snake about. To take evasive action: RAF aircrews' coll. (1939) >, by 1943, j. Ex prec., 1.

snake bite. Lager and cider mixed: N.E. England drinkers'. *New Society*, 17 Nov. 1983.

snake-charmers. A dance band: RAF: since ca. 1930. (Jackson.) Ex snake-charming by music, and cf. **snake**, n., 1. There may be a ref. to 'Snake Hips' Johnson, the dance-band leader.—2. Plate-layers: Aus. railwaymen's. B., 1942.

Snake Gully (course). A country racecourse: Aus. sporting: since 1930s. (B., 1953.) Imaginary country town. From the 1930s radio-comedy series 'Dad and Dave' (Wilkes). Cf. **woop woop**.

snake-headed. Spitefully angry; vindictive: Aus. C.J. Dennis.

snake-hips. 'Ironic for man with middle-aged spread' (L.A.): mostly RAF: from ca. 1935. Cf. **snake**, v., 1, and **snake-charmers**, 1.

snake-juice. 'Any improvised alcoholic drink; strong liquor generally' (Wilkes): Aus. Hence *snake-juicer*, an addict to bad liquor (Baker): since early 1920s.

snake off. To slip quietly away: Aus. coll.: since ca. 1910. (Brockman, 1947.) See also **snake**, v., 2.

Snake-Pit, the. The haunt mentioned at **fishing fleet**, 2, q.v.: RN. Granville.—2. Perhaps hence, the Maymo Club lounge: Burma: ca. 1925–41.—3. Sergeants' mess: Aus. Services': WW2 and since. B., 1943.

snake yarn. A tall story: Aus. juvenile: since ca. 1935. B., 1953.

snakes. A prison warder's felt-shod shoes or slippers: c.:—1923 (Manchon). So he snakes along silently.

snake's hiss. (To) piss: Aus. r.s. Franklyn.

snake's (or **snakes'**) **honeymoon.** A tangled mass of, e.g., ropes: RN: since ca. 1950. (Peppitt.)

snaky, -ey. Bad-tempered: Aus.: since early C.20. (Wilkes' earliest quot'n is dated 1919.) Cf. **snake-headed**, of which it is perhaps a shortening (P.B.).—2. Jealous: Aus.: since ca. 1939. Cusack, 1931.

snap. Packed food; hence, *snap tin*, a container for a packed meal: railwaymen's: since ca. 1920 (*Railway*). P.B.: ex N. Midlands dial. for mid-morning snack; cf. **bait**, another synon. regional word spread by the railways.—2. 'An ampoule of amyl nitrate sewn into cotton-wool pads': drug addicts': since ca. 1950. Because 'broken with a sharp sound under the nose and inhaled' (Cook, 1962).

snap! Exclam. called forth by any (usu. minor) coincidence: coll. Ex the parlour/nursery card-game so called.

snap out of it! Go away quick!: low: adopted, ex US, ca. 1925; superseded by:—2. Wake up! (e.g., out of a day-dream); Realise the truth!; 'Be your age!': coll.: adopted, ex US, ca. 1933.

snapper. 'A railway ticket inspector, so called because he "snaps" holes in tickets' (Culotta): Aus.: since ca. 1930.—2. 'A vagina that its proud possessor can tighten at will' (Hollander); loosely, any vagina (W. & F.) [P.B.: I think E.P.'s pun here is unintentional]: C.20 in US; since ca. 1950 in Brit.—3. 'One night we got bounced by a snapper (fighter) and the rear gunner was hit' (a bomber pilot, quoted in Edwards, 1974): RAF: WW2.

snappin. A packed lunch; hence, any packed food: Merseyside workers': since ca. 1910. A var. of **snap**, n., 1, q.v.

snappy. Short-tempered; irritable; apt to 'snap' at people: coll.: since late C.19. 'Taffrail', 1916, 'Don't act so snappy'.—2. In *make it snappy!*, look lively!; be quick!; coll., adopted ex US. Cf. **snap out of it!**

snappy undercut; or merely **undercut.** A smart sexually attractive girl: butchers' >, by 1935, fairly gen. Cf. *snazzy undercut*, a raffish, later C.20, var. (L.A., 1976).

snaps. (Or *Snaps.*) A Naval photographer: RN: since ca. 1940. (Granville, 1962.) Cf. synon. **smudger**.

snare. 'To acquire; to seize; to win' (Dennis): Aus.: late C.19–20. Ex snaring animals. In Public and Grammar Schools' coll. also 'to steal' (Lambert, 1968). Cf.:—2. To cheat; hence, *snare sheet*, a slip of paper with notes for use in an examination: schools'. Lambert, 1968.

snargasher. A training aircraft: Can. airmen's: 1939+. (H. & P.) A corruption—perhaps rather a deliberate distortion—of 'tarmac-smasher'.

snarge. An ugly or an unpleasant person: lower classes' and military: early C.20. (F. & G.) Perhaps ex *snitch*, n. + *nark* (s. sense). Cf. **snurge**.

snarl. To steal; acquire illicitly—or even lawfully: circus: since ca. 1920. (Seago, 1934.) Perhaps ex American *snarl*, a tangle.

snarler. A bad discharge: Aus. Services': since ca. 1919. 'Services *no longer required*.' (L.D.M. Roberts.)

snarl(e)y goster (usu. pl.). A sausage: RN. Heard, late 1950s, from a petty officer who had been through RN training school HMS *Ganges* as a boy seaman. (P.B.)

snatch. A hasty or illicit or mercenary copulation: coll.: C.17–20.—2. Hence, ultimately, though imm. ex Yorkshire dial.: the female pudend: late C.19–20. Cf. **snatch-blatch**, **-block**, **-box**, and:—3. Hence, girls viewed collectively as 'fun': coll. since ca. 1930. Chamberlain, 'Yet another couple of "snatch".'

snatch-blatch. The female pudend: ca. 1890–1915. On **snatch**, 2. Cf.:-

snatch-block. MN var. of **snatch**, 2. Ex the technical snatch block, 'a block that can have a rope clipped rather than threaded' (Peppitt), whence the anatomical sense. Yet, even there, *snatch* is the more usual term. Cf.:-

snatch-box. A further punning elab., cf. prec., on **snatch**, 2: low. Prob. suggested by *match-box*, but cf. also **box** in this sense.

snatch game, the. Kidnapping: c.: from ca. 1920. Brandon, 1936.

snatch (one's) time. To resign from a job: Aus.: since ca. 1920. (B., 1943; Casey, 1945.) Hence also *snatch it* (Marshall, 1946).

snatched (car or **cab).** A car taken back from an owner-driver who has failed with his payments: taxi-drivers': since ca. 1925. (Hodge, 1938.) Cf.:-

snatcher. One who, when hire-purchasers fail to pay installments, seizes (part of) the furniture: trade: from ca. 1920. (*Daily Telegraph*, 19 Oct. 1934.) Abbr. of an assumed *furniture-snatcher*. Cf. prec.—2. An assistant conductor: busmen's: since ca. 1945.

snazzy. Fashionable, smart: Aus.: adopted, ca. 1943, ex US servicemen. (Cusack, 1951, 'A couple of snazzy little cameras'; Niland, 1955.) Also, by 1954, English s.—Perhaps a blend of *snappy* + *jazzy*.—2. 'Smooth': see CANADIAN ADO-LESCENTS, in Appx.

snazzy chassis. A girl's good figure, esp. in *lassie with a snazzy chassis*: Aus.: since ca. 1945. Cf. prec., and **snappy undercut**, q.v.; partly rhyming. (B.P.)

sneak. One who informs or peaches on his fellow(s): schoolboys' s: since late C.19 >, by mid-C.20, gen. coll. verging on informal S.E. Ex late C.19 v., to bear tales.

snelt. A sneak-thief; a term of abuse: NZ and Aus. c. (B., 1941, 1942.) ?Yiddish.

snerge. See **snurge**.

snibbet. Sexual intercourse: low. Prob. ex Scottish and Northumberland dial. *snibbet* (or *-it*), a mechanical device involving an 'eye' and an insertion (*EDD*, *snibbit*, sense 1). Cf.:-

snibley, esp. *a bit of snibley*, as in ' 'Ad a nice bit of snibley last night'. Sexual intercourse, mostly from the male angle: low. Cf. prec.

snicket, a bit of. A girl: since ca. 1945. (Gordon, 1953.) Ex Lancashire dial. *snicket*, a forward girl. R.S.: 'The Lancashire dial. meaning, "a forward girl", contrasts with the W. Riding dial. meaning of *snicket*—a "passage-way" or "short cut between houses" (cf. W. Riding "ginnel"), apparently derived from *snick*, v. Perhaps this Lancashire lass kept her assignments in Yorkshire back-alleys, unless the allusion is to a biological passage.' Cf. **snippet**.

snide. 'The business of passing counterfeit half-crowns and other imitation silver coins': c.: from ca. 1920. (Spenser, 1934.) Abbr. earlier c. (since mid-C.19), *snide-pitching*, where *snide* = spurious, sham.

snide shop. An agency for the selling of counterfeit notes: c.: from ca. 1920. Wallace.

snidget. Excellent: Aus. juvenile: since the 1930s. B., 1953.

snie; occ. **sny.** A hole filled with water; a hidden pool, even if large: Can. coll. (Beames.) Leechman: ex Can. Fr. *chenal*, a canal-like watercourse.

sniff. To drink (strong liquor): from ca. 1920. (Harrison, 1934.) Cf.:—2. To 'inhale fumes (e.g. glue) for "kicks" ' (Home Office): orig. teenage and other addicts, > gen. coll.: later C.20. Ex the lit. S.E., as is the earlier *sniff coke*, where *coke* (= cocaine) is used generically, and the phrase = to take drugs: adopted ex US ca. 1930.—3. 'Used to describe the desire to have sexual relations, particularly oral, with a female. E.g., "I'd like to *sniff* her", "I had a *sniff* of her" ' (Turner, 1986): Merseyside raffish.

sniff of the barmaid's apron. See smell of the barman's . . .

sniffer. A sexually desirable female, as in 'She's a gorgeous little sniffer': Merseyside raffish. (Turner, 1986.)—2. 'A male renowned for attempting to achieve sexual relations with any female' (Ibid.): id. Both ex **sniff**, 3.

sniftem. An inhalant: fair-grounds'. This *-em* is a characteristic (minor yet determinant) of fair-ground slang—cf. **stickem** below. Perhaps a var. or even a perversion of the mock-Latin *-um*; cf. the mock-Latin *-us* of *bonus* and *hocus-pocus*.

snifty conner. Good food: Services' (esp. RAF): ca. 1925–45. (Jackson.) See **conner**.

snig. A policeman: urban schoolchildren's, mostly boys'. (Naughton, 1966.) A dial. form of *sneak*?

sninny. A girl or young woman: Aus. low: since ca. 1920. (B., 1942.) A perversion of synon. Aus. *skinny*.

snip. A good tip: racing: from ca. 1890.—2. Hence, a bargain; a certainty; an easy win or acquisition: 1894 (*OED*).—3. Hence, an easy job: B. & P.—4. A ticket collector: railwaymen's. (*Railway*.) Cf. **snapper**, 1.

snipcock. A Jew: 'Ardent national romantics, [the earlier C.20. Brit. secret service officers] looked down on "snipcocks" and intellectuals . . . ' (Ascherson, 1985). An insulting ref. to circumcision.

snipe, n. (Gen. in pl.) A cigarette-end: vagrants c. (Gape, 1936.) Cf. the **v.**—2. A trimmer (stoke-hold): Aus.: since ca. 1910. Cusack, 1953.—3. A small poster glued—for political purposes—to a telegraph pole or a wall: Aus.: since ca. 1945. (B.P.)—4. A sniper'shide; ' "a snipe", as the Provos [q.v.] euphemistically called their murderous ambushes' (Hawke): N. Ireland: since late 1960s.

snipe, v. To pilfer: low:—1923 (Manchon). Prob. ex shooting. Also since ca. 1920, low Aus. s. (Ronan, 1954).

sniper. 'A non-union wharf labourer' (B., 1943): Aus.: since ca. 1930.

snipes. A pair of scissors: c.: ca. 1810–1910. (Vaux.) But as *snips*, its use continues in this sense among market traders: 1978 (*M.T.*).

snipey or **snipy.** Crafty, esp. of a hiding-place: prison officers'. Phelan, 1954.

snippet. The female pudend: Liverpool: late C.19–20.—2. Hence, intercourse with a girl: Liverpool.

snippy. Snappy; captious; coll. Ex dial. Lit., cutting. (*EDD.*) R.S.: 'Cf. S. Ger. *schnippisch* used precisely in this sense by Goethe: *Faust*, Part I, 1808, referring to Gretchen's first curt refusal of Faust's advances.'

snips. See **snipes.**

snitch. To purloin: 1933, Sayers, 'He . . . snitched other people's ideas without telling them.' Ex Lancashire dial. (*EDD*).

snitcher, n. A person or thing remarkably good, strong, attractive, etc.: NZ and Aus.:—1935.

snitcher, adj. Excellent; attractive: Aus.: since ca. 1930. (Baker.) Ex prec.

sniv. An attention-seeking ploy, undertaken in order that it could be 'written up' in the journal compulsorily kept for periodical inspection by officer-instructors: RN officer cadets': mid-C.20. (*Heart*, 1962.) Prob. ex *sniveller*. (P.B.)

snizzle. To fornicate: lower classes':—1923 (Manchon). Origin? Possibly cognate with dial. *sniggle* (see *EDD*, at *sniggle*, v., 2).

snodder. One who dislikes spending: grafters'. (*Cheapjack*, 1934.) Perhaps ex Yiddish *shnorrer*, one of whose meanings is 'a compulsive bargain-hunter' (Rosten).

snodger, n. and adj. Excellent (person or thing), attractive (etc.): Aus.: since ca. 1925. (B., 1942.) Arbitrary; yet cf. **snitcher** and **snidget.** Ob. by 1978 (Wilkes).

snog, n. A flirtation; a courting: esp. among beatniks: since ca. 1959. (Anderson.) P.B.: but as in, e.g., *have a snog*, earlier, a var. of:-

snog, v. 'To make love with repletion of kissing and cuddling; hence *snogging session*, making love' (L.A., 1977): very common throughout WW2 [and still, 1983, not ob.: P.B.]. I surmise a dial. alteration of *snug*, cosy, notably as in that *snuggling-up* which so often preludes a warmer conjunction.—2. Hence, to flirt, or to court, esp. in *be* or *come* or *go snogging*: beatniks', adopted, ca. 1959, ex gen. s. (Anderson.) The term, esp. as *be* or *go snogging*, seems to have orig. in the RAF, late 1930s (Partridge, 1945).

snogged up. Smartened up; 'all dressed up': RAF: WW2.

snogging. Vbl n. corresponding to **snog,** v.

snood. 'A knitted, wool warmer for a man's private parts' (Leech, 1985): Can. P.B.: joc. on old S.E. for a hair-ribbon or -band.

snooks. 'A term of endearment for a small child' (B.P.): Aus.: since ca. 1925. Cf. **snookums.** Cf.:—2. In *be (dead) snooks on*, to be in love with: Aus.: earlier C.20. Franklin, 1931.

snookums. A trivial endearment; esp. applied to a lap-dog: coll.: 1928. (*OED* Sup.) Cf. *diddums*, and prec.

snooky. Critical; pernickety: Aus.: since ca. 1910; by 1960, ob. Clunes, 1933. 'There was a snooky guy up in the corner listening to all I had to say.' P.B.: prob. a var. of *snoopy*; see:-

snoop; gen. snoop around. To pry; go about slyly: orig. (ca. 1830) US; anglicised as a coll. ca. 1905; by 1935, gen. considered virtually S.E. Ex the Dutch *snoepen.* (Thornton.) Hence *snooper, snooping*, one who does this, and the action; also *snoopy*, adj.: all anglicised ca. 1920.—2. Hence v.t. *snoop*, to 'appropriate', steal on the sly: coll.: 1924 (Galsworthy).—3. To be a Service policeman: RAF: 1939+. (Partridge, 1945.) Ex sense 1.

Snoops, the. Service (>, in late 1944, RAF) Police: RAF: since ca. 1939. (E.P., 1942.) Short for *snooper*, ex **snoop.**

snoopy. See **snoop,** 1.

snoot. Superciliousness; affected superiority: coll.: prob. a back-formation ex **snooty,** q.v. (L.A., 1976.) Cf.:—2. A disagreeable, or a supercilious, person: Aus.: since ca. 1930. B., 1942.—3. See **droop-snoot.**

snooter. In a poorly-executed landing, 'you are miserably easing up the nose and trying to "make it" by snootering over the hedge half a mile ahead of you by hanging on the "slots".

No sticking on a little discreet engine and doing an imperceptible "rumble" when there's an A1 instructor in the back' (Tredrey, 1939): RAF: 1930s.

snootful, have a. To be tipsy: Can.: adopted, ca. 1940, ex US.

snooty. (Of persons) unpleasant; cross, irritable; supercilious: Society and near-Society: from ca. 1930. (Mackail, 1934.) Perhaps on *snoopy* (see **snoop**) but ex *snorty*: cf. Lancashire *snoot*, v.i. to sneak, hang round. Adopted ex US; used in Can. from ca. 1920. P.B.: E.P. noted at *snoot*, 1, 'Ex turning up one's nose or *snout* (dial. *snoot*)'; perhaps rather 'looking down one's nose at', than the Lancs. dial. which is not really relevant.

snore. (A) sleep: low: since ca. 1920. Curtis, 1938, 'He had not had much snore the night before.' Extension of S.E. sense.

snore-bag. A sleeping-bag: Army officers': 1939+. P-G-R.

snore-off. A short sleep: low Aus. (Park, 1950); adopted, ca. 1925, in NZ (Slatter). Cf. **snore.**

snoring, be. Thomas Skeats, barrow-boy (as in the *Daily Mail* of 24 July 1963), says, 'What you gotta watch is that your pears don't go "sleepy", as we say, in the 'eat. When it's very 'ot and they get real soft, we say they are "snoring" ': barrow boys': since ca. 1910. (*Sleepy* has long been S.E.)

snork. A baby: Aus. and NZ. (B., 1941.) Perversion of *stork*, the baby-carrier.—2. Hence, a youth, a stripling: Aus. coll.: later C.20. McNeil.—3. See:-

snorker. (Usu. in pl.) A sausage: Public Schools' and Aus. coll. (L.A.; B., 1941.) In Aus. also as *snork.*

snorrer. 'A difficult customer' (*M.T.*); 'a scrounger' (Powis, who spells it *snorer*): low. Ex Yiddish *shnorrer*, a beggar: see esp. Rosten, 1968, and cf. **snodder.**

snort, n. A 'pull'—a drink—of spirits: Society: since late 1920s. Wodehouse, 1936, 'He produced his flask and took a sharp snort.' Ex the snorting cough induced by a large 'pull' at a brandy, whisky, rum. P.B.: in Hemingway, 1942, applied even to tea: RAF in Burma: 1942.

snort, v. To take drugs through the nose (cf. **sniff**): drugs world: adopted, ex US, mid-1960s. *Time Out*, 15 Feb. 1980, 'those already into snorting cocaine or amphetamine sulphate': cf. synon. **toot.**

snorter. 'A single rope, used mostly on paper reels, [which] was capable of holding 15 cwt. Up to 15 cwt could be used at one time when unloading bacon' (Ash): London dockers'.

snorting-pole. A foot-brace at the end of a bed: Can. lumbermen's.

snot. See **slicker than snot.**

snot-gobbler; -gobbling, n. and adj. 'Very commonly heard in the Army. Usually abusive, it seems to cover all forms of personal dirtiness, uncouthness, unkemptness, filth and so on, both physical and mental. Also used of talking filth' (P.B., 1974): low coll.: since mid-C.20.

snot, n. Tobacco: c.:—1896 (*OED*). Tempest, 1950: 'The word originates from the days when smoking was prohibited in prison. When smoking, the lag [q.v.] cupped his hand and pretended to rub his nose while taking a "draw" on his cigarette.'—2. A betrayer; an informer to the police: c.: from ca. 1920. (Wallace; Leach.) Cf. older s. *nose.*—3. Hence, a detective: low Glasgow:—1934.—4. A cigarette: low London. (Norman.) In 1950s, much used by Teddy-boys and National Servicemen. See v., 5.—5. In *have a snout on* (someone), to bear him a grudge: Aus.: since ca. 1920. (B., 1942.) Ex v., 1. See **take a snout.**

snout, v. 'To bear [a person] a grudge' (Dennis): military and Aus. Ex pigs.—2. Whence, *snouted*, 'treated with disfavour' (id.): ibid.: id.—3. To be an informer; to lay information: c.: since ca. 1925; by 1940 at latest, also police s. Ex **snout,** n., 2. Warner, 1961, 'Thereafter Ruskin snouted and snouted good.'—4. (Also *snout around.*) To discover, spot, 'nose out': police s.: later C.20. Hunter, 1962.—5. In phrase *snout us out!*, a request to a friend for a cigarette: Army Other Ranks': since early 1950s. See the n., 4. (P.B.)

snout baron. In prison, a major trafficker in tobacco: since ca. 1930. (Tempest, 1950.) See **baron,** 2, and **snout,** n., 1.

snout day. Tobacco-issue day: prison c. Ibid.

snouter. A tobacconist: c., whence police s.: since late 1940s. Ex **snout**, n., 1.

snouting. Giving information to the police: c.: from ca. 1920. Wallace.

snouty, n. Var. of **snout**, n., 1. Sharpe, 1938.

snouty, adj. Overbearing; haughty; insolent: coll.: 1858 (*OED*); somewhat ob. Cf. *sniffy*, and **snooty**, which has superseded it.

snow, n. Cocaine: adopted, ex US, ca. 1920 as c. >, ca. 1930, s. (Wallace, *passim*; Irwin; Home Office, 1978.) Ex appearance.—2. Silver; silver money: Services' and low. (F. & G.; Tempest, 1950.) Cf. c. adj. *white*, of silver. McKenna, 1970, glosses it as 'Small silver, i.e. sixpences', in railwaymen's coll.—3. 'A blond inferior schoolboy, a bully's victim, as in "*What* did you say to me, snow?" ' (Humphries, 1981): Aus.: later C.20.

snow, v. To deceive; to try to throw (someone) 'off the scent': police s.: later C.20. (Hunter, 1977.) See **snow job**.

snow-bunny. A Royal Marine trained in Arctic warfare; also as v.: 'They intend to snow-bunny the whole Corps eventually': RM: late 1970s. Ex the white camouflage suit. (Glynn, 1978.)—2. A young girl companion of winter-sportsmen: Aus. coll.: ca. 1950s. One of the 'characters' popularised by Barry Humphries (Raab, 1982).

snow-drop. See **snowdrop**.

snow job. Deception, 'flannel', insincere charm (US since 1940s: W. & F.); hence applied to any public relations exercise, and then, as on BBC Radio 4, 19 Oct. 1983, to jaunts abroad on 'fact-finding missions' at tax-payers' expense, by members of Parliament.

snowball, v., usu. in passive. To return (a car) to its original owner: secondhand-car dealers': since ca. 1950. Ex the throwing of snow-balls?

snowball hitch. A knot that easily loosens: RN. (Granville.) It comes *adrift*.

snowbirds. Women that bring clients to dope-pedlars: c.: since ca. 1938. Ex **snow**, cocaine.

snowdrop. An American military policeman: 1942+. (*Daily Express*, 12 June 1944.) Ex his white helmet and pipe-clayed equipment.—2. But, earlier, 'On duty the [RAF] police wore white blancoed belt and white cap cover with, occasionally, white gaiters, which uniform gained them the name of "snowdrop". And this in the 1920s' (Adkin, 1983).—3. 'Among the female guests there were few if any snowdrops' (Bonham-Carter, 1965): Society term for 'a drooping white flower of early spring'.

snowed in. 'The condition of the table or board when the shearers are working too fast for the shed hands to keep up' (*Straight Furrow*, 21 Feb. 1968): NZ: since ca. 1920. Ex the piles of fleeces.

snowed under; snowed up. Over-burdened with work; having a heavy back-log of work to attend to: coll.: the *under* version prob. adopted ex US: since ca. 1930.

snozzler. Any person or thing remarkable for excellence, skill, strength, etc.: NZ (—1935); Aus. (B., 1942). Prob. suggested by such terms as *snifter* and *bobby-dazzler*, of which pair it may be a blend.

snuck. A sol. past tense of S.E. *sneak* (*in*), used joc.: adopted ex US earlier C.20. 'I just snuck in and took a look' or 'I craftily snuck a dekko at . . .' (P.B.)

snuff and butter (maiden). A Eurasian girl: Anglo-Indian: since early 1920s; ob. by mid-C.20.

snuff-bottle. 'Anything shocking, mortifying or destroying, e.g. a tax demand . . . "That put the snuff-bottle on him/it" = "That put an end to him/it" ', thus *M.T.*, which neatly indicates its semantics thus: 'One takes an animal for a sniff of the snuff bottle, i.e. to be destroyed . . . Cf. "to snuff it" [q.v.]'. Occ. var. *snuff-box*.

snuff-box. A gas-mask: mostly civilians': 1939+. *New Statesman*, 30 Aug. 1941.—2. A newspaper's list of deaths; its obituaries: Aus. journalists': since ca. 1920. (Baker.) A list of those who have 'snuffed out'.

snuff film or **movie.** A film in which a victim is actually murdered: US since mid-1970s (Barnhart, 2); adopted in UK by early 1980s (*Daily Mail*, 13 Aug. 1983). 'ITN [TV] have booked themselves up to film [a cow] walk up the plank to the slaughter house . . . Clare is a star, even if it is to be a snuff movie' (Toynbee, 1984). Ex:-

snuff it. To die: s. (—1874) >, ca. 1900, coll. H., 5th ed., 'Term very common among the lower orders of London . . . Always to die from disease or accident.' Ex **snuff out**, q.v.

snuff out. To die: s. (—1864) >, ca. 1900, S.E. (H., 3rd ed.) Prob. ex snuffing out a candle. Cf. prec.

snuffler. A veterinary surgeon: market-traders'. (*M.T.*) See etym. at **snuff-bottle**.

snuggy. A woman's muff: since ca. 1940. (Meynell, 1950.) It keeps one's hands snug and warm.

snugly moored in Sot's Bay. Dead drunk: RN: since mid-C.20 (?earlier, perhaps much earlier). Baynham, 1969.

snurge, n. A Poor Law Institution: from ca. 1920. *Answers*, 21 Sep. 1940.—2. An objectionable, contemptible person: Services' and schoolboys': mid-C.20. One reputed to 'go around sniffing girls' cycle-seats'; cf. **twerp**, and the (prob.) var. **snarge**. Prob. ex the v. (P.B.)—3. See GREMLINS, in Appx.

snurge, v. 'To get out of doing some unpopular job': nautical. (Bowen.) Prob. ex dial., *snudge*, to sneak, to sulk, curry favour (*EDD*). In the RAF, 'to lose surreptitiously' (H.W., 1942, when spelt *snerge*).

snurgle. 'When the Marines [were] sneaking up on an unsuspecting enemy [it] was [called] "snurgling" ' (*Don't Cry*, 1983): RM: Falkland Is. campaign, 1982.

so-and-so. Objectionable person, as in 'that old so-and-so': coll.: C.20; but gen. and frequent only since ca. 1945. Euph. for *bastard* or *bugger* or *bitch*, as the context determines. In later C.20 usu. qualified, as 'he's a right so-and-so', or 'Watch her! She's a bit of a so-and-so, she is.'

soak, n. A heavy fall of rain: Aus. coll. (B., 1942.) P.B.: ex Eng. dial., as in the old weather-lore, 'Ash before oak, we're in for a soak'.—2. A drunkard: Aus. and Eng.: since ca. 1910. But see **soaks**.

soak, v. To borrow money from: ca. 1925. Sayers, 1932, 'Poor, but not mercenary or dishonest, since he refused to soak Mrs W.'

soaking glass . . . As in 'A soaking glass of wet Booth and blimey', glossed in H.W., 1942, as 'a gin and lime': RAF: WW2.

soaks. 'Folks' in the convivial sense; usu. in address, by one joining a drinking session: r.s., with pun on S.E. *soak*, a tippler.

Soanly Ranger. 'That slightly lesser social breed of girls known as "Soanly Rangers"—these are Sloanes who find it cheaper to live in places like Clapham and Stockwell (they got their name because they explain their location by saying, "It's only 10 minutes from Sloane Square")' (*Observer*, 6 Mar. 1988). See **Sloane Rangers**, and cf. **twirlies**.

soap. A simpleton; a dupe: Aus.: since ca. 1925. (B., 1953.) As soft as soap. P.B.: the dating is E.P.'s; by Baker's listing date, it could derive ex **Joe Soap**, q.v.—2. Later C.20 abbr. of **soap opera**.

soap-and-baccy pay(master). An accountant officer of the Victualling Branch: RN: earlier C.20. Bowen.

soap and flannel. Bread and cheese: RN lowerdeck. (Granville.) Cf:-

soap and towel. 'A bread and cheese meal' (McKenna, 1): railwaymen's. Cf. prec.

soap opera. 'Daytime radio serials for women. As in operas, the plot is less important than characters who attract emotional involvement. Often sponsored by soap manufacturers' (B.P.): coll.: adopted ex US, in Aus. by mid-1950s, Eng. since late 1950s.

soapie. Later C.20 Aus. coll. for prec. Harris, 1985.

S

S

soapy. Silly, stupid; effeminate: Aus.: since ca. 1920. (B., 1942.) See **soap,** n., 1.

soapy bubble. Trouble: Glasgow r.s., as in 'You're gauny end up in a soapy bubble, pal' (Munro, 1985).

soash. See sosh.

sob sister. A writer of articles for the more emotional, sensation-mongering newspapers, esp. a woman journalist replying to women readers' inquiries: journalistic, adopted ca. 1930 from US. Cf. **sob stuff.**

sob story. A hard-luck story: coll. >, by 1940, S.E.

sob stuff. Intentional and, gen., excessive sentimentality (to appeal to the emotions—and often the pocket): orig. (ca. 1919) US; anglicised by 1921, as a coll., verging on S.E. by late 1930s. *OED* Sup.; Lyell.

sobbing sisters. German six-barrelled mortars: military: 1940–5. 'The bombs came over in broken volleys of six with a peculiar slow, sobbing wail' (Peniakoff, 1950).

sober-gradge fight. A fight arising out of a long-standing quarrel: Can. coll.:—1932 (Beames).

Sobs. Senior observer: FAA: later C.20. (Knight, 1985.)

social secretary. A joc. ref. to one's spouse when one has been given an invitation; e.g. 'I shall have to consult my . . . ': later C.20. (P.B.)

social tit. A 'poodle-faker'; an officer fond of dancing: RN: since ca. 1925. P-G-R.

sock. To save up, put aside, deposit in the bank: Aus.: since ca. 1930. Cusack, 1951, 'I bet he's socked a pretty packet away.' Ex a sock used as bank.

sock a boot into. To take advantage of the misfortunes of (a person): lower classes'. (F. & G.) Cf. **put the boot in.**

sock the rocks to. 'To have sex with and ejaculate, as in "I'm gonna sock the rocks to the old lady tonight": N. Am.: since ca. 1960' (Leech, 1986).

socked out. Out of commission, as in 'To add to our [pilots'] problems, Scotland is socked out with weather . . . ' (*Phantom*): RAF: later C.20. N. Am. prefers *socked in* (Leech, 1986, for Can.).

socko-boffo. Absolutely outstanding, as in 'risking the production's chances of being a socko-boffo hit' (Stott, 1981): entertainments world: adopted ex US, later C.20. A blend of *sock*, v., (since late C.17) to hit hard, + echoic of impact. (P.B.)

sod. A sodomist: low coll.: C.19–20.—2. Hence, a pej., orig. and gen. violent: since early C.19. *Sessions*, June 1818, 'As he passed me he said the other was a bloody sod.' In later C.20, often applied to circumstances, as 'It's a proper sod, it really is!' (P.B.) Often used in ignorance of its origin: cf. **bugger.**—3. Non-pej. for 'chap, fellow' or even for 'girl, woman': Eng. and Aus.: late C.19–20. 'Good on yer, Martha, yer old sod!' (O'Connor, 1962).

sod all. Nothing: orig. mostly RN, since ca. 1920; by 1950 at latest, gen. low. Var. of *bugger all, damn all, fuck all.*

sod-buster. An agricultural (not a pastoral) farmer: Can. (and US). R.C., 1976, 'Originally, a *pioneer* farmer in the US or Canadian prairies, the dense, tough, native sod of which took a lot of busting.'

sod off! Go away!: low. An exact semantic equivalent of *bugger off!*

soda. Something easy to do; someone easy to do: Aus. low: since ca. 1925. Palmer 1930, ' "Just one more guess, Lew . . ." Lew chuckled. "Umph, that's a soda. Must be the old doctor." '

sodding. A vague pej., as in 'I've been in your sodding country' (Hesling, 1963): late C.19–20.

sodge. 'Short for *sodger*, a soldier, and applied to a Royal Marine. Also a term for a lubberly deck-hand; from a seaman's traditional attitude towards a Royal Marine' (Granville): RN lowerdeck: C.20 (?earlier).

sods, odds and. See odds and sods.

sods' holiday. 'Everybody doing something they didn't ought to be' (Tansey, 1984); a complete confusion. Cf. **buggers' muddle.**

Sod's law. That 'law' which decrees that if something *can* go wrong, it will; and that if it doesn't, it might: coll., gen. since early 1970s, although Garstin, 1984, claims that the term was 'already well known when I went to sea in 1942'. Applied perhaps mostly to trivial inconveniences and mishaps. Cf. synon. **Murphy's law, Spode's law.**

sods' opera. 'An unofficial and extremely low concert, usually held in barracks' (Granville): Services' (I heard it in late 1915). Hence, from ca. 1925, RAF for 'the din of jollification; a drunken party' (L.A., 1950). R.C., 1976: 'The reference is, I believe, to a (probably mythical) work of that name, late C.19, slanderously ascribed to Gilbert & Sullivan.' P.B.: R.C. is perhaps citing an ex. of *The Buggers' Opera*—an obvious pun on Gay's *Beggar's Opera*, 1728—of which all that now remains in Service memories is the list of *dramatis personae*, including, among others, 'Penis, The Count: a young upstart; Test and Ickles, hangers-on to the Count; Anus, a little brown fellow, usually tight; Scrotum: an aged and wrinkled retainer; etc.'

soft cop, (be) on a. To have an easy job; be on 'a good thing': Aus.: since ca. 1925. (B.P.) A var. is *a sweet cop.*

soft ha'porth. A 'softy'; a person easily imposed upon or duped: mostly working-classes'.

soft mick. In Army usage, mid-C.20, a gen. intensive, as in *drunk as soft mick*; 'as stupid as' or 'stupider than soft mick'; and, e.g., 'There's more ammo in the bottom of that swamp [Kota Tinggi training area, W. Malaysia] than soft mick'. (P.B., with thanks to Ronald Pearsall, late WO1, R. Signals.)

soft-nosed. Stupid: RN. Contrast **hard-nosed.**

soft number. An easy task or job, 'a cushy billet': orig. Army, since ca. 1910 (F. & G.); by ca. 1916, also RN (Harling, 1946). Perhaps ex music.

soft option. The easier, or easiest, of choices in any given circumstances; a 'soft number', q.v.: coll., usu. derogatory: since early 1970s. L.A. noted the term in 1974. 'Stanley [Falkland Islands' capital] is regarded by the islanders who live outside it as a kind of soft option, a place of bright lights, idleness and decadence' (Jack, 1979).

soft-pedal. To subdue; tone down; proceed circumspectly in an affair: coll.: later C.20. Hunter, 1969, 'The best we can do is soft-pedal it, play it down, stick with the book.' Ex piano or organ pedals controlling volume. (P.B.)

soft roll. A girl easily persuaded to coït: since late 1940s. Easy to 'roll in the hay': *roll*, an act of coïtion from the male point of view, comes ex US.

soft-skinned vehicle. An unarmoured vehicle: Army coll. (1940) >, by 1944, j. As an apple is to a coconut, so . . .

soft stuff. Unarmoured vehicles: Army s. (1940) >, by 1941, coll. (P-G-R.) Cf., perhaps ex, prec.

soft touch. 'A person easy to borrow from or sponge on' (Petch): coll.: since ca. 1910.

softers. 'Soft soap', i.e. flattery: RN (mostly lowerdeck): since ca. 1930. (P-G-R.) The 'OXFORD/RN -*ER*(*s*)'.

soggies. Breakfast cereals: upper-middle-class s.: later 1970s. York, 1980.

soggy type. A dull-witted and slow-moving person: RAF: since ca. 1937. (Jackson.) See **wet,** adj., 1–2, which prob. suggested it.—2. One who drinks excessively: RAF: since ca. 1938. (Hinde, 1945.)

soixante-neuf, adopted from French, is a term diagrammatically descriptive (69) of a reciprocal sexual act: late C.19–20: orig., upper and middle classes', but by 1914 or 1915 fairly common in the Forces, esp. the Navy, as *swaffonder* or *swassonder* (or -*ander*); by 1920, *soixante-neuf* was coll.—and, by 1960, virtually S.E.

solarist. The main aim of 'the solarists . . . is not to actually *see* anything [while on package tours overseas], but just go and shove themselves down on a bit of beach, get brick red and come home' (Hudson, 1979).

sold on (something), **be.** To be enthusiastic about, very much attracted by, it: coll.: since late 1940s. 'She's very taken, of course, but I'm not exactly sold on it myself.' Cf. 'I'll *buy* it/ that': I agree—that seems a sensible idea. (Petch, 1969; P.B.)

sold out. To be temporarily utterly exhausted: London club cyclists': early 1930s. (*Fellowship*, 1984.) Cf. **the bonk**.

soldier. An upright (often, in j., termed a 'runner') of 9 inches by 3, gen. used as a support for 'shuttering': Public Works':—1935. They are usually placed at intervals, edge on to the shuttering: and thus they resemble a rank of soldiers.

soldier on. To persevere against peril and/or hardship: military coll.: esp. 1916–18. Often as a c.p. in form *soldier on, chum* (B. & P.). P.B.: the phrase > gen. coll. and is still very much alive, 1988.

soldiers. 'Fingers' of buttered bread: nursery and domestic coll. 'He cut his buttered bread into soldiers to dip into the yolk' (Scott, 1977). Prob. orig. so named as a ruse in urging reluctant children to 'eat up' (P.B.).—2. Tinned sausages: intercontinental lorry drivers': later C.20. Wilce, 1977.

soldiers bold. Cold: Aus. r.s. Often shortened to *soldiers*.

soldier's farewell, a. 'Go to bed!', with ribald additions and/or elaborations: military:—1909 (Ware). Cf. **sailor's farewell**.—2. Also (in WW1, and after) = 'Good-bye and bugger (*or* fuck) you!' Lincoln, 1933, ' "Goodbye . . . !" he yelled . . . "Soldier's farewell", he said amiably.'—3. 'By WW2 it had come to mean the 7*s* 6*d* weekly maintenance payable by the father of an illegitimate child' (Bishop, 1978). (= 37½p.)

soldier's privilege. Complaining: WW1 Army coll. >, in later C.20, almost proverbial as 'grumbling (or grousing) is the soldier's privilege'. (E.P.; P.B.)

soldier's wash, a. 'Cupping water in the hands instead of using a flannel' (*Muvver*): Cockneys'.

solid, n. A road: tramps' and Romanies' s. (Dawson.)

solid, adj. Severe; difficult: Aus.:—1916 (Dennis); also gen. coll.—2. (?)Hence, extortionate; unreasonable: Aus.: since ca. 1918. B., 1942.—3. Stupid; 'thick': RN, since (?)ca. 1925, > gen. s. (Granville.) Solid ivory above the ears.—4. Staunch; 'unbreakable in a tough situation' (Grindley, 1977): Aus. c.: since ca. 1945. P.B.: but this nuance is not far off S.E. as exemplified in *SOD*.—5. See JAZZ, in Appx.

sollicker, n. and adj. (Some thing or person) very big or remarkable: Aus.: since ca. 1920. B., 1942.

solo creeper. 'Sneak thief operating absolutely alone' (Powis): c., and police coll.: later C.20.

Solomon. In *do a Solomon*, to pretend to be very wise: earlier C.20. Lowell, 1929.

solus. An advertisement on a page containing no other advertisement: advertising coll. (from ca. 1926) verging on j. by 1935.

some. Both as adverb of quantity and as an intensive adjective—equivalent respectively to *much*, or *very*, and *great*, *lovely*, etc.—*some* was orig., and still is, an Americanism that has contributed laudably to the gaiety of nations and enabled the English to take their pleasures less sadly. As an adjective, e.g. *some girl!*, it is an importation (rare before WW1) into England, but as an adverb, e.g. *going some*, it was known at least as early as 1890 in Brit. In America, the earliest examples are 'I hunt some and snake a little', 1834, or in a slightly different sense, 'He stammers some in his speech', 1785; and 'She's some woman now, that is a fact', 1848. Nevertheless, the Americans prob. adopted both the adj. and adv. from English dial.: see *EDD*. Cf. the French, 'Ça c'est quelque chose'. *OED* and Sup.; Ware; Thornton; Weekley; Fowler.

something above the ears, have. To be intelligent: since ca. 1925. P.B.: seldom heard in later C.20. Contrast **dead from the neck up**, and **solid**, adj. 3.

something else. 'So cool [i.e. excellent; abreast of contemporary music] it defies description' ('Basic Beatnik'): Can. jazz-lovers': since ca. 1956. P.B.: some use in UK, 1960s–early 70s, for (usu. joc.) admiration, not necessarily to do with music: 'Well, now, JP [Jet Provost training aircraft] pilots are something else', heard 1972, meaning 'they're good—but

probably quite mad!' By late 1970s, wider still: 'Prices were something else' (*Guardian*, 1 Aug. 1979), i.e. outrageously high.

something good. A good racing tip: s. (from ca. 1890) >, ca. 1920, coll.—2. Hence, a profitable affair, a safe but not generally known investment, venture, etc.: coll. E.g. 'I'm on something good.'

something in socks. A bachelor, or what a girl wants: joc.: since ca. 1910.

something in the City. In lit. vagueness, obviously S.E.; but, pointedly coll. from ca. 1890, it denotes a shady financier, a nondescript and none too honest agent, and esp. a criminal or even a burglar. Ware.

sommie. (In gymnastics) a somersault: sporting: prob. since early C.20. Orig. a children's term; I head it ca. 1905.

son of . . . Successor of, as in, e.g., 'Cheaper seats likely if "Son of Concorde" flies', a *Daily Telegraph* headline of 29 Mar. 1979. A joc. derivation from a number of Hollywood sequel-film titles: coll. usage by late 1970s. (Playfair, 1979.) An early UK use is in Stuart, 1971: 'the camera team dedicated to the production of yet another Son-of-Woodstock', i.e., of the film made of the mass youth/hippy pop festival held at Woodstock, NJ, Aug. 1969 (P.B.).

song. In *on song*, in good form: sporting, esp. Association Football: since ca. 1960. Football report in the *Observer*, 1 Dec. 1974, 'Any side on song would have given them the run-around early'. Cf. S.E. *in good voice*.

song and dance; occ., as in Vachell, 1914, *little* . . . Anyone's 'performance' in the course of doing his job. A salesman, e.g., reels off his patter.—2. A homosexual: r.s., on *Nance*: since ca. 1910; by 1940, ob. and by 1960, †. Franklyn.

sonkey or **sonky.** Silly, stupid; idiotic: Aus. low. Drake Brock-man, 1938, 'Mrs Abbott and her sonky ideas!'

Soo. Staff Officer Operations: RN: since ca. 1914. ('Sea Lion', 1946.) Ex the official abbreviation *S.O.O.* Cf. **Sobs**.

soogan. A cowboy's bed-roll: Can.: adopted, ca. 1920, ex S.W. US.—2. Hence, any bed-roll, but esp. a transient worker's: Can.: since ca. 1930. As Leechman has suggested, *soogan*, a blanket roll, may have originated in the *soogun*, or hay rope, once used to tie the roll.

sook, sook(e)y, sookie, n. A coward; a timorous person; 'a mother's boy' (McNeil): 'an Aus. cry-baby' (Humphries, 1981): Aus.: since ca. 1920. B., 1942.—2. A calf: Aus. (B., 1943.) Ex *suck*?

sookey, adj. Sentimental: Aus.: since ca. 1925. Cusack, 1953.

sool. To set (a dog) on: Aus. coll.: from ca. 1890. (Morris.) Also *sool on*.—2. Hence, to run: Aus. juvenile: since ca. 1930. B., 1953.—3. *Sool after*, to pursue (a person, esp. of the opposite sex): Aus.: since ca. 1935 (Casey, 1942).—4. To wheedle; to bamboozle: Aus. (Campion, 1942.) Hence, *soo-lin' sod*, a hypocrite (male): Aus. Campion, 1942.

sooner, n. A shirker; one who would 'sooner loaf than work': in Brit., perhaps mostly RN; also Aus.: since late C.19. (Moe; B., 1942.) Cf.:—2. A dog, esp. one that would 'sooner feed than fight': since (?)late C.19. Leechman glosses Can. use as 'a dog that would rather defecate indoors than out'. Cf.:—3. 'I once asked my father why cats were called "sooners". "Sooner shit than eat", the old man replied. (Oh well, curiosity killed the cat.)' (*Muvver*): Cockney.—4. 'A jibbing horse (one that would sooner go backward than forward)' (Alexander, 1939): NZ; Aus. (Baker.) Hence, as in Smith, a worn-out locomotive (Wilkes).—5. A swindler; a trickster: Aus.: since ca. 1920. Palmer, 1931.

sooner, adv. Better, as in 'You had sooner go,' you had better go, you would do well to go: lower classes' coll.: 1923 (Manchon). Ex S.E. *sooner*, 'more readily as a matter of choice' (*OED*).

sooner dog. See **sooner**, n., 2.

soop. An occ. var. (from ca. 1910; e.g. in Brandon, 1934) of:-

sooper. A var. (—1909) of older **super**, n., with various meanings. (Ware.) P.B.: it is also used to represent a certain emphatic way of saying **super**, adj., esp. as exclam. Also occ. *soopah*.

sootie or **-y.** 'There is a difference between calling people "wing-nut" [q.v.] and "Jock", and calling people "nigger", "coon", "spade", and "sootie" ' (Holdaway, 1986). The last four are racialist insults. Cf. *sooty-tunes*, reggae music: joc. or mildly derog. (Hibbert, 1983, who notes humorous association with the well-known glove puppet.)

soppy. Foolishly sentimental, 'soft': coll.: since early C.20. Wells, 1918, 'What Joan knew surely to be lovely, Highmorton denounced as "soppy". "Soppy" was a terrible word in boys' schools and girls' schools alike, a flail for all romance.' (Cf. **wet**.) Lit., wet with sentiment.—2. Hence, *be soppy on*, to be foolishly fond of (a person): coll.: from ca. 1924.

soppy date. See **date**, n., 5.

soppy (h)a'p'orth. Var. of *soppy date* (perhaps its orig.), a 'soft' and silly person: coll., children's and proletarian: since (?)1930s. (P.B.) See **soppy**, and cf. **soft ha'porth**.

sore as a boil, as. Angry, resentful ('sore'): Aus. Tennant, 1956.

sore as a snouted sheila. As resentful as a girl who has been 'stood up': Aus.: since ca. 1940. B., 1959.

sore finger or **toe.** Esp. in *dressed up, dolled up, done up like a . . .*, too elaborately or conspicuously over-dressed, with an implication of discomfort: Aus.: since early C.20. Cf. Eng. coll. *stand out* or *stick out like a sore thumb*. Wilkes.

sorority siren. See **frat rat**.

sorry? 'Used to indicate that one has not heard or not understood; for many people it seems to have replaced "I beg your pardon?" ' (P.B., 1974, who says, 'I first heard it early 1960s'.) But it goes back to before WW2; was at first coll., but by 1965, at latest, informal S.E.

sorry and sad. Bad: r.s.

sort, n. A companion of the opposite sex; thus, 'All the girls and their sorts are going to the pictures' (Baker): Aus.: since ca. 1925. Sorts, good or bad, of people.—2. In England, a girl: low: since ca. 1945. (Norman.) Prob. ex Aus., where this sense existed since ca. 1910: cf. Chine, 1933, 'I've a great little sort to meet' (in 1911 or 1912).

sort, v. To shoot up; to attack fiercely: Army: since ca. 1940. 'We went to Div. H.Q., which had been well and truly sorted' (Dawson, 1946). Cf. **sort out**, 2 and 3.

sort-out, n. A fight, a mellay; workers':—1935. Ex v., 2 and 3.

sort out, v. To tease; leg-pull (v.t.): Cockney. Also to *take on*, as, e.g., 'I took him on' or 'sorted him out'; 'Why are you taking *me* on, I'd like to know!'—2. To fight: low.—3. To pick a quarrel with and use force upon someone: Services': since ca. 1934. (H. & P.) Cf. n., 1.—4. To choose (someone) for a job, esp. if it be unpleasant or arduous: Services' (esp. RAF): since ca. 1938. H. & P., 'Who sorted me out for this one?' Ex, e.g., wool-sorting.—5. In Aus., to reprove or reprimand (someone): since ca. 1930. (B., 1942.) P.B.: by 1950, Services' Eng.; cf. **sort**, v.; and sense 3.

sorts. In *of sorts*, inferior; unsatisfactory: coll. E.g. 'He's certainly a writer—of sorts.' Ex the ob. *of sorts*, of various kinds. P.B.: cf. the Army quartermasters' j. in, e.g., 'One cases [sic], wooden, packing, local pattern, of sorts.'

Sosh (long *o*). Socialism: political writers', mostly: since ca. 1918.

sosh, adj. Used to express annoyance at, e.g., something unnecessary; also as in 'Sosh on you!' = Thanks for nothing! (always heavily sarcastic): Loughborough Grammar School: mid-1970s. Ex *sociable*, used ironically. (Reed, 1979.)

soul-case. The body: late C.18–20; ob. by 1900. Grose, 3rd ed.—2. Hence, a person, as 'those poor soul-cases down in the engine-room': MN. (Hardy, 1979.)—3. In *belt* or *worry* or *work the soul(-)case out of* (someone), 'To subject to extreme hardship or punishment' (Wilkes): Aus.

soul-hunter was, ca. 1900–14, a Cambridge undergraduates' term for 'a man intent on saving the souls of others' (Marples, 2).

soul-searcher. A drink: 1909 (Gibbs); † by 1920.

soul-smiter. A sensational novel (of the sentimental sort): book-world coll.:—1923 (Manchon); ob. by 1930. The 1980s prefer to speak of 'a sloppy thriller'.

sound, v. To knock or ring to see if the occupants of a house to be robbed are at home: c.:—1933 (Leach). Cf. **drum**, v.

sound, adj. Sound asleep: domestic coll.

sound as a pound. ' "That's (as) sound . . . !" means "That's right, that's OK, correct, etc." ' (Turner, 1986): Cheshire.

sound egg. A very 'decent' fellow. Mackail, Apr. 1934, 'Another and infinitely superior sex still remained, full of stout fellows, sound eggs, and great guys.'

sound (one's) flute. To blow one's whistle: police: since ca. 1925. *Free-Lance Writer*, Apr. 1948.

sound off. To become (very) angry about a particular topic or on a particular occasion: adopted, ca. 1955, ex US.—2. To boast; talk too much: Aus. c. and low s.: since ca. 1950. (Grindley, 1977.) Brit. usage also, ex US. R.C.'s comment, 1976, fits both senses: 'From the U.S. Army command to "Sound off!" while marching, i.e. to count in cadence "Hup, two, three, four" . . . Its U.S. meaning is merely "to speak one's mind".'

sounds. Music; esp. in, e.g. 'Hit me with the sounds!'—play me some music: teenagers': early 1980s. (James Williamson, 1982.)

sounds man. 'Person providing amplified reggae music at illegal drinking establishment' (Powis): later C.20.

soup. 'Any material injected into a horse with a view to changing its speed or temperament' (Webster, 1911); low s., orig. and mainly US.—2. Bad weather: RAF: since ca. 1915. Jackson.—3. 'The broken part of a wave' (*Pix*, 28 Sep. 1963): Aus. surfers'.

soup and fish. 'Formal attire: prob. post WW1 in the US, and then to Can., with widespread usage' (Leech, 1985). I.e., dressed for a formal many-coursed dinner. Cf. **penguin suit**.

Soup and Gravy, the. The Navy: r.s.

soup plate. A taxicabman's badge: taxidrivers': since ca. 1910. Hodge, 1939.

soup-plate track. A small race-course: Aus.: since ca. 1920. B., 1942.

souped(-)up. Kilduff, 1985: 'the term was originally (and should be spelt) "suped-up" and "supered-up". [It originated] in the [WW2] years to exemplify and extol the supercharged aero engines of the day. We Air Force chaps from then on applied the term extensively to cars and other propelled things as well as aircraft.' The writer goes on to deplore the post-war corruption, through ignorance, to *souped*. Follow-up letters, however, suggested earlier orig. in older s. *soup* (—1905), nitro-glycerine or gelignite, and in **soup**, 1.

sour-dook; Scottish **soor dook.** Buttermilk: c.:—1932 (Mackenzie). Adopted from Scots.

sour(-)puss. A morose person: adopted in 1942 from US. (*John Bull*, 14 Aug. 1943.) Ex US *sour puss*, a sour face.

sourdough. An experienced old-timer in the northwest: Can.: late C.19–20. It arose during the Yukon gold-rush and Robert Service's *Songs of a Sourdough*, 1907, popularised the term; by 1910, it was coll. Leechman, 'The sourdough was used as a yeast in making bread. At each baking, a portion of the dough was retained and allowed to go sour or ferment. It was essential that the sour dough be kept warm and so the old timers took it to bed with them in cold weather.'

souse, n. A getting drunk: from late 1920s; † by 1950. OED Sup.—2. A drunkard: Aus.: since ca. 1925. B., 1942.

souse, v. To drink to intoxication: ca. 1920–80. (OED Sup.) Ex *souse*, to drench, or perhaps a back-formation from:-

soused. Tipsy: coll.: mid-C.19–20. Ex *soused*, soaked in liquor. Cf. *sozzled*.

south. In *dip south*, to put one's hand in one's pocket for money, esp. if it is running low: Aus. and NZ.—2. See **north**.

south, v. To put (something) into one's (esp. trouser) pocket: Aus.: since ca. 1920. (B., 1959.) Elliptical for prec.

South Ken, the. The Victoria and Albert Museum, London: coll.: from ca. 1905. (Allingham, 1932.) Situated in South Kensington.

South of France. A dance: r.s.: late C.19–20.

south-paw. See **southpaw**.

Southend. A score of 26: darts-players': earlier C.20. (London *Evening News*, 2 July 1937.) Once upon a time *2s 6d* was the fare from London. Cf. **bed and breakfast**.

Southend kiss. A form of assault: 'A "butt", known colloquially as "a Southend kiss", is delivered with the head . . . [two kinds] "the flick butt" or "side-header".. [and] the front butt, or the "full nod" ' (Lynch, 1987): the perpetrators'. The correspondence arose from a query about the tautologous use of v. *head-butt*, which had suddenly > common.

southpaw (earlier, hyphenated). A left-handed boxer: pugilistic: US, anglicised in 1934: *Daily Telegraph*, Sep. 21, concerning Freddie Miller, 'He is, in boxing parlance, a "southpaw".' Ex US baseball s. (—1918). An American correspondent of Mr John Moore's has sent him, ca. 1967, this convincing explanation—'On regulation baseball fields, the batter faces East, so that the afternoon sun won't be in his eyes; the pitcher, therfore, must face West, which in the case of the lefthander puts his throwing arm and hand (or "paw") on the South side of his body.'—2. Hence, a car with left-hand drive: car dealers': since mid-1940s. *Woman's Own*, 28 Feb. 1968.

souvenir. A French girl's illegitimate child by a 'Tommy' father: ca. 1916–39. (Petch, 1974.)

sov. A sovereign: coll.: since mid-C.19. Also *half-sov*. (OED.) Since the departure of the coin as currency, it denoted a £1 note (Newman, 1977).

sow. To lay (mines): Army coll.: 1940–5. P-G-R.

sow's ear. In *make a sow's ear* (*of*), to blunder, to mess something up: since ca. 1946. Ex the proverb 'you can't make a silk purse out of a sow's ear'. Cf. synon. var. *make a pig's ear of*.

space cadet. See **air head**.

space-pusher. An advertisement-canvasser working on a periodical: from ca. 1925.

spaced. Short for next, 1 and 2: adopted, ca. 1970, ex US.

spaced out. 'Very high on a hallucinogen or psychedelic' (Janssen, 1968): drugs world: adopted, latish 1960s, ex US. 'Spaced out of her mind on hash and speed' (Stuart, 1971). Loosely, exhilarated on any drug. Cf. **spacy**.—2. Hence, unrealistic, tending to theoretical analysis and exposition, but based upon insufficient data and a lack of understanding and sympathy: among young people: adopted, ca. 1971, ex US. 'Noted among clients of a pop festival on Exmoor in June 1976. "What did the participants think of the Melchett Report on pop festivals?"—"Just spaced out" ' (*Observer*, 13 June 1976).

spacers. '[He]'s a walking cornucopia of drugs; downers and lifters and speeders and freaked-out spacers' (Stuart, 1971): drugs world: adopted, late 1960s, ex US. Ex prec., 1.

spacy. Under the influence of narcotic drug: drugs world: since late 1970s; prob. adopted ex US. Ex **spaced out**, 1. 'Some spacy kid . . . appeared stoned on American TV' (*New Scientist*, 7 Aug. 1980).

spade. A Negro: low: from ca. 1920. Since ca. 1954, it has mostly designated a West Indian. Ex the colour of the card suit; cf. 'as black as the ace of spades'.—2. In *go for a walk with a spade*; *take a spade for a walk*: to defecate: Army in N. Africa: WW2. Ex the earthing-over in a latrineless land. P-G-R.

spag. 'Plastic tubing used to insulate wire in electronic equipment' (B.P.): radio s., esp. Aus.: since late 1950s. Ex *spaghetti*—from the resemblance.—2. (Also *Spaggie*.) An Italian: Aus. derogatory: since early 1960s. (Wilkes.) Abbr. *spaghetti*, *the* Italian dish.—3. A spastic; hence, an idiot, foolish person: E. Midlands schoolboys' var. of **spaz**: later 1970s. Derivatives: *spag-chariot*; occ. *spagmobile*, a wheel-chair. (McPheely, 1978.) See **spastic**. (P.B.)

spag bol. The dish *spaghetti Bolognese*: later C.20. A natural contraction. (P.B., 1988.) Cf.:-

spaggers; loosely **spraggers**. Spaghetti: smart young set: ca. 1955–60. (Gilderdale, 2.) The 'OXFORD -ER(s)'.

spaggie. See **spag**, 2.

Spaghetti Junction. The convoluted motorway interchange at Gravelly Hill, near Birmingham, was already known by this nickname in late 1971, even before it opened for use later in 1972. *Drive: AA Motorists' Magazine*, New Year 1972. (P.B.)

spaghetti Western. 'A western (cowboy film about the American West) produced by the Italian movie industry' (Barnhart): coll.: adopted ex US s. early 1970s; also in Aus. (B.P.).

spam can. Midland Region railwaymen's derogatory term for Southern Region 4–6–2 express passenger locomotives of the 'West Country' class: mid-C.20.—2. 0–6–0 Class 'Q' 'austerity' freight locomotive: railwaymen's: WW2—ca. 1968. Like 1, ex shape; also called a *biscuit-box*. (Both: Hardy, 1979.) '*Spam*, 1939 [from initial and final letters of *spiced ham*]. Proprietary name for a type of tinned meat' (*SOD* Sup.).—3. Derogatory term among pilots of veteran, fabric-covered aircraft, e.g. D.H. Tiger Moth, for the more modern, enclosed, all-metal type of light aircraft: flying clubs': since ca. 1970. (Huston, 1979.)

spam medal. RN version of **Naffy gong**, q.v.

spandule. See GREMLINS, in Appx.

Spanish customs or **practices**. Shady, money-making, subversive or downright illegal practices among compositors and printers: the term was much publicised when the newspaper world of Fleet Street 'went electronic', notably when *The Times* moved to Wapping in 1987.

spanjer. See GREMLINS, in Appx.

spanner. A girl whose appearance is sexually exciting: Aus.: since ca. 1950. A spanner tightens nuts; in s., *nuts* = testicles.

spanner man. A mechanic or pit assistant: motorcycle racers': later C.20. (Dunford, 2.)

spara. Rubbish: Northumberland teenagers': later C.20. (Blyth Ridley, 1984.)

Sparagras, the. That express freight train which 'takes Asparagus during the Season from Worcester to Crewe': railwaymen's: from ca. 1905. (*Daily Telegraph*, 15 Aug. 1936.) Cf. **the Spud**.

spare. Idle; loafing: low: from ca. 1919. (*Gilt Kid*, 1936.) Ex *look spare*, 'To be idle: not engaged on any particular job' (F. & G.): Army: WW1. Cf. dial. *spare*, dilatory.—2. Absent, esp. without leave, as in 'The Old Man turned down my compassionate, so I went spare': Army: 1939+.—3. Angry, as in 'When the sarnt sees this, he'll go fucking spare': Army: since ca. 1940.—4. Hence, crazy; (almost) mad: mostly teenagers': since late 1950s. 'They send me spare' = they drive me crazy.

spare boy. Treacle; golden syrup: Aus., mostly rural: since ca. 1920. B., 1943.

spare file. A man with no definite job to do: Army: WW2. (P-G-R.) The file of 'rank and file'.

spare prick. A useless fellow: Services', orig. Army: since 1939. It shortens *spare prick at a wedding*, ex the phrase *standing about like a* . . . May be used elliptically and allusively, as in, 'Wherever we went, I continued to stand out like a spare prick' (Taylor, 1982). Cf. **spare wank**.

spare tyre. A roll of fat around one's middle: coll.: since late 1940s. *Woman's Realm*, 11 Mar. 1967.

spare whank (or **wank**). A spare man; (among gunners) a spare gunner: Army: since ca. 1930. See **wank**, and cf. **spare prick**.

spark. To send a wireless message to (ship or person): nautical and wireless operators': since ca. 1920. Shaw, 1932, 'If Scotland Yard . . . spark a ship that wanted people are aboard'.—2. To court (a girl): Can.: earlier C.20. (Leechman.) Adopted ex US.—3. To react to a stimulus, to respond: coll.: since ca. 1955. Ex electricity. (P.B.)

spark out; gen. **pass spark out**. Utterly; to become unconscious through liquor, to faint, to die: pugilistic. (*Gilt Kid*, 1936.) Ex dial. *spark out*, utterly extinguished (*EDD*), which has itself, in later C.20, > coll. (P.B.) See **sparkers**.

sparker. A wireless-telegraphist rating: RN. (Granville.) Cf. **sparks**, 1.

sparkers. 'Unconscious or deeply asleep: "She was sparkers" ' (Powis, 1977). By 'OXFORD -ER(s)' on the *spark* of **spark out**. (P.B.)

sparkle. A diamond: low:—1923 (Manchon).—2. Hence(?), generic for jewellery: c.:—1935 (Hume).

sparkler. An electric train: railwaymen's: since ca. 1939. (*Railway*, 2nd.) Ex the sparks emitted from the live rails.

sparklers (rare in sing.). Sparkling gems; esp., diamonds: since ca. 1820: S.E. until mid-C.19, then coll.; in C.20, virtually s. Tempest, 1950, writes, 'Obsolete word once used for diamonds, which today are mostly referred to as *ice*'; but Powis, 1977, lists it without qualification as 'diamonds'.—2. Flares from enemy aircraft: RN: WW2. (P-G-R.) Ironic on the children's fireworks (P.B.).

sparko. Later C.20 coll. var. of **sparkers**. See quot'n at **tincture**.—2. Var. of next, 1. 'Taffrail', 1916.

sparks. A nickname, mostly in vocative, for a wireless operator: Services': since ca. 1916. ('Taffrail', 1917.) Ex electric sparks.—2. The X-ray department: medical students':—1933 (*Slang*).—3. Precious stones: c. Manchon, 1923; Leach, 1933.—4. (Ex 1.) Electrical apparatus repairer in REME: Army: 1943+.—5. An electrician: builders': since ca. 1945.

Sparks Theory, the; the Stinks Theory. The theories that nerve impulses are transmitted electrically or (*Stinks*) chemically: medical coll.: since ca. 1940. (B.P.)

sparky. A wireless operator: Services': since ca. 1918. Cf. **sparker,** and **sparks**, 1.

sparring partner, (one's). One's companion or friend: coll. Ex pugilism. Wife; occ., husband: joc. domestic coll.: late C.19–20.

sparrow-bill maker. A workman that 'forges wrought-iron nails from iron rod' (*Evening News*, 28 Sep. 1955): industrial s. (C.20) > industrial obsol. >, by 1945 at latest, official j.

sparrow-crow, at. A joc. Aus. euph. for **sparrow-fart**, 2. (Baker.) Cf. **sparrow's cough**.

sparrow-fart (or solid). A person of no consequence; a 'twerp': Anglo-Irish. Joyce, 1922, 'Miss This That Miss Theother lot of sparrowfarts skitting around talkin about politics they know as much about as my backside.'—2. In *at sparrow-fart*, at daybreak: dial. >, ca. 1910, coll.: popularised by WW1. Cf. prec., **sparrow's cough**, and **beetle-belch**.

sparrow-starver. A collector of dung from off the streets: lower classes':—1923 (Manchon).

sparrow's cough, at. At dawn: a polite Eng. var. of 'at *sparrow-fart*': since late 1930s. Gordon, 1950.

sparrow's knee-caps. Applied to, e.g., a small boy's almost non-existent arm muscles: coll. Ex the parody of 'The Village Blacksmith': 'The muscles of his brawny arms stood out like—sparrow's kneecaps!' (P.B.)

sparrow's ticket, (e.g.) **come in on a**. To gain an illicitly free admission to a match, contest, competition, show, what-have-you: Aus. Baker.

spastic, n. and adj. 'An unkind and utterly tasteless epithet for a maladroit or his clumsiness. Favoured by the more animal type of drill instructor. But cf., I suppose, the earlier synon. use of cretin' (P.B., 1974): Services': since mid-1950s. Cf. **spag, spaz**. But see also the quot'n at **Sloane Rangers** for evidence of wider usage.

spat, n., a quarrel, a smart blow, a smacking sound,—all C.1920,—is, when not US, rather dial. than coll.—2. See **spats**.

spat, v. To cane: Public Schools': from ca. 1910. (Beeding, 1932.) Ex prec., 1.

spats. Those stream-lined covers over landing-wheels which are in aircraft designed to reduce air-resistance: aviators': from 1934. (*Daily Telegraph*, 9 Feb. 1935.) 'If the wheels of a

"spatted" 'plane do not retract, it is said to have permanent "spats" ' (H. & P.): RAF: since ca. 1935.—2. Slabs of bread and butter to assuage hunger about 4 p.m.: Marlborough College.—3. Hence, butter: Public and Grammar Schools': later C.20. (Lambert, 1968.) Prob. influenced by S.E. *pats of butter*.

spatted. See prec., 1.

spatter. To strike (somebody); 'make a mess' of him: low: since ca. 1945. (Wilson, 1956.) Ex S.E.

spawny. (Very) lucky: RAF: since ca. 1930. Jackson. 'Thus, "You're spawny to get your promotion so soon." ' Perhaps ex the near-cliché, *the best ever spawned*. P.B.: in later C.20, also Army. Usu. in phrase *spawny git*, and envious.

spaz(z). Schoolboys' var. of **spastic**, q.v. (Parsons, 1977; *New Society*, 31 Jan. 1980.) Cf. **spag**.

speak fancy waistcoats. To speak with the utmost accuracy: RN. Granville.

speak French. (Of a horse) to be an excellent steeplechaser: turf:—1923 (Manchon).

speak in (someone's) **knuckle.** To interrupt someone's conversation or story: N. Country. Ex the game of marbles, where the boy about to shoot may be 'advised' to do this or that and say 'I wish you wouldn't speak in my knuckle.'

speak proper. To speak Standard Received English: var. of **talk proper**, q.v.

speak the same language. To have the same sort of upbringing, hence the same general ideas: coll.: since ca. 1930. P-G-R.

speak white. 'Boorish English-speaking people sometimes instruct French Canadians, speaking French, to "speak white" ' (i.e. English): Can. *Maclean's Magazine*, 2 Nov. 1963.

speakers, on. On speaking terms (with someone): since ca. 1950. (J. Mitford, 1960; Simmonds, 1987.) By the 'OXFORD -ER(s)'.

speakie. Ephemeral coll. term for a motion picture with sound-track, a 'talkie': 1928–9. (*OED* Sup.) Cf. **audies**.

spear, n. In *get the spear*, 'to be sacked from a job' (Wilkes): Aus. Hence *give the spear*, to dismiss (B., 1959), an elab. of next.—2. See **hold a spear**.

spear, v. To dismiss: Aus.:—1911 (Rudd).—2. To throw (someone) out of a shop, a pub, etc.: Aus. c. and low, > gen s.: since early C.20. See AUSTRALIAN, in Appx.

spear a job. To obtain employment: Aus.: since early C.20. Baker.

spear-carrier. A 'walk-on' part in a play, with no words to speak: actors' coll. (Raab.) Cf. **hold a spear**.

spear flounders. To conduct an orchestra: Aus.: since ca. 1925. Baker, 'Whence, "flounder-spearing".'

speci. Abbr. *specimen*: s. (—1923) rather than coll., for it is infelicitous. (Manchon.) Cf. **spess**.

special, v. To act as a special nurse to (a person): nurses' coll.: from ca. 1910. 'She came to special me.' By abbr.

specilate. To invest money, in the hope of bringing good luck: Romanies', hence a few tramps', s.: since ca. 1930. (Dawson.) Ex *speculate*.

speckled. 'Demoted': Rugby: since ca. 1916. (Marples.) To revert to a *speckled* straw hat.

speckled potato. A spectator: early C.20. A joc. perversion.

specs. Specifications; detailed requirement: coll.: since mid-C.20. Also sing., as in *job spec*, the details of a post. (P.B.)

speed. An amphetamine, esp. methedrine: drugs world: adopted, ca. 1965, ex US. (*Groupie*, 1968.) Hence, as v.i., to 'use' these drugs: since ca. 1967 (*Jagger*), and *speed(-) freak*, 'One who takes amphetamine, usually addictively' (Cutland, 1985).

speed-cop. A policeman observing the speed of motorists: coll., orig. (ca. 1924) US, anglicised by 1929. *OED* Sup.

speed-merchant. One who cycles or, esp., motors at high speed: US; anglicised ca. 1920. Cf. *road-hog*. (The forms *speed-bug* and *speed-hog* are hardly eligible, for they have not 'caught on'.)—2. Whence, from ca. 1926, a very fast bowler: cricketers'. In this compound, *merchant* = chap, fellow.

speed the wombats! Aus. synon. of *stone the crows!, starve the lizards!*, etc.; a mainly humorous exclam.: since ca. 1925. B., 1942.

speedballing. Injecting or sniffing a mixture of cocaine and heroin; also snowballing: drugs c. (Stockley, 1986.) *Speedballing* US since—1936 (Spears).

speedo. A speedometer: motorists': since ca. 1920. *Passing Show*, 21 July 1934.

speedo lurk, the. The used-car-dealers' trick of turning back the odometer: Aus. dealers', hence also motorists': since ca. 1920. (B.P.) A *speedo* is strictly a speedometer. See **clock**, v., 6.

speedy. Living a loose life; apt to be amorous: joc. coll.:—1923 (Manchon). Punning *fast*.

spell-binder, spellbinder. A 'spiller of rhetorical dope' (Laing): journalistic coll., verging on rank j.: adopted, ca. 1910, ex US, where it was earlier applied to Theodore Roosevelt.

spend a penny. To urinate: euph. coll. Strictly, to use the w.c. in a public convenience: mostly feminine. (Lewis, 1945.) *Daily Telegraph*, 8 Mar. 1977, had a brief news item headed '2p to spend a penny'. The first public convenience to charge one penny was opened outside the Royal Exchange, London, in 1855.

speng. A fool: Black youth, London: mid-1980s. (Rowbotham, 1987.)

spew (one's) **guts** (up). To vomit violently and comprehensively: low. (P.B.)—2. Hence, to inform the police on one's friends: c.: from ca. 1930. Cf. **spill** (one's) **guts** or **the works,** and synon. **come** (one's) **cocoa.**

spew it. To leave one's job on a ship, go home, report again in the afternoon and try for another job, there or elsewhere: London docks': since ca. 1930. (*New Statesman*, 31 Dec. 1965.) 'It' = the ship, hence also the job.

spew (one's) **ring** (up). To vomit violently: low: since ca. 1920. (The BBC let this pass on 1 Mar. 1963.) The *ring* = the anus.

Spic. Spanish, as in 'I'm doing this because I can speak Spic . . . Not very well, got most of it from Fawlty Towers' (*Don't Cry*, 1983, quoting a lieutenant in charge of disarming Argentinian prisoners after the Falkland Is. armistice): adopted ex US, where *spic* (and variants) has = Central or Latin American, n. and adj., since ca. 1915 (W. & F.). Fawlty Towers: a BBC TV comedy series in which a comic Spanish waiter appears. *Spic* perhaps a contraction of Hispanic.

spice. Spicy sex-items in the newspapers: newsagents' coll.—2. Joc. pl. of *spouse*: since (?)ca. 1950. Cf. *grice*, joc. pl. of *grouse*, etc. (P.B.)

spicey or **spicy.** Usu. in pl. *spicies*, spicy books or magazines: booksellers' and newsagents' coll.: since ca. 1910.

spider. A wireless operator's badge: RAF: since ca.1935. Emanuel, 'From the shape'.

spiel, n. A hard-luck story: tramps' c.:—1932 ('Stuart Wood'). Ex sense 2 or 3 of the v.—2. A grafter's patter: late C.19-20. P. Allingham, 1934.—3. Set or formal advice: Aus. B., 1959.—4. 'A wordy explanation' (B., 1959): Aus.—5. A drinking club: c.: later C.20. (*Now!*, 10 Apr. 1981.) Prob. a shortening of **spieler**, 4, with a widened meaning. (P.B.)

spiel, v. To talk glibly, plausibly; to patter: mostly Aus.: from ca. 1870. Perhaps a back-formation ex *spieler*.—2. Hence, to 'tell the tale': tramps' c.:—1932 ('Stuart Wood').—3. To race 'all out'—at full speed: Aus. sporting: B.,1942.

spiel off. To 'spout', utter plausibly: vagrants' c. Gape, 1936, 'When my turn came I was not ready to "spiel" off the answers.'

spieler; occ. **speeler** or **speiler.** A gambler, esp. a cardsharper; a professional swindler: Aus. and NZ: 1886, *New Zealand Herald*, 1 June, 'A fresh gang of "speelers" are operating in the town' (*OED*). Ex Ger. *Spieler*, player, esp. at cards, a gamester.—2. Hence, a glib and crafty fellow: Aus.: from ca.

1905.—3. A 'weaver of hard luck stories': tramps' c.:—1932 ('Stuart Wood'). Cf. **spiel**, v., 3.—4. A gambling-den: c.: from ca. 1925. (Leach.) But also any room in which card-games are habitually played: London's East End: since ca. 1945. (Herd, 1957.)—5. A 'barker': grafters'. (*Cheapjack*, 1934.) Cf. sense 2.—6. A fast horse (usually *speeler*): Aus. sporting: (B., 1942.) Ex **spiel**, v., 3.—7. A welsher: Aus. sporting: since ca. 1910.

spike, n. A needle: lower classes':—1923 (Manchon).—2. Hence, a needle, or a syringe, for injecting a drug: drugs world: adopted, ca. 1960, ex US. Wyatt, 1973.

spike, v. To hit or strike; to knock (someone) down: Aus. low: since ca. 1920. Baker.—2. To render a drink dangerous, either by surreptitiously adding strong(er) alcohol, or by actually poisoning it: (?c. >) s. > gen. coll.: adopted ex US mid-C.20 (?earlier). W. & F. give 1900 as an early US date, and indicate gen. use by ca. 1920, orig. simply 'to fortify a drink with alcohol'. Perhaps ex 'spiking a gun', rendering it useless. (P.B.)

spill, n. 'A declaration that all offices are vacant and that new elections will be held. Mostly in the Labor Party' (B.P.): Aus. political: since ca. 1930; by 1950, coll.: by 1966, virtually S.E.

spill, v. To confess, divulge: c. (—1932) now verging on low s. ('Stuart Wood'). Ex U.S. P.B.: prob. a shortening of *spill the beans*, or (one's) *guts*, or *the works*, rather than these being elaborations. Cf.:—2. Hence, used frequently in Aus. by women when engaged in slander or in mere gossip: since ca. 1945. 'You know that I won't tell a living soul. Do tell! Spill!' (B.P.)

spill (one's) **guts.** To inform on one's friends to the police: low s.: adopted, ex US, ca. 1930. More usu. than synon. *spew* (one's) *guts*; cf. **spill the works.**

spill over. That part of a newspaper or magazine contribution which has been deferred to the end of the periodical: journalistic coll. (for the S.E. *turn-over*).

spill the beans. To blab; to divulge, whether unintentionally or not, important facts; to confess; to lay information: US, anglicised by 1928 (Sayers); Brophy, 1932. Orig., to 'make a mess' of things.

spill the works. A c. var., from ca. 1929, of prec. Brandon, 1934.

spin. 'A piece of experience (always with an adjective: "rough spin", "fair spin", etc.) [?From *spin* for the toss of a coin, *OED* 1882, or *spin* in various uses implying duration, *OED* 1856, 1875]' (Wilkes): Aus. With *tough spin*, a bad time or a spoiled chance, cf. synon. **lean trot.** Hence *get* or *give a* (e.g. *fair*) *spin*, to get, give a fair chance.—2. (Also *spinnaker*.) £5, whether note or sum: Aus. (Partridge, 1938; B., 1942.) Used esp. in two-up.—3. In *go for a spin*, to go for a drive in a motor-car; occ. on a motor-cycle or in its side-car: coll.: ca. 1905-55.—4. 'A cab rank. Authorised taxi stand' (Tempest, 1950): c.: mid-C.20.—5. 'Search by officers for contraband, etc.' (Clayton, 1970): prisons'. Cf. **spin** (someone's) **drum.**—6. See **flat spin.**

spin dits. 'Talking or yarning . . . is "spinning dits" ' (*You*, 13 Nov. 1983): RN submariners'. A *dit* was noted in use for a story, a yarn, in R. Aus. N., 1943; perhaps it shortened *ditty*, dial. for a fit, a long and circumstantial tale (*EDD*), but there may have been later influence from the 'dits' of the Morse Code. *Spin* in this sense has been nautical s. since late C.18.

spin (someone's) **drum.** 'To search a house' (Powis): police and c.: later C.20.

spin for. To court (a woman): Aus.: since ca. 1930. (Marshall, 1946.) Ex the game of two-up? P.B.: or ex fishing?

spin-off (later, written solid). An important secondary result, esp. the final, most significant, consequence: adopted, late 1940s, ex US.—2. Hence, loosely, *any* result, however minor or irrelevant, of something bigger, as 'of course, non-sticking frying-pans are a useful spin-off from the US space programme': since the early 1960s, when that programme started giving rise to so much j.—3. Fig., 'A benefit, either anticipated or gratuitous' (R.S., quoting BBC, Nov. 1970).

spin the dope. To tell a (good) story, e.g. in chiromancy: Aus.: since ca. 1920. Prichard, 1930.

spin the fanny. To 'tell the tale', to spin a good yarn or deliver a good, set 'spiel': fairground grafters': since ca. 1925. (Merry.) Cf. **fanny**, n., 3.

spine-bashing. Sleeping or, at least, lying down: Aus. army: WW2+. (*Rats*, 1944.) Hence, *spine-basher*, a lazy man. Cf. *charpoy-* or *pit-bashing*, the Brit. Service synons.

Spinifex wire, the. A N. Aus. version of the bush telegraph: since ca. 1930. (Brockman, 1938.) Hence, *a spinifex wire*, a rumour, esp. if well-founded (Ibid.). Cf. synon. **mulga wire.**

spinner. £50: Aus. low: since ca. 1910. (B., 1942.) Cf. **spin**, n., 2.—2. A parachutist with twisted rigging lines in his parachute: RAF: 1939+. (Jackson.) He spins as he descends.—3. 'Chris has just finished a rotating shift, "a spinner" they all call it, filling in for other [air traffic] controllers when they're having their tea break' (*New Society*, 23 Apr. 1981).

spinning jenny. A prismatic compass, early model: Royal Artillery: ca. 1915–50. Ex the way in which the card spun.

Spion Kop. City Road: London taxi-drivers': early C.20. Ex a battle in the S. African war.

Spirit, the. A Melbourne-Sydney train: Aus. coll.: 1962+. Short for *the Spirit of Progress*. (B.P.) Cf. **Roarer, the.**

spit. A (distinguished or remarkable or attractive) manner of spitting: coll. Wade, 1934.—2. A smoke (of a cigarette): low. 'Some of them had bits of cigarettes, and asked us if we'd like a "spit" ' (Behan, 1958). P.B.: prob. shortening of **spit and a drag**, q.v.—3. As *Spit*, a Spitfire fighter plane: since 1938 in RAF: since 1940 (Berrey) among civilians. Spitfires and Hurricanes saved Britain in Aug.–Sep. 1940.—4. In *the big* (less commonly, *the long*) *spit*, a vomiting: Aus., esp. among drinkers: since mid-C.20. (Hardy, 1967, where it is made clear that this is the most used of the numerous Aus. s. terms for a vomiting.)

spit and a drag, a. A smoke on the sly: RN >, by ca. 1920, gen. s.: late C.19–20. (Ibid.) Ex *spit and drag*, a cigarette: r.s., on *fag*: late C.19–20. (B. & P.) P.B.: is this really rhyming, or simply coincidence? Shreds of tobacco from a badly-rolled cigarette are often spat away, while the smoke is dragged, or drawn (see next) into the lungs.

spit and a draw, a. Var. of prec.: proletarian: prob. since late C.19. Paterson, 1911.

Spit and Cough, the. The Athenæum Club: London taxi-drivers': since ca. 1910. (Hodge, 1939.) Ex the high incidence of asthma and bronchitis among members?

spit and sawdust. A general saloon in a public-house. Ex the sawdust sprinkled on the floor and the spitting on to the sawdust. (Chamberlain.)

spit-and-scratch game. A hair-pulling fight: lower classes' coll.: early C.20. Lyons, 1914; Manchon.

spit chips. (Usu. *spitting* . . .) 'To be in a state of anger and frustration' (Wilkes): Aus.: since mid-C.20.

spit (one's) guts. To tell or confess everything: low s. verging on c.: from not later than 1931. Cf. later synon. **come** (one's) **cocoa**, and **spill** (one's) **guts.**

spit in the bag and stand up. (Of a bookmaker on the course) to occupy his stand and accept bets without the money to honour them if they are successful: Aus. racing: since ca. 1925. (Glassop, 1949.) He spits in his bag for luck.

spit out. To confess: gen. as *spit it out!*: coll. (Lyell.) Ex S.E. *spit out*, to utter plainly, bravely, or proudly.

spitcher. To sink (an enemy submarine): RN: from 1916. (*OED* Sup.) Hence, *spitchered*, done for, 'sunk'; mortally wounded, etc. (Granville). It derives from Italianate Maltese *spizzia*, finished, done for, itself from It. *spezzare*, to break into small pieces.

spitfire. A contraceptive: RN lowerdeck: 1945+. A usu. effective interceptor: see **spit**, n., 3.

Spitfire kitten. A woman munition-worker. See **whistler**, 4.

Spitfires. 'Ration cigarettes with R.A.F. roundels on the packet. A fair description'; Forces' in N. Africa: 1940–3. (Sanders, 1967.) Ex the famous fighter aircraft.

Spithead pheasant. A bloater: RN. (*Birmingham Mail*, 24 Feb. 1939; Granville.) Cf. *Yarmouth capon*.—2. A kipper: since ca. 1950. *News Chronicle*, 4 Nov. 1954.

Spitter, -y. Occ. var. of **spit**, 3: 1941–5. H. & P.

spiv. One who lives by his wits—within the law, for preference; esp. by 'the racing game': c.: since ca. 1890; by 1940 low s. Seccombe, 1936; Worby, 1937 (the 'locus classicus'); Hoby, 1946, ' "Spivs"—the small town touts and racketeers'; a definition enunciated in June 1947 was 'One who earns his living by not working'. In the *Daily Telegraph*, 29 and 30 July 1947, Lord Rosebery and 'Peterborough' clearly established that the term had been in use by and among racecourse gangs since the 1890s and had been known to a few police detectives since 1920 or so. *Spiv* is of the same orig. as dialectal *spif* or *spiff*, 'neat, smart, dandified; excellent'; compare Scottish and Northern *spiffer*, 'anything first-rate'. The adj. *spif* becomes a noun (compare **phoney**) and *spif* becomes *spiv* because the latter is easier to pronounce. Whence *spivvish*: 'of or like a spiv': 1946+.

spiv days (singular rare). Rest days: railwaymen's: since ca. 1945. *Railway.*

spiv-knot. 'The "Windsor" knotting of the tie: knotted double to emphasize the shoulders and waist of tie-knot. Of Cockney origin' (L.A.): late 1947+. See **spiv.**

splash, n. A small quantity of soda-water (added to whisky, etc.): coll.:—1927 (Collinson).—2. In *have a splash*, (of men) to urinate. A blend of synon. *splash* (one's) *boots* and *have a slash*.—3. Amphetamine: drugs c. (Stockley, 1986.) US since—1966 (Spears).

splash, v.i. To be actively extravagant with money: coll.: from ca. 1912. Ex *splash money about*. Whence *splasher*.—2. V.t., to expend: Aus.: –1916 (Dennis).—3. (Of men) to masturbate: low: since ca. 1930. (L.A.)

splash out. An extension of **splash**, v., 1: coll.: later C.20. 'He splashed out on a new car.' (P.B.)

splasher. A person very extravagant with money: coll.: from ca. 1919.

splat. Imit. of something soft being dashed against something hard, e.g. an insect against a moving car's windscreen. Hence as n., as in 'We apologise for the various clicks and splats on the line from Birmingham . . . ' (BBC Radio 3 announcers after the marred relay of the broadcast of a live concert, 14 Jan. 1988.) Occ., in narrative, *ker-splat!* Ex W. Country dial. for splash (*EDD*).

splattered, get. To lose heavily: racing, esp. bookies': since ca. 1920. *Sunday Telegraph*, 7 May 1967.

splice. In *sit on* (or *upon*) *the splice*, to play a strictly defensive bat: cricket s. >, by 1935, coll.: from ca. 1905. (Lewis.) As if to sit on the shoulder of the bat.

spliff. 'Hand-rolled cigarette' (Home Office): prisons' c.: later C.20. Ex:—2. 'A marijuana cigarette' (Ibid.): drugs world: id. Spears, giving US, 1967, specifies Jamaican marijuana.

split, n. 'A division of profits' (*OED* Sup.): low:—1919.—2. A ten-shilling currency note (i.e. half a £1 note): low: ca. 1920–40.—3. A safety match: Aus. B., 1959.

split, v. To copulate: low: C.18–20. P.B.: in later C.20, also v.t., as in 'when [an army vehicle] passes a girl, aged sixteen years old upwards, the usual [soldierly] remark is "Cor, I'd like to split that one" ' (*New Statesman*, 2 Oct. 1981).—2. To run away; to escape: adopted, ca. 1960, ex US. Reid, 1970. Cf.:—3. Hence, simply, to depart; go away; to leave one person or a group: orig. US hippies' >, by 1970, gen. Stuart, 1971; Powis.—4. V.i., to divide, or share in, profits: low:—1919 (*OED* Sup.).

split-arse, n. (?Usu. pl.) 'Dumplings that had burst open (also vulgarly applied to nuns' (Butcher, 1979): naval.

split-arse, adj. 'He's a pukka split-arse pilot'—i.e. stunt pilot: RAF: since ca. 1915. (Jackson.) Cf. **split-arse turn.** White, 1970: 'A cavalry term before the R.A.F. came up. A horse, at its fullest gallop and seen from behind, visibly splays its legs.'—2. Hence, addicted to stunting: RAF since ca.1920.—3. 'Used by the South Africans (in the Air Force) to indicate very good or very clever, e.g. "split-arse navigator" ' (Hinde, 1945).

split-arse, adv. A low var. of (*at*) *full split*, full speed:—1923 (Manchon).

split-arse cap. The (former) RFC cap, rather like a Glengarry: Air Force: 1915–ca. 1920. (B. & P.) It has been kept alive by the RAF for the field-service cap as distinct from the peaked dress-service cap. (Jackson.) Cf. **cunt cap.**

split-arse landing. A daring landing at speed: RAF: since ca. 1925. Jackson.

split-arse turn. A flat turn, without banking; it is caused by using the rudder instead of rudder and ailerons: RFC/RAF: prob. from ca. 1917.

split-arsing. 'Stunting low and flying near the roofs of billets or huts': Air Force: from 1918. B. & P.

split-arsing about. Elab. of prec.: since ca. 1916.—2. Hence, acting the fool in a dangerous way: all three Services': since ca. 1925. P-G-R.

split beaver. See **beaver,** 3.

split stuff. Women collectively: low Aus. (B., 1942.) Physiological; cf. **slotted jobs.**

split the difference. A punning elab. of **split,** v., 1: ca. 1960. (L.A., 1974.)

split-up. A division of booty: c., and low. *Gilt Kid,* 1936.

split yarn, on a. 'Ready for instant anchor' (Foster, 1931): RN. Granville has simply, of *have everything on a split yarn,* 'to be ready to carry out an evolution'.—2. Hence, to have a plan worked out: RN: since ca. 1925.

splits. Split peas or lentils: domestic and grocers' coll.

sploshing it on, adj. or n. Betting heavily; heavy betting: racing, esp. bookies': since ca. 1920. (*Sunday Telegraph,* 7 May 1967.) Ex heavy (and careless) application of any thick liquid, paint, cosmetics, etc.

Splot. Senior pilot: FAA: later C.20. (Knight, 1985.) Cf. **Sobs** and **spo.**

splutter. A 'shindy' or 'dust'; a scandal: low:—1923 (Manchon). Ex C.19–20 dial.

splutterbug. 'People are even becoming nostalgic about early diesel engines [locomotives] ("splutterbugs", as the enthusiasts call them, with schoolboy humour)' (Godfrey, 1979). Perhaps modelled on *shutterbug.* (P.B.)

spo. Stoker *Petty Of*ficer; 'One word. Like **Polto** [q.v.] it was just another way of hanging on to the old ranks. When it was changed to Petty Officer Mechanic (Engineering) they were also known as *Pommy*' (Malin, 1979): RN submariners': 1960s.—2. A spot: Charterhouse. Cf. **squo** for the form.

Spode's law. 'If something *can* go wrong, it *will*'—esp. in scientific research: scientists', pharmaceutical chemists', technologists': since ca. 1930. (Rogers, 1967.) Cf. the rather earlier scientific dictum about the mythical fourth general law of the physicists, 'the cussedness of the universe tends to a maximum'. P.B.: E.P. may have back-dated this too far: it sounds like a bowdlerisation of *Sod's law,* q.v. Cf. **Murphy's law.**

spodiodi. A 'mixture of cheap port and bar whisky' affected by the jazz world ('Basic Beatnik'): Can. jazz-lovers' and musicians': since ca. 1955. Origin? Apparently arbitrary—perhaps after such a name as *asti spumante.*

Spokeshay. Shakespeare: joc. Aus. By perverted reversal: perhaps on *spokeshave.* Cf. **Waggle-dagger.**

spon; spons. Money: Aus.: from ca. 1920. (B., 1942.) Ex later C.19 s. *spondulicks.*

spongged. Struck, assaulted: joc. coll.: since mid-late 1950s. Ex BBC Radio comedy series 'The Goon Show', a recurring line, 'Ooh, mate, I bin spongged!', said in a pained, 'common' voice. Hence, it came to mean 'hit in the pocket; grossly overcharged'. Echoic. (P.B.)

sponk. Infatuated. Public School girls': since late 1940s; by 1967, ob. Winton, 1960, ' "I had a crush on my games mistress," Mary said. "I was absolutely *sponk* on her." '

spons. See **spon.**

spoof, n. Misleading or 'planted' information: Army, esp. Intelligence: since ca. 1940. (Sanders.)

spoof, v. To practise hoaxing or humbugging, gen. with present ppl. ('You're not spoofing, are you?'): from ca. 1920.

spook, n. A drug addict: c.: since ca. 1943. (Norman.) Such addicts tend to look ghastly.—2. A Negro, esp. a West Indian: adopted, ca. 1965, ex US. But even in 1977, **spade,** q.v., was by far the commoner throughout the British Commonwealth. W. & F. offer no date earlier than 1947, neither do they explain its origin. Prob. it comes from the fear shown by many young white children at their first sight of a Negro. (Crisp, 1976.) Hence the adj. *spooky,* as in Norman, 1959.—3. A cloak-and-dagger man, spy or political agent: espionage: since (?)ca. 1950, familiarised by the efforts of the American CIA. Whence *spook house,* a headquarters of a department of military intelligence. Le Carré, 1977.

spook, v. To render (a horse or other quadruped) nervous: Can.: since ca. 1930. 'Don't show him the whip, you'd spook him'—'You'll never catch him now, he's spooked.' To cause to shy or to gallop away, as if at sight of a *spook* or ghost. Perhaps of US orig. (cf. W. & G.); Leechman thinks not. By later C.20 also Brit., as v.i., (of a horse) to shy away from insignificant or unseen things, e.g. a reed shaken by the wind: horsemen's. (Littmoden, 1980.)

spoon. $\frac{1}{16}$th oz. of drug: drugs c. (Stockley, 1986.) US since—1969 (Spears).

spoon and gravy. Full-dress evening clothes (men's): early C.20. Cf. **soup and fish.**

sport. A 'good sport', either one who subordinates his or her own personality or abilities to the gen. enjoyment; or, of women only, one who readily accords the sexual favour: coll. Hence, *be a sport!* = don't be a spoil-sport! Abbr. *a good sport,* ex *sport,* a sportsman: cf. *sporty. Be a Sport!* occurs in, e.g., *Punch,* 21 May 1913. As a term of address, it has been current in Aus. since before WW1.

Spo's, the. The School Sports meeting: Charterhouse. For the form cf. **spo** and **squo.**

sposh. Excellent: mainly theatrical: ca. 1929+. Milne, 1931, 'Sposh . . . I should adore to.' Perhaps a blend of *spiffing + posh.* P.B.: ?simply (*it*)' *Sposh.*

spot. A small amount of. Gen. *a spot of* . . . , e.g. lunch, hence of rest, work, pleasure, music, etc. C.20, but common only since ca. 1915: s. >, ca. 1930, coll. Sayers, 1932.—2. A detective: low: early C.20. Lyons, 1912; Manchon.—3. In (*be*) *in a spot,* occ. later, *in a bit of a spot,* to be in a difficult or dangerous position or condition: c., from ca. 1930, > by 1939, s.; esp. in the Services. (*Gilt Kid,* 1936; Partridge, 1945.) Perhaps ex *be put on the spot.*—4. A worn patch on the pitch: cricketers' coll. Cardus, 1934, concerning the third test match, 'It is the duty of all loyal subjects to talk about "a spot" in loud voices so that the Australians will hear.'—5. A guess: from ca. 1932. Gorell, 1935, 'My spot is that after baiting his poor victim, he had a fancy for the melodramatic.'—6. £10: Aus. low: since ca. 1930. (B., 1942.) Ex US *ten-spot,* 10 dollars; and cf. **spotter,** 3.—7. A spotlight: cinematic, since ca. 1925; TV since ca. 1945. By 1960, coll.—8. (Cf. 6.) Since ca. 1965, 100 dollars Aus. See AUSTRALIAN, in Appx.—9. An allotted space in a programme, church service, agenda, etc., as 'They've given me a 5-minute spot near the end': coll.: later C.20. (P.B.)—10. In *on the spot,* a US c. sense, anglicised ca. 1930 as s. rather than as c.: in the place (and position) pre-arranged for one's murder. The rapidity of the anglicising, once it started, was largely owing to the popularity of Edgar Wallace's play (*On the Spot*), an excellent 'thriller', and of the ensuing novel (1931). Merely a special application of the S.E. sense, 'at the very place or locality in question'. Hence *to put on the spot,* to determine and arrange the murder of: adopted, ex US, ca. 1930. The meaning soon weakened, as in, e.g., 'They've rather put you on the spot, haven't they!' = you've been left in an awkward, embarrassing, but not necessarily dangerous, predicament: coll.: since mid-C.20 at latest (P.B.).

spot-joint. A booth for the presentation of a form of amusement popular at fairs: grafters'. *Cheapjack*, 1934.

spot(-)on. An, orig. occ., var. of **bang on:** RAF: 1940–5. Since late 1940s, the usu. term in Aus. (B.P.) P.B.: in UK it has completely superseded the dated *bang on*, to mean 'absolutely accurate, precise, exact', as 'she arrived spot on 6 o'clock', or 'just what is required', as 'How was that graph paper I sent you?'—'Spot on, thanks—lovely.'

spots on burnt(, e.g. two). (E.g. two) poached eggs on toast: low:—1923 (Manchon).

spotter. He who 'spots' a likely victim for a 'mob' to rob: police s. Leach.—2. A man on the look-out for military police: Army: WW2. (P-G-R.) Ex, e.g., *plane-spotter*, one on watch for enemy aircraft.—3. As suffix: 'Financial embarrassment. . . . puts me under the necessity of borrowing a five-spotter [5 francs]' (*Punch*, 30 Apr. 1919): Army in France. Cf. **spot**, 6 and 8.

sprag, n. A goods guard: Eastern Railway employees': ca. 1890–1925. (*Railway*, 2nd.) Perhaps ex dial. *sprag*, to put a brake on something.—2. 'A good sized cod' (Piper): trawlermen's. Butcher, 1980, glosses it 'Halfgrown cod'.

sprag, v. 'To accost truculently' (Dennis): Aus.:—1916. Prob. same deriv. as n., 1.—2. To deny employment to (a man): trawlermen's coll. 'He used to be one of the best of hands but they've spragged him. They said he was the ringleader of a strike we had here' (Piper). Peppitt noted the var. *spraggled*, in the ITV programme, 'A Life Apart', 13 Feb. 1973.

spraggers. Var. of **spaggers**.

sprang. Tea; any drink: Army: early C.20. (F. & G.) A corruption, prob. of Southern dial. *sprank*, a sprinkling, a slight shower (*EDD*).

sprarser, -sey, -sie, -zer, -zy; spraser, sprasey; sparsie; spowser; sprowsie, -sy. All variants of a word for (a) sixpence: among grafters, market-traders; the last, nautical: ob. by 1980. (The 2nd, *Muvver*; 4th, *M.T.*; 5th, Daniells; 6th, 7th, P. Allingham; 8th, Tempest; 10th, 11th, Orwell.) Perhaps ex C.19 synon. s. *sprat*, on **susie**, 1.

sprauncy. As in 'At the darkest end of the wardrobe there was this Flash Suit. A real sprauncy whistle' (Daniells, 1980). *Whistle*, a shortening of later C.19 r.s., *whistle and flute*, suit.

spread. 'A herbalist who sells a mixture of dried plants. He spreads these herbs out in front of him and lectures on the health-giving value of each'; *work the spread*, 'to graft as a herbalist': grafters': late C.19–20. *Cheapjack*, 1934.—2. A plasterer: builders'.—3. In *in a spread*, making money: young London financiers'. Taylor, 1987.

spread (one's) **custard.** To vomit: Army: later C.20. (Jones, 1979.)

spread for (someone). (Of a woman) to dispose her body for sexual intercourse: low. (L.A., 1978.) Cf. older synon. *do a spread*.

spread it thick or **thin.** To live expensively; poorly: coll.:—1923 (Manchon). Ex spreading butter, or margarine, thick or thin.

spread the royal. (Gen. as vbl n.) To give evidence against confederates: c.:—1935 (Hume). Ex 'turn *King's* evidence.'

spread-worker. A herbalist: showmen's: late C.19–20. See **spread**, 1.

spreading broads. 'Playing or cheating at cards. Manipulating the three-card trick' (Powis): c.:—1886 (*Underworld*).

spridgy – sproggy – spudgy. Aus., esp. juvenile, terms for a sparrow. (B., 1953.) With the first, cf. the Scottish dial. *sprig*; with the second, cf. Scottish and N. Country dial. *sprog* (and *sprug*); with the third, cf. the Scottish and N. Country dial. *spug* and Sussex *spudger*.

spring. To see: Aus., esp. Sydneyites: since ca. 1945. 'I've never sprung him before' (Morrisby, 1958).—2. To get a man released from prison, esp. on a technicality: Can.: adopted, ca. 1935, ex US. (Leechman.) In gen. use in UK by 1950, at

latest.—3. Hence, to get a man out of prison by plot or even by violence: since ca. 1960.

spring-sides. Elastic-sided boots: Aus. B., 1942.

springer. A 'dark' horse so much an outsider that no odds are quoted until just before the race: turf c.:—1932. Ex springing a surprise.—2. A physical-training officer: (lower-deck): since ca. 1920. P-G-R.—3. A planner of a prison escape: since ca. 1960. Ex **spring**, 3.

sprog, n. A recruit: RAF: since ca. 1930; by ca. 1939, also—via the FAA—used occ. by the Navy. (H. & P.) By later C.20 also Army: 'punched, kicked and beat the "sprogs"—Army slang for rookie soldiers' (Daily Telegraph, 14 May 1988; Kipling used *rookie* in 1893). Origin obscure and debatable (see esp. Partridge, 1945); but perhaps a reversal of 'frog-spawn' (very, very green) or, more prob., the adoption of a recruit's *sprog*, a confusion of 'sprocket' and 'cog', a sprocket being, like the recruit, a cog in a wheel. R.C. suggests that the word might just be a distortion of S.E. sprout.—2. Hence, an aircraftman: R Aus. AF: WW2. B., 1943.—3. A baby, as in 'Nobby Clarks's gone on leave, his wife's just had a *sprog*' (Granville); a child, esp. in relation to its parents: RAF; FAA; RN: since late 1930s. Cf. the adj.—4. A new, young prisoner: prisons': later C.20. Clement, 1977.—5. 'According to the Home Office, a graver problem than political flak are the "spurious emissions" (known in the trade as "sprogs"), which interfere with emergency services' (*New Society* article on pirate radio stations, 19 May 1983).

sprog, adj. New ('sprog tunic'); recently promoted ('sprog corporal'); recently created or become ('Two sprog fathers in the room in two days,' Brickhill, 1946). Ex the n.

sproggie. See **spridgey**.

sprogster. RN var. of **sprog**, n., 3. Bolster, 1945.

spronger. A multi-pronged underwater fishing spear. (Crapp, 1944.) P.B.: perhaps simply echoic: *sprong* is sometimes used to represent the sound of spring uncoiling.

sprout wings. To become angelic, extremely upright, chaste, etc.: joc. coll.

sprowsie, -y. See **sprarser**.

spruce. A field: c.—1933 (Leach). Perhaps ex spruce growing there.

spruce, v.i. To tell lies or 'tall stories'; v.t., to deceive thus: military: from 1916. (F. & G.) Either ex *spruce up*, or a corruption of **spruik**, q.v.—2. Hence, *sprucer*, one who does any, or all, of those things: from 1916. Also *sprucing*, these, and leg-pulling (P-G-R). Cf.:-

spruce, adj. Make-believe, as a practical joke; 'We worked a spruce arrest on X— one night' (Hatton, 1930): coll.: earlier C.20. Cf. prec.

spruik. 'To deliver a speech, as a showman': Aus. (Dennis.) Presumably ex Dutch *spreken*, to speak.—2. Whence *spruiker*, a plausible 'spouter': id.: id. Hence, a platform speaker: Aus.:—1926 (Doone).

sprung out. 'Feeling ill from lack of narcotics' (Home Office): drugs world: later C.20. Contrast **spaced out**.

spud. A friend, pal, chum: Services': since ca. 1930; † by 1950. (H. & P.; P.B.) Cf. **mucking-in spud**.—2. A large hole in (usu. the heel of) one's stocking or sock: since late C.19. Ex synon. *tater*; *spud* = s. potato since ca. 1845. Naughton, 1966.—3. As *the Spud*, a fast goods-train carrying potatoes to London: railwaymen's. (Daily Telegraph, 15 Aug. 1936.) Cf. **the Sparagras** and **the Flying Pig**, and see **the Bacca**.

spud-barber. A man on cookhouse fatigue, esp. potato-peeling: Services', esp. NZ in WW1; current in RN mid-C.20 (Granville).

spud-basher. 'A man on cookhouse fatigue for potato-peeling' (H. & P.): Services': since ca. 1919.—2. Hence, a lorry carrying potatoes. Cf. HAULIERS' SLANG, in Appx.

spud-bashing. Kitchen fatigues: Services': since ca. 1920. (Daily Mail, 7 Sep. 1940.) Cf. **jungle-bashing, square-bashing**, etc.

spud-grinder (or solid). The gullet; e.g. in the ferocious threat 'Shut your crunch or I'll shove your choppers [teeth] down your spudgrinder' (*Undercurrents*, Dec. 1978): low.

spud line or **locker, in the.** Pregnant: RN lowerdeck: the 1st (since ca. 1946) perhaps ex the 2nd.

spud net. 'String bag carried by Naval husbands on shopping expeditions with their wives ashore. 2. Scrambling net, as used in assault vessels for descending into boats and for climbing back on board' (Granville): RN: WW2+.

spud-oosh (or solid). 'Kind of stew in which rather sodden potatoes predominate' (Granville): RN. Cf. **oos-me-goosh** and **oosh.** Harling, 1946: 'Lower-deck "spudoosh", that dismal diet of many-eyed potatoes mashed with corned beef into a mockery of a meal.'

spud-skinner. RN var. of **spud-basher.** Granville.

spud-walloping. Services' var. of **spud-bashing:** ca. 1930–45. P-G-R.

spud(d)ler. An indirect cause of trouble: West Country railwaymen's. (*Railway.*) Ex dial. *spuddle,* to 'mess about' or to 'make a mess of things'. More precisely, 'one who causes trouble indirectly' (*Railway,* 2nd).

spudgy. See **spridgy.**

spudoosh. See **spud-oosh.**

spuds. Preparation of potatoes for cooking: Kelham Theological College: 1960s. (Towler, 1979.) Cf. **spud-bashing,** etc.

spun. Exhausted, tired out: 1924 (*SOD*).—2. Checkmated; at a loss. Burton, 1934, policeman speaking, 'We know our way about . . . the underworld . . . But when it's a case . . . of the overworld, as one might say, then we're spun.'

spun from the winch. (Of a story that has been) invented: nautical: earlier C.20. (Bowen.) Punning *yarn.*

spun in. Crash-landed (plane or pilot): RAF: since ca. 1930. H. & P.; Jackson, 'Failed to recover from a spin.'—2. Hence, applied to one who has committed a technical error: since ca. 1938. Partridge, 1945.

spun-yarn major. A lieutenant-commander: RN. (Bowen.) Granville points out that the *major* refers to the Marine officer of equivalent rank; this is prob., therefore, another RN 'dig' at the RM (P.B.).

spun-yarn Sunday. 'Sabbath when there are no Divisions and church is voluntary' (Granville): RN.

spunk-bubble; -dust. Terms of genial abuse between men: mostly Services'. Cf. **fuck-dust.** (L.A.; P.B.) *Spunk,* low coll. = semen, since early C.19.

spurge. An effeminate male: Aus.: low: since ca. 1920. (B., 1942.) Ex the rather weedy plant thus named.

Spurs, the. See ASSOCIATION FOOTBALL, in Appx.—2. In *dish up the spurs,* to cause guests to feel that it is time for them to depart: coll.: early C.20. (Manchon.) I.e. spurs to speed them on their way.

spurter. A blood-vessel severed in an operation: medical students':—1933 (*Slang*). It spurts blood.

squab-job. A job for (young) girls: ca. 1910–15. (Klickman, 1919.) A *squab* is a newly-hatched or young bird, esp. a pigeon.

squabbling bleeder. A Squadron Leader: RAF r.s.: WW2, then mainly historical. (Franklyn 2nd.) Cf. **squadron** or **squalid bleeder:** all perversions rather than rhyming (P.B.).

squad-father. NCO in charge of a squad of recruits or trainees: Army: early 1970s. An ephemeral pun attendant on the publicity accorded to *The Godfather,* a film about the Mafia. (P.B.)

squadded, be. To be, on first joining up, put into a squad: Army coll. > j.: since ca. 1910. P-G-R.

squaddie, -y. A term 'generally applied mock self-deprecatingly by private soldiers to or about one another' (Fassnidge, 1981): an early occurrence in print is in Ingram, 1933, but it > gen. Army usage only with WW2, superseding the much older *swaddy.* E.P. suggested that it is an 'occ. perversion' of the latter, but I consider that, though perhaps influenced by *swaddy, squaddie* stands in its own right for 'a man who has been squadded' (see prec.)—and, like Mr Fassnidge, I was

one. Like *erk* or *sprog,* it implies anonymity in a crowd; perhaps cf. also the US *grunt,* an infantryman. (P.B.)

Squadron, the. Headquarters of the Royal Yacht Squadron at Cowes, I.o.W.: RN coll.

squadron bleeder. Squadron-Leader: RAF: since ca. 1925. (Jackson.) By an entirely inoffensive pun.

Squadron-Leader Swill. Squadron-Leader 'A' (Administration) on a station: RAF coll.: since ca. 1930. Jackson, 'The disposal of waste food-scraps . . . for use as pig-swill is one of [his] numerous responsibilities.'

squaff, squoff. Var. of **squo.** (McDouall, 1945.)

squalid. A pej., synon. with and prob. suggested by **filthy:** upper classes': from ca. 1933. Blake, 1936, 'Squalid fellow'.

squalid bleeder. A Squadron Leader: RAF: WW2. 'An inoffensive pun' (R.S.); cf. **squabbling bleeder.**

square, n. An old-fashioned person, esp. about dancing and music; later, concerning culture and customs in gen.: younger generations': adopted, ca. 1938, ex US, but in widespread use only since mid-C.20. (E.P.; P.B.)—2. An honest citizen: adopted ex US, in Can. ca. 1955, in Brit., ca. 1958. Cf. Aus. synon. **squarehead.**—3. In *on the square,* on the tramp: beggars' and vagrants' c.:—1926 (Jennings).—4. A non-addict: drugs c. (Stockley, 1986.) US since—1944 (Spears).

square, adj. Corresponding to senses 1 and 2 of the n.: old-fashioned; esp., decent and honest; with connotation 'reactionary': since late 1950s. Opp. *swinging.*

square away. To arrange: R Aus. N, hence also Army, coll.: since ca. 1940. See quot'n at **head off.**

square-bashing. Drill, esp. by recruits on the parade ground. Army and post-1930 RAF. (H. & P., at *gravel-bashing.*) The recruits, *square-bashers,* 'bash' their feet down on the *square,* the parade ground; hence *square-bashing camp,* recruit-training camp: Army and RAF: esp. during National Service period, late-1940s–early 1960s (P.B.).

square-eyed. Reputed to be the effect of watching too much TV: contemptuous, 'Yah, they've all gone square-eyed at home'; also *square-eyes,* one who indulges in over-much viewing of 'the goggle-box': since mid-C.20. Also Aus. (B.P.; P.B.)

square-head, squarehead. 'One who has never been in prison, or who lives by the norms of society outside prison' (McNeil): Aus. low: late C.20. Cf.:—2. A timid, or an amateurish, thief with a conscience: Aus. low: since ca. 1920. (B., 1943.)—3. Hence, an unconvicted crook: Aus. c.: since ca. 1945.—4. Elab. of **square,** n., 1: teenagers'. Heard in Forest of Dean, W. Glos., 1988.

square Jane and no nonsense. A respectable, intensely self-respecting girl: Aus.: since ca. 1925. Baker.

square meal. A dog biscuit: joc.: since the 1930s. (Petch, 1974.) Ex shape and a pun on S.E. sense.

square number. An easy billet: RN. Bowen, 'the "number" refers to the station bill in which every man's job is entered.' Cf. **cushy number,** the Army equivalent.

square-off, n. An apology; a concocted excuse: Aus.: since ca. 1910. (B., 1943.) Ex sense 1 of:-

square off, v. To placate (a person): Aus.: from ca. 1905.—2. V.i. and t. 'To make things ship-shape' (Granville): RN coll.—3. To prepare to fight: Aus. B., 1943.

square peg in a round hole. One who, for whatever reason, is badly suited to the job or post he or she occupies: coll. Hence, occ., *round peg in . . . ,* used of one ideally suited to his occupation.

square shepherd. An old-fashioned but essentially honest, decent, kindly person, esp. among the beatniks: beatniks': since ca. 1959. (Anderson.) An elab. of **square,** n., 1; ephemeral.

square tack. A girl; girls in general: Guards': since ca. 1918. Grinstead, 1946.

square up the job; often as n., **squaring up . . .** To conclude an investigation by making an arrest: police coll.: since ca. 1910. *Free-Lance Writer,* April 1948.

square wheels. 'Wheels with worn running surface' (*Railway*): railwaymen's: late C.19–20.—2. Often used in adverse comment on a bumpy ride in any vehicle, as 'Cor strewth! Has this heap got square wheels?': since mid-C.20. In the early 1970s the Automobile Association produced 'The square wheel award', a booby-prize for the new car found to have the most and worst faults after sale to its first owner. (P.B.)

square (one's) **yardarm.** To protect oneself in a manner inspectable by one's seniors: RN wardroom.

squarehead. To prepare to fight, adopting a suitable stance: Aus.: since ca. 1910. B., 1942.

Squareville. 'The *fons et origo* of all "squares" and conventional people and conduct. "Him! Oh, he's strictly from Squareville!" ' Can.: adopted in 1960–1 ex US, where orig. it was jazz s. (Leechman.) Also var. *squaresville*.

squarey. A crook not yet convicted or not yet even interrogated: Aus.: c.: since ca. 1945. (B., 1953.) Cf. **square-head**, 3.

Squariel. An Ariel 'Square Four [cylinder]' motorcycle, in production from 1931: motorcyclists'. (Partridge, 1979.)

squash. A youth-movement gathering, many persons crowded into a small room: Church coll.: since ca. 1930.

squat, n. A premises in which squatters have settled: coll.: since later 1970s. A back-formation ex S.E. *squatter* and v. *squat* in this sense.

squat, v. Medical s., as in Lillingston, 1936, an agent to a young doctor: 'You may become someone's assistant . . . , or you may squat—put up your plate in a likely district and wait for patients.' Hence *squatter*, mentioned also by Lillingston. Ex land squatting.

squat loo. A privy that has no seat, and is merely a hole in the floor: in my memory, since early 1920s, when I heard the term and used the convenience in France.

squattage. A squatter's station; his homestead: Aus.: since ca. 1930. (B., 1943.) A blend of *squatter* + *cottage*.

squatter's daughter. Water: Aus. r.s. (Baker.) Cf. older Cockney *fisherman's daughter*.

squawk, n. and v. A complaint; to complain: Can.: adopted, ca. 1935, ex US P.B.: also Brit., as in 'put up a squawk'.—2. As v., 'When a plane sends signals to ground radar stations, deliberately identifying itself as it flies, it's said in the trade to be "squawking" ' (*Listener*, 29 July 1982): air traffic controllers' s. verging on j.: later C.20.

squawk-box. An office intercommunication system: Can.: since ca. 1945. (Leechman.)—2. 'Now applied to an intercom on an office desk, but specifically to the Admiralty desks' (Granville, 1963).—3. A walkie-talkie set: police: since early 1960s. John Wainwright's police novels, *passim*.—4. 'Ship's public-address system . . . The *tannoy*' (Granville): RN: prob. WW2+.

squawk-horn. A bulb horn: motorcyclists'. (Dunford, 2.)

squeak, n. A piece of information to the police: c. (Wallace.) Esp. *put in the squeak*, to turn informer: c.:—1935 (Hume). Ex v., 1.—2. A sergeant: Aus. Army: WW2. (B., 1943.) Prob. ex *pip-squeak*.

squeak, v. To turn informer: c.: C.18–earlier 20. Ex:—2. To confess (v.i.): s.: late C.17–earlier 20. In C.19–20, rare except as in sense 1. In construction, *squeak on* (a person), as in Wallace, 1924.

squeaker. In card-playing, either a low-value card that takes a trick or a trump that unnecessarily takes a trick.

squeaky-clean. Patently honest and above-board, mostly of persons obviously (young and) innocent, occ., of their activities and dealings: journalistic and coll.: since ca. 1987. An intensification on the US *clean* in this sense, in use since mid-1930s (W. & F.).

squeakies, the. The cinema: ca. 1931–5. (Vivian, 1933.) Cf. **talkies**.

squealer. A pork sausage: tramps' c. Gape, 1936.

Squealers, the. The Australian Provost Corps: Aus. soldiers': 1939+. (B., 1942.) P.B.: ?with a glance at *pig* = policeman, as well as C.19 s. for informers.

squee-pee. Nestlé's tinned milk: Scottish Public Schools', or at least at that of which Miller writes, 1935: from ca. 1905. Perhaps a reduplication of *squish* on *pee*. R.S., 'May I suggest an origin based on *squee*zing the punctured (not conventionally "opened") tin & thus producing a thin trickle (or jet, depending on the pressure applied) from the hole?'

squeeze, n. An illegal exaction: Anglo-Chinese coll.: from ca. 1880. (Y. & B.) Hence, 'Ship's stewards' term for a gratuity. Cf. the Cockney slang *dropsy*' (Granville): MN.—2. An impression: police coll. Cole, 1930; Keverne, 1933, 'Parry's "squeeze" of the key to the Bruges warehouse.'—3. A woman's waist: Aus.: since ca. 1925. B., 1943.—4. 'To threaten a thief with arrest unless he informed on his friends' (Gosling, 1959): police s.—5. Economy, esp. *a credit squeeze*: since ca. 1958: coll. >, by 1966, S.E.

squeeze, v. To defecate: domestic coll. Cf. **squeeze** (one's) **head**.

squeeze-box. A ship's harmonium: RN:—1909. Ware, 'From the action of the feet.'—2. A concertina: Services', > gen. s.: WW1 and since. H. & P.—3. Hence, a piano-accordion: id.: WW2 and since. Ibid.—4. A gas-respirator: Army: 1939. (*Daily Mail*, 7 Sep. 1940.) Prob. ex fancied resemblance to 2 and 3.

squeeze(-)gun. An anti-tank gun of small calibre: Army: 1941+.—2. A gun with a slightly tapering bore: artillerymen's: ca. 1941–5. P-G-R.

squeeze (one's) **head.** To defecate: low, mostly Services'. Prob. self-deprecatory ref., in 'Well, I must go an squeeze me 'ead', to the abusive 'He's got shit for brains'.

squeeze (someone, e.g. the taxpayer) **like a lemon.** To charge, to tax, very severely; even more intensively, *squeeze until the pips squeak*, a phrase first used, concerning German reparations, in late 1918, and revived in the mid-1970s (*Daily Mirror*, 7 Oct. 1976, *pips*; *New Statesman*, 26 Nov. 1976, *lemon*).

squeeze off a fish. To fire a torpedo: RN: since ca. 1939. Cf. synon. **squirt a mouldy**.

squeeze-pigeon or **-pidgin.** Blackmail: mostly RN: since ca. 1910. See **squeeze**, n., 1. Here, *pidgin* (wrongly *Pigeon*) = business, affair.

squeeze the lemon. To urinate: low euph.; as in 'I must go and . . . ' or 'He's gone to . . . ': C.19–20. Cf. **squeeze** (one's) **head**.

squeeze the teat or **tit.** See **tit**, 3.

squeeze up. To ejaculate: low. L.A., 1974, prefers 'intromit penis; "to ejaculate" is not, to my belief, physiological'.

squeeze-wax. An accommodating sort of fellow: c.:—1923 (Manchon).

squeezable. Easy to make speak: lower classes' coll.:—1923 (Manchon).

squelch. A blunder, a *faux-pas*, a 'putting one's foot in it': Aus.: since late 1950s. (B.P.)

squib, n. A professional punter: turf c.:—1932. Ex his often 'pyrotechnic' gains.—2. One who backs out; a faint-heart: Aus. *Truth*, 6 Apr. 1924: Wilkes.—3. A plan that fails: Aus.: since ca. 1910. (B., 1942.) Ex a damp squib.—4. A small, weedy person: Aus.: since ca. 1912. Baker.

squib, v. To be afraid; to be a coward: Aus. (B., 1943.) Cf. n., 2, and:-

squib it. To turn coward, to 'chicken out': Aus.: since ca. 1950. Cf. the fig. uses of *squib*, n. and v., in English dial., and prec.

squib on. To betray (someone); to fail (him): Aus.: since ca. 1910. (Baker, 1938.) To go out, fail to explode, like a damp squib.

Squibbley. Esquimalt and Royal Naval College: R. Can. N: since ca. 1930. (P-G-R.) 'This distortion of the pronunciation of Esquimalt reminds me of Slackers, which I believe to be a distortion of Halifax, something like *Pompey* [for Portsmouth]. Two Navy types I have asked (but yesterday) say that they were not aware of any slackness while they were there. See also *Uckers*' (Leechman, 1967).

squid. See **grimbo**.

squidge-off; squidger. See TIDDLYWINKS, in Appx.

squiff. A drunkard: Aus.: since ca. 1920. B., 1942.—2. In *on the squiff*, on a drinking bout: Aus.: since ca. 1925. B., 1943.

squiff it. To die: Aus.: since ca. 1945. (B.P.) Cf. **snuff it.**

squiffer. A concertina: rather low: prob. dating from ca. 1890, for it was orig. a nautical term (Bowen). Perhaps a perversion of *squeezer*: cf. dial. *squidge* for *squeege*.—2. 'By a process of excusable exaggeration, an organ-bellows, or even the organ itself. By a characteristic confusion of ideas, a person who blows an organ' (Hay, 1934): Public Schools'.

squiffy. Slightly drunk: from ca.. 1873. H., 5th ed.—2. Hence, unwell: Aus. Baker.—3. Silly; stupid: Aus.: since ca. 1920–4. Crooked; askew: Aus.: since ca. 1920. (Baker.) Prob., as R.S. suggests, a contraction of *skew-whiff*.—5. Menstruating: schoolgirls': since the 1930s. (Kersh, 1958.) Cf. 2.

squint. 'A man who hangs about the market with a paltry order, and who will not deal fairly': Stock Exchange:—1909 (Ware). Cf. Fr. *louche*.

Squire. A joc. term of address among men: coll. P.B.: in later C.20, raffish and rather low, e.g. the false jollity of car-salesmen.

squirms, the; esp. in 'It'll give you the squirms'—horribly embarrass or irritate you: since ca. 1930.

squirrel. See **secret squirrel.**

squirreled away. 'Hidden away' (Powis): c.: later C.20 (?earlier in rural Eng.). As a squirrel hides nuts. (P.B.)

squirrely. 'Mentally unbalanced, crazy, *nutty*: widespread Can.: prob. ex US [W. & F. have *squirrel*, an eccentric, 1943]; used as in "He went squirrely during the winter" ' (Leech, 1986).

squirt, n. A revolver: Aus. c. (—1926) >, by 1930, low s. (Doone); in NZ c. by not later than 1932. It sprays bullets.—2. The cheapest (and worst) beer: low: from ca. 1920. Ex its effect: cf. **squitters.**—3. A quick burst of machine-gun fire: mostly RAF: since late 1930s. H. & P.—4. A jet-propelled aircraft: RAF: from May 1944; by 1950, ob. A pun on *jet*. P-G-R.

squirt, v. To shoot at: RAF: WW2. (Forbes, 1942.) Cf. prec., 1.—2. To accelerate; also *give it a squirt*: motorcyclists': later C.20. (Dunford, 2.)

squirt a mouldy. To fire a torpedo. See **mouldy,** and cf. synon. **squeeze off a fish.**

squit. 'A late-arriving IBM personal computer has all but squitted the promising British microcomputer industry' (*New Society*, 21 Feb. 1986); i.e., extinguished, frustrated, 'shit all over'. Cf.:-

squitters. Diarrhœa: mid-C.17–20: S.E. till C.19, then dial.; in late C.19–20, also schoolboys' s. Cognate with **squirt.**

squiz, n. 'A brief glance' (Dennis); a sly glance: (low) Aus. Ex *squint* + *quiz*. P.B.: by 1940, also English schoolboys', esp. 'Let's have a squiz', Let me have a look. Cf.:-

squiz, v. To regard; to inspect: Aus.: since ca. 1910 (the n., dating since late C.19: see prec.). B., 1942. Ex the n.—2. Hence, to peep slyly: Aus.: since ca. 1925. Park, 1950.

squo. (Also *squoff.*) A Squadron-Officer (WAAF equivalent of S/Ldr): WAAF and RAF: 1940+. (Jackson.)

squop. See TIDDLYWINKS, in Appx.

squoff. See **squo.**

stab. An attempt, as in 'Let's have a stab at it!': Services': since ca. 1930. (H. & P.) Adopted from US: Flynt, 1901, has it. Cf. Fr. > S.E. *coup*.—2. A medical inoculation: Aus. Services': 1939–45 (and after). B., 1943. Cf. synon. Brit. **jab.**

stable-companion. A member of the same club, clique, etc.: coll. Ex lit. sense, a horse from the same stable.

stable pea. The horse fancied by the members of its stable: racing: since ca. 1920. (Sarl, 1938.) With a pun on *sweet pea*.

stack. As v.i., to stand down from duty: RAF: later C.20. *Phantom.*

stack on a blue. To start a brawl or fight: Aus. (mostly soldiers'): since ca. 1920. *Rats*, 1944. Cf.:-

stack on an act. Var. of **bung on an act:** Aus.: since ca. 1925. B., 1959.

stack (one's) **drapery.** To place one's hat and coat on the ground prior to fighting: Aus.: since ca. 1920. B., 1942.

stack-up. A synon. of **pile-up,** n., 2: racing cyclists': since ca. 1945.

stacked. Esp. *well stacked*: (of a girl) having large and shapely breasts: Can.: adopted, ca. 1942, ex US. B.P., 1963, commented, 'the shorter form seems to have displaced *well-stacked* in Aus.' P.B.: both forms have been common in Brit. since the early 1960s. R.C., 1976, in ref. to E.P.'s comparison, in earlier edd. of this *Dict.*, with stacked playing-cards, adds, 'The semantics are merely those of "well built", referring not just to breasts but to other interesting parts of the anatomy. From US–Can. *stacked like a brick shithouse*, where the reference is not . . . to shape but rather to excellence of construction.' Cf. synon. **well-endowed.**—2. Wealthy. Also *well-stacked*: coll. Cf. synon. **well-heeled** or **-breeched,** and *stacks*, its prob. orig.

staff. A staff-sergeant, in address or ref.: Army. (F. & G.) Also, loosely, a colour-sergeant or a quartermaster sergeant (P-G-R), but never in address, these latter being equivalent rank appointments (P.B.).—2. As *the Staff*, or in address, the staff nurse in a ward: hospitals' coll.: since mid-C.20 at latest.

staffy. A staff officer: RN officers'.

stag, n. Sentry-go: orig. Army, since late C.19; whence RN, RAF. Usu. *on stag*, on sentry-duty; H. & P. have 'as a roving picket; on the prowl', but by 1950, *on stag* = simply standing guard, e.g., at the camp gate (P.B.).—2. In *go stag*, to go to, e.g., a party, without a female companion: Can.: adopted, ca. 1925, ex US.—3. As *the stag*, *nystagmus* (a succession of involuntary eyeball-twitchings): miners': late C.19–20. Forster, 1970, says 'an eye disease once common among miners. Scots: *glenny-blink*.'

stag, v. To make fun of, to deride, to 'rib': Anglo-Irish. Gardner cites the end of a letter from an Irish labourer, read out on RTE Radio, 31 May 1978, 'Please don't read me name on the air. I'd get a desperate staggin' on the building site.'

stag-night. A Services' mess-function, e.g. a games evening, to which the ladies are not invited: since mid-C.20, at latest.

stage, the. The privilege-period of a convict's imprisonment; gained by a certain number of good-conduct (or remission) marks: c.:—1932 (*Dartmoor*). I.e. the final stage.

stage, v. To do or accomplish, esp. if unexpectedly or very effectively or effectually: mainly sporting: from ca. 1920. E.g., Crawford was, in the Wimbledon semi-finals, 1934, said to have staged a come-back against Shields after being two, and very nearly three, sets down. Cf. s. use of **show.**

stage fright. A (glass of) light (ale): r.s.: later C.20. Powis.

stagger, n. In *do a stagger*, to walk: Oxford University: 1918+. Cf. the v.

stagger, v. To go: among young men-about-town: from ca. 1908. (Wodehouse; Sayers.) Hence, *stagger off* (e.g. to bed), to depart.

stagger-juice. Strong liquor: Cockney and Aus.: earlier C.20. In the RN, it = Navy rum (Granville). Manchon has *staggering juice* as gen. low s.

stagger out. To depart: joc. coll.: earlier C.20. (Wodehouse, 1909.) Cf. **stagger,** n. and v.

stagger-through. A preliminary, slap-dash dress rehearsal: show business: later C.20. In 'Kaleidoscope' on BBC Radio 4, 17 Feb. 1975. (P.B.)

staggering juice. See **stagger-juice.**

staggers. In *get the staggers*, to lose one's touch, temporarily lose one's skill; to be making mistakes: sporting: 1933 (*Passing Show*, 15 July).

stain. One not in the social swim with the elite at Oxford University, i.e. the great majority of its undergraduates: the self-elected elite of monied socialites. *Daily Telegraph*, 15 June 1988, reviewing *The Oxford Myth*, ed. R. Johnson.

S

S

staining. An effusion of blood: hospitals' euph. coll. (Cusack, 1951.) Strictly, it is medical coll. for a slight discharge of blood. Cf. *under-stain*, a later C.20 feminine euph. for menstruation: lower-middle-class coll. (Cooper, 1980).

stair-steps, -steppers. Children at regular intervals, as one sees by (e.g.) their height: coll.: both in Copper, 1925 (*OED* Sup.).

stairs. In *up the stairs*, the Assize Court: c.: mid-C.20. Tempest, 1950.

stake (one's) **lot.** To gamble all: orig. Glasgow coll.:—1934.

stake out. To place, e.g. a building, under surveillance in the hope of obtaining information: adopted, ca. 1955, ex US. Ex the tying of a goat in order to attract a tiger (R.C.).

stakes, the –. The [specified] 'line', way of life: coll. As in *Gilt Kid*, 1936, 'Both men looked as if they might be on the Jo Roncing stakes' (q.v. at **Joe Ronce**). Prob. ex racing j.

stakey. Carrying money; solvent: Can.: since ca. 1950, if not earlier. St Pierre, 1970.

stal; stallie. Stalactite/stalagmite formations: cavers', potholers'. (Bliss, 1980.)

stale. (Of freight) overdue: railwaymen's: since ca. 1920, but esp. since ca. 1940. (*Railway*.) Proleptic.

Stalin's barrel organ. A Russian multi-barrelled rocket-launcher copied by the Germans: Army: 1942–5. Ex. the deafening noise it made. (Sanders.) The term is still extant, 1978, as *Stalin organ*, for the 40-barrelled 122 mm rocket-launcher. (*Sunday Times* mag., 10 Sep. 1978, article on the guerrilla warfare in Angola.) The original was also known as a *Stalin organ* on the WW2 Murmansk convoys (Hartog, 1966).

stalk, n. A tie-pin: c. Sharpe, 1938.—2. An erection: low: since ca. 1910.—3. ?Hence, 'Male sexual propensity, courage or cheek: "He's got plenty of stalk" ' (Powis): low: later C.20.—4. As *the stalk*, 'The flag is "the stalk" and to "do a stalker" is to carry a passenger without pulling the flag down. "Stalking a job" is doing the same thing' (Hodge, 1939): taxi-drivers': since ca. 1910; since 1918 the phrases. Powis, however, in 1977 defines *stalking* as 'The practice by unscrupulous owner cab-drivers . . . of leaving their meters set "hired" while unhired, so that they can cruise or loiter about "stalking" worth-while hirings'.

stalk a job. See prec., 4.

stallie. See **stal.**

stallion. A prostitute's customer: prostitutes' c. Cf. *mare*.

stamping-ground. Esp, in (one's) *old stamping-ground*, the place where one has formerly been active or made one's mark, as in 'Well? what's it feel like—to be back in your old stamping-ground after all these years, then?': coll. (P.B.)—2. 'Parade ground in Naval barracks' (Granville): RN. The literal truth!

stamps. A person of no account, esp. of no relevant status: RN: since ca. 1945. If, for instance, an assistant issues stores to another while the storekeeper himself is present, the storekeeper might well exclaim, 'What am I, stamps?'—usu. 'fucking stamps'.

Stamshaw nanny-goat. See **Torpoint chicken.**

stana shwaya! Wait a moment!: soldiers' Arabic: late C.19–20. See **schwaya.**

stanchion. See **barrack stanchion.**

stand a bar of, cannot. To dislike (someone) intensely: Aus.: since ca.. 1920. Stivens, 1944.—2. To refuse to tolerate (e.g. an act): Aus.: since ca. 1920. Durack, 1955.

stand-by. An optimistic air passenger in the habit of standing by, in the hope that a reservation will lapse: Can. air-travel coll., verging on j.: since ca. 1954. (Leechman.) P.B.: soon, if not already by 1954, international airlines' j.

stand (one) **down.** To cost: Aus. coll.: since ca. 1925. Brockman, 1940, 'Only stand you down eighty quid.'

stand for. To endure, tolerate; agree to: adopted, ex US, early 1920s: coll. *OED* Sup.

stand-in. A deputy; one who takes your turn of duty: Services' coll.: since ca. 1925. (H. & P.) Ex:-

stand in for. To take (someone's) turn of duty; to stand by for him: Services' coll.: since ca. 1925. (Partridge, 1945.) Ex the theatre.

stand on everything! Hold it!; Await further orders!: RAF: since ca. 1938. H. & P., 'To put the brakes on'. Perhaps a development from 'Tread on everything', applied to the model-T Ford, with its rapid deceleration accomplished best by the driver pressing down all the foot controls.

stand on (one's) **hind legs.** 'To take an obstinate stand on opinion, preference; above all, not to budge from it; cf. S.E. *stand on one's dignity*' (L.A., 1976): since ca. 1910.

stand (or **be standing**) **on one leg.** To be caught—*caught standing . . .* is the usual form—doing something unofficial in official hours; to be in an awkward position: Services': since ca. 1935. (H. & P.) Cf. **caught with one's trousers down,** and *caught bending.*

stand on the stones. See **standing on the stones.**

stand over (a person). Menacingly to demand money from: c., and low: from ca. 1910. See also **standover.**

stand (one's) **peggy.** To take one's turn in fetching food and cleaning the fo'c'sle: nautical. (Springer, 1923.) See **peggy,** 1.

stand sam to. To promise (a person something). Bell, 1931.

stand to. A shortening of next. Powis, 1977.

stand-to-attention. A pension: r.s.: since ca. 1919.

stand up. To keep waiting; to deceive: c.: from ca. 1925. *Gilt Kid*, 1936, 'He didn't want Maisie to think that he was standing her up.' Hence also v.i., to fail to 'keep a date' (with someone): since ca. 1943; and as n., since ca. 1945.—2. To coït with (a girl), as in 'He stood her up three times in one evening': low. Orig. of perpendicular conjunction.

stand up drinks. 'To set out drinks' (B., 1942): Aus. coll.

stand up in. To be wearing at that moment: coll. 'I can't very well stay the night, I've only the things I stand up in.'

stand-up seat, have a. To (be obliged to) stand, e.g. in a train: joc. coll.

standard NATO. 'One milk and one sugar'—i.e., a teaspoonful of each in one's tea or coffee: Services': since ca. 1970. (Peppitt.)

standing on the stones. Omitted from the list of those 'wanted' (for work): dockers': from ca. 1930. *Daily Herald*, late July 1936.

standing up for fine weather. 'Phrase loosely applicable to anything that is standing up (e.g. a man's hair) that can and should be lying down. The scabrous innuendo goes back to late C.19–early 20' (L.A., 1976).

standing up in a hammock. Orig. synon. with 'trying to do the impossibly difficult': RN lowerdeck: mid-C.19–early 20. Thence, it came to mean 'anything fantastically and impossibly funny. An allusion to the [impossible and] humorous aspect of attempting sexual intercourse in such a [position and] situation: RN: 1940s [later > fairly gen.]' (Peppitt). As if it were not difficult and ludicrous enough *in* a hammock to start with!

standover. A piece of criminal intimidation: *standover man*, one who practises this sort of intimidation (for money): low Aus.: since ca. 1920. (Tennant, 1939.) Ex **stand over,** q.v.—2. Short for next. Hence *work the standover*: Aus. c.: since ca. 1920. B., 1942.

standover man. See prec., 1: Aus. c. (since ca. 1920) >, ca. 1930, low s. Baker.

standover merchant. Var. of prec.: Aus. c. (since ca. 1925) >, by 1935, low s. B., 1959.

staph. Staphylococcus, a common type of bacteria: medical students':—1933 (*Slang*). Cf. **strep.**

star-back. An expensive seat: circus s.:—1933 (Seago). I.e. a seat with a back, not a mere plank.

star-dust. Cocaine: drugs c. (Stockley, 1986.) US since—1954 (Spears).

Star-Hotel. Esp. *sleep in*, or *at, the Star Hotel*, or *the Inn of Stars*, or *the Moon and Stars Hotel, ground floor*: to sleep in the open: Aus. and NZ. (Wilkes.) Cf. **sleep with Mrs Green.**

star in the East, a. A fly-button showing: Public Schools': since ca. 1915.

star man. A prisoner on first conviction: c. and police s.:—1933 (Leach). Ex the official mark against his name.

star turn. The central or most important person: coll. (Merrick, 1911.) Ex the music hall.—2. Hence, as in 'He's a star turn'—someone admirably good, esp. at his job and much admired therefor: working-class coll.: since ca. 1930. (Petch, 1969.)

starboard light. Crème de menthe: since ca. 1920. (Macdonald, 1930.) Both are green.

starbolic naked. A corruption of *stark-ballock naked*, utterly naked: low (esp. Aus.): since ca. 1870. Penton, 1936, 'Is it true he makes the miners strip starbolic naked in front of him to show they ain't pinching any of his gold?'

starched collars. Game birds: poachers': since ca. 1920.

stare at the ceiling over a man's shoulder. (Of women) to coït: feminine, but joc. rather than euph. Cf. C.19 synon. *stargazing*.

stares, the. The 'fixed, glassy-eyed look of unwilling divers who realize what they have let themselves in for. They know that they have to go, but delay it to the last' (Granville, 1964): skin-divers': since the late 1940s.

stark ballock. Shortening of next. Burgess, 1977.

stark-ballock naked. See **starbolic naked**.

stark-bol(l)ux. Stark-naked: Aus.: since ca. 1890. (Mann, 1937.) Ex prec.

stark staring bonkers. Utterly mad: coll.: since mid-C.20. A s. var. of S.E. *stark raving mad*.

starkers; starko. Stark-naked: from ca. 1910: resp. Oxford University s. and low coll. (Manchon.) I.e. *stark* + the 'OXFORD -ER(s)', and *stark* + the lower-class suffix *o* (as in *wido*).

starry, do a. To sleep in the open: tramps' c.

star's nap. To borrow (money from): theatrical r.s., on synon. *tap*. Franklyn 2nd.

start off the button. (Of a car) to begin running immediately: motor trade: since ca. 1918. Press the button and off she goes.

start something, as, e.g., 'Now you've started something!' To set afoot, deliberately or unwittingly, something that will have important or exciting consequences, coll.: adopted (via the cinema) ca. 1938 from US.—2. To render a girl pregnant: raffish: since ca. 1940. (Petch, 1966.)

starters. An apéritif; an hors d'oeuvres; a first course: non-cultured. Thus, 'Right, then! We'll have soup for starters . . .'—2. (Prob.) hence, to begin with; in the first, or most important, place: coll.: since mid-C.20. 'For starters, I want to know why you . . .' Cf. **fyfas**. (P.B.)

starter's orders. See under **starter's . . .**

starvation buoys. Buoys used for laying up ships: since ca. 1920. (Gladwin, 1973.) So called because quayside mooring is expensive.

starve, do a. To be starving: (mostly lower classes') coll.: from ca. 1910 at the latest. Also Aus. (Tennant, 1956).

starve the bardies or **lizards** or **mopokes** or **wombats!** Aus. expletives, the 1st esp. W. Aus. (a *bardy* is a wood-grub). *Wombats* may also be *speede*d. Cf. *stone the crows!* B., 1942.

starver. Person, fellow, chap: Cockney: earlier C.20. Cf. older synon. *perisher* (since mid-C.19), which has lasted better. 'You bleed'n ol' starver!'—2. A saveloy: Aus.: since ca. 1910. B., 1942.

starving mush. See **instalment mixture**.

stash, n. 'A hidden supply of drugs or the hiding place' (Cutland, 1985): drugs c. Ex v.; a specialisation of sense 'cache', applied to anything illicit, and hence, joc., to anything hidden, as 'He keeps a stash of cans [of beer] in the frig'.

stash, v. (Usu. with *away*.) To hide (something); to put money into a bank account: Can.: adopted, ca. 1925, ex US. 'He's got thousands stashed away!' (Leechman.) Clearly influenced by 'to *cache*'. Barltrop adds, 1981, that it 'has been common among Cockneys [and more widely] for the

last 40 years for hoarding, secreting or safe-keeping something. "The old lady keeps her best crockery stashed away in a cupboard"; "let's stash our tools here ready to start work tomorrow".' P.B. suggests a blend of *stack*, v.t. + *cache*. E.P. notes later that, 'by the late 1940s the term had > common throughout the Commonwealth'.—2. Hence, merely 'to place': coll.: later C.20. Blake, 1964, 'Well, Leake stashed the wheel [car] in the car park'; 'He stashed his dib behind his ear'ole' (P.B.).

stash up. To terminate abruptly, as in the earliest record, Wells, 1909, 'She brought her [piano-]playing to an end by—as schoolboys say—"stashing it up" ' (*OED*). Among dockers, from ca. 1920, *to have stashed the game up* is to have stopped the job (*Daily Herald*, 1936).

stat. A statutory tenant: landlords' and property speculators': since ca. 1954. See the quot'n at **schwarz**.

stat dec. A statutory declaration: Aus. spoken, esp. legal and journalistic: since ca. 1940. (B.P.)

state! Elliptical ex *what a state to get into!*, > *state to get into!*: teenagers' (usu.) joc. pej.: early 1980s. (James Williamson, 1982.)

state of chassis. See **chassis**.

Stater. A member of the Irish Free State Army: Anglo-Irish coll.: from 1922.

static. Back talk; face-saving objections: since late 1960s. Prob. ex US (*DCCU*). P.B.: ex radio operators' j. for mere noise, meaningless crackle from loudspeaker or earphones.

station bicycle. A sexually generous girl employed on a RAF station: RAF: since ca. 1940. Cf. **town bike**.

station bloke. The police officer in charge of a station: police: since ca. 1920. (*Free-Lance Writer*, Apr. 1948.) Also *station-master*.

stationery. Cigarettes: early C.20.

stationmaster. Station Commander: RAF: since ca. 1930. (Berrey; H. & P.) Ex the railway title.—2. See **station bloke**.

stationmaster's hat. 'The cap with gilt peak worn by commanders and above' (Bowen): RN officers': from ca. 1916. Cf. prec., 1, and **scrambled egg**.

stats. Statistics: familiar coll. of anyone using or learning them: since ca. 1945.

staunch. 'A person who is exceedingly keen on games and other house activities, and makes it unpleasant for those who do not wish to participate' (Lambert, 1968): Public and Grammar Schools' s. P.B.: ironic perversion of S.E. adj.; cf. **keeno**, and—for the type—the older *heartie*.

stay-put, n. One who holds his ground ('stays put'): coll., esp. Aus.: since ca. 1950. (B.P.)

stay put, v.i. To remain, in time of emergency (e.g. invasion), where one lives: 1940+; by 1942, familiar S.E.

stay with. To keep up with (a competitor, a rival, in any contest): coll.: adopted, ex US, ca. 1920.—2. To copulate with (a woman): coll., orig. euph.: since ca. 1940.

staying at Mrs Greenfield's. Hauliers' var. of **Greenfields**, 1, q.v. See also HAULIERS', in Appx.

steady. 'In the Guards, son, "Steady" means "Absolutely lousy". If you want to sort of spit in a man's eye, call him Steady' (Kersh, 1941). An extension of S.E. nuance 'dependable but slow'.—2. Easy-going; 'decent': non-Guards units of the Army: since ca. 1939. P-G-R.

steady as a crock, as. Applied to someone hardly 'as steady as a rock': since ca. 1940. (Petch, 1966.)

steady man. 'One who is so slow as to be practically useless' (H. & P.): Services': since ca. 1930. Sarcastic. Cf. **steady**. P.B.: † by 1950.

steak and bull's eyes. Steak-and-kidney pudding: low eating-house. Jennings, 1932.

steak and kid. Steak-and-kidney pudding or pie: mostly eating-house employees' and their imitators': since ca. 1910.

Steak and Kidney. Sydney: Aus. r.s. B., 1945.

steak and kidney pie. A theatrical (late C.19–20) var. of *mince pie*, eye. Franklyn.

steal (someone) **blind.** 'To steal everything he has. A coll. expression common to the U.S. and Canada' (Barr, 1976): Can., since ca. 1960; but in Brit., heard occ. since ca. 1930 and fairly gen. since ca. 1950. Not coll., but s. In a way, an illiteracy for *rob* (him) *blind*.

steal the show. To gain most of the applause; greatly to outshine other performers: music-hall and variety s. *New Zealand Free Lance*, late June or early July 1934 (reprinted in *Everyman*, 24 Aug. 1934), in an article entitled 'The Star Turn', represents a British Lion batsman saying to an Australian Kangaroo bowler, 'It seems we've stolen the show, Aussie.'

stealy. Liable to be stolen: (?esp. booksellers') coll.: later C.20. See quot'n at **walk**, v., 2.

steam, n. Cheap, fiery liquor (esp. 'plonk'—Australian brand): Aus., orig. Sydney c.; whence also NZ: from ca. 1930. (B., 1941.) By 1945, no longer low. (B.P.)—2. Hence, any wine: Aus.: since ca. 1945. (Culotta, 1960.) McNeil, 1973, however, still defines *steam* as 'cheap wine'.—3. In *like steam*, fast, vigorously; easily; excellently: Aus. coll.: since ca. 1920. *Rats*, 1944, 'We reefed watches and rings off 'em like steam.' P.B.: not unknown in Brit. Eng.—4. In *under* (one's) *own steam*, unaided: coll. Prob. ex locomotives not using a shunter. 'I have always thought this, as applied to ships or locomotives and, by extension, any moving or should-be moving object, meant "Damaged but still able to raise enough steam to proceed slowly" ' (Leechman, 1967).

steam, v. To work at high pressure; to hustle oneself: orig. RN, then to Army and RAF, for which Jackson glosses the nuance 'to work hard and pertinently': since late 1920s.—2. To go, applied to forms of transport other than steam-driven, as in 'We steamed across the airfield in battle four-ship [a fighting formation of four aircraft]' (*Phantom*); it may also be applied joc. to a person moving in a purposeful, poss. angry, way towards an encounter, as 'the old lady heard the row and came steaming across the road': coll.: prob. since earlyish C.20. (P.B.)—3. As in, 'Steaming, which involves large groups of muggers running through crowds and robbing anyone in their path' (*Daily Telegraph*, 17 Feb, 1988, concerning events at the 1987 Notting Hill Carnival): orig. Black usage. Hence the agent, a *steamer* (Ibid.).

steam, adj. Old-fashioned and 'honest', as opp. to 'hi-tech' and new-fangled: a coll. metaphor, transferrable from **steam radio**, as in 'The honest-to-God steam spy is probably in greater demand now than ever . . . Within the intelligence community the steam spy won't die out' (Le Carré, 1983). Cf. **steam navigation**.

steam chickens. Carrier-borne aircraft: RN: 1943+. (P-G-R.) 'Ex the British invented steam-propelled launching catapult above R.N. carriers?' (R.S.) P.B.: not necessarily; cf. such fancies as **paraffin budgie** and **electricial string.**

steam navigation. Aerial navigation that depends not upon radar and radio, but upon the old-fashioned methods of map-reading and eyesight: airmen's derogatory: ca. 1960. (Mead, 1967.) Cf. **steam radio**. Cf.:–

steam Navy, the. 'The Royal Navy during the coal-burning era between the "tar and spunyarn" days of sail and modern oil-burning' (Granville). Perhaps one orig. of *steam* = old-fashioned (P.B.).

steam pig. Anybody—or, come to that, anything—either not defined or not easily definable: railwaymen's: since ca. 1930. *Railway*.

steam radio. Radio (sound only): coined by the BBC in 1958, as Mr Val Gielgud tells me; gen. since ca. 1961. In a sense, radio was outmoded by TV, much as the steam-engine was outmoded by the internal-combustion engine. (E.P.) If not 're-invented', the term was borrowed from the RAF, where it was used by the operators of the second generation of radar, '*beam* radio', ca. 1941, as a jibe against the original 'Range and Direction Finding' system known officially as Chain Home. (Carter, 1988.)

steam tug. A 'mug', a simpleton or easy dupe: low: r.s. See **steamer**, 1.

steamboat course. 'The direct, easy way; a semi-contemptuous form (or method): cruising yachtsmen's: 1970 . . . A steamboat does not need to steer as the wind directs' (Peppitt).

steamboats. 'A picturesque if somewhat inexplicable word for drunk: "Look at the state of him—steamboats again!" ' (Munro, 1985): Glasgow. Cf.:–

steamed-up. Tipsy: Glasgow:—1934. Because heated.—2. Heated; angry: since ca. 1925; Aus. by late 1920s (B., 1942).—3. Ready for sexual congress: Can.: since ca. 1930.

steamer. A 'mug': turf c.:—1932. Ex **steam tug**, q.v. Also gen. c.: witness *Gilt Kid*, 1936. Curtis writes, 1937: 'A steamer can, I think, be differentiated from a mug. A steamer wants something back for his money. He is a bookmaker's or a prostitute's client or a "con"-man's victim.' Cf. 'Wherever I look I see steamers [homosexuals prepared to pay boys money] and suckers', quoted by Simon Raven in *Encounter*, Nov. 1960 (P.B.).—2. A cigarette: young peoples'. (James Williamson, 1984.)—3. See **steam**, v. 3.

steamie, -y. A public wash-house with stone sinks, a boiler, a dryer: Scots s. > coll.: ca. 1890–1930. *Woman*, 20 Dec. 1969; Crawford, 1966; Munro, 1985, who notes, '[the steamies'] reputation for being hotbeds of gossip lives on . . . *the talk of the steamie* describes somebody or something that is (or deserves to be) the subject of gossip or scandal.'

steaming. 'Used in mild abuse; cf. **bleeding**. Schoolchildren's invective, "You great steaming nit!" Popularised by radio comedy series "The Goon Show" and still very widespread' (P.B., 1975): since ca. 1955.

steaming, or **scram, bag.** A small bag, containing toilet and other necessary gear, drawn from the purser's stores by a sailor suddenly dispatched to a troopship where heavy gear is forbidden: RN: since the mid-1940s. Probably *scram* = scramble; *steaming* perhaps refers to 'in a steaming hurry'.

steaming covers. 'Spats worn with plain clothes ashore when spats were fashionable. Steaming covers, made of canvas, protect the paint or mast yards from funnel smoke. They were abolished in 1902, though the slang senses remain' (Granville, 1962): RN. Cf.:—2. 'Official bloomers issued as underwear to Wrens' (Ibid.): RN: WW2.

steaming revvy. 'Any working cap, usually handmade: Merchant Navy stokers': 1970s' (Peppitt)—and, I think, earlier. Perhaps ex 'reversible'.

steamy. See **steamie**.

steamy side of life, the. A housewife's or washer-woman's life in scullery or wash-house: joc. domestic: earlier C.20. On *seamy side*.

steel helmet. An Anderson shelter: esp. Londoners': late 1940+. (Langford, 1941.)

steel jockey. A train-jumper: Aus.: since ca. 1925. (B., 1942.) He *rides* free; *steel* wheels, etc., of the train.

Steele Rudds. Potatoes: Aus. r.s., on *spuds*. (B., 1945.) Steele Rudd's *On Our Selection* and *Our New Selection* were famous in the Australia of ca. 1900–14 and, indeed, since.

steelie or **-ly,** n.; mostly in pl. *steelies*. 'Not real marbles, but large ball-bearings' (B.P.): Aus. schoolchildren's: since ca. 1920.—2. A steel guitar: since ca. 1955. Marsh, 1967.

steely, adj. Heroic, indomitable: RAF aircrews' ironic: later C.20. 'Call it a day and climb out? No way! How can a steely Phantom operator [pilot] call it a day after such a screw up' (*Phantom*). Prob. shortened version of:–

steely-eyed. A 'self-derogatory RAF term applied to keenness and professionalism. I heard it a lot while on detachment to the RAF in 1972' (P.B., 1974). Ex journalistic cliché.

steeped. Homosexual in practice or tendency: Society: ca. 1890–1905. (*Listener*, 10 Mar. 1937.) Ex *steeped in the higher philosophy*.

steeplechaser. 'A "ropey" landing, going across the airstrip in a succession of bounces' (John Bebbington): RAF: since mid-1930s.

steepling. 'Putting [one's] fingers together to form a church steeple . . . apparently "indicates confidence, sometimes with a smug, pontifical, egotistical outlook" ' (*The Times*, 4 Dec. 1975): coll.

steer. To pick up (a 'mug'): c.

steer-decorating, since ca. 1945; **bull-dogging,** ca. 1910–45. A rodeo method of throwing a steer by grasping one horn and the muzzle and twisting the neck: Can.

steever. As *M.T.* shows, this is the predominant market-trading form of *stever*, a shilling, var. of much older (C.18–20) *stiver*, itself ex Dutch: late C.19–20. Still (1976) current—for, of course, 5 new pence.

Stella. Egyptian beer: Services in N. Africa: WW2+. Ex a well-known brand.

Stella by Starlight. Alliterative nickname for girls named Stella (L. *stella*, a star): Aus.: since ca. 1925. (B.P.)

stengah. A small drink, at any time of the day, of spirit with soda; e.g. *a whisky stengah* or *brandy stengah*: Anglo-Indian and in Malaya: since later C.19. Ex Malay *sa tengah*, a half. Also occ. *stingah* or *stinger*. (E.P.; P.B.)

steno; stenog; stenoggy. A shorthand writer: office coll. for stenographer: adopted ex US, where orig. ca. 1905 (the 2nd). The 2nd var. ca. 1920 (*OED* Sup.); the 3rd occurs in Ferguson, 1939; the 1st since ca. 1945, and by 1970 the predominant non-standard form of the S.E. word.

step. A step-brother or -sister: coll. Heyer, 1933.

step-ins. Women's knickers that require no fastening: since ca. 1918: feminine coll. >, by 1940, S.E. Cf. **pull-ons.**

step off. To die: 1926 (Edgar Wallace: *OED* Sup.).

step on it. To hurry: from ca. 1929. (*OED* Sup.) Ex:–

step on the gas. To accelerate: s. > coll.: adopted ex US ca. 1926. Ex motor-driving, *gas* being gasolene, hence the accelerator pedal.

stepney. A white-slaver's fancy girl: white-slave c.: earlier C.20. (Londres, 1928.) At first applied, raffish upper class, to a mistress: a pun on the Stepney [wheel], a makeshift spare wheel carried in early motorcars, and manufactured by a firm in Stepney Street, Llanelli (*OED*, 1933 Supp.).

stepper. A smart, good-looking girl: mostly Londoners': early C.20. Lyons, 1912.

steps. In *up the steps*, at the Old Bailey: c.: late C.19–20.—2. Hence, *up the steps*, committed to Sessions or Assizes: c. (Sharpe, 1938.) Cf. **stairs.**

stereo. Stereophonic: coll. > j.: since mid-C.20. Hence, as n. = short for 'stereophonic reproduction of sound'; usu. *in stereo*, as in (of a recording) 'available in stereo or cassette' (P.B.).

sterks, give (someone) **the.** To annoy, to infuriate; to render low-spirited: Aus.: since ca. 1920. Prob. *sterks = sterics =* hysterics. Wilkes notes var. spelling *sturks*.

sterky. Afraid, frightened: Aus.: since ca. 1939. Devanney, 1944, 'He's a bit sterky, too'; B., 1953, says that it comes ex *stercocoraceous*, faecal; perhaps rather ex prec.

stern approach. Buggery: educated bawdy: since ca. 1945.

stern over appetite. Head over heels: Aus.: since ca. 1930. Stivens, 1951, 'I hit him on the chin and he went stern over appetite.' 'Euphemistic for *arse over appetite* and its numerous variants (*arse over tip, base over apex*, etc.)' (R.C., 1976).

Steve. A gen. term of address, esp. in *believe me, Steve!*: mostly Aus. Cf. the generic use of **George** and **Jack.**

stew. A 'fixed' boxing-match or horse-race: Aus. sporting: since ca. 1920. B., 1943.—2. Hence, a case framed against a serviceman: Aus Forces': WW2. B., 1953.

stew zoo. As in 'just one of many beach communities known as "stew zoos" where stewardesses . . . colonize' (Victoria, BC, *Daily Colonist*, 4 Sep. 1977): Can. s.

stewed to the eyeballs (or **to the gills).** Exceedingly drunk. Quite common: R.S. has reminded me that I've often heard it since 1921. An intensification of older (since early C.18) *stewed*, drunk.

stewkeeper. An army cook: Aus. Army: WW2. (B., 1943.) Perhaps orig. a pun on *storekeeper*.

stews. Fellows, chaps, strictly if crowded together or closely associated: Can.: adopted, early in C.20, ex US. From '*students*'. Munroe, 1918.

stewy (of tea) that has stewed too long: Aus. coll.: since ca. 1920. Trist, 1944.

stick. A dull, stupid, awkward, or (in the theatre) incompetent person: C.19–20: S.E. until mid-C.19, then coll. Via *wooden*. P.B.: since mid-C.20 at latest, not necessarily stupid or awkward, though the dullness, perhaps reinforced by a certain stuffy respectability, remains, as in, 'Oh, I don't know—he (*or* she) isn't such a bad old stick (*or* is quite a decent old stick), really.' Prob. sometimes a shortening of *stick-in-the-mud.*—2. Short for *joy stick*, 1: RAF coll.: since ca. 1925. Jackson.—3. Short for **sticky-beak,** n.: Aus.: since ca. 1930. B., 1942.—4. A column of newsprint: journalistic and compositors'. Leechman, 1967: 'When I was setting type by hand (ca. 1910) a stick of type was about thirteen lines, which was all my composing stick would hold. When the stick was full the contents were transferred to a galley. An unimportant news item was quickly disposed of: "Don't give it more than a stick," the editor would say.'—5. A small glass of beer: since ca. 1925. Cf. *finger* of spirits.—6. Short for *stick of bombs*, 'the entire load released in one operation so that the bombs hit the ground in a straight line' (Jackson): RAF coll.: since ca. 1939.—7. A wireless mast: RAF: since ca. 1930. Emanuel, 1945.—8. A 'joint' or 'reefer', i.e. a marijuana cigarette: drugs world: since ca. 1965. Wyatt, 1973.—9. In WW2 *a bit of stick* = a (heavy) shelling; cf. **stonk**, and see **give stick.** P.B.: in later C.20, *stick* has come to mean, esp. in the phrases *to give* or *get stick*, 'to dole out, *or* to be victim of, violence, or indeed unpleasantness, cruelty of any sort', as in 'Town foxes . . . come in for a lot of unnecessary stick' (*Guardian*, 2 July 1982) = 'are caused unnecessary suffering by human beings'.—10. In *on the stick*, (of a conductor) using the baton: musical coll.—11. As in 'When [he] is off stick his scores zoom up to the 78–79 levels' (*Observer*, 13 July 1980); i.e. not playing one's best at golf.

stick (someone) **a length.** To reprimand, or to punish, severely: Army: since ca. 1925. P-G-R.

stick a tail on (a woman). (Of a man) to coït, as in the wishful-thinking expression of admiration, 'Cor, I could stick a tail on *that!*', where *that* = an attractive girl: raffish, M.C.P.: since ca. 1960. ?Ex US; an elab. of older synon. v. *stick*. (P.B.) See **tail**, n., 1.

stick (someone) **for** (a thing, a price or charge). To charge someone too much; make someone pay so much.

stick in. To work steadily at one's job; to keep it: Glasgow coll. (MacArthur.) Cf. *get stuck in*, to start working hard.

stick in promise land for (a prison sentence). To threaten, minatorily assure of: c.: since late 1940s (or a decade earlier). Norman, 1959.

stick in the mud occurs as coll. nickname as early as *Sessions*, 7th session, 1733, 'James Baker, alias, *Stick-in-the-Mud*'. In late C.19–earlier 20 Brit. Eng., it epitomised the concept later termed *square*, n. and v. Leech, 1986, notes that in N. Am. it more gen. = a *party-pooper*, one who would spoil others' fun (presumably by his sheer dullness).

stick it into (someone). To ask (someone), esp. if surprisingly or abruptly, for a loan or other favour: Aus. Cf. **put the bite on.**

stick it on. To strike (someone): low (?orig. c.): since ca. 1945. (Norman.) Cf. *stick one on*, the more usual later C.20 synon.

stick-jaw. Something extremely boring: lower classes':—1923 (Manchon). Ex C.19 use of the term for anything difficult to chew, and hence, take. Cf. **sticking-plaster.**

stick job. A motor vehicle with manually operated (via a lever or *stick*), as opp. automatic, gears: drivers': since later 1970s. (D. Beale, from a busman, 1981.)

stick man, stickman. A male constantly lustful: later C.20. (*Observer*, 5 Jan. 1975.) Ex centuries-old *stick* = penis.

stick (one's) neck out. To ask for trouble: since early 1930s: perhaps orig. Army. (P-G-R.) P.B.: to expose oneself to sniper-fire, or to the executioner's axe?

stick (someone) on. To warn (a policeman) for disciplinary proceedings: police: later C.20. (Seabrook, 1987.) Cf. the older Armed Forces' synon. *stick him on a fizzer,* put him on a charge (summary justice); and see quot'n at **paper-tearer.**

stick one on. As in 'He threatened to stick one on me' or 'Go on—stick him one on!': to hit someone, esp. on the chin: low: later C.20. Cf. **stick it on.** (P.B.)

stick-up. A delay; a quandary: Aus. B., 1942.—2. A hold-up robbery: c. > coll.: Can., then Brit., ex US; but ultimately ex Aus.: in Brit., since mid-C.20.

stick with it! A farewell exhortation of generalised encouragement: coll.: later C.20. Cf. the US *hang in there, baby!* (P.B.)

stickability. The ability to preserve and/or endure: coll.: from ca. 1920. *OED* Sup. 1933.

sticked(, be). (To be) caned: Wembley County School: from ca. 1925.

stickem. Cement or gum: fair-grounds'. 'He had grafted the tubed stickem for years. (He had sold *a special cement in tubes,* used for sticking on rubber soles and dozens of other household repairs.)' (Buchanan-Taylor, 1943).

sticker. A good worker: Glasgow:—1934.—2. A supporter of a mob-'king': Glasgow c. MacArthur.—3. A small, sticky-backed poster: coll.—4. Usu. pl. *stickers,* such goods in short supply as are slow in coming from manufacturers or wholesalers: trade: since ca. 1941.—5. 'A prisoner who must remain in custody while on remand or awaiting appearance at court' (Powis): police coll.: later C.20.

sticker licker. See **brown bomber.**

sticking-plaster. An extremely boring visit (made by another person on oneself): from ca. 1920. (Manchon.) Ex its adhesiveness. Cf. **stick-jaw.**

sticks. A drummer: Army:—1909 (Ware). Knock, 1932, ref. 1903–24, defines it as 'Marine drummer'. Granville, 'Paradoxically, the ship's bugler, even though he may not play the drum': RN.—2. A ship's derricks: London dockers':—1935. Perhaps by the suggestion of rhyme. P.B.: or by an extension of older *stick* = mast. Ash, 'Name given to the winches. The stevedores preferred to work on the "sticks" as they maintained they could work faster.'—3. Always *the sticks,* the outback: adopted, in Aus., ca. 1945, and in UK, ca. 1950 (for 'the provinces, the countryside'), ex US. ' "People will think that you come from the sticks" is often heard from parents admonishing their children' (B.P.). Leechman, however, recalls that, 'When I was in South Wales, at Llanstefan, it was quite common for the people of the village to gather in the evenings to sing together in "the sticks", by which they meant a patch of trees just below the ruined castle. And that was some seventy years [i.e., late C.19] ago, but I can still hear them.'—4. Cannabis: drugs c. (Stockley, 1986.) US since—1938 (Spears).

sticks and whistles. A parade of warders coming on duty for the day: prison coll. They are inspected, to see whether they are carrying their batons and whistles. Norman.

sticksing, vbl n.; agent, **sticksman.** '[An 18-year old West Indian girl] talks about the London "sticksing" or "dropstick" scene—West Indian terms for pickpocketing or "dipping"—like a veteran' (Weightman, 1977, where also *sticksman*): c.: since ca. 1955.

sticky, n. Sticking-plaster: lower- and lower-middle-class coll.: late C.19–20. Since late 1940s, usu. cellulose tape (Sellotape, Scotch tape, etc.).—2. A 'sticky', i.e. damp and difficult, pitch: cricketers' coll., esp. Aus.—3. A free pass on the buses: London busmen's: since ca. 1930.—4. A **sticky-beak,** q.v.: Aus.: since ca. 1930. (B.P.) Hence, *have a sticky,* to have an inquisitive look-round: id.—5. Usu. in pl., *the stickies,* the official Irish Republican Army: N. Ireland: since late 1960s. Hawke.—6. A sticky bun: coll.: since the 1920s, as in 'tea and stickies', joc. for a formal afternoon refreshment.

sticky, adj. (Of persons) not easy to interview; unpleasant and/or obstinate; difficult to placate: from ca. 1919. Ex:—2. Of situation, incident, work, duty: unpleasant; very difficult: 1915 ('A sticky time in the trenches': *OED* Sup.); Eliot, 1935, '[St Thomas of Canterbury] came to a sticky end.'—3. Inquisitive: Aus. (B., 1942.) Cf. n., 4.—4. In *play sticky,* to hold fast to one's money or goods; esp. of one who has recently done well: since ca. 1920.

sticky at or **on, be.** To be 'potty' on (a member of the opposite sex): lower classes':—1923 (Manchon). Ex earlier synon. *stuck on.*

sticky-back. A very small photograph with gummed back: from ca. 1910. Dawson, 1913.

sticky-beak, n. An inquisitive person: Aus:—1926 (Doone). Ex a bird that, in searching for food, gets its beak sticky. Cf. **sticky-fingered.**

sticky-beak (or solid), v. To pry; to snoop: Aus.: since ca. 1930. Wilkes quotes Tennant, 1935. Ex n.

sticky dog. A sticky wicket: cricketers': from ca. 1930. (London) *Evening News,* 19 June 1934.

sticky-fingered. Thievish; covetous: proletarian: from ca. 1870. (B. & L.) P.B.: also as in 'I suspect he's a bit of a sticky-fingers' or 'Watch out! There's sticky fingers about.' Cf. **sticky palm.**

sticky on. See **sticky at.**

sticky palm, have a. To be a habitual thief; esp., to be constitutionally susceptible to bribes: coll.: late (?mid-) C.19–20. The latter sense, a reminder from Thomas, 1976.

sticky toffee. Coffee: later C.20. Barker, 1979.

sticky Willie. A long iced roll or similar confectionery: Sussex young people's: later C.20. (Martin, 1985.)

stiff, n. Esp in Aus. (ex US) a term of (often joc.) contempt, as *you stiff!, the big stiff:* ob. by later C.20. Cf.:—2. 'An unlucky man; one always in trouble' (F. & G.): Army: earlier C.20. Cf. adj., 5.—3. An unskilled dockhand: working-men's: 1914 (*OED* Sup.). 'Because he works stiffly.—4. A non-tipper: ships' stewards'. (Marlowe, 1937.) Also in the hotel trade (Green, 1984).—5. A police summons: Aus. low. B., 1942.—6. A newspaper used to push or prod the intended victim: pickpockets': since ca. 1930. Moynahan, 15 May 1969.—7. A conformist, a 'square', q.v.: teenagers': early 1980s. (James Williamson, 1982.) Cf. **wackie,** n., 2.—8. 'An illicit, probably smuggled communication' (Green, 1984): prisons'. Cf. C.19 s. for any document or paper.

stiff, v. (Of a man) to coït: raffish: since (?)1930s. Newman, 1977, where it is used in both the active and the passive.—2. To extort from: since (?)ca. 1950. 'Every time the old man's on the phone, stiff him for all you can get. I'll bet that's what she's telling them' (Busby, 1978).—3. To kill: c.: later C.20. (Powis.) Cf. later C.19 synon. **stiffen.**—4. A restaurant customer 'who leaves without tipping is said to have "stiffed" the waiter' (Mars, 1984): hotel and catering industry. Cf. **stiff,** n., 4, and late C.19 s. *stiff,* a penniless man, cramped for lack of means.—5. Also *stiff out.* To fail to appeal to an audience; of e.g., a performer, a book, etc.: 'pop' world. Hibbert, 1983.

stiff, adj. (Of an event), certain to be won: sporting: 1912, *Punch,* 21 Aug., 'He ought to have this event absolutely stiff at the next Olympic Games' (*OED* Sup.).—2. Penniless: Aus.—3. ?Hence, unlucky: mostly Aus. and NZ: since ca. 1910. Hence *stiff!* or *stiff luck!,* 'An ironic expression of sympathy' (McNeil): Aus. coll.—4. Hard, severe towards someone: Aus.: since ca. 1910. B., 1942.—5. (Of liquor) potent: coll.: late (?mid- or earlier) C.18–20. (*Blackwood's,* July 1823, 'Idyl': Moe.) P.B.: 'I couldn't half do with a stiff whisky!'

stiff, adv. Greatly. Only in *bore (one) stiff:* coll.: from ca. 1910. (Cf. the US *scared stiff.*) Lit., to death. P.B.: by 1940, at latest, *scared stiff* had > Brit. coll.

stiff as a crutch. Destitute: Aus. (B., 1942.) An intensive of **stiff,** adj., 2.

stiff-box. Obituary list in newspaper: Aus. journalistic: since ca. 1915. (B., 1942.) Ex later C.19 s. *stiff*, a corpse, itself a shortening of early C.19 *stiff 'un*.

stiff for. Certain for, certain to win: Aus. sporting: since ca. 1920. (Baker.) Ex **stiff,** adj., 1.

stiff 'un; occ. **stiff one.** A ticket already cancelled, i.e. 'dead': busmen's.—2. An erection: schoolboys': late C.19–20. Cf. **stiff, v.,** 1.

stiffen. To kill: 1888.—2. Hence to prevent (a horse) from doing its best: the turf: 1900 (*Westminster Gazette*, 19 Dec.). *OED* both senses.—3. Hence, to buy over (a person): low Aus.:—1916 (Dennis). Mostly as passive ppl.—4. To swindle (someone): Aus.: since ca. 1920. The usu. passive is *get stiffened*. B., 1943.

stiffen the crows – lizards – snakes! Aus. exclam.: in later C.20, mostly joc. (Baker.) Cf. **starve the lizards!; speed the wombats!**

stiffener. A pick-me-up drink: 1928 (Sayers). In Glasgow, it is used of any heavy drink. Now coll. [ca. 1930].—2. A cigarette card: earlier C.20. Originally inserted to stiffen paper packets of cigarettes.—3. A (very) boring person: RAF (mostly officers'): since ca. 1937. Jackson, 'He bores you to death, i.e., stiff.'

stiffy. A horse that is losing: Glasgow sporting:—1934.—2. An engraved invitation card: Sloane Rangers', q.v. *Sunday Express* supp., 11 Oct. 1982.

stift. One—usu. a male—who won't work: Romanies' s.: since ca. 1920. (Dawson.)

still and all. Nevertheless: coll. Browne, 1934, 'Still and all . . . the average politician does no great harm to anybody.'

still in a bottle of stout, often particularized as . . . *a bottle of Guinness.* (Of a person) unborn: smokeroom wit: since ca. 1945. Ex the body-building virtues of good stout. P.B.: 'Guinness and oysters' is said to be a powerful aid to procreation.

stimmt. See PRISONER-OF-WAR SLANG, para. 1, in Appx.

sting, n. Penis: lowish: late C.19–20. Cf. synon. **prick.**—2. Dope, esp. if by hypodermic, administered to a horse; hence *give* (it) *a sting*: Aus. sporting: since ca. 1945.—3. Strong drink: Aus. (Prichard, 1920.) Ex *stingo*. By later C.20, cheap wine (McNeil, 1973), or even methylated spirits (1972 quot'n in Wilkes).—4. A short blare on, e.g., trumpet, trombone, etc. to point up a comedian's joke: show business.—5. (?Hence) 'Any short burst of music used as part of the links between programmes, station identification, etc.' (Green, 1984): broadcasters'. By specialisation, 'a brief . . . station identification theme used for weather, news, [or for] a particular programme or presenter' (Ibid.).

sting, v. (Gen. in passive.) To snub: Charterhouse.—2. To inoculate with a hypodermic: Services' s. (1930) >, 1940, coll. (H. & P.) P.B.: † by 1950, when *jab* had become the commonest synon.

stingah. See **stengah.**

stink, n. In *like stink*, a var. of *like stinking hell*, desperately hard or fast or much: from not later than 1915. Ex *stinking hell!*, an asseveration. Sayers, 1930, 'Toiling away like stink'.

stink, v.t. To smell the stink of or from: Public Schools'. Benson, 1916.

stink boat. (Usu. in pl.) A small power-boat: RN: 1970s' (Peppitt).

stink of money. To be 'lousily' or 'filthily' rich: middle and upper classes':—1929 (*COD*, 2nd ed.). Cf. **stinking with . . .**

stink-wagon. 'Any car or lorry: very prevalent [among club cyclists] in the [19]30s' (*Fellowship*, 1984). P.B.: and still, from a cyclists' angle, a well-merited pej., esp. for diesel-engined vehicles, and those using unleaded petrol (1989).

stinker. A very sharp or an offensive letter, a stinging criticism, a pungent comment or a crushing argument: from ca. 1916, it being orig. military.—2. Anything (very) difficult to do: since later C.19. R.C., 'used by Kipling in "Regulus" [1908]: "The next passage was what was technically [i.e. slangily] known as a stinker"—hence, presumably in use in Kipling's school-

days, ca. 1880.'—3. A sultry or very hot, humid, day: Aus. (B., 1942.) Also *stonkers*.—4. A police informer: low Aus.: since ca. 1920. B., 1942.—5. A delayed wagon 'remaining for several days in a marshalling yard' (*Railway*): railwaymen's. Cf. **stale,** adj.—6. As *Stinker*, Steinkier, Norway: Army: 1940–1. By Hobson-Jobson.—7. As *the Stinker*, a fortune-telling device, often called 'the Mystic Writer' or 'the Gypsy Queen': grafters': from ca. 1910. *Cheapjack*, 1934.

stinkeries. A set of cages for a (silver-)fox farm: middle-class rural: from ca. 1920. E. Waugh, 1934.

stinkeroo. A poor show-place (town, etc.), with few customers: Can. carnival s.: since ca. 1920. It 'stinks'. Contrast **lulu.**

stinking. Disgusting; contemptible: C.13–20: S.E. until C.19, then a vulgarism.—2. (Of a blow, criticism, repartee, etc.) sharp. See **stinker,** 1.—3. Extremely drunk: Society: from ca. 1929 (E. Waugh, 1934); by 1939, gen. middle-class s. (P-G-R). Also Aus. (Niland, 1958). Abbr. *stinking drunk.*—4. Either absolute, as in 'Are they rich?'—'Oh, stinking!', or as **stinking with,** q.v.

stinking hell!; like stinking hell. See **stink, n.**

stinking with (esp. money). Possessed of much (e.g. money): coll.: since ca. 1916. Cf. **lousy with,** and **stink of . . .**

stinko, n. Liquor; esp., wine: Aus.: since ca. 1925. Niland, 1958, 'This is a little bottle of stinko to go with it'. Cf. the adj.

stinko, adj. Exceedingly drunk: mostly clerks': from ca. 1928. Ex *stinking drunk* on *blotto*. Hence *stinko paralytico*, as in E. Waugh, 1942, and *stinko profundo*, as in Rattigan, 1943.

stipe. A *stipe*ndiary racecourse steward: Aus. sporting. (B., 1942.) By 1930, also Brit. ' "Stipe" is short for stipendiary steward or stewards' secretary' (Lawrence, 1961).

stir-happy. Adversely affected by prison-life, whether at the time or afterwards: since ca. 1940 (see *Underworld*): orig. c., but by 1950 also police s. (Gosling, 1959.) *Stir* ex abbr. Romany *stariben, steripen*.

stir shit out of. To scold bitterly; reprimand severely: NZ: since ca. 1940. 'Wait till I get hold of him! I'll stir shit out of him.'

stir the pudding. '[The pilot] "stirs the pudding" as he lands, an agitated control column moving all round the cockpit as he "feels" his ailerons to tell him when the stall is coming near' (Tredrey, 1939): RAF.

stir the shit. To stir up trouble in a general way: low, ?mostly Forces': since ca. 1950, at latest. (P.B.)

stir the stew. To copulate with (a woman): early C.20. (R.S.)

stitch. 'To overcome, to beat in a fight or contest' (B., 1953): Aus.: since ca. 1930. Prob. suggested by *sewn up*. Cf.:-

stitch up. (Usu. in the passive, *be stitched up*.) To fleece; to intimidate into submission by virtual, or real, complete bribery: c. and low s.: since ca. 1950. Weightman, 1977, 'Both Sheila and Gary have many stories of being "stitched up" by the police or being fleeced.'—2. 'To deal effectively with a situation, but usually unscrupulously. "Let's stitch up old Bill" might be "Let's give overwhelming but perjured evidence against that policeman". See also *fit up*.' (Powis): id.—3. To complete a task satisfactorily, and not necessarily with any suggestion of underhand methods; e.g. 'Once we've got *that* angle stitched up, we can go on and . . .': coll.: since ca. 1970. (P.B.) The later C.20 var. of *sewn up*.

stitched. Tipsy: Services': since ca. 1925. H. & P.—2. Beaten, defeated: Aus.: since ca. 1920. (B., 1942.) All sewn up.

stitched up. 'Charge found proved at adjudication' (Home Office): prisoners' c.: later C.20. See **stitch up,** 1.

stitches. See **in stitches.**

stiver. A small standard of value; esp. in *not a stiver*, not a penny: coll.: mid-C.18–20. See **coal,** 1.

stoater. 'A superb and impressive event, experience, etc.' (Hibbert, 1983); a brilliant inspiration: pop musicians'. Ex Edinburgh s. says Hibbert, but the word has meant a sharp, heavy blow (a 'stunner') since C.17, Munro, 1985: 'Most commonly used [of] an attractive woman, "a wee stoater": Glasgow.

stock. Repertory (n.); esp. *in stock*: theatrical coll. (Lincoln, 1933). Ex *stock piece*.

S

stock-bubbling. Stockbroking: money-market s.:—1923 (Manchon). Ex causing stocks and shares to rise and fall.

stockbanger; stockbanging. A stockman; mustering (e.g. cattle): Aus. Russell, 1934.

Stockbrokers' Belt, the. See **gin and Jaguar Belt.** Also *stockbroker belt.*

stockbroker's taxi. A 'showy' motorcar, e.g. the Jaguar: since ca. 1960. *New Statesman*, 5 Feb. 1965.

Stockbrokers' Tudor. Bogus Tudor architecture: since ca. 1950; by 1960, coll.; 1966, virtually S.E. Cf. **North Oxford Gothic.** (Sanders.) R.C., 'the term was coined by Osbert Lancaster, in his classic *Pillar to Post*', pub. 1938, a light-hearted but penetrating review of English architectural styles.

stocker-bait. 'Money made by the fishing crews over and above their wages (done by selling surplus fish, net cleanings, etc.' (Butcher, 1979): nautical. Also known as *stockie* (Ibid.).

stocking-tops! A joc. parody of children's 'naughty' words, used, almost as a c.p., among adults, perhaps esp. among National Servicemen: 1950s. As a mock-erotic stimulant, with '*and* men's hairy legs!' Cf. *knickers!* (P.B.)

stockyard confetti. See **confetti,** 2, and cf. **meadow mayonnaise.**

Stodger, the. 'The "tuck-shop" at Osborne or Dartmouth, a *Britannia* survival until WW2 and the change of regime at Dartmouth' (Granville): RN cadets'.

stoke; gen. **stoke up.** To eat; nourish oneself: coll. Ex stoking a boiler.

stoked. Thrilled, as in 'He's stoked on [*or* about] surfing': Aus. teenagers', esp. surfers': since the late 1950s. (*Pix*, 28 Sep. 1963.) Semantically 'hot and excited'.

stokehold bosun. Warrant Engineer of the Engine-Room: RN: since 1925. Granville.

stoker. The rider on the back seat of a tandem bicycle: club cyclists'. *Fellowship*, 1984.

stokers. 'Smuts and cinders flying from a ship's funnels at high speed': nautical. Bowen.

stokes. 'Anyone employed in the stoking side of the ship' (H. & P.): RN: earlier C.20.

stomp. To dance: Aus. teenagers', esp. surfies': since ca. 1956. Ex US dial. *stomp*, to stomp one's feet, walk heavily. Hence *stomping*, n. and adj., dancing. (*Sunday Mirror*, 22 Sep. 1963.) Hence also *stomp*, a dance; whence *stomp hall*, a dance-hall.—2. To attack savagely, esp. by 'putting the boot in': teenage thugs' and hooligans': copied ex US later 1960s. Stuart, 1971, *passim*; e.g. '[He] has a big opinion of himself; he is just about due for a stomping administered by the whole Chapter [of Hell's Angels], he's full of shit . . . '—3. Hence (also as *stomp on* or *stomp all over*), fig., as to suppress; to out-argue; to attack verbally and win: Services': ca. 1970. (P.B.)

stomping, n. and adj. See prec.

stomping ground. A 'stamping ground'—one's habitat or district or *milieu*: Aus. teenagers', esp. surfies': since 1959. Cf. **stomp,** 1.

stone, n. A drug-taking, esp. of one of the less harmful drugs: addicts': since ca. 1955. (Diment, 1963.) Cf. **stoned,** 2.

stone is a common Aus. coll. intensive, sometimes adjectival, sometimes adverbial; as in *stone cert*, a dead-certainty, and its synon. *stone moral*, and *stone motherless broke*, penniless and alone: late C.19–20. (B., 1942–3.) P.B.: prob. ex the S.E. usage in, e.g., *stone blind*; cf. **stone lakes.**

stone-ache. Synon. with **blue balls;** see also **stones,** 1.

stone-blinder. A sure winner: horse-racing: since ca. 1910. (Sarl, 1938.) Cf. **stone-ginger.**

stone-bonker. Var. of prec., and a shortening of **stone-wall bonker,** since ca. 1945. 'Stone-bonker certainties' occurs in *The Boundary Book*, 1962. Contrast:-

stone bonkers. Utterly mad: coll.: since mid-C.20. A blend of *stone lakes*, or *winnick*, + *stark bonkers*. See **bonkers.**

stone coals and coke. See **coals (and coke).**

stone finish, the. The very end: Aus. coll. (Tennant, 1947.) See note at **stone.**

stone frigates. 'Naval Barracks or Shore Establishments . . . usually named after the old frigates' (P-G-R.): RN coll.: late C.19–20.

stone-ginger, a. A certainty: Aucklandites' (NZ): from ca. 1910; ob. By 1930, however, it was gen.: *Gilt Kid*, 1936. Ex a horse that won virtually every hurdle-race for which it was entered.

Stone House, the. Prison: since ca. 1930. (BBC, 22 Sep. 1963.) Ex dial.

stone-jug. A fool, an easy dupe: low r.s., on *mug*:—1923 (Manchon); † by 1960 (Franklyn 2nd). Ex much older s., *prison*.

stone lakes. Stone-mad: low, esp. among grafters. (*Cheapjack*, 1934.) See **lakes.**

stone me! A mild expletive or exclam.: since ca. 1920. Popularised by the comedian Tony Hancock, in the BBC radio-comedy series 'Hancock's Half-Hour', 1950s. Perhaps a blend of *stone the crows* + *stap me!*

stone-rich. Wealthy: c.: later C.20. (Elliott, 1988.) Contrast older *stone-broke*, penniless.

stone-wall bonker. A 'stone' (= absolute) certainty: 1930s. See **stone-bonker.**

stone-wall horrors, in the. Suffering from *delirium tremens*: Anglo-Irish. Also *cast-iron horrors*.

stone(-)waller. A certainty: Glasgow sporting:—1934. Cf. **stone-ginger, stone-wall bonker.**

stone winnick, gone. Muddled; out of one's wits: military: from 1914. (F. & G.) See **winnick,** adj.

stoned. Very drunk: adopted, ca. 1950, ex US.—2. Drug-exhilarated: (mostly teenage) drug addicts': adopted, ca. 1960, ex US. Fryer, 1967, defines it as 'very high on cannabis'.

stones. Testicles: C.12–20: S.E. until ca. 1850, then—except of a horse—a vulgarism.—2. As the **Stones,** Caledonian Market, London: pitch-holders': late C.19–20. (Brown, 1946.) Ex the cobble-stones that characterized the Market, which closed ca. 1954. Cf.:—3. In *on the stones*, selling goods laid out on the pavement, not from a stall: pedlars' and street vendors': since ca. 1910. 'Originally Caledonian market, now anywhere' (Franklyn, 1962).—4. By specialisation, *on the stones* also = engaged in selling hired paintings from a pavement pitch or series of pitches: pedlars' and street vendors': since ca. 1925 (prob. much earlier). Fane, 1936.—5. In *on the stones*, on the street, i.e. destitute: coll.:—1923 (Manchon). Cf. **standing on the stones.**—6. As the *Stones*, 'A 20-mile belt of desert between Mechili and Msus entirely covered with boulders; the most uncomfortable "going" in Libya' (Sanders, 1967): Army in N. Africa: 1940–43.

stonie. A stone-mason: builders'. (Clifton-Taylor, 1983.) Cf. *brickie*, a bricklayer.

stonikey. A cosh: c. (Powis, 1977.) Ex RN term for a rope's end as an instrument of punishment; there were several early spellings.

stonk, n. A heavy shelling, as in 'giving 'em a stonk' (or 'a bit of stick'): Army: 1940+. (Gander, 1949.) Hence also as v., usu. in passive, as *be stonked*, to be shelled by artillery. Prob. echoic, but cf.:-

stonkered, be. To be put out of action: military: 1914 or 1915; ob. (F. & G.) Perhaps ex dial. *stonk(s)*, the game of marbles, *on stonkers*.—2. Hence, to be outwitted: Aus.: since ca. 1918. B., 1942.—3. Hence, to be in a fix, a dilemma: Aus. and NZ Services' in WW2 (Fullarton, 1942), > gen throughout Australasia (B.P., 1963). But the v. *stonker* is also used actively, as in 'He stepped on a bloody mine. Stonkered the poor bastard properly' (Slatter): NZ: since ca. 1917.—4. To be dead drunk: Aus.: since mid-1940s. Vickers, 1955.—5. (Perhaps ex prec.) Surfeited: Aus.: later C.20. Humphries, 1981.

stony blind. Blind-drunk: Aus.: since ca. 1920. Palmer, 1930.

stooge, n. A learner (as in 'Q learner') at a divisional or a corps HQ in the Army: since ca. 1935. (E.P., 1942.) Either ex *student* or perhaps ex US *stooge*, a comedian's butt or a conjurer's assistant, a 'feed', itself either ex *stool pigeon* via *studious* (mispronounced *stew-djus*) or ex *student*.—2.

Hence, a deputy; a stand-in: since late 1940. H. & P.—3. Hence, 'an over-willing chap' (H. & P.): since early 1941. B.P. notes the post-1945 Aus. nuance, a servile underling.—4. 'A second-rater, one without importance' (Jackson): since late 1941. Ex sense 1.—5. (Ex sense 1.) 'One of our own sentries to warn escape workers whenever ferrets [q.v. at **ferret**] approached' (Brickhill, 1946): prisoners-of-war in Germany: 1940–5.—6. The pilot of a taxi-aircraft, picking up other pilots after they had delivered operational aircraft to squadrons; the second pilot on a large aircraft (cf. 2): Air Transport Auxiliary: WW2. Phelps, 1946.—7. 'A select social gathering in a study' (Marples): Lancing College: since mid-1930s. Perversion of *study*.—8. Hard work: Reading undergraduates':—1940 (Marples, 2). Cf. sense 1.—9. In *put in a stooge*, to act as a spare man (i.e. standing by to a bomber crew): RAF: 1940+. (Lewis, 1943.) Ex 2.

stooge, v. To fly over the same old ground as before; esp. to be on patrol: RAF: since 1938. (H. & P.) Ex n., 1.

stooge around. To 'hang about', waiting to land (1940+); hence (also *about*), 'to idle about, on the ground, or in the air' (Jackson): RAF: since 1940. *Observer*, 4 Oct. 1942, 'We stooged about a bit above our target'. Cf. prec., and **stooge**, n., 4.—2. Also, with var. *stooge about*, a synon. of **stooge**, v.: since 1938 or 1939. Partridge, 1945.—3. As in **stooging**.

stooge patrol. 'A patrol on which one has [not seen] or does not expect to see the enemy' (Forbes, 1942): RAF: WW2.

stooge pilot. A pilot engaged on flying-training 'planes carrying untrained navigators and/or gunners: RAF: 1940+. (Hinde, 1945.) See also **stooge**, n., 6.

stooging. 'General for non-operational flying' (Rhodes, 1942): RAF: WW2.

stook. A cigarette: Aus. RMC, Duntroon: mid-C.20. B., 1953.—2. Gen. *in stook*, and usu. pron. *shtook* (later C.20), in trouble, in difficulties: orig. London proletarian, since late C.19, > gen. low; by ca. 1920, also Aus. 'From Yiddish, where it means "difficulties" and is pronounced *stooch*. "He took all the money and left Abe in stooch," ' (Franklyn, 1962.)—3. (?Hence), something illegal: Aus. c.: later C.20. (Grindley, 1977.)

stool-pigeon. A cardsharper's decoy: c.: from ca. 1880. R.C.: ex pigeons tied to wooden frames (*stools*) to attract wild birds within range of gunners.—2. Hence, an informer: c., orig. US; anglicised by 1916. Wallace, *passim*.

stoolie or **-y.** A spy upon criminals: c.: from ca. 1920. (Brandon, 1934.) By 1939 also Aus. c. >, ca. 1946, low. (Park, 1946.) Ex prec., 2. Cf.:-

stoolie job. An informer's or a spy's giving of information to the police: since ca. 1930: c. >, by 1940, low s. From US: see 'stoolie' in *Underworld*.

stooper. A cigarette-end picked off the street: London: since ca. 1930.

stop. In a fisticuffs fight, to knock out; to kill (a quarry): Aus. B., 1942.

stop a pot. 'To quaff ale' (Dennis): Aus. low: earlier C.20. Cf. **stop one**.

stop-gap. The last-born child: lower classes':—1923 (Manchon).

stop one. To take a drink of liquor: Aus. (Prichard, 1929; Russell, 1936.) Ex *stop a pot*.

stop ticking. To cease being of importance; to die: from ca. 1930. Ex a watch.

stopped for bobbins. Unable to proceed with job in hand because some vital spare part is not immediately available: Lancashire, orig. in the cotton mills, thence to other trades and industries. Extra bobbins were needed on occasion to deal with extra heavy yarn, and were always in supply. (Rogerson, 1984.) Also *stuck for bobbins*.

stopper. A brake: motor-racers': from ca. 1925. (Chamberlain.)

stoppo. A 'spello', or rest from work. (Phelan, *Lifer*, 1938.)—2. Hence, as exclam., 'Stop!': c.: since late 1930s. (Norman, 1959.) Cf. **nark it!** and **nitto!**

store, the. A branch store of a co-operative society: coll.

store-basher. An Equipment assistant: RAF: since ca. 1925. (H. & P.) Cf. **basher**, 3 and 4.

store-basher's Bible, the. Air Publication no. 830, vol. I being *Equipment Regulations*; II, *Storage and Packing*; III, *Scales of R.A.F. Equipment*: RAF: since ca. 1930. Jackson; Partridge, 1945.

storm and strife. Can. var. of later C.19 r.s. *trouble and strife*, a wife.

storm(-)stick. An umbrella: Aus. joc.: since ca. 1925. B., 1942.

stoush, n. Fighting, violence; anything from fisticuffs to a great battle: Aus. (Wilkes' 1st quot'n is from Henry Fletcher, 1908.) Perhaps cognate with *stash*; cf. dial. *stashie*, *stushie*, an uproar, a quarrel (*EDD*).—2. In *put in the stoush*, to fight vigorously, spiritedly, esp. with the fists: Aus.: since ca. 1910. B., 1942.—3. In *the Big Stoush*, WW1: Aus.: since ca. 1919. B., 1943.

stoush, v. To hit, clout, punch: Aus.: since late C.19. Wilkes cites J.A. Barry, 1893—Eric Lambert, 1965. Cf. the n.

stoush merchant. A boxer; one good with his fists; a bully: Aus.: since ca. 1918. Baker.

stoush-up. Var. of **stoush**, n.: Aus.: since ca. 1910. Cf. Brit. **punch-up**.

stout fellow. A reliable, courageous, and likable fellow: coll. (B. & P.) Abbr. *stout-hearted fellow*. See the quot'n at **sound egg**, and cf. *stout*, Eton s. for 'strong and expert' (e.g. a stout bowler): *Spy*, 1825.

stove. A car-heater: car-dealers': later C.20. Graham-Ranger, 1981.

stove up, v.; stove-up, n. To disinfect—the disinfecting of—clothes in a casual ward: tramps' c.: from ca. 1919. Also *bake up*, v., and *bake-up*, n. Ex the disinfector, which resembles a stove.

stow on their edges. To save money: MN: early C.20. Bowen.

stowaway. A pocket-sized magazine: book world and newsagents': since ca. 1939.

straddle-legged patents. 'Patent reefing gear' (Bowen): nautical coll.

strafe, n.; occ. straff. A fierce assault: military: from 1915. *Blackwood's*, Feb. 1916. 'Intermittent strafes we are used to' (*OED*). Ex the v.—2. Hence, a severe bombardment: military: from late 1915.—3. Hence, a severe reprimand: 1916: military >, by 1919, gen. B. & P.—4. An efficiency campaign: RAF: since ca. 1930. 'The C.O. is going to have a gas-mask strafe.' (Hinde, letter, 1945). P.B.: this may rather have been a coinage of WW2, in which *strafe* developed a specialised, verging on j. meaning: 'to attack, from the air, targets on the ground, with weapons other than bombs, i.e. with machine-gun, cannon, or rocket fire.' This was the last echo of what had been an extremely popular and useful piece of s.; the j. sense has >, in later C.20, informal S.E. See:-

strafe (occ. straff), v. To attack fiercely; to bombard: military: from 1915. *TLS*, 10 Feb. 1916, 'The Germans are [but after 1916 they were not] called the Gott-strafers, and strafe is becoming a comic English word' (*OED*). Ex the Ger. salutation and toast, *Gott strafe England*, 'may God punish England!'—2. Hence, to punish; to damage: military: from early 1916.—3. Hence, from mid-1916, to swear at, to reprimand severely: military >, by 1918, gen. An early occurrence is in 'Taffrail', 1916.

straight, n. A cigarette of Virginia tobacco: from ca. 1920. (Manchon.) Ex *straight-cut*. Also *straighter*.—2. 'Ordinary cigarette tobacco' (Home Office)—as opp. marijuana, etc.: drugs world: later C.20. Cf. **civvy**, n., 4. Prob. cf. adj., 2, rather then sense 1.—3. A heterosexual person: homosexuals': later C.20; adopted ex US. Ex adj., 1.

straight, adj. Not homosexual: Brit. and US homosexuals'.—2. Not using drugs: addicts' and hippies' and their like: since ca. 1960. (Fryer, 1967.) Cf. n., 2.—3. In *lay* (someone) *straight*, to operate on him: medical students':—1923 (Manchon).

straight and level. See **get some straight . . .**

straight and narrow, the. The straight and narrow path of virtue or honour: coll.: since ca. 1925. 'Sometimes misapprehended as "the straight and narrow path between right and wrong" ' (Leechman).

straight as a corkscrew. 'Prone to ethical deviation' (Parsons, 1973): since ca. 1920. Emphasis through irony.

straight bake. A roast joint: RN. (Bowen.) Cf. **straight rush.**

straight-cut. A respectable girl; a girl in no way connected with the underworld: c.: from ca. 1920. (*Gilt Kid*, 1936.) An elab. of *straight*, honest, virtuous. Cf. **straight, n., 1,** for poss. imm. orig.

straight down the line. An elab. of 'telling someone straight', directly and without frills or prevarication, as 'so I gave it them, straight down the line: either . . . ': coll.: later C.20. (P.B.)

straight goer. A dependable—esp. an honest—person: Aus. coll.: since ca. 1925. Caddie, 1953.

straight Jane and no nonsense. 'Said of, or claimed by, a woman of sober taste and scruples and strict principles' (L.A., 1974): later C.19–early 20. Also *plain Jane . . .*

straight-laced. See **straight-striper.**

straight Navy, the. The Royal Navy: since ca. 1920. Prompted by 'the *Wavy Navy*', q.v.

straight off the turnips. Applied to one who is a country bumpkin or very green: NZ:—1932. P.B.: but Weighell, 1983, remembers this as a true Yorkshirism; and its opp. is *sharp as a box of monkeys*. Cf. *straight out of the trees.*

straight oil. Var. of **dinkum oil,** influenced by **straight wire:** Aus.: since ca. 1920. B., 1942.

straight out of the egg. 'The manning demands of the [Submarine Service] have been so enormous that the Navy has had to "press" men from general service . . . some "straight out of the egg": there are now many young sailors whose first sea-going ship was a bomber [= a Polaris missile submarine]' (Winton, 1976).

straight out of the trees. Applied to coloured people, esp. Negroes, by those who resent their presence in UK: later C.20. This sort of insult is not new: cf. the older *straight from the bog* or **straight off the turnips,** of Irish, or of country bumpkins generally.

straight prop (man). A genuine builder specialising in house-repair work: since ca. 1963. (Bournemouth *Evening Echo*, 20 Apr. 1966.) Cf. **prop game.**

straight rush. 'Meat and potatoes prepared for cooking which are rushed straight to the galley from the ship's butcher' (Granville): RN and R Can. N: earlier C.20. The Victoria, BC, *Daily Colonist*, 19 June 1960, adds that it was 'the simplest preparation of a joint of beef, employed when time was short.' Cf. **straight bake.**

straight screw. A warder that traffics with the prisoners: c. Ingram, 1933.

straight-set. To defeat in the minimum number of sets (i.e. in *straight sets*): lawn-tennis coll.: 1935 (*Daily Telegraph*, 4 Apr.). Hence, such a match is called a *straight-setter*: lawn-tennis s.: June, 1935.

straight-striper. A R Aus. N regular: R Aus. N: since ca. 1938. (B., 1943.) P.B.: this presumably applied to an officer: cf. 'straight-laced. RN officer, from his straight stripes of rank. Obsolete, since all officers, active service or reserve, now [1962] wear straight stripes' (Granville). See **Wavy Navy.**

straight-up. Correct; the truth: low: from ca. 1925. *Gilt Kid*, 1936, 'Maisie was the only girl he had ever loved. That was straight-up.'—2. As exclam., 'honestly!': since ca. 1905. Cf. synon. *straight!*, and S.E. *straight* = honest. Since ca. 1935, occ. elab. to *straight up on my eyesight!* (Norman).—3. 'Precisely noon or midnight from the position of the hands of a clock. "It's twelve o'clock, straight up!": that is, exactly'. (Leechman.)—4. To *be straight up* = up-to-date in one's work: coll.

straight walk-in. An easy entry; esp. of a girl or woman easily 'made' or obviously wearing very little clothing: among would-be Lotharios, Lovelaces, Romeos, Don Juans: since ca. 1925.

straight wire(, the), n.; also as adj. and adv. The genuine thing; esp., authentic news; 'on the level': Aus. and NZ version of **straight-up,** adj., 1: later C.19–earlier 20. (Wilkes, whose 1st citation is William Lane, 1892.) E.P. quotes Lancaster, 1904, for NZ: 'Walt, you are a smeller, straight wire'.

straighten. To set right: Aus. coll.: since ca. 1910. (Prichard, 1932.) Ex 'put, or set, *straight*'.—2. To bribe, try to bribe; applied at first to policemen: c.: since ca. 1920. Wallace, *passim*; Gosling, 1959.—3. To avenge (an affront); to take revenge upon (a rival gang): Teddy-boys': mid-C.20. (*Observer*, 1 Mar. 1959.) Cf. sense 1, and **straightener.**

straighten (someone) **out.** To 'stop someone taking liberties or being overbearing or bumptious, or unconsciously being a nuisance' (L.A.): coll. 'Oh, he'll be all right when he's been straightened out—he just needs taking in hand' (P.B.).

straighten up. To become honest or honourable: s. (ca. 1906) >, ca. 1930, coll. Ex lit. sense, to assume an upright posture.

straightener. A fisticuffs fight between two rival gangs: Teddy-boys', esp. in London: since ca. 1955. (*Daily Mail*, 7 Feb. 1959.) It is fought in order to 'straighten things out' between them. Cf. **straighten, 3,** and:—2. A discussion or argument tending to become angry or bitter: coll.: since ca. 1950, if not considerably earlier. Newman, 1977.

straighter and **topper.** One who drinks his beer *straight*; one who *tops* it with, e.g., lemonade: Army, esp. in India: earlier C.20. (Mays, 1969.) P.B.: beer diluted thus was still known, in the Army in Hong Kong, 1960s, as *tops*.—2. See **straight, n., 1.**

strain (one's) greens. '(Of a man) to have sexual intercourse' (L.A., 1974): low: earlier C.20.—2. To urinate: lowish coll. (Clarke, 1980.) See:-

strain off. To urinate: lowish coll. (L.A.) Ex prec., 2, or:-

strain (one's) taters. Synon. of prec.: ca. 1880–1930. Ex the colour of the water in which potatoes have been washed or strained.

strained through a silk handkerchief. Esp. 'You must have been . . .', applied to a very undersized child: since ca. 1930. (P.B. heard it, addressed to himself, during WW2.)

Straits, the. The Mediterranean: nautical. (Bowen.) Ex the S.E. sense, the Straits of Gibraltar.—2. In *up the Straits*, 'into the Mediterranean' (Goodenough, 1901); 'serving on the Mediterranean Station in the Straits of Gibraltar' (Granville, 1962): RN coll.

strangle. To get something from (someone) for nothing: RN lowerdeck: since ca. 1930. Mostly applied to 'runs ashore'. (Granville.) Cf. **jam-strangling . . .** —2. To prevent (a horse) from winning: Aus. racing: since ca. 1935. (Glassop, 1949.) Strictly, to pull (a horse) back so strongly that it's almost strangled, as one of the 'dodges' employed by jockeys in order to lose a race, as in Francis, 1962, 'The general opinion among the jockeys was that Sandy had "strangled" a couple [of horses] at one stage, but not during the past few months.'

strangler. A neck-tie: c., and low. *Gilt Kid*, 1936.

strap, n. Credit: dial. (—1828) >, ca. 1880, s. Esp. *on strap*, occ. *on the strap*. Slightly ob. by 1935. But *on the strap* was still in use among car-dealers, later C.20, for 'on hire purchase' (Graham-Ranger, 1981). Contrast:—2. In *on the strap*, penniless: Aus.: since ca. 1910. (B., 1942.) Cf. **strapped, 2.**

strap, v. To allow credit for (goods): dial. (—1862) >, ca. 1890, s. Ex **strap, n.,** 1.—2. Hence, *strap it* (gen. as vbl n.), to get goods on credit: Glasgow.—3. To obtain an advance on one's weekly pay: workmen's: (? late C.19–) C.20. Ex senses 1 and 2. Lewis, 2, 1976.—4. 'To interrogate strongly' (Powis): police and c.: later C.20.

strap on. (Of a male) to copulate with: RM: later C.20. ' "Cor, I could strap *that* bint on any time, no problem!" ' (Hawke).

Cf. synon. s. strap (C.17–19), though *strap on* is prob. conjunctive rather than percussive. (P.B.)

strap up. 'To wash up the saloon table gear. A steward is said to be "*on the Crockery Strap-up*" ' (Bowen): nautical. Prob. because so many articles have then to be firmly secured.—2. To obtain (goods) or drinks at a hotel) on credit: Aus.: since ca. 1919. (B., 1942.) Cf. **strap**, v., 1, 2, and n. 1.

strapped. (Of goods, etc., had) on credit: Glasgow. See **strap**, v., 1 and 2.—2. Penniless: Eng. and Can.: late C.19–20. (Leechman.) Prob. ex rural *strap*, to strip (a cow), hence to draw (anything) dry, hence (London) to work to the limit. Cf. **strap**, n., 2. R.C., 'More likely, with one's belt pulled tight against hunger; cf. the coll. *tighten one's belt*'.

strapper. A stable lad: Aus. racing: since ca. 1925. Glassop, 1949.

strapping it. See **strap**, v., 2.

straw-basher. A boater, a straw hat for man or boy: 1930. (*OED* Sup.) Prob. suggested by *hard-hitter*. P.B.: Mrs D. Birkett tells me that the term was in use among girls in Edinburgh private schools, 1940s, for their boaters.

straw in her ear, wear a. To seek re-marriage. Manchon.

strawberry. A red nose: Cockneys': Cf. **grog-blossom.**—2. A compliment, praise from a superior: Army officers': since ca. 1930. (H. & P.) In contrast to **raspberry.**—3. A frequent shortening of **strawberry tart.**

strawberry ripple. 'He spent months in a wheelchair . . . living in a "strawberry ripple" residential school. ("Ripple, cripple—see?" says Vincent)' (Roberts, 1982): r.s.: later C.20. A type of ice-cream.

strawberry tart. The heart: r.s. Mrs R. Pearsall reports hearing frequently, in late 1978, the expression *don't do that—you'll give me a dickey strawberry!* [i.e. a bad heart].

strawbs. Strawberries. A var. of later C.19 *straws*, by analogy with **rasbs.** (Raab, 1982.)

strawing. Putting children on straw in front of seating stand: circus coll.: late C.19–20. Cochran, 1945.

strawmen. '[The author] makes a great deal of thunder in the dressing room and peoples too much of his stage with strawmen' (Crick, 1980). Elliptical for S.E. *men of straw*.

stray. A sausage: R Aus. N: since ca. 1930. (B., 1943.) Ex '*stray dog*.'

streak, n. A very thin person: mostly Aus. and NZ when unqualified. Cf. **streak of piss.**—2. A 'locomotive Class A4 (N.E.)' (*Railway*): railwaymen's: mid-C.20.

streak, v. 'To scurry stark-naked through a public place or assembly ostensibly as a form of protest against some grievance' (R.S., 1974), or 'trying to prove a point, or out of sheer exhibitionism' (P.B.); whence *streaking*, the vbl n., and *streaker*, one who does this: s. in 1973; both nn. and v. were, by 1975, coll. and, by 1976, S.E. It was a phenomenon of the early 1970s, with subsequent echoes.

streak of piss. (Usu. *long streak . . .*) Someone who overestimates his own importance or ability: low: earlier C.20.—2. Applied to any tall, thin person, esp. of a rather droopy or 'wet' nature: perhaps mostly Services': since mid-C.20, if not earlier. (P.B.)

streaker; -ing. See **streak**, v.

stream. A heavy air-raid; strictly the 'stream' of bombers delivering it: RAF coll.: 1940+.

stream-line. A tall, thin man: Army: from 1917. (F. & G.) Cf.:-

stream-line(d). Slim and graceful (of persons): from ca. 1932. Ex stream-lined motor-cars, designed to offer small resistance to the atmosphere. (Of clothes) neatly and closely tailored: coll.: since ca. 1940. ' "Yes," Jeffrey said, "slap-happy", and he laughed, but the colloquialism disturbed him. He was suddenly tired of all the new words— "stream-lined", "blitzed", "three-point programme", "blue-print" ' (Marquand, 1943, but written in late 1941–2). Cf. the RN *streamline(d) piece*, a very attractive girl: ca. 1941–6. P-G-R.

streamer. A severe head-cold: coll.: since 1920s. (Petch, 1974, 'Often heard'.) Elliptical for 'a streaming cold'.

Street, the. The money-market held outside the Stock Exchange after 4 p.m.: Stock Exchange coll.—2. Archer Street, London, W1: musicians' coll. Ex the agencies there.—3. Wardour Street: film industry coll.: since ca. 1918.

street accident. A mongrel dog: joc. coll.: later C.20. (P.B.)

street credibility. 'The ability to communicate with ordinary, working-class folk; a quality of not flaunting one's riches or displaying pretentiousness' (Hibbert, 1983); pop musicians', politicians', and others who live by image-projection. Simmonds, 1985, noting abbr. *street cred*, defines it as a sense of style and *savoir faire*, and quotes a London teenager, 'A lad with a lot of street cred may be described, "Yeah, 'e thinks 'e's Jack the Biscuit".' Green, 1984, on the idea of the 'artist' being able to relate genuinely to the 'real people', calls it 'punk rock's answer to a social conscience'.

streetwise. Imbued with city cunning: coll. verging on informal S.E.: adopted ex US ca. 1980. 'Maybe law-abiding America is getting as streetwise as its criminal class' (Smith, 1981).

strel(l). A banjo; hence *strell-homey* (or *homie*), a banjoist: Parlyaree: late C.19–20. Compare and contrast *strill homey*, earlier for a pianist.

strength of it or **this** or **that** or **the other, the.** The 'real'—i.e. the hidden or ulterior or most important—meaning or significance (of some act or thing specified or implied), as in 'What's the strength of him (*or* his) coming here?': coll., perhaps first in Aus., where it is much used. (F. & G.) Cf. C.15–early 17 S.E. *strength*, the tenor or import (of a document). E.P. later added: app. earliest in NZ: 1871 (C.L. Money, *Knocking About in New Zealand*). B., 1941, 'Highly popular, throughout both New Zealand and Australia.' Often absolutely, as 'That's about the strength of it.' See **strong**, n.

strenuous. Excited; angry: upper classes': from ca. 1930. See the quot'n at **crashing bore.** Ex the S.E. sense.

strep. Streptococcus, a common type of bacteria: medical students':—1933 (*Slang*). Cf. **staph.**

strepto. Streptomycin: medical coll.: since ca. 1940. (Cusack, 1951.) Cf. **strep.**

stretch. To outstay (one's furlough): RN coll. Ware; Bowen.—2. To outstay an opponent, e.g. at fisticuffs: Anglo-Irish: Blake, 1968, ref. the year 1939, ' "You're out of condition," Seumus told him. "If that fella'd persevered, he'd have stretched you." ' P.B.: E.P. may have misinterpreted this sense: R.C., 1976, draws attention to Kipling's 'So I stretched Peg Barney', where it means to knock flat, to 'stretch on the canvas': late C.19–earlier 20.

stretch off the land. 'A short sleep. A "masts and yards" era survival. When a sailing ship was moving towards the shore nobody was allowed to sleep, but when she was making an off-shore tack, or *stretch off the land*, those so disposed, if not on watch, could have a short sleep' (Granville): nautical. Goodenough, 1901, has it as 'an afternoon nap'.

stretch-out. 'The extra-long multi-seat limousines beloved of show business celebrities' (Green, 1984): entertainments world.

stretcher. A long journey, or stretch of road: coll. Manchon.

stretcher case. A liar: since ca. 1942. Ex *lying*. Also 'because he is stretching the truth' (R.C.).

stretchers. Laces: tramps' c.:—1935.

strict pusser. A ship noted for very strict—even harsh—discipline: RN: since late C.19 (Knock). See **pusser.**

strides. Trousers: theatrical (—1904), and prob. market-traders' as early as this; ex dial. (1895: *EDD*.) Aus. by 1924 (Wilkes), and Can., 1949: 'Recent name for trousers worn by zoot-suiters' (Priestley); by 1930 at latest, common in Brit. underworld and its fringes, e.g. in Borstals and detention centres, strides = 'Civilian trousers (civvies)' (Home Office, 1978).—2. Hence, women's drawers or knickers: Colonial: from ca. 1919. *M.T.* has 'the monnisher's flashing her strides', which may indicate that the term has been thus used in Brit. low coll. since early C.20. Gosling, 1959, records this sense for 1930 at latest.

strike, n. Short for **strike-me-dead,** 2. Kersh, 1941, in nuance 'bread-and-butter'.

strike, v. To *strike a horse* is to feed it immediately before it runs in a race and therefore spoil its chance: Aus. sporting. B., 1942.—2. To go on strike at the location of: Can. coll.: 1959+. 'Four hundred men struck the King Lumber Company this morning.' (Leechman.)

strike! An Aus. ejaculation: since ca. 1925. (Baker.) Short for *strike a light!* or *strike me dead!*

strike a blow. To start work: Aus.: since ca. 1945. 'I must go now. It's half past nine—and I haven't struck a blow.' (B.P.)

strike a light. To commence work: sheet-metal workers'. (*Daily Herald,* 11 Aug. 1936.) Ex a job of welding.

strike it down. To drink heavily, either on one occasion or in general: RN: since ca. 1920. P-G-R.

strike-me. Bread: 'I . . . had a quick bite of strike-me and sweet evening' (bread and cheese). Lester. Short for next:-

strike-me-dead. Bread: military r.s.: from ca. 1899. (F. & G.) As gen. s. in Kersh, 1938. See **strike,** n., and prec.—2. Head: r.s. B. & P.

strike me handsome! An Aus. exclam. of the politer sort. B., 1942.

strill. A piano: Parlyaree: late C.19–20. (Lester.) It app. derives ex It. *strillo,* a shrill cry, a piercing note, etc.; cf. It. *strillare,* to shriek, to scream.—2. A portable harmonium: esp. among pierrots: late C.19–20. Cf. **strel(l)**.

string, n. A surgical ligature: medical students':—1933 (*Slang*).—2. As (*the*) *String,* short for **String o(f) Beads.** McShane, 1961, 'Used to be a good fight town, the old String.'—3. The published material that, each week, a writer 'on space rates' gets paid for. He pastes 'clips' of all his published work in one long 'string' and is paid on this evidence: Can. journalists'. (Leechman.)—4. See **electricial string.**

string, v. See **BIRD-WATCHERS,** in Appx.

string along. A var. of *string* (*on*), to deceive or 'lead up the garden path': since ca. 1920. (Gray, 1969.)—2. To accompany, as v.i. of next: 'We're just going down to Bill's—you want to string along?': coll.: adopted, ex US, mid-C.20. (P.B.)

string along with. To go along with; agree with; support: Can. coll.: adopted, ca. 1930, ex US.

string and glitter boys. Men detailed for guard-duty: Army: ca. 1905–20.

String o(f) Beads. Leeds: r.s.; railwaymen's, ex N. Country. (*Daily Herald,* 5 Aug. 1936.) See also **string,** n., 2.

string of ponies. A 'stable' of prostitutes 'owned' by one man: white-slave traffic: since ca. 1925. (BBC, 22 Sep. 1963.)

string up. To keep waiting: low: from ca. 1920. 'He strung me up.' See also **stringing up.**—2. 'In the back alleys [of London's East End] there was garotting—some of the brides would lumber a seaman while he was drunk and then he would be dropped—"stringing someone up" was the slang phrase for it' (Samuel, 1981): early C.20.

Stringbag. The Fairey Swordfish torpedo-spotter-reconnaissance biplane: mainly FAA: ca. 1934–45, then nostalgically. Rhodes, 1942; H. & P., 1943, note *Stringbag the Sailor.* The blurb to Lamb, *War in a Stringbag,* 1977, instructively begins: 'Practically obsolete even before [WW2], the robust, inelegant "Stringbags" . . . unbelievably were flying against the enemy at the end of it. Their cruising speed was 90 knots, yet they could outmanoeuvre almost every other aircraft'. Jackson records that the nickname was applied also to the Swordfish's successor, the Fairey Albacore, of similar appearance: 1943–5.

stringer. A reporter paid for what is published: mostly journalists': since ca. 1925. Cf. **string,** n., 3.

stringing up. A strong admonition, severe reprimand: 1925, F. Lonsdale (*OED* Sup.). P.B.: ?ex *string up,* to hang.

strip off. See **tear a strip off.**

strip-tease. A gradual, leisurely, teasing removal of clothes by a female in US vaudeville or variety; adopted in Brit. during the 1940s, orig. as s. soon elevated to coll. and, by 1970 at latest, to S.E. Not quite so old as time, yet well established in AD C.1 by Salome, skilled in the seven veils technique.

stripe. 'One who is no longer a first offender' (Ingram): c.:—1933. Cf. **striping.**—2. A long, esp. if narrow, scar: c.: since ca. 1915. Norman.

striped. 'When another did you a wrong turn [and] the other dockers found out, they would say "You're being striped" ' (Ash): London dockers': mid-C.20.

striper, two – two and a half – three. A lieutenant; lieutenant-commander; commander, RN: RN coll. (F. & G.) *Two-and-a-half striper* occurs in 'Taffrail', 1916. Ex the indications of rank.—2. Only *striper,* any naval officer: RN wardroom. (Granville.) See quot'n at **ringer,** 5.

stripey. 'A rating with one or more Good Conduct Badges (a *Stripey*) awarded for long years of undetected crime' (Bolster, 1945); Granville specifies 'a three-badge able seaman': RN lowerdeck.—2. 'Marines called lance-corporals "stripeys", but always knew sergeant-majors as "sir" '(*Don't Cry* 1983).

striping. Punishment, esp. in the form of an arrest, a conviction: c.: since ca. 1945. (Norman, 1959, in the first of the two poems.) ?Ex **stripe,** 1.

stripper. A strip-tease performer: coll.: adopted late 1940s, ex US.

stripping. 'The process of opening a safe with a . . . *jemmy*. This is a long process . . . it is first necessary to find a crack into which the jemmy can be wedged and with the modern safe this is improbable' (Tempest, 1950): c.: earlier C.20.

strobe. A stroboscope (an electronic flash unit): photographers': since ca. 1950. (B.P.)

stroke. 'To save detailing an officer to supervise them, one of the men was chosen as leader and made responsible for the general running of the mess. Such leaders are called "strokes", the word being taken from rowing parlance' (Merrow Smith, 1962): prison officers': since ca. 1930.—2. An unfair action, esp. in **pull a stroke,** q.v.

stroll on! A comment on what seems very hard to believe: Army and RAF: since ca. 1950. (Hall, 1959.) Pretend you haven't noticed! P.B.: by mid-1970s, some use among civilians also. In low use, often intensified, e.g. *fucking stroll on!* Perhaps ex *roll on* [demob, Christmas, my twelve, etc.]! As well as mild surprise, it may also express disgusted disbelief.

strong, n. Esp. in *the strong of* (something), the truth; the essential point or the especial importance of, e.g., a message, instruction, news: Aus.: since early C.20. (Baker.) Var. of the **strength of . . . ,** q.v.

strong, v. To impose a heavy sentence: c.: later C.20. 'The offender might observe [to the judge], "Hang on gov, you're *strongin'* it a bit." The judge, however, may not agree: "Don't come the *acid.* Have *six moon* for being *flash*" (six months is added to the sentence for being cheeky)' (McConville, 1980).

strong, adv. In *go it strong,* to act recklessly or energetically: coll.: from ca. 1840. 'I thought it was a bit strong you not wearing a coat and tie for the funeral' (McVicar, 1982): underworld.

strong-arm, v. To bully; to manhandle: Aus. c.: since late 1920s. (B., 1942.) Adopted from US.—2. Hence, to act as bully to (a prostitute): c.: since ca. 1930. Baker.

strong-arm, adj. Esp. in *strong-arm tactics,* the use of force, usu. against people: coll.: later C.20. Ex the US v.; see prec.

strong man. A confidence trickster: Aus. c.: since ca. 1920. (Baker.) He 'comes it strong'.

strongers. Any powerful cleanser such as spirits of salts: RN officers'. (Bowen.) Ex *strong,* by the 'OXFORD -ER'.

stronk. Sexual effusions, male and female: low Scots. 'The Ballad of Kirriemuir' in Page, 1976.

stropper. (Often *young*, or *old*, *s*.) One who is 'stroppy' (see next): coll.: later C.20. P.B.: heard from Aus. servicemen, 1960s.

stroppy. Obstreperous: orig. RN (Granville); > by 1970s very widespread and popular (P.B.). Via *obstropolous*, and various other spellings, s. since early C.18 (*EDD*, which lists also Scots var. *outstropolous*, early C.19).—2. Hence, 'to *get stroppy*' or become very angry: gen.: since ca. 1946. (Gilderdale, 2.) Cf. 'You'll get me stroppy if you start bullying' (Blake, 1964).

struggle and strife. Wife: r.s.; not very gen. (cf. *trouble . . .*). Franklyn. Often shortened to *struggle*.

struggling! 'A frequent answer to "How are you going [*or* doing]?" ': mostly Aus.: since ca. 1925. Either ex *'struggling* along' or ex *'struggling* to make ends meet'. (B.P.)

strung(-)out. Emaciated; weak and wits-wandering, esp. thus affected by drugs: adopted, late 1960s, ex US. (*Jagger*.) Cf. **spaced out**.

stubbie, -y. 'The key word is "stubbies", slang for both the shorts they [the Australian men] wear . . . and the bottles from which they drink' (*Guardian*, 18 Dec. 1982): Aus.: later C.20. P.B.: *stubbie* is used of a bottle in UK also, but of a squat bottle of—milk.

stubble jumper. 'Someone from the Can. Prairies, esp. Alberta and Saskatchewan; a farmer, or country person: either affectionate or derog.: since mid-C.20' (Leech, 1986).

stubs. Teeth: c.: since ca. 1945. (Cook, 1962.) Ex S.E. *stub*, a butt-end.

stuck. In *be stuck*, to be confirmed; *sticking-parade*, Confirmation: Charterhouse. I.e., fixed in one's Faith.

stuck away. In pawn: Glasgow:—1934. Euph.

stuck for. Lacking; at a loss how to obtain: from ca. 1870. See **stopped for bobbins**.

stud. A virile man: Anglo-Irish, since ca. 1925; since ca. 1955, gen. throughout the Commonwealth. (Moore, 1960.) Short for S.E. 'stud stallion' or 'stallion at *stud*'.—2. A mistress, esp. if available whenever required: Aus.: since ca. 1920. (Ronan, 1954), 'the boss's stud'. Short for S.E. *stud mare*.—3. As *Stud*, a *Stud*ebaker motorcar: since ca. 1950. (Freeborn, 1976.)

studying for Staff College, be. To sleep in the afternoon, esp. in hot countries: Army officers': since ca. 1920.

stuff, n. Drugs; esp. cocaine (*the stuff*): c.: earlier C.20. Since mid-C.20, marijuana (Home Office).—2. An anæsthetic; *give stuff* is to anæsthetise at an operation; *do stuffs* is to take a course in the administration of anæsthetics: medical:—1933 (*Slang*).—3. Aircraft collectively, as in 'There's a lot of stuff going across (to, e.g., Germany)': RAF coll.: 1940+. Partridge, 1945, 'And in "Heavy stuff" (heavy bombers)'.—4. A copulation: low, mostly Aus. 'She's had more stuffs than you've had twins'—almost a c.p. The Brit. version would be ' . . . hot dinners'. Ex the older v. Hence, woman regarded as sex object: 'I bet she'd make a smashing little stuff' (P.B.).

stuff, v. (Of man) to copulate with: late (?mid-) C.19–20. Ex upholstery. Hence the defiant c.p., *go and get stuffed*.—2. Hence, to defeat severely: NZ: since ca. 1920. Slatter, 'Wait till we clean up Otago [at Rugby Football]. We'll stuff 'em!'

stuff it! Dispose of it as you will!; get rid of it, but don't bother me; as in 'Tell them they can stuff it—we don't want it': low coll.: since ca. 1930. I.e. 'stuff it up your arse!', with perhaps a glance at **stuff**, v., 1. (Petch; P.B.)

stuff-jacket. An earlier, ca. 1910–35, var. of **stuffed shirt**.

stuffed rat. In gambling, a loaded die: Aus. c., since ca. 1930; by ca. 1945, low sporting s. Glassop, 1949.

stuffed shirt. A pompous fool: upper and middle classes': from ca. 1920.

stuffer. ' "Stuffers and blockers", thieves who seize small sums of money after jamming coin return slots [in telephone kiosks]' (*Daily Telegraph*, 8 Apr. 1988): British Telecom employees'.

stuffing. Superfluous matter included to fill the required space: journalistic coll. (—1904) >, ca. 1920, S.E.

stuffs. See **stuff**, n., 2.

stuffy. Angry, irritable; sulky; obstinate, 'difficult': US, anglicised ca. 1895 as a coll.; Kipling, 1898 (*get stuffy*). Cf. **sticky**, adj., 1. *OED*.—2. Hence, secretive: schools':—1923 (Manchon).—3. (Also ex sense 1.) Easily shocked; strait-laced: from ca. 1925. Galsworthy, 1926.—4. Wealthy: c.: adopted, ca. 1930, ex US. (Gardner, 1932; Powis, 1977.) Cf. C.18 s. *stuff*, money.—5. Stand-offish: orig. Services', from ca. 1926 (H. & P.) >, in later C.20, gen. coll.

Stuka Valley. The plain around Souk el Khemis (Tunisia), notorious for the attentions of German *Stuka* dive-bombers: Army in N. Africa: 1942–3. P-G-R.

stumer. A 'dud' person: from not later than 1913. (Manchon.) Perhaps orig. at Harrow School, for it appears in Lunn's *The Harrovians*. Ex late C.19 sense, a worthless cheque.—2. Hence, a bankrupt; a defaulter; (of a plan or enterprise) a failure: Aus. sporting and gambling: since ca. 1920. (B., 1942.) Cf. Aus. and NZ *come a stumer*, to crash financially. (B., 1941.)—3. A fool: Cockney. Ex Yiddish. Cf.:—4. A deaf-mute: id.: since ca. 1910. Also ex Yiddish (Franklyn).—5. A difficult customer; a naughty child' (*M.T.*, where spelt *stewmer*): market-traders'.—6. In *in a stumer*, in a 'mess' or hopeless confusion, as 'He's in a "stumer" ': Aus. and NZ. Cf. sense 2.—7. In *on a stumer*: 'If they don't want a cab when he gets there, he's "been on a stumer" ' (Hodge, 1939): taxi-drivers': since ca. 1920.—8. A blunder, mess, mistake: later C.20. 'He made a bit of a stumer of that.' (Helen Burt, 1983.) Cf. sense 6.

stumm (and crum). See **shtoom**.

stump jockey. A wicket-keeper: Aus.: since ca. 1930; by 1960, archaic.

stumpy. See PRISONER-OF-WAR SLANG, §12, in Appx.

Stun, the. The daily tabloid newspaper *The Sun*. (Watts, 1988.) Ex its style and approach.

stun, n. In *on the stun*, engaged in drinking heavily: Aus.: since ca. 1920. B., 1942.

stung. '(1) drunk; (2) having been induced to lend' (Wilkes): Aus.: since WW1.

stung for, be. To be cheated in a mild way, over (usu.) quite small matters; to be overcharged; as in 'I was stung for six quid for those tickets', or 'They tried to sting me for six quid': coll.—2. (?)Hence to be at a loss for: Aus.: from ca. 1925. B., 1943.

stunned. Tipsy: NZ, from ca. 1910; Aus. by 1918 (Baker); and, by 1933 at latest, Glaswegians'. Ex effects of liquor. Cf. **stun**, n.

stunned mullet, like a. 'Stupid, silly' (B., 1959): Aus.: since mid-C.20.

stute. An institute; a club: mostly proletarian. By aphesis and conflation of *institute*: that is, *in* dropped, *stitute* is telescoped from two syllables to one.

stuvac (pron. *stoó-vac*). A study vacation; a holiday from lectures before an examination: Aus. universities', since ca. 1945; then any students': since ca. 1960. Always coll. rather than s. (B.P., 1977.)

style. See **cramp** (one's) **style**.

stymied. Awkwardly placed; nonplussed: from ca. 1920: sporting coll. >, by 1933, S.E. Ex golf; golf sense ex *stymie*, a person partially blind (W.).

suave. 'Always pron. *swave*. Adj. of approbation with very wide application: Army in Cyprus: late 1950s' (P.B., 1974).

sub, n. A submarine: orig. RN coll., from 1914, soon > widespread and gen. *OED* Sup.—2. A sub-machine-gun (strictly a modified light machine-gun): Army coll.: since ca. 1942. Trevor, 1967.—3. A sub-editor: journalists'. Campbell, 1960, 'I'd a considerable battle with the chief sub to stop him cutting this paragraph out.'—4. Substantive rank: Army coll.: since mid-1940s, prob. earlier. Shortening of *sub rank*, equally common. (P.B.)

sub, v. See TIDDLYWINKS in Appx.

sub, adj. Mentally sub-normal; of low intelligence. Allingham, 1963: 'There was a woman who was slightly "sub", they said.

They didn't call her that but they made it perfectly clear' (P.B.).—2. See n., 4.

sub-fusc. The 1931–6 var. of **dim** (insignificant, lacking character), q.v.: Oxford University. This, however, is a revival, for the term existed in 1864, *Fun*, 21 May, 'Anon I saw a gentle youth (no '*sub fusc*' undergrad)./'*Toga virilis*' he had none, no mortar-board he had' (F. & H.). It existed at Harrow School in first decade of C.20: Lunn, 1913. Lit., *sub-fusc*, *subfusc*, *subfusk* = dusky; sombre (lit. and fig.).—2. Hence, (of dress) modest, of quiet colour: Ibid.: from ca. 1932. Sayers, 1935, 'I notice that we are both decently sub-fusc. *Have* you seen Trimmer in that frightful frock like a canary lampshade?'

sub-line. A printed form enabling a man to get an advance of wages: Public Works':—1935.

sub rank. See **sub**, n., 4.

subbie, -y. A sub-lieutenant: RN lowerdeck. Granville.—2. A sub-contractor: workmen's, esp. bricklayers': since ca. 1950. (*Sunday Citizen*, 29 Jan. 1969.) By early 1980s, more widely used; e.g. of agricultural sub-contractors (Littmoden, 1984).—3. Someone mentally or educationally sub-normal: 'Not that I've got anything against the cons [convicts] . . . most of them are barely above being out-and-out subbies' (a prison officer, quoted in *Guardian*, 5 Sep. 1987). Cf. **sub**, adj.

subcheese or **sub-cheese.** Everything, all there is, 'the whole shoot': Indian Army: Forces in India: mid-C.19–20; 1939–45. As in 'We saw a lot of Nips and gave 'em the sub-cheese' or, in a shop, 'Tighai, Mohammed, I'll take the sub-cheese' (All right, M., I'll take the rest). With thanks to John Bebbington, librarian. Here, *cheese* is probably Hindustani *chīz*, thing.

subfusc. See **sub-fusc.**

submarine, n. An after-hours drinking session: Old Scholars' Rugby Clubs': 1970s (Peppitt)—and prob. a decade earlier.

submarine, v.; mostly as vbl n. *submarining*, riding through tall grass: Northern Territory, Aus.: since ca. 1942. Hill, 1951.

submarine dandruff. 'Cork particles shaken off deck-head insulation—a common failing, a real snowstorm if under depth-charge attack: RN: 1950s' (Peppitt).

Submarine Lancers, the. A fictitious unit: WW1 and 2. To an undersized would-be enlister, the recruiting sergeant might say, 'Try the . . .'

submariners. 'Officers and men of the submarine service; it rhymes with *mariners*' (Granville): RN: since ca. 1941.

subs. In *pair o(f) subs*, a pair of shoes: Glasgow lower classes':—1934. ?Ex submarines.

subscribe to the Bookies' Benefit; esp., **be subscribing . . .** To throw money away by betting recklessly or haphazardly on horses. (Petch, 1966.)

suck (one's) **forefinger.** To suck it and then, with it, draw a line round one's neck as a form of oath: lower classes' coll.—1923 (Manchon).

suck-hole. To toady, as in 'He won't suck-hole to anyone'; hence, to cringe: low Can.

suck-holer. A toady: NZ low coll. Cf. prec.

suck the mop. In later C.20 coll., to be *left sucking the mop* is to be left, helpless and hopeless, the victim of any trick; to be left at a complete disadvantage. (P.B.)

sucked orange. A very silly fellow: lower classes' coll.:— 1923 (Manchon).

sucker. A greenhorn; a simpleton: coll.: US (1857), partly anglicised ca. 1895. Thornton.—2. Hence, in C.20, among tramps, one who gives money (*not* always derisive: Jennings); and among criminals, a prospective victim (Leach).— 3. A person easily taken in or gulled; often, one who is aware of what is happening, as in 'Come on, let's go in! I always was a sucker for fairs and circuses': coll., the predominant sense since mid-C.20. (P.B.)

suckered, be. To be gulled (cf. prec.): later C.20. 'It's impossible to find a [snooker hall] hustler who will admit to being suckered' (*Sunday Express*, 2 Aug. 1987). Cf. earlier (since mid-C.19) s. *sucked-in*, deceived, cheated.

suckers. 'Without music . . . life is incomplete. You know, it is . . . suckers' (McCartney, II, 1980, song 'Bogey Music'): cited by Janssen, who comments: 'This seems to be a Brit. var. of US s. "It sucks" (= to be a failure; be of poor quality; be unpleasant: W. & F., 1975).'

sucking the hindtit. (Esp. in pool-rooms; but also gen. sporting.) Well behind or in arrears: low Can.: since ca. 1930.—2. To have a low priority: since the late 1930s. Monsarrat, 1951.

sucks! An 'expression of derision': schools' (?mostly boys'): since late C.19. Often *sucks to you*. Benson, 1924, has *sucks for ——!*, that's a disappointment for so-and-so! P.B.: *sucks to* . . . may also be directed at others, e.g., 'Well, sucks to them! They can jolly well go without!'

sucky. Very painful: Scottish Public Schools': ca. 1915. (Marshall, 1934.) P.B.: causing one to suck in one's cheeks?

suction raid. Such a bombing attack on enemy concentrations just ahead of the Allied armies as was 'designed to create a vacuum and suck the *brown jobs* forward' (P-G-R.): RAF: 1943–5.

sudden. Swift; efficient; esp., swift and efficient: Aus. coll.: since ca. 1940. (B., 1953.) 'This use is pure Shakespeare. *Julius Caesar*, III, i, "Casca, be sudden, for we fear prevention" ' (R.S.).—2. Hence, brutally drastic; brutal: Aus.: since ca. 1940. (B., 1959.) See **sudden death on.**

sudden death. A decision by one throw (not, e.g., by two out of three): 1834 (Maginn).—2. Hence, a decision by one game, as in lawn tennis when the set-score is 5-all: s. >, by 1930, coll. Collinson.—3. ' "Sudden death" had two meanings. A front living-room that opens [directly] on to the street, and . . . a quick curtain' (Warwick, 1968): theatrical, esp. among touring-company actors: the former sense, ca. 1880–1930; the latter, since ca. 1870 and not yet (1976) †.

sudden death on. Expert at (something); brutal or unnecessarily or extremely severe towards (someone): Aus.: since ca. 1920. (B., 1942.) Ex prec., 1, 2. See **sudden**, 2, prob. a shortening of this.

suds. Ale; beer: Army, early C.20 (F. & G.); by ca. 1930, Aus. (B.P.) Ex 'bubbles on ale likened to soap-suds' or from C.18 s. *in the suds*, slightly drunk.

sudser, sudster. A 'soap opera', q.v.: the 2nd, BBC, hence world of entertainment in gen., since early 1970s; the 1st in *Listener*, 11 May 1972 (Barnhart, 2). Ex 'soap suds'.

suffer a recovery. 'To recover from a drinking bout' (Baker): Aus. joc.

sugar. North(wards): Wood Wharf (West India Dock, London) dockers':—1935. E.g. 'a little more sugar, Tom (or Bill or Jack)!', called by the piler to the driver of the electric gantry. Ex the fact that the *North* quay of the West India Dock is regarded as 'the natural home for *sugar* storage.' (Very local, this: but included for the light it throws on the origin of s.)—2. Gen. *a sugar*, a cube or lump of sugar: coll.—3. A term of address to a girl: from ca. 1930. Ex US. *Gilt Kid*, 1936.—4. Worthless banknotes.—5. 'The ski-ing was quite excellent in granulated snow, what is sometimes called Sugar, formed by one day of hot spring sun' (Walker, 1968): skiers'.—6. (Also *sugar lump*.) The drug LSD 25, lysergic acid: drugs world: adopted, ca. 1965, ex US. Orig. taken on loaf-sugar. Wyatt, 1973; Home Office (the longer version).

sugar! A euph. exclam., used instead of *shit* or *bugger it*, and owing something to both.

sugar along. See **shovel along.**

sugar(-)baby. A member of the Aus. militia: Aus. soldiers': 1940+. (B., 1942.) No service overseas: perhaps imm. ex:— 2. A child averse from going outside the house while it's raining: domestic: late C.19–20. P.B.: from the taunt *You're not make of sugar—you won't melt* [in the rain]*!*

sugar-basin. A marble mason: builders' and masons': r.s. (A master-builder, 1963.)

sugar candy. Handy: r.s.

sugar daddy. An oldish man spending lavishly on a young woman: US, anglicised, via the 'talkies', ca. 1931. It may

sugar (a man's) **milk for him.** To harm a person under the pretext of doing his work: workmen's:—1923 (Manchon).

sugar up. To flatter (a person): coll.:—1923 (Manchon). Cf. synon. *butter up*.

suicide. In Aus. the word has, to motorists, borne, since ca. 1945, the meaning treated by B.P. in this note, written in June 1963: 'The "cide" of a truck which should not be used for overtaking. In Australia and in Britain, this is the left. "Suicide" and "Passing Side" are often painted on the back of a truck. Also "Undertaker" on the left and "Overtaker" on the right. "Undertaker" is not used in Australia, but it is universally known . . . Another motorists' phrase is, "Look out for the driver on your right and the fool on your left".'

suicide blonde. Dyed by her own hand: Aus. joc.: since ca. 1950. (B.P.) The pun is quite well known in Brit. too. (P.B.)

suicide brigade, the. Those fielders who stand very close to the man batting: cricketers': since ca. 1930. (Not, however, to Hammond, Constantine, Bradman, Compton, Nourse.)

sulph. Amphetamine sulphate; sulphates, amps in powder form: drugs c. Stockley, 1986.

summer-blink. A gleam of sunlight on a day of bad weather: nautical coll. Bowen.

summer soup. 'Non-specific soup, i.e. "some o' this and some o' that" ' (Martin, 1983): RN Submariners'. Cf. *bitser*.

summer uniform. 'Mackintosh and leggings' (McKenna, 1): railwaymen's ironic: mid-C.20.

sump oil. Hair oil: Aus., esp. Sydney, motor mechanics': since ca. 1940. (B.P.)

sun. Short form of **sunflower** (Anderson).—2. As *Sun*, a Short *Sun*derland flying-boat: RAF: 1939+. Jackson.

sun-arc. See MOVING-PICTURE SLANG, §3, in Appx.

sun-bonnet. A type of steel helmet, esp. designed for fireguards and other civilian anti-air-raid services, which came into use 1941. Illus. in Longmate, 1971, about civilian life in Brit. during WW2.

sun-dodger. An extremely lazy tramp: Aus.: since ca. 1910. B., 1942.

sun over the foreyard. 'Time for drinking in the wardroom. Eight bells in the forenoon watch: mid-day. It is a traditional Naval convention never to drink before the sun clears the foreyard' (Granville): RN. P.B.: ignorant civilians sometimes substitute *yardarm*, in mock-navalese: 'Sun's over the yardarm—break open the gin!' for 'let's have a drink'.

sunbeam. Crockery and cutlery that, placed on the table, hasn't been used and therefore doesn't need to be washed: domestic, mainly feminine, Aus.: since ca. 1950; s. >, by 1970, coll. (*Aus. Pocket Ox. Dict.*, 1976.) A ray of sunshine in the midst of drudgery.

Sunday; morning; midday; evening. Newspaper (and -vendors') coll. for a Sunday paper; one issued in the early morning, at noon, after noon: late C.19–20.

Sunday dog. 'An indolent sheep or cattle dog' (B., 1941): Aus. and NZ rural coll. Every day a Sunday.

Sunday Graffiti, the. The *Sunday Graphic*, a pictorial newspaper: ca. 1945–60. This defunct newspaper was more reputable than its nickname would imply.

Sunday-mopper. An employee that, to increase his earnings, does others' Sunday work: workmen's:—1923 (Manchon).

Sunday Pic, the. The *Sunday Pictorial*: journalists' coll.

Sunday sidings. 'Sidings compelling Sunday clearance' (*Railway*, 2nd): railwaymen's coll.

sunflower. A girl; a young lady: beatniks': since ca. 1959. (Anderson.) Perhaps 'flowering for the sons'.

sunny side up. 'An egg fried so that it is done on one side only, the yolk not broken, and not turned over' (Leechman): since ca.1920: Can. >, by 1942, also Eng.

sun's high lad. A smart fellow: tailors': 1928 (*Tailor and Cutter*, 29 Nov.). An elab. of *bright lad*.

Sunset Strip. See TOMBOLA, in Appx.

sunshade. 'A superstructure on a tank to disguise it as a truck. It was "ditched" before going into action' (Sanders, 1967): Army in N. Africa: 1940–43.

sunshine. A cheerful form of address to a child, or an ironic one to a gloomy person: coll. (P.B.)

sup. A supplement: coll.:—1923 (Manchon). Cf.:-

sup ben. *Sup*plementary *bene*fit, to the income of the country's lowest paid: s., an inevitable abbr., soon > j.: used in discussion programme on BBC Radio 4, 5 Nov. 1987, but current well before then.

supe. A supervisor, as in, e.g. *set-room supe*: Army signals units': later C.20. (P.B.) Cf. **super**, 2.

suped-up. The prob. correct orig. of **souped-up**, q.v.

super, n. Superphosphate: farmers' and seed-merchants'.—2. *Super* has, increasingly throughout C.20, been used of any superintendent or supervisor: coll.—3. Superannuation pension: Aus. coll.: later C.20. Buzo, 1969, 'Oh, I'm with the public service . . . it's a pretty soft cop. The money's good. Plenty of super.' Cf. **super-ann**.

super, adj. Extremely strong, capable, intelligent: from ca. 1910. Ex *superman*. Cf. **wizard**.—2. Hence excellent, 'swell': from ca. 1925. Keverne, 1930, 'He was staying at the "Beach". Very super.' Since WW2 it has been immensely popular among school children and teenagers—and even [?esp.: P.B.] among 'debs', as in Haden-Guest, 1971: 'Now . . . that deb slang ("Soopah!") is only heard in the glummest of bedsitters.' P.B.: a mainly middle- and upper-class usage; working classes prefer *smashing*.

super-ann. Superannuation pension contributions: coll.: later C.20. 'All these things taking bites out of your pay: PAYE, super-ann, union dues . . .' (P.B.)

super-duper (pron. *sooper-dooper*). An intensive of **super**, adj., 2: schoolgirls' and teenagers': 1947+; by 1957, slightly ob. P.B.: but still extant, 1983.

super-grass. 'In the late 1970s the variant [of **grass**, n., 2] *super-grass* has emerged in the media for an informer instrumental in breaking up large and powerful criminal rings' (R.S., 1978).

super-snooper. 'There are also the periodic purges by the "super-snoopers", as the special [Dept. of Health & Social Services] inspectors are called' (*New Society*, article on unemployed young people in N.E. England, 2 June 1983).

super-snoopy. 'A helicopter with a camera which can take close-up pictures of people's faces from one kilometre away' (*Time Out*, 25 July 1980): security forces', N. Ireland.

super sorrow. Very sorry, as in 'Oh! super sorrow': several Brit. preparatory schools': ca. 1960–5.

super-super bastard. A mean, bullying, tyrannical fellow: c., and low s.: from ca. 1910. Spenser, 1934, 'This warder was another of the variety known amongst prison populations as super-super bastards.'

super-trooper. 'Large spotlight in the theatre, used to illuminate the major artiste prominently, mostly in variety shows' (Watts, 1988).

supercharged. Drunk: aircraft engineers' and RAF: from late 1920s. *Daily Herald*, 1 Aug. 1936; Jackson.

superintendent (or **supervisor**) **of the sidewalk.** A pedestrian standing, esp. if habitually standing, on the sidewalk (or pavement or footpath and what-have-you) and gazing up at a new building in the course of construction: Aus.: adopted, ca. 1956, ex US. (B.P.)

superjam. 'Slackers were likely to be asked to leave—"super-jammed", in the Wykehamist vocabulary' (Pound, 1976, writing of the 1900s): Winchester.

supped all (one's) **porridge, have.** No longer to suffer with one's teeth: lower classes' coll.:—1923 (Manchon).

Supply Chief. A Supply Chief Petty Officer: since ca. 1920: RN coll.: by 1940, virtually j. Granville.

suppo. A suppository, whether anal or vaginal: medical and pharmaceutical coll.: since ca. 1935.

Supreme Examples of Allied Confusion. *South-East Asia Command (SEAC):* coined by the Americans, adopted, 1944, by the RN.

sure-fire. Certain; infallible: coll.: US anglicised ca. 1918. Sayers, 1933, 'He thought it was a sure-fire mascot.'

sure pop! Certainly!; 'sure': children's:—1923 (Manchon).

surface. To wake: Wrens' (?after submariners'): since ca. 1939. Ex a submarine surfacing. P.B.: in later C.20 > widespread coll.; also as 'to get up, and appear', as 'Old Freddie doesn't usually surface till about noon.'

surface raiders. 'Southern Railway electrical multiple units' (*Railway*, 2nd): since ca. 1946.

surfie. A surfer, esp. a surfboard rider: 'not heard before 1961', says B.P., who, in mid-1963, adds that it's 'a term rarely used by genuine surfers'.

surgeon's bugbear. Adipose tissue: medical:—1933 (*Slang*). Because, when cut, it bleeds in a way difficult to check.

Surrey Docks. Pox (syphilis): r.s.: later C.20. Ex the large complex of commercial wharves at Rotherhithe in S.E. London. (Hillman, 1974.)

surveyor's friend, the. Whitewash: RN. Bowen. Ex 'the amount used for marking points on shore'.

sus. (N. and adj.) A being *sus*pected; suspected; (on) suspicion: c.: from ca. 1920. *Gilt Kid*, 1936, 'What you nick me for? Sus?' Cf. **suspect.**—2. Hence, arrest 'on suspicion': police and underworld >, by early 1970s, gen. coll. See **sus law.**—3. Hence, 'a person arrested for "being a suspected person loitering . . . " ' (Powis): police: later C.20.—4. See **suss,** n.

sus, v. See **suss.**

sus, adj. and adv. Suspicious(ly): c.: since ca. 1925. (Norman.)—2. (Adj.) suspect, esp. by the police: since ca. 1925; by 1960, also s. Cook, 1962.

sus law, the. Later C.20 coll. for the Vagrancy Act, Section 4: 'Every suspected person or reputed thief frequenting or loitering about in any place of public resort . . . with intent to commit an arrestable offence . . . shall be deemed a rogue and a vagabond.' (P.B.)

susie. A sixpence, whether coin or value: turf c.:—1932. Perhaps *Susie*: by personification suggested by *bob*, a shilling. More prob. ex dial. *suse*, six: cf. the Lancashire *susepence*, sixpence (*EDD*).—2. (Or *Suzie*.) A Suzuki motorcycle, in production since 1936, but popular in UK only since ca. 1960: motorcyclists'. (Dunford.)

suspect, for. For being a suspicious character; on suspicion of crime: c.: from ca. 1920. *Gilt Kid*, 1936, 'He got nicked for suspect.' Cf. **sus,** n.

suspish (accent on *pish*, unlike the pron. of, e.g., *waspish*). A *suspic*ion. (Manning, 1930.) Esp. *under suspish*, under suspicion (by the police): Aus.: from ca. 1925. Cf. *ambish* for *ambition*.

suss, n. See **sus.** But *suss* has since WW2, been the prevalent spelling. In *New Society*, 7 July 1977, Weightman uses *suss* thus: 'She is always liable to be arrested for "suss" (suspected person); when he has been arrested, it has mostly been on "suss" [= **sus,** n., 2]; [three West Indian pickpockets] are all frightened of "suss" '.—2. Knowledge, as in 'The kids up there, they'd never seen anything like it. I mean, they've got a lot of suss and all that, but they all surged to the front of the stage, went mad' (a young Londoner's comment on 'Spandau Ballet's' perfomance in Birmingham, quoted in *New Society*, 8 Jan. 1981). Ex **suss out.**

suss, v. To suspect: c.: from ca. 1920.—2. To put right; to repair, as 'Got a puncture on the M1, but I soon sussed it': later C.20. Loosely ex next, 1. (P.B.)—3. 'When your sins find you out you are *well sussed*, or *sussed badly*' (Simmonds, 1985): teenagers'. Cf.:-

suss out. To puzzle out, work out (an explanation of): mostly teenagers': since 1965 or 1966. *The Queen*, 28 Sept. 1966, 'Youth susses things out on its own.' Cf. **sus,** adj.—2. Hence, to ascertain, to spy out (e.g., site of a planned outrage): since latish 1960s. *Daily Telegraph*, 5 Oct. 1974 (R.S.).

sussed. 'Arrested as a suspected person loitering' (Powis). See **sus,** n., 1.

Sussex weed(s). Oaks: Southern (esp. Sussex) coll. Cooke, 1911, 'Among the "Sussex weed".' (Apperson.)

susso. The dole; esp. *on the susso*, 'in receipt of unemployment *sus*tenance' (B., 1942): Aus.: since ca. 1925.

sussy. Suspicious: since ca. 1940. Cunliffe, 1965, 'It seemed a bit sussy to me.'

suzie. See **susie.**

swab (one's) **tonsils.** To kiss passionately: adopted, ex low US, ca. 1920.

swag, n. A 'packet' of money: Aus.: since ca. 1925. Mann, 1942, 'I've got a chance to get a swag on commission.' Cf. synon. use of **loot.**—2. In *a swag of*, many; much: NZ: since ca. 1930. 'There's swag of 'em in this joint' (Slatter). A re-emergence of C.19 c.; recorded by Vaux, 1812.—3. Punning acronym on 'Sophisticated Wild Ass Guess': UN in Middle East: 1982. (Mindel.)

swag, v. To hustle or hurry (someone, e.g., into a room): low s.: since ca. 1930. (Norman, 1959.) Cf. **swag away.**

swag and plunder. See MOCK-AUCTION SLANG, in Appx.

swag away. To abduct or kidnap (someone): police and underworld: since (?)ca. 1955. Barnett, 1978: 'The object is to see if the Commissioner was swagged away by anyone during the demo.'

swag in. To cause to enter secretly: c.:—1923. (Manchon.)

swailer. A cosh: c.: later C.20. (Powis.) P.B.: this has a dial. sound to it. *EDD* lists Herefordshire v. *swale*, to cleave, split asunder, while almost countrywide is *sweal*, with various meanings of scorch, singe, etc.

swain. A theatrical term of contempt: 1912, Lyons, 'They're a silly set o' swain, the General Public' (Manchon); ob. Ex the sense of yokel. P.B.: or ex affected pron. of *swine*.

swak. A superscription, SWAK, q.v. in Appx., at LOVERS' ACRONYMS, on the envelope of a letter to a sweetheart, i.e. *sealed with a kiss*. Hence, *swakking*, censoring mail: RN officers': WW2. P-G-R.

swallow, n. A quick draw at a cigarette. Ex 'swallowing' the smoke and exhaling it through the nostrils.—2. In *have a spiral swallow*, to have a taste for liquor: from ca. 1920 (Manchon); ephemeral. ?Ex corkscrew.

swallow, v. To cancel (an appointment or arrangement or plan): low, esp. Londoners'. La Bern, 1947, 'We were all tired, so we decided to swallow it' (a visit to the racecourse). Cf.:-

swallow it. 'Only a few weeks ago he told me he "had swallowed it"—got out of crime' (Gosling, 1959): since ca. 1920: orig. and still mainly c. Prob. ex:-

swallow the anchor. To settle down—above all, to loaf—on shore, esp. if one is still active: nautical: late C.19–20. (Ware.)—2. To surrender or yield: c.: from ca. 1919. Ingram, 1933.

swamp, v. To exchange or barter: Aus. (B., 1942.) Perversion of *swap*?—2. To spend (money), esp. on drink: Aus.: since ca. 1920. (Baker.) Perhaps ex the next.—3. The v.i. (with var. *swamp it*) of *swamper*, 1 and 2. B., 1959.

swamp down. To swallow, gulp down (a drink): Aus.: since ca. 1910. (Baker.) Cf. **swamp,** v. and **swamped.**

swamp (one's) **way** (**with**). To travel along (with someone), esp. in the outback. (Ronan, 1961.) Cf. **swamp,** v., 1, and **swamper,** 1.

swamped. Tipsy: Services' (little in Army): since ca. 1920. (H. & P.) Cf. US *tanked*.

swamper. A tramp; one who walks to his destination but has a teamster carry his 'swag': Aus. rural. (B., 1942.) Ex a bullock-driver's assistant: Aus. bullock-drivers'. (Prichard, 1926.) (There we also find *swamp*, v.i., to be such an assistant.)—2. 'A man, often partially incapacitated, who keeps the bunkhouses clean (*swamped out*) in a logging camp or on a ranch' (Leechman): Can. coll.

swan, n. 'The migratory habits of the swan have provided us with one of the most expressive of all Korean words. The act

S

of "swanning" (going purposefully anywhere without a pur- pose) is one of the most favoured pastimes of the theatre. If one were to "swan" southward with the purpose of moving on from the enemy, the act would be called "bugging out" ' (*Iddiwah*, July 1953): United Nations troops in and during the Korean War. Ex the next two entries.—2. Earlier, as used by the Army in France and Germany, 1944–5 and esp. in *a good swan*, a rapid advance. (Sanders, 1965.) Ex *swan around*.—3. In *on a* or *the swan*, on an excursion, ostensibly duty, but just as much pleasure, as e.g., 'a tour of inspection of our units in Hong Kong [at the pleasantest time of the year]': Services', perhaps mainly Army: since ca. 1950. Ex *swan around*. (P.B.)

swan, v. To parade, perhaps rather self-consciously, as swans often appear to do: may be used in contempt, tinged with envy, as in 'I was there in my jeans and jersey and they began swanning in in black ties and long dresses like Glyndebourne [Opera House]' (*Guardian*, Feb. 1979). Influenced by prec., 3. (P.B.)

swan about the blue. 'To drive about aimlessly, with more than a suspicion that one is lost' (Sanders): Army: 1940–3, *the blue* being the desert; then loosely in, or concerning, regions other than N. Africa.

swan around. (Of tanks) to circle about; (of persons) to wander either in search of a map reference or aimlessly: Army: 1940+. Ex the manœuvres of swans queening it on pond or stream. P-G-R.—2. Hence, to 'tour', deviate from a set route, unauthorised: Army: since ca. 1944. (P-G-R.) See **swan**.

Swanee. As in 'Lots of the textile firms round here are going down the Swanee—let's hope ours isn't next'; headed for bankruptcy, 'going down the drain': coll.: later C.20. Also var. *up the Swanee*, which by 1988 had come to mean 'out of order, not working', as in 'There'll be no phones today— switchboard's up the Swanee'. Perhaps influenced by *swan*. (P.B.)

swank, v. To pretend: Powis, 1977, 'Let's swank that Tommy here isn't married'. Ex N.W. Midlands dial.; *EDD* has a citation for 1900.

swank, adj. Var. of **swank(e)y**, adj.: since ca. 1917. (Joyce, 1922.) Common in N. America, which has reinforced its Brit. use; as in 'a swank car', an expensive automobile.

swank(e)y. Showy; conceited; pretentious; pretentiously grand: dial. >, ca. 1910, s. The *OED*'s earliest record is of 1912. Ex v. *swank*, to show off, behave conceitedly.

swankiness. The rather rare abstract n. ex **swank(e)y**, adj.: from ca. 1914.

swanks. One's best clothes: Services': ca. 1925–45. Cf. **swank(e)y**.—2. Sausages: Army: 1940+. P-G-R, 'They pretend to be meat and are mostly bread.' See **swank**, v.

swanner. One 'on a swan': see **swan**, n., 3; v.; and **swan around**, 2: Army: since late WW2.

swap spit(s). (Of a couple) to kiss passionately: low. (L.A., 1978.) Cf. **swab (one's) tonsils**.

swartzer. See **schwartz(e)**.

swassander or **-onder**. See **sixty-niner**.

swatched. Tipsy: since ca. 1950. Perhaps cf. Warwickshire dial. *swatched*, (of a woman) untidily dressed.

swear and cuss. A bus: Cockney rhyming: since ca. 1910. Ort-zen, 1938.

swear-up. A vigorous altercation, involving (usu.) the use of 'bad language': since early C.20. Cf. **punch-up**, a physical fight. (P.B.)

sweat blood. To make unsparing effort on behalf of oneself, a friend, or a cause; to work extremely hard: coll.: since WW2. (L.A., 1974.) Cf. **sweat (one's) guts out**.

sweat-box. 'A sluing or aligning jack requiring much human energy' (*Railway*): railwaymen's: late C.19–20.

sweat cobs. To perspire heavily and freely: lowish coll.: since mid-C.20, prob. earlier. *Cobs* = dial. lumps. (P.B.)

sweat it out. To keep on trying hard, esp. in order to 'survive', as in, say, cricket or football: coll.

sweat like a bull. To perspire freely: coll. orig. mostly Cockneys': from ca. 1880. Cf. **sweat cobs**.

sweat machine. A bicycle: Aus., esp. Sydney, motor mechanics': since ca.1945. (B.P.)

sweat on is short for **sweat** (or **be sweating**) **on the top line**, q.v.

sweat on promotion. To make oneself conspicuous with a view to advancement: military: from ca. 1920. Ex:-

sweat on the top line; be sweating . . . , the more gen. form. 'To be in eager anticipation' (of promotion, or posting), or 'on the eve of obtaining something much wanted': military. (F. & G.) Ex the game of House: a player with four or five numbers on the top line anxiously awaits the call of one more number to win. Hence the n., in *get* or *have a sweat-on*.

sweat pads. Pancakes: Can.: since ca. 1945. (Leechman.)

sweat-room. Interrogation room at a police station: police s.: mid-C.20. (Hunter, 1974.) Cf. *sweat-box*, since ca. 1875, the cell where prisoners waiting to go before a magistrate are kept.

sweater girl. A girl, a young woman, with a well-developed bust: adopted, ex US, early 1940s; s. > coll. A sweater or other tightly-fitting upper garment exhibits such a female to considerable advantage. The style was very much in vogue in early 1940s for 'pin-ups'—the influence of WW2.

sweating. See **sweat on** . . .

Sweatipore. India: Army officers': from ca. 1920. A pun on *paw* (hand) and *pores* of the hand, and also on such names of military stations as *Barrackpore*.

sweaty. Hard, difficult, severe: coll., esp. schoolboys': earlier C.20. Lunn, 1919, ' "It's a sweaty house for new men." Cluff shook his head sadly. "Yes, it's a hard life for new men." ' Also of persons, as in Ibid.: 'These Blues [as schoolmasters] are sometimes rather sweaty. They think it lip if you cut your work for a man who's been a Blue.' *Lip* = impudence. Cf. later **hairy**, which implies also dangerous.

swede. A farm labourer: urban. Ex S.E. *swede*, a kind of turnip. See also **swedey**, 3.—2. 'A raw recruit, i.e. one just from the country; or an airman with a rural, countrified manner' (Jackson): RAF: since ca. 1930. Short for **swede-basher**.—3. The head, esp. in *set the swede down; crash down the swede*, or simply **crash the swede**, q.v., all = lie down to sleep.

swede-basher. An agricultural labourer; a country bumpkin: Services': since ca. 1925. (H. & P.) He 'bashes about'—walks heavily—among the turnips. Cf. *gravel-basher* at **basher**, 4.—2. Hence, since ca. 1930, the agent in:-

swede-bashing. Field training, as opposed to *square-bashing* (parade work, drill): since ca. 1930: Army and RAF: Partridge, 1945, 'Field training . . . often takes recruits into the fields and hedgerows.' In the RN *swede-bashing* means sleeping: Granville.

Swedeland. Country parts: urban derogatory: since ca. 1950. (L.A., 1967.) Ex **swede**, 1.

swedey or **swedy.** An employee of the Great Eastern Railway: ca. 1890–1925. (*Railway*.) It passed through much agricultural country.—2. As *the Swed(e)y*, it = the old Great Eastern Railway.—3. During 'Operation Countryman', when provincial police were drafted to London to investigate alleged corruption in the Metropolitan force, 1979, '[the former] have been derisively nicknamed the "Swedey"—a pun on "Sweeney", the rhyming slang for Sweeney Todd/Flying Squad. "Swede" is a long-established arrogant Met. word for people they see as bumbling country coppers, totally at sea in the world of serious villainy' (*New Statesman*, 1 Jan. 1980). See **swede**, 1, and **Sweeney Todd**.

sweedle. To trick with cajolery: from 1912; ob. by 1935. In Henry Arthur Jones' comedy, *Dolly Reforming Herself* (pub. in 1913), extravagant featherhead Dolly was played by Marie Lohr; her long-suffering husband accused her of 'sweedling' him, and the phrase caught on. Obviously a blend of *swindle* + *wheedle*.

Sweeney Todd, the. The Flying Squad: low London r.s.: since ca. 1925. (Sharpe, *The Flying Squad*, 1938.) Often shortened to *the Sweeny*, as in Gosling, 1959. See **swedey**, 3, and:-

sweenies. Members of the Flying Squad: c., since ca. 1930; hence, since ca. 1940, also police s. (Carr, 1956.) Ex prec.

sweep under the carpet. To conceal or hide (something), esp. in the hope that it (a project or plan—also, a grave blunder) will be overlooked or forgotten: coll.: since ca. 1955; by ca. 1975, informal S.E. (Petch, 1969.) It is recorded in *OED* Sup., 1972, first as *push under* . . . , 1936, and then as *sweep* . . . , 1966. Ex idle servants sweeping dust under the carpet instead of into a dustpan, to save time and effort.

sweet, adj. Arranged, settled; gen. *It's* (or *she's*) *sweet*, all right because fixed: Aus.—2. Hence, correct; in order: Aus.: since ca. 1910. Glassop, 1949.—3. Egregious; (ref.) great, thorough: coll.: C.19–20; by ca. 1930, slightly ob. 'The ship was at this time refitting, and . . . a sweet mess she was in' (Marryat, 1829).

sweet, adv. Without difficulty or trouble: c. Sharpe, 1938.

sweet and sours. Flowers: r.s.: mid-C.20. (Barnes, 1976.) The influence of Chinese cuisine.

sweet B.A. Nothing: low: since ca. 1940. 'You can do sweet B.A. about it' (Norman). Cf. *sweet F.A.* at **Fanny Adams**, 2, and esp. the exact semantic parallel, *sod all*, for *B.A.* here stands for *bugger all*. *Sweet bugger all* prob. goes back to early C.20, and may orig. have been mainly Can. (Leech, 1974). P.B.: I have heard the Can. prairieland described, without the Mesopotamian distinction of 'a river running through it', as 'miles and miles of sweet bugger all'.

sweet cop. See **soft cop**.

sweet damn all. A mild synon. of **sweet B.A.** Lyell.

sweet evening breeze. Cheese: r.s.: earlier C.20. (Lester.) Often shortened to *sweet(-)evening*; cf. **strike-me**.

sweet Jane (or **jane**). A complaisant girl: Teddy boys': since ca. 1948. (*News of the World*, 26 Sep. 1954.) Contrast **straight Jane**.

sweet-pea ward. See **lily-pond**.

sweet savagery. See **bodice ripper**.

sweet sixteen. See TOMBOLA, in Appx.

sweet tweet. 'Valueless, as in "It's not worth sweet tweet." App. double neg., but the usage does mean that the thing in question is worthless: widespread N. Am. W. Coast: since early 1950s' (Leech, 1986).

sweeten. To increase (the collateral of a loan) by furnishing additional securities: financial:—1919 (*OED*).

sweetie. A sweetheart: coll.: from ca. 1920; much earlier in US. Also, since ca. 1945, in ref., e.g. 'He's been an absolute sweetie to me' (kind, considerate, generous).—2. Ironically, of anyone particularly unpleasant or disgusting: later C.20. (P.B.)

sweetie (or **-y**) **pie.** In address: dear; 'sweet': since ca. 1930. (Bell, 1942.) Elab. of prec., 1.

sweetness and light. Whisky: Aus. joc.: since early C.20. Niland, 1958.

sweets. Amphetamines: drugs world: later C.20. Home Office.

swell mob. In C.20 c., 'the "kite" men, the confidence artists, and . . . fashionably dressed young men who lie in wait for gullible strangers' (Wallace, 1928).

swep. Joc. coll. past tense of *sweep*, usu. in *swep out* and applied to a female retiring with a great show of (often, offended) dignity. Middle-class mockery of servants' slovenly pron., at conclusion of narrative, e.g., 'an' with that [remark], she swep' out'. Used to good effect in column 'Dear Mary . . . ', *Guardian*, 11 Oct. 1982: '[a retort], said Jane grandly and swep off. Swep in again sharpish, though, when she got a whiff of food.' (Raab; P.B.)

swerve, n. and v. (To stop at a) *coïtus interruptus*: Aus. motorists': since ca. 1950. An evasive action to avoid a child.

swi (or **swy**). Two-up, the gambling game: Aus. and NZ low or c.: since ca. 1920, perhaps earlier. Hence *swi(-up) school*; *swy-game*. Ex Ger. *zwei* = two. E.P. (NZ); B., 1942; Wilkes.—2. A florin, i.e. two shillings: low Aus.: late C.19–20.—3. Hence, a sentence, or a term, of two years' imprisonment: Aus. c.: since ca. 1925. (B., 1942.) See **swy** at AUSTRALIAN UNDERWORLD, in Appx.

swift. In *a bit swift*: 'Unfair advantage was taken: "Guv'nor, now that was a bit swift" ' (Powis, who lists also *very swift*, 'grossly unfair'): c.: later C.20. Cf.:-

swift 'un, a. 'An arrest for "being a suspected person loitering [see also **sus law**] with undertones of unfair advantage being taken" ' (Powis): c. and underworld: later C.20. Cf. prec., and:-

swiftie, -y. An illegal trick: Aus.: since early C.20. Caddie, 1953, ' "You didn't work a swiftie on them, did you?" I asked suspiciously.' Perhaps a semantic blend of *swift*, fast, and *fast one*. It is 'most commonly heard in the phrase *to pull a swiftie*' (B.P., 1963).—2. As *Swifty*, 'Derisive nickname for slow-moving rating' (Granville): RN coll.: late C.19–20. Cf. *Curly* and *Tiny*, for a bald or a large man respectively.—3. A quick drink: public houses': later C.20. Also *a swift one*. Glover, 1985.

swilge. Weak, black, instant coffee, with just enough sugar to render it tasteless: Westfield College, Univ. of London: early 1960s. A blend of *swig* or *swill* + *bilge*; also dim., *swiggle*. (Huston, 1980.)

swillery. A non-temperance hotel: Aus.: since ca. 1945. (B., 1953.) Cf. S.E. *swill*, to drink deeply and heavily, as swine: since C.16 (*SOD*).

swim. In *go for a swim*, to be capsized, or otherwise bereft of one's canoe: wild-water racers': later C.20. The documentary film *Travelin' Light*, 1980.

swindle. 'A cunning contrivance, a wangle' (Jackson): RAF: since ca. 1930. Esp. in *tea swindle*, 'arrangement by section for co-operative purchase of tea and refreshments' (Emanuel). P.B.: *tea* or *coffee swindle* >, later C.20, widespread, esp. office, etc., coll.

swindle sheet. An expense sheet: perhaps orig. RN humorous, since early C.20; by late 1940s gen. and, by 1970, coll. E.P.; *COD*, 1976.

swine mixture. 'At Bishop Stortford College, between the wars, there was something called "swine mixture", composed of sardines mashed with cocoa and a minute tin of Nestlés milk' (R.S.).

swing, n. A sexual orgy: Anglo-American: since ca. 1955. (Hollander.) Cf. *swing party*, a party at which this is the central activity (Landy, 1971). See **swing**, v., 6.

swing, v. To play 'swing' music: musicians': from 1936. E.g. 'Hear our Orchestra. They will swing for you', in an advertisement, seen in a MS. novel on 1 July 1937.—2. To postpone, put off, defer: RN: since late C.19. Granville, 'Confronted with a pile of paper work, one occasionally "swings it till Monday".' Brock, 1973, notes Granville's phrase as 'the motto of the Torpedo School, HMS *Vernon*, [where it] really meant "switch on and chance it" ' (*DCpp*.): late C.19–early 20.—3. To boast about: Army: since ca. 1930. Esp. in *swinging one's service*. (P-G-R.)—4. (Cf. sense 1.) 'To get the feel of, to comprehend the truth or beauty of anything worth digging; to impart the same truth or beauty to others' ('Basic Beatnik'): Can. jazz-lovers' and musicians': adopted, 1956 or 1957, ex US. Hinton, 1958, defines *swing* as 'to play well in all senses, technically and otherwise, but especially to have the basic feel for jazz rhythms'.—5. Hence, mostly as in 'These times are more swinging'—livelier: since ca. 1961. P.B.: whence the term *the swinging sixties*, applied, in later, gloomier, recession times of 'the sombre seventies' and onwards, nostalgically to the 1960s.—6. V.i.: *swinger*; *swinging*, vbl n. To indulge in group sexual activities: since ca. 1965; one who does this—since ca. 1966; the practice, since ca. 1965. In a way, they were orig. euph.; and always they have tended to be applied to married couples (or those who might just as well be) interchanging partners, 'wife-swapping'. All three terms are Anglo-American, and not indisputably US before Brit.

swing a bag (whence the n. **bag-swinger**). Of a prostitute: to walk the streets: Aus. c.: since ca. 1925. B., 1953.

swing a free leg; (be) swinging a . . . To be free, i.e. unmarried: mostly N. Country. 'Oh, are you married? I thought you were swinging a free leg' (overheard in Liverpool, 1966). A leg, whether male or female, to swing over in sexual intercourse.

swing at (someone), **take a.** To punch (him): mostly children's and teenagers', esp. in Aus.: since ca. 1925. (B.P.) Since mid-C.20, if not earlier, gen. coll. in Brit.; also occ. as v., 'He swung at me'. (P.B.)

swing coconuts at (one). To 'shoot a line', q.v.: Services': later C.20. (Huston, 1982.)

swing it on. To deceive slyly; to impose on; do (one) a bad turn: at first, perhaps mostly Aus. where it = to malinger with, as in *swing it on a sore foot*: military: from 1915. B. & P. (at *swinging the lead*).

swing it till Monday. See **swing**, v., 2.

swing o' the door. 'Publand . . . first round is known as "one", second as "the other half", third as "same again", fourth as "a final", fifth as "one for the road", sixth as "a binder", and seventh as "swing o' the door" ' (*Sunday Dispatch*, 3 July 1938).

swing on the ear; usu. as vbl n., *swinging* . . . , requesting a loan: Army: earlier C.20.

swing round the buoy. To hold on to a soft job: RN: since ca. 1920. Ex RN coll. sense 'to ride at anchor'. P-G-R.

swing the billy. To put the kettle on the fire in order to make a pot of tea: Aus.: since ca. 1920. Niland, 1958.

swing the dolphin. To indulge in masturbation: low: earlier C.20. (Lawrence, about RAF life in the early 1920s.) Here, *dolphin* clearly = penis; cf., e.g., **gallop** (one's) **maggot**.

swing the hambone. 'To use a sextant': RN: 1970s' (Peppitt)—also earlier; Granville, 1962, lists *hambone*, sextant. Ex shape.

swing the hammer. To malinger: Army: earlier C.20. (F. & G.) A var. of:-

swing the lead. To loaf; malinger, evade duty: orig. and mainly Army. By folk-etymology corruption ex earlier synon. nautical *swing the leg*, the issue being confused by the sailors' technical phrase for taking the soundings, *heave* (never *swing*) *the lead*. Actually, this duty, assumed by soldiers to be easy and to admit of loafing, is both arduous and skilful, for its performer is 'bang under the [chief] officer's eye—and usually the captain's and pilot's as well, and in a tight spot of navigation at that' (Dixey, 1934). Whence **lead-swinger**, q.v. A Glasgow var. is *sling the lead*.—2. Hence, loosely, to 'tell the tale'; to boast: from ca. 1919.

swinger. Short for *lead-swinger*, a malingerer: Brit. Army, from ca. 1916; thence, by 1918, to Aus. (B., 1942).—2. An unscheduled extra bus: London busmen's: from ca. 1925. It has been 'swung' on them.—3. 'An additional train coach' (*Railway*): railwaymen's coll. At the end of the train, and esp. on a curve, it tends to swing. Cf. **tail-wag**.—4. A fine and delightful person: Aus.: since ca. 1925. Devanney, 1938.—5. One 'who is modern in his or her thinking' (B.P.): Aus., and some Brit. use: since late 1960s. Ex **swing**, v., 5, but cf.:—6. One 'who engages in group sexual activities (B.P.): since ca. 1972. Ex **swing**, v., 6.—7. See:-

swingers. Self-supporting breasts that swing as the owner walks: Aus.: since ca. 1930.—2. Hence, any female breasts: Aus.: since ca. 1940.

swinging, vbl n. Corresponds to all senses of **swing**, v. Also, the 'swapping' of marital partners in sexual activity: since late 1960s. Thomas, 1976.

swinging, adj. Lively and alert and progressive, with a connotation of success: since ca. 1963. Lejeune, 1967, 'The words "swinging" and "square" are like "progressive" and "reactionary", vague value judgements disguised as descriptions.' Perhaps ex *swinging along*—of, e.g., pedestrians.

swining. A pej.: later C.20. (*Sunday Express* mag., 1 Nov. 1981.) Cf. **cowing**.

swipe. A term of reproach or scornful condemnation: from ca. 1920. *OED* Sup.: 'Cf. *swipes* [bad beer].'—2. A kind of jersey used for games: Marlborough College.—3. An objectionable person: Aus. and NZ: since ca. 1920. Devanney, 1944; Park, 1952.

swish, v. To beat, to cane: Public Schools'. Hence, *swishing*, a caning.—2. See **swish-tail**.

swish, adj. Smart; fashionable: s. > coll. Ex dial. *swish*, the same: cognate with dial. *swash*, gaudy or showy. Also Aus. (Tennant, 1939).—2. (?Hence) effeminate: since the late 1930s and mostly theatrical. 'A male making "pansy" gestures is "swish" ' (Merry).

swish! Oh, is that all?!: ironic:—1923 (Manchon).

swish-tail. 'To check speed by a yaw before landing' (*New Statesman and Nation*, 20 Feb. 1937): ca. 1920-40.

switch, at the. 'Stealing property from a shop and subsequently exchanging it for cash at the same shop' (Powis): c.: later C.20.

switch off! Stop talking!, 'shut up!': s. >, by 1930, coll. (Manchon.) Ex disconnecting a 'phone and/or turning off an electric light.

switched. 'Known in the [watchmaking] trade as a "switched" watch—with trashy works put into a case bought up for the purpose' (Newspaper cutting of 25 Mar. 1944). Cf. **patacca**.

switched on. In the fashion; well-informed; 'with it': since ca. 1960. Ex electric lighting.—2. 'Aroused by music or by sexual overtures. Can be used in female company' (Powis): coll.: later C.20.

swivel-headed. Applied to a man constantly looking around at passing girls: Services': 1950s-60s. (P.B.)

swoffer, swaffer. A pupil either good at his work or, at the least, hard-working; a 'swotter': Public Schools'. Van Greenaway, 1978.

swoman. A station warrant officer (S.W.O.): RAF: since ca. 1925; slightly ob. since ca. 1955. P.B.: usu. *the swoman* (there is only one per station); pron. to rhyme with, and prob. orig. a pun on, snowman.

sword and medals. A ceremonial occasion: RN officers' coll. Hence, adj., as in 'This will be a sword-and-medals "do" '. Granville.

sword swallowing. 'The practice of eating with one's knife' (Baker): Aus. joc.

swosh. Nonsense; drivel: 1924, Galsworthy, 'And anyway sentiment was swosh'. It lived only ca. 1923-5. A blend of *swindle* + *bosh* (or perhaps *tosh*).

swy. See **swi**.

syl-slinger. An actor that mouths his words: theatrical:—1913 (A.H. Dawson); ob. by 1930.

sympathy. A man's intimate caressing of a woman. Ex that indelicate definition of sympathy which arose from Byron's 'A fellow-feeling . . .'

sync (pron. *sink*), n. and v. Synchronization; to synchronize: filmland: since ca. 1931. McCabe, 1937, 'To get them synced' and 'Put them both in sync'. But, since ca. 1940, used in all technical fields. (B..P.) Also *synch*, in *out of synch*, uncoordinated in time [P.B.: or merely unco-ordinated].

synch. See prec.

synthetic. 'Often applied to news which is suspect, or to a person who seems to pretend to be something more than he really is' (H. & P.): Services': since ca. 1935. In the RAF it is often applied to the theory as opposed to the practice of flying. Cf. **pseud**, a later version.

sypho. Syphilis: Aus.: since ca. 1920. B., 1953.

syphon. A British Rail Class 37 locomotive: engine-spotters' and haulage bashers'. (Allison, 1986.) Ex Great Western's Syphon-G refrigerator wagon, with grill-work sides; its code name was 'syphon' (Irwin).

syrup. A wig: r.s., on *syrup of figs*: later C.20. 'A common criminal expression, as wigs are not infrequently used as disguises and are often worn by prostitutes. (Term originates from the name of a commercial laxative)' (Powis); Daniells, 1980, assigns the term to show-business. Cf. **Irish.**

T

T.A. Tel Aviv: coll.: since ca. 1939. (Jeffries, 1958.)

t.b.; loosely **t.-b.** (or **T.-b.**). *Tuberculosis*: coll. (orig. medical).—2. '*Two beauts*' (large and shapely breasts, of course): Aus. joc.: since ca. 1920.

T-bird. A two-seater training aircraft: RAF: 1970s. (P.B., 1977.) Obviously *bird* is a plane. Contrast US *T-bird*, a Thunderbird.

T.D.H. Tall, dark and handsome (applied to a hero): romance-writers'. (Raab, 1986.) Cf. **bodice ripper**.

T.G. Represents 'Thank God!', and is applied to cutlery and crockery left unused at table and therefore not needing to be washed up; hence, *T.G.s*, the articles themselves: domestic: since ca. 1940. (Short, 1978.) Cf. synon. **sunbeam**.—2. See **temporary gentleman**.

T.L.C. *Tender Loving Care*; as in, e.g., 'She should be OK with a bit of TLC': the 'caring' professions': since ca. 1965. (Raab, 1980.) By the early 1980s could be used, joc., by a turkey-farmer with ref. to care of his stock (P.B.).

T.M. A 'tailor-made'—i.e., ready-made—cigarette: Aus.: since ca. 1935.

ta muchly! Thank you very much!: a deliberately sol. elab. of two centuries older *ta!*, usu. for humorous effect. Cf. *ta very much!*, another exaggerated form of *ta!*: 'non-U' coll. (P.B., 1980; Petch, 1969.)

tab, n. A Can*tab* or Cambridge University man: coll.: from ca. 1910. (*SOD*.) But see **Tab-socking**.—2. A customer that, after giving an infinity of trouble, buys precisely nothing: drapers' and hosiers':—1935. Perhaps ex **tab**, v.—3. A cigarette: Northern: from ca. 1920. Also among grafters (*Cheapjack*). Hunter, 1955, has 'tab-end of a Woodbine'.—4. *Tablet*, a drug compressed flat or flattish: medical and pharmaceutical coll.: since early C.20. Hence, used in drugs' c. (Stockley, 1986, 'usually LSD'): US since—1969 (Spears, who notes esp. LSD on a tablet of sugar or saccharine).—5. See **pick up the tab; tabs**.

tab, v.i. (Of a customer) to give much trouble: drapery and kindred trades':—1935. Perhaps ex C.18–early 20 *tab(bie)*, an old maid; perhaps ex *keep (a) tab*. Whence *tabber*, a customer hard to please.—2. To walk, hence *tabbing*, walking, and as in 'that night he set out on a "tab" for Goose Green': Parachute Regt in the Falkland Is. campaign, 1982. (Fox.) See:-

Tab Guards, the. 'In the Household Cavalry the Foot Guards are known as the "Tab Guards", because in the Household Cavalry a man's feet are his "tabs" ' (Carew).

tab-nabs. 'Little delicacies, tab-nabs . . . little hot cakes of cheese and potato or some sort of savoury tart' (Piper, 1974):

nautical, MN and trawlermen's. Peppitt defines them as 'Sweet biscuits or small cakes to go with a cup of tea'.

Tab-socking. A boxing contest against Cambridge University ('the Can*tabs*'): Oxford University boxers': ca. 1895–1914. But cf. Bartlett, 1986: 'We're going to skin the Tabs [at orienteering].'

tab (up) on. See **keep tabs on**.

tabber. See **tab**, v.

tabhole. Ear: an extension of C.19 tailors' synon. *tab*, with which cf. dial. *tab-* or *waste-end* cut from cloth. Callow, 1968.

table. As *the table*, the pitch: cricketers': since ca. 1920. Ex the frequent description of Aus. and S. African pitches being 'as hard and smooth as a billiard table'.—2. In *on the table*, adj. and adv., on the operating table: medical coll.: mid-C.19–20. Brand, 1945.—3. In *under the table*, adj. and adv., applied to 'something given as a bribe' (Sharpe, 1938): low. Cf. the commercial *under the counter* of 1941–8.

tabloid sports. A 'miniature' sports meeting: Army officers' joc. coll.: ca. 1930–70. P-G-R; P.B.

tabs. Feet: military. See **Tab Guards**.—2. See **keep tabs on**.

tacho (pron. *takko*). A tachometer; tachograph: coll.: since ca. 1955. (B.P., 1977.) Cf. **speedo**.

tackety boots. Boots steel-tipped and -heeled: RN: since ca. 1960. (Peppitt.) Reinforced as if with large *tacks*, perhaps influenced by *attack*. P.B.: or merely echoic, of their clatter on board ship? Also railwaymen's: McKenna, 2, has 'Dungarees, a uniform glazed cap, and a tackety pair of boots, the essential apparel for cleaning engines.' In Glasgow *tackety boots* are hob-nailed boots (Munro, 1985).

tackiness. N. ex **tacky**. 'The pictures [in a book about late 1970s Teddy-boys] reveal a world where tackiness and style lock together' (*Time Out*, 23 Nov. 1979).

tackline. A hyphen, as in a hyphenated name: RN signalmen's: since the 1930s. A tackline 'joins' a set of flags.

tacky. Vulgar, unrefined; gen. adj. of contempt: coll.: adopted, ex US, early 1970s. *Time Out*, 9 May 1980, '[The film] is as subtle as a two-bob hairpiece and just as tacky'. See also quot'ns at **feisty** and **naff**, adj., 1. Whence *tackiness, tackily*.

taddler. A sausage: low:—1923 (Manchon). Perhaps *tiddler* corrupted or perverted.

taffy horse. 'A chestnut with a much lighter (often silver) mane and tail' (B., 1942): Aus. sporting and rural. Ex the colour of toffee (dial. *taffy*).

tag. Synon. with **tail**, n., 4.

tag along. To go along; to go. (Spenser, 1934.) Perhaps ex *tag (oneself) on to a person and go along with him*. Cf.:-

tag around with. To frequent; follow about. Sayers, 1933, 'He used to tag around with that de Momerie crowd.'

tag on. To comprehend, or merely to hear what is said; to 'twig' what is going on: coll.: later C.20. Often neg., 'I didn't tag on quite soon enough'. (L.A.; P.B.)

tagger. 'The antics of the graffiti artists [on the London Underground], known in vandal subculture as "taggers" ' (*Daily Telegraph*, 16 Feb. 1988).

taggie, -y. A girl or woman; occ. women in gen.; sometimes 'a bit of taggy': Services'; perhaps mostly RN: mid-C.20. (P.B.)

Taig. A Roman Catholic. (Powis.) Var. of *Teague*, since C.17 a nickname for any Irishman, and hence, by ca. 1900, in Ulster for a Roman Catholic.

tail, n. The penis; more gen., the female pudend: mid-C.14–20: S.E. until C.18, then coll.; in C.19–20, low coll. See **stick a tail on**. Ex this sense, and C.18–19, a harlot, comes Powis' 1977 definition: 'Tail. Sexual intercourse in a general sense: "He loves tail" ', with which cf. *give* (a girl) *tail*, to copulate with (her): raffish: since ca. 1965. Thomas, 1976.—2. A political following in the House of Commons: Parliamentary: late C.19–20.—3. A rear gunner in an aircraft: RAF: since ca. 1938. (P-G-R.) Cf. **tail-end Charlie.**—4. A person who 'tails', follows, another: police, espionage, etc.: since mid-C.20. Ex the v., 2. 'However hard he tried, he couldn't shake his "tail" off'. (P.B.)—5. In *be* [gen. *shall* or *will*] *on* (someone's) *tail*, to look for, to pursue, a person with a view to punishing or severely scolding him.—6. In *get on* (one's) *own tail*, to grow angry—but also, to grow afraid: Aus.: since ca. 1918. B., 1942.

tail, v.i. To coït: C.18–20.—2. V.t., to follow, as a detective a criminal: coll.: late C.19–20. Perhaps ex Aus. sense, *tail* (*up*), (drive or tend) sheep or cattle, for an early occurrence is in Money, 1871 (B., 1941). P.B.: perhaps simply ex 'to stay behind'; cf. the old reproof 'You're all behind—like the cow's tail.'—3. See **tail it.**

tail arse Charlie. A confusion between **arse-end Charlie** and next. Granville, 'Junior ship in a squadron or the last in the line.'

tail-end Charlie. The rear gunner on a bomber: RAF: since ca. 1938. (*Weekly Telegraph*, 25 Jan. 1941; H. & P.) A fellow at the rear.—2. Hence, the rear plane in a formation: since ca. 1939. Jackson. Cf. **arse-end Charlie.**—3. (Ex senses 1 and 2.) A goods guard: railwaymen's: since ca. 1945. *Railway*, 2nd.—4. Hence, loosely, one who brings up the rear of anything, e.g. a group of ramblers, or a sponsored walk, where a 'shepherd' is needed: coll.: since WW2. (P.B.)

tail it, occ. merely *tail*. To die: c. and low s.: since ca. 1920. 'The old dear "tailed" meant the old lady died' (Bournemouth *Evening Echo*, 20 Apr. 1966).

Tail Light Alley. A street frequented by amorous couples using parked cars at night: low Aus.: since late 1940s. With a pun on **tail,** n., 1.

tail puff. See **fluter.**

tail-wag. The motion of the rearmost coach or truck of a train: railwaymen's coll.: late C.19–20. *Railway*.

tail-wagger. A dog: joc. coll. 'The "Tail-Waggers' Club" was started for publicity purposes by a manufacturer of "canine condition-powders" in, I think, the 1920s' (R.S., 1967).—2. 'A "dog" [see **dog**, n., 5 and 6] with added connotations of obsequiousness' (McNeil): Aus. c.: later C.20. (B.P.)

tailgate. To follow on the heels of: c.: later C.20. (Clement, 1977.) An elab. of **tail,** v., 2.

tailie; headie. A player consistently backing tails or heads: Aus. two-up-players': since ca. 1920. Glassop, 1949.

tailor. 'Term of abuse addressed to an unhandy seaman and used by mates in the Merchant Navy' (Granville).—2. See:-

tailor-made, n. and adj. (A) machine-made (cigarette), as opp. a *roll-up*: RN: since ca. 1910. (*Weekly Telegraph*, 13 Sep. 1941.) Fairly gen. by ca. 1920; current in Aus. and NZ since ca. 1925. (Devanney, 1930.) In Aus. sometimes abbr. *tailors* (B., 1942.) Cf. synon. **civvy,** n., 4.

tailor's Tarzan. A man whose bulk is manifestly emphasised by sartorial devices, e.g. padded shoulders: coll.:—1947. Ex the 'beefcake' Tarzans of the films.

tails. A dress-suit, esp. and properly the coat only: coll.

tainted money. Money belonging to a third party; or at least neither to the speaker nor to his 'audience': joc.: since ca. 1930. '*Taint* yours and '*taint* mine.

taipan. (Occ. spelt, and usu. pron., *typan*.) A boss; in later C.20 usu. refers to the heads of the great Far Eastern commercial houses: China Coast Europeans': since earlier C.19. Pidgin, directly ex Cantonese, lit. 'big board', pron. *dye barn*, the boss of, e.g., a shop. (P.B.)

take, n. A cheater at cards; esp. a professional card-sharp: Aus.: since ca. 1930. B., 1953.—2. Esp. a confidence trickster: Aus. c.: since ca. 1935. Ibid.—3. A gross deception; a swindle: Aus.: since ca. 1935. (B.P.) Ex the v., 1.—4. Money received, esp. on one occasion, at, e.g., a theatre, cinema: coll.: adopted, ca. 1960, ex US. (*DCCU*.) By 1975, informal S.E. P.B.: but, e.g., 'the day's take' of a shop, stall, etc., prob. goes back, in commercial coll., several decades.—5. A theft. Cf. 3, and see AUSTRALIAN UNDERWORLD, in Appx.—6. See MOVING-PICTURE SLANG, §6, in Appx.

take, v. To swindle (someone): c.: since ca. 1920. Kersh, 1946.—2. An Army, esp. a Guards', usage perhaps best exemplified by these examples from Grinstead, 1943: 'It'll take you instead of me'—you, not I, will be on duty: 'It takes you for a casual day'—you'll be on this duty for a day, in addition to your usual work; 'Soon be taking us to storm the shores of France'—we'll soon be due to invade France. P.B.: by ca. 1954, at latest, widespread in the Army; I first heard it in Malaya then, among the 15/19 King's Royal Hussars, in such contexts as 'Is it my crash?' (Is it my turn to offer my cigarettes around?)—'It just about takes you!' (Yes, indeed; we thought you were never going to ask!)—3. To accept; to endure: see **take it** below.—4. To overtake: mostly motorists': since ca. 1950.

take! All right; all correct!; certainly!: Can. (B. & P.) P.B.: ?ex cinematography.

take a bend out of. To reduce the high spirits of; to quieten (beasts) by wearying: Aus. (Prichard, 1926.) Cf. **take a stretch . . .**

take a dim view of. To disapprove; think silly, inefficient, objectionable: Services': since ca. 1937. (Finn-Smith, 1942.) Cf. **dim,** 2, and **take a poor view.**

take a dive. To lose a boxing match—for a (considerable) bribe: sporting world: since ca. 1920. On to the canvas.

take a figure out of the air. 'To estimate without details of calculation . . . more from feeling and experience than from detailed calculation' (L.A., 1976): coll.: later C.20. Also *pluck a figure . . .* , giving the impression that the figure so chosen is random.

take a flier. To fall heavily: coll.:—1931 (Lyell). Ex the lit. S.E. sense, to take a flying leap.

take a handful. Open the throttle on a motorcycle: motorcyclists': later C.20. (Dunford.) Operated by a twist-grip.

take a heebee. To lose one's temper, as in 'Divvent tek [don't take] a heebee': 'This originates from "epileptic fit", an alternative being "divvent tek an eppi" ' (Blyth Ridley, 1984): Northumberland teenagers'. But see also **heebie-jeebies.**

take a hike! Go away!: N. Am. since 1930s–40s. (Leech, 1986.)

take a holiday. To jump bail: since ca. 1950—if not a decade earlier. (Petch, 1974.)

take a lunar. To glance, look, keenly; properly upwards: late C.19–20. Galsworthy, 1926, ' "Taking a lunar" at flying grouse.' Ex *take a lunar observation*.

take a (or the) mike out of. To insult or annoy (a person) with a direct or an indirect verbal attack: Cockneys': since mid-C.20. Var. of **take the mick(e)y.**

take a piece out of. To reprimand or reprove (someone): Aus.: since ca. 1925. (B., 1942.) Cf. **tear a strip off.**

take a piss out of. A rare var. of **take the piss**: E.P. may have heard the often slovened response, ' 'ere—you takin' de piss?' (P.B.)

take a poor view is slightly milder than . . . *dim* . . . : Services': since ca. 1938. (Finn-Smith, 1942.)

take a powder. To disappear without paying the rent: Can. s.: adopted, ca. 1940, ex US. In the sense simply of 'to depart', it has had some use in UK, mid-C.20: again, US influence at work. Ex the 'moving' powers of a laxative powder. Cf. *do a fade*. P.B.: also explained as ex women 'going to powder their noses', euph. for a visit to the toilet.

take a punt at. To 'have a go' at, to attempt, something: Aus.: since the late 1940s. O'Grady, 1965.

take a rick view. To view with pleasure, the opp. of *take a dim view*: RAF: WW2. (H.W., 1942.) P.B.: rare; ?misprint for *rich*.

take a screw at. To glance or look at: mostly Aus., but also low. B., 1942.

take a sight. (Gen. as vbl n.) As skipper, to engage a hand without knowing him: nautical (Can.). Bowen.

take a snout. To take offence: low Aus. Niland, 1959.

take a stretch out of (esp. a horse). To exercise: Aus. coll.: late C.19–20. (Prichard, 1929.) To cause to stretch its limbs. Cf. **take a bend** . . .

take a swab! Hold an investigation!—of any sort: Aus.: since ca. 1950. 'Ex swab taken to detect drugs in the saliva of race-horses' (B.P.).

take a toss. To 'fall for' a person: coll.—2. As in Barr, 1935, 'In her set, the word adultery was not often mentioned. One went even off the deep end about somebody; one took a toss, one even dropped a brick; one slid off the rails.' Ex hunting.

take a turn in the barrel or **at the bung-hole.** To sodomise: RN lowerdeck, hence other Services', low. Masked sodomy. P.B.: in later C.20 surviving mainly in the facetious cry, 'whose turn in the barrel?'

take a whirl at. See **birl**, latter part.

take advantage. '(Of a man) seduce a woman, in the convention that women are innocent while men are "carnal" ' (L.A., 1974): euph. or joc.

take and . . . (Gen. imperative.) To go and (do something): lower-class coll. (Manchon.) Ex dial.

take apart. To defeat in physical combat; to reprimand severely: low coll.: since mid-C.20. 'Never tangle with the fuzz—they'll fuckin' take you apart!' (P.B.)

take care of. To eliminate by murdering: prob. orig. c.; also in espionage, where less a euph. than a sardonic meiosis.

take-down, n. A gross deception; a swindle, trivial or grave: coll.—2. Hence, a thief, a cheat: Aus.: from ca. 1910. Doone.—3. The person 'taken down': Aus.: since ca. 1920. B., 1942.—4. A swindler: Aus.: since ca. 1925. B., 1943.

take-down, v.t. To deceive grossly; to swindle: coll. (orig. Aus.): 1895, Melbourne *Argus*, 5 Dec., '[The defendant] accused him of having taken him down, stigmatised him as a thief and a robber.'

take evasive action. To avoid a difficulty or a danger; to depart tactfully, or prudently escape: in Michie, 1941, Mary Monks: 'Fighter pilots' combat reports include "I took evasive action", and the W.A.A.F.s adopted it in describing their adventures on dates. It is heard in powder rooms everywhere now.' Since 1943 applied also to evasion of debt-payment and to non-performance of unpleasant tasks.

take (a person's) eye. To be appreciated by (a person): tailors' coll. *The Tailor and Cutter*, 29 Nov. 1928.

take felt. To be retired or superseded from the Service: Fighting Services': since ca. 1941. H. & P.—2. To be demobilised: mostly RAF: 1945+. Often as vbl n.: *taking felt*. P.B.: i.e., to exchange one's Service cap for a civilian felt hat; perhaps orig. a pun on the legal *take silk*.

take five (or **ten**)! Take five (or ten) minutes off: radio studios' coll.: since ca. 1945. 'The omission of *minutes* for short periods of time is becoming quite common' (B.P.) in Aus., as in 'I'll be back in about ten': coll.: since ca. 1945.

take (a person) **for.** To impose on to the extent of (getting); to 'sting' for: low. *Gilt Kid*, 1936, 'Good kid that Molly even if she had taken him for a oncer' (£1).

take (one) **for a ride.** To take a person in a motor-car and then, at a convenient spot, shoot him dead: US (C.20), anglicised ca. 1930, often loosely (i.e. in order to thrash). (Fellowes, 1934.) Cf. the old US *ride* (one) *on a rail*, to expel forcibly (Thornton).—2. To dupe, to 'con'; to swindle: c. > coll.: since mid-C.20. (P.B.)

take gas. To get caught in the curl of a wave—its curved crest as it breaks—and lose one's board: Aus. (teenage) surfers': since ca. 1961. *Pix*, 28 Sep. 1963.

take in (a statement, a story, etc.) **like a dustbin.** To believe it all: N. Country Grammar Schools': since ca. 1950. (*New Society*, 22 Aug. 1963.)

take in the slack of (one's) **pants.** 'To turn over a new leaf' (Carr, ref. to WW1); in the shortened *take in the slack*, to get a grip of oneself, to 'get organised': mid-C.20: RN lowerdeck. *Heart*, 1962.

take it. To accept, endure, punishment courageously or cheerfully: boxing: since ca. 1933. Adopted from US.—2. Hence, since 1939: to endure trial and adversity without whining or cowardice.

take it green. (Of a boat) to take water: oarsmen's. *Daily Telegraph*, 4 Apr. 1938, 'The Oxford boat took it "green" and was half full of water.' Surface water is green. P.B.: a borrowing from older nautical, deep-sea term, applied to a ship ploughing through high seas; also *ship it green*.

take it in the neck and **punch the breeze.** Of hoboes sitting on a bar of a truck that supports the (railway) carriage, 'If you sit . . . facing ahead, that's called "punching the breeze". If you sit . . . looking back, it's called "taking it in the neck" ' (Niven, 1927): Can. hoboes': late C.19–20.

take it off your back! Don't worry about it!: RN lowerdeck. Granville, 'borrowed from dock lumpers' (stevedores working at a fish dock).

take it on. (Of an aircraft) to climb rapidly: RAF: since ca. 1930. H. & P.

take it on the chin. To take misfortune, distress or disappointment, as unflinchingly as possible, to 'take it like a man': coll.: since ca. 1930. Ex boxing.

take it on (one's) **toes.** To run away; escape: c.: later C.20. (*Time Out*, 27 June 1980.) Cf. synon. **have it on** (one's) **dancers.**

take it out. 'To undergo imprisonment in lieu of a fine' (Dennis): low (?c.) Aus.

take it out in trade. To have sexual intercourse with the girl one entertains: Can.: since ca. 1946. Joc.

take (something) **lying down.** To submit tamely: coll. Either ex boxing or ex cowed dogs.—2. Esp., a feminine coll. for submitting to sexual intercourse—not necessarily passively: since the late 1940s; commoner in the 1950s than in the 1960s.

take man. See AUSTRALIAN UNDERWORLD, in Appx.

take off. To 'get going', to start, to depart, as in 'Let's take off!' or 'He took off at a rate of knots': s. > coll.: since late 1940s. In Aus. and Can., a forcible order to depart, 'take off!' (B.P.; Leech). Ex aircraft *taking off*; cf.:-

take-off any minute now!, he'll. He's very angry—likely to 'hit the ceiling'; but more often, 'He's in a flap' (exceedingly excited): RAF c.p.: 1938+. (L.A.)

take-on, n. A fight, esp. with fists; a contest: Aus.: since ca. 1920. (B., 1942.) Ex v., 3.

take on, v. To engage (a person, or army) in a fight, a battle: coll. Dennis.—2. As v.i., to re-engage, in the Services, for a further period, esp. for a pension; e.g. 'Are you going to take on again after you've done your twelve [years]?': orig. RN, thence to Army and RAF: since ca. 1925. Granville.—3. See **sort out; take on with.**

take on board. To comprehend, as in 'At last he took on board that I was speaking seriously': since ca. 1970. (R.S., 1974.) Orig. nautical—to accept as passenger or cargo?—2. To adopt an idea, assume responsibility for, as in (Chairman speaking) 'We've had a look at this proposal and, suffice it to say, we've agreed to take it on board': vogue phrase in committees, etc.: 1980s. (P.B.)

take on with. To take up with (a woman): proletarian coll.:—1923 (Manchon). Ex dial.

take one. To be open to bribery, to accept bribes: c., and police s. Newman, 1970.

take out. To kill: Services', police: since ca. 1970. (Hawke; Hunter, 1977.) Copied from one of the many disgustingly clinical euphs. invented by the US military to whitewash the Vietnam War. (P.B.)

take (one)self in hand. (Of a man) to masturbate: nautical > gen.:—1953. A low pun.

take sights. To have a look, to glance; v.t. with *of*: low. *Cheapjack*, 1934.

take (one's) snake for a gallop. To urinate: RAF joc.: ca. 1925–45. Cf synon. *water one's nag.*

take tea with. To 'act with covert impertinence towards someone (usually someone in authority), or to take advantage of someone; to outwit a clever person (not used in respect of "mugs")' (Powis): c.: later C.20.

take the bent stick. 'Descriptive of a woman who, getting past the marrying age and having missed her chance with the man she wanted, decides to marry the elderly and faithful admirer who has been hanging around so long' (Alan Smith, 1939): earlier C.20.

take the can back. To be reprimanded; see **carry the can (back)**: nautical and military: late C.19–20. (Bowen.) Perhaps ex illicit usage of its contents.—2. To be held responsible for a mishap: Services', railwaymen's: from ca. 1919. *Daily Herald*, 11 Aug. 1936.—3. To be imposed on: road-transport workers': from ca. 1925. Ibid.

take the cherry. See **cherry**, 5.

take the dairy off. To take the best of—or off—something. Ex the late C.19–20 coll. sense 'take the cream off the milk'.

take the (or a) day off to carry bricks. To take a working holiday: NZ: later C.20. (Davies, 1974.)

take the drop. To accept a bribe: c. >, by 1930, taxi-drivers', as in Hodge, 1939. See **drop**, n., 2–4.

take the heat off. To relieve the pressure on someone, as in 'The aim is that the escorts take the heat off the bombers by engaging the CAP [combat air patrol] fighters' (*Phantom*): coll.: later C.20. Opp. the earlier *put the heat on*, to menace, threaten.

take the knock on. See **knocker**, 4.

take the mick(e)y; . . . Mike. Variants, via r.s., on *Mickey*, or *Mike Bliss*, of **take the piss**, and used in exactly the same way: since ca. 1950 (*Mickey*); *Mike* perhaps a little earlier. *Mickey* is by far the commoner in gen. use; the phrase may be elab., as in 'Are you by any chance extracting the Michael?'

take the pen. To sign for a voyage as a seaman: MN: 'I have never enjoyed this ceremony of "taking the pen" for I do not see the need of special laws to float by' (Piper, 1974).

take the piss out of. To pull someone's leg: low.—2. More commonly, to jeer at, deride: id. Ex the idea of deflation, as a bladder, of conceit (Franklyn). Variants: **take a piss out of**, q.v.; and, among the literary, *pass* (someone) *the catheter*. Also absolutely, as in the victim's 'Are you trying to take the piss? Because if you are . . . !', and in Behan, 1958, ' "Don't mind me, Kid," said Tubby. "I just can't help taking the piss." ' Hunter, 1984, uses the euph. *take the juice.* See also **take the mick(e)y**, and cf. **pull (one's) pisser.**

take the stripes out. To remove, with acid, the crossing on a cheque: c.:—1933 (Leach).

take the weight off (one's) feet, mostly in the imperative. To sit down; properly, to put one's feet up: joc.: since ca. 1945.

take (one) to the cleaners. To swindle (someone) thoroughly, esp. in a 'con game' or at gambling: adopted, ca. 1945, ex US. (W. & F.) A late Brit. example, *Observer*, 7 Dec. 1975. Ex the lit. S.E. sense.

take to the hills. 'To remove oneself from the danger zone' (Granville, 1969): adopted, ca. 1930, ex American films, notably 'Westerns'. P.B.: sometimes uttered as a joc. exhortation in the face of trivial peril.

take too much on (one's) plate. To act presumptuously; to 'bite off more than one can chew'; to overload oneself with work or responsibilities—even girl/boy friends: since ca. 1939. Cf., e.g., 'he's got enough in his plate already, as it is.'

take water. To leave (esp. from a bar, a hotel) penniless after a 'spree': Aus. B., 1942.

taken to see the cups. Up before the superintendent: police: since ca. 1930. (*Free-Lance Writer*, April 1948.) The cups that, won by the division, are displayed in the superintendent's room.

talc. In (*be*) *on the talc*, to be informed of strategy or tactics: Army officers': 1941+. Maps were protected with a talc covering. R.S. explains: 'Military maps were (and are) not so much "protected" with a talc covering as given a convenient (talc) overlay on which dispositions, situations, movements, etc., can be quickly marked with coloured chinograph pencils, and just as quickly erased and amended at need. This saves time and makes for clarity—much more important than merely economising maps.' Ex *put in the picture.*

Tale of Two Cities. Breasts (the two female): r.s., on *titties.* Often spoonerised as *Sale of Two Titties.* (Franklyn.) Cf. the, in later C.20 much commoner, synon. **Bristols.**

talent, the. Backers of horses as opp. the bookmakers: sporting coll. >, ca. 1910, j.: from the early 1880s. Clever because they make a horse a favourite. In Aus., however, it = the bookmakers' ring, bookmakers collectively. B., 1942.—2. The underworld in general: Aus. low: since ca. 1910. Baker.—3. The girls, as in 'Let's look into the Pally and see what the talent's like': raffish: since ca. 1930. P.B.: this is, in Brit. and esp. in the Services, the predominant sense. Often *the local talent*, the available girls.

Taliano. An Italian: mostly lower classes', esp. London. Ex It. *Italiano. Muvver* spells it phonetically, *Taliarner.*

talk. To talk about, discuss: late C.14–20: S.E. until ca. 1850, then coll. P.B.: after decades of disuse, this idiom re-emerged in the early 1980s, perhaps via US, and usu. concerning money, as in 'Spends enormous sums in Bond Street. And I'm talking money . . . He has some Persian illuminated manuscripts that would make you drool' (Moody, 1984); and, 'We're not talking hundreds and thousands here, Squire – we're talking telephone numbers [q.v.]'.

talk BBC. To talk politely, to speak in a clear, precise and cultured manner: coll.: since ca. 1930. Gray, 1946.

talk funny. To speak oddly or strangely: Aus.: since ca. 1920. Applied, e.g., to any speech, even English, other than their own. P.B.: but the intensely parochial attitude implied is by no means confined to Aus.; the phrase has been and is very gen. in Brit., prob. throughout C.20, if not earlier.

talk into the big white telephone. To vomit, esp. drunkenly: 'Heard recently from a Loughborough University student' (P.J. Emrys Jones, 1978). Poss. a nonce-usage, or ephemeral parochialism, but it has a certain coarse poetry (P.B.).

talk it under. 'To get rid of some problem, generally political, by plausible argument' (Petch, 1969): coll.: since ca. 1960. A confusion of '*talk* (someone) *down*' and 'sweep *under* the carpet'? P.B.: or to drown in a meaningless sea of words?

talk last commission. To tend to talk glowingly of one's preceding ship: RN officers'. Granville.

talk like the back of a cigarette card. To speak pseudo-learnedly or with an unusual syntax: coll.: lower classes': 1930s.

talk Miss Nancy. To talk very politely: since ca. 1910. (Riley, 1916.) With the implication that such politeness is effeminate.

talk of the devil! Usu. as an ungracious, though not necessarily unfriendly, greeting: C.20 shortening of the coll. proverb, current since C.17, *talk of the devil and you'll see his horns* or *tail*, applied to a person who, being spoken of, unexpectedly appears.

talk off the top of (one's) **head.** To speak extempore, with truth of statement not guaranteed, references unchecked: coll.: later C.20. Cf. **off the cuff.** (P.B.)

talk proper. To speak Standard Received English: coll.; usu. joc. as a deliberate sol. Var. *speak proper*; cf. **talk funny.** (P.B.)

talk through (one's) **fly-buttons.** 'To talk *cock*, to argue from a base of fancy ideas or false claims.—2. To talk randy' (L.A., 1969).

talk through (the back of) one's) **neck.** To talk extravagantly, catachrestically: 1904 (*OED* Sup.).—2. Hence, to talk nonsense: from ca. 1920. Both senses had, by 1930, > coll. Occ. *talk out of the back* . . .

talk to. To discuss as being likely to reach (a certain figure or price): Stock Exchange coll.: from ca. 1920. 'Securitas', *Time and Tide*, 22 Sep. 1934, 'Local loans are up to the new high level (post-war) of $93\frac{11}{16}$, and are being talked to 100.'

talk turkey. To talk business; to talk sense: Can. (ex US) coll.: since ca. 1890; adopted, as coll., in England ca. 1930. Kersh, 1938. 'Just for the moment, let's talk turkey.' Also, since ca. 1935, Aus. (B., 1942). The substantial and succulent part of a (Christmas) dinner.

talk up. To advertise by word of mouth, perhaps indirectly; to bring to notice by repetitious suggestion rather than by **hype**, q.v.: coll. 'For the past six months the "talking up" of new titles . . . has been dominated by one book' (*Bookseller*, 6 May 1988).

talk wet. To speak sentimentally, foolishly; talk 'soft': from ca. 1910. ('Taffrail'.) See **wet**, adj., 1.

talkee-talkee. Serious conversation or discussion on or of Service matters; a conference: RN. Ex pidgin English. (P-G-R.) Cf.:–

talkies. An audience with a VIP, a conversation among VIPs, at a state function, mostly in India—until the end of 'the Raj'. Allen, 1977.—2. (Occ., but rare, in sing.) A moving picture with words: 1928 (*SOD*): coll. >, by 1935, S.E. On **movie**, q.v.

talking. See **talk**.

talking head. A person appearing on TV, who merely talks to the audience, or at an audience through discussion with others in the studio, in an attempt to inform rather than to entertain; therefore, perhaps, boring to those conditioned to simply being amused by TV: media world: since late 1970s. Hence, it may be loosely applied to, e.g., political party spokesmen. ' "Talking heads" seem to be a pervasive and popular form of television . . .' (Dyer, 1978). Cf. **noddy**, 3.

talking-Tommy (or **-tommy**). A comb-and-paper, serving as a musical instrument: secondary schools'. Poole, 1935.

talky. See **talkies**, 2.

talky-talk. Idle or pointless or trivial talk: coll. *OED* Sup., 1933.

tall poppy. A very important person, such as a senior Public Servant (English: Civil Servant): Aus.: since early 1930s. Ex a savage threat made in the early 1930s by, and during the *régime* of, Mr J. Lang: taxation that would have 'cut off the heads of the tall poppies'. (B.P.)

tall-water man. A blue-water (or deep-sea) seaman: nautical coll. Bowen.

tallahwah. 'Decent, straightforward and honourable. Complimentary adj. (West Indian)' (Powis, 1977).

tallie. A tall story: Aus.: since ca. 1930. B., 1953.

tally. A name: nautical. (*Musings*, 1912.) Ex *tally*, a mark, label, or tab.—2. Hence, *cap tally*, name of ship on cap ribbon: RN coll.:–

tally-band. WRNS term for cap ribbon (or **tally**, 2): later C.20. 'The use of this term by the girls used to make the sailors fall about [with laughter]' (Wood, 1977).

taloia. *T*here's *a l*ot *of* it *about*: friends' or even doctor's diagnosis of unspecific minor sickness: mostly middle-class coll.: mid-C.20. (Raab.)

tampax. Filter-tipped cigarette(s): Services' and low: since ca. 1955. Ex the trade-name of a well-known brand of women's sanitary tampons. (P.B.)

tampi. Marijuana: prisoners' c. (and, presumably, drugs world): later C.20. Home Office.

tan; tan (one's) **hide.** To beat severely; to thrash: resp. s., mid-C.19–20 (H., 1859); and coll., mid-C.17–20. In C.20, of a quite mild beating: preparatory schools'.—2. Hence, to overwork (a means of livelihood): grafters'. *Cheapjack*, 1934.

tan-track. Rectum: proletarian: late C.19–20.

tangi, n. and v. *Tangi*, a Maori word for 'a tribal gathering at a funeral; a dirge': 'Now very commonly adopted here [NZ] by the upper classes, especially as an equivalent of the outmoded "beano". E.g., Harold and I were on the tangi (or were tangi-ing) last night; or there is a big tangi on tonight' (Alexander, 1939); and earlier in Devanney's novels.—2. In *holding a tangi*, faced with a problem or a set-back: NZ. (B., 1941.) Cf. 1.

tangle foot. Whisky: US (—1860), partly anglicised ca. 1900. Ex effect. P.B.: some later use, mostly joc., for other strong drinks, e.g., W. Country cider. In Aus., beer or bad liquor (B., 1942).

tangle, or **get tangled**, **in the soup.** To become lost in a fog: RAF: since 1939. Berrey (the former).

tangle with. To become involved in a fight with; to get into trouble with: coll.: since mid-C.20. Also as in 'Oh, he got tangled with the police over something fairly trivial.' (P.B.)

tank, n. A wet canteen: Army: late C.19–early 20. (F. & G.) In later C.20, also police: 'The Tank was the ground-floor bar, used by the police and civilian personnel who worked in the building' (Newman, 1977). Cf. *on the tank*, engaged in beer-drinking, often with implications of 'heavy drinking': id.: since ca. 1890. (*The Regiment*, 1900.) The early use, almost simultaneous in Brit. and US, could have risen from joint service—e.g. in the Peking expedition of 1900, with Americans adopting it from Britons. Cf. the Aus. var., since ca. 1920, *on a tank* (Baker), and v. **tank up**. Also cognate is:—2. A pint of beer: Aus. (Baker.) Short for *tankard*.—3. An old, battered whore: Cockneys': from 1918 or 1919. Ex the appearance of tanks derelict on sodden plains. See **Jodrell Bank**.—4. A safe: NZ c.:—1932—5. A hammock: R Aus. N: WW2 (?and before). B., 1943.—6. In *do* one's *tank*, to become extremely annoyed: Services', prisons', etc.: since mid-1940s. (*Daily Telegraph*, 4 June 1958, 'Bacon Bonces . . .') Cf. **do** (one's) **crunch**, **nut**, etc.

tank, v. To drink, a shortening of **tank up**; usu. as a continuous activity, e.g., 'He went tanking steadily on all through the evening': mostly Services': since mid-C.20. (P.B.)—2. To travel at high speed, esp. in a motor vehicle, as in 'tanking down (*or* along) the motorway at a fair old rate of knots': later C.20.

tank-busting. Shooting up tanks, whether from the air or with field anti-tank guns: RAF and Army coll.: 1940+.

tank-slapper. Speed wobble on a motorcycle: 'It causes the handlebars to flail against the fuel tank sides, often cutting the rider's thumbs' (Dunford): motorcyclists': since mid-C.20.

tank up. To drink much liquor: adopted, ex US, ca. 1916, esp. in Army. (*OED* Sup.; F. & G.) Cf. **tank**, v., and **tanked**.

tanked. Tipsy: from early 1917. Prob. ex **tank**, n., 1; perhaps suggested by **canned**, q.v.

tanker wanker. 'Someone who flies in air-to-air refuellers' (Wilson, 1979): RAF: later 1970s. The airborne *tanker* would naturally attract the rhyming **wanker**, 2. (P.B.)

tanking. A severe physical, hence occ. fig. mental, assault; usu. *a proper* or *real* or *right tanking*: Army: since ca. 1950, at latest. Ex dial. *tank*, a blow.

tankman. A safe-breaker: Aus. c.: since ca. 1935. (Grindley, 1977.) Ex **tank**, n, 4. Cf. **peter-man**.

Tanks. As *the Tanks*, coll. term for the Royal Tank Regiment, formed in 1917 and already operating in the latter half of that year.

tanky. The navigator's assistant: RN: from ca. 1912. (Bowen.) Because responsible for the fresh water. Cf.:—2. A seaman that helps the storekeeper (*Jack Dusty*) to handle his stores equipment: RN: since ca. 1950. (P-G-R.) 'Now used almost exclusively for the seaman rating who helps the Supply Dept with daily issues and the rum. The rating responsible for the fresh-water supply is always from the engine-room branch, and is alluded to as the *fresh-water tanky*' (Granville, 1962).—3. A member of the Royal Armoured Corps, esp. a man of the Royal Tank Regiment: Army: WW2 and since. Cf. **Tanks.**—4. A UK Communist Party pej. term for a 'hard-liner' who supported the entry of Soviet tanks into Czechoslovakia in 1968. R. Falber, who used the word in a letter to *7 Days*, 18 June 1988: 'Intolerance and contempt for others' opinions [are] the hallmark of the "tankies".' (Via Raab.)

tanner organs. Scallops: trawlermen's. Butcher, 1980.

tap. In *on tap*, 'Available at a moment's notice' (H. & P.): much used by the Fighting Services in 1939–45. 'All modern conveniences, including h. and c.' or as R.C. adds, 1976, 'Perhaps rather from beer, a hardly less essential convenience.'—2. In *on the tap*, begging for money: c.: 1933 (Leach). Cf.:-

tap (a person) **for.** To ask (him) for (money). Among ships' stewards, used absolutely (i.e. *tap*, v.i.), it has the nuance 'to suggest or imply that one would not refuse a tip' (Marlow, 1937).

tap in. 'R.A.F. slang in France [1939–40] for "have a good time" ' (Monks, 1940). Perhaps 'to *tap* on the door, go right *in*, and make oneself at home'. P.B.: or ex *tap in* to conversation on telephone or radio.

tap the boards. To be brought before the Officer Commanding: Army: ca. 1925–50. Ex smart steps on the barrack-room floor. (P-G-R.) P.B.: ?and influenced by the variety stage, e.g. tap-dancing.

tap up. Synon with *date*, and **chat up**, v., 2: RN, and hence Army and RAF: since mid-C.20. P.B.: the Army was using the term by 1900. Cf.:—2. To approach (someone) in order to solicit his help, as 'Nip round [to] the QM's stores and tap him up for a couple of sheets': Army: id. A blend of **chat up**, v., 2, and **tap for.** (P.B.)

tape off. To set in order, put in place, prepare: Aus.: since ca. 1920. (B., 1942.) Ex **taped.**—2. To reprimand: Aus.: since ca. 1925. (Baker.) To measure rightly: reduce to the correct size.

tape-worm. An airman expecting—or, at the least, hoping and working for—promotion: RAF: since ca. 1935. Cf. **tapes.**—2. 'The Chief Officer; sometimes a Principal Officer (because of the amount of braid sewn on coat and trousers)' (Tempest): prisons': mid-C.20.

taped, be; gen. have or **have got** (one) **taped.** In these phrases, *taped* = sized-up; detected; so seen-through as to be rendered incapable of harm, mischief, etc.: orig. (1916), military >, 1920, gen. (B. & P.; Lyell.) Ex *tape*, to measure (something) with a tape, with esp. ref. to the Engineer-laid tapes along which the Infantry lay waiting for the signal to attack when there was no trench or sunken road convenient as a jumping-off place.—2. Hence, from ca. 1920, *taped* often = arranged, or settled, as in Knox, 1933, 'Let's get the whole thing taped.' Also *taped up* (Cole, 1927).

tapes. Rank-stripes: Army and RAF coll. (H. & P.) Hence, *get one's tapes*, to be promoted to corporal; *get one's third tape*, to be promoted from corporal to sergeant; *swing one's tapes*, 'to overdo one's N.C.O. authority' (L.A.).—2. See **run the tapes.**

tapioca. As in 'A day spent in a warm studio with a perfumed houri or two is bound to . . . send you home with a touch of the tapioca, I shouldn't wonder' (Daniells, 1980): low.

tapped. Eccentric; slightly mad: military: earlier C.20. (B. & P.) Ex Hindustani *tap*, fever, taken as brain fever, prob.

influenced by synon. *cracked* and S.E. *touched*. Cf. earlier *tap*, sunstroke. See also **doolally.**

tapper. A beggar: Glasgow (—1934); tramps' c. (—1936: Gape). Ex *tap for*: cf.:—2. A habitual borrower: low coll.: earlier C.20. Cf. 'although he associated with the rest of the gang, [he] never took part in stealing or pickpocketing . . . He was a "tapper", that is he expected the gang to give him money like most of the street bookies did' (Samuel, 1981).— 3. A hard-hitting batsman: cricketers'. Gordon, 1939.—4. 'A man who gives you false or useless information in return for a small loan' (Gosling, 1959): police s.: since ca. 1930.—5. A 'carriage and wagon examiner' (*Railway*, 2nd): railwaymen's coll. P.B.: short for *wheel-tapper*.

tappers. Overtime, as in, e.g., 'five hours' tappers': Post Office employees'. (L.A., 1967.)

tapping. Asking for, or implying readiness to accept, a tip: ships' stewards'. See **tap for,** and cf. earlier C.20 Glasgow meaning of straightforward begging.

taps. 'The controls and gadgets of a modern aircraft' (H. & P.): RAF: since ca. 1936. In *open the taps*, the sense is 'to open the throttle': since ca. 1940, usu. *hit the taps*. The term 'probably originated in the old Bristol Fighter, where there were a multitude of taps in the petrol system that had to be manipulated to keep the feed system clear of air'—a certain RAF officer, telling me (1949) of a collective opinion formed, appropriately in an RAF bar, by a number of officers discussing the entry *taps* in P-G-R.

tar. Opium or morphine: drugs c. (Stockley, 1986.) US since −1936 (Spears).

tar-sprayer. See **Bescot** . . .

tara. See **tarrer.**

Taranaki gate. 'One made from several strands of barbed wire, strengthened with two or three saplings set in vertically' (Griffiths, 1970): NZ rural. Cf.:-

Taranaki top-dressing. Cattle dung: NZ (mostly South Island). (Alexander, 1939.) Taranaki, in the middle and western North Island, is famous for its dairy cattle. 'Among the sheep-farming communities, Taranaki is usually referred to as a land of cows and cow cockies up to their knees in mud and cow dung' (Ibid.).

tararabit (accent on 2nd syllable, *ra*). Au revoir!: low coll.: later C.20, esp. 1970s. Liverpudlian elab. of *ta-ta*, slovened to *tarrah*: I suspect the comedian Ken Dodd as the agent of its popularity and spread.

target for tonight, (one's). One's girl friend: RAF (esp. aircrews'): 1939+. Jackson.

tarp or **Tarp.** An ecclesiastical (Anglican) c.p., of ca. 1920 onwards, 'used of those ministrants who take the Ablutions immediately after the Communion instead of after the Blessing' (Roberts, 1933). I.e. 'take Ablutions in right place'.—2. Tarpaulin: late C.19–20.

tarrer or **tara.** The Regimental Sergeant-Major: Army: esp. common in early 1950s; ob. by ca. 1960. Prob. ex N. Country pron. *t'RSM*. Spelling is arbitrary; I have never seen it written. (P.B.)

tarry rope. 'A woman or girl who frequents the Sydney waterfront to consort with sailors' (B., 1942): Aus. nautical and Sydney low.

tart. The young favourite of one of the older boys; not necessarily a catamite: Scottish Public Schools'. (Miller, 1935.) Whence *tarting*, this practice.

tart up. To dress up smartly; in later C.20, with the implication of tastelessness or tawdriness. See:-

tarted(-)up. Dressed like a *tart*, later C.19–20 s. for a 'fast' woman or a prostitute; very smartly (and brightly) dressed: since early 1920s. Buckley, 1947.—2. The term has, since ca. 1960, been applied, usu. in a derogatory way, to things, e.g., a public house or a private residence, meretriciously dressed up or presented. Hence, since ca. 1970, *untarted*, restored to original simplicity and lack of pretentiousness (L.A.); or, of course, never *tarted-up* in the first place. (P.B.) Cf. **tarty.**

tarting. See **tart.**

tart's delight. A certain frilly, fussy, looped-up way of hanging lace net curtains at windows: middle-class contemptuous: later C.20. (P.B.)

tarty. Of or like a prostitute (see **tarted-up**): coll.: since ca. 1920. Wilson, 1949.—2. (Of a girl) sexy: coll.: since ca. 1930. Laski, 1944.

Tas. Tasmania: Aus. coll. *Aus. Pocket Oxford Dict.*

tash. Moustache: Services': since ca. 1920. (H. & P.) Also *tache.*

tassie. An intaglio: antique dealers'. Gash, 1977.

taste. '(A taste of.) Taking a small amount of a drug and only just feeling it' (Home Office): drugs world: later C.20.

tasty bit of pastry. A girl with a shapely body eminently beddable: since late 1940s. Often simply *tasty pastry.* (L.A., 1976.)

Tasty Blues, the. The Life Guards' nickname for the Royal Horse Guards (the Blues), who retaliated with *Ticky Tins*: both tasty and ticky meant the same, 'insect-ridden, dirty, verminous, scruffy, unhygienic, unwashed and unshaved, coated with verdigris' (Carew): earlier C.20. A case of 'pot and kettle'—and quite unjustified.

Taswegian. A Tasmanian seaman: R Aus. N: since ca. 1930. (B., 1943.) Also someone born in *Tasmania*: Aus. joc. *Aus. Pocket Oxford Dict.* A blend of Tasmanian and e.g. Glaswegian.

tat. Mediocre (or worse) art or craft, e.g., painting or pottery: upper- and middle-class: since the 1920s. (E.P.; P..B.) Cf.:—2. 'Ecclesiastical paraphernalia, *objets religieux*, fondness of [sic] same' (Towler, 1979): theological colleges': 1960s. Hence, adj. *tatty.* (P.B.) See also **tatt**, and **tatty.**

tata. A silly person: since ca. 1920. An adult of the kind that would use such baby-talk as 'go (for) a *ta-ta*' or walk. (Shaw.)

Tate and Lyle. The Royal Arms badge worn on lower sleeve by a warrant Officer, first class: Army: since (?)ca. 1950. Ex the Royal Arms indicating 'By appointment' on the packets of Tate & Lyle sugar products, esp. the golden syrup tins. Cf. synon. **fighting cats** or **dogs**. (P.B.)—2. A smile: r.s. East, 1989.

tatered. 'Fed up with having no luck or with unproductive patrols': RAF: 1939+. H. & P.; Partridge, 1945, 'A potato, though—like the patrol—exceedingly useful, can become monotonous.'

taters. Shortening of **taters** or **taties** or **potatoes in the mould**, r.s. for cold, adj: much more frequent than the full version in later C.20.

tatie oggy. A Cornish pasty: RN. (*Weekly Telegraph*, Nov. 1942.) Prob. the orig., or perhaps merely a rationalised var., of *tiddey* or *tiddy oggy. Tatie*, dial. potato.

tatt. Odds and ends of (dress or furnishing) material: mostly theatrical: since ca. 1920. 'She turned out a whole mass of the old tatt . . . to see what there was in the way of material. She found that old pair [of gloves] over there and a lot of old embroidery, silks and gold wire and some fake jewellery that was near enough for the props' (Marsh, 1967). Cf. **tat.**

tattie (or **-y**) **-bye!** A form of farewell 'inherited . . . from Ken Dodd's dad' (Rees, 1980) and popularised by the Liverpool comedian: in widespread use by mid-1970s. Presumably a conflation of *ta-ta* and *bye-bye.* Cf. **tararabit**, itself sometimes shortened to *t'ra.* (P.B.)

Tatts. Tattersall's horse-market in London: coll.: mid-C.19–20, but, since ca. 1940, a mere nostalgic memory. Not only among riders to hounds and the country gentry, but among all Londoners.—2. Tattersall's lottery, Melbourne: Aus. coll. ' "Take a ticket in Tatts": to chance. "Fair as Tatts": absolutely fair' (B., 1942). 'In Sydney, *Tatts* is more likely to refer to Tattersall's Club, where the "big-time punters" settle their debts on settling day' (B.P.).

tatty. 'Fussy, especially as applied to clothes and decoration' (Mortimer, 1937).—2. Inferior; cheap: Aus.: since ca. 1920. (B., 1942.) Ex C.19 *tat*, an old rag.—3. (Of persons) hopeless, or helpless, at something or other: certain Public

Schools': since ca. 1925.—4. Of things, e.g. goods in a shop: trifling, insignificant: since ca. 1945.—5. Hence, since late 1940s, unkempt, dishevelled; of things, dilapidated, obviously neglected, as of a building, a vehicle, a garment. (P.B.)

tatty-bye! See **tattie-bye!**

taut. A favourite RN adj. 'In "a taut drop of skin" of shapely female, the "taut" as applied to development of breasts and buttocks is a classic'—as I'm assured by a notably well-informed Naval correspondent.

taut ship. 'One run by a taut-handed captain' (Granville): RN. I.e., highly efficient and with no disciplinary problems.

tax. See **taxing.**

taxi, n.; occ. **taxy**, rare after 1909. Abbr. *taxi-meter*: 1907 (*OED*): coll. and ob.—2. Abbr. *taxi-cab*: 1907 (Ibid.): coll. >, ca. 1933, S.E. (Late in 1934, the latter sense was received into standard Fr.)—3. An aircraft that can carry a small number of passengers: RAF: since ca. 1940. (Jackson.) P.B.: cf. *taxiplane*, recorded by *SOD* for 1920, as a light aircraft for hire.

taxi, v. To go by taxi-cab: coll.: from ca. 1915. Ex **taxi**, n., 2. P.B.: soon ob., superseded by S.E. use of taxi, applied to aircraft moving under their own power on the ground.

taxi-cabs. Body-lice: low r.s., on *crabs*: fringe of underworld: since ca. 1910. (Norman, 1959.) Cf. synon. **Sandy McNabs.**

taxi († **taxy**)**-driver.** A driver of a taxi-cab: coll. (1907) >, ca. 1934, S.E. (*OED*.) Ex **taxi**, n., 2.—2. A staff pilot at a navigation school: RAF: since ca. 1940. H. & P.—3. 'A rating "not dressed as seaman"; not however, the petty officers. Men of the Supply and Secretariat branch, also engine-room artificers and sick-berth attendants . . . wear suits of civilian cut, with black buttons and a peaked-cap, like a taxi-driver's, with a red badge' (Granville): RN.

taxi-rank. To masturbate: r.s., on *wank*: homosexuals': current ca. 1970. Cf. synon. **Barclay's Bank.**

taxing. 'In Borstals, the collecting of "protection money" by threatening weaker prisoners with violence' (Green, 1984). ?Ex, or hence:—2. 'Lone individuals being picked off by juvenile hoods working in hit squads of two or three. The target? A kid's clothes . . . some of the tracksuits worn by the kids cost £60 or more' (*New Society*, 19 Apr. 1984); 'This is known as "taxing" in my area of London [Harrow], and is a common problem for "Casuals" [q.v.]' (Ibid., follow-up letter, 3 May 1984). Term noted earlier in *You*, 4 Dec. 1983.

taz. A beard: Cockneys'.—2. An immature moustache; youthful down, wherever growing: mostly Cockneys': since ca. 1920. (L.A.) Ex *tache.*

tazz. To go, as in 'the girl had . . . tazzed off' (Mitchell, 1930) = gone away: (?)mainly feminine. I have also heard, late 1970s, the var. *tazzie*, 'Let's just tazzie over to your place'. Perhaps a 'perversion' of C.19–20 nursery *go tatis*, or *ta-tas*, to go for a little walk. (P.B.)

tea. Marijuana: drug addicts': adopted, ca. 1945, ex US. US since—1930 (Spears, who explains, 'tea-leaves and marijuana leaves look much alike'). Cf. **tea-head.**—2. In *go for* (one's) *tea*, to die: c.: later C.20. Powis.—3. In *be* (someone's) *tea*, to be attractive to; esp., to be suitable to and for: 'smart young things': 1920s. (E. Waugh, 1932.) Prob. elliptical for *be* (one's) **cup o(f) tea**, q.v., but see also **ticket**, 5.—4. See **take tea with; tea's wet.**

tea and a wad. See **wads.**

tea and cocoa. See **coffee and cocoa.**

tea-and-sugar burglar. 'A swagman who begs or "borrows" tea and sugar; a minor predator' (Wilkes): Aus. s.: since late C.19. Cf. Brit. police **gas-meter bandit** for a 'minor predator'.

Tea and sugar, the. A supply train for the builders of the Trans-continental Railway: Aus.: since ca. 1920(?).

tea-and-tattle. An afternoon tea; a minor social gathering: Aus. coll.: since ca. 1925. B., 1942.

tea-blow. A taxi-cab rank where refreshments can be obtained: taxi-drivers': from ca. 1926. Ex **blow**, n., 3.

tea-boardy. (Of a picture) inferior: studio s.: from ca. 1870; ob. (B. & L.) Ex 'old-fashioned lacquered tea-trays with landscapes on them'. Cf. *chocolate-box* in this sense, and derog. *cheese-label*, applied to garish postage stamps.

tea-boat. 'A tea-making firm on the lower deck. Anyone who decides to brew a pot of tea is said to run the tea-boat' (Granville): RN. Bowen.

tea-cosy mob, the. Young unemployed West Indians roaming the streets around the Bullring in Birmingham shop-keepers': mid-1970s. Ex tam-o'-shanters, their 'badge'. BBC 4 'In Britain Now', 7 Apr. 1976. (P.B.)

tea for two and a bloater. A motor-car: derisive r.s.: early C.20. Franklyn.

tea gardens. 'Somers Town goods yard' (*Railway*, 2nd): London railwaymen's: since ca. 1920(?).—2. 'The cells or place of punishment' (*Daily Telegraph*, 4 June 1958): Borstal: since ca. 1920. Ironic.

tea grout. A boy scout: r.s. Cf. **Brussels Sprout**.

tea-head (or solid). 'User of cannabis' (Home Office): drugs world: later C.20. Ex *tea*, n., 1; cf. *acid-head*, *piss-head*, etc.

tea is wet. See **tea's wet.**

tea-leaf. The Chief Officer: prisons' r.s.: mid-C.20. Tempest.

tea-pot, n. A male baby: Aus. domestic: since ca. 1930. A married woman loq., 'We want one with a spout next time'—cited by B.P., who comments this, 'A male baby is called a "teapot" in such a conversation and a female baby is called a "jug" ' (1963).—2. (Usu. prec. by *old*, sometimes by *regular*; occ. *r.o.t.*) An inveterate tea-drinker: domestic: (lower- and) middle-class: latish C.19–20. I have no printed records—and I don't remember it earlier than ca. 1904. Cf. *tea-bottle*.—3. See **tea-pot lid.**

tea-pot, v. Short for **tea-pot lid,** v. *New Statesman*, 29 Nov. 1941.

tea-pot lid, n. A Jew: Cockney. Rhyming *Yid*, often shortened to *tea-pot*.—2. A child. Rhyming *kid*. Cf. next, 1.—3. £1: r.s., on *quid*. Jones, 1971.

tea-pot lid, v. To 'kid' (pretend): r.s.: late C.19–20. (*John o' London's Weekly*, 9 June 1934.) Hence vbl n. *tea-pot lidding*.

tea swindle. See **swindle.**

tea-trays. Flat handlebars: club cyclists': earlier C.20. *Fellowship*, 1984.

tea, two, and a bloater. Var of **tea for two ...**

tea-wad. A cup of tea and bun(s): military:—1935. See **wads, buns.**

teach. A teacher, a coach: adopted, ca. 1944, ex US servicemen. (Norman.) R.C., 1976, 'In US, almost invariably in vocative, "Hey, teach!" ' P.B.: but still, 1980, felt to be more US than Brit.

Teague. See **Taig.**

teaks. Pieces of bread, served at table: Cheltenham College: earlier C.20. Ex their dryness or hardness? P.B.: or ironic, short for tea-cakes?

team. A gang: Teddy-boys': since ca. 1947. The district where it lives is a *manor* (Sigal, 1959).

teapot. See **tea-pot.**

tear. See **shed a tear.**

tear a strip off (someone); as v.i., usu. *tear off a strip*. To reprimand: RAF: since ca. 1938. Bolitho, 1941, 'Hope that they won't have a strip torn off them'; Jackson, 1943, 'If you tear off a strip of cloth quickly and decisively, the noise caused thereby will not be unlike what has been referred to colloquially ... as a raspberry'; Partridge, 1945, ' "The 'Stationmaster' tore him off a strip for dressing in so slovenly a way." Off his self-satisfaction'; 1945, Granville records it as an RN phrase—which it had, via the FAA, > as early as 1941.—2. In the RN, *to tear off a strip* denotes sexual intercourse: WW2+. Cf. **tear off a piece.**

tear-arse, n. Cheese: low. Costive.—2. One who works devilish hard, who 'tears into' his work: proletarian: since—1923 (Manchon).—3. An excitable man: tailors': 1928 (*Tailor and Cutter*, 29 Nov.). P.B.: later, also Services', for one who 'goes tear-arsing about'.—4. Treacle; golden syrup: Aus. rural: since ca. 1920. (B., 1953.) Ex aperient effect.

tear-arse, v. (usu. with **about**). To rush about; behave in a violent way, recklessly: Services' coll. There is also adj. *tear-arsing*. Cf. **tear the arse** (P.B.).

tear (one's) **arse off.** To work furiously: low. Manchon.

tear 'em up. To delight the audience: music-halls': from ca. 1920. Lincoln, 1933, 'A number ... that simply "tore 'em up".'

tear into. To attack vigorously, whether with fists or with words: Aus. B., 1942.

tear-jerker. A very sentimental book or story or film: adopted, ca. 1954, ex US.

tear off a piece. To coït with a woman: Aus., Can., US: late C.19–20. (Baker.) Cf. **tear a strip off,** 2.

tear-over. See **rip,** n.

tear the arse, v.i.; v.t., *... out of it* (or **things**). To overdo anything; to exaggerate: Services': since early 1950s. Cf. synon. **kick the arse out of it**; and Carew, 1967, 'being done out of R and R [rest and recuperation] leave was bad enough, but to be put on the peg [charged] because a couple of Chinks died was "tearing it a bit".'

tear the end off. To finish; to finish with: coll.:—1923 (Manchon).

tear the tartan. (Gen. as vbl n.) To speak in Gaelic: Glasgow:—1934 (Baxter).

tear-up. ' ... which with "beat-up" occurs when a local [cycling] club meets another from the same area a few miles from home at the finish of a club run' (*Fellowship*, 1984). See **blind,** n., 3.

tear up the ground. 'Anxious to get moving or going, as in "I'm gonna tear up the ground" ' (cf. *rarin'* to go); full of vigour, wanting very keenly to do something. "If I got that opportunity, I'd really tear up the ground": widespread in W. Can. since mid-1950s. Ex large male animal in the rutting season(?)' (Leech, 1986).

tearaway. A would-be rough, esp. in *ladies' tearaway*, a man specialising in snatching handbags from women: low, verging on c.: late C.19–20. (Norman.)—2. 'Bobby Twist, a tearaway (or strongarm man), now dead' (Gosling, 1959): orig. c., but by 1930 also police s. and by ca. 1960 fairly gen. s.—3. Anyone who, esp. with a criminal record, tends to violence: since ca. 1960.

tearing. (Of work) exhausting: coll.:—1923 (Manchon). Cf. Aus. *ball-tearing*, adj., q.v. at **ball-tearer.**

tearing up pound notes in a gale. Engaging in something very expensive, e.g. modern grand prix motor-racing: later 1970s. Phillips, 1979.

tea's wet, the tea is ready; **wet the tea,** to make the tea: RN: coll.: since ca. 1910. (Mallalieu, 1944.) Cf. the army's **brew up.**

teased out. Exhausted: RAF (esp. aircrews'): since ca. 1938. (H. & P.) Ex S.E. *teased* (out): 'with fibres pulled asunder'.

teaser. A preliminary advertisement (specifying neither article nor advertiser, or, loosely, specifying only the one or the other), prior to an advertising campaign: advertising (esp. publicity) coll.: from ca. 1920.

tech. A technician: coll. abbr.: since ca. 1950. E.g. the RAF ranks Senior and Junior Tech[nician]. Cf. **mech** = mechanic(al). (P.B.)—2. (Often *the Tech* for one's local one) a *technical* college or institution: from ca. 1910, s.; by ca. 1930 verging on coll. (*OED* Sup.) Earlier sometimes written *tec*. Cf. *uni*(versity), *poly*(technic).

technicolour spit or **yawn.** Vomit; a vomiting: the 1st, RN, 1970s (Peppitt), prob. ex the 2nd: Aus. joc.: since ca. 1965; by very early 1970s, fairly well known in UK, thanks to the Aus. Barry Humphries' satirical cartoon-strip running, 1971 or 1972, in *Private Eye*.

tecker. A teacher: Northumberland teenagers'. (Blyth Ridley, 1984.) Prob. a local (deliberate) mispronun., but cf.:-

teckery. Detection of crime: coll.: earlier C.20.

T

Ted, n. usu. in pl. A German soldier: Army in Italy: 1943–5. Ex It. *Tedesco* (pl. *Tedeschi*), 'a German'.—2. A Teddy-boy: orig., among Teddy-boys: since ca. 1954. Gilderdale, 2.

Ted, adj. Characteristic of a Teddy-boy: mostly teenagers': since ca. 1956. Anderson.

Ted Frazer. A cut-throat razor: r.s.: later C.20. (Powis.) Cf. **hoosie**.

Ted Heath. A thief: r.s.: ca. 1970. (Haden-Guest, 1972.) Fairly ephemeral—it failed to oust *tea-leaf*. Ex the Conservative Prime Minister.

Teddy. A combination flying suit used by airship crews: aeronautical engineers' and airship crews': 1920s and 1930s. (Shute, 1954.) P.B.: prob. a shortening of **teddy bear**, 1.—2. (Usu. *teddy*.) A woman's garment, consisting of camisole and (loose) panties in one: Can., ex US: ca. 1920–40. Named after 'Teddy' Roosevelt.—3. Familiar shortening of teddy-bear: mostly domestic.

teddy bear. A shaggy goatskin or fur coat 'issued for winter wear in the trenches in 1915' (F. & G.): Army. Ex the toy, which was named after Theodore ('Teddy') Roosevelt who, from one of his big-game hunting expeditions, returned with some baby bears for the Bronx Zoo. Hence, in 1939–45, an RAF term for the fleece-lined jacket issued to aircrews. Cf. prec., 1.—2. A koala—the little native bear: Aus.: since ca. 1919. B., 1942.—3. A flashily dressed man: Aus. c.: since ca. 1930. (B., 1953.) Rhyming on *lair*. Wilkes quotes Huelin, 1973: '*Teddy-bears*, *Lairs*: Brash, vain young hoboes.' Wilkes also notes its specialised use, among cricketers, for 'a show-off . . . given to antics on the field': Aus.: since early 1960s.

Teddy-boy. A youth imitating a garb (stovepipe trousers and short jacket) supposed to characterize Edward VII's reign (1901–10): since ca. 1949; by 1960, coll.; by 1965, virtually S.E.

tee-heeing. 'This currying favour with superiors—tee-heeing, as we call it' (Grinstead, 1946): Guards'. 'Ex the sound of sycophantic sniggering' (R.S.). P.B.: also RAF, WW2. A humorous article in *Punch*, 17 Jun. 1942, on the dangers, from the erk's [q.v.] point of view, of the activity, contains also *tee-heer* and *tee-hee*, n. and v. Cf. **pee-hee**.

tee up; mostly as in 'It's (all) teed up' or fully arranged and virtually assured: Army officers': since ca. 1935. Ex outgoing. Compare **lay on** and **organise**.—2. '*Tee up* . . . adopted in the R.A.F. to denote "Time to get ready" for a flight or for a parade' (H. & P.): since ca. 1940.—3. Among Aus. soldiers (since 1940): to make arrangements (B., 1943). Hence, since ca. 1946, gen. s. (Culotta.)

teedle. An earlier RAF term for **stooge around**, q.v. 'Last week we were teedling round the air in overalls and shoes . . . ' (Tredrey, 1939, writing of 1935). Cf. much older S.E. *tiddle*, to potter about, fidget.

teek-hi! All right!: Army, esp. men with service in India: earlier C.20. In Malaya, in the 1950s, men of the Gurkha Regiments were still sometimes greeted by 'Ram ram, Johnnie! Teek-hi!' Ex Hindustani *thik*, precise, exact (Y. & B.). Also written *tickeye*, and, ca. 1930–50, often shortened to *tig*. I have altered E.P.'s orig. entry: P.B. Cf. **ticketty-boo**.

teeming and lading. 'Using cash received today to make up cash embezzled yesterday' (Chenhalls): accountants'. Lit., unloading and loading.

teen-ager. A person aged from thirteen to nineteen, especially 15–17: coll., adopted in 1945 from US, but not at all gen. until the latter half of 1947. Since ca. 1955, has usu. been written as one word—and, since ca. 1960, has been regarded as S.E.

teeny bopper. 'A teenager, esp. a teenage girl, who follows enthusiastically the latest trends in pop music, clothes, etc.' (Chambers' *C.20th Dict.*, 1977 ed.): adopted, ex US, ca. 1966, as s. >, by 1980, coll. and slightly ob. An early occurrence is in *Observer*, 3 Dec. 1967. P.B.: a blend of *teenager*, perhaps influenced by nursery *teeny* = tiny, + an exponent of **bop**, n., 2.

Teeny-Weeny Airlines. Liaison flights of the Army Air Corps, using light 'taxiplanes': Army, since ca. 1960; also, of small civilian air companies. By a joc. ironic pun on the large US Trans World Airline, usu. abbr. TWA. (P.B., 1975.)

teepee creep. 'To be unfaithful to one's wife or girlfriend; to visit the bedroom(s) of one or more women: Can.: later C.20.' (Leech, 1985). 'I am told that when a [N. Am.] Indian man married he had also to "take care of" his wife's sister(s) if they were unmarried. Thus, he would sneak from one teepee (tipi) to another, then return home' (Ibid., 1986).

teepee duck. 'The "ducking" flinch that taller men often have when they enter a room, even though there is no possibility that their heads will hit the lintel. A teepee has a low entrance' (Leech, 1985): Can.

teesy-weesy. Very small: mostly feminine: since ca. 1930. (Wilson, 1952.) Ex *teeny-weeny*, influenced by such locutions as *palsy-walsy*. Also, occ., *teensy-weensy*.

teeth. The dental department of a hospital: medical coll.:—1933 (*Slang*).

teething troubles. Such noises given out by a wireless set as indicate derangement: from 1935. *Daily Telegraph*, 16 or 17 Oct. 1936.—2. Applied to initial troubles with any new invention or device, as in 'Once we've got over the teething troubles, got the bugs ironed out a bit, she'll be fine': coll.: later C.20. (P.B.)

teg. A tooth, esp. a baby tooth; 'Ah, is he losing his little milk-tegs then!': domestic coll. Perhaps an ellision of *toothy-peg*. (P.B.)

tel. A telegraphist rating: RN: since ca. 1925. (Granville.) Cf. **telist**, **telt**, and **Pots**, 1.

tele. See **telly**.

telegraph. Elliptical for **bush telegraph**: B., 1943.

telephone numbers. 'Large amounts [of money]; rich: financial circles' (Mann, 1985). See quot'n at **talk**.

telist; telt. A telegraphist: telegraphists' coll.:—1923 (Manchon). Ex these two words written as official abbr.

tell a picture. To tell the story a film consists of: mostly Anglo-Irish coll. Behan, 1958.

tell all. To tell everything; esp. in the imperative: Aus. c.p.: since ca. 1945. (B.P.) PB.: in Brit., often *do tell all!*: mostly arch feminine curiosity.

tell (someone) **his birthright** dates from ca. 1910 and has prob. prompted the next. (L.A., 1976.)

tell (someone) **his fortune**. To threaten with reprisal; to let (him) know what a bastard he is: ?esp. Forces': since ca. 1945. (L.A., 1967.)

tell off. To scold, blame, rebuke severely: coll., prob. orig. Services', and since late C.19; by 1919, > gen. 'Taffrail', 1917.—2. Hence, to sentence (an incriminated person): c.: since ca. 1920. Ingram, 1933.

tell-tale. An indicator light (or lamp): Aus. motorists': since ca. 1950. *The Open Road*, 1 July 1963.

tell the tale. To tell a begging-story; to make love.—2. To tell an incredible or a woeful tale: from ca. 1910. (Esp. among soldiers.)—3. To be a confidence trickster: mostly Aus.: since ca. 1910. Hence the verbal noun *telling the tale*, as in Kelly, 1955.

tell (one) **where he gets off**. To rebuke; to scold: see **get off**, 2.

telling. In *I'm telling you!*: there's no argument necessary or possible: coll. Prob. abbr. 'I'm not arguing; I'm *telling* you.' Contrast *don't tell me!*, and cf. *you're telling me!*, I agree with you wholeheartedly.

telling-off. A scolding; a reprimand: coll.:—1923 (Manchon). Ex **tell off**, 1.

Telly, The. *The Daily Telegraph*: newsagents' and newsboys' coll.: late C.19–20. Among Sydneyites, *The* (Sydney) *D.T.*: since ca. 1920. B., 1942.—2. Television: coll., since ca. 1947; in later C.20 often as in 'I saw it on telly' and 'We haven't got a telly, remember!': at first non-cultured, but soon > gen., coll. Properly but rarely *tele*, as in Wilson, 1956, 'I seen him on the Tele.' Cf. **goggle-box**, **idiot's lantern**, and the mainly US *flickering blue parent*. (E.P., P.B.)

T

tellywag. A telegram: Public Schools': early C.20. (Benson, 1916.) In dial. as early as 1867 (*EDD*).

telt. See **telist.**

temp. Temperature: doctors' and nurses' coll.: late C.19–20. Graham, 1967.—2. A temporary employee, esp. a typist or secretary: office girls' and employment agencies': since ca. 1950, but *very* common since ca. 1960. Contrast **perm,** n., 3.

temperament. See **throw temperament.**

temperance. A rating that does not draw his tot of rum: RN coll. (Granville.) But among RN officers, it indicates 'a man who doesn't drink ashore but regularly takes his tot, the equivalent of three large rums ashore, in the middle of the forenoon' (Osmond, 1948).

temperature, have a. To be feverish: coll.: from late 1890s. Benson, 1904, 'He has . . . had a temperature for nearly a week' (*OED*). Abbr. *have a temperature higher than normal.*

temple balls. Cannabis: drugs c. (Stockley, 1986.) Prob. a pun on *temple bells.*

temporary gentleman. An officer for the duration of the War [i.e. WW1] or until demobilised: Regular Army pej. coll.: 1916; ob. Manchon, who notes the occ. abbr. *t.g.* (or *T.G.*). The term caused much justifiable resentment. Rolph, 1980, writing of police constables in the City of London force, 1920s, who had been commissioned Service officers in WW1, says that they would refer to themselves, bitterly, as 'gorblimey officers'.

ten, v. To play lawn tennis: 1906 (Wodehouse); Collinson.

ten, adj. First-class, very good, as in 'The disco was pretty ten': teenagers': ca. 1977. Ex school marks, ten out of ten; only this top rating is ever used. (McPheely, 1977.)

ten-bob bit. A 50 pence coin: Glasgow. (Munro, 1985.) Since decimalisation of UK currency, 1971; usage lingers more widely than just Glasgow, among the older generation to whom 'pounds, shillings and pence' remains '*real* money' (P.B., 1988).

ten(-)foot. 'Middle space between four rows of tracks' (*Railway*, 2nd): railwaymen's coll.

ten o'clock girls. Prostitutes: Londoners': since ca. 1930. (Stokes, 1950.) At that hour, a.m., they have to surrender to their bail in the Magistrates' Court.

ten-ogg. A ten-shilling note: market-traders': prob. since ca. 1920, but since 1971 merely nostalgic. (*M.T.*) See **ogg.**

ten-one (or **10–1**). Broken: teenagers': early 1980s. Ex Citizens' Band radio j. (James Williamson, 1982.)

ten penn'orth. A sentence of 10 years: c. Ingram, 1933.

ten points. 'Sarcastic comment on a mistake, as when someone misses a shot in basketball, you say, "You get ten points for that, Joe"': W. Can.: mid-1980s' (Leech, 1985). Cf. **ten,** adj.

ten stone eight. A '10' and an '8' in one's hand: Aus. pokerplayers': since ca. 1920. B., 1953.

ten to two. A Jew: r.s. Less usual than **four by two.** *The Leader*, Jan. 1939.

ten-ton Tessie. 'The R.A.F.'s latest and biggest bomb . . . yesterday . . . was used for the first time by specially equipped Lancasters . . . The new . . . bomb—the R.A.F. calls it "Ten-ton Tessie"—weighs 22,000 lb' (*Daily Herald*, 15 Mar. 1945). The 4,000, 8,000, 12,000 pounders received the name *block-buster*. It was named after 'Ten Ton' Tessie O'Shea, the famous variety artist.

tence; esp. in *false tences*, false pretences. Phelan, 1939.

tenderfoot. A tramp always looking for conveyance along the road: tramps' c.:—1932 (Jennings). A pun on the S.E. term.

tennis ball. See **sharp as a tennis ball.**

terminally unwell. See **sloughed.**

termite. A political (esp. Labour) saboteur: Aus. political since ca. 1925. (B., 1943.) Cf. **white-ant.**

ter(r). A member of any terrorist organisation: Services': later C.20. (Beevor, 1983.) See also RHODESIAN, in Appx.

Terrier, terrier. A member of the Territorial Army: coll.: 1908 (*OED*). Punningly. Cf.:-

Terries, the. The Territorial Army: NZ: since ca. 1930. (Slatter.)

terror. Used extensively in Samuel, 1981, as late C.19–earlier 20 term for a dangerous, armed criminal.

terse. Abrupt in manner: Society coll.: from ca. 1928. (Lincoln, 1933.) Suggested by 'terse style' and '*short*-tempered'.

test-tube wallahs. See **whiz.**

testiculating, adj. and vbl n. 'Defined to me in 1972 as "waving one's arms about and talking a lot of balls" ' (P.B., 1974). Blending *testicles* and *gesticulate*. Cf. my adjectival neologism (latish 1975): *totitesticular*, 'all balls' or 'utter nonsense' and 'notably virile'.

tetchy as a cat with a wet tail. Bad-tempered; extremely 'touchy' or sensitive: coll., esp. Essex: late C.19–20. (*The Times*, Sep. 1977.) Cf. **mad as a wet hen.**

tether (one's) **nag.** To coit: low Scots: C.19–20.

tewt. *T*actical *e*xercises *w*ithout *t*roops: Army officers': from ca. 1934; by 1942, j. Also *toot.*

Texas mickey. 'A 130-ounce bottle of rye (a northern speciality known as a "Texas mickey")' (*Maclean's*, Toronto, 7 May 1976: Leechman): Can.: since ca. 1930.

Thai sticks. Cannabis: drugs c. (Stockley, 1986.) US since mid-1970s (Spears).

thalidomide. Unarmed combat: a cruel pun. attrib. to the SAS, in Beevor, 1983; the ref. is to the appalling effects of the drug so named.

thanker. A 'thank-you' letter: girls' Public Schools': since ca. 1950; by late 1950s, rather more gen. Halliday, 1970, 'Anyone who knew Janey would be apt to meet Daddy, and perhaps get a thanker or something from him that would do.'

thanks! (I) thank you: coll.: late C.16–20. Ex *my thanks to you*, etc. Likewise *many* or *best thanks*, rare before C.19, though Shakespeare has *great thanks*. (*OED*.) Raab: in Aus., it combines economically 'please' and 'thank you', for a small request, as in 'I'll have a choc malted, thanks', from 1950s at least: gen. coll., used by all age-groups.

thanks a bunch! A deliberate intensification of prec., but meaning 'thank you for nothing': young peoples': later C.20. (Fraser, 1986.)

thanks a million. Thank you very much: coll.: since ca. 1950. Cf. Fr. *mille fois merci.*

that. 'Mildly derogatory "prefix" to a (usually proper) noun, as "You going out with that Harry again?" ' (R.C., 1976): coll.: since when?—mid-C.19, or much earlier?

that and this. A urination; to urinate: racing r.s., on *piss*. (Franklyn 2nd.) Contrast **this and that.**

that kind of money, as in 'I don't earn'—or 'have'—'that kind of money, I'm not well off': coll.: since the late 1940s.

that there. Esp. *a bit of* . . . , sexual intercourse: proletarian euph.

that thing is wild. That aircraft is much faster than I thought: RAF: 1939+. H. & P.

that way. Homosexual: since ca. 1920; by 1966 slightly ob. Mackenzie, 1956, 'She didn't want to believe the stories about Henry Fortesque being that way as he was obviously *épris* with his pretty sister-in-law.' Short for euph. *that way inclined.*

thataway. As in 'He's gone thataway', in that direction, often very vaguely indicated: since ca. 1955. Adopted ex US, where orig. dial.—very common in 'Western' films.

thee and me. Occ. used, in later C.20, for humorous effect—the influence of rhyme: e.g., one of only two people left to carry out some plan may say to the other , 'Well! That only leaves thee and me . . . !' A deliberate use of dial. (P.B.)

theirs. The enemy's: military coll.: by WW2, also civilian, esp. of aircraft, 'That's one of theirs—I can tell by the engine-noise'. A natural extension from 'Them versus Us'.

theolog. A student of Theology: Durham undergraduates'. Marples, 2.

there you are! A coll. var. of the *there you go!* of surprise, disgust, or approval: app. unrecorded before 1907.—2. A bar (for drinking): r.s. Franklyn.

there you go! A term of approbation, gen. of a specific action, method, etc.; a phrase of agreement: coll.: borrowed back, ex US, late 1970s, esp. popular 1980–1—but see prec., 1. Leech recalls the phrase as Can. coll. since ca. 1940 at latest. I have heard, as thanks for correct amount in change, 'There you go, lovely!'; and by later 1980s it had almost ousted the older *here* or *there you are*, which used to be said when handing something to somebody, as 'Here you are, then—mind you don't drop it!', etc. To plagiarise a source I regretfully cannot remember, *Here you are* is welcoming, *There you go* is dismissive. (P.B., 1988.)

thereoa. Other: back s. (Norman, 1959.) See quot'n at **ouya.**

thermos. An Italian bomb shaped like a thermos flask; hence *Thermos Bottle Flats*, an area where these bombs were dropped in large numbers: Army in N. Africa: WW2. P-G-R.

these and those. Nose; toes: Aus. r.s.

thick. A blockhead; a foolish person: coll., mostly schools'; ob. Hughes, 1857, 'What a thick I was to come!' Ex *thick*, stupid. Also Anglo-Irish: late C.19–20. (Moore, 1960.) This *thick* may be for '*thick*-headed person'. Cf. **thickie.**—2. A *thick* is a letter-card [E.P. used hundreds of them: P.B.], a *thin* a post-card: Post Office staffs'. I first heard the term in 1947.—3. In *in the thick*, in, esp. caught in, a thick fog: RAF (operational 'types'): ca. 1930–50. Cf. **shit** in this sense.

thick boot. A term of abuse: N. Country Grammar Schools': since late 1940s. *New Society*, 22 Aug. 1963.

thick dick (or **D-**). A stupid person: teenagers': early 1980s. (Joanna Williamson, 1982.) Opp. *smart Alec*. Cf. **dipstick.**

thick on the ground. Abundant: the natural, subsequent opp. of **thin on the ground.** (P.B.)

thick one; gen. **thick 'un.** In *do* (one) *a thick 'un*, to play a dirty trick upon: mostly Londoners': since ca. 1920. Proctor, 1958.

thickening for something. Visibly pregnant: since late 1950s. A pun on S.E. *sickening for something*. (Petch, 1966.)

thickers. Strong mess-deck tea: RN lowerdeck: since ca. 1925. (P-G.R.) The 'OXFORD/RN-*ER*(*s*)'.

thickie, -y; thicko. Variants of **thick,** n., 1: resp. since early C.20, mid-C.20. The latter in Craig, 1976.

thieve. A theft: since ca. 1945. Cunliffe, 1965, 'There was no other way into the drum. (Which . . . is what we call a place we've got in line for a thieve.)'

thieved, be. To be arrested: c.: from ca. 1925. *Gilt Kid*, 1936.

Thieves' Kitchen, the. The City Athenæum Club: City of London joc.:—1923 (Manchon: 'cercle des financiers de la Cité'.)—2. The London Stock Exchange: taxi-drivers': since ca. 1920. *Weekly Telegraph*, 6 Apr. 1946.

thimble and thumb. Rum: r.s. *Weekly Telegraph*, 6 Apr. 1946.

thin, v. To deceive, dupe, 'catch out', swindle: from ca. 1922. Manchon. Cf.:-

thin, adj. Disappointing; unpleasant; distressing. Gen. (*have*) *a thin time*, to go through hardship, spend a disappointing holiday, have a thoroughly disagreeable or distasteful experience. From ca. 1922. Mainly ex S.E. *thin*, feeble (as in *thin story*), slight, almost worthless, but partly proleptic ('enough to make one thin').

thin miner. 'A hewer working in thin seams of coal' (*Evening News*, 28 Sep. 1955): miners' coll. (late C.19–20) >, by 1945, official j.

thin(-)oil engine. A 'diesel locomotive, particularly during transitory period, when a driver may have had to perform duties on either steam or diesel locomotives' (*Railway*, 2nd): coll.: since late 1950s.

thin on the ground. Sparse; sparsely: coll., middle and upper classes'. Of agricultural (or forestry) origin—cf. the S.E. sense, 'not dense, not bushy'? Or, less likely, of sport (shooting). As applied to human beings, it was used first by the Higher Command, in WW1, of the disposition of troops. 'We are very thin on the ground' occurs in a signal from 'A.P. Wavell to Chiefs of Staff' dated 7 Mar. 1942, quoted in Connell, 1969. [The then Major-Gen. A.P. Wavell gave 'extensive' help to E.P. by contributing items for the 2nd ed. of *DSUE*, 1937.]

thing. Penis; pudend: when not used euph. but carelessly (cf. **affair**) or lightly, it is low coll.: since C.17.—2. In e.g. *Mrs Thing*, in ref. to someone whose name has slipped the memory: coll. Heard in the street, 3 May 1935.—3. A fad; a moral, or an intellectual, kink; an obsession: since ca. 1935. Marsh, 1945, 'She hated bits on the carpet. She had a "thing" about them and always picked them up.' Prob. short for *thingummy*, used for 'obsession' or 'complex', words too learned for the commonalty of everyday speech.—4. 'In the 1960s [and later] an activity or interest . . . "Stamp collecting is his thing", without any implication that it is carried to excess' (R.S., 1969).—5. Heroin: drugs c. (Stockley, 1986.) US since—1971 (Spears).—6. See **do** (one's) **thing.**

thingie, -y. The sexual organs: later C.20. Cf. prec., 1. Dim. of *thing*, or abbr. much older *thingummy*(*-bob*), etc.—2. Var. of prec. 2, e.g. 'Mrs Thingy down at the shop': mainly feminine usage: since later 1970s.

think (one)**self.** To be conceited: Aus.: since ca. 1930. Trist, 1944, 'Thinks herself, that girl.' Elliptical for '*Think* well of (one)self'. Cf. **reckon** (one)**self.**

think-in. A poetry session or a discussion group: among the more intelligent jazz 'fans' and drug addicts and hippies: since ca. 1965. (Fryer, 1967.) Cf. **love-in.**

think-piece. A serious article: journalists': since ca. 1946. It causes one to think, not merely to proliferate at the mouth. 'Also an article that the writer was able to "think up" out of his head without doing any research or "leg work" ' (Leechman, 1960).

think-tank. Gen., as in 'What useful idea ever came out of a think-tank?' (Trevor-Roper, 1980); specifically, the Central Policy Review Staff: coll., adopted ex US, mid-1970s, very soon > journalistic S.E., as in a *Guardian*, 18 Feb. 1981, headline: 'Ministers refuse Think Tank's advice on random B[reathalyser]-tests'. A gathering of highly-intelligent people who, by pooling their ideas, may or may not come up with the best idea. Influenced by alliteration. (P.B.) See next, and cf.:—2. In *have bubbles in* (one's) *think-tank*, to be crazy: motorists': ca. 1908–15.

Think-Tankers. The 'brains' in prec., 1: Winchester, 1977, 'a short wave radio [on which] if the Think Tankers leave it alone, we can listen to the [BBC] World Service' (Mindel, Kfar Tabor). There was (as usual) a funding threat to the BBC.

think to do (something). Think of doing: coll. Gen. in past, as 'Did he think to close the door, I wonder.' (*OED*; Fowler.) Ex † Scottish.

thinners. In the Portsmouth Royal Dockyard, a joc. insult, '*e needs a dose of* [paint] *thinners*, implying 'thickness' of brain. Patterson.

thirteence. A shilling: since ca. 1920. '*Twelve* pence' > a baker's dozen. P.B.: † by 1950, if not earlier.

thirty, but in form **30.** The end: Can. journalists' and freelance writers': since ca. 1910. 'I believe this to be one of the few remaining traces of a telegraphers' code (Philips?) in which numbers stood for words or sentences, thus economizing space and time' (Leechman, 1959). In a note written a year later, Leechman says, 'Two years ago, in the interior [of British Columbia], I dug up another remnant of this code: "73s"—which meant kind regards.' P.B.: *73*, kind regards, and *88*, 'love and kisses', continue to be used by radio operators, civilian, Service, and 'ham', and have now, ca. 1980, been adopted by the 'breakers' (operators) on CB, or Citizens' Band, radio.

thirty days. Three '10' cards: Aus. poker-players': since ca. 1920. B., 1953.

thirty-first of May. A simpleton; a dupe: Aus. c.: since ca. 1925. (B., 1953.) Rhyming on older sense of *gay*, n.

this. This . . . now fashionable or recently invented (or introduced): coll. The *OED* instances, in 1916, 'What do you think of this wireless telegraphy?'—2. In later C.20, *this* has supplanted *a* as the indefinite article in many people's speech, or has become, at best, a halfway between indefinite

T

and demonstrative: e.g., 'So we went down this street, see, and came to this house, and this guy said . . .', where the listener cannot possibly be expected to know *which* street, *which* house, *which* man. (P.B., 1988.)

this and that. (Mostly in pl. *thises and thats*.) Spats: Cockney r.s.: early C.20.—**2.** A hat: Aus. r.s. Martin, 1937; B., 1942.—**3.** To bat (in cricket): r.s.: since ca. 1946. Franklyn 2nd.

Thomas Tilling. A shilling: r.s.: early C.20. (Harrison, 1936.) 'T.T. was famous for his service of horses and horse-drawn vehicles . . . He also ran buses, coaches, and the like' (Franklyn).

thongs. 'Flip-flop' flat slippers: Aus. coll.: since mid-1950s. (Raab.)

thora. A thoracoplasty: medical coll.: since ca. 1930. Cusack, 1951.

Thorny. A Thornycroft motor-truck: coll., mostly Aus.: from ca. 1920. Idriess, 1931.

thorny wire. A quick-tempered person: Anglo-Irish.

those, one of. See **one of those**.

thou (with *th* light, unvoiced, as in *thin*). A thousandth of an inch: technical coll.: since ca. 1930. (B.P.) As in 'accurate to within a couple of thou' (P.B.).

thousand fathoms deep, a, n. and adj. Sleep; asleep: RN lower-deck. (Peppitt.)

thrash. A party, with drinks, supper, dancing: Services', perhaps orig. RN: since late 1930s. Winton, 1967; P.B.—**2.** A 'slog' or bout of hard-hitting, whether by one batsman or more: cricketers': since ca. 1960. Brian Close, England's captain at that time, in an interview reported in the *Daily Express* of 14 Aug. 1967.

thread. (Of the man) to coït with: Anglo-Irish. (Behan, 1958.) Cf.:-

thread the needle. Synon. with prec.: C.19–early 20 in England; current mid-C.20 in Anglo-Irish. (Ibid.) Cf. the joc. Aus. low synon. *thread the eye of the golden doughnut*.

threaders. Bored and disgruntled; 'fed-up': RM: later C.20. (*Mail on Sunday*, 8 Nov. 1987.) RN *–ers*, on 'patience worn *thread*bare'; or perhaps a perversion of *fedders*.

threads. Garments, esp. if fashionable: s. 'Maybe their minds were blown by the crazy threads' (Burchill, 1986) = Perhaps they were excited by the bizarre costumes.

Three-Be (or, **By**)**-Two.** A Jew: low. A var. of **four by two,** 2.

three-card monte. 'The three-card trick' (Powis): c.

three cheers and a tiger. Three cheers and a very hearty additional cheer: adopted, ca. 1918, from US. A tiger is ferocious.

three-cross double (or **treble**). A glass of beer, a half-glass of rum, and a gill of red wine: Glasgow public houses':—1934. Cf. **roll-up,** 1.

three-handed. Three (adj.): c.:—1933 (Leach). Cf. **mob-handed**.

three-hole woman. 'Description of a female who is known to, or is likely to, participate in oral, vaginal, and anal sexual congress' (Turner, 1986).

three-island ship. 'A steamer with forecastle, bridge deck and poop': nautical coll.: earlier C.20. Bowen.

three-kidney man. A pimp in whose service there are three women: white-slavers' c.: early C.20. Londres.

three months' bumps. (A course of) three months' flying training: RAF: since ca. 1938. (Jackson.) Cf. **circuit and bumps**.

three nines agreement. A lease for 999 years: house-agents' coll.:—1927 (Collinson).

three-o; two-o. Third officer; second officer: nautical. Ex the abbrr. *3 o* and *2 o*. In WW2 the terms were applied esp. to a third and second officer in the WRNS: RN (P-G-R).

three of the best. Three condoms: Aus.: since ca. 1925. 'Gis [Give us] three of the best, mate.' In Aus., condoms are usu. sold in packets of three. Cf. **three screws,** and **packet of three**.

three on the hook, three on the book. Half-a-week's work: dockers': since ca. 1925. The *book* refers to the dole; the *hook* is a tool of the stevedore's trade.

three-op packet. A passenger ship carrying three operators: 'nautical' wireless operators': from ca. 1925. Bowen.

three-or-four-point drinker. 'A man who calls for *6d.* gin with bitters, limejuice and soda' (B., 1942): since ca. 1925; by end of 1945, ob.

three parts seven-eights. Tipsy: nautical. (Bowen.) Prob. ex *three sheets in the wind*. In F. & G. it is . . . *five-eighths*.

three pennorth. Three years' penal servitude: c. (Sharpe, 1938.) And see **penn'orth**.

three pennorth of God help us. A weakling; a spiritless, unprepossessing fellow: Aus. B., 1942.

three-piece suite. The male genitals: joc., perhaps mainly boxers': later C.20. Luckham, 1982.

three-pipper. A captain: Army. Ex the three stars indicating his rank. P-G-R.

three-pointer. A perfect, a three-point landing, i.e. with the two wheels and the tail-skid (or wheel) simultaneously touching down: from early 1930s. RAF coll.>, by 1944, j. Whence *three-pointer on the deck*, a heavy fall, noted by *Daily Herald*, 1 Aug. 1936, as aircraft engineers' s. Cf.:-

three-pricker. Var. of prec.: RAF: early 1930s.

three-ringer. A Commander, RN, or Wing Commander, RAF: see **ringer,** 5, and cf. **three-pipper**.

three-rounder. A petty criminal; a small operator: since ca. 1950: c. >, by 1965, low s. (Warner, 1961.) Ex the three-round bouts of junior and novice boxing.

three screws. 'An aluminum box containing three condoms. Three Screws was the brand name' (Leechman): Can.: since ca. 1920. A pun on s. *screw*, a copulation. Cf. **three of the best**.

three-striper. See **striper**.

three-tone. (Of a car) 'Badly repaired after an accident' (Graham-Ranger, 1981): car-dealers'. Worse still: *four-tone*. Punning the advertisers' 'two-tone', of a car painted in two colours.

three whippets, the. Explained as 'Whip it in, whip it out, and wipe it': N. Country low, and Services'. Wainwright, 1975, a Northern policeman's veiled threat to his 'nark', 'You're also tailing [sleeping with] one of the waitresses at *The Golden Slipper*. Surprise! Surprise! You thought nobody knew. Wednesdays and Fridays . . . Right! Just a quick job . . . whip it in, whip it out and wipe it.' *It*, of course = the penis. P.B.: L.A., 1974, recalls its service use in WW2, and I, since then.

three'd up. 'Three inmates in a cell' (Home Office): prisons'.

threes. 'Second landing above ground floor' (Home Office): prisons'.

threepenny bits, the. Diarrhœa: r.s., on *the shits*. Often shortened to *the threepennies*.—**2.** Hence, irritation, disgust, as in 'He gives me the *threepennies*': since ca. 1920.

threepenny dodger; t. Johnnie. A threepenny piece: Cockneys': earlier C.20. The former ex its elusiveness: the ref. is to the silver coin.

threepenny (pronounced *thruppenny*) **vomit.** Fish and chips: low Glasgow:—1934.

thrifty. A threepenny piece, esp. the 12-sided one minted 1937–52, which bore a representation of the plant thrift on the reverse. Not a common term. (E.P.; P.B.)

thrill. An orgasm; esp., *give* (one) *a thrill*: euph. coll.: since ca. 1910.

thrilled. Pleased; content; quite satisfied: Society coll.: from ca. 1915. E.g. Mackail, *passim*. Cf. **thrilling**. Hence, *thrilled to bits* as intensive, utterly delighted: since late 1940s; perhaps ob. by 1970: both *thrilled* and . . . *to bits* > much more widespread than just 'Society' (P.B.).

thriller merchant. A writer of 'thrillers': publishers' and authors': since ca. 1919. Lorac, 1935.

thrilling. Pleasing; pleasant; suitable, apt: Society coll.: from ca. 1915. Cf. **thrilled**.

thrips. Incorrectly treated as a pl., with erroneous singular *thrip*. A genus of the family *Thripidæ*, or an insect belonging thereto. Late C.18–20. *OED*; CSIRO, *The Insects of Australia*, 1970.

throat. As *the throat*, 'frenulum or G-string; underside of neck of penis; play it on the throat, of coïtion' (L.A., 1974): low or raffish.—2. In *have a game by the throat*, 'to be in full control, in a position of advantage' (Wilkes): Aus.: since 1940s. Sometimes *have it by . . .*

throb. Such a person as, usu. of the opposite sex, mightily appeals to someone: schoolgirls': since ca. 1945. Short for *heart-throb*. Franklin, 1951.

thrombosis. A traffic apprentice: railwaymen's: since ca. 1945. *Railway*, 2nd, records the witty professional definition, 'a bloody clot wandering round the system'.

throne, the. Lavatory-seat; esp. *be on the t.*, as in 'Sometimes he's on the throne for half an hour, reading the paper' (L.A., 1974): grandiosely joc.: since ca. 1920. P.B.: it used to occur as a *double entendre* in the BBC's famous radio-comedy series, 'The Goon Show', of the 1950s.

through, be. To have finished (a job, etc.): Can. (and US) coll.: since ca. 1910. (Leechman.)

through the lights. (Of a punch) that is an uppercut: low, and boxing:—1935.

throw, n. A vomit: see v., 6.—2. In (so much) *a throw*, such and such a price or charge at a time (each time), as in 'two bob a throw': NZ: since ca. 1956. Griffiths, 1962, 'From the old side-shows of the fair'. P.B.: coll. Brit. since long before 1956.

throw, v. To throw away, i.e. lose deliberately, a game, a set in order to obtain service or to conserve energy: lawn tennis coll.: from 1933, or early 1934. *Lowe's Annual*, 1935.—2. To bring as wages: lower-class Glaswegians'. MacArthur, 'His job "threw him" forty-eight shillings for the week of forty-eight hours.'—3. To fail to extract the full meaning or emotional content out of one's lines as one might: theatrical coll.: since ca. 1945. Ex 'to *throw* away'. Cf. sense 1.—4. Hence, to deliberately fail in this: theatrical: since ca. 1950.—5. To disconcert; to upset: since ca. 1961. 'Your unexpected arrival threw him.' P.B.: ?elliptical for **thrown for a loop**, q.v.—6. To vomit: low coll.: short for, e.g., *throw a map, sixers*, etc. Cf. **big spit**.—7. May be substituted in many of the phrases at **chuck**, q.v.

throw a fit. To become very angry or agitated: s. >, ca. 1930, coll. Sometimes intensified to *throw forty fits*.

throw a map. To vomit: Aus. joc.: since ca. 1925. B., 1943.

throw a party. To give a party: adopted, ex US, ca. 1925. Prob. ex such US phrases as *throw* (have) *a fit*: cf. *chuck a dummy*. Beatnik variants, noted by Anderson in the late 1950s, and soon ob., were *throw a rave*, occ. *a shake* or *a percolator*.

throw a seven. To die: Aus.: late C.19–early 20. (Sutherland, 1940.) A die has no '7'. R.C., however, says, 'More likely, I think, from craps, where to throw a seven (when one is trying to make a point) is to lose—to "crap out", itself occ. used in U.S. as synonym. for "die" (more commonly, to depart, to withdraw).' B., 1942, notes the variants . . . *six, sixer, willy*. Also *chuck . . .*—2. To faint: Aus.: Wilkes cites Upfield, 1932.

throw a six. See prec., 1.

throw a wap. To indulge in a tantrum, lose one's temper; with *at*, to get angry with, as in 'Mum just threw a wap at me' (Burt, 1986): teenagers'. See **wappy**, 2.

throw a willy. See prec., 1, and **Willie**, 4.

throw a wobbly. See **wobbly**.

throw-away. A leaflet, esp. if of only one sheet: coll.: since ca. 1930. It is usu. thrown away as soon as read—if not before. Cf. **dodger**, 5.—2. Short for *throw-away line, remark*, etc., an aside, often extempore, memorably witty or unemphatically trenchant, which may pass unnoticed at time of utter-

ance, only to be recalled later, as 'Do you remember that marvellous throwaway of his at Celia's party . . .', or 'So he said, almost as throw-away . . . ': coll.: since mid-C.20. (P.B.) Contrast **throw-off**, n.

throw for a loop. See **thrown for . . .**

throw forty fits. See **throw a fit**.

throw it in. To give up, to desist: Aus. coll.: since ca. 1910. 'They might be ready to throw it in' (Harris, 1958). Short for boxing *throw in the towel*.

throw it up the road. To come off one's motorcycle accidentally: motorcyclists': later C.20. (Dunford.) *It* is the machine.

throw (one's) **money about like a man with no arms.** To be tight-fisted, mean with one's money: joc.: since ca. 1950. Sometimes . . . *with no hands*. (L.A.)

throw-off. A depreciative remark or allusion. Manchon.

throw off. To deduct (so much) from (a stated sum): lower classes':—1923 (Manchon). Perhaps suggested by *cast accounts*.—2. To vomit: coll.

throw-off practice. 'Gunnery practice where an actual ship is used as the target': RN coll. Bowen.

throw one up. To salute in a neat, efficient, regulation manner: Services': since ca. 1925. H. & P.

throw out the anchors. 'Popular way of saying "stop in a hurry [i.e. abruptly]", although it is technically incorrect: anchors do not stop a vessel—they hold it after it has stopped' (Sayers, 1985).

throw sixers. To vomit heartily: Aus. (G.D. Mitchell). Wilkes cites Ronan, 1966, for *chucking sevens*: Aus. Cf. **throw a seven**.

throw temperament. (Mostly *throwing . . .*) To lose one's temper: theatrical: from ca. 1930. (*The Times*, 15 Feb. 1937.) On *throw a party*.

throw the baby out with the bath-water. To overdo something, carry it too far, e.g. a political measure or a commercial practice or a sociological activity, often as a warning to theorists 'Don't throw . . . ': since ca. 1946. 'Cf. the Ger. proverbial *Das Kind mit dem Bad ausgiessen*' (R.S.).

throw the book at (someone). Of the police, a magistrate, a judge: to sentence to the full penalty of the law: adopted, ca. 1944, ex US. 'The book of rules' or 'the law book'.

throw up. To abandon hope completely. Milne, 1931, 'When it became definitely mottled, there was really nothing for a girl to do but to "throw up".' Perhaps ex *throw up the sponge*.

throw (one's) **weight about.** To boast, swagger, unduly stress one's authority: orig. Services': since ca. 1910. (F. & G.) Prob. ex boxing or circus. Also *chuck . . .*

throwing temperament. See **throw temperament**.

thrown for a loop. Startled; shocked: RAF: 1939+. 'That posting to the Med. threw me for a loop.' Ex aerobatics. 'Much earlier, I think, in US. I suspect from cowboy roping, but also influenced by "thrown for a loss" (US football)' (R.C., 1966). Cf. **throw**, v., 5.

thruster. One who in the field, thrusts himself forward or rides very close to the hounds: hunting s. >, ca. 1920, coll.: from 1885. Ex usual sense. (*OED*.) Also *thrusting*, n. and adj.—2. Hence, among motorists, one who thrusts his car—thrusting one's car—ahead of others: coll.: since ca. 1910.

thud, n. A figurative fall: Aus. Casey, 1945, 'You're heading for a thud with the yellow stuff, too.'

thud, v. To strike (a person) resoundingly: Aus. coll.: since ca. 1919. (Park, 1950.) Echoic.

thud and blunder. A happy spoonerism, used joc., for 'blood-and-thunder' entertainment, film, novel, play, etc.: since mid-C.20. (P.B.)

thumb, n. For *travel on the thumb*, see **hitch-hike** and:-

thumb, v. To ask (someone) for a 'lift' or free ride: coll.: 1940+. Ex *thumb a lift from* (someone). P.B.: still current, 1983: 'They thumbed their way to Paris and back'.

thumb crusher. Motorcycle speed wobble. See **tank-slapper**.

thumbs up!, occ. prec. by **put your**. Be cheerful. Ex the gesture that spared the life of gladiators at Rome. Cf. *tails up!*—2. In *give the thumbs up*, to make this gesture, as a sign of agreement, that all is going well, etc.: coll.: since mid-C.20 (?earlier). (P.B.)

thump, n. In *have a thump*, to have one's chest finger-tapped; to be examined by the sanatorium doctor: TB patients': since ca. 1920.

thump! 'I *don't* think'; it's very improbable: an ejaculation of dissent modifying the preceding statement: military in WW1. (Raymond, 1930.) Hence, among the lower and lower middle classes, as in Raymond, 1931, 'Call me a business man! Am I? *Thump!* I'm going in for gardening.'

thump seven kinds (occ. **shades**) **of shit out of** (someone). (Sometimes *knock* . . .) To 'lay into someone with the intention of really hurting him' (P.B., 1974): Army, > gen. low: since ca. 1950.

thump-up. A var. of, but much less common than, **punch-up**, a fight: since ca. 1960. (P.B.)

thumped-in. (A landing that is) badly effected, necessitating the use of the engine: RAF: from 1932.

thumper. A large, four-stroke motorcycle engine: motorcyclists': 1950s. (Dunford, 2.) Cf. synon. **plonker**, 4.

thunder-bowl. Lavatory: Sloane Rangers', q.v. (*Sunday Express* supp., 11 Oct. 1982). Cf.:-

thunder-box. A commode: esp. in India, or among those with service in India: since later C.19; slightly ob. by mid-C.20. Note, however, that it has, since ca. 1925, been common among submariners (P-G-R.).

thunder-thighs. 'At 15 stone, [she] is no shrinking violet wilting under the fusillade of "thunderthighs, fatso and porky" insults that frequently assail her' (*You*, 24 Nov. 1985). Prob. ex US: it is listed in *New DAS*, 1986.

Thunderbirds. See quot'n at **trog**, 3.

thunk. A facetious past participle of 'to *think*': Can.: since ca. 1935. 'Who'd have thunk it?' (Leechman.) *EDD* notes it as Yorkshire dial.

tib and fib. Tibia and fibula: medical coll.: late C.19–20. Brand, 1945.

tibby, n. A 'tabloid' newspaper: Aus.: since ca. 1930. (B., 1943.) P.B.: ?*tabby* thinned by Aus. pron.

tibby, adj. Very eccentric; mad: Charterhouse School: earlier C.20.

Tic. A member of *the Tics* or Authentics' Cricket Club: Oxford. (Marples, 2.) Cf. **Tics**.

tic-tac, tick-tack. Phencyclidine, PCP: drugs c. (Stockley, 1986, has *tic and tac*.) US since early 1970s (Spears, who gives also *tic* and *tac*).

Tich. A nickname given to any small man. E.g. 'Tich' Freeman, Kent's googly bowler. Ex 'Little Tich', stage-name of the comedian Harry Relph, 1867–1928. It has also, since ca. 1925, been a nickname conferred by females upon a female.

tichy, titchy. Little, small: mostly children's. Ex prec. (P.B.)

tick, n. Esp. in *have a tick on*, to be monotonously or constantly complaining: Army: since ca. 1920. Ex v., 1. P-G-R.—2. A professional shadower: espionage: since (?)ca. 1945. Hall, 1975, 'The opposition-in-place in whatever city are very watchful and you can pick up ticks just by stopping to do up your shoe-lace.'—3. See BIRD-WATCHERS, in Appx.

tick, v. To grumble: military: from 1916 or 1917. (F. & G.) Prob. ex **tick off**, 2. P.B.: or from an unexploded bomb ticking menacingly? Cf. **tick like fuck.**—2. To salute (a master): Rugby: since mid-1920s. Marples.—3. See **tick off; tick over; tick up; what makes** (someone) **tick.**

tick-jammer. The man that presses wool into bales: Aus. (B., 1942.) I.e. sheep-ticks.

tick like fuck. To grumble like the very devil: Army: since ca. 1940. Cf. **tick**, v., 1. 'The degrees of disgruntledness among troops of the 8th Army were, *brassed off, browned off, cheesed off,* and ticking *like fuck*' (a correspondent, 1965). P.B.: a gentler version, in 1950s–60s, was *tick like a meter*, usu. 'they were ticking like meters.'

tick off. To identify: coll. Ex *tick off a person's name on a list.*—2. Hence, from ca. 1916 (orig. military), to reproach, upbraid, blame; esp. to reprimand, 'I ticked him off good and proper.' Partly influenced by **tell off**, q.v.

tick over. To come; to act, function: from ca. 1930. Clarke, 1934, of water-divining, 'How shall I know when the influence is ticking over?' Ex motoring j.—2. Hence, in *be ticking over* (often with *nicely* added), to be feeling, moving, progressing, satisfactorily: since ca. 1939. (R.C., 1977.)

tick-tack. In *give the tick-tack*, to give the agreed word, or notice or warning: Glasgow c. (MacArthur.) Ex *tic-tac* and *give the tip* or *word.*

tick-tock. A clock: children's coll.: C.19–20.—2. As n. or adj., as in 'Real tick-tock he was—proper little action-man [q.v.]': Army s. implying a brainless, well-drilled automatism: mid-1960s–mid-70s. (P.B.)

tick up. Of, e.g., a taxi-meter, 'It had already ticked up a couple of quid, and we'd only just started!'; of any mechanical device for marking increase: coll. (P.B.)

ticker. An account; an invoice or a statement: from ca. 1910: esp. among publishers. Ex S.E. *ticker*, a stock-indicator.—2. A taxi-meter: taxi-drivers': since ca. 1910. Cf. **clock**, n., 1.—3. One who is constantly, esp. if monotonously, complaining: Army: since ca. 1920. (P-G-R.) Cf. **tick**, v., 1.—4. A telephone: Army: ca. 1930–45. Ibid.—5. A cyclometer: club cyclists'. *Fellowship*, 1984.—6. 'An off-hand expression for an Inspector's Assistant, whose primary function is to certify the accuracy of entries in a Branch's records: "Is X an inspector now?" "No, he's still only a ticker" ' (Taylor, 1986): bank clerks'.

ticket. A certificate: nautical s. (late 1890s) >, ca. 1920, coll. Chiefly *captain's* or *mate's ticket.* Ex *ticket*, a licence. Also, since ca. 1919, an RAF or civil pilot's certificate (Jackson).—2. A trade union contribution card: industrial coll.: since ca. 1910.—3. (Usu. pl.) A playing card: card-, esp. bridge-, players': since ca. 1935.—4. 'Warrant to arrest or search' (Powis): police and underworld: later C.20.—5. In *be* (one's) *ticket*, to appeal to one, be of his kind: from ca. 1920. (E. Waugh, 1934.) Often abbr. to *tea* (properly *t*).—6. In *be on the straight ticket*, to live respectably: lower classes':—1923 (Manchon). Perhaps ex:—7. In *on ticket*, on ticket-of-leave (from prison): police coll. Carlin, 1927.—8. 'A person, as in a hard ticket (a tough guy) or a useless ticket (a shiftless person, good-for-nothing)' (Munro, 1985): Glasgow.—9. In, e.g., 'He just ain't the ticket', he is either physically not completely fit, or, more usu., somewhat mentally deficient: coll.—10. See **meal ticket.**

ticket man. A distributor of tickets for a meal and/or a bed: tramps' c.:—1933.

ticket(-)snapper. A ticket collector: railwaymen's. *Railway.*

tickets. 'A play, musical, concert, rock band, film, etc. which has box office potential, e.g.: "ET has tickets" ' (Green, 1984): entertainments. I.e., a lot of people will buy tickets to see the show.

tickets on (one)**self, have.** To be vain or conceited: Aus. (B.P.) Ex lotteries, raffles, sweepstakes, etc., 'fancied to win'.

ticketty-boo; tickety-boo; tiggerty-boo. Correct; arranged; safe; satisfactory: Services', perhaps orig. RAF: since early 1920s. The 3rd is perhaps the oldest form: Jackson derives it ex 'the Hindustani *teega*'; this has prob. been influenced by older *ticket*, as in *just the ticket*, absolutely correct; Partridge, 1945, 'For the second element, cf. **peek-a-boo** [a sketchy salute]'. Also Civil Service since ca. 1945. All forms are occ. written solid. 'A Guards officer was in charge of all the correspondents [for the funeral of King George VI, 1952] . . . his voice half-strangled with grief, he just said, "I'm quite sure that everything must be tickety-boo on the day of the race" ' (Russell, 1979). Another suggested etym. is ex Hindi *tikai babu*, 'it's all right, sir'. Cf. **teek-hi**, with its variants *tickeye* and *tig*. E.P.; P.B.

ticking. Disgruntled in the ultimate degree: Army in N. Africa: 1940–3. (Sanders, 1967.) Cf. **tick like fuck.**

ticking-off. A reprimand: coll.: see **tick off,** v., 2.

ticking spider. 'Sturmey-Archer [cycle 3-speed] gear (the hub being the spider and the spokes the web' (*Fellowship*, 1984): club cyclists'. Cf. **milk-tin gear.**

tickle, n. A robbery; esp. a burglary: c.: since ca. 1920. (Sharpe, 1938; Scott, 1979, 'planning a big tickle', a big robbery.) A joc. meiosis. Cf. v., 1, and:—2. 'Successful crime or a worthwhile arrest, especially if unexpected. Sometimes, a medium-sized betting success: "A nice little tickle!"' (Powis): police and underworld: later C.20.

tickle, v. To steal from, to rob, as in *tickle a peter*, to rob the till: NZ c., –1932; Aus. (Baker, letter, 1946). Perhaps ex *to tickle trout*, but cf. prec.—2. Prob. hence, to ask (someone) for a loan: Aus.: since ca. 1925. B., 1942.

tickle (someone's) ears. To flatter him: coll.: earlier C.20. Lyell.

tickle (a, or the) peter. See **tickle,** v., 1; *peter*, since C.19, a safe or till.

tickle the tintinabulum. Ring the bell (for the servant): joc.—pedantic domestic: 1920s. (Aldiss, 1978.)

tickle your fancy. A male homosexual: r.s., on *Nancy*. Franklyn 2nd.

tickled. Amused, as 'She was very tickled when I told her': coll. Ex the physical effect. (P.B.) Cf.:-

tickled pink. Immensely pleased: late C.19–20. 'I'll be tickled pink to accept the offer.' To the point of blushing with pleasure.

tickler. 'Anything worn on the penis to increase friction during *coitus*' (B.P., 1974): low coll.—2. A cigarette 'made from the monthly issue of naval tobacco' (Bowen): RN: since ca. 1910. 'It is tinned by the firm of Tickler's . . . To roll a tickler is to make a cigarette from Navy tobacco' (Granville). The effect on the throat may also be relevant.—3. Hence, a cigarette-smoker: RN: from ca. 1912. Bowen.

tickler's. Tinned tobacco, whether for pipe or for cigarette: RN: since ca. 1920.

ticky. Verminous: Army coll. (F. & G.) Ex Lancashire dial. (*EDD*). Cf.:-

Ticky Tins, the. Royal Horse Guards' nickname for the Life Guards. See quot'n at **Tasty Blues.**

Tics. Peripatetics (a team within the School): Charterhouse. By abbr. Cf. **Tic.**

tid. A drunkard: Aus. low: since ca. 1925. (B., 1942.) Ex *tiddly*, drunk.—2. The D-Day, 6 June 1944, invasion fleet 'included the most powerful tugs in the world and also the "tids" (short for tiddlers)—prefabricated little fellows mass-produced in Yorkshire' (Ministry of Information, *News Clip*, 15 Nov. 1944). Also short for **tiddler,** 4 (Granville).—3. 'Must be in a good tid, the W.O. No bellowing, no binding' (Macadam): RAF: since ca. 1935. Meaning 'temper, mood', *tid* may derive ex *tide*, 'time'.—4. (A) Chinese: Army in Hong Kong, esp. Middlesex Regt: mid-C.20. Abbr. r.s. **Tiddlywink,** 3. See also **chogey.** (P.B.)

tidapathy. Indifference: among Britons in Malaya: since ca. 1925. 'Tid'apa: it does not matter. Tidapathy' (Godfrey, 1949). A punning blend: cf. **scapathy.**

tiddle. To urinate: children's and joc. Cf. synon. **widdle.**

tiddled. Tipsy: from ca. 1920. Cf. **tiddly,** drunk, and prec.

tiddled off. Annoyed, cross, 'fed up'; euph. for *pissed off* (cf. **tiddle**): Pickering, quoting RAF NCO's disgruntled wife, in *New Society*, 4 Aug. 1977. (P.B.)

tiddler. A stickleback, or minnow: children's coll.: 1885 (*OED*). Ex *tittlebat, tiddlebat*, a popular form. In Aus., any small fish (B.P.). P.B.: hence, anything small, e.g. child, small animal, 'He's only a tiddler'.—2. 'Thingamy', 'thingummy bob': lower classes': 1912, Lyons, 'Clara, steady on with that tiddler!'—3. A £1 note: Aus.: from ca. 1920. (Baker.) Cf. *fiddly did*, a quid.—4. A midget submarine: RN: 1942. Ex sense 1; often abbr. *tid* (Granville). Cf. **tid,** 2.—5. An easy, short putt: golfers': since ca. 1920. Devine, 1968.—6. A small motorcycle: motorcyclists': later C.20. (Dunford.) Cf. sense 1.

tiddler's bait. Late: r.s. Franklyn.

tiddlies. A rating's best clothes: RN. See **tiddly,** adj.

tiddling. A vbl n. ex *tiddler*, q.v.: nursery coll.

tiddly, n. A threepenny bit: Aus.: since ca. 1920. (Baker.) Ex its smallness; cf. **tiddler,** 1; but see **tiddler,** 3.—2. A 'tailor-made' cigarette: RN: WW2.—3. See **tiddlywink,** 1.

tiddly, adj. Drunk: low >, by earlier C.20, gen.: since late C.19.—2. Little: dial. and nursery coll.: C.19–20.—3. 'Naval adjective meaning the acme of smartness and efficiency, hence *tiddley ship*, one that is **pusser** [q.v.] to the *n*th degree . . . from *tidy*, influenced by *titivate*' (Granville): since late C.19. Bowen. Cf.:-

tiddly bull. 'Ceremony; Service etiquette; preparation to receive some exalted person on board' (Granville): RN: since ca. 1930. Ex prec., 3, and *bullshit*.

Tiddly Chats. 'Chatham Depot and Naval barracks, known as HMS *Pembroke* . . . This historic establishment closed down in 1961' (Granville): RN. 'Taffrail'.

Tiddl(e)y Dike (Railway), the. The Midland and South-Western Railway: railwaymen's: ca. 1890–1925. (*Railway*.) Cf. **Chidley Dyke.**

tiddly oggy. Occ. var. of **tiddy oggy.** H. & P.

tiddly push! A nonsense-word meaning *au revoir*: ca. 1920–40. (Petch, 1974.) Cf. earlier synon. *tinkety-tonk, toodle-oo* (or *–pip*).—2. Usu. *old tiddly-push*, male equivalent of 'Mrs Thing', a 'shorthand' for someone whose name momentarily escapes one: coll. (P.B.) Cf.:-—3. In *and tiddly* (or *tidderly*) *push*, and the rest of it; and so on: a c.p. (—1923) 'used to replace any statement . . . considered . . . too long or too involved to be expressed in full' (Kastner & Marks, cf. the Fr. equivalent, *et patati et patata*). Manchon.

Tiddly Quid, the. HMS *Royal Sovereign*: RN: she was in commission 1915–49. (Bowen; P-G-R.) A pun on *quid* = a sovereign. See **tiddly,** adj., 3.

tiddly suit. 'Best shore-going uniform' (Granville): RN. Cf. **tiddlies; tiddly,** adj., 3.

tiddlywink. A drink: r.s.: since later C.19. (Barrett, 1880.) Jones, 1971, 'Come for a little tiddly'. Franklyn remarks, 'It is applied more frequently to "shorts" (short drinks, wines and spirits), than to beer', and suggests that it may be the orig. of *tiddly*, drunk.—2. A sickly, very thin child: lower classes':—1923 (Manchon).—3. A Chinese: r.s., on *Chink*. See **tid,** 4.—4. See:-

tiddlywinks. Twins: since 1960 at latest. Petch cites ITV, 24 Nov. 1974.—2. In *play tiddlywinks*, to copulate: euph. or trivial.—3. For terms used in the game, see TIDDLYWINKS, in Appx.

tiddy. (Of clothes) pretty; pretty-pretty: Society: ca. 1930–9. (Allingham, 1938.) Ex *tiddyvated* = titivated.

tiddy oggie or **oggy.** A Cornish pastie made of meat and potatoes: RN. Often simply *oggie*, as in the naval chorus: 'Carry me back to the West Countree, where the oggies grow on trees: cor, bugger!, Janner.' Perhaps orig. *tatie oggy*, as that var. suggests; or ex *tidbit* (= titbit); *oggie* seems to be a fanciful arbitrariness, it does not appear in *EDD*. (E.P.; P.B.)

tidgen. Night: back s. Esp. *on tidgen*, on night-work: 'Working from 5 p.m. until midnight' (London *Evening News*, 13 Nov. 1936); 'Night work done by tugmen and lightermen on the river [Thames]' (Granville). Cf. **midties.**

tie. The need of constant attendance (e.g. on invalids or children); restraint, or deficiency, of freedom: coll. and dial.

tie in with. To link up with (plans, or disposition of forces): Army coll.: since ca. 1930. P-G-R.

tie one on. To get (very) drunk: adopted, ex US, later C.20. 'You have your problem drinker who ties one on in the evenings and at weekends' (*Now!*, 16 Apr. 1981). Cf. synon. **hang one on.**

tie up a dog. To obtain credit for drinks at a hotel: Aus. (B., 1942.) Cf. **dog,** n., 8, a drinking debt, and the occ. early C.20 var. *chain up a pup*. 'A [British] farmer would use *dog tied up* to explain why he always bought from the same merchant; in other words, he owed him a lot of money so couldn't go else-where' (M. Beale, 1985): earlier C.20.

tied up. Hanged: low:—1923 (Manchon).—2. Thoroughly pre-pared; in perfect order: Services': since ca. 1925. Cf. **but-toned up**; **sewn up.**

tiffic(k)s. Odds and ends of iron (e.g. screws): nautical:—1923 (Manchon). Origin? P.B.: has it perhaps some connection with artificer? See:-

tiffy. An engine-room ar*tificer*: nautical: from late 1890s. F.T. Bullen, 1899 (*OED*).—2. Hence, any artificer or fitter: mechanics'. Blaker.—3. Hence, 'a carpenter's term of con-tempt for a botching incompetent fellow-carpenter—i.e., one fit only to work with metals. Heard ca. 1967' (R.S.).—4. An artificer of the Royal Army Ordnance Corps; applied loosely to a gun fitter of the Royal Artillery: Army: since ca. 1910. H. & P.—5. As *Tiffy*, a Hawker *Typhoon* fighter air-craft: RAF: 1943+.

tiffy bloke. An engine-room artificer: RN. (H. & P.) An elab. of prec., 1.

tig. All right. See **teek-hi.**

tiger. 'The steward who acts as personal servant to the captain of a liner': nautical. (Bowen.) Ex C.19 s. for a boy-groom, or servant.—2. A formidable opponent, esp. at lawn tennis: coll.:—1934 (*COD*, 3rd ed., Sup.). Opp. *rabbit.*—3. A diesel locomotive: railwaymen's: later C.20. 'Ex its roar of power' (Granville, letter, 1967).—4. A wife: Cockney s. (Daniells, 1980.) See quot'n at **six-and-eight.**—5. In *on the tiger*, on a heavy drinking-bout: Aus.: since ca. 1910. B., 1942.—6. Heroin: drugs c. (Stockley, 1986.) P.B.: perhaps, like 5, ex 'to have a tiger by the tail' (unable to let go, and doomed).—7. See **three cheers and a tiger**; **turn you inside out.**

tiger-box. See PRISONER-OF-WAR SLANG, §1, in Appx.

tiger country. 'Rough, thickly wooded terrain feared by air-men; any primitive area' (Wilkes): Aus.: WW2 and since.

tiger-hunter. A mat-mender, the trade gen. being learnt in gaol: c.:—1932 ('Stuart Wood'). Prob. ex rugs of tiger-skin.

tiger piss. 'Lowerdeck name for beer sold on a certain foreign station. (From the picture of a tiger on the bottle)': RN: since ca. 1930. (Granville.) Cf. **panther's piss.** P.B.: *Tiger* beer is brewed in Singapore; cf. Burgess' use of the brewers' slogan as the title of his novel set in Malaya, *Time for a Tiger*, 1956.

tiger tank. 'Wank. Usually in the sense of "not worth a . . ." rather than masturbation' (Daniells, 1980): r.s.: 1970s. Ex the 1960s oil company's slogan, *put a tiger in your tank*; a change from the usu. r.s. use of the names of various banks in this context. (P.B.)

tigering. 'Working hard under adverse conditions; roughing it' (Wilkes): Aus.: since later C.19.

Tigerschmitt. A De Havilland *Tiger Moth* training biplane: R Aus. AF joc.: WW2. (B., 1943.) The Messerschmitt 109 was the German Air Force's equivalent of the British Spitfire fighter.

tight-arsed. Stingy, money-mean: low. 'Tight-arsed with his purse strings' (Keyes, 1966).

tight as a drum. Extremely drunk. (Hutchinson, 1908.) An elab. on s. *tight* = drunk (since earlier C.19).—2. 'Said of a boy's belly or "tummy" after eating his fill of cakes as a birth-day or Christmas indulgence' (L.A., 1976): since ca. 1930.

tight as a fart. Exceedingly tipsy: low: since ca.1925.

tight as, or **tighter than, a fish's arsehole.** Exceedingly mean: low; with **and that's watertight** sometimes added. Other creatures thus watertight are *crabs* and *ducks*: Peppitt records the former as MN; in *Heart*, 1962, occurs the ellipti-cal *tight as a fish's*.

tight as a gnat's arse. Cockney var. of prec. (Muvver): later C.20. Cf. **within a gnat's.**

tight as a mouse's ear 'ole. Very tight, applied to a vagina: raf-fish M.C.P.: mid-C.20. (P.B.)

tight as a tick. Extremely drunk: low and Forces'. 'Presumably from the appearance of a tick gorged with blood' (Philip Gas-kell). See also **tighter than a tick.**

tight section. 'Water made rough and hard to ride by rips or cross-currents' (*Sun-Herald*, 22 Sep. 1963): Aus. surfers' coll.: since ca. 1955.

tight ship. See **run a tight ship.**

tight-wad. A person mean with money: adopted, ca. 1934, from US. (Kersh, 1938.) I.e. he keeps his hand closed tight upon his wad of notes.

tighten (one's) **galabieh.** To tighten one's belt: Egyptian-service military coll.: from ca. 1920. The n. is direct ex Arabic.—2. Hence, from ca. 1925, to make the best of a bad job.

tighter than a crab's arsehole. Var. of **tight as a fish's . . .**

tighter than a tick. Excessively mean; also close-mouthed: Can.: later C.20. 'You can't get secrets from him, he's tighter than a tick' (Leech, 1981). Cf. **tight as a tick.**

tighter than a witch's cunt. 'Very tight, as in hard to get off; usu. in ref. to jar lids, nuts or bolts, etc. For Protestant use, say "nun's cunt" ' (Leech, 1981): Can.: later C.20.

tighties. Women's drawers that fit very tight: feminine coll.: from ca. 1933. See quot'n at **neathie-set.**

tightified. (Rendered) tight; close-fitting: (low) coll. Macken-zie, 1933.

tike, gen. **tyke; T.** A Roman Catholic: Aus. (B., 1942.) A pun —or a rhyme—on *Mike*, but cf. **Taig.**

tiller. Steering wheel of a motorcar: Aus. motorists': since ca. 1930. (B.P.) 'Mostly likely a metaphor from boats—but some [early] autos did have tillers rather than steering wheels' (R.C., 1976).

tillikum. A friend: Can. West Coast: since ca. 1930. Chinook; lit., 'people, friends'. (Leechman.)

tilly or, by personification, **Tilly.** A utility van or truck: Army: since ca. 1939. H. & P., 'See also **ute** or doodle-bug'. I.e. *util-ity*.

Tilly Bates. An illiteracy for **tiddler's bait.** Franklyn.

Tim. 'A nickname for a Roman Catholic' (Munro, 1985): Glas-gow. Cf. synon. **Dan.**

timber! (with stress on the 2nd syllable, which is prolonged). An exclam. uttered when something is about to fall: Aus.: since ca. 1920, 'Ex tree-fellers' use of the word when tree is about to fall' (B.P.). The word has long been 'in daily use in North American lumber camps' (Leechman), and the Aus. usage may well have derived from that of Can. and the US. P.B.: some use also in UK, since mid-C.20 at latest.

time. A redundant suffix, e.g., 'I'll see you twelve o'clock time' = at about 12 o'clock: coll. (L.A.)—2. In (it's) *time I* (you, we) *wasn't* (*weren't*) *here*, I (etc.) ought to have departed already: (usu. joc.) coll.: since mid-C.20 (?earlier). (P.B.)

time bomb. Is 'a useful device for the [computer] fraudster who does not want to be around when his crime is actually com-mitted. He uses the computer's clock to activate his program when he himself is far away from the scene' (*Telegraph Sun-day Mag.*, 10 June 1984). A *logic bomb* is similar, but uses a combination of events rather than the computer's clock as a trigger (Ibid.).

time out. Time set aside for specific purpose, for something that one wants to do, (usu.) outside one's normal routine: adopted, ex US, early 1970s, by advertising copywriters, as in, e.g., 'Give yourself a treat—take time out to . . .'; >, by late 1970s, gen. coll., superseding the older Brit. *time off*. The *out* is redundant. (P.B.)

Times Lit., The. *The Times Literary Supplement*: book-world coll.: from 1901.

timesing. See **share-bys.**

timothy. A brothel: Aus. c.: since ca. 1930. B., 1953.

Timothy's. A branch of the Timothy White chain of stores in southern England: coll.: ca. 1910–1970s.

timp. A *timpano* or orchestral kettledrum; usually the pl. *timps*, the timpani: musicians'.

tin, the. Tin-mining country: Aus. coll. Devanney, 1944.

tin-arse; -back; -bum. A lucky person: Aus. s.: resp. C.20; since late C.19; since mid-C.20 (to judge from the quot'ns in my source, Wilkes, who suggests '?from being impervious to kicks in the backside. Apparently unrelated to *tin* = money'). Hence *tin-arsed* = lucky. Cf. **tinny**.

tin(-)basher. A metalworker or coppersmith metalworker: RAF: since ca. 1930. Jackson, 1943; Brickhill, 1946.

tin beard. A crêpe-hair beard that, unpainted at edges, has a metallic look: actors': late C.19–20. Granville.

tin-bitser. See **Rolls-can-hardly** and **bitser**.

tin-bum. See **tin-arse.**

tin can. A destroyer, esp. one of the fifty obsolete American destroyers that came to Britain in 1940: RN.

Tin-can Alley. The London street that specialises in second-hand cars: since ca. 1955. A pun on *Tin Pan Alley*.

tin can (on wheels). An old, esp. if noisy, car: Aus., mostly teenagers': since mid-1950s. P.B.: also Brit.: cf. **banger; bomber.**

tin dog. Tinned meat: Aus.: since ca. 1905. B., 1942.

tin ear. An eavesdropper: Aus. Baker.—2. A fool; a simpleton: Aus.: since ca. 1920. Baker.—3. In *have a tin ear*, or *have tin ears*, or *tin-eared*, to be unmusical, tone-deaf: since ca. 1945. Hence, in e.g. literature, a dearth of feeling for what is consonant with a particular style, as in 'Nothing betrays [i.e. spoils the work of] a writer [of fantasy] more quickly and completely than a tin-ear' (Edwards, 1983). Cf. **cloth ears**, 2.

Tin-Ear Alley. See **Cauliflower Alley**. Perhaps suggested by America's *Tin Pan Alley*.

tin fish, n. A torpedo: RN: it arose just before WW1 (Carr, 1939). Adopted by the RAF ca. 1937 (Jackson). Cf. synon. **mouldy**, and **paraffin budgie**, a helicopter.

tin-fish or **tinfish,** v. To torpedo: RN: 1939+. (Harling, 1946.) Ex the n.

tin hare. The mechanical quadruped used in dog-racing: coll.: since late 1920s.

tin hat, n. A helmet: theatrical. Cf. **tin beard**.—2. A soldier's steel helmet: from late 1915. In WW2, also civilians', in the home defence services.—3. In *put a* or *the tin hat on* (*it*, or something), to finish, in a manner regarded as objectionable by the speaker: from ca. 1900.

tin-hat, v. To show contempt for; to talk down to and at: Aus.: since ca.1919. (B., 1942.) E.P. recorded a second sense of *put a* or *the tin hat on* (see n., 3), as Glasgow s. for 'to "talk big" ':—1934.

tin lid. A child: r.s., on *kid*. Cf. synon. *God forbid*, and **teapot-lid**.

tin Lizzie. A Ford motor-car: from ca. 1915. Occ. *Lizzie*.—2. Hence, any (cheap) motor-car: from ca. 1920.

tin man. See **come the tin man.**

tin off. 'The stuff [viz. honey] we sold was "tinned off" into four-gallon tins from a tap at the base of the tank' (Tennant, 1956): Aus. coll.: since ca. 1920.

tin-opener. A steel-cutting tool used in safe-breaking: Aus. Kelly, 1955.—2. A tank-destroying aircraft: Army: 1944–5. P-G-R.

Tin Pan Alley. The Charing Cross Road district, where song publishers flourish: since ca. 1935. 'Probably [I would say 'undoubtedly': P.B.] adopted from US, where it refers to the centre of popular music publishing, recording, etc., near Times Square, New York City. W. & F. date its US use from ca. 1925. The reference was to the alleged sound of the compositions in question' (R.C., 1976).

tin plate. A companion: r.s., on *mate*. An occ. var. of **china**, q.v.

tin-pot. (Of a place, a town, etc.) Small; insignificant: NZ coll. (Slatter.) Ex the S.E. sense, 'cheap, inferior'.

tin pound. 'In 1983 we shall have two new coins—a £1 piece made out of a yellow alloy, already nicknamed "the tin pound", and a seven-sided 20p piece' (*Now!*, 6 Feb. 1981). The term did not 'catch on', but see **Maggie**, 8.

tin-scratcher, -scratching. Tin-miner, -mining: Aus. (Idriess, 1932.) Ex 'to scratch for tin'.

tin soldier. 'A voyeur-type male, usually of middle- or upper-class background, who voluntarily acts as a prostitute's

"slave" or companion for no apparent reward (prostitutes' slang)' (Powis): later C.20.—2. See **come the tin man.**

tin tack. A sack: r.s.: from ca. 1879. (P.P., 1932.) Hence, as *the tin tack*, 'the sack' = dismissal; *get the tin tack*, to lose one's job: C.20. (Gardner, 1967.) Franklyn classes it 'not of frequent occurrence—"the sack" seems to be sufficiently slangy in itself.'—2. See:-

tin tacks. Esp. *come* (or *get*) *down to t.t.*, an occ. coll. var. of . . . *brass tacks*: both are r.s. on Cockney pron. of *facts*.

tin termites. Rust: motorists', engineers', etc., joc.: since late 1960s. ''Fraid the dreaded tin termites have got into me little Old Min [Austin Mini]' (heard 1972: P.B.).

tin tit. A steel helmet: RAF: mid-1930s. (R.S.) Short for:-

tin titfa (or **-fer** or **-for**). A steel helmet: nautical, esp. RN: since mid-1930s. (H. & P.) Var. of *tin hat*; *titfer*, later C.19–20 r.s. *tit-for-tat*, hat.

tin town. A hutment of corrugated iron: Army coll.: since 1915. (B. & P.) P.B.: esp., in mid-C.20, the huge army camp at Bulford, Wiltshire.

tincture. A light drug in liquid form: joc. euph.: since ca. 1960; ob. by 1975. *Groupie*, 1968.—2. (?)Hence, by late 1970s, a drink of liquor: raffish joc.: since late 1970s. 'He'd be sparko after his usual lunchtime tincture' (Burn, 1980). But this may be a revival (?inspired by the magazine *Private Eye*), and sense 1 the derivative, for it has an Edwardian flavour (P.B.).

ting-ting-bang. 'The equivalent of the Army's "One-One-Two" to illustrate swiftness and precision of action. It represents the ringing of a fire-buzzer followed by the discharge of a gun, e.g., "I ordered 'out boom' and ting-ting-bang, there it was." ' (Bolster, 1945): RN: WW2. Cf. **ching! ching! ching!**

tingalairy. A hand-worked auger: railwaymen's. (*Railway*.) Ex the West Yorkshire dial. *tingerlary*, a street organ. Echoic. Cf. **wimbler**.

tingle. A 'tinkle' on the telephone: Aus.: since ca. 1945. By assimilation of 'tin*k*le' to 'ring'. (B.P.)

tingloo. A corrugated iron clad Nissen hut banked up all over the outside with packed earth to keep it on the ground during the winter gales: RAF in Iceland: WW2. Adkin, 1983.

tinhorn gambler. A petty gambler: Can. since ca. 1912, Aus. since ca. 1920, NZ since ca. 1922. Adopted from US: for US, see *Underworld*; for Can., see Mason, 1924.

tinies. Very small children: coll.: since ca.1920. Ex *tiny tots*.

tinker. A child, esp. in exasperated address by adult: 'You little *tinker!*': domestic coll.: since late C.19, perhaps much earlier. Ex the reputed mischief and mischievousness of *tinkers*, S.E. for itinerant repairers of pots and pans. E.P. recalls its use in NZ, ca. 1904, and Aus., ca. 1910; P.B. was thus admonished by his grandmothers in the early 1940s.—2. Penis: Can. schoolchildren's: since mid-C.20. (Barr, 1968.)

tinker's. Tinker's curse: Aus. coll. Park, 1950, 'Nobody caring a tinker's.' Cf. **not care a . . .** , esp. the shortening of *not give a monkey's* (toss).

tinker's mufti. A dress half military, half civilian: military coll.:—1923 (Manchon). Tinkers frequently wore very odd garments.

tinkety-tonk! 'A farewell current among "bright young people" . . . Wodehouse, *passim*, Macdonell, 1933' (R.S.): ca. 1920–35. Artificial echoic. Cf. **ticketty-boo**, and *toodle-pip*.

tinkle, n. A telephone-call; mostly *give* (someone) *a tinkle*, to phone them: trivial coll.: since ca. 1910. Also, since ca. 1925, NZ (Slatter).—2. Money: raffish: mid-C.20. Wollaston, 1965, 'She married a bit of tinkle'. Echoic, perhaps suggested by *tin*. (P.B.)—3. A urination: trivial, domestic: since ca.1930. Ex:-

tinkle, v. To urinate: children's, hence also nannies' and parents': since 1920 (?much earlier). Ex the sound of urine falling into a light metal chamberpot. Leechman compares the similarly echoic Ger. *pinkeln*, to pee.—2. 'When I was young [mid-C.20] this meant to make a telephone number

465

ring [e.g.] twice, then ring off, so as to pass on a pre-arranged message without having to pay for the call, e.g. "I'll tinkle when I reach the station" ' (Sayers, 1985).

tinkler. A spoon: nautical, esp. RN. Ex the RN lowerdeck jingle, 'Tinkle, tinkle little spoon; knife and fork will follow soon', uttered as any piece of cutlery is accidentally tipped over the ship's side with the dishwater. Has var. *tinkly*. (Peppitt, 1977.)

tinned. Tipsy: since ca. 1940. (Bell, 1946.) A pun on *canned*.

tinned air. Artificial ventilation: nautical: from ca. 1910. Bowen.

tinned dog. Bully beef: Aus.: since late C.19. Wilkes.

tinner. Afternoon *t*ea and *d*inner combined. P.B.: not common, and prob. † by mid-C.20. Cf. later C.20 *brunch*: breakfast + lunch.

tinnie. 'We call beer cans tinnies now that everybody's caught on to "tubes" ' (*New Society*, 5 Aug. 1982): drinking-places'. Prob. ex Aus., where current since mid-1960s.

tinny. Lucky: Aus. and NZ. Ex **tin-arse**, q.v.—2. Cheap: Aus.: since ca. 1925. Made of tin, not of iron, or steel.—3. Mean, close-fisted: Aus.: since ca. 1935. (B.P.) Money-minded.

tins, on the. On the scoring-board: cricketers' coll. (*OED* Sup.) Ex the tin plates on which the numbers are painted.

tinted folk. People with 'coloured' or black skins. Aus. joc. coll.: popularised by Barry Humphries' monologues: since ca. 1950s. (Raab.)

tip. Applied to a place, esp. a room, that is very untidy, as 'Your bedroom is an absolute tip! If you don't do something . . . ' (any mother to teenage offspring): mainly domestic: later C.20. I.e., it looks like the municipal rubbish-dump. (P.B.)

tip and run, n. and v. 'Used during the Great War of German naval dashes at seaside resorts' (W.). Ex the *tip* (hit lightly) *and run* of cricket. P.B.: during WW2 applied more to German air raiders, usu. crossing the Channel or North Sea singly or in small numbers: coll., or j.; also as adj., *tip and run raid*(er)*s*: a var. of S.E. *hit-and-run*.

tip-off, n. A police informer: Aus. police: since ca. 1915. Kelly, 1955, 'Information supplied by underworld informers . . . variously known as "shelfs, tip-offs, stool-pigeons, phiz-gigs".' Immediately ex *tip off*, a piece of information, itself current since ca. 1905 and derived from **tip off**, v., 1. P.B.: this latter has >, in later C.20, informal S.E., e.g., in BBC news broadcasts, frequently, 'Police (or customs, etc.) acting on a tip-off . . . '

tip off, v. To give private information, or a friendly hint or warning: coll.: since ca. 1900. Expansion of synon. s. *tip* (since early 1880s).—2. To kill; low:—1928 (*OED* Sup., 1933).

tip-slinger. A racecourse tipster. Hence, by back-formation, *tip-sling*, v., whence *tip-slinging*, vbl n.: since ca. 1930. Doone; B., 1953.

tip them out. (Of railway officials) to clear a train of public passengers: railwaymen's, esp. underground railway guards': since mid-1940s. *Daily Telegraph*, 14 May 1960.

tipply. Unsteady: coll.: 1906 (*OED*). Lit., apt to tipple over.—2. Hence, drunk: from ca. 1910. Burton, 1932.

tippy. Generous with *tips* (of money): servants' and subordinate staffs'. Brandon, 1931.

tiptoe on the bow caps. 'Hitting the sea-bottom. Rarely used' (Malin, 1979): RN, esp. HM submarine *Astute*: mid-1960s.

tired. (Of a picture, or rather of the painting thereof) over-worked: artists'. Virtually synon. with the longer-established *tight*. Also *hard*. (Lobley,—1937.)

Tired Tim. See **Weary Willie**.

tisdalling. 'Tisdalling civil servants' (Guardian, 15 May 1984): ephemeral. Ex Sarah Tisdall, who leaked information about the arrival of *Cruise* missiles at USAF airbase Greenham Common to the press, and was jailed for 6 months.

tishy. Drunk: ca. 1910–40. (Horne, 1923.) A drunken pron. of *tipsy*.

tisket. A bastard, lit. and fig.: ca. 1940–50. Ex the popular song words, 'A tisket, a tasket, A little yellow basket', where *basket* euphemises *bastard*. Franklyn.

tissied up. Dressed up; smartly dressed: Aus.: since ca. 1925. (Courtier, 1964.) Perhaps a blend of *tit*ivated + *sissi*fied. P.B.: but see **tizz up**.

tissue. A racing list: racing men's and racecourse workers'. (Henry, 1942.) Ex the flimsy paper used therefor.

tiswas. See **all of a tiswas**, and cf. **tizzy**.

tit. A sol. spelling and pron. of *teat*: prob. from C.17 or even earlier. P.B.: so can it still be called 'a sol.'? I think not: it is rather 'Standard Low Eng.'—2. Hence, a female breast: low, esp. Aus., coll.: late C.19–20. 'In Australia, *tit* always = breast, not nipple' (B.P.). P.B.: in later C.20, unless firmly specified, B.P.'s comment is true also of low coll. in UK, so that *tit*, in this sense, has come to mean 'woman in general', as in 'I fancy a bit of tit tonight', and 'Lovely bit of tit, she was' = she was a fine and shapely girl, without necessarily emphasising appreciation of her bust.—3. It does, however, = 'nipple' in its RAF sense, a gun-button: since ca. 1930. (H. & P.) Esp. in *squeeze the tit* (in firing a machine-gun).—4. Hence, any finger-pressed 'button' (of, e.g., an electric bell): RAF: since ca. 1938. (Jackson.) Whence, loosely and in gen. coll. by 1955, any button-like or knobby protuberance that vaguely resembles a nipple.

tit about or **around.** To act ineffectually and trivially or irritatingly; to play about at doing something, instead of really tackling it; to potter uselessly or time-wastingly: low.

tit-for-tats. Female breasts: Aus. low. (*Rats*, 1944.) An elab. of **tit**, 2.

tit-hammock. A brassière: sailors': since ca. 1920. By 1950, fairly gen. low s. Cf. **titbag**.

tit-head. A policeman, exp. uniformed with helmet: Nottingham youths' (prob, more widespread). (Fraser, 1986.) Graphic.

tit in a tight crack, have (one's). To find oneself in an awkward and uncomfortable position, whether physical or emotional: low Can.: since ca. 1920.

tit in a trance. Usu. in (standing there) *like a . . .* , dreamy; abstracted: low (mostly Londoners). (L.A.) John Smith, Bath, supplies, 1981, the variants *like a tom tit on a blather o' lard* or *on a side o' beef*, which show that the tit in question is prob. the bird rather than earlier s. *tit*, a fool.

tit(s)-man. A male more interested in a woman's breasts than in, e.g., her legs: low: since ca. 1910. Cf. **arse man**.

tit-show. A vaudeville act in which uncovered female breasts are to be seen: raffish coll.: since ca. 1930.

tit ticklers. Metal studs decorating the back of a young male motorcyclist's riding jacket: motorcyclists': since ca. 1965. (Dunford.) Cf. **peach-perch**.

titbag. A brassière: low: since ca. 1945. Cf. **tit-hammock**.

titless wonder. 'A flat-chested woman' (Parsons, 1973): RN officers': since ca. 1930. Cf. the equally factual *chinless wonder*.

titley (or **tiddley**) **and binder.** A drink of beer and a piece of bread-and-cheese (cf. **binder**, 1): public-house phrase. Ryan, 1935.

tits. As exclam., an expression of anger or annoyance: later C.20. Cf. similar use of *arseholes!*, *ballocks!*, etc. (P.B., 1988.)—2. See **get on** (one's) **tit(s)**.

tits like a young heifer. As in 'She's got tits on her like a young heifer': raffish, M.C.P. (Raper, 1973.) Of rural orig.

tits-man. See **tit(s)-man**.

tits off! Go away!: low: since ca. 1955. Cf. **piss off!**, **sod off!**

tits-up. 'Unserviceable, out of action (used of aeroplanes, cars, plans, people: tits-up on the runway)' (*Fighter Pilot*, 1981): RAF: later C.20. Formed on comparable *balls-up*, *ballsed up*. (P.B.)

tittle-tat. A tittle-tattle; a tale-bearer: Aus. juvenile: since ca. 1930. (B.P.) Cf. older *tell tale tit*.

titty. Synon. with **tit**, 2, 3, q.v. P-G-R.—2. In *hard* or *tough titty!*, bad luck!: sometimes genuine consolation, but often ironic, as 'Well, that's *your* tough titty!': low. Also, just as common, *hard* or *tough tit*. (P.B.)

titty-bag; -bottle. Resp., a small linen bag containing bread sprinkled with sweetened milk, given by some nurses to their charges; a bottle (of milk) with teat attached: children's:—1923 (Manchon).

tizwas. See **all of a tiswas**.

tizz. A shortened form of **tizzy**, n.: since ca.1930. Gaye, 1959.

tizz (or **tiz**) **up.** To dress up, esp. flashily; to furbish or smarten (some object): Aus.: since ca. 1938. (B., 1953.) Apparently ex **tizzy**, adj. See also **tissied up**, and cf. synon. **tart up**.

tizzy, n. A 'state': esp. *get into a tizzy*, to get 'all worked up'. Perhaps ex S.E. *hysteria*. Cf. **all of a tiswas**.

tizzy, adj. Ostentatiously or flashily dressed: Aus.: since ca. 1935. (B., 1953.) A thinning and a disguising of S.E. *tidy*. Or perhaps rather ex S.E. *tidy* + s. *jazzy*; or, more prob., ex older *titivated*.—2. Hence, flashy, ostentatious, showy but cheaply made, as, e.g., an inferior Espresso coffee machine: Aus.: since ca. 1945. (B.P.)

tizzy-snatcher. An assistant-paymaster: RN: earlier C.20. 'Taffrail', 1916. Granville, 1962, however, glosses it 'Naval paymaster'. Ex *tizzy*, C.19 s., 'sixpence', and the C.19 RN sense, 'a purser'.

to-and-fro'ing. A constant moving-about; work that necessitates much getting-about: coll.: since ca. 1945. P.B.: just as common is *to'ing-and-fro'ing*, as in 'There was a great deal of to'ing-and-fro'ing before everybody got settled down.'

to-and-from. A concertina: since ca. 1910. Ex the movements of the player's arms.—2. An English serviceman: Aus. prisoners of war in the Far East: 1942–5. Rhyming on *pom*. B., 1953.

toad. One who has done wrong yet is none the less popular: Marlborough College: since the late 1920s.

toast. To blush: Shrewsbury: since mid-1930s. Marples.

toast-rack. A term applied, since ca. 1910, to the horse-trams at Douglas, Isle of Man. (Chamberlain.)—2. 'One of the old-style footboard trams still used in Sydney' (B., 1943): Aus.: since ca. 1920. 'Discontinued by 1960' (Wilkes)—but the term continues nostalgically.

tobacco road. Cadgers taking payment in tobacco for odd favours, from trawlermen going off to sea: trawlermen's coll.: later C.20. (Piper, 1974.) Prob. suggested by Erskine Caldwell's 1932 novel of the same name, later dramatised and running for over 3,000 performances on Broadway. (P.B.)

tober. A road: tramps' c. and Romany, the former in 1845 in '*No.747*'.—2. Hence, a circus-field: Parlyaree (?)and circus s.:—1933 (Seago).—3. Among grafters, it is a fair-ground or market; hence, one's pitch thereon or therein. *Cheapjack*, 1934.—4. Hence, 'rent for stallholder's or caravan site' (*M.T.*): market-traders': since 1930s.

tober-mush. A market-inspector: market-traders' (e.g. Petticoat Lane). Ex prec., 3, 4 + **mush**, 4: cf. **coring mush** and **rye mush**.—2. Fair-ground official; collective for such officials: grafters'. *News of the World*, 28 Aug. 1938.

toby. A tramp: c. (Orwell, 1933.) Ex C.19 c., the highway.—2. A (young) child, often in address, as 'You little (or young) toby!': domestic: late C.19–earlier 20. One of my grandmother's epithets for me, late 1930s–40s. Cf. synon. use of **tinker** or **Turk**. (P.B.)—3. A weak-witted, clumsy-handed, but very willing, obliging fellow: Aus. B., 1942.—4. A dissolute girl or young woman: Aus. low: from ca. 1920. B.—5. A man servant: Haileybury: since ca. 1920. (Marples.) Common-property of a familiar male given name.—6. In *have a toby on*, to be well disposed towards: Aus.: since ca. 1925. Alan Marshall, 1944, 'I'm not much chop on pies, but I'm a toby on puddins.' Opp. *have a grape on*.

tod. On (one's) *tod*, alone: r.s.: since late C.19. (*Cheapjack*, 1934.) A shortening of earlier Tod Sloan, famous late-Victorian jockey. Cf. synon. **Jack Jones** and **Jack** or **Pat Malone**, and see **pea pod**.

toddle, to go, walk, depart, is, by the *OED*, considered S.E.; but its C.20. use, esp. in the upper and upper-middle classes (see, e.g., Sayers' *Lord Peter Wimsey* novels), seems to me to be coll. *Sunday Express Mag.*, 11 Oct. 1982, notes its later C.20. use among Sloane Rangers, q.v.; and Nash, 1985, gives an example of the merely facetious 'What say we toddle down to my humble abode for drinkies?'

todge. To walk slowly, with an effort, but with some purpose, as an elderly person might, even if only window-shopping: domestic coll. Perhaps suggested by prec., with the stoutness of *podge*. (P.B.)

toe-biter. 'If there is a long wait, without a job, the cabmen on the rank are "having a binder"—or, in cold weather, a "toe-biter". Some of them may decide to "run away"; that is, drive off without a job' (Hodge, 1939); taxi-drivers': since ca. 1910.

toe-face. An objectionable or dirty fellow: low:—1923 (Manchon). Cf. **toe-rag**.

toe-nail poisoning. Ptomaine poisoning: joc.: from 1934.

toe-rag. Morlock, 1965, writing of 1864, 'Stockings being unknown, some luxurious men wrapped round their feet a piece of old shirting, called, in language more expressive than elegant, a "toe-rag"' (Wilkes). In pl., those windings of cotton-wool about the ball of the foot and the toes which, to displace socks, prevent blistering: tramps' c. Jennings, 1932.—2. Hence, a beggar: provincial s.:—1909 (Ware).—3. 'A London docker who works bulk grain ex-ship': nautical: earlier C.20. Bowen.—4. A term of contempt for a person; a 'dog's-body': Aus.: since ca. 1905. (B., 1942.) Cf. **toe-ragger**. But current in Brit. Army, WW1; in Glasgow University and schools in 1927, and prob. for some years earlier. It occurs as a Cockney usage in Kersh, 1958. The term 'enjoyed' a revival in schools in the mid-1970s, perhaps influenced by some TV show.—5. A £1 note: Aus.: earlier C.20. B., 1943.—6. 'In the Merchant Navy (at any rate up to the 1920s) dried Newfoundland cod—a singularly unappetising Friday dish aboard ship. (On the authority of a retired sea-captain friend)' (R.S., 1969).—7. A dirty thing; rubbish, as in 'I'm not fencing that toe-rag' = I'm not selling that rubbish: market-traders'. *M.T.*—8. A cigarette: r.s., on *fag*. Barnes, 1976.

toe-ragger. 'Name applied to corn porters. When working down the ship's hold they would tie sacking round their boots to stop the corn from getting into them' (Ash): London dockers': earlier C.20.

Toe-Rags, the. The Tuareg (Saharan tribesmen): Army: since ca. 1942. (Sanders.) By the process of Hobson-Jobson.

toe the line. To appear in an identification parade: c.: from ca. 1910.—2. To conform: coll. 'If you join the Army you'll have to toe the line.' Ex infantry drill. P.B.: since mid-C.20, in very gen. use, and with specified application, as in 'these place-seeking MPs are all the same—no independence, just toeing the party line all through.'

toey. (Of a horse) speedy: Aus. B., 1953.—2. But also: restive, unsettled: since ca. 1925. At first of horses, then also of persons. (Ibid.) Cf. **towy**.

toff, n. A 'brick', a person behaving handsomely: 1898 (*OED*); slightly ob.—2. Hence, in Aus. c., a dependable fellow-prisoner, or even a warder who's as good as his (good) word: since ca. 1945. (Grindley, 1977.)

toff, v. Esp. *be toffed up*, to be dressed like a 'toff': low: 1928 (*OED* Sup.).

toffee. Tobacco: c.:—1932 ('Stuart Wood'). Ex its colour.—2. (A stick of) gelignite: since mid-1940s. (BBC, 'Z Cars', 11 Mar. 1964.) Gelignite looks rather like soft toffee.—3. 'Nonsense or flattery: "You don't believe that load of toffee, do you?", or "He's full of the old toffee!"' (Powis): since mid-C.20. L.A., 1967, supplies 'Don't give me that toffee', from RAF, Malta, 1960, and glosses 'wrapped-up glib explanation'.—4. In *not for toffee*, not at all; by no manner of means; not in any circumstances: uncultured: late C.19–20. 'Taffrail', 1917; Walpole, 1933; 'That fellow X. can't bat for toffee', of a Test cricketer in 1934. Raab, 1979: 'Also *not for toffee-nuts*: London schoolchildren's: since 1930s; not yet quite†.'

toffee-apple. A Very light, or a tracer bullet, fired as a guide to motor transport moving in the dark: 8th Army: 1942–3.—2. A cask of either asphalt or pitch: railwaymen's: since ca. 1945. (*Railway*, 2nd.) Ironic.

Toffee Men, the. See ASSOCIATION FOOTBALL, in Appx.

toffee-nosed. Supercilious; too proud; conceited; snobbish: 'lower classes'. (F. & G.) It was very popular, as was its var. *toffee-nose* (H. & P.), with the RAF and WAAF in WW2. With a pun on *toffy*.

toffee ration. Marital sexual intercourse: RN: since mid-1940s.

Toffs, the. See ASSOCIATION FOOTBALL, in Appx.

together. Having one's life, one's career, emotions, under control; knowing what one wants and how to get it: adopted, ex US, mid-1960s. 'And . . . sensible Davey, together Davey, making sure he's not left in lurch without a career' (*Groupie*, 1968). Of US usage, W. & F., 1975, notes 'Often in phrases "get it all together" and "have it all together".'

toggy. A small boy's penis: nursery, whence some joc. adult use. (Burt, 1984.)

to'ing and fro'ing. See to-and-fro'ing.

Tojo. A var. of **Private Tojo:** P-G-R.

toke, n. See:-

toke, v. 'To inhale the smoke of a drug-infested cigarette, usually while making "tiff-tiff" noises. *n.* A puff of such a cigarette. Ex 1940s US s. *toke*, drag of a cigarette' (Hibbert, 1983).

tole. A street-corner fight: Teddy-boys': 1954+. Perhaps ex dial. *toll*, a clump (of, e.g., trees). See quot'n at **lamp**, v., 2.

tolly(-)whacker. A roll of paper that, in the form of a club, is used by boys in rough play: Cockneys': from ca. 1920. Ex *tolly*, a candle.

tolo. 'A dance at which the girls pay the admission fee rather than the men' (Leechman): Can.: since ca. 1955. Perhaps ex S.E. *toll*, a tax; perhaps, however, cf. the Newfoundland *tole*, to entice with bait.

tom, n. A tomato: a trade abbr. >, by 1925, a lower-class coll.—2. Any prostitute: police. (*Free-Lance Writer*, Apr. 1948.) Cf. v., and **Toms Patrol.**—3. Jewellery. Short for **tomfoolery**, q.v. Gash, 1983, extends the meaning to anything precious but stolen.—4. Short also for **Tom Mix**, 2; **tom-tits**; **Tom Thumb**, qq.v. See also **Toms.**

tom, v. To be a prostitute: since ca. 1935. 'They were perfectly willing to go "tomming" on the streets to earn a few quid, but I never could' (*Progl*, 1964).—2. 'She's tomming a bit— you know, Uncle Tomming—putting it on [over-acting]' (*Amis*, 1986).

Tom and Dick. Var. of **Tom, Harry and Dick**, sick. (Jones, 1971.) P.B.: this version trips more easily off the tongue. Powis instances 'Where's Roy?'—'He's Tom and Dick.'

Tom Beet. Feet: r.s., mostly itinerant entertainers'. (Lester, 1937.) Much less common than *plates (of meat)*.

Tom Browns. See **Billy Browns.**

tom-cat. A door-mat: r.s. Franklyn 2nd.

tom-catting, n. and adj. Roaming about in search of sexual gratification. Acting like a tom-cat on the prowl. (L.A., 1976.)

Tom, Harry and Dick. Sick: r.s., esp. busmen's: since ca. 1940. (London *Evening News*, 27 Apr. 1954.) See also **Tom and Dick.**

Tom Mix. The number 6: darts- and tombola-players' r.s.: from ca. 1932. (London *Evening News*, 2 July 1937.) From the name of a famous 'Westerns' film-actor.—2. A difficult situation: r.s., on older synon. s. *fix*: since ca. 1935. Franklyn 2nd.—3. 'An injection of a narcotic' (Home Office): drugs world; rhyming on *fix*, n., 1: later C.20. Often shortened to *Tom*.

Tom Pudding or **Tompudding.** A 'compartment boat', worked in 'trains' with other such boats: canal-men's. Rolt, 1944.

tom-tart. 'A girl or woman. Not derogatory, but not used by women of themselves: obsolescent' (Wilkes): Aus.: prob.

r.s., on *sweetheart*: since later C.19. Wilkes quotes *The Sydney Slang Dictionary*, ca. 1882. In C.20, shortened to *Tom*.

Tom Thumb. The human posterior, the buttocks: r.s., on *bum*: since ca. 1920.

tom-tit. To defecate; defecation: r.s., on *shit*: since late C.19 (B. & P.); since mid-C.20 usu. the n., as 'I must have (or go for) a tom-tit' (Llewellyn, 1943; Powis, 1977). Cf. synon. *pony and trap*, (to) crap. See also:-

tom(-)tits. Also used fig., as in 'You give me the tom-tits' = 'the shits'; you disgust me, or irritate me beyond endurance. But *get the tom-tits* = to 'become demoralized with fear' (Culotta). Wilkes quotes Keneally, 1964: 'this silence business. It gives me the toms.'

tom-tom. An accordion: RN lowerdeck: earlier C.20. Knock.

tomato. A girl: Aus.: adopted, 1943, ex US servicemen. (Park, 1950.) Luscious. R.C. adds, 1976, 'Also smooth and well-rounded'.

tomato-can tramp. A tramp that, to sleep, will curl up anywhere: tramps' c.:—1932 (Jennings). Prob. derives ex the utensil being carried as a cooking-tin (Leechman).

tombola. For the calls used in this game, whether known as *house*, *housey-housey*, or *bingo*, see TOMBOLA, in Appx.

tomfoolery. Jewellery: r.s.: late C.19–20. (Harrison, 1943.) Since ca. 1940, and esp. in the underworld, it has often been shortened to *Tom*. Gosling, 1958.

tommy, n. A bookmaker: Aus.: since ca. 1925. B., 1943.—2. Hence, his ledger: since ca. 1930. B., 1953.—3. A 'small shunting disc ground signal' (*Railway*): railwaymen's: since ca. 1920. Cf. **Tommy Dodd.**—4. A Curtiss *Tomahawk* fighter (US P-40), in use with RAF mid-WW2: mostly RAF.—5. A 'Tommy gun' (Thompson sub-machine gun): Aus.: adopted, ca. 1940, ex US. Drake Brockman, 1947, concerning early 1942.

tommy, v. To depart; to make off, decamp: Aus. low. Baker.

Tommy Dodd. A calling, or a call, on a warning signal: railwaymen's r.s., on *nod*: from ca. 1930. (*Railway*, 2nd.) Cf. **tommy**, 3.

Tommy-toes. (Or as one word.) Tomatoes: London joc. Also as *tommy-ay-toes*.

tomorrow. In *on for t.*, (of a clock) very fast: coll., almost a c.p.

Toms, the. The privates in the Parachute Regiments: Army: 1950s. Cavanagh, 1965.

Toms Patrol, the. The Vice Squad: police: since late 1940s. (Newman, 1970.) See **tom**, n., 2.

ton. £100; *half a ton*, £50: gamblers' c.: since ca. 1940. Hoby, 1946.—2. Usu. *the ton*, a speed of 100 m.p.h.: motorcyclists': since ca. 1948. See also **ton-up.**—3. A score of 100 runs: cricketers', ex cricket reporters': since ca. 1955.

ton of bricks. Usu. in *be* (or *come*) *down on* (someone) *like a ton of bricks*, to reprimand very severely; to punish heavily; to be extremely and adversely critical of, as 'he soon spotted my mistake, and was down on it like . . . ': coll. (P.B.)

ton-up, n. and adj. 100 m.p.h., as in *doing the ton-up* (an elab. of **ton**, 2), and in *ton-up boys*, those who have achieved this speed on a motorcycle; hence, young 'tearaway' motorcyclists in general: since ca. 1955; less common, but still current, in 1983. (P.B.)

tonge. Penis: low (esp. in RAF of ca. 1930–50). Cf. **toggy.**

tongue job. Cunnilingus, whether gen. or particular: since ca. 1960. Hollander.

tongue-pie, get or **give.** To be scolded; to scold: lower classes':—1923 (Manchon). Cf. earlier *rag-sauce*.

tongue wrestling. Kissing, as in 'couples on the [park-] benches . . . some old geezer tongue-wrestling with his secretary in the lunch break' (M. Harris, quoting a punk [q.v.] girl in London, in *New Society*, 24 May 1984). Cf. **swap spit**, and Mann, 1985, notes synon. *tongue sandwich*.

tonk, n. 'A man with unmasculine characteristics; a male homosexual, esp. in the passive role: derogatory' (Wilkes): Aus.: since ca. 1960. A specialisation of the B., 1941, definitions, 'a simpleton or fool; a dude or fop; a general term of contempt,' which E.P. dated from early 1920s, suggesting that 'dude or fop' was the orig. nuance, and that it might be a perversion of *tony* (person).—2. A term of abuse: N. Country Grammar Schools': from ca. 1945.—3. A hit, at cricket: *have a tonk*: ex v., 1. BBC 3 cricket commentary, 15 Aug. 1981. Cf.:-

tonk, v. At cricket, to hit a ball into the air: Charterhouse and Durham (schools): late C.19–20. Cf. *tonkabout*, the corresponding n. Ex the mainly Midland dial. *tank*, n., a blow; v., to strike.—2. Hence, gen. in passive, to defeat utterly: from ca. 1920. Galsworthy, 1926, 'He seems to enjoy the prospect of getting tonked.'—3. To punish, e.g. to cane: Aus.: since ca. 1920. Baker. To *get tonked* is the usu. passive (B., 1943).

tonky. Fashionable: NZ: since ca. 1935. Slatter, 'She's probably been to a tonky school.' Perhaps a blend of *tony* + *swanky*.

tons of soil. 'Sons of Toil. Strictly a Spoonerism. At the turn of the century [ca. 1900], "Goin' dahn da tons o' soil" meant the local working men's club, such establishments being open to "fellow Workers and Sons of Toil" ' (Hillman, 1974).

tonsil-snatcher. A ship's surgeon: RN. Granville.

tonsil-varnish. 'Messdeck tea' (Granville): RN.

tonsorials. See **touch of the tonsorials.**

too-a-roo! Good-bye!: Aus.: ca. 1919–39. (MacInnes, 1952.) Cf. **tooraloo.**

too bad. Familiar S.E. when used as genuine commiseration, either alone or as 'that's too bad!'; but coll. when used ironically, with derisive lack of sympathy. ?Orig. US. (P.B.)—2. In *not too bad*, really quite good: coll. Cf. *not bad*; *not half*.

too funny for words. Extremely funny: coll.: late C.19–20. Prob. suggested by *too funny for anything*, which was orig. (the late 1860s) US (Thornton).

too much, adj.; always in predicate, as 'The tubes are too much' (excellent or wonderful): Aus. teenagers', esp. surfers': since late 1950s. (B.P.) But also, by 1960, Eng., as in 'Isn't she too much?' [= good at something or other.] (Lejeune, 1967.)

too much on (one's) **plate**(, esp. **have**). (To have) too much to do: since mid-C.20. Fairly gen. throughout UK and the Commonwealth. More than one can eat. P.B.: an East Midlands var. is *too much on* (one's) *wheel*.

too slow to catch cold. Said of a person mentally or physically sluggish: coll. Dent, 1917.

toodle em buck. Teetotum; to gamble with cherry stones: Victorian (Aus.) State School children: ca. 1880–1910. (Innes, 1944.)—2. The game of Crown and Anchor: Can. B. & P.

toodle-oo! See **tootle-oo!**

toofer. An expensive cigar: ?mainly Cockney: ca. 1910–20. (*Green Envelopes*, 1929.) A mere guess: *two for* a crown, i.e. a half crown each. See also **twofer.**

took. Taken by surprise: joc. use of a common sol.: RAF: later C.20. 'We had been "took"; took good too' (*Phantom*).

tool, n. A pickpocket: c. London *Evening News*, 9 Dec. 1936.—2. A weapon: prison c.: since ca. 1942. (Norman.) Senses 1 and 2 prob. really since mid-C.19.—3. 'A jemmy' (Powis): c.—4. See **tools.**

tool, v. To cut, to slash, a person with a razor: c.: since ca. 1945. Norman, 1959.

tool about or **around.** To do nothing in particular: upper classes': from ca. 1910. Iles, 1932, ' "What are you doing with yourself?" "Me, eh? Oh, tooling round, you know. Nothing much." ' Cf. C.19 use of s. *tool*, to drive a coach, > merely, to go; perhaps influenced also by *fool around*. Cf.:-

tool along. To fly without a fixed objective: RAF: since ca. 1925. H. & P.—2. Hence, to walk aimlessly: RAF: since ca. 1938. (Partridge, 1945.) Cf. prec.

tool around. See **tool about.**

tool check. A venereal inspection: RAF mechanics': since ca. 1930. By a pun on C.16–20 s. *tool* = penis.

tool up. (Of a man) to prepare for copulation: low: since ca. 1920. Cf. prec.; see also:-

tooled up, ppl adj. Equipped with weapons: c.: since ca. 1946. (*Observer*, 1 Mar. 1959.) Since ca. 1970, or poss. earlier, also

police usage. Publicised in such BBC programmes as 'The Sweeney', later 1970s (R. Pearsall). Esp. *be*, or *get, tooled up*, as in 'You're to be tooled up, men: these particular villains are dangerous and they carry firearms.'—2. 'In possession of house-breaking implements' (Powis): c.: later C.20. Cf. **tool**, n., 3.

tools. 'Knives, forks and spoons' (Bowen): nautical, late C.19–20; since ca. 1935, also RAF. Cf. synon. **eating**, or **fighting, irons.**—2. Equipment for injecting drugs: drugs c. (Stockley, 1986.) US since—1967 (Spears).

tooniopperty or **tuniopperty.** Opportunity: centre s: early C.20. Manchon.

tooraloo! Goodbye for now!; I'll be seeing you: a mainly Anglo-Irish var. of **tootle-oo**, q.v.: since ca. 1910. Joyce, 1922, ' "Tooraloo," Lenehan said, "see you later." ' Cf. **too-a-roo!** P.B.: both prob. ex pron. rather than genuine var.

toosh. A sovereign, coin or value: c. (esp. tramps'): from before 1935. Ex C.19 *tusheroon*, c., half-a-crown.

toot, n. Money: RN: earlier C.20. (F. & G.) Prob. short for *whistle and hoot* or *toot*, r. on *loot*. Cf. synon. **hoot.**—2. A var. of **tewt.** H. & P.—3. A complaint; a 'moan': Services': since ca. 1930. H. & P.—4. A water-closet: Aus., orig. feminine: since ca. 1950. Ex *toilet*. (B.P.) Rhymes with *hoot*; contrast:—5. (Rhyming with *foot*,) excrement; occ. 'a lump of toot', fig. 'in the shit' = in (deep) trouble: low coll.: since (?)mid-C.20. Also *tooty*; cf. synon. **too-too(s)**. (P.B.)—6. In *have a toot*, to have a drink: since ca. 1930; ob. by 1950. Prompted by 'to wet one's *whistle*'. Cf. the v., 1.—7. 'A line of cocaine for snorting up the nasal passages' (Hibbert, 1983): drugs c. Cf. v., 2.

toot, v. To drink heavily (at one session): RN: since ca. 1939. Granville, '*Exercise toot* is the Wardroom description of a mild "pubcrawl"; on the other hand, *Operation toot* is a monumental drinking party'. Cf. n., 6.—2. Synon. with **snort**, v. (Cutland, 1985.) ?Influence of sense 1, with s. *hooter*, nose.

tooter. 'One who "drinks between drinks", a seasoned performer' (Granville): RN: since ca. 1930. Ex **toot**, v., 1.

tooth-brush. A tooth-brush moustache, so named because, at most one and often only a half-inch laterally, and short and bristly vertically, it closely resembles the hairy part of a small tooth-brush: coll.: from 1915.

toothful. A drink: joc. coll.: from ca. 1920. (Benson, 1924.) Cf. Scot. *toothful*, to tipple.

Toothy. A ship's dental surgeon: RN wardrooms': since ca. 1920. Granville.

tootle. To go; esp. *tootle off*, to depart: dial (C.19–20) form of *toddle* >, in late 1890s, US and reintroduced, as s. or coll., ca. 1920. (Wodehouse, *passim*.) Prob. on *toddle*.

tootle-oo!; loosely, **toodle-oo!** Good-bye!: from ca. 1905, according to Collinson; the *OED* Sup. records it at 1907. Ob. Perhaps ex prec., or maybe, as has been most ingeniously suggested, a Cockney corruption of the French equivalent of '(I'll) see you soon': *à tout à l'heure*.

tootoo(s). 'Excrement' (Powis): domestic and joc.: later C.20. See **toot,** n., 5.

tootsie, tootsy; tootsie (or **-y**)**-wootsie.** (And in voc., *toots*, r. *hoots*.) A young woman; a girl-friend, sweetheart: coll.: adopted, ex US, prob. from Al Jolson's famous chorus 'Toots, toots, tootsie, Goodbye . . . ', composed 1924, and immortalised by him in the first commercially shown 'talkie', *The Jazz Singer*, 1927. By 1965, ob. Hunter, 1957.

tooty, n. See **toot,** n., 5.

tooty, adj. Supercilious, 'superior': (mostly upper-) middle-class: since ca. 1960. O'Donnell, 1978, 'Clarissa's smile became frosty . . . Her voice held the lofty admonition of the Head Prefect. "But if you don't mind my saying so, you're not exactly in a position to get tooty about anything." ' Perhaps an altered blend of *hoity-toity* and *snooty*.

top, n. Abbr. *top gear* in motoring; gen. *on top*, very rarely—and by 1930, †—*on the top*; 1906, *on the top*; 1909, *on top*. (*OED*.) P.B.: since mid-C.20, ?earlier, usu. *in top*.—2.

(Gen. pl.) Counterfoil of a divided warrant: accountants' coll., verging on j.—3. In *on top*, 'The odds on the horse at the top of the bookie's board' (*Weekend*, 11 Oct. 1967): racing coll.—4. See **over the top.**

top, v. To behead, to hang: c.: C.18–20, in C.20, mostly in the passive. P.B.: in later C.20, other methods of killing are subsumed, and the active voice is again in use, e.g. 'The IRA topped him—said he was a traitor'. Also in *top* (one)*self*, to commit suicide, no matter how.

top and tail. To wash a patient's face and fundament, clean teeth, check for bedsores, etc.: nurses': later C.20. (D. Beale, 1984.) Ex domestic coll., to *top and tail*, e.g. gooseberries, before cooking or preserving.

top brass (and collective n., *the top brass*). High-ranking officers in the Fighting Services; hence in civilian uniformed organisations, and even, joc., the Church: orig. US; Can., 1939; and soon afterwards, Brit. without *the*, used as adj. Cf. **brass,** n., 4. (P.B.)

top brick off the chimney. Term used to describe the acme of generosity, with implication that foolish spoiling, or detriment to the donor may result, as in 'his parents'd give that boy the . . . ', or 'she's that soft-hearted, she'd give you . . .': heard by me only in early 1980s, but prob. in use much earlier. (P.B.)

Top Cat. 'Thames Conservancy—and latterly any personal body with *T.C.* as initials, after 1960s cartoon character: 1970s' (Peppitt, 1976). P.B.: e.g., Town Clerk. The cartoons were US, made by Hanna & Barbera for TV: 'Top Cat' was leader of a gang of alley cats, and addressed by his gang as 'TC'.

top deck, the. The head: Aus. nautical (C.20) >, by 1925, gen. B., 1942.

top drawer, out of the. (Mostly in negative.) Well-bred; gentlemanly, ladylike: coll., by 1935 verging on S.E. Gen. *come out of . . .* Vachell, 1905 (*OED*).

Top End, the. The northern part of the Northern Territory; *Top Ender*, a resident there: Aus. coll. Baker.

top hush. 'Top Secret': Service officers', esp. RAF: WW2. P-G-R.

top-kick. A high-ranking officer: Aus. Services': WW2. (Tennant, 1953.) P.B.: ex US Army usage, where, since WW1, it has = a first sergeant.—2. Hence (as also in US), the head man, the leader, of a gang or criminal team: later C.20. (Hall, 1976.) In US, more gen. = anyone in authority. (W. & F.) Both senses are prob. an extension of the earlier **side-kick,** q.v., now promoted above one.

top kiker. Breast pocket of coat or jacket: pickpockets': since (?)mid-C.20. Palmer, 1974.

top laddies. Senior officers of the RN; senior civil servants': wardrooms': since late 1930s. (Granville, letter, 1967.)

top line. In *be on the top line*, to be ready and eager: lowerdeck: ca. 1905–30. ('Taffrail', 1916.) See also **sweat on the top line,** which is perhaps relevant. The phrase *be on . . .* has had a more gen. use than E.P. allows, and is still extant, 1983 (P.B.).

top mag. See AUSTRALIAN UNDERWORLD, in Appx.

top man. Auctioneer for a rigged auction: mock-auction world: since ca. 1945. *Sunday Chronicle*, 28 June 1953.

top of the bill. First-rate; the best of all: coll. (1934, ' "She's wonderful," I breathed. "Marvellous. Top of the bill, in fact." ') Ex theatrical and music-hall advertisements, 'stars' being at the top. Cf. S.E. *top-liner*.

top of the bleeding bungalow; . . . of the box, house, shop. See TOMBOLA, in Appx.

top of the world, (be or sit) on. (To be) prospering, prosperous; esp. to be it and show it, to be very confident and highspirited: adopted, ca. 1930, ex US. Cf. **sit pretty.**

top-off, n. An informer to the police: Aus. c. (B., 1942.) By 1948, low s. (Park, 1950.) Also as v. (Baker.)

top-off merchant. A low Aus. var. of **top-off,** n. *Rats*.

top people, the. Tic-tac men signalling from high in the stands: racing: since ca. 1920. *Sunday Telegraph*, 7 May 1967, anon. article on bookies' s.

top set. Female breasts: since mid-C.20. (Petch, 1969.) A pun on dentists' j.

top step. ' "He's standing on the top step." Said of a man standing trial; this means that there is every prospect of his being given the maximum sentence' (Tempest, 1950): c.: mid-C.20.

top ten, in the. 'In use in "Pop" circles [in the "pop" song chart of the week]'—ineligible thus, of course—'but is used in other ways, as when somebody is becoming successful in any line of business' (Petch, 1969): since ca. 1966.

top 'uns. Breasts: low. (Norman.) Cf. late C.19 synon. *top bal-locks* or *buttocks*.

top up. To bring a liquid to the necessary level; hence, to fill a drinking-glass or a fuel tank: coll. (?orig. Army): since ca. 1930. (P-G-R.) Also as n., 'May I give you a top-up?' = recharge your glass.

topcoat warmer, a. Warmer by a topcoat, i.e. much warmer: coll.: since ca. 1930.

topes. Latrine: Imperial Service College: early C.20. (Marples.) Ex *topos*.

topnobber. Someone first-class or even pre-eminent: Anglo-Irish. Joyce, 1922.

topo. A topographical map: Aus.: since ca. 1940. B., 1953.

topos. Latrine(s): university undergraduates':—1884; ob. by 1930 (E.P.), but extant in theological colleges, 1960s (Towler, 1979). It may have come from Rugby School (Marples). At Rugby School, always in the pl. *topoi*, except in *topos bumf*, toilet paper—a term current since ca. 1920. Ex Gr. τόπος, a place.

topped. Hanged. See **top,** v.

topped up. 'Any container full "to the brim" and, by extension, drunkenness' (Powis). See **top up.**

topper. A public hangman: c.: earlier C.20. Wallace, 1927, speaks of 'Mr Topper Wells—public executioner of England'. Ex **top,** v.—2. A sovereign (coin): tramps' and beggars' c.:—1926 (Jennings).—3. An unamusing so-called 'funny story': since ca. 1950. (*Evening Standard*, 20 July 1963.) It '*tops* the lot'.—4. See **straighter.**

tops, n. Important persons; persons in the news: journalistic: since ca. 1925. Ex *top-liners*.—2. As *the tops*, as in 'He's the tops'—admirable, the best possible; most likeable: coll.: adopted, ca. 1943, from US.—3. See **straighter,** 1; **top,** n., 2.

tops, adj. First-class: Army: 1944+. (P-G-R.) Adapted ex n., 2.

tops and bottoms. 'In his pockets were bundles of "tops and bottoms"—rolls of "notes" with genuine fivers on top and bottom and sheets of toilet paper or telephone directory pages, their edges trimmed to look like notes, in between' (Gosling, 1959): c. >, by ca. 1930, also police s.

tops gen. See HAULAGE, in Appx.

topside. Fig., on top; in control: coll.: from late 1890s. (*OED*) P.B.: prob. an adaptation of pidgin usage.—2. Hence, lit., in the air; airborne; flying: RAF: since ca. 1918. Jackson.—3. In *go topside*, i.e. heaven, to die: id. ' "Major McCudden's gone west, sir," [the fitter] said . . . "I hear Jimmy McCudden's gone topside," I said' (Johns, 1933).

topsider. A lazy dog: Aus.: since ca. 1910. (B., 1942.) Prob. ex prec., 1.

topsides. Those at the head of a specialist corps or of a branch of the Service: Army. E.P., 1942.—2. WW2 RAF var. of **topside,** 2. H.W., 1942.

torch up. Light up a cannabis cigarette: drugs c. (Stockley, 1986.) US since—1955 (Spears).

tore out. A small boat (up to about 15 tons T.M.) converted from cargo-boat to yacht: Essex coast s. rather than Essex dial. I.e. *torn out* 'because the internals have been torn out' (Boycott, 1938).

torn off a strip. See **tear a strip off.**

torn thumb. An inferior form of **Tom Thumb.** Franklyn.

torp. A torpedo. (Berrey, 1940.) Cf. **torps.**

torpedo, n. The penis: Services': WW2. Ex shape—and an unofficial, anecdotal poster. (R.S.)

torpedo, v. To steal: R Aus. N: WW2. B., 1953.

Torpedo Jack. A torpedo lieutenant: RN coll. ('Taffrail', 1916.) Cf. **torps.**

Torpoint chicken; also **Stamshaw nanny-goat.** A very quick-tempered messmate: RN. Torpoint is that township which lies across from Devonport. Stamshaw is in the Portsmouth area. The chickens of the former were noted for their 'testiness', and the nanny-goats on Stamshaw Common, noted 'butters', usually attacked on sight. Granville.

torps. A torpedo officer; often as vocative: RN. ('Taffrail'; Bowen.) Cf. *chips* and *sparks*, carpenter and radio-operator.

Tory wet. See **wet,** adj., 3.

tosh. A term of address, to male friend or stranger, as in 'Wotcher, Tosh!': proletarian; common in Army, WW2, and much affected by spivs in the imm. post-war years: from late 1930s; ob. by 1960. Perhaps related to Scot. dial. *tosh*, neat, smart, whence the n. = a smart fellow. Cf. **mush,** 4 and 6; used in exactly the same way as 6. (E.P.; P.B.)—2. As *the Tosh*, it = the school swimming-bath: Rugby School. (Wharton, 1965.)—3. See **tush.**

tosh and waddle. Utter nonsense: Aus. r.s., on *twaddle*: since ca. 1950. (B.P.) Cf. older *tosh* = nonsense.

tosh up. To fake an effect by 'tarting up' something: car dealers': later C.20. See quot'n at **pudden.**

tosher. A painter/decorator: coll., ?mainly south-east England. (Malin, 1979.) Cf. E. Anglian dial. *toshy*, muddy, sticky (*EDD*).

toss, v. To throw away, esp. as useless or worthless: Aus.: since ca. 1930. 'Do you want to keep this?'—'No, you can toss it' (B.P.).—2. Hence, as v.i., to give up, throw in: Aus. coll.: later C.20. (McNeil.) A shortening of *toss in the alley*, . . . **towel.**—3. In *toss a party*, to 'throw' (give) one: Aus.: since ca. 1950. (B.P.)—4. To search a person or premises: drugs c. (Stockley, 1986.) US since—1968 (Spears). Cf. **spin** (someone's) **drum.**

Toss an' Joss. The T. and J. Harrison Steamship Company: HMS *Conway.* (Granville, 1962.) *Joss* rhymes with *Toss*; *Toss = Thos,* Thomas.

toss bag. 'An irritating and stupid person; sometimes an affected person' (Hibbert, 1983, who says ex Aus. s., 'meaning "rubbish receptacle", by extension "condom"'): 'pop' world. Also *tosser* and *toss pot.* Ibid.

toss (one's) **cookies.** To vomit: Can.: ca. 1920–55. (Leechman.)

toss in the alley or **the towel.** To give up, to 'throw in the towel': Aus. (B., 1942, *alley*; Dennis, 1916, *towel*.) *Alley* prob. ex the game of marbles; *towel* from boxing j.

toss it up airy. To 'show off', put on 'side': lower classes':—1923 (Manchon).

toss off. To show off; to be pretentious and boring; to display ego-trip symptoms' (Hibbert, 1983): 'pop' world. Perhaps ex s. *toss off*, to masturbate, since C.18.

toss the balls up. To put forward several options: commercial coll.: late 1970s. (Raab: 'heard 1979'.)

tosser. A penny used in pitch-and-toss: Glasgow:—1934.—2. Also, any coin, esp. a sovereign: from ca. 1910. Harrison, 1935.—3. See **toss bag.**

tosspot. 'Used as a jocular affectionate term of address [to men] in Australia' (B.P.): Aus. coll.: late C.19–20. Ex the † S.E. *toss-pot*, a heavy and habitual toper. Cf. **soaks.**

tossy. Proud, haughty, supercilious: proletarian coll.:—1923 (Manchon). An extension of the rare S.E. sense, pert or contemptuous.

total loss, a. 'He's a total loss', i.e. useless: RAF: since ca. 1939. Ex aircraft thus classified. Cf. synon. **dead loss.**

total wreck. A cheque: Aus. r.s. Baker.

totalled, be. 'To be killed outright, as in a road smash. (*Observer* TV review, 27 Apr. 1975)' (R.S.): copied ex US s. Barnhart quotes an advertisement in *Scientific American,* Apr. 1968, 'An accident serious enough to "total" a car

generally "totals" the occupants as well', and defines *total*, v.t. 'to wreck beyond repair; destroy totally.' Cf. **total loss.** Prob. ultimately ex insurance-brokers' j. (P.B.)

tote. A woman's large bag, used for carrying groceries or baby's napkins, etc.: Aus. coll. rather than s.: since ca. 1930. (B.P.)

tote up. To add up: Aus.: since ca. 1920. (B.P.) Ex *total.*

totem pole. 'An item of airfield lighting equipment, so called from its shape' (Jackson): RAF: since ca. 1925. By 1943, j.

totsie. Var. of **Tottie,** a girl. Greene, 1938, *passim.*

totterman, whence the elab. **totterman's mate.** Habitual drinker, even unto the stage of tottering: 'very common in the same sense as piss-head' (Parsons, 1973): mostly RN.

Tottie. A girl, a young woman, esp. if of a compliant nature, but not a whore: RN. 'That mad pusser. Gone native. Shacking up with a Japanese tottie somewhere' (Winton, 1960). Cf. later C.19 meaning, a high-class whore.

Tottie (or **-y**) **fie.** A smart young woman given to 'throwing her weight about'; a prostitute or near-prostitute with such tendencies: Londoners', esp. Cockneys': early C.20. The *fie* is of exclamatory origin ('Oh my!'); see prec. Hence, *Totty Fay* (pronounced *Fye*), alternatively *Tottie Hardbake*, a female assuming a haughty air: derisive Cockney: since ca. 1890. (L.A.)

touch. The sum of money obtained at one time, esp. by cadging or theft: low.—2. 'In these rounds or . . . "walks", we have our "touches"—regular places of call where we pick up letters and, in certain cases, leave them', from 'You're in My Bag!' by a Postman, *Passing Show,* 24 Dec. 1932.—3. A simpleton; a dupe: Aus. (orig. c.): since ca. 1910. (B., 1953.) Prob. a shortening of **soft touch,** q.v., a person easily imposed upon for money loan or gift.—4. 'A pick-up or girl got acquainted with casually' (Petch, 1969): slightly raffish: since ca. 1955.—5. In *get a touch.* 'To come into personal contact with a live rail' (*Railway,* 2nd): railwaymen's: since ca. 1950. A pun on sense 1.

touch and goes. '[The] aircraft were . . . trainers . . . [and] in the late 'fifties and early 'sixties, could be seen carrying out touch and goes (or circuits and bumps!) as part of the training procedure for fledgling pilots' (Jarram, 1978). I.e. practising landing and taking-off. Mrs B. Huston adds, 'also used of aircraft demonstrations, which include landing and immediate take-off, at flying shows'. Later C.20.

touch-bottom. A forced landing, esp. a crash-landing: RAF: since ca. 1925. (H. & P.) Also a v. (unhyphenated), 'to crash-land': since ca. 1925. (Jackson.) By meiosis.

touch down. To land: RAF coll. (by 1944, j.): since ca. 1918. (Jackson.) Ex Rugby football.

touch for. To get, incur, catch (gen. something unpleasant): from ca. 1910.

touch ground. Of an argument, to make sense; to be relevant to a plan, as in, e.g., 'See which of these ideas touches ground with you': coll.: later C.20. Clark, 1981.

touch of 'em. See **give** (someone) **a touch of 'em** ['the shits'], to annoy intensely.

touch of the . . . , a. Lit. 'characteristic of', but > an almost meaningless qualifier, of manifold use, as in, e.g., 'A touch of the fruitcakes' = slightly nutty [crazy], ex *nutty as a fruit-cake;* 'A touch of the Harvey Smiths' = contemptuously giving the vulgar two-finger signal, as H.S. did to the judges (see **Harvey Smith sign**); 'A touch of the GTs' (headline of a motoring article in *Guardian,* 30 Apr. 1970), to describe a car with sporting lines: adapted from lit. S.E. early 1970s, but with the difference that the thing qualified is always pluralised: gen. coll. (P.B.)

touch of the seconds, a. See **seconds.**

touch of the tonsorials, a. 'Haircut' (Powis): joc. elab.: later C.20. See **touch of the . . .**

touchables, the. The corruptible; those open to bribes: since ca. 1939. Punning on India's *untouchables.*

tough, v.t. To support, bear, face up to (esp. a difficulty, a hardship): Can.: from ca. 1905. (Beames, 1930.) Prob. ex US *tough it*, to rough it: cf. **tough it out.**

tough, adj. Morally callous and/or commercially unscrupulous: also n. From ca. 1910: coll. Ex two US senses: *tough*, criminal, vicious, and *tough*, a rough, esp. a street bully.—2. Unfortunate; severe: from ca. 1928. Wodehouse, 1929, ' "Tough!" 'You bet it's tough. A girl can't help her appearance" ' (*OED* sup.). Ex US *tough luck*.

tough it out. An elab. of **tough,** v., to endure to the finish (Leech, 1986, notes 'widespread N. Am.'): adopted in UK mid-1980s, e.g. *Guardian,* 31 May, 1986, 'A handful of London boroughs still toughing it out along with Liverpool [against the government's ratecapping scheme]'.

toughie, n. A tough: since ca. 1945. (Blake, 1954.) 'Officials up to and including the permanent secretary, a Whitehall toughie' (*New Society,* 12 Aug. 1982). Ex **tough,** n., at adj., 1.—2. Something very difficult to do, e.g. an examination, or in relationships, as in '[for a woman] producing a condom and asking for its use can be a toughie' (*Time Out,* 1 Feb. 1980): coll.: later C.20.

toughie, adj. Behaving as a **toughie,** n., 1: 'part of the Anglo-American toughie response to Afghanistan' (*New Society,* 14 Feb. 1980).

tour of miseries. 'The day's work when one is feeling down in the mouth' (H. & P.): Services' (esp. Army): since ca. 1930. Ex military j. *tour* (as in *tour in the trenches, tour of duty*).

tourist ('officer' understood, orig. expressed). 'Army and RAF. One who, by virtue of a special skill (e.g., language) is seconded for employment in a specialist trade or branch for one tour of duty, to the annoyance and possible detriment to promotion of those whose permanent job it is, before returning to, e.g., the "real" Army' (P.B., 1974): sarcastic: since late 1940s.

touristy. Full of tourists: coll.: later C.20. 'It used to be such a nice quiet place, and now it's awfully touristy, full of shops flogging cheap nasties and so on' (P.B.).

tout. An informer, to the police, etc.: N. Ireland: 1970s. Hawke, 1979.

towel up. To beat or defeat, fig. rather than lit.: Aus. B., 1942; Buzo, 1969.

towering. A superlative, as in 'Oh, there's no towering hurry—tomorrow will do': early 1980s. Perhaps here an echo of 'tearing', and influenced by the film title *The Towering Inferno,* 1974. (P.B.)

town bike. A loose woman: Aus.: since ca. 1920. (Stivens, 1951; Niland, 1955.) So often and generally ridden. P.B.: the term is well known also in Brit.; cf. synon. **camp bicycle,** *garrison bike.*

townie. 'Anyone not connected with the circus' (Victoria, BC, *Islander,* 19 Dec. 1971): Can. circus s.: adopted, 1930s, ex US.

Towns. A vocative, cf. **wings;** not necessarily a fellow-townsman: RN: later C.20. *Heart,* 1962.

towy. Agitatedly obstreperous, 'stroppy': NZ. (Heffernan, 1984.) Cf. **toey,** 2.

toy. A trainer aircraft: RAF: since ca. 1930. (Jackson.) For the 'new boys' to play with.—2. See **def.**

toy-box. The engine-room: RN (not very gen.): earlier C.20. (Bowen.) Cf. **toys.**

toy-boy. A cicisbeo, an older woman's young lover or recognised escort: since ca. 1985. The influence of rhyme.

toys. 'The mechanical parts of a 'plane so beloved by the armourers and flight mechanics who care for the machine' (H. & P.): RAF: since ca. 1920.—2. Equipment, vehicles, etc.; to a Gunner his guns: Army: since ca. 1925.

toys in the attic. Crazy, perhaps, in a child-like way, 'bats in the belfry'. Simmonds, in *Guardian,* 15 Apr. 1985.

trachy. Tracheotomy: medical students':—1933 (*Slang*).

track, n. 'A warder who will carry contraband messages or goods out of or into jail for a prisoner' (B., 1959): Aus. c.: since ca. 1930. A *way* in or out.—2. In (*go*) *on the track,* (to go) tramping the back country in search of work: Aus. coll.: since late C.19. Wilkes.—3. In *go down the track,* to go down south on leave: Aus. servicemen's: 1940–5. (B., 1943.) From

Darwin.—4. In *up the track* and *quickie up the t.,* q.v. at HAULIERS', in Appx.

track, v. See **tracks.**

track mitts. Leather mittens: (racing) cyclists': since ca. 1930.

track record. Someone's personal record, assessed on the relevant facts: 'primarily business usage' (Playfair, 1977): adopted, ca. 1970, ex US. P.B.: it can apply also to a firm: e.g., an advertisement in *The Times,* 29 Sep. 1978, 'Hutchison Whampoa has a proven track record of successful business dealings in the People's Republic of China . . . ' By 1980, commercial, hence political, j.

track square. See:-

track with. 'To associate with, to cohabit with' (Wilkes): Aus., rather derogatory; 'To pursue an amorous enterprise with honourable intentions' (Downing, 1919) is *track square with* (a girl), hence to deal fairly with a person: since early C.20. Dennis, 1915.

tracking. Injecting intravenously along a vein: drugs c. (Stockley, 1986.) Cf.:-

tracks. Needle marks: drugs world: ca. 1955–65: adopted, yet never very common in UK, ex US. Landy, 1971.

tractor. A car: pej.: since ca. 1950. (*New Statesman,* 5 Feb. 1965.) Cf. synon. use of **lorry.**

trad, n. Traditional or 'hot' jazz music: mostly teenagers': since ca. 1959, but not common until 1961. (*Sunday Telegraph,* 3 Dec. 1961.) See also JAZZ, in Appx.

trad, adj. Traditional; may be applied to almost anything: coll.: since ca. 1960. Ex prec. Cf.:-

trad rags. 'Traditional dress of a people' (Granville, letter, 1962). A pun on **glad rags,** q.v.

trade, the. The Submarine Service: RN coll.: WW1-WW2 (P-G-R). '[Pre-1914] a term of opprobrium coined by the pukka navy to describe officers who looked more like plumbers' assistants while on duty than spic-and-span naval officers, the name took on a different significance during [WW1], and was accepted throughout the under-water branch of the service with a certain affectionate regard' (Carr, 1930).—2. In homosexual circles, it is the normal word for sexual commerce, as in 'Did you have any trade last night?' See also **rough trade.**

trade-in. A car 'traded in' as part of the purchase money for a new car. A motor-trade coll., esp. in Aus.: since ca. 1930. (Casey, 1947.) P.B.: by mid-C.20, gen. motor-trade j.; also as adj., e.g. 'Did you get a good trade-in price on your old one?'

Tradesmen's Entrance, the. That entrance and narrow passage to the Grand Fleet anchorage at Scapa Flow which was used by destroyers and smaller craft: RN: WW2. (Granville.)—2. The anus: low: later C.20. Cf. **servant's entrance.**

traffic. Wireless messages sent or received: wireless operators' (esp. at sea) coll.: from ca. 1926. (Bowen.) P.B.: soon, and anyway by WW2, > j.

traffic cop. A policeman controlling the traffic: adopted ex US, ca. 1935 in Can., ca. 1945 elsewhere; by 1945 in Can., by 1955 elsewhere, virtually coll.

tragic. No good; opp. of **magic,** q.v.: teenagers': ca. 1979. E.g., in the East Midlands, if Nottingham Forest Football team win, the chant is 'Nottingham Forest are magic'; if they lose, ' . . . are tragic'. (Paterson.)

trail boss. A stationmaster: railwaymen's: since ca. 1935. (*Railway,* 2nd.) Joc., ex 'Western' films.

train. In *going like a train,* 'Moving very fast; in a great hurry' (Griffiths, 1970): NZ.

train(-)driver. 'The leader of a large formation (of aircraft)' (H. & P.): RAF since ca. 1938.

train lines. 'East and west course of steamships in the English Channel' (Granville): nautical.

train(-)smash. 'Fried tomatoes' (Granville; *Weekly Telegraph,* 13 Sep. 1941); 'tinned tomatoes' (Peppitt, 1976; Malin, 1979): RN lowerdeck. Ex the colour of flowing gore, the aspect of mangled limbs. Thus do brave men deride their own secret dreads.

traitors' gate. 'The portcullis on H.M. Customs officers' caps: MN: 1940s' (Peppitt).

tram, n. British Rail, Southern Region's DC train, working, with an electrical multiple unit, exactly like a tram: railwaymen's and spotters'. (Irwin, 1987.) See also HAULAGE, in Appx.—2. See **fish-horn**.

tram, v. To run or walk very fast and urgently: E. Midlands': earlier C.20. 'She's tramming it!' (Ryott, 1985.) Cf. C.19 synon. *train-up*.

tram basher. See HAULAGE, in Appx.

tram-driver. A Coastal Command pilot on patrols: RAF: 1940–5. Contrast **train-driver**.

tram-handle. 'Applied to the handle which adjusted the variable gear on Zenith motorcycles . . . also used for any similarly shaped control handle needing movement in the horizontal plane' (Partridge, 1980): motorcyclists': early C.20. Ex resemblance to a tram-driver's control-handle.

tram-lined. (Of trousers) having a double crease: joc. coll.: since ca. 1925.

tram-lines. The 4½-ft-wide area on each side of a (doubles) lawn-tennis court: sporting: from ca. 1929. Esp. *down the tram-lines*, i.e. more or less straight along this strip of the court.—2. Convoy or patrol routes: RN: WW2. (Granville.) Cf. RAF **milk round** for a regular route.—3. Parallel brushmarks: builders' and house-painters': since ca. 1910. (A master builder, 5 Dec. 1953.)—4. 'Ruts cut into the snow by constant use of the same area by skiers' (*LAM*, 4 Feb. 1986): skiers'.

tram-walloper. One who pickpockets on tramcars: c.: from ca. 1910. *Yorkshire Post*, latish May, 1937.

trammy or **-ie.** A tram conductor or driver: Aus. coll. B., 1943; Trist, 1946.

tramp. A girl or woman willing to copulate with almost any man: adopted, ca. 1955, ex US.—2. A trampolinist: since late 1940s. *Weekend*, 8 Nov. 1969.—3. A master: Imperial Service College: earlier C.20.

tramped, adj. (in predicate only). Dismissed from employment: Aus. Labour: since ca. 1920. (B., 1942.) I.e. rendered a tramp.

trams. Legs: underworld (and 'fringe'): r.s., on *gams*, synon. c. or s. since C.18. Franklyn 2nd.

tranks (pl.; also, by journalists, spelt *tranx*). Tranquillising drugs, anxiolytics: addicts', users': later C.20.

trannie, -y. A transistor radio set: since ca. 1965.—2. A male transvestite: raffish: later C.20.—3. A transparent slide film: photographers'. *Amateur Photographer*, 29 June 1985, 'How to salvage those rejected trannies.'—4. A heart-transplant patient: 'Writing about what it is like to be "a tranny", as the staff at Papworth [Hospital, Cambridgeshire] affectionately call us . . . ' (Rawnsley, 1986).

tranx. See **tranks**.

trap, n. A mould used in coining counterfeit: c.:—1929 (*OED* Sup.).—2. See **traps**.

trap, v.i. To obtain a fare: taxicabmen's: from ca. 1925. ' "Did you trap off the Museum?" "Yes, I puts on there and I traps in ten minutes." ' This *put on*, v.i., is also cabmen's (same date): i.e. I put my car on the rank at ('the Museum' being the rank in front of the British Museum). Perhaps cf. C.19 omnibus-men's *net a load of rabbits*.—2. (Of both sexes, and by them.) To meet a desirable person, as in, e.g., with ref. to previous night's dance, 'Did you trap last night?': WRNS: later C.20. (Wood, 1978.)

trappers, the. 'The Examining teams, described less respectfully by the units as "The Trappers", made a fairly detailed assessment of the Army Air Corps' flying and technical efficiency' (Mead, 1967): AAC: 1960s.

traps. Personal effects; belongings; baggage: coll.: 1813 (*OED*). Abbr. *trappings*.—2. Hence, *cleaning-traps*, one's cleaning-materials (polish, buttonstick, brushes, etc.): Army, esp. Artillery: earlier C.20. Cf. C.19 *mess-traps*, cooking utensils.—3. See **around the traps**.

trash. To frighten: market-traders'. (*M.T.*) Directly ex Romany.—2. To destroy, to smash up: 'pop' world. (Hibbert, 1983.) I.e., to make trash of.

trasher. A thriller (film, novel, etc.): ex prec., 1. Ibid.

trashing. 'The young call looting [from shops] "trashing", and the word suggests what is happening. The status of goods changes from something with a price to trash' (*New Society*, 9 July 1981): adopted ex US (W. & F., 1975 Sup., defined but undated).

travel. To take stage properties and important accessories on tour: theatrical coll.: late C.19–20. 'Theatrical people, on the road, may or may not "travel" all their "props" and accessories' (Leechman).

travel on the (or one's) **thumb.** To hitch-hike: s.: ca. 1925–40. E.P. noted that it was a 'more English phrase [than hitch-hike, which has, however, predominated]'. Mostly as vbl n., *travelling* . . . (P.B.)

traveller. A walking ganger, a man in charge of a section of the job on which are working gangs of navvies under the charge of ordinary gangers, or gangs of bricklayers, etc.: Public Works coll.:—1935.—2. A loafer: Aus. (B., 1942.) Ex coll., since C.18, a tramp.

travelling by rail. So tipsy that one has to hang onto things. Slater heard it in Sydney, 1960s; but it dates from ca. 1930. P.B.: e.g., a comic postcard signed 'Comicus', reproduced in *Sauce*, 1978, shows a drunk clutching the street railings. The caption is 'I'm coming home by rail.'

travelling the bees. Migratory bee-keeping; hence, *travel the bees*, to be a migratory bee-keeper: Aus. coll.: since ca. 1945. Tennant's novel, *The Honey Flow*, 1956, forms the 'locus classicus' of the subject.

tray, trey. Three, whether as number or set: c. >, ca. 1910, low s.: from mid-1890s. Ex *tray, trey*, the 3 at dice or cards.—2. Hence, a shortening of **tray-bit**, q.v., a threepenny piece: low: 1907 (*OED*), but prob. several years earlier. Norman, 1959, notes its (rare) use for £3. See PARLYAREE, in Appx.

tray-bit. See prec., 2, a threepenny piece.—2. Hence, a term of contempt for an insignificant person: Aus. B., 1941.—3. (Usu. in pl.) A female breast: Aus. c.: since ca. 1920. (B., 1963.) Rhyming on *tit*.—4. (Always in pl.) 'The shits' = diarrhoea: Aus. r.s. Wilkes.

traysalties. Female breasts: Parlyaree, ex r.s. on *threepenny bits*. (Hollis, 1983.) Synon. with **tray-bit**, 3; *saltie* = It *soldi*.

treacle, the. A hanger-on; one who is neither a constant nor an accepted member of a gang: Teddy boys': since ca. 1950. *Observer*, 1 Mar. 1959.

treacle, v. To flatter (esp. a superior): Services': since ca. 1930. H. & P., 'To administer soothing syrup'.

treacle-stick, the. '(Used contemptuously for) Social Security (formerly National Assistance). "Slinks and slags on the Treacle-Stick". The term is now in common use amongst Boston market-traders. The late Charles Ashton [the compiler's father-in-law] claimed to have invented it. He would explain that once "they" were on the Treacle-Stick, "they" stuck' (*M.T.*, 1979).

treacle toffee. Welsh coal: railwaymen's. *Railway*, 2nd.

tread on the gas. See **step on the gas**.

treadler. A bicycle: earlier C.20. Short for synon. *treadling-machine*. (P.B.)

treat (a person) **like shit.** To treat humiliatingly, contemptuously: low coll. (Leech.)

treat with ignore. To overrule (someone): Aus., since 1930s but esp. Army, WW2. (B., 1943.) A var. of S.E. *treat with contempt, disdain*, etc., in which sense it has had some later, more gen. use.

Treble One Tremblers, the. No. 111 (Fighter) Squadron, RAF: later C.20. *Listener*, 13 July 1978.

tree. See **out of** (one's) **tree**.

tree-rat. A native prostitute: Army, Other Ranks, in India: late C.19–1947. Allen, 1947.

trees. Creases in carbon-paper: typists': since ca. 1910. Stevens, 1942.

trekkie, -y. A devotee of the American science-fiction space serial 'Star Trek': fans'. *New Statesman*, 23 July 1982.

Trenchard brat. An RAF apprentice: 1920+; by 1940, ob. Jackson, 'After Marshal of the Air the Viscount Trenchard who, in 1920, introduced the apprenticeship system into the Service.'

trendiness. The natural abstract n. ex **trendy**, adj.: coll.: since late 1960s. For the idea ': expresses, not the word itself, cf. the quot'n at **kinky**, adj., 5. (P.B.)

trendy, n. One who is 'trendy': since 1967. Fleming, 1968, 'the Chelsea Set . . . there are trendies and *personae non gratae* amongst them'.

trendy, adj. Following the social or intellectual or artistic or literary or musical or sartorial or other trend; up-to-the-minute smart or fashionable: since 1966; by end of 1967, already verging on coll. *New Statesman*, 24 Mar. 1967.

Trent otter, **stink** or **smell like a.** 'In Doncaster, at least, . . . applied as often to an excess of pleasant aroma, e.g. too much after-shave lotion, as to unpleasant smells' (Taylor, 1987, who notes that in *EDD*, a *Trent otter* is listed as a Yorks and Notts name for 'one of the huge steam tugs that ply between Hull and Nottingham').

trezzie. A threepenny piece: Aus.: since ca. 1920. (B., 1942.) Ex *trey*: see **tray**, 2. Wilkes spells it *trizzie*.

tri. A tricycle: coll.

tri-car. A motor-car with only one wheel at rear: coll.: since ca. 1930.

trick. A customer: prostitutes': adopted, ca. 1944, ex US (where current since WW1); by 1960, also gen. low, s. Hence, *be on a trick*, to be 'entertaining' a customer. Powis, 1977, 'Prostitutes' term for one transaction with a client: "I've done six tricks so far today." ' Cf. C.19 nautical s. > j., a tour of duty, a turn at the controls.

trick cyclist. A psychiatrist: Army: 1943+. By Hobson-Jobson. (Hastings, 1947.) 'At least as early as 1938 in civilian slang. Also used as a verb in the Forces towards the end of the war [of 1939–45]. "He got himself trick-cycled out of the Army" ' either legitimately or fraudulently: Sanders.

trick up. To baffle; to get the better of: Aus.: since ca. 1920. Devanney, 1944.

trickle, n. Sweat: Scottish Public Schools'. Miller, 1935, has it also as a v.i. Whence *trickle-bags*. The sense 'to perspire' has been current at Harrow School since before 1913: witness Lunn.

trickle, v. To go: joc. coll.: 1920 (Wodehouse: *OED* Sup.); ob. Cf. *filter*.—2. See prec.

trickle-bags. A coward: see **trickle**, n.

tricks. In *be in* (one's) *tricks*, to be in a bad temper: market-traders': since ca. 1920. (*M.T.*) Perhaps orig. in ref. to tantrums.

tricksy. Occ. var. of S.E. *tricky*, esp. in sense sly, cunning.—2. See **trixy**.

trier, tryer (try-er). An unsuccessful thief: c.

triff. A superlative: teenagers': early 1980s. A contraction of 'terrific'. (Joanna Williamson, 1982.) Cf. synon. **brill** ex 'brilliant'.

trig. To pull the trigger of a camera in taking a snapshot: from ca. 1925. Collinson.

trigger-happy. Likely to use a firearm on the slightest excuse, or on none: adopted, early 1940s, ex US. A fairly late example occurs in Clark, 1964 (P.B.).

trim. A back trouser pocket: pickpockets' c.: since ca. 1930. Palmer, 1974.

trim your language! Cease swearing!: Aus. (B., 1942.) I.e. render it less shaggy—less rough.

Trinco. Trincomalee, a seaport of Sri Lanka: coll.: late C.19–20 nautical; 1942–5 Services' (Chapman, 1949).

trip, n. A harlot; a thief's woman: c.: from mid-1870s; slightly ob. by 1930. (Horsley, 1977.) Esp. as in 'Trips: Women who decoy and rob drunken persons' (Sharpe, 1938). Cf. **tripper-up**.—2. Hence, an affectionate term of address: lower classes':—1923 (Manchon). Cf. Fr. *cocotte*.—3. As *Trip*, Tri-

pos: Cambridge University coll.: from ca. 1920. *OED* Sup.—4. An experience of drug-taking: drug addicts': since ca. 1966. *Daily Colonist* (Victoria, BC), 29 Mar. 1967. 'A Vancouver youth who had a nightmare ride on an L.S.D. "trip", said Tuesday he never wants to make the journey again.' (Leechman.) By early 1967, also Brit. (Fryer, 1967). Esp. in *take a trip*: late 1960s.—5. Hence, any (profound) experience, as in 'It was more of a psychological trip than a physical one' (Hollander): adopted, ca. 1970, ex US (*DCCU*; W. & F.). Cf. **ego-trip**.—6. 'Single (cubic: sugar) measure of LSD' (Home Office): drugs world. Ex sense 4.—7. A triplicate of a form, as 'One for them, one for you, and we file the trips': offices', etc., coll., verging on j. (P.B.)

trip, v. 'To take a trip' as in n., 4 and 5: 1970s. *Jagger*.

trip round the horn. ' "Tripping round the horn" is the way the clandestine radio operator checks his set for activity' (*Daily Telegraph*, 22 Feb. 1988): espionage. Prob. ex US: *horn*, s., telephone (W. & F., 1975); ?pun on Cape Horn, or old-fashioned gramophone horn.

trip up the Rhine, a. Sexual intercourse: Forces': 1945+. Cf. the barmaids' *a bike ride to Brighton*.

tripe. Filth, dirt: Army, esp. in the Guards' regts. Kersh, 1941.—2. Tissues for microscopic examination: medical students':—1933 (*Slang*). Also **meat**.—3. Very easy bowling: cricketers' coll.: since ca. 1920. Ex older s. sense, non-sense.—4. In *in tripe*, in trouble: army: ca. 1920–50. Kersh, 1942, 'He was in tripe . . . and about forty hours pushed [late]'. Ex sense 1.—5. In *up to tripe*, q.v.

tripe-hound. A foul, an objectionable fellow: lower classes': earlier C.20. Manchon.—2. A reporter: orig. and mainly newspapermen's: from ca. 1924. Sayers, 1936.—3. A sheep-dog: NZ and Aus. farmers'. (B., 1941, 1942.) P.B.: in UK, may be applied affectionately—or unkindly—to any dog.

Tripe Shop, the. Broadcasting House, London: taxi-drivers': since ca. 1930. (*Weekly Telegraph*, 6 Apr. 1946.) See **tripe**, 3.

tripe-writer. A typewriter: joc. perversion. Whence *triping* = typing. (P.B., 1980.)

triplets. See **have kittens**.

Tripoli gallop, the. The advance towards Tripoli (N. Africa)—an advance that happened twice before the 8th Army captured it: Army: 1942–3. P-G-R.

tripper-up. A woman preying on drunken men: c. Sweeney, 1904 (*OED*).

trippy. Going on a 'trip' (n., 4, q.v.), indulging in a bout, an experience, of drug-taking: since late 1960s. *Jagger*.—2. Exciting; pleasurable: since early 1970s. Both senses app. ex US.

trips. Triplets: mostly lower-middle class: since ca. 1910. (Macaulay, 1937.) Cf. **quads** and **quins**.

triss. An objectionable fellow; esp. a pathic: Aus. c.: since ca. 1930. (Tennant, 1953.) Origin? A 'siss' or 'sissie': r.s.: by 1950, no longer low.—2. A var. of *trizzie* or *trezzie*, q.v.: Aus.: since ca. 1925. (B.P.)

triv quiz. 'Shortened name of the popular board game "Trivial Pursuit", by Parker Games' (Turner, 1986): players'—and their detractors'.—2. Hence, generic name for trivia-based video games (Ibid.).

trixy. A quirk, a personal oddity: ca. 1910–40. Deeping, 1925, 'But why should I feel flattered because certain physical trix-ies of mine happen to pique you?' A diminutive of S.E. *trick*, perhaps influenced by S.E. *pixy*.

trizzer. A lavatory: Aus. low: since ca. 1922. (B., 1942.) The charge for a wash and brush-up is a:-

trizzie. A threepenny piece. See **trezzie**, and **triss**, 2.

trog, n. A cadet: Royal Naval College, Dartmouth, and gen. RN s.: since ca. 1950. (Winton, 1959) A midshipman, a newly appointed officer: Winton, 1960, 'Now I must . . . introduce the rest of the trogs to the captain.'—2. 'An army recruit in basic training—he was "the lowest form of animal life"; I heard the term in the Intelligence Corps Depot, early 1950s, but it was widely understood throughout the army at the time. The abbr. *trg* [= training], which appeared so frequently on orders, may have suggested *troglodyte*' (P.B., 1974).—3. 'We are "Trogs"—sort of "Mods" who go potholing. We were having a "do" at the "Thunderbirds"—they're a sort of "Rockers" ': thus a youth of 20, as reported in *The Times* of 8 June 1965. Obviously ex S.E. *troglodyte*, a cave-dweller, it dates since ca. 1961.—4. A 'stuffy', old-fashioned person (a very cubical 'square'): since ca. 1950. (Bickers, 1965.) Ex the *Troglodytes* or cave-dwellers of the Ancient World.—5. 'It is the considered view of this observer that much of the chaos on our weekend roads is caused by the proliferation of Trogs. A Trog, by our family tradition, is a driver who is dedicated to the principle that all road journeys should be made to last the longest possible time' (Gardner, 1972). Cf. sense 4, and **conker**, 2.

trog, v. To walk; depart (*trog off*, or 'Well, I'll be trogging along, then'): Army, (?orig. esp. Intelligence Corps), since ca. 1950; current at RMA Sandhurst, 1970, where *trog along* = to march heavily laden. *Trog* for walk, as in 'he was just trogging along, minding his own business', had, by late 1970s, > gen. Perhaps a blend of *trudge* + *slog* or *jog*, or ex the n., 1 and 2. Cf. centuries-old synon. *shog*. (P.B.)

trog boots. 'Especially heavy, cleated, rubber-soled boots used in bad-weather conditions by certain tradesmen and outdoor workers' (Farley, 1967): RAF: since ca. 1960. Cf. n., 2, and v., **trog**.

troll. To look for 'trade': prostitutes', since ca. 1930; hence also male homosexuals' (current ca. 1970).—2. Hence, to wander, saunter, rather aimlessly, as in 'just trolling around looking in shop-windows and that': gen. coll.: since mid-1970s. Cf. 'All [fighter aircraft] will be trolling up and down on various CAPs [combat air patrols]' (*Phantom*): RAF: 1970s. Both senses prob. ex S.E. *trawl*. (P.B.)

trolley. RN shortening, 1950s, of next. (Malin, 1980.) But cf. **trolleys**.

trolley and truck. Coïtion; to coït: low r.s.: since ca. 1910. Franklyn.

trolley-oggling. Watching sexual intercourse: RN: 1950s. (Malin, 1980.) See prec.

trolleys. Underpants: since ca. 1950, poss. orig. RN, but by 1970s gen. (Malin, 1980.) Used also in girls' schools. (Wober, 1971.) Prob. a shortening of mid-Victorian *trolly-wags*, trousers, but cf. **shreddies**, and the just possibly relevant definition of a tom-cat as 'a ball-bearing mouse-trap'. (P.B.)

trolling. Streetwalking by a prostitute: prostitutes': since ca. 1930. I.e. *trawling*. See **troll**, 1.

trombone, the. The telephone: defective r.s.: since ca. 1930. Warner, 1961.

tromboning, n. and adj. (The) being on half- or part-time work: N. Country, esp. Yorkshire: since ca. 1931. By a musical pun. Cf. **laking** and **playing**.(Hillaby, 1950.)

tronk. An idiot, a foolish person; also *tronk-head*: East Midlands' teenagers': later 1970s. (McPheely, 1977.)

tronker. A long-distance lorry-driver: hauliers': since late 1950s. (*Daily Telegraph*, 4 Feb. 1964.) Perhaps, ex *trunk*-route driver, influenced by French *tronc*.

troop. To convey in a troop-ship: coll.: since ca. 1940. (Gordon, 1950.) P.B.: but *the trooping season*, the term for the time of year when new drafts were conveyed by troop-ship to India, and the time-expired men brought home, dates back to late C.19.—2. To cause (a defaulter) to be brought before a superior officer: coll.: Services', esp. RN: since ca. 1930. Winton, 1960.

troopie groupie. War correspondent, or other civilian, become enthusiastically military-minded. (Bishop, 1982.) Cf. **groupie**.

troops, the. 'The Ship's Company' (H. & P.): RN. 'Not quite correct, the truth being that this is the Wardroom's term for the lowerdeck' (Granville).

trophy. A convert: Salvation Army j. >, by 1920, coll. Manchon.

tropical. (Of language) blasphemous; obscene: from ca. 1920. Ex *tropical*, very hot.

troppo. 'Term used by men serving during World War II in the Pacific area = one who has had long service in tropical areas and, by inference, ought to be repatriated' (W. Colgan): NZ and Aus.: since ca. 1941. (B., 1942, *troppo*; Cusack, 1951, *half-troppo*, partly, or as if, crazy.) Ex '*tropical*', with Aus. suffix *-o*.—2. Hence, *go troppo*, to go crazy: since ca. 1942; by late 1940s, common throughout the Pacific; cf. 'He had the look of men Hurst had seen in the tropics, when they were going "troppo"—off their heads' (Trevor, 1966).

tross. (Mostly as vbl. n., *trossing*.) Walking: Post Office employees', esp. telegraph messenger boys'. (L.A., 1967.) ?A perversion of *stroll* or *trot*.

trot, n. 'A sequence of chance events, esp. betokening good or ill fortune' (Wilkes): Aus. and NZ, mostly sporting: since late C.19. Orig. ex a succession of heads thrown at two-up, 'a good trot'; hence *do a trot*, to have a successful run (Palmer, 1955), with its opp., *a bad, lean, rough* or *tough trot*, of gen. application. I.e. *trot* = run.—2. A fellow, chap: mostly University: from ca. 1919. Blake, 1936, Oxford don speaking: 'He's quite a decent old trot, but definitely in the Beta class.' Perhaps ironically ex † S.E. *trot*, a whore.—3. A woman: NZ: since ca. 1925. Cf. 2., and see quot'n at **mocker**, 2.—4. A lavatory: RAF: since ca. 1950. See **trots, the**.—5. Nonsense, a 'flannelling' tale, as in 'Don't give me that load of old trot!': low coll. Perhaps a tale 'trotted out', to be tried on the gullible—but cf. the v. (P.B.)—6. As *Trot*, a Trotskyite extremist: political pej.: since mid-C.20. (*Observer*, 23 Nov. 1975.) London University students, late 1970s, would attend political meetings to play 'Spot the Trot'. (P.B.)—7. In *on the trot*, in succession: Services' in WW2; > gen. use. Cf. sense 1, and the familiar S.E. *running*.—8. See **trots**.

trot, v. To lead someone 'up the garden path': printers'. Rowles, 1948.

trot(-)boat. 'A duty boat plying between ship and shore': RN. (Granville.) A *trot* is a line of buoys and the *trot-boat* serves ships moored on the *trot*.

trot-boat queen. 'Wren member of a trot-boat's crew' (Granville): RN: 1941+. Ex prec.

trot fob. The moving of submarines in the 'trot' alongside their parent ship to make way for a submarine that is to be victualled or ammunitioned: submariners': since ca. 1930. P-G-R.

trots, the. Diarrhœa: Can., since ca. 1910; Aus., since ca. 1912 (I heard it in Gallipoli in 1915); and (P.B.) in later C.20, if not earlier, Brit.—2. A horse-trotting meeting: Aus. coll. 'Betting on the Harold Park trots' (B.P.).

trotter. 'A deserter from HM Armed Forces' (Powis): police and underworld: later C.20.—2. For *the Trotters*, see ASSOCIATION FOOTBALL, in Appx.

troub (pron. *trub*). A coll. shortening of *trouble*, as in, e.g., 'he found himself in dead [= great] troub': since mid-C.20. (P.B.)—2. A tram conductor: Aus.: since ca. 1925. (B., 1943.) Ex *trouble* or perhaps *troublesome*.

trouble(-)box. Fuse in mine or bomb: RN: 1939+.

trouble-shooter. A public relations man: coll.: since late 1950s. A sense-adaptation of an American term; a word so useful that, by 1966, it has > S.E.

trough, n. A school dinner: N. Country Grammar Schools'. *New Society*, 22 Aug. 1963.—2. 'In a students' hostel it would have been called the commonroom. In building workers' lodging it was known as the "trough" ' (Ward, 1976).

trough, v. To eat: RM. (*Mail on Sunday*, 8 Nov. 1987.) Cf. n., 1.

trouncer. Somebody extremely expert or capable; something excellent or astounding: Aus. coll. (B., 1942.) Ex S.E. *trounce*, to thrash.

trouser. To put (money) into one's trouser-pocket, hence to pocket (it): from ca. 1890.—2. To steal a rare book or document from a library or bookshop, and to smuggle it out stuffed down the front of one's trousers (or equivalent): perpetrators' and bereft: later C.20. (Lyons, 1986.)

trouser-brown. Cider: West Country s.: later C.20. (Patten, 1979.) Ex effect. Cf. **cripple-cock.**

trouser-ferret. Penis: joc.: later C.20. Cf. C.19–early 20 low s. *ferreting*, copulation (from the male angle), and:-

trouser-snake. Penis: RN joc.: mid-C.20. (Malin, 1979.) Cf. synon. **one-eyed t.-s.**

trousered; trousers. *'Trousers*. The stream-line covering in which the undercarriage legs of some 'planes are enclosed; such planes being *trousered*. (Cf. **spats**)' (H. & P.): RAF: since ca. 1930.

trousers full of pockets. No money: proletarian. (Malin, 1979.)

trout. In (*be*) *all about trout*, alert or watchful: c.: mid-C.20. (Cook, 1962.) Prob. mere play on rhyme.—2. See **salmon and trout.**

truck. 'To walk around in a state of relaxation; to "cruise" [go in search of a sexual partner]' (Hibbert, 1983): ex US.

truck drivers. Amphetamines: drugs c. (Stockley, 1986.) US since—1967 (Spears).

truckie (-ky). A railroad truck: Aus., mostly juvenile: since ca. 1920. (Dick.)—2. A truck (lorry) driver: Aus.: since ca. 1950. Hesling, 1963.—3. See:-

Truckies, the. The Royal Corps of Transport (formed 1965): Army nickname. *New Society*, 24 Apr. 1980.—2. The RAF Transport Command aircrews: RAF joc.: later 1970s. (Wilson, 1979.) Both senses ex prec., 2. Cf. *driver* = pilot.

trudge. A trudgen stroke (ex John Trudgen, British swimmer, † 1902): since ca. 1905. Garden, 1949.

trumpet. A telephone: c.: later C.20. Powis.—2. In *on the trumpet*, objectionable; disliked: Aus. Army: 1939+. (B., 1942.) ?Ex one who 'blows his own trumpet'.—3. A *Triumph* motorcycle: motorcyclists': later C.20. (Bishop, 1984.)

trumps. In *turn up* (occ., in C.20, *come up*) *trumps*, to turn out well, prove a success: coll.: 1862 (Collins: *OED*). Ex game of cards. P.B.: in C.20, often applied to a person, particularly one who, almost unexpectedly, does a favour and does it well, as 'You'd never think it of her, but when the time came, the old girl turned up trumps—really did us proud!'

trumpy. Dear in price: since ca. 1960. (London *Evening Standard*, 17 Oct. 1969.) 'That *trumps* everything!'

trunch. 'All those slags who support the system got some trunch as well' (*Time Out*, 29 Feb. 1980: an article on Wormwood Scrubs) = 'those despicable people . . . were also bludgeoned with truncheons'. Foreshadowed in Max Beerbohm's parody of Kipling, a cruel police story published in *A Christmas Garland*, 1912; the tale is prefaced, *à la* Kipling, by a verse which ends 'Then yer've got ter give 'im 'Ell,/An' it's trunch, trunch, truncheon does the trick.' (P.B.)

trundlie. A shopping trolley: 'Heard from a London bus conductor, June 1985' (Raab).

trunk, n. A trunk call: coll., among telephonists and constant telephone-users: since ca. 1930.

trunk, v.t. To coït: RN lowerdeck: 1950s. (Malin, 1980.) ?Ex hyperbolic equation: penis = elephant's trunk (P.B.).

trunnions. 'Hair over the ears which curls over a sailor's cap' (Granville): RN: since ca. 1920. Ex the lit. nautical S.E. sense.

trust you! An ironic and pej. ellipsis of 'Trust you to do that!', e.g. to bungle something; to act in an unhelpful way; or, even, 'to come up smelling of violets': since late C.19. Also, of course, with other pronouns or names: 'Trust her!', 'Trust old Smudger!', etc.

trut. A threepenny-piece: Aus.: since ca. 1930. (B., 1943.) Origin? 'Perhaps from broad pronunciation of "trupenny bit" ' (B.P.); with I suggest, the *p* of 'trupenny' influenced by the *t* of 'bit'—in short, by assimilation.

truth chamber. See **confessional.**

try-out. A selective trial: coll.: US (—1900), anglicised ca. 1910.

trying to open an oyster with a bus-ticket (usu. **, like**). (Like) trying to perform the excessively difficult or the impossible: orig. and mainly RN: since ca. (?)1930. (Peppitt.) P.B.: cf. the equally graphic *like a man with diarrhœa trying to pick a lavatory lock with a bus-ticket* or *a blade of grass*, for frantic haste with inadequate tools, which I heard in the Army, 1960s.

tub. An omnibus: c.,—1933 (Leach); >, by 1950 at latest, busmen's. See **barrow,** 2.—2. A cathode-ray tube: RAF technicians': WW2. Emanuel, 1945, 'From "tube" '.—3. A brake: railwaymen's: since ca. 1920. *Railway*, 2nd.

tubber; usu. in pl. A difficult question asked in a *viva voce* examination: RN. (Granville.) It comes like a cold douche.

tube, n. A cigarette: Cambridge undergraduates': ca. 1925–40. Hence, 1940+, among Leeds undergraduates. Marples, 2.—2. A submarine: RN: since ca. 1918. Ex its torpedo tubes.—3. Penis: Anglo-Irish feminine: late C.19–20. Joyce, 1922.—4. A drinking glass, orig. and strictly a tall, narrowish one: Aus.: since ca. 1950, ?rather earlier. *Aus. POD*, 1976.—5. 'A can of beer; given currency by the Barry Mackenzie [cartoon-]strip in the 1960s' (Wilkes); hence the drink itself: Wilkes quotes Johnston, 1971, ' "A beer'd be just the shot," said the Ocker. "Never bin known to say no to a tube." '—6. 'A hollow piped wave' (*Pix*, 28 Sep. 1963): Aus. surfers': from ca. 1961. Hence, *ride in a tube; shoot the tube*: the 2nd phrase occurs in *Pix*'s definition of *shooting the tube* as 'crouching on the nose of the board, shooting through the hollow portion of the curl'; the 1st phrase, in the *Sun-Herald*, 22 Sep. 1963, 'Riding "in a tube" is the ultimate aim of all surfers—shooting along the tube formed by a perfect wave as its crest curls over.' Also known as a *tunnel*.—7. 'Officer who listens to information given by "squealers"; a "screw" who listens to a "bubble" (or rumour). "To put the bubble in the tube" is to give information to those in authority, in the knowledge that it will get someone into trouble' (Tempest, 1950; he adds 'of medium usage'): prison c. See also **put the bubble in.**—8. 'A contemptuous term for a stupid or otherwise despicable person' (Munro, 1985): Glasgow. Perhaps ex sense 3: cf. synon. use of **prick.**

tube, v. (And hence agent *tuber*, and *tubing*, n.) To toady; a toady; toadying: University of Alberta: ca. 1925–40. P.B.: ?a ref. to the rectum; cf. *arse-lick.*—2. See quot'n at **bag,** v., 4.

tuber. A race-horse with a *tube* inserted in the air-passage: turf: 1922 (*OED* Sup.).—2. See **tube,** v., 1.

tubs. Tubular tyres: cyclists' and motorcyclists': later 1930s.

tuck in. As a cyclist, to manoeuvre to a position behind the rider in front, using him as a windshield: racing cyclists'. (*Fellowship*, 1984.) Also called **hook in.** Cf. **bit-and-bit.**

tuck strands. 'Curry favour, usually as a verbal noun, tucking strands, ingratiating oneself with Authority; from the technical sense of tucking strands of rope over and under other strands so that all of them fit snugly' (Granville): RN.

tucked away. Dead and buried: Aus. coll.: early C.20. Dennis.

tuckerbox. 'A dog [see **dog,** n., 6], a reference to the Jack Moses poem of which the chorus is: "The dog sat on the tuckerbox, Nine miles from Gundagai" ' (McNeil): Aus. c. or low s.: early 1970s. (Raab: except in ultra-polite circles, an *h* was inserted into *sat* whenever I heard the song.)

tuckertin. A metal pannier box on a motorcycle: motorcyclists': since mid-C.20. (Dunford.) An anglicisation of Aus. coll. *tucker-bag* or *-box.*

tudgy yarn. Spun-yarn: RNC, Dartmouth: since ca. 1930. 'After a Seamanship Instructor of that name' (P-G-R.).

Tudorbethan (or **t-**). Applied to a house possessing either no particular, or every, style; architecturally a 'mess': cultured coll.: since ca. 1950. Price, 1957.

tuffler. A cigarette: market-traders'. (*M.T.*) P.B.: perhaps, as this term was recorded at Boston, ex the Lincolnshire dial. v. *tuffle*, to bind flax (*EDD*).

tuft. Female pubic hair: low coll.: later C.20. James, 1980, '[The Degas drawings] are all brothel scenes and show plenty of tuft.'

tug, n. In *have a tug*, (of males) to masturbate: (low) Aus. Buzo, 1968.—2. See AUSTRALIAN . . . , in Appx.

tug, v. To eat (greedily): proletarian:—1923 (Manchon). Ex tugging with one's teeth.—2. See AUSTRALIAN . . . , in Appx.

tug pilot. 'The pilot of the aeroplane towing a glider' (P-G-R): RAF coll.: ca. 1942–5.

tuggies. Clothes: market-traders'. (*M.T.*) Ultimately ex older synon. *togs*. P.B.: ?blended with the idea of their being *tugged on*.

tugging. Dealing cards from the bottom of the pack: Aus. card-players': since ca. 1920. B., 1953.

tuggo. A tyro cyclist: club cyclists' derog. *Fellowship*, 1984.

tum-jack. The stomach: lower-middle-class: Crispin, 1950, 'Upsets the old tum-jack to mix [drinks]'.

tumble, n. A failure: c.: from ca. 1910. *Gilt Kid*, 1936.—2. A rough sea: Aus. nautical: since ca. 1915. (Parkman, 1946.) Proleptic.—3. In *give it a tumble*, 'Try it; experiment with it' (Powis): coll.: later C.20. Var. of *give it a whirl*.—4. Short for **tumble down . . .** , q.v.

tumble, v. To confuse; to upset the balance: Aus. coll.: later C.20. McNeil.—2. Abbr. next. Phillips, 1931.

tumble down the sink. A drink; to drink: r.s.: late C.19–20. B. & P.

tumble in the hay, n. A sexual serendipity; *joie-de-vivre* expressed in copulation. Orig. rural.

tummy. Stomach: coll.: 1868 (W.S. Gilbert: *OED* Sup.). Prob., orig., a children's corruption of *stomach*.—2. Hence, *tummy-tickling*, copulation, and *tummy-ache*: the former s.; the latter, coll.—3. 'A chronic though perhaps slight abdominal pain' (*Slang*): medical:—1933.

tummy banana. Penis: joc. or nursery. Bell, 1986.

tumour. A term of abuse, ca. 1930–4, at several Public Schools. Hay, 1936, 'Smear is the very latest word here. Last year it was tumour.'

tump. Rubbish; nonsense: from ca. 1930. Murray, 1933, 'Did you ever read such tump as our parish magazine?' Perhaps ex *tush* + *dump*.

Tunbridge Wells Fargos. 'Southern Railway old type Pullman trains' (McKenna, 1970): railwaymen's joc.: mid-C.20. A pun on T.W. and the famous US carriers Wells Fargo.

tune-and-toe show. A musical song-and-dance entertainment, e.g. *My Fair Lady*; as in 'public money has for a long time now been subsidising tune-and-toe shows' (*Guardian*, 29 Jan. 1979).

tunk. To dip (e.g. bread) in a liquid (esp. gravy or tea or coffee): coll.: adopted, ca. 1944, from US servicemen. The US coll. *tunk* comes ex the synon. Pennsylvania Ger. *dunken* (past p., *gedunkt*) a deviation from Ger. *tunken*. Cf. the more familiar Cockney ex Yiddish *dunk*, since mid-C.19.

tunnel. Synon. of *tube*, n., 6: since ca. 1961. *Pix*, 28 Sep. 1963.

tunnel motor. '0–6–0 Pannier tank fitted with condensing apparatus for working over the Inner Circle and Metropolitan lines' (*Railway*, 2nd): London railwaymen's: since ca. 1950.

tup. 'Butt, strike with the head' (*M.T.*): market-traders'. Perhaps ex *tup*, the head of a steam-hammer.

tuppence-ha'penny. A squadron-leader: RAF: ca. 1920–50. A pun on *two-and-a-half* ringer; ex his badge of rank.

tuppence on the can. Slightly drunk: lower classes'. (Raymond, 1930.) Ex public-house j.

Turbot. A Talbot car: Cambridge undergraduates': ca. 1925–40. Pun.

turd. A lump of excrement: C.11–20: S.E., but in mid-C.18–20 a vulgarism. Ex A.-S. *tord*, from a Germanic radical: cf. L. *tordere*.—2. A term of contempt, as in 'You are a turd': S. African coll.: since ca. 1925. P.B.: also Brit., prob. for as long, if not longer.

turd-burglar. An active male homosexual: Army, low, Other Ranks': since mid-C.20 at latest. (P.B.)

turf, n. One's own home territory: police s., and c.: later C.20. 'What are you doing at seven o'clock in the morning so far from your turf?' (Clement, 1978). Cf. synon. **patch, manor,** *bailiwick*.

turf, v. As exclam. or imperative, used by senior to junior schoolfellow: 'You have been turfed off from doing that, because I, your senior, say so and want it!': Public and Grammar Schools' s.: later C.20. Lambert, 1968.—2. (Also *turf up*.) To throw up—abandon—a job: Aus.: since ca. 1920. (B., 1942.) Cf. **pack it up** and *turn it in*.

turf it! Stow it!; Be quiet!: Aus.: since ca. 1930. (B.P.)

turf off. To remove, either by orders or bodily, someone from somewhere; e.g. 'The RSM turfed him off the square very smartly—his feet didn't touch!', or ' . . . off his bed [where he had been lying on top of it]': coll. (P.B.) Cf.:-

turf out. To kick out; to expel: from ca. 1912. Manchon.—2. Hence, to throw away or out, to discard: coll.: since ca. 1920. 'I've turfed out all that old rubbish from your cupboard.' Also Aus. (B., 1953).

Turk. 'An ill-natured surly boorish fellow' (Joyce, 1910): Anglo-Irish: late C.19–20. Cf. **toby,** 2.—2. A turkey: Aus. (B., 1942.) Cf. similarly shortened *donk* and *monk*.—3. See **Cape Turk; Turks.**

turk, v. (Properly **T-**.) Of the male, to copulate with, orig. esp. if brutally: C.20—but prob. going back a generation or two longer. Cf. **Cape Turk.** I suspect influence from synon. *firk*, itself prob. orig. euph. (Naughton, 1966.) Powis, 1977, writes, of *turking*: 'Low expression for sexual intercourse, not used in mixed company.'

turkey. A tramp's swag: Aus.; in Can., a lumberman's bag. B., 1943; Beames.—2. 'A disaster or resounding failure' (Powis): orig. US theatrical, since ca. 1944 (W. & F.), > gen.; adopted in UK later C.20. Felton, 1975.—3. Poor quality drugs or non-drug substance used to deceive: drugs c. (Stockley, 1986.) US since—1936 (Spears).—4. See **cold turkey; talk turkey.**

Turkey Trots. Traveller's diarrhœa: s., punning on the name of a dance; cf. **Aztec two-step.** *Daily Telegraph*, 17 May 1988.

Turks. The Irish: Teddy-boys': mid-C.20. (*Observer*, 1 Mar. 1959.) Cf. **Turk,** n., 1.

turn. An act of copulation: low: C.19–20. P.B.: cf. the C.20 simple *do a turn*, (of girls) to coït, esp. without fuss: s. >, by 1940, coll. M.C.P. loq.: 'Yes, nice kid—does she do a turn?'—2. A party, whether formal or informal: Aus.: since mid-C.20, prob. earlier. Buzo, 1969: 'BENTLEY: How do you think the turn went?—GARY: It was a beauty. Best house-warming party I've been to.' See **turn it on,** 1, for poss. orig.

turn a drum. Var. of **spin** (someone's) **drum**: drugs c. Stockley, 1986.

turn an honest penny. To be a pimp, a harlot's bully: low:—1923 (Manchon). Ironic.

turn copper. To inform the police: c. (Hume.)

turn in. To bring (someone) before the Officer Commanding: Army: since ca. 1930. Ex underworld. P-G-R.

turn it on. To provide, to pay for, drinks, esp., to give a party: Aus. B., 1942.—2. To fight—to begin to fight—with one's fists: Aus.: since ca. 1920. Baker.—3. (Of a woman) to agree to coït: Aus. low: since ca. 1920. (Baker.) Cf. *do a turn* at **turn,** n.—4. To enliven, as in 'I think the game is strong enough to stand a disappointing world championship. And, anyway, you know something will happen . . . Somebody's going to go out there and turn it on' (quot'n in Burn, 1983).

turn milky. See **milky,** adj.

turn-off, n. Opp. of **turn-on,** 3; as in 'Nor will [young] students be impressed by smartness. Nylon shirts and string vests are the biggest turn-offs' (Thirsk, 1979): adopted, early 1970, ex US. Ex:-

turn off, v. To disgust; esp. in ppl adj., *turned off*: adopted, ca. 1960, ex US. (*DCCU*; Hollander; W. & F.) Prompted by *turn on*, to exhilarate.

turn-on, n. A 'gag' or joke, a bogus jazz conversation intended to shock 'square' tourists: Can. jazz musicians' and lovers': since ca. 1956. (1959, 'Basic Beatnik').—2. An exhilarating or exciting or inspiring person or thing: adopted, ca. 1970, ex US. Hollander.—3. An exciting or exhilarating or inspiring experience: id. (W. & F.) By specialisation, 'a single particular drug occasion' (Home Office, which lists also *turning on* for this nuance). Cf. v., 2 and 3.

turn on, v. To inspire (someone): Can. jazz musicians' and lovers': since ca. 1955. (1959, 'Basic Beatnik'.) Esp., to excite, to thrill—a nuance that, ca. 1956, > popular among English teenagers, and thence, gen. Also as v.i., in 'More and more teen-agers are turning on with alcohol' (*Maclean's*, 17 May 1976): Can. and Brit. Prob. suggested by turning on a light (P.B.). Dempster, 1979, lists *turn on* as 'out' [= old-fashioned]—presumably he meant this sense, but that didn't stop its use: witness 'Being turned on by a film isn't the same process as being turned on by your lover' (Milne, 1987). See **turned-on.**—2. A specialisation of sense 1 as v.i. is 'to smoke a Marijuana cigarette' (Home Office): drugs world: 1970s. Cf.:—3. To introduce to drugs; to supply with a drug: drug addicts' and hippies': since ca. 1961. Fryer, 1967.

turn on a cabbage-leaf. (Of a horse) to respond promptly to guidance: Aus. coll. (Baker.) P.B.: cf. the Brit. version, as in, e.g. 'London taxis'll turn on a sixpence'.

turn-out. A suit of clothes, as in 'a smart turn-out': late C.19–20. Perhaps orig. RN lowerdeck (Knock). P.B.: the phrase 'a smart turn-out' may also be applied to, e.g., a vehicle, horse-drawn or mechanical: 'There will be a prize for the smartest turn-out'; by later C.20 coll., and verging on informal S.E. in, e.g., Service orders, 'A high standard of turn-out is expected.'

turn over, n. (Also as v.) A search of one's cell or belongings: prisons': since ca. 1920. (Phelan, 1940; Norman.) Cf. **turned over.**—2. Robbery from an accomplice one has just done a 'job' with: c.: since ca. 1945. Norman, 1959.

turn over, v. To raid (a building): Aus. police. (Kelly, 1955.) Cf. prec., 1.—2. To cross-question, examine severely: c.:—1930 (*OED* Sup.).—3. To set upon and beat up: teenage gangsters': since ca. 1950. *Observer*, 15 July 1962, reporting a fight between the 'Mussies' (Muswell Hill) and the Finchley Mob.—4. See **turned over.**

turn the corner. (Gen. as vbl. n. *turning* . . .) To round the Grand Banks on the trans-Atlantic passage: nautical coll. Bowen.

turn up the wick. To open the throttle: RAF: since ca. 1920. Cf. **go through the gate.** Partridge, 1945, 'It's an easy transition from getting a better light to getting a better speed.' Since 1945, esp. of a jet engine. P.B.: 'Oh, the wick blew out' is an occ. joc. ref. to jet-engine failure, among e.g. airline passengers stranded by such a mishap: later C.20. Also joc. coll. applied to motor vehicles: Hebden, 1973, 'Things do [fall off] when you turn the wick up', with ref. to an old car.

turn you inside out like a tiger, I'll. A threat to a naughty child, 'If you don't behave, I'll . . . ' (Reynolds.) Presumably from the striped effect that would result.

turnabout. Sodomy: Aus. low coll. McNeil.

turned off. Withdrawn from drugs: drugs c. (Stockley, 1986.) US since—1966 (Spears). Contrast next.—2. See **turn off,** v.

turned-on. Having taken an exhilarating drug, esp. marijuana; hence, aware, 'with it': drug addicts', beatniks', hippies': since early 1960s (Fryer, 1967); also common among teen-agers, and by 1970, gen. Cf.:—2. Hence, 'Aroused by music or by sexual overtures. Can be used in female company' (Powis): 1970s. Cf. **bring on; switched on.** See **turn on,** v., 1.

turned over, be. 'To be stopped by the police and searched' (F. & H.): c.: from ca. 1850. H., 1st ed.; Horsley, 1877, 'What catch would it be if you was to turn me over?' Exactly a century later, Powis has: 'A house search or a search in the street of a person or vehicle: "My motor was turned over by the Law today".' See **turn over,** n., 1.

turnip basher. 'Term applied to the dockers at Tilbury' (Ash): London dockers': Rural: cf.:-

turnip-bashing. A var. of swede-bashing, q.v.: RAF: 1940+. (Partridge, 1945.) In the King's Royal Rifle Corps, however, *turnip-bashing* is ordinary drill and *turnip-bashers* is the name for County regiments, both because they are regarded as country bumpkins and because they bang their rifles on the ground, whereas the KRRC put theirs down quietly. (Chamberlain, 1942.)

Turpentine, the. The Serpentine: Cockney r.s. Often—cf. **turps**—reduced to *the Turps.* Franklyn.

turps. Beer: Aus.: since ca. 1935. (B.P.) Ex shortening, since early C.19, of *turpentine*.—2. 'Any alcoholic drink. Whence, *be on the turps* and *get on the turps*' (B., 1959): Aus.: since late 1930s. Hollis, 1983, for London, specifies 'whisky'.

turret down, esp. **get . . .** See **hull down.**

turret rat. 'A sweeper in a ship's turret' (Bowen); 'Turret sweeper in a tramp steamer' (Granville): nautical.

turtle. A girl, a young woman, esp. regarded sexually; a (young) prostitute: Aus. low. (B., 1942.) 'A turtle on its back is not unlike a girl in the same position, and they are both in a vulnerable state', as a shrewd observer has remarked.

turtle dove. '*Love.* A term of endearment as in, "me ole turtle dove!" and probably inspired by the opening lines of the still popular song "Lily of Laguna" [written and composed by Leslie Stuart, i.e. Thomas A. Barrett; pub. 1898]' (Hillman, 1974): r.s.: (Raab: 'O fare thee well, my little turtle dove' is the first line of a well-known Eng. folksong—the term is prob. very old.)—2. See:-

turtle doves. (A pair of) gloves: r.s.—1857 ('Ducange Anglicus'). Also *turtles.* Powis, 1977, notes 'commoner than may be expected, used to refer to housebreakers' and safe-cutters' gloves.'

tush or **tosh.** A half-crown: mostly showmen's. (*Night and Day,* 22 July 1937.) Abbr. C.19 *tusheroon* or *tosheroon.*

tushery. Deliberate archaism or 'Wardour Street English': since late 1940s. (P.B., 1975.) Ex archaic S.E. *tush!*, non-sense. Cf. the use of archaic *pshaw!*

tussies. See **pussies and tussies.**

Tutbury Jinnie. 'Passenger train between Tutbury and Burton on Trent' (*Railway,* 2nd): railwaymen's: since ca. 1930(?).

tute (loosely written *tut*). A tutorial: universities'. Marples, 2.

tuts. Articles; possessions; 'bits and bobs'; as in 'Get your tuts together': market-traders'. (*M.T.*) Perhaps a var. of synon. *duds.*

tux. A tuxedo or dinner-jacket: Aus.: adopted, ca. 1945, ex US. (B.P.)

twag. To 'skive', q.v.: Lincolnshire; poss. dial., but not in *EDD.* (S. Williams, 1983.)

twallop (or *twollop*). Pej. term for a fool: 'I have heard the two terms coupled—twerps and twallops—on several occasions' (Bruckshaw, 1987): mid-C.20. Cf. **twat** and **twizzit.**

twam or **twammy.** The female pudend: low. Perhaps a blend of '*twat*' + 'qui*m*' Cf. synon. **twim.**

twang. Opium: Aus. c.: since late C.19. Wilkes.

twank. The quarry of a homosexual prostitute (male); a man willing and ready to become any dominant man's 'partner': 1920s; prob. also 1930s. Ackerley, 1968; he also says that it has, since 1930, been common among Guardsmen. P.B.: ?ex *Widow Twankey,* a pantomime 'dame' part played 'in drag'.

twat. Pej. term for a fool: low: since late C.19. Abusive: 'You stupid twat!'; cf. synon. use of *cunt, pratt*; and the Liverpool street arabs' use of the word, contemptuously, for an idler, a loafer (*Arab*). P.B.: I have heard *twat* defined, joc., as 'the back-end of a tram'.

twat-faker. A prostitute's bully: c.:—1923 (Manchon).

twat(-)hooks. Fingers; hence, loosely, hands: low: since ca. 1950. (Heard on BBC, 18 Jan. 1973.) Cf. synon. **cunt hooks.**

twat-masher. Low s. var. of **twat-faker** (Ibid.).

tweak. 'An expression often used to describe opening the throttle-twistgrip [of a motorcycle] . . . to decelerate is "to tweak it off" ' (Dunford): motorcyclists': later C.20. Cf. **demon tweak.**

tweaker; occ. **tweeker.** (Also *tweeker.*) A leg-break spinner: cricketers': from ca. 1932. *The Times,* 6 July 1937, 'R.C.M. Kimpton came on with his "tweekers" at the Nursery end.'

twee. Dainty; chic; pleasing: coll.: 1905 (*SOD*). ob. Ex *tweet,* affected or childish *sweet*: coll.: late C.19–20.—2. '(Of men) pernickety over standard of neatness; concerned over niceties; suspected of disdain for run of the mill standards' (L.A., 1974): coll.: since mid-C.20.—3. Hence, applied to artistic effort, the term has developed, since WW2, an undertone of slight contempt, for finickiness, or over-daintiness, as in *TLS*, 14 Feb. 1975, 'Commentary', on Laurence Housman's illustrations: 'They are neatly and coolly executed, though there are a few lapses into the twee' (P.B.).

tweedle. 'A Brummagem ring of good appearance used for fraudulent purposes' (F. & H.): c.: late C.19–20.—2. Hence, a trick involving dummy diamonds: c. ' "A bloke's tried to pull a tweedle on me with a load of jargoons" ' (Gosling, 1959). Also as *the tweedle*, the selling of 'dud' diamonds. (Sharpe, 1938.) There is prob. no connection with S.E. *tweedle*; *tweedle* is a var. of *twiddle*, cognate with *twist*, and there is perhaps a humorous side-glance at *wheedle*. Cf.:-

tweedler, agent, and **tweedling,** activity, can be applied to 'the **tweedle**', 2. Usu., however, a *tweedler* is a very minor, petty sort of 'con man'. Gosling, 1959, 'The tweedler will flog you sawdust cigarettes or dummy diamond rings'—a nuance dating, like sense 1 (of which, clearly, it forms a mere extension), from early C.20. 'The terms "conning" and "tweedling" cover virtually everything in the crime known as obtaining money by false pretences.' They derive, ultimately, ex **tweedle**, 1. Cf.—2. 'A stolen vehicle disguised for "honest" sale to a respectable dupe' (Powis): c.: later C.20.

tweedly. High-pitched and fidgetty, esp. of violin music: coll. (P.B.)

tweeker. See **tweaker**.

tweezie, -y (mostly in pl.). A twinge: (?)late C.19–earlier 20. Kipling, in a letter to Rider Haggard, 25 Mar. 1925, writes of 'tweezies in the trash-bag', i.e. stomach pains (quoted in Cohen, 1965).

twenty-spot(ter). A £20 bank-note: since ca. 1965. (*Spectator*, 19 June 1976.) Cf. **spot**, n., 6.

twenty-two carat. Utterly trustworthy: since ca. 1930: c. >, by ca. 1950, also s. Cook, 1962.

twerp. An unpleasant or objectionable or foolish or 'soft' person (rarely female): from ca. 1910. (F. & G.; Brown, 1934.) P.B.: very common, mid-C.20, but ob. by ca. 1970.

twi. (Very) old age; senility: since ca. 1960. (Travers, 1973.) Prob. an abbr. of the cliché *the twilight of one's years*.

twice. To cheat (somebody): low. (Hume, 1940.) Double-dealing.

twicer. One who asks for two helpings; hence, one who persistently tries to get more than his due: Aus.: esp. in WW1.—2. A cheat, a liar, a twister, a crook: Aus.; in Brit. mostly commercial, and for the first two. (Lancaster, 1910.) P.B.: prob. ex *double*-cross.—3. (?Hence), a sycophant: Aus.: since ca. 1918. (Baker.) Or ex 'two-faced'.—4. A widow or widower remarrying: lower classes': earlier C.20. F. & G.—5. A two-year prison sentence: police and c.: later C.20. Hunter, 1974.—6. A tandem bicycle: cyclists'. *Fellowship*, 1984.

Twickers. Twickenham Rugby Football ground: sporting: since ca. 1920. *Twicken*ham + the 'OXFORD-*ER*(s)'. L.A. noted an ITV interview of 5 Nov. 1969 in which it was stated that 'the people who call it "Twickers" don't play Rugby, but just call it Headquarters'—but E.P. felt that this was 'too sweeping'.

twiddler. A paperback book: RN: since early 1940. (*Observer*, 18 Aug. 1940.) One can twiddle them about in one's hands.

twig. Mostly in pl. *twigs*, matches: Borstal boys': since ca. 1945. (*Daily Telegraph*, 4 June 1958.) Ex the rough, 'twiggy' quality of inferior safety matches.

twig and berries. A child's penis and testicles: lower-class euph. Cf. **pencil and tassel**.

Twiggy. 'A nickname sometimes given to a stout girl or woman. Of course, Twiggy the model was very slim' (Petch, 1976): ironic: early 1970s. It is the professional name of Lesley Hornby.

twilight zone. 'The period whilst awaiting promotion from fireman to driver' (McKenna, 1970): railwaymen's: mid-C.20.

twilights. Summer-weight knickers worn by the WAAF: among WAAF and RAF: 1940+. (Jackson.) Ex their pale-blue colour. Cf. **black-outs** and **passion-killers**.

twillies. Sympathy between twins: medical: since ca. 1920. Ex *twinly feelings*? The German for 'twins' is *Zwillinge* (from *zwei*, two), so prob. imm. ex Yiddish (R.S.).

twillip. A foolish, weak man; a 'twerp', an objectionable and/or insignificant person: since ca. 1919, among London youths (L.A., 1974); thence Guards' Regts (Kersh, 1941) and RAF, WW2 (L.A.); ob. by 1950. Cf. **twallop**.

twim. Female pudend: low. A blend of *tw*at and qu*im*. Cf. synon. **twam**.

twin-set. A two-bottle aqualung: skin divers': since ca. 1950. Ex the terminology of women's clothing.

twine. To grumble: c. and low: from ca. 1925. Cf. synon. **bind**, v., 2.

twink. A moment: proletarian: Connington, 1937, 'I just pressed the electric light switch for a twink—to make sure—an' the current was off.' Abbr. *twinkle* or *twinkling*. P.B.: often as *two twinks*, as in 'Just hang on a mo—I shan't be two twinks.'—2. (Also adj.) Homosexual: one of Society's 'in' words, according to Dempster, 1984. Poss. ex US (listed in W. & F., 1975): but cf. **twank**.

twinkle. Diamonds; jewellery in general: c.: later C.20. Scott, 1982.

twirl. A warder: prisoners' c.:—1933 (Ingram). Ex his bunch of keys.—2. In *on the twirl*, adj. and adv., a-thieving professionally: c. (*Gilt Kid*, 1936.) Ex skeleton keys.

twirler. A skeleton key: c.: C.20 var. of later C.19 *twirl*. *Now!*, 10 Apr. 1981.

twirlies. 'Busmen particularly loathe the daily hassle with the "twirlies" at around 9.30 am as senior citizens ask conductors whether they are "too early" to use their free passes' (*New Society*, 13 Nov. 1980.).—2. See **twirly**.

twirling. The dishonest substitution of a winning betting slip for a losing one: bookmakers': since ca. 1925. *Bournemouth Echo*, 18 Aug. 1960.

twirly. A cigarette: R Aus. N: since ca. 1920. (B., 1943.) One twirls it in one's fingers.—2. See **twirlies**.

twirp. Var. spelling of **twerp**. Cf.:-

twirt. (Also *twirp* or *twerp*.) A cheeky small boy: Shrewsbury: since mid-1930s. (Marples.) Cf. **twillip**.

twist, n. *The twist* is 'sharp practice, in gen. or in particular': c. (Sharpe, 1938.) Cf. **twist**, v., 1, and **twister**, 1. As '*a twist*' it = esp. 'A swindle', as in 'I thought the betting slip a twist'—a bookmaker's remark quoted by *Bournemouth Echo*, 18 Aug. 1960.—2. A habitual criminal: Aus. c.: since ca. 1910. B., 1942.—3. A girl: low Can.: adopted, ca. 1940, from US—as also were *bim, broad, frail*. All four US terms orig. in the underworld. R.C., 1966, commented, from USA, 'This is rhyming slang: "twist-and-twirl"—one of the few bits of r.s. that ever became fairly gen. in U.S.: cf. E.E. Cummings, "To be a feller's twist-and-twirl". Now ob. here.'—4. In *at the twist*, adj. and adv., (by) double-crossing: c.:—1933 (Leach).—5. See **round the twist; knickers in a twist**.

twist, v. To swindle, to cheat: Aus., from not later than 1914; and by mid-C.20 at latest, also Brit. coll. Perhaps by back-formation ex **twister**, 1.—2. In passive, to be convicted of a crime: Aus. low (?c.). B., 1942.

twist (someone's) arm. To persuade; strictly, to persuade forcibly, hence with lengthy argument: since the late 1950s. L.A. adds, 1976, 'also to use threat (of revealing disreputable fact, etc.) in order to ensure compliance.' P.B.: often used joc., esp. in, e.g., 'Have another drink?', which may be answered eagerly by a fellow-toper, 'Well, if you twist me arm perhaps I could manage to force one down!'

twist joint. Any cheap dance-hall for twist (a form of dance) sessions: since ca. 1961; by late 1965, already slightly ob. P.B.: by 1980 so ob. that the term might be understood as synon. with *clip-joint*, a place where one might *be twisted*, as in **twist**, v., 1.

twist the book (on). To turn the tables (on a person): c.: from early 1920s. Wallace.

twister. A 'shady' fellow, a swindler, a crook; a shuffler, a prevaricator; a person of no decided opinions: low: from not later than 1912 in Aus., not later than 1914 in England. P.B.: *SOD* records this fig. use from 1834.—2. One who cannot be tricked or swindled: c.: from ca. 1920. See esp. Wallace, *The Twister*, 1928. Ironic ex sense 1, or direct ex **twist the book**, q.v.—3. A whirlwind: Aus., esp. Western. (Elliott, 1970.) P.B.: but known also elsewhere in the world, in places afflicted by tornadoes, williwaws, dust-devils, and the like.—4. A key. Cf. **twirler**; and see CANADIAN . . . and JIVE, in Appx.

twisty. Odd, strange, esp. in 'a *twisty* look': low. (Phelan, 1957.) Semantically cf. *twist*, a strange turn of mood or bent of character.

twit. A contemptible—or a very insignificant—person: since ca. 1925. (Linklater, 1934.) A blend of *twerp* and *twat*.—2. A simpleton, a fool: Aus.: late 1920s. (B., 1942.) Very prob. orig. in Brit.; by 1973 somewhat ob. in Aus. 'In slang, I think the basic meaning is one who is twitted or [here's the crux] deserves to be twitted' (Mainprice, 1972). The v. is S.E. for 'to reproach, to taunt.'—3. A term of abuse: N. Country Grammar Schools': since late 1940s. (*New Society*, 22 Aug. 1963.) Ex sense 1. P.B.: in later C.20 much more gen.

twitch, n. A bout of nerves, esp. if noticeable by others: RAF: since the late 1930s. (Bickers, 1965.) Cf. *twitchety*, **twitters** and 'Have you ever used that old service slang and said that someone has a "bit of a twitch on"? You don't mean it literally, of course. You're merely implying that the person concerned is in a highly emotional state and somewhat "het up" about something' (*Woman's Own*, 16 Jan. 1965). Synon. adj. in post-WW2 RAF: *twitched-up* and *twitchy*.—2. Also *twitchable*, *twitcher*, *twitching*. See BIRD-WATCHERS', in Appx.

twitter. In *have a (bit of a) twitter on*, to be rather tipsy: mostly RN: mid-C.20. Prob. ex drunken twittering, as of birds, but cf. 2. (P.B.)—2. Short for *ring-twitter*. See **twittering ringpiece.**

twittering. Paying court to other sex: University of Alberta: ca. 1925–40.—2. (N. and adj.) Menstruating: schoolgirls': since ca. 1930. Kersh, 1958.

twittering ringpiece; also **ring-twitter** and **ring-twitch.** A state of extreme nervousness: RAF: since ca. 1939. Ex a physiological symptom.

twitters, the. Nervousness: Scottish Public Schools'. Miller, 1935, 'I played my best game in the match *v.* the Academy, in spite of a bad attack of the twitters before going on to the field.'

twittishness. As in ' . . . her tantrums, her empty socialising, her twittishness has been exposed to view' (Johnson, 1987). See **twit.**

twizzit. Mild reproof for a fool, 'You silly twizzit!'; 'a bit of an ass': De Bunsen, 1960, writing of the ATA [see **Ancient and Tattered**] in WW2, 'I remember her [a fellow pilot] saying of a rather dim-looking batch of recruits, "Well, they *are* Twizetts, *aren't* they!" The word was new to me but it described them rather well.' Cf. all the other mild pej. beginning *tw-*, twerp, twillip, etc. (P.B.)

two-and-a-half bloke. A lieutenant-commander: RN: since ca. 1930. (H. & P.) A var. of **two-and-a-half-striper.** Cf.:-

two-and-a-half ringer. See **ringer,** 5.

two-and-a-half striper. See **striper** . . .

two-and-eight. (Often *in a* . . .) A fluster, a confusion, emotional state, attack of nerves: r.s., on *state*, arose during WW1 (Franklyn). Franklyn forecast that it would not supersede synon. *Harry Tate*, but time has proved him wrong (P.B.). See also **six-and-eight.**

two bastards on bikes. See **two ladies** . . .

two-bit. Insignificant: Can., since ca. 1930; Aus. and Brit. since ca. 1945, but not common: ex US *two bits*, *two-bit*, 25 cents (R.C.). However, by 1929, at latest, its US meaning was 'cheap' or 'inferior' (W. & F.). P.B.: some Brit. use, aping US, in *two-bit chiseller*, a 'small-time' cheat. Cf. **two-bob,** 2.

two blocks. See **blocks.**

two-bob. A blonde: Aus. Army: WW2. B., 1943.—2. 'The sum of money most often used in derogatory expressions like "not worth two bob", "silly as a two bob watch" ' (Wilkes): Aus.: since ca. 1940, or earlier. Cf.:-

two-bob hop. A cheap evening's dancing: Aus.: since ca. 1920. (B.P.) Cf. *twopenny hop*, the earlier Brit. version.

two crows for a banker. 'Code whistles exchanged between engine and second [or] banking engine when ready to move' (*Railway*): railwaymen's: since ca. 1920.

two-dog night. A very cold night: Aus.: later C.20. 'Evidently Aborigines used to describe the cold by counting how many dogs they had to sleep with in order to keep warm' (*Guardian*, 1 Oct. 1982).

two draws and a spit. Smoking half a cigarette; hence, any short smoke at convenient intervals: mostly in factories and workshops: from ca. 1915. Cf. **spit and a draw,** and **whiffs** . . .

two-ender. A florin: Cockneys'. (*Evening News*, 20 Jan. 1936.) Also grafters': witness *Cheapjack*, 1934.

two eyes of blue! Too true!: r.s.: since ca. 1925. Franklyn 2nd.

two fat ladies or **Waafs.** See TOMBOLA, in Appx.

two-fer. See **twofer.**

two five two. Esp. *be put on a* . . . , to be 'crimed': Army coll. verging on j.: from ca. 1912. (F. & G.) The charge-sheet was officially known as Form 252.

two, four, six, eight, bog in, don't wait! A secular grace before meals: Aus.: since ca. 1920; perhaps much earlier. (B.P.) Cf. **bog in.**

two-four-six-eight! whom do we appreciate? A chanted equivalent of 'For he's a jolly good fellow!', but may be applied also to, e.g., the name of a team; the object of the 'appreciation' is shouted after the question, as in 'Two-four-six-eight! Who(m) do we appreciate? Ee-goles! [*Eagles* = the Bedford Town Association Football Club]': since 1940s (?earlier); prob. adopted ex US. (P.B.)

two-hander. A stage play with only two characters: theatrical and literary: since ca. 1960 or a little earlier. *The Times* Saturday Review, 9 Oct. 1976.

two ha'pennies to rub together, have not. To be very poor; occ., to lack any spare money whatsoever: coll. 'He hasn't . . . ' (Petch, 1966.) P.B.: cf. earlier C.20 (e.g. *he*) *hasn't got a ha'penny to jingle on a tombstone*.

two i.c. (A spoken abbr.) A second *in* command or charge: Services', esp. Army: since ca. 1945 (?earlier). Ex the written abbr. *2 i/c*. (P.B.; B.P.)

two Labour gains. 'Two yellow lights at a colour signal' (*Railway*, 2nd): since 1945 or 1946. Cf. **one Labour gain.**

two ladies on bikes. The figure of Britannia on the obverse of the two pennies: two-up players', esp. NZ. I.e. when both turned up tails; the 'heads' betters call them the *two bastards on bikes*.

two little ducks. See TOMBOLA, in Appx.

two-o. See **three-o.**

two of eels, (standing there) like. 'Abstracted, indecisive, at a loss' (L.A., 1948).

two of fat and one of lean. The marking on the ships' funnels of the Harrison Line: nautical: earlier C.20.

two of that. Something much better, esp. as in Walpole, 1933, '[Mr Childers] had forestalled the Conservatives, . . . but Gladstone knew two of that': coll.: late C.19–20. Abbr. a *trick worth two of that*.

two old ladies. See TOMBOLA, in Appx.

two-one. A second class, upper division, grading in the bachelors' degree examinations, as 'She was hoping for a first [q.v.], but she got only a two-one. Still that's not bad': universities' and polytechnics'. Similarly *two-two*, second class, lower division. Cf. **Desmond.** (P.B.)

two ones. At two-up, a 'head' and a 'tail' when two coins are used: Aus. coll.: late C.19–20. B., 1942.

two-peg. A florin: Aus. B., 1942.

two-pence-ha'penny. See **tuppence ha'penny.**

two pennorth of tripe, like. (Of something) contemptible or worthless.

two-pot screamer. One who very easily becomes drunk: Aus.: since ca. 1950. Slater, 'heard in the Northern Territory in 1957–62'.

two-ringer. See **ringer**, 5.

two-six, do a. To do something very speedily and promptly, e.g. in bombing-up: RAF, esp. armourers': since ca. 1930. Davison, 1942, ' "To do a two-six out of camp" (to leave camp immediately or very quickly)—"a two-six into a shelter".' Cf. a *one-two*, two quick, successive punches in boxing. But *two-six*, or *two*, *six*, also occurs alone, to urge speed or a spurt of energy, as in 'a spot of two, six'. P.B.: also, and perhaps orig., RN; esp. in exhortation, e.g. at rope-hauling: 'Two-Six . . . Heave!' It may even date back to earlier C.19 gun-drill.

two-striper. See **striper** . . .

two-thirder. A printer's apprentice that has served two-thirds of his time; hence, loosely, someone fairly well-advanced in the trade: printers' coll.

two-three-five-nine; written **2359.** See PRISONER-OF-WAR SLANG, § 15, in Appx.

two ticks, in. Very quickly; in just a moment: coll. Cf. *in two twinks* (at **twink**) and *in two twos.* (P.B.)

two-time, to double-cross (someone); **two-timer,** a double-crosser, or merely one who doesn't 'play the game': adopted, in 1939, from US. R.C., 1976, adds, 'the US nuance is mainly sexual', the deceived 'thinking he (she) is "the one and only".'

two-tone. 'Groups are . . . now called two-tone because they put black and white musicians together to play ska' (Walker, 26 June 1980). Contrast **three-tone.**

two-two. See **two-one.**

two-year-old, like a. In a very lively manner; vigorous(ly): coll. (*Punch,* 19 June 1912.) Ex race-horses.

two'd up. 'Two inmates in a cell' (Home Office): prisons': later C.20. Also *three'd up,* etc.

twoer. £200: c. and fringe of underworld: since late 1940s, if not a decade or two earlier. (Newman, 1970.)

twofer. 'Yacht with sails and an auxiliary engine' (Granville): nautical.—2. 'Combined bathroom and toilet in a liner' (Ibid.): id.—3. A cigarette: mostly RN: from ca. 1950. 'For *two for a penny*'—the penny 'that one once put into a slot machine' (L.A., 1967).

two's, the. The second floor: prison c. (and prison officers' s.). Cook, 1962.

two's up. 'Let *me* have it next, please', as in 'Good book, this!'—'Is it? Two's up, then!' or 'Two's up on your blanco brush, mucker': Services', very widely used: since ca. 1950 or a little earlier. (P.B.)—2. Hence, 'Sharing—usually butt-ends' (Home Office): Borstals' and detention centres': later C.20.

ty. Typhoid fever: Aus. Prichard, 1929.

typ. Typical: uncultured and trivial: since ca. 1930. Allingham, 1948.

type has since WW1, been increasingly used very loosely for 'kind', 'category', 'character', 'nature'.—2. 'An officer whether of the R.A.F. or another service' (H. & P., early 1943): RAF since ca. 1920. Jackson (late 1943), however, does not confine it to officers: *'Type.* Classification of person. Thus, "He's a poor type, a ropey type, a dim type, a brown type." In the R.A.F. the word is universal in this sense, and derives from its common use in connection with aircraft. Used since the Great War' (1914–18). This 'etymology' is correct; I think, however, that there has been some influence by the French-slang use of *type* for 'chap, fellow'.—3. A typewriting machine: makers', dealers', repairers': since ca. 1920.

typed. (Of actors, theatrical or cinematic) kept in one type of role: theatrical and cinematic: since ca. 1937.

typewrite. To fire a Bren, or other, machine-gun in bursts: Army: WW2. (P-G-R.) Cf. **typewriters.**

typewriter. A fighter, boxer: r.s.: from ca. 1920. Phillips, 1931.

typewriters. Machine-guns in action: Army: WW1 and WW2. (Pound, 1964.) Ex the crisp tapping [P.B.: E.P. heard them when he was on the Somme].

typogremlin. See GREMLINS, in Appx.

481

U

U.F.O. A hippy club: drug addicts' and hippies': ephemeral pun, mid-1960s, on *un*limited *f*reak-*o*ut (see **freak-out**, n.) and the more durable *un*identified *f*lying *o*bject (a 'flying saucer'). Fryer, 1967.—2. Another ephemeral pun on *UFO*, ca. 1979, was *U.F.O.S.* = the 'Unacceptable face of Socialism', coined during the widespread industrial [in]action early in that year. It refers back to an earlier 1970s phrase 'the unacceptable face of capitalism'. (P.B.)

u-jeep. 'Two-man submarine; a play on U-boat [Ger., *Unterseeboot*]. What the jeep is to a lorry, so is the two-man boat to the orthodox submarine' (Granville): RN: later WW2.

u/s or **U/S** or **u.s.** or **U.S.** (Of persons) unhelpful, helpless, useless: (of things) unavailable: RAF coll.: since ca. 1935. Jackson, 'I'm in dock. I'm afraid I shall be u/s for some time'; Partridge, 1945, 'From the official abbreviation, u/s (or U/S), "unserviceable" '—esp. as applied to aircraft or aircraft parts; Brickhill, 1946. P.B.: from ca. 1950 at latest, also army.

U.T.C.A.A. Uncle Tom Cobley and all [of Widdicombe Fair fame], i.e. everybody; 'all the world and his dog': Services': WW2 and after. Ex its use by signallers for 'inform all parties concerned'. (Bishop.)

U-turn. Esp, *do a . . . ,* or *there will be no . . . :* 'political coll., from mid-1970s, for a sudden reversal of policy. Ex motorists' j.' (R.S., 1975). It has been Australianised as *do a uey* or *youee* or *u-ie*, etc. (Raab, 1979). B.P., 1976, prefers *yewie*. See **uie**.

uckers. The game of ludo, played large-scale on ship's deck: RN. (Granville.) Ex *uck*, an RN lowerdeck term, from later C.19 and dial., = to heave, hoist + 'OXFORD/RN -*ER*(*s*)': 'one of the objects is to remove one's opponent's pieces from the board by landing [one's own piece, by throw of dice] in the same square' (Ibid.). The game has its own c.p., 'Uckers, you fuckers—take six!'

ugly pills. 'Anyone who manifests a surly disposition is apt to be accused of having taken ugly pills' (Leechman): Can.: since late 1950s.—2. Hence, perhaps by a misapprehension of the N. Am. meaning, used in the Brit. Army as a—usu. joc.—gratuitously offensive remark, as in 'Been at the ugly pills again then, have you?' = 'I don't like your face!': late 1950s–early 60s. (P.B.)

ugsome. Thoroughly unpleasant: coll.: later C.20. (HRH Prince Philip, quoted in *The Times*, 17 July 1982.) *SOD* records it as a literary revival (by Sir Walter Scott) of Scot. and Northern Middle Eng.

uie. A u-turn. 'If the law isn't up my arse I'll hang a Uie' (Humphries, 1981). Sayers, 1985, cites 'Do a uey in the ute at the uni'.

uke. Ukelele: musicians' >, ca. 1930, gen.—2. As *Uke*, a Ukrainian immigrant settled in Halifax, Yorkshire: local coll.: later C.20. White, 'The Ukes of Halifax', *New Society*, 12 June 1980.

ukelele. A type J. 39 locomotive: railwaymen's, esp. North Eastern. *Railway.*

Ukers (pron. *yukers*). The United Kingdom: sometimes among servicemen overseas: later C.20. By the 'OXFORD -*ER*(*s*)' on U.K. (P.B.)

Ukrainian suitcase. 'A cardboard box, or thick paper bag, tied with string: W. Can., esp. Prairie States: since 1920s or '30s during large immigration of Ukrainians and Poles to the Prairies. Usu. derog. or put-down' (Leech, 1986). Cf **Mexican drag-line**.

ulu. Malay for 'upstream', hence applied to jungle, it was adopted by the post-WW2 Army serving in Malaya; thence it >, in other parts of the world, a wilderness of any sort, paradoxically even that of Arabia Deserta or the strife-torn streets of central Belfast. Often in the phrase 'out in the ulu'. (P.B.)

umbiginga. Umbrella: domestic coll., by joc. perversion. (Reed, 1980.)

umbrella. A parachute: Services', esp. RAF: since ca. 1934 (?earlier: cf. **brolly**, 2). Partridge, 1945.

Umbrella Brigade. 'Ironic police term for the Special Branch' (Powis): later C.20.

umbrella club, the. 'If a Maltese girl marries but has no children in the first two years, the priest visits her to fix it. Whilst performing the necessary servicing, the priest hangs his umbrella on the bedroom door, so that neither husband nor other visitors intrude, RN [scurrilous], 1950s' (Peppitt).

umbrella man. A parachutist: RAF since ca. 1935, Army since ca. 1942. (Jackson.) See **umbrella**.

umbrella regulations. 'The National Security Regulations—"they cover everything". (War slang.)' (B., 1943): Aus.: WW2.

umbrella treatment, the. 'A particularly nasty and now almost legendary way of treating venereal disease': Army: since ca. 1945 (prob. much earlier). (P.B.)

umgeni, umgenis. See SWAHILI, in Appx.

ump. An umpire: sporting, esp. cricketers': from ca. 1919. 'Ah, here comes the umps', heard in the Oval Pavilion on 19 June 1937.

umpie. Umpire: Aus. Palmer, 1955.

um(p)teen, umpty, nn.; um(p)teenth, umptieth, adj. An undefined number; of an undefined number: Dennis, (and heard by editor in) 1916: WW1 Army, to disguise the number of a brigade, division, etc.; orig. signallers' s., says F. & G. Whereas *umpty, umptieth*, are ob. and were never sen. gen., *umpteen*(*th*) is still common, though rather in the sense of '(of) a considerable number', as in *for the umpteenth time*, a change of sense implicit from the beginning. Ex *um*, a noncommittal sound aptly replacing an unstated number, + *-teen*; the later *umpty, -ieth*, ex the same *um* + *-ty* as in *twenty, thirty*, etc. Possibly *um* represents *any*.

umpty (**iddy**). Esp. *feel* . . . , (to feel) indisposed, off colour; the shorter form also = 'unsuccessful': Services'; the full, from 1915 (F. & G.); *umpty* alone, since ca. 1916 (Kersh, 1938). Prob. ex *umpty iddy* as the reverse form of signallers' **iddy umpty**, q.v.: 'all backwards', hence 'queer, ill' (Leechman). P.B.: but perhaps influenced also by late C.19-early 20 *humpy*, depressed, dispirited.

umpty-poo. Just a little more: Army: 1915–18. (F. & G.) Ex Fr. *un petit peu*.—2. As in Rattigan, 1950, Act I (set in 1917):

> DAPHNE . . . (In *a confidential manner*): I say, old bean, where's the oojah?
> MARK: The oojah?
> DAPHNE: The om-tiddly-om-pom.
> MARK: *Still looks baffled*.
> DAPHNE: The umpti-poo.
> MARK (*Light breaking*): Oh, the umpti-poo. How foolish of me. It's through the door here, and then on the right.

All three words, euph. for a w.c., prob. arose among civilians in WW1, who would have heard these strange, almost nonsensical words from soldiers home on leave: *oojah* short for **ooja-ka-piv**, q.v.; *om-tiddly-om-pommers* were machine-gunners, ex the 'tune' of a burst fired with rhythm; and *umpti-poo* ex sense 1. (E.P. supplied the quot'n, I the suggested etym.; he had dated *umpti-poo* in this sense from 'ca. 1910', which, for want of other evidence, seems unlikely. P.B.)

umpty show. An inferior play, or inferior acting of a play: theatrical: since ca. 1917. (Marsh, 1938.) Ex *umpty iddy*.

umses (or **U-**). The 'boss': tailors'. *Tailor and Cutter*, 29 Nov. 1928.

unan. Unanimous: (mostly) upper classes'. Brandon, 1933.

unappropriated blessing. An old maid: cultured joc. coll.:— 1923 (Manchon).

Unbleached Australians. Aborigines: Aus. joc. (B., 1942.) Contrast *Smoked Welshmen*.

unblock. See BIRD-WATCHERS', in Appx.

unbridle. 'When he saw the thief he was to "unbridle" (take off his hat). Then it was up to us' (Gosling, 1959): c.: since ca. 1925.

unbutton. 'Decode a signal. 2. Cast off a ship in the convoy' (Granville): RN: WW2. Cf **uncork!**.

unbuttoned. Upset; unprepared: Army: WW2. (P-G-R.) Ex **come unbuttoned**, q.v.

unc. A steward in the MN: nautical. (*Bournemouth Echo*, 21 Oct. 1943.) ?Ex:—2. Uncle, esp. in address: domestic coll. Cf. earlier *nunky*, a pet form of (*my*) *nuncle* (SOD). P.B.: from mid-1930s it was used in address, and in ref., to a favourite uncle in our family; we spelt it *Unk*.

uncle. One's—esp. one's Hollywood—film agent: cinematic world: since ca. 1925.—2. A theatrical backer: since ca. 1925. Moseley, 1952.—3. Short for **Uncle Ned**. Lester.—4. In *go and see uncle*, an earlier C.20 euph. for 'to visit the privy'.

Uncle Ben. See TOMBOLA, in Appx.

Uncle Bert. A shirt: (not very common) r.s. Franklyn 2nd.

Uncle Bill. The police: since ca. 1935: c. >, by ca. 1955, low s. (Cook, 1962.) Cf. **Old Bill** in this sense, and:-

Uncle Bob. A policeman: since ca. 1945. (Cunliffe, 1965.) Prompted by the synon. *bobby*.

Uncle Charlie. A German long-distance gun firing from Le Havre in June–July 1944: invasion forces'. (Jordan, 1946.)

Uncle Dick. Sick: r.s.: late C.19–20.—2. Penis: r.s., on *prick*. Both are recorded by Franklyn in his *Rhyming Slang*.

Uncle Fred. Bread: r.s. (P.P., 1932.) Franklyn comments, 'This is used chiefly by, and to, children.'

Uncle Ned. Bed: r.s.: late C.19–20. (F. & G.) 'It refers to the article of furniture itself, and to the act of going there' (Franklyn).—2. The head: id. Rare.

Uncle Tim's Cabin. The Vice-Regal Lodge of the Irish Free State during *Tim* Healy's governorship: Anglo-Irish: 1922–8. Timothy Healy: 1855–1931. Mrs. H. B. Stowe's famous anti-slavery novel, *Uncle Tom's Cabin*, appeared serially in 1851–2, and in book form in 1852.

Uncle Tom. A Negroes', a West Indians', pej. for such a man of their own race as is deferential towards white people: adopted in the British Commonwealth, ca. 1965, ex US, where the sense and the feeling are, among Negroes, somewhat stronger. See prec. for etym. Also as v., to act thus; and the abstract *Uncle Tomism*. Cf. **coconut** in this sense, brown outside, white within.

Uncle Willie. Silly: r.s. from ca. 1870. P.P., 1932.—2. Chilly: r.s.: since ca. 1920. Franklyn 2nd.

uncling. See **go uncling**.

uncomfy. Uncomfortable. It occurs in print in, e.g., a letter written by Kipling in 1907, quoted in Birkenhead, 1978. The natural opp. of *comfy*, s. since early C.19.

unconscious. A daydreamer; a dreamy person: from ca. 1926. Cf. **romance**.

uncool. Excitable; tending to show one's feelings more than is prudent or advisable: adopted, ex US, mid-1960s. (*Groupie*, 1968.) Opp. of **cool**, adj.

uncork!; cork! 'Decode': 'Code'—as orders: RN: since ca. 1920. (Occ. used in other grammatical moods.) Granville. Cf synon. **unbutton**.

under, n. Sexual intercourse: c. (*Gilt Kid*, 1936; Hunter, 1963.) Often as *a bit of under*. Cf. **under-petticoating** and **undercut**, of which this is perhaps a shortening.

under, adv. Under (the influence of) a narcotic: medical coll., now verging on S.E. Blaker, 1934.

under-arm. Pornographic, 'blue': low. Nuttall, 1979, 'One of the first things Randle asked him was did he make any . . . under-arm films' Cf. **under the arm**, 2.

under book. Lower-priced (car) than as shown in *Glass's Guide to Secondhand Car Prices*: car-dealers' coll.: since ca. 1950.

under-cart. The undercarriage of an aircraft: RAF: from 1932.

under (someone's) **neck, get** or **go.** 'To forestall an action contemplated by another, usurp someone else's prerogative' (Wilkes, whose 1st quot'n is from Hungerford, 1953): Aus. (?racing) s. > coll.

under starter's orders, be. To be, or to have been, arrested: since ca. 1945: orig. and still mainly c.; by ca. 1950, also police s. (Gosling, 1959.) Ex horse–racing.

under the arm. (Of a job) additional: tailors':—1903 (F. & H.).—2. No good: tramps' c.,—1935; by 1940, low s. (Norman). Implication: it stinks. Cf. synon. **under the crutch**.

under the cosh, to have (someone). To have him at one's mercy: prisoners': since 1945. Norman.

under the crutch. See **under the arm**, 2.

under the gun. 'Under pressure; working to a deadline; to put someone under pressure in order to obtain information. E.g., "I'm sorry to have to put you under the gun, but we have to have the paper out by tomorrow." Widespread N. Am.: since early C.20' (Leech, 1986).

under the hammer. (Of a train) 'accepted at caution' (Railway, 1964).

under the influence. Tipsy: coll. Abbr. *under the influence of alcohol*, which is sometimes joc. spoonerised to *under the affluence of incohol*.—2. Under an anaesthetic: since ca. 1925.

under the lamp. Underhand; illicit: nautical. With ref. to an arrangement for payment.

under the lap. Confidentially: Aus.: since ca. 1920. (B., 1942.) Cf.:—2. 'Clandestinely, e.g. a book printed with a false place of publication' (Raab, 1977): Aus.: since late 1940s.

undercart. See **under-cart**.

undercut. See **snappy undercut**.—2. Female pudend: low.

underfug. An under-vest. de Sélincourt, 1924.

undergraduette. A girl 'undergrad': s. >, by 1930, coll.: 1919, *Observer*, 23 Nov., 'The audience was chiefly composed of undergraduates and undergraduettes' (W.).

underground, the. 'The subculture rebelling against the straight society [the *squares*] or the Establishment' (Wolfe, 1968; cf. Landy's title, 1971): since ca. 1965: coll. >, by 1970, S.E. Prompted by the always S.E. *the underworld*. Hence *undergrounders* (Jagger, 1974) and adj., e.g. *the underground press*: since late 1960s.

underground fruit. Potatoes; hence, other vegetables: RN lowerdeck: since ca.1925.

underground mutton. 'Rabbit, as edible meat' (Wilkes): Aus.: since early 1940s.

undergrounder. See **underground**.

underneaths. Female legs: Welsh coll.: late C.19–20. Evans, 1923.

underpants like St Paul's. Underpants very tight in the crutch: Aus.: since late 1940s. (B.P.) P.B.: perhaps cf. the raffish English comment on tight trousers or underpants, *they're like the Edgware Road*, explained by 'that's got no ball-room either'.

undershoot. To fail to land at the intended spot: RAF coll., soon > j.: since 1932.

undertaker's job. A horse running *dead* (not intended to win): Aus. sporting: since ca. 1930. Powis, 1977, 'Specifically, a horse or greyhound not intended to win; generally, any hopeless proposition.' Was the Brit. adopted ex Aus., or *vice versa*?

underweight. A girl under 21 sent out as prospective harlot to the Argentine: white-slave traffickers' c. Londres.

undesertworthy. (Of a soldier) utterly useless: Army in N. Africa: 1940–3. Ex vehicles and equipment classified *desertworthy* or *undesertworthy*, fit or unfit for use in the desert—j. dating from 1938 or 1939. (Sanders.)

undies. Women's, women's occ. children's, underclothes: (orig. euph.) coll.: 1918, 'Women's under-wear or "undies" as they are coyly called' (*Chambers' Journal*, Dec.: *OED*); 1934, *Books of To-Day* (Nov.), 'I like my daily paper,/ But one thing gets me curl'd,/ And that's the morning caper / Of London's "undie"-world.'—with which cf. the quotations at **briefs** and **neathie-set**.

unexploded portion of the day's ration. A pun on *the unexpired portion . . .* , given to a soldier in the form of haversack rations when he goes on a journey, posting, to hospital, etc.: Army: 1950s–60s. Ex the ammunition remaining unfired, after a day on the ranges. (P.B.)

unflappable. Imperturbable: coll.: since ca. 1944. Ex **flap**, n., 2.

unfledged. (Of persons) naked: joc. coll.:—1923 (Manchon). Extended from 'featherless'.

unfrocked. One, usu. an officer, who is unpopular with his branch of the Service: RN: since ca. 1948. (Granville, letter, 1962.)—2. 'Also of F.A.A. embryo pilots who fail their basic flying course' (Granville, Ibid.): id.: since ca. 1950. Ex ecclesiastical j.

unh unh. Sex appeal: since ca. 1940. Echoic of amorous utterance: cf. **oomph** and *yumph*.

unhealthy. (Of area) exposed to gun-fire; unsafe: orig. Army in WW1 (W.; B. & P.); since > gen.

unhook. To borrow (something) without asking the owner's permission: RN: since ca. 1920. (Granville.) One merely takes it off the hook and strolls away.

unhorse. 'To deprive an owner of his car by means of long-drawn-out repairs' (B.P.): Aus. motor trade: since ca. 1950.

uni; gen. the Uni. A, one's own, university: Aus. coll.: later C.20. P.B.: in later C.20, also Brit.—2. Uniform, e.g. Cadet Corps uniform: Public Schools' (but see FELSTED, in Appx.): mid-C.20. (P.B.)

union card or **ticket.** Credentials: common in Can., early 1950s-late 70s. (Leech, 1985.)

Univ. University College, Oxford: Oxford University coll.: mid-C.19–20.—2. University College, London: London undergraduates'. Marples, 2.

universal subject, the. (The subject of) smutty talk: Can. coll., verging on S.E.: since ca. 1930. By ca. 1935, fairly gen. coll.; by 1960, S.E. everywhere.

university of hard knocks, the. Experience: coll., esp. among those who haven't been to one: since ca. 1910. Cf. the sententious cliché, *the University of Life*.

unkermesoo (or **-zoo**). Stupid: tailors'. A fanciful word.

unload. To drop (bombs) on the enemy: RFC/RAF joc. coll.: WW1. (F. & G.) And since.

unlucky for some. The number 13 in tombola; hence, as a tag when 13 is mentioned, in gen. coll. See TOMBOLA, in Appx.

unmonkeyable. (Of a person or thing) that one cannot play tricks with: coll.:—1923 (Manchon).

unpack. To vomit: 'pop' world. (Hibbert, 1983.) Cf. later C.19 *unspit*.

unprovoke, n. and v. Unprovoked assault; to commit one upon (esp. a warder): prison: since ca. 1920. Phelan, 1943.

unquote! Quotation ends here: US journalistic coll. >, by 1951, Can. and, by 1955, English. 'Now I quote: "Five thousand pounds each." Unquote', with the emphasis upon *un*-. (Leechman.) P.B.: later C.20 > more gen. Used to give emphasis to reported speech, and not always logically placed, as in ' . . . and that's all she had to say. Unquote!' Cf. *end of story*; **period!**.

unship (e.g. a grin). To remove: RN: since ca. 1910. (Granville.) Cf. **ship**, v., 3.

unshop. To dismiss (a workman): lower classes':—1923 (Manchon).

unstick. To extricate (a vehicle) from the desert sand: Army coll. (N. Africa): ca. 1940–3; hence in other, although analogous, contexts. P-G-R.

unstuck, come. To go amiss; to fail: from ca. 1919. Sayers, 1931, 'The plan came rather unstuck at this point.'

unswallow. To vomit: euph.: 'current in the 30s, but (mercifully) not heard since' (Sanders). Cf. **unpack**.

untarted. See **tarted-up**, 2.

untidy as a Javanese brothel, as. Extremely untidy: Aus.: brought back, ca. 1942, by Servicemen. (B.P.)

untogether. The negative of **together**, it denotes 'all mixed up', not integrated: from ca. 1970. ob. by 1980. *Jagger*.

untouchables, the. 'The "Charity begins at home" types that are too mean to give anything even though they are well provided for' (Petch, 1974): later C.20. A pun on *touch*, older coll. for to ask (someone) for money, and the Indian caste.

unwell. See **sloughed**.

unwind. 'To relax after the cares of the day, or after some tensing experience' (L.A., 1974): orig. coll. >, by 1975, informal S.E.

unzymotic. Synon. with **fab** (or *fabulous*), i.e. an adj. of high approbation: ephemeral teenage vogue-word of early 1960s. (Anderson, 1965.) Cf. **zymotic**, its opp.

up, n. (Mostly in pl., *ups*.) A stimulating drug, esp. amphetamine: adopted, latish 1960s, ex US (noted by *6000 Words*). Ex the Am. adj. *up*, drug-exhilarated (since very early 1960s). Janssen cites *Apple*.

up, adv. Up to specifications; esp. *not up*, not up to specifications; hence, no good: Aus.: since ca. 1925. B., 1942.—2. Up to date, conversant, well-informed, expert: undergraduate coll.

up against. Confronted by (a difficulty): coll.: US (1896, George Ade: *OED* Sup.) >, by 1914, anglicised. Esp. in the phrase *up against it*, in serious difficulties: 1910, *Chambers' Journal*, April, 'In Canadian phraseology, we were "up against it" with a vengeance!' (*OED*).

up and down. A rough-and-tumble fight: Cockney. (*Sessions*, 9 June 1902; Ingram, 1935.) Ex:-

up-and-downer. A violent quarrel: lower classes': late C.19–20. (MacDonald, 1932.) Since mid-1930s, much in RN use for 'a fierce argument' (Granville). Cf. **upper-and-downer**.—2. An unimaginative, usu. medium paced bowler of 'straight up-and-down stuff' (without break or swerve or spin): cricketers': since ca. 1925. Cary, 1948.

up and up, on the. Dependable; 'straight' in the crooks' sense: c.: from ca. 1919. Ex US. P.B.: by mid-C.20 > gen. s. for 'genuine', esp. of information.

up for office. On a charge; due to appear before the Officer Commanding: Services', esp. Army, coll.: earlier C.20. P-G-R.

up front. 'Straightforward and honest. "He's up front" is a great compliment' (Powis): later C.20. Cf. **out front**. Also written solid; see quot'n at **closet**.

up homers, as in 'He's up homers', applied to a rating welcome at home of a family in the port where he happens to be stationed: RN. Peppitt, dating the phrase from ca. 1939, notes that it applies esp. to a girl-friend's home.

up in the flies. Prosperous: theatrical. (George, 1914.) Ex the *flies* of the theatrical j.: the space over the proscenium.

up on one. On a charge or accusation: police coll. Newman, 1974.

up-stage. Haughty, supercilious; conceited: theatrical coll. (from ca. 1920) >, by 1933, gen. S.E. (*OED* Sup.) Ex *play up-stage*, a foremost role. The v., when not theatrical j. but used fig. for 'to overshadow, to usurp attention', is S.E. (*SOD*, 1977).

up stick. As in *up stick* or *up the stick* (even, occ., *up stickers*), pregnant: Public Schools': mid-C.20. Cf. **up the pole**, 4.

up the chute. Worthless; (persons and plans, acts, etc.) stupid; wrong: Aus.: since ca. 1920. B., 1942.

up the dirt road. A low Can. ref. to sodomy:—1950.

up the duff. (Of a woman) pregnant: low Aus. (B., 1942.) Prob. suggested by *pudden club*; cf. **up stick**.

up the Gulf. 'Serving in the Persian Gulf (Granville): RN coll., since ca. 1915—but more and more widely understood and gen. as the C.20 progressed, and the Gulf's importance with it. Cf. **up the Straits**.

up the line; esp. *go . . .* (To go) on leave: RN. 'The phrase originated in Naval depots and referred to the railway line leading from the port to London or home' (Granville).—2. Hence, as in ' "He went up the line on his tod," — "Deserted?"—"Yes. They caught him three weeks later in Blackpool. Clewed up in a dosshouse, he was, stone broke" ' (*Heart*, 1962): RN: mid-C.20.

up the mad house, adv. and adj. 'Working trains into London' (*Railway*, 2nd): Southern Region railwaymen's: since late 1940s.

up the pole. Half-witted; mad: low. —2. In Aus., 'distraught through anger, fear, etc.; also, disappeared, vanished' (Dennis): late C.19–20.—3. Hence, 'Wrong, worthless, stupid' (B., 1942): Aus.: since ca. 1918.—4. Pregnant: low, esp. Cockneys': from ca. 1908.—5. In *go up the pole*, to behave circumspectly.

up the road. 'Committed for trial before a judge and jury' (Powis): police and c.: later C.20. Also *up the steps*.

up the spout. (Of a bullet) in the rifle-barrel and ready to be fired: military: from 1914. (B. & P.) P.B.: in later C.20, often *one up the spout*.

up the stick. (Very) eccentric; crazy, mad: workers':—1935. Ex synon. *up the pole*. P.B.: perhaps orig. suggested by *monkey up a stick*.—2. Pregnant: low, esp. Cockneys' and N. Country: from ca. 1920. Cf. **up stick**.

up the Straits. On the Mediterranean Station: RN coll.: late C.19–20. Granville, 'Through the Straits of Gibraltar'. Cf. **up the Gulf**.

up the wall, adv.: hence, also, an adj. (in the predicate). Orig. of persons, 'out of one's wits' (not congenitally, but driven so by others or by circumstances); hence, awry; (of supposed facts, calculations, premises) fallacious; crazy: since ca. 1944, but gen. only since ca. 1950. 'It's'—'He's'—'enough to drive'—or 'send'—'you up the wall.' Adopted, I suspect, from the slang of American drug addicts and transmitted by US servicemen. But cf. **run up the wall**.

up the way. (Of women) pregnant: Aus. low. Also *up the wop*. (B., 1942.) Cf. S.E. *in the family way*.

up to. Obligatory (up)on; (one's) duty; the thing one should, in decency, do: US (1896, Ade: *OED* Sup.), anglicised ca. 1910. *East London Dispatch* (S. Africa), 10 Nov. 1911; Dennis, 1916; Walpole, 1933. Orig. in poker, as Greenough & Kittredge remark.—2. See **upta**.

up to (one's) **arse in alligators.** In deep trouble; extremely busy with demanding problems: adopted ex US. Simmonds, 1983.

up to here. To an unspecified but considerable degree, as in 'I've had it—I'm choked off—up to here', which may be accompanied by a gesture indicating one's throat, top of head, etc.; or simply as in 'You're in trouble up to here' (Hunter, 1969): coll.: later C.20. (P.B.)

up to mud. Worthless: mostly Aus. (B., 1942.) Cf. *clear as mud*.

up to tripe. Worthless; thoroughly objectionable: lower classes': earlier C.20. (F. & G.) Ex *tripe*, s., nonsense. Cf. **up to mud**.

up top. 'Flying at high altitude' (Jackson): RAF coll.: since ca. 1925.—2. High ranked; among the high-ranked officers: adv. and adj.: RN coll. P-G-R.

up topsides. 'On the upper-deck; aloft' (Granville): RN coll. P.B.: perhaps a relic of China Stations' pidgin. Cf. **topside**.

up you! The orig. form of the **up your . . .** entries: C.19–20 (and prob. much earlier). This expression of rudest contempt forms the verbal equivalent of the world-wide extended-middle-finger gesture, indicating also derision and defiance. P.B.: but cf. also mid-C.19-20 *up*, v., to coït, which would make it = simply a brutal 'fuck you!' A mid-C.20 Services' 'catch' was to say to some innocent, 'Do you know (such-and-such a place)?', and, on the affirmative, to mention some prominent landmark; then, taking the listener along in imagination, 'Well, go a hundred yards down the left-hand side—and *up* you from there!'

up you for the rent! Aus. elab. of **up you!**: since ca. 1930. B., 1959.

up your arse! See **up your pipe!** and cf.:-

up your ass, with a hard-wire brush (or **crooked stick** or **red-hot poker**)! A low Can. c.p., uttered 'just for something to say; fellow doesn't mean anything uncomfortable when he says it' (Can. correspondent, who adds the post-1945 var *. . . with a charged condenser*): common among Can. soldiers of WW2. Cf. **up your pipe!**, the Brit. version.

up your gonga or **jacksie,-y!** Variants of **up your pipe!**

up your jumper! A c.p. of either defiance or derision: Aus.: since ca. 1920. (Cleary, 1950.) P.B.: either elliptical for (*oompah, oompah*) *stick it up your jumper!* or euph. for:-

up your pipe! A var. of the classic vulgar derisive retort *up your arse!* = 'Get away with you!', 'Of course I won't do it!', etc.: orig. Services', mostly Army: since ca.1930. Cf. synon. **up your gonga** or **jacksie, -y!** Often simply:-

up yours! Abbr. *up your arse*, etc. late C.19–20. Still current in later C.20, often as semi-joc. expression of greeting or for lack of something to say. Cf. **fyfas** and **up your ass**. In Can. usage, 'a contemptuous way of saying "No!" ' (Leech, 1985).

uplift. An auxiliary spring: Aus. motorists': since ca. 1950. A ref. to brassières. (B.P.)

upness for inspection. Ready and prepared for inspection: Army: mid-C.20. Mead, 1967.

uppard twizzle or, by deliberate alternation, **ozzletwizzle.** An upward—strictly, a vertical—climbing roll in flying: RAF: since ca. 1950 at latest.

upped. Raped: lower. (Cowan, 1937.)

upper-and-downer. A wrestling-match: lower classes':—1909 (Ware). Cf. **up-and-downer**.

upper deck. (Female) bosom; breasts: mostly Aus. (*Rats.*) Cf. synon. **flight deck**.

upper yardman. 'Active service rating who is a candidate for commissioned rank. In Nelson's time the upper yardmen were the pick of the lower deck who could be relied upon to perform the most difficult jobs aloft' (Granville): RN.

uppers. Loafers aboard a warship: R Aus. N.: WW2. B., 1943.—2. Amphetamines (rare in sing.): drugs world: adopted, ca. 1960, ex US. (Wyatt, 1973.) Cf. **downer**, 5.—3. As *the uppers*, the upper classes: coll., mostly lower-middle class: since ca. 1920.

uppers and downers. 'In casual use for the teeth, otherwise "choppers" ' (Petch, 1969): since mid-C.20. They move up and down.

uppity. Above oneself; conceitedly recalcitrant or arrogant: coll.: adopted ex US. R.C., 1976, cites Mark Twain, *Huckleberry Finn*, 1884, and notes 'esp. of Negroes'.—2. Hence, socially grand: beatniks': since ca. 1959. Anderson, '*He was carrying such weight at that uppity shake. He was so bored by that grand reception . . .* '

upright grand. Perpendicular copulation: Aus. urban: since ca. 1925. (B., 1942.) Prob. an elab. on earlier (since C.18) synon. *upright*, with a pun on playing the piano, upright or grand (P.B.).

uproar. See **balls in an uproar**.

uprooted. See **sloughed**.

upstairs, adj. In pawn: Glasgow:—1934. Euph. Cf. **stuck away**.

upstairs, adv. Up in, up into, the air: airmen's coll.: from ca. 1918. (*OED* Sup.) Hence, in *come* or *go upstairs*, to ascend, to gain height. An RAF S/Ldr, ' "Nasty Messerschmitts." And the answer came back, "Okay, pals, keep them busy. I'm coming upstairs" ' (Michie, 1940). In contrast, *downstairs* is in the air but near the ground or, at the least, at a low altitude, as in Ibid., 'We were fighting upstairs and downstairs between 1,000 and 1,500 feet.'

upta or **upter**. Inferior; worthless, no good; contemptible: Aus.:—1919 (Downer: Wilkes, who glosses 'No good at all [abbr. of "up to putty" or "up to shit"]').

uptight. Tense; nervous: adopted, ca. 1967, ex US, orig. as Black or hippy s., but very soon > gen. coll. (Wolfe, 1968.) Janssen remarks of two quot'ns from *Jagger*, 1974, that in the first, p. 175, the sense is as above, but that, in the second, p. 209, it has shifted to 'shy; introverted'. Ex *wound up tight*. Other nuances following from these are 'embarrassed', 'angry', 'anxious'.

upward Charlie. Upward slow roll: RAF: WW2. Forbes, 1942.

urge, n. As in 'powered by the 180-horsepower engine—and that's some urge': used by the commentator at an aerobatic display, 1976. (P.B.)

urge, v. 'To hint (for something)': Aus. coll. B., 1942.

urger. A racecourse tipster: Aus.:—1926 (Doone). Amplified in Kimmins, 1960, ' "An urger, " explained Lugs patiently, "is a man who looks around for suckers like you—and tips each one a different horse. Someone's *got* to win." ' Wilkes' earliest quot'n is from *Truth*, 6 Apr. 1924, and he adds the important comment, 'a race tipster who seeks a bonus from the winnings of others.' Cf.:—2. A confidence-trickster's accomplice: Aus. c.: since ca. 1920. B., 1942.—3. Tout for a brothel: Aus. c.: since ca. 1925. *Rats*, 1944.—4. A chap, a fellow: Aus. ('not particularly pejorative': B.P.): since ca. 1940. 'What are you urgers up to?' Ex senses 1 and perhaps 2 and 3.—5. A sponger: Aus. (Ronan, 1961.) He urges you to stand him a drink. Prob. the earliest sense.

urky-purky (or **-perky**)! An Aus. children's exclam. of disgust; also used attributively, as in 'I don't want to eat that urky-purky porridge': since ca. 1930. (B.P.) A defective reduplication of *dirty*—or, at the least, prompted by *dirty*. P.B.: *yurkies* also occurs in Brit. domestic coll.: cf. **yuk!**

urn. In *carry the urn*, RN joc. var. of **carry the can**, q.v.: WW2. P-G-R.

usby. See **Wosby**.

use, n. Esp. in *have no use for* (person or thing), to consider (him, it) superfluous or tedious or objectionable: coll.: orig. (1887), US; anglicised ca.1900.

use, v. To enjoy—if only one could get it, as in 'I could use a beer right now!': since ca. 1935, perhaps 10 or 20 years earlier. Gray, 1969, dates NZ usage as current since ca. 1950. Meiosis.—2. Elliptical for 'using drugs', as in 'You're so out of your box when you're using' (*New Society*, 11 Aug. 1983), and 'Junkies will always exaggerate how much they are into using' (Cape, 1982): drugs c. Cf. **user**.

use frightening powder. 'The defending solicitor produced a recording machine at the lower court—a move which we call "using frightening powder" ' (Gosling, 1959): police s.: since ca. 1935.

use (one's) loaf. To think (esp., hard or clearly); to be ingenious, exercise ingenuity; to use one's commonsense, with, if necessary, a certain amount of cunning as well: esp. Services' in WW2, and gen. since. Often in imperative or exhortation, 'Oh, come on! Use your loaf!' *Loaf* (of bread), r.s. = head.

use your teeth! A taunt, 'to annoy anyone who is having difficulty in accomplishing a task, particularly if it involves digital dexterity' (Roberts, 1985).

used-beer department. The latrine in a drinking establishment: Can.: since ca. 1925.

used to was. Used to be: joc.: since ca. 1910; by 1960, ob. ' "Losing y'r dash, Fin," grinned Ryan. "Not the family man yer useter was".' (Brockman, 1948; earlier in her play, *Men Without Wives*, 1938.) Earlier yet in Maugham, 1930. 'I'm not so young as I used to was.'

useful. Very good or capable; (extremely) effective or effectual: from ca. 1929. E.g. 'He's a pretty useful boxer.'

user. Specifically, a 'taker of narcotics' (Home Office): drugs world coll. or j.: later C.20.

Ushant-eyed. 'A man with a fixed eye. Ushant lights were once one fixed and the other revolving' (Bowen): nautical coll.: early C.20.

usher. A naval instructor: RN. (P-G-R.) Joc. use of C.19 S.E. term for 'assistant schoolmaster'; cf. **schoolie**.

ute. A utility truck (a light van): Army: since ca.1936. (H. & P.) Also, since ca. 1945, common in Aus., as in 'Till You Come to a Green Ute' (Dark, 1959).

utter. To speak; to make any vocal sound (e.g. of pain or pleasure): mostly Society: since early C.20. Kipling, 1910. Marsh, 1938, 'If you stare like a fish and never utter.' Short for *utter a word* or *a sound*. Cf. the almost-c.p., *is it my turn to utter?*, is it my turn to speak now?

uxib. Unexploded fire bomb: Fire Services': WW2. (Franklyn.) Cf. **incy**.

uzby. See **Wosby**.

V

V. See **vee.**

V. and A. Anything worth stealing: RAF: since ca. 1945. Ex stores marked 'V. and A.'—valuable and attractive, e.g. watches and cameras.—2. Always *the V. and A.*, the Victoria and Albert Museum: since late C.19.—3. As *the V. & A.*, the Royal yacht the *Victoria and Albert*: RN coll.: early C.20. F. & G.

V.D. and scar. The Volunteer Reserve Decoration (VRD) and bar: RN: later C.20 (Peppitt). P.B.: but this is also an imaginary decoration, used to parody those who carry many 'letters after their name', as in, 'Sir Somebody Something, D.S.O. [q.v.], BSA two and three-quarter [a type of motorcycle], VD and scar'; among Servicemen since mid-C.20 at latest. Sayers, 1985, adds *W.C. and chain*.

v.d.t. Valuable drinking time, as in 'Let's get down to the pub quick, we're wasting v.d.t.' (Turner, 1986): 'serious' drinkers'.

V.I.P. Lit. 'very important person' (popularised during the latter half of WW2), has, since the late 1940s, often been used ironically, esp. of a self-important person.

vac. A vacuum cleaner: Aus. domestic, since ca. 1948 (B.P.); by ca. 1950, common among women in Britain.—2. (Or spelt *vacc.*) Vaccination: medical world: late C.19–20.—3. See **vack.**

vacation. An imprisonment; a prison: tramps' c.:—1932 (Jennings).

vack (rare after 1940); **vackie,** better **vacky.** A person, esp. a child, evacuated overseas or from city to country: since Sep. (ca. the 10th) 1939. *Daily Telegraph*, 4 Oct. 1939 (*vack* and *vacky*); Berrey, 9 Nov. 1940 (the longer form). Ex *evacuee*.—2. (Only *vack*.) An old woman: Aus. low: since ca. 1925. (B., 1942.) A corruption of '*vag*abond'?—3. See **vac.**

vacuum cleaner. A sports car: Londoners': since ca. 1947. Used for *picking up bits of fluff*: an ephemeral pun.

valise. A bed-roll: Army officers' coll. P-G-R.

vallie. The tranquilliser drug Valium: Aus. Humphries, 1981.

vamp, n. A woman that makes it her habit or business to captivate men by an unscrupulous display of her sexual charm: coll.: 1918 (*OED* Sup.). Abbr. *vampire*.

vamp, v.t. and i. To attract (men) by one's female charms; to attempt so to attract (them): coll.: 1927 (*OED* Sup.). Ex prec.

vampire. One who, in a hospital, draws off, for testing, a little of a patient's blood: Forces': 1940+. Ex the activities of the traditional vampire. (L.A.) Cf.—2. (Usu. pl., *the Vampires*.) Joc., usu. affectionate and admiring, nickname for the collecting teams of the National Blood Transfusion Service: later C.20. (P.B.)

vampire's bagmeal. Cold tinned veal: RN lowerdeck: mid-C.20. *Heart*, 1962.

van. (Ad)vantage: lawn tennis.

Van der Merwe story. A 'pointless or naïve humorous joke at the expense of a mythical, foolish, Afrikaans-speaking person, typified by the commonest name in South Africa, van der Merwe: since 1965' (A.C. Partridge, 1968): S. African. P.B.: but, as the Rev. Kenneth Cracknell pointed out to me, after a visit to S. Africa, 1981, the jokes are not necessarily foolish or pointless; unlike in 'Irish' or 'Polish' jokes, the eponymous hero sometimes makes his point—he is not always the loser; e.g.: Van der M. applied for a job as a tree-feller. Asked for references, he replied that he had worked in the Kalahari Desert. 'But', said his interviewers, 'it is a wilderness, a waste land. There are no trees there at all!' 'So . . . !', says Van der M.

Van-Dooze, the. Nickname of the Royal Vingt-Deuxième Regiment of the Canadian Army: Army. (P.B.)

van-dragger. 'One who steals parcels from vans' (Hume): c.

vanboy. A conductor: busmen's: since ca. 1930.

Vandyke. In *be no Vandyke*, to be plain-looking. Applied esp. to men, in ref. to the handsome fellows in Vandyke's portraits. P.B.: to which a coll. retort might justifiably be 'well, you're no ruddy oil-painting, yourself!'

vanilla. ' "Vanilla", as a synonym for ordinary, is catching on [among Brit. computer enthusiasts, from US usage]' (*Guardian*, 16 Feb. 1984). Cf. **plain-vanilla.**

vap. A rather rare schoolboys' term dating from ca. 1905 and now ob. As in Lunn, 1919: 'He distrusted the female sex because they seemed to indulge in an undue amount of "vap"—as he called it—chat which said one thing and meant another. Maurice hated "vap". ' I.e. vapouring.

varicose. A varicose vein; (collectively with pl. v.) one's varicose veins: coll.

various veins. Varicose veins: coll. when the sol. is used humorously. (Park, 1950.) Other versions are *very coarse* or *very close veins*.

varnish. Sauce: coffee-stall frequenters'. Cf. synon. **disinfectant.**

varnish (one's) cane. (Of the male) to coït: Can. low.

Vasco. A navigating officer: RN submariners': mid-C.20. (Bryant, 1958.) Vasco da Gama, 1469–1524, famous Portuguese navigator.

Vatican roulette. The so-called 'safe period' which immediately precedes menstruation and is regarded as a means of birth control: Catholics': 1960 (the date of a famous encyclical) and after. On the analogy of the dicing-with-death Russian *roulette*.

vaudevillian. A vaudeville 'villain': joc. coll.: since ca. 1930.

Vaux. A *Vaux*hall car: since ca. 1930. Trevor, 1968.

've. Have: coll. (*he've*, e.g., is sol.): C.19–20. Rather rare in the infinitive, as in Fielding, 1932, 'My road sense seems to've deserted me for the time being.' It may occur even at the beginning of a sentence, as in ' 've you done much?' (Bell, 1946), where *'ve you* is pronounced *view*.

Vee Dub. A *VW*, i.e. Volkswagen car or bus: motorists' coll.: since ca. 1960. (B.P., 1977.) See next.

Vee Wee. A Volkswagen vehicle: motorists': later C.20. Raab cites the name of a London Volkswagen spare parts firm, Vee Wee Ltd. Cf. *Peewee* as nickname for people whose initials are P.W., e.g. the jazz player Peewee Hunt.

veegle. A car: Aus. joc.: since ca. 1950. (B.P.) Ex childish pron. of S.E. *vehicle*.

veg. Vegetable(s): eating-houses' coll.: mid-C.19–20. E.g. 'Meat and two veg.' Ex abbr. P.B.: variant plurals are *veggies* (Tweedie, 1979) and *vegets*: both gen. domestic coll.—2. 'A sea-mine. (Bomber command.) Short for *vegetable* in the same sense; *vegetable* was suggested by the fact that the mines were sown in areas known by such code-names as *Onions* and *Nectarine*' (P-G-R.): mostly RAF: WW2.—3. Both n. and adj., vegetarian: since ca. 1920.

vegetarian. A spinster averse from 'exchanging flesh': since ca. 1925.

vegets. See veg, 1, and cf.:-

veggie, -y. Var. of veg, 3.—2. 'A person whose brain appears to be non-functional; . . . often due to prolonged drug usage' (Hibbert, 1983): drugs c.

vegy. Vegetable: domestics': late C.19–20. Vachell, 1914.

velvet. Elliptical for *black velvet*, any dark-skinned woman: in Australia, a lubra, a gin. Ronan, 1954, 'It was a case of black velvet or no material, and the pioneers took to the velvet.' Cf.:-

velvet glove or **vice, the.** The female pudend: MCP raffish. (Van Dulken, 1987.) Cf. **bearded clam.**

vent. A ventriloquist; ventriloquism; ventriloquial; esp. in *vent act*: music halls', variety, light entertainment world. Brett, 1975.—2. A Lockheed-Vega *Ventura* bomber used by the Allied Air Forces, WW2. Beede, 1970.

Vera Lynn. A (drink of) gin: r.s.: since ca. 1940. (*Weekly Telegraph*, 6 Apr. 1946.) Often shortened to *Vera*, as in Cook, 1962. Ex the singer immensely popular during WW2—and after. Cf. earlier synon. *Ralph Lynn*.

verbals. 'Oral statements of admission made at the time of arrest by criminals, and very frequently denied in court. It is often said that police invent them. However, they are usually not denied until legal aid is granted to the criminals' (Powis); cf. 'If you are a City of London mover, you get a fair investigation and a fair trial . . . but if you are the type of criminal I was [i.e. violent and dangerous] . . . something like verballing and fitting up [q.v.] is something you expect' (McVicar, 1979): police coll., verging on j.; also Aus.: later C.20.—2. See **dancing about.**

Vernon's private navy. A flotilla of five East Coast herring drifters—*Lord Cavan, Silver Dawn, Fisher Boy, Jacketa*, and *Fidget*: RN: 1939+. They were wooden ships, and so were used in the anti-magnetic-mine operations of 1939. They also did excellent work bringing off troops from Dunkirk, and again on the return to Normandy, 1944. (Granville.) P.B.: cf. the equally diverse names in Kipling's poem 'Mine Sweepers', of similar craft in WW1, 'Sweepers—*Unity, Claribel, Assyrian, Stormcock*, and *Golden Gain*.'

vertical breeze, draught or **gust.** See **wind vertical.**

vertical à la. See **à la.**

very close; very coarse. See **various veins.**

very dead. Applied to a soldier, or to a quadruped, left unburied on the battlefield: a WW1 c.p. Not so tautological as it sounds, the connotation being the squalor and the stink. Later > gen. coll.

very grave. 'When finances are low you will often hear, in reply to a question, the words, "Very grave", or "The position is critical" . . . merely a polite way of letting the world know

that you are broke' (H. & P.): Service officers': since June 1940. Ex the Allied military position in May–June 1940.

Very Little Water Society, the. 'A most informal and fluid group of North American anthropologists, who take their liquor "on the rocks". A play on the name of a real secret society of the Iroquois tribe, the "Little Water Society". Since ca. 1950' (Leechman): Can.

very 'oh my!' Smug: Glasgow:—1934.

very, very. A ca. 1919–39 coll. equivalent of the earlier (1880s—) superlative *too* (*utterly*) *too*. 'That's very *very*' usu. connotes blame, esp. for indecency. Short for, e.g., 'very *very* naughty'.

vet, n. A veteran: coll.: later C.20. Prob. adopted ex US. *Time Out*, 9 May 1980.

vet, v. To cause (an animal) to be examined by a *vet*erinary surgeon: coll.: from ca. 1890. Hence, soon applied to medical treatment of human beings (1898, *OED*).—2. Hence, to revise (a manuscript): a book-world coll., orig. and mainly publishers': from ca. 1910.—3. Also, to sound, or ask questions of (a person), in order to discover his abilities or opinions: coll.: from ca. 1920. Keverne, 1928, 'I brought you here so that I might "vet" you. I do things like that—and then trust my instinct.' P.B.: by ca. 1950, perhaps earlier, security services' j. for 'to make enquiries about a person's character and suitability for employment in "delicate posts" ' [esp., behind his or her back].

vibe out. To intimidate; to frighten; to emit heavy vibes: 1960s–70s' 'pop' world. (Hibbert, 1983.) Ex:-

vibes. Emotional 'vibrations' from a person's aura and general character; the atmosphere generated by any event; mood; and nuances intimately related to all three senses: adopted ca. 1960 ex US, although not very frequent until ca. 1965. (Wolfe, 1968.) Ex next, and orig. from same milieu, but by 1977 Powis could quote 'She gave me the old vibes, all right'; by 1980, slightly ob. Hence, *vibed up*, excited; alert; mentally prepared (Hibbert, 1983), with which cf. later synon. **psych-up.**

vibrations. 'Atmosphere; reactions, with sexual overtones' (Fryer, 1967): jazz devotees', drug addicts', beatniks' and hippies': since ca. 1965. Quickly shortened to prec.

Vic, vic. The *Vic*kers *Vic*toria; the *Vic*kers Valencia; troop-carrying aircraft: RAF: 1930s. Jackson.—2. A V-shaped formation of aircraft: RAF: since ca. 1940. (P-G-R.) Ex signallers' phonetic for letter V; see relevant section of the Appx.—3. As the Vic, HMS *Victorious*: RN. She was commissioned on 14 Sep. 1939 and scrapped 30 years later (Knight, 1984).—4. See **Vicky.**

Vic and Alb, the. The *Vic*toria and *Alb*ert Museum in South Kensington, London: arty. (Marsh, 1967.) P.B.: more gen. known as *the V. and A.*

Vic Eddy. 'The night signal given on the headlights (if working) or horn by a truck "swanning" round a "laager" but unable to find it. The reply was anything recognisable as friendly' (Sanders, 1967): Army in N. Africa: 1940–3. Ex the Morse letters *V* and *E*. P.B.: but the official phonetic for *E* was *easy*: see PHONETIC ALPHABET, in Appx.

vicarage, the. The chaplain's cabin: RN: since ca. 1930. Ex *the vicar*, the chaplain. Granville.

vicking. Services signallers' term for sending out a series of *V*s in Morse code, for receiving stations to tune in on: coll. > j.: WW2 and since. (P.B.)

Vicky. A shortening of *Vic*toria (cf. **Vic,** 1); used in later C.19 for Queen Victoria († 1901), and then reminiscently; in later C.20 in, e.g. *Vicky Park* (Leicester), *Vicky Barracks* (Hong Kong), etc. (P.B.)

vicky-verky. *Vice versa*: Merseyside: late C.19–20. But perhaps sol. or dial. rather than s. or coll. P.B.: since early C.20 a fairly widespread joc. usage.

Victor Trumper. A 'bumper' or cigarette-butt: Aus. r.s.: since ca. 1905. (B., 1945.) Ex an Aus. cricketer (Franklyn).

victualled up, be. 'To have a good time ashore as guest of friends or relatives' (Granville): RN: since ca. 1920.

video nasties. See **nasty**, n.

vidiot. A constant, mindless looker-in at TV: Aus.: since ca. 1960. A blend of *video* + id*iot*. (B.P.)

view. 'R.A.F. types do not "have an opinion", but instead "take a view". Thus, "He took a poor view when Bert snaffled his popsie" ' (Jackson): RAF coll. since ca. 1925; later, gen. coll. Ex the aerial view they get of things.

vig. Vigilance: anti-aircraft: WW2. Michie, 1941, ' "Special vig," says John. "That means keep a special vigilance," he explains to me.'

vile. As a mere intensive (cf. **foul**) = 'unpleasant', 'objectionable': coll.

Vill, the. Pentonville Prison: c. Norman.

Villa(, the). See **Casey's Court**, and ASSOCIATION FOOTBALL, in Appx.

villain. A criminal; anyone with a criminal record: police coll.: since ca. 1935. Allingham, 1945.

-ville. Adopted, ca. 1960, ex US. 'Beat—and, indeed, gen. American—jargon has crept in, including the habit of adding "ville" on the end of an adjective: "Cor, man, this prep is dead cinchyville" '—i.e. dead easy, a 'cinch' (*New Society*, 22 Aug. 1963, a short article on N. Country grammar school slang). The earliest example I've seen of the comic, often slangy, use of *-ville* occurs on the title page of T.C. Haliburton, *The Clockmaker; the Sayings and Doings of Sam Slick of Slicksville*, 1837. Very common in US since mid-1950s, it has exercised only a slight influence in Brit. R.C., 1976, 'The -ville suffix in U.S. is now obsolescent, being replaced by city, as in fat city, great prosperity, and fruitcake city, an insane situation or person.'

Viney bones. Rubber bands: motorcyclists'. 'Originated with the famous [motorcycle] trials rider Hugh Viney of the '30s, who used to cut up old inner tubes and supply his mates with bands to fix their riding numbers' (Dunford, 1979).

vingty. Vingt-et-un: gamblers' coll. Whaley, 1936.

Vinnie. A *Vin*cent motorcycle, in production 1928–56: motorcyclists'. (Dunford.)

vino. Italian wine: Army: 1942+. It. *vino* 'any wine'. Cf. **demon vino.**

violent evasive action; the v. being *take* . . . To avoid an undesirable task or a boring person: RAF: 1940+. P-G-R.—2. Hence, *coïtus interruptus*: Aus.: since c. 1943. (B.P.)

violet; garden-violet. An onion; gen. in pl. as = spring onions eaten as a salad. The usu. term among RN lowerdeck (Granville).

vip. A very close-fisted, cheese-paring person: Aus.: since ca. 1925. (B., 1942.) A thinning of *vipe* (short for viper)?

viper. A marijuana-smoker: c.: adopted, ca. 1943, ex US. (Norman.—see *Underworld*.) Hence:-

viper's drag. Marijuana: drugs world: mid-C.20. A pun on prec., *drag*, 'a smoke', and the jazz-tune/dance *the viper's drag*. (P.B.)

virgin, n. A cigarette made of *Virgin*ia tobacco: smokers':— 1923 (Manchon).—2. A mixture of *ver*mouth and *gin*: topers': id. (Ibid.).—3. A term of reproach among chorus-girls: from ca. 1920.—4. As *the Virgin*, the Petty Officers' Mess: RN. Screened off, at meal-times, from the vulgar gaze of the lowerdeck.

virgin, adj. Excellent; very attractive; indeed, a general superlative: Oxford undergraduates': late 1930s. Ex the idea of purity.

virgin bride. A ride: Aus. r.s.: since ca. 1890. B., 1945, citing Sydney *Bulletin*, 18 Jan. 1902.

virginity curtain. The canvas screen secured to the underside of a warship's accommodation gangway to conceal from prying eyes in the boat below the legs of those who go up and down the gangway' (Laffin, 1969): since ca. 1920.

vis. Visibility: esp. among skin-divers: since ca. 1950. (Granville.)

vis aids. (Pron. *viz*.) Visual aids to teaching: teachers' and instructors' coll.: since early 1950s, but not gen. until ca. 1965. (P.B.; E.P.'s dating.)

visit Lady Perriam. To go to the underground lavatory: Balliol College, Oxford. Lord Bacon's sister, Lady Perriam, presented a new building to Balliol; on its site now stands this convenience. Hobhouse, 1939.

visiting cards. See **leave visiting cards.**

vital statistics. A woman's bust, waist, hip measurements (e.g. 36, 23, 35 inches): since ca. 1945: joc. coll. >, by 1965, S.E. P.B.: a pun on the orig. S.E. sense, statistics of births, deaths, etc.

Vits, the. A Licensed Victuallers' (Protective) Association. In e.g., *Essex Chronicle*, 17 Mar. 1939, where a caption reads, 'Rochford "Vits" '.

vittles. 'An accountant officer, R.N., borne for victualling duties': RN. Bowen.

vocab. A vocabulary; a glossary or dictionary: Charterhouse (—1904) >, by 1920, gen. Public School coll. P.B.: and, of course, language students anywhere. In the Services, ?mostly Army, applied esp. to the standard 'Vocabulary of Stores', the quartermaster's list of every piece of equipment in existence.—2. In *watch your vocab!*, mind your language!: Aus., orig. undergraduates': since ca. 1930. (B.P.)

vodeodo. Money, cash; booty: c.: from ca. 1930. (*Gilt Kid*, 1936.) This has the appearance of being a rhyming fantasy on *dough*, money, possibly suggested or influenced by Romany *vongar*, money. See also *DCpp*.

voker. To speak: tramps' c. and low s.:—1859 (H., 1st ed.). This is a debased form of **rocker**, q.v., of which it is prob. a mere misapprehension. Powis, 1977, lists 'Voker?: Do you understand?', which seems to show a sense-shift.

vol. Volume (of a book): book-world coll.: late C.19–20. Ex the abbr., as in 'Gibbon, vol. 2'.

Volks. A *Volks*wagen motor-vehicle: coll. abbr.: since ca. 1945. Cf. **Vee Dub.** (P.B.)

vomiting viper, the. Penis: a consciously 'amusing' expression; cf. *the one-eyed guardsman, milkman, trouser-snake*, etc.: mid-C.20. (P.B.)

vulch. To avail oneself of the excellent 'left-overs' from classes at the Catering School of Loughborough College, sold off cheaply: 1980s. (Allow me one advertisement, and parochial coinage: P.B., 1988.) Ex:-

vulture. To borrow without permission from someone else's collection of, e.g., books: coll., among, e.g., librarians: later C.20. The predators' work. (P.B.)

W. 'a W, a warrant to arrest or search' (Powis): c. and police coll.: later C.20. Norman, 1959.

w.a.f.u. (or solid). 'Wet and fucking useless': an insult applied by the 'sea-level Navy' to members of the FAA: later C.20. (A seaman on the carrier HMS *Invincible*, quoted in a BBC Radio 4 programme, 13 Jan. 1985—but not in full.) Influence of *snafu*.

w.a.w.a. See **wawa**.

W.C. A C.W. candidate: RN. Granville, 'The C.W. Branch, Admiralty, deals with the awarding of "commissions and warrants" '.

W.C. and chain. See **V.D. and scar**.

W.O.S.ers. Overseas British authors: authors': since ca. 1919. (*The Writer*, May 1939.) Ex 'the *wide open spaces*' + the agential *-er*.

Waaf. A member of the *Woman's Auxiliary Air Force*: since 1939: coll. >, by mid-1943, j. Ex the initials, *W.A.A.F.* Pronounced *Waff*, which is, however, to be regarded as an incorrect spelling. The W.A.A.F. became the Women's Royal Air Force in Feb. 1949.

waaf-basher. A male fornicator: RAF: 1941+. See **basher**, 5.

Waafery. 'The part of the camp frequented, or the billets occupied, by members of the W.A.A.F.' (H. & P.): RAF: since 1939. See **Waaf**.

waafise. 'To substitute airwomen for airmen. I believe the term originated in Balloon Command, which was waafised in a big way' (Jackson): RAF coll. (by 1943, j.): 1941+. See **Waaf**.

waas or **wass.** To run; to hurry; to exercise oneself vigorously: Uppingham: since ca. 1912. (Marples.) Echoic. See also **wass**.

Wack-Eyes, the. The *Women's Auxiliary Corps* (*I*ndia): 1942–5. (Mather, 1977.) Cf. **Wasbees**.

wacker, n. and adj. See **whacker, n.** and adj.

wacko! A var. of—and inferior to—*whacko!*

wackie, -y, n. A typical male member of the working classes ('wears flat hat, muffler, carries lunchbox'): teenagers': early 1980s. (James Williamson, 1982.) Perhaps cf. **whacker**, 1.—2. ?Hence, a conformist, a 'square'; someone with 'old-fashioned' standards: id. (Ibid.)

wacky. Unusual, out of the way, little known; esp. *wacky news*: adopted from US by journalists ca. 1942. I.e. not ordinary 'straight' news.—2. Also, in gen. use, since 1944, for 'incorrect, unreliable' (news) and 'eccentric' (persons).—3. See **wackie**.

Waco, Big and **Little.** The first two aircraft of the Long Range Desert Group: RAF in N. Africa: 1942–3. Ex *Western Aircraft Corporation of Ohio*.

wad. A roll of banknotes: c. > low s. (Leach.) Hence, a fortune: id. Cf. **cake**, 1.—2. A drink of liquor: since ca. 1910. (Jordan, 1935.) It comfortingly fills a void.—3. A (large) quantity of anything: Aus.: since ca. 1920. (B., 1942.)—4. A bun. See **wads**, and:-

wad-scoffer. A bun-eater; esp., a teetotaller: Services': from ca. 1904. (F. & G.) Also *wad-shifter*: Army: from ca. 1910. (Richards.) Both † by 1950 (P.B.). See **wads**.

wad that would choke a wombat, a. Alliterative var. of *a roll that would choke a bullock*, a large roll of banknotes: Aus.:—1959 (Baker). Cf. **roll, n.**, 4, and **wad**, 1.

wadi-bashing. Service flying over Middle Eastern deserts: RAF: later C.20. (*Phantom*.) Ex Arabic *al-wadi*, a usu. dry water course in ravine or valley. Cf. **jungle-bashing**.

wads (less usu. in sing.). Buns; occ., small cakes sold at a canteen: Services'. (F. & G.) Ex shape; also ex 'What doesn't fatten, fills'. Hence *char and wads* (Army) or *tea and a wad* (RAF), a snack, esp. that at the mid-morning break: earlier C.20.

Waff. See **Waaf**.

Waffery. See **waafery**.

waffle, v. (Of an aircraft) to be out of control (usu. as vbl n. or participial adj. *waffling*, 'spinning, losing height'); to fly in a damaged condition and/or uncertainty: RAF: since ca. 1930. (H. & P.) McDouall, 1945, 'Waffling precedes spinning'.—2. Hence(?), to dither: Services' (mostly officers'): since ca. 1930. (H. & P.) But cf. older s., to talk nonsense.—3. 'To cruise along unconcernedly and indecisively' (Jackson): RAF: since ca. 1925. Cf. 1 and 2; also **stooge** in this sense.

waffler. 'Snobs, Hooray Henrys [q.v.] who talk wah-wah [q.v., sense 2]: we call them a bunch of wafflers' (Isobel Williamson, 1984): young people's. A specialised use of the s. term, since late C.19, one who talks nonsense.

waft; wafty, n. General madness or wildness, lack of tact and/or gumption; the corresponding adj.: Oundle: since late 1920s. (Marples.) Perhaps suggested by excessive *breeziness*.

wafty, adj. 'Of poor quality' (*M.T.*): market-traders': since late C.19. Prob. ex Romany *wafedo*, bad.

wafu. See **w.a.f.u.**

wag, the. The humorous *tail*-piece that appears at the end of a newspaper gossip-column: orig., and still mainly, journalistic.

wag (one's) **bottom.** To be a harlot: mostly Cockney: late C.19–20. Cf.:-

wag (one's) **bum.** (Of men) to coït: mostly Services'. See **prec.**

wag (one's) **knickers at everybody.** 'To be extremely sociable and "out-going". A BBC panel-game, 29 Oct. 1975' (R.S.).

wages. Illegal or illicit or shady or disreputable income: as, e.g., thief's, race-gang's, whore's: c., and low (mostly Londoners'): from ca. 1925.—2. 'There is occasional use of this among Retired Pensioners, who, when they go to a post office to draw their pension, may say "I am going to draw my wages" ' (Petch, 1966): coll.: since late 1940s.

waggle. To wield (a bat, stick, oar): joc. coll. Ex lit. sense.

Waggle-dagger; Waggle-spear. Shakespeare: schoolchildren's. Punning *Shakespeare;* cf. the surname *Wagstaff*. (Raab; E.P.)

waggon. A bunk (bed): ships' stewards':—1935.—2. An omnibus: busmen's: from ca. 1928. *Daily Herald*, 5 Aug. 1936.—3. A battleship: RN: 1940+. (Granville.) Short for **battle waggon**.

wags. Signallers: R Aus. AF: WW2. (B., 1943.) Ex *flag-wagging*, signalling, morse or semaphore, by flag (P.B.).

wahiné. A woman: NZ coll.: late C.19–20. Direct ex Maori.—2. Hence, esp. a girl surfer: Aus. surfers': since ca. 1962. The word is also Hawaiian.

wahwah (or hyphenated). Esp. *a bit* . . . , of a car, or a car's starter, that is rather sluggish: car-dealers': since ca. 1950. (*Woman's Own*, 28 Feb. 1968.) Echoic.—2. 'Sloane Ranger [q.v.] men speak Wahwah, their expression for their particular hooray tone of voice' (York, 1977): upper-middle-class coll.: later 1970s. Also echoic: cf. mid-C.19 *Punch* cartoons of similar men interspersing their utterances with 'Haw-haw!' (P.B.)

Wailing Winnie. Synon. with and echoically comparable to **Mona**, an air-raid-warning siren: civilians': WW2. E.P., 1942.—2. 'The broadcast system aboard ships' (H. & P.): nautical: WW2.

wait one! Just wait for one moment (or minute) while I, e.g., deal with something else: Services' coll.: since ca. 1950. Ex voice signals procedure. Cf. **just hold one!** (P.B.)

waiter. A horse that, started in a race, is not meant to win: Aus. turf. B., 1942. See:-

waiters. As *full waiters* = men's full evening dress, so *half waiters* = dinner-jacket (a tuxedo): Society: since ca. 1930. Ex restaurant waiters' garb.

wake. To 'wake up' to a trick, a racket, etc.: Aus. since ca. 1925. Glassop, 1949, ' "Lay off some of the others [= horses]," whispered Max. "I tell you, somebody'll wake." '

wake-up. A wide-awake person: Aus.: coll.: from ca. 1910. Howard, 1934, 'Well, I'm a wake-up; they don't get nothing out of *me*!' P.B.: Wilkes' quot'ns make it clear that the full phrase is *a wake-up to* (a trick, dodges, etc.).—2. (Usu. pl.) Amphetamines: drugs c. (Stockley, 1986.) US since—1967 (Spears).

wake your ideas up! Pull yourself together: Services' coll.: since ca. 1930. I.e. *wake up!* P.B.: sometimes indirect, as in the criticism, 'He wants to wake his ideas up a bit', of a man 'dozy' and unco-operative.

waker (or **W-**). A sleeping train running between Paddington and Penzance: (mostly West Country) railwaymen's: since ca. 1910; by 1960, ob. (*Railway*, 2nd.)

walk. To be a prostitute on the streets: white-slavers' c. Londres, 1928.—2. To disappear: mostly Army, as when a part of one's kit has disappeared: since ca. 1910. P.B.: since ca. 1950, at latest, gen., and usu. implying theft, as in 'large expensive coffee-table books also "walk", and Hilary Lee at Hammick's Covent Garden Bookshop finds occult and humour very "stealy" sections' (*Bookseller*, 18 Apr. 1981).—3. In *go for a walk*, to go to the separate cells ('separates'): c.: from ca. 1920. Ingram, 1933.—4. In *on the walk*, (of bank clerks and/or messengers) taking money round to other banks and to business-houses: commercial.

walk (a girl) **home.** To accompany her back to her home: coll.: since ca. 1943. Ex US. R.C., 1976, recalls the popular song 'Walking My Baby Back Home', composed by Fred Ahlert & Harry Richmond in 1930.

walk it. (Of racehorse or dog) to win easily: turf. Hence, also of a person.

walk out, v.i. and n. (To have) an affair: Society: from ca. 1930. (E. Waugh, 1934.) Ex dial. v.t. *walk out*, to take one's fiancée out. Cf. **walking-out** . . .—2. To bale out of an aircraft: RAF: WW2. Forbes, 1942.

walk the plank. To move up and down one's surfboard: Aus. surfers': since ca. 1961. (B.P.) With a pun on the pirates' practice of making their victims walk the plank.

walk-up fuck; also simply *walk-up*. 'She's . . . All you have to do is walk up and ask': low Aus.

walkabout. A mid-C.19–20 term as in a book-review in *The Times* of 8 Sep. 1936: 'Under the title "Walkabout"—the pidgin word for "journey" in the Western Pacific—Lord Moyne has written a book on his latest expedition in his yacht *Rosaura* to little-known lands between the Pacific and Indian Oceans.'—2. A walking tour, a riding (and walking) tour: Aus. coll. Russell, 1934.—3. An outback road: Aus. coll. B., 1942.—4. The term was adopted, as *do a*, or *go*, *walkabout*, by Brit. politicians and journalists, for any informal tour on foot by an important person 'to meet the people': late 1970s. E.g., as a picture-caption, 'Queen goes walkabout in city centre'. (P.B.)

walked off, be. To be led to prison: proletarian:—1923 (Manchon).

walkie(s). (Going out for) a walk with a very small child or, esp., with a dog: nursery, and childish address to animals. Although in use for many decades previously, the exclam. *walkies!* achieved sudden c.p. status ca. 1980, e.g. as a jeer from rude boys to people exercising their dogs, from the popularity of Mrs Barbara Woodhouse's dog-training classes broadcast on TV. Cf. **outy!** (P.B.)

walkie-talkie. 'A wireless set, carried by one man, with both receiving and transmitting equipment' (P-G-R): Army: 1940–5; then civilian (e.g. police); by 1950, coll.

walking, go. To go rotten: mostly Londoners'. Ex the prospective maggots.

walking disaster area, a. A person particularly inept and accident-prone: since late 1960s. Prob. ex the US use in, e.g., '(Such-and-such a place) has been declared a disaster area following last night's tornado.' (P.B.)

walking-out finger. A man's middle finger: poss. mainly military. (Beevor, 1983.) The term is sexual: see **walk out**.

wall. In *up against the wall*, in serious difficulties: Services', since 1916 (F. & G.), > in later C.20, gen. coll. Perhaps ex being put up against a wall to be shot for cowardice.—2. In *drive* or *send up the wall*, to send crazy, to drive to distraction: coll.: since late 1940s. Cf. **round the bend; up the pole**. Ex the pains of enforced drug-withdrawal.—3. See **off the wall**.

wall-to-wall. Abundant, 'thick on the ground'; all over the place: copied, esp US, esp. on Citizens' Band radio, since late 1970s. E.g., *wall-to-wall bears* = police much in evidence. Ex carpets so laid. (P.B.)

wallflower. 'Escapee. One who talks of nothing else but (*a*) escaping, (*b*) "how nice it will be when he gets outside". Usually applied to the (*a*) class, who are convinced that one day they will make the perfect getaway' (Tempest, 1950): prisons': mid-C.20.

wallop, n. A resounding, esp. if severe, blow: coll.:—1823 ('Jon Bee').—2. Hence, the strength to deliver such a blow: boxing: from ca. 1910. *Varsity*, 24 Feb. 1914, '[He] has a prodigious "wallop", but no great amount of skill.'—3. Liquor, usu. (and in the Services, always) beer: low s. > coll.: since ca. 1930. H. & P.; *Gilt Kid*, 1936, 'He could not stand his wallop as well as he had been able to.' Ex its potency.—4. Strictly, the proprietary Walpamur; 'but now [1953] often used for any washable distemper': builders' and housepainters' and -decorators' (A master builder).—5. In *get* (or *give*) *the wallop*, to be dismissed—to dismiss—from a job: Aus.: since ca. 1920. B., 1942.

wallop, v. To dance, esp. tap-dance: buskers'. (Hollis, 1983.) Cf. next, 2.

walloper. A hotel; drinking-den: c.: from ca. 1930. (*Gilt Kid*, 1936.) Ex **wallop**, n., 3. Cf. **boozer** in this sense.—2. A dancer: itinerant entertainers': late C.19–20. (Lester.) Perhaps influenced by It. *galoppo*, a lively dance, and *galoppare*, to gallop, and *galoppatore*, a galloper. P.B.: or is it simply that he wallops the stage with his feet?—3. A policeman: Aus. c., since ca. 1945; soon > low s. (B., 1945.) Prob. of sadistic origin; cf. synon. **paddler**.

Wallsy. A Wall's ice-cream man: coll.: from ca. 1925. *Gilt Kid*, 1936.

wally (pron. *wolly*); **shock-a-lolly**, n. Cockney terms (quite distinct one from the other) for cucumber pickled in brine, the second term being rare: from ca. 1880. Hence, a century later, used abusively, '[wally]'s just another way of saying "You pr[ick]!"' (Dean, 1985.)—2. A uniformed policeman, esp. a constable: much used by detectives—and also by the underworld—mostly in the Metropolitan Police area of London: later C.20. (Newman, 1970.) P.B.: perhaps ex 1, influenced by *Wallie*, *-y*, a diminutive: cf. **charlie**, in the sense of a fool, a buffoon. See esp. Rees, 1987, for a number of almost as plausible derivations, particularly in:—3. A moron, a fool (usu. a young male): since late 1970s. 'He thinks a lot of recent skin [i.e. **skinhead**, q.v.] converts [to the National Front Party] are "just a bunch of wallies who've learnt how to chant *Sieg Heil* at gigs"' (Ian Walker, 1980).—4. (Gen. pl.) An olive: E. Londoners':—1909 (Ware, who spells *wollies*, and suggests ex street-cry, *Oh! Olives!*). Cf. sense 1, and *nana*, ex banana.—5. (Pron. to rhyme with 'rallies'.) False teeth: Glasgow. (Munro, 1985.) Or just teeth: 'Belt up, or I'll kick yeer wallies in!' (Brinklow, 1967).—6. One who 'wallies': See:-

wally, v. To 'send up' the disco 'scene' by deliberate bad dancing or outrageous dressing; a term of approval for 'to parody': late 1970s. (Raab, 1979.)

walrus. A large, bushy moustache; hence, its wearer: the former coll. (elliptical for *'walrus* moustache'); the latter, s.: since ca. 1917; virtually extinct by 1960.

waltz into. To attack, 'walk into' (a person): coll.:—1923 (Manchon).

wampo. Intoxicating liquor: RAF: from ca. 1930. (Jackson.) Prob. ex Scot. *wampish*, 'to wave one's arms about'.

wampo coupons. Pound notes, regarded as fair exchange for liquor: RAF: ca. 1930–50. Cf. prec.

Wan. A member of the Women's Royal Australian Naval Service: Aus. Services': WW2.

Wanch, the (pron. *wonch*), n. Wan Chai, in its aspect as the red light district of Hong Kong: Services': later C.20. Cf. next two entries. (P.B.)

wanch, v. To go to Wan Chai (see prec.) as a prospective or actual customer; to go drinking in the bars there: Army: 1960s. A pun on 'to wench'. (P.B.)

Wanchai burberry. A Chinese oiled-paper umbrella: RN: mid-C.20. Wan Chai is the waterside district of Hong Kong Island in which the China Fleet Club is situated. (Malin; P.B.)

wandering Willie. An 'escaped' barrage balloon: RAF: ca. 1938–45.

wang. Penis: low. Prob. ex older *whang*, a strike or blow.—2. Disgusting food served at mealtimes: Duke of York's Army boys' school, Dover: later 1940s. (Paine, 1988.) P.B.: perhaps cognate with *wank*, or perhaps ex *w(h)ang*, to hurl, fit only for defenestration?

wangle, n. A 'wangling'; some favour illicitly obtained: from 1915: orig. military. Ex the v.—2. Hence (—1935), a swindle.

wangle, v.t. To arrange to suit oneself; contrive or obtain with sly cunning, insidiously or illicitly; to manipulate, to 'fake': printers' s. (—1888) >, before or by 1911, fairly gen.; in WW1, a very common soldiers' word; since WW1, very gen. indeed. (Jacobi, 1888; esp. B. & P.) Esp. *wangle a job*, *wangling leave* (of absence).—2. Hence as v.i.: 1920 (*OED* Sup.).—3. To persuade (one) to do something: 1926 (ibid.). Possibly ex dial. *wangle*, to shake, as W. suggests; perhaps

(*OED*) ex *waggle*; in either case, perhaps influenced by **wanky**, q.v.

wangler. One who 'wangles' (see prec.): from ca. 1910. Wallace, 1912, 'A wangler is . . . a nicker, a shirker, a grouser—any bloomin' thing that talks a lot an' don't do much work' (W.).—2. Hence, from ca. 1915, a schemer (cf. **wangle**, n.).

wangling. The n. ex **wangle**, v. (q.v.): from ca. 1915. Cf. **wangler**.

wank, n. An act of masturbation: low. I remember a fellow recruit, a man from Birmingham, exclaiming, in a very 'Brummy' accent, 1952, 'Ooh! A letter from me tart! I'm off to the lats for a wank!' Prob. ex the v., rather than *vice versa*. (P.B.)—2. In, e.g. *a load of old wank*, nonsense: Services', ?esp. Army, late 1960s–early 70s. As in 'that's just a load . . . !'; cf. the exclam. *wank! wank!* (pron. almost as if quacked), greeting any announcement or declaration considered to be rubbish: id. (P.B.)—3. See **spare wank**, with which cf. **wonk**, 1.

wank, v. (Until early 1970s, usu. spelt *whank*.) To masturbate: low: since late C.19. Also *wank off*.

wank-pit. A bed: RAF: since ca. 1920. Ex prec. Also *wanking-pit*.

wank-stain. An idiot; stupid person: teenagers' term of mild abuse: mid-1970s. (McPheely.)

wanker. A masturbator: low: since late C.19.—2. 'The great working-class swear-word of today: over the last 8 to 10 years, I would say. It equals "cunt" in its weight as an insult, and revives that word's original implication of effeminacy and unworthiness' (Barltrop, 1981). In Weightman, 1977, a youth interviewed describes a police squad on the look-out for pickpockets as 'a bunch of wankers'; and Woddis, 1977, has 'Wile werds of lernid lenf an thundrin sahnd/Amazed the gazin wankers sittin rahnd.' Comparable is the generalisation, and gradual weakening, of such words as *bugger* and *fucker*. *Fighter Pilot*, 1981, defines its RAF use as '(fig.) universal derogatory term for someone not trusted or thought little of'. (P.B.)—3. Var. of **wank-pit**: RAF: since ca. 1925.

wanker's colic. An undiagnosed visceral pain: RAF: since early 1920s. Cf.:-

wanker's doom. Debility: orig. RAF, since ca. 1925; by 1945 > fairly common and gen. low s.; also prison s., as in Tempest, 1950: 'A man suspected of excessive masturbation is said to be suffering from "whanker's doom".' R.C., 1976, 'Ex the myth of ensuing insanity'.

wankersauros. An elderly person (i.e. anyone over 30): teenagers': ca. 1984 (Cross).

wanking-pit. Army var. of **wank-pit**: since early 1920s.

wanking-spanner. An imaginary tool like a 'sky-hook': low. Ex **wank**, v.—2. The hand: low: since ca. 1920.—3. Hence, the badge of the Royal Armoured Corps, 1941–55; its main feature was a mailed fist: Army: mid-C.20.

wanks. Strong liquor: RAF: ca. 1930–45. (Partridge, 1945.) P.B.: perhaps because stronger than *piss* (= weak beer)?

wanky; wonky (by mid-C.20 the usu. form). Spurious, inferior, wrong, damaged or injured: printers',—1890 (B. & L.), >, by 1914, gen. 'A *wanky* tanner = a **snide** [q.v.] sixpence'. (F. & H.) Prob. ex dial. *wankle*, unsteady, precarious; delicate in health; sickly. In East Anglian dial., *wanky* is 'feeble': *EDD*.—2. Pornographic; i.e. conducive to masturbation (see **wank**, v., 1): ?esp. Oxford undergraduates': later C.20. In Stewart, 1976, of a picture.

wannabee. Someone who 'want(s) to be' like a current idol in showbusiness, sport, etc.; orig. of fans of the singer 'Madonna', but soon more widespread: media j. Kipper Williams, in *Time Out*, 26 Aug. 1987.

Wanstead Flats. Spats: Londoner's r.s.: since ca. 1920.

want in; want out. To wish to enter; to wish to go out: from ca. 1840: coll. of Scotland, N. Ireland, and US. Abbr. *want to go in* or *out*. (*OED*.) P.B.: by 1960s, at latest, to 'want out' had come to mean a desire for a complete change of circumstances: 'I'm sick and tired of this [my present situation]! I want out!' Poss. a return of the usage from N. Am.: see:-

want in, down, off, out, up, etc. 'There is an extraordinary locution used here which omits "to get". "I want down" means "I want to get down". Cf. also "I want out, I want in, I want out of here, I want on (a tram), I want off"—and countless others.' Thus Leechman, 1959, concerning a Can. usage that was, ca. 1954, adopted ex US. Prob. a development of prec.

want jam on it. To desire something over and above what is reasonable, as in 'Huh! Bloody HQ are always the same—they want effing jam on it!': a natural extension of the Services' c.p. *what do you want (then)—jam on it?*, in response to a grumble about poor commons. (P.B.)

want (something) like a baby wants its titty. 'To want with insistent call to satisfy, e.g., a deep inner need of heart or soul, even if, to an outsider, superficial' (L.A., who, 1976, notes that the expression goes 'close to the heart language of poetry'): prob. since later C.19.

want to piss like a dressmaker. 'A Cockney figure of speech for urgent need, perhaps originating in sweated-labour days' (L.A.): late C.19–20. P.B.: cf. the more rural *want to pee like a rabbit.*

want-to-was(s)er, n. and adj. (An athlete or a boxer) hopeful but past his prime: Can., rare: early C.20. Beames; Leechman.

wap. See **throw a wap.**

wappy. Idealistic; sentimental; 'soppy': since ca. 1950. Sillitoe, 1959, 'Just like the governor of this Borstal who spouts to us about Borstal and all that wappy stuff.' Perhaps a blend of *wet* + *soppy.*—2. In *to go wappy*, to get angry, mad, 'lose one's cool', 'go spare': teenagers'. (J. Burt, 1984.) Cf. **throw a wap.**

War Box, the. The War Office (> the Ministry of Defence): Army: since ca. 1919. Cf. *War House.*

warb. A simpleton or a fool: Aus.: since ca. 1905. B., 1943.—2. An odd-job youth in a circus; a badly paid manual worker: Aus.: since ca. 1910. B., 1942.—3. 'A dirty or untidy person' (B., 1959): Aus.: since ca. 1920.—4. A 'derelict, drunkard, "no-hoper" ' (Grindley, 1977): Aus. c.: since ca. 1960. With all senses, cf.:-

warby. Unwell; (of things) insecure: Aus.: since ca. 1905. B., 1942.—2. Unattractive; inferior: Aus.: since ca. 1910. B., 1953.—3. Silly, daft: Aus. Tennant, 1941, 'Of all the warby ideas . . . ' Ex Scottish *warback*, or † *warbie*, 'a maggot': cf. prec.

warbling on the topmost bough, be left. To be left with one's stocks and shares and unable to sell them: joc. Stock Exchange:—1923 (Manchon).

warco. A *war* correspondent: mostly journalistic: 1939+.

ward-room joints as lower-deck hash. 'Officers' conversation or information which finds its way forward': RN. (Bowen.) P.B.: this refers to food, not to marijuana: Granville substitutes *stew* for *hash*: since ca. 1930.

warm and runny, be or **feel** or **get (all).** To 'become excited over a musician's improvisation, esp. rhythm': early 1970s' (L.A.). A 'pop' fans' hyperbole that implies either wetting oneself or even experiencing an orgasm.

warm shop or **show.** A brothel: low:—1923 (Manchon). Cf. **hot stuff** in its sexual sense.

warmed-up corpse, feel like a. To feel half-dead: low:—1923 (Manchon).

warmer. A smart person: Glasgow:—1934. Cf. *hot*, expert.—2. Hence, by ironic use > predominant sense (cf. **charming!**), 'a term for someone who exasperates or disgusts you' (Munro, 1985): Glasgow.

warming the whole of (one's) **body.** A punning c.p. (on *hole*) applied to someone standing with back to a coal, gas, etc., fire: C.20, perhaps earlier. (P.B.)

warrant officers' champagne. Rum and ginger-ale mixed: RN joc. coll. Bowen.

warriors bold, n. and adj. (A) cold: r.s. (Franklyn 2nd.) Cf. synon. **soldiers bold,** and **taters.**

warry. See **ruggsy.**

wart. An objectionable fellow: upper classes': from ca. 1919.

Warthog. A *Wartburg* motor vehicle (manufactured in the German Democratic Republic): coll. joc.: later C.20. (P.B.)

Warwicks. In *bloke* or *chap* or *fellow out o' the Warwicks*, a joc. ref. to someone whose name the speaker has momentarily forgotten, as in 'You know 'im—whatsisname—old oojamaflip. You know, bloke out of the Warwicks': Army: 1940s–50s. (P.J. Emrys Jones, 1980.) Perhaps orig. a ref. to F.M. Viscount Montgomery of Alamein, who was commissioned into the Royal Warwickshire Fusiliers in 1908, and who was the Regt's last colonel. (P.B.)

Warwick Farms. Arms: Aus. r.s. (B., 1945.)

Wasbees (or **Wasbies**), **The.** The *Women's Auxiliary Service, Burma*: 1942–6. (Disbanded in July 1946.) Cf. **Wack-eyes.**

waser or **wasser.** A girl: Cockneys': early C.20. Fr. *oiseau*, a bird.

wash. Garage s., from ca. 1920, as in Blaker, 1934, 'Hales went . . . through the workshop to the "wash", where finished jobs were left, ready for collection or delivery.'—2. In c., *the wash* is the theft of money in public lavatories while the owner is washing. See **wash-up**, 2. Hence, as in Powis, 1977, *at the wash*, stealing as a pickpocket from public washrooms.—3. As *the wash*, 'Shebeen proprietors' term for the mash of cheap grain and sugar (for example) cooked before distillation into illegal drinking spirit alcohol' (Powis): later C.20.—4. Beer: young people's: earlier 1980s. (James Williamson, Eastbourne, 1985.)

wash about. (Of stocks and shares) to be in (rapid) circulation: Stock Exchange coll.:—1923 (Manchon).

wash-deck. Mediocre, as in 'wash-deck musician': RN. (Granville.) ?Ex, or hence:-

wash-deck boatswain. 'A non-specialist warrant officer' (Bowen): RN.

wash-house ghost. Toasted bread: Army: early C.20. (B. & P.) P.B.: ?r.s., on *toast.*

wash out. 'Cancel. The term dates from the period when slates were used by signalmen for taking messages, a cancelled message being washed out with a damp sponge' (Granville): RN, since C.19; >, by 1919, gen. coll. Phelps, 1946, (of WW2 flying) 'If there was no chance of [the weather] becoming flyable we were usually washed out for the day' (P.B.).

wash out (one's) **mouth.** Usu. either *get your mouth washed out* or *go and wash out your mouth* (or *why don't you wash out your mouth?*—or *wash your mouth out?*), a virtual c.p. addressed to a dirty-tongued, foul-mouthed person: since ca. 1910.

wash-up. A scrubbing and sterilising of the hands before an operation: medical coll.:—1933 (*Slang*).—2. 'Wash Up (the): Stealing from clothing hung up in wash-houses. A thief engaged in this sort of crime would be . . . "at the wash" or "at the wash-up" ' (Sharpe, 1938): c.: since ca. 1910.—3. A post-exercise analytical discussion attended by officers during Fleet exercises: RN: since ca. 1950. (Granville, 1965.) Soon also other Services' (P.B.).

washed-up. Withdrawn from drugs: drugs c. (Stockley, 1986.) US since—1938 (Spears).

washer. A face-flannel: coll.

washers. Playing to an almost empty tent: circus- and showmen's: from ca. 1920. (*John o'London's Weekly*, 19 Mar. 1937.) Perhaps ex *wash-out*. P.B.: more prob. ex (playing for) *washers*, derisory for coins in small change; cf. **shirt-buttons.**

washing the tiles. Pouring out the Mah Jong tiles: Mah-Jong-players': from late 1923; ob. by 1933. Christie, 1926.

wasp. A traffic warden: since ca. 1960. 'From the yellow pipings on the uniform's hat and sleeves' (Petch, citing an article in the *Christchurch* (Hampshire) *Times*, 14 Oct. 1966).—2. Acronym from *White Anglo-Saxon Protestant*, hence an important and influential person: adopted, ex US, ca. 1975. *DCCU*.

wass. To urinate: Felstead School. Ex Essex dial. P.B.: but also Lancashire usage (where pron. *wazz*); also fig., as of rain, 'It's wazzin' it down'. (I. Pearsall, 1980.) Perhaps cf. Lakeland dial. *wass*, sour or acid (*EDD*).

waste. To knock out (someone): coll.: early C.20. (*Punch*, 26 July 1916.) With thanks to Mrs B. Huston, who points out that, in the late 1970s, the term is frequently heard in imported American TV 'entertainment', for 'to kill'. Barnhart records it as s. from the Vietnam War. (P.B.)

wasted. Drunk, tipsy: teenagers': early 1980s. (James Williamson, 1982.) Cf. prec. Ex:—2. Under the influence of drugs: drugs c. (Stockley, 1986.) US since—1967 (Spears).

watch. To guard against; refrain from: lowerclass. Gape, 1936, 'They're jealous because we won't use their lousy "kips". I'll watch getting lousy and paying eightpence for it too.' Cf. **watch it!**

watch(-)basher. See **clock basher**.

watch it! Be careful, you're running a risk; often uttered in threatening, resentful tone, implying 'Look out—mind what you're saying or I shall use violence on you', or as a dismissive, after a scolding, 'Just watch it, that's all!': coll.: since 1920s.

watch-out. In *keep a watch-out*, to be on one's guard: coll.: since ca. 1910.

watch (one's) six o'clock. See **six o'clock**.

watch-works. See CANADIAN, in Appx.

Watcher, the. See **Chad**.

watchkeepers' union, the. Junior Officers of the Watch: RN: since ca. 1920.

water, n. In *on the water*, 'The machinery is on the water'—will arrive soon: Aus. coll. (B.P.) Arriving by ship.—2. See **dead in the water**; **water hen**.

water, v. To paint in water-colours: artistic: since ca. 1920. Marsh, 1940.

water bill. See **going to pay** . . .

water(-)boiler. A fireman: railwaymen's. *Railway*, 2nd.

water carnival, the. 'Cleaning down a warship after coaling' (Bowen): RN: early C.20; superseded by:—2. 'The weekly orgy of hosing, scrubbing and general "chamfering-up" which takes place on Saturday in order that the ship may be "tiddley" for Captain's inspection and Sunday Divisions' (Granville): RN: since ca. 1920.

water-cart, n. 'A 15-cwt truck, fitted with a tank for bringing water from the waterpoint to the unit' (P-G-R): Army coll.: ca. 1940–5.—2. In *on the water-cart*, an occ. var. of *on the water-wagon*, abstaining from strong liquor.

water-cart, v.i. To weep: 1921 (W. de Morgan: *OED* Sup.); ob. by 1930. Ex S.E. n.

water hen. Ten: r.s., esp. in horse-racing world. (Drummond, 1969.) Often shortened to *water*.

water jerry. At a harvesting, he who looks after the water-tank: Aus. B., 1942.

water-logged. Dead drunk: coll.:—1923 (Manchon).

water wren. 'A Wren member of a boat's crew' (Granville): RN: 1940+.

waterbag. A teetotaller; a temperance fanatic: Aus.: since ca. 1920. B., 1942.

waterborne. See **inland navy**.

Waterbury watch. Scotch: r.s. P.P., 1932.

watering-hole. Often (one's) *favourite* . . . , a pub or club to which one habitually resorts for liquid refreshment: drinkers' joc.: later C.20. 'Strand Hotel, the Raffles of Burma, a somewhat down-market version of the great colonial watering-hole' (Hulme, 1984). A var. occurs in Seabrook, 1987, 'If you know that So-and-so uses the King's Arms as his regular waterhole . . . '

waterproof sailors. 'Generic for officers and men of the submarine branch' (Granville): RN.

waterworks. Rain: Sayers, 1931, 'You'd think they turned on the water-works yesterday on purpose to spoil my sketching-party.'

wattle, n. 'A dirty or untidy person. Truncated from *wattle and daub*, r.s. based on *warb*' (B., 1959): Aus.: since ca. 1950. Cf. **warb**, 3.

wattle, v.i. To drink (an intoxicant). Ex 'What'll you have?' A certain Oxford college has its Watling Club.

Waussie. A female member of any of the Aus. fighting Services: Aus.: 1940–5. (B., 1943.) A blend of *women* + *Aussie*.

wavelength. Esp. *be*, or *not be*, *on the same wavelength*. Way of thinking about, looking at, or tackling things, as in 'Yes, driving's very dodgy in Hong Kong—the Chinese drive on quite a different wavelength', or 'I just can't work with him, he's not on my wavelength at all': coll.: since late 1960s. Ex radio operators' j. (P.B.)

waves. See **make waves**, stir up trouble.

Wavies, the. RNVR personnel: mostly RN: since ca. 1918. Ex **Wavy Navy**, q.v. Granville. Cf:-

Wavy Bill. A RNVR officer in a ship for training: RN: earlier C.20. (Bowen.) See **Wavy Navy**.

Wavy Navy, the. The Royal Naval Volunteer Reserve. Bowen, 'Seldom heard afloat'. Granville, 'When the first uniform was issued to the Reserve, the three white tapes on the jean collar were wavy to distinguish them from the Active Service rating. To-day, only R.N.V.R. officers have wavy lace on their sleeves.'

wavy ringer or **striper.** An officer of the RNVR (see prec.): RN, resp. lowerdeck and wardroom. Granville.

wawa. 'Wawa is the acronym for West Africa Wins Again . . . The past tense is, "We've been wawaed" ' (*Economist*, 9 Feb. 1985: 'Wawa on the road to Kaduna'): expression coined to cover all the inevitable frustrations suffered by travellers from other places where they have been 'accustomed to standards of speed and efficiency not found in [West] Africa' (Ibid.).

wax. 'You're sitting there watching them drop shells on [Beirut] airport. You can see everything happening and you can just imagine the people out there getting waxed' (*Guardian*, quoting a USMC private in Lebanon, 31 Aug. 1983). Here US, but see **waxed**.

wax-borer. A long-winded bore: Aus.: since ca. 1935. (B., 1953.) The wax is that of the auditor's ears.

waxed. In *have* (a person) *waxed*, a Cockney and Services' var. of *have someone cold*: early C.20. (Pugh, 1906; F. & G.) Hence, in later C.20 RAF s., beaten, as in 'if you were vanquished [in aerial mock-combat], to secretly choke over it while sitting with a fixed grin—"Waxed again!" ' (*Phantom*).

waxer. A little drink: MN. Perhaps from 'a drop of *wax*'.

Waxies. Wellingborough men: railwaymen's. (*Railway*, 2nd.) P.B.: Wellingborough is a footwear-manufacturing town: *Waxy* was a C.19 nickname for a cobbler. Cf:-

waxy. A saddler: Army: early C.20. F. & G.—2. (?)Hence, an equipment-repairer: Army: 1939+.

way. In horse-racing, a double—a bet on two races: Aus. sporting: since ca. 1930. (B., 1953.) Perhaps ex 'two-*way* bet' as opposed to 'each-*way* bet'.—2. In *this*, or *that*, *way*, crooked; criminal, engaged in crime: c.: from ca. 1910.—3. In *on the way out*, (of a person) due for retirement or, esp., for dismissal: coll.: since ca. 1935. Hence, (of things) wearing out, coming to end of useful 'life': coll.: since ca. 1939.

way-out, n. (Or *wayout*.) One who is 'way-out' (see next): 1960s. In the *Sunday Telegraph*, 6 July 1969, front-page article about 'The Rolling Stones' pop-group, 'There were Kings Road [Chelsea] trendies, hippies and wayouts.'

way out; way out with the birds. Living in a world of fantasy; hence, extremely eccentric: resp. jazz-lovers' (esp. teenagers') and beatniks': since ca. 1954 and, the latter, since ca. 1959. The beatnik phrase is recorded in Rachel & Verily Anderson's *Guide to The Beatniks*; for the jazz phrase, cf. the entry at JAZZ, in Appx. By early 1960s, gen. usage in Can.; since ca. 1965, in Brit.; then, almost immediately, in Aus., NZ, S. Africa. P.B.: *way out* = away out, far distant, and occurs in other phrases, e.g. *way out in the sticks*, in the provinces.

wazz, wozz, v.i. and v.t. To accompany (another messenger) unofficially on delivery: Post Office telegraph-messengers':—1935. Perhaps ex *wangle*: cf. *swiz* ex *swindle*.—2. See **wass**.

wazz, adj. See:-

wazzer. 'Marines called anything good "wazzer" or just "wazz", a term which caught on with some Paras [see **para**, 3] by the time they landed' (*Don't Cry*, 1983): Falkland Is. campaign, 1982. P.B.: ?an affected pron. of synon. *wiz*, ex *wizard*.

wazzock. A fool, a 'twit', a term of (usu. fairly mild) abuse, 'You stupid wazzock!', with no real meaning: suddenly popular early 1980s, ephemeral. Perhaps a blend of **wass** + e.g., *pillock*, rather than ex dial. *wassock*, a protective pad (*EDD*). Cf.:-

wazzocked. Drunk. Jack, 1983, cites young London secretaries. Ex prec.

wazzums; or **w., then.** Were you [e.g. hurt], then?: joc. Ex baby talk.

we lie anywhere. A members' pun on the initials WLA, the Women's Land Army: WW2. (P.M.C. Pearsall, 1980.)

weakheart. 'West Indian slang for police. Meant to be offensive' (Powis): later C.20.

weakie (or **-ky**). A weak person; esp., a coward: Aus., mostly juvenile: since ca. 1920. (Dick.)

wear. To tolerate, put up with; usu. (?always) in the negative or implied negative, as 'Do you think they'll wear it?', or 'The old man'll never wear *this* one!': Services', prob. orig. Army. F. & G.—2. 'The verb *to wear* is used in extraordinary senses in the US and Canada. Women *wear* perfume, cripples *wear* a cane, and sandwich men *wear* placards' (Leechman, 1959). This coll. usage—by 1955, Standard in US; by 1960, virtually Standard in Can.—originated in the US and began to affect Can. during the 1930s. Note, however, that 'wear a cane' derives from the idea implicit in 'wear a sword'. Leechman, 1967: 'I caught an even better one some years ago. Margaret Mead, the anthropologist, spoke of a woman "wearing a baby on her back".'

wear (someone's) **balls for a necktie.** 'To inflict a most drastic punishment or revenge. "You pull that trick again and I'll wear your balls for a necktie."' (Leechman.) Mostly Can.: since ca. 1920. P.B.: an updated version of the old threat 'I'll have your guts for garters!'

wear (one's) **hair out against the head of the bed.** A joc. explanation of 'thinness on top'. Implication of abundant sexual intercourse.

wear more than one hat. To hold more than one post, or position of responsibility, simultaneously, as in, e.g. 'He was actually wearing three different hats by then': Services', soon also gen. usage: since ca. 1960. 'I haven't got the documents here. Come and see me this afternoon when I shall be wearing my other hat anyway.' (P.B.)

wear the gaiters. To be a convict: c. Sharpe, 1938, 'Convicts wear breeches and cloth gaiters, while short-term prisoners wear trousers.'

wear the kilt. To be a pathic: euph.

wear two (or more) **hats.** See **wear more . . .**

Weary Willie and Tired Tim. Two tramps, esp. if they resemble the famous cartoons: since ca. 1902. Created by artist Tom Browne (1870–1910).—2. Hence, lazy, loafing males: coll.: since ca. 1935.

weasel. A tip: railway porters': since ca. 1945. (*Radio Times*, 21 Jan. 1965.) Perhaps ex 'to *weasel* (something) out of somebody'.—2. See **weasel and stoat**.

weasel(l)ing, adj. and n. 'Extracting tips' (*Railway*, 2nd): since ca. 1945. Cf. prec. P.B.: but E.P. overlooked an entry in the 1st ed. of *DSUE*, at *weazling*: Manchon, 1923, defines it as 'The act of depriving a comrade of his tip': low.

weasel and stoat. 'Coat. *It's a bit parky—I'll put on me weasel*' (Jones, 1971; Powis). Cf. synon. *I'm afloat*, which it appears to have superseded. (P.B.)

weasel-pee. Any weak, insipid drink, but esp. tea: ?mostly Yorkshire derogatory. (C. Pearsall, 1957.)

weather breaker. 'The term in the [TV broadcasting] trade for entertainers who keep the viewers indoors even when the sun is shining' (Rodd, 1981).

weather-lorist. A meteorologist: joc.:—1923 (Manchon).

weaving, get. To hurry, act with urgency, as 'Come on, we must get weaving!'; often in the imperative: orig. RAF, ex j. for an aerial manoeuvre in which aircraft 'weave' in and out of each other's paths; > s. during WW2; by 1945 common also among other Servicemen and civilians; like much other wartime s., it soon > dated. (E.P.; Jackson; R.S.) Cf. synon. **get cracking**.

weazling. See **weaselling**.

web-foot. 'Any rating whose port Division is Devonport' (Granville): RN.

webbing. Web equipment, i.e. belt, shoulder-straps, haversacks, holsters, etc., made out of tough woven material: Army coll. > j. P-G-R; P.B.

webs. (A sailor's) feet: RN. (F. & G.) Cf. **web-foot**.

Wedding Cake, the. 'The Victoria Memorial (in front of Buckingham Palace)' (Hodge, 1939): London taxi-drivers': since ca. 1910. Shape and ornament.—2. Hence, the Vittorio Emanuele monument in Rome: since ca. 1944.

wedding kit or **tackle.** Genitals: mostly Army and RAF: since ca. 1918. Cf. **family jewels**.

wedge, n. A sandwich: RN: since (?)late 1930s. (Granville, letter, 1967; Winton, 1967.) Cf. the Army and RAF **wad**.

wedge, v. To hit (someone) hard: N. Country miners'. Ex driving-in a wedge.

wedgies. Wedge-heeled shoes: since ca. 1945. (Boswell, 1959.) Cf. **flatties**.

wee. A 'wee-wee': nursery coll.; and adult joc.; used as alternative for *pee*.

wee Danny. A glass of Aitkin's ale: Falkirk: from ca. 1930. Ex Mr *Dan* Robertson, JP, for many years the head brewer of Messrs James Aitkin, the Falkirk Brewery.

Wee Free Kirk, the. The Free Church of Scotland minority remaining after the majority, in 1900, joined with the U.P. Church to constitute the United Free Church. Hence, from 1904, *Wee Frees* and, from 1905, *Wee Kirkers*, the members of that minority. Coll. nicknames. *OED*.

wee Georgie. See **any wee Georgie?.**

wee-oh. A W.E.O., Weapons Electrical Officer: RN. The appointment was introduced in the 1930s. (Knight, 1984.) Cf. **wem**.

wee-poh. Among 'children of Welsh descent in Canada, ca. 1912, the penis' (Leechman): ob. by ca. 1950.

wee small hours, the. An intensification of S.E. *the small hours*, the period immediately after midnight: coll. Dent, 1917.

wee-wee. A urination; esp. *do* or *have a wee-wee*: nursery coll.: since late C.19. Cf. synon. *pee* = piss, since C.18. Also absolute, as v.i.

weed, n. 'Tobacco, cigarette, snout, burn smoke and herbal cannabis' (Home Office): prison c.: later C.20. *Weed* = 'marijuana' is an adoption ex US.—2. In *have a weed on*, to have a 'grouse'; to be grumbling: RN: since ca. 1920. Cf. **bitter weed**.—3. In *at the weed*, thieving, as in 'He's been at the weed again': market-traders' (*M.T.*) and c. Cf.:-

weed, v. To pilfer or steal part of, or a small amount from: c.: since early C.19, and still current later C.20. Powis, 1977, has 'Weeding: Stealing, especially from an employer, or at the scene of a crime already committed.'

weed head (or **solid**). 'Cannabis user' (Home Office): drugs c.: later C.20. Cf. *acid-head*, **pot-head**, etc. US since—1933 (Spears).

weeds. Trees, and vegetation generally: RAF aircrews': later C.20. 'I need to smoke my way into the distance down in the "weeds" at zero feet or thereabouts' (*Phantom*).

weedy chizz. Injustice: preparatory schools': mid-C.20. *Weedy*: a gen. pej. in such schools at that time.

weegie, weejie. See **widgie**.

Weekend Air Force, the. The Auxiliary Air Force: RAF coll.: from 1925 (year of its inception). (Jackson.) Only at weekends could most of these selfless men do their flying. P.B.: The AAF became 'Royal' after WW2, but was disbanded, as an 'economy measure', in 1957. Cf. **Saturday night sailors.**

weekend habit. A pattern of occ. drug use: drugs c. (Stockley, 1986.) US since—1938 (Spears).

week's Navy, a. 'Seven tots of rum bottled by the drawer in order to barter for a special favour: "I'll give you *a week's Navy* if you'll swap weekend leave with me" ' (Granville): RN lowerdeck: ca. 1895–1950. (Knock.) Abbr. *Navy rum.*

weelikies. Sausages: Glasgow:—1934.

weeno. Wine: Can. carnival s. I.e. a blend of 'wine' + It. 'vino' (pron. *veeno*). 'In Aus., this is undergraduate jocularity' (B.P., who, prob. rightly, thinks the Aus. use orig. in the Latin *in vino veritas* pron. *in weeno weritas*).

weeny-bopper. In the *Universe*, 10 Nov. 1972, 'Justin' writes, 'The word Weeny-bopper . . . means [one of those] girls between 8 and 12 who assemble in screaming multitudes to greet visiting pop-groups': heyday, 1971–5. A sub-teenage *teeny-bopper.*

weeper. A sentimental problem-novel: journalists': from ca. 1925. (Bell, 1934.) Cf.:-

weepie. A sentimental film; occ. of play or novel: coll.: since ca. 1930.

Weetabix Junction. Burton Latimer, Northamptonshire: railwaymen's: since ca. 1950. (*Railway*, 2nd.) The breakfast cereal so named is produced nearby (P.B.).

weevil bosun. Var. of **jam bosun.** Granville.

weff. A vocalisation of the Services' j. initials *w.e.f.* = with effect from (a certain time or date): Services' coll.: since ca. 1950. 'We've got to move.'—'Weff when?'—'Weff now, he says.' (P.B.)

weigh in with. To produce (something additional), introduce (something extra or unexpected): coll.: 1885 (*Daily News*, Nov.). Ex a jockey *weighing in*, being weighed after a race.—2. Hence, *weigh in*, v.i. to appear (on the scene): sporting coll.: from ca. 1920.—3. To 'stump up' or 'fork out': low:—1923 (Manchon).

weigh into (someone). To attack; to punch vigorously: Aus. sporting: since ca. 1910. (B., 1942.) Ex the boxers' *weighing-in* before a fight.

weigh off. To sentence (someone) to imprisonment: c.: since ca. 1920. (*Daily Express*, 25 Mar. 1938.) Cf. **weighed off**.—2. (Of the prison governor) to reprimand (a prisoner) and sentence (him) to the solitary cell: prisons': since ca. 1930. The process, from the receiving end, is known as *getting weighed off*. (Both in Norman.)—3. To get one's own back on, to take revenge on, someone, as in 'You do want to weigh off Brodie for the stroke he pulled' (Newman, 1977): c.—whence police s.: since the 1930s.

weighed off, be or **get**. 'To be brought up before an officer and punished' (F. & G.): Services': since ca. 1910. Occ. shortened to *get weighed.* (McDouall, 1945.) Cf. **weigh off**.—2. To be received into prison: prison c.: since ca. 1925. Norman.

weight. In (*a bit*) *above* one's *weight*, (a little) beyond one's class, too expensive, fashionable, highbrow, or difficult: coll., orig. (ca. 1910) racing. Ex a horse's handicap of weight.—2. 'A "weight" is half a kilo, it used to be a pound, but dope has gone metric' (Taylor, 1982): drugs c.—3. See **fancy** (one's) **weight.**

weird (frequently, by the way, misspelt *wierd*). Odd; unusual; wonderful: from the middle 1920s, and mostly upper classes'.

weirdo, n. and adj. A later C.20 var., Brit., Aus., and US, of:-

weirdy. A very odd person; an eccentric; since ca. 1947 'The Chelsea set' of 1959 was—at least, then—described as 'the weirdies'. It appears as *weerdie*, 'an odd, uncanny person' in Scots dial., 1894 (*EDD* Sup.). Also, in later C.20, adj., as 'He's a right weirdy character.'—2. A beatnik: journalists' and teenagers': since ca. 1959. Anderson.—3. (Also *weirdie.*) 'One who affects weird dress, such as a beatnik; often found in company with beardies' (Leechman,

1967): mostly Can.: since ca. 1950. Note that, in this sense, it is predominantly male.—4. A homosexual, usu. male: since ca. 1960. (Petch, 1969.)

well. Satisfactory, very good, capital: Society coll.: ca. 1860–1900. Ware.—2. Suddenly, in mid-1980s, teenagers were using *well* = very, as in 'I got well out of my box last night' [very drunk]; ' . . . well out of my tree'; and, paradoxically: 'It was well bad' (Simmonds, 1985). Kipper Williams' Christmas cartoon in *Time Out*, 20 Dec. 1984, shows a stocking labelled 'well empty'; Hibbert, 1983, notes that it is usu. to emphasise negative qualities.

well away, be. To be rather drunk: coll. (Lyell.) Has later C.20 var. *well on* (Munro, 1985).—2. To prosper, be doing splendidly: coll.: from ca. 1912. 'He's well away with that girl.' Orig. sporting: ex a horse that has, from the start, got well away.

well-bottled. Tipsy: Services' (mostly officers'): since ca. 1920. H. & P.

well-bushed. (Mostly of women) 'with plentiful pubic hair'; (of men) 'endowed with robust-looking sex' (L.A., 1976): raffish.

well-cemented. Well-off, rich: Aus.: since ca. 1945. (B., 1953.) Prob. suggested by the US coll. *well-fixed.*

well-endowed. (Of a woman) having well-developed breasts: coll., often joc.: since ca. 1925.—2. (Of a man) equipped with ample genitals: since late 1920s. (Montsarrat, 1951.) By 1977, > informal S.E.; prob. rather playfully joc. (and cultured) than merely euph. Cf.:-

well-furnished. (Of a man—well, mostly) to be largely genital'd: since ca. 1935: s. >, by 1970, coll. Cf. prec., and older (since C.18) *well-hung.*

well-gone. Much in love, infatuated: NZ, from ca. 1913; Aus. by ca. 1920: coll. E.P.; B., 1942.

well-heeled. Rich, either temporarily or permanently: Can.: adopted, ca. 1910, ex US. (Leechman.) P.B.: by mid-C.20, at latest, Brit. coll. Cf. older (C.19) synon. *well-breeched.*

well have! Well played!; well done!: proletarian coll.:—1923 (Manchon).

well-in. An Aus. var. of well-off, well to do: 1891 ('Rolf Boldrewood'); coll. >, by 1910, S.E.—2. Hence, engaged in profitable business: Aus. coll. B., 1943.—3. (Of a person) popular: coll.

well-loaded. Synon. with **well-endowed**: perhaps since ca. 1920. L.A., 1974.—2. Rich: since ca. 1930. *Loaded* with money.

well-sprung. Tipsy: ca. 1910–40. Muir, 1917.

well under. Drunk: Aus.: from ca. 1916. Prob. an abbr. of *well under water.* P.B.: more likely ex *under the influence.*

wellie, -y, n. (Usu. in pl.) Wellington boot(s) (in the modern, i.e. rubber or plastic, form): domestic. In the 1970s used in phrases where previously *boot* occurred, e.g., 'The welly's on the other foot now'; 'he's getting too big for his wellies': perhaps started by 'The Great Northern Welly Boot Show', put on by Billy Connolly at the Edinburgh Festival, early 1970s. Hence, *give it some welly*, really 'belt it out', put all one's effort into something; cf. '[The motorcycle] goes like hell and it likes plenty of Wellie though I haven't had it flat out yet' (letter to *Which Bike?*, Sep. 1980)—but with this quot'n cf. **clog down.** See also **green wellie brigade**, and **yellow wellie.**

wellie, v. To smash or defeat: RM, in the Falkland Is.: 1982. (Fox, 1982.) Ex *put the boot in.* Cf. synon. Paratroopers' **banjo** and SAS **mallet**. Earlier in Liverpool (MacClure, 1980).

wellie-whanging. A popular street-party, fête or gala sport, the competitive hurling of a rubber boot to the greatest distance: joc. coll.: later 1970s. See **whang**, v. (P.B.)

wellied. Tipsy, drunk: Glasgow: later C.20. (Munro, 1985.) Cf. **wellie**, v.

welligogs. Elab. of **wellie**(s): domestic coll., ?mostly Midlands: later C.20.

Wells Fargo. 'Old Pullman coaching stock named after the Television Western Programme' (*Railway*, 2nd): railwaymen's: since ca. 1960; by 1966, slightly ob. Ex the *Wells*

Fargo coaching company of the US. Cf. **Tunbridge Wells Fargos**.

Welly B. Wellington Barracks: Army, mostly Guards': late C.19–20. (Sinclair, 1959.) Cf. **wellie**.

Welsh Navy. Holt's Blue Funnel Line: nautical: earlier C.20. (Bowen.) Ex its numerous executive officers from Wales. Cf. **Blue Flue Boats**.

welt, n. A self-awarded period of loafing or absence: Liverpool labourers'. See **work a welt.**—2. A large penis: Forces'. Sadistic?

welt, v. To punch or strike (someone): Aus. B., 1942.

welter. Anything unusually big or heavy of its kind: dial. (—1865) >, by ca. 1890, coll.—2. (?)Hence, *in make a welter of it*, to go to extremes or to excess: Aus.: since early C.20. Cleary, 1952; Niland, 1958, has *make it a welter*. Or perhaps ex, e.g., *in a welter of excitement*.

Welwyn. Nickname for a slow or lazy fellow: RAF: 1941+. Cf. *take your finger out*. The relevant finger is *well in*.

wem. A wireless and electrical mechanic (as a 'trade'): RAF: since ca. 1934. (Emanuel, 1945.) Ex the abbr. *W.E.M.* or *W/E/M*.—2. A weapons engineering mechanic: RN. (Knight, 1984.) The trade was introduced in the 1960s. Cf. **wee-oh**.

wenneyes. 'In retaliation [for being called *Bennies*, q.v. at **Benny**, 4] the [Falkland Islanders] have named the soldiers "wenneyes" after their constant references to past exploits: "When I was in Belize; when I was in Cyprus . . . " ' (Lustig, 1984.) Cf. **wiwol**. The US *Time* magazine, 7 May 1984, spells it *whennies*.

Wentworth Falls; Wentworth's Balls. Testicles: Aus. r.s., not widely used: since 1920. Wentworth Falls is a resort, near Katoomba, in the Blue Mountains of NSW. (B.P.)

Werris Creek. A Greek: Aus. r.s. (Qantas advert., 3 Aug. 1986.) Cf. the Aus. cardplayers' c.p. of despair at a bad hand, 'Things is weak at Werris Creek'.

Wessy. A London North-*Western* employee: railwaymen's: (prob.) late C.19–1923, then nostalgic. (*Railway*.) McKenna, 2, adds that the term was also applied to the company itself. Cf. **Lanky**.

west. In (*that*) *gets* (e.g. *me*) *west*, (that) puzzles (me); (I) can't understand it: earlier C.20. Mitchell, 1930.

West Country. 'Its Naval use stemmed from the fact that nearly all H.M. ships used to be manned by ratings drawn from one Port Division:—Devonport, "West Country"; Portsmouth— no colloquial variant [but see **Pompey**]; Chatham—occasionally "East Country" . . . Portsmouth and Chatham thought of West Countrymen as being rather simple, noisy, easy-going, greedy, mechanically inept, "full of ignorance and brute force" . . . "West Country" as a seaman's adjectival phrase implied an unsatisfactory makeshift.' Hence, *West Country argument*, a fight; *West Country compliment*, 'The gift of something not wanted by the donor'. Kipling, 'RAF Bathurst', reprinted in *Traffics and Discoveries*, 1904: 'Some pride of the West Country had sugared up [euph. for 'buggered up', ruined] a gyroscope.' (Brock, 1969.) Cf. **Westo**.

West Ham reserves. Nerves: Londoners' r.s. 'That sod gets on me West Hams.' Cf. **Queen's Park Ranger**. Powis instances 'Mum's got the West Hams'.

Western. An American cowboy film or novel: coll.: since ca. 1910; by 1940, S.E. The action takes place in the south-west of the US.—2. As *the Western*, the Atlantic Ocean: nautical coll.: late C.19–20. (Gape, 1936.) See next.—3. See **spaghetti Western**.

Western Ocean relief. 'An overdue relief at the end of a watch': nautical. (Bowen.) In sailors' j., the *Western Ocean* = the Atlantic.

Westminster Palace of Varieties. The Admiralty: sea-going RN officers'. Bowen.

Westo. A Devon or Cornish ship or seaman: nautical coll.: late C.19–20. (Bowen.) Ex *West Country*.

wet, n. A drink: coll.: 1703 (Steele). In RN, a sip, esp. of rum (Granville), and in later C.20 coll., always alcoholic, as

'Fancy coming round for a couple of wets?' (P.B.).—2. A dull, stupid, futile, 'soft', or incompetent person: coll. pej.; perhaps orig., later C.19, Public Schools'—hence Service officers (for RN,—1914: Knock); by ca. 1950, gen. Cf. the adj., 1–3.—3. As *the wet*, the rainy season, esp. in NW. Aus. but also in N. Queensland: coll.: late C.19–20. Idriess, 1932 (N. Queensland); B., 1942; Devanney, 1944 (N. Queensland); Cleary, 1955, 'You know our work starts when the Wet finishes.' Contrast *the dry*.

wet, adj. 'Soft', silly, dull, stupid, 'dud'. (*Musings*, 1912; 'Taffrail', 1916.) Unheard by me before 1928, except in **talk wet**, q.v.; but see the n., 2.—2. (Excessively) sentimental: since ca. 1930. Partly ex 1., and partly ex the idea of *'tearfully sentimental'*.—3. P.B.: in politics, unrealistic, visionary—often, additionally, ineffectual: since ca. 1980 [E.P.'s estimate, ca. 1975—contrast the quot'n]. A natural development ex 1, aided by 2. In his 'The Tory Wets Stand and Wait', 1980, Taylor writes, 'Mrs Thatcher has coined the word "wet" to denounce those Conservatives who fail to share her assertive and abrasive convictions.' The term *Tory Wets* was much bandied about in earlier 1980s.—4. In *all wet*, all wrong; esp. 'You're all wet': NZ,—1934, and also, by 1935, Aus. This sense also very common in Can. (Leech, 1986). But the predominating Aus. sense is 'very foolish, or very stupid' (B., 1942), with which cf. sense 1.

wet and fucking useless. See **w.a.f.u.**

wet as a scrubber. 'An incalculably stupid rating' (Granville): RN: since ca. 1930. I.e. as a scrubbing-brush. In the R Aus. N, since the 1930s, such a rating would have been, would be, described as (*as*) *wet as piss*. P.B.: perhaps influenced by synon. *daft as a brush*.

wet-bed. One who, esp. while asleep, wets his bed: coll. Spenser, 1934.

wet behind the ears. Ignorant, untrained, inexperienced; youthful: orig. Services' (B. & P.); by 1930 > gen. Cf. the Fr. *avoir encore du lait derrière les oreilles*.

wet dream. An amorous dream accompanied by sexual emission: coll.: C.19–20—and prob. from at least a century earlier.—2. Hence, a dull, stupid person: Public Schools': late C.19–20. ' "He's a frightful wet; he's an absolute wet dream: he's so wet that he positively drips: oh him, he drips!" ' (Clifton, 1914, and I should think all schools since the beginning of time)': thus a valued correspondent. J.B.Smith, 1979, recalled the elab. *like a wet dream in technicolor*, 'Said of someone ineffectual and generally "wet" . . . [also] scathingly, of a person who tended to boast of his sexual prowess': Army and RAF National Servicemen's: 1950s.

wet foot. 'Naïve and innocent person' (Powis): c.: later C.20.

wet head. A law-enforcement officer, esp. a prison guard: Can. c.: since ca. 1960. (Schroeder, 1976.) Merely derogatory: cf. the US sense, 'A simpleton'.

wet list. Officers listed for sea appointments, as opp. to 'the dry list', listed for shore service only: RN. (Granville, 1967.)

wet Nelly. 'A dough cake, the size of a small plate, baked in the oven and served with syrup: Liverpool: earlier C.20' (L.A.).

wet ship. 'A ship whose wardroom has a great drinking reputation' (Granville): RN.

wet smack. A dull, ineffectual person, usu. male: low London: since ca. 1950. Gloag, 1962.

wet-suit. A plastic suit for protection against cold: Aus. surfers' coll.: since ca. 1961. (B.P.) P.B.: soon >, if not always, j.

wet week. In *look like a* (hence, *feel like a*) *wet week*, to look, to feel, miserable or wretched: coll. Obviously because a wet week tends to cause people to look miserable.

wetness. A foolish, hence dangerous, sentimentality: since ca. 1930. (*The Times*, 29 Sep. 1977.) Ex **wet**, adj., 1–3.

wets roster. 'The list of those whose turn it is to make the wets' (Hawke): RN; RM: later C.20. I.e. the drinks, not necessarily alcoholic: see **wet**, n., 1.

wetter. A 'wet dream' (q.v.): orig. Public Schools' >, by early C.20, gen low (Manchon), by the 'OXFORD -ER'.

wetty, have a. To be, or to become, angry or over-excited or worked-up: Aus.: since ca. 1945, or perhaps a decade earlier. Buzo, 1968: 'NORM: Eh, Ahmed, don't have a wetty. No offence meant.' Ex excitement causing urination.

Weymouth splashers. 'Paddle-steamers running pleasure-trips from Weymouth to adjacent ports' (Granville): coll.: since ca. 1925.

whack, n. 'Food, sustenance:—"He gets 2s. 6d. a day and his *whack*" ' (Joyce, 1910): Anglo-Irish: late C.19–20. Perhaps ex s., since C.18, a share.—2. Anxiety; dilemma: from ca. 1925; ob. by 1950. Frome, 1934, 'I was in a frightful whack . . . I thought I was blotto.'—3. Hence, a rage; a bad state of nerves: from ca. 1925. Frome, 1935.—4. In *out of whack*, not working properly; 'off colour'. 'His mind's out of whack'; 'Our wireless is out of whack'.

whack, v. To sell illicitly: Army: ca. 1910–40. Prob. suggested by the synon. *flog*.

whack down. To put (e.g. money) down; to write (e.g. names) down, to note: coll.

whack it out. To defend or support successfully: proletarian:—1923 (Manchon).

whack it up. To deal severely with (a prisoner): c.:—1933 (Ingram).

whack off. To masturbate. (Watts, 1988.) Ex US (W. & F., 1975).

whack out. To distribute (e.g. rations) equitably: military: early C.20. (B. & P.) Cf. **whack,** n., 1.

whack (one's) own donkey. To be occupied, or preoccupied, with one's own affairs: lower classes' coll.:—1923 (Manchon).

whack the illy. See **illywhacker.**

Whacker. (Also spelt *Wacker*.) A Merseyside term of address to a man. 'Most of the stokers we passed [at Scapa Flow, in Jan. 1944] seemed to be from Liverpool, for cries of "Hey, *Whacker!*" (a local expression) greeted Tommy Handley [himself from Liverpool] on all sides' (Worsley, 1948). P.B.: often abbr. to *Wack*, and perhaps ex dial. v. *wack*, to share out, divide (*EDD*); hence, one who does this, a friend: cf. the Services' *mucker*, one who 'mucks in' with another. Contrast:—2. A fellow, esp. a poor sort of fellow: Aus.: since ca. 1946. Dick, 1965.

whacker, adj. (Also spelt *wacker*.) Fine; excellent; wonderful: Aus., esp. Melbourne, children's: since ca. 1946. (Dick.) Prob. a var. of:-

whacko! Splendid! Good!: Aus.: since ca. 1920. (B., 1942.) Hence, since ca. 1930, an ordinary adj., as in 'a whacko time' (Cusack). Campion, 1940. By 1945, at latest, also English—popularised by Mr Jimmy Edwards.

whacko-the-diddle-o. (Of a girl) extremely attractive: Aus. (esp. Sydney) youths': since ca. 1938. (Park, 1950.) An elab. of *whacko!*, perhaps aided by the refrain of an Irish or dial. song.—2. Indeed, 'an elaboration of *whacko* in all its senses' (B.P.): Aus.: since ca. 1940.

whale and whitewash. Fish and sauce: tramps' c.:—1932 (Jennings).

whale into. To attack, punch, vigorously and spiritedly: Aus. (B., 1942.) Also some Brit. use (P.B.). 'The obsolescent US sense of *whale* is "beat" (v.)—hence, perhaps, corruption of S.E. *wale*' (R.C., 1976)—to mark the, or someone's, flesh with *wales* or weals.

whale of a . . . , a. 'No end of a . . . ': coll.: US (—1913), partly anglicised ca. 1918. Ex the whale's huge size. P.B.: by mid-C.20 at latest, familiar coll.; esp. in *a whale of a party* and *. . . a time.*

Whaley. The Whale Island Gunnery School (Portsmouth): RN. Bowen.

whang, n. A piece, portion, share: Aus. low: since ca. 1918. (B., 1942.) Echoic: cf. **whack out.**—2. A drive around in a vehicle, as in 'I'm off for a whang in the car (*or* on my bike)': Leicestershire teenagers': later 1970s. (McPheely.)—3. See **wang.**

whang, v. To throw violently; to fling: dial. > low coll. 'He whanged a stone at me'. Cf. **wellie-whanging.**

whangam, whangdoodle. An imaginary animal: rather nonce-words than coll. [E.P.'s entry in early edd. of this *Dict*.] P.B.: in later C.20 *whangdoodle* is an occ. joc. euph. for penis.

whanger. Alarm bell: RN. Wingate, 1981.

whank. For all senses, tenses, and compounds, see **wank,** the predominant later C.20 spelling.

wharfie, -y. A docker, stevedore: Aus. Wilkes' first citation is 1912. Ex '*wharf*-labourer'.

what ever. For *or whatever* see **or what-have-you.**

what for, what-for. Trouble; a great fuss, e.g. *raise what-for*, to 'raise Cain'. (Frome, 1932.) Ex *give* (one) *what-for*, to punish or hurt severely: from ca. 1870. Du Maurier, 1894, 'Svengali got "what for" ' (*OED*). Ex *what for?*, why: 'to respond to [one's] remonstrant *what for?* by further assault' (W.). Hence, to reprimand, reprove severely: from 1890s (F. & H.). As 'why' it may either stand alone, or be as in, e.g., 'what did you want to go and do a silly thing like that for?': coll.: mid-C.19.

what-have-we, a. An eccentrically dashing person, whether male or female: ca. 1912–18. Applied by Tom Pocock in *The Times*, 13 Aug. 1977, to the Sybil Thorndike of 1916 (Playfair). In short, a 'What have we here?' Cf. *what-shall-call-um.*

what it takes. Esp., courage, fortitude, perseverance; ability; (in Aus.) money: coll., adopted ca. 1935 from US. (B., 1942.) Lit., what the situation requires.

what makes (someone) **tick.** (His) chief interest in life, his driving-force: since ca. 1930. 'I've never discovered what makes him tick.' Ex watches and clocks.

what-o(h). As in 'She is a what-oh', a lively or fast piece: proletarian coll.:—1923 (Manchon).

what the devil. An intensive of *what*: coll. Oppenheim, 1934, 'What the devil concern is it of yours, anyway?'

what the fuck. Orig. a stronger intensive of prec., and perhaps a shortening of next: since mid-C.20 at latest. Not necessarily a straight question: 'It's hopeless! Nobody knows what the fuck's going on anywhere.' (P.B.)

what the fucking hell! A very common lowerclass expletive: mid-C.19–20. A mere elab. of:-

what the hell. One of the commonest intensifiers of *what*, as in 'What the hell do you think you're doing?': coll. Standing on its own, as in the American columnist Don Marquis' *archy and mehitabel* series, 1927+, 'what the hell, archy, what the hell', it is elliptical for 'What do I care? (I don't)'; 'What does it matter?', sentiments either resigned, or challenging as in 'What the hell! I'll show the bastards . . . ' (P.B.) Manchon, 1923, listed the euph. *what the fiery furnace . . .* A further var. is *what the Llanfairfechan hell*, euph., ca. 1920–50, for 'what the effing [q.v.] hell!'

whatever. For *or whatever* see **or what-have you.**

what's with (someone or -thing)? In *what's with* (e.g. him)?, it is a version of *what's up with* (him); but in *what's with* (e.g. the dinner-jacket)? it = Why are you (e.g. wearing one)?: adopted ex US, this idiosyncratic s. usage > gen. only ca. 1970, but I've heard it a decade or two earlier. R.S. cites the *Daily Telegraph* mag., 7 Dec. 1974, and adds, 'A literal translation of coll. Ger. *was ist mit . . .* , presumably via Yiddish.'

whatter (occ. **what-er** or **whater**), a. A what, a what-did-you-say. ' "Yesterday I saw a dinosaurus, Jim." "You saw a—a whatter, Bill?" '

wheat belt. A prostitute: Aus.: since ca. 1920. (B., 1942.) With an erotic pun on harvesting. Cf. **endless belt.**

wheel. A motorcar: since ca. 1959. Blake, 1964, 'The Leake character gave us a ride in his wheel.' Cf. more usu. **wheels.**—2. Someone important, esp. in an enterprise, whether licit or illicit: Can.: adopted, in late 1940s, ex US. *Daily Colonist*, 16 Apr. 1967, 'Poor old Robin Hood may have been a wheel in Sherwood Forest, but he would have had to call it quits [nowadays]'. By later C.20 also Brit. (*Phantom*, 1979). See also **big wheel,** which it shortens.

wheel-man. 'Expert driver of a motor car' (Powis): c., as also is the sense 'driver of a getaway car' (*Underworld*): since 1930s.

wheeler. A landing on the front wheel: RAF from ca. 1938. P-G-R.

wheeler-dealer. In the sense of 'an adroit, quick-witted, scheming person; a person with many business or social interests' (W. & F.) it has been adopted ex US: later C.20. (L.A., 1974.) Also adj., *wheeling-dealing*, and the activity *wheeling-and-dealing*.

wheelie, -y. Esp. in *do a wheelie*, as in 'three youths on mopeds . . . were doing "wheelies"—revving up their engines and using the power to lift the front wheels' (*Loughborough Echo*, 12 Mar. 1976): later C.20. Also, of course, applied to motorcycles, and even to pedal-cycles. Mrs B. Huston told me, 1979, that she had heard a child describe a kitten up on its hind legs as 'doing cat-wheelies'. (P.B.)—2. Such a rapid acceleration of a motorcar as to cause the driving wheels to slip: Aus. motorists': since ca. 1965. (B.P.)

wheelman. See **wheel-man.**

wheels. A motorcar: var. of **wheel,** n., 1: coll.: since late 1960s. (Hawke.) Also Aus. (B.P., 1977.)

wheels down! Get ready; esp., ready to leave train, tram, bus: RAF: since ca. 1937. H. & P., 'Taken from the lowering of the undercarriage . . . necessary to enable a modern 'plane to make a good landing.' Cf. *land wheels up*, to slip, lit. or fig.: id: 1941+.

wheeze, n. A 'tip' (information); gen. *the wheeze*, esp. in *give* (a person) *the wheeze*: c. >, by 1930, low s. Cf. the v., which is the possibly imm. origin.—2. Anything remarkable: Seaford Preparatory School: from ca. 1930. Also *weeze*.—3. A smart idea: RN: early C.20. (*Musings*, 1912; 'Taffrail', 1916.) P.B.: but also schoolboys': earlier C.20. E.g. 'I say, what a cracking good wheeze!, Cf. **Wheezers . . .**

wheeze, v. To give information, to peach: c.: later C.19–early 20. B. & L.; F. & H.

Wheezers and Dodgers, the. The Admiralty's Department of Miscellaneous Weapons Development: RN: WW2. (Pawle, 1976.) Ex **wheeze,** n., 3. and the initials. (P.B.)

wheezy; occ. **weezy.** Remarkable, very fine: Seaford Preparatory School: from ca. 1930. Ex **wheeze,** n., 2.

whelks behind a window-pane(, like). Phrase applied to the appearance of the eyes of anyone unfortunate enough to have to wear very thick-lensed spectacles: earlier C.20. Cf. **bottle-bottoms.** (P.B.)

whelpie. A child: market traders'. *M.T.*

when ever; loosely **whenever.** In *or whenever*: either a shortening of 'or whenever you like', as 'We could go on Friday—or whenever', or, used like *or whatever*, an avoidance of a tedious listing of suggested times: since mid-1970s. Prob. ex the pattern of *or whatever*; cf. **or what-have-you.** (P.B.)

whennies. See **wenneyes.**

where the five'n'arf . . . ? Where in the name of God (e.g. have you been?): r.s., on *rod* (pole, or perch) = 5½ yards. (Petch, 1976.) 'Where the five'n'arf you been, y' little skunk?' (Strange, 1930).

whereabouts. Men's underpants: Aus.: since ca. 1920. (B., 1942.) A pun on *wear-abouts*.

whiff. (A whiff of) oxygen: RAF coll.: since ca. 1935. Jackson.

whiff out. To cause (e.g. a room) to stink: mostly Aus.: since ca. 1920. (Campbell, 1964.)

whiffled. Tipsy: ca. 1930. R.S., 1973, suggests, 'perhaps ex S.E. *whiffle*, to veer, to shift about haphazardly. Influenced by *whistled.*' P.B.: or a drunken attempt at synon. *whistled*, or merely fanciful.

whiffs and a spit, take two. To smoke a little, have a short smoke, a pull: lower classes' coll.:—1923 (Manchon). Cf. **a spit and a drag** or **draw,** and **two draws . . .**

whine, (be) on the. (To be) querulous, given to whining: coll. Heard in conversation, early 1979—and that reminded me of

its existence since as early as 1904. P.B.: this was one of E.P.'s last 'home-grown', as opp. 'book-found', entries for *DSUE8*. He sent the note to me in Jan. 1979, when he was already almost bed-ridden, and I'm sure a friend must have said to him, 'I've never heard you be on the whine', for he was uncomplaining and stoical to the very end.

whingding. See **wing-ding.**

whinge; -ger; -ging. See **winge.**

whingey. See **wingey.**

whiny. Given to whining: NZ coll.: late C.19–20. (Park, 1952.) P.B.: also Brit. Often applied to a whining voice.

whip, n. A bustle, busyness: nautical coll.:—1923 (Manchon). Cf. S.E. v., *whip around* (v.i.).—2. Rum, the drink: Aus.: since ca. 1920. Culotta, 1963.

whip, v. To swindle (v.t.): c.: late C.19–earlier 20. Cf. military *flog* and *whip off*. Superseded by:—2. Hence, to steal: since ca. 1917. (Kersh, 1946.) P.B.: in later C.20 > gen. coll., though still rather low.

whip (someone) **a cripple,** as in 'The C.O.'ll whip him a cripple all right', pass a heavy sentence on: Army: since ca. 1930. Proleptic. (P-G-R.) Contrast *slip her a crippler*, to coït with a woman.

whip-and-ginger man. A horse-dealer: Leicestershire s. (not dial.): earlier C.20. Ex two 'dodges' used by horse-copers as enliveners of the horses they wish to sell.

whip up a smart one. To salute smartly; merely to salute: mostly RAF: since ca. 1925. (L.A.) Also *sling up; fling up*.

whip with a wet boot-lace. To apply an antidote to recalcitrance of the flesh: men's low.

whirligig. A gadget, a 'what-d'ye-call-it': coll.:—1923 (Manchon). Cf. **jigger.**—2. A Westland *Whirlwind* fighter: RAF: ca. 1941–5. H. & P.

whirling spray. A *Wirraway* aircraft: R. Aus. AF. WW2. (B., 1943.) By Hobson-Jobson.—2. A long-winded bore: Aus.: since ca. 1940. (B., 1953.) A fanciful elab. of the idea informing synon. *drip*.

whirly-bird (or **solid**). A helicopter: Can. (RCAF and commercial airlines'): since ca. 1950. (Leechman.) By late 1950s, also Brit., esp. RAF. Superseded during 1960s by *chopper*.—2. A 'Matisa tamping machine' (*Railway*, 2nd): railwaymen's: since late 1950s.

whisker. A girl or young woman: Aus.: since ca. 1921. (B., 1942.) Antiphrastically, but also because 'she's the *cat's whiskers*'.—2. See **shagged to a thin whisker.**

whiskers. See **all my whiskers.**

whisky MacDonald. A whisky-and-ginger-wine: orig. Scot.: since ca. 1920. 'And by the 1960s, almost invariably abbreviated to *whisky Mac*' (R.S., 1967).

whisky racket, the. The offer of printing machinery (and accessories) without the production of bona fides: printers': 1945 +. (*World Press News*, 10 Jan. 1946.) So often made over a whisky offered by a crook.

whisper, n. In *get it on the whisper*, 'To buy on hire purchase (because at one time you didn't tell the neighbours you couldn't afford to pay cash)' (Gosling, 1959): lower and lower-middle classes': since ca. 1920.

whisper, v.i. To make water: preparatory schools': from ca. 1920. Echoic.

whisper and talk. (Often shortened to *whisper*.) A walk: r.s.: late C.19–20. (Lardner, 1951.)

whisperer. A racing tipster: Aus. turf. B., 1942.

Whispering Death. A sobriquet bestowed upon the Bristol Beaufighter fighter-bomber by the Japanese forces in WW2; ex its ability to deal destruction by approaching fast and low, and so unheard until too late: journalistic, and some RAF use, 1943–5, then historical. (Frank G. Bunn, sometime Beaufighter navigator, 603 (City of Edinburgh) Squadron, 1981.) The more gen. RAF name was *Beau*.

Whispering Giant, the. The Bristol *Britannia* airliner: rather journalistic nickname—but the aircraft was indeed very quiet for its power and size: 1950s–60s. (P.B.)

whistle. 'To hurry away, to scram' (Jackson): RAF: 1940+. Ex the speed of the going.

whistle and flute. A suit (of clothes): r.s.: late C.19–20. (B. & P.; Powis.) Gen. abbr. *whistle* (Gilt Kid, 1936).

whistle and toot. Money, esp. cash: r.s., on *loot*. Usu. shortened to *toot*—see **toot,** n., 1. Franklyn 2nd.

whistler-blower, -ing. See **blow the whistle on.**

whistle-stop. A very small town (at which the train stops only if signalled by a whistle): Can., adopted ex US: since ca. 1925. Hence, as adj. in *whistle-stop tour*, a vote-catching progress by a politician through a succession of such places: orig. and mainly US, but some Brit. use in later C.20.

whistle up. To send for (esp. reinforcements) in a hurry: Army coll.: since ca. 1925. P-G-R.—2. Hence, to arrange for, e.g., food, usu. at short notice, as 'In no time at all they had whistled us up some supper': coll. Cf. synon. **rustle up.** (P.B.)

whistled. Tipsy: upper classes': since ca. 1920; then Services' (esp. RAF) since ca. 1925. (March-Phillipps, 1938; Jackson.) M.H. MacAlpine, however, in a letter pub'd in *TLS*, 28 Nov. 1980, claims that the term was in use in Scotland, esp. Glasgow, very early in C.20. Cf. mid-C.18 *whistle-drunk* = very drunk.

whistler. A revolver: low:—1923 (Manchon). Ex *whistler*, a bullet.—2. Something big: coll.:—1923 (Manchon). Recorded in dial. for 1895 (*EDD*).—3. 'A high-explosive bomb as it descends' (H. & P.): Services', from 1939, very soon > also civilian. Cf. **screamer,** 2.—4. As in the following quot'n from *Weekly Telegraph*, 28 Feb, 1942: 'The war has brought into being many nicknames, which often mystify the uninitiated. Thus, women railway porters are known as "whistlers", female bus conductors as "Annie Lauries", women van drivers as "Gerties", girl munition workers as "Spitfire kittens", female "milk-roundsmen" as "dairy dots", women window-cleaners as "climbing Marys" and women fire-watchers as "pouncers", while land-girls are known as "dainty diggers" and women employed in the building trade as "kilted brickies".'—5. A British Rail Class 40 locomotive: gricers' (q.v.). 'Because of the engine noise' (Watts, 1988).

Whistling Wheelbarrow. An Armstrong-Whitworth *Argosy* freight aircraft, a 'flying box-car' type: 1950s–60s. (Commentator at Duxford Air Show, 17 June 1984.)

white. A £5 note: low sporting: mid-C.20. (*Daily Express*, 20 Mar. 1946.) Tempest, 1950, glosses this sense, 'Five pounds and upwards'. Ex colour of the note, impressive black print on white; this form ceased in 1961.—2. 'Where jewellery is concerned "White" is used to refer to platinum' (Tempest, 1950): c.: mid-C.20.—3. Silver; silver coins, e.g. 'A pony [25 shillings in silver] in white' (Tempest, 1950): c.: as *whites, white stuff*, since earlier C.19.

white-ant. To sabotage; to undermine: Australian labour movement: since ca. 1920. Hence, *white-anter*, a saboteur, and *white-anting*, sabotage. (B., 1942.) White ants are wood-destructive.

white ants. In *have* or *get the w.a.*, to be or to become exceedingly silly, or insane: Aus. B., 1942, 'also "in one's attic" '; or, as in Hill, 1951, *have white ants in the billy* (= billycan). Applied orig. to men gone crazy or, at the least, eccentric through isolation and solitude.

white-bag man. A pickpocket: c.:—1923 (Manchon).

white-bearded boys, the. 'People who establish unintelligible principles and prove them, like the ballisticians of Woolwich' (H. & P.): Services' (mostly Army): since ca. 1938.

white blackboard. An instructional film: schoolteachers': since ca. 1930.

white blow. Semen: literary or cultured.

white coat. A hospital attendant in prison: c.:—1932 (*Dartmoor*).—2. As *Whitecoat*, 'The senior examiner at the (taxi) Police Public Carriage Office' (Powis): taxi-drivers': later C.20.

white elephant. A boat that did not pay its way: drifter-men's. (Butcher, 1979.) A specialisation of S.E.

white girl. Cocaine: drugs c. (Stockley, 1986.) US since—1971 (Spears). Cf. **girl,** 2.

White Highlands, the. The affluent suburbs—often on higher ground—surrounding a multi-racial, deprived inner city, e.g. Nottingham, Glasgow, etc.: coll.: 1980s. Ex the prosperous and salubrious 'White Highlands' in what was formerly British colonial East Africa.

white it out. To serve a prison sentence: Aus. c. B., 1942.

white lady. Methylated spirits drunk as an intoxicant: Aus.: since ca. 1920. (B., 1953.) Because it turns white in water.—2. Cocaine: drugs c. (Stockley, 1986.) US since—1969 (Spears). Cf. **white girl.**

white man's burden, the. Work: joc. coll.: from ca. 1929. Punning the S.E. sense.

white mice. Lice: low Aus. r.s. Prichard, 1930.—2. Dice: English spivs': from late 1940s. *Picture Post*, 2 Jan. 1954.

white money. Silver money: low. (Jackson, 1946.)

White Paper candidate. A candidate for a temporary commission in the RNVR: RN: 1940+. Granville.

white rat. 'A sycophant; a tale-bearer': RN: since ca. 1925. (Granville.) Cf. the c. use of *rat*, esp. for 'informer'.

white stuff. Morphine: drugs c. (Stockley, 1986.) US since—1936 (Spears).

white turtle-neck brigade. Male homosexuals: (London) *Evening Standard*, 16 Oct. 1969, 'The leader of a Council estate Tenants' association said " . . . [Wimbledon] Common has become an international stamping ground for what are known as the white turtle-neck brigade" ' (L.A.). Ex current gay vogue at the time for this type of sweater.

white wings. A dinner-table steward: ships' stewards':—1935. Ex dress.

white wogs. Brit. and Continental European residents in Near and Middle East countries: Army and RAF: since ca. 1930. See **wog,** 1.—2. A derogatory term, usu. joc., for a Welshman: Services': since ca. 1950. Ex prec.

Whitehaven Docks. The pox: r.s.: later C.20. (Daniells, 1980.) Cf. **Albert Docks.**

whites. Amphetamine sulphate tablets: drugs. c. (Stockley, 1986.) US since—1967 (Spears).—2. See **white,** 3.

whitewash. To coït with (a woman).—2. To beat (an opponent) before he has scored an opening double: darts players': since ca. 1930.

whitewash-worker. A seller of 'a liquid alleged to replate silverware at home' (Allingham, 1934): grafters'.

Whitey; or w-. A white person, whether individually or collectively; hence, the Establishment as represented by the whites: orig. and still (1977) predominantly Negroes', in Brit. usu. West Indians': adopted, ex US, ca. 1955. (*DCCU*.) Powis: 'A racist Negro term for a white person (usually male), not said in a pleasant manner.'

whittle; wittle. To talk, chatter; aimlessly, to 'rabbit on': coll. Perhaps a var. of *witter*, q.v. (P.B.)

whiz, whizz, n. Pocket-picking: c.: from ca. 1920. (Leach.) Powis, 1977, has 'Tom has been at the whiz these last ten years at least.' Cf. the v., and compounds below, q.v.—2. Energy, 'go': Aus.: since ca. 1910. Stivens, 1951.—3. A lively, energetic, go-ahead type: coll.: late 1950s. (Campbell, 1960.) Perhaps an abbr. of *wizard*, as in 'She's an absolute whizz at making meringues'; an adaptation of sense 2; or an early shortening of **whizz-kid,** q.v. (P.B.)

whizz, v. To be actively a pickpocket: c.: from ca. 1920. Cf. **buz** in the same sense. Ex his speed.—2. See **beetle off.**

whizz-bang. 'A Fighter on the tail of an enemy aircraft' (H. & P.): RAF: 1939+.

whizz-boy. A pickpocket: c. (Allingham, 1931.) Also among grafters: witness *Cheapjack*, 1934. Cf.:-

whizz-game. The jostling of persons by one criminal to enable another to pick their pockets: c.: from ca. 1920. Spenser, 1934.

whizz-kid. A precociously bright boy shining at radio or TV knowledge tests: adopted ca. 1960, ex US, where formed on the *quiz-kids* of the 1930s (W. & F.).—2. Hence, a 'bright boy' (young man) rising rapidly, by intelligence and determination, in a firm, an organisation: likewise adopted ex US, later 1960s. Here, the *whizz* is more indicative of rapidity of rise through the ranks, and of energy (cf. **whizz**, n., 2), than any tenuous connection with *quiz*. The term is often used disparagingly, because enviously. (P.B.)—3. See:-

Whizz Kids, the. Wainwright, 1971 (2), lists the following police nicknames, all prec. by *the*, for the Forensic Chemists: *Baubles, Bangles and Beads Mob*; *Brain Drain*; *Clever Creeps*; *Egg-Head Brigade*; *Quackery*; *Test-Tube Wallahs*; *Whizz Kids*. None of these arose earlier than 1930 and none later than mid-1960s. The sixth is, I think, the earliest—and the fourth the latest. *Quackery* contains a pun on *quack*, a charlatan; for *whizz kids* see prec., 1. *Brain Drain* alludes ironically to the drift of scientists to America; and an *egghead* has been adopted ex US s. for an intellectual. The first, from the title of a song in the US musical show *Kismet*, later (1955) is perhaps an allusion to witch-doctors.

whizz-man; whizzer. A pickpocket: c.: from ca. 1920. 'Stuart Wood', both forms. Ex **whiz**, n., 2.

whizz-mob. A gang of pickpockets: c. Also among grafters: witness *Cheapjack*, 1934. See **whiz**, n., 1.

whizzer. A ship's propeller: RN: since ca. 1918. Cf. **fan**, n., 3.—2. Anything superlative, whether good or bad: since ca. 1945. Trevor, 1956, ' "Rather windy." —'I'll bet it's a real whizzer on deck." '—3. A drinking bout: Can.: since latish 1960s. Dempsey, 1975, 'He was only off on a little bit of a whizzer'.—4. See **put on the rattle; whizz-man.**

whizzo, adj. Perhaps corresponds to **whizz-kid,** 2, with a suggestion of too much too fast, as in 'The Banks-Livingstone whizzo scheme was thrown out by the [Greater London Council]' (*New Society* editorial, 23 July 1981). But cf.:-

whizzo! (esp. as exclam.) Splendid: mostly children's: since ca. 1944. Ex the adj. *wizard*. Blake, 1954.

whizzuck. See GREMLINS, in Appx.

who. Occ. used without v., e.g., *who dat?* [= that], as mock-Pidgin, for humorous effect: later C.20. *New Society*, 23 July 1981, in an editorial on recent European election results, 'They all said that Mitterand would lose . . . and they thought that Franz-Josef Strauss (who he?) might finally make it'—a joc. implication that 'nobody's ever heard of' the latter. Earlier, in Jennings, 1959, quoting the *Classification of Occupations*, 1950: 'Articulator of Bones and Skeletons, Cadman (who he?), Clock Winder . . . ' This use of 'who he?' is reliably attrib. to Harold Ross, ed. of *The New Yorker*, in 1920s. (P.B.)

who(-)done(-)it; usu. **whodunit.** A murder story; a detective novel; a murder-story cartoon: coll.: adopted in 1942 from US, where current since ca. 1934. (*Writer*, Jan. 1944.) R.C., 1976: 'Because the central problem in any detective story is, in fact, "who [has] done it?" '—i.e., committed the crime.

whole box and dice, the. The whole lot, everything; (of persons) all: Aus.: since ca. 1930. Durack, 1955, 'The boys tossed it in . . . and the whole box and dice clears out to Jericho.'

whole caboose, the. The whole lot; everyone and everything: Aus.: since ca. 1930. (B., 1943.) But *the whole cabush* occurs in a dialogue between two demobilised Brit. army subalterns, *Punch*, 5 Mar. 1919 (P.B.). See **whole shebang.**

whole issue, the. See **issue.**

whole kit and caboodle, the. The lot; everything: Can.: adopted, ca. 1920, ex US. (Leechman.) P.B.: by 1950, at latest, also Brit.

whole schmear, or **schmeer, the.** Same as prec.: N. Am.; in E. Can. since 1950s at latest. (Leech, 1986.) W. & F. give a citation dated 1970, and derive ex Yiddish for 'Smear or spread'. Cf.:-

whole shebang, the. The whole matter, affair, collection of things: coll.: adopted, ex US, later C.20. Cf. **whole caboose** or earlier *caboodle*; like them, orig. = a cabin, and hence, the contents thereof.

whole shooting-match, the. The whole thing, affair, etc.: from ca. 1915. (Blaker, 1934.) Ex earlier *whole shoot*, by influence of WW1.

whoop it up. To 'live it up'; have a riotous time; go on the spree: since late 1940s. 'A great section of the nation is still whooping it up' (Bournemouth *Echo*, 27 Dec. 1968, concerning a prolonged Christmastide holiday). Cf.—perhaps ex:-

whoopee; esp. **make whoopee,** to enjoy oneself, rejoice hilariously: coll.: US (from ca. 1927) anglicised by 1933 at latest. Clarke, 1934, 'Sitting on molehills and counting grasshoppers isn't my idea of rural whoopee.' Ex *whoop with joy.*

whoopsie. A mistake, usu. an embarrassing one, and usu. minor; a 'bloomer' or *faux pas*; a 'hiccup in the system': coll.: later C.20. Ex exclam. *whoops!*; cf. synon. **boo-boo.** (P.B., 1984.)

whoor (pron. *hoo-er*). See **whore,** 2.

whoosh. To move rapidly, emitting a dull, usu. soft, always sibilant sound; eligible only when used fig.; coll.: since ca. 1920. 'He whooshed through the house without even saying goodbye.' Ex the lit., echoic S.E. sense, as in 'Miserable passengers huddled back against the wall while passing vehicles "whooshed" through the inches-deep roadway puddles' (*Sydney Morning Herald*, 30 Aug. 1963). The lit. sense is admitted by *Webster's International* without comment; in Brit.—esp. Scot.—dial., it has long been common as an interjection expressive of a dull, rushing, hissing sound, as noted by the *EDD*.

whop it up. (Of men) to coït; esp. in, e.g. 'Cor! I could (*or* I'd like to) whop it up *her!*', among young men ogling an attractive girl: since mid-C.20. (L.A., 1974.)

whop-whop-whop! See **ching-ching-ching!** and **whoppity . . .**

whopcacker or **wopcacker.** Anything astounding, notable, excellent; hence as an adj.: Aus.: since ca. 1925. (B., 1942.) Cf. also **woopknacker.**

whopper-chopper. Nickname for a man known to be 'well-endowed', q.v.: Services': since mid-C.20. (P.B.)

whoppity-whop-whop-cockin'-'andle. 'At the end of a sentence this phrase means "and so on and so forth". It's a gibe at Gunnery jargon' (Bolster, 1945): RN wardroom: WW2.

whore is, in mid-C.19–20, considered a vulgarism; *harlot* is considered preferable, but in C.20, archaic; *prostitute*, however, is now quite polite.—2. Hence, a term of opprobrium even for a man: coll.: late C.19–20. Gen. pron. *hoor* or *hoó-er*.—3. A semi-affectionate term (cf. **bastard**) for a man: Anglo-Irish. O'Neill, 1959, 'Brian was one of the best—the cute whore.'

whore-shop. A brothel: coll.: C.19–20.—2. Hence, a house or flat where behaviour is dissolute.

Whore's Gazette – Red Light News – Piccadilly Part Two Orders – Screws of the World. National Servicemen's names, all in common use, for a famous newspaper: since ca. 1947. The 1st and the 2nd were common in the Services in 1939–45, and presumably date from much earlier. Affectionate, not (except very rarely) derogatory. 'Part Two Orders' give details of servicemen's personal occurrences, promotions, qualifications, marriage, etc., that affect pay.

whore's get. A white-slaver: c., and low. Gen. *hoorsget*.

whore's musk. Scented cosmetics; esp., their odour when advertising the presence of women: military coll.: earlier C.20.

whore's robber. See **messer.**

whosermybob or **whosermyjig.** 'Whatsit' or 'thingummy (bob)' or 'whatsisname': Aus.: since ca. 1930. (B.P.)

whosit. An occ. var. of *whatsit*, for *whatsisname*, a person whose name is momentarily forgotten: coll.: later C.20. Perhaps ex US. (P.B.)

why the devil or **the fuck** or **the hell . . . ?** Mere intensifications of 'why': cf. **what the hell.**

wick. See **dip** (one's) **wick; get on** (one's) **wick; turn up the wick.**

wicked. '(That's) wicked!' = excellent!: young people's adj., exclam. of approval. (Cockitt, 1988.) Complete reversal of earlier sense; cf. the fate of *rum* since C.16, and the later C.20 counter-culture use of *bad* = excellent. In print, *Sunday Telegraph*, 10 Apr. 1988.

wicked enemy, the. The Germans; esp. German aircraft (sing. or pl.): ca. Sep.–Dec. 1940. Bolitho, 1941, 'Fashionable for a time'. Ex the Press.

wicked lady, the. The cat-o'-nine tails: London's East End: since ca. 1945. (Herd, 1957.)

wicked sod. A liar: proletarian.

Wid; usu. in pl. *Wids*. A member of the Women's Division of the RCAF: Can. airmen's: 1942–5.

widdle, v. To make water: children's. Ex *wee-wee* + *piddle*. Also as n., in *have a widdle*.

wide, n. Elliptical for **wide boy:** from ca. 1940.—2. In *to the wide*, utterly; esp. in *done* or *whacked to the wide*, utterly exhausted: coll.: from ca. 1912. Very gen. among soldiers in WW1. (F. & G.) I.e. to the wide world: for all to see.—3. Hence, in *dead* or *done to the wide*, utterly drunk. Lyell.

wide, adv. Outside the harbour: Sydney anglers': since ca. 1930. 'Have you been fishing wide?' (B.P.)

wide boy. A man living by his wits: c. > by 1935, s. Ex earlier C.19 c. *wide-awake*, > by later C.19 *wide* = alert, well-informed, shrewd.

widger. A small boy: RN: since late 1950s. (Peppitt.) Perhaps ex dial.; or ex *wee*, (very) small + the *-dger* of such words as *bodger*, *codger*.—2. RAF var. of next, 1: late 1970s. (Wilson.)

widget. A mechanical contraption or device, usu. small: coll.: 1970s. Perhaps a contraction of older *wifflow-gadget*. (P.B.) 'A . . . one off service to iron out particular [engineering] problems, or as English workshop slang puts it, making widgets fit wodgets' (*Guardian*, 1983).—2. 'The original widget was probably the cigarette card. The traditional widget is the toy submarine in the cornflakes packet . . . [Widgets] are, in fact, any gewgaws which are given away free in packets of something else [as sales promotion 'gimmicks']' (Barber, 'Making Widgets Come True', 1979). Whence n., *widgetry*, the design and manufacture of widgets, and *widgeteer*, one who designs them. (P.B.)—3. See GREMLINS, in Appx.

widgie (or **-gy**). 'Girl with horse-tail hair-do and bobby-socks, also playing juke-box in milk-bar' (*Sunday Chronicle*, 6 Jan. 1952): Aus.: ca. 1950–60. Orig. also spelt *weegie* (Wilkes' quot'ns, dated 1950 and 1951). The female counterpart of *bodgie*. Ex *wigeon*, q.v.—2. Esp. in *have (got) a widgy on*, to be in a bad temper: RN: mid-C.20. L.A., 1961.

widow maker. 'a) Cut tree that hangs up or does not fall, b) a broken branch hanging in a tree': W. Can. and US forestry industry' (Leech, 1985). P.B.: cf. Kipling's 'the old grey widow-maker', the sea.

Widows, the. The Scottish Widows' Society: insurance coll.: late C.19–20. Cf. **the Pru**.

widows and orphans. A railwaymen's term, applied to the suicidal practice of walking along a railway line with one's back to the approaching traffic. *Railway*.

widow's balls, the. That weekly dance in Hull which is attended by wives of fishermen at sea: RN lowerdeck: since ca. 1970 or a little earlier. (Peppitt.)

widow's wink. A Chinese: r.s., on *chink*: later C.20. (Barker, 1979.) Cf. **Tid**.

wife. Fiancée; one's girl; one's mistress: Services' (esp. RAF): since ca. 1930. (Partridge, 1945.) Cf. **bride**.—2. The passive member of a homosexual partnership: homosexuals': late C.19–20. Complement: **husband**. *Lavender Lexicon*, 1965.

wife-in-law. A girl belonging to a 'stable' of prostitutes: the world of prostitution: since ca. 1920. Gosling, 1960.

wife-preserver. A rolling pin: joc. (Petch.) A pun on S.E. *life-preserver*.

wig, n. A scene, an act; such playing as will render the audience ecstatic: Can. jazz-lovers' and musicians': since ca. 1956. ('Basic Beatnik', 1959.) Cf. the US jazzmen's **flip** one's **wig** (later *flip*), to approve ecstatically (Hinton, 1958).

wig, v. To eavesdrop; to listen to (person or persons) surreptitiously, as 'Is he wigging us?': market traders'. (*M.T.*) Abbr., synon. *earwig*. Among trawlermen, to listen on the radio (Butcher, 1980).

wigeon. An endearment for a little girl or a female teenager or a young woman: Aus.: since ca. 1946. This—the source of **widgie**, q.v.—derives ex S.E. *pigeon* (used occ. as endearment) + piggy-*wiggy*, as B.P. informs me.

wigga-wagga. A flexible walking-cane: ca. 1895–1912.—2. Hence, penis: low: earlier C.20. Perhaps influenced by an early C.20 popular song, 'With my little wigga-wagga in my hand', the protagonist being represented as walking down the Strand: cf. Harry Randall's gag, 'There *is* such a thing as love at first sight, but, young man, if you meet it in the Strand, *walk on!*'

wigged-out. 'So high on drugs that one is removed from reality' (Janssen, 1968): adopted, ca. 1972, ex US. Prob. ex *flip* (one's) *wig*: cf. **wig**, n.

wigger. An eavesdropper: market traders'. Ex **wig**, v. (*M.T.*) Cf. **earwigger**.

wiggle, a wriggle; esp. in *get a wiggle on*, to hurry: Can. (Beames.) P.B.: since ca. 1950, at latest, also Brit.

wilco! Strictly, Services' telephonic j. (often used to complement **roger!**, q.v.), it telescopes '(message understood and) *will co*mply!': used loosely in ordinary conversation, it is Services' coll., civilian s.: WW2 and since; ob. by 1970.

wild. See MOVING-PICTURE SLANG, §6, in Appx.

wild-cat. Elliptical for *wild-cat strike*, an unofficial strike, called at short notice: industrial coll.: since ca. 1950.—2. In the petroleum industry, since ca. 1910, thus, 'Indications are sought of [geological] structures which might act as oil traps, and the most promising of these are tested by the drilling of deep wells, known in the industry as "wild cats"' (Colonial Report no. 1930, *State of Borneo*, 1938, pub. in 1940). R.C., 1976, '*Pace* the Colonial Office, a wild cat well has nothing to do with depth, but rather *risk* . . . This is in contrast with a "producer well", drilled to exploit a known oil field.' These terms apply world-wide.

Wild Cats and Tigers Union. The NZ Women's Christian Temperance Union: since ca. 1950. A pun on the initials.

wilderness. In *be in the wilderness*, to be in need of 99 points: darts-players': since ca. 1930. Also the adj. *cracked* and *split*.

wilf. An ephemeral var., among Leics teenagers, of **wally**, 2. (Burt, 1984.)

Wilfred Pickles, do a. To 'have a go': ca. 1947–60. An allusion to the famous radio star's most famous programme.

Wilkie Bards. A pack of cards: r.s.: earlier C.20. (F. & G.) Ex Wilkie Bard, comedian and 'card'.—2. (In sing.) A race card: racecourse r.s. Franklyn.

will do! I will obey your order, follow your advice, suggestion, etc.: gen. coll.: 1970s. Perhaps spontaneous elliptical, but more prob. influenced by *wilco*. (P.B.)

will I buggery! (or . . . **fuck!; hell!**) No, I certainly will not!: low emphatic. Cf. **is it fuck!**

William. Weak tea: lower classes':—1923 (Manchon).—2. An occ. synon. of *John Thomas*, the penis: low: mid-C.19–20. Cf. **Willie**.

William Powell. A towel: convicts' r.s.: since ca. 1935. (Franklyn 2nd.) Ex the famous American film star.

Willie, -y. A (child's) penis: N. Country s.:—1905 (*EDD* Sup.); not dial. Often *little Willie*. By later C.20, much more widespread and sometimes used by adults as joc., childish. (Franklin, 1982.) ' "ET hasn't got a willie," observes Linda' (Hennessy, article on children viewing the film *ET* [Extra Terrestrial], 1982).—2. A supply of betting money: Aus. sporting (Glassop, 1949); also Aus. c. for any money, money in the till; hence, the till itself. Neil James spells it *willy*.—3. A ball: Shrewsbury: since mid-1930s. Marples, 'Perhaps *pill, bill, willy*.'—4. In *chuck* or *throw a willy*, to throw a fit: Aus. (B., 1942.) Cf. **willies**.—5. See **sticky willie**; **wandering Willie**.

Willie wellie. A condom: joc. (*New Society*, 20 Mar. 1987.) Cf. prec., 1, and **wellie**.

willies, the. A feeling of nervousness, discomfort, vague fear: US (1900), anglicised ca. 1925. (*OED* Sup.) Esp. in *give one the willies*, to induce this feeling in a person, as in 'I don't know what it is about (e.g. a person, a place), but (he, it) gives me the willies.' Cf. **heebie-jeebies**.

Willy. See **Willie**.

Willy Lee. A flea; mostly in pl. *Willy Lees*: Aus. r.s.: since ca. 1925. B., 1953.

Willy Wag or **W.w.** or **w.w.** A swag: Aus. r.s. Durack, 1955.

wimbler. A hand-worked auger: railwaymen's coll. (*Railway*.) Ex S.E. 'to *wimble*', itself ex the n. *wimble*.

wimp. A (young) woman, a girl: perhaps orig. Cambridge undergraduates', from ca. 1909 (R.M. Williamson, 1939; >, by 1923, more gen. (Manchon); ob. by 1930. Perhaps ex *whimper* or—a long shot—*wimpel*.—2. One who is old-fashioned and behind the times, a 'square': teenagers': adopted, late 1970s, ex US. Hennessy, 1979.—3. Hence, 'a creepy, spotty youth; a drip' (Wallinger, 1979): id. Walker, 1980, 'Mark [a skinhead, q.v.] says he has no time for mods ("just a load of wimps")'; 'Weeds and wimps cluster pallidly around the Ultimate Nutrition Products stand . . . ' (*New Society*, 4 June 1981). Watkins, 1987, draws attention to the Wymps, 'characters in a series of children's books of the 1890s, written by Evelyn Sharp . . . Wymps were fond of playing jokes but were apt to cry when jokes were played on them'.

Wimpey. A Vickers *Wellington* bomber aircraft: RAF: ca. 1938–52, then nostalgic. (*New Statesman*, 30 Aug. 1941.) Ex J. Wellington Wimpey, Popeye the Sailor's esteemed partner, in a very popular series of comic cartoons.—2. Humorously reputed to be an acronym of 'We Import Millions of Paddies Every Year', an allusion to the number of Irishmen employed by the very large construction firm of this name: 1970s. Cf. **McAlpine Fusilier**. (P.B.)

wimpish, adj. From **wimp**, 2, 3.

wimp-out. Elab. of **wimp**, 3, prob. influenced by *drop-out*. 'He was a loser, a wimp-out, and at thirty-five [the army] had all just got too much for him' (Kavanagh, 1987).

win(-)on. To 'get off' with a girl: Aus.: since ca. 1945. (Dick.)

wincey. Very small: Aus.: since ca. 1930. 'I would class this word as mainly feminine and juvenile . . . Not a recent introduction' (B.P., 1969). Perhaps, as B.P. proposes, ex Ger. *winzig*, tiny, itself ex *wenig*, few or little. P.B.: but cf. the old finger-game, played for very young children, with its rhyme 'Incey-wincey spider, climbing up the waterspout'.

winchin'. Courting; courtship: Glasgow. I.e. *wenching* in favourable sense: cf. † Scots *winchie*, a young woman. See:-

winching. An Army var. of prec.: 1930s–40s. Perhaps contaminated, purposely, by '*winching* a vehicle'. For a specialised var., see **wanch**, v.

winco or **winko.** Wing commander: RAF: since before 1930. (Michie, 1941 ('winko'); Jackson, 1943.) Ex *Wing Co.*, a frequent abbr.

wind. A wind instrument: musicians': coll. >, by 1945, S.E.

wind(-)hammer. A pneumatic riveter: RN: since ca. 1930. Granville.

wind-pills. Beans: joc. 'I first heard it about 1908' (Leechman). Ex the flatulence they tend to cause; cf. **musical fruit**.

wind-splitters. 'Lean and scraggy cattle' (B., 1943): Aus. rural.

wind up, n. Orig. in *get* or *have (got) the wind up*, to get frightened or alarmed: from 1915; whence, *put the wind up* (someone), to scare or greatly frighten, from 1916; and so, independent, *the wind up*, nervousness, anxious excitement, from not later than 1918: all orig. Services' >, post-WW1, gen. Hay, 1915 (*OED* Sup.); Gibbs, (late) 1916, 'It was obvious that the blinking Boche had got the wind up'; C. Alington, 1922, *put* . . . (*OED*.) Cf. **wind vertical**, and var. *breeze up*. See **windy**. Wall, 1939: 'A favourite marching tune in the Army was "The British Grenadiers", of which a

rude parody had been made [perhaps soon after the Peninsular War] . . . and the marching soldiers would sing it right up to the time of the war of 1914–1918. One verse ran: "Father was a soldier, at the battle of Waterloo, The wind blew up his trousers, and he didn't know what to do." It was natural that when a man was flustered . . . , he was said to have "got the wind up his trousers", later shortened to "got the wind up". This bears the obvious stamp of truth . . . The wedding of the words to a well known tune doubtless aided the vitality of the expression.' Professor Wall is probably right.—2. Dempster, 1979, notes that *wind-up* (as a clock) 'is replacing the démodé *hassle* [q.v., the n.]' Cf.:-

wind (someone) **up,** v. 'The kids . . . will "wind you up" (take the piss [q.v.]) as much as they can, [but] the conversation becomes deadly serious on certain topics' (*Time Out*, 30 Nov. 1979): Londoners': late 1970s. Perhaps ex the fig. use of, e.g., *winding* someone *up* (like a mechanical toy), priming him to argue with bureaucracy. (P.B.) Cf. prec., 2, and the title of a pop song, 1982, 'It's only a Wind-up'.—2. As in '*winding up*': a gradual acceleration, as on a club run': club cyclists': from late 1920s. (*Fellowship*, 1984.) 'If you wind [a motorcycle] up and you hit something . . . ' (Police advice, on BBC Radio Leicester, 14 June 1984).

wind vertical; with vertical breeze. 'Wind up', i.e. frightened, very nervous: military, mostly officers': from 1916. (B. & P.) Also *suffer from a vertical breeze* or, occ., *gust*, to be 'windy' (F. & G.). See **wind up**, n. P.B.: a further var. occurs in Tennant, 1920, 'With reinforcements of pilots we began to feel our strength, and determined, in the jargon of the air, "to keep a vertical draught up the enemy".'

windbag. A mystery packet: grafters'. (*Cheapjack*, 1934.) The contents are worth little more than those of an empty bag.

windbag-blower. Market traders' term for the next: *M.T.*, 1978.

windbag man. A seller of sealed envelopes: grafters': from ca. 1910. (P. Allingham, 1934.) See **windbag**, and cf. prec.

winder. Short for *Sidewinder*, the name of an air-to-air missile: RAF coll.: later C.20. *Phantom*.

Windies, the. The West Indies test cricket team: Aus. sports writers': since mid-1960s. *Australasian Express*, 2 Feb. 1982.

windmill. An autogyro: RAF: since ca. 1935. (H. & P.) Cf. **egg-whisk**.—2. A propeller: RAF: since ca. 1938. (Jackson.) Both senses † by 1950 (P.B.).

window-pane. A monocle: joc. coll.—1923 (Manchon).

windward. In *get to windward of*, to get the better of (a person): nautical, esp. RN: coll.: late C.19–20. *Musings*, 1912.—2. 'To get on the right side of authority, especially dockyard officials, from whom is obtained paint and other materials for smartening a ship' (Granville): RN.

windy. Afraid or very nervous; apt to 'get the wind up': Army >, post-WW1, gen. See **wind up**, n.—2. 'Long-winded, prosey, etc., as in a windy bore' (Granville): HM submariners': mid-C.20.—3. (Of matter or of type) set very open: Aus. printers'—1950 (B., 1953).

Windy Corner. Northern Germany, esp. the coast near Kiel: RAF pilots': since 1939. (Michie, 1940.) Cf. prec., 1.

windyburbs. A wind-proof jacket: RN: later C.20. 'Presumably a blend of *wind*cheater + *Burb*erry' (Wood).

wine grape. A Roman Catholic: Glasgow r.s. on *pape* (i.e. papist). Cf. **Jungle Jim**. Munro, 1985.

wine-mopper. 'A down and out alcoholic who drinks cheap strong wine. Sometimes shortened to **mopper**' (Munro, 1985): Glasgow.

wing, n. A sandwich-man's boards: c.—1932 (Jennings).

wing, v.t. 'To run in or report a sailor for an offence against Naval regulations. Lower deck, from the shooting sense of "winging" a bird' (Granville): RN.—2. Eric Idle, concerning the early years of the surrealist TV comedy series 'Monty Python's Flying Circus', in *Listener*, 28 June 1979: 'It's such a tight, anal little group. You can't wing or busk anything. It's always "Get it right, get it right".'

wing-ding. A party, a celebration: Aus. and Can. (spelt *whingding*), adopted ex US, where orig. it = a fit (epileptic or drug-induced), hence of anger, hence any ruckus: since mid-C.20. (W. & F.; P.B.) See CANADIAN, in Appx., and **ding,** 1.

Wing-nut. Nickname for a boy or man with large, protruding ears. Bishop, 1986; *Sunday Express mag.*, 24 Aug. 1986, for use among policemen.

wingco is a var. of **winco.**

winge. To complain frequently or habitually: Aus.: since ca. 1910. (Baker, 1938.) A perversion—or perhaps merely a corruption of—*to wince.* Also *whinge.* Hence, *winger* or *whinger,* a grouser, and *w(h)inging,* grousing (g pron. *dj*). But orig. Eng.—esp. Lancashire and Yorkshire—dial.; whence presumably the Aus. usage. P.B.: in common use in the British Army since mid-1950s, at latest. During later C.20, much play has been made in Australia with the derogatory generalisation *wingeing Poms.* Also as n., in e.g., 'having a whinge'; 'What's his whinge?' = what is he complaining about?

winger. A steward at table: nautical: early C.20. Bowen.—2. Hence, a sneak, an underhand fellow: RN: from ca. 1915. (Bowen.) Cf. **wing,** v., 1.—3. 'A young sailor; an old tar's protégé' (Knock); hence, an assistant, a 'mucker': RN lower-deck. Variants of the latter nuance are (usu. vocative): *wings* (from ca. 1930) and *wingsy-bash* (from ca. 1940), a joc. elab.—4. As *the Winger,* the Commander (Flying): FAA: since ca. 1920. Cf. **Wings,** 2.—5. A ship's steward, or a sailor, habitually allowing himself to be used passively: homosexuals': since ca. 1930.—6. Hence, fig., as in 'She seems to think she's the admiral's winger' = He thinks a lot of himself: since ca. 1935: orig., RN; by ca. 1950, fairly gen. homosexual.—7. In *do a winger,* to take unfair advantage in a bargain: Services': since ca. 1916. (F. & G.) Cf. sense 2, and the Army **work a flanker.** (P.B.)—8. See **winge.**

wingey or **whingey;** inferior forms in -*gy.* Querulous; cantankerous: Aus.: since ca. 1930. (B., 1953.) See **winge.**

wingless wonder. An officer on ground duties, i.e., one not wearing pilot's 'wings', or aircrew brevet: RAF: since ca. 1930. (Emanuel, 1945.) Cf. synon. **kiwi** and **penguin.**

Wings, wings. A wing commander: RAF: since ca. 1935. (Kee, 1947.) Cf. **winco.** Perhaps ex, or poss. influenced by:—2. A commander in the FAA: RN: since ca. 1925. (Granville.) Cf. **winger,** 4.—3. Hence, commander (Air) 'responsible for the flying routine or operations in an aircraft carrier' (Granville, 1967): RN: since late 1930s. Cf. earlier **guns, torps.**—4. A pilot's badge, worn on the left breast, showing that he is qualified; hence, *have* (one's) *wings,* to be qualified to fly: since 1916 (B. & P.), and *get* (one's) *wings,* to complete one's flying training and qualify as an operational pilot: RAF coll. >, by 1943, j. The pilot's badge is a double spread of wings, but the term is also applied, loosely, to the single wing, or brevet, of other aircrew: observer, navigator, air electronics officer, etc.; also, among commercial airlines, to, e.g., stewardesses of the cabin staff. (E.P.; P.B.)—5. See **winger,** 3.

winick. See **winnick.**

wink. A sixpence: Aus.: since ca. 1920. B., 1942, 'One and a wink'. Cf. Eng. **kick** in this sense.

winker. The female pudend: low: later C.20. Bailey, 1970.—2. See sense 2 of:-

winkers. Spectacles: Aus. Caddie, 1953.—2. Directional indicators in the form of flashing lights, on an automobile: motorists' coll., verging on j.: since late 1950s. Occ. in sing., as in 'the offside front winker isn't working'; even, paradoxically, 'my winker's on the blink' (= isn't working properly). P.B.

winkle, n. Penis: children's; (young) schoolboys': late C.19–20. But since ca. 1960, it has been also adults': joc. or disparaging ('his little winkle'). (L.A., 1974; 'Jonathan Thomas', 1976.) P.B.: at nursery stage applied also to little girls' vulva: domestic. It may be diminished even further by nursery var. *winkie, -y.*—2. In *have* (got some-

thing) *on the winkle,* to be obsessed by it: since ca. 1920. Amis, 1969. 'Look, Dad, for some reason you've got death on the winkle.' Ex sense 1: cf. **get on** (one's) **wick** (= penis). (Gardner.)—3. See **winkle-bags.**

winkle, v.t. To steal: lower classes': from ca. 1910. (F. & G.) Ex prising a winkle out of its shell.

winkle-bags (or solid). Cigarettes: r.s., on *fags:* later C.20. ' "Seize a winkle", from "Gi'e us a winkle . . . " ' (Daniells, 1980.)

winkle barge. An anti-aircraft ship, esp. a Landing Craft (Flak): RN: ca. 1941–5. P-G-R.

winkle-fishing. Putting fingers in nose: proletarian:—1923 (Manchon).

winkle out; winkling. To hunt out, house by house or 'fox-hole' by 'fox-hole', esp. with rifle and bayonet: bayonet exercises: resp. since 1940 (military) and ca. 1930 (RN). The latter: Granville. The former: *People,* 31 Oct. 1943. (RN). Cf.:—2. *Winkling.* attacks by Typhoon aircraft on small enemy strongpoints, 500-or-so yards ahead of the troops: RAF: 1944–5.

winkle-pickers. 'Winkle-picker' shoes—shoes with very pointed toecaps: since ca. 1959. Cf.:-

winkle-pin. A bayonet: Army, esp. Cockney: WW1+. (F. & G.) Meiosis; cf. *toasting-fork,* a sword. See **winkle out.**

winkle(-)piss. 'A term of contempt for *any* insipid drink and not solely for alcoholic ones.' Apparently current mostly in the Hampshire–Dorset region. '?Ex the pallid outflowings of childhood compared with the more [darkly coloured and] pungent effluxions of maturity' (R.S.). P.B.: but cf. **weasle-pee.**

winkle-trip. Strip-tease act by male(s) for an all-female audience, performed on a Thames pleasure-boat; 'the boys [strippers] on the trip call it a "winkle trip" or 'ladies' dingdong night" ' (Weir, 1980). Cf. **winkle,** n., 1. (P.B.)

winko. See **winco.**

winky. In *my winky!,* a trivial oath, disapproved of for children's use in Kipling, 1906. Perhaps cf. **winkle,** n., 1. (P.B.)

winner. A thing, e.g. a play, that scores a success: since ca. 1912. Ex *winner,* a horse that wins.—2. Hence, from ca. 1920, something esteemed to be certain to score a success. (But many a publishing 'winner' is a 'flop'.) P.B.: E.P. writes with feeling; he was himself a publisher, ca. 1926–32.

winners and losers. Trousers: Glasgow r.s., on local pron. *troosers.* (Munro, 1985.) Cf. London **round the houses,** 1.

winnet (or perhaps **winnit**). 'A dull, unimaginative student who is always studying; that is, he is a "grind" ': St Catherine's College, Oxford. (Apt, 1978.) Later C.20.—2. Sense 1 *may* poss. derive ex a term heard, used by a Scottish drill instructor, 1953: he amplified it thus: 'Ye're a load o' winnits! That's turds. Turds that winnit stay in—an' they winnit come oot!' (Obviously, 'will not'.) Or it may be sheer coincidence, merely a homophone. (P.B.)

winnick, v.i. To giggle, snigger: market traders'. (O'Shaughnessy, 1979.) Perhaps derived ex *whinny; whinnick* is recorded in *EDD* as 'to whimper or cry'. (P.B.)

winnick, adj. Crazy; mad, in any degree: Army, from 1915; some later gen. use. (B. & P.) Ex the lunatic asylum at Winwick (pron. *winnick*), Lancashire. Also in *gone stone winnick,* (to have) gone clean out of one's mind, insane: id.

Winnipeg. Leg: r.s. Hollis, 1983, where spelt *winnypeg.*

winny-popper. The penis: Can. schoolchildren's: since ca. 1950. (Barr, 1968.) Cf. **winkle,** n., 1.

wino. A drunkard on wine: Can.: adopted, ca. 1925, ex US. (Leechman.) Adopted also in UK, ca. 1945, for an 'Alcoholic, particularly one who drinks cheap domestic wine' (Powis).

winter blossoms (or one word). Seabrook, 1977, writes of Bournemouth in the spring, when 'The few old ladies, who still live in hotels—the "Winterblossoms" as they are sometimes called—begin their journey to . . . cheaper hotels inland'.

Winter Headquarters. Devon and Cornwall: tramps' c. Gape, 1936.

winter-hedge. A clothes-horse: proletarian:—1904 (F. & H.). Sayers, 1984, recalled that his grandmother († 1960) used the term all her life, pronouncing it *winteredge*.

winter woolies. See **woollies,** 1.

wipe. To refuse (a loan): c.: from ca. 1921.—2. To do without, dispense with: Aus.: since ca. 1920. (B., 1942.) I.e. 'wipe off the plate'.—3. To have nothing to do with; to refuse to see or to speak to (someone): Aus.: since ca. 1940. Cleary, 1959.—4. Hence, to ignore (someone) coldly; to snub severely: Aus.: since the middle 1940s. Culotta, 1957, adduces 'He got wiped' and 'I've wiped him'. Also NZ Army: 'to dismiss cursorily', noted by Erik de Mauny in his diary, 8 Dec. 1944, quoted in *Oasis*.—5. To 'wipe out', i.e. to kill, esp. to effect the killing of (someone): espionage: since (?)ca. 1950. Thomas, 1978.

wipe (a person's) **eye for** (something). To rob him of it: Army: since ca. 1930. P-G-R.

wipe hell out of (someone). To thrash, or defeat soundly: Aus. B., 1942.

wipe-off, n. A dismissal: Aus.: since ca. 1930. (Drake Brockman, 1940.) Ex:-

wipe off, v. To say a final good-bye; to decide to see no more of (e.g. a locality): Aus. coll.: since ca. 1925. (Niland, 1955.) Probably elliptical for *wipe off the slate*.

wipe-out, n. A violent dumping of a surfer by a wave: Aus. surfboard riders': since ca. 1960. *Sun-Herald*, 22 Sep. 1963.—2. Crash: skiers': later C.20. (*LAM*, 4 Feb. 1986.) Also as v.; perhaps ex 1.

wipe out, v. To kill: Fighting Services', prob. since ca. 1850; by 1919, also in civilian use; by mid-C.20, verging on S.E. Carr, 1939.

wipe the deck with. To defeat utterly: RN. ('Taffrail', 1916.) P.B.: by mid-C.20, this phrase had been 'civilianised' as *wipe the floor with*: orig. low coll. > gen. and sporting.

wipe up. To steal: Army, from ca. 1908 (F. & G.); police s. (*Freelance Writer and Photographer*, Apr. 1948).—2. To arrest: c.:—1935 (Hume).

wiped-out. Very 'high' on drugs; hence incapable, unaware of one's surroundings, bewildered: adopted, ex US, late 1960s. (*Jagger*; W. & F.) But cf. **wipe-out,** n.

wire. A wire-haired terrier: dog-dealers': from ca. 1890. London *Evening News*, 2 July 1937.—2. The penis: low. Ex **pull** (one's) **wire,** q.v.—3. A reprimand: Aus.: since ca. 1930. B., 1943.—4. In *give* (one) *the wire*, to warn secretly: low (pre-WW1) and Services' (WW1). (F. & G.) Revived in WW2, mostly Army, for 'to give advance information' (P-G-R).—5. As the *Wire*, the wire fence built by Mussolini on the frontier of Libya and Egypt: Army coll.: 1940–3. 'It kept out nothing but the gazelles' (Sanders, 1967).—6. As *the wire*, a var. of *the straight wire*, genuine information: c.: from ca. 1918. (*Gilt Kid*, 1936.) Perhaps ex 4.

wire-happy. (Of prisoners of war) depressed and slightly unbalanced mentally by the constant sight of the surrounding barbed wire and mess: WW2. Used also in Cyprus, late 1950s, by non-combatant troops confined to camp because of terrorist activities in the surrounding countryside. Cf. **stir-happy.** (P.B.)

wire into. To understand and enjoy; to be at one with: students of technology: later C.20. 'I really wire into Beethoven's later quartets' (Harrison, 1978). Cf. **dig,** v., 2 and 3.

wire-puller. A Royal Engineer: Army. They're forever handling wire.—2. An electrician: ca. 1900–25.—3. A male masturbator: low: late C.19–20. Ex *pull* (one's) *wire*.—4. A manipulator of people and events: coll.: later C.20. Ex *pull wires*, var. of *pull strings*, as a puppeteer does. (P.B.)

wired. Tense; anxious: Dempster, 1979, reports it as 'replacing the démodé "uptight" [q.v.]': therefore, Society: later 1970s. But it did not replace *uptight* for 'ordinary people'. (P.B.)

wired for sound. (Of a person) wearing an earpiece of any kind: Aus.: since late 1950s. (B.P.) Ex radio mechanics' j.

wireless or **message by wireless.** A baseless rumour, a report without ascertainable origin: since ca. 1925.

wireman. A telegraphist: coll.: early C.20. Manchon.

wires crossed. In *get* or *(have) got* (one's) . . . , to talk at cross-purposes (since ca. 1935); to fall or be under a misapprehension (?since ca. 1950): orig. s. >, very soon, coll. Ex mishaps with the telephone; occ. *lines* for *wires*. Cf. *get one's knitting twisted*; *have a leg over*. (Petch; P.B.)

-wise. Suffix = concerning, or 'in the manner of'; but often virtually meaningless: some Brit. copying of the US vogue usage: later C.20. (P.B.)—2. See **streetwise.**

wise as a dockyard pigeon(, as). Keen-witted: nautical. 'The Liver Birds', episode broadcast on BBC TV, 1 May 1976 (Peppitt).

Wise Boy's Paradise, the. 'This very apt term is used in the services to describe the *unimportant* jobs which seem to keep so many eligible men out of uniform, and the places overseas to which men have gone to avoid conscription' (H. & P., early 1943): since 1939.

wise-crack. See **wisecrack.**

wise (to). Aware (of); warned (about). Esp. *be* (or *get*), or *put* a person, *wise* (*to*): US coll. (ca. 1900), anglicised ca. 1910. Cf.:-

wise up, v.i. To 'get wise'; v.t., to 'put (a person) wise': US (C.20), anglicised ca. 1918, but 'Australianised' by 1916 (Dennis): Buchan, 1919; Wodehouse, 1922. Ex prec. (*OED*.) But adopted in Can. by 1905 at latest. 'You've got a little way to hike alone . . . and you're not wised up in everything' (Niven, 1927).

wisecrack. A smart, pithy saying: adopted, ex US, ca. 1932; it had, by ca. 1950, and so for some time in US, an often pej. connotation. Earlier, hyphenated.

wish (a person) **on** (occ. **upon**). To recommend a person to another: rare before C.20. Many knowledgeable persons think (and several have written to tell me so) that this term should be included: but at lowest it is coll. and I myself believe it to be familiar S.E. E.g. 'That officer was wished on us by the -th Brigade.' 'Ultimately, I think, from the Witch Doctor's ability to transfer evil wishes from his client to his client's enemy, and it prob. comes into English slang via the Colonial Service' (Franklyn).

wished on, as in 'I had this job wished on me', i.e. foisted upon me: coll.: late C.19–20. Ex prec.

wiskideon. A waistcoat: ca. 1945+. Fanciful; ex the now dial. pron., *weskit*.

witch-piss. An inferior, or an unpopular, beverage, ranging from 'Naffy' tea to thin beer: RAF: ca. 1940–60. Also *witch's piss*. Cf. synon. **winkle-piss** and **weasle-pee.**

witch tit (or **teat**). (Of weather) very, esp. if bitterly, cold: since ca. 1960. (Granville.) R.C., 1976, proposes, 'abridged from the (?US) phrase, "cold as a witch's tit" (at midnight)—which presumably arose through some confusion between witch and *revenant* [ghost]'.

witches' hats. The portable, coloured, safety cones used by police or workmen to guide traffic around and away from obstacles on the road: coll.: since late 1960s. Ex shape, like that of the traditional witch's pointed hat. (P.B.)

witch's cunt. See **tighter than . . .**

witch's tit. See **witch tit.**

with book. In the 'throes' of writing a book. I've heard it only rarely since ca. 1960. Prob. of medical orig., on *with child*. Deeping, 1925, 'and that people who write books have a way of disappearing while they were "with book".'

with – but afters. 'Officers of the Naval Reserves who rank *with, but after*, officers of the Royal Navy' (Granville): RN wardroom.

with it. As agreement, *with it!*, or *with you!*; 'I understand you—I have grasped what it is you require of me': coll.: from ca. 1970. (P.B.) Prob. ex sense 3.—2. In *be with it*, to understand and appreciate and enjoy music: jazz-lovers': since the late 1930s. (*Observer*, 16 Sep. 1956.) This perhaps derives from the Can. (and US) carnival employees' to *be with it*, to be one of carnival or fairground crew. (Leechman.) P.B.: or is it ex 'in sympathy with'? See also JAZZ, in Appx., for *get with it*.—3. Hence, to be alert or well-informed and up-to-date: since ca. 1959. Cf. the quot'n at **Rockers** . . . 'Even "with-it" might be acceptable as a kind of sociological onomatopoeia, an expression with overtones which match the thing described' (Lejeune, 1967). P.B.: also as adj., e.g., 'They were a very with-it lot in my class.'

with or without?; positive: **with or without.** 'Often heard in cafés and snack bars. The server at the counter, where sugar is put in tea at the counter, will say "With or without?" The person ordering often asks for tea and adds "With" or "Without". People who have heard German or Swiss say "mit" sometimes use this. They seldom say "With sugar" ' (Petch, 1966): coll.: since ca. 1920. P.B.: occ., joc. domestic: *with or without with?*

within a gnat's(, to). A very short distance indeed; 'a fit to within, say, a "thou" [1000th of an inch]: the distance between a gnat's piss'ole and its arse'ole—but not to be measured with a micrometer' (Irwin, 1979): engineers' and technicians': later C.20.

within a hair of. Almost: coll.:—1933 (Lyell). 'He came within a hair of being dismissed'. Abbr. S.E. *within a hair's breadth of*.

within the four seas. In the British Isles, it refers to a bird's breeding-range: coll.: since (?)ca. 1920. Fitter, 1966.

without a mintie. Penniless: Aus. sporting: since ca. 1920. (Glassop, 1949.) I.e. without a *minted* coin.

witter. To annoy (someone) by talking nonsense: Leeds undergraduates':—1940 (Marples, 2). P.B.: in later C.20, fairly gen. coll.; used in the same way as **rabbit**, v., q.v.: 'He went wittering on, a great long spiel about how he'd . . . ' Ex dial. (*EDD*, which compares *twitter*).

wittle. To talk at length to little point; to talk nonsense, to 'witter' q.v.: later C.20. Heard in E. Midlands; poss. ex dial., though not recorded in this sense in *EDD*, but more prob. a var. of *witter*. It might also be spelt **whittle**, q.v (P.B.)

wiwol. 'A pilot that keeps telling people that he flew Lightnings [jet fighters]—"when I was on Lightnings" ' (Wilson, 1980): RAF joc.: late 1970s.

wizard. Excellent, first-rate: from ca. 1924. ('Ganpat', 1933, 'A perfectly wizard week!') Ex *wizard*, magical. (*Dict*. 1st ed., 1937.) E.P. later added this note: it was immensely popular in the RAF (and the WAAF) in WW2: witness, e.g., Bolitho, 1940; Jackson, who postulates RAF currency before 1930; Partridge, 1945. Via the FAA, it > popular in the RN by 1942 (Granville). The term became gen. civilian s.; after ca. 1952, however, it was little used except by schoolchildren and—such things reach them after they've reached everyone else—by the lower-middle class. Pearson-Rogers, 1981, confirms that the RAF was using *wizard* in 1929–30, dating it by the Schneider Cup victories.

wizz, the. Var. of **whiz(z)**, n., 1. Sharpe, 1938, where also occurs *wizzer* for *whizzer* (see **whizz-man**).

wizzo, usu. exclam. Splendid!: RAF: 1942+. (Partridge.) Ex **wizard.**—2. See **whizzo.**

wobbegong. Anything notable or excellent: Aus.: since ca. 1920. (B., 1942.) Ironic ex *woebegone*? P.B.: *Aus. POD* gives *wobbegong* as Aboriginal name for a carpet-shark.—2. (Pron. halfway between *wobbegong* and *woebegone*.) A 'thingummy' (Baker); esp. an insect, a 'creepy-crawly', centipede, cranefly, etc. (P.B.): Aus.: since (?)ca. 1925.

Wobbie or **-y.** A member of the International Workers of the World: Can. workers': from ca. 1910. (Gape, 1936.) In US, it is *Wobbly* or *Wabbly*. In Brit. and Aus., *Wobbly*.

wobbler. 'A soldier toadying for stripes' (B., 1942): Aus. Army: WW2.—2. A staid, dull conformist, a 'square', q.v.: teenagers': early 1980s. (James Williamson, 1982.) Cf. **wackie**, 2.—3. Var. of **wobbly**, n.

Wobblies. Members of the International Workers of the World: since ca. 1910. See **Wobbie.**

wobbly, n. In *throw a w.*, to become mentally unbalanced, have a nervous breakdown: Services': later C.20. *Guardian*, 30 Oct. 1982, quotes a naval psychiatrist, Surgeon Cdr Morgan O'Connell, reporting his experience in the Falkland Is. campaign: 'If the men heard my name called on the public address system all kinds of stories would go round. They'd say "Someone's thrown a wobbly again" '. Cf. the coll. *throw a fit*, and similar entries at **chuck a** . . . —2. Hence, a short indisposition of any sort, as in 'A brief wobbly . . . which kept me off duty for precisely ten hours sleeping-time' (Cole, 1987).—3. As *Wobbly*, a member of the **wobblies.**

wobbly, adj. Uncertain, risky, likely to fail: coll.: late 1970s. Leitch, 1979, article about the Radio 4 one o'clock news programme; right up to the last minute, the exact details of the broadcast are uncertain, so 'It gets very wobbly sometimes'. (P.B.)

woebegone. See **wobbegong.**

woefuls, got the. Sad; wretched: coll.:—1909 (Ware); still heard occ., 1980: sometimes *a touch of the woefuls* (P.B.). Cf. **mis.**

Woff. A member of the Women's Auxiliary Australian Air Force: Aus. Services': WW2. (B., 1943.) Cf. the English **Waff.**

wog (or **W.**). A lower-class babu shipping-clerk: nautical: late C.19–20. (Bowen.) Soon, any Indian, Pakistani, etc. from the Indian Subcontinent; an Arab; 'A native. Someone once called enlightened natives "Westernised Oriental gentlemen" and the name caught on' (Jackson), via the initials: RAF: since ca. 1930. But Emanuel goes nearer the mark, I think, when (1945) he asks, 'Surely the derivation is from "golliwog"'?—with ref. to the frizzy or curly hair; *wog*, indeed, is a nursery shortening of *golliwog*. See also **white wogs.** P.B.: in later C.20 the term has > gen. and, although patronising, is not *always* used with rabid xenophobia—it's often a matter of 'Well, what else can you call them?' Also as adj; see compounds below.—2. A baby; a very young child: Aus. nursery. Also *pog-wog, poggy-wog, pog-top, poggle-top*, etc. (Baker.) Of the *diddums* variety of affectionate idiocy. P.B.: I suggest that these 'idiocies' are all variants or perversions of the common Eng. dial. *pollywog*, a tadpole (*EDD*).—3. Hence, a germ or parasite; anything small (e.g. tealeaf floating on cup of tea): Aus B., 1942.—4. As *the wog*, tubercular infection: Aus.: since ca. 1920. (Trist, 1945.) Hence, *wog*, a person with tuberculosis: since ca. 1925. (Cusack, 1951.) But B.P., 1963, amends: 'I have made extensive enquiries and everybody agrees with my belief that *the wog* is used of tuberculosis only by those in sanatoria or during a discussion concerning tuberculosis. Ten million Australians regard *the wog* as influenza, or loosely as a heavy cold with aches and pains, running nose, headache, etc.' P.B.: I have heard it used (1960s) also for a stomach-ache: Aus.: 'I've got a wog in my belly this morning!' seemed to refer to the pain rather than the germ of sense 3. Cf.:-

wog gut. (Acute) diarrhoea: Aus. Army: mostly 1940–2. (*Rats*, 1944.) Also *Palestine ache*. Ex their training period in Palestine. See prec. 1, 4.

wog music. 'In the late [19]40s and early 50s "Wog music" was the common term for the Middle-East strains often picked up on the radio . . . Obviously it came from returned soldiers; it was not used offensively; and it seems to have been dropped when the immigrants started arriving.' Barltrop is writing (1981, to P.B.) of London; but the term was more widespread and, in the Services, still current until at least ca. 1975. See **wog**, 1.

woggery. An Arab village: Army and RAF: since ca. 1930. (P-G-R.) P.B.: used of the 'native quarter' of Port Said, during the invasion of Egypt by Anglo-French forces, late 1956.

Woggins. Worcester College: Oxford undergraduates': earlier C.20. (Collinson.) Also **Wuggins.**

woggling. Waggling one's club for a long time before making the stroke: golfers' coll.: since ca. 1920. (Darwin.) Ex *waggle + jog*.

wogs. See **white wogs.**

wolf. A philanderer: adopted, ca. 1944, ex US servicemen. One of the linguistic consequences of the American occupation of London during 1943–5. Cf. S.E. *wolfish*, predatory. 'The word "wolf" has softer meanings in Australia, particularly when used by girls, as in "I don't trust your father, he's a wolf" ' (B.P.).

Wolf of Tuscany. An Italian soldier: Brit. Army in N. Africa: 1940–3. Sanders, 1967, adds that 'one of the Italian formations in the desert was the Wolves of Tuscany division'. P.B.: this sounds like Brit. Army ironic, 'taking the mickey'.

wolf-whistle. 'A whistle to show awareness of, approval of, and sometimes an invitation to, a sexually attractive woman . . . Commonly a brief rising note followed immediately by a longer descending note' (W. & F.): coll.: adopted, ex US, ca. 1944. See **wolf.** *SOD*; P.B.

wolly. See **wally**, n. and v.

Wolver. Penis: Midland and Northern English r.s.: since ca. 1945. Short for *Wolverhampton*, clearly an elab. of *Hampton*, itself elliptical for **Hampton Wick**, q.v. (Hjort, 1967.)

Wolves, the. See ASSOCIATION FOOTBALL, in Appx.

wom. A wireless operator (mechanic): RAF: since ca. 1935. (E.P., 1942.) Ex the initials *W.O.M.* Distinct from **Wop.**

women's-lib;-libber;-libby. See **lib**, n., 2.

womming. A 'GW/GC joint line expression for rail turning' (*Railway*, 2nd): ca. 1890–1925. Ex dial. *wam*ble, or *wom*ble to revolve. I.e. Great Western and Great Central Railways.

wonch. See **wanch**, n. and v.

wonder. See **chinless wonder; ninety days' wonder; titless wonder; wingless wonder.**

wong. A catapult: Aus.: since ca. 1920. (B., 1943.) P.B.: perhaps a corruption of synon. *shanghai.*

wongi. 'A friendly yarn, a chat; esp. in N.W. Australia. Ex Aboriginal' (Wilkes).

wonk. 'Yellow dog. A term commonly applied by foreigners to the ordinary chinese [mongrel, pi] dog. From the Ningpo pronunciation of the two characters [for y.d.]' (Giles, 1900). Still in use among 'Old China hands' in Hong Kong in the 1960s, for any scruffy mongrel. (P.B.)—2. A useless seaman; a very inexperienced naval cadet: RN: from ca. 1917. (Bowen.) Since ca. 1930, predominantly a junior midshipman. Granville derives the term ex sense 1, suggesting that it originated on 'China Stations'; E.P. prefers 'ex *wonky*'.—3. An Aus. Aborigines' pej. for a white person—cf. the Aus. whites' use of *boong* for an Aboriginal. B., 1959.—4. In *all of a wonk*, upset, very nervous: ca. 1918–28. (*OED* Sup.) Ex *wanky*.—5. Occ. earlier spelling of *whank*, q.v. at **wank.**

wonky. See **wanky.**

woo. A 'petting session', a bout of mild love-making: NZ: since ca. 1930. Slatter, 'Having a woo with some joker.' Directly ex S.E. 'to *woo*'.

wood. In *have the wood on* (someone), 'to hold an advantage' over him: NZ (B., 1941), soon >, if not there already, Aus. (Glassop, 1949). Also, in *Sunday Telegraph*, 16 Sep. 1973, *hold the wood on.* Wilkes. E.P.: prob. ex the game of bowls.—2. As *Mr Wood*, a truncheon: police. *Free-Lance Writer*, Apr. 1948.

Woodbine. A British soldier: Aus. and NZ Services': WW1 (B. & P.); WW2 (B., 1943). Because the Tommies smoked so many Wills 'Wild Woodbine' cigarettes, among the cheapest to be had.—2. Any cheap cigarette: coll.: from 1916. ('Taffrail'). By ca. 1950, if not much earlier, *Woodbine* was shortened to *Wood*, as 'A packet of Woods', or 'It's only a Wood, I'm afraid' (P.B.). Cf. **Woods.**

Woodbine funnel. 'Long, narrow funnel above Elliott pot engine' (Butcher, 1979): driftermen's: earlier C.20.

wooden, n. One month's imprisonment: c., and grafters' s. (*Cheapjack*, 1934.) Prob. abbr. or postulated *wooden spoon* = *moon* = month. P.B.: but cf. **woodman.**

wooden, v. 'To fell, knock out' (Wilkes: 'cf. stiffen'): Aus. Cf. **wooden out.**

wooden ears on, have, as 'I had wooden ears on', I couldn't hear: since ca. 1920. Cf. **cloth ears** and **tin ear.**

wooden out. To floor (someone) with a punch: NZ var. of **wooden,** v., q.v. Slatter, 'You bloody piker. A man oughta wooden you out.' Perhaps, as E.P. suggests, ex stretching out on the wooden floor.

wooden pegs. Legs: r.s. An occ. var. of older *Scotch pegs*. Franklyn 2nd.

wooden swear. An ill-tempered slamming of a door.

Wooden Tops (or as one word), **the.** The Guards Regiments: *non*-Guards Army: since late 1940s. An amiably derogatory nickname, based on an alleged lack of intelligence, and the military legend that the cobblestones in St James's Palace courtyard are actually the tops of the heads of Guardsmen buried upright. (P.B.) And **Woodentops:**—2. As in 'Smart Metropolitan detectives refer to their flatfoot colleagues in blue as Woodentops. In the wake of the latest Countryman trial for corruption the Woodentops have taken to calling their errant detective colleagues Bananas: yellow, bent and hanging around in bunches' (*Guardian*, mid-1982).

woodener. A punch, a blow: Aus.: 1908 (Wilkes). Hence, *woodener of five*, a fist: Aus. low. (B., 1942.) See **wooden,** v.; cf. **bunch of fives.**

woodie. An 'old wood-panelled station wagon' (*Pix*, 28 Sep. 1963) or 'an old car, partly constructed, or reconstructed, of wood' (B.P., mid-1963); hence, 'any old car having surfboard racks' (B.P., late 1963): Aus.; the latter, surfers': since ca. 1950, 1961, resp.—2. See **Woods,** 1.

woodman. A prison sentence of one month: c. 'From the fact that years ago in prison you slept on wooden boards for the first month' (Gosling, 1959). Cf. **wooden,** n.

Woods. A Wills Wild *Wood*bine cigarette: Army (1914) >, by 1919, lower classes'. (B. & P.) Also *wood; woodie, -y.*

woodser. See **Jimmy Woodser.**

woodwork. In such phrases as 'crept out of the woodwork' (York, 1977), 'he must have just crawled out . . . ' (Burchill, 1978), and 'They're probably hiding in the woodwork', comparing persons with woodworm, deathwatch beetle, dry-rot, etc. for (usu.) humorous effect. (P.B.)

woof. 'To eat fast (from "to wolf")' (Jackson): RAF, since ca. 1925; by mid-C.20, also Army. Often as *woof it back.*—2. Hence(?), 'to open the throttle quickly' (Ibid.): id.: since ca. 1930. P.B.: or perhaps echoic, ex the resultant *whoof* of energy and sound; cf. **woofle.**

woof run. A hash-house; a cheap restaurant: R Aus. N: WW2. (B., 1943.) Cf. prec., 1.

Woofers, the. The Worcestershire and Sherwood Foresters Regiment (29th/45th), 'now conveniently abbreviated to "The Woofers" ' (*Soldier Magazine*, June 1980): Army nickname. The regts amalgamated in 1970. (P.B.)

woofits, the; esp. *get the woofits*, to be moodily depressed: from ca. 1916; ob. by 1930. Perhaps = *woeful fits?*

woofle. The syncopated beat of a twin-cylinder engine: motorcyclists': later C.20. (Dunford.) Echoic; cf. **woof,** 2.

woofter. Var. of **poofter,** q.v., a male homosexual: teenagers': early 1980s. (Joanna Williamson, 1982.)

wool. In *have* (one) *by the wool*, by infatuation to control: Aus. (Baker.) R.C. comments, 1976: 'Surely the "wool" here is the genital hair—thus related to *get* [or *have*] *someone by the short hairs*, which I continue to believe must originally have referred *only* to genital hair, as shown by the paraphrase *short and curlies*. Hair on the nape may be short, but it is not necessarily so.'

wool(-)barber. A sheep-shearer: Aus. joc. (Ronan, 1961.) Cf.:-

wool-bug. 'He pictured the shearers, the "wool-bugs", in their dirt and grease' (Devanney, 1926): NZ: ca. 1890–1940.

wool-classer. A sheep-biting dog: Aus. joc.: since ca. 1910. (Baker.) A wool-classer 'pecks at' the wool he classifies.

wool, or woollen, king. A sheep 'king' or owner of a very large sheep-station or of numerous stations: Aus.: since ca. 1920. B., 1943.

Woolies. A Woolworth's store: urban Aus.: since ca. 1930. (Brewster.) Also Brit. Cf. **Marks.**

woollies. Woollen underwear: domestic coll.: late C.19–20. P.B.: esp. *winter woollies*, warm underwear (or jersey, cardigan, etc.), whether made of wool, or of any other material.—2. As *the woollies*, esp. in *give one the woollies*, an occ. var. of *the willies*: Army officers' (prob. joc.): Feb. 1935—ca. (?)1945.

Woolly. 'Woollongong (popularly pronounced Woollengong)': Aus.: since ca. 1920. B., 1953.—2. (*w-.*) A sheep: Aus.: late C.19–20. B., 1942.

woolly-back. 'A thesis [about Skelmersdale, Lancashire] by Inspector Roy Yates produced last month speaks of tribal tensions between "scousers" (former Liverpudlians there) and "woolly-backs" (locals)' (*The Times*, 16 July 1981). But McKenna, 1980, lists *woolley-backs* as a railwaymen's nickname for Leeds men, and Cross, 1984, claims it for Leicester people.

woolly-headed, go at. To attack furiously, most vigorously, very rashly: Aus. Baker.

woolly pully. The standard army-issue heavy jumper (*pull-over*), worn as part of barrack dress since ca. 1960: Army, and perhaps the other Services', who wear their own coloured versions. (P.B.)

Woolly's. See **woollies** and **Woolies.**

Woolworth carrier. 'Ships of the "Attacker" class, 11,420 tons . . . 18 aircraft . . . Known as "Woolworth" carriers, they were built in the USA, being adapted from uncompleted mercantile hulls' (Rendell, 1980): RN and RAF: ca. 1940–5. P-G-R.

Woolworth marriage or **wedding.** A fictitious one, as feigned by the week-end couples that buy a 'wedding-ring' at 'Woolly's': coll.: since ca. 1925.

woop. A rustic simpleton, a 'hick': Aus.: earlier C.20. Ex:-

woop woop (or **W-.**). The country districts: NSW joc. coll.:—1926 ('Jice Doone'). In later C.20, often *the woop woop*. Satirising the Aus. Aboriginal names, so often reduplicatory. Also NZ, where pron. *wop-wop* (Kendall, 1984).—2. Hence, 'the hypothetically most rustic of all rustic townships in Australia' (B., 1959): Aus.: since ca. 1930.

woop-woop pigeon. A kookaburra: Aus.: since ca. 1920. (B., 1942.) See prec.—2. A swamp pheasant: Aus.: since ca. 1925. B., 1943.

woopknacker. A decided 'hard case': NZ: since ca. 1920. Slatter, 'He's a hard shot. Yeah, he's a woopknacker all right.' Arbitrary? P.B.: cf. **whopcacker.**

woosey. Alt. spelling of **woozy**, as in 'A bit woosey round the eyes' (Hunter, 1964), where it = bleary, having the appearance of being 'hung over'. (P.B.)

woozled. Tipsy: ca. 1905–30. Benstead, 1930, 'Collett had a bit of a newt party. Everybody got pleasantly woozled . . .' See **pissed**, and cf.:-

woozy. Fuddled (with drink); muzzy: US (1897), anglicised by Conan Doyle (*OED*) in 1917. ?Ex *woolly* + *muzzy* (or *dizzy* or *hazy*).—2. Hence, dizzy, as from, e.g., a blow on the head, sunstroke, etc.: perhaps orig. Can. (ex US); Brit. by (prob.) ca. 1920. See **woosey.**

Wop; w-. An Italian: adopted, ex US, early 1920s. (George, 1924.) Ex Sp. *guapo*, 'a dandy'—via Sicilian dialect. Thrasher, 1912, 'There is a society of criminal young men in New York City, who are almost the exact counterpart of the Apaches of Paris. They are known by the euphonious name of "Waps" or "Jacks". These are young Italian-Americans who allow themselves to be supported by one or two women, almost never of their own race . . . They form one variety of the many gangs that infest the city.' Hence as adj., and in such extensions as 'an Italian aircraft': 'It's a Wop!': WW2.—2. Hence, an Italian prostitute: Aus.: since ca. 1925.—3. Hence, any prostitute: since ca. 1930, but never very gen. Whence *wop-shop*, a brothel, ob. by 1960. B., 1953.—4. A wireless operator: RAF: since ca. 1930. (Rhodes, 1942.) Ex abbr. W/Op. Cf. next.

wopag. 'An airman of the trade of wireless operator/air gunner' (Jackson): RAF: ca. 1937–43, then ob. Ex the unofficial abbr. *W.Op./A.G.*, the official one being W/O/AG.

wopcacker. See **whopcacker.**

woppity-wop-wop . . . See **whoppity . . .**

word. To warn or to prime (a person): s. >, ca. 1935, coll. Prob. ex *give* (a person) *the word*, to indicate the password. Also Aus., where sometimes elab. *word up* (B., 1941).

words. A wordy dispute or quarrel: coll.: late C.19–20. Christie, 1934, 'What is called in a lower walk of life "words".' P.B.: usu. *have words*, as in 'She and I had words, I'm afraid—and now she's not speaking [sc. to me].'

work. To ply one's trade of prostitution: white-slavers' c. Londres.—2. To *work* a (stolen) cheque book, credit card, etc. is to make fraudulent use of it: c. Dovkants, 1988.

work a door. To ply prostitution by sitting or standing at the door of one's premises: Aus. c.: since ca. 1920. (B., 1953.) Hence, loosely, *door*, a brothel.

work a flanker; . . . a ginger; . . . a ready. See **flanker; ginger, v.; ready.**

work a slinter. To play a mean or illicit trick; tell a false story: Aus. low: C.20. (B., 1942.) See **schlenter.**

work a swindle. To accomplish something by devious or irregular means: RAF: since ca. 1930. Jackson.

work a welt. See **working a welt.**

work it. To 'work one's ticket' (q.v.), for release from the Services: RN: mid-C.20. (*Heart*, 1962.) See quot'n at **shot-away.**—2. Often as exclam., *work it* (occ. *up you*)!: go to the devil with!; expressly, 'You know what you can do with it!'—brutally, 'thrust it up your arse!' (cf. synon. **stuff it!**): low. Also in other grammatical moods; e.g., 'So that's what they intend, is it? Well, they can bloody well work it!' (E.P.; P.B.)

work-out. A wholesale dismissal of employees: lower classes':—1935. Also *slaughter.*

work over, v.; **a work(ing)-over.** To beat up; a beating-up: low: since ca. 1930.

work Pompey. Var., since ca. 1920, of **dodge Pompey.**

work the halls. (Gen. as vbl n.) To steal from hall-stands, having called as a pedlar: c.:—1935 (Hume).

work the mark. To handle or operate mail-bag apparatus: (mail-train) railwaymen's: from ca. 1926. (*Daily Herald*, 5 Aug. 1936.) Ex the Government mark on the bags.

work (one's; occ. the) ticket. To obtain one's discharge from the Army by having oneself adjudged physically unfit: from late 1890s: s. >, ca. 1910, coll. (The phrase *get one's ticket*, to be, in the ordinary way, discharged from the service, is military j.) Wyndham, 1899, 'It is a comparatively easy matter for a discontented man to work his ticket.' In Aus., from ca. 1918, *get a ticket* = to catch a venereal disease (bad cases were dismissed the Service): B., 1942.

workaholic. 'A person having an uncontrollable urge to work incessantly [e.g., E.P.!: P.B.] . . . coined by pastoral counsellor Wayne Oates [ca. 1971]' (Barnhart): adopted, ex US, early 1970s.

worker. A prostitute: Aus. low: later C.20. McNeil.

workhouse. A hard, ill-found ship: nautical. Bowen.

working a welt, pres. ppl and ppl adj. 'Skiving' or 'miking'; 'wangling'—dishonestly contriving—a break from work: Liverpool dockers', hence, many dockers having changed over to the car factories, Liverpool car workers': since ca. 1900 (?earlier), the former; mid-C.20 the latter. Mr Lew Lloyd, the dockers' leader, explains the origin: 'In the old days, if a docker wanted a bit of time off, he used to pretend that the sole [of his boot] had come away from the welt [that part of boot or shoe to which the sole is attached]. He then got time off, ostensibly to go to the cobbler, but in fact usually went for a pint of beer' (*Sun*, 30 Aug. 1976).

working by. Work on the wharves or from wharf to ship: stewards' coll. Gape, 1936.

working for Street, Walker & Co. Out of work, and walking the streets in search of it: Aus.: since ca. 1920. B., 1942.

workingman's solo. A Solo Whist hand (almost) impossible to beat: Aus. card-players'.

workoholic. Perhaps a more logical form of **workaholic**, q.v., since the latter is presumably derived ex *alcoholic*.

works. See **get on** (one's) **works**.

works, the. All the equipment needed for injecting drugs: syringe, spoon, etc.: drugs world: later C.20; adopted ex US. Wyatt, 1973. Ex 'the works' of, e.g., a clock.—2. In *give* (one) *the works*, to give (or inflict) the complete treatment; to cure, as a doctor; or to harm, beat up, or even to kill (occ. here *to give the whole works*, although this phrase too may also be beneficent, as 'Yes, they gave me the whole works, X-ray, heat-treatment, massage—the lot'): adopted, ex US, ca. 1930: s. > coll.—3. As *give* (them) *the works*, to address a political, or 'hot-gospel', meeting: tub-thumpers': since ca. 1936. Perhaps, here, short for 'fire*works*', but prob. ex 2.—4. In, e.g. 'Is that the works?': is that all, is that the whole thing?: Can. (Dickey, 1986.)

Works and Bricks. The Air Ministry Works Directorate, and its successors: RAF coll.: since ca. 1920. (Jackson.) Cf. **Bricks and Sticks**.

worm. A *bookworm*, an ardent student or reader: since mid-C.20. (Petch, 1969.)

worms. (Mostly as nickname.) That rating who, in an RN Establishment, attends to the gardens: since ca. 1910. Ex the worm-casts. P-G-R.—2. In *give* (one's) *works* or **wick**. Baker.—3. Macaroni: RN lowerdeck; schoolchildren's: late C.19–20. Knock; P.B.

worry and strife. A wife: r.s. (Ortzen, 1938.) Much less used than older *trouble and strife*, which it varies.

worry wart. A chronic worrier: N. Am.: since 1920s. (Leech, 1986.)

worse for wear, be (the). Tipsy: coll. (P.B.)

Worst End, the. The West End (London): among those who (e.g. waiters, taxicabmen, 'con' men, whores) go there for profit rather than pleasure: from ca. 1928. I.e. worst for the pleasure-seekers.

worth a bob or two. With ref. to persons, (fairly) wealthy; to things, (fairly) valuable: joc. (envious) coll. In 'After the old man snuffed it, they, and that grotty old cottage, must be worth . . . ' In Hunter, 1981, a police inspector says, 'A few bobs'-worth here, sir', of an expensive-looking house. Still in common use, even though now almost two decades since decimalisation, when the old *bob* (shilling) became 'five pee'. Cf. **couple of bob**.

worthy. Much used as the concomitant of both 'decent fellow' and 'stout fellow': Public Schools'; hence upper classes': ca. 1920–39. Although this usage approximates to that in S.E., yet it may well be classified rather as s. than as coll., for it is glib and somewhat vague. It is also applied to things: e.g. of a remark, one says 'That is not worthy' instead of 'not worthy of you'.—2. Hence, trustworthy and honest and good-natured, but rather dull: middle- and upper-class coll.: since ca. 1944.

wory. Any military reminiscence: Army: since ca. 1950. Ex 'War st*ory*', and thus pronounced. (P.B.) Cf. **warry**.

Wosby. The *W*ar *O*ffice *S*election *B*oard, that all who aspire to an army commission must pass: Army: WW2 and since. A preliminary to 'going on Wosby', for men already operational in the ranks, was *uzby*, the *U*nit *S*election *B*oard (P.B.). Adopted by civilians, as in *spiritual Wosby*, an extended interview and tests for intending clerics.

wossname. A mere written var. of *wassname*, itself a slovening of 'what's his (*or* its) name'. Cf. the writing of *wot* to represent *what*, and:-

wotcher! is the predominant Cockney shape, in C.20, of *what cheer!* as a greeting: coll. Often elab., in C.20, to, e.g., *wotcher cock*, . . . *me old cock-sparrer*, . . . *me old brown son*, etc. + *how's yerself* or *how are yer?*: used other than by genuine Cockneys, joc. coll.; by Cockneys, dial.

would be none the worse for. (Of person or thing) he, it, etc., would be (much) improved by: coll.

wow, be a; rare except in **it's a wow**. To be a great success or most admirable, 'really' excellent: US (1927), partly anglicised by 1929, esp. in theatrical s. Prob. ex a dog's bark: cf. '*howling* success'.

woz. A deliberate mis-spelling of *was*, in juvenile graffiti of the 1970s +, as in '(e.g. Gaz) woz ere' = Gary was here. (P.B.) See **-z**.

wozz. See **wazz**.

Wraf. A member of the *W*omen's *R*oyal *A*ir *F*orce: from 1917: (mainly military) coll. Cf. **Wren**. Disbanded in 1919, the WRAF was re-formed in June 1939 as the Women's Auxiliary Air Force; it again became Royal in Feb. 1949. See also **Waaf** and associated entries.

wrap. Shortening of next, 2. Stockley, 1986, 'Street quantity of drugs (heroin, amphetamine, cocaine) sold in small folded paper bag or foil packet'.—2. See next, 3.

wrap-up, n. A girl willing, ready and available—on a vague yet firm understanding: raffish: since late 1940s. Naughton, 1970, 'I can always accommodate a second wrap-up.' Distinct from a **set-up**, 2.—2. 'Brown paper packet containing cannabis' (Home Office): drugs world: later C.20.—3. 'A flattering account (interchangeable with *rap up*)' (Wilkes): Aus. coll.: since mid-C.20. Occ. just *wrap*.

wrap up (usu. in imperative), v. To cease talking; also, stop making a row or a noisy fuss: Services': since ca. 1930. (Finn-Smith, 1942.) Prob. ex *wrapping up* preparatory to cold-weather departure. L.A., 1978, 'Still current and in widespread use.'—2. To crash-land (an aircraft): RAF: since ca. 1938. Jackson, 'Thus, "I'm afraid I've wrapped her up, sir".' I.e. to cause to *fold up*.—3. (Contrast sense 1.) Only as *wrap up!*, 'a cry of despair at the imbecility of one's superior or at one's own state of boredom' (P-G-R.): Army: since ca. 1935. Cf. **roll on!** and **stroll on!**, used on similar provocation.—4. Thoroughly to understand: R. Aus. AF: WW2. (B., 1943.) Prob. ex **wrapped-up**, q.v.—5. 'To praise (interchangeable with *rap up*)' (Wilkes): Aus. coll.: since ca. 1970. Cf. **wrapped**.

wrapped. Enthralled: Aus.: since ca. 1955. Buzo, 1969, 'Richard took me to a turn [a party] and I was really wrapped.' A sort of emotive blend of *wrapped up* in a subject = *rapture*; not an illiteracy for *rapt*.—2. See:-

wrapped-up. Carefully arranged; carefully prepared; entirely in order: Services': since ca. 1935. H. & P., 'Don't worry; it's all wrapped up!' Often shortened to *wrapped*. Cf. **buttoned up** and **sewn up**.

wrath of God, like the. 'The wrath of God . . . To my children it is just a phrase, like "nothing on earth". I hear Christine and her friends saying that a dress or a play is "like the wrath of God" [i.e. terrible]. It seems to me to be one of the catch-words of 1936' (McKenna, 1937): Society. Still common in Can. at least as late as 1959. (Leechman.) Nor, even in Brit., did it quite disappear; have myself heard it, occ., during the 1950s.—2. Feeling very ill, esp. if from a bad hangover: since ca. 1950. (Sanders.)

wreath of roses. A chancre: lower classes' euph. (*Slang*.) Cf. synon. **ring of roses**.

wreck. A recreation ground: Cockneys'. A deliberate perversion of *rec*.—2. A 'dud' boy: Public Schools': since ca. 1925. (Marples.) Ex *total wreck*.

Wrecker's Retreat, the. The RN School of Navigation: RN: since 1941, merely reminiscent. Granville, 'This building, perhaps the oldest in Portsmouth Dockyard, was destroyed by enemy action during the Hitler War.'

Wren. A member of the Women's Royal Naval Service, which 'came into existence in 1939, taking its name from an earlier organisation estab. between 1917 and 1919' (*Everyman's Encyclopaedia*, 3rd ed.): in WW1, Services' coll.; in and since WW2, gen. coll. and, in the Service, j. Cf. **Waff**, and:-

wren-pecked. Wren-beset; Wren-harassed: RN: 1940+. (Granville.) Poor, *poor* fellow!

Wrenlin. See GREMLINS, in Appx.

wrennery. Quarters or billets of the Wrens: Services' (esp. RN and WRNS). See **Wren**, for dates. H. & P.

wriggle-diggle. Heavy petting; also, copulation; 'a spot of wriggle-diggle': mid-C.20. The girl does the wriggling, the man the digging. (P.B., 1974.) A reduplication more apt than most.

wriggle like a cut snake. To be evasive, shifty; to toady: Aus. B., 1942.

wring (one's) **sock out.** (Of men) to urinate: joc. rather than euph. Cf. synon. **strain** (one's) **greens**; **shed a tear**; etc.

wrinkly. An old person—as applied to anyone over the venerable age of thirty: teenagers', and the underground: later C.20. (Weightman, 1977.) Cf. **groanies/grownies**.

wrist. In *have one off the wrist*, to masturbate: prisons: later C.20. McVicar, 1987.

write-off. A completely wrecked aircraft: orig. RFC, from 1914. (F. & G.) The machine could be written off the inventory as useless.—2. Hence, any machine, vehicle, etc., smashed beyond economic repair: orig. mainly Services' >, in later C.20, insurance, hence motorists', j.—3. Hence, a useless or worthless person, as in 'As a rugger-player, I say he's pretty much of a write-off'—not worth listing: mostly Services': since mid-C.20. (P.B.)

write (one)**self off.** To get killed, esp., through carelessness or impetuousness: RAF: since 1939. Jackson. Cf. prec. and **written off**.

write-up. A eulogistic paragraph or 'feature' or article: journalists' coll.: since ca. 1945.

write (an account) **with a fork.** To charge three times as much: N.T., Aus., since ca. 1925. (Hill, 1951.) Ex a fork's three tines.

written all over. As in 'The job has [e.g. 'Small time Sid'] written all over it', i.e. it is obvious that (e.g. the crime) has been done by him: coll. Cf. **map of England**, 2.

written off. (Of aircraft) damaged, esp. crashed, beyond repair; (or a person) killed, esp. through carelessness: RAF, resp. coll. and, for persons, s.: resp. ca. 1930 and ca.

1939. (Jackson.) Cf. **write-off**. P.B.: by ca. 1950, also Army, and prob. more widespread still; in later C.20, esp. of vehicles, j.

wrong. Silly, foolish; extremely eccentric, or slightly mad: Aus.: since early 1920s. B., 1942, 'I.e., wrong in the head'.—2. In *get* (someone) *wrong*, to mistake his spoken meaning or unexpressed intentions: coll.: since the early 1920s. 'Don't get me wrong, I mean you no harm.'—2. In *get* (a girl or woman) *wrong*, to render her pregnant; also v.i.: N. Country. Mostly among women and girls, as in 'Don't do that, or you'll get me wrong' (render me pregnant).

wrong fount. An ugly human face: printers':—1933 (*Slang*). Ex the technical term. P.B.: also 'a shady kind of fellow' (Rowles, 1948).

wrong with. In *what's wrong with*, what's the objection to?; why not have?: coll.: from early 1920s. Knox, 1925, 'I want to know what's wrong with a game of bridge?' (*OED*).

wrought. 'Wroughts . . . are situations in which something dramatic happens' (Taylor, 1982): later C.20. 'And don't forget. I'm not in on the wrought. I'm there dwelling up; changing up some money' (Ibid.: a con-man on working a bank fraud). See **rort**; but this *wrought* is perhaps rather from 'wrought up' than ex 'riot'. (P.B.)

wuff. To shoot (a person) dead; to blast with gunfire: Guards': 1940–5. (Grinstead, 1946.) Echoic.

Wuggins. See **Woggins**.

wump; occ. **whump.** A hard blow: coll.:—1931 (Lyell). Perhaps a blend of *whack* (or *wallop*) + *clump* (or *thump*).

wurl; yurse. Defective pron. of *well* and *yes*, esp. in emphasis or reflection: C.19–20. Raymond, 1930, 'Many casualties in the battalion? *Wurl*, no—not too bad.' See also **yurse**.

Wyatt Earp. The penis: r.s., on *curp*, itself strictly *kcirp*, back s. (Daniells, 1980.) The influence of 'Westerns'.

Wyckers. Wyclffe Hall, Oxford: undergraduates':—1940 (Marples, 2). The 'OXFORD -ER(S)'.

wylocks. 'Vicious horse; naughty child. "Give the little wylocks his clatters" ' (*M.T.*): market-traders'. Orig.?

X

X. Annoyed, irritated: since ca. 1945: c. >, by 1960, also s. (Cook, 1962). By a pun on S.E. *cross*, n., and *cross*, irritable, angry.

x-chaser. 'A naval officer with high theoretical qualifications' (Bowen): RN: from early C.20. ('Taffrail', 1916.) The *x* is that *x* which figures so disturbingly in mathematics. Also RAF (prob. via RNAS): in a discussion on the theory of flight, 'Damned if I know. Chasing X has never been my strong suit' (Tredrey, 1939). Hence, an ardent mathematician: RN: since ca. 1910. Granville.

X-ray art. 'A form of Aboriginal bark and cave painting which shows internal parts of human and animal anatomy' (B., 1959): Aus. artists' and art-critics' coll.: since ca. 1950. Technically known as *mimi art*.

xawfully. Thanks awfully: slovenly coll.: from ca. 1919. Mackail, 1930, ' "Good-bye, old thing. Good luck, and all that." "Xawfully." ' P.B.: better, ' 'ks awfully.'

X's. (Often *X-es*.) 'Atmospheric or static interference with wireless': wireless-operators', esp. on ships: from ca. 1926. Bowen.

Y

Y, the. The YMCA: Services': WW2. (Jackson.) Used elsewhere since ca. 1919: see, e.g., Archer, 1946. Short for **Y.M.**

Y Dub. The YWCA: since mid-C.20 (?earlier). See:-

Y.M.; Y.W. (Pron. *wy em, wy double you.*) The Young Men's and the Young Women's Christian Association, frequently abbr. *YMCA, YWCA*: coll. P.B.: in Services' coll. these usu. refer to the canteen or the accommodation provided by these organisations, as 'I stayed a night or two at the Y.M.'

yabbie, -y, n. A freshwater crayfish: Aus. coll.: since late C.19. ('Tom Collins', 1903.) Ex Aboriginal. Hence also as v., to fish for them: id. Tennant, 1941.—2. 'Also [as well as 1] a wicket-keeper—well, there is a vague resemblance to a crayfish . . . isn't there?' (Qantas advert., 3 Aug. 1986): Aus.

yachtie. A yachtsman: RN Search & Rescue teams'. *You*, 22 May 1983.

yack, n. Food, esp. in *hard yack* (= hard tack): Aus.: since ca. 1955.

yack, v., often **yak**; in full, **ya(c)kety-ya(c)k.** Both n. and v.: voluble talk; to talk volubly and either idly or stupidly or both: adopted, in the late 1950s, ex US. Clearly echoic of idle chatter: *yack-yack-yack.*—2. Hence, a or to talk, or even a, or to, lecture: since ca. 1962. Early in 1964, the late Nancy Spain, in a *News of the World* article, said, 'I was to yak' [deliver a talk] 'in Spennymoor (or some such place) that night.'

yacker. A catapult: Leicester: earlier C.20. ('Crosstalk', 20 June, 1984.) Ex dial. *yack,* to throw with a jerk.

yackers. Money: teenagers': early 1980s. (Joanna Williamson, 1982.) Ex *akka(s).* Cf. synon. **beans.**

yag. Yttrium *a*luminium *g*arnet: diamond trade coll.: since ca. 1930(?). Lambert, 1975.

yak, yakety-yak. See **yack,** v.

yakker; occ. **yacka, yacker, yakka.** (Correctly **yakka.**) To work; work at: Aus. 'pidgin': late C.19–20. Ex Aboriginal. Morris.—2. Whence as n., hard toil: id. Dennis.—3. Food: Aus. B., 1942.—4. Talk: Aus. (Baker.)—5. Hence, a contract: Aus. rural: since ca. 1925. (Campion.)

Yammie, -y. A Japanese-made *Yamaha* motorcycle, in production since 1954: motorcyclists'. (Dunford.)

Yank. Yankee (n. and adj.): coll.: 1778 (*OED*): in orig. US sense, C.19–20 for '(an) American'; the adj. *Yank* (of the US), app. not before the 1830s. Abbr. *Yankee.*—2. An American motor-car: esp. in the secondhand-car business: since ca. 1945. (Cowdy, 1965.) Cf. next.—3. See BIRD-WATCHERS'; also **yankee shout; Yanks.**

Yank iron. An American motorcycle: motorcyclists': since ca. 1950. (Dunford.)

Yankee. 'Slide hammer. Sometimes called a "slam hammer" [q.v.] . . . or "Yankee" . . . (these types of "push and pull" screwdrivers are often called "Yankees" by English tradesmen)' (Powis): later C.20. Because from USA; or ex the action? Perhaps both. (P.B.)—2. Aus. coll. for *American* in its nuance 'equal for all', as in *Yankee shout,* and *tournament:* since ca. 1930. B., 1943.—3. As *yankee.* 'An increasingly popular form of bet in which four horses are backed in six doubles, four trebles and one accumulator' (Evans, 1983): turf: later C.20.

Yankee-bashing. See **Yanking.**

Yankee dish-up. 'To throw a dirty plate through the open scuttle instead of washing it' (Granville): RN.

yankee shout. A drinking bout or party or rendezvous at which everyone pays for his own drinks: Aus.: 1940+. (B., 1942.) Also *a yank.* Ex next.

yankee tournament. An American tournament (everyone playing everyone else): sporting coll.: since ca. 1930. Baker.

Yanking. 'Popular expression to describe the activities of girls who specialise in picking up American soldiers' (or, come to that, sailors or airmen): since 1943; by 1966, slightly ob. (Tempest, 1950.) P.B.: this activity was known, among WRAC girls in Hong Kong, 1960s, where the scope was ample, as *Yankee-bashing.*

Yanks. Cheap American magazines flooding Brit. bookstalls ca. 1930–9: coll.: since ca. 1930.

yap. A chat: WW1+. Weldon, 1925.

yapper. A Bofors anti-aircraft gun: Army and Civil Defence: 1940+. It 'barks' very loudly.

yappies, the; or **the puppies.** 'The dogs'—greyhound racing or coursing: Aus.: since ca. 1946. (B.P.)

yappy. Foolishly generous; foolish, soft: from ca. 1870. H., 5th ed. Cf.:—2. Among market-traders, it is both n. 'idiot' and adj. 'idiotic'. The adj. may be elab. *yappified. M.T.*

Yarco. A Yarmouth man: nautical. Butcher, 1979.

yard. To 'corral' or 'round up', to get hold of: Can.: since late 1950s. 'We yarded Harry and Alice and tooled off to the dance' (Leechman, 1961).

yard ape. See **curtain-climber.**

Yardies. 'Criminal gangs calling themselves Yardies, who are using the threat of violence to try to gain Mafia style control of black communities in Britain . . . the term . . . originated [from] a word to describe one's home in Jamaica: the yard around the house' (Guardian, 25 Feb. 1988): since ca. 1986. Cf. **Back-ah-Yard.**

Yarmouth. Esp. in *go* (mostly *have gone*) *Yarmouth* or *quite Yarmouth,* to go—chiefly, to have gone—(quite) mad: RN:

earlier C.20. 'From the RN Hospital, Great Yarmouth, where mental cases are treated' (Granville).

Yarmouth bloater. A *motor*-car: r.s.: since ca. 1910. Franklyn, 'Merely a contracted and less derisive form of **tea for two and . . .** [q.v.]'.

yarn. In *have a* (*bit of a*) *yarn with*, simply 'to chat with', e.g. over a drink at a bar: coll. (P.B.) Ex older s. sense, a (long) story, a romance.

yarra. Stupid; eccentric or even crazy: Aus.: since ca. 1910. (B., 1943.) The intensive is '*stone yarra*, completely mad' (B., 1959). 'From the mental asylum at Yarra Bend, Victoria' (Wilkes). Cf. Eng. **winnick** and **Yarmouth**.

Yarra-bankers. Loafers and down-and-outs idling on the banks of the Yarra River: Melbourne coll.: B., 1942.—2. Melbourne soap-box orators: Melbournites': since ca. 1914. (B., 1943.) On the banks of the Yarra river.

yasmé; Yasmé Villa. See PRISONER-OF-WAR SLANG, §7, in Appx.

yassoo (occ. **yasu**). A greeting among troops serving, or having served, in Cyprus: since ca. 1950. Ex Greek *giasou!*, an all-purpose word for 'Hello', 'Goodbye', 'Cheers!' Sometimes elab. into mock Scots: *yassoo the noo!* (P.B.)

Yawpies. See **Jaapies**.

year dot, the. A date long ago: coll.: late C.19–20. Lit., 'the year 0'. Esp. as in 'Ganpat', 1933, 'He's been in every frontier show [battle or skirmish] since the year dot.' Cf. 'I reckon *he* was born in the year dot, that 'orse was' (Ridge, 1895). At that point in historical times which lies between the last year BC and the first year AD. The var. *in the year one* occurs in 'Taffrail', 1916.

-yearer. A pupil in his first, second, etc., year: Public School coll.: late C.19–20. A. Waugh, 1934, 'He was a third yearer at a public school.' P.B.: in later C.20 comprehensive schools the suffix is *-years*, as 'I'm taking the third years for maths', or 'She was one of the third years'.

yearling. A boy that has been at the School for three terms: Charterhouse. There, a new boy is a *new-bug*; a boy that has been at the School for a term is an *ex new bug*; for two terms, an *ex new bug*: the second and the third are rather j. than eligible.—2. Simply a boy in his first year: Charterhouse. (Sanders.)

yegg. A travelling burglar or safe-breaker: US c., anglicised by 1932, as s., among cinema-'fans'. (Irwin; *COD*, 1934, Sup.) Possibly ex Scottish and English dial. *yark* or *yek*, to break.

Yehudi; usu. in pl. A Jew: Army officers' (esp. in Palestine): since ca. 1941. Ex a Jewish given-name.

yell. A (tremendous) joke: mostly theatrical: since late 1950s. 'Of course Harry made it sound a bit of a yell' (Marsh, 1967). Cf. synon. **hoot, scream**, etc.

yellow, n. (Pl. *yellow*.) A pound sterling: c.: from ca. 1910. Brandon, 1936, 'Five hundred "yellow" to pay for it.' Ex the colour of a sovereign.—2. Ordinary-issue yellow soap: RN lowerdeck coll.: (?mid-) C.19–20. Goodenough, 1901.—3. See **baby's yellow**.

yellow, adj. Cowardly though perhaps not app. so: coll.: from ca. 1910. Orig. US; prob. ex *yellow* as applied to a writer on the *yellow press* (1898).

yellow-back. 'A gob of phlegm' (B., 1942): Aus. low.

Yellow Belly, or **y.b.** A coward: low: from ca. 1925. Ex US.—2. A Central American: Brit. and Am. in C. America: late C.19–20.—3. A Japanese: Aus.: 1942–5, then historical. Cusack, 1953.—4. A Yorkshire and Lancashire Railway tank engine: railwaymen's: ?ca. 1910–25. (*Railway*.) Cf.:—5. 'These trains [connecting Leicester and Nottingham with Norwich and Lowestoft, *via* the Fen country] introduced the [Midland and Great Northern] "Yellowbellies" (a nickname derived from their distinctive livery) to the East Midlands' (Anderson, 1973): railwaymen's: late C.19–early 20. P.B.: but Fenlanders have been known as *Yellow Bellies* since C.18.

yellow doughnut. The small collapsible dinghy carried by modern aircraft: RAF: since ca. 1936. H. & P., 'It looks like a doughnut from the air'.

yellow fever. Spy-mania: Singapore: ca. 1930–41. How enthusiastically we Britons succeeded in shutting our eyes to the obvious danger! Cf. **yellow belly**, 3.

yellow-jacket. (Usu. pl.) Nembutal: drugs c. (Stockley, 1986.) US since—1952 (Spears).

Yellow-Legs, the. The Royal Canadian Mounted Police: Can., esp. in the Yukon: since ca. 1950. Hunt, 1974. ?Ex yellow gaiters or some such part of their uniform.

yellow peril; or with capitals. A Gold Flake cigarette: from ca. 1910. Ex the yellow packets, with a pun on journalistic *y.p.*, the Chinese menace. P.B.: the scare about the expansion of the East Asian races was whipped up in Germany in the 1890s. Since this first(?) s. application the term has been applied joc. to all sorts of things with 'yellow' connections; the next four senses are by no means exhaustive.—2. A trainer aircraft: RAF: WW2. (Jackson, 1943.) In the 1930s–40s all RAF training planes were painted overall yellow.—3. Any slab cake that, yellowish and not notably edible, is served in institutions or sold in canteens: Services', school children's, etc.: since early C.20.—4. A haddock: RN: since mid-C.20.—5. A traffic warden: motorcyclists': later C.20. (Dunford.) Ex yellow flashes on the uniform.—6. Hepatitis: drugs c. Cutland, 1985.—7. See **bolshies**.

yellow stuff. Gold: c.: mid-C.19–20. B. & L.—2. Hence, gold stolen by miners from the company's mine they're working: Aus. miners'. Casey, 1945.

yellow wellie. 'A civilian "Sunday sailor" [yachtsman type]; from the yellow Wellington boots worn by this sort: usu. derog.' (Knight, 1984): Portsmouth professional seamen's.

yelper. 'Railway dog used for catching rats' (McKenna, 1; he explains why certain areas of railway property are infested with rats): railwaymen's.

Yen, the. The *Yorkshire Evening News*: journalists': since ca. 1933.—2. As *yen*, a male homosexual: Liverpool street arabs': late C.19–20. *Arab*.

yen(h)ams. Free cigarettes: mostly Cockneys': from ca. 1925. (E.P.) '*Yenams* is Yiddish for "his", and in Hebrew slang also it is used for "free cigarettes" ' (Mindel, 1971). A straight 'borrowing' by the Cockneys.

yen(n)ep. A penny: back s.:—1851 (Mayhew, 1); still current, late 1970s, (Powis, who spells it *yennap*).

yer actual (pron. *ackch'll* or *acksh'll*). Truly somebody or something, with *yer* (your) as familiar, button-holing, *the* —the real or true; popularised by Peter Cooke, mid-1960s, and by the character Alf Garnett in the very successful TV comedy-series 'Till Death Do Us Part'. For instance, Philip Jenkinson in *Radio Times*, 1 Mar. 1975, 'yer actual cast in Bill Naughton's very funny play'; and P.B., 1975 (to me), 'I heard an actress on the radio not long ago describing how she had been presented to "yer actual royals", i.e., the Royal Family.' I didn't particularly notice it until the early 1970s, but suspect that it has been a Cockneyism since (at a guess) ca. 1955.

yes(-)girls. Girls very easily persuaded to participate in sexual intimacy: since ca. 1960. After:-

yes man, yes-man, yesman. One who cannot say 'no': coll.: from 1933. (*COD*, 3rd ed., Sup. 1934; Langmaid, *The Yes Man*, 1935.) Ex American *yes man*, a private secretary, an assistant (film-)director, a parasite. P.B.: but the US sense, 'a sycophantic parasite', has prevailed in Brit. since mid-C.20.

yet to be. Usu., costing nothing; occ., unrestrained: r.s., on *free*. Franklyn 2nd.

yewie. See **U-turn**.

Yid. (Also *yid*, and in *half a yid*.) A sovereign, £1; a half-sovereign, 10 shillings: Aus. r.s., on *quid*: earlier C.20. (Stivens, 1951.) Cf. **fiddley**.

Yiddified. Anti-Semitic: Jewish: since 1934. I.e. Yiddish *Yiddenfeint*, itself = *Yid* + Ger. *Feind*, an enemy. Therefore, lit., inimical to the 'Yids'. Possibly in ironic contrast with the usual sense.

Yiddisher fiddle. A minor cheating or illegality: since ca. 1925; by 1960, ob. Franklyn 2nd.

Yiddisher piano. A cash-register: Cockney street-boys': from ca. 1910. Cf. Aus. synon. **Jewish pianola**.

Yiddle. A Jew; esp. a Jewish boxer: mainly pugilistic: from ca. 1930. An elab. of **Yid**.

Yidsbury. See **Abrahampstead**.

yike. A hot argument; a quarrel; a fight: Aus. low: since ca. 1920. (B., 1942.) A perversion of *fight*?

yikes! An exclam. of surprise or excitement or shock or pain: Aus., adopted, ca. 1945, ex US, and common esp. among children. Ex *yoicks!*—or is it a euph. for *Christ* (cf. *crikey!*). P.B.: in later C.20 some Brit. use also, ex US comics and TV cartoons.

Yim, Yoe and Yesus. Three knaves: Aus. poker-players': since ca. 1930. B., 1953.

yimkin (Arabic, anglicised as *yimpkin*). Perhaps: Brit. Forces in Middle-East: WW1 and 2. F. & G., WW1; Sanders, 1967: 'Expressive of extreme scepticism. "When Tunis falls, we're all going home, yimp-kin!" '—of WW2.

yip, n. 'It's the moment that all sports stars dread—when victory is snatched away from them because they make a silly mistake. Missing an open goal . . . dropping a simple catch . . . These moments of failure are known in the sports business as "yips". . . . [The word] was first used by golfers when they failed to get a simple putt into the hole—and is now used worldwide in every sport' (*Radio Times*, 15 June 1985).

yip, v.i. To inform, to 'split': Liverpool street arabs': late C.19–mid-20. (*Arab.*) Derogatory comparison with a small dog's noise, a thinning of *yap*. Cf. **yop**.

yippee! An exclam. of delight: since ca. 1930. (Michie, 1940.) R.C., 1976, confirms *SOD*'s 'US': 'Much earlier in US, where it was a variant of *whoopee*—both may have originated as cowboys' cries for moving cattle.' Cf.:-

yippee beans. Baked beans: Aus. Army: early 1960s. As L/Cpl Dick Shaeffer explained it to me: 'That's all cowboys eat!' Cf. prec. (P.B.)

yo-yo children. 'Children who become pawns in a violent matrimonial battle and are constantly changing home' (Barefoot, 1977): social workers': later C.20.

yob. A boy: back s.:—1895 (H., 1st ed.).—2. Hence, a youth: from ca. 1890.—3. ?Hence, a lout, a stupid fellow (rarely girl or woman): low (orig. East End). Lyons, 1908; F. & G. By ca. 1930, fairly gen. London s.; by ca. 1960, widespread and gen. See quot'n at **scrote**.—4. 'A raw recruit; a very much countrified airman (cf. **swede**)' (Partridge, 1945): RAF: since ca. 1937. Earliest dictionary-recording: Jackson, 1943. Ex senses 1 and 3.

yobbo. A post-1910 var. of **yob**, 3. (London *Evening News*, 7 Mar. 1938; Hodge, 1939.) P.B.: Eager, 1922, has *yobo*. In later C.20, *yob* (sense 3) is often thought of as a shortening.—2. Hence, an arrogant and resentful, loutish and violent Teddy boy: low, mostly London: since ca. 1948. An extension of *yob*, as Anglo-Irish *boyo* is of S.E. *boy*. P.B.: in later C.20 generic for any gang-lout, be he Teddy-boy, mod, rocker, skinhead or any other of that type. And, by mid-1980s, 'the international word for Brit' (*LAM*, 4 Feb. 1986, article on skiers' j.).

yock. An eye: c. and market-traders'. (*Gilt Kid*, 1936; *M.T.*) Directly ex Romany *yok*.—2. See:-

yog. A Gentile: East London back s., on *goy* 'Pronounced *yock* for euphony' (the *Leader*, Jan. 1939)—but Powis lists 'Yock-ele: East End Yiddish for Christian (commoner than "goy"), often used in a slightly derogatory sense.'—2. (Also spelt *yogg.*) 'Fire (in the hearth)' (*M.T.*): market-traders'. Ex Romany.—3. Yoghurt; a carton, or a helping of yoghurt: domestic; students'; etc.: since ca. 1955.

yogis, the. The uniformed staff (commissionaires, security staff, *et al.*) at Nottingham University: early 1970s. Ex the popular US cartoons featuring the amiable 'Yogi Bear'.

yoke. A riding horse, whether ordinary or racehorse: Anglo-Irish: latish C.19–20. Joyce, 1916, 'I couldn't get any kind of

a yoke to give me a lift.' Cf. **green-yoke**.—2. Hence, by metonymy, a horse-drawn carriage: id. Joyce, 1922.—3. (?Hence), an apparatus; almost any gadget: Anglo-Irish: since ca. 1925. Fitzgerald, 1958, applies it to a revolver.

yomp. 'Earlier this month [May 1982] . . . the *Daily Telegraph*'s man in the Falklands report[ed] that British troops were "yomping" towards Port Stanley—"marching, humping anything up to 120lb of equipment and all the arms needed for attack at the end of the trek" ' (Silverlight, 1982): RM. The picturesque term of course soon > a vogue-word, and its orig. meaning considerably loosened, to the extent that the *Guardian* could, 24 Oct. 1982, write of the miners' president doing 'a fortnight's yomp round Britain, campaigning for a "yes" vote [in a forthcoming ballot on pay, etc.]'. J.S. suggests ex Scandinavian pron. of *jump*; I prefer a perversion of *hump*. Cf. **trog** in this sense. Poss. ex Scandinavian rally-drivers' term for driving over rough country; this is the view held by the Oxford Word and Language Service. (P.B.)

yonks. Ages; an indefinitely long time; often in *yonks ago* or *it'll take yonks before* . . . : perhaps orig. Army, in Cyprus, where I first heard it in 1957; since > widespread, esp. student use. I propose ex 'years, months and weeks'; my contemporary at the Signals Regiment in Cyprus, Capt. E.W. Bishop, prefers a telescoping of *donkey's years*. (P.B.)

yoof, yufe. A person; also used voc.: Leicestershire teenagers': later 1970s. (McPheely, 1977.) A deliberate mispron. of *youth*; cf. Hampshire 'a rare youth' (rhymed with *south*) of mid-C.20. (P.B.)

yop. To tell tales, to inform on someone: Glasgow schools'. A *yop* or *yopper* is an informer. (Munro, 1985.) Cf. **yip**, v.

yorer. An egg: market-traders'. *M.T.*

Yorkshire Penny Bank. 'Wank [q.v.]. Usually in the sense of "not worth a . . . " rather than masturbation' (Daniells, 1980): r.s. Cf. synon. **Barclay's Bank**.

Yorkshire tyke. (Often shortened to *Yorkshire*.) A microphone: r.s., on *mike*: since ca. 1945. (Bower, 1957.)

you. Short for next, 1: since ca. 1910. Kersh, 1941.

you and me. Tea: r.s. (F. & G.; Powis.) Cf. older synon. *Rosy Lea*. Powis glosses it as 'the evening meal: "I'm off for my you and me." '—2. A urination: id. On *pee*.—3. A pea: Aus. r.s.

you reckon. Either as statement or as question, with some degree of incredulity or irony implied: coll.: since (?)ca. 1930. (P.B.)

you ring the bell. You're accepted by the chaps: Services' (esp. RAF): since 1939. (H. & P.) See **ring a bell**.

young blood. A youthful and vigorous member of a political party: political coll.

young fogey. A man below the age of about 40 who deliberately acts, dresses, and appears to think like someone of the previous generation: journalistic s. > gen. coll.: 1980s. See **yuppie**. Deliberate opp. to much earlier *old fogey*.

young kipper. A very poor meal: East End of London: earlier C.20. Punning the Jewish holy day, *Yom Kippur*.

young strop. (Gen. pl.) A newly joined ordinary seaman: nautical. (Bowen.) Cf. **stropper, -py**.

your. A coll. 'personalising' and familiarising, humanising, of the subject, as in ' "Rain coming down in your genuine buckets" ' for mock comic overtones (L.A., 1977). This usage—Cockney, I think, in origin—has prob. existed since late or, even, mid-C.19, but it has, since early 1970s, > much more widely used because of its popularisation by the TV comedy series, 'Steptoe and Son'. P.B.: see also **yer actual**.

Yous, occ. **youse.** (Pron. *yews*.) You: dial > Services' coll.: late (?mid-) C.19–20. Lit., *you* + *-s*, the sign of the pl. With this illiteracy, cf. *you-uns* and the US *you-all* and *yous guys*, all = pl. you.

yow. See **keep yow**.

yowl. The exhaust note of a twin two-stroke motorcycle engine: motorcyclists'. (Dunford.) Cf.:-

Yowler. The Scott two-stroke motorcycle, in production 1909–50: motorcyclists'. (Dunford.) Cf. prec., a derivative.

yoyo. A fool, an idiot, as in 'Don't be a yoyo' (Mackenzie, 1980): police coll. (? more widespread): later C.20.

yuck!, yuk! An exclam. of disgust: since early 1960s. Ex the sound of vomiting, and perhaps an intensification of *ugh!* Whence *yuck-yuck*, unpalatable food: schoolchildren's. B.P., 1969, notes use of the exclam. in Aus. Hence *yuck*, and derivative *yucky*, adj. = revolting or nauseating (e.g. of food, a stench, etc.); hence, unduly or excessively sentimental. '15-year old Brenda de Wilde . . . provides some non-yucky juvenile appeal' (Jenkinson, 1975). *The Times*, 12 Oct. 1976, spelt it *yukky*. E.P.; R.S.; P.B.

yug. Deviation from intended flight-path: RAF aircrews': later C.20. *Phantom*, 1979: 'a small "yug" develops which whiplashes down the line [of aircraft] and I . . . fight to damp out the oscillations.'

Yugers. Yugoslavia: prob. since ca. 1941. By 'the OXFORD -ER(*s*)'. Ob. by 1970s.

yuk!, yukky. See **yuck!**

yuletide log(s). Dog(s): r.s.: later C.20. Normally abbr. *Yuletide*(*s*); sometimes rendered *Christmas log*(*s*). (Hillman, 1974.)

yum-yum! Excellent; first rate: orig. and mostly low and juvenile:—1890 (B. & L.). Ex *yum-yum!*, an exclam. of animal satisfaction (with, e.g., exquisite or delicious food).—2. Hence, as n.: love-letters: RN: since ca. 1920. H. & P.; Granville.

yummy. Delicious, scrumptious, of food; attractive, of e.g., a dress, a handsome male: mostly children's and feminine: later C.20. Ex prec.

yunk. A piece, a portion; a lump: Aus.: since ca. 1910. (B., 1943.) Ex Aboriginal? P.B.: or simply a corruption of S.E. *hunk*. Cf.:-

yunk of dodger. A slice of bread: Aus.: since ca. 1919. (B., 1959.) Cf. prec., and see **dodger**, 4.

yuppie. Perhaps the most obtrusive and contagious of all the vogue unconventional English terms coined in the 1980s, and it came inexorably—and inevitably—from New York. Young, 1985, 'The letters [acronyms] and labels invented by people-watchers to describe the under-25s today—Yuppies, . . . Sloane Rangers, Young Fogies—share one common characteristic [rather, the people so labelled do]: the abandonment of youth by the young. A Yuppie is someone who tries to be like his older brother; a Sloane is someone who tries to be like his [but Sloane Rangers are essentially female] families; and a Young Fogey is someone who tries to be like his grandparents.' Rimmer, 1986, 'When the term [*yuppie*] first surfaced in America around 1983, it was used to identify a new breed of young, ambitious, obsessively hard-working high-fliers in finance, advertising, the hi-tech industries or the professions. It came from "young urban professional", though many wrongly thought the "u" stood for "upwardly mobile" (you occasionally hear people referring to "yumpies").' UK *yuppies* are sometimes referred to as *Thatcher's children*, as they appear to embody the ideals attributed to the Prime Minister, Mrs Margaret Thatcher. The term *yuppie* is still as popular (1988) but is becoming threadbare. It soon > adj., as in, e.g.:-

yuppie deaf-aids. A Sony Walkman (and imitations), a miniature, personal cassette-player with light-weight earphones. (Raybold, 1987.)

yurse. See **wurl**. Raymond, 1930, ' "We're *for* it, boys, if you arst me . . . *Yurse*," he concluded with rich appreciation, "that means we're for it." ' P.B.: this is one of the many phonetic renderings of the different dial. or slovenly forms of *yes* that E.P. included in earlier edd. of this *Dict*., e.g., *yeah, yep, yum, yus*(*s*), etc.

Y

Z

-z. During the 1970s, particularly, it was fashionable among teenagers to truncate one's forename to it first open syllable, and add a *z*; thus Gary > *Gaz*, Jeremy > *Jez*, Sharon > *Shaz*, etc. Popular graffiti stated that '(e.g. Gaz) woz ere'. Just as common, by the mid-1980s, was the graffito, e.g. 'Jez 4 Shaz', where *4* by a visual pun replaces the traditional pierced heart symbol of true love. (P.B.)

zac, zack. Sixpence: Aus. and NZ: since ca. 1890; ob. by 1977 (Wilkes). Orig. *zack*; in C.20 usu., but not always, *zac*. Hence *not worth a zack*, utterly worthless: Aus. Perhaps a perversion of *six*; but cf. Dutch *zaakje*, 'small affair'.—2. Hence, a six-month prison sentence: Aus. c. B., 1942.

zaftig. See zoftig.

zambuck. 'A first-aid man in attendance at a sporting contest' (B., 1943): Aus.: since ca. 1925. Ex a famous embrocation. Ob. by 1977 (Wilkes).

zap, n. Impact; sting; effectiveness, of article, book, play, etc.: adopted, ex US, early 1970s. (*Daily Telegraph*, 26 July 1973.) Ex the next, v.—2. A self-adhesive sticker badge, esp. one sold for charity, 'zapped' on to one's coat by the vendor: heard at Duxford Air Show, 1982. (Huston.)

zap, v. To defeat heavily, perhaps orig. in boxing, hence in any activity: adopted, ca. 1966, ex US. (Janssen, 1968; W. & F.) Ex:—2. To strike, or punch, heavily; hence, to criticise with almost inhuman severity: adopted, ca. 1967, ex US. Echoic. *DCCU*.—3. Usu. in jest (?rather, 'sick' humour), to kill (orig., however, to shoot (someone), esp. to shoot dead): again ex US, 1968 (Wolfe). It occurs in the song 'The Continuing Story of Bungalow Bill', part of the Beatles' 'White Album', released in Nov. 1968 (Janssen). P.B.: the word became hideously familiar in late 1960s–earlier 70s from its use by the American Forces in Vietnam and their efforts to 'zap Charlie Cong' [their Communist opponents there]. It prob. orig. in the 'sound-effects' of US 'comic' magazines; cf. zot.—4. To destroy an entire computer program: computer criminals' c. *Telegraph Sunday Mag.*, 10 June 1984.

zap over. To change one's mind, allegiance, etc. very rapidly, as in 'Often you get very respectable pin-striped men who zap over and buy something very occult' (*Observer* colour sup., 1 Oct. 1972.).

zappy. Full of impact on the senses, as in 'It's an absolutely marvellous, zappy series' (a critic, on BBC Radio 'Kaleidoscope', 10 Mar. 1983): early 1980s. Prob. adopted ex US, and ex *zap*, to strike or kill.

zeck. Var. of zac, 2. B., 1942.

zeds. Sleep: RM. (*Mail on Sunday*, 8 Nov. 1987.) Cf. **push up Z's**, and **zizz**, n. and v. Hence *zed out*, to fall asleep.—2. Depressant drugs': drugs c. (Hibbert, 1983.) Ex 1. Hence

clock up some zeds (BBC Radio 4, 'The Archers', 17 June 1988), to get some sleep.

zeiger. See Jewish piano, 2.

zen. '(Instant Zen) Lysergic Acid Diethylamide (LSD 25) (US)' (Home Office): drugs world: later C.20.

zep; rarely zepp. (Gen. with capital.) A *Zeppelin* airship: coll.: 1915, Pope, 'The night those Zeps bombarded town' (*OED*).

Zeppelins. 'Railway canteen sausages' (McKenna, 1); cf. *Zeppelin(s)* (or *Zepps*) *in a cloud* or *in a fog* or *in a smoke screen*, sausage(s) and mashed potatoes: resp.; orig. Army, since ca. 1917 at latest, > gen. lower-class or joc. s. and still, 1983, not quite † (F. & G.; Lawrence, for the RAF, ca. 1925); RN, from ca. 1917 (Bowen); Army > gen. (Allingham, 1931).

ziff. A beard: Aus., orig. Army: since WW1. Downing, 1919 (Wilkes).—2. See ziph.

zift. No good; inferior; ineffectual: Army. Arabic for 'pitch, tar, dirt'. (L.A.) Perhaps the E. *zift* contracts Ar. *zefut*, weak. (McQueen.)

zig. See catch the zig.

zilch. Nothing: RAF: since ca. 1948. W. & F., 1960, define the US meaning as 'gibberish', hence presumably 'nonsense', and remark 'Never common'; but *6,000 Words*, 1976, defines it as 'nothing, zero' and states, 'Origin unknown'. R.C., 1976, 'Orig., I think, US. In this sense ['meaningless language'] it dates from at least ca. 1930. Perhaps Yiddish— or pseudo-Yiddish double-talk.' Not German, to judge by its absence from the admirable 1972 ed. of Wildhagen & Heraucourt *German–English Dictionary*. It would, therefore, appear that Mr. Claiborne's 'pseudo-Yiddish' could well be right, and than my orig. 'wild guess', that *zilch* could be a blend of *zero* + *nil* + *nichts*, although prob. condemned by the professional philologists, may not, after all, be so very 'wild'.

zinfandel. Grave trouble, esp. as jail: Can., esp. Brit. Columbia: since (?)ca. 1950. 'There was the prisoner of the morning, deep in the zinfandel again' (St Pierre, 1970). Orig.? When a word is orig. underworld, the etym. can be almost impossible to establish. There is a Californian grape so named, itself presumably ex the original grower's name.

zing, n. Sex-appeal: coll.: adopted, ex US, ca. 1943. Echoic: it 'rings a bell'. Cf. **oomph**.—2. Earlier, however, it has been current in the Guards Regt for 'vigour, energy'. Kersh, 1941, records it as having been used in 1940 by a PT instructor, 'I'll soon get that paleness off your faces and put some zing into those limbs.' Cf.:-

zing, v. 'Mostly their minds are zinging with the alert restlessness and near tremor of methedrine or several yellowbellies'

516

(Stuart, 1971); i.e., presumably, a sort of 'electric singing': ex US. (P.B.)

zip. An echoic word indicative of the noise made by (say) a bullet or a mosquito in its passage through the air: coll.: 1875 (Fogg: *OED*).—2. Hence, adj., as in *zip* (lightning) *fastener*: 1925 (*SOD*): coll. >, by 1930, S.E. Also *zipper*, n.: from ca. 1926: coll. >, by 1930, S.E.

ziph. That ancient linguistic aberration which consists in saying, e.g., *shagall wege gogo* for *shall we go*.

zipper. See **zip**.

zipper (**up** one's) **lip.** Widespread N. Am. var., since mid-C.20, of **button** (**up** one's) **lip.** (Leech, 1986.)

zippo. Nothing: 'He's the man from nowhere. I have absolutely zippo on him,' admitted Mr Peter Hennessy of the Institute of Contemporary British History [concerning the new Director General of Security Services]' (*Observer*, 17 Jan. 1988). Cf. synon. **zilch**, and *zippo* as brandname of a cheap, expendable cigarette-lighter.

zippy. Lively, bright; energetic, vigorous: coll.: 1923 (Wodehouse: *OED* Sup.). Ex **zip**.—2. Hence, fast, speedy: since ca. 1930. 'My idea . . . was to get a zippy load into Richon, and then move on to T.A.' (Jeffries, 1958).

zit. An acne pimple or spot: teenagers': 1982. (Burt.) Barnhart, 2, cites US use in 1979.

zizz, n. A rest period: Services': since ca. 1925. (H. & P.) RN var., WW2, *dizz*. Echoic ex the hissing and whistling noises made by those who fall off to sleep; but more prob. deriving ex the fact that newspaper cartoons (e.g. Felix) have long used a string of *z*'s issuing from the mouths of their somnolent characters. Cf. **zeds**.

zizz, v. To sleep: orig. mostly RAF, since ca. 1930; by 1940, via the FAA, it was fairly common in the RN (Granville); by 1950 > fairly gen. Ex prec.

zizz-pud(ding). A heavy suet-pudding: RN: since ca. 1940. Granville, 'Because of its sleep-inducing properties'.

zizzer. A bed: Services', esp. RAF: ca. 1930–50. Ex **zizz**, n., v.

zizzy. (Of, e.g., a tie or a pullover, or of material, fabric, patterns in general) gaudy; bizarre; angular and very brightly coloured: from early 1970s. (L.A., 1976.) Prob. ex streaks of lightning (P.B.).

zob. To curse, and to exchange abuse: RN. Perhaps ex Maltese. Brock, who adds that there was a gunroom—or junior officers' messroom—game called *zobbing*, from a Maltese game called *zob*.

zobbit. An officer: RAF lower ranks': later C.20. (Farley, 1967.) Mindel, 1971, 'From Arabic *dabat*, also pronounced *zabat*, an officer'.

zoftig. 'Yiddish term literally meaning "juicy". Often used to describe a curvaceous and attractive woman. Not used in mixed company, but not completely taboo' (Powis, 1977, spelling *zaftig*). By 1981 > fairly gen., and with wider application. Cf. **lush**, adj., 1. (P.B.)

zombie. A conscript: Can. Army: WW2. Cf.:—2. A Can. 'Home Guard' not allowed to serve outside N. America: ca. 1940–5. 'After the Voodoo cult which insists that dead men can be made to walk and act as if they were alive' (*Daily Express*, 16 Sep. 1943).—3. 'A "zombie" as the trade calls suspicious unidentified [flying] objects' (*Listener*, 29 July 1982): air traffic controllers' s. verging on j.: later C.20.—4. See:-

zombies. (Rare in sing.) Policewomen: c., since ca. 1949; then, since ca. 1952, also police s. (Carr, 1956.) Cf. prec.—2. Basutoland and Bechuanaland companies of Pioneers in E. Africa and Near East: Army: ca. 1940–6.

zone, the. 'The coveted promotion zone, the goal of the two-and-a-half striper. If one is outside the zone one is said to have "been" ' (Granville): RN officers': since ca. 1925. Compare the Army's **sweat on the top line**. P.B.: the usage spread to the Army. I remember, as a Warrant Officer 2 in the late 1960s, being told by a visiting Brigadier, 'You're in

the zone, y'know—you're in the zone.' I didn't know, and the phrase was new to me at the time.

zonked. Extremely intoxicated, on alcohol or drugs: adopted, at first by teenagers, in Can., mid-1960s, (Leechman); in UK, late 1960s, ex US (Janssen, 1968). Either echoic or arbitrary (*DCCU*). The v. *zonk* is recorded by Wolfe, 1968. Hence, in 1970s, > gen., as in 'Getting zonked by the Holy Spirit is a confusing experience at first . . . ' (Canon Michael Green, of Oxford, quoted in *The Times*, 30 Jan. 1980, under the headline 'Oxford faces a zonking from the Holy Spirit'). Cf.:-

zonked(-)out. Drug-high, esp. on a hallucinogen or a psychedelic: adopted, ca. 1968, ex US, at first by addicts and then by teenagers in general. Janssen remarks, 1968, that the term implies a long euphoric, followed by a comatose, period.—2. Hence, merely deeply asleep, as from physical exhaustion: later 1970s. (P.B.)

zonks. A superlative, as in 'People have been here for zonks of years' (BBC archaeological programme 'Hot Air', 4 July 1982). Cf. **yonks**.

Zoo, zoo, the. The Montreal immigration hall for those immigrants who wish to return to their own country: Can.: from ca. 1929. Ex the variety of dress and language.—2. 29th Armoured Division's name for 'the funnies', q.v.: ca. 1942–5. P-G-R.—3. As *zoo*, zoology: schoolboys' and -girls': since ca. 1925.

zoo box. A messing van: railwaymen's. *Railway*.

zoom. An abrupt hauling-up and forcing-up of an aeroplane when it is flying level: aviation. Also, and slightly earlier, a v.i. Both, 1917 (*Daily Mail*, 19 July: *OED*). Ex *zoom*, 'to make a continuous low-pitched humming or buzzing sound' (*OED*).—2. Hence, as v.i., to 'make a hit'; v.t. to boost by publicity: mid-C.20.—3. A mixture of cocaine, heroin and amphetamine which is either sniffed or injected: drugs c. Stockley, 1986.—4. See **beetle**, v.

zoomer. A member of an aircrew: R Aus. AF: WW2. (B., 1943.) Ex prec., 1.

zoon-bat. Funny-looking. See CANADIAN . . . , in Appx.

zooped (up). Applied to anything enhanced, 'tarted up', q.v.: teenagers': early 1980s. (Joanna Williamson, 1982.) Ex *souped up*, itself from S.E. 'supercharged'.

zoot canary. A fashion model (the person): beatniks' and teenagers': ca. 1959+. (Anderson.) Ex:-

zoot suit. A flashy suit of clothes: adopted, ca. 1950, from US. Mexican immigrant youths in California were among the first to affect the fashion: Terkel, 1984, has a section on the 'Zoot-suit riots' in Los Angeles, 1943, when US servicemen fought pitched battles with the young Mexicans. Leechman comments thus: This is a bit complicated. In the first place, the New York ruffians corresponding to the Teddy-boys pronounce 'suit', as 'soot', rhyming with 'boot', not as we do, rhyming with 'cute'. When zoot suits became fashionable, it was 'the thing' to duplicate words, thus the 'zoot soot', which had a fashionable 'drape shape'. R.C., 1976, 'The original zoot suit, popular among "tough" adolescents in US, 1940s, consisted of a long jacket with immensely padded shoulders, its skirts reaching halfway down the thighs (the "drape shape"), and baggy trousers with pleats at waist (a "reet pleat") and sharply pegged cuffs. It was said of the true "zoot suiter" that he had to grease his feet to get his pants on.'—2. 'Special wind- and water-proof clothing which, issued to the crews of armoured vehicles in Europe in Nov. 1944, could also be used as sleeping bags' (Sanders): late 1944–5. P.B. This sense shows an earlier Brit. awareness of the term, prob. borrowed from US servicemen; E.P.'s '1950' in sense 1 should, I think, be amended to 'ca. 1945'—as a schoolboy I knew about zoot suits in the later 1940s.

zot. 'Like **zap** [q.v.], a very useful import from USA, principally, I think, from the excellent cartoons of Johnny Hart; used to express suddenness of movement, a swift surprise strike, as of lightning. Sometimes used alone simply as a very expressive noise, sometimes as a verb: "There I was, zotting down the motorway at a rate of knots, when all of a sudden there was this fuzz . . . " ' (P.B., 1974): since ca. 1965. Purely echoic.

zowie. 'A new import from San Francisco, meaning hippy language' (Fryer, 1967): hippies': since (?May) 1967. In US s., since ca. 1920 (Lewis, 1922), *zowie* has signified 'energy' or 'zest' or the two combined (W. & F.); itself ex the exclamatory *zowie!*, *biff!* or *bang!*

zubric(k). Penis: Services', mainly Army and RAF in, or ex-, Middle East; also Aus.: since early C.20. Esp. in 'soldiers' Arabic', *shufti zubrick* or *shufti zoob*, let's see (or show) the penis. (L.A.; P.B.; Morrisby.)

zurucker. A police trooper: Aus. Used by John Manifold in his 'Ballad of Ned Kelly', which I set to music ca. 1947. (' "Come out o' that, Ned Kelly", the head zurucker calls.') 'Presumably ex Ger. *zurück*, adv., backwards, but [semantics] not clear' (R.C., 1976). I hazard that a *zurucker* is, lit., a back-tracker, the detective following of a trail or other clue. There may even by a punning ref. to those remarkable *black* (Aboriginal) trackers who have done such wonderful work, with the white police, in the Australian 'bush'.

zyders. The washing places: Felsted School: since ca. 1925. Marples, 'Probably from Zuyder Zee'.

zymotic, whence the even slangier *zymy*, 'Lousy': teenagers': since ca. 1963. (Anderson, 1963.) Contrast **unzymotic**.

Z

Appendix

THE EVOLUTION OF THE PHONETIC ALPHABET

	ROYAL NAVY WW1	— IN		USE	IN —		INTER-NATIONAL since 1956
		1904	1914	1927	1938	1941	
A	APPLES	ACK	ACK	ACK	ACK	ABLE	ALFA
B	BUTTER	BEER	BEER	BEER	BEER	BAKER	BRAVO
C	CHARLIE	C	C	CHARLIE	CHARLIE	CHARLIE	CHARLIE
D	DUFF	D	DON	DON	DON	DOG	DELTA
E	EDWARD	E	E	EDWARD	EDWARD	EASY	ECHO
F	FREDDY	F	F	F	FREDDIE	FOX	FOXTROT
G	GEORGE	G	G	G	GEORGE	GEORGE	GOLF
H	HARRY	H	H	HARRY	HARRY	HOW	HOTEL
I	INK	I	I	INK	INK	ITEM	INDIA
J	JOHNNIE	J	J	JOHNNY	JOHNNIE	JIG	JULIETT
K	KING	K	K	K	KING	KING	KILO
L	LONDON	L	L	L	LONDON	LOVE	LIMA
M	MONKEY	EMMA	EMMA	MONKEY	MONKEY	MIKE	MIKE
N	NUTS	N	N	N	NUTS	NAN	NOVEMBER
O	ORANGE	O	O	O	ORANGE	OBOE	OSCAR
P	PUDDING	PIP	PIP	PIP	PIP	PETER	PAPA
Q	QUEENIE	Q	Q	QUEEN	QUEEN	QUEEN	QUEBEC
R	ROBERT	R	R	R	ROBERT	ROGER	ROMEO
S	SUGAR	ESSES	ESSES	SUGAR	SUGAR	SUGAR	SIERRA
T	TOMMY	TOC	TOC	TOC	TOC	TARE	TANGO
U	UNCLE	U	U	U	UNCLE	UNCLE	UNIFORM
V	VINEGAR	VIC	VIC	VIC	VIC	VICTOR	VICTOR
W	WILLIAM	W	W	W	WILLIAM	WILLIAM	WHISKEY
X	XERXES	X	X	X	X-RAY	X-RAY	X-RAY
Y	YELLOW	Y	Y	Y	YORKER	YOKE	YANKEE
Z	ZEBRA	Z	Z	Z	ZEBRA	ZEBRA	ZULU

References:
Signalling Regulations, 1904, ch. 13, p. 187; *Training Manual, Signalling*, part II, 1914, p. 96. 1915, p. 194; *Signal Training*, vol. V, part I, 1927; *Signal Training, All Arms*, 1938; *Signal Training, All Arms*, 1952.

My thanks for the above information are to the Royal Signals Museum at Blandford Forum, and in particular to its Librarian, Mr L.L. 'Les' Evans, for his ready help. (P.B.)

APPENDIX

ASSOCIATION FOOTBALL

Here follow the nicknames by which some of the British Soccer teams have been known at some time during C.20, with explanations where possible, and not obvious. All names are usu. prec. by *the*.

Addicks	Charlton Athletic
Bank of England Team	Aston Villa: briefly, from late 1935, when the club paid what were then very large transfer fees for star players in an attempt to avoid relegation
Bees	Brentford
Biscuit Men	Reading. Headquarters of Huntley & Palmer's biscuit manufacture
Bishops	Bishop Auckland
Blades	Sheffield Wednesday: in late C.19–early 20, 'used to be called "The Blades" and their rivals . . . Sheffield United . . . "The Cutlers". Now, however, Wednesday are known as "The Owls" . . . The district in which the Wednesday ground is situated is divided into localities known as Hillsborough and Owlerton. In 1907, there was first published in the city the *Sports Special* and the cartoonist fastened on the first three letters of Owlerton and in his sketches depicted Wednesday as an Owl. His cartoons appeared regularly year after year . . . until the crowd cried, "Play up the Owls". Further, Sheffield United have been nicknamed "The Blades" and "The Cutlers" has died out' (Sparling, 1946)
Borough	Middlesbrough
Calies, or Callies	Caledonian
Canaries	Norwich. Ex yellow 'strip'
Cestrians	Chester
Cherries	Boscombe
Citizens	Leicester (Observer, 29 Oct. 33); Manchester City
Cobblers	Northampton. A centre of boot and shoe manufacture
Cottagers	Fulham, whose ground is Craven Cottage
Cutlers	See *Blades*
Dons	Wimbledon; Aberdeen
Eagles	Bedford: ex the town's crest
Fifers	East Fife
Filberts	Leicester City: their home ground is at Filbert Street
Forest	Nottingham Forest
Gills	Gillingham
Glaziers	Crystal Palace
Grecians	Exeter City
Gunners	(Woolwich) Arsenal
Hammers	West Ham United
Imps	Lincoln City: ex the famous carved imp which lurks high in the Cathedral
Latics	Oldham Athletic
Lions	Colchester(?)
Magpies	Newcastle United: ex black and white 'strip'
Mariners	Grimsby Town, once a great fishing harbour
Moorites	Burnley
O's	Clapton Orient
Orient	Leyton Orient
Owls	See *Blades*
Paraders	Bradford(?)
Peacocks	Leeds United: ex a well-known player (–1937)
Pensioners	Chelsea: ex the hospital for military pensioners
Pilgrims	Plymouth: whence the 'Pilgrim Fathers' set sail for America
Posh	Peterborough: 'There are several local versions as to the origin of this name, the most widely accepted being that supporters referred to the team as looking "posh" when they kicked off in the Southern League against Gainsborough on 1 Sept. 1934 wearing a new strip'. The club became professional in that year
Potteries	Stoke City
Railway Men	Swindon Town: formerly noted for its extensive workshops
Rams	Derby County: ex the famous, hyperbolic Derby ram
Rangers	Queen's Park Rangers
Reds	Manchester United
Robins	Bristol City
Saddlers	Walsall(?)
Saints	Southampton: the team was orig. Southampton St Mary's Church
Seasiders	Blackpool
Shakers	Bury
Spurs	Tottenham Hotspurs
Tangerines	Blackpool(?)
Toffee Men	Everton
Toffs	Corinthian Casuals
Trotters	Bolton Wanderers
Villa or Villains	Aston Villa. See *Bank of England*
Wolves	Wolverhampton Wanderers

AUSTRALIAN SURFING SLANG AND COLLOQUIALISMS

The terms cited in the main text come notably from four sources: J.R. Westerway ('The Surfies') in the (Sydney) *Bulletin* of 30 Mar. 1963; a brief, unsigned article ('Language of Their Own') in the *Sun-Herald* of 22 Sep. 1963; Dick Dennison, 'The World of the Surfies'—a valuable article, with a glossary, containing, however, much that is sheer jargon (technicalities); and the comments, and several additions, made by Mr Barry Prentice, who sent me the articles.

As a sport, surf-board riding became extremely popular soon after WW2; it erupted as a passion, a rage, a cult, almost a way of life, among teenagers, in 1960–1. All its jargon and some of its slang have been imported from Hawaii. P.B.: and many of the terms associated with surfboarding made their way to Britain in the later 1970s, borrowed and adapted by skateboarders.

AUSTRALIAN UNDERWORLD TERMS CURRENT IN 1975

In the (Sydney) *Bulletin* of 26 Apr. 1975, Neil James, who had been a member of the underworld for some thirty years, published a long article titled 'Nodding the Nut for a Swy and One', which means 'pleading guilty and being sentenced to a term of two years, with remission of one year for good behaviour'. This fascinating article generalises upon the underworld itself, the *knock-about* or *knock-around* (composed of *knock-abouts*, or *-arounds*), a term that promptly became low and, finally, gen. s., and upon its speech, its idiom, its vocabulary. The vocabulary used here is, as it must inevitably be, selective, but the selection is truly representative.

Most of the terms go back to just after WW2 (1939–45); a few arose not long before it; a very few of them arose late, or latish, in the C.19. From the following alphabetical list, I have omitted those terms which appeared in *DSUE7*, 1970, except where a ref. seemed necessary. Many terms belong also to the fringes of the underworld, and a very few even to mere low slang; it's occ. impossible to decide which stratum has influenced which. Moreover, many of the true cant (or underworld) words and phrases are known and used outside Aus.: especially in near-by NZ; fewer in Can. and the US; a few have been adopted from the UK, notably London.

I have put the terms treated by Mr James into alphabetical order, defined them, and, where advisable, cross-referenced. But the credit for the terms themselves belongs to him; and I'm most grateful to the *Bulletin*, Australia's greatest weekly, for their courteous permission to use the article.

Items in bold type are references to the main text of the Dictionary; 'above' and below' to the entries within this section.

arse, n. Anyone the speaker rates as objectionable; a 'shit'; any place he thinks poorly of; a 'dump': although most used in the underworld and its fringes, also low s.: prob. since ca. 1930. James employs it in both these nuances. See also *put on the arse bit*, below.

back-up. 'A friend or ally willing to defend another man in trouble': since ca. 1920: c. > low s. > gen. s.

bagman. That member of a shoplifting team who carries away the stolen goods: since ca. 1930.

bake, n. 'He [a prisoner] went on to say that the jacks [i.e. the police] gave him the best bake in history (a malicious description of his character to the court). A bake is a verbal assault, also known as a roast, or "being on the griller" ': since ca. 1945.

balk, v. To cover up, as in 'balk with a molly', to use a girl as cover or shield.

barrel, v. To deliver (a punch): also low s.: since ca. 1945. 'Some mug . . . barrelled a king at him' (i.e., a *king-hit*, a hard, unexpected punch).

bow the crumpet. 'To plead guilty in court', is also known as *get one's head down*.

brass, v. To steal from a fellow thief, esp. a mate: since early 1920s.

comics. Short for *comic cuts*, r.s. for 'guts' or belly.

dip, v. Cf. **dip out**, to fail: in Aus. c. it = to fail in committing a crime, esp. of theft or robbery.

dolly, v. To interrogate (a suspect): since ca. 1930.

drag, n. = **drag**, n., 1: in Aus. c. prob. since late C.19.

dud, n. (the dud) and v.; vbl n. *dudding*. 'He had been charged with dudding, that is, misrepresenting the origin, quality and value of goods he sold': since ca. 1935, or a decade earlier. Ex 'dud' goods—of inferior quality or performance—orig., duds, clothes.

earn. Money obtained illicitly by the police for granting a thief, or other criminal, leniency or other privilege; hence, a (mild) degree of bribery: since ca. 1930. Cf. **earn**, v.

egg. A pimp: short for r. *egg and spoon*, on synon. Aus c. *hoon*.

fall, v. To arrive, esp. if suddenly; applied esp. to police or store detectives: since late 1940s. Often in 'the law falls (*or* fell)!', the police arrive or make a raid.

fix, n. A well thought out plan, the *locus* carefully reconnoitred: since ca. 1945.

fizz-gig. A busybody: orig.—late 1930s—c., but soon also low s. Cf. **fizz-gig**.

fly the flag. 'To appeal the case to a higher court in the hope of having the sentence reduced': since early 1940s. P.B.: ?the flag of distress.

front, n. ' "The Limp" [a man with one] had front (boldness and self-confidence)': since ca. 1940. Ex **front**, n., 1.

gather (usu. in passive, *be gathered*). To be arrested: since ca. 1930. Also *lumbered*.

gear, n. Anything (esp. if illicit) intentionally undefined: since 'long before the word became popular'; therefore, since ca. 1945, if not ca. 1930. Peculiarly Aus. c.

get (one's) *head down (to it)*. Slightly less common than *nod the nut*: since, at latest, 1945; prob. since the 1920s.

give (a place) *a peg*. To 'case it', reconnoitre it: since ca. 1930.

give (the accused) *the book*. Aus. var. of the much more widely distributed *throw the book at*; to condemn to the maximum term of imprisonment: since late 1940s.

goose, n. A shop assistant: esp. shoplifters' c.: since (?)late 1930s.

Gregory Peck. Often shortened to *Gregory*: the neck: r.s., esp. in Aus., and there mostly in the lowest stratum: since ca. 1950. P.B.: also Brit., later C.20.

griller. See *bake*, above.

head. See *pullaway*, below.

heavy, n. (usu. in pl.). An intimidator used by money-lenders, bookmakers, *et al.*, for the collection of dues from reluctant clients: both in Brit. and in other Commonwealth countries: since ca. 1930: c., hence also low s. Cf. **standover man.**

junk, n. Short for **junkie,-y**, a drug addict: since latish 1950s.

king, n. Short for **king hit**: a knock-out, esp. if unexpected, punch: since ca. 1930. Also v., as in 'he kinged a floor-walker'.

kite blue. A worthless cheque: since ca. 1930. See **kite**, n., 2.

knock-about, less often *knock-around*; the former, derivatively, also an adj. 'A guy who is appalled at the idea of an honest day's work', but rather more than a mere 'layabout', for it virtually means a crook, esp. a professional thief: since ca. 1930 or perhaps a decade earlier.

live square. To be an honest citizen: c. and low s.: since ca. 1950.

load, n. and v. Fabricated evidence; to fabricate evidence against (a suspect): since ca. 1930.

loiter, n. 'Loitering with intent to commit a felony': c., and police s.: since ca. 1920, perhaps since ca. 1910.

lumbered. See *gather*, above—but prob. considerably older than it.

monkey. **Monkey**, n., 1 has naturally become applied to 500 Aus. dollars.

Moreton. Short for *Moreton Bay*, itself short for *Moreton Bay fig*, q.v. at **gig**, n., 4. James wrongly spells it *Morton*. Moreton Bay is situated at the mouth of the Brisbane River and is enclosed on the north-east by Moreton Island. In the early days of transportation, one of the harshest of the penal settlements was sited there. Moreton Bay, and its notorious governor, Logan, frequently crop up in Aus. 'convict' ballads. (Raab.)

nod the nut is much commoner than *bow the crumpet*. Commoner also—though less so than *nod the nut*—is *get one's head down (to it)*. James mentions only the *get . . .* and *nod . . .* forms. All four obviously refer to nodding, or ducking, one's head in voiceless affirmative.

onkaparinga, often shortened to *onka*. A finger: app. of Aus. orig., and certainly underworld r.s. P.B.: Wilkes gives only the short form, notes 'rare', and explains 'from the place-name'.

peg, n. See *give a peg*, above.

post, v. 'There's no way he'll post you on the job'—leave in the lurch, abandon you to the police in order to secure his own freedom or safety: since the 1930s.

pullaway (or *pull-away*). 'The terms "pullaway"—"tugging a head", "pulling away" or "slewing a head" [or "pulling a head"] mean simply diverting someone's attention from the scene of operations': since ca. 1930, if not 20–25 years earlier.

pussy, esp. *pussy in*. To move, to enter, very quietly or unobtrusively: since ca. 1930: c. >, by ca. 1940, s. Like a cat. P.B.: cf. synon. S.E. *pussyfoot*, v.

put (someone) *on the arse bit*. To tell another indignantly what one thinks of him: c. and low s.: since mid-1940s.

put on the griller; mostly *being put* . . . See *bake*, above.

rave. To talk fluently and loudly, with connotation of craziness; hence *raver*, one who does this as a role in a crime: since latish 1940s.

raver. See prec.

red-penny man. A pimp: since late 1930s. Less common than synon. **hoon.**

roast, n. See *bake*, above.

rorter. A petty confidence trickster: since ca. 1910. A specialisation of **rorter**, 1.

serve, n.; *serve up*, v. Unpleasant or painful or unjust 'service' or treatment; to beat up, to assault or to attack: c.

shoppy; *shoppying*; *shoppying job*. A shoplifter; shoplifting in general; shoplifting in particular: since the 1930s; by 1950, also low s.

slewing a head. See *pullaway*, above. But also 'to slew', as in 'Marg pussies in to slew the manager.'

sling, n. In *beat it for the sling*, to fail to appear in court, e.g., at the end of one's bail: since ca. 1950.

slot. A prison cell: c.: since ca. 1950. A prisoner is put into a (strictly, small) cell or a cell for two. He is *slotted* into his allocated niche.

smother. To use something to conceal a movement, a trick, an object, as in 'Marg and Ratty Jack was gonna smother with a box while [a shoplifting was in progress]': since ca. 1920. As an Aus. usage, recorded by Baker 35 years earlier.

snag, n. It survives, in its main text sense, but it seems to be s., not coll.; I suspect that it is mainly Sydney-siders'.

spear, v. To throw (someone) out of a shop, a pub, etc.: since ca. 1910: c. and low, then gen., 'I got speared through the front door.' Cf. *get* and *give the spear* at **spear,** n.

spot, n. 100 dollars Aus.: since ca. 1965. James has 'the police had asked for two spot ($200) in return for the no-bake [see *bake*, above]'. It is only fair to the Australian police to remark that he seems to have encountered an exceptionally high amount of corruption.

swinging, be. (Of a case) 'adjourned to a further date': c. and low s.: since ca. 1920.

swy with one. A sentence, or a term, of two years' imprisonment, with one year remitted for good behaviour: c., esp. convicts' and ex-convicts': since ca. 1925. See **swi,** 3.

take, n. A theft: c.: since latish 1940s.

take man (or hyphenated). 'The man who [in a gang] actually steals the money': since ca. 1930.

tank. **Tank,** 4, a safe for money, is also, as James shows, Aus.—clearly adopted ex NZ. But as a prison cell it has, since ca. 1940, been Aus. c.—adopted ex US where, however, it denotes a large cell for temporary detention of, e.g. drunk-and-disorderlies.

tea-leaf. The Brit. r.s. for 'thief' is common also in the Aus. underworld, and James notes it.

tidy (someone) *up.* To deal with someone thoroughly, to complete his (e.g. police) examination, esp. of detectives interrogating a suspect: since ca. 1930. Ironic.

top mag. A fast-talking 'con man' or other crook: prob ex older s. *mag,* to chatter.

tug, n. See next. It derives straight from the v.—and prob. did so almost immediately.

tug, v. To warn, as one crook (or a beggar, a 'layabout') warns another of imminent or immediate danger: since the 1930s. Sometimes *tug* (one's) *coat* and sometimes *give* (one) *the tug*: both in James. 'The expression derives from the system of signals shoppies [shoplifters] use in large stores . . . One of these signals is tugging at the lapels of the signaller's coat, signifying danger.'

verbal, n. and v. An official police interrogation, ending in a signed statement: police j. > semi-c. Whence, prob., the specifically c. sense, as in 'because the police had . . . verballed him (perjured themselves giving testimony)': since ca. 1950. See **verbals,** for Brit. usage.

willy. See **Willie,** 2: money, whether in gen. or, as of that in a till, in particular, or indeed the till itself.

BACK SLANG

Back s. dates from the first half of C.19: the earliest ref. I've seen occurs in G.W.M. Reynolds's *Pickwick Abroad,* 1839, p. 587 (footnote). It would be fair to say that back s. is slowly disappearing from general low-level s., but that it actively persists among minor criminals and near-criminals. See, e.g., Frank Norman's article in *Encounter,* 1959, reprinted in Len Deighton's *London Dossier,* and in Frank Norman's own *Norman's London.* Several back s. terms adduced by F.N. occur in this Dictionary. The situation remains the same in 1977 as it was in 1959. (E.P., 2 May 1977.) P.B.: another group making considerable use of back s., at least until mid-C.20, were retail butchers, and not only in London, to judge by C.S. Upton's comprehensive article 'Language Butchered: Back-Slang in the Birmingham Meat Trade', *Lore & Language,* vol. 2, no. 1, July 1974. Further evidence is provided in a 1981 letter to me from Robert Barltrop, co-author of *The Muvver Tongue:* 'Many years ago I worked for Sainsbury's as a shop porter . . . There was a butchering staff, from whom the use of backslang spread through the place. Some of them were quite clever at it: cries of "Kay-rop poches!" and "Sheep's dee-aitch!" (pork chops, sheep's head) answered by "Ee-mocing pu!" Scales were "ee-lacs", "nam-oh" for a woman, "exobs" boxes, "ee-fink" a knife, "ee-nobs" bones. The call "Nav pu!" to me meant a delivery van to be unloaded; and a thorough muddle was a "slabs-pu" ("pu" pronounced *pew*).'

BIRD-WATCHERS' SLANG

Although scientific and semi-scientific and informed-amateur bird-watching (in the S.E. sense) has existed since earth knows when, it has at the pursuit-of-knowledge level been a very serious matter, hardly conducive to levity. As a popular hobby, especially among the youthful, it arose, I'd have thought, only since WW2 (1939–45). Not until 1977 did I become aware that there existed a small but healthy group of bird-watching slangy and colloquial terms; on 17 Nov. *New Society* published an article by Gavin Weightman, 'To Twitch a Dowitcher' (a real American bird roughly equivalent to a UK sandpiper, esp. the red-breasted snipe, and in Brit., first dictionaried in the 2nd Sup. of *OED*, vol. I, 1972). Here are listed terms from that article '(G.W.)'; other sources are recorded below.

bananabill. A white-billed diver. Collins, 1987.

bird. v. To bird-watch. BBC, 1985.

birder. A bird-watcher: perhaps coll. rather than s.

clinch, v.t.; whence vbl n. *clinching.* 'Clinching is identifying a rarity' (G.W.).

crippling. 'Birds are graded according to rarity value and range from merely "worth having" through "crippling" up to a "megatick" or—every twitcher's dream—a "cosmic mind-blower" ' (Cable). Hence also *crippler,* 'a rare and colourful bird' (Collins).

dip in. 'They were on their way back from the Scilly Isles where they had dipped in on an alpine accentor (a European bird like a dunnock or hedge-sparrow). In twitcher talk, to be dipped in is to go on a successful twitch (trip to see a rarity)' (G.W.). Cf.:-

dip out. To fail, on a bird-watching trip, as in 'we nearly dipped out when two water authority men walked past in the open and sent the birds up.' P.B.: see **dip out** in the main text, and cf. use of *dip* in children's counting-out songs.

dude. 'At Wilstone, I was clearly among dudes (rather staid non-twitchers)'; serious, experienced, usually rather older bird-watchers.

flicker. A fly-catcher; *R.B. flicker* = red-breasted fly-catcher. BBC.

grip off, usu. *be gripped off,* as in 'If you miss a rarity a fellow twitcher sees, you are gripped off'; annoyed, bitterly disappointed. P.B.: *grip* and *gripped,* in various forms and with various meanings akin to the one given here, were common among National Servicemen, WW2—early 1960s.

gropper. A grasshopper warbler. BBC.

lancey. A lanceolated warbler. Collins.

lifer. A particular species of bird seen for the first time in one's life. Cable.

lister. An enthusiastic bird-watcher, listing in his little notebook every rarity or, to him, new bird he has ever seen (cf. train- or plane-spotters). Cf. *tick-hunter.*

Med. A Mediterranean bird.

megatick. See *crippling,* above, and **megatick,** in main text.

sibe. A Siberian bird.

string, v. 'Confuse rare bird with common species' (Collins).

tick. Sighting a rare bird, to be noted on one's *tick-list.* (BBC.) Hence also *tick-hunter,* an ardent, usu. excitable bird-watcher. Cf. *lister.*

twitch; twitchable; twitcher; twitching, n. and adj. A group based on the fact that many bird-watchers tend to twitch with excitement, whether at the sight of a bird new to them or of a genuine rarity. (Contrast *dude.*) The n. *twitch,* the earliest derivative, signifies a trip to see a rarity; then comes *twitcher,* one who reacts thus, also called a *lister* or *tick-hunter,* and

G.W. refers to the 'hard-core twitcher'; *twitching* = either 'excited' or 'being a twitcher' or 'pertaining to such bird-watching'—and, as n., 'the practice of excitable, enthusiastic bird-watching'; and *twitchable* = likely to cause such ardour and excitement, as in 'looking at a Blyth's reed-warbler, "the first twitchable one for years" ' (G.W.). R.E. Emmett claims to have coined *twitcher* in mid-1950s to describe the behaviour of well-known bird-watcher Howard Medhurst when on the trail of a rare bird. Green adds that H.M. 'rode to rare sightings on a motorbike in all weathers, often shivering and twitching with cold.'

unblock. 'If you miss a rarity a fellow twitcher sees you are gripped off. You can unblock him by seeing one he misses'— that is, you can get even with him and dampen his triumph.

Yank. Also *yank* (as in G.W.'s article): 'It might be a yank (American bird)'.

Other sources are:

Cable, M.C., in *Sunday Express Magazine*, 4 Oct. 1987.
Collins. W.C., in *Observer*, 30 Aug. 1987.
Green. E.G., in *You*, 26 Feb. 1984.

CANADIAN ADOLESCENTS' SLANG, 1946

'Mother! Do you want to be able to converse easily with your teenagers? Here is the glossary: alligator, swing fan: Ameche, telephone: blitz-buggy, automobile: bone-box, mouth: crumb-hunting, house work: dazzle dust, face powder: dig the drape, buy a new dress: droolin with schoolin, a grind: fag hag, a girl who smokes: give with the goo, explain in detail: in a gazelle, I'm feeling good: junior wolf, kid brother: make like a boid, go away: pucker paint, lipstick: Red Mike, a woman hater: riffs, music: slab, sandwich: slide your jive, talk freely: snazzy, smooth: square, a person who doesn't dance: ticks, moments: twister to the turner, a door key: watch works, brains: whing ding, head covering: you shred it, Wheat, you said it: zoon bat, funny looking' (A Toronto newspaper, 24 Oct, 1946). *Teen-agers* = *teen-agers* = those in their teens.

'Practically all this is now obsolescent or obsolete' (Leechman, May 1959).

COCKNEY SPEECH

Edwin Pugh, one of the best of all writers on Cockney life, wrote at the beginning of *Harry the Cockney*, 1912: 'There is no such being . . . as a typical Cockney. But there are approximations to a type. There are men and women, the sons and daughters of Cockneys, born and bred within sound of Bow bells, and subject to all the common influences of circumstance and training and environment that London brings into play upon their personalities, who may be said to be . . . typical. The average Cockney is not articulate. He is often witty; he is sometimes eloquent; he has a notable gift of phrase-making and nicknaming. Every day he is enriching the English tongue with new forms of speech, new clichés, new slang, new catchwords. The new thing and the new word to describe the new thing are never very far apart in London. But the spirit, the soul, of the Londoner is usually dumb.'

Considerable space is given in this work to peculiarities of Cockney speech, because it is in itself important; it is important, too, for the influence it has exercised on the everyday language of Colonials—and, it must not be forgotten, that of Americans. Moreover, back slang and rhyming slang were invented by Cockneys; they are still used widely by costermongers. In 1908 Clarence Rook, in *London Side Lights*, could say: 'I will back the costermonger . . . to . . . talk to a Regius Professor of English for half an hour, tell him the most amusing stories, and leave that Professor aghast in darkest ignorance.'

One of the best-informed *aperçus* on the Cockney is that on pp. 42–3 of Michael Harrison's *Reported Safe Arrival*, 1943—a book containing many vivid, and accurate, transcripts of the Cockney speech of the 20th century.

But the best and most comprehensive study of the Cockney and his speech is Julian Franklyn's *The Cockney*, 1953, 2nd ed. revised, 1954. P.B.: to which must now be added Robert Barl-trop & Jim Wolveridge, *The Muvver Tongue*, 1980, and Jim Wolveridge's pamphlet *He Don't Know 'A' from a Bull's Foot*, [n.d.].

DROP A BRICK

To make a *faux pas*, esp. of tact or speech: C.20; by ca. 1935, coll. I am credibly informed that this phrase arose among a group of third-year undergraduates of Trinity College, Cambridge, in the May term, 1905; that it soon > university s.; and that it spread very rapidly. The guarantor's account of the origin of the phrase is this: H.S. was Sergeant-Major of the Trinity College Company of the University Volunteers—a pre-Territorial force renowned neither for discipline nor for efficiency. Whilst leading his company—small in numbers—along Trumpington Road on a route march, H.S. had to give an order, the road being under repair and building operations in progress on one or both sides. This H.S. did, in his best form and voice. Result: (1) on the troops, *nil*; (2) on the builders, *some in alarm dropped their bricks*. The order was repeated with the same result. H.S. told us that after that he felt that each time he gave an order he too was going to drop a brick—hence the phrase meaning to 'make a mistake'. In a few days the phrase was all over Cambridge and in a few months had gone round the world and returned to us.

ECHOISM IN SLANG

Many of the most vivid slangy neologisms originate as echoic words, seen at their most immediate as nouns of impact, more or less synonymous with such exclamations as *smash!—crash!—bang!—whack!* Some of those nouns become or, at the least, give rise to nouns of enthusiastic approval. A long essay or even a monograph could very easily be written on the subject. The Appendix, however, is not in any sense, nor to any degree, a collection of essays, large or small.

The point can by illustrated, briefly yet perhaps adequately, with three passages from William Golding's masterpiece, *Lord of the Flies*, published in 1954 and dealing with a miscellaneous group of boys aged 6–13. (The edition used is the Faber paperback, 1962.)

> The great rock . . . leapt droning through the air and smashed a deep hole in the canopy of the forest. Echoes and birds flew, white and pink dust floated, the forest further down shook as with the passage of an enraged monster: and then the island was still.
> 'Wacco!'
> 'Like a bomb!'
> 'Whee-aa-oo!' (p. 37)
> Jack was on his feet.
> 'We'll have rules!' he cried excitedly. 'Lots of rules! Then when anyone breaks 'em—'
> 'Whee-oh!'
> 'Wacco!'
> 'Bong!'
> 'Doink!' (p. 44)
> Immured in these tangles, at perhaps their most difficult moment, Ralph turned with shining eyes to the others.
> 'Wacco.'
> 'Wizard.'
> 'Smashing.'
> The cause of their pleasure was not obvious. (p. 35)
> Again came the solemn communion of shining eyes in the gloom.
> 'Wacco.'
> 'Wizard.' (p. 36)

Strictly, no comments are necessary. Yet perhaps one should note that *wacco* is better written *whacko* and that the echoic *bong* has the same root as *bonkers*, crazy, and that *doink* occurs, with its intensively echoic prefix *ger* or *ker*, in *ger-doying*, *kerdoying*, qq.v. at **kerdoying,** in main text.

FELSTED

Felsted School has a considerable body of slang. In *The Felsted-*

ian of Dec. 1947, there appeared an excellent glossary of current slang, arranged by subject. I have re-arranged the material in alphabetical order, shortened the definitions, and omitted certain terms belonging to the main body of slang.

arge. A sergeant, e.g. a Gym Instructor. Amputated *sarge*. Hence *argery*, mostly the gymnasium.

bang-on or *bash-on*. Terms of approval, 'recent importations, but rapidly passing into common speech', as in 'It's absolutely bang-on'. From the Forces: *bang on the target*.

Billy boy; Billy man. A House boy; man.

blitch or *blotch*. Blotting-paper. The former is a thinning of the latter, and the latter is a proleptic.

bog. A bicycle. A shortening of *bog-wheel*.

bumming. A caning, a beating. Ex **bum.**

butch. A sturdy fellow; also in address. Cinematic influence.

cheery. Excellent; e.g. 'a cheery pudding'. By humorous transference.

cheese off. To annoy. Cf. **cheesed-off.**

chigger. To cheat; *chigger notes*, notes used in cheating, or a crib; *chiggerer*, a cheat (person). By the 'OXFORD -ER'.

clothers. Clothes-room (?).

coffins. A particular set of deep and ancient baths in the main block.

Confirmaggers. Confirmation; *Confirmagger pragger* (prayers), a confirmation class. By the 'Oxford -agger(s)'.

debaggers. A debate. Cf. prec.

dip. A light; an electric bulb. Hence, *dips*, lights in general or 'Lights out!'

Div (not *Divvers*). A Divinity period.

dockets. Cigarettes. Cf. **docker**, 2.

drive, esp. in 'am I driving?'—Must I hurry?, and in *Drive in!*, Get a move on! Ex *drive*, energy.

Duck. Matron; *Under-Duck*, Under-Matron.

ex. Exercise, games. See *vol ex*.

fugs. A radiator; also *fug-pipes*; *under-fugs*, underpants.

grass. Lettuce; watercress; any green salad.

Headman. Headmaster.

hook. To take—not necessarily to filch.

hot, as in *half-hot*, halfpenny; *six hots*, sixpence; *hots*, pennies, cash; *trav. hots*, travelling expenses; *hot ice*, an ice-cream costing a penny.

ipe. A rifle. Ex army *(h)ipe*.

jack. As v.i., to cease (cf. **jack in**); as v.t., to shirk.

knockers. Cigarettes.

Ma (e.g. Smith). A master's wife; a lady on the staff.

mooners. A manservant who cleans classrooms.

new nip. A new *nip* or small boy, a new boy. Cf. **nipper.**

quagger-pragger. Choir practice. By the 'Oxford -agger'.

razz up. To reprimand severely.

rollers. Roll-call. By the 'OXFORD -ER(s)'.

shants. Lavatories.

Siggers. The JTC Signals Hut. 'OXFORD -ER(s)'. [JTC = Junior Training Corps, a post-WW2 title of the army branch of the Combined Cadet Force.]

skiv. A maidservant. Short for **skivvy.**

smut. A person one happens to dislike.

snitch. To take—not necessarily to filch.

stodge. A steamed pudding.

stooge. A School steward. Ex the Services' sense.

stub. To kick (a ball), esp. at Rugger.

swipe. To take—not necessarily to filch.

swot. A lesson period.

tabby. A bedside cupboard. *The Felstedian* proposes deriv. ex *tabernacle*.

tolly mug. A tooth mug or glass.

tonk. To hit (a ball) with a stick, e.g. at hockey.

tough. A fight; *toughing*, fighting, fisticuffs.

toys. Desks with bookcase attached. Adopted from Winchester.

trav tie. A (too) smart tie, not worn in School. I.e. for travelling.

Tuckers. The School tuck-shop. By the 'OXFORD -ER(s)'.

Underling. Nickname for the under-butler. By pun on Ling, the butler.

uni (pron. *unny*). A uniform.

Vic! A warning cry, in Lower School only and gradually going out of use.

Vill. Felsted village.

vol. 'An afternoon free from prescribed games'; *vol ex*, an afternoon when exercise—of one's own choice—must be taken.

wagger-pagger. Short for older, univ. s. *wagger-pagger-bagger*, a waste-paper basket.

Washes. The ablution rooms.

wasses. Lavatories. Ex Ger. *Wasser*, water. But see **wass,** in main text.

wonker. A kipper.

GRAFTERS' AND MARKET-TRADERS' SLANG

This is that argot used by those who work a line at fair or market, e.g. as fortune-teller or quack doctor. Some of it is Parlyaree, some Romany, some Yiddish, some r.s.; some of it, too, verges on c. The authority on the subject is Mr Philip Allingham: see his fascinating *Cheapjack*, 1934. [E.P.'s note in the 1st ed.; in the manuscript notes for the 8th ed., he wrote:] It should be aligned with market-traders' s.; clearly the two overlap. The best glossary I've seen of market-traders' occurs in *Lore & Language*, July 1975; it was compiled by Mr Patrick O'Shaughnessy and was based upon the recollections of Mrs Grace Lilian Ashworth (1899–1975), with a brief supplement of words added by her surviving children. P.B.: even a cursory scan through this Dictionary will show the extent to which I am indebted to Mr O'Shaughnessy: all entries attributed to him are tagged '(M.T.)'. His glossary was published in booklet form, with a short introduction, in 1979, by Richard Kay, Boston (ISBN 902662–20–1).

GREMLINS

Gremlins did not emerge as part of C.20 folklore until WW2, although they had been known to the RAF since ca. 1923. They were (probably still are) those modern goblins, elves, or fairies to whom could be attributed all mechanical misfortunes that befall flyers; they were an anthropomorphised manifestation of Sod's Law. Gremlins were regarded mostly not as malevolent and destructive devils, but as mischievous imps, some of them moved occasionally by malicious glee rather than by pure fun: Pucks responsible for minor mishaps otherwise unaccountable, and dangerous only when the sheer aggregate of mishaps caused bewilderment. Gremlins must always, like 'the little folk' of earlier centuries, be referred to as *them*, because mere *he*, *she* or *it* does not fully convey a due feeling of their immanence and nameless power. Main journalistic, hence public, interest centred on them in early 1942–43.

Various attempts have been made to provide an etymology; none has been really satisfactory. One fanciful explanation is that a gremlin is a goblin that lives in a Fremlin beer-bottle (Fremlins were brewers in Kent, lost in the big mergers of mid-C.20); more seriously (or academically), derivations have been suggested from Danish, Old Norse, or Erse. Most likely, someone invented the word in a flash of genius and wit, and his hearers finding it so completely apt, it spread unimpeded as instantly acceptable. *Gremlin* itself was the keyword, but it gave rise to variations on the theme; I list here all those noted in *DSUE8*, with their sources where given: an article from the *Glasgow Herald*, 7 Mar. 1942 (GH); an undatable contemporary piece from *Men Only* (MO); Charles Graves, *Seven Pilots*, 1943 (CG); H & P, 1943.

Fifinella. A female g. MO.

Ground Walloper. That fat little g. who is in charge of flying: perhaps a perversion of *Grand W*., the Gremlin King. GH.

Petrol Booser or *Boozer*. Mentioned in GH. Perhaps a pun on petrol bowser, and applied to gremlins infesting a refuelling wagon; or perhaps one that caused aircraft to run out of fuel.

Phagassies. 'Those gremlins which sit on the wings and blow on the aileron and send it down' (CG).

Pigeon Gremlin. A patronising g., active only in hot weather.

Retired Gremlin. Wears a yellow hat and a fancy waistcoat, and behaves in a Blimpish manner.

Snurge. Unspecified. (GH.) See **snurge**, n., 2, for the type.

Spandule. A g. that—but only at 9,999 feet—enjoys being tangled up with the propellers.

Spanjer. A g. that lives above 20,000 feet—an anti-fighter type. H & P.

Typogremlin. What printers, borrowing from the RAF, blamed for printing errors.

Whizzuck. A g. that lives on the outskirts of enemy aerodromes. H & P.

Widget. A baby g. (MO.) See **widget** in main text for later developments.

Wrenlin. A **Wren** (q.v.) g.: FAA.

Yehudi. Unspecified. (GH.) As *Yohodi*, it appears in D. Charlwood, *No Moon Tonight*, Sydney, 1956: it kept guns from freezing up.

My thanks to Mr Richard Hawkins, of Dublin 14, who has made an exhaustive study of the subject. Gremlins, like the Radio comedy show ITMA, helped to keep spirits up when such encouragement was so needed. (P.B.)

HARRY, as a meaningless prefix.

With the support of Wilfred Granville's note in his *Dictionary of Sailors' Slang*, 1962, I propose that the evolution of this originally RN 'in-word' went something like this: from *drink at* [Henry] *Freeman's Quay*, to drink at another's expense (— 1811), the RN had, by ca. 1870, produced 'It's Harry Freeman's' for anything on which there was nothing to pay (F. & G.; Bowen), a blending of the name and the idea of 'free', e.g. free cigarettes or, as 'Harry Frees', fruit and vegetables donated by the civilian public. There may also have been incidental influence by the use of **Harry Tate** and **Harry Wragg'**, qq.v. *Harry* then became 'free' of *Freeman's* (?during WW1) and began, now always accompanied by the '-ers' suffix, to be attached to various other terms; e.g. the English Channel off Dunkirk in the fateful weeks of early summer 1940 was said to be *Harry flatters*, dead calm. By the late 1950s, however, the RAF had adopted *Harry flatters* to mean 'flat out', at full speed; but 'flat out' on one's back through exhaustion or intoxication was already (ca. 1918, according to E.P.) *Harry flakers*—ex **'flaked out'**. (Note that what E.P. designated 'the Oxford *-er*' suffix is equally common in RN s.) These terms then gave rise to numerous others on the same pattern, e.g.: *H. booters*, 'boot-faced'; *H. clampers*, weather completely overcast; *H. crashers*, 'crashed out' asleep; *H. roughers*, opp. of *H. flatters*, calm; *H. screechers* or *shriekers*, drunk; and in Colin Evans' naval novel, *The Heart of Standing*, 1962, are *H. shakers*, extreme nervousness, and 'I'm harry starkers [naked], and freezing bastard solid.' Sanders notes that *H. starkers* may also = stark mad, and adds *H. skinters*, penniless. In the later 1950s there was a revival and extension of the usage, as Gilderdale, 1958, wrote concerning the smart young set: 'One verbal affectation (not new, but still in circulation) is the habit of saying "Harry" in conjunction with a host of words. Thus: Harry champers (champagne), Harry bangers (sausages), Harry redders (red wine), Harry spraggers (spaghetti), Harry Blissington (absolutely wonderful).' Gilderdale's last example harks back to a suffix even older than *-ers*; cf. *Alderman Lushington is concerned*, an early C.19 c.p. applied to drunkenness. The form was popular not only in what E.P. called 'the smart young set'; it plagued the Intelligence Corps unit I served with in Cyprus at this time, and, when flying home on leave in 1959 I felt at once 'on the same wavelength' with the BEA stewardess who was amused by a pilot's coinage: he had been trying on a seat-belt, only to become, as he groaned, 'Harry trappers', entangled in it—a good example of the usage's instant adaptability. (P.B.)

HAULAGE-BASHERS' SLANG

Among the many and various strange hobbies and obsessions in UK, home of such things, one of the strangest and most demanding is perhaps that of the *haulage-bashers*, or *bashers* for short (see **basher**, 3 and 4). These are people, nearly all male, whose self-imposed mission is to ride, in due course, behind as many different locomotives (*locos*) as they possibly can, and who devote all their spare time, thought and money to that object. (Who is a compiler of such a dictionary as this to wonder at others' weird obsessions!) What is not so strange is that they have evolved a private jargon or slang, although some of it, I surmise, is common also to professional railwaymen. Here are listed some examples, and my thanks go to Lincoln Allison, from whose article in *New Society*, 8 Aug. 1986, they are taken with his permission.

baglet. A woman: ' "Baglets" are not greatly liked and The Baglet (Margaret Thatcher) is profoundly disliked, principally because of her extreme reluctance to travel by train).' Dim. of *bag*, low s. since later C.19; gen. *old bag*, in certain contexts a slatternly prostitute or part-time prostitute.

bert. 'The great bulk of mankind are mere "berts" (as in Bert 'n' Ada), people whose only interest in getting on a train is to arrive at a particular destination.'

coffin. A British Rail air-conditioned coach.

druid. A Welsh train guard on British Rail.

Duff. A British Rail Class 47 locomotive, 'the common all-purpose BR workhorse'.

Egg-timer. A BR Class 58 locomotive: ex shape, the engine in the middle, with a cab at both ends.

Elmer. A 'US citizen travelling around UK on Britrail passes, much resented because the passes are a good deal, which is not available to the natives.' Ex once-common US forename.

Goyle. ' "Goyles" are widely considered to be [BR's] ugliest train (as in gargoyle)'.

Hoover. A BR Class 50 locomotive, 'which sounds like a vacuum-cleaner'.

insects. 'Occasional railway enthusiasts; they swarm all over the place at certain times of the year.' Cf. *crocus*, 3, and its synon. *daffodil.*

kettle. A steam locomotive. In earlier use,—1931, among Can. railwaymen. Hence *kettle-bashers*, 'who are looked on as effete sentimentalists'.

Laser. A BR Class 87 locomotive, 'electric train with brilliant headlights'.

Rat. A BR Class 25 locomotive.

tops gen. 'Information from the Total Operations Processing System on [BR]'s computer. This contains "diagrams", separate but related plans for the deployment of engines, crew and rolling stock.' See also **gen**, n.

tram. A fully electric train. See **tram** in main text.

tram basher. One who specialises in travelling on trains on electrified lines.

HAULIERS' SLANG

The British Road Services have a slang of their own: and much of it—that is, many of the printable terms—has been recorded in *British Road Services Magazine*, Dec. 1951.

Aberdeen booster. See *Scotsman's fifth.*

anchor. A brake: since ca. 1930.

Billy Bunter. A shunter: r.s.: since ca. 1925.

Chinese dominoes. A load of bricks: since ca. 1930.

Chinese gunpowder. Cement: since ca. 1930.

dangler or *pup.* A trailer: since ca. 1920.

hook, on the; on the ribs. On tow; very old; since ca. 1925 and 1920.

jockey or *pilot.* The driver of any heavy-load vehicle: since ca. 1925 and 1945.

load of wind. A light load: since ca. 1920.

monkey. 'Two-wheeled trailer used for carrying very long loads': since ca. 1930.

Mrs Greenfield's, staying at. See below.

pilot. See *jockey.*

pimple. A steep hill: since ca. 1925.

pipe. A telephone: since ca. 1925.

poodler. A small vehicle: since ca. 1935.

pup. See *dangler*.

ribs, on the. See *hook, on the*.

roller skate. A small, light waggon: since ca. 1945.

round the houses. (Adj. and adv.) Of or for or in or by 'multiple delivery work': coll.

Scotsman's fifth or *Aberdeen booster*. Coasting (n.): since ca. 1930.

showboat. A large eight-wheeled van (Fisher Renwick type): since ca. 1946.

skull. A passenger: since ca. 1945.

smoke, up the, adj. and adv. Going to London.

spud-basher. A lorry carrying potatoes: since ca. 1920.

staying at Mrs Greenfield's. Sleeping in the cab of one's vehicle: since ca. 1925. [See **Greenfields**, in main text.]

track, up the, adj. and adv. Travelling along a depot's particular trunk route: since ca. 1940.

In *Drive*, a motorists' magazine, there appeared in 1968, at p. 113, an article that appears to 'catch up' and add to the list given above. The only new terms, including modifications, are these:—

bookie. A Scottish lorry-drivers' term for the office where he books in and receives his instructions and documents.

crime-sheet. A log-sheet.

gunpowder. Short for *Chinese gunpowder*.

junk pile. A lorry in exceedingly poor condition: a 'pile' fit only for the 'junk heap'.

quickie up the track. A return journey made during one night and along the usual route—cf. *track, up the*.

stiff 'un, the. A person given a lift: he just sits there while the driver does all the work and takes all the responsibility.

JAZZ TERMS

An attempt has been made to include the best-known, most widely used British Commonwealth s. terms of jazz. Most of them come ultimately from the US. A sane, judicious article on the 'Language of Jazz Musicians', written by Norman D. Hinton, appeared in *American Dialect Society*, Nov. 1958. For Can. usage, I owe almost everything to Priestley and Leechman.

Jazz slang current in May 1963: in that month, Mr Rex Harris sent me a selected—and select—list of s. words and phrases popular and general at that time. Several, it will be noticed, were, well before that date, already used widely; and since, several others have gained a wide currency.

all that jazz. All that sort of thing: since ca. 1958, orig. jazz-lovers'.

bundle on, go a. To be wildly enthusiastic about (something): since ca. 1955, esp. among jazz-lovers.

gasser. Something quite breath-taking: adopted by jazz-lovers, in 1960, ex US.

gate. A form of greeting, esp. in *Hiya, gate!*: adopted by jazz-lovers, in 1962, ex US.

get sent. See *sent, get*, below.

get the message. See *message, get the*, below.

get with it. See *with it, get*, below.

give out. To do one's utmost, esp. in playing a musical instrument: adopted, ca. 1960, ex US, by jazz-lovers. Elliptical for *give out one's best*?

grab (oneself) a ball. To have a very good time: adopted, ca. 1959 and orig. by jazz-lovers, ex US.

groove, in the. 'Firmly established in the situation: musically integrated' (Rex Harris); adopted ex US, ca. 1955, by jazz-lovers.

jumping, adj. Moving, musically, in a fine, esp. an exciting, rhythm: jazz-lovers': since ca. 1959.—2. Hence, (very) successful, as in 'The joint is jumping'—the club, or the café, is happily excited: since ca. 1960.

message, get the. To understand the gist of an argument, the point of a warning, a hint: since ca. 1957. Cf. the Fighting Services' j. *message received*.

out of this world. Very beautiful; wonderful; superlative; perfect; although heard occasionally since ca. 1956, it has been common only since 1960. Applied orig.—and, of course, still—to consummate playing by an instrumentalist or to consummate singing.

sent, get. To become *en rapport* with, or enthusiastic about, the music (esp. jazz) that is being played, whether one is listener or performer: jazz-lovers': since ca. 1950.

solid. Satisfactory; (solidly) good; since ca. 1960, orig. jazz-lovers'.

trad. 'Abbreviation of traditional (jazz)': since ca. 1961. Rex Harris.

way out. Of jazz music: 'extremely advanced; complicated; esoteric' (Rex Harris): jazz-lovers': adopted, ca. 1950, ex US.

with it, get. (Cf. **with it**.) To appreciate a situation or a quality: since ca. 1957, orig. among jazz-lovers.

With these terms, cf.:

JIVE AND SWING

This slang reached Britain from the US in 1945; still in July 1947 it was very little known except among the *hep cats* or addicts of jive and swing, early called 'hot jazz'. All of it is American, most of it ephemeral. In mid-1947 Vic Filmer compiled a glossary of jive and swing. Almost the only terms that have the least importance and look at all likely to survive more than a year or two are these, culled from that glossary:

beat up (one's) chops. To be loquacious.

blow (one's) wig. To go crazy; hence, to act crazily. Prompted by that other Americanism, *blow (one's) top*. Cf. later *flip (one's) wig*.

fin. £1 (sum or note); *mash me a fin*, give me one pound. See **finnif**, in the main text.

gravy. Money. Hence *get (one)self some gravy for grease*, to obtain money for food.

neigho, pops! No (or, nothing doing), pal! Ex *nay!*, no!

razz-ma-tazz. Ordinary jazz, old-fashioned jazz, also called *ricky-tick* or *rooty-toot*.

twister. A key, esp. in *twister to the slammer*, a door key.

Priestley, 1965, amends the foregoing paragraph thus, 'I have a record I bought ca. 1934, made by the Negro bandleader and pianist Fats Waller, with the title "Don't try your jive on me", which suggests that it did not then mean the same as jazz. May mean "tricks", whence *jive* as a "tricky" form of playing. When the term *jive* came in, it denoted the sort of music that jitter-bugs danced to. This was a different style from the traditional "hot jazz". Jive and swing are not the same thing as what was before called "hot jazz".' He adds that *fin* and *gravy* are not, of course, jive talk; that *razz-ma-tazz* refers esp. to Cab Calloway's singing and conducting, ca. 1925–35; and that *ricky-ticky* or *rooty-toot* is old-fashioned New Orleans jazz.

KNOW

Here are listed some of the slang or colloquial ways of expressing the idea that a person is well-informed, experienced, wide-awake, equal to an emergency. Some are used in admiration (even if grudgingly given), but most, included because they *may* be (though seldom are) used positively, are predominantly negative and derogatory; the latter are generally used contemptuously of someone who, in the speaker's opinion, is stupid, ignorant, brash, incompetent, etc. This list makes no claim to being complete.

know A (or B) from a bull's foot: coll.: since C.18.

know a thing or two: since late C.18. A Cockney elab. of late C.19–early 20 was *know a thing or two or six* (Pugh, 1912 and 1914). Not to be confused with the emphatic *I know one thing—and that ain't two*, as prefix to a firm declaration.

know (one's) age(, gen. not): Petch, 1966.

know (one's) anus from (one's) ankle(, gen. not): BBC Radio 4 play, *Broken Fences*, by Ivor Wilson, 26 June 1982.

know (one's) arse from a hole in the ground or *from (one's) elbow(, gen. not)*: Can. and Brit. (Leechman). Cf. the most polite var. *know (one's) ears from (one's) elbows* (Blaker), and the version attrib. to Sir Thomas Beecham, the great conductor, 'He doesn't know his brass [*or* bass] from his oboe'.

know (one's) *boxes*: printers' coll. Rowles, 1948.

know (one's) *eccer*: Aus. (Baker). Ex *eccer*, school homework or exercise

know enough to come in out of the rain(, gen. *not*): later C.20.

know if . . . See *know whether . . .*

know (one's) *kit*: Army: since ca. 1950

know (one's) *onions*: s. > coll.: adopted ex US mid-1930s. Weekley.

know (one's) *stuff*: coll.: adopted ex US ca. 1930.

know the score: adopted ex US ca. 1950. Ex games, or music?

know where (one's) *arse hangs*(, gen. *not*): since early C.20. 'For a man who has got on in the world and become greedy in the process: "Since he's come into money he doesn't know where his arse hangs" ' (Muvver); L.A., on the other hand, wrote, 'Applied to a (usually) young man who hasn't "grown up" and who retains his boyhood's delusions of being a "hero" ': the two are not mutually exclusive.

know where (one) *is at* or *where* (one) *lives*(, gen. *not*): esp. later C.20; since ca. 1920.

know whether (one) *has* got *Arthur or Martha*(, *not*): to be in a state of confusion; dithering: (?mainly) Aus.

know whether (or *if*) *it's Pancake Tuesday or half-past break-fast-time*(, *not*): since ca. 1945: orig. euph. for any of the more vulgar examples in this list, but by 1955, it had > independent and gen.

know whether (one) *is on* (one's) *arse or* (one's) *elbow*(, *not*): to be utterly incompetent, or in a state of confusion.

KOREAN WAR SLANG

During this war, 1950–3 (but the period here is ca. 1951–5), the British Commonwealth troops, occasionally in collusion with the Americans, evolved a slang of their own. I owe all the examples given in this dictionary to Staff Sergeant C.R. O'Day of the Royal Army Educational Corps, four from his letter (18 Feb. 1955) and the rest from 'Slanguage', an article in the New Zealand contingent's magazine, *Iddiwah*, issue of July 1953. These terms are: **bring on**, (?)**Britcom, bug-out, chop-chop, Gook, grog on, hachi, hava no** and **hava yes,** *hills are closing in,* **hoochie, moose, Noggies, number one—ten—ninety-nine, sexy** (n.), **skoshi, slickee-slick** and **slickee-slickee, swan,** qq.v. in main text.

J.R. Elting, et al., *Dict. of Soldier Talk*, N.Y., 1984: '**idewa, iddiwa.** (Mostly 1950s on, although earlier use during the US occupation of Korea in 1945–49). Come here! . . . Most sources regard it as of Korean origin, but no comparable Korean form has been found. In all probability, it is pidgin Japanese, a corruption of *o-ide nasai* 'come here', in which *nasai* has been dropped and the nominative particle *wa* has (incorrectly) been added in its place.'

LOO

E.P.'s first suggested etym. was ex either Fr. *l'eau* or *gardy-loo*, but he later amended this: 'Far more prob. suggested by *Waterloo* station in London, itself named after the battle. In Fr. colloquialism, "le water" is elliptical for *water*-closet; and the *loo* part of *Waterloo* suggests Fr. *l'eau*, water.' But as R.S. has remarked, 1977, there is still another theory worth consideration: 'The bordalou, much used in C.18 by ladies travelling or in other privy difficulties on drawn-out social occasions. Portable in a muff, its artistic quality and its shape have sometimes led to its being mistaken nowadays for a sauce-boat. The name is said to derive from Louis Bourdaloue, the fashionable and prolix Jesuit preacher of Louis XIV's reign. The first known example, made in Delft, dates from 1710—and the article became very much "the thing". (*The Penguin Dictionary of the Decorative Arts*, 1977.)' A case can also be made that *loo* is cognate with 'leeward', since on board a small boat that is the side one would use (see G. Nixon's article 'Loo', *Lore and Language*, Jan. 1978, pp. 27–8); or might it simply be an anglicised *lieu*, 'the place', as in the frequently mispronounced 'time

off in lieu/*loo* [of time worked]'? Dempster, 1979, notes the term as 'out' in fashionable circles, being replaced by *lav*. But in ordinary, unfashionable circles it is still going strong in 1988. See also Rees, 1987, for half a dozen further explanations. (P.B.)

LOVERS' ACRONYMS or CODE-INITIALS

Mostly lower and lower-middle class, and widely used by Servicemen. Usu. at the foot, or on the envelope, of letters. The commonest of all is *SWALK*, sealed with a loving kiss; perhaps earlier, and less demonstratively, merely *SWAK*, as in F. & G., who also note the var. *SWANK*, . . . nice kiss; a joc. elab. is *SWALCAKWS*, sealed with a lick 'cos a kiss won't stick. Common also are [E.P. writing ca. 1950] BOLTOP, better on lips than on paper (set over against *X*, a 'paper kiss'), and ILUVM, I love you very much. The next three occur in Winton, 1960, but are, of course, very much older: *ITALY*, I trust and love you; *BURMA*, be undressed, ready, my angel (dating from WW2); *NORWICH*, (k)nickers off ready when I come home (prob. since WW1). The phonetic element is worth noting; also note the symbol ( ), an embrace. (With thanks to L.A., 1967, who cautiously adds that there are doubtless others.) P.B.: L.A. was right to be cautious! Two other examples are *HOLLAND,* here our love lies and never dies, and the somewhat more earthy *EGYPT,* eager to grab your pretty tits. I have heard the theory put forward that these 'code-words' were at first less demonstrations of affection than, used in their expanded form, indications to a girl-friend of the writer's location if this were officially secret. My uncle, Max Beale, 1985, adds 'Sometimes as a postscript by teenagers when asking a girl to a party: *LYKAH* = Leave your knickers at home.'

MAH-JONG

A player writes, late in 1961: We have the White Dragon referred to as 'soup' (being a completely blank—or clean—tile). There are three suits commonly referred to as (*a*) woods, bamboos, sticks; (*b*) balls, circles; (*c*) characters, ricks or 'icks. These are numbered 1 to 9, and some have nicknames:

Woods:	1 bird or shitehawk or hawk
	2 Long Annie
	3 tripod, hence tripe
	8 garden-gate, hence gate
	9 all the wood
Circles:	1 plate
	2 dog's (for dog's balls)
	3 'broker (for pawnbroker's three balls)
	4 taxi (four wheels or circles)
	5 spare wheel
	7 main crane
	8 scrubber
	9 all the balls
Ricks:	1 Eric (from 'a rick')
	6 spew (from 'seasick' through 'six 'ick')

P.B.: there must be many, many variations on these themes, wherever mah-jong is played in the English-speaking world. In our family games the 'dragons' are reduced to *drag*; the 'red dragon', actually the Chinese character for 'centre', is sometimes called *Dettol*, from its fancied resemblance to the trademark of that well-known antiseptic; and the 'South wind' is *candlesticks*, from its appearance when viewed upside down.

MOCK AUCTION SLANG

A few examples occur, scattered about the main text: e.g. **gazump** (there are other spellings), **nailers.** But here is a passage reported, in the section headed 'Parliament' (dealing with the Mock Auctions Bill) in *Daily Telegraph*, 25 Feb. 1961:

Sir Tufton [Beamish] told members that he had been to mock auctions in Britain and America. He gave an example of the jargon used:

'The top man operates his joint by nailing the steamers among the plunder-snatchers in the pitch got by his frontman running out the flash gear or hinton lots as N.S. lots to ricks and gees or to hinton, and gazoomphing the sarkers with swag and plunder, while the raving Noahs are silenced with bung-ons and the bogies are smitzed to hinton to noise the edge . . .'

He gave the translation:

'The mock auctioneer operates a stall by ensuring attendance until the end of the sale of those who are mugs rather than those who are just about for free gifts among the crowd collected by his men.

'He pretends to sell, as bait to his victims, genuine goods, which are in fact never sold, to accomplices among the crowd or to non-existent bidders at the back and tricking those of the mugs who have enough money to buy his cheap trash.

'Anyone who tries to warn the crowd is given a present. Dissatisfied customers who are likely to complain about previous sales are taken behind the rostrum to avoid trouble.'

The 'translation' is not a translation but a very free paraphrase. The following little glossary may help, even though, through my ignorance, I cannot render it either complete or 'watertight'. Refs. in bold type are to the main text.

bogies. Dissatisfied customers. See **bogey,** n., 3.
bung-ons. Gifts. Cf. **bung,** v., 2–4.
edge. See *noise the edge,* below.
flash gear. Showy, yet superior goods. Cf. **flash,** n., 1.
frontsman. That member of the gang who attracts the crowds.
gazoomphing. Swindling. See **gazump.**
gees. Auctioneer's accomplices. See **gee,** n., 1.
hinton-lots. Goods offered as bait; usu. genuine. Cf. *hinting-gear* in the para. below.
joint. A stall; the room where the auction is held. See **joint,** n., 1.
nailing. Successfully attracting. See **nailers,** and para. below.
noise the edge. To avoid trouble: app. since ca. 1945.
pitch. The crowd around the stall or in the auction room.
plunder-snatchers. Seekers after free gifts—and the real bargains.
raving Noahs. Trouble-makers. (Noahs prophesying floods.) P.B.: more prob. a shortening of rhyming *Noah's ark,* 'nark'.
ricks. Accomplices. See **rick.**
sarkers. ?Those tending to be sarcastic, yet, for all that, 'mugs'. P.B.: or perhaps a var. of (*raving*) *Noahs: Noah's arkers.*
smitzed. ?Reduced to silence. Perhaps on '*smith*ereens', but prob. Yiddish ex Ger. *schmitzen,* to lash, to whip.
steamers. Simpletons (natural victims) or 'mugs'. See **steamer,** 1.
swag and plunder. Cheap goods.
topman. Auctioneer. See **top man.**

Earlier, in Bournemouth *Evening Echo,* 18 Feb. 1960, had appeared the following:

'Mr Rudling said part of his duty'—at a mock-auction—'was to front up at the "hinting gear" table for the purpose of getting people into the shop'; *hinting gear* occurs thus, 'The selling was done by gathering an audience. There was a table put inside the shop on which was what was called "hinting gear". To passers-by it was said that alarm clocks were going at a shilling each or even sixpence. Among the "hinting gear" were such things as electric shavers and musical boxes'; 'articles sold for sixpence or a shilling were called "nailers" and were such things as after-shave lotions and ornamental poodle dogs'.

MOVING-PICTURE SLANG

Most of the terms in the following short article, 'It is Said in Filmland: "Slanguage" the "Movies" Have Made', reprinted—with many thanks to the proprietors and the editor—from *Tit-Bits,* 31 Mar. 1934, date, in England, from ca. 1930:-

The visitor to a foreign country expects to hear the natives speaking a tongue which is unlike his own, but it comes as a surprise to a visitor to a modern studio to find the technicians and artists speaking one of the strangest languages ever evolved.

2. Every trade and profession has its own jargon, but the film world has a colourful compilation of expressions unlike those in other walks of life.

3. 'Niggers' are not men of colour, but blackboards used to 'kill' unwanted reflections from the powerful lights. The latter, however, are not called lights but 'inkies' (short for incandescent), or 'sun arcs' (searchlights), or 'baby spots' (powerful lamps giving a very narrow beam), or 'broads' (lights which give flat, over-all lighting). 'Spiders' are the switches into which connections are plugged. When it is bristling with cables on all sides it is not unlike a giant spider. The 'organ' is not a musical instrument but a control panel which enables the technicians to start up the cameras and sound-recording apparatus, switch on red warning lamps outside the doors, and cut out all telephones.

4. 'Gertrude' is not a young lady, but a giant steel crane, with a camera at its head, which enables shots to be taken of players going up staircases or along balconies. 'Dollies', too, have nothing to do with femininity; they are the low trucks, with pneumatic-tyred wheels, on which cameras follow stars as they hurry through hotel foyers or along the decks of liners.

5. Here are some more studio terms. 'Juicers' are electricians; 'lens hogs' are stars who are over-anxious to hold the dead centre of the picture. A 'wild' scene has nothing to do with Hollywood parties, it is the terse description of scenes, usually of cars, aeroplanes or trains, which have appropriate fake sounds added in the laboratory after they have been photographically recorded.

6. When a film is completed it is 'in the can'. Every time a scene is successfully 'shot' it is called 'a take'; the whole of the day's 'takes' are then assembled and shown to the producer in a private projection room, but are then known as 'the rushes' or 'the dailies'. Exposed film is 'stuff'; unexposed film is 'raw stock'. If too much film has been shot on a scene, the surplus is known as 'grief'. The chemicals in which film is developed are known as 'soup'.

7. But not all studio terms are coined; as in other walks of life, many of the expressions used owe nothing to slang and everything to tradition.

8. For instance, a broadly funny situation is known as 'a Mack Sennett'; a film cheaply and hurriedly made is known as 'A Poverty Row Picture', in commemoration of the days when Gower Street, Hollywood (nicknamed Poverty Row), was the home of small independent companies turning out pictures quickly and cheaply.

9. 'To do a Gaynor' means to smile upwards through eyes swimming with tears, a tribute to Janet Gaynor's ability to switch on the 'sunshine through the tears'.

10. 'To do a Garbo', on the other hand, means to be proud, aloof, and unbending.

11. But perhaps the most picturesque phrase of all is 'the lot', which is always used to describe the company's land surrounding the studio. It has been in use since the days when, before studios were thought of, all 'interior' scenes were made in the open air (sunlight being the only satisfactory illuminant thirty years ago), and for which purpose hard-pressed pioneers rented vacant building lots.

OCKER

ocker, a constant disparager, whose assurance matches his ignorance and prejudice: Aus.: since ca. 1965 (or, perhaps, even a decade or two earlier), but not widely used until 1968. It derives, I believe, from **knocker,** an inveterate adverse-criticiser: *a knocker* has > *an ocker* by a well-known phonetic process: in originally careless pronunciation, *knocker = nocker,* therefore *a nocker* > *an ocker,* and the noun is apprehended as *ocker*; cf. *a nadder* (M.E. *naddr*), which duly > *an adder*. The process is discussed in 'Articled Nouns', an essay in my *From Sanskrit to Brazil*, 1952.

That origination was prompted by Mr John B. Gadson of New South Wales in a letter he wrote to me on 26 Dec. 1975: and I show my grateful appreciation by mentioning that it was he who drew my attention to the semantic equivalence of *ocker* to the earlier *knocker* (in its sense 'constant disparager'). To render him full justice, I quote from his letter:

There is the added attraction that this peculiarly Australian word . . . can be uttered in a peculiarly Australian way; i.e. with unmoving lips, relaxed throat and the head slightly back as if looking into the sun or into a raised glass of beer.

This type of person, who drinks regularly with his mates at his favourite pub after a hard day's 'yakka' [i.e. work], has few but highly self-centred interests. He tends to disparage what he has not, what he cannot have. He is Master Sour-Grapes of classical vintage. He 'knocks' almost everything with an accomplished inverted snobbery. A 'knocker' is an 'ocker' . . .

This figure has pervaded TV commercials . . . and is exemplified by such entertainers as Bazza McKenzie and Paul Hogan. As a possible reproach to a deteriorating national image it may be justifiable for local consumption, but attempts to foist it on the unsuspecting foreigner make one wonder anew at the pretensions of ockerdom.

The word has now come to the attention of the academics because of its . . . application to a new situation and . . . to a type of person receiving more prominence than hitherto in the mass media . . .

The word serves its new purpose admirably; it conveys a distinct, recognisable and verifiable concept.

Academic and scholarly, and indeed all literate, men and women both in Australia and in Britain were initiated, not as fully as necessary, into the word when, in 1976, the late Professor Graham Johnstone defined *ocker* thus: 'A boorish person who is aggressively Australian in speech and behaviour, often for humorous effect.' Hence, *ockerism*.

Jack Fingleton, famous Australian batsman and fielder and later an excellent writer on cricket, defined *ocker* (*Sunday Times*, 20 Mar. 1974) very succinctly as 'a cheerful, abrasive type who likes to be tough and throw his weight about.'

The type is also known as *Alf*, perhaps because it typifies a cheerful moron or virtual moron [P.B.: cf. 'Alfred E. Neuman' of the American magazine *Mad*].

'OXFORD -ER(s)'

At Oxford, it began late in 1875 and came from Rugby School (*OED* Sup.). By this process, the original word is changed and gen. abridged; then *-er* is added. Thus, *memorial* > *memugger*, the *Radcliffe* Camera > *the Radder* (for *the* is prefixed where the original has *the*). Occ. the word is pluralised, where the original ends in *s*: as in *Adders*, Addison's Walk, *Jaggers*, Jesus College. This *-er* has got itself into gen. upper-middle-class s. [E.P.'s note in 1st ed.; later he added:] Mr Vernon Rendall, himself an old Rugby School boy, rejects the Rugby School origin; he is supported by Fischer Williams, in his *Harrow*, 1901.

P.B.: the RN seems to have taken enthusiastically to the custom from quite early in C.20; see HARRY.

It should be noted that the suffixes *-agger(s)* and *-ugger(s)* (other initial vowels are seldom, if ever, used) are elaborated variations on the original *-er(s)* theme. They seem to have occurred where the original word was a monosyllable, e.g. the *Pragger Wagger* being preferred to the possible *Princers* of *Walers* for ease of pronunciation; *Jaggers* for 'Jesus' above because the possible *Jesers* makes little difference verbally; and they occur when a simple *-er(s)* suffix seems feeble or unsatisfactory: *indijaggers* rolls more easily off the tongue than mere *indigers* or *indigesters* for 'indigestion', and the same applies to *memugger* above. These are merely observations; I am in no way attempting to explain the phenomenon, for I cannot.

PARLYAREE

The 'Lingua Franca'—but actually as to 90% of its words, Italianate—vocabulary of C.18–20 actors and mid-C.19–20 costermongers and showmen: (orig. low) coll. verging, after ca. 1930, on S.E. (How long the word itself has existed, I do not know: prob. not before ca. 1850, when the vocabulary was much enlarged and the principal users changed so radically, though itinerant and inferior actors supply the link.) Ex It. *pargliare*, to speak. See *Slang*, *passim*, and at 'Circus Slang,' and P. Allingham's *Cheapjack*, 1934. [E.P.'s note in 1st ed.; later he added:]

In line 8, *pargliare* is a misprint for *parlare*, which accounts for the *Parlaree* (*-ry*) form; the *Parlyaree* form has been influenced either by C.19 spelling *palarie* or by, e.g., *parliamo*, 'let us speak'.

A full account of this Cinderella among languages appears in my book of essays and studies upon language, *Here, There and Everywhere*, 1949.

Parlyaree is both less general and less serviceable than *Parlary* or *parlary*. In late C.19–early 20, *palarey* or *palary* was very common, esp. among music-hall artists; after ca. 1945, *palary* is demotic, *parlary* hieratic. Lester's title for his glossary means 'Know Parlary'. In this work, ca. 1937, he enumerates the old, pre-decimal coins thus: halfpenny, *medza*; a penny, or (so many) pence, *soldi*; threepence, *tray-bit*, adopted from gen.—orig., low—s. and elab. from **tray**, 2; sixpence, *say soldi*; a shilling, *bionk*; a florin, *dewey bionk*; a half-crown, *medza(-)caroon*; a crown (piece) or 5 shillings, *caroon*; 10 shillings, *daiture bionk* or *medza(-)funt*; £1, *funt*. Lester cites the numerals: *una*, 1; *dewey*, 2; *tray*, 3; *quattro*, 4; *chi(n)qua*, 5; *say*, 6; *setta*, 7; *otta*, 8; *nobba*, 9; *daiture*, 10; *lepta*, 11; *kenza*, 12. The greatest deviation from the Italian originals are exhibited by *daiture*, *kenza*, *lepta*, which aren't Italian at all.

Mr Herbert Seaman, learned in the ways of theatre, music-hall, side-show, tells me (letter, 1950) that 'Mr Dai Griffith, a singer, once sang to me this song, which he said was current among buskers.

Nantee dinarly; the omee of the carsey
Says due bionc peroney, manjaree on the cross.
We'll all have to scarper the letty in the morning
Before the bonee omee of the carsey shakes his doss.

The tune is simple, in 6/8 time, and should have a guitar accompaniment.'

Since ca. 1970, as L.A. notes, 1976, 'gay' slang has come to be known, in raffish, homosexual circles, as *polari*.

PIP-SQUEAK

Amplification of the entry at **pip-squeak**, 4: 'Forgetting to switch off his "pip-squeak" (radio contactor), Nicky climbed thankfully out on to the wing' (Brickhill, 1946). H. & P., 1943, 'Radio telephony set': RAF (aircrews') since ca. 1935. Cf. sense 2. At short intervals, it goes *pip squeak*.

' "Radio-telephony set" is perhaps misleading. The pip-squeak was an automatic transmitter *only*, whose once-a-minute signals enabled ground direction-finding stations to fix the aircraft's position accurately for the benefit of the Fighter Controller in the Operations Room. But for those seconds when it was transmitting, ordinary radio-telephonic communication with the pilot was not possible. The Controller's occasional query: "Is your pip-squeak in (i.e. switched on)?" soon acquired sexual connotations.'

'An equivalent equipment' in homing bombers was I.F.F. (Identification, Friend or Foe), which, however, imparted a characteristic pulse to the visual echo on radar screens' (R.S., 1967).

PRISONER-OF-WAR SLANG

There is a valuable note on the prisoners-of-war-in-Germany slang at the beginning of Brickhill, 1946: see entry at **kriegy**. Morgan, 1945, contains these additional terms: *big eats!*: How are you?—Ger. *Wie geht's?*, How goes it?; *bunker*, solitary-confinement cell; *fish-paste?*, What time is it?—Ger. *Wie spät ist es?*; **goon** (see main text), 'after that dumb top-heavy ham-handed race of giants in the "Pop-Eye" comic strip'; hence, *goon up!*—a warning that a German (soldier) is near-by or approaching; *millet*, 'porridge-like soup'; *Nix fish-tins*, I don't understand—Ger. *Nicht verstehen; stimmt*, genuine, true—from Ger. *alles stimmt*, all correct; *tiger-box*, a square box that, on a pole at each corner of the barbed wire, contained search-light, machine-gun, telephone and a sentry.

2. For the POW slang of the Far East, there was published in a ship's news-sheet of late 1945, an excellent and delightful article by H.W. Fowler & I.P. Watt, who have generously allowed me to make full use of it. Here are some few of the terms they list; the quotations come from that article.

3. A rumour: *borehole* (ex a rough-and-ready latrine); *griff* (see **griff,** n., in main text); and *latrin(e)o-gram*.

4. 'Anyone thought to run a wireless set, or to have other sources of information, was "in the cloak and dagger club".' The word *canary* was officially suggested for 'radio' or 'wire-less'; thence 'came "dicky bird", "birdsong" and "bird-seed" . . . Trouble in getting batteries to work the sets was "trouble about birdseed".'

5. At Changi camp, the Sikh guards did not behave well: hence *sikhery*, 'brutality; bloody-mindedness'; *Sikh's beard*, a local tobacco, coarse, tough, wiry.

6. Terms from Malay were *go buso*, 'to turn septic'—from *busok*, 'rotten'; *lagi*, often mispronounced *leggy*, superseding the synon. *baksheesh*; *Nazi Goering*, 'fried rice'—from *nasi goreng*; and a number of direct adoptions. [E.P. later added:] Concerning *leggy*, another Far East POW—Mr R.H. Pant-ling—tells me (1960) that 'its far more general use was for a second helping of our very inadequate rations. The frequent cry, towards the end of a meal, of "Any more leggies?" made pedantic scholars of Malay wince.' (P.B.: Malay *lagi* = more, another.)

7. Japanese supplied *benjo*, lit. 'a convenient place'—a water closet or latrine; *byoki*, sick; *yasmé*, lit. 'rest', which did duty for 'rest'—'sleep'—'holiday'—'peace'; camp headquarters being *Yasmé Villa*; and, remotely, *Nip*, a Japanese. To which Cdr C. Parsons, RN ret., added in 1973, '*Yasmé* (phonetic) derives from Japanese *yasumi*, rest, recess, etc.'

8. From Aus. slang, or from association with Australian sol-diers, came *jokers*, 'chaps', 'fellows'; *'bronzies* (Aussies, the "bronzed gods" of Singapore ballyhoo journalism)'; '*Bungs* (for Dutch half-castes), originally Australian slang for their own Aboriginals'.

9. Dutch yielded *eten halen*, lit. 'to fetch food', and *Got(t)-fordommers*, from *Gott verdomme* (Dutch version of *God damn!*), both as nicknames for the Dutch themselves.

10. Some names for food were these: 'The staple stew, taste-less, meatless . . . was dubbed "jungle stew"—anything bad was "jungle"—jungle sores, jungle camps, jungle fever, jungle bananas'; 'various types of dried fish . . . "Cheese fish"—"Bengofish"—"Picture-frame fish" or "Tennis-racket fish" '; the various disguises of rice were generically *doovers* (see **doover;** though perhaps ironically ex 'hors d'œuvre') or *efforts*, the latter having, at Changi, been a rissole. A *gas-cape stew* was a dried vegetable soup.

11. Canteen cries and names: *hot, sweet and filthy*, concern-ing coffee or for 'coffee'; *nutty nutty*, 'a local concoction of sugar, peanuts and newspaper'; *lime slime*, a sweetened version of *gu-gu* (tapioca gruel); *limo-limo*, a hot lime drink.

12. Medical terms: 'Amputations were so frequent that two abbreviations, "amputs" and "stumpies", were required; and "amput cigarettes" were on sale'—rolled by those men who had had a limb amputated; *avit*, an avitaminosis patient; *the diary*, diarrhœa.

13. References to Japanese influence occur in *Jap-happy*, 'for those who were thought to "collaborate" in any way or to do well out of the Nips . . . coined early in Singapore. But it became current in Thailand when the lucky few were the recipi-ents of Japanese clothing—rubber boots were "Jap-happies",

and a loin cloth was a "Jap-happy" (or sometimes a "G-string").'

14. Phrases: Anyone who was in a constipated mental con-dition 'had his finger up', and was expected to 'pull it out'. 'One phrase . . . stands out . . . ; it will live to describe an aspect of human nature seen very clearly in the bad times, when selfish-ness and greed were matched by the envy and malice of the less fortunate, in the utter lack of privacy of the camps in Thailand. It was developed from the phrase "Pull the ladder up, Jack, I'm all right!" which had long been current, as had "fuck you, Jack, I'm all right!" It was abbreviated, however, by frequency of use to the P.O.W. forms "A Jack Club", "a ladder club" or "Lad-der", "a ladder job", "Got your ladder", "Mine's up", and so on all to describe whatever was considered a "cushy" job for which the usual term could have been "administration" as opposed to "work". On the other hand, our officers spurred themselves to greater efforts in hut-building with the cry, "Up guards and atap!" (*Note*. All our huts were atap-roofed.)'

15. Miscellaneous: *Bangkok bowler*, a Thailander's bamboo hat; *bamboo presento*, a beating-up with a bamboo; *Gordon Thailanders*, Gordon Highlanders; *2359 (hours)*, a coloured officer—usually as a nickname—the time, on the very verge of midnight, when all is dark.

16. P.B.: in Drage, 1954, is noted *Mimi Lau's* for bricks and concrete used as a bed: in Stanley Prison civilian internment camp, Hong Kong, WW2: 'origin unknown'.

PUBLIC AND GRAMMAR SCHOOL SLANG IN 1968

On 1 Sep. 1968, 'Atticus' in the *Sunday Times* published a short article on the slang vocabulary of 'a typical school', based on the findings of sociologists Royston Lambert and Spencer Mill-ham. Apart from words or phrases merely variants of S.E. and from those common in many English Public and Grammar Schools, I have listed a few that seemed note-worthy, either because apt and picturesque or because they have since gained a wider, several a much wider, currency; on the other hand, several clearly belonged also to other schools.

basic. Simple-minded; (of acts) stupid.

brace, n. A snub; *brace up*, to snub (someone)—*brace up!*, 'You have been snubbed.'

bugger. 'A type of rugger with no rules played in the water-meadows'.

bushy. Annoyed.

crease, v. Esp. in the vbl n., *creasing*. 'To make oneself pleas-ant to [someone] with the idea of getting somewhere oneself.'

kick up, v. To 'make a fuss (especially applied to masters who complain about a boy's behaviour).'

oil, n. Gravy.

pseud. 'One who holds pretentious or unorthodox opinions'; a cynic; an insincere person; a would-be or, 'for the hell of it' pre-tending to be, an intellectual and tending to incomprehensible conversation; a dry intellectual; a socialist or any other non-Conservative. Mostly used pej.—'almost the exact opposite of *staunch*'.

shag, adj. Shaggy in appearance; but usu., 'bad'—with a derog-atory connotation.

staunch, n. 'A person who is exceedingly keen on games and other house activities, and makes it unpleasant for those who do not wish to participate.'

turf! Senior to junior schoolfellow, 'You have been turfed off from doing that, because I, your senior, say so and want it.'

RAILWAYMEN'S SLANG AND NICKNAMES

Many items of railwaymen's s. are to be found scattered through the main text. Most are taken from Harvey Sheppard's *Dictionary of Railway Slang*, 1964, and later edd., or from Frank McKenna's *Glossary of Railwaymen's Talk*, 1970. The latter was the basis of his admirably informative book *The Rail-way Workers, 1840–1970*, pub'd 1980 by Messrs Faber & Faber Ltd, and I am most grateful to Mr McKenna and to the pub-lishers for permission to draw on the book both to support entries in the main text, and for the lists, which I append here without additional comment, from pp. 239–41:

Signalling Terms

back 'un	Distance signal
big dipper	High semaphore
biscuit	Signal line token
blackboard	Oblong ground signal
bullseye	Signal light
Christmas tree	Multiple aspect signal
clear pop	Clear signal
dolly, dodd, dummy	Ground signals
double yolk	Two yellows
fairy land	Multiple aspect signals
feathers	Lunar lights
Forever Amber	Fixed distant signals
gun	Radar speed trap
harbour lights	Lunar lights
Hitler salute	Upraised semaphore
iron man	IBS post
on the block	In the loop
orange peel	Plate-layers' orange jackets
peg, stick, board	Semaphore signals
persecuted minority	Employed, over-65s
pounded	Inside clear
spider	Signal apparatus in four foot
stairway to the stars	Ladder to signal's arm
triple crown	Three headlamps

Places of Interest

Back Pan, the	Washwood Heath
Big Stacks, the	Brickfield Chimneys, Bedford
Block all Junction	Watford
Cupboard, the	Coppermill Junction, Eastern Region
Drain, the	Waterloo
Fernando's Hideaway	Plate-layers' cabin
Goal Post, the	Cricklewood
Hostile Territory	Another region
Indian Country	Eastern region
Land of Plenty	Overtime
Maze, the	Clapham Junction
Orchard, the	Cricklewood sidings
Plywood Sidings	Barking, Essex
Ponderosa, the	Kentish Town to Barking
Rat Hole, the	Euston Tunnel
Shanty, the; also *Library*	Messroom
Tea Gardens, the	Somers Town Sidings, St Pancras

Nicknames

Abadan	Excessive oil user
College of Knowledge	The depot union representative
Dead-end kid	Person not taking promotion
Desk jockey	Clerk
Florence Nightingale	Shunter with lamp
Genial Menial	Shed labourer
Gruesome twosome	Joint chairmen
Gutta percha	Bird on shed roof
Jumping Jack	Lively chargehand
Mistletoe Men, Out Riders	Non-union men
Pail hands	Office cleaner
Set of grinders	Sheffield men
Siamese twins	Branch and LDC secretaries
Syndicate, the	Full meeting, management—unions
Talkies, the	Local negotiating meeting
Talking machine	Branch secretary
Traps	Guard's equipment
Whispering Baritone	Noisy person

Wigan blind	A grey puddeny mass. Dross, a mixture of dust found in coal wagons emanating from briquettes, cobbles, slack and nuts.

I have permission to reprint the following from p. 234 of *The Railway Workers:* 'an example of railway talk which could have been heard almost anywhere on the railways of Britain in the days of steam':

We were humping the bricks with a short of puff Black Five. It was as thick as a bag. At Stone Crossing both squirters packed in, but we got inside without blocking the fast. A set of Huns with a tender first crab hooked up but we still made a rounder.

Translation

Humping the bricks	Working a brick train
Short of puff	An engine steaming poorly
Black Five	A Class 5 Mixed Traffic Engine, LMS
Thick as a bag	Very foggy. [P.B.: cf. **black as a bag.**]
Squirters	Water injector mechanism, taking water from tender to boiler
Getting inside	Entering a loop or siding
Blocking the fast	Blocking the main line
Set of Huns	Engine-men from another depot
Tender first crab	'Crab' was a freight engine; tender first meant that the engine was wrong way round for train working
Making a rounder	A twelve-hour shift—halfway round the clock

Another example is the skill with which railway workers gave new titles to the companies that employed them:

Staff Nickname	Railway Company
The Clog and Knocker	Grand Central
Let Me Sleep	
Lord, My Shephard	London, Midland and Scottish
Elleva Mess	
Go When Ready	
Greatest Way Round	Great Western
God's Wonderful Railway	
Late, Never Early	London and North-Eastern
Muddle, Goes Nowhere	Midland, and Great Northern
Slow and Dirty	Somerset and Dorset
Languish and Yawn	Lancashire and Yorkshire.

Simon Watts, 1988, adds these:

Slow Mouldy and Jolting	Stratford and Midland Junction
Lose 'em, Mix 'em and Smash 'em	LMS
Got Nowhere	Great Northern (its northern terminus was an end on junction in a field north of Doncaster)
Gone Completely	Great Central: because it is the only main railway that has

and Andrew Poole, 1988:

Money Sunk and Lost	Manchester, Sheffield and Lincoln

RHODESIAN ARMY (LIGHT INFANTRY) SLANG CURRENT IN NOV. 1976

In the *Star*, Johannesburg, 22 Nov. 1976, as my friend Ashley Cooper Partridge tells me, appeared an entertainingly light-hearted anonymous article, 'Tune Me a Glide, Toppie'. Because of its ephemeral nature, emphasised by Capt. Colin

Dace of the Rhodesian Light Infantry, I here alphabetise the terms therein treated, but do not insert them separately into the main text. Several, however, will be recognised as of a venerable antiquity or of a much wider distribution—or as of both: 'see above' means 'see at this entry in the main text of the *Dict.*'

babalas. Tipsy. [P.B.: should perhaps be *babarasi*, which means 'drunk' or 'with a hangover', in the Ndebele language. With thanks to Mr Eshialwa D. Obati, of Nairobi.]

bend. To damage (a car): coll. rather than s. [P.B.: Brit. Forces' s.]

burg. A town. This, however, was orig. US, then by ca. 1925, fairly gen. Brit. s. [P.B.: but may it not have arisen independently, under Afrikaans influence, in Southern Africa?]

buzz. Esp. *give* (someone) *a buzz*, to cause (him) trouble.

catch a gonk. See *gonk*.

chibuli. See *flatten*.

chick. A girl. Gen. s., ex US. See above.

clobber. Clothes. Gen s. See above.

cream into. To collide, as one car with another. See *cream*, v., above.

fade. To leave (a locality or position), i.e. to fade away from it, as in 'Let's fade this possy (*or* loc)'. Adopted ex US.

flat dog, or *flatdog*. A crocodile; cf. *mobile handbag*.

flatten (or *kill* or *slay*) *a chibuli*. To 'down' one's beer. [*Chibuli*, perhaps a corruption of *chibuku*, a word for beer, and also a well-known brand-name for it in East Africa. With thanks to Mr E.D. Obati. P.B.]

floppy. ' "Floppies"—Terrorists . . . because of a noted tendency to flop down when shot.' Cf. *ter*.

gangen. The bush or outback. Cf. the Aus. *walkabout*. [P.B.: perhaps one of the words absorbed into Swahili from the former German East Africa: Ger. *gangen*, to go.]

give a buzz. See *buzz*.

glide. A lift in a vehicle, as in *tune me a glide*, formally 'Kindly give me a lift'. Semantics: *accord* a lift.

gonk. In *catch a gonk*, to have a nap or a full sleep, but also to take a look.

gook. See *rev*, 2. [P.B.: the former sense also Brit. Forces' s. See above.]

graze, n. and v. Food or 'a bite to eat', a meal; to eat, to have a meal. Ex livestock grazing.—2. To injure or wound, as 'I was grazed by a flatdog.'

grimmy. An unattractive girl, as in 'Who was that grimmy I saw you with last night?' [P.B.: cf. Brit. Public Schools' **grimmer.**]

hit out to the gomos. To climb and search a hill, a group of hills, e.g. in search of terrorists. *Gomo* is presumably a native word. [P.B.: Mr E.D. Obati tells me that *gomos* means 'hill' in the Ndebele language.]

hooli. A lively party or a night on the town, esp. in *lekker hooli*, a successful one. [E.P. surmised a shortening of *hooligan*, but cf. **hooley**, 1, above.]

kill a chibuli. See *flatten*.

lekker. Excellent or delightful, as in *lekker chick* (girl) and *lekker hooli*. Afrikaans. [P.B.: cf. the lowish German 'Hast du geschmeckt?' (Have you enjoyed your meal?)—'Lecker, lecker!' (Yes, indeed!)]

loc. A locality—place—(military) position: as in 'Let's fade this loc.'

mobile handbag. A crocodile. Ex use of crocodile skin in making women's handbags.

owen. 'Among themselves the troopies often refer to one another as owens': at a guess I'd say that here is a pun on the given name and surname *Owen* and 'our *own* fellows'.

possy. A *position*, esp. if military; a post, trench, site: a WW1 term.

pull, v.i. To 'pull out' or depart.

rev. 'A "rev" (dressing down) from the commanding officer'. [—2. To kill. *Listener*, 9 Nov. 1978, quotes 'rev gooks' as Rhodesian Army s. for 'to shoot terrorists', and adds, 'the word "gooks" is courtesy of Vietnam.']

Saints, the. The nickname bestowed, by themselves, on men of the Rhodesian L.I.: joc. ironic.

scale, v.i. To dress in one's best clothes, for instance in order to meet a girl. [P.B.: ex 'full scale of issue'?]

slay a chibuli. See *flatten*.

ter. A *ter*rorist, esp. a member of a terrorist striking force.

toppie. An old man; in address, 'old fellow', as in the title of the article. Cf. the writer's 'and the toppie bit? If that's what your troopy's thinking, you may as well . . . quietly fade. You're past it, over the hill, too long in the tooth. Over 30 anyway.' ?Afrikaans.

troopy. A trooper, i.e. a private, occ. a non-commissioned officer, in the Rhodesian Light Infantry.

tune. To accord—to agree to give or grant (a kindness) to someone, as in *tune* (*me*) *a glide*, to oblige with a lift in car or jeep. [*zap*. To shoot and kill. *Listener*, 9 Nov. 1978, quotes 'zap CTs' as Rhodesian Army s. for 'to kill terrorists'. 'Zap' has been taken over from US Forces' usage in the Vietnam war (cf. *gook*, q.v. at *rev*, 2), while *CT*, standing for 'Communist Terrorist', was in common use during the war in Malaya, 1948–60. P.B.]

SPANGLISH

Writing from Argentina in 1960, Mrs Daphne Hobbs remarks, 'You would be quite interested in the sort of lingua franca spoken in Argentina—in Buenos Aires particularly—among the Argentine-born children of English parents. We call it 'Spanglish'. . . . The custom is to anglicise Spanish verbs and use them as if they were English—and also to do the same to some of the Argentine (Criollo) slang. For instance, 'to iron' is *planchar* in Spanish and this becomes *planchate*, e.g. 'I must heat the iron to planchate my dress.' In Criollo slang, *canchero* means someone rather smart, good-looking, exciting, etc., so we get *canch*, meaning, roughly, 'super' as the English schoolboy or -girl would use it. Again, in Criollo patois, we have *cacho*, a small chunk, and this becomes *catch*, meaning 'a small piece' or even 'slightly', e.g. 'Now I understand a catch.'

R.C. adds, 1976, that in US Spanglish is 'the dialect spoken by Hispanic (mostly Puerto Rican) immigrants in New York City. Educated Puerto Ricans dislike the term because [it implies] that their countrymen do not speak "correct" Spanish—which most of them don't, and what difference does it make?'

STONYHURST

Marples lists *atramentarius*, a 'fag'; *bonk*, *bunker*, a cad; *cob*, to 'cop' (take); *crow*, a master; *haggory*, 'a garden used for discussion . . . from *agora*, market-place'; *heavy*, important (or self-important), impressive; *oil*, to take (a culprit) by surprise, and *oilers*, rubber-soled shoes; *pin*, to enjoy—hence *pinning* or *pinnable*, enjoyable; *shouting cake*, a currant cake; *squash*, a football scrum; *stew*, to 'swot'; *swiz*, a crib; *taps*, a caning; *tolly*, an improvised cane.

STRINE

Despite Mr R.W. Burchfield's stricture (*New Statesman*, 17 Mar. 1967, p. 376): 'Australiana abound but *Strine* has escaped notice', it has nothing to do with slang: it doesn't mean 'Australian slang': it does concern the way in which Australians, esp. of the larger State capitals, run words together—and mispronounce them—in conversation; its true unit is not the word but the colloquial group, usually a phrase. *Let Stalk Strine*, Alistair Morrison's biting satire published in 1965, mean's 'Let's talk Australian.' P.B.: A.M. later, and again under the pseudonym 'Afferbeck Lauder', compiled an equally witty collection entitled *Fraffly* (= frightfully), following his sojourn among the upper-class inhabitants of Mayfair.

SURNAMES, TRUNCATED

'Always in the plural, thus, "*The Partri*: The Partridges; *the Prenti*: the Prentices". This practice has some currency among schoolboys and undergraduates' (B.P.): Aus.: since the late 1940s. I'd say that it originated as undergraduate wit, on the analogy of Ancient Roman *gens* (or clan) names ending in *-i*, reinforced by Latin plurals in *-i*, e.g. 'the *Gracchi*'. P.B.: similar affectionate perversions are not unknown in UK: the next-door neighbours of my childhood, 1930s, a family surnamed Foot, were always known as 'The Feet', and inevitably surnames ending in *-man*, e.g. Portman, Chapman, become 'The Portmen', etc.

SWAHILI

Swahili words used by the Armed Forces in E. Africa (and S. Africa) in 1939–45 include *pesi-pesi* (pronounced *pacey-pacey*), quickly, get a move on!, and *pole-pole* (pronounced *poley-poley*), slowly, take it easy; *pombī*, native beer, hence any brew obtained in the East; *shauri* or *shauria*, trouble, a row or fracas; *umgeni*, more, again, hence *umgenis*, 'afters'.

TIDDLYWINKS

P.B.: although, strictly speaking, the terms that follow ought to be considered jargon, they are colourful and slangy enough to qualify for entry in this Dictionary. I was made aware of their existence by a short article in the *Sunday Times* mag., 9 Mar. 1980, and am very grateful to Mr C.W. Edwards, sometime Secretary of the English Tiddlywinks Association, for this Glossary which he compiled for me in 1980:

'blitz, v.i. and n. To pot all six winks of one colour before the 20-minute time-limit has elapsed and thus score an easy victory (American).

bomb, v.t. To play a wink at a pile of winks with destructive intent.

boondock, v.t. To send an opponent's wink (lying beneath one's own) a long way away, preferably off the table. (Amer. 'in the boondocks') [P.B. See **boondocks**.]

bridge, v.t. and n. To cover further winks of the opponent's colours with a wink that is already covering at least one.

bristol, v.i. and n. To play a shot with one's own wink, taking with it an underlying opponent's wink that thus remains squopped [see below]. (Difficult to describe, but ought to be effective over long distance.) From Bristol University Tiddlywinks Society in the 1960s. Most recent derivatives include 'a John O'Groats'—a disastrous attempt at a Bristol shot that loses the opponent's wink.

carnovsky, v.i. and n. To pot a wink or several winks from the baseline, a distance of 3 feet. This usually happens by accident, and is to be avoided in the early stages in the game, but the name derives from the feat of Steve Carnovsky at Harvard in 1962 of potting four winks in succession from the baseline in his very first game. He immediately retired from the game. (Amer.)

doubleton, an. A shot which results in one of one's own winks squopping two enemy winks.

murgatroyd, n. A badly manufactured wink which is flat on both sides. Etymology unknown, but very probably Oxford Univ. T.S.

nurdle, v.t. To play a wink into a position so near the pot it cannot be potted. (No such position really exists, in my view!)

pile-jump, v.t. and n. To play a shot which involves placing at least two winks on at least two more, with one's own winks preferably on top and in command. (Amer.)

pot, v.t. and n. To play one's wink(s) into the pot. Hence to *pot-out*, to place all six winks of one's colour in the pot, thus gaining a bonus point. *Pot-squop* is a strategy which involves one of the two partners attempting to pot his winks, while the other keeps the opponents tied up by covering them. The alternative strategies are *double-pot* (bordering on the insane) and *double-squop* (the most commonly practised and effective strategy).

round(s), n. The last five shots of the four players after the time-limit has elapsed.

scrunge, v.t. To pot a wink which then bounces out of the pot again.

squidger, n. A circular plastic counter of between 1 and 2 inches in diameter used to play one's (smaller) winks with. Hence to *squidge*, *squidging*.

squidge-off, n. and v.i. The action of playing a wink to the middle to determine who commences the game. (Etym. from kick-off.)

squop, v.t. and n. To cover one's opponent's wink with one's own (Cambridge, 1950s).

squopped up, p. ppl. The state of having all one's winks covered, and thus being unable to play a shot.

sub, v.i. To play one's wink under an opponent's wink or pile, inadvertently (from 'submarine').

tiddlywinks, n. See *OED*. The adult game was devised by Cambridge undergraduates in 1955.

wink(s), n. Abbr. of above, but also the six plastic counters, two 3/32 in. thick and 7/8 in. diameter and four 1/16 in. thick and 5/8 in. diameter, which each player has.

There are doubtless many more terms which I have forgotten or do not employ myself, but these I think are the most commonly used. There is, I believe, an American linguistics thesis on winks terminology, but I've just had a vain hunt for a reference to it. The American terminology has influenced our British terminology, and of the two theirs is—not untypically—the more colourful and creative language. I restrict myself to those terms in current usage on the mainland. Putting a date to the terms is difficult, but none of them is likely to be older than 1955 and the founding of modern tiddlywinks in Cambridge.'

TOMBOLA

P.B.: I have here concentrated all the notes about the game that were scattered through *DSUE* 7. They were drawn mostly from three sources: Laurie Atkinson, ca. 1950 (= A); Michael Harrison, *Reported Safe Arrival*, 1943, p. 85 (= H); and Frank Richards, dealing with Services, mainly Army, early C.20 (= R). To these have been added my own observations, Army calls, later 1950s (= B); and the later C.20 Bingo calls, some rhyming, listed in Peter Wright, *Cockney Dialect and Slang*, 1981 (= W). P = unannotated, from earlier editions of the *Dict*.

The game was known originally, in later C.18, as *Lotto* (1778: *SOD*); in late C.19–early 20 Services it was *House* or *Housey-Housey*, from the call shouted by the winner on completing his *card* or *ticket*; by mid-C.20 it had become *Tombola* (*SOD*: 1880, as 'a kind of lottery'); and finally, when it became a widespread craze ca. 1960, the game was called *Bingo* (although *SOD* has 1936). It appears that earlier the highest number to be marked off was 100, but by 1950, if not before, this had been reduced to 90. Nearly every number has its nickname, some have several; in Service messes the numbers have to be inferred from the nicknames shouted by the caller, they are not included in the calls every time; in civilian Bingo halls however the game has to be made as simple as possible.

The traditional call to attention on the game, at the start or resumption of play, is 'Eyes down—look in! And the first number is . . . ' If, as must occasionally happen, the first number drawn out of the bag to be marked off by the holders of those cards on which it is printed is actually the number 1, the caller will continue, 'as it should be: number one!' Otherwise, the numbers may be called as follows. Note that the single numbers are usually prefaced, 'On its own . . . '; 'q.v.' references are to the main text of the Dict., where most of the nicknames are listed anyway, some with further explanation.

1. Kelly's eye (R) *or* (rare) wonk (P); Buttered scone (W); Little Jimmy (R).

2. Dirty old Jew (A); Baby's done it (B); Me an' you *or* Doctor Who (from children's TV) (both W); One little duck (see 22) (B); Buckle < buckle me < buckle-my-shoe: r.s. (H).

3. Goodness me (P); Dearie me (B); One little feather *or* fevver (see 33) (B).

4. Knock at the door; Door to door; 'The one next door—it's number four' (all W).

5. Jack's alive (P); Dead alive (W).

6. Spot below (P): the counter has a spot below the figure to distinguish it from 9; Tom Mix; Chopping sticks *or* Chopsticks (all W).

7. One little crutch (see 77) (B); Gawd's in 'eaven (W).

8. Garden gate (A); One fat lady *or* waaf (see 88) (B); 'Arry Tate (W).

9. The doctor (P). The 'number 9' pill was the Service medical officer's standby, especially to cure constipation, in early C.20, and gave rise to variants: Doctor's chum (B); Doctor Foster (P); Doctor's favourite *or* orders (H); Doctor's shop (P); Medicine and duty (P); 'Orspital (W).

10. May be preceded 'One oh . . . ': Shiny ten, q.v. (H); occ. Blind ten (cf. 20); Downing Street (A), ex the Prime Minister's official residence, when [name of incumbent]'s den (B); Cock(s) an' 'en (W); Uncle Ben (H).

11. Legs eleven (R), Kelly's legs (P), *or* Legs—they're lovely (B); Marine's breakfast (H). (The number resembles a pair of legs, and was given this extra syllable to distinguish it from 7 and avoid mistakes.)

From here on, the double numbers, except in multiples of 10 and 11, are called with 'and' between tens and digits, e.g.:

12. One and two—one duzz (= dozen) (B); Monkey's cousin (W).

13. Unlucky for some (R); or simply 'Unlucky'.

15. Rugby team (W).

16. Sweet sixteen *or* lovely (B); Sweet sixteen and never been kissed (R).

17. Never been kissed *or* Never had it (A); How I like 'em (B, who adds, 'if followed by a much higher number, e.g. 87, the latter would then be called "8 and 7—how I get 'em!" ').

20. Blind twenty (A).

21. Key of the door (R), ex the former legal coming-of-age; Age o' mi ol' dutch (W); Royal salute (H).

22. Dinkie doo(s) (A); All the twos (A); Two little, *or* A couple of, ducks (B), ex shape, also: Ducks in the, *or* on a, pond *or* in the water (P).

24. Two duzz (= dozen) (B); Pompey [= Portsmouth] (wh)ore (A).

26. Bed and breakfast (A, who adds 'half-a-crown being evidently the accepted traditional charge').

28. The Old Brags (R), q.v.

30. Blind thirty (A); Speed limit (W).

33. All the threes (A); occ. elab. All the threes—fevvers, or simply Fevvers!, an allusion to the Cockneyism 'firty-free-fah-sand fevvers on a frush's froat' (B); Gertie Lee (P).

34. Dirty 'ore (A).

36. Three duzz (= dozen) (B).

39. All the steps (A: from the title of John Buchan's novel *The Thirty-Nine Steps*).

40. Blind forty (A); Life begins (B: from the advertising slogan of that tonic which claims to 'fortify the over-forties').

44. All the fours (A); Open the door (R); Menopause (W); Diana Dors (B); Pompey (r.s. = 'whores' understood), whence var. Grant Road (also B: the brothel district of Bombay, an Army call inherited from those with service in India), and Aldershot ladies (P).

45. Halfway house (B: for the later-style card).

48. Four duzz (B).

49. Copper (ex *PC49* of radio police series); Cannock-nuff (also W: from WW1 attempts at French *quarante-neuf*); Rise and shine (r.s., in Hastings, 1947).

50. Blind fifty (A); Halfway house (A: the old-style card); Change hands (B).

51. The Highland Div[ision] (B).

52. The Lowland Div[ision] (B).

53. The Welsh Div[ision] (B: these three refer to WW2 military formations).

55. All the fives (A).

57. Heinz *or* Beans *or* All the beans (A: from Heinz's well-known 57 varieties).

59. The Brighton Line (B: hearsay tells me that the first engine used to pull the old *Brighton Belle* was locomotive number 59—or this may be simply r.s.).

60. Blind sixty (A).

62. Ticketty-boo (r.s., in *Punch*, 14 Oct. 1942, p. 312. Cf *ticketty-boo* in main text.)

65. Old age pension (P); Stop work (W: men's retirement age).

66. All the sixes (A); Clickety-click (R), whence Clicketies (B).

70. Blind seventy (A).

72. Six duzz (B).

76. Was she? (B: i.e. worth the cost of the marriage certificate; or, as A has it more positively) She was worth it!; Trombones (W: from the song about 'seventy-six trombones in the big parade').

77. All the sevens (A); Crutches (B: from the shape); Sunset Strip.

80. Blind eighty (A).

88. All the eights (A); Two fat ladies *or* Two old ladies *or* Two fat waafs (B: ex shape); The Connaught Rangers (B, the old 88th Regt. of Foot, disbanded in 1922, with other Irish Regts).

90, 99, 100. The highest number in the game may be called Top of the house *or* shop (P) *or* . . . the bleeding bungalow (R) *or* . . . the ship. Lt Cdr J. Irving, *Royal Navalese*, 1946, has '90: Top of the Grot'; Petch notes Top of the box as a Bingoism, and W has Top of the tree.

After the call of 'House' for the claim of a won game, the usual call is 'Eyes down for a check'. For resumption after a trivial query, players are warned of the resumption by 'Eyes down'. If someone 'has a sweat on' and calls 'House!' prematurely out of nervous anticipation, and his card is found on checking to be wrong or incomplete, then the caller announces, amid jeers, 'House a bogey!', and the game continues.

In order to break the monotony of always playing for a 'full house', there are various subsidiary forms. The simplest is 'a jildi five', covering the first five numbers of the card in any order. 'A Nelson's column' requires one number on the top line, one on the middle, and one on the bottom, as near vertical as possible on the card.

Atkinson defines 'a NAAFI sandwich' as 'covering, for example, two in the top line of the card, one in the next line, and two on the following line, or any three lines in this order.' Whereas B remembers it as a round in which the winning ticket has all the numbers in the top and bottom lines marked off as having been called, but none in the middle line. Atkinson contrasts with his version, an 'Officers' Mess sandwich', in which 'the middle term' is thicker, e.g. two, three, two. B knew A's version of the NAAFI sandwich as 'a Union Jack', with all four corner numbers marked off, and the centre one of the middle line.